# Oxford American Large Print Dictionary

# Oxford American Large Print Dictionary

OXFORD
UNIVERSITY PRESS

OXFORD UNIVERSITY PRESS

Oxford University Press, Inc., publishes works that further
Oxford University's objective of excellence
in research, scholarship, and education.

Oxford   New York
Auckland   Cape Town   Dar es Salaam   Hong Kong   Karachi
Kuala Lumpur   Madrid   Melbourne   Mexico City   Nairobi
New Delhi   Shanghai   Taipei   Toronto

With offices in
Argentina   Austria   Brazil   Chile   Czech Republic   France   Greece
Guatemala   Hungary   Italy   Japan   Poland   Portugal   Singapore
South Korea   Switzerland   Thailand   Turkey   Ukraine   Vietnam

The *Oxford American Large Print Dictionary* is based on the *Oxford American Minidictionary*, 2004

Published by Oxford University Press, Inc.
198 Madison Avenue, New York, New York, 10016
www.oup.com/us
www.askoxford.com

**Library of Congress Cataloging-in-Publication Data**
Oxford American large print dictionary.
    p. cm.
  ISBN 0-19-530078-5
  1. English language—United States—Dictionaries.   2. Large type books.   I. Oxford University
Press

  PE1628.0265 2006
  423—dc22
                                2005025391

ISBN-10: 0-19-530078-5
ISBN-13: 978-0-19-530078-9

10   9   8   7   6   5   4   3   2   1
Printed in the United States of America on acid-free paper

# Contents

# Staff

| | |
|---|---|
| *Editor in Chief* | Erin McKean |
| *Managing Editor* | Constance Baboukis |
| *Senior Editor* | Christine Lindberg |
| *Editors* | Carol Braham |
| | Georgia Maas |
| | Katherine Sietsema |
| | Deborah Posner |
| *Assistant Editor* | Grant Barrett |
| *Editorial Assistant* | Elizabeth Jerabek |

# Preface

The *Oxford American Large Print Dictionary* is intended as a helpful, easy-to-read dictionary for the home, school, or office. The dictionary covers the essential vocabulary of American English, with features that include syllabification, pronunciation, derivatives and inflected forms, and clear, concise definitions. Special sections at the back of the book provide clear and helpful information on grammar and usage, composition, capitalization, and spelling.

This book's clear page layout, designed in association with Lighthouse International, offers enlarged fonts, larger margins, generous line spacing, and good quality paper for minimum glare and show-through.

The *Oxford American Large Print Dictionary*, with its attention to quality, thoroughness, and currency, continues the tradition of Oxford—the world's most trusted name in dictionaries.

This dictionary has been produced in cooperation with Lighthouse International, which made recommendations on design and layout. A percentage from the sale of each dictionary will be made to Lighthouse International to support its work helping people with vision loss remain productive and independent. For more information about Lighthouse International, please visit www.lighthouse.org.

# Abbreviations

| | | | |
|---|---|---|---|
| abbr. | abbreviation | inf. | informal |
| adj. | adjective | interj. | interjection |
| adv. | adverb | lit. | literary |
| Anat. | anatomy | Med. | medical |
| approx. | approximately | Mus. | music |
| aux. | auxiliary | n. | noun |
| Brit. | British | orig. | originally |
| c. | century; circa | part. | participle |
| Chem. | chemistry | pl. | plural |
| comb. | combination; combining | poet. | poetic |
| conj. | conjunction | prep. | preposition |
| contr. | contraction | pron. | pronoun |
| derog. | derogatory | pronunc. | pronunciation |
| e.g. | for example | sing. | singular |
| esp. | especially | symb. | symbol |
| etc. | et cetera (and so on) | usu. | usually |
| fem. | feminine | v. | verb |
| Gram. | grammar | var. | variant |

# Pronunciations Key

| | | | | |
|---|---|---|---|---|
| a | hat /hat/ | | ŏŏ | foot /fŏŏt/ |
| ā | day /dā/ | | o͞o | too /to͞o/ |
| ä | far /fär/, lot /lät/ | | ou | mouse /mous/ |
| b | big /big/ | | p | pin /pin/ |
| CH | chew /CHo͞o/ | | r | run /rən/ |
| d | dog /dôg/ | | s | sit /sit/ |
| e | let /let/ | | SH | she /SHē/ |
| ē | be /bē/ | | t | top /täp/ |
| e(ə)r | air /e(ə)r/ | | TH | thin /THin/ |
| f | fee /fē/ | | T͟H | then /T͟Hen/ |
| g | go /gō/ | | v | very /verē/ |
| h | he /hē/ | | w | we /wē/ |
| i | if /if/ | | (h)w | why /(h)wī/ |
| ī | tie /tī/ | | y | you /yo͞o/ |
| i(ə)r | ear /i(ə)r/ | | z | zoo /zo͞o/ |
| j | joy /joi/ | | ZH | vision /'viZHən/ |
| k | key /kē/ | | ə | soda /'sōdə/, but /bət/, fir /fər/ |
| l | lap /lap/ | | | |
| m | me /mē/ | | | |
| n | no /nō/ | | | |
| NG | sing /siNG/ | | **Foreign Sounds** | |
| ō | go /gō/ | | KH | Hanukkah /'KHänəkə/ |
| ô | law /lô/ | | N | en route /äN 'ro͞ot/ |
| oi | toy /toi/ | | OE | oeuvre /'OEvrə/ |

Stress Marks are placed before the syllable. Primary stress [ ' ] indicates greater emphasis and secondary stress [ ˌ ] indicates weaker emphasis.

# Oxford American Large Print Dictionary

# Aa

**A**¹ /ā/ (also **a**) ▸*n.* (*pl.* **As** or **A's**; **a's**) **1** first letter of the alphabet. **2** *Mus.* sixth note of the diatonic scale of C major. **3** first hypothetical person or example. **4** highest class or category (of academic grades, etc.). **5** human blood type.

**A**² (also **A.**) ▸*abbr.* **1** ampere(s). **2** answer. **3** atomic (energy, etc.).

**a**¹ /ə; ā/ (also **an** before a vowel) ▸*adj.* [called the *indefinite article*] **1** one; some; any. **2** one like: *a Judas.* **3** one single: *not a thing in sight.* **4** the same. **5** in, to, or for each: *twice a year.*

**a**² ▸*prep.* [usu. as *prefix*] **1** to; toward: *ashore.* **2** in the process of; in a specified state: *a-wandering* | *abuzz.* **3** on: *afire.*

**Å** ▸*abbr.* ångström(s).

**a-** ▸*prefix* not; without: *amoral.*

**AA** ▸*abbr.* Alcoholics Anonymous.

**aard·vark** /'ärd,värk/ ▸*n.* ant-eating nocturnal mammal of southern Africa.

**AB** ▸*n.* **1** human blood type. **2** Bachelor of Arts.

**ab-** ▸*prefix* off; away; from: *abduct* | *abnormal* | *abuse.*

**ABA** ▸*abbr.* **1** American Bar Association. **2** American Basketball Association.

**a·back** /ə'bak/ ▸*adv.* (in phrase **take someone aback**) surprise; disconcert: *your request took me aback.*

**ab·a·cus** /'abəkəs/ ▸*n.* (*pl.* **ab·a·cus·es**) oblong frame with wires along which beads are slid, used for calculating.

**ab·a·lo·ne** /,abə'lōnē/ ▸*n.* saltwater mollusk with a shallow ear-shaped shell.

**a·ban·don** /ə'bandən/ ▸*v.* **1** give up completely or before completion. **2** forsake, desert, or leave.
▸*n.* lack of inhibition or restraint. **—a·ban·don·ment** *n.*

**a·ban·doned** ▸*adj.* **1** deserted; forsaken. **2** unrestrained; profligate.

**a·base** /ə'bās/ ▸*v.* humiliate or degrade. **—a·base·ment** *n.*

**a·bash** /ə'baSH/ ▸*v.* [usu. as *adj.* **abashed**] cause to feel embarrassed or disconcerted.

**a·bate** /ə'bāt/ ▶v. make or become less strong, severe, intense, etc. —**a·bate·ment** n.

**ab·at·toir** /'abə,twär/ ▶n. slaughterhouse.

**ab·bess** /'abis/ ▶n. head of a community of nuns.

**ab·bey** /'abē/ ▶n. (pl. **-beys**) 1 building(s) occupied by a community of monks or nuns. 2 the community itself.

**ab·bot** /'abət/ ▶n. head of a community of monks.

**abbr.** (also **abbrev.**) ▶abbr. abbreviation.

**ab·bre·vi·ate** /ə'brēvē,āt/ ▶v. shorten, esp. represent (a word, etc.) by a part of it. —**ab·bre·vi·a·tion** n.

**ABC** ▶n. 1 the alphabet. 2 (**ABCs**) rudiments of any subject.

**ab·di·cate** /'abdi,kāt/ ▶v. 1 give up or renounce (esp. a throne). 2 renounce (a responsibility, duty, etc.). —**ab·di·ca·tion** n.

**ab·do·men** /'abdəmən/ ▶n. 1 part of the body containing digestive and reproductive organs. 2 hind part of an insect, crustacean, etc. —**ab·dom·i·nal** adj.

**ab·duct** /ab'dəkt/ ▶v. carry off or kidnap (a person) illegally. —**ab·duc·tion** n. —**ab·duc·tor** n.

**a·be·ce·dar·i·an** /,ābēsē-'de(ə)rēən/ ▶adj. 1 arranged alphabetically. 2 rudimentary; elementary.

**ab·er·rant** /'abərənt; ə'ber-/ ▶adj. departing from an accepted standard.

**ab·er·ra·tion** /,abə'rāsHən/ ▶n. 1 departure from what is normal or regarded as right. 2 moral or mental lapse. —**ab·er·rant** adj.

**a·bet** /ə'bet/ ▶v. (**a·bet·ted, a·bet·ting**) (usu. in phrase **aid and a·bet**) encourage or assist (an offender or offense).

**a·bey·ance** /ə'bāəns/ ▶n. state of temporary disuse or suspension: matters were held in abeyance pending further investigation.

**abhor** /ab'hôr/ ▶v. (**-horred, -hor·ring**) detest; regard with disgust and hatred. —**ab·hor·rence** n.

**a·bide** /ə'bīd/ ▶v. (past **a·bode** or **a·bid·ed**) 1 tolerate; endure. 2 (**abide by**) act in accordance with.

**a·bid·ing** ▶adj. enduring; permanent: an abiding sense of loss.

**a·bil·i·ty** /ə'bilitē/ ▶n. (pl. **-ties**)

1 capacity or power.
2 cleverness; talent; mental power.

**-ability** ▸*suffix* forming nouns of quality from, or corresponding to, adjectives in *-able*: *capability* | *vulnerability.*

**ab·ject** /ˈabˌjekt/ ▸*adj.* 1 miserable; wretched: *abject poverty.* 2 self-abasing: *abject apology.* 3 absolute and humiliating: *abject failure.*

**ab·jure** /abˈjo͝or/ ▸*v.* renounce under oath. **—ab·ju·ra·tion** *n.*

**ab·la·tive** /ˈablətiv/ ▸*n. Gram.* case (esp. in Latin) of nouns and pronouns indicating an agent, instrument, or location.

**ab·laut** /ˈabˌlout/ ▸*n.* change of vowel in related words or forms (e.g., in *sing, sang, sung*).

**a·blaze** /əˈblāz/ ▸*adj. & adv.* 1 on fire. 2 glittering; glowing; radiant. 3 greatly excited.

**a·ble** /ˈābəl/ ▸*adj.* (**a·bler**, **a·blest**) 1 having the capacity or power: *able to come.* 2 having great ability; clever.

□ **able-bodied** fit; healthy.

**-able** /əbəl/ ▸*suffix* forming adjectives meaning: 1 that may or must be: *eatable.* 2 that can be made the subject of: *dutiable* | *objectionable.* 3 relevant to or in accordance with: *fashionable.*

**ab·lu·tion** /əˈblo͞oshən/ ▸*n.* (usu. **ablutions**) ceremonial washing of hands, sacred vessels, etc.

**ab·ne·gate** /ˈabniˌgāt/ ▸*v.* 1 give up or deny oneself (a pleasure, etc.). 2 renounce or reject (a right or belief). **—ab·ne·ga·tion** *n.* **—ab·ne·ga·tor** *n.*

**ab·ne·ga·tion** /ˌabniˈgāshən/ ▸*n.* act of renouncing or rejecting something.

**ab·nor·mal** /abˈnôrməl/ ▸*adj.* deviating from the norm; exceptional. **—ab·nor·mal·i·ty** *n.* **—ab·nor·mal·ly** *adv.*

**a·board** /əˈbôrd/ ▸*adv. & prep.* 1 on or into (a ship, aircraft, etc.). 2 into an organization as a new member: *coming aboard as the new chairman.*

**a·bode** /əˈbōd/ ▸past of **ABIDE**.
▸*n.* dwelling; one's home.

**a·bol·ish** /əˈbälish/ ▸*v.* put an end to (esp. a custom or institution).

**ab·o·li·tion** /ˌabəˈlishən/ ▸*n.* 1 abolishing or being abolished. 2 the ending of a practice or institution, esp. (in U.S. hist.) slavery. **—ab·o·li·tion·ist** *n.*

**A-bomb** /ˈā ˌbäm/ ▸*n.* **ATOM BOMB**.

**a·bom·i·na·ble** /əˈbäm(ə)nəbəl/
▸*adj.* **1** detestable; loathsome;
morally reprehensible. **2** *inf.*
very unpleasant.
—**a·bom·i·na·bly** *adv.*

**a·bom·i·nate** /əˈbämə͵nāt/ ▸*v.*
detest; loathe.
—**a·bom·i·na·tion** *n.*

**ab·o·rig·i·ne** /͵abəˈrijənē/ ▸*n.*
**1** inhabitant from earliest times.
**2** (**Aborigine**) original inhabitant
of Australia. **3** indigenous plant
or animal. —**ab·o·rig·i·nal** *adj.*

**a·bort** /əˈbôrt/ ▸*v.* **1** miscarry.
**2** effect abortion. **3** (cause to)
end fruitlessly or prematurely.
▸*n.* **1** prematurely terminated
space flight or other
undertaking. **2** termination of
such an undertaking.

**a·bor·tion** ▸*n.* expulsion of a
fetus (naturally or esp. by
medical induction) from the
womb before it is able to survive
independently.

**a·bound** /əˈbound/ ▸*v.* **1** be
plentiful. **2** (**abound in/with**) be
rich in; teem or be infested with.

**a·bout** /əˈbout/ ▸*prep.* **1 a** on the
subject of. **b** relating to. **c** in
relation to. **d** so as to affect. **2** at
a time near to. **3** in; around.
▸*adv.* **1** approximately. **2** at

points nearby: *a lot of flu about.*
**3** in every direction.

**a·bove** /əˈbəv/ ▸*prep.* **1** over; on
the top of; higher than. **2** more
than: *above average.* **3** higher in
rank, importance, etc., than.
▸*adv.* **1** at or to a higher point;
overhead. **2** upstairs. **3** (of a text
reference) further back on a
page or in a book: *as noted above.*
▸*adj.* preceding.
▸*n.* what is mentioned above.
□ **above all** more than anything
else.

**a·bove·board** ▸*adj. & adv.*
without concealment; fair or
fairly; open or openly.

**ab o·vo** /ab ˈō͵vō; äb/ ▸*adv.* from
the very beginning.

**a·brade** /əˈbrād/ ▸*v.* scrape or
wear away (something) by
friction or erosion.

**ab·ra·sion** /əˈbrāzʜən/ ▸*n.*
**1** result of abrading. **2** damaged
area resulting from this.
—**a·brade** *v.*

**ab·ra·sive** /əˈbrāsiv/ ▸*adj.*
**1 a** tending to rub or abrade.
**b** capable of polishing by
rubbing or grinding. **2** harsh or
hurtful in manner.
▸*n.* abrasive substance.

**ab·re·ac·tion** /͵abrēˈaksʜən/ ▸*n.*
expression and consequent

release of a previously repressed emotion, achieved through reliving the experience that caused it (typically through hypnosis or suggestion).

**a·breast** /əˈbrest/ ▶*adv.* **1** side by side and facing the same way. **2 a** up to date. **b** well-informed.

**a·bridge** /əˈbrij/ ▶*v.* **1** shorten (a book, movie, etc.). **2** curtail. —**a·bridg·ment** or **a·bridge·ment** *n.*

**a·broad** /əˈbrôd/ ▶*adv.* **1** in or to a foreign country or countries. **2** over a wide area. **3** in circulation.

**ab·ro·gate** /ˈabrəˌgāt/ ▶*v.* repeal, annul, or abolish (a law or custom). —**ab·ro·ga·tion** *n.*

**ab·rupt** /əˈbrəpt/ ▶*adj.* **1** sudden; hasty. **2** (of speech, manner, etc.) curt. **3** steep: *an abrupt drop.*

**ab·scess** /ˈabˌses/ ▶*n.* swelling containing pus. —**ab·scessed** *adj.*

**ab·scis·sion** /abˈsizHən/ ▶*n.* natural detachment of parts of a plant, typically dead leaves and ripe fruit.

**ab·scond** /abˈskänd/ ▶*v.* depart hurriedly and furtively, esp. unlawfully or to avoid arrest.

**ab·sent** ▶*adj.* /ˈabsənt/ **1** not present. **2** not existing. **3** inattentive.
▶*v.* /abˌsent/ (**absent oneself**) stay or go away. —**ab·sence** *n.*

**ab·sen·tee** /ˌabsənˈtē/ ▶*n.* person not present.

**ab·sent·mind·ed** ▶*adj.* forgetful or inattentive.

**ab·sinthe** /ˈabˌsinTH/ (also **ab·sinth**) ▶*n.* potent green aniseed-flavored liqueur prepared from wormwood that turns milky when water is added.

**ab·so·lute** /ˈabsəˌlo͞ot/ ▶*adj.* **1** complete; utter. **2** unconditional. **3** despotic. **4** (of a standard or other concept) not relative or comparative. **5** (of a legal decree, etc.) final. —**ab·so·lute·ly** *adv.* —**ab·so·lute·ness** *n.*

**ab·so·lute pitch** ▶*n. Mus.* **1** pitch according to a standard defined by frequency of sound vibration. **2** ability to recognize or sound any given note.

**ab·so·lute ze·ro** ▶*n.* theoretical lowest possible temperature, calculated as −273.15° C (or 0° K).

**ab·so·lu·tion** /absəˈlo͞osHən/ ▶*n.* formal forgiveness from guilt, sin, etc.

**ab·so·lut·ism** /'absəlōō,tizəm/
▶n. acceptance of or belief in
absolute principles in political,
philosophical, ethical, or
theological matters.

**ab·solve** /əb'zälv/ ▶v. **1 a** free
from blame or obligation, etc.
**b** acquit; pronounce not guilty.
**2** pardon or give absolution for
(a sin, etc.).

**ab·sorb** /əb'zôrb/ ▶v.
**1** incorporate as part of itself or
oneself. **2** take in; suck up.
**3** reduce the effect or intensity
of. **4** consume. **5** engross the
attention of. **—ab·sorb·en·cy** n.
**—ab·sorb·ent** adj.
**—ab·sorp·tion** n.

**ab·stain** /əb'stān; ab-/ ▶v.
**1** refrain from doing something.
**2** formally decline to use one's
vote. **—ab·sten·tion** n.

**ab·ste·mi·ous** /ab'stēmēəs/
▶adj. moderate, esp. in eating
and drinking.

**ab·sti·nence** /'abstənəns/ ▶n.
abstaining, esp. from food,
alcohol, or sexual relations.
**—ab·sti·nent** adj.

**ab·stract** ▶adj. /'ab,strakt/
**1 a** of or existing in thought or
theory rather than matter or
practice; not concrete. **b** (of a
word, esp. a noun) denoting a
quality, condition, etc., not a
concrete object. **2** (of art)
achieving its effect by shapes
and colors rather than by
realism.
▶v. /əb'strakt/ **1** extract; remove.
**2** summarize.
▶n. /'ab,strakt/ summary.
**—ab·stract·ly** adj.
**—ab·strac·tion** n.

**ab·struse** /əb'strōōs/ ▶adj. hard
to understand; obscure;
profound.

**ab·surd** /əb'sərd/ ▶adj. wildly
illogical or inappropriate.
**—ab·surd·i·ty** n.

**a·bu·li·a** /ə'bōōlēə/ ▶n. absence
of willpower or an inability to
act decisively, as a symptom of
mental illness.

**a·bun·dance** /ə'bəndəns/ ▶n.
very great quantity; more than
enough. **—a·bun·dant** adj.

**a·buse** ▶v. /ə'byōōz/ **1 a** use
improperly; misuse. **b** take (a
drug) for a purpose other than a
therapeutic one; be addicted to
(a substance). **2** insult verbally.
**3** maltreat; assault (esp.
sexually).
▶n. /ə'byōōs/ **1** improper use.
**2** insulting language. **3** unjust or
corrupt practice.

**4** maltreatment. —**a·bused** *adj.*
—**a·bus·er** *n.* —**a·bu·sive** *adj.*

**a·but** /ə'bət/ ▶*v.* (**a·but·ted,
a·but·ting**) border (upon).

**a·bys·mal** /ə'bizməl/ ▶*adj.* **1** *inf.*
extremely bad. **2** profound;
utter. —**a·bys·mal·ly** *adv.*

**a·byss** /ə'bis/ ▶*n.* **1** deep chasm.
**2** immeasurable depth.

**a·byss·al** /ə'bisəl/ ▶*adj.* relating
to or denoting the depths or bed
of the ocean, esp. between about
10,000 and 20,000 feet (3,000
and 6,000 meters) down.

**AC** ▶*abbr.* **1** (also **ac**) alternating
current. **2** air conditioning.

**Ac** ▶*symb.* actinium.

**ac-** ▶*prefix* assim. form of **AD-**
before *c, k, q*.

**-ac** ▶*suffix* forming adjectives
often (or only) used as nouns:
*cardiac* | *maniac*.

**a·ca·cia** /ə'kāSHə/ ▶*n.* tree with
yellow or white flowers, esp. one
yielding gum arabic.

**ac·a·deme** /ˌakə'dēm; 'akəˌdēm/
▶*n.* academic environment or
community; academia.

**ac·a·dem·ic** /ˌakə'demik/ ▶*adj.*
**1** scholarly; of learning.
**2** theoretical; not of practical
relevance.
▶*n.* teacher or scholar in a
university, etc.
—**ac·a·dem·i·cal·ly** *adv.*

**a·cad·e·my** /ə'kadəmē/ ▶*n.* (*pl.*
**-mies**) **1 a** place of specialized
training. **b** secondary school.
**2** (usu. **Academy**) society or
institution of distinguished
scholars, artists, scientists, etc.

**a cap·pel·la** /ˌä kə'pelə/ ▶*adj. &
adv.* (of choral singing)
unaccompanied.

**ac·cede** /ak'sēd/ ▶*v.* **1** assent or
agree. **2** assume an office.

**ac·cel·er·an·do** /äkˌselə'rändō;
ak-; äˌCHelə-/ ▶*adj. & adv.* with a
gradual increase of speed (used
chiefly as a musical direction).

**ac·cel·er·ate** /ak'seləˌrāt/ ▶*v.*
move or begin to move more
quickly; increase the speed (of).
—**ac·cel·er·a·tion** *n.*

**ac·cel·er·a·tor** ▶*n.* **1** device for
increasing speed, esp. the pedal
that controls the speed of a
vehicle's engine. **2** *Physics*
apparatus for imparting high
speeds to charged particles.

**ac·cent** /'akˌsent/ ▶*n.*
**1** particular mode of
pronunciation, esp. local or
national. **2** prominence given to
a syllable by stress or pitch.
**3** mark on a letter or word to
indicate pitch, stress, or vowel

quality. **4** distinctive feature or emphasis.

▶*v.* **1** emphasize (a word or syllable). **2** accentuate.

**ac·cen·tu·ate** /ak'senCHŌŌ,āt/ ▶*v.* emphasize; make prominent. —**ac·cen·tu·a·tion** *n.*

**ac·cept** /ak'sept/ ▶*v.* **1** willingly receive. **2** answer affirmatively. **3** regard favorably; treat as welcome. **4** believe.

**ac·cess** /'ak,ses/ ▶*n.* **1** way of approach or entry. **2** right or opportunity to reach or use or visit; admittance.

▶*v. Computing* gain access to (data, a file, etc.).

**ac·ces·si·ble** /ak'sesəbəl/ ▶*adj.* **1** readily reached, entered, or used. **2** readily available. **3** easy to understand. —**ac·ces·si·bil·i·ty** *n.*

**ac·ces·sion** ▶*n.* **1** taking office (esp. the throne). **2** thing added (e.g., a book to a library); increase.

▶*v.* record the addition of (a new item) to a library, etc.

**ac·ces·so·ry** /ak'ses(ə)rē/ ▶*n.* (*pl.* **-ries**) **1** additional or extra thing. **2 a** small attachment or fitting. **b** (**accessories**) small items of (esp. a woman's) dress (e.g., shoes, gloves, etc.). **3** *Law*

person who helps in or knows the details of an (esp. illegal) act.

▶*adj.* additional; contributing or aiding in a minor way; dispensable.

**ac·ci·dent** /'aksidənt/ ▶*n.* **1** event that is without apparent cause or that is unexpected. **2** unfortunate event, esp. one causing physical harm or damage. **3** occurrence of things by chance. —**ac·ci·den·tal** *adj.* —**ac·ci·den·tal·ly** *adv.*

□ **accident-prone** (of a person) subject to frequent accidents.

**ac·claim** /ə'klām/ ▶*v.* welcome or applaud enthusiastically; praise publicly.

▶*n.* applause; welcome; public praise. —**ac·claim·er** *n.*

**ac·cla·ma·tion** /,aklə'māSHən/ ▶*n.* loud and enthusiastic approval, typically to welcome or honor someone or something.

**ac·cli·mate** /'aklə,māt/ ▶*v.* acclimatize.

**ac·cli·ma·tize** /ə'klīmə,tīz/ ▶*v.* accustom or become accustomed to new surroundings.

**ac·cliv·i·ty** /ə'klivitē/ ▶*n.* (*pl.* **-ties**) upward slope.

**ac·co·lade** /'akə,lād/ ▶*n.* awarding of praise; acknowledgment of merit.

**ac·com·mo·date** /əˈkäməˌdāt/ ▸v. **1** provide lodging or room for. **2** adapt; harmonize; reconcile. **3** do a favor for.

**ac·com·mo·dat·ing** /əˈkäməˌdātiNG/ ▸adj. obliging; compliant.

**ac·com·mo·da·tion** /əˌkäməˈdāsHən/ ▸n. **1** act or process of accommodating or being accommodated. **2** (**accomodations**) **a** lodgings; place to live. **b** room and board. **3 a** adjustment or adaptation. **b** settlement or compromise.

**ac·com·mo·da·tion·ist** /əˌkäməˈdāsHənist/ ▸n. person who seeks compromise with an opposing point of view, typically a political one.

**ac·com·pa·ni·ment** /əˈkəmp(ə)nimənt/ ▸n. **1** instrumental or orchestral support for a solo instrument, voice, or group. **2** accompanying thing. —**ac·com·pa·nist** n.

**ac·com·pa·ny** ▸v. (-nies, -nied) **1** go with; escort. **2** Mus. support or partner with accompaniment.

**ac·com·plice** /əˈkämplis/ ▸n. partner in a crime.

**ac·com·plish** /əˈkämplisH/ ▸v. perform; complete; succeed in doing.

**ac·com·plished** ▸adj. clever; skilled.

**ac·com·plish·ment** ▸n. **1** completion (of a task, etc.). **2** thing achieved.

**ac·cord** /əˈkôrd/ ▸v. be in harmony; be consistent. ▸n. **1** agreement; consent. **2** harmony. **3** formal treaty or agreement. —**ac·cord·ance** n. □ **of one's own accord** voluntarily.

**ac·cord·ing·ly** ▸adv. **1** as suggested or required by the (stated) circumstances. **2** consequently.

**ac·cor·di·on** /əˈkôrdēən/ ▸n. musical reed instrument with bellows, keys, and buttons. —**ac·cor·di·on·ist** n.

**ac·cost** /əˈkôst/ ▸v. approach and address (a person), esp. boldly.

**ac·couche·ment** /ˌäkо̄о̄sHˈmäN; əˈko̅o̅sHmənt/ ▸n. action of giving birth to a baby.

**ac·count** /əˈkount/ ▸n. **1** narration or description. **2** arrangement at a bank, etc., for commercial or financial transactions, esp. for depositing and withdrawing money. **3** (often **accounts**) record or statement of financial transactions.

▶ *v.* consider; regard as: *account it a misfortune.*

□ **account for 1** serve as or provide an explanation for. **2 a** give a reckoning of (money, etc., entrusted). **b** answer for (one's conduct). □ **take into account** consider along with other factors: *took their age into account.*

**ac·count·a·ble** ▶*adj.*
**1** responsible; required to account for (one's conduct). **2** understandable.
—**ac·count·a·bil·i·ty** *n.*

**ac·count·ant** /əˈkount(ə)nt/ ▶*n.* professional keeper or inspector of accounts.

**ac·count·ing** ▶*n.* process or practice of keeping and verifying accounts.

**ac·cou·tre** /əˈko͞otər/ (also **ac·cou·ter**) ▶*v.* (**-tred, -tring; -tered, -ter·ing**) clothe or equip, typically in something noticeable or impressive.

**ac·cou·tre·ment** /əˈko͞otərmənt; -trə-/ (also **ac·cou·ter·ment**) ▶*n.* (usu. **accoutrements**) additional items of dress or equipment, or other items carried or worn by a person or used for a particular activity.

**ac·cred·it** /əˈkredit/ ▶*v.*
**1** attribute. **2** send (an ambassador, etc.) with credentials. **3** make credible (an adviser, a statement, etc.). **4** certify (esp. an educational institution) as maintaining professional standards.
—**ac·cred·i·ta·tion** *n.*
—**ac·cred·it·ed** *adj.*

**ac·cre·tion** /əˈkrēsʜən/ ▶*n.*
**1** process of growth or increase, typically by the gradual accumulation of additional layers or matter. **2** coming together and cohesion of matter under the influence of gravitation to form larger bodies.

**ac·crue** /əˈkro͞o/ ▶*v.* (**-crued, -cru·ing**) come as a natural increase or advantage, esp. financial. —**ac·cru·al** *n.*

**ac·cu·mu·late** /əˈkyo͞omyəˌlāt/ ▶*v.* **1** acquire an increasing number or quantity of. **2** produce or acquire (a resulting whole) in this way.
—**ac·cu·mu·la·tion** *n.*
—**ac·cu·mu·la·tive** *adj.*

**ac·cu·rate** /ˈakyərit/ ▶*adj.*
**1** careful; precise; lacking errors.

**2** conforming exactly with a qualitative standard, physical or quantitative target, etc.
—**ac·cu·ra·cy** *n.*

**ac·curs·ed** /əˈkərst/ ▶*adj.* **1** under a curse. **2** *inf.* detestable; annoying.

**ac·cu·sa·tive** /əˈkyo͞ozətiv/ *Gram.* ▶*n.* case of nouns, pronouns, and adjectives expressing the object of an action.
▶*adj.* of or in this case.

**ac·cuse** /əˈkyo͞oz/ ▶*v.* **1** charge with a fault or crime; indict: *he was accused of larceny.* **2** blame.
—**ac·cu·sa·tion** *n.*
—**ac·cu·sa·to·ry** *adj.*
—**ac·cus·er** *n.*

**ac·cus·tom** /əˈkəstəm/ ▶*v.* make (a person or thing) used to: *the army accustomed him to discipline.*

**ac·cus·tomed** ▶*adj.* **1** used to: *accustomed to the rainy weather.* **2** customary; usual: *on the accustomed route.*

**ace** /ās/ ▶*n.* **1** playing card with a single spot and generally having the highest value. **2** person who excels in some activity.
▶*adj. inf.* excellent.

**a·ce·di·a** /əˈsēdēə/ ▶*n.* spiritual or mental sloth; apathy.

**a·cer·bic** /əˈsərbik/ ▶*adj.* **1** astringently sour; harsh-tasting. **2** bitter in speech, manner, or temper.
—**a·cer·bi·cal·ly** *adv.*
—**a·cer·bi·ty** *n.*

**a·ce·ta·min·o·phen** /əˌsētə-ˈminəfən/ ▶*n.* common drug used to reduce fever and pain.

**ac·e·tate** /ˈasiˌtāt/ ▶*n.* **1** salt or ester of acetic acid. **2** fabric made from this.

**a·ce·tic** /əˈsētik/ ▶*adj.* of or like vinegar.
□ **acetic acid** clear liquid acid that gives vinegar its characteristic taste.

**ac·e·tone** /ˈasiˌtōn/ ▶*n.* colorless, volatile liquid that dissolves organic compounds, esp. paints, varnishes, etc.

**a·cet·y·lene** /əˈsetl-ēn/ ▶*n.* colorless hydrocarbon gas, burning with a bright flame, used esp. in welding.

**ache** /āk/ ▶*n.* **1** continuous dull pain. **2** mental distress.
▶*v.* **1** suffer an ache. **2** feel intense sadness or compassion: *my heart ached for her.* **3** desire greatly: *she ached for his touch.*
—**ach·y** *adj.*

**a·chieve** /əˈCHēv/ ▶*v.* **1** attain by effort. **2** accomplish. **3** be

successful. —**a·chiev·a·ble** *adj.*
—**a·chieve·ment** *n.*
—**a·chiev·er** *n.*

**A·chil·les heel** /ə'kilēz/ ▶*n.*
person's weak or vulnerable
point.

**ac·id** /'asid/ ▶*n.* **1 a** any of a class
of substances that liberate
hydrogen ions in water, are usu.
sour and corrosive, and have a
pH of less than 7. **b** any
compound or atom donating
protons. **2** any sour substance.
**3** *inf.* the drug LSD.
▶*adj.* **1** sour. **2** biting; sharp.
**3** having the properties of an
acid. —**a·cid·ic** *adj.* —**a·cid·i·fy** *v.*
—**a·cid·i·ty** *n.*
□ **acid test** severe or conclusive
test.

**ac·id rain** ▶*n.* rain made acidic
by atmospheric pollution.

**a·cid·u·lous** /ə'sijələs/ ▶*adj.*
**1** sharp-tasting or sour. **2** (of a
person's remarks or tone) bitter
or cutting.

**ac·knowl·edge** /ak'nälij/ ▶*v.*
**1** recognize; accept as truth.
**2** confirm the receipt of:
*acknowledged her letter.* **3** express
appreciation for. **4** recognize
the validity of.
—**ac·knowl·edg·ment** or
**ac·knowl·edge·ment** *n.*

**ac·me** /'akmē/ ▶*n.* highest point.

**ac·ne** /'aknē/ ▶*n.* skin condition
characterized by pimples.

**ac·o·lyte** /'akə,līt/ ▶*n.* **1** person
assisting a priest; altar boy or
girl. **2** assistant; beginner.

**a·corn** /'ā,kôrn/ ▶*n.* fruit of the
oak, with a smooth nut in a
rough cuplike base.

**a·cous·tic** /ə'kōōstik/ ▶*adj.*
**1** relating to sound or the sense
of hearing. **2** (of a musical
instrument) not having electrical
amplification. **3** (of building
materials) used for
soundproofing.
▶*n.* **1** [*pl. n.*] (**acoustics**) properties
or qualities (esp. of a room, etc.)
in transmitting sound: *the new
hall's acoustics are outstanding.*
**2** (**acoustics**) science of sound:
*acoustics is his specialty.*
—**a·cous·ti·cal** *adj.*
—**a·cous·ti·cal·ly** *adv.*
—**ac·ous·ti·cian** *n.*

**ac·quaint** /ə'kwānt/ ▶*v.* make
aware of or familiar with.

**ac·quaint·ance** ▶*n.* **1** slight
knowledge (of a person or thing).
**2** person one knows slightly.

**ac·qui·esce** /,akwē'es/ ▶*v.*
**1** agree, esp. tacitly. **2** raise no
objection. **3** accept (an
arrangement, etc.).

—ac·qui·es·cence *n.*
—ac·qui·es·cent *adj.*

**ac·quire** /ə'kwī(ə)r/ ▶*v.* **1** gain by and for oneself. **2** come into possession of.

**ac·qui·si·tion** /ˌakwi'zisHən/ ▶*n.* **1** something acquired. **2** act of acquiring.

**ac·quis·i·tive** /ə'kwizitiv/ ▶*adj.* eager to acquire things.

**ac·quit** /ə'kwit/ ▶*v.* (**-quit·ted, -quit·ting**) **1** declare not guilty. **2** conduct oneself or perform in a specified way. —**ac·quit·tal** *n.*

**a·cre** /'ākər/ ▶*n.* measure of land, 4,840 sq. yds. —**acre·age** *n.*

**ac·rid** /'akrid/ ▶*adj.* bitterly pungent.

**ac·ri·mo·ni·ous** /ˌakrə'mōnēəs/ ▶*adj.* bitter in manner or temper. —**ac·ri·mo·ny** *n.*

**ac·ro·bat** /'akrə,bat/ ▶*n.* performer of gymnastic feats. —**ac·ro·bat·ic** *adj.*

**ac·ro·bat·ics** /ˌakrə'batiks/ ▶*pl. n.* **1** acrobatic feats. **2** art of performing these. **3** skill requiring ingenuity: *mental acrobatics.*

**ac·ro·nym** /'akrə,nim/ ▶*n.* word formed from the initial letters of other words (e.g., *laser*, *NATO*).

**ac·ro·pho·bi·a** /ˌakrə'fōbēə/ ▶*n.* abnormal dread of heights. —**ac·ro·pho·bic** *adj.*

**a·cross** /ə'krôs/ ▶*prep.* **1** to or on the other side of. **2** from one side to another side of. **3** at or forming an angle (esp. a right angle) with.
▶*adv.* **1** to or on the other side. **2** from one side to another.
□ **across the board** generally; applying to all.

**a·cros·tic** /ə'krôstik/ ▶*n.* poem, word puzzle, or other composition in which certain letters in each line form a word or words.

**a·cryl·ic** /ə'krilik/ ▶*adj.* **1** of synthetic material made from an organic substance. **2** of or derived from this substance.
▶*n.* acrylic fiber.

**act** /akt/ ▶*n.* **1** something done; deed. **2** process of doing. **3 a** piece of entertainment. **b** performer(s) of this. **4** pretense. **5** main division of a play or opera. **6** statute law.
▶*v.* **1** behave. **2** perform actions or functions; take action. **3** (also **act on**) exert energy or influence. **4** perform a part in a play, movie, etc.
□ **act up** misbehave; become troublesome.

**act·ing** ▶*n.* art or occupation of an actor.
▶*adj.* serving temporarily.

**ac·tin·i·um** /ak'tinēəm/ ▶*n.* radioactive metallic element. (Symb.: **Ac**)

**ac·tion** /'aksHən/ ▶*n.* **1** process of doing or acting. **2** forcefulness or energy. **3** exertion of energy or influence. **4** deed or act. **5** series of events in a story, play, etc. **6** armed conflict; fighting. **7** way in which a machine, instrument, etc., works. **8** lawsuit.

**ac·tion·a·ble** ▶*adj.* giving cause for legal action. —**ac·tion·a·bly** *adv.*

**ac·ti·vate** /'aktə,vāt/ ▶*v.* **1** make active or operative. **2** convert (a substance) into a reactive form.

**ac·tive** /'aktiv/ ▶*adj.* **1** marked by action; energetic. **2** working; operative: *active volcano.* **3** originating action: *active support.* **4** *Gram.* designating the voice that attributes the action of a verb to the person or thing from which it logically proceeds (e.g., of the verb in *guns kill*).
▶*n. Gram.* active form or voice of a verb. —**ac·tive·ly** *adv.*

**ac·tiv·ism** ▶*n.* policy of vigorous action in a cause, esp. in politics. —**ac·tiv·ist** *n.*

**ac·tiv·i·ty** /ak'tivitē/ ▶*n.* (*pl.* **-ties**) **1 a** condition of being active or moving about. **b** exertion of energy; vigorous action. **2** (often **activities**) particular occupation or pursuit.

**ac·tor** /'aktər/ ▶*n.* performer in a play, movie, etc.

**ac·tress** /'aktris/ ▶*n.* female performer in a play, movie, etc.

**ac·tu·al** /'akcHo͞oəl/ ▶*adj.* **1** existing in fact; real. **2** current. —**ac·tu·al·ly** *adv.*

**ac·tu·ar·y** /'akcHo͞o,erē/ ▶*n.* (*pl.* **-ies**) person who calculates insurance risks and premiums. —**ac·tu·ar·i·al** *adj.*

**ac·tu·ate** /'akcHo͞o,āt/ ▶*v.* **1** cause the operation of (an electrical device, etc.). **2** cause to act.

**a·cu·i·ty** /ə'kyo͞oitē/ ▶*n.* sharpness; acuteness.

**a·cu·men** /ə'kyo͞omən/ ▶*n.* keen insight or discernment.

**ac·u·punc·ture** /'akyə-,pəNGkcHər/ ▶*n.* method (orig. Chinese) of treating various conditions by pricking the skin with needles. —**ac·u·punc·tur·ist** *n.*

**a·cute** /ə'kyo͞ot/ ▶*adj.* (**-cut·er,**

-cut·est) **1** (of senses, pain, etc.) keen; penetrating. **2** (of a disease) coming sharply to a crisis; not chronic. **3 a** (of an angle) less than 90°. **b** sharp; pointed. —**a·cute·ly** adv.
□ **acute accent** mark (´) placed over letters in some languages to show vowel length, pronunciation (e.g., maté), etc.

**A.D.** ▸abbr. (of a date) of the Christian era (Latin Anno Domini, 'in the year of the Lord').

**ad** /ad/ inf. ▸n. advertisement.

**ad-** ▸prefix with the sense of motion or direction to; reduction or change into; addition, adherence, increase, or intensification.

**ad·age** /'adij/ ▸n. traditional maxim; proverb.

**a·da·gio** /ə'däjēō/ Mus. ▸adv. & adj. in slow time.
▸n. (pl. **-gios**) adagio movement or passage.

**ad·a·mant** /'adəmənt/ ▸adj. stubbornly resolute; resistant to persuasion.

**ad·a·man·tine** /ˌadə'man,tīn/ ▸adj. unbreakable.

**a·dapt** /ə'dapt/ ▸v. **1** make suitable for a new purpose; modify. **2** become adjusted to new conditions: they adapted

quickly to life in Paris.
—**a·dapt·a·ble** adj. —**ad·ap·ta·tion** n. —**a·dapt·er** or **a·dap·tor** n. —**a·dap·tive** adj.

**add** /ad/ ▸v. **1** join (one thing to another) as an increase or supplement. **2** put together (numbers) to find their total value. **3** say further.
□ **add up 1** find the total of. **2** amount to: adds up to a disaster.

**ad·den·dum** /ə'dendəm/ ▸n. (pl. **-da**) **1** thing to be added, esp. as additional matter at the end of a book. **2** appendix; addition.

**ad·der** /'adər/ ▸n. any of various small venomous snakes, esp. the common viper.

**ad·dict** ▸v. /ə'dikt/ devote or apply habitually or compulsively; make addicted.
▸n. /'adikt/ **1** person addicted to a habit, esp. to a drug. **2** inf. devotee. —**ad·dic·tion** n. —**ad·dic·tive** adj.

**ad·di·tion** /ə'dishən/ ▸n. **1** adding or being added. **2** person or thing added. —**ad·di·tion·al** adj. —**ad·di·tion·al·ly** adv.
□ **in addition** moreover; furthermore. □ **in addition to** as well as; as something added to.

**ad·di·tive** /'aditiv/ ▸*n.* substance added to another so as to give it specific qualities.

**ad·dle** /'adl/ ▸*v.* muddle; confuse.

**ad·dress** /ə'dres/ ▸*n.* **1 a** place where a person lives or an organization is situated. **b** *Computing* location of an item of stored information. **2** discourse delivered to an audience.
▸*v.* **1** write postal directions on (an envelope, package, etc.). **2** speak or write to, esp. formally: *addressed the audience.* **3** direct one's attention to. —**ad·dress·ee** *n.*

**ad·duce** /ə'd(y)o͞os/ ▸*v.* cite as evidence.

**ad·duc·tor** /ə'dəktər/ (also **adductor muscle**) ▸*n.* muscle whose contraction moves a limb or other part of the body toward the midline of the body or toward another part.

**a·dept** /ə'dept/ ▸*adj.* thoroughly proficient. —**a·dept·ly** *adv.* —**a·dept·ness** *n.*

**ad·e·quate** /'adikwit/ ▸*adj.* sufficient; satisfactory. —**ad·e·qua·cy** *n.*

**ad·here** /ad'hi(ə)r/ ▸*v.* **1** stick fast to: *paint won't adhere to that surface.* **2** believe in and follow the practices of: *adhere to Islam.* —**ad·her·ence** *n.* —**ad·her·ent** *n.*

**ad·he·sive** /ad'hēsiv/ ▸*adj.* able to stick fast to a surface; sticky. ▸*n.* adhesive substance. —**ad·he·sion** *n.*

**ad hoc** /'ad 'häk/ ▸*adv. & adj.* for one particular (usu. exclusive) purpose: *an ad hoc appointment.*

**a·dieu** /ə'd(y)o͞o/ ▸*interj.* good-bye.
▸*n.* (*pl.* **a·dieus** or **a·dieux**) a good-bye.

**ad in·fi·ni·tum** /ˌad infə'nītəm/ ▸*adv.* without limit; forever.

**ad·i·pose** /'adəˌpōs/ ▸*adj.* (esp. of body tissue) used for the storage of fat.

**ad·ja·cent** /ə'jāsənt/ ▸*adj.* lying near or adjoining: *adjacent rooms | adjacent to the police station.*

**ad·jec·tive** /'ajiktiv/ ▸*n.* word used to modify or describe a noun or pronoun. —**ad·jec·ti·val** *adj.*

**ad·join** /ə'join/ ▸*v.* be next to and joined with.

**ad·journ** /ə'jərn/ ▸*v.* break off (a meeting, etc.) temporarily. —**ad·journ·ment** *n.*

**ad·judge** /ə'jəj/ ▸*v.* decide judicially.

**ad·ju·di·cate** /ə'jo͞odiˌkāt/ ▸*v.*

**1** act as judge. **2** decide judicially regarding (a claim, etc.). —**ad·jud·i·ca·tion** *n.* —**ad·ju·di·ca·tive** *adj.* —**ad·ju·di·ca·tor** *n.*

**ad·junct** /ˈajəNGkt/ ▸*n.* **1** subordinate or incidental thing. **2** subordinate person, esp. one with a temporary appointment only.

**ad·just** /əˈjəst/ ▸*v.* **1** put in the correct order or position. **2** make suitable. **3** adapt or become used to: *my eyes adjusted to the darkness.* —**ad·just·a·ble** *adj.* —**ad·just·ment** *n.*

**ad·ju·tant** /ˈajətənt/ ▸*n.* **1** officer who assists superior officers. **2** assistant. —**ad·ju·tan·cy** *n.*

**ad lib** /ˈad ˈlib/ ▸*v.* (**libbed**, **lib·bing**) improvise.
▸*adj.* improvised.
▸*adv.* as one pleases.
▸*n.* something spoken or played extempore.

**ad li·tem** /ad ˈlītəm/ ▸*adj.* (esp. of a guardian) appointed to act in a lawsuit on behalf of a child or other person who is not considered capable of representing themselves.

**ad·min·is·ter** /ədˈministər/ ▸*v.* **1** manage. **2** be responsible for the implementation of (the law, justice, punishment, etc.). **3** (of a priest) perform the rites of (a sacrament, esp. the Eucharist). **4** provide; give; deliver. —**ad·min·is·tra·ble** *adj.*

**ad·min·is·tra·tion** /əd͵miniˈstrāSHən/ ▸*n.* **1** process or activity of running a business, organization, etc. **2** executive branch officials under a certain chief executive: *the Kennedy administration.* **3** action of dispensing, giving, or applying something: *administration of the oath | administration of the vaccine.* —**ad·min·is·tra·tive** *adj.*

**ad·min·is·tra·tor** /ədˈmini͵strātər/ ▸*n.* **1** manager. **2** *Law* person appointed to manage the estate of one who has died intestate.

**ad·mi·ra·ble** /ˈadmərəbəl/ ▸*adj.* **1** deserving admiration. **2** excellent. —**ad·mi·ra·bly** *adv.*

**ad·mi·ral** /ˈadmərəl/ ▸*n.* **1** commander in chief of a fleet. **2** naval officer of high rank.

**ad·mire** /ədˈmī(ə)r/ ▸*v.* **1** regard with approval, respect, or satisfaction. **2** express one's high regard for. —**ad·mi·ra·tion** *n.* —**ad·mir·er** *n.* —**ad·mir·ing** *adj.* —**ad·mir·ing·ly** *adv.*

**ad·mis·si·ble** /ədˈmisəbəl/ ▸*adj.*

**1** (of an idea or plan) worth accepting or considering. **2** *Law* allowable as evidence. —**ad·mis·si·bil·i·ty** *n.*

**ad·mis·sion** /əd'miSHən/ ▸*n.* **1** acknowledgment. **2 a** process or right of entering. **b** charge for this.

**ad·mit** /əd'mit/ ▸*v.* (**-mit·ted**, **-mit·ting**) **1** confess to be true: *I have to admit I was delighted when they left.* **2** confess to (a crime). **3** allow (a person) entrance or access. **4** (**admit of**) allow the possibility of. —**ad·mit·tance** *n.*

**ad·mit·ted·ly** /əd'mitidlē/ ▸*adv.* as an acknowledged fact.

**ad·mon·ish** /əd'mäniSH/ ▸*v.* **1** warn or reprimand firmly. **2** advise or urge. —**ad·mo·ni·tion** *n.* —**ad·mon·i·to·ry** *adj.*

**ad nau·se·am** /ad 'nôzēəm/ ▸*adv.* to an excessive or disgusting degree.

**a·do** /ə'do͞o/ ▸*n.* (*pl.* **a·dos**) fuss; busy activity; trouble; difficulty.

**a·do·be** /ə'dōbē/ ▸*n.* **1** sun-dried brick of clay and straw. **2** clay used for making this.

**ad·o·les·cent** /ˌadl'esənt/ ▸*adj.* between childhood and adulthood. ▸*n.* adolescent person. —**ad·o·les·cence** *n.*

**a·dopt** /ə'däpt/ ▸*v.* **1** legally take another's child as one's own. **2** choose to follow (a course of action, etc.). **3** take over (a name, idea, etc.). —**a·dop·tion** *n.* —**a·dop·tive** *adj.*

**a·dore** /ə'dôr/ ▸*v.* **1** regard with honor and deep affection. **2** worship as divine. —**ad·o·ra·tion** *n.*

**a·dorn** /ə'dôrn/ ▸*v.* add beauty to; decorate. —**a·dorn·ment** *n.*

**ad rem** /'ad 'rem/ ▸*adv. & adj.* relevant to what is being done or discussed at the time.

**a·dre·nal** /ə'drēnl/ ▸*adj.* **1** at or near the kidneys. **2** of the adrenal glands. ▸*n.* (also **adre·nal gland**) either of two ductless glands above the kidneys, secreting adrenaline.

**a·dren·al·ine** /ə'drenl-in/ ▸*n.* stimulant hormone produced by the adrenal glands.

**a·drift** /ə'drift/ ▸*adv. & adj.* **1** (of a boat or its passengers) floating without guidance. **2** powerless; aimless.

**a·droit** /ə'droit/ ▸*adj.* dexterous; skillful.

**ad·sci·ti·tious** /ˌadsi'tiSHəs/ ▸*adj.* forming an addition or supplement; not integral or intrinsic.

**ad·u·late** /ˈajəˌlāt/ ▶v. praise (someone) excessively or obsequiously.

**ad·u·la·tion** /ˌajəˈlāsʜən/ ▶n. excessive flattery.

**a·dult** /əˈdəlt/ ▶adj. **1** mature; grown-up. **2** of or for adults. ▶n. adult person. —**a·dult·hood** n.

**a·dul·ter·ate** /əˈdəltəˌrāt/ ▶v. debase (esp. foods) by adding other or inferior substances. ▶adj. spurious; debased; counterfeit. —**a·dul·ter·a·tion** n.

**a·dul·tery** /əˈdəlt(ə)rē/ ▶n. voluntary sexual intercourse between a married person and a person (married or not) other than his or her spouse. —**a·dul·ter·er** n. —**a·dul·ter·ous** adj.

**ad·um·brate** /ˈadəmˌbrāt; əˈdəm-/ ▶v. **1** report or represent (something) in outline. **2** foreshadow or symbolize something. **3** overshadow something.

**ad va·lo·rem** /ˌad vəˈlôrəm/ ▶adv. & adj. (of the levying of tax or customs duties) in proportion to the estimated value of the goods or transaction concerned.

**ad·vance** /ədˈvans/ ▶v. **1** move or put forward. **2 a** pay (money) before it is due. **b** lend (money). **3** promote (a person, cause, or plan). ▶n. **1** progress. **2** prepayment. **3** loan. **4** (usu. **advances**) amorous approach. **5** rise in price. ▶adj. beforehand: *advance warning.* —**ad·vance·ment** n. □ **in advance** ahead in place or time.

**ad·van·tage** /ədˈvantij/ ▶n. **1** beneficial feature. **2** benefit; profit. **3** superiority. **4** (in tennis) the next point won after deuce. ▶v. be beneficial or favorable to. —**ad·van·ta·geous** adj. □ **take advantage of 1** make good use of. **2** exploit, esp. unfairly.

**ad·vec·tion** /adˈveksʜən/ ▶n. transfer of heat or matter by the flow of a fluid, esp. horizontally in the atmosphere or the sea.

**Ad·vent** /ˈadˌvent/ ▶n. **1** season before Christmas. **2** (**advent**) important arrival.

**adven·ti·tious** /ˌadvenˈtisʜəs/ ▶adj. accidental; casual.

**ad·ven·ture** /adˈvencʜər/ ▶n. **1** unusual and exciting experience. **2** daring enterprise. —**ad·ven·tur·er** n. —**ad·ven·tur·ous** adj.

**ad·verb** /ˈadvərb/ ▶n. word or

phrase that modifies or qualifies an adjective, verb, or other adverb (e.g., *gently*, *quite*, *then*, *there*). —**ad·ver·bi·al** *adj.*

**ad·ver·sar·y** /'advər,serē/ ▸*n.* (*pl.* **-ies**) **1** enemy. **2** opponent.
▸*adj.* opposed; antagonistic. —**ad·ver·sar·i·al** *adj.*

**ad·verse** /ad'vərs/ ▸*adj.* **1** unfavorable. **2** harmful.

**ad·ver·si·ty** /ad'vərsitē/ ▸*n.* (*pl.* **-ties**) difficulties; misfortune.

**ad·ver·tise** /'advər,tīz/ ▸*v.* **1** promote (goods or services) publicly to increase sales. **2** make generally known. **3** place an advertisement: *advertise for a pastry chef.* —**ad·ver·tise·ment** *n.* —**ad·ver·tis·er** *n.*

**ad·vice** /əd'vīs/ ▸*n.* **1** recommendation about future action or behavior. **2** information given; news.

**ad·vis·a·ble** /əd'vīzəbəl/ ▸*adj.* to be recommended; sensible. —**ad·vis·a·bil·i·ty** *n.*

**ad·vise** /əd'vīz/ ▸*v.* **1** offer suggestions about the best course of action. **2** recommend. **3** inform about a fact or situation. —**ad·vis·er** or **ad·vi·sor** *n.*

**ad·vi·so·ry** /əd'vīzərē/ ▸*adj.* giving advice.
▸*n.* (*pl.* **-ries**) information, esp. warning about bad weather, etc.

**ad·vo·cate** ▸*n.* /'advəkit/ **1** person who supports or speaks in favor. **2** professional pleader in a court of justice.
▸*v.* /'advə,kāt/ **1** recommend. **2** plead for; defend. —**ad·vo·ca·cy** *n.*

**adz** /adz/ (also **adze**) ▸*n.* ax with a blade at right angles to the handle.

**ae·gis** /'ējis/ ▸*n.* protection; impregnable defense.

**ae·o·li·an** /ē'ōlēən; ā'ō-/ ▸*adj.* characterized by a sighing or moaning sound as if produced by the wind.

**aer·ate** /'e(ə)rāt/ ▸*v.* **1** charge a liquid with carbon dioxide. **2** expose to air. —**aer·a·tion** *n.*

**aer·i·al** /'e(ə)rēəl/ ▸*n.* radio or TV antenna.
▸*adj.* **1** by, in, or from the air. **2** existing, moving, or happening in the air. **3** thin as air; ethereal.

**aer·ie** /'e(ə)rē/ (also **ey·rie**) ▸*n.* **1** lofty nest of a bird of prey. **2** house, etc., perched high up.

**aer·o·bic** /ə'rōbik/ ▸*adj.* **1** existing or active only in the presence of oxygen. **2** of or relating to aerobics.

**aer·o·bics** ▶*pl. n.* vigorous exercises designed to increase the body's heart rate and oxygen intake.

**aer·o·dy·nam·ics** /ˌe(ə)rōdī-ˈnamiks/ ▶*n.* study of solid bodies moving through air.
—**aer·o·dy·nam·ic** *adj.*
—**aer·o·dy·nam·i·cal·ly** *adv.*

**aer·o·nau·tics** /ˌe(ə)rəˈnôtiks/ ▶*n.* science or practice of motion in the air. —**aer·o·nau·tic** *adj.*

**aer·o·sol** /ˈe(ə)rəˌsôl/ ▶*n.* **1** pressurized container for releasing a substance as a fine spray. **2** system of colloidal particles dispersed in a gas (e.g., fog or smoke).

**aer·o·space** /ˈe(ə)rōˌspās/ ▶*n.* **1** earth's atmosphere and outer space. **2** technology of aviation in this region.

**aes·thete** /ˈesˌTHēt/ ▶*n.* person who has or affects to have a special appreciation of art and beauty.

**aes·thet·ic** /esˈTHetik/ (also **es·thet·ic**) ▶*adj.* **1** concerned with beauty or the appreciation of beauty. **2** sensitive to beauty. ▶*n.* **1** (**aesthetics**) philosophy of the beautiful, esp. in art. **2** set of principles of good taste and the appreciation of beauty.
—**aes·thet·i·cal·ly** *adv.*
—**aes·thet·i·cism** *n.*

**aes·the·ti·cian** /ˌesTHəˈtisHən/ ▶*n.* **1** person who is knowledgeable about the nature and appreciation of beauty, esp. in art. **2** beautician.

**a·far** /əˈfär/ ▶*adv.* at or to a distance.

**af·fa·ble** /ˈafəbəl/ ▶*adj.* friendly.
—**af·fa·bil·i·ty** *n.*

**af·fair** /əˈfe(ə)r/ ▶*n.* **1** concern, business, or matter to be attended to. **2** celebrated or notorious happening. **3** amorous relationship. **4** (**affairs**) **a** ordinary pursuits of life. **b** business dealings. **c** public matters.

**af·fect** ▶*v.* /əˈfekt/ **1 a** have an effect on. **b** (of a disease, etc.) attack. **2** touch the feelings of. **3** pretend to have or feel (something): *affected a complete lack of concern.*
▶*n.* /ˈafekt/ *Psychol.* feeling or emotion. —**af·fect·ing** *adj.*
—**af·fect·ing·ly** *adv.*

**af·fec·ta·tion** /ˌafekˈtāsHən/ ▶*n.* **1** assumed or contrived manner of behavior. **2** pretense.

**af·fect·ed** /əˈfektid/ ▸*adj.*
1 influenced or touched.
2 artificial or pretentious.
3 disposed; inclined.

**af·fec·tion** /əˈfekSHən/ ▸*n.*
feeling of fondness or liking.

**af·fec·tion·ate** /əˈfekSHənit/
▸*adj.* loving; tender; showing
love or tenderness.

**af·fi·da·vit** /ˌafiˈdāvit/ ▸*n.*
written statement confirmed
under oath, for use as evidence
in court.

**af·fil·i·ate** ▸*v.* /əˈfilēˌāt/ connect
or be connected with a larger
organization.
▸*n.* /əˈfilēit/ affiliated person or
organization. —**af·fil·i·a·tion** *n.*

**af·fin·i·ty** /əˈfinitē/ ▸*n.* (*pl.* **-ties**)
1 liking for or attraction to a
person or thing. 2 relationship,
esp. by marriage. 3 similarity of
character suggesting a
relationship.

**af·firm** /əˈfərm/ ▸*v.* assert
strongly; state as a fact.
—**af·fir·ma·tion** *n.*
—**af·firm·a·to·ry** *adj.*

**af·fir·ma·tive** /əˈfərmətiv/ ▸*adj.*
1 affirming; asserting that a
thing is so. 2 (of a vote)
expressing approval.
▸*n.* 1 affirmative statement,
reply, or word. 2 (**the**

affirmative) positive or affirming
position.
□ **affirmative action** action
favoring minorities, etc., who
have been discriminated against.

**af·fix** ▸*v.* /əˈfiks/ 1 attach; fasten.
2 add in writing.
▸*n.* /ˈafiks/ 1 addition. 2 *Gram.*
prefix or suffix.

**af·fla·tus** /əˈflātəs/ ▸*n.* divine
creative impulse or inspiration.

**af·flict** /əˈflikt/ ▸*v.* inflict bodily
or mental suffering on.
—**af·flic·tion** *n.*

**af·flu·ent** /ˈaflo͞oənt/ ▸*adj.*
wealthy; rich. —**af·flu·ence** *n.*

**af·flux** /ˈaˌfləks/ ▸*n.* flow of
something, esp. water or air.

**af·ford** /əˈfôrd/ ▸*v.* 1 have
enough money, means, time,
etc., for; be able to spare. 2 yield
a supply of. —**af·ford·a·ble** *adj.*
—**af·ford·a·bil·i·ty** *n.*

**af·fray** /əˈfrā/ ▸*n.* loud public
brawl.

**af·front** /əˈfrənt/ ▸*n.* open insult.
▸*v.* 1 insult openly. 2 offend the
modesty or self respect of: *she
was affronted by his familiarity.*

**Af·ghan** /ˈafˌgan/ ▸*n.* 1 **a** native
or inhabitant of Afghanistan.
**b** person of Afghan descent.
2 official language of

Afghanistan. **3** (**afghan**) knitted or crocheted shawl or throw.

▸*adj.* of or relating to Afghanistan or its people or language.

□ **Afghan hound** tall hunting dog with long silky hair.

**a·fi·ci·o·na·do** /əˌfisн(ē)əˈnädō; əˌfisyə-/ ▸*n.* (*pl.* **-dos**) person who is very knowledgeable and enthusiastic about an activity, subject, or pastime.

**a·field** /əˈfēld/ ▸*adv.* **1** away from home. **2** to or on a field. **3** astray.

**a·flame** /əˈflām/ ▸*adv. & adj.* in flames.

**a·float** /əˈflōt/ ▸*adv. & adj.* **1** floating in water or on air. **2** at sea; on board ship.

**a·foot** /əˈfŏŏt/ ▸*adv. & adj.* **1** in operation; progressing. **2** astir; on the move.

**a·fraid** /əˈfrād/ ▸*adj.* alarmed; frightened.

**a·fresh** /əˈfresн/ ▸*adv.* anew; with a fresh beginning.

**Af·ri·can** /ˈafrikən/ ▸*n.* **1** native of Africa (esp. a black person). **2** person of African descent.

▸*adj.* of or relating to Africa.

**Af·ri·can-A·mer·i·can** ▸*n.* American citizen of black African origin or descent.

▸*adj.* of or relating to American blacks or their culture.

**Af·ri·can vi·o·let** ▸*n.* houseplant with heart-shaped velvety leaves and blue, purple, or pink flowers.

**Af·ri·kaans** /ˌafrəˈkänz/ ▸*n.* language derived from Dutch, spoken in S. Africa.

**Af·ri·ka·ner** /ˌafrəˈkänər/ ▸*n.* Afrikaans-speaking white person in S. Africa.

**Afro-** ▸*comb. form* African: *Afro-Asian.*

**aft** /aft/ ▸*adv.* at or toward the stern of a ship or tail of an aircraft.

**af·ter** /ˈaftər/ ▸*prep.* **1 a** following in time; later than. **b** in specifying time. **2** in view of. **3** in spite of: *after all my efforts I'm no better off.* **4** behind: *shut the door after you.* **5** in pursuit or quest of. **6** about; concerning. **7** in allusion to: *named after his uncle.* **8** in imitation of. **9** next in importance to. **10** according to: *after a fashion.*

▸*conj.* later than.

▸*adv.* **1** later in time: *soon after.* **2** behind.

**af·ter·birth** ▸*n.* placenta and fetal membranes discharged from the womb after childbirth.

**af·ter·care** ▸*n.* care of a patient after a stay in the hospital or of a person on release from prison.

**af·ter·ef·fect** ▸*n.* delayed effect following an accident, trauma, etc.

**af·ter·life** ▸*n.* **1** life after death. **2** life at a later time.

**af·ter·math** ▸*n.* consequences; aftereffects.

**af·ter·noon** ▸*n.* time from noon to evening.

**af·ter·thought** ▸*n.* thing thought of or added later.

**af·ter·ward** /'aftərwərd/ (also **af·ter·wards**) ▸*adv.* later; subsequently.

**a·gain** /ə'gen/ ▸*adv.* **1** another time; once more. **2** in addition. **3** further; besides. **4** on the other hand.

**a·gainst** /ə'genst/ ▸*prep.* **1** in opposition to: *arson is against the law.* **2** into collision or in contact with. **3** to the disadvantage of. **4** in contrast to.

**a·gape** /ə'gāp/ ▸*adv. & adj.* gaping; open-mouthed.

**ag·ate** /'agit/ ▸*n.* **1** an ornamental stone streaked with bands of color. **2** colored toy marble resembling this.

**age** /āj/ ▸*n.* **1 a** length of time that a person or thing has existed. **b** particular point in or part of one's life. **2** distinct historical or geological period. **3** old age. ▸*v.* (**ag·ing, age·ing**) **1** show signs of advancing age. **2** grow old. **3** mature.

**-age** /ij/ ▸*suffix* forming nouns denoting: **1** action: *breakage.* **2** condition: *bondage.* **3** aggregate or number of: *acreage.* **4** cost: *postage.* **5** product of an action: *wreckage.* **6** place; abode: *anchorage | orphanage.*

**a·ged** ▸*adj.* **1** /ājd/ **a** of the age of. **b** allowed to reach maturity or ripeness in storage. **2** /'ājid/ old.

**age·ism** /'āj,izəm/ (also **ag·ism**) ▸*n.* prejudice or discrimination on the grounds of age. —**age·ist** *adj. & n.*

**age·less** ▸*adj.* **1** never growing or appearing old or outmoded. **2** eternal; timeless.

**a·gen·cy** /'ājənsē/ ▸*n.* (*pl.* **-cies**) **1** business or establishment of an agent. **2** intervention. **3** governmental department.

**a·gen·da** /ə'jendə/ ▸*n.* **1** list of

items of business to be considered at a meeting. **2** things to be done. **3** underlying motivation.

**a·gent** /ˈājənt/ ▸n. **1 a** a person who acts for another in business, etc. **b** a spy. **2 a** a person or thing that exerts power or produces an effect. **b** cause of a natural force or effect on matter.

**ag·glom·er·ate** ▸v. /əˈglämə-ˌrāt/ **1** collect into a mass. **2** accumulate in a disorderly way.
▸n. /əˈglämərit/ **1** mass or collection of things. **2** mass of large volcanic fragments bonded under heat.
▸adj. /əˈglämərit/ collected into a mass.

**ag·glu·ti·na·tive** /əˈgloōtn-ətiv/ ▸adj. (of a language) forming words predominantly by combining simple words or parts of words, rather than by inflection or by using isolated elements. Examples include Hungarian, Turkish, Korean, and Swahili.

**ag·gran·dize** /əˈgranˌdīz/ ▸v. **1** increase the power, rank, or wealth of (a person or nation). **2** cause to appear greater than is the case. **—ag·gran·dize·ment** n.

**ag·gra·vate** /ˈagrəˌvāt/ ▸v. **1** increase the seriousness of (an illness, offense, etc.). **2** inf. annoy; exasperate (a person). **—ag·gra·va·tion** n.

**ag·gre·gate** /ˈagrəgit/ ▸n. **1** total amount assembled. **2** crushed stone, gravel, etc., used in making concrete. **3** mass of minerals formed into solid rock.
▸adj. **1** (of disparate elements) collected into one mass. **2** constituted by the collection of many units into one body.
▸v. combine into one mass.
**—ag·gre·ga·tion** n.
**—ag·gre·ga·tive** adj.

**ag·gres·sion** /əˈgreSHən/ ▸n. **1** hostile or violent behavior. **2** unprovoked attack. **3** self-assertiveness; forcefulness.
**—ag·gres·sor** n.

**ag·gres·sive** /əˈgresiv/ ▸adj. **1** (of a person) **a** given to aggression; hostile. **b** forceful; self-assertive. **2** (of an act) offensive; hostile.

**ag·grieved** /əˈgrēvd/ ▸adj. having a grievance.

**a·ghast** /əˈgast/ ▸adj. filled with dismay or consternation.

**ag·ile** /ˈajəl/ ▸adj. quick-moving; nimble; active. **—a·gil·i·ty** n.

**ag·i·tate** /ˈajiˌtāt/ ▸v. **1** disturb

or excite (a person or feelings). **2** shake or move, esp. briskly. —**ag·i·ta·tion** *n.* —**ag·i·ta·tor** *n.*

**ag·it·prop** /'ajit‚präp/ ▸*n.* political (originally communist) propaganda, esp. in art or literature.

**ag·let** /'aglit/ ▸*n.* metal or plastic tube fixed tightly around each end of a shoelace.

**ag·nate** /'ag‚nāt/ ▸*adj.* descended from the same male ancestor as a specified or implied subject, esp. through the male line.

**ag·nos·tic** /ag'nästik/ ▸*n.* person who believes that the existence or nature of God cannot be proven. ▸*adj.* of this theory or belief. —**ag·nos·ti·cism** *n.*

**a·go** /ə'gō/ ▸*adv.* earlier; before the present.

**a·gog** /ə'gäg/ ▸*adv.* eagerly; expectantly. ▸*adj.* eager; expectant.

**a·go·go** /ə'gōgō/ ▸*n.* small bell made of two metal cones, used as a percussion instrument in African and Latin music.

**ag·o·nize** /'agə‚nīz/ ▸*v.* suffer or cause agony to. —**ag·o·niz·ing·ly** *adv.*

**ag·o·ny** /'agənē/ ▸*n.* (*pl.* **-nies**) extreme mental or physical suffering.

**ag·o·ra·pho·bi·a** /‚agərə'fōbēə/ ▸*n.* abnormal fear of open spaces or public places. —**ag·o·ra·pho·bic** *adj. & n.*

**a·grar·i·an** /ə'gre(ə)rēən/ ▸*adj.* **1** of the land or its cultivation. **2** relating to the ownership of land.

**a·gree** /ə'grē/ ▸*v.* (**-greed, -gree·ing**) **1** hold a similar opinion. **2** consent. **3** become or be in harmony. **4** *Gram.* have the same number, gender, case, or person as.

**a·gree·a·ble** ▸*adj.* **1** pleasing. **2** willing to agree.

**a·gree·ment** ▸*n.* **1** act of agreeing. **2** mutual understanding. **3** arrangement or contract.

**ag·ri·busi·ness** /'agrə‚biznis/ ▸*n.* large-scale farming and related commerce, e.g., food processing, etc.

**ag·ri·cul·ture** /'agri‚kəlcHər/ ▸*n.* cultivating the soil and rearing animals. —**ag·ri·cul·tur·al** *adj.* —**ag·ri·cul·tur·al·ly** *adv.*

**a·gron·o·my** /ə'gränəmē/ ▸*n.* science of soil management and crop production. —**ag·ro·nom·ic** *adj.* —**a·gron·o·mist** *n.*

**a·ground** /əˈground/ ▸*adj. & adv.* (of a ship) on or on to the bottom of shallow water: *run aground.*

**ah** /ä/ ▸*interj.* expressing surprise, pleasure, realization, etc.

**a·head** /əˈhed/ ▸*adv.* **1** further forward in space or time. **2** in the lead.

**a·him·sa** /əˈhimˌsä/ ▸*n.* (in the Hindu, Buddhist, and Jain tradition) the principle of nonviolence toward all living things.

**a·hoy** /əˈhoi/ ▸*interj.* call used by sailors in hailing.

**aid** /ād/ ▸*n.* **1** help. **2** financial or material help. **3** person or thing that helps.
▸*v.* **1** help. **2** promote or encourage.

**aide** /ād/ ▸*n.* **1** aide-de-camp. **2** assistant.

**aide-de-camp** /ˈād də ˈkamp/ ▸*n.* (*pl.* **aides-de-camp** *pronunc.* same) officer acting as a confidential assistant to a senior officer.

**aide-me·moire** /ˈād memˈwär/ ▸*n.* (*pl.* **aides-me·moires** or **aides-me·moire** *pronunc.* same) aid to the memory, esp. a book or document.

**AIDS** /ādz/ ▸*n.* acquired immune deficiency syndrome, a viral disorder marked by severe loss of resistance to infection.
☐ **AIDS-related complex** symptoms of a person affected with the AIDS virus who has not developed the disease.

**ail** /āl/ ▸*v.* make or be ill: *her father has been ailing for more than a year.*

**ai·le·ron** /ˈāləˌrän/ ▸*n.* hinged surface in the trailing edge of an airplane wing, used to control lateral balance, etc.

**ail·ment** /ˈālmənt/ ▸*n.* minor or chronic illness.

**aim** /ām/ ▸*v.* **1** direct or point (a weapon, blow, remark, action, etc.) at something or someone. **2** intend to achieve: *we aim to provide excellent service.*
▸*n.* **1** purpose or object. **2** directing of a weapon, etc., at an object. —**aim·less** *adj.* —**aim·less·ly** *adv.*
☐ **take aim** direct a weapon, etc., at an object.

**ain't** /ānt/ ▸*contr. inf.* **1** am not; are not; is not. **2** has not; have not.

**air** /e(ə)r/ ▸*n.* **1** invisible gaseous mixture, mainly of oxygen and nitrogen, surrounding the earth. **2** this substance as needed for breathing: *get some fresh air*. **3** free space above the surface of the earth. **4** (**air of**) distinctive impression given by something or someone. **5** (**airs**) pretentious or condescending manner: *put on airs*. **6** tune.

▶*v.* **1** expose (a room, etc.) to the open air; ventilate. **2** express publicly. **3** broadcast. —**air·less** *adj.*

**air bag** ▶*n.* safety device that fills with nitrogen on impact to protect the occupants of a vehicle in a collision.

**air·borne** ▶*adj.* **1** transported by air. **2** (of aircraft) in the air after taking off.

**air·brush** /ˈe(ə)r,brəSH/ ▶*n.* artist's device for spraying paint by means of compressed air.

▶*v.* alter or conceal (a photograph or a detail in one) using an airbrush.

**air con·di·tion·ing** ▶*n.* system for regulating the humidity, ventilation, and temperature in a building. —**air-con·di·tioned** *adj.* —**air con·dition·er** *n.*

**air·craft** ▶*n.* (*pl.* same) machine capable of flight, esp. an airplane or helicopter.

□ **aircraft carrier** warship that carries and serves as a base for airplanes.

**air force** ▶*n.* branch of the armed forces concerned with fighting or defense in the air.

**air·lift** ▶*n.* emergency transport of supplies by air.

▶*v.* transport in this way.

**air·line** ▶*n.* organization providing a regular public service of air transport on one or more routes.

**air·lin·er** ▶*n.* passenger aircraft, esp. a large one.

**air·mail** ▶*n.* **1** system of transporting mail by air. **2** mail carried by air.

**air·man** ▶*n.* (*pl.* **-men**) **1** pilot or member of the crew of an aircraft. **2** member of the U.S.A.F. below commissioned rank.

**air·plane** ▶*n.* powered heavier-than-air flying vehicle with fixed wings.

**air·port** ▶*n.* complex of runways and buildings for the takeoff, landing, and maintenance of civil aircraft, with facilities for passengers.

**air raid** ▶*n.* attack by aircraft.

**air ri·fle** ▶*n.* rifle that fires BBs using compressed air.

**air·ship** ▸*n.* power-driven aircraft lighter than air.

**air·space** ▸*n.* air above a country and subject to its jurisdiction.

**air·tight** ▸*adj.* **1** not allowing air to pass through. **2** having no visible or apparent weaknesses: *an airtight alibi.*

**air·waves** ▸*pl. n.* radio waves used in broadcasting.

**air·y** /ˈe(ə)rē/ ▸*adj.* (-i·er, -i·est) **1** well ventilated; breezy. **2** flippant; superficial. **3** graceful; delicate. —**air·i·ly** *adv.* —**air·i·ness** *n.*

**aisle** /īl/ ▸*n.* **1** passage between rows of pews, seats, etc. **2** passageway in a supermarket, etc.

**a·jar** /əˈjär/ ▸*adv. & adj.* (of a door) slightly open.

**AK** ▸*abbr.* Alaska (in official postal use).

**a.k.a.** ▸*abbr.* also known as.

**a·kim·bo** /əˈkimbō/ ▸*adj. & adv.* (of the arms) with hands on the hips and elbows turned outwards.

**a·kin** /əˈkin/ ▸*adj.* of similar or kindred character: *a feeling akin to joy.*

**a·ki·ne·sia** /ˌākiˈnēzнə; ˌākī-/ ▸*n.* loss or impairment of the power of voluntary movement.

**AL** ▸*abbr.* Alabama (in official postal use).

**Al** ▸*symb. Chem.* aluminum.

**-al** /əl/ ▸*suffix* **1** forming adjectives meaning 'relating to; of the kind of': **a** from Latin or Greek words: *central* | *tropical.* **b** from English nouns: *tidal.* **2** forming nouns, esp. of verbal action: *arrival* | *trial.*

**Ala.** ▸*abbr.* Alabama.

**à la** /ˈä ˌlä/ ▸*prep.* after the manner of: *à la russe.*

**al·a·bas·ter** /ˈaləˌbastər/ ▸*n.* translucent usu. white form of gypsum, often carved. ▸*adj.* **1** of alabaster. **2** white or smooth.

**à la carte** /kärt/ ▸*adv. & adj.* ordered as separately priced item(s) from a menu, not as part of a set meal.

**a·lac·ri·ty** /əˈlakritē/ ▸*n.* briskness or cheerful readiness.

**à la mode** ▸*adv. & adj.* **1** in fashion. **2** served with ice cream.

**a·larm** /əˈlärm/ ▸*n.* **1** warning of danger, etc. **2** warning sound or device. **3** apprehension. ▸*v.* **1** frighten or disturb. **2** warn.

**a·larm clock** ▶*n.* clock that rings at a set time.

**Alas.** ▶*abbr.* Alaska.

**a·las** /əˈlas/ ▶*interj.* expression of grief, pity, or concern.

**al·ba·tross** /ˈalbəˌtrôs/ ▶*n.* **1** long-winged, web-footed, stout-bodied sea bird. **2** source of frustration or guilt.

**al·be·do** /alˈbēdō/ ▶*n.* (*pl.* **-dos**) proportion of the incident light or radiation that is reflected by a surface, typically that of a planet or moon.

**al·be·it** /ôlˈbēit/ ▶*conj.* though.

**al·bi·no** /alˈbīnō/ ▶*n.* (*pl.* **-nos**) **1** person or animal lacking pigment in the skin and hair (which are white), and the eyes (usu. pink). **2** plant lacking normal coloring.

**al·bum** /ˈalbəm/ ▶*n.* **1** blank book for photographs, stamps, etc. **2** long-playing phonograph, audio cassette, or compact disc recording.

**al·bu·men** /alˈbyo͞omən/ ▶*n.* egg white.

**al·bu·min** /alˈbyo͞omən/ ▶*n.* *Biochem.* water-soluble proteins found in egg white, milk, blood, etc. **—al·bu·min·ous** *adj.*

**al·che·my** /ˈalkəmē/ ▶*n.* (*pl.* **-mies**) medieval forerunner of chemistry, esp. attempts to turn base metals into gold. **—al·che·mist** *n.*

**al·co·hol** /ˈalkəˌhôl/ ▶*n.* **1** colorless volatile flammable liquid forming the intoxicating element in wine, beer, liquor, etc., and also used as a solvent, as fuel, etc. **2** any liquor containing this. **3** any of a large class of organic compounds that contain one or more hydroxyl groups attached to carbon atoms.

**al·co·hol·ic** ▶*adj.* of, relating to, containing, or caused by alcohol. ▶*n.* person suffering from alcoholism.

**al·co·hol·ism** ▶*n.* addiction to the consumption of alcoholic liquor; condition resulting from this.

**al·cove** /ˈalˌkōv/ ▶*n.* recess, esp. in the wall of a room.

**al den·te** /äl ˈdentā; al/ ▶*adj.* & *adv.* (of food, typically pasta) cooked so as to be still firm when bitten.

**al·der** /ˈôldər/ ▶*n.* tree related to the birch.

**al·der·man** ▶*n.* (*pl.* **-men**) elected municipal official serving on the governing council of a city.

**ale** /āl/ ▸*n.* type of beer with bitter flavor and higher alcoholic content.

**a·lert** /ə'lərt/ ▸*adj.* **1** watchful or vigilant. **2** quick (esp. of mental faculties); attentive.
▸*n.* **1** alarm. **2** state or period of special vigilance.
▸*v.* warn.
□ **on the alert** vigilant.

**a·lex·i·a** /ə'leksēə/ ▸*n.* inability to see words or to read, caused by a defect of the brain.

**al·fal·fa** /al'falfə/ ▸*n.* cloverlike plant used for fodder.

**al·fres·co** /al'freskō/ ▸*adv. & adj.* in the open air.

**al·gae** /'aljē/ ▸*n.* (*sing.* **al·ga**) nonflowering stemless water plants, esp. seaweed and phytoplankton. —**al·gal** *adj.* —**al·goid** *adj.*

**al·ge·bra** /'aljəbrə/ ▸*n.* branch of mathematics that uses letters, etc., to represent numbers and quantities. —**al·ge·bra·ic** *adj.*

**Al·gon·qui·an** /al'gäNGk(w)ēən/ ▸*n.* any of the languages or dialects used by the Algonquin peoples, native to eastern N. America.

**al·go·rithm** /'algə,riᴛʜəm/ ▸*n. Math.* process or set of rules used for calculation or problem-solving, esp. with a computer. —**al·go·rith·mic** *adj.*

**a·li·as** /'ālēəs/ ▸*adv.* also named or known as.
▸*n.* false or assumed name.

**al·i·bi** /'alə,bī/ ▸*n.* (*pl.* **-bis**) **1** claim or proof that when an alleged act took place one was elsewhere. **2** excuse.
▸*v.* (**-bis**, **-bied**, **-bi·ing**) *inf.* provide an alibi or offer an excuse for (a person).

**al·ien** /'ālyən/ ▸*adj.* **1** belonging to a foreign country. **2 a** unfamiliar; unacceptable or repugnant. **b** different or separated. **3** of or relating to beings supposedly from other worlds.
▸*n.* **1** foreigner, esp. one who is not a citizen of the country where he or she is living. **2** being supposedly from another world.

**al·ien·ate** /'ālēə,nāt/ ▸*v.* cause (a person) to become unfriendly or hostile. —**al·ien·a·tion** *n.*

**a·light** /ə'līt/ ▸*v.* **1** descend from a horse or a vehicle. **2** settle; come to earth from the air.
▸*adj.* **1** on fire. **2** lit up; excited.

**a·lign** /ə'līn/ ▸*v.* **1** put or bring into line. **2** bring (oneself, etc.) into agreement or alliance with

(a cause, party, etc.).
—**a·lign·ment** *n.*

**a·like** /ə'līk/ ▸*adj.* similar; like.
▸*adv.* in a similar way.

**al·i·men·ta·ry** /ˌalə'men(ə)rē/
▸*adj.* of or providing
nourishment or sustenance.
—**al·i·men·ta·tion** *n.*
□ **alimentary canal** passage along
which food is passed during
digestion.

**al·i·mo·ny** /'alə,mōnē/ ▸*n.*
money payable to a spouse after
divorce or legal separation.

**a·live** /ə'līv/ ▸*adj.* **1** living; not
dead. **2 a** (of a thing) existing;
continuing. **b** under discussion.
**3** lively; active. **4** (**alive to**) aware
of; responsive to: *always alive to
new ideas.* **5** (**alive with**)
swarming or teeming with: *the
area was alive with mosquitoes.*
—**a·live·ness** *n.*

**al·ka·li** /'alkə,lī/ ▸*n.* (*pl.* **-lis**)
chemical compound that reacts
with or neutralizes acids.
—**al·ka·line** *adj.* —**al·ka·lin·i·ty** *n.*

**al·ka·line** /'alkəlin; -,līn/ ▸*adj.*
having the properties of an
alkali, or containing alkali;
having a pH greater than 7.

**al·ka·loid** /'alkə,loid/ ▸*n.*
nitrogenous organic compound
of plant origin, e.g., morphine,
quinine.

**all** /ôl/ ▸*adj.* **1** whole amount,
quantity, or extent of. **2** any
whatever: *beyond all doubt.*
**3** greatest possible: *with all speed.*
▸*n.* the whole of one's
possessions, energy, or interest.
▸*adv.* used for emphasis:
completely.
□ **all but** very nearly: *it was all but
impossible.* □ **all in all** everything
considered. □ **all right**
**1** satisfactory; in good condition.
**2** satisfactorily; as desired.

**Al·lah** /'älə/ ▸*n.* name of God in
Islam.

**al·lay** /ə'lā/ ▸*v.* diminish (fear,
suspicion, etc.).

**al·lege** /ə'lej/ ▸*v.* declare, esp.
without proof. —**al·leged** *adj.*
—**al·leg·ed·ly** *adv.*

**al·le·giance** /ə'lējəns/ ▸*n.*
**1** loyalty (to a person or cause,
etc.). **2** the duty of a subject to
his or her government.

**al·le·go·ry** /'alə,gôrē/ ▸*n.* (*pl.*
**-ries**) story, etc., whose
characters are represented
symbolically.

**al·le·gro** /ə'legrō/ ▸*adv. & adj.*
*Mus.* in a brisk tempo.
▸*n.* (*pl.* **-gros**) such a passage or
movement.

**al·lele** /ə'lēl/ ▶n. one of two or more alternative forms of a gene that arise by mutation and are found at the same place on a chromosome.

**al·le·lu·ia** /ˌalə'lōōyə/ (also **hal·le·lu·jah**) ▶interj. God be praised.
▶n. praise to God.

**al·ler·gen** /'alərjən/ ▶n. any substance that causes an allergic reaction. —**al·ler·gen·ic** adj.

**al·ler·gy** /'alərjē/ ▶n. (pl. **-gies**) adverse reaction to certain substances, as particular foods, pollen, fur, or dust. —**al·ler·gic** adj. —**al·ler·gist** n.

**al·le·vi·ate** /ə'lēvē ̩āt/ ▶v. lessen or make less severe (pain, suffering, etc.). —**al·le·vi·a·tive** adj. —**al·le·vi·a·tion** n.

**al·ley** /'alē/ ▶n. (pl. **-leys**) **1** narrow streetlike passageway, esp. between or behind buildings. **2** place for bowling, etc.

**al·li·ance** /ə'līəns/ ▶n. **1** union or agreement to cooperate, esp. of nations by treaty or families by marriage. **2** the parties involved.

**al·lied** /ə'līd/ ▶adj. **1 a** associated in an alliance. **b** (**Allied**) of or relating to the U.S. and its allies in World War I and World War II. **2** connected or related.

**al·li·ga·tor** /'ali ̩gātər/ ▶n. large reptile of the crocodile family native to the Americas and China, with a head broader and shorter than that of the crocodile.

**al·lit·er·a·tion** /ə ̩litə'rāsнən/ ▶n. occurrence of the same letter or sound at the beginning of adjacent or closely connected words (e.g., *calm, cool, and collected*). —**al·lit·er·ate** v. —**al·lit·er·a·tive** adj.

**al·lo·cate** /'alə ̩kāt/ ▶v. assign, apportion, or devote to (a purpose, person, or place). —**al·lo·ca·tion** n.

**al·lot** /ə'lät/ ▶v. (**-lot·ted, -lot·ting**) apportion or distribute to (a person) as a share or task. —**al·lot·ment** n.

**al·low** /ə'lou/ ▶v. **1** permit. **2** provide or set aside for a purpose. **3** admit; concede. —**al·low·a·ble** adj.

**al·low·ance** /ə'louəns/ ▶n. **1** amount allowed. **2** sum of money paid regularly.
□ **make allowances** be tolerant or lenient.

**al·loy** /'a ̩loi/ ▶n. **1** mixture of two or more metals. **2** inferior metal mixed esp. with gold or silver.

▶*v.* **1** mix (metals). **2** moderate.

**All Saints' Day** ▶*n.* Christian festival honoring the saints, celebrated November 1.

**all·spice** ▶*n.* aromatic spice obtained from the ground berry of a tropical American tree.

**al·lude** /ə'lood/ ▶*v.* refer, esp. indirectly, covertly, or briefly to. —**al·lu·sion** *n.*

**al·lure** /ə'loor/ ▶*n.* attractiveness; personal charm; fascination.

**al·lu·vi·um** /ə'loovēəm/ ▶*n.* (*pl.* **-vi·ums** or **-vi·a**) deposit of usu. fine fertile soil left behind by a flood. —**al·lu·vi·al** *adj.*

**al·ly** ▶*n.* /'alī/ (*pl.* **-lies**)
**1** government formally cooperating or united with another, esp. by a treaty.
**2** person or organization that cooperates with or helps another.
▶*v.* /ə'lī/ (**-lied**) combine or unite in alliance.

**-ally** /əlē/ ▶*suffix* forming adverbs from adjectives in *-al*.

**al·ma ma·ter** /'älmə 'mätər/ (also **Al·ma Ma·ter**) ▶*n.*
**1** university, school, or college one attends or attended.
**2** official school anthem or song.

**al·ma·nac** /'ôlmə,nak/ ▶*n.* calendar, usu. with astronomical data and other reference information.

**al·might·y** /ôl'mītē/ ▶*adj.*
**1** having complete power; omnipotent. **2** (**the Al·might·y**) God.

**al·mond** /'ämənd/ ▶*n.* nutlike seed (kernel) of a fruit related to the peach and plum.

**al·most** /'ôlmōst/ ▶*adv.* all but; very nearly.

**alms** /ämz/ ▶*pl. n.* charitable donation of money or food to the poor.

**a·loft** /ə'lôft/ ▶*adj. & adv.* **1** high up; overhead. **2** upwards.

**a·lo·ha** /ə'lō,hä/ ▶*interj.* Hawaiian salutation at meeting or parting.

**a·lone** /ə'lōn/ ▶*adj. & adv.*
**1** having no one else present.
**2** only; exclusively.

**a·long** /ə'lôNG/ ▶*prep.* **1** from one end to the other end of.
**2** on, beside, or through any part of the length of.
▶*adv.* **1** onward. **2** arriving.
**3** with oneself or others.

**a·long·side** ▶*adv.* at or to the side.
▶*prep.* close to the side of.

**a·loof** /ə'loof/ ▶*adj.* distant; unsympathetic.

▶*adv.* away; apart. —**a·loof·ness** *n.*

**a·loud** /ə'loud/ ▶*adv.* audibly; not silently or in a whisper.

**al·pac·a** /al'pakə/ ▶*n.* **1** S. American mammal related to the llama, with long shaggy hair. **2** wool from the animal.

**al·pha** /'alfə/ ▶*n.* **1** first letter of the Greek alphabet (A, α). **2** beginning.
□ **alpha and omega** beginning and end.

**al·pha·bet** /'alfə,bet/ ▶*n.* set of letters used in writing a language. —**al·pha·bet·i·cal** or **al·pha·bet·ic** *adj.* —**al·pha·bet·ize** *v.*

**al·pha·nu·mer·ic** /,alfən(y)ōō-'merik/ (also **al·pha·nu·mer·i·cal**) ▶*adj.* containing both alphabetical and numerical symbols.

**al·pine** /'al,pīn/ ▶*adj.* **1** of, relating to, or found in high mountains. **2** (**Alpine**) of or relating to the Alps.

**al·read·y** /ôl'redē/ ▶*adv.* **1** before the time in question. **2** as early or as soon as this.

**al·so** /'ôlsō/ ▶*adv.* in addition; likewise; besides.
□ **also-ran 1** one who does not win a competition. **2** undistinguished person.

**alt.** ▶*abbr.* **1** alternate. **2** altimeter. **3** altitude.

**al·tar** /'ôltər/ ▶*n.* **1** table or flat block for sacrifice or offering to a deity. **2** raised surface or table used in a Christian service.

**al·ter** /'ôltər/ ▶*v.* **1** make or become different; change. **2** castrate or spay. —**al·ter·a·tion** *n.*

**al·ter·ca·tion** /,ôltər'kāsHən/ ▶*n.* noisy dispute.

**al·ter e·go** ▶*n.* **1** intimate and trusted friend. **2** person's secondary or alternative personality.

**al·ter·nate** ▶*v.* /'ôltər,nāt/ **1** (of two things) succeed each other in turn. **2** change repeatedly (between two conditions). ▶*adj.* /'ôltərnit/ **1** every other. **2** (of things of two kinds) each following and succeeded by one of the other kind. ▶*n.* /'ôltərnit/ alternative; deputy or substitute. —**al·ter·nate·ly** *adv.* —**al·ter·na·tion** *n.*
□ **alternating current** electric current that reverses its direction at regular intervals.

**al·ter·na·tive** /ôl'tərnətiv/ ▶*adj.* **1** available or usable instead of another. **2** unconventional. ▶*n.* **1** any of two or more

possibilities. **2** choice.
—**al·ter·na·tive·ly** adv.

**al·ter·na·tor** /'ôltər,nātər/ ▸n. generator that produces an alternating current.

**al·though** /ôl'тнō/ ▸conj. despite the fact that; even though.

**al·tim·e·ter** /al'timitər/ ▸n. instrument for showing height above sea or ground level.

**al·ti·tude** /'alti,t(y)ōod/ ▸n. height of an object in relation to a given point, esp. sea level or the horizon.

**al·to** /'altō/ ▸n. (pl. **-tos**) **1** lowest female singing voice; contralto. **2** instrument pitched next below a soprano of its type: alto saxophone.

**al·to·geth·er** /,ôltə'geтнər/ ▸adv. **1** totally; completely. **2** on the whole. **3** in total.

**al·tru·ism** /'altrōo,izəm/ ▸n. unselfishness as a principle of action. —**al·tru·ist** n. —**al·tru·is·tic** adj.

**al·um** /'aləm/ ▸n. sulfate of aluminum and potassium.

**a·lu·mi·num** /ə'lōominəm/ ▸n. silvery light and malleable metallic element. (Symb.: **Al**)

**a·lum·nus** /ə'ləmnəs/ ▸n. (pl. **-ni**; fem. **-na**, pl. **-nae**) former pupil or

student of a particular school, college, or university.

**al·ways** /'ôl,wāz/ ▸adv. at all times; on all occasions.

**Alz·hei·mer's dis·ease** /'älts-,hīmərz/ ▸n. brain disorder causing premature senility.

**AM** ▸abbr. **1** amplitude modulation. **2** Master of Arts.

**Am** ▸symb. Chem. americium.

**am** /am/ ▸1st person sing. present of **BE**.

**a.m.** (also **A.M.** or **AM**) ▸abbr. ante meridiem; between midnight and noon.

**AMA** ▸abbr. American Medical Association.

**a·mal·gam** /ə'malgəm/ ▸n. **1** mixture or blend. **2** alloy of mercury with one or more other metals.

**a·mal·ga·mate** /ə'malgə,māt/ ▸v. combine or unite. —**a·mal·ga·ma·tion** n.

**am·a·ryl·lis** /,amə'rilis/ ▸n. bulbous lilylike plant with white, pink, or red flowers.

**a·mass** /ə'mas/ ▸v. gather or heap together.

**am·a·teur** /'amə,снōor/ ▸n. **1** person who engages in a pursuit as a pastime rather than

a profession. **2** person who does something unskillfully.
▶*adj.* for or done by amateurs; amateurish; unskillful.
—**am·a·teur·ish** *adj.*

**am·a·to·ry** /ˈaməˌtôrē/ ▶*adj.* relating to sexual love or desire.

**a·maze** /əˈmāz/ ▶*v.* surprise greatly; overwhelm with wonder. —**a·maze·ment** *n.*
—**a·maz·ing** *adj.*

**Am·a·zon** /ˈaməˌzän/ ▶*n.* **1** female warrior of a mythical race. **2** (**amazon**) tall, strong, or athletic woman.

**am·bas·sa·dor** /amˈbasədər/ ▶*n.* **1** accredited diplomat sent by a nation as its representative in a foreign country. **2** representative or promoter.
—**am·bas·sa·do·ri·al** *adj.*
—**am·bas·sa·dor·ship** *n.*

**am·ber** /ˈambər/ ▶*n.* yellowish translucent fossilized resin deriving from extinct (esp. coniferous) trees and used in jewelry.

**am·ber·gris** /ˈambərˌgrē(s)/ ▶*n.* waxlike secretion of the sperm whale, used in perfumes.

**am·bi·dex·trous** /ˌambi-ˈdekst(ə)rəs/ ▶*adj.* able to use either hand equally well.
—**am·bi·dex·ter·i·ty** *n.*

**am·bi·ence** /ˈambēəns/ (also **am·bi·ance**) ▶*n.* surroundings or atmosphere of a place.

**am·bi·ent** /ˈambēənt/ ▶*adj.* of or relating to the immediate surroundings of something.

**am·big·u·ous** /amˈbigyo͞oəs/ ▶*adj.* **1** having an obscure or double meaning. **2** difficult to classify. —**am·big·u·i·ty** *n.*
—**am·big·u·ous·ly** *adv.*

**am·bit** /ˈambit/ ▶*n.* scope, extent, or bounds of something.

**am·bi·tion** /amˈbiSHən/ ▶*n.* **1** determination to succeed. **2** object of this. —**am·bi·tious** *adj.*

**am·biv·a·lence** /amˈbivələns/ ▶*n.* simultaneous conflicting feelings. —**am·biv·a·lent** *adj.*

**am·ble** /ˈambəl/ ▶*v.* move at an easy pace.
▶*n.* such a pace.

**am·bro·sia** /amˈbrōZHə/ ▶*n.* **1** (in Greek and Roman mythology) food of the gods. **2** anything very pleasing to taste or smell. —**am·bro·sial** *adj.*

**am·bu·lance** /ˈambyələns/ ▶*n.* vehicle equipped for conveying the sick or injured to and from a hospital.

**am·bu·la·to·ry** /ˈambyələˌtôrē/
▸*adj.* **1** (of a patient) able to walk
about. **2** of or for walking.

**am·bus·cade** /ˈambəˌskād;
ˌambəˈskād/ ▸*n.* ambush.

**am·bush** /ˈambo͝osH/ ▸*n.*
surprise attack from a concealed
position.
▸*v.* **1** attack by ambush. **2** lie in
wait for.

**a·me·ba** /əˈmēbə/ (also
**a·moe·ba**) ▸*n.* (*pl.* **-bas, -bae**) any
usu. aquatic microscopic one-
celled animal capable of
changing shape.

**a·me·lio·rate** /əˈmēlyəˌrāt/ ▸*v.*
make or become better;
improve. —**a·mel·io·ra·tion** *n.*
—**am·el·io·ra·tive** *adj.*

**a·men** /äˈmen/ ▸*interj.* word
uttered at the end of a prayer,
etc., meaning 'so be it.'

**a·me·na·ble** /əˈmēnəbəl/ ▸*adj.*
responsive.

**a·mend** /əˈmend/ ▸*v.* **1** make
minor improvements in (a text,
etc.). **2** correct an error in (a
document). **3** modify formally,
as a legal document.

**a·mend·ment** ▸*n.* **1** minor
change in a document (esp. a
legal or statutory one). **2** article
added to the U.S. Constitution.

**a·mends** ▸*n.* (in phrase **make
amends**) compensate or make
up (for).

**a·men·i·ty** /əˈmenitē/ ▸*n.* (*pl.*
**-ties**) **1** (usu. **amenities**) pleasant
or useful feature. **2** pleasantness
(of a place, etc.).

**Am·er·a·sian** /ˌamərˈāzHən/ ▸*n.*
person of American and Asian
descent.

**A·mer·i·can** /əˈmerikən/ ▸*adj.*
**1** of, relating to, or characteristic
of the United States or its
inhabitants. **2** of or relating to
the continents of America: *Latin-
American.*
▸*n.* **1** native or citizen of the
United States. **2** native or
inhabitant of the continents of
America. **3** (also **Amer·ican
Eng·lish**) the English language as
it is used in the United States.
—**A·mer·i·can·ize** *v.*
□ **American Indian** member of the
aboriginal peoples of America or
their descendants.

**A·mer·i·can·ism** ▸*n.* **1** word,
sense, or phrase peculiar to or
originating from the United
States. **2** attachment to or
sympathy for the United States.

**am·e·thyst** /ˈaməTHəst/ ▸*n.*
semiprecious stone of a violet or
purple variety of quartz.

**a·mi·a·ble** /ˈāmēəbəl/ ▸*adj.*

friendly and pleasant, likable.
—**a·mi·a·bil·i·ty** *n.*

**am·i·ca·ble** /ˈamikəbəl/ ▸*adj.* showing or done in a friendly spirit. —**am·i·ca·bly** *adv.*

**a·mid** /əˈmid/ (also **a·midst**) ▸*prep.* **1** in the middle of. **2** in the course of.

**a·mi·no ac·id** /əˈmēnō/ ▸*n.* any of a group of nitrogenous organic acids forming the basic constituents of proteins.

**a·miss** /əˈmis/ ▸*adj.* not quite right; out of order.

**am·i·ty** /ˈamitē/ ▸*n.* friendship; friendly relations.

**am·me·ter** /ˈa(m)ˌmētər/ ▸*n.* instrument for measuring electric current in amperes.

**am·mo·nia** /əˈmōnyə/ ▸*n.* **1** pungent, strongly alkaline gas. **2** solution of ammonia gas in water.

**am·mu·ni·tion** /ˌamyəˈnisHən/ ▸*n.* **1** supply of bullets, shells, grenades, etc. **2** points usable to advantage in an argument.

**am·ne·sia** /amˈnēzHə/ ▸*n.* partial or total loss of memory.

**am·nes·ty** /ˈamnistē/ ▸*n.* (*pl.* **-ties**) general pardon, esp. for political offenses.

**am·ni·o·cen·te·sis**
/ˌamnēōsenˈtēsis/ ▸*n.* (*pl.* **-ses**) sampling of amniotic fluid to determine the health of a fetus.

**am·ni·on** /ˈamnēˌän; -ən/ ▸*n.* (*pl.* **-** or **-ni·a** /-nēə/) innermost membrane that encloses the embryo of a mammal, bird, or reptile.

**am·ni·ot·ic flu·id** /ˌamnēˈätik/ ▸*n.* fluid surrounding the fetus in the uterus.

**a·mok** /əˈmək/ (also **a·muck**) ▸*adv.* (in phrase **run amok**) run about wildly in an uncontrollable violent rage.

**a·mong** /əˈməNG/ (also **a·mongst**) ▸*prep.* **1** surrounded by; in the company of. **2** included in. **3** in the class or category of: *is among the richest men alive.* **4** shared by. **5** with one another. **6** as distinguished from: *she is one among many.*

**a·mor·al** /āˈmôrəl/ ▸*adj.* **1** having no moral principles. **2** not concerned with or outside the scope of morality. —**a·mo·ral·i·ty** *n.*

**am·o·rous** /ˈamərəs/ ▸*adj.* **1** showing, feeling, or inclined to sexual love. **2** of or relating to sexual love. —**am·o·rous·ly** *adv.* —**am·o·rous·ness** *n.*

**a·mor·phous** /əˈmôrfəs/ ▶adj. shapeless. —**a·mor·phous·ly** adv.

**am·or·tize** /ˈamərˌtīz/ ▶v. gradually extinguish (a debt) by regular payments. —**am·or·ti·za·tion** n.

**a·mount** /əˈmount/ ▶n. quantity, esp. the total in number, size, value, extent, etc. ▶v. (**amount to**) **1** come to be (the total) when added together. **2** be the equivalent of. **3** (of a person) develop into; become.

**a·mour** /əˈmo͝or/ ▶n. love affair, esp. a secret one.

**a·mour pro·pre** /äˌmo͝or ˈprôpr(ə)/ ▶n. sense of one's own worth; self-respect.

**amp·er·age** /ˈamp(ə)rij/ ▶n. strength of an electric current in amperes.

**am·pere** /ämˈpi(ə)r/ ▶n. base unit of electric current. (Symb.: **A**).

**am·per·sand** /ˈampərˌsand/ ▶n. character (&) representing the word *and*.

**am·phet·a·mine** /amˈfetəˌmēn/ ▶n. synthetic drug used esp. as a stimulant.

**am·phib·i·an** /amˈfibēən/ ▶adj. **1** of a class of vertebrates living both on land and in water. **2** (of a vehicle) able to operate on land and water.

▶n. **1** class of vertebrates including frogs, toads, newts, and salamanders. **2** vehicle that can operate on land and in water. —**am·phib·i·ous** adj. —**am·phib·i·ous·ly** adv.

**am·phi·the·a·ter** /ˈamfəˌTHēətər/ ▶n. round, usu. unroofed building with tiers of seats surrounding a central space.

**am·pho·ra** /ˈamfərə/ ▶n. (pl. **-rae** /-ˌrē/ or **-ras**) tall ancient Greek or Roman jar with two handles and a narrow neck.

**am·ple** /ˈampəl/ ▶adj. (**-pler, -plest**) **1** plentiful; abundant; extensive. **2** (esp. of a person) large; stout. —**am·ply** adv.

**am·pli·fy** /ˈampləˌfī/ ▶v. (**-fied**) **1** increase the strength of (sound, electrical signals, etc.). **2** enlarge upon or add detail to (a story, etc.). —**am·pli·fi·ca·tion** n.

**am·pli·tude** /ˈampliˌt(y)o͞od/ ▶n. **1** *Physics* maximum extent of a vibration or oscillation from the position of equilibrium. **2** *Physics* maximum departure of the value of an alternating current or wave from the average value. **3** spaciousness; breadth; wide range.

□ **amplitude modulation**

**1** modulation of a wave by variation of its amplitude. **2** system using such modulation.

**am·pule** /'am,p(y)ool/ ▶*n.* sealed capsule holding a solution for injection.

**am·pu·tate** /'ampyə,tāt/ ▶*v.* cut off by surgical operation (a limb, etc.). —**am·pu·ta·tion** *n.*

**am·u·let** /'amyəlit/ ▶*n.* charm worn against evil.

**a·muse** /ə'myooz/ ▶*v.* **1** cause to laugh or smile. **2** interest or occupy; keep entertained. —**a·muse·ment** *n.*

**an** /an; ən/ ▶*adj.* form of the indefinite article. See **A.**

**an-** ▶*prefix* not; without: *anarchy.*

**-an** (also **-ean, -ian**) ▶*suffix* forming adjectives and nouns, esp. from names of places, systems, classes or orders, and founders: *Mexican | Anglican | crustacean | Lutheran.*

**a·nach·ro·nism** /ə'nakrə,nizəm/ ▶*n.* **1 a** attribution of a custom, event, etc., to the wrong period. **b** thing attributed in this way. **2** out-of-date person or thing. —**a·nach·ro·nis·tic** *adj.*

**an·a·con·da** /,anə'kändə/ ▶*n.* large nonpoisonous snake that kills its prey by constriction.

**an·a·gram** /'anə,gram/ ▶*n.* word or phrase formed by transposing the letters of another word or phrase.

**a·nal** /'ānl/ ▶*adj.* of or near the anus. —**a·nal·ly** *adv.*

□ **anal retentive** (of a person) excessively orderly and fussy.

**an·al·ge·sic** /,anl'jēzik/ ▶*adj.* relieving pain.
▶*n.* analgesic drug.

**an·a·log** /'anl,ôg/ ▶*n.* **1** person or thing comparable to another. **2** (of an electronic process) using physical variables (e.g., voltage, weight, etc.) to represent numbers.

**a·nal·o·gous** /ə'naləgəs/ ▶*adj.* partially similar or parallel.

**a·nal·o·gy** /ə'naləjē/ ▶*n.* (*pl.* **-gies**) **1** correspondence or partial similarity. **2** *Logic* arguing from parallel cases.

**a·nal·y·sis** /ə'naləsis/ ▶*n.* (*pl.* **-ses**) **1 a** detailed examination of elements or structure. **b** statement of the result of this. **2** *Chem.* determination of the constituent parts of a mixture or compound. **3** psychoanalysis. —**an·a·lyt·ic** *adj.* —**an·a·lyt·i·cal** *adj.* —**an·a·lyt·i·cal·ly** *adv.*

**an·a·lyze** /'anl,īz/ ▶*v.* **1** examine in detail. **2** break down into constituent parts.

**an·ar·chy** /'anərkē/ ▸n.
**1** disorder, esp. political or
social. **2** lack of government in a
society. —**an·ar·chic** adj.
—**an·ar·chist** n.

**a·nas·tro·phe** /ə'nastrəfē/ ▸n.
inversion of the usual order of
words or clauses.

**a·nath·e·ma** /ə'naTHəmə/ ▸n.
(pl. -**mas**) **1** detested thing or
person. **2** rejection of a person
or doctrine by a church.

**a·nat·o·my** /ə'natəmē/ ▸n. (pl.
-**mies**) **1** science of the bodily
structure of animals and plants.
**2** this structure. **3** analysis.
—**an·a·tom·i·cal** adj.
—**a·nat·o·mist** n.

**-ance** ▸suffix forming nouns
expressing: **1** quality or state or
an instance of: appearance |
resemblance. **2** action: assistance.

**an·ces·tor** /'an,sestər/ ▸n.
**1** any (esp. remote) person from
whom one is descended. **2** early
type of animal or plant from
which others have evolved.
**3** prototype or forerunner.
—**an·ces·tral** adj.

**an·chor** /'aNGkər/ ▸n. **1** heavy
metal weight used to moor a
ship or a balloon. **2** thing
affording stability. **3** source of
confidence. **4** (also **anc·hor·man,**

**an·chor·per·son,**
**an·chor·wom·an**) **a** news
broadcaster who introduces
segments and reads
news.**b** person who plays a vital
part, as the last member of a
relay team, etc.

▸v. **1** secure or be secured by
means of an anchor. **2** fix
firmly.

**an·cho·vy** /'an,CHōvē/ ▸n. (pl.
-**vies**) small strong-flavored fish
of the herring family.

**an·cient** /'ānCHənt/ ▸adj. **1** of
long ago. **2** having lived or
existed long.

▸n. very old person.

**an·cil·lar·y** /'ansə,lerē/ ▸adj.
**1** providing necessary support to
the operation of an institution,
industry, etc. **2** additional;
subsidiary.

▸n. (pl. -**ies**) **1** person whose work
provides necessary support: the
employment of specialist teachers
and ancillaries. **2** something
functioning in a supplementary
role.

**and** /and/ ▸conj. **1** connecting
words, clauses, or sentences to
be taken jointly: buy and sell.
**2** implying: **a** progression.
**b** causation. **c** great duration.
**d** great number. **e** addition.

**an·dan·te** /än'dän‚tā/ *Mus.* ▸*adv. & adj.* in a moderately slow tempo.
▸*n.* andante passage or movement.

**an·dro·gen** /'andrəjən/ ▸*n.* male sex hormone or other substance that reinforces certain male sexual characteristics.
—**an·dro·gen·ic** *adj.*

**an·drog·y·nous** /an'dräjənəs/ ▸*adj.* **1** partly male and partly female. **2** having the appearance or attributes of both sexes.
—**an·drog·y·ny** *n.*

**an·droid** /'an‚droid/ ▸*n.* robot with a human appearance.

**an·ec·dote** /'anik‚dōt/ ▸*n.* short account of an entertaining or interesting incident.
—**an·ec·do·tal** *adj.*

**a·ne·mi·a** /ə'nēmēə/ ▸*n.* deficiency of red cells or their hemoglobin.

**a·nem·o·ne** /ə'nemənē/ ▸*n.* plant akin to the buttercup, with flowers of various vivid colors.

**an·es·the·sia** /‚anəs'тнēzнə/ ▸*n.* absence of sensation, esp. artificially induced before surgery. —**an·es·the·si·ol·o·gist** *n.* —**an·es·the·si·ol·o·gy** *n.* —**an·es·thet·ic** *n. & adj.*

—**an·es·the·tist** *n.*
—**an·es·the·tize** *v.*

**an·eu·rysm** /'anyə‚rizəm/ (also **an·eu·rism**) ▸*n.* excessive localized enlargement of an artery caused by a weakening of the artery wall.

**a·new** /ə'n(y)o͞o/ ▸*adv.* **1** again. **2** in a different way.

**an·gel** /'ānjəl/ ▸*n.* **1** attendant or messenger of God. **2** very virtuous person. **3** *inf.* financial backer of an enterprise, esp. in the theater. —**an·gel·ic** *adj.*

**an·ger** /'aNGgər/ ▸*n.* extreme or passionate displeasure.
▸*v.* make angry; enrage.

**an·gle** /'aNGgəl/ ▸*n.* **1 a** space between two meeting lines or surfaces. **b** inclination of two lines or surfaces to each other. **2** corner. **3 a** point of view. **b** approach, technique, etc.
▸*v.* **1** move or place obliquely. **2** present (information) from a particular viewpoint. **3** fish with hook and line. **4** seek an objective by devious means: *angled for a pay raise.* —**an·gled** *adj.* —**an·gler** *n.*

**An·gli·can** /'aNGglikən/ ▸*adj.* of or relating to the Church of England or any church in communion with it.

▶*n.* member of an Anglican Church. **—An·gli·can·ism** *n.*

**An·gli·cize** /ˈaNGgliˌsīz/ ▶*v.* make English in form or character.

**an·glo·phone** /ˈaNGgləˌfōn/ ▶*adj.* English-speaking.

▶*n.* English-speaking person.

**An·glo-Sa·xon** /ˈaNGlō ˈsaksən/ ▶*adj.* **1** of the English Saxons (as distinct from the Old Saxons of the European continent, and from the Angles) before the Norman Conquest. **2** of English descent.

▶*n.* **1** Anglo-Saxon person. **2** Old English. **3** *inf.* plain (esp. crude) English.

**an·go·ra** /aNGˈgôrə/ ▶*n.* **1** long-haired variety of cat, goat, or rabbit. **2** fabric or wool made from the hair of the angora goat or rabbit.

**an·gry** /ˈaNGgrē/ ▶*adj.* (**-gri·er, -gri·est**) **1** feeling or showing anger. **2** (of a wound, sore, etc.) inflamed; painful. **3** stormy: *an angry sky.* **—an·gri·ly** *adv.*

**angst** /aNG(k)st/ ▶*n.* anxiety.

**an·guish** /ˈaNGgwiSH/ ▶*n.* severe mental suffering.

▶*v.* [often as *adj.* **anguished**] cause to suffer physical or mental pain.

**an·gu·lar** /ˈaNGgyələr/ ▶*adj.* **1** having angles or sharp corners. **2** forming an angle.

**an·i·mad·vert** /ˌanəmadˈvərt/ ▶*v.* criticize; censure. **—an·i·mad·ver·sion** *n.*

**an·i·mal** /ˈanəməl/ ▶*n.* living organism that feeds on organic matter, usu. one with specialized sense organs and a nervous system, and able to respond rapidly to stimuli.

▶*adj.* characteristic of animals.

**an·i·mate** /ˈanəˌmāt/ ▶*adj.* **1** having life. **2** lively.

▶*v.* **1** enliven. **2** inspire; encourage.

**an·i·ma·tion** ▶*n.* **1** vivacity; ardor. **2** technique of filming successive drawings, positions of puppets, etc., to create an illusion of movement.

**an·i·mism** /ˈanəˌmizəm/ ▶*n.* attribution of a living soul to plants, inanimate objects, and natural phenomena. **—an·i·mist** *n.*

**an·i·mos·i·ty** /ˌanəˈmäsitē/ ▶*n.* (*pl.* **-ties**) spirit or feeling of strong hostility.

**an·i·mus** /ˈanəməs/ ▶*n.* **1** hostility or ill feeling. **2** motivation to do something.

**an·ise** /ˈanis/ ▶*n.* plant having

aromatic seeds, used to flavor liqueurs and candy.

**an·kle** /ˈaNGkəl/ ▶n. **1** joint connecting the foot with the leg. **2** this part of the leg.

**ank·let** /ˈaNGklit/ ▶n. **1** ornament worn around the ankle. **2** short sock.

**an·nals** /ˈanlz/ ▶pl. n. **1** narrative of events year by year. **2** historical records.

**an·neal** /əˈnēl/ ▶v. **1** heat (metal or glass) and cool slowly, esp. to toughen it. **2** toughen.

**an·nex** ▶v. /əˈneks/ **1** add as a subordinate part. **2** incorporate (territory of another) into one's own. ▶n. /ˈaneks/ **1** separate or added building, esp. for extra accommodations. **2** addition to a document. **—an·nex·a·tion** n.

**an·ni·hi·late** /əˈnīə,lāt/ ▶v. destroy completely. **—an·ni·hi·la·tion** n.

**an·ni·ver·sa·ry** /ˌanəˈvərsərē/ ▶n. (pl. **-ries**) **1** date on which an event took place in a previous year. **2** celebration of this.

**an·no·tate** /ˈanə,tāt/ ▶v. add explanatory notes to (a book, document, etc.). **—an·no·ta·tion** n. **—an·no·ta·tive** adj. **—an·no·ta·tor** n.

**an·nounce** /əˈnouns/ ▶v. **1** make publicly known. **2** make known the arrival or imminence of (a guest, etc.). **—an·nounc·er** n. **—an·nounce·ment** n.

**an·noy** /əˈnoi/ ▶v. irritate; make a little angry: *she was annoyed at being wakened.* **—an·noy·ance** n. **—an·noy·ing** adj.

**an·nu·al** /ˈanyo͞oəl/ ▶adj. **1** reckoned by the year. **2** occurring every year. **3** living or lasting for one year. ▶n. **1** book, etc., published once a year; yearbook. **2** plant that lives only for a year or less. **—an·nu·al·ly** adv.

**an·nu·i·ty** /əˈn(y)o͞oitē/ ▶n. (pl. **-ties**) **1** yearly grant or allowance. **2** investment yielding a fixed annual sum. **3** sum paid.

**an·nul** /əˈnəl/ ▶v. (**-nulled, -nul·ling**) **1** declare (a marriage, etc.) invalid. **2** cancel; abolish. **—an·nul·ment** n.

**An·nun·ci·a·tion** /əˌnənsē-ˈāSHən/ ▶n. **1** announcement of the Incarnation, made by the angel Gabriel to the Virgin Mary. **2** Christian festival commemorating this.

**an·ode** /ˈanōd/ ▶n. positive

electrode in an electrolytic cell.
**—an·od·ic** *adj.*

**a·noint** /ə'noint/ ▶*v.* apply oil or ointment to, esp. as part of a religious ceremony.

**a·nom·a·ly** /ə'näməlē/ ▶*n.* (*pl.* **-lies**) something that deviates from what is standard or expected. **—a·nom·a·lous** *adj.*

**an·o·mie** /'anə,mē/ (also **an·o·my**) ▶*n.* lack of the usual social or ethical standards in an individual or group.

**a·non** /ə'nän/ ▶*adv. archaic* soon; shortly.

**anon.** ▶*abbr.* anonymous; anonymous author.

**a·non·y·mous** /ə'nänəməs/ ▶*adj.* **1** of unknown name. **2** of unknown or undeclared authorship. **3** without character; featureless. **—an·o·nym·i·ty** *n.*

**an·o·rak** /'anə,rak/ ▶*n.* warm jacket, usu. with a hood; parka.

**an·o·rex·i·a** /,anə'reksēə/ ▶*n.* **1** lack of appetite for food. **2** (also **an·o·rex·ia ner·vo·sa**) psychological illness, esp. in young women, characterized by an obsessive desire to lose weight by refusing to eat. **—an·o·rex·ic** *adj.*

**an·oth·er** /ə'nəT͟Hər/ ▶*adj.* **1** additional: *have another piece of* cake. **2** person like: *another Lincoln.* **3** a different: *quite another matter.*

▶*pron.* **1** additional one. **2** different one. **3** some or any other one: *I love another.*

**an·swer** /'ansər/ ▶*n.* **1** something said or done in reaction to a question, statement, or circumstance. **2** solution to a problem.

▶*v.* **1** make an answer to: *answer me.* **2** respond to the summons or signal of: *answer the door.* **3** be satisfactory for (a purpose or need). **4** be responsible or to blame for: *people who failed to vote have a lot to answer for.* **5** report to: *I answer to the vice president.* **—an·swer·a·ble** *adj.*

□ **answer back** answer impudently.

**an·swer·ing ma·chine** ▶*n.* device that supplies a recorded answer to a telephone call and usu. records incoming messages.

**ant** /ant/ ▶*n.* small insect living in complex social colonies, usu. wingless, and proverbial for industry.

**-ant** ▶*suffix* **1** forming adjectives denoting attribution of an action or state: *repentant | arrogant.*

**2** forming nouns denoting an agent: *assistant.*

**ant·ac·id** /ant'asid/ ▸*n.* substance that prevents or corrects acidity.

**an·tag·o·nism** /an'tagə,nizəm/ ▸*n.* active opposition or hostility. —**an·tag·o·nize** *v.*

**an·tag·o·nist** /an'tagə,nist/ ▸*n.* opponent or adversary. —**an·tag·o·nis·tic** *adj.*

**Ant·arc·tic** /ant'är(k)tik/ ▸*adj.* of the south polar regions. ▸*n.* this region. □ **Antarctic Circle** parallel of latitude 66° 33− S., delimiting this region.

**an·te** /'antē/ ▸*n.* stake put up by a player in poker, etc., before receiving cards. □ **up the ante** increase what is being discussed: *he decided to up the ante in the contract dispute.*

**ante-** ▸*prefix* forming nouns and adjectives meaning 'before; preceding': *anteroom.*

**ant·eat·er** /'ant,ētər/ ▸*n.* any of various mammals feeding on ants and termites.

**an·te·bel·lum** /,antē'beləm/ ▸*adj.* before the U.S. Civil War.

**an·te·ced·ent** /,anti'sēdnt/ ▸*n.* **1** preceding thing or circumstance. **2** *Gram.* word, phrase, etc., to which another word (esp. a relative pronoun) refers. **3** (**antecedents**) person's family or ancestors. ▸*adj.* previous.

**an·te·date** /'anti,dāt/ ▸*v.* precede in time; come before (something) in date.

**an·te·di·lu·vi·an** /,antēdə-'lōōvēən/ ▸*adj.* **1** of the time before the biblical flood. **2** *inf.* ridiculously old-fashioned.

**an·te·lope** /'antl,ōp/ ▸*n.* (*pl.* same or **-lopes**) swift-moving deerlike ruminant, e.g., the gazelle and impala.

**an·ten·na** /an'tenə/ ▸*n.* (*pl.* **-nae**) **1** one of a pair of feelers on the heads of insects, crustaceans, etc. **2** (*pl.* **-nas**) metal rod, wire, or other structure by which broadcast signals are transmitted or received.

**an·te·pe·nul·ti·mate** /,antēpə-'nəltəmit/ ▸*adj.* last but two in a series; third last.

**an·te·ri·or** /an'ti(ə)rēər/ ▸*adj.* **1** nearer the front. **2** earlier; prior.

**an·te·room** ▸*n.* small room leading to a main one.

**an·them** /'anTHəm/ ▸*n.* **1** choral composition usu. based on a biblical passage. **2** rousing song identified with a particular group. **3** (also **national anthem**) solemn patriotic song expressing a country's national identity.

**an·ther** /ˈanTHər/ ▸*n.* the part of a flower's stamen containing pollen.

**an·thol·o·gy** /anˈTHäləjē/ ▸*n.* (*pl.* **-gies**) published collection of passages from literature, songs, reproductions of paintings, etc.
—**an·thol·o·gist** *n.*
—**an·thol·o·gize** *v.*

**an·thra·cite** /ˈanTHrəˌsīt/ ▸*n.* coal of a hard variety burning with little flame and smoke.

**an·thrax** /ˈanˌTHraks/ ▸*n.* disease of sheep and cattle transmissible to humans.

**an·thro·poid** /ˈanTHrəˌpoid/ ▸*adj.* **1** human in form. **2** *inf.* (of a person) apelike.
▸*n.* anthropoid ape.

**an·thro·pol·o·gy** /ˌanTHrəˈpäləjē/ ▸*n.* study of humankind, esp. its societies and customs.
—**an·thro·pol·og·i·cal** *adj.*
—**an·thro·pol·og·ist** *n.*

**an·thro·po·mor·phic** /ˌanTHrəpəˈmôrfik/ ▸*adj.* attributing human form or character to an animal or god.
—**an·thro·po·mor·phism** *n.*

**an·thro·poph·a·gy** /ˌanTHrə-ˈpäfəjē/ ▸*n.* eating of human flesh by human beings.

**an·ti** /ˈanˌtī; ˈantē/ ▸*prep.* opposed to: *is anti everything.*
▸*n.* (*pl.* **-tis**) person opposed to a particular policy, etc.

**anti-** /ˈantē; ˈantī/ (also **ant-** before a vowel) ▸*prefix* forming nouns and adjectives meaning: **1** opposed to; against: *antivivisectionism.* **2** preventing: *antiscorbutic.* **3** opposite of: *anticlimax.* **4** rival: *antipope.* **5** unlike the conventional form: *antihero.*

**an·ti·bi·ot·ic** /-bīˈätik-/ ▸*n.* substance (e.g., penicillin) that can inhibit or destroy susceptible microorganisms.

**an·ti·bod·y** /ˈantiˌbädē/ ▸*n.* (*pl.* **-ies**) blood protein produced in response to and then counteracting antigens.

**an·tic** /ˈantik/ ▸*n.* (usu. **antics**) absurd or foolish behavior or action; prank.

**an·tic·i·pate** /anˈtisəˌpāt/ ▸*v.* **1** deal with or use before the proper time. **2** expect; foresee. **3** forestall (a person or thing). **4** look forward to.
—**an·tic·i·pa·tion** *n.*
—**an·tic·i·pa·tor·y** *adj.*

**an·ti·cli·max** ▶*n.* disappointingly trivial conclusion to something significant. —**an·ti·cli·mac·tic** *adj.*

**an·ti·de·pres·sant** ▶*n.* drug that alleviates depression.

**an·ti·dote** /ˈantiˌdōt/ ▶*n.* **1** medicine, etc., used to counteract poison. **2** anything that counteracts something unpleasant.

**an·ti·freeze** /ˈantiˌfrēz/ ▶*n.* substance added to water to lower its freezing point, esp. in the radiator of a motor vehicle.

**an·ti·gen** /ˈantijən/ ▶*n.* toxin or other foreign substance that induces an immune response in the body, esp. the production of antibodies.

**an·ti·he·ro** /ˈantēˌhi(ə)rō; ˈantī-/ ▶*n.* central character in a story, movie, or drama who lacks conventional heroic attributes.

**an·ti·his·ta·mine** /-ˈhistəmən/ ▶*n.* substance used esp. in the treatment of allergies.

**an·ti·mat·ter** /ˈantēˌmatər; ˈantī-/ ▶*n.* molecules formed by atoms consisting of antiparticles.

**an·ti·mo·ny** /ˈantəˌmōnē/ ▶*n.* brittle silvery metallic element used esp. in alloys. (Symb.: **Sb**)

**an·ti·par·ti·cle** /ˌantēˈpärtikəl; ˌantī-/ ▶*n.* subatomic particle having the same mass as a given particle but opposite electric or magnetic properties. Every kind of subatomic particle has a corresponding antiparticle, e.g., the positron has the same mass as the electron but an equal and opposite charge.

**an·ti·pas·to** /ˌantiˈpästō/ ▶*n.* (*pl.* **-tos** or **-ti**) (in Italian cooking) appetizer of olives, marinated vegetables, cheese, etc.

**an·tip·a·thy** /anˈtipəTHē/ ▶*n.* (*pl.* **-thies**) strong or deep-seated aversion or dislike.

**an·ti·per·spi·rant** /ˌantiˈpərspərənt/ ▶*n.* substance applied to the skin to prevent or reduce perspiration.

**an·tip·o·des** /anˈtipədēz/ ▶*pl. n.* (also **Antipodes**) places diametrically opposite to one another, esp. Australasia in relation to N. America or Europe. —**an·tip·o·de·an** *adj. & n.*

**an·ti·quar·i·an** /ˌantiˈkwe(ə)rēən/ ▶*adj.* of or dealing in antiques or rare books. ▶*n.* antiquary.

**an·ti·quar·y** /ˈantiˌkwerē/ ▶*n.* (*pl.*

-ies) student or collector of antiques or antiquities.

**an·ti·quat·ed** /ˈantiˌkwātid/ ▶adj. old-fashioned; out of date.

**an·tique** /anˈtēk/ ▶n. old object, item of furniture, etc., esp. one valued for its beauty or quality. ▶adj. of or existing from an early date.

**an·tiq·ui·ty** /anˈtikwitē/ ▶n. (pl. -ties) **1** ancient times, esp. before the Middle Ages. **2** great age. **3** (**antiquities**) relics from ancient times, esp. buildings and works of art.

**an·ti-Sem·ite** /-ˈsemīt/ ▶n. person prejudiced against Jews. —**an·ti-Se·mit·ic** adj. —**an·ti-Sem·i·tism** n.

**an·ti·sep·tic** /ˌantiˈseptik/ ▶adj. **1** counteracting sepsis, esp. by preventing the growth of disease-causing microorganisms. **2** free from contamination. **3** lacking character. ▶n. antiseptic agent.

**an·ti·so·cial** ▶adj. **1** contrary to laws and customs of the existing social order. **2** not wanting the company of others.

**an·tith·e·sis** /anˈtiTHəsis/ ▶n. (pl. -ses) **1** person or thing that is the direct opposite. **2** contrast or opposition between two things. —**an·ti·thet·i·cal** adj. —**an·ti·thet·i·cal·ly** adv.

**an·ti·tox·in** /ˌantiˈtäksn/ ▶n. antibody that counteracts a toxin.

**ant·ler** /ˈantlər/ ▶n. each of the branched horns of a stag or other (usu. male) deer.

**an·to·nym** /ˈantəˌnim/ ▶n. word opposite in meaning to another.

**a·nus** /ˈānəs/ ▶n. excretory opening at the end of the alimentary canal.

**an·vil** /ˈanvil/ ▶n. block (usu. of iron) on which metals are shaped.

**anx·i·e·ty** /aNGˈzī-itē/ ▶n. (pl. -ties) **1** worry, nervousness, or unease. **2** anxious desire.

**anx·ious** /ˈaNG(k)SHəs/ ▶adj. **1** feeling worried, uneasy, or nervous. **2** causing or marked by worry or nervousness: *some anxious moments.* **3** wanting something very much: *anxious to avoid further problems.* —**anx·ious·ly** adv.

**an·y** /ˈenē/ ▶adj. & pron. **1 a** one, no matter which, of several. **b** some, no matter how much or many or of what sort. **2** anyone: *ceased payments to any but the most severely disabled.* **3** whichever of a specified class might be chosen: *any fool knows that.*

▸*adv.* at all; in some degree: *no one would be any the wiser.*

**an·y·bod·y** ▸*n. & pron.* person of any kind.

**an·y·how** ▸*adv.* **1** ANYWAY. **2** in a careless way: *does his work anyhow.*

**any·one** ▸*pron.* anybody.

**an·y·thing** ▸*pron.* **1** thing, no matter which. **2** thing of any kind.

**an·y·way** ▸*adv.* **1** in any way or manner. **2** at any rate. **3** in any case.

**an·y·where** ▸*adv.* in or to any place.
▸*pron.* any place: *anywhere will do.*

**a·or·ta** /ā'ôrtə/ ▸*n.* (*pl.* **-tas**) main artery through which oxygenated blood is supplied to the body from the heart.
—**a·or·tic** *adj.*

**a·pace** /ə'pās/ ▸*adv.* swiftly; quickly.

**A·pach·e** /ə'pacHē/ ▸*n.* member of a N. American Indian tribe of the southwestern U.S.

**a·part** /ə'pärt/ ▸*adv.* **1** separately; not together. **2** into pieces. **3** to or at a distance.

**a·part·heid** /ə'pär‚tāt/ ▸*n. hist.* (in S. Africa) racial segregation or discrimination.

**a·part·ment** /ə'pärtmənt/ ▸*n.* room or suite of rooms, usu. on one floor, used as a residence.

**ap·a·thy** /'apəтHē/ ▸*n.* lack of interest or feeling; indifference.
—**ap·a·thet·ic** *adj.*
—**ap·a·thet·i·cal·ly** *adv.*

**ape** /āp/ ▸*n.* **1** monkeylike primate characterized by the absence of a tail, e.g., the gorilla, chimpanzee, etc. **2** (in general use) any monkey.
▸*v.* imitate; mimic.

**a·per·çu** /äper'soo/ ▸*n.* (*pl.* **-çus** *pronunc.* same) comment or brief reference that makes an illuminating or entertaining point.

**a·pe·ri·tif** /ä‚peri'tēf/ ▸*n.* alcoholic drink taken before a meal to stimulate the appetite.

**ap·er·ture** /'apər‚cHər/ ▸*n.* opening; gap.

**a·pex** /'āpeks/ ▸*n.* (*pl.* **-pex·es** or **-pi·ces**) **1** highest point. **2** climax. **3** tip or pointed end.

**a·pha·sia** /ə'fāzHə/ ▸*n.* loss of ability to understand or express speech, caused by brain damage.

**a·phid** /'āfid/ ▸*n.* small insect that feeds by sucking sap from leaves, stems, or roots of plants.

**aph·o·rism** /ˈafəˌrizəm/ ▸n. short pithy maxim. —**aph·o·rist** n. —**aph·o·ris·tic** adj.

**aph·ro·di·si·ac** /ˌafrəˈdizēˌak/ ▸adj. arousing sexual desire. ▸n. aphrodisiac drug.

**a·pi·ar·y** /ˈāpēˌerē/ ▸n. (pl. -ies) place where bees are kept. —**a·pi·a·rist** n.

**a·piece** /əˈpēs/ ▸adv. for each one; severally; individually.

**a·plomb** /əˈpläm/ ▸n. assurance; self-confidence.

**a·poc·a·lypse** /əˈpäkəˌlips/ ▸n. 1 (**the Apocalypse**) Revelation, the last book of the New Testament. 2 grand or violent event resembling those described in the Apocalypse. —**a·poc·a·lyp·tic** adj. —**a·poc·a·lyp·ti·cal·ly** adv.

**A·poc·ry·pha** /əˈpäkrəfə/ ▸pl. n. 1 biblical writings not forming part of the accepted canon of Scripture. 2 (**apocrypha**) writings or reports not considered genuine.

**a·poc·ry·phal** /-fəl/ ▸adj. of doubtful authenticity.

**ap·o·gee** /ˈapəjē/ ▸n. 1 point in an orbit farthest from the earth. 2 point in a celestial body's orbit where it is farthest from the body being orbited. —**ap·o·ge·an** adj.

**a·po·lit·i·cal** /ˌāpəˈlitikəl/ ▸adj. not interested in or concerned with politics.

**ap·o·lo·gi·a** /ˌapəˈlōj(ē)ə/ ▸n. formal written defense of one's opinions or conduct.

**a·pol·o·gist** /əˈpäləjist/ ▸n. person who defends something by argument.

**a·pol·o·gize** /əˈpäləˌjīz/ ▸v. make an apology for an offense or failure; express regret.

**a·pol·o·gy** /əˈpäləjē/ ▸n. (pl. -gies) 1 regretful acknowledgment of an offense or failure. 2 assurance that no offense was intended. 3 explanation or defense. 4 poor or scanty specimen of: *this apology for a letter.*

**ap·o·plex·y** /ˈapəˌpleksē/ ▸n. sudden loss of consciousness, voluntary movement, and sensation caused by blockage or rupture of a brain artery; stroke.

**a·pos·ta·sy** /əˈpästəsē/ ▸n. abandonment or renunciation of a religious or political belief.

**a·pos·tate** /əˈpäsˌtāt/ ▸n. person who renounces a former belief, adherence, etc. ▸adj. engaged in apostasy.

**a pos·te·ri·o·ri** /ˈä pä̩ˌsti(ə)rēˈô-̩rē/ ▸*adj.* (of reasoning) inductive; empirical; proceeding from effects to causes. ▸*adv.* inductively.

**a·pos·tle** /əˈpäsəl/ ▸*n.* **1** (**Apostle**) any of the twelve men first sent out by Christ to preach the gospel. **2** leader or outstanding figure, esp. of a reform movement.

**a·pos·tro·phe** /əˈpästrəfē/ ▸*n.* punctuation mark used to indicate: **1** omission of letter or numbers: (e.g., *can't*; *Class of '92*). **2** possessive case (e.g., *Harry's book*).

**a·poth·e·car·y** /əˈpäтнiˌkerē/ ▸*n.* (*pl.* **-ies**) *archaic* pharmacist.

**ap·o·thegm** /ˈapəˌтнem/ ▸*n.* concise saying or maxim; an aphorism.

**a·po·the·o·sis** /əˌpäтнēˈōsis/ ▸*n.* (*pl.* **-ses**) **1** elevation to divine status; deification. **2** glorification of a thing; sublime example.

**ap·pall** /əˈpôl/ ▸*v.* greatly dismay or horrify. —**ap·pal·ling·ly** *adv.*

**ap·pa·rat·chik** /ˌäpəˈrächik/ ▸*n.* (*pl.* **-chiks** or **-chi·ki** /-chiˌkē/) or official in a large organization, typically a political one.

**ap·pa·rat·us** /ˌapəˈratəs/ ▸*n.* **1** equipment for a particular function, esp. scientific or technical. **2** political or other complex organization.

**ap·par·el** /əˈparəl/ ▸*n.* clothing; dress.
▸*v.* (**-eled**, **-el·ing**; **-elled**, **-el·ling**) clothe.

**ap·par·ent** /əˈparənt/ ▸*adj.* **1** readily visible or perceivable. **2** seeming.

**ap·pa·ri·tion** /ˌapəˈrishən/ ▸*n.* sudden or dramatic appearance, esp. of a ghost or phantom; visible ghost.

**ap·peal** /əˈpēl/ ▸*v.* **1** make a serious or urgent request: *the police appealed to the public for help | appealed to Canada for asylum.* **2** address oneself to: *I appealed to his sense of fairness.* **3** *Law* apply (to a higher court) for a reconsideration of a decision. **4** be attractive or of interest; be pleasing: *the play will appeal to children.*

▸*n.* **1** act or instance of appealing. **2** formal or urgent request for public support, esp. financial. **3** *Law* referral of a case to a higher court. **4** attractiveness.

**ap·pear** /əˈpi(ə)r/ ▸*v.* **1** become or be visible or evident. **2** seem.

**3** present oneself publicly or formally.

**ap·pear·ance** ▸*n.* **1** act or instance of appearing. **2** outward form as perceived: *gives the appearance of trying hard.* **3** semblance. □ **keep up appearances** maintain an impression or pretense. □ **put in an appearance** be present, esp. briefly.

**ap·pease** /ə'pēz/ ▸*v.* **1** make calm or quiet, esp. conciliate (a potential aggressor) by making concessions. **2** satisfy (an appetite, scruples, etc.). —**ap·pease·ment** *n.*

**ap·pel·late** /ə'pelit/ ▸*adj.* (esp. of a court) concerned with or dealing with appeals.

**ap·pel·la·tion** /ˌapə'lāsHən/ ▸*n.* name or title.

**ap·pend** /ə'pend/ ▸*v.* attach, affix, or add, esp. to a written document, etc.: *the new research is appended to the final chapter.*

**ap·pend·age** /ə'pendij/ ▸*n.* something attached; addition.

**ap·pen·dec·to·my** /ˌapən-'dektəmē/ ▸*n.* (*pl.* **-mies**) surgical removal of the appendix.

**ap·pen·di·ci·tis** /ə,pendi'sītis/ ▸*n.* inflammation of the appendix.

**ap·pen·dix** /ə'pendiks/ ▸*n.* (*pl.* **-di·ces**; **-dix·es**) **1** (also **verm·i·form ap·pen·dix**) small outgrowth of tissue attached to the large intestine. **2** subsidiary matter at the end of a book or document.

**ap·per·tain** /ˌapər'tān/ ▸*v.* (**appertain to**) relate to; concern.

**ap·pe·tite** /'api,tīt/ ▸*n.* **1** natural desire to satisfy bodily needs, esp. for food or sexual activity. **2** inclination or desire.

**ap·pe·tiz·er** /'api,tīzər/ ▸*n.* small amount of food served before a meal, to stimulate the appetite.

**ap·plaud** /ə'plôd/ ▸*v.* express approval or praise, esp. by clapping. —**ap·plause** *n.*

**ap·ple** /'apəl/ ▸*n.* **1** rounded firm edible fruit with a crisp flesh. **2** tree bearing this.

**ap·ple·jack** ▸*n.* brandy distilled from fermented apple cider.

**ap·pli·ance** /ə'plīəns/ ▸*n.* device for a specific task, esp. a household device for washing, drying, cooking, etc.

**ap·pli·ca·ble** /'aplikəbəl/ ▸*adj.* **1** that may be applied. **2** having reference; appropriate.

**ap·pli·cant** /'aplikənt/ ▸*n.* person who applies for something, esp. a job.

**ap·pli·ca·tion** /ˌapliˈkāsHən/ ▸n.
**1** act or instance of applying.
**2** formal request, usu. in writing.
**3 a** relevance. **b** use. **4** diligence.

**ap·pli·ca·tor** ▸n. device for
applying a substance to a
surface.

**ap·pli·qué** /ˌapliˈkā/ ▸n.
attachment of cut-out fabric
patterns to the surface of
another fabric to form pictures
or patterns.

**ap·ply** /əˈplī/ ▸v. (-plies, -plied)
**1** (**apply for**) formally request.
**2** have relevance. **3** make use of;
employ. **4** put or spread on.

**ap·point** /əˈpoint/ ▸v. **1** assign a
job or office to: *appoint him
governor.* **2** fix (a time, place,
etc.). **—ap·point·ee** *n.*
**—ap·poin·tive** *adj.*

**ap·point·ment** ▸n.
**1** arrangement to meet at a
specific time and place. **2 a** job
or office, esp. one available for
applicants. **b** person appointed.
**c** act or instance of appointing.
**3** (**appointments**) furniture;
fittings.

**ap·por·tion** /əˈpôrsHən/ ▸v.
portion out; assign as a share.

**ap·po·site** /ˈapəzit/ ▸adj. **1** apt;
well chosen. **2** well expressed.
**—ap·pos·ite·ly** *adv.*

**ap·praise** /əˈprāz/ ▸v. **1** estimate
the value or quality of. **2** (esp.
officially) set a price on.
**—ap·prais·al** *n.* **—ap·prais·er** *n.*

**ap·pre·cia·ble** /əˈprēsH(ē)əbəl/
▸adj. significant; considerable.
**—ap·pre·cia·bly** *adv.*

**ap·pre·ci·ate** /əˈprēsHē͟ˌāt/ ▸v.
**1 a** esteem highly; value. **b** be
grateful for. **2** understand;
recognize. **3** (of property, etc.)
rise in value. **—ap·pre·ci·a·tion** *n.*
**—ap·pre·cia·tive** *adj.*

**ap·pre·hend** /ˌapriˈhend/ ▸v.
**1** seize; arrest. **2** understand;
perceive.

**ap·pre·hen·sion** /ˌapri-
ˈhensHən/ ▸n. **1** uneasiness;
dread. **2** understanding;
perception. **3** arrest; capture.

**ap·pre·hen·sive** ▸adj. uneasily
fearful; dreading.
**—ap·pre·hen·sive·ly** *adv.*
**—ap·pre·hen·sive·ness** *n.*

**ap·pren·tice** /əˈprentis/ ▸n.
person learning a trade by being
employed in it usu. at low wages.
**—ap·pren·tice·ship** *n.*

**ap·prise** /əˈprīz/ ▸v. inform.
□ **be apprised of** be aware of.

**ap·proach** /əˈprōcH/ ▸v. **1** come
near or nearer (to). **2** make a
tentative proposal or suggestion
to. **3** be similar to.

▸*n.* **1** way of dealing with a person or thing. **2** act of speaking to someone for the first time: *the developer made an approach to the landowner.* **3** action of coming nearer to something in place or time: *the approach of the holidays.* **4** way to a place: *all the approaches to the city.* —**ap·proach·a·ble** *adj.*

**ap·pro·ba·tion** /ˌaprəˈbāsHən/ ▸*n.* approval; consent.

**ap·pro·pri·ate** ▸*adj.* /əˈprōprēit/ suitable or proper.
▸*v.* /əˈprōprēˌāt/ **1** take possession of, esp. without authority. **2** devote (money, etc.) to special purposes. —**ap·pro·pri·ate·ly** *adv.* —**ap·pro·pri·ate·ness** *n.* —**ap·pro·pri·a·tion** *n.*

**ap·prove** /əˈpro͞ov/ ▸*v.* **1** confirm; sanction. **2** give or have a favorable opinion. **3** commend. —**ap·prov·al** *n.* —**ap·prov·ing·ly** *adv.*

**approx.** ▸*abbr.* **1** approximate. **2** approximately.

**ap·prox·i·mate** /əˈpräksəmit/ ▸*adj.* fairly correct; near to the actual.
▸*v.* /əˈpräksəˌmāt/ bring or come near (esp. in quality, number, etc.). —**ap·prox·i·mate·ly** *adv.* —**ap·prox·i·ma·tion** *n.*

**ap·pur·te·nance** /əˈpərtn-əns/ ▸*n.* (usu. **appurtenances**) accessory, etc., associated with an activity.

**APR** ▸*abbr.* annual or annualized percentage rate.

**Apr.** ▸*abbr.* April.

**ap·ri·cot** /ˈapriˌkät/ ▸*n.* small, juicy, soft fruit of an orange-yellow color.

**A·pril** /ˈāprəl/ ▸*n.* fourth month of the year.
□ **April Fool's Day** April 1.

**a pri·o·ri** /ˈā prīˈôrī/ ▸*adj.* **1** (of reasoning) deductive; proceeding from causes to effects. **2** (of concepts, etc.) logically independent of experience.
▸*adv.* **1** deductively. **2** as far as one knows.

**a·pron** /ˈāprən/ ▸*n.* **1** garment covering and protecting the front of a person's clothes. **2** part of a stage in front of the curtain in a theater. **3** paved area of an airfield for maneuvering or loading aircraft.

**ap·ro·pos** /ˌaprəˈpō/ ▸*adj.* to the point; appropriate.
▸*adv.* appropriately.
▸*prep.* in respect to.

**apse** /aps/ ▸*n.* large semicircular or polygonal recess, arched or with a domed roof, at the eastern end of a church.

**ap·sis** /ˈapsis/ ▸*n.* (*pl.* **-si·des** /-siˌdēz/) either of two points on the orbit of a planet or satellite that are nearest to or furthest from the body around which it moves.

**apt** /apt/ ▸*adj.* **1** appropriate; suitable. **2** (**apt to**) having a tendency. **3** clever; quick to learn. —**apt·ly** *adv.* —**apt·ness** *n.*

**apt.** ▸*abbr.* apartment.

**ap·ti·tude** /ˈaptiˌt(y)o͞od/ ▸*n.* **1** natural talent. **2** ability or suitability.

**aq·ua·cul·ture** /ˈäkwəˌkəlCHər; ˈak-/ ▸*n.* rearing of aquatic animals or the cultivation of aquatic plants for food.

**aq·ua·ma·rine** /ˌäkwəməˈrēn; ˌak-/ ▸*n.* **1** light bluish-green precious stone. **2** (also **aq·ua**) bluish-green color.

**aq·ua·plane** /ˈäkwəˌplān; ˈak-/ ▸*n.* board for riding on water, pulled by a speedboat.
▸*v.* (of a vehicle) slide uncontrollably on a wet surface.

**a·quar·i·um** /əˈkwe(ə)rēəm/ ▸*n.* (*pl.* **-i·ums** or **-i·a**) **1** tank of water with transparent sides for keeping live aquatic plants and animals. **2** building where aquatic plants and animals are kept for study and exhibition.

**a·quat·ic** /əˈkwätik/ ▸*adj.* **1** growing or living in water. **2** (of a sport) played in or on water.
▸*n.* (**aquatics**) aquatic sports.

**aq·ue·duct** /ˈakwiˌdəkt/ ▸*n.* artificial channel for conveying water, esp. in the form of a bridge supported by tall columns across a valley.

**a·que·ous** /ˈākwēəs/ ▸*adj.* of, containing, or like water.

**aq·ui·line** /ˈakwəˌlīn/ ▸*adj.* **1** (of a nose) curved like an eagle's beak. **2** of or like an eagle.

**AR** ▸*abbr.* Arkansas (in official postal use).

**Ar** ▸*symb.* argon.

**-ar** ▸*suffix* **1** forming adjectives: *angular* | *linear* | *nuclear* | *titular.* **2** forming nouns: *scholar* | *pillar* | *bursar* | *mortar.* **3** assim. form of **-ER, -OR**: *liar* | *beggar.*

**Ar·ab** /ˈarəb/ ▸*n.* member of a Semitic people inhabiting Saudi Arabia and the Middle East generally.
▸*adj.* of Arabia or the Arabs.

**ar·a·besque** /ˌarəˈbesk/ ▸*n.* posture in which the body is supported on one leg, with the other leg extended horizontally backward.

**Ar·a·bic** /ˈarəbik/ ▶n. Semitic language of the Arabs.

▶adj. of or relating to Arabia.

☐ **Arabic numeral** any of the numerals 0, 1, 2, 3, 4, 5, 6, 7, 8, and 9.

**ar·a·ble** /ˈarəbəl/ ▶adj. (of land) suitable for crop production.

**a·rach·nid** /əˈraknid/ ▶n. any arthropod of a class comprising scorpions, spiders, etc.

▶adj. of or pertaining to the arachnids.

**A·rap·a·ho** /əˈrapəˌhō/ ▶n.
**1 a** N. American people native to the central plains of Canada and the U.S. **b** member of this people. **2** language of this people.

**ar·bi·ter** /ˈärbitər/ ▶n. arbitrator; judge.

**ar·bi·trage** /ˈärbiˌträzн/ ▶n. simultaneous buying and selling of securities, currency, or commodities in different markets or in derivative forms in order to take advantage of differing prices for the same asset.

▶v. buy and sell assets in such a way.

**ar·bi·trar·y** /ˈärbiˌtrerē/ ▶adj.

**1** random; capricious. **2** (of power) unrestrained and autocratic. —**ar·bi·trar·i·ly** adv. —**ar·bi·trar·i·ness** n.

**ar·bi·trate** /ˈärbiˌtrāt/ ▶v. decide by or as an arbitrator. —**ar·bi·tra·tion** n. —**ar·bi·tra·tor** n.

**ar·bor** /ˈärbər/ ▶n. shady garden alcove enclosed by trees or climbing plants; bower.

**ar·bo·re·al** /ärˈbôrēəl/ ▶adj. of or living in trees.

**ar·bo·re·tum** /ˌärbəˈrētəm/ ▶n. (pl. -**tums** or -**ta**) botanical garden devoted to trees, shrubs, etc.

**ar·bor·i·cul·ture** /ˈärbəriˌkəlcнər; ärˈbôri-/ ▶n. cultivation of trees and shrubs.

**arc** /ärk/ ▶n. **1** part of the circumference of a circle or any other curve. **2** luminous discharge between two electrodes.

▶v. (**arced, arc·ing**) form an arc or move in a curve.

**ar·cade** /ärˈkād/ ▶n. **1** passage with an arched roof. **2** covered walk, esp. lined with shops. **3** series of arches supporting or set along a wall. **4** entertainment establishment with coin-operated games, etc.

**ar·ca·na** /ärˈkānə/ ▶pl. n. [treated

as *sing.* or *pl.*] (*sing.* **-num** /-nəm/) secrets or mysteries.

**ar·cane** /är'kān/ ▶*adj.* mysterious; secret.

**arch** /ärch/ ▶*n.* **1** curved structure as an opening or a support for a bridge, roof, floor, etc. **2** any arch-shaped curve. ▶*v.* form or span like an arch. ▶*adj.* self-consciously or affectedly playful or teasing. —**arch·ly** *adv.*

**arch-** ▶*comb. form* chief; principal: *archbishop | archenemy.*

**ar·chae·ol·o·gy** /ˌärkē'äləjē/ (also **ar·che·ol·o·gy**) ▶*n.* study of ancient cultures, esp. through the excavation and analysis of physical remains. —**ar·chae·o·log·i·cal** *adj.* —**ar·chae·ol·o·gist** *n.*

**ar·cha·ic** /är'kāik/ ▶*adj.* **1** antiquated. **2** (of a word, etc.) no longer in ordinary use. **3** primitive.

**ar·cha·ism** /'ärkēˌizəm; 'ärkā-/ ▶*n.* **1** thing that is very old or old-fashioned. **2** use or conscious imitation of very old or old-fashioned styles or features in language or art.

**arch·an·gel** /'ärˌkānjəl/ ▶*n.* angel of the highest rank.

**arch·bish·op** /'ärch'bishəp/ ▶*n.*

bishop of the highest rank. —**arch·bish·op·ric** *n.*

**arch·di·o·cese** /ärch'dīəsis/ ▶*n.* diocese of an archbishop. —**arch·di·oc·e·san** *adj.*

**arch·en·e·my** /'ärch'enəmē/ ▶*n.* (*pl.* **-mies**) **1** chief enemy. **2** the Devil.

**arch·er** /'ärchər/ ▶*n.* person who shoots with a bow and arrows.

**ar·che·type** /'ärk(ə)ˌtīp/ ▶*n.* **1** typical example of a person or thing. **2** original that has been imitated. **3** recurrent symbol or motif. —**ar·che·typ·al** *adj.*

**ar·chi·pel·a·go** /ˌärkə'peləˌgō/ ▶*n.* (*pl.* **-gos** or **-goes**) **1** group of islands. **2** sea with many islands.

**ar·chi·tect** /'ärkiˌtekt/ ▶*n.* **1** designer of buildings, ships, etc., supervising their construction. **2** person who brings about a specified thing: *the architect of the tax reform bill.*

**ar·chi·tec·ture** /'ärkiˌtekchər/ ▶*n.* **1** design and construction of buildings. **2** style of a building. **3** buildings collectively. —**ar·chi·tec·tur·al** *adj.*

**ar·chive** /'arˌkīv/ ▶*n.* (usu. **archives**) collection of historical documents or records or the place where they are kept: *the National Archives.*

▸*v.* **1** store in an archive.
**2** *Computing* transfer (data) to a less frequently used file or less easily accessible medium.
—**ar·chi·val** *adj.* —**ar·chi·vist** *n.*

**arch·way** ▸*n.* **1** vaulted passage. **2** arched entrance.

**Arc·tic** /'är(k)tik/ ▸*adj.* **1** of the north polar regions. **2** (**arctic**) very cold.
▸*n.* Arctic regions.
□ **Arctic Circle** parallel of latitude 66° 33– N, forming an imaginary line around this region.

**ar·cu·ate** /'ärkyo͞oit; -ˌāt/ ▸*adj.* shaped like a bow; curved.

**ar·dent** /'ärdnt/ ▸*adj.* eager; zealous; fervent; passionate.

**ar·dor** /'ärdər/ ▸*n.* zeal; burning enthusiasm; passion.

**ar·du·ous** /'ärjo͞oəs/ ▸*adj.* hard to achieve or overcome; difficult; laborious.

**are** /är/ ▸2nd sing. present & 1st, 2nd, 3rd pl. present of BE.

**a·re·a** /'e(ə)rēə/ ▸*n.* **1** extent or measure of a surface: *3 acres in area.* **2** region. **3** space for a specific purpose.

**a·re·a code** ▸*n.* three-digit number that identifies a telephone service region.

**a·re·na** /ə'rēnə/ ▸*n.* **1** central part of an amphitheater, etc. **2** scene of conflict; sphere of action or discussion.

**aren't** /är(ə)nt/ ▸*contr.* are not.

**ar·go·sy** /'ärgəsē/ ▸*n.* (*pl.* **-sies**) large merchant ship, originally one from Ragusa (now Dubrovnik) or Venice.

**ar·got** /'ärgət/ ▸*n.* jargon of a group or class.

**ar·gue** /'ärgyo͞o/ ▸*v.* (**-gued, -gu·ing**) **1** exchange views or opinions heatedly or contentiously. **2** indicate; maintain by reasoning.
—**ar·gu·a·ble** *adj.* —**ar·gu·a·bly** *adv.*

**ar·gu·ment** /'ärgyəmənt/ ▸*n.* **1** exchange of views, esp. a contentious and prolonged one. **2** reason advanced; reasoning process.

**ar·gu·men·ta·tive** /ˌärgyə-'mentətiv/ ▸*adj.* fond of arguing.

**a·ri·a** /'ärēə/ ▸*n.* solo in an opera, etc.

**-arian** ▸*suffix* forming adjectives and nouns meaning '(one) concerned with or believing in': *agrarian | antiquarian | humanitarian | vegetarian.*

**ar·id** /'arid/ ▸*adj.* **1 a** dry; parched. **b** barren. **2** uninteresting. —**a·rid·i·ty** *n.*

**a·rise** /əˈrīz/ ▸v. (past **a·rose**; past part. **a·ris·en**) **1** come into existence or be noticed. **2** rise.

**a·ris·to·cra·cy** /ˌariˈstäkrəsē/ ▸n. (pl. **-cies**) **1 a** highest class in society; the nobility. **b** the nobility as a ruling class. **2 a** government by a privileged group. **b** nation so governed.

**a·ris·to·crat** /əˈristəˌkrat/ ▸n. member of the aristocracy. —**a·ris·to·crat·ic** adj.

**a·rith·me·tic** /əˈriTHmiˌtik/ ▸n. **1** science of numbers. **2** use of numbers; computation. ▸adj. (also **a·rith·met·i·cal**) of arithmetic.

**Ariz.** ▸abbr. Arizona.

**Ark.** ▸abbr. Arkansas.

**ark** /ärk/ ▸n. **1** (**the ark**) (in the Bible) ship used by Noah to save his family and the animals from the flood. **2** (also **Holy Ark**) chest housing the Torah scrolls in a synagogue.

**arm** /ärm/ ▸n. **1** each of the upper limbs of the human body from shoulder to hand. **2** forelimb or tentacle of an animal. **3 a** sleeve of a garment. **b** arm support of a chair. **c** thing resembling an arm in branching from a main stem. **4** (usu. **arms**) weapon. ▸v. **1** supply with weapons.

**2** make (a bomb, etc.) able to explode.

**ar·ma·da** /ärˈmädə/ ▸n. fleet of warships, esp. that sent by Spain against England in 1588.

**ar·ma·dil·lo** /ˌärməˈdilō/ ▸n. (pl. **-los**) tropical American mammal with a body covered in bony plates.

**Ar·ma·ged·don** /ˌärməˈgedn/ ▸(also **ar·ma·ged·don**) n. any huge bloody battle or struggle.

**ar·ma·ment** /ˈärməmənt/ ▸n. **1** (also **ar·ma·ments**) military weapons and equipment. **2** process of equipping for war. **3** force equipped for war.

**arm·chair** ▸n. chair with arm supports.

**ar·mi·stice** /ˈärmistis/ ▸n. truce, esp. permanent. □ **Armistice Day** former name of Veteran's Day.

**ar·mor** /ˈärmər/ ▸n. **1** defensive covering, usu. of metal. **2** armored vehicles collectively. ▸v. [usu. as adj. **armored**] provide with armor and often with guns.

**ar·mor·y** ▸n. (pl. **-ies**) **1** arsenal. **2** arms factory.

**arm·pit** ▸n. hollow under the arm at the shoulder.

**ar·my** /ˈärmē/ ▸n. (pl. **-mies**)

**1** organized armed land force.
**2** very large number.

**a·ro·ma** /əˈrōmə/ ▸ *n.* distinctive and esp. pleasing smell.
—**ar·o·mat·ic** *adj.*

**ar·o·mat·ic** /ˌarəˈmatik/ ▸ *adj.* having a pleasant and distinctive smell.
▸ *n.* substance or plant emitting a pleasant and distinctive smell.

**a·round** /əˈround/ ▸ *adv.* **1** on every side; on all sides. **2** in various places; here and there: *shop around.* **3** approximately. **4** in existence or in active use. **5** near at hand.
▸ *prep.* **1** on or along the circuit of. **2** on every side of. **3** here and there; in or near. **4** about; at a time near to.

**a·rouse** /əˈrouz/ ▸ *v.* **1** awake from sleep. **2** stir into activity. **3** stimulate sexually.
—**a·rous·al** *n.*

**ar·peg·gi·o** /ärˈpejēˌō/ ▸ *n.* (*pl.* **-os**) notes of a chord played in succession, either ascending or descending.

**ar·raign** /əˈrān/ ▸ *v.* indict; formally accuse.
—**ar·raign·ment** *n.*

**ar·range** /əˈrānj/ ▸ *v.* **1** put into order; classify. **2** plan or provide for. **3** adapt (a composition) for

performance with instruments or voices. —**ar·rang·er** *n.*
—**ar·range·ment** *n.*

**ar·rant** /ˈarənt/ ▸ *adj.* complete, utter.

**ar·ray** /əˈrā/ ▸ *n.* **1** imposing or well-ordered series or display. **2** ordered arrangement, esp. of troops.
▸ *v.* **1** deck; adorn. **2** set in order; marshal (forces).

**ar·rears** /əˈri(ə)rz/ ▸ *pl. n.* money owed that should have been paid earlier.
□ **in arrears** behind in paying money that is owed: *two of the tenants are in arrears.*

**ar·rest** /əˈrest/ ▸ *v.* **1** lawfully seize (a person, ship, etc.). **2** stop or check (esp. a process or moving thing). **3** attract (a person's attention).
▸ *n.* **1** arresting or being arrested. **2** stoppage.
□ **under arrest** in custody.

**ar·rhyth·mi·a** /āˈriTHmēə; əˈriTH-/ ▸ *n.* condition in which the heart beats with an irregular or abnormal rhythm.

**ar·rière-pen·sée** /äˌryer pänˈsā/ ▸ *n.* concealed thought or intention; an ulterior motive.

**ar·rive** /əˈrīv/ ▸ *v.* **1** reach a destination: *arrived at his house |*

*arrived in Geneva.* **2** reach (a conclusion, etc.): *they arrived at the same conclusion.* —**ar·riv·al** *n.*

**ar·ri·viste** /ˌärēˈvēst/ ▶*n.* ambitious or ruthlessly self-seeking person, esp. one who has recently acquired wealth or social status.

**ar·ro·gant** /ˈarəgənt/ ▶*adj.* aggressively assertive or presumptuous. —**ar·ro·gance** *n.*

**ar·ro·gate** /ˈarəˌgāt/ ▶*v.* claim (power, responsibility, etc.) without justification.

**ar·row** /ˈarō/ ▶*n.* **1** sharp pointed wooden or metal missile shot from a bow. **2** representation of an arrow indicating a direction.

**ar·row·head** ▶*n.* pointed end of an arrow.

**ar·row·root** ▶*n.* **1** type of nutritious starch. **2** plant yielding this.

**ar·se·nal** /ˈärs(ə)nl/ ▶*n.* **1** store of weapons. **2** government establishment for the storage and manufacture of weapons and ammunition. **3** resources regarded collectively: *the U.S. arsenal of nuclear weapons.*

**ar·se·nic** /ˈärs(ə)nik/ ▶*n.* **1** nonscientific name for arsenic trioxide, a poisonous white powder used in weed killers, rat poison, etc. **2** brittle semimetallic element. (Symb.: **As**)
▶*adj.* of or containing arsenic.

**ar·son** /ˈärsən/ ▶*n.* act of maliciously setting fire to property. —**ar·son·ist** *n.*

**art** /ärt/ ▶*n.* **1 a** human creative skill or its application. **b** work exhibiting this. **2** (**the arts**) various branches of creative activity concerned with the production of imaginative designs, sounds, or ideas, e.g., painting, music, writing, etc. **3** creative activity, esp. painting and drawing, resulting in visual representation. **4** human skill as opposed to nature. **5** skill, aptitude, or knack.
▶2nd sing. present of BE.

**ar·te·rio·scle·ro·sis** /ärˌti(ə)rēōskləˈrōsis/ ▶*n.* loss of elasticity and thickening of the walls of the arteries, esp. in old age; hardening of the arteries. —**ar·te·ri·o·scle·rot·ic** *adj.*

**ar·te·ry** /ˈärtərē/ ▶*n.* (*pl.* **-ries**) **1** any of the blood vessels carrying oxygen-enriched blood from the heart. **2** main road or railroad line. —**ar·te·ri·al** *adj.*

**ar·thri·tis** /ärˈТHrītis/ ▶*n.*

inflammation of a joint or joints. —**ar·thrit·ic** *adj. & n.*

**ar·thro·pod** /'ärThrə,päd/ ▶*n.* invertebrate with a segmented body, jointed limbs, and an external skeleton, e.g., a spider, crustacean, etc.

**ar·ti·choke** /'ärti,CHōk/ ▶*n.* plant related to the thistle, having an edible flower head.

**ar·ti·cle** /'ärtikəl/ ▶*n.* **1** particular item or object. **2** piece of writing in a newspaper, magazine, etc. **3** separate clause or portion of any document. **4** *Gram.* word (e.g., *a, an, the*) preceding a noun and signifying a specific instance (*the*) or any of several instances (*a, an*).
▶*v.* bind by the terms of a contract, as one of apprenticeship.

**ar·ti·cu·late** ▶*adj.* /är'tikyəlit/ **1** able to speak fluently and coherently. **2** (of sound or speech) having clearly distinguishable parts. **3** having joints.
▶*v.* /är'tikyə,lāt/ **1** pronounce clearly and distinctly. **2** express (an idea, etc.) coherently: *was unable to articulate her emotions.* **3** connect by joints. —**ar·tic·u·la·tion** *n.*

**ar·ti·fact** /'ärtə,fakt/ ▶*n.* man-made object.

**ar·ti·fice** /'ärtifis/ ▶*n.* clever or cunning device.

**ar·ti·fi·cial** /,ärtə'fisHəl/ ▶*adj.* **1** produced by human art or effort; not natural. **2** imitation; fake. **3** affected; insincere. —**ar·ti·fi·ci·al·i·ty** *n.* —**ar·ti·fi·cial·ly** *adv.*

**ar·ti·fi·cial in·tel·li·gence** ▶*n.* application of computers to areas normally regarded as requiring human intelligence.

**ar·ti·fi·cial res·pir·a·tion** ▶*n.* restoration or initiation of breathing by manual or mechanical methods.

**ar·til·ler·y** /är'tilərē/ ▶*n.* (*pl.* -**ies**) **1** large-caliber guns used in warfare on land. **2** branch of the armed forces that uses these.

**ar·ti·san** /'ärtizən/ ▶*n.* skilled manual worker or craftsman.

**art·ist** ▶*n.* **1** person who creates works of art. **2** professional performer, esp. a singer or dancer. **3** habitual or skillful practitioner of a specified activity. —**ar·tis·tic** *adj.* —**ar·tis·ti·cal·ly** *adv.* —**art·ist·ry** *n.*

**ar·tiste** /är'tēst/ ▶*n.* professional entertainer, esp. a singer or dancer.

**art·less** ▸*adj.* guileless; ingenuous. —**art·less·ly** *adv.*

**art·y** ▸*adj.* (**-i·er**, **-i·est**) *inf.* pretentiously or affectedly artistic.

**As** ▸*symb.* arsenic.

**as** /az/ ▸*adv. & conj.* [*adv.* as antecedent in main sentence; *conj.* in relative clause expressed or implied] . . . to the extent to which . . . is or does, etc.: *I am as tall as he* | *it is not as easy as you think.*

▸*conj.* **1** expressing result or purpose: *came early so as to meet us.* **2** although: *good as it is = although it is good.* **3 a** in the manner in which. **b** in the capacity or form of. **c** during or at the time that. **d** since.

▸*pron.* **1** that; who; which: *I had the same trouble as you.* **2** a fact that: *he lost, as you know.*

▸*prep.* in the role of: *he works as a cook.*

□ **as for** with regard to. □ **as if** (or **as though**) as would be the case if: *acts as if she were in charge.* □ **as it is** (or **as is**) in the existing circumstances or state. □ **as it were** in a way; to a certain extent.

**a.s.a.p.** (also **ASAP**) ▸*abbr.* as soon as possible.

**as·bes·tos** /as'bestəs/ ▸*n.* fibrous silicate mineral, esp. used as a heat-resistant or insulating material.

**as·cend** /ə'send/ ▸*v.* move upwards; rise; climb.

**as·cen·dan·cy** /ə'sendənsē/ (also **as·cen·den·cy**) ▸*n.* superior or dominant condition or position. —**as·cen·dant** *adj.*

**as·cen·sion** /ə'sensHən/ ▸*n.* **1** ascent. **2** (**Ascension**) ascent of Christ into heaven.

**as·cent** ▸*n.* **1** ascending; rising. **2** upward slope.

**as·cer·tain** /ˌasər'tān/ ▸*v.* find out as a definite fact. —**as·cer·tain·a·ble** *adj.* —**as·cer·tain·ment** *n.*

**as·cet·ic** /ə'setik/ ▸*n.* person who practices severe self-discipline and abstains from all forms of pleasure, esp. for religious or spiritual reasons.

▸*adj.* relating to or characteristic of ascetics or their practices; abstaining from pleasure. —**as·cet·i·cism** *n.*

**ASCII** /'askē/ ▸*abbr. Computing* American Standard Code for Information Interchange.

**a·scor·bic ac·id** /ə'skôrbik/ ▸*n.* vitamin C.

**as·cot** /'as,kä/ ▸*n.* scarflike item

of neckwear with broad ends worn looped to lie flat one over the other against the chest.

**as·cribe** /əˈskrīb/ ▶v. attribute or impute. —**a·scrib·a·ble** adj. —**a·scrip·tion** n.

**a·sep·sis** /āˈsepsis/ ▶n. **1** absence of harmful microorganisms. **2** exclusion of such microorganisms, esp. in surgery. —**a·sep·tic** adj.

**a·sex·u·al** /āˈseksHŌŌəl/ ▶adj. **1** without sex or sexuality. **2** (of reproduction) not involving the fusion of gametes. —**a·sex·u·al·ly** adv.

**ash** /asH/ ▶n. **1** powdery residue left after burning. **2** (**ashes**) ruins. **3** (**ashes**) remains of the human body after cremation. **4** tree with silvery-gray bark and hard, pale wood. —**ash·y** adj.

**a·shamed** /əˈsHāmd/ ▶adj. **1** embarrassed by shame. **2** hesitant; reluctant (but usu. not actually refusing or declining): *ashamed to admit I was wrong.*

**ash·en** /ˈasHən/ ▶adj. pale or gray.

**a·shore** /əˈsHôr/ ▶adv. toward or on the shore or land.

**ash·tray** ▶n. small receptacle for cigarette ashes, butts, etc.

**Ash Wednes·day** ▶n. first day of Lent.

**A·sian** /ˈāzHən/ ▶n. **1** native of Asia. **2** person of Asian descent. ▶adj. of or relating to Asia or its people, customs, or languages.

**a·side** /əˈsīd/ ▶adv. **1** to or on one side; away. **2** out of consideration: *joking aside.* ▶n. **1** words spoken in a play for the audience to hear, but supposed not to be heard by the other characters. **2** incidental remark.

**as·i·nine** /ˈasəˌnīn/ ▶adj. like an ass, esp. stubborn or stupid.

**ask** /ask/ ▶v. **1** call for an answer to or about. **2** seek to obtain from another person. **3** invite; request the company of. **4 a** seek to obtain, meet, or be directed to. **b** bring upon oneself.

**a·skance** /əˈskans/ ▶adv. (in phrase **look askance at**) regard with suspicion.

**as·ke·sis** /əˈskēsis/ (also **as·ce·sis** /əˈsēsis/) ▶n. practice of severe self-discipline, typically for religious reasons.

**a·skew** /əˈskyŌŌ/ ▶adv. & adj. **1** not in a straight or level position. **2** wrong; awry: *the plan went sadly askew.*

**a·sleep** /əˈslēp/ ▶adj. & adv.

**1 a** in or into a state of sleep. **b** inactive; inattentive. **2** (of a limb, etc.) numb.

**asp** /asp/ ▶n. small venomous snake of North Africa and southern Europe.

**as·par·a·gus** /əˈsparəgəs/ ▶n. plant of the lily family having shoots that are edible when young.

**as·pect** /ˈaspekt/ ▶n. **1 a** particular component or feature of a matter. **b** particular way in which a matter may be considered. **2** appearance.

**as·pen** /ˈaspən/ ▶n. poplar tree with especially tremulous leaves.

**as·per·i·ty** /əˈsperitē/ ▶n. (pl. -ties) **1** harshness or sharpness of temper or tone. **2** roughness. **3** rough excrescence.

**as·per·sion** /əˈspərzʜən/ ▶n. slander; false insinuation.

**as·phalt** /ˈasfôlt/ ▶n. **1** dark bituminous pitch occurring naturally or made from petroleum. **2** mixture of this with sand, gravel, etc., for surfacing roads, etc. ▶v. surface with asphalt.

**as·phyx·i·ate** /asˈfiksēˌāt/ ▶v. suffocate. —**as·phyx·i·a·tion** n.

**as·pi·rate** /ˈaspəˌrāt/ ▶v. **1** pronounce (a sound) with an exhalation of breath. **2** draw (fluid) from the body by suction.

**as·pi·ra·tion** /ˌ▶n. **1** hope or ambition: *the gap between aspiration and reality.* **2** pronouncing a sound with an exhalation of breath. **3** drawing fluid from the body by suction.

**as·pire** /əˈspī(ə)r/ ▶v. have ambition or strong desire.

**as·pi·rin** /ˈasp(ə)rin/ ▶n. (pl. same or **as·pir·ins**) white powder, acetylsalicylic acid, used to relieve pain and reduce fever.

**ass** /as/ ▶n. **1 a** four-legged long-eared mammal related to the horse. **b** donkey. **2** inf. stupid person. **3** vulgar, inf. buttocks.

**as·sail** /əˈsāl/ ▶v. attack physically or verbally. —**as·sail·ant** n.

**as·sas·sin** /əˈsasin/ ▶n. killer, esp. of a political or religious leader. —**as·sas·si·nate** v. —**as·sas·si·na·tion** n.

**as·sault** /əˈsôlt/ ▶n. **1** violent physical or verbal attack. **2** Law act that threatens physical harm. ▶v. make an assault on.

**as·say** /aˈsā/ ▶n. testing of a metal or ore to determine its ingredients and quality. ▶v. make an assay of (a metal or ore).

**as·sem·blage** /ə'semblij/ ▶*n.*
**1** bringing or coming together.
**2** assembled group.

**as·sem·ble** /ə'sembəl/ ▶*v.*
**1** gather together; collect.
**2** arrange in order. **3** fit together
the parts of.

**as·sem·bly** /ə'semblē/ ▶*n.* (*pl.*
**-blies**) **1** assembling. **2 a** group
of persons gathered together,
esp. as a deliberative body.
**b** gathering of the entire
membership of a school.
**3** assembling of a machine or
structure or its parts.

**as·sent** /ə'sent/ ▶*v.* **1** express
agreement. **2** consent.
▶*n.* **1** mental or inward
acceptance or agreement.
**2** consent or sanction, esp.
official.

**as·sert** /ə'sərt/ ▶*v.* **1** declare;
state clearly. **2** insist on (one's
rights, etc.): *it was time to assert
her authority.* —**as·ser·tion** *n.*
—**as·ser·tive** *adj.* —**as·ser·tive·ly**
*adv.*

**as·sess** /ə'ses/ ▶*v.* **1** estimate
the size or quality of. **2** estimate
the value of (a property) for
taxation. —**as·sess·ment** *n.*
—**as·ses·sor** *n.*

**as·set** /'aset/ ▶*n.* **1 a** useful or
valuable quality. **b** person or

thing possessing such a quality.
**2** (usu. **assets**) property; thing
owned.

**as·sev·er·a·tion** /ə,sevə-
'rāsHən/ ▶*n.* solemn or emphatic
declaration or statement of
something.

**as·si·du·i·ty** /,asi'd(y)o͞oitē/ ▶*n.*
(*pl.* **-ties**) constant or close
attention to what one is doing.

**as·sid·u·ous** /ə'sijo͞oəs/ ▶*adj.*
**1** persevering; hardworking.
**2** attending closely.
—**as·sid·u·ous·ly** *adv.*
—**as·sid·u·ous·ness** *n.*

**as·sign** /ə'sīn/ ▶*v.* **1 a** allot as a
share or responsibility.
**b** appoint to a position, task, etc.
**2** fix (a time, place, etc.) for a
specific purpose. **3** ascribe or
refer to.
▶*n.* person to whom property or
rights are legally transferred.
—**as·sign·a·ble** *adj.*
—**as·sign·ment** *n.*

**as·sig·na·tion** /,asig'nāsHən/
▶*n.* appointment to meet, esp. in
secret.

**as·sim·i·late** /ə'simə,lāt/ ▶*v.*
absorb or cause to be absorbed
into the body, mind, or a larger
group. —**as·sim·i·la·tion** *n.*

**as·sist** /ə'sist/ ▶*v.* help.

▶*n.* act of helping. —**as·sis·tance** *n.* —**as·sis·tant** *n.*

**assn.** ▶*abbr.* association.

**as·so·ci·ate** ▶*v.* /əˈsōsēˌāt/ **1** connect in the mind. **2** join or combine. **3** declare oneself in agreement: *want to associate ourselves with the plan.* **4** meet frequently or have dealings. ▶*n.* /əˈsōsēit/ **1** business partner or colleague. **2** friend or companion. **3** subordinate member of a body, institute, etc. ▶*adj.* /əˈsōsēit/ **1** joined or allied. **2** of less than full status. —**as·so·ci·a·tive** *adj.*

**as·so·ci·a·tion** ▶*n.* **1** group organized for a joint purpose. **2** connection between people or organizations. **3** mental connection between ideas.

**as·so·nance** /ˈasənəns/ ▶*n.* resemblance of sound (often of vowels) between two syllables in nearby words, e.g., *saw, caught; cold, culled.* —**as·so·nant** *adj.*

**as·sort·ed** /əˈsôrtid/ ▶*adj.* of various kinds put together. —**as·sort** *v.*

**as·sort·ment** /əˈsôrtmənt/ ▶*n.* diverse group or mixture.

**Asst.** ▶*abbr.* Assistant.

**as·suage** /əˈswāj/ ▶*v.* **1** calm or soothe. **2** appease (an appetite).

**as·sume** /əˈsoōm/ ▶*v.* **1** take or accept as being true. **2** simulate or pretend (ignorance, etc.). **3** undertake (an office or duty). **4** take or put on (an aspect, attribute, etc.).

**as·sump·tion** /əˈsəm(p)SHən/ ▶*n.* **1** assuming. **2** accepting without proof.

**as·sure** /əˈSHoŏr/ ▶*v.* **1** confirm confidently. **2** make safe. —**as·sur·ance** *n.*

**as·sured** ▶*adj.* **1** guaranteed. **2** self-confident.

**as·ter** /ˈastər/ ▶*n.* plant with bright daisylike flowers.

**as·ter·isk** /ˈastəˌrisk/ ▶*n.* symbol (*) used in printing and writing to mark words, etc., for reference, to stand for omitted matter, etc. ▶*v.* mark with an asterisk.

**a·stern** /əˈstərn/ ▶*adv.* **1** aft; away to the stern. **2** backward.

**as·ter·oid** /ˈastəˌroid/ ▶*n.* any of the small celestial bodies revolving around the sun, mainly between the orbits of Mars and Jupiter.

**asth·ma** /ˈazmə/ ▶*n.* usu. allergic respiratory disorder, often with paroxysms of difficult breathing. —**asth·mat·ic** *adj. & n.*

**a·stig·ma·tism** /əˈstigməˌtizəm/

▶*n.* defect in the eye or lens resulting in distorted images. —**as·tig·mat·ic** *adj.*

**a·stir** /əˈstər/ ▶*adj. & adv.* in motion.

**as·ton·ish** /əˈstänisʜ/ ▶*v.* amaze; surprise greatly. —**as·ton·ish·ing** *adj.* —**as·ton·ish·ment** *n.*

**as·tound** /əˈstound/ ▶*v.* shock with alarm or surprise; amaze. —**as·tound·ing** *adj.*

**as·tral** /ˈastrəl/ ▶*adj.* of or resembling the stars.

**a·stray** /əˈstrā/ ▶*adv. & adj.* **1** in or into error or sin: *lead astray.* **2** out of the right way.

**a·stride** /əˈstrīd/ ▶*adv.* with a leg on each side of.
▶*prep.* with a leg on each side of; extending across.

**as·trin·gent** /əˈstrinjənt/ ▶*adj.* **1** causing the contraction of body tissues. **2** severe or severe in manner: *her astringent words had an effect.* **3** sharp or bitter: *an astringent smell of rotting fruit.*
▶*n.* astringent substance or drug. —**as·trin·gen·cy** *n.*

**as·trol·o·gy** /əˈsträləjē/ ▶*n.* study of the movements and relative positions of celestial bodies interpreted as an influence on human affairs. —**as·trol·o·ger** *n.* —**as·tro·log·i·cal** *adj.*

**as·tro·naut** /ˈastrəˌnôt/ ▶*n.* person trained to travel in a spacecraft. —**as·tro·nau·tics** *n.*

**as·tro·nom·i·cal** /ˌastrə-ˈnämikəl/ (also **as·tro·nom·ic**) ▶*adj.* **1** of astronomy. **2** extremely large. —**as·tro·nom·i·cal·ly** *adv.*
□ **astronomical unit** unit of measurement equal to the mean distance from the center of the earth to the center of the sun, $1.496 \times 10^{11}$ meters or 92.9 million miles.

**as·tron·o·my** /əˈstränəmē/ ▶*n.* scientific study of celestial bodies. —**as·tron·o·mer** *n.*

**as·tro·phys·ics** /ˌastrōˈfiziks/ ▶*n.* branch of astronomy concerned with the physics and chemistry of celestial bodies. —**as·tro·phys·i·cist** *n.*

**as·tute** /əˈst(y)o͞ot/ ▶*adj.* shrewd.

**a·sun·der** /əˈsəndər/ ▶*adv.* *poet./lit.* apart.

**a·sy·lum** /əˈsīləm/ ▶*n.* **1** sanctuary; protection, esp. for those pursued by the law. **2** *hist.* institution for the mentally ill or destitute.

**a·sym·me·try** /āˈsimitrē/ ▶*n.* lack of symmetry. —**a·sym·met·ric** *adj.* —**a·sym·met·ri·cal** *adj.* —**a·sym·met·ri·cal·ly** *adv.*

**At** ▸*symb. Chem.* astatine.

**at** /at/ ▸*prep.* **1** expressing position: *at the corner.* **2** expressing a time: *at dawn.* **3** expressing a point in a scale: *at his best.* **4** expressing engagement in a state or activity: *at war.* **5** expressing a value or rate: *sell at $10 each.* **6 a** with or with reference to. **b** by means of. **7** expressing: **a** motion toward. **b** aim toward or pursuit of.

**at·a·vism** /'atə,vizəm/ ▸*n.* **1** (in plants or animals) resemblance to remote ancestors rather than to parents. **2** reversion to an earlier type. —**at·a·vis·tic** *adj.* —**at·a·vis·ti·cal·ly** *adv.*

**at·a·vis·tic** /,atə'vistik/ ▸*adj.* relating to or characterized by reversion to something ancient or ancestral.

**ate** /āt/ ▸past of EAT.

**-ate** ▸*suffix* **1** forming nouns denoting status or office: *doctorate* | *episcopate.* **2** forming nouns denoting state or function: *curate* | *mandate.* **3** forming verbs: *associate* | *duplicate* | *hyphenate.*

**a·te·lier** /,atl'yā/ ▸*n.* workshop or artist's studio.

**a·the·ism** /'āTHē,izəm/ ▸*n.* belief that God does not exist. —**a·the·ist** *n.*

**ath·e·nae·um** /,aTHə'nēəm/ (also **ath·e·ne·um**) ▸*n.* **1** used in the names of libraries or institutions for literary or scientific study. **2** used in the titles of periodicals concerned with literature, science, and art.

**ath·lete** /'aTH,lēt/ ▸*n.* skilled performer in sports and physical activities. —**ath·let·ic** *adj.* —**ath·let·ics** *pl. n.*

**ath·lete's foot** ▸*n.* fungal foot condition.

**a·thwart** /ə'THwôrt/ ▸*prep.* **1** from side to side of; across. **2** in opposition to; counter to. ▸*adv.* **1** across from side to side; transversely. **2** so as to be perverse or contradictory.

**at·las** /'atləs/ ▸*n.* book of maps or charts.

**ATM** ▸*abbr.* automated teller machine.

**at·mo·sphere** /'atmə,sfi(ə)r/ ▸*n.* **1** gases surrounding the earth, any other planet, or any substance. **2** air in any particular place. **3** pervading tone or mood of a place or situation. **4** feelings or emotions evoked by a work of art, a piece of music, etc. —**at·mos·pher·ic** *adj.* —**at·mos·pher·i·cal·ly** *adv.*

**at·oll** /ˈatôl/ ▸*n.* ring-shaped coral reef enclosing a lagoon.

**at·om** /ˈatəm/ ▸*n.* **1** smallest particle of a chemical element that can take part in a chemical reaction. **2** this as a source of nuclear energy. —**a·tom·ic** *adj.*

□ **atom bomb** bomb involving the release of energy by nuclear fission.

**at·om·iz·er** /ˈatəˌmīzər/ ▸*n.* instrument for emitting liquids as a fine spray.

**a·ton·al** /āˈtōnl/ ▸*adj. Mus.* not written in any key or mode. —**a·to·nal·i·ty** *n.*

**a·tone** /əˈtōn/ ▸*v.* make amends.

**at·ra·bil·ious** /ˌatrəˈbilēəs; -ˈbilyəs/ ▸*adj.* melancholy or ill-tempered.

**a·tri·um** /ˈātrēəm/ ▸*n.* (*pl.* **-ums** or **-a**) **1** central court of an ancient Roman house. **2** usu. skylit central court rising through several stories. **3** (in a modern house) central hall or courtyard with rooms opening off it. **4** one of the two upper cavities of the heart. —**a·tri·al** *adj.*

**a·tro·cious** /əˈtrōsHəs/ ▸*adj.* **1** very bad or unpleasant. **2** extremely savage or wicked.

**at·ro·phy** /ˈatrəfē/ ▸*v.* (**-phied**) waste away or cause to waste away through lack of use; become emaciated. ▸*n.* wasting away.

**at·tach** /əˈtaCH/ ▸*v.* **1** fasten; affix; join. **2** attribute; assign. **3** (of a thing) adhere; (of a person) join. **4** *Law* seize by legal authority.

**at·ta·ché** /ˌatəˈsHā/ ▸*n.* person appointed to an ambassador's staff, usu. with a special sphere of activity.

□ **attaché case** small flat rectangular case for carrying documents, etc.

**at·tach·ment** ▸*n.* **1** thing attached, esp. for a special function. **2** affection; devotion. **3** means of attaching. **4** attaching or being attached.

**at·tack** /əˈtak/ ▸*v.* **1** act against with (esp. armed) force. **2** seek to hurt or defeat. **3** criticize adversely. **4** act harmfully upon. **5** vigorously apply oneself to. ▸*n.* **1** act of attacking. **2 a** offensive operation. **b** severe criticism. **3** sudden occurrence of an illness. —**at·tack·er** *n.*

**at·tain** /əˈtān/ ▸*v.* **1** reach (a

goal, etc.). **2** gain; accomplish.
—**at·tain·a·ble** *adj.*
—**at·tain·a·bil·i·ty** *n.*
—**at·tain·ment** *n.*

**at·tempt** /əˈtem(p)t/ ▸*v.* seek to achieve, complete, or master.
▸*n.* attempting; endeavor.

**at·tend** /əˈtend/ ▸*v.* **1 a** be present at. **b** go regularly to. **2 a** be present. **b** wait on. **3 a** turn or apply one's mind. **b** deal with.

**at·ten·dance** /əˈtendəns/ ▸*n.* **1** attending or being present. **2** number present.

**at·ten·dant** ▸*n.* person employed to wait on others or provide a service.
▸*adj.* **1** accompanying. **2** waiting on; serving.

**at·ten·tion** /əˈtensHən/ ▸*n.* **1** act or faculty of applying one's mind. **2 a** consideration. **b** care. **3** erect stance in military drill.
—**at·ten·tive** *adj.* —**at·ten·tive·ly** *adv.* —**at·ten·tive·ness** *n.*

**at·ten·u·ate** /əˈtenyo͞oˌāt/ ▸*v.* **1** make thin. **2** reduce in force, value, etc.
▸*adj.* **1** slender. **2** tapering gradually. —**at·ten·u·at·ed** *adj.*
—**at·ten·u·a·tion** *n.*

**at·test** /əˈtest/ ▸*v.* **1** certify the validity of. **2** (**attest to**) bear witness to.

**At·tic** /ˈatik/ ▸*adj.* of ancient Athens or Attica, or the form of Greek spoken there.
▸*n.* form of Greek used by the ancient Athenians.

**at·tic** ▸*n.* uppermost story in a house, usu. under the roof.

**at·tire** /əˈtī(ə)r/ ▸*n.* clothes.
▸*v.* dress.

**at·ti·tude** /ˈatiˌt(y)o͞od/ ▸*n.* **1 a** opinion or way of thinking. **b** behavior reflecting this. **2** bodily posture. **3** position of an aircraft, spacecraft, etc., in relation to specified directions.
—**at·ti·tu·di·nal** *adj.*

**at·tor·ney** /əˈtərnē/ ▸*n.* (*pl.* **-neys**) **1** lawyer. **2** person, esp. a lawyer, appointed to act for another in business or legal matters.
□ **attorney general** chief legal officer in the U.S. and some other countries.

**at·tract** /əˈtrakt/ ▸*v.* **1** draw or bring to oneself or itself. **2** be attractive to; fascinate.
—**at·trac·tion** *n.*

**at·trac·tive** ▸*adj.* **1** pleasing to the senses. **2** appealing to look at. —**at·trac·tive·ly** *adv.*
—**at·trac·tive·ness** *n.*

**at·tri·bute** ▸*v.* /əˈtribyo͞ot/
**1** regard as belonging or
appropriate. **2** ascribe to a
cause.
▸*n.* /ˈatrəˌbyo͞ot/ **1** characteristic
quality ascribed to a person or
thing. **2** material object
recognized as appropriate to a
person, office, or status.
—**at·trib·ut·a·ble** *adj.*
—**at·tri·bu·tion** *n.*

**at·tri·tion** /əˈtriSHən/ ▸*n.*
**1** gradual reduction, as by
retirement, etc., in a work force.
**2 a** gradual wearing out, esp. by
friction. **b** abrasion.

**at·tune** /əˈt(y)o͞on/ ▸*v.* make or
become sensitive.

**atty.** ▸*abbr.* attorney.

**ATV** ▸ *abbr.* all-terrain vehicle.

**a·typ·i·cal** /āˈtipikəl/ ▸*adj.* not
typical. —**a·typ·i·cal·ly** *adv.*

**au·burn** /ˈôbərn/ ▸*adj.* reddish
brown (usu. of a person's hair).

**au cou·rant** /ˌō ˈko͞oräN/ ▸*adj.*
**1** aware of what is going on; well
informed. **2** fashionable.

**auc·tion** /ˈôkSHən/ ▸*n.* sale in
which articles are sold to the
highest bidder.
▸*v.* sell at auction.
—**auc·tion·eer** *n.*

**au·da·cious** /ôˈdāSHəs/ ▸*adj.*
**1** daring; bold. **2** impudent.

—**au·da·cious·ly** *adv.*
—**au·dac·i·ty** *n.*

**au·di·ble** /ˈôdəbəl/ ▸*adj.* capable
of being heard. —**au·di·bil·i·ty** *n.*
—**au·di·bly** *adv.*

**au·di·ence** /ˈôdēəns/ ▸*n.*
**1** assembled listeners or
spectators at an event, esp. a
stage performance, concert, etc.
**2** people addressed by a movie,
book, play, etc. **3** formal
interview with a person in
authority: *the prime minister had
an audience with the pope.*

**au·di·o** /ˈôdēˌō/ ▸*n.* sound or its
reproduction.
□ **audio frequency** frequency
perceivable by the human ear.

**au·di·o·vi·su·al** ▸*adj.* (esp. of
teaching methods) using both
sight and sound.

**au·dit** /ˈôdit/ ▸*n.* official
examination of accounts.
▸*v.* **1** conduct an audit of.
**2** attend (a college-level class) for
no credit.

**au·di·tion** /ôˈdiSHən/ ▸*n.* test for
a performer's ability or
suitability.
▸*v.* assess or be assessed at an
audition.

**au·di·to·ri·um** /ˌôdiˈtôrēəm/ ▸*n.*
(*pl.* **-ums** or **-a**) **1** large room or
building for meetings, etc.

**2** part of a theater, etc., in which the audience sits.

**au·di·to·ry** /ˈôdiˌtôrē/ ▸adj. concerned with hearing.

**au fait** /ˌō ˈfe/ ▸adj. (**au fait with**) having a good or detailed knowledge of something.

**Aug.** ▸abbr. August.

**au·ger** /ˈôgər/ ▸n. tool resembling a large corkscrew, for boring holes in wood, the ground, etc.

**aught** /ôt/ ▸pron. anything at all. ▸n. inf. zero.

**aug·ment** /ôgˈment/ ▸v. **1** make or become greater; increase. **2** add to; supplement. —**aug·men·ta·tion** n. —**aug·men·ta·tive** adj.

**au·gur** /ˈôgər/ ▸v. **1** (of an event, circumstance, etc.) suggest a specified outcome: *augur well* or | *ill.* **2** portend; bode.

**au·gu·ry** /ˈôgyərē/ ▸n. (pl. **-ries**) sign of what will happen in the future; an omen.

**Au·gust** /ˈôgəst/ ▸n. eighth month of the year.

**au·gust** /ôˈgəst/ ▸adj. inspiring reverence and admiration; venerable; impressive. —**au·gust·ly** adv. —**au·gust·ness** n.

**auk** /ôk/ ▸n. black and white diving bird, e.g., the puffin and razorbill.

**auld lang syne** /ôld laNG ˈzīn/ ▸n. times long past.

**au na·tu·rel** /ˌō ˌnaCHəˈrel/ ▸adj. & adv. **1** with no elaborate treatment, dressing, or preparation. **2** (humorous) naked.

**aunt** /ant; änt/ ▸n. **1** sister of one's father or mother. **2** uncle's wife.

**au pair** /ˌō ˈpe(ə)r/ ▸n. young foreign person who helps with child care, housework, etc., in exchange for room and board.

**au·ra** /ˈôrə/ ▸n. (pl. **-rae** or **-ras**) **1** distinctive atmosphere. **2** subtle emanation or aroma.

**au·ral** /ˈôrəl/ ▸adj. of the ear; of hearing. —**au·ral·ly** adv.

**au·re·ate** /ˈôrē-it; -ˌāt/ ▸adj. denoting, made of, or having the color of gold.

**au·re·ole** /ˈôrēˌōl/ (also **au·re·o·la**) ▸n. **1** halo, esp. around the head in a religious painting. **2** corona around the sun or moon.

**au re·voir** /ˌō rəvˈwär/ ▸interj. & n. good-bye (until we meet again).

**au·ri·cle** /ˈôrikəl/ ▸n. **1 a** small

muscular pouch on the surface of each atrium of the heart. **b** the atrium itself. **2** external ear of animals.

**au·ro·ra** /əˈrôrə/ ▸*n.* (*pl.* **-ras** or **-rae**) luminous phenomenon, usu. of streamers of light in the night sky above the northern or southern magnetic pole.
□ **aurora australis** southern occurrence of an aurora.
□ **aurora borealis** northern occurrence of an aurora.

**aus·cul·ta·tion** /ˌôskəlˈtāsHən/ ▸*n.* action of listening to sounds from the heart, lungs, or other organs, typically with a stethoscope, as a part of medical diagnosis.

**aus·pice** /ˈôspis/ ▸*n.* (in phrase **under the auspices of**) with the support or help of: *the visit was arranged under UN auspices.*

**aus·pi·cious** /ôˈspisHəs/ ▸*adj.* conducive to success: *it was not the most auspicious moment to hold an election.* —**aus·pi·cious·ly** *adv.* —**aus·pi·cious·ness** *n.*

**aus·tere** /ôˈsti(ə)r/ ▸*adj.* (**-ter·er,** **-ter·est**) severe or simple in manner, attitude, or appearance. —**aus·ter·i·ty** *n.*

**aus·ter·i·ty** /ôˈsteritē/ ▸*n.* (*pl.* **-ties**) **1** sternness or severity of manner or attitude. **2** extreme plainness and simplicity of style or appearance. **3** difficult economic condition created by government measures to reduce a budget deficit, esp. by reducing public expenditure.

**Aus·tral·i·an** /ôˈstrālyən/ ▸*n.* **1** native or inhabitant of Australia. **2** person of Australian descent. **3** any of the aboriginal languages of Australia.
▸*adj.* of or relating to Australia.

**au·then·tic** /ôˈтнentik/ ▸*adj.* **1** of undisputed origin; genuine. **2** reliable or trustworthy.
—**au·then·ti·cal·ly** *adv.*
—**au·then·ti·cate** *v.*
—**au·then·tic·i·ty** *n.*

**au·then·ti·cate** /ôˈтнenti‚kāt/ ▸*v.* prove or show (something, esp. a claim or an artistic work) to be true or genuine.

**au·thor** /ˈôтнər/ ▸*n.* **1** writer, esp. of books. **2** originator of an event, condition, etc.
▸*v.* be the author of (a book, plan, idea, etc.). —**au·tho·ri·al** *adj.* —**au·thor·ship** *n.*

**au·thor·i·tar·i·an** /ə‚тнôri-ˈte(ə)rēən/ ▸*adj.* **1** favoring or enforcing strict obedience to authority. **2** tyrannical or domineering.

▶*n.* person favoring absolute obedience to a constituted authority. —**au·thor·i·tar·i·an·ism** *n.*

**au·thor·i·ta·tive** /əˈTHôriˌtātiv/ ▶*adj.* **1** recognized as true or dependable. **2** (of a person, behavior, etc.) commanding or self-confident. **3** (of a text) considered to be the best of its kind. —**au·thor·i·ta·tive·ly** *adv.* —**au·thor·i·ta·tive·ness** *n.*

**au·thor·i·ty** /əˈTHôritē/ ▶*n.* (*pl.* -**ties**) **1** power or right to enforce obedience. **2** right to act in a specified way: *the legal authority to arrest trespassers.* **3** (often **authorities**) person or body having control. **4 a** influence based on recognized knowledge or expertise. **b** such an influence expressed in a book, etc. **c** expert.

**au·thor·ize** /ˈôTHəˌrīz/ ▶*v.* give official permission for: *the government authorized the use of force.* —**au·thor·i·za·tion** *n.*

**au·tism** /ˈôˌtizəm/ ▶*n.* mental condition, usu. present from childhood, characterized by complete self-absorption and social withdrawal. —**au·tis·tic** *adj.*

**au·to** /ˈôtō/ ▶*n.* (*pl.* -**tos**) *inf.* automobile.

**auto-** (usu. **aut-** before a vowel) ▶*comb. form* **1** self: *autism.* **2** one's own: *autobiography.* **3** by oneself or spontaneous: *autosuggestion.* **4** by itself or automatic: *automobile.*

**au·to·bi·og·ra·phy** ▶*n.* (*pl.* -**phies**) **1** written account of one's own life. **2** this as a literary form. —**au·to·bi·o·graph·i·cal** *adj.*

**au·toch·thon** /ôˈtäkTHən/ ▶*n.* (*pl.* -**thons** or -**tho·nes** /-THəˌnēz/) original or indigenous inhabitant of a place; an aborigine.

**au·toc·ra·cy** /ôˈtäkrəsē/ ▶*n.* (*pl.* -**cies**) **1** absolute government by one person; tyranny. **2** country, etc., governed in such a way. —**au·to·crat** *n.* —**au·to·crat·ic** *adj.* —**au·to·crat·i·cal·ly** *adv.*

**au·to·crat** /ˈôtəˌkrat/ ▶*n.* **1** ruler who has absolute power. **2** someone who insists on complete obedience from others; an imperious or domineering person.

**au·to·da·fé** /ˈôtō də ˈfā/ ▶*n.* (*pl.* **au·tos·da·fé**) burning of a heretic by the Spanish Inquisition.

**au·to·graph** ▸*n.* **1** signature, esp. that of a celebrity. **2** manuscript in an author's own handwriting.
▸*v.* sign (a photograph, autograph album, etc.).

**au·to·im·mune** ▸*adj.* (of a disease) caused by antibodies produced against substances naturally present in the body. —**au·to·im·mu·ni·ty** *n.*

**au·to·mate** /ˈôtəˌmāt/ ▸*v.* convert to or operate by automation.

**au·to·ma·ted tel·ler ma·chine** (also **automatic teller machine**) ▸*n.* electronic machine that allows customers to deposit or withdraw funds, etc. (Abbr.: **ATM**.)

**au·to·mat·ic** /ˌôtəˈmatik/ ▸*adj.* **1** (of a machine, etc.) working by itself, without direct human intervention. **2 a** done spontaneously. **b** necessary and inevitable. **3** *Psychol.* performed unconsciously or subconsciously. **4** (of a firearm) able to be loaded and fired continuously. **5** (of a motor vehicle or its transmission) using gears that change automatically.
▸*n.* **1** automatic device, esp. a gun or transmission. **2** vehicle with automatic transmission. —**au·to·mat·i·cal·ly** *adv.*

**au·to·mat·ic pi·lot** ▸*n.* device for keeping an aircraft on a set course.

**au·to·ma·tion** /ˌôtəˈmāsHən/ ▸*n.* use of automatic manufacturing equipment.

**au·tom·a·ton** /ôˈtämətən/ ▸*n.* (*pl.* **-ta** or **-tons**) **1** mechanism with concealed motive power. **2** person who behaves like a robot.

**au·to·mo·bile** /ˌôtəmōˈbēl/ ▸*n.* motor vehicle for road use with an enclosed passenger compartment; car.

**au·ton·o·mous** /ôˈtänəməs/ ▸*adj.* **1** (of a country or region) having self-government, at least to a significant degree. **2** acting independently or having the freedom to do so.

**au·ton·o·my** /ôˈtänəmē/ ▸*n.* (*pl.* **-mies**) **1** self-government. **2** personal freedom. —**au·ton·o·mous** *adj.*

**au·top·sy** /ˈôˌtäpsē/ ▸*n.* (*pl.* **-sies**) postmortem examination to determine cause of death, etc.

**au·tumn** /ˈôtəm/ ▸*n.* **1** season between summer and winter. (Also called **fall**). **2** time of

maturity or incipient decay.
—**au·tum·nal** adj.

**aux·il·ia·ry** /ôg'zilyərē/ ▸adj.
**1** (of a person or thing) that gives help. **2** (of services or equipment) subsidiary; additional.
▸n. (pl. **-ries**) auxiliary person or thing.
□ **auxiliary verb** Gram. verb used in forming tenses or moods of other verbs, e.g., have in I have seen.

**a·vail** /ə'vāl/ ▸v. **1** use or take advantage of: my son did not avail himself of my advice. **2** help; benefit: no amount of struggle availed him. **3** be of use, value, or profit: the hiding place did not avail to save them.
▸n. use; profit: to no avail.

**a·vail·a·ble** ▸adj. **1** capable of being used; at one's disposal. **2** within one's reach. **3** (of a person) **a** free. **b** able to be contacted. —**a·vail·a·bil·i·ty** n.

**av·a·lanche** /'avə,lanCH/ ▸n.
**1** mass of snow and ice tumbling rapidly down a mountain.
**2** sudden appearance or arrival of anything in large quantities.

**a·vant-garde** /'ävänt 'gärd/ ▸n. pioneers or innovators, esp. in art and literature.

▸adj. (of ideas, etc.) new; progressive.

**av·a·rice** /'avəris/ ▸n. extreme greed for money or gain; cupidity. —**av·a·ri·cious** adj. —**av·a·ri·cious·ly** adv. —**av·a·ri·cious·ness** n.

**av·a·tar** /'avə,tär/ ▸n. movable icon representing a person in cyberspace or virtual reality graphics.

**Ave.** ▸abbr. Avenue.

**a·venge** /ə'venj/ ▸v. **1** inflict retribution on behalf of. **2** take vengeance for (an injury). —**a·veng·er** n.

**av·e·nue** /'avə,n(y)o͞o/ ▸n.
**1** broad, often tree-lined road or street. **2** approach: there are three possible avenues of research.

**a·ver** /ə'vər/ ▸v. (**-verred, -ver·ring**) assert; affirm; declare.

**av·er·age** /'av(ə)rij/ ▸n.
**1** amount obtained by dividing the total of given amounts by the number of amounts in the set. **2 a** usual amount, extent, or rate. **b** ordinary standard.
▸adj. **1 a** usual; typical. **b** mediocre. **2** estimated by average.
▸v. **1** amount on average to: sales averaged $1000 a day. **2** do on

average. **3** estimate the average of.

☐ **average out at** result in an average of. ☐ **on average** as an average rate or estimate.

**a·verse** /ə'vərs/ ▸*adj.* opposed; disinclined: *as a former CIA director, he is not averse to secrecy.*

**a·ver·sion** /ə'vərzнən/ ▸*n.* **1** dislike or unwillingness. **2** object of dislike.

**a·vert** /ə'vərt/ ▸*v.* **1** turn away (one's eyes or thoughts). **2** prevent or ward off (an undesirable occurrence).

**avg.** ▸*abbr.* average.

**a·vi·ar·y** /'āvē,erē/ ▸*n.* (*pl.* **-ies**) large enclosure or building for keeping birds.

**a·vi·a·tion** /,āvē'āsнən/ ▸*n.* **1** skill or practice of operating aircraft. **2** aircraft manufacture.

**a·vi·a·tor** /'āvē,ātər/ ▸*n.* person who pilots an aircraft.

**av·id** /'avid/ ▸*adj.* eager; greedy. —**a·vid·i·ty** *n.* —**a·vid·ly** *adv.*

**av·o·ca·do** /,avə'kädō/ ▸*n.* (*pl.* **-dos**) pear-shaped fruit with rough leathery skin, smooth flesh, and a large stone.

**av·o·ca·tion** /,avə'kāsнən/ ▸*n.* hobby.

**a·void** /ə'void/ ▸*v.* **1** refrain or keep away from. **2** escape; evade. **3** *Law* nullify or render void. —**a·void·a·ble** *adj.* —**a·void·a·bly** *adv.* —**a·void·ance** *n.*

**av·oir·du·pois** /,ävərdə'poiz/ ▸*n.* system of weights based on a pound of 16 ounces or 7,000 grains.

**a·vow** /ə'vow/ ▸*v.* admit; confess. —**a·vow·al** *n.* —**a·vow·ed·ly** *adv.*

**a·vun·cu·lar** /ə'vənGkyələr/ ▸*adj.* **1** of or relating to an uncle. **2** kind and friendly toward a younger or less experienced person.

**a·wait** /ə'wāt/ ▸*v.* **1** wait for. **2** be in store for.

**a·wake** /ə'wāk/ ▸*v.* (*past* **a·woke**; *past part.* **a·wok·en**) **1 a** cease to sleep. **b** become active. **2** become aware of: *finally awoke to the immensity of the problem.* **3** rouse, esp. from sleep. ▸*adj.* **1** not asleep. **2** aware of: *few are awake to the dangers.*

**a·wak·en** /ə'wākən/ ▸*v.* **1** rouse or be roused from sleep. **2** (**awaken someone to**) make someone aware of.

**a·ward** /ə'wôrd/ ▸*v.* **1** give or order to be given as a payment or prize. **2** grant; assign. ▸*n.* **1** payment, compensation, or prize awarded.  **2** the act or process of awarding.

**a·ware** /ə'we(ə)r/ ▶*adj.* **1** conscious; having knowledge: *are you aware of the danger?* **2** well-informed: *a politically aware electorate.*
—**a·ware·ness** *n.*

**a·wash** /ə'wôSH/ ▶*adj.* flooded or covered with water.

**a·way** /ə'wā/ ▶*adv.* **1** to or at a distance from.  **2** at a specified distance: *an explosion a short distance away.*  **3** at a specified future distance in time: *the wedding is only two weeks away.* **4** downward: *the land fell away to the river.*  **5** into a place for storage or safekeeping: *put the silver away.*  **6** constantly; persistently: *she kept clicking away with her new camera.*

**awe** /ô/ ▶*n.* reverential fear or wonder.
▶*v.* inspire with awe.
□ **awe-inspiring** causing awe; magnificent.

**awe·some** ▶*adj.* **1** inspiring awe.  **2** *inf.* excellent; superb.
—**awe·some·ly** *adv.*
—**awe·some·ness** *n.*

**aw·ful** /'ôfəl/ ▶*adj.* **1** very bad or unpleasant.  **2** extremely shocking.  **3** used to emphasize the extent of something: *I've made an awful fool of myself.*

**aw·ful·ly** ▶*adv.* **1** unpleasantly, badly.  **2** very: *I'm awfully sorry to bother you.*

**a·while** /ə'(h)wīl/ ▶*adv.* for a short time.

**awk·ward** /'ôkwərd/ ▶*adj.* **1** difficult to use or deal with. **2** clumsy or bungling.  **3** causing or feeling embarrassment.
—**awk·ward·ly** *adv.*
—**awk·ward·ness** *n.*

**awl** /ôl/ ▶*n.* small pointed tool used for piercing holes.

**awn·ing** /'ôniNG/ ▶*n.* sheet of canvas or similar material stretched on a frame and used as a shelter from the sun or rain.

**AWOL** ▶*abbr.* absent without leave.

**a·wry** /ə'rī/ ▶*adv. & adj.* **1** away from the planned or expected course; amiss.  **2** out of the correct position; askew.

**ax** /aks/ (also **axe**) ▶*n.* **1** chopping tool, usu. of iron with a steel edge at a right angle to a wooden handle.  **2** drastic cutting or elimination of expenditure, staff, etc.
▶*v.* (**ax·ing**) **1** use an ax.  **2** cut (esp. costs or services) drastically.  **3** remove or dismiss.

☐ **an ax to grind** private or selfish purpose to serve.

**ax·i·om** /'aksēəm/ ▸n. established or widely accepted principle. —**ax·i·o·mat·ic** adj.

**ax·is** /'aksis/ ▸n. (pl. **ax·es**) **1 a** imaginary line about which a body rotates. **b** line that divides a regular figure symmetrically. **2** Math. fixed reference line for the measurement of coordinates, etc. **3 (the Ax·is)** alliance of Germany and Italy during World War II, later also Japan.

**ax·le** /'aksəl/ ▸n. spindle on which a wheel is fixed.

**a·ya·tol·lah** /ˌīə'tōlə/ ▸n. Shiite religious leader in Iran.

**aye** /ī/ (also **ay**) ▸interj. **1** archaic yes. **2** (in voting) I assent: all in favor say, "aye." ▸n. affirmative answer or assent, esp. in voting: the ayes have it.

**a·za·lea** /ə'zālyə/ ▸n. flowering shrub with brightly colored flowers.

**az·i·muth** /'azəməTH/ ▸n. angular distance from a north or south point of the horizon to the intersection with the horizon of a vertical circle passing through a given celestial body.

**AZT** ▸n. drug used against the AIDS virus.

**Az·tec** /'az,tek/ ▸n. **1** member of the native people dominant in Mexico before the Spanish conquest of the 16th century. **2** language of the Aztecs. ▸adj. of the Aztecs or their language (Nahuatl).

**az·ure** /'azHər/; ▸adj. of a bright blue color: white beaches surrounded by azure seas. ▸n. **1** deep sky-blue color. **2** poet./lit. clear sky.

# Bb

**B**[1] /bē/ (also **b**) ▶*n.* (*pl.* **Bs** or **B's**; **b's**) **1** second letter of the alphabet. **2** *Mus.* seventh note of the diatonic scale of C major. **3** second class or category (of sizes, academic marks, etc.). **4** *Algebra* (usu. **b**) second known quantity. **5** human blood type. □ **B movie** low-budget movie.

**B**[2] ▶*symb.* **1** *Chem.* boron. **2** *Physics* magnetic flux density.

**B**[3] (also **B.**) ▶*abbr.* **1** bachelor. **2** bishop. **3** black (pencil lead). **4** *Baseball* base; baseman.

**b.** ▶*abbr.* **1** born. **2** billion.

**BA** ▶*abbr.* **1** Bachelor of Arts. **2** *Baseball* batting average.

**Ba** ▶*symb. Chem.* barium.

**bab·ble** /ˈbabəl/ ▶*v.* **1** talk inarticulately or incoherently. **2** (of a stream, etc.) murmur. ▶*n.* murmur of voices, water, etc. —**bab·bler** *n.*

**babe** /bāb/ ▶*n.* **1** baby: *a babe in arms.* **2** innocent or helpless person. **3** *inf.* affectionate form of address for someone with whom one has an intimate relationship. **4** *derog. inf.* young woman.

**ba·boon** /baˈbo͞on/ ▶*n.* monkey having a long doglike snout, large teeth, and a short tail.

**ba·by** /ˈbābē/ ▶*n.* (*pl.* **-bies**) **1** very young child or infant. **2** childish person: *is a baby about injections.* **3** youngest member of a family, team, etc. **4** young or newly born animal. ▶*v.* (**-bied**) treat like a baby. —**ba·by·hood** *n.* —**ba·by·ish** *adj.*

**ba·by boom** ▶*n. inf.* temporary marked increase in the birthrate, esp. that after World War II. —**ba·by boom·er** *n.*

**ba·by car·riage** ▶*n.* four-wheeled carriage for pushing a baby.

**ba·by·sit** ▶*v.* look after a child while the parents are out. —**ba·by·sit·ter** *n.*

**bac·ca·lau·re·ate** /ˌbakəˈlôrēit/ ▶*n.* **1** college or university bachelor's degree. **2** religious service held before commencement.

**bac·cha·nal** /ˌbakəˈnäl/ ▶*n.* **1** wild and drunken revelry. **2** priest, worshiper, or follower of Bacchus, the Greek or Roman god of wine.

▸*adj.* (also **bac·cha·nal·i·an**) **1** of or like Bacchus or his rites. **2** riotous.

**bach·e·lor** /ˈbaCH(ə)lər/ ▸*n.* **1** unmarried man. **2** man or woman who has earned the degree of Bachelor of Arts or Science, etc.
—**bach·e·lor·hood** *n.*

**ba·cil·lus** /bəˈsiləs/ ▸*n.* (*pl.* **-li**) **1** any disease-causing bacterium. **2** any rod-shaped bacterium.

**back** /bak/ ▸*n.* **1** rear surface of the human body from shoulders to hips. **2** upper surface of an animal's body. **3** spine. **4** any backlike surface, e.g., of the head, a chair, etc. **5** part of a garment that covers the back. **6** less active or visible or important part: *write it on the back.* **7** player or position in some games.

▸*adv.* **1** to the rear. **2 a** in or into an earlier or normal position or condition: *went back home.* **b** in return: *pay back.* **3** in or into the past: *back in June.* **4** at a distance: *stand back from the road.* **5** in check: *hold him back.* **6** (**in back of**) behind.

▸*v.* **1** help with moral or financial support. **2** bet on. **3** move, or cause (a vehicle, etc.) to move, backward. **4** put or serve as a back or support to. **5** *Mus.* accompany. **6** lie at the back of: *a beach backed by steep cliffs.*

▸*adj.* **1** situated behind, esp. as remote or subsidiary: *back entrance.* **2** past; not current: *back pay.* **3** reversed: *back flow.*
—**back·er** *n.* —**back·less** *adj.*

▢ **back and forth** to and fro.
▢ **back down** withdraw one's claim; concede defeat in an argument. ▢ **back off 1** draw back; retreat. **2** abandon one's intention, stand, etc. ▢ **back out** withdraw from a commitment. ▢ **back talk** *inf.* rude or impudent response. ▢ **back up 1** give (esp. moral) support to. **2** *Computing* copy (a file, disk, etc.). **3** (of running water, etc.) accumulate behind an obstruction. **4** move (a vehicle) backward. ▢ **get off a person's back** stop troubling a person. ▢ **turn one's back on 1** abandon. **2** disregard; ignore.

**back·bite** ▸*v.* speak badly of. —**back·bit·er** *n.*

**back·bone** ▸*n.* **1** spine. **2** main support. **3** firmness of character.

**back·break·ing** ▸*adj.* extremely hard.

**back·drop** ▸*n.* painted cloth at the back of the stage as a main part of the scenery.

**back·fire** ▸*v.* **1** undergo a mistimed explosion in the cylinder or exhaust of an internal combustion engine. **2** (of a plan, etc.) have the opposite effect to that intended.
▸*n.* instance of backfiring.

**back·gam·mon** /ˈbakˌgamən/ ▸*n.* board game for two with pieces moved according to throws of the dice.

**back·ground** ▸*n.* **1** part of a scene or picture farthest from the observer. **2** inconspicuous or obscure position, esp. as: *in the background.* **3** person's education, knowledge, or social circumstances. **4** explanatory or contributory information or circumstances.

**back·hand** *Tennis* ▸*n.* stroke played with the back of the hand turned toward the opponent.
▸*adj.* of or made with a backhand: *backhand volley.*

**back·hand·ed** ▸*adj.* **1** (of a blow, etc.) delivered with the back of the hand. **2** indirect; ambiguous: *backhanded compliment.*

**back·lash** ▸*n.* **1** excessive or marked adverse reaction. **2** sudden recoil in a mechanism.

**back·log** ▸*n.* **1** accumulation of uncompleted work, etc. **2** reserve; reserves: *backlog of goodwill.*

**back·pack** ▸*n.* bag with shoulder straps for carrying on the back.
▸*v.* travel or hike with this.
**—back·pack·er** *n.*

**back·ped·al** ▸*v.* (-ped·aled, -ped·al·ing) **1** pedal backward. **2** reverse one's previous action or opinion.

**back·side** ▸*n. inf.* buttocks.

**back·slide** ▸*v.* (*past* -slid; *past part.* -slid or -slid·den) relapse into bad ways or error.
**—back·slid·er** *n.*

**back·stage** ▸*n.* area of a theater out of view of the audience.
▸*adj. & adv.* referring to or in the area behind the stage.

**back·stroke** ▸*n.* swimming stroke performed on the back.

**back·track** ▸*v.* **1** retrace one's steps. **2** reverse one's previous action or opinion.

**back·up** ▸*n.* **1** moral or

technical support. **2** reserve.
**3** *Computing* security copies of
data.

**back·ward** /ˈbakwərd/ ▸*adv.*
(also **back·wards**) **1** away from
one's front. **2 a** with the back
foremost. **b** in reverse of the
usual way. **3** into the past.
▸*adj.* **1** directed to the rear or
starting point. **2** reversed.
**3** slow to progress. **4** reluctant;
shy. —**back·ward·ness** *n.*

**back·wa·ter** ▸*n.* **1** place
remote from the center of
activity. **2** stagnant water.

**back·woods** ▸*pl. n.* **1** remote
uncleared forest land. **2** any
remote or sparsely inhabited
region. —**back·woods·man** *n.*

**ba·con** /ˈbākən/ ▸*n.* cured meat
from the back or sides of a pig.

**bac·te·ri·a** /bakˈti(ə)rēə/ ▸pl. of
BACTERIUM.

**bac·te·ri·ol·o·gy** /bak͵ti(ə)rē-
ˈäləjē/ ▸*n.* the study of bacteria.
—**bac·te·ri·o·log·i·cal** *adj.*
—**bac·te·ri·o·log·i·cal·ly** *adv.*
—**bac·te·ri·ol·o·gist** *n.*

**bac·te·ri·um** /bakˈti(ə)rēəm/ ▸*n.*
(*pl.* **-ri·a**) unicellular
microorganism lacking an
organized nucleus, esp. one that
can cause disease. —**bac·te·ri·al**
*adj.*

**bad** /bad/ ▸*adj.* (**worse**; **worst**)
**1** inferior; inadequate; defective.
**2** incompetent: *I'm so bad at
numbers.* **3** unsatisfactory;
unfortunate. **4** harmful: *too
much salt is bad for his blood
pressure.* **5 a** (of food) decayed;
putrid. **b** polluted: *bad air.*
**6** unwell: *She's feeling bad this
morning.* **7** regretful; guilty: *I feel
bad about leaving her alone.*
**8** serious; severe: *a bad case of the
flu.* **9** morally unacceptable.
**10** disobedient. **11** not valid: *a
bad check.*

▸*adv. inf.* badly. —**bad·ly** *adv.*
—**bad·ness** *n.*

□ **not bad** (or **not so bad**) *inf.*
fairly good. □ **too bad** *inf.*
regrettable.

**bad blood** ▸*n.* ill feeling.

**badge** /baj/ ▸*n.* **1** distinctive
emblem worn as a mark of
office, membership,
achievement, etc. **2** thing that
reveals a condition or quality.

**bad·ger** /ˈbajər/ ▸*n.* omnivorous
gray-coated nocturnal mammal
with a black and white striped
head.

▸*v.* pester; harass; tease.

**bad·min·ton** /ˈbadmintn/ ▸*n.*
game with rackets in which a

shuttlecock is volleyed back and forth across a net.

**bad-mouth** ▶*v.* subject to malicious gossip or criticism.

**baf·fle** /'bafəl/ ▶*v.* **1** confuse. **2** frustrate; hinder. ▶*n.* device that checks the flow of fluid, gas, sound, etc. —**baf·fle·ment** *n.* —**baf·fling** *adj.*

**bag** /bag/ ▶*n.* **1** receptacle of flexible material with an opening at the top. **2 a** piece of luggage. **b** handbag. **3** amount of game shot or allowed. **4** loosely hanging skin under the eyes. ▶*v.* (**bagged, bag·ging**) **1** put in a bag. **2** *inf.* catch. **3** hang loosely or cause to do so. —**bag·ful** *n.* —**bag·gy** *adj.* □ **in the bag** *inf.* achieved; secured.

**bag·a·telle** /ˌbagə'tel/ ▶*n.* mere trifle.

**ba·gel** /'bāgəl/ ▶*n.* hard bread roll in the shape of a ring.

**bag·gage** /'bagij/ ▶*n.* luggage.

**bagn·io** /'banyō; 'bän-/ ▶*n.* (*pl.* **-ios**) **1** brothel. **2** oriental prison. **3** bathhouse in Turkey or Italy.

**bag·pipe** ▶*n.* (usu. **bagpipes**) musical instrument consisting of a windbag connected to reeded pipes. —**bag·pip·er** *n.*

**bail** /bāl/ ▶*n.* money, etc., required as security for the temporary release of a person in custody pending trial. ▶*v.* **1** release or secure the release of (a prisoner) on payment of bail. **2** scoop water out of (a boat, etc.). □ **bail out 1** parachute from an aircraft. **2** leave or desert a difficult situation. □ **bail someone out** rescue someone.

**bai·liff** /'balif/ ▶*n.* official in a court of law who keeps order, looks after prisoners, etc.

**bai·li·wick** /'bāləwik/ ▶*n.* **1** district or jurisdiction of a bailiff. **2** person's particular area of interest.

**bail·out** ▶*n.* a rescue from a dire situation: *a financial bailout for an ailing company.*

**bait** /bāt/ ▶*n.* **1** food used to entice prey, esp. a fish or an animal. **2** allurement. ▶*v.* **1** harass or annoy. **2** put bait on (a hook, trap, etc.).

**bake** /bāk/ ▶*v.* **1** cook or process (food, etc.) by dry heat in an oven or on a hot surface, without direct exposure to a flame. **2** undergo the process of being baked.

►*n.* act or an instance of baking. —**bak·er** *n.*

**bak·er's doz·en** ►*n.* thirteen.

**bak·er·y** ►*n.* (*pl.* **-ies**) place where bread and cakes are made or sold.

**bak·ing pow·der** ►*n.* mixture of sodium bicarbonate, cream of tartar, etc., used as a leavening agent.

**bak·ing so·da** ►*n.* sodium bicarbonate.

**bak·sheesh** /'bakSHēSH; bak-'SHēSH/ ►*n.* (in parts of Asia) a small sum of money given as alms, a tip, or a bribe.

**bal·ance** /'baləns/ ►*n.* **1** even distribution of weight or amount. **2** stability of body or mind. **3** apparatus for weighing, esp. one with a central pivot, beam, and two scales. **4 a** counteracting weight or force. **b** (also **bal·ance wheel**) regulating device in a clock, etc. **5 a** agreement between or the difference between credits and debits in an account. **b** amount outstanding. **6** *Art* harmony and proportion. **7** *Mus.* relative volume of sources of sound. ►*v.* **1** counteract, equal, or neutralize the weight or importance of. **2** bring into, keep in, or be in equilibrium. **3** make well-proportioned and harmonious. **4** (of the debits and credits of an account) equalize or be equalized. —**bal·anc·er** *n.*

□ **balance of payments** difference in value between payments into and out of a country. □ **balance of power** situation in which the chief nations of the world have roughly equal power. □ **balance of trade** difference in value between imports and exports. □ **balance sheet** statement giving the balance of an account.

**bal·co·ny** /'balkənē/ ►*n.* (*pl.* **-nies**) **1** usu. balustraded platform on the outside of a building, with access from an upper floor window or door. **2** upper tier of seats in a theater, etc. —**bal·co·nied** *adj.*

**bald** /bôld/ ►*adj.* **1** with the scalp wholly or partly lacking hair. **2** lacking the usual hair, feathers, leaves, etc. **3** *inf.* with the surface worn away: *a bald tire.* **4** blunt; unelaborated: *a bald statement.* **5** marked with white, esp. on the face: *a bald horse.* —**bald·ing** *adj.* —**bald·ly** *adv.* —**bald·ness** *n.*

**bald ea·gle** ►*n.* white-headed

eagle used as the emblem of the United States.

**bal·der·dash** /ˈbôldər,dasH/ ▸n. nonsense.

**bale** /bāl/ ▸n. tightly bound bundle of merchandise or hay.
▸v. make up into bales.

**ba·leen** /bəˈlēn/ ▸n. whalebone.

**bale·ful** /ˈbālfəl/ ▸adj. **1** (esp. of a manner, look, etc.) gloomy; menacing. **2** harmful; malignant; destructive.
—**bale·ful·ly** adv.
—**bale·ful·ness** n.

**balk** /bôk/ ▸v. **1** hesitate or be unwilling to accept an idea or proposal: *she balked at cutting down the lilac bush.* **2** Baseball (of a pitcher) make an illegal motion.
▸n. **1** Baseball illegal action made by a pitcher. **2** hindrance; stumbling block. —**balk·er** n.

**ball** /bôl/ ▸n. **1 a** sphere, esp. for use in a game. **b** game played with such a sphere. **2** ball-shaped object; material forming the shape of a ball: *ball of snow.* **3** rounded part of the body: *ball of the foot | ball of the thumb.* **4** Baseball pitched ball that is not swung at by the batter and that does not pass through the strike zone. **5** formal social gathering for dancing. **6** inf. enjoyable time, esp. as: *have a ball.*
▸v. form into a ball.
□ **ball game 1** game played with a ball, esp. a game of baseball. **2** inf. affair or concern: *a whole new ball game.* □ **on the ball** inf. alert.

**bal·lad** /ˈbaləd/ ▸n. **1** poem or song narrating a popular story. **2** slow sentimental song.
—**bal·lad·eer** n. —**bal·lad·ry** n.

**bal·last** /ˈbaləst/ ▸n. **1** any heavy material placed in a ship's hold, etc., for stability. **2** coarse stone, etc., used to form the bed of a railroad track or road.

**ball bear·ing** ▸n. **1** bearing in which friction is relieved by a ring of metal balls. **2** one of these balls.

**bal·le·ri·na** /ˌbaləˈrēnə/ ▸n. female ballet dancer.

**bal·let** /baˈlā/ ▸n. **1** dramatic or representational style of dancing to music. **2** particular piece or performance of ballet.
—**bal·let·ic** adj.

**bal·lis·tic** /bəˈlistik/ ▸adj. **1** of or relating to projectiles or their flight. **2** moving under the force of gravity only.

**bal·lis·tic mis·sile** /bəˈlistik/ ▸n. missile that is initially powered and guided but falls under gravity on its target.

**bal·lis·tics** ▸*n.* science of projectiles and firearms.

**bal·loon** /bəˈloon/ ▸*n.* **1** small inflatable rubber pouch with a neck, used as a toy or decoration. **2** large bag inflatable with hot air or gas to make it rise in the air, often carrying a basket for passengers. **3** balloon shape enclosing dialogue in a comic strip or cartoon.

▸*v.* swell out or cause to swell out like a balloon. —**bal·loon·ist** *n.*

**bal·lot** /ˈbalət/ ▸*n.* **1** process of recorded voting, usu. secret. **2** list of candidates or issues to be voted on. **3** total of votes recorded in a ballot. **4** paper or ticket, etc., used in voting.

▸*v.* elicit a secret vote from: *the union balloted its members.*

□ **ballot box** sealed box into which voters put completed ballot papers.

**ball·park** ▸*n.* baseball field.

□ **ballpark figure** *inf.* approximate or rough amount. □ **in the ballpark** *inf.* approximately correct.

**ball·point** (also **ballpoint pen**)

▸*n.* pen with a tiny ball as its writing point.

**ball·room** ▸*n.* large room for dancing.

**bal·ly·hoo** /ˈbaleˌhoo/ ▸*n.* **1** loud noise or fuss; confused state or commotion. **2** extravagant or sensational publicity.

**balm** /bäm/ ▸*n.* aromatic soothing ointment or oil.

**balm·y** /ˈbämē/ ▸*adj.* (**-i·er, -i·est**) **1** mild; soothing. **2** fragrant. —**balm·i·ness** *n.*

**ba·lo·ney** /bəˈlōnē/ ▸*n.* (*pl.* **-neys**) *inf.* **1** nonsense. **2** BOLOGNA.

**bal·sa** /ˈbôlsə/ ▸*n.* tough lightweight wood from a tropical American tree, used for making models, etc.

**bal·sam** /ˈbôlsəm/ ▸*n.* **1** resin exuded from various trees and shrubs. **2** ointment, esp. containing oil or turpentine. **3** any of various trees or shrubs that yield balsam. —**bal·sam·ic** *adj.*

**bal·us·ter** /ˈbaləstər/ ▸*n.* short post or pillar supporting a rail.

**bal·us·trade** /ˈbaləˌsträd/ ▸*n.* railing supported by balusters.

**bam·boo** /ˌbamˈboo/ ▸*n.* **1** tropical giant woody grass with hollow jointed stem. **2** its stem used for canes, furniture, etc.

**bam·boo·zle** /bam'bōōzəl/ ▶*v. inf.* cheat; hoax; mystify.

**ban** /ban/ ▶*v.* (**banned, ban·ning**) forbid; prohibit, esp. formally. ▶*n.* formal or authoritative prohibition.

**ba·nal** /bə'nal/ ▶*adj.* trite; feeble; commonplace. —**ba·nal·i·ty** *n.*

**ba·nan·a** /bə'nanə/ ▶*n.* long curved tropical fruit with soft pulpy flesh and yellow skin.

**band** /band/ ▶*n.* **1** flat, thin strip or loop of material (e.g., paper, metal, or cloth) put around something esp. to hold or decorate it. **2** strip of material forming part of a garment. **3** stripe. **4** range of frequencies or wavelengths in a spectrum (esp. of radio frequencies). **5** range of values within a series. **6** organized group, esp. of nonclassical musicians. ▶*v.* unite: esp. as *band together.*

**band·age** /'bandij/ ▶*n.* strip of material for binding up a wound, etc. ▶*v.* bind with a bandage.

**Band-Aid** /'band ˌād/ ▶*trademark.* adhesive strip with a gauze pad for covering minor wounds.

▶*n.* (**band-aid**) stopgap solution to a problem.

**ban·dan·na** /ban'danə/ (also **ban·dan·a**) ▶*n.* large patterned handkerchief.

**ban·dit** /'bandit/ ▶*n.* robber; outlaw. —**ban·dit·ry** *n.*

**band·stand** ▶*n.* covered outdoor platform for a band to play on, usu. in a park.

**band·wag·on** ▶*n.* (in phrase **jump on the bandwagon**) join a popular or successful cause, etc.

**ban·dy** /'bandē/ ▶*adj.* (**-di·er, -di·est**) **1** (of the legs) curved so as to be wide apart at the knees. **2** (also **ban·dy-legged**) (of a person) having bandy legs. ▶*v.* (**-died**) pass (a story, rumor, insults, etc.) back and forth.

**bane** /bān/ ▶*n.* **1** cause of ruin or trouble. **2** ruin; woe. —**bane·ful** *adj.* —**bane·ful·ly** *adv.*

**bang** /baNG/ ▶*n.* **1** loud short sound. **2** sharp blow. **3** (**bangs**) fringe of hair cut straight across the forehead. ▶*v.* **1** strike or shut noisily. **2** make or cause to make a bang. ▶*adv.* with a bang.

**ban·gle** /'baNGgəl/ ▶*n.* rigid bracelet or anklet.

**ban·ish** /'baniSH/ ▶*v.* **1** condemn to exile. **2** dismiss from one's

presence or mind.
—**ban·ish·ment** *n.*

**ban·is·ter** /ˈbanəstər/ (also **ban·nis·ter**) ▶*n.* uprights and handrail at the side of a staircase.

**ban·jo** /ˈbanjō/ ▶*n.* (*pl.* **-jos** or **-joes**) guitarlike stringed instrument with a circular body.
—**ban·jo·ist** *n.*

**bank** /baNGk/ ▶*n.* **1** area of sloping land alongside a river. **2** raised shelf of ground; slope. **3** mass of cloud, fog, snow, etc. **4** row of similar objects, e.g., lights, switches, oars, etc. **5** establishment for depositing, withdrawing, and borrowing money. **6** kitty in some gambling games. **7** storage place.
▶*v.* **1** heap or rise into banks. **2** heap up (a fire) tightly so that it burns slowly. **3** (of a vehicle or aircraft or its occupant) travel or cause to travel with one side higher than the other in rounding a curve. **4** deposit (money or valuables) in a bank.

**bank·rupt** /ˈbaNGkrəpt/ ▶*adj.* **1** insolvent; declared in law unable to pay debts. **2** exhausted or drained (of some quality, etc.); deficient; lacking.
▶*n.* insolvent person.
▶*v.* make bankrupt.
—**bank·rupt·cy** *n.*

**ban·ner** /ˈbanər/ ▶*n.* **1** large sign bearing a slogan or design used esp. in a demonstration or procession. **2** flag.
▶*adj.* outstanding: *a banner year.*

**banns** /banz/ ▶*pl. n.* notice in a parish church announcing an intended marriage.

**ban·quet** /ˈbaNGkwit/ ▶*n.* elaborate usu. extensive feast.

**ban·shee** /ˈbanSHē/ ▶*n.* female spirit whose wailing warns of a death in a house.

**ban·tam** /ˈbantəm/ ▶*n.* **1** any of several small breeds of domestic fowl. **2** small but aggressive person.

**ban·ter** /ˈbantər/ ▶*n.* good-humored teasing.
▶*v.* talk humorously or teasingly.

**ban·yan** /ˈbanyən/ ▶*n.* Indian fig tree with self-rooting branches.

**ban·zai** /ˈbanˈzī/ ▶*exclam.* **1** Japanese battle cry. **2** form of greeting used to the Japanese emperor.

**bap·tism** /ˈbaptizəm/ ▶*n.* **1** religious rite symbolizing admission to the Christian Church, with water and usu.

name giving. **2** any initiation.
—**bap·tis·mal** *adj.*

**Bap·tist** /'baptist/ ▶*n.* Christian advocating baptism by total immersion.

**bap·tize** /'baptīz/ ▶*v.* **1** administer baptism to. **2** give a name or nickname to.

**bar** /bär/ ▶*n.* **1** long piece of rigid material used to confine, obstruct, or support. **2** barrier or restriction. **3 a** counter in a restaurant, etc., for serving alcohol or refreshments. **b** room or establishment in which alcohol is served and customers may sit and drink. **4** *Mus.* any of the sections of usu. equal time value into which a musical composition is divided by vertical lines. **5** (**the Bar**) lawyers. **6** unit of pressure, $10^5$ newtons per square meter, approx. one atmosphere.

▶*v.* (**barred, bar·ring**) **1** fasten (a door, window, etc.) with a bar or bars. **2** prohibit (someone) from doing something: *journalists were barred from the courtroom.* **3** exclude (something) from consideration. **4** mark (something) with stripes.

▶*prep.* except: *all were there bar a few.*

□ **behind bars** in prison.

**barb** /bärb/ ▶*n.* **1** secondary, backward-facing projection from an arrow, fishhook, etc. **2** hurtful remark.
▶*v.* **1** provide (an arrow, fishhook, etc.) with a barb or barbs. **2** [as *adj.* **barbed**] (of a remark, etc.) make deliberately hurtful.

**bar·bar·i·an** /bär'be(ə)rēən/ ▶*n.* **1** uncultured or brutish person. **2** member of a primitive community or tribe.
▶*adj.* **1** rough and uncultured. **2** uncivilized.

**bar·bar·ic** ▶*adj.* **1** savagely cruel. **2** primitive; unsophisticated.

**bar·ba·rism** /'bärbə,rizəm/ ▶*n.* **1** absence of culture and civilized standards; rudeness. **2** nonstandard word or expression.

**bar·bar·i·ty** ▶*n.* (*pl.* **-ties**) **1** savage cruelty. **2** example of this.

**bar·ba·rous** ▶*adj.* BARBARIC.
—**bar·ba·rous·ly** *adv.*
—**bar·ba·rous·ness** *n.*

**bar·be·cue** /'bärbi,kyoo/ ▶*n.* **1 a** meal cooked over an open fire, often out of doors.

**b** marinated or seasoned meat prepared for cooking this way. **2** grill used for this.

▶*v.* (**-cued, -cuing**) cook on a barbecue.

**bar·ber** /ˈbärbər/ ▶*n.* person who cuts men's hair as an occupation.

▶*v.* cut the hair of; shave or trim the beard of. —**bar·ber·shop** *n.*

**bar·bi·tu·rate** /bärˈbicʜərit/ ▶*n.* sedative or sleep-inducing drug derived from an organic, white crystalline acid.

**bar code** ▶*n.* machine-readable striped code on packaging.

**bard** /bärd/ ▶*n.* poet. —**bard·ic** *adj.*

**bare** /be(ə)r/ ▶*adj.* **1** unclothed or uncovered. **2** leafless; unfurnished; empty. **3** unadorned. **4** scanty; mere.

▶*v.* uncover; reveal. —**bare·ness** *n.*

**bare·back** ▶*adj. & adv.* without a saddle.

**bare·faced** ▶*adj.* undisguised; impudent: *barefaced lie.*

**bare·ly** ▶*adv.* **1** only just; scarcely. **2** scantily.

**bar·gain** /ˈbärgən/ ▶*n.* **1** agreement on the terms of a transaction or sale. **2** something acquired or offered cheaply.

▶*v.* negotiate the terms of a transaction. —**bar·gain·er** *n.*

**barge** /bärj/ ▶*n.* **1** long flat-bottomed cargo boat on canals, rivers, etc. **2** long ornamental pleasure boat.

▶*v.* **1** move forcefully. **2** (**barge in**) intrude or interrupt rudely.

**bar·i·tone** /ˈbariˌtōn/ ▶*n.* **1 a** second-lowest adult male singing voice. **b** singer with this voice. **2** instrument pitched second-lowest in its family.

**bar·i·um** /ˈbe(ə)rēəm/ ▶*n. Chem.* white, reactive, soft metallic element of the alkaline earth group. (Symb.: **Ba**)

**bark** /bärk/ ▶*n.* **1** sharp explosive cry of a dog, fox, etc. **2** sound resembling this. **3** tough protective outer sheath of tree trunks, branches, etc.

▶*v.* (of a dog, fox, etc.) give a bark.

**bark·er** ▶*n.* person at an auction, sideshow, etc., who calls out to passersby as advertising.

**bar·ley** /ˈbärlē/ ▶*n.* cereal widely used as food and in malt liquors and spirits.

**bar mitz·vah** /ˌbär ˈmitsvə/ ▶*n.* **1** religious initiation ceremony of a Jewish boy who has reached the age of 13. **2** boy undergoing this ceremony.

**barn** /bärn/ ▸*n.* large farm building for storing grain, housing livestock, etc.

**bar·na·cle** /'bärnəkəl/ ▸*n.* **1** any of various species of small marine crustaceans that cling to rocks, ships' hulls, etc. **2** tenacious attendant or follower. —**bar·na·cled** *adj.*

**barn·storm** ▸*v.* **1** tour rural districts as an entertainer or political campaigner. **2** *Aeron.* give informal flying exhibitions; do stunt flying. —**barn·storm·er** *n.*

**ba·rom·e·ter** /bə'rämitər/ ▸*n.* **1** instrument measuring atmospheric pressure, esp. in forecasting the weather. **2** anything that reflects change. —**bar·o·met·ric** *adj.* —**bar·o·met·ri·cal** *adj.* —**ba·rom·e·try** *n.*

**bar·on** /'barən/ ▸*n.* **1** member of the lowest order of the British nobility. **2** important businessman or other powerful or influential person: *newspaper baron.*

**bar·on·et** /'barənet/ ▸*n.* member of the lowest hereditary titled British order.

**ba·roque** /bə'rōk/ ▸*adj.* **1** highly ornate and extravagant in style, esp. of European art, architecture, and music of the 17th and 18th c. **2** of or relating to this period. ▸*n.* baroque style or art.

**bar·racks** /'barəks/ ▸*pl. n.* [often treated as *sing.*] **1** large building for housing soldiers. **2** large bleak building.

**bar·ra·cu·da** /,barə'koodə/ ▸*n.* (*pl.* same or **-das**) large voracious tropical marine fish.

**bar·rage** /bə'räzн/ ▸*n.* **1** concentrated artillery bombardment. **2** rapid succession of questions or criticisms.

**bar·rel** /'barəl/ ▸*n.* **1** cylindrical container usu. bulging out in the middle. **2** its contents. **3** measure of capacity, usu. varying from 30 to 40 gallons. **4** cylindrical tube forming part of an object such as a gun or pen. ▸*v.* (**-reled, -rel·ing; -relled, -rel·ling**) **1** *inf.* drive or move fast: *barreling along the freeway.* **2** put into a barrel or barrels.

**bar·ren** /'barən/ ▸*adj.* **1** unable to produce fruit or vegetation. **2** unable to bear young.

**3** showing no results. **4** (of a place) bleak. **5** empty, esp. of meaning.
▸*pl. n.* (**barrens**) barren tract of land: *the pine barrens.*
—**bar·ren·ly** *adv.*
—**bar·ren·ness** *n.*

**bar·rette** /bəˈret/ ▸*n.* hair clip.

**bar·ri·cade** /ˈbarəˌkād/ ▸*n.* improvised barrier across a street.
▸*v.* block or defend with a barricade.

**bar·ri·er** /ˈbarēər/ ▸*n.* **1** fence, etc., that bars advance or access. **2** obstacle: *language barrier.*

**bar·ring** /ˈbäriNG/ ▸*prep.* except; not including.

**bar·ri·o** /ˈbärēˌō/ ▸*n.* (*pl.* **-os**) the Spanish-speaking quarter of a town or city.

**bar·ris·ter** /ˈbärəstər/ ▸*n.* in Britain, a trial lawyer.

**bar·row** /ˈbarō/ ▸*n.* **1** two-wheeled handcart. **2** ancient burial mound.

**bar·tend·er** ▸*n.* person serving behind the bar of a tavern, bar, etc.

**bar·ter** /ˈbärtər/ ▸*v.* exchange (goods or services) without using money.
▸*n.* trade by exchange of goods.

**ba·salt** /bəˈsôlt/ ▸*n.* dark volcanic rock.

**base** /bās/ ▸*n.* **1** part supporting from beneath or serving as a foundation. **2** notional structure or entity: *power base.* **3** principle or starting point. **4** headquarters. **5** main or important ingredient. **6** *Chem.* substance capable of combining with an acid to form a salt. **7** *Math.* number in terms of which other numbers or logarithms are expressed. **8** *Baseball* one of the four stations that must be reached in turn to score a run.
▸*v.* **1** found or establish. **2** station: *troops were based in Malta.*
▸*adj.* **1** without moral principles: *the electorate's baser instincts of greed and selfishness.* **2** (of coins, etc.) not made of precious metal.

**base·ball** ▸*n.* **1** game played with a bat and ball, and a circuit of four bases that must be completed to score. **2** ball used in this game.

**base·board** ▸*n.* narrow board, etc., along the bottom of the wall of a room.

**base·less** ▸*adj.* unfounded; groundless.

**base·line** ▶*n.* **1** line used as a base or starting point. **2** (in tennis, basketball, etc.) line marking each end of a court. **3** *Baseball* either of the lines leading from home plate and determining the boundaries of fair territory.

**base·ment** /ˈbāsmənt/ ▶*n.* lowest floor of a building, usu. at least partly below ground level.

**bash** /basH/ ▶*v. inf.* strike bluntly or heavily.

▶*n.* **1** heavy blow. **2** party.

**bash·ful** ▶*adj.* **1** shy; diffident; self-conscious. **2** sheepish.

**BASIC** /ˈbāsik/ ▶*n.* computer programming language using familiar English words and designed for beginners.

**bas·ic** ▶*adj.* **1** serving as a base. **2** fundamental.

▶*pl. n.* (**basics**) fundamental facts or principles. **—ba·si·cal·ly** *adv.*

**ba·sil** /ˈbāzəl/ ▶*n.* aromatic annual herb of the mint family, used as a flavoring.

**ba·sil·i·ca** /bəˈsilikə/ ▶*n.* **1** ancient Roman public hall used as a court of law, etc. **2** similar building used as a Christian church.

**ba·sin** /ˈbāsən/ ▶*n.* **1** shallow, open container for holding water; sink. **2** hollow depression. **3** any sheltered mooring area. **4** area drained by rivers and tributaries.

**ba·sis** /ˈbāsis/ ▶*n.* (*pl.* **-ses**) **1** foundation or support. **2** main or determining principle or ingredient. **3** starting point for a discussion, etc.

**bask** /bask/ ▶*v.* **1** relax in warmth and light. **2** (**bask in**) revel in (something pleasing): *he was basking in the glory of his first novel.*

**bas·ket** /ˈbaskit/ ▶*n.* **1** container made of interwoven cane, etc. **2** amount held by this. **3** goal in basketball, or a goal scored. **—bas·ket·ful** *n.*

**bas·ket·ball** ▶*n.* **1** game between two teams in which points are scored by making the ball drop through hooped nets fixed at each end of the court. **2** ball used in this game.

**bas mitz·vah** /ˌbäs ˈmitsvə/ (also **bat mitzvah**) ▶*n.* **1** initiation ceremony for a Jewish girl who has reached the age of 13. **2** girl undergoing this ceremony.

**bas-re·lief** /ˌbä rəˈlēf/ ▶*n.* sculpture or carving in which the figures project slightly from the background.

**bass**[1] /bās/ ▶*n.* **1 a** lowest adult male singing voice. **b** singer with this voice. **2** instrument pitched lowest in its family. **3** *inf.* bass guitar or double bass. **4** low-frequency output of a radio, CD player, etc.

▶*adj.* **1** lowest in musical pitch. **2** deep sounding. —**bass·ist** *n.*

**bass**[2] /bas/ ▶*n.* (*pl.* same or **bass·es**) any of various edible fishes including the common perch.

**bas·si·net** /ˌbasəˈnet/ ▶*n.* baby's wicker cradle, usu. hooded.

**bas·soon** /bəˈsoōn/ ▶*n.* bass instrument of the oboe family.

**bas·tard** /ˈbastərd/ ▶*n.* **1** *archaic* person born of parents not married to each other. **2** *inf.* unpleasant or despicable person. **3** *inf.* difficult or awkward thing, undertaking, etc.

▶*adj.* **1** *archaic* illegitimate by birth. **2** (of things) unauthorized; counterfeit; hybrid. —**bas·tard·y** *n.*

**baste** /bāst/ ▶*v.* **1** moisten (meat) with gravy or melted fat during cooking. **2** stitch loosely together in preparation for sewing; tack.

**bas·tion** /ˈbasCHən/ ▶*n.* **1** projecting part of a fortification. **2** thing regarded as protecting: *bastion of freedom.*

**bat** /bat/ ▶*n.* **1** implement with a handle, used for hitting balls in games. **2** player's turn with this. **3** nocturnal flying mammal.

▶*v.* (**bat·ted**, **bat·ting**) **1** hit with or as with a bat. **2** take a turn at batting. **3** flutter one's eyelashes.

□ **not bat an eye** *inf.* show no reaction.

**batch** /bacH/ ▶*n.* **1** group of things or persons dealt with together. **2** loaves, panfuls, etc., produced at one baking. **3** *Computing* group of records processed as a single unit.

▶*v.* arrange or deal with in batches.

**bat·ed** /ˈbātid/ ▶*adj.* (in phrase **with bated breath**) very anxiously.

**bath** /baTH/ ▶*n.* **1** act of washing the body in a tub. **2** liquid in which something is immersed, treated, etc.

**bathe** /bāTH/ ▶*v.* **1** immerse oneself in water, esp. to wash. **2** soak. **3** (of sunlight, etc.) envelop.

**bath·ing suit** /ˈbāTHiNG/ ▸*n.* garment worn for swimming.

**ba·thos** /ˈbāTHäs/ ▸*n.* lapse in mood from the sublime to the absurd or trivial. —**ba·thet·ic** *adj.*

**bath·robe** ▸*n.* loose robe worn before and after taking a bath.

**bath·room** ▸*n.* room with a toilet and sink and usu. a bathtub or shower.

**bath·tub** ▸*n.* container for water used for bathing the body.

**ba·tik** /bəˈtēk/ ▸*n.* method of producing colored designs on textiles by applying wax to the parts to be left uncolored; piece of cloth treated in this way.

**bat mitz·vah** /bät ˈmitsvə/ ▸var. of BAS MITZVAH.

**ba·ton** /bəˈtän/ ▸*n.* **1** thin stick used by a conductor to direct an orchestra. **2** *Sports* short stick carried and passed on in a relay race. **3** stick carried by a drum major. **4** staff of office or authority.

**bat·tal·ion** /bəˈtalyən/ ▸*n.* army unit, part of a division.

**bat·ten** /ˈbatn/ ▸*n.* **1** narrow flat strip of wood used as a stiffener, etc. **2** strip of wood used for clamping the boards of a door, etc. **3** *Naut.* strip for securing tarpaulin over a ship's hatchway.

▸*v.* strengthen or fasten with battens.

☐ **batten down the hatches 1** *Naut.* secure a ship's tarpaulins. **2** prepare for a difficulty or crisis.

**bat·ter** /ˈbatər/ ▸*v.* **1 a** strike repeatedly with hard blows. **b** pound heavily and insistently: *batter at the door.* **2** handle roughly, esp. over a long period.

▸*n.* **1** mixture of flour, egg, and liquid used in cooking, esp. for cakes, etc. **2** player batting, esp. in baseball. —**bat·ter·er** *n.* —**bat·ter·ing** *n.*

**bat·ter·y** /ˈbatərē/ ▸*n.* (*pl.* -**ies**) **1** cell or cells carrying an electric charge, as a source of current. **2** set of similar units of equipment, esp. connected. **3** series of tests. **4** fortified emplacement for heavy guns. **5** *Law* unlawful personal violence on another (See ASSAULT).

**bat·tle** /ˈbatl/ ▸*n.* **1** prolonged fight between armed forces. **2** contest; difficult struggle.

▸*v.* **1** struggle; fight. **2** engage in battle with. —**bat·tler** *n.*

☐ **battle cry** cry or slogan used in a battle. ☐ **battle royal 1** battle of many combatants; free fight. **2** heated argument.

**bat·tle·ment** ▸*n.* (usu. **battlements**) recessed parapet along the top of a fortification.

**bat·tle·ship** ▸*n.* heaviest armored warship.

**bat·ty** ▸*adj.* (**-ti·er**, **-ti·est**) *inf.* crazy.

**bau·ble** /ˈbôbəl/ ▸*n.* showy trinket or toy of little value.

**baud** /bôd/ ▸*n.* (*pl.* same or **bauds**) *Computing* unit to express the speed of electronic code signals, corresponding to one information unit or one bit per second.

**baux·ite** /ˈbôksīt/ ▸*n.* claylike ore, the source of aluminum.

**bawd** /bôd/ ▸*n.* woman in charge of a brothel.

**bawd·y** /ˈbôdē/ ▸*adj.* (**-i·er**, **-i·est**) indecent; raunchy. **—bawd·i·ly** *adv.* **—bawd·i·ness** *n.*

**bawl** /bôl/ ▸*v.* **1** speak or call out noisily. **2** weep loudly. **—bawl·er** *n.*

□ **bawl out** *inf.* reprimand angrily.

**bay** /bā/ ▸*n.* **1** broad inlet of the sea where the land curves inward. **2** laurel having deep green leaves and purple berries. **3** space created by a window line projecting outward from a wall. **4** recess; alcove. **5** compartment: *bomb bay.* **6** area specially allocated: *loading bay.* **7** bay horse with a black mane and tail.

▸*adj.* (esp. of a horse) dark reddish brown.

▸*v.* **1** bark or howl loudly and plaintively. **2** bay at.

□ **at bay** cornered; unable to escape. □ **bay leaf** aromatic (usu. dried) leaf of the bay tree, used in cooking. □ **hold** (or **keep**) **at bay** hold off (a pursuer).

**bay·ber·ry** ▸*n.* (*pl.* **-ries**) N. American plants bearing waxy berries.

**bay·o·net** /ˈbāənit/ ▸*n.* stabbing blade attachable to the muzzle of a rifle.

▸*v.* stab with a bayonet.

**bay·ou** /ˈbīo͞o/ ▸*n.* marshy offshoot of a river, etc.

**bay win·dow** ▸*n.* window projecting from an outside wall.

**ba·zaar** /bəˈzär/ ▸*n.* **1** market in an Eastern or Middle Eastern country. **2** fund-raising sale, esp. for charity.

**ba·zoo·ka** /bəˈzo͞okə/ ▸*n.* antitank rocket launcher.

**BB** ▸*abbr.* pellet about .18 inch in diameter, for use in a BB gun.

**BB gun** ▶*n.* air rifle that fires BBs.

**BC** ▶*abbr.* **1** (of a date) before Christ. **2** British Columbia.

**Be** ▶*symb. Chem.* beryllium.

**be** /bē/ (*sing. present* **am**, **is**; *pl. present* **are**; *1st and 3rd sing. past* **was**; *2nd sing. past and pl. past* **were**; *present subj.* **be**; *past subj.* **were**; *pres. part.* **be·ing**; *past part.* **been**) ▶*v.* **1** exist; live: *I think, therefore I am.* **2** occur; take place: *that was before the war.* **3** occupy a position in space. **4** remain; continue. **5** linking subject and predicate, expressing: **a** identity: *she is the person.* **b** condition: *he is ill.* **c** state or quality: *he is kind.* **d** opinion: *I am against hanging.* **e** total: *two and two are four.* **f** cost or significance: *it is nothing to me.*
▶*aux. v.* **1** with a past participle to form the passive mood: *it was done.* **2** with a present participle to form continuous tenses: *we are coming.* **3** with an infinitive to express duty or commitment, intention, possibility, destiny, or hypothesis: *we are to wait here.*

**be-** ▶*prefix* forming verbs:
**1 a** all over; all around: *beset.* **b** thoroughly; excessively: *begrudge* | *belabor.* **2** (added to intransitive verbs) expressing transitive action: *bemoan.* **3** (added to adjectives and nouns) expressing transitive action: *befoul.* **4** (added to nouns) **a** affect with: *befog.* **b** treat as: *befriend.* **5** (forming adjectives ending in -*ed*) having: *bejeweled.*

**beach** /bēCH/ ▶*n.* pebbly or sandy shore.
▶*v.* **1** run or haul up (a boat, etc.) onto a beach. **2** (of a whale, etc.) become stranded out of the water.

**beach·comb·er** ▶*n.* vagrant who lives by searching beaches for articles of value.

**beach·head** *Mil.* ▶*n.* fortified position established on a beach by landing forces.

**bea·con** /ˈbēkən/ ▶*n.* **1** visible warning or guiding device (e.g., a lighthouse, navigation buoy, etc.). **2** radio transmitter whose signal helps fix the position of a ship or aircraft.

**bead** /bēd/ ▶*n.* **1** small usu. rounded and perforated piece of glass, stone, etc., for threading with others or sewing on to fabric, etc. **2** (**beads**) necklace made of a string of beads. **3** (**beads**) rosary. **4** drop of liquid. **5** small knob in the foresight of a gun.

▶ *v.* decorate with beads.
—**bead·ed** *adj.*

□ **draw a bead on** take aim at.

**bea·gle** /'bēgəl/ ▶ *n.* small short-haired hound.

**beak** /bēk/ ▶ *n.* **1** bird's horny projecting jaws; bill. **2** similar jaw of a turtle, etc. —**beaked** *adj.* —**beak·y** *adj.*

**beak·er** ▶ *n.* **1** tall drinking vessel. **2** lipped cylindrical vessel for scientific experiments.

**beam** /bēm/ ▶ *n.* **1** long sturdy piece of timber or metal spanning an opening or room, usu. to support the structure above. **2** ray or shaft of light. **3** series of radio or radar signals as a guide to a ship or aircraft. **4** crossbar of a balance. **5** ship's breadth at its widest point.

▶ *v.* **1** emit or direct (light, radio waves, etc.). **2 a** shine. **b** look or smile radiantly.

□ **off** (*or* **off the**) **beam** *inf.* mistaken. □ **on the beam** *inf.* on the right track.

**bean** /bēn/ ▶ *n.* **1 a** plant with edible seeds in long pods. **b** one of these seeds. **2** similar seed of coffee, etc. **3** *inf.* the head, esp. as a source of common sense.

▶ *v. inf.* hit on the head.

□ **bean counter** *inf.* accountant.

**bear** /be(ə)r/ ▶ *v.* (*past* **bore**; *past part.* **borne, born**) **1** carry, bring, or take. **2** show; have as an attribute or characteristic: *bear marks of violence.* **3 a** produce; yield (fruit, etc.). **b** give birth to. **4 a** sustain (a weight, responsibility, cost, etc.). **b** endure (an ordeal, difficulty, etc.). **5 a** tolerate. **b** admit of. **6** veer in a given direction: *bear left.*

▶ *n.* **1** large heavy mammal having thick fur and walking on its soles. **2** rough or uncouth person. **3** person who sells shares of stocks hoping to buy them back later at a lower price. —**bear·a·ble** *adj.* —**bear·a·bly** *adv.* —**bear·er** *n.*

□ **bear down** exert downward pressure. □ **bear down on** approach rapidly or purposefully. □ **bear on** (or **upon**) be relevant to. □ **bear out** support or confirm (an account or the person giving it). □ **bear with** tolerate. □ **bear witness** testify.

**beard** /bi(ə)rd/ ▶ *n.* **1** facial hair growing on the chin, etc. **2** similar tuft on an animal.

▶*v.* boldly confront, esp. someone formidable. —**beard·ed** *adj.* —**beard·less** *adj.*

**bear·ing** ▶*n.* **1** person's bodily attitude or outward behavior. **2** relevance: *has no bearing on the subject.* **3** part of a machine that supports a rotating or other moving part. **4** direction or position relative to a fixed point. **5** sense of one's orientation: *get my bearings.*

**beast** /bēst/ ▶*n.* **1** animal, esp. a wild quadruped. **2** brutal, objectionable person.

**beast·ly** ▶*adj.* (-**li·er**, -**li·est**) **1** *inf.* objectionable; unpleasant. **2** like a beast; brutal. —**beast·li·ness** *n.*

**beat** /bēt/ ▶*v.* (*past* **beat**; *past part.* **beat·en**) **1** strike persistently or repeatedly, esp. to harm or punish. **2** strike (a thing) repeatedly, e.g., to remove dust from (a carpet, etc.), or to sound (a drum, etc.). **3** overcome; surpass. **4** complete an activity before (another person, etc.). **5** be too hard for; perplex. **6** stir (eggs, etc.) vigorously. **7** shape (metal, etc.) by blows. **8** (of the heart, etc.) pulsate rhythmically. **9 a** indicate (a tempo or rhythm) by tapping, etc. **b** sound (a signal, etc.) by striking a drum.

**10** move or cause (wings) to move up and down. **11** make (a path, etc.) by trampling.
▶*n.* **1 a** main stress accent in music or verse. **b** indication of rhythm by a conductor. **2** stroke, blow, or measured sequence of strokes. **3** route or area allocated to a police officer, etc.
▶*adj. inf.* exhausted; tired out: *I'm beat.* —**beat·a·ble** *adj.*
□ **beat it** *inf.* go away. □ **beat off** drive back (an attack, etc.). □ **beat up** give a beating to, esp. with punches and kicks. □ **beat-up** *inf.* dilapidated; in a state of disrepair.

**be·a·tif·ic** /ˌbēəˈtifik/ ▶*adj.* **1** *inf.* blissful: *beatific smile.* **2 a** of or relating to blessedness. **b** making blessed. —**be·a·tif·i·ca·lly** *adv.*

**be·at·i·fy** /bēˈatəˌfī/ ▶*v.* (-**fied**) (in the Roman Catholic Church) announce the beatification of someone.

**be·at·i·tude** /bēˈatəˌt(y)ōōd/ ▶*n.* **1** blessedness. **2** (**the Beatitudes**) declarations of blessedness in Matt. 5:3-11.

**beat·nik** /ˈbētnik/ ▶*n.* disillusioned young person, esp. in the 1950s, who rejected conventional dress, habits, and beliefs.

**beau** /bō/ ▶*n.* (*pl.* **beaux** or **beaus**) boyfriend.

**beau geste** /ˌbō ˈzHest/ ▶*n.* (*pl.* **beaux gestes** *pronunc.* same) noble and generous act.

**beau monde** /ˌbō ˈmônd/ ▶*n.* (**the beau monde**) fashionable society.

**beau·te·ous** /ˈbyo͞otēəs/ ▶*adj.* *poet.* beautiful.

**beau·ti·cian** /byo͞oˈtisHən/ ▶*n.* specialist in beauty treatment.

**beau·ti·ful** /ˈbyo͞otifəl/ ▶*adj.* **1** delighting the aesthetic senses. **2** pleasant; enjoyable: *had a beautiful time.* **3** excellent: *beautiful specimen.* —**beau·ti·ful·ly** *adv.*

**beau·ti·fy** ▶*v.* (**-fied**) make beautiful; adorn.
—**beau·ti·fi·ca·tion** *n.*
—**beau·ti·fi·er** *n.*

**beau·ty** /ˈbyo͞otē/ ▶*n.* (*pl.* **-ties**) **1** combination of shape, color, etc., that pleases the senses. **2** excellent example of something. **3** best feature of something.

**beau·ty par·lor** (or **salon** or **shop**) ▶*n.* establishment for manicure, hairdressing, makeup, etc.

**bea·ver** /ˈbēvər/ ▶*n.* (*pl.* same or **bea·vers**) amphibious broad-tailed rodent native to N. America, Europe, and Asia able to cut down trees and build dams.

**be·cause** /biˈkôz/ ▶*conj.* for the reason that; since.
☐ **because of** on account of; by reason of.

**beck** /bek/ ▶*n.* (in phrase **at a person's beck and call**) having constantly to obey a person's orders.

**beck·on** /ˈbekən/ ▶*v.* **1** summon by gesture. **2** make a signal to attract a person's attention.

**be·come** /biˈkəm/ ▶*v.* (*past* **be·came**; *past part.* **be·come**) **1** begin to be; come to be; turn into: *tadpoles become frogs.* **2 a** look well on; suit. **b** befit: *it ill becomes you to complain.* **3** flattering; suitable; decorous. —**be·com·ing·ly** *adj.*
☐ **become of** happen to: *what will become of me?*

**bed** /bed/ ▶*n.* **1** piece of furniture or padding, etc. for sleeping on. **2** garden plot, esp. for flowers. **3** bottom of the sea or a river. **4** foundations of a road or railroad. **5** stratum; layer.
▶*v.* (**bed·ded, bed·ding**) **1** put or

go to bed. **2** plant in a garden bed. **3 a** arrange as a layer. **b** be or form a layer.

□ **bed and board** lodging and food. □ **bed and breakfast** establishment that provides lodging and breakfast.

**bed·bug** ▸*n.* biting parasite infesting beds, etc.

**bed·clothes** ▸*pl. n.* coverings for a bed, such as sheets, blankets, etc.

**bed·ding** ▸*n.* **1** mattress and bedclothes. **2** geological strata.

**be·dev·il** /bi'devəl/ ▸*v.* **1** plague; afflict. **2** confound; confuse. **3** bewitch. —**be·dev·il·ment** *n.*

**bed·fel·low** ▸*n.* **1** person who shares a bed. **2** associate.

**be·di·zened** /bi'dīzənd/ ▸*adj.* dressed up or decorated gaudily.

**bed·lam** /'bedləm/ ▸*n.* scene of uproar and confusion.

**Bed·ou·in** /'bedo͞oin/ (also **Bed·u·in**) ▸*n.* (*pl.* same) **1** nomadic Arab of the desert. **2** wanderer; nomad.

**bed·pan** ▸*n.* toilet for a bedridden patient.

**be·drag·gled** /bi'dragəld/ ▸*adj.* dirty and disheveled.

**bed·rid·den** ▸*adj.* confined to bed by infirmity.

**bed·rock** ▸*n.* **1** solid underlying rock. **2** underlying principles or facts.

**bed·room** ▸*n.* room for sleeping in.

**bed·sore** ▸*n.* sore developed by lying in bed.

**bed·spread** ▸*n.* decorative cover for a bed.

**bed·stead** ▸*n.* framework of a bed.

**bee** /bē/ ▸*n.* **1** any four-winged social insect that collects nectar and pollen and produces wax and honey. **2** meeting for communal work or amusement: *quilting bee.*

□ **bee in one's bonnet** obsession.

**beech** /bēcH/ ▸*n.* **1** large tree with smooth gray bark and glossy leaves. **2** its wood.

**beef** /bēf/ ▸*n.* **1** flesh of the ox, bull, or cow for eating. **2** *inf.* well-developed male muscle. **3** *inf.* (*pl.* **beefs**) complaint. ▸*v. inf.* complain.

□ **beef up** *inf.* strengthen; reinforce.

**bee·hive** ▸*n.* structure in which bees live.

**bee·line** ▸*n.* straight line between two places.

**beep** /bēp/ ▸*n.* **1** sound of an

automobile horn. **2** any similar high-pitched noise.

▶*v.* emit a beep.

**beep·er** ▶*n.* portable electronic device that receives signals and emits a beep to page the person carrying it.

**beer** /bi(ə)r/ ▶*n.* **1** alcoholic drink made from yeast-fermented malt, etc., flavored with hops. **2** fermented nonalcoholic drink, e.g., ginger beer or root beer.

**bees·wax** ▶*n.* yellow substance secreted by bees, used in candles and as polish.

**beet** /bēt/ ▶*n.* plant with an edible root, such as the sugar beet.

**bee·tle** /ˈbētl/ ▶*n.* insect with modified front wings forming hard protective cases closing over the back wings.

▶*v.* (of brows, cliffs, etc.) project or overhang threateningly.

▶*adj.* (esp. of the eyebrows) projecting; shaggy; scowling.

**be·fall** /biˈfôl/ ▶*v.* (*past* **be·fell**; *past part.* **be·fall·en**) happen (to).

**be·fit** /biˈfit/ ▶*v.* (**-fit·ted, -fit·ting**) be appropriate for; suit. —**be·fit·ting** *adj.* —**be·fit·ting·ly** *adv.*

**be·fore** /biˈfôr/ ▶*conj.* **1** earlier than the time when. **2** rather than that.

▶*prep.* **1** in front of; ahead of. **2** earlier than; preceding. **3** rather than. **4 a** in the presence of. **b** for the attention of.

▶*adv.* **1** earlier than the time in question; already. **2** ahead.

**be·fore·hand** ▶*adv.* in advance; in readiness.

**be·fud·dle** /biˈfədl/ ▶*v.* confuse.

**beg** /beg/ ▶*v.* (**begged, beg·ging**) **1** ask for food, money, etc., as charity. **2** ask (for) earnestly or humbly. **3** (of a dog, etc.) sit up with the front paws raised expectantly.

□ **beg off 1** decline to take part in or attend. **2** get (a person) excused from a penalty, etc.

**be·get** /biˈget/ ▶*v.* (**be·get·ting**; *past* **be·got**; *past part.* **be·got·ten**) **1** father; procreate. **2** cause: *success begets further success.*

**beg·gar** /ˈbegər/ ▶*n.* **1** person who lives by begging. **2** poor person.

▶*v.* **1** reduce to poverty. **2** cause one's ability for (description, etc.) to be inadequate. —**beg·gar·ly** *adj.*

**be·gin** /biˈgin/ ▶*v.* (**be·gin·ning**; *past* **be·gan**; *past part.* **be·gun**)

**1** perform the first part of; start. **2** come into being. —**be·gin·ner** n.

**be·go·nia** /bɪˈgōnyə/ ▶n. plant with brightly colored sepals and no petals, and often having brilliant glossy foliage.

**be·grudge** ▶v. **1** envy (a person) the possession of: *he begrudged Martin his wealth.* **2** give resentfully. —**be·grudg·ing·ly** adv.

**be·guile** ▶v. **1** charm, esp. deceitfully. **2** spend time pleasantly.

**be·half** ▶n. (in phrase **on behalf of** or **on a person's behalf**) representing or in the interests of (a person, principle, etc.).

**be·have** /bɪˈhāv/ ▶v. **1** act or react (in a specified way). **2** (esp. to or of a child) conduct oneself properly.

**be·hav·ior** /bɪˈhāvyər/ ▶n. **1** way one conducts oneself; manners. **2** way in which a ship, machine, etc., acts or works. —**be·hav·ior·al** adj.

**be·head** ▶v. cut off the head.

**be·he·moth** /bɪˈhēməTH; ˈbēəməTH/ ▶n. **1** huge or monstrous creature. **2** something enormous, esp. a big and powerful organization.

**be·hest** /bɪˈhest/ ▶n. poet./lit. command; entreaty.

**be·hind** /bɪˈhīnd/ ▶prep. **1 a** in, toward, or to the rear of. **b** hidden by. **2** in the past in relation to. **3** inferior to; weaker than. **4** in support of.
▶adv. **1 a** in or to the rear; farther back. **b** on the farther side: *a high wall with a field behind.* **2** remaining. **3** farther back than other members of a group. **4** late in accomplishing a task, etc.: *behind in my work.*
▶n. inf. buttocks.

**be·hold** ▶v. (past & past part. **be·held**) poet./lit. see; observe. —**be·hold·er** n.

**be·hold·en** ▶adj. under obligation.

**be·hoove** /bɪˈhoov/ ▶v. formal **1** be incumbent on: *it behooves any president to study history.* **2** it is appropriate: *it ill behooves the candidate to criticize her opponent's family.*

**beige** /bāzH/ ▶n. pale sandy color.
▶adj. of this color.

**be·ing** /ˈbēɪNG/ ▶n. **1** existence. **2** nature or essence. **3** human being. **4** anything that exists or is imagined.

**be·la·bor** ▶v. **1** argue or

elaborate (a subject) in excessive detail. **2** attack or assault.

**be·lat·ed** /bi'lātid/ ▸*adj.* late or too late. **—be·lat·ed·ly** *adv.* **—be·lat·ed·ness** *n.*

**belch** /belCH/ ▸*v.* **1** emit wind noisily from the stomach through the mouth. **2** (of a chimney, gun, etc.) send (smoke, etc.) out or up.
▸*n.* act of belching.

**be·lea·guer** /bi'lēgər/ ▸*v.* **1** besiege. **2** vex; harass.

**bel·fry** /'belfrē/ ▸*n.* (*pl.* **-fries**) space for bells in a tower.

**be·lie** /bi'lī/ ▸*v.* (**-lied, -ly·ing**) **1** give a false notion of. **2** fail to fulfill or justify.

**be·lief** /bi'lēf/ ▸*n.* **1 a** religious conviction. **b** firm opinion. **c** acceptance. **2** trust or confidence.

**be·lieve** /bi'lēv/ ▸*v.* **1** accept as true or as conveying the truth. **2** think; suppose. **3 a** have faith in the existence of. **b** have confidence in. **4** have (esp. religious) faith. **—be·liev·a·ble** *adj.* **—be·liev·er** *n.*
□ **make believe** pretend.

**be·lit·tle** ▸*v.* disparage. **—be·lit·tle·ment** *n.*

**bell** /bel/ ▸*n.* **1** hollow usu. metal object in the shape of a cup usu.

widening at the lip, made to sound a clear musical note when struck. **2** sound or stroke of a bell, esp. as a signal. **3** anything that sounds like or functions as a bell.
▸*v.* provide with a bell or bells.
□ **bells and whistles** *inf.* attractive but unnecessary additional features.

**bel·la·don·na** /ˌbelə'dänə/ ▸*n.* **1** *Bot.* poisonous plant with purple flowers and purple-black berries. (Also called **deadly nightshade**). **2** *Med.* drug from this.

**belle** /bel/ ▸*n.* beautiful woman.

**belle é·poque** /ˌbel ā'pək/ ▸*n.* period of settled and comfortable life preceding World War I.

**bell·hop** ▸*n.* person who carries luggage, runs errands, etc., in a hotel or club.

**bel·li·cose** /'beliˌkōs/ ▸*adj.* eager to fight; warlike. **—bel·li·cos·i·ty** *n.*

**bel·lig·er·ent** /bə'lijərənt/ ▸*adj.* **1** engaged in war or conflict. **2** given to constant fighting; pugnacious.
▸*n.* nation or person engaged in war or conflict. **—bel·lig·er·ence** *n.* **—bel·lig·er·ent·ly** *adv.*

**bell jar** ▸*n.* bell-shaped glass cover or container.

**bel·low** /ˈbelō/ ▸*v.* emit or utter with a deep loud roar.

▸*n.* bellowing sound.

**bel·lows** ▸*pl. n.* **1** device that emits a stream of air when squeezed, esp. (**pair of bel·lows**) a kind with two handles used for blowing air onto a fire. **2** expandable component, e.g., of a camera.

**bell·weth·er** /ˈbelˌweᴛʜər/ ▸*n.* **1** indicator of something: *university campuses are often the bellwether of change.* **2** leading sheep of a flock.

**bel·ly** /ˈbelē/ ▸*n.* (*pl.* **-lies**) **1** part of the human body below the chest, containing the stomach and bowels. **2** stomach. **3** front of the body from the waist to the groin. **4** underside of a four-legged animal. **5** cavity or bulging part.

▸*v.* (**-lied**) swell or cause to swell; bulge.

□ **belly button** *inf.* navel. □ **belly dance** Middle Eastern dance performed by a woman, involving voluptuous movements. □ **belly laugh** loud unrestrained laugh.

**be·long** /biˈlôNG/ ▸*v.* **1** be the property of: *the house belongs to my mother.* **2** be rightly assigned to: *place where it belongs.* **3** be a member of: *she belongs to the garden club.* **4** fit socially: *I don't belong here.*

**be·long·ings** ▸*pl. n.* movable possessions or luggage.

**be·lov·ed** /biˈləv(i)d/ ▸*adj.* much loved.

▸*n.* much loved person.

**be·low** /biˈlō/ ▸*prep.* **1 a** lower in position than. **b** south of. **2** beneath the surface of. **3** unworthy of.

▸*adv.* **1** at or to a lower point or level. **2** (of a text reference) further forward on a page or in a book: *as noted below.*

**belt** /belt/ ▸*n.* **1** strip of leather, etc., esp. worn around the waist. **2 a** circular band of material used as a driving medium in machinery. **b** conveyor belt. **3** distinct region or extent. **4** *inf.* heavy blow.

▸*v.* **1** fasten with or put a belt around. **2** *inf.* hit hard.

□ **below the belt** unfair or unfairly. □ **tighten one's belt** live more frugally. □ **under one's belt** satisfactorily achieved: *he needs to get more experience under his belt.*

**belt·way** ▸*n.* highway skirting a metropolitan region.

**bel·ve·dere** /ˈbelviˌdi(ə)r/ ▸*n.* summerhouse or open-sided gallery, usually at rooftop level, commanding a fine view.

**be·moan** ▸*v.* complain about.

**be·muse** /biˈmyo͞oz/ ▸*v.* puzzle, confuse, or bewilder (someone).

**bench** /bencH/ ▸*n.* **1** long seat of wood, stone, etc. **2** strong worktable. **3** (**the bench**) **a** office of judge or magistrate. **b** judges and magistrates collectively. **4** *Sports* **a** seating to the side of a field for coaches and players not taking part. **b** those players not taking part in a game. ▸*v. Sports* keep (a player) on the bench.

**bench·mark** ▸*n.* standard or point of reference. ▸*v.* evaluate by comparison with a standard: *benchmark our performance against an external standard.*

**bend** /bend/ ▸*v.* (*past* and *past part.* **bent**) **1** make or become curved. **2** (**bend down/over**) incline or cause to incline from the vertical; stoop. **3** interpret or modify (a rule) to suit oneself. **4** (**bend to**) direct or devote (oneself or one's attention, energies, etc.) to: *bent all her energy to completing her degree.* **5** turn (one's steps or eyes) in a new direction. **6** (force to) submit. ▸*n.* **1** curve. **2** departure from a straight course. **3** bent part. —**bend·a·ble** *adj.*

**be·neath** /biˈnēTH/ ▸*prep.* **1** not worthy of. **2** below; under. ▸*adv.* below; underneath.

**ben·e·dic·tion** /ˌbeniˈdiksHən/ ▸*n.* **1** blessing, esp. as part of a religious service. **2** state of being blessed.

**ben·e·fac·tor** /ˈbenəˌfaktər/ (*fem.* **ben·e·fac·tress**) ▸*n.* person who gives support (esp. financial) to a person or cause.

**be·nef·i·cent** /bəˈnefisənt/ ▸*adj.* doing good; generous; actively kind. —**be·nef·i·cence** *n.* —**be·nef·i·cent·ly** *adv.*

**ben·e·fi·cial** /ˌbenəˈfisHəl/ ▸*adj.* advantageous; having benefits. —**ben·e·fi·cial·ly** *adv.*

**ben·e·fi·ci·ar·y** /ˌbenəˈfisHēˌerē/ ▸*n.* (*pl.* **-ies**) person who benefits, esp. from a will.

**ben·e·fit** /ˈbenəfit/ ▸*n.* **1** favorable or helpful factor or circumstance. **2** (often **benefits**) insurance, social security, welfare, etc., payment. **3** public performance or game in aid of a charitable cause.

▶ *v.* (**-fit·ed**, **-fit·ing**; **-fit·ted**, **-fit·ting**) **1** do good to; bring advantage to. **2** receive an advantage.

**be·nev·o·lent** /bəˈnevələnt/ ▶ *adj.* wishing to do good; actively friendly and helpful.
—**be·nev·o·lence** *n.*
—**be·nev·o·lent·ly** *adv.*

**be·night·ed** /biˈnītid/ ▶ *adj.* intellectually or morally ignorant: *they saw themselves as bringers of culture to poor, benighted peoples.*

**be·nign** /biˈnīn/ ▶ *adj.* **1** gentle; kindly. **2** (of an environment) mild and favorable. **3** *Med.* (of a tumor, etc.) not malignant.
—**be·nign·ly** *adv.*

**be·nig·nant** /biˈnignənt/ ▶ *adj.* kindly and benevolent.
—**be·nig·nan·cy** *n.*
—**be·nig·nant·ly** *adv.*

**bent** /bent/ ▶ past and past part. of **BEND**.
▶ *adj.* **1** curved; having an angle. **2** determined to do or have: *he is bent on becoming a millionaire.*
▶ *n.* **1** inclination or bias. **2** talent for something specified: *bent for mimicry.* **3** any of various grasslike reeds, rushes, or sedges. **4** stiff stalk of a grass usu. with a flexible base.

**ben·thos** /ˈbenˌTHäs/ ▶ *n.* flora and fauna found on the bottom, or in the bottom sediments, of a sea, lake, or other body of water.

**be·numb** /biˈnəm/ ▶ *v.* **1** make numb; deaden. **2** paralyze (the mind or feelings).

**ben·zene** /ˈbenˌzēn/ ▶ *n.* colorless carcinogenic volatile liquid found in coal tar, petroleum, etc., and used as a solvent and in the manufacture of plastics, etc.

**be·queath** /biˈkwēTH/ ▶ *v.* **1** leave (a personal estate) to a person by a will. **2** hand down to posterity. —**be·queath·al** *n.* —**be·queath·er** *n.*

**be·quest** /biˈkwest/ ▶ *n.* **1** legacy. **2** action of bequeathing something.

**be·rate** /biˈrāt/ ▶ *v.* scold; rebuke.

**be·reaved** /biˌrēv/ ▶ *adj.* deprived of a relative, friend, etc., by death.

**be·reft** /biˈreft/ ▶ *adj.* deprived (esp. of a non-material asset).

**be·ret** /bəˈrā/ ▶ *n.* round, flattish, visorless cap of felt or cloth.

**beri·beri** /ˈberēˈberē/ ▶ *n.* nerve

disease caused by a deficiency of vitamin B$_1$.

**berm** /bərm/ ▸*n.* flat strip of land, raised bank, or terrace bordering a river or canal.

**ber·ry** /'berē/ ▸*n.* (*pl.* **-ries**) **1** any small roundish juicy fruit without a stone. **2** *Bot.* fruit with its seeds enclosed in a pulp (e.g., banana, tomato). —**ber·ried** *adj.*

**ber·serk** /bər'sərk/ ▸*adj.* wild; frenzied; in a violent rage: *he went berserk when he heard the news.*

**berth** /bərth/ ▸*n.* **1** fixed bunk on a ship, train, etc. **2** ship's place at a wharf.
▸*v.* moor (a ship) in its berth.
□ **give a wide berth to** stay away from.

**ber·yl** /'berəl/ ▸*n.* transparent precious stone, esp. emerald and aquamarine.

**be·seech** /bi'sēch/ ▸*v.* (*past* and *past part.* **be·sought** or **be·seeched**) ask earnestly. —**be·seech·ing** *adj.*

**be·set** ▸*v.* (**be·set·ting**; *past* and *past part.* **be·set**) **1** trouble persistently. **2** surround and harrass. —**be·set·ment** *n.*

**be·side** ▸*prep.* **1** at the side of; near. **2** compared with. **3** irrelevant to.

□ **beside oneself** overcome with worry, anger, etc.

**be·sides** ▸*prep.* in addition to; apart from.
▸*adv.* also; as well; moreover.

**be·siege** /bi'sēj/ ▸*v.* **1** lay siege to. **2** crowd around oppressively. **3** harass with requests. —**be·sieg·er** *n.*

**be·smirch** /bi'smərch/ ▸*v.* **1** soil. **2** dishonor.

**be·sot·ted** /bi'sätid/ ▸*adj.* infatuated.

**be·speak** ▸*v.* (*past* **-spoke**; *past part.* **-spo·ken** or **-spoke**) **1** be evidence of. **2** engage in advance.

**be·spoke** /bi'spōk/ ▸*adj.* (of goods, esp. clothing) made to order.

**best** /best/ ▸*adj.* (superl. of **GOOD**) of the most excellent or desirable kind.
▸*adv.* (superl. of **WELL**). **1** in the best manner. **2** to the greatest degree. **3** most usefully.
▸*n.* **1** that which is best. **2** chief merit or advantage. **3** winning majority of (games, etc., played).
▸*v. inf.* defeat, outwit, outbid, etc.
□ **at best** on the most optimistic view. □ **get the best of** defeat; outwit. □ **make the best of** derive what limited advantage

one can from (something unsatisfactory or unwelcome).

**best boy** ▶*n.* assistant to the chief electrician of a movie crew.

**bes·tial** /'bēsCHəl/ ▶*adj.* **1** brutish; cruel; savage. **2** of or like a beast. —**bes·tial·ly** *adv.*

**bes·ti·al·i·ty** /ˌbēsCHē'alitē; ˌbes-/ ▶*n.* **1** savagely cruel or depraved behavior. **2** sexual intercourse between a person and an animal.

**bes·ti·ar·y** /'bēsCHēˌerē; 'bes-/ ▶*n.* (*pl.* **-ar·ies**) descriptive or anecdotal treatise on various real or mythical kinds of animals, esp. a medieval work with a moralizing tone.

**be·stir** ▶*v.* (**-stirred, -stir·ring**) exert or rouse (oneself).

**be·stow** ▶*v.* confer (a gift, right, etc.). —**be·stow·al** *n.*

**be·strew** ▶*v.* (*past part.* **-strewed** or **-strewn**) lie scattered over (a surface).

**be·stride** /bi'strīd/ ▶*v.* (*past* **-strode;** *past part.* **-strid·den**) stand astride over; span or straddle.

**bet** /bet/ ▶*v.* (**bet·ting;** *past* and *past part.* **bet** or **bet·ted**) **1** risk (money, etc.), on the outcome of an event (esp. a race, game, etc.). **2** *inf.* feel sure.

▶*n.* **1** act of betting. **2** money, etc., staked. —**bet·tor** or **bet·ter** *n.*

**bet.** ▶*abbr.* between.

**bête noire** /ˌbāt 'nwär/ ▶*n.* (*pl.* **bêtes noires** *pronunc.* same) person or thing one particularly dislikes or fears.

**be·to·ken** /biˌtōkən/ ▶*v.* be a sign of.

**be·tray** /bi'trā/ ▶*v.* **1** be disloyal or treacherous to (another person, etc.). **2** reveal involuntarily or treacherously; be evidence of. —**be·tray·al** *n.* —**be·tray·er** *n.*

**be·troth** /bə'trōTH/ ▶*v.* bind with a promise to marry. —**be·troth·al** *n.*

**bet·ter** /'betər/ ▶*adj.* (compar. of GOOD). **1** of a more excellent or desirable kind. **2** partly or fully recovered from illness.

▶*adv.* (compar. of WELL). **1** in a better manner. **2** to a greater degree. **3** more usefully or advantageously.

▶*n.* **1** that which is better. **2** (**betters**) one's superiors.

▶*v.* **1** surpass. **2** improve.

□ **better off** in a better (esp. financial) position. □ **get the better of** defeat; outwit.

**be·tween** /bi'twēn/ ▶*prep.* **1** at

or to a point in the area or interval bounded by two points in space, time, etc.: *broke down between Boston and Providence.* **2** separating. **3** shared by. **4** to and from.

▶*adv.* (also **in be·tween**) at a point or in the area bounded by two or more other points in space, time, sequence, etc.: *not fat or thin but in between.*

□ **between ourselves** (or **you and me**)  in confidence.

**be·twixt** /bi'twikst/ ▶*prep. & adv.* between.

□ **betwixt and between** *inf.* neither one thing nor the other.

**bev·el** /'bevəl/ ▶*n.* **1** slope from the horizontal or vertical; sloping surface or edge. **2** (also **bev·el square**) tool for marking angles.

▶*v.* (**-eled, -el·ing; -elled, -el·ling**) **1** reduce (a square edge) to a sloping edge. **2** slope at an angle.

□ **bevel gear** gear working another gear at an angle.

**bev·er·age** /'bev(ə)rij/ ▶*n.* drink.

**bev·y** /'bevē/ ▶*n.* (*pl.* **-ies**) **1** large group of people of a particular kind. **2** flock of quails or larks.

**be·wail** ▶*v.* lament.

**be·ware** /bi'we(ə)r/ ▶*v.* be cautious (of).

**be·wil·der** /bi'wildər/ ▶*v.* utterly perplex or confuse.
—**be·wil·der·ment** *n.*

**be·witch** ▶*v.* **1** enchant; greatly delight. **2** cast a spell on.
—**be·witch·ing** *adj.*

**be·yond** /bē'änd/ ▶*prep.* **1** at or to the farther side of. **2** outside the scope or understanding of. **3** more than.

▶*adv.* **1** at or to the farther side. **2** farther on.

▶*n.* (**the beyond**) the unknown after death.

**Bi** ▶*symb. Chem.* bismuth.

**bi-** /bī/ (often **bin-** before a vowel) ▶*comb. form* forming nouns and adjectives meaning: **1** having two; thing having two: *bilateral.* **2 a** occurring twice in every one or once in every two: *biweekly.* **b** lasting for two: *biennial.*

**bi·an·nu·al** ▶*adj.* occurring, appearing, etc., twice a year.
—**bi·an·nu·al·ly** *adv.*

**bi·as** /'bīəs/ ▶*n.* **1** predisposition or prejudice. **2** edge cut obliquely across the weave of a fabric.

▶*v.* influence (usu. unfairly); prejudice.

□ **on the bias** obliquely; diagonally.

**bi·ath·lon** /bī'aтHlän/ ▶n. *Sports* athletic contest in skiing and shooting. —**bi·ath·lete** n.

**bib** /bib/ ▶n. **1** piece of cloth fastened around a child's neck while eating. **2** top front part of an apron, overalls, etc.

**Bi·ble** /'bībəl/ ▶n. **1 a** Christian scriptures consisting of the Old and New Testaments. **b** Jewish scriptures. **2** (**bible**) any authoritative book: *the woodworker's bible.* —**bib·li·cal** *adj.* —**bib·li·cal·ly** *adv.*

□ **Bible belt** area of the southern and central U.S. where fundamentalist Protestant beliefs prevail.

**bib·li·og·ra·phy** /ˌbiblē'ägrəfē/ ▶n. (*pl.* **-phies**) **1 a** list of books referred to in a scholarly work, usu. as an appendix. **b** list of books by a specific author or publisher, or on a specific subject, etc. **2** history or description of books, including authors, editions, etc. —**bib·li·og·ra·pher** n. —**bib·li·o·graph·ic** *adj.* —**bib·li·o·graph·i·cal** *adj.* —**bib·li·o·graph·i·cal·ly** *adv.*

**bib·li·o·phile** /'biblēəˌfīl/ ▶n.

person who collects or has a great love of books.

**bib·u·lous** /'bibyələs/ ▶*adj.* excessively fond of drinking alcohol.

**bi·cam·er·al** /bī'kamərəl/ ▶*adj.* (of a legislative body) having two chambers. —**bi·cam·er·al·ism** n.

**bi·car·bo·nate** /bī'kärbənit/ ▶n. (also **bicarbonate of soda**) sodium bicarbonate used as an antacid or in baking powder.

**bi·cen·ten·ni·al** ▶n. two-hundredth anniversary.
▶*adj.* lasting two hundred years or occurring every two hundred years.

**bi·ceps** /'bīseps/ ▶n. muscle having two heads or attachments, esp. the one that bends the elbow.

**bick·er** /'bikər/ ▶v. quarrel pettily; wrangle.

**bi·cus·pid** /bī'kəspid/ ▶*adj.* having two cusps.
▶n. the premolar in humans. —**bi·cus·pi·date** *adj.*

**bi·cy·cle** /'bīsikəl/ ▶n. two-wheeled vehicle propelled by pedals and steered with handlebars attached to the front wheel.
▶v. ride a bicycle.

**bid**[1] /bid/ ▶v. (**bid·ding**; *past* and

*past part.* **bid**) **1** (esp. at an auction) offer (a certain price): *bid $20.* **2** offer to do work, etc., for a stated price. **3** *Cards* state before play how many tricks one intends to make.
▶*n.* **1 a** offer (of a price). **b** offer (to do work, etc.) at a stated price. **2** attempt; effort. —**bid·da·ble** *adj.* —**bid·der** *n.*

**bid**² ▶*v.* (**bid·ding;** *past* **bid, bade;** *past part.* **bid**) **1** utter (greeting or farewell) to. **2** *archaic* or *poet.* **a** command or order. **b** invite: *he bade them enter.*

**bid·da·ble** /'bidəbəl/ ▶*adj.* meekly ready to accept and follow instructions; docile and obedient.

**bide** /bīd/ ▶*v.* (in phrase **bide one's time**) await one's best opportunity.

**bi·det** /bi'dā/ ▶*n.* low, oval, basinlike bathroom fixture used esp. for washing the genital area.

**bi·en·ni·al** /bī'enēəl/ ▶*adj.* **1** lasting two years. **2** recurring every two years.
▶*n.* **1** *Bot.* plant that takes two years to grow from seed to fruition and die. **2** event celebrated or taking place every two years. —**bi·en·ni·al·ly** *adv.*

**bier** /bi(ə)r/ ▶*n.* movable frame for a coffin.

**bi·fo·cal** /'bī,fōkəl/ ▶*adj.* having two focuses, esp. of a lens with a part for distant vision and a part for near vision.
▶*pl. n.* (**bifiocals**) bifocal eyeglasses.

**bi·fur·cate** ▶*v.* /'bīfər,kāt/ divide into two branches or forks.

**big** /big/ ▶*adj.* (**big·ger, big·gest**) **1 a** of considerable size, amount, intensity, etc. **b** of a large or the largest size. **2** important; significant; outstanding. **3 a** grown up. **b** elder.
□ **big bang theory** theory that the universe began with the explosion of dense matter. □ **Big Dipper** constellation of seven bright stars in Ursa Major in the shape of a dipper. □ **big top** main tent in a circus.

**big·a·my** /'bigəmē/ ▶*n.* (*pl.* **-mies**) crime of marrying when one is lawfully married to another person. —**big·a·mist** *n.* —**big·a·mous** *adj.*

**big·horn** ▶*n.* American wild sheep, esp. native to the Rocky Mountains.

**bight** /bīt/ ▶*n.* **1** curve or recess in a coastline, river, etc. **2** loop of rope.

**big·ot** /'bigət/ ▸*n.* person convinced of the superiority of his or her own opinions and prejudiced against those who hold different opinions. —**big·ot·ed** *adj.* —**big·ot·ry** *n.*

**big·ot·ed** /'bigətid/ ▸*adj.* obstinately convinced of the superiority or correctness of one's own opinions and prejudiced against those who hold different opinions.

**bi·jou** /'bēzhōō/ ▸*adj.* (esp. of a residence or business establishment) small and elegant.

▸*n.* (*pl.* **-joux** /-zhōō(z)/) jewel or trinket.

**bike** /bīk/ ▸*n. inf.* bicycle or motorcycle.

▸*v.* ride a bicycle or motorcycle. —**bik·er** *n.*

**bi·ki·ni** /bi'kēnē/ ▸*n.* brief two-piece swimsuit for women.

**bi·lat·er·al** ▸*adj.* **1** of, on, or with two sides. **2** affecting or between two parties, countries, etc.: *bilateral negotiations.* —**bi·lat·er·al·ly** *adv.*

□ **bilateral symmetry** symmetry about a plane.

**bile** /bīl/ ▸*n.* **1** bitter fluid that aids digestion and is secreted by the liver. **2** bad temper; peevish anger.

**bilge** /bilj/ ▸*n.* **1 a** almost flat part of a ship's bottom, inside or out. **b** (also **bilge·wa·ter**) filthy water that collects there. **2** *inf.* nonsense; worthless ideas.

**bi·lin·gual** ▸*adj.* **1** able to speak two languages. **2** spoken or written in two languages. —**bi·lin·gual·ism** *n.*

**bil·ious** /'bilyəs/ ▸*adj.* **1** affected by a disorder of the bile. **2** bad-tempered. —**bil·ious·ly** *adv.* —**bil·ious·ness** *n.*

**bilk** /bilk/ ▸*v. inf.* **1** cheat. **2** avoid paying (a creditor or debt).

**bill** /bil/ ▸*n.* **1 a** statement of charges for goods or services rendered. **b** amount owed: *ran up a bill of $300.* **2** draft of a proposed law. **3** poster; placard. **4** printed list, esp. a theater program. **5** piece of paper money. **6** bird's beak.

▸*v.* **1** list in a program: *they were billed to appear but didn't show up.* **2** send a note of charges to.

□ **bill and coo** *inf.* behave in a very loving way. □ **bill of exchange** written order to pay a sum of money on a given date to the drawer or to a named payee. □ **bill of goods 1** shipment of merchandise, often for resale. **2** *inf.* item that is misrepresented, fraudulent, etc. □ **bill of sale** certificate of transfer of personal property.

**bill·board** ▶*n.* large outdoor advertising sign.

**bil·let** /'bilit/ ▶*n.* place where troops, etc., are lodged. ▶*v.* quarter (soldiers, etc.): *the regiment was billeted at the hotel.*

**bil·let-doux** /'bilā 'doo/ ▶*n.* (*pl.* **bil·lets-doux**) love letter.

**bill·fold** ▶*n.* wallet for keeping paper money.

**bil·liards** /'bilyərdz/ ▶*n.* any of several games played on an oblong cloth-covered table, esp. one with three balls struck with cues into pockets around the edge of the table.

**bil·lion** /'bilyən/ ▶*n.* (*pl.* same or **bil·lions**) [in *sing.* prec. by *a* or *one*] **1** a thousand million (1,000,000,000 or $10^9$). **2** *inf.* very large number: *billions of years.* —**bil·lionth** *adj. & n.*

**bil·lion·aire** /'bilyə,ne(ə)r/ ▶*n.* person possessing over a billion dollars, pounds, etc.

**bil·low** /'bilō/ ▶*n.* **1** wave. **2** any large soft mass. —**bil·low·y** *adj.*

**bil·ly goat** ▶*n.* male goat.

**bi·month·ly** /bī'mənTHlē/ ▶*adj.* occurring twice a month or every two months. ▶*adv.* twice a month or every two months. ▶*n.* (*pl.* **-lies**) periodical produced bimonthly.

**bin** /bin/ ▶*n.* large receptacle for storage or garbage.

**bi·na·ry** /'bī,nerē/ ▶*adj.* **1 a** dual. **b** of or involving pairs. **2** of the arithmetical system using 2 as a base. ▶*n.* (*pl.* **-ries**) **1** something having two parts. **2** binary number. □ **binary code** *Computing* coding system using the binary digits 0 and 1 to represent a letter, digit, or other character. □ **binary star** system of two stars orbiting each other.

**bind** /bīnd/ ▶*v.* (*past* and *past part.* **bound**) **1** tie or fasten tightly. **2 a** restrain. **b** [as *comb. form*] constricted; obstructed: *snowbound.* **3** cause to cohere. **4** fasten or hold together as a single mass. **5** compel; impose. **6 a** edge (fabric, etc.) with braid, etc. **b** fasten (the pages of a book) in a cover. **7** ratify (a bargain, agreement, etc.). **8** be required by an obligation or duty: *am bound to answer.*

**9** bandage: *she bound up the injury.*

▸*n.* tight or difficult situation: *in a political bind.*

**bind·ing** ▸*n.* something that binds, esp. the covers, glue, etc., of a book.

▸*adj.* obligatory.

**binge** /binj/ ▸*n.* spree; period of uncontrolled eating, drinking, etc.

▸*v.* indulge in a binge.

**bin·go** /ˈbiNGgō/ ▸*n.* game in which each player has a card of squares with numbers that are marked off as they are randomly drawn and called.

**bin·oc·u·lars** /biˈnäkyələrz/ ▸*pl. n.* optical instrument with a lens for each eye, for viewing distant objects.

**bi·no·mi·al** /bīˈnōmēəl/ ▸*n.* **1** algebraic expression of the sum or the difference of two terms. **2** two-part name, esp. the Latin name of a species of living organism (consisting of the genus followed by the specific epithet).

**bi·o** /ˈbīō/ ▸*n.* **1** biology. **2** biography.

▸*adj.* biological.

**bio-** ▸*comb. form* **1** life: *biography.*

**2** biological: *biomathematics.* **3** of living beings: *biophysics.*

**bi·o·chem·is·try** ▸*n.* study of the chemical and physicochemical processes of living organisms.
—**bi·o·chem·i·cal** *adj.*
—**bi·o·chem·ist** *n.*

**bi·o·de·grad·a·ble** ▸*adj.* capable of being decomposed by bacteria or other living organisms.
—**bi·o·de·grad·a·bil·i·ty** *n.*
—**bi·o·deg·ra·da·tion** *n.*

**bi·o·eth·ics** /ˌbīōˈeTHiks/ ▸*pl. n.* [treated as *sing.*] ethics of medical and biological research.

**bi·o·feed·back** ▸*n.* technique of using the feedback of a normally automatic bodily response to a stimulus in order to acquire voluntary control of that response.

**bi·o·gen·e·sis** /ˌbīōˈjenəsis/ ▸*n.* synthesis of substances by living organisms.

**bi·og·ra·phy** /bīˈägrəfē/ ▸*n.* (*pl.* -phies) **1** written account of a person's life, usu. by another. **2** such writing as a branch of literature. —**bi·og·ra·pher** *n.*
—**bi·o·graph·i·cal** *adj.*

**biol.** ▸*abbr.* **1** biologic.

**2** biological. **3** biologist. **4** biology.

**bi·ol·o·gy** /bī'äləjē/ ▸*n.* the study of living organisms.
—**bi·o·log·i·cal** *adj.*
—**bi·o·log·i·cal·ly** *adv.*
—**bi·ol·o·gist** *n.*

**bi·o·mass** /'bīō,mas/ ▸*n.* **1** total mass of organisms in a given area or volume. **2** organic matter used as a fuel, esp. in a power station for the generation of electricity.

**bi·ome** /'bī,ōm/ ▸*n.* large naturally occurring community of flora and fauna occupying a major habitat, e.g., forest or tundra.

**bi·on·ics** /bī'äniks/ ▸*n.* the study of mechanical systems that function like living organisms.

**bi·op·sy** /'bī,äpsē/ ▸*n.* (*pl.* **-sies**) examination of tissue removed for diagnosis.

**bi·o·rhythm** ▸*n.* any recurring biological cycle thought to affect a person's emotional, intellectual, and physical activity.

**bi·o·sphere** ▸*n.* regions of the earth's crust and atmosphere occupied by living organisms.

**bi·o·tech·nol·o·gy** ▸*n.* exploitation of biological processes in industry, medicine, etc.

**bi·par·ti·san** /bī'pärtəzən/ ▸*adj.* of or involving two (esp. political) parties.
—**bi·par·ti·san·ship** *n.*

**bi·par·tite** /bī'pärtīt/ ▸*adj.* **1** consisting of two parts. **2** involving two groups.

**bi·ped** /'bīped/ ▸*n.* two-footed animal.
▸*adj.* two-footed. —**bi·ped·al** *adj.*

**birch** /bərCH/ ▸*n.* **1** hardwood tree with thin peeling bark. **2** (also **birch rod**) bundle of birch twigs used for flogging.

**bird** /bərd/ ▸*n.* egg-laying feathered vertebrate with a beak, two wings, and two feet, and usu. able to fly.
□ **bird in the hand** something secured or certain. □ **bird's-eye view** general view from above. □ **birds of a feather** people of like character.

**bird·ie** /'bərdē/ ▸*n. Golf* score of one stroke less than par at any hole.

**birth** /bərTH/ ▸*n.* **1** emergence of an infant or other young from the body of its mother. **2** beginning: *birth of socialism.* **3** origin; descent; ancestry: *of noble birth.*

☐ **birth control** contraception.

**birth·day** ▶*n.* day on which one was born or the anniversary of this.

**birth·mark** ▶*n.* brown or red mark on one's body at or from birth.

**birth·right** ▶*n.* right of possession or privilege one has from birth.

**bis·cuit** /'biskit/ ▶*n.* **1** small leavened bread or cake. **2** *Brit.* cookie.

**bi·sect** /bī'sekt/ ▶*v.* divide into two (equal) parts. —**bi·sec·tion** *n.* —**bi·sec·tor** *n.*

**bi·sex·u·al** ▶*adj.* **1** sexually attracted to persons of both sexes. **2** *Biol.* having characteristics of both sexes. **3** of or concerning both sexes. ▶*n.* bisexual person. —**bi·sex·u·al·i·ty** *n.*

**bish·op** /'bishəp/ ▶*n.* **1** senior member of the Christian clergy usu. in charge of a diocese. **2** chess piece that is moved diagonally.

**bish·op·ric** /'bishəprik/ ▶*n.* office or diocese of a bishop.

**bi·son** /'bīsən/ ▶*n.* (*pl.* same) humpbacked shaggy-haired oxen of N. America or Europe.

**bis·tro** /'bistrō/ ▶*n.* (*pl.* -**tros**) small restaurant.

**bit** /bit/ ▶*n.* **1** small piece or quantity. **2 a** fair amount: *quite a bit of gossip.* **b** somewhat: *am a bit tired.* **3** short time or distance. **4** *Computing* unit of information; 0 or 1 in binary notation. **5** metal mouthpiece on a bridle. **6** (usu. metal) tool or piece for boring or drilling. ☐ **bit by bit** gradually. ☐ **do one's bit** *inf.* make a useful contribution. ☐ **two bits** 25 cents.

**bitch** /bich/ ▶*n.* **1** female dog or other canine animal. **2** *inf.* spiteful woman. **3** *inf.* very unpleasant or difficult thing. ▶*v. inf.* complain; grumble: *they bitched about the boss all through lunch.*

**bite** /bīt/ ▶*v.* (*past* **bit**; *past part.* **bit·ten**) **1** cut or puncture using the teeth. **2** (of an insect, etc.) sting. **3** (of a wheel, screw, etc.) grip; penetrate. **4** accept bait or an inducement: *the fish aren't biting today.* ▶*n.* **1** act of biting. **2** wound made by biting. **3** mouthful of food. **4** taking of bait by a fish. **5** pungency (esp. of flavor). **6** incisiveness; sharpness.

□ **bite the bullet** *inf.* behave bravely or stoically. □ **bite the dust** *inf.* **1** die. **2** fail; break down.

**bit·ing** /ˈbītiNG/ ▸*adj.* **1** stinging; intensely cold. **2** sharp; effective. —**bit·ing·ly** *adv.*

**bit·ter** /ˈbitər/ ▸*adj.* **1** having a sharp pungent taste; not sweet. **2** caused by, feeling, or showing mental pain or resentment. **3** harsh; virulent. ▸*pl. n.* (**bitters**) liquor with a bitter flavor used as an additive in cocktails. —**bit·ter·ly** *adv.* —**bit·ter·ness** *n.*

**bit·tern** /ˈbitərn/ ▸*n.* wading bird of the heron family.

**bit·ter·sweet** ▸*adj.* **1** sweet with a bitter aftertaste. **2** arousing pleasure tinged with sadness. ▸*n.* scarlet-berried climbing nightshade of N. America.

**bi·tu·men** /biˈt(y) o͞omən/ ▸*n.* any of various tarlike mixtures of hydrocarbons derived from petroleum. —**bi·tu·mi·nous** *adj.*

**bi·valve** ▸*n.* any of a group of aquatic mollusks with two hinged shells, e.g., oysters.

**biv·ou·ac** /ˈbivo͞o,ak/ ▸*n.* temporary open encampment without tents.

▸*v.* (**-acked, -ack·ing**) camp in a bivouac.

**bi·zarre** /biˈzär/ ▸*adj.* strange; eccentric; grotesque.

**blab** /blab/ ▸*v.* (**blabbed, blab·bing**) **1** talk foolishly or indiscreetly. **2** reveal secrets. ▸*n.* person who blabs.

**black** /blak/ ▸*adj.* **1** having no color from the absorption of all or nearly all incident light (like coal or soot). **2** completely dark. **3** of the human group having dark-colored skin, esp. of African descent. **4** (of the sky, etc.) dusky; heavily overcast. **5** angry; threatening. **6** wicked; sinister; deadly. **7** gloomy; depressed; sullen: *a black mood.* **8** with sinister or macabre, as well as comic, import: *black comedy.* **9** (of coffee or tea) without milk. ▸*n.* **1** black color or pigment. **2** credit side of an account: *in the black.* **3** member of a dark-skinned human group, esp. one of African descent. —**black·ness** *n.*

**black and blue** ▸*adj.* discolored by bruises.

**black·ball** ▸*v.* **1** reject (a candidate) in a ballot (orig. by voting with a black ball). **2** exclude; ostracize.

**black·ber·ry** ▸*n.* (*pl.* **-ries**) black fleshy edible fruit of certain brambles.

**black·bird** ▸*n.* **1** common thrush of which the male is black with an orange beak. **2** any of various birds, esp. a grackle, with black plumage.

**black·board** ▸*n.* board with a smooth, usu. dark surface for writing on with chalk.

**black box** ▸*n.* flight recorder in an aircraft.

**black·en** ▸*v.* **1** make or become black or dark. **2** speak evil of; defame.

**black Eng·lish** ▸*n.* any of various nonstandard forms of English spoken by black people, esp. as an urban dialect in the U.S.

**black·guard** /ˈblagərd/ ▸*n.* villain; scoundrel. —**black·guard·ly** *adj.*

**black·head** ▸*n.* black-topped pimple on the skin.

**black hole** ▸*n.* region of space possessing a strong gravitational field from which matter and radiation cannot escape.

**black ice** ▸*n.* thin, hard transparent ice, esp. on a road surface.

**black·jack** ▸*n.* **1** card game in which players try to acquire cards with a face value totaling 21 and no more. **2** flexible leaded bludgeon.

**black·list** ▸*n.* list of people in disfavor, etc. ▸*v.* put on a blacklist.

**black ma·gic** ▸*n.* magic involving supposed invocation of evil spirits.

**black·mail** ▸*n.* **1** extortion of payment in return for not disclosing a secret, etc. **2** any payment extorted in this way. ▸*v.* extort money, etc., by blackmail. —**black·mail·er** *n.*

**black mar·ket** ▸*n.* illicit traffic in officially controlled or scarce commodities. —**black mar·ke·teer** *n.*

**black·out** ▸*n.* **1** temporary loss of consciousness or memory. **2** temporary loss of power, etc. **3** compulsory darkness as a precaution against air raids. **4** suppression of news. **5** sudden darkening of a theater stage.

**black·smith** ▸*n.* smith who works in iron.

**black·thorn** ▸*n.* thorny shrub bearing white flowers and small blue-black fruits.

**black tie** ▸*n.* **1** black bow tie

worn with a dinner jacket.
**2** man's formal evening dress.

**black·top** ▶*n.* type of surfacing material for roads, playgrounds, etc.

**black wid·ow** ▶*n.* venomous spider, of which the female has an hourglass-shaped red mark on her abdomen.

**blad·der** /'bladər/ ▶*n.*
**1** membranous sac in some animals, esp. that which stores urine. **2** inflatable bag.

**blade** /blād/ ▶*n.* **1 a** cutting edge of a knife, etc. **b** flat piece of metal with a sharp edge or edges used in a razor. **2** flattened part of an oar, propeller, etc. **3** flat, narrow leaf of grass and cereals. —**blad·ed** *adj.*

**blame** /blām/ ▶*v.* **1** assign the responsibility for a wrong: *blamed the engineer for the accident.* **2** assign the responsibility for something bad to (a person or thing): *blamed the explosion on faulty maintenance.*
▶*n.* **1** responsibility for a bad result. **2** blaming or attributing responsibility. —**blam·a·ble** or **blame·a·ble** *adj.* —**blame·less** *adj.*
□ **be to blame** be responsible;

deserve censure: *human error is to blame for the crash.*

**blanch** /blanCH/ ▶*v.* **1** make or become white or pale. **2** prepare (a vegetable, etc.) by briefly immersing in boiling water.

**bland** /bland/ ▶*adj.* **1 a** mild; not irritating. **b** tasteless; insipid. **2** gentle in manner; smooth. —**bland·ly** *adv.* —**bland·ness** *n.*

**bland·ish·ment** /'blandisHmənt/ ▶*n.* flattering or pleasing statement or action used to persuade someone gently to do something.

**blank** /blaNGk/ ▶*adj.* **1 a** (of paper) not written or printed on. **b** (of a document) with spaces left for a signature or details. **2** empty. **3** puzzled; nonplussed.
▶*n.* **1** unfilled space in a document. **2** cartridge containing gunpowder but no bullet.
▶*v.* screen; obscure: *electronic countermeasures blanked out the radar signal.* —**blank·ly** *adv.* —**blank·ness** *n.*
□ **blank check 1** check with the amount left for the payee to fill in. **2** *inf.* freedom of action.
□ **blank verse** unrhymed verse.

**blan·ket** /'blaNGkit/ ▶*n.* **1** large piece of woolen or other

material used for warmth, esp. as a bed covering. **2** thick covering mass or layer: *the lawn was covered with a blanket of snow.*
▶*adj.* covering all cases or classes; inclusive.
▶*v.* **1** cover. **2** stifle; keep quiet.

**blare** /ble(ə)r/ ▶*v.* sound or utter loudly.
▶*n.* loud sound.

**blar·ney** /ˈblärnē/ ▶*n.* cajoling talk; flattery.
▶*v.* (**-neys, -neyed**) flatter; cajole.

**blasé** /bläˈzā/ ▶*adj.* bored; indifferent.

**blas·pheme** /blasˈfēm/ ▶*v.* **1** talk profanely, making use of religious names, etc. **2** talk profanely about; revile.
—**blas·phem·er** *n.*

**blas·phe·my** /ˈblasfəmē/ ▶*n.* profane talk about sacred things.
—**blas·phe·mous** *adj.*
—**blas·phe·mous·ly** *adv.*

**blast** /blast/ ▶*n.* **1** strong gust of wind, heat, etc. **2 a** explosion. **b** destructive wave of air from this. **3** loud note of a wind instrument, car horn, etc. **4** *inf.* severe reprimand.
▶*v.* **1** blow up with explosives. **2** wither; shrivel. **3** make or cause to make a loud noise. **4** *inf.* reprimand severely.

☐ **at full blast** *inf.* working at maximum speed, etc. ☐ **blast off** (of a rocket, etc.) take off from a launching site.

**bla·tant** /ˈblātnt/ ▶*adj.* **1** flagrant; unashamed. **2** offensively obtrusive.
—**bla·tan·cy** *n.* —**bla·tant·ly** *adv.*

**blath·er** /ˈblaTHər/ ▶*v.* talk long-windedly without making very much sense.

**blath·er·skite** /ˈblaTHər,skīt/ ▶*n.* person who talks at great length without making much sense.

**blaze** /blāz/ ▶*n.* **1** bright flame or fire. **2** bright glaring light. **3** violent outburst (of passion, etc.). **4** white mark on an animal's face. **5** mark cut on a tree, esp. to mark a route.
▶*v.* **1** burn with a bright flame. **2** be brilliantly lit. **3** be consumed with anger, excitement, etc. **4** mark (a tree or path) with blazes. —**blaz·ing** *adj.* —**blaz·ing·ly** *adv.*

**blaz·er** ▶*n.* solid-color jacket.

**bldg.** ▶*abbr.* building.

**bleach** /blēCH/ ▶*v.* whiten by sunlight or chemical process.
▶*n.* bleaching substance.

**bleak** /blēk/ ▶*adj.* **1** exposed; windswept: *bleak and barren moor.* **2** dreary: *he looked around* *the bleak little room.* —**bleak·ly** *adv.* —**bleak·ness** *n.*

**blear·y** /ˈbli(ə)rē/ ▸*adj.* (**-i·er, -i·est**) (of the eyes) unfocused from sleep or tiredness. —**blear·i·ly** *adv.* —**blear·i·ness** *n.*

**bleat** /blēt/ ▸*v.* **1** (of a sheep, goat, or calf) make a wavering cry. **2** speak feebly, foolishly, or plaintively.
▸*n.* **1** sound made by a sheep, goat, etc. **2** weak cry.

**bleed** /blēd/ ▸*v.* (*past* and *past part.* **bled**) **1** emit blood. **2** extort money from. **3** allow (fluid or gas) to escape from a closed system through a valve, etc.

**bleep** /blēp/ ▸*n.* intermittent high-pitched sound made electronically.
▸*v.* **1** make such a sound, esp. as a signal. **2** obliterate obscenities with a bleep, as on a broadcast.

**blem·ish** /ˈblemiSH/ ▸*n.* defect; stain; flaw.
▸*v.* spoil; stain.

**blend** /blend/ ▸*v.* **1** mix together. **2** harmonize; become one. **3** (esp. of colors): **a** merge imperceptibly. **b** go well together; harmonize.
▸*n.* mixture.

**blend·er** ▸*n.* kitchen appliance for liquefying, chopping, or puréeing food.

**bless** /bles/ ▸*v.* (*past* and *past part.* **blessed, blest**) **1** (of a priest, etc.) pronounce words, esp. in a religious rite, asking for divine favor. **2** consecrate (something) by a religious rite. **3** endow (someone) with a cherished attribute: *God has blessed us with free will.* **4** thank: *silently blessed the premonition that had sent her home early.*
—**bless·ed·ly** *adv.*
—**bless·ed·ness** *n.*

**blight** /blīt/ ▸*n.* **1** plant disease caused by mildew, insects, etc. **2** harmful or destructive force. **3** unsightly or neglected urban area: *urban blight.*
▸*v.* **1** infect with blight. **2** spoil, harm, or destroy.

**blimp** /blimp/ ▸*n.* small nonrigid airship.

**blind** /blīnd/ ▸*adj.* **1** lacking the power of sight. **2 a** without discernment. **b** unwilling or unable to appreciate (a circumstance, etc.): *she is blind to his faults.* **3** not governed by purpose or reason. **4 a** concealed. **b** closed at one end. **5** *Aeron.* (of flying) using instruments only.

▸*v.* **1** deprive of sight. **2** rob of judgment: *we were blinded to the truth.*

▸*n.* **1** shade for a window. **2** pretext. **3** obstruction to sight or light. **4** camouflaged shelter used for observing wildlife or hunting animals. —**blind·ly** *adv.* —**blind·ness** *n.*

☐ **blind date 1** social engagement between two people who have not previously met. **2** either of such people.

**blind·fold** ▸*v.* **1** cover the eyes with a cloth, etc. **2** deprive of understanding; hoodwink.

▸*n.* cloth used to blindfold.

▸*adj. & adv.* with eyes covered.

**blind·side** ▸*v.* strike or attack unexpectedly.

**blink** /bliNGk/ ▸*v.* **1** shut and open the eyes quickly. **2** look with eyes opening and shutting. **3** prevent (tears) by blinking: *blinked back tears.* **4** ignore; condone.

▸*n.* **1** act of blinking. **2** momentary gleam or glimpse.

**blip** /blip/ ▸*n.* **1** small image of an object on a radar screen. **2** minor deviation or error.

▸*v.* (**blipped**, **blip·ping**) make a blip.

**bliss** /blis/ ▸*n.* perfect joy;

gladness. —**bliss·ful** *adj.* —**bliss·ful·ly** *adv.* —**bliss·ful·ness** *n.*

**blis·ter** /ˈblistər/ ▸*n.* **1** small bubble on the skin filled with fluid and caused by friction, etc. **2** similar swelling on any surface.

▸*v.* **1** raise a blister on. **2** form blisters: *the paint blistered in the heat.* —**blis·ter·y** *adj.*

**blithe** /blīTH/ ▸*adj.* **1** careless; casual: *blithe disregard for the rules.* **2** joyous: *a blithe comedy.* —**blithe·ly** *adv.* —**blithe·ness** *n.*

**blitz** /blits/ *inf.* ▸*n.* **1** intensive or sudden (esp. aerial) attack. **2** (**the Blitz**) German air raids on London in 1940 during World War II.

▸*v.* attack, damage, or destroy by a blitz.

**blitz·krieg** /ˈblits·krēg/ ▸*n.* intense military campaign intended to bring about a swift victory.

**bliz·zard** /ˈblizərd/ ▸*n.* severe snowstorm with high winds.

**bloat** /blōt/ ▸*v.* swell with gas, liquid, fat, etc.

**blob** /bläb/ ▸*n.* **1** small drop of matter. **2** drop; spot.

**bloc** /bläk/ ▸*n.* combination of

parties, governments, etc., sharing a common purpose.

□ **bloc vote** vote proportional in power to the number of people a delegate represents.

**block** /bläk/ ▸n. **1** solid piece of hard material, esp. of stone or wood. **2** this as a base for chopping, etc. **3** area bounded by four streets in a town. **4** obstruction. **5** pulley or system of pulleys mounted in a case. **6** (**blocks**) any of a set of solid cubes, etc., used as a child's toy. **7** piece of wood or metal engraved for printing. ▸v. obstruct. —**block·age** n. —**block·er** n.

□ **block and tackle** system of pulleys and ropes, esp. for lifting.

**block·ade** /blä'kād/ ▸n. blocking of a place, esp. a port, by an enemy to prevent entry and exit. ▸v. subject to a blockade.

**block·bust·er** ▸n. inf. extremely popular movie or book.

**block·head** ▸n. inf. stupid person. —**block·head·ed** adj.

**blond** /bländ/ ▸adj. (also fem. **blonde**) (of hair) light-colored; fair. ▸n. person with fair hair and skin. —**blond·ish** adj. —**blond·ness** n.

**blood** /bləd/ ▸n. **1** red fluid circulating in the arteries and veins of vertebrates. **2** corresponding fluid in invertebrates. **3** bloodshed. **4** passion; temperament. **5** race; descent; parentage. **6** relationship; relations. ▸v. **1** give (a hound) a first taste of blood. **2** initiate (a person) by experience. —**blood·y** adj.

**blood count** ▸n. number of red and white blood cells in a volume of blood.

**blood·cur·dling** ▸adj. horrifying.

**blood·hound** ▸n. **1** large hound used in tracking, having a keen sense of smell. **2** this breed.

**blood·mo·bile** ▸n. van, truck, or bus equipped and staffed to take blood from donors.

**blood pres·sure** ▸n. pressure of the blood in the circulatory system.

**blood·shed** ▸n. **1** spilling of blood. **2** slaughter.

**blood·shot** ▸adj. (of an eyeball) inflamed.

**blood·stream** ▸n. blood in circulation.

**blood·suck·er** ▸n. **1** animal or insect that sucks blood, esp. a leech. **2** extortionist. **3** person

who lives off others.
—**blood·suck·ing** *adj.*

**blood·thirst·y** ▶*adj.* (**-i·er, -i·est**)
eager for bloodshed.
—**blood·thirst·i·ly** *adv.*
—**blood·thirst·i·ness** *n.*

**blood ves·sel** ▶*n.* tube carrying
blood through the tissues and
organs.

**bloom** /bloom/ ▶*n.* **1 a** flower,
esp. cultivated. **b** state of
flowering. **2** one's prime. **3 a** (of
the complexion) glow. **b** delicate
powder on fruits, leaves, etc.
▶*v.* **1** bear flowers; be in flower.
**2** flourish.

**bloom·ers** /'bloomərz/ ▶*pl. n.*
women's loose, almost knee-
length underpants or knee-
length trousers.

**blos·som** /'bläsəm/ ▶*n.* **1** flower
or mass of flowers, esp. of a fruit
tree. **2** promising stage.
▶*v.* **1** open into flower. **2** mature;
thrive.

**blot** /blät/ ▶*n.* **1** spot or stain,
esp. of ink. **2** disgraceful act or
quality. **3** any blemish.
▶*v.* (**blot·ted, blot·ting**) **1** spot or
stain, esp. with ink. **2 a** use
blotting paper to absorb excess
liquid, esp. ink. **b** (of blotting
paper, etc.) soak up (esp. ink).
□ **blot out 1** obliterate (writing).

**2** obscure (a view, sound, etc.).
□ **blotting paper** absorbent paper
for drying excess ink.

**blotch** /bläCH/ ▶*n.* **1** discolored
or inflamed patch on the skin.
**2** irregular patch of color.
▶*v.* cover with blotches.
—**blotch·y** *adj.*

**blot·ter** /'blätər/ ▶*n.* **1** sheet of
blotting paper. **2** logbook, esp. a
police charge sheet.

**blouse** /blous/ ▶*n.* **1** woman's
loose upper garment, usu.
buttoned and collared. **2** upper
part of a military uniform.
▶*v.* make (a shirt, etc.) full like a
blouse.

**blow** /blō/ ▶*v.* (*past* **blew**; *past part.*
**blown**) **1 a** (of the wind or air)
move rapidly. **b** drive or be
driven by an air current. **2** send
a directed air current from the
mouth. **3** sound or be sounded
by blowing. **4** clear (the nose) by
blowing. **5** puff; pant. **6** *inf.*
depart suddenly (from): *blew
town yesterday.* **7** shatter by an
explosion. **8** make or shape
(glass or a bubble) by blowing.
**9** melt or cause to melt from
overloading: *the fuse has blown.*
**10** break into (a safe, etc.) with
explosives. **11** *inf.* **a** squander;
spend recklessly: *blew $20 on a*

*meal.* **b** spoil; bungle (an opportunity, etc.). **c** reveal (a secret, etc.).

▶*n.* **1** act of blowing (e.g., one's nose, a wind instrument, etc.). **2 a** gust of wind or air. **b** exposure to fresh air. **3** hard stroke with a hand or weapon. **4** sudden shock or misfortune.

□ **blow-by-blow** (of a description, etc.) giving all the details in sequence. □ **blow over** (of trouble, etc.) fade away. □ **blow up 1 a** shatter or destroy by an explosion. **b** explode; erupt. **2** inflate (a tire, etc.). **3 a** enlarge (a photograph). **b** exaggerate. **4** *inf.* lose one's temper.

**blow·out** ▶*n.* **1** burst tire. **2** melted fuse. **3** large party. **4** victory by a wide margin.

**blows·y** /ˈblouzē/ (also **blowz·y**) ▶*adj.* (of a woman) coarse, untidy, and red-faced.

**blow·torch** ▶*n.* portable device with a very hot flame used for burning off paint, soldering, etc.

**blub·ber** /ˈbləbər/ ▶*n.* **1** whale fat. **2** thick or excessive fat.

▶*v. inf.* **1** sob loudly. **2** sob out (words). —**blub·ber·er** *n.* —**blub·ber·ing·ly** *adv.* —**blub·ber·y** *adj.*

**blud·geon** /ˈbləjən/ ▶*n.* heavy club.

▶*v.* **1** beat with a bludgeon. **2** force or bully: *he bludgeoned me into taking the assignment.*

**blue** /blo͞o/ ▶*adj.* **1** having the color of a clear sky. **2** sad; depressed. **3** pornographic.

▶*n.* **1** blue color or pigment. **2** blue clothes or material: *looks good in blue.*

**blue·ber·ry** ▶*n.* (*pl.* **-ries**) small, blue-black edible fruit of various plants.

**blue·bird** ▶*n.* any of various blue songbirds.

**blue blood** ▶*n.* noble birth. —**blue-blood·ed** *adj.*

**blue cheese** ▶*n.* cheese with veins of blue mold.

**blue-chip** ▶*adj.* **1** (of a stock) sound and usu. paying a dividend. **2** high quality.

**blue-collar** ▶*adj.* manual; industrial: *blue-collar workers.*

**blue jay** ▶*n.* common crested bird with a blue back and head.

**blue jeans** ▶*pl. n.* pants made of blue denim.

**blue·print** ▶*n.* **1** photographic print of plans in white on a blue background. **2** detailed plan.

▶*v.* work out (a program, plan, etc.).

**blue·rib·bon** ▸*adj.* of the highest quality.

**blues** ▸*pl. n.* **1** (often **the blues**) melancholic music of African-American folk origin. **2** *inf.* (**the blues**) feelings of sadness or depression. —**blues·y** *adj.*

**blue·stock·ing** /ˈblo͞oˌstäkiNG/ ▸*n.* intellectual or literary woman.

**bluff** /bləf/ ▸*v.* **1** feign strength, confidence, etc. **2** mislead by bluffing.
▸*n.* **1** act of bluffing. **2** steep cliff or headland.
▸*adj.* good-naturedly direct in speech or manner. —**bluff·er** *n.* —**bluff·ly** *adv.* —**bluff·ness** *n.*
□ **call a person's bluff** challenge a person to prove a claim.

**blun·der** /ˈbləndər/ ▸*n.* serious or foolish mistake.
▸*v.* make a blunder; act clumsily or ineptly.

**blunt** /blənt/ ▸*adj.* **1** (of a knife, pencil, etc.) not sharp or pointed. **2** (of a person or manner) direct; outspoken.
▸*v.* make less sharp. —**blunt·ly** *adv.* —**blunt·ness** *n.*

**blur** /blər/ ▸*v.* (**blurred, blur·ring**) **1** make or become unclear or less distinct. **2** smear.
▸*n.* something that appears or

sounds indistinct or unclear. —**blur·ry** *adj.*

**blurb** /blərb/ ▸*n.* promotional description of a book.

**blurt** /blərt/ ▸*v.* (**blurt out**) utter abruptly, thoughtlessly, or tactlessly.

**blush** /bləSH/ ▸*v.* **1 a** become pink in the face from embarrassment. **b** (of the face) redden thus. **2** feel embarrassed or ashamed. **3** become red or pink.
▸*n.* **1** act of blushing. **2** pink tinge.
□ **at first blush** on the first glance.

**blush·er** ▸*n.* cosmetic for the cheeks.

**blus·ter** /ˈbləstər/ ▸*v.* **1** behave pompously and boisterously. **2** (of the wind, etc.) blow fiercely.
▸*n.* **1** noisily self-assertive talk. **2** empty threats. —**blus·ter·y** *adj.*

**blvd.** ▸*abbr.* boulevard.

**bo·a** /ˈbōə/ ▸*n.* **1** large snake that kills its prey by crushing and suffocating. **2** long scarf of feathers or fur.

**boar** /bôr/ ▸*n.* **1** wild pig. **2** male pig.

**board** /bôrd/ ▸*n.* **1** long, flat, thin piece of sawn lumber. **2** provision of regular meals for payment. **3** directors of a company; committee or group of councilors, etc. **4** (**boards**) stage of a theater. **5** *Naut.* side of a ship.

▶*v.* **1** go on board (a ship, train, etc.). **2** receive or provide regular meals for payment. **3** cover with boards. —**board·er** *n.*

□ **go by the board** be neglected or discarded. □ **on board** on or onto a ship, aircraft, etc.

**board·ing·house** ▶*n.* establishment providing board and lodging.

**board·walk** ▶*n.* promenade, esp. of wood, along a beach.

**boast** /bōst/ ▶*v.* talk about oneself with indulgent pride.

▶*n.* **1** act of boasting. **2** thing one is proud of. —**boast·ful** *adj.* —**boast·ful·ly** *adv.* —**boast·ful·ness** *n.*

**boat** /bōt/ ▶*n.* **1** small vessel propelled on water by an engine, oars, or sails. **2** (in general use) any ship. **3** elongated boat-shaped container used for sauce, gravy, etc.

▶*v.* go in a boat, esp. for pleasure.

□ **in the same boat** sharing the same problems.

**boat·swain** /'bōsən/ (also

**bo·sun**, **bo'·sun**) ▶*n.* ship's officer in charge of equipment and the crew.

**bob** /bäb/ ▶*v.* (**bobbed**, **bob·bing**) **1** move quickly up and down. **2** emerge suddenly.

▶*n.* movement up and down.

**bob·bin** /'bäbin/ ▶*n.* cylinder for thread.

**bob·by pin** ▶*n.* flat, closed hairpin.

**bob·cat** ▶*n.* small N. American lynx with a spotted reddish-brown coat and a short tail.

**bob·sled** ▶*n.* mechanically steered and braked sled used for racing down a steep ice-covered run.

▶*v.* race in a bobsled.

**bob·white** ▶*n.* American quail.

**bo·da·cious** /bō'dāsHəs/ ▶*adj.* excellent, admirable, or attractive.

**bode** /bōd/ ▶*v. tr.* portend; foreshadow.

□ **bode well** (or **ill**) be a good (or bad) sign.

**bod·ice** /'bädis/ ▶*n.* part of a woman's dress above the waist.

**bod·i·ly** /'bädl-ē/ ▶*adj.* of the body.

▶*adv.* **1** as a whole. **2** in the body; as a person.

**bod·y** /ˈbädē/ ▶n. (pl. **-ies**)
**1** physical structure, including the bones, flesh, and organs, of a person or animal. **2** corpse.
**3** physical aspect of a person as opposed to the soul. **4** trunk apart from the head and limbs: *the blow nearly severed his head from his body.* **5** main or central part. **6** large amount of something: *a rich body of Canadian folklore.* **7** group with a common purpose: *regulatory body.* **8** full or substantial quality of flavor, tone, etc.

**bod·y·guard** ▶n. person or group of persons escorting and protecting another person (esp. a dignitary).

**body lan·guage** ▶n. communication through gestures and poses.

**bod·y pol·i·tic** ▶n. nation or government as a corporate body.

**bod·y shop** ▶n. workshop where bodies of vehicles are repaired.

**bog** /bäg/ ▶n. wet, spongy ground.
▶v. (**bogged, bog·ging**) **1** (usu. **be bogged down**) cause (a vehicle) to become stuck in mud. **2** (**be bogged down**) be unable to make progress: *don't get bogged down in detail.* —**bog·gy** adj. —**bog·gi·ness** n.

**bog·gle** /ˈbägəl/ inf. ▶v. **1** be startled or baffled, esp. as: *the mind boggles.* **2** (**boggle at**) hesitate or demur at: *she didn't boggle at the price.*

**bo·gus** /ˈbōgəs/ ▶adj. sham; fictitious; spurious. —**bo·gus·ly** adv. —**bo·gus·ness** n.

**Bo·he·m·ian** /bōˈhēmēən/ ▶n. **1** native of Bohemia; Czech. **2** (also **bo·he·mi·an**) socially unconventional person, esp. an artist or writer.
▶adj. **1** of Bohemia or its people. **2** socially unconventional. —**bo·he·mi·an·ism** n.

**boil** /boil/ ▶v. **1 a** (of a liquid) start to bubble up and turn into vapor; reach a temperature at which this happens. **b** (of a vessel) contain boiling liquid. **2 a** cause to boil. **b** cook or be cooked by boiling. **3** be very angry.
▶n. **1** act or process of boiling; boiling point. **2** inflamed pus-filled swelling caused by infection of a hair follicle, etc.
□ **boil down 1** reduce volume by boiling. **2** reduce to essentials. **3** (**boil down to**) amount to.

**boil·er** ▶n. **1** apparatus for

heating a hot water supply. **2** tank for turning water to steam.

**bois·ter·ous** /ˈboist(ə)rəs/ ▸*adj.* **1** (of a person) rough; noisily exuberant. **2** (of the sea, etc.) stormy. —**bois·ter·ous·ly** *adv.* —**bois·ter·ous·ness** *n.*

**bold** /bōld/ ▸*adj.* **1** confidently assertive; adventurous; courageous. **2** impudent. **3** vivid. —**bold·ly** *adv.* —**bold·ness** *n.*

**bo·le·ro** /bəˈle(ə)rō/ ▸*n.* (*pl.* **-ros**) **1** Spanish dance in simple triple time. **2** woman's short open jacket.

**boll** /bōl/ ▸*n.* rounded seedpod of flax or cotton.

**bo·lo·gna** /bəˈlōnē/ ▸*n.* large meat sausage sold ready for eating.

**Bol·she·vik** /ˈbōlSHəˌvik/ ▸*n. hist.* member of the radical faction of the Russian Social Democratic party, which became the Communist party in 1918.

**bol·ster** /ˈbōlstər/ ▸*n.* long, thick pillow. ▸*v.* encourage; reinforce: *the fall in interest rates is bolstering confidence | he bolstered up his theory with solid facts.* —**bol·ster·er** *n.*

**bolt** /bōlt/ ▸*n.* **1** sliding bar and socket used to fasten a door, etc. **2** threaded pin, usu. metal, used with a nut to hold things together. **3** discharge of lightning. **4** act of bolting. **5** roll of fabric, wallpaper, etc. ▸*v.* **1** fasten with a bolt. **2 a** dash suddenly away. **b** (of a horse) suddenly gallop out of control. **3** gulp down (food) unchewed. ▸*adv.* rigidly; stiffly: esp. as *bolt upright.*

**bomb** /bäm/ ▸*n.* **1** container with explosive, incendiary material, etc., designed to explode and cause damage. **2** small pressurized container that sprays liquid, foam, or gas. **3** *inf.* failure (esp. a theatrical one). ▸*v.* **1** attack with or drop bombs. **2** *inf.* fail badly.

**bom·bard** /bämˈbärd/ ▸*v.* **1** attack with heavy guns or bombs. **2** subject to persistent questioning. **3** *Physics* direct a stream of high-speed particles at (a substance). —**bom·bard·ment** *n.*

**bom·bast** /ˈbämbast/ ▸*n.* pompous, pretentious, or extravagant language. —**bom·bas·tic** *adj.*

**bomb·er** ▸*n.* **1** aircraft equipped to drop bombs. **2** person using bombs.

**bomb·shell** ▸*n.* **1** overwhelming surprise. **2** *inf.* very attractive woman.

**bo·na fi·de** /ˈbōnə ˌfīd/ ▸*adj.* genuine; sincere.
▸*adv.* genuinely; sincerely.

**bo·na fi·des** /ˈbōnə ˌfīdz; ˈfīdēz; ˈbänə/ ▸*n.* person's honesty and sincerity of intention.

**bo·nan·za** /bəˈnanzə/ ▸*n.* **1** source of wealth. **2** rich lode. **3** prosperity.

**bon·bon** /ˈbänˌbän/ ▸*n.* piece of candy.

**bond** /bänd/ ▸*n.* **1 a** thing that fastens another down or together. **b** (**bonds**) thing restraining bodily freedom. **2** uniting force. **3** restraint; responsibility. **4** binding agreement. **5** *Commerce* certificate issued by a government or a company promising to repay borrowed money at a fixed rate of interest. **6** (also **bail bond**) money deposited to guarantee appearance in court.
▸*v.* **1** adhere; hold together. **2** connect with a bond. **3** place (goods) in bond.

**bond·age** /ˈbändij/ ▸*n.* **1** slavery. **2** subjection to constraint, influence, etc.

**bond·ed** /ˈbändid/ ▸*adj.* **1** (of a thing) joined securely to another thing, esp. by an adhesive, a heat process, or pressure. **2** emotionally or psychologically linked. **3** (of a person or company) bound by a legal agreement, in particular: **a** (of a debt) secured by bonds.**b** (of a worker or workforce) obliged to work for a particular employer, often in a condition close to slavery. **4** (of dutiable goods) placed in bond.

**bonds·man** ▸*n.* (*pl.* **-men**) **1** person who provides bond. **2** *archaic* slave.

**bone** /bōn/ ▸*n.* **1** any piece of hard tissue making up the skeleton in vertebrates. **2** the body, esp. as a seat of intuitive feeling: *felt it in my bones.* **3 a** material of which bones consist. **b** similar substance such as ivory, dentine, or whalebone.
▸*v.* take out bones from (meat or fish). —**bone·less** *adj.* —**bon·y** *adj.*

□ **bone of contention** source of dispute. □ **bone up** *inf.* study (a subject) intensively: *bone up on Latin for the exam.*

**bone chi·na** ▸*n.* fine china made of clay mixed with bone ash.

**bone-dry** ▸*adj.* extremely dry.

**bon·fire** /ˈbänˌfī(ə)r/ ▸*n.* large open-air fire.

**bon·go** /ˈbäNGgō/ ▸*n.* (*pl.* **-gos** or **-goes**) either of a pair of small connected drums usu. held between the knees and played with the fingers.

**bon·kers** /ˈbäNGkərz/ ▸*adj. inf.* crazy.

**bon mot** /ˈbän ˈmō; ˌbôN ˈmō/ ▸*n.* (*pl.* **bons mots** *pronunc.* same or /ˈmōz/) witty remark.

**bon·net** /ˈbänit/ ▸*n.* woman's or child's hat tied under the chin.

**bon·sai** /bänˈsī; ˈbänsī/ ▸*n.* (*pl.* same) (also **bonsai tree**) **1** ornamental tree or shrub grown in a pot and artificially prevented from reaching its normal size. **2** art of growing trees or shrubs in such a way.

**bo·nus** /ˈbōnəs/ ▸*n.* **1** extra benefit. **2** usu. seasonal gratuity to employees beyond their normal pay.

**bon vi·vant** /ˈbän vēˈvänt; ˌbôN vēˈväN/ ▸*n.* (*pl.* **bon vi·vants** or **bons vi·vants** *pronunc.* same or

/-ˈvänts/) person who enjoys a sociable and luxurious lifestyle.

**boo** /boō/ ▸*interj.* **1** expression of disapproval or contempt. **2** sound intended to surprise. ▸*v.* (**boos, booed**) **1** utter boos. **2** jeer at by booing.

**boob·oi·sie** /ˌboōbwäˈzē/ ▸*n.* stupid people as a class.

**boo·boo** ▸*n. inf.* **1** mistake. **2** (esp. by or to a child) minor injury.

**boo·by** /ˈboōbē/ ▸*n.* (*pl.* **-bies**) **1** stupid or childish person. **2** large tropical seabird with a bright bill and bright feet.

**boo·by prize** ▸*n.* prize given to the least successful competitor in any contest.

**boo·by trap** ▸*n.* something designed to catch the unwary.

**book** /boŏk/ ▸*n.* **1** written or printed work consisting of pages glued or sewn together along one side and bound in covers. **2** literary composition intended for publication: *working on her book.* **3** bound set of tickets, stamps, matches, etc. **4** (**books**) set of records or accounts. **5** main division of a literary work, or of the Bible. **6** libretto, script of a play, etc. **7** telephone directory. **8** record of bets.

▸*v.* **1 a** reserve (a seat, etc.) in advance. **b** engage (a guest, musical act, etc.) for some occasion. **2** record the personal details of (esp. a criminal offender).

□ **go by the book** proceed according to the rules.

**book·end** ▸*n.* usu. ornamental prop used to keep a row of books upright.

**book·ie** *inf.* ▸*n.* BOOKMAKER.

**book·ing** ▸*n.* reservation or engagement.

**book·ish** ▸*adj.* **1** studious; fond of reading. **2** acquiring knowledge mainly from books. —**book·ish·ly** *adv.* —**book·ish·ness** *n.*

**book·keep·er** ▸*n.* person who keeps accounts for a business, etc. —**book·keep·ing** *n.*

**book·let** ▸*n.* small book, usu. with paper covers.

**book·mak·er** ▸*n.* professional taker of bets. —**book·mak·ing** *n.*

**book·mark** ▸*n.* strip of leather, cardboard, etc., used to mark one's place in a book.

**boom** /bo͞om/ ▸*n.* **1** deep resonant sound. **2** period of economic prosperity or activity. **3** *Naut.* pivoted spar to which a sail is attached. **4** long pole over a movie or television stage set, carrying microphones and other equipment.

▸*v.* **1** make or speak with a boom. **2** be suddenly prosperous.

□ **boom box** *inf.* portable stereo with powerful speakers.

**boo·mer·ang** /ˈbo͞oməˌraNG/ ▸*n.* **1** curved flat missile able to return to the thrower. **2** plan that recoils on its originator.

▸*v.* (of a plan, etc.) backfire.

**boon** /bo͞on/ ▸*n.* advantage; blessing.

▸*adj.* intimate; favorite: esp. as *boon companions.*

**boon·docks** (also **boon·ies** *inf.*) ▸*n.* rough, remote, or isolated country.

**boon·dog·gle** /ˈbo͞onˌdägəl/ ▸*n.* **1** trivial work done to appear busy. **2** questionable public project that typically involves political patronage and graft.

▸*v.* participate in a boondoggle.

**boor** /bo͝or/ ▸*n.* rude, unmannerly person. —**boor·ish** *adj.* —**boor·ish·ly** *adv.* —**boor·ish·ness** *n.*

**boost** /bo͞ost/ *inf.* ▸*v.* **1 a** promote by praise or advertising; push; increase. **b** push from below.

**2** increase or amplify (voltage, a radio signal, etc.).
▶*n.* act or result of boosting.

**boot** /boot/ ▶*n.* **1** outer foot covering reaching above the ankle. **2** (in phrase **to boot**) as well; in addition.
▶*v.* **1** kick. **2** (**boot out**) dismiss (a person) forcefully. **3** put (a computer) in a state of readiness. —**boot·ed** *adj.*
□ **you bet your boots** *inf.* it is quite certain.

**booth** /booTH/ ▶*n.* (*pl.* **booths**) **1** small temporary structure used esp. for sale or display of goods at a market, etc. **2** enclosure for telephoning, voting, etc. **3** set of a table and benches in a restaurant or bar.

**boot·leg** ▶*adj.* (esp. of liquor) smuggled; illicitly sold.
▶*v.* (**-legged, -leg·ging**) make, distribute, or smuggle (illicit goods). —**boot·leg·ger** *n.*

**boot·less** ▶*adj.* unavailing; useless.

**boo·ty** ▶*n.* plunder gained, esp. in war or by piracy.

**booze** /booz/ *inf.* ▶*n.* alcohol, esp. hard liquor.
▶*v.* drink alcohol, esp. excessively or habitually. —**booz·er** *n.*

**bo·rax** /'bôraks/ ▶*n.* mineral salt, sodium borate, used in making glass and china, and as an antiseptic.

**bor·der** /'bôrdər/ ▶*n.* **1** edge or boundary, or the part near it. **2 a** line separating two countries. **b** district on each side of this. **3** edging around anything.
▶*v.* **1** form an edge along (something). **2** (of an area) be adjacent to (another area). **3** (**border on**) adjoin: *the mountains border on Afghanistan.* **4** (**border on/upon**) approximate; resemble: *excitement bordering on hysteria.*

**bore** /bôr/ ▶past of BEAR.
▶*v.* **1** make a hole, esp. with a revolving tool. **2** hollow out (a tube, etc.). **3** weary by tedious talk or dullness.
▶*n.* **1** hollow of a firearm barrel or of a cylinder in an internal combustion engine. **2** diameter of this; caliber. **3** tiresome or dull person or thing. —**bore·dom** *n.* —**bor·ing** *adj.*

**bo·re·al** /'bôrēəl/ ▶*adj.* **1** of the North or northern regions. **2** relating to or characteristic of the climatic zone south of the Arctic, esp. the cold temperate region dominated by forests of birch, poplar, and conifers.

**born** /bôrn/ ▶*adj.* **1** existing as a result of birth. **2 a** of natural ability or quality. **b** destiny. **3** of a certain status by birth: *French-born* | *well-born.*

□ **born-again** converted (esp. to fundamentalist Christianity): *born-again Christian.*

**bo·ron** /'bôrän/ ▶*n.* nonmetallic crystalline element. (Symb.: **B**)

**bor·ough** /'bərō/ ▶*n.* **1** (in some states) incorporated municipality. **2** each of five political divisions of New York City. **3** (in Alaska) a county equivalent.

**bor·row** /'bärō/ ▶*v.* **1 a** acquire temporarily with the promise or intention of returning. **b** obtain money in this way. **2** use (an idea, etc.) originated by another; plagiarize. —**bor·row·er** *n.* —**bor·row·ing** *n.*

**bos·cage** /'bäskij/ (also **bos·kage**) ▶*n.* massed trees or shrubs.

**bo·som** /'bŏŏzəm/ ▶*n.* **1 a** person's breast. **b** enclosure formed by the breast and arms. **2** emotional center: *the bosom of the family.*

▶*adj.* (esp. in **bos·om friend**) close; intimate.

**boss** /bôs; bäs/ ▶*n.* **1** employer; manager; overseer. **2** one who controls a political organization. **3** round knob, stud, or other protuberance, esp. in the center of a shield or in ornamental work.

▶*v.* **1** treat domineeringly. **2** be the master or manager of.

**bo·sun** (also **bo'·sun**) ▶ variant spelling of BOATSWAIN.

**bo·tan·i·cal** /bə'tanikəl/ ▶*adj.* of or relating to plants.

▶*n.* (usu. **botanicals**) substance obtained from a plant and used as an additive, esp. in gin or cosmetics.

**bot·a·ny** /'bätn-ē/ ▶*n.* the study of plants. —**bo·tan·ic** *adj.* —**bo·tan·i·cal** *adj.* —**bot·a·nist** *n.*

**botch** /bäCH/ ▶*v.* **1** bungle; do badly. **2** repair clumsily.

▶*n.* bungled or spoiled work.

**both** /bōTH/ ▶*adj. & pron.* the two; not only one: *both boys* | *both the boys* | *both of the boys* | *the boys are both here.*

▶*adv.* with equal truth in two cases: *both angry and sad.*

**both·er** /'bäTHər/ ▶*v.* **1** take the trouble to do something: *nobody bothered to lock the door.* **2** worry, disturb, or upset (someone): *I don't want to bother her with the letter.* **3** feel concern about. **4 (bother oneself)** concern oneself.

▶*n.* **1** person or thing that bothers; nuisance. **2** trouble; worry; fuss. —**both·er·some** *adj.*

**bot·tle** /ˈbätl/ ▶*n.* **1** container, usu. of glass or plastic, for storing liquid. **2** amount filling it.

▶*v.* **1** put into bottles or jars. **2 (bottle up) a** conceal or restrain (esp. a feeling). **b** keep (an enemy force, etc.) contained or entrapped. —**bot·tle·ful** *n.* —**bot·tler** *n.*

□ **hit the bottle** *inf.* drink heavily.

**bot·tle·neck** ▶*n.* **1** point at which the flow of traffic, production, etc., is constricted. **2** any impedance to progress.

**bot·tom** /ˈbätəm/ ▶*n.* **1 a** lowest point or part. **b** base. **c** underside. **2** *inf.* buttocks. **3** seat of a chair, etc. **4** ground under the water of a lake, etc. **5** basis; origin.

▶*adj.* **1** lowest. **2** last. —**bot·tom·most** *adj.*

□ **at bottom** basically; essentially.
□ **bottom line** *inf.* ultimate, esp. financial, criterion.

**bot·tom·less** ▶*adj.* **1** without a bottom. **2** (of a supply, etc.) inexhaustible.

**bot·u·lism** /ˈbächə,lizəm/ ▶*n.* poisoning caused by a bacillus growing in spoiled food.

**bou·doir** /ˈbo͞odwär/ ▶*n.* woman's private room or bedroom.

**bouf·fant** /bo͞oˈfänt/ ▶*adj.* (of a dress, hair, etc.) puffed out.

**bough** /bou/ ▶*n.* branch of a tree, esp. a main one.

**bouil·lon** /ˈbo͞olyən/ ▶*n.* clear soup; broth.

**boul·der** /ˈbōldər/ ▶*n.* large rock.

**bou·le·vard** /ˈbo͞olə,värd/ ▶*n.* **1** broad, tree-lined avenue. **2** broad main road.

**bou·le·var·dier** /,bo͞oləvärˈdi(ə)r/ ▶*n.* wealthy, fashionable socialite.

**bounce** /bouns/ ▶*v.* **1** (of a ball, etc.) rebound or cause to rebound. **2** *inf.* (of a check) be returned by a bank when there are insufficient funds to meet it. **3** jump, spring, or rush noisily, enthusiastically, etc.

▶*n.* **1 a** rebound. **b** power of rebounding. **2** *inf.* **a** liveliness. **b** resilience. —**bounc·i·ness** *n.* —**bounc·y** *adj.*

**bounc·ing** ▶*adj.* (esp. of a baby) big and healthy.

**bound**[1] /bound/ ▸*v.* **1 a** spring; leap. **b** walk or run with leaping strides. **2** (of a ball, etc.) bounce. ▸*n.* **1** springy leap. **2** bounce. ▸*adj.* **1** on one's way: *trains bound for Chicago.* **2** [*comb. form*] moving in a specified direction: *northbound.*

**bound**[2] ▸*n.* (often **bounds**) **1** border; boundary. **2** limitation; restriction. ▸*v.* **1** form the boundary of: *the property was bounded by the sea on one side and the forest on the other.* **2** restrict: *freedom of action is bounded by law.* □ **out of bounds 1** outside a permitted area. **2** beyond what is acceptable.

**bound**[3] ▸past and past part. of BIND. □ **bound to** certain to: *he's bound to come.*

**bound·a·ry** /'bound(ə)rē/ ▸*n.* (*pl.* **-ries**) real or notional line marking the limits of an area, territory, etc.

**bound·less** ▸*adj.* unlimited; immense: *boundless enthusiasm.* —**bound·less·ly** *adv.* —**bound·less·ness** *n.*

**boun·te·ous** /'bountēəs/ ▸*adj. archaic* generously given or giving. —**boun·te·ous·ly** *adv.* —**boun·te·ous·ness** *n.*

**boun·ti·ful** /'bountifəl/ ▸*adj.* **1** large in quantity. **2** giving generously.

**boun·ty** /'bountē/ ▸*n.* (*pl.* **-ties**) **1** generosity. **2** reward; premium.

**bou·quet** /bō'kā/ ▸*n.* **1** bunch of flowers. **2** scent of wine, etc. **3** compliment.

**bour·bon** /'bŏŏrbən/ ▸*n.* whiskey distilled from corn mash.

**bour·geois** /bŏŏr'zнwä/ ▸*adj.* of or characteristic of the middle class, esp. referring to its materialistic values or conventional attitudes. ▸*n.* bourgeois person.

**bour·geoi·sie** /ˌbŏŏrzнwä'zē/ ▸*n.* middle class.

**bourse** /bŏŏrs/ ▸*n.* stock market in a non-English-speaking country, esp. France.

**bou·stro·phe·don** /ˌbōōstrə'fēdn/ ▸*adj. & adv.* (of written words) from right to left and from left to right in alternate lines.

**bout** /bout/ ▸*n.* **1** limited period. **2 a** wrestling or boxing match. **b** trial of strength.

**bou·tique** /bōō'tēk/ ▸*n.* small

shop, esp. one selling fashionable goods.

**bou·ton·nière** /ˌbo͞otn'i(ə)r/ ▶*n.* spray of flowers worn in a buttonhole.

**bo·vine** /ˈbōvīn/ ▶*adj.* **1** of or relating to cattle. **2** stupid; dull. —**bo·vine·ly** *adv.*

**bow**[1] /bō/ ▶*n.* **1 a** slipknot with a double loop. **b** ribbon, shoelace, etc., tied with this. **2** device for shooting arrows with a taut string joining the ends of a curved piece of wood, etc. **3** rod with horsehair stretched along its length, used for playing the violin, cello, etc. **4** shallow curve or bend.
▶*v.* use a bow on (a violin, etc.).

**bow**[2] /bou/ ▶*v.* **1** incline the head or trunk, esp. in greeting or acknowledgment. **2** submit. **3** cause to bend downwards.
▶*n.* **1** act of bowing. **2** forward end of a boat or ship.
□ **take a bow** acknowledge applause.

**bow·el** /ˈbou(ə)l/ (also **bow·els**) ▶*n.* **1** intestine. **2** depths; innermost parts.
□ **bowel movement** defecation.

**bow·er** /ˈbou(ə)r/ ▶*n.* secluded place enclosed by foliage; arbor. —**bow·er·y** *adj.*

**bowl** /bōl/ ▶*n.* **1** round deep basin for food or liquid. **2** contents of such a container. **3** any deep-sided container shaped like a bowl. **4** bowl-shaped part of a tobacco pipe, spoon, balance, etc.
▶*v.* **1** play a game where a ball is rolled to knock over pins. **2** (**bowl along**) go along rapidly. —**bowl·ing** *n. & adj.*
□ **bowl over 1** knock down. **2** *inf.* **a** impress greatly. **b** overwhelm.

**bowl·er** ▶*n.* hard felt hat with a rounded top.

**box** /bäks/ ▶*n.* **1** container, usu. flat sided and firm. **2** separate seating area in a theater, etc. **3** facility at a post office, etc., for receiving mail or messages. **4** enclosed area for a jury or witnesses in a courtroom. **5** space or area of print on a page, enclosed by a border. **6** small evergreen tree with glossy dark green leaves.
▶*v.* **1** put in or provide with a box. **2** confine. **3** fight (an opponent) at boxing. **4** slap (esp. a person's ears).
□ **box office 1** ticket office at a theater, etc. **2** the commercial aspect of a performance.

**box·car** ▸*n.* enclosed railroad freight car.

**box·er** ▸*n.* **1** person who boxes. **2** medium-sized dog with a smooth brown coat and pug-like face.

**boy** /boi/ ▸*n.* **1** male child or youth. **2** young man. **3** (**the boys**) group of men mixing socially. —**boy·hood** *n.* —**boy·ish** *adj.* —**boy·ish·ly** *adv.* —**boy·ish·ness** *n.*

□ **boy scout** (also **Boy Scout**) member of an organization of boys, esp. the Boy Scouts of America, that promotes character, outdoor activities, community service, etc.

**boy·cott** /ˈboiˌkät/ ▸*v.* refuse social or commercial relations with (a person, country, etc.). ▸*n.* such a refusal.

**boy·friend** ▸*n.* person's regular male companion or lover.

**bra** /brä/ ▸*n.* undergarment worn by women to support the breasts.

**brace** /brās/ ▸*n.* **1** device that clamps or fastens tightly. **2** (**braces**) wire device for straightening the teeth. **3** (*pl.* same) pair (esp. of game). **4** connecting mark { or } in printing.

▸*v.* **1** give strength or support to. **2** [usu. as *adj.* **bracing**] invigorate; refresh. —**brac·ing·ly** *adv.* —**brac·ing·ness** *n.*

**brace·let** /ˈbrāslit/ ▸*n.* ornamental band or chain worn on the wrist or arm.

**bra·chi·al** /ˈbrākēəl; ˈbrak-/ ▸*adj.* of or relating to the arm, specifically the upper arm, or an armlike structure.

**brack·et** /ˈbrakit/ ▸*n.* **1** support projecting from a vertical surface. **2 a** each of a pair of marks [ ] (**square brack·ets**) or < > (**an·gle brack·ets**) used to enclose words or figures. **b** PARENTHESIS. **c** BRACE. **3** group or classification. ▸*v.* **1 a** combine within brackets. **b** imply a connection or equality between. **2** enclose in brackets.

**brack·ish** /ˈbrakiSH/ ▸*adj.* (of water, etc.) slightly salty. —**brack·ish·ness** *n.*

**bract** /brakt/ ▸*n.* brightly colored leaflike part of a plant.

**brad** /brad/ ▸*n.* thin flat nail with a small head.

**brae** /brā/ ▸*n. Scottish & N. Irish* steep bank or hillside.

**brag** /brag/ ▸*v.* (**bragged**, **brag·ging**) talk boastfully. ▸*n.* boastful statement or talk.

**brag·ga·do·ci·o** /ˌbragəˈdōSHē-ˌō/ ▸n. boastful or arrogant behavior.

**Brah·man** /ˈbrämən/ (also **Brah·min** /-min/) ▸n. (pl. **-mans** also **-mins**) member of the highest Hindu caste, that of the priesthood.

**Brah·min** /ˈbrämin/ ▸n. socially or culturally superior person, esp. a wealthy, influential person from New England.

**braid** /brād/ ▸n. **1** woven band as edging or trimming. **2** length of hair, straw, etc., in three or more interlaced strands.
▸v. intertwine. **—braid·ing** n.

**Braille** /brāl/ ▸n. system of writing and printing for the blind with patterns of raised dots.

**brain** /brān/ ▸n. **1** organ of soft nervous tissue contained in the skull of vertebrates, the center of sensation and of intellectual and nervous activity. **2** (**brains**) the substance of the brain, esp. as food. **3** (**brains**) person's intellectual capacity. **4** inf. intelligent person.
□ **brain wave 1** (usu. **brain waves**) electrical impulse in the brain. **2** inf. sudden bright idea.

**brain death** ▸n. irreversible ending of brain function, regarded as indicating death. **—brain-dead** adj.

**brain·storm** ▸n. spontaneous ingenious idea or invention. ▸v. discuss ideas spontaneously and openly. **—brain·storm·ing** n.

**brain·wash** ▸v. subject (a person) to a process by which ideas are implanted in the mind. **—brain·wash·ing** n.

**braise** /brāz/ ▸v. sauté lightly and then stew slowly with a little liquid in a closed container.

**brake** /brāk/ ▸n. **1** device for stopping or slowing a wheel, vehicle, etc. **2** something that slows progress.
▸v. apply a brake.

**bram·ble** /ˈbrambəl/ ▸n. any of various thorny shrubs bearing fleshy red or black berries. **—bram·bly** adj.

**bran** /bran/ ▸n. grain husks separated from the flour.

**branch** /branCH/ ▸n. **1** limb of a tree. **2** lateral extension or subdivision, esp. of a river or railroad. **3** conceptual extension or subdivision, as of a family, knowledge, etc. **4** local office, etc., of a large business.
▸v. **1** diverge: the road branched off just before the town. **2** (of a plant)

divide into branches.
**—branched** *adj.*

□ **branch out** extend one's field of interest.

**brand** /brand/ ▸*n.* **1 a** a particular make of goods. **b** identifying trademark, label, etc.
**2** characteristic kind.
**3** identifying mark burned on livestock, etc. **4** iron used for this. **5** piece of burning, smoldering, or charred wood.
**6** stigma; mark of disgrace.
▸*v.* **1** mark with a hot iron.
**2** stigmatize: *was branded for life.*
**3** impress unforgettably on one's mind.

□ **brand-new** completely new.

**bran·dish** /'brandiSH/ ▸*v.* wave or flourish as a threat or in display.

**bran·dy** /'brandē/ ▸*n.* (*pl.* **-dies**) strong alcoholic spirit distilled from wine or fermented fruit juice.

**brash** /brasH/ ▸*adj.* **1** vulgarly self-assertive. **2** hasty; rash.
**3** impudent. **—brash·ly** *adv.*
**—brash·ness** *n.*

**brass** /bras/ ▸*n.* **1** yellow alloy of copper and zinc. **2** *Mus.* brass wind instruments. **3** (also **top brass**) persons of high (esp. military) rank. **4** *inf.* effrontery.
▸*adj.* made of brass.

□ **brass tacks** *inf.* actual details: *let's get down to brass tacks.*

**bras·siere** /brə'zi(ə)r/ ▸*n.* bra.

**brass·y** /'brasē/ ▸*adj.* (**brass·i·er**, **brass·i·est**) resembling brass, in particular: **a** bright or harsh yellow. **b** sounding like a brass musical instrument; harsh and loud. **c** (of a person, typically a woman) tastelessly showy or loud in appearance or manner.

**brat** /brat/ ▸*n.* child, esp. a badly-behaved one. **—brat·ty** *adj.*

**bra·va·do** /brə'vädō/ ▸*n.* show of boldness.

**brave** /brāv/ ▸*adj.* **1** able or ready to face and endure danger or pain. **2** splendid; spectacular.
▸*v.* defy; encounter bravely.
**—brave·ly** *adv.* **—brav·er·y** *n.*

**bra·vo** /'brävō/ ▸*interj.* expressing approval.
▸*n.* (*pl.* **-vos**) cry of bravo.

**bra·vu·ra** /brə'v(y)o͞orə/ ▸*n.* great technical skill and brilliance shown in a performance or activity.

**brawl** /brôl/ ▸*n.* noisy quarrel or fight.
▸*v.* quarrel noisily or roughly.
**—brawl·er** *n.*

**brawn** /brôn/ ▸*n.* **1** muscular strength. **2** muscle; lean flesh.
**—brawn·y** *adj.* **—brawn·i·ness** *n.*

**bray** /brā/ ▸*n.* cry of a donkey.
▸*v.* make such a sound.

**bra·zen** /'brāzən/ ▸*adj.* **1** (also
**bra·zen-faced**) shameless;
insolent. **2** of or like brass.
▸*v.* (**brazen it** (or **something**) **out**)
face or undergo defiantly.
—**bra·zen·ly** *adv.*
—**bra·zen·ness** *n.*

**bra·zier** /'brāzʜər/ ▸*n.* metal pan
or stand for holding lighted coals.

**breach** /brēcʜ/ ▸*n.* **1** breaking of
or failure to observe a law,
contract, etc. **2 a** breaking of
relations. **b** quarrel. **3** gap;
opening.
▸*v.* **1** break through; make a gap
in. **2** break (a law, contract, etc.).

**bread** /bred/ ▸*n.* baked dough of
flour and liquid usu. leavened
with yeast.
▸*v.* coat with breadcrumbs for
cooking.

**bread·crumb** ▸*n.* (usu.
**breadcrumbs**) small fragment of
bread.

**breadth** /bredTʜ/ ▸*n.* **1** distance
or measurement from side to
side of a thing. **2** extent;
distance; room.

**bread·win·ner** ▸*n.* person who
earns the money to support a
family.

**break** /brāk/ ▸*v.* (*past* **broke**; *past*
*part.* **bro·ken**) **1** separate into
pieces, as from a blow; shatter.
**2** make or become inoperative.
**3** interrupt. **4** fail to keep (a law,
promise, etc.). **5** make or
become subdued or weakened;
yield or cause to yield. **6** weaken
the effect of (a fall, etc.): *the yew
tree broke her fall.* **7** defeat;
destroy. **8** surpass (a record,
etc.). **9** (**break with**) quarrel or
cease association with (another
person, etc.). **10** be no longer
subject to (a habit). **11** reveal or
be revealed. **12** (of the weather)
change suddenly: *the weather
broke just in time for the picnic.*
**13** (of waves) curl over and foam.
**14** (of the day) begin with the
sun rising: *dawn was just
breaking.* **15** *Electr.* disconnect (a
circuit). **16 a** (of the voice)
change with emotion. **b** (of a
boy's voice) change at puberty.
**17** decipher (a code).

▸*n.* **1 a** act or instance of
breaking. **b** gap; split. **2** interval;
interruption; pause. **3** sudden
dash (esp. to escape). **4** *inf.* piece
of good luck. —**break·a·ble** *adj.*

□ **bad break** *inf.* **1** piece of bad
luck. **2** mistake or blunder.
□ **break down 1** fail; cease to
function. **2** be overcome by

emotion. **3** demolish. **4** analyze into components. □ **break even** make neither profit nor loss. □ **break in 1** enter by force. **2** interrupt. **3** accustom to a habit, etc. □ **break-in** illegal forced entry into premises, esp. with criminal intent. □ **break into 1** enter forcibly. **2 a** burst forth with. **b** suddenly change one's pace for (a faster one). **3** interrupt. □ **break off 1** detach by breaking. **2** bring to an end. □ **break out 1** escape by force, esp. from prison. **2** begin suddenly; burst forth. **3** become covered in (a rash, etc.). □ **break up 1** disperse; disband. **2** terminate a relationship.

**break·age** /ˈbrākij/ ▸*n.* **1** act or instance of breaking. **2** something broken.

**break·down** ▸*n.* **1 a** mechanical failure. **b** loss of (esp. mental) health. **2** detailed analysis.

**break·er** ▸*n.* heavy breaking wave.

**break·fast** /ˈbrekfəst/ ▸*n.* first meal of the day. ▸*v.* have breakfast.

**break·ing and en·ter·ing** ▸*n.* crime of entering a building by force so as to commit burglary.

**break·neck** ▸*adj.* (of speed) dangerously fast.

**break·through** ▸*n.* **1** major advance or discovery. **2** act of breaking through an obstacle, etc.

**break·up** ▸*n.* **1** disintegration; collapse. **2** dispersal.

**break·wa·ter** ▸*n.* barrier built out into the sea to break the force of waves.

**breast** /brest/ ▸*n.* **1 a** either of two milk-secreting organs on a woman's chest. **b** corresponding part of a man's body. **2** chest. **3** part of a garment that covers the breast. ▸*v.* face and move forward against: *he breasted the wave.* —**breast·ed** *adj.*

**breast·bone** ▸*n.* thin, flat vertical bone and cartilage in the chest connecting the ribs.

**breast·stroke** ▸*n.* stroke made while swimming face down by extending arms forward and sweeping them back in unison.

**breath** /breTH/ ▸*n.* **1 a** air taken into or expelled from the lungs. **b** respiration. **2 a** breeze. **b** whiff of perfume, etc. **3** whisper. **4** spirit; vitality. □ **under one's breath** in a whisper. □ **catch one's breath**

**1** cease breathing momentarily in surprise, suspense, etc. **2** rest to restore normal breathing. □ **hold one's breath 1** cease breathing temporarily. **2** *inf.* wait in eager anticipation.

**breathe** /brēᴛʜ/ ▸v. **1** take air into and expel it from the lungs. **2** be or seem alive.

**breath·er** /'brēᴛʜər/ ▸n. *inf.* brief pause for rest.

**breath·less** /'breᴛʜlis/ ▸adj. out of breath. —**breath·less·ly** adv. —**breath·less·ness** n.

**breath·tak·ing** /'breᴛʜ,tākiNG/ ▸adj. astounding; awe-inspiring. —**breath·tak·ing·ly** adv.

**brec·ci·a** /'brecHēə; 'bresH-/ ▸n. rock consisting of angular fragments cemented together.

**breech·es** /'bricHiz/ (also **pair of breeches**) ▸pl. n. short trousers, esp. fastened below the knee, now used esp. for riding.

**breed** /brēd/ ▸v. (*past* and *past part.* **bred**) **1** generate (offspring); reproduce. **2** produce; result in. **3** bring up; train. ▸n. **1** stock of genetically similar animals or plants. **2** race; lineage. **3** sort; kind. —**breed·er** n.

**breed·ing** ▸n. **1** developing or propagating (animals, plants, etc.). **2** generation; childbearing. **3** good manners: *has no breeding.*

**breeze** /brēz/ ▸n. **1** gentle wind. **2** *inf.* easy task. ▸v. *inf.* come or go casually: *she breezed in shortly after dinner.* —**breez·y** adj.

**breth·ren** /'breᴛʜ(ə)rin/ ▸see **BROTHER.**

**bre·vi·ar·y** /'brēvē,erē/ ▸n. (*pl.* **-ies**) book containing the service for each day, to be recited in the Roman Catholic Church.

**brev·i·ty** /'brevitē/ ▸n. **1** conciseness. **2** shortness (of time, etc.).

**brew** /broō/ ▸v. **1 a** make (beer, etc.) by infusion, boiling, and fermentation. **b** make (tea, etc.) by infusion. **2** gather force; threaten: *there is a storm brewing.* ▸n. kind of beer. —**brew·er** n. —**brew·er·y** n.

**bri·ar** /'brīər/ ▸var. of **BRIER.**

**bribe** /brīb/ ▸v. persuade to act improperly by a gift of money, etc. ▸n. money or services offered in bribing. —**brib·a·ble** adj. —**brib·er·y** n.

**bric-à-brac** /'brik ə ,brak/ ▸n. (also **bric-a-brac, bric·a·brac**) miscellaneous cheap ornaments.

**brick** /brik/ ▸*n.* **1 a** block of fired or sun-dried clay, used in building. **b** similar block of concrete, etc. **2** brick-shaped solid object.
▸*v.* close, pave, or block with bricks.
▸*adj.* built of brick.

**brick·bat** ▸*n.* **1** piece of brick, esp. when used as a missile. **2** critical and insulting remark.

**bri·co·lage** /ˌbrēkōˈläzн; ˌbrikə-/ ▸*n.* (*pl.* same or **-lag·es**) (in art or literature) construction or creation from a diverse range of available things.

**bride** /brīd/ ▸*n.* woman on her wedding day or just before and after it. —**brid·al** *adj.*

**bride·groom** ▸*n.* man on his wedding day or just before and after it.

**brides·maid** ▸*n.* girl or woman attending a bride at her wedding.

**bridge** /brij/ ▸*n.* **1 a** structure providing a way across a river, ravine, road, etc. **b** thing joining or connecting. **2** operational superstructure on a ship. **3** upper bony part of the nose. **4** *Mus.* upright piece of wood on a violin, etc., over which the strings are stretched.

**5** BRIDGEWORK. **6** card game derived from whist.
▸*v.* **1 a** be a bridge over. **b** make a bridge over. **2** span as if with a bridge. —**bridge·a·ble** *adj.*

**bridge·work** ▸*n.* dental structure used to cover a gap.

**bri·dle** /ˈbrīdl/ ▸*n.* **1** headgear to control a horse, including reins and bit. **2** restraining thing.
▸*v.* **1** put a bridle on. **2** bring under control; curb. **3** express offense, etc., esp. by throwing up the head: *she bridled at his insensitive remark.*
□ **bridle path** rough path or road suitable for horseback riding.

**brief** /brēf/ ▸*adj.* **1** of short duration. **2** concise. **3** abrupt; brusque. **4** scanty.
▸*n.* **1** (**briefs**) short underpants. **2** *Law* summary of a case.
▸*v.* instruct in preparation for a task; inform in advance. —**brief·ly** *adv.*

**brief·case** ▸*n.* flat, rectangular document case.

**bri·er** /ˈbrīər/ (also **bri·ar**) ▸*n.* **1** any prickly bush, esp. of a wild rose. **2** white heath native to S. Europe. **3** tobacco pipe made from its root.

**brig** /brig/ ▸*n.* **1** two-masted

square-rigged ship. **2** prison, esp. in the navy.

**bri·gade** /bri'gād/ ▶n. **1** subdivision of an army consisting usu. of three battalions and forming part of a division. **2** organized or uniformed band of workers: *fire brigade.*

**brig·a·dier** /ˌbrigə'di(ə)r/ ▶n. (also **brig·a·dier gen·er·al**) officer ranking between colonel and major general.

**brig·and** /'brigənd/ ▶n. member of a robber band. **—brig·and·age** n.

**bright** /brīt/ ▶adj. **1** emitting or reflecting much light; shining. **2** intense; vivid. **3** talented. **4 a** (of a person) cheerful; vivacious. **b** (of prospects, etc.) promising; hopeful. **—bright·en** v. **—bright·ly** adv. **—bright·ness** n.

**bril·liant** /'brilyənt/ ▶adj. **1** very bright; sparkling. **2** outstandingly talented. **3** showy. ▶n. diamond of the finest cut with many facets. **—bril·liance** n. **—bril·liant·ly** adv.

**brim** /brim/ ▶n. **1** edge or lip of a glass, etc. **2** projecting edge of a hat.

▶v. (**brimmed, brim·ming**) fill or be full to the point of overflowing. **—brim·less** adj. **—brimmed** adj.

**brim·stone** ▶n. sulfur.

**brin·dled** /'brindld/ (also **brin·dle**) ▶adj. (esp. of domestic animals) brownish or tawny with streaks of other color(s).

**brine** /brīn/ ▶n. **1** water saturated or strongly impregnated with salt. **2** sea water. **—brin·y** adj.

**bring** /briNG/ ▶v. (*past* and *past part.* **brought**) **1 a** come carrying or leading. **b** come with. **2** cause to come or be present. **3** cause or result in: *war brings misery.* **4** be sold for; produce as income.
☐ **bring about** cause to happen.
☐ **bring forth** give birth to.
☐ **bring off** achieve successfully.
☐ **bring up 1** rear (a child). **2** call attention to.

**brink** /briNGk/ ▶n. **1** extreme edge. **2** furthest point before something dangerous or exciting is discovered.
☐ **on the brink of** about to experience or suffer.

**brink·man·ship** /'briNGkmən-ˌSHip/ (also **brinks·man·ship** /'briNGksmən-/) ▶n. art or practice of pursuing a dangerous policy to the limits of safety before stopping, typically in politics.

**bri·quette** /bri'ket/ (also **bri·quet**) ▸*n.* block of compressed coal dust or charcoal used as fuel.

**brisk** /brisk/ ▸*adj.* **1** quick; lively. **2** enlivening. **3** curt; peremptory. —**brisk·ly** *adv.* —**brisk·ness** *n.*

**bris·ket** /'briskit/ ▸*n.* animal's breast, esp. as a cut of meat.

**bris·tle** /'brisəl/ ▸*n.* **1** short stiff hair, esp. one of those on an animal's back. **2** this, or an artificial substitute, used in brushes. ▸*v.* **1** (of the hair) stand or cause to stand upright. **2** show irritation. **3** be covered or abundant (in): *the roof bristled with antennas.* —**bris·tly** *adj.*

**Brit·i·cism** /'briti,sizəm/ (also **Brit·ish·ism** /'britisH,izəm/) ▸*n.* idiom used in Britain but not in other English-speaking countries.

**Brit·ish** /'britisH/ ▸*adj.* **1** of Great Britain or the United Kingdom, or its people or language. **2** of the British Commonwealth. ▸*n.* (**the British**) the British people.

**Brit·ish ther·mal u·nit** ▸*n.* amount of heat needed to raise 1 lb. of water at maximum density through one degree Fahrenheit, equivalent to 1.055 x $10^3$ joules.

**Brit·on** /'britn/ ▸*n.* **1** one of the people of S. Britain before the Roman conquest. **2** native or inhabitant of Great Britain.

**brit·tle** /'britl/ ▸*adj.* **1** hard and fragile; apt to break. **2** frail; weak; unstable. ▸*n.* brittle confection made from nuts and hardened melted sugar. —**brit·tle·ness** *n.*

**broach** /brōcH/ ▸*v.* **1** raise for discussion. **2** pierce (a cask) to draw liquor, etc.

**broad** /brôd/ ▸*adj.* **1** large in extent from one side to the other; wide. **2** spacious or extensive: *broad plain.* **3** full and clear: *broad daylight.* **4** explicit. **5** not taking account of detail. —**broad·ly** *adv.* —**broad·ness** *n.*
□ **broad-minded** tolerant; liberal. □ **broad spectrum** (of a drug) effective against many microorganisms.

**broad·cast** /'brôd,kast/ ▸*v.* (*past* -**cast** or -**cast·ed**; *past part.* -**cast**) **1 a** transmit by radio or television. **b** disseminate widely. **2** undertake or take part in a radio or television transmission. **3** scatter (seed, etc.) widely.

▶*n.* radio or television program or transmission.

▶*adj.* **1** transmitted by radio or television. **2** scattered widely.

▶*adv.* over a large area.
—**broad·cast·er** *n.*
—**broad·cast·ing** *n.*

**broad·cloth** ▶*n.* fine cloth of wool, cotton, or silk.

**broad·en** /'brôdn/ ▶*v.* make or become broader.

**broad·loom** ▶*adj.* (esp. of carpet) woven in broad widths.

**broad·side** ▶*n.* **1** firing of all guns from one side of a ship. **2** vigorous verbal onslaught. **3** side of a ship above the water.

**bro·cade** /brō'kād/ ▶*n.* rich fabric woven with a raised pattern.
▶*v.* weave with this design.

**broc·co·li** /'bräk(ə)lē/ ▶*n.* green vegetable with edible flower heads.

**bro·chure** /brō'sHŏŏr/ ▶*n.* pamphlet or leaflet.

**bro·gan** /'brogən/ ▶*n.* coarse, stout leather shoe reaching to the ankle.

**brogue** /brōg/ ▶*n.* **1** strong outdoor shoe with ornamental perforated bands. **2** marked dialect or accent, esp. Irish.

**broil** /broil/ ▶*v.* **1** cook (meat) on a rack or a grill. **2** make or become very hot. —**broil·er** *n.*

**broke** /brōk/ ▶*adj. inf.* having no money; financially ruined.
□ **go for broke** *inf.* risk everything in a strenuous effort.

**bro·ken** /'brōkən/ ▶*adj.* **1** that has been broken. **2** reduced to despair. **3** (of language) badly spoken, as by a foreigner. **4** interrupted. **5** uneven: *broken ground.* **6** tamed. —**bro·ken·ly** *adv.* —**bro·ken·ness** *n.*
□ **broken-down 1** worn out by age, use, etc. **2** out of order.

**bro·ken·heart·ed** ▶*adj.* overwhelmed with sorrow or grief.

**brok·er** /'brōkər/ ▶*n.* **1** agent who buys and sells for others; intermediary. **2** member of the stock exchange dealing in stocks and bonds. —**bro·ker·age** *n.*

**bro·me·li·ad** /brō'mēlē,ad/ ▶*n.* plant of tropical and subtropical America, usu. having short stems with rosettes of stiff, usually spiny, leaves.

**bro·mide** /'brōmīd/ ▶*n.* **1** *Chem.* any binary compound of bromine. **2** trite remark.

**bro·mine** /'brōmēn/ ▶*n. Chem.* poisonous liquid element with an irritating smell. (Symb.: **Br**)

**bron·chi·al** /ˈbräNGkēəl/ ▸*adj.* of or relating to the bronchi.

**bron·chi·tis** /bräNGˈkītis/ ▸*n.* inflammation of the mucous membrane in the bronchial tubes. —**bron·chit·ic** *adj. & n.*

**bron·chus** /ˈbräNGkəs/ ▸*n.* (*pl.* -**chi**) either of the two main divisions of the windpipe.

**bron·co** /ˈbräNGkō/ ▸*n.* (*pl.* -**cos**) wild or half-tamed horse of western N. America.

**bronze** /bränz/ ▸*n.* **1** alloy of copper and tin. **2** its brownish color. **3** thing of bronze, esp. a sculpture.
▸*adj.* made of or colored like bronze.
▸*v.* **1** give a bronzelike surface to. **2** make or become brown; tan.

**brooch** /brōCH/ ▸*n.* ornamental pin.

**brood** /brood/ ▸*n.* **1** young of an animal (esp. a bird) produced at one time. **2** *inf.* children in a family.
▸*v.* **1** think about something that makes one unhappy: *he brooded over his need to find a wife.* **2** sit as a hen on eggs to hatch them. **3** (of silence, a storm, etc.) hang or hover closely. —**brood·ing·ly** *adv.*

**brook** /brook/ ▸*n.* small stream.

▸*v. formal* tolerate; allow: *I shall brook no interference.*
—**brook·let** *n.*

**broom** /broom; broŏm/ ▸*n.* **1** long-handled brush for sweeping. **2** any of various shrubs bearing bright yellow flowers.

**broom·stick** ▸*n.* handle of a broom.

**Bros.** ▸*abbr.* Brothers (esp. in the name of a business).

**broth** /brôTH/ ▸*n.* thin soup of meat or fish stock.

**broth·el** /ˈbräTHəl/ ▸*n.* house where men visit prostitutes.

**broth·er** /ˈbrəTHər/ ▸*n.* **1** male sibling. **2** close male friend or associate. **3** (*pl.* also **breth·ren**) **a** a member of a male religious order, esp. a monk. **b** fellow member of a congregation, religion, or (formerly) guild, etc.
—**broth·er·ly** *adj. & adv.*
—**broth·er·li·ness** *n.*

☐ **brother-in-law 1** brother of one's wife or husband. **2** husband of one's sister or sister-in-law.

**broth·er·hood** ▸*n.* **1** relationship between brothers. **2** association of people linked by a common interest.

**brou·ha·ha** /ˈbrо̄о̄häˌhä/ ▶n. commotion; sensation.

**brow** /brou/ ▶n. 1 forehead. 2 eyebrow. 3 summit of a hill or pass. 4 edge of a cliff, etc. —**browed** adj.

**brow·beat** ▶v. (past **-beat**; past part. **-beat·en**) intimidate with stern looks and words.

**brown** /broun/ ▶adj. 1 having the color as of dark wood or rich soil. 2 dark-skinned or suntanned. ▶n. 1 brown color or pigment. 2 brown clothes or material. ▶v. make or become brown by cooking, sunburn, etc. —**brown·ish** adj. —**brown·ness** n. □ **brown-bag** take one's lunch to work, etc., in a brown paper bag. □ **brown rice** unpolished rice.

**brown·ie** ▶n. 1 (**Brownie**) member of the junior branch of the Girl Scouts. 2 small square of rich, usu. chocolate, cake with nuts. 3 benevolent elf. □ **Brownie point** inf. notional credit for something done to please.

**brown·out** ▶n. period during which electrical voltage is reduced to avoid a blackout.

**browse** /brouz/ ▶v. 1 read or survey desultorily. 2 feed (on leaves, twigs, etc.). ▶n. 1 twigs, young shoots, etc., as fodder. 2 act of browsing. —**brows·er** n.

**bruise** /brо̄о̄z/ ▶n. 1 injury appearing as a discoloration of the skin. 2 similar damage on a fruit, etc. ▶v. 1 inflict a bruise on. 2 be susceptible to bruising.

**bruis·er** ▶n. inf. tough-looking person.

**bruit** /brо̄о̄t/ ▶v. spread (a report or rumor) widely. ▶n. 1 report or rumor. 2 sound, typically an abnormal one, heard through a stethoscope; a murmur.

**brume** /brо̄о̄m/ ▶n. mist or fog.

**brunch** /brənCH/ ▶n. late-morning meal eaten as the first meal of the day.

**bru·nette** /brо̄о̄ˈnet/ (also masc. **bru·net**) ▶n. person with dark hair. ▶adj. having dark hair.

**brunt** /brənt/ ▶n. chief impact of an attack, task, etc., esp as: bear the brunt of.

**brush** /brəSH/ ▶n. 1 implement with bristles, hair, wire, etc., set into a handle, for arranging the hair, cleaning, painting, etc.

**2** application of a brush; brushing. **3** short, esp. unpleasant encounter: *brush with death.* **4** bushy tail of a fox. **5** *Electr.* piece of carbon or metal serving as an electrical contact, esp. with a moving part. **6** (also **brushwood**) undergrowth.

▸*v.* **1** sweep, scrub, or put in order with a brush. **2** remove or apply with a brush. **3** graze in passing. **4** perform a brushing action or motion.

□ **brush aside** dismiss curtly. □ **brush-off** abrupt dismissal. □ **brush up** revive one's former knowledge of (a subject).

**brusque** /brəsk/ ▸*adj.* abrupt or offhand. —**brusque·ly** *adv.* —**brusque·ness** *n.*

**brut** /broot/ ▸*adj.* (of sparkling wine) unsweetened; very dry.

**bru·tal** /'brootl/ ▸*adj.* **1** savagely or viciously cruel. **2** harsh; merciless. —**bru·tal·i·ty** *n.* —**bru·tal·ly** *adv.*

**bru·tal·ize** ▸*v.* treat brutally. —**bru·tal·i·za·tion** *n.*

**brute** /broot/ ▸*n.* **1** brutal or violent person or animal. **2** animal as opposed to a human being.

▸*adj.* **1** not possessing the capacity to reason. **2** merely physical. **3** harsh. —**brut·ish** *adj.* —**brut·ish·ly** *adv.* —**brut·ish·ness** *n.*

**BS** ▸*abbr.* Bachelor of Science.

**BTU** (also **B.t.u.**) ▸*abbr.* British thermal unit(s).

**bub·ble** /'bəbəl/ ▸*n.* **1 a** thin sphere of liquid enclosing air, etc. **b** air-filled cavity in a liquid or a solidified liquid such as glass or amber. **c** (**bubbles**) froth; foam. **2** sound or appearance of boiling. **3** semicylindrical or domed structure. **4** visionary or unrealistic project.

▸*v.* **1** rise in or send up bubbles. **2** make the sound of boiling.

□ **bubble gum** chewing gum that can be blown into bubbles. □ **bubble memory** *Computing* type of memory that stores data as a pattern of magnetized regions in a thin layer of magnetic material. □ **bubble wrap** clear plastic wrap with air bubbles in it.

**buc·cal** /'bəkəl/ ▸*adj.* of or relating to the mouth or cheek

**buc·ca·neer** /ˌbəkə'ni(ə)r/ ▸*n.* **1** pirate. **2** unscrupulous adventurer. —**buc·ca·neer·ing** *n. & adj.*

**buck** /bək/ ▸*n.* **1** male deer, hare, rabbit, etc. **2** dollar.

**3** article placed as a reminder before a player whose turn it is to deal at poker.

▶*v.* **1** (of a horse) jump upward with back arched and feet drawn together. **2** oppose; resist. **3** (**buck up**) make or become more cheerful. —**buck·er** *n.*

□ **pass the buck** *inf.* shift responsibility (to another).

**buck·et** /ˈbəkit/ ▶*n.* **1 a** a roughly cylindrical open container with a handle, for carrying, catching, or holding water, etc. **b** amount contained in this. **2** (**buckets**) large quantities, esp. rain or tears. **3** compartment on the outer edge of a waterwheel. **4** scoop of a dredger or a grain elevator.

□ **bucket seat** seat with a rounded back to fit one person, esp. in a car.

**buck·et shop** ▶*n.* unauthorized office for speculating in stocks or currency using the funds of unwitting investors.

**buck·le** /ˈbəkəl/ ▶*n.* **1** clasp with a hinged pin, used for securing a belt, strap, etc. **2** similarly shaped ornament, esp. on a shoe.

▶*v.* **1** fasten with a buckle. **2** give way or cause to give way under longitudinal pressure; crumple.

□ **buckle down** make a determined effort.

**buck·ram** /ˈbəkrəm/ ▶*n.* coarse linen or other cloth stiffened with gum or paste.

**buck·shot** ▶*n.* large-sized lead shot.

**buck·skin** ▶*n.* **1** leather made from a buck's skin. **2** thick, smooth cotton or wool cloth.

**buck·tooth** ▶*n.* upper tooth that projects.

**buck·wheat** ▶*n.* cereal plant with triangular seeds used for fodder and flour.

**bu·col·ic** /byōōˈkälik/ ▶*adj.* of or concerning the pleasant aspects of rural life. —**bu·col·i·cal·ly** *adv.*

**bud** /bəd/ ▶*n.* **1 a** a shoot from which a stem, leaf, or flower develops. **b** flower or leaf not fully open. **2** anything still undeveloped.

▶*v.* (**bud·ded, bud·ding**) **1** *Bot.* & *Zool.* form a bud. **2** begin to grow or develop.

**Bud·dhism** /ˈbōōdizəm/ ▶*n.* widespread Asian religion or philosophy, founded by Gautama Buddha in India in the 5th c. BC. —**Bud·dhist** *n. & adj.*

**bud·dy** /ˈbədē/ ▶*n. inf.* (*pl.* **-dies**) close friend or companion.

**budge** /bəj/ ▶*v.* move slightly.

**bud·get** /'bəjit/ ▶n. **1** amount of money needed or available. **2** estimate or plan of revenue and expenditure.
▶v. allow or arrange for in a budget. —**budg·et·ar·y** adj.

**buff** /bəf/ ▶adj. of a yellowish beige color.
▶n. **1** this color. **2** velvety dull yellow ox leather. **3** enthusiast.
▶v. **1** polish (metal, etc.). **2** make (leather) velvety.
□ **in the buff** inf. naked.

**buf·fa·lo** /'bəfə,lō/ ▶n. (pl. same or **-loes**) **1** N. American bison. **2** wild ox of Africa or Asia.

**buf·fer** /'bəfər/ ▶n. **1 a** device that deadens an impact, etc. **b** such a device on the front and rear of a railroad vehicle or at the end of a track. **2** Biochem. substance that maintains the hydrogen ion concentration of a solution when an acid or alkali is added. **3** Computing temporary memory area for data.
▶v. **1** act as a buffer to. **2** Biochem. treat with a buffer.
□ **buffer state** small nation situated between two larger ones regarded as reducing friction. □ **buffer zone** any area separating those in conflict.

**buf·fet**[1] /bə'fā/ ▶n. **1** meal consisting of several dishes set out on a table from which guests serve themselves. **2** restaurant or counter where light meals or snacks may be bought. **3** sideboard.
□ **buffet car** railroad car serving refreshments.

**buf·fet**[2] /'bəfit/ ▶v. strike repeatedly: buffeted by fate.
▶n. **1** blow, esp. of the hand or fist. **2** shock.

**buf·foon** /bə'fōōn/ ▶n. **1** jester; mocker. **2** stupid person. —**buf·foon·er·y** n. —**buf·foon·ish** adj.

**buf·foon·er·y** /bə'fōōnerē/ ▶n. (pl. **-er·ies**) behavior that is ridiculous but amusing.

**bug** /bəg/ ▶n. **1** any of various insects with mouthparts modified for piercing and sucking. **2** inf. virus; infection. **3** concealed microphone. **4** error in a computer program or system, etc. **5** inf. obsession, enthusiasm, etc.
▶v. (**bugged, bug·ging**) **1** conceal a microphone in. **2** inf. annoy. **3** inf. (**bug off**) go away.
□ **bug-eyed** with bulging eyes.

**bug·a·boo** /'bəgə,bōō/ ▶n. object of fear or alarm; a bugbear.

**bug·bear** ▶n. **1** cause of

annoyance; bête noire. **2** object of baseless fear.

**bug·ger·y** /ˈbəgərē; ˈbŏŏg-/ ▶n. anal intercourse.

**bug·gy** /ˈbəgē/ ▶n. (pl. **-gies**) **1** small light, horse-drawn vehicle. **2** small, sturdy, esp. open, motor vehicle: beach buggy. **3** baby carriage.

**bu·gle** /ˈbyoōgəl/ ▶n. (also **bu·gle horn**) brass military instrument like a small trumpet.
▶v. sound a bugle. **—bu·gler** n.

**build** /bild/ ▶v. (past & past. part. **built**) **1 a** construct. **b** commission, finance, and oversee the building of. **2 a** establish, develop, make, or accumulate. **b** (**build on**) base (hopes, theories, etc.) on.
▶n. **1** physical proportions. **2** style of construction.
**—build·er** n.
□ **build in** incorporate. □ **build on** add (an extension, etc.). □ **build up** **1** increase in size or strength. **2** praise; boost. **3** gradually become established. □ **built-in** integral. □ **built-up** **1** (of a locality) densely developed. **2** increased in height, etc., by the addition of parts.

**build·ing** ▶n. **1** permanent structure with roof and walls. **2** process or business of constructing such structures.

**build·up** ▶n. **1** favorable advance publicity. **2** gradual approach to a climax.

**built** /bilt/ ▶adj. (of a person) having a specified physical size or build.

**bulb** /bəlb/ ▶n. **1** underground fleshy-leaved storage organ of some plants (e.g., lily or onion) sending roots downward and leaves upward. **2** LIGHTBULB. **3** any object or part shaped like a bulb. **—bul·bous** adj.

**bulge** /bəlj/ ▶n. **1** irregular swelling; lump. **2** inf. temporary increase in quantity or number.
▶v. **1** swell. **2** be full or replete.
**—bulg·y** adj.

**bu·lim·i·a** /boō'lēmēə/ ▶n. Med. **1** insatiable overeating as a medical condition. **2** (also **bu·lim·ia ner·vo·sa**) emotional disorder in which bouts of overeating are followed by self-induced vomiting, etc.
**—bu·lim·ic** adj. & n.

**bulk** /bəlk/ ▶n. **1 a** magnitude (esp. large). **b** large mass. **c** large quantity. **2** large shape, body, or person. **3** [treated as pl.] the

greater part or number.
**4** roughage.

▶*v.* **1** seem in respect to size or importance; loom. **2** make (a book, etc.) seem thicker: *bulked it with irrelevant stories.*

□ **in bulk** in large quantities.

**bulk·head** ▶*n.* **1** upright partition separating compartments in a ship, aircraft, etc. **2** embankment, esp. along a waterfront.

**bulk·y** /ˈbəlkē/ ▶*adj.* (**-i·er**, **-i·est**) awkwardly large; unwieldy. —**bulk·i·ly** *adv.* —**bulk·i·ness** *n.*

**bull** /bo͝ol/ ▶*n.* **1 a** uncastrated male bovine animal. **b** male of the whale, elephant, etc. **2** person who buys shares of stock hoping to sell them at a higher price. **3** a papal edict.
▶*adj.* like that of a bull.
▶*v.* push or drive violently. —**bull·ish** *adj.*

□ **bull pen** (also **bull·pen**) **1** *Baseball* **a** area where relief pitchers warm up. **b** relief pitchers on a team. **2** large temporary holding cell for prisoners. □ **bull's-eye** center of a target; direct hit.

**bull·dog** ▶*n.* **1 a** dog of a sturdy powerful breed with a large head and smooth hair. **b** this

breed. **2** tenacious and courageous person.

**bull·doz·er** /ˈbo͝olˌdōzər/ ▶*n.* powerful tractor with a broad curved vertical blade at the front for clearing ground.

**bul·let** /ˈbo͝olit/ ▶*n.* small missile fired from a rifle, revolver, etc.

**bul·le·tin** /ˈbo͝olitn/ ▶*n.* **1** short official statement of news. **2** regular periodical issued by an organization.

□ **bulletin board 1** board for posting notices, information, etc. **2** *Computing* public computer file serving the function of a bulletin board.

**bull·fight** ▶*n.* sport of baiting and (usu.) killing bulls. —**bull·fight·er** *n.*

**bull·frog** ▶*n.* large frog native to eastern N. America, with a deep croak.

**bull·head·ed** ▶*adj.* obstinate; impetuous; blundering. —**bull·head·ed·ly** *adv.* —**bull·head·ed·ness** *n.*

**bul·lion** /ˈbo͝olyən/ ▶*n.* gold or silver in bulk before coining, or valued by weight.

**bull mar·ket** ▶*n.* market in which share prices are rising, encouraging buying.

**bul·lock** /ˈbo͝olək/ ▸n. castrated bull; steer.

**bul·ly** /ˈbo͝olē/ ▸n. (pl. **-lies**) person intimidating others. ▸v. (**-lied**) **1** persecute. **2** pressure (a person) to do something: *bullied him into agreeing.*

**bul·ly·rag** /ˈbo͝olēˌrag/ ▸v. (**-ragged, -rag·ging**) treat (someone) in a scolding or intimidating way.

**bul·rush** /ˈbo͝olˌrəSH/ ▸n. **1** rushlike water plant. **2** (in biblical use) papyrus.

**bul·wark** /ˈbo͝olˌwərk/ ▸n. **1** defensive wall, esp. of earth; a rampart. **2** person, principle, etc., that acts as a defense. **3** (usu. **bulwarks**) ship's side above deck. ▸v. serve as a bulwark to; protect.

**bum** /bəm/ *inf.* ▸n. habitual loafer or tramp; lazy dissolute person. ▸v. (**bummed, bum·ming**) **1** loaf or wander around. **2** cadge: *may I bum a cigarette?* ▸adj. **1** of poor quality. **2** false; fabricated. **3** not entirely functional: *bum ankle.*

**bum·ble** /ˈbəmbəl/ ▸v. move or act in an awkward manner. —**bum·bler** n.

**bum·ble·bee** ▸n. any large loud humming bee.

**bump** /bəmp/ ▸n. **1** dull-sounding blow or collision. **2** swelling or dent so caused. **3** uneven patch on a road, etc. ▸v. **1** knock or collide with. **2** hurt or damage by striking. **3** (**bump along**) move with much jolting. ▸adv. with a bump. —**bump·y** adj.

**bump·er** ▸n. **1** horizontal bar across the front or back of a vehicle, at the end of a track, etc., to reduce damage in a collision. **2** unusually large or fine: *a bumper crop.*

**bump·kin** /ˈbəmpkin/ ▸n. rustic or socially inept person.

**bun** /bən/ ▸n. **1** small bread, roll, or cake. **2** hair worn in the shape of a bun.

**bunch** /bənCH/ ▸n. **1** things growing or fastened together: *bunch of grapes.* **2** collection. **3** *inf.* group of people. ▸v. form or be formed into a group or crowd. —**bunch·y** adj.

**bun·co** /ˈbəNGkō/ (also **bun·ko**) ▸n. (pl. **-cos**) swindle or confidence trick. ▸v. (**-coes, -coed**) swindle or cheat.

**bun·dle** /ˈbəndl/ ▸n. **1** things tied or fastened together. **2** set

of nerve fibers, etc. **3** *inf.* large amount of money.
▶*v.* **1** tie or make into a bundle. **2** move or push quickly or confusedly: *he was bundled into a van.*

**bun·ga·low** /ˈbəNGgəˌlō/ ▶*n.* one-storied house.

**bun·gle** /ˈbəNGgəl/ ▶*v.* mismanage or fail at (a task).
▶*n.* mistake or failure.
—**bun·gler** *n.*

**bun·ion** /ˈbənyən/ ▶*n.* swelling on the foot, esp. at the base of the big toe.

**bunk** /bəNGk/ ▶*n.* **1** shelflike bed against a wall, e.g., in a ship. **2** *inf.* nonsense.
◻ **bunk bed** each of two or more beds one above the other, forming a unit.

**bunk·er** ▶*n.* **1** large container or compartment for storing fuel. **2** reinforced underground shelter. **3** sand-filled hollow as an obstacle in a golf course.

**bun·kum** /ˈbəNGkəm/ ▶*n.* nonsense; humbug.

**bun·ny** /ˈbənē/ ▶*n.* (*pl.* **-nies**) child's word for a rabbit.

**bunt** /bənt/ ▶*v.* **1** push with the head or horns; butt. **2** *Baseball* tap or push (a ball) with the bat without swinging.
▶*n.* act of bunting.

**bun·ting** /ˈbəntiNG/ ▶*n.* **1** any of numerous seed-eating birds related to the finches and sparrows. **2** flags and other decorations. **3** loosely woven fabric.

**buoy** /ˈbo͞oē/ ▶*n.* **1** anchored float as a navigation mark, etc. **2** life buoy.
▶*v.* **1** (**buoy up**) **a** keep afloat. **b** uplift; encourage. **2** mark with a buoy.

**buoy·ant** /ˈboiənt/ ▶*adj.* **1 a** able or apt to keep afloat. **b** (of a liquid or gas) able to keep something afloat. **2** lighthearted; resilient.
—**buoy·an·cy** *n*  —**buoy·ant·ly** *adv.*

**bur** /bər/ ▶*n.* var. of BURR.

**bur.** ▶*abbr.* bureau.

**bur·den** /ˈbərdn/ ▶*n.* **1** load, esp. a heavy one. **2** oppressive duty, expense, emotion, etc. **3** ship's carrying capacity; tonnage.
▶*v.* load with a burden; oppress.
—**bur·den·some** *adj.*
—**bur·den·some·ness** *n.*

**bur·dock** /ˈbərdäk/ ▶*n.* plant with prickly flowers and leaves.

**bu·reau** /ˈbyoŏrō/ ▶*n.* (*pl.* **-reaus** or **-reaux**) **1** chest of drawers. **2 a** office or department for specific business. **b** government department.

**bu·reau·cra·cy** /byoŏ'räkrəsē/ ▶*n.* (*pl.* **-cies**) **1 a** government by central administration. **b** nation so governed. **2** officials of such a government, esp. regarded as oppressive and inflexible. **3** conduct typical of these. —**bu·reau·crat** *n.* —**bu·reau·crat·ic** *adj.* —**bu·reau·crat·i·cal·ly** *adv.*

**bur·geon** /'bərjən/ ▶*v.* grow or increase rapidly; flourish.

**burg·er** /'bərgər/ ▶*n.* hamburger.

**burgh** /bərg; 'bərə/ ▶*n.* or *Scottish* borough or chartered town.

**bur·glar** /'bərglər/ ▶*n.* person who commits burglary.

**bur·gla·ry** ▶*n.* (*pl.* **-ries**) entry into a building illegally with intent to commit a felony.

**bur·gun·dy** /'bərgəndē/ (also **Burgundy**) ▶*n.* (*pl.* **-dies**) **1 a** wine of Burgundy in E. France. **b** similar wine from another place. **2** dark red color of burgundy wine.

**bur·i·al** /'berēəl/ ▶*n.* burying of a dead body.

**bu·rin** /'byoŏrin/ ▶*n.* steel tool used for engraving in copper or wood.

**bur·lesque** /bər'lesk/ ▶*n.*

**1 a** comic imitation; parody. **b** performance or work of this kind. **2** variety show, often including striptease. ▶*adj.* of or in the nature of burlesque. ▶*v.* (**-lesqued, -lesqu·ing**) parody.

**bur·ly** /'bərlē/ ▶*adj.* (**-li·er, -li·est**) of stout sturdy build; big and strong. —**bur·li·ness** *n.*

**burn** /bərn/ ▶*v.* (*past* and *past part.* **burned** or **burnt**) **1** be or cause to be consumed or destroyed by fire. **2** blaze or glow with fire. **3** be or cause to be injured or damaged by fire, heat, or radiation. **4** use or be used as fuel. **5** char in cooking. **6** produce (a hole, a mark, etc.) by fire or heat. **7** make, be, or feel hot, esp. painfully. **8** make or be passionate; feel or cause to feel great emotion. ▶*n.* mark or injury caused by burning. □ **burn down** destroy or be destroyed by fire. □ **burn out 1** be reduced to nothing by burning. **2** suffer exhaustion. □ **burn up 1** get rid of by fire. **2** *inf.* be or make furious.

**burn·er** ▶*n.* part of a gas stove, lamp, etc., that emits and shapes the flame.

□ **on the back** (or **front**) **burner**
*inf.* having low (or high) priority.

**bur·nish** /ˈbərniSH/ ▶*v.* polish by
rubbing.

**burn·out** ▶*n.* **1** physical or
emotional exhaustion.
**2** extinguishing of a rocket
motor when fuel is exhausted.

**burp** /bərp/ *inf.* ▶*v.* **1** belch.
**2** make (a baby) belch.
▶*n.* belch.

**burr** /bər/ ▶*n.* **1** whirring sound.
**2** rough sounding of the letter *r*.
**3** rough edge on cut metal or
paper. **4** surgeon's or dentist's
small drill. **5 a** prickly clinging
seedcase or flowerhead. **b** any
plant producing these.
▶*v.* make a whirring sound.

**bur·ri·to** ▶*n.* (pl. **-tos**) tortilla
rolled around a usu. meat or
bean filling.

**bur·ro** /ˈbərō/ ▶*n.* (pl. **-ros**) small
donkey.

**bur·row** /ˈbərō/ ▶*n.* hole or
tunnel dug by a small animal as
a dwelling.
▶*v.* **1** make a burrow. **2** make (a
hole, etc.) by digging. **3** (**burrow
into**) investigate; search.
—**bur·row·er** *n.*

**bur·sa** /ˈbərsə/ ▶*n.* (pl. **bursae** or
**bursas**) *Anat.* fluid-filled sac or
cavity that eases friction.

**bur·sar** /ˈbərsər/ ▶*n.* treasurer,
esp. of a college.

**bur·sa·ry** /ˈbərsərē/ ▶*n.* (pl. **-ries**)
treasury of an institution, esp. a
religious one.

**bur·si·tis** /bərˈsītis/ ▶*n.*
inflammation of a bursa.

**burst** /bərst/ ▶*v.* (*past* and *past
part.* **burst**) **1** (cause to) break
suddenly apart from within.
**2** open or be opened forcibly.
**3** make one's way suddenly,
dramatically, or by force. **4** fill
or be full to overflowing.
**5** appear or come suddenly: *burst
into flame.* **6** suddenly begin to
utter: *burst into tears* or *laughter*
or *song*. **7** feel a very strong
emotion or impulse: *burst with
excitement*.
▶*n.* **1** act of bursting; split.
**2** sudden issuing forth.
**3** sudden outbreak. **4** sudden
effort; spurt. **5** explosion.

**bur·y** /ˈberē/ ▶*v.* (**-ied**) **1** place (a
dead body) in the earth, a tomb,
or the sea. **2** put under ground.
**3** cover up; submerge. **4** involve
deeply: *he buried himself in work.*

**bus** /bəs/ ▶*n.* (pl. **bus·es** or
**bus·ses**) **1** large passenger
vehicle, usu. on a fixed route.
**2** *Computing* defined set of
conductors carrying data and

control signals within a computer.

▶ *v.* (**bused, bus·ing; bussed, bus·sing**) go or transport by bus.

**bus.** ▶ *abbr.* business.

**bus·boy** ▶ *n.* assistant to a restaurant waiter who fills water glasses, removes dirty dishes, etc.

**bush** /bŏŏsн/ ▶ *n.* **1** shrub or clump of shrubs. **2** thing resembling this, esp. a clump of hair or fur. —**bush·i·ly** *adv.* —**bush·i·ness** *n.* —**bush·y** *adj.*

**bushed** ▶ *adj. inf.* tired out.

**bush·el** /'bŏŏsнəl/ ▶ *n.* measure of capacity equivalent to 64 pints.

**bu·shi·do** /'bŏŏsнēdō/ ▶ *n.* code of honor and morals developed by the Japanese samurai.

**busi·ness** /'biznis/ ▶ *n.* **1** one's regular occupation, profession, or trade. **2** one's own concern. **3 a** task or duty. **b** reason for coming. **4** commercial firm. □ **the business end** *inf.* functional part of a tool or device. □ **has no business to** has no right to. □ **in business 1** trading or dealing. **2** able to begin operations. □ **in the business of 1** engaged in. **2** intending to: *we are not in the business of*

*surrendering.* □ **mind one's own business** not meddle.

**busi·ness·like** ▶ *adj.* efficient; systematic; practical.

**bus·kin** /'bəskin/ ▶ *n.* calf-high or knee-high boot of cloth or leather.

**bust** ▶ *n.* **1** human chest, esp. that of a woman; bosom. **2** sculpture of a person's head, shoulders, and chest.

▶ *v.* (*past* and *past part.* **bust·ed** or **bust**) burst; break.

▶ *n.* **1** sudden failure. **2 a** police raid. **b** arrest.

▶ *adj.* (also **bust·ed**) **1** broken; burst. **2** bankrupt. **3** arrested.

**bus·tle** /'bəsəl/ ▶ *v.* **1 a** work, etc., showily and energetically. **b** hasten. **2** [as *adj.* **bustling**] be full of activity.

▶ *n.* excited activity; fuss. —**bus·tler** *n.*

**bus·y** /'bizē/ ▶ *adj.* (**-i·er, -i·est**) **1** occupied or engaged. **2** full of activity; fussy. **3** (of a telephone line) in use.

▶ *v.* (**-ied**) keep busy; occupy. —**bus·i·ly** *adv.* —**bus·y·ness** *n.*

□ **busy signal** intermittent buzzing sound indicating that a telephone line is in use.

**bus·y·bod·y** ▸n. (pl. -ies)
**1** meddlesome person.
**2** mischief maker.

**but** /bət/ ▸conj. **1 a** nevertheless; however. **b** on the other hand; on the contrary. **2** except; other than; otherwise than: *what could we do but run?* **3** without the result that: *it never rains but it pours.*
▸prep. except; apart from; other than: *everyone went but me.*
▸adv. **1** only; no more than; only just: *we can but try | did it but once.* **2** introducing emphatic repetition; definitely: *wanted to see nobody, but nobody.*
▸rel.pron. who not; that not: *there is not a man but feels pity.*
▸n. objection: *ifs and buts.*
☐ **but for** without the help or hindrance, etc., of: *but for you I'd be rich by now.*

**bu·tane** /ˈbyo͞oˌtān/ ▸n. Chem. gaseous hydrocarbon used as fuel.

**butch** /bo͞oCH/ inf. ▸adj. masculine; tough-looking.
▸n. mannish woman.

**butch·er** ▸n. **1 a** person who deals in meat. **b** person who slaughters animals for food. **2** person who kills indiscriminately or brutally.
▸v. **1** slaughter or cut up (an animal) for food. **2** kill (people) wantonly or cruelly. **3** ruin through incompetence.

**but·ler** /ˈbətlər/ ▸n. principal manservant of a household.

**butt** /bət/ ▸v. **1** push with the head or horns. **2** meet end to end with; abut.
▸n. **1** a push with the head. **2** joining of two edges. **3** person or thing at which ridicule, criticism, etc., is directed. **4** (also **butt end**) thicker end, esp. of a tool or a weapon. **5** stub of a cigar or a cigarette. **6** inf. buttocks.
☐ **butt in** interrupt; meddle.

**but·ter** /ˈbətər/ ▸n. solidified churned cream used as a spread and in cooking.
☐ **butter up** inf. flatter excessively.

**but·ter·cup** ▸n. plant with bright yellow, cup-shaped flowers.

**but·ter·fin·gers** ▸n. inf. clumsy person.

**but·ter·fly** ▸n. (pl. -flies)
**1** insect with four usu. brightly colored wings erect when at rest. **2** (**butterflies**) nervous sensation felt in the stomach.
☐ **butterfly stroke** stroke in

swimming, with both arms raised out of the water and lifted forward together.

**but·ter·milk** ▸*n.* slightly acid liquid left after churning butter.

**but·ter·scotch** ▸*n.* **1** brittle candy made from butter, brown sugar, etc. **2** this flavor in desserts, etc.

**but·tock** /ˈbətək/ ▸*n.* **1** either of two fleshy protuberances on the lower rear part of the human trunk. **2** the corresponding part of an animal.

**but·ton** /ˈbətn/ ▸*n.* **1** small disk or knob sewn to a garment as a fastener or as an ornament. **2** knob on electronic equipment that is pressed to operate it.
▸*v.* fasten with buttons.

**but·ton·hole** ▸*n.* **1** slit in a garment for a button. **2** flower worn in a lapel buttonhole.
▸*v. inf.* accost and detain (a reluctant listener).

**but·tress** /ˈbətris/ ▸*n.* **1** projecting support of stone or brick, etc., built against a wall. **2** source of help or encouragement.
▸*v.* **1** support with a buttress. **2** support by argument, etc.

**bu·xom** /ˈbəksəm/ ▸*adj.* (esp. of a woman) plump and healthy-looking; large bosomed.

**buy** /bī/ ▸*v.* (*past* and *past part.* **bought**) **1 a** obtain in exchange for money. **b** serve to obtain: *money can't buy happiness.* **2** bribe. **3** get by sacrifice, great effort, etc. **4** *inf.* accept; believe in; approve of. **5** purchase goods for a store, etc.: *she buys for Bloomingdale's.*
▸*n. inf.* purchase. —**buy·er** *n.*
□ **buy off** get rid of by payment.
□ **buy out** pay (a person) to give up an ownership, interest, etc.
□ **buy up** buy as much as possible of.

**buy·out** ▸*n.* purchase of a controlling share in a company, etc.

**buzz** /bəz/ ▸*n.* **1** hum of a bee, etc. **2** sound of a buzzer. **3 a** murmur, as of conversation. **b** stir; hurried activity. **c** *inf.* rumor. **4** *inf.* telephone call. **5** *inf.* thrill; euphoric sensation.
▸*v.* **1** make a humming sound. **2** signal or signal to with a buzzer. **3 a** (**buzz about**) move busily. **b** (of a place) have an air of excitement or purposeful activity. **4** *Aeron.* fly fast and

very close to (another aircraft, the ground, etc.).
▢ **buzz off** *inf.* go or hurry away.
▢ **buzz saw** circular saw.

**buz·zard** /ˈbəzərd/ ▶*n.* turkey vulture.

**buzz·er** ▶*n.* electrical device that makes a buzzing noise.

**buzz·word** ▶*n. inf.* **1** fashionable technical or computer jargon. **2** catchword; slogan.

**by** /bī/ ▶*prep.* **1** near; beside. **2** through the agency or means of. **3** not later than. **4 a** past; beyond. **b** passing through; via. **5** in the circumstances of: *by day.* **6** to the extent of. **7** according to. **8** with the succession of. **9** concerning; in respect of. **10** placed between specified lengths in two directions: *three feet by two.* **11** inclining to: *north by northwest.*
▶*adv.* **1** near. **2** aside; in reserve: *put $5 by.* **3** past: *marched by.*
▶*interj.* BYE.
▢ **by and by** before long; eventually. ▢ **by and large** on the whole. ▢ **by the by** (or **bye**) incidentally.

**by-** (also **bye-**) ▶*prefix* subordinate; incidental: *byroad.*

**bye** ▶*interj. inf.* GOOD-BYE.

**by·gone** ▶*adj.* past; antiquated.

▶*pl. n.* (**bygones**) past offenses: *let bygones be bygones.*

**by·law** (also **bye·law**) ▶*n.* regulation made by a society or corporation.

**by·line** ▶*n.* line in a newspaper, etc., naming the writer of an article.

**by·pass** ▶*n.* **1** road passing around a town or its center. **2** secondary channel or pipe, etc., used in emergencies. **3** alternative passage for the circulation of blood to the heart.
▶*v.* avoid; go around.

**by-prod·uct** ▶*n.* **1** incidental product of the manufacture of something else. **2** secondary result.

**by·road** ▶*n.* minor road.

**by·stand·er** ▶*n.* person who stands by but does not take part; mere spectator.

**byte** /bīt/ ▶*n. Computing* group of eight binary digits, often used to represent one character.

**by·way** ▶*n.* small seldom-traveled road.

**by·word** ▶*n.* **1** person or thing as a notable example: *a byword for luxury.* **2** familiar saying; proverb.

**Byz·an·tine** /ˈbizənˌtēn/ ▸*adj.*
**1** of Byzantium or the E. Roman Empire. **2** (of a political situation, etc.): **a** extremely complicated. **b** inflexible. **c** underhand. **3** *Archit. & Painting* of Byzantium's highly decorated style.
▸*n.* citizen of Byzantium or the E. Roman Empire. —**By·zan·tin·ism** *n.* —**Byz·an·tin·ist** *n.*

# Cc

**C**[1] /sē/ (also **c**) ▸*n.* (*pl.* **Cs** or **C's**; **c's**) **1** third letter of the alphabet. **2** *Mus.* first note of the diatonic scale of C major. **3** third hypothetical person or example. **4** third highest class or category. **5** (as a Roman numeral) 100. **6** (also ©) copyright.

**C**[2] ▸*symb. Chem.* carbon.

**C**[3] (also **C.**) ▸*abbr.* Celsius; centigrade.

**c.** ▸*abbr.* **1** century; centuries. **2** chapter. **3** cent(s). **4** cubic. **5** circa; about.

**CA** ▸*abbr.* California (in official postal use).

**Ca** ▸*symb. Chem.* calcium.

**cab** /kab/ ▸*n.* **1** taxi. **2** driver's compartment in a truck, train, crane, etc.

**ca·bal** /kə'bäl/ ▸*n.* secret intrigue.

**cab·a·ret** /ˌkabə'rā/ ▸*n.* **1** entertainment in a nightclub or restaurant. **2** such a nightclub, etc.

**cab·bage** /'kabij/ ▸*n.* vegetable with thick green or purple leaves forming a round heart or head.

**ca·bil·do** /kə'bildō/ ▸*n.* (*pl.* **-dos**) (in Spain and Spanish-speaking countries) a town council or local government council.

**cab·in** /'kabin/ ▸*n.* **1** small shelter or house, esp. of wood. **2** room or compartment in an aircraft or ship.
□ **cabin fever** state of restlessness and irritability from having been confined for an extended period.

**cab·i·net** /'kabənit/ ▸*n.* **1** cupboard or case for storing or displaying articles. **2** (**Cabinet**) committee of senior government advisers.

**ca·ble** /'kābəl/ ▸*n.* **1** thick rope of wire or hemp. **2** encased group of insulated wires for transmitting electricity or electrical signals. **3** cablegram.
□ **cable-ready** (of a TV, VCR, etc.) designed for direct connection to a coaxial cable TV system.
□ **cable television** broadcasting system with signals transmitted by cable to subscribers' sets.

**ca·ble·gram** /ˈkābəlˌgram/ ▸n. telegraph message sent by undersea cable, etc.

**ca·boose** /kəˈboos/ ▸n. crew car at the rear of a freight train.

**ca·ca·o** /kəˈkāō/ ▸n. (pl. **-os**) seed pod from which cocoa and chocolate are made.

**cache** /kasH/ ▸n. **1** collection of items of the same type stored in a hidden place: *cache of gold coins.* **2** hidden storage place. **3** *Computing* (also **cache memory**) auxiliary memory from which high-speed retrieval is possible. ▸v. put in a cache.

**ca·chet** /kaˈsHā/ ▸n. **1** distinguishing mark or seal. **2** prestige.

**cach·in·nate** /ˈkakəˌnāt/ ▸v. laugh loudly.

**ca·cique** /kəˈsēk/ ▸n. **1** (in Latin America or the Spanish-speaking Caribbean) a native chief. **2** (in Spain or Latin America) a local political boss.

**cack·le** /ˈkakəl/ ▸n. **1** clucking sound as of a hen or a goose. **2** loud, silly laugh. **3** noisy, inconsequential talk. ▸v. **1** emit or utter with a cackle. **2** talk noisily and inconsequentially.

**ca·cog·ra·phy** /kəˈkägrəfē/ ▸n. bad handwriting or spelling.

**ca·col·o·gy** /kəˈkäləjē/ ▸n. bad choice of words or poor pronunciation.

**ca·coph·o·ny** /kəˈkäfənē/ ▸n. (pl. **-nies**) harsh discordant mixture of sound. **—ca·coph·o·nous** adj.

**cac·tus** /ˈkaktəs/ ▸n. (pl. **-ti** or **-tus·es**) succulent plant with a thick fleshy stem and usu. spines but no leaves.

**CAD** ▸abbr. computer-aided design.

**cad** /kad/ ▸n. man who behaves dishonorably toward women. **—cad·dish** adj.

**ca·dav·er** /kəˈdavər/ ▸n. corpse.

**cad·die** /ˈkadē/ (also **cad·dy**) ▸n. (pl. **-dies**) person who assists a golfer during a match, by carrying clubs, etc. ▸v. (**-died**, **-dy·ing**) act as caddie.

**ca·dence** /ˈkādns/ ▸n. **1** modulation or inflection of the voice: *famous for the measured cadences of his speeches.* **2** rhythm. **3** *Mus.* close of a musical phrase. **—ca·denced** adj.

**ca·det** /kəˈdet/ ▸n. young trainee, as in the armed services or police force.

**cadge** /kaj/ ▸v. get or seek by

begging: *he eats whenever he can cadge a meal.* —**cadg·er** *n.*

**cad·mi·um** /ˈkadmēəm/ ▸*n.* soft, bluish-white metallic element. (Symb.: **Cd**)
□ **cadmium yellow** intense yellow pigment.

**cad·re** /ˈkadrē/ ▸*n.* basic unit, esp. of servicemen.

**Cae·sar·e·an** /siˈze(ə)rēən/ (also **Cae·sar·i·an**) ▸*var.* of CESAREAN.

**cae·su·ra** /siˈzʜoŏrə; -ˈzoŏrə/ ▸*n.* **1** (in modern verse) a pause near the middle of a line. **2** any interruption or break.

**ca·fé** (also **ca·fe**) ▸*n.* **1** small coffeehouse; simple restaurant. **2** bar.
□ **café au lait 1** coffee with milk. **2** color of this. □ **café noir** black coffee.

**caf·e·te·ri·a** /ˌkafəˈti(ə)rēə/ ▸*n.* restaurant in a school or business in which customers select their food at a counter and pay before eating.

**caf·feine** /kaˈfēn/ ▸*n.* alkaloid drug with stimulant action found in tea leaves and coffee beans.

**caf·tan** (also **kaf·tan**) ▸*n.* **1** long tunic worn in the Near East. **2** long, loose dress or shirt.

**cage** /kāj/ ▸*n.* **1** structure of bars or wires, esp. for confining animals or birds. **2** any similar open framework, as in a freight elevator, etc.
▸*v.* place or keep in a cage.

**cag·ey** /ˈkājē/ (also **cag·y**) *inf.* ▸*adj.* (**-i·er**, **-i·est**) cautious and uncommunicative; wary. —**cag·i·ly** *adv.*

**cais·son** /ˈkāˌsän/ ▸*n.* **1** watertight chamber in which underwater construction work can be done. **2** wagon for carrying ammunition.

**cai·tiff** /ˈkātif/ ▸*n.* contemptible or cowardly person.

**ca·jole** /kəˈjōl/ ▸*v.* persuade by flattery, deceit, etc. —**ca·jole·ment** *n.* —**ca·jol·ery** *n.*

**cake** /kāk/ ▸*n.* **1** baked mixture of flour, butter, eggs, sugar, etc., often iced. **2** other food in a flat round shape. **3** flattish compact mass.
▸*v.* form into a compact mass.
□ **piece of cake** *inf.* something easily achieved.

**Cal** ▸*abbr.* large calorie(s).

**cal** ▸*abbr.* small calorie(s).

**cal·a·bash** /ˈkaləˌbasʜ/ ▸*n.* **a** gourd-bearing evergreen tree native to tropical America. **b** gourd from this tree.

**cal·a·boose** /ˈkaləˌbo͞os/ ▸*n.* prison.

**cal·a·mine** /ˈkaləˌmīn/ ▸*n.* pink powder consisting of zinc carbonate and ferric oxide, used in lotion or ointment.

**ca·lam·i·ty** /kəˈlamətē/ ▸*n.* (*pl.* **-ties**) disaster; great misfortune. —**ca·lam·i·tous** *adj.*

**cal·car·e·ous** /kalˈke(ə)rēəs/ ▸*adj.* containing calcium carbonate; chalky.

**cal·ci·fy** /ˈkalsəˌfī/ ▸*v.* (**-fied**) **1** harden or become hardened by deposition of calcium salts; petrify. **2** convert or be converted to calcium carbonate. —**cal·cif·ic** *adj.* —**cal·ci·fi·ca·tion** *n.*

**cal·ci·um** /ˈkalsēəm/ ▸*n.* soft, gray metallic element of the alkaline earth group occurring naturally in limestone, marble, chalk, etc. (Symb.: **Ca**)
□ **calcium carbonate** white, insoluble solid occurring naturally as chalk, limestone, and marble.

**cal·cu·late** /ˈkalkyəˌlāt/ ▸*v.* **1** determine mathematically. **2** determine by reasoning. **3** intend (an action) to have a certain effect: *his words were calculated to make her angry.*

—**cal·cu·la·ble** *adj.*
—**cal·cu·la·tion** *n.* —**cal·cu·la·tive** *adj.*

**cal·cu·lat·ing** ▸*adj.* shrewd; scheming.

**cal·cu·la·tor** ▸*n.* device (esp. a small electronic one) used for making mathematical calculations.

**cal·cu·lus** /ˈkalkyələs/ ▸*n.* (*pl.* **-li** or **-lus·es**) **1** *Math.* particular method of calculation or reasoning: *calculus of probabilities.* **2** *Med.* stone or concretion of minerals formed within the body.

**cal·de·ra** /kalˈderə/ ▸*n.* large volcanic crater, typically one formed by a major eruption leading to the collapse of the mouth of the volcano.

**cal·dron** /ˈkôldrən/ ▸var. of CAULDRON.

**cal·en·dar** /ˈkaləndər/ ▸*n.* **1** system by which the beginning, length, and subdivisions of the year are fixed. **2** chart or series of pages showing the days, weeks, and months of a particular year. **3** timetable of appointments, special events, etc.

**cal·ends** /ˈkaləndz; ˈkā-/ (also **kal·ends**) ▸*pl. n.* first day of the month in the ancient Roman calendar.

**calf** /kaf/ ▶*n.* (*pl.* **calves**) **1** young bovine animal. **2** young of other animals, e.g., elephant, deer, and whale. **3** fleshy hind part of the human leg below the knee.

**cal·i·ber** /ˈkaləbər/ ▶*n.* **1 a** internal diameter of a gun or tube. **b** diameter of a bullet or shell. **2** strength or quality of character; ability; importance.

**cal·i·brate** /ˈkaləˌbrāt/ ▶*v.* **1** mark (a gauge) with a scale of readings. **2** correlate the readings of (an instrument) with a standard. —**cal·i·bra·tion** *n.* —**cal·i·bra·tor** *n.*

**cal·i·co** /ˈkaliˌkō/ ▶*n.* (*pl.* **-coes** or **-cos**) printed cotton fabric. ▶*adj.* **1** made of calico. **2** multicolored; piebald: *calico cat.*

**cal·i·pers** /ˈkaləpərz/ ▶*pl. n.* compasses for measuring diameters or internal dimensions.

**ca·liph** /ˈkālif/ ▶*n.* chief Muslim civil and religious ruler. —**ca·liph·ate** *n.*

**cal·is·then·ics** /ˌkaləsˈtнeniks/ ▶*pl. n.* fitness exercises. —**cal·is·then·ic** *adj.*

**calk** ▶/kôk/ var. of CAULK.

**call** /kôl/ ▶*v.* **1 a** cry; shout; speak loudly. **b** (of a bird or animal) emit its characteristic note or cry. **2** communicate with by telephone or radio. **3** summon. **4** pay a brief visit: *called at the house.* **5** announce or order to take place: *called a meeting of the board.* **6** name; describe as. **7** order; demand: *called for silence.*

▶*n.* **1** shout or cry. **2 a** characteristic cry of a bird or animal. **b** imitation of this. **c** instrument for imitating it. **3** brief visit: *paid them a call.* **4** act of telephoning. **5** invitation; appeal. **6** duty, need, or occasion: *no call to be rude.* **7** signal on a bugle, etc.

□ **call off 1** cancel (an arrangement, etc.). **2** order (an attacker or pursuer) to desist. □ **call to order 1** request to be orderly. **2** declare (a meeting) open. □ **call up 1** reach by telephone. **2** imagine; recollect. **3** summon, esp. to military duty. □ **on call** (of a doctor, etc.) available if required.

**call girl** ▶*n.* female prostitute who accepts appointments by telephone.

**cal·lig·ra·phy** /kə'ligrəfē/ ▸ *n.* art of fine handwriting.
—**cal·lig·ra·pher** *n.*
—**cal·li·graph·ic** *adj.*

**call·ing** ▸ *n.* profession or occupation.

**call·ing card** ▸ *n.* **1** card with a person's name, etc., sent or left in lieu of a formal visit. **2** identifying mark, etc., left behind (by someone). **3** card used to pay for a telephone call.

**cal·li·pyg·i·an** /ˌkalə'pijēən/ (also **cal·li·pyg·e·an**) ▸ *adj.* having well-shaped buttocks.

**cal·los·i·ty** /kə'läsitē/ ▸ *n.* (*pl.* **-ties**) thickened and hardened part of the skin; a callus.

**cal·lous** /'kaləs/ ▸ *adj.* **1** unfeeling; insensitive. **2** (of skin) hardened. —**cal·lous·ly** *adv.* —**cal·lous·ness** *n.*

**cal·low** /'kalō/ ▸ *adj.* inexperienced; immature.

**cal·lus** /'kaləs/ ▸ *n.* hard thick area of skin or tissue.

**calm** /käm/ ▸ *adj.* **1** tranquil; quiet; windless. **2** settled; not agitated.
▸ *n.* **1** state of being calm; stillness; serenity. **2** period without wind or storm.

▸ *v.* make or become calm.
—**calm·ly** *adv.* —**calm·ness** *n.*

**ca·lo·ric** /kə'lôrik/ ▸ *adj.* of heat or calories.

**cal·o·rie** /'kalərē/ ▸ *n.* **1** unit of quantity of heat: **2** (also **small calorie**) amount needed to raise the temperature of 1 gram of water through 1°C. (Abbr.: **cal**) **3** (also **large calorie**) amount needed to raise the temperature of 1 kilogram of water through 1°C, often used to measure the energy value of foods. (Abbr.: **Cal**)

**cal·u·met** /'kalyə,met/ ▸ *n.* North American Indian peace pipe.

**ca·lum·ni·ate** /kə'ləmnē,āt/ ▸ *v.* slander. —**ca·lum·ni·a·tion** *n.* —**ca·lum·ni·a·tor** *n.*

**cal·um·ny** /'kaləmnē/ ▸ *n.* (*pl.* **-nies**) **1** making of false and defamatory statements in order to damage someone's reputation; slander. **2** false and slanderous statement.

**calve** /kav/ ▸ *v.* give birth to a calf.

**ca·lyp·so** /kə'lipsō/ ▸ *n.* (*pl.* **-sos**) W. Indian musical style with syncopated rhythm.

**ca·lyx** /'kāliks/ ▸ *n.* (*pl.* **-lyx·es** or **-ly·ces**) **1** *Bot.* sepals collectively, forming the protective layer of a flower in bud. **2** *Biol.* any cuplike cavity or structure.

**cam** /kam/ ▶*n.* projection on a rotating part in machinery, shaped to impart a particular motion.

**ca·ma·ra·de·rie** /ˌkäm(ə)ˈrädərē/ ▶*n.* mutual trust and sociability among friends.

**cam·ber** /ˈkambər/ ▶*n.* slightly convex or arched shape.

**cam·bric** /ˈkāmbrik/ ▶*n.* a fine white linen or cotton fabric.

**cam·cor·der** /ˈkamˌkôrdər/ ▶*n.* combined video camera and sound recorder.

**came** /kām/ ▶past of COME.

**cam·el** /ˈkaməl/ ▶*n.* large, long-necked desert mammal having slender legs and one hump (**A·ra·bi·an cam·el**) or two humps (**Bac·tri·an cam·el**).

**ca·mel·li·a** /kəˈmēlyə/ ▶*n.* evergreen shrub native to E. Asia, with shiny leaves and showy flowers.

**cam·e·o** /ˈkamēˌō/ ▶*n.* (*pl.* **-os**) **1** relief carving with a background of a different color. **2** small character part in a play or film played by a distinguished actor.

**cam·er·a** /ˈkam(ə)rə/ ▶*n.* device for recording visual images as photographs, movie film, etc.

**cam·i·sole** /ˈkaməˌsōl/ ▶*n.* an upper-body undergarment.

**cam·o·mile** /ˈkaməˌmēl/ ▶var. of CHAMOMILE.

**cam·ou·flage** /ˈkaməˌfläzн/ ▶*n.* **1** disguising of soldiers, vehicles, aircraft, etc., so that they blend with their surroundings. **2** such a disguise. **3** misleading or evasive precaution or expedient. ▶*v.* hide by camouflage.

**camp** /kamp/ ▶*n.* **1** place where troops are lodged or trained. **2** temporary accommodations, as huts or tents. **3** adherents of a particular party or doctrine regarded collectively. ▶*v.* set up or spend time in a camp. ▶*adj.* done in an exaggerated way for effect. —**camp·i·ness** *n.* —**camp·ing** *n.* —**camp·y** *adj.*

**cam·paign** /kamˈpān/ ▶*n.* **1** organized course of action to achieve a specific goal: *her campaign for president.* **2** series of military operations. ▶*v.* conduct or take part in a campaign. —**cam·paign·er** *n.*

**cam·pa·ni·le** /ˌkampəˈnēlē; -ˈnēl/ ▶*n.* Italian bell tower, esp. a freestanding one.

**camp·er** ▶*n.* **1** person who camps. **2** large motor vehicle with beds, etc.

**cam·pe·si·no** /ˌkampəˈsēnō; ˌkäm-/ ▶*n.* (*pl.* **-nos**) (in Spanish-speaking regions) a peasant farmer.

**cam·phor** /ˈkamfər/ ▶*n.* white, crystalline volatile substance with aromatic smell used to make celluloid and in medicine.

**cam·pus** /ˈkampəs/ ▶*n.* grounds of a university or other institution.

**cam·shaft** /ˈkamˌSHaft/ ▶*n.* shaft with one or more cams.

**can**¹ /kan/ ▶*aux. v.* (*past* **could**) **1 a** be able to; know how to: *I can run fast* | *can you speak German?* **b** be potentially capable of: *you can do it if you try.* **2** be permitted to: *can we go to the party?*

**can**² ▶*n.* **1** metal vessel for liquid. **2** metal container in which food or drink is sealed. **3** (**the can**) *inf.* **a** prison. **b** toilet. ▶*v.* (**canned, can·ning**) put or preserve in a can.

**ca·nal** /kəˈnal/ ▶*n.* **1** artificial waterway for inland navigation or irrigation. **2** tubular duct in a plant or animal: *ear canal.*

**ca·na·pé** /ˈkanəˌpā/ ▶*n.* small piece of bread or pastry with a savory food on top, often served as an hors d'oeuvre.

**ca·nard** /kəˈnär(d)/ ▶*n.* **1** unfounded rumor or story. **2** small winglike projection attached to an aircraft forward of the main wing to provide extra stability or control, sometimes replacing the tail.

**ca·nar·y** /kəˈne(ə)rē/ ▶*n.* (*pl.* **-ies**) songbird native to the Canary Islands, with mainly yellow plumage.

**can·cel** /ˈkansəl/ ▶*v.* (**-celed, -cel·ing; -celled, -cel·ling**) **1** withdraw, revoke, or discontinue (an arrangement). **2** obliterate; delete; invalidate. **3** neutralize; counterbalance. **4** *Math.* strike out (an equal factor) on each side of an equation, etc. **—can·cel·la·tion** *n.*

**can·cer** /ˈkansər/ ▶*n.* **1** malignant growth or tumor of body cells. **2** evil influence or corruption spreading uncontrollably. **— can·cer·ous** *adj.*

**can·de·la·brum** /ˌkandəˈläbrəm/ (also **can·de·la·bra**) ▶*n.* (*pl.* **-bra, -brums, -bras**) large branched candlestick or lamp holder.

**can·did** /ˈkandid/ ▶*adj.* **1** frank. **2** (of a photograph) taken informally. —**can·did·ly** *adv.* —**can·did·ness** *n.*

**can·di·date** /ˈkandiˌdāt/ ▶*n.* nominee, office seeker, or entrant. —**can·di·da·cy** *n.*

**can·dle** /ˈkandəl/ ▶*n.* cylinder or block of wax or tallow with a central wick, for giving light when burning.

**can·dle·stick** ▶*n.* holder for one or more candles.

**can·dor** /ˈkandər/ ▶*n.* candid behavior or action.

**can·dy** /ˈkandē/ ▶*n.* (*pl.* **-dies**) sweet confection, usu. containing sugar, chocolate, etc. ▶*v.* (**-died**) preserve by coating and impregnating with a sugar syrup: *candied fruit.* □ **candy stripe** pattern consisting of alternate stripes of white and a color (usu. pink).

**cane** /kān/ ▶*n.* **1** stem of giant reeds or grasses. **2** material of cane used for wickerwork, etc. **3** cane used as a walking stick or an instrument of punishment. ▶*v.* **1** beat with a cane. **2** weave cane into (a chair, etc.). —**can·ing** *n.*

**ca·nine** /ˈkāˌnīn/ ▶*adj.* of a dog or dogs. ▶*n.* **1** dog. **2** (also **canine tooth**) pointed tooth between incisors and premolars.

**can·is·ter** /ˈkanəstər/ ▶*n.* **1** rigid container for storage. **2** cylinder of shot, tear gas, etc.

**can·ker** /ˈkaNGkər/ ▶*n.* **1** destructive fungus disease of trees and plants. **2** *Zool.* ulcerous ear disease of animals, esp. cats and dogs. **3** corrupting influence. —**can·ker·ous** *adj.*

**can·na·bis** /ˈkanəbəs/ ▶*n.* **1** hemp plant. **2** parts of this used as an intoxicant or hallucinogen.

**canned** /kand/ ▶*adj.* **1** prerecorded. **2** supplied in a can.

**can·ner·y** /ˈkanərē/ ▶*n.* (*pl.* **-ies**) canning factory.

**can·ni·bal** /ˈkanəbəl/ ▶*n.* **1** person who eats human flesh. **2** animal that feeds on flesh of its own species. —**can·ni·bal·ism** *n.* —**can·ni·bal·is·tic** *adj.*

**can·ni·bal·ize** ▶*v.* use (a machine, etc.) as a source of spare parts for others.

**can·non** /ˈkanən/ ▶*n.* (*pl.* same) heavy gun installed on a carriage or mounting.

**can·non·ade** /ˌkanəˈnād/ ▶*n.* period of continuous heavy gunfire.

▶*v.* bombard with a cannonade.

**can·not** /ˈkanˌät/ ▶*v.* can not.

**can·ny** /ˈkanē/ ▶*adj.* (**-ni·er, -ni·est**) shrewd; worldly-wise. —**can·ni·ly** *adv.* —**can·ni·ness** *n.*

**ca·noe** /kəˈnoō/ ▶*n.* narrow boat with pointed ends usu. propelled by paddling.

▶*v.* (**-noed, -noe·ing**) travel in a canoe. —**ca·noe·ist** *n.*

**can·on** /ˈkanən/ ▶*n.* **1** general law, rule, principle, or criterion. **2** church decree or law. **3** member of the clergy who is on the staff of a cathedral, esp. a member of the cathedral chapter. **4** works of an author that are accepted as genuine. **5** body of esp. literary works considered to be of the highest quality and of enduring value. **6** *Mus.* piece with different parts taking up the same theme successively. □ **canon law** ecclesiastical law.

**can·on·ize** ▶*v.* declare officially to be or regard as a saint. —**can·on·i·za·tion** *n.*

**can·o·py** /ˈkanəpē/ ▶*n.* (*pl.* **-pies**) **1** covering hung or held up over a throne, bed, person, etc. **2** rooflike projection or shelter.

**cant** /kant/ ▶*n.* **1** insincere pious or moral talk. **2** language peculiar to a class, profession, sect, etc.; jargon.

**can't** /kant/ ▶*contr.* can not.

**can·ta·loupe** /ˈkantlˌōp/ ▶*n.* variety of melon with orange flesh.

**can·tan·ker·ous** /kanˈtaNGkərəs/ ▶*adj.* bad-tempered; quarrelsome. —**can·tan·ker·ous·ly** *adv.* —**can·tan·ker·ous·ness** *n.*

**can·ta·ta** /kənˈtätə/ ▶*n.* short composition with vocal solos and usu. chorus and orchestral accompaniment.

**can·teen** /kanˈtēn/ ▶*n.* **1** restaurant for employees in an office or factory, etc. **2** store selling provisions or liquor in a barracks or camp. **3** water flask.

**cant·er** /ˈkantər/ ▶*n.* gentle gallop.

▶*v.* (of a horse or its rider) go at a canter.

**can·ti·cle** /ˈkantikəl/ ▶*n.* song or chant with a biblical text.

**can·ti·le·ver** /ˈkantlˌēvər/ ▶ **1** long bracket or beam, etc., projecting from a wall to support a balcony, etc. **2** beam or girder fixed at only one end.

☐ **cantilever bridge** bridge made of cantilevers projecting from the piers and connected by girders.

**can·to** /ˈkanˌtō/ ▶*n.* (*pl.* **-tos**) division of a long poem.

**can·ton** /kanˈtän/ ▶*n.* **1** subdivision of a country. **2** state of the Swiss confederation.

**can·tor** /ˈkantər/ ▶*n.* person who sings liturgical prayers in a synagogue.

**can·vas** /ˈkanvəs/ ▶*n.* **1 a** strong coarse kind of cloth used for sails and tents, etc., and as a surface for oil painting. **b** piece of this. **2** painting on canvas, esp. in oils.

**can·vass** /ˈkanvəs/ ▶*v.* **1** solicit votes. **2** ascertain opinions of. ▶*n.* canvassing, esp. of electors: *house-to-house canvass.* —**can·vass·er** *n.*

**can·yon** /ˈkanyən/ ▶*n.* deep gorge, often with a stream or river.

**caou·tchouc** /ˈkouˌCHŏŏk; -ˌCHŏŏ(k)/ ▶*n.* unvulcanized natural rubber.

**cap** /kap/ ▶*n.* **1** covering for the head, often soft and with a visor.

**2** device to seal a bottle or protect the point of a pen, lens of a camera, etc. **3** artificial protective covering for a tooth. **4** upper limit on spending, etc. ▶*v.* (**capped, cap·ping**) **1 a** put a cap on. **b** cover the top or end of. **c** set a limit to: *rate-capping.* **2 a** lie on top of; form the cap of. **b** surpass; excel.

**cap.** ▶*abbr.* **1** capital. **2** capital letter. **3** chapter.

**ca·pa·ble** /ˈkāpəbəl/ ▶*adj.* **1** competent; able. **2 a** having the ability, fitness, etc., for. **b** susceptible or admitting of (explanation, improvement, etc.). —**ca·pa·bil·i·ty** *n.* —**ca·pa·bly** *adv.*

**ca·pa·cious** /kəˈpāSHəs/ ▶*adj.* roomy; able to hold much. —**ca·pa·cious·ness** *n.*

**ca·pac·i·tance** /kəˈpasitəns/ ▶*n.* **1** ability of a system to store an electric charge. **2** ratio of the change in an electric charge in a system to the corresponding change in its electric potential.

**ca·pac·i·tor** /kəˈpasitər/ ▶*n.* device used to store an electric charge.

**ca·pac·i·ty** /kəˈpasitē/ ▶*n.* (*pl.* **-ties**) **1** power of containing, receiving, experiencing, or producing: *capacity for heat, pain,* etc. **2** maximum amount that can be contained or produced, etc. **3** mental power. **4** position or function: *in a civil capacity.* **5** legal competence.

**ca·par·i·son** /kə'parəsən/ ▶*n.* ornamental covering spread over a horse's saddle or harness.

▶*v.* (**be caparisoned**) (of a horse) be decked out in rich decorative coverings.

**cape** /kāp/ ▶*n.* **1** sleeveless cloak. **2** headland or promontory.

**ca·per** /'kāpər/ ▶*v.* skip or dance about playfully.

▶*n.* **1** playful jump or leap. **2** silly escapade.

**ca·pers** ▶*pl. n.* buds of a bramblelike shrub that are pickled for use as flavoring.

**cap·il·lar·y** /'kapə,lerē/ ▶*n.* (*pl.* **-ies**) any of the very fine branching blood vessels between arteries and veins.

☐ **capillary action** rise or depression of a liquid in contact with a solid, owing to surface tension, etc.

**cap·i·tal** /'kapitl/ ▶*n.* **1** most important town or city of a country, state, or region. **2 a** money or other assets with which a company starts in business. **b** accumulated wealth. **3** capital letter. **4** head of a pillar or column.

▶*adj.* **1** principal; most important. **2** involving or punishable by death. **3** (of letters of the alphabet) large in size and of the form used to begin sentences and names, etc. —**cap·i·tal·ly** *adv.*

**cap·i·tal gain** ▶*n.* profit from the sale of investments or property.

**cap·i·tal·ism** ▶*n.* economic system in which the production and distribution of goods depend on invested private capital and profit making. —**cap·i·tal·ist** *n.*

**cap·i·tal·ize** ▶*v.* **1** convert into or provide with capital. **2 a** write (a letter of the alphabet) as a capital. **b** begin (a word) with a capital letter. **3** (**capitalize on**) use to one's advantage; profit from. —**cap·i·tal·i·za·tion** *n.*

**cap·i·tol** /'kapitl/ ▶*n.* **1** building housing a legislative assembly. **2** (**the Capitol**) seat of the U.S. Congress in Washington, DC.

**ca·pit·u·late** /kə'piCHə,lāt/ ▶*v.* surrender, esp. on stated conditions. —**ca·pit·u·la·to·ry** *adj.*

**ca·pon** /'kā,pän/ ▶*n.* domestic cock castrated and fattened for eating.

**cap·puc·ci·no** /,käpə'CHēnō/ ▶*n.* (*pl.* **-nos**) espresso coffee with milk made frothy with pressurized steam.

**ca·price** /kə'prēs/ ▶*n.* **1** unaccountable or whimsical change of mind or conduct. **2** work of lively fancy in painting, drawing, or music.

**ca·pri·cious** /kə'prishəs/ ▶*adj.* subject to whim; unpredictable.

**cap·size** /'kap,sīz/ ▶*v.* (of a boat) overturn.

**cap·stan** /'kapstən/ ▶*n.* revolving cylinder with a vertical axis, for winding cable, tape, etc.

**cap·sule** /'kapsəl/ ▶*n.* **1** small gelatinous case enclosing a dose of medicine and swallowed with it. **2** detachable compartment of a spacecraft or nose cone of a rocket. **3** enclosing membrane in the body. **4** dry fruit that releases its seeds when ripe. **5** concise; highly condensed: *a capsule history.* —**cap·su·lar** *adj.* —**cap·su·late** *adj.*

**Capt.** ▶*abbr.* Captain.

**cap·tain** /'kaptən/ ▶*n.* **1** chief, leader, or commander. **2 a** army or air force officer next above lieutenant. **b** navy officer in command of a warship; one ranking below commodore or rear admiral and above commander. ▶*v.* be captain of; lead. —**cap·tain·cy** *n.*

**cap·tion** /'kapshən/ ▶*n.* **1** title or brief explanation appended to an illustration, cartoon, etc. **2** heading of a chapter or article, etc. ▶*v.* provide with a caption.

**cap·tious** /'kapshəs/ ▶*adj.* given to finding fault or raising petty objections. —**cap·tious·ly** *adv.* —**cap·tious·ness** *n.*

**cap·ti·vate** /'kaptə,vāt/ ▶*v.* charm; fascinate. —**cap·ti·vat·ing** *adj.* —**cap·ti·vat·ing·ly** *adv.*

**cap·tive** /'kaptiv/ ▶*n.* person or animal that has been taken prisoner or confined. ▶*adj.* **1** taken prisoner. **2** kept in confinement or under restraint. —**cap·tiv·i·ty** *n.*

**cap·ture** /'kapcHər/ ▶*v.* **1** take prisoner; seize. **2** portray in permanent form. **3** cause (data) to be stored in a computer. ▶*n.* act of capturing.

**car** /kär/ ▶*n.* **1** automobile. **2** vehicle that runs on rails, esp.

a railroad car or a streetcar. **3** passenger compartment of an elevator, cable railway, balloon, etc. —**car·ful** *n.*

**ca·rafe** /kəˈraf/ ▶*n.* glass container for water or wine.

**car·a·mel** /ˈkarəməl/ ▶*n.* **1** sugar or syrup heated until it turns brown, then used as a flavoring or coloring. **2** kind of soft toffee made with sugar, butter, etc., melted and further heated. —**car·a·mel·ize** *v.*

**car·at** /ˈkarət/ ▶*n.* unit of weight for precious stones, now equivalent to 200 milligrams.

**car·a·van** /ˈkarəˌvan/ ▶*n.* company of merchants or pilgrims, etc., traveling together, esp. across a desert.

**car·a·van·sa·ry** /ˌkarəˈvansərē/ ▶*n.* (*pl.* **-sa·ries** or **-se·rais** /-sə-ˌrīz/) **1** inn with a central courtyard for travelers in the desert regions of Asia or North Africa. **2** group of people traveling together; a caravan.

**car·a·vel** /ˈkarəˌvel; -vəl/ (also **car·vel** /ˈkärvəl/) ▶*n.* small, fast Spanish or Portuguese ship of the 15th–17th centuries.

**car·a·way** /ˈkarəˌwā/ ▶*n.* umbelliferous plant, bearing clusters of tiny white flowers.

□ **caraway seed** its fruit used as flavoring and as a source of oil.

**car·bide** /ˈkärˌbīd/ ▶*n.* binary compound of carbon.

**car·bine** /ˈkärˌbīn/ ▶*n.* lightweight firearm, usu. a rifle, orig. for cavalry use.

**car·bo·hy·drate** /ˌkärbəˈhīˌdrāt/ ▶*n.* energy-producing organic compound containing carbon, hydrogen, and oxygen, e.g., starch, glucose, and other sugars.

**car·bon** /ˈkärbən/ ▶*n.* nonmetallic element occurring naturally as diamond, graphite, and charcoal, and in all organic compounds. (Symb.: **C**)

**car·bon·ate** *Chem.* ▶*n.* /ˈkärbənit/ salt of a carbon-containing acid.

▶*v.* /ˈkärbəˌnāt/ **1** dissolve carbon dioxide in; aerate. **2** convert into a carbonate. —**car·bon·a·tion** *n.*

**car·bon cop·y** ▶*n.* **1** copy made with carbon paper. **2** person or thing identical or similar to another: *is a carbon copy of his father.*

**car·bon di·ox·ide** /dīˈoksīd/ ▶*n.* colorless, odorless gas produced by respiration and by burning carbon and organic compounds.

**car·bon mon·ox·ide** /məˈnoksīd/ ▶*n.* colorless, odorless toxic flammable gas formed by incomplete combustion of carbon.

**car·bon pa·per** ▶*n.* paper coated with pigment for making a copy.

**car·bun·cle** /ˈkärˌbəNGkəl/ ▶*n.* **1** severe abscess in the skin. **2** bright red gem. —**car·bun·cu·lar** *adj.*

**car·bu·ret·or** /ˈkärb(y)əˌrātər/ (also **car·bu·rat·or**) ▶*n.* apparatus for mixing fuel and air in an internal combustion engine to make an explosive mixture.

**car·cass** /ˈkärkəs/ ▶*n.* **1** dead body of an animal. **2** framework of a building, ship, etc.

**car·cin·o·gen** /kärˈsinəjən/ ▶*n.* any substance that produces cancer. —**car·ci·no·gen·ic** *adj.*

**car·ci·no·ma** /ˌkärsəˈnōmə/ ▶*n.* (*pl.* **-mas** or **-ma·ta**) cancerous tumor. —**car·ci·no·ma·tous** *adj.*

**card** /kärd/ ▶*n.* **1** thick, stiff paper or thin pasteboard. **2** rectangular piece of paper or plastic for identity, etc. **3** playing card. **4** (**cards**) card playing; a card game.
□ **card-carrying** being a registered member of an organization, esp. a political party or labor union.
□ **in the cards** possible or likely.
□ **put one's cards on the table** reveal one's resources, intentions, etc.

**card·board** ▶*n.* pasteboard or stiff paper, esp. for making cards or boxes.

**car·di·ac** /ˈkärdēˌak/ ▶*adj.* of or relating to the heart.

**car·di·gan** /ˈkärdigən/ ▶*n.* sweater fastening down the front.

**car·di·nal** /ˈkärdnəl; ˈkärdn-əl/ ▶*n.* **1** small scarlet American songbird. **2** leading dignitary of the Roman Catholic Church, one of the college electing the pope.
▶*adj.* **1** of the greatest importance; fundamental. **2** of deep scarlet.
□ **cardinal numbers** those numbers denoting quantity (one, two, three, etc.), as opposed to ordinal numbers (first, second, third, etc.). □ **cardinal points** four main points of the compass (N., S., E., W.).

**car·di·o·graph** /ˈkärdēəˌgraf/ ▶*n.* instrument for recording heart muscle activity. —**car·di·og·ra·phy** *n.*

**car·di·ol·o·gy** /ˌkärdēˈäləjē/ ▶*n.* branch of medicine concerned

with the heart.
—**car·di·ol·o·gist** n.

**car·di·o·vas·cu·lar** /ˌkärdēō-ˈvaskyələr/ ▸adj. of or relating to the heart and blood vessels.

**card·sharp** (also **card·shark**) ▸n. swindler at card games.

**care** /ke(ə)r/ ▸n. **1** worry; anxiety. **2** occasion for this. **3** serious attention; heed; caution; pains: *assembled with care.* **4** protection; charge.
▸v. **1** feel concern or interest. **2** wish or be willing to: *do not care to be seen with him.*
▢ **care for** provide for; look after. ▢ **care of** at the address of: *sent it care of his sister.* ▢ **have a care 1** take care; be careful. **2** have worries or responsibilities: *don't have a care in the world.* ▢ **take care** be careful. ▢ **take care of** look after.

**ca·reen** /kəˈrēn/ ▸v. **1** (cause to) tilt or lean over. **2** move swiftly in an uncontrolled way: *bike careened around the corner.*

**ca·reer** /kəˈri(ə)r/ ▸n. **1** one's advancement through life, esp. in a profession. **2** profession; occupation.
▸v. move swiftly in an uncontrolled way: *car careered across the road and into the hedge.*

**ca·reer·ist** /kəˈri(ə)rist/ ▸n. person whose main concern is for professional advancement, esp. one willing to achieve this by any means.

**care·free** ▸adj. free from anxiety or responsibility; lighthearted.

**care·ful** ▸adj. **1** painstaking; thorough. **2** cautious. **3** taking care; not neglecting.
—**care·ful·ly** adv.

**care·giv·er** ▸n. person who provides care for children, the sick, the elderly, etc.

**care·less** ▸adj. **1** not taking care nor paying attention. **2** unthinking; insensitive. **3** lighthearted. —**care·less·ly** adv. —**care·less·ness** n.

**ca·ress** /kəˈres/ ▸v. touch or stroke gently or lovingly.
▸n. loving or gentle touch.

**car·et** /ˈkarət/ ▸n. mark (∧) indicating a proposed insertion in printing or writing.

**care·tak·er** ▸n. person employed to look after something, esp. a house in the owner's absence.

**car·go** /ˈkärgō/ ▸n. (pl. **-goes** or **-gos**) goods carried on a ship or aircraft.

**car·i·bou** /ˈkarəˌbo͞o/ ▶n. (pl. same) N. American reindeer.

**car·i·ca·ture** /ˈkarikəCHər/ ▶n. **1** usu. comic representation of a person by exaggeration of characteristic traits. **2** ridiculous or grotesque version: *he was a caricature of himself.*
▶v. make a caricature of. —**car·i·ca·tur·ist** n.

**car·ies** /ˈke(ə)rēz/ ▶n. (pl. same) decay of a tooth or bone.

**car·il·lon** /ˈkarəˌlän/ ▶n. set of bells.

**car·jack·ing** /ˈkärˌjakiNG/ ▶n. theft of an automobile whose driver is forced to leave the vehicle, kept captive while the thief drives, or forced to drive while at gunpoint, etc. —**car·jack·er** n.

**car·min·a·tive** /kärˈminətiv; ˈkärməˌnātiv/ ▶adj. (chiefly of a drug) relieving flatulence.
▶n. drug of this kind.

**car·mine** /ˈkärmən/ ▶adj. of a vivid crimson color.
▶n. this color.

**car·nage** /ˈkärnij/ ▶n. great slaughter, esp. in battle.

**car·nal** /ˈkärnl/ ▶adj. **1** of the body or flesh; worldly. **2** sensual; sexual. —**car·nal·ly** adv.

□ **carnal knowledge** *Law* sexual intercourse.

**car·nal know·ledge** ▶n. sexual intercourse.

**car·na·tion** /kärˈnāsHən/ ▶n. variously colored clove-scented flower.

**car·ni·val** /ˈkärnəvəl/ ▶n. **1** festivities usual during the period before Lent in Roman Catholic countries. **2** merrymaking; revelry. **3** traveling fair or circus.

**car·niv·o·rous** /kärˈnivərəs/ ▶adj. **1** (of an animal) feeding on other animals. **2** (of a plant) able to trap and digest small animals, esp. insects. —**car·ni·vore** /ˈkärnəˌvôr/ n.

**car·ob** /ˈkarəb/ ▶n. **1** evergreen tree native to the Mediterranean, bearing edible pods. **2** brown floury powder made from the carob bean, used as a substitute for chocolate.

**car·ol** /ˈkarəl/ ▶n. joyous song, esp. a Christmas hymn.
▶v. sing carols. —**car·ol·er** n.

**ca·rot·id** /kəˈrätid/ ▶n. each of the two main arteries carrying blood to the head and neck.
▶adj. of or relating to either of these arteries.

**ca·rouse** /kəˈrouz/ ▶v. have a

noisy or lively drinking party.
—**ca·rous·al** *n.* —**ca·rous·er** *n.*

**carp** ▶*n.* (*pl.* same) freshwater food fish.

▶*v.* find fault; complain pettily: *he was constantly carping at me.*
—**carp·er** *n.*

**car·pal** /ˈkärpəl/ ▶*adj.* of or relating to the bones in the wrist.

▶*n.* any of the bones forming the wrist.

☐ **carpal tunnel syndrome** painful condition of the hand and fingers caused by compression of a major nerve where it passes over the carpal bones through a passage at the front of the wrist.

**car·pe di·em** /ˌkärpā ˈdē,em/ ▶*exclam.* used to urge someone to make the most of the present time and give little thought to the future.

**car·pel** /ˈkärpəl/ ▶*n. Bot.* female reproductive organ of a flower.
—**car·pel·lar·y** *adj.*

**car·pen·ter** /ˈkärpəntər/ ▶*n.* person skilled in woodwork, esp. of a structural kind.
—**car·pen·try** *n.*

**car·pet** /ˈkärpit/ ▶*n.* **1** thick fabric for covering a floor or stairs. **2** expanse or layer resembling a carpet in being smooth, soft, bright, or thick: *carpet of snow.*

▶*v.* cover with or as with a carpet.

**car·pet·bag·ger** /ˈkärpit,bagər/ ▶*n.* **1** political candidate who seeks election in an area where they have no local connections. **2** a person from the northern states who went to the South after the Civil War to profit from the Reconstruction. **3** person perceived as an unscrupulous opportunist.

**car·pool** ▶*n.* (also **car pool**) **1** arrangement by which a group of commuters travel to and from their destination in a single vehicle. **2** commuters taking part in such an arrangement: *there are four people in our carpool.*

▶*v.* (also **car-pool**) participate in or organize a carpool.

**car·port** ▶*n.* shelter with a roof and open sides for a car, usu. beside a house.

**car·pus** /ˈkärpəs/ ▶*n.* (*pl.* **-pi**) small bones between the forelimb and metacarpus in terrestrial vertebrates, forming the wrist in humans.

**car·rack** /ˈkarək/ ▶*n.* large merchant ship of a kind

operating in European waters in the 14th to the 17th c.

**car·rel** /'karel/ ▶*n.* small cubicle for a reader in a library.

**car·riage** /'karij/ ▶*n.* **1** wheeled vehicle, esp. one pulled by horses. **2** carrying part of a machine (e.g., a typewriter). **3** gun carriage. **4** bearing; deportment.

**car·ri·er** /'karēər/ ▶*n.* **1** person or thing that carries. **2** transport or freight company. **3** person or animal that may transmit a disease or hereditary characteristic.

**car·ri·on** /'karēən/ ▶*n.* dead putrefying flesh.

**car·rot** /'karət/ ▶*n.* **1** tapering orange-colored root eaten as a vegetable. **2** plant of the parsley family with feathery leaves, which yields this vegetable. —**car·rot·y** *adj.*

**car·ry** /'karē/ ▶*v.* (**-ried**) **1** support or hold up, esp. while moving. **2** convey with one or have on one's person. **3** conduct or transmit: *pipe carries water.* **4** take (a process, etc.) to a specified point; continue: *carry into effect | carry a joke too far.* **5** involve; imply; entail as a feature or consequence: *principles carry consequences.* **6** (in reckoning) transfer (a figure) to a column of higher value. **7** publish or broadcast esp. regularly. **8** keep a regular stock of. **9** be audible at a distance: *her voice carried into the hall.* **10 a** win victory or acceptance for (a proposal, etc.). **b** gain (a state or district) in an election. **11** be pregnant with.

□ **carry away 1** remove. **2** inspire; affect emotionally or spiritually. **3** deprive of self-control: *got carried away.* □ **carry the day** be victorious or successful. □ **carry off 1** take away, esp. by force. **2** win (a prize). **3** (esp. of a disease) kill. **4** render (something) acceptable or passable: *I never thought she'd carry it off.* □ **carry on 1** continue. **2** engage in (a conversation or a business). **3** *inf.* behave excitedly or in a specified way. **4** advance (a process) by a stage. □ **carry something out** put (ideas, instructions, etc.) into practice.

**car·sick** ▶*adj.* affected with nausea caused by the motion of a car. —**car·sick·ness** *n.*

**cart** /kärt/ ▶*n.* **1** strong vehicle with two or four wheels for carrying loads, usu. drawn by a horse. **2** light vehicle for pulling by hand.

▶*v.* convey in or as in a cart. —**cart·er** *n.*

□ **cart off** remove, esp. by force.

**carte blanche** /ˈkärt ˈbläNCH/ ▶*n.* full discretionary power given to a person.

**car·tel** /kärˈtel/ ▶*n.* informal association of manufacturers or suppliers to maintain prices at a high level.

**car·ti·lage** /ˈkärtl-ij/ ▶*n.* gristle; firm flexible connective tissue. —**car·ti·lag·i·nous** *adj.*

**car·tog·ra·phy** /kärˈtägrəfē/ ▶*n.* science or practice of drawing maps. —**car·tog·ra·pher** *n.* —**car·to·graph·ic** *adj.*

**car·to·man·cy** /ˈkärtə,mansē/ ▶*n.* fortune-telling by interpreting a random selection of playing cards.

**car·ton** /ˈkärtn/ ▶*n.* light box or container, esp. one made of cardboard.

**car·toon** /kärˈto͞on/ ▶*n.* **1** humorous drawing in a newspaper, magazine, etc., esp. as a topical comment. **2** sequence of drawings telling a story. **3** motion picture using animation techniques. —**car·toon·ist** *n.*

**car·tridge** /ˈkärtrij/ ▶*n.* **1** case containing a charge of propelling explosive for firearms or blasting, with a bullet or shot if for small arms. **2** spool of film, magnetic tape, etc., in a sealed container ready for insertion. **3** ink container for insertion in a pen.

**cart·wheel** /ˈkärt,(h)wēl/ ▶*n.* circular sideways handspring.

**carve** /kärv/ ▶*v.* **1** produce or shape (a statue, representation in relief, etc.) by cutting into a hard material: *carved a figure out of rock.* **2** cut patterns, designs, letters, etc., in (hard material). **3** cut (meat, etc.) into slices for eating. —**carv·er** *n.*

□ **carve out 1** take from a larger whole. **2** establish (a career, etc.) purposefully: *carved out a name for themselves.*

**cas·cade** /kasˈkād/ ▶*n.* **1** small waterfall, esp. one in a series. **2** material, etc., draped in descending folds.

▶*v.* fall in or like a cascade.

**case** /kās/ ▶*n.* **1** instance of something occurring. **2** state of affairs, hypothetical or actual. **3 a** instance of a person receiving professional guidance, e.g., from a doctor or social worker. **b** such a person. **4** matter under official investigation, esp. by the police. **5** *Law* cause or suit for trial. **6** *Gram.* any of the inflected forms of a noun, adjective, or pronoun that expresses the relation of the word to other words in a sentence: *the accusative case.* **7** container or covering serving to enclose or contain. **8** container with its contents.

▶*v. inf.* reconnoiter (a house, etc.), esp. with a view to robbery.

□ **in any case** whatever the truth is; whatever may happen. □ **in case** in the event that; if.

**case·ment** ▶*n.* window or part of a window hinged to open on its outer frame.

**cash** /kaSH/ ▶*n.* **1** money in coins or bills. **2** (also **cash down**) full payment at the time of purchase, as distinct from credit.

▶*v.* give or obtain cash for (a note, check, etc.).

□ **cash flow** movement of money into and out of a business. □ **cash in 1** obtain cash for. **2** *inf.* profit (from); take

advantage (of). **cash machine 3** AUTOMATED TELLER MACHINE.

**ca·shew** /ˈkaSH,o͞o/ ▶*n.* **1** bushy evergreen tree native to Central and S. America, bearing kidney-shaped nuts. **2** (also **cashew nut**) edible nut of this tree.

**cash·ier** /kaˈSHi(ə)r/ ▶*n.* person dealing with cash transactions in a store, bank, etc.

**cash·mere** /ˈkazH,mi(ə)r/ ▶*n.* **1** fine soft wool, esp. that of a Kashmir goat. **2** material made from this.

**cas·ing** /ˈkāsiNG/ ▶*n.* protective or enclosing cover or shell.

**ca·si·no** /kəˈsēnō/ ▶*n.* (*pl.* **-nos**) place for gambling.

**cask** /kask/ ▶*n.* **1** large barrellike container made of wood, metal, or plastic, esp. one for alcoholic liquor. **2** its contents.

**cas·ket** /ˈkaskit/ ▶*n.* **1** coffin. **2** small, often ornamental box or chest for jewels, letters, etc.

**casque** /kask/ ▶*n.* **1** helmet. **2** helmetlike structure, such as that on the beak of certain birds.

**cas·sa·va** /kəˈsävə/ ▶*n.* **1** plant with starchy tuberous roots. **2** starch or flour obtained from these roots. (Also called **tapioca** or **manioc**).

**cas·se·role** /ˈkasəˌrōl/ ▸*n.*
**1** covered dish for baking.
**2** food cooked in a casserole.

**cas·sette** /kəˈset/ ▸*n.* sealed case containing a length of tape, film, etc., ready for insertion in tape recorder, camera, etc.

**cas·sock** /ˈkasək/ ▸*n.* long garment worn by clergy, members of choirs, etc.

**cast** /kast/ ▸*v.* (*past* and *past part.* **cast**) **1** throw, esp. deliberately or forcefully. **2 a** direct or cause to fall (one's eyes, a glance, light, a shadow, a spell, etc.). **b** express (doubts, aspersions, etc.).
**3** throw out (a fishing line) into the water. **4** let down (an anchor, etc.). **5** record, register, or give (a vote). **6 a** shape (molten metal or plastic material) in a mold. **b** make (a product) in this way. **7 a** assign (an actor) to play a particular character. **b** allocate roles in (a play, motion picture, etc.).
▸*n.* **1** the throwing of a missile, dice, line, etc. **2 a** object of metal, clay, etc., made in a mold. **b** rigid case to support an injured limb. **3** the actors in a play, motion picture, etc.
□ **cast aside** give up using; abandon. □ **cast off 1** abandon.

**2** loosen and throw off (rope, etc.). □ **cast-off** abandoned; discarded. □ **cast out** expel.

**cas·ta·nets** /kastəˈnets/ ▸*pl. n.* pair of hand-held concave pieces of hardwood, ivory, etc., clicked together, esp. by Spanish dancers.

**cast·a·way** ▸*n.* shipwrecked person.
▸*adj.* **1** shipwrecked. **2** cast aside; rejected.

**caste** /kast/ ▸*n.* **1** Hindu hereditary class. **2** more or less exclusive social class. **3** system of dividing society into such classes.

**cas·tel·lat·ed** /ˈkastəˌlātid/ ▸*adj.* **1** having battlements. **2** (of a nut or other mechanical part) having grooves or slots on its upper face. **3** having a castle or several castles.

**cast·er** ▸*n.* **1** small swiveled wheel as on furniture. **2** small container with holes in the top for sprinkling the contents.

**cas·ti·gate** /ˈkastiˌgāt/ ▸*v.* rebuke or punish severely.
—**cas·ti·ga·tion** *n.* —**cas·ti·ga·tor** *n.* —**cas·ti·ga·to·ry** *adj.*

**cast i·ron** ▸*n.* hard alloy of iron, carbon, and silicon cast in a mold. —**cast-i·ron** *adj.*

**cas·tle** /ˈkasəl/ ▸n. **1** large fortified building or group of buildings; stronghold. **2** *Chess* ROOK. —**cas·tled** *adj.*
□ **castles in the air** visionary unattainable scheme; daydream.

**cast·or oil** /ˈkastər/ ▸n. oil from the seeds of a plant, used as a purgative and lubricant.

**cas·trate** /ˈkasˌtrāt/ ▸v. **1** remove the testicles of; geld. **2** deprive of vigor. —**cas·tra·tion** *n.*

**cas·u·al** /ˈkazHo͞oəl/ ▸adj. **1** accidental; due to chance. **2** not regular or permanent: *casual work*. **3** unconcerned or careless: *was very casual about it*. **4** (of clothes) informal. —**cas·u·al·ly** *adv.* —**cas·u·al·ness** *n.*

**ca·su·al·ty** /ˈkazHo͞oəltē/ ▸n. (pl. **-ties**) **1** person killed or injured in a war or accident. **2** thing lost or destroyed.

**cas·u·ist** /ˈkazHo͞oist/ ▸n. person who uses clever but unsound reasoning, esp. in relation to moral questions; a sophist.

**CAT** ▸abbr. *Med.* computerized axial tomography.

**cat** /kat/ ▸n. **1** small, soft-furred, four-legged domesticated animal. **2** any wild animal of the same family, e.g., a lion, tiger, or leopard.
□ **cat burglar** burglar who enters by climbing to an upper story.
□ **cat's-paw** person used as a tool by another.

**cat·a·chre·sis** /ˌkatəˈkrēsis/ ▸n. (pl. **-ses** /-sēz/) use of a word in a way that is not correct, for example, the use of *mitigate* for *militate*.

**cat·a·clysm** /ˈkatəˌklizəm/ ▸n. sudden violent upheaval or disaster. —**cat·a·clys·mic** *adj.* —**cat·a·clys·mi·cal·ly** *adv.*

**cat·a·comb** /ˈkatəˌkōm/ ▸n. (usu. **catacombs**) underground cemetery, esp. in Rome.

**cat·a·lep·sy** /ˈkatlˌepsē/ ▸n. trance or seizure with loss of sensation or consciousness. —**cat·a·lep·tic** *adj.*

**cat·a·logue rai·son·né** /katlˌôg ˌrāzəˈnā; -ˌäg/ ▸n. (pl. **cat·a·logues rai·son·nés** /ˈkatlˌôg(z) ˌrāzəˈnā; -ˌäg(z)/) descriptive catalog of works of art with explanations and scholarly comments.

**cat·a·lyst** /ˈkatl-ist/ ▸n. **1** *Chem.* substance that increases the rate of a reaction. **2** person or thing that precipitates a change.

**cat·a·lyt·ic** /ˌkatl'itik/ ▸*adj.* relating to or involving the action of a catalyst.

**cat·a·ma·ran** /'katəməˌran/ ▸*n.* boat with parallel twin hulls.

**cat·a·pult** /'katəˌpəlt/ ▸*n.* mechanical device for launching a glider, an aircraft from the deck of a ship, etc.
▸*v.* hurl from or as from a catapult.

**cat·a·ract** /'katəˌrakt/ ▸*n.* **1** large waterfall or cascade. **2** *Med.* condition in which the lens of the eye becomes progressively opaque.

**ca·tarrh** /kə'tär/ ▸*n.* inflammation of a mucous membrance, esp. the nose.

**ca·tas·tro·phe** /kə'tastrəfē/ ▸*n.* great and usu. sudden disaster. —**cat·a·stroph·ic** *adj.* —**cat·a·stroph·i·cal·ly** *adv.*

**cat·a·to·ni·a** /ˌkatə'tōnēə/ ▸*n.* **1** abnormality of movement and behavior arising from a disturbed mental state (typically schizophrenia). **2** state of immobility and stupor. —**cat·a·ton·ic** /ˌkatə'tänik/ *adj.*

**cat·call** ▸*n.* shrill whistle of disapproval.

**catch** /kaCH/ ▸*v.* (*past* and *past part.* **caught**) **1** lay hold of so as to restrain; capture in a trap, in one's hands, etc. **2** detect or surprise (esp. a guilty person). **3 a** contract (a disease) by infection or contagion. **b** acquire (a quality or feeling). **4** reach in time and board (a train, bus, etc.). **5** apprehend with the mind (esp. a thing occurring quickly or briefly). **6** become fixed or entangled. **7** draw the attention of; captivate.
▸*n.* **1** act of catching. **2 a** amount of a thing caught, esp. of fish. **b** thing or person caught or worth catching. **3 a** question, trick, etc., intended to deceive, incriminate, etc. **b** unexpected or hidden difficulty or disadvantage. **4** device for fastening a door or window, etc. —**catch·a·ble** *adj.* —**catch·er** *n.*

□ **catch on** *inf.* **1** (of a practice, fashion, etc.) become popular. **2** (of a person) understand what is meant. □ **catch up 1 a** reach a person who is ahead of one. **b** do tasks that one should have done earlier. **2** (**be/get caught up in**) become involved or entangled in.

**catch·ing** ▸*adj. inf.* infectious.

**catch·word** ▸*n.* word or phrase in common, often temporary, use.

**catch·y** ▸*adj.* (**-i·er, -i·est**) (of a tune) easy to remember; attractive. —**catch·i·ly** *adv.* —**catch·i·ness** *n.*

**cat·e·chism** /ˈkatiˌkizəm/ ▸*n.* **1 a** principles of a religion in the form of questions and answers. **b** book containing this. **2** series of questions put to anyone. —**cat·e·chis·mal** *adj.*

**cat·e·chize** /ˈkatəˌkīz/ ▸*v.* instruct (someone) in the principles of Christian religion by means of question and answer, typically by using a catechism.

**cat·e·gor·i·cal** /ˌkatiˈgôrikəl/ (also **cat·e·gor·ic**) ▸*adj.* unconditional; absolute; explicit. —**cat·e·gor·i·cal·ly** *adv.*

**cat·e·go·ry** ▸*n.* (*pl.* **-ries**) class or division. —**cat·e·go·ri·al** *adj.*

**cat·e·nar·y** /ˈkatnˌerē/ ▸*n.* (*pl.* **-nar·ies**) curve formed by a wire, rope, or chain hanging freely from two points that are on the same horizontal level.

▸*adj.* having the form of, involving, or denoting a curve of this type.

**cat·e·nat·ed** /ˈkatnˌātid/ ▸*adj.* connected in a chain or series.

**ca·ter** /ˈkātər/ ▸*v.* **1** provide (food and drink): *cater a party.* **2** (**cater to**) provide with what is needed or required: *the school caters to children with learning disabilities.* **3** (**cater to**) try to satisfy: *she caters to his every whim.*

**ca·ter·cor·nered** /ˈkātēˌkôrnərd/ (also **cat·er·cor·ner, cat·ty·cor·nered, kit·ty·cor·ner**) ▸*adj.* placed or situated diagonally.

▸*adv.* diagonally.

**cat·er·pil·lar** /ˈkatə(r)ˌpilər/ ▸*n.* larva of a butterfly or moth.

**cat·er·waul** /ˈkatərˌwôl/ ▸*v.* make the shrill howl of a cat.

▸*n.* caterwauling noise.

**cat·fish** ▸*n.* any of various esp. freshwater fish, usu. having whiskerlike barbels around the mouth.

**cat·gut** ▸*n.* material used for surgical sutures, etc., made of animal intestine (but not of the cat).

**ca·thar·sis** /kəˈTHärsis/ ▸*n.* (*pl.* **-ses**) release of strong emotion or tension. —**ca·thar·tic** *adj.*

**ca·the·dral** /kəˈTHēdrəl/ ▶n. principal church of a diocese.

**cath·e·ter** /ˈkaTHitər/ ▶n. tube inserted into a body cavity for introducing or removing fluid. —**cath·e·ter·ize** v.

**cath·ode** /ˈkaTH‚ōd/ *Electr.* ▶n. **1** negative electrode in an electrolytic cell or electronic valve or tube. **2** positive terminal of a primary cell such as a battery. □ **cathode ray** beam of electrons emitted from the cathode of a high-vacuum tube.

**cath·o·lic** /ˈkaTH(ə)lik/ ▶adj. **1** all-embracing; of wide sympathies or interests: *has catholic tastes.* **2** of or including all Christians. ▶n. (**Catholic**) Roman Catholic. —**Ca·thol·i·cism** n. —**cath·o·lic·i·ty** n.

**cat·kin** /ˈkatkin/ ▶n. spike of usu. downy or silky flowers hanging from a willow, hazel, etc.

**cat·nap** ▶n. short sleep. ▶v. (**-napped**, **-nap·ping**) have a catnap.

**cat·nip** ▶n. white-flowered plant that attracts cats.

**CAT scan** /kat/ ▶n. X-ray image of the body made using a computerized technique. —**CAT scan·ner** n.

**cat·sup** /ˈkecHəp/ ▶var. of KETCHUP.

**cat·tle** /ˈkatl/ ▶pl. n. domesticated bovine animals bred for meat and milk.

**cat·ty** /ˈkatē/ ▶adj. (**-ti·er**, **-ti·est**) sly; spiteful; deliberately hurtful in speech. —**cat·ti·ness** n.

**cat·walk** ▶n. narrow footway or platform.

**Cau·ca·sian** /kôˈkāzHən/ ▶adj. **1** of or relating to the white or light-skinned division of mankind. **2** of or relating to the Caucasus. ▶n. Caucasian person.

**cau·cus** /ˈkôkəs/ ▶n. meeting of a political party, esp. in a legislature or convention, to decide policy.

**caul** /kôl/ ▶n. amniotic membrane enclosing a fetus, or part of this membrane occasionally found on a child's head at birth, thought to bring good luck.

**caul·dron** /ˈkôldrən/ (also **cal·dron**) ▶n. large, deep, bowl-shaped vessel for boiling over an open fire.

**cau·li·flow·er** /ˈkôli‚flouər/ ▶n. cabbage with a large flower head of small usu. creamy-white buds.

**caulk** /kôk/ (also **calk**) ▶v. stop up

(the seams of a boat, etc.) with a pliable sealant.

**cause** /kôz/ ▶*n.* **1** person or thing that produces an effect. **2** reason or motive; ground that may be held to justify something: *no cause for complaint.* **3** principle, belief, or purpose: *faithful to the cause.* **4** matter to be settled at law. ▶*v.* be the cause of; produce; make happen: *caused a commotion.* —**caus·a·tion** *n.*

**cause cé·lè·bre** /ˈkôz sə-ˈleb(rə)/ ▶*n.* (*pl.* **causes cé·lè·bres** *pronunc.* same) trial or case that attracts much attention.

**cause·way** ▶*n.* raised road or track across low or wet ground or a stretch of water.

**caus·tic** /ˈkôstik/ ▶*adj.* **1** corrosive; burning. **2** sarcastic; biting. —**caus·ti·cal·ly** *adv.* —**caus·tic·i·ty** *n.*

**cau·ter·ize** /ˈkôtəˌrīz/ ▶*v.* burn or coagulate (tissue), esp. to stop bleeding. —**cau·ter·i·za·tion** *n.*

**cau·tion** /ˈkôSHən/ ▶*n.* **1** attention to safety; prudence; carefulness. **2** warning. ▶*v.* warn or admonish.

**cau·tion·ar·y** /ˈkôSHəˌnerē/ ▶*adj.* giving or serving as a warning.

**cau·tious** /ˈkôSHəs/ ▶*adj.* careful; prudent; attentive to safety. —**cau·tious·ly** *adv.*

**cav·al·cade** /ˌkavəlˈkād/ ▶*n.* procession or formal company of riders, motor vehicles, etc.

**cav·a·lier** /ˌkavəˈli(ə)r/ ▶*n.* courtly gentleman. ▶*adj.* showing a lack of proper concern; offhand. —**cav·a·lier·ly** *adv.*

**cav·al·ry** /ˈkavəlrē/ ▶*n.* (*pl.* **-ries**) [usu. treated as *pl.*] soldiers on horseback or in armored vehicles.

**cave** /ˈkāv/ ▶*n.* large hollow in the side of a cliff, hill, etc., or underground. —**cave·like** *adj.* □ **cave in 1** (of a wall, earth over a hollow, etc.) collapse or cause to collapse. **2** yield; give up.

**ca·ve·at** /ˈkavēˌät/ ▶*n.* warning or proviso.

**ca·ve·at emp·tor** /ˈempˌtôr/ ▶*n.* principle that the buyer alone is responsible for checking the quality and suitability of goods before a purchase is made.

**cave·man** ▶*n.* (*pl.* **-men**) prehistoric human living in a cave.

**cav·ern** /ˈkavərn/ ▶*n.* cave, esp. a large or dark one. —**cav·ern·ous** *adj.*

**cav·i·ar** /ˈkavēˌär/ ▶*n.* pickled

roe of sturgeon or other large fish, eaten as a delicacy.

**cav·il** /ˈkavəl/ ▸v. make petty objections.
▸n. trivial objection.

**cav·i·ta·tion** /ˌkavəˈtāsHən/ ▸n. 1 formation of an empty space within a solid object or body. 2 formation of bubbles in a liquid, typically by the movement of a propeller through it.

**cav·i·ty** /ˈkavitē/ ▸n. (pl. -ties) 1 hollow within a solid body. 2 decayed part of a tooth.

**ca·vort** /kəˈvôrt/ ▸v. leap around excitedly.

**caw** /kô/ ▸n. harsh cry of a crow, etc.
▸v. utter this cry.

**cay** /kē; kā/ ▸n. low bank or reef of coral, rock, or sand.

**cay·enne** /kīˈen/ ▸n. (also **cay·enne pep·per**) powdered red pepper.

**CB** ▸abbr. citizens' band.

**CCU** ▸abbr. 1 cardiac care unit. 2 coronary care unit. 3 critical care unit.

**CD** ▸abbr. 1 compact disc. 2 certificate of deposit.

**Cd** ▸symb. Chem. cadmium.

**CD-ROM** /ˌsē ˌdē ˈräm/ ▸abbr.

compact disc read-only memory, a medium for data storage and distribution.

**cease** /sēs/ ▸v. stop; bring or come to an end: ceased breathing.

**cease-fire** ▸n. temporary suspension of fighting.

**ce·dar** /ˈsēdər/ ▸n. spreading evergreen conifer that yields fragrant durable wood.

**cede** /sēd/ ▸v. give up one's rights to or possession of.

**ce·dil·la** /siˈdilə/ ▸n. mark written under the letter c (ç), esp. in French, to show that it is sibilant.

**cei·lidh** /ˈkālē/ ▸n. social event at which there is Scottish or Irish folk music and singing, traditional dancing, and storytelling.

**ceil·ing** /ˈsēliNG/ ▸n. 1 upper interior surface of a room or other similar compartment. 2 upper limit. 3 Aeron. maximum altitude a given aircraft can reach.

**cel·a·don** /ˈseləˌdän/ ▸n. willow-green color.

**cel·e·brate** /ˈseləˌbrāt/ ▸v. 1 mark with or engage in festivities. 2 perform publicly and duly (a religious ceremony,

etc.). —**cel·e·bra·tion** *n.*
—**cel·e·bra·to·ry** *adj.*

**ce·leb·ri·ty** /sə'lebrətē/ ▶*n.* (*pl.* -ties) **1** well-known person. **2** fame.

**cel·er·y** /'sel(ə)rē/ ▶*n.* plant of the parsley family with closely packed succulent leafstalks used as a vegetable.

**ce·les·tial** /sə'leschəl/ ▶*adj.* **1** of the sky or heavenly bodies. **2** belonging or relating to heaven. **3** supremely good.

**ce·les·tial sphere** ▶*n.* imaginary sphere of which the observer is the center and on which all celestial objects are considered to lie.

**cel·i·bate** /'seləbət/ ▶*adj.* **1** abstaining from marriage and sexual relations, typically for religious reasons. **2** having or involving no sexual relations. ▶*n.* person who abstains from marriage and sexual relations.

**cell** /sel/ ▶*n.* **1** small room, esp. in a prison or monastery. **2** small compartment, e.g., in a honeycomb. **3** small group as a nucleus of political activity. **4** microscopic unit of living matter. **5** device for producing electric current chemically. —**celled** *adj.*

**cel·lar** /'selər/ ▶*n.* storage room below ground level.

**cel·lo** /'CHelō/ ▶*n.* (*pl.* -los) bass instrument of the violin family, held between the legs of the seated player. —**cel·list** *n.*

**cel·lo·phane** /'selə,fān/ ▶*n.* thin transparent wrapping material.

**cell·phone** ▶*n.* small portable telephone that uses radio transmission.

**cel·lu·lar** /'selyələr/ ▶*adj.* consisting of cells; of open texture; porous.

□ **cellular telephone** system of mobile communication over an area divided into "cells," each served by its own small transmitter.

**cel·lu·lite** /'selyə,līt/ ▶*n.* lumpy fat, esp. on the hips and thighs.

**cel·lu·loid** /'selyə,loid/ ▶*n.* **1** transparent plastic made from camphor and cellulose nitrate. **2** motion-picture film.

**cel·lu·lose** /'selyə,lōs/ ▶*n.* **1** carbohydrate forming the main constituent of plant cell walls, used in textile fibers. **2** paint or lacquer containing cellulose acetate or nitrate.

**Cel·si·us** /'selsēəs/ ▶*adj.* of a scale of temperature on which water freezes at 0° and boils at 100°.

**Celt** /kelt; selt/ ▶n. member of a group of W. European peoples, including inhabitants of Ireland, Wales, Scotland, Cornwall, Brittany, and the Isle of Man. —**Celt·ic** adj., n.

**ce·ment** /si'ment/ ▶n. **1** powdery substance made of lime and clay, mixed with water to form mortar or used in concrete. **2** similar substance that hardens and fastens on setting. **3** uniting factor or principle. **4** substance for filling cavities in teeth.
▶v. **1** unite with or as with cement. **2** establish or strengthen (a friendship, etc.). —**ce·ment·er** n.

**cem·e·ter·y** /'semi,terē/ ▶n. (pl. **-ies**) burial ground.

**cen·a·cle** /'senikəl/ ▶n. **1** group of people, such as a discussion group or literary clique. **2** room in which the Last Supper was held.

**ce·no·bite** /'senə,bīt/ ▶n. member of a monastic community.

**cen·o·taph** /'senə,taf/ ▶n. tomblike monument, esp. a war memorial, to a person whose body is elsewhere.

**Ce·no·zo·ic** /,senə'zōik/ Geol. ▶adj. of or relating to the most recent era of geological time, marked by the evolution and development of mammals, birds, and flowers.
▶n. this era.

**cen·ser** /'sensər/ ▶n. vessel in which incense is burned.

**cen·sor** ▶n. person who examines printed matter, movies, news, etc., to suppress any parts on the grounds of obscenity, security, etc.
▶v. examine and make deletions or changes in. —**cen·so·ri·al** adj. —**cen·sor·ship** n.

**cen·so·ri·ous** /sen'sôrēəs/ ▶adj. severely critical of others.

**cen·sure** /'sensHər/ ▶v. criticize harshly; reprove.
▶n. harsh criticism; expression of disapproval. —**cen·sur·a·ble** adj.

**cen·sus** /'sensəs/ ▶n. (pl. **-sus·es**) official count of a population or of a class of things.

**cent** /sent/ ▶n. **1** monetary unit valued at one-hundredth of a dollar. **2** coin of this value.

**cen·taur** /'sen,tôr/ ▶n. (in Greek mythology) creature with the head, arms, and torso of a man and the body and legs of a horse.

**cen·te·na·ry** /'sentn,erē/ ▶*n.* (*pl.* **-ries**) CENTENNIAL.
▶*adj.* **1** of or relating to a centenary. **2** occurring every hundred years.

**cen·ten·ni·al** /sen'tenēəl/ ▶*adj.* **1** lasting for a hundred years. **2** occurring every hundred years.
▶*n.* **1** hundredth anniversary. **2** celebration of this.

**cen·ter** /'sentər/ ▶*n.* **1** middle point. **2** pivot or axis of rotation. **3** place or group of buildings forming a central point or a main area for an activity. **4** point of concentration or dispersion; nucleus or source. **5** political party or group holding moderate opinions.
▶*v.* **1** have or cause to have something as a major theme. **2** place in the center. —**cen·tered** *adj.* —**cen·ter·most** *adj.*
□ **center of gravity** point at which the weight of a body may be considered to act.

**cen·ter·fold** ▶*n.* printed and usu. illustrated sheet folded to form the center spread of a magazine, etc.

**cen·ter·piece** ▶*n.* **1** ornament for the middle of a table. **2** principal item.

**cen·ti·grade** /'sentə,grād/ ▶*adj.* CELSIUS.

**cen·ti·gram** /'senti,gram/ ▶*n.* one-hundredth of a gram.

**cen·ti·li·ter** /'sentə,lētər/ ▶*n.* one-hundredth of a liter.

**cen·ti·me·ter** /'sentə,mētər/ ▶*n.* one-hundredth of a meter.

**cen·ti·pede** /'sentə,pēd/ ▶*n.* arthropod with a wormlike body of many segments each with a pair of legs.

**cen·to** /'sentō/ ▶*n.* (*pl.* **-tos**) literary work made up of quotations from other authors.

**cen·tral** /'sentrəl/ ▶*adj.* **1** of, at, or forming the center. **2** from the center. **3** chief; essential; most important. —**cen·tral·i·ty** *n.* —**cen·tral·ly** *adv.*

**cen·tral·ize** ▶*v.* **1** bring or come to a center. **2** concentrate (administration) at a single center. —**cen·tral·i·za·tion** *n.*

**cen·tral ner·vous sys·tem** ▶*n.* brain and spinal cord.

**cen·tral proc·ess·ing u·nit** (also **cen·tral proc·es·sor**) ▶*n.* principal operating part of a computer. (Abbr.: **CPU**)

**cen·trif·u·gal** /sen'trif(y)əgəl/ ▸*adj.* moving or tending to move from a center. —**cen·trif·u·gal·ly** *adv.*

☐ **centrifugal force** apparent force that acts outward on a body moving about a center.

**cen·tri·fuge** /'sentrə,fyoōj/ ▸*n.* machine with a rapidly rotating device designed to separate liquids from solids or other liquids (e.g., cream from milk).

**cen·trip·e·tal** /sen'tripətl/ ▸*adj.* moving or tending to move toward a center. The opposite of CENTRIFUGAL.

**cen·trist** /'sentrist/ ▸*n.* person who holds moderate political views. —**cen·trism** *n.*

**cen·tu·ry** /'senchərē/ ▸*n.* (*pl.* -ries) **a** period of one hundred years. **b** any of the centuries calculated from the birth of Christ: twentieth century = 1901–2000. In modern use often calculated as, e.g., 1900–1999.

**CEO** ▸*abbr.* chief executive officer.

**ce·phal·ic** /sə'falik/ ▸*adj.* of, in, or relating to the head.

**ceph·a·lo·pod** /'sefələ,päd/ ▸*n.* mollusk having a distinct tentacled head, e.g. the octopus, squid, etc.

**ce·ram·ic** /sə'ramik/ ▸*adj.* **1** made of clay and permanently hardened by heat: *ceramic bowl.* **2** of or relating to ceramics: *ceramic arts.* ▸*n.* ceramic article or product.

**ce·re·al** /'s(ə)rēəl/ ▸*n.* **1 a** grain used for food. **b** any grass producing this, e.g., wheat, corn, rye, etc. **2** breakfast food made from a cereal. ▸*adj.* of edible grain or products of it.

**cer·e·bel·lum** /,serə'beləm/ ▸*n.* (*pl.* -**lums** or -**la**) part of the brain at the back of the skull.

**ce·re·bral** /sə'rēbrəl/ ▸*adj.* **1** of the brain. **2** intellectual rather than emotional. —**ce·re·bral·ly** *adv.*

**ce·re·bral pal·sy** ▸*n.* spastic paralysis from brain damage before or at birth, with jerky or uncontrolled movements.

**cer·e·bra·tion** /,serə'brāsʜən/ ▸*n.* working of the brain; thinking.

**ce·re·brum** /sə'rēbrəm/ ▸*n.* (*pl.* -**brums** or -**bra**) principal part of the brain in vertebrates, located in the front area of the skull.

**cer·e·mo·ni·ous** /,serə-'mōnēəs/ ▸*adj.* **1** relating or appropriate to grand and formal occasions. **2** excessively polite; punctilious.

**cer·e·mo·ny** /'serə,mōnē/ ▸*n.* (*pl.* **-nies**) **1** formal religious or public occasion, esp. celebrating a particular event or anniversary. **2** formalities, esp. of an empty or ritualistic kind. **3** excessively polite behavior. —**cer·e·mo·ni·al** *adj., n.* —**cer·e·mo·ni·al·ly** *adv.*
□ **stand on ceremony** insist on the observance of formalities.

**ce·rise** /sə'rēs/ ▸*adj.* of a light, clear red.
▸*n.* this color.

**cer·tain** /'sərtn/ ▸*adj.* **1 a** confident; convinced. **b** indisputable. **2 a** that may be relied on to happen: *it is certain to rain.* **b** destined: *certain to become a star.* **3** unfailing; reliable. **4** that might be specified, but is not: *a certain lady.* **5** some though not much: *a certain reluctance.*
▸*pron.* some but not all: *certain of them were wounded.*
□ **for certain** without doubt.

**cer·tain·ly** /'sərtnlē/ ▸*adv.* **1** undoubtedly; definitely. **2** (as an answer) yes; of course.

**cer·tain·ty** /'sərtntē/ ▸*n.* (*pl.* **-ties**) **1** undoubted fact.

**2** absolute conviction. **3** person or thing that can be relied on.

**cer·ti·fi·a·ble** /,sərtə'fīəbəl/ ▸*adj.* **1** able or needing to be certified. **2** officially recognized as needing treatment for a mental disorder. **3** *inf.* crazy.

**cer·tif·i·cate** /sər'tifikit/ ▸*n.* formal document attesting a fact, esp. birth, marriage, death, a medical condition, a level of achievement, etc. —**cer·ti·fi·ca·tion** *n.*

**cer·ti·fy** /'sərtə,fī/ ▸*v.* (**-fied**) **1** make a formal statement of; attest; attest to. **2** declare by certificate (that a person is qualified or competent): *certified as a trained bookkeeper.* **3** officially declare insane.

**cer·ti·tude** /'sərti,t(y)ōōd/ ▸*n.* feeling of absolute certainty.

**ce·ru·le·an** /sə'rooleən/ ▸*adj.* *poet./lit.* deep blue like a clear sky.
▸*n.* this color.

**cer·vine** /'sər,vīn; -vin/ ▸*adj.* of or relating to deer; deerlike.

**cer·vix** /'sərviks/ ▸*n.* (*pl.* **-vic·es** or **-vix·es**) any necklike structure, esp. the neck of the womb. —**cer·vi·cal** *adj.*

**ce·sar·e·an** /si'ze(ə)rēən/ (also **cae·sar·e·an** or **Cae·sar·e·an**)

▶*adj.* (of a birth) effected by cesarean section.

▶*n.* cesarean section.

**ce·sar·e·an sec·tion** ▶*n.* operation for delivering a child by cutting through the wall of the mother's abdomen.

**ces·sa·tion** /se'sāsHən/ ▶*n.* **1** ceasing. **2** pause.

**ces·sion** /'sesHən/ ▶*n.* **1** ceding (of rights, property, and esp. of territory by a nation). **2** the territory, etc., so ceded.

**cess·pool** /'ses,po͞ol/ ▶*n.* pit for waste or sewage.

**Cf** ▶*symb. Chem.* californium.

**cf.** ▶*abbr.* compare.

**cg** ▶*abbr.* centigram(s).

**c.h.** (also **C.H.**) ▶*abbr.* **1** clearinghouse. **2** courthouse.

**Cha·blis** /sHa'blē/ ▶*n.* (*pl.* same) type of dry white wine.

**chad·or** /'cHədər; 'cHäd,ôr/ (also **chad·ar**) ▶*n.* large piece of dark-colored cloth, typically worn by Muslim women, wrapped around the head and upper body to leave only the face exposed.

**chafe** /cHāf/ ▶*v.* **1** make or become sore or damaged by rubbing. **2** make or become

annoyed; fret: *was chafed by the delay.*

**chaff** /cHaf/ ▶*n.* **1** husks of grain or other seed. **2** chopped hay and straw used as fodder. **3** lighthearted joking.

▶*v.* tease; banter. **—chaff·y** *adj.*

□ **separate the wheat from the chaff** distinguish good from bad.

**chaf·ing dish** /'cHāfiNG/ ▶*n.* **1** cooking pot with an outer pan of hot water, used for keeping food warm. **2** dish with an alcohol lamp, etc., for cooking at table.

**cha·grin** /sHə'grin/ ▶*n.* acute vexation or mortification.

▶*v.* affect with chagrin.

**chain** /cHān/ ▶*n.* **1 a** connected flexible series of esp. metal links. **b** something resembling this: *formed a human chain.* **2** (**chains**) fetters, restraining force. **3** sequence, series, or set: *chain of events* | *mountain chain.* **4** group of associated restaurants, newspapers, etc.

▶*v.* secure or confine with a chain.

**chain re·ac·tion** ▶*n.* **1** *Physics* self-sustaining nuclear reaction. **2** *Chem.* self-sustaining molecular reaction.

**chain saw** ▶*n.* motor-driven

saw with teeth on an endless chain.

**chair** /CHe(ə)r/ ▶*n.* **1** separate seat for one person, of various forms, usu. having a back and four legs. **2** professorship. **3 a** chairperson. **b** seat or office of a chairperson: *I'm in the chair.*

▶*v.* act as chairperson of or preside over (a meeting).

**chair·man** /'CHe(ə)rmən/ ▶*n.* (*pl.* **-men**; *fem.* **chair·wom·an**, *pl.* **-wom·en**) **1** person chosen to preside over a meeting. **2** permanent president of a committee, board of directors, etc. —**chair·man·ship** *n.*

**chair·per·son** ▶*n.* chairman or chairwoman.

**chaise longue** /'SHāz 'lôNG/ ▶*n.* reclining chair with a lengthened seat forming a leg rest.

**chal·ced·o·ny** /kal'sedn,ē; CHal-; 'kalsə,dōnē; 'CHalsə-/ ▶*n.* (*pl.* **-nies**) type of quartz occurring in several different forms, including onyx, agate, and jasper.

**cha·let** /SHa'lā/ ▶*n.* **1** small house, bungalow, or hut, esp. with an overhanging roof. **2** Swiss cowherd's hut, or

wooden cottage, with overhanging eaves.

**chal·ice** /'CHalis/ ▶*n.* **1** wine cup used in the Christian Eucharist. **2** goblet.

**chalk** /CHôk/ ▶*n.* **1** white, soft, earthy limestone. **2** similar substance (calcium sulfate), sometimes colored, used for writing or drawing.

▶*v.* **1** rub, mark, draw, or write with chalk. **2** (**chalk up**) **a** write or record with chalk. **b** register (a success, etc.). —**chalk·i·ness** *n.* —**chalk·y** *adj.*

**chal·lenge** /'CHalənj/ ▶*n.* **1 a** summons to take part in a contest or a trial of strength, etc. **b** summons to prove or justify something. **2** demanding or difficult task. **3** *Law* objection made to a jury member.

▶*v.* **1 a** invite to take part in a contest, game, debate, duel, etc. **b** invite to prove or justify something. **2 a** stretch; stimulate: *challenges him to produce his best.* **b** [as *adj.* **challenging**] be demanding; be stimulatingly difficult. **3** *Law* object to (a jury member, evidence, etc.). —**chal·leng·er** *n.*

**chal·lis** /'SHalē/ ▶*n.* soft

lightweight clothing fabric made from silk and worsted.

**cha·lyb·e·ate** /kə'lēbēət; -'lib-/ ▶*adj.* of or denoting natural mineral springs containing iron salts.

**cham·ber** /'CHāmbər/ ▶*n.* **1 a** hall used by a legislative or judicial body. **b** body that meets in it. **2** (**chambers**) judge's room. **3** enclosed space in machinery, etc. (esp. the part of a gun bore that contains the charge). **4 a** cavity in a plant or in the body of an animal. **b** compartment in a structure. **5** *archaic* room, esp. a bedroom. □ **chamber of commerce** association to promote local commercial interests.

**cham·ber·maid** ▶*n.* housemaid who cleans bedrooms, esp. in a hotel, etc.

**cham·ber mu·sic** ▶*n.* instrumental music played by a small ensemble.

**cha·me·le·on** /kə'mēlyən/ ▶*n.* small lizard having the power of changing color. **—cha·me·le·on·ic** *adj.*

**cham·ois** /'SHamē/ ▶*n.* (*pl.* same) **1** agile goat antelope native to Europe and Asia. **2 a** soft leather from sheep, goats, deer, etc. **b** a piece of this or similar soft material used for polishing, etc.

**cham·o·mile** /'kamə,mēl/ (also **cam·o·mile**) ▶*n.* aromatic plant with daisylike flowers. □ **chamomile tea** infusion of its dried flowers used as a tonic.

**champ** /CHamp/ ▶*v.* another term for **CHOMP.** ▶*n. inf.* champion.

**cham·pagne** /SHam'pān/ ▶*n.* white sparkling wine associated with celebration, originally from Champagne in France.

**cham·per·ty** /'CHampərtē/ ▶*n.* illegal agreement in which a person with no previous interest in a lawsuit finances it with a view to sharing the disputed property if the suit succeeds.

**cham·pi·on** /'CHampēən/ ▶*n.* **1** person, animal, plant, etc., that has defeated or surpassed all rivals in a competition, etc. **2** person who fights or argues for a cause or on behalf of another person. ▶*v.* support the cause of; defend; argue in favor of. **—cham·pi·on·ship** *n.*

**champ·le·vé** /,SHänlə'vā/ ▶*n.* enamelwork in which hollows made in a metal surface are filled with colored enamel.

**chance** /CHans/ ▶*n.*
**1 a** possibility. **b** probability: *the chances are against it.*
**2** opportunity: *didn't have a chance to speak.* **3** the way things happen; fortune; luck: *we'll just leave it to chance.*

▶*adj.* fortuitous; accidental: *a chance meeting.*

▶*v.* **1** *inf.* risk: *we'll chance it and go.* **2** happen without intention: *I chanced to find it.*

☐ **by any chance** as it happens; perhaps. ☐ **by chance** without design; unintentionally. ☐ **stand a chance** have a prospect of success, etc.

**chan·cel** /ˈCHansəl/ ▶*n.* part of a church near the altar.

**chan·cel·ler·y** /ˈCHansəl(ə)rē/ ▶*n.* (*pl.* **-ies**) **1 a** position, office, staff, department, etc., of a chancellor. **b** official residence of a chancellor. **2** office attached to an embassy or consulate.

**chan·cel·lor** /ˈCHans(ə)lər/ ▶*n.*
**1** government official of various kinds; head of the government in some European countries, e.g., Germany. **2** chief administrator at certain universities.
—**chan·cel·lor·ship** *n.*

**chanc·y** /ˈCHansē/ ▶*adj.* (**-i·er, -i·est**) *inf.* uncertain; risky.

**chan·de·lier** /ˌSHandəˈli(ə)r/ ▶*n.* ornamental branched hanging support for several candles or electric light bulbs.

**change** /CHānj/ ▶*n.* **1 a** making or becoming different. **b** alteration or modification. **2 a** money given in exchange for money in larger units or a different currency. **b** money returned as the balance of that given in payment. **3** new experience; variety: *for a change.* **4** substitution of one thing for another: *change of scene.*

▶*v.* **1** undergo, show, or subject to change; make or become different. **2** take or use another instead of: *changed trains.* **3** give or get change in smaller denominations for: *can you change a ten-dollar bill?* **4** put fresh clothes or coverings on: *changed into something loose.* **5** give and receive; exchange: *we changed places.* —**change·a·ble** *adj.*

☐ **change hands 1** pass to a different owner. **2** substitute one hand for another.

**change·ling** /ˈCHānjliNG/ ▶*n.* child believed to have been secretly substituted by fairies for the parents' real child in infancy.

**change·o·ver** ▶*n.* change from one system or situation to another.

**chan·nel** /ˈCHanl/ ▶*n.* **1 a** length of water wider than a strait, joining two larger areas, esp. seas. **b** (**the Channel**) the English Channel. **2** medium of communication; agency. **3** band of frequencies used in radio and television transmission, esp. as used by a particular station. **4** course in which anything moves; direction. **5 a** natural or artificial hollow bed of water. **b** navigable part of a waterway. ▶*v.* guide; direct.

**chant** /CHant/ ▶*n.* **1** repeated rhythmic phrase, typically shouted by a crowd. **2** *Mus.* **a** short musical passage in two or more phrases used for singing unmetrical words, e.g., psalms, canticles, etc. **b** song, esp. monotonous or repetitive. ▶*v.* **1** say or shout repeatedly in a singsong tone. **2** sing or intone (a psalm, etc.).

**chan·teuse** /ˌSHänˈto͞oz; ˈtœz/ ▶*n.* female singer of popular songs, esp. in a nightclub.

**chant·ey** /ˈSHantē/ (also **chant·y**) ▶*n.* song with alternating solo and chorus, of a kind originally sung by sailors while performing physical labor together.

**Cha·nu·kah** ▶*n.* variant spelling of **HANUKKAH**

**cha·os** /ˈkāˌäs/ ▶*n.* utter confusion. —**cha·ot·ic** *adj.* —**cha·ot·i·cal·ly** *adv.* □ **chaos theory** *Math.* the study of the apparently random behavior of deterministic systems.

**chap** /CHap/ ▶*v.* (**chapped**, **chap·ping**) (esp. of the skin; also of dry ground, etc.) crack in fissures, esp. because of exposure and dryness. ▶*n. inf.* man; boy; fellow.

**chap.** ▶*abbr.* chapter.

**chap·ar·ral** /ˌSHapəˈral/ ▶*n.* vegetation consisting chiefly of tangled shrubs and thorny bushes.

**chap·el** /ˈCHapəl/ ▶*n.* **1** place for private Christian worship in a large church or esp. a cathedral, with its own altar and dedication. **2** place of worship attached to a private house or institution.

**chap·er·one** /ˈSHapəˌrōn/ (also **chap·er·on**) ▶*n.* **1** person who

takes charge of esp. young people in public. **2** person, esp. an older woman, who ensures propriety by accompanying a young unmarried woman on social occasions.
▶*v.* act as a chaperon to. —**chap·er·on·age** *n.*

**chap·fall·en** /ˈCHapˌfôlən/ ▶*adj.* with one's lower jaw hanging due to extreme exhaustion or dejection.

**chap·lain** /ˈCHaplən/ ▶*n.* member of the clergy attached to a private chapel, institution, ship, regiment, etc. —**chap·lain·cy** *n.*

**chap·let** /ˈCHaplət/ ▶*n.* **1** garland or wreath for a person's head. **2** string of 55 beads (one third of the rosary number) for counting prayers, or as a necklace. **3** metal support for the core of a hollow casting mold.

**chaps** ▶*pl. n.* leather pants worn by cowboys.

**chap·ter** /ˈCHaptər/ ▶*n.* **1** main division of a book. **2** period of time (in a person's life, a nation's history, etc.). **3** local branch of a society. **4** governing body of a religious community.

**char** /CHär/ ▶*v.* (**charred**, **char·ring**) **1** make or become black by burning; scorch. **2** burn to charcoal.

**char·ac·ter** /ˈkeriktər/ ▶*n.* **1** collective qualities or characteristics, esp. mental and moral, that distinguish a person or thing. **2** person in a novel, play, etc. **3** printed or written letter, symbol, or distinctive mark: *Chinese characters.* **4** *inf.* person, esp. an eccentric or outstanding individual: *he's a real character.* —**char·ac·ter·less** *adj.*

**char·ac·ter·is·tic** ▶*adj.* typical; distinctive: *with characteristic expertise.*
▶*n.* distinguishing feature or quality. —**char·ac·ter·is·ti·cal·ly** *adv.*

**char·ac·ter·ize** ▶*v.* **1** describe the character of. **2** be characteristic of. —**char·ac·ter·i·za·tion** *n.*

**char·coal** /ˈCHärˌkōl/ ▶*n.* **1 a** amorphous form of carbon consisting of a porous black residue from partially burned wood, bones, etc. **b** piece of this used for drawing. **2** drawing in charcoal. **3** (also **charcoal gray**) dark gray color.

**charge** /CHärj/ ▶*v.* **1 a** ask (an

amount) as a price. **b** ask (a person) for an amount as a price. **2 a** debit the cost of to (a person or account). **b** debit (a person or an account). **3** accuse (of an offense): *charged him with theft.* **4** instruct or urge. **5** entrust with. **6** make a rushing attack (on). **7** give an electric charge to (a body). **8** load or fill, as with fuel, emotion, etc.

▶*n.* **1** price asked for goods or services. **2** accusation, esp. against a defendant. **3 a** task, duty, or commission. **b** care, custody, responsible possession. **4** impetuous rush or attack, esp. in a battle. **5** appropriate amount of material to be put into a receptacle, mechanism, etc. **6** property of matter causing electrical phenomena. **7** exhortation; directions; orders. —**charge·a·ble** *adj.*

□ **charge account** credit account at a store, etc. □ **charge card** credit card for which the account must be paid in full when a statement is issued. □ **in charge** having command. □ **take charge** assume control or direction.

**char·gé d'af·faires** /SHär,ZHā dä'fer/ ▶*n.* (*pl.* **char·gés**

**d'af·faires**) **1** diplomatic official who temporarily takes the place of an ambassador. **2** state's diplomatic representative in a minor country.

**char·ger** ▶*n.* **1** cavalry horse. **2** apparatus for charging a battery. **3** person or thing that charges.

**char·i·ot** /'CHarēət/ ▶*n.* two-wheeled vehicle drawn by horses, used in ancient warfare and racing. —**char·i·o·teer** *n.*

**cha·ris·ma** /kə'rizmə/ ▶*n.* (*pl.* **-ma·ta**) **1** ability to inspire followers with devotion and enthusiasm. **2** attractive aura; great charm. —**char·is·mat·ic** *adj.* —**char·is·mat·ic·al·ly** *adv.*

**char·is·mat·ic** /ˌkariz'matik/ ▶*adj.* **1** exercising a compelling charm that inspires devotion in others. **2** of or relating to a movement in the Christian Church that emphasizes gifts believed to be conferred by the Holy Spirit, such as speaking in tongues and healing of the sick.

**char·i·ta·ble** /'CHaritəbəl/ ▶*adj.* **1** generous in giving to those in need. **2** relating to charities. **3** apt to judge persons, acts, etc., favorably.

**char·i·ty** /'CHaritē/ ▶*n.* (*pl.* **-ties**)

**1** giving voluntarily to those in need. **2** institution or organization for helping those in need. **3 a** kindness; benevolence. **b** tolerance.

**chari·va·ri** /ˌSHivə'rē; 'SHivəˌrē/ (also **shiv·a·ree**) ▶*n.* (*pl.* **-va·ris**) cacophonous mock serenade, typically performed by a group of people in derision of an unpopular person or in celebration of a marriage.

**char·la·tan** /'SHärlətən/ ▶*n.* person falsely claiming a special knowledge or skill.

**charm** /CHärm/ ▶*n.* **1 a** power or quality of giving delight or arousing admiration. **b** attractive or enticing quality. **2** trinket on a bracelet, etc. **3** object, act, or word(s) supposedly having occult or magic power; spell.
▶*v.* **1** delight; captivate. **2** influence or protect as if by magic: *leads a charmed life.* **3** gain or influence by charm. —**charm·er** *n.*
□ **like a charm** perfectly; wonderfully.

**char·meuse** /SHär'm(y)o͞oz/ ▶*n.* soft, silky dress fabric.

**chart** /CHärt/ ▶*n.* **1** geographical map or plan, esp. for navigation by sea or air. **2** sheet of information in the form of a table, graph, or diagram. **3** (usu. **charts**) *inf.* listing of the currently most popular music recordings.
▶*v.* make a chart of; map.

**char·ter** ▶*n.* **1** written grant of rights, by a sovereign or legislature, esp. the creation of a city, company, university, etc. **2** written constitution or description of an organization's functions, etc.
▶*v.* **1** grant a charter to. **2** hire (an aircraft, ship, etc.).
□ **charter member** original member of a society, corporation, etc.

**ohar·treuse** /SHär'tro͞oz/ ▶*n.* **1** pale green or yellow liqueur made from brandy. **2** pale yellow or pale green color of this.

**char·y** /'CHe(ə)rē/ ▶*adj.* (**-i·er, -i·est**) **1** cautious; wary. **2** sparing; ungenerous. —**char·i·ly** *adv.* —**char·i·ness** *n.*

**chase** /CHās/ ▶*v.* **1** pursue in order to catch. **2** drive or cause to go. **3** emboss or engrave (metal).
▶*n.* pursuit.

**chasm** /'kazəm/ ▶*n.* **1** deep fissure or opening in the earth, rock, etc. **2** wide difference; gulf.

**chas·sé** /SHaˈsā/ ▸*n.* gliding step in dancing in which one foot displaces the other.

**chas·sis** /ˈCHasē; ˈSHasē/ ▸*n.* (*pl.* same) **1** base frame of a motor vehicle, carriage, etc. **2** frame to carry radio, etc., components.

**chaste** /CHāst/ ▸*adj.* **1** abstaining from extramarital, or from all, sexual intercourse. **2** (of behavior, speech, etc.) pure; virtuous; decent. **3** (of artistic, etc., style) simple; unadorned. —**chaste·ly** *adv.* —**chas·ti·ty** *n.*

**chas·ten** /ˈCHāsən/ ▸*v.* **1** [usu. as *adj.* **chastening, chastened**] subdue; restrain. **2** discipline; punish.

**chas·tise** /CHasˈtīz/ ▸*v.* **1** rebuke or reprimand severely. **2** punish, esp. by beating. —**chas·tise·ment** *n.*

**chat** /CHat/ ▸*v.* (**chat·ted, chat·ting**) talk in a light familiar way. ▸*n.* informal conversation or talk. —**chat·ty** *adj.* —**chat·ti·ly** *adv.* —**chat·ti·ness** *n.*

**châ·teau** /SHaˈtō/ ▸*n.* (*pl.* **-teaus** or **-teaux**) large French country house or castle.

**chat·tel** /ˈCHatl/ ▸*n.* moveable possession; any possession or piece of property other than real estate or a freehold.

**chat·ter** /ˈCHatər/ ▸*v.* **1** talk quickly, incessantly, trivially, or indiscreetly. **2** (of a bird) emit short, quick notes. **3** (of the teeth) click repeatedly together (usu. from cold). ▸*n.* chattering talk or sounds.

**chat·ter·box** ▸*n.* talkative person.

**chauf·feur** /ˈSHōfər/ ▸*n.* person employed to drive a private or rented automobile or limousine. ▸*v.* drive (a car or a person) as a chauffeur.

**chau·vin·ism** /ˈSHōvə,nizəm/ ▸*n.* **1** exaggerated or aggressive patriotism. **2** excessive or prejudiced support or loyalty.

**cheap** /CHēp/ ▸*adj.* **1** low in price; worth more than its cost: *cheap labor.* **2** charging low prices; offering good value: *a cheap restaurant.* **3** of poor quality; inferior. **4** costing little effort and hence of little worth: *a cheap joke.* ▸*adv.* cheaply: *got it cheap.* —**cheap·ly** *adv.* —**cheap·ness** *n.* ☐ **dirt cheap** very cheap.

**cheap·skate** ▸*n. inf.* stingy person.

**cheat** /CHēt/ ▶*v.* **1** deceive; trick. **2** gain unfair advantage by deception or breaking rules.
▶*n.* **1** person who cheats. **2** trick, fraud, or deception.
—**cheat·er** *n.*

**check** /CHek/ ▶*v.* **1** examine the accuracy, quality, or condition of. **2** stop or slow the motion of; curb. **3** *Chess* directly threaten (the opposing king). **4** agree or correspond when compared. **5** mark with a check mark, etc. **6** deposit (luggage, etc.) for storage or dispatch.
▶*n.* **1** means or act of testing or ensuring accuracy, quality, etc. **2 a** stopping or slowing of motion. **b** rebuff or rebuke. **c** person or thing that restrains. **3** written order to a bank to pay the stated sum from one's account. **4** *Chess* exposure of a king to direct attack. **5** bill in a restaurant. **6** pattern of small squares.
▶*interj.* expressing assent or agreement.
☐ **check in 1** arrive or register at a hotel, airport, etc. **2** record the arrival of. ☐ **check mark** a mark (√) to denote correctness, check items in a list, etc. ☐ **check off** mark on a list, etc., as having been examined or dealt with.
☐ **check on** examine carefully; keep a watch on (a person, work done, etc.). ☐ **check out 1** leave a hotel, etc., after paying. **2** *inf.* investigate; examine for authenticity or suitability. ☐ **in check** under control; restrained.

**check·er** ▶*n.* **1** person or thing that examines, esp. in a factory, etc. **2** cashier in a supermarket, etc. **3 a** (**checkers**) game for two played with 12 pieces each on a checkerboard. **b** red and black pieces used in a game of checkers.

**check·er·board** ▶*n.* checkered board, identical to a chessboard, used in the game of checkers.

**check·ered** ▶*adj.* marked with varied fortunes: *a checkered career.*

**check·mate** ▶*n. Chess* check from which a king cannot escape.
▶*v.* **1** *Chess* put into checkmate. **2** defeat; frustrate.

**check·out** ▶*n.* **1** act of checking out. **2** point at which goods are paid for in a supermarket, etc.

**check·point** ▶*n.* barrier or gate for inspection.

**check·up** ▸*n.* thorough (esp. medical) examination.

**ched·dar** /ˈCHedər/ ▸*n.* kind of firm smooth cheese orig. made in Cheddar in S. England.

**cheek** /CHēk/ ▸*n.* **1 a** side of the face below the eye. **b** sidewall of the mouth. **2** impertinence; cool confidence. **3** *inf.* either buttock.

**cheer** /CHi(ə)r/ ▸*n.* **1** shout of encouragement or applause. **2** mood; disposition: *full of good cheer.*
▸*interj.* (**Cheers!**) expressing good wishes on parting or before drinking.
▸*v.* **1** shout for joy. **2** applaud or encourage with shouts. —**cheer·ful** *adj.* —**cheer·ful·ly** *adv.* —**cheer·ful·ness** *n.*

**cheese** /CHēz/ ▸*n.* a food made from the pressed curds of milk.

**cheese·burg·er** ▸*n.* hamburger with cheese on it.

**cheese·cloth** ▸*n.* thin loosely woven cloth, used orig. for wrapping cheese.

**chee·tah** /ˈCHētə/ ▸*n.* swift, spotted leopardlike feline.

**chef** /SHef/ ▸*n.* cook, esp. the chief cook in a restaurant, etc.

**chef-d'œu·vre** /SHā ˈdœv(rə); ˈdə(r)v/ ▸*n.* (*pl.* **chefs-d'œu·vre** /SHāz ˈdœv(rə); ˈdə(r)v/) masterpiece.

**chem·i·cal** /ˈkemikəl/ ▸*adj.* of, made by, or employing chemistry or chemicals.
▸*n.* substance obtained or used in chemistry. —**chem·i·cal·ly** *adv.*

**chem·i·cal war·fare** ▸*n.* warfare using poison gas and other chemicals.

**che·mise** /SHəˈmēz/ ▸*n.* woman's loose-fitting undergarment or dress hanging straight from the shoulders.

**chem·is·try** /ˈkeməstrē/ ▸*n.* (*pl.* **-tries**) **1** the study of the elements and the compounds they form and the reactions they undergo. **2** chemical composition and properties of a substance or body. **3** emotional or psychological interaction between two people.

**che·mo·ther·a·py** /ˌkēmō-ˈTHerəpē/ ▸*n.* treatment of disease, esp. cancer, by chemical substances. —**che·mo·ther·a·pist** *n.*

**che·nille** /SHəˈnēl/ ▸*n.* tufted velvety cord or yarn, used for trimming furniture and making carpets and clothing, or fabric made from such yarn.

**cher·ish** /ˈCHeriSH/ ▸*v.* **1** protect

and care for (someone) lovingly.
**2** hold (something) dear.

**cher·no·zem** /ˈCHərnəˌzHôm;
-ˌzem/ ▶*n.* fertile black soil rich
in humus, with a lighter lime-
rich layer beneath. Chernozem
is found on the North American
prairies.

**Cher·o·kee** /ˈCHerəkē/ ▶*n.*
**1 a** N. American Indian people
formerly inhabiting much of the
southern U.S. **b** member of this
people. **2** language of this
people.

**cher·ry** /ˈCHerē/ ▶*n.* (*pl.* **-ries**)
**1** small, soft, round stone fruit.
**2** tree bearing this, also grown
for its wood and its ornamental
flowers.
▶*adj.* of a light red color.

**cher·ub** /ˈCHerəb/ ▶*n.* **1** (*pl.*
**-u·bim, -ubs**) angelic being, usu.
depicted as a winged child or the
head of a winged child.
**2** beautiful or innocent child.
—**che·ru·bic** *adj.*

**chess** /CHes/ ▶*n.* game for two
with 16 pieces each, played on a
chessboard.

**chess·board** ▶*n.* checkered
board used in the game of
chess.

**chest** /CHest/ ▶*n.* **1** large strong
box. **2 a** part of a human or
animal body enclosed by the
ribs. **b** front surface of the body
from neck to waist. **3** small
cabinet for medicines, etc.
□ **get something off one's chest**
*inf.* disclose a fact, secret, etc., to
relieve one's anxiety about it.

**chest·nut** /ˈCHes(t)ˌnət/ ▶*n.*
**1 a** glossy, hard, brown edible
nut. **b** tree bearing it. **2** horse
chestnut. **3** the heavy wood of
any chestnut tree. **4** horse of a
reddish-brown or yellowish-
brown color. **5** *inf.* stale joke or
anecdote. **6** reddish-brown
color.

**chest·y** /ˈCHestē/ ▶*adj.* **1** (of a
sound) produced deep in the
chest. **2** (of a woman) having
large or prominent breasts.
**3** conceited and arrogant.

**chev·ron** /ˈsHevrən/ ▶*n.* **1** V-
shaped line or stripe. **2** badge,
etc., of such lines or stripes.

**chew** /CHo͞o/ ▶*v.* work (food, etc.)
between the teeth.
▶*n.* **1** act of chewing.
**2** something for chewing, esp. a
chewy candy. —**chew·a·ble** *adj.*
—**chew·er** *n.*
□ **chewing gum** flavored gum, for
chewing. □ **chew out** *inf.*
reprimand.

**chew·y** ▸*adj.* (**-i·er, -i·est**)
**1** needing much chewing.
**2** suitable for chewing.
—**chew·i·ness** *n.*

**Chey·enne** /SHī'an/ ▸*n.* **1 a** N. American Indian people formerly living between the Missouri and Arkansas rivers. **b** member of this people. **2** language of this people.

**chez** /SHā/ ▸*prep.* at the home of (used in imitation of French, often humorously).

**Chi·an·ti** /kē'äntē/ ▸*n.* (*pl.* **-tis**) dry, red wine, orig. produced in Tuscany.

**chi·a·ro·scu·ro** /kē,ärə-'sk(y)o͝orō; kē,arə-/ ▸*n.* **1** treatment of light and shade in drawing and painting. **2** effect of contrasted light and shadow created by light falling unevenly or from a particular direction on something.

**chi·as·mus** /kī'azməs/ ▸*n.* inversion in a second clause or phrase of the word order of the first; e.g. 'Poetry is the record of the best and happiest moments of the happiest and best minds.'

**chic** /SHēk/ ▸*adj.* (**-er, -est**) stylish; elegant.
▸*n.* stylishness; elegance.
—**chic·ly** *adv.*

**chi·ca·ner·y** /SHi'kānərē/ ▸*n.* (*pl.* **-ies**) **1** clever but misleading talk; false argument. **2** trickery; deception.

**Chi·ca·no** /CHi'känō/ ▸*n.* (*pl.* **-nos**; *fem.* **Chi·ca·na**, *pl.* **-nas**) American of Mexican origin.

**chick** /CHik/ ▸*n.* **1** young bird. **2** *inf.* young woman.

**chick·a·dee** /'CHikə,dē/ ▸*n.* small gray titmouse with a black cap.

**Chick·a·saw** /'CHikə,sô/ ▸*n.* **1 a** N. American Indian people native to Mississippi and Alabama. **b** member of this people. **2** language of this people.

**chick·en** /'CHikən/ ▸*n.* (*pl.* same or **chick·ens**) **1** common breed of domestic fowl kept for its meat and eggs. **2** coward.
▸*adj. inf.* cowardly.
▸*v.* (**chicken out**) *inf.* withdraw through fear or lack of nerve.

**chick·en pox** ▸*n.* infectious disease, esp. of children, with a rash of small blisters.

**chick·en wire** ▸*n.* light wire netting with a hexagonal mesh.

**chick·pea** ▸*n.* round yellowish seed, used as food. (Also called **garbanzo**)

**chic·o·ry** /ˈCHikərē/ ▸n. (pl. -ries)
**1** blue-flowered plant cultivated for its salad leaves and its root.
**2** its root, roasted and ground for use with or instead of coffee.

**chide** /CHīd/ ▸v. (past **chid·ed** or **chid**; past part. **chid·ed** or **chid** or **chid·den**) scold; rebuke.
—**chid·er** n. —**chid·ing·ly** adv.

**chief** /CHēf/ ▸n. **1 a** leader or ruler. **b** head of a tribe, clan, etc. **2** head of a department; highest official.
▸adj. **1** most important. **2** having the highest rank.
☐ **chief executive officer** highest ranking executive in a corporation, organization, etc. (Abbr.: **CEO**)

**chief·ly** ▸adv. mainly.

**chief·tain** /ˈCHēftən/ (fem. **chief·tain·ess**) ▸n. leader of a tribe, clan, etc. —**chief·tain·cy** n.

**chif·fon** /SHiˈfän/ ▸n. light, diaphanous fabric of silk, nylon, etc.
▸adj. **1** made of chiffon. **2** light-textured: chiffon cake.

**chig·ger** /ˈCHigər/ ▸n. harvest mite with parasitic larvae.

**chi·gnon** /ˈSHēn,yän; SHēnˈyän/ ▸n. knot or coil of hair arranged on the back of a woman's head.

**child** /CHīld/ ▸n. (pl. **chil·dren**)
**1 a** young human being below the age of puberty. **b** unborn or newborn human being. **2** one's son or daughter. **3** descendant, follower, or product (of): child of God. **4** childish person.
—**child·hood** n. —**child·ish** adj.
—**child·less** adj.
—**child·less·ness** n.
☐ **child care** care of children, esp. by someone other than a parent.
☐ **child's play** easy task.

**child·birth** ▸n. act of giving birth to a child.

**chil·i** /ˈCHilē/ ▸n. (pl. -ies) small, hot-tasting dried pod of a certain red pepper, used as a spice.
☐ **chili con carne** stew of chili-flavored ground meat and usu. beans.

**chill** /CHil/ ▸n. **1** moderate but unpleasant cold sensation.
**2** (**chills**) lowered body temperature, accompanied by shivering. **3** unpleasant coldness (of air, water, etc.). **4** depressing influence: cast a chill over.
**5** coldness of manner.
▸v. **1** make or become cold.
**2** horrify or frighten: the city was chilled by the violence.
☐ **chill out** inf. become calm or less agitated.

**chill·y** ▸*adj.* (**-i·er, -i·est**)
**1** uncomfortably cool or cold.
**2** unfriendly: *a chilly reception.*

**chime** /CHīm/ ▸*n.* **a** any of a set of bells tuned to produce melodious sounds when struck. **b** sound made by such an instrument.
▸*v.* (of a clock) indicate (the time) by chiming.
□ **chime in** interject a remark.

**chi·me·ra** /kī'mi(ə)rə/ (also **chi·mae·ra**) ▸*n.* **1** (in Greek mythology) fire-breathing female monster with a lion's head, a goat's body, and a serpent's tail. **2** fantastic or grotesque product of the imagination.
—**chi·mer·i·cal** *adj.*

**chim·ney** /'CHimnē/ ▸*n.* (*pl.* **-neys**) **1** vertical channel conducting smoke or combustion gases, etc., up and away from a fire, furnace, etc. **2** part of this that projects above a roof. **3** glass tube protecting the flame of a lamp. **4** narrow vertical crack in a rock face.

**chim·pan·zee** /ˌCHimˌpan'zē/ (also **chimp**) ▸*n.* small African anthropoid ape.

**chin** /CHin/ ▸*n.* front of the lower jaw.
□ **chin-up** exercise in which the chin is raised up to the level of an overhead bar that one grasps.

**chi·na** /'CHīnə/ ▸*n.* **1** fine white or translucent ceramic ware, porcelain, etc. **2** things made from ceramic, esp. household tableware.
▸*adj.* made of china.
—**chi·na·ware** *n.*

**chin·chil·la** /CHin'CHilə/ ▸*n.* **1** S. American small rodent having soft, silver-gray fur. **2** its highly valued fur.

**chine** /CHīn/ ▸*n.* **1** backbone, esp. that of an animal as it appears in a cut of meat. **2** mountain ridge.
▸*v.* cut (meat) across or along the backbone.

**Chi·nese** /CHī'nēz/ ▸*adj.* **1** of or relating to China. **2** of Chinese descent.
▸*n.* **1** the Chinese language. **2 a** native or national of China. **b** person of Chinese descent.

**chink** ▸*n.* narrow opening; slit.
▸*v.* (cause to) make a slight ringing sound, as of glasses or coins striking together.
▸*n.* this sound.

**chi·noi·se·rie** /ˌSHēnˌwäz(ə)'rē; ˌSHēn'wäzərē/ ▸*n.* (*pl.* **-ries**) **1** imitation or evocation of Chinese motifs and techniques in Western art, furniture, and architecture, esp. in the 18th c. **2** objects or decorations in this style.

**Chi·nook** /SHə'nŏŏk/ ▶*n.* **1 a** N. American people native to the northwestern coast of the U.S. **b** member of this people. **2** language of this people.

**chintz** /CHints/ ▶*n.* printed multicolored cotton fabric with a glazed finish.

**chintz·y** ▶*adj.* (-i·er, -i·est) **1** like chintz. **2** gaudy; cheap. —**chintz·i·ly** *adv.* —**chintz·i·ness** *n.*

**chip** /CHip/ ▶*n.* **1** small piece removed by or in the course of chopping, cutting, or breaking. **2** hole or flaw where such a chip has been made. **3** thin slice of food made crisp by frying, baking, etc.: *potato chip* | *tortilla chip.* **4** MICROCHIP. **5** counter used in some gambling games to represent money: *poker chip.*
▶*v.* (**chipped, chip·ping**) **1** cut or break (a piece) from a hard material. **2** (of stone, china, etc.) be apt to break at the edge: *will chip easily.*
□ **chip in** contribute (money or resources) to a joint activity.
□ **chip on one's shoulder** *inf.* deeply ingrained resentment or

grievance. □ **when the chips are down** *inf.* when a difficult situation arises.

**chip·munk** /'CHip,məNGk/ ▶*n.* small ground squirrel having alternate light and dark stripes.

**chip·per** ▶*adj. inf.* cheerful.

**chi·rog·ra·phy** /kī'rägrəfē/ ▶*n.* handwriting, esp. as distinct from typography.

**chi·rop·o·dy** /kə'räpədē/ ▶PODIATRY. —**chi·rop·o·dist** *n.*

**chi·ro·prac·tic** /,kīrə'praktik/ ▶*n.* manipulative treatment of mechanical disorders, esp. of the spinal column. —**chi·ro·prac·tor** *n.*

**chirp** /CHərp/ ▶*v.* (usu. of small birds, grasshoppers, etc.) utter a short, sharp note.
▶*n.* chirping sound.

**chis·el** /'CHizəl/ ▶*n.* hand tool with a squared, beveled blade.
▶*v.* **1** cut or shape with a chisel. **2** *inf.* cheat; swindle. —**chis·el·er** *n.*

**chit** /CHit/ ▶*n.* short official note, memorandum, or voucher, typically recording a sum owed.

**chiv·al·ry** /'SHivəlrē/ ▶*n.* **1** medieval knightly system with its religious, moral, and social code. **2** courteous behavior, esp. of a man toward women.

—**chi·val·ric** *adj.* —**chi·val·rous** *adj.*

**chive** /CHĪv/ ▸*n.* plant with onion-flavored tubular leaves.

**chiv·vy** /ˈCHivē/ (also **chiv·y** ) ▸*v.* (**-vied**) tell (someone) repeatedly to do something.

**chlo·ride** /ˈklôrīd/ ▸*n.* *Chem.* compound of chlorine with another element or group.

**chlo·rine** /ˈklôrˌēn/ ▸*n.* poisonous gaseous element used for purifying water, bleaching, etc. (Symb.: **Cl**)

**chlo·ro·fluor·o·car·bon** /ˌklôrōˌflo͝orōˈkärbən/ ▸*n.* any of a class of compounds of carbon, hydrogen, chlorine, and fluorine, typically gases used chiefly in refrigerants and aerosol propellants. They are known to damage the ozone layer and their use is being phased out.

**chlo·ro·form** /ˈklôrəˌfôrm/ ▸*n.* colorless, volatile, sweet-smelling liquid used as a solvent and formerly used as a general anesthetic.

**chlo·ro·phyll** /ˈklôrəˌfil/ ▸*n.* green pigment found in most plants.

**chock** /CHäk/ ▸*n.* block or wedge of wood to check motion, esp. of a cask or a wheel.
▸*v.* fit or make fast with chocks.

**choc·o·late** /ˈCHäk(ə)lit/ ▸*n.* food preparation made from roasted and ground cacao seeds, usually sweetened.
▸*adj.* made from or of chocolate. —**choc·o·lat·y** *adj.*

**cho·co·la·tier** /ˌCHôk(ə)ləˈti(ə)r/ ▸*n.* maker or seller of chocolate.

**Choc·taw** /ˈCHäkˌtô/ ▸*n.* (*pl.* same or **-taws**) **1 a** N. American people originally from Alabama. **b** member of this people. **2** language of this people.

**choice** /CHois/ ▸*n.* **1 a** act or instance of choosing. **b** thing or person chosen: *not a good choice.* **2** range from which to choose. **3** power or opportunity to choose: *what choice have I?*
▸*adj.* of superior quality; carefully chosen. —**choice·ly** *adv.*

**choir** /ˈkwī(ə)r/ ▸*n.* **1** group of singers, esp. taking part in church services. **2** part of a cathedral or large church used by the choir and clergy.

**choke** /CHōk/ ▸*v.* **1** hinder or impede the breathing of (a person or animal), esp. by

constricting the windpipe or (of gas, smoke, etc.) by being unbreathable. **2** suffer a hindrance or stoppage of breath. **3** make or become speechless from emotion. **4** retard the growth of or kill (esp. plants).
▸*n.* valve of an internal combustion engine that controls the intake of air.
☐ **choke up** become overly anxious or emotionally affected.

**chol·er** /ˈkälər/ ▸*n.* **1** (in medieval science and medicine) one of the four bodily humors, identified with bile, believed to be associated with a peevish or irascible temperament. **2** anger or irascibility.

**chol·er·a** /ˈkälərə/ ▸*n.* infectious and often fatal bacterial disease of the small intestine.

**chol·er·ic** /ˈkälərik; kəˈle(ə)rik/ ▸*adj.* bad-tempered or irritable.

**cho·les·ter·ol** /kəˈlestəˌrôl/ *Biochem.* ▸*n.* fatty animal substance found in most body tissues, including the blood, where high concentrations promote arteriosclerosis.

**chomp** /CHämp/ ▸*v.* **1** munch or chew noisily. **2** (of a horse, etc.) work (the bit) noisily between the teeth.

**choose** /CHo͞oz/ ▸*v.* (*past* **chose**; *past part.* **chos·en**) **1** select out of a greater number. **2** decide; be determined: *chose to stay behind.* —**choos·er** *n.*

**choos·y** ▸*adj.* (**-i·er, -i·est**) *inf.* overly fastidious in making a choice. —**choos·i·ly** *adv.* —**choos·i·ness** *n.*

**chop** /CHäp/ ▸*v.* (**chopped, chop·ping**) **1** cut or fell by a blow, usu. with an ax. **2** cut into small pieces.
▸*n.* **1** cutting blow. **2** thick slice of meat (esp. pork or lamb) usu. including a rib.

**chop·per** ▸*n.* **1** person or thing that chops. **2** *inf.* helicopter.

**chop·py** ▸*adj.* (**-pi·er, -pi·est**) (of the sea, etc.) fairly rough. —**chop·pi·ly** *adv.* —**chop·pi·ness** *n.*

**cho·ral** /ˈkôrəl/ ▸*adj.* of, for, or sung by a choir or chorus.

**cho·rale** /kəˈral/ (also **cho·ral**) ▸*n.* stately and simple hymn tune; harmonized version of this.

**chord** /kôrd/ ▸*n.* **1** group of (usu. three or more) notes sounded together, as a basis of harmony. **2** straight line joining the ends of an arc.

□ **strike a chord** affect or stir someone's emotions.

**chore** /CHôr/ ▶*n.* tedious or routine task, esp. domestic.

**cho·re·og·ra·phy** /ˌkôrēˈägrəfē/ ▶*n.* design or arrangement of a ballet or other staged dance. —**cho·re·o·graph** *v.* —**cho·re·og·ra·pher** *n.*

**cho·ris·ter** /ˈkôrəstər/ ▶*n.* a member of a choir.

**cho·rog·ra·phy** /kəˈrägrəfē/ ▶*n.* systematic description and mapping of regions or districts.

**chor·tle** /ˈCHôrtl/ ▶*v.* chuckle gleefully.
▶*n.* gleeful chuckle.

**cho·rus** /ˈkôrəs/ ▶*n.* (*pl.* **-rus·es**) **1** group (esp. a large one) of singers; choir. **2** refrain or main part of a popular song. **3** group of singers and dancers performing in concert in a musical comedy, opera, etc. **4** in ancient Greek tragedy, a group of performers who comment on the main action.
▶*v.* (of a group) speak or utter simultaneously.

**chow** /CHou/ ▶*n.* **1** *inf.* food. **2** (also **chow chow**) dog of a Chinese breed with long hair and a bluish-black tongue.

**chow·der** /ˈCHoudər/ ▶*n.* rich soup or stew usu. containing fish, clams, or corn with potatoes, onions, etc.

**chres·tom·a·thy** /kreˈstäməTHē/ ▶*n.* (*pl.* **-thies**) selection of passages from an author or authors, designed to help in learning a language.

**chrism** /ˈkrizəm/ ▶*n.* mixture of oil and balsam, consecrated and used for anointing at baptism and in other rites of Catholic, Orthodox, and Anglican Churches.

**chris·om** /ˈkrizəm/ ▶*n.* white robe put on a child at baptism.

**Christ** /krīst/ ▶*n.* **1** title, also now treated as a name, given to Jesus of Nazareth. **2** Messiah as prophesied in the Old Testament. —**Christ·like** *adj.*

**chris·ten** /ˈkrisən/ ▶*v.* **1** give a baby a Christian name at baptism. **2** give a name to. —**chris·ten·ing** *n.*

**Chris·ten·dom** /ˈkrisəndəm/ ▶*n.* Christians worldwide.

**Chris·tian** /ˈkrisCHən/ ▶*adj.* **1** of Christ's teachings or religion. **2** believing in or following the religion based on the teachings of Jesus Christ. **3** showing the qualities associated with Christ's teachings.

▶*n.* adherent of Christianity.
□ **Christian name** first name, esp. as given at baptism.

**Chris·ti·an·i·ty** /ˌkrisCHē'anitē/ ▶*n.* **1** Christian religion. **2** being a Christian. **3** CHRISTENDOM.

**Christ·mas** /'krisməs/ ▶*n.* (*pl.* **-mas·es**) **1** (also **Christmas Day**) annual festival of Christ's birth, celebrated on Dec. 25. **2** season in which this occurs.

**chro·mat·ic** /krō'matik/ ▶*adj.* **1** *Mus.* (of a scale) ascending or descending by semitones. **2** of or produced by color. —**chro·mat·i·cal·ly** *adv.*

**chrome** /krōm/ ▶*n.* **1** chromium, esp. as plating. **2** (also **chrome yellow**) yellow pigment obtained from lead chromate. □ **chrome steel** hard, fine-grained steel containing much chromium and used for tools, etc.

**chro·mi·um** /'krōmēəm/ ▶*n.* hard, white metallic element used as a shiny electroplated coating. (Symb.: **Cr**)
□ **chromium steel** CHROME STEEL.

**chro·mo·some** /'krōmə,sōm/ *Biochem.* ▶*n.* threadlike cellular structures that carry the genetic information in the form of genes. —**chro·mo·so·mal** *adj.*

**chron·ic** /'kränik/ ▶*adj.* **1** persisting for a long time (usu. of an illness or a personal or social problem). **2** having a chronic complaint. **3** having a particular bad habit: *a chronic liar.* —**chron·i·cal·ly** *adv.*

**chron·i·cle** /'känikəl/ ▶*n.* register of events in order of their occurrence.
▶*v.* record (events) in the order of their occurrence.
—**chron·i·cler** *n.*

**chro·nol·o·gy** /krə'näləjē/ ▶*n.* (*pl.* **-gies**) arrangement of events, dates, etc., in the order of their occurrence. —**chron·o·log·i·cal** *adj.* —**chron·o·log·i·cal·ly** *adv.*

**chro·nom·e·ter** /krə'nämətər/ ▶*n.* time-measuring instrument, esp. one keeping accurate time at all temperatures.
—**chro·nom·e·try** *n.*
—**chron·o·met·ric** *adj.*
—**chron·o·met·ri·cal** *adj.*
—**chron·o·met·ri·cal·ly** *adv.*

**chro·nom·e·try** /krə'nämətrē/ ▶*n.* science of accurate time measurement.

**chrys·a·lis** /'krisələs/ (also **chrys·a·lid**) ▶*n.* (*pl.* **-a·lis·es** or **-al·i·des**) **1** quiescent pupa of a butterfly or moth. **2** hard outer case enclosing it.

**chry·san·the·mum** /kri-'saNTHəməm/ ▶*n.* garden plant of the daisy family having brightly colored flowers.

**chthon·ic** /'THänik/ ▶*adj.* concerning, belonging to, or inhabiting the underworld.

**chub·by** /'CHəbē/ ▶*adj.* (**-bi·er, -bi·est**) plump and rounded. —**chub·bi·ness** *n.*

**chuck** /CHək/ ▶*v. inf.* **1** fling or throw carelessly or with indifference. **2** give up; reject; abandon; jilt: *chucked my job.* **3** touch playfully, esp. under the chin.
▶*n.* cut of beef between the neck and the ribs.

**chuck·le** /'CHəkəl/ ▶*v.* laugh quietly or inwardly.
▶*n.* quiet or suppressed laugh.

**chum** /CHəm/ ▶*n. inf.* close friend. —**chum·my** *adj.*

**chump** /CHəmp/ ▶*n. inf.* foolish person.

**chunk** /CHəNGk/ ▶*n.* **1** thick, solid slice or piece of something firm or hard. **2** substantial amount or piece.

**chunk·y** ▶*adj.* (**-i·er, -i·est**) **1** containing or consisting of chunks. **2** short and thick; small and sturdy. —**chunk·i·ness** *n.*

**church** /CHərCH/ ▶*n.* **1** building for public (usu. Christian) worship. **2** meeting for public worship in such a building: *go to church.* **3** (**the Church**) body of all Christians. **4** (**the Church**) the clergy or clerical profession. **5** institutionalized religion as a political or social force: *church and state.*

**churl·ish** /'CHərlisH/ ▶*adj.* surly; mean. —**churl·ish·ly** *adv.* —**churl·ish·ness** *n.*

**churn** /CHərn/ ▶*n.* machine for making butter.
▶*v.* **1** agitate (milk or cream) or make (butter) in a churn. **2** (of a liquid) seethe; foam violently: *the churning sea.*
□ **churn out** produce routinely or mechanically, esp. in large quantities.

**chur·ri·gue·resque** /ˌCHŏŏrigə-'resk/ (also **Chur·ri·gue·resque**) ▶*adj.* of or relating to the lavishly ornamented late Spanish baroque style.

**chute** /SHŏŏt/ ▶*n.* sloping channel or slide, for conveying things to a lower level.

**chut·ney** /'CHətnē/ ▶*n.* (*pl.* **-neys**)

pungent condiment made of fruits or vegetables, vinegar, spices, sugar, etc.

**chutz·pah** /'ho͝otspə; 'ᴋʜo͝otspə; -spä/ ▶n. shameless audacity; impudence.

**chyle** /kīl/ ▶n. milky fluid consisting of fat droplets and lymph. It drains from the small intestine into the lymphatic system during digestion.

**chyme** /kīm/ ▶n. pulpy acidic fluid that passes from the stomach to the small intestine, consisting of gastric juices and partly digested food.

**CIA** ▶abbr. Central Intelligence Agency.

**ci·ca·da** /si'kādə/ ▶n. (pl. **-das** or **-dae**) transparent-winged large insect that makes a loud, rhythmic, chirping sound.

**cic·a·trix** /'sikə,triks/ (also **cic·a·trice** /-,tris/) ▶n. (pl. **cic·a·tri·ces** /,sikə'trīsēz; sə'kātrə-,sēz/) 1 scar of a healed wound. 2 scar on the bark of a tree.

**cic·e·ro·ne** /,sisə'rōnē; ,ᴄʜēᴄʜə-/ ▶n. (pl. **-ro·ni** pronunc. same) guide who gives information about antiquities and places of interest to sightseers.

**-cide** ▶suffix forming nouns meaning: 1 person or substance that kills: regicide. 2 killing of: suicide.

**ci·der** /'sīdər/ ▶n. usu. unfermented drink made from crushed apples.

**ci·de·vant** /,sē də'väN/ ▶adj. from or in an earlier time (used to indicate that someone or something once possessed a specified characteristic but no longer does so).

**ci·gar** /si'gär/ ▶n. tight roll of tobacco leaves for smoking.

**cig·a·rette** /,sigə'ret/ (also **cig·a·ret**) ▶n. thin cylinder of finely cut tobacco rolled in paper for smoking.

**cinch** /sinᴄʜ/ ▶n. 1 inf. very easy task. 2 inf. sure thing; certainty. 3 girth for a saddle or pack. ▶v. 1 secure (a garment) with a belt. 2 fix (a saddle) securely with a girth. 3 inf. make certain of.

**cin·der** /'sindər/ ▶n. small piece of coal or wood, etc., after burning. □ **cinder block** concrete building block.

**cin·e·ma** /'sinəmə/ ▶n. production of films as an art or industry; cinematography. —**cin·e·mat·ic** adj.

**cin·e·ma·tog·ra·phy** /ˌsinəmə-ˈtägrəfē/ ▶n. art of making motion pictures.
—**cin·e·ma·tog·ra·pher** n.

**cin·e·rar·i·um** /ˌsinəˈre(ə)rēəm/ ▶n. (pl. **-ums**) place where the ashes of the cremated dead are kept.

**cin·na·mon** /ˈsinəmən/ ▶n. aromatic spice from the peeled, dried, and rolled bark of a SE Asian tree.

**ci·pher** /ˈsīfər/ ▶n. **1** secret or disguised way of writing using letters or numbers. **2** arithmetical symbol (0; zero). **3** person or thing of no importance.

**cir·ca** /ˈsərkə/ ▶prep. (preceding a date) about.

**cir·ca·di·an** /sərˈkādēən/ ▶adj. (of biological processes) recurring naturally on a twenty-four-hour cycle, even in the absence of light fluctuations.

**cir·cle** /ˈsərkəl/ ▶n. **1** round plane figure whose circumference is everywhere equidistant from its center. **2** roundish enclosure or structure. **3** persons grouped around a center of interest. **4** set or class or restricted group: *literary circles.*
▶v. **1** move in a circle. **2** revolve or form a circle around.

**cir·cuit** /ˈsərkit/ ▶n. **1** line or course enclosing an area; circumference. **2** *Electr.* **a** path of a current. **b** apparatus through which a current passes.
□ **circuit breaker** automatic device for stopping the flow of current in an electrical circuit.

**cir·cu·i·tous** /sərˈkyo͞oitəs/ ▶adj. longer than the most direct way.
—**cir·cu·i·tous·ly** adv.
—**cir·cu·i·tous·ness** n.

**cir·cuit rid·er** ▶n. clergyman who traveled on horseback from church to church, esp. within a rural Methodist circuit.

**cir·cu·lar** /ˈsərkyələr/ ▶adj. **1** forming, moving, or taking place along a circle; indirect; circuitous: *circular route.* **2** *Logic* (of an argument) already containing an assumption of what is to be proved.
▶n. letter, leaflet, etc., distributed to a large number of people.
—**cir·cu·lar·ly** adv.

**cir·cu·late** /ˈsərkyəˌlāt/ ▶v. **1** (cause to) go around an area; put into or be in circulation. **2** be actively sociable at a party, gathering, etc. —**cir·cu·la·tor** n.
—**cir·cu·la·to·ry** adj.

**cir·cu·la·tion** ▸*n.* **1** movement within or around, esp. of blood from and to the heart. **2 a** transmission or distribution (of news, etc.). **b** number of copies sold, esp. of journals and newspapers.
□ **in** (or **out**) **of circulation** participating (or not participating) in activities, etc.

**circum-** ▸*comb. form* round; about; around.

**circum.** ▸*abbr.* circumference.

**cir·cum·am·bi·ent** /ˌsərkəm-ˈambēənt/ ▸*adj.* surrounding.

**cir·cum·cise** /ˈsərkəmˌsīz/ ▸*v.* cut off the foreskin or clitoris. —**cir·cum·ci·sion** *n.*

**cir·cum·fer·ence** /sər-ˈkəmf(ə)rəns/ ▸*n.* **1** enclosing boundary, esp. of a circle. **2** distance around.

**cir·cum·flex** /ˈsərkəmˌfleks/ ▸*n.* mark (^) placed over a vowel in some languages to indicate a contraction or a special quality.

**cir·cum·lo·cu·tion** /ˌsərkəmˌlō-ˈkyo͞oSHən/ ▸*n.* roundabout expression; evasive talk. —**cir·cum·loc·u·to·ry** *adj.*

**cir·cum·nav·i·gate** /ˌsərkəm-ˈnaviˌgāt/ ▸*v.* sail around (esp. the world). —**cir·cum·nav·i·ga·tion** *n.* —**cir·cum·nav·i·ga·tor** *n.*

**cir·cum·scribe** /ˈsərkəmˌskrīb/ ▸*v.* **1** enclose or outline. **2** lay down the limits of; confine. —**cir·cum·scrib·a·ble** *adj.* —**cir·cum·scrip·tion** *n.*

**cir·cum·spect** /ˈsərkəmˌspekt/ ▸*adj.* wary; cautious. —**cir·cum·spec·tion** *n.* —**cir·cum·spect·ly** *adv.*

**cir·cum·stance** /ˈsərkəm-ˌstans/ ▸*n.* **1 a** fact, occurrence, or condition. **b** (**circumstances**) external conditions. **2** (**circumstances**) one's state of financial or material welfare. **3** ceremony; fuss: *pomp and circumstance.*
□ **in** (or **under**) **the** (or **these**) **circumstances** the state of affairs being what it is. □ **under no circumstances** not at all; never.

**cir·cum·stan·tial** /ˌsərkəm-ˈstanCHəl/ ▸*adj.* **1** (of evidence or a legal case) pointing indirectly toward someone's guilt but not conclusively proving it. **2** (of a description) containing full details. —**cir·cum·stan·tial·ly** *adv.*

**cir·cum·vent** /ˌsərkəmˈvent/ ▸*v.* **1** find a way around (an obstacle). **2** evade (a difficulty). —**cir·cum·ven·tion** *n.*

**cir·cus** /ˈsərkəs/ ▶n. (pl. **-cus·es**) **1** traveling show of performing animals, acrobats, clowns, etc. **2** inf. scene of lively action; a disturbance.

**cir·rho·sis** /səˈrōsəs/ ▶n. chronic disease of the liver, a result of alcoholism, hepatitis, etc. —**cir·rhot·ic** adj.

**cir·rus** /ˈsirəs/ ▶n. (pl. **-ri**) white wispy cloud, esp. at high altitude.

**cis·tern** /ˈsistərn/ ▶n. **1** tank or container for storing water, etc. **2** underground reservoir for rainwater.

**cit·a·del** /ˈsitədl/ ▶n. fortress, usu. on high ground protecting or dominating a city.

**ci·ta·tion** /sīˈtāsHən/ ▶n. **1** quotation from or reference to a book, paper, or author, esp. in a scholarly work. **2** mention of a praiseworthy act or achievement in an official report, esp. that of a member of the armed forces in wartime. **3** note accompanying an award, describing the reasons for it. **4** reference to a former tried case, used as guidance in the trying of comparable cases or in support of an argument. **5** summons.

**cite** /sīt/ ▶v. **1** adduce as an instance. **2** quote (a passage, etc.) in support. **3** summon to appear in a court of law. —**cit·a·tion** n.

**cit·i·zen** /ˈsitizən/ ▶n. member of a country, state, city, etc. —**cit·i·zen·ry** n. —**cit·i·zen·ship** n.

**cit·ron** /ˈsitrən/ ▶n. **1** shrubby tree bearing large lemonlike fruits with thick fragrant peel. **2** this fruit.

**cit·ro·nel·la** /ˌsitrəˈnelə/ ▶n. scented oil used in insect repellent, perfume, and soap manufacture.

**cit·rus** /ˈsitrəs/ ▶n. **1** tree of a group including citron, lemon, lime, orange, and grapefruit. **2** (also **cit·rus fruit**) fruit from such a tree.

**cit·y** /ˈsitē/ ▶n. (pl. **-ies**) **1** large town. **2** state-chartered municipal corporation occupying a definite area.

**civ·et** /ˈsivət/ ▶n. (also **civet cat**) **1** slender nocturnal carnivorous mammal with a barred and spotted coat and well-developed anal scent glands, native to Africa and Asia. **2** strong musky perfume obtained from the secretions of the civet's scent glands.

**civ·ic** /ˈsivik/ ▶adj. **1** of a city;

municipal. **2** of or proper to citizens: *civic virtues.*

**civ·ics** ▶*n.* the study of the rights and duties of citizenship.

**civ·il** /ˈsivəl/ ▶*adj.* **1** of or belonging to citizens. **2** of ordinary citizens and their concerns, as distinct from military or ecclesiastical matters. **3** polite; obliging; not rude. **4** *Law* concerning private rights and not criminal offenses. —**civ·il·ly** *adv.*

☐ **civil disobedience** refusal to comply with certain laws or to pay taxes, etc., as a peaceful form of political protest. ☐ **civil liberty** freedom of action and speech subject to the law. ☐ **civil rights** rights of citizens to political and social freedom and equality. ☐ **civil servant** member of the civil service. ☐ **civil service** nonelected civilian branches of governmental administration. ☐ **civil war** war between citizens of the same country.

**ci·vil·ian** /səˈvilyən/ ▶*n.* person not in the armed services or the police force.
▶*adj.* of or for civilians.

**ci·vil·i·ty** /səˈvilətē/ ▶*n. (pl.* **-ties)**

formal politeness and courtesy in behavior or speech.

**civ·i·li·za·tion** /ˌsivələˈzāsHən/ ▶*n.* **1** advanced stage or system of social development. **2** those peoples of the world regarded as having this. **3** a people or nation (esp. of the past) regarded as an element of social evolution.

**civ·i·lize** /ˈsivəˌlīz/ ▶*v.* **1** bring out of a less developed stage of society. **2** refine and educate.

**civ·il law** ▶*n.* **1** system of law concerned with private relations between members of a community rather than criminal, military, or religious affairs. **2** system of law predominant on the European continent and of which a form is in force in Louisiana, historically influenced by the codes of ancient Rome.

**Cl** ▶*symb. Chem.* chlorine.

**cl** ▶*abbr.* **1** centiliter(s). **2** class.

**cla·dis·tics** /kləˈdistiks/ ▶ *n.* method of classification of organisms according to the proportion of measurable characteristics that they share.

**claim** /klām/ ▶*v.* **1** demand as one's due or property. **2** represent oneself as having or achieving: *claim victory.* **3** assert; contend: *claim that one knows.* **4** have as an achievement or a consequence: *the fire claimed many victims.*

▸*n.* **1** demand or request for something considered one's due: *lay claim to.* **2** right or title. **3** contention or assertion. **4** thing claimed. —**claim·a·ble** *adj.* —**claim·ant** *n.*

**clair·voy·ance** /kle(ə)r'voiəns/ ▸*n.* supposed faculty of perceiving things or events in the future or beyond normal sensory contact. —**clair·voy·ant** *adj.*

**clam** /klam/ ▸*n.* edible bivalve mollusk.
▸*v.* (**clammed, clam·ming**) **1** dig for clams. **2** (**clam up**) refuse to talk.

**cla·mant** /'klāmənt; 'klam-/ ▸*adj.* forcing itself urgently on the attention.

**clam·ber** /'klambər/ ▸*v.* climb with hands and feet, esp. with difficulty or laboriously.
▸*n.* difficult climb.

**clam·my** /'klamē/ ▸*adj.* (**-mi·er, -mi·est**) unpleasantly damp and sticky. —**clam·mi·ness** *n.*

**clam·or** /'klamər/ ▸*n.* **1** loud or vehement shouting or noise. **2** protest; demand.
▸*v.* **1** shout loudly. **2** protest or demand vehemently. —**clam·or·ous** *adj.*

**clamp** /klamp/ ▸*n.* device, esp. a brace or band of iron, etc., for strengthening other materials or holding things together.
▸*v.* **1** strengthen or fasten with a clamp. **2** place or hold firmly.
□ **clamp down on** put a stop to.

**clan** /klan/ ▸*n.* **1** group of people with a common ancestor. **2** group with a strong common interest. —**clan·nish** *adj.*

**clan·des·tine** /klan'destin/ ▸*adj.* surreptitious; secret. —**clan·des·tine·ly** *adv.*

**clang** /klaNG/ ▸*n.* loud, resonant, metallic sound.
▸*v.* make a clang.

**clang·or** /'klaNGər/ ▸*n.* continuous loud banging or ringing sound.

**clank** /klaNGk/ ▸*n.* sound as of heavy pieces of metal meeting or a chain rattling.
▸*v.* make a clanking sound.

**clap** /klap/ ▸*v.* (**clapped, clap·ping**) strike the palms of one's hands together as a signal or repeatedly as applause.
▸*n.* **1** act of clapping, esp. as

applause. **2** explosive sound, esp. of thunder. **3** slap; pat.

**clap·board** /ˈklabərd/ ▸n. overlapping long, thin, flat pieces of wood, used to cover the outer walls of buildings.

**clap·trap** ▸n. insincere or pretentious talk.

**clar·et** /ˈklarit/ ▸n. red wine, esp. from Bordeaux.

**clar·i·fy** /ˈklarəˌfī/ ▸v. (**-fied**) make or become clearer. —**clar·i·fi·ca·tion** n.

**clar·i·net** /ˌklarəˈnet/ ▸n. woodwind instrument with a single-reed mouthpiece. —**clar·i·net·ist** n.

**clar·i·on** /ˈklarēən/ ▸n. clear, rousing sound.

**clar·i·ty** /ˈklaritē/ ▸n. state or quality of being clear, esp. of sound or expression.

**clash** /klasH/ ▸n. **1** violent confrontation. **2** incompatibility leading to disagreement. **3** mismatch of colors. **4** loud, jarring sound as of metal objects being struck together. ▸v. **1** come into conflict or be discordant. **2** collide; coincide awkwardly. **3** make a clashing sound.

**clasp** /klasp/ ▸n. **1** device with interlocking parts for fastening.
**2 a** embrace. **b** grasp or handshake.
▸v. **1** fasten with or as with a clasp. **2** grasp; hold closely.

**class** /klas/ ▸n. **1** any set of persons or things grouped together, or graded or differentiated from others. **2** *Biol.* grouping of organisms, below a division or phylum. **3** *inf.* distinction; high quality. **4 a** group of students taught together. **b** occasion when they meet.
▸v. assign to a class or category: *conduct that is classed as criminal.*
□ **class-conscious** aware of one's place in a system of social class.

**clas·sic** /ˈklasik/ ▸adj. **a** of the first class; of acknowledged excellence. **b** remarkably typical; outstandingly important: *a classic case.* **c** having enduring worth; timeless.
▸n. **1** work of art of recognized or established value. **2** (usu. **Classics**) school subject that involves the study of ancient Greek and Latin literature and history. **3** thing that is a good example of its kind.

**class·i·cal** ▸adj. **1** of ancient Greek or Roman civilization.

**2** following traditional principles of form and style.

**clas·si·cism** /'klasə₁sizəm/ ▸*n.* following of ancient Greek or Roman principles and style in art and literature, esp. from the Renaissance to the 18th c.

**clas·si·fy** ▸*v.* (**-fied**) **1** arrange in classes or categories. **2** designate (information, etc.) as officially secret. —**clas·si·fi·able** *adj.* —**clas·si·fi·ca·tion** *n.* —**clas·si·fied** *adj.*

**class·ism** /'klas₁izəm/ ▸*n.* prejudice against or in favor of people belonging to a particular social class.

**class·y** ▸*adj.* (**-i·er**, **-i·est**) *inf.* superior; stylish.

**clat·ter** /'klatər/ ▸*n.* rattling sound as of many hard objects struck together.

**clause** /klôz/ ▸*n.* **1** *Gram.* distinct part of a sentence, including a subject and predicate. **2** single statement in a treaty, law, bill, or contract.

**claus·tro·pho·bi·a** /₁klôstrə-'fōbēə/ ▸*n.* abnormal fear of confined places. —**claus·tro·pho·bic** *adj.*

**clav·i·chord** /'klavi₁kôrd/ ▸*n.* small keyboard instrument with a very soft tone.

**clav·i·cle** /'klavikəl/ ▸*n.* collarbone.

**claw** /klô/ ▸*n.* **1** pointed horny nail on an animal's foot. **2** pincers of a shellfish. ▸*v.* scratch, maul, or pull with claws or fingernails.

**clay** /klā/ ▸*n.* stiff, sticky earth, used for making bricks, pottery, ceramics, etc.

**clean** /klēn/ ▸*adj.* **1** free from dirt or contaminating matter; unsoiled. **2** clear; unused or unpolluted; pristine. **3** free from obscenity or indecency. **4** attentive to personal hygiene. **5** complete: *make a clean break.* **6** streamlined; well-formed. **7** free from any record of a crime, offense, etc. ▸*adv.* **1** completely; outright; simply: *clean forgot.* **2** in a clean manner. ▸*v.* make or become clean. —**clean·er** *n.*
▫ **clean-cut** **1** sharply outlined. **2** neatly groomed. ▫ **clean out 1** clean or clear thoroughly. **2** *inf.* empty or deprive (esp. of money). ▫ **clean up 1 a** clear (a mess) away. **b** make (things) neat. **c** make (oneself) clean. **2** restore order or morality to. **3** *inf.* make a substantial profit.

□ **come clean** *inf.* confess everything.

**clean·ly**[1] /ˈklēnlē/ ▸*adv.* **1** in a clean way. **2** efficiently; without difficulty.

**clean·ly**[2] /ˈklenlē/ ▸*adj.* (**-li·er, -li·est**) habitually clean; with clean habits. —**clean·li·ness** *n.*

**cleanse** /klenz/ ▸*v.* make clean or pure. —**cleans·er** *n.*

**clear** /ˈkli(ə)r/ ▸*adj.* **1** easy to perceive, understand, or interpret. **2** free from dirt or contamination. **3** (of weather, the sky, etc.) not dull or cloudy. **4** transparent: *the clear glass of the French windows.* **5** free of obstructions: *I had a clear view in both directions.* **6** (of a person) free of something undesirable: *after 5 years, she is free of cancer.* **7** (of a person's conscience) free of guilt. **8** without deduction; net: *a clear $1,000.* **9** (of a period of time) free of commitments.
▸*adv.* **1** clearly. **2** completely: *he got clear away.* **3** apart; out of contact: *keep clear.*
▸*v.* **1** make or become clear. **2** show or declare (a person) to be innocent. **3** give official approval for. **4** pass over or by safely or without touching. **5** make (an amount of money) as a net gain. —**clear·ly** *adv.* —**clear·ness** *n.*

□ **clear the air** disperse suspicion, tension, etc. □ **clear-cut 1** sharply defined. **2** obvious. □ **clear out 1** empty. **2** remove. **3** *inf.* go away. □ **in the clear** free from suspicion or difficulty.

**clear·ance** ▸*n.* **1** removal of obstructions, etc. **2** clear space allowed for the passing of two objects or two parts in machinery, etc. **3** special authorization or permission.

□ **clearance sale** sale to get rid of superfluous stock.

**clear·ing** ▸*n.* area in a forest cleared for cultivation.

**clear·ing·house** ▸*n.* **1** bankers' establishment where checks and bills are exchanged and resolved. **2** agency for collecting and distributing information.

**cleat** /klēt/ ▸*n.* **1** fixed piece of metal, wood, etc., for fastening ropes to, or to strengthen woodwork, etc. **2** projecting piece to give footing or prevent slipping. **3** (**cleats**) athletic shoes with cleated soles.

**cleav·age** /ˈklēvij/ ▸*n.* **1** hollow between a woman's breasts. **2** division; splitting.

**cleave**[1] /klēv/ ▶*v.* (*past* **cleaved** or **cleft** or **clove**; *past part.* **cleaved** or **cleft** or **clo·ven**) split; divide.

**cleave**[2] ▶*v.* (*past* **cleaved** or **clove** or **clave**) *poet.* stick fast to; adhere.

**cleav·er** ▶*n.* heavy tool for cutting or chopping.

**clef** /klef/ ▶*n. Mus.* symbol placed at the beginning of a staff, indicating the pitch of the notes written on it.

**cleft** /kleft/ ▶*adj.* split; partly divided.
▶*n.* split; fissure.
□ **cleft lip** (or **cleft palate**) congenital split in the lip or the roof of the mouth.

**cle·ma·tis** /ˈklemətəs; kləˈmatəs/ ▶*n.* erect or climbing plant bearing white, pink, or purple flowers and feathery seeds.

**clem·ent** /ˈklemənt/ ▶*adj.* **1** mild: *clement weather.* **2** merciful. —**clem·en·cy** *n.*

**clench** /klenCH/ ▶*v.* **1** close (teeth or fingers) tightly. **2** grasp firmly.
▶*n.* clenching action or state.

**clep·sy·dra** /ˈklepsədrə/ ▶*n.* (*pl.* **-dras** or **-drae** /-ˌdrē; -ˌdrī/) ancient time-measuring device worked by a flow of water.

**cler·gy** /ˈklərjē/ ▶*n.* (*pl.* **-gies**) (**the clergy**) the body of all persons ordained for religious duties.

**cler·ic** /ˈklerik/ ▶*n.* member of the clergy.

**cler·i·cal** ▶*adj.* **1** of the clergy or a member of the clergy. **2** of or done by a clerk or clerks.

**cler·i·hew** /ˈklerəˌhyoo/ ▶*n.* short comic or nonsensical verse, typically in two rhyming couplets with lines of unequal length and referring to a famous person.

**clerk** /klərk/ ▶*n.* **1** person employed to keep records, accounts, etc. **2** secretary, agent, or record keeper of a municipality, court, etc. **3** person employed by a judge or being trained by a lawyer.
▶*v.* work as a clerk. —**clerk·ship** *n.*

**clev·er** /ˈklevər/ ▶*adj.* (**-er·er, -er·est**) skillful; talented; quick; adroit; ingenious; cunning. —**clev·er·ly** *adv.* —**clev·er·ness** *n.*

**cli·ché** /klēˈSHā/ (also **cli·che**) ▶*n.* phrase or opinion that is overused and shows no original thought. —**cli·chéd** *adj.*

**click** /klik/ ▶*n.* **1** slight, sharp sound. **2** *Computing* pressing a mouse button.

▶*v.* **1** make a click. **2** cause (one's tongue, heels, etc.) to click. **3** *Computing* press (a mouse button). —**click·er** *n.*

**cli·ent** /ˈklīənt/ ▶*n.* person using the services of a lawyer, architect, social worker, or other professional person.

**cli·en·tele** /ˌklīənˈtel/ ▶*n.* clients collectively.

**cliff** /klif/ ▶*n.* steep rock face, as at the edge of the sea. —**cliff·like** *adj.*

**cliff·hang·er** ▶*n.* very suspenseful story, ending, etc.

**cli·mac·ter·ic** /klīˈmaktərik; ˌklīmakˈterik/ ▶*n.* **1** critical period or event. **2** period of life when fertility and sexual activity are in decline; (in women) menopause.

▶*adj.* having extreme and far-reaching implications or results; critical.

**cli·mac·tic** /klīˈmaktik; klə-/ ▶*adj.* (of an action, event, or scene) exciting or thrilling and acting as a climax to a series of events.

**cli·mate** /ˈklīmit/ ▶*n.* **1** prevailing weather conditions. **2** region with particular weather conditions: *vacationing in a warm climate.* **3** prevailing trend of an aspect of public life: *the current economic climate.* —**cli·mat·ic** *adj.*

**cli·max** /ˈklīˌmaks/ ▶*n.* **1** event or point of greatest intensity or interest; culmination or apex. **2** sexual orgasm. —**cli·mac·tic** *adj.*

**climb** /klīm/ ▶*v.* ascend; mount; go or come up.

▶*n.* **1** ascent by climbing. **2** place, esp. a hill, climbed or to be climbed. —**climb·a·ble** *adj.* —**climb·er** *n.*

**clime** /klīm/ ▶*n.* (usu. **climes**) region considered with reference to its climate.

**clinch** /klinCH/ ▶*v.* **1** confirm or settle (an argument, bargain, etc.) conclusively. **2** secure (a nail or rivet) by driving the point sideways when through.

▶*n.* **1** clinching action or state. **2** *inf.* embrace.

**cling** /kliNG/ ▶*v.* (*past* and *past part.* **clung**) **1** adhere, stick, or hold on. **2** remain persistently or stubbornly faithful (to a friend, habit, idea, etc.). **3** maintain one's grasp; keep hold; resist separation. —**cling·y** *adj.* —**cling·i·ness** *n.*

**clin·ic** /'klinik/ ▶n. **1** private or specialized hospital. **2** place or occasion for giving specialist medical treatment or advice. **3** instructional session: *ski clinic.* —**cli·ni·cian** *n.*

**cli·ni·cian** /klə'nisHən/ ▶n. doctor having direct contact with and responsibility for patients, rather than one involved with theoretical or laboratory studies.

**clink** /kliNGk/ ▶n. sharp ringing sound.

▶v. (cause to) make such a sound.

**clink·er** ▶n. **1** mass of slag or lava. **2** stony residue from burned coal. **3** *inf.* mistake or blunder.

**cli·o·met·rics** /ˌklīə'metriks/ ▶n. technique for the interpretation of economic history, based on the statistical analysis of large-scale numerical data from population censuses, parish registers, and similar sources.

**clip** /klip/ ▶n. **1** device for holding objects together or in place. **2** piece of jewelry fastened by a clip. **3** short sequence from a motion picture. **4** *inf.* speed, esp. rapid.

▶v. cut with shears or scissors, esp. cut short or trim (hair, wool, etc.).

**clip·per** ▶n. **1** (usu. **clippers**) instrument for clipping hair, hedges, etc. **2** fast sailing ship.

**clique** /klēk/ ▶n. small exclusive group of people. —**cli·quish** *adj.* —**cli·quish·ness** *n.*

**cli·to·ris** /'klitərəs/ ▶n. small erectile part of the female genitals at the upper end of the vulva.

**clo·a·ca** /klō'ākə/ ▶n. (*pl.* **-cae** /-ˌkē; -ˌsē/) common cavity at the end of the digestive tract for the release of both excretory and genital products in birds, reptiles, amphibians, most fish, and monotremes.

**cloak** /klōk/ ▶n. **1** outdoor overgarment, usu. sleeveless, that hangs loosely from the shoulders. **2** covering: *cloak of snow.*

▶v. cover; conceal.

**clob·ber** /'kläbər/ ▶v. *inf.* **1** hit hard. **2** defeat.

**cloche** /klōsH/ ▶n. **1** small translucent cover for protecting or forcing outdoor plants. **2** (also **cloche hat**) woman's close-fitting, bell-shaped hat.

**clock** /kläk/ ▶n. **1** instrument for measuring and showing time.

**2** any measuring device resembling a clock.

▶*v.* attain or register (a stated time, distance, or speed, esp. in a race).

**clock·wise** ▶*adj. & adv.* in a curve corresponding in direction to the movement of the hands of a clock.

**clock·work** ▶*n.* mechanism of or like that of a clock.

□ **like clockwork** smoothly; regularly; automatically.

**clod** /kläd/ ▶*n.* **1** lump of earth, clay, etc. **2** *inf.* silly or foolish person.

**clog** /kläg/ ▶*n.* **1** shoe with a thick wooden sole. **2** impediment.

▶*v.* (**clogged, clog·ging**) obstruct or become obstructed; choke.

**cloi·son·né** /ˌkloizəˈnā/ ▶*n.* enamel work in which the different colors are separated by strips of flattened wire placed edgeways on a metal backing.

**clois·ter** /ˈkloistər/ ▶*n.* **1** covered walk, often open to a courtyard on one side. **2** convent or monastery.

▶*v.* seclude.

**clois·tered** ▶*adj.* **1** kept away from the outside world;

sheltered. **2** having or enclosed by a cloister, as in a monastery.

**clone** /klōn/ ▶*n.* **1** group of organisms produced asexually from one stock or ancestor. **2** person or thing regarded as identical with another.

▶*v.* (produce) a clone (of).

**close**¹ /klōs/ ▶*adj.* **1** situated at only a short distance or interval. **2 a** having a strong or immediate relation or connection: *close friend.* **b** corresponding almost exactly: *close resemblance.* **3** dense; compact. **4** in which competitors are almost equal: *close contest.* **5** concentrated; searching: *close attention.* **6** (of air, etc.) stuffy or humid.

▶*adv.* at only a short distance or interval: *they live close to us.* —**close·ly** *adv.*

□ **close-knit** tightly bound or interlocked; closely united in friendship. □ **close shave** *inf.* narrow escape. □ **close-up 1** photograph, etc., taken at close range. **2** intimate description.

**close**² /klōz/ ▶*v.* **1** shut or become shut. **2** bring or come to an end. **3** bring or come closer or into contact.

▸*n.* conclusion; end. —**clos·a·ble** *adj.* —**clos·er** *n.*

□ **close down** discontinue business. □ **close in** **1** enclose. **2** come nearer.

**closed shop** ▸*n.* place of work where membership in a union is a condition for being hired and for continued employment.

**clos·et** /ˈkläzit/ ▸*n.* small room or cupboard for storing things. ▸*adj* secret; covert: *closet drinker*. ▸*v.* (**clos·et·ed**, **clos·et·ing**) shut away.

**clo·sure** /ˈklōzhər/ ▸*n.* **1** act or process of closing something, esp. an institution, thoroughfare, or frontier, or of being closed. **2** thing that closes or seals something, such as a cap or zipper. **3** resolution or conclusion to a work or process.

**clot** /klät/ ▸*n.* thick mass of coagulated liquid, esp. of blood. ▸*v.* (**clot·ted**, **clot·ting**) form into clots.

**cloth** /klôth/ ▸*n.* (*pl.* **cloths**) **1** woven or felted material. **2** piece of this. **3** (**the cloth**) the clergy.

**clothe** /klōth/ ▸*v.* (*past* and *past part.* **clothed** or **clad**) **1** provide with clothes. **2** cover as with clothes.

**clothes** /klō(th)z/ ▸*pl. n.* garments worn to cover the body and limbs.

**cloth·ier** /ˈklōthyər; -thēər/ ▸*n.* person or company that makes, sells, or deals in clothes or cloth.

**cloth·ing** /ˈklōthing/ ▸*n.* clothes collectively.

**cloud** /kloud/ ▸*n.* **1** visible mass of condensed watery vapor floating above the ground. **2** mass of smoke, dust, etc. **3** state of gloom, trouble, or suspicion. ▸*v.* become covered with clouds or gloom or trouble. —**cloud·less** *adj.* —**cloud·y** *adj.*

□ **under a cloud** out of favor, under suspicion. □ **with one's head in the clouds** daydreaming; unrealistic.

**cloud cham·ber** ▸*n.* device that contains air or gas supersaturated with water vapor and that is used to detect charged particles, X-rays, and gamma rays by the condensation trails that they produce.

**clout** /klout/ ▸*n.* **1** heavy blow. **2** *inf.* influence; power: *I knew he carried a lot of clout.* ▸*v.* hit hard.

**clove** /klōv/ ▸*n.* **1** dried flower bud of a tropical plant used as a pungent aromatic spice. **2** any of the small bulbs making up a compound bulb of garlic, shallot, etc.

▶past of CLEAVE.

**clo·ver** /ˈklōvər/ ▶n. plant with dense globular flowerheads and typically three-lobed leaves, used for fodder.

□ **in clover** in ease and luxury.

**clown** /kloun/ ▶n. **1** comic entertainer, esp. in a pantomime or circus. **2** silly, foolish, or playful person.

▶v. behave like a clown.

**cloy** /kloi/ ▶v. disgust or sicken (someone) with an excess of sweetness, richness, or sentiment. —**cloy·ing** adj.

**club** /kləb/ ▶n. **1** association of persons meeting periodically. **2** members' organization or premises. **3** organization offering subscribers certain benefits: *book club*. **4** heavy stick with a thick end, used as a weapon, etc. **5** headed stick used in golf. **6** (**clubs**) suit of playing cards marked with black clover leaves.

▶v. (**clubbed**, **club·bing**) beat with or as with a club.

**club·ba·ble** /ˈkləbəbəl/ ▶adj. suitable for membership of a club because of one's sociability or popularity.

**club·by** ▶adj. (-**bi·er**, -**bi·est**) friendly and sociable with fellow members of a group or organization but not with outsiders.

**club·foot** ▶n. congenitally deformed foot.

**cluck** /klək/ ▶n. **1** guttural sound like that of a hen. **2** similar sound made by a person to express annoyance.

▶v. emit a cluck or clucks.

**clue** /kloo/ ▶n. **1** fact or idea that serves as a guide, or suggests a line of inquiry, in a problem or investigation. **2** piece of evidence. **3** verbal hint in a crossword.

**clump** /kləmp/ ▶n. cluster or mass.

▶v. **1** form into a clump. **2** (also **clomp**) walk with a heavy tread. —**clump·y** adj.

**clum·sy** /ˈkləmzē/ ▶adj. (-**si·er**, -**si·est**) **1** awkward in movement or shape. **2** difficult to handle or use. —**clum·si·ly** adv. —**clum·si·ness** n.

**clus·ter** /ˈkləstər/ ▶n. aggregated or close group or bunch.

▶v. be or come into a cluster or clusters.

**clutch** /kləCH/ ▶v. seize eagerly; grasp tightly.

▶n. **1** tight grasp. **2** set of eggs for hatching. **3** brood of chickens. **4** (**clutches**) cruel or relentless grasp or control: *he narrowly escaped the clutches of the Nazis.* **5 a** (in a vehicle) device for connecting and disconnecting the engine from the transmission. **b** control operating this.

**clut·ter** /ˈklətər/ ▶n. **1** collection of things lying about untidily. **2** untidy state.

▶v. crowd untidily: *luggage cluttered the hallway.*

**Cm** ▶*symb. Chem.* curium.

**cm** ▶*abbr.* centimeter(s).

**CO** ▶*abbr.* **1** carbon monoxide. **2** Colorado (in official postal use). **3** commanding officer.

**Co** ▶*symb. Chem.* cobalt.

**Co.** ▶*abbr.* **1** company. **2** county.

**c/o** ▶*abbr.* care of.

**co-** ▶*prefix* **1** nouns, with the sense 'joint, mutual, common': *coauthor.* **2** adjectives and adverbs, with the sense 'jointly, mutually': *coequal | coequally.* **3** verbs, with the sense 'together with another or others': *coauthor.*

**coach** /kōCH/ ▶n. **1** bus, usu. comfortably equipped for longer journeys. **2** railroad car. **3** horse-drawn carriage, usu. closed. **4** instructor or trainer in a sport, etc.

▶v. train or teach as a coach.

**co·ag·u·late** /kōˈagyəˌlāt/ ▶v. change or cause to change from a fluid to a solid or semisolid state: *blood had coagulated around the edges of the wound.*
—**co·ag·u·lant** *n.*
—**co·ag·u·la·tion** *n.*

**coal** /kōl/ ▶n. **1** hard black mineral used as fuel. **2** red-hot piece of coal, wood, etc., in a fire.

**co·a·lesce** /ˌkōəˈles/ ▶v. come together and form one whole.

**co·a·li·tion** /ˌkōəˈlisHən/ ▶n. temporary alliance for combined action, esp. of political parties.

**coarse** /kôrs/ ▶adj. **1** rough or loose in texture or grain; made of large particles. **2** lacking refinement; crude; obscene.
—**coarse·ly** *adv.*
—**coarse·ness** *n.*

**coast** /kōst/ ▶n. border of the land near the sea; seashore.

▶v. **1** ride or move, usu. downhill, without use of power. **2** make progress without much effort.
—**coast·al** *adj.*

**coast·er** ▶n. small tray or mat for a bottle or glass.

**coat** /kōt/ ▸n. **1** outer garment with sleeves and often extending below the hips. **2** animal's fur, hair, etc. **3** single covering of paint, etc.
▸v. **1 a** provide with a layer or covering. **b** [as adj. **coated**] cover with. **2** (of paint, etc.) form a covering to.

**coat·ing** ▸n. thin layer or covering of paint, etc.

**coat of arms** ▸n. heraldic bearings or shield of a person, family, or corporation.

**coax** /kōks/ ▸v. **1** persuade (a person) gradually or by flattery. **2** manipulate (a thing) carefully or slowly. —**coax·ing·ly** adv.

**co·ax·i·al** /kō'aksēəl/ ▸adj. **1** having a common axis. **2** Electr. (of a cable or line) transmitting by means of two concentric conductors separated by an insulator.

**cob** /käb/ ▸n. **1** (also **corn·cob**) central woody part of the corn ear to which the kernels are attached. **2** sturdy riding or driving horse with short legs. **3** male swan.

**co·balt** /'kō,bôlt/ ▸n. silvery-white, magnetic metallic element. (Symb.: **Co**)
□ **cobalt blue 1** pigment

containing a cobalt salt. **2** deep-blue color of this.

**cob·ble** /'käbəl/ ▸n. (also **cob·ble·stone**) small rounded stone of a size used for paving.
▸v. **1** pave with cobbles. **2** mend or patch up (esp. shoes). **3** (**cobble something together**) join or assemble roughly. —**cob·bler** n.

**co·bra** /'kōbrə/ ▸n. venomous snake of Africa and Asia.

**cob·web** /'käb,web/ ▸n. **1** fine network of threads spun by a spider from a liquid secreted by it. **2** thread of this. —**cob·webbed** adj.

**co·ca** /'kōkə/ ▸n. **1** tropical American shrub that is widely grown for its leaves, which are the source of cocaine. **2** dried leaves of this shrub, chewed as a stimulant by the native people of western South America.

**co·caine** /kō'kān/ ▸n. drug used illegally as a stimulant.

**coc·cyx** /'käksiks/ ▸n. (pl. **coc·cy·ges** /'käksə,jēz/ or **coc·cyx·es** small, triangular bone at the base of the spinal column in humans and some apes, formed of fused vestigial vertebrae.

**coch·i·neal** /'käcHə,nēəl; 'kō-/

▶*n.* **1** scarlet dye used chiefly for coloring food. **2** scale insect that is used to make cochineal, native to Mexico and formerly widely cultivated on cacti.

**cock** /käk/ ▶*n.* **1** male bird, esp. of a domestic fowl. **2** firing lever in a gun. **3** tap or valve controlling flow. ▶*v.* **1** turn or move (the eye or ear) attentively or knowingly. **2** set aslant, or turn up the brim of (a hat). **3** raise the cock of (a gun). □ **cock-and-bull story** absurd or incredible account.

**cock·a·hoop** /ˌkäk ə ˈho͞op; ˈho͞op/ ▶*adj.* extremely and obviously pleased, esp. about a triumph or success.

**cock·a·lo·rum** /ˌkäkəˈlôrəm/ ▶*n.* (*pl.* **-rums**) self-important little man.

**cock·a·ma·mie** /ˈkäkəˌmāmē/ ▶*adj.* ridiculous; implausible.

**cock·a·too** /ˈkäkəˌto͞o/ ▶*n.* crested parrot.

**cock·eyed** *inf.* ▶*adj.* **1** crooked; askew; not level. **2** (of a scheme, etc.) absurd; not practical.

**cock·le** /ˈkäkəl/ ▶*n.* **1** bivalve edible mollusk. **2** (also **cock·le·shell**) its shell.

**cock·ney** /ˈkäknē/ ▶*n.* (*pl.* **-neys**) **1** native of London, esp. of the East End. **2** dialect or accent typical of this area.

**cock·pit** ▶*n.* compartment for the pilot (or the pilot and crew) of an airplane or other craft.

**cock·roach** ▶*n.* flat brown verminous insect.

**cock·tail** ▶*n.* **1** usu. alcoholic drink made by mixing various spirits, fruit juices, etc. **2** dish of mixed ingredients: *fruit cocktail*. **3** any hybrid mixture.

**cock·y** ▶*adj.* (**-i·er, -i·est**) conceited; arrogant. —**cock·i·ly** *adv.* —**cock·i·ness** *n.*

**co·coa** /ˈkōkō/ ▶*n.* **1** powder made from crushed cacao seeds, often with other ingredients. **2** hot drink made from this. □ **cocoa butter** fatty substance obtained from cocoa beans.

**co·co·nut** /ˈkōkəˌnət/ ▶*n.* large ovate brown seed of a tropical palm, with a hard shell and edible white fleshy lining enclosing a milky juice.

**co·coon** /kəˈko͞on/ ▶*n.* **1** silky case spun by many insect larvae for protection as pupae. **2** protective covering.

**co·cotte** /kôˈkôt/ ▶*n.* **1** (usu. **en cocotte**) covered, heatproof dish or casserole in which food can be both cooked and served; Dutch oven. **2** fashionable prostitute.

**COD** ▶*abbr.* cash or collect on delivery.

**cod** /käd/ ▶*n.* (*pl.* same) large marine fish used as food.

□ **cod-liver oil** oil pressed from the fresh liver of cod, which is rich in vitamins D and A.

**co·da** /ˈkōdə/ ▶*n. Mus.* concluding passage of a piece or movement.

**cod·dle** /ˈkädl/ ▶*v.* **1** treat as an invalid; protect attentively. **2** cook (an egg) in water below boiling point.

**code** /kōd/ ▶*n.* **1** system of words, letters, figures, or symbols, used to represent others for secrecy or brevity. **2** system of laws, etc. **3** standard of moral behavior.
▶*v.* put into code.

**co·deine** /ˈkōˌdēn/ ▶*n.* analgesic alkaloid from morphine.

**co·dex** /ˈkōˌdeks/ ▶*n.* (*pl.* **co·di·ces** /ˈkōdəˌsēz; ˈkäd-/ or **co·dex·es**) **1** ancient manuscript text in book form. **2** official list of medicines, chemicals, etc.

**cod·ger** /ˈkäjər/ ▶*n.* elderly man, esp. one who is eccentric: *old codgers always harp on about yesteryear.*

**cod·i·cil** /ˈkädəˌsil/ ▶*n.* addition explaining, modifying, or revoking a will or part of one.

**cod·i·fy** /ˈkädəˌfī/ ▶*v.* (**-fied**) arrange (laws, etc.) systematically.
—**cod·i·fi·ca·tion** *n.*

**cod·piece** ▶*n.* pouch, esp. a conspicuous and decorative one, attached to a man's breeches or close-fitting hose to cover the genitals, worn in the 15th and 16th c.

**co·ed** /ˈkōˌed/ *inf.* ▶*n.* female student at a coeducational institution.
▶*adj.* coeducational.

**co·ed·u·ca·tion** /ˌkōˌejə-ˈkāsHən/ ▶*n.* education of pupils of both sexes together.
—**co·ed·u·ca·tion·al** *adj.*

**co·ef·fi·cient** /ˌkōəˈfisHənt/ ▶*n.* **1** *Math.* quantity placed before and multiplying an algebraic expression (e.g., 4 in $4xy$). **2** *Physics* multiplier or factor that measures some property: *coefficient of expansion.*

**co·erce** /kōˈərs/ ▶*v.* persuade or restrain by force: *coerced you into signing.* —**co·er·cion** *n.*
—**co·er·cive** *adj.*

**co·e·ter·nal** /ˌkō-iˈtərnl/ ▶*adj.* equally eternal; existing with something else eternally.

**co·e·val** /kōˈēvəl/ ▸*adj.* having the same age or date of origin; contemporary.
▸*n.* person of roughly the same age as oneself; a contemporary.

**co·ex·ist** /ˌkōigˈzist/ ▸*v.* 1 exist together (in time or place). 2 (esp. of nations) exist in mutual tolerance.
—**co·ex·ist·ence** *n.*
—**co·ex·is·tent** *adj.*

**cof·fee** /ˈkôfē/ ▸*n.* drink made from the roasted and ground beanlike seeds of a tropical shrub.
□ **coffee break** short rest from work. □ **coffee cake** type of cake or sweetened bread, often served with coffee. □ **coffee shop** small informal restaurant. □ **coffee table** small low table.

**cof·fer** /ˈkôfər/ ▸*n.* 1 large strongbox for valuables. 2 (**coffers**) treasury or store of funds: *the state government's empty coffers.*

**cof·fin** /ˈkôfin/ ▸*n.* long, narrow, usu. wooden box in which a corpse is buried or cremated.

**cof·fle** /ˈkôfəl; ˈkäfəl/ ▸*n.* line of animals or slaves fastened or driven along together.

**cog** /käg/ ▸*n.* 1 each of a series of projections on the edge of a wheel or bar transferring motion by engaging with another series. 2 unimportant worker.

**co·gent** /ˈkōjənt/ ▸*adj.* (of arguments, reasons, etc.) convincing; compelling.
—**co·gen·cy** *n.* —**co·gent·ly** *adv.*

**cog·i·tate** /ˈkäjiˌtāt/ ▸*v.* ponder; meditate. —**cog·i·ta·tive** *adj.*

**cog·nac** /ˈkōnˌyak/ ▸*n.* high-quality brandy, properly that distilled in Cognac in W. France.

**cog·nate** /ˈkägˌnāt/ ▸*adj.* 1 related to or descended from a common ancestor. 2 (of a word) having the same derivation.
▸*n.* cognate word.

**cog·ni·tion** /ˌkägˈnisHən/ ▸*n.* 1 knowing, perceiving, or conceiving as an act or faculty. 2 a result of this. —**cog·ni·tion·al** *adj.* —**cog·ni·tive** *adj.*

**cog·ni·tive** /ˈkägnətiv/ ▸*adj.* of or relating to cognition.

**cog·ni·tive dis·so·nance** ▸*n.* state of having inconsistent thoughts, beliefs, or attitudes, esp. as relating to behavioral decisions and attitude change.

**cog·ni·tive sci·ence** ▸*n.* study of thought, learning, and mental organization, which draws on aspects of psychology, linguistics, philosophy, and computer modeling.

**cog·ni·za·ble** /'kägnəzəbəl; käg-'nīz-/ ▶*adj.* **1** perceptible; clearly identifiable. **2** within the jurisdiction of a court.

**cog·ni·zance** /'kägnəzəns/ ▶*n.* knowledge or awareness; perception; sphere of one's observation or concern.

**co·gno·scen·ti** /ˌkänyō'sнentē; ˌkägnə-/ ▶*pl. n.* people who are considered to be especially well informed about a particular subject.

**co·hab·it** /kō'habit/ ▶*v.* (**-it·ed,** **-it·ing**) live together, esp. as an unmarried couple.

**co·here** /kō'hl(ə)r/ ▶*v.* **1** (of parts or a whole) stick together; remain united. **2** (of reasoning, etc.) be logical or consistent.

**co·her·ent** /kō'hi(ə)rənt/ ▶*adj.* **1** intelligible and articulate. **2** (of an argument, etc.) consistent. **3** *Physics* (of waves) having a fixed phase relationship. —**co·her·ence** *n.* —**co·her·ent·ly** *adv.*

**co·he·sion** /kō'hēzнən/ ▶*n.* tendency to cohere. —**co·he·sive** *adj.*

**co·hort** /'kō,hôrt/ ▶*n.* **1** persons banded or grouped together, esp. in a common cause. **2** supporter or companion.

**coif·fure** /kwä'fyo͝or/ ▶*n.* hairstyle.
▶*v.* (also **coif**) provide a coiffure.

**coign** /koin/ ▶*n.* projecting corner or angle of a wall or building.

**coil** /koil/ ▶*n.* **1** anything arranged in a joined sequence of concentric circles, e.g., rope, wire, etc. **2** *Electr.* device consisting of a coiled wire for converting low voltage to high voltage. **3** piece of wire, piping, etc., wound in circles or spirals.
▶*v.* twist or be twisted into a circular or spiral shape.

**coin** /koin/ ▶*n.* piece of flat, usu. round metal stamped and issued by authority as money.
▶*v.* **1** make (coins) by stamping. **2** invent or devise (esp. a new word or phrase). —**coin·age** *n.*

**co·in·cide** /ˌkōən'sīd/ ▶*v.* **1** occur at or during the same time. **2** occupy the same portion of space.

**co·i·tus** /'kōətəs/ ▶*n.* sexual intercourse. —**co·i·tal** *adj.*

**co·i·tus in·ter·rup·tus** /intə-'rəptəs/ ▶*n.* sexual intercourse in which the penis is withdrawn before ejaculation.

**coke** /kōk/ ▶*n.* **1** solid substance

left after the gases have been extracted from coal. **2** *inf.* cocaine.

**Col.** ▶*abbr.* **1** colonel. **2** Colossians (New Testament).

**col-** ▶*prefix* assim. form of COM- before l.

**co·la** /ˈkōlə/ (also **ko·la**) ▶*n.* **1** small tree, native to W. Africa, bearing seeds containing caffeine. **2** carbonated drink usu. flavored with these seeds.

**col·an·der** /ˈkələndər/ ▶*n.* perforated vessel used to strain off liquid from food after cooking.

**cold** /kōld/ ▶*adj.* **1** of or at a low or relatively low temperature. **2** lacking ardor, friendliness, or affection. **3** (in games) far from finding what is sought. ▶*n.* **1 a** prevalence of a low temperature, esp. in the atmosphere. **b** cold weather or environment. **2** infection of the nose or throat, causing sneezing, sore throat, etc. ▶*adv.* completely; entirely: *stopped cold.* —**cold·ness** *n.* □ **cold feet** *inf.* loss of nerve. □ **in cold blood** without feeling or passion; deliberately. □ **out in the cold** ignored; neglected.

**cold-blood·ed** ▶*adj.* **1** having a body temperature varying with that of the environment. **2** callous; deliberately cruel.

**cold cream** ▶*n.* ointment for cleansing and softening the skin.

**cold cuts** ▶*pl. n.* slices of cold cooked meats.

**cold shoul·der** ▶*n.* intentional unfriendliness.

**cold sore** ▶*n.* viral inflammation and blisters in and around the mouth.

**cold tur·key** ▶*n. inf.* abrupt withdrawal from something to which one is addicted.

**cold war** ▶*n.* state of hostility between nations without actual fighting.

**cole·slaw** /ˈkōlˌslô/ ▶*n.* dressed salad of sliced raw cabbage.

**col·ic** /ˈkälik/ ▶*n.* severe spasmodic abdominal pain. —**col·ick·y** *adj.*

**col·i·se·um** /ˌkäləˈsēəm/ ▶*n.* large stadium.

**co·li·tis** /kəˈlītis/ ▶*n.* inflammation of the lining of the colon.

**col·lab·o·rate** /kəˈlabəˌrāt/ ▶*v.* **1** work jointly. **2** cooperate traitorously with an enemy. —**col·lab·o·ra·tion** *n.*

—**col·lab·o·ra·tive** adj.

—**col·lab·o·ra·tor** n.

**col·lage** /kəˈläzʜ/ ▶n. work of art in which various materials are arranged and glued to a backing.

**col·la·gen** /ˈkäləjən/ ▶n. main structural protein found in animal connective tissue.

**col·lapse** /kəˈlaps/ ▶v. 1 (of a structure) (cause to) fall down or in. 2 (of a person) fall down and become unconscious. 3 (of an institution, etc.) fail suddenly and completely.

▶n. 1 tumbling down or falling in of a structure. 2 sudden failure. 3 physical or mental breakdown.

—**col·lap·si·ble** adj.

**col·lar** /ˈkälər/ ▶n. 1 part of a garment that goes around the neck. 2 band of leather or other material put around an animal's neck. 3 encircling part, device, etc.

▶v. capture; apprehend.

—**col·lar·less** adj.

**col·lar·bone** ▶n. either of two bones joining the breastbone and the shoulder blades; the clavicle.

**col·late** /kəˈlāt; ˈkōˌlāt/ ▶v. 1 collect and combine (texts, information, or sets of figures) in proper order. 2 compare and analyze (texts or other data).

**col·lat·er·al** /kəˈlatərəl/ ▶n. 1 security pledged as a guarantee for repayment of a loan. 2 person having the same descent as another but by a different line.

▶adj. 1 descended from the same stock but by a different line. 2 additional but subordinate.

—**col·lat·er·al·ly** adv.

**col·la·tion** /kəˈlāsʜən; kō-/ ▶n. light, informal meal.

**col·league** /ˈkälˌēg/ ▶n. fellow official or worker.

**col·lect** /kəˈlekt/ ▶v. 1 bring or come together; assemble; accumulate. 2 systematically seek and acquire, esp. as a hobby. 3 obtain (taxes, contributions, etc.). 4 a regain control of oneself. b [as adj. **collected**] not be perturbed or distracted.

▶adj. & adv. to be paid for by the receiver (of a telephone call, parcel, etc.). —**col·lect·a·ble** adj.

—**col·lec·tor** n.

**col·lec·ta·ne·a** /ˌkälekˈtānēə/ ▶pl. n. [treated as sing. or pl.] passages, remarks, and other pieces of text collected from various sources.

**col·lect·i·ble** /kə'lektəbəl/ ▸adj. worth collecting. ▸n. item sought by collectors.

**col·lec·tion** ▸n. **1** collecting or being collected. **2** things collected. **3** money collected, esp. in church or for a charity.

**col·lec·tive** ▸adj. **1** taken as a whole; aggregate. **2** of or from several or many individuals; common. ▸n. cooperative enterprise. —**col·lec·tive·ly** adv. —**col·lec·tive·ness** n.

**col·lec·tive bar·gain·ing** ▸n. negotiation of wages, etc., by an organized body of employees.

**col·lec·tive noun** ▸n. Gram. noun that denotes a collection or number of individuals (e.g., *assembly*, *family*, *troop*).

**col·lec·tive un·con·scious** ▸n. the part of the unconscious mind that is derived from ancestral memory and experience and is common to all humankind, as distinct from the individual's unconscious.

**col·lec·tiv·ism** /kə'lektə,vizəm/ ▸n. theory and practice of the collective ownership of land and the means of production.

**col·lege** /'kälij/ ▸n. **1** establishment for further or higher education, sometimes part of a university. **2** organized body of persons with shared functions and privileges: *college of cardinals.* —**col·le·gi·al** adj.

**col·le·gi·al** /kə'lēj(ē)əl/ ▸adj. relating to or involving shared responsibility, as among a group of colleagues.

**col·le·giate** /kə'lējit/ ▸adj. constituted as or belonging to a college.

**col·le·gi·um** /kə'lējēəm/ ▸n. (pl. **-le·gi·a** /-'legēə/) (in full **col·le·gi·um mu·si·cum** /'m(y)o͞ozikəm/) (pl. **col·le·gi·a mu·si·ca** /'m(y)o͞ozikə/) society of amateur musicians, esp. one attached to a college.

**col·lide** /kə'līd/ ▸v. come into collision or conflict.

**col·lie** /'kälē/ ▸n. longhaired dog orig. of a Scottish breed.

**col·li·sion** /kə'lizнən/ ▸n. **1** violent impact of a moving body with another or with a fixed object. **2** clashing of opposed interests or considerations.

**col·lo·cate** /'kälə,kāt/ ▸v. **1** (of a word) be habitually juxtaposed with another with a frequency greater than chance. **2** place side by side or in a particular relation.

▶*n.* word that is habitually juxtaposed with another with a frequency greater than chance.

**col·lo·qui·al** /kəˈlōkwēəl/ ▶*adj.* of ordinary or familiar conversation. —**col·lo·qui·al·ism** *n.* —**col·lo·qui·al·ly** *adv.*

**col·lo·qui·um** /kəˈlōkwēəm/ ▶*n.* (*pl.* **-ums** or **-a**) academic conference or seminar.

**col·lo·quy** /ˈkäləkwē/ ▶*n.* (*pl.* **-quies**) conversation; talk.

**col·lude** /kəˈlood/ ▶*v.* come to an understanding or conspire together. —**col·lu·sion** *n.*

**col·lu·sion** /kəˈloozHən/ ▶*n.* secret or illegal cooperation or conspiracy, esp. in order to cheat or deceive others.

**col·ly·wob·bles** /ˈkälē,wäbəlz/ ▶*pl. n.* [treated as *sing.* or *pl.*] *inf.* stomach pain or queasiness.

**Colo.** ▶*abbr.* Colorado.

**co·logne** /kəˈlōn/ ▶*n.* perfumed water.

**co·lon** /ˈkōlən/ ▶*n.* **1** punctuation mark (:) used esp. to set off something to follow. **2** lower and greater part of the large intestine. —**co·lon·ic** *adj.*

**col·o·nel** /ˈkərnl/ ▶*n.* military officer, just below a brigadier general in rank. —**colo·nel·cy** *n.*

**co·lo·ni·al** /kəˈlōnēəl/ ▶*adj.* of a colony or colonies.

▶*n.* inhabitant of a colony.

**co·lo·ni·al·ism** ▶*n.* policy of acquiring or maintaining colonies, esp. for economic advantage. —**co·lo·ni·al·ist** *n.*

**co·lon·ic** /kōˈlänik; kə-/ ▶*adj.* of, relating to, or affecting the colon.

▶*n.* (also **colonic irrigation**) a water enema given to flush out the colon, performed for its supposed therapeutic benefits.

**col·o·nize** /ˈkälə,nīz/ ▶*v.* establish a colony or colonies in (an area).

**col·on·nade** /ˌkäləˈnād/ ▶*n.* row of columns, esp. supporting a roof, arcade, etc. —**col·on·nad·ed** *adj.*

**col·o·ny** /ˈkälənē/ ▶*n.* (*pl.* **-nies**) **1** group of settlers or settlement in a new country fully or partly subject to the mother country. **2** people of one nationality, race, occupation, etc., forming a community. **3** *Biol.* collection of animals, plants, etc., connected, in contact, or living close together. —**col·o·nist** *n.*

**col·o·phon** /ˈkäləfən; -ˌfän/ ▶*n.* publisher's emblem or imprint, esp. one on the title page or spine of a book.

**color** /ˈkələr/ ▶n. **1** sensation produced by visible wavelengths of light. **2** one, or any mixture, of the constituents into which light can be separated as in a spectrum or rainbow. **3** pigmentation of the skin, esp. when dark. **4** appearance or aspect: *see things in their true colors.* **5** flag, insigna, etc.: *show the colors.* **6** quality or mood in art, speech, etc. ▶v. **1** apply color to. **2** influence. —**col·or·a·tion** *n.*

□ **show one's true colors** reveal one's true character or intentions.

**col·or·a·tu·ra** /ˌkələrəˈt(y)o͝orə/ ▶n. **1** elaborate ornamentation of a vocal melody. **2** soprano skilled in this.

**col·or·blind** (also **col·or·blind**) ▶adj. **1** unable to distinguish certain colors. **2** ignoring racial prejudice. —**col·or·blind·ness** *n.*

**col·ored** ▶adj. having color(s).

**col·or·ful** ▶adj. **1** having much or varied color; bright. **2** vivid; lively. —**col·or·ful·ly** adv.

**col·or·less** ▶adj. **1** without color. **2** lacking character or interest. **3** dull or pale in hue.

—**col·or·less·ly** adv.

**co·los·sal** /kəˈläsəl/ ▶adj. extremely large.

**co·los·sus** /kəˈläsəs/ ▶n. (pl. **-si** or **-sus·es**) **1** gigantic statue. **2** gigantic or important person or thing.

**col·por·teur** /ˈkälˌpôrtər; ˌkälpôrˈtər/ ▶n. **1** peddler of books, newspapers, and similar literature. **2** someone employed by a religious society to distribute Bibles and other religious tracts.

**colt** /kōlt/ ▶n. young, uncastrated male horse.

**colt·ish** ▶adj. energetic but awkward in one's movements or behavior.

**col·umn** /ˈkäləm/ ▶n. **1** upright, usu. cylindrical pillar. **2** column-shaped structure or part. **3** vertical cylindrical mass of liquid or vapor. **4** vertical division of a page, etc., containing a sequence of figures or words. **5** regular newspaper feature devoted to a particular subject. **6** arrangement of troops or ships in successive lines, with a narrow front. —**co·lum·nar** adj. —**col·umned** adj.

**com-** (also **co-, col-, con-, cor-**)
▶*prefix* with; together; jointly.

**co·ma** /'kōmə/ ▶*n.* prolonged
deep unconsciousness.

**Co·man·che** /kə'manchē/ ▶*n.*
**1 a** N. American Indian people
native to the western plains.
**b** member of this people.
**2** language of this people.

**com·a·tose** /'kōmə,tōs; 'kämə-/
▶*adj.* of or in a state of deep
unconsciousness for a prolonged
or indefinite period, esp. as a
result of severe injury or illness.

**comb** /kōm/ ▶*n.* **1** toothed strip
of rigid material for grooming
hair. **2** tool having a similar
design. **3** red, fleshy crest of esp.
male fowl.
▶*v.* **1** groom (hair) with a comb.
**2** dress (wool or flax) with a
comb. **3** search (a place)
thoroughly.

**com·bat** /'käm,bat/ ▶*n.* **1** armed
conflict; battle. **2** struggle;
contest.
▶*v.* /kəm'bat/ **1** engage in combat.
**2** oppose. —**com·bat·ant** *n.*
□ **combat fatigue** mental disorder
caused by stress in wartime
combat.

**comb·er** /'kōmər/ ▶*n.* **1** long
curling sea wave. **2** person or
machine that separates and
straightens the fibers of cotton
or wool.

**com·bi·na·tion** /,kämbə-
'nāshən/ ▶*n.* **1** a combining;
process of being combined.
**2** combined state or set.
**3** sequence of numbers used to
open a combination lock.
□ **combination lock** lock that
opens only by a specific
sequence of movements.

**com·bine** ▶*v.* /kəm'bīn/ **1** join
together; unite. **2** possess
(qualities usually distinct)
together. **3** form or cause to
form a chemical compound.
▶*n.* /'käm,bīn/ combination of esp.
commercial interests.

**com·bin·ing form** ▶*n. Gram.*
linguistic element used with
another element to form a word
(e.g., *bio-* = life, *-graphy* =
writing).

**com·bo** /'kämbō/ ▶*n.* (*pl.* **-bos**) *inf.*
small jazz or dance band.

**com·bus·ti·ble** /kəm'bəstəbəl/
▶*adj.* capable of or used for
burning.
▶*n.* combustible substance.
—**com·bus·ti·bil·i·ty** *n.*

**com·bus·tion** /kəm'bəschən/
▶*n.* **1** burning; consumption by
fire. **2** development of light and
heat from the chemical

combination of a substance with oxygen.

**come** /kəm/ ▶ v. (past **came**; past part. **come**) **1** move, be brought toward, or reach a place, situation, or result. **2** traverse or accomplish: *have come a long way.* **3** occur; happen: *how did you come to break your leg?* **4** take or occupy a specified position in space or time: *it comes on the third page.* **5** become perceptible or known: *the news comes as a surprise.* **6** become: *the handle has come loose.* **7 a** be descended from: *comes from a rich family.* **b** be the result of: *that comes of complaining.*

□ **come about** happen; take place. □ **come across 1 a** be effective or understood. **b** appear or sound in a specified way: *the ideas came across clearly.* **2** meet or find by chance. □ **come around 1** pay an informal visit. **2** recover consciousness. **3** be converted to another opinion. □ **come between 1** interfere with the relationship of. **2** separate; prevent contact between. □ **come by 1** pass; go past. **2** call on; visit. **3** acquire; obtain. □ **come down 1** lose position or wealth. **2** reach a decision or recommendation: *the report came down against change.* **3** signify; be dependent on (a factor): *it comes down to who is willing to go.* **4** criticize harshly: *she came down on me like a ton of bricks.* **5** begin to suffer from (a disease): *I think I'm coming down with a cold.* □ **come in 1** take a specified position in a race, etc.: *came in third.* **2 a** have a useful role or function. **b** prove to be: *came in very handy.* **3** begin speaking, esp. in radio transmission. □ **come into** receive, esp. as heir. □ **come off 1** *inf.* (of an action) succeed; be accomplished. **2** fare; turn out: *came off badly | came off the winner.* **3** be detached or detachable (from). □ **come-on** *inf.* lure or enticement. □ **come out 1 a** emerge; become known. **b** end; turn out. **2** appear or be published. **3 a** declare oneself; make a decision: *came out in favor of joining.* **b** openly declare that one is a homosexual. **4** turn out in a specified way (esp. the subject of a photograph). **5** (of a stain, etc.) be removed. □ **come over** (of a feeling, etc.) overtake or affect (a person). □ **come through 1** be successful; survive.

**2** survive or overcome (a difficulty). □ **come to 1** recover consciousness. **2** *Naut.* bring a vessel to a stop. **3** reach in total; amount to. **4** have as a destiny; reach: *what is the world coming to?* **5** be a question of: *when it comes to wine, he is an expert.* □ **come to pass** happen; occur. □ **come to rest** cease moving. □ **come up 1** (of an issue, problem, etc.) arise; present itself. **2** produce (an idea, etc.): *come up with a solution.* □ **come up against** be faced with or opposed by. □ **come upon 1** meet or find by chance. **2** attack by surprise. □ **come what may** no matter what happens.

**come·back** ▶*n.* **1** return to a previous (esp. successful) state. **2** *inf.* retaliation or retort.

**co·me·di·an** /kəˈmēdēən/ ▶*n.* humorous entertainer.

**com·e·dy** /ˈkämidē/ ▶*n.* (*pl.* **-dies**) **1** amusing or satirical play, film, etc. **2** dramatic genre of such works.

**com·e·dy of man·ners** ▶*n.* comedy that satirizes behavior in a particular social group, esp. the upper classes.

**come·ly** /ˈkəmlē/ ▶*adj.* (**-li·er**, **-li·est**) pleasant to look at; lovely. —**come·li·ness** *n.*

**co·mes·ti·ble** /kəˈmestəbəl/ ▶*n.* (usu. **comestibles**) item of food. ▶*adj.* edible.

**com·et** /ˈkämit/ ▶*n.* celestial tailed object of ice, dust, and gas, orbiting the sun.

**com·fit** /ˈkəmfit; ˈkämfit/ ▶*n.* candy consisting of a nut, seed, or other center coated in sugar.

**com·fort** /ˈkəmfərt/ ▶*n.* **1** consolation; relief in affliction. **2** state of physical or mental well-being. **3** (**comforts**) things that make life easy or pleasant. **4** cause or provider of satisfaction. ▶*v.* console.

**com·fort·a·ble** /ˈkəmf(ər)təbəl/ ▶*adj.* **1** providing or enjoying physical or mental well-being. **2** free from financial worry.

**com·fort·er** /ˈkəmfərtər/ ▶*n.* **1** person who comforts. **2** quilt.

**com·ic** /ˈkämik/ ▶*adj.* **1** of, or in the style of, comedy. **2** funny. ▶*n.* **1** comedian. **2** (**comics**) comic-strip section of a newspaper. —**com·i·cal** *adj.* —**com·i·cal·ly** *adv.*

□ **comic book** magazine of comic strips. □ **comic strip** sequence of drawings in a newspaper, etc., telling a story.

**com·i·ty** /ˈkämitē/ ▸n. (pl. **-ties**) **1** courtesy and considerate behavior toward others. **2** association of nations for their mutual benefit.

**com·ma** /ˈkämə/ ▸n. punctuation mark (,) indicating pause or division.

**com·mand** /kəˈmand/ ▸v. **1** give formal order to. **2** have authority or control over. **3** gain or have the use of (a skill, resources, etc.). **4** deserve and get (respect, etc.).
▸n. **1** authoritative order. **2** mastery; possession: *a good command of languages.* **3** exercise of authority, esp. naval or military: *has command of this ship.* **4** *Computing* **a** instruction causing a computer to perform a function. **b** signal initiating such an operation.
□ **command performance** performance given at the request of a head of state or sovereign.

**com·man·dant** /ˈkämənˌdant; -ˌdänt/ ▸n. commanding officer.

**com·man·deer** /ˌkämənˈdi(ə)r/ ▸v. **1** seize for military purposes.

**2** take possession of without authority.

**com·mand·er** ▸n. person who commands, esp. a naval officer next in rank below captain.
□ **commander in chief** supreme commander, esp. of a nation's forces.

**com·mand·ment** ▸n. divine command.
□ **Ten Commandments** divine rules of conduct given by God to Moses (Exod. 20:1–17).

**com·man·do** /kəˈmanˌdō/ ▸n. (pl. **-dos**) member of a unit trained for raids.

**com·me·dia dell'ar·te** /kəˈmädēə del ˈärtē/ ▸n. improvised kind of popular comedy in Italian theaters in the 16th–18th c. Actors played stock characters in a few basic plots and improvised dialogue to address topical issues.

**com·mem·o·rate** /kəˈmeməˌrāt/ ▸v. **1** preserve in memory by ceremony or celebration. **2** be a memorial of.
—**com·mem·o·ra·tive** adj.
—**com·mem·o·ra·tion** n.

**com·mence** /kəˈmens/ ▸v. begin.

**com·mence·ment** ▸n. **1** a beginning. **2** ceremony in which degrees or diplomas are awarded.

**com·mend** /kəˈmend/ ▶v.
**1** entrust. **2** praise.
—**com·men·da·tion** n.

**com·men·sal** /kəˈmensəl/ ▶adj.
of, relating to, or exhibiting commensalism.
▶n. commensal organism, such as many bacteria.

**com·men·sal·ism** /kəˈmensə-ˌlizəm/ ▶n. association between two organisms in which one benefits and the other derives neither benefit nor harm.

**com·men·su·ra·ble** /kəˈmensərəbəl; kəˈmensHərəbəl/ ▶adj. **1** measurable by the same standard. **2** (**commensurable to**) proportionate to. **3** (of numbers) in a ratio equal to a ratio of integers.

**com·men·su·rate** /kəˈmensərət; -ˈmensHə-/ ▶adj.
**1** having the same size, duration, etc. **2** proportionate.

**com·ment** /ˈkämˌent/ ▶n.
**1** remark, esp. critical.
**2** explanatory note (e.g., on a written text). **3** (of a play, book, etc.) critical illustration: *his art is a comment on society.*
▶v. **1** make (esp. critical) remarks.
**2** write explanatory notes.

**com·men·tar·y** /ˈkämənˌterē/
▶n. (pl. **-ies**) **1** set of critical notes on a text, etc.
**2** descriptive spoken account of an event or a performance as it happens.

**com·men·ta·tor** /ˈkämənˌtātər/
▶n. person who provides commentary.

**com·merce** /ˈkämərs/ ▶n. large-scale business transactions.

**com·mer·cial** /kəˈmərsHəl/ ▶adj.
**1** engaged in, or concerned with, commerce. **2** having profit as a primary aim.
▶n. broadcast advertisement.
—**com·mer·cial·ism** n.
—**com·mer·cial·i·za·tion** n.
—**com·mer·cial·ize** v.

**com·mi·na·tion** /ˌkämə-ˈnāsHən/ ▶n. action of threatening divine vengeance.

**com·min·gle** /kəˈmiNGgəl; kä-/
▶v. mingle together.

**com·mis·er·ate** /kəˈmizəˌrāt/
▶v. express or feel pity.
—**com·mis·er·a·tion** n.

**com·mis·sar** /ˈkäməˌsär/ ▶n.
**1** official of the Communist Party, esp. in the former Soviet Union or present-day China, responsible for political education and organization.

**2** strict or prescriptive figure of authority.

**com·mis·sar·y** /ˈkämə,serē/ ▶n. (pl. **-ies**) **1** store for the supply of food, etc., to soldiers. **2** restaurant in a movie studio, etc.

**com·mis·sion** /kəˈmiSHən/ ▶n. **1 a** authority to perform a task or certain duties. **b** person or group entrusted with such authority. **c** instruction or duty given. **2** order for something, esp. a work of art, to be produced. **3** warrant conferring the rank of a military officer. **4 a** authority to act as agent for a company, etc., in trade. **b** percentage paid to the agent from profits obtained. **5** act of committing (a crime, sin, etc.). ▶v. **1** authorize by a commission. **2** order (an artistic or musical work) to be created. **3 a** give (an officer) command of a ship. **b** prepare (a ship) for active service. □ **out of commission** not in service.

**com·mis·sion·er** ▶n. leader appointed by a commission.

**com·mit** /kəˈmit/ ▶v. (**-mit·ted**, **-mit·ting**) **1** entrust or consign for safekeeping, treatment, etc.

**2** perpetrate, do (esp. a crime or blunder). **3** pledge or bind (esp. oneself) to a certain course.

**com·mit·ment** ▶n. **1** dedication. **2** obligation. **3** binding pledge.

**com·mit·tal** /kəˈmitl/ ▶n. **1** action of sending a person to an institution, esp. prison or a psychiatric hospital. **2** burial of a corpse.

**com·mit·tee** /kəˈmitē/ ▶n. **1** body of persons appointed for a specific function by, and usu. out of, a larger body. **2** *Law* person entrusted with the charge of another person or another person's property.

**com·mode** /kəˈmōd/ ▶n. **1** chest of drawers. **2** TOILET.

**com·mod·i·fy** /kəˈmädə,fī/ ▶v. (**-fies, -fied**) turn into or treat as a commodity.

**com·mo·di·ous** /kəˈmōdēəs/ ▶adj. roomy and comfortable.

**com·mod·i·ty** /kəˈmäditē/ ▶n. (pl. **-ties**) **1** article or raw material that can be bought and sold. **2** useful thing.

**com·mo·dore** /ˈkämə,dôr/ ▶n. **1** naval officer just above captain. **2** commander of a fleet division. **3** president of a yacht club.

**com·mon** /ˈkämən/ ▶*adj.*
**1 a** occurring often. **b** overused; trite. **c** ordinary; without special rank. **2** shared by or coming from more than one: *common knowledge.* **3** *Math.* belonging to two or more quantities: *common denominator.*
▶*n.* piece of open public land. —**com·mon·ly** *adv.*
▢ **common ground** argument accepted by both sides in a dispute.

**com·mon·er** ▶*n.* one of the common people, as opposed to the aristocracy.

**com·mon law** ▶*n.* law derived from custom and judicial precedent rather than statutes.

**com·mon·place** ▶*adj.* lacking originality; trite.
▶*n.* **1 a** everyday saying; platitude. **b** ordinary topic of conversation. **2** anything usual or trite.

**com·mons** ▶*pl. n.* **1** dining hall at a university, etc. **2** central public park or ground.

**com·mon sense** ▶*n.* sound practical sense.

**com·mon·weal** /ˈkämən‚wēl/ ▶*n.* (**the commonweal**) welfare of the public.

**com·mon·wealth** ▶*n.*

**1 a** independent state or community, esp. a democratic republic. **b** designation of four U.S. states (Ky., Mass., Penna., Va.). **2** (**the Commonwealth**) association of the UK with nations previously part of the British Empire. **3** federation of states.

**com·mo·tion** /kəˈmōsHən/ ▶*n.* confused and noisy disturbance.

**com·mu·nal** /kəˈmyo͞onl/ ▶*adj.* relating to or benefiting a community; for common use. —**com·mu·nal·ly** *adv.*

**com·mu·nal·ism** /kəˈmyo͞onl‚izəm/ ▶*n.* **1** principle of political organization based on federated communes. **2** principle or practice of living together and sharing possessions and responsibilities. **3** allegiance to one's own ethnic group rather than to the wider society.

**com·mu·nard** /‚kämyəˈnär(d)/ ▶*n.* member of a commune.

**com·mune**[1] /ˈkäm‚yo͞on/ ▶*n.* group of people sharing living accommodation, goods, etc.

**com·mune**[2] /käˈmyo͞on/ ▶*v.* **1** speak confidentially and intimately. **2** feel in close touch (with nature, etc.).

**com·mu·ni·cate** /kəˈmyo͞onə-

,kāt/ ▶v. **1** transmit (information) by speaking or writing. **2** impart (feelings, etc.) nonverbally.
—**com·mu·ni·ca·tor** *n.*

**com·mu·ni·ca·tion** ▶*n.* **1** act of imparting, esp. news. **2** information communicated. **3** (**communications**) science and practice of transmitting information.

**com·mu·ni·ca·tive** /kä-'myo͞onə,kātiv/ ▶*adj.* open; talkative.

**com·mu·nion** /kə'myo͞onyən/ ▶*n.* **1** sharing, esp. of thoughts, etc.; fellowship. **2** (**Communion, Holy Communion**) the Eucharist. **3** Christian denomination: *the Methodist communion.*

**com·mu·ni·qué** /kə,myo͞onə'kā/ ▶*n.* official communication.

**com·mu·nism** /'kämyə,nizəm/ ▶*n.* **1** political theory advocating public ownership of property. **2** (**Communism**) communistic form of society, as established in the former USSR.

**com·mu·ni·tar·i·an·ism** /kə-,myo͞oni'te(ə)rēə,nizəm/ ▶*n.* **1** theory or system of social organization based on small self-governing communities. **2** ideology that emphasizes the responsibility of the individual to the community and the social importance of the family unit.

**com·mu·ni·ty** /kə'myo͞onitē/ ▶*n.* (*pl.* **-ties**) **1** body of people living in one locale or united by religion, profession, etc. **2** locality, including its inhabitants. **3** the public.

**com·mu·ni·ty col·lege** ▶*n.* nonresidential junior college offering college courses to a local community or region.

**com·mute** /kə'myo͞ot/ ▶*v.* **1** travel to and from one's daily work. **2** *Law* change (a judicial sentence, etc.) to another less severe.

▶*n.* trip made by one who commutes. —**com·mut·er** *n.*

**com·pact**[1] /kəm'pakt/ ▶*adj.* **1** closely or neatly packed together. **2** (of a piece of equipment, a room, etc.) well-fitted and practical though small.

▶*v.* **1** join or press firmly together. **2** condense.

▶*n.* /'käm,pakt/ **1** small, flat case for face powder, a mirror, etc. **2** medium-sized automobile.
—**com·pact·ly** *adv.*
—**com·pact·ness** *n.*

**com·pact**[2] /'käm‚pakt/ ▶n. agreement; contract.

**com·pact disc** ▶n. disk on which information or sound is recorded digitally and reproduced by laser reflection.

**com·pa·dre** /kəm'pädrä/ ▶n. (pl. **-pa·dres**) way of addressing or referring to a friend or companion.

**com·pan·ion** /kəm'panyən/ ▶n. **1** person who accompanies or associates with another. **2** handbook on a particular subject. **3** thing that matches another. —**com·pan·ion·ship** n.

**com·pan·ion·a·ble** /kəm-'panyənəbəl/ ▶adj. **1** (of a person) friendly and sociable. **2** (of a shared situation) relaxed and pleasant.

**com·pa·ny** /'kəmpənē/ ▶n. (pl. **-nies**) **1 a** number of people assembled; crowd. **b** guest(s). **2** state of being a companion or fellow; companionship, esp. of a specific kind: *do not care for his company.* **3** commercial business. **4** troupe of entertainers. **5** subdivision of a battalion.

**com·pa·ra·ble** /'kämp(ə)rəbəl/ ▶adj. able to be compared.

**com·par·a·tive** /kəm'parətiv/ ▶adj. **1** perceptible by or involving comparison; relative. **2** *Gram.* (of an adjective or adverb) expressing a higher degree (e.g., *braver, more fiercely*). ▶n. *Gram.* comparative expression or word. —**com·par·a·tive·ly** adv.

**com·pare** /kəm'pe(ə)r/ ▶v. **1** express similarities in; liken. **2** be equivalent to. **3** *Gram.* form comparative and superlative degrees of (an adjective or adverb).

**com·par·i·son** ▶n. **1** comparing. **2** similarity.

**com·part·ment** /kəm'pärtmənt/ ▶n. **1** partitioned space within a larger space. **2** watertight division of a ship.

**com·part·men·tal·ize** /kəm-‚pärt'mentl‚īz/ ▶v. divide into sections or categories.

**com·pass** /'kəmpəs/ ▶n. **1** instrument showing the direction of magnetic north and bearings from it. **2** instrument within two hinged legs for taking measurements and describing circles. **3** circumference or boundary.

**com·pas·sion** /kəm'paSHən/ ▶n. pity inclining one to be merciful. —**com·pas·sion·ate** adj.

**com·pat·i·ble** /kəm'patəbəl/

▸*adj.* **1 a** able to coexist; mutually tolerant. **b** consistent. **2** (of equipment, etc.) able to be used in combination. —**com·pat·i·bil·i·ty** *n.*

**com·pa·tri·ot** /kəmˈpātrēət/ ▸*n.* fellow countryman.

**com·peer** /ˈkämˌpi(ə)r; kämˈpi(ə)r/ ▸*n.* person of equal rank, status, or ability.

**com·pel** /kəmˈpel/ ▸*v.* (**-pel·led, -pel·ling**) force; constrain: *compelled them to admit it.*

**com·pel·ling** ▸*adj.* rousing strong interest.

**com·pen·di·ous** /kəmˈpendēəs/ ▸*adj.* comprehensive but brief.

**com·pen·di·um** /kəmˈpendēəm/ ▸*n.* (*pl.* **-ums** or **-a**) concise summary or abridgment.

**com·pen·sate** /ˈkämpənˌsāt/ ▸*v.* **1** pay. **2** make amends. **3** counterbalance or offset. —**com·pen·sa·tion** *n.* —**com·pen·sa·to·ry** *adj.*

**com·pen·sa·to·ry** /kəmˈpensəˌtôrē/ ▸*adj.* providing, effecting, or aiming at compensation, in particular: **a** (of a payment) intended to recompense someone who has experienced loss, suffering, or injury. **b** reducing or offsetting the unpleasant or unwelcome effects of something.

**com·pete** /kəmˈpēt/ ▸*v.* **1** contend; vie. **2** take part in a contest.

**com·pe·tent** /ˈkämpətənt/ ▸*adj.* adequately qualified or skilled. —**com·pe·tent·ly** *adv.*

**com·pe·ti·tion** /ˌkämpəˈtiSHən/ ▸*n.* **1** competing. **2** event in which people compete. **3** the others competing; opposition.

**com·pet·i·tive** ▸*adj.* **1** involving competition. **2** eager to win.

**com·pet·i·tor** ▸*n.* one who competes.

**com·pile** /kəmˈpīl/ ▸*v.* **1** collect (material) into a list, volume, etc. **2** accumulate (a large number of). —**com·pi·la·tion** *n.* —**com·pil·er** *n.*

**com·pla·cent** /kəmˈplāsənt/ ▸*adj.* smugly self-satisfied. —**com·pla·cence** *n.*

**com·plain** /kəmˈplān/ ▸*v.* express dissatisfaction or pain. —**com·plain·er** *n.* —**com·plain·ing·ly** *adv.*

**com·plaint** ▸*n.* **1** complaining. **2** grievance. **3** ailment.

**com·plai·sant** /kəmˈplāsənt/ ▸*adj.* willing to please; acquiescent. —**com·plai·sance** *n.*

**com·ple·ment** /ˈkämpləmənt/ ▸n. **1** thing that completes; counterpart. **2** full number needed.

▸v. form a complement to. —**com·ple·men·ta·ry** adj.

**com·plete** /kəmˈplēt/ ▸adj. **1** having all its parts; entire. **2** finished. **3** of the maximum extent: *a complete surprise.*

▸v. **1** finish. **2** make whole. —**com·plete·ly** adv. —**com·plete·ness** n. —**com·ple·tion** n.

**com·plex** ▸n. /ˈkäm,pleks/ **1** building, series of rooms, etc., of related parts. **2** group of unconscious feelings or thoughts that influence behavior.

▸adj. /kämˈpleks/ complicated. —**com·plex·i·ty** n.

**com·plex·ion** /kəmˈplekSHən/ ▸n. **1** natural appearance of skin, esp. of the face. **2** aspect; interpretation.

**com·pli·cate** /ˈkämplə,kāt/ ▸v. make difficult or complex. —**com·pli·ca·tion** n.

**com·plic·i·ty** /kəmˈplisitē/ ▸n. partnership in wrongdoing.

**com·pli·ment** /ˈkämpləmənt/ ▸n. **1** polite expression of praise. **2** (**compliments**) formal greetings or praise.

▸v. congratulate; praise.

**com·pli·men·ta·ry** /ˌkämpləˈment(ə)rē/ ▸adj. **1** expressing a compliment. **2** given free.

**com·ply** /kəmˈplī/ ▸v. (**-plied**) act in accordance (with a wish, command, etc.).

**com·po·nent** /kəmˈpōnənt/ ▸n. part of a larger whole.

▸adj. being part of a larger whole. —**com·po·nen·tial** adj.

**com·port** /kəmˈpôrt/ ▸v. (**comport oneself**) behave.

**com·pose** /kəmˈpōz/ ▸v. **1** create in music or writing. **2** constitute; make up. **3** calm; cause to appear calm. **4** prepare (text) for printing. —**com·pos·er** n.

**com·pos·ite** /kəmˈpäzit/ ▸adj. **1** made up of various parts. **2** (of a plant) having a bloom head of many flowers.

▸n. composite thing or plant.

**com·po·si·tion** ▸n. **1** putting together; composing. **2** work of music, literature, or art. **3** constitution of a substance. **4** compound artificial substance.

**com·post** /ˈkäm,pōst/ ▸n. organic fertilizing mixture.

▸v. make into or treat with compost.

**com·po·sure** /kəmˈpōzʜər/ ▸n. tranquil manner; calmness.

**com·pote** /ˈkämˌpōt/ ▸n. fruit preserved or cooked in syrup.

**com·pound** ▸n. /ˈkämˌpound/ **1** mixture of two or more things. **2** word made up of two or more existing words. **3** substance chemically formed from two or more elements. **4** enclosure or fenced-in space.
▸adj. /ˈkämˌpound/ **1** made up of several ingredients. **2** combined; collective.
▸v. /kəmˈpound/ **1** mix or combine (ingredients, elements, etc.). **2** increase or complicate (difficulties, etc.).

**com·pre·hend** /ˌkämprˌhend/ ▸v. understand.
—**com·pre·hen·si·bil·i·ty** n.
—**com·pre·hen·si·ble** adj.
—**com·pre·hen·si·bly** adv.
—**com·pre·hen·sion** n.

**com·pre·hen·si·ble** /ˌkämpri-ˈhensəbəl/ ▸adj. able to be understood; intelligible.

**com·pre·hen·sive** /ˌkämpri-ˈhensiv/ ▸adj. **1** including all or nearly all. **2** (of insurance) providing complete protection.
—**com·pre·hen·sive·ly** adv.
—**com·pre·hen·sive·ness** n.

**com·press** ▸v. /kəmˈpres/ **1** squeeze together. **2** bring into a smaller space or shorter extent.
▸n. /ˈkämˌpres/ pad applied to a wound. —**com·pres·sion** n.

**com·prise** /kəmˈprīz/ ▸v. **1** include. **2** consist of. **3** make up, compose.

**com·pro·mise** /ˈkämprəˌmīz/ ▸n. **1** mutual settlement of a dispute. **2** intermediate state between conflicting opinions, actions, etc.
▸v. **1** mutually settle a dispute. **2** modify one's opinions, demands, etc. **3** bring into disrepute or danger, esp. by indiscretion.

**comp·trol·ler** /kənˈtrōlər/ ▸n. financial officer.

**com·pul·sion** /kəmˈpəlsʜən/ ▸n. **1** constraint; obligation. **2** irresistible urge.

**com·pul·sive** /kəmˈpəlsiv/ ▸adj. **1** resulting or acting (as if) from compulsion. **2** irresistibly interesting. —**com·pul·sive·ly** adv. —**com·pul·sive·ness** n.

**com·pul·so·ry** /kəmˈpəlsərē/ ▸adj. required; essential.

**com·punc·tion** /kəmˈpəNG(k)sʜən/ ▸n. feeling of guilt or moral scruple: *spent the money without compunction.*

**com·pur·ga·tion** /ˌkämpərˈgāsʜən/ ▸n. acquittal from a

charge or accusation, obtained by statements of innocence given by witnesses under oath.

**com·pute** /kəm'pyo͞ot/ ▸v. reckon or calculate. —**com·pu·ta·tion** n.

**com·put·er** ▸n. electronic device for storing and processing data.

**com·put·er·ize** ▸v. **1** equip with a computer. **2** store or produce by computer. —**com·put·er·i·za·tion** n.

**com·pu·ter vi·rus** ▸n. hidden code within a computer program intended to corrupt a system.

**com·rade** /'käm,rad/ ▸n. **1** associate or companion. **2** fellow socialist or communist. —**com·rade·ly** adj. —**com·rade·ship** n.

**con** /kän/ inf. ▸n. confidence trick. ▸v. (**conned, con·ning**) **1** swindle; deceive. **2** reason against: list the pros and cons. ▸prep. & adv. against.

**con-** ▸prefix assim. form of COM-.

**co·na·tion** /kō'nāsHən/ ▸n. & mental faculty of purpose, desire, or will to perform an action; volition.

**con·cave** /kän'kāv; 'kän,kāv/ ▸adj. curved like the interior of a circle or sphere.

**con·ceal** /kən'sēl/ ▸v. keep secret; hide. —**con·ceal·ment** n.

**con·cede** /kən'sēd/ ▸v. **1** admit to be true. **2** admit defeat in. **3** grant (a right, privilege, etc.).

**con·ceit** /kən'sēt/ ▸n. **1** personal vanity; pride. **2 a** elaborate metaphoric comparison. **b** fanciful notion.

**con·ceit·ed** ▸adj. vain; proud.

**con·ceive** /kən'sēv/ ▸v. **1** become pregnant (with). **2** imagine; formulate.

**con·cen·trate** /'känsən,trāt/ ▸v. **1** focus one's attention. **2** bring together to one point. **3** make less dilute. ▸n. concentrated substance. —**con·cen·tra·tion** n.

**con·cen·tric** /kən'sentrik; kän-/ ▸adj. (esp. of circles) having a common center. —**con·cen·tri·cal·ly** adv. —**con·cen·tric·i·ty** n.

**con·cept** /'kän,sept/ ▸n. general notion; abstract idea. —**con·cep·tu·al** adj.

**con·cep·tion** /kən'sepsHən/ ▸n. **1** act or instance of conceiving. **2** idea; plan.

**con·cep·tu·al·ize** /kən'sepCHo͞oə,līz/ ▸v. form a concept or idea of. —**con·cep·tu·al·i·za·tion** n.

**con·cern** /kən'sərn/ ▸v. **1 a** be relevant or important to. **b** relate to; be about. **2** interest or involve oneself. **3** worry; affect.
▸n. **1** anxiety; worry. **2** matter of interest or importance. **3** business; firm.

**con·cerned** ▸adj. **1** involved; interested. **2** troubled; anxious.

**con·cern·ing** ▸prep. about; regarding.

**con·cert** /'kän,sərt; 'känsərt/ ▸n. musical performance.

**con·cert·ed** /kən'sərtəd/ ▸adj. jointly arranged or planned.

**con·cer·to** /kən'CHertō/ ▸n. (pl. **-ti** or **-tos**) composition for solo instrument(s) and orchestra.

**con·ces·sion** /kən'seSHən/ ▸n. **1 a** conceding. **b** thing conceded. **2** right to sell goods in a particular territory.

**conch** /käNGk; känCH/ ▸n. (pl. **conchs** or **conches**) spiral shell.

**con·cil·i·ate** /kən'silē,āt/ ▸v. make calm and amenable; pacify. **—con·cil·i·a·tory** adj.

**con·cil·i·a·to·ry** /kən'silēə,tôrē/ ▸adj. intended or likely to placate or pacify.

**con·cin·ni·ty** /kən'sinitē/ ▸n. **1** skillful and harmonious arrangement or fitting together of the different parts of something. **2** studied elegance of literary or artistic style.

**con·cise** /kən'sīs/ ▸adj. brief but comprehensive. **—con·cise·ly** adv. **—con·cise·ness** n.

**con·clave** /'kän,klāv/ ▸n. **1** private meeting. **2** assembly of cardinals for the election of a pope.

**con·clude** /kən'klo͞od/ ▸v. **1** bring or come to an end. **2** settle (a treaty, etc.).

**con·clu·sion** ▸n. **1** final result. **2** judgment reached by reasoning. **3** summing-up. **4** settling (of peace, etc.).

**con·clu·sive** ▸adj. decisive; convincing.

**con·coct** /kən'käkt/ ▸v. **1** make by mixing ingredients. **2** invent. **—con·coc·tion** n.

**con·com·i·tant** /kən'kämitənt/ ▸adj. going together; associated. **—con·com·i·tant·ly** adv.

**con·cord** /'käNGkərd/ ▸n. agreement; harmony.

**con·cor·dance** /kən'kôrdns/ ▸n. **1** agreement. **2** book or book part containing an index of important words used in a book or by an author.

**con·course** /'kän,kôrs/ ▸n. large

open area in a building for public use.

**con·crete** ▸*adj.* /kän'krēt/ **1 a** existing in a material form. **b** specific; definite. **2** *Gram.* (of a noun) denoting a material object as opposed to a quality, state, action, etc.

▸*n.* /'kän,krēt/ mixture of gravel, sand, cement, and water, used for building. —**con·crete·ly** *adv.*

**con·cre·tion** /kən'krēsHən/ ▸*n.* hard, solid mass.

**con·cu·bine** /'käNGkyoo,bīn/ ▸*n.* **1** (in some societies) secondary wife. **2** mistress.

**con·cur** /kən'kər/ ▸*v.* (-**curred**, -**cur·ring**) **1** coincide. **2** agree (with). —**con·cur·rent** *adj.*

**con·cur·rent** /kən'kərənt/ ▸*adj.* **1** existing, happening, or done at the same time. **2** (of two or more prison sentences) to be served at the same time. **3** (of three or more lines) meeting at or tending toward one point.

**con·cuss** /kən'kəs/ ▸*v.* hit the head of (a person or animal), causing temporary unconsciousness or confusion.

**con·cus·sion** /kən'kəsHən/ ▸*n.* temporary unconsciousness caused by a blow to the head.

**con·demn** /kən'dem/ ▸*v.* **1** express utter disapproval of. **2** find guilty; convict. **3** pronounce (a building, etc.) unfit for use. **4** doom or assign (to something unpleasant). —**con·dem·na·tion** *n.* —**con·dem·na·to·ry** *adj.*

**con·dense** /kən'dens/ ▸*v.* **1** make denser or more concentrated. **2** express in fewer words. **3** reduce or be reduced to a liquid.

**con·de·scend** /,kändə'send/ ▸*v.* **1** be gracious enough (to do a thing unworthy of one). **2** behave as if one is on equal terms with (an inferior). —**con·de·scend·ing·ly** *adv.* —**con·de·scen·sion** *n.*

**con·dign** /kən'dīn/ ▸*adj.* (of punishment or retribution) appropriate to the crime or wrongdoing; fitting and deserved.

**con·di·ment** /'kändəmənt/ ▸*n.* seasoning or relish for food.

**con·di·tion** /kən'disHən/ ▸*n.* **1** stipulation; term(s). **2 a** state of fitness. **b** ailment; abnormality. **3** (**conditions**) circumstances.

▸*v.* **1 a** bring into a good or desired state. **2** teach or accustom.

**con·dole** /kən'dōl/ ▸v. (**condole with**) express sympathy for (someone); grieve with.

**con·dom** /'kändəm/ ▸n. prophylactic or contraceptive sheath worn on the penis.

**con·do·min·i·um** /ˌkändə'minēəm/ ▸n. **1** building or complex containing individually owned apartments. **2** joint sovereignty.

**con·done** /kən'dōn/ ▸v. forgive or overlook.

**con·dor** /'kän,dôr/ ▸n. **1** large S. American vulture. **2** smaller vulture of California.

**con·duce** /kən'd(y)o͞os/ ▸v. (**conduce to**) help to bring about (a particular situation or outcome).

**con·du·cive** /kən'd(y)o͞osiv/ ▸adj. contributing or helping (toward something).

**con·duct** ▸n. /'kän,dəkt/ **1** behavior. **2** action or manner of directing or managing.
▸v. /kən'dəkt/ **1** direct or manage (business, etc.). **2** be the conductor of (an orchestra, etc.). **3** transmit (heat, electricity, etc.).

**con·duc·tor** ▸n. **1** person who directs an orchestra, choir, etc. **2** official in charge of passengers on a train, etc. **3** thing that conducts heat or electricity.

**con·duit** /'kän,d(y)o͞oit/ ▸n. **1** channel or pipe conveying liquids. **2** tube protecting electric wires.

**cone** /kōn/ ▸n. **1** solid figure with a circular (or other curved) plane base, tapering to a point. **2** thing or holder of similar shape. **3** dry fruit of a conifer.

**con·fab·u·late** /kən'fabyə,lāt/ ▸v. **1** engage in conversation; talk. **2** fabricate imaginary experiences as compensation for loss of memory.

**con·fec·tion** /kən'fekSHən/ ▸n. sweet dish; candy.

**con·fed·er·a·cy** /kən'fedərəsē/ ▸n. (pl. **-cies**) **1** league or alliance. **2** (**the Confederacy**) the 11 Southern states that seceded from the U.S. in 1860–61.

**con·fed·er·ate** /kən'fedərət/ ▸adj. allied.
▸n. **1** ally; accomplice. **2** (**Confederate**) supporter of the Confederacy.
▸v. bring or come into alliance. —**con·fed·er·a·tion** n.

**con·fer** /kən'fər/ ▸v. (**-ferred, -fer·ring**) **1** grant or bestow. **2** converse; consult.

**con·fer·ence** /ˈkänf(ə)rəns/ ▶n.
**1** consultation. **2** meeting.

**con·fess** /kənˈfes/ ▶v.
**1 a** acknowledge or admit.
**b** admit (to). **2** declare (one's
sins) to a priest. —**con·fes·sion**
n.

**con·fes·sion·al** /kənˈfeSHənl/
▶n. enclosed stall in a church in
which a priest hears confessions.

**con·fes·sor** ▶n. priest who
hears confessions.

**con·fet·ti** /kənˈfetē/ ▶n. bits of
colored paper thrown during
celebrations, etc.

**con·fi·dant** /ˈkänfəˌdant/ (fem.
**con·fi·dante**) ▶n. person trusted
with knowledge of one's private
affairs.

**con·fide** /kənˈfīd/ ▶v. **1** tell in
confidence. **2** entrust (an object,
a task, etc.) to. **3** (**confide in**)
talk confidentially to.

**con·fi·dence** /ˈkänfədəns/ ▶n.
**1** firm trust. **2** feeling of
reliance or certainty.
**3** something told confidentially.
—**con·fi·dent** adj.
□ **confidence game** swindle in
which the victim is persuaded to
trust the swindler. □ **confidence
man** swindler in a confidence
game.

**con·fi·den·tial** /ˌkänfəˈdenCHəl/

▶adj. spoken or written in
confidence. —**con·fi·den·ti·al·i·ty**
n. —**con·fi·den·tial·ly** adv.

**con·fig·u·ra·tion** /kənˌfig(y)ə-
ˈrāSHən/ ▶n. arrangement in a
particular form.

**con·fine** ▶v. /kənˈfīn/ **1** keep or
restrict (within certain limits,
etc.). **2** imprison.
▶n. /ˈkänˌfīn/ (usu. **confines**) limit;
boundary.

**con·fine·ment** ▶n. confining;
being confined.

**con·firm** /kənˈfərm/ ▶v. **1** settle
the truth or correctness of.
**2** make formally valid.
**3** encourage (a person) in (an
opinion, etc.).
—**con·fir·ma·tion** n.

**con·firmed** ▶adj. firmly settled
in some habit or condition: *a
confirmed bachelor.*

**con·fis·cate** /ˈkänfəˌskāt/ ▶v.
take or seize by authority.
—**con·fis·ca·tion** n.

**con·fla·gra·tion** /ˌkänflə-
ˈgrāSHən/ ▶n. great and
destructive fire.

**con·flict** ▶n. /ˈkänˌflikt/ **1** state
of opposition. **2** fight; struggle.
▶v. /ˈkänˌflikt/ clash; be
incompatible.

**con·flu·ence** /ˈkänˌflo͞oəns/ ▶n.

**1** place where two rivers meet.
**2** coming together.

**con·form** /kən'fôrm/ ▶v. comply with; be in accordance with. —**con·form·i·ty** n.

**con·form·ist** /kən'fôrmist/ ▶n. person who conforms to accepted behavior or established practices. ▶adj. (of a person or activity) conforming to accepted behavior or established practices; conventional.

**con·found** /kən'found/ ▶v. perplex.

**con·fra·ter·ni·ty** /ˌkänfrə'tərnitē/ ▶n. (pl. **-ties**) brotherhood, esp. with a charitable or religious purpose.

**con·frère** /'kän,fre(ə)r/ (also **con·frere**) ▶n. fellow member of a profession; a colleague.

**con·front** /kən'frənt/ ▶v. **1** face in hostility or defiance. **2** present itself to. **3** bring (a person) face to face with. —**con·fron·ta·tion** n. —**con·fron·ta·tion·al** adj.

**con·fuse** /kən'fyo͞oz/ ▶v. **1** perplex; bewilder. **2** mix up in the mind; mistake (one for another).

**con·fute** /kən'fyo͞ot/ ▶v. prove to be in error. —**con·fu·ta·tion** n.

**con·gé** /kôN'zHā 'kän,jā/ ▶n. unceremonious dismissal of someone; a leavetaking.

**con·geal** /kən'jēl/ ▶v. make or become semisolid by cooling.

**con·ge·nial** /kən'jēnyəl/ ▶adj. **1** pleasantly sociable. **2** agreeable. —**con·ge·ni·al·i·ty** n. —**con·gen·ial·ly** adv.

**con·gen·i·tal** /kən'jenətl/ ▶adj. (esp. of a disease, defect, etc.) existing from birth.

**con·ge·ries** /'känjərēz/ ▶n. (pl. same) disorderly collection; a jumble.

**con·gest·ed** /kən'jestəd/ ▶adj. over full; blocked up. —**con·ges·tive** adj.

**con·glom·er·ate** /kən'glämərət/ ▶n. **1** group or corporation. **2** heterogeneous mass. ▶adj. gathered into a rounded mass. —**con·glom·er·a·tion** n.

**con·grat·u·late** /kən'graCHə,lāt; -'grajə-/ ▶v. express pleasure at the good fortune or excellence of (a person). —**con·grat·u·la·to·ry** adj.

**con·gre·gate** /'käNggrə,gāt/ ▶v. collect or gather into a crowd or mass.

**con·gre·ga·tion** ▶n. people gathered for a church service. —**con·gre·ga·tion·al** adj.

**con·gre·ga·tion·al** /ˌkäNGgrə-ˈgāSHənl/ ▸*adj.* of a congregation.

**con·gress** /ˈkäNGgrəs/ ▸*n.* **1** formal meeting of delegates for discussion. **2** (**Congress**) national legislative body of the U.S. —**con·gres·sion·al** *adj.*

**con·gru·ent** /kənˈgrōōənt; ˈkäNGgrōōənt/ ▸*adj.* **1** suitable; agreeing. **2** *Geom.* coinciding when superimposed. —**con·gru·ence** *n.*

**con·ic** /ˈkänik/ ▸*adj.* of a cone. —**con·i·cal** *adj.* —**con·i·cal·ly** *adv.*

**co·ni·fer** /ˈkänəfər; kō-/ ▸*n.* any cone-bearing tree or shrub, usu. evergreen.

**con·jec·ture** /kənˈjekCHər/ ▸*n.* formation of an opinion on incomplete information. ▸*v.* guess. —**con·jec·tur·al** *adj.*

**con·join** /kənˈjoin/ ▸*v.* join; combine.

**con·ju·gal** /ˈkänjəgəl/ ▸*adj.* of or relating to marriage.

**con·ju·gate** /ˈkänjəˌgāt/ ▸*v.* *Gram.* give the different forms of (a verb). ▸*adj.* joined together; fused.

**con·junc·tion** /kənˈjəNGkSHən/ ▸*n.* **1** joining; connection. **2** *Gram.* connective word (e.g., *and, but, if*). **3** combination (of events or circumstances).

**con·junc·ti·va** /kənˌjəNG(k)tə-ˈvə/ ▸*n.* mucous membrane covering the front of the eye and lining the inside of the eyelid.

**con·junc·ti·vi·tis** /kən-ˌjəNG(k)təˈvītis/ ▸*n.* inflammation of the conjunctiva.

**con·jure** /ˈkänjər/ ▸*v.* evoke. —**con·jur·or** *n.* □ **conjure up** produce as if by magic.

**Conn.** ▸*abbr.* Connecticut.

**con·nate** /ˈkänˌāt; käˈnāt/ ▸*adj.* (esp. of ideas or principles) existing in a person or thing from birth; innate.

**con·nect** /kəˈnekt/ ▸*v.* **1** join or be joined. **2** associate mentally or practically. **3** (of a train, etc.) be timed such that passengers can transfer. —**con·nec·tive** *adj.* —**con·nec·tor** *n.*

**con·nec·tion** ▸*n.* **1** connecting or being connected. **2** meeting point. **3** link. **4** connecting train, flight, etc. **5** (**connections**) influential acquaintances or relatives.

**con·nive** /kəˈnīv/ ▸*v.* conspire.

**con·nois·seur** /ˌkänəˈsər; -ˈsŏŏr/ ▸*n.* expert judge in matters of taste.

**con·no·ta·tion** /ˌkänəˈtāSHən/ ▸*n.* idea or feeling that a word invokes in a person in addition to its literal or primary meaning.

**con·note** /kə'nōt/ ▸*v.* imply in addition to the literal or primary meaning. —**con·no·ta·tion** *n.* —**con·no·ta·tive** *adj.*

**con·nu·bi·al** /kə'n(y)ōōbēəl/ ▸*adj.* of or relating to marriage.

**con·quer** /'käNGkər/ ▸*v.* overcome militarily or by effort. —**con·quer·or** *n.*

**con·quest** /'käNGkwest/ ▸*n.* **1** conquering or being conquered. **2** something won.

**con·quis·ta·dor** /kôNG'kēstə-ˌdôr/ ▸*n.* (*pl.* -**dor·es** or -**dors**) conqueror, esp. a 16th-c. Spanish conqueror of Mexico and Peru.

**con·san·guin·e·ous** /ˌkän-ˌsaNG'gwinēəs/ ▸*adj.* relating to or denoting people descended from the same ancestor.

**con·science** /'känCHəns/ ▸*n.* moral sense of right and wrong.

**con·sci·en·tious** /ˌkänCHē-'enCHəs/ ▸*adj.* diligent and scrupulous. —**con·sci·en·tious·ly** *adv.*

□ **conscientious objector** person who refrains from military service on moral grounds.

**con·scious** /'känCHəs/ ▸*adj.* awake and aware of one's surroundings and identity. —**con·scious·ly** *adv.* —**con·scious·ness** *n.*

**con·script** ▸*v.* /kən'skript/ summon for compulsory (esp. military) service.
▸*n.* /'känˌskript/ conscripted person. —**con·scrip·tion** *n.*

**con·se·crate** /'känsiˌkrāt/ ▸*v.* **1** make or declare sacred: *the church was consecrated in 1908.* **2** (in Christian belief) make (bread and wine) into the body or blood of Christ. —**con·se·cra·tion** *n.*

**con·sec·u·tive** /kən'sekyətiv/ ▸*adj.* following continuously; in unbroken or logical order. —**con·sec·u·tive·ly** *adv.*

**con·sen·su·al** /kən'senCHōōəl/ ▸*adj.* relating to or involving consent, esp. mutual consent.

**con·sen·sus** /kən'sensəs/ ▸*n.* general agreement or opinion.

**con·sent** /kən'sent/ ▸*v.* express willingness; agree.
▸*n.* voluntary agreement; permission.

**con·se·quence** /'känsikwəns/ ▸*n.* **1** result or effect of an action or condition. **2** importance: *he didn't say anything of great consequence.*

**con·se·quent** /ˈkänsikwənt/ ▸*adj.* following as a result or consequence.

**con·serv·an·cy** /kənˈsərvənsē/ ▸*n.* (*pl.* **-cies**) **1** body concerned with the preservation of nature, specific species, or natural resources. **2** conservation of something, esp. wildlife and the environment.

**con·ser·va·tion** /ˌkänsər-ˈvāsʜən/ ▸*n.* preservation, esp. of the natural environment.

**con·ser·va·tive** /kənˈsərvətiv/ ▸*adj.* **1** holding to traditional attitudes and values, esp. in relation to politics or religion. **2** (of an estimate, etc.) purposely low. ▸*n.* person who holds to traditional attitudes. —**con·ser·va·tism** *n.* —**con·ser·va·tive·ly** *adv.*

**con·ser·va·tor** /kənˈsərvətər; -ˌtôr; ˈkänsərˌvātər/ ▸*n.* person responsible for the repair and preservation of works of art, buildings, or other things of cultural or environmental interest.

**con·ser·va·to·ry** /kənˈsərvə-ˌtôrē/ ▸*n.* (*pl.* **-ries**) **1** greenhouse. **2** music school.

**con·serve** ▸*v.* /kənˈsərv/ **1** keep from harm or damage, esp. for later use. **2** *Physics* maintain a quantity of (heat, etc.). **3** preserve (food, esp. fruit), usu. with sugar. ▸*n.* /ˈkänˌsərv/ fresh fruit jam.

**con·sid·er** /kənˈsidər/ ▸*v.* **1** contemplate; weigh and evaluate. **2** examine the merits of. **3** give attention to. **4** take into account. **5** regard as. □ **all things considered** taking everything into account.

**con·sid·er·a·ble** /kənˈsidərəbəl/ ▸*adj.* **1** much; a lot of. **2** notable; important. —**con·sid·er·a·bly** *adv.*

**con·sid·er·a·tion** ▸*n.* **1** careful thought. **2** thoughtfulness. **3** fact or thing taken into account.

**con·sid·er·ing** ▸*prep.* in view of; because of.

**con·sign** /kənˈsīn/ ▸*v.* **1** hand over; deliver. **2** assign; commit. —**con·sign·ee** *n.* —**con·sign·or** *n.*

**con·sist** /kənˈsist/ ▸*v.* be composed; have as ingredients or essential features.

**con·sis·ten·cy** /kənˈsistənsē/ ▸*n.* (*pl.* **-cies**) **1** degree of density, viscosity, etc., esp. of liquids. **2** being consistent.

**con·sis·tent** ▸*adj.* **1** compatible or in harmony. **2** constant.

**con·sole**[1] /kən'sōl/ ▸*v.* comfort, esp. in grief or disappointment. —**con·sol·a·ble** *adj.* —**con·sol·ing·ly** *adv.*

**con·sole**[2] /'kän,sōl/ ▸*n.* **1** panel for switches, controls, etc. **2** cabinet for an organ's keyboards, etc.

**con·sol·i·date** /kən'sälə,dāt/ ▸*v.* **1** make or become strong or solid. **2** combine into one whole. —**con·sol·i·da·tion** *n.*

**con·som·mé** /,känsə'mā/ ▸*n.* clear soup from meat stock.

**con·so·nant** /'känsənənt/ ▸*n.* **1** speech sound in which the breath is at least partly obstructed. **2** letter(s) representing this. ▸*adj.* consistent; in agreement or harmony.

**con·sort**[1] ▸*n.* /'kän,sôrt/ **1** spouse, esp. of royalty. **2** group of players, singers, etc. ▸*v.* /kən'sôrt/ keep company; associate.

**con·sor·tium** /kən'sôrsH(ē)əm; -'sôrtēəm/ ▸*n.* (*pl.* **-ti·a** or **-ti·ums**) association, esp. of several firms.

**con·spic·u·ous** /kən'spikyo͞oəs/ ▸*adj.* clearly visible; attracting notice. —**con·spic·u·ous·ly** *adv.* —**con·spic·u·ous·ness** *n.*

**con·spir·a·cy** /kən'spirəsē/ ▸*n.* secret plan to commit a crime.

**con·spire** /kən'spī(ə)r/ ▸*v.* collude for an unlawful or harmful act.

**con·sta·ble** /'känstəbəl/ ▸*n.* peace officer, esp. in a small town.

**con·stab·u·lar·y** /kən'stabyə,lerē/ ▸*n.* (*pl.* **-ies**) constables, collectively.

**con·stant** /'känstənt/ ▸*adj.* **1** continuous. **2** occurring frequently. **3** faithful; dependable. ▸*n.* anything that does not vary. —**con·stant·ly** *adv.*

**con·stel·la·tion** /,känstə'lāsHən/ ▸*n.* **1** group of associated stars. **2** assemblage of persons, ideas, etc.

**con·ster·na·tion** /,känstər'nāsHən/ ▸*n.* anxiety; dismay.

**con·sti·pa·tion** /'känstə,pāsHən/ ▸*n.* difficulty in emptying the bowels.

**con·sti·tu·en·cy** /kən'sticHo͞oənsē/ ▸*n.* **1** body of voters who elect a representative. **2** area so represented.

**con·stit·u·ent** /kənˈstiCHo͞oənt/ ▸*adj.* composing; constituting.
▸*n.* **1** member of a constituency. **2** component.

**con·sti·tute** /ˈkänstəˌt(y)o͞ot/ ▸*v.* be the components or essence of; make up.

**con·sti·tu·tion** /ˌkänstə-ˈt(y)o͞osHən/ ▸*n.* **1** body of fundamental governing principles or a written record of this: *the Constitution of the United States.* **2** composition of something. **3** person's health, strength, etc.

**con·stitu·tion·al** ▸*adj.* **1** of or relating to a constitution: *a constitutional amendment.* **2** in accordance with the principles of a constitution: *the court ruled that the law is constitutional.*

**con·strain** /kənˈstrān/ ▸*v.* **1** severely restrict the scope or activity of. **2** compel (someone) toward a particular course of action.

**con·straint** ▸*n.* **1** restriction. **2** stiffness; embarrassment.

**con·strict** /kənˈstrikt/ ▸*v.* make narrow or tight; compress. —**con·stric·tion** *n.*

**con·struct** ▸*v.* /kənˈstrəkt/ make by fitting together; build.

▸*n.* /ˈkänˌstrəkt/ thing constructed, esp. by the mind.

**con·struc·tive** ▸*adj.* **1** tending to form a basis for ideas. **2** helpful; positive. —**con·struc·tive·ly** *adv.*

**con·strue** /kənˈstro͞o/ ▸*v.* interpret.

**con·sue·tude** /ˈkänswiˌt(y)o͞od/ ▸*n.* established custom, esp. one having legal force.

**con·sul** /ˈkänsəl/ ▸*n.* official appointed by a government to protect its citizens and interests in a foreign city. —**con·sul·ar** *adj.* —**con·sul·ate** *n.*

**con·sult** /kənˈsəlt/ ▸*v.* seek information or advice from. —**con·sul·tant** *n.* —**con·sul·ta·tion** *n.* —**con·sul·ta·tive** *adj.*

**con·sume** /kənˈso͞om/ ▸*v.* **1** eat or drink. **2** destroy. **3** possess: *consumed with rage.* **4** use up. —**con·sum·a·ble** *adj. & n.*

**con·sum·er** ▸*n.* person who consumes, esp. one who uses a product or service.

**con·sum·er·ism** ▸*n.* protection or promotion of consumers' interests.

**con·sum·mate** /ˈkänsəˌmāt/ ▸*v.* **1** complete; make perfect.

**2** complete (a marriage) by sexual intercourse. ▸*adj.* complete; perfect. —**con·sum·ma·tion** *n.*

**con·sump·tion** /kən-ˈsəm(p)sHən/ ▸*n.* **1** consuming; being consumed. **2** purchase and use of goods, etc.

**con·sump·tive** /kənˈsəm(p)tiv/ ▸*adj.* **1** affected with a wasting disease, esp. pulmonary tuberculosis. **2** of or relating to the using up of resources. ▸*n.* person with a wasting disease, esp. pulmonary tuberculosis.

**cont.** ▸*abbr.* **1** contents. **2** continued.

**con·tact** /ˈkänˌtakt/ ▸*n.* **1** state or condition of touching, meeting, or communicating. **2** person useful to deal with. **3** connection for electric current. **4** *inf.* contact lens. ▸*v.* get in touch with.

**con·tact lens** ▸*n.* small lens placed directly on the eyeball to correct vision.

**con·ta·gion** /kənˈtājən/ ▸*n.* communication of disease by bodily contact. —**con·ta·gious** *adj.*

**con·tain** /kənˈtān/ ▸*v.* **1** hold or be capable of holding within itself. **2** prevent from moving or extending. **3** control or restrain (feelings, etc.). —**con·tain·er** *n.*

**con·tam·i·nate** /kənˈtaməˌnāt/ ▸*v.* pollute. —**con·tam·i·nant** *n.* —**con·tam·i·na·tion** *n.*

**con·te** /kôNt/ ▸*n.* short story as a form of literary composition.

**con·temn** /kənˈtem/ ▸*v.* treat or regard with contempt.

**con·tem·plate** /ˈkäntəmˌplāt/ ▸*v.* **1** survey visually or mentally. **2** regard (an event) as possible. **3** intend. **4** meditate. —**con·tem·pla·tion** *n.* —**con·tem·pla·tive** *adj.*

**con·tem·po·ra·ne·ous** /kən-ˌtempəˈrānēəs/ ▸*adj.* existing or occurring in the same period of time.

**con·tem·po·rar·y** /kənˈtempə-ˌrerē/ ▸*adj.* **1** living or occurring at the same time. **2** modern. ▸*n.* (*pl.* **-ies**) contemporary person or thing.

**con·tempt** /kənˈtem(p)t/ ▸*n.* **1** feeling of scorn or extreme reproach. **2** being so regarded. **3** disrespect shown to a court, etc. —**con·temp·ti·ble** *adj.*

□ **beneath contempt** utterly despicable. □ **hold in contempt** despise.

**con·tempt·i·ble** /kən-'tem(p)təbəl/ ▶*adj.* deserving contempt; despicable.

**con·temp·tu·ous** /kən-'tem(p)CHo͞oəs/ ▶*adj.* showing contempt; scornful.

**con·tend** /kən'tend/ ▶*v.* **1** strive; fight. **2** assert; maintain. —**con·tend·er** *n.*

**con·tent**[1] /kən'tent/ ▶*adj.* **1** satisfied; adequately happy. **2** willing. ▶*v.* satisfy. ▶*n.* contented state. —**con·tent·ment** *n.*

**con·tent**[2] /'kän,tent/ ▶*n.* **1** (**contents**) what is contained, as in a vessel, book, or house. **2** amount contained.

**con·tent·ed** ▶*adj.* happy; satisfied.

**con·ten·tion** /kən'tenCHən/ ▶*n.* **1** dispute or argument; rivalry. **2** point contended.

**con·ter·mi·nous** /kän-'tərmənəs; kən-/ ▶*adj.* sharing a common boundary.

**con·test** ▶*n.* /'kän,test/ **1** contending; competition. **2** dispute. ▶*v.* /kən'test/ **1** dispute. **2** contend or compete for. —**con·test·ant** *n.*

**con·tes·ta·tion** /,käntəs-'tāsHən/ ▶*n.* action or process of disputing or arguing.

**con·text** /'kän,tekst/ ▶*n.* **1** parts that surround and clarify a word or passage. **2** relevant circumstances. —**con·tex·tu·al** *adj.*

**con·tex·tu·al·ize** /kən-'teksCHo͞oə,līz/ ▶*v.* place or study in context.

**con·tig·u·ous** /kən'tigyo͞oəs/ ▶*adj.* touching; in contact. —**con·tig·u·ous·ly** *adv.*

**con·ti·nent** /'käntn-ənt; -tənənt/ ▶*n.* any of earth's main land masses. ▶*adj.* **1** able to control one's bowels and bladder. **2** exercising self-restraint. —**con·ti·nence** *n.*

**con·ti·nen·tal** /,käntn'entl/ ▶*adj.* **1** forming or belonging to a continent. **2** coming from or characteristic of mainland Europe. **3** (also **Continental**) pertaining to the 13 original colonies of the US. ▶*n.* **1** inhabitant of mainland Europe. **2** (**Continental**) member of the colonial army in the American Revolution. **3** (also **Continental**) piece of paper currency used at the time of the American Revolution.

**con·tin·gen·cy** /kən'tinjənsē/ ▶*n.* (*pl.* **-cies**) **1** event that may or may not occur. **2** uncertainty; chance.

**con·tin·gent** ▶*adj.* **1** conditional; dependent (on an uncertain circumstance). **2** that may or may not occur. ▶*n.* body (of troops, ships, etc.) forming part of a larger group.

**con·tin·u·al** /kən'tinyōōəl/ ▶*adj.* constantly or frequently recurring. —**con·tin·u·al·ly** *adv.*

**con·tin·ue** /kən'tinyōō/ ▶*v.* **1** maintain; not stop. **2** resume or prolong (a narrative, journey, etc.). **3** remain.

**con·ti·nu·i·ty** /ˌkäntn'(y)ōōətē/ ▶*n.* (*pl.* **-ties**) **1** state of being continuous. **2** logical sequence.

**con·tin·u·ous** /kən'tinyōōəs/ ▶*adj.* unbroken; uninterrupted. —**con·tin·u·ous·ly** *adv.*

**con·tin·u·um** /kən'tinyōōəm/ ▶*n.* (*pl.* **-ua** or **-u·ums**) thing having a continuous structure.

**con·tort** /kən'tôrt/ ▶*v.* twist or force out of normal shape. —**con·tor·tion** *n.*

**con·tour** /'kän,tŏŏr/ ▶*n.* outline.

**contra-** ▶*comb. form* against; opposite.

**con·tra·band** /'käntrə,band/ ▶*n.* smuggled goods. ▶*adj.* forbidden from import or export.

**con·tra·cep·tion** /ˌkäntrə'sepsHən/ ▶*n.* prevention of pregnancy esp. by artificial means. —**con·tra·cep·tive** *adj. & n.*

**con·tract** ▶*n.* /'kän,trakt/ **1** written or spoken agreement, esp. one enforceable by law. **2** document recording this. ▶*v.* /ˌkən'trakt/ **1** make or become smaller. **2** make a contract. **3** catch or develop (a disease). —**con·trac·tion** *n.*

**con·tract·a·ble** /kən'traktəbəl/ ▶*adj.* (of a disease) able to be caught.

**con·tract·i·ble** /kən'traktəbəl/ ▶*adj.* able to be shrunk or capable of contracting.

**con·trac·tor** /'kän,traktər/ ▶*n.* person who makes a contract, as to provide services.

**con·tra·dict** /ˌkäntrə'dikt/ ▶*v.* **1** deny (a statement). **2** be in opposition to or in conflict with. —**con·tra·dic·tion** *n.* —**con·tra·dic·to·ry** *adj.*

**con·tra·in·di·cate** /ˌkäntrə'ində,kāt/ ▶*v.* (usu. **be contraindicated**) (of a condition or circumstance) suggest or indicate that (a particular technique or drug) should not be used in the case in question.

**con·tral·to** /kən'traltō/ ▶n. (pl. **-tos**) **1** lowest female singing voice. **2** singer with this voice.

**con·tra·po·si·tion** /ˌkäntrəpə-'ziSHən/ ▶n. conversion of a proposition from *all A is B* to *all not-B is not-A*.

**con·trap·tion** /kən'trapSHən/ ▶n. machine or device, esp. a strange one.

**con·tra·pun·tal** /ˌkäntrə'pəntl/ ▶adj. **1** of or in counterpoint. **2** (of a piece of music) with two or more independent melodic lines.

**con·trar·i·an** /kən'tre(ə)rēən; kän-/ ▶n. person who opposes or rejects popular opinion, esp. in stock exchange dealing. ▶adj. opposing or rejecting popular opinion; going against current practice.

**con·trar·y** /'kän,tre(ə)rē/ ▶adj. **1** opposite in nature, direction, or meaning. **2** perversely inclined to disagree. ▶n. (pl. **-ies**) the opposite.

**con·trast** ▶n. /'kän,trast/ **1 a** juxtaposition or comparison showing differences. **b** difference so revealed. **2** range of color or tone in a picture. ▶v. /kən'trast/ set together so as to reveal a contrast.

**con·tra·vene** /ˌkäntrə'vēn/ ▶v. **1** violate (a law, etc.). **2** conflict with (a right, principle, etc.). —**con·tra·ven·tion** n.

**con·trib·ute** /kən'tribyōōt/ ▶v. **1** give (money, help, etc.) toward a common purpose. **2** supply (an article, etc.) for publication. —**con·trib·u·tor** n.

**con·trite** /kən'trīt/ ▶adj. penitent; feeling remorse. —**con·tri·tion** n.

**con·trive** /kən'trīv/ ▶v. devise; plan or make resourcefully. —**con·tri·vance** n.

**con·trol** /kən'trōl/ ▶n. **1** power of directing. **2** power of restraining, esp. self-restraint. **3** means of restraint. **4** means of regulating. **5** (**controls**) switches, etc., by which a machine is controlled. **6** place where something is overseen: *mission control.* **7** standard of comparison in an experiment. ▶v. (**-trolled, -trol·ling**) **1** have control of; regulate. **2** hold in check. —**con·trol·la·ble** adj.

**con·trol·ler** ▶n. **1** person or thing that controls. **2** person in charge of expenditures.

**con·tro·ver·sy** /ˈkäntrəˌvərsē/ ▸n. (pl. **-sies**) prolonged argument or dispute. —**con·tro·ver·sial** adj.

**con·tro·vert** /ˈkäntrəˌvərt/ ▸v. dispute; deny. —**con·tro·vert·i·ble** adj.

**co·nun·drum** /kəˈnəndrəm/ ▸n. riddle.

**con·ur·ba·tion** /ˌkänərˈbāsHən/ ▸n. extended urban area.

**con·va·lesce** /ˌkänvəˈles/ ▸v. recover health after illness. —**con·va·les·cence** n. —**con·va·les·cent** adj.

**con·vec·tion** /kənˈveksHən/ ▸n. heat transfer by upward movement of a heated and less dense medium.

**con·vene** /kənˈvēn/ ▸v. 1 summon or arrange (a meeting, etc.). 2 assemble.

**con·ven·ient** /kənˈvēnyənt/ ▸adj. serving one's comfort or interests; suitable. —**con·ven·ience** n.

**con·vent** /ˈkänˌvent/ ▸n. religious community, esp. of nuns.

**con·ven·tion** /kənˈvencHən/ ▸n. 1 general custom or customary practice. 2 assembly for a common purpose. 3 formal agreement, esp. between nations.

**con·verge** /kənˈvərj/ ▸v. come together or toward the same point. —**con·ver·gence** n. —**con·ver·gent** adj.

**con·ver·sant** /kənˈvərsənt/ ▸adj. well acquainted (with).

**con·ver·sa·tion** /ˌkänvərˈsāsHən/ ▸n. informal spoken communication. —**con·ver·sa·tion·al** adj.

**con·ver·sa·zi·o·ne** /ˌkänvərˌsätsēˈōnē; -ˈōˌnä/ ▸n. (pl. **-nes** or **-ni** /-nē/) scholarly social gathering held for discussion of literature and the arts.

**con·verse**[1] /kənˈvərs/ ▸v. talk.

**con·verse**[2] /ˈkänˌvərs/ ▸adj. opposite; contrary; reversed. ▸n. something opposite or contrary. —**con·verse·ly** adv.

**con·vert** ▸v. /kənˈvərt/ 1 change or be changed in form or function. 2 change one's religious beliefs, etc. ▸n. /ˈkänˌvərt/ person converted to a different belief, etc. —**con·ver·ter** n.

**con·vert·i·ble** /kənˈvərtəbəl/ ▸adj. that may be converted. ▸n. car with a folding roof.

**con·vex** /känˈveks/ ▸adj. curved

like the exterior of a circle or sphere.

**con·vey** /kən'vā/ ▸*v.* **1** transport or carry. **2** communicate or transmit (an idea, meaning, etc.). —**con·vey·or** *n.*

**con·vey·ance** /kən'vāəns/ ▸*n.* **1** conveying; being conveyed. **2** means of transport.

**con·vict** ▸*v.* /kən'vikt/ declare guilty by legal process.

▸*n.* /'kän,vikt/ prison inmate.

**con·vic·tion** /kən'vikSHən/ ▸*n.* **1** convicting; being convicted. **2 a** being convinced. **b** firm belief.

**con·vince** /kən'vins/ ▸*v.* firmly persuade. —**con·vinc·ing** *adj.*

**con·viv·i·al** /kən'vivēəl/ ▸*adj.* fond of good company; sociable; lively. —**con·viv·i·al·i·ty** *n.*

**con·voke** /kən'vōk/ ▸*v.* call together. —**con·vo·ca·tion** *n.*

**con·vo·lu·tion** /,känvə'looSHən/ ▸*n.* **1** coiling; twisting. **2** complexity.

**con·voy** /'kän,voi/ ▸*n.* group of ships, vehicles, etc., traveling together or under escort.

**con·vulse** /kən'vəls/ ▸*v.* **1** affect with convulsions. **2** cause to laugh uncontrollably.

**con·vul·sion** ▸*n.* **1** (usu. **convulsions**) violent body spasm. **2** violent disturbance. **3** (**convulsions**) uncontrollable laughter.

**coo** /koo/ ▸*n.* soft murmuring sound as of a dove.

▸*v.* emit a coo.

**cook** /kook/ ▸*v.* **1** prepare (food) by heating it. **2** (of food) undergo cooking. **3** *inf.* falsify (accounts, etc.): *cook the books.*

▸*n.* person who cooks.

**cook·ie** /'kookē/ (also **cook·y**) ▸*n.* (*pl.* **-ies**) small sweet cake.

**cool** /kool/ ▸*adj.* **1** of or at a fairly low temperature. **2** calm; unexcited. **3** lacking enthusiasm. **4** unfriendly. **5** calmly audacious. **6** *inf.* excellent.

▸*n.* **1** coolness. **2** calmness; composure: *she kept her cool.*

▸*v.* make or become cool.

**coop** /koop/ ▸*n.* cage for keeping poultry.

▸*v.* (**coop up**) confine (a person, etc.).

**co-op** /'kō,äp/ ▸*n.* cooperative business, apartment building, etc.

**co·op·er·ate** /kō'äpə,rāt/ ▸*v.* **1** work or act together; assist.

**2** (of things) concur in producing an effect. —**co·op·er·a·tion** *n.*

**co·op·er·a·tive** /kō'äp(ə)rətiv/ ▶*adj.* **1** of or affording cooperation. **2** willing to cooperate. **3** (of a business) owned and run jointly by its members, with profits shared. **4** (of an apartment building) with individual units owned by tenants. ▶*n.* cooperative farm, society, or business.

**co-opt** /kō'äpt/ ▶*v.* appoint to membership of a body by invitation.

**co·or·di·nate** ▶*v.* /kō'ôrdn,āt/ (cause to) function together effectively. ▶*adj.* /kō'ôrdn-it/ equal in rank or importance. ▶*n.* /kō'ôrdn-it/ *Math.* value used to fix the position of a point, line, or plane. —**co·or·di·na·tion** *n.*

**cop** /käp/ ▶*n. inf.* police officer. ▶*v.* (**copped, cop·ping**) catch or arrest (an offender). □ **cop out** withdraw; renege.

**cope** /kōp/ ▶*v.* deal effectively or contend with; manage. ▶*n.* priest's or bishop's cloaklike vestment.

**cop·i·er** /'käpēər/ ▶*n.* machine that copies (esp. documents).

**co·pi·lot** /'kō,pīlət/ ▶*n.* second pilot in an aircraft.

**cop·ing** ▶*n.* top (usu. sloping) course of wall masonry.

**co·pi·ous** /'kōpēəs/ ▶*adj.* abundant. —**co·pi·ous·ly** *adv.* —**co·pi·ous·ness** *n.*

**cop·per** /'käpər/ ▶*n.* malleable, red-brown metallic element. (Symb.: **Cu**).

**cop·per·head** ▶*n.* venomous N. American or Australian snake.

**copse** /käps/ ▶*n.* small dense forest.

**cop·u·la** /'käpyələ/ ▶*n.* connecting word, in particular a form of the verb *be* connecting a subject and complement.

**cop·u·late** /'käpyə,lāt/ ▶*v.* have sexual intercourse. —**cop·u·la·tion** *n.*

**cop·y** /'käpē/ ▶*n.* (*pl.* **-ies**) **1** thing made to imitate another. **2** issue of a publication. **3** matter to be printed: *scandals make good copy.* ▶*v.* (**-ied**) **1** make a copy of. **2** do the same as; imitate.

**cop·y·cat** ▶*n. inf.* imitator.

**cop·y·right** ▶*n.* exclusive legal right to print, publish, perform, film, or record material. ▶*v.* secure copyright for (material).

**co·quet·ry** /ˈkōkətrē; kōˈketrē/ ▸n. flirtatious behavior or a flirtatious manner.

**co·quette** /kōˈket/ ▸n. woman who flirts. —**co·quet·tish** adj.

**cor·al** /ˈkôrəl/ ▸n. hard stony red, pink, or white substance secreted by marine polyps, forming large reefs in warm seas.

**cord** /kôrd/ ▸n. **1** long, thin, flexible material made from several twisted strands. **2** body structure resembling a cord: *spinal cord*. **3** ribbed fabric, esp. corduroy. **4** unit of cut firewood (usu. 128 cu.ft.).

**cor·dial** /ˈkôrjəl/ ▸adj. heartfelt; warm; friendly: *he gave us a cordial welcome.*
▸n. liqueur. —**cor·di·al·i·ty** n. —**cor·dial·ly** adv.

**cord·less** ▸adj. (of an electrical appliance, etc.) not connected by wire to an external source of energy, data, etc.

**cor·don** /ˈkôrdn/ ▸n. protective line or circle of police, soldiers, guards, etc.
▸v. (**cordon off**) enclose or separate with a cordon.

**cor·du·roy** /ˈkôrdəˌroi/ ▸n. thick cotton fabric with velvety ribs.

**core** /kôr/ ▸n. **1** central part of various fruits, containing the seeds. **2** central or most important part of anything. **3** central region of the earth.
▸v. remove the core from.

**co·re·spond·ent** (also **co·re·spond·ent**) ▸n. **1** joint defendant in a lawsuit, esp. one on appeal. **2** person cited in a divorce case as having committed adultery with the respondent.

**co·ri·an·der** /ˈkôrēˌandər/ ▸n. aromatic herb of the carrot family whose seeds are used for flavoring.

**cork** /kôrk/ ▸n. **1** buoyant light-brown bark of a S. European oak. **2** bottle stopper, esp. of cork.
▸v. stop up, as with a cork.

**cork·age** /ˈkôrkij/ ▸n. charge made by a restaurant or hotel for serving wine that has been brought in by a customer.

**cork·screw** ▸n. **1** spiral device for extracting corks from bottles. **2** thing with a spiral shape.
▸v. move spirally; twist.

**cor·mo·rant** /ˈkôrmərənt/ ▸n. diving black sea bird.

**corn** /kôrn/ ▸n. **1 a** cereal plant bearing kernels on a long ear (cob). **b** cobs or kernels of this plant. **2** *inf.* something tritely sentimental. **3** tender area of horny skin, esp. on the toe.

**corn·cob** ▶*n.* cylindrical center of a corn ear.

**cor·ne·a** /ˈkôrnēə/ ▶*n.* transparent covering of the front of the eyeball. **—cor·ne·al** *adj.*

**cor·ner** /ˈkôrnər/ ▶*n.* **1** place where sides or edges meet. **2** difficult position. **3** secluded or remote place. **4** monopoly on a stock or commodity. ▶*v.* force into a difficult or inescapable position.

**cor·ner·stone** ▶*n.* **1** foundation stone at the corner of a building. **2** indispensable part or basis.

**cor·net** /kôrˈnet/ ▶*n.* brass instrument resembling a trumpet but shorter and wider.

**cor·nice** /ˈkôrnis/ ▶*n.* ornamental molding just below the ceiling.

**cor·niche** /ˈkôrnisH; kôrˈnēsH/ ▶*n.* road cut into the edge of a cliff, esp. one running along a coast.

**corn·meal** ▶*n.* coarsely ground corn.

**corn·starch** ▶*n.* fine-ground flour from corn.

**cor·nu·co·pi·a** /ˌkôrn(y)əˈkōpēə/ ▶*n.* **1** symbol of plenty consisting of a goat's horn overflowing with flowers, fruit, etc. **2** abundant supply.

**corn·y** ▶*adj.* (**-i·er, -i·est**) *inf.* **1** feebly humorous. **2** tritely sentimental. **—corn·i·ly** *adv.* **—corn·i·ness** *n.*

**co·rol·la** /kəˈrōlə/ ▶*n.* petals forming a flower.

**cor·ol·lar·y** /ˈkôrəˌlerē/ ▶*n.* (*pl.* **-ies**) **1** proposition that follows from one already proved. **2** natural consequence.

**co·ro·na** /kəˈrōnə/ ▶*n.* (*pl.* **-nas** or **-nae**) halo around the sun or moon.

**cor·o·nar·y** /ˈkôrəˌnerē/ ▶*adj.* of the arteries supplying blood to the heart. ▶*n.* (*pl.* **-ies**) **1** CORONARY THROMBOSIS. **2** heart attack. □ **coronary artery** artery supplying blood to the heart. □ **coronary thrombosis** blockage caused by a blood clot in a coronary artery.

**cor·o·na·tion** /ˌkôrəˈnāsHən/ ▶*n.* ceremony of crowning.

**cor·o·ner** /ˈkôrənər/ ▶*n.* officer holding inquests on deaths thought to be violent or accidental.

**cor·o·net** /ˌkôrəˈnet/ ▸ *n.* small crown or band worn on the head.

**Corp.** ▸ *abbr.* **1** corporal. **2** corporation.

**cor·po·ral** ▸ *n.* noncommissioned officer ranking next below sergeant. ▸ *adj.* of the human body. —**cor·po·ral·ly** *adv.*

☐ **corporal punishment** physical punishment.

**cor·po·ra·tion** /ˌkôrpəˈrāsʜən/ ▸ *n.* group of people authorized to act as an individual, esp. in business.

**cor·po·re·al** /kôrˈpôrēəl/ ▸ *adj.* bodily; physical; material. —**cor·po·re·al·i·ty** *n.* —**cor·po·re·al·ly** *adv.*

**cor·po·sant** /ˈkôrpəˌsant/ ▸ *n.* appearance of St. Elmo's fire on a mast, rigging, or other structure.

**corps** /kôr/ ▸ *n.* (*pl.* **corps** /kôrz/) **1** military body or subdivision with special duties. **2** body of people engaged in a special activity.

**corps de bal·let** /ˌkôr də baˈlā/ ▸ *n.* **1** members of a ballet company who dance together as a group. **2** members of the lowest rank of dancers in a ballet company.

**corpse** /kôrps/ ▸ *n.* dead body.

**cor·pu·lent** /ˈkôrpyələnt/ ▸ *adj.* bulky in body; fat. —**cor·pu·lence** *n.*

**cor·pus** /ˈkôrpəs/ ▸ *n.* (*pl.* **-po·ra** or **-pus·es**) body or collection of writings, texts, etc.

**cor·pus·cle** /ˈkôrˌpəsəl/ ▸ *n.* minute body in an organism, esp. a red or white cell in the blood of vertebrates. —**cor·pus·cu·lar** *adj.*

**cor·pus de·lic·ti** /dəˈlikˌtī; -tē/ ▸ *n.* **1** facts and circumstances constituting a breach of a law. **2** concrete evidence of a crime, such as a corpse.

**cor·ral** /kəˈral/ ▸ *n.* pen for cattle, horses, etc. ▸ *v.* (**-ralled, -ral·ling**) **1** put or keep in a corral. **2** *inf.* gather in; acquire.

**cor·rect** /kəˈrekt/ ▸ *adj.* true; right; accurate; proper. ▸ *v.* **1** set right; amend. **2** mark errors in. **3** counteract (a harmful quality). —**cor·rect·ly** *adv.* —**cor·rect·ness** *n.*

**cor·re·late** /ˈkôrəˌlāt/ ▸ *v.* have or bring into a mutual relation. ▸ *n.* each of two complements. —**cor·re·la·tion** *n.*

**cor·re·spond** /ˌkôrəˈspänd/ ▸v.
**1 a** be analogous or similar (to).
**b** be in agreement with.
**2** exchange letters with.
—**cor·re·spond·ing·ly** adv.

**cor·re·spon·dence** ▸n.
**1** agreement or harmony.
**2 a** communication by letters.
**b** letters written.

**cor·re·spond·ent** ▸n. **1** person who writes letters. **2** reporter or news source.
—**cor·re·spond·ent·ly** adv.

**cor·ri·da** /kôˈrēdə/ ▸n. bullfight.

**cor·ri·dor** /ˈkôrədər/ ▸n.
**1** passage in a building from which doors lead into rooms.
**2** belt of land between giving access to somewhere.

**cor·rob·o·rate** /kəˈräbəˌrāt/ ▸v. confirm or give support to (a statement or belief, etc.).
—**cor·rob·o·ra·tion** n.
—**cor·rob·o·ra·tive** adj.

**cor·rode** /kəˈrōd/ ▸v. wear away or be worn away, esp. by chemical action. —**cor·rod·i·ble** adj. —**cor·ro·sive** adj.

**cor·ru·gate** /ˈkôrəˌgāt/ ▸v. [usu. as adj. **corrugated**] form into ridges and grooves.
—**cor·ru·ga·tion** n.

**cor·rupt** /kəˈrəpt/ ▸adj.
**1** morally depraved; wicked.
**2** influenced by or using bribery or fraudulent activity. **3** (of a text, etc.) harmed by errors or alterations.
▸v. make or become corrupt.
—**cor·rupt·i·ble** adj.
—**cor·rup·tion** n.

**cor·sage** /kôrˈsäzH/ ▸n. small bouquet worn by a woman.

**cor·sair** /ˈkôrˌse(ə)r/ ▸n.
**1** privateer. **2** pirate ship.

**cor·set** /ˈkôrsit/ ▸n. closely fitting undergarment worn for support. —**cor·set·ed** adj.

**cor·tex** /ˈkôrˌteks/ ▸n. (pl. **-ti·ces** or **-tex·es**) outer part of an organ, esp. of the brain (**ce·re·bral cor·tex**) or kidneys (**re·nal cor·tex**). —**cor·ti·cal** adj.

**cor·ti·sone** /ˈkôrtəˌsōn/ ▸n. hormone used esp. against inflammation and allergy.

**cor·vée** /ˈkôrˌvā; kôrˈvā/ ▸n.
**1** day's unpaid labor owed by a vassal to his feudal lord.
**2** forced labor exacted in lieu of taxes, in particular that on public roads.

**cor·vine** /ˈkôrˌvīn/ ▸adj. of or like a raven or crow, esp. in color.

**cor·y·phée** /ˌkôrəˈfā/ ▸n. leading dancer in a corps de ballet.

**co·ry·za** /kəˈrīzə/ ▸n. catarrhal inflammation of the mucous membrane in the nose, caused esp. by a cold or by hay fever.

**cos·met·ic** /käz'metik/ ▶*adj.* **1** enhancing; beautifying. **2** only superficially improving. ▶*n.* cosmetic preparation, esp. for the face. —**cos·met·i·cal·ly** *adv.*

**cos·mic** /'käzmik/ ▶*adj.* of the universe or cosmos, esp. as distinct from the earth.

**cos·mog·o·ny** /käz'mägənē/ ▶*n.* (*pl.* **-nies**) branch of science that deals with the origin of the universe, esp. the solar system.

**cos·mol·o·gy** /käz'mäləjē/ ▶*n.* science or theory of the universe.

**cos·mo·pol·i·tan** /ˌkäzmə-'pälətn/ ▶*adj.* of, from, or knowing many parts of the world. ▶*n.* cosmopolitan person.

**cos·mos** /'käzməs/ ▶*n.* the universe, esp. as a well-ordered whole.

**cost** /kôst/ ▶*v.* (*past* and *past part.* **cost**) **1** be obtainable for (a sum); have as a price. **2** involve as a loss or sacrifice: *it cost me my job.* ▶*n.* **1** what a thing costs; price. **2** loss or sacrifice. □ **at all costs** (or **at any cost**) no matter what. □ **cost of living**

level of prices, esp. of the basic necessities of life.

**cos·tive** /'kästiv; 'kôstiv/ ▶*adj.* **1** constipated. **2** slow or reluctant in speech or action; unforthcoming.

**cos·tume** /'käs,t(y)oōm/ ▶*n.* **1** style of dress, esp. of a particular place, time, or class. **2** clothing for a particular activity or role. ▶*v.* provide with a costume. □ **costume jewelry** jewelry made of artificial or inexpensive materials.

**cot** /kät/ ▶*n.* small folding or portable bed.

**co·tan·gent** /kō'tanjənt/ ▶*n.* *Math.* ratio of the side adjacent to an acute angle (in a right triangle) to the opposite side.

**cote** /kōt/ ▶*n.* shelter, esp. for animals or birds.

**co·te·rie** /'kōtərē/ ▶*n.* exclusive clique or circle.

**co·til·lion** /kə'tilyən/ ▶*n.* **1** formal ball. **2** ballroom dance resembling a quadrille.

**cot·tage** /'kätij/ ▶*n.* small, simple house, esp. in the country.

**cot·tage cheese** ▶*n.* soft white cheese made from milk curds.

**cot·tage in·dus·try** ▸*n.* business activity carried on at home.

**cot·ton** /'kätn/ ▸*n.* **1** soft, white fibrous substance covering the seeds of a plant. **2** this plant. **3** thread or fabric made from cotton.
▸*v.* (**cotton to**) be attracted by.

**cot·ton gin** ▸*n.* machine for separating cotton from its seeds.

**cot·ton·mouth** ▸*n.* venomous pit viper of the southeastern U.S.

**couch** /kouсн/ ▸*n.* upholstered piece of furniture for several people; sofa.
▸*v.* express in words of a specified kind: *couched in simple language.*

**couch·ant** /'kouснənt/ ▸*adj.* (of an animal) lying with the body resting on the legs and the head raised.

**couch po·ta·to** ▸*n. inf.* person who likes lazing, esp. watching television.

**cou·gar** /'kōōgər/ ▸*n.* puma.

**cough** /kôf/ ▸*v.* **1** expel air from the lungs with a sudden, sharp sound. **2** (of an engine, etc.) make a similar sound.
▸*n.* **1** act of coughing. **2** illness causing coughing.
□ **cough drop** medicated lozenge to relieve a cough. □ **cough up**

*inf.* bring out or give (money or information) reluctantly.

**could** /kŏŏd/ ▸past of **CAN**.

**cou·lee** /'kōōlē/ ▸*n.* **1** deep ravine. **2** a lava flow.

**cou·lisse** /kōō'lēs/ ▸*n.* **1** flat piece of scenery at the side of the stage in a theater. **2** groove, or a grooved timber, in which a movable partition slides up and down.

**coun·cil** /'kounsəl/ ▸*n.* advisory, deliberative, or administrative body.

**coun·sel** /'kounsəl/ ▸*n.* **1** advice, esp. formally given. **2** legal adviser.
▸*v.* **1** advise (a person). **2** give advice on personal problems, esp. professionally.
**3** recommend (a course of action). —**coun·sel·ing** *n.*

**coun·se·lor** ▸*n.* **1** person trained to give guidance on personal, etc., problems: *marriage counselor.* **2** person supervising children at a camp. **3** trial lawyer.

**count** /kount/ ▸*v.* **1** determine, esp. one by one, the total number of. **2** repeat numbers in order. **3** include or be included. **4** consider (a thing or a person) to be (lucky, etc.). **5** have value;

matter: *his opinion counts for a great deal.*

▶*n.* **1 a** counting; reckoning. **b** total of a reckoning: *pollen count.* **2** *Law* each charge in an indictment. **3** noble corresponding to a British earl.

□ **count down** recite numbers backward to zero. □ **count on** (or **upon**) depend on.

**count·down** ▶*n.* **1** act of counting numerals in reverse order. **2** final moments before any significant event.

**coun·te·nance** /ˈkountn-əns/ ▶*n.* **a** the face. **b** facial expression.

▶*v.* give approval to: *I cannot countenance the use of force.*

**count·er** /ˈkountər/ ▶*n.* **1** long, flat-topped fixture in a store, etc., across which business is conducted or food is served. **2 a** small disk used in board games. **b** token representing a coin. **3** apparatus used for counting.

▶*v.* **1** oppose; contradict. **2** make an opposing statement.

▶*adv.* in the opposite direction or manner.

▶*adj.* **1** opposite. **2** duplicate; serving as a check.

□ **over the counter 1** (of stock) sold through a broker directly. **2** by ordinary retail purchase.

□ **run counter to** act contrary to.

□ **under the counter** surreptitiously, esp. sold illegally.

**counter-** ▶*comb. form* denoting: **1** retaliation, opposition, or rivalry: *counterthreat.* **2** opposite direction: *counterclockwise.* **3** correspondence: *counterpart.*

**coun·ter·act** ▶*v.* hinder or neutralize by contrary action.

**coun·ter·at·tack** ▶*n.* attack in reply to an attack.

▶*v.* attack in reply.

**coun·ter·bal·ance** ▶*n.* weight or influence balancing another.

▶*v.* act as a counterbalance to.

**coun·ter·clock·wise** ▶*adv. & adj.* circling in a direction opposite to the movement of the hands of a clock.

**coun·ter·cul·ture** ▶*n.* way of life, etc., opposed to that usually considered normal.

**coun·ter·feit** /ˈkountərˌfit/ ▶*adj.* made in imitation; not genuine; forged.

▶*n.* forgery; imitation.

▶*v.* imitate fraudulently; forge.
—**coun·ter·feit·er** *n.*

**coun·ter·in·tel·li·gence** ▶*n.* activities to prevent spying, sabotage, etc., by an enemy.

**coun·ter·mand** /ˌkountər'mand/ ▶*v.* revoke (an order or command).
▶*n.* order revoking a previous one.

**coun·ter·pane** /'kountər,pān/ ▶*n.* bedspread.

**coun·ter·part** ▶*n.*
**1** complement or equivalent to another. **2** duplicate, esp. of a document.

**coun·ter·point** ▶*n.* **1** *Mus.* **a** art or technique of combining melodies according to fixed rules. **b** melody played in conjunction with another.
**2** contrasting argument, theme, etc., used to set off the main element.
▶*v.* **1** *Mus.* add counterpoint to (a melody). **2** set (an argument, etc.) in contrast to (a main element).

**coun·ter·poise** /'kountər,poiz/ ▶*n.* factor, force, or influence that balances or neutralizes another.

**coun·ter·pro·duc·tive** ▶*adj.* having the opposite of the desired effect.

**coun·ter·sign** ▶*v.* add a ratifying signature to (a document).
—**coun·ter·sig·na·ture** *n.*

**count·ess** /'kountis/ ▶*n.* **1** wife or widow of a count or an earl. **2** woman holding the rank of count or earl.

**count·less** ▶*adj.* too many to be counted.

**coun·try** /'kəntrē/ ▶*n.* (*pl.* **-tries**)
**1** nation or its territory. **2** rural area. **3** region associated with a particular person, feature, etc. **4** national population, esp. as voters.
□ **country club** golfing and social club.

**coun·ty** /'kountē/ ▶*n.* (*pl.* **-ties**)
**1** political and administrative division of a state, as in the U.S. **2** administrative divisions of some countries.
□ **county seat** administrative capital of a county.

**coup** /ko͞o/ ▶*n.* (*pl.* **coups** /ko͞oz/)
**1** (also **coup d'é·tat** /ˌko͞o dā'tä/) violent or illegal seizure of power. **2** successful stroke or move.

**coup de fou·dre** /ˌko͞o də 'fo͞od(rə)/ ▶*n.* (*pl.* **coups de fou·dre** *pronunc.* same) sudden unforeseen event, in particular an instance of love at first sight.

**coup de maî·tre** /ˌkoo də 'met(rə)/ ▶n. (pl. **coups de maî·tre** pronunc. same) master stroke.

**coupe** /koop/ ▶n. two-door car with a hard top.

**cou·ple** /ˈkəpəl/ ▶n. **1** two or about two. **2 a** married or engaged pair. **b** pair of partners in a dance, etc.
▶v. **1** link together. **2** copulate.

**cou·plet** /ˈkəplit/ ▶n. two successive lines of verse, usu. rhyming and of the same length.

**cou·pon** /ˈk(y)oo͞oˌpän/ ▶n. **1** discount voucher presented at purchase. **2** detachable ticket or form entitling holder to payment, goods, a discount, services, etc.

**cour·age** /ˈkərij/ ▶n. ability to disregard fear; bravery. —**cou·ra·geous** adj.

**cou·ri·er** /ˈkoor͞ēər; ˈkərēər/ ▶n. special messenger.

**course** /kôrs/ ▶n. **1** route or direction followed by a ship, road, river, etc. **2** way in which something progresses. **3** ground on which a race, etc., takes place. **4** series of lessons, etc., in a particular subject. **5** each successive part of a meal. **6** water channel.
▶v. (esp. of liquid) run, esp. fast.

□ **in the course of** during. □ **of course** naturally; as is or was to be expected. □ **run its course** (esp. of an illness) complete its natural development.

**cours·er** /ˈkôrsər/ ▶n. swift horse.

**court** /kôrt/ ▶n. **1** (also **court of law**) **a** judicial body hearing legal cases. **b** place where such a tribunal meets. **2** quadrangular area for games. **3** quadrangular area surrounded by a building. **4** milieu or attendants of a sovereign. **5** attention paid to a person for favor.
▶v. **1** try to win affection or favor of. **2** seek to win (applause, fame, etc.). **3** invite (misfortune) by one's actions.

**cour·te·ous** /ˈkərtēəs/ ▶adj. polite or respectful.

**cour·te·san** /ˈkôrtəzən/ ▶n. prostitute, esp. one with wealthy clients.

**cour·te·sy** /ˈkərtəsē/ ▶n. (pl. **-sies**) courteous behavior or act.

**cour·ti·er** /ˈkôrtēər/ ▶n. person who attends or frequents a sovereign's court.

**court·ly** ▶adj. (**-li·er, -li·est**) polished or refined in manners. —**court·li·ness** n.

**court·mar·tial** ▸*n.* (*pl.* **courts-mar·tial**) military judicial court. ▸*v.* try by court-martial.

**cous·in** /ˈkəzin/ ▸*n.* **1** (also **first cousin**) child of one's uncle or aunt. **2** person of kindred race or nation. □ **second cousin** child of one's parent's first cousin.

**couth** /kōōTH/ *inf.* ▸*adj.* cultured, refined, and well mannered. ▸*n.* good manners; refinement.

**cou·ture** /kōōˈtōōr/ ▸*n.* design and manufacture of fashionable clothes to a client's specific requirements and measurements, the business of designing and making such clothes, or the clothes themselves.

**cou·tu·ri·er** /kōōˈtōōrē,ā/ ▸*n.* fashion designer.

**cou·vade** /kōōˈväd/ ▸*n.* custom in some cultures in which a man takes to his bed and goes through certain rituals when his child is being born, as though he were physically affected by the birth.

**cove** /kōv/ ▸*n.* **1** small, esp. sheltered, bay or creek. **2** sheltered recess.

**co·ven** /ˈkəvən/ ▸*n.* assembly of witches.

**cov·e·nant** /ˈkəvənənt/ ▸*n.* **1** agreement; contract. **2** (**Covenant**) in the Old Testament, the agreement between God and the Israelites. ▸*v.* agree, esp. by legal covenant.

**cov·er** /ˈkəvər/ ▸*v.* **1** protect or conceal with a cloth, lid, etc. **2** extend over the surface of. **3** include; comprise; deal with. **4** travel (a specified distance). **5** investigate or describe as a reporter. **6 a** protect oneself. **b** stand in for: *will you cover for me?* **7 a** aim a gun, etc., at. **b** protect (an exposed person, etc.) with a gun, etc. ▸*n.* **1** something that covers, esp.: **a** lid. **b** binding of a book. **c** envelope or wrapping. **d** (**covers**) bedclothes. **2** shelter. **3 a** pretense; screen. **b** force protecting an advance party from attack. □ **cover charge** charge levied per head in a restaurant, nightclub, etc. □ **cover crop** crop grown for protection and enrichment of the soil. □ **cover letter** explanatory letter sent with an enclosure. □ **cover story** news story in a magazine, as illustrated on the front cover. □ **cover up** conceal (circumstances, etc., esp. illicitly). □ **cover-up** act of concealing circumstances, esp. illicitly. □ **take cover** find shelter, esp. against an attack.

**cov·er·age** /ˈkəv(ə)rij/ ▸n. **1** area or amount covered. **2** amount of publicity received by a particular story, person, event, etc.

**cov·er crop** ▸n. crop grown for the protection and enrichment of the soil.

**cov·er·let** /ˈkəvərlit/ ▸n. bedspread.

**co·vert** /ˈkōvərl/ ▸adj. secret or disguised: *covert glance.*

**cov·er·ture** /ˈkəvər,CHo͝or; -CHər/ ▸n. **1** protective or concealing covering. **2** legal status of a married woman, considered to be under her husband's protection and authority.

**cov·et** /ˈkəvit/ ▸v. desire greatly (another's possession, attribute, etc.).

**cov·ey** /ˈkəve/ ▸n. (pl. **-eys**) **1** brood of partridges. **2** small group of people, etc.

**cow** /kou/ ▸n. **1** grown female of any bovine animal, used esp. as a source of milk and beef. **2** female of other large animals, esp. the elephant, whale, and seal.
▸v. intimidate.

**cow·ard** /ˈkouərd/ ▸n. person easily frightened or intimidated.

**cow·boy** ▸n. (fem. **cow·girl**) person who tends cattle.

**cow·er** ▸v. crouch or shrink in fear.

**cowl** /koul/ ▸n. **1** monk's hood or hooded habit. **2** hood-shaped covering.

**cow·lick** ▸n. projecting lock of hair.

**cox·swain** /ˈkäksən/ ▸n. person who steers and directs the crew, esp. in a rowboat.

**coy** /koi/ ▸adj. (**coy·er, coy·est**) **1** modestly or affectedly shy. **2** irritatingly reticent. —**coy·ly** adv. —**coy·ness** n.

**coy·o·te** /kīˈōtē/ ▸n. (pl. same or **-tes**) N. American wolflike wild dog.

**coz·en** /ˈkəzən/ ▸v. trick or deceive.

**co·zy** /ˈkōzē/ ▸adj. (**-zi·er, -zi·est**) comfortable and warm; snug.
▸n. (pl. **-zies**) cover to keep something hot, esp. a teapot. —**co·zi·ly** adv. —**co·zi·ness** n.

**CPA** ▸abbr. certified public accountant.

**CPI** ▶*abbr.* consumer price index.

**CPR** ▶*abbr.* cardiopulmonary resuscitation.

**CPU** ▶*abbr. Computing* central processing unit.

**crab** /krab/ ▶*n.* **1** crustacean with four pairs of legs and two pincers. **2** (also **crab louse**) parasitic louse, infesting hairy parts of the body. **3** *inf.* irritable person. —**crab·like** *adj.*

**crab ap·ple** (also **crab apple**) ▶*n.* small, sour applelike fruit.

**crab·by** ▶*adj.* (**-bi·er**, **-bi·est**) *inf.* irritable. —**crab·bi·ly** *adv.* —**crab·bi·ness** *n.*

**crack** /krak/ ▶*n.* **1 a** sharp, explosive noise. **b** (in a voice) sudden change in pitch. **2** sharp blow. **3** narrow opening; break; partial fracture. **4** *inf.* mischievous or malicious remark. **5** *inf.* attempt: *I'll have a crack at it.* **6** exact moment: *the crack of dawn.* **7** *inf.* (also **crack cocaine**) potent crystalline form of cocaine broken into small pieces and smoked.

▶*v.* **1** break without separating the parts. **2** make or cause to make a sharp, explosive sound. **3** break or cause to break with a sharp sound. **4** (of the voice) become dissonant; break. **5** *inf.* find a solution to. **6** say (a joke, etc.) in a jocular way. **7** break (grain) into coarse pieces.

▶*adj.* excellent; first-rate: *he is a crack shot.*

□ **crack down on** *inf.* take severe measures against.

**crack·down** ▶*n. inf.* severe measures (esp. against lawbreakers, etc.).

**crack·er** ▶*n.* **1** thin, crisp wafer. **2** firework exploding with a sharp noise.

**crack·le** /ˈkrakəl/ ▶*v.* make repeated slight cracking sound.

▶*n.* **1** such a sound. **2** paintwork, china, or glass decorated with a pattern of minute surface cracks.

**crack·pot** *inf.* ▶*n.* eccentric person.

▶*adj.* mad; unworkable: *crackpot scheme.*

**cra·dle** /ˈkrādl/ ▶*n.* **1** baby's bed, esp. on rockers. **2** place in which a thing begins or is nurtured in its infancy. **3** supporting structure or framework.

▶*v.* contain or shelter as if in a cradle.

**craft** /kraft/ ▶*n.* **1** skill, esp. in practical arts. **2** trade or art.

**3 a** boat or vessel. **b** aircraft or spacecraft.

▸*v.* make in a skillful way.

**craft·y** ▸*adj.* (-i·er, -i·est) cunning; artful; wily. —**craft·i·ly** *adv.* —**craft·i·ness** *n.*

**crag** /krag/ ▸*n.* steep or rugged rock.

**cram** /kram/ ▸*v.* (**crammed, cram·ming**) **1** fill to bursting; stuff. **2** prepare for an exam by intensive study.

**cramp** /kramp/ ▸*n.* painful involuntary muscle contraction.

▸*v.* **1** affect with cramp. **2** confine narrowly. **3** [as *adj.* **cramped**] crowd (a room, etc.) uncomfortably.

**cran·ber·ry** /ˈkranˌberē/ ▸*n.* (*pl.* -ries) **1** N. American evergreen shrub yielding edible small, red, acid berries. **2** berry from this.

**crane** /krān/ ▸*n.* **1** machine with long hoisting arm. **2** tall wading bird with long legs, long neck, and straight bill.

▸*v.* stretch out (one's neck) to see.

**cra·ni·um** /ˈkrānēəm/ ▸*n.* (*pl.* -ums or -a) skull, esp. the part enclosing the brain. —**cra·ni·al** *adj.*

**crank** /kraNGk/ ▸*n.* **1** part of an axle or shaft bent at right angles for interconverting reciprocal and circular motion. **2** eccentric or bad-tempered person.

▸*v.* cause to move by means of a crank.

**crank·y** ▸*adj.* (-i·er, -i·est) ill-tempered; crotchety. —**crank·i·ly** *adv.* —**crank·i·ness** *n.*

**cran·ny** /ˈkranē/ ▸*n.* (*pl.* -nies) chink; crevice; crack. —**cran·nied** *adj.*

**crap** /krap/ *vulgar, inf.* ▸*n.* **1** nonsense; rubbish. **2** excrement.

▸*v.* (**crapped, crap·ping**) defecate. —**crap·py** *adj.*

**crape** /krāp/ ▸*n.* crepe, usu. of black silk, formerly used for mourning.

**craps** ▸*pl. n.* gambling game played with dice.

**crap·u·lent** /ˈkrapyələnt/ ▸*adj.* of or relating to the drinking of alcohol or drunkenness.

**crash** /kraSH/ ▸*v.* **1** make or cause to make a loud smashing noise. **2** throw, drive, move, or fall with a loud smashing noise. **3 a** collide or cause (a vehicle, etc.) to collide violently. **b** fall or cause (an aircraft) to fall and land violently. **4** undergo financial ruin. **5** *inf.* enter without permission: *crashed the* party. **6** *Computing* (of a system) fail suddenly.

▶*n.* **1** loud and sudden smashing noise. **2 a** violent collision, esp. of a vehicle. **b** violent fall and landing of an aircraft. **3** ruin, esp. financial. **4** *Computing* sudden failure (of a system). **5** done rapidly or urgently: *crash course in first aid.*

**crass** /kras/ ▶*adj.* lacking sensitivity or intelligence. —**crass·ly** *adv.* —**crass·ness** *n.*

**crate** /krāt/ ▶*n.* **1** slatted wooden case for transporting goods. **2** any similar case. ▶*v.* pack in a crate.

**cra·ter** ▶*n.* **1** mouth of a volcano. **2** bowl-shaped cavity, esp. from a shell or bomb. **3** hollow on the surface of a planet or moon.

**cra·ton** /ˈkrāˌtän/ ▶*n.* large, stable block of the earth's crust forming the nucleus of a continent.

**cra·vat** /krəˈvat/ ▶*n.* scarf worn inside an open-necked shirt.

**crave** /krāv/ ▶*v.* long or beg for.

**cra·ven** ▶*adj.* cowardly.

**crav·ing** ▶*n.* strong desire or longing.

**crawl** /krôl/ ▶*v.* **1** move on the hands and knees with the body close to the ground. **2** walk or move slowly. **3** *inf.* behave obsequiously. **4** be covered or filled with crawling or moving things, people, etc. ▶*n.* **1** crawling. **2** slow rate of movement. **3** high-speed overarm swimming stroke.

**cray·fish** /ˈkrāˌfiSH/ ▶*n.* (*pl.* same) small, lobsterlike freshwater crustacean.

**cray·on** /ˈkrāˌän/ ▶*n.* stick or pencil of colored wax, chalk, etc.

**craze** /krāz/ ▶*v.* [usu. as *adj.* **crazed**] make insane. ▶*n.* fad; rage.

**cra·zy** ▶*adj.* (**-zi·er, -zi·est**) *inf.* **1** insane; mad; foolish. **2** extremely enthusiastic. —**cra·zi·ness** *n.*

**creak** /krēk/ ▶*n.* harsh scraping or squeaking sound. ▶*v.* **1** move with a creaking noise. **2** move stiffly. —**creak·y** *adj.*

**cream** /krēm/ ▶*n.* **1** fatty content of milk. **2** (usu. **the cream**) best part of something. **3** creamlike cosmetic, etc. **4** pale yellow or off-white color. ▶*v.* work (butter, etc.) to a creamy consistency. —**cream·y** *adj.*

**cream·er·y** /ˈkrēm(ə)rē/ ▶*n.* (*pl.* **-ies**) factory or store for dairy products.

**cream of tar·tar** ▶*n.* crystallized potassium hydrogen tartrate, used chiefly in baking powder.

**crease** /krēs/ ▶*n.* line caused by folding; wrinkle.
▶*v.* **1** make creases in. **2** become creased.

**cre·ate** /krē'āt/ ▶*v.* **1** bring into existence; cause. **2** originate.
—**cre·a·tion** *n.* —**cre·a·tor** *n.*

**cre·a·tion sci·ence** ▶*n.* interpretation of scientific knowledge in accord with belief in the literal truth of the Bible, esp. regarding the creation of matter, life, and humankind in six days.

**cre·a·tive** ▶*adj.* inventive; imaginative.

**crea·ture** /'krēcHər/ ▶*n.* **1** any living being. **2** person of a specified kind: *poor creature.*

**crèche** /kresH/ ▶*n.* model or tableau representing the scene of Jesus Christ's birth, displayed in homes or public places at Christmas.

**cre·dence** /'krēdns/ ▶*n.* belief.

**cre·den·tial** /krə'denCHəl/ ▶*n.* (usu. **credentials**) evidence of a person's qualifications, etc., usu. in the form of certificates, references, etc.

**cre·den·za** /krə'denzə/ ▶*n.* sideboard or cupboard.

**cred·i·ble** /'kredəbəl/ ▶*adj.* believable; worthy of belief.
—**cred·i·bly** *adv.*

**cred·it** /'kredit/ ▶*n.* **1** source of honor, pride, etc. **2** acknowledgment of merit. **3** good reputation. **4** person's financial standing. **5** (usu. **credits**) acknowledgment of a contribution. **6** entry in an account of a sum paid into it.
▶*v.* **1** enter on the credit side of an account. **2** ascribe a good quality or achievement to. **3** believe: *cannot credit it.*
▫ **to one's credit** in one's praise, commendation, or defense.

**cred·it·a·ble** ▶*adj.* bringing credit or honor.
—**cred·it·a·bil·i·ty** *n.*
—**cred·it·a·bly** *adv.*

**cred·i·tor** ▶*n.* person to whom a debt is owed.

**cre·du·li·ty** /krə'd(y)ōōlitē/ ▶*n.* tendency to be too ready to believe that something is real or true.

**cred·u·lous** /'krejələs/ ▶*adj.* too ready to believe; gullible.
—**cre·du·li·ty** *n.*

**creed** /krēd/ ▶*n.* **1** system of Christian or other religious beliefs. **2** (**the Creed**) formal statement of Christian beliefs. **3** set of beliefs that guide someone's actions.

**Creek** /krēk/ ▸*n.* **1 a** confederacy of N. American peoples formerly of Alabama and Georgia. **b** member of these peoples. **2** language of these peoples.

**creek** ▸*n.* stream.

**creep** /krēp/ ▸*v.* (*past* and *past part.* **crept**) **1** move with the body prone and close to the ground. **2** move stealthily or timidly. **3** (of a plant) grow along the ground or up a wall, etc. **4** (of flesh) shiver; shudder. ▸*n.* **1** act or instance of creeping. **2** (**the creeps**) feeling of revulsion or fear. **3** *inf.* detestable person.

**creep·y** ▸*adj.* (**-i·er, -i·est**) *inf.* producing a feeling of horror or revulsion.

**cre·mate** /ˈkrēˌmāt/ ▸*v.* consume (a corpse, etc.) by fire. —**cre·ma·tion** *n.* —**cre·ma·to·ri·um** *n.*

**cren·el·la·tions** /ˌkrenlˈāsHənz/ ▸*pl. n.* battlements of a castle or other building.

**Cre·ole** /ˈkrēˌōl/ ▸*n.* **1** person of mixed European and black descent, esp. in the Caribbean.

**2** language formed from a European language (esp. English, French, or Portuguese) and another (esp. African) language. ▸*adj.* **1** of Creoles. **2** (usu. **creole**) of Creole origin: *creole cooking.*

**cre·o·sote** /ˈkrēəˌsōt/ ▸*n.* distillate of wood or coal tar, used as wood preservative, antiseptic, etc.

**crepe** /krāp/ (also **crêpe**) ▸*n.* **1** fine, gauzelike wrinkled fabric. **2** thin pancake, usu. with a filling. **3** hard-wearing wrinkled rubber used for the soles of shoes, etc. □ **crepe paper** thin crinkled paper.

**crep·i·tate** /ˈkrepəˌtāt/ ▸*v.* make a crackling sound.

**cre·pus·cu·lar** /krəˈpəskyələr/ ▸*adj.* of, resembling, or relating to twilight.

**cre·scen·do** /krəˈsHendō/ ▸*n.* (*pl.* **-dos**) *Mus.* **1** gradual increase in loudness. **2** progress toward a climax. ▸*adv. & adj.* increasing in loudness. ▸*v.* (**-doed**) increase gradually in loudness or intensity.

**cres·cent** /ˈkresənt/ ▸*n.* **1** curved sickle shape, as of the waxing or waning moon. **2** anything of this shape.

**cress** /kres/ ▶*n.* plant of the cabbage family with pungent edible leaves.

**cres·set** /ˈkresit/ ▶*n.* metal container of oil, grease, wood, or coal burned as a torch and typically mounted on a pole.

**crest** /krest/ ▶*n.* **1 a** comb, tuft, etc., on a bird's or animal's head. **b** plume, etc., on a helmet, etc. **2** top of a mountain, wave, roof, etc. **3** heraldic device, as on seals, etc.

**crest·fall·en** ▶*adj.* dejected; dispirited.

**cre·tin** /ˈkrētn/ ▶*n.* stupid person.

**cre·vasse** /krəˈvas/ ▶*n.* deep open crack, esp. in a glacier.

**crev·ice** /ˈkrevis/ ▶*n.* narrow opening or fissure, esp. in a rock.

**crew** /krōō/ ▶*n.* **1 a** people manning a ship, aircraft, train, etc. **b** these as distinct from the captain or officers. **c** people working together; team. **2** *inf.* company of people; gang: *a motley crew.*

▶*v.* **1** supply or act as a crew or crew member for. **2** act as a crew or crew member.

**crew cut** ▶*n.* very short haircut.

**crib** /krib/ ▶*n.* **1** baby's bed with high sides. **2** rack for animal fodder. **3** *inf.* translation of a text for use by students.

▶*v.* (**cribbed**, **crib·bing**) **1** *inf.* copy without acknowledgment. **2** confine in a small space.

**crib·bage** /ˈkribij/ ▶*n.* card game for up to four players.

□ **cribbage board** board with pegs for scoring at cribbage.

**crib death** ▶*n.* SUDDEN INFANT DEATH SYNDROME.

**crick** /krik/ ▶*n.* painful stiffness in the neck or back.

**crick·et** /ˈkrikit/ ▶*n.* **1** team game played with ball, bats, and wickets. **2** grasshopperlike chirping insect.

□ **not cricket** underhand behavior.

**cri·er** /ˈkrīər/ (also **cry·er**) ▶*n.* official making public announcements, as in a court of law.

**crime** /krīm/ ▶*n.* **1** offense punishable by law. **2** illegal acts.

**crim·i·nal** /ˈkrimənl/ ▶*n.* person who has committed a crime.

▶*adj.* of or relating to a crime.

**crim·i·nal·ize** /ˈkrimənlˌīz/ ▶*v.* turn (an activity) into a criminal offense by making it illegal.

**crimp** /krimp/ ▶*v.* **1** compress into small folds. **2** corrugate. **3** make waves in (hair).

▶*n.* crimped thing or form.

□ **put a crimp in** *inf.* thwart.

**crim·son** /ˈkrimzən/ ▶*adj.* of a rich, deep red.

▶*n.* this color.

**cringe** /krinj/ ▶*v.* shrink in fear; cower.

**crin·kle** /ˈkriNGkəl/ ▶*n.* wrinkle or crease on the surface of something.

▶*v.* form crinkles (in). **—crin·kly** *adj.*

**crin·o·line** /ˈkrinl-in/ ▶*n.* stiffened or hooped petticoat.

**cri·ol·lo** /krēˈō(l)yō/ (also **Cri·ol·lo**) ▶*n.* (*pl.* **-los**) person from Spanish South or Central America, esp. one of pure Spanish descent.

**crip·ple** /ˈkripəl/ ▶*n.* lame person or animal.

▶*v.* disable; impair.

**cri·sis** /ˈkrīsis/ ▶*n.* (*pl.* **-ses**) **1** time of intense difficulty or danger. **2** decisive moment. **3** turning point of a disease.

**crisp** /krisp/ ▶*adj.* **1** hard but brittle. **2 a** (of air) bracing. **b** (of a style or manner) lively; brisk and decisive. **c** (of paper) stiff and crackling.

▶*v.* make or become crisp.

**cris·pate** /ˈkris,pāt; -pət/ ▶*adj.* (esp. of a leaf) having a wavy or curly edge.

**criss·cross** /ˈkris,krôs/ ▶*n.* pattern of crossing lines.

▶*adj.* crossing; in cross lines.

▶*adv.* crosswise; at cross purposes.

▶*v.* **1 a** intersect repeatedly. **b** move crosswise. **2** mark or make with a crisscross pattern.

**cri·te·ri·on** /krīˈti(ə)rēən/ ▶*n.* (*pl.* **-a** or **-ons**) principle or standard that a thing is judged by.

**crit·ic** /ˈkritik/ ▶*n.* **1** person who censures or criticizes. **2** person who reviews literary, artistic, etc. works.

**crit·i·cal** /ˈkritikəl/ ▶*adj.* **1** involving adverse comments; faultfinding. **2** of literary or artistic criticism. **3** of or at a crisis; crucial. **—crit·i·cal·ly** *adv.*

**crit·i·cal mass** ▶*n.* **1** minimum amount of fissile material needed to maintain a nuclear chain reaction. **2** minimum size or amount of something required to start or maintain a venture.

**crit·i·cism** /ˈkritə,sizəm/ ▶*n.* **1** finding fault; censure. **2** critical remark. **3** evaluation of a literary or artistic work.

**crit·i·cize** /ˈkritə,sīz/ ▶*v.* **1** find

fault with; censure. **2** discuss critically.

**cri·tique** /kri'tēk/ ▶n. expression of critical analysis.

▶v. (**-tiqued, -ti·quing**) discuss critically.

**crit·ter** /'kritər/ ▶n. inf. living creature.

**croak** /krōk/ ▶n. deep, hoarse sound, as of a frog.

▶v. utter (with) a croak.

**cro·chet** /krō'shā/ ▶n. handicraft in which yarn is hooked into a patterned fabric.

▶v. make in such a way.

**crock** /kräk/ ▶n. earthenware pot or jar.

**croc·o·dile** /'kräkə,dīl/ ▶n. **1** large, long-jawed tropical amphibious reptile. **2** leather from its skin.

□ **crocodile tears** insincere grief.

**cro·cus** /'krōkəs/ ▶n. (pl. **-cus·es**) small plant bearing white, yellow, or purple flowers in early spring.

**crois·sant** /k(r)wä'sänt/ ▶n. crescent-shaped pastry.

**crone** /krōn/ ▶n. withered old woman.

**cro·ny** /'krōnē/ ▶n. (pl. **-nies**) close friend or companion.

**cro·ny·ism** /'krōnē,izəm/ ▶n. appointment of friends and associates to positions of authority, without proper regard to their qualifications.

**crook** /krŏŏk/ ▶n. **1** hooked staff of a shepherd or bishop. **2** bend; curve; hook. **3** inf. swindler; criminal.

▶v. bend; curve.

**croon** /krōōn/ ▶v. hum or sing in a low sentimental voice.
—**croon·er** n.

**crop** /kräp/ ▶n. **1** produce of cultivated plants. **2** group or amount produced or appearing at one time. **3** handle of a whip. **4** predigestive pouch in a bird's gullet.

▶v. (**cropped, crop·ping**) **1** cut off. **2** cut (hair, etc.) short.

□ **crop circle** circular depression in a standing crop. □ **crop-dusting** sprinkling of insecticide or fertilizer, esp. from the air.

□ **crop up** occur unexpectedly.

**cro·quet** /krō'kā/ ▶n. lawn game with hoops, mallets, and wooden balls.

**cro·quette** /krō'ket/ ▶n. fried, breaded ball of mashed potato or ground meat, etc.

**cro·sier** /'krōzнər/ (also **cro·zier**) ▶n. bishop's hooked staff.

**cross** /krôs/ ▶*n.* **1** upright post with a transverse bar. **2 a** (**the Cross**) cross on which Christ was crucified. **b** representation of this. **3** thing or mark like a cross. **4** hybrid. **5** (**a cross between**) mixture or compromise of two things. **6** trial; affliction.

▶*v.* **1** go across. **2** (cause to) intersect. **3** draw a line or lines across, esp. to delete. **4** make the sign of the cross on or over. **5** pass in opposite or different directions. **6** cross-fertilize (plants). **7** oppose or stand in the way of.

▶*adj.* **1** annoyed. **2** transverse; reaching from side to side. **3** intersecting.

□ **at cross purposes** misunderstanding; conflicting. □ **cross-dress** wear clothing typically worn by the opposite sex.

**cross·bar** ▶*n.* horizontal bar.

**cross·bow** /bō/ ▶*n.* bow fixed on a wooden stock, with a groove for an arrow.

**cross·breed** ▶*n.* hybrid breed of animals or plants.

▶*v.* (*past* and *past part.* **-bred**) produce by crossing.

**cross·coun·try** ▶*adj. & adv.* **1** across open country. **2** not keeping to main roads.

**cross·ex·am·ine** ▶*v.* examine (esp. a witness in a court of law) to check or extend testimony already given. —**cross·ex·am·in·a·tion** *n.*

**cross·hatch** /'krôsˌhaCH/ ▶*v.* (in drawing or graphics) shade (an area) with intersecting sets of parallel lines.

**cross·patch** /'krôsˌpaCH/ ▶*n.* bad-tempered person.

**cross·ref·er·ence** ▶*n.* reference from one part of a book, etc., to another.

▶*v.* provide with cross-references.

**cross sec·tion** ▶*n.* **1 a** cutting across a solid. **b** plane surface produced in this way. **2** representative sample.

**cross·walk** ▶*n.* pedestrian crossing.

**cross·word** (also **cross·word puz·zle**) ▶*n.* grid of squares and blanks for words crossing vertically and horizontally to be filled in from clues.

**crotch** /kräCH/ ▶*n.* place where something forks, esp. the legs of the human body or a garment.

**crotch·et** /'kräCHət/ ▶*n.* perverse or unfounded belief or notion.

**crotch·et·y** /ˈkräCHitē/ ▸*adj.* peevish.

**crouch** /krouCH/ ▸*v.* lower the body with limbs close to the chest; be in this position. ▸*n.* crouching; crouching position.

**croup** /kro͞op/ ▸*n.* inflammation of the larynx and trachea in children, with a hard cough.

**crou·pi·er** /ˈkro͞opēˌā/ ▸*n.* person in charge of a gaming table.

**crou·ton** /ˈkro͞oˌtän/ ▸*n.* cube of toasted bread served with soup, etc.

**Crow** /krō/ ▸*n.* **1 a** N. American people native to eastern Montana. **b** member of this people. **2** language of this people.

**crow** ▸*n.* large black bird having a powerful black beak. ▸*v.* **1** (of a cock) utter a loud cry. **2** express glee. □ **crow's-foot** wrinkle at the outer corner of the eye. □ **crow's nest** lookout platform at the masthead of a sailing vessel.

**crow·bar** ▸*n.* iron bar with a flattened end, used as a lever.

**crowd** /kroud/ ▸*n.* **1** large gathering of people. **2** spectators; audience. **3** *inf.* particular set of people. ▸*v.* **1** (cause to) come together in a crowd. **2 a** (**crowd into**) force or compress into (a confined space). **b** fill or make abundant with. **3** come aggressively close to.

□ **crowd out** exclude by crowding.

**crown** /kroun/ ▸*n.* **1** monarch's jeweled headdress. **2** (**the Crown**) **a** monarch, esp. as head of state. **b** power or authority of the monarchy. **3 a** wreath worn on the head, esp. as an emblem of victory. **b** award or distinction, esp. in sport. **4** crown-shaped device or ornament. **5** highest or top part. **6 a** part of a tooth projecting from the gum. **b** artificial replacement for this. ▸*v.* **1** put a crown on. **2** invest with royal authority. **3** be a crown to; rest on top of. **4** [as *adj.* **crowning**] be or cause to be the reward or finishing touch to: *the crowning glory.* **5** promote (a piece in checkers) to king.

**CRT** ▸*abbr.* cathode-ray tube.

**cru·cial** /ˈkro͞oSHəl/ ▸*adj.* **1** decisive; critical. **2** very important.

**cru·ci·ate** /ˈkro͞oSH(ē)ət; -SHēˌāt/ ▸*adj.* cross-shaped.

**cru·ci·ble** /ˈkrōōsəbəl/ ▸*n.*
1 melting pot for metals, etc.
2 severe test or trial.

**cru·ci·fix** /ˈkrōōsəˌfiks/ ▸*n.* image
of a cross with a figure of Christ
on it. —**cru·ci·fix·ion** *n.*

**cru·ci·fy** /ˈkrōōsəˌfī/ ▸*v.* (**-fied**)
1 put to death by fastening to a
cross. 2 persecute; torment.

**crude** /krōōd/ ▸*adj.* 1 a in the
natural state; not refined.
b unpolished; lacking finish.
2 a rude; blunt. b offensive;
indecent. 3 inexact; rough: *a
crude estimate.*
▸*n.* natural petroleum.
—**cru·di·ty** *n.*

**cru·di·tés** /ˌkrōōdəˈtā/ ▸*pl. n.*
hors d'oeuvre of mixed raw
vegetables.

**cru·el** /ˈkrōōəl/ ▸*adj.* 1 harsh;
severe. 2 causing pain or
suffering, esp. deliberately.
—**cru·el·ly** *adv.* —**cru·el·ty** *n.*

**cru·et** /ˈkrōōt/ ▸*n.* small
container (esp. for oil or vinegar)
for use at the table.

**cruise** /krōōz/ ▸*v.* 1 make a
journey by sea, esp. for pleasure.
2 travel at a moderate or steady
speed. 3 achieve an objective,
win a race, etc., with ease. 4 *inf.*
search for a sexual partner, esp.
on streets, in bars, etc.

▸*n.* pleasure voyage on a ship.
□ **cruise control** device for
automatically maintaining the
speed of an automobile, etc.
□ **cruise missile** low-flying, self-
guiding missile.

**cruis·er** ▸*n.* 1 high-speed
warship. 2 police patrol car.

**crumb** /krəm/ ▸*n.* small
fragment, esp. of bread.

**crum·ble** /ˈkrəmbəl/ ▸*v.* 1 break
or fall into fragments. 2 (of
power, reputation, etc.)
gradually disintegrate.
—**crum·bly** *adj.*

**crum·my** /ˈkrəmē/ ▸*adj.* (**-mi·er,
-mi·est**) *inf.* squalid; worthless.

**crum·ple** /ˈkrəmpəl/ ▸*v.* 1 crush
or become crushed into creases.
2 collapse; give way.
▸*n.* crease or wrinkle.

**crunch** /krənCH/ ▸*v.* 1 crush
noisily with the teeth. 2 grind
under foot, wheels, etc.
▸*n.* 1 crunching; crunching
sound. 2 *inf.* decisive event;
moment of pressure.
—**crunch·i·ness** *n.* —**crunch·y**
*adj.*

**cru·sade** /krōōˈsād/ ▸*n.* 1 (often
**Crusade**) any of several
medieval military expeditions
made by Europeans to recover
the Holy Land from the Muslims.

**2** vigorous campaign in favor of a cause.

▸*v.* engage in a crusade.
—**cru·sad·er** *n.*

**cruse** /krōōz/ ▸*n.* earthenware pot or jar.

**crush** /krəsH/ ▸*v.* **1** compress with force or violence, so as to break, bruise, etc. **2** reduce to powder by pressure. **3** defeat or subdue completely.

▸*n.* **1** act of crushing. **2** crowded mass of people. **3** *inf.* infatuation. **4** drink made from crushed fruit.

**crust** /krəst/ ▸*n.* **1** hard outer part of bread. **2** pastry covering of a pie. **3** hard casing of a softer thing. **4** outer portion of the earth. **5** hard residue or deposit.

▸*v.* **1** cover or become covered with a crust. **2** form into a crust.

**crus·ta·cean** /krəs'tāsHən/ ▸*n.* hard-shelled, esp. aquatic arthropod, e.g., crab, lobster, and shrimp.

**crutch** /krəCH/ ▸*n.* **1** support for walking used by a lame person, usu. with a crosspiece fitting under the armpit. **2** support or object of dependency.

**crux** /krəks/ ▸*n.* (*pl.* **crux·es** or **cru·ces**) decisive point at issue.

**cry** /krī/ ▸*v.* (**cried**) **1** make a loud or shrill sound, esp. to express pain, appeal for help, etc. **2** shed tears; weep.

▸*n.* (*pl.* **cries**) **1** loud shout of grief, pain, joy, etc. **2** spell of weeping. **3** public demand. **4** call of an animal.

□ **cry out for** demand as a self-evident requirement or solution.
□ **far cry 1** long way. **2** very different thing.

**cry·o·gen·ics** /ˌkrīə'jeniks/ ▸*n.* branch of physics dealing with very low temperatures.
—**cry·o·gen·ic** *adj.*

**crypt** /kript/ ▸*n.* underground vault, used usu. for burial.

**cryp·tic** ▸*adj.* obscure in meaning; secret; mysterious.
—**cryp·ti·cal·ly** *adv.*

**crys·tal** /'kristl/ ▸*n.* **1** clear transparent mineral. **2** highly transparent glass. **3** substance with a definite internal structure and a solid form enclosed by symmetrical plane faces.

▸*adj.* made of, like, or clear as crystal.

**crys·tal·line** /'kristl-in/ ▸*adj.* **1** of, like, or clear as crystal. **2** having the structure and form of a crystal.

**crys·tal·lize** ▸*v.* **1** form or cause to form crystals. **2** (of ideas or plans) become or make definite. —**crys·tal·li·za·tion** *n.*

**crys·tal·log·ra·phy** /ˌkristl-ˈägrəfē/ ▸*n.* branch of science concerned with the structure and properties of crystals.

**CST** ▸*abbr.* central standard time.

**CT** ▸*abbr.* Connecticut (in official postal use).

**ct.** ▸*abbr.* **1** carat. **2** cent.

**Cu** ▸*symb. Chem.* copper.

**cu.** ▸*abbr.* cubic.

**cub** /kəb/ ▸*n.* **1** young of a fox, bear, lion, etc. **2** (also **cub reporter**) young newspaper reporter.

**cube** /kyōōb/ ▸*n.* **1** solid of six equal square sides. **2** product of a number multiplied by its square.
▸*v.* **1** find the cube of (a number). **2** cut (food, etc.) into small cubes.
□ **cube root** number for which a given number is the cube.

**cu·bic** ▸*adj.* **1** cube-shaped. **2** of three dimensions. **3** involving the cube of a number.

**cu·bi·cle** /ˈkyōōbikəl/ ▸*n.* small partitioned space; compartment.

**cub·ism** /ˈkyōōˌbizəm/ ▸*n.* geometric style in art, esp. painting. —**cub·ist** *n. & adj.*

**cu·bit** /ˈkyōōbit/ ▸*n.* ancient measure of length, approx. equal to the length of a forearm. It was typically about 18 inches or 44 centimeters.

**cuck·old** /ˈkəkəld/ ▸*n.* man whose wife commits adultery.
▸*v.* make a cuckold of.

**cuck·oo** /ˈkōōkōō/ ▸*n.* bird with a characteristic cry, known to lay its eggs in the nests of other birds.
▸*adj. inf.* crazy; foolish.

**cu·cum·ber** /ˈkyōōˌkəmbər/ ▸*n.* long, green, fleshy fruit, used in salads and for pickles.

**cud** /kəd/ ▸*n.* half-digested food returned from the first stomach of ruminants to the mouth for further chewing.

**cud·dle** /ˈkədl/ ▸*v.* **1** hug lovingly. **2** nestle together.
▸*n.* gentle hug. —**cud·dly** *adj.*

**cud·gel** /ˈkəjəl/ ▸*n.* short, thick stick used as a weapon.
▸*v.* beat with a cudgel.

**cue** /kyōō/ ▸*n.* **1 a** last words of an actor's line as a signal to another to enter or speak. **b** similar signal to a musician, etc. **2** signal for action. **3** long rod for striking the ball in billiards or pool.

▶ v. (**cued**, **cu·ing** or **cue·ing**) give a signal to.

**cues·ta** /ˈkwestə/ ▶ n. ridge with a gentle slope on one side and a steep slope on the other.

**cuff** /kəf/ ▶ n. **1** end part of a sleeve. **2** turned-up hem on pants.

▶ v. strike with an open hand.

□ **off-the-cuff** inf. impromptu.

**cui bo·no?** /kwē ˈbōnō/ ▶ exclam. who stands, or stood, to gain (from a crime, and so might have been responsible for it)?

**cui·sine** /kwiˈzēn/ ▶ n. style or method of cooking.

**cu·li·nar·y** /ˈkələˌnerē/ ▶ adj. pertaining to cooking.

**cull** /kəl/ ▶ v. pick selectively.

**cul·mi·nate** /ˈkəlməˌnāt/ ▶ v. reach or bring to its highest or final point. —**cul·mi·na·tion** n.

**cul·pa·ble** /ˈkəlpəbəl/ ▶ adj. deserving blame.
—**cul·pa·bil·i·ty** n.

**cul·prit** /ˈkəlprit/ ▶ n. guilty person.

**cult** /kəlt/ ▶ n. **1** ritualistic religious system. **2** devotion to a person or thing: cult of aestheticism. **3** denoting a fashionable person or thing: cult film.

**cul·ti·vate** /ˈkəltəˌvāt/ ▶ v. **1** prepare and use (soil, etc.) for crops or gardening. **2 a** raise (crops). **b** culture (bacteria, etc.). **3 a** [often as adj. **cultivated**] adj. improve or develop (the mind, manners, etc.). **b** nurture (a person, friendship, etc.).
—**cul·ti·va·tion** n.

**cul·ture** /ˈkəlCHər/ ▶ n. **1** artistic and intellectual achievement. **2** customs, achievements, etc., of a particular civilization. **3** cultivation of plants; rearing of bees, silkworms, etc. **4** quantity of microorganisms and the nutrient material supporting their growth.

▶ v. maintain (bacteria, etc.) in suitable growth conditions.
—**cul·tur·al** adj. —**cul·tured** adj.

**cul·vert** /ˈkəlvərt/ ▶ n. channel carrying water under a road, etc.

**cum·ber·some** /ˈkəmbərsəm/ ▶ adj. inconvenient in size, weight, or shape; unwieldy.

**cu·mu·la·tive** /ˈkyo͞omyələtiv/ ▶ adj. **1** increasing progressively in amount, force, etc. **2** formed by successive additions.
—**cu·mu·la·tive·ly** adv.

**cu·mu·lus** /ˈkyo͞omyələs/ ▶ n. (pl.

-li) cloud formation of heaped, rounded masses. —**cu·mu·lous** *adj.*

**cu·ne·i·form** /kyoō'nēə,fôrm/ ▸*adj.* **1** wedge-shaped. **2** of or using wedge-shaped writing, as in ancient Babylonian, etc., inscriptions.

▸*n.* cuneiform writing.

**cun·ning** /'kəniNG/ ▸*adj.* **1** deceitful; clever; crafty. **2** ingenious.

▸*n.* **1** craftiness; skill in deceit. **2** skill; ingenuity.

**cup** /kəp/ ▸*n.* **1** small bowl-shaped container for drinking from. **2** its contents. **3** cup-shaped thing. **4** cup-shaped trophy.

▸*v.* (**cupped, cup·ping**) **1** form (esp. one's hands) into the shape of a cup. **2** take or hold as in a cup.

**cup·board** /'kəbərd/ ▸*n.* recess or piece of furniture with a door and (usu.) shelves.

**Cu·pid** /'kyoōpid/ ▸*n.* **1** Roman god of love, represented as a naked winged archer. **2** (also **cupid**) representation of Cupid.

**cu·pid·i·ty** /kyoō'piditē/ ▸*n.* greed for gain; avarice.

**cu·po·la** /'kyoōpələ/ ▸*n.* dome forming or adorning a roof.

**cu·pre·ous** /'k(y)oōprēəs/ ▸*adj.* of or like copper.

**cur** /kər/ ▸*n.* **1** mongrel. **2** *inf.* contemptible man.

**cu·rate** /'kyoōrit/ ▸*n.* assistant to a rector or parish priest.

**cu·ra·tor** /'kyoō,rātər/ ▸*n.* keeper or custodian of a museum, etc. —**cu·ra·to·ri·al** *adj.* —**cu·ra·tor·ship** *n.*

**curb** /kərb/ ▸*n.* **1** street edge or sidewalk border. **2** check; restraint. **3** strap, etc., to restrain a horse. **4** enclosing border.

▸*v.* restrain.

**curd** /kərd/ ▸*n.* coagulated milk product, often made into cheese.

**cur·dle** /'kərdl/ ▸*v.* make into or become curds; (of milk) turn sour; congeal.

**cure** /kyoōr/ ▸*v.* **1** restore to health. **2** eliminate (disease, evil, etc.). **3** preserve (meat, fruit, etc.) by salting, drying, etc.

▸*n.* **1** restoration to health. **2** thing that effects a cure. **3** course of treatment.

□ **cure-all** panacea.

**cur·few** /'kər,fyoō/ ▸*n.* regulation requiring people to remain indoors between specified hours, usu. at night.

**cu·ri·o** /'kyo͞orē,ō/ ▸n. (pl. **-os**) rare or unusual object.

**cu·ri·o·sa** /,kyo͞orē'ōsə; -'ōzə/ ▸pl. n. curiosities, esp. erotic or pornographic books or articles.

**cu·ri·os·i·ty** /,kyo͞orē'äsitē/ ▸n. (pl. **-ties**) **1** eager desire to know; inquisitiveness. **2** strange, rare, or interesting thing.

**cu·ri·ous** /'kyo͞orēəs/ ▸adj. **1** eager to learn; inquisitive. **2** strange; surprising; odd.

**curl** /kərl/ ▸v. bend or coil into a spiral; form or cause to form curls.
▸n. **1** lock of curled hair. **2** anything spiral or curved inward. **3 a** curling movement. **b** being curled. —**curl·y** adj.

**cur·lew** /'kər,lo͞o/ ▸n. wading bird, usu. with long, slender bill.

**cur·li·cue** /'kərli,kyo͞o/ ▸n. decorative curl or twist.

**cur·mud·geon** /kər'məjən/ ▸n. bad-tempered person.

**cur·rant** /'kərənt/ ▸n. **1** small seedless dried grape. **2 a** any of various shrubs producing red, white, or black berries. **b** such a berry.

**cur·ren·cy** /'kərənsē/ ▸n. (pl. **-cies**) **1 a** money in use in a country. **b** other commodity used as money. **2** being current; prevalence.

**cur·rent** /'kərənt/ ▸adj. belonging to the present time; happening now.
▸n. **1** narrow stream of water, air, etc., moving in a definite direction. **2 a** ordered movement of electrically charged particles. **b** quantity representing the intensity of this.

**cur·ric·u·lum** /kə'rikyələm/ ▸n. (pl. **-la** or **-lums**) subjects in a course of study. —**cur·ric·u·lar** adj.

**cur·ric·u·lum vi·tae** /kə-'rik(y)ələm 've̅,tī; 'vītē/ (abbr.: **CV**) ▸n. (pl. **cur·ric·u·la vi·tae** /kə-'rik(y)ələ/) brief account of a person's education, qualifications, and previous experience, typically sent with a job application.

**cur·ry** /'kərē/ ▸n. (pl. **-ries**) dish prepared with curry powder.
▸v. (**-ried**) **1** flavor with curry powder. **2** groom (a horse) with a currycomb. **3** treat (tanned leather) to improve it.
□ **curry favor** ingratiate oneself.

**cur·ry·comb** ▸n. metal serrated device for grooming horses.

**cur·ry pow·der** ▸n. usu. hot-tasting preparation of various spices such as turmeric, ginger, and coriander.

**curse** /kərs/ ▶*n.* **1** solemn invocation of supernatural wrath. **2** evil supposedly resulting from a curse. **3** violent exclamation of anger; profane oath. **4** thing that causes evil or harm.
▶*v.* **1** utter a curse against. **2** afflict (with). **3** utter expletive curses.

**cur·sive** /ˈkərsiv/ ▶*adj.* (of writing) done with joined characters.
▶*n.* cursive writing. —**cur·sive·ly** *adv.*

**cur·sor** /ˈkərsər/ ▶*n.* Computing positional indicator on a screen.

**cur·so·ry** ▶*adj.* hasty; hurried: *cursory glance.* —**cur·so·ri·ly** *adv.*

**curt** /kərt/ ▶*adj.* rudely brief.

**cur·tail** /kərˈtāl/ ▶*v.* cut short; reduce. —**cur·tail·ment** *n.*

**cur·tain** /ˈkərtn/ ▶*n.* **1** piece of cloth, etc., hung as a screen, esp. at a window. **2** partition or cover.
▶*v.* shut off with curtains.
□ **curtain call** audience's summons to actor(s) to take a bow.

**curt·sy** /ˈkərtsē/ (also **curt·sey**)

▶*n.* (*pl.* **-sies** or **-seys**) woman's or girl's formal greeting or salutation made by bending the knees and lowering the body.
▶*v.* (**-sied** or **-seys**, **-seyed**) make a curtsy.

**cur·va·ture** /ˈkərvəcHər/ ▶*n.* curving or degree of curve.

**curve** /kərv/ ▶*n.* **1** line or surface of which no part is straight or flat. **2** curved form or thing.
▶*v.* bend or shape to form a curve. —**curved** *adj.* —**cur·vi·ness** *n.* —**curv·y** *adj.*

**cur·vet** /kərˈvet/ ▶*n.* (of a horse) a graceful or energetic leap.

**cur·vi·lin·e·ar** /ˌkərvəˈlinēər/ ▶*adj.* contained by or consisting of a curved line or lines.

**cush·ion** /ˈkŏŏsHən/ ▶*n.* **1** bag stuffed with soft material, for sitting or leaning on, etc. **2** protection against shock.
▶*v.* **1** provide or protect with a cushion or cushions. **2** mitigate the adverse effects of.

**cush·y** ▶*adj.* (**-i·er**, **-i·est**) *inf.* easy and pleasant.

**cusp** /kəsp/ ▶*n.* **1** point or pointed end. **2** point at which two arcs meet.

**cus·pi·dor** /ˈkəspəˌdôr/ ▶*n.* spittoon.

**cus·tard** /ˈkəstərd/ ▶*n.* pudding

or sweet sauce made with milk, eggs, and flavored cornstarch.

**cus·to·di·an** /kəsˈtōdēən/ ▶*n.* caretaker, esp. of a public building, etc.

**cus·to·dy** /ˈkəstədē/ ▶*n.* **1** guardianship; protective care. **2** imprisonment. —**cus·to·di·al** *adj.*
□ **take into custody** arrest.

**cus·tom** /ˈkəstəm/ ▶*n.* **1 a** usual behavior. **b** particular established way of behaving. **2** *Law* established usage having the force of law.

**cus·tom·ar·y** /ˈkəstəˌmerē/ ▶*adj.* usual. —**cus·tom·ar·i·ly** *adv.*

**cus·tom·er** ▶*n.* **1** person who buys goods or services. **2** person one has to deal with: *tough customer.*

**cus·tom·ize** ▶*v.* make or modify according to individual requirements.

**cus·toms** ▶*n.* **1** department that administers and collects duties levied by a government on imported goods. **2** place at a port, frontier, etc., where officials check incoming goods.

**cut** /kət/ ▶*v.* (**cut·ting**; *past* and *past part.* **cut**) **1** penetrate or wound with a sharp-edged instrument. **2** divide or be divided with a knife, etc. **3** reduce the length of or detach by cutting. **4** reduce (wages, prices, time, etc.) or cease (services, etc.). **5 a** make (a coat, gem, key, record, etc.) by cutting. **b** make (a path, tunnel, etc.) by removing material. **6** perform; make: *cut a deal.* **7** cross; intersect. **8** deliberately miss (a class, etc.). **9** *Cards* divide (a deck) into two parts. **10** switch off (an engine, etc.). **11** dilute.

▶*n.* **1** cutting. **2** division or wound made by cutting. **3** reduction or excision. **4** wounding remark or act. **5** style in which a garment, the hair, etc., is cut. **6** piece of butchered meat. **7** *inf.* share of profits.

□ **cut-and-dried** completely decided; inflexible. □ **cut corners** do a task, etc., perfunctorily, esp. to save time. □ **cut in 1** interrupt. **2** pull in closely in front of another vehicle. **3** give a share of profits, etc., to. **4** interrupt a dancing couple to take over from one partner. □ **cut into** interfere with and reduce: *cuts into my free time.* □ **cut short** terminate

prematurely: *cut short his visit.*
□ **cut a tooth** have a tooth appear through the gum.

**cu·ta·ne·ous** /kyoo'tānēəs/ ▶*adj.* of the skin.

**cut·back** ▶*n.* cutting back, esp. a reduction in expenditure.

**cute** /kyoot/ ▶*adj.* **1** attractive in a pretty or endearing way. **2** *inf.* superficially clever.

**cu·ti·cle** /'kyootikəl/ ▶*n.* dead skin at the base of a fingernail or toenail.

**cut·lass** /'kətləs/ ▶*n.* short sword with a slightly curved blade.

**cut·ler·y** /'kətlərē/ ▶*n.* **1** knives, etc., for kitchen use. **2** knives, forks, and spoons for use at table.

**cut·let** /'kətlit/ ▶*n.* small piece of veal, etc., for frying.

**cut·off** ▶*n.* **1** point at which something is cut off. **2** device for stopping a flow. **3** (**cutoffs**) shorts made from jeans, etc.

**cut·throat** ▶*n.* murderer.
▶*adj.* ruthless and intense.

**cut·tle·fish** /'kətl,fisн/ ▶*n.* mollusk with ten arms that ejects a black fluid when threatened.

**cy·a·nide** /'sīə,nīd/ ▶*n.* highly

poisonous substance used in mineral extraction.

**cy·ber·net·ics** /,sībər'netiks/ ▶*n.* science of communications and control systems in machines and living things. —**cy·ber·net·ic** *adj.*

**cy·ber·space** ▶*n.* the perceived virtual environment in which communication over computer networks occurs.

**cy·borg** /'sī,bôrg/ ▶*n.* fictional or hypothetical person whose physical abilities are extended beyond normal human limitations by mechanical elements built into the body.

**cy·cle** /'sīkəl/ ▶*n.* **1** recurrent round or period (of events, phenomena, etc.). **2** series of related songs, poems, etc. **3** bicycle, tricycle, etc.
▶*v.* **1** ride a bicycle, etc. **2** move in cycles.

**cy·clone** /'sī,klōn/ ▶*n.* violent, low-pressure hurricane of limited diameter.

**cy·clo·tron** /'sīklə,trän/ ▶*n.* apparatus for acceleration of charged atomic and subatomic particles revolving in a magnetic field.

**cyg·net** /'signit/ ▶*n.* young swan.
**cyl·in·der** /'siləndər/ ▶*n.*

**1** uniform solid or hollow body with straight sides and a circular cross section. **2** thing of this shape. —**cy·lin·dri·cal** *adj.*

**cym·bal** /'simbəl/ ▶*n.* brass or bronze plate struck to make a ringing sound. —**cym·bal·ist** *n.*

**cyn·ic** /'sinik/ ▶*n.* person with little faith in human nature. —**cyn·i·cal** *adj.* —**cyn·i·cism** *n.*

**cy·no·sure** /'sīnə,SHŏŏr/ ▶*n.* **1** center of attraction or admiration. **2** guiding star.

**cy·press** /'sīpris/ ▶*n.* conifer with hard wood and dark foliage.

**cyst** /sist/ ▶*n.* sac formed in the body, containing liquid or semiliquid.

**czar** /zär/ (also **tsar**; *fem.* **cza·ri·na**, **tsa·ri·na**) ▶*n.* **1** *hist.* title of the former emperor of Russia. **2** person with great authority.

**Czech** /CHek/ ▶*n.* **1** native or national of the Czech Republic. **2** language of the Czech people. ▶*adj.* of the Czechs or their language.

# Dd

**D**[1] /dē/ (also **d**) ▸*n.* (*pl.* **Ds** or **D's**; **d's**) **1** fourth letter of the alphabet. **2** *Mus.* second note of the diatonic scale of C major. **3** (as a Roman numeral) 500.

**D**[2] ▸*symb. Chem.* deuterium.

**D**[3] ▸*abbr.* **1** (also **D.**) Democrat. **2** dimension: *3-D.*

**d.** ▸*abbr.* **1** daughter. **2** departs. **3** delete. **4** depth. **5** died.

**'d** *inf.* ▸*v.* had; would: *I'd | he'd.*

**DA** ▸*abbr.* district attorney.

**dab** /dab/ ▸*v.* (**dabbed**, **dab·bing**) **1** press (a surface) briefly with a cloth, etc., without rubbing. **2** (**dab on**) apply (a substance). ▸*n.* **1** brief application of a cloth, etc., to a surface. **2** small amount applied in this way.

**dab·ble** /ˈdabəl/ ▸*v.* **1** take a casual interest (in an activity, etc.). **2** move the feet, hands, etc., in liquid.

**dachs·hund** /ˈdäksənd/ ▸*n.* dog of a short-legged, long-bodied breed.

**da·coit** /dəˈkoit/ ▸*n.* member of a band of armed robbers in India or Myanmar (Burma).

**dad** /dad/ ▸*n. inf.* father.

**dad·dy** /ˈdadē/ ▸*n.* (*pl.* **-dies**) *inf.* father.

**dad·dy long·legs** ▸*n.* arachnid with globular body and long thin legs.

**da·do** /ˈdādō/ ▸*n.* (*pl.* **-dos**) **1** lower part of the wall of a room, below about waist height, if it is a different color or has a different covering than the upper part. **2** groove cut in the face of a board, into which the edge of another board is fixed. **3** part of a pedestal between the base and the cornice.

**daf·fo·dil** /ˈdafə,dil/ ▸*n.* bulbous plant with a yellow trumpet-shaped flower.

**dag·ger** /ˈdagər/ ▸*n.* short pointed knife for stabbing.

**da·guerre·o·type** /dəˈge(ə)rə-ˌtīp/ (also **da·guer·ro·type**) ▸*n.* photograph taken by an early photographic process employing an iodine-sensitized silvered plate and mercury vapor.

**dahl·ia** /ˈdalyə/ ▸*n.* composite garden plant of Mexican origin, cultivated for its many-colored flowers.

**dai·ly** /ˈdālē/ ▸*adj.* done or occurring every day.

▸*adv.* every day.

▸*n.* (*pl.* **-lies**) newspaper published every day.

**dai·myo** /ˈdīmyō/ (also **dai·mio**) ▸*n.* (*pl.* **-myos**) (in feudal Japan) one of the great lords who were vassals of the shogun.

**dain·ty** /ˈdāntē/ ▸*adj.* (**-ti·er**, **-ti·est**) 1 delicately pretty. 2 delicate. 3 (of food) choice. 4 fastidious.

▸*n.* (*pl.* **-ties**) choice morsel; delicacy. —**dain·ti·ly** *adv.* —**dain·ti·ness** *n.*

**dair·y** /ˈde(ə)rē/ ▸*n.* (*pl.* **-ies**) 1 place for the storage, processing, and distribution of milk and its products. 2 store where milk and milk products are sold.

▸*adj.* pertaining to milk and its products (and sometimes eggs).

**da·is** /ˈdāis/ ▸*n.* low platform, usu. at the front of a hall, used to support a table, lectern, etc.

**dai·sy** /ˈdāzē/ ▸*n.* (*pl.* **-sies**) small composite plant bearing white-petaled flowers.

**Da·ko·ta** /dəˈkōtə/ ▸*n.* 1 N. American Indian people native to the northern Mississippi valley. 2 language of this people. —**Da·ko·tan** *adj.*

**dale** /dāl/ ▸*n.* valley.

**dal·li·ance** /ˈdalēəns; ˈdalyəns/ ▸*n.* 1 casual romantic or sexual relationship. 2 brief or casual involvement with something.

**dal·ly** /ˈdalē/ ▸*v.* (**-lied**) 1 delay; waste time. 2 flirt.

**Dal·ma·tian** /dalˈmāsʜən/ ▸*n.* dog of a large, white, short-haired breed with dark spots.

**dam** /dam/ ▸*n.* 1 barrier constructed to hold back water, forming a reservoir or preventing flooding. 2 mother, esp. of a four-footed animal.

▸*v.* (**dammed**, **dam·ming**) 1 furnish or confine with a dam. 2 block up; obstruct.

**dam·age** /ˈdamij/ ▸*n.* 1 harm or injury. 2 (**damages**) financial compensation for a loss or injury.

▸*v.* inflict damage on.

**dam·a·scened** /ˈdaməˌsēnd; ˌdaməˈsēnd/ ▸*adj.* 1 (of iron or steel) given a wavy pattern by hammer-welding and repeated heating and forging. 2 (of a metal object) inlaid with gold or silver decoration.

**dam·ask** /ˈdaməsk/ ▸*n.* woven

fabric (esp. silk or linen) with a pattern visible on both sides.

**dam·ask rose** ▸*n.* sweet-scented variety of rose with very soft petals.

**dame** /dām/ ▸*n.* **1** (**Dame**) (in the UK) honorific title given to a woman. **2** *inf.* a woman.

**damn** /dam/ ▸*v.* **1** curse (a person or thing). **2** doom to hell. **3** condemn; censure. **4** [often as *adj.* **damning**] (of evidence, etc.) show or prove to be guilty.
▸*adj. inf.* used to express anger.

**dam·na·ble** /'damnəbəl/ ▸*adj.* hateful; annoying.

**dam·na·tion** /dam'nāsʜən/ ▸*n.* eternal punishment in hell.

**damp** /damp/ ▸*adj.* slightly wet.
▸*n.* moisture, esp. inconvenient or dangerous.
▸*v.* **1** dampen; moisten. **2 a** take the force or vigor out of. **b** make (a fire) burn less strongly by reducing the flow of air.
—**damp·ly** *adv.* —**damp·ness** *n.*

**damp·en** ▸*v.* make or become damp.

**damp·er** ▸*n.* **1** person or thing that discourages. **2** metal plate in a flue to control the draft, and so the rate of combustion.
☐ **put a damper on** take the enjoyment out of.

**dam·sel** /'damzəl/ ▸*n. archaic poet./lit.* young unmarried woman.

**dance** /dans/ ▸*v.* **1** move about rhythmically, usu. to music, for pleasure or as entertainment. **2** move in a lively way; skip or jump about. **3** perform (a specified dance or a role in a ballet).
▸*n.* **1** piece of dancing; sequence of steps in dancing. **2** social gathering for dancing. **3** piece of music for dancing. **4** lively motion. —**danc·er** *n.*

**dan·de·lion** /'dandl,īən/ ▸*n.* composite plant with jagged leaves and a yellow flower, then a head of seeds with downy tufts.

**dan·der** /'dandər/ ▸*n.* **1** *inf.* (in phrase **get one's dander up**) lose one's temper. **2** skin flakes in an animal's fur.

**dan·dle** /'dandl/ ▸*v.* dance (a child) on one's knees.

**dan·druff** /'dandrəf/ ▸*n.* dead skin in small scales among the hair.

**dan·dy** /'dandē/ ▸*n.* (*pl.* -**dies**) man unduly devoted to style and fashion.

**Dane** /dān/ ▸*n.* native or national of Denmark.

**dan·ger** /'dānjər/ ▶n. **1** liability or exposure to harm. **2** thing that causes or may cause harm. **—dan·ger·ous** adj.
□ **in danger of** likely to incur or to suffer from.

**dan·gle** /'daNGgəl/ ▶v. **1** hold, carry, or be loosely suspended. **2** hold out (hope, temptation, etc.) enticingly.

**Dan·ish** /'dāniSH/ ▶adj. of or relating to Denmark or the Danes.
▶n. **1** Danish language. **2** (**the Danish**) the Danish people.

**Da·nish pas·try** ▶n. sweetened yeast pastry topped with icing, fruit, nuts, etc.

**dank** /daNGk/ ▶adj. disagreeably damp and cold.

**dan·seur** /dän'sər/ ▶n. male ballet dancer.

**dan·seuse** /dän'sŏŏz; -'sœz/ ▶n. female ballet dancer.

**dap** /dap/ ▶v. (**dapped, dap·ping**) fish by letting the fly bob lightly on the water without letting the line touch the water.

**dap·per** /'dapər/ ▶adj. neat and precise, esp. in dress or movement.

**dap·ple** /'dapəl/ ▶v. mark or be marked with spots.

▶n. **1** dappled effect. **2** dappled horse.

**dare** /de(ə)r/ ▶v. **1** have the courage or impudence (to): *I dare not speak | I do not dare to jump.* **2** defy or challenge (a person).
▶n. **1** act of daring. **2** challenge, esp. to prove courage.

**dare·dev·il** ▶n. recklessly daring person.
▶adj. recklessly daring.

**dark** /därk/ ▶adj. **1** with little or no light. **2** of deep or somber color. **3** gloomy; depressing; dismal. **4** evil; sinister.
▶n. **1** absence of light. **2** nightfall. **—dark·en** v. **—dark·ly** adv. **—dark·ness** n.
□ **in the dark** lacking information.

**dark horse** ▶n. little-known person who is unexpectedly prominent.

**dark·ling** /'därkliNG/ ▶adj. of or relating to growing darkness.

**dark·room** ▶n. room for photographic work, with normal light excluded.

**dar·ling** /'därliNG/ ▶n. **1** beloved or lovable person or thing. **2** favorite.
▶adj. **1** beloved; lovable. **2** favorite. **3** *inf.* charming or pretty.

**darn**[1] /därn/ ▶v. mend (esp.

knitted material) by filling a hole with stitching.
▶*n.* darned area in material.

**darn**[2] ▶*v., adj., adv. inf.* euphemism for **DAMN.**

**dart** /därt/ ▶*n.* **1** small pointed missile used as a weapon or in a game. **2** (**darts**) indoor game of throwing these at a target to score points. **3** sudden rapid movement. **4** tapering tuck stitched in a garment.
▶*v.* **1** move or go suddenly or rapidly. **2** direct suddenly (a glance, etc.).

**dash** /dasH/ ▶*v.* **1** rush. **2** strike or fling with force, esp. to shatter.
▶*n.* **1** rush; sudden advance. **2** horizontal stroke in writing or printing to mark a pause, break in sense, etc. **3** showy appearance or behavior. **4** sprinting race. **5** small amount of something added to something else. **6** DASHBOARD. **7** longer signal of the two in Morse code.
□ **dash off** depart or write hurriedly.

**dash·board** ▶*n.* instrument panel of a vehicle.

**dash·ing** ▶*adj.* **1** spirited; lively. **2** stylish.

**da·ta** /'datə/ ▶*pl. n.* (*sing.* **da·tum**) [also treated as *sing.*] **1** known facts used as a basis for conclusions. **2** quantities or characters operated on by a computer, etc.

**da·ta·base** ▶*n.* structured set of data held in a computer.

**da·ta pro·cess·ing** ▶series of operations on data, esp. by a computer, to retrieve or classify information.

**date** /dāt/ ▶*n.* **1** day of the month, esp. as a number. **2** particular day or year. **3** statement in a document, etc., of the time of composition or publication. **4** period to which a work of art, etc., belongs. **5** *inf.* **a** social or romantic appointment. **b** person with whom one has such an appointment. **6** **a** oval, single-stoned fruit. **b** (in full **date palm**) tall tree native to W. Asia and N. Africa, bearing this fruit.
▶*v.* **1** mark with a date. **2** assign a date to (an object, etc.). **3** have its origins at a particular time. **4** be recognizable as from the past. **5** *inf.* **a** arrange with (a person) to meet socially. **b** meet socially by agreement.
□ **out of date** old-fashioned;

obsolete. □ **to date** until now. □ **up to date** fashionable; current.

**dat·ed** ▸*adj.* **1** showing or having a date: *dated letter.* **2** old-fashioned; out-of-date.

**da·tive** /ˈdātiv/ *Gram.* ▸*n.* case of nouns and pronouns indicating an indirect object or recipient. ▸*adj.* of or in the dative.

**daub** /dôb/ ▸*v.* **1** spread (paint, etc.) crudely or roughly. **2** coat (a surface) with paint, etc. **3** paint crudely or unskillfully. ▸*n.* paint, etc., daubed on a surface.

**daugh·ter** /ˈdôtər/ ▸*n.* **1** girl or woman in relation to her parents. **2** female descendant. **3** female member of a family, nation, etc. □ **daughter-in-law** wife of one's son.

**daunt** /dônt/ ▸*v.* discourage; intimidate. —**daunt·ing** *adj.* —**daunt·ing·ly** *adv.*

**daunt·less** ▸*adj.* intrepid; persevering.

**dav·en·port** /ˈdavənˌpôrt/ ▸*n.* large, heavily upholstered sofa.

**daw·dle** /ˈdôdl/ ▸*v.* **1** delay; waste time. **2** walk slowly and idly.

**dawn** /dôn; dän/ ▸*n.* **1** daybreak.

**2** beginning or incipient appearance of something. ▸*v.* **1** (of a day) begin; grow light. **2** begin to appear or develop.

**day** /dā/ ▸*n.* **1** time between sunrise and sunset. **2** 24 hours as a unit of time. **3** daylight: *clear as day.* **4 a** period of the past or present: *the old days.* **b** present time: *issues of the day.* **5** prime of a person's life: *in my day.* **6** a point of time: *will do it one day.* **7** day of a particular event. □ **day after day** without respite. □ **day and night** all the time. □ **day by day** gradually. □ **day-to-day** mundane; routine.

**day·break** ▸*n.* first appearance of morning light.

**day care** ▸*n.* supervision and care of young children or the elderly: *family issues such as day care | day-care center.*

**day·dream** ▸*n.* pleasant fantasy or reverie. ▸*v.* indulge in this.

**day·light** ▸*n.* **1** light of day. **2** dawn. **3** visible gap or interval.

**day·light sav·ing time** (also **day·light sav·ings time**) ▸*n.* achieving longer evening daylight, esp. in summer, by setting the time an hour ahead of standard time.

**day·time** ▸*n.* part of the day when there is natural light.

**daze** /dāz/ ▸*v.* stupefy; bewilder. ▸*n.* state of bewilderment: *in a daze.*

**daz·zle** /ˈdazəl/ ▸*v.* **1** blind or confuse temporarily by an excess of light. **2** impress or overpower with knowledge, ability, etc. ▸*n.* bright confusing light.

**DC** ▸*abbr.* **1** (also **d.c.**) direct current. **2** District of Columbia.

**DD** ▸*abbr.* doctor of divinity.

**D.D.S.** ▸*abbr.* **1** doctor of dental science. **2** doctor of dental surgery.

**DDT** ▸*abbr.* dichlorodiphenyl-trichloroethane, a colorless chlorinated hydrocarbon used as an insecticide.

**DE** ▸*abbr.* Delaware (in official postal use).

**de-** /dē/ ▸*prefix* **1** forming verbs and their derivatives: **a** down; away: *descend.* **b** completely: *denude.* **2** added to form verbs and nouns implying removal or reversal: *decentralize.*

**dea·con** /ˈdēkən/ ▸*n.* **1** (in Catholic, Anglican, and Orthodox churches) ordained person of an order ranking below that of priest. **2** (in some Protestant churches) lay officer assisting a minister.

**de·ac·ti·vate** ▸*v.* make inactive or less reactive.

**dead** /ded/ ▸*adj.* **1** no longer alive. **2** numb: *my fingers are dead.* **3** no longer current, relevant, effective or in use: *a dead issue.* **4 a** lacking force or vigor. **b** (of sound) not resonant. **5** quiet; lacking activity; motionless. **6 a** (of a microphone, etc.) not transmitting sound, esp. because of a fault. **b** (of a circuit, etc.) carrying no current; not connected to a source of electricity. **7** (of the ball in a game) out of play. **8** abrupt; complete; exact: *come to a dead stop | dead certainty.*
▸*adv.* absolutely; exactly: *dead on target.*
▸*n.* **1** (**the dead**) those who have died. **2** time of silence or inactivity: *dead of night.*
—**dead·en** *v.*

**dead·beat** ▸*n. inf.* person who tries to evade paying debts.

**dead end** ▸*n.* **1** closed end of a road, passage, etc. **2** situation offering no prospects of progress or advancement: *dead-end job.*

**dead heat** ▸*n.* **1** race in which two or more competitors finish in a tie. **2** result of such a race.

**dead·line** ▸*n.* latest time by which something must be completed.

**dead·lock** ▸*n.* situation, esp. one involving opposing parties, in which no progress can be made.
▸*v.* bring or come to a standstill.

**dead·ly** ▸*adj.* (**-li·er, -li·est**) **1** causing or able to cause fatal injury or serious damage. **2** intense; extreme. **3** (of aim, etc.) extremely accurate or effective. **4** deathlike.
▸*adv.* **1** as if dead. **2** extremely; intensely: *deadly serious.*

**dead·pan** ▸*adj. & adv.* deliberately lacking expression or emotion: *deadpan humor.*

**dead·wood** ▸*n.* **1** dead trees or branches. **2** *inf.* useless people or things.

**deaf** /def/ ▸*adj.* **1** wholly or partly without hearing. **2** refusing to listen or comply: *she is deaf to all complaints.*
—**deaf·en** *v.* —**deaf·ness** *n.*
□ **fall on deaf ears** be ignored.

□ **turn a deaf ear** be unresponsive.

**deal** /dēl/ ▸*v.* (*past* and *past part.* **dealt**) **1** (**deal with**) **a** take measures concerning (a problem, etc.), esp. to resolve. **b** do business with; associate with. **c** discuss or treat (a subject). **2** behave in a specified way: *dealt honorably by them.* **3** (**deal in**) to sell or be concerned with commercially. **4** (often **deal out**) distribute to several people, etc. **5** distribute (cards) to players. **6** administer: *deal a heavy blow.*
▸*n.* **1** (usu. **a good** or **great deal**) large amount. **2** *inf.* business arrangement. **3** specified treatment: *gave them a bad deal.* **4 a** distribution of cards by dealing. **b** player's turn to do this. **c** set of hands dealt to players.

**deal·er** ▸*n.* **1** person dealing in retail goods. **2** player dealing in a card game. **3** person who sells illegal drugs.

**dean** /dēn/ ▸*n.* **1** head of a college or university faculty or department. **2** college or university official with disciplinary and advisory functions. **3** head of the chapter of a cathedral or collegiate church.

**dear** /di(ə)r/ ▶*adj.* **1** beloved or esteemed. **2** as a formula of address, esp. beginning a letter: *Dear Sir.* **3** precious; cherished. **4** earnest; deeply felt: *my dearest wish.* **5** high-priced.

▶*n.* (esp. as a form of address) dear person.

▶*adv.* at great cost.

▶*interj.* expressing surprise, dismay, pity, etc.: *oh dear!* —**dear·ly** *adv.*

**dearth** /dərTH/ ▶*n.* scarcity or lack, esp. of food.

**death** /deTH/ ▶*n.* **1** irreversible ending of life. **2** event that terminates life. **3 a** being killed or killing. **b** being dead. **4** destruction or permanent cessation: *the death of our hopes.*
□ **at death's door** close to death. □ **be the death of 1** cause the death of. **2** be very harmful to. □ **death trap** *inf.* dangerous or unhealthy building, vehicle, etc.

**de·ba·cle** /di'bäkəl/ (also **dé·bâ·cle**) ▶*n.* utter defeat, failure, or collapse.

**de·bar** ▶*v.* (**de·barred**, **de·bar·ring**) exclude; prohibit. —**de·bar·ment** *n.*

**de·bark** ▶*v.* land from a ship. —**de·bar·ka·tion** *n.*

**de·base** ▶*v.* lower in quality, value, or character. —**de·base·ment** *n.*

**de·bate** /di'bāt/ ▶*v.* **1** discuss or dispute, esp. formally. **2** consider.
▶*n.* **1** formal discussion, esp. in a legislature, etc. **2** discussion. —**de·bat·a·ble** *adj.*

**de·bauch** /di'bôCH/ ▶*v.* **1** corrupt; pervert. **2** make intemperate or sensually indulgent.
▶*n.* bout of sensual indulgence. —**de·bauch·er·y** *n.*

**de·bauch·er·y** /di'bôCHərē/ ▶*n.* excessive indulgence in sensual pleasures.

**de·bil·i·tate** /di'bilə,tāt/ ▶*v.* make weak and infirm. —**de·bil·i·ta·tion** *n.*

**de·bil·i·ty** ▶*n.* physical weakness.

**deb·it** /'debit/ ▶*n.* **1** entry in an account recording a sum owed. **2** total of such sums. **3** debit side of an account.
▶*v.* enter on the debit side of an account.

**deb·o·nair** /,debə'ne(ə)r/ ▶*adj.* **1** carefree; self-assured. **2** having pleasant manners.

**de·bouch** /di'bouCH; -'bōōSH/ ▸ v. emerge from a narrow or confined space into a wide, open area.

**de·bride·ment** /di'brēdmənt/ ▸ n. removal of damaged tissue or foreign objects from a wound.

**de·brief** ▸ v. interrogate (a diplomat, pilot, etc.) about a mission or undertaking. —**de·brief·ing** n.

**de·bris** /də'brē/ ▸ n. scattered fragments, esp. of something wrecked or destroyed.

**debt** /det/ ▸ n. 1 something owed, esp. money. 2 state of owing: in debt. —**debt·or** n.

**de·bug** ▸ v. (**de·bugged, de·bug·ging**) 1 identify and remove defects from (a computer program, etc.). 2 remove concealed listening devices from (a room, etc.).

**de·bunk** ▸ v. expose the falseness of (a claim, etc.).

**de·but** /dā'byōō/ ▸ n. (also **dé·but**) first public appearance. ▸ v. make a debut.

**deb·u·tante** /'debyōō,tänt/ ▸ n. wealthy young woman making her first formal appearance in society.

**Dec.** ▸ abbr. December.

**dec·ade** /'dekād/ ▸ n. 1 period of ten years. 2 set, series, or group of ten.

**dec·a·dence** /'dekədəns/ ▸ n. 1 moral or cultural deterioration. 2 immoral behavior. —**dec·a·dent** adj.

**de·caf·fein·at·ed** /dē'kafə-,nātəd/ ▸ adj. with caffeine removed or reduced.

**de·cal** /'dēkal/ ▸ n. design made on special paper for transfer onto another surface.

**Dec·a·logue** /'dekə,lôg/ ▸ n. Ten Commandments.

**de·camp** ▸ v. 1 break up or leave a camp. 2 depart suddenly; abscond.

**de·cant** /di'kant/ ▸ v. gradually pour off (liquid, esp. wine), esp. without disturbing the sediment.

**de·cant·er** ▸ n. stoppered glass container for wine.

**de·cap·i·tate** /di'kapi,tāt/ ▸ v. behead. —**de·cap·i·ta·tion** n.

**de·cath·lon** /di'kaTH,län/ ▸ n. athletic contest in which each competitor takes part in ten events. —**de·cath·lete** n.

**de·cay** /di'kā/ ▸ v. 1 (cause to) rot or decompose. 2 decline or cause to decline in quality, power, etc. ▸ n. 1 rotten state. 2 decline in health, quality, etc. **3** *Physics* change by radioactivity.

**de·ceased** /di'sēst/ ▸*adj.* dead. ▸*n.* (**the deceased**) person who has died, esp. recently.

**de·ce·dent** /di'sēdnt/ ▸*n.* person who has died.

**de·ceit** /di'sēt/ ▸*n.* **1** deception, esp. by concealing the truth. **2** dishonest trick or stratagem. **3** willingness to deceive.

**de·ceive** /di'sēv/ ▸*v.* make (a person) believe what is false; mislead purposely. —**de·ceiv·er** *n.* □ **deceive oneself** persist in a mistaken belief.

**De·cem·ber** /di'sembər/ ▸*n.* twelfth month of the year.

**de·cen·cy** /'dēsənsē/ ▸*n.* (*pl.* **-cies**) **1** correct and tasteful behavior. **2** (**decencies**) the requirements of correct behavior. —**de·cent** *adj.*

**de·cen·tral·ize** ▸*v.* transfer (power, etc.) from central to local authority. —**de·cen·tral·i·za·tion** *n.*

**de·cep·tion** /di'sepSHən/ ▸*n.* **1** deceiving or being deceived. **2** thing that deceives; trick or sham.

**de·cep·tive** ▸*adj.* misleading.

**dec·i·bel** /'desə,bel/ ▸*n.* unit used to measure electrical signals or sound intensities. (Abbr.: **dB**).

**de·cide** /di'sīd/ ▸*v.* resolve or settle (an issue) after consideration.

**de·cid·ed** ▸*adj.* **1** definite; unquestionable: *today's weather is a decided improvement.* **2** (of a person) resolute, not vacillating.

**de·cid·u·ous** /di'sijo͞oəs/ ▸*adj.* **1** (of a tree) shedding leaves annually. **2** (of leaves, horns, teeth, etc.) shed periodically.

**dec·i·mal** /'des(ə)məl/ ▸*adj.* (of a system of numbers, measures, etc.) based on the number ten. ▸*n.* decimal fraction. □ **decimal fraction** fraction whose denominator is a power of ten, esp. when expressed positionally by units to the right of a decimal point. □ **decimal point** period placed before a numerator in a decimal fraction.

**dec·i·mate** /'desə,māt/ ▸*v.* destroy a large proportion of. —**dec·i·ma·tion** *n.*

**de·ci·pher** /di'sīfər/ ▸*v.* **1** convert (text written in code) into an intelligible language. **2** determine the meaning of (anything unclear). —**de·ci·pher·a·ble** *adj.*

**de·ci·sion** /di'siZHən/ ▸n. **1** act or process of deciding. **2** conclusion or resolution reached after consideration. **3 a** settlement of a question. **b** formal judgment.

**de·ci·sive** /di'sīsiv/ ▸adj. **1** that decides an issue; conclusive. **2** (of a person, esp. as a characteristic) able to decide quickly and effectively. —**de·ci·sive·ly** adv. —**de·ci·sive·ness** n.

**deck** /dek/ ▸n. **1** flooring on a ship. **2** platformlike structure, usu. made of lumber, attached to a house, etc. **3** component for playing (disks, tapes, etc.) in sound-reproduction equipment. **4** pack of cards.

**de·claim** ▸v. speak rhetorically or affectedly. —**dec·la·ma·tion** n. —**de·clam·a·to·ry** adj.

**de·clare** /di'kle(ə)r/ ▸v. **1** announce openly or formally. **2** pronounce: *declared it invalid.* **3** assert emphatically. **4** acknowledge possession of (dutiable goods, etc.). **5** [as adj. **declared**] admit to being: *a declared atheist.*

**dé·clas·sé** /ˌdäklä'sā/ (also **dé·clas·sée**) ▸adj. having fallen in social status.

**de·clen·sion** /di'klenSHən/ ▸n. *Gram.* class of nouns, etc., with the same inflections.

**de·cline** /di'klīn/ ▸v. **1** deteriorate; lose strength or vigor. **2** refuse, esp. formally and courteously. **3** slope or bend downward. **4** *Gram.* state the forms of (a noun, pronoun, or adjective). ▸n. **1** gradual loss of vigor or excellence. **2** decay; deterioration. **3** setting; the last part of the course (of the sun, of life, etc.).

**de·cliv·i·ty** /di'klivitē/ ▸n. (pl. **-ties**) downward slope.

**de·coct** /di'käkt/ ▸v. extract the essence from (something) by heating or boiling it.

**de·code** ▸v. decipher.

**de·col·late** /di'kä,lāt/ ▸v. behead (someone).

**dé·colle·tage** /dā,käl(ə)'täzH ,dekələ-/ ▸n. low neckline on a woman's dress or top.

**de·com·mis·sion** ▸v. **1** close down (a nuclear reactor, etc.). **2** take (a ship) out of service.

**de·com·pose** ▸v. decay; rot. —**de·com·po·si·tion** n.

**de·con·ges·tant** /ˌdēkən-'jestənt/ ▸n. medicinal agent that relieves congestion.

**de·con·tam·i·nate** ▶*v.* remove contamination from.
**—de·con·tam·i·na·tion** *n.*

**de·cor** /dā'kôr/ (also **dé·cor**) ▶*n.* furnishing and decoration of a room, stage, etc.

**dec·o·rate** /'dekə,rāt/ ▶*v.* **1** adorn; beautify. **2** paint, wallpaper, etc. **3** serve as an adornment to. **4** confer an award or distinction on.
**—dec·o·ra·tion** *n.* **—dec·o·ra·tive** *adj.*

**dec·o·rous** /'dekərəs/ ▶*adj.* having or showing decorum.
**—dec·o·rous·ly** *adv.*
**—dec·o·rous·ness** *n.*

**de·co·rum** /di'kôrəm/ ▶*n.* appropriate or dignified behavior.

**de·cou·page** /,dākoo'päzн/ ▶*n.* decoration of the surface of an object with paper cut-outs, which is then usu. varnished or lacquered.

**de·coy** /'dēkoi/ ▶*n.* person or thing used as a lure, bait, or enticement.
▶*v.* allure or entice, esp. using a decoy.

**de·crease** /di'krēs/ ▶*v.* make or become smaller or fewer.
▶*n.* **1** decreasing. **2** amount by which a thing decreases.

**de·cree** /di'krē/ ▶*n.* **1** official order. **2** legal judgment or decision.
▶*v.* ordain by decree.

**de·crep·it** /di'krepit/ ▶*adj.* **1** (of a person) weakened by age or infirmity. **2** worn out and ruined. **—de·crep·i·tude** *n.*

**de·cres·cent** /di'kresənt/ ▶*adj.* (of the moon) waning.

**de·cre·tal** /di'krētl/ ▶*n.* papal decree concerning a point of canon law.
▶*adj.* of the nature of a decree.

**de·crim·i·nal·ize** /dē'kriminə,līz/ ▶*v.* cease to treat (an action, etc.) as criminal.
**—de·crim·i·nal·i·za·tion** *n.*

**de·cry** ▶*v.* (**-cried**) disparage; belittle.

**ded·i·cate** /'dedi,kāt/ ▶*v.* **1** devote (esp. oneself) to a special task or purpose. **2** cite (a book, etc.) as being issued or performed in someone's honor. **3** devote (a building, etc.) to an honored person, cause, etc. **4** [as *adj.* **dedicated**] **a** (of a person) be devoted single-mindedly to a goal, etc. **b** (of equipment) be designed for a specific purpose.
**—ded·i·ca·tion** *n.* **—ded·i·ca·to·ry** *adj.*

**de·duce** /di'd(y)o͞os/ ▶v. infer logically. —**de·duc·i·ble** adj.

**de·duct** /di'dəkt/ ▶v. subtract, take away, or withhold (an amount, portion, etc.).

**de·duc·tion** ▶n. **1 a** deducting. **b** amount deducted. **2 a** inferring of particular instances from a general law. **b** conclusion deduced.

**de·duc·tive** ▶adj. of or reasoning by deduction.

**deed** /dēd/ ▶n. **1** thing done intentionally or consciously. **2** brave, skillful, or conspicuous act. **3** action. **4** Law document used for transferring ownership of property. ▶v. convey or transfer by legal deed.

**deem** /dēm/ ▶v. regard or consider in a specific way: the event was deemed a great success.

**deep** /dēp/ ▶adj. **1** extending far down or in. **2 a** to or at a specified depth: 6 feet deep. **b** in a specified number of ranks: soldiers drawn up six deep. **3** situated or coming from far down, back, or in: deep in his pockets | deep sigh. **4** low-pitched; full-toned: deep voice. **5** intense; extreme: deep disgrace. **6** heartfelt; absorbing: deep affection. **7** fully absorbed or overwhelmed: deep in debt. **8** profound; difficult to understand: deep thought. ▶n. **1** (**the deep**) the sea. **2** abyss, pit, or cavity. ▶adv. deeply; far down or in: read deep into the night. —**deep·en** v. —**deep·ly** adv.

**deep freeze** ▶n. **1** refrigerator in which food can be quickly frozen and kept for long periods. **2** suspension of activity. ▶v. (**deep-freeze**) freeze or store (food) in a deep freeze.

**deep-fry** ▶v. fry (food) in fat or oil sufficient to cover it.

**deer** /di(ə)r/ ▶n. (pl. same) four-hoofed grazing animal, the males of which usu. have antlers.

**de·face** ▶v. disfigure. —**de·face·ment** n.

**de fac·to** /di 'faktō/ ▶adv. in fact, whether by right or not. ▶adj. existing in fact: de facto ruler.

**de·fame** /di'fām/ ▶v. libel; slander. —**def·a·ma·tion** n. —**de·fam·a·to·ry** adj.

**de·fault** /di'fôlt/ ▶n. **1** failure to appear, pay, or act in some way. **2** preselected option adopted by a computer program when no alternative is specified.

▶*v.* fail to fulfill an obligation, esp. to pay money or to appear in court.

□ **by default** because of a lack of an alternative or opposition.

**de·fea·sance** /di'fēzəns/ ▶*n.* **1** action or process of rendering something null and void. **2** clause or condition which, if fulfilled, renders a deed or contract null and void.

**de·feat** /di'fēt/ ▶*v.* **1** overcome in battle, contest, etc. **2** prevent an aim from being achieved or prevent (someone) from achieving an aim. **3** reject (a motion, etc.) by voting. ▶*n.* defeating or being defeated.

**de·feat·ism** ▶*n.* excessive readiness to accept defeat. —**de·feat·ist** *n.*

**def·e·cate** /'defi,kāt/ ▶*v.* discharge feces from the body. —**def·e·ca·tion** *n.*

**de·fect**[1] /'dēfekt/ ▶*n.* imperfection; shortcoming; blemish. —**de·fec·tive** *adj.*

**de·fect**[2] /di'fekt/ ▶*v.* leave one's country or cause in favor of another. —**de·fec·tion** *n.* —**de·fec·tor** *n.*

**de·fend** /di'fend/ ▶*v.* **1** resist an attack made on; protect. **2** support or uphold by

argument. **3** conduct the defense in a lawsuit. —**de·fend·er** *n.*

**de·fend·ant** ▶*n.* person, etc., sued or accused in a court of law.

**de·fense** /di'fens/ ▶*n.* **1** defending from or resisting attack. **2** something that defends. **3** justification; vindication. **4** defendant's case or counsel in a lawsuit. —**de·fense·less** *adj.* —**de·fense·less·ness** *n.*

□ **defense mechanism 1** body's reaction against disease. **2** usu. unconscious mental process to avoid anxiety.

**de·fen·si·ble** ▶*adj.* **1** justifiable. **2** able to be defended.

**de·fen·sive** ▶*adj.* **1** done or intended for defense. **2** overreacting to criticism.

**de·fer** /di'fər/ ▶*v.* (**de·ferred, de·fer·ring**) **1** postpone. **2** (**defer to**) yield or make concessions: *I defer to your superior knowledge.* —**def·er·en·tial** *adj.* —**de·fer·ment** *n.* —**de·fer·ral** *n.*

**def·er·ence** /'defərəns/ ▶*n.* **1** courteous regard; respect. **2** compliance.

□ **in deference to** out of respect for.

**de·fi·ance** /di'fīəns/ ▸n. open disobedience; bold resistance. —**de·fi·ant** adj.

**de·fi·cien·cy** /di'fishənsē/ ▸n. (pl. -cies) **1** being deficient. **2** lack or shortage. **3** thing lacking.

**de·fi·cient** ▸adj. incomplete; insufficient.

**def·i·cit** /'defəsit/ ▸n. **1** amount by which a thing (esp. money) is too small. **2** excess of liabilities over assets.

**de·file** ▸v. make dirty; pollute; befoul.
▸n. narrow gorge or pass.

**de·fine** ▸v. **1** describe or explain the scope of. **2** give the meaning of (a word, etc.). **3** mark out the boundary of. —**de·fin·a·ble** adj.

**def·i·n·ite** /'defənit/ ▸adj. **1** having exact and discernible limits. **2** clear and distinct; not vague.
□ **definite article** the word the.

**def·i·ni·tion** ▸n. **1** meaning of a word or nature of a thing. **2** distinctness in outline of an image.

**de·fin·i·tive** /di'finitiv/ ▸adj. **1** (of an answer, verdict, etc.) decisive; unconditional; final. **2** (of a book, etc.) most authoritative.

**def·la·grate** /'deflə,grāt/ ▸v.

burn away or cause (a substance) to burn away with a sudden flame and rapid, sharp combustion.

**de·flate** /di'flāt/ ▸v. **1** (of a tire, balloon, etc.) empty or be emptied of air or gas. **2** lose or cause to lose confidence. **3** bring about a general reduction of price levels in (an economy).

**de·fla·tion** ▸n. **1** deflating or being deflated. **2** reduction of the general level of prices in an economy. —**de·fla·tion·ar·y** adj.

**de·flect** /di'flekt/ ▸v. **1** bend or turn aside from a course or purpose. **2** (cause to) deviate. —**de·flec·tion** n. —**de·flec·tor** n.

**de·flow·er** /dē'flou(-ə)r/ ▸v. **1** deprive (a woman) of her virginity. **2** strip (a plant or garden) of flowers.

**de·fo·li·ate** /dē'fōlē,āt/ ▸v. remove leaves from, esp. as a military tactic. —**de·fo·li·ant** n. & adj. —**de·fo·li·a·tion** n.

**de·form** ▸v. **1** distort the shape or form of. **2** become distorted or misshapen. —**de·formed** adj. —**de·for·mi·ty** n.

**de·fraud** ▸v. cheat by fraud.

**de·fray** ▸v. pay (a cost or expense). —**de·fray·al** n.

**de·frost** ▸v. **1** remove frost or

ice from (esp. a refrigerator, windshield, etc.). **2** unfreeze or become unfrozen.

**deft** /deft/ ▶*adj.* neat; dexterous; adroit.

**de·funct** /di'fəNGkt/ ▶*adj.* no longer existing or functioning.

**de·fuse** ▶*v.* **1** remove the fuse from (a bomb, etc.). **2** reduce tensions in (a crisis, difficulty, etc.).

**de·fy** /di'fī/ ▶*v.* (**-fied**) **1** resist openly; refuse to obey. **2** (of a thing) present insuperable obstacles to: *defies solution.* **3** challenge (a person) to do or prove something.

**dé·ga·gé** /ˌdāgä'zHā/ ▶*adj.* unconcerned or unconstrained; relaxed. ▶*n.* (*pl.* same) (in ballet) pointing of the foot to an open position with an arched instep slightly off the floor.

**de·gauss** /dē'gous/ ▶*v.* remove unwanted magnetism from (a television or monitor) in order to correct color disturbance.

**de·gen·er·ate** ▶*adj.* /di'jenərit/ fallen from former normality or goodness. ▶*n.* /di'jenərit/ degraded person. ▶*v.* /di'jenə,rāt/ become degenerate. —**de·gen·er·a·cy** *n.*

**de·grade** ▶*v.* **1** reduce to a lower rank. **2** dishonor; humiliate. —**de·grad·a·ble** *adj.* —**deg·ra·da·tion** *n.*

**de·gree** /di'grē/ ▶*n.* **1** amount, level, or extent to which something is present. **2** unit of measurement of angles or arcs, with 360 degrees comprising a circle. (Symb.: °). **3** stage in scale, series, or process. **4** unit in a scale of temperature. **5** grade used to classify severity of burns. **6** legal grade of crime. **7** academic rank conferred by a college or university: *master's degree.*

**de·hisce** /di'his/ ▶*v.* (of a pod or seed vessel, or of a cut or wound) gape or burst open.

**de·hu·man·ize** ▶*v.* **1** deprive of human characteristics. **2** make impersonal. —**de·hu·man·i·za·tion** *n.*

**de·hy·drate** ▶*v.* **1 a** remove water from (esp. foods). **b** make dry. **2** lose water. —**de·hy·dra·tion** *n.* —**de·hy·dra·tor** *n.*

**de·i·fy** /'dēə,fī/ ▶*v.* (**-fied**) **1** make a god of. **2** regard or worship as a god. —**de·i·fi·ca·tion** *n.*

**deign** /dān/ ▶*v.* think fit; condescend.

**de·ism** /'dē,izəm/ ▶n. reasoned belief in the existence of a god. —**de·ist** n.

**de·i·ty** /'dēitē/ ▶n. (pl. **-ties**) **1** god or goddess. **2** divine status, quality, or nature. **3** (**the Deity**) God.

**dé·jà vu** /,däzHä 'voo/ ▶n. feeling of having already experienced a situation.

**de·ject** /di'jekt/ ▶v. [as adj. **dejected**] make sad or dispirited; depress.

**de ju·re** /di 'joŏrē/ ▶adj. rightful: *he had been de jure king since his father's death.* ▶adv. rightfully; by right.

**Del.** ▶abbr. Delaware.

**de·lay** /di'lā/ ▶v. **1** postpone; defer. **2** make or be late. ▶n. **1** delaying. **2** time lost by inaction. **3** hindrance.

**de·le** /'dēlē/ ▶v. (**de·led**, **de·le·ing**) delete or mark (a part of a text) for deletion. ▶n. proofreader's sign indicating matter to be deleted.

**de·lec·ta·ble** /di'lektəbəl/ ▶adj. delightful; pleasant. —**de·lec·ta·bil·i·ty** n. —**de·lec·ta·bly** adv.

**de·lec·ta·tion** /,dēlek'tāsHən/ ▶n. pleasure and delight.

**del·e·gate** ▶n. /'deligit/ **1** elected representative sent to a conference. **2** member of a committee or deputation. ▶v. /'deli'gāt/ **1 a** commit (authority, etc.) to an agent or deputy. **b** entrust (a task) to another. **2** send or authorize (a person) as a representative. —**del·e·ga·tion** n.

**de·lete** /di'lēt/ ▶v. remove (written or printed matter), esp. by striking out. —**de·le·tion** n.

**del·e·te·ri·ous** /,deli'ti(ə)rēəs/ ▶adj. harmful (to mind or body).

**del·i** /'delē/ ▶n. (pl. **-is**) inf. delicatessen.

**de·lib·er·ate** ▶adj. /di'libərit/ **1 a** intentional. **b** fully considered. **2** slow in deciding; cautious. **3** (of movement, etc.) leisurely and unhurried. ▶v. /di'libə,rāt/ consider; think or discuss carefully. —**de·lib·er·ate·ly** adv. —**de·lib·er·a·tive** adj.

**del·i·ca·cy** /'delikəsē/ ▶n. (pl. **-cies**) **1** (esp. in craftsmanship or beauty) fineness or intricacy of structure or texture. **2** susceptibility to injury or disease. **3** quality of requiring discretion or sensitivity. **4** choice food.

**del·i·cate** /'delikit/ ▶adj. **1 a** fine

in texture, quality, etc. **b** slender or slight. **c** subtle or subdued. **2 a** (of a person) susceptible to injury or illness. **b** (of a thing) easily spoiled or damaged. **3 a** requiring care; tricky. **b** (of an instrument) highly sensitive.

**del·i·ca·tes·sen** /ˌdelikəˈtesən/ ▶*n.* **1** store selling cooked meats, cheeses, prepared foods, etc. **2** such foods.

**de·li·cious** ▶*adj.* highly enjoyable to the taste or smell.

**de·lict** /diˈlikt/ ▶*n.* violation of the law; a tort.

**de·light** /diˈlīt/ ▶*v.* **1** please greatly. **2** take great pleasure. ▶*n.* **1** great pleasure. **2** something giving pleasure. —**de·light·ed** *adj.* —**de·light·ful·** *adj.*

**de·lim·it** ▶*v.* fix the limits or boundary of. —**de·lim·i·ta·tion** *n.*

**de·lin·e·ate** /diˈlinēˌāt/ ▶*v.* portray by drawing, etc., or in words. —**de·lin·e·a·tion** *n.*

**de·lin·quent** /diˈliNGkwənt/ ▶*n.* offender. ▶*adj.* **1** guilty of a minor crime or a misdeed. **2** failing in one's duty. **3** in arrears: *delinquent account.* —**de·lin·quen·cy** *n.*

**de·lir·i·um** /diˈli(ə)rēəm/ ▶*n.* **1** disorder involving incoherence, hallucinations, etc., caused by intoxication, fever, etc. **2** great excitement; ecstasy.
□ **delirium tremens** psychosis of chronic alcoholism involving tremors and hallucinations.

**de·liv·er** /diˈlivər/ ▶*v.* **1** distribute (letters, goods, etc.) to the addressee or purchaser. **2** save, rescue, or set free. **3 a** give birth to. **b** assist at the birth of. **4 a** utter or recite (an opinion, speech, etc.). **b** (of a judge) pronounce (a judgment). **5** launch or aim (a blow, ball, or attack). —**de·liv·er·ance** *n.* —**de·liv·er·y** *n.*

**dell** /del/ ▶*n.* small usu. wooded hollow or valley.

**del·phin·i·um** /delˈfinēəm/ ▶*n.* garden plant with tall spikes of usu. blue flowers.

**del·ta** /ˈdeltə/ ▶*n.* **1** triangular tract of earth, alluvium, etc., at the mouth of a river. **2** fourth letter of the Greek alphabet (Δ, δ).

**de·lude** /diˈlo͞od/ ▶*v.* deceive or mislead.

**del·uge** /ˈdel(y)o͞oj/ ▶*n.* **1** great flood. **2** heavy fall of rain. **3** (**the Deluge**) biblical Flood (Gen. 6–8).

**4** great outpouring (of words, paper, etc.).
▸ *v.* **1** flood. **2** inundate with a great number or amount.

**de·lu·sion** /diˈlo͞ozHən/ ▸*n.* **1** false belief or impression that is firmly maintained despite being contradicted by evidence. **2** this as a symptom or form of mental disorder. —**de·lu·sion·al** *adj.*

**de·lu·sive** ▸*adj.* giving a false impression.

**de·luxe** /diˈləks/ ▸*adj.* **1** luxurious or sumptuous. **2** of a superior kind.

**delve** /delv/ ▸*v.* search or research energetically or deeply.

**Dem.** ▸*abbr.* Democrat.

**dem·a·gogue** /ˈdeməˌgäg/ (also **dem·a·gog**) ▸*n.* political agitator appealing to mob instincts. —**dem·a·gogu·er·y** *n.*

**de·mand** /diˈmand/ ▸*n.* **1** insistent and peremptory request. **2** desire for a commodity, service, etc. **3** pressing requirements: *she's got enough demands on her time.*
▸*v.* **1** ask for (something) insistently and urgently. **2** require or need. **3** insist on. **4** [as *adj.* **demanding**] require skill, effort, etc.

□ **in demand** sought after. □ **on demand** as soon as a demand is made: *a check payable on demand.*

**de·mar·ca·tion** /ˌdēmärˈkāSHən/ ▸*n.* marking a boundary or limits.

**de·mean** ▸*v.* lower the dignity of.

**de·mean·or** /diˈmēnər/ ▸*n.* behavior or bearing.

**de·ment·ed** /diˈmentid/ ▸*adj.* mad; crazy.

**de·men·tia** /diˈmenSHə/ ▸*n.* chronic or persistent disorder of the mental processes caused by brain disease, injury, or age and marked by memory disorders, impaired reasoning, etc.

**de·mer·it** ▸*n.* **1** fault. **2** mark given to an offender.

**de·mesne** /diˈmān/ ▸*n.* land attached to a manor and retained for the owner's own use.

**demi-** ▸*prefix* **1** half. **2** partially or imperfectly such.

**dem·i·god** /ˈdemēˌgäd/ ▸*n.* **1** partly divine being. **2** person of compelling beauty, powers, or personality.

**dem·i·john** /ˈdemēˌjän/ ▸*n.* bulbous, narrow-necked bottle holding from 3 to 10 gallons of liquid, typically enclosed in a wicker cover.

**de·mil·i·ta·rize** /dē'militə,rīz/ ▶v. remove military forces from (a frontier, zone, etc.).
—**de·mil·i·ta·ri·za·tion** n.

**de·mise** /di'mīz/ ▶n. **1** person's death. **2** end or failure of something. **3** transfer (of property, title, etc.) by demising. ▶v. **1** convey or grant (an estate) by will or lease. **2** transmit (a title, etc.) by death.

**de·mit** /di'mit/ ▶v. (**-mit·ted**, **-mit·ting**) resign from (an office or position).

**dem·i·tasse** /'demē,täs/ ▶n. small coffee cup, esp. for strong coffee.

**dem·o** /'demō/ ▶n. (pl. **-os**) inf. DEMONSTRATION.

**de·mo·bi·lize** ▶v. disband (troops, ships, etc.).
—**de·mo·bi·li·za·tion** n.

**de·moc·ra·cy** /di'mäkrəsē/ ▶n. (pl. **-cies**) **1** government by the whole population, usu. through elected representatives. **2** nation or organization so governed.

**dem·o·crat** /'demə,krat/ ▶n. **1** advocate of democracy. **2** (**Democrat**) supporter of the Democratic Party.

**dem·o·crat·ic** ▶adj. **1** of, like, practicing, advocating, or constituting democracy. **2** favoring social equality.
—**dem·o·crat·i·cal·ly** adv.

□ **Democratic Party** U.S. political party, considered to support social reform and greater federal powers.

**de·mog·ra·phy** /di'mägrəfē/ ▶n. study of statistics such as births, deaths, income, or the incidence of disease, which illustrate the changing structure of human populations.

**de·mol·ish** /di'mälisH/ ▶v. **1** pull or knock down. **2** destroy.
—**dem·o·li·tion** n.

**de·mon** /'dēmən/ ▶n. **1** evil spirit or devil. **2** malignant supernatural being; the Devil. **3** forceful, fierce, or skillful performer: *she's a demon cook | she's a demon for work.*
—**de·mon·ic** adj. —**de·mon·ize** v.

**de·mon·e·tize** /dē'mäni,tīz/ ▶v. deprive (a coin or precious metal) of its status as money.

**de·mo·ni·ac** /di'mōnē,ak/ ▶adj. of, like, or characteristic of a demon or demons. ▶n. person believed to be possessed by an evil spirit.

**dem·on·strate** /'demən,strāt/ ▶v. **1** show (feelings, etc.).

**2** describe and explain (a proposition, machine, etc.) by experiment, use, etc. **3** logically prove or be proof of. **4** take part in or organize a public demonstration.
—**dem·on·stra·tor** *n.*

**dem·on·stra·tion** ▶*n.*
**1** showing the existence or truth of something by giving proof. **2** practical exhibition or explanation of how something works. **3** outward showing of feeling. **4** public meeting or march protesting something or expressing political views.

**de·mon·stra·tive** /di-ˈmänstrətiv/ ▶*adj.* **1** showing feelings readily; affectionate. **2** logically conclusive; giving proof: *the work is demonstrative of their skill.* **3** *Gram.* (of an adjective or pronoun) indicating the person or thing referred to (e.g., *this, that, those*).
▶*n. Gram.* demonstrative adjective or pronoun.

**de·mor·al·ize** /diˈmôrəˌlīz/ ▶*v.* destroy (a person's) morale; make hopeless.
—**de·mor·al·iz·ing** *adj.*

**de·mote** /diˈmōt/ ▶*v.* reduce to a lower rank or class.
—**de·mo·tion** *n.*

**de·mur** /diˈmər/ ▶*v.* (-**murred**, -**mur·ring**) raise objections or show reluctance.
▶*n.* objection: *agreed without demur.*

**de·mure** /diˈmyo͝or/ ▶*adj.* (-**mur·er**, -**mur·est**) **1** (of a woman or her behavior) composed, quiet, and reserved; modest. **2** (of clothing) lending such an appearance.

**den** /den/ ▶*n.* **1** wild animal's lair. **2** place of crime or vice. **3** homey, informal room.

**de·na·ture** /dēˈnāCHər/ ▶*v.* **1** change the properties of (a protein, etc.) by heat, acidity, etc. **2** make (alcohol) unfit for drinking.

**den·dro·chro·nol·o·gy** /ˌdendrōkrəˈnäləjē/ ▶*n.* science or technique of dating events, environmental change, and archaeological artifacts by using the characteristic patterns of annual growth rings in timber and tree trunks.

**de·ni·al** /diˈnīəl/ ▶*n.* **1** denying the truth or existence of. **2** refusal of a request or wish. **3** disavowal of a person as one's leader, etc.

**den·i·grate** /ˈdeniˌgrāt/ ▶*v.* defame or disparage the

reputation of (a person); blacken. —**den·i·gra·tion** *n.*

**den·im** /'denəm/ ▶*n.* **1** usu. blue, hard-wearing, cotton twill fabric used for jeans, overalls, etc. **2** clothing made of this.

**den·i·zen** /'denəzən/ ▶*n.* **1** inhabitant or occupant. **2** foreigner admitted to certain rights in an adopted country.

**de·nom·i·nate** /di'nämə,nāt/ ▶*v.* **1** give a name to. **2** call or describe (a person or thing) as.

**de·nom·i·na·tion** ▶*n.* **1** church or religious sect. **2** class of units of numbers, weights, money, etc. **3** name or designation. —**de·nom·i·na·tion·al** *adj.*

**de·nom·i·na·tor** ▶*n.* number below the line in a fraction; divisor.
□ **common denominator 1** common multiple of the denominators of several fractions. **2** common feature of members of a group. □ **lowest common denominator** lowest common multiple as above.

**de·no·ta·tion** /,dēnō'tāsHən/ ▶*n.* literal or primary meaning of a word, in contrast to the feelings or ideas that the word suggests.

**de·note** ▶*v.* **1** be a sign of; indicate. **2** stand as a name for; signify.

**de·noue·ment** /,dānoo'män/ (also **dé·noue·ment**) ▶*n.* final unraveling of a plot or complicated situation.

**de·nounce** /di'nouns/ ▶*v.* **1** publicly declare to be wrong or evil. **2** inform against.

**de no·vo** /dā 'nōvō; di/ ▶*adv. & adj.* starting from the beginning; anew.

**dense** /dens/ ▶*adj.* **1** closely compacted; thick. **2** crowded together. **3** *inf.* stupid. —**den·si·ty** *n.*

**dent** /dent/ ▶*n.* **1** slight hollow made by a blow or pressure. **2** noticeable effect.
▶*v.* mark with a dent.

**den·tal** /'dentl/ ▶*adj.* **1** of the teeth or dentistry. **2** *Phonet.* (of a consonant) produced with the tongue's tip against the upper front teeth (as *th*) or the ridge of the teeth (as *n, s, t*).
□ **dental floss** thread used to clean between the teeth.
□ **dental hygienist** person trained to clean and examine teeth.

**den·ti·frice** /'dentəfris/ ▶*n.* paste or powder for cleaning teeth.

**den·til** /'dentl; -til/ ▶*n.* (in classical

architecture) one of a number of small, rectangular blocks resembling teeth and used as a decoration under the soffit of a cornice.

**den·tin** /'dentin/ (also **den·tine**) ▶*n.* dense, bony tissue forming the bulk of a tooth.

**den·tist** /'dentist/ ▶*n.* person qualified to treat diseases and conditions that affect the mouth, jaws, teeth, and their supporting tissues, and to repair and extract teeth.
—**den·tist·ry** *n.*

**den·ture** /'denCHər/ ▶*n.* removable artificial tooth or teeth.

**de·nude** /di'n(y)o͞od/ ▶*v.* make naked or bare.

**de·nun·ci·a·tion** /di,nənsē-'āSHən/ ▶*n.* denouncing (a person, policy, etc.); public condemnation.
—**de·nun·ci·ate** *v.*

**de·ny** /di'nī/ ▶*v.* (**-nied**) **1** declare untrue or nonexistent. **2** repudiate or disclaim. **3** refuse (a person or thing, or something to a person).

**de·o·dor·ant** /dē'ōdərənt/ ▶*n.* substance applied to the body or sprayed into the air to remove or conceal unpleasant smells.

**de·o·dor·ize** ▶*v.* remove or destroy the smell of.

**De·o vo·len·te** /'dāō və'lentē/ ▶*adv.* God willing; if nothing prevents it.

**de·part** ▶*v.* **1 a** go away; leave. **b** start; set out. **2** diverge; deviate. —**de·par·ture** *n.*

**de·part·ment** ▶*n.* separate part of a complex whole, esp.: **a** branch of municipal or federal administration. **b** division of a university, school, etc., by subject. **c** section of a large store. —**de·part·men·tal** *adj.*
—**de·part·men·tal·ize** *v.*
—**de·part·men·tal·ly** *adv.*
□ **department store** retail store stocking many varieties of goods by departments.

**de·pend** /di'pend/ ▶*v.* **1** be controlled or determined by. **2** be unable to do without. **3** rely on. —**de·pen·dence** *n.*
—**de·pen·dent** *adj., n.*

**de·pend·a·ble** ▶*adj.* reliable.
—**de·pend·a·bil·i·ty** *n.*

**de·pict** /di'pikt/ ▶*v.* **1** represent in a drawing, painting, etc. **2** portray in words; describe.
—**de·pic·tion** *n.*

**de·pil·a·to·ry** /di'pilə,tôrē/ ▶*adj.* that removes unwanted hair.
▶*n.* (*pl.* **-ries**) depilatory substance.

**de·plete** /di'plēt/ ▸v. **1** reduce in numbers or quantity. **2** exhaust. —**de·ple·tion** n.

**de·plor·a·ble** /di'plôrəbəl/ ▸adj. **1** deserving strong condemnation. **2** shockingly bad in quality.

**de·plore** /di'plôr/ ▸v. **1** grieve over; regret. **2** find exceedingly bad. —**de·plor·a·ble** adj.

**de·ploy** /di'ploi/ ▸v. **1** cause (troops) to spread out from a column into a line. **2** use (arguments, forces, etc.) effectively. —**de·ploy·ment** n.

**de·po·lit·i·cize** /ˌdēpə'liti,sīz/ ▸v. make (a person, an organization, etc.) nonpolitical. —**de·po·lit·i·ci·za·tion** n.

**de·pop·u·late** ▸v. **1** reduce the population of. **2** decline in population. —**de·pop·u·la·tion** n.

**de·port** /di'pôrt/ ▸v. expel (a foreigner) from a country. —**de·por·ta·tion** n.

**de·port·ment** ▸n. bearing or manners.

**de·pose** /di'pōz/ ▸v. **1** remove from office suddenly and forcefully. **2** Law testify or give (evidence) on oath, typically in a written statement. —**dep·o·si·tion** n.

**de·pos·it** /di'päzit/ ▸n. **1 a** money in a bank account. **b** anything stored for safekeeping. **2** payment made as a first installment on the purchase of something or as a pledge for a contract. **3** returnable sum payable on a rental. **4** natural layer of accumulated matter. ▸v. **1** put or lay down. **2** pay (a sum) into a bank account. **3** pay (a sum) as a first installment or as a pledge.

**dep·o·si·tion** /ˌdepə'ziSHən/ ▸n. **1** action of deposing someone, esp. a monarch. **2** process of giving sworn evidence. **3** formal, usually written, statement to be used as evidence outside court.

**de·pos·i·to·ry** /di'päzi,tôrē/ ▸n. (pl. -ries) **1** storehouse for furniture, etc. **2** store (of wisdom, knowledge, etc.).

**de·pot** /'dēpō/ ▸n. **1** storehouse, esp. for military supplies. **2** railroad or bus station.

**de·prave** /di'prāv/ ▸v. corrupt, esp. morally. —**de·praved** adj. —**de·prav·i·ty** n.

**dep·re·cate** /'depiə,kāt/ ▸v. express disapproval of or a wish against; deplore. —**dep·re·cat·ing·ly** adv.

—**dep·re·ca·tion** n.

—**dep·re·ca·to·ry** adj.

**de·pre·ci·ate** /di'prēshē,āt/ ▶v.
**1** diminish in value. **2** belittle.

—**de·pre·ci·a·tion** n.

**dep·re·da·tion** /,deprə'dāshən/
▶n. despoiling, ravaging, or
plundering.

**de·press** ▶v. **1** make dispirited
or dejected. **2** reduce the level
of strength or activity in. **3** push
or pull down; lower.

—**de·press·ing** adj.

—**de·press·ing·ly** adv.

**de·pres·sion** ▶n. **1** severe
despondency and dejection.
**2** reduction in vitality, vigor, or
spirits. **3** long period of
financial and industrial decline.
**4** (**the Depression**) the economic
decline of the 1930s. **5** lowering
of atmospheric pressure.
**6** hollow on a surface.
**7** lowering or reducing of
something.

**de·prive** /di'prīv/ ▶v. **1** strip,
dispossess; debar from enjoying.
**2** [as adj. **deprived**] **a** (of a child,
etc.) suffer from the effects of a
poor or loveless home. **b** (of an
area) to have inadequate
housing, facilities, employment,
etc. —**dep·ri·va·tion** n.

**Dept.** ▶abbr. department.

**depth** /depth/ ▶n. **1 a** deepness.
**b** measurement from the top
down, surface inward, or front
to back. **2** difficulty;
abstruseness. **3** intensity of
emotion, color, etc. **4** (**depths**)
**a** abyss. **b** low, depressed state.
**c** lowest or inmost part: depths of
the country. **5** middle: in the
depth of winter.
□ **in depth** comprehensively,
thoroughly, or profoundly. □ **in-
depth** thorough.

**dep·u·ta·tion** /,depyə'tāshən/
▶n. delegation.

**dep·u·ty** /'depyətē/ ▶n. (pl. **-ties**)
person appointed to act for
another.

**de·rac·in·ate** /di'rasə,nāt/ ▶v.
tear (something) up by the roots.

**de·rail** ▶v. (of a train, etc.) leave
or cause to leave the rails
accidentally. —**de·rail·ment** n.

**de·rail·leur** /di'rālər/ ▶n. bicycle
mechanism that moves the
chain out and up, allowing it to
shift to different cogs.

**de·range** /di'rānj/ ▶v. **1** throw
into confusion; disorganize.
**2** [usu. as adj. **deranged**] make
insane: deranged by tragic events.
—**de·range·ment** n.

**der·by** /'dərbē/ ▶n. (pl. **-bies**)
**1** any of several annual horse

races, esp. for three-year-olds. **2** sporting contest. **3** bowler hat.

**de·reg·u·late** ▸*v.* remove regulations or restrictions from. —**de·reg·u·la·tion** *n.*

**der·e·lict** /'derə,likt/ ▸*adj.* **1** (esp. of property) ruined; dilapidated. **2** negligent (of duty, etc.). ▸*n.* social outcast; person without a home, job, or property.

**der·e·lic·tion** /,derə'liksHən/ ▸*n.* **1** neglect; failure to carry out obligations. **2** abandoning; being abandoned.

**de·ride** ▸*v.* mock; ridicule. —**de·ri·sion** *n.* —**de·ri·sive** *adj.*

**de·rive** /di'rīv/ ▸*v.* **1** get, obtain, or form. **2** arise from; originate in; be descended or obtained from. **3 a** trace the descent of (a person). **b** show the origin of (a thing). —**de·riv·a·tive** *adj. & n.*

**der·ma·ti·tis** /,dərmə'tītis/ ▸*n.* inflammation of the skin.

**der·ma·tol·o·gy** /,dərmə'täləjē/ ▸*n.* the study of skin disorders. —**der·ma·to·log·i·cal** *adj.* —**der·ma·tol·o·gist** *n.*

**der·o·gate** /'derə,gāt/ ▸*v.* **1** disparage. **2** (**derogate from**) detract from: *this does not*

*derogate from his duty to act responsibly.* **3** (**derogate from**) deviate from: *one country has derogated from the Geneva Convention.* —**de·rog·a·tive** *adj.*

**de·rog·a·to·ry** /di'rägə,tôrē/ ▸*adj.* showing a critical or disrespectful attitude.

**der·rick** /'derik/ ▸*n.* **1** pivoting crane for moving or lifting heavy weights. **2** framework over an oil well, etc., holding the drilling machinery.

**der·ri·ere** /,derē'e(ə)r/ (also **der·ri·ère**) ▸*n. inf.* buttocks.

**der·vish** /'dərvisH/ ▸*n.* Muslim (specifically Sufi) religious man who has taken vows of poverty. Some orders (especially the **whirling dervishes**) are noted for their wild or ecstatic rituals.

**de·scend** /di'send/ ▸*v.* **1** go or come down (a hill, etc.). **2** (of a thing) sink; fall: *rain descended heavily.* **3** slope downward. **4** (**descend on**) **a** attack. **b** make an unexpected and usu. unwelcome visit. **5** (**descend from**) (of property, rights, etc.) be passed by inheritance. **6** sink in rank, quality, etc. —**de·scend·ent** *adj.* —**de·scent** *n.*

☐ **be descended from** have as an ancestor.

**de·scend·ant** ▸*n.* person or thing descended from another: *a descendant of John Adams.*

**de·scribe** /di'skrīb/ ▸*v.* **1 a** state the characteristics, appearance, etc., of. **b** assert to be: *described him as a habitual liar.* **2** outline; delineate.

**de·scrip·tion** /di'skripSHən/ ▸*n.* **1** describing or being described. **2** representation (of a person, object, etc.), esp. in words. **3** sort, kind, or class. —**de·scrip·tive** *adj.*

**de·scry** /di'skrī/ ▸*v.* (**-scried**) *poet./lit.* catch sight of; discern.

**des·e·crate** /'desi,krāt/ ▸*v.* violate (a sacred place or thing) with violence, profanity, etc. —**des·e·cra·tion** *n.*

**de·seg·re·gate** ▸*v.* abolish racial segregation in (schools, etc.). —**de·seg·re·ga·tion** *n.*

**de·sen·si·tize** ▸*v.* reduce or destroy the sensitiveness of (an allergic person, etc.). —**de·sen·si·ti·za·tion** *n.*

**de·sert**[1] /di'zərt/ ▸*v.* **1** give up; leave: *deserted the sinking ship.* **2** forsake or abandon (a cause, person, etc.): *deserted his children.*

**3** run away (esp. from military service).

▸*n.* (**deserts**) person's worthiness or entitlement to reward or punishment. —**de·sert·er** *n.* —**de·ser·tion** *n.*

☐ **get** (or **receive**) **one's just deserts** receive the appropriate reward or punishment for one's actions.

**des·ert**[2] /'dezərt/ ▸*n.* dry, barren, often sand-covered area of land; uninteresting or barren subject, period, etc.: *a cultural desert.*

▸*adj.* **1** uninhabited; desolate. **2** uncultivated; barren.

**de·serve** /di'zərv/ ▸*v.* **1** be worthy of (reward, punishment, etc.): *deserves to be imprisoned.* **2** [as *adj.* **deserved**] rightfully merit or earn: *a deserved win.* —**de·serv·ed·ly** *adv.* —**de·serving** *adj.*

**de·sex** /dē'seks/ ▸*v.* **1** deprive (someone) of sexual qualities or attraction. **2** castrate or spay (an animal).

**des·ic·cate** /'desi,kāt/ ▸*v.* **1** remove the moisture from something to preserve it. **2** [as *adj.* **desiccated**] lack passion or energy. —**des·ic·ca·tion** *n.*

**de·sid·er·a·tum** /diˌsidəˈrätəm/ ▸n. (pl. **-ta**) something lacking but needed or desired.

**de·sign** /diˈzīn/ ▸n. **1** plan or sketch for making a building, machine, garment, etc. **2** lines or shapes forming a pattern or decoration. **3** plan, purpose, or intention. **4** arrangement or layout.
▸v. **1** produce a design for. **2** intend, plan, or propose. **3** be a designer. —**de·sign·er** n.
□ **by design** on purpose. □ **have designs on** plan to harm or appropriate.

**des·ig·nate** /ˈdezigˌnāt/ ▸v. **1** appoint: *designated him as postmaster general.* **2** specify. **3** describe as; style.
▸adj. appointed but not yet installed: *bishop designate.* —**des·ig·na·tion** n.
□ **designated driver** member of a group who abstains from alcohol in order to drive the others safely. □ **designated hitter** *Baseball* batter in the lineup who hits for the pitcher. (Abbr.: **DH**).

**de·sign·ing** ▸adj. crafty or scheming.

**de·sire** /diˈzī(ə)r/ ▸n. **1 a** longing or craving. **b** expression of this. **2** lust. **3** something desired.
▸v. **1** long for; crave. **2** request. —**de·sir·a·ble** adj.

**de·sist** /diˈsist/ ▸v. abstain; cease: *desist from interrupting.*

**desk** /desk/ ▸n. **1** piece of furniture with a writing surface and often drawers. **2** counter in a hotel, bank, etc., at which a customer may check in or obtain information.

**des·o·late** ▸adj. /ˈdesəlit/ **1** left alone; solitary. **2** (of a building or place) uninhabited; ruined; dreary. **3** forlorn; wretched.
▸v. /ˈdesəˌlāt/ **1** devastate; lay waste to. **2** [usu. as adj. **desolated**] make wretched. —**des·o·la·tion** n.

**de·spair** /diˈspe(ə)r/ ▸n. complete loss or absence of hope.
▸v. lose or be without hope (about).

**des·per·a·do** /ˌdespəˈrädō/ ▸n. (pl. **-does** or **-dos**) desperate or reckless person, esp. a criminal.

**des·per·ate** /ˈdespərit/ ▸adj. **1** reckless or dangerous from despair. **2** extremely dangerous or serious. **3** needing or desiring very much. —**des·per·ate·ly** adv. —**des·per·a·tion** n.

**des·pi·ca·ble** /diˈspikəbəl/ ▸adj. vile; contemptible, esp. morally.

**de·spise** /diˈspīz/ ▸v. look down

on as inferior, worthless, or contemptible.

**de·spite** /di'spīt/ ▸*prep.* in spite of.

**de·spoil** /di'spoil/ ▸*v.* plunder; rob; deprive: *despoiled the roof of its lead.* —**de·spo·li·a·tion** *n.*

**de·spond·ent** /di'spändənt/ ▸*adj.* in low spirits; dejected. —**de·spond·en·cy** *n.* —**de·spond·ent·ly** *adv.*

**des·pot** /'despət/ ▸*n.* absolute ruler; tyrant. —**des·pot·ic** *adj.* —**des·pot·ism** *n.*

**des·pot·ism** /'despə,tizəm/ ▸*n.* **1** exercise of absolute power, esp. in a cruel and oppressive way. **2** country or political system where the ruler holds absolute power.

**des·sert** /di'zərt/ ▸*n.* sweet course of a meal, served at or near the end.

**des·ti·na·tion** /,destə'nāsHən/ ▸*n.* place to which a person or thing is going.

**des·tine** /'destin/ ▸*v.* preordain; intend: *destined him for the navy.* □ **be destined to** be fated or preordained to.

**des·ti·ny** /'destinē/ ▸*n.* (*pl.* **-nies**) **1** predetermined course of events; fate. **2** particular person's fate or lot.

**des·ti·tute** /'desti,t(y) o͞ot/ ▸*adj.* **1** completely impoverished. **2** lacking. —**des·ti·tu·tion** *n.*

**de·stroy** /di'stroi/ ▸*v.* **1** pull or break down; demolish. **2** end the existence of; kill (esp. an animal). **3** make useless; spoil utterly. **4** defeat: *destroyed the enemy.*

**de·stroy·er** ▸*n.* **1** person or thing that destroys. **2** fast warship used to protect other ships.

**de·struct** /di'strəkt/ ▸*v.* cause deliberate, irreparable damage to.

**de·struc·tion** ▸*n.* **1** destroying or being destroyed. **2** cause of ruin. —**de·struct·i·ble** *adj.* —**de·struc·tive** *adj.* —**de·struc·tive·ness** *n.*

**des·ue·tude** /'deswi,t(y)o͞od/ ▸*n.* state of disuse.

**des·ul·to·ry** /'desəl,tôrē/ ▸*adj.* **1** without enthusiasm or purpose. **2** going from one subject to another, esp. halfheartedly. —**des·ul·to·ri·ly** *adv.*

**de·tach** /di'taCH/ ▸*v.* **1** unfasten or disengage and remove. **2** [as *adj.* **detached**] be impartial or unemotional: *a detached viewpoint.* —**de·tach·a·ble** *adj.*

**de·tach·ment** ▸*n.*
**1 a** aloofness; indifference.
**b** impartiality. **2** detaching or
being detached. **3** troops, etc.,
used for a specific purpose.

**de·tail** /di'tāl/ ▸*n.* **1** small
particular; item; minor element.
**2 a** these collectively: *has an eye
for detail.* **b** treatment of them:
*the detail was insufficient.* **3** small
detachment.
▸*v.* **1** give particulars or
circumstances of. **2** assign for
special duty. **3** [as *adj.* **detailed**]
itemize.
□ **in detail** item by item, minutely.

**de·tain** /di'tān/ ▸*v.* **1** keep (a
person) in custody. **2** keep
waiting; delay. —**de·tain·ee** *n.*
—**de·tain·ment** *n.*

**de·tect** /di'tekt/ ▸*v.* discover or
perceive. —**de·tect·a·ble** *adj.*
—**de·tec·tion** *n.*

**de·tec·tive** ▸*n.* person who
investigates crime.
□ **private detective** detective
carrying out investigations for a
private employer.

**dé·tente** /dā'tänt/ ▸*n.* easing of
tension, esp. between nations.

**de·ter** /di'tər/ ▸*v.* (**-terred**,
**-ter·ring**) discourage or prevent
(a person), esp. through fear.

**de·ter·gent** /di'tərjənt/ ▸*n.*
cleaning agent.
▸*adj.* cleansing.

**de·te·ri·o·rate** /di'ti(ə)rēə,rāt/ ▸*v.*
make or become bad or worse.
—**de·te·ri·o·ra·tion** *n.*

**de·ter·mi·na·tion** /di,tərmə-
'nāsHən/ ▸*n.* **1** firmness of
purpose. **2** process of deciding,
determining, or calculating.

**de·ter·mine** /di'tərmin/ ▸*v.*
**1** find out or establish precisely.
**2** decide or settle. **3** be a
decisive factor in regard to:
*demand determines supply.*
—**de·ter·mi·nant** *n.*
□ **be determined** be resolved: *was
determined not to give up.*

**de·ter·mined** ▸*adj.* **1** showing
determination; resolute;
unflinching. **2** fixed in scope or
character.

**de·ter·rent** ▸*n.* thing that
discourages.
▸*adj.* intended to deter: *the
deterrent effect of heavy prison
sentences.* —**de·ter·rence** *n.*

**de·test** /di'test/ ▸*v.* hate; loathe.
—**de·test·a·ble** *adj.*

**de·throne** ▸*v.* remove from the
throne; depose.

**det·o·nate** /'detn,āt/ ▸*v.* explode
with a loud noise.

—**det·o·na·tion** *n.*

—**det·o·na·tor** *n.*

**de·tour** /'dē,tŏor/ ▶*n.* divergence from a direct or intended route. ▶*v.* make or cause to make a detour.

**de·tox·i·fy** /dē'täksi,fī/ ▶*v.* remove the poison from. —**de·tox·i·fi·ca·tion** *n.*

**de·tract** /di'trakt/ ▶*v.* take away (a part of something); reduce: *self-interest detracted nothing from their victory.* —**de·trac·tor** *n.*

**det·ri·ment** /'detrəmənt/ ▶*n.* **1** harm; damage. **2** something causing this. —**det·ri·men·tal** *adj.*

**det·ri·men·tal** /,detrə'mentl/ ▶*adj.* tending to cause harm.

**de·tri·tus** /di'trītəs/ ▶*n.* **1** gravel, sand, etc., from erosion. **2** debris.

**de trop** /də 'trō/ ▶*adj.* not wanted; unwelcome.

**deuce** /d(y)ōōs/ ▶*n.* two on dice or playing cards.

**de·us ex ma·chi·na** /'dāəs eks 'mäkənə/ ▶*n.* unexpected power or event saving a seemingly hopeless situation, esp. as a contrived plot device in a play or novel.

**deu·te·ri·um** /d(y)ōō'ti(ə)rēəm/ ▶*n.* *Chem.* stable isotope of hydrogen with a mass approx. twice that of the usual isotope. (Symb.: **D**)

**de·val·ue** ▶*v.* reduce the worth of.

**dev·as·tate** /'devə,stāt/ ▶*v.* **1** cause great destruction to. **2** overwhelm with shock or grief: *we were devastated by the announcement of the company's bankruptcy.* —**dev·as·tat·ing** *adj.* —**dev·as·ta·tion** *n.*

**de·vel·op** /di'veləp/ ▶*v.* **1 a** make or become bigger or fuller, etc. **b** bring or come to an active, visible, or mature state. **2 a** begin to exhibit or suffer from. **b** come into existence; originate; emerge. **3 a** build on (land). **b** convert (land) to a new use. **4** treat (film, etc.) to make the image visible. —**de·vel·op·er** *n.* —**de·vel·op·ment** *n.*

□ **developing country** poor or undeveloped country that is becoming more advanced economically and socially.

**de·vi·ant** /'dēvēənt/ ▶*adj.* departing from accepted standards, esp. social or sexual: *deviant behavior.* ▶*n.* deviant person or thing. —**de·vi·ance** *n.*

**de·vi·ate** /'dēvē,āt/ ▶*v.* depart

from an established course or usual standards. —**de·vi·a·tion** *n.*

**de·vice** /di'vīs/ ▸*n.* **1** thing made or adapted for a particular purpose. **2** plan, scheme, or trick. **3** emblematic or heraldic design.

**dev·il** /'devəl/ ▸*n.* **1** (usu. **the Devil**) (in Christian and Jewish belief) supreme spirit of evil; Satan. **2** evil spirit; demon. **3 a** wicked or cruel person. **b** mischievous person. **4** *inf.* person of a specified nature: *lucky devil.*

▸*v.* (**-iled, -il·ing; -illed, -il·ling**) **1** prepare (food) with hot seasoning. **2** harass; worry. —**dev·il·ish** *adj. & adv.*

□ **devil-may-care** cheerful and reckless. □ **devil's advocate** person who tests a proposition by arguing against it.

**dev·il's ad·vo·cate** ▸*n.* person who expresses a contentious opinion in order to provoke debate or test the strength of the opposing arguments.

**de·vi·ous** /'dēvēəs/ ▸*adj.* **1** (of a person, etc.) not straightforward; underhand. **2** winding; circuitous.

**de·vise** /di'vīz/ ▸*v.* **1** plan or invent carefully. **2** *Law* leave (real estate) to someone by will.

▸*n.* *Law* clause in a will leaving real estate to someone.

**de·void** /di'void/ ▸*adj.* lacking or free from: *a book devoid of all interest.*

**de·voir** /dəv'wär/ ▸*n.* person's duty.

**dev·o·lu·tion** /,devə'loosHən/ ▸*n.* **1** transfer or delegation of power to a lower level, esp. by central government to local or regional administration. **2** evolutionary degeneration.

**de·volve** /di'välv/ ▸*v.* **1** pass (power) to a lower level: *measures to devolve power to the provinces.* **2** (**devolve on/upon/to**) (of duties or responsibility) pass to (a deputy, etc.): *his duties devolved on a comrade.*

**de·vote** /di'vōt/ ▸*v.* apply or give over (resources, etc., or oneself) to (a particular activity, purpose, or person): *devoted himself to his guests.*

**de·vot·ed** ▸*adj.* very loving or loyal: *a devoted husband.*

**dev·o·tee** /,devə'tē/ ▸*n.* **1** zealous enthusiast or supporter: *devotee of medieval music.* **2** zealously pious person: *devotees thronged to the temple.*

**de·vo·tion** ▸n. **1** enthusiastic loyalty (to a person or cause); great love. **2** (**devotions**) prayers. —**de·vo·tion·al** adj.

**de·vour** /di'vour/ ▸v. **1** eat hungrily or greedily. **2** (of fire, etc.) engulf; destroy.

**de·vout** /di'vout/ ▸adj. **1** earnestly religious. **2** earnestly sincere: devout hope.

**dew** /d(y)oo/ ▸n. **1** atmospheric vapor condensing on cool surfaces at night. **2** beaded moisture resembling this. —**dew·y** adj.
□ **dew point** the temperature at which dew forms.

**dew·lap** /'d(y)oo,lap/ ▸n. fold of loose skin hanging from the neck or throat of an animal or bird, esp. that present in many cattle.

**dew point** ▸n. atmospheric temperature (varying according to pressure and humidity) below which water droplets begin to condense and dew can form.

**dex·ter·i·ty** /dek'sterite/ ▸n. **1** skill in handling. **2** manual or mental adroitness.

**dex·ter·ous** /'dekst(ə)rəs/ ▸adj. demonstrating skill with the hands.

**dex·trose** /'dekstros/ ▸n. form of glucose.

**di·a·be·tes** /ˌdīə'bētēz/ ▸n. any disorder of the metabolism with excessive thirst, increased urine production, and high blood sugar. —**di·a·bet·ic** adj. & n.

**di·a·bol·ic** /ˌdīə'bälik/ (also **di·a·bol·i·cal**) ▸adj. **1** of the Devil. **2** devilish; inhumanly cruel or wicked. **3** fiendishly clever or cunning or annoying. —**di·a·bol·i·cal·ly** adv.

**di·a·crit·ic** /ˌdīə'kritik/ ▸n. sign (e.g., an accent, cedilla, etc.) indicating different sounds or values of a letter. —**di·a·crit·i·cal** adj.

**di·a·dem** /'dīə,dem/ ▸n. crown or ornamental headband.

**di·ag·nose** /ˌdīəg'nōs/ ▸v. make a diagnosis of (a disease, fault, etc.) from its symptoms.

**di·ag·no·sis** /ˌdīəg'nōsis/ ▸n. (pl. **-ses**) identification of a disease, mechanical fault, etc., after observing its symptoms.

**di·ag·nos·tic** /ˌdīəg'nästik/ ▸adj. **1** concerned with the diagnosis of illness or other problems. **2** (of a symptom) distinctive, and so indicating the nature of an illness. **3** characteristic of a

particular species, genus, or phenomenon.
▸*n.* **1** distinctive symptom or characteristic. **2** computer program or routine that helps a user to identify errors.

**di·ag·o·nal** /dī'agənl/ ▸*adj.*
**1** crossing a straight-sided figure from corner to corner.
**2** slanting; oblique.
▸*n.* straight line joining two nonadjacent corners.
—**di·ag·o·nal·ly** *adv.*

**di·a·gram** /'dīə,gram/ ▸*n.* drawing showing the general scheme or outline of an object and its parts.
▸*v.* (**-gramed, -gram·ing; -grammed, -gram·ming**) represent by means of a diagram.

**di·al** /'dī(ə)l/ ▸*n.* **1** face of a clock or watch, marked to show the hours, etc. **2** flat plate with a scale for measuring weight, volume, etc., indicated by a pointer. **3** adjustment control on a radio, appliance, etc. **4** movable disk on a telephone, with finger holes and numbers for making a call.
▸*v.* select (a telephone number) by means of a dial or set of buttons: *dialed 911.*

□ **dial tone** sound indicating that a telephone is ready for dialing.

**di·a·lect** /'dīə,lekt/ ▸*n.*
**1** regional form of speech.
**2** variety of language with nonstandard vocabulary, pronunciation, or grammar.

**di·a·lec·tic** ▸*n.* (often **dialectics**) art of investigating the truth of opinions; testing of truth by discussion.
▸*adj.* of or relating to logical disputation.

**di·a·logue** /'dīə,lôg/ (also **di·a·log**) ▸*n.* **1** conversation. **2** conversation in written form.

**di·al·y·sis** /dī'aləsis/ ▸*n.* (*pl.* **-ses**) separation of particles in a liquid by use of a membrane, esp. for purification of blood.

**di·am·e·ter** /dī'amitər/ ▸*n.*
**1** straight line through the center of a circle or sphere.
**2** length of this line.

**di·a·met·ri·cal** /,dīə'metrikəl/ (also **di·a·met·ric**) ▸*adj.* **1** of or along a diameter. **2** (of opposites, etc.) absolute.
—**di·a·met·ri·cal·ly** *adv.*

**di·a·mond** /'dī(ə)mənd/ ▸*n.*
**1** precious stone of pure carbon crystallized in octahedrons, etc., the hardest naturally occurring substance. **2** figure shaped like

the cross section of a diamond; rhombus. **3 a** playing card of a suit denoted by a red rhombus. **b** (**diamonds**) this suit. **4** *Baseball* the playing field, esp. the infield. ▸*adj.* **1** made of or set with diamonds or a diamond. **2** rhombus-shaped.

**di·a·mond·back** ▸*n.* **1** edible freshwater terrapin, native to N. America, with diamond-shaped markings on its shell. **2** rattlesnake, native to N. America, with diamond-shaped markings.

**di·a·per** /'dī(ə)pər/ ▸*n.* absorbent material wrapped around a baby to retain urine and feces.

**di·aph·a·nous** /dī'afənəs/ ▸*adj.* (of fabric, etc.) light and delicate, and almost transparent.

**di·a·phragm** /'dīə,fram/ ▸*n.* **1** muscular partition separating the thorax from the abdomen in mammals. **2** vibrating disk that produces sound in acoustic systems, etc. **3** device for varying the aperture of a camera lens. **4** contraceptive cap fitting over the cervix.

**di·ar·rhe·a** /,dīə'rēə/ ▸*n.* condition of excessively frequent and loose bowel movements.

**di·a·ry** /'dīərē/ ▸*n.* (*pl.* **-ries**) **1** daily record of events or thoughts. **2** book for this.

**di·as·po·ra** /dī'aspərə/ ▸*n.* (often **the Diaspora**) **1** Jews living outside Israel. **2** dispersion of the Jews beyond Israel. **3** dispersion of any people from their original homeland, or the people so dispersed.

**di·a·ton·ic** /dīə'tänik/ ▸*adj. Mus.* relating to a standard major or minor scale of eight notes.

**di·a·tribe** /'dīə,trīb/ ▸*n.* forceful verbal attack or bitter criticism.

**dib·ble** /'dibəl/ ▸*n.* hand tool for making holes in the ground for seeds or young plants.

**dice** /dīs/ ▸*pl. n.* **1 a** small cubes with faces bearing 1–6 spots used in games of chance. **b** one of these cubes (See note at **DIE**[2]). **2** game played with dice. ▸*v.* cut (food) into small cubes.

**dic·ey** ▸*adj.* (**-i·er, -i·est**) *inf.* risky; unreliable.

**di·chot·o·my** /dī'kätəmē/ ▸*n.* (*pl.* **-mies**) division into two, esp. a sharply defined one.

**dick·er** /'dikər/ ▸*v.* bargain; haggle.

**dic·tate** /'dik,tāt/ ▸*v.* **1** say or read aloud (words to be written down or recorded). **2** prescribe

or lay down authoritatively (terms, etc.).
▶*n.* authoritative instruction: *dictates of conscience.*
—**dic·ta·tion** *n.*

**dic·ta·tor** ▶*n.* **1** ruler with unrestricted authority. **2** person with supreme authority in any sphere. —**dic·ta·tor·ship** *n.*

**dic·ta·tor·i·al** /ˌdiktə'tôrēəl/ ▶*adj.* **1** of or like a dictator. **2** imperious; overbearing.

**dic·tion** /'dikSHən/ ▶*n.* **1** choice and use of words in speech or writing. **2** manner of enunciation in speaking or singing.

**dic·tion·ar·y** /'dikSHə,nerē/ ▶*n.* (*pl.* **-ies**) **1** publication that lists (usu. alphabetically) and explains the words of a language or gives equivalents in another language. **2** reference publication on any subject, arranged alphabetically: *dictionary of architecture.* **3** *Computing* ordered list of words, codes, etc., used by a program.

**dic·tum** /'diktəm/ ▶*n.* (*pl.* **-ta** or **-tums**) **1** formal utterance or pronouncement. **2** saying or maxim.

**di·dac·tic** /dī'daktik/ ▶*adj.* **1** meant to instruct. **2** (of a

person) tediously pedantic.
—**di·dac·ti·cal·ly** *adv.*
—**di·dac·ti·cism** *n.*

**did·n't** /'didnt/ ▶*contr.* did not.

**die¹** /dī/ ▶*v.* (**died, dy·ing**) **1** (of a person, animal, or plant) cease to live; expire. **2 a** come to an end; fade away. **b** cease to function. **c** (of a flame) go out. □ **be dying** wish for longingly or intently: *am dying to see you.* □ **die down** become less loud or strong. □ **die hard** die reluctantly: *old habits die hard.*

**die²** ▶*n.* **1** sing of DICE. *Dice* is now standard in general use in this sense. **2** (*pl.* **dies**) engraved stamping device.

**die·hard** ▶*n.* conservative or stubborn person.

**di·er·e·sis** /dī'erəsis/ (also **di·aer·e·sis**) ▶a mark placed over a vowel (as in *naïve*) to indicate that it is sounded separately.

**die·sel** /'dēzəl/ ▶*n.* **1** (also **die·sel engine**) internal combustion engine that burns fuel ignited by compression. **2** vehicle driven by a diesel engine. **3** fuel for a diesel engine.

**di·et** /'dīit/ ▶*n.* **1** kinds of food that a person or animal habitually eats. **2** food to which a person is restricted, esp. for medical reasons or to control weight. **3** legislative assembly in certain countries.

▶ *v.* restrict oneself to small amounts or special kinds of food, esp. to control weight. —**di·e·ta·ry** *adj.* —**di·et·er** *n.*

**di·e·tet·ics** /ˌdīiˈtetiks/ ▶*n.* scientific study of diet and nutrition.

**di·e·ti·tian** /ˌdīiˈtisHən/ (also **di·e·ti·cian**) ▶*n.* expert in dietetics.

**dif·fer** /ˈdifər/ ▶*v.* **1** be unlike or distinguishable. **2** disagree; be at variance (with a person).

**dif·fer·ence** /ˈdif(ə)rəns/ ▶*n.* **1** being different or unlike. **2** distinction. **3** quantity by which amounts differ; deficit: *will have to make up the difference.* **4 a** disagreement, quarrel, or dispute. **b** grounds of disagreement: *put aside their differences.*

**dif·fer·ent** ▶*adj.* **1** unlike; not the same. **2** distinct; separate.

**dif·fer·en·ti·ate** /ˌdifəˈrensHē-ˌāt/ ▶*v.* **1** recognize what makes (someone or something) different. **2** identify differences between. **3** make or become different while growing or developing (species, word forms, etc.). —**dif·fer·en·ti·a·tion** *n.*

**dif·fi·cult** /ˈdifikəlt/ ▶*adj.* **1 a** needing much effort or skill. **b** troublesome; perplexing. **2** (of a person): **a** not easy to please. **b** uncooperative; troublesome. **3** characterized by hardships or problems: *a difficult period in his life.*

**dif·fi·cul·ty** ▶*n.* (*pl.* **-ties**) **1** being difficult. **2 a** difficult thing; problem; hindrance. **b** distress or hardship: *in financial difficulties.*

**dif·fi·dent** /ˈdifidənt/ ▶*adj.* shy; lacking self-confidence. —**dif·fi·dence** *n.*

**dif·fuse** ▶*adj.* /diˈfyo͞os/ **1** (of light, inflammation, etc.) spread out; not concentrated. **2** (of prose, speech, etc.) not concise; long-winded; verbose.

▶*v.* /diˈfyo͞oz/ **1** disperse or be dispersed. **2** spread or be spread widely; reach a large area. —**dif·fu·sion** *n.*

**dig** /dig/ ▶*v.* (**dig·ging**; *past* and *past part.* **dug**) **1** break up and remove or turn over soil, etc. **2** break up the soil of. **3** make (a hole, grave, tunnel, etc.) by digging. **4 a** obtain or remove by digging. **b** find or discover after searching. **5** thrust or poke into or down into. **6** (**dig into**) investigate or study closely; probe.

▶*n.* **1** piece of digging. **2** thrust or poke: *a dig in the ribs.* **3** pointed or critical remark. **4** archaeological excavation. —**dig·ger** *n.*

**di·gest** ▶*v.* /di'jest/ **1** assimilate (food) in the stomach and bowels. **2** understand and assimilate mentally. **3** reduce to a systematic or convenient form; classify; summarize.

▶*n.* /'dījest/ **1** compendium or summary of information; résumé. **2** periodical synopsis of current literature or news. —**di·gest·i·ble** *adj.* —**di·gest·i·bil·i·ty** *n.* —**di·ges·tion** *n.* —**di·ges·tive** *adj.*

**di·git** /'dijit/ ▶*n.* **1** any numeral from 0 to 9. **2** finger, thumb, or toe.

**dig·i·tal** ▶*adj.* **1** of or using a digit or digits. **2** (of a clock, watch, etc.) that gives a reading by displayed digits. **3** (of a computer) operating on data represented by digits. **4** (of a recording) with sound

electronically represented by digits. —**dig·it·al·ly** *adv.*

**dig·i·tize** ▶*v.* convert (data, etc.) into digital form, esp. for a computer.

**dig·ni·fied** /'dignə‚fīd/ ▶*adj.* having or expressing dignity; noble or stately in appearance or manner.

**dig·ni·fy** ▶*v.* (**-fied**) **1** give dignity or distinction to. **2** ennoble. **3** give the appearance of dignity to: *dignified the house with the name of mansion.*

**dig·ni·tar·y** /'digni‚terē/ ▶*n.* (*pl.* **-ies**) person of high rank or office.

**dig·ni·ty** /'dignitē/ ▶*n.* (*pl.* **-ties**) **1** composed and serious manner or style. **2** worthiness; excellence. **3** high or honorable rank or position. **4** high regard. **5** self-respect. □ **beneath one's dignity** not considered worthy enough for one to do.

**di·graph** /'dī‚graf/ ▶*n.* **1** combination of two letters representing one sound, as in *ph* and *oo*. **2** character consisting of two joined letters; a ligature.

**di·gress** /dī'gres/ ▶*v.* depart from the main subject in speech or

writing. —**di·gres·sion** n.
—**di·gres·sive** adj.

**dike** /dīk/ (also **dyke**) ▶n.
**1** embankment built to prevent flooding from the sea.
**2** causeway. **3** ditch or watercourse.

**di·lap·i·dat·ed** /di'lapi‚dātid/ ▶adj. in disrepair or ruin.

**di·late** /'dī‚lāt/ ▶v. make or become wider or larger: *dilated pupils.* —**di·la·tion** n.

**dil·a·to·ry** /'dilə‚tôrē/ ▶adj. given to or causing delay.

**di·lem·ma** /di'lemə/ ▶n. situation in which a choice has to be made between two equally undesirable alternatives.

**dil·et·tante** /‚dili'tant/ ▶n. (pl. **-tantes** or **-tan·ti**) person who studies a subject or area of knowledge superficially.

**dil·i·gent** /'dilijənt/ ▶adj.
**1** hardworking. **2** showing care and effort. —**dil·i·gence** n.

**dill** /dil/ ▶n. herb with aromatic seeds and leaves, used for flavoring and medicinal purposes.
□ **dill pickle** pickled cucumber, etc., flavored with dill.

**dil·ly·dal·ly** /'dilē‚dalē/ ▶v. (**-lied**) *inf.* waste time through aimless wandering or indecision.

**di·lute** /di'lōōt/ ▶v. **1** reduce the strength of (a fluid) by adding water, etc. **2** weaken or reduce in effect.

**dim** /dim/ ▶adj. (**dim·mer**, **dim·mest**) **1 a** faintly luminous or visible; not bright. **b** obscure; ill-defined. **2** not clearly perceived or remembered.

▶v. (**dimmed**, **dim·ming**) make or become dim.

□ **take a dim view of** disapprove of.

**dime** /dīm/ ▶n. ten-cent coin.

**di·men·sion** /di'menchən/ ▶n.
**1** measurable extent, as length, breadth, etc. **2** (**dimensions**) size; scope; extent. **3** aspect or facet of a situation, etc.

**di·min·ish** /di'minish/ ▶v.
**1** make or become smaller or less. **2** lessen the reputation or influence of (a person).

**di·min·u·en·do** /di‚minyōō'endo/ *Mus.* ▶adv. gradual decrease in loudness.

▶n. (pl. **-dos**) passage played in this way.

**di·min·u·tive** /di'minyətiv/ ▶adj.
**1** remarkably small; tiny.
**2** *Gram.* (of a word or suffix) implying smallness or affection (e.g., -*let*, -*kins*).

▶*n. Gram.* diminutive word or suffix.

**dim·ple** /'dimpəl/ ▶*n.* small hollow, esp. in the cheeks or chin.

▶*v.* produce or show dimples (in).

**dim·wit** /'dim,wit/ ▶*n. inf.* stupid person. —**dim·wit·ted** *adj.*

**din** /din/ ▶*n.* prolonged loud and distracting noise.

**dine** /dīn/ ▶*v.* eat dinner.

□ **dining room** room in which meals are eaten.

**din·er** /'dīnər/ ▶*n.* **1** person who is eating, esp. in a restaurant. **2** small restaurant. **3** railroad dining car.

**di·nette** /dī'net/ ▶*n.* **1** small room or part of a room used for eating meals. **2** (also **di·nette set**) table and chairs designed for such a room.

**din·ghy** /'diNGē/ ▶*n.* (*pl.* **-ghies**) small boat for rowing or sailing.

**din·gle** /'diNGgəl/ ▶*n.* deep wooded valley or dell.

**din·gy** /'dinjē/ ▶*adj.* (**-gi·er**, **-gi·est**) dirty-looking; drab; dull-colored. —**din·gi·ness** *n.*

**din·ner** /'dinər/ ▶*n.* **1** main meal of the day, either at midday or in the evening. **2** formal evening meal or banquet.

**di·no·saur** /'dīnə,sôr/ ▶*n.* **1** extinct reptile of the Mesozoic era, often of enormous size. **2** large, unwieldy system or organization.

**di·o·cese** /'dīəsis/ ▶*n.* district administered by a bishop. —**di·oc·e·san** *adj.*

**di·o·ram·a** /,dīə'ramə/ ▶*n.* three-dimensional scenic display with a painted backdrop.

**di·ox·ide** /dī'äk,sīd/ ▶*n.* oxide containing two atoms of oxygen which are not linked together: *carbon dioxide.*

**dip** /dip/ ▶*v.* (**dipped**, **dip·ping**) **1** put or let down briefly into liquid, etc.; immerse. **2 a** go below a surface or level. **b** (of a level of income, activity, etc.) decline slightly. **3** extend or slope downward.

▶*n.* **1** dipping or being dipped. **2** liquid or sauce into which something is dipped. **3** brief swim. **4** brief downward slope in a road, skyline, etc.

**diph·the·ri·a** /dif'THi(ə)rēə/ ▶*n.* acute infectious bacterial disease with inflammation, esp. of the throat.

**diph·thong** /'dif,THäNG/ ▶*n.* speech sound in one syllable in which the articulation begins as for one vowel and moves as for another (as in *coin*, *loud*, and *side*). —**diph·thon·gal** *adj.*

**di·plo·ma** /di'plōmə/ ▶*n.* (*pl.* -mas) certificate awarded by an education institution indicating that a course of study has been completed.

**di·plo·ma·cy** ▶*n.* **1** management of international relations. **2** adroitness in personal relations; tact.

**dip·lo·mat** /'diplə,mat/ ▶*n.* **1** official representing a country abroad. **2** person who can deal tactfully with others. —**dip·lo·mat·ic** *adj.*

**dip·so·ma·ni·a** /,dipsə'mānēə/ ▶*n.* alcoholism. —**dip·so·ma·ni·ac** *n.*

**dire** /dī(ə)r/ ▶*adj.* **1** extremely serious or urgent. **2** ominous.

**di·rect** /di'rekt/ ▶*adj.* **1** extending or moving in a straight line or by the shortest route. **2 a** straightforward. **b** frank. **3** without intermediaries: *direct rule.* **4** (of descent) lineal; not collateral. **5** exact; complete; greatest possible (esp. where contrast is implied): *the direct opposite.*
▶*adv.* in a direct way or manner: *dealt with them direct.*

▶*v.* **1** control; guide; govern the movements of. **2** order or command. **3** tell or show (a person) the way to. **4** aim (something) in a particular direction or at a particular person: *his smile was directed at Laura.* **5** address a comment to: *I suggest he direct his remarks to the council.* **6 a** supervise the performing, staging, etc., of (a movie, play, etc.). **b** supervise the performance of (an actor, etc.). —**di·rect·ly** *adv.* —**di·rect·ness** *n.*

**di·rect cur·rent** ▶*n.* electric current flowing in one direction only. (Abbr.: **DC, d.c.**)

**di·rec·tion** ▶*n.* **1** directing; supervision. **2** (usu. **directions**) instructions on how to get somewhere or how to do something: *do you have directions to the party?* **3** course or line of movement, sight, etc. **4** tendency or scope of a theme, subject, or inquiry. —**di·rec·tion·al** *adj.* —**di·rec·tion·less** *adj.*

**di·rec·tive** ▶*n.* instruction from an authority.
▶*adj.* serving to direct.

**di·rect ob·ject** ▶*n.* *Gram.* primary object of the action of a transitive verb.

**di·rec·tor** ▶*n.* **1** person who directs or controls something, esp. a member of the board of a corporation. **2** person who directs a movie, play, etc.

**di·rec·to·ry** ▶*n.* (*pl.* **-ries**) alphabetical or thematic listing of a particular group of individuals (e.g., telephone subscribers) or organizations.

**dirge** /dərj/ ▶*n.* lament for the dead.

**dir·i·gi·ble** /dəˈrijəbəl/ ▶*n.* rigid-frame airship.

**dirk** /dərk/ ▶*n.* long dagger.

**dirt** /dərt/ ▶*n.* **1** unclean matter that soils. **2** earth; soil. **3 a** foul or malicious words or talk. **b** scurrilous information; scandal; gossip; the lowdown. **4** person or thing considered worthless.

**dirt·y** ▶*adj.* (**-i·er, -i·est**) **1** soiled; unclean. **2** causing dirtiness: *a dirty job.* **3** sordid; lewd; morally illicit or questionable: *dirty joke.* **4** unpleasant; nasty. **5** dishonest; dishonorable; unfair: *dirty play.* **6** (of weather) rough; stormy. **7** (of a color) not pure nor clear; dingy.
▶*v.* (**-ied**) make or become dirty.
□ **dirty work 1** unpleasant tasks.

**2** dishonorable or illegal activity, esp. done clandestinely.

**dis** /dis/ ▶*v. inf.* act or speak disrespectfully toward.

**dis-** ▶*prefix* forming nouns, adjectives, and verbs indicating: **1** negation: *dishonest.* **2** reversal or absence of an action or state: *disengage* | *disbelieve.* **3** removal of a thing or quality: *dismember* | *disable.* **4** separation: *distinguish* | *dispose.* **5** completeness or intensification: *disembowel* | *disgruntled.* **6** expulsion from: *disbar.*

**dis·a·ble** ▶*v.* render unable to function; deprive of an ability. —**dis·a·bil·i·ty** *n.*

**dis·a·buse** /ˌdisəˈbyo͞oz/ ▶*v.* free from a mistaken idea: *he quickly disabused me of my fanciful notions.*

**dis·ad·van·tage** ▶*n.* unfavorable circumstance or condition.
▶*v.* cause disadvantage to. —**dis·ad·van·ta·geous** *adj.*
□ **at a disadvantage** in an unfavorable position or aspect.

**dis·ad·van·taged** ▶*adj.* placed in unfavorable circumstances (esp. of a person lacking normal opportunities).

**dis·af·fect·ed** ▶*adj.* dissatisfied with those in authority: *a* *military plot by disaffected elements in the army.*

**dis·a·gree** ▶*v.* (**-greed, -gree·ing**) **1** hold a different opinion. **2** quarrel. **3** (of factors or circumstances) not correspond. **4** have an adverse effect upon (a person's health, digestion, etc.).
—**dis·a·gree·ment** *n.*

**dis·a·gree·a·ble** ▶*adj.* **1** unpleasant. **2** rude or bad-tempered.
—**dis·a·gree·a·ble·ness** *n.*
—**dis·a·gree·a·bly** *adv.*

**dis·al·low** ▶*v.* refuse to allow or accept as valid; prohibit.
—**dis·al·low·ance** *n.*

**dis·ap·pear** ▶*v.* **1** cease to be visible. **2** cease to exist or be in circulation or use.
—**dis·ap·pear·ance** *n.*

**dis·ap·point** ▶*v.* **1** fail to fulfill a desire or expectation of. **2** frustrate (hopes, plans, etc.).
—**dis·ap·point·ing** *adj.*
—**dis·ap·point·ingly** *adv.*
—**dis·ap·point·ment** *n.*

□ **be disappointed** fail to have one's expectation, etc., fulfilled: *was disappointed in you | am disappointed to be last.*

**dis·ap·pro·ba·tion** ▶*n.* strong disapproval.

**dis·ap·prove** ▶*v.* **1** have or express an unfavorable opinion. **2** be displeased with.
—**dis·ap·prov·al** *n.*
—**dis·ap·prov·ing** *adj.*
—**dis·ap·prov·ingly** *adv.*

**dis·arm** ▶*v.* **1** take weapons away from (a person, nation, etc.). **2** (of a nation, etc.) disband or reduce its armed forces. **3** remove the fuse from (a bomb, etc.). **4** render harmless. **5** charm; mollify; placate.
—**dis·ar·ma·ment** *n.*
—**dis·arm·ing** *adj.*
—**dis·arm·ing·ly** *adv.*

**dis·ar·range** ▶*v.* bring into disorder. —**dis·ar·range·ment** *n.*

**dis·ar·ray** ▶*n.* disorder; confusion (esp. among people).

**dis·as·so·ci·ate** /ˌdisəˈsōSHēˌāt/ ▶*v.* DISSOCIATE.
—**dis·as·so·ci·a·tion** *n.*

**dis·as·ter** /diˈzastər/ ▶*n.* **1** great or sudden misfortune. **2** complete failure.
—**dis·as·trous** *adj.*

**dis·a·vow** ▶*v.* disclaim knowledge of, responsibility for, or belief in. —**dis·a·vow·al** *n.*

**dis·band** ▶*v.* **1** (of an organized group, etc.) cease to work or act together. **2** cause (such a group) to disband.

**dis·bar** ▸*v.* (-barred, -bar·ring) deprive (an attorney) of the right to practice. —**dis·bar·ment** *n.*

**dis·be·lieve** ▸*v.* be unable or unwilling to believe (a person or statement). —**dis·be·lief** *n.*

**dis·burse** /dis'bərs/ ▸*v.* 1 expend (money). 2 pay money. —**dis·burs·al** *n.* —**dis·burse·ment** *n.*

**disc** /disk/ ▸var. of DISK.

**dis·card** ▸*v.* 1 reject as unwanted. 2 *Cards* remove (a card) from one's hand. ▸*n.* /'dis,kärd/ discarded item, esp. a card in a card game.

**dis·cern** /di'sərn/ ▸*v.* perceive clearly with the mind or the senses. —**dis·cern·i·ble** *adj.* —**dis·cern·i·bly** *adv.* —**dis·cern·ment** *n.*

**dis·cern·ing** /di'sərniNG/ ▸*adj.* having or showing good judgment.

**dis·charge** ▸*v.* /dis'CHärj/ 1 release, esp. from a duty, commitment, or confinement. 2 dismiss from office, employment, etc. 3 (of liquid) flow or allow to flow out. 4 carry out; perform (a duty). 5 relieve oneself of (a financial commitment): *discharged his* debt. 6 *Physics* release an electrical charge from. ▸*n.* /'dis,CHärj/ 1 discharging or being discharged. 2 dismissal, esp. from the armed services. 3 written certificate of release, etc. 4 an act of firing a gun, etc. 5 matter (pus, liquid, etc.) discharged. 6 *Physics* release of an electric charge.

**dis·ci·ple** /di'sīpəl/ ▸*n.* 1 follower of a leader, teacher, philosophy, etc.: *a disciple of Zen Buddhism.* 2 early believer in Christ, esp. one of the twelve Apostles.

**dis·ci·pline** /'disəplin/ ▸*n.* 1 a control or order exercised over people or animals, esp. children, prisoners, military personnel, church members, etc. b rules used to maintain this control. c behavior of groups subjected to such rules: *poor discipline in the ranks.* 2 mental, moral, or physical training. 3 branch of learning. ▸*v.* 1 train in obedience; drill. 2 punish. —**dis·ci·plin·ar·y** *adj.*

**dis·claim** ▸*v.* 1 deny or disown. 2 *Law* renounce legal claim to (property, etc.). —**dis·claim·er** *n.*

**dis·close** /dis'klōz/ ▸*v.* 1 make

known. **2** expose to view.
—**dis·clo·sure** *n.*

**dis·co** /'diskō/ ▶*n.* (*pl.* **-cos**) *inf.*
DISCOTHEQUE.

**dis·color** ▶*v.* spoil or cause to
spoil the color of; stain; tarnish.
—**dis·col·or·a·tion** *n.*

**dis·com·bob·u·late** /ˌdiskəm-
'bäbyəˌlāt/ ▶*v.* disconcert or
confuse (someone).

**dis·com·fit** /dis'kəmfit/ ▶*v.*
disconcert or baffle.
—**dis·com·fi·ture** *n.*

**dis·com·fort** ▶*n.* **1** lack of ease;
slight pain. **2** lack of comfort.

**dis·com·mode** /ˌdiskə'mōd/ ▶*v.*
inconvenience (a person, etc.).
—**dis·com·mo·di·ous** *adj.*

**dis·com·pose** ▶*v.* disturb or
agitate (someone).
—**dis·com·po·sure** *n.*

**dis·con·cert** /ˌdiskən'sərt/ ▶*v.*
disturb the composure of
(someone): *the abrupt change of
subject disconcerted her* [as *adj.*
**disconcerted**] *she was amused to
see a disconcerted expression on his
face.* —**dis·con·cert·ing** *adj.*

**dis·con·nect** ▶*v.* break the
connection or functioning of
(things, ideas, etc.).
—**dis·con·nec·tion** *n.*

**dis·con·so·late** /dis'känsəlit/

▶*adj.* **1** forlorn. **2** unhappy or
disappointed.

**dis·con·tent** /ˌdiskən'tent/ ▶*n.*
lack of contentment;
restlessness, dissatisfaction.

▶*adj.* dissatisfied.
—**dis·con·tent·ment** *n.*

**dis·con·tin·ue** ▶*v.* **1** come or
bring to an end. **2** give up; cease
from. —**dis·con·tin·u·a·tion** *n.*

**dis·cord** /'disˌkôrd/ ▶*n.*
**1** disagreement; strife. **2** harsh
noise. **3** *Mus.* lack of harmony.
—**dis·cord·ance** *n.*
—**dis·cord·ant** *adj.*

**dis·cord·ant** /dis'kôrdnt/ ▶*adj.*
**1** disagreeing or incongruous.
**2** (of sounds) harsh and jarring
because of a lack of harmony.

**dis·co·theque** /'diskəˌtek/ ▶*n.*
club, etc., for dancing to
recorded popular music.

**dis·count** /'disˌkount/ ▶*n.*
amount deducted from a
customary price.

▶*v.* **1** disregard as unreliable or
unimportant: *discounted his story.*
**2** detract from; lessen; deduct
(esp. an amount from a bill, etc.).
—**dis·count·a·ble** *adj.*

**dis·coun·te·nance** ▶*v.*
**1** disconcert: *was discountenanced
by his abruptness.* **2** refuse to

countenance; show disapproval of.

**dis·cour·age** ▶*v.* **1** deprive of courage, confidence, or energy. **2** dissuade: *discouraged her from going.* **3** show disapproval of; oppose: *smoking is discouraged.* —**dis·cour·age·ment** *n.* —**dis·cour·ag·ing·ly** *adv.*

**dis·course** /'dis,kôrs/ ▶*n.* **1** conversation; talk. **2** dissertation or treatise on an academic subject. **3** lecture or sermon.
▶*v.* **1** talk; converse. **2** speak or write learnedly or at length (on a subject).

**dis·cour·te·ous** ▶*adj.* impolite; rude. —**disc·cour·te·sy** *n.*

**dis·cov·er** ▶*v.* **1** find out or become aware of: *discovered a new entrance.* **2** be the first to find or find out: *Fleming discovered penicillin early in the twentieth century.* **3** devise or pioneer: *discover new techniques.*

**dis·cred·it** ▶*n.* **1** harm to reputation. **2** person or thing causing this: *he is a discredit to his family.* **3** doubt; disbelief.
▶*v.* **1** harm the good reputation of. **2** cause to be disbelieved.

**dis·creet** /dis'krēt/ ▶*adj.* (**-er**, **-est**) **1** careful and circumspect

in speech or action. **2** unobtrusive.

**dis·crep·an·cy** /dis'krepənsē/ ▶*n.* (*pl.* **-cies**) difference; failure to correspond; inconsistency.

**dis·crete** /dis'krēt/ ▶*adj.* individually distinct; separate; discontinuous. —**dis·crete·ly** *adv.* —**dis·crete·ness** *n.*

**dis·cre·tion** /dis'kreSHən/ ▶*n.* **1** being discreet. **2** freedom to act and think as one wishes, usu. within legal limits: *it is within his discretion to leave.* —**dis·cre·tion·ary** *adj.*

**dis·crim·i·nate** /dis'krimə,nāt/ ▶*v.* **1** make or see a distinction. **2** treat unfavorably, esp. on the basis of race, color, or sex. **3** [usu. as *adj.* **discriminating**] observe distinction carefully; have good judgment. —**dis·crim·i·na·tion** *n.* —**dis·crim·i·na·to·ry** *adj.*

**dis·crim·i·nat·ing** /dis'krimə-,nātiNG/ ▶*adj.* (of a person) having or showing refined taste or good judgment.

**dis·crim·i·na·tion** /dis,krimə-'nāSHən/ ▶*n.* **1** unjust or prejudicial treatment of different categories of people or things, esp. on the grounds of race, age, or sex. **2** recognition and understanding of the difference between one thing and another. **3** ability to discern what is of high quality; good judgment or taste.

**dis·cur·sive** /dis'kərsiv/ ▶*adj.* rambling or digressive.

**dis·cus** /'diskəs/ ▶*n.* (*pl.* **-cus·es**) heavy disk thrown in competition.

**dis·cuss** /dis'kəs/ ▶*v.* talk or write about; debate. —**dis·cus·sion** *n.*

**dis·dain** /dis'dān/ ▶*n.* scorn; contempt.
▶*v.* **1** regard with disdain. **2** think oneself superior to; reject: *disdained to enter* | *disdained answering.* —**dis·dain·ful** *adj.*

**dis·ease** /di'zēz/ ▶*n.* **1** unhealthy condition of the body or the mind; illness; sickness. **2** corresponding condition of plants. **3** particular kind of illness. —**dis·eased** *adj.*

**dis·em·bark** ▶*v.* put or go ashore or land from a ship or an aircraft. —**dis·em·bar·ka·tion** *n.*

**dis·em·bod·ied** /ˌdisemˌbädēd/ ▶*adj.* **1** separated from the body. **2** (of a sound) lacking any obvious physical source.

**dis·em·bogue** /ˌdisem'bōg/ ▶*v.* (**-bogued, -bogu·ing**) (of a river or stream) emerge or be discharged in quantity; pour out.

**dis·em·bow·el** /ˌdisem'bouəl/ ▶*v.* remove the bowels or entrails of.

**dis·en·chant** ▶*v.* disillusion. —**dis·en·chant·ment** *n.*

**dis·en·gage** ▶*v.* **1 a** detach, free, loosen, or separate (parts, etc.): *disengaged the clutch.* **b** detach oneself; get loose: *disengaged ourselves from their company.* **2** become detached. —**dis·en·gage·ment** *n.*

**dis·en·gaged** ▶*adj.* emotionally detached.

**dis·en·tan·gle** ▶*v.* **1** unravel; untwist. **2** free from complications.

**dis·fa·vor** ▶*n.* **1** disapproval or dislike. **2** being disliked: *fell into disfavor.*

**dis·fig·ure** ▶*v.* spoil the appearance of; deform; deface. —**dis·fig·ure·ment** *n.*

**dis·fran·chise** /dis'franchīz/ (also **dis·en·fran·chise**) ▶*v.* deprive of the right to vote, be represented, etc. —**dis·fran·chise·ment** *n.*

**dis·gorge** /dis'gôrj/ ▶*v.* **1** pour

forth; discharge (contents, ill-gotten gains, etc.). **2** vomit.

**dis·grace** ▸*n.* **1** shame; ignominy. **2** dishonorable, inefficient, or shameful person, thing, state of affairs, etc. ▸*v.* bring shame or discredit on. □ **in disgrace** having lost respect or reputation; out of favor.

**dis·grun·tled** /ˌdisˈgrəntld/ ▸*adj.* discontented; moody; sulky.

**dis·guise** /disˈgīz/ ▸*v.* alter the appearance, sound, smell, etc., of, so as to conceal the identity; make unrecognizable: *disguised herself as a police officer* | *disguised the taste by adding sugar.* ▸*n.* **1** costume, makeup, action, etc., used to conceal or deceive. **2** act or practice of disguising; concealment of reality. □ **in disguise 1** wearing a concealing costume, etc. **2** appearing to be the opposite: *a blessing in disguise.*

**dis·gust** /disˈgəst/ ▸*n.* strong aversion; repugnance. ▸*v.* cause disgust in: *their behavior disgusts me.*

**dish** /disH/ ▸*n.* **1 a** shallow, flat-bottomed container for cooking or serving food. **b** food served in a dish: *all the dishes were delicious.* **2** (**dishes**) plates, cooking pots, etc., used for a meal. **3 a** dish-shaped receptacle, object, or cavity. **b** SATELLITE DISH. ▸*v.* put (food) into a dish for serving.

**dis·ha·bille** /ˌdisəˈbēl/ ▸*n.* state of being only partly or scantily clothed.

**dis·heart·en** /disˈhärtn/ ▸*v.* cause to lose courage or confidence.

**dis·hon·est** ▸*adj.* fraudulent or insincere. **—dis·hon·es·ty** *n.*

**dis·hon·or** ▸*n.* **1** shame or disgrace; discredit. **2** something that causes dishonor: *a dishonor to her profession.* ▸*v.* **1** treat without honor or respect. **2** disgrace. **—dis·hon·or·a·ble** *adj.*

**dish·wash·er** ▸*n.* **1** machine for automatically washing dishes. **2** person employed to wash dishes.

**dis·il·lu·sion** ▸*v.* rid of illusions; disenchant. ▸*n.* freedom from illusions; disenchantment. **—dis·il·lu·sion·ment** *n.*

**dis·in·cline** ▸*v.* **1** make reluctant. **2** [as *adj.* **disinclined**] be unwilling or averse. **—dis·in·cli·na·tion** *n.*

**dis·in·fect** ▸*v.* cleanse (a wound,

a room, clothes, etc.) of infection. **—dis·in·fect·ant** *n. & adj.*

**dis·in·for·ma·tion** ▶*n.* false information, intended to mislead.

**dis·in·gen·u·ous** ▶*adj.* having secret motives; insincere.

**dis·in·her·it** ▶*v.* reject as one's heir; deprive of the right of inheritance. **—dis·in·her·i·tance** *n.*

**dis·in·te·grate** ▶*v.* **1** separate into component parts or fragments. **2** lose or cause to lose cohesion. **—dis·in·te·gra·tion** *n.*

**dis·in·ter** /ˌdisin'tər/ ▶*v.* (-**terred**, -**ter·ring**) remove (esp. a corpse) from the ground; unearth; exhume. **—dis·in·ter·ment** *n.*

**dis·in·ter·est·ed** ▶*adj.* not influenced by one's own advantage; impartial.

**dis·joint·ed** /dis'jointid/ ▶*adj.* lacking a coherent sequence or connection.

**disk** /disk/ (also **disc**) ▶*n.* **1 a** flat thin circular object. **b** round, flat or apparently flat surface: *the sun's disk.* **2** layer of cartilage between vertebrae. **3 a** phonograph record. **b** compact disc. **4 a** (also magnetic disk) round, flat computer storage device. **b** (also optical disk) smooth nonmagnetic disk with large storage capacity for data recorded and read by laser.

□ **disk brake** brake employing the friction of pads against a disk.
□ **disk drive** *Computing* mechanism for reading or writing data from a disk on which it is stored digitally.
□ **disk** (also **disc**) **jockey** presenter of a selection of phonograph records, compact discs, etc., of popular music, esp. in a broadcast.

**disk·ette** /dis'ket/ ▶*n. Computing* FLOPPY DISK.

**dis·like** ▶*v.* have an aversion to; not like.
▶*n.* **1** feeling of repugnance or not liking. **2** object of dislike.

**dis·lo·cate** ▶*v.* **1** disturb the normal connection of (esp. a joint in the body). **2** disrupt; put out of order. **3** displace. **—dis·lo·ca·tion** *n.*

**dis·lodge** ▶*v.* disturb or move.

**dis·loy·al** ▶*adj.* not loyal; unfaithful.

**dis·mal** /'dizməl/ ▶*adj.* **1** gloomy; miserable; dreary. **2** *inf.* feeble or

inept: *a dismal performance.*
**—dis·mal·ly** *adv.*

**dis·man·tle** /dis'mantl/ ▶*v.* take to pieces; pull down.

**dis·may** /dis'mā/ ▶*v.* discourage or depress; reduce to despair.
▶*n.* **1** anxiety. **2** depression or despair.

**dis·mem·ber** ▶*v.* **1** remove the limbs from. **2** partition or divide up. **—dis·mem·ber·ment** *n.*

**dis·miss** ▶*v.* **1** send away; cause to leave one's presence.
**2** discharge from employment, etc., esp. dishonorably. **3** put out of one's thoughts. **4** treat (a subject) summarily: *dismissed his application.* **5** *Law* refuse further hearing to (a case).
**—dis·mis·sal** *n.*

**dis·mount** ▶*v.* **1** alight from a horse, bicycle, etc. **2** cause to fall or alight.
▶*n.* /'dis,mount/ dismounting.

**dis·o·be·di·ent** ▶*adj.* disobeying; rebellious.
**—dis·o·be·di·ence** *n.*

**dis·o·bey** ▶*v.* fail to obey (rules, a person, etc.).

**dis·or·der** ▶*n.* **1** lack of order; confusion. **2** riot; commotion. **3** ailment or disease.

**dis·or·gan·ize** ▶*v.* **1** destroy the system or order of; throw

into confusion. **2** [as *adj.* **disorganized**] lack organization or system.
**—dis·or·gan·i·za·tion** *n.*

**dis·o·ri·ent** ▶*v.* confuse (a person) as to his or her bearings.

**dis·own** ▶*v.* **1** repudiate; disclaim. **2** renounce one's connection with or allegiance to.

**dis·par·age** /dis'parij/ ▶*v.* **1** criticize; belittle. **2** bring discredit on. **—dis·par·age·ment** *n.* **—dis·par·ag·ing·ly** *adv.*

**dis·pa·rate** /'dispərit/ ▶*adj.* essentially different; without comparison or relation.

**dis·par·i·ty** /di'sparitē/ ▶*n.* (*pl.* **-ties**) great difference.

**dis·pas·sion·ate** ▶*adj.* free from passion; calm; impartial.

**dis·patch** /dis'pacH/ ▶*v.* **1** send off to a destination or for a purpose. **2** perform (business, a task, etc.) promptly; finish off.
▶*n.* /'dis,pacH/ **1** sending (a messenger, letter, etc.).
**2 a** official message on state or esp. military affairs. **b** news report. **3** promptness; efficiency: *done with dispatch.*
**—dis·patch·er** *n.*

**dis·pel** /dis'pel/ ▶*v.* (**-pelled, -pel·ling**) dissipate; disperse; scatter.

**dis·pen·sa·ry** /dis'pensərē/ ▶n. (*pl.* **-ries**) place where medicines, etc., are dispensed.

**dis·pen·sa·tion** /ˌdispən-'sāsʜən/ ▶n. **1** exemption from a rule or duty. **2** system of order or organization of a nation, community, etc., at a particular time. **3** dispensing or distributing something.

**dis·pense** /dis'pens/ ▶v. **1** distribute or provide to a number of people. **2** make up and give out (medicine, etc.). **3** (**dispense with**) do without; render needless. **4** give exemption from (a rule).

**dis·perse** /dis'pərs/ ▶v. **1** go, send, drive, or distribute in different directions or widely. **2** (of people at a meeting, etc.) leave and go their various ways. **3** put in circulation; disseminate. —**dis·pers·al** *n.* —**dis·per·sion** *n.*

**dis·place** ▶v. **1** shift from its accustomed place. **2** remove from office. **3** take the place of; oust.

**dis·play** ▶v. **1** expose to view; exhibit; show. **2** show ostentatiously. **3** allow to appear; reveal; betray. ▶n. **1** displaying. **2** exhibition or show. **3** ostentation; flashiness.

**4** mating rituals of some birds, fish, etc. **5** presentation of signals or data on a visual display unit, etc.

**dis·please** ▶v. make indignant or angry; offend; annoy. —**dis·plea·sure** *n.*

**dis·pose** ▶v. **1 a** make willing; incline: *was disposed to release them.* **b** give a tendency to: *the wheel was disposed to buckle.* **2** [as *adj.* **disposed**] have a specified mental inclination: *ill-disposed.* **3** determine the course of events: *man proposes, God disposes.* —**dis·po·sa·ble** *adj.* —**dis·po·sal** *n.*
□ **dispose of 1 a** deal with. **b** get rid of. **c** finish. **d** kill. **e** distribute; dispense; bestow. **2** sell.

**dis·po·si·tion** ▶n. **1 a** natural tendency; inclination. **b** temperament or attitude. **2 a** setting in order. **b** arrangement.

**dis·pos·sess** ▶v. **1** deprive (someone) of something they own: *they were dispossessed of their lands during the revolution.* **2** dislodge; oust (a person): *he dispossessed all of his tenants.* —**dis·pos·ses·sion** *n.*

**dis·pro·por·tion** ▶n. lack of

proportion. —**dis·pro·por·tion·al** *adj.* —**dis·pro·por·tion·ate** *adj.*

**dis·prove** ▶*v.* prove false; refute.

**dis·pu·ta·tious** /ˌdispyŏŏ-'tāsHəs/ ▶*adj.* **1** (of a person) fond of having heated arguments. **2** (of an argument or situation) motivated by or causing strong opinions.

**dis·pute** /dis'pyŏŏt/ ▶*v.* **1** debate; argue. **2** discuss, esp. heatedly. **3** question the truth or correctness or validity of (a statement, alleged fact, etc.). **4** contend for; strive to win: *disputed the crown.* ▶*n.* **1** controversy; debate. **2** quarrel. —**dis·put·a·ble** *adj.* —**dis·pu·tant** *n.* —**dis·put·ta·tion** *n.* —**dis·pu·ta·tious** *adj.* □ **beyond dispute** certain or certainly; without a doubt. □ **open to dispute** not definitely decided.

**dis·qual·i·fy** ▶*v.* (-fied) pronounce ineligible, unsuitable, or unqualified. —**dis·qual·i·fi·ca·tion** *n.*

**dis·qui·et** ▶*v.* deprive of peace; worry. ▶*n.* anxiety; unrest.

**dis·qui·si·tion** /ˌdiskwə'zisHən/ ▶*n.* long or elaborate essay or discussion on a particular subject.

**dis·re·gard** ▶*v.* pay no attention to; ignore. ▶*n.* indifference; neglect.

**dis·re·pair** ▶*n.* poor condition due to neglect.

**dis·re·pute** /ˌdisrə'pyŏŏt/ ▶*n.* lack of good reputation or respectability; discredit, esp. as: *fall into disrepute.* —**dis·rep·u·ta·ble** *adj.*

**dis·re·spect** ▶*n.* lack of respect; discourtesy.

**dis·robe** ▶*v.* undress.

**dis·rupt** /dis'rəpt/ ▶*v.* interrupt (an event, activity, or process): *the rail strike disrupted both freight and passenger service* | *protesters disrupted the meeting.* —**dis·rup·tion** *n.* —**dis·rup·tive** *adj.*

**dis·sat·is·fy** ▶*v.* (-fied) [often as *adj.* **dissatisfied**] make discontented; fail to satisfy. —**dis·sat·is·fac·tion** *n.*

**dis·sect** /di'sekt/ ▶*v.* **1** cut up, esp. a plant or animal, to examine its parts, structure, etc., or a corpse for a post mortem. **2** analyze; criticize in detail. —**dis·sec·tion** *n.*

**dis·sem·ble** /di'sembəl/ ▶v. conceal one's true motives, feelings, and beliefs.

**dis·sem·i·nate** /di'semə,nāt/ ▶v. scatter about; spread (esp. ideas) widely.
—**dis·sem·i·na·tion** n.

**dis·sen·sion** /di'sensHən/ ▶n. disagreement.

**dis·sent** /di'sent/ ▶v. **1** disagree. **2** differ, esp. from established or official opinion.
▶n. **1** difference of opinion. **2** refusal to accept established opinion; nonconformity.
—**dis·sent·er** n.

**dis·ser·ta·tion** /ˌdisər'tāsHən/ ▶n. long essay on a particular subject, esp. one written as a requirement for the degree of Doctor of Philosophy.

**dis·serv·ice** ▶n. harmful action.

**dis·si·dent** /'disidənt/ ▶n. person who opposes official policy.
▶adj. in opposition to official policy. —**dis·si·dence** n.

**dis·sim·i·lar** ▶adj. unlike; not similar. —**dis·sim·i·lar·i·ty** n.

**dis·si·pate** /'disə,pāt/ ▶v. **1** disperse; scatter; disappear. **2** squander (money, energy, etc.).
—**dis·si·pa·tion** n.

**dis·so·ci·ate** /di'sōsHē,āt/ ▶v. disconnect or become disconnected; separate: *dissociated her from their guilt.*
□ **dissociate oneself from 1** declare that one is not connected with. **2** decline to support or agree with (a proposal, etc.).

**dis·so·lute** /'disə,lo͞ot/ ▶adj. lax in morals; licentious.

**dis·solve** /di'zälv/ ▶v. **1** make or become liquid, esp. by dispersion in a liquid. **2** disappear or cause to disappear gradually. **3** dismiss (an assembly, esp. parliament). **4** annul or put an end to (a partnership, marriage, etc.).

**dis·so·nant** /'disənənt/ ▶adj. **1** *Mus.* lacking harmony. **2** incongruous; clashing.
—**dis·so·nance** n.

**dis·suade** /di'swād/ ▶v. discourage (a person); persuade against: *was dissuaded from his belief.* —**dis·sua·sion** n.

**dis·taff** /'distaf/ ▶n. stick onto which wool or flax is wound for spinning.
□ **distaff side** female side of the family.

**dis·tance** /'distəns/ ▶n. **1** space or interval between two things

or people. **2** being far off; remoteness. **3** distant point or place: *came from a distance.* **4** avoidance of familiarity; aloofness; reserve: *there was a certain distance between them.*
▶*v.* place far off.
□ **go the distance** complete, esp. a hard task; endure an ordeal.
□ **keep one's distance** maintain one's reserve.

**dis·tant** ▶*adj.* **1** far away; remote. **2** at a specified distance: **3** reserved; cool: *a distant nod.*

**dis·taste** ▶*n.* dislike; repugnance; aversion, esp. slight. —**dis·taste·ful** *adj.*

**dis·tem·per** ▶*n.* disease of some animals, esp. dogs, causing fever, coughing, and catarrh.

**dis·tend** /dis'tend/ ▶*v.* swell out by pressure from within: *distended stomach.*

**dis·till** /dis'til/ ▶*v.* **1** purify (a liquid) by vaporizing it and condensing it. **2** come as or give forth in drops; exude. **3** extract the essential meaning or implications of (an idea, etc.). **4** make (whiskey, essence, etc.) by distilling raw materials. —**dis·til·late** *n.* —**dis·til·la·tion** *n.* —**dis·till·er** *n.*

**dis·tinct** /dis'tiNGkt/ ▶*adj.* **1** not identical; separate; different. **2** clearly perceptible; definite. **3** unmistakable, decided: *had a distinct impression of being watched.* —**dis·tinc·tive** —**dis·tinct·ly** *adv.*

**dis·tinc·tion** ▶*n.* **1 a** discriminating or distinguishing. **b** difference made by distinguishing. **2** thing that differentiates. **3** honor, award, title, etc. **4** distinguished character; excellence; eminence: *a film of distinction.*

**dis·tin·gué** /ˌdistaNG'gā/ ▶*adj.* (*fem.* **dis·tin·guée** *pronunc.* same) having a distinguished manner or appearance.

**dis·tin·guish** /dis'tiNGgwiSH/ ▶*v.* **1** see or draw distinctions between; differentiate. **2** be a mark or property of; characterize: *distinguished by her greed.* **3** discern: *could distinguish two voices.* **4** make prominent or noteworthy: *distinguished himself by winning.* —**dis·tin·guish·a·ble** *adj.*

**dis·tin·guished** ▶*adj.* **1** eminent; famous. **2** dignified, elegant.

**dis·tort** /dis'tôrt/ ▶*v.* **1** put out of shape. **2** misrepresent (motives,

facts, statements, etc.).
**—dis·tor·tion** n.

**dis·tract** /dis'trakt/ ▶v. **1** draw away the attention of (a person, the mind, etc.). **2** bewilder; perplex. **3** amuse, esp. to take attention from pain or worry.

**dis·traught** /dis'trôt/ ▶adj. extremely agitated.

**dis·tress** /dis'tres/ ▶n. **1** severe pain, sorrow, anguish, etc. **2** poverty.
▶v. **1** subject to distress; exhaust; afflict. **2** cause anxiety to; make unhappy; vex.
□ **in distress 1** suffering or in danger. **2** (of a ship, aircraft, etc.) in danger or damaged.

**dis·trib·u·tar·y** /dis'tribyoͦo,terē/ ▶n. (pl. **-tar·ies**) branch of a river that does not return to the main stream after leaving it (as in a delta).

**dis·tri·bu·te** /dis'tribyoͦot/ ▶v. **1** give shares of; deal out. **2** spread about; scatter: *distributed the seeds evenly over the garden.* **—dis·tri·bu·tion** n. **—dis·trib·u·tor** n.

**dis·trict** /'distrikt/ ▶n. **1** territory marked off for special administrative purposes. **2** area that has common characteristics; region.

▶v. divide into districts.
□ **district attorney** prosecuting officer of a district.

**dis·trust** ▶n. lack of trust; doubt; suspicion.
▶v. have no trust in.

**dis·turb** /dis'tərb/ ▶v. **1** break the rest, calm, or quiet of. **2** agitate; worry. **3** move from a settled position.
**—dis·turb·ance** n.

**dis·use** /dis'yoͦos/ ▶n. **1** lack of use or practice; discontinuance. **2** disused state.
□ **fall into disuse** cease to be used.

**ditch** /dicH/ ▶n. **1** long, narrow excavated channel, esp. for drainage. **2** watercourse, stream, etc.
▶v. **1** make or repair ditches. **2** *inf.* get rid of.

**dith·er** /'diTHər/ ▶v. be indecisive.
▶n. **1** indecisive behavior. **2** state of agitation or apprehension.

**dit·to** /'ditō/ ▶n. (pl. **-tos**) **1** (in accounts, inventories, lists, etc.) aforesaid; same. **2** *inf.* (replacing a word or phrase to avoid repetition) the same: *came in late last night and ditto the night before.*
▶v. (**-toed**) repeat (another's action or words).

▫ **ditto marks** quotation marks representing 'ditto'.

**dit·ty** /ˈditē/ ▸*n.* (*pl.* **-ties**) short simple song.

**di·u·ret·ic** /ˌdīəˈretik/ ▸*adj.* causing increased output of urine.

▸*n.* diuretic drug.

**di·ur·nal** /dīˈərnl/ ▸*adj.* of or during the day; not nocturnal.

**div.** ▸*abbr.* division.

**di·va** /ˈdēvə/ ▸*n.* (*pl.* **-vas** or **-ve**) woman opera singer; prima donna.

**di·van** /ˌdəˈvan/ ▸*n.* long, low, backless sofa, often used as a bed.

**di·var·i·cate** ▸*v.* /dīˈvariˌkāt; di-/ stretch or spread apart; diverge widely.

▸*adj.* /-kit; -ˌkāt/ (of a branch) coming off the stem almost at a right angle.

**dive** /dīv/ ▸*v.* (**dived** or **dove**) **1** plunge head first into water. **2** plunge steeply downward.

▸*n.* **1** diving; plunge. **2** steep descent. **3** sudden darting movement. **4** *inf.* disreputable nightclub, bar, etc. —**div·er** *n.*

▫ **diving board** elevated board used for diving from.

**di·verge** /diˈvərj/ ▸*v.* **1 a** spread out from a point: *diverging rays.*

**b** take a different course. **2** depart from a set course. **3** cause to diverge; deflect. —**di·ver·gence** *n.* —**di·ver·gent** *adj.*

**di·vers** /ˈdīvərz/ ▸*adj.* more than one; sundry; several.

**di·verse** /diˈvərs/ ▸*adj.* unlike; varied. —**di·ver·si·fy** *v.* —**di·ver·si·ty** *n.*

**di·vert** /diˈvərt/ ▸*v.* **1** turn aside; deflect. **2** distract (attention). **3** entertain; amuse.

**di·ver·tisse·ment** /diˈvərtismənt/ ▸*n.* minor entertainment or diversion.

**di·vest** /diˈvest/ ▸*v.* **1** unclothe; strip: *divested himself of his jacket.* **2** free; rid: *cannot divest herself of the idea.* —**di·vest·i·ture** *n.* —**di·vest·ment** *n.*

**di·vide** /diˈvīd/ ▸*v.* **1** separate or be separated into parts; break up; split. **2** distribute; deal; share. **3 a** mark into parts: *ruler divided into inches.* **b** specify different kinds of; classify: *people can be divided into two types.* **4** cause to disagree. **5 a** find how many times (a number) contains another: *divide 20 by 4.* **b** (of a number) be contained in (a number) without a remainder: *4 divides into 20.*

▸*n.* **1** dividing or boundary line. **2** watershed.

**div·i·dend** /ˈdiviˌdend/ ▸*n.* **1** money to be divided among a number of persons, esp. that paid by a company to shareholders. **2** number to be divided. **3** benefit: *their long training paid dividends.*

**div·i·na·tion** /ˌdivəˈnāsHən/ ▸*n.* practice of seeking knowledge of the future or the unknown by supernatural means.

**di·vine** /diˈvīn/ ▸*adj.* (**-vin·er, -vin·est**) **1 a** of, from, or like God or a god. **b** sacred. **2** more than humanly excellent.
▸*v.* discover by intuition or magic.
▸*n.* **1** theologian or clergyman. **2** (**the Divine**) God.
—**div·i·na·tion** *n.* —**di·vine·ly** *adv.*

**di·vin·ing rod** ▸*n.* stick used for dowsing.

**di·vin·i·ty** /diˈvinitē/ ▸*n.* (*pl.* **-ties**) **1** being divine. **2 a** god; divine being. **b** (as **the Divinity**) God. **3** theology.

**di·vis·i·ble** /ˌdiˈvizəbəl/ ▸*adj.* capable of being divided.

**di·vi·sion** /diˈvizHən/ ▸*n.* **1** dividing; being divided. **2** dividing one number by another. **3** disagreement or discord: *division of opinion.*
**4 a** one of two or more parts into which a thing is divided. **b** point at which a thing is divided. **5** unit of administration or organization.
☐ **division sign** sign (÷) indicating that one quantity is to be divided by another.

**di·vi·sor** /diˈvīzər/ ▸*n.* number by which another is divided.

**di·vorce** /diˈvôrs/ ▸*n.* **1** legal dissolution of a marriage. **2** severance or separation: *divorce between thought and feeling.*
▸*v.* **1 a** legally dissolve the marriage of (a person) by divorce. **2** separate: *divorced from reality.*

**di·vor·cé** /diˌvôrˈsā/ ▸*n.* divorced man.

**di·vor·cée** /diˌvôrˈsā/ ▸*n.* divorced woman.

**div·ot** /ˈdivət/ ▸*n.* piece of turf cut out by a golf stroke.

**di·vulge** /diˈvəlj/ ▸*v.* disclose; reveal (a secret, etc.).
—**di·vul·gence** *n.*

**Dix·ie** /ˈdiksē/ ▸*n.* southern states of the U.S.

**Dix·ie·land** ▸*n.* jazz with a strong, two-beat rhythm and collective improvisation.

**diz·zy** /'dizē/ ▸*adj.* (**-zi·er**, **-zi·est**)
**1** giddy. **2** causing giddiness.
▸*v.* **1** make dizzy. **2** bewilder.
—**diz·zi·ness** *n.*

**DJ** ▸*abbr.* **1** disk jockey.
**2** district judge.

**djinn** /jin/ ▸*n.* variant spelling of
JINN.

**DNA** ▸*abbr.* deoxyribonucleic
acid, the material that carries
genetic information in
chromosomes.
☐ **DNA fingerprinting**
identification, esp. in a legal
case, by analysis of DNA from
body tissue, hair, blood, etc.

**do**¹ /doo/ ▸*v.* (*past* **did**; *past part.*
**done**) **1** perform; carry out;
complete (work, etc.): *did his
homework | there's a lot to do.*
**2** produce; make: *I did a
translation.* **3** bestow; grant: *do
me a favor.* **4** act; behave;
proceed: *do as I do.* **5** work at;
study: *what does your father do?*
**6** be suitable or acceptable (for);
suffice. **7** deal with; put in
order. **8** fare; perform.
**9 a** solve; work out: *we did the
puzzle.* **b** be competent at: *can
you do cartwheels?* **10 a** traverse
(a certain distance): *we did fifty
miles today.* **b** travel at a specified
speed: *he overtook us doing about*
eighty. **11 a** *inf.* finish: *I'm done in
the bathroom.* **b** be over: *the day is
done.* **12** *inf.* take (a drug): *do
cocaine.* **13** in questions and
negative statements or
commands: *do you understand? | I
don't smoke | don't be silly.*
**14** forming emphasis: *I do want
to | they did go.*
▸*n.* (*pl.* **dos** or **do's**) *inf.* elaborate
event, party, or operation.
—**do·a·ble** *adj.*
☐ **do away with** *inf.* **1** abolish.
**2** kill. ☐ **do in** *inf.* **1** kill.
**2** exhaust; tire out. ☐ **dos and
don'ts** rules of behavior. ☐ **do
with** would be glad to have;
would profit by: *I could do with a
rest.*

**do**² /dō/ (also **doh**) ▸*n. Mus.* (in
tonic sol-fa) the first and eighth
notes of a major scale.

**DOA** ▸*abbr.* dead on arrival (at a
hospital, etc.).

**do·cent** /'dōsənt/ ▸*n.* person
who acts as a guide, typically on
a voluntary basis, in a museum,
art gallery, or zoo.

**doc·ile** /'däsəl/ ▸*adj.* submissive;
easily managed. —**do·cil·i·ty** *n.*

**dock** /däk/ ▸*n.* **1** structure
extending alongshore or out
from shore to which boats may
be moored. **2** enclosed area of

water for loading, unloading, and repairing ships. **3** (**docks**) group of such areas with wharves and offices. **4** enclosure in a criminal court for the accused.

▶*v.* **1** bring or come into a dock. **2** (of spacecraft) join or be joined in space. **3** cut short (an animal's tail). **4** deduct (a part) from wages, supplies, etc.

**dock·et** ▶*n.* **1** schedule of cases in a court of law. **2** list of things to be done.

**doc·tor** /'däktər/ ▶*n.* **1** qualified practitioner of medicine; physician. **2** qualified dentist or veterinarian. **3** person who holds a doctorate.

▶*v.* tamper with; falsify.

**doc·tor·ate** /'däktərit/ ▶*n.* highest university degree. —**doc·tor·al** *adj.*

**Doc·tor of Phi·los·o·phy** ▶*n.* doctorate in a discipline other than law, medicine, or sometimes theology. (Abbr.: **Ph.D.**)

**doc·tri·naire** /ˌdäktrə'ner/ ▶*adj.* seeking to impose a doctrine in all circumstances without regard to practical considerations.

▶*n.* person who seeks to impose a theory in such a way.

**doc·trine** /'däktrin/ ▶*n.* **1** what is taught; body of instruction. **2** religious, political, etc., belief. —**doc·tri·nal** *adj.*

**doc·u·ment** /'däkyəmənt/ ▶*n.* written evidence of events, agreement, ownership, etc.

▶*v.* **1** prove by or support with documents. **2** record in a document. —**doc·u·men·ta·tion** *n.*

**doc·u·men·ta·ry** /ˌdäkyə-'ment(ə)rē/ ▶*adj.* **1** consisting of documents: *documentary evidence.* **2** providing a factual record or report.

▶*n.* (*pl.* -**ries**) documentary film, etc.

**dod·der** /'dädər/ ▶*v.* tremble or totter, esp. from age.

**dodge** /däj/ ▶*v.* **1** move quickly to elude a pursuer, blow, etc.: *dodged behind the chair.* **2** evade by cunning or trickery.

▶*n.* **1** quick movement to avoid something. **2** clever trick or expedient. —**dodg·er** *n.*

**do·do** /'dōdō/ ▶*n.* (*pl.* -**does** or -**dos**) **1** extinct flightless bird. **2** old-fashioned, stupid, or inactive person.

**DOE** ▶*abbr.* Department of Energy.

**doe** /dō/ ▶*n.* female deer, reindeer, hare, or rabbit.

**does** /dəz/ ▶3rd sing. present of DO.

**does·n't** /'dəzənt/ ▶*contr.* does not.

**doff** /däf/ ▶*v. dated* take off (one's hat).

**dog** /dôg/ ▶*n.* **1** four-legged, flesh-eating animal of many breeds domesticated and wild, kept as pets or for work or sport. **2** *inf.* unpleasant or despicable person. **3** mechanical device for gripping.
▶*v.* (**dogged**, **dog·ging**) follow closely and persistently; pursue; track.
□ **dog-eared** (of a book, etc.) with the corners worn or battered with use. □ **dog paddle** elementary swimming stroke like that of a dog. □ **dog tag** **1** usu. metal plate attached to a dog's collar, giving owner's address, etc. **2** identification tag, esp. as worn by a member of the military.

**doge** /dōj/ ▶*n.* chief magistrate of Venice or Genoa.

**dog·ged** /'dôgid/ ▶*adj.* tenacious; grimly persistent. —**dog·ged·ly** *adv.*

**dog·ger·el** /'dôgərəl; 'däg-/ ▶*n.* **1** comic verse composed in irregular rhythm. **2** verse or words that are badly written or expressed.

**dog·house** ▶*n.* dog's shelter.
□ **in the doghouse** *inf.* in disgrace or disfavor.

**dog·ma** /'dôgmə/ ▶*n.* **1** principle, tenet, or creed, esp. of a church or political party. **2** arrogant declaration of opinion.

**dog·mat·ic** /dôg'matik/ ▶*adj.* **1** (of a person) asserting or imposing opinions; arrogant. **2** of or in the nature of dogma; doctrinal. —**dog·mat·i·cal·ly** *adv.*

**dog·ma·tism** /'dôgmə,tizəm/ ▶*n.* tendency to be dogmatic. —**dog·ma·tist** *n.*

**dogs·bod·y** /'dôgz,bädē/ ▶*n.* (*pl.* -**bod·ies**) person who is given boring, menial tasks to do.

**dog·wood** ▶*n.* type of flowering tree or shrub.

**doi·ly** /'doilē/ ▶*n.* (*pl.* -**lies** or -**leys**) small ornamental mat of paper, lace, etc., on a plate for cakes, etc.

**dol·ce far nien·te** /'dōlchā fär nē'entä/ ▶*n.* pleasant idleness.

**dol·ce vi·ta** /ˌdōlCHā ˈvētə/ ▸*n.* (usu. **la dolce vita**) life of heedless pleasure and luxury.

**dol·drums** /ˈdōldrəmz/ ▸*pl. n.* **1** low spirits. **2** period of inactivity. **3** equatorial ocean region of calms, sudden storms, and light winds.

**dole** /dōl/ ▸*v.* (**dole out**) deal out sparingly.
▸*n. Brit.* unemployment benefits.

**dole·ful** ▸*adj.* **1** mournful; sad. **2** dreary; dismal.

**doll** /däl/ ▸*n.* **1** small model of a human figure, as a child's toy. **2** *inf.* young woman, esp. an attractive one.
▸*v.* dress up smartly: *she got all dolled up for the party.*

**dol·lar** /ˈdälər/ ▸*n.* chief monetary unit in the U.S., Canada, Australia, etc.
□ **dollar sign** sign ($) used to indicate currency in dollars.

**dol·lop** /ˈdäləp/ ▸*n.* shapeless lump of food, etc.

**dol·ly** /ˈdälē/ ▸*n.* (*pl.* **-lies**) **1** small cart for freight. **2** movable platform for a movie camera.

**dol·men** /ˈdōlmən; ˈdäl-/ ▸*n.* megalithic tomb with a large flat stone laid on upright ones, found chiefly in Britain and France.

**dol·or·ous** /ˈdōlərəs/ ▸*adj.* *poet./lit.* feeling or showing great sorrow.

**dol·phin** /ˈdälfin/ ▸*n.* small, gregarious sea mammal having a slender, beaklike snout and curved fin on the back.

**dolt** /dōlt/ ▸*n.* stupid person.
—**dolt·ish** *adj.*

**-dom** ▸*suffix* forming nouns denoting: **1** state or condition: *freedom.* **2** rank or status: *earldom.* **3** domain: *kingdom.* **4** class of people (or their attitudes, etc.): *officialdom.*

**do·main** /dōˈmān/ ▸*n.* **1** area under one rule; realm. **2** sphere of control or influence. **3** *Computing* subset of the Internet with addresses sharing a common suffix.

**dome** /dōm/ ▸*n.* **1** rounded vault as a roof; large cupola. **2** natural vault or canopy (of the sky, trees, etc.). **3** *Geol.* dome-shaped structure.
▸*v.* [usu. as *adj.* **domed**] cover with or shape as a dome.

**do·mes·tic** /dəˈmestik/ ▸*adj.* **1** of the home, household, or family affairs. **2 a** of one's own country. **b** homegrown or homemade. **3** (of an animal) tamed.

▸*n.* household servant.

**do·mes·ti·cate** ▸*v.* **1** tame (an animal) to live with humans. **2** accustom to home life and management. —**do·mes·ti·ca·tion** *n.*

**do·mes·ti·ci·ty** /ˌdōmeˈstisitē/ ▸*n.* **1** being domestic. **2** home or family life.

**dom·i·cile** /ˈdäməˌsīl/ (also **dom·i·cil**) ▸*n.* dwelling place; one's home; residence.

**dom·i·nate** /ˈdäməˌnāt/ ▸*v.* **1** command; control. *dominates over his friends.* **2** be the most influential or conspicuous. —**dom·i·nance** *n.* —**dom·i·nant·** *adj.* —**dom·i·na·tion** *n.*

**dom·i·na·trix** /ˌdäməˈnātriks/ ▸*n.* (*pl.* **-tri·ces** /-trəˌsēz/ or **-trix·es**) dominating woman, esp. one who takes the sadistic role in sadomasochistic sexual activities.

**dom·i·neer** /ˌdäməˈni(ə)r/ ▸*v.* behave in an arrogant and overbearing way: *his domineering manner caused great resentment.*

**do·min·ion** /dəˈminyən/ ▸*n.* **1** sovereignty; control. **2** territory of a sovereign or government; domain.

**dom·i·no** /ˈdäməˌnō/ ▸*n.* (*pl.* **-noes** or **-nos**) **1 a** small oblong piece marked with 0–6 dots in each half. **b** (**dominoes**) game played with these. **2** mask for the eyes.

□ **domino theory** theory that one event will cause similar events, like a row of falling dominoes.

**don** /dän/ ▸*v.* (**donned, don·ning**) put on (clothing).

▸*n.* **1** university teacher, esp. a senior member of a college at Oxford or Cambridge. **2** (**Don**) Spanish title of respect.

**do·nate** /ˈdōnāt/ ▸*v.* give (money, etc.), esp. voluntarily to charity. —**do·na·tion** *n.*

**don·jon** /ˈdänjən; ˈdən-/ ▸*n.* great tower or innermost keep of a castle.

**don·key** /ˈdôNGkē/ ▸*n.* (*pl.* **-keys**) **1** domesticated mammal of the horse family with long ears and a braying call. **2** *inf.* stupid or foolish person.

**don·née** /däˈnā/ (also **don·né**) ▸*n.* **1** subject or theme of a narrative. **2** basic fact or assumption.

**don·ny·brook** /ˈdänēˌbrŏŏk/ ▸*n.* scene of uproar and disorder; a heated argument.

**do·nor** /ˈdōnər/ ▸*n.* **1** person who

gives or donates something (e.g., to a charity). **2** one who provides blood for a transfusion, semen for insemination, or an organ or tissue for transplantation.

**doo·dle** /ˈdo͞odl/ ▶v. scribble or draw, esp. absentmindedly.
▶n. scrawl or drawing made.

**doom** /do͞om/ ▶n. **1 a** grim fate or destiny. **b** death or ruin. **2** condemnation; judgment or sentence.
▶v. **1** condemn or destine: *city doomed to destruction.* **2** [usu. as *adj.* **doomed**] consign to misfortune or destruction.

**dooms·day** /ˈdo͞omzˌdā/ ▶n. day of the Last Judgment.

**door** /dôr/ ▶n. **1** movable barrier for closing and opening an entrance to a building, room, cupboard, etc. **2** this as representing a house, etc.: *lives two doors away.* **3** entrance or exit; means of access.
□ **door prize** prize awarded usu. by lottery at a dance, charity event, etc. □ **door-to-door** (of selling, etc.) done at each house in turn.

**door·way** ▶n. opening filled by a door.

**dope** /dōp/ *inf.* ▶n. **1** narcotic; stupefying drug. **2** stupid person. **3** information.
▶v. take or administer addictive drugs to.

**dope·y** (also **dop·y**) ▶adj. (**-i·er**, **-i·est**) *inf.* **1** stupefied by sleep or a drug: *she was still dopey from the anesthesia.* **2** stupid; silly.

**dop·pel·gäng·er** /ˈdäpəlˌɡaNGər/ ▶n. apparition or double of a living person.

**dor·mant** /ˈdôrmənt/ ▶adj. **1** inactive; sleeping. **2 a** (of a volcano, etc.) temporarily inactive. **b** (of faculties, etc.) in abeyance. **3** (of plants) alive but not growing. —**dor·man·cy** n.

**dor·mer** /ˈdôrmər/ (in full **dor·mer win·dow**) ▶n. projecting upright window in a sloping roof.

**dor·mi·to·ry** /ˈdôrmiˌtôrē/ ▶n. (pl. **-ries**) group sleeping area or building, esp. in a school or institution.

**dor·mouse** /ˈdôrˌmous/ ▶n. (pl. **-mice**) small, mouselike hibernating rodent having a long, bushy tail.

**dor·sal** /ˈdôrsəl/ ▶adj. of, on, or near the back of an animal, plant, or organ.

**do·ry** /ˈdôrē/ ▶n. (pl. **-ries**) flat-bottomed fishing boat with high bow and flaring sides.

**DOS** /dôs/ ▶*abbr.* disk operating system: software operating system for personal computers.

**dose** /dōs/ ▶*n.* **1** single portion of medicine. **2** quantity of something experienced (e.g., work, praise, punishment, etc.). **3** amount of radiation received.
▶*v.* **1** administer a dose to. **2** blend (a substance) with another substance.

**dos·si·er** /'dôsē,ā/ ▶*n.* file of specific information about a person, event, or subject.

**DOT** ▶*abbr.* Department of Transportation.

**dot** /dät/ ▶*n.* **1 a** small spot, speck, or mark. **b** such a mark as part of an *i* or *j*, as a diacritical mark, as one of a series of marks to signify omission, or as a period. **c** decimal point. **2** shorter signal of the two in Morse code. **3** tiny or apparently tiny object: *a dot on the horizon.*
▶*v.* (**dot·ted, dot·ting**) **1** mark with a dot or dots. **2** partly cover as with dots: *an ocean dotted with ships.*
□ **dotted line** line of dots on a document, esp. to show a place

for a signature. □ **on the dot** exactly on time.

**dot·age** /'dōtij/ ▶*n.* senility.

**dote** /dōt/ ▶*v.* (**dote on/upon**) be excessively and uncritically fond of. —**dot·ing·ly** *adv.*

**dou·ble** /'dəbəl/ ▶*adj.* **1** consisting of two parts, things, levels, etc. **2** twice as much or many. **3** twice the usual size, quantity, strength, etc. **4** designed for two people: *double bed.*
▶*adv.* **1** at or to twice the amount, etc. **2** two together.
▶*n.* **1** double quantity. **2** counterpart; person who looks exactly like another. **3** (**doubles**) game between two pairs of players.
▶*v.* **1** make or become double; multiply by two. **2 a** fold or bend (paper, cloth, etc.) over on itself. **b** become folded. **3** play a twofold role. —**dou·bly** *adv.*
□ **double agent** one who spies simultaneously for two rival countries, etc. □ **double-cross** deceive or betray (a person one is supposedly helping).
□ **double-dealing** deceit, esp. in business. □ deceitful; practicing deceit. □ **double-decker** *inf.* anything consisting of two

layers. □ **double play** *Baseball* putting out two runners. □ **double standard** rule or principle applied more strictly to some people than to others (or to oneself). □ **double take** delayed reaction to a situation, etc., immediately after one's first reaction. □ **double-talk** verbal expression that is (usu. deliberately) ambiguous or misleading. □ **on the double** running; hurrying.

**dou·ble-breast·ed** ▸*adj.* (of a coat or jacket) overlapping in front and showing two rows of buttons.

**dou·ble en·ten·dre** /än'tändrə/ ▸*n.* word or phrase open to two interpretations, one usu. risqué or indecent.

**dou·ble jeop·ard·y** ▸*n.* prosecution of a person twice for the same offense.

**dou·ble·think** /'dəbəl,THiNGk/ ▸*n.* acceptance of or mental capacity to accept contrary opinions or beliefs at the same time, esp. as a result of political indoctrination.

**doubt** /dout/ ▸*n.* **1** uncertainty; undecided state of mind. **2** inclination to disbelieve.

**3** uncertain state of things. **4** lack of full proof.

▸*v.* **1** feel uncertain or undecided (about). **2** hesitate to believe or trust.

□ **doubting Thomas** skeptical person (after John 20:24–29). □ **no doubt** certainly; probably. □ **without a doubt** certainly.

**doubt·ful** ▸*adj.* feeling or causing doubt.

**douche** /do͞oSH/ ▸*n.* **1** jet of liquid applied to a body part for cleansing or medicinal purposes. **2** device for producing this.

▸*v.* treat with or use a douche.

**dough** /dō/ ▸*n.* **1** thick mixture of flour, etc., and liquid for baking **2** *inf.* money. —**dough·y** *adj.*

**dough·nut** (also **do·nut**) ▸*n.* small fried cake of sweetened dough, usu. ring-shaped.

**dour** /do͞or/ ▸*adj.* severe, stern, or sullenly obstinate in manner or appearance.

**douse** /dous/ ▸*v.* **1** pour water over; drench. **2** extinguish (a light).

**dove**[1] /dəv/ ▸*n.* **1** bird with short legs, a small head, and a cooing voice. **2** advocate of peace.

**dove**[2] /dōv/ ▸past and past part. of **DIVE**.

**dove·tail** /ˈdəvˌtāl/ ▸n. mortise and tenon joint shaped like a dove's spread tail.
▸v. **1** join by means of a dovetail. **2** fit readily together; combine neatly.

**dow·a·ger** /ˈdouəjər/ ▸n. **1** widow with a title or property from her late husband. **2** dignified elderly woman.

**dow·dy** /ˈdoudē/ ▸adj. (**-di·er**, **-di·est**) **1** (of clothes) unattractively dull. **2** dressed in such clothes. —**dow·di·ness** n.

**dow·el** /ˈdouəl/ ▸n. headless peg of wood, metal, or plastic for holding together components.

**dow·er** /ˈdou(ə)r/ ▸n. widow's share for life of her husband's estate.

**down**[1] /doun/ ▸adv. (superl. **down·most**) **1** into or toward a lower place, esp. to the ground. **2** in a lower place or position: *blinds were down.* **3** to or in a place regarded as lower, esp. southward. **4** in or into a low or weaker position, mood, or condition: *many down with colds.* **5** (of a computer system) not operating. **6** from an earlier to a later time: *customs handed down.* **7** to a finer or thinner consistency or a smaller amount or size. **8** lower in price or value. **9** into a more settled state: *calm down.* **10** in or into recorded or listed form: *copy it down.* **11** (of part of a larger whole) paid.

▸prep. **1** downward along, through, or into. **2** from top to bottom of. **3** along: *cut down the middle.*

▸adj. (superl. **down·most**) **1** directed downward. **2** inf. unhappy; depressed.

▸v. **1** knock or bring down. **2** swallow.

▸n. **1** act of putting down. **2** reverse of fortune. **3** Football one of a series of plays.

□ **be down on** inf. disapprove.
□ **down-and-out** destitute.
□ **down-at-the-heels** shabby; slovenly. □ **down on one's luck** inf. dispirited by misfortune.
□ **down payment** partial payment at time of purchase.
□ **down-to-earth** practical; realistic.

**down**[2] ▸n. **1** fine, soft feathers or hair. **2** (usu. **downs**) open rolling land. —**down·y** adj.

**down·cast** ▸adj. **1** (of eyes) looking downward. **2** dejected.

**down·er** ▸n. inf. **1** depressant or

tranquilizing drug. **2** depressing person or experience; failure.

**down·fall** ▸*n.* **1** fall from prosperity or power. **2** cause of this: *his stubbornness will be his downfall.*

**down·grade** ▸*v.* **1** reduce in rank or status. **2** speak disparagingly of.
▸*n.* **1** descending slope. **2** deterioration.

**down·heart·ed** ▸*adj.* dejected; in low spirits.

**down·hill** ▸*adv.* toward the bottom of an incline.
▸*adj.* sloping down; descending.
□ **go downhill** *inf.* decline; deteriorate (in health, state of repair, moral state, etc.).

**down·play** ▸*v.* minimize the importance of.

**down·pour** ▸*n.* heavy fall of rain.

**down·right** ▸*adj.* **1** plain; straightforward; blunt. **2** utter; complete: *a downright lie.*
▸*adv.* thoroughly.

**down·size** ▸*v.* (**-sized, -siz·ing**) **1** (esp. of personnel) reduce in size. **2** (of a company) eliminate staff positions.

**down·stage** ▸*n.* frontmost portion of the stage.
▸*adj. & adv.* at or to the front of the stage.

**down·stairs** ▸*adv.* **1** down a flight of stairs. **2** to or on a lower floor.
▸*adj.* situated downstairs.
▸*n.* a lower floor.

**down·stream** ▸*adv.* in the direction of the flow of a stream, etc.
▸*adj.* moving downstream.

**Down syn·drome** (also **Down's syndrome**) ▸*n.* congenital disorder with mental retardation and physical abnormalities.

**down·town** ▸*adj.* of esp. the central part of a town or city.
▸*n.* downtown area.
▸*adv.* in or into a downtown area.

**down·trod·den** ▸*adj.* oppressed; badly treated.

**down·turn** ▸*n.* decline, esp. economic.

**dow·ry** /'dourē/ ▸*n.* (*pl.* **-ries**) property or money brought by a bride to her husband.

**dowse** /dous/ ▸*v.* search for underground water, etc., using a rod that dips when over the right spot. —**dows·er** *n.*

**dox·y** /'däksē/ ▸*n.* (*pl.* **dox·ies**) **1** lover or mistress. **2** prostitute.

**doz.** ▸*abbr.* dozen.

**doze** /dōz/ ▶ v. sleep lightly; be half asleep.

▶ n. short, light sleep.

□ **doze off** fall lightly asleep.

**doz·en** /'dəzən/ ▶ n. 1 (pl. **doz·en**) twelve, regarded collectively: *two dozen eggs.* 2 set of twelve. 3 very many: *made dozens of mistakes.*

□ **by the dozen** in large quantities.

**Dr.** ▶ abbr. 1 Doctor. 2 Drive.

**drab** /drab/ ▶ adj. (**drab·ber, drab·best**) 1 dull; uninteresting. 2 of a dull brownish color.

**dra·co·ni·an** /drə'kōnēən; drā-/ ▶ adj. (of laws or their application) excessively harsh and severe.

**draft** /draft/ ▶ n. 1 preliminary written version of a speech, document, etc. 2 a written order for payment by a bank. b drawing of money by means of this. 3 military conscription. 4 current of air. 5 pulling; traction. 6 depth of water needed to float a ship. 7 drawing of liquor from a cask, etc. 8 amount of liquid drunk at one time.

▶ v. 1 prepare a draft of (a document, etc.). 2 select for a special duty or purpose.

3 conscript for military service. —**draft·ee** n.

**draft horse** ▶ n. horse used for pulling heavy loads.

**drafts·man** ▶ n. (pl. **-men**) person who makes drawings, plans, or sketches. —**drafts·man·ship** n.

**drag** /drag/ ▶ v. (**dragged, drag·ging**) 1 pull along with difficulty. 2 (allow to) trail along the ground. 3 (of time, etc.) pass slowly or tediously. 4 search the bottom of (a river, etc.) with grapnels, nets, or drags. 5 take (an unwilling person to a place, etc.): *she dragged him to the party.* 6 draw on (a cigarette, etc.).

▶ n. 1 obstruction to progress. 2 *inf.* tiresome person, duty, performance, etc. 3 *inf.* inhalation of smoke from a cigarette. 4 clothing conventionally worn by the opposite sex. 5 *inf.* street or road: *the main drag.*

□ **drag out** protract. □ **drag queen** man who dresses in women's clothes.

**drag·gle** /'dragəl/ ▶ v. make (something) dirty or wet, typically by trailing it through mud or water.

**drag·net** ▶ n 1 net drawn

through water or across land to trap fish or game. **2** systematic hunt for criminals, etc.

**drag·on** /'dragən/ ▶*n.* mythical monster, usu. depicted as a fire-breathing winged reptile.

**drag·on·fly** ▶*n.* (*pl.* **-flies**) insect with a long body and two pairs of transparent wings.

**dra·goon** /drə'goon/ ▶*n.* cavalryman.
▶*v.* coerce; bully: *they dragooned her into helping with the housework.*

**drain** /drān/ ▶*v.* **1** draw off liquid from. **2** draw off (liquid). **3** flow or trickle away. **4** become dry as liquid flows away. **5** exhaust. **6** drink all of; empty.
▶*n.* **1 a** channel or pipe carrying off liquid. **b** tube for drawing off discharge, etc. **2** constant outflow or expenditure: *the lawsuit was a drain on the company's finances.* —**drain·age** *n.*

**drake** /drāk/ ▶*n.* male duck.

**dram** /dram/ ▶*n.* **1** small drink of liquor. **2** measure of weight (apothecaries' one-eighth ounce; avoirdupois one-sixteenth ounce).

**dra·ma** /'drämə/ ▶*n.* **1** play for stage or broadcasting. **2** art of writing and presenting plays.

**3** exciting or emotional event, circumstances, etc. **4** dramatic quality.

**dra·mat·ic** /drə'matik/ ▶*adj.* **1** relating to drama. **2** sudden and striking: *a dramatic decline in recorded crime.* **3** intended to create an effect: *with a dramatic gesture, she put her hand to her brow.*

**dra·mat·ics** ▶*n.* **1** performance of plays. **2** [*n. pl.*] exaggerated behavior.

**dram·a·tist** /'drämə,tist/ ▶*n.* writer of dramas.

**dram·a·tize** ▶*v.* **1** adapt (a novel, etc.) to a stage play. **2** make a dramatic scene of. —**dram·a·ti·za·tion** *n.*

**dram·a·tur·gy** /'drämə,tərjē/ ▶*n.* theory and practice of dramatic composition.

**drape** /drāp/ ▶*v.* hang, cover loosely, or adorn with cloth, etc. ▶*n.* (**drapes**) curtains. —**dra·per·y** *n.*

**dras·tic** /'drastik/ ▶*adj.* having a far-reaching effect; severe. —**dras·ti·cal·ly** *adv.*

**draught** /draft/ ▶*Brit.* DRAFT.

**draw** /drô/ ▶*v.* (*past* **drew**; *past part.* **drawn**) **1** pull or cause to move toward or after one. **2** pull (a thing) up, over, or across.

**3** attract; bring; take in: *drew a deep breath.* **4** take out; remove. **5** obtain or take from a source: *draw a salary.* **6** produce (a picture) by tracing lines and marks. **7** reach (a conclusion) by deduction or inference. **8** induce (someone) to reveal or do something. **9** bring out or extract (liquid). **10** (of a chimney, etc.) promote or allow a draft. **11** call on (a person, a person's skill, etc.). **12** write out or compose (a check, document, etc.). **13** formulate or perceive (a comparison or distinction).
▸*n.* **1** act of drawing. **2** attraction. **3** raffle, lottery, etc. **4** game ending in a tie.
□ **draw the line** set a limit (of tolerance, etc.). □ **draw out 1** prolong. **2** elicit. □ **draw up 1** draft (a document, etc.). **2** come to a halt.

**draw·back** ▸*n.* disadvantage.

**draw·bridge** ▸*n.* bridge that may be raised or moved aside.

**draw·er** /ˈdrô(ə)r/ ▸*n.* **1** person or thing that draws. **2** lidless, boxlike storage compartment, sliding in and out of a desk, table, etc. **3** (**drawers**) underpants.

**draw·ing** ▸*n.* **1** the art of representing by line with pencils, crayons, etc. **2** picture produced in this way.

**drawl** /drôl/ ▸*v.* speak with drawn-out vowel sounds.

**drawn** /drôn/ ▸*adj.* **1** looking strained and tense. **2** (of butter) melted.

**draw·string** / ▸*n.* a string in the seam of the material of a garment or a bag, which can be pulled to tighten or close it.

**dray** /drā/ ▸*n.* low cart without sides for heavy loads.

**dread** /dred/ ▸*v.* **1** fear greatly. **2** look forward to with great apprehension.
▸*n.* great fear; apprehension.

**dread·ful** ▸*adj.* **1** terrible; inspiring fear or awe. **2** *inf.* very bad. —**dread·ful·ly** *adv.*

**dread·locks** ▸*pl. n.* hair twisted into tight braids hanging down on all sides.

**dread·nought** /ˈdred,nôt/ (also **dread·naught**) ▸*n.* **1** type of battleship introduced in the early 20th century, larger and faster than its predecessors and equipped entirely with large-caliber guns. **2** heavy overcoat for stormy weather.

**dream** /drēm/ ▸*n.* **1** pictures or events in the mind of a sleeping

person. **2** daydream or fantasy.
**3** ideal; aspiration. **4** beautiful
or ideal person or thing.

▸*v.* (*past* and *past part.* **dreamed** or
**dreamt**) **1** experience a dream.
**2** imagine as in a dream.
**3** contemplate the possibility
(of).

**drear·y** /ˈdri(ə)rē/ ▸*adj.* (**-i·er,
-i·est**) dismal; dull; gloomy.
**—drear·i·ly** *adv.* **—drear·i·ness** *n.*

**dredge** /drej/ ▸*n.* apparatus used
to scoop up objects or mud from
a riverbed or seabed.

▸*v.* **1** clear out the bed of (a river,
harbor, etc.) by scooping up
mud, rubbish, etc., with a
dredge. **2** bring up (lost or
hidden material) as if with a
dredge. **3** (**dredge something
up**) bring to people's attention
something unpleasant that had
been forgotten: *I don't know why
you had to dredge up that old story.*
**4** sprinkle (food) with flour,
sugar, etc.

**dregs** /dregz/ ▸*pl. n.* **1** sediment;
grounds. **2** most worthless part.

**drench** /drenCH/ ▸*v.* wet
thoroughly; soak.

**dress** /dres/ ▸*v.* **1** put on or wear
clothes. **2** decorate or adorn.
**3** treat (a wound) with ointment,
etc. **4 a** clean and prepare

(poultry, etc.) for cooking or
eating. **b** add a dressing to (salad,
etc.). **5** finish the surface of
(fabric, building stone, etc.).
**6** curry (leather, etc.).

▸*n.* **1** woman's garment of a
bodice and skirt. **2** clothing, esp.
a whole outfit.

□ **dress code** set of rules for
acceptable dress, as at a school,
restaurant, etc. □ **dress down**
*inf.* **1** reprimand or scold.
**2** dress casually. □ **dress up**
**1** dress in fancy dress. **2** disguise
(unwelcome facts) by
embellishment.

**dres·sage** /drəˈsäzH/ ▸*n.*
training of a horse in obedience
and deportment.

**dress·er** ▸*n.* **1** chest of drawers.
**2** person who assists actors to
dress. **3** person who dresses in a
specified way: *a snappy dresser.*

**dress·ing** ▸*n.* **1** sauce for
salads. **2** stuffing, esp. for
poultry. **3** bandage for a wound.
**4** stiffening used to finish
fabrics.

**dress re·hear·sal** ▸*n.* final
rehearsal of a play, etc., wearing
costumes.

**dress·y** ▸*adj.* (**-i·er, -i·est**) (of
clothes or a person) stylish;
elaborate. **—dress·i·ness** *n.*

**drib·ble** /'dribəl/ ▶v. **1** flow or allow to flow in drops. **2** move (a ball, etc.) with slight touches or taps.
▶n. **1** act of dribbling. **2** trickling flow.

**dri·er** /'drīər/ ▶compar. of DRY.
▶n. machine for drying hair, laundry, etc.

**drift** /drift/ ▶v. **1** be carried by or as if by a current. **2** progress passively or aimlessly: *drifted into teaching.* **3** pile or be piled into drifts.
▶n. **1** slow movement or variation. **2** deviation of a ship, aircraft, etc., from its course. **3** general intention, meaning, etc., of what is said, etc. **4** mass of windblown snow, etc. —**drift·age** n.

**drift·er** ▶n. aimless or rootless person.

**drill** /dril/ ▶n. **1** tool or machine for boring holes. **2** such a machine used by a dentist for cutting away part of a tooth before filling it. **3** military marching. **4** rigorous discipline or methodical instruction. **5** routine procedure in an emergency: *fire drill.* **6** coarse twilled cotton or linen fabric.
▶v. **1** make a hole with a drill through or into. **2** make (a hole) with a drill. **3** (of a dentist) cut away part of (a tooth) before filling it. **4** undergo discipline by drill. **5** impart (knowledge, etc.) by drill.

**drink** /driNGk/ ▶v. (*past* **drank**; *past part.* **drunk**) **1** swallow (liquid). **2** take alcohol, esp. to excess.
▶n. **1** liquid for drinking. **2** alcoholic liquor. —**drink·a·ble** adj. —**drink·er** n.
☐ **drink in** listen to eagerly.
☐ **drink to** toast (a person, event, etc.).

**drip** /drip/ ▶v. (**dripped**, **drip·ping**) **1** let fall or be so wet as to shed drops: *the faucet won't stop dripping.* **2** (cause or allow to) fall in small drops.
▶n. **1 a** dripping: *steady drip of rain.* **b** drop of liquid. **c** sound of dripping. **2** *inf.* weak or ineffectual person.

**drive** /drīv/ ▶v. (*past* **drove**; *past part.* **driv·en**) **1** urge in some direction, esp. forcibly. **2 a** compel. **b** force into a specified state. **3 a** operate and direct (a vehicle, etc.). **b** convey or be conveyed in a vehicle. **4** (of wind, water, etc.) carry along, propel, or cause to go in some direction. **5** force (a stake, nail, etc.) into place. **6** effect or conclude forcibly: *drove a hard bargain.* **7** set or keep (machinery) going.

▶*n.* **1** journey or excursion in a vehicle. **2** motivation and energy. **3** usu. landscaped street or road. **4** driving stroke of a bat, club, etc. **5** organized effort: *famine-relief drive.* **6** the transmission of power to machinery, wheels, etc.

□ **drive at** intend; mean: *what is he driving at?* □ **drive-by** (of a crime, etc.) carried out from a moving vehicle. □ **drive-in** (of a bank, movie theater, etc.) used while sitting in one's car. □ such a bank, movie theater, etc.

**driv·el** /'drivəl/ ▶*n.* silly nonsense; twaddle.

**drive·way** ▶*n.* usu. private road from a public street, etc., to a house, garage, etc.

**driz·zle** /'drizəl/ ▶*n.* very fine rain.

▶*v.* (esp. of rain) fall in very fine drops. —**driz·zly** *adj.*

**drogue** /drōg/ ▶*n.* device, typically conical or funnel-shaped with open ends, towed behind a boat, aircraft, or other moving object to reduce speed or improve stability.

**droll** /drōl/ ▶*adj.* **1** quaintly amusing. **2** odd; surprising.

**drom·e·dar·y** /'drämi,derē/ ▶*n.* (*pl.* **-ies**) one-humped camel, bred for riding and racing.

**drone** /drōn/ ▶*n.* **1** nonworking male of certain bees. **2** idler. **3** deep humming sound. **4** monotonous speech or speaker.

▶*v.* **1** make a deep humming sound. **2** speak or utter monotonously.

**drool** /drool/ ▶*v.* **1** slobber. **2** show much pleasure or infatuation.

▶*n.* slobbering.

**droop** /droop/ ▶*v.* **1** sag; hang down; languish. **2** lose heart; be dejected.

▶*n.* **1** drooping. **2** loss of spirit or enthusiasm.

**drop** /dräp/ ▶*n.* **1 a** globule of liquid. **b** very small amount of liquid. **2 a** abrupt slope. **b** degree of this. **c** act of falling or dropping. **d** fall in prices, temperature, etc. **e** deterioration. **3** globular gemstone, piece of candy, etc. **4** curtain or scenery let down on to a stage. **5** (**drops**) liquid medicine used in drops.

▶*v.* (**dropped, drop·ping**) **1** fall or

let fall in drops. **2** relinquish.
**3 a** sink from exhaustion, a
wound, etc. **b** die. **4 a** cease or
cause to cease; lapse or let lapse;
abandon. **b** *inf.* stop associating
with. **5** deposit (a passenger,
etc.). **6** utter or be uttered
casually. **7** send casually: *drop
me a postcard.* **8** fall or allow to
fall in direction, amount,
condition, degree, pitch, etc.
**9** *inf.* lose (money, esp. in
gambling). **10** omit. **11** give
birth to (esp. a lamb, a kitten,
etc.). **12** lose (a game, point,
etc.). **13** *inf.* dismiss or exclude:
*was dropped from the team.*
—**drop·let** *n.*
□ **drop in** (or **by**) visit casually.
□ **drop-leaf** (of a table, etc.)
having a hinged flap. □ **drop off**
fall asleep.

**drop·out** ▶*n. inf.* a person who
has dropped out, esp. from
school.

**dross** /drôs/ ▶*n.* **1** refuse.
**2** scum from melted metals.

**drought** /drout/ ▶*n.* **1** prolonged
absence of rain. **2** prolonged
lack of something. —**drought·y**
*adj.*

**drove** /drōv/ ▶past of DRIVE.
▶*n.* large number (of people,
animals, etc.) moving together.

**drown** /droun/ ▶*v.* **1** kill or be
killed by submersion in liquid.
**2** submerge; flood; drench.
**3** (**drown out**) make (a sound)
inaudible by means of a louder
sound.

**drow·sy** /'drouzē/ ▶*adj.* (**-si·er**,
**-si·est**) **1** half asleep; dozing.
**2** sluggish. —**drow·si·ly** *adv.*
—**drow·si·ness** *n.*

**drub** /drəb/ ▶*v.* (**drubbed**,
**drub·bing**) **1** thump; belabor.
**2** beat in a fight. —**drub·bing** *n.*

**drudge** /drəj/ ▶*n.* servile worker,
esp. at menial tasks.
—**drudg·er·y** *n.*

**drug** /drəg/ ▶*n.* **1** medicinal
substance. **2** (esp. addictive)
narcotic, hallucinogen, or
stimulant.
▶*v.* (**drugged**, **drug·ging**) **1** add a
drug to (food or drink).
**2** administer a drug to. **3** take
drugs as an addict.

**drug·gist** ▶*n.* pharmacist.

**Dru·id** /'drōōid/ ▶*n.* member of an
ancient Celtic religion.

**drum** /drəm/ ▶*n.* **1 a** hollow,
cylindrical percussion
instrument covered at one or
both ends. **b** percussion section.
**c** sound made by or like that of a
drum. **2** thing resembling a
drum, esp. a container.

▸ *v.* (**drummed**, **drum·ming**) **1** play a drum. **2** beat, tap, or thump (fingers, etc.) continuously (on something). —**drum·mer** *n.*

□ **drum into** drive (a lesson) into (a person) by persistence. □ **drum out** expel or dismiss for wrongdoing. □ **drum up** summon, gather, or call up.

**drum ma·jor** ▸ *n.* leader of a marching band.

**drum·stick** ▸ *n.* **1** stick for beating a drum. **2** lower leg of a dressed fowl.

**drunk** /drəNGk/ ▸ *adj.* **1** rendered incapable by alcohol. **2** overcome with joy, success, power, etc. ▸ *n.* drunkard.

**drunk·ard** /'drəNGkərd/ ▸ *n.* person who is habitually drunk.

**dry** /drī/ ▸ *adj.* (**dri·er**; **dri·est**) **1** without moisture or liquid. **2** (of wine, etc.) not sweet. **3** meager; plain; uninteresting. **4** (of humor) subtle; ironic. **5** prohibiting the sale of alcohol: *this county is dry.* ▸ *v.* (**dried**) make or become dry. —**dry·ly**, **dri·ly** *adv.* —**dry·ness** *n.*

□ **dry out 1** become fully dry. **2** (of a drug addict, alcoholic, etc.) undergo treatment for addiction. □ **dry up 1** make or become utterly dry. **2** (of supplies) run out.

**dry·ad** /'drī,ad/ ▸ *n.* wood nymph.

**dry cell** ▸ battery cell in which the electrolyte is dry.

**dry-clean** ▸ *v.* clean (clothes, etc.) with solvents and no water.

**dry dock** ▸ *n.* enclosure for the building or repairing of ships.

**dry goods** ▸ *pl. n.* fabric, thread, clothing, etc., esp. as distinct from hardware, groceries, etc.

**dry ice** ▸ *n.* solid carbon dioxide.

**dry rot** ▸ *n.* decay of wood caused by certain fungi.

**dry run** ▸ *n. inf.* rehearsal.

**DST** ▸ *abbr.* daylight saving(s) time.

**du·al** /'d(y)o͞oəl/ ▸ *adj.* **1** of two; twofold. **2** double: *dual ownership.* —**du·al·i·ty** *n.* —**du·al·ly** *adv.*

**dub** /dəb/ ▸ *v.* (**dubbed**, **dub·bing**) **1** give (a person) a name, nickname, etc. **2** make (a person) a knight by touching his shoulders with a sword. **3** provide (a movie, etc.) with an alternative soundtrack. **4** add (sound effects or music) to a movie or broadcast.

**du·bi·e·ty** /d(y)o͞o'bī-itē/ ▸ *n.* state

or quality of being doubtful; uncertainty.

**du·bi·ous** /ˈd(y)o͞obēəs/ ▸*adj.* **1** hesitating; doubting. **2** questionable. **3** unreliable; suspicious.

**du·cal** /ˈd(y)o͞okəl/ ▸*adj.* of or like a duke.

**duch·ess** /ˈdəCHis/ ▸*n.* **1** duke's wife or widow. **2** woman holding the rank of duke.

**duch·y** /ˈdəCHē/ ▸*n.* (*pl.* **-ies**) territory of a duke or duchess.

**duck** /dək/ ▸*n.* (*pl.* same or **ducks**) **1** swimming bird, esp. the domesticated mallard or wild duck. **2** strong linen or cotton fabric.
▸*v.* **1** plunge, dive, or dip under water and emerge. **2** bend quickly, esp. to avoid a blow or being seen. **3** *inf.* avoid or dodge: *ducked the meeting.*
□ **like a duck to water** adapting very readily. □ **like water off a duck's back** (of remonstrances, etc.) producing no effect.

**duck·bill** (also **duck-billed plat·ypus**) ▸*n.* PLATYPUS.

**duct** /dəkt/ ▸*n.* channel or tube for conveying fluid, cable, etc.

**duc·tile** /ˈdəktl; -ˌtīl/ ▸*adj.* **1** (of metal) capable of being drawn into wire; pliable. **2** (of a substance) easily molded.

**duct tape** ▸*n.* strong, cloth-backed, waterproof adhesive tape.

**dud** /dəd/ ▸*n. inf.* **1** futile or ineffectual person or thing. **2** shell, etc., that fails to explode. **3** (**duds**) clothes.

**dude** /do͞od/ ▸*n. inf.* **1** fellow; guy. **2** dandy. **3** city-dweller vacationing on a ranch.

**dudg·eon** /ˈdəjən/ ▸*n.* feeling of resentment or offense: *she stormed out in high dudgeon.*

**due** /d(y)o͞o/ ▸*adj.* **1** owing or payable. **2** merited; appropriate. **3** to be ascribed to (a cause, an agent, etc.). **4** intended to arrive or occur at a certain time.
▸*n.* **1** (**one's due**) what is owed to a person. **2** (**dues**) obligatory payment or fee.
▸*adv.* (of a direction) exactly; directly.
□ **due process** legal procedures to ensure individual rights. □ **in due course 1** at about the appropriate time. **2** in the natural order.

**du·el** /ˈd(y)o͞oəl/ ▸*n.* **1** armed contest between two people, usu. to settle a point of honor. **2** any contest between two.

▶*v.* fight a duel. —**du·el·ist** *n.*

**du·et** /d(y)o͞o'et/ ▶*n.*
**1** performance by two performers. **2** composition for two performers.

**dug·out** /'dəg,out/ ▶*n.* **1** roofed shelter, esp. for troops or at a baseball field. **2** canoe made from a tree trunk.

**du jour** /də 'ZHo͞or; ,d(y)o͞o/ ▶*adj.* (of food in a restaurant) available and being served on this day.

**duke** /d(y)o͞ok/ ▶*n.* **1 a** person holding the highest hereditary title of nobility. **b** prince ruling a duchy. **2** *inf.* hand; fist: *put up your dukes!*

**dul·cet** /'dəlsit/ ▶*adj.* (esp. of sound) sweet and soothing (often used ironically).

**dul·ci·mer** /'dəlsəmər/ ▶*n.* stringed musical instrument played by being struck with hammers.

**dull** /dəl/ ▶*adj.* **1** slow to understand; stupid. **2** tedious; boring. **3** (of the weather) overcast; gloomy. **4 a** (esp. of a knife edge, etc.) not sharp; blunt. **b** (of color, light, sound, etc.) not bright, vivid, or keen. **5** (of pain, etc.) not acute. **6** (of a person, an animal, trade, etc.) sluggish; slow-moving.

▶*v.* make or become dull.
—**dull·ness** *n.* —**dul·ly** *adv.*

**du·ly** /'d(y)o͞olē/ ▶*adv.* **1** in due time or manner. **2** rightly; properly; fitly.

**dumb** /dəm/ ▶*adj.* **1** unable to speak; mute. **2** silenced by surprise, shyness, etc. **3** *inf.* stupid.

**dumb·bell** ▶*n.* **1** short bar with a weight at each end, used for muscle-building, etc. **2** *inf.* stupid person.

**dumb·found** (also **dum·found**) ▶*v.* strike dumb; confound; nonplus.

**dumb·wait·er** ▶*n.* small elevator for carrying food, plates, etc., between floors.

**dum·my** /'dəmē/ ▶*n.* (*pl.* **-mies**) **1** model of a human, esp.: **a** ventriloquist's doll. **b** figure used to model clothes. **2** imitation or stand-in object. **3** *inf.* stupid person.
▶*adj.* sham; counterfeit.

**dump** /dəmp/ ▶*n.* **1** place for depositing trash, garbage, etc. **2** *inf.* unpleasant or dreary place. **3** temporary store of ammunition, etc.
▶*v.* **1** deposit or dispose of (rubbish, etc.). **2** put down firmly or clumsily. **3** *inf.*

abandon or desert (someone.
**4** sell off (excess goods) to a
foreign market at a low price.
**5** *Computing* copy (stored data) to
a different location.

**dump·ling** ▸*n.* **1** ball of boiled
or steamed dough, usu. eaten
with stew, etc. **2** dough filled
with fruit, etc.

**dump truck** ▸*n.* truck with a
body that tilts or opens at the
back for unloading.

**dump·y** ▸*adj.* (**-i·er, -i·est**) short
and stout.

**dun** ▸*adj.* dull grayish brown.
▸*n.* demand for payment.
▸*v.* (**dunned, dun·ning**) importune
for payment of a debt; pester.

**dunce** /dəns/ ▸*n.* ignorant
person.

**dune** /d(y)o͞on/ ▸*n.* bank of sand
formed by the wind.

**dung** /dəNG/ ▸*n.* excrement of
animals; manure.

**dun·ga·ree** /ˌdəNGəˈrē/ ▸*n.*
**1** coarse cotton cloth.
**2** (**dungarees**) pants made of
this.

**dun·geon** /ˈdənjən/ ▸*n.*
underground prison cell.

**dunk** /dəNGk/ ▸*v.* **1** dip (food)
into liquid before eating.
**2** immerse.

**du·o** /ˈd(y)o͞o-ō/ ▸*n.* (*pl.* **-os**) **1** pair
of performers. **2** duet.

**du·o·de·num** /ˌd(y)o͞oəˈdēnəm/
▸*n.* first part of the small
intestine below the stomach.
—**du·o·de·nal** *adj.*

**dupe** /d(y)o͞op/ ▸*n.* victim of
deception.
▸*v.* make a fool of; cheat.

**du·plex** /ˈd(y)o͞opleks/ ▸*n.*
**1** apartment on two levels.
**2** house subdivided for two
families.
▸*adj. Computing* (of a circuit)
allowing the transmission of
signals in both directions
simultaneously.

**du·pli·cate** ▸*adj.* /ˈd(y)o͞oplikit/
exactly like something else.
▸*n.* /ˈd(y)o͞oplikit/ identical thing,
esp. a copy.
▸*v.* /ˈd(y)o͞opliˌkāt/ **1** make or be
an exact copy of. **2** repeat (an
action, etc.), esp. unnecessarily.
—**du·pli·ca·tion** *n.*

**du·plic·i·ty** /d(y)o͞oˈplisitē/ ▸*n.*
deceitfulness. —**du·plic·i·tous**
*adj.*

**du·ra·ble** /ˈd(y)o͞orəbəl/ ▸*adj.*
lasting; hard-wearing.
—**du·ra·bil·i·ty** *n.*

**du·ra ma·ter** /ˈd(y)o͞orə ˈmätər/
▸*n. Anat.* the tough outermost

membrane enveloping the brain and spinal cord.

**du·ra·tion** /d(y)oo'rāsHən/ ▶*n.* length of time for which something continues.

**du·ress** /d(y)oo'res/ ▶*n.* **1** coercive circumstances. **2** forcible restraint or imprisonment.

**dur·ing** /'d(y)ooriNG/ ▶*prep.* throughout or at some point in.

**du·rum** /'d(y) oorəm/ ▶*n.* hard seeded wheat used in the manufacture of pasta, etc.

**dusk** /dəsk/ ▶*n.* darker stage of twilight.

**dust** /dəst/ ▶*n.* **1** finely powdered earth, dirt, etc. **2** dead person's remains.
▶*v.* **1** clear (furniture, etc.) of dust. **2** sprinkle with powder, dust, sugar, etc.

**dust bowl** ▶*n.* area denuded of vegetation by drought or erosion.

**dust dev·il** ▶*n.* whirlwind visible as a column of dust.

**dust jack·et** ▶*n.* paper cover on a book.

**Dutch** /dəcH/ ▶*adj.* of the Netherlands.
▶*n.* **1** language of the

Netherlands. **2** (**the Dutch**) people of the Netherlands.
□ **go Dutch** share expenses.

**Dutch door** ▶*n.* door horizontally divided allowing one part to be shut and the other open.

**Dutch elm dis·ease** ▶*n.* fungus disease affecting elms.

**Dutch ov·en** ▶*n.* heavy, covered cooking pot for braising, etc.

**Dutch treat** ▶*n.* outing, etc., at which people pay for themselves.

**Dutch un·cle** ▶*n.* kind but firm adviser.

**du·ti·ful** /'d(y)ootəfəl/ ▶*adj.* doing one's duty; obedient.

**du·ty** /'d(y)ootē/ ▶*n.* (*pl.* **-ties**) **1** moral or legal obligation; responsibility. **2** tax on certain imports, etc. **3** job or function.
□ **on** (or **off**) **duty** engaged (or not engaged) in one's work.

**dwarf** /dwôrf/ ▶*n.* (*pl.* **dwarfs** or **dwarves**) **1** (in folklore or fairy tales) small mythological being with supernatural powers. **2** person of abnormally small stature. **3** animal or plant much below ordinary size. **4** (also **dwarf star**) small usu. dense star.
▶*v.* cause to seem small or insignificant.

**dwell** /dwel/ ▸v. (*past* and *past part.* **dwelled** or **dwelt**) live; reside. —**dwell·er** n.

□ **dwell on** (or **upon**) linger over; write, brood, or speak at length on.

**dwin·dle** /'dwindl/ ▸v. become gradually less or smaller.

**dye** /dī/ ▸n. substance used to change the color of hair, fabric, wood, etc.

▸v. (**dye·ing**) color with dye.

□ **dyed-in-the-wool** out-and-out; unchangeable.

**dy·nam·ic** /dī'namik/ ▸adj. **1** energetic; active. **2** *Physics* of force producing motion. —**dy·nam·i·cal·ly** adv.

**dy·nam·ics** ▸n. **1** branch of mechanics studying the motion of bodies under the action of forces. **2** [*n. pl.*] varying levels of volume in a musical performance.

**dy·na·mite** /'dīnə,mīt/ ▸n. **1** high explosive containing nitroglycerin. **2** potentially dangerous person, situation, etc.

▸v. charge or shatter with dynamite.

**dy·na·mo** /'dīnə,mō/ ▸n. (*pl.* **-mos**) **1** electric generator. **2** *inf.* energetic person.

**dy·nast** /'dī,nast; -nəst/ ▸n.

member of a powerful family, esp. a hereditary ruler.

**dy·nas·ty** /'dīnəstē/ ▸n. (*pl.* **-ties**) **1** line of hereditary rulers. **2** succession of leaders in any field. —**dy·nas·tic** adj.

**dyne** /dīn/ ▸n. *Physics* a unit of force that, acting on a mass of one gram, increases its velocity by one centimeter per second every second along the direction that it acts.

**dys-** /dis/ ▸comb. form bad; difficult.

**dys·en·ter·y** /'disən,terē/ ▸n. inflammation of the intestines, causing severe diarrhea. —**dys·en·ter·ic** adj.

**dys·func·tion** ▸n. abnormality or impairment of function. —**dys·func·tion·al** adj.

**dys·func·tion·al** /dis-'fəNGksHənl/ ▸adj. **1** not operating normally or properly. **2** deviating from the norms of social behavior in a way regarded as bad.

**dys·gen·ic** /dis'jenik/ ▸adj. exerting a detrimental effect on later generations through the inheritance of undesirable characteristics.

**dys·lex·i·a** /dis'leksēə/ ▸n. general term for disorders

involving difficulty in learning to read or interpret words, letters, etc., but not affecting intelligence. —**dys·lex·ic** *adj. & n.*

**dys·pep·sia** /dis'pepsēə/ ▶*n.* indigestion. —**dys·pep·tic** *n.*

**dys·pep·tic** /dis'peptik/ ▶*adj.* of or having indigestion or consequent irritability or depression.

▶*n.* person who suffers from indigestion or irritability.

**dys·phe·mism** /'disfə,mizəm/ ▶*n.* derogatory or unpleasant term used instead of a pleasant or neutral one, such as "loony bin" for "mental hospital." The opposite of EUPHEMISM.

**dz.** ▶*abbr.* dozen.

# Ee

**E**[1] /ē/ (also **e**) ▸*n.* (*pl.* **Es** or **E's**; **e's**) **1** fifth letter of the alphabet. **2** *Mus.* third note of the diatonic scale of C major.

**E**[2] (also **E.**) ▸*abbr.* **1** east; eastern. **2** energy. **3** English.

**e-** ▸*prefix* form of **EX-** before some consonants.

**ea.** ▸*abbr.* each.

**each** /ēCH/ ▸*adj.* every one of two or more persons or things, regarded separately.
▸*pron.* each person or thing.
□ **each other** one another: *they wore each other's hats.*

**ea·ger** /ˈēgər/ ▸*adj.* enthusiastic; keen. —**ea·ger·ly** *adv.* —**ea·ger·ness** *n.*

**ea·gle** /ˈēgəl/ ▸*n.* **a** large bird of prey with keen vision and powerful flight. **b** this as a symbol, esp. of the U.S.
□ **eagle-eyed** keen-sighted; watchful.

**Ea·gle Scout** ▸*n.* highest Boy Scout rank.

**ear** /i(ə)r/ ▸*n.* **1** organ of hearing, esp. its external part. **2** faculty for discriminating sounds: *an ear for music.* **3** listening; attention. **4** seed-bearing head of a cereal plant: *he ate three ears of corn.*
□ **all ears** listening attentively.
□ **have a person's ear** receive a favorable hearing. □ **in one ear and out the other** heard but disregarded or quickly forgotten.
□ **up to one's ears** deeply involved or occupied.

**ear·drum** ▸*n.* membrane of the middle ear.

**earl** /ərl/ ▸*n.* British nobleman ranking between marquess and viscount. —**earl·dom** *n.*

**ear·ly** /ˈərlē/ ▸*adj. & adv.* (**-li·er, -li·est**) **1** before the usual or expected time. **2** not far on in the day or night, or in time. **3** not far on in a period or process. —**ear·li·ness** *n.*

**ear·mark** ▸*n.* identifying mark.
▸*v.* **1** set aside for a special purpose. **2** mark (sheep, etc.) with an earmark.

**earn** /ərn/ ▸*v.* **1** bring in as interest or income. **2** deserve; be entitled to; obtain as reward.

**ear·nest** /ˈərnist/ ▸*adj.* intensely serious. —**ear·nest·ly** *adv.* —**ear·nest·ness** *n.*

□ **in earnest** serious(ly), not joking(ly); with determination.

**earn·ings** ▸*pl. n.* money earned.

**ear·phone** ▸*n.* device applied to the ear to receive radio, etc., communications.

**ear·ring** ▸*n.* jewelry worn on the ear.

**ear·shot** ▸*n.* hearing range.

**ear·split·ting** ▸*adj.* excessively loud.

**earth** /ərTH/ ▸*n.* **1** (**Earth**) the planet on which we live. **2** land and sea, as distinct from sky. **3** the ground; soil.

**earth·en** ▸*adj.* **1** made of earth. **2** made of baked clay.

**earth·ly** ▸*adj.* of the earth; terrestrial.

**earth·quake** ▸*n.* convulsion of the earth's surface due to underground faults or volcanic action.

**earth·work** ▸*n.* **1** artificial bank of earth in fortification, road building, etc. **2** process of excavating soil in civil engineering work.

**earth·worm** ▸*n.* common worm living and burrowing in the ground.

**earth·y** ▸*adj.* (**-i·er, -i·est**) **1** of or like earth or soil. **2** somewhat coarse or crude; unrefined: *earthy humor.* **3** down-to-earth. —**earth·i·ness** *n.*

**ease** /ēz/ ▸*n.* **1** facility; effortlessness. **2** freedom or relief from pain, anxiety, hardship, etc.

▸*v.* **1 a** relieve from pain, anxiety, etc. **b** help; facilitate. **2** become less painful or burdensome. **3** move or be moved carefully into place.

**ea·sel** /'ezəl/ ▸*n.* frame to hold an artist's work, a blackboard, etc.

**east** /ēst/ ▸*n.* **1 a** point of the horizon where the sun rises at the equinoxes. **b** compass point corresponding to this. **c** direction in which this lies. **2** eastern part of a country, town, etc.

▸*adj.* **1** toward, at, near, or facing the east. **2** from the east: *east wind.*

▸*adv.* **1** toward, at, or near the east. **2** (**east of**) further east than. —**east·er·ly** *adj. & adv.* —**east·ern** *adj.* —**east·ward** *adj.*

**Eas·ter** ▸*n.* festival (held on a Sunday in March or April) of Christ's resurrection.

**eas·y** ▸*adj.* (**-i·er, -i·est**) **1** not

difficult; achieved without great effort. **2** relaxed and pleasant.
▸*adv.* with ease; in an effortless or relaxed manner.
□ **take it easy 1** proceed calmly. **2** relax.

**eas·y chair** ▸*n.* large comfortable chair.

**eas·y·go·ing** ▸*adj.* placid and tolerant.

**eas·y street** ▸*n. inf.* situation of ease or affluence.

**eat** /ēt/ ▸*v.* (*past* **ate**; *past part.* **eat·en**) **1** take into the mouth, chew, and swallow. **2** consume food; have a meal. **3** destroy gradually.
□ **eat one's heart out** suffer from excessive longing or envy. □ **eat up 1** consume completely. **2** use rapidly or wastefully: *eats up time.* **3** encroach upon. □ **eat one's words** admit that one was wrong.

**eat·er·y** ▸*n.* (*pl.* **-ies**) *inf.* informal restaurant.

**eaves** /ēvz/ ▸*pl. n.* underside of a projecting roof.

**eaves·drop** ▸*v.* (**-dropped, -drop·ping**) listen secretly to a private conversation.
—**eaves·drop·per** *n.*

**ebb** /eb/ ▸*n.* movement of the tide out to sea.

▸*v.* **1** flow out to sea; recede. **2** decline.
□ **ebb and flow** continuing process of decline and upturn in circumstances.

**eb·on** /'ebən/ ▸*n.* dark brown or black; ebony.

**eb·on·y** /'ebənē/ ▸*n.* (*pl.* **-ies**) **1** heavy, hard, dark wood. **2** any of various trees producing this.
▸*adj.* **1** made of ebony. **2** black like ebony.

**e·bul·lient** /i'bōolyənt/ ▸*adj.* exuberant. —**e·bul·lience** *n.* —**e·bul·lient·ly** *adv.*

**ec·cen·tric** /ik'sentrik/ ▸*adj.* **1** (of a person) odd or capricious in behavior or appearance. **2** (of a circle) not centered on the same point as another. **3** (of an orbit) not circular.
▸*n.* **1** eccentric person. **2** *Mech.* disk for changing rotation into backward-and-forward motion.
—**ec·cen·tri·cal·ly** *adv.* —**ec·cen·tric·i·ty** *n.*

**ec·cle·si·as·tic** /i‚klēzē'astik/ ▸*n.* clergyman.
▸*adj.* ECCLESIASTICAL.

**ec·cle·si·as·ti·cal** ▸*adj.* of or relating to the Christian Church or its clergy.

**ec·dys·i·ast** /ek'dizēəst/ ▸*n.* striptease performer.

**ech·e·lon** /ˈesHəˌlän/ ▶n. 1 level in an organization, in society, etc.; those occupying it. 2 formation of troops, ships, aircraft, etc., in staggered parallel rows.

**ech·o** /ˈekō/ ▶n. (pl. **-oes** or **-os**) 1 a repetition of a sound by reflection of sound waves. b sound so produced. 2 reflected radio or radar beam. 3 close imitation or repetition of something already done. ▶v. (**-oed**) 1 a (of a place) resound with an echo. b (of a sound) be repeated; resound. 2 repeat (a sound) by an echo. 3 repeat or imitate the words, opinions, or actions of (a person).

**ech·o·la·li·a** /ˌekōˈlālēə/ ▶n. 1 meaningless repetition of another person's spoken words as a symptom of psychiatric disorder. 2 repetition of speech by a child learning to talk.

**echt** /ekt/ ▶adj. authentic and typical. ▶adv. authentically and typically.

**é·clair** /āˈkle(ə)r/ ▶n. small, elongated light pastry filled with whipped cream or custard.

**é·clat** /āˈklä/ ▶n. 1 brilliant display; dazzling effect. 2 conspicuous success.

**ec·lec·tic** /iˈklektik/ ▶adj. deriving ideas, style, etc., from various sources. —**ec·lec·ti·cal·ly** adv. —**ec·lec·ti·cism** n.

**e·clipse** /iˈklips/ ▶n. 1 obscuring of light from one celestial body by another. 2 loss of light, importance, or prominence. ▶v. 1 (of a celestial body) obscure the light from or to (another). 2 outshine; surpass.

**e·clip·tic** /iˈkliptik/ ▶n. sun's apparent path among the stars during the year.

**ec·logue** /ˈekˌlôg; ˈekˌläg/ ▶n. short poem, esp. a pastoral dialogue.

**eco-** ▶comb. form ecology, ecological.

**e·col·o·gy** /iˈkäləjē/ ▶n. 1 study of the relations of organisms to one another and to their physical surroundings. 2 study of the interaction of people with their environment. —**ec·o·log·i·cal** adj. —**ec·o·log·i·cal·ly** adv. —**e·col·o·gist** n.

**e·con·o·met·rics** /iˌkänəˈmetriks/ ▶pl. n. branch of economics concerned with the use of mathematical methods (esp. statistics) in describing economic systems.

**ec·o·nom·ic** /ˌekəˈnämik; ˌēkə-/
▶*adj.* **1** of economics.
**2** profitable; cost-effective.

**ec·o·nom·i·cal** ▶*adj.* sparing in the use of resources; avoiding waste. —**ec·o·nom·i·cal·ly** *adv.*

**ec·o·nom·ics** ▶*n.* **1** science of the production and distribution of wealth. **2** [*pl. n.*] application of this to a particular subject.

**e·con·o·mism** /iˈkänəˌmizəm/ ▶*n.* belief in the primacy of economic causes or factors.

**e·con·o·mize** /iˈkänəˌmīz/ ▶*v.* spend less; reduce one's expenses: *I have to economize as much as possible.*

**e·con·o·my** /iˈkänəmē/ ▶*n.* (*pl.* -mies) **1 a** wealth and resources of a community. **b** particular kind of this: *capitalist economy.* **2** careful management of (esp. financial) resources; frugality. **3** sparing or careful use.

**ec·o·sys·tem** /ˈekōˌsistəm; ˈēkō-/ ▶*n.* biological community of interacting organisms and their physical environment.

**ec·ru** /ˈekrōō/ ▶*n.* color of unbleached linen.

**ec·sta·sy** /ˈekstəsē/ ▶*n.* (*pl.* -sies) overwhelming joy or rapture. —**ec·stat·ic** *adj.* —**ec·stat·i·cal·ly** *adv.*

**ec·to·plasm** /ˈektəˌplazəm/ ▶*n.* supernatural viscous substance that is supposed to exude from the body of a medium during a spiritualistic trance and form the material for the manifestation of spirits.

**ec·u·men·i·cal** /ˌekyəˈmenikəl/ ▶*adj.* **1** of or representing the whole Christian world. **2** seeking worldwide Christian unity. —**ec·u·me·nism** *n.* —**ec·u·men·i·cal·ly** *adv.*

**ec·ze·ma** /ˈeksəmə/ ▶*n.* inflammation of the skin, with itching and discharge.

**E·dam** /ˈēdəm/ ▶*n.* round Dutch cheese, usu. pale yellow with a red rind.

**ed·dy** /ˈedē/ ▶*n.* (*pl.* -dies) **1** circular movement of water causing a small whirlpool. **2** similar movement of wind, smoke, etc. ▶*v.* (-died) whirl around in eddies.

**e·del·weiss** /ˈādlˌwīs; -ˌvīs/ ▶*n.* white-flowered Alpine plant.

**e·de·ma** /iˈdēmə/ ▶*n.* accumulation of excess fluid in body tissues.

**E·den** /ˈēdn/ (also **Garden of Eden**) ▶*n.* place of great happiness; paradise (with reference to the abode of Adam and Eve in the biblical account of Creation).

**edge** /ej/ ▶*n.* **1** boundary line or margin of an area or surface. **2** area close to a steep drop. **3** point before something happens: *the economy was on the edge of recession.* **4** sharpened side of the blade. **5** narrow surface of a thin object. **6** meeting line of surfaces. **7** sharp or threatening tone in the voice: *she was smiling, but there was an edge to her voice.* **8** intense or striking quality. **9** quality that gives superiority: *he had an edge in sheer strength.*

▶*v.* **1** advance gradually or furtively. **2** provide with an edge or border.

□ **on edge 1** tense and irritable. **2** eager; excited. □ **set a person's teeth on edge** (of a taste, sound, etc.) cause an unpleasant nervous sensation. □ **take the edge off** make less effective or intense.

**edg·y** ▶*adj.* (**-i·er, -i·est**) irritable; nervously anxious. —**edg·i·ly** *adv.* —**edg·i·ness** *n.*

**ed·i·ble** /'edəbəl/ ▶*adj.* fit or suitable to be eaten. —**ed·i·bil·i·ty** *n.*

**e·dict** /'ēdikt/ ▶*n.* order proclaimed by authority.

**ed·i·fice** /'edəfis/ ▶*n.* building, esp. an imposing one.

**ed·i·fy** /'edə,fī/ ▶*v.* (**-fied**) improve morally or intellectually. —**ed·i·fi·ca·tion** *n.*

**ed·it** /'edit/ ▶*v.* **1** assemble, prepare, or modify (written material) for publication. **2** be editor of (a newspaper, etc.). **3** take extracts from and collate (movies, etc.) to form a unified sequence. **4** reword; correct. —**ed·i·tor** *n.*

**e·di·tion** /i'dishən/ ▶*n.* **1** edited or published form of a book, etc. **2** copies of a book, newspaper, etc., issued at one time. **3** particular version or instance of a broadcast. **4** person or thing resembling another.

**ed·i·to·ri·al** /,edi'tôrēəl/ ▶*adj.* of editing or editors.

▶*n.* article giving a newspaper's opinion on a topical issue. —**ed·i·to·ri·al·ize** *v.* —**ed·i·to·ri·al·ly** *adv.*

**ed·u·cate** /'ejə,kāt/ ▶*v.* give intellectual, moral, or social instruction to; teach. —**ed·u·ca·tion** *n.* —**ed·u·ca·tion·al** *adj.* —**ed·u·ca·tor** *n.*

**e·duce** /i'd(y)o͞os/ ▸v. **1** bring out or develop (something latent or potential). **2** infer (something) from data.

**EEG** ▸abbr. electroencephalogram.

**eel** /ēl/ ▸n. **1** snakelike fish. **2** evasive person or thing.

**e'er** /e(ə)r/ ▸contr. poet. EVER.

**ee·rie** /'i(ə)rē/ ▸adj. (-ri·er, -ri·est) gloomy and strange; weird. —**ee·ri·ly** adv. —**ee·ri·ness** n.

**ef·face** /i'fās/ ▸v. **1** rub or wipe out. **2** treat or regard oneself as unimportant: *self-effacing.* —**ef·face·ment** n.

**ef·fect** /i'fekt/ ▸n. **1** result; consequence. **2** impression produced on a spectator, hearer, etc. **3** (**effects**) property. **4** (**effects**) lighting, sound, etc., used to accompany a movie, etc. **5** physical phenomenon: *Doppler effect.* ▸v. bring about. □ **in effect** for practical purposes; in reality. □ **take effect** become operative.

**ef·fec·tive** ▸adj. **1** having a definite or desired effect. **2** impressive. **3** actual; existing. **4** operative. —**ef·fec·tive·ly** adv. —**ef·fec·tive·ness** n.

**ef·fec·tu·al** /i'fekCHo͞oəl/ ▸adj. **1** producing the required result or effect. **2** valid. —**ef·fec·tu·al·ly** adv.

**ef·fem·i·nate** /i'femənət/ ▸adj. (of a man) feminine in appearance or manner. —**ef·fem·i·na·cy** n.

**ef·fen·di** /i'fendē/ ▸n. (pl. **-dis** /-dēz/) **1** man of high education or social standing in an eastern Mediterranean or Arab country. **2** title of respect or courtesy in Turkey.

**ef·fer·vesce** /ˌefər'ves/ ▸v. **1** give off bubbles of gas. **2** be lively. —**ef·fer·ves·cence** n. —**ef·fer·ves·cent** adj.

**ef·fete** /i'fēt/ ▸adj. **1 a** feeble. **b** effeminate. **2** exhausted of its essential quality or vitality. —**ef·fete·ness** n.

**ef·fi·ca·cious** /ˌefi'kāSHəs/ ▸adj. (of something abstract or inanimate) producing the desired effect. —**ef·fi·ca·cy** n.

**ef·fi·ca·cy** /'efikəsē/ ▸n. ability to produce a desired or intended result.

**ef·fi·cient** /i'fiSHənt/ ▸adj. **1** productive with minimum waste or effort. **2** capable; acting effectively. —**ef·fi·cien·cy** n.

**ef·fi·gy** /'efijē/ ▸n. (pl. **-gies**) sculpture or model of a person.

**ef·fleu·rage** /ˌeflə'räzɦ/ ▸*n.* form of massage involving a circular stroking movement made with the palm of the hand. ▸*v.* massage with such a circular stroking movement.

**ef·flo·resce** /ˌeflə'res/ ▸*v.* **1** (of a substance) lose moisture and turn to a fine powder upon exposure to air. **2** reach an optimum stage of development; blossom.

**ef·flu·ent** /'efloo͞ənt/ ▸*adj.* flowing forth or out. ▸*n.* waste discharged into a river, etc. —**ef·flu·ence** *n.*

**ef·fort** /'efərt/ ▸*n.* **1** physical or mental exertion. **2** determined attempt. **3** force exerted. —**ef·fort·less** *adj.*

**ef·fron·ter·y** /i'frəntərē/ ▸*n.* (*pl.* **-ies**) impudent audacity.

**ef·fuse** /i'fyoo͞z; i'fyoo͞s/ ▸*v.* talk in an unrestrained, excited manner.

**ef·fu·sion** /i'fyoo͞zɦən/ ▸*n.* outpouring.

**ef·fu·sive** ▸*adj.* expressing emotion in an unrestrained manner. —**ef·fu·sive·ly** *adv.* —**ef·fu·sive·ness** *n.*

**e.g.** ▸*abbr.* for example.

**e·gal·i·tar·i·an** /i,galə'terēən/ ▸*adj.* of or advocating the principle of equal rights and opportunities for all. ▸*n.* egalitarian person. —**e·gal·i·tar·i·an·ism** *n.*

**egg** /eg/ ▸*n.* **1 a** spheroidal reproductive body produced by females of animals such as birds, reptiles, fish, etc., enclosed in a protective layer and capable of developing into a new individual. **b** egg of the domestic hen, used for food. **2** ovum. ▸*v.* (**egg someone on**) urge or encourage someone to do something.

**egg·head** ▸*n. inf.* intellectual.

**egg·nog** /'eg,näg/ ▸*n.* drink made with eggs, cream, and often alcohol.

**egg·plant** ▸*n.* plant bearing edible purple or white egg-shaped fruit.

**e·go** /'ēgō/ ▸*n.* (*pl.* **-gos**) **1** the part of the mind that has self-awareness. **2** self-esteem.

□ **ego trip** *inf.* activity, etc., devoted entirely to one's own interests or feelings.

**e·go·cen·tric** /ˌēgō'sentrik/ ▸*adj.* self-centered. —**e·go·cen·tric·i·ty** *n.*

**e·go·ism** /'ēgō,izəm/ ▸*n.* self-interest as the foundation of

morality. —**e·go·ist** *n.*
—**e·go·is·tic** *adj.*

**e·go·tism** /'ēgə‚tizəm/ ▸*n.*
**1** conceit. **2** selfishness.
—**e·go·tist** *n.* —**e·go·tis·tic** *adj.*
—**e·go·tis·ti·cal** *adj.*

**e·gre·gious** /i'grējəs/ ▸*adj.*
outstandingly bad; shocking.
—**e·gre·gious·ness** *n.*

**e·gress** /'ē‚gres/ ▸*n.* exit.

**e·gret** /'ēgrit/ ▸*n.* heron with
long white feathers.

**E·gyp·tian** /i'jipsʜən/ ▸*adj.* of
Egypt.
▸*n.* **1** native of Egypt. **2** language
used in ancient Egypt.

**eight** /āt/ ▸*n.* **1** one more than
seven. **2** symbol for this (8, viii,
VIII).

**eight·een** /ā(t)'tēn/ ▸*n.* **1** one
more than seventeen. **2** symbol
for this (18, xviii, XVIII).
—**eight·eenth** *adj. & n.*

**eight·y** /'ātē/ ▸*n.* (*pl.* **-ies**) **1** eight
times ten. **2** symbol for this (80,
lxxx, LXXX). **3** (**eighties**)
numbers from 80 to 89, esp. as
years. —**eight·i·eth** *adj. & n.*

**eis·tedd·fod** /ī'steʇʜ‚väd/ ▸*n.* (*pl.*
**-fods** or **-fo·dau** /-'vädī/)
competitive festival of music
and poetry in Wales, in
particular the annual National
Eisteddfod.

**ei·ther** /'ēʇʜər; 'īʇʜər/ ▸*adj. &
pron.* **1** one or the other of two.
**2** each of two.
▸*adv. & conj.* **1** as one possibility
or alternative. **2** any more than
the other: *I didn't like it either.*
□ **either-or** unavoidable choice
between alternatives. □ **either
way** in either case.

**e·jac·u·late** ▸*v.* /i'jakyə‚lāt/
**1** exclaim. **2** eject (fluid, etc.,
esp. semen) from the body.
▸*n.* /-‚lit/ ejaculated semen.
—**e·jac·u·la·tion** *n.*

**e·ject** /i'jekt/ ▸*v.* **1** expel; compel
to leave. **2** cause to be removed.
—**e·jec·tion** *n.* —**e·jec·tor** *n.*

**eke** /ēk/ ▸*v.* (**eke out**) contrive to
make (a livelihood) or support
(an existence).

**EKG** ▸*abbr.* electrocardiogram.

**e·lab·o·rate** ▸*adj.* /i'lab(ə)rit/
**1** minutely worked out.
**2** complicated.
▸*v.* /i'labə‚rāt/ work out or explain
in detail. —**e·lab·o·rate·ly** *adv.*
—**e·lab·o·ra·tion** *n.*

**é·lan** /ā'län; ā'lan/ ▸*n.* vivacity;
dash.

**e·lapse** /i'laps/ ▸*v.* (of time) pass
by.

**e·las·tic** /i'lastik/ ▸*adj.* **1** able to
resume its normal bulk or shape

after contraction, dilatation, or distortion. **2** springy.

▶*n.* elastic cord or fabric. —**e·las·tic·i·ty** *n.* —**e·las·ti·cize** *v.*

**e·lat·ed** /i'lātəd/ ▶*adj.* very happy and excited. —**e·la·tion** *n.*

**el·bow** /'el‚bō/ ▶*n.* **1** joint between the forearm and the upper arm. **2** elbow-shaped bend.

▶*v.* thrust or jostle (a person or oneself): *people elbowed past each other to the exit | he elbowed his way through the crowd.*

**el·bow grease** ▶*n. inf.* vigorous polishing; hard work.

**el·bow·room** ▶*n.* plenty of room to move or work in.

**el·der** /'eldər/ ▶*adj.* (of persons, esp. when related) senior; of a greater age.

▶*n.* **1** older of two (esp. related) persons. **2** (**elders**) persons older and usu. venerable. **3** church official. **4** tree with white flowers and dark berries.

**eld·er·ly** ▶*adj.* rather old; past middle age.

▶*n.* (**the elderly**) elderly people.

**eld·est** /'eldəst/ ▶*adj. & n.* first-born; oldest.

**el·dritch** /'eldrich/ ▶*adj.* weird and sinister or ghostly.

**e·lect** /i'lekt/ ▶*v.* **1** choose. **2** choose by vote.

▶*adj.* **1** chosen. **2** select; choice. **3** chosen but not yet in office: *president elect.*

**e·lec·tion** ▶*n.* **1** electing or being elected. **2** formal and organized instance of this.

**e·lec·tion·eer** /i‚leksHə'ni(ə)r/ ▶*v.* take part in an election campaign.

▶*n.* person who electioneers.

**e·lec·tor** ▶*n.* person who has the right of voting.

**e·lec·tor·ate** ▶*n.* body of electors.

**e·lec·tric** /i'lektrik/ ▶*adj.* **1** of, worked by, or charged with electricity; producing electricity. **2** causing or charged with excitement. —**e·lec·tri·cal** *adj.*

**e·lec·tri·cian** /ilek'trisHən/ ▶*n.* person who installs or maintains electrical equipment.

**e·lec·tric·i·ty** /ilek'trisitē-/ ▶*n.* **1** form of energy resulting from the existence of charged particles (electrons, protons, etc.). **2** science of electricity. **3** supply of electric current. **4** excitement.

**e·lec·tro·car·di·o·gram** /i‚lektrō'kärdēə‚gram/ ▶*n.* record of the heartbeat traced by an electrocardiograph.

**e·lec·tro·car·di·o·graph** /i‚lektrō'kärdiə‚graf/ ▶*n.* instrument recording electric currents generated by a heartbeat.

**e·lec·tro·cute** /i'lektrə‚kyo͞ot/ ▶*v.* kill by electric shock.
—**e·lec·tro·cu·tion** *n.*

**e·lec·trode** /i'lektrōd/ ▶*n.* conductor through which electricity enters or leaves an electrolyte, gas, vacuum, etc.

**e·lec·tro·en·ceph·a·lo·gram** /i‚lektrōən'sefələ‚gram/ ▶*n.* record of the brain's activity traced by an electroencephalograph.

**e·lec·tro·en·ceph·a·lo·graph** /i‚lektrōən'sefələ‚graf/ ▶*n.* instrument recording electrical activity of the brain.

**e·lec·trol·y·sis** /ilek'träləsis/ ▶*n.* **1** decomposition by electric current. **2** destruction of tumors, hair roots, etc., by this process.

**elec·tro·lyte** /i'lektrə‚līt/ ▶*n.* **1** substance that conducts electricity when molten or in solution, esp. in a battery. **2** solution of this.

**e·lec·tro·mag·net** /i‚lektrō'magnit/ ▶*n.* soft metal core made into a magnet by the passage of electricity through a surrounding coil.
—**e·lec·tro·mag·net·ic** *adj.*
—**e·lec·tro·mag·net·ism** *n.*

**e·lec·tron** /i'lekträn/ ▶*n.* stable elementary particle with a charge of negative electricity.

**e·lec·tron·ic** /ilek'tränik/ ▶*adj.* **1** (of a device) having, or operating with the aid of, many cmall components, esp. microchips and transistors, that control and direct an electric current. **2** of electrons. **3** relating to or using a computer. **4** (of music) produced by electronic means.
—**e·lec·tron·i·cal·ly** *adv.*

**e·lec·tron·ic mail** ▶*n.* another term for E-MAIL.

**e·lec·tron·ics** ▶*n.* science concerned with the behavior and movement of electrons.

**el·ee·mos·y·nar·y** /‚elə'mäsə‚nerē; ‚elēə-/ ▶*adj.* of, relating to, or dependent on charity; charitable.

**el·e·gant** /'eləgənt/ ▶*adj.* **1** graceful. **2** tasteful; refined. **3** ingeniously simple.
—**el·e·gance** *n.*

**el·e·gi·ac** /‚elə'jīək; e'lējē‚ak/ ▶*adj.* (esp. of a work of art) having a mournful quality.

**el·e·gy** /ˈeləjē/ ▶n. (pl. **-gies**) song or poem of lament, esp. for the dead.

**el·e·ment** /ˈeləmənt/ ▶n. **1** component part; contributing factor or thing. **2** any of the substances that cannot be resolved by chemical means into simpler substances. **3** any of the four substances (earth, water, air, and fire) in ancient and medieval philosophy. **4** wire that heats up in an electric appliance. **5** (**elements**) atmospheric agencies, esp. wind and storm. **6** (**elements**) rudiments of learning. □ **in** (or **out of**) **one's element** in (or out of) one's accustomed or preferred surroundings.

**el·e·men·ta·ry** /ˌeləˈment(ə)rē/ ▶adj. rudimentary; simple. —**el·e·men·tar·i·ly** adv.

**el·e·men·ta·ry school** ▶n. school in which elementary subjects are taught to young children.

**el·e·phant** /ˈeləfənt/ ▶n. (pl. same or **-phants**) largest land animal, with a trunk and ivory tusks.

**el·e·phan·tine** /ˌeləˈfantēn/ ▶adj. huge.

**el·e·vate** /ˈeləˌvāt/ ▶v. **1** bring to a higher position. **2** exalt in rank, etc. **3** [usu. as adj. **elevated**] **a** raise the spirits of; elate. **b** raise morally or intellectually.

**el·e·va·tion** /ˌeləˈvāSHən/ ▶n. **1** elevating or being elevated. **2** height above a given level, esp. sea level. **3** raised area. **4** loftiness; grandeur; dignity. **5** diagram showing one side of a building.

**el·e·va·tor** /ˈeləˌvātər/ ▶n. **1** platform or compartment for raising and lowering persons or things between floors. **2** tall building used for storing grain. **3** device on an airplane's tail for changing pitch.

**e·lev·en** /iˈlevən/ ▶n. **1** one more than ten. **2** symbol for this (11, xi, XI). —**e·lev·enth** adj.

**elf** /elf/ ▶n. (pl. **elves**) supernatural being, esp. one that is small and mischievous. —**elf·in** adj.

**e·lic·it** /iˈlisit/ ▶v. **1** draw out; evoke (a response, etc.). **2** draw forth (what is latent). —**e·lic·i·ta·tion** n.

**e·lide** /iˈlīd/ ▶v. omit (a vowel or syllable) when speaking. —**e·li·sion** n.

**el·i·gi·ble** /ˈeləjəbəl/ ▶adj. **1** fit or entitled to be chosen.

**2** desirable or suitable, esp. for marriage. —**el·i·gi·bil·i·ty** *n.*

**e·lim·i·nate** /i'limə,nāt/ ▶*v.* **1** remove; get rid of. **2** kill; murder. **3** exclude from consideration. **4** excrete. —**e·lim·i·na·tion** *n.*

**e·lite** /ə'lēt/ ▶*n.* **1** choice part of a body or group. **2** size of letter in typewriting (12 per inch). ▶*adj.* exclusive.

**e·lit·ism** ▶*n.* advocacy of or reliance on leadership or dominance by a select group. —**e·lit·ist** *n. & adj.*

**e·lix·ir** /i'liksər/ ▶*n.* **1** preparation supposedly able to change metals into gold or to prolong life. **2** aromatic medicinal solution. **3** quintessence of a thing.

**elk** /elk/ ▶*n.* (*pl.* same or **elks**) large deer of N. Europe and Asia.

**el·lipse** /i'lips/ ▶*n.* closed symmetrical oval figure. —**el·lip·tic** (also **el·lip·ti·cal**) *adj.* —**el·lip·ti·cal·ly** *adv.*

**el·lip·sis** /i'lipsis/ ▶*n.* (*pl.* **-ses**) **1** omission of words within or at the end of a construction or sense. **2** set of three dots, etc., indicating such.

**el·lip·tic** /i'liptik/ ▶*adj.* **1** of, relating to, or having the form of an ellipse. **2** (of speech or writing) lacking a word or words, esp. when the sense can be understood from contextual clues.

**elm** /elm/ ▶*n.* tall shade tree with rough serrated leaves.

**el·o·cu·tion** /ˌelə'kyo͞osHən/ ▶*n.* art of clear and expressive speech. —**el·o·cu·tion·ar·y** *adj.* —**el·o·cu·tion·ist** *n.*

**e·lon·gate** /i'lôNG,gāt/ ▶*v.* lengthen; prolong. ▶*adj.* long in proportion to width. —**e·lon·ga·tion** *n.*

**e·lope** /i'lōp/ ▶*v.* run away to wed secretly. —**e·lope·ment** *n.*

**el·o·quence** /'eləkwəns/ ▶*n.* fluent and effective use of language. —**el·o·quent** *adj.*

**else** /els/ ▶*adv.* **1** besides: *someone else.* **2** instead: *what else could I say?* **3** otherwise; if not: *or else you will be late.*

**else·where** ▶*adv.* in or to some other place.

**e·lu·ci·date** /i'lo͞osi,dāt/ ▶*v.* throw light on; explain. —**e·lu·ci·da·tion** *n.*

**e·lude** /i'lo͞od/ ▶*v.* **1** escape adroitly; dodge. **2** avoid compliance with. —**e·lu·sive** *adj.*

**e·ma·ci·at·ed** /iˈmāsHēˌātəd/ ▸*adj.* very thin from starvation or illness.

**e-mail** /ˈē ˌmāl/ (also **e-mail, E-mail**) ▸*n.* messages distributed by electronic means.

**em·a·nate** /ˈeməˌnāt/ ▸*v.* issue; originate. —**em·a·na·tion** *n.*

**e·man·ci·pate** /iˈmansəˌpāt/ ▸*v.* free from restraint, esp. social or political; liberate.
—**e·man·ci·pa·tion** *n.*
—**e·man·ci·pa·tor** *n.*
—**e·man·ci·pa·to·ry** *adj.*

**e·mas·cu·late** /iˈmaskyəˌlāt/ ▸*v.*
**1** deprive of force or vigor.
**2** castrate. —**e·mas·cu·la·tion** *n.*

**em·balm** /emˈbäm/ ▸*v.* preserve (a corpse) from decay.
—**em·balm·er** *n.*

**em·bank·ment** /emˈbaNGkmənt/ ▸*n.* earth or stone bank for keeping back water, or for carrying a road or railroad.

**em·bar·go** /emˈbärgō/ ▸*n.* (*pl.* **-goes**) **1** order forbidding foreign ships access to ports. **2** official suspension of commerce.
▸*v.* (**-goed**) place under embargo.

**em·bark** /emˈbärk/ ▸*v.* **1** put or go on board a ship or aircraft (to a destination). **2** (**embark on** or **upon**) engage in an undertaking.
—**em·bar·ka·tion** *n.*

**em·bar·rass** /emˈbarəs/ ▸*v.* cause (a person) to feel awkward or ashamed.
—**em·bar·rass·ment** *n.*

**em·bas·sy** /ˈembəsē/ ▸*n.* (*pl.* **-sies**) **1 a** residence or offices of an ambassador. **b** ambassador and staff. **2** deputation to a foreign country.

**em·bat·tled** /emˈbatld/ ▸*adj.* **1** involved in or prepared for war. **2** beset by difficulties.

**em·bed** /emˈbed/ (also **im·bed**) ▸*v.* (**-bed·ded, -bed·ding**) fix firmly in; implant.

**em·bel·lish** /emˈbelisH/ ▸*v.* **1** beautify; adorn. **2** add interest to (a narrative) with fictitious additions: *she had difficulty telling the truth because she liked to embellish things.*
—**em·bel·lish·ment** *n.*

**em·ber** /ˈembər/ ▸*n.* **1** small piece of glowing coal or wood in a dying fire. **2** almost extinct residue of a past activity, feeling, etc.

**em·bez·zle** /emˈbezəl/ ▸*v.* divert (money, etc.) fraudulently to one's own use.
—**em·bez·zle·ment** *n.*
—**em·bez·zler** *n.*

**em·bit·ter** /em'bitər/ ▸v. arouse bitter feelings in.

**em·bla·zon** /em'blāzən/ ▸v. 1 portray or adorn conspicuously. 2 adorn (a heraldic shield).

**em·blem** /'embləm/ ▸n. 1 symbol. 2 heraldic device. —**em·blem·at·ic** adj.

**em·bod·i·ment** / em'bädēmənt; im-/ ▸n. tangible or visible form of an idea, quality, or feeling.

**em·bod·y** /em'bädē/ ▸v. (-ied) 1 give a concrete or discernible form to (an idea, concept, etc.). 2 (of a thing or person) be an expression of (an idea, etc.). —**em·bod·i·ment** n.

**em·bol·ism** /'embə,lizəm/ ▸n. obstruction of an artery by a clot of blood, air bubble, etc.

**em·bon·point** /,äNbôN'pwaN/ ▸n. plump or fleshy part of a person's body, in particular a woman's bosom.

**em·boss** /em'bôs/ ▸v. carve or mold in relief.

**em·bou·chure** /,ämbōō'SHŏŏr/ ▸n. way in which a player applies the mouth to the mouthpiece of a brass or wind instrument.

**em·brace** /em'brās/ ▸v. 1 hold closely in the arms as a sign of affection; hold one another in this way. 2 accept eagerly. 3 adopt (a course of action, etc.). 4 include; comprise. ▸n. act of embracing; hug.

**em·broi·der** /em'broidər/ ▸v. 1 decorate (cloth, etc.) with needlework. 2 embellish (a narrative). —**em·broi·der·er·y** n.

**em·broil** /em'broil/ ▸v. involve (a person) in conflict or difficulties.

**em·bry·o** /'embrē,ō/ ▸n. (pl. -os) 1 a unborn or unhatched offspring. b human offspring in the first eight weeks from conception. 2 rudimentary plant in a seed. 3 thing in a rudimentary stage. —**em·bry·on·ic** adj.

**em·bry·on·ic** /,embrē'änik/ ▸adj. 1 of or relating to an embryo. 2 (of a system, idea, or organization) in a rudimentary stage with potential for further development.

**em·cee** /,em'sē/ ▸n. master of ceremonies. ▸v. (-ceed) act as an emcee.

**e·mend** /i'mend/ ▸v. edit (a text, etc.) to make corrections. —**e·men·da·tion** n.

**em·er·ald** /'em(ə)rəld/ ▸n. 1 bright-green precious stone, a variety of beryl. 2 color of this.

**e·merge** /i'mərj/ ▸v. 1 come up

or out into view. **2** come to light; become known, esp. as a result of inquiry, etc. **3** become recognized or prominent. —**e·mer·gence** *n.* —**e·mer·gent** *adj.*

**e·mer·gen·cy** /i'mərjənsē/ ▶*n.* (*pl.* **-cies**) sudden state of danger, etc., requiring immediate action.

**em·er·y** /'em(ə)rē/ ▶*n.* coarse abrasive for polishing metal, etc.

□ **emery board** emery-coated strip of thin wood, etc., used as a nail file.

**e·met·ic** /i'metik/ ▶*adj.* causing vomiting.

▶*n.* emetic medicine.

**em·i·grate** /'emi,grāt/ ▶*v.* leave one's own country to settle in another. —**em·i·grant** *n.* —**em·i·gra·tion** *n.*

**é·mi·gré** /'emə,grā/ (also **e·mi·gré**) ▶*n.* emigrant, esp. a political exile.

**em·i·nence** /'emənəns/ ▶*n.* **1** fame; distinction; recognized superiority. **2** important person. **3** *formal* piece of rising ground. —**em·i·nent** *adj.*

**é·mi·nence grise** /,āmēnäns 'grēz/ ▶*n.* (*pl.* **é·mi·nences grises** *pronunc.* same) person who exercises power or influence in a certain sphere without holding an official position.

**em·i·nent do·main** ▶*n.* right of a government or its agent to expropriate private property for public use, with payment of compensation.

**em·is·sar·y** /'emə,serē/ ▶*n.* (*pl.* **-ies**) person sent on a diplomatic mission.

**e·mit** /i'mit/ ▶*v.* (**-mit·ted**, **-mit·ting**) send out (heat, sound, light, etc.); discharge. —**e·mis·sion** *n.*

**e·mol·lient** /i'mälyənt/ ▶*adj.* softening or soothing the skin. ▶*n.* emollient agent. —**e·mol·lience** *n.*

**e·mol·u·ment** /i'mälyəmənt/ ▶*n.* salary or fee from employment.

**e·mote** /i'mōt/ ▶*v.* show excessive emotion.

**e·mo·tion** /i'mōsHən/ ▶*n.* strong mental or instinctive feeling such as love or fear. —**e·mo·tional** *adj.*

**e·mo·tive** /i'mōtiv/ ▶*adj.* **1** arousing or able to arouse intense feeling. **2** expressing a person's feelings rather than being neutrally or objectively descriptive.

**em·pa·thy** /'empəTHē/ ▶*n.* capacity to identify with a

person or object. **—em·pa·thet·ic** *adj.*

**em·per·or** /ˈemp(ə)rər/ ▸*n.* sovereign of an empire.

**em·pha·sis** /ˈemfəsis/ ▸*n.* (*pl.* **-ses**) **1** importance or prominence given to a thing. **2** stress laid on a word or words to indicate special meaning or importance. **—em·pha·size** *v.* **—em·phat·ic** *adj.*

**em·phy·se·ma** /ˌemfəˈsēmə; -ˈzēmə/ ▸*n.* disease of the lungs causing breathlessness.

**em·pire** /ˈemˌpī(ə)r/ ▸*n.* **1** extensive group of lands or countries under a single authority. **2** supreme dominion. **3** large commercial organization, etc., directed by one person or group.

**em·pir·i·cal** /emˈpirikəl/ (also **em·pir·ic**) ▸*adj.* based on observation or experiment, not on theory. **—em·pir·i·cal·ly** *adv.* **—em·pir·i·cism** *n.* **—em·pir·i·cist** *n.*

**em·ploy** /emˈploi/ ▸*v.* **1** use the services of (a person) in return for payment. **2** use to good effect. **3** keep (a person) occupied. **—em·ploy·a·ble** *adj.* **—em·ploy·ee** *n.* **—em·ploy·er** *n.* **—em·ploy·ment** *n.*

**em·po·ri·um** /emˈpôrēəm/ ▸*n.* (*pl.* **-ums** or **-a**) store selling a wide variety of goods.

**em·pow·er** /emˈpouər/ ▸*v.* **1** authorize, license. **2** give power to; make able. **—em·pow·er·ment** *n.*

**emp·ty** /ˈem(p)tē/ ▸*adj.* (**-ti·er, -ti·est**) **1** containing nothing. **2** unoccupied; uninhabited; deserted; unfurnished. **3** hollow; insincere.

▸*v.* (**-tied**) **1** remove the contents of. **2** become empty. **3** (of a river) discharge itself (into the sea, etc.). **—emp·ti·ness** *n.*

**em·py·re·an** /emˈpirēən; ˌempəˈrēən/ (also **em·py·re·al** /-əl/) ▸*adj.* belonging to or deriving from heaven.

**EMT** ▸*abbr.* emergency medical technician.

**e·mu** /ˈēm(y)o͞o/ ▸*n.* large flightless bird of Australia.

**em·u·late** /ˈemyəˌlāt/ ▸*v.* **1** try to equal or excel. **2** imitate. **—em·u·la·tion** *n.*

**e·mul·si·fy** /iˈməlsəˌfī/ ▸*v.* (**-fied**) convert into an emulsion. **—e·mul·si·fi·ca·tion** *n.* **—e·mul·si·fi·er** *n.*

**e·mul·sion** /iˈməlSHən/ ▸*n.* fine dispersion of one liquid in another, esp. as paint, medicine, etc.

**en-**[1] (also **em-** before *b*, *p*) ▶*prefix* forming verbs, = **IN-**: **1** from nouns, meaning 'put into or on': *engulf* | *entrust* | *embed*. **2** from nouns or adjectives, meaning 'bring into the condition of': *enslave*. **3** from verbs: **a** in the sense 'in, into, on': *enfold*. **b** as an intensifier: *entangle*.

**en-**[2] (also **em-** before *b*, *p*) ▶*prefix* in; inside: *energy*.

**-en**[1] ▶*suffix* forming verbs: **1** from adjectives, usu. meaning 'make or become so or more so': *deepen* | *fasten* | *moisten*. **2** from nouns: *happen* | *strengthen*.

**-en**[2] (also **-n**) ▶*suffix* forming adjectives from nouns, meaning: **1** made or consisting of (often with extended and figurative senses): *wooden*. **2** resembling; of the nature of: *golden* | *silvern*.

**-en**[3] (also **-n**) ▶*suffix* forming past participles of strong verbs: **1** as a regular inflection: *spoken* | *sworn*. **2** with restricted sense: *drunken*.

**-en**[4] ▶*suffix* forming the plural of a few nouns: *children* | *brethren* | *oxen*.

**-en**[5] ▶*suffix* forming diminutives of nouns: *chicken* | *maiden*.

**en·a·ble** /en'ābəl/ ▶*v.* **1** give (a person, etc.) the means or authority. **2** make possible. —**en·a·bler** *n.*

**en·act** /en'akt/ ▶*v.* **1 a** ordain; decree. **b** make (a bill, etc.) law. **2** play (a part). —**en·act·ment** *n.*

**e·nam·el** /i'naməl/ ▶*n.* **1** glasslike opaque coating for metal, etc. **2 a** smooth, hard coating. **b** hard gloss paint. **3** hard coating of a tooth.

▶*v.* inlay or encrust with enamel.

**en·am·ored** /i'namərd/ ▶*adj.* filled with a feeling of love or admiration for.

**en·camp** /en'kamp/ ▶*v.* **1** settle in a military camp. **2** lodge in the open in tents. —**en·camp·ment** *n.*

**en·cap·su·late** /en'kaps(y)ə,lāt/ ▶*v.* **1** enclose in or as in a capsule. **2** summarize; express briefly.

**en·case** /en'kās/ ▶*v.* **1** put into a case. **2** surround as with a case.

**-ence** ▶*suffix* forming nouns: **1** denoting a quality or an instance of it: *patience*. **2** denoting an action: *reference*.

**en·ceph·a·li·tis** /en,sefə'lītis/ ▶*n.* inflammation of the brain. —**en·ceph·a·lit·ic** *adj.*

**en·chant** /en'CHant/ ▸v.
1 charm; delight. 2 bewitch.
—**en·chant·er** n.
—**en·chant·ment** n.

**en·chi·la·da** /ˌenCHə'lädə/ ▸n.
rolled tortilla filled with meat,
etc.

**en·cir·cle** /en'sərkəl/ ▸v.
1 surround. 2 form a circle
around. —**en·cir·cle·ment** n.

**en·clave** /'enˌklāv; 'äNG-/ ▸n.
1 portion of territory
surrounded by larger, foreign
territory. 2 group of people who
are culturally, intellectually, or
socially distinct from those
surrounding them.

**en·clit·ic** /en'klitik/ ▸n. word
pronounced with so little
emphasis that it is shortened
and forms part of the preceding
word, e.g., *n't* in *can't*.

**en·close** /en'klōz/ ▸v.
1 surround with a wall, fence,
etc. 2 put in an envelope along
with a letter. —**en·clo·sure** n.

**en·code** /en'kōd/ ▸v. put into
code.

**en·co·mi·ast** /en'kōmēˌast/ ▸n.
person who publicly praises or
flatters someone else.

**en·co·mi·um** /en'kōmēəm/ ▸n.
(*pl.* **-ums** or **-a**) formal or high-
flown praise.

**en·com·pass** /en'kəmpəs/ ▸v.
1 surround. 2 contain.

**en·core** /'änˌkôr/ ▸n. repeated or
additional performance, as
called for by an audience.
▸*interj.* called out by an audience
to request such a performance.

**en·coun·ter** /en'kounər/ ▸v.
1 meet unexpectedly. 2 meet as
an adversary. 3 meet with;
experience (problems,
opposition, etc.).
▸*n.* 1 meeting by chance.
2 confrontation or struggle.

**en·coun·ter group** ▸n. group
of persons seeking psychological
benefit through contact with
one another.

**en·cour·age** /en'kərij/ ▸v. 1 give
courage, confidence, or hope to.
2 urge; advise. 3 promote.
—**en·cour·age·ment** n.

**en·croach** /en'krōCH/ ▸v.
(**encroach on/upon**) intrude on.
—**en·croach·ment** n.

**en·crypt** /en'kript/ ▸v. convert
(information or data) into a
cipher or code, esp. to prevent
unauthorized access.

**en·cum·ber** /en'kəmbər/ ▸v.
1 be a burden to. 2 hamper;
impede. —**en·cum·brance** n.

**en·cyc·li·cal** /en'siklikəl/ ▸n.
papal letter to bishops.

▶*adj.* (of a letter) for wide circulation.

**en·cy·clo·pe·di·a** /en͵sīklə'pēdēə/ (also **en·cy·clo·pae·di·a**) ▶*n.* book or set of books giving information on many subjects, or on many aspects of one subject.

**end** /end/ ▶*n.* **1 a** extreme limit. **b** extremity. **2** extreme part or surface of a thing. **3 a** conclusion; finish. **b** latter or final part. **c** death; destruction. **d** result; outcome. **4** goal; purpose. **5** piece left over.

▶*v.* **1** bring or come to an end. **2** (**end in**) result.

□ **at the end of the day** *inf.* when everything is taken into consideration. □ **end of the road** point at which hope has to be abandoned. □ **end result** final outcome. □ **end up** reach a specified state, action, or place eventually: *ended up a drunk.* □ **make (both) ends meet** live within one's income. □ **on end** **1** upright. **2** continuously: *for three weeks on end.*

**en·dan·ger** /en'dānjər/ ▶*v.* place in danger.

**en·dear** /en'di(ə)r/ ▶*v.* make dear to. —**en·dear·ment** *n.*

**en·deav·or** /en'devər/ ▶*v.* try earnestly.

▶*n.* earnest attempt.

**en·dem·ic** /en'demik/ ▶*adj.* regularly or only found among a particular people or in a certain region.

**end·ing** ▶*n.* **1** end or final part, esp. of a story. **2** inflected final part of a word.

**en·dive** /'en͵dīv; 'än͵dēv/ ▶*n.* **1** bitter, curly-leaved salad green. **2** (also **Belgian endive**) young, blanched chicory plant, eaten cooked or in salads.

**en·do·crine** /'endəkrin/ ▶*adj.* (of a gland) secreting directly into the blood; ductless.

**en·dog·a·my** /en'dägəmē/ ▶*n.* custom of marrying only within the limits of a local community, clan, or tribe.

**en·dorse** /en'dôrs/ ▶*v.* **1** approve. **2** sign or write on (a document), esp. the back of (a bill, check, etc.). —**en·dor·see** *n.* —**en·dorse·ment** *n.* —**en·dors·er** *n.*

**en·dow** /en'dou/ ▶*v.* **1** bequeath or give a permanent income to (a person, institution, etc.). **2** provide with talent, ability, etc. —**en·dow·ment** *n.*

**en·dure** /en'd(y)o͝or/ ▸v.
1 undergo (a difficulty, etc.).
2 tolerate. 3 last. **—en·dur·a·ble**
*adj.* **—en·dur·ance** *n.*

**en·e·ma** /'enəmə/ ▸n. injection
of liquid into the rectum, esp. to
expel its contents.

**en·e·my** /'enəmē/ ▸n. (*pl.* **-mies**)
person or group actively hostile
to another.

**en·er·gize** /'enər,jīz/ ▸v.
1 infuse energy into. 2 provide
energy for the operation of (a
device).

**en·er·gy** /'enərjē/ ▸n. (*pl.* **-gies**)
1 force; vigor; capacity for
activity. 2 property of matter
and radiation that is manifest as
the ability to do work.
**—en·er·get·ic** *adj.*
**—en·er·get·i·cal·ly** *adv.*

**en·er·vate** /'enər,vāt/ ▸v.
deprive of vigor or vitality.
**—en·er·va·tion** *n.*

**en·fee·ble** /en'fēbəl/ ▸v. make
feeble. **—en·fee·ble·ment** *n.*

**en·fi·lade** /'enfə,lād; -,läd/ ▸n.
1 volley of gunfire directed along
a line from end to end. 2 suite
of rooms with doorways in line
with each other.
▸v. direct a volley of gunfire along
the length of (a target).

**en·fold** /en'fōld/ ▸v. 1 wrap;
envelop. 2 clasp; embrace.

**en·force** /en'fôrs/ ▸v. 1 compel
observance of (a law, etc.).
2 impose (an action, conduct,
one's will). **—en·force·a·ble** *adj.*
**—en·force·ment** *n.* **—en·forc·er**
*n.*

**en·fran·chise** /en'fran,CHīz/ ▸v.
1 give (a person) the right to
vote. 2 free (a slave, etc.).
**—en·fran·chise·ment** *n.*

**en·gage** /en'gāj/ ▸v. 1 occupy or
attract (someone's interest).
2 a (**engage someone in**) cause
someone to become involved in.
b (**engage in**) become involved
in. 3 employ or hire. 4 pledge
or enter into a contract: *he
engaged to pay them $10,000
against a bond.* 5 (of a part, gear,
etc.) interlock. 6 come or bring
(troops) into battle.

**en·gaged** ▸*adj.* 1 having
formally agreed to marry.
2 busy; occupied.

**en·gage·ment** ▸*n.* 1 engaging
or being engaged. 2 promise to
marry a specific person.
3 appointment. 4 battle.

**en·gag·ing** ▸*adj.* attractive;
charming. **—en·gag·ing·ly** *adv.*

**en·gen·der** /en'jendər/ ▸v. give
rise to; bring about.

**en·gine** /'enjən/ ▶*n.*
**1** mechanical contrivance, esp. as a source of power.
**2** locomotive.

**en·gi·neer** /ˌenjəˈni(ə)r/ ▶*n.*
**1** person qualified in a branch of engineering. **2 a** person in charge of engines. **b** operator of an engine, esp. a railroad locomotive. **3** contriver.
▶*v.* **1** contrive; bring about. **2** act as an engineer.

**en·gi·neer·ing** ▶*n.* application of science to the design, building, and use of machines, etc.

**Eng·lish** /'ɪNG(g)lɪSH/ ▶*adj.* of England or its people or language.
▶*n.* **1** language of England, now used in the UK, U.S., Canada, etc. **2** (**the English**) the people of England. **3** spin given to a ball in pool or billiards.
□ **the Queen's** (or **King's**) **English** English language as correctly written or spoken in Britain.

**Eng·lish horn** ▶*n.* alto woodwind instrument of the oboe family.

**Eng·lish muf·fin** ▶*n.* flat round bread-dough muffin, usu. served sliced and toasted.

**en·gorge** /enˈgôrj/ ▶*v.* (cause to) swell with blood, water, etc.

**en·gram** /'engram/ ▶*n.* hypothetical permanent change in the brain accounting for the existence of memory; a memory trace.

**en·grave** /enˈgrāv/ ▶*v.* **1** carve (a text or design) on a hard surface. **2** inscribe (a surface) in this way. **3** impress deeply on a person's memory, etc. —**en·grav·er** *n.*

**en·gross** /enˈgrōs/ ▶*v.* absorb the attention of; occupy fully: *engrossed in studying.*

**en·gulf** /enˈgəlf/ ▶*v.* flow over and swamp; overwhelm.

**en·hance** /enˈhans/ ▶*v.* intensify (qualities, value, etc.); improve (something already of good quality). —**en·hance·ment** *n.*

**e·nig·ma** /iˈnigmə/ ▶*n.*
**1** puzzling thing or person.
**2** riddle; paradox. —**en·ig·mat·ic** *adj.* —**en·ig·mat·i·cal·ly** *adv.*

**en·join** /enˈjoin/ ▶*v.* **1** command; order (a person). **2** *Law* prohibit (a person) by order.

**en·joy** /enˈjoi/ ▶*v.* **1** take pleasure in. **2** have the use or benefit of. **3** experience. —**en·joy·a·ble** *adj.* —**en·joy·ment** *n.*

**en·large** /enˈlärj/ ▶*v.* make or

become larger or wider.
—**en·large·ment** *n.*

**en·light·en** /en'lītn/ ▶*v.* **1** inform
(a person) about a subject or
situation. **2** [as *adj.* **enlightened**]
have a rational, well-informed
outlook: *the more enlightened
employers offer better terms.*
—**en·light·en·ment** *n.*

**en·list** /en'list/ ▶*v.* **1** enroll in
the armed services. **2** secure as a
means of help or support.

**en·liv·en** /en'līvən/ ▶*v.* **1** give life
or spirit to. **2** make cheerful;
brighten (a picture or scene).

**en masse** /än 'mas/ ▶*adv.* **1** all
together. **2** in a mass.

**en·mesh** /en'mesн/ ▶*v.* entangle
in or as in a net.

**en·mi·ty** /'enmitē/ ▶*n.* (*pl.* **-ties**)
**1** state of being an enemy.
**2** feeling of hostility.

**en·nui** /än'wē/ ▶*n.* mental
weariness; boredom.

**e·nor·mi·ty** /i'nôrmitē/ ▶*n.* (*pl.*
**-ties**) **1** extreme wickedness.
**2** great size.

**e·nor·mous** /i'nôrməs/ ▶*adj.* very
large; huge.

**e·nough** /i'nəf/ ▶*adj. & pron.* as
much or as many as required:
*too much work and not enough
people to do it | they ordered more
than enough for five people.*

▶*adv.* **1** to the required extent:
*she's not old enough to drive.*
**2** fairly: *he seems nice enough.*
**3** used for emphasis: *oddly
enough, we have not heard from
her.*

**en·quire** /en'kwī(ə)r/ ▶var. of
INQUIRE.

**en·rage** /en'rāj/ ▶*v.* make
furious.

**en·rap·ture** /en'rapcнər/ ▶*v.* give
intense delight to.

**en·rich** / en'ricн/ ▶*v.* **1** make
rich or richer. **2** increase the
strength, value, or contents of.
—**en·rich·ment** *n.*

**en·roll** /en'rōl/ (also **en·rol**) ▶*v.*
(**-rolled, -rol·ling**) **1** enlist.
**2 a** write the name of (a person)
on a list. **b** incorporate as a
member. —**en·roll·ee** *n.*
—**en·roll·ment** *n.*

**en route** /än 'rōōt; en; äN/ ▶*adv.*
on the way.

**en·sconce** /en'skäns/ ▶*v.*
establish or settle comfortably.

**en·sem·ble** /än'sämbəl/ ▶*n.*
**1** group of musicians, etc.,
working together. **2** thing
viewed as the sum of its parts.
**3** set of clothes worn together.

**en·shrine** /en'sнrīn/ ▶*v.*
**1** enclose in a shrine. **2** preserve
or cherish.

**en·shroud** /en'sнroud/ ▶v.
**1** cover with or as with a shroud.
**2** cover completely; hide from view.

**en·sign** /'ensən/ ▶n. **1** banner or flag, esp. the military or naval flag of a nation. **2** lowest commissioned officer in the U.S. Navy or U.S. Coast Guard.

**en·slave** /en'slāv/ ▶v. make (a person) a slave.

**en·snare** /en'sne(ə)r/ ▶v. catch in or as in a snare; entrap.

**en·sue** /en'sōō/ ▶v. happen afterward or as a result.

**en·sure** /en'sнŏŏr/ ▶v. make certain.

**-ent** ▶suffix **1** forming adjectives denoting attribution of an action or state: *consequent* | *existent*. **2** forming nouns denoting an agent: *coefficient* | *president*.

**en·tail** /en'tāl/ ▶v. involve as a necessary part or consequence.

**en·tan·gle** /en'taNGgəl/ ▶v.
**1** cause to get caught in a snare or among obstacles. **2** cause to become tangled. **3** involve in difficulties. **4** complicate.
—**en·tan·gle·ment** n.

**en·tente** /än'tänt/ ▶n. friendly relationship between nations.

**en·ter** /'entər/ ▶v. **1** go or come in(to). **2** penetrate. **3** write (a name, details, etc.) in a list, book, etc. **4** register or announce oneself as a competitor (in an event).
**5** enroll in a society, school, etc.
**6** present for consideration: *entered a protest.* **7** (**enter into**) **a** engage in (conversation, an undertaking, etc.). **b** bind oneself by (an agreement, etc.).

**en·ter·prise** /'entər,prīz/ ▶n.
**1** undertaking, esp. a bold or difficult one. **2** initiative and resourcefulness. **3** business or company.

**en·ter·pris·ing** ▶adj. having initiative and resourcefulness.

**en·ter·tain** /,entər'tān/ ▶v.
**1** amuse; occupy agreeably.
**2 a** receive as a guest. **b** receive guests: *they entertain a great deal.*
**3** consider (an idea, feeling, etc.).
—**en·ter·tain·er** n.
—**en·ter·tain·ment** n.

**en·thrall** /en'тнrôl/ ▶v. captivate; please greatly.

**en·throne** /en'тнrōn/ ▶v. place on a throne.

**en·thuse** /en'тнōōz/ ▶v. *inf.* be or make enthusiastic.

**en·thu·si·asm** /en'тнōōzē-,azəm/ ▶n. strong interest; great eagerness. —**en·thu·si·ast** n.
—**en·thu·si·as·tic** adj.

**en·tice** /enˈtīs/ ▸v. persuade by the offer of pleasure or reward. —**en·tice·ment** n. —**en·tic·ing·ly** adv.

**en·tire** /enˈtī(ə)r/ ▸adj. whole; complete; unbroken. —**en·tire·ly** adv.

**en·ti·tle** /enˈtītl/ ▸v. **1** give just claim or right. **2** give a title to. —**en·ti·tle·ment** n.

**en·ti·ty** /ˈentitē/ ▸n. (pl. **-ties**) **1** thing with distinct existence. **2** existence; being: *entity and nonentity.*

**en·tomb** /enˈtoōm/ ▸v. place in or as in a tomb.

**en·to·mol·o·gy** /ˌentəˈmäləjē/ ▸n. study of insects. —**en·to·mo·log·i·cal** adj. —**en·to·mol·o·gist** n.

**en·tou·rage** /ˌäntoōˈräzн/ ▸n. people attending an important person.

**en·tr'acte** /ˈän,trakt; änˈtrakt/ ▸n. interval between two acts of a play or opera, or a piece of music or a dance performed during such an interval.

**en·trails** /ˈentrālz/ ▸pl. n. **1** bowels; intestines. **2** innermost parts.

**en·trance¹** /ˈentrəns/ ▸n. **1** going or coming in. **2** door, passage, etc., by which one enters. **3** right of admission. **4** coming of an actor on stage.

**en·trance²** /enˈtrans/ ▸v. **1** enchant; delight. **2** put into a trance.

**en·trant** /ˈentrənt/ ▸n. person who enters (esp. a competition, profession, etc.).

**en·trap** /enˈtrap/ ▸v. (**-trapped**, **-trap·ping**) **1** catch in or as in a trap. **2** beguile or trick.

**en·treat** /enˈtrēt/ ▸v. ask earnestly; beg. —**en·treat·y** n.

**en·tre·chat** /ˌäntrəˈsнä/ ▸n. vertical jump during which the dancer repeatedly crosses the feet and beats them together.

**en·trée** /ˈän,trā ˌänˈtrā/ (also **en·tree**) ▸n. **1** main dish of a meal. **2** right of admission.

**en·trench** /enˈtrencн/ ▸v. establish firmly (in a position, office, etc.): *ageism is entrenched in our society* | *her political opponents had been entrenched in power for years.* —**en·trench·ment** n.

**en·tre·pre·neur** /ˌäntrəprəˈnoōr/ ▸n. person who undertakes a commercial risk for profit. —**en·tre·pre·neur·i·al** adj. —**en·tre·pre·neur·ship** n.

**en·tro·py** /ˈentrəpē/ ▸n. quantity representing the amount of a system's thermal energy not available for conversion into mechanical work, often interpreted as the degree of disorder in the system.

**en·trust** /en'trəst/ ▸*v.* give into the care of another.

**en·try** /'entrē/ ▸*n.* (*pl.* **-tries**) **1** going or coming in. **2** liberty to go or come in. **3** place of entrance. **4** item entered (in a diary, list, etc.). **5** registered competitor.

**en·twine** /en'twīn/ ▸*v.* **1** twine together. **2** interweave.

**e·nu·mer·ate** /i'n(y)ōōmə,rāt/ ▸*v.* specify (items) one by one. —**e·nu·mer·a·tion** *n.*

**e·nun·ci·ate** /i'nənsē,āt/ ▸*v.* **1** pronounce clearly. **2** express in definite terms. —**e·nun·ci·a·tion** *n.*

**en·vel·op** /en'veləp/ ▸*v.* **1** wrap up or cover completely. **2** completely surround.

**en·ve·lope** /'envə,lōp; 'änvə-/ ▸*n.* **1** folded paper container, usu. with a sealable flap, for a letter, etc. **2** wrapper; covering.

**en·vi·a·ble** /'envēəbəl/ ▸*adj.* likely to excite envy.

**en·vi·ous** ▸*adj.* feeling or showing envy.

**en·vi·ron·ment** /en'vīrənmənt/ ▸*n.* **1** surroundings, esp. as affecting lives. **2** conditions or circumstances of living. **3** (**the environment**) natural world, esp. as affected by human activity. —**en·vi·ron·men·tal** *adj.* —**en·vi·ron·men·tal·ly** *adv.*

**en·vi·ron·men·tal·ist** ▸*n.* person concerned with the protection of the natural environment. —**en·vi·ron·men·tal·ism** *n.*

**en·vi·rons** ▸*pl. n.* surrounding district, esp. around an urban area.

**en·vis·age** /en'vizij/ ▸*v.* have a mental picture of (a thing or conditions not yet existing).

**en·voy** /'en,voi; 'än,voi/ ▸*n.* **1** messenger or representative. **2** diplomat ranking below ambassador.

**en·vy** /'envē/ ▸*n.* (*pl.* **-vies**) **1** discontent aroused by another's better fortune, etc. **2** object of this feeling. ▸*v.* (**-vied**) feel envy of (a person, etc.): *I envy you your position.*

**en·zyme** /'enzīm/ ▸*n.* protein catalyst in a specific biochemical reaction. —**en·zy·mat·ic** *adj.*

**e·on** /'ēən; 'ē,än/ (also **ae·on**) ▸*n.* **1** very long or indefinite period.

**2** age of the universe. **3** an eternity.

**EPA** ▶*abbr.* Environmental Protection Agency.

**ep·au·let** /ˈepəˌlet; ˌepəˈlet/ (also **ep·au·lette**) ▶*n.* ornamental shoulder piece, esp. on a uniform.

**e·phem·er·al** /əˈfem(ə)rəl/ ▶*adj.* lasting for only a short time; transitory.

**ep·ic** /ˈepik/ ▶*n.* **1** long narrative poem of heroic deeds. **2** grand or extended story, film, etc. ▶*adj.* **1** of or like an epic. **2** grand; heroic.

**ep·i·cene** /ˈepiˌsēn/ ▶*adj.* having characteristics of both sexes or no characteristics of either sex; of indeterminate sex.

**ep·i·cen·ter** /ˈepiˌsentər/ ▶*n.* **1** point at which an earthquake reaches the earth's surface. **2** central point of a difficulty.

**ep·i·cure** /ˈepiˌkyo͝or/ ▶*n.* person with refined tastes, esp. in food and drink.

**ep·i·dem·ic** /ˌepiˈdemik/ ▶*n.* **1** widespread occurrence of a disease at a particular time. **2** such a disease. ▶*adj.* in the nature of an epidemic.

**ep·i·der·mis** /ˌepiˈdərmis/ ▶*n.* outer layer of the skin. —**ep·i·der·mal** *adj.*

**ep·i·du·ral** /ˌepiˈd(y)o͝orəl/ ▶*adj.* on or around the dura mater, in particular, (of an anesthetic) introduced into the space around the dura mater of the spinal cord. ▶*n.* epidural anesthetic, used esp. in childbirth to produce loss of sensation below the waist.

**ep·i·glot·tis** /ˌepiˈglätəs/ ▶*n.* flap of cartilage at the root of the tongue, depressed during swallowing to cover the windpipe.

**ep·i·gram** /ˈepiˌgram/ ▶*n.* pointed or witty saying. —**ep·i·gram·mat·ic** *adj.* —**ep·i·gram·ma·tist** *n.*

**ep·i·graph** /ˈepiˌgraf/ ▶*n.* **1** inscription on a building, statue, or coin. **2** short quotation or saying at the beginning of a book or chapter, intended to suggest its theme.

**ep·i·lep·sy** /ˈepəˌlepsē/ ▶*n.* nervous disorder with convulsions and often loss of consciousness.

**ep·i·logue** /ˈepəˌlôg/ (also **ep·i·log**) ▶*n.* concluding narrative part, speech, etc.

**e·piph·a·ny** /i'pifənē/ ▸n. (pl. -nies) 1 (Epiphany) a manifestation of Christ to the Magi. b festival of this on January 6. 2 moment of profound insight.

**ep·i·phyte** /'epəˌfīt/ ▸n. plant that grows on another plant but is not parasitic, such as the numerous ferns, bromeliads, air plants, and orchids growing on tree trunks in tropical rain forests.

**e·pis·co·pal** /i'piskəpəl/ ▸adj. of or headed by a bishop or bishops.

**E·pis·co·pal Church** ▸n. Anglican Church in the U.S. and Scotland. —E·pis·co·pa·lian adj. & n.

**ep·i·sode** /'epiˌsōd/ ▸n. 1 event or period as part of a sequence. 2 dramatic installment. 3 incident or set of incidents in a narrative. —ep·i·sod·ic adj.

**e·pis·tle** /i'pisəl/ ▸n. 1 letter, esp. a long one on a serious subject. 2 (Epistle) any of the letters of the apostles in the New Testament.

**e·pis·to·lar·y** /i'pistəˌlerē/ ▸adj. relating to or denoting the writing of letters or literary works in the form of letters.

**ep·i·taph** /'epiˌtaf/ ▸n. words written in memory of a person who has died, esp. as a tomb inscription.

**ep·i·the·li·um** /ˌepəˌTHēlēəm/ ▸n. (pl. -ums or -a) tissue forming the outer layer of the body and lining many hollow structures. —ep·i·the·li·al adj.

**ep·i·thet** /'epəˌTHet/ ▸n. 1 characterizing adjective, etc. 2 such a word as a term of abuse.

**e·pit·o·me** /i'pitəmē/ ▸n 1 person or thing embodying a quality, etc. 2 thing representing another in miniature.

**ep·och** /'epək/ ▸n. 1 notable period in history or a person's life. 2 beginning of an era. —ep·och·al adj.

**ep·ox·y** /i'päksē/ ▸adj. designating a resin used in adhesives, insulation, etc.

**Ep·som salts** /'epsəm/ ▸n. magnesium sulfate used as a purgative or for other medicinal use.

**eq·ua·ble** /'ekwəbəl/ ▸adj. 1 (of a person) not easily angered; even-tempered. 2 not varying; uniform.

**e·qual** /'ēkwəl/ ▸adj. 1 the same in quantity, quality, size, degree, level, etc. **2** evenly balanced. **3** having the same rights or status.

▶*n.* person or thing equal to another.

▶*v.* **1** be equal to. **2** achieve something that is equal to. —e·**qual·i·ty** *n.* —e·**qual·ize** *v.* —e·**qual·ly** *adv.*

□ **equal opportunity** opportunity to be employed, paid, etc., without discrimination on grounds of sex, race, etc. □ **equal** (or **equals**) **sign** the symbol =.

e·**qua·nim·ity** /ˌēkwəˈnimitē/ ▶*n.* mental composure; evenness of temper.

e·**quate** /iˈkwāt/ ▶*v.* **1** regard as equal or equivalent. **2** be equal or equivalent to. —e·**quat·a·ble** *adj.*

e·**qua·tion** /iˈkwāzʜən/ ▶*n.* **1** statement that the values of two mathematical expressions are equal. **2** process of equating or making equal.

e·**qua·tor** ▶*n.* imaginary line around the earth or other body, equidistant from the poles. —e·**qua·to·ri·al** *adj.*

e·**ques·tri·an** /iˈkwestrēən/ ▶*adj.* of horses and horseback riding.

▶*n.* (*fem.* e·**ques·tri·enne**) rider or performer on horseback.

e·**qui·dis·tant** /ˌēkwiˈdistənt/ ▶*adj.* at equal distances.

e·**qui·lat·er·al** /ˌēkwəˈlatərəl/ ▶*adj.* having all sides equal in length.

e·**qui·lib·ri·um** /ˌēkwəˈlibrēəm/ ▶*n.* (*pl.* -**ums** or -**a**) **1** state of balance of opposing forces or influences. **2** calm state of mind.

e·**quine** /ˈēˌkwīn/ ▶*adj.* of or like a horse.

e·**qui·nox** /ˈēkwəˌnäks/ ▶*n.* time or date (about March 20 (*vernal equinox*) and September 22 (*autumnal equinox*) each year) at which the sun crosses the celestial equator, when day and night are of equal length. —e·**qui·noc·tial** *adj.* & *n.*

e·**quip** /iˈkwip/ ▶*v.* (-**quipped**, -**quip·ping**) supply with what is needed.

e·**quip·ment** ▶*n.* necessary articles, clothing, etc., for a purpose.

eq·**ui·ta·ble** /ˈekwitəbəl/ ▶*adj.* fair; just. —eq·**ui·ta·bly** *adv.*

eq·**ui·ty** /ˈekwitē/ ▶*n.* (*pl.* -**ties**) **1** fairness. **2** net value of property after the deduction of any debts. **3** ownership, as in shares of stock, etc.

**e·quiv·a·lent** /iˈkwivələnt/ ▸*adj.* **1** equal in value, amount, importance, etc. **2** corresponding. ▸*n.* equivalent thing, amount, word, etc. —**e·quiv·a·lence** *n.*

**e·quiv·o·cal** /iˈkwivəkəl/ ▸*adj.* **1** of double or doubtful meaning. **2** uncertain; questionable.

**e·quiv·o·cate** /iˈkwivəˌkāt/ ▸*v.* use ambiguity to conceal the truth. —**e·quiv·o·ca·tion** *n.* —**e·quiv·o·ca·tor** *n.*

**ER** ▸*abbr.* **1** Elizabeth Regina (Queen Elizabeth). **2** emergency room.

**Er** ▸*symb. Chem.* erbium.

**-er**[1] ▸*suffix* forming nouns from nouns, adjectives, and many verbs, denoting: **1** person, animal, or thing that performs a specified action or activity: *cobbler* | *lover* | *computer.* **2** person or thing that has a specified attribute or form: *foreigner.* **3** person concerned with a specified thing or subject: *geographer.* **4** person belonging to a specified place or group: *villager.*

**-er**[2] ▸*suffix* forming the comparative of adjectives (*wider*) and adverbs (*faster*).

**-er**[3] ▸*suffix* forming iterative and frequentative verbs: *blunder* | *glimmer* | *twitter.*

**-er**[4] ▸*suffix* **1** forming nouns and adjectives through Old French or Anglo-French, corresponding to: **a** Latin *-aris*: *sampler.* **b** Latin *-arius, -arium*: *butler* | *carpenter* | *danger.* **c** (through Old French *-ëure*) Latin *-atur* or (through Old French *-ëor*) Latin *-atorium.* **2** = **-OR.**

**-er**[5] *esp. Law* ▸*suffix* forming nouns denoting verbal action or a document effecting this: *disclaimer* | *misnomer.* The same ending occurs in *dinner* and *supper.*

**ERA** ▸*abbr.* **1** *Baseball* earned run average. **2** Equal Rights Amendment.

**e·ra** /ˈi(ə)rə; ˈerə/ ▸*n.* **1** period reckoning from a noteworthy event: *the Christian era.* **2** large distinct period of time, esp. regarded historically: *the pre-Roman era.*

**e·rad·i·cate** /iˈradiˌkāt/ ▸*v.* root out; destroy completely. —**e·rad·i·ca·ble** *adj.* —**e·rad·i·ca·tion** *n.*

**e·rase** /iˈrās/ ▸*v.* **1** rub out;

obliterate. **2** remove recorded material from (a magnetic tape or medium). **—e·ras·a·ble** *adj.* **—e·ra·sure** *n.*

**ere** /e(ə)r/ ▸*prep. & conj. poet.* before (of time): *ere noon.*

**e·rect** /i'rekt/ ▸*adj.* **1** upright; vertical. **2** enlarged and rigid. ▸*v.* **1** raise; set upright. **2** build. **—e·rec·tion** *n.*

**e·rec·tile** /ē'rektl; -ˌtīl/ ▸*adj.* capable of becoming erect.

**er·e·mite** /'erəˌmīt/ ▸*n.* Christian hermit or recluse.

**erg** /ərg/ ▸*n. Physics* unit of work or energy, equal to the work done by a force of one dyne when its point of application moves one centimeter in the direction of the force.

**er·go** /'ərgō/ ▸*adv.* therefore.

**er·go·nom·ics** /ˌərgə'nämiks/ ▸*n.* study of the efficiency of persons in their working environment. **—er·go·nom·ic** *adj.*

**er·mine** /'ərmən/ ▸*n.* (*pl.* same or **-mines**) stoat, esp. when in its white winter fur.

**e·rode** /i'rōd/ ▸*v.* wear away; destroy or be destroyed gradually.

**e·rog·e·nous** /i'räjənəs/ ▸*adj.* (of a part of the body) sensitive to sexual stimulation.

**e·ro·sion** /ē'rōzнən/ ▸*n.* **1** process of eroding or being eroded. **2** gradual destruction of something: *erosion of public confidence.*

**e·rot·ic** /i'rätik/ ▸*adj.* of or causing sexual desire or excitement. **—e·rot·i·cal·ly** *adv.*

**e·rot·i·ca** ▸*n.* erotic literature or art.

**err** /ər; er/ ▸*v.* **1** be mistaken or incorrect. **2** do wrong; sin. □ **err on the side of** act with a specified bias: *errs on the side of generosity.*

**er·rand** /'erənd/ ▸*n.* short outing for a specific purpose.

**er·rant** /'erənt/ ▸*adj.* deviating from an accepted standard.

**er·rat·ic** /i'ratik/ ▸*adj.* **1** inconsistent in conduct, opinions, etc.; unpredictable; eccentric. **2** uncertain in movement. **—er·rat·i·cal·ly** *adv.*

**er·ra·tum** /i'rätəm/ ▸*n.* (*pl.* **-ta**) error in printing or writing.

**er·ro·ne·ous** /i'rōnēəs/ ▸*adj.* incorrect; arising from error.

**er·ror** /'erər/ ▸*n.* **1** mistake. **2** state or condition of being wrong.

**er·satz** /ˈerˌsäts; -ˌzäts/ ▸*adj.* substitute; imitation.

**erst·while** /ˈərstˌ(h)wīl/ ▸*adj.* former; previous.

**er·u·dite** /ˈer(y)əˌdīt/ ▸*adj.* having or showing great learning. —**er·u·di·tion** *n.*

**e·rupt** /iˈrəpt/ ▸*v.* **1** break out suddenly or dramatically. **2** (of a volcano) become active and eject lava, etc. **3** (of a rash, boil, etc.) appear on the skin. —**e·rup·tion** *n.*

**-ery** ▸*suffix* forming nouns denoting: **1** class or kind: *greenery | machinery.* **2** employment; state or condition: *dentistry | slavery.* **3** place of work or cultivation or breeding: *brewery | rookery.* **4** behavior: *mockery.*

**es·ca·late** /ˈeskəˌlāt/ ▸*v.* **1** increase or develop (usu. rapidly) by stages. **2** cause to become more intense. —**es·ca·la·tion** *n.*

**es·ca·la·tor** ▸*n.* moving staircase consisting of a circulating belt forming steps.

**es·ca·pade** /ˈeskəˌpād/ ▸*n.* daring or reckless caper.

**es·cape** /iˈskāp/ ▸*v.* **1** get free of restriction, control, a person, etc. **2** (of a gas, liquid, etc.) leak. **3** succeed in avoiding danger, punishment, etc. **4** avoid. ▸*n.* **1** act or instance of escaping. **2** temporary relief from reality or worry. —**es·cap·ee** *n.*

**es·cape·ment** ▸*n.* part of a clock, etc., that connects and regulates the motive power.

**es·cap·ism** ▸*n.* tendency to seek distraction and relief from reality, esp. in the arts or through fantasy. —**es·cap·ist** *n. & adj.*

**es·carp·ment** /iˈskärpmənt/ (also **es·carp**) ▸*n.* long, steep slope at the edge of a plateau, etc.

**es·chew** /esˈCHo͞o/ ▸*v.* avoid; abstain from: *he appealed to the crowd to eschew violence.*

**es·cort** ▸*n.* /ˈesˌkôrt/ **1** one or more persons, vehicles, etc., accompanying a person, vehicle, etc., for protection or as a mark of status. **2** person accompanying a person of the opposite sex socially. ▸*v.* /iˈskôrt/ act as an escort to.

**es·crow** /ˈeskrō/ ▸*n.* **1** bond, deed, or other document kept in the custody of a third party, taking effect only when a specified condition has been fulfilled. **2** deposit or fund held in trust or as a security.

**es·cu·lent** /ˈeskyələnt/ ▶*adj.* fit to be eaten; edible.

▶*n.* thing, esp. a vegetable, fit to be eaten.

**es·cutch·eon** /iˈskəCHən/ ▶*n.* **1** shield or emblem bearing a coat of arms. **2** protective plate around a keyhole or door handle.

**ESL** ▶*abbr.* English as a second language.

**e·soph·a·gus** /iˈsäfəgəs/ ▶*n.* (*pl.* **-gi**) passage for food from the mouth to the stomach; gullet. —**e·soph·a·ge·al** *adj.*

**es·o·ter·ic** /ˌesəˈterik/ ▶*adj.* intelligible only to those with special knowledge.

**es·o·ter·i·ca** /ˌesəˈterikə/ ▶*n.* esoteric or highly specialized subjects or publications.

**ESP** ▶*abbr.* extrasensory perception.

**es·pa·drille** /ˈespəˌdril/ ▶*n.* light canvas shoe with a plaited fiber sole.

**es·pe·cial** /iˈspeSHəl/ ▶*adj.* notable; exceptional. —**es·pe·cial·ly** *adv.*

**es·pi·o·nage** /ˈespēəˌnäzH/ ▶*n.* spying or use of spies.

**es·pla·nade** /ˈespləˌnäd; -ˌnād/ ▶*n.* long, open level area for walking.

**es·pouse** /iˈspouz/ ▶*v.* **1** adopt or support (a cause, doctrine, etc.). **2** *archaic* (**be espoused to**) (of a woman) be engaged to.

**es·pres·so** /eˈspresō/ ▶*n.* (*pl.* **-sos**) strong black coffee made under steam pressure.

**esprit de corps** /eˌsprē də ˈkôr/ ▶*n.* feeling of pride, loyalty, etc., shared by members of a group.

**es·prit de l'es·ca·lier** /eˌsprē də ˌleskalˈyā/ ▶*n.* used to refer to the fact that a witty remark or retort often comes to mind after the opportunity to make it has passed.

**es·py** /iˈspī/ ▶*v.* (**-pied**) *poet./lit.* catch sight of; perceive.

**es·quire** /ˈeskwī(ə)r/ ▶*n.* **1** title appended to a man's surname, esp. as a form of address for letters. **2** title placed after the name of an attorney.

**es·say** /ˈesā/ ▶*n.* **1** short piece of writing on a given subject. **2** attempt.

▶*v.* attempt. —**es·say·ist** *n.*

**es·sence** /ˈesəns/ ▶*n.* **1** fundamental nature; inherent characteristics. **2 a** extract

obtained by distillation, etc.
**b** perfume.
□ **in essence** fundamentally. □ **of the essence** indispensable; vital.

**es·sen·tial** /i'sensʜəl/ ▶*adj.*
**1** necessary; indispensable. **2** of or constituting the essence of a person or thing.
▶*n.* (**essentials**) basic or indispensable element or thing: *we sent out on the trip with only the bare essentials.*

**EST** ▶*abbr.* eastern standard time.

**est.** ▶*abbr.* **1** established. **2** estimate.

**-est** ▶*suffix* forming the superlative of adjectives (*widest, nicest, happiest*) and adverbs (*soonest*).

**es·tab·lish** /i'stablisʜ/ ▶*v.* **1** set up on a permanent basis. **2** achieve permanent acceptance for (a custom, belief, etc.). **3** validate; place beyond dispute.

**es·tab·lish·ment** ▶*n.*
**1** establishing; being established. **2 a** business organization or public institution. **b** site of such. **3** (**the Establishment**) social group or authority exerting influence and resisting change.

**es·tate** /i'stāt/ ▶*n.* **1** property consisting of much land usu.
with a large house. **2** person's assets and liabilities, esp. at death. **3** class or order.

**es·teem** /i'stēm/ ▶*v.* have a high regard for.
▶*n.* high regard; respect; favor.

**es·ter** /'estər/ ▶*n.* chemical produced by replacing the hydrogen of an acid by an organic radical.

**es·ti·ma·ble** /'estəməbəl/ ▶*adj.* worthy of esteem.

**es·ti·mate** ▶*n.* /'estə,mit/
**1** approximate judgment, esp. of cost, value, size, etc.
**2** statement of approximate charge for work to be undertaken.
▶*v.* /'estə,māt/ **1** form an estimate or opinion of. **2** make a rough calculation. —**es·ti·ma·tion** *n.*

**es·ti·vate** /'estə,vāt/ ▶*v.* (of an animal, particularly an insect, fish, or amphibian) spend a hot or dry period in a prolonged state of torpor or dormancy.

**es·trange** /i'strānj/ ▶*v.* cause (a person or group) to turn away; alienate. —**es·trange·ment** *n.*

**es·tro·gen** /'estrəjən/ ▶*n.* sex hormone controlling female characteristics of the body.

**es·trus** /'estrəs/ ▶*n.* recurring period of sexual receptivity and fertility in many female mammals; heat.

**es·tu·ar·y** /'eschŏŏ,erē/ ▶n. (pl. **-ies**) tidal course or mouth of a river.

**e·su·ri·ent** /i'sŏŏrēənt/ ▶adj. hungry or greedy.

**ETA** ▶abbr. estimated time of arrival.

**et al.** ▶abbr. and others.

**et cet·er·a** /et 'set(ə)rə/ ▶adv. and the rest; and so on.

**etch** /ech/ ▶v. **1 a** reproduce (a picture, etc.) by engraving it on a metal plate with acid. **b** engrave (a plate) in this way. **2** practice this craft. **3** impress deeply (esp. on the mind). —**etch·er** n. —**etch·ing** n.

**e·ter·nal** /i'tərnl/ ▶adj. **1** existing always. **2** essentially unchanging: *eternal truths.* —**e·ter·nal·ly** adv.

**e·ter·ni·ty** ▶n. **1** infinite time. **2** endless life after death. **3** timelessness.

**eth·ane** /'eth,ān/ ▶n. colorless, odorless flammable gas, occurring in petroleum and natural gas.

**e·ther** /'ēthər/ ▶n. **1** colorless volatile organic liquid used as an anesthetic or solvent. **2** clear sky; upper regions of air beyond the clouds. **3** medium formerly assumed to permeate space.

**e·the·re·al** /i'thi(ə)rēəl/ ▶adj. **1** light; airy. **2** highly delicate, esp. in appearance. **3** heavenly.

**eth·ics** /'ethiks/ ▶n. **1** science of morals in human conduct. **2** [pl. n.] moral principles. —**eth·i·cist** n.

**eth·nic** /'ethnik/ ▶adj. **1** having a common national or cultural tradition. **2** denoting origin by birth or descent rather than nationality. **3** relating to race or culture. —**eth·nic·i·ty** n.
□ **ethnic cleansing** mass expulsion or killing of people from opposing ethnic groups.

**eth·no·cen·tric** /,ethnō'sentrik/ ▶adj. evaluating other peoples and cultures according to the standards of one's own culture.

**eth·nol·o·gy** /eth'näləjē/ ▶n. comparative study of peoples. —**eth·no·log·i·cal** adj. —**eth·nol·o·gist** n.

**e·thos** /'ēthäs/ ▶n. characteristic spirit or attitudes of a community, etc.

**eth·yl** /'ethəl/ ▶n. radical derived from ethane by removal of a hydrogen atom: *ethyl alcohol.*

**e·ti·o·lat·ed** /'ētēə,lātid/ ▶adj. **1** (of a plant) pale and drawn out due to a lack of light. **2** having lost vigor or substance; feeble.

**et·i·quette** /ˈetikit/ ▶*n.* conventional rules of social behavior or professional conduct.

**et seq.** (also **et seqq.**) ▶*abbr.* and the following (pages, etc.).

**é·tude** /āˈt(y)o͞od/ ▶*n.* musical composition designed to improve the technique of the player.

**et·y·mol·o·gy** /ˌetəˈmäləjē/ ▶*n.* (*pl.* -**gies**) **1 a** verifiable sources of the formation and development of a word. **b** account of these. **2** study of etymologies. —**et·y·mo·log·i·cal** *adj.* —**et·y·mol·o·gist** *n.*

**et·y·mon** /ˈetəˌmän/ ▶*n.* (*pl.* -**mons** or -**ma** /-mə/) word or morpheme from which a later word is derived.

**Eu** ▶*symb. Chem.* europium.

**eu-** ▶*comb. form* well; easily.

**eu·ca·lyp·tus** /ˌyo͞okəˈliptəs/ ▶*n.* (*pl.* -**tior** -**tus·es**) **1** tree of Australasia, cultivated for its wood and the oil from its leaves. **2** this oil used as an antiseptic, etc.

**Eu·cha·rist** /ˈyo͞okərist/ ▶*n.* **1** Christian sacrament commemorating the Last Supper, in which bread and wine are consecrated and consumed. **2** consecrated elements, esp. the bread. —**Eu·cha·ris·tic** *adj.*

**eu·gen·ics** /yo͞oˈjeniks/ ▶*n.* belief that the (esp. human) population can be improved by controlling inherited characteristics. —**eu·gen·ic** *adj.* —**eu·gen·i·cal·ly** *adv.* —**eu·gen·i·cist** *n.*

**eu·lo·gy** /ˈyo͞oləjē/ ▶*n.* (*pl.* -**gies**) speech or writing in praise of a person.

**eu·nuch** /ˈyo͞onək/ ▶*n.* castrated man.

**eu·pep·tic** /yo͞oˈpeptik/ ▶*adj.* of or having good digestion or a consequent air of healthy good spirits.

**eu·phe·mism** /ˈyo͞ofəˌmizəm/ ▶*n.* **1** mild or vague expression substituted for a harsher, more direct one (e.g., *pass away* for *die*). **2** use of such expressions. —**eu·phe·mis·ti·cal·ly** *adv.*

**eu·pho·ny** /ˈyo͞ofənē/ ▶*n.* (*pl.* -**nies**) pleasantness of sound, esp. of a word or phrase; harmony. —**eu·pho·ni·ous** *adj.*

**eu·pho·ri·a** /yo͞oˈfôrēə/ ▶*n.* intense feeling of well-being. —**eu·phor·ic** *adj.*

**Eur·a·sian** /yŏŏr'āzнən/ ▶*adj.*
1 of mixed European and Asian parentage. 2 of Europe and Asia.
▶*n.* Eurasian person.

**eu·re·ka** /yə'rēkə; yŏŏ-/ ▶*interj.* I have found it! (announcing a discovery, etc.).

**Eu·ro·pe·an** /ˌyŏŏrə'pēən/ ▶*adj.*
1 of or in Europe. 2 a descended from natives of Europe.
b originating in or characteristic of Europe.
▶*n.* 1 native or inhabitant of Europe. 2 person descended from natives of Europe.

**Eu·ro·pe·an Com·mun·i·ty**
▶*n.* confederation of certain European countries as a unit with internal free trade and common external tariffs. (Abbr.: **EC**)

**Eu·ro·pe·an Un·ion** ▶*n.* official name of the European Community from November 1993. (Abbr.: **EU**)

**Eu·sta·chian tube** /yŏŏ-'stāsн(ē)ən; -kēən/ ▶*n.* tube from the pharynx to the middle ear.

**eu·tha·na·sia** /ˌyŏŏтнə'nāzнə/ ▶*n.* bringing about of a gentle death in the case of incurable and painful disease.

**e·vac·u·ate** /i'vakyŏŏ,āt/ ▶*v.*
1 a remove (people) from a place of danger. b empty or leave (a place). 2 make empty.
3 withdraw from (a place).
4 empty (the bowels, etc.).
—**e·vac·u·a·tion** *n.*

**e·vade** /i'vād/ ▶*v.* 1 escape from; avoid, esp. by guile or trickery.
2 avoid doing, answering, etc.

**e·val·u·ate** /i'valyŏŏ,āt/ ▶*v.*
1 assess; appraise. 2 determine the number or amount of.
—**e·val·u·a·tion** *n.*

**ev·a·nes·cent** /ˌevə'nesənt/
▶*adj.* (of an impression or appearance, etc.) quickly fading.
—**ev·a·nes·cence** *n.*

**e·van·gel·i·cal** /ˌivan'jelikəl/
▶*adj.* 1 of or according to the teaching of the gospel or the Christian religion.
2 maintaining the doctrine of salvation by faith.
▶*n.* believer in this.

**e·van·ge·list** ▶*n.* 1 any of the writers of the four Gospels (Matthew, Mark, Luke, John).
2 preacher of the gospel.
—**e·van·ge·lism** *n.*

**e·vap·o·rate** /i'vapə,rāt/ ▶*v.*
1 turn from solid or liquid into vapor. 2 lose or cause to lose moisture as vapor. 3 disappear or cause to disappear: *our courage evaporated.* —**e·vap·o·ra·tion** *n.*

**e·va·sion** /i'vāzʜən/ ▶*n.*
1 evading. 2 evasive answer.

**e·va·sive** ▶*adj.* 1 seeking to
evade. 2 not direct in one's
answers, etc. —**e·va·sive·ly** *adv.*
—**e·va·sive·ness** *n.*

**eve** /ēv/ ▶*n.* 1 evening or day
before a holiday, etc. 2 time just
before anything: *eve of the
election.* 3 evening.

**e·ven** /'ēvən/ ▶*adj.* (**-ven·er,
-ven·est**) 1 level; flat and
smooth. 2 **a** uniform in quality;
constant. **b** equal in amount or
value, etc. **c** equally balanced.
3 in the same plane or line. 4 (of
a person's temper, etc.) equable;
calm. 5 (of a number) divisible
by two without a remainder.

▶*adv.* 1 not so much as: *never even
opened the letter.* 2 used to
introduce an extreme case: *it
might even cost $100.* 3 in spite
of; notwithstanding: *even with
the delays, we arrived on time.*

▶*v.* make or become even.
—**e·ven·ly** *adv.*

□ **even now** 1 now as well as
before. 2 at this very moment.
□ **even so** nevertheless.

**e·ven·hand·ed** ▶*adj.* impartial;
fair.

**eve·ning** /'ēvniɴɢ/ ▶*n.* close of
the day, esp. from about 6 p.m.
to bedtime.

**eve·ning star** ▶*n.* planet
Venus, conspicuous in the west
after sunset.

**e·vent** /i'vent/ ▶*n.* 1 thing that
happens, esp. one of importance.
2 fact or outcome of a thing's
occurring. 3 item in a
competitive program.

□ **in any event** (or **at all events**)
whatever happens. □ **in the
event of** if (a specified thing)
happens. □ **in the event that** if it
happens that.

**e·ven·tu·al** /i'vencʜōōəl/ ▶*adj.*
occurring in due course;
ultimate. —**e·ven·tu·al·ly** *adv.*

**e·ven·tu·al·i·ty** /i,vencʜōō'alitē/
▶*n.* (*pl.* **-ties**) possible event or
outcome.

**ev·er** /'evər/ ▶*adv.* 1 at all times;
always. 2 at any time. 3 (as an
emphatic word) in any way; at
all. 4 constantly: *ever-present.*
5 (**ever so**) very; very much.

□ **ever since** throughout the
period since.

**ev·er·glade** ▶*n.* marshy land
with tall grass.

**ev·er·green** ▶*adj.* retaining
green leaves year round.

▶*n.* evergreen plant.

**ev·er·last·ing** ▸*adj.* lasting forever or for a long time.

**eve·ry** /'ev(ə)rē/ ▸*adj.* **1** each single. **2** each at a specified interval. **3** all possible; the utmost degree of.
□ **every other** each second in a series. □ **every so often** occasionally. □ **every which way** *inf.* **1** in all directions. **2** in a disorderly manner.

**eve·ry·bod·y** ▸*pron.* every person.

**eve·ry·day** ▸*adj.* **1** used on ordinary days. **2** commonplace; usual.

**eve·ry·one** ▸*pron.* every person.

**eve·ry·thing** ▸*pron.* **1** all things; all the things of a group or class. **2** essential consideration.

**eve·ry·where** ▸*adv.* in every place.

**e·vict** /i'vikt/ ▸*v.* expel (a tenant, etc.) by legal process. —**e·vic·tion** *n.*

**ev·i·dence** /'evədəns/ ▸*n.* **1** available facts, circumstances, etc., determining truth or validity. **2** statements, information, etc., admissible as testimony in a court of law.

**ev·i·dent** /'evədənt/ ▸*adj.* **1** plain or obvious; manifest.

**2** seeming; apparent: *his evident anxiety.*

**ev·i·dent·ly** ▸*adv.* **1** as shown by evidence. **2** seemingly; as it appears.

**e·vil** /'ēvəl/ ▸*adj.* **1** morally bad; wicked. **2** harmful.
▸*n.* **1** evil thing. **2** wickedness.

**e·vince** /i'vins/ ▸*v.* **1** indicate or make evident. **2** show that one has (a quality).

**e·vis·cer·ate** /i'visə,rāt/ ▸*v.* disembowel. —**e·vis·cer·a·tion** *n.*

**e·voke** /i'vōk/ ▸*v.* **1** inspire or draw forth (memories, feelings, a response, etc.). **2** summon (a supposed spirit from the dead). —**ev·o·ca·tion** *n.* —**ev·o·ca·tive** *adj.*

**ev·o·lu·tion** /evə'loōsHən/ ▸*n.* **1** gradual development. **2** development of species from earlier forms, as an explanation of origins. **3** unfolding of events, etc. —**ev·o·lu·tion·ar·y** *adj.*

**e·volve** /i'välv/ ▸*v.* develop gradually and naturally.

**ewe** /yoō/ ▸*n.* female sheep.

**ew·er** ▸*n.* water jug with a wide mouth.

**ex** /eks/ *inf.* ▸*n.* former husband or wife.

**ex-**[1] (also **e-** before some

consonants, **ef-** before *f*) ▸*prefix*
**1** forming verbs meaning: **a** out;
forth: *exclude*. **b** upward: *extol*.
**c** thoroughly: *exacerbate*. **d** bring
into a state: *exasperate*. **e** remove
or free from: *expatriate*.
**2** forming nouns meaning
'former': *ex-convict*.

**ex-**[2] ▸*prefix* out: *exodus*.

**ex·ac·er·bate** /ig'zasər,bāt/ ▸*v.*
**1** make (pain, etc.) worse.
**2** irritate.

**ex·act** /Ig'zakt/ ▸*adj.* **1** accurate;
correct in all details. **2** precise.
▸*v.* **1** enforce payment of (money,
etc.). **2** demand; insist on.
—**ex·act·ly** *adv.*

**ex·act·ing** ▸*adj.* **1** making great
demands. **2** calling for much
effort.

**ex·ag·ger·ate** /ig'zajə,rāt/ ▸*v.*
give an impression of (a thing)
that makes it seem larger or
greater. —**ex·ag·ger·a·tion** *n.*

**ex·alt** /ig'zôlt/ ▸*v.* **1** raise in rank
or power, etc. **2** praise highly.
**3** [usu. as *adj.* **exalted**] **a** make
lofty or noble. **b** make
rapturously excited.
—**ex·al·ta·tion** *n.*

**ex·am** /ig'zam/ ▸*n.* EXAMINATION.

**ex·am·i·na·tion** /ig,zamə-
'nāsHən/ ▸*n.* **1** examining; being
examined. **2** detailed inspection.

**3** test. **4** formal questioning in
court.

**ex·am·ine** /ig'zamən/ ▸*v.*
**1** inquire into the nature or
condition, etc., of. **2** look closely
at. **3** test by examination.
**4** check the health of (a patient).
—**ex·am·i·nee** *n.* —**ex·am·in·er** *n.*

**ex·am·ple** /ig'zampəl/ ▸*n.*
**1** thing characteristic of its kind
or illustrating a rule. **2** model.
**3** circumstance or treatment
seen as a warning to others.
**4** illustrative problem or
exercise.
□ **for example** by way of
illustration.

**ex·as·per·ate** /ig'zaspə,rāt/ ▸*v.*
irritate intensely.
—**ex·as·per·a·tion** *n.*

**ex·ca·vate** /'ekskə,vāt/ ▸*v.*
**1 a** make (a hole or channel) by
digging. **b** dig out material from
(the ground). **2** reveal or extract
by digging. —**ex·ca·va·tion** *n.*
—**ex·ca·va·tor** *n.*

**ex·ceed** /ik'sēd/ ▸*v.* **1** be more
or greater than. **2** go beyond or
do more than is warranted.
**3** surpass; excel.

**ex·ceed·ing·ly** ▸*adv.* extremely.

**ex·cel** /ik'sel/ ▸*v.* (-**celled**,
-**cel·ling**) **1** be superior to. **2** be
preeminent.

**Ex·cel·len·cy** /ˈeksələnsē/ ▶*n.* (*pl.* **-cies**) title used in addressing or referring to certain high officials.

**ex·cel·lent** ▶*adj.* extremely good. —**ex·cel·lence** *n.*

**ex·cept** /ikˈsept/ ▶*prep.* not including; other than.
▶*conj.* unless.
▶*v.* exclude.

**ex·cep·tion** ▶*n.* **1** excepting; being excepted. **2** thing to be excepted. **3** instance that does not follow a rule.
□ **take exception** object. □ **with the exception of** except; not including.

**ex·cep·tion·a·ble** ▶*adj.* open to objection.

**ex·cep·tion·al** ▶*adj.* **1** forming an exception. **2** unusual. **3** outstanding.
—**ex·cep·tion·al·ly** *adv.*

**ex·cerpt** /ˈek,sərpt/ ▶*n.* extract from a book, film, etc.
▶*v.* take excerpts from (a book, etc.).

**ex·cess** /ˈekses/ ▶*n.*
**1** exceeding. **2** amount by which one thing exceeds another. **3 a** overstepping of accepted limits. **b** (**excesses**) immoderate behavior.
▶*adj.* that exceeds a prescribed amount: *excess weight.*
—**ex·ces·sive** *adj.*

□ **in excess of** more than; exceeding.

**ex·change** /iksˈCHānj/ ▶*n.* **1** giving of one thing and receiving of another in its place. **2** giving of money for its equivalent in a different currency. **3** place where merchants, bankers, etc., transact business. **4** short conversation.
▶*v.* **1** give or receive (one thing) in place of another. **2** give and receive as equivalents. **3** make an exchange. —**ex·change·a·ble** *adj.*

□ **in exchange** as a thing exchanged (for).

**ex·cheq·uer** /eksˈCHekər; iks-/ ▶*n.* royal or national treasury.

**ex·cise**[1] /ˈeksīz/ ▶*n.* **1** tax levied on goods produced or sold within the country of origin. **2** tax levied on certain licenses.

**ex·cise**[2] /ekˈsīz/ ▶*v.* remove; cut out. —**ex·ci·sion** *n.*

**ex·cite** /ikˈsīt/ ▶*v.* **1 a** rouse the emotions of (a person). **b** arouse (feelings, etc.). **2** provoke.
—**ex·cit·a·ble** *adj.*
—**ex·cite·ment** *n.*

**ex·claim** /ik'sklām/ ▶v. cry out suddenly.

**ex·cla·ma·tion** /eksklə-'māsʜən/ ▶n. **1** exclaiming. **2** words exclaimed.

**ex·cla·ma·tion point** ▶n. punctuation mark (!) indicating exclamation.

**ex·clam·a·to·ry** /eks'klamə-,torē/ ▶adj. of or serving as an exclamation.

**ex·clude** /ik'sklōōd/ ▶v. **1** keep out (a person or thing) from a place, group, privilege, etc. **2** remove from consideration. —**ex·clud·ing** prep. —**ex·clu·sion** n.

**ex·clu·sive** /ik'sklōōsiv/ ▶adj. **1** excluding other things. **2** (**exclusive of**) not including; excepting: *prices are exclusive of tax and delivery.* **3** tending to exclude others, esp. socially; select. **4** high-class. **5** not obtainable or published elsewhere. ▶n. article, etc., published by only one newspaper, etc. —**ex·clu·siv·i·ty** n.

**ex·com·mu·ni·cate** /ˌekskə-'myōōni,kāt/ ▶v. officially exclude (a person) from membership in and sacraments of the church. —**ex·com·mu·ni·ca·tion** n. adj.

**ex·co·ri·ate** /ik'skôrē,āt/ ▶v. **1** censure or criticize severely. **2** strip or peel off (skin). —**ex·co·ri·a·tion** n.

**ex·cre·ment** /'ekskrəmənt/ ▶n. feces.

**ex·cres·cence** /ik'skresəns/ ▶n. **1** abnormal or morbid outgrowth. **2** ugly addition.

**ex·crete** /ik'skrēt/ ▶v. (of an animal or plant) expel (waste matter). —**ex·cre·to·ry** adj.

**ex·cru·ci·at·ing** /ik'skrōōsʜē-,ātiNG/ ▶adj. extremely painful or unpleasant.

**ex·cul·pate** /'ekskəl,pāt/ ▶v. free from blame; clear of a charge. —**ex·cul·pa·to·ry** adj.

**ex·cur·sion** /ik'skərzʜən/ ▶n. **1** short pleasure trip. **2** digression.

**ex·cuse** /ik'skyōōz/ ▶v. **1** attempt to lessen the blame attaching to (a person, act, or fault). **2** (of a fact or circumstance) serve in mitigation of (a person or act). **3** obtain exemption for (a person or oneself). **4** (**excuse from**) release (a person) from a duty, etc. **5** forgive. ▶n. /ik'skyōōs/ **1** reason put forward to justify an offense, fault, etc. **2** apology. **3** (**excuse**

**for**) poor or inadequate example of.

**ex·e·crate** /'eksi,krāt/ ▸*v.* express or feel loathing for: *they were execrated as dangerous and corrupt.* —**ex·e·cra·tion** *n.*

**ex·e·cute** /'eksi,kyōōt/ ▸*v.* **1** carry out a death sentence on. **2** carry out; perform. **3** carry out a design for (a product of art or skill). **4** make valid by signing, sealing, etc. —**ex·e·cu·tion** *n.* —**ex·e·cu·tion·er** *n.*

**ex·ec·u·tive** /ig'zekyətiv/ ▸*n.* **1** person or body with managerial or administrative responsibility. **2** branch of government concerned with executing laws, agreements, etc. ▸*adj.* concerned with executing laws, agreements, etc., or with other administration or management.

**ex·ec·u·tor** /ig'zekyətər/ ▸*n.* (*fem.* **-trix**, *pl.* **-tri·ces** or **-trix·es**) person appointed to fulfill provisions of a will.

**ex·e·ge·sis** /,eksi'jēsis/ ▸*n.* (*pl.* **-ses** /-sēz/) critical explanation or interpretation of a text, esp. of scripture.

**ex·em·plar** /ig'zemplər; -plär/ ▸*n.* **1** model. **2** typical instance.

**ex·em·pla·ry** ▸*adj.* **1** fit to be imitated; outstandingly good. **2** serving as a warning. **3** illustrative; representative.

**ex·em·pli·fy** /ig'zemplə,fī/ ▸*v.* (**-fied**) serve as an example of.

**ex·empt** /ig'zem(p)t/ ▸*adj.* free from an obligation imposed on others. ▸*v.* (**exempt from**) free from an obligation. —**ex·emp·tion** *n.*

**ex·er·cise** /'eksər,sīz/ ▸*n.* **1** activity requiring physical effort, done to sustain or improve health. **2** mental or spiritual activity, esp. to develop a skill. **3** task devised as exercise. **4** use or application of a mental faculty, right, etc. **5** (often **exercises**) military drill or maneuvers. ▸*v.* **1** use or apply (a faculty, right, etc.). **2** perform (a function). **3 a** do exercises. **b** provide with exercise. **4 a** tax the powers of. **b** perplex; worry.

**ex·ert** /ig'zərt/ ▸*v.* **1** exercise; bring to bear (a quality, force, etc.). **2** (**exert oneself**) strive: *he needs to exert himself to improve his grades.* —**ex·er·tion** *n.*

**ex·hale** /eks'hāl; 'eks,hāl/ ▸*v.* **1** breathe out. **2** give off or be given off in vapor. —**ex·ha·la·tion** *n.*

**ex·haust** /igˈzôst/ ▸v.
**1** consume or use up the whole of. **2** [often as *adj.* **exhausted, exhausting**] tire out. **3** study or expound on (a subject) completely.
▸*n.* **1** waste gases, etc., expelled from an engine after combustion. **2** (also **ex·haust pipe**) pipe or system by which these are expelled.
—**ex·haus·tion** *n.*

**ex·haus·tlve** ▸*adj.* thorough; comprehensive.

**ex·hib·it** /igˈzibit/ ▸*v.* **1** show or reveal publicly. **2** display (a quality, etc.).
▸*n.* **1** thing or collection displayed. **2** item produced in court as evidence. —**ex·hi·bi·tion** *n.* —**ex·hib·i·tor** *n.*

**ex·hi·bi·tion·ism** /ˌeksəˈbisHə-ˌnizəm/ ▸*n.* tendency toward display or extravagant behavior. —**ex·hi·bi·tion·ist** *n.*

**ex·hil·a·rate** /igˈzilə,rāt/ ▸*v.* enliven; raise the spirits of. —**ex·hil·a·ra·tion** *n.*

**ex·hort** /igˈzôrt/ ▸*v.* urge strongly or earnestly. —**ex·hor·ta·tion** *n.* —**ex·hort·a·tive** *adj.*

**ex·hume** /igˈz(y)o͞om; ek-ˈs(y)o͞om/ ▸*v.* dig out; unearth (esp. a buried corpse). —**ex·hu·ma·tion** *n.*

**ex·i·gen·cy** /ˈeksijənsē/ (also **ex·i·gence**) ▸*n.* (*pl.* **-cies**) urgent need or demand. —**ex·i·gent** *adj.*

**ex·i·gent** /ˈeksijənt/ ▸*adj.* pressing; demanding.

**ex·ile** /ˈeg,zīl; ˈek,sīl/ ▸*n.*
**1** expulsion from one's native land. **2** long absence abroad. **3** exiled person.
▸*v.* send into exile.

**ex·ist** /igˈzist/ ▸*v.* **1** have a place in objective reality. **2** occur; be found. **3** continue in being; live. —**ex·is·tence** *n.* —**ex·is·tent** *adj.*

**ex·is·ten·tial** /ˌegziˈstenCHəl/ ▸*adj.* **1** of or relating to existence. **2** *Phllos.* concerned with human existence as viewed by existentialism. —**ex·is·ten·tial·ly** *adv.*

**ex·is·ten·tial·ism** ▸*n.* philosophical theory emphasizing the existence of the individual as a free and self-determining agent. —**ex·is·ten·tial·ist** *n.*

**ex·it** /ˈegzit; ˈeksit/ ▸*n.* **1** passage or door by which to leave a room, etc. **2** act or right of going out. **3** place to leave a highway. **4** actor's departure from the stage.

▶*v.* go out of a room, etc.

□ **exit poll** survey of voters leaving voting booths, used to predict an election's outcome, etc.

**exo-** ▶*comb. form* external.

**ex·o·bi·ol·o·gy** /ˌeksōbī'äləjē/ ▶*n.* branch of science that deals with the possibility and likely nature of life on other planets or in space.

**ex·o·dus** /'eksədəs/ ▶*n.* **1** mass departure. **2** (**Exodus**) **a** departure of the Israelites from Egypt. **b** the book of the Old Testament relating this.

**ex of·fi·cio** /'eks ə'fiSHēō/ ▶*adv. & adj.* by virtue of one's office.

**ex·og·a·my** /ek'sägəmē/ ▶*n.* custom of marrying outside a community, clan, or tribe.

**ex·on·er·ate** /ig'zänəˌrāt/ ▶*v.* free or declare free from blame, etc. —**ex·on·er·a·tion** *n.* —**ex·on·er·a·tive** *adj.*

**ex·or·bi·tant** /ig'zôrbitənt/ ▶*adj.* (of a price, etc.) grossly excessive. —**ex·or·bi·tance** *n.* —**ex·or·bi·tant·ly** *adv.*

**ex·o·sphere** /'eksōˌsfi(ə)r/ ▶*n.* furthermost layer of earth's atmosphere.

**ex·ot·ic** /ig'zätik/ ▶*adj.* **1** introduced from a foreign country. **2** attractively strange or unusual.

▶*n.* exotic person or thing.

**ex·pand** /ik'spand/ ▶*v.* **1** make or become larger or more important. **2** give a fuller account. —**ex·pand·a·ble** *adj.* —**ex·pan·sion** *n.*

**ex·panse** /ik'spans/ ▶*n.* wide continuous area.

**ex·pan·sive** ▶*adj.* **1** able or tending to expand. **2** extensive. **3** (of a person, etc.) effusive; open. —**ex·pan·sive·ly** *adv.* —**ex·pan·sive·ness** *n.*

**ex·pa·ti·ate** /ik'spāSHēˌāt/ ▶*v.* speak or write at length. —**ex·pa·ti·a·tion** *n.*

**ex·pa·tri·ate** /eks'pātrēit/ ▶*adj.* **1** living abroad. **2** exiled.

▶*n.* expatriate person.

▶*v.* expel (a person) from his or her native country. —**ex·pa·tri·a·tion** *n.*

**ex·pect** /ik'spekt/ ▶*v.* **1** regard as likely. **2** look for as appropriate or one's due. **3** *inf.* think; suppose. —**ex·pec·tant** *adj.* —**ex·pec·ta·tion** *n.*

□ **be expecting** *inf.* be pregnant.

**ex·pec·to·rate** /ik'spektəˌrāt/ ▶*v.* cough or spit out (phlegm, etc.). —**ex·pec·to·rant** *n.*

**ex·pe·di·ent** /ik'spēdēənt/ ▸*adj.* advantageous; advisable.
▸*n.* means of attaining an end.
—**ex·pe·di·ence** *n.*

**ex·pe·dite** /'ekspə,dīt/ ▸*v.* assist the progress of.

**ex·pe·di·tion** /,ekspə'disHən/ ▸*n.* **1** journey or voyage for a particular purpose, esp. exploration. **2** personnel undertaking this. **3** promptness.

**ex·pe·di·tious** ▸*adj.* acting or done with speed and efficiency.

**ex·pel** /ik'spel/ ▸*v.* (**-pelled**, **-pel·ling**) **1** deprive of membership, etc. **2** force out; eject.

**ex·pend** /ik'spend/ ▸*v.* spend or use up (money, time, etc.).
—**ex·pen·di·ture** *n.*

**ex·pend·a·ble** ▸*adj.* that may be sacrificed or dispensed with; not worth saving.
—**ex·pend·a·bil·i·ty** *n.*

**ex·pense** /ik'spens/ ▸*n.* **1** cost incurred. **2** amount paid to reimburse this. **3** thing that is a cause of expense.
□ **at the expense of** so as to cause damage, discredit, etc., to.

**ex·pen·sive** ▸*adj.* costing or charging much.

**ex·pe·ri·ence** /ik'spi(ə)rēəns/ ▸*n.* **1** observation of or practical acquaintance with facts or events. **2** knowledge or skill resulting from this. **3** activity participated in or observed.
▸*v.* have experience of; undergo.
—**ex·pe·ri·en·tial** *adj.*

**ex·pe·ri·enced** ▸*adj.* **1** having had much experience. **2** skilled from experience: *an experienced driver.*

**ex·per·i·ment** /ik'sperəmənt/ ▸*n.* procedure for testing a hypothesis, etc.
▸*v.* make an experiment.
—**ex·per·i·men·tal** *adj.*
—**ex·per·i·men·ta·tion** *n.*

**ex·pert** /'ek,spərt/ ▸*adj.* **1** having special knowledge or skill. **2** involving or resulting from this.
▸*n.* person having special knowledge or skill.

**ex·per·tise** /,ekspər'tēz/ ▸*n.* expert skill, knowledge, or judgment.

**ex·pi·ate** /'ekspē,āt/ ▸*v.* **1** pay the penalty for (wrongdoing). **2** make amends for.
—**ex·pi·a·to·ry** *adj.*
—**ex·pi·a·tion** *n.*

**ex·pire** /ik'spī(ə)r/ ▸*v.* **1** (of a period of time, validity, etc.)

come to an end. **2** cease to be valid. **3** die. —**ex·pi·ra·tion** *n.*

**ex·plain** /ik'splān/ ▶*v.* **1** make clear or intelligible. **2** say by way of explanation. **3** account for (one's conduct, etc.). —**ex·pla·na·tion** *n.* —**ex·plan·a·to·ry** *adj.*
□ **explain away** minimize the significance of by explanation.
□ **explain oneself** give an account of one's meaning, motives, etc.

**ex·ple·tive** /'eksplitiv/ ▶*n.* swearword or exclamation.

**ex·pli·cate** /'ekspli,kāt/ ▶*v.* **1** develop the meaning of (an idea, etc.). **2** explain (esp. a text). —**ex·pli·ca·tion** *n.*

**ex·plic·it** /ik'splisit/ ▶*adj.* **1** expressly stated; not merely implied. **2** definite; clear. **3** outspoken.

**ex·plode** /ik'splōd/ ▶*v.* **1** (cause to) expand suddenly with a loud noise owing to a release of internal energy. **2** give vent suddenly to emotion, esp. anger. **3** increase suddenly or rapidly. **4** show (a theory, etc.) to be false or baseless. —**ex·plo·sion** *n.* —**ex·plo·sive** *adj. & n.*

**ex·ploit** ▶*n.* /'ek,sploit/ daring feat.

▶*v.* /ik'sploit/ **1** make use of (a resource, etc.). **2** take advantage of (esp. a person) for one's own ends. —**ex·ploi·ta·tion** *n.* —**ex·ploit·a·tive** *adj.*

**ex·plore** /ik'splôr/ ▶*v.* **1** travel through (a country, etc.) to learn about it. **2** inquire into. —**ex·plo·ra·tion** *n.* —**ex·plor·a·to·ry** *adj.* —**ex·plor·er** *n.*

**ex·po·nent** /ik'spōnənt; 'ekspōnənt/ ▶*n.* **1** person who promotes an idea, etc. **2** practitioner of an activity, profession, etc. **3** type or representative. **4** *Math.* raised symbol beside a numeral indicating how many times it is to be multiplied by itself (e.g., $2^3$ = 2 x 2 x 2).

**ex·port** /ik'spôrt; 'ekspôrt/ ▶*v.* sell or send to another country. ▶*n.* **1** exporting. **2** exported article or service. —**ex·port·a·ble** *adj.* —**ex·por·ta·tion** *n.* —**ex·port·er** *n.*

**ex·pose** /ik'spōz/ ▶*v.* **1** leave uncovered or unprotected. **2** (**expose to**) **a** put at risk of. **b** introduce to: *exposed to the arts.* **3** subject (film) to light. **4** reveal. **5** exhibit; display. —**ex·po·sure** *n.*

**ex·po·sé** /ˌekspō'zā/ ▶n. revelation of something discreditable.

**ex·po·si·tion** /ˌekspə'zishən/ ▶n. **1** explanatory account. **2** explanation or commentary. **3** large public exhibition.

**ex·pos·i·to·ry** /eks'pəziˌtôrē/ ▶adj. intended to explain something: *expository prose*.

**ex·pos·tu·late** /ik'späschəˌlāt/ ▶v. make a protest; remonstrate.

**ex·pound** /ik'spound/ ▶v. **1** set out in detail. **2** explain or interpret.

**ex·press** /ik'spres/ ▶v. **1** represent or make known in words or by gestures, conduct, etc. **2** communicate. **3** represent by symbols. **4** squeeze out (liquid or air). ▶adj. **1** operating at high speed. **2** definitely stated. **3 a** done, made, or sent for a special purpose. **b** delivered by a special service. ▶adv. **1** at high speed. **2** by express shipment. ▶n. **1** fast train, etc. **2** service for rapid package delivery. —**ex·press·ly** adv.

**ex·pres·sion** ▶n. **1** expressing or being expressed. **2** word or phrase expressed. **3** manner of expressing. **4** person's facial appearance, indicating feeling. **5** depiction or conveyance of feeling, movement, etc., in art.

**ex·press·way** ▶n. high-speed highway.

**ex·pro·pri·ate** /ˌeks'prōprēˌāt/ ▶v. take away (property) from its owner. —**ex·pro·pri·a·tion** n.

**ex·pul·sion** /ik'spəlshən/ ▶n. expelling; being expelled.

**ex·punge** /ik'spənj/ ▶v. erase; remove.

**ex·pur·gate** /'ekspərˌgāt/ ▶v. remove objectionable matter from (a book, etc.). —**ex·pur·ga·tion** n.

**ex·qui·site** /ek'skwizit; 'ekskwizit/ ▶adj. **1** extremely beautiful or delicate. **2** keenly felt. **3** highly discriminating: *exquisite taste*.

**ex·tant** /'ekstənt/ ▶adj. still existing.

**ex·tem·po·ra·ne·ous** /ikˌstempə'rānēəs/ ▶adj. spoken or done without preparation.

**ex·tend** /ik'stend/ ▶v. **1** lengthen or make larger in space or time. **2** stretch or lay out at full length. **3** (cause to) stretch or span over a period of time. **4** reach or encompass. —**ex·ten·sion** n.

□ **extended family** family that includes nearby relatives.

**ex·ten·sive** /ik'stensiv/ ▶*adj.* **1** covering a large area. **2** far-reaching.

**ex·tent** /ik'stent/ ▶*n.* **1** space over which a thing extends. **2** degree; scope.

**ex·ten·u·ate** /ik'stenyo͞o,āt/ ▶*v.* [often as *adj.* **extenuating**] lessen the seeming seriousness of (guilt or an offense).

**ex·te·ri·or** /ik'stirēər/ ▶*adj.* **1** of or on the outer side. **2** coming from outside.
▶*n.* **1** outward aspect or surface. **2** outward demeanor.

**ex·ter·mi·nate** /ik'stərmə,nāt/ ▶*v.* destroy (a living thing) completely. **—ex·ter·mi·na·tion** *n.* **—ex·ter·mi·na·tor** *n.*

**ex·ter·nal** /ik'stərnl/ ▶*adj.* **1 a** of or on the outside or visible part. **b** coming or derived from the outside or an outside source. **2** foreign. **3** outside the conscious subject: *the external world.* **4** for use on the outside of the body.
▶*pl. n.* (**externals**) **1** outward features or aspect. **2** external circumstances. **3** inessentials. **—ex·ter·nal·ly** *adv.*

**ex·tinct** /ik'stiNG(k)t/ ▶*adj.* **1** that has died out. **2** (of a volcano) that no longer erupts. **—ex·tinc·tion** *n.*

**ex·tin·guish** /ik'stiNGgwisH/ ▶*v.* **1** cause (a flame, light, etc.) to die out. **2** destroy. **—ex·tin·guish·er** *n.*

**ex·tir·pate** /'ekstər,pāt/ ▶*v.* root out; destroy completely. **—ex·tir·pa·tion** *n.*

**ex·tol** /ik'stōl/ ▶*v.* (**-tolled, -tol·ling**) praise enthusiastically.

**ex·tort** /ik'stôrt/ ▶*v.* obtain by coercion. **—ex·tor·tion** *n.*

**ex·tra** /'ekstrə/ ▶*adj.* additional; more than usual, necessary, or expected.
▶*adv.* **1** more than usually. **2** additionally: *was charged extra.*
▶*n.* **1** extra thing. **2** thing for which an extra charge is made. **3** performer in a minor role.

**extra-** ▶*comb. form* **1** outside; beyond: *extragalactic.* **2** beyond the scope of: *extracurricular.*

**ex·tract** ▶*v.* /ik'strakt/ **1** remove or take out. **2** obtain (money, an admission, etc.) by pressure. **3** obtain (a natural resource) from the earth. **4** select (a passage of writing, music, etc.). **5** obtain (juice, etc.) by pressure, distillation, etc. **6** derive (pleasure, etc.).

▶ *n.* /'ek,strakt/ **1** short passage from a book, etc. **2** concentrated ingredient.

**ex·tra·cur·ric·u·lar** /,ekstrəkə-'rikyələr/ ▶ *adj.* (of a subject of study) not included in the normal curriculum.

**ex·tra·dite** /'ekstrə,dīt/ ▶ *v.* hand over (a person accused or convicted of a crime) to the country, state, etc., in which the crime was committed. —**ex·tra·di·tion** *n.*

**ex·tra·ne·ous** /ik'strānēəs/ ▶ *adj.* **1** of external origin. **2** separate; irrelevant; unrelated.

**ex·tra·or·di·nar·y** /ik'strôrdn-,erē/ ▶ *adj.* **1** unusual or remarkable. **2** unusually great. **3** (of a meeting, official, etc.) additional; special. —**ex·tra·or·di·nar·i·ly** *adv.*

**ex·trap·o·late** /ik'strapə,lāt/ ▶ *v.* calculate or derive approximately from known data, etc. —**ex·trap·o·la·tion** *n.*

**ex·tra·sen·so·ry** /,ekstrə-'sensərē/ ▶ *adj.* outside the known senses.

**ex·tra·ter·res·tri·al** /,ekstrətə-'restrēəl/ ▶ *adj.* outside the earth or its atmosphere.
▶ *n.* (in science fiction) being from outer space.

**ex·trav·a·gant** /ik'stravəgənt/ ▶ *adj.* **1** spending (esp. money) excessively. **2** costing much. **3** unreasonable; absurd. —**ex·trav·a·gance** *n.*

**ex·trav·a·gan·za** /ik,stravə-'ganzə/ ▶ *n.* spectacular theatrical production.

**ex·treme** /ik'strēm/ ▶ *adj.* **1** of a high or the highest degree: *in extreme danger.* **2** severe. **3** outermost. **4** on the far left or right of a political party. **5** risking life or injury: *extreme sports.*

▶ *n.* **1** one or other of two opposite things. **2** highest degree. **3** *Math.* first or last term of a ratio or series.

□ **go to extremes** take an extreme course of action. □ **go to the other extreme** take an opposite course of action.

**ex·trem·i·ty** /ik'stremitē/ ▶ *n.* (*pl.* -**ties**) **1** extreme point; end. **2** (**extremities**) the hands and feet. **3** extreme adversity.

**ex·tri·cate** /'ekstri,kāt/ ▶ *v.* free or disentangle from a difficulty, etc.

**ex·trin·sic** /ik'strinzik; -sik/ ▶ *adj.* **1** not inherent or intrinsic. **2** extraneous. **3** from without.

**ex·tro·vert** /'ekstrə,vərt/ ▶n. outgoing or sociable person. —**ex·tro·ver·sion** n. —**ex·tro·vert·ed** adj.

**ex·trude** /ik'strood/ ▶v. thrust or force out. —**ex·tru·sion** n.

**ex·u·ber·ant** /ig'zoobərənt/ ▶adj. **1** lively; high-spirited. **2** (of a plant, etc.) prolific. —**ex·u·ber·ance** n.

**ex·ude** /ig'zood/ ▶v. **1** ooze out. **2** display (an emotion, etc.) freely.

**ex·ult** /ig'zəlt/ ▶v. be joyful. —**ex·ul·ta·tion** n. —**ex·ult·ant** adj.

**ex·urb** /'eksərb/ ▶n. district outside a city, esp. a prosperous area beyond the suburbs.

**eye** /ī/ ▶n. **1** organ of sight. **2** eye characterized by the color of the iris. **3** region around the eye: *eyes red from crying.* **4** sight. **5** particular visual faculty. **6** leaf bud of a potato. **7** calm region at the center of a hurricane. **8** hole of a needle, etc. ▶v. (**eyed**, **eye·ing** or **ey·ing**) watch or observe closely. □ **all eyes 1** watching intently. **2** general attention: *all eyes were on us.* □ **eye for an eye** retaliation in kind. □ **have one's eye on** wish or plan to procure. □ **have an eye for** be partial to.

□ **keep an eye on 1** pay attention to. **2** take care of. □ **see eye to eye** be in agreement.

**eye·brow** ▶n. line of hair on the ridge above the eye socket.

**eye·ful** ▶n. (*pl.* **-fuls**) *inf.* **1** long, steady look. **2** visually striking person or thing.

**eye·lash** ▶n. each of the hairs growing on the edges of the eyelids. □ **by an eyelash** by a very small margin.

**eye·let** /'īlit/ ▶n. **1** small hole for string or rope, etc., to pass through. **2** metal ring reinforcement for this.

**eye·lid** ▶n. either of the skin folds closing to cover the eye.

**eye·o·pen·er** ▶n. *inf.* enlightening experience.

**eye·shad·ow** ▶n. cosmetic applied to the skin around the eyes.

**eye·sore** ▶n. visually offensive or ugly thing.

**eye·tooth** ▶n. canine tooth in the upper jaw.

**eye·wash** ▶n. *inf.* nonsense; insincere talk.

**eye·wit·ness** ▶n. person who saw thing happen.

**ey·rie** /'e(ə)rē/ ▶var. of AERIE.

# Ff

**F¹** /ef/ (also **f**) ▶*n.* (*pl.* **Fs** or **F's; f's**)
**1** sixth letter of the alphabet.
**2** *Mus.* fourth note of the
diatonic scale of C major.
**3** grade indicating failure.

**F²** (also **F.**) ▶*abbr.* **1** Fahrenheit.
**2** farad(s). **3** female.

**F³** ▶*symb. Chem.* fluorine.

**f** (also **f.**) ▶*abbr.* **1** female.
**2** feminine. **3** *Mus.* forte. **4** folio.
**5** focal length.

**FAA** ▶*abbr.* Federal Aviation
Administration.

**fa·ble** /ˈfābəl/ ▶*n.* **1** tale, esp.
with animals as characters,
conveying a moral. **2** lie.

**fab·ric** /ˈfabrik/ ▶*n.* **1** woven
material; textile. **2** essential
structure.

**fab·ri·cate** ▶*v.* **1** construct, esp.
from prepared components.
**2** invent (a story, etc.).
—**fab·ri·ca·tion** *n.*

**fab·u·late** /ˈfabyəˌlāt/ ▶*v.*
**1** relate (an event or events) as a
fable or story. **2** relate untrue or
invented stories.

**fab·u·list** /ˈfabyəlist/ ▶*n.*
**1** person who composes or
relates fables. **2** liar, esp. a
person who invents elaborate,
dishonest stories.

**fab·u·lous** /ˈfabyələs/ ▶*adj.*
**1** incredible; exaggerated;
absurd. **2** *inf.* marvelous.

**fa·çade** /fəˈsäd/ ▶*n.* **1** face of a
building, esp. its principal front.
**2** outward appearance or front,
esp. a deceptive one.

**face** /fās/ ▶*n.* **1** front of the head
from the forehead to the chin.
**2** expression of the facial
features. **3** surface; side. **4** dial
of a clock, etc. **5** outward
appearance or aspect.

▶*v.* **1** look or be positioned
toward or in a certain direction:
*facing the window.* **2** meet
resolutely or defiantly; confront:
*face one's critics.* **3** cover the
surface of (a thing) with a
coating, extra layer, etc.

□ **face the music** *inf.* put up with
or stand up to unpleasant
consequences. □ **face up to**
accept bravely; confront. □ **in
the face of 1** despite.
**2** confronted by. □ **save face**
avoid humiliation.

**face·less** ▶*adj.* **1** without

identity; purposely not identifiable. **2** without a face.

**face-lift** (also **face·lift**) ▸*n.* cosmetic surgery to remove wrinkles, etc.

**fac·et** /ˈfasət/ ▸*n.* **1** particular aspect of a thing. **2** one side of a cut gem. —**fac·et·ed** *adj.*

**fa·ce·tious** /fəˈsēSHəs/ ▸*adj.* characterized by flippant or inappropriate humor. —**fa·ce·tious·ly** *adv.* —**fa·ce·tious·ness** *n.*

**fa·cial** /ˈfāSHəl/ ▸*adj.* of or for the face.
▸*n.* beauty treatment for the face.

**fa·cile** /ˈfasəl/ ▸*adj.* **1** easily achieved but of little value. **2** fluent; ready; glib.

**fa·cil·i·tate** /fəˈsiləˌtāt/ ▸*v.* ease (a process, etc.). —**fa·cil·i·ta·tor** *n.*

**fa·cil·i·ty** ▸*n.* (*pl.* **-ties**) **1** ease. **2** fluency; dexterity; aptitude. **3** (**facilities**) **a** opportunity, equipment, or resources for doing something. **b** *inf.* (public) toilet.

**fac·ing** /ˈfāsiNG/ ▸*n.* **1** garment lining. **2** outer layer on the surface of a wall.

**fac·sim·i·le** /fakˈsiməlē/ ▸*n.* exact copy, esp. of writing, printing, etc., often one

produced by electronic scanning and transmission of data.

**fact** /fakt/ ▸*n.* **1** thing that is known to have occurred, to exist, or to be true. **2** truth; reality. —**fac·tu·al** *adj.*

**fac·tion** /ˈfakSHən/ ▸*n.* small organized dissenting group within a larger one. —**fac·tion·al** *adj.*

**fac·tious** ▸*adj.* of, characterized by, or inclined to faction.

**fac·toid** /ˈfakˌtoid/ ▸*n.* **1** brief or trivial item of news or information. **2** assumption or speculation that is reported and repeated so often that it becomes accepted as fact.

**fac·tor** /ˈfaktər/ ▸*n.* **1** circumstance, fact, or influence contributing to a result. **2** whole number, etc., that when multiplied with another produces a given number or expression.
▸*v.* resolve into factors or components.

**fac·to·ry** ▸*n.* (*pl.* **-ries**) building containing equipment for manufacturing machinery or goods.

**fac·ul·ta·tive** /ˈfakəlˌtātiv/ ▸*adj.* occurring optionally in response to circumstances rather than by nature.

**fac·ul·ty** /ˈfakəltē/ ▸*n.* **1** aptitude or ability for a particular activity. **2** inherent mental or physical power. **3** teaching staff.

**fad** /fad/ ▸*n.* craze; short-lived fashion. —**fad·dish** *adj.*

**fade** /fād/ ▸*v.* **1** lose or cause to lose color, light, or sound. **2** lose freshness or strength; droop. **3** (**fade in/out**) (of a photographic image, recorded sound, etc.) to appear or disappear gradually. ▸*n.* action or an instance of fading. □ **fade away** languish; grow thin.

**fa·er·ie** /ˈfe(ə)rē/ ▸*n.* **1** fairyland. **2** fairy. ▸*adj.* imaginary; mythical.

**fag·ot** /ˈfagət/ ▸*n.* **1** bundle of sticks or twigs bound together as fuel. **2** bundle of iron rods for heat treatment.

**Fahr·en·heit** /ˈferən,hīt/ ▸*adj.* of a scale of temperature on which water freezes at 32° and boils at 212°.

**fa·ience** /fīˈäns; fā-/ ▸*n.* glazed ceramic ware, in particular decorated tin-glazed earthenware.

**fail** /fāl/ ▸*v.* **1** not succeed; not pass: *failed to qualify* | *failed the exam.* **2** neglect to do something: *he failed to appear.* **3** disappoint. **4** (of crops) become lacking or insufficient. **5** become weaker; cease functioning: *her health is failing.* **6** (of an enterprise) collapse; come to nothing. —**fail·ure** *n.* □ **without fail** for certain; whatever happens.

**fail·ing** ▸*n.* fault; weakness. ▸*prep.* in default of; if not.

**fail-safe** ▸*adj.* reverting to a safe condition in the event of a breakdown, etc.

**fai·né·ant** /ˈfānēənt/ ▸*adj.* idle or ineffective.

**faint** /fānt/ ▸*adj.* **1** indistinct; dim; quiet. **2** weak or dizzy. **3** slight; remote: *a faint chance.* **4** feeble; halfhearted: *faint praise.* **5** timid: *a faint heart.* ▸*v.* lose consciousness. ▸*n.* sudden loss of consciousness.

**faint-hearted** ▸*adj.* cowardly; timid.

**fair** /fe(ə)r/ ▸*adj.* **1** just; unbiased; in accordance with the rules. **2** blond; light or pale. **3 a** of (only) moderate quality or amount; average. **b** considerable; satisfactory: *a fair chance of success.* **4** (of weather) fine and

dry; (of the wind) favorable.
**5** beautiful; attractive.
▶*adv.* in a fair manner: *play fair.*
▶*n.* **1** gathering of stalls,
amusements, etc., for public
(usu. outdoor) entertainment.
**2** exhibition, esp. commercial.

**fair game** ▶*n.* thing or person
one may legitimately pursue,
exploit, etc.

**fair play** ▶*n.* reasonable
treatment or behavior.

**fair·y** ▶*n.* (*pl.* **-ies**) small
imaginary being with magical
powers.
▶*adj.* of fairies; delicate; small.

**fair·y god·moth·er** ▶*n.*
benefactress.

**fair·y tale** (or **story**) ▶*n.* **1** tale
about fairies or other fantastic
creatures. **2** incredible story;
fabrication.

**fait ac·com·pli** /'fet əkäm'plē;
'fāt/ ▶*n.* thing that has already
happened or been decided
before those affected hear about
it, leaving them with no option
but to accept.

**faith** /fāтн/ ▶*n.* **1** complete trust
or confidence. **2** firm belief, esp.
without logical proof. **3** system
of religious belief. **4** duty to
fulfill a trust, promise, etc.: *keep
faith.*

**faith·ful** ▶*adj.* **1** showing faith.
**2** loyal; trustworthy; constant.
**3** accurate; true to fact.
—**faith·ful·ly** *adv.*
—**faith·ful·ness** *n.*

**fake** /fāk/ ▶*n.* **1** thing or person
that is not genuine. **2** trick.
**3** *Sports* feint.
▶*adj.* counterfeit; not genuine.
▶*v.* make a fake or imitation.
—**fak·er** *n.* —**fak·er·y** *n.*

**fa·kir** /fə'ki(ə)r; 'fākər/ ▶*n.* Muslim
(or, loosely, Hindu) religious
ascetic who lives solely on alms.

**fal·con** /'falkən; 'fôl-/ ▶*n.* bird of
prey having long pointed wings,
and sometimes trained to hunt
small game for sport.

**fall** /fôl/ ▶*v.* (*past* **fell**; *past part.*
**fall·en**) **1** go or come down
freely; descend. **2** cease to stand;
come to the ground. **3 a** (of hair,
clothing, etc.) hang down. **b** (of
ground, etc.) slope. **4** sink lower;
decline. **5** occur: *darkness fell.*
**6** (of the face) show dismay or
disappointment. **7** yield to
temptation. **8** (**fall under/within**)
be classed among. **9** pass into a
specified condition: *fall into
decay.* **10** die. **11** begin: *fell to
wondering.*
▶*n.* **1** act or instance of falling.
**2** that which has fallen, e.g.,

snow, rocks, etc. **3** decline in price, value, etc. **4** overthrow; downfall: *the fall of Rome.* **5** (**the Fall**) the biblical sin of Adam and its consequences. **6** (also **Fall**) autumn. **7** (**falls**) waterfall.

□ **fall apart** (or **to pieces**) **1** break into pieces. **2** be reduced to chaos. **3** lose one's capacity to cope. □ **fall back** retreat. □ **fall back on** have recourse to in difficulty. □ **fall into place** begin to make sense or cohere. □ **fall out** quarrel. □ **fall short** be or become inadequate. □ **fall through** fail; come to nothing.

**fal·la·cy** /ˈfaləsē/ ▶n. (pl. **-cies**) **1** mistaken belief. **2** faulty reasoning; unsound argument. —**fal·la·cious** adj.

**fall guy** ▶n. inf. **1** easy victim. **2** scapegoat.

**fal·li·ble** /ˈfaləbəl/ ▶adj. **1** capable of making mistakes. **2** liable to be erroneous. —**fal·li·bil·i·ty** n. —**fal·li·bly** adv.

**fall·ing star** ▶n. meteor.

**Fal·lo·pi·an tube** /fəˈlōpēən/ ▶n. either of two tubes along which ova travel from the ovaries to the uterus.

**fall·out** ▶n. **1** radioactive nuclear debris. **2** adverse side effects or results of a situation.

**fal·low** /ˈfalō/ ▶adj. **1** (of land) plowed but left unsown. **2** uncultivated.

**fal·set·to** /fôlˈsetō/ ▶n. (pl. **-tos**) male singing voice above the normal range.

**fal·ter** /ˈfôltər/ ▶v. **1** stumble; stagger; go unsteadily. **2** waver; lose courage. **3** stammer; speak hesitatingly. —**fal·ter·ing·ly** adv.

**fame** /fām/ ▶n. renown; state of being famous.

**fa·mil·iar** /fəˈmilyər/ ▶adj. **1 a** well acquainted. **b** often encountered or experienced. **2** excessively informal; impertinent. —**fa·mil·i·ar·i·ty** n.

**fam·i·ly** /ˈfam(ə)lē/ ▶n. (pl. **-lies**) **1** set of parents and children, or of relations. **2** descendants of a common ancestor. **3** brotherhood of persons or nations united by political or religious ties. **4** group of objects distinguished by common features. **5** *Biol.* group of related genera of organisms.

**fam·i·ly plan·ning** ▶n. birth control.

**fam·i·ly tree** ▶n. chart showing relationships and lines of descent.

**fam·ine** /ˈfamən/ ▶n. extreme scarcity, esp. of food.

**fam·ished** /ˈfamisʜt/ ▸*adj. inf.* very hungry.

**fa·mous** /ˈfāməs/ ▸*adj.*
**1** celebrated; well known. **2** *inf.* excellent.

**fam·u·lus** /ˈfamyələs/ ▸*n.* (*pl.* **-li** /-ˌlē; -ˌlī/) assistant or servant, esp. one working for a magician or scholar.

**fan** /fan/ ▸*n.* **1** apparatus, usu. with rotating blades, for ventilation, etc. **2** wide, flat device, waved to cool oneself. **3** devotee; follower.
▸*v.* (**fanned, fan·ning**) **1** blow a current of air on, with or as with a fan. **2** spread out in the shape of a fan.

**fa·nat·ic** /fəˈnatik/ ▸*n.* person filled with excessive and often misguided enthusiasm for something.
▸*adj.* excessively enthusiastic.
—**fa·nat·i·cal** *adj.*
—**fa·nat·i·cism** *n.*

**fan·ci·er** /ˈfansēər/ ▸*n.* connoisseur.

**fan·ci·ful** /ˈfansəfəl/ ▸*adj.* **1** (of a person or their thoughts and ideas) overimaginative and unrealistic. **2** designed to be exotically ornamental rather than practical.

**fan·cy** /ˈfansē/ ▸*adj.* (**-ci·er,** **-ci·est**) **1** decorative; elaborate. **2** (esp. of foodstuffs) high quality.
▸*v.* (**-cied**) **1** be inclined to suppose. **2** *inf.* feel a desire for: *do you fancy a drink?*
▸*n.* (*pl.* **-cies**) **1** individual taste or inclination. **2** whim. **3** supposition. **4 a** faculty of imagination. **b** mental image.

**fan·cy-free** ▸*adj.* free from emotional attachments.

**fan·fare** /ˈfanˌfe(ə)r/ ▸*n.* **1** short showy or ceremonious sounding of trumpets, bugles, etc. **2** elaborate display.

**fang** /faNG/ ▸*n.* **1** canine tooth, esp. of a dog or wolf. **2** tooth of a venomous snake, by which poison is injected. —**fanged** *adj.*

**fan·ny** /ˈfanē/ ▸*n.* (*pl.* **-nies**) *inf.* the buttocks.

**fan·ny pack** ▸*n.* pouch worn on a belt around the waist or hips.

**fan·ta·sia** /fanˈtāzʜə; fantəˈzēə/ ▸*n.* **1** musical composition with a free form and often an improvisatory style. **2** thing that is composed of a mixture of different forms or styles.

**fan·ta·size** /ˈfantəˌsīz/ ▸*v.* have or create a fantasy or fanciful vision (about). —**fan·ta·sist** *n.*

**fan·tas·tic** /fanˈtastik/ (also

**fan·tas·ti·cal**) ▸*adj.* **1** *inf.* excellent; extraordinary. **2** extravagantly fanciful. **3** grotesque. —**fan·tas·ti·cal·ly** *adv.*

**fan·ta·sy** /ˈfantəsē/ ▸*n.* (*pl.* **-sies**) **1** faculty of inventing images, esp. extravagant or visionary ones. **2** fanciful mental image; daydream. **3** fiction genre that features supernatural, magical, or otherworldly elements.

**far** /fär/ ▸*adv.* (**far·ther, far·thest** or **fur·ther, fur·thest**) **1** at or to or by a great distance: *far off.* **2** a long way (off) in space or time: *are you traveling far?* **3** to a great extent or degree; by much: *far better.*

▸*adj.* (**far·ther, far·thest** or **fur·ther, fur·thest**) **1** remote; distant: *a far cry.* **2** more distant: *the far end of the hall.* **3** extreme: *far right militants.*

□ **as far as 1** to the distance of (a place). **2** to the extent that: *travel as far as you like.* □ **by far** by a great amount. □ **so far 1** to such an extent or distance; to this point. **2** until now. □ **so far, so good** progress has been satisfactory up to now.

**far·a·way** ▸*adj.* **1** remote; long past. **2** (of a look) dreamy. **3** (of a voice) sounding as if from a distance.

**farce** /färs/ ▸*n.* **1 a** broadly comic dramatic work based on ludicrously improbable events. **b** this type of drama. **2** absurdly futile proceedings; pretense; mockery. —**far·ci·cal** *adj.*

**fare** /fe(ə)r/ ▸*n.* **1** price a passenger has to pay to be conveyed by bus, train, etc. **2** food.

▸*v.* progress; get on: *the party fared badly in the general election.*

**fare·well** ▸*interj.* good-bye; adieu.

▸*n.* leave-taking.

**far-fetched** ▸*adj.* (of an explanation) unconvincing; unlikely.

**far-flung** ▸*adj.* distant or remote.

**fa·ri·na** /fəˈrēnə/ ▸*n.* flour or meal of cereal, nuts, or starchy roots. —**far·i·na·ceous** *adj.*

**farm** /färm/ ▸*n.* **1** area of land and its buildings used under one management for growing crops, rearing animals, etc. **2** place or establishment for breeding a particular type of animal, growing fruit, etc.: *trout farm.*

▸*v.* **1 a** use (land) for growing crops, rearing animals, etc. **b** be

a farmer; work on a farm.
**2** (**farm out**) delegate or
subcontract (work) to others.
—**farm·a·ble** *adj.* —**farm·er** *n.*
—**farm·ing** *n.*

**farm hand** ▸*n.* worker on a
farm.

**fa·rouche** /fəˈro͞oSH/ ▸*adj.* sullen
or shy in company.

**far·row** /ˈfarō/ ▸*n.* **1** litter of
pigs. **2** birth of a litter.
▸*v.* (of a sow) produce (pigs).

**far·sight·ed** ▸*adj.* **1** having
foresight; prudent. **2** able to see
clearly only what is
comparatively distant.
—**far·sight·ed·ness** *n.*

**far·ther** /ˈfärT͟Hər/ (also **fur·ther**)
▸*adv.* **1** to or at a more advanced
point in space or time: *unsafe to
proceed farther.* **2** at a greater
distance: *nothing was farther from
his thoughts.*
▸*adj.* more distant or advanced: *on
the farther side.* —**far·ther·most**
*adj.*

**far·thest** (also **fur·thest**) ▸*adj.*
most distant.
▸*adv.* to or at the greatest
distance.

**fas·ces** /ˈfas,ēz/ ▸*pl. n.* **1** (in
ancient Rome) a bundle of rods
with a projecting ax blade,
carried by a lictor as a symbol of

a magistrate's power. **2** (in
Fascist Italy) such items used as
emblems of authority.

**fas·ci·cle** /ˈfasikəl/ ▸*n.*
separately published installment
of a book or other printed work.

**fas·ci·nate** /ˈfasə,nāt/ ▸*v.*
**1** capture the interest of; attract
irresistibly. **2** (esp. of a snake)
paralyze (a victim) with fear.
—**fas·ci·na·tion** *n.*

**Fas·cism** /ˈfasH,izəm/ ▸*n.*
extreme totalitarian right-wing
nationalist movement or
philosophy, as instituted in Italy
(1922–43). —**Fas·cist** *n. & adj.*

**fash·ion** /ˈfasHən/ ▸*n.* **1** current
popular custom or style, esp. in
dress. **2** manner or style of
doing something.
▸*v.* make or form.

**fash·ion·a·ble** ▸*adj.*
**1** following, suited to, or
influenced by the current
fashion. **2** characteristic of or
favored by those who are leaders
of social fashion.
—**fash·ion·a·bly** *adv.*

**fast** /fast/ ▸*adj.* **1** rapid; quick-
moving. **2** capable of or
intended for high speed: *a fast
car.* **3** ahead of the correct time.
**4** (of a photographic film)
needing only a short exposure.

**5** firmly fixed or attached. **6** (of a color) not fading. **7** immoral; dissipated.

▸*adv.* **1** quickly; in quick succession. **2** firmly; fixedly; tightly; securely. **3** soundly; completely: *fast asleep.*

▸*v.* abstain from all or some kinds of food or drink.

▸*n.* act or period of fasting.

**fast·en** /ˈfasən/ ▸*v.* **1** make or become fixed or secure. **2** lock securely; shut in. **3 a** direct (a look, thoughts, etc.) fixedly or intently. **b** focus or direct the attention fixedly upon. —**fas·ten·er** *n.*

**fast food** ▸*n.* food that can be prepared and served quickly and easily, esp. in a snack bar or restaurant.

**fas·tid·i·ous** /fasˈtidēəs/ ▸*adj.* **1** very careful in matters of choice or taste; fussy. **2** easily disgusted; squeamish. —**fas·tid·i·ous·ly** *adv.* —**fas·tid·i·ous·ness** *n.*

**fast·ness** ▸*n.* **1** stronghold or fortress. **2** state of being secure.

**fat** /fat/ ▸*n.* **1** natural oily or greasy substance occurring esp. in animal bodies. **2** part of anything containing this. **3** overabundance or excess.

▸*adj.* (**fat·ter**, **fat·test**) **1** corpulent; plump. **2** containing much fat. **3** (of land or resources) fertile; yielding abundantly. **4** thick; substantial. —**fat·ty** *adj.*

**fa·tal** /ˈfātl/ ▸*adj.* **1** causing or ending in death: *fatal accident.* **2** ruinous: *made a fatal mistake.* —**fa·tal·ly** *adv.*

**fa·tal·ism** ▸*n.* **1** belief that all events are predetermined and therefore inevitable. **2** submissive acceptance. —**fa·tal·ist** *n.* —**fa·tal·is·tic** *adj.*

**fa·tal·i·ty** /fāˈtalətē/ ▸*n.* (*pl.* **-ties**) occurrence of death by accident or in war, etc.

**fat cat** ▸*n. inf.* **1** wealthy person, esp. as a benefactor. **2** highly paid executive or official.

**fate** /fāt/ ▸*n.* **1** a power regarded as predetermining events unalterably. **2 a** the future regarded as determined by such a power. **b** an individual's appointed lot. **3** death; destruction.

▸*v.* (**be fated**) be destined to happen: *the relationship was fated to end badly.*

**fate·ful** ▸*adj.* **1** important; decisive. **2** controlled as if by fate. —**fate·ful·ly** *adv.*

**fa·ther** /ˈfäT͟Hər/ ▸*n.* **1** male

parent. **2** (**fathers**) progenitors or forefathers. **3** originator, designer, or early leader. **4** (also **Father**) (often as a title or form of address) priest. **5** (**the Father**) (in Christian belief) the first person of the Trinity. **6** elders: *city fathers.*

▶*v.* **1** beget; be the father of. **2** originate (a scheme, etc.). —**fa·ther·hood** *n.* —**fa·ther·less** *adj.*

☐ **fa·ther-in-law** father of one's husband or wife.

**fa·ther fig·ure** ▶*n.* older man who is respected like a father.

**fa·ther·land** ▶*n.* one's native country.

**fath·om** /ˈfaTHəm/ ▶*n.* measure of six feet, esp. used in taking depth soundings.

▶*v.* **1** grasp or comprehend. **2** measure the depth of. —**fath·om·a·ble** *adj.* —**fath·om·less** *adj.*

**fa·tigue** /fəˈtēg/ ▶*n.* **1** extreme tiredness. **2** weakness in materials, esp. metal. **3 a** menial, nonmilitary duty in the army. **b** (**fatigues**) clothing worn for this.

▶*v.* (**-tigued**, **-tigu·ing**) cause fatigue in.

**fat·ten** /ˈfatn/ ▶*v.* make or become fat.

**fat·u·ous** /ˈfaCHo͞oəs/ ▶*adj.* vacantly silly; purposeless; idiotic. —**fa·tu·i·ty** *n.* —**fat·u·ous·ly** *adv.*

**fat·wa** /ˈfätwä/ ▶*n.* ruling on a point of Islamic law given by a recognized authority.

**fau·cet** /ˈfôsit/ ▶*n.* device by which a flow of liquid from a pipe or vessel can be controlled.

**fault** /fôlt/ ▶*n.* **1** defect or imperfection. **2** misguided or dangerous action. **3** responsibility for wrongdoing, error, etc. **4** *Geol.* extended break in the continuity of strata or a vein.

▶*v.* find fault with; blame. —**fault·less** *adj.*

☐ **at fault 1** responsible for a misfortune. **2** mistaken or defective. ☐ **find fault** make an adverse criticism; complain: *he finds fault with everything I do.* ☐ **to a fault** excessively.

**faun** /fôn/ ▶*n.* Roman rural deity with a human face and torso and a goat's horns, legs, and tail.

**fau·na** /ˈfônə/ ▶*n.* (*pl.* **-nas** or **-nae**) animal life of a region or geological period.

**faux pas** /fō ˈpä/ ▶*n.* (*pl.* same)

**1** tactless mistake; blunder. **2** social indiscretion.

**fa·vor** /ˈfāvər/ ▸n. **1** act of kindness. **2** esteem; liking; approval; goodwill; friendly regard: *gained their favor.* **3** partiality. **4** small present or token given out, as at a party. ▸v. **1** regard or treat with favor or partiality. **2** give support or approval to; promote; prefer. **3 a** be to the advantage of (a person). **b** facilitate (a process, etc.). **4** *inf.* resemble in features.

**fa·vor·a·ble** ▸adj. **1** expressing approval. **2** giving consent. **3** advantageous. **4** (of weather) fine. **5** (of a wind) blowing in the right direction.

**fa·vor·ite** /ˈfāv(ə)rit/ ▸adj. preferred to all others: *my favorite book.* ▸n. **1** particularly favored person. **2** competitor thought most likely to win.

**fa·vor·it·ism** ▸n. unfair partiality.

**fawn** /fôn/ ▸n. **1** young deer in its first year. **2** light yellowish brown. ▸v. **1** (of a person) behave servilely in an attempt to win favor. **2** (of an animal, esp. a dog) show extreme affection.

**fax** /faks/ ▸n. **1** exact copy of a document made by electronic scanning and transmitted as data by telecommuncation links. **2** production or transmission of documents in this way. ▸v. transmit in this way.

**faze** /fāz/ ▸v. *inf.* disconcert; perturb; disorient.

**FBI** ▸abbr. Federal Bureau of Investigation.

**FCC** ▸abbr. Federal Communications Commission.

**FDA** ▸abbr. Food and Drug Administration.

**FDIC** ▸abbr. Federal Deposit Insurance Corporation.

**fear** /fi(ə)r/ ▸n. **1** panic or distress caused by exposure to danger, expectation of pain, etc. **2** cause of fear: *all fears removed.* **3** danger. ▸v. **1** feel fear about or toward (a person or thing). **2** (**fear for**) feel anxiety about. —**fear·ful** adj. —**fear·less** adj.

**fear·some** /ˈfi(ə)rsəm/ ▸adj. frightening, esp. in appearance.

**fea·si·ble** /ˈfēzəbəl/ ▸adj. practicable; possible. —**fea·si·bil·i·ty** n.

**feast** /fēst/ ▸n. **1** large or sumptuous meal, esp. with entertainment. **2** gratification to the senses or mind. **3** religious festival.

▶ *v.* partake of a feast; eat and drink sumptuously.

□ **feast one's eyes on** take pleasure in beholding.

**feat** /fēt/ ▶*n.* noteworthy act or achievement.

**feath·er** /ˈfeT͟Hər/ ▶*n.* any of the appendages growing from a bird's skin, with a horny hollow stem and fine strands.

▶ *v.* **1** cover or line with feathers. **2** turn (an oar) so that it passes through the air edgewise. **3** cause (propeller blades) to rotate in such a way as to lessen the air or water resistance. —**feath·ered** *adj.* —**feath·er·y** *adj.*

□ **feather in one's cap** achievement to one's credit. □ **feather one's nest** enrich oneself. □ **as light as a feather** extremely light.

**fea·ture** /ˈfēCHər/ ▶*n.* **1** distinctive or characteristic part of a thing. **2** (**features**) (distinctive parts of) the face. **3** distinctive or regular article in a newspaper or magazine. **4** (also **fea·ture film**) full-length movie intended as the main attraction at a showing.

▶ *v.* **1** make a special display or attraction of; give special prominence to. **2** star. —**fea·ture·less** *adj.*

**Feb.** ▶*abbr.* February.

**feb·ri·fuge** /ˈfebrəˌfyo͞oj/ ▶*n.* medicine used to reduce fever.

**fe·brile** /ˈfebˌrīl; ˈfēˌbrīl/ ▶*adj.* **1** having or showing the symptoms of a fever. **2** having or showing a great deal of nervous excitement or energy.

**Feb·ru·ar·y** /ˈfebro͞oˌerē; ˈfeb(y)o͞o-/ ▶*n.* (*pl.* **-ies**) second month of the year.

**fe·ces** /ˈfēsēz/ ▶*pl. n.* waste matter discharged from the bowels. —**fe·cal** *adj.*

**feck·less** /ˈfekləs/ ▶*adj.* **1** feeble; ineffective. **2** unthinking; irresponsible.

**fe·cund** /ˈfekənd; ˈfē-/ ▶*adj.* **1** prolific; fertile. **2** fertilizing. —**fe·cun·di·ty** *n.*

**fed** /fed/ ▶past and past part. of FEED.

□ **fed up** discontented; bored.

**fed·er·al** /ˈfed(ə)rəl/ ▶*adj.* **1** of a system of government in which several states or provinces, etc., form a union but remain independent in internal affairs. **2** of such a federation: *federal laws.* —**fed·er·al·ism** *n.*

—**fed·er·al·ist** *n.* —**fed·er·al·ly** *adv.*

**Fed·er·al Re·serve Sys·tem** ▸*n.* federal banking authority in the U.S. that controls credit and money flow and supervises member banks.

**fed·er·ate** /ˈfedəˌrāt/ ▸*v.* unite on a federal basis. —**fed·er·a·tion** *n.*

**fe·do·ra** /fəˈdôrə/ ▸*n.* soft felt hat with a curled brim.

**fee** /fē/ ▸*n.* **1** payment made for professional advice or services. **2** entrance or access charge.

**fee·ble** /ˈfēbəl/ ▸*adj.* **1** weak; infirm. **2** lacking energy, effectiveness, etc. —**fee·ble·ness** *n.* —**fee·bly** *adv.*

**feed** /fēd/ ▸*v.* (*past* and *past part.* **fed**) **1** give food to. **2** eat. **3** nourish. **4 a** maintain supply of raw material, fuel, etc., to (a fire, machine, etc.). **b** supply or send (an electronic signal) for broadcast, etc. **c** flow into. **5** (**feed on**) **a** be nourished by. **b** derive benefit from. ▸*n.* food, esp. for animals. —**feed·er** *n.*

**feed·back** ▸*n.* **1** information about the result of an experiment, etc.; response. **2** return of a fraction of the output signal to the input.

**feel** /fēl/ ▸*v.* (*past* and *past part.* **felt**) **1** examine, search, or perceive by touch. **2** experience, exhibit, or be conscious of (an emotion, conviction, etc.). **3** have a vague or unreasoned impression. **4** consider; think. **5** seem. **6** be consciously; consider oneself: *I feel happy.* **7** have sympathy or pity. ▸*n.* **1** feeling; testing by touch. **2** attendant sensation. **3** sense of touch. □ **feel like** have a wish for; be inclined toward. □ **feel up to** be ready to face or deal with. □ **feel one's way** proceed carefully; act cautiously.

**feel·er** ▸*n.* **1** organ in certain animals for sensing or for searching for food. **2** tentative proposal.

**feel·ing** ▸*n.* **1** capacity to feel; sense of touch. **2** belief not based on reason. **3** emotion. **4** (**feelings**) emotional susceptibilities or sympathies.

**feign** /fān/ ▸*v.* simulate; pretend.

**feint** /fānt/ ▸*n.* **1** sham attack or diversionary blow. **2** pretense. ▸*v.* make a feint.

**feist·y** /ˈfīstē/ ▶*adj.* (**feist·i·er, feist·i·est**) **1** having or showing exuberance and strong determination. **2** touchy and aggressive.

**fe·lic·i·tate** /fəˈlisəˌtāt/ ▶*v.* congratulate.
—**fe·lic·i·ta·tions** *pl. n.*

**fe·lic·i·tous** ▶*adj.* strikingly apt; pleasantly ingenious: *a felicitous phrase.*

**fe·lic·i·ty** ▶*n.* (*pl.* **-ties**) **1** intense happiness. **2 a** capacity for apt expression. **b** well-chosen phrase.

**fe·line** /ˈfēˌlīn/ ▶*adj.* **1** of the cat family. **2** catlike.
▶*n.* animal of the cat family.

**fell** /fel/ ▶ past of FALL *v.*
▶*v.* **1** cut down (esp. a tree). **2** strike or knock down (a person or animal).
▶*n.* hill or stetch of moorland.
▶*adj. poet.* ruthless; destructive.
□ **at** (or **in**) **one fell swoop** in a single (orig. deadly) action.

**fel·loes** /ˈfelōz/ ▶*pl. n.* outer rim of a wheel, to which the spokes are fixed.

**fel·low** /ˈfelō/ ▶*n.* **1** *inf.* man or boy. **2** (usu. **fellows**) **a** person of the same rank or otherwise associated with another: *the defense counsel conferred with her fellows.* **b** thing of the same kind as another; other of a pair: *the page has been torn away from its fellows.* **3** holder of a fellowship for a period of research. **4** member of a learned society.

**fel·low·ship** ▶*n.* **1** companionship; friendliness. **2** body of associates. **3** financial grant to a scholar.

**fel·on** /ˈfelən/ ▶*n.* person who has committed a felony.

**fel·o·ny** ▶*n.* (*pl.* **-nies**) serious, often violent, crime.
—**fe·lo·ni·ous** *adj.*

**felt**[1] /felt/ ▶*n.* cloth of matted and pressed fibers of wool, etc.

**felt**[2] ▶past and past part. of FEEL.

**fe·male** /ˈfēˌmāl/ ▶*adj.* **1** of the sex that can bear offspring or produce eggs. **2** (of plants) fruit-bearing. **3** of women or female animals or female plants. **4** (of a screw, socket, etc.) hollow to receive an inserted part.
▶*n.* female person, animal, or plant.

**fem·i·nine** /ˈfemənin/ ▶*adj.* **1** of women. **2** having womanly qualities. **3** *Gram.* of or denoting the gender proper to women's names.
▶*n. Gram.* feminine gender or word. —**fem·i·nin·i·ty** *n.*

**fem·i·nism** /ˈfeməˌnizəm/ ▶*n.* advocacy of women's rights on the ground of political, social, and economic equality of the sexes. —**fem·i·nist** *n.*

**fem·i·nize** /ˈfeməˌnīz/ ▶*v.* **1** make (something) more characteristic of or associated with women. **2** induce female sexual characteristics in (a male).

**fe·mur** /ˈfēmər/ ▶*n.* (*pl.* **fe·murs** or **fem·o·ra**) thigh bone. —**fem·o·ral** *adj.*

**fen** /fen/ ▶*n.* low and marshy or often flooded land.

**fence** /fens/ ▶*n.* **1** barrier, railing, etc., enclosing an area of ground. **2** *inf.* receiver of stolen goods.
▶*v.* **1** surround with or as with a fence. **2** *inf.* deal in (stolen goods). **3** practice the sport of fencing; use a sword. **4** evade answering. —**fenc·er** *n.*

**fend** /fend/ ▶*v.* **1** (**fend for**) look after (esp. oneself). **2** (**fend off**) keep away; ward off (an attack, etc.).

**fend·er** ▶*n.* **1** low frame bordering a fireplace. **2** shieldlike device or enclosure over or around the wheel of a motor vehicle, bicycle, etc.

**feng shui** /ˈfəNG ˈSHwē; -ˈSHwā/ ▶*n.* (in Chinese thought) a system of laws considered to govern spatial arrangement and orientation in relation to the flow of energy, and whose effects are taken into account when siting and designing buildings.

**fen·nel** /ˈfenl/ ▶*n.* yellow-flowered fragrant plant of the parsley family, used as flavoring.

**fe·ral** /ˈfi(ə)rəl; ˈferəl/ ▶*adj.* **1** (of an animal or plant) wild; untamed; uncultivated. **2** savage; brutal.

**fer·ment** /fərˈment/ ▶*n.* **1** agitation; excitement; tumult. **2 a** fermentation. **b** fermenting agent or leaven.
▶*v.* **1** undergo or subject to fermentation. **2** effervesce or cause to effervesce. **3** excite; stir up; foment. —**fer·ment·a·ble** *adj.* —**fer·ment·er** *n.*

**fer·men·ta·tion** /ˌfərmənˈtāSHən/ ▶*n.* **1** breakdown of a substance by microorganisms, such as yeasts and bacteria, usu. in the absence of oxygen, esp. of sugar in making alcohol. **2** agitation; excitement.

**fern** /fərn/ ▶*n.* (*pl.* same or **ferns**) flowerless plant reproducing by spores and usu. having feathery fronds.

**fe·ro·cious** /fəˈrōSHəs/ ▶*adj.* fierce; savage; wildly cruel. —**fe·roc·i·ty** *n.*

**fer·ret** /ˈferət/ ▶*n.* small domesticated polecat, used in catching rabbits, rats, etc. ▶*v.* search tenaciously.

**fer·ric** /ˈferik/ ▶*adj.* of or containing iron.

**Fer·ris wheel** /ˈferis/ ▶*n.* carnival ride consisting of a tall revolving vertical wheel with passenger cars.

**fer·rous** /ˈferəs/ ▶*adj.* containing iron.

**fer·ry** /ˈferē/ ▶*n.* (*pl.* **-ries**) boat or ship for conveying passengers and goods, esp. across water. ▶*v.* (**-ried**) **1** convey or go in a ferry. **2** transport from one place to another, esp. as a regular service.

**fer·tile** /ˈfərtl/ ▶*adj.* **1** (of soil) producing abundant vegetation or crops. **2 a** (of a seed, egg, etc.) capable of becoming a new individual. **b** (of animals and plants) able to reproduce. **3** producing new and inventive ideas. —**fer·til·i·ty** *n.*

**fer·til·ize** /ˈfərtl̩ˌīz/ ▶*v.* **1** make (soil, etc.) fertile or productive.

**2** cause (an egg, female animal, or plant) to develop or gestate by mating. —**fer·ti·liz·er** *n.* —**fer·ti·li·za·tion** *n.*

**fer·vent** /ˈfərvənt/ ▶*adj.* **1** ardent; impassioned; intense: *fervent hatred.* **2** hot; glowing. —**fer·ven·cy** *n.* —**fer·vent·ly** *adv.*

**fer·vid** /ˈfərvid/ ▶*adj.* intensely enthusiastic. —**fer·vid·ly** *adv.*

**fer·vor** ▶*n.* intensity of feeling.

**fes·ter** /ˈfestər/ ▶*v.* **1** make or become septic. **2** cause continuing annoyance. **3** rot; stagnate.

**fes·ti·val** /ˈfestəvəl/ ▶*n.* **1** day or period of celebration, religious or secular. **2** series of cultural events.

**fes·tive** ▶*adj.* **1** of or suitable for a festival. **2** joyous. —**fes·tiv·i·ty** *n.*

**fes·toon** /fesˈtoōn/ ▶*n.* chain of flowers, leaves, ribbons, etc., hung in a curve as a decoration. ▶*v.* (often **be festooned with**) adorn with or form into festoons; decorate elaborately.

**fet·a** /ˈfetə/ ▶*n.* crumbly white Greek cheese made of sheep's or goat's milk.

**fetch** /feCH/ ▶*v.* **1** go for and

bring back (a person or thing). **2** be sold for; realize (a price).

**fetch·ing** ▸*adj.* attractive.

**fête** /fāt; fet/ ▸*n.* **1** great entertainment; festival. **2** saint's day.

▸*v.* (usu. **be fêted**) honor or entertain lavishly.

**fet·id** /'fetid/ ▸*adj.* stinking. —**fet·id·ness** *n.*

**fe·tish** /'fetiSH/ ▸*n.* **1 a** inanimate object worshiped as magic. **b** thing evoking irrational devotion or respect. **2** thing abnormally stimulating or attracting sexual desire.

**fet·lock** /'fet,läk/ ▸*n.* **1** part of the back of a horse's leg above the hoof where a tuft of hair grows. **2** such a tuft of hair.

**fe·tor** /'fētər/ ▸*n.* strong, foul smell.

**fet·ter** /'fetər/ ▸*n.* **1** shackle for holding a prisoner by the ankles. **2** restraint or check.

▸*v.* **1** put into fetters. **2** restrict.

**fet·tle** /'fetl/ ▸*n.* condition or trim: *in fine fettle.*

**fe·tus** /'fētəs/ ▸*n.* unborn or unhatched offspring of a mammal, esp. a human one more than eight weeks after conception. —**fe·tal** *adj.*

**feud** /fyo͞od/ ▸*n.* prolonged mutual hostility, esp. between two families, tribes, etc.

▸*v.* conduct a feud.

**feu·dal** /'fyo͞odl/ ▸*adj.* according to or resembling feudalism.

**feu·dal·ism** ▸*n.* medieval social system whereby a vassal held land from a superior in exchange for allegiance and service.

**fe·ver** /'fēvər/ ▸*n.* **1 a** abnormally high body temperature, often with delirium, etc. **b** disease characterized by this: *scarlet fever.* **2** nervous excitement; agitation. —**fe·vered** *adj.* —**fe·ver·ish** *adj.*

**fe·ver pitch** ▸*n.* state of extreme excitement.

**few** /fyo͞o/ ▸*adj.* not many.

▸*n.* **1** (**a few**) some but not many. **2** not many. **3** (**the few**) **a** the minority. **b** the elect.

□ **not a few** considerable number.

**fey** /fā/ ▸*adj.* **1** strange; otherworldly; elfin; whimsical. **2** clairvoyant.

**fez** /fez/ ▸*n.* (*pl.* **fez·zes**) flat-topped conical red cap, worn by men in some Muslim countries.

**fi·an·cé** /,fēän'sā; fē'änsā/ (*fem.* **fi·an·cée**) ▸*n.* person to whom another is engaged to be married.

**fi·as·co** /fē'askō/ ▶*n.* (*pl.* **-cos**) ludicrous or humiliating failure or breakdown; ignominious result.

**fi·at** /'fē‚ät/ ▶*n.* **1** authorization. **2** decree or order.

**fib** /fib/ ▶*n.* trivial or venial lie. ▶*v.* (**fibbed, fib·bing**) tell a fib.

**fi·ber** /'fībər/ ▶*n.* **1** threads or filaments forming a tissue or textile. **2** piece of glass in the form of a thread. **3** substance formed of fibers or able to be spun, woven, or felted. **4** structure; character. —**fi·brous** *adj.*

**fi·ber·glass** ▶*n.* **1** textile fabric made from woven glass fibers. **2** plastic reinforced by glass fibers.

**fi·ber op·tics** ▶*n.* optics employing thin glass fibers, usu. for the transmission of light, esp. modulated to carry signals.

**fi·bril·la·tion** /‚fibrə'lāsHən/ ▶*n.* (of the heart muscle) uncoordinated contractions causing rapid and irregular heartbeat.

**fib·u·la** /'fibyələ/ ▶*n.* (*pl.* **-lae** or **-las**) smaller and outer of the two bones between the knee and the ankle in terrestrial vertebrates. —**fib·u·lar** *adj.*

**FICA** ▶*abbr.* Federal Insurance Contributions Act.

**fiche** /fēsH/ ▶*n.* (*pl.* same or **fiches**) microfiche.

**fick·le** /'fikəl/ ▶*adj.* inconstant or changeable, esp. in loyalty. —**fick·le·ness** *n.*

**fic·tion** /'fiksHən/ ▶*n.* **1** literature, esp. novels, describing imaginary events and people. **2** invented idea, thing, etc. —**fic·tion·al** *adj.* —**fic·tion·al·i·za·tion** *n.*

**fic·ti·tious** /fik'tisHəs/ ▶*adj.* **1** imaginary; unreal. **2** counterfeit; not genuine.

**fic·tive** /'fiktiv/ ▶*adj.* creating or created by imagination.

**fid·dle** /'fidl/ *inf.* ▶*n.* stringed instrument played with a bow, esp. a violin. ▶*v.* **1** play restlessly; fidget. **2** make minor adjustments; tinker. **3** play (on) the fiddle. —**fid·dler** *n.* □ **as fit as a fiddle** in very good health. □ **play second fiddle** take a subordinate role.

**fi·del·i·ty** /fi'delitē/ ▶*n.* **1** faithfulness; loyalty. **2** strict accuracy. **3** precision in reproduction of sound or video.

**fid·get** /ˈfijit/ ▸v. move or act restlessly or nervously. —**fid·get·y** adj.

**fi·du·ci·ar·y** /fiˈdōōSHē͞eˌerē/ ▸adj. **1** of a trust, trustee, or trusteeship. **2** held or given in trust.

▸n. (pl. **-ies**) trustee.

**fief** /fēf/ ▸n. **1** estate of land, esp. one held on condition of feudal service. **2** person's sphere of operation or control.

**field** /fēld/ ▸n. **1** area of open land, esp. one used for pasture or crops. **2** area rich in some natural product: *gas field.* **3** piece of land for a specified purpose. **4** participants in a contest, race, or sport. **5** expanse of ice, snow, sea, sky, etc. **6** area of activity or study. **7** region in which a force is effective: *magnetic field.* **8** range of perception: *field of view.*

▸v. **1** *Baseball* **a** act as a fielder. **b** catch (and return) (the ball). **2** deal with (a succession of questions, etc.).

☐ **play the field** *inf.* avoid exclusive attachment to one person or activity, etc.

**field·er** ▸n. *Baseball* player who occupies a defensive position in the field while the other team is batting.

**field glas·ses** ▸pl. n. binoculars for outdoor use.

**fiend** /fēnd/ ▸n. **1** evil spirit; demon. **2** very wicked or cruel person. **3** *inf.* person who is excessively fond of or addicted to something. —**fiend·ish** adj. —**fiend·ish·ly** adv.

**fierce** /fi(ə)rs/ ▸adj. (**fierc·er,** **fierc·est**) **1** vehemently aggressive or frightening. **2** eager; intense; ardent. **3** unpleasantly strong or intense. —**fierce·ly** adv.

**fi·er·y** /ˈfī(ə)rē/ ▸adj. (**-i·er, -i·est**) **1** consisting of or flaming with fire. **2** like fire in appearance; bright red. **3** hot; burning. **4** spirited.

**fi·es·ta** /fēˈestə/ ▸n. **1** (in Spanish-speaking regions) religious festival. **2** festivity or celebration.

**fife** /fīf/ ▸n. kind of small, shrill flute used with the drum in military music. —**fif·er** n.

**fif·teen** /fifˈtēn; ˈfifˌtēn/ ▸n. **1** one more than fourteen. **2** symbol for this (15, xv, XV). **3** size, etc., denoted by fifteen.

▸adj. that amount to fifteen. —**fif·teenth** adj. & n.

**fifth** /fifтн/ ▶*n.* **1** next after fourth. **2** any of five equal parts of a thing. **3** *Mus.* interval or chord spanning five consecutive notes in the diatonic scale (e.g., C to G). **4** (**the Fifth**) Fifth Amendment to the U.S. Constitution.
▶*adj.* that is the fifth. —**fifth·ly** *adv.*
□ **take the Fifth** exercise the right guaranteed by the Fifth Amendment to the Constitution of refusing to answer questions in order to avoid incriminating oneself.

**fif·ty** /'fiftē/ ▶*n.* (*pl.* **-ties**) **1** product of five and ten. **2** symbol for this (50, L). **3** (**fifties**) numbers from 50 to 59, esp. the years of a century or of a person's life.
▶*adj.* that amount to fifty. —**fif·ti·eth** *adj. & n.*
□ **fifty-fifty** equal; equally.

**fig** /fig/ ▶*n.* **1** soft pear-shaped fruit with many seeds, eaten fresh or dried. **2** (**fig tree**) deciduous tree having broad leaves and bearing figs.

**fig.** ▶*abbr.* figure.

**fight** /fīt/ ▶*v.* (*past* and *past part.* **fought**) **1** contend or struggle (against) in war, battle, single combat, etc. **2** argue; quarrel.
**3** strive determinedly to achieve or overcome something.
▶*n.* **1** battle; conflict; struggle. **2** argument. **3** power or inclination to fight. —**fight·er** *n.*
□ **fight off** repel with effort.

**fight·ing chance** ▶*n.* opportunity to succeed by great effort.

**fig·ment** /'figmənt/ ▶*n.* invented or imaginary thing.

**fig·u·ra·tive** /'figyərətiv/ ▶*adj.* **1** metaphorical, not literal. **2** of pictorial or sculptural representation. —**fig·u·ra·tive·ly** *adv.*

**fig·ure** /'figyər/ ▶*n.* **1** external form or bodily shape. **2 a** person as seen in outline but not identified. **b** person as contemplated mentally. **3** two-dimensional space enclosed by a line or lines, or a three-dimensional space enclosed by a surface or surfaces; any of the classes of these, e.g., the triangle, the sphere, etc. **4 a** numerical symbol or number, esp. any of the ten in Arabic notation. **b** amount of money; value. **5** (**figure of speech**) recognized form of rhetorical expression giving variety, force, etc., esp. a metaphor or hyperbole.

▶*v.* **1** calculate. **2** appear or be mentioned, esp. prominently. **3** *inf.* be likely or understandable.

□ **figure out 1** work out by arithmetic or logic. **2** estimate. **3** understand.

**fig·ure·head** ▶*n.* **1** nominal leader. **2** carving, usu. a bust or a full-length figure, at a ship's prow.

**fig·ure ska·ting** ▶*n.* sport of performing jumps, spins, patterns, etc., while ice skating. —**fig·ure ska·ter** *n.*

**fig·u·rine** /ˌfigyəˈrēn/ ▶*n.* statuette.

**fil·a·ment** /ˈfiləmənt/ ▶*n.* **1** threadlike body or fiber. **2** conducting wire or thread with a high melting point in an electric bulb.

**fil·bert** /ˈfilbərt/ ▶*n.* **1** cultivated hazel, bearing edible ovoid nuts. **2** this nut.

**filch** /filCH/ ▶*v.* pilfer; steal.

**file** /fīl/ ▶*n.* **1** folder, box, etc., for holding loose papers. **2** set of papers kept in this. **3** *Computing* collection of (usu. related) data stored under one name. **4** line of people or things one behind another. **5** tool with a roughened surface or surfaces, usu. of steel, for smoothing or shaping wood, fingernails, etc.

▶*v.* **1** place (papers) in a folder, box, etc., for reference. **2** submit a legal document, application, etc., to be placed on record. **3** walk in a file: *the children filed into the auditorium.* **4** smooth or shape with a file.

**fil·i·al** /ˈfilēəl/ ▶*adj.* **1** of or due from a son or daughter. **2** bearing the relation of offspring.

**fil·i·bus·ter** /ˈfiləˌbəstər/ ▶*v.* delay passage of a bill, approval of a nomination, etc., by making long speeches.

▶*n.* obstruction of progress in a legislative assembly by prolonged speaking.

**fil·i·gree** /ˈfiləˌgrē/ (also **fil·a·gree**) ▶*n.* **1** fine ornamental work of gold or silver or copper wire. **2** anything delicate resembling this.

**Fil·i·pi·no** /ˌfiləˈpēnō/ ▶*n.* (*pl.* **-nos**) native or inhabitant of the Philippines, a group of islands in the SW Pacific.

▶*adj.* of the Philippines or the Filipinos.

**fill** /fil/ ▶*v.* **1** make or become full. **2** occupy completely; spread over or through; pervade. **3** drill and put a filling into (a decayed tooth). **4** appoint a person to hold (a vacant post). **5** hold (a position). **6** carry out or supply (an order, commission, etc.). **7** occupy (vacant time). **8** (esp. of food) satisfy.

▶*n.* **1** as much as one wants or can bear. **2** enough to fill something.

☐ **fill in 1** add information to complete. **2** fill (a hole, etc.) completely. **3** (**fill in for**) act as a substitute for (someone). **4** inform (a person) more fully: *I'll fill you in on the details tomorrow.* ☐ **fill out 1** enlarge to the required size. **2** become enlarged or plump. **3** add information to complete (a document, etc.).

**fil·let** /fi'lā/ ▶*n.* **1** (usu. **fi·let**) **a** fleshy boneless piece of meat from near the loins or the ribs. **b** (**fillet steak**) tenderloin. **c** boned longitudinal section of a fish. **2** strip; band.

▶*v.* remove bones from (fish or meat).

**fil·lip** /'filəp/ ▶*n.* stimulus or incentive.

**fil·ly** /'filē/ ▶*n.* (*pl.* **-lies**) young female horse.

**film** /film/ ▶*n.* **1** strip or sheet of plastic or other flexible base coated with light-sensitive emulsion for exposure in a camera. **2** motion picture; movie. **3** thin coating or covering layer. **4** slight veil or haze, etc.

▶*v.* **1** make a movie or television film of (a book, etc.). **2** cover or become covered with or as with a film.

**film·strip** ▶*n.* series of transparencies in a strip for projection as still pictures.

**film·y** ▶*adj.* (**-i·er, -i·est**) **1** thin and translucent. **2** covered with or as with a film. —**film·i·ness** *n.*

**fil·ter** /'filtər/ ▶*n.* **1** porous device for removing impurities or solid particles from a liquid or gas passed through it. **2** screen or attachment for absorbing or modifying light, X rays, etc. **3** device for suppressing electrical or sound waves of frequencies not required.

▶*v.* **1** pass or cause to pass through a filter to remove unwanted material. **2** make way gradually: *people filtered out of the concert during the last set* **3** (of information) gradually become known: *the news began to filter in from the hospital.*

**filth** /filTH/ ▸*n.* **1** repugnant or extreme dirt; excrement; refuse. **2** vileness; corruption; obscenity. —**filth·y** *adj.*

**fin** /fin/ ▸*n.* **1** thin projection on the body of a fish, used for propelling and steering. **2** similar projection on an aircraft, car, etc.

**fi·na·gle** /fə'nāgəl/ ▸*v. inf.* obtain by devious means.

**fi·nal** /'finl/ ▸*adj.* **1** situated at the end; coming last. **2** conclusive; decisive.
▸*n.* **1** (also **finals**) last or deciding heat or game. **2** examination at the end of an academic course. —**fi·nal·ly** *adv.*

**fi·na·le** /fə'nalē; -'nälē/ ▸*n.* last movement or section of a piece of music or drama, etc.

**fi·nance** /'finans; fə'nans/ ▸*n.* **1** management of large amounts of (esp. public) money. **2** monetary support for an enterprise. **3** (**finances**) money resources.
▸*v.* provide funding for (a person or enterprise). —**fi·nan·cial** *adj.* —**fi·nan·cial·ly** *adv.*

**fi·nan·cier** /fə'nan,si(ə)r/ ▸*n.* capitalist.

**finch** /finCH/ ▸*n.* small seed-eating songbird having a stout bill and colorful plumage.

**find** /find/ ▸*v.* (*past* and *past part.* **found**) **1** discover by chance or effort: *found a key.* **2** succeed in obtaining. **3** seek out and provide or supply. **4** (of a jury, judge, etc.) decide and declare: *found him guilty | the jury found for the defendant.* **5** reach by a natural or normal process: *water finds its own level.*
▸*n.* **1** discovery of treasure, minerals, etc. **2** thing or person discovered, esp. when of value.
□ **find out** **1** discover or detect (a wrongdoer, etc.). **2** get information. **3** discover.

**fine**[1] /fin/ ▸*adj.* **1** of high quality: *they sell fine fabrics.* **2 a** excellent; of notable merit: *a fine painting.* **b** good; satisfactory: *that will be fine.* **3** pure; refined. **4** in good health. **5** (of weather, etc.) bright and clear. **6 a** thin; sharp. **b** in small particles.
▸*adv.* **1** finely. **2** *inf.* very well: *suits me fine.* —**fine·ness** *n.*
□ **fine-tune** make small adjustments to.

**fine**[2] ▸*n.* sum of money exacted as a penalty.

▸*v.* punish by a fine: *fined him $5.*
—**fin·a·ble** *adj.*

**fine arts** ▸*pl. n.* poetry, music, and esp. painting, sculpture, and architecture.

**fin·er·y** /ˈfīnərē/ ▸*n.* showy dress or decoration.

**fi·nesse** /fəˈnes/ ▸*n.*
**1** refinement. **2** subtle or delicate manipulation.
**3** artfulness, esp. in handling a difficulty tactfully.
▸*v.* use or achieve by finesse.

**fin·ger** /ˈfiNGgər/ ▸*n.* **1** any of the terminal projections of the hand (esp. other than the thumb).
**2** part of a glove, etc., intended to cover a finger. **3** finger-like object or structure.
▸*v.* **1** touch, feel, or handle with the fingers. **2** *Mus.* **a** play (a passage) with fingers used in a particular way. **b** play upon (an instrument) with the fingers.
—**fin·gered** *adj.*
□ **put one's finger on** locate or identify exactly.

**fin·ger·nail** ▸*n.* nail at the tip of each finger.

**fin·ger·print** ▸*n.* impression made on a surface by the fine ridges on the fingertips, esp. as used for identifying individuals.
▸*v.* record the fingerprints of.

**fin·i·al** /ˈfinēəl/ ▸*n.* **1** distinctive ornament at the apex of a roof, pinnacle, canopy, or similar structure in a building.
**2** ornament at the top, end, or corner of an object.

**fin·ick·y** /ˈfinikē/ ▸*adj.* **1** overly particular; fastidious. **2** detailed.
—**fin·ick·i·ness** *n.*

**fi·nis** /ˈfinis; fiˈnē/ ▸*n.* the end (used esp. at the end of a book, movie, etc.).

**fin·ish** /ˈfiniSH/ ▸*v.* **1** bring to an end; come to the end of; complete. **2** consume or get through the whole or the remainder of (food or drink): *finish your dinner.* **3** reach or come to the end. **4** treat the surface of (cloth, woodwork, etc.).
▸*n.* **1** end; last stage; completion. **2** method, material, or texture used for surface treatment of wood, cloth, etc. —**fin·ish·er** *n.*
□ **finish with** have no more to do with; complete one's use of or association with.

**fi·nite** /ˈfīnīt/ ▸*adj.* **1** limited; not infinite. **2** (of a part of a verb) having a specific number and person. —**fi·nite·ly** *adv.*
—**fin·i·tude** *n.*

**Finn** /fin/ ▸*n.* native or inhabitant

of Finland; person of Finnish descent.

**Finn·ish** ▸*adj.* of the Finns or their language.

▸*n.* language of the Finns.

**fiord** /fē'ôrd/ ▸var. of **FJORD**.

**fir** /fər/ ▸*n.* (also **fir tree**) evergreen coniferous tree with needles borne singly on the stems.

**fire** /fī(ə)r/ ▸*n.* **1 a** combustion of substances with oxygen, giving out bright light and heat. **b** flame or incandescence. **2** conflagration; destructive burning: *forest fire.* **3** burning fuel in a fireplace, furnace, etc. **4** fervor; spirit; vivacity. **5** burning heat; fever. ▸*v.* **1** discharge (a gun, etc.). **2** propel (a missile) from a gun, etc. **3** deliver or utter in rapid succession: *fired insults at us.* **4** *inf.* dismiss (an employee). **5** (of an engine) undergo ignition. **6** stimulate. **7 a** bake or dry (pottery, bricks, etc.). **b** cure (tea or tobacco) by artificial heat. □ **catch fire** begin to burn. □ **under fire 1** being shot at. **2** being rigorously criticized or questioned.

**fire·arm** ▸*n.* gun, esp. a pistol or rifle.

**fire·bomb** ▸*n.* incendiary bomb.

**fire·brand** /'fīr,brand/ ▸*n.* **1** person who is passionate about a particular cause, typically inciting change and taking radical action. **2** piece of burning wood.

**fire·crack·er** ▸*n.* explosive firework.

**fire de·part·ment** ▸*n.* organized body of firefighters trained and employed to extinguish fires.

**fire drill** ▸*n.* rehearsal of the procedures to be used in case of fire.

**fire en·gine** ▸*n.* vehicle carrying equipment for fighting large fires.

**fire es·cape** ▸*n.* emergency staircase or apparatus for escape from a building on fire.

**fire ex·tin·guish·er** ▸*n.* apparatus with a jet for discharging liquid chemicals, water, or foam to extinguish a fire.

**fire·fight·er** ▸*n.* person employed to extinguish fires.

**fire·fly** ▸*n.* (*pl.* **-flies**) soft-bodied beetle that emits phosphorescent light.

**fire·man** ▶*n.* (*pl.* **-men**)
**1** member of a fire department.
**2** person who tends a furnace.

**fire·place** ▶*n.* **1** place for a domestic fire, esp. a grate or hearth at the base of a chimney.
**2** structure surrounding this.
**3** area in front of this.

**fire·plug** ▶*n.* hydrant for a fire hose.

**fire·pow·er** ▶*n.* destructive capacity of guns, etc.

**fire·proof** ▶*adj.* able to resist fire or great heat.
▶*v.* make fireproof.

**fire·storm** ▶*n.* high wind or storm following a very intense fire.

**fire·trap** ▶*n.* building difficult to escape from in case of fire.

**fire·works** ▶*pl. n.* devices containing chemicals that explode with spectacular effects, used for display or celebration.

**fir·kin** /ˈfərkin/ ▶*n.* **1** small cask used chiefly for liquids, butter, or fish. **2** unit of liquid volume (about 11 gallons or 41 liters).

**firm** /fərm/ ▶*adj.* **1 a** of solid or compact structure. **b** fixed; stable. **2 a** resolute; determined. **b** steadfast; constant. **3** (of an offer, etc.) not liable to cancellation after acceptance.
▶*adv.* firmly.
▶*v.* make or become firm, secure, compact, or solid.
▶*n.* business concern, esp. one involving a partnership.
—**firm·ly** *adv.* —**firm·ness** *n.*

**fir·ma·ment** /ˈfərməmənt/ ▶*n.* the sky regarded as a vault or arch.

**first** /fərst/ ▶*adj.* **1** earliest in time or order. **2** foremost in position, rank, or importance. **3** most willing or likely. **4** basic or evident.
▶*n.* **1** person or thing first mentioned or occurring. **2** first gear. **3** first place in a race.
▶*adv.* **1** before any other person or thing. **2** before someone or something else. **3** for the first time.
□ **at first** at the beginning.

**first aid** ▶*n.* emergency medical treatment.

**first-born** ▶*adj.* eldest.
▶*n.* eldest child of a person.

**first class** ▶*n.* **1** set of persons or things grouped together as the best. **2** best accommodations in a train, ship, etc. **3** mail given priority.
▶*adj. & adv.* **1** of the best quality;

very good: *a large city should have a first-class orchestra.* **2** belonging to or traveling by first class: *first-class accommodations.*

**first cous·in** ▸*n.* see COUSIN.

**first gear** ▸*n.* see GEAR.

**first·hand** ▸*adj. & adv.* from the original source; direct.

**first la·dy** ▸*n.* wife of the U.S. president.

**first name** ▸*n.* personal name other than a family name.

**first per·son** ▸*n. Gram.* see PERSON.

**first-rate** ▸*adj.* of the highest class; excellent. ▸*adv.* **1** very well. **2** excellently.

**fis·cal** /ˈfiskəl/ ▸*adj.* of public revenue; of financial matters. —**fis·cal·ly** *adv.*
□ **fiscal year** year as reckoned for taxing or accounting.

**fish** /fiSH/ ▸*n.* (*pl.* same or **fish·es**) **1** vertebrate cold-blooded animal with gills and fins living wholly in water. **2** any animal living wholly in water, e.g., a cuttlefish, shellfish, jellyfish, etc. **3** flesh of fish as food. ▸*v.* **1** try to catch fish, esp. with a line or net. **2** fish for (a certain kind of fish) or in (a certain stretch of water). **3 a** search for in water or a concealed place

fishing for bluefish. **b** seek by indirect means: *fishing for compliments.* **4** (**fish something out**) retrieve something with careful or awkward searching.

**fish stor·y** ▸*n. inf.* exaggerated account.

**fish·y** ▸*adj.* (**-i·er, -i·est**) **1** of or like fish. **2** *inf.* of dubious character; questionable; suspect.

**fis·sile** /ˈfisəl; ˈfisˌīl/ ▸*adj.* (of an atom or element) able to undergo nuclear fission.

**fis·sion** /ˈfiSHən; ˈfiZHən/ ▸*n.* **1** splitting of a heavy atomic nucleus with a release of energy. **2** division of a cell as a mode of reproduction.

**fis·sure** /ˈfiSHər/ ▸*n.* opening, usu. long and narrow, made esp. by cracking, splitting, or separation of parts.

**fist** /fist/ ▸*n.* **1** tightly closed hand. **2** *inf.* handwriting.

**fist·i·cuffs** /ˈfistiˌkəfs/ ▸*pl. n.* fighting with the fists.

**fis·tu·la** /ˈfisCHələ/ ▸*n.* (*pl.* **-las** or **-lae** /-lē/) abnormal or surgically made passage between a hollow or tubular organ and the body surface, or between two hollow or tubular organs.

**fit** /fit/ ▸*adj.* (**fit·ter, fit·test**) **1 a** well adapted or suited.

**b** qualified; competent; worthy. **c** in a suitable condition; ready. **d** good enough. **2** in good health or athletic condition. **3** proper; becoming; right.

▶*v.* (**fit·ted, fit·ting**) **1 a** be of the right shape and size for: *the dress fits her* | *do the shoes fit?* **b** make the right size or shape. **2** (usu. **be fitted with**) supply; furnish; equip. **3** be in harmony with; befit; become: *it fits the occasion.*

▶*n.* **1** way in which a garment, component, etc., fits *that's a good fit.* **2** sudden seizure of epilepsy, hysteria, apoplexy, fainting, or paralysis, with unconsciousness or convulsions. **3** sudden short bout or burst. **—fit·ness** *n.* **—fit·ter** *n.*

☐ **fit in 1** be (esp. socially) compatible or accommodating. **2** find space or time for.

**fit·ful** ▶*adj.* active or occurring spasmodically or intermittently. **—fit·ful·ly** *adv.*

**fit·ting** ▶*n.* **1** process or an instance of having a garment, etc., fitted: *needed several fittings.* **2** (**fittings**) fixtures and furnishings of a building. ▶*adj.* proper; becoming; right.

**five** /fīv/ ▶*n.* **1** one more than four. **2** symbol for this (5, v, V).

▶*adj.* that amount to five.

**fix** /fiks/ ▶*v.* **1** make firm or stable; fasten; secure. **2** decide; specify (a price, date, etc.). **3** repair. **4** implant (an idea or memory) in the mind. **5** (**fix on/upon**) direct (one's eyes, attention, etc.) toward. **6** place definitely or permanently. **7** determine the exact nature, position, etc., of. **8** (of eyes, features, etc.) make or become rigid. **9** *inf.* secure or arrange fraudulently. **10** castrate or spay (an animal).

▶*n.* **1** *inf.* dilemma or predicament. **2** position found by bearings or astronomical observations. **3** *inf.* dose of a narcotic drug. **4** *inf.* bribery. **—fix·a·ble** *adj.* **—fix·ed·ly** *adv.* **—fix·er** *n.*

☐ **fix up 1** arrange; organize; prepare. **2** accommodate. **3** provide (a person) with. **4** restore; refurbish.

**fix·ate** /ˈfiksāt/ ▶*v.* **1** direct one's gaze on. **2** cause (a person) to become abnormally attached to persons, things, ideas, etc.

**fix·a·tion** ▶*n.* **1** obsession; concentration on a single idea. **2** act or an instance of being fixated.

**fixed in·come** ▸*n.* income deriving from a pension, investment at fixed interest, etc.: *most elderly people live on a fixed income.*

**fix·ings** ▸*pl. n.* **1** apparatus or equipment. **2** trimmings for a dish. **3** trimmings of a dress, etc.

**fix·i·ty** /ˈfiksitē/ ▸*n.* state of being unchanging or permanent.

**fix·ture** /ˈfikscʜər/ ▸*n.* something fixed in position.

**fizz** /fiz/ ▸*v.* **1** make a hissing or spluttering sound. **2** (of a drink) effervesce.
▸*n.* effervescence.

**fiz·zle** /ˈfizəl/ ▸*v.* make a feeble hissing or spluttering sound.
▸*n.* such a sound.
□ **fizzle out** end feebly.

**fjord** /fēˈôrd/ (also **fiord**) ▸*n.* long narrow inlet of the sea between high cliffs, as in Norway.

**FL** ▸*abbr.* Florida (in official postal use).

**fl.** ▸*abbr.* **1** floor. **2** floruit. **3** fluid.

**Fla.** ▸*abbr.* Florida.

**flab** /flab/ ▸*n. inf.* fat; flabbiness.

**flab·ber·gast** /ˈflabər,gast/ ▸*v. inf.* [usu. as *adj.* **flabbergasted**] overwhelm with astonishment; dumbfound.

**flab·by** ▸*adj.* (**-bi·er, -bi·est**) **1** (of flesh, etc.) hanging down; limp; flaccid. **2** (of language or character) feeble. —**flab·bi·ly** *adv.* —**flab·bi·ness** *n.*

**flac·cid** /ˈfla(k)sid/ ▸*adj.* limp; flabby; drooping. —**flac·cid·i·ty** *n.* —**flac·cid·ly** *adv.*

**flag** /flag/ ▸*n.* **1** piece of cloth, usu. oblong or square, used as a country's emblem or as a standard, signal, etc. **2** (also **flag·stone**) **a** flat, usu. rectangular stone slab used for paving.**b** (**flags**) pavement made of these.
▸*v.* (**flagged, flag·ging**) **1** grow tired; lose vigor; lag. **2** inform (a person) by flag signals. **3** mark (an item) for attention.
□ **flag down** signal to stop.

**flag**[3] ▸*n.* plant with a bladed leaf, esp. the iris.

**flag·el·late** /ˈflajə,lāt/ ▸*v.* scourge; flog. —**flag·el·la·tion** *n.*

**fla·gi·tious** /fləˈjisʜəs/ ▸*adj.* (of a person or their actions) criminal; villainous.

**flag·on** /ˈflagən/ ▸*n.* large vessel usu. with a handle, spout, and lid, to hold wine, etc.

**fla·grant** /ˈflāgrənt/ ▸*adj.* glaring; notorious; scandalous.

—**fla·gran·cy** *n.* —**fla·grant·ly** *adv.*

**flag·ship** ▸*n.* **1** ship having an admiral on board. **2** best or most important member, office, etc., of its kind.

**flail** /flāl/ ▸*n.* threshing tool consisting of a wooden staff with a short heavy stick swinging from it.
▸*v.* **1** beat. **2** wave or swing wildly or erratically.

**flair** /fle(ə)r/ ▸*n.* **1** instinct for selecting or performing what is excellent, useful, etc.; a talent: *has a flair for languages.* **2** talent or ability, esp. artistic or stylistic.

**flak** /flak/ (also **flack**) ▸*n.* **1** antiaircraft fire. **2** adverse criticism; abuse.

**flake** /flāk/ ▸*n.* **1 a** small thin light piece of snow. **b** similar piece of another material. **2** thin broad piece of material peeled or split off. **3** *inf.* crazy or eccentric person.
▸*v.* take off or come away in flakes.

**flak·y** ▸*adj.* (**-i·er, -i·est**) **1** of, like, or in flakes. **2** *inf.* crazy; eccentric. —**flak·i·ness** *n.*

**flam·bé** /fläm'bā/ ▸*v.* (**-béed**

/-'bād/, **-bé·ing**) cover (food) with liquor and set it alight briefly.

**flam·beau** /'flam,bō/ ▸*n.* (*pl.* **-beaus** or **-beaux** /-,bōz/) **1** flaming torch, esp. one made of several thick wicks dipped in wax. **2** large candlestick with several branches.

**flam·boy·ant** /flam'boiənt/ ▸*adj.* **1** ostentatious; showy. **2** floridly decorated. **3** gorgeously colored. —**flam·boy·ance** *n.* —**flam·boy·ant·ly** *adv.*

**flame** /flām/ ▸*n.* **1** ignited gas. **2** (usu. **flames**) visible combustion.
▸*v.* burn; blaze.
□ **old flame** *inf.* former boyfriend or girlfriend.

**fla·men·co** /flə'meNGkō/ ▸*n.* (*pl.* **-cos**) **1** style of Spanish gypsy guitar music. **2** dance performed to this music.

**fla·min·go** /flə'miNGgō/ ▸*n.* (*pl.* **-gos** or **-goes**) tall, long-necked, web-footed wading bird with crooked bill and pink, scarlet, and black plumage.

**flam·ma·ble** /'flaməbəl/ ▸*adj.* easily set on fire; inflammable. —**flam·ma·bil·i·ty** *n.*

**flâ·neur** /flä'nər; -'nœr/ (also **fla·neur**) ▸*n.* (*pl.* **flâ·neurs** *pronunc.* same) idler or lounger.

**flange** /flanj/ ▶n. projecting flat rim, etc., used for strengthening or attachment. —**flanged** adj.

**flank** /flaNGk/ ▶n. **1** side of the body between the ribs and the hip. **2** side of a mountain, building, etc. **3** side of an array of troops.
▶v. be situated at both sides of.

**flan·nel** /'flanl/ ▶n. woven wool fabric, usu. napless.

**flap** /flap/ ▶v. (**flapped**, **flap·ping**) **1** move (wings, the arms, etc.) up and down when flying, or as if flying. **2** swing or sway about; flutter.
▶n. **1** piece of cloth, wood, paper, etc., hinged or attached by one side only, e.g., the folded part of an envelope or a table leaf. **2** one up-and-down motion of a wing, an arm, etc. **3** inf. agitation; panic. **4** hinged or sliding section of a wing used to control lift and drag.

**flap·doo·dle** /'flap,doodl/ ▶n. nonsense.

**flap·per** /'flapər/ ▶n. **1** (in the 1920s) a fashionable young woman intent on enjoying herself and flouting conventional standards of behavior. **2** thing that flaps, esp.

a movable seal inside a toilet tank.

**flare** /fle(ə)r/ ▶n. **1 a** dazzling irregular flame or light. **b** sudden outburst of flame. **2** signal light, bright light, or firework used as a signal. **3** gradual widening, esp. of a skirt or trousers.
▶v. **1** burn suddenly with a bright unsteady flame. **2** burst into anger; burst forth. **3** widen, esp. toward the bottom.
□ **flare up** burst into a sudden blaze, anger, activity, etc.
□ **flare-up** sudden outburst.

**flash** /flasH/ ▶v. **1** emit or reflect or cause to emit or reflect light briefly, suddenly, or intermittently; gleam or cause to gleam. **2** send or reflect like a sudden flame. **3** burst suddenly into view or perception. **4 a** send (news, etc.) by radio, telegraph, etc. **b** signal to (a person) by shining lights or headlights briefly. **5** inf. show ostentatiously.
▶n. **1** sudden bright light or flame, e.g., of lightning. **2** very brief time; an instant. **3** brief, sudden burst of feeling, understanding, wit, etc.

**4** breaking news story. **5** bright patch of color.

**flash·back** ▸*n.* scene in a movie, novel, etc., set in a time earlier than the main action.

**flash·light** ▸*n.* battery-operated portable light.

**flash point** (or **flash·point**) ▸*n.* **1** temperature at which vapor from oil, etc., will ignite in air. **2** point at which anger, indignation, etc., becomes uncontrollable.

**flash·y** ▸*adj.* (**-i·er, -i·est**) showy; gaudy; cheaply attractive.

**flask** /flask/ ▸*n.* **1** narrow-necked bulbous bottle for wine, etc., or as used in chemistry. **2** pocket-sized beverage container.

**flat** /flat/ ▸*adj.* (**flat·ter, flat·test**) **1** horizontally level. **2** even; smooth; unbroken. **3** unqualified; plain; downright: *a flat denial.* **4** dull; monotonous: *spoke in a flat tone.* **5** (of a carbonated drink) having lost its effervescence; stale. **6** *Music* **a** below true or normal pitch: *the violins are flat.* **b** lowered a half step. **7** (of a tire) punctured; deflated. ▸*adv.* **1** lying at full length; spread out: *she was lying flat on the floor.* **2** *inf.* completely; absolutely. **3** *Music* below the true or normal pitch.

▸*n.* **1** flat part of anything; something flat. **2** apartment on one floor. **3** (usu. **flats**) level ground, esp. a plain or swamp. **4** *Music* **a** note lowered a half step below natural pitch. **b** sign (♭) indicating this. **5** *inf.* flat tire. —**flat·ly** *adv.* —**flat·ness** *n.* —**flat·ten** *v.*

□ **flat out 1** at top speed. **2** without hesitation or delay. **3** using all one's strength, energy, or resources.

**flat·fish** ▸*n.* any marine fish having both eyes on one side of a flattened body, including the sole, turbot, plaice, etc.

**flat·foot** ▸*n.* (*pl.* **-foots** or **-feet**) **1** (also **flat foot**) foot with a less than normal arch. **2** *inf.* police officer. —**flat·foot·ed** *adj.*

**flat·ter** /ˈflatər/ ▸*v.* **1** compliment unduly; overpraise, esp. for gain or advantage. **2** please, congratulate, or delude (oneself, etc.). **3** make (a person) appear to the best advantage: *that blouse flatters you.* **4** make (a person) feel honored. —**flat·ter·er** *n.* —**flat·ter·y** *n.*

**flat·u·lent** /ˈflaCHələnt/ ▶*adj.*
**1** having or producing intestinal gas. **2** (of speech, etc.) inflated; pretentious. —**flat·u·lence** *n.*

**fla·tus** /ˈflātəs/ ▶*n.* gas in or from the stomach or intestines, produced by swallowing air or by bacterial fermentation.

**flat·ware** ▶*n.* **1** forks, knives, spoons, etc. **2** plates, saucers, etc.

**flaunt** /flônt/ ▶*v.* display ostentatiously; show off.

**fla·ves·cent** /fləˈvesənt/ ▶*adj.* yellowish or turning yellow.

**fla·vor** /ˈflāvər/ ▶*n.* **1** distinctive mingled sensation of smell and taste. **2** indefinable characteristic quality.
▶*v.* give flavor to; season. —**fla·vor·ful** *adj.* —**fla·vor·less** *adj.*

**flaw** /flô/ ▶*n.* imperfection; blemish.
▶*v.* (usu. **be flawed**) (of an imperfection) mar, weaken, or invalidate (something). —**flawed** *adj.* —**flaw·less** *adj.* —**flaw·less·ly** *adv.* —**flaw·less·ness** *n.*

**flax** /flaks/ ▶*n.* **1** blue-flowered plant, cultivated for its textile fiber and its seeds. **2** dressed or undressed flax fibers.

**flay** /flā/ ▶*v.* **1** strip the skin or hide off, esp. by beating. **2** criticize severely.

**flea** /flē/ ▶*n.* small wingless jumping insect that feeds on human and other blood.

**flea mar·ket** ▶*n.* market selling secondhand goods, etc.

**fleck** /flek/ ▶*n.* **1** small particle or speck, esp. of dust. **2** spot.
▶*v.* mark with flecks.

**fledge** /flej/ ▶*v.* **1** (of a young bird) develop wing feathers that are large enough for flight. **2** provide (an arrow) with feathers.

**fledg·ling** /ˈflejliNG/ ▶*n.* **1** young bird. **2** inexperienced person.

**flee** /flē/ ▶*v.* (*past* and *past part.* **fled**) run away (from).

**fleece** /flēs/ ▶*n.* **1** woolly covering of a sheep or a similar animal. **2** soft warm fabric.
▶*v.* strip (a person) of money, valuables, etc.; swindle. —**fleeced** *adj.*

**fleet** /flēt/ ▶*n.* **1** navy; ships sailing together. **2** aircraft or vehicles operating under one command or proprietor.
▶*adj.* swift; nimble. —**fleet·ly** *adv.* —**fleet·ness** *n.*

**fleet·ing** ▶*adj.* transitory; brief.

**flense** /flens/ (also **flench** /flenCH/) ▸*v.* slice or strip the skin or fat from (a carcass, esp. that of a whale).

**flesh** /fleSH/ ▸*n.* **1** soft, esp. muscular, substance between the skin and bones of an animal or human. **2** the body as opposed to the mind or the soul, esp. considered as sinful. **3** pulpy substance of a fruit or a plant. **4** (also **flesh col·or**) yellowish pink color. □ **flesh and blood 1** the body or its substance. **2** humankind. **3** human nature, esp. as being fallible. **4** actually living, not imaginary or supernatural. □ **in the flesh** in bodily form; in person.

**flex** /fleks/ ▸*v.* **1** bend (a joint, limb, etc.) or be bent. **2** move (a muscle) or (of a muscle) be moved to bend a joint.

**flex·i·ble** /'fleksəbəl/ ▸*adj.* **1** able to bend without breaking; pliable. **2** adaptable; variable. —**flex·i·bil·i·ty** *n.*

**flib·ber·ti·gib·bet** /'flibərtē‚jibit/ ▸*n.* frivolous, flighty, or excessively talkative person.

**flick** /flik/ ▸*n.* **1 a** light, sharp, quickly retracted blow with a whip, etc. **b** sudden release of a bent finger or thumb. **2** sudden movement or jerk, esp. of the wrist. **3** *inf.* **a** a movie. **b** (**the flicks**) the movies. ▸*v.* strike or move with a flick.

**flick·er** ▸*v.* **1** shine or burn unsteadily. **2** flutter; quiver; vibrate. **3** appear briefly. ▸*n.* flickering movement, light, thought, etc.

**fli·er** /'flīər/ (also **fly·er**) ▸*n.* **1** aviator. **2** thing that flies. **3** (usu. **fly·er**) small handbill or circular.

**flight** /flīt/ ▸*n.* **1** swift movement or passage through the air. **2** journey made through the air or in space. **3** series, esp. of stairs. **4** fleeing; hasty retreat.

**flight at·ten·dant** ▸*n.* airline employee who attends to passengers' safety and comfort during flights.

**flight·less** ▸*adj.* (of a bird, etc.) naturally unable to fly.

**flight·y** ▸*adj.* (**-i·er, -i·est**) frivolous; fickle; changeable. —**flight·i·ness** *n.*

**flim·flam** /'flim‚flam/ ▸*n.* **1** nonsensical or insincere talk. **2** confidence game. ▸*v.* (**-flammed, -flam·ming**) swindle (someone) with a confidence game.

**flim·sy** /'flimzē/ ▸*adj.* (**-i·er, -i·est**) **1** insubstantial; easily damaged. **2** (of an excuse, etc.) unconvincing. **3** (of clothing) thin. —**flim·si·ness** *n.*

**flinch** /flinCH/ ▸*v.* **1** make a quick, nervous movement in instinctive reaction to fear, pain, etc. **2** (**flinch from**) avoid doing through fear or anxiety.

**fling** /fliNG/ ▸*v.* (*past* and *past part.* **flung**) **1** throw, rush, or let go of forcefully or hurriedly. **2** put or send suddenly or violently.

▸*n.* **1** spell of wild behavior: *he's had his fling.* **2** brief romance.

**flint** /flint/ ▸*n.* **1** hard gray stone of nearly pure silica. **2** piece of hard alloy used to give an igniting spark. —**flint·y** *adj.*

**flip** /flip/ ▸*v.* (**flipped, flip·ping**) **1** flick or toss (a coin, ball, etc.) with a quick movement so that it spins in the air. **2** turn or turn over; flick.

▸*n.* act of flipping.

▸*adj. inf.* glib; flippant.

**flip-flop** /'flip,flap/ ▸*n.* **1** usu. rubber sandal with a thong between the toes. **2** esp. sudden change of direction, attitude, policy, etc.

▸*v.* (**-flopped, -flop·ping**) change direction, attitude, policy, etc., esp. suddenly.

**flip·pant** /'flipənt/ ▸*adj.* treating serious things lightly; disrespectful. —**flip·pan·cy** *n.* —**flip·pant·ly** *adv.*

**flip·per** /'flipər/ ▸*n.* **1** broadened limb of a tortoise, penguin, etc., used in swimming. **2** attachment worn on the foot for underwater swimming.

**flirt** /flərt/ ▸*v.* **1** behave in a frivolously amorous or sexually enticing manner. **2** superficially interest oneself (with an idea, etc.). **3** trifle (with danger, etc.).

▸*n.* person who indulges in flirting. —**flir·ta·tion** *n.* —**flir·ta·tious** *adj.*

**flit** /flit/ ▸*v.* (**flit·ted, flit·ting**) move lightly, softly, or rapidly: *flitted from one room to another.*

**flitch** /flicH/ ▸*n.* side of bacon.

**float** /flōt/ ▸*v.* **1** rest or move or cause (a buoyant object) to rest or move on the surface of a liquid. **2** move or hover lightly in the air. **3 a** bring (a company, scheme, etc.) into being; launch. **b** offer (stock, shares, etc.) on the stock market. **4** circulate or cause (a rumor or idea) to circulate.

▸*n.* **1** thing that floats, esp.:

a raft. **b** cork or other buoyant object on a fishing line. **c** floating device on the surface of water, fuel, etc., controlling the flow. **2** platform mounted on a truck or trailer and carrying a display in a parade, etc.

**flock** /fläk/ ▸n. **1 a** number of animals of one kind, esp. birds, feeding or traveling together. **b** number of domestic animals, esp. sheep, goats, or geese, kept together. **2** large crowd of people. **3** Christian congregation or body of believers, esp. in relation to one minister.
▸v. **1** congregate; mass. **2** go together in a crowd; troop.

**floe** /flō/ ▸n. sheet of floating ice.

**flog** /fläg/ ▸v. (**flogged, flog·ging**) beat with a whip, stick, etc.

**flood** /fləd/ ▸n. **1 a** overflowing or influx of water, esp. over land; inundation. **b** the water that overflows. **2 a** outpouring of water; torrent. **b** abundance or excess. **3** (**the Flood**) the biblical flood brought by God upon the earth (Gen. 6 ff.). **4** inflow of the tide: *flood tide.*
▸v. **1** cover with or overflow in a flood. **2** irrigate, deluge, or overfill.

**flood·light** ▸n. large powerful light to illuminate a building, stage, etc.
▸v. illuminate with floodlights.

**floor** /flôr/ ▸n. **1** lower surface of a room. **2** bottom of the sea, a cave, a cavity, etc. **3** one level of a building; story. **4 a** (in a legislative assembly) the part of the house where members meet. **b** right to speak next in a debate: *gave him the floor.* **5** minimum of prices, wages, etc.
▸v. **1** furnish with a floor. **2** bring or knock (a person) down. **3** *inf.* confound; baffle.
□ **take the floor 1** begin to dance on a dance floor, etc. **2** speak in a debate, at a meeting, etc.

**floor·ing** ▸n. material to make or cover a floor.

**floor show** ▸n. entertainment presented at a nightclub, etc.

**flop** /fläp/ ▸v. (**flopped, flop·ping**) **1** sway about loosely. **2** sit, kneel, lie, or fall awkwardly or suddenly. **3** *inf.* fail; collapse. **4** make a dull sound as of a soft body landing.
▸n. **1** flopping movement or sound. **2** *inf.* failure.

**flop·py** ▸adj. (**-pi·er, -pi·est**) tending to flop; not firm or rigid.
▸n. (also **flop·py disk**) (*pl.* **-pies**)

*Computing* removable disk on a flexible magnetic medium for the storage of data.

**flo·ra** /'flôrə/ ▶*n.* (*pl.* **-ras** or **-rae**) plants of a particular region, geological period, or environment.

**flo·ral** ▶*adj.* **1** of or depicting flowers. **2** of flora or floras.

**flor·id** /'flôrid/ ▶*adj.* **1** ruddy; flushed. **2** elaborately ornate. —**flo·rid·i·ty** *n.*

**flo·rist** ▶*n.* person who deals in or grows flowers.

**floss** /flôs/ ▶*n.* **1** silk thread used in embroidery. **2** DENTAL FLOSS. ▶*v.* clean (teeth) with dental floss.

**flo·til·la** /flō'tilə/ ▶*n.* small fleet of boats or naval vessels.

**flot·sam** /'flätsəm/ ▶*n.* wreckage floating at sea.
□ **flotsam and jetsam** **1** odds and ends; rubbish. **2** vagrants, etc.

**flounce** /flouns/ ▶*v.* go or move with an agitated, violent, or impatient motion. ▶*n.* **1** flouncing movement. **2** deep frill on a skirt, etc.

**floun·der** /'floundər/ ▶*v.* **1** struggle in mud, or as if in mud, or when wading. **2** become confused. ▶*n.* type of edible flatfish.

**flour** /'flou(ə)r/ ▶*n.* **1** meal or powder obtained by grinding grain, esp. wheat. **2** any fine powder. —**flour·y** *adj.*

**flour·ish** /'flərisH/ ▶*v.* **1** grow vigorously; thrive; prosper. **2** wave (a weapon, one's limbs, etc.) vigorously. ▶*n.* **1** ostentatious gesture with a weapon, a hand, etc. **2** ornamental curving decoration of handwriting. **3** fanfare or ornate musical passage.

**flout** /flout/ ▶*v.* express contempt for (the law, rules, etc.) by word or action; mock; insult.

**flow** /flo/ ▶*v.* **1** glide along as a stream. **2** move smoothly or steadily. **3** (of hair, etc.) hang easily or gracefully. **4** be supplied and drunk in large quantities. **5** result from; be caused by. ▶*n.* **1** flowing movement. **2** copious outpouring; stream. **3** rise of a tide or a river: *ebb and flow.*

**flow chart** (also **flow·chart** or **flow diagram**) ▶*n.* diagram of the movement or action of things or persons engaged in a complex activity.

**flow·er** /'flouər/ ▶*n.* **1** part of a plant from which the fruit or seed is developed. **2** blossom, esp. on a stem and used in bunches for decoration. **3** plant cultivated or noted for its flowers.

▶*v.* **1** bloom or blossom. **2** reach a peak.

□ **the flower of** the best or best part of.

**flu** /flo͞o/ ▶*n.* influenza.

**fluc·tu·ate** /'fləkCHo͞oˌāt/ ▶*v.* vary irregularly; be unstable; vacillate; rise and fall. **—fluc·tu·a·tion** *n.*

**flue** /flo͞o/ ▶*n.* **1** smoke duct in a chimney. **2** channel for conveying heat, esp. a hot-air passage in a wall.

**flu·ent** /'flo͞oənt/ ▶*adj.* **1** flowing naturally and readily. **2** verbally facile, esp. in a foreign language. **—flu·en·cy** *n.* **—flu·ent·ly** *adv.*

**fluff** /fləf/ ▶*n.* **1** soft, light, feathery material coming off blankets, etc. **2** soft fur or feathers. **3** *inf.* mistake in a performance, etc.

▶*v.* **1** shake into or become a soft mass. **2** *inf.* make a mistake in; blunder: *fluffed his opening line.*

**flu·id** /'flo͞oid/ ▶*n.* substance, esp. a gas or liquid, whose shape is determined by its container.

▶*adj.* **1** able to flow and alter shape freely. **2** constantly changing. **—flu·id·i·ty** *n.* **—flu·id·ly** *adv.*

□ **fluid ounce** see OUNCE.

**fluke** /flo͞ok/ ▶*n.* **1** lucky accident. **2** flat parasitic worm. **3** flatfish, esp. a flounder. **4** barbed arm of an anchor. **5** lobe of a whale's tail.

**flume** /flo͞om/ ▶*n.* **1** artificial channel conveying water, etc. **2** ravine with a stream.

**flum·mer·y** /'fləmərē/ ▶*n.* (*pl.* **-mer·ies**) empty compliments; nonsense.

**flunk** /fləNGk/ ▶*v. inf.* **1 a** fail (an examination, etc.). **b** fail (an examination candidate). **2** fail utterly; give up.

**flun·ky** (also **flun·key**) ▶*n.* (*pl.* **-kies** or **-keys**) **1** liveried servant. **2** toady; underling.

**flu·o·res·cence** /flo͞o(ə)'resəns; flôr'esəns/ ▶*n.* **1** light radiation from certain substances. **2** property of absorbing light of short (invisible) wavelength and emitting light of longer (visible) wavelength. **—flu·o·res·cent** *adj.*

**flu·o·ride** /'flo͞orˌīd; 'flôr-/ ▶*n.* any binary compound of fluorine.

**flu·o·rine** /'flo͞orˌēn; flôr-/ ▶*n.* poisonous pale yellow gaseous element of the halogen group. (Symb.: **F**).

**flur·ry** /ˈflərē/ ▶*n.* (*pl.* **-ries**) **1** gust or squall (esp. of snow). **2** sudden burst of activity.
▶*v.* (**-ried**) confuse by haste or noise; agitate.

**flush** /fləSH/ ▶*v.* **1** make or become red; blush. **2** cleanse by a flow of water. **3** drive out from cover.
▶*n.* **1** blush. **2** rush of emotion. **3** cleansing with a rush of water.
▶*adj.* **1** in the same plane; even. **2** *inf.* having plenty of money.

**flus·ter** /ˈfləstər/ ▶*v.* make or become nervous or confused.
▶*n.* confused or agitated state.

**flute** /flo͞ot/ ▶*n.* **1** high-pitched wind instrument of metal or wood, having holes along it stopped by the fingers or keys. **2** cylindrical groove. —**flut·ist** *n.*

**flut·ter** /ˈflətər/ ▶*v.* **1 a** flap the wings in flying or trying to fly. **2** fall with a quivering motion. **3** move or cause to move irregularly or tremblingly. **4** go about restlessly; flit; hover.
▶*n.* **1** act of fluttering. **2** tremulous state of excitement. —**flut·ter·y** *adj.*

**flux** /fləks/ ▶*n.* **1** process of flowing or flowing out. **2** continuous change: *in a state of flux.* **3** substance mixed with a metal, etc., to promote fusion.

**fly¹** /flī/ ▶*v.* (*past* **flew**; *past part.* **flown**) **1** move through the air under control, esp. with wings. **2** travel through the air or through space. **3** wave or flutter. **4** hasten or spring violently. **5** flee (from). **6** *Baseball* hit a fly ball.
▶*n.* (*pl.* **-ies**) **1** flap on a garment, esp. trousers, to contain or cover a fastening. **2** (**flies**) space over the proscenium in a theater. **3** *Baseball* batted ball hit high in the air.
□ **fly off the handle** *inf.* lose one's temper suddenly and unexpectedly.

**fly²** ▶*n.* (*pl.* **flies**) **1** insect with two usu. transparent wings. **2** natural or artificial fly used as bait in fishing.
□ **fly in the ointment** minor irritation that spoils enjoyment.

**fly-by-night** ▶*adj.* **1** unreliable. **2** short-lived.

**fly-fishing** ▶*n.* fishing using a rod and an artificial fly as bait.

**fly·leaf** ▶*n.* (*pl.* **-leaves**) blank leaf at the beginning or end of a book.

**fly·wheel** ▶*n.* heavy wheel on a

revolving shaft used to regulate machinery or accumulate power.

**foal** /fōl/ ▶*n.* young of a horse or related animal.

▶*v.* (of a mare, etc.) give birth to (a foal).

**foam** /fōm/ ▶*n.* **1** mass of small bubbles formed on or in liquid. **2** froth of saliva or sweat. **3** substance resembling these, e.g., rubber or plastic in a cellular mass.

▶*v.* **1** emit foam; froth. **2** run with foam. —**foam·y** *adj.*

**fob** /fäb/ ▶*n.* **1** (also **fob chain**) chain of a pocket watch. **2** small pocket. **3** tab on a key ring.

▶*v.* (**fobbed, fob·bing**) cheat; deceive.

☐ **fob off** deceive into accepting something inferior.

**fo·cus** /ˈfōkəs/ ▶*n.* (*pl.* **-cus·es** or **-ci**) **1 a** point at which rays or waves meet after reflection or refraction. **b** the point from which diverging rays or waves appear to proceed. (Also called **focal point**). **2 a** point at which an object must be situated for an image of it given by a lens or mirror to be well defined: *bring into focus.* **b** adjustment of the eye or a lens necessary to produce a clear image. **3** center of interest or activity.

▶*v.* (**-cused, -cus·ing; -cussed, -cus·sing**) **1** bring into or adjust the focus (of). **2** concentrate or be concentrated on.

**fo·cus group** ▶*n.* group that meets to discuss a particular problem, issue, etc.

**fod·der** /ˈfädər/ ▶*n.* dried hay, straw, etc., for cattle, horses, etc.

**foe** /fō/ ▶*n.* enemy or opponent.

**fog** /fôg/ ▶*n.* **1** thick cloud of water droplets or smoke suspended in the atmosphere at or near the earth's surface. **2** uncertain or confused position or state.

▶*v.* (**fogged, fog·ging**) **1** cover with or confuse as if with a fog. **2** become covered with fog or condensed vapor.

**fo·gey** /ˈfōgē/ (also **fo·gy**) ▶*n.* (*pl.* **-geys** or **-gies**) person, typically an old one, who is considered to be old-fashioned or conservative in attitude or tastes.

**fo·gy** /ˈfōgē/ (also **fo·gey**) ▶*n.* (*pl.* **-gies** or **-geys**) dull old-fashioned person, esp. as: *old fogy.*

**foi·ble** /ˈfoibəl/ ▶*n.* minor weakness or idiosyncrasy.

**foil** /foil/ ▸*v.* frustrate; baffle; defeat.

▸*n.* **1** metal hammered or rolled into a thin sheet. **2** person or thing setting off another by contrast. **3** light blunt sword used in fencing.

**foist** /foist/ ▸*v.* impose (an unwelcome person or thing).

**fold** /fōld/ ▸*v.* **1** bend or close (a flexible thing) over upon itself. **2** become or be able to be folded. **3** make compact by folding. **4** *inf.* collapse; disintegrate. **5** clasp (the arms); wrap; envelop.

▸*n.* **1** line made by or for folding. **2** folded part. **3** SHEEPFOLD. **4** body of believers or members of a church.

**-fold** ▸*suffix* forming adjectives and adverbs from cardinal numbers, meaning: **1** in an amount multiplied by: *repaid tenfold.* **2** consisting of so many parts: *threefold blessing.*

**fold·er** ▸*n.* **1** folding cover or holder for loose papers. **2** folded leaflet.

**fo·ley** /'fōlē/ ▸*n.* relating to or concerned with the addition of recorded sound effects after the shooting of a film.

**fo·li·age** /'fōl(ē)ij/ ▸*n.* leaves; leafage.

**fo·lic ac·id** /'fōlik/ ▸*n.* vitamin of the B complex, found in leafy green vegetables, liver, and kidney.

**fo·li·o** /'fōlē,ō/ ▸*n.* (*pl.* **-os**) **1** leaf of paper, etc., esp. one numbered only on the front. **2** page number of a book. **3** sheet of paper folded once, making two leaves of a book. **4** book made of such sheets.

**folk** /fōk/ ▸*n.* (*pl.* **folk** or **folks**) **1** people in general or of a specified class: *rich and poor folks alike.* **2** (usu. **folks**) one's parents or relatives. **3** a people.

▸*adj.* of popular origin; traditional: *folk art.*

☐ **folk dance** dance of traditional origin. ☐ **folk singer** singer of folk songs. ☐ **folk song** song of popular or traditional origin or style. ☐ **folk tale** popular or traditional story.

**folk·lore** ▸*n.* traditional beliefs and stories of a people; the study of these. **—folk·lor·ic** *adj.* **—folk·lor·ist** *n.*

**folk·sy** ▸*adj.* (**-si·er, -si·est**) **1** friendly; informal. **2** of or like folk art, culture, etc.

**fol·li·cle** /'fälikəl/ ▸*n.* **1** small sac

or vesicle. **2** small sac-shaped secretory gland or cavity. —**fol·lic·u·lar** *adj.* —**fol·lic·u·late** *adj.*

**fol·low** /ˈfälō/ ▶*v.* **1** go or come after (a person or thing proceeding ahead). **2** go along (a route, path, etc.). **3** come after in order or time: *dessert followed the main course.* **4** take as a guide or leader. **5** conform to. **6** practice or undertake. **7** understand. **8** provide with a sequel or successor. **9** be a result of.

□ **follow-up** subsequent or continued action.

**fol·low·er** ▶*n.* **1** adherent or devotee. **2** person or thing that follows.

**fol·low·ing** ▶*prep.* after in time; as a sequel to.

▶*n.* adherents or devotees.

▶*adj.* that follows or comes after.

**fol·ly** /ˈfälē/ ▶*n.* (*pl.* **-lies**) **1** foolishness; lack of good sense. **2** foolish act, behavior, idea, etc.

**fo·ment** /ˈfōˌment/ ▶*v.* instigate or stir up (trouble, sedition, etc.).

**fond** /fänd/ ▶*adj.* **1** (**fond of**) having affection or a liking for. **2** affectionate; loving; doting. **3** (of beliefs, etc.) foolishly

credulous; naive. —**fond·ly** *adv.* —**fond·ness** *n.*

**fon·dant** /ˈfändənt/ ▶*n.* soft creamy candy of flavored sugar.

**fon·dle** /ˈfändl/ ▶*v.* caress.

**fon·due** /fänˈd(y)o͞o/ ▶*n.* dish of flavored melted cheese.

**fons et o·ri·go** /ˈfänz et ōˈrīgō; -ˈrē-/ ▶*n.* source and origin of something.

**font** /fänt/ ▶*n.* **1** receptacle in a church for baptismal water. **2** reservoir for oil in a lamp. **3** set of type of one face or size.

**food** /fo͞od/ ▶*n.* **1** nutritious substance, esp. solid in form, ingested to maintain life and growth. **2** mental stimulus.

**food chain** ▶*n.* series of organisms each dependent on the next for food.

**food pro·ces·sor** ▶*n.* machine for chopping and mixing food.

**fool** /fo͞ol/ ▶*n.* **1** person who acts unwisely or imprudently; stupid person. **2** *hist.* jester; clown. **3** dupe.

▶*v.* **1** deceive; trick. **2** act in a joking or teasing way. —**fool·ish** *adj.*

**fool·har·dy** ▶*adj.* (**-di·er, -di·est**) rashly or foolishly bold; reckless. —**fool·har·di·ness** *n.*

**fool·proof** ▸*adj.* (of a procedure, mechanism, etc.) incapable of misuse or mistake.

**foot** /foŏt/ ▸*n.* (*pl.* **feet**) **1 a** lower extremity of the leg below the ankle. **b** part of a sock, etc., covering the foot. **2** lowest or endmost part. **3** (*pl.* **feet** or **foot**) unit of linear measure equal to 12 inches (30.48 cm). **4** group of syllables constituting a unit in verse.
▸*v.* pay (a bill).
□ **have one's** (or **both**) **feet on the ground** be practical. □ **on foot** walking; not riding, etc. □ **put one's foot down** *inf.* **1** be firmly insistent or repressive. **2** accelerate a motor vehicle.

**foot-and-mouth disease** ▸*n.* contagious viral disease of cattle, etc.

**foot·ball** ▸*n.* **1** team game played with an inflated oval ball. **2** ball used in this.

**foot·hill** ▸*n.* any of the low hills around the base of a mountain.

**foot·hold** ▸*n.* **1** place, esp. in climbing, where a foot can be supported securely. **2** secure initial position.

**foot·ing** ▸*n.* **1** foothold; secure position: *lost his footing.* **2** basis on which an enterprise is established or operates; relative position or status.

**foot·lights** ▸*pl. n.* row of lights along the front of a stage at the level of the actors' feet.

**foot·ling** /ˈfoŏtliNG/ ▸*adj.* trivial and irritating.

**foot·lock·er** ▸*n.* small trunk usu. kept at the foot of a soldier's or camper's bunk.

**foot·loose** ▸*adj.* free to act as one pleases.

**foot·note** ▸*n.* note printed at the foot of a page.

**foot·step** ▸*n.* **1** step taken in walking. **2** sound of this.

**foot·stool** ▸*n.* stool for resting the feet on when sitting.

**fop** /fäp/ ▸*n.* affectedly elegant or fashionable man; dandy.
—**fop·pish** *adj.*

**for** /fôr; fər/ ▸*prep.* **1** in the interest or to the benefit of; intended to go to. **2** in defense, support, or favor of. **3** suitable or appropriate to. **4** regarding. **5** representing or in place of. **6** in exchange against. **7** at the price of. **8** as a consequence of. **9 a** with a view to; in the hope or quest of. **b** on account of. **10** to reach; toward: *ran for home.* **11** through or over (a distance or period). **12** as being: *for the last* *time.* **13** in spite of. **14** considering or making due allowance in respect of. ▸*conj.* because; since.

**for-** ▸*prefix* forming verbs and their derivatives, meaning: **1** away; off: *forget.* **2** prohibition: *forbid.* **3** abstention or neglect: *forgo.* **4** excess or intensity: *forlorn.*

**for·age** /'fôrij/ ▸*n.* **1** food for horses and cattle. **2** act or an instance of searching for food. ▸*v.* **1** go searching; rummage (esp. for food). **2** obtain food from; plunder. —**for·ag·er** *n.*

**for·ay** /'fôr,ā/ ▸*n.* sudden attack; raid or incursion. ▸*v.* make or go on a foray.

**for·bear** /fôr'be(ə)r/ ▸*v.* (*past* **-bore**; *past part.* **-borne**) abstain or desist (from): *forbore to mention it.*

**for·bid** /fər'bid/ ▸*v.* (**-bid·ding**; *past* **-bade** or **-bad**; *past part.* **-bid·den**) **1** order not: *I forbid you to go.* **2** refuse to allow.

**for·bid·ding** ▸*adj.* uninviting; repellent; stern. —**for·bid·ding·ly** *adv.*

**force** /fôrs/ ▸*n.* **1** power; exerted strength or impetus; intense effort. **2** coercion; compulsion. **3** organized body of soldiers, police, etc. **4** binding power; validity. **5** mental or moral strength; efficacy. **6** influence tending to cause the motion of a body. ▸*v.* **1** compel or coerce. **2** break open or into by force. **3** drive or propel violently or against resistance. **4** cause, produce, or attain by effort: *forced a smile.* —**force·ful** *adj.*

□ **in force 1** valid; effective. **2** in great strength or numbers.

**for·ceps** /'fôrsəps; -,seps/ ▸*n.* (*pl.* same) surgical pincers.

**for·ci·ble** /'fôrsəbəl/ ▸*adj.* done by or involving force; forceful. —**for·ci·bly** *adv.*

**ford** /fôrd/ ▸*n.* shallow water crossing, as in a river. ▸*v.* cross (water) at a ford.

**fore** /fôr/ ▸*adj.* situated in front. ▸*n.* front part, esp. of a ship; bow. ▸*interj. Golf* warning to a person in the path of a ball.

□ **fore-and-aft** (of a sail or rigging) set lengthwise, not on the yards.

**fore-** ▸*prefix* forming: **1** verbs meaning: **a** in front: *foreshorten.* **b** beforehand: *forewarn.* **2** nouns meaning: **a** situated in front of: *forecourt.* **b** front part of: *forehead.*

**fore·arm** ▸*n.* part of the arm

from the elbow to the wrist or the fingertips.

**fore·bear** ▸*n.* ancestor.

**fore·bode** ▸*v.* **1** betoken; be an advance warning of. **2** have a presentiment of (usu. evil).

**fore·cast** ▸*v.* (*past* and *past part.* **-cast** or **-cast·ed**) predict. ▸*n.* calculation or estimate of something future, esp. coming weather. —**fore·cast·er** *n.*

**fore·cas·tle** /ˈfōksəl; ˈfôrˌkasəl/ (also **fo'c's'le**) ▸*n.* forward part of a ship where the crew has quarters.

**fore·close** ▸*v.* **1** repossess mortgaged property when a loan is not duly repaid. **2** exclude. —**fore·clo·sure** *n.*

**fore·fa·ther** ▸*n.* ancestor.

**fore·fin·ger** ▸*n.* finger next to the thumb.

**fore·front** ▸*n.* **1** foremost part. **2** leading position.

**fore·go·ing** ▸*adj.* preceding; previously mentioned.

**fore·ground** ▸*n.* **1** part of a view that is nearest the observer. **2** most conspicuous position.

**fore·hand** ▸*n.* *Tennis, etc.* stroke played with the palm of the hand facing the opponent.

**fore·head** ▸*n.* part of the face above the eyebrows.

**for·eign** /ˈfôrən/ ▸*adj.* **1** of, from, in, or characteristic of a country or a language other than one's own. **2** unfamiliar; strange. **3** coming from outside: *foreign body.* —**for·eign·er** *n.* —**for·eign·ness** *n.*

**fore·knowl·edge** ▸*n.* awareness of something before it happens.

**fore·leg** ▸*n.* each of the front legs of a quadruped.

**fore·man** ▸*n.* (*pl.* **-men**) **1** worker supervising others. **2** presiding juror in a legal trial.

**fore·most** ▸*adj.* **1** chief or most notable. **2** first; front. ▸*adv.* most importantly: *first and foremost.*

**fore·name** ▸*n.* first name.

**fo·ren·sic** /fəˈrenzik; -sik/ ▸*adj.* of or used in courts of law. —**fo·ren·si·cal·ly** *adv.*

**fore·play** ▸*n.* stimulation preceding sexual intercourse.

**fore·run·ner** ▸*n.* predecessor.

**fore·see** ▸*v.* (*past* **-saw**; *past part.* **-seen**) see or be aware of beforehand. —**fore·see·a·ble** *adj.*

**fore·shad·ow** ▸*v.* be a warning or indication of (a future event).

**fore·sight** ▶*n.* regard or provision for the future.

**fore·skin** ▶*n.* fold of skin covering the end of the penis. (Also called **prepuce**).

**for·est** /ˈfôrəst/ ▶*n.* large area of trees and undergrowth.
▶*v.* plant with trees.
—**for·est·er** *n.*

**fore·stall** ▶*v.* **1** act in advance of in order to prevent. **2** anticipate.

**fore·tell** ▶*v.* (*past* and *past part.* **-told**) predict; prophesy.

**fore·thought** ▶*n.* care or provision for the future.

**for·ev·er** ▶*adv.* continually; persistently.

**fore·warn** ▶*v.* warn beforehand.

**fore·word** ▶*n.* introductory remarks at the beginning of a book, often by a person other than the author.

**for·feit** /ˈfôrfit/ ▶*n.* **1** penalty. **2** something surrendered as a penalty.
▶*adj.* lost or surrendered as a penalty.
▶*v.* lose the right to; have to pay as a penalty. —**for·fei·ture** *n.*

**for·gath·er** (also **fore·gath·er**) ▶*v.* assemble; meet together; associate.

**forge** /fôrj/ ▶*v.* **1** make or write in fraudulent imitation. **2** shape (esp. metal) by heating in a fire and hammering. **3** move forward gradually or steadily.
▶*n.* furnace or workshop for melting or refining metal.
—**forg·er** *n.*
□ **forge ahead** **1** take the lead. **2** strive and progress.

**for·get** /fərˈget/ ▶*v.* (**-get·ting**; *past* **-got**; *past part.* **-got·ten** or **-got**) **1** lose the remembrance of. **2** overlook; neglect. **3** cease to think of: *forgive and forget.*
—**for·get·ta·ble** *adj.*

**for·get·ful** ▶*adj.* **1** apt to forget; absent-minded. **2** forgetting; neglectful.

**for·get-me-not** ▶*n.* plant with small yellow-eyed bright blue flowers.

**for·give** /fərˈgiv/ ▶*v.* (*past* **-gave**; *past part.* **-giv·en**) cease to feel angry or resentful toward; pardon. —**for·giv·a·ble** *adj.*
—**for·give·ness** *n.*

**for·go** /fôrˈgō/ (also **fore·go**) ▶*v.* (*past* **-went**; *past part.* **-gone**) go without; relinquish.

**fork** /fôrk/ ▶*n.* **1** instrument with two or more prongs used in eating or cooking. **2** similar much larger instrument used for

digging, lifting, etc.
**3 a** divergence of anything, e.g., a stick, road, or river, into two parts. **b** either of the two parts. ▸*v.* **1** diverge into two parts. **2** dig, lift, etc., with a fork.

**fork·lift** ▸*n.* vehicle with a horizontal fork in front for lifting and carrying loads.

**for·lorn** /fôrˈlôrn/ ▸*adj.* sad and abandoned or lonely.
—**for·lorn·ly** *adv.*

**form** /fôrm/ ▸*n.* **1** shape; arrangement of parts. **2** person or animal as visible or tangible. **3** species, kind, or variety. **4** document to be filled in. **5** correct procedure. **6** (of an athlete, horse, etc.) condition of health and training. **7** general state or disposition: *in great form.* **8** arrangement; style. ▸*v.* **1** make or fashion. **2** take a certain shape; be formed. **3** train or instruct. **4** develop or establish. —**form·less** *adj.*

**-form** (usu. as **-iform**) ▸*comb. form* forming adjectives meaning 'having the form of': *cruciform | cuneiform.*

**for·mal** /ˈfôrməl/ ▸*adj.* **1** in accordance with rules, convention, or ceremony. **2** precise or symmetrical: *formal garden.* **3** stiff in manner. **4** explicit or official. ▸*n.* **1** evening dress. **2** occasion on which evening dress is worn. —**for·mal·ly** *adv.*

**form·al·de·hyde** /fôrˈmaldəˌhīd/ ▸*n.* colorless pungent gas used as a disinfectant and preservative.

**for·mal·i·ty** /fôrˈmalətē/ ▸*n.* (*pl.* **-ties**) **1** formal procedure or custom. **2** thing done simply to comply with a rule.

**for·mat** /ˈfôrˌmat/ ▸*n.* **1** shape and size of a book, periodical, etc. **2** style or arrangement. ▸*v.* (**-mat·ted, -mat·ting**) arrange or put into a format.

**for·ma·tion** /fôrˈmāsHən/ ▸*n.* **1** forming. **2** thing formed. **3** particular arrangement.

**form·a·tive** ▸*adj.* serving to form or fashion; of formation.

**for·mer** ▸*adj.* **1** of the past; earlier; previous. **2** the first or first mentioned of two. —**for·mer·ly** *adv.*

**for·mi·da·ble** /ˈfôrmədəbəl/ ▸*adj.* **1** inspiring fear, dread, or awe. **2** hard to overcome or deal with.

**for·mu·la** /ˈfôrmyələ/ ▸*n.* (*pl.* **-las** or esp. in senses 1, 2 **-lae**) **1** chemical symbols showing the constituents of a substance. **2** mathematical rule expressed in symbols. **3** fixed form, esp. of words used on social or ceremonial occasions. **4** list of ingredients. **5** infant's liquid food preparation. —**for·mu·la·ic** *adj.*

**for·mu·late** /ˈfôrmyəˌlāt/ ▸*v.* **1** express in a formula. **2** express clearly and precisely. —**for·mu·la·tion** *n.*

**for·ni·cate** /ˈfôrniˌkāt/ ▸*v.* (of people not married to each other) have sexual intercourse voluntarily. —**for·ni·ca·tion** *n.*

**for·sake** /fərˈsāk; fôr-/ ▸*v.* (*past* -**sook**; *past part.* -**sak·en**) **1** give up; break off from; renounce. **2** desert; abandon.

**for·swear** /fôrˈswe(ə)r/ ▸*v.* (*past* -**swore**; *past part.* -**sworn**) **1** renounce. **2** commit perjury.

**for·syth·i·a** /fərˈsiT͟Hēə/ ▸*n.* ornamental shrub bearing bright yellow flowers in early spring.

**fort** /fôrt/ ▸*n.* fortified building or position.

**for·te**[1] /fôrt/ ▸*n.* person's strong point; a thing in which a person excels.

**for·te**[2] /ˈfôrˌtā/ ▸*adv. Music* loudly.

**forth** /fôrT͟H/ ▸*adv.* **1** forward; into view. **2** onward in time: *henceforth.*

**forth·com·ing** ▸ *adj.* **1** coming or available soon. **2** produced when wanted. **3** (of a person) informative; responsive.

**forth·right** ▸*adj.* direct and outspoken; straightforward.

**forth·with** ▸*adv.* without delay.

**for·ti·fy** /ˈfôrtəˌfī/ ▸*v.* (-**fied**) **1** provide or equip with military defense. **2** strengthen or invigorate physically, mentally, or morally. **3** strengthen (wine) with alcohol. **4** increase the nutritive value of (food, esp. with vitamins). —**for·ti·fi·ca·tion** *n.*

**for·tis·si·mo** /fôrˈtisəˌmō/ ▸*adv. Music* very loudly.

**for·ti·tude** /ˈfôrtəˌto͞od/ ▸*n.* courage in pain or adversity.

**fort·night** ▸*n.* period of fourteen days; two weeks.

**for·tress** /ˈfôrtrəs/ ▸*n.* fortified building or town.

**for·tu·i·tous** /fôrˈto͞oətəs/ ▸*adj.* due to or characterized by chance; accidental; casual. —**for·tu·i·tous·ly** *adv.*

**for·tu·nate** /ˈfôrCHənət/ ▸*adj.* **1** favored by fortune; lucky; prosperous. **2** auspicious; favorable. —**for·tu·nate·ly** *adv.*

**for·tune** /ˈfôrCHən/ ▸*n.* **1 a** chance or luck as a force in human affairs. **b** person's destiny. **2** good or bad luck that befalls a person or an enterprise. **3** good luck. **4** prosperity; riches.

**for·tune-tel·ler** ▶*n.* person who claims to predict future events in a person's life. —**fortune-telling** *n.*

**for·ty** /ˈfôrtē/ ▶*n.* (*pl.* **-ties**) **1** product of four and ten. **2** symbol for this (40, xl, XL). **3** (**forties**) numbers from 40 to 49, esp. as years. ▶*adj.* that amount to forty. —**for·ti·eth** *adj. & n.*

**fo·rum** /ˈfôrəm/ ▶*n.* **1** place, agency, or meeting for public discussion. **2** public square in an ancient Roman city.

**for·ward** /ˈfôrwərd/ ▶*adj.* **1** lying in one's line of motion. **2** onward or toward the front. **3** precocious; bold in manner; presumptuous. **4** relating to the future: *forward contract.*
▶*n.* attacking player positioned near the front of a team in football, soccer, hockey, etc.
▶*adv.* **1** to the front; into prominence. **2** in advance; ahead: *sent them forward.* **3** onward. **4** (also **for·wards**) **a** toward the front in the direction one is facing. **b** in the normal direction of motion.
▶*v.* **1** send (a letter, etc.) on to a further destination. **2** help to advance; promote.

**fos·sil** /ˈfäsəl/ ▶*n.* **1** remains or impression of a (usu. prehistoric) plant or animal hardened in rock. **2** *inf.* antiquated or unchanging person or thing.
▶*adj.* **1** of or like a fossil. **2** antiquated; out of date. —**fos·sil·ize** *v.*

**fos·sil fuel** ▶*n.* natural fuel such as coal or gas.

**fos·ter** /ˈfôstər/ ▶*v.* **1** promote the growth or development of. **2** (of circumstances) be favorable to. **3** bring up (a child that is not one's own by birth).
▶*adj.* **1** having a family connection by fostering: *foster child.* **2** concerned with fostering a child: *foster care.*

**foul** /foul/ ▶*adj.* **1** offensive; loathsome; stinking. **2** dirty; soiled; filthy. **3** *inf.* very disagreeable or unpleasant. **4** noxious. **5** disgustingly abusive or offensive. **6** against the rules. **7** (of weather) rough; stormy.
▶*n.* *Sports* unfair or invalid stroke or action.

▸*adv.* unfairly.

▸*v.* **1** make or become foul or dirty. **2** *Sports* commit a foul against (a player). **3** (cause to) become entangled or blocked. **4** bungle.

**foul mouth** ▸*n.* person who uses offensive language.

**foul play** ▸*n.* **1** unfair play in games. **2** treacherous or violent activity, esp. murder.

**foul-up** ▸*n.* muddle or bungle.

**found**[1] /found/ ▸past and past part. of FIND.

**found**[2] ▸*v.* **1** establish; originate; initiate. **2** set on a base or basis. **3 a** melt and mold (metal). **b** fuse (materials for glass).

**foun·da·tion** /foun'dāsHən/ ▸*n.* **1** solid ground or base on which a building rests. **2** basis or underlying principle. **3** establishment (esp. of an endowed institution). **4** institution established with an endowment, such as a body devoted to financing research or charity.

**found·er** ▸*v.* **1** (of a ship) sink. **2** fail completely. **3** stumble or fall.
▸*n.* person who has founded an institution, etc.

**found·ling** /'foundliNG/ ▸*n.* abandoned infant of unknown parentage.

**found·ry** /'foundrē/ ▸*n.* (*pl.* **-ries**) workshop for or a business of casting metal.

**foun·tain** /'fountn/ ▸*n.* **1** jet or jets of water made to spout for ornamental purposes or for drinking. **2** natural spring of water. **3** source.

**foun·tain·head** ▸*n.* source.

**foun·tain pen** ▸*n.* pen with a reservoir or cartridge holding ink.

**four** /fôr/ ▸*n.* **1** one more than three. **2** symbol for this (4, iv, IV, iiii, IIII).
▸*adj.* that amount to four. —**fourth** *adj.* & *n.*
□ **on all fours** on hands and knees.

**four-let·ter word** ▸*n.* any of several short words referring to sexual or excretory functions, regarded as coarse or offensive.

**four·score** ▸*n.* eighty.

**four·some** ▸*n.* group of four persons.

**four·square** ▸*adj.* **1** solidly based. **2** steady; resolute. **3** square shaped.
▸*adv.* steadily; resolutely.

**four·teen** /ˌfôr'tēn/ ▸*n.* **1** one

more than thirteen. **2** symbol for this (14, xiv, XIV).
▸*adj.* that amount to fourteen. —**four·teenth** *adj. & n.*

**four-wheel drive** ▸*n.* drive powering all four wheels of a vehicle.

**fowl** /foul/ ▸*n.* (*pl.* same or **fowls**) **1** domestic birds, esp. chickens, kept for eggs and flesh. **2** flesh of these birds as food.

**Fox** /fäks/ ▸*n.* **1 a** N. American Indian people native to the northeastern U.S. **b** member of this people. **2** language of this people.

**fox** ▸*n.* **1** canine animal with a bushy tail and red or gray fur. **2** cunning or sly person.
▸*v.* deceive; trick. —**fox·like** *adj.*

**fox·glove** ▸*n.* tall plant with erect spikes of purple or white flowers like glove fingers.

**fox·hole** ▸*n.* hole in the ground used as a shelter against enemy fire or as a firing point.

**fox ter·ri·er** ▸*n.* kind of short-haired terrier.

**fox·trot** ▸*n.* ballroom dance with slow and quick steps.
▸*v.* (**-trot·ted**, **-trot·ting**) perform this dance.

**fox·y** ▸*adj.* (**-i·er**, **-i·est**) foxlike; sly; cunning.

**foy·er** /ˈfoiər/ ▸*n.* **1** entrance hall or other open area in a hotel, theater, etc. **2** entrance hall in a house or apartment.

**FPO** ▸*abbr.* **1** field post office. **2** fleet post office.

**Fr** ▸*symb. Chem.* francium.

**Fr.** (also **Fr**) ▸*abbr.* **1** Father. **2** French.

**fr.** ▸*abbr.* franc(s).

**fra·cas** /ˈfrākəs/ ▸*n.* (*pl.* same) noisy disturbance or quarrel.

**frac·tion** /ˈfrakSHən/ ▸*n.* **1** numerical quantity that is not a whole number (e.g., 0.5, $1/2$). **2** small part, piece, or amount. —**frac·tion·al** *adj.*

**frac·tious** ▸*adj.* **1** irritable; peevish. **2** unruly.

**frac·ture** /ˈfrakCHər/ ▸*n.* breakage, esp. of a bone.
▸*v.* break or cause to break.

**frag·ile** /ˈfrajəl/ ▸*adj.* easily broken; delicate; weak. —**fra·gil·i·ty** *n.*

**frag·ment** /ˈfragmənt/ ▸*n.* **1** part broken off; a detached piece. **2** isolated or incomplete part (of a book, etc.).
▸*v.* break or separate into fragments. —**frag·men·ta·tion** *n.*

**fra·grance** /ˈfrāgrəns/ ▸n.
**1** sweetness of smell. **2** sweet
scent. —**fra·grant** adj.

**frail** /frāl/ ▸adj. **1** fragile; delicate.
**2** in weak health.

**frame** /frām/ ▸n. **1** case or border
enclosing a picture, window,
door, etc. **2** basic rigid
supporting structure of
anything, e.g., of a building,
motor vehicle, or aircraft.
**3** (**frames**) structure of spectacles
holding the lenses. **4** human or
animal body structure.
**5** established order, plan, or
system. **6** single image on film,
tape, etc.
▸v. **1** set in or serve as a frame
for. **2** construct; devise. **3** adapt;
fit. **4** inf. concoct a false charge
or evidence against; devise a plot
with regard to. **5** articulate
(words). —**frame·less** adj.
—**fram·er** n.
□ **frame-up** inf. conspiracy, esp. to
make an innocent person appear
guilty.

**franc** /fraNGk/ ▸n. chief monetary
unit of Switzerland and several
other countries, and formerly of
France, Belgium, and
Luxembourg.

**fran·chise** /ˈfranˌCHīz/ ▸n.
**1** right to vote in elections;
citizenship. **2** authorization
granted by a company to sell its
goods or services in a particular
way.
▸v. grant a franchise to.

**fran·gi·ble** /ˈfranjəbəl/ ▸adj.
fragile; brittle.

**Frank** /fraNGk/ ▸n. member of
the Germanic nation or coalition
that conquered Gaul in the 6th
c. —**Frank·ish** adj.

**frank** ▸adj. **1** candid; outspoken:
frank opinion. **2** undisguised;
avowed: frank admiration.
▸v. stamp (a letter) with an official
mark to record the payment of
postage.
▸n. franking signature or mark.
—**frank·ly** adv. —**frank·ness** n.

**frank·furt·er** /ˈfraNGkˌfərtər/ ▸n.
seasoned smoked sausage.

**frank·in·cense** /ˈfraNGkən-
ˌsens/ ▸n. aromatic gum resin
used for burning as incense.

**fran·tic** /ˈfrantik/ ▸adj. **1** wildly
excited. **2** hurried or anxious;
desperate. —**fran·ti·cal·ly** adv.

**fra·ter·nal** /frəˈtərnl/ ▸adj. **1** of a
brother or brothers. **2** brotherly.
**3** (of twins) developed from
separate ova and not necessarily
closely similar. —**fra·ter·nal·ism**
n. —**fra·ter·nal·ly** adv.

**fra·ter·ni·ty** /frə'tərnətē/ ▶n. (pl. **-ties**) **1** male students' society. **2** group or company with common interests, or of the same professional class. **3** being fraternal; brotherliness.

**frat·er·nize** /'fratər,nīz/ ▶v. associate with someone, esp. when one is not supposed to. —**frat·er·ni·za·tion** n.

**frat·ri·cide** /'fratrə,sīd/ ▶n. **1** killing of one's brother or sister. **2** person who does this. —**frat·ri·cid·al** adj.

**fraud** /frôd/ ▶n. **1** criminal deception. **2** dishonest artifice or trick. **3** impostor. —**fraud·u·lent** adj.

**fraud·u·lent** /'frôjələnt/ ▶adj. **1** obtained, done by, or involving deception, esp. criminal deception. **2** unjustifiably claiming or being credited with particular accomplishments or qualities.

**fraught** /frôt/ ▶adj. filled or attended with.

**fray** /frā/ ▶v. **1** wear through or become worn, esp. (of woven material) unweave at the edges. **2** (of nerves, temper, etc.) become strained; deteriorate. ▶n. brawl.

**fraz·zle** /'frazəl/ ▶n. inf. worn or exhausted state. ▶v. [usu. as adj. **frazzled**] wear out; exhaust.

**freak** /frēk/ ▶n. **1** (also **freak of nature**) monstrosity; abnormally developed individual or thing. **2** inf. enthusiast: *health freak.* ▶v. inf. **1** become or make very angry: *she freaked out when I came home late.* **2** undergo or cause to undergo hallucinations or a strong emotional experience, esp. from use of narcotics. —**freak·ish** adj.

**freck·le** /'frekəl/ ▶n. light brown spot on the skin. ▶v. spot or be spotted with freckles. —**freck·ly** adj.

**free** /frē/ ▶adj. (**fre·er**; **fre·est**) **1** not under the control of another; at liberty. **2** autonomous; democratic. **3** unrestricted; not restrained or fixed. **4** released from duties, etc. **5** independent. **6** (**free of/from**) **a** exempt from. **b** not containing: *free of preservatives.* **7** permitted to: *free to choose.* **8** costing nothing. **9** not occupied or in use. **10** lavish: *he is always very free with his money.* **11** frank; unreserved. **12** (of a translation) not literal.

▶*adv.* **1** in a free manner. **2** without cost or payment.

▶*v.* **1** make free; liberate. **2** relieve. **3** disengage; disentangle. —**free·dom** *n.* —**free·ly** *adv.*

**-free** ▶*comb. form* free of or from: *duty-free* | *trouble-free.*

**free·base** /ˈfrēˌbās/ ▶*n.* cocaine that has been converted from its salt to its base form by heating with ether or boiling with sodium bicarbonate, taken by inhaling the fumes or smoking the residue.

▶*v.* prepare or take (cocaine) in such a way.

**free·boot·er** /ˈfrēˌbo͞otər/ ▶*n.* pirate.

**free en·ter·prise** ▶*n.* system of private business operating free from government control.

**free fall** ▶*n.* **1** part of a parachute descent before the parachute opens. **2** movement of a spacecraft in space without thrust from the engines.

**free-for-all** ▶*n.* chaotic fight, unrestricted discussion, etc.

**free hand** ▶*n.* freedom to act at one's own discretion.

**free-hand·ed** ▶*adj.* generous.

**free·hold** ▶*n.* **1** complete ownership of property for life. **2** such property. —**free·hold·er** *n.*

**free·lance** ▶*adj.* (also **free-lance**) working on particular assignments for different companies at different times.

▶*adv.* earning one's living in such a way: *I work freelance.*

▶*n.* (also **free·lanc·er**) person who earns a living in such a way.

▶*v.* earn one's living as a freelance.

**free·load·er** ▶*n. inf.* person who eats, drinks, or lives at others' expense.

**free mar·ket** ▶*n.* market with unrestricted competition.

**free speech** ▶*n.* right to express opinions freely.

**free-stand·ing** ▶*adj.* not supported by another structure.

**free·think·er** ▶*n.* person who rejects dogma or authority, esp. in religious belief.

**free trade** ▶*n.* international trade without import or export restrictions.

**free verse** ▶*n.* verse without a fixed metrical pattern.

**free·way** ▶*n.* express highway, esp. with controlled access.

**free will** ▶*n.* power of acting at one's own discretion.

**freeze** /frēz/ ▶*v.* (*past* **froze**; *past part.* **fro·zen**) **1** turn or be turned into ice or another solid by cold. **2** be or feel very cold. **3** cover or become covered with ice: *the roads froze overnight.* **4** preserve (food) by refrigeration below the freezing point. **5** make or become motionless or powerless through fear, surprise, etc.: *he froze when she walked into the room.* **6** make (credits, assets, etc.) temporarily or permanently unrealizable. **7** fix or stabilize (prices, wages, etc.) at a certain level. **8** arrest (a movement in a movie, video, etc.).

▶*n.* **1** period or state of frost. **2** fixing or stabilization of prices, wages, etc. **3** film shot in which movement is arrested by the repetition of a frame.
—**freez·er** *n.*

**freeze-dry** ▶*v.* (**-dried**) freeze and dry by the sublimation of ice in a high vacuum.

**freez·ing point** ▶*n.* temperature at which a liquid, esp. water, freezes.

**freight** /frāt/ ▶*n.* **1** transport of goods. **2** goods transported; cargo. **3** charge for transportation of goods.

▶*v.* **1** transport (goods) as freight. **2** load with freight.

**freight·er** ▶*n.* ship designed to carry freight.

**French** /frenCH/ ▶*adj.* **1** of France or its people or language. **2** having the characteristics attributed to the French people.
▶*n.* **1** language of France. **2** (**the French**) the people of France.
—**French·man** *n.*
—**French·wom·an** *n.*

**French bread** ▶*n.* white bread in a long crisp loaf.

**French Ca·na·di·an** ▶*n.* Canadian whose principal language is French.
▶*adj.* of French-speaking Canadians.

**French cuff** ▶*n.* double cuff formed by turning back a long cuff and fastening it.

**French door** ▶*n.* door with glass panes throughout its length.

**French dress·ing** ▶*n.* **1** salad dressing of vinegar and oil, usu. seasoned. **2** creamy orange salad dressing.

**French fries** ▶*pl. n.* strips of potato, deep fried.

**French horn** ▶*n.* coiled brass wind instrument with a wide bell.

**French kiss** ▸*n.* openmouthed kiss.

**French win·dow** ▸*n.* one of a pair of casement windows extending to the floor in an outside wall, serving as both window and door.

**fre·net·ic** /frə'netik/ ▸*adj.* frantic; frenzied.

**fren·zy** /'frenzē/ ▸*n.* (*pl.* **-zies**) wild or delirious excitement, agitation, or fury. **—fren·zied·ly** *adv.*

**fre·quen·cy** /'frēkwənsē/ ▸*n.* (*pl.* **-cies**) **1** commonness of occurrence. **2** *Physics* rate of recurrence of a vibration, etc.

**fre·quen·cy mod·u·la·tion** ▸*n.* modulation in which the frequency of the carrier wave is varied.

**fre·quent** /'frēkwənt/ ▸*adj.* **1** occurring often or in close succession. **2** habitual; constant. ▸*v.* attend or go to habitually. **—fre·quent·er** *n.* **—fre·quent·ly** *adv.*

**fres·co** /'freskō/ ▸*n.* (*pl.* **-cos** or **-coes**) painting done in watercolor on wet plaster. **—fres·coed** *adj.*

**fresh** /fresH/ ▸*adj.* **1** newly made or obtained. **2** other; different; new. **3** lately arrived. **4** not stale or musty or faded: *fresh flowers.* **5** (of food) not preserved. **6** not salty: *fresh water.* **7** pure; untainted; refreshing. **8** (of the wind) brisk. **9** *inf.* impudent. **10** inexperienced. ▸*adv.* newly; recently: *fresh-cut.* **—fresh·ly** *adv.* **—fresh·ness** *n.*

**fresh·et** /'fresHət/ ▸*n.* **1** flood of a river from heavy rain or melted snow. **2** rush of fresh water flowing into the sea.

**fresh·man** ▸*n.* (*pl.* **-men**) **1** first-year student at a high school, college, or university. **2** newcomer or novice: *freshman senator.*

**fresh·wa·ter** ▸*adj.* not of the sea: *freshwater fish.*

**fret** /fret/ ▸*v.* (**fret·ted, fret·ting**) **1** (cause to) be worried or distressed. **2** ornamental pattern made of straight lines joined usu. at right angles. ▸*n.* **1** ornamental pattern made of straight lines joined usu. at right angles. **2** each of a sequence of bars or ridges on the fingerboard of a guitar, etc.

**Freud·i·an** /'froidēən/ ▸*adj.* of or relating to Sigmund Freud or his methods of psychoanalysis. ▸*n.* follower of Freud or his methods.

**Freud·ian slip** ▸*n.* unintentional error regarded as revealing subconscious feelings.

**Fri.** ▸*abbr.* Friday.

**fri·a·ble** /ˈfrīəbəl/ ▸*adj.* easily crumbled. —**fri·a·bil·i·ty** *n.*

**fri·ar** /ˈfrīər/ ▸*n.* member of any of certain religious orders of men, esp. the four mendicant orders.

**frib·ble** /ˈfribəl/ ▸*n.* **1** frivolous or foolish person. **2** thing of no great importance.
▸*v.* (**fribble away**) part with lightly and wastefully; fritter.

**fric·as·see** /ˈfrikəˌsē/ ▸*n.* dish of stewed pieces of meat served in a thick white sauce.

**fric·tion** /ˈfrikSHən/ ▸*n.* **1** rubbing of one object against another. **2** the resistance encountered in moving an object. **3** clash of wills, temperaments, or opinions.

**Fri·day** /ˈfrīdā/ ▸*n.* day of the week following Thursday.

**friend** /frend/ ▸*n.* **1** person with whom one enjoys mutual affection and regard. **2** sympathizer, helper. —**friend·less** *adj.* —**friend·ship** *n.*

**friend·ly** ▸*adj.* (**-li·er, -li·est**) **1** well-disposed; kindly; cordial. **2** on amicable terms.
▸*adv.* in a friendly manner. —**friend·li·ness** *n.*

**frieze** /frēz/ ▸*n.* horizontal decorative or sculpted band, esp. along a wall near the ceiling.

**frig·ate** /ˈfrigit/ ▸*n.* naval vessel between a destroyer and a cruiser in size.

**fright** /frīt/ ▸*n.* **1 a** sudden or extreme fear. **b** instance of this: *gave me a fright.* **2** person or thing looking grotesque or ridiculous.

**fright·en** ▸*v.* **1** make (someone) afraid. **2** become afraid: *she doesn't frighten easily.* **3** (**frighten off**) drive or force by fright. —**fright·en·ing** *adj.* —**fright·en·ing·ly** *adv.*

**fright·ful** ▸*adj.* **1** dreadful; shocking; revolting. **2** *inf.* extreme. —**fright·ful·ly** *adv.*

**frig·id** /ˈfrijid/ ▸*adj.* **1** very cold. **2** lacking friendliness or enthusiasm. **3** (esp. of a woman) sexually unresponsive. —**fri·gid·i·ty** *n.* —**frig·id·ly** *adv.* —**frig·id·ness** *n.*

**frill** /fril/ ▸*n.* **1** strip of material with one side gathered or pleated, used as an ornamental edging. **2** (**frills**) unnecessary extra features or embellishments. —**frill·y** *adj.*

**fringe** /frinj/ ▸*n.* **1** ornamental bordering of threads left loose or formed into tassels or twists. **2** outer edge or margin; outer limit of an area, population, etc.: *fringe theater.* **3** thing, part, or area of secondary or minor importance.
▸*v.* adorn with or serve as a fringe.

**fringe ben·e·fit** ▸*n.* employee benefit supplementing a money wage or salary.

**frip·per·y** /ˈfripərē/ ▸*n.* (*pl.* **-ies**) showy, tawdry, or unnecessary finery or ornament, esp. in dress.

**frisk** /frisk/ ▸*v. inf.* feel over or search (a person) for a weapon, etc. (usu. rapidly).

**frisk·y** ▸*adj.* (**-i·er, -i·est**) lively; playful. **—frisk·i·ly** *adv.* **—frisk·i·ness** *n.*

**fris·son** /frēˈsôN/ ▸*n.* sudden strong feeling of excitement or fear; a thrill.

**frit·ter** /ˈfritər/ ▸*v.* (**fritter something away**) waste (money, time, etc.) on trifling matters.
▸*n.* piece of fruit, meat, etc., coated in batter and deep-fried: *apple fritter.*

**friv·o·lous** /ˈfrivələs/ ▸*adj.* **1** paltry; trifling; trumpery.

**2** lacking seriousness; given to trifling; silly. **—fri·vol·i·ty** *n.*

**frizz** /friz/ ▸*v.* form (hair, etc.) into a mass of small curls.
▸*n.* **1 a** frizzed hair. **b** row of curls. **2** frizzed state. **—friz·zy** *adj.*

**fro** /frō/ ▸*adv.* back (now only in *to and fro*: see **TO**).

**frock** /fräk/ ▸*n.* **1** woman's or girl's dress. **2** monk's or priest's long gown with loose sleeves. **3** smock.

**frog** /frôg; fräg/ ▸*n.* **1** small amphibian having a tailless smooth-skinned body with legs developed for jumping. **2** ornamental coat fastening of a spindle-shaped button and loop.

**froi·deur** /frwäˈdər/ ▸*n.* coolness or reserve between people.

**frol·ic** /ˈfrälik/ ▸*v.* (**-icked, -ick·ing**) play cheerfully.
▸*n.* **1** cheerful play. **2** merriment.

**from** /frəm/ ▸*prep.* expressing separation or origin, followed by: **1** person, place, time, etc., that is the starting point: *rain comes from the clouds.* **2** place, object, etc., whose distance or remoteness is reckoned or stated: *ten miles from Los Angeles.* **3 a** source. **b** giver or sender. **4** reason, cause, or motive: *died *from fatigue.* **5** thing distinguished or unlike: *know black from white.* **6** lower limit: *saw from 10 to 20 boats.* **7** state changed for another.

**frond** /fränd/ ▶*n.* foliage leaf in various flowerless plants, esp. ferns and palms.

**front** /frənt/ ▶*n.* **1** side or part normally nearer or toward the spectator or the direction of motion. **2** any face of a building, esp. that of the main entrance. **3** foremost line or part of an army, etc. **4** sector of activity regarded as resembling a military front. **5** demeanor; bearing: *put on a bold front.* **6** forward or conspicuous position: *come to the front.* **7** pretext. **8** person, etc., serving to cover subversive or illegal activities. **9** forward edge of an advancing mass of cold or warm air.

▶*adj.* **1** of the front: *the front page of the newspaper.* **2** situated in front: *she was in the front yard.*

▶*v.* **1** have the front facing or directed toward. **2** act as a front or cover for: *he fronted for them in illegal property deals.* **3** furnish with a front: *fronted with stone.*

—**fron·tal** *adj.* —**front·ward** *adj. & adv.* —**front·wards** *adv.*

□ **in front of** **1** ahead of; in advance of. **2** in the presence of; confronting.

**front·age** /'frəntij/ ▶*n.* **1** front of a building. **2** land abutting on a street or on water.

**fron·tier** /frən'ti(ə)r/ ▶*n.* **1 a** the border between two countries. **b** district on each side of this. **2** extreme limit of settled country. **3** limits of attainment or knowledge in a subject.

**fron·tis·piece** /'frəntis,pēs/ ▶*n.* illustration facing the title page of a book or of one of its divisions.

**front of·fice** ▶*n.* management or administration of an organization.

**front run·ner** ▶*n.* contestant most likely to succeed.

**front-wheel drive** ▶*n.* automobile drive system in which power is transmitted to the front wheels.

**frost** /frôst/ ▶*n.* **1** white frozen dew. **2** consistent temperature below freezing point causing frost to form.

▶*v.* **1** become covered with frost. **2** cover with or as if with frost, powder, etc. **3** give a roughened or finely granulated surface to (glass, metal). **4** decorate (a cake, etc.) with icing.

**frost·bite** ▸*n.* injury to skin due to freezing and often resulting in gangrene.

**frost·ing** ▸*n.* icing.

**froth** /frôTH/ ▸*n.* **1** foam. **2** anything unsubstantial or of little worth.
▸*v.* emit or gather froth. —**froth·y** *adj.*

**frou·frou** /ˈfroōˌfroō/ (also **frou-frou**) ▸*n.* **1** rustling noise made by someone walking in a dress. **2** frills or other ornamentation, particularly of women's clothes.

**frown** /froun/ ▸*v.* **1** wrinkle one's brows, esp. in displeasure or deep thought. **2** express disapproval.
▸*n.* look expressing severity, disapproval, or deep thought. —**frown·ing·ly** *adv.*

**frow·zy** /ˈfrouzē/ (also **frow·sy**) ▸*adj.* (**-zi·er, -zi·est**) scruffy and neglected in appearance; dingy. —**frow·zi·ness** *n.*

**fruc·ti·fy** /ˈfrəktəˌfī/ ▸*v.* (**-fied**) bear fruit or become productive.

**fruc·tose** /ˈfrəkˌtōs/ ▸*n.* simple sugar found in honey and fruits. (Also called **fruit sugar**).

**fru·gal** /ˈfroōgəl/ ▸*adj.* **1** sparing; thrifty. **2** meager; slight; costing little. —**fru·gal·i·ty** *n.*

**fruit** /froōt/ ▸*n.* **1** usu. sweet and fleshy edible product of a plant or tree, containing seed. **2** seed of a plant or tree with its covering, e.g., an acorn, pea pod, cherry, etc. **3** vegetables, grains, etc., used for food: *fruits of the earth.* **4** the result of action, etc., esp. as financial reward: *they are enjoying the fruits of years of hard work.*
▸*v.* bear or cause to bear fruit.

**fruit·ar·i·an** /froō'te(ə)rēən/ ▸*n.* person who eats only fruit.

**fruit·ful** ▸*adj.* **1** producing much fruit; abundant. **2** successful; remunerative. —**fruit·ful·ly** *adv.* —**fruit·ful·ness** *n.*

**fru·i·tion** /froō'isHən/ ▸*n.* **1 a** bearing of fruit. **b** production of results. **2** realization of aims or hopes. **3** enjoyment.

**fruit·less** ▸*adj.* useless; unsuccessful; unprofitable.

**frump** /frəmp/ ▸*n.* dowdy, old-fashioned woman. —**frump·ish** *adj.* —**frump·y** *adj.*

**frus·trate** /ˈfrəsˌtrāt/ ▸*v.* **1** make (efforts) ineffective. **2** prevent (a person) from achieving a purpose. **3** disappoint (a hope). —**frus·tra·tion** *n.*

**fry**[1] /frī/ ▶v. (**fried**) cook or be cooked in hot fat.
▶n. **1** social gathering serving fried food. **2** (**fries**) FRENCH FRIES.

**fry**[2] ▶pl. n. **1** young or newly hatched fishes. **2** young of other creatures produced in large numbers, e.g., bees or frogs.

**ft.** ▶abbr. foot, feet.

**FTC** ▶abbr. Federal Trade Commission.

**fuch·sia** /ˈfyo͞osHə/ ▶n. shrub with drooping red, purple, pink, or white flowers.

**fud·dle** /ˈfədl/ ▶v. confuse or stupefy (someone), esp. with alcohol.

**fudge** /fəj/ ▶n. soft toffee-like candy made with milk, sugar, butter, chocolate, etc.
▶v. **1** deal with (something) in a vague or inadequate way. **2** adjust or manipulate (facts) in order to present a desired picture.

**fu·el** /ˈfyo͞oəl/ ▶n. **1** material burned or used as a source of heat or power. **2** food as a source of energy. **3** anything that sustains or inflames emotion or passion.
▶v. (**-eled, -el·ing**) **1** supply with fuel. **2** sustain or inflame (a feeling or activity).

**fu·el in·jec·tion** ▶n. direct introduction of fuel into the combustion units of an internal combustion engine.

**fu·el oil** ▶n. oil used as fuel in an engine or furnace.

**fu·gi·tive** /ˈfyo͞ojətiv/ ▶n. person who flees, esp. from justice, an enemy, danger, or a master.
▶adj. **1** fleeing. **2** transient; fleeting; of short duration.

**fugue** /fyo͞og/ ▶n. musical composition in which a short melody or phrase is introduced by one part and successively taken up and developed by others.

**-ful** /fo͝ol; fəl/ ▶comb. form **1** forming adjectives from nouns, meaning: **a** full of: *beautiful*. **b** having the qualities of: *masterful*. **2** forming adjectives from adjectives or Latin stems: *direful*. **3** forming adjectives from verbs, meaning 'apt to': *forgetful*. **4** (pl. **-fuls**) forming nouns from nouns, meaning 'the amount needed to fill': *handful*.

**ful·crum** /ˈfo͝olkrəm/ ▶n. (pl. **-cra** or **-crums**) point against which a lever is placed to get a purchase or on which it turns or is supported.

**ful·fill** /foõl'fil/ ▸*v.* (-filled, -fill·ing) **1** carry out (a prophecy or promise). **2** satisfy (a desire or prayer). **3** perform (a task). **4** bring to an end; finish; complete. —**ful·fill·ment** *n.*

**ful·gu·ra·tion** /ˌfoõlg(y)ə'rāsHən/ ▸*n.* flash like that of lightning.

**full** /foõl/ ▸*adj.* **1** holding all its limits will allow: *full of water.* **2** having eaten to one's limits or satisfaction. **3** abundant; copious; satisfying; sufficient. **4** having or holding an abundance of. **5** (of tone or color) deep and clear. **6** plump; rounded; protuberant: *full figure.* **7** (of clothes) made of much material arranged in folds or gathers.
▸*adv.* **1** very: *you know full well.* **2** quite; fully: *full six miles.*
▸*v.* cleanse and thicken (cloth). —**full·ness** *n.* —**ful·ly** *adv.*
□ **in full swing** at the height of activity. □ **in full view** entirely visible.

**full·back** ▸*n.* **1** offensive player in the backfield in football. **2** defensive player, or a position near the goal, in soccer, field hockey, etc.

**full-blood·ed** ▸*adj.* **1** vigorous; hearty; sensual. **2** of unmixed race.

**full-blown** ▸*adj.* fully developed; complete.

**full-fledged** ▸*adj.* **1** fully developed. **2** of full rank or standing.

**full house** ▸*n.* **1** maximum or large attendance at a theater, etc. **2** *Poker* hand with three of a kind and a pair.

**full moon** ▸*n.* moon with its whole disk illuminated.

**full-scale** ▸*adj.* not reduced in size; complete.

**full-time** ▸*adj.* occupying or using the whole of the available working time.

**ful·mi·nate** /'foõlməˌnāt/ ▸*v.* express protest loudly and forcefully.

**ful·some** /'foõlsəm/ ▸*adj.* excessive; cloying.

**fum·ble** /'fəmbəl/ ▸*v.* use the hands awkwardly; grope about.
▸*n.* act of fumbling.

**fume** /fyoõm/ ▸*n.* (usu. **fumes**) gas, smoke, or vapor, esp. when harmful or unpleasant.
▸*v.* **1** emit gas, smoke, or vapor. **2** feel or show great anger: *was fuming at their inefficiency.*
—**fume·less** *adj.*

**fu·mi·gate** /ˈfyoomə,gāt/ ▶v. disinfect or purify with fumes of certain chemicals.
—**fu·mi·ga·tion** n.
—**fu·mi·ga·tor** n.

**fun** /fən/ ▶n. **1** amusement, esp. lively or playful. **2** source of this.
▶adj. inf. amusing; entertaining; enjoyable: *a fun thing to do.*
□ **make fun of** tease; ridicule.

**fu·nam·bu·list** /fyoōˈnambyəlist/ ▶n. tightrope walker.

**func·tion** /ˈfəNGKSHən/ ▶n. **1** activity proper to a person or institution. **2** mode of action or activity by which a thing fulfills its purpose. **3** public or social occasion. **4** *Math.* quantity whose value depends on the varying values of others.
▶v. fulfill a function; operate; be in working order. —**func·tion·al** adj.

**func·tion·ar·y** ▶n. (pl. -ies) person who has to perform official functions or duties; an official.

**fund** /fənd/ ▶n. **1** permanently available supply. **2** stock of money, esp. for a specific purpose. **3** (**funds**) money resources.
▶v. **1** provide with money.

**2** make (a debt) permanent at fixed interest.

**fun·da·ment** /ˈfəndəmənt/ ▶n. **1** foundation or basis of something. **2** buttocks.

**fun·da·men·tal** /ˌfəndəˈmentl/ ▶adj. of, affecting, or serving as a base or foundation; essential; primary.
▶n. (usu. **fundamentals**) primary rule or principle on which something is based.
—**fun·da·men·tal·ly** adv.

**fun·da·men·tal·ism** ▶n. strict maintenance of traditional religious beliefs.
—**fun·da·men·tal·ist** n.

**fund-rais·er** ▶n. **1** person who seeks financial support for a cause, enterprise, etc. **2** activity, event, etc., to raise money, as for charity, etc. —**fund-rais·ing** n.

**fu·ner·al** /ˈfyoonərəl/ ▶n. ceremonies honoring a dead person, usu. involving burial or cremation. —**fu·ner·ar·y** adj.

**fu·ner·al di·rec·tor** ▶n. undertaker.

**fu·ner·al par·lor** (also **fu·ner·al home**) ▶n. establishment where the dead are prepared for burial or cremation.

**fu·ne·re·al** /fyə'ni(ə)rēəl/ ▸adj.
**1** gloomy; dismal; dark. **2** of or
appropriate to a funeral.

**fun·gus** /'fəNGgəs/ ▸n. (pl. -gi or
-gus·es) any of a group of
nonphotosynthetic organisms
feeding on organic matter,
which include molds, yeast,
mushrooms, and toadstools.
—**fun·gi·form** adj.
—**fun·gous** adj.

**fu·nic·u·lar** /fyoo̅'nikyələr/ ▸adj.
**1** (of a railroad, esp. one on a
mountainside) operating by
cable with ascending and
descending cars
counterbalanced. **2** of or
relating to a rope or its tension.
▸n. railroad operating in such a
way.

**funk** /fəNGk/ ▸n. inf. **1** depression.
**2** funky music. **3** strong smell.
□ **in a funk** dejected.

**funk·y** ▸adj. (-i·er, -i·est) inf.
**1** (esp. of jazz or rock music)
earthy and bluesy, with a heavy
rhythmical beat. **2** fashionable.
**3** odd; unconventional. **4** having
a strong smell.

**fun·nel** /'fənl/ ▸n. **1** narrow tube
or pipe widening at the top, for
pouring liquid, powder, etc.,
into a small opening. **2** metal
chimney on a steam engine or
ship.
▸v. (-neled, -nel·ing; -nelled,
-nel·ling) guide or move through
or as through a funnel.

**fun·ny** ▸adj. (-ni·er, -ni·est)
**1** amusing; comical. **2** strange;
perplexing; hard to account for.

**fun·ny bone** ▸n. inf. **1** part of
the elbow over which a very
sensitive nerve passes. **2** sense
of humor: *tickle one's funny bone.*

**fur** /fər/ ▸n. **1** short, fine, soft
hair of certain animals. **2** skin
of such an animal with the fur
on it; pelt. —**fur·ry** adj.
□ **make the fur fly** inf. cause a
disturbance; stir up trouble.

**fur·bish** /'fərbiSH/ ▸v. give a new
look to; renovate.

**fu·ri·ous** /'fyoo̅rēəs/ ▸adj.
**1** extremely angry. **2** full of fury.
**3** raging; violent; intense.
—**fu·ri·ous·ly** adv.

**furl** /fərl/ ▸v. roll up and secure (a
sail, umbrella, flag, etc.).

**fur·long** /'fər,lôNG/ ▸n. unit of
measurement equal to an eighth
of a mile or 220 yards.

**fur·lough** /'fərlō/ ▸n. leave of
absence, esp. granted to a
member of the armed services.
▸v. grant furlough to.

**fur·nace** /'fərnəs/ ▶*n.* enclosed structure for intense heating.

**fur·nish** /'fərniSH/ ▶*v.* **1** provide with furniture. **2** provide; afford; yield. —**fur·nished** *adj.*

**fur·ni·ture** /'fərniCHər/ ▶*n.* movable equipment of a house, room, etc., e.g., tables, chairs, and beds.

**fu·ror** /'fyŏŏrər/ ▶*n.* **1** uproar; outbreak of fury. **2** wave of enthusiastic admiration; craze.

**fur·ri·er** /'fərēər/ ▶*n.* dealer in or dresser of furs.

**fur·row** /'fərō/ ▶*n.* **1** narrow trench made in the ground by a plow. **2** rut, groove, or deep wrinkle. **3** ship's track. ▶*v.* **1** plow. **2** make furrows, grooves, etc., in. **3** mark with wrinkles.

**fur·ther** /'fərTHər/ ▶*adv.* **1** FARTHER. **2** to a greater extent; more. **3** in addition. ▶*adj.* **1** FARTHER. **2** more; additional: *threats of further punishment.* ▶*v.* promote; favor (a plan, etc.). —**fur·ther·most** *adj.*

**fur·ther·more** ▶*adv.* in addition; besides.

**fur·thest** /'fərTHəst/ ▶var. of FARTHEST.

**fur·tive** /'fərtiv/ ▶*adj.* **1** done by stealth. **2** sly; stealthy. —**fur·tive·ly** *adv.* —**fur·tive·ness** *n.*

**fu·ry** /'fyŏŏrē/ ▶*n.* (*pl.* **-ries**) **1** wild and passionate anger; rage. **2** violence of a storm, disease, etc. **3** (**Fury**) (in Greek myth) each of three avenging goddesses.

**fuse** /fyŏŏz/ ▶*n.* **1** safety device or component for protecting an electric circuit when an excessive current passes through. **2** (also **fuze**) device of combustible matter for igniting an explosive. ▶*v.* **1** melt with intense heat. **2** blend or amalgamate into one whole by or as by melting.

**fu·se·lage** /'fyŏŏsə,läzH/ ▶*n.* the body of an airplane.

**fu·sil·lade** /'fyŏŏsə,läd/ ▶*n.* continuous discharge of firearms.

**fu·sion** /'fyŏŏzHən/ ▶*n.* **1** act or instance of fusing or melting. **2** (also **nuclear fusion**) union of atomic nuclei to form a heavier nucleus with the release of energy.

**fuss** /fəs/ ▶*n.* **1** excited commotion; bustle. **2** excessive concern about a trivial thing. **3** sustained protest or dispute.

▶*v.* **1** make a fuss. **2** busy oneself restlessly with trivial things.

□ **make a fuss** complain vigorously. □ **make a fuss over** treat (a person or animal) with great or excessive attention.

**fus·tian** /ˈfəsCHən/ ▶*n.* **1** thick, twilled cotton cloth. **2** pompous speech or writing.

**fus·ty** /ˈfəstē/ ▶*adj.* (**-ti·er, -ti·est**) **1** musty; moldy. **2** antiquated. —**fus·ti·ness** *n.*

**fu·tile** /ˈfyo͞otl/ ▶*adj.* useless; ineffectual, vain. —**fu·til·i·ty** *n.*

**fu·ton** /ˈfo͞oˌtän/ ▶*n.* **1** Japanese quilted mattress rolled out on the floor for use as a bed. **2** type of low wooden sofa bed having such a mattress.

**fu·ture** /ˈfyo͞oCHər/ ▶*adj.* **1** going or expected to happen or be or become. **2** of time to come: *future years.* **3** *Gram.* (of a tense or participle) describing an event yet to happen.

▶*n.* **1** time to come. **2** what will happen in the future. **3** future condition of a person, country, etc. **4** prospect of success, etc.: *there's no future in it.* **5** *Gram.* future tense.

**fu·ture per·fect** ▶*n. Gram.* tense giving the sense 'will have done'.

**fu·ture shock** ▶*n.* inability to cope with rapid progress.

**fuzz** /fəz/ ▶*n.* **1** fluff. **2** fluffy or frizzled hair.

**fuzz·y** ▶*adj.* (**-i·er, -i·est**) **1** like fuzz; fluffy. **2** blurred; indistinct. —**fuzz·i·ly** *adv.* —**fuzz·i·ness** *n.*

**FYI** ▶*abbr.* for your information.

**fyl·fot** /ˈfilˌfät/ ▶*n.* swastika.

# Gg

**G**[1] /jē/ (also **g**) ▶ *n.* (*pl.* **Gs** or **G's**; **g's**) **1** seventh letter of the alphabet. **2** *Mus.* fifth note in the diatonic scale of C major.

**G**[2] (also **G.**) ▶ *abbr.* **1** gauss. **2** giga-. **3** gravitational constant.

**g** (also **g.**) ▶ *abbr.* **1** gram(s). **2** gravity.

**GA** ▶ *abbr.* Georgia (in official postal use).

**Ga** ▶ *symb. Chem.* gallium.

**Ga.** ▶ *abbr.* Georgia (U.S.).

**gab** /gab/ *inf.* ▶ *n.* talk; chatter. ▶ *v.* talk incessantly and trivially; chatter. —**gab·by** *adj.*

**gab·ar·dine** /ˈgabərˌdēn/ ▶ *n.* smooth durable twilled cloth, esp. of worsted or cotton.

**gab·ble** /ˈgabəl/ ▶ *v.* talk inarticulately or too fast. ▶ *n.* fast unintelligible talk.

**ga·ble** /ˈgābəl/ ▶ *n.* triangular upper part of a wall at the end of a ridged roof. —**ga·bled** *adj.*

**gad** /gad/ ▶ *v.* (**gad·ded**, **gad·ding**) go about idly or in search of pleasure: *gadding about the countryside.*

**gad·a·bout** ▶ *n.* person who gads about.

**gad·fly** ▶ *n.* (*pl.* **-flies**) **1** cattle-biting fly. **2** irritating person.

**gadg·et** /ˈgajit/ ▶ *n.* mechanical or electronic device or tool.

**gaff** /gaf/ ▶ *n.* **1** stick with an iron hook for landing large fish. **2** spar to which the head of a fore-and-aft sail is bent.

**gaf·fer** ▶ *n.* chief electrician in a movie or television production unit.

**gag** /gag/ ▶ *n.* **1** piece of cloth thrust into or covering the mouth to prevent speaking. **2** something restricting free speech. **3** a joke. ▶ *v.* (**gagged**, **gag·ging**) **1** apply a gag to. **2** silence; deprive of free speech. **3 a** choke or retch. **b** cause to do this.

**gage** /gāj/ ▶ var. of **GAUGE**.

**gag·gle** /ˈgagəl/ ▶ *n.* flock (of geese).

**gai·e·ty** /ˈgāitē/ (also **gay·e·ty**) ▶ *n.* **1** state of being lighthearted. **2** merrymaking.

**gai·ly** /ˈgālē/ ▶ *adv.* in a lighthearted manner.

**gain** /gān/ ▶*v.* **1** obtain or secure. **2** acquire; earn. **3** (**gain in**) make a specified advance or improvement. **4** (of a clock, etc.) display a later time. **5** come closer to.
▶*n.* **1** something gained, achieved, etc. **2** increase of possessions, etc.; profit, advance, or improvement.

**gain·say** ▶*v.* (*past* and *past part.* **gain·said**) deny; contradict.

**gait** /gāt/ ▶*n.* manner of running or walking.

**gal** /gal/ ▶*n. inf.* girl.

**gal.** ▶*abbr.* gallon(s).

**ga·la** /ˈgālə/ ▶*n.* festive or special occasion: *a black-tie gala.*
▶*adj.* festive: *a gala affair.*

**gal·ax·y** /ˈgaləksē/ ▶*n.* (*pl.* **-ies**) **1** any of many independent systems of stars, gas, dust, etc., held together by gravitational attraction. **2** (often **the Galaxy**) the Milky Way.

**gale** /gāl/ ▶*n.* **1** very strong wind. **2** *Naut.* storm. **3** outburst, esp. of laughter.

**gall** /gôl/ ▶*n.* **1** impudence. **2** rancor. **3** bitterness; anything bitter. **4** bile. **5** sore made by chafing. **6** growth produced by insects or fungus, etc., on plants and trees, esp. on oak.
▶*v.* **1** rub sore. **2** vex; annoy; humiliate.

**gal·lant** ▶*adj.* /ˈgalənt/ **1** brave; chivalrous. **2** grand; fine; stately. **3** very attentive to women.
▶*n.* /gəˈlänt/ ladies' man.
—**gal·lant·ly** *adv.*

**gal·lant·ry** /ˈgaləntrē/ ▶*n.* (*pl.* **-ries**) **1** courageous behavior, esp. in battle. **2** polite attention or respect given by men to women. **3** (**gallantries**) actions or words used when paying such attention.

**gall·blad·der** /ˈgôlˌbladər/ (also **gall blad·der**) ▶*n.* organ that stores bile.

**gal·le·on** /ˈgalēən/ ▶*n. hist.* **1** war ship (usu. Spanish). **2** large Spanish merchant ship.

**gal·ler·y** /ˈgalərē/ ▶*n.* (*pl.* **-ies**) **1** room or building for showing works of art. **2** balcony, esp. in a church, hall, etc. **3 a** highest balcony in a theater. **b** its occupants. **4** portico or colonnade. **5** long narrow room or corridor. **6** group of spectators.

**gal·ley** /ˈgalē/ ▶*n.* **1** ship's or aircraft's kitchen. **2** (also **galley proof**) typeset copy before division into pages. **3** low, flat single-decked vessel using sails and oars, and usu. rowed by slaves or criminals.

**gal·li·vant** /ˈɡaləˌvant/ ▶v. inf. gad about.

**gal·lon** /ˈɡalən/ ▶n. measure of capacity equivalent to four quarts (3.785 liters), used for liquids.

**gal·lop** /ˈɡaləp/ ▶n. fastest pace of a horse, with all the feet off the ground together in each stride.
▶v. (-**loped**, -**lop·ing**) **1** (of a horse or its rider) go at the pace of a gallop. **2** move very rapidly.

**gal·lows** /ˈɡalōz/ ▶pl. n. [usu. treated as *sing.*] structure formerly used for the hanging of criminals.
□ **gallows humor** grim humor.

**gall·stone** /ˈɡôlˌstōn/ ▶n. small hard mass that sometimes forms in the gallbladder.

**ga·lore** /ɡəˈlôr/ ▶adv. in abundance: *decorated with flowers galore.*

**ga·losh** /ɡəˈläsH/ ▶n. (usu. **galoshes**) waterproof rubber overshoe.

**gal·van·ic** /ɡalˈvanik/ ▶adj. **1** relating to or involving electric currents produced by chemical action. **2** sudden and dramatic.

**gal·va·nize** /ˈɡalvəˌnīz/ ▶v.

**1** coat (iron) with zinc as a protection against rust. **2** rouse forcefully, esp. by shock or excitement.

**gam·bit** /ˈɡambit/ ▶n. **1** chess opening in which a player sacrifices a piece or pawn to secure an advantage. **2** opening move in a discussion, etc. **3** trick or device.

**gam·ble** /ˈɡambəl/ ▶v. **1** play games of chance for money. **2** bet (a sum of money). **3** take risks in the hope of gain. **4** act in the hope or expectation of: *gambled on fine weather.*
▶n. risky undertaking or attempt. —**gam·bler** n.

**gam·bol** /ˈɡambəl/ ▶v. (-**boled**, -**bol·ing**) skip or frolic playfully.
▶n. playful frolic.

**game** /ɡām/ ▶n. **1 a** form of play or sport, esp. a competitive one played according to rules. **b** specific instance of playing such a game; a match. **2** (**games**) meeting for athletic, etc., contests: *Olympic Games.* **3 a** fun; jest. **b** (**games**) jokes; tricks: *none of your games!* **4** scheme. **5** wild animals or birds hunted for sport or food.
▶adj. **1** spirited; eager and

willing. **2** (of a leg, arm, etc.) lame; crippled.

▸*v.* gamble.

□ **game plan 1** winning strategy worked out in advance. **2** plan of campaign, esp. in politics.

**ga·mete** /ˈgamēt/ ▸*n.* mature germ cell able to unite with another in sexual reproduction.

**gam·ine** /ˈgamēn/ ▸*n.* girl with mischievous or boyish charm.

▸*adj.* characteristic of or relating to such a girl.

**gam·mon** /ˈgamən/ ▸*n.* **1** ham that has been cured or smoked like bacon. **2** bottom piece of a side of bacon, including a hind leg.

**gam·ut** /ˈgamət/ ▸*n.* whole range or scope of anything: *the whole gamut of crime.*

**gam·y** /ˈgāmē/ ▸*adj.* (**-i·er, -i·est**) **1** having the flavor or odor of game. **2** scandalous.
—**gam·i·ness** *n.*

**gan·der** /ˈgandər/ ▸*n.* **1** male goose. **2** *inf.* a look; a glance.

**gang** /gaNG/ ▸*n.* **1 a** band of persons associating for criminal or asocial purposes. **b** *inf.* group of people who associate with one another: *the whole gang gets together after work on Fridays.* **2** set of workers or prisoners.

□ **gang up on** combine against.

**gan·gling** /ˈgaNGgliNG/ ▸*adj.* (of a person) loosely built; lanky.

**gan·gli·on** /ˈgaNGglēən/ ▸*n.* (*pl.* **-gli·a** or **-gli·ons**) structure containing an assemblage of nerve cells.

**gang·plank** ▸*n.* movable plank usu. with cleats nailed on it for boarding or disembarking from a ship, etc.

**gan·grene** /ˈgaNGgrēn/ ▸*n.* death and decomposition of a part of the body tissue, usu. resulting from obstructed circulation.
—**gan·gre·nous** *adj.*

**gang·ster** ▸*n.* member of a gang of violent criminals.

**gang·way** ▸*n.* **1** opening in a ship's bulwarks. **2** bridge laid from ship to shore.

**gan·try** /ˈgantrē/ ▸*n.* (*pl.* **-tries**) **1** overhead structure supporting a traveling crane, or railroad or road signals. **2** structure supporting a space rocket prior to launching.

**gap** /gap/ ▸*n.* **1** unfilled space; break in continuity. **2** wide divergence in views, etc.

□ **fill** (or **close**) **a gap** make up a deficiency.

**gape** /gāp/ ▶v. **1 a** open one's mouth wide. **b** be or become wide open. **2** (**gape at**) stare curiously or wonderingly.
▶n. **1** openmouthed stare. **2** yawn.

**ga·rage** /gə'räzн/ ▶n. **1** building or shed for the storage of motor vehicles. **2** establishment for repairing and servicing motor vehicles.
▶v. put or keep (a motor vehicle) in a garage.

**garb** /gärb/ ▶n. clothing, esp. of a distinctive kind. —**garbed** adj.

**gar·bage** /'gärbij/ ▶n. domestic waste, esp. food wastes.

**gar·ble** /'gärbəl/ ▶v. unintentionally distort or confuse (facts, messages, etc.).

**gar·den** /'gärdn/ ▶n. **1** piece of ground used for growing esp. flowers or vegetables. **2** (esp. **gardens**) ornamental grounds laid out for public enjoyment: *botanical gardens.*
▶v. cultivate or work in a garden. —**gar·den·er** n. —**gar·den·ing** n.

**gar·de·nia** /gär'dēnyə/ ▶n. tree or shrub with large white or yellow flowers and usu. a fragrant scent.

**gar·gan·tu·an** /gär'ganchooən/ ▶adj. enormous; gigantic.

**gar·gle** /'gärgəl/ ▶v. wash (one's mouth and throat), esp. for medicinal purposes, with a liquid kept in motion by breathing through it.
▶n. liquid used for gargling.

**gar·goyle** /'gärgoil/ ▶n. grotesque carved human or animal face or figure, esp. as a spout from the gutter on a building.

**gar·ish** /'ge(ə)rish/ ▶adj. **1** overly bright; showy. **2** gaudy; overdecorated. —**gar·ish·ly** adv.

**gar·land** /'gärlənd/ ▶n. wreath of flowers and leaves. —**gar·land·ed** adj.

**gar·lic** /'gärlik/ ▶n. plant of the onion family with flavorful bulb used in cooking.

**gar·ment** /'gärmənt/ ▶n. article of dress.

**gar·ner** /'gärnər/ ▶v. **1** collect. **2** store.

**gar·net** /'gärnit/ ▶n. a transparent deep red mineral used as a gem.

**gar·nish** /'gärnish/ ▶v. decorate (esp. food).
▶n. (also **gar·nish·ing**) decoration, esp. to food.

**gar·ret** /'garit/ ▶n. **1** top floor or attic room. **2** attic.

**gar·ri·son** /'garəsən/ ▸n.
**1** troops stationed in a fortress or town to defend it. **2** the building they occupy.

▸v. provide with or occupy as a garrison.

**gar·rote** /gə'rät; -'rōt/ (also **ga·rotte**; **gar·rotte**) ▸v. kill by strangling with a wire, usu. with handles.

▸n. this apparatus.

**gar·ru·lous** /'garələs/ ▸adj.
**1** talkative. **2** wordy.
—**gar·ru·li·ty** n. —**gar·ru·lous·ly** adv. —**gar·ru·lous·ness** n.

**gar·ter** /'gärtər/ ▸n. band worn to keep a sock or stocking or shirt sleeve up.

**gas** /gas/ ▸n. (pl. **gas·es**) **1** any airlike substance that moves freely to fill any space available, irrespective of its quantity.
**2** such a substance used as fuel: *gas stove.* **3** gasoline.

▸v. (**gassed**, **gas·sing**) **1** expose to gas, esp. to kill or make unconscious. **2** fill (the tank of a motor vehicle) with gasoline.
—**gas·e·ous** adj.

□ **gas chamber** room for execution by gas. □ **gas mask** respirator used as a defense against poison gas.

**gash** /gasH/ ▸n. long and deep slash, cut, or wound.

▸v. make a gash in; cut.

**gas·ket** /'gaskit/ ▸n. sheet or ring of rubber, etc., shaped to seal the junction of metal surfaces.

**gas·o·line** /ˌgasə'lēn/ ▸n. flammable liquid made from petroleum and used as fuel.

**gasp** /gasp/ ▸v. **1** catch one's breath with an open mouth as in exhaustion or astonishment. **2** utter with gasps.

▸n. convulsive catching of breath.

**gas·tric** /'gastrik/ ▸adj. of the stomach.

**gate** /gāt/ ▸n. **1** barrier used to close an entrance through a wall, fence, etc. **2** means of entrance or exit. **3** numbered place of access to aircraft at an airport. **4** number of people entering a sports stadium, concert, etc.; the proceeds taken for admission.

□ **gated community** residential area protected by gates, fences, etc.

**-gate** ▸suffix forming nouns denoting a scandal comparable in some way to the Watergate scandal of 1972: *Irangate.*

**gate·way** ▸n. entrance or exit.

*fourth-generation computers.* **4** procreation.

**gen·er·a·tor** /ˈjenəˌrātər/ ▸*n.* machine for converting mechanical into electrical energy.

**ge·ner·ic** /jəˈnerik/ ▸*adj.* **1** characteristic of a class; general, not specific or special. **2** (of goods, esp. a drug) having no trade or brand name. —**ge·ner·i·cal·ly** *adv.*

**gen·er·ous** /ˈjenərəs/ ▸*adj.* **1** giving or given freely. **2** noble-minded; unprejudiced. **3** abundant. —**gen·er·os·i·ty** *n.* —**gen·er·ous·ly** *adv.*

**gen·e·sis** /ˈjenəsis/ ▸*n.* **1** origin. **2** (**Genesis**) first book of the Old Testament.

**ge·net·ics** /jəˈnetiks/ ▸*n.* the study of heredity and inherited characteristics. —**ge·net·i·cist** *n.*

**gen·ial** /ˈjēnyəl; -nēəl/ ▸*adj.* sociable; kindly; cheerful. —**ge·ni·al·i·ty** *n.* —**ge·nial·ly** *adv.*

**ge·nie** /ˈjēnē/ ▸*n.* (*pl.* usu. **ge·ni·i**) spirit of Arabian folklore.

**genital** /ˈjenitl/ ▸*adj.* of or relating to human or animal reproductive organs. ▸*pl. n.* (**genitals**) external reproductive organs.

**gen·i·ta·li·a** /ˌjeniˈtālēə/ ▸*pl. n.* genitals.

**gen·i·tive** /ˈjenitiv/ ▸*n.* grammatical case indicating possession or association. ▸*adj.* of or in the genitive.

**gen·ius** /ˈjēnyəs/ ▸*n.* **1** exceptional intellectual or creative power or other natural ability or tendency. **2** person having this.

**gen·o·cide** /ˈjenəˌsīd/ ▸*n.* deliberate extermination of a people or nation. —**gen·o·ci·dal** *adj.*

**ge·nome** /ˈjēˌnōm/ ▸*n.* complete set of genes or genetic material present in a cell or organism.

**gen·re** /ˈzhänrə/ ▸*n.* kind or style of art, literature, etc.

**gen·teel** /jenˈtēl/ ▸*adj.* **1** affectedly or ostentatiously refined or stylish. **2** well-bred; upper-class. —**gen·teel·ly** *adv.*

**gen·tian** /ˈjenchən/ ▸*n.* mountain plant usu. with violet or vivid blue flowers.

**Gen·tile** /ˈjentīl/ ▸*adj.* not Jewish; heathen. ▸*n.* person who is not Jewish.

**gen·tle** /ˈjentl/ ▸*adj.* (**-tler, -tlest**) **1** not rough; mild or kind, esp. in temperament. **2** moderate;

**gath·er** /ˈgaᴛʜər/ ▸*v.* **1** bring or come together; assemble. **2** acquire by gradually collecting; amass. **3** harvest. **4** infer or understand. **5** increase: *gather speed.* **6** summon up (one's thoughts, energy, etc.) for a purpose. **7** draw (material, or one's brow) together in folds or wrinkles. ▸*n.* (**gathers**) part of a garment that is gathered or drawn in. —**gath·er·er** *n.*

**gauche** /gōsh/ ▸*adj.* **1** lacking ease or grace; socially awkward. **2** tactless.

**gau·cho** /ˈgouchō/ ▸*n.* (*pl.* **-chos**) cowboy of the South American pampas.

**gaud·y** /ˈgôdē/ ▸*adj.* (**-i·er, -i·est**) tastelessly or extravagantly bright or showy. —**gaud·i·ly** *adv.* —**gaud·i·ness** *n.*

**gauge** /gāj/ (also **gage**) ▸*n.* **1** standard measure to which certain things must conform, esp. in thickness or diameter. **2** instrument for measuring. **3** distance between a pair of rails or the wheels on one axle. ▸*v.* **1** measure exactly. **2** estimate.

**gaunt** /gônt/ ▸*adj.* **1** lean; haggard. **2** grim or desolate in appearance. —**gaunt·ly** *adv.* —**gaunt·ness** *n.*

**gaunt·let** /ˈgôntlit/ ▸*n.* stout glove with a long loose wrist. □ **run the gauntlet** be subjected to harsh criticism. □ **throw down the gauntlet** make a challenge.

**gauze** /gôz/ ▸*n.* thin transparent fabric of silk, cotton, etc. —**gauz·y** *adj.*

**ga·vage** /gəˈväzh/ ▸*n.* administration of food or drugs by force, esp. to an animal, typically through a tube leading down the throat to the stomach.

**gav·el** /ˈgavəl/ ▸*n.* small hammer used by an auctioneer, or for calling a meeting, courtroom, etc., to order.

**gawk** /gôk/ ▸*v.* stare stupidly.

**gawk·y** /ˈgôkē/ ▸*adj.* (**-i·er, -i·est**) awkward or ungainly. —**gawk·i·ly** *adv.*

**gay** /gā/ ▸*adj.* **1 a** homosexual. **b** intended for or used by homosexuals: *gay bar.* **2** lighthearted and carefree; cheerful **3** brightly colored. ▸*n.* homosexual, esp. male.

**gaze** /gāz/ ▸*v.* look fixedly. ▸*n.* intent look. —**gaz·er** *n.*

**ga·ze·bo** /gəˈzēbō/ ▸*n.* (*pl.* **-bos** or **-boes**) open-sided structure giving a wide view.

**ga·zelle** /gəˈzel/ ▸*n.* any of various graceful soft-eyed antelopes of Asia or Africa.

**ga·zette** /gəˈzet/ ▸*n.* newspaper, esp. the official one of an organization or institution: *University Gazette.*

**gaz·et·teer** /ˌgazəˈti(ə)r/ ▸*n.* geographical index or dictionary.

**gaz·pa·cho** /gäˈspäCHō/ ▸*n.* (*pl.* -chos) Spanish soup made with tomatoes, oil, garlic, onions, etc., and served cold.

**gear** /gi(ə)r/ ▸*n.* 1 (**gears**) set of toothed wheels that work together, as in a vehicle. 2 particular setting of these: *low gear.* 3 equipment or tackle for a special purpose. 4 possessions in general. ▸*v.* 1 adjust or adapt (something) to. 2 (**gear up**) make ready or prepared.

**gear·shift** ▸*n.* lever used to engage or change gear.

**geck·o** /ˈgekō/ ▸*n.* (*pl.* -os or -oes) tropical lizard.

**gee** /jē/ (also **gee whiz**) ▸*interj.* mild expression of surprise, discovery, etc.

**geek** /gēk/ ▸*n.* 1 unfashionable or socially inept person. 2 person with an eccentric devotion to a particular interest.

3 carnival performer who does wild or disgusting acts.

**gee·zer** /ˈgēzər/ ▸*n. inf.* person, esp. an old man.

**Gei·ger count·er** /ˈgīgər/ ▸*n.* device for measuring radioactivity by detecting and counting ionizing particles.

**gei·sha** /ˈgāSHə/ ▸*n.* (*pl.* same or **gei·shas**) Japanese hostess trained in entertaining men with dance and song.

**gel** /jel/ ▸*n.* 1 semisolid colloidal suspension or jelly. 2 gelatinous hairstyling preparation. ▸*v.* (**gelled, gel·ling**) form a gel.

**gel·a·tin** /ˈjelətn/ (also **gel·a·tine**) ▸*n.* transparent water-soluble protein derived from collagen and used in food preparation, photography, etc. —**ge·lat·i·nous** *adj.*

**geld** /geld/ ▸*v.* castrate.

**geld·ing** ▸*n.* gelded animal, esp. a male horse.

**gel·id** /ˈjelid/ ▸*adj.* icy; extremely cold.

**gem** /jem/ ▸*n.* 1 precious stone, esp. when cut and polished. 2 object or person of great beauty or worth. —**gem·like** *adj.*

**ge·müt·lich·keit** /gəˈmootlik-ˌkīt/ (also **Ge·müt·lich·keit**) ▸*n.* geniality; friendliness.

**Gen.** ▸*abbr.* 1 General. 2 Genesis (Old Testament).

**-gen** ▸*comb. form* 1 *Chem.* that which produces: *hydrogen | antigen.* 2 *Bot.* growth: *endogen | exogen | acrogen.*

**gen·der** /ˈjendər/ ▸*n.* 1 a grammatical classification corresponding to the two sexes and sexlessness. b each of these classes of nouns. 2 a person's sex.

**gene** /jēn/ ▸*n.* unit of heredity composed of DNA or RNA and forming part of a chromosome, that alone or in conjunction with other genes determines a particular characteristic of an individual.

**ge·ne·al·o·gy** /ˌjēnēˈäləjē; -ˈal-/ ▸*n.* (*pl.* -gies) 1 descent traced continuously from an ancestor. 2 study of family descent. —**ge·ne·a·log·i·cal** *adj.* —**ge·ne·a·log·i·cal·ly** *adv.* —**ge·ne·al·o·gist** *n.*

**gen·er·al** /ˈjen(ə)rəl/ ▸*adj.* 1 completely or almost universal; including or affecting all or nearly all parts or cases of things. 2 prevalent; widespread; usual. 3 not limited in application; not restricted,

specialized, or detailed: *a general idea.* ▸*n.* 1 commander of an army. 2 tactician or strategist of specified merit: *a great general.* —**gen·er·al·ly** *adv.* □ **in general** 1 as a normal rule; usually. 2 for the most part.

**gen·er·al·is·si·mo** /ˌjenərəˈlisə-ˌmō/ ▸*n.* (*pl.* -mos) commander of a combined military force consisting of army, navy, and air force units.

**gen·er·al·i·ty** /ˌjenəˈralitē/ ▸*n.* (*pl.* -ties) 1 statement or principle having general validity or force. 2 vagueness; lack of detail.

**gen·er·al·ize** ▸*v.* 1 speak in general or indefinite terms. 2 infer (a law or conclusion) by induction. —**gen·er·al·i·za·tion** *n.*

**gen·er·ate** /ˈjenəˌrāt/ ▸*v.* 1 bring into existence; produce; evolve. 2 produce (electricity). —**gen·er·a·tive** *adj.*

**gen·er·a·tion** /ˌjenəˈrāSHən/ ▸*n.* 1 all the people born at a particular time, regarded collectively: *my generation.* 2 single step in descent or pedigree. 3 stage in (esp. technological) development:

not severe: *gentle rebuke.*
—**gen·tle·ness** *n.* —**gen·tly** *adv.*

**gen·tle·man** ▶*n.* (*pl.* -men)
**1** man (in polite or formal use).
**2** chivalrous or well-bred man.
**3** (**gentlemen**) form of address to men in an audience.
—**gen·tle·man·ly** *adj.*

**gen·tri·fi·ca·tion** /ˌjentrəfi-'kāsHən/ ▶*n.* improvement of an urban area by the fixing of buildings and arrival of affluent residents who displace poorer inhabitants. —**gen·tri·fy** *v.*

**gen·try** /ˈjentrē/ ▶*pl. n.* (in aristocratic societies) people next below the nobility in position and birth.

**gen·u·flect** /ˈjenyə,flekt/ ▶*v.* bend the knee, esp. in worship.
—**gen·u·flec·tion** *n.*

**gen·u·ine** /ˈjenyo͞oin/ ▶*adj.*
**1** really coming from its stated, advertised, or reputed source; not fake. **2** sincere.
—**gen·u·ine·ly** *adv.*
—**gen·u·ine·ness** *n.*

**ge·nus** /ˈjenəs/ ▶*n.* (*pl.* **gen·er·a**) taxonomic grouping of organisms, usu. of several species, with common structural characteristics.

**geo-** ▶*comb. form* earth: *geology.*

**ge·ode** /ˈjēōd/ ▶*n.* **1** small cavity lined with crystals. **2** rock containing this.

**ge·og·ra·phy** /jēˈägrəfē/ ▶*n.*
**1** the study of the earth's physical features, resources, and climate. **2** main physical features of an area.
—**ge·og·ra·pher** *n.*
—**ge·o·graph·ic** *adj.*
—**ge·o·graph·i·cal** *adj.*
—**ge·o·graph·i·cal·ly** *adv.*

**ge·ol·o·gy** /jēˈäləjē/ ▶*n.* science of the earth, including the composition, structure, and origin of its rocks. —**ge·o·log·ic** *adj.* —**ge·o·log·i·cal** *adj.*
—**ge·o·log·i·cal·ly** *adv.*
—**ge·ol·o·gist** *n.*

**ge·om·e·try** /jēˈämitrē/ ▶*n.* the study of the properties and relations of points, lines, surfaces, and solids.
—**ge·o·met·ric** *adj.*
—**ge·om·e·tri·cian** *n.*

**ge·o·phys·ics** /ˌjēōˈfiziks/ ▶*n.* the physics of the earth.
—**ge·o·phys·i·cal** *adj.*
—**ge·o·phys·i·cist** *n.*

**ge·ra·ni·um** /jəˈrānēəm/ ▶*n.* one of many widely cultivated flowering garden plants.

**ger·bil** /ˈjərbəl/ ▶*n.* mouselike desert rodent with long hind legs.

**ger·i·at·rics** /ˌjerē'atriks/ ▶n. branch of medicine or social science dealing with the health and care of old people. —**ger·i·at·ric** adj. —**ger·i·a·tri·cian** n.

**germ** /jərm/ ▶n. 1 microorganism, esp. one that causes disease. 2 seed. 3 original idea, etc., from which something may develop. —**germ·y** adj.

**Ger·man** /'jərmən/ ▶n. 1 native or inhabitant of Germany; person of German descent. 2 language of Germany. ▶adj. of Germany or its people or language.

**ger·mane** /jər'mān/ ▶adj. relevant: *that is not germane to our discussion.*

**Ger·man mea·sles** ▶ n. contagious disease, rubella, with symptoms like mild measles.

**Ger·man shep·herd** ▶n. breed of large dog bred from the wolfhound.

**ger·mi·cide** /'jərmə,sīd/ ▶n. substance destroying germs.

**ger·mi·nate** /'jərmə,nāt/ ▶v. 1 sprout, bud, or put forth shoots. 2 cause to sprout or shoot. —**ger·mi·na·tion** n.

**ger·on·tol·o·gy** /ˌjerən'täləjē/ ▶n. study of old age and aging. —**ge·ron·to·log·i·cal** adj. —**ger·on·tol·o·gist** n.

**ger·ry·man·der** /'jerē,mandər/ ▶v. manipulate the boundaries of (a constituency, etc.) for political advantage.

**ger·und** /'jerənd/ ▶n. verbal noun, in English ending in -ing: *asking* in *do you mind my asking?* and *skiing* in *skiing is fun.*

**ge·stalt** /gə'sHtält; -'sHtôlt/ (also **Ge·stalt**) ▶n. (pl. **-stalt·en** /-'sHtältn; -'sHtôltn/ or **-stalts**) organized whole that is perceived as more than the sum of its parts.

**ges·ta·tion** /je'stāsHən/ ▶n. 1 process of carrying or being carried in the womb between conception and birth. 2 this period.

**ges·tic·u·late** /je'stikyə,lāt/ ▶v. 1 use gestures instead of or in addition to speech. 2 express with gestures. —**ges·tic·u·la·tion** n.

**ges·ture** /'jescHər/ ▶n. 1 significant movement of a limb or the body. 2 use of such movements, esp. to convey feeling or as a rhetorical device.

**ghastly**

3 action to evoke a response or convey intention, usu. friendly.
▶*v.* gesticulate. —**ges·tur·al** *adj.* —**ges·tur·er** *n.*

**get** /get/ ▶*v.* (**get·ting**; *past* **got**; *past part.* **got** or **got·ten**) **1** come into the possession of; receive or earn. **2 a** fetch; procure. **b** get hold of (a person). **3** go to catch (a bus, train, etc.). **4** prepare (a meal, etc.). **5** reach or cause to reach a certain state; become or cause to become: *get rich | got them ready.* **6** contract (a disease, etc.). **7** establish contact with by telephone or radio. **8** experience or suffer; have inflicted on one: *got four years in prison.* **9 a** succeed in bringing, placing, etc.: *get it onto the agenda.* **b** succeed or cause to succeed in coming or going: *get you there somehow.* **10 a** (**have got**) possess. **b** (**have got to**) be bound or obliged to. **11** induce; prevail upon: *got them to help me.* **12** *inf.* understand (a person or an argument): *have you got that?* **13** *inf.* punish; retaliate: *I'll get you for that.*
▶*n.* **1** act of begetting (of animals). **2** an offspring (of animals).
☐ **get about** (or **around**) **1** travel extensively or fast. **2** manage to walk, etc. (esp. after illness). **3** (of news) be circulated, esp. orally. ☐ **get at 1** reach; get hold of. **2** *inf.* imply. ☐ **get away with 1** escape blame or punishment for. **2** steal. ☐ **get back at** retaliate against. ☐ **get by** just manage. ☐ **get off 1** *inf.* be acquitted; escape with little or no punishment. **2** leave. **3** alight from (a bus, etc.). ☐ **get out 1** leave or escape. **2** manage to go outdoors. **3** alight from a vehicle. **4** become known. ☐ **get over** recover from (an illness, upset, etc.). ☐ **get through 1** pass or assist in passing (an examination, etc.). **2** manage; survive. **3** make contact. **4** (**get through to**) succeed in making (a person) listen or understand. ☐ **get-up** *inf.* style or arrangement of dress, etc., esp. an elaborate one.

**get·a·way** ▶*n.* escape, esp. after a crime.

**gey·ser** /ˈgīzər/ ▶*n.* intermittently gushing hot spring.

**ghast·ly** /ˈgastlē/ ▶*adj.* (**-li·er, -li·est**) **1** horrible; frightful. **2** deathlike; pallid. —**ghast·li·ness** *n.*

**gher·kin** /ˈgərkin/ ▸n. small cucumber, used for pickling.

**ghet·to** /ˈgetō/ ▸n. (pl. **-tos**) part of a city, esp. a slum area, occupied by a minority group or groups.

**ghost** /gōst/ ▸n. **1** supposed apparition of a dead person or animal. **2** shadow or mere semblance.
▸v. **1** act as ghostwriter. **2** act as ghostwriter of (a work).
—**ghost·like** adj.

**ghost town** ▸n. deserted town with few or no remaining inhabitants.

**ghost·writ·er** ▸n. person who writes material for another person who is named as the author.

**ghoul** /gool/ ▸n. **1** person morbidly interested in death, etc. **2** in Muslim folklore, an evil spirit preying on corpses.
—**ghoul·ish** adj. —**ghoul·ish·ly** adv.

**GI** ▸n. soldier in the U.S. armed forces, esp. the army.

**gi·ant** /ˈjīənt/ ▸n. **1** imaginary or mythical being of human form but superhuman size.
**2** abnormally tall or large person, animal, or plant.
▸adj. very large.

**gib·ber** /ˈjibər/ ▸v. speak fast and inarticulately.

**gib·bet** /ˈjibit/ ▸n. hist. gallows.

**gib·bon** /ˈgibən/ ▸n. small ape having a slender body and long arms, native to SE Asia.

**gibe** /jīb/ (also **jibe**) ▸v. (often **gibe at**) jeer; mock.
▸n. a taunt.

**gib·lets** /ˈjiblits/ ▸pl. n. liver, gizzard, neck, etc., of a bird.

**gid·dy** /ˈgidē/ ▸adj. (**-di·er, -di·est**) **1** having a sensation of whirling and a tendency to fall, stagger, or spin around. **2** excitable; frivolous. **3** tending to make one giddy. —**gid·di·ly** adv. —**gid·di·ness** n.

**gift** /gift/ ▸n. **1** thing given; a present. **2** natural ability or talent.

**gift·ed** ▸adj. exceptionally talented or intelligent.
—**gift·ed·ness** n.

**gig** /gig/ ▸n. **1** light, two-wheeled one-horse carriage. **2** inf. engagement to play popular music, jazz, etc.

**gi·gan·tic** /jīˈgantik/ ▸adj. enormous.

**gig·gle** /ˈgigəl/ ▸v. laugh in half-suppressed spasms, esp. in an affected or silly manner.

▶*n.* such a laugh. —**gig·gler** *n.*
—**gig·gly** *adj.*

**GIGO** /'gɪˌgō/ ▶*n. Computing* abbr. for *garbage in, garbage out*, an informal rule stating that the quality of the data input determines the quality of the results.

**gig·o·lo** /'jɪgəˌlō/ ▶*n.* (*pl.* **-los**) young man paid by an older woman to be her escort or lover.

**gild** /gɪld/ ▶*v.* (*past part.* **gild·ed** or (in sense 1) **gilt**) **1** cover thinly with gold. **2** give a specious or false brilliance to. —**gild·ing** *n.*

**gill** /gɪl/ [usu. in *pl.*] ▶*n.* respiratory organ in fishes and other aquatic animals. —**gilled** *adj.*

**gilt** /gɪlt/ ▶*adj.* **1** covered thinly with gold. **2** gold-colored.
▶*n.* gilding.

**gilt-edged** ▶*adj.* (of securities, stocks, etc.) very reliable.

**gim·bal** /'gɪmbəl; 'jɪm-/ ▶*n.* (often **gimbals**) contrivance, typically consisting of rings pivoted at right angles, for keeping an instrument such as a compass or chronometer horizontal in a moving vessel or aircraft.

**gim·let** /'gɪmlɪt/ ▶*n.* **1** small tool with a screw tip for boring holes. **2** cocktail, usu. of gin and lime juice.

**gim·mick** /'gɪmɪk/ ▶*n.* trick or device, esp. to attract attention or publicity. —**gim·mick·ry** *n.* —**gim·mick·y** *adj.*

**gin** /jɪn/ ▶*n.* **1** distilled alcoholic spirit flavored with juniper berries. **2** machine for separating cotton from its seeds.
□ **gin rummy** form of the card game rummy.

**gin·ger** /'jɪnjər/ ▶*n.* **1** hot spicy root used as a spice or flavoring. **2** light reddish yellow color.
▶*adj.* of a ginger color. —**gin·ger·y** *adj.*

**gin·ger ale** ▶*n.* carbonated nonalcoholic clear drink flavored with ginger extract.

**gin·ger beer** ▶*n.* carbonated sometimes mildly alcoholic cloudy drink, made from ginger and syrup.

**gin·ger·bread** ▶*n.* cake made with molasses or syrup and flavored with ginger.

**gin·ger·ly** ▶*adv.* carefully or cautiously.
▶*adj.* showing great care or caution.

**ging·ham** /'gɪNGəm/ ▶*n.* plain-woven cotton cloth, esp. striped or checked.

**gin·gi·vi·tis** /ˌjɪnjəˈvītis/ ▶*n.* inflammation of the gums.

**gink·go** /ˈgiNGkō/ (also **ging·ko**) ▸*n.* (*pl.* **-gos** or **-goes**) tree with fan-shaped leaves, native to China.

**gin·seng** /ˈjinseNG/ ▸*n.* medicinal root of a plant found in E. Asia and N. America.

**gi·raffe** /jəˈraf/ ▸*n.* (*pl.* same or **gi·raffes**) ruminant African mammal, with a long neck and forelegs.

**gir·an·dole** /ˈjirənˌdōl/ ▸*n.* **1** branched support for candles or other lights, which either stands on a surface or projects from a wall. **2** earring or pendant with a large central stone surrounded by small ones.

**gird** /gərd/ ▸*v.* (*past* and *past part.* **gird·ed** or **girt**) **1** encircle or secure with a belt or band. **2** enclose or encircle.

**gird·er** ▸*n.* large iron or steel support beam.

**gir·dle** /ˈgərdl/ ▸*n.* **1** belt or cord worn around the waist. **2** woman's corset. **3** thing that surrounds.
▸*v.* surround with a girdle.

**girl** /gərl/ ▸*n.* **1** female child or young woman. **2** *inf.* girlfriend or sweetheart. —**girl·hood** *n.* —**girl·ish** *adj.* —**girl·ish·ly** *adv.*

**girl·friend** ▸*n.* **1** regular female companion or lover. **2** female friend.

**Girl Scout** ▸*n.* member of an organization of girls, esp. the Girl Scouts of America, that promotes character, outdoor activities, community service, etc.

**girth** /gərTH/ ▸*n.* **1** distance around a thing. **2** band around the body of a horse to secure the saddle, etc.

**gist** /jist/ ▸*n.* essence of a matter.

**give** /giv/ ▸*v.* (*past* **gave**; *past part.* **giv·en**) **1** transfer the possession of freely; hand over as a present. **2 a** bequeath. **b** transfer temporarily; provide with. **c** administer (medicine). **d** deliver (a message). **3 a** pay: *gave him $30 for the bicycle.* **b** sell: *gave him the bicycle for $30.* **4 a** confer; grant. **b** bestow. **c** award. **d** pledge: *gave his word.* **5 a** perform; execute. **b** utter: *gave a shriek.* **6** yield as a product or result. **7 a** yield to pressure. **b** collapse: *the roof gave under the pressure.* **8** devote; dedicate. **9** offer; show. **10** impart; be a source of.
▸*n.* capacity to yield; elasticity. —**giv·er** *n.*

□ **give and take 1** exchange of

words, etc.; compromise.
**2** exchange (words, blows, or concessions). □ **give away 1** transfer as a gift. **2** hand over (a bride) ceremonially to a bridegroom. **3** betray or expose to ridicule or detection. □ **give in** cease fighting; yield. □ **give off** emit (vapor, etc.). □ **give or take** *inf.* more or less. □ **give out 1** announce; emit. **2** break down from exhaustion, etc. **3** run short. □ **give rise to** cause. □ **give up 1** resign; surrender. **2** part with. **3** deliver (a wanted person, etc.). **4** renounce hope of. **5** renounce or cease (an activity).

**giv·en** /ˈgivən/ ▸*adj.* assumed; granted; specified: *a given number of people.*
▸*n.* known fact or situation.

**giz·zard** /ˈgizərd/ ▸*n.* part of a bird's stomach, for grinding food usu. with grit.

**gla·cé** /glaˈsā/ ▸*adj.* **1** (of fruit) having a glossy surface due to preservation in sugar. **2** (of cloth or leather) smooth and highly polished.

**gla·cial** /ˈglāSHəl/ ▸*adj.* **1** of ice; icy. **2** exceptionally slow.
—**gla·cial·ly** *adv.*

**gla·cier** /ˈglāSHər/ ▸*n.* mass of land ice formed by the accumulation of snow.

**gla·cis** /ˈglāsis; ˈglas-/ ▸*n.* (*pl.* same or **-cis·es**) gently sloping bank, in particular one that slopes down from a fort, exposing attackers to the defenders' missiles.

**glad** /glad/ ▸*adj.* (**glad·der**, **glad·dest**) **1** pleased; willing: *glad to be here.* **2 a** marked by, filled with, or expressing, joy: *a glad smile.* **b** (of news, events, etc.) giving joy: *glad tidings.*
—**glad·den** *v.* —**glad·ly** *adv.*
—**glad·ness** *n.*
□ **glad rags** *inf.* best clothes; evening dress.

**glade** /glād/ ▸*n.* open space in a forest.

**glad·i·a·tor** /ˈglādēˌātər/ ▸*n.* trained fighter at ancient Roman shows.

**gla·di·o·lus** /ˌglādēˈōləs/ ▸*n.* (*pl.* **-li** or **-lus·es**) plant with sword-shaped leaves and spikes of brightly colored flowers.

**glam·or·ize** /ˈglaməˌrīz/ (also **glam·our·ize**) ▸*v.* make glamorous or attractive.
—**glam·or·i·za·tion** *n.*

**glam·our** /ˈglamər/ (also **glam·or**) ▸*n.* **1** physical or cosmetic attractiveness. **2** excitement;

adventure: *the glamour of New York.* —**glam·or·ous** *adj.* —**glam·or·ous·ly** *adv.*

**glance** /glans/ ▶*v.* **1** cast a brief look or read quickly. **2** (of talk or a talker) pass quickly over a subject. **3** (of a bright object or light) flash, dart, or gleam; reflect: *the sun glanced off the knife.* ▶*n.* **1** brief look. **2** flash or gleam. □ **at a glance** immediately upon looking.

**gland** /gland/ ▶*n.* organ in an animal that secretes substances. —**gland·u·lar** *adj.*

**glare** /gle(ə)r/ ▶*v.* **1** look fiercely or fixedly. **2** express (hate, defiance, etc.) by a look. ▶*n.* **1 a** strong fierce light. **b** oppressive public attention: *the glare of fame.* **2** fierce or fixed look: *a glare of defiance.*

**glar·ing** ▶*adj.* **1** conspicuous: *a glaring error.* **2** shining oppressively. —**glar·ing·ly** *adv.*

**glass** /glas/ ▶*n.* **1** hard, brittle, usu. transparent substance. **2** object made from glass, esp. a drinking vessel. **3** (**glasses**) **a** eyeglasses. **b** binoculars; opera glasses. ▶*adj.* of or made from glass. —**glass·ful** *n.* —**glass·like** *adj.*

**glass ceil·ing** *n.* barrier hindering promotion, esp. of women and minorities, to executive positions.

**glass cut·ter** ▶*n.* tool for cutting glass.

**glass·y** ▶*adj.* (**-i·er, -i·est**) **1** of or resembling glass. **2** (of the eye, expression, etc.) dull; fixed: *fixed her with a glassy stare.* —**glass·i·ly** *adv.*

**glau·co·ma** /glôˈkōmə/ ▶*n.* eye condition causing gradual loss of sight.

**glaze** /glāz/ ▶*v.* **1** fit or cover with glass. **2** cover (pottery) with a shiny finish. **3** cover (pastry, meat, etc.) with a glaze. **4** (of the eyes) become fixed or glassy: *his eyes glazed over.* ▶*n.* **1** vitreous substance used to glaze pottery. **2** shiny coating.

**gla·zier** /ˈglāzʜər/ ▶*n.* person whose trade is glazing windows, etc.

**gleam** /glēm/ ▶*n.* faint or brief light; trace: *a gleam of sunlight* | *not a gleam of hope.* ▶*v.* **1** emit gleams. **2** shine.

**glean** /glēn/ ▶*v.* collect (grain) after the harvest; collect (news, gossip, etc.) in small quantities. —**glean·ings** *pl. n.*

**glee** /glē/ ▸n. mirth; delight.
—**glee·ful** adj. —**glee·ful·ly** adv.

**glee club** ▸n. group that sings choral compositions.

**glen** /glen/ ▸n. narrow valley.

**glib** /glib/ ▸adj. (**glib·ber, glib·best**) articulate but insincere or superficial. —**glib·ly** adv.

**glide** /glīd/ ▸v. **1** (of a stream, snake, skater, etc.) move with a smooth continuous motion. **2** (of an aircraft, esp. a glider) fly without engine power. **3** move quietly or stealthily.
▸n. **1** gliding movement. **2** flight in a glider.

**glid·er** ▸n. **1** aircraft that flies without an engine. **2** porch swing with a gliding motion.

**glim·mer** /'glimər/ ▸v. shine faintly or intermittently.
▸n. **1** feeble or wavering light. **2** faint sign (of hope, understanding, etc.).
—**glim·mer·ing·ly** adv.

**glimpse** /glimps/ ▸n. **1** momentary or partial view. **2** faint transient appearance: *glimpses of the truth.*
▸v. **1** see faintly or partly: *glimpsed her in the crowd.* **2** cast a passing glance.

**glint** /glint/ ▸v. flash or cause to flash; glitter; sparkle.

▸n. flash; sparkle.

**glis·ten** /'glisən/ ▸v. shine, esp. like a wet object or snow.

▸n. glitter; sparkle.

**glitch** /glicH/ inf. ▸n. sudden irregularity or malfunction.

**glit·ter** /'glitər/ ▸v. shine with a bright reflected light; sparkle.

▸n. **1** sparkle. **2** sparkling material as decoration.
—**glit·ter·y** adj.

**glit·te·ra·ti** /ˌglitəˈräte/ ▸pl. n. fashionable set of people engaged in show business or some other glamorous activity.

**glitz·y** /'glitsē/ ▸adj. (**glitz·i·er, glitz·i·est**) ostentatiously attractive (often used to suggest superficial glamour).

**gloam·ing** /'glōmiNG/ ▸n. poet. twilight.

**gloat** /glōt/ ▸v. consider with greed, malice, triumph, etc.
▸n. act of gloating. —**gloat·ing·ly** adv.

**glob** /gläb/ ▸n. soft mass or lump.

**glob·al** /'glōbəl/ ▸adj. worldwide or affecting an entire group.
—**glob·al·ly** adv.

**glob·al warm·ing** ▸n. increase in the temperature of the earth's atmosphere.

**globe** /glōb/ ▸n. **1** (**the globe**) the earth. **2** spherical representation of earth with a map on the surface. —**glob·u·lar** adj.

**globe-trot·ter** ▸n. inf. person who travels widely. —**globe-trot·ting** n. & adj.

**glob·ule** /'gläbyōōl/ ▸n. small round particle; drop.

**gloom** /glōōm/ ▸n. **1** darkness; obscurity. **2** melancholy; despondency.

**gloom·y** /'glōmē/ ▸adj. (-i·er, -i·est) **1** dark; unlighted. **2** depressed or depressing. —**gloom·i·ly** adv. —**gloom·i·ness** n.

**glo·ri·fy** /'glôrə,fī/ ▸v. (-fied) **1** exalt; make glorious. **2** extol; praise. **3** [as adj. **glorified**] seem or pretend to be better than in reality: just a glorified office boy. —**glo·ri·fi·ca·tion** n.

**glo·ry** /'glôrē/ ▸n. (pl. -ries) **1** renown or fame; honor. **2** adoring praise and thanksgiving: glory to the Lord. **3** resplendent majesty, beauty, etc.: the glory of Versailles. **4** heavenly bliss and splendor. ▸v. (-ried) pride oneself; exult: glory in their skill. —**glo·ri·ous** adj. —**glo·ri·ous·ly** adv.

**gloss** /gläs; glôs/ ▸n. **1** surface shine or luster. **2** (also **gloss paint**) paint formulated to give a hard glossy finish. **3** explanatory comment inserted between the lines or in the margin of a text. ▸v. make glossy. □ **gloss over** conceal or evade by mentioning briefly or misleadingly.

**glos·sa·ry** /'gläsərē; 'glô-/ ▸n. (pl. -ries) alphabetical list of terms relating to a specific subject or text; brief dictionary.

**glos·sy** ▸adj. having a shiny or lustrous surface. —**glos·si·ness** n.

**glot·tis** /'glätis/ ▸n. space between the vocal cords.

**glove** /gləv/ ▸n. **1** hand covering, worn esp. for protection against cold or dirt, usu. with separate fingers. **2** padded protective glove, as one used for boxing, baseball, etc. ▸v. cover or provide with a glove(s).

**glove com·part·ment** ▸n. compartment in the dashboard of an automobile.

**glow** /glō/ ▸v. **1** emit light and heat without flame; be incandescent. **2** express or feel strong emotion: glow with pride.

**3** show a warm color: *the painting glows with warmth.* **4** [as *adj.* **glowing**] express pride or satisfaction: *glowing praise.*

▶*n.* **1** glowing state. **2** feeling of satisfaction or well-being.

**glow·er** /ˈglouər/ ▶*v.* stare or scowl, esp. angrily.

▶*n.* glowering look.

**glow·worm** /ˈglō‚wərm/ ▶*n.* beetle whose wingless female emits light from the end of the abdomen.

**glu·cose** /ˈglo͞okōs/ ▶*n.* **1** simple sugar found in blood, fruit juice, etc. **2** syrup containing glucose sugars.

**glue** /glo͞o/ ▶*n.* adhesive substance.

▶*v.* (**glued**, **glu·ing** or **glue·ing**) **1** fasten or join with glue. **2** keep or put very close: *an eye glued to the keyhole.* —**glue·like** *adj.* —**glue·y** *adj.*

**glum** /gləm/ ▶*adj.* (**glum·mer**, **glum·mest**) dejected; sullen; displeased. —**glum·ly** *adv.* —**glum·ness** *n.*

**glut** /glət/ ▶*v.* (**glut·ted**, **glut·ting**) indulge (an appetite, a desire, etc.) to the full; fill to excess.

▶*n.* supply exceeding demand: *a glut in the market.*

**glu·ten** /ˈglo͞otn/ ▶*n.* mixture of proteins in cereal grains.

**glu·te·us** /ˈglo͞otēəs/ ▶*n.* (*pl.* **-te·i** /-tē‚ī/) any of three muscles in each buttock that move the thigh, the largest of which is the **gluteus maximus.**

**glu·ti·nous** /ˈglo͞otn-əs/ ▶*adj.* sticky; like glue.

**glut·ton** /ˈglətn/ ▶*n.* **1** greedy eater. **2** insatiably eager person: *a glutton for work.* —**glut·ton·y** *n.* —**glut·ton·ous** *adj.* —**glut·ton·ous·ly** *adv.*
□ **glutton for punishment** person eager to take on hard or unpleasant tasks.

**glyc·er·in** /ˈglisərin/ (also **glyc·er·ol**, **glyc·er·ine**) ▶*n.* colorless sweet viscous liquid used as medicine, ointment, etc., and in explosives, etc.

**glyph** /glif/ ▶*n.* **1** hieroglyphic character or symbol. **2** small graphic symbol.

**glyp·tic** /ˈgliptik/ ▶*adj.* of or concerning carving or engraving.

▶*n.* (usu. **glyptics**) art of carving or engraving, esp. on precious stones.

**gnarled** /närld/ (also **gnarl·y**) ▶*adj.* (of a tree, hands, etc.) knobby; twisted.

**gnarl·y** /ˈnärlē/ ▶*adj.* (**gnarl·i·er**, **gnarl·i·est**) **1** gnarled. **2** difficult, dangerous, or challenging. **3** unpleasant; unattractive.

**gnash** /nasH/ ▶*v.* **1** grind (the teeth). **2** (of teeth) strike together; grind.

**gnat** /nat/ ▶*n.* **1** small two-winged biting fly. **2** insignificant annoyance.

**gnaw** /nô/ ▶*v.* (*past part.* **gnawed** or **gnawn**) **1 a** bite persistently; wear away by biting. **b** bite; nibble. **2 a** (of pain, fear, etc.) corrode; waste away; consume; torture. **b** corrode, consume, torture, etc., with pain, fear, etc.: *was gnawed by doubt.* —**gnaw·ing** *adj.*

**gnome** /nōm/ ▶*n.* dwarfish legendary creature or goblin, living under ground.

**gno·mic** /ˈnōmik/ ▶*adj.* **1** expressed in or of the nature of short, pithy maxims or aphorisms. **2** enigmatic; ambiguous.

**gno·mon** /ˈnōmän/ ▶*n.* projecting piece on a sundial that shows the time by the position of its shadow.

**gno·sis** /ˈnōsis/ ▶*n.* knowledge of spiritual mysteries.

**GNP** ▶*abbr.* gross national product.

**gnu** /n(y)o͞o/ ▶*n.* antelope, native to S. Africa, with brown stripes on the neck and shoulders. (Also called **wildebeest**)

**go** /gō/ ▶*v.* (*past* **went**; *past part.* **gone**) **1** start moving or be moving; travel; proceed. **2** make a special trip for; participate in; proceed to do: *went skiing* | *often goes running.* **3** lie or extend to; lead to: *the road goes to the shore* | *where does that door go?* **4 a** leave; depart: *they had to go.* **b** disappear: *my bag is gone.* **5** move, act, work, etc.: *the clock doesn't go.* **6 a** make a specified movement: *go like this with your foot.* **b** make a sound: *the gun went bang.* **c** *inf.* say: *so he goes to me "Why didn't you like it?"* **7** be in a specified state: *go hungry.* **8 a** pass into a specified condition: *went mad.* **b** *inf.* die. **c** proceed or escape in a specified condition: *the crime went unnoticed.* **9** (of time or distance) pass; elapse; be traversed: *ten days to go.* **10 a** (of a document, verse, song, etc.) have a specified content or wording; run: *the tune goes like this.* **b** be suitable; fit; match: *the* *shoes don't go with the hat.* **c** be regularly kept or put: *the forks go here.* **d** find room; fit: *it goes in the cupboard.* **11 a** turn out; proceed in a certain way: *things went well.* **b** be successful: *make the party go.* **c** progress: *a long way to go.* **12 a** be sold: *went cheap.* **b** (of money) be spent: *$200 went for a new jacket.* **13 a** be relinquished, dismissed, or abolished: *the car will have to go.* **b** fail; decline; give way; collapse: *his sight is going.* **14** be acceptable or permitted; be accepted without question: *what I say goes.* **15** be guided by; judge or act on or in harmony with: *have nothing to go on | a good rule to go by.* **16** attend regularly: *goes to church.* **17** *inf.* proceed (often foolishly) to do: *don't go making him angry.* **18** act or proceed to a certain point: *will go so far and no further.* **19** (of a number) be capable of being contained in another: *6 goes into 12 twice.* **20** be allotted or awarded; pass: *first prize went to her.* **21** be known or called: *goes by the same name.* **22** apply to; have relevance for: *that goes for me, too.* **23** *inf.* expressing annoyance: *they've gone and broken it.*

▶*n.* (*pl.* **goes**) **1** *inf.* success: *made a go of it.* **2** *inf.* turn; attempt: *I'll have a go at it.* **3** permission; approval; go-ahead: *gave us a go on the new project.* **4** Japanese board game of territorial possession and capture.

▶*adj. inf.* functioning properly: *all systems are go.*

□ **go ahead** proceed without hesitation. □ **go-ahead 1** permission to proceed. **2** enterprising. □ **go along with** agree to. □ **go back on** fail to keep (one's word, promise, etc.). □ **go-between** intermediary. □ **go down 1 a** (of an amount) become less: *your weight has gone down.* **b** subside: *the flood went down.* **c** decrease in price; lose value. **2 a** (of a ship or aircraft) sink or crash. **b** (of the sun) set. **3** deteriorate; fail; (of a computer, etc.) cease to function. **4** (of an event, person, etc.) be recorded or remembered: *go down in history.* **5** be swallowed. □ **go for 1** go to fetch. **2** be accounted as or achieve: *went for nothing.* **3** prefer; choose: *that's the one I go for.* **4** *inf.* strive to attain: *go* *for it!* **5** *inf.* attack: *the dog went for him.* □ **go into 1** enter (a profession, etc.). **2** take part in; be a part of. **3** investigate. □ **go off 1** explode. **2 a** leave the stage. **b** leave; depart. **3** sound, as an alarm, siren, etc. □ **go on 1** continue; persevere: *decided to go on with it.* **2** *inf.* **a** talk at great length. **b** admonish: *went on and on at him.* **3** proceed: *went on to become a star.* □ **go out 1** leave a room, house, etc. **2** be broadcast. **3** be extinguished. **4** be courting. **5** cease to be fashionable. **6** (of workers) strike. □ **go over 1** inspect; rehearse; retouch. **2** [often foll. by *to*] change one's allegiance or religion. **3** (of a play, etc.) be received in a specified way: *went over well in Dallas.* □ **go through 1** be dealt with or completed. **2** discuss in detail; scrutinize in sequence. **3** perform (a ceremony, a recitation, etc.). **4** undergo. **5** *inf.* use up; spend (money, etc.). **6** make holes in. □ **on the go** *inf.* **1** in constant motion. **2** constantly working.

**goad** /gōd/ ▸*n.* **1** spiked stick used for urging cattle forward. **2** anything that incites.
▸*v.* **1** urge on with a goad.

**2** irritate; stimulate: *goaded him to rage.*

**goal** /gōl/ ▸*n.* **1** object of a person's ambition or effort; destination; aim. **2 a** area at which a ball, puck, etc., is directed for a score. **b** point(s) won: *scored 2 goals.*

**goal·ie** /ˈgōlē/ ▸*n.* goalkeeper.

**goal·keep·er** ▸*n.* player defending the goal in various sports.

**goat** /gōt/ ▸*n.* **1** hardy, agile mammal, having horns and (in the male) a beard, and kept for its milk and meat. **2** lecherous man.

**goa·tee** /gōˈtē/ ▸*n.* small pointed beard.

**gob** /gäb/ *inf.* ▸*n.* **1** lump or clot of slimy matter. **2** (**gobs**) large amounts.

**gob·bet** /ˈgäbit/ ▸*n.* piece or lump of flesh, food, or other matter.

**gob·ble** /ˈgäbəl/ ▸*v.* **1** eat hurriedly and noisily. **2** (of a male turkey) make a swallowing sound in the throat.
—**gob·bler** *n.*

**gob·let** /ˈgäblit/ ▸*n.* drinking vessel with a foot and a stem, usu. of glass.

**gob·lin** /ˈgäblin/ ▸*n.* mischievous,

ugly, dwarflike creature of folklore.

**god** /gäd/ ▸*n.* **1 a** (in many religions) superhuman being or spirit worshiped as having power over nature, human fortunes, etc.; deity. **b** image, idol, animal, or other object worshiped as divine or symbolizing a god. **2** (**God**) (in Christian and other monotheistic religions) creator and ruler of the universe; supreme being. **3 a** adored, admired, or influential person. **b** something worshiped like a god: *makes a god of success.* —**god·like** *adj.*

**god·dess** /ˈgädis/ ▸*n.* female deity.

**god·ly** ▸*adj.* religious; pious; devout. —**god·li·ness** *n.*

**god·par·ent** ▸*n.* person who sponsors a child at baptism.

**god·send** ▸*n.* unexpected but welcome event or acquisition.

**go·fer** /ˈgōfər/ *inf.* ▸*n.* person who runs errands, esp. on a movie set or in an office.

**gog·gle** /ˈgägəl/ ▸*v.* **1** look with wide-open eyes. **2** (of the eyes) be rolled about; protrude. ▸*adj.* (of the eyes) protuberant or rolling.

▸*pl. n.* (**goggles**) eyeglasses for protecting the eyes from dust, water, etc.

**goi·ter** ▸*n.* swelling of neck from enlarged thyroid gland.

**gold** /gōld/ ▸*n.* **1** yellow, malleable, ductile, metallic element resistant to chemical reaction and precious as a monetary medium, in jewelry, etc. (Symb.: **Au**) **2** color of gold. **3 a** coins or articles made of gold. **b** wealth. ▸*adj.* (also **gold·en**) **1** made of gold. **2** colored like gold.

**gold·en·rod** /ˈgōldənˌräd/ ▸*n.* plant with a rodlike stem and small, bright yellow flower heads.

**gold·finch** ▸*n.* American finch with yellow feathers.

**gold·fish** ▸*n.* small reddish golden Chinese carp kept for ornament.

**gold·fish bowl** ▸*n.* round glass container for goldfish.

**gold leaf** ▸*n.* thin sheet of beaten gold.

**gold med·al** ▸*n.* medal of gold, usu. awarded as first prize.

**gold mine** ▸*n.* **1** place where gold is mined. **2** *inf.* source of wealth.

**gold stand·ard** ▸*n.* system

valuing currency in terms of gold, for which the currency may be exchanged.

**go·lem** /'gōləm/ ▶*n.* **1** (in Jewish legend) a clay figure brought to life by magic. **2** automaton or robot.

**golf** /gälf/ ▶*n.* game in which a small ball is driven with clubs into a series of 18 or 9 holes with the fewest possible strokes. ▶*v.* play golf. —**golf·er** *n.*

**golf club** ▶*n.* **1** club used in golf. **2** organization for playing golf. **3** premises used by such an organization.

**gol·li·wog** /'gälē,wäg/ (also **gol·li·wogg**) ▶*n.* **1** soft doll with bright clothes, a black face, and fuzzy hair. **2** grotesque person.

**go·nad** /'gōnad/ ▶*n.* animal organ producing gametes, e.g., the testis or ovary.

**gon·do·la** /'gändələ/ ▶*n.* **1** flat-bottomed boat used on Venetian canals, with a high point at each end. **2** car suspended from an airship, balloon, or cable.

**gone** /gôn/ ▶ past part. of GO.

**gon·er** /'gônər/ ▶*n. inf.* person or thing that is doomed, ended, etc.; dead person.

**gon·fa·lon** /'gänfələn/ ▶*n.* banner or pennant, esp. one with streamers, hung from a crossbar.

**gong** /gäNG/ ▶*n.* **1** metal disk giving a resonant note when struck. **2** saucer-shaped bell. ▶*v.* summon with a gong.

**gon·or·rhea** /,gänə'rēə/ ▶*n.* venereal disease with discharge.

**gon·zo** /'gänzō/ ▶*adj.* **1** of or associated with journalistic writing of an exaggerated, subjective, and fictionalized style. **2** bizarre or crazy.

**goo** /gōō/ *inf.* ▶*n.* **1** sticky or viscous substance. **2** sickening sentiment.

**good** /gŏŏd/ ▶*adj.* (**bet·ter**, **best**) **1** having the right or desired qualities; satisfactory; adequate. **2 a** (of a person) efficient; competent: *a good driver.* **b** (of a thing) reliable; efficient: *good brakes.* **c** (of health, etc.) strong: *good eyesight.* **3 a** kind; benevolent: *good of you to come.* **b** morally excellent; virtuous: *a good deed.* **c** charitable: *good works.* **d** well-behaved. **4** enjoyable, agreeable: *a good party.* **5** thorough; considerable: *gave it a good wash.* **6** not less than: *waited a good hour.* **7** valid; sound: *a good reason.* ▶*n.* **1** that which is good; what is beneficial or morally right: *only good can come of it* | *did it for your own good*. **2** (**goods**) **a** movable property or merchandise. **b** (**the goods**) *inf.* what one has undertaken to supply, esp as: *deliver the goods*. **3** (**the goods**) proof, esp. of guilt.

▶*adv. inf.* well: *doing pretty good*.

□ **as good as** practically: *he as good as told me*. □ **good for 1** beneficial to; having a good effect on. **2** able to perform; inclined for: *good for a ten-mile walk*. **3** able to be trusted to pay: *is good for $100*.

**good·bye** (also **good·bye, good·by, good·by**) ▶*interj.* expressing good wishes on parting or ending a telephone conversation.

▶*n.* parting; farewell.

**Good Friday** ▶*n.* Friday before Easter, commemorating Christ's Crucifixion.

**good·ly** ▶*adj.* (**-li·er, -li·est**) of imposing size, quantity, etc.

**good·will** ▶*n.* **1** kindly feeling. **2** established reputation of a business, etc., as enhancing its value.

**good·y** (also **good·ie**) ▶*n.* (*pl.* **-ies**) *inf.* (usu. **goodies**) something good or attractive, esp. to eat.

▶*interj.* expressing childish delight.

**good·y-good·y** ▶*n.* smugly virtuous person.

▶*adj.* smugly virtuous.

**goof** /go͞of/ *inf.* ▶*n.* **1** foolish or stupid person. **2** mistake.

▶*v.* **1** blunder; make a mistake. **2** (**goof off**) idle; waste time.

**goon** /go͞on/ *inf.* ▶*n.* **1** stupid or playful person. **2** person hired by racketeers, etc.

**goose** /go͞os/ ▶*n.* (*pl.* **geese**) **1** large edible water bird with short legs and webbed feet. **2** female of this.

**goose·ber·ry** ▶*n.* (*pl.* **-ries**) edible yellowish green berry with juicy flesh.

**goose bumps** (also **goose pimples**) ▶*pl. n.* bristling state of the skin produced by cold or fright.

**goose egg** ▶*n. inf.* **1** zero score in a game. **2** lump, esp. on the head.

**goose step** ▶*n.* military marching step in which the knees are kept stiff.

**GOP** ▶*abbr.* Grand Old Party (Republican Party).

**go·pher** /ˈgōfər/ ▶*n.* (also **pock·et go·pher**) burrowing rodent, native to N. America, having sharp front teeth; ground squirrel.

**gore** /gôr/ ▸n. **1** shed and clotted blood. **2** violence. **3** wedge-shaped piece in a garment, umbrella, etc.

▸v. pierce with a horn, tusk, etc.

**gorge** /gôrj/ ▸n. **1** narrow opening between hills or a rocky ravine. **2** contents of the stomach.

▸v. feed greedily.

**gor·geous** /ˈgôrjəs/ ▸adj. **1** strikingly beautiful. **2** richly colored; magnificent. **3** *inf.* very pleasant; splendid: *gorgeous weather.* —**gor·geous·ly** *adv.*

**go·ril·la** /gəˈrilə/ ▸n. largest anthropoid ape, native to Central Africa.

**gos·ling** /ˈgäzliNG/ ▸n. young goose.

**gos·pel** /ˈgäspəl/ ▸n. **1** teaching of Christ. **2** (**Gospel**) the first four books of the New Testament. **3** thing regarded as absolutely true: *take my word as gospel.* **4** (**gos·pel mu·sic**) African-American evangelical religious singing.

□ **gospel truth** something considered to be unquestionably true.

**gos·sa·mer** /ˈgäsəmər/ ▸n. **1** filmy substance of small spiders' webs. **2** delicate filmy material.

▸adj. light and flimsy.

**gos·sip** /ˈgäsip/ ▸n. **1 a** unconstrained talk or writing, esp. about persons or social incidents. **b** groundless rumor. **2** person who indulges in gossip.

▸v. (**-siped, -sip·ing**) engage in gossip.

**Goth** /ˈgäTH/ ▸n. member of Germanic people who invaded the Roman Empire between the 3rd and 5th centuries.

**Goth·ic** ▸adj. **1** of the Goths. **2** in the style of architecture prevalent in W. Europe in the 12th–16th c., characterized by pointed arches. **3** (of a novel, etc.) with supernatural or horrifying events.

**gouache** /gwäSH; gooˈäSH/ ▸n. **1** method of painting using opaque pigments ground in water and thickened with a gluelike substance. **2** paint of this kind; opaque watercolor.

**Gou·da** /ˈgoodə/ ▸n. mild Dutch cheese.

**gouge** /gouj/ ▸n. **1** chisel with a concave blade, used in

woodworking, sculpture, etc.
**2** indentation made with or as with this.

▶*v.* **1** cut with or as with a gouge. **2** *inf.* swindle; extort money from.

**gou·lash** /ˈgoo͞ˌläsʜ/ ▶*n.* highly seasoned Hungarian stew flavored with paprika.

**gourd** /gôrd/ ▶*n.* **1** fleshy usu. large fruit with a hard skin, often used as containers, ornaments, etc. **2** hollow gourd shell used as a drinking vessel, etc.

**gour·mand** /goo͞rˈmänd/ ▶*n.* person who is fond of eating and often eats too much.

**gour·met** /ˌgôrˈmā; ˌgoo͞r-/ ▶*n.* connoisseur of good food.

**gout** /gout/ ▶*n.* inflammation of the smaller joints, esp. the big toe. —**gout·y** *adj.*

**gov·ern** /ˈgəvərn/ ▶*v.* **1 a** rule or control (a nation, subject, etc.) with authority; conduct the affairs of. **b** be in government. **2 a** influence or determine (a person or a course of action). **b** be the predominating influence. **3** be a standard or principle for; constitute a law for; serve to decide (a case). **4** check or control (esp. passions

and machinery). —**gov·ern·a·ble** *adj.*

**gov·er·ness** /ˈgəvərnis/ ▶*n.* woman employed to teach children at home.

**gov·ern·ment** /ˈgəvər(n)mənt/ ▶*n.* **1** system of governing. **2** body of persons governing a nation. —**gov·ern·ment·al** *adj.*

**gov·er·nor** /ˈgəvə(r)nər/ ▶*n.* **1** executive head of each state of the U.S. **2** person who governs; ruler.

**govt.** ▶*abbr.* government.

**gown** /goun/ ▶*n.* **1** loose flowing garment, esp. a woman's long dress or nightgown. **2** official or academic robe. **3** members of a university as distinct from other residents of the university town: *conflict between town and gown.*

▶*v.* (**be gowned**) be attired in a gown: *gowned in red silk.*

**goy** /goi/ ▶*n.* (*pl.* **goy·im** /ˈgoi-im/ or **goys**) (sometimes offensive) Jewish name for a non-Jew.

**GP** ▶*abbr.* general practitioner.

**grab** /grab/ ▶*v.* (**grabbed, grab·bing**) **1** seize suddenly; capture. **2** take greedily or unfairly. **3** snatch at.

▶*n.* sudden clutch or attempt to seize.

□ **up for grabs** *inf.* easily obtainable.

**grab bag** ▸*n.* container from which one removes a mystery gift, as at a party.

**grace** /grās/ ▸*n.* **1** attractiveness in proportion, manner, or movement; elegance. **2** courteous good will: *had the grace to apologize.* **3 a** (in Christian belief) favor of God. **b** state of receiving this. **4** goodwill; favor: *fall from grace.* **5** delay granted as a favor: *a year's grace.* **6** short prayer before or after a meal.
▸*v.* honor with one's presence. —**grace·ful** *adj.* —**grace·ful·ly** *adv.* —**grace·less** *adj.*

**grac·ile** /'grasəl; 'gras,īl/ ▸*adj.* (of a person) slender or thin, esp. in a charming or attractive way.

**gra·cious** /'grāsʜəs/ ▸*adj.* **1** kind; good to others. **2** (of God) merciful. **3** elegant; luxurious.
▸*interj.* expressing surprise. —**gra·cious·ly** *adv.* —**gra·cious·ness** *n.*

**grack·le** /'grakəl/ ▸*n.* American blackbird with iridescent black feathers.

**gra·da·tion** /grā'dāsʜən/ ▸*n.* **1** stage of transition or advance.

**2** certain degree in rank, intensity, merit, divergence, etc. **3** (of color) gradual passing from one shade or tone to another.

**grade** /grād/ ▸*n.* **1 a** certain degree in rank, merit, proficiency, quality, etc. **b** class of persons or things of the same grade. **2** mark indicating the quality of a student's work. **3** class in school, concerned with a particular year's work and usu. numbered from the first upward. **4** gradient or slope.
▸*v.* **1** arrange in or allocate to grades; class; sort. **2** give a grade to (a student). **3** lessen the slope of.

**grade cross·ing** ▸*n.* crossing of a roadway, etc., with a railroad track at the same level.

**grade point av·er·age** ▸*n.* scholastic average obtained by dividing the number of earned points (for grades) by the number of credits taken. (Abbr.: **GPA**)

**grad·ual** /'grajōōəl/ ▸*adj.* **1** progressing by degrees. **2** not rapid, steep, or abrupt. —**grad·u·al·ly** *adv.*

**grad·u·ate** ▸*n.* /'grajōōit/ person who has been awarded an academic degree.

▸v. /'grajoo͞,āt/ **1 a** receive an academic degree. **b** grant an academic degree. **2** (**graduate from**) be a graduate of a specified university. **3** (**graduate to**) move up to (a higher status, etc.). **4** (**graduate in**) gain qualification in a particular subject. **5** mark out in degrees or parts. —**grad·u·a·tion** n.

**grad·u·ate school** ▸n. division of a university offering advanced programs beyond the bachelor's degree.

**graf·fi·ti** /grə'fētē/ ▸pl. n. (sing. **-to**) writing or drawing scribbled, scratched, or sprayed on a surface.

**graft** /graft/ ▸n. **1** plant scion inserted into a slit of stock, from which it receives sap. **2** tissue, organ, etc., transplanted surgically. **3** practices, esp. bribery, used to secure illicit gains in politics or business.
▸v. **1** insert (a scion) as a graft. **2** transplant (tissue). **3** insert or fix (a thing) permanently to another.

**Grail** /grāl/ (also **Ho·ly Grail**) ▸n. (in medieval legend) cup or platter used by Christ at the Last Supper.

**grain** /grān/ ▸n. **1** fruit or seed of a cereal. **2 a** wheat or other cereal used as food. **b** their fruit. **3** small hard particle of salt, sand, etc. **4** smallest unit of weight in the troy or avoirdupois system. **5** smallest possible quantity: *a grain of truth.* **6 a** roughness of surface. **b** granular appearance on a photograph or negative. **7** pattern of lines of fiber in wood or paper. —**grain·y** adj.

□ **against the grain** contrary to one's natural inclination or feeling.

**gram** /gram/ ▸n. metric unit of mass equal to one-thousandth of a kilogram.

**-gram** ▸comb. form forming nouns denoting a thing written or recorded (often in a certain way): *monogram | telegram.*

**gram·mar** /'gramər/ ▸n. **1** study or rules of a language's inflections, forms, etc. **2** observance or application of such rules: *bad grammar.* —**gram·mat·i·cal** adj. —**gram·mat·i·cal·ly** adv.

**gram·mar school** ▸n. elementary school.

**gran·a·ry** /'grānərē/ ▸n. (pl. **-ries**) storehouse for threshed grain.

**grand** /grand/ ▸*adj.*
**1** magnificent; imposing; dignified. **2** main; of chief importance: *grand staircase | grand entrance.* **3** *inf.* excellent; enjoyable: *had a grand time.* **4** upper class; wealthy. **5** in names of family relationships, denoting the second degree of ascent or descent: *granddaughter.*
▸*n.* (*pl.* same) *inf.* thousand dollars. —**grand·ly** *adv.*

**grand·child** ▸*n.* (*pl.* **-chil·dren**) child of one's son or daughter.

**gran·deur** /'granjər/ ▸*n.* splendor.

**gran·dil·o·quent** /gran-'diləkwənt/ ▸*adj.* pompous in language or manner. —**gran·dil·o·quence** *n.*

**gran·di·ose** /'grandē͵ōs/ ▸*adj.*
**1** producing or meant to produce an imposing effect. **2** ambitious in scale. —**gran·di·ose·ly** *adv.* —**gran·di·os·i·ty** *n.*

**grand ju·ry** ▸*n.* jury selected to examine the validity of an accusation prior to trial.

**grand mas·ter** ▸*n.* chess player of the highest class.

**grand·pa·rent** ▸*n.* parent of one's father or mother.

**grand pi·an·o** ▸*n.* large piano standing on three legs, with horizontal strings.

**grand slam** ▸*n.* **1** *Sports* winning of all of a group of major championships. **2** *Bridge* winning of all 13 tricks. **3** *Baseball* home run with bases loaded.

**grand·stand** ▸*n.* main stand for spectators at a racetrack, etc.
▸*v.* seek to attract favorable attention from spectators: *guilty of political grandstanding.*

**grange** /grānj/ ▸*n.* **1** farm. **2** (**Grange**) farmer's social organization.

**gran·ite** /'granit/ ▸*n.* granular crystalline igneous rock of quartz, mica, etc., used for building.

**gra·no·la** /grə'nōlə/ ▸*n.* breakfast or snack food consisting of a mixture of rolled oats, nuts, dried fruits, etc.

**grant** /grant/ ▸*v.* **1 a** consent to fulfill (a request, wish, etc.): *granted all he asked.* **b** allow (a person) to have (a thing): *granted me my freedom.* **2** give (rights, property, etc.) formally; transfer legally. **3** admit as true; concede, esp. as a basis for argument.
▸*n.* **1** process of granting or thing

granted. **2** sum of money officially given, esp. to finance education. —**gran·tee** *n.* —**grant·er** *n.* —**gran·tor** *n.*

□ **take for granted 1** assume something to be true or valid. **2** cease to appreciate through familiarity.

**gran·u·lat·ed** /ˈgranyəˌlātid/ ▶*adj.* formed into grains. —**gran·u·la·tion** *n.*

**gran·ule** /ˈgranyo͞ol/ ▶*n.* small grain. —**gran·u·lar** *adj.* —**gran·u·lar·i·ty** *n.*

**grape** /grāp/ ▶*n.* berry (usu. green, purple, or black) growing in clusters on a vine, used as fruit and in making wine.

**grape·fruit** ▶*n.* (*pl.* same) large round yellow citrus fruit.

**grape·vine** ▶*n.* **1** vine bearing grapes. **2** *inf.* means of transmission of rumor: *heard it through the grapevine.*

**graph** /graf/ ▶*n.* **1** diagram showing the relation between variable quantities, usu. along two axes. **2** *Math.* collection of points whose coordinates satisfy a given relation. ▶*v.* plot or trace on a graph.

**-graph** ▶*comb. form* **1** in nouns denoting something written, drawn, etc., in a specified way:

*autograph.* **2** in nouns denoting an instrument that records: *seismograph* | *telegraph.*

**graph·eme** /ˈgrafēm/ ▶*n.* smallest meaningful contrastive unit in a writing system.

**graph·ic** ▶*adj.* **1** of or relating to the visual or descriptive arts, esp. writing and drawing. **2** vividly descriptive; conveying all (esp. unwelcome or unpleasant) details. ▶*n.* product of the graphic arts. —**graph·i·cal·ly** *adv.*

**-graphic** (also **-graphical**) ▶*comb. form* forming adjectives corresponding to nouns in *-graphy.*

**graph·ic arts** ▶*pl. n.* visual and technical arts involving design, writing, drawing, printing, etc.

**graph·ics** ▶*pl. n.* [usu. treated as *sing.*] **1** products of the graphic arts. **2** use of diagrams in calculation and design. **3** (in full **com·pu·ter graph·ics**) mode of processing and output in which information is in pictorial form.

**graph·ite** /ˈgraˌfīt/ ▶*n.* form of carbon used as a lubricant, in pencils, etc.

**gra·phol·o·gy** /graˈfäləjē/ ▶*n.* the study of handwriting, esp. as

a supposed guide to character.
—**graph·ol·o·gist** *n.*

**graph pa·per** ▶*n.* paper printed with a network of lines, used for drawing graphs.

**-graphy** ▶*comb. form* **1** in nouns denoting a descriptive science: *geography.* **2** in nouns denoting a technique of producing images: *photography.* **3** in nouns denoting a style or method of writing, drawing, etc.: *calligraphy.*

**grap·nel** /ˈgrapnl/ ▶*n.* **1** device with iron claws, for dragging or grasping. **2** small anchor with several flukes.

**grap·ple** /ˈgrapəl/ ▶*v.* **1** fight at close quarters or in close combat. **2** try to manage a difficult problem, etc. **3** seize with or as with a grapnel; grasp. ▶*n.* **1** hold or grip in or as in wrestling. **2** clutching instrument; grapnel.

**grap·pling hook** (or **iron**) ▶*n.* grapnel.

**grasp** /grasp/ ▶*v.* **1 a** clutch at; seize greedily. **b** hold firmly; grip. **2** try to seize. **3** understand or realize (a fact or meaning). ▶*n.* **1** firm hold; grip. **2 a** mastery or control: *a grasp of the situation.*

**b** mental hold or understanding: *a grasp of the facts.* **3** mental agility: *a quick grasp.*

**grasp·ing** ▶*adj.* avaricious; greedy.

**grass** /gras/ ▶*n.* **1 a** small plants with green blades that are eaten by cattle, horses, sheep, etc. **b** plant that includes cereals, reeds, and bamboos. **2** pasture land. **3** lawn: *keep off the grass.* **4** *inf.* marijuana. ▶*v.* **1** cover with turf. **2** provide with pasture. —**grass·y** *adj.*

**grass·hop·per** ▶*n.* jumping insect.

**grass·land** ▶*n.* large open area covered with grass, esp. used for grazing.

**grass roots** ▶*pl. n.* **1** fundamental level or source. **2** ordinary people, esp. as voters; rank and file of an organization, esp. a political party.

**grate** /grāt/ ▶*v.* **1** reduce to particles by rubbing on a serrated surface. **2** rub with a harsh scraping sound. **3** utter in a harsh tone. **4 a** sound harshly or discordantly. **b** have an irritating effect. ▶*n.* **1** metal frame confining fuel in a fireplace. **2** (also **grat·ing**) framework of parallel or crossed

bars that prevent access.
—**grat·er** *n.* —**grat·ing** *adj.*

**grate·ful** ▶*adj.* **1** thankful; feeling or showing gratitude: *grateful for your help.* **2** pleasant; acceptable. —**grate·ful·ly** *adv.* —**grate·ful·ness** *n.*

**grat·i·fy** /ˈgratəˌfī/ ▶*v.* (-**fied**) **1** please. **2** indulge in or yield to (a feeling or desire). —**grat·i·fi·ca·tion** *n.*

**grat·is** /ˈgratis/ ▶*adv. & adj.* free; without charge.

**grat·i·tude** /ˈgratəˌt(y) o͞od/ ▶*n.* being thankful; appreciation.

**gra·tu·i·tous** /grəˈt(y)o͞oitəs/ ▶*adj.* **1** uncalled-for; for no reason. **2** given or done free of charge. —**gra·tu·i·tous·ly** *adv.*

**gra·tu·i·ty** /grəˈt(y)o͞oitē/ ▶*n.* (*pl.* -**ties**) money given for service; tip.

**gra·va·men** /grəˈvāmən/ ▶*n.* (*pl.* -**vam·i·na** /-ˈvamənə/) essence or most serious part of a complaint or accusation.

**grave** /grāv/ ▶*n.* **1** trench for the burial of a corpse. **2** something compared to or regarded as a grave.
▶*adj.* **1** serious; important. **2** solemn: *a grave look.*

**grave ac·cent** /grāv/ ▶*n.* mark (`) placed over a vowel to denote pronunciation, length, etc.

**grav·el** /ˈgravəl/ ▶*n.* mixture of coarse sand and small stones, used for paths, roads, etc.

**grav·el·ly** ▶*adj.* **1** of or like gravel. **2** (of a voice) deep and rough sounding.

**grav·id** /ˈgravid/ ▶*adj.* **1** pregnant; carrying eggs or young. **2** full of meaning or a specified quality.

**grav·i·tas** /ˈgraviˌtäs/ ▶*n.* dignity, seriousness, or solemnity of manner.

**grav·i·ta·tion** /ˌgraviˈtāsHən/ *Physics* ▶*n.* **1** force of attraction between particles of matter in the universe. **2** effect of this, esp. the falling of bodies to the earth. —**grav·i·ta·tion·al** *adj.*

**grav·i·ty** /ˈgravitē/ ▶*n.* **1** force that attracts a body to the center of the earth. **2** property of having weight. **3 a** importance; seriousness. **b** solemnity.

**gra·vy** /ˈgrāvē/ ▶*n.* (*pl.* -**vies**) **1** fat and juices exuded from meat during cooking, and made into a sauce for food. **2** *inf.* unearned or unexpected gains, esp. money.

**gra·vy boat** ▶*n.* vessel for serving gravy.

**gra·vy train** ▶*n. inf.* source of easy financial benefit.

**gray** /grā/ (also **grey**) ▶*adj.* **1** of a color intermediate between black and white. **2** (of the weather, etc.) dull; overcast; bleak. **3** (of hair) turning white with age, etc. ▶*n.* **1 a** gray color or pigment. **b** gray clothes or material: *dressed in gray.* **2** gray or white horse. —**gray·ish** *adj.* —**gray·ness** *n.*

**gray a·re·a** ▶*n.* situation or topic not clearly defined.

**gray mat·ter** ▶*n.* **1** darker tissues of the brain and spinal cord. **2** *inf.* intelligence.

**graze** /grāz/ ▶*v.* **1** (of cattle, sheep, etc.) eat growing grass. **2** feed (cattle, etc.) on growing grass. **3** scrape (part of the body). **4** touch lightly in passing. ▶*n.* abrasion.

**grease** /grēs/ ▶*n.* **1** oily or fatty matter esp. as a lubricant. **2** melted animal fat. ▶*v.* smear or lubricate with grease. —**greas·y** *adj.*

**great** /grāt/ ▶*adj.* **1 a** of a size, amount, or intensity much above the normal: *take great care.* **b** reinforcing other words denoting size, quantity, etc.: *a great big hole* | *a great many.* **2** important; preeminent; worthy. **3** grand; imposing: *a great occasion* **4** (esp. of a public or historic figure) distinguished; prominent. **5 a** (of a person) remarkable in ability, character, achievement, etc.: *a great thinker.* **b** (of a thing) outstanding of its kind: *the Great Depression.* **6** *inf.* **a** very enjoyable or satisfactory; attractive; fine: *had a great time.* **b** (as an exclam.) fine; very good. **7** (in names of family relationships) denoting one degree further removed upward or downward: *great-uncle* | *great-great-grandmother.* ▶*n.* great or outstanding person or thing. —**great·ly** *adv.* —**great·ness** *n.*

**Great Dane** ▶*n.* dog of a very large, short-haired breed.

**grebe** /grēb/ ▶*n.* diving bird with a long neck, lobed toes, and almost no tail.

**greed** /grēd/ ▶*n.* excessive desire, esp. for food or wealth. —**greed·y** *adj.* —**greed·i·ly** *adv.* —**greed·i·ness** *n.*

**Greek** /grēk/ ▶*n.* **1** native or inhabitant of Greece; person of Greek descent. **2** language of Greece.

▸*adj.* of Greece or its people or language.

**green** /grēn/ ▸*adj.* **1** of the color between blue and yellow in the spectrum; colored like grass, emeralds, etc. **2** covered with leaves or grass. **3** (of fruit, etc., or wood) unripe or unseasoned. **4** inexperienced; naive; gullible. **5** young; flourishing. **6** vegetable: *green salad.* **7** (also **Green**) concerned with or supporting protection of the environment.

▸*n.* **1** green color or pigment. **2** green clothes or material: *dressed in green.* **3 a** piece of public grassy land: *village green.* **b** grassy area used for a special purpose: *putting green.* **4** (**greens**) green vegetables. —**green·ish** *adj.* —**green·ness** *n.*

**green bean** (or **string bean**) ▸*n.* the green pods of a young kidney bean, eaten as a vegetable.

**green belt** ▸*n.* area of open land around a city, designated for preservation.

**Green Be·ret** ▸*n.* member of the U.S. Army Special Forces.

**green card** ▸*n.* work and residence permit issued to permanent resident aliens in the U.S.

**green·er·y** ▸*n.* green foliage or growing plants.

**green-eyed mon·ster** ▸*n. inf.* jealousy.

**green·horn** ▸*n.* inexperienced person.

**green·house** ▸*n.* structure with sides and roof mainly of glass, for growing plants.

**green·house effect** ▸*n.* trapping of the sun's warmth in the earth's atmosphere caused by an increase in carbon dioxide.

**green light** ▸*n.* **1** signal to proceed on a road, railroad, etc. **2** *inf.* permission to go ahead with a project.

**green pep·per** ▸*n.* unripe bell or sweet pepper, eaten green as a vegetable.

**green thumb** ▸*n.* skill in growing plants.

**greet** /grēt/ ▸*v.* **1** address politely or welcomingly on meeting or arrival. **2** receive or acknowledge in a specified way: *everyone greeted the suggestion warmly.* **3** (of a sight, sound, etc.) become apparent to or noticed by: *cheers greeted the miners when they emerged.* —**greet·er** *n.*

**gre·gar·i·ous** /gri'ge(ə)rēəs/ ▶*adj.* **1** fond of company. **2** living in flocks or communities. —**gre·gar·i·ous·ly** *adv.*

**grem·lin** /'gremlin/ *inf.* ▶*n.* imaginary mischievous sprite regarded as responsible for mechanical faults, esp. in aircraft.

**gre·nade** /grə'nād/ ▶*n.* small bomb thrown by hand (**hand gre·nade**) or shot from a rifle.

**grey** /grā/ ▶var. of GRAY.

**grey·hound** ▶*n.* dog of a tall slender breed that is capable of high speed, used in racing and coursing.

**grid** /grid/ ▶*n.* **1** framework of spaced parallel bars; grate. **2** system of squares printed on a map for reference. **3** network of lines, electrical power connections, etc. **4** arrangement of city streets in a rectangular pattern.

**grid·dle** /'gridl/ ▶*n.* iron plate that can be heated for baking, toasting, etc.

**grid·i·ron** ▶*n.* **1** football field (with parallel lines marking the area of play). **2** utensil of metal bars for broiling or grilling.

**grid·lock** ▶*n.* **1** traffic jam in which vehicular movement is blocked by stoppage of cross traffic. **2** complete standstill in action or progress. —**grid·locked** *adj.*

**grief** /grēf/ ▶*n.* **1** deep or intense sorrow or mourning. **2** cause of this.

□ **come to grief** meet with disaster.

**griev·ance** /'grēvəns/ ▶*n.* cause for complaint.

**grieve** /grēv/ ▶*v.* cause or suffer grief or distress.

**griev·ous** /'grēvəs/ ▶*adj.* **1** (of pain, etc.) severe. **2** causing grief. **3** flagrant; heinous. —**griev·ous·ly** *adv.*

**grif·fin** /'grifin/ (also **gryph·on**, **grif·fon**) ▶*n.* mythical creature with an eagle's head and wings and a lion's body.

**grift** /grift/ ▶*v.* engage in petty swindling.

▶*n.* petty swindle. —**grift·er** *n.*

**grill** /gril/ ▶*n.* **1** GRIDIRON. **2** food cooked on a grill.

▶*v.* **1** cook or be cooked under a broiler or on a gridiron. **2** subject to severe questioning. —**grill·ing** *n.*

**grille** /gril/ (also **grill**) ▶*n.* **1** grating or latticed screen.

**2** metal grid protecting the radiator of a motor vehicle.

**grim** /grim/ ▶*adj.* (**grim·mer, grim·mest**) **1** of stern or forbidding appearance. **2 a** harsh; merciless; severe. **b** resolute: *grim determination.* **3** joyless; sinister: *has a grim truth in it.* **4** unpleasant; unattractive. —**grim·ly** *adv.* —**grim·ness** *n.*

**grim·ace** /ˈgriməs/ ▶*n.* distortion of the face made in disgust, etc., or to amuse.

▶*v.* make a grimace.

**grime** /grīm/ ▶*n.* soot or dirt ingrained in a surface.

▶*v.* blacken with grime; befoul.

**grin** /grin/ ▶*v.* (**grin·ned, grin·ning**) smile broadly, showing the teeth.

▶*n.* act of grinning.

□ **grin and bear it** take pain or misfortune stoically.

**grind** /grīnd/ ▶*v.* (*past* and *past part.* **ground**) **1** reduce to particles or powder by crushing. **2 a** reduce, sharpen, or smooth by friction. **b** rub or rub together gratingly: *grind one's teeth.* **3** produce with effort: *grinding out verses.*

▶*n.* **1** act or instance of grinding.

**2** *inf.* hard dull work: *the daily grind.* **3** size of ground particles.

**grin·go** /ˈgriNGgō/ ▶*n.* (*pl.* **-gos**) (sometimes offensive term for) a white person from an English-speaking country (used in Spanish-speaking regions, chiefly Latin America).

**grip** /grip/ ▶*v.* (**gripped, grip·ping**) **1 a** grasp tightly. **b** take a firm hold. **2** (of a feeling or emotion) deeply affect (a person): *was gripped by fear.* **3** compel the attention of: *a gripping story.*

▶*n.* **1** firm hold; tight grasp. **2 a** intellectual control. **b** control of a situation or one's behavior, etc.: *lose one's grip.* **3 a** part of a machine that grips. **b** handle.

□ **come to grips with** begin to deal with.

**gripe** /grīp/ ▶*v. inf.* complain; grumble.

▶*n.* **1** *inf.* complaint. **2** colic.

**grippe** /grip/ ▶*n.* old-fashioned term for INFLUENZA.

**gris·ly** /ˈgrizlē/ ▶*adj.* (**-li·er, -li·est**) causing horror, disgust, or fear.

**grist** /grist/ ▶*n.* grain to grind.

□ **grist for the mill** something to take advantage of.

**gris·tle** /ˈgrisəl/ ▶*n.* tough flexible animal tissue; cartilage.

**grit** /grit/ ▸n. **1** particles of stone or sand. **2** pluck; endurance.
▸v. (**grit·ted**, **grit·ting**) clench (the teeth). —**grit·ty** adj. —**grit·ti·ness** n.

**grits** /grits/ ▸pl. n. coarsely ground hulled grain, esp. hominy.

**griz·zly** /'grizlē/ ▸adj. (**-zli·er**, **-zli·est**) gray; grayish; gray-haired.
▸n. (pl. **-zlies**) (**griz·zly bear**) variety of large brown bear found in N. America.

**groan** /grōn/ ▸v. **1 a** make a deep sound expressing pain, grief, or disapproval. **b** utter with groans. **2** complain inarticulately. **3** (**groan under/beneath**) fig. be loaded or oppressed by.
▸n. sound made in groaning.

**gro·cer** /'grōsər/ ▸n. dealer in food and household provisions.

**gro·cer·y** ▸n. (pl. **-ies**) **1** grocer's trade or store. **2** (**groceries**) provisions, esp. food, sold by a grocer.

**grog** /gräg/ ▸n. drink of liquor (orig. rum) and water.

**grog·gy** ▸adj. (**-gi·er**, **-gi·est**) unsteady; dazed. —**grog·gi·ly** adv.

**groin** /groin/ ▸n. **1** depression between the belly and the thigh.
**2** Archit. **a** edge formed by intersecting vaults. **b** arch supporting a vault.

**grom·met** /'grämit/ ▸n. metal, plastic, or rubber eyelet placed in a hole to protect or insulate a rope or cable, etc., passed through it.

**groom** /groom/ ▸n. **1** BRIDEGROOM. **2** caretaker of horses.
▸v. **1 a** curry or tend (a horse). **b** give a neat appearance to (a person, etc.). **2** prepare or train (a person) for a particular purpose: *was groomed for the top job*. **3** (of an animal) clean and comb the fur of.

**grooms·man** /'groomzmən; 'groomz-/ ▸n. (pl. **-men**) male friend officially attending the bridegroom at a wedding.

**groove** /groov/ ▸n. **1** channel or hollow. **2** established routine or habit.
▸v. make a groove or grooves in.

**grope** /grōp/ ▸v. **1** feel about or search blindly or uncertainly with the hands. **2** (**grope for/after**) search mentally for: *groping for an answer*. **3** feel (one's way) toward something.
▸n. process or instance of groping.

**gross** /grōs/ ▸*adj.* **1** overfed; bloated; repulsively fat. **2** (of a person, manners, or morals) coarse, unrefined, or indecent. **3** flagrant: *gross negligence.* **4** total; without deductions; not net. **5** *inf.* repulsive; disgusting. ▸*v.* produce or earn as gross profit or income. ▸*n.* (*pl.* same) amount equal to twelve dozen things. —**gross·ly** *adv.*

□ **gross out** *inf.* disgust, esp. by repulsive or obscene behavior.

**gross do·mes·tic prod·uct** ▸*n.* total value of goods produced and services provided in a country in one year. (Abbr.: **GDP**)

**gross na·tion·al prod·uct** ▸*n.* gross domestic product plus the total of net income from abroad. (Abbr.: **GNP**)

**gro·tesque** /grō'tesk/ ▸*adj.* **1** repulsively distorted. **2** incongruous; absurd. ▸*n.* decorative form combining human and animal features. —**gro·tesque·ly** *adv.*

**grot·to** /'grätō/ ▸*n.* (*pl.* **-toes** or **-tos**) small, esp. picturesque cave.

**grouch** /grouCH/ ▸*n.* habitually discontented person.

▸*v.* grumble. —**grouch·y** *adj.*

**ground**[1] /ground/ ▸*n.* **1 a** surface of the earth. **b** part of this specified in some way: *low ground.* **2** substance of the earth's surface; soil; earth: *stony ground* | *dug deep into the ground.* **3 a** position, area, or distance on the earth's surface. **b** extent of activity, etc., achieved or of a subject dealt with: *the book covers a lot of ground.* **4** (**grounds**) foundation, motive, or reason: *there are some grounds for concern.* **5** designated area: *fishing-grounds.* **6** (**grounds**) land attached to a house, etc. **7** area or basis for consideration, agreement, etc.: *common ground.* **8** (**grounds**) solid particles, esp. of coffee, forming a residue. **9** *Electr.* connection to the ground that completes an electrical circuit.

▸*v.* **1 a** refuse authority for (a pilot or an aircraft) to fly. **b** restrict (esp. a child) from certain activities, places, etc., esp. as a form of punishment. **2 a** run (a ship) aground; strand. **b** (of a ship) run aground. **3** instruct thoroughly (in a subject). **4** (usu. **be grounded in**) give a firm theoretical or practical basis to: *the study of history must be grounded in a thorough knowledge of the past.* **5** *Electr.* connect to the ground.

□ **break new** (or **fresh**) **ground** treat a subject previously not dealt with. □ **get off the ground** make a successful start. □ **hold one's ground** not retreat or give way. □ **on the grounds of** because of.

**ground²** ▶past and past part. of GRIND.

**ground con·trol** ▶*n.* personnel directing the landing, etc., of aircraft or spacecraft.

**ground cov·er** ▶*n.* plants covering the surface of the soil, esp. low-growing spreading plants that inhibit the growth of weeds.

**ground floor** ▶*n.* floor of a building at ground level.

**ground·hog** ▶*n.* burrowing rodent found in N. America; woodchuck.

**ground·less** ▶*adj.* without motive or foundation.

**ground·ling** /'groundliNG/ ▶*n.* **1** spectator or reader of inferior taste, such as a member of a theater audience who traditionally stood in the pit beneath the stage. **2** person on

the ground as opposed to one in a spacecraft or aircraft.

**ground speed** ▶*n.* aircraft's speed relative to the ground.

**ground·swell** ▶*n.* surge of feeling or support.

**ground·work** ▶*n.* **1** preliminary or basic work. **2** foundation or basis.

**group** /groop/ ▶*n.* persons or things located close together, or considered together. ▶*v.* **1** form or be formed into a group. **2** place in a group or groups. **3** classify. —**group·ing** *n.*

**group·er** ▶*n.* large warm-water sea bass.

**group·ie** ▶*n. inf.* ardent follower of touring music groups, celebrities, or activities.

**group ther·a·py** ▶*n.* therapy in which patients are brought together to assist one another psychologically.

**group·think** /'groop,THiNGk/ ▶*n.* practice of thinking or making decisions as a group in a way that discourages creativity or individual responsibility.

**grouse** /grous/ ▶*n.* (*pl.* same) **1** game bird with a plump body and feathered legs. **2** complaint. ▶*v.* grumble or complain pettily.

**grout** /grout/ ▶*n.* thin mortar for filling gaps in tiling, etc.
▶*v.* provide or fill with grout. —**grout·er** *n.*

**grove** /grōv/ ▶*n.* small group of trees.

**grov·el** /ˈgrävəl; ˈgrə-/ ▶*v.* (**-eled**, **-el·ing**) **1** behave obsequiously. **2** lie prone in abject humility. —**grov·el·ing** *adj.*

**grow** /grō/ ▶*v.* (*past* **grew**; *past part.* **grown**) **1** increase in size, height, quantity, etc. **2 a** develop or exist as a living plant or natural product. **b** germinate; sprout; spring up. **3** be produced; come naturally into existence; arise. **4 a** produce (plants, fruit, wood, etc.) by cultivation. **b** bring forth. —**grow·er** *n.*
□ **grow on** become gradually more favored by. □ **grow up** **1** mature. **2** [usu. as *interj.*] begin to behave sensibly.

**growl** /groul/ ▶*v.* **1** (esp. of a dog) make a low guttural sound. **2** murmur angrily. **3** rumble.
▶*n.* growling sound; rumble.

**grown-up** ▶*adj.* adult.
▶*n.* adult person.

**growth** /grōTH/ ▶*n.* **1** act or process of growing. **2** increase in size or value. **3** something that has grown or is growing. **4** *Med.* abnormal mass of tissue, e.g., a tumor, wart, etc.

**grub** /grəb/ ▶*n.* **1** larva of an insect. **2** *inf.* food.
▶*v.* (**grubbed**, **grub·bing**) **1** dig superficially in the soil. **2** rummage.

**grub·by** ▶*adj.* (**-bi·er**, **-bi·est**) dirty. —**grub·bi·ly** *adv.* —**grub·bi·ness** *n.*

**grudge** /grəj/ ▶*n.* persistent feeling of ill will or resentment.
▶*v.* be resentfully unwilling to give or allow (a thing). —**grudg·ing** *adj.* —**grudg·ing·ly** *adv.*

**gru·el** /ˈgrōōəl/ ▶*n.* liquid food of oatmeal, etc., chiefly for invalids.

**gru·el·ing** ▶*adj.* extremely demanding, severe, or tiring. —**gruel·ing·ly** *adv.*

**grue·some** /ˈgrōōsəm/ ▶*adj.* horrible; grisly; disgusting. —**grue·some·ly** *adv.*

**gruff** /grəf/ ▶*adj.* **1** (of a voice) low and harsh. **2** surly. —**gruff·ly** *adv.* —**gruff·ness** *n.*

**grum·ble** /ˈgrəmbəl/ ▶*v.* **1** complain peevishly. **2 a** growl faintly. **b** rumble.
▶*n.* **1** complaint. **2** rumble. —**grum·bler** *n.* —**grum·bling** *adj.*

**grump·y** /ˈgrəmpē/ ▸*adj.* (-**i·er**, -**i·est**) morosely irritable; surly. —**grump·i·ly** *adv.* —**grump·i·ness** *n.*

**grunge** /grənj/ ▸*n.* **1** grime; dirt. **2** (also **grunge rock**) style of rock music characterized by a raucous guitar sound and lazy vocal delivery. **3** fashion associated with this music, including loose, layered clothing and ripped jeans.

**grunt** /grənt/ ▸*n.* **1** low guttural sound made by a pig. **2** similar sound.
▸*v.* **1** (of a pig) make a grunt or grunts. **2** (of a person) make a low inarticulate sound resembling this, esp. to express discontent, dissent, fatigue, etc.

**gua·no** /ˈgwänō/ ▸*n.* (*pl.* -**nos**) excrement of sea birds, bats, etc., used as fertilizer.

**guar·an·tee** /ˌgarənˈtē/ ▸*n.* formal promise or assurance, esp. of quality or performance.
▸*v.* (-**teed**) **1** give or serve as a guarantee for. **2** provide with a guarantee.

**guar·an·ty** /ˈgarənˌtē/ (also **guar·an·tee**) ▸*n.* (*pl.* -**ties**) **1** formal pledge to pay another person's debt or to perform another person's obligation in the case of default. **2** thing serving as security for a such a pledge.

**guard** /gärd/ ▸*v.* **1** watch over and defend or protect. **2** supervise (prisoners, etc.) and prevent from escaping. **3** keep (thoughts or speech) in check. **4** provide with safeguards. **5** take precautions.

▸*n.* **1** state of vigilance. **2** person who protects or keeps watch. **3** soldiers, etc., protecting a place or person; escort. **4** part of an army detached for some purpose: *advance guard.* **5** thing that protects or defends. **6** in some sports: **a** protective or defensive player. **b** defensive posture or motion.

**guard·ed** ▸*adj.* cautious; avoiding commitment. —**guard·ed·ly** *adv.*

**guard·i·an** /-ēən/ ▸*n.* **1** defender, protector, or keeper. **2** legal custodian of another, esp. a minor. —**guard·i·an·ship** *n.*

**gua·va** /ˈgwävə/ ▸*n.* edible pale yellow fruit with pink juicy flesh.

**gu·ber·na·to·ri·al** /ˌgoobərnəˈtôrēəl/ ▸*adj.* of or relating to a governor.

**guer·don** /'gərdn/ ▶*n.* reward or recompense.

▶*v.* give a reward to (someone).

**guer·ril·la** /gə'rilə/ (also **gue·ril·la**) ▶*n.* member of a small, independent (usu. political) group taking part in irregular fighting.

**guess** /ges/ ▶*v.* **1** estimate without calculation or measurement, or on the basis of inadequate data. **2** form a hypothesis or opinion about; conjecture; think likely: *cannot guess how you did it.* **3** conjecture or estimate correctly: *guess my weight.* **4** make a conjecture about.

▶*n.* estimate or conjecture.

**guess·work** ▶*n.* process of or results achieved by guessing.

**guest** /gest/ ▶*n.* **1** person invited to visit, have a meal, etc., at the expense of the inviter. **2** person lodging at a hotel, boardinghouse, etc. **3 a** outside performer invited to take part with regular performers. **b** [as *adj.*] describing a person who takes part by invitation in a radio or television program: *guest artist.*

▶*v.* be a guest on a radio or television show or in a theatrical performance, etc.

**guf·faw** /gə'fô/ ▶*n.* loud or boisterous laugh.

▶*v.* utter a guffaw.

**guid·ance** /'gīdəns/ ▶*n.* **1 a** advice or helpful direction. **b** leadership or direction. **2** guiding or being guided.

**guide** /gīd/ ▶*n.* **1** person who leads or shows the way. **2** person who conducts tours, etc. **3** adviser. **4** book with essential information on a subject, esp. a GUIDEBOOK. **5** thing marking a position.

▶*v.* **1** act as guide to. **2** be the principle, motive, or ground of (an action, judgment, etc.).

□ **guided missile** missile directed to its target by remote control or by equipment within itself.

□ **guide dog** dog trained to guide a blind person.

**guide·book** ▶*n.* book of information about a place for visitors, tourists, etc.

**guide·line** ▶*n.* principle directing action.

**guild** /gild/ ▶*n.* **1** association of people for mutual aid or the pursuit of a common goal. **2** medieval association of craftsmen or merchants.

**guile** /gīl/ ▸n. deceit; cunning or sly behavior. —**guile·ful** adj. —**guile·less** adj.

**guil·lo·tine** /ˈgilə,tēn; ˈgēə-/ ▸n. machine with a heavy knife blade that drops vertically, used for beheading.

**guilt** /gilt/ ▸n. **1** fact of having committed a specified or implied offense. **2 a** culpability. **b** feeling of this. —**guilt·i·ly** adv. —**guilt·i·ness** n. —**guilt·less** adj. —**guilt·y** adj.

**guin·ea fowl** ▸n. African fowl with slate-colored, white-spotted plumage.

**guin·ea pig** ▸n. **1** S. American rodent kept as a pet or for research in biology, etc. **2** subject used in an experiment.

**guise** /gīz/ ▸n. **1** assumed appearance; pretense: *in the guise of* | *under the guise of*. **2** garb.

**gui·tar** /giˈtär/ ▸n. usu. six-stringed musical instrument played with the fingers or a plectrum. —**gui·tar·ist** n.

**gulch** /gəlCH/ ▸n. ravine, esp. one in which a torrent flows.

**gulf** /gəlf/ ▸n. **1** deep ocean inlet with a narrow mouth. **2** (**the Gulf**) **a** Gulf of Mexico. **b** Persian Gulf. **3** deep hollow; chasm or abyss. **4** wide difference of feelings, opinion, etc.

**Gulf Stream** ▸n. warm ocean current flowing from the Gulf of Mexico toward Europe.

**gull** /gəl/ ▸n. long-winged sea bird, usu. white with a mantle varying from pearly gray to black.
▸v. dupe; fool.

**gul·let** /ˈgəlit/ ▸n. **1** esophagus. **2** throat.

**gul·li·ble** /ˈgələbəl/ ▸adj. easily persuaded or deceived; credulous. —**gul·li·bil·i·ty** n. —**gul·lib·ly** adv.

**gull·y** /ˈgəlē/ ▸n. (pl. **-ies**) ravine or channel created by water.

**gulp** /gəlp/ ▸v. **1** swallow hastily or greedily. **2** swallow with difficulty.
▸n. **1** act of gulping: *drained it at one gulp*. **2** large mouthful of a drink.

**gum** /gəm/ ▸n. **1 a** viscous secretion of some trees and shrubs. **b** adhesive substance. **2** chewing gum. **3** firm flesh around the roots of the teeth.
▸v. (**gummed**, **gum·ming**) **1** smear or cover with gum. **2** fasten with gum. —**gum·my** adj.
□ **gum up 1** (of a mechanism, etc.) become clogged or

obstructed with stickiness.
**2** interfere with the smooth running of: *gum up the works.*

**gum ar·a·bic** ▶*n.* gum exuded by some acacias and used as glue and in incense.

**gum·bo** /ˈgəmbō/ ▶*n.* (*pl.* **-bos**) soup thickened with okra pods.

**gum·drop** ▶*n.* soft, flavored candy made with gelatin or gum arabic.

**gump·tion** /ˈgəmpSHən/ ▶*n. inf.* resourcefulness; initiative.

**gum·shoe** ▶*n. inf.* detective.

**gun** /gən/ ▶*n.* **1** weapon consisting of a metal tube and with a grip at one end, from which bullets are propelled with explosive force. **2** device imitative of this, e.g., a starting pistol. **3** device for discharging grease, electrons, etc. **4** gunman: *a hired gun.*
▶*v.* (**gunned, gun·ning**) **1** (**gun down**) shoot (a person) with a gun. **2** *inf.* accelerate. **3** seek out determinedly to attack or rebuke.
☐ **go great guns** *inf.* proceed vigorously or successfully.
☐ **stick to one's guns** *inf.* maintain one's position under attack.

**gun·fire** ▶*n.* **1** firing of a gun or guns. **2** the noise from this.

**gung-ho** /ˈgəNG ˈhō/ ▶*adj.* enthusiastic; eager.

**gunk** /gəNGk/ *inf.* ▶*n.* viscous or liquid material.

**gun·man** ▶*n.* (*pl.* **-men**) man armed with a gun, esp. during a crime.

**gun·ny** /ˈgənē/ ▶*n.* (*pl.* **-nies**) **1** coarse sacking, usu. of jute fiber. **2** sack made of this.

**gun·pow·der** ▶*n.* explosive made of saltpeter, sulfur, and charcoal, used in cartridges, fireworks, etc.

**gun·shot** ▶*n.* **1** shot fired from a gun. **2** range of a gun: *within gunshot.*

**gun·smith** ▶*n.* person who makes, sells, and repairs small firearms.

**gun·wale** /ˈgənl/ (also **gun·nel**) ▶*n.* upper edge of the side of a boat or ship.

**gup·py** /ˈgəpē/ ▶*n.* (*pl.* **-pies**) popular freshwater fish of the W. Indies and S. America, that give birth to live young.

**gur·gle** /ˈgərgəl/ ▶*v.* make a bubbling sound.
▶*n.* gurgling sound.

**gu·ru** /ˈgo͝oro͞o/ ▶*n.* **1** Hindu

spiritual teacher or head of a religious sect. **2 a** influential teacher. **b** revered mentor.

**gush** /gəSH/ ▸*v.* **1** emit or flow in a sudden and copious stream. **2** speak or behave effusively. ▸*n.* **1** sudden or copious stream. **2** effusive or sentimental manner. —**gush·ing** *adj.* —**gush·y** *adj.*

**gush·er** ▸*n.* oil well from which oil flows without being pumped.

**gus·set** /ˈgəsit/ ▸*n.* piece inserted into a garment, etc., to strengthen or enlarge it.

**gus·sy** /ˈgəsē/ ▸*v.* (-**sied**) (**gussy up**) *inf.* decorate in a showy way.

**gust** /gəst/ ▸*n.* **1** sudden strong rush of wind; burst of rain, smoke, noise, etc. **2** passionate outburst. ▸*v.* blow in gusts. —**gust·y** *adj.*

**gus·ta·to·ry** /ˈgəstəˌtôrē/ ▸*adj.* concerned with tasting.

**gus·to** /ˈgəstō/ ▸*n.* (*pl.* -**toes**) zest; enjoyment or vigor.

**gut** /gət/ ▸*n.* **1** intestine. **2** (**guts**) the bowel or entrails. **3** (**guts**) *inf.* personal courage. **4** *inf.* stomach; belly. **5** (**guts**) **a** internal parts: *the guts of a computer.* **b** essence, e.g., of an issue. **6 a** material for violin or racket strings or surgical use. **b** material for fishing lines. ▸*adj.* **1** instinctive: *gut reaction.* **2** fundamental: *a gut issue.* ▸*v.* (**gut·ted, gut·ting**) **1** remove or destroy the interior of (a house, etc.). **2** take out the guts of (a fish, etc.).

**gut·sy** /ˈgətsē/ ▸*adj.* (-**si·er, -si·est**) *inf.* courageous. —**gut·si·ness** *n.*

**gut·ter** /ˈgətər/ ▸*n.* shallow trough along the eaves of a house, or channel at the side of a street, to carry off rainwater. ▸*v.* (of a candle) melt away rapidly.

**gut·tur·al** /ˈgətərəl/ ▸*adj.* throaty; harsh sounding. —**gut·tur·al·ly** *adv.*

**guy** /gī/ ▸*n.* **1** *inf.* **a** man; fellow. **b** (**guys**) people of either sex. **2** rope or chain to secure a tent or steady a load, etc. ▸*v.* secure with a guy or guys.

**guz·zle** /ˈgəzəl/ ▸*v.* consume greedily or in great amounts. —**guz·zler** *n.*

**gym·na·si·um** /jimˈnāzēəm/ ▸*n.* (*pl.* -**si·ums** or -**si·a**) room or building equipped for indoor sports or training.

**gym·nas·tics** /jimˈnastiks/ ▸*pl. n.* [also treated as *sing.*] **1** exercises developing or displaying physical agility and coordination. **2** other forms of physical or mental agility. —**gym·nast** *n.* —**gym·nas·tic** *adj.*

**gy·ne·col·o·gy** /ˌgīnəˈkäləjē; ˌjinə-/ ▶*n.* branch of medicine concerned with the functions and diseases of the female reproductive system. —**gy·ne·co·log·i·cal** *adj.* —**gy·ne·col·o·gist** *n.*

**gyp** /jip/ *inf.* ▶*v.* (**gypped, gyp·ping**) cheat; swindle. ▶*n.* a swindle.

**gyp·sum** /ˈjipsəm/ ▶*n.* form of calcium sulfate used to make plaster of Paris and in the building industry.

**Gyp·sy** /ˈjipsē/ ▶*n.* (*pl.* **-sies**) **1** member of a nomadic people of Hindu origin with dark skin and hair. **2** (**gypsy**) person resembling or living like a Gypsy.

**gyp·sy moth** ▶*n.* tussock moth of which the larvae are very destructive to foliage.

**gy·rate** /ˈjīrāt/ ▶*v.* go in a circle or spiral; revolve; whirl. —**gy·ra·tion** *n.*

**gyre** /ˈjī(ə)r/ ▶*v.* whirl; gyrate. ▶*n.* spiral; a vortex.

**gy·ro·scope** /ˈjīrəˌskōp/ ▶*n.* rotating wheel whose axis is free to turn but maintains a fixed direction despite change of position, esp. used for stabilization or with the compass in an aircraft, ship, etc.

# Hh

**H**[1] /āCH/ (also **h**) ▸*n.* (*pl.* **Hs** or **H's**; **h's**) **1** eighth letter of the alphabet. **2** anything having the form of an H: *H-bar*.

**H**[2] ▸*symb. Chem.* hydrogen.

**h** *symb.* ▸Planck's constant.

**h.** ▸*abbr.* **1** height. **2** hour(s). **3** *Baseball* hit(s).

**Ha** ▸*symb. Chem.* hahnium.

**ha** /hä/ (also **hah**) ▸*interj.* expressing surprise, suspicion, triumph, etc.

**ha·be·as cor·pus** /ˈhābēəs ˈkôrpəs/ ▸*n.* writ requiring a person to be brought before a court, esp. to investigate the lawfulness of the detention.

**ha·bil·i·tate** /həˈbiləˌtāt/ ▸*v.* **1** make (someone) competent to lead a normal life or knowledgeable enough to do a particular task. **2** clothe or dress.

**hab·it** /ˈhabit/ ▸*n.* **1** regular tendency or practice, esp one that is hard to give up. **2** *inf.* addiction. **3 a** dress, esp. of a religious order. **b** (**riding habit**) woman's riding dress. □ **habit-forming** addictive.

**hab·it·a·ble** ▸*adj.* suitable for living in. —**hab·it·a·bil·i·ty** *n.*

**hab·i·tat** /ˈhabiˌtat/ ▸*n.* natural home of an organism.

**hab·i·ta·tion** /ˌhabiˈtāSHən/ ▸*n.* **1** inhabiting. **2** house or home.

**ha·bit·u·al** /həˈbiCHo͞oəl/ ▸*adj.* done constantly or as a habit. —**ha·bit·u·al·ly** *adv.*

**ha·bit·u·ate** /həˈbiCHo͞oˌāt/ ▸*v.* accustom; make used to something. —**ha·bit·u·a·tion** *n.*

**ha·bit·u·é** /həˈbiCHo͞oˌā/ ▸*n.* habitual visitor or resident.

**ha·ček** /ˈhaˌCHek/ (also **há·ček**) ▸*n.* diacritic mark ( ˇ ) placed over a letter to indicate modification of the sound in Slavic and other languages.

**hack** /hak/ ▸*v.* **1** cut or chop roughly. **2** *inf.* gain unauthorized access to (data in a computer). **3** *inf.* **a** manage; cope. **4** drive a taxi.
▸*n.* **1** person hired to do dull routine work, esp. writing. **2** taxi. **3** horse for ordinary riding, esp. one for hire.
▸*adj.* uninspired: *a hack performance.*

**hack·er** ▸*n. inf.* **1** person who gains unauthorized access to computer data. **2** person adept at working with computers.

**hackles** /ˈhakəlz/ ▸*pl. n.* **1** hairs on an animal's back that rise when it is angry. **2** similar hairs on the back of a person's neck.

**hack·neyed** ▸*adj.* (of a phrase, etc.) made commonplace or trite by overuse.

**hack·saw** ▸*n.* saw with a narrow blade set in a frame, for cutting metal.

**had·dock** /ˈhadək/ ▸*n.* (*pl.* same) N. Atlantic marine fish used as food.

**Ha·des** /ˈhādēz/ ▸*n. Gk. mythol.* the underworld; abode of the spirits of the dead.

**haft** /haft/ ▸*n.* handle of a dagger, knife, etc.

**hag** /hag/ ▸*n.* **1** witch. **2** ugly old woman.

**hag·gard** /ˈhagərd/ ▸*adj.* looking exhausted and distraught, esp. from fatigue, worry, etc. —**hag·gard·ness** *n.*

**hag·gle** /ˈhagəl/ ▸*v.* dispute or bargain persistently: *haggled over water rights.* —**hag·gler** *n.*

**hag·i·ol·o·gy** /ˌhagēˈäləjē; ˌhāgē-/ ▸*n.* literature dealing with the lives and legends of saints.

**ha-ha** /ˈhä ˌhä/ ▸*n.* ditch with a wall on its inner side below ground level, forming a boundary to a park or garden without interrupting the view.

**hail** /hāl/ ▸*n.* **1** pellets of frozen rain. **2** barrage or onslaught (of missiles, curses, etc.).
▸*v.* **1** shower down hail: *it is hailing.* **2** pour down (blows, words, etc.). **3** attract the attention of: *hail a taxi.* **4** acclaim: *hailed him king* | *hailed as a prodigy.*

**hair** /he(ə)r/ ▸*n.* **1** fine threadlike strands growing from the skin of mammals, esp. from the human head. **2** anything resembling a hair. **3** very small extent: *a hair to the left.* —**hair·less** *adj.* —**hair·y** *adj.*
□ **let one's hair down** *inf.* abandon restraint; behave freely or wildly. □ **make a person's hair stand on end** alarm or horrify a person.

**hair·cut** ▸*n.* style or act of cutting the hair.

**hair·do** ▸*n.* (*pl.* -dos) *inf.* style or act of styling hair.

**hair·piece** ▸*n.* piece of

detached hair used to augment a person's natural hair.

**hair·rais·ing** ▶*adj.* alarming; terrifying.

**hair's breadth** ▶*n.* very small amount or margin.

**hair·style** ▶*n.* particular way of arranging or dressing the hair. —**hair·styl·ist** *n.*

**hake** /hāk/ ▶*n.* marine food fish.

**hal·cy·on** /'halsēən/ ▶*adj.* **1** calm; peaceful: *halcyon days at the beach.* **2** (of a period) happy; prosperous.

**hale** /hāl/ ▶*adj.* strong and healthy (esp. in phrase **hale and hearty**).

**half** /haf/ ▶*n.* (*pl.* **halves**) **1** either of two equal or corresponding parts or groups into which a thing is or might be divided. **2** *Sports* either of two equal periods of play.
▶*adj.* of or being an amount or quantity equal to a half, or loosely to a part thought of as a half: *take half the men* | *half a pint* | *a half pint* | *half-price.*
▶*adv.* **1** to the extent of half; partly: *only half cooked* | *half-frozen.* **2** to a certain extent; somewhat; esp. in phrases: *half dead.* **3** (in reckoning time) by

the amount of half (an hour, etc.): *half past two.*
□ **not half 1** not nearly: *not half long enough.* **2** *inf.* not at all: *not half bad.*

**half-and-half** ▶*adv. & adj.* in equal parts.
▶*n.* mixture of milk and cream.

**half·back** ▶*n.* (in some sports) player between the linemen and fullbacks, or behind the forward line.

**half-baked** ▶*adj.* **1** incompletely considered or planned. **2** foolish.

**half brother** ▶*n.* brother with only one parent in common.

**half·heart·ed** ▶*adj.* lacking enthusiasm. —**half·heart·ed·ly** *adv.*

**half-life** ▶*n.* time needed for the radioactivity or some other property of a substance to fall to half its original value.

**half-mast** ▶*n.* position of a flag halfway down the mast, as a mark of respect for a person who has died.

**half sister** ▶*n.* sister with only one parent in common.

**half·time** ▶*n.* time at which half of a game or contest is completed.

**half-truth** ▶*n.* statement that

conveys (esp. deliberately) only part of the truth.

**half·way** ▶*adv.* **1** at a point equidistant between two others: *halfway to Troy.* **2** to some extent; more or less: *halfway decent.*
▶*adj.* situated halfway: *a halfway point.*

**half·way house** ▶*n.* facility for assisting ex-prisoners, mental patients, etc., in readjusting to society.

**half·wit** ▶*n. inf.* extremely foolish or stupid person.
—**half·wit·ted** *adj.*

**hal·i·but** /'haləbət/ ▶*n.* (*pl.* same) large marine flatfish used as food.

**hal·i·to·sis** /ˌhaliˈtōsəs/ ▶*n.* bad breath.

**hall** /hôl/ ▶*n.* **1 a** space or passage into which the front entrance of a house, etc., opens. **b** corridor or passage in a building. **2** large room or building for meetings, meals, concerts, etc. **3** university residence for students.

**hal·le·lu·jah** /ˌhaləˈlōōyə/ ▶var. of ALLELUIA.

**hall·mark** /'hôlˌmärk/ ▶*n.* **1** mark of purity, as stamped

into gold, silver, and platinum. **2** distinctive feature.

**hal·low** /'halō/ ▶*v.* **1** make holy; consecrate. **2** honor as holy.

**Hal·low·een** /ˌhaləˈwēn/ (also **Hal·low·e'en**) ▶*n.* eve of All Saints' Day, Oct. 31, esp. as celebrated by children dressing in costumes and collecting treats door-to-door.

**hal·lu·ci·nate** /həˈlōōsəˌnāt/ ▶*v.* experience a seemingly real perception of something not actually present.

**hal·lu·ci·na·tion** ▶*n.* perception of sights, sounds, etc., not actually present.

**hal·lu·ci·no·gen** /həˈlōōsənəˌjən/ ▶*n.* drug causing hallucinations.
—**hal·lu·ci·no·gen·ic** *adj.*

**hall·way** /'hôlˌwā/ ▶*n.* entrance hall or corridor.

**ha·lo** /'hālō/ ▶*n.* (*pl.* **-loes, -los**) **1** disk or circle of light shown in art surrounding the head of a sacred person. **2** circle of light around a luminous body, esp. the sun or moon. **3** circle or ring.
▶*v.* (**-loed**) surround with a halo.

**hal·o·gen** /'haləjən/ ▶*n.* Any of a group of non-metallic elements including chlorine and iodine.

▸*adj.* denoting a lamp using a filament surrounded by halogen vapor.

**halt** /hôlt/ ▸*n.* stop (usu. temporary): *come to a halt.*

▸*v.* **1** stop; come or bring to a halt. **2** hesitate:

**halt·er** ▸*n.* **1** bridle and rope for leading or tying up a horse. **2 a** strap around the back of a woman's neck holding her dress top or blouse and leaving her shoulders and back bare. **b** garment held by this.

▸*v.* put a halter on (a horse, etc.).

**halt·ing** ▸*adj.* slow and hesitant. —**halt·ing·ly** *adv.*

**halve** /hav/ ▸*v.* **1** divide into two halves. **2** reduce by half.

**ham** /ham/ ▸*n.* **1** upper part of a pig's leg salted and dried or smoked for food. **2** back of the thigh. **3** inexpert or unsubtle actor. **4** *inf.* amateur radio operator.

▸*v.* (**hammed**, **ham·ming**) *inf.* overact.

**ham·burg·er** /'ham,bərgər/ ▸*n.* round patty of fried or grilled ground beef.

**ham·let** /'hamlit/ ▸*n.* small village.

**ham·mer** /'hamər/ ▸*n.* **1 a** tool with a heavy metal head used for driving nails, etc. **b** similar contrivance, as for exploding the charge in a gun, striking the strings of a piano, etc. **2** metal ball attached to a wire for throwing in an athletic contest. **3** bone of the middle ear.

▸*v.* **1** hit or beat with or as with a hammer; strike violently. **2 a** drive in (nails). **b** fasten or secure by hammering: *hammered the lid down.* **3** inculcate (ideas, knowledge, etc.) forcefully. **4** utterly defeat; inflict heavy damage on. **5** (**hammer away at**) work hard or persistently at.

□ **hammer out 1** make flat or smooth by hammering. **2** work out the details of (a plan or agreement) laboriously.

**ham·mer and sick·le** ▸*n.* emblem of the former USSR and of international communism.

**ham·mock** /'hamək/ ▸*n.* bed of canvas or rope network, suspended by cords.

**ham·per** /'hampər/ ▸*n.* basket, often with a hinged lid, for laundry, etc.

▸*v.* hinder.

**ham·ster** /'hamstər/ ▸*n.* rodent having a short tail and large cheek pouches, kept as a pet or laboratory animal.

**ham·string** *Anat.* ▶*n.* **1** each of five tendons at the back of the knee in humans. **2** great tendon at the back of the hock in quadrupeds.

▶*v.* (*past* and *past part.* **ham·strung** or **ham·stringed**) **1** cripple by cutting the hamstrings of (a person or animal). **2** prevent the activity or efficiency of (a person or enterprise).

**hand** /hand/ ▶*n.* **1 a** end part of the human arm beyond the wrist, including the fingers and thumb. **b** in other primates, end part of a forelimb, also used as a foot. **2** control; management; custody; disposal: *in good hands.* **3** the pointer of a clock or watch. **4** right or left side or direction. **5** skill: *a hand for making pastry.* **6** individual's writing or the style of this: *a legible hand.* **7** source of information, etc.: *at first hand.* **8** person as a manual laborer, esp. on a farm, on board ship, etc. **9 a** playing cards dealt to a player. **b** round of play. **10** *inf.* applause: *got a big hand.* **11** [as *adj.* or in *comb.*] held or done by hand: *hand brake | hand-stitched quilt.*

▶*v.* deliver; transfer by hand or otherwise.
□ **by hand** by a person and not a machine. □ **hand in hand** in close association. □ **hands down** with no difficulty. □ **hands-on** involving active participation: *a hands-on workshop.* □ **hands off!** used as a warning not to touch something. □ **on hand** available. □ **out of hand** out of control.

**hand·bag** ▶*n.* woman's small bag, used to hold a wallet, cosmetics, etc.

**hand·ball** ▶*n.* game in which a ball is struck with an open hand against a wall.

**hand·bill** ▶*n.* printed notice distributed by hand.

**hand·book** ▶*n.* short manual.

**hand·cuff** ▶*n.* (**handcuffs**) lockable linked metal rings for securing a person's wrists.
▶*v.* put handcuffs on.

**hand·ful** ▶*n.* (*pl.* **-fuls**) **1** quantity that fills the hand. **2** small number or amount. **3** *inf.* troublesome person or task.

**hand grenade** ▶*n.* see GRENADE.

**hand·gun** ▶*n.* small firearm.

**hand·i·cap** /ˈhandēˌkap/ ▶*n.* **1 a** disadvantage imposed on a superior competitor to make

chances more equal. **b** race, etc., in which this is imposed.
**2** number of strokes by which a golfer normally exceeds par.
**3** physical or mental disability.
▸ *v.* (**-capped, -cap·ping**) **1** impose a handicap on. **2** place (a person) at a disadvantage.
—**hand·i·capped** *adj.*

**hand·i·craft** ▸*n.* work requiring manual and artistic skill.

**hand·i·work** ▸*n.* work done or a thing made by hand, or by a particular person.

**hand·ker·chief** /ˈhaNGkərCHif/ ▸*n.* (*pl.* **-chiefs** or **-chieves**) cloth for wiping one's nose, etc.

**han·dle** /ˈhandl/ ▸*n.* part by which a thing is held, carried, or controlled.
▸*v.* **1** touch, feel, operate, or move with the hands. **2** manage or deal with. **3** deal in (particular goods).

**hand·made** ▸*adj.* made by hand, not by machine.

**hand-me-down** ▸*n.* article of clothing, etc., passed on from another person.

**hand·out** ▸*n.* **1** something given free to a needy person.
**2** printed information given out.

**hand·shake** ▸*n.* clasping of a person's hand as a greeting, etc.

**hand·some** ▸*adj.* (**-som·er, -som·est**) **1** (of a person) good-looking. **2** (of an object, etc.) imposing; attractive.
**3** generous; liberal: *a handsome present.* —**hand·some·ly** *adv.*

**hand·spring** ▸*n.* acrobatic flip in which one lands first on the hands and then on the feet.

**hand-to-hand** ▸*adj.* (of fighting) at close quarters.

**hand·writ·ing** ▸*n.* **1** writing with a pen, pencil, etc.
**2** individual's style of writing.
—**hand·writ·ten** *adj.*

**hand·y** /ˈhandē/ ▸*adj.* (**-i·er, -i·est**)
**1** convenient to handle or use; useful. **2** placed or occurring conveniently. **3** clever with the hands. —**hand·i·ly** *adv.*
—**hand·i·ness** *n.*

**hand·y·man** ▸*n.* (*pl.* **-men**) person who does odd jobs.

**hang** /haNG/ ▸*v.* (*past* and *past part.* **hung** except in sense 5)
**1** secure or cause to be supported from above, esp. with the lower part free. **2** set up (a door, gate, etc.) on hinges.
**3** place (a picture) on a wall or in an exhibition. **4** attach (wallpaper) to a wall. **5** (*past* and *past part.* **hanged**) suspend or be suspended by the neck, usu.

with a noosed rope, until dead.
**6** let droop: *hang one's head.* **7** be present or imminent: *a hush hung over the room.*
▶*n.* way a thing hangs or falls.
☐ **hang around** loiter or dally.
☐ **hang back 1** show reluctance. **2** remain behind. ☐ **hang in** *inf.* persist; persevere. ☐ **hang on** *inf.* **1** continue or persevere. **2** cling; retain. **3 a** (in telephoning) continue to listen during a pause in the conversation. ☐ **hang out 1** *inf.* spend time; frequent. **2** (**hang out with**) *inf.* accompany; be friends with. **3** loiter; dally. ☐ **hang up 1** hang from a hook, etc. **2** end a telephone conversation, esp. abruptly: *then he hung up on me.*

**hang·ar** /ˈhaNGər/ ▶*n.* building for aircraft.

**hang·dog** ▶*adj.* dejected; shamefaced.

**hang·er** ▶*n.* shaped piece of plastic, wood, etc., with a hook at the top, from which clothes are hung.

**hang glid·er** ▶*n.* kitelike glider controlled by a person suspended beneath it.

**hang·nail** ▶*n.* torn skin near a fingernail.

**hang·over** ▶*n.* headache, upset stomach, etc., caused by too much alcohol.

**hang-up** ▶*n. inf.* emotional problem or inhibition.

**hank** /haNGk/ ▶*n.* coil or skein of yarn or thread, etc.

**han·ker** ▶*v.* (**hanker after/for/to do something**) long for; crave. —**han·ker·ing** *n.*

**han·ky-pan·ky** /ˈhaNGkē-ˈpaNGkē/ *inf.* ▶*n.* naughtiness, esp. sexual misbehavior.

**Ha·nuk·kah** /ˈKHänəkə; ˈhä-/ (also **Cha·nu·kah**) ▶*n.* Jewish festival of lights, commemorating the purification of the Temple in 165 B.C.

**hap·haz·ard** /ˌhapˈhazərd/ ▶*adj.* done, etc., by chance; random.
▶*adv.* at random. —**hap·haz·ard·ly** *adv.*

**hap·less** /ˈhaplis/ ▶*adj.* unlucky.

**hap·log·ra·phy** /hapˈlägrəfē/ ▶*n.* inadvertent omission of a repeated letter or letters in writing (e.g., writing *philogy* for *philology*).

**hap·pen** /ˈhapən/ ▶*v.* **1** occur. **2** have (good or bad) fortune: *I happened to meet her.* **3** be the (esp. unwelcome) fate or experience of: *what happened to you?* **4** (**happen on**) meet or discover by chance.

□ **as it happens** in fact; in reality: *as it happens, it turned out well.*

**hap·py** /ˈhapē/ ▸*adj.* (**-pi·er**, **-pi·est**) **1** feeling or showing pleasure or contentment. **2 a** fortunate; lucky. **b** (of words, behavior, etc.) apt; pleasing. **3** *inf.* inclined to use excessively or at random: *trigger-happy.* —**hap·pi·ly** *adv.* —**hap·pi·ness** *n.*

**happy-go-lucky** ▸*adj.* cheerfully casual.

**hap·py hour** ▸*adj.* time when alcoholic drinks are sold at reduced prices.

**hap·tic** /ˈhaptik/ ▸*adj.* of or relating to the sense of touch, in particular relating to the perception and manipulation of objects using the sense of touch.

**ha·rangue** /həˈraNG/ ▸*n.* lengthy and earnest speech. ▸*v.* make a harangue to.

**ha·rass** /həˈras; ˈharəs/ ▸*v.* **1** trouble and annoy continually. **2** make repeated attacks on. —**ha·rass·ment** *n.*

**har·bin·ger** /ˈhärbinjər/ ▸*n.* person or thing that announces or signals the approach of another.

**har·bor** /ˈhärbər/ ▸*n.* **1** place of shelter for ships. **2** shelter. ▸*v.* **1** give shelter to (esp. a criminal or wanted person). **2** keep in one's mind, esp. resentfully: *harbor a grudge.*

**hard** /härd/ ▸*adj.* **1** firm and solid. **2 a** difficult to understand or explain: *hard problem.* **b** difficult to accomplish: *hard decision.* **c** not easy: *hard to believe.* **3** difficult to bear; severe or harsh: *a hard life | hard winter.* **4** (of a person) unfeeling; severely critical. **5** enthusiastic; intense: *hard worker | a hard night.* **6 a** (of liquor) strongly alcoholic. **b** (of drugs) potent and addictive. **7** not disputable: *hard facts | had data.* ▸*adv.* **1** strenuously; intensely; copiously; with one's full effort: *try hard | look hard at | hardworking.* **2** so as to be hard or firm: *hard-baked.* —**hard·en** *v.* —**hard·ness** *n.*

□ **be hard on 1** be difficult for. **2** be severe in one's treatment or criticism of. □ **hard up** short of money.

**hard·bit·ten** ▸*adj. inf.* cynical.

**hard-boiled** ▸*adj.* **1** (of an egg) boiled until solid. **2** (of a person) tough; shrewd.

**hard cop·y** ▸*n.* printed material produced by computer, usu. on paper.

**hard core** ▸*n.* most active or committed members of a society or movement.

▸*adj.* (**hard-core**) **1** blatant; uncompromising. **2** (of pornography) explicit.

**hard disk** ▸*n. Computing* large-capacity, rigid, usu. magnetic storage disk.

**hard hat** ▸*n.* protective helmet worn on building sites, etc.

**hard·head·ed** ▸*adj.* practical; not sentimental.

**hard-heart·ed** ▸*adj.* unfeeling; unsympathetic.

**hard-lin·er** ▸*n.* person who adheres rigidly to a policy.

**hard·ly** ▸*adv.* **1** scarcely; only just: *we hardly knew them.* **2** only with difficulty: *could hardly speak.*

**hard-nosed** ▸*adj. inf.* realistic and determined.

**hard-pressed** ▸*adv.* burdened; put-upon.

**hard sell** ▸*n.* aggressive salesmanship or advertising.

**hard·ship** ▸*n.* **1** severe suffering or privation. **2** circumstance causing this.

**hard·tack** /ˈhärdˌtak/ ▸*n.* hard dry bread or biscuit, esp. as rations for sailors.

**hard·ware** ▸*n.* **1** tools and household articles of metal, etc. **2** heavy machinery or armaments. **3** mechanical and electronic components of a computer, etc.

**hard·wood** ▸*n.* wood from a deciduous broad-leaved tree as distinguished from that of conifers.

**hard·y** ▸*adj.* (**-i·er, -i·est**) **1** robust; enduring. **2** (of a plant) able to grow in the open air all year.

**hare** /he(ə)r/ ▸*n.* mammal like a large rabbit.

**hare·brained** ▸*adj.* rash; foolish; wild.

**hare·lip** ▸*n.* congenital fissure of the upper lip.

**har·em** /ˈhe(ə)rəm/ ▸*n.* **1** women of a Muslim household, living in a separate part of the house. **2** their quarters.

**har·le·quin** /ˈhärlək(w)in/ ▸*n.* (**Harlequin**) mute character in pantomime, usu. masked and dressed in a diamond-patterned costume.

▸*adj.* in varied colors.

**har·lot** /ˈhärlət/ ▸*n. archaic* prostitute.

**harm** /härm/ ▸*n.* hurt; damage.

▸*v.* cause harm to. —**harm·ful** *adj.*

□ **out of harm's way** in safety.

**harm·less** ▸*adj.* **1** not able or likely to cause harm. **2** inoffensive.

**har·mon·i·ca** /här'mänikə/ ▸*n.* small rectangular wind instrument played by blowing or sucking air through it.

**har·mo·ny** /'härmənē/ ▸*n.* (*pl.* **-nies**) **1** simultaneously sounded musical notes that produce chords. **2** agreement; concord. —**har·mo·ni·ous** *adj.* —**har·mo·nize** *v.*

**har·ness** /'härnis/ ▸*n.* **1** straps by which a horse is fastened to a cart and controlled. **2** similar arrangement for fastening a thing to a person's body, for restraining a young child, etc. ▸*v.* **1 a** put a harness on (esp. a horse); attach by a harness. **2** make use of (natural resources), esp. to produce energy.

**harp** /härp/ ▸*n.* upright stringed instrument plucked with the fingers. ▸*v.* (**harp on**) talk repeatedly about. —**harp·ist** *n.*

**har·poon** /ˌhär'po͞on/ ▸*n.* barbed spear with a rope attached, for killing whales, etc. ▸*v.* spear with a harpoon.

**harp·si·chord** /'härpsiˌkôrd/ ▸*n.* keyboard instrument in which strings are plucked mechanically.

**har·ri·dan** /'haridn/ ▸*n.* bad-tempered woman.

**har·ri·er** /'harēər/ ▸*n.* hound used for hunting hares.

**har·row** /'harō/ ▸*n.* heavy frame with iron teeth dragged over plowed land to break up clods, remove weeds, etc. ▸*v.* draw a harrow over (land).

**har·ry** /'harē/ ▸*v.* (**-ried**) persisently ravage or despoil; harrass or worry.

**harsh** /härSH/ ▸*adj.* **1** unpleasantly rough or sharp, esp. to the senses. **2** severe; cruel. —**harsh·ly** *adv.* —**harsh·ness** *n.*

**har·vest** /'härvist/ ▸*n.* **1 a** process of gathering in crops, etc. **2** season's yield or crop. ▸*v.* gather as harvest; reap. —**har·ves·ter** *n.*

**har·vest moon** ▸*n.* full moon nearest to the autumnal equinox (Sept. 22 or 23).

**has** /haz/ ▸3rd sing. present of **HAVE**.

**has-been** ▸*n. inf.* person who

has lost his or her former importance.

**hash** /hasʜ/ ▸*n.* **1** dish of cooked meat and potatoes cut into small pieces and recooked. **2 a** mixture; jumble. **b** mess. **3** *inf.* hashish.

▸*v.* settle by conferring or debating.

**hash·ish** /ˈhaˌsʜēsʜ/ ▸*n.* resinous product of hemp, smoked as a narcotic.

**has·n't** /ˈhazənt/ ▸*contr.* has not.

**hasp** /hasp/ ▸*n.* hinged metal clasp that can be secured by a padlock.

**has·sle** /ˈhasəl/ *inf.* ▸*n.* **1** trouble or inconvenience. **2** argument.

▸*v.* **1** harass; annoy. **2** argue; quarrel.

**has·sock** /ˈhasək/ ▸*n.* **1** thick firm cushion for kneeling on or used as a footrest. **2** tuft of matted grass.

**haste** /hāst/ ▸*n.* **1** urgency of movement or action. **2** excessive hurry. —**hast·i·ly** *adv.* —**hast·y** *adj.*

**hast·en** /ˈhāsən/ ▸*v.* **1** hurry. **2** bring about sooner.

**hat** /hat/ ▸*n.* **1** covering for the head, often with a brim. **2** person's occupation or capacity, esp. one of several: *wearing his managerial hat.*

□ **pass the hat** collect contributions of money.

**hatch** /hacʜ/ ▸*v.* **1 a** (of a young bird, fish, etc.) emerge from the egg. **b** (of an egg) produce a young animal. **c** (of a bird, etc.) incubate (an egg). **2** devise (a plot, etc.).

▸*n.* **1** act or instance of hatching. **2** brood hatched. **3** opening or door in an aircraft, spacecraft, etc. **4** *Naut.* **a** HATCHWAY. **b** cover for this: *batten the hatches.*

**hatch·et** /ˈhacʜit/ ▸*n.* light short-handled ax.

**hatch·et man** ▸*n. inf.* person employed to harm or dismiss another.

**hatch·way** ▸*n.* opening in a ship's deck for cargo.

**hate** /hāt/ ▸*v.* **1** feel intense dislike for or aversion to. **2** be reluctant (to do something): *I hate to disturb you.*

▸*n.* **1** intense or passionate dislike. **2** hated person or thing.

**hate·ful** ▸*adj.* arousing hatred.

**ha·tred** /ˈhātrid/ ▸*n.* intense or passionate dislike.

**haugh·ty** /ˈhôtē/ ▸*adj.* (**-ti·er**, **-ti·est**) arrogant and disdainful.

—**haugh·ti·ly** *adv.*

—**haugh·ti·ness** *n.*

**haul** /hôl/ ▸*v.* **1** pull or drag forcibly. **2** transport by truck, cart, etc.

▸*n.* **1** act or instance of hauling. **2** distance to be traversed: *a short haul.* —**haul·er** *n.*

**haunch** /hônCH/ ▸*n.* **1** fleshy part of the buttock with the thigh. **2** leg and loin of a deer, etc., as food.

**haunt** /hônt/ ▸*v.* **1** (of a ghost) visit (a place) regularly. **2** (of a person) frequent. **3** (of a memory, etc.) be persistently in the mind of.

▸*n.* place frequented: *my old haunts in Paris.*

**haunt·ing** ▸*adj.* (of a memory, melody, etc.) poignant; wistful; evocative.

**haute cui·sine** /ˌōt ˌkwəˈzēn/ ▸*n.* cooking of a high standard, esp. of the French traditional school.

**hau·teur** /hōˈtər/ ▸*n.* haughtiness of manner; disdainful pride.

**haut monde** /ō ˈmôND; ˈmänd/ ▸*n.* (**the haut monde**) fashionable society.

**have** /hav/ ▸*v.* (*3rd sing. present* **has**; *past* and *past part.* **had**) **1** own or be able to use: *has a car* | *had no time to read* | *has nothing to wear.* **2** hold in a certain relationship: *has a sister.* **3** contain as a part or quality: *house has two floors* | *has green eyes.* **4 a** experience: *had a good time* | *has a headache.* **b** be subjected to a specified state: *had my car stolen* | *the book has a page missing.* **c** cause (a person or thing) to be in a particular state or take a particular action: *had him dismissed* | *had us worried* | *had my hair cut.* **5 a** engage in (an activity): *had an argument.* **b** hold (a meeting, party, etc.). **6** eat or drink: *had a beer.* **7** accept or tolerate; permit to: *I won't have it* | *will not have you say such things.* **8 a** let (a feeling, etc.) be present: *have no doubt* | *has a lot of sympathy for me.* **b** show or feel (mercy, pity, etc.): *have pity on him* | *have mercy!* **9 a** give birth to (offspring). **b** conceive mentally (an idea, etc.). **10** receive; obtain: *not a ticket to be had.* **11** *inf.* **a** get the better of: *I had him there.* **b** (usu. **be had**) cheat; deceive: *you were had.*

▸*aux. v.* used with a past participle to form the perfect, pluperfect, and future perfect tenses, and the conditional mood: *have worked | had seen | will have been | had I known, I would have gone | have you met her? yes, I have.*

▶*pl. n.* (**the haves**) people who have wealth or resources.

□ **have it in for** *inf.* be hostile or ill-disposed toward. □ **have on** be wearing (clothes). □ **have to** be obliged to; must.

**ha·ven** /ˈhāvən/ ▶*n.* **1** harbor or port. **2** place of refuge.

**have-nots** ▶*pl. n.* people lacking wealth or resources.

**have·n't** /ˈhavənt/ ▶*contr.* have not.

**hav·er·sack** /ˈhavərˌsak/ ▶*n.* strong bag carried on the back or over the shoulder.

**hav·oc** /ˈhavək/ ▶*n.* widespread destruction or disorder.

**hawk** /hôk/ ▶*n.* **1** diurnal bird of prey having a curved beak, rounded short wings, and a long tail. **2** person who advocates an aggressive or warlike policy, esp. in foreign affairs.

▶*v.* **1** hunt game with a hawk. **2** carry about or offer (goods) for sale. **3** clear the throat to remove phlegm.

□ **hawk-eyed** keen-sighted.

**haw·thorn** /ˈhôˌTHôrn/ ▶*n.* thorny shrub or tree with white,

red, or pink blossoms and small dark red fruit.

**hay** /hā/ ▶*n.* grass mown and dried for fodder.

▶*v.* make hay.

□ **make hay (while the sun shines)** seize opportunities for profit or enjoyment.

**hay fe·ver** ▶*n.* common allergy with respiratory symptoms, caused esp. by pollen.

**hay·wire** *inf.* ▶*adj.* **1** badly disorganized; out of control. **2** (of a person) erratic.

**haz·ard** /ˈhazərd/ ▶*n.* **1** danger or risk. **2** source of this.

▶*v.* dare to make or take; risk: *hazard a guess.* —**haz·ard·ous** *adj.*

**haze** /hāz/ ▶*n.* thin atmospheric vapor.

▶*v.* force (fraternity initiates) to perform humiliating or dangerous tasks. —**haz·i·ness** *n.* —**haz·y** *adj.*

**ha·zel** /ˈhāzəl/ ▶*n.* **1** shrub or small tree bearing round edible nuts. **2** greenish brown eye color.

**H-bomb** ▶*n.* HYDROGEN BOMB.

**HDTV** ▶*abbr.* high-definition television.

**He** ▶*symb. Chem.* helium.

**he** /hē/ ▶*pron.* (*obj.* **him**; *poss.* **his**;

*pl.* **they**) **1** the man or boy or male animal previously named or in question. **2** person, etc., of unspecified sex.

▸*n.* **1** male; man. **2** male: *he-goat.*

**head** /hed/ ▸*n.* **1** upper part of the human body, or foremost or upper part of an animal's body, containing the brain, mouth, and sense organs. **2 a** seat of intellect. **b** mental aptitude or tolerance: *good head for business | no head for heights.* **3** thing like a head in form or position; top. **4** person in charge. **5** front or forward part of something, e.g., a line. **6** upper end of something, e.g., a table or bed. **7** top or highest part of something, e.g., a page, stairs, etc. **8** individual person or animal regarded as a numerical unit: *$10 per head | 20 head of cattle.* **9 a** side of a coin bearing the image of a head. **b** (**heads**) this side as a choice in a coin toss. **10** source of a river, etc. **11** height or length of a head as a measure. **12** promontory (esp. in place-names): *Diamond Head.* **13** *Naut.* **a** bow of a ship. **b** toilet on ship or boat. **14** culmination, climax, or crisis. **15** habitual taker of drugs; drug addict.

▸*adj.* chief or principal: *head gardener | head office.*

▸*v.* **1** be at the head or front of. **2** be in charge of: *headed a small team.* **3 a** face or move in a specified direction or toward a specified result: *is heading for trouble.* **b** direct in a specified direction.

▢ **come to a head** reach a crisis. ▢ **go to one's head 1** (of liquor) make one dizzy or slightly drunk. **2** (of success) make one conceited. ▢ **head off 1** get ahead of so as to intercept. **2** forestall. ▢ **head-on 1** with the front foremost: *a head-on crash.* **2** in direct confrontation. ▢ **head start** advantage granted or gained at an early stage. ▢ **keep one's head** remain calm. ▢ **lose one's head** lose self-control; panic. ▢ **over one's head** beyond one's ability to understand.

**head·ache** ▸*n.* continuous pain in the head. —**head·ach·y** *adj.*

**head·dress** ▸*n.* ornamental covering for the head.

**head·ing** ▸*n.* **1** title at the head of a page, chapter, etc. **2** course of an aircraft, ship, etc.

**head·light** ▸*n.* **1** strong light at

the front of a motor vehicle, etc. **2** beam from this.

**head·line** ▸*n.* **1** heading at the top of an article in a newspaper. **2** (**headlines**) most important items in a news bulletin.

**head·long** ▸*adv. & adj.* **1** with head foremost. **2** in a rush.

**head·phones** ▸*pl. n.* pair of earphones fitting over the head.

**head·quar·ters** ▸*n.* [treated as *sing.* or *pl.*] administrative center of an organization.

**head·stone** ▸*n.* stone set up at the head of a grave.

**head·strong** ▸*adj.* self-willed; obstinate.

**head·wait·er** ▸*n.* person in charge of waiters, busboys, and other staff in a restaurant.

**head·way** ▸*n.* **1** progress. **2** ship's rate of progress.

**head·wind** ▸*n.* wind blowing from directly in front.

**head·y** ▸*adj.* (-i·er, -i·est) intoxicating; exhilarating

**heal** /hēl/ ▸*v.* **1** become sound or healthy again. **2** cause to heal or be healed. —**heal·er** *n.*

**health** /helTH/ ▸*n.* **1** state of being well in body or mind. **2** person's mental or physical condition: *in poor health.*

**health food** ▸*n.* food thought to have health-giving or -sustaining qualities.

**health main·te·nance or·ga·ni·za·tion** ▸*n.* organization that provides medical care to subscribers who have paid in advance, usu. through a health insurance plan. (Abbr.: **HMO**)

**health·y** ▸*adj.* (-i·er, -i·est) **1** having or showing good health. **2** substantial. —**health·i·ness** *n.*

**heap** /hēp/ ▸*n.* **1** disorderly pile. **2** (**heaps**) *inf.* large number or amount: *there's heaps of time.* **3** *inf.* old or dilapidated thing, esp. a motor vehicle or building. ▸*v.* **1** collect or be collected in a heap. **2** load copiously.

**hear** /hi(ə)r/ ▸*v.* (*past* and *past part.* **heard**) **1** perceive with the ear. **2** listen to: *heard them on the radio.* **3** judge (a case, etc.). **4** be told or informed. —**hear·er** *n.*

**hear·say** ▸*n.* rumor; gossip.

**hearse** /hərs/ ▸*n.* vehicle for conveying the coffin at a funeral.

**heart** /härt/ ▸*n.* **1** hollow muscular organ maintaining the circulation of blood by rhythmic contraction and dilation. **2 a** center of thought, feeling, and emotion (esp. love).

**b** capacity for feeling emotion: *has no heart.* **3 a** courage or enthusiasm: *take heart.* **b** mood or feeling: *change of heart.* **4** central or essential part of something. **5 a** heart-shaped thing. **b** conventional representation of a heart with two equal curves meeting at a point at the bottom and a cusp at the top.

□ **at heart 1** in one's inmost feelings. **2** basically; essentially. □ **break a person's heart** overwhelm a person with sorrow. □ **by heart** from memory. □ **take to heart** be much affected or distressed by.

**heart·ache** ▶*n.* mental anguish or grief.

**heart at·tack** ▶*n.* sudden failure of the heart to function normally.

**heart·break** ▶*n.* overwhelming distress. —**heart·break·er** *n.* —**heart·break·ing** *adj.* —**heart·bro·ken** *adj.*

**heart·burn** ▶*n.* burning sensation in the chest resulting from indigestion.

**heart·en** /ˈhärtn/ ▶*v.* make or become more cheerful. —**heart·en·ing** *adj.*

**heart·felt** ▶*adj.* sincere; deeply felt.

**hearth** /härTH/ ▶*n.* floor of a fireplace or area in front of it.

**heart·sick** ▶*adj.* very despondent.

**heart·y** /ˈhärtē/ ▶*adj.* (**-i·er, -i·est**) **1** vigorous. **2** (of a meal or appetite) large. **3** warm; friendly. —**heart·i·ly** *adv.* —**heart·i·ness** *n.*

**heat** /hēt/ ▶*n.* **1** condition of being hot. **2** energy arising from the motion of molecules. **3** hot weather: *succumbed to the heat.* **4 a** warmth of feeling. **b** anger or excitement: *the heat of the argument.* **5** most intense part or period of an activity: *in the heat of battle.* **6** preliminary round in a race or contest.
▶*v.* **1** make or become hot or warm. **2** inflame; excite or intensify. —**heat·ing** *n.*
□ **in heat** (of mammals, esp. females) sexually receptive.

**heat·ed** ▶*adj.* **1** angry; impassioned. **2** made hot. —**heat·ed·ly** *adv.*

**heath** /hēTH/ ▶*n.* area of flattish uncultivated land with low shrubs.

**hea·then** /ˈhēTHən/ ▶*n.* **1** person who does not belong to a widely held religion as regarded by those that do. **2** person regarded as lacking culture or moral principles.

▸*adj.* **1** of or relating to heathens. **2** having no religion.

**heath·er** /ˈheT͟Hər/ ▸*n.* purple-flowered shrub growing on moorland and heath.

**heat light·ning** ▸*n.* flashes of lightning without thunder.

**heat·stroke** ▸*n.* severe feverish condition caused by excessive exposure to high temperature.

**heat wave** ▸*n.* period of very hot weather.

**heave** /hēv/ ▸*v.* **1** lift or haul (a heavy thing) with great effort. **2** utter with effort or resignation: *heaved a sigh.* **3** *inf.* throw. **4** retch.

▸*n.* **1** instance of heaving. **2** (**heaves**) respiratory disease of horses.

**heav·en** /ˈhevən/ ▸*n.* **1** place regarded in some religions as the abode of God and of the good after death. **2** place or state of supreme bliss. **3** *inf.* something delightful. **4** (**the heav·ens**) the sky as seen from the earth, esp. at night.
—**heav·en·ly** *adj.*

**heav·y** /ˈhevē/ ▸*adj.* (**-i·er**, **-i·est**)

**1** of great or exceptionally high weight; difficult to lift. **2** of great density; abundant:

**3** severe; intense: *heavy fighting.* **4** doing something to excess: *heavy drinker.* **5** (of machinery, artillery, etc.) very large of its kind. **6** needing much effort: *heavy work.* **7** (of food) hard to digest.

▸*n.* (*pl.* **-ies**) **1** *inf.* large violent person; thug. **2** villainous role or actor in a play, etc.
—**heav·i·ly** *adv.* —**heav·i·ness** *n.*

**heav·y-du·ty** ▸*adj.* **1** intended to withstand hard use. **2** serious; grave.

**heav·y go·ing** ▸*n.* slow or difficult progress.

**heav·y-hand·ed** ▸*adj.* **1** clumsy. **2** overbearing; oppressive.

**heav·y-hearted** ▸*adj.* sad; doleful.

**heav·y in·dus·try** ▸*n.* industry producing metal, machinery, etc.

**heav·y met·al** ▸*n.* **1** highly amplified rock music with a strong beat. **2** metal of high density.

**heav·y·set** ▸*adj.* stocky; thickset.

**heav·y wa·ter** ▸*n.* water in

which the hydrogen in the molecules is partly or wholly replaced by the isotope deuterium, used esp. as a moderator in nuclear reactors.

**heb·dom·a·dal** /heb'dämədl/ ▸*adj.* weekly (used esp. of organizations that meet weekly).

**heb·e·tude** /'hebə,t(y)ŏod/ ▸*n.* state of being dull or lethargic.

**He·brew** /'hēbrŏo/ ▸*n.* **1** member of a Semitic people orig. centered in ancient Palestine. **2 a** language of this people. **b** modern form of this used esp. in Israel. ▸*adj.* **1** of or in Hebrew. **2** of the Hebrews or the Jews.

**heck·le** /'hekəl/ ▸*v.* interrupt and harass (a public speaker, entertainer, etc.); badger. —**heck·ler** *n.*

**hec·tic** /'hektik/ ▸*adj.* **1** busy and confused; excited. **2** feverish.

**hec·tor** /'hektər/ ▸*v.* bully; intimidate. ▸*n.* bully.

**hedge** /hej/ ▸*n.* **1** fence or boundary of dense bushes or shrubs. **2** protection against possible loss. ▸*v.* **1** surround or bound with a hedge. **2** enclose. **3 a** reduce one's risk of loss on (a bet, etc.)

by compensating transactions. **b** avoid a definite decision or commitment.

**hedge·hog** ▸*n.* **1** small nocturnal Old World mammal having a coat of spines and rolling itself into a ball for defense. **2** American porcupine or other animal similarly covered with spines.

**heed** /hēd/ ▸*v.* attend to; take notice of. ▸*n.* careful attention. —**heed·ful** *adj.* —**heed·less** *adj.* —**heed·less·ly** *adv.*

**heed·less** /'hēdlis/ ▸*adj.* showing a reckless lack of care or attention.

**heel** /hēl/ ▸*n.* **1** back part of the foot below the ankle. **2 a** part of a sock, etc., covering the heel. **b** part of a shoe or boot supporting the heel. **3** crust end of a loaf of bread. **4** *inf.* person regarded with contempt or disapproval. **5** command to a dog to walk close to its owner's heel. ▸*v.* **1** fit or renew a heel on (a shoe or boot). **2** (of a dog) follow closely. **3** (of a ship) lean over. ☐ **at** (or **on**) **the heels of** following closely after (a person or event). ☐ **down at (the) heel** see DOWN.

□ **kick up one's heels** have fun or go on a spree.  □ **take to one's heels** run away.

**heft·y** /ˈheftē/ ▸*adj.* (**-i·er, -i·est**) **1** (of a person) big and strong. **2** (of a thing) large; heavy; powerful.

**he·ge·mo·ny** /həˈjemənē; ˈhejə-ˌmōnē/ ▸*n.* rule, esp. by one nation over another.

**heif·er** /ˈhefər/ ▸*n.* young cow.

**height** /hīt/ ▸*n.* **1** measurement from base to top or from head to foot.  **2** elevation above ground. **3** considerable elevation.  **4** high place or area.  **5 a** most intense part or period. **b** extreme example.

**Heim·lich ma·neu·ver** /ˈhīmlik; -liкн/ ▸*n.* emergency procedure to aid a choking victim by applying sudden pressure against the victim's upper abdomen to dislodge the object.

**hei·nous** /ˈhānəs/ ▸*adj.* odious or wicked.

**heir** /e(ə)r/ ▸*n.* person entitled to inherit property or rank: *heir to the throne.*

**heir·loom** ▸*n.* piece of personal property that has been in a family for several generations.

**heist** /hīst/ *inf.* ▸*n.* robbery. ▸*v.* rob.

**hel·i·cal** /ˈhelikəl; ˈhē-/ ▸*adj.* having the shape or form of a helix; spiral.

**he·li·cop·ter** /ˈheliˌkäptər/ ▸*n.* aircraft without fixed wings, obtaining lift and propulsion from horizontally revolving overhead blades, and capable of moving vertically and horizontally. ▸*v.* transport or fly by helicopter.

**he·li·um** /ˈhēlēəm/ ▸*n. Chem.* light, inert, gaseous element used in airships and balloons and as a refrigerant. (Symb.: **He**)

**he·lix** /ˈhēliks/ ▸*n.* (*pl.* **-li·ces**) spiral curve (like a corkscrew) or a coiled curve (like a watch spring).

**hell** /hel/ ▸*n.* **1** place regarded in some religions as the abode of dead sinners and devils.  **2** place or state of misery or wickedness. □ **come hell or high water** no matter what the difficulties. □ **hell of a** *inf.* extremely: *hell of a hot day.*

**he'll** /hēl/ ▸*contr.* he will; he shall.

**hel·lo** /həˈlō; he-/ ▸*interj.* **1** expression of informal greeting. **2** cry used to call attention.

▶*n.* (*pl.* **-los**) cry of "hello."

**helm** /helm/ ▶*n.* tiller or wheel for controlling a ship's rudder. □ **at the helm** in control; at the head (of an organization, etc.).

**hel·met** /ˈhelmit/ ▶*n.* protective head covering worn by soldiers, police officers, firefighters, cyclists, etc.

**help** /help/ ▶*v.* **1** provide with the means toward what is needed or sought: *helped me with my work.* **2** be of use or service to (a person): *does that help?* **3** contribute to alleviating (a pain or difficulty). **4** prevent or remedy: *it can't be helped.* **5 a** refrain from: *can't help it.* **b** refrain from acting: *couldn't help himself.* **6** serve (a person with food): ▶*n.* **1** helping or being helped: *we need your help.* **2** person or thing that helps. **3** domestic servant or employee, or several collectively. **4** remedy or escape. —**help·er** *n.* —**help·ful** *adj.* □ **help oneself 1** serve oneself (with food). **2** take without permission; steal.

**help·ing** ▶*n.* portion of food, esp. at a meal.

**help·less** ▶*adj.* **1** lacking help or protection. **2** unable to act without help. —**help·less·ly** *adv.* —**help·less·ness** *n.*

**help·mate** (also **help·meet**) ▶*n.* helpful companion or partner.

**hel·ter-skel·ter** /ˈheltər ˈskeltər/ ▶*adv.* in disorderly haste. ▶*adj.* disorderly.

**helve** /helv/ ▶*n.* handle of a weapon or tool.

**hem** /hem/ ▶*n.* **1** border of cloth, esp. a cut edge turned under and sewn down. **2** a slight cough or clearing of the throat expressing hesitation. ▶*v.* (**hemmed, hem·ming**) **1** turn and sew the edge of (cloth, etc.). **2** say *hem*; hesitate in speech. ▶*interj.* (also **a·hem**) calling attention or expressing hesitation by a slight cough or clearing of the throat. □ **hem in** confine; restrict. □ **hem and haw** hesitate, esp. in speaking.

**he-man** /ˈhē ˌman/ ▶*n.* masterful or virile man.

**hem·i·sphere** /ˈheməˌsfi(ə)r/ ▶*n.* **1** half a sphere. **2** half of the earth, esp. as divided by the equator or by a line passing through the poles: *northern hemisphere* | *eastern hemisphere.* **3** either lateral half of the brain.

**hem·lock** /ˈhemˌläk/ ▸n.
**1** poisonous plant with fernlike leaves and small white flowers.
**2** poison made from this.

**he·mo·glo·bin** /ˈhēməˌglōbin/ ▸n. oxygen-carrying substance containing iron in red blood cells.

**he·mo·phil·i·a** /ˌhēməˈfilēə/ ▸n. hereditary disorder with a tendency to bleed severely from even a slight injury, through the failure of the blood to clot normally.
—**he·mo·phil·i·ac** adj., n.

**hem·or·rhage** /ˈhem(ə)rij/ ▸n. profuse loss of blood from a ruptured blood vessel.
▸v. undergo a hemorrhage.

**hem·or·rhoid** /ˈhem(ə)ˌroid/ ▸n. (usu. **hemorrhoids**) swollen veins at or near the anus.

**hemp** /hemp/ ▸n. **1** (in full **In·di·an hemp**) plant native to Asia. **2** narcotic drug made from it. **3** its fiber used to make rope and strong fabrics.

**hen** /hen/ ▸n. female bird, esp. of a domestic fowl.

**hence** /hens/ ▸adv. **1** from this time: *two years hence.* **2** for this reason: *hence we seem to be wrong.*

**hence·forth** (also **hence·for·ward**) ▸adv. from this time onward.

**hench·man** /ˈhenCHmən/ ▸n. (pl. **-men**) trusted supporter or attendant.

**hen·di·a·dys** /henˈdīədəs/ ▸n. expression of a single idea by two words connected with "and," e.g., *nice and warm*, when one could be used to modify the other, as in *nicely warm*.

**hen·na** /ˈhenə/ ▸n. **1** tropical shrub having small pink, red, or white flowers. **2** reddish hair dye made from this.

**hep·a·ti·tis** /ˌhepəˈtitis/ ▸n. disease characterized by inflammation of the liver.

**her** /hər/ ▸pron. **1** objective case of SHE: *I like her.* **2** inf. she: *it's her all right | am older than her.*
▸poss. pron. of or belonging to her or herself: *her house | her own business.*

**her·ald** /ˈherəld/ ▸n. **1** official messenger. **2** forerunner: *spring is the herald of summer.*
▸v. proclaim the approach of; usher in: *the storm heralded trouble.*

**her·ald·ry** /ˈherəldrē/ ▸n. art or knowledge of coats of arms, genealogies, etc.

**herb** /(h)ərb/ ▶*n.* **1** any nonwoody seed-bearing plant. **2** plant with leaves, seeds, or flowers used for flavoring, food, medicine, scent, etc. —**her·ba·ceous** *adj.* —**herb·al** *adj.* —**herb·al·ist** *n.*

**her·bi·cide** /'(h)ərbə,sīd/ ▶*n.* poison used to destroy unwanted vegetation.

**her·biv·o·rous** /'(h)ər'bivərəs/ ▶*adj.* (of an animal) feeding on plants. —**her·bi·vore** /'(h)ərbə,vôr/ *n.*

**Her·cu·le·an** /,hərkyə'lēən/ ▶*adj.* having or requiring great strength or effort.

**herd** /hərd/ ▶*n.* a number of animals, esp. cattle, feeding, traveling, or kept together. ▶*v.* **1** go or cause to go in a herd: *herded the cattle into the field.* **2** tend (sheep, cattle, etc.): *herding goats.* —**herd·er** *n.*

**here** /hi(ə)r/ ▶*adv.* **1** in or at or to this place or position: *put it here.* **2** indicating a person's presence or a thing offered: *here is your coat | my son here.* **3** at this point. ▶*n.* this place: *get out of here.* ▶*interj.* **1** calling attention: short for *come here, look here,* etc. **2** indicating one's presence in a roll call: short for *I am here.*

□ **neither here nor there** of no importance.

**here·af·ter** ▶*adv.* from now on; in the future. ▶*n.* **1** the future. **2** life after death.

**here·by** ▶*adv.* by this means; as a result of this.

**he·red·i·tar·y** /hə'redi,terē/ ▶*adj.* **1** (of disease, instinct, etc.) able to be passed down genetically. **2** descending by inheritance.

**he·red·i·ty** /hə'reditē/ ▶*n.* **1** passing on of physical or mental characteristics genetically. **2** genetic constitution.

**here·in** ▶*adv. formal* in this matter, book, etc.

**he·re·si·arch** /hə'rēzē,ärk; 'herəsē-/ ▶*n.* founder of a heresy or the leader of a heretical sect.

**her·e·sy** /'herəsē/ ▶*n.* (*pl.* -**sies**) **1** belief or practice contrary to orthodox doctrine, esp. of the Christian church. **2** nonconforming opinion: *it's heresy to say that instant tea is as good as brewed tea.*

**here·to·fore** /'hi(ə)rtə,fôr/ ▶*adv. formal* before this time.

**here·with** ▶*adv.* with this (esp. of an enclosure in a letter, etc.).

**her·i·tage** /ˈheritij/ ▸n.
1 anything that is or may be inherited. 2 historic buildings, traditions, etc., deemed valuable.

**her·maph·ro·dite** /hərˈmafrə-ˌdīt/ ▸n. person, animal, or plant having both male and female reproductive organs.
▸adj. combining aspects of both sexes. —**her·maph·ro·dit·ic** adj.

**her·me·neu·tics** /ˌhərmə-ˈn(y)o͞otiks/ ▸n. branch of knowledge that deals with interpretation, esp. of the Bible or literary texts.

**her·met·ic** /hərˈmetik/ ▸adj. with an airtight closure.
—**her·met·i·cal·ly** adv.

**her·mit** /ˈhərmit/ ▸n. 1 early Christian recluse. 2 any person living in solitude. —**her·mit·ic** adj.

**her·mit·age** /ˈhərmitij/ ▸n.
1 hermit's dwelling.
2 monastery.

**her·mit crab** ▸n. crab that lives in a cast-off mollusk shell.

**her·ni·a** /ˈhərnēə/ ▸n. protrusion of part of an organ through the wall of the cavity containing it, esp. of the abdomen.
—**her·ni·at·ed** adj.

**he·ro** /ˈhi(ə)rō/ ▸n. (pl. **-roes**)
1 person noted or admired for nobility, courage, outstanding achievements, etc. 2 chief male character in a poem, play, story, etc. 3 (also **hero sandwich**) SUBMARINE SANDWICH (see SUBMARINE). —**he·ro·ic** adj.
—**he·ro·ism** n.

**her·o·in** /ˈherōin/ ▸n. highly addictive narcotic drug derived from morphine.

**her·on** /ˈherən/ ▸n. large wading bird with long legs and a long S-shaped neck.

**her·pes** /ˈhərpēz/ ▸n. virus disease causing skin blisters.

**her·pes zos·ter** /ˈzästər/ ▸n. SHINGLES.

**her·ring** /ˈheriNG/ ▸n. N. Atlantic food fish.

**her·ring·bone** ▸n. stitch with a zigzag pattern.

**hers** /hərz/ ▸poss. pron. the one(s) belonging to or associated with her: *it is hers* | *hers are over there.*
□ **of hers** of or belonging to her: *friend of hers.*

**her·self** ▸pron. 1 a emphatic form of SHE or HER: *she herself will do it.* b reflexive form of HER: *she has hurt herself.* 2 in her normal state of body or mind: *does not feel quite herself.*

**hertz** /hərts/ ▸n. (pl. same) unit of

frequency, equal to one cycle per second. (Abbr.: **Hz**)

**hes·i·tate** /ˈheziˌtāt/ ▶v. **1** show or feel indecision or uncertainty; pause in doubt. **2** be reluctant: *hesitate to say.* —**hes·i·tant** *adj.* —**hes·i·tant·ly** *adv.* —**hes·i·ta·tion** *n.*

**he·tae·ra** /hiˈti(ə)rə/ (also **he·tai·ra** /-ˈtīrə/) ▶n. (*pl.* **-tae·ras** or **-tae·rae** /-ˈti(ə)rē/) courtesan or mistress, esp. one in ancient Greece akin to the modern geisha.

**het·er·o·dox** /ˈhetərəˌdäks/ ▶adj. (of a person, opinion, etc.) not orthodox. —**het·er·o·dox·y** *n.*

**het·er·o·ge·ne·ous** /ˌhetərə-ˈjēnēəs/ ▶adj. **1** diverse in character. **2** varied in content. —**het·er·o·ge·ne·i·ty** *n.*

**het·er·o·nym** /ˈhetərəˌnim/ ▶n. **1** each of two or more words that are spelled identically but have different sounds and meanings, such as *tear* meaning "rip" and *tear* meaning "liquid from the eye." **2** each of two or more words that are used to refer to the identical thing in different geographical areas of a speech community, such as *submarine sandwich, hoagie,* and *grinder.* **3** each of two words having the same meaning but

derived from unrelated sources, for example *preface* and *foreword.*

**het·er·o·sex·u·al** ▶adj. feeling or involving sexual attraction to persons of the opposite sex. ▶n. heterosexual person. —**het·er·o·sex·u·al·i·ty** *n.* —**het·er·o·sex·u·al·ly** *adv.*

**hew** /hyo͞o/ ▶v. (*past part.* **hewn** or **hewed**) **1** chop or cut (a thing) with an ax, sword, etc. **2** strike cutting blows.

**hex** /heks/ ▶v. practice witchcraft; bewitch. ▶n. magic spell; curse.

**hex·a·gon** /ˈheksəˌgän/ ▶n. plane figure with six sides and angles. —**hex·ag·o·nal** *adj.*

**hey·day** /ˈhāˌdā/ ▶n. time of one's greatest strength, vigor, prosperity, etc.

**hgt.** ▶abbr. height.

**hgwy.** ▶abbr. highway.

**HI** ▶abbr. Hawaii (in official postal use).

**hi** /hī/ ▶interj. expression of greeting or to call attention.

**hi·a·tus** /hīˈātəs/ ▶n. (*pl.* **-tus·es**) break or gap, esp. in a series, account, or chain of proof.

**hi·ba·chi** /hiˈbäCHē/ ▶n. portable charcoal-burning grill.

**hi·ber·nate** /ˈhībərˌnāt/ ▶v. (of

some animals) spend the winter in a dormant state. —**hi·ber·na·tion** n.

**hi·bis·cus** /hī'biskəs/ ▶n. cultivated tree or shrub with large bright-colored flowers.

**hic·cup** /'hikəp/ (also **hic·cough**) ▶n. **1** involuntary spasm of the diaphragm causing a coughlike sound. **2** temporary or minor stoppage or difficulty. ▶v. make a hiccup.

**hick** /hik/ ▶n. inf. country dweller; provincial.

**hick·o·ry** /'hik(ə)rē/ ▶n. (pl. -ries) **1** N. American tree yielding wood and nutlike edible fruits. **2** the wood of these trees.

**hid·den a·gen·da** ▶n. secret motive.

**hide** /hīd/ ▶v. (past **hid**; past part. **hid·den**) **1** put or keep out of sight: hid it under the cushion. **2** keep secret: hid his real motive from her. **3** conceal: trees hid the house. ▶n. skin of an animal, esp. when tanned or dressed. —**hid·den** adj. —**hid·er** n.

**hide-and-seek** ▶n. children's game in which players hide and another searches for them.

**hide·a·way** ▶n. hiding place or a retreat.

**hide·bound** ▶adj. **1** narrow-minded; bigoted. **2** (of the law, rules, etc.) constricted by tradition.

**hid·e·ous** /'hidēəs/ ▶adj. frightful, repulsive, or revolting: hideous monster. —**hid·e·ous·ly** adv. —**hid·e·ous·ness** n.

**hide-out** ▶n. hiding place.

**hi·er·arch** /'hī(ə)ˌrärk/ ▶n. chief priest, archbishop, or other leader.

**hi·er·ar·chy** /'hī(ə)ˌrärkē/ ▶n. (pl. -chies) **1** system in which grades of status are ranked one above the other: ranks third in the hierarchy. **2** hierarchical system (of government, management, etc.). —**hi·er·ar·chi·cal** adj.

**hi·er·o·glyph·ic** /ˌhī(ə)rə'glifik/ ▶adj. depicted with pictures representing words or sounds, as used in ancient Egypt. ▶pl. n. (**hieroglyphics**) hieroglyphic writing.

**hi·er·o·phant** /'hī(ə)rəˌfant/ ▶n. person, esp. a priest in ancient Greece, who interprets sacred mysteries or esoteric principles.

**hi-fi** /'hī 'fī/ inf. ▶adj. of high fidelity. ▶n. (pl. **hi-fis**) set of equipment for high fidelity sound reproduction.

**high** /hī/ ▸*adj.* **1 a** of great vertical extent: *high building.* **b** of a specified height: *one inch high* | *waist-high.* **2** far above ground or sea level, etc.: *high altitude.* **3** above the normal level: *high boots.* **4** of exalted, esp. spiritual, quality: *high art.* **5** of exalted rank: *in high society.* **6 a** great; intense; extreme; powerful: *high praise* | *high temperature.* **b** greater than normal: *high prices.* **7** excited; euphoric. **8** intoxicated. **9** (of a sound or note) of high frequency; shrill; at the top end of the scale. **10** (of a period, an age, a time, etc.) at its peak: *high noon* | *High Renaissance.*

▸*n.* **1** high, or the highest, level or figure. **2** area of high barometric pressure. **3** *inf.* state of high spirits or euphoria.

▸*adv.* **1** far up; aloft: **2** in or to a high degree. **3** at a high price. **4** (of a sound) at or to a high pitch:

☐ **high and low** everywhere: *searched high and low.*

**high·ball** ▸*n.* drink of liquor (esp. whiskey) and soda, etc., served with ice in a tall glass.

**high beam** ▸*n.* brightest setting of a motor vehicle's headlight.

**high·brow** ▸*adj. often derog.* intellectual; cultural.

**high chair** ▸*n.* infant's chair with long legs and a tray for meals.

**high-class** ▸*adj.* **1** of high quality. **2** characteristic of the upper class.

**high fi·del·i·ty** ▸*n.* reproduction of sound with little distortion.

**high five** ▸*n.* gesture in which two people slap each other's raised palm, esp. out of elation.

**high-flown** ▸*adj.* (of language, etc.) extravagant; bombastic.

**high fre·quen·cy** ▸*n.* frequency, esp. in radio, of 3 to 30 megahertz.

**high-hand·ed** ▸*adj.* overbearing.

**high-lev·el** ▸*adj.* **1** (of negotiations, etc.) conducted by high-ranking people. **2** (of a computer programming language) at a level of abstraction close to natural language.

**high·light** ▸*n.* **1** moment or detail of vivid interest; outstanding feature. **2** (in a painting, etc.) light area, or one seeming to reflect light.
▸*v.* **1** bring into prominence;

draw attention to. **2** mark with a highlighter pen.

**high·light·er** /ˈhīˌlītər/ ▸*n.* **1** a broad felt-tipped pen used to mark text with transparent color. **2** a cosmetic used to emphasize features.

**high·ly** ▸*adv.* **1** in or to a high degree: *highly amusing | commend it highly.* **2** honorably; favorably: *think highly of him.*

**high·mind·ed** ▸*adj.* having high moral principles.

**high·ness** ▸*n.* title used of a prince or princess.

**high-pitched** ▸*adj.* **1** (of a sound) high. **2** (of a roof) steep. **3** intense.

**high-pow·ered** ▸*adj.* **1** having great power or energy. **2** important or influential.

**high-pres·sure** ▸*adj.* **1** stressful. **2** (of a salesperson) insistent. **3** involving much physical force. **4** denoting atmospheric pressure that is above average.

**high priest** ▸*n.* **1** chief priest, esp. in early Judaism. **2** head of any cult.

**high-rise** ▸*adj.* (of a building) having many stories.
▸*n.* such a building.

**high school** ▸*n.* secondary school.

**high seas** ▸*pl. n.* open seas not within any country's jurisdiction.

**high spir·its** ▸*pl. n.* lively and cheerful mood. —**high-spir·i·ted** *adj.*

**high-strung** ▸*adj.* very sensitive or nervous.

**high-tech** ▸*adj.* involving high technology.
▸*n.* (**high tech**) see HIGH TECHNOLOGY.

**high tech·nol·o·gy** ▸*n.* advanced technological development, esp. in electronics.

**high tide** ▸*n.* time or level of the tide at its peak.

**high·way** ▸*n.* **1 a** large public road. **2** main route.

**high·way·man** ▸*n.* (*pl.* -men) *hist.* robber of passengers, travelers, etc.

**high wire** ▸*n.* high tightrope.

**hi·jack** /ˈhīˌjak/ ▸*v.* **1** seize control of (an aircraft in flight, etc.), esp. to force it to a different destination. **2** seize (goods) in transit.
▸*n.* instance or act of hijacking. —**hi·jack·er** *n.*

**hike** /hīk/ ▸*n.* **1** long walk, esp. in

the country with a backpack.
**2** increase (of prices, etc.).

▸*v.* **1** go for a hike. **2** pull up (clothing, etc.). **3** increase sharply (prices, etc.). —**hik·er** *n.*

**hi·lar·i·ous** /hə'le(ə)rēəs/ ▸*adj.* **1** exceedingly funny. **2** boisterously merry. —**hi·lar·i·ous·ly** *adv.* —**hi·lar·i·ty** *n.*

**hill** /hil/ ▸*n.* **1** naturally raised area of land, lower than a mountain. **2** heap; mound: *anthill | dunghill.* **3** sloping piece of road. —**hil·li·ness** *n.* —**hill·y** *adj.*

**hill·bil·ly** /'hil,bilē/ ▸*n.* (*pl.* **-lies**) *inf., usu. derog.* person from a remote or mountainous area, esp. in the Appalachian mountains of the eastern U.S.

**hilt** /hilt/ ▸*n.* handle of a sword, dagger, tool, etc.

□ **to the hilt** completely.

**him** /him/ ▸*pron.* **1** objective case of HE: *I saw him.* **2** *inf.* he: *it's him again | taller than him.*

**him·self** ▸*pron.* **1 a** emphatic form of HE or HIM: *he himself will do it.* **b** reflexive form of HIM: *he has hurt himself.* **2** in his normal state of body or mind: *does not feel quite himself.*

**hind** /hīnd/ ▸*adj.* (esp. of parts of the body) at the back: *hind leg.*

**hin·der** /'hindər/ ▸*v.* impede; delay.

**hind·most** ▸*adj.* farthest behind; most remote.

**hin·drance** /'hindrəns/ ▸*n.* thing that provides resistance, delay, or obstruction to something or someone.

**hind·sight** ▸*n.* wisdom after the event.

**Hin·du** /'hindoo/ ▸*n.* follower of Hinduism.

▸*adj.* of Hindus or Hinduism.

**Hin·du·ism** ▸*n.* main religious and social system of India.

**hinge** /hinj/ ▸*n.* **1** movable joint on which a door, lid, etc., turns or swings. **2** central point or principle on which everything depends.

▸*v.* **1** depend (on a principle, event, etc.): *it hinges on the weather.* **2** attach with or as if with a hinge.

**hint** /hint/ ▸*n.* **1** slight or indirect indication or suggestion: *took the hint and left.* **2** bit of practical information; tip **3** trace: *a hint of perfume.*

▸*v.* suggest: *hinted that they were wrong.*

**hin·ter·land** /ˈhintərˌland/ ▸n. **1** deserted or uncharted areas beyond a coast or a river's banks. **2** remote area.

**hip** /hip/ ▸n. **1** projection of the pelvis and upper thigh bone on each side of the body. **2** fruit of a rose. **3** (also **hep**) **a** stylish. **b** understanding; aware.

**hip-hop** ▸n. style of popular music of U.S. black and Hispanic origin, featuring rap with an electronic backing.

**hip·pie** /ˈhipē/ (also **hip·py**) ▸n. (pl. **-pies**) inf. (esp. in the 1960s) person of unconventional appearance, typically with long hair, jeans, beads, etc., often associated with hallucinogenic drugs.

**hip·po** /ˈhipō/ ▸n. (pl. **-pos**) inf. hippopotamus.

**hip·po·drome** /ˈhipəˌdrōm/ ▸n. **1** arena used for equestrian or other sporting events. **2** (in ancient Greece or Rome) a course for chariot or horse races.

**hip·po·pot·a·mus** /ˌhipəˈpätəməs/ ▸n. (pl. **-mus·es** or **-mi**) large thick-skinned mammal of Africa, inhabiting rivers, lakes, etc.

**hir·cine** /ˈhərˌsīn; -sən/ ▸adj. of or resembling a goat.

**hire** /hī(ə)r/ ▸v. employ (a person) for wages or a fee.
▸n. hiring or being hired.

**hire·ling** ▸n. person who works for hire usu. at a menial job.

**hir·sute** /ˈhərˌso͞ot/ ▸adj. hairy; shaggy. —**hir·sut·ism** n.

**his** /hiz/ ▸poss. pron. **1** of or belonging to him or himself: *his house* | *his own business*. **2** the one or ones belonging to or associated with him: *it is his* | *his are over there*.
□ **of his** of or belonging to him: *friend of his*.

**His·pan·ic** /hiˈspanik/ ▸adj. **1** of or being a person of Latin-American or Spanish or Portuguese descent in the U.S. **2** of or relating to Spain or to Spain and Portugal. **3** of Spanish-speaking countries.
▸n. person of Spanish descent living in the U.S.

**hiss** /his/ ▸v. make a sharp sibilant sound, esp. as a sign of disapproval or derision: *audience booed and hissed* | *water hissed on the hotplate*.
▸n. sharp sibilant sound as of the letter *s*.

**his·tor·ic** /hiˈstôrik/ ▸adj. famous or important in history or potentially so: *a historic moment*.

**his·tor·i·cal** ▸*adj.* of or concerning history or past events: *historical background* | *historical figures.*

**his·to·ric·i·ty** /ˌhistəˈrisitē/ ▸*n.* historical authenticity.

**his·to·ry** /ˈhist(ə)rē/ ▸*n.* (*pl.* **-ries**) **1** continuous record of important or public events. **2 a** study of past events. **b** accumulation of past events: *our nation's history* | *history of astronomy.* **3** account of or research into a past event or events, etc.

**hit** /hit/ ▸*v.* (**hit·ting**; *past* and *past part.* **hit**) **1** strike with a blow or missile. **2** cause to suffer or affect adversely. **3** direct a blow. **4** knock; bang: *hit his head on the table.* **5** *inf.* **a** encounter: *hit a snag.* **b** arrive at: *hit town.* **c** indulge in, esp. liquor, etc.: *hit the bottle.* **6** occur forcefully to: *the seriousness of the situation hit him later.* **7** *Sports* **a** propel (a ball, etc.) with a bat, etc. **b** score (runs, etc.) in this way.
▸*n.* **1 a** blow; stroke. **b** collision. **2** shot, etc., that hits its target. **3** popular success in entertainment. **4** *Computing* identifying data that matches search requirements.

□ **hit and run** cause damage and escape or leave the scene before being discovered. □ **hit it off** agree or be congenial. □ **hit the nail on the head** state the truth exactly. □ **hit the road** (or **trail**) *inf.* depart. □ **hit the spot** *inf.* be satisfying.

**hitch** /hiCH/ ▸*v.* **1 a** fasten or be fastened with a loop, hook, etc.; tether. **2** move (a thing) with a jerk. **3** *inf.* **a** HITCHHIKE. **b** obtain (a ride) by hitchhiking.
▸*n.* **1** temporary obstacle. **2** abrupt pull or push; jerk. **3** noose or knot of various kinds. **4** *inf.* free ride in a vehicle. **5** *inf.* period of military service.
□ **get hitched** *inf.* marry.

**hitch·hike** ▸*v.* travel by seeking free rides in passing vehicles. —**hitch·hiker** *n.*

**hith·er** /ˈhiTHər/ ▸*adv. archaic* or *poet.* to or toward this place.
□ **hither and thither** in various directions; to and fro.

**hith·er·to** /ˈhiTHərˌtoo/ ▸*adv.* until this time; up to now.

**hit man** ▸*n. inf.* hired assassin.

**HIV** ▸*abbr.* human immunodeficiency virus, any of several retroviruses causing AIDS.

**hive** /hīv/ ▸*n.* **1** beehive. **2** busy

swarming place. **3** (**hives**) [treated as *sing.* or *pl.*] allergic skin eruption.

**HMO** ▸*abbr.* health maintenance organization.

**hoa·gie** /ˈhōgē/ (also **hoa·gy**) ▸*n.* (*pl.* **-gies**) SUBMARINE SANDWICH.

**hoar** /hôr/ ▸*adj.* grayish white; gray or gray-haired with age. ▸*n.* hoarfrost.

**hoard** /hôrd/ ▸*n.* stock or store (esp. of money or food) laid by. ▸*v.* accumulate more than one's current requirements of food, etc., in a time of scarcity; amass. —**hoard·er** *n.* —**hoard·ing** *n.*

**hoarse** /hôrs/ ▸*adj.* **1** (of the voice) rough and deep; croaking. **2** having such a voice. —**hoarse·ly** *adv.* —**hoarse·ness** *n.*

**hoar·y** /ˈhôrē/ ▸*adj.* (**-i·er**, **-i·est**) gray or white with age.

**hoax** /hōks/ ▸*n.* humorous or malicious deception. ▸*v.* deceive with a hoax.

**hob·ble** /ˈhäbəl/ ▸*v.* **1** walk lamely; limp; proceed haltingly. **2** tie the legs of (a horse, etc.) to prevent it from straying. ▸*n.* **1** uneven or infirm gait. **2** rope for hobbling a horse, etc.

**hob·ble·de·hoy** /ˈhäbəldēˌhoi/ ▸*n.* clumsy or awkward youth.

▸*adj.* awkward or clumsy.

**hob·by** /ˈhäbē/ ▸*n.* (*pl.* **-bies**) leisure time activity pursued for pleasure.

**hob·by·horse** ▸*n.* **1** child's toy consisting of a stick with a horse's head. **2** favorite topic of conversation.

**hob·gob·lin** /ˈhäbˌgäblən/ ▸*n.* mischievous imp; bogy.

**hob·nob** /ˈhäbˌnäb/ ▸*v.* (**-nobbed**, **-nob·bing**) mix socially or informally.

**ho·bo** /ˈhōˌbō/ ▸*n.* (*pl.* **-boes** or **-bos**) tramp; vagrant.

**hock** /häk/ ▸*n.* **1** joint of a quadruped's hind leg between the knee and fetlock. **2** knuckle of pork; lower joint of a ham. ▸*v. inf.* pawn. □ **in hock 1** in pawn. **2** in debt.

**hock·ey** /ˈhäkē/ ▸*n.* team sport played on skates or on a field, with angled sticks and a puck (when played on ice) or ball.

**ho·cus-po·cus** /ˌhōkəsˈpōkəs/ ▸*n.* **1** deception; trickery. **2** language intended to mystify.

**hod** /häd/ ▸*n.* **1** V-shaped trough on a pole used for carrying bricks, etc. **2** portable receptacle for coal.

**hodge·podge** /ˈhäjˌpäj/ ▸*n.* confused mixture; jumble.

**hoe** /hō/ ▶*n.* long-handled tool with a thin metal blade, used for weeding, etc.
▶*v.* (**hoed, hoe·ing**) use a hoe to weed (crops) or loosen (earth).

**hog** /hôg/ ▶*n.* **1 a** large domesticated pig. **2** *inf.* greedy person.
▶*v.* (**hogged, hog·ging**) *inf.* take greedily; hoard selfishly.
□ **go whole hog** *inf.* do something completely or thoroughly.

**hogs·head** ▶*n.* large cask.

**hog·wash** ▶*n. inf.* nonsense; rubbish.

**hoi pol·loi** /ˈhoi pəˌloi/ ▶*pl. n.* (usu. **the hoi polloi**) *derog.* the masses; the common people.

**hoist** /hoist/ ▶*v.* raise or haul up, esp. with ropes, pulleys, etc.
▶*n.* **1** act of hoisting; lift. **2** apparatus for hoisting.

**hoi·ty-toi·ty** /ˈhoitē ˈtoitē/ ▶*adj.* **1** haughty; snobbish. **2** frolicsome.

**hok·ey** /ˈhōkē/ (also **hok·y**) *inf.*
▶*adj.* (**-i·er, -i·est**) sentimental; contrived.

**hold** /hōld/ ▶*v.* (*past* and *past part.* **held**) **1 a** keep fast; grasp (esp. in the hands or arms). **b** keep or sustain in a particular position: *held himself erect.* **c** grasp so as to control: *hold the reins.* **2** contain or be capable of containing: *holds two pints.* **3** possess, gain, or have, esp.: **a** be the owner or tenant of (land, property, etc.). **b** gain or have gained (a degree, record, etc.). **c** have the position of (a job or office). **d** keep possession of (a place, a person's thoughts, etc.) esp. against attack. **4** remain intact: *the roof held under the storm.* **5** observe; celebrate; conduct (a meeting, festival, conversation, etc.). **6 a** keep (a person, etc.) in a specified condition, place, etc.: *held her prisoner | held him at arm's length.* **b** detain, esp. in custody. **7 a** engross: *the book held him for hours.* **b** dominate: *held the stage.* **8** make (a person, etc.) adhere to (a promise, etc.). **9** (of weather) continue as is. **10** think; believe: *held that the earth was flat.* **11** regard with a specified feeling: *held him in contempt.* **12 a** cease; restrain: *hold your fire.* **b** *inf.* withhold; not use: *a burger please, and hold the onions!* **13** be able to drink (liquor) without effect. **14** (of a judge, a court, etc.) lay down; decide.

▶*n.* **1** grasp: *catch hold of him.* **2** (**have a hold over**) influence over: *has a strange hold over them.* **3** cargo area in a ship or aircraft. —**hold·er** *n.*

☐ **hold off 1** delay; not begin. **2** keep one's distance. ☐ **hold on 1** keep one's grasp on something. **2** wait a moment. **3** (when telephoning) not hang up. ☐ **hold out 1** stretch forth (a hand, etc.). **2** offer (an inducement, etc.). ☐ **hold out on** *inf.* refuse something to (a person). ☐ **hold up 1 a** support; sustain. **b** maintain (the head, etc.) erect. **c** last; endure. **2** exhibit; display. **3** arrest the progress of; obstruct. **4** stop and rob by force.

**hold·ing** ▸*n.* **1 a** land held by lease. **2** (**holdings**) stocks, property, etc., held.

**hold·ing com·pa·ny** ▸*n.* company created to hold the shares of other companies, which it then controls.

**hold·up** ▸*n.* **1** stoppage or delay. **2** robbery, esp. with threats or violence.

**hole** /hōl/ ▸*n.* **1 a** empty space in a solid body. **b** aperture in or through something. **2** animal's burrow. **3** *inf.* awkward situation.

▸*v.* make a hole or holes in. —**hol·ey** *adj.*

☐ **hole up** *inf.* hide oneself.

**hol·i·day** /ˈhäləˌdā/ ▸*n.* day of festivity or recreation when no work is done, esp. a national or religious festival, etc.

**ho·li·ness** /ˈhōlēnis/ ▸*n.* **1** sanctity; being holy. **2** (**Holiness**) title used when referring to or addressing the pope.

**hol·low** /ˈhälō/ ▸*adj.* **1 a** having a cavity. **b** sunken: *hollow cheeks.* **2** (of a sound) echoing or muffled. **3** empty; hungry. **4** insincere: *hollow promises.* ▸*n.* **1** hollow place. **2** valley. ▸*v.* make hollow; excavate. —**hol·low·ly** *adv.* —**hol·low·ness** *n.*

**hol·ly** /ˈhälē/ ▸*n.* (*pl.* -**lies**) evergreen shrub with glossy green leaves and red berries.

**hol·ly·hock** ▸*n.* tall plant with large showy flowers of various colors.

**ho·lo·caust** /ˈhäləˌkôst/ ▸*n.* **1** large-scale destruction, esp. by fire or nuclear war. **2** (**the Holocaust**) mass murder of Jews by the Nazis in World War II.

**ho·lo·gram** /ˈhäləˌgram/ ▸*n.* three-dimensional photographic image made with laser technology.

**ho·log·ra·phy** /hō'lägrəfē/ ▸*n.* study of holograms.
—**hol·o·graph·ic** *adj.*

**hol·ster** /'hōlstər/ ▸*n.* leather case for a pistol or revolver, worn on a belt, etc.

**ho·ly** /'hōlē/ ▸*adj.* (**-li·er, -li·est**) **1** morally and spiritually excellent. **2** devoted to God. **3** sacred.

**Ho·ly Com·mun·ion** ▸*n.* see **COMMUNION**.

**Ho·ly Fa·ther** ▸*n.* the Pope.

**Ho·ly Ghost** ▸*n.* **HOLY SPIRIT**.

**Ho·ly Grail** ▸*n.* see **GRAIL**.

**Ho·ly Land** ▸*n.* **1** in Christianity, region on the E. shore of the Mediterranean Sea in what is now Israel and Palestine. **2** region similarly revered in non-Christian religions.

**Ho·ly See** ▸*n.* papacy or papal court.

**Ho·ly Spir·it** ▸*n.* third person of the Christian Trinity.

**ho·ly war** ▸*n.* war waged in support of a religious cause.

**Ho·ly Week** ▸*n.* the week before Easter.

**hom·age** /'(h)ämij/ ▸*n.* dutiful reverence: *pay homage.*

**home** /hōm/ ▸*n.* **1** place where one lives; fixed residence. **2** one's family background: *comes from a good home.* **3** native land. **4** institution caring for people or animals. **5** place where a thing originates or is native or most common.

▸*adj.* **1** of or connected with one's home: *I don't have his home address.* **2** carried on or produced in one's own country: *home industries | the home market.* **3** *Sports* played on one's own field, etc.: *home game.*

▸*adv.* **1 a** to one's home or country: *go home.* **b** arrived at home: *is he home yet?.* **c** at home: *stay home.* **2 a** to the point aimed at: *the thrust went home.* **b** as far as possible: *drove the nail home | pressed his advantage home.*

▸*v.* **1** (esp. of a trained pigeon) return home. **2** (of a vessel, missile, etc.) be guided toward a destination or target.
—**home·less** *adj.*

□ **at home 1** in one's own house or native land. **2** at ease as if in one's own home: *make yourself at* *home.* **3** familiar or well informed.

**home ec·o·nom·ics** ▸*pl. n.* [often treated as *sing.*] cooking and other aspects of household management.

**home·ly** /ˈhōmlē/ ▸*adj.* (**-li·er, -li·est**) **1** (of people or their features) not attractive in appearance. **2** simple; plain. —**home·li·ness** *n.*

**home·made** ▸*adj.* made at or as if at home.

**home·maker** ▸*n.* person who manages a household, esp. as a full-time occupation.

**ho·me·op·a·thy** /ˌhōmēˈäpəтHē/ ▸*n.* treatment of disease by minute doses of drugs that in a healthy person would produce symptoms of the disease. —**ho·me·o·path** *n.* —**ho·me·o·path·ic** *adj.*

**ho·me·o·sta·sis** /ˌhōmēə-ˈstāsis/ ▸*n.* (*pl.* **-ses** /-sēz/) maintenance of a relatively stable equilibrium, esp. by physiological processes.

**home plate** ▸*n. Baseball* plate beside which the batter stands and which the runner must cross to score a run.

**home·sick** ▸*adj.* longing for home.

**home·spun** ▸*adj.* **1** made or spun at home. **2** plain; simple.

**home·stead** ▸*n.* house and adjoining land.

**home·work** ▸*n.* work to be done at home, esp. by a student.

**hom·ey** /ˈhōmē/ (also **hom·y**) ▸*adj.* (**-i·er, -i·est**) suggesting home; cozy. —**hom·ey·ness** *n.*

**ho·mi·cide** /ˈhäməˌsīd/ ▸*n.* killing of a human being by another. —**ho·mi·ci·dal** *adj.*

**hom·i·let·ic** /ˌhäməˈletik/ ▸*adj.* of the nature of or characteristic of a homily. ▸*n.* (**homiletics**) art of preaching or writing sermons.

**hom·i·ly** /ˈhäməlē/ ▸*n.* (*pl.* **-lies**) **1** sermon. **2** moralizing discourse.

**hom·i·nid** /ˈhäməˌnid/ ▸*n.* primate of a family that includes humans and their fossil ancestors.

**hom·i·ny** /ˈhämənē/ ▸*n.* coarsely ground corn kernels, usu. boiled for food.

**ho·mo·e·rot·ic** /ˌhōmō-iˈrätik/ ▸*adj.* concerning or arousing sexual desire centered on a person of the same sex.

**ho·mo·ge·ne·ous** /ˌhōmə-ˈjēnēəs/ ▸*adj.* **1** of the same kind. **2** consisting of parts all of

the same kind; uniform.
—**ho·mo·ge·ne·i·ty** *n.*
—**ho·mo·ge·ne·ous·ly** *adv.*

**ho·mog·en·ize** /həˈmäjəˌnīz/ ▶*v.*
**1** make or become
homogeneous. **2** treat (milk) so
that the fat is emulsified and the
cream does not separate.

**hom·o·graph** /ˈhäməˌgraf/ ▶*n.*
word of the same spelling as
another but of different
meaning and origin (e.g., BOW[1]
and BOW[2]).

**hom·o·nym** /ˈhäməˌnim/ ▶*n.*
word of the same pronunciation
as another but of different
meaning, origin, or spelling (e.g.,
DOWN[1] and DOWN[2]).

**ho·mo·pho·bi·a** /ˌhōməˈfōbēə/
▶*n.* hatred or fear of
homosexuals. —**ho·mo·phobe** *n.*
—**ho·mo·pho·bic** *adj.*

**ho·mo·phone** /ˈhäməˌfōn/ ▶*n.*
word of the same pronunciation
as another but of different
spelling and meaning (e.g., KNEW
and NEW).

**Ho·mo sa·pi·ens** /ˈhōmō
ˈsāpēənz/ ▶*n.* modern humans
regarded as a species.

**ho·mo·sex·u·al** /ˌhōmə-
ˈseksHŌŌəl/ ▶*adj.* feeling or
involving sexual attraction only
to persons of the same sex.

▶*n.* homosexual person.
—**ho·mo·sex·u·al·i·ty** *n.*
—**ho·mo·sex·u·al·ly** *adv.*

**hon·cho** /ˈhänCHō/ ▶*n.* (*pl.* **-chos**)
*inf.* leader or manager; person in
charge.

**hone** /hōn/ ▶*v.* **1** sharpen with a
whetstone. **2** (usu. **be honed**)
make sharper or more focused:
*their appetites were honed by the
fresh air.*

**hon·est** /ˈänist/ ▶*adj.* **1** fair and
just. **2** fairly earned: *an honest
living.*

▶*adv. inf.* used to persuade
someone of the truth of
something: *you'll like it when you
get there, honest.* —**hon·est·ly** *adv.*
—**hon·es·ty** *n.*

**hon·ey** /ˈhənē/ ▶*n.* (*pl.* **-eys**)
**1** sweet sticky yellowish fluid
made by bees from nectar.
**2** color of this. **3** (usu. as a form
of address) darling; sweetheart.

**hon·ey·comb** ▶*n.* structure of
hexagonal cells of wax, made by
bees to store honey and eggs.

**hon·ey·moon** ▶*n.* vacation
taken by a newly married
couple.

▶*v.* spend a honeymoon.
—**hon·ey·moon·er** *n.*

**hon·ey·suck·le** ▶*n.* climbing

shrub with fragrant yellow, pink, or red flowers.

**honk** /häNGk/ ▶n. **1** cry of a wild goose. **2** sound of a car horn. ▶v. emit or cause to emit a honk.

**hon·or** /ˈänər/ ▶n. **1** high respect; reputation. **2** adherence to what is right or accepted conduct. **3** nobleness of mind: *honor among thieves*. **4** official award. **5** privilege: *had the honor of being invited*. **6 a** exalted position. **b** (**Honor**) title of a judge, mayor, etc. **7** person or thing that brings honor: *she is an honor to her profession*. **8** *dated* **a** (of a woman) chastity. **b** reputation for this. **9** (**honors**) **a** special distinction in academics. **b** specialized course of degree studies. ▶v. **1** respect highly. **2** confer honor on. **3** accept or pay (a bill or check) when due. **4** acknowledge.
□ **do the honors** perform the duties of a host to guests, etc.

**hon·or·a·ble** ▶adj. **1** worthy of honor. **2** showing honor. **3** consistent with honor. —**hon·or·a·bly** adv.

**hon·o·rar·i·um** /ˌänəˈre(ə)rēəm/ ▶n. (pl. **-rar·i·ums** or **-rar·i·a** /-ˈre(ə)rēə/) payment given for professional services that are rendered nominally without charge.

**hon·or·ar·y** /ˈänəˌrerē/ ▶adj. **1** conferred as an honor: *honorary degree*. **2** holding such a title or position: *honorary colonel*.

**hood** /ho͝od/ ▶n. **1** covering for the head and neck, as part of a garment. **2** cover over the engine of a motor vehicle. **3** canopy to protect users of machinery or to remove fumes, etc. **4** hoodlike part of a cobra, seal, etc. **5** gangster or gunman.

**hood·lum** /ˈho͝odləm/ ▶n. **1** ruffian; hooligan. **2** gangster.

**hood·wink** ▶v. deceive; delude.

**hoof** /ho͝of/ ▶n. (pl. **hoofs** or **hooves**) horny part of the foot of a horse, antelope, etc.

**hook** /ho͝ok/ ▶n. **1** bent or curved piece of metal, etc., for catching or hanging things on. **2** fishhook. ▶v. **1** grasp or secure with a hook or hooks. **2** attach or become attached with or as with a hook. **3** catch with or as with a hook: *he hooked a fish | she hooked a husband*.
□ **off the hook 1** *inf.* no longer in difficulty or trouble. **2** (of a

telephone receiver) not on its rest, and so preventing incoming calls.

**hook·er** ▸*n. inf.* prostitute.

**hook·up** ▸*n.* connection, esp. electronic.

**hoo·li·gan** /ˈho͞oligən/ ▸*n.* hoodlum; ruffian.

**hoop** /ho͞op/ ▸*n.* **1** circular band of metal, wood, etc., esp. as part of a framework. **2** arch through which the balls are hit in croquet; wicket. **3** *inf.* (**hoops**) [treated as *sing.*] game of basketball.

**hoop·la** /ˈho͞oˌplä/ ▸*n. inf.* commotion; excitement.

**hoo·ray** /həˈrā; ho͞o-/ ▸*interj. & n.* HURRAH.

**hoose·gow** /ˈho͞osˌgou/ ▸*n.* prison.

**hoot** /ho͞ot/ ▸*n.* **1** owl's cry. **2** shout expressing scorn or disapproval. **3** *inf.* **a** laughter. **b** cause of this.
▸*v.* **1** utter or make a hoot. **2** make loud sounds, esp. of scorn or disapproval or merriment: *hooted with laughter.*
□ **not give a hoot** (or **two hoots**) *inf.* not care at all.

**hop** /häp/ ▸*v.* (**hopped, hop·ping**) **1** (of a bird, frog, etc.) spring with two or all feet at once. **2** (of

a person) jump on one foot. **3** *inf.* **a** make a quick trip. **b** make a quick change of position or location. **4** *inf.* **a** jump into (a vehicle). **b** obtain (a ride) in this way.
▸*n.* **1** hopping movement. **2** informal dance. **3** short journey, esp. a flight. **4** climbing plant cultivated for its cones. **5** (**hops**) ripe cones of this, used to flavor beer.

**hope** /hōp/ ▸*n.* **1** expectation and desire combined, e.g., for a thing: *hope of getting the job.* **2** person, thing, or circumstance that gives cause for hope. **3** what is hoped for.
▸*v.* **1** feel hope; feel confident. **2** expect and desire. —**hope·ful** *adj.* —**hope·less** *adj.*

**hope·ful·ly** /ˈhōpfəlē/ ▸*adv.* **1** in a hopeful manner. **2** it is to be hoped that.

*USAGE* The traditional sense of **hopefully**, 'in a hopeful manner', has been used since 1593. The first recorded use of **hopefully** as a sentence adverb, meaning 'it is to be hoped that', appears in 1702. This use of **hopefully** is now the most common one. However, most traditionalists continue to withhold approval of **hopefully** as a sentence adverb.

**hop·head** ▸n. inf. drug addict.

**Ho·pi** /'hōpē/ ▸n. **1 a** N. American people native to northeastern Arizona. **b** member of this people. **2** language of this people.

**hop·lite** /'häp‚līt/ ▸n. heavily armed foot soldier of ancient Greece.

**hop·per** ▸n. **1** hopping insect. **2 a** container tapering downward (orig. having a hopping motion) through which grain passes into a mill. **b** similar device in various machines.

**hop·sack** ▸n. coarse fabric of a loose plain weave, used for clothing.

**horde** /hôrd/ ▸n. **1** usu. derog. large group. **2** moving swarm or pack (of insects, wolves, etc.).

**ho·ri·zon** /hə'rīzən/ ▸n. **1** line at which earth and sky appear to meet. **2** limit of mental perception, experience, interest, etc.
□ **on the horizon** about to happen or becoming apparent.

**hor·i·zon·tal** /‚hôrə'zäntl/ ▸adj. parallel to the plane of the horizon; at right angles to the vertical: *horizontal plane.*
▸n. horizontal line, plane, etc. —**hor·i·zon·tal·ly** adv.

**hor·mone** /'hôrmōn/ ▸n. **1** substance produced in an organism and transported in tissue fluids such as blood or sap to stimulate cells or tissues into action. **2** similar synthetic substance. —**hor·mon·al** adj.

**horn** /hôrn/ ▸n. **1** hard outgrowth, often curved and pointed, on the head of cattle, rhinoceroses, giraffes, and other esp. hoofed mammals. **2** hornlike projection, or thing shaped like a horn. **3** substance of which horns are composed. **4** Mus. **a** FRENCH HORN. **b** brass wind instrument. **c** horn player. **5** device sounding a warning: *car horn | foghorn.*
□ **horn in** inf. intrude; interfere.

**hor·net** /'hôrnit/ ▸n. large wasp with a brown and yellow striped body, and capable of inflicting a serious sting.

**horn of plen·ty** ▸n. cornucopia.

**horn·pipe** ▸n. lively dance, usu. by one person (esp. associated with sailors).

**horn-rimmed** ▸adj. having rims

made of horn or a similar substance.

**hor·o·scope** /'hôrə,skōp/ *Astrol.* ▸*n.* forecast of a person's future based on a diagram showing the relative positions of the stars and planets at that person's birth.

**hor·ren·dous** /hə'rendəs/ ▸*adj.* horrifying.

**hor·ri·ble** /'hôrəbəl/ ▸*adj.* **1** causing or likely to cause horror. **2** *inf.* unpleasant; excessive: *horrible weather | horrible noise.* —**hor·ri·bly** *adv.*

**hor·rid** /'hôrid/ ▸*adj.* **1** horrible; revolting. **2** *inf.* unpleasant; disagreeable: *horrid weather | horrid children.*

**hor·ri·fy** /'hôrə,fī/ ▸*v.* (**-fied**) fill with horror.

**hor·ror** /'hôrər/ ▸*n.* **1** painful feeling of loathing and fear. **2** person or thing causing horror. **3** intense dislike. ▸*adj.* (of literature, movies, etc.) designed to attract by arousing pleasurable feelings of horror.

**hors d'oeuvre** /ôr 'dərv; 'dœvrə/ ▸*n.* (*pl.* same or **hors d'oeuvres**) appetizer served at the beginning of a meal.

**horse** /hôrs/ ▸*n.* **1** solid-hoofed plant-eating quadruped with flowing mane and tail, used for riding and to carry and pull loads. **2** gymnastic apparatus for vaulting. **3** *inf.* heroin. □ **horse around** fool around.

**horse chest·nut** ▸*n.* **1** large ornamental tree with upright conical clusters of white or pink or red flowers. **2** inedible dark brown fruit of this.

**horse·play** ▸*n.* boisterous play.

**horse·power** (abbr.: **h.p.**) ▸*n.* (*pl.* same) **1** unit of power equal to 550 foot-pounds per second (about 750 watts). **2** power of an engine, etc., measured in terms of this.

**horse race** ▸*n.* race between horses with riders.

**horse·rad·ish** ▸*n.* **1** plant with long, lobed leaves. **2** pungent root of this scraped or grated as a condiment.

**horse sense** ▸*n.* *inf.* common sense.

**horse·shoe** ▸*n.* **1** U-shaped iron plate nailed to a horse's hoof for protection. **2** thing of this shape. **3** (**horseshoes**) [treated as *sing.*] game in which horseshoes are tossed to encircle a stake.

**hors·y** (also **hors·ey**) ▸*adj.* (**-i·er, -i·est**) **1** of or like a horse.

**2** interested in horses or horse racing. **3** large; clumsy.

**hor·ta·to·ry** /ˈhôrtəˌtôrē/ ▸*adj.* tending or aiming to exhort.

**hor·ti·cul·ture** /ˈhôrtiˌkəlCHər/ ▸*n.* art of garden cultivation. —**hor·ti·cul·tur·al** *adj.* —**hor·ti·cul·tur·ist** *n.*

**ho·san·na** /hōˈzanə/ ▸*n. & interj.* shout of adoration to God.

**hose** /hōz/ ▸*n.* **1** flexible tube for conveying a fluid. **2** [treated as *pl.*] stockings and socks. ▸*v.* spray with a hose.

**ho·sier·y** /ˈhōZHərē/ ▸*n.* stockings and socks.

**hos·pice** /ˈhäspis/ ▸*n.* home for people who are terminally ill.

**hos·pi·ta·ble** /häˈspitəbəl; ˈhäspi-/ ▸*adj.* giving hospitality. —**hos·pi·ta·bly** *adv.*

**hos·pi·tal** /ˈhäˌspitl/ ▸*n.* institution providing medical and surgical treatment and nursing care for ill or injured people. —**hos·pi·tal·i·za·tion** *n.* —**hos·pi·tal·ize** *v.*

**hos·pi·tal·i·ty** /ˌhäspiˈtalitē/ ▸*n.* friendly and generous reception and entertainment of guests or strangers.

**host** /hōst/ ▸*n.* **1** person who receives another as a guest. **2** animal or plant having a

parasite. **3** person who introduces or interviews guests on a show, esp. on radio or TV. **4** large number of people or things. **5** bread consecrated in the Eucharist. ▸*v.* act as host to (a person) or at (an event).

**hos·tage** /ˈhästij/ ▸*n.* person held as security for the fulfillment of a condition.

**hos·tel** /ˈhästl/ ▸*n.* inexpensive lodging esp. for travelers, hikers, etc.

**host·ess** /ˈhōstis/ ▸*n.* woman entertaining guests.

**hos·tile** /ˈhästl/ ▸*adj.* **1** of an enemy. **2** unfriendly. —**hos·til·i·ty** *n.*

**hot** /hät/ ▸*adj.* (**hot·ter, hot·test**) **1** having a relatively high temperature. **2** producing the sensation of heat: *hot flash.* **3** (of pepper, spices, etc.) pungent; piquant. **4** (of a person) feeling heat. **5 a** passionate; excited. **b** eager: *in hot pursuit.* **6** (of news, etc.) fresh; recent. **7** (of a competitor) strongly favored to win: *a hot favorite.* **8** *inf.* (of goods) stolen.

**hot air** ▸*n. inf.* boastful or excited talk.

**hot·bed** ▸*n.* environment

promoting the growth of something, esp. something unwelcome: *hotbed of vice.*

**hot-blooded** ▶*adj.* ardent; passionate.

**hot·cake** ▶*n.* pancake.
□ **like hotcakes** (be sold, etc.) quickly: *the new CD is selling like hotcakes.*

**hot dog** ▶*n.* FRANKFURTER.

**ho·tel** /hō'tel/ ▶*n.* establishment providing accommodations and meals for payment.

**ho·te·lier** /ˌôtel'yā; ˌhōtl'i(ə)r/ ▶*n.* person who owns or manages a hotel.

**hot flash** (also **hot flush**) ▶*n.* sudden feeling of feverish heat, typical of menopause.

**hot·head** ▶*n.* impetuous person. —**hot·head·ed** *adj.* —**hot·head·ed·ness** *n.*

**hot·house** ▶*n.* **1** heated building for rearing plants out of season or in a climate colder than is natural for them. **2** environment that encourages the rapid growth or development of something.

**hot·line** ▶*n.* direct exclusive line of communication, esp. for emergencies.

**hot plate** ▶*n.* heated metal plate for cooking food or keeping it hot.

**hot po·ta·to** ▶*n. inf.* controversial or awkward matter or situation.

**hot rod** ▶*n.* motor vehicle modified to have extra power and speed.

**hot seat** ▶*n. inf.* **1** position of difficult responsibility. **2** electric chair.

**hot-tem·pered** ▶*adj.* easily angered.

**hot tub** ▶*n.* tub of heated, circulating water for therapy or recreation, usu. able to accommodate several people.

**hot-water bottle** ▶*n.* container, usu. made of rubber, filled with hot water, esp. to warm the feet, a bed, etc.

**hound** /hound/ ▶*n.* dog used for hunting.
▶*v.* harass or pursue relentlessly.

**hour** /ou(ə)r/ ▶*n.* **1** twenty-fourth part of a day and night; 60 minutes. **2** period set aside for some purpose: *lunch hour.* **3** present time: *question of the hour.* **4** time for action, etc.: *the hour has come.* **5** time of day specified as an exact number of hours from midnight or midday:

buses leave on the hour | on the half hour.

□ **after hours** after closing time.

**hour·glass** ▸n. reversible device with two connected glass bulbs containing sand that takes a specified time to pass from the upper to the lower bulb.

**hou·ri** /ˈho͞orē/ ▸n. (pl. **-ris**) beautiful young woman, esp. one of the virgin companions of the faithful in the Muslim paradise.

**house** ▸n. /hous/ **1** building for human habitation. **2** [as adj.] (of an animal) kept in, frequenting, or infesting houses: house cat | housefly. **3** building for a special purpose: opera house | summer house. **4** royal family or dynasty: House of York. **5 a** legislative or deliberative assembly. **b (the House)** the House of Representatives.
▸v. /houz/ **1** provide (a person, a population, etc.) with a house or other accommodations. **2** store (goods, etc.). **3** enclose or encase (a part or fitting).
□ **on the house** at the management's expense; free.

**house·bro·ken** ▸adj. (of pets) trained to excrete only in specified places.

**house·fly** ▸n. common fly.

**house·hold** ▸n. occupants of a house regarded as a unit. **—house·hold·er** n.

□ **household word** (or **name**) familiar name, person, or thing.

**house·hus·band** ▸n. married man whose main job is managing household duties.

**house·keep·er** ▸n. person employed to manage a household. **—house·keep·ing** n.

**House of Rep·re·sent·a·tives** ▸n. lower house of the U.S. Congress and other legislatures.

**house·plant** ▸n. plant grown indoors.

**house·warm·ing** ▸n. party celebrating a move to a new home.

**house·wife** ▸n. (pl. **-wives**) woman (usu. married) whose main job is managing household duties. **—house·wife·ly** adj.

**house·work** ▸n. housekeeping chores.

**hous·ing** /ˈhouziNG/ ▸n. **1** dwellings collectively. **2** shelter; lodging. **3** rigid casing, esp. for machinery, etc.

**hov·el** /ˈhəvəl; ˈhäv-/ ▸n. small miserable dwelling.

**hov·er** /ˈhəvər/ ▸v. **1** (of a bird, helicopter, etc.) remain in one place in the air. **2** wait close at hand; linger.

**hov·er·craft** ▸n. (pl. same) vehicle that travels over land or water on a cushion of air provided by a downward blast.

**how** /hou/ ▸adv. **1** by what means; in what way: *how do you do it?* **2** in what condition, esp. of health: *how is the patient?* **3** to what extent: *how far is it?* | *how did they play?* **4** in whatever way. ▸conj. inf. that: *told us how he'd been in Canada.*

□ **how about** would you like: *how about a game of chess?* □ **how do you do?** formal greeting.

**how·ev·er** /houˈevər/ ▸adv. **1 a** in whatever way: *do it however you want.* **b** to whatever extent: *must go however inconvenient.* **2** nevertheless.

**how·it·zer** /ˈhouitsər/ ▸n. short cannon for high-angle firing of shells at low velocities.

**howl** /houl/ ▸n. **1** long, doleful cry of a dog, wolf, etc. **2** prolonged wailing noise, as of a stong wind. **3** loud cry of pain or rage. ▸v. **1** emit a howl. **2** weep loudly.

**how·so·ev·er** /ˌhousōˈevər/ ▸adv. **1** in whatever way. **2** to whatever extent.

**hoy·den** /ˈhoidn/ ▸n. boisterous girl.

**h.p.** (also **hp**) ▸abbr. horsepower.

**HQ** ▸abbr. headquarters.

**HR** (also **H.R.**) ▸abbr. **1** House of Representatives. **2** home run.

**hr.** ▸abbr. hour.

**HS** ▸abbr. high school.

**Hs** ▸symb. Chem. hassium.

**hub** /həb/ ▸n. **1** central part of a wheel, rotating on or with the axle. **2** center of interest, activity, etc.

**hub·bub** /ˈhəbəb/ ▸n. **1** confused noise. **2** disturbance.

**hu·bris** /ˈ(h)yo͞obris/ ▸n. arrogant pride.

**huck·le·ber·ry** /ˈhəkəlˌberē/ ▸n. (pl. **-ries**) **1** low-growing N. American shrub. **2** blue or black fruit of this.

**huck·ster** /ˈhəkstər/ ▸n. peddler or hawker.

**HUD** ▸abbr. (Department of) Housing and Urban Development.

**hud·dle** /ˈhədl/ ▸v. **1** crowd together. **2** coil one's body into a small space. ▸n. **1** confused or crowded mass. **2** inf. close or secret conference.

**3** *Football* gathering of the players of one team to receive instructions about the next play.

**hue** /(h)yōō/ ▸*n.* **1** color or tint. **2** variety or shade of color.

**huff** /həf/ ▸*v.* give out loud puffs of air, steam, etc.
▸*n.* fit of petty annoyance.
□ **in a huff** annoyed and offended.

**hug** /həg/ ▸*v.* (**hugged, hug·ging**) **1** squeeze tightly in one's arms, esp. with affection. **2** keep close to (the shore, curb, etc.).
▸*n.* strong clasp with the arms.

**huge** /(h)yōōj/ ▸*adj.* very large or great. —**huge·ly** *adv.*

**hug·ger-mug·ger** /ˈhəgər ˌməgər/ ▸*adj.* **1** confused; disorderly. **2** secret; clandestine.
▸*n.* **1** confusion; muddle. **2** secrecy.

**hu·la** /ˈhōōlə/ (also **hu·la-hu·la**) ▸*n.* Polynesian dance with flowing arm and rhythmic hip movements.

**hulk** /həlk/ ▸*n.* **1** body of a old or unwieldy vessel. **2** *inf.* large clumsy-looking person or thing.

**hulk·ing** ▸*adj. inf.* bulky; large and clumsy.

**hull** /həl/ ▸*n.* **1** body of a ship, airship, flying boat, etc. **2** outer covering of a fruit, esp. the pod of peas and beans, husk of grain, or calyx of a strawberry.
▸*v.* remove the hulls from (fruit, etc.).

**hul·la·ba·loo** /ˈhələbəˌlōō/ ▸*n.* (*pl.* **-loos**) uproar; clamor.

**hum** /həm/ ▸*v.* (**hummed, hum·ming**) **1** make a low steady buzzing sound. **2** sing (a wordless tune) with closed lips. **3** *inf.* be active: *really made things hum.*
▸*n.* humming sound.

**hu·man** /ˈ(h)yōōmən/ ▸*adj.* **1** consisting of human beings: *the human race.* **2** of or characteristic of people: *is only human | proved to be very human.*
▸*n.* human being.

**hu·man be·ing** ▸*n.* man or woman or child of the species *Homo sapiens.*

**hu·mane** /(h)yōōˈmān/ ▸*adj.* benevolent; compassionate. —**hu·mane·ly** *adv.*

**hu·man·ism** /ˈ(h)yōōməˌnizəm/ ▸*n.* progressive nonreligious philosophy emphasizing human values. —**hu·man·ist** *n.* —**hu·man·is·tic** *adj.*

**hu·man·i·tar·i·an** /(h)yōō-ˌmanəˈte(ə)rēən/ ▸*n.* person who seeks to promote human welfare.

▸*adj.* relating to humanitarians. —**hu·man·i·tar·i·an·ism** *n.*

**hu·man·i·ty** /(h)yŏŏ'manitē/ ▸*n.* (*pl.* **-ties**) **1 a** humankind. **b** being human. **2** humane quality. **3** (**humanities**) learning concerned with human culture.

**hu·man·ize** /'(h)yŏŏmə,nīz/ ▸*v.* **1** make human. **2** make humane.

**hu·man·kind** ▸*n.* human beings collectively.

**hu·man·ly** ▸*adv.* **1** by human means: *I will do it if it is humanly possible.* **2** from a human point of view: *they can grow both humanly and spiritually.*

**hu·man na·ture** ▸*n.* general characteristics and feelings of human beings.

**hu·man·oid** /'(h)yŏŏmə,noid/ ▸*adj.* having an appearance or character resembling that of a human. ▸*n.* (esp. in science fiction) a being resembling a human in its shape.

**hu·man right** ▸*n.* (usu. **human rights**) right that is believed to belong justifiably to every person.

**hum·ble** /'həmbəl/ ▸*adj.* **1** having or showing low self-esteem. **2** of low social rank:

humble origins. **3** (of a thing) of modest pretensions, size, etc. ▸*v.* make humble; abase. —**hum·ble·ness** *n.* —**hum·bly** *adv.*

**hum·bug** /'həm,bəg/ ▸*n.* **1** deception or lying. **2** impostor.

**hum·drum** /'həm,drəm/ ▸*adj.* **1** commonplace; dull. **2** monotonous.

**hu·mid** /'(h)yŏŏmid/ ▸*adj.* (of the air or climate) warm and damp. —**hu·mid·i·ty** *n.*

**hu·mil·i·ate** /(h)yŏŏ'milē,āt/ ▸*v.* injure the dignity or self-respect of. —**hu·mil·i·at·ing** *adj.* —**hu·mil·i·a·tion** *n.*

**hu·mil·i·ty** /(h)yŏŏ'militē/ ▸*n.* humbleness; meekness.

**hum·ming·bird** /'həmiNG,bərd/ ▸*n.* tiny nectar-feeding bird that makes a humming sound with its wings.

**hum·mock** /'həmək/ ▸*n.* hillock, knoll, or hump.

**hu·mon·gous** /(h)yŏŏ'mäNGgəs; -'məNG-/ (also **hu·mun·gous**) *inf.* ▸*adj.* extremely large or massive.

**hu·mor** /'(h)yŏŏmər/ ▸*n.* **1** condition of being amusing. **2** (**sense of humor**) ability to perceive or express humor or take a joke. **3** mood or state of mind: *bad humor.*

▶*v.* gratify or indulge (a person or taste, etc.). —**hu·mor·ous** *adj.* —**hu·mor·ous·ly** *adj.*

**hu·mor·ist** ▶*n.* humorous writer or performer.

**hump** /həmp/ ▶*n.* **1** rounded protuberance on a camel's back, or as an abnormality on a person's back. **2** rounded raised mass of earth, etc.

▶*v. inf.* lift or carry (heavy objects, etc.) with difficulty.

□ **over the hump** over the worst.

**hump·back** ▶*n.* **1** baleen whale with a dorsal fin forming a hump. **2** person having a back with a hump. —**hump·backed** *adj.*

**hu·mus** /'(h)yo͞oməs/ ▶*n.* organic part of soil, formed by decayed vegetation.

**hunch** /hənCH/ ▶*v.* **1** bend or arch into a hump. **2** sit with the body hunched.

▶*n.* **1** intuitive feeling or conjecture. **2** hump.

**hun·dred** /'həndrid/ ▶*n.* (*pl.* **hun·dreds** or **hun·dred**) **1** product of ten and ten (100). **2** set of a hundred things. **3** (**hundreds**) the years of a specified century: *the seventeen hundreds.* —**hun·dredth** *adj. & n.*

**Hun·gar·i·an** /həNG'ge(ə)rēən/ ▶*n.* **1 a** native or inhabitant of Hungary. **b** person of Hungarian descent. **2** Finno-Ugric language of Hungary.

▶*adj.* of Hungary or its people or language.

**hun·ger** /'həNGgər/ ▶*n.* **1** discomfort caused by lack of food. **2** strong desire.

▶*v.* crave or desire. —**hun·gry** *adj.* —**hun·gri·ly** *adv.*

**hunk** /həNGk/ ▶*n.* **1** large piece cut off: *hunk of bread.* **2** *inf.* sexually attractive man. —**hunk·y** *adj.*

**hunt** /hənt/ ▶*v.* **1 a** pursue and kill (wild animals, esp. game) for sport or food. **b** (of an animal) chase (its prey). **2** seek; search: *hunting for a pen.*

▶*n.* **1** practice or instance of hunting. **2** search. —**hunt·er** *n.* —**hunt·ress** *n.* —**hunt·ing** *n.* —**hunts·man** *n.*

**hur·dle** /'hərdl/ ▶*n.* **1** obstacle or difficulty. **2 a** a light frame to be cleared by athletes in a race. **b** (**hurdles**) a hurdle race.

▶*v.* **1** overcome (a difficulty). **2** clear (a hurdle). —**hur·dler** *n.*

**hurl** /hərl/ ▶*v.* **1** throw with great

force. **2** utter (abuse, etc.) vehemently.

▶*n.* forceful throw.

**hur·ly-bur·ly** /'hərlē 'bərlē/ ▶*n.* boisterous activity; commotion.

**hur·rah** /hoo'rä/ (also **hur·ray**) ▶*interj. & n.* exclamation of joy or approval.

**hur·ri·cane** /'həri,kān/ ▶*n.* storm with a violent wind, esp. in the W. Atlantic.

**hur·ri·cane lamp** ▶*n.* oil lamp designed to resist a high wind.

**hur·ry** /'hərē/ ▶*n.* (*pl.* **-ries**) **1** great haste: *in a hurry.* **2** need for haste: *what's the hurry?*

▶*v.* (**-ried**) **1** move or cause to move hastily. **2** [as *adj.* **hurried**] be hasty; do rapidly owing to lack of time. **—hur·ried·ly** *adv.*

**hurt** /hərt/ ▶*v.* (*past* and *past part.* **hurt**) **1** cause pain, injury, or distress to. **2** suffer pain or harm: *my arm hurts.*

▶*n.* **1** injury. **2** harm; wrong.

▶*adj.* expressing emotional pain. **—hurt·ful** *adj.*

**hur·tle** /'hərtl/ ▶*v.* move or hurl rapidly or noisily.

**hus·band** /'həzbənd/ ▶*n.* married man, esp. in relation to his wife.

▶*v.* manage thriftily; use (resources) economically.

**hus·band·ry** ▶*n.* **1** farming. **2** management of resources.

**hush** /həsH/ ▶*v.* [often as *adj.* **hushed**] make or become quiet.

▶*interj.* calling for silence.

▶*n.* expectant silence.

**hush pup·py** ▶*n.* deep-fried ball of cornmeal dough.

**husk** /həsk/ ▶*n.* dry outer covering of some fruits or seeds.

▶*v.* remove husk(s) from.

**husk·y** /'həskē/ ▶*adj.* (**-i·er, -i·est**) **1** dry in the throat; hoarse. **2** strong; hefty.

▶*n.* (*pl.* **-ies**) dog of a powerful breed used in the Arctic for pulling sleds. **—husk·i·ly** *adv.* **—husk·i·ness** *n.*

**hus·sy** /'həsē; -zē/ ▶*n.* (*pl.* **-sies**) *derog.* impudent or immoral girl or woman.

**hus·tle** /'həsəl/ ▶*v.* **1** push roughly; jostle; hurry; bustle. **2** coerce or deal with hurriedly or unceremoniously: *hustled them out of the room.* **3** *inf.* **a** swindle. **b** engage in prostitution.

▶*n.* **1** act or instance of hustling. **2** *inf.* fraud or swindle. **—hus·tler** *n.*

**hut** /hət/ ▶*n.* small crude house or shelter.

**hutch** /həcH/ ▶*n.* **1** cage with a

wire mesh front, for keeping rabbits. **2** cupboard.

**hwy.** ▸*abbr.* highway.

**hy·a·cinth** /ˈhīəˌsinTH/ ▸*n.* plant with clusters of bell-shaped fragrant flowers.

**hy·brid** /ˈhīˌbrid/ ▸*n.* **1** offspring of two plants or animals of different species or varieties. **2** thing composed of diverse elements.

**hy·brid·ize** ▸*v.* interbreed or subject to cross-breeding. —**hy·brid·i·za·tion** *n.*

**hy·dran·gea** /hīˈdranjə/ ▸*n.* shrub with globular clusters of white, pink, or blue flowers.

**hy·drant** /ˈhīdrənt/ ▸*n.* pipe (esp. in a street) with a nozzle for a hose, for drawing water from a main.

**hy·drau·lic** /hīˈdrôlik/ ▸*adj.* **1** operated by liquid moving under pressure: *hydraulic brakes.* **2** of or concerned with hydraulics: *hydraulic engineer.* —**hy·drau·li·cal·ly** *adv.*

**hy·drau·lics** ▸*pl. n.* [usu. treated as *sing.*] the science of the conveyance of liquids through pipes, etc., esp. as motive power.

**hy·dro·car·bon** /ˈhīdrəˌkärbən/ ▸*n.* compound of hydrogen and carbon.

**hy·dro·e·lec·tric** /ˌhīdrōiˈlektrik/ ▸*adj.* generating electricity by waterpower.

**hy·dro·foil** /ˈhīdrəˌfoil/ ▸*n.* **1** boat with finlike members on struts for lifting its hull out of the water to increase speed. **2** this device.

**hy·dro·gen** /ˈhīdrəjən/ ▸*n.* colorless gaseous element, without taste or odor, the lightest element and occurring in water and all organic compounds. (Symb.: **H**) —**hy·dro·gen·ous** *adj.*

**hy·drog·e·nate** /ˈhīdrəjəˌnāt; hīˈdräj-/ ▸*v.* charge with or cause to combine with hydrogen. —**hy·drog·en·a·tion** *n.*

**hy·dro·gen bomb** ▸*n.* immensely powerful bomb utilizing the explosive fusion of hydrogen nuclei. (Also called **H bomb**).

**hy·dro·gen per·ox·ide** ▸*n.* colorless liquid used as an antiseptic and bleach.

**hy·drog·ra·phy** /hīˈdrägrəfē/ ▸*n.* science of surveying and charting bodies of water, such as seas, lakes, and rivers.

**hy·dro·pho·bi·a** /ˌhīdrəˈfōbēə/ ▸*n.* **1** morbid aversion to water.

**2** rabies, esp. in humans.
—**hy·dro·pho·bic** *adj.*

**hy·dro·plane** ▸*n.* **1** light fast motorboat designed to skim over water. **2** seaplane.
▸*v.* **1** (of a boat) skim over the surface of water with its hull lifted. **2** (of a vehicle) glide uncontrollably on a wet road surface.

**hy·dro·pon·ics** /ˌhīdrəˈpäniks/ ▸*pl. n.* process of growing plants in sand, gravel, or liquid, with added nutrients but without soil.

**hy·dro·ther·a·py** ▸*n.* use of water, esp. swimming, as a medical treatment.

**hy·e·na** /hīˈēnə/ ▸*n.* doglike flesh-eating mammal with hind limbs shorter than forelimbs.
□ **laughing hyena** hyena whose howl is compared to a fiendish laugh.

**hy·giene** /ˈhīˌjēn/ ▸*n.* conditions or practices, esp. cleanliness, for maintaining health.
—**hy·gi·en·ic** *adj.*

**hy·grom·e·ter** /hīˈgrämitər/ ▸*n.* instrument for measuring humidity.

**hy·men** /ˈhīmən/ ▸*n.* membrane at the opening of the vagina.

**hy·me·ne·al** /ˌhīməˈnēəl/ ▸*adj.* of or concerning marriage.

**hymn** /him/ ▸*n.* song of praise, esp. to God in Christian worship.

**hym·nal** /ˈhimnəl/ ▸*n.* book of hymns.

**hype** /hīp/ *inf.* ▸*n.* **1** extravagant or intensive publicity promotion. **2** cheating; trick.
▸*v.* **1** promote (a product) with extravagant publicity. **2** cheat; trick.

**hy·per** /ˈhīpər/ ▸*adj. inf.* excessively excited, nervous, stimulated, etc.

**hyper-** ▸*prefix* meaning: **1** over; beyond; above: *hyperphysical.* **2** exceeding: *hypersonic.* **3** excessively; above normal: *hyperbole* | *hypersensitive.*

**hy·per·ac·tive** ▸*adj.* abnormally active.
—**hy·per·ac·tiv·i·ty** *n.*

**hy·per·bo·le** /hīˈpərbəlē/ ▸*n.* exaggerated statement not meant to be taken literally.
—**hy·per·bol·ic** *adj.*

**hy·per·cor·rec·tion** /ˌhīpərkəˈrekSHən/ ▸*n.* erroneous use of a word form or pronunciation based on a false analogy with a correct or prestigious form, such as *between you and I* for the standard *between you and me.*

**hy·per·crit·i·cal** ▸*adj.*

excessively critical, esp. of small faults.

**hy·per·gly·ce·mi·a** /ˌhīpərglī-ˈsēmēə/ ▶*n.* excess of glucose in the bloodstream, often associated with diabetes mellitus.

**hy·per·son·ic** /ˌhīpərˈsänik/ ▶*adj.* **1** relating to speeds of more than five times the speed of sound. **2** relating to sound frequencies above about a thousand million hertz.

**hy·per·ten·sion** ▶*n.* abnormally high blood pressure. —**hy·per·ten·sive** *adj.*

**hy·per·ven·ti·la·tion** ▶*n.* abnormally rapid breathing.

**hy·phen** /ˈhīfən/ ▶*n.* sign (-) used to join words semantically or syntactically (as in *pick-me-up*, *rock-forming*), to indicate the division of a word at the end of a line, or to indicate a missing or implied element (as in *man- and womankind*).

**hy·phen·ate** ▶*v.* write or join with a hyphen.

**hyp·na·gog·ic** /ˌhipnəˈgäjik; -ˈgō-/ (also **hyp·no·gog·ic**) ▶*adj.* of or relating to the state immediately before falling asleep.

**hyp·no·sis** /hipˈnōsis/ ▶*n.* state like sleep in which the subject acts only on external suggestion. —**hyp·not·ic** *adj.* —**hyp·no·tism** *n.* —**hyp·no·tist** *n.* —**hyp·no·tize** *v.*

**hy·po** /ˈhīpō/ ▶*n.* (*pl.* **-pos**) *inf.* HYPODERMIC.

**hypo-** (usu. **hyp-** before a vowel or h) ▶*prefix* **1** under: *hypodermic.* **2** below normal: *hypoxia.*

**hy·po·al·ler·gen·ic** /ˌhīpōalər-ˈjenik/ ▶*adj.* having little likelihood of causing an allergic reaction: *hypoallergenic foods.*

**hy·po·chon·dri·a** /ˌhīpə-ˈkändrēə/ ▶*n.* abnormal anxiety about one's health. —**hy·po·chon·dri·ac** *n.*

**hy·poc·ri·sy** /hiˈpäkrisē/ ▶*n.* (*pl.* **-sies**) **1** false claim to virtue; insincerity; pretense. **2** instance of this.

**hy·po·crite** /ˈhipəˌkrit/ ▶*n.* person given to hypocrisy. —**hy·po·crit·i·cal** *adj.*

**hy·po·der·mic** /ˌhīpəˈdərmik/ ▶*adj.* injected beneath the skin or used to do this. ▶*n.* hypodermic injection or syringe.

**hy·po·gly·ce·mi·a** /ˌhīpōglī-ˈsēmēə/ ▶*n.* deficiency of glucose in the bloodstream. —**hy·po·gly·ce·mic** *adj.*

**hy·pot·e·nuse** /hī'pätn͵(y)o͞os/ ▶*n.* side opposite the right angle of a right triangle.

**hy·po·ther·mi·a** /͵hīpə-'THərmēə/ ▶*n. Med.* abnormally low body temperature.

**hy·poth·e·sis** /hī'päTHəsis/ ▶*n.* (*pl.* **-ses**) supposition made as a basis for reasoning or as a starting point for further investigation. —**hy·poth·e·size** *v.*

**hys·ter·ec·to·my** /͵histə-'rektəmē/ ▶*n.* (*pl.* **-mies**) surgical removal of the uterus.

**hys·te·ri·a** /hi'sterēə; -'sti(ə)r-/ ▶*n.* wild uncontrollable emotion or excitement. —**hys·ter·i·cal** *adj.* —**hys·ter·ics** *pl. n.*

**Hz** ▶*abbr.* hertz.

# Ii

**I**[1] /ī/ (also **i**) ▶*n.* (*pl.* **Is** or **I's**; **i's**) ninth letter of the alphabet.

**I**[2] ▶*pron.* (*obj.* **me**; *poss.* **my, mine**; *pl.* **we**) used by a speaker or writer to refer to himself or herself.

**I**[3] ▶*symb. Chem.* iodine.

**I**[4] (also **I.**) ▶*abbr.* **1** independent. **2** interstate. **3** Island(s). **4** Isle(s). **5** (as a Roman numeral) 1.

**i** (also **i.**) ▶*abbr.* **1** incisor. **2** interest. **3** intransitive. **4** island. **5** isle.

**IA** ▶*abbr.* Iowa (in official postal use).

**Ia.** ▶*abbr.* Iowa.

**i·am·bic** /ī'ambik/ ▶*adj.* (of verse) having metrical feet of one short and one long syllable.

**i·at·ro·gen·ic** /ī,atrə'jenik/ ▶*adj.* of or relating to illness caused by medical examination or treatment.

**i·bex** /'ī,beks/ ▶*n.* (*pl.* same or **i·bex·es**) wild mountain goat of Europe, N. Africa, and Asia, with curved ridged horns.

**ibid.** (also **ib.**) ▶*abbr.* in the same book or passage, etc.

**i·bis** /'ībis/ ▶*n.* (*pl.* same or **i·bis·es**) wading bird with a long neck and long legs.

**-ible** ▶*suffix* forming adjectives meaning 'that may or may be' (See **ABLE**): *terrible*.

**i·bu·pro·fen** /,ībyoo'prōfən/ ▶*n.* anti-inflammatory medication used to relieve pain and reduce fever.

**-ic** ▶*suffix* forming adjectives (*Arabic*) and nouns (*critic*).

**ICC** ▶*abbr.* Interstate Commerce Commission.

**ice** /īs/ ▶*n.* **1** frozen water. **2** *inf.* diamonds.

▶*v.* **1** mix with or cool in ice. **2** (**ice over/up**) cover or become covered with ice. **3** cover with icing. —**i·cy** *adj.*

□ **on ice** *inf.* held in reserve; awaiting further attention. □ **on thin ice** in a risky situation.

**ice·berg** /'īs,bərg/ ▶*n.* large floating mass of ice.

**ice cap** ▶*n.* permanent covering of ice, e.g., in polar regions.

**ice cream** ▶*n.* sweet creamy frozen food.

**ice cube** ▶*n.* small block of ice made in a freezer.

**ice hock·ey** ▶*n.* form of hockey played on ice.

**ice skate** ▶*n.* boot with a blade beneath, for skating on ice. —**ice-skate** *v.*

**ich·thy·ol·o·gy** /ˌikтнē'äləjē/ ▶*n.* study of fishes. —**ich·thy·ol·o·gist** *n.*

**i·ci·cle** /'īsikəl/ ▶*n.* hanging tapering piece of ice, formed by the freezing of dripping water.

**i·cing** ▶*n.* sweet coating on a cake or cookie.

**i·con** /'ī,kän/ ▶*n.* **1** (also **i·kon**) devotional painting, esp. in the Eastern Church. **2** image or statue. **3** respected person. **4** *Computing* symbol that appears on the monitor in a program, option, or window, esp. one of several for selection. —**i·con·ic** *adj.*

**i·con·o·clast** /ī'känə,klast/ ▶*n.* person who attacks cherished beliefs.

**-ics** ▶*suffix* [treated as *sing.* or *pl.*] forming nouns denoting arts or sciences or branches of study or action: *athletics* | *politics*.

**ICU** ▶*abbr.* intensive care unit.

**ID** ▶*abbr.* **1** identification: *ID card.* **2** Idaho (in official postal use).

**I'd** /īd/ ▶*contr.* **1** I had. **2** I should. **3** I would.

**id** /id/ ▶*n. Psychol.* inherited instinctive impulses of the individual as part of the unconscious.

**i·de·a** /ī'dēə/ ▶*n.* **1 a** mental impression or notion; concept. **b** opinion; outlook. **2** intention, purpose, or essential feature.

**i·de·al** /ī'dē(ə)l/ ▶*adj.* **1** answering to one's highest conception. **2** existing only in idea. ▶*n.* **1** perfect type, or a conception of this. **2** moral principle or standard of behavior. —**i·de·al·ly** *adv.*

**i·de·al·ism** ▶*n.* **1** forming or following after ideals, esp. unrealistically. **2** representation of things in ideal or idealized form. —**i·de·al·ist** *n.* —**i·de·al·is·tic** *adj.*

**i·de·al·ize** /ī'dēə,līz/ ▶*v.* consider or represent as ideal. —**i·de·al·i·za·tion** *n.*

**i·den·ti·cal** /ī'dentikəl/ ▶*adj.* **1** (of different things) agreeing in every detail. **2** (of twins) developed from a single fertilized ovum. —**i·den·ti·cal·ly** *adv.*

**i·den·ti·fy** /ī'dentə,fī/ ▶v. (-fied)
**1** establish the identity of;
recognize. **2** establish or select.
—**i·den·ti·fi·ca·tion** n.

**i·den·ti·ty** /ī'dentitē/ ▶n. (pl. -ties)
**1 a** condition of being a
specified person or thing.
**2** identification or the result of
it: *mistaken identity.*

**i·de·o·logue** /'īdēə,lôg; -,läg;
'idēə-/ ▶n. adherent of an
ideology, esp. one who is
uncompromising and dogmatic.

**id·e·ol·o·gy** /,īdē'äləjē/ ▶n. (pl.
-gies) **1** ideas at the basis of an
economic or political theory.
**2** the manner of thinking
characteristic of a class or
individual. —**i·de·o·log·i·cal** adj.

**ides** /īdz/ ▶pl. n. (in the ancient
Roman calendar) a day falling
roughly in the middle of each
month (the 15th day of March,
May, July, and October, and the
13th of other months), from
which other dates were
calculated.

**id·i·om** /'idēəm/ ▶n. phrase
established by usage whose
meaning cannot be deduced
from the individual words (e.g.,
*at the drop of a hat*).

**id·i·o·mat·ic** /,idēə'matik/ ▶adj.
**1** using, containing, or denoting
expressions that are natural to a
native speaker. **2** appropriate to
the style of art or music
associated with a particular
period, individual, or group.

**id·i·o·syn·cra·sy** /,idēə-
'siNGkrəsē/ ▶n. (pl. -sies) mode of
behavior peculiar to a person.
—**id·i·o·syn·crat·ic** adj.

**id·i·ot** /'idēət/ ▶n. inf., derog.
stupid person. —**id·i·ot·ic** adj.

**id·i·ot box** ▶n. inf. television set.

**id·i·ot sa·vant** ▶n. (pl. **id·i·ot
sa·vants** or **id·i·ots sa·vants**
*pronunc.* same) person who is
considered to be mentally
handicapped but displays
brilliance in a specific area, esp.
one involving memory.

**i·dle** /'īdl/ ▶adj. (-dler, -dlest)
**1** lazy; indolent. **2** not in use;
unemployed. **3** (of an action,
thought, or word) not effective;
worthless.

▶v. **1** (of an engine) run slowly.
**2** (**idle away**) pass (time, etc.) in
idleness. —**i·dle·ness** n. —**i·dly**
adv.

**i·dol** /'īdl/ ▶n. **1** image of a deity,
etc., as an object of worship.
**2** the object of excessive
adulation: *movie idol.*
—**i·dol·ize** v.

**i·dol·a·try** /ī'dälətrē/ ▶n. the worship of idols.

**i·dyll** /'īdl/ (also **i·dyl**) ▶n. picturesque or romantic scene or incident or a description of this, esp. in verse.

**IE** ▶abbr. **1** Indo-European. **2** industrial engineer(ing).

**i.e.** ▶abbr. that is to say.

**-ie** ▶suffix var. of **-Y**: *dearie* | *nightie*.

**if** /if/ ▶conj. **1** introducing a conditional clause: **a** on the condition or supposition that; in the event that: *if he comes, I will tell him.* **b** [with *past tense*] implying that the condition is not fulfilled: *if I knew, I would say.* **2** even though: *I'll finish it if it takes me all day.* **3** whenever: *if I am not sure, I ask.* **4** whether: *see if you can find it.* **5 a** expressing a wish or surprise: *if I could just try!* **b** expressing a request: *if you wouldn't mind opening the door?* **6** with implied reservation; perhaps not: *very rarely if at all.* ▶n. condition or supposition: *too many ifs about it.*

□ **if only** **1** even if for no other reason than: *I'll come if only to see her.* **2** expression of regret: *if only I could swim!*

**if·fy** /'ifē/ ▶adj. inf. (**-fi·er**, **-fi·est**) uncertain; doubtful.

**ig·loo** /'igloō/ ▶n. dome-shaped Eskimo dwelling, esp. one built of snow.

**ig·ne·ous** /'ignēəs/ ▶adj. (esp. of rocks) produced by volcanic or magmatic action.

**ig·nite** /ig'nīt/ ▶v. **1** catch or set on fire. **2** excite (feelings, etc.).

**ig·ni·tion** /ig'niSHən/ ▶n. **1** act of igniting. **2** device for igniting, esp. for an internal-combustion engine.

**ig·no·ble** /ig'nōbəl/ ▶adj. (**-bler**, **-blest**) **1** dishonorable. **2** of low birth or position. —**ig·no·bly** *adv.*

**ig·no·min·i·ous** /ˌignə'minēəs/ ▶adj. causing or deserving public disgrace: *the party suffered ignominious defeat in the last election.* —**ig·no·min·i·ous·ly** *adv.*

**ig·no·mi·ny** /'ignəˌminē/ ▶n. public disgrace.

**ig·no·ra·mus** /ˌignə'rāməs/ ▶n. (*pl.* **-mus·es**) ignorant or stupid person.

**ig·no·rance** /'ignərəns/ ▶n. lack of knowledge. —**ig·no·rant** *adj.*

**ig·nore** /ig'nôr/ ▶v. intentionally disregard.

**i·gua·na** /i'gwänə/ ▶n. any of

various large lizards native to tropical America and the Pacific islands, with a dorsal crest.

**IL** ▶*abbr.* Illinois (in official postal use).

**il-** ▶*prefix* assim. form of **IN-** before *l*.

**ilk** /ilk/ ▶*n.* family, class, or set: *not of the same ilk as you.*

**Ill.** ▶*abbr.* Illinois.

**ill.** ▶*abbr.* **1** illustrated. **2** illustration. **3** illustrator.

**I'll** /īl/ ▶*contr.* **1** I shall. **2** I will.

**ill** /il/ ▶*adj.* **1** not healthy; sick: **2** wretched; unfavorable: *ill fortune | ill luck.* **3** harmful: *ill effects.*
▶*adv.* **1** badly; wrongly; unfavorably. **2** scarcely: *can ill afford to do it.*
▶*n.* **1** injury; harm. **2** evil.
□ **ill-advised** foolish or imprudent. □ **ill at ease** embarrassed; uneasy.

**ill-bred** ▶*adj.* badly brought up; rude.

**il·le·gal** /i(l)ˈlēgəl/ ▶*adj.* not legal.

**il·leg·i·ble** /i(l)ˈlejəbəl/ ▶*adj.* not legible.

**il·le·git·i·mate** /ˌi(l)ləˈjitəmit/ ▶*adj.* **1** (of a child) born of parents not married to each other. **2** unlawful. **3** improper. —**il·le·git·i·ma·cy** *n.*

**ill-fat·ed** ▶*adj.* destined to fail.

**ill-fa·vored** ▶*adj.* unattractive.

**ill-got·ten** ▶*adj.* gained by wicked or unlawful means.

**ill hu·mor** ▶*n.* irritability.

**il·lib·er·al** /i(l)ˈlib(ə)rəl/ ▶*adj.* **1** intolerant; narrow-minded. **2** not generous; stingy.

**il·li·cit** /i(l)ˈlisit/ ▶*adj.* unlawful; forbidden. —**il·li·cit·ly** *adv.*

**il·lim·it·a·ble** ▶*adj.* without limits.

**il·lit·er·ate** /i(l)ˈlitərit/ ▶*adj.* **1** unable to read. **2** uneducated.
▶*n.* illiterate person. —**il·lit·er·a·cy** *n.*

**ill-man·nered** ▶*adj.* rude.

**ill-na·tured** ▶*adj.* mean and irritable.

**ill·ness** ▶*n.* **1** disease. **2** being ill.

**il·lo·cu·tion** /ˌiləˈkyoōsHən/ ▶*n.* action performed by saying or writing something, e.g., ordering, warning, or promising.

**il·log·i·cal** /i(l)ˈläjikəl/ ▶*adj.* devoid of or contrary to logic. —**il·log·i·cal·ly** *adv.*

**ill-tem·pered** ▶*adj.* irritable; angry.

**ill-treat** (or **-use**) ▸*v.* treat badly; abuse.

**il·lu·mi·nate** /iˈlo͞oməˌnāt/ ▸*v.*
**1** light up; make bright.
**2** decorate (a manuscript, etc.) with gold, silver, etc. **3** help to explain. —**il·lu·mi·nat·ing** *adj.*
—**il·lu·mi·na·tion** *n.*

**il·lu·sion** /iˈlo͞ozHən/ ▸*n.*
**1** deception; delusion. **2 a** faulty perception. **3** figment of the imagination. **4 OPTICAL ILLUSION.**
—**il·lu·so·ry** *adj.*

**il·lu·so·ry** /iˈlo͞osərē; -zərē/ ▸*adj.* based on illusion; not real.

**il·lus·trate** /ˈiləˌstrāt/ ▸*v.*
**1** provide (a book, etc.) with pictures. **2** serve as an example of. **3** explain by examples.
—**il·lus·tra·tion** *adj.*
—**il·lus·tra·tive** *adj.*

**il·lus·tri·ous** /iˈləstrēəs/ ▸*adj.* distinguished; renowned.

**ill will** ▸*n.* bad feeling; animosity.

**I'm** /īm/ ▸*contr.* I am.

**im-** ▸*prefix* assim. form of **IN-** before *b*, *m*, *p*.

**im·age** /ˈimij/ ▸*n.*
**1** representation of an object.
**2** character or reputation of a person as generally perceived.
**3** appearance in a mirror.
**4** simile or metaphor. **5** mental representation.

**im·age·ry** /ˈimij(ə)rē/ ▸*n.*
**1** images collectively. **2** mental images collectively.

**i·mag·in·ar·y** /iˈmajəˌnerē/ ▸*adj.* not real; existing only in the imagination.

**i·mag·ine** /iˈmajin/ ▸*v.* **1** form a mental image or concept of.
**2** guess. **3** suppose.
—**i·mag·in·a·tive** *adj.*

**i·ma·go** /iˈmāgō; iˈmä-/ ▸*n.* (*pl.* **i·ma·gos**, **i·ma·goes** or **i·ma·gi·nes** /iˈmāgəˌnēz/) **1** final and fully developed adult stage of an insect, typically winged.
**2** unconscious, idealized mental image of someone, esp. a parent, that influences a person's behavior.

**i·mam** /iˈmäm/ ▸*n.* **1** leader of prayers in a mosque. **2** title of various Islamic leaders.
—**i·mam·ate** *n.*

**im·bal·ance** /imˈbaləns/ ▸*n.*
**1** lack of balance.
**2** disproportion.

**im·be·cile** /ˈimbəˌsil/ ▸*n. inf., derog.* stupid person.
—**im·be·cil·ic** *adj.*
—**im·be·cil·i·ty** *n.*

**im·bibe** /imˈbīb/ ▸*v.* drink (esp. alcoholic liquor).

**im·bro·glio** /im'brōlyō/ ▶n. (pl. **-glios**) confused or complicated situation.

**im·bue** /im'byoo/ ▶v. (**-bued, -bu·ing**) **1** inspire or permeate (with feelings, opinions, or qualities). **2** saturate.

**im·i·tate** /'imi,tāt/ ▶v. **1** follow the example of; copy. **2** be like. —**im·i·ta·tion** n. —**im·i·ta·tive** adj.

**im·mac·u·late** /i'makyəlit/ ▶adj. **1** pure; perfectly clean. **2** perfect. —**im·mac·u·late·ly** adv. —**im·mac·u·late·ness** n.

**im·ma·nent** /'imənənt/ ▶adj. **1** inherent. **2** (of the Supreme Being) omnipresent. —**im·ma·nence** n.

**im·ma·te·ri·al** ▶adj. **1** unimportant. **2** incorporeal.

**im·ma·ture** ▶adj. **1** not mature. **2** emotionally undeveloped. **3** unripe. —**im·ma·tu·ri·ty** n.

**im·mea·sur·a·ble** ▶adj. not measurable; immense. —**im·mea·sur·a·bil·i·ty** n.

**im·me·di·ate** /i'mēdēit/ ▶adj. **1** occurring or done at once. **2** nearest; next; not separated by others. **3** most pressing or urgent. —**im·me·di·a·cy** n. —**im·me·di·ate·ly** adv. & conj.

**im·me·mo·ri·al** ▶adj. **1** beyond memory or record. **2** very old.

**im·mense** /i'mens/ ▶adj. extremely large or great. —**im·men·si·ty** n.

**im·mense·ly** ▶adv. extremely.

**im·merse** /i'mərs/ ▶v. **1** dip; plunge; submerge. **2** absorb or involve deeply (in). —**im·mer·sion** n.

**im·mi·grant** /'imigrənt/ ▶n. person who immigrates. ▶adj. of or concerning immigrants.

**im·mi·grate** /'imi,grāt/ ▶v. come as a permanent resident into a country. —**im·mi·gra·tion** n.

**im·mi·nent** /'imənənt/ ▶adj. impending; about to happen. —**im·mi·nence** n.

**im·mo·bile** ▶adj. **1** not moving. **2** not able to move or be moved. —**im·mo·bil·i·ty** n.

**im·mod·er·ate** ▶adj. excessive; lacking moderation. —**im·mod·er·ate·ly** adv. —**im·mod·er·a·tion** n.

**im·mod·est** ▶adj. lacking humility or decency. —**im·mod·es·ty** n.

**im·mo·late** /'imə,lāt/ ▶v. kill or offer as a sacrifice, esp. by burning. —**im·mo·la·tion** n.

**im·mor·al** ▶adj. morally wrong. —**im·mo·ral·i·ty** n.

**im·mor·tal** ▸*adj.* **1 a** living forever. **b** divine. **2** famous for all time.

▸*n.* **1** immortal being. **2** (**the immortals**) gods of antiquity.
—**im·mor·tal·i·ty** *n.*
—**im·mor·tal·ize** *v.*

**im·mov·a·ble** ▸*adj.* **1** not able to be moved. **2** unyielding. **3** motionless.
—**im·mov·a·bil·i·ty** *n.*

**im·mune** /i'myo͞on/ ▸*adj.* **1 a** protected against infection through inoculation or inherited or acquired resistance. **b** relating to immunity: *immune mechanism.* **2** (**immune to**) not influenced by: *immune to his charm.*
—**im·mu·nize** *v.*
—**im·mu·ni·za·tion** *n.*

**im·mu·ni·ty** ▸*n.* (pl. **-ties**) **1** *Med.* ability of an organism to resist infection by means of antibodies and white blood cells. **2** freedom or exemption from an obligation, penalty, etc.

**im·mu·nol·o·gy** /ˌimyə'näləjē/ ▸*n.* scientific study of immunity.
—**im·mu·no·log·i·cal** *adj.*
—**im·mu·nol·o·gist** *n.*

**im·mure** /i'myo͝or/ ▸*v.* enclose within walls; imprison.

**im·mu·ta·ble** /i'myo͞otəbəl/ ▸*adj.* unchangeable.
—**im·mu·ta·bil·i·ty** *n.*

**imp** /imp/ ▸*n.* **1** mischievous child. **2** small devil or sprite.

**im·pact** /'im,pakt/ ▸*n.* **1** forceful contact. **2** strong effect or influence.

▸*v.* **1 a** come forcibly into contact with a (larger) body or surface. **b** have a pronounced effect on. **2** [as *adj.* **impacted**] (of a tooth) wedged between another tooth and the jaw. —**im·pac·tion** *n.*

**im·pair** /im'pe(ə)r/ ▸*v.* damage or weaken. —**im·pair·ment** *n.*

**im·pale** /im'pāl/ ▸*v.* fix or pierce with a sharp instrument.
—**im·pale·ment** *n.*

**im·pal·pa·ble** ▸*adj.* **1** not easily grasped by the mind; intangible. **2** imperceptible to the touch.
—**im·pal·pa·bil·i·ty** *n.*

**im·pan·el** /im'panl/ ▸*v.* officially establish (a jury).
—**im·pan·el·ment** *n.*

**im·part** ▸*v.* **1** make (information) known; communicate. **2** bestow (a quality).

**im·par·tial** ▸*adj.* unprejudiced; fair. —**im·par·ti·al·i·ty** *n.*
—**im·par·tial·ly** *adv.*

**im·pass·a·ble** ▸*adj.* that cannot

be traversed.
—**im·pass·a·bil·i·ty** *n.*

**im·passe** /'im‚pas/ ▶*n.* deadlock.

**im·pas·sioned** /im'pasʰənd/ ▶*adj.* deeply felt; ardent.

**im·pas·sive** ▶*adj.* deficient in or incapable of showing emotion.
—**im·pas·sive·ly** *adv.*
—**im·pas·siv·i·ty** *n.*

**im·pa·tient** ▶*adj.* **1 a** lacking patience or tolerance. **b** (of an action) showing a lack of patience. **2** restlessly eager.
—**im·pa·tience** *n.* —**im·pa·tient·ly** *adv.*

**im·peach** ▶*v.* charge (a public official) with misconduct.
—**im·peach·a·ble** *adj.*
—**Im·peach·ment** *n.*

**im·pec·ca·ble** /im'pekəbəl/ ▶*adj.* faultless; exemplary.
—**im·pec·ca·bly** *adv.*

**im·pe·cu·ni·ous** /‚impə-'kyoŏnēəs/ ▶*adj.* having little or no money.

**im·pede** /im'pēd/ ▶*v.* retard by obstructing; hinder.

**im·ped·i·ment** /im'pedəmənt/ ▶*n.* **1** hindrance or obstruction. **2** defect in speech.

**im·ped·i·men·ta** /im‚pedə-'mentə/ ▶*pl. n.* equipment for an activity or expedition, esp. when considered as bulky or an encumbrance.

**im·pel** /im'pel/ ▶*v.* (**-pelled, -pel·ling**) **1** drive, force, or urge. **2** propel.

**im·pend** /im'pend/ ▶*v.* **1** be about to happen. **2** (of a danger) be threatening. —**im·pend·ing** *adj.*

**im·pen·e·tra·ble** ▶*adj.* **1** not able to be penetrated. **2** incomprehensible.
—**im·pen·e·tra·bil·i·ty** *n.*
—**im·pen·e·tra·bly** *adv.*

**im·per·a·tive** /im'perətiv/ ▶*adj.* **1** urgent. **2** obligatory. **3** commanding. **4** *Gram.* expressing a command (e.g., *come here!*).
▶*n.* **1** *Gram.* the imperative mood. **2** command. —**im·per·a·ti·val** *adj.*
—**im·per·a·tive·ly** *adv.*

**im·per·cep·ti·ble** ▶*adj.* **1** not perceptible. **2** very slight, gradual, or subtle.
—**im·per·cep·ti·bil·i·ty** *n.*
—**im·per·cep·ti·bly** *adv.*

**im·per·fect** ▶*adj.* **1** faulty; incomplete. **2** *Gram.* denoting action in progress but not completed at the time of action.
▶*n.* imperfect tense.
—**im·per·fect·ly** *adv.*
—**im·per·fec·tion** *n.*

**im·pe·ri·al** /im'pi(ə)rēəl/ ▸*adj.*
**1** of or characteristic of an
empire or an emperor.
**2** majestic. —**im·pe·ri·al·ly** *adv.*

**im·pe·ri·al·ism** ▸*n.* policy of
extending a country's power and
influence through diplomacy or
military force. —**im·pe·ri·al·ist** *n.*
& *adj.* —**im·pe·ri·al·is·tic** *adj.*

**im·per·il** ▸*v.* bring or put into
danger.

**im·pe·ri·ous** /im'pi(ə)rēəs/ ▸*adj.*
overbearing; domineering.
—**im·pe·ri·ous·ly** *adv.*

**im·per·ish·a·ble** ▸*adj.* that
cannot perish.

**im·per·me·a·ble** ▸*adj.* that
cannot be penetrated by fluids.
—**im·per·me·a·bil·i·ty** *n.*

**im·per·son·al** ▸*adj.* **1** not
influenced by, showing, or
involving personal feelings.
**2** *Gram.* **a** (of a verb) used esp.
with *it* as a subject (e.g., *it is
snowing*). **b** (of a pronoun)
INDEFINITE. —**im·per·son·al·ly** *adv.*

**im·per·son·ate** /im'pərsə,nāt/
▸*v.* pretend to be (another
person). —**im·per·son·a·tion** *n.*

**im·per·turb·a·ble** ▸*adj.* not
excitable; calm.
—**im·per·turb·a·bil·i·ty** *n.*
—**im·per·turb·a·bly** *adv.*

**im·per·vi·ous** /im'pərvēəs/ ▸*adj.*

**1** not responsive to argument,
etc. **2** impermeable.
—**im·per·vi·ous·ly** *adv.*

**im·pe·ti·go** /,impi'tīgō/ ▸*n.*
contagious skin infection
forming pustules.

**im·pet·u·ous** /im'pecho͞oəs/
▸*adj.* **1** acting or done rashly or
with sudden energy. **2** moving
forcefully or rapidly.
—**im·pet·u·os·i·ty** *n.*

**im·pe·tus** /'impitəs/ ▸*n.* **1** force
or energy with which a body
moves. **2** driving force or
impulse.

**im·pi·et·y** ▸*n.* (*pl.* **-ies**) **1** lack of
piety or reverence. **2** an act, etc.,
showing this.

**im·pinge** /im'pinj/ ▸*v.* **1** make an
impact; have an effect.
**2** encroach.

**im·pi·ous** /'impēəs/ ▸*adj.* **1** not
showing piety or reverence.
**2** wicked. —**im·pi·ous·ly** *adv.*

**im·pla·ca·ble** /im'plakəbəl/ ▸*adj.*
unable to be appeased.
—**im·pla·ca·bil·i·ty** *n.*

**im·plant** ▸*v.* /im'plant/ **1** insert
or fix. **2** instill; plant. **3 a** insert
(tissue, etc.) in a living body.
**b** (of a fertilized ovum) become
attached to the wall of the
womb.

▸*n.* /'implant/ thing implanted.
—**im·plan·ta·tion** *n.*

**im·plau·si·ble** /im'plôzəbəl/
▸*adj.* not plausible.
—**im·plau·si·bil·i·ty** *n.*
—**im·plau·si·bly** *adv.*

**im·ple·ment** /'impləmənt/ ▸*n.*
tool, instrument, or utensil.
▸*v.* **a** put (a decision, plan, etc.)
into effect. **b** fulfill (an
undertaking).
—**im·ple·men·ta·tion** *n.*

**im·pli·cate** /'impli,kāt/ ▸*v.* show
(a person) to be involved (in a
crime, etc.).

**im·pli·ca·tion** ▸*n.* **1** conclusion
that can be drawn from
something although it is not
explicitly stated. **2** consequence
of something: *political
implications.*

**im·plic·it** /im'plisit/ ▸*adj.*
**1** implied though not plainly
expressed. **2** absolute;
unquestioning; unreserved.
—**im·plic·it·ly** *adv.*

**im·plode** /im'plōd/ ▸*v.* burst or
cause to burst inward.
—**im·plo·sion** *n.* —**im·plo·sive**
*adj.*

**im·plore** /im'plôr/ ▸*v.* beg
earnestly for; entreat.
—**im·plor·ing** *adj.*

**im·ply** /im'plī/ ▸*v.* (**-plied**)

**1** strongly suggest the truth or
existence of (a thing not
expressly asserted). **2** insinuate;
hint: *what are you implying?*
**3** signify. —**im·plied** *adj.*

**im·po·lite** ▸*adj.* ill-mannered;
uncivil; rude.

**im·pol·i·tic** ▸*adj.* inexpedient or
unwise.

**im·pon·der·a·ble** ▸*n.*
something difficult to assess:
*there are many imponderables.*
—**im·pon·der·a·bil·i·ty** *n.*
—**im·pon·der·a·bly** *adv.*

**im·port** ▸*v.* /im'pôrt/ **1** bring in
(goods) to a country. **2** indicate;
signify.
▸*n.* /'im,pôrt/ **1** process of
importing. **2** imported article.
**3** meaning; importance.
—**im·por·ta·tion** *n.* —**im·port·er** *n.*

**im·por·tant** /im'pôrtnt/ ▸*adj.*
**1** of great effect or consequence;
momentous. **2** having high rank
or great authority.
—**im·por·tance** *n.*
—**im·por·tant·ly** *adv.*

**im·por·tu·nate** /im'pôrchənit/
▸*adj.* persistent, esp. to the point
of annoyance or intrusion.

**im·por·tune** /,impôr't(y)ōōn/ ▸*v.*
solicit (a person) pressingly.

**im·pose** /im'pōz/ ▸*v.* **1** lay (a tax,
duty, charge, or obligation) on.

**2** enforce compliance with.
**3** demand the attention or commitment of a person: *I hate to impose on you.* —**im·po·si·tion** *n.*

**im·pos·ing** ▸*adj.* impressive or formidable, esp. in appearance.

**im·pos·si·ble** ▸*adj.* **1** not possible. **2** (loosely) not easy, convenient, or believable. **3** *inf.* (of a person) outrageous; intolerable. —**im·pos·si·bil·i·ty** *n.* —**im·pos·si·bly** *adv.*

**im·post** /'im‚pōst/ ▸*n.* tax; duty; tribute.

**im·pos·tor** /im'pästər/ (also **im·pos·ter**) ▸*n.* person who pretends to be someone else.

**im·pos·ture** /im'päsCHər/ ▸*n.* instance of pretending to be someone else in order to deceive others.

**im·po·tent** /'impətənt/ ▸*adj.* **1** powerless. **2** (of a male) unable to achieve an erection or orgasm. —**im·po·tence** *n.*

**im·pound** ▸*v.* **1** take possession of. **2** shut up (animals) in a pound.

**im·pov·er·ish** /im'päv(ə)riSH/ ▸*v.* **1** make poor. **2** exhaust the strength or natural fertility of. —**im·pov·er·ish·ment** *n.*

**im·prac·ti·ca·ble** ▸*adj.* impossible in practice. —**im·prac·ti·ca·bil·i·ty** *n.* —**im·prac·ti·ca·bly** *adv.*

**im·prac·ti·cal** ▸*adj.* **1** not sensible or realistic. **2** impossible to do. —**im·prac·ti·cal·i·ty** *n.* —**im·prac·ti·cal·ly** *adv.*

**im·pre·cate** /'impri‚kāt/ ▸*v.* utter (a curse) or invoke (evil) against someone or something.

**im·pre·ca·tion** /‚impri'kāSHən/ ▸*n.* curse.

**im·pre·cise** ▸*adj.* not precise. —**im·pre·cise·ly** *adv.* —**im·pre·ci·sion** *n.*

**im·preg·na·ble** /im'pregnəbəl/ ▸*adj.* (of a fortified position) that cannot be taken by force. —**im·preg·na·bil·i·ty** *n.*

**im·preg·nate** /im'preg‚nāt/ ▸*v.* **1** fill or saturate. **2** make (a female) pregnant. —**im·preg·na·tion** *n.*

**im·pre·sa·ri·o** /‚imprə'särē‚ō/ ▸*n.* (*pl.* **-os**) organizer of public entertainments, esp. a theatrical, etc., manager.

**im·press** ▸*v.* /im'pres/ **1 a** affect or influence deeply. **b** affect (a person) favorably. **2** emphasize (an idea, etc.). **3 a** imprint or stamp. **b** apply (a mark, etc.) with pressure.

▸*n.* /'impres/ **1** instance of impressing. **2** mark made by a seal, stamp, etc. **3** IMPRESSION.

**im·pres·sion** ▸*n.* **1** effect produced (esp. on the mind or feelings). **2** vague notion or belief. **3** imitation of a person or sound, esp. done to entertain. **4 a** impressing of a mark. **b** mark impressed.

**im·pres·sion·a·ble** ▸*adj.* easily influenced. —**im·pres·sion·a·bil·i·ty** *n.* —**im·pres·sion·a·bly** *adv.*

**im·pres·sion·ism** ▸*n.* style or movement in art, music, etc., that seeks to convey a brief impression or emotion without close, realistic detail. —**im·pres·sion·ist** *n.* —**im·pres·sion·is·tic** *adj.*

**im·pres·sive** ▸*adj.* causing approval or admiration. —**im·pres·sive·ly** *adv.*

**im·pri·ma·tur** /ˌimprə'mätərr/ ▸*n.* **1** official license by the Roman Catholic Church to print (a religious book, etc.). **2** official approval.

**im·print** ▸*v.* /im'print/ **1** impress or establish firmly, esp. on the mind. **2 a** make a stamp or impression of (a figure, etc.) on a thing.

▸*n.* /'im,print/ **1** impression or stamp. **2** printer's or publisher's name, etc., printed in a book.

**im·pris·on** ▸*v.* **1** put into prison. **2** confine. —**im·pris·on·ment** *n.*

**im·prob·a·ble** /im'präbəbəl/ ▸*adj.* **1** unlikely. **2** difficult to believe. —**im·prob·a·bil·i·ty** *n.* —**im·prob·a·bly** *adv.*

**im·promp·tu** /im'präm(p),t(y)oo/ ▸*adj. & adv.* not planned or rehearsed.

**im·prop·er** ▸*adj.* **1** not in accordance with accepted rules of behavior. **2** inaccurate; wrong. —**im·prop·er·ly** *adv.*

**im·pro·pri·e·ty** /ˌimprə'prī-itē/ ▸*n.* (*pl.* **-ties**) failure to observe standards or show due honesty or modesty; improper language, behavior, or character.

**im·prove** ▸*v.* make or become better. —**im·prove·ment** *n.*

**im·prov·i·dent** ▸*adj.* **1** lacking foresight. **2** wasteful. —**im·prov·i·dence** *n.* —**im·prov·i·dent·ly** *adv.*

**im·pro·vise** /'imprə,vīz/ ▸*v.* compose or perform (music, verse, etc.) spontaneously. —**im·pro·vi·sa·tion** *n.* —**im·pro·vi·sa·to·ry** *adj.*

**im·pru·dent** ▸*adj.* rash; indiscreet. —**im·pru·dence** *n.*

**im·pu·dent** /ˈimpyəd(ə)nt/ ▸*adj.* impertinent. —**im·pu·dence** *n.*

**im·pugn** /imˈpyo͞on/ ▸*v.* challenge or call in question (a statement, action, etc.).

**im·pulse** /ˈimˌpəls/ ▸*n.* **1** sudden desire or tendency to act without reflection: *did it on impulse.* **2** tendency to act in this way. **3** impetus. **4** pulse of electrical energy; brief current.

**im·pul·sive** /imˈpəlsiv/ ▸*adj.* acting or done on impulse. —**im·pul·sive·ly** *adv.*

**im·pu·ni·ty** /imˈpyo͞onitē/ ▸*n.* exemption from punishment, bad consequences, etc. □ **with impunity** without punishment.

**im·pure** ▸*adj.* **1** adulterated. **2** unchaste; morally wrong. —**im·pure·ly** *adv.* —**im·pure·ness** *n.*

**im·pute** /imˈpyo͞ot/ ▸*v.* attribute (a fault, etc.) to. —**im·pu·ta·tion** *n.*

**IN** ▸*abbr.* Indiana (in official postal use).

**In** ▸*symb. Chem.* indium.

**in** /in/ ▸*prep.* **1** expressing inclusion or position within limits of space, time, circumstance, etc.: *in Nebraska | in bed | in the rain.* **2** during the time of. **3** within the time of: *will be back in two hours.* **4 a** with respect to: *blind in one eye.* **b** as a kind of: *the latest thing in luxury.* **5** as a proportionate part of: *one in three failed.* **6** with the form or arrangement of: *packed in tens.* **7** as a member of: *in the army.* **8** concerned with: *is in politics.* **9** as the content of: *there is something in what you say.* **10** having the condition of; affected by: *in bad health.* **11** having as a purpose: *in reply to.* **12** by means of or using as material: *drawn in pencil.* **13** into: with a verb of motion or change: *put it in the box.*

▸*adv.* expressing position within limits, or motion to such a position: **1** into a room, house, etc.: *come in.* **2** at home, in one's office, etc.: *is not in.* **3** so as to be enclosed or confined: *locked in.* **4** in a publication: *is the advertisement in?* **5** in or to the inward side: *rub it in.* **6** in fashion or season: *long skirts are in.*

▸*adj.* **1** internal; inside. **2** fashionable. **3** confined to a small group: *in-joke.*

□ **in on** privy to (a secret, etc.).
□ **in that** because; in so far as.

**in.** ▸*abbr.* inch(es).

**in-** (also **il-, im-, ir-**) ▸*prefix*
**1** added to adjectives, meaning 'not': *inedible* | *insane*. **2** added to nouns, meaning 'without; lacking': *inaction*. **3** in, on, into, toward, within: *induce* | *influx* | *insight* | *intrude*.

**in ab·sen·tia** /ˌin əb'sensʜ(ē)ə/ ▸*adv.* in (his, her, or their) absence.

**in·ad·ver·tent** /ˌinəd'vərtnt/ ▸*adj.* (of an action) unintentional. —**in·ad·ver·tence** *n.* —**in·ad·ver·tent·ly** *adv.*

**in·a·lien·a·ble** /in'ālēənəbəl/ ▸*adj.* that cannot be transferred to another. —**in·a·lien·a·bly** *adv.*

**in·ane** /ɪ'nan/ ▸*adj.* silly; stupid. —**in·ane·ly** *adv.* —**in·an·i·ty** *n.*

**in·ar·tic·u·late** /ˌinär'tikyəlit/ ▸*adj.* **1** unable to express oneself clearly. **2** (of speech) indistinctly pronounced. —**in·ar·tic·u·late·ly** *adv.*

**in·au·gu·rate** /in'ôg(y)ə,rāt/ ▸*v.* **1** admit formally to office. **2** initiate the public use of (a building, etc.). **3** begin; introduce. —**in·au·gu·ra·tion** *n.*

**in·board** ▸*adv.* within the sides of or toward the center of a ship, aircraft, or vehicle.
▸*adj.* situated inboard.

**in·born** ▸*adj.* existing from birth.

**inc.** ▸*abbr.* **1** (esp. **Inc.**) Incorporated. **2** incomplete.

**in·can·des·cent** /ˌinkən-'desənt/ ▸*adj.* **1** glowing with heat. **2** shining brightly. —**in·can·des·cence** *n.* —**in·can·des·cent·ly** *adv.*

**in·can·ta·tion** /ˌinkan'tāsʜən/ ▸*n.* words used as a magical spell or charm.

**in·ca·pac·i·tate** /ˌinkə'pasi,tāt/ ▸*v.* prevent from functioning normally. —**in·ca·pac·i·ta·tion** *n.*

**in·car·cer·ate** /in'kärsə,rāt/ ▸*v.* imprison or jail. —**in·car·cer·a·tion** *n.*

**in·car·na·dine** /in'kärnə,dīn; -,dēn/ ▸*n.* bright crimson or pinkish-red color.
▸*adj.* of a crimson or pinkish-red color.
▸*v.* color (something) a bright crimson or pinkish-red.

**in·car·nate** /in'kärnit/ ▸*adj.* **1** embodied in human form: *the devil incarnate.* **2** represented in a recognizable or typical form: *folly incarnate.*

**in·car·na·tion** /ˌinkär'nāsʜən/ ▸*n.* **1** embodiment in human flesh of an idea, deity, etc. **2** (**the Incarnation**) embodiment of God the Son in human flesh as Jesus Christ.

**in·cen·di·ar·y** /in'sendē,erē/ ▸*adj.* **1** (of a bomb) designed to cause fires. **2** tending to stir up strife.

▸*n.* (*pl.* **-ies**) fire bomb or device.

**in·cense**[1] /'in,sens/ ▸*n.* **1** gum or spice producing a sweet smell when burned. **2** the smoke or perfume of this.

▸*v.* perfume with incense, etc.

**in·cense**[2] /in'sens/ ▸*v.* enrage; make angry: *she was incensed by the accusation.*

**in·cen·tive** /in'sentiv/ ▸*n.* **1** motive or incitement to action. **2** payment or concession to stimulate greater output by workers.

▸*adj.* serving to motivate or incite.

**in·cep·tion** /in'sepsHən/ ▸*n.* beginning.

**in·ces·sant** /in'sesənt/ ▸*adj.* unceasing; continual. —**in·ces·sant·ly** *adv.*

**in·cest** /'in,sest/ ▸*n.* sexual intercourse between persons regarded as too closely related to legally marry each other.

**inch** /incH/ ▸*n.* unit of linear measure equal to one-twelfth of a foot (2.54 cm).

▸*v.* move gradually: *inched forward.*

**in·cho·ate** /in'kōit/ ▸*adj.* **1** just begun. **2** undeveloped; rudimentary; unformed.

**in·ci·dence** /'insidəns/ ▸*n.* **1** fact, manner, or rate of occurrence or action. **2** range, scope, or extent of influence of a thing.

**in·ci·dent** ▸*n.* **1** occurrence. **2** hostile clash, esp. of warring troops.

▸*adj.* **1** apt or liable to happen; naturally attaching: **2** (of light, etc.) falling on or upon.

**in·cin·er·ate** /in'sinə,rāt/ ▸*v.* burn to ashes. —**in·cin·er·a·tion** *n.* —**in·cin·er·a·tor** *n.*

**in·cip·i·ent** /in'sipēənt/ ▸*adj.* **1** beginning. **2** in an initial stage. —**in·cip·i·ence** *n.* —**in·cip·i·ent·ly** *adv.*

**in·cise** /in'sīz/ ▸*v.* **1** make a cut in. **2** engrave. —**in·ci·sion** *n.*

**in·ci·sive** /in'sīsiv/ ▸*adj.* **1** mentally sharp. **2** clear; penetrating. —**in·ci·sive·ly** *adv.*

**in·ci·sor** /in'sīzər/ ▸*n.* cutting tooth, esp. at the front of the mouth.

**in·cite** /in'sīt/ ▸*v.* urge or stir up. —**in·cite·ment** *n.*

**in·clem·ent** /in'klemənt/ ▸*adj.* (of the weather) unpleasantly cold or wet.

**in·cline** ▸*v.* /in'klīn/ **1** have a tendency to; be disposed to: **2** lean or slope.
▸*n.* /'in,klīn/ slope.
—**in·cli·na·tion** *n.*

**in·clude** /in'klood/ ▸*v.* **1** comprise or reckon in as part of a whole; place in a class or category. **2** [as *prep.* **including**] if we include: *six members, including the chairperson.* —**in·clu·sion** *n.*

**in·clu·sive** /in'kloosiv/ ▸*adj.* **1** including; comprising. **2** including all the normal services, etc. **3** (of language or programs) designed to appeal to both sexes, all races, etc.

**in·cog·ni·to** /,inkäg'nētō/ ▸*adj. & adv.* with one's name or identity kept secret.

**in·come** /'in,kəm/ ▸*n.* money received from one's work, investments, etc.

**in·com·mu·ni·ca·do** /,inkə-,myoōni'kädō/ ▸*adj.* **1** without means of communication. **2** in solitary confinement.

**in·com·pa·ra·ble** /in-'kämp(ə)rəbəl/ ▸*adj.* without equal. —**in·com·pa·ra·bly** *adv.*

**in·con·nu** /,inkə'n(y)oō; аnkô'ny/ ▸*n.* unknown person or thing.

**in·con·sid·er·ate** /,inkən-'sidərit/ ▸*adj.* **1** thoughtless. **2** lacking regard for others. —**in·con·sid·er·ate·ly** *adv.*

**in·con·ti·nent** /in'käntənənt/ ▸*adj.* unable to control the bowels or bladder. —**in·con·ti·nence** *n.*

**in·cor·po·rate** /in'kôrpə,rāt/ ▸*v.* **1** unite; form into one body. **2** combine (ingredients) into one substance. **3 a** constitute as a legal corporation. **b** [as *adj.* **incorporated**] forming a legal corporation. —**in·cor·po·ra·tion** *n.*

**in·cor·po·re·al** /,inkôr'pôrēəl/ ▸*adj.* not composed of matter.

**in·cor·ri·gi·ble** /in'kôrijəbəl/ ▸*adj.* **1** (of a person or habit) incurably bad. **2** not readily improved. —**in·cor·ri·gi·bil·i·ty** *n.* —**in·cor·ri·gi·bly** *adv.*

**in·crease** ▸*v.* /in'krēs/ **1** make or become greater or more numerous. **2** intensify (a quality).
▸*n.* /'in,krēs/ **1** growth; enlargement. **2** amount or extent of an increase. —**in·creas·ing·ly** *adv.*

**in·cred·i·ble** /in'kredəbəl/ ▸adj.
**1** not believable. **2** inf. amazingly
good or beautiful. —**in·cred·i·bly**
adv.

**in·cred·u·lous** /in'krejələs/ ▸adj.
unwilling to believe.
—**in·cre·du·li·ty** n.
—**in·cred·u·lous·ly** adv.

**in·cre·ment** /'iNGkrəmənt; 'in-/
▸n. **1** increase, esp. one of a
series on a fixed scale. **2** a small
additional amount.
—**in·cre·men·tal** adj.

**in·crim·i·nate** /in'krimə,nāt/ ▸v.
tend to prove the guilt of:
*incriminating evidence.*
—**in·crim·i·na·tion** n.
—**in·crim·i·na·to·ry** adj.

**in·cu·bate** /'iNGkyə,bāt/ ▸v. sit
on or artificially heat (eggs) in
order to hatch them.

**in·cu·ba·tor** ▸n. warming
apparatus for protecting a
premature baby, hatching eggs,
etc.

**in·cul·cate** /in'kəl,kāt/ ▸v. urge
or impress (a fact, habit, or idea)
persistently. —**in·cul·ca·tion** n.

**in·cum·bent** /in'kəmbənt/ ▸adj.
**1** (**incumbent on/upon**) resting
as a duty of: *incumbent on you to
warn them.* **2** currently holding
office.
▸n. holder of an office or post.

**in·cur** /in'kər/ ▸v. (**-curred**,
**-cur·ring**) suffer or experience
(something unpleasant) as a
result of one's own behavior,
etc.: *incurred huge debts.*

**in·cur·sion** /in'kərzHən/ ▸n.
invasion or attack, esp. when
sudden or brief. —**in·cur·sive**
adj.

**Ind.** ▸abbr. **1** Independent.
**2** Indiana. **3 a** India. **b** Indian.

**in·debt·ed** /in'detid/ ▸adj. owing
gratitude or money.
—**in·debt·ed·ness** n.

**in·de·ci·pher·a·ble** ▸adj. that
cannot be deciphered.

**in·de·ci·sion** ▸n. lack of
decision; hesitation.

**in·deed** ▸adv. **1** in truth; really;
yes; that is so: *they are, indeed,
remarkable.* **2** expressing
emphasis or intensification: *I'm
very glad indeed.* **3** admittedly:
*there are indeed exceptions.*
▸interj. expressing irony,
contempt, incredulity, etc.

**in·de·fat·i·ga·ble** /,ində-
'fatigəbəl/ ▸adj. unwearying;
unremitting.

**in·def·i·nite** ▸adj. **1** vague;
undefined. **2** unlimited. **3** *Gram.*
not determining the person, etc.,
referred to. —**in·def·i·nite·ly** adv.

□ **indefinite article** the word *a* or *an*.

**in·del·i·ble** /in'deləbəl/ ▶*adj.* that cannot be erased or removed. —**in·del·i·bly** *adv.*

**in·dem·ni·fy** /in'demnə,fī/ ▶*v.* (**-fied**) **1** protect or secure from harm, a loss, penalties, etc. **2** compensate for a loss. —**in·dem·ni·fi·ca·tion** *n.*

**in·dent** ▶*v.* /in'dent/ start (a line of print or writing) further from the margin than other lines, e.g., to mark a new paragraph. ▶*n.* /'in,dent/ **1** space left by indenting a line. **2** notch or dent. —**in·den·ta·tion** *n.*

**in·den·ture** /in'denCHər/ ▶*n.* **1** formal legal contract or document. **2** agreement binding an apprentice to a master. ▶*v. hist.* bind by indentures, esp. as an apprentice.

**in·de·pen·dent** /,ində'pendənt/ ▶*adj.* **1** not subject to authority or control. **2** (of income or resources) making it unnecessary to earn one's living. **3** unwilling to be under an obligation to others. **4** *Polit.* (usu. **Independent**) not belonging to or supported by a party. ▶*n.* (usu. **Independent**) person who is politically independent. —**in·de·pen·dence** *n.* —**in·de·pen·dent·ly** *adv.*

**in·de·struc·ti·ble** /,indi-'strəktəbəl/ ▶*adj.* unable to be destroyed. —**in·de·struc·ti·bil·i·ty** *n.* —**in·de·struc·ti·bly** *adv.*

**in·dex** /'in,deks/ ▶*n.* (*pl.* **-dex·es** or esp. in technical use **-di·ces**) **1** alphabetical list of names, subjects, etc., with references, usu. at the end of a book. **2** (also **card in·dex**) index with each item entered on a separate card. **3** (also **in·dex num·ber**) number showing the variation of prices or wages as compared with a chosen base period: *Dow-Jones index.* **4 a** pointer, esp. on an instrument. **b** indicator. ▶*v.* **1** provide with or enter in an index. **2** relate (wages, etc.) to a price index. —**in·dex·er** *n.*

**in·dex fin·ger** ▶*n.* the forefinger.

**In·di·an** /'indēən/ ▶*adj.* **1** of or relating to India, or to the subcontinent comprising India, Pakistan, and Bangladesh. **2** of or relating to the indigenous peoples of America. ▶*n.* **1 a** native or national of India. **b** person of Indian descent. **2** American Indian.

**In·di·an sum·mer** ▸*n.* dry, warm weather in late autumn after a frost.

**in·di·cate** /'indi,kāt/ ▸*v.* **1** point out; show. **2** express the presence of. **3** suggest; require. **4** (of a gauge, etc.) give as a reading. —**in·di·ca·tion** *n.*

**in·dic·a·tive** /in'dikətiv/ ▸*adj.* **1** serving as an indication. **2** *Gram.* stating a fact. ▸*n. Gram.* indicative mood.

**in·dict** /in'dīt/ ▸*v.* accuse formally by legal process. —**in·dict·a·ble** *adj.* —**in·dict·ment** *n.*

**in·dif·fer·ent** ▸*adj.* **1** having no partiality for or against; having no interest in or sympathy for. **2** neither good nor bad; average. —**in·dif·fer·ence** *n.* —**in·dif·fer·ent·ly** *adv.*

**in·dig·e·nous** /in'dijənəs/ ▸*adj.* **1** (esp. of flora or fauna) originating naturally in a region. **2** (of people) born in a region.

**in·di·gent** /'indijənt/ ▸*adj.* needy; poor. —**in·di·gence** *n.*

**in·di·ges·tion** ▸*n.* pain or discomfort in the stomach caused by difficulty in digesting food.

**in·dig·nant** /in'dignənt/ ▸*adj.* angry at supposed injustice; resentful. —**in·dig·na·tion** *n.*

**in·dig·ni·ty** ▸*n.* (*pl.* -ties) **1** humiliating treatment, condition, or position. **2** slight or insult.

**in·di·go** /'indi,gō/ ▸*n.* (*pl.* -gos) deep blue dye obtained from a plant, or this color.

**in·dis·crim·i·nate** /,indi-'skrimənit/ ▸*adj.* done without careful judgment. —**in·dis·crim·i·nate·ly** *adv.*

**in·dis·pen·sa·ble** /,indis-'pensəbəl/ ▸*adj.* absolutely essential.

**in·dis·posed** /,indi'spōzd/ ▸*adj.* slightly unwell. —**in·dis·po·si·tion** *n.*

**in·dis·sol·u·ble** /,indi'sälyəbəl/ ▸*adj.* unable to be destroyed; lasting.

**in·di·vid·u·al** /,ində'vijōōəl/ ▸*adj.* **1** single. **2** particular; special; not general. **3** having a distinct character. **4** designed for use by one person. ▸*n.* **1** single member of a class. **2** single human being. —**in·di·vid·u·al·i·ty** *n.* —**in·di·vid·u·al·ly** *adv.*

**in·di·vid·u·ate** /,ində'vijōō,āt/ ▸*v.* distinguish from others of the same kind; single out.

**in·doc·tri·nate** /in'däktrə,nāt/ ▸*v.* teach to accept certain (esp.

partisan) ideas uncritically.
—**in·doc·tri·na·tion** *n.*

**in·do·lent** /ˈindlənt/ ▸*adj.* lazy.
—**in·do·lence** *n.* —**in·do·lent·ly**
*adv.*

**in·dom·i·ta·ble** /inˈdämitəbəl/
▸*adj.* **1** that cannot be subdued;
unyielding. **2** stubbornly
persistent.

**in·door** ▸*adj.* situated, carried
on, or used within a building or
under cover: *indoor antenna* |
*indoor games.* —**in·doors** *adv.*

**in·du·bi·ta·ble** /inˈd(y)o͞obitəbəl/
▸*adj.* that cannot be doubted.

**in·duce** /inˈd(y)o͞os/ ▸*v.* **1** prevail
on; persuade. **2** *Med.* bring on
(labor) artificially.
—**in·duce·ment** *n.*

**in·duct** /inˈdəkt/ ▸*v.* enlist (a
person) for military service.
—**in·duc·tee** *n.*

**in·duc·tion** ▸*n.* **1** act or an
instance of inducting or
inducing. **2** *Logic* inference of a
general law from particular
instances. **3** *Electr.* production of
an electric or magnetic state, or
an electric current, by the
proximity (without contact) of
an electrified or magnetized
body. **4** enlistment for military
service.

**in·dulge** /inˈdəlj/ ▸*v.* **1** (**indulge
in**) allow oneself to enjoy the
pleasure of. **2** yield freely to (a
desire, esp. to drink alcohol).
**3** allow someone to enjoy a
desired pleasure. —**in·dulg·ent**
*adj.* —**in·dulg·ence** *n.*

**in·du·rate** /ˈind(y)əˌrāt/ ▸*v.*
harden.

**in·dus·tri·al·ist** /inˈdəstrēəlist/
▸*n.* person engaged in the
management of industry.

**in·dus·tri·al·ize** ▸*v.* introduce
industries to (a country or
region, etc.).
—**in·dus·tri·a·li·za·tion** *n.*

**in·dus·tri·ous** /inˈdəstrēəs/ ▸*adj.*
diligent; hardworking.

**in·dus·try** /ˈindəstrē/ ▸*n.* (*pl.*
**-tries**) **1 a** branch of trade or
manufacture. **b** these
collectively. **2** concerted or
copious activity: *the building was
a hive of industry.* **3** diligence.
**4** habitual employment in useful
work. —**in·dus·tri·al** *adj.*

**in·e·bri·ate** /iˈnēbrēˌāt/ ▸*v.* make
drunk.
▸*adj.* tending to drink; drunken.
—**in·e·bri·a·tion** *n.*

**in·ef·fa·ble** /inˈefəbəl/ ▸*adj.*
unutterable; too great for
description in words.
—**in·ef·fa·bly** *adv.*

**in·ef·fec·tu·al** /ˌiniˈfekCHŌŌəl/ ▸adj. **1** without effect. **2** (of a person) unable to achieve results. —**in·ef·fec·tu·al·i·ty** n. —**in·ef·fec·tu·al·ly** adv.

**in·ept** /iˈnept/ ▸adj. without skill; clumsy. —**in·ep·ti·tude** n. —**in·ept·ly** adv.

**in·ert** /iˈnərt/ ▸adj. **1** lacking the ability or strength to move. **2** chemically inactive. —**in·ert·ly** adv.

**in·ev·i·ta·ble** /inˈevitəbəl/ ▸adj. **1** unavoidable. **2** bound to occur. —**in·ev·i·ta·bil·i·ty** n. —**in·ev·i·ta·bly** adv.

**in·ex·o·ra·ble** /inˈeksərəbəl/ ▸adj. relentless. —**in·ex·o·ra·bil·i·ty** n. —**in·ex·o·ra·bly** adv.

**in·ex·pert** /inˈekspərt/ ▸adj. unskillful; lacking expertise. —**in·ex·pert·ly** adv.

**in·ex·pli·ca·ble** /ˌinekˈsplikəbəl/ ▸adj. that cannot be explained. —**in·ex·pli·ca·bly** adv.

**in·ex·tri·ca·ble** /ˌinikˈstrikəbəl/ ▸adj. impossible to untangle, separate, or escape from. —**in·ex·tri·ca·bly** adv.

**in·fal·li·ble** /inˈfaləbəl/ ▸adj. **1** incapable of error. **2** unfailing; sure to succeed. —**in·fal·li·bil·i·ty** n. —**in·fal·li·bly** adv.

**in·fa·mous** /ˈinfəməs/ ▸adj. notoriously bad. —**in·fa·mous·ly** adv. —**in·fa·my** n.

**in·fant** /ˈinfənt/ ▸n. child during the earliest period of its life. —**in·fan·cy** n.

**in·fan·ta** /inˈfantə/ ▸n. daughter of the ruling monarch of Spain or Portugal, esp. the eldest daughter who was not heir to the throne.

**in·fan·te** /inˈfantā/ ▸n. second son of the ruling monarch of Spain or Portugal.

**in·fan·try** /ˈinfəntrē/ ▸n. body of foot soldiers; foot soldiers collectively. —**in·fan·try·man** n.

**in·farct** /ˈinˌfärkt/ ▸n. Med. area of dead tissue caused by an inadequate blood supply. —**in·farc·tion** n.

**in·fat·u·at·ed** /inˈfaCHŌŌˌātid/ ▸adj feeling intense, usu. transitory passion or admiration. —**in·fat·u·ate** v. —**in·fat·u·a·tion** n.

**in·fect** /inˈfekt/ ▸v. contaminate with harmful organisms or noxious matter. —**in·fec·tion** n.

**in·fec·tious** /inˈfekSHəs/ ▸adj. **1** transmissible by infection. **2** (of emotions, etc.) quickly affecting others. —**in·fec·tious·ly** adv.

**in·fer** /in'fər/ ▸v. (-ferred, -fer·ring) deduce or conclude from evidence.

**in·fe·ri·or** /in'fi(ə)rēər/ ▸adj. **1 a** below. **b** of lower rank, quality, etc. **2** poor in quality. ▸n. person inferior to another. —**in·fe·ri·or·i·ty** n.

**in·fer·nal** /in'fərnl/ ▸adj. **1** of or like hell. **2** irritating. —**in·fer·nal·ly** adv.

**in·fer·no** /in'fərnō/ ▸n. (pl. -nos) **1** raging fire. **2** hell.

**in·fest** /in'fest/ ▸v. (esp. vermin) overrun (a place). —**in·fes·ta·tion** n.

**in·fi·del** /'infidl/ ▸n. unbeliever in a particular religion. ▸adj. of unbelievers.

**in·field** ▸n. Baseball **1** area enclosed by the three bases and home plate. **2** the four fielders stationed near the bases. —**in·field·er** n.

**in·fight·ing** ▸n. hidden conflict within an organization. —**in·fight·er** n.

**in·fil·trate** /'infil,trāt;/ ▸v. **1** gain entrance or access surreptitiously (as spies, etc.). **2** permeate by filtration. —**in·fil·tra·tion** n.

**in·fi·nite** /'infənit/ ▸adj. **1** endless. **2** very great or many.

**in·fin·i·tes·i·mal** /ˌinfini-'tesəməl/ ▸adj. extremely small.

**in·fin·i·tive** /in'finitiv/ Gram. ▸n. form of a verb without a particular subject, tense, etc. as see in we came to see | let him see. ▸adj. having this form.

**in·firm** /in'fərm/ ▸adj. weak, esp. through age. —**in·firm·i·ty** n.

**in·fir·ma·ry** /in'fərm(ə)rē/ ▸n. (pl. -ries) place for those who are ill, as at school, etc.

**in fla·gran·te de·lic·to** /ˌin flə'gräntā də'liktō/ (also **in fla·gran·te**) ▸adv. in the very act of wrongdoing, esp. in an act of sexual misconduct.

**in·flame** ▸v. **1** provoke or become provoked to strong feeling, esp. anger. **2** Med. become or cause to become hot, red, and sore. **3** aggravate. —**in·flam·ma·tion** n.

**in·flam·ma·ble** /in'flaməbəl/ ▸adj. **1** easily set on fire. **2** easily excited.

**in·flam·ma·to·ry** /in'flamə,tôrē/ ▸adj. tending to cause anger.

**in·flate** /in'flāt/ ▸v. **1** distend with air or gas. **2** puff up (with pride, etc.). **3** raise (prices) artificially. **4** [as adj. **inflated**] (esp. of language) bombastic. —**in·flat·ed·ly** adv.

**in·fla·tion** /in'flāsHən/ ▸*n.* **1** act, instance, or condition of inflating. **2** general increase in prices and fall in the purchasing value of money. —**in·fla·tion·ar·y** *adj.*

**in·flect** /in'flekt/ ▸*v.* **1** change the pitch of (the voice, etc.). **2** *Gram.* change the form of (a word) to express tense, gender, number, mood, etc. —**in·flec·tion** *n.*

**in·flict** /in'flikt/ ▸*v.* **1** deal (a stroke, wound, etc.). **2** impose (suffering, oneself, etc.) on.

**in·flu·ence** /'inflо̄о̄əns/ ▸*n.* **1** effect a person or thing has on another. **2** moral ascendancy or power. ▸*v.* exert influence on. □ **under the influence** *inf.* affected by alcoholic drink.

**in·flu·en·tial** ▸*adj.* having great power or influence.

**in·flu·en·za** /ˌinflо̄о̄'enzə/ ▸*n.* highly contagious virus infection often occurring in epidemics; the flu.

**in·flux** /'inˌfləks/ ▸*n.* continual stream of people or things.

**in·fo·mer·cial** /'infōˌmərsHəl/ ▸*n.* TV program promoting a product.

**in·form** /in'fôrm/ ▸*v.* **1** give (someone) information; tell. **2** make an accusation. —**in·form·ant** *n.* —**in·form·a·tive** *adj.*

**in·for·ma·tion** /ˌinfər'māsHən/ ▸*n.* **1** knowledge; facts. **2** *Computing* data stored or generated by a program.

**in·fo·tain·ment** /ˌinfō'tānmənt/ ▸*n.* **1** factual information presented in dramatized form on TV. **2** TV program mixing news and entertainment.

**in·frac·tion** /in'fraksHən/ ▸*n.* violation or infringement of a law, etc.

**in·fra·red** /ˌinfrə'red/ ▸*adj.* of or using a wavelength just greater than the red end of the visible spectrum.

**in·fra·struc·ture** /'infrəˌstrəkcHər/ ▸*n.* basic structural foundations, esp. roads, bridges, sewers, etc.

**in·fringe** /in'frinj/ ▸*v.* **1** violate (a law, an oath, etc.). **2** (**infringe on/upon**) encroach; trespass. —**in·fringe·ment** *n.*

**in·fu·ri·ate** /in'fyо̄о̄rēˌāt/ ▸*v.* fill with fury; enrage.

**in·fuse** /in'fyо̄о̄z/ ▸*v.* **1** fill; pervade; instill. **2** steep (herbs, tea, etc.) in liquid. —**in·fu·sion** *n.*

**in·ge·nious** /in'jēnyəs/ ▶*adj.*
**1** clever, original, and inventive.
**2** (of a machine) cleverly
contrived. —**in·ge·ni·ous·ly** *adv.*

**in·ge·nue** /'anzHə,n(y)ōō/ (also
**in·gé·nue**) ▶*n.* **1** unsophisticated
young woman. **2 a** such a part
in a play. **b** actress who plays
this part.

**in·ge·nu·i·ty** /ˌinjə'n(y)ōōitē/ ▶*n.*
quality of being clever, original,
and inventive.

**in·gen·u·ous** /in'jenyōōəs/ ▶*adj.*
(of a person) innocent and
unsuspecting. —**in·gen·u·ous·ly**
*adv.*

**in·gest** /in'jest/ ▶*v.* take in (food,
etc.); eat. —**in·ges·tion** *n.*

**in·got** /'iNGgət/ ▶*n.* bar of cast
metal, esp. of gold.

**in·grained** /in'grānd/ ▶*adj.*
**1** deeply rooted. **2** (of dirt)
deeply embedded.

**in·grate** /'in,grāt/ ▶*n.* ungrateful
person.

**in·gra·ti·ate** /in'grāsHē,āt/ ▶*v.*
bring oneself into favor: *she
ingratiated herself with the
professor.*

**in·gre·di·ent** /in'grēdēənt/ ▶*n.*
component part or element in a
recipe, mixture, or combination.

**in·gress** /'in,gres/ ▶*n.* **1** act or
right of entering. **2** means of
entrance. —**in·gres·sion** *n.*

**in·hab·it** /in'habit/ ▶*v.* dwell in;
occupy (a region, town, house,
etc.). —**in·hab·it·ant** *n.*

**in·hal·ant** /in'hālənt/ ▶*n.*
medicine for inhaling.

**in·hale** /in'hāl/ ▶*v.* breathe in (air,
gas, tobacco smoke, etc.).
—**in·ha·la·tion** *n.*

**in·hal·er** ▶*n.* device for
administering an inhalant.

**in·here** /in'hi(ə)r/ ▶*v.* be inherent.

**in·her·ent** /in'hi(ə)rənt/ ▶*adj.*
**1** existing in something, esp. as a
permanent or characteristic
attribute. **2** vested in (a person,
etc.) as a right or privilege.

**in·her·it** /in'herit/ ▶*v.* **1** receive
(property, rank, etc.) by legal
succession. **2** derive (a quality or
characteristic) genetically from
one's ancestors. **3** succeed as an
heir: *a younger son rarely inherits.*
—**in·her·it·a·ble** *adj.*
—**in·her·i·tance** *n.*

**in·hib·it** /in'hibit/ ▶*v.* **1** hinder,
restrain, or prevent. **2** [as *adj.*
**inhibited**] subject to inhibition.
**3** forbid or prohibit.
—**in·hib·i·tion** *n.* —**in·hib·i·to·ry**
*adj.*

**in·hu·man** /in'(h)yōōmən/ ▶*adj.*
**1** brutal; unfeeling; barbarous.

**2** not of a human type.
—**in·hu·man·i·ty** *n.*
—**in·hu·man·ly** *adv.*

**in·im·i·cal** /i'nimikəl/ ▸*adj.*
**1** hostile. **2** harmful.
—**in·im·i·cal·ly** *adv.*

**in·im·i·ta·ble** /i'nimitəbəl/ ▸*adj.*
impossible to imitate.

**in·iq·ui·ty** /i'nikwitē/ ▸*n.* (*pl.* **-ties**)
**1** wickedness; unrighteousness.
**2** gross injustice. —**in·iq·ui·tous**
*adj.*

**in·i·tial** /i'nisHəl/ ▸*adj.* of,
existing, or occurring at the
beginning.
▸*n.* (usu. **initials**) the first letter of
a (esp. a person's) name.
▸*v.* mark or sign with one's
initials. —**in·i·tial·ly** *adv.*

**in·i·ti·ate** ▸*v.* /i'nisHē,āt/
**1** begin; set going. **2** admit (a
person) into a society, an office,
a secret, etc., esp. with a ritual.
▸*n.* /i'nisHēit/ initiated person.
—**in·i·ti·a·tion** *n.*

**in·i·ti·a·tive** /i'nisH(ē)ətiv/ ▸*n.*
**1** ability to initiate things;
enterprise. **2** right of citizens
outside the legislature to
originate legislation.

**in·ject** /in'jekt/ ▸*v.* **1** drive or
force (a solution, medicine, etc.)
into a person's or animal's body
by or as if by a syringe.

**2** introduce (a new element) into
something. —**in·jec·tion** *n.*

**in·junc·tion** /in'jəNG(k)sHən/ ▸*n.*
**1** authoritative warning or order.
**2** *Law* judicial order restraining
or compelling some action.
—**in·junc·tive** *adj.*

**in·jure** /'injər/ ▸*v.* **1** harm;
damage. **2** impair. **3** do wrong
to. —**in·jured** *adj.*

**in·ju·ry** /'injərē/ ▸*n.* (*pl.* **-ries**)
harm or damage. —**in·ju·ri· ous**
*adj,*

**ink** /iNGk/ ▸*n.* colored fluid or
paste used for writing, printing,
etc.
▸*v.* cover (type, etc.) with ink
before printing.

**ink-jet print·er** (also **ink·jet
print·er**) ▸*n.* computer-controlled
printer in which minute
droplets of ink are projected
onto the paper.

**ink·ling** /'iNGkliNG/ ▸*n.* slight
knowledge or suspicion; hint.

**in·land** ▸*adj. & adv.* in, toward, or
situated in the interior of a
country.
▸*n.* interior parts of a country.

**in-law** ▸*n.* relative by marriage.

**in·lay** ▸*v.* (*past* and *past part.*
**in·laid**) **1** embed (a thing in
another) so that the surfaces are
even. **2** [as *adj.* **inlaid**] (of a piece

of furniture, etc.) ornamented by inlaying.

▶ *n.* **1** inlaid work. **2** filling shaped to fit a tooth cavity.

**in·let** ▶ *n.* small arm of the sea, lake, or river.

**in·line skate** ▶ *n.* roller skate with wheels in a single line.

**in lo·co pa·ren·tis** /in ˌlōkō pə-ˈrentis/ ▶ *adv.* & *adj.* (of a teacher or other adult responsible for children) in the place of a parent.

**in·mate** /ˈinˌmāt/ ▶ *n.* occupant of a prison.

**in mem·o·ri·am** /ˌin mə-ˈmôrēəm/ ▶ *prep.* in memory of (a dead person).

**in·most** ▶ *adj.* most inward.

**inn** /in/ ▶ *n.* **1** small hotel. **2** restaurant or tavern.

**in·nards** /ˈinərdz/ ▶ *pl. n. inf.* entrails.

**in·nate** /iˈnāt/ ▶ *adj.* inborn; natural.

**in·ner** /ˈinər/ ▶ *adj.* **1** inside; interior. **2** (of thoughts, feelings, etc.) deeper; more secret. —**in·ner·most** *adj.*

**in·ner ci·ty** ▶ *n.* central most densely populated area of a city: *inner-city housing.*

**in·ner tube** ▶ *n.* separate inflatable tube inside a pneumatic tire.

**in·ning** ▶ *n. Baseball* **1** division of a game during which both teams bat. **2** single turn at bat for a team.

**in·no·cent** /ˈinəsənt/ ▶ *adj.* **1** free from moral wrong. **2** not guilty (of a crime, etc.). **3** simple; guileless; harmless. —**in·no·cence** *n.*

**in·noc·u·ous** /iˈnäkyōōəs/ ▶ *adj.* **1** harmless. **2** inoffensive.

**in·no·vate** /ˈinəˌvāt/ ▶ *v.* bring in new methods, ideas, etc. —**in·no·va·tion** *n.* —**in·no·va·tive** *adj.*

**in·nu·en·do** /ˌinyōōˈendō/ ▶ *n.* (*pl.* **-dos** or **-does**) allusive remark or hint, usu. disparaging or suggestive.

**in·nu·mer·a·ble** /i-ˈn(y)ōōmərəbəl/ ▶ *adj.* too many to be counted.

**in·oc·u·late** /iˈnäkyəˌlāt/ ▶ *v.* treat with a vaccine or serum to promote immunity against disease. —**in·oc·u·la·tion** *n.*

**in·or·di·nate** /iˈnôrdn-it/ ▶ *adj.* disproportionately large; excessive. —**in·or·di·nate·ly** *adv.*

**in·pa·tient** /ˈinˌpāsHənt/ ▶ *n.* patient who stays in the hospital while under treatment.

**in·put** ▸*n.* **1** what is put in or taken in, or operated on by any process or system. **2** information fed into a computer. **3** contribution of information, etc. ▸*v.* (**-put·ting**; *past* and *past part.* **-put** or **-put·ted**) *Computing* supply (data, programs, etc., to a computer, program, etc.). —**in·put·ter** *n.*

**in·quest** /'in,kwest/ ▸*n. Law* inquiry by a coroner into the cause of a death.

**in·quire** /in'kwī(ə)r/ ▸*v.* **1** make a formal investigation. **2** ask. —**in·qui·ry** *n.*

**in·qui·si·tion** /ˌinkwi'zishən/ ▸*n.* **1** prolonged and intensive questioning or investigation. **2** (**the Inquisition**) ecclesiastical tribunal for the violent suppression of heresy, esp. in Spain. —**in·qui·si·tor** *n.*

**in·qui·si·tive** /in'kwizitiv/ ▸*adj.* **1** unduly curious. **2** seeking knowledge.

**in re** /ˌin 'rā/ ▸*prep.* in the legal case of; with regard to.

**in rem** /ˌin 'rem/ ▸*adj.* made or availing against or affecting a thing, and therefore other people generally; imposing a general liability.

**in·road** /'in,rōd/ ▸*n.* **1** (usu. **inroads**) progress: *made inroads in controlling spending.* **2** hostile attack.

**INS** ▸*abbr.* Immigration and Naturalization Service.

**in·sane** /in'sān/ ▸*adj.* **1** not of sound mind; mad. **2** *inf.* extremely foolish. —**in·san·i·ty** *n.*

**in·sa·tia·ble** /in'sāsHəbəl/ ▸*adj.* **1** unable to be satisfied. **2** extremely greedy.

**in·scape** /'in,skāp/ ▸*n.* unique inner nature of a person or object as shown in a work of art, esp. a poem.

**in·scribe** /in'skrīb/ ▸*v.* **1** write or carve (words, etc.) on stone, paper, etc. **2** write an informal dedication in (a book). —**in·scrip·tion** *n.*

**in·scru·ta·ble** /in'skrōōtəbəl/ ▸*adj.* mysterious; impenetrable. —**in·scru·ta·bly** *adv.*

**in·sect** /'in,sekt/ ▸*n.* **1** any arthropod having a head, thorax, abdomen, two antennae, three pairs of thoracic legs, and usu. one or two pairs of thoracic wings. **2** (loosely) any other small segmented invertebrate animal.

**in·sec·ti·cide** /in'sekti,sīd/ ▸n. substance used for killing insects.

**in·sem·i·nate** /in'semə,nāt/ ▸v. introduce semen into. —**in·sem·i·na·tion** n.

**in·sen·si·ble** /in'sensəbəl/ ▸adj. 1 unconscious. 2 unaware of; indifferent to. 3 callous.

**in·sert** ▸v. /in'sərt/ place, fit, or thrust (a thing) into another. ▸n. /'in,sərt/ something inserted, e.g., a loose page in a magazine. —**in·ser·tion** n.

**in·shore** ▸adv. & adj. at sea but close to the shore.

**in·side** ▸n. 1 inner side; inner part. 2 (**insides**) inf. stomach and bowels. ▸adj. situated on or in the inside; (of information, etc.) available only to those on the inside. ▸adv. 1 on, in, or to the inside. 2 inf. in prison. ▸prep. 1 on the inner side of; within. 2 in less than: inside an hour. □ **inside out** with the inner surface turned outward.

**in·sid·er** ▸n. 1 person who is within a society, organization, etc. 2 person privy to a secret.

**in·sid·er trad·ing** ▸n. illegal practice of stock trading while having access to confidential information.

**in·sid·i·ous** /in'sidēəs/ ▸adj. 1 proceeding inconspicuously but harmfully. 2 treacherous. —**in·sid·i·ous·ly** adv. —**in·sid·i·ous·ness** n.

**in·sight** ▸n. 1 capacity of understanding hidden truths, etc. 2 instance of this. —**in·sight·ful** adj.

**in·sig·ni·a** /in'signēə/ ▸n. [treated as sing. or pl.] 1 badge. 2 distinguishing mark.

**in·sin·u·ate** /in'sinyoō,āt/ ▸v. 1 convey indirectly. 2 (**insinuate oneself into**) introduce (oneself, a person, etc.) into favor, etc., by subtle manipulation. —**in·sin·u·a·tion** n.

**in·sip·id** /in'sipid/ ▸adj. 1 lacking vigor; dull. 2 lacking flavor.

**in·sist** /in'sist/ ▸v. maintain or demand assertively. —**in·sist·ent** adj.

**in·sole** ▸n. inner sole of a boot or shoe.

**in·so·lent** /'insələnt/ ▸adj. offensively contemptuous or arrogant; insulting. —**in·so·lence** n. —**in·so·lent·ly** adv.

**in·sol·vent** ▸adj. unable to pay one's debts. —**in·sol·ven·cy** n.

**in·som·ni·a** /in'sämnēə/ ▸n. habitual sleeplessness; inability to sleep. —**in·som·ni·ac** n. & adj.

**in·so·much** ▸adv. **1** (**insomuch that**) to such an extent. **2** in (**insomuch as**) as much as.

**in·sou·ci·ance** /in'sōōsēəns; ˌʌnsōō'syäns/ ▸n. casual lack of concern; indifference.

**in·sou·ci·ant** /in'sōōsēənt/ ▸adj. carefree; unconcerned. —**in·sou·ci·ance** n. —**in·sou·ci·ant·ly** adv.

**in·spect** /in'spekt/ ▸v. **1** look closely at or into. **2** examine (a document, etc.) officially. —**in·spec·tion** n.

**in·spec·tor** ▸n. **1** person who inspects. **2** police officer usu. ranking just below a superintendent.

**in·spire** /in'spī(ə)r/ ▸v. **1** fill (someone) with the urge or ability to do something. **2** create (a positive feeling) in someone: *inspire confidence*. **3** [as adj. **inspired**] a (of a work of art, etc.) as if prompted by a supernatural source. **4** inhale. —**in·spir·a·tion** n. —**in·spir·ing** adj.

**inst.** ▸abbr. **1** instance. **2** institute. **3** institution. **4** instrument.

**in·stall** /in'stôl/ ▸v. (**-stalled, -stall·ing**) **1** place (equipment, etc.) in position ready for use. **2** establish in a place. —**in·stal·la·tion** n.

**in·stall·ment** ▸n. **1** any of several usu. equal payments. **2** any of several parts, as of a TV or radio serial.

**in·stall·ment plan** ▸n. payment by installments.

**in·stance** /'instəns/ ▸n. **1** example or illustration of. **2** particular case. □ **for instance** as an example.

**in·stant** /'instənt/ ▸adj. **1** occurring immediately. **2 a** (of food, etc.) processed for quick preparation. ▸n. **1** precise moment. **2** short space of time.

**in·stan·ta·ne·ous** /ˌinstən-'tānēəs/ ▸adj. occurring or done in an instant.

**in·stant re·play** ▸n. immediate repetition of part of a videotaped sports event.

**in·stead** /in'sted/ ▸adv. **1** (**instead of**) as an alternative to: *instead of this one*. **2** as an alternative: *took me instead*.

**in·step** ▸n. **1** inner arch of the foot between the toes and the ankle. **2** part of a shoe, etc., over or under this.

**in·sti·gate** /ˈinstiˌgāt/ ▶v. bring about by incitement or persuasion. —**in·sti·ga·tion** n. —**in·sti·ga·tive** adj.

**in·still** ▶v. (**-stilled, -still·ing**) introduce (a feeling, idea, etc.) gradually.

**in·stinct** /ˈinstiNG(k)t/ ▶n. **1** innate pattern of behavior, esp. in animals. **2** unconscious skill; intuition. —**in·stinc·tive** adj. —**in·stinc·tu·al** adj.

**in·sti·tute** /ˈinstiˌt(y)o͞ot/ ▶n. society or organization for the promotion of science, education, etc.
▶v. **1** establish; found. **2** initiate (an inquiry, etc.).

**in·sti·tu·tion** ▶n. **1** society or organization founded esp. for a particular purpose. **2** established law, practice, or custom. **3** (of a person, a custom, etc.) familiar object. **4** establishment of a cleric, etc., in a church. —**in·sti·tu·tion·al** adj.

**in·struct** /inˈstrəkt/ ▶v. **1** teach. **2** command.

**in·struc·tion** ▶n. **1** direction; order. **2** teaching; education.

**in·struc·tor** ▶n. **1** teacher.

**2** university teacher below assistant professor.

**in·stru·ment** /ˈinstrəmənt/ ▶n. **1** tool or implement, esp. for delicate or scientific work. **2** (**mu·sic·al in·stru·ment**) device for producing musical sounds.

**in·su·lar** /ˈins(y)ələr/ ▶adj. **1** separated or remote. **2** narrow-minded. —**in·su·lar·i·ty** n.

**in·su·late** /ˈins(y)əˌlāt/ ▶v. **1** prevent the passage of electricity, heat, or sound by interposing nonconductors. **2** protect from unpleasant effects of something. —**in·su·la·tion** n. —**in·su·la·tor** n.

**in·su·lin** /ˈinsəlin/ ▶n. hormone regulating the amount of glucose in the blood, the lack of which causes diabetes.

**in·sult** ▶v. /inˈsəlt/ speak to or treat with scornful abuse.
▶n. /ˈinˌsəlt/ insulting remark or action. —**in·sult·ing·ly** adv.

**in·su·per·a·ble** /inˈso͞op(ə)rəbəl/ ▶adj. (of a barrier or difficulty) impossible to surmount. —**in·su·per·a·bil·i·ty** n.

**in·sur·ance** /inˈSHo͝orəns/ ▶n. **1** insuring. **2 a** sum paid for this. **b** sum paid out as compensation for theft, damage, loss, etc.

□ **insurance policy** contract of insurance.

**in·sure** /inˈSHŏŏr/ ▶v. arrange for compensation in the event of damage to or loss of (property, life, etc.) in exchange for regular advance payments to a company or the government.
—**in·sur·a·ble** adj. —**in·sur·er** n.

**in·sur·gent** /inˈsərjənt/ ▶adj. rising in active revolt.
▶n. rebel. —**in·sur·gence** n. —**in·sur·gen·cy** n.

**in·sur·rec·tion** /ˌinsəˈrekSHən/ ▶n. rebellion.
—**in·sur·rec·tion·ist** n.

**in·tact** /inˈtakt/ ▶adj. **1** entire. **2** untouched.

**in·take** ▶n. **1** action of taking in. **2** amount taken in. **3** place where water, fuel, or air is taken in.

**in·te·ger** /ˈintijər/ ▶n. whole number.

**in·te·gral** /ˈintigrəl/ ▶adj. **1 a** of or necessary to a whole. **b** forming a whole. **c** complete. **2** Math. of or denoted by an integer. —**in·teg·ral·ly** adv.

**in·te·grate** /ˈintiˌgrāt/ ▶v. **1** combine (parts) into a whole. **2** bring or come into equal participation in society, a school, etc. **3** desegregate, esp. racially.
—**in·te·gra·tion** n.

**in·te·grat·ed cir·cuit** ▶n. Electronics small chip, etc., of material replacing several separate components in a conventional electrical circuit.

**in·teg·ri·ty** /inˈtegritē/ ▶n. **1** uprightness; honesty. **2** wholeness; soundness.

**in·teg·u·ment** /inˈtegyəmənt/ ▶n. natural outer covering, as a skin, husk, rind, etc.

**in·tel·lect** /ˈintlˌekt/ ▶n. **1** faculty of reasoning, knowing, and thinking, as distinct from feeling. **2** clever or knowledgeable person.

**in·tel·lec·tu·al** /ˌintlˈekCHŏŏəl/ ▶adj. **1** of or relating to the intellect. **2** possessing a high level of intelligence.
▶n. person possessing a highly developed intellect.
—**in·tel·lec·tu·a·lize** v.
—**in·tel·lec·tu·al·ly** adv.

**in·tel·li·gence** /inˈtelijəns/ ▶n. **1 a** intellect; understanding. **b** quickness of understanding. **2 a** collection of information, esp. of military or political value. **b** information; news.

**in·tell·i·gence quo·tient** (Abbr.: **IQ**) ▶n. number denoting the ratio of a person's intelligence to the normal or average, considered to be 100.

**in·tel·li·gent** /in'telijənt/ ▸*adj.* having or showing intelligence, esp. of a high level. —**in·tel·li·gent·ly** *adv.*

**in·tel·li·gi·ble** /in'telijəbəl/ ▸*adj.* able to be understood. —**in·tel·li·gi·bil·i·ty** *n.*

**in·tend** /in'tend/ ▸*v.* **1** have as one's purpose; plan. **2** mean: *I intended no offense.*

**in·tend·ed** ▸*adj.* **1** done on purpose. **2** designed; meant. ▸*n.* one's fiancé or fiancée.

**in·tense** /in'tens/ ▸*adj.* (**-tens·er, -tens·est**) **1** existing in a high degree; violent; forceful. **2** very emotional. —**in·tense·ly** *adv.*

**in·ten·sive** ▸*adj.* **1** thorough; vigorous. **2** *Gram.* (of an adjective, adverb, etc.) expressing intensity, as *really* in *my feet are really cold.* —**in·ten·sive·ly** *adv.*

**in·ten·sive care** ▸*n.* **1** medical treatment with constant monitoring, etc., of a dangerously ill patient. **2** special unit of a hospital for such treatment: *he has been in intensive care since last night.*

**in·tent** /in'tent/ ▸*n.* intention; purpose.
▸*adj.* **1** (**intent on**) resolved; determined. **2** attentively occupied. **3** (esp. of a look) earnest. —**in·tent·ly** *adv.*
□ **to** (or **for**) **all intents and purposes** practically; virtually.

**in·ten·tion** /in'tenCHən/ ▸*n.* thing intended; aim or purpose. —**in·ten·tion·al** *adj.*

**in·ter** /in'tər/ ▸*v.* (**-terred, -ter·ring**) bury (a corpse, etc.).

**inter-** /'intər/ ▸*comb. form* **1** between; among: *intercontinental.* **2** mutually; reciprocally: *interbreed.*

**in·ter·act** ▸*v.* act on each other. —**in·ter·ac·tion** *n.*

**in·ter a·li·a** /'intər 'ālēə; 'älēə/ ▸*adv.* among other things.

**in·ter·breed** ▸*v.* (*past* and *past part.* **-bred**) **1** breed or cause to breed with members of a different race or species to produce a hybrid. **2** breed within one family, etc.

**in·ter·cede** /ˌintər'sēd/ ▸*v.* intervene on behalf of another. —**in·ter·ces·sion** *n.*

**in·ter·cept** /ˌintər'sept/ ▸*v.* seize, catch, or stop (a person or thing) going from one place to another. —**in·ter·cep·tion** *n.*

**in·ter·change** ▶v. /ˌintərˈcHānj/ 1 (of two people) exchange (things) with each other. 2 put each of (two things) in the other's place; alternate.
▶n. /ˈintərˌcHānj/ 1 reciprocal exchange between two people, etc. 2 alternation. 3 road junction designed on several levels so that traffic streams do not intersect.
—in·ter·change·a·ble adj.

**in·ter·con·ti·nen·tal** ▶adj. connecting or traveling between continents.

**in·ter·course** ▶n.
1 communication or dealings between individuals, nations, etc. 2 SEXUAL INTERCOURSE.

**in·ter·de·nom·i·na·tion·al** ▶adj. concerning more than one (religious) denomination.

**in·ter·de·pend·ent** ▶adj. (of two or more people or things) dependent on each other: *interdependent economies.*
—in·ter·de·pend·ence n.

**in·ter·dict** /ˈintərˌdikt/ ▶n. formal or authoritative prohibition.
▶v. 1 prohibit (an action); restrain from. 2 forbid the use of.
—in·ter·dic·tion n.

**in·ter·est** /ˈint(ə)rist/ ▶n.
1 a curiosity; concern. b quality exciting curiosity, etc. 2 subject, hobby, etc., in which one is concerned. 3 money paid for the use of money lent. 4 financial stake (in an undertaking, etc.).
▶v. 1 excite the curiosity or attention of. 2 [as adj. **interested**] not impartial: *an interested party.*

**in·ter·est·ing** ▶adj. causing curiosity; holding the attention.

**in·ter·face** ▶n. 1 point where interaction occurs between two systems, etc. 2 *Computing* a apparatus for connecting two pieces of equipment so that they can be operated jointly. b means by which a user interacts with a program or application.
▶v. (**interface with**) connect with.

**in·ter·fere** /ˌintərˈfi(ə)r/ ▶v. 1 a (of a person) meddle; obstruct a process, etc. b (of a thing) be a hindrance. 2 intervene, esp. without invitation or necessity. 3 molest or assault sexually.

**in·ter·im** /ˈintərəm/ ▶n. intervening time.
▶adj. provisional; temporary.

**in·te·ri·or** /inˈti(ə)rēər/ ▶adj.
1 inner. 2 inland. 3 internal; domestic. 4 situated further in or within.
▶n. 1 inner or inside part of

something. **2** inland part of a country. **3** internal affairs. —**in·te·ri·or·ize** *v.* —**in·te·ri·or·ly** *adv.*

**in·ter·ject** /ˌintərˈjekt/ ▶*v.* interrupt someone speaking.

**in·ter·jec·tion** /ˌintərˈjeksHən/ ▶*n. Gram.* exclamation, esp. as a part of speech, e.g., *ah!* | *dear me!*

**in·ter·lace** ▶*v.* bind or wind intricately together.

**in·ter·lock** ▶*v.* **1** engage with each other by overlapping. **2** lock or clasp within each other.

**in·ter·loc·u·tor** /ˌintərˈläkyətər/ ▶*n.* person who takes part in a conversation. —**in·ter·lo·cu·tion** *n.*

**in·ter·loc·u·to·ry** /ˌintərˈläkyəˌtôrē/ ▶*adj. Law* (of a decree, etc.) given provisionally.

**in·ter·lop·er** /ˈintərˌlōpər/ ▶*n.* **1** intruder. **2** person who interferes in others' affairs, esp. for profit. —**in·ter·lope** *v.*

**in·ter·lude** /ˈintərˌlood/ ▶*n.* **1** intervening time, space, or event that contrasts with what goes before or after. **2** pause between the acts of a play.

**in·ter·mar·ry** ▶*v.* (**-ried**) become connected by marriage. —**in·ter·mar·riage** *n.*

**in·ter·me·di·ar·y** /ˌintərˈmēdēˌerē/ ▶*n.* (*pl.* **-ies**) mediator; go-between. ▶*adj.* acting as mediator; intermediate.

**in·ter·me·di·ate** /ˌintərˈmēdēit/ ▶*adj.* coming between two things in time, place, order, etc. ▶*n.* intermediate thing. ▶*v.* act as intermediary. —**in·ter·me·di·a·tion** *n.* —**in·ter·me·di·a·tor** *n.*

**in·ter·ment** /inˈtərmənt/ ▶*n.* burial.

**in·ter·mi·na·ble** /inˈtərmənəbəl/ ▶*adj.* **1** endless. **2** tediously long. —**in·ter·mi·na·bly** *adv.*

**in·ter·mis·sion** /ˌintərˈmisHən/ ▶*n.* **1** pause or break. **2** interval between parts of a play, concert, etc.

**in·ter·mit·tent** /ˌintərˈmitnt/ ▶*adj.* occurring at irregular intervals; not continuous. —**in·ter·mit·tent·ly** *adv.*

**in·tern** /ˈinˌtərn/ ▶*n.* **1** recent medical school graduate receiving supervised training in a hospital. **2** trainee who works at an occupation, often without pay, to gain work experience. ▶*v.* **1** confine; oblige (a prisoner, alien, etc.) to reside within prescribed limits. **2** serve as an

intern. —in·tern·ment *n.*
—in·tern·ship *n.*

**in·ter·nal** /in'tərnl/ ▸*adj.* **1** of or situated on the inside. **2** of the inside of the body: *internal injuries.* **3** of a nation's domestic affairs. —in·ter·nal·ize *v.*
—in·ter·nal·i·za·tion *n.*
—in·ter·nal·ly *adv.*

**in·ter·nal com·bus·tion en·gine** ▸*n.* engine powered by the explosion of gases or vapor with air in a cylinder.

**in·ter·na·tion·al** ▸*adj.* **1** existing, involving, or carried on between or among nations. **2** agreed on or used by all or many nations: *international date line.* —in·ter·na·tion·al·ism *n.*
—in·ter·na·tion·al·ize *v.*
—in·ter·na·tion·al·ly *adv.*

**in·ter·ne·cine** /ˌintər'nesēn/ ▸*adj.* mutually destructive.

**In·ter·net** ▸*n.* communications network enabling the linking of computers worldwide for data interchange.

**in·tern·ist** /in'tərnist/ ▸*n.* specialist in internal medicine.

**in·ter·per·son·al** ▸*adj.* occurring between persons, esp. reciprocally.
—in·ter·per·son·al·ly *adv.*

**in·ter·plan·e·tar·y** ▸*adj.* between planets.

**in·ter·play** ▸*n.* reciprocal action.

**in·ter·po·late** /in'tərpə,lāt/ ▸*v.* **1** insert (words) in a book. **2** estimate (values) from known ones in the same range.
—in·ter·po·la·tion *n.*

**in·ter·pose** /ˌintər'pōz/ ▸*v.* **1** place or insert (a thing) between others; intervene. **2** say (words) as an interruption.
—in·ter·po·si·tion *n.*

**in·ter·pret** /in'tərprit/ ▸*v.* **1** explain the meaning of (words, a dream, etc.). **2** translate orally the words of someone speaking a foreign language.
—in·ter·pret·er *n.*
—in·ter·pre·ta·tion *n.*
—in·ter·pre·tive *adj.*

**in·ter·ra·cial** ▸*adj.* existing between or affecting different races.

**in·ter·ro·gate** /in'terə,gāt/ ▸*v.* ask questions of, esp. closely, thoroughly, or formally.
—in·ter·ro·ga·tion *n.*
—in·ter·ro·ga·tor *n.*

**in·ter·rupt** /ˌintə'rəpt/ ▸*v.* break the continuous progress of (an action, speech, a person speaking, etc.). **—in·ter·rup·tion** *n.* **—in·ter·rup·tive** *adj.*

**in·ter se** /ˈintər ˈsē; ˈsā/ ▶*adv.* between or among themselves.

**in·ter·sect** /ˌintərˈsekt/ ▶*v.* **1** divide by passing or lying across something. **2** (of lines, roads, etc.) pass or lie across each other.

**in·ter·sec·tion** ▶*n.* **1** place where two or more roads cross each other. **2** act of intersecting.

**in·ter·sperse** /ˌintərˈspərs/ ▶*v.* scatter among or between other things.

**in·ter·state** ▶*adj.* existing or carried on between states, esp. of the U.S. ▶*n.* highway that is part of the U.S. Interstate Highway System.

**in·ter·stel·lar** ▶*adj.* between stars.

**in·ter·stice** /inˈtərstis/ ▶*n.* **1** intervening space. **2** chink or crevice. **—in·ter·sti·tial** *adj.*

**in·ter·twine** ▶*v.* **1** twist together. **2** connect or link.

**in·ter·val** /ˈintərvəl/ ▶*n.* **1** intervening time or space. **2** difference in pitch between two musical sounds. □ **at intervals** here and there; now and then.

**in·ter·vene** /ˌintərˈvēn/ ▶*v.* **1** come between so as to prevent or modify events. **2** (of an event) occur as a delay to something being done. **3** be situated between things: *the intervening months.* **—in·ter·ven·tion** *n.*

**in·ter·view** ▶*n.* **1** meeting face to face, esp. for consultation. **2** conversation between a reporter, etc., and a person of public interest, used as a basis of a broadcast or publication. **3** examination of an applicant. ▶*v.* hold an interview with. **—in·ter·view·ee** *n.*

**in·ter vi·vos** /ˈintər ˈvē,vōs; ˈvī-,vōs/ ▶*adv. & adj.* (esp. of a gift as opposed to a legacy) between living people.

**in·tes·tate** /inˈtestāt/ ▶*adj.* not having made a will before death. **—in·tes·ta·cy** *n.*

**in·tes·tine** /inˈtestən/ ▶*n.* [in *sing.* or *pl.*] lower part of the alimentary canal. **—in·tes·tin·al** *adj.*

**in·ti·mate** ▶*adj.* /ˈintəmit/ **1** closely acquainted. **2** private; personal. **3** having sexual relations. **4** detailed; thorough. ▶*n.* /ˈintəmit/ very close friend. ▶*v.* /ˈintə,māt/ imply; hint.

—**in·ti·ma·cy** *n.* —**in·ti·mate·ly** *adv.* —**in·ti·ma·tion** *n.*

**in·ti·mi·date** /in'timi,dāt/ ▶*v.* frighten or overawe, esp. to subdue or influence. —**in·ti·mi·da·tion** *n.*

**in·to** /'intōō/ ▶*prep.* **1** expressing motion or direction to a point on or within: *ran into the house.* **2** expressing direction of attention. **3** *inf.* interested in; knowledgeable about: *is really into art.*

**in·tol·er·a·ble** ▶*adj.* that cannot be endured.

**in·tol·er·ant** /in'tälərənt/ ▶*adj.* not tolerant of views, etc., differing from one's own.

**in·tone** ▶*v.* recite with prolonged sounds, esp. in a monotone.

**in·tox·i·cate** /in'täksikāt/ ▶*v.* make drunk; excite. —**in·tox·i·ca·tion** *n.*

**in·trac·ta·ble** /in'traktəbəl/ ▶*adj.* **1** hard to control. **2** stubborn.

**in·tra·mu·ral** /,intrə'myōōrəl/ ▶*adj.* **1** situated or done within walls. **2** forming part of normal university or college studies.

**in·tra·net** ▶*n.* computer network within an organization, available only to members.

**in·tran·si·gent** /in'transijənt/ ▶*adj.* uncompromising; stubborn. —**in·tran·si·gent·ly** *adv.*

**in·tran·si·tive** /in'transitiv/ ▶*adj.* *Gram.* (of a verb or sense of a verb) that does not take a direct object (whether expressed or implied), e.g., *look* in *look at the sky.* —**in·tran·si·tiv·i·ty** *n.*

**in·tra·ve·nous** /,intrə'vēnəs/ ▶*adj.* in or into a vein or veins.

**in·trep·id** /in'trepid/ ▶*adj.* fearless; brave.

**in·tri·cate** /'intrikit/ ▶*adj.* very complicated; perplexingly detailed. —**in·tri·ca·cy** *n.* —**in·tri·cate·ly** *adv.*

**in·trigue** /in'trēg/ ▶*v.* (**-trigued, -trigu·ing**) **1** carry on an underhand plot. **2** arouse the curiosity of.
▶*n.* **1** underhand plot or plotting. **2** secret arrangement. —**in·tri·guing** *adj.*

**in·trin·sic** /in'trinzik/ ▶*adj.* inherent; essential; belonging naturally: *intrinsic value.* —**in·trin·si·cal·ly** *adv.*

**in·tro·duce** /,intrə'd(y)ōōs/ ▶*v.* **1** bring (a custom, idea, etc.) into use for the first time. **2** make (a person or oneself) known by name to another, esp. formally.

**3** announce or present. **4** insert or bring into.

**in·tro·spec·tion** /ˌintrə-'speksHən/ ▶n. examination or observation of one's own mental and emotional processes, etc. —**in·tro·spec·tive** adj.

**in·tro·vert** /'intrə,vərt/ ▶n. **1** shy, reticent person. **2** Psychol. person chiefly concerned with their own thoughts rather than with external things. ▶adj. (also **in·tro·vert·ed**) Psychol. typical or characteristic of an introvert. —**in·tro·ver·sion** n.

**in·trude** /in'trōod/ ▶v. come uninvited or unwanted; force oneself abruptly on others. —**in·tru·sion** n.

**in·tu·it** /in't(y)ōo-it/ ▶v. understand or work out by instinct.

**in·tu·i·tion** /ˌint(y)ōo'isHən/ ▶n. immediate insight or understanding without conscious reasoning. —**in·tu·i·tive** adj.

**in·tu·mesce** /ˌint(y)ōo'mes/ ▶v. swell up.

**in·un·date** /'inən,dāt/ ▶v. **1** flood. **2** overwhelm. —**in·un·da·tion** n.

**in·ure** /i'n(y)ōor/ ▶v. accustom to something esp. unpleasant.

**in u·ter·o** /in 'yōotərō/ ▶adv. & adj. in a woman's uterus; before birth.

**in·vade** /in'vād/ ▶v. **1** enter (a country, etc.) with hostility. **2** swarm into. **3** encroach upon. —**in·va·sion** n. —**in·vas·ive** adj.

**in·val·id**[1] ▶n. /'invəlid/ **1** person enfeebled or disabled by illness or injury. **2** [as adj.] of or for invalids. —**in·va·lid·ism** n.

**in·val·id**[2] /in'valid/ ▶adj. not valid. —**in·val·id·ly** adv.

**in·val·i·date** ▶v. make invalid. —**in·val·i·da·tion** n.

**in·val·u·a·ble** ▶adj. above valuation; inestimable.

**in·vec·tive** /in'vektiv/ ▶n. abusive language.

**in·veigh** /in'vā/ ▶v. (**inveigh against**) speak or write about with strong hostility.

**in·vei·gle** /in'vāgəl/ ▶v. entice; persuade by guile.

**in·vent** /in'vent/ ▶v. **1** create by thought; originate (a new method, instrument, etc.). **2** concoct (a false story, etc.). —**in·vent·ive** adj. —**in·ven·tor** n.

**in·ven·to·ry** /'invən,tôrē/ ▶n. (pl. **-ries**) **1** complete list of goods, etc. **2** goods listed in this. ▶v. (**-ried**) **1** make an inventory of. **2** enter (goods) in an inventory.

**in·verse** /ˈinvərs/ ▶*adj.* inverted in position, order, or relation.
▶*n.* thing that is the opposite or reverse of another. —**in·verse·ly** *adv.*

**in·verse pro·por·tion** (or **ratio**) ▶*n.* relation between two quantities such that one increases in proportion as the other decreases.

**in·vert** /inˈvərt/ ▶*v.* **1** turn upside down. **2** reverse the position, order, or relation of.
—**in·ver·sion** *n.*

**in·ver·te·brate** /inˈvərtəbrit/ ▶*adj.* (of an animal) not having a backbone.
▶*n.* invertebrate animal.

**in·vest** /inˈvest/ ▶*v.* **1** expend money with the expectation of receiving a profit by putting it into stocks, financial schemes, etc.: *he invested $10,000 in his friend's business.* **2** devote (time, effort, etc.) to an undertaking with the expectation of a worthwhile result. **3** endow with a quality. —**in·vest·ment** *n.*
—**in·ves·tor** *n.*

**in·ves·ti·gate** /inˈvestiˌgāt/ ▶*v.* inquire into; examine.
—**in·ves·ti·ga·tion** *n.*
—**in·ves·ti·ga·tive** *adj.*
—**in·ves·ti·ga·to·ry** *adj.*

**in·vet·er·ate** /inˈvetərit/ ▶*adj.* **1** confirmed in a habit, etc. **2** (of a habit, etc.) long-established; habitual. —**in·vet·er·a·cy** *n.*

**in·vid·i·ous** /inˈvidēəs/ ▶*adj.* likely to excite resentment or indignation.

**in·vig·o·rat·ing** /inˈvigəˌrāt/ ▶*adj.* giving strength to; energizing. —**in·vig·or·ate** *v.*
—**in·vig·or·a·tion** *n.*

**in·vin·ci·ble** /inˈvinsəbəl/ ▶*adj.* unconquerable.
—**in·vin·ci·bil·i·ty** *n.*

**in·vi·o·la·ble** /inˈvīələbəl/ ▶*adj.* not to be violated or profaned.

**in·vi·o·late** /inˈvīəlit/ ▶*adj.* not violated or profaned.

**in·vite** ▶*v.* /inˈvīt/ **1** ask courteously to come or to do something. **2** attract.
▶*n.* /ˈinˌvīt/ *inf.* invitation.

**in·vit·ing** ▶*adj.* **1** attractive. **2** tempting.

**in vi·tro** /in ˈvēˌtrō/ ▶*adv.* taking place in a test tube or other laboratory environment.

**in·vo·ca·tion** /ˌinvəˈkāsHən/ ▶*n.* **1** invoking, esp. in prayer. **2** summoning a source of inspiration, e.g., the Muses. **3** *Eccl.* the words "In the name of the Father," etc., used as the preface to a sermon, etc.

**in·voice** /'in,vois/ ▸*n.* itemized bill for goods or services.

▸*v.* make or send an invoice.

**in·voke** /in'vōk/ ▸*v.* **1** call on (a deity, etc.) in prayer or as a witness. **2** appeal to (the law, a person's authority, etc.). **3** summon (a spirit) by charms.

**in·vol·un·tar·y** ▸*adj.* **1** done without the exercise of the will; unintentional. **2** (of a limb, muscle, or movement) not under conscious control.

**in·volve** /in'välv/ ▸*v.* **1** cause to participate, or share the experience or effect (in a situation, activity, etc.). **2** include or affect in its operations. —**in·volve·ment** *n.*

**in·ward** /'inwərd/ ▸*adj.* **1** directed toward the inside; going in. **2** situated within. **3** mental; spiritual.

▸*adv.* (also **in·wards**) **1** toward the inside. **2** in the mind or soul.

**I/O** *Computing* ▸*abbr.* input/output.

**i·o·dine** /'īə,dīn/ ▸*n.* **1** element forming black crystals and a violet vapor when heated. (Symb.: **I**) **2** solution of this as a mild antiseptic.

**i·on** /'īən/ ▸*n.* atom or group of atoms that has lost or gained one or more electrons. —**i·on·ic** *adj.*

**-ion** (usu. as **-sion**, **-tion**, **-xion**) ▸*suffix* forming nouns denoting: **1** verbal action: *excision.* **2** instance of this: *suggestion.* **3** resulting state or product: *vexation | concoction.*

**i·on·ize** /'īə,nīz/ ▸*v.* convert or be converted into an ion or ions, typically by removing one or more electrons.

**i·on·o·sphere** /ī'änə,sfi(ə)r/ ▸*n.* ionized region of the atmosphere above the stratosphere, reflecting radio waves. —**i·on·o·spher·ic** *adj.*

**i·o·ta** /ī'ōtə/ ▸*n.* **1** ninth letter of the Greek alphabet (I, ι). **2** smallest possible amount: *not an iota of common sense.*

**IOU** ▸*n.* signed document acknowledging a debt.

**ip·se dix·it** /'ipsē 'diksit/ ▸*n.* dogmatic and unproven statement.

**ip·so fac·to** /'ipsō 'faktō/ ▸*adv.* **1** by that very fact or act. **2** thereby.

**IQ** ▸*abbr.* intelligence quotient.

**IRA** ▸*abbr.* **1** individual retirement account. **2** Irish Republican Army.

**I·ra·ni·an** /i'rānēən/ ▸*adj.* **1** of or

relating to Iran (formerly Persia) in the Middle East. **2** of the Indo-European group of languages including Persian, Pashto, Avestan, and Kurdish.

▸*n.* native or national of Iran.

**I·ra·qi** /iˈräkē/ ▸*adj.* of or relating to Iraq in the Middle East.

▸*n.* (*pl.* **I·ra·qis**) **1** native or national of Iraq. **2** form of Arabic spoken in Iraq.

**i·ras·ci·ble** /iˈrasəbəl/ ▸*adj.* irritable; hot-tempered. —**i·ras·ci·bil·i·ty** *n.*

**ire** /ī(ə)r/ ▸*n.* anger.

**ir·i·des·cent** /ˌiriˈdesənt/ ▸*adj.* showing rainbowlike luminous colors that change with angle of view. —**ir·i·des·cence** *n.*

**i·ris** /ˈīris/ ▸*n.* **1** flat, circular colored membrane behind the cornea of the eye, with a circular opening (pupil) in the center. **2** herbaceous plant of a family with tuberous roots, sword-shaped leaves, and showy flowers.

**I·rish** /ˈīriSH/ ▸*adj.* of or relating to Ireland; of or like its people.

▸*n.* **1** Celtic language of Ireland. **2** (**the Irish**) the people of Ireland.

**irk** /ərk/ ▸*v.* irritate; annoy.

**i·ron** /ˈīərn/ ▸*n.* **1** gray metallic element used for tools and implements, and found in some foods. (Symb.: **Fe**) **2** implement with a flat base which is heated to smooth clothes, etc. **3** golf club with a metal sloping face. **4** (**irons**) fetters.

▸*adj.* **1** made of iron. **2** robust. **3** unyielding; merciless.

▸*v.* smooth (clothes, etc.) with an iron. —**i·ron·ing** *n.*

**i·ron·clad** ▸*adj.* **1** clad or protected with iron. **2** impregnable; rigorous.

**I·ron Cur·tain** ▸*n.* notional barrier to the passage of people and information between the former Soviet bloc and the West.

**i·ro·ny** /ˈīrənē/ ▸*n.* (*pl.* **-nies**) **1** humorous or sarcastic use of language of a different or opposite meaning. **2** ill-timed arrival of an event or circumstance that is in itself desirable. —**i·ron·ic** *adj.*

**Ir·o·quois** /ˈirəˌkwoi/ ▸*n.* [*pl.* same] **1 a** Native American confederacy of five (later six) peoples formerly inhabiting New York State. **b** member of any of these peoples. **2** any of the languages of these peoples.

▸*adj.* of or relating to the Iroquois

or their languages.
—Ir·o·quoi·an *n. & adj.*

**ir·ra·di·ate** /i'rādē,āt/ ▸*v.*
**1** subject to radiation. **2** shine upon; light up. —**ir·ra·di·a·tion** *n.*

**ir·ra·tion·al** /i'rasHənl/ ▸*adj.*
**1** illogical; unreasonable. **2** not endowed with reason.
—**ir·ra·tion·al·i·ty** *n.*

**ir·rec·on·cil·a·ble** /i,rekən-'sīləbəl/ ▸*adj.* **1** implacably hostile. **2** incompatible.
—**ir·rec·on·cil·a·bly** *adv.*

**ir·re·deem·a·ble** /,iri'dēməbəl/ ▸*adj.* hopeless; absolute.

**ir·re·duc·i·ble** /,iri'd(y)o͞osəbəl/ ▸*adj.* that cannot be reduced or simplified.

**ir·re·fut·a·ble** /,irə'fyo͞otəbəl/ ▸*adj.* that cannot be refuted.

**ir·reg·u·lar** /i'regyələr/ ▸*adj.* **1** not regular; unsymmetrical; uneven. **2** contrary to a rule, moral principle, or custom; abnormal. —**ir·reg·u·lar·i·ty** *n.*

**ir·rel·e·vant** /i'reləvənt/ ▸*adj.* not relevant. —**ir·rel·e·vance** *n.*

**ir·re·li·gious** /,irə'lijəs/ ▸*adj.* indifferent or hostile to religion.

**ir·rep·a·ra·ble** /ir'rep(ə)rəbəl/ ▸*adj.* that cannot be rectified or made good.

**ir·re·press·i·ble** /,irə'presəbəl/ ▸*adj.* that cannot be repressed or restrained. —**ir·re·press·i·bly** *adv.*

**ir·re·proach·a·ble** /,irə-'prōcHəbəl/ ▸*adj.* faultless; blameless.

**ir·re·sist·i·ble** /,irə'zistəbəl/ ▸*adj.* **1** too strong or convincing to be resisted. **2** delightful; alluring.

**ir·res·o·lute** /i(r)'rezə,lo͞ot/ ▸*adj.* hesitant; undecided.

**ir·re·spec·tive** /,iri'spektiv/ ▸*adj.* not taking into account; regardless of. —**ir·re·spec·tive·ly** *adv.*

**ir·re·spon·si·ble** /,irə-'spänsəbəl/ ▸*adj.* **1** acting or done without due sense of responsibility. **2** not responsible for one's conduct.
—**ir·re·spon·si·bil·i·ty** *n.*

**ir·re·triev·a·ble** /,iri'trēvəbəl/ ▸*adj.* that cannot be retrieved or restored.

**ir·rev·er·ent** /i'rev(ə)rənt/ ▸*adj.* lacking reverence.
—**ir·rev·er·ence** *n.*

**ir·re·vo·ca·ble** /,i'revəkəbəl/ ▸*adj.* **1** unalterable. **2** gone beyond recall.

**ir·ri·gate** /'irigāt/ ▸*v.* **1** water (land) by means of channels. **2** clean (a wound, etc.) with a

constant flow of liquid.
—**ir·ri·ga·tion** n.

**ir·ri·ta·ble** /ˈiritəbəl/ ▶adj.
**1** easily annoyed. **2** (of an organ, etc.) very sensitive to contact.
—**ir·ri·ta·bil·i·ty** n.

**ir·ri·tate** /ˈiriˌtāt/ ▶v. **1** annoy.
**2** stimulate discomfort in (a part of the body). —**ir·ri·tat·ing** adj.
—**ir·ri·ta·tion** n.

**IRS** ▶abbr. Internal Revenue Service.

**Is.** ▶abbr. **1 a** Island(s). **b** Isle(s).
**2** (also **Isa.**) Isaiah (Old Testament).

**is** /iz/ ▶3rd sing. present of BE.

**-ish** /iSH/ ▶suffix forming adjectives: **1** from nouns, meaning: **a** having the qualities or characteristics of: boyish. **b** of the nationality of: Danish.
**2** from adjectives, meaning 'somewhat': thickish. **3** inf. denoting an approximate age or time of day: fortyish | six-thirtyish.
**4** forming verbs: vanish | finish.

**Is·lam** /isˈläm/ ▶n. **1** religion of the Muslims, a monotheistic faith regarded as revealed by Muhammad as the Prophet of Allah. **2** the Muslim world.
—**Is·lam·ic** adj.

**is·land** /ˈīlənd/ ▶n. **1** land surrounded by water.

**2** anything compared to an island. **3** detached or isolated thing.

**isle** /īl/ ▶n. island or peninsula, esp. a small one.

**is·let** /ˈīlət/ ▶n. **1** small island.
**2** Anat. portion of tissue structurally distinct from surrounding tissues.

**-ism** /ˈizəm/ ▶suffix forming nouns, esp. denoting: **1** action or its result: baptism. **2** system, principle, or ideological movement: feminism. **3** state or quality: heroism | barbarism.
**4** basis of prejudice or discrimination: racism | sexism.
**5** peculiarity in language: Americanism. **6** pathological condition: alcoholism.

**i·so·bar** /ˈīsəˌbär/ ▶n. line on a map connecting positions having the same atmospheric pressure. —**i·so·bar·ic** adj.

**i·so·late** /ˈīsəˌlāt/ ▶v. **1** place apart or alone; cut off from society. **2 a** identify and separate for attention. **b** Chem. separate (a substance) from a mixture. —**i·so·lat·ed** adj.
—**i·so·la·tion** n.

**i·so·la·tion·ism** ▶n. policy of holding aloof from the affairs of

other countries or groups.
—**i·so·la·tion·ist** *n.*

**i·so·met·rics** /ˌīsə'metriks/ ▸*pl. n.* system of physical exercises in which muscles act against each other or a fixed object.

**i·sos·ce·les** /ī'säsə,lēz/ ▸*adj.* (of a triangle) having two sides equal.

**i·so·tope** /'īsə,tōp/ ▸*n.* one of two or more forms of an element differing from each other in atomic mass.
—**i·so·top·ic** *adj.*

**Is·rae·li** /iz'rālē/ ▸*adj.* of or relating to the modern state of Israel in the Middle East.
▸*n.* native or national of Israel.

**is·sue** /'ishoo/ ▸*n.* **1 a** giving out or circulation of notes, stamps, etc. **b** item or amount given out or distributed. **c** each of a regular series of a magazine, etc.: *the May issue.* **2** point in question; important subject of debate. **3** result. **4** *Law* children.
▸*v.* (**-sued, -su·ing**) **1** go or come out. **2** publish; put into circulation. **3** be derived or result. —**is·su·ance** *n.*
□ **at issue** in dispute. □ **take issue** disagree.

**-ist** /ist/ ▸*suffix* forming personal nouns (and in some senses related adjectives) denoting: **1** adherent of a system, etc., in -ism (see **-ISM**): *Marxist.* **2** member of a profession: *pathologist.* **3** person who uses a thing: *violinist.* **4** person who does something expressed by a verb in -ize: *plagiarist.* **5** person who subscribes to a prejudice or practices discrimination: *racist.*

**isth·mus** /'isməs/ ▸*n.* narrow piece of land connecting two larger bodies of land.

**it** /it/ ▸*pron.* (*poss.* **its**; *pl.* **they**) **1** thing previously named or in question: *took a stone and threw it.* **2** person in question: *Who is it?* **3** as the subject of an impersonal verb: *it is raining.* **4** as a substitute for a deferred subject or object: *it is silly to talk like that.* **5** (in children's games) player who has to catch the others.

**I·tal·ian** /i'talyən/ ▸*n.* **1** native or national of Italy. **2** language of Italy.
▸*adj.* of or relating to Italy or its people or language.

**i·tal·ic** /i'talik/ ▸*adj.* slanting type used esp. for emphasis and in foreign words.

**itch** /ich/ ▸*n.* **1** irritation in the skin. **2** impatient desire.

▶*v.* feel an irritation in the skin. —**itch·y** *adj.*

**i·tem** /ˈītəm/ ▶*n.* **1** any of a number of enumerated things. **2** article, esp. one for sale. **3** piece of news, etc.

**i·tem·ize** ▶*v.* state or list item by item. —**i·tem·i·za·tion** *n.*

**i·tin·er·ant** /īˈtinərənt/ ▶*adj.* traveling from place to place. ▶*n.* itinerant person.

**i·tin·er·ar·y** /īˈtinəˌrerē/ ▶*n.* (*pl.* -ies) route; list of places to visit.

**-itis** /ˈītis/ ▶*suffix* forming nouns, esp.: **1** names of inflammatory diseases: *appendicitis.* **2** *inf.* with ref. to conditions compared to diseases: *electionitis.*

**its** /its/ ▶*pron.* of it; of itself: *can see its advantages.*

**it's** /its/ ▶*contr.* it is.

**it·self** ▶*pron.* emphatic and refl. form of IT. □ **in itself** viewed in its essential qualities: *not in itself a bad thing.*

**IV** ▶*abbr.* intravenous(ly).

**I've** /īv/ ▶*contr.* I have.

**-ive** /iv/ ▶*suffix* forming adjectives meaning 'tending to, having the nature of,' and corresponding nouns: *suggestive* | *corrosive* | *palliative* | *coercive* | *talkative.*

**i·vo·ry** /ˈīv(ə)rē/ ▶*n.* (*pl.* -ries) **1** hard substance of the tusks of an elephant, etc. **2** color of this. **3** (**ivories**) keys of a piano or a person's teeth.

**i·vo·ry tow·er** ▶*n.* privileged seclusion or separation from the practicalities of the real world.

**i·vy** /ˈīvē/ ▶*n.* (*pl.* -vies) climbing evergreen shrub with dark-green, shining five-angled leaves.

**-ize** /īz/ ▶*suffix* forming verbs, meaning: **1** make or become such: *Americanize* | *realize.* **2** treat in such a way: *monopolize* | *pasteurize.* **3 a** follow a special practice: *economize.* **b** have a specified feeling: *sympathize.* — **-ization** *suffix* — **-izer** *suffix*

# Jj

**J¹** /jā/ (also **j**) ▶*n.* (*pl.* **Js** or **J's; j's**) tenth letter of the alphabet.

**J²** (also **J.**) ▶*abbr.* **1** *Cards* jack. **2** joule(s). **3** Judge. **4** Justice.

**jab** /jab/ ▶*v.* (**jabbed, jab·bing**) **1 a** poke roughly. **b** stab. **2** thrust (a thing) hard or abruptly.
▶*n.* abrupt blow with one's fist or a pointed implement.

**jab·ber** /'jabər/ ▶*v.* chatter volubly.
▶*n.* meaningless jabbering.

**jack** /jak/ ▶*n.* **1** device for lifting heavy objects, esp. vehicles. **2** playing card with a picture of a soldier, page, etc. **3** ship's flag, esp. showing nationality. **4** device to connect an electrical circuit. **5 a** small piece of metal, etc., used with others in tossing games. **b** (**jacks**) [treated as *sing.*] game with a ball and jacks.
▶*v.* (**jack up**) **1** raise with or as with a jack. **2** *inf.* raise, e.g., prices.

**jack·al** /'jakəl/ ▶*n.* a wild doglike mammal found in Africa and S. Asia.

**jack·ass** /'jak,as/ ▶*n.* **1** male ass. **2** stupid person.

**jack·et** /'jakit/ ▶*n.* **1 a** sleeved, short outer garment. **b** thing worn esp. around the torso for protection or support: *life jacket.* **2** casing or covering. **3** DUST JACKET.

**jack·ham·mer** ▶*n.* pneumatic hammer or drill.

**jack-in-the-box** ▶*n.* toy figure that springs out of a box.

**jack·knife** ▶*n.* (*pl.* **-knives**) **1** large pocket knife. **2** dive in which the body is first bent at the waist and then straightened.
▶*v.* (**-knifed, -knif·ing**) (of an articulated vehicle) fold against itself in an accidental skidding movement.

**jack·leg** /'jak,leg/ ▶*n.* incompetent, unskillful, or dishonest person.

**jack-o'-lan·tern** ▶*n.* lantern made from a pumpkin with holes for facial features, made at Halloween.

**jack·pot** ▶*n.* large prize, esp. accumulated in a game or lottery, etc.

□ **hit the jackpot** *inf.* **1** win a large prize. **2** have remarkable luck or success.

**jack·rab·bit** ▸*n.* large prairie hare.

**jac·que·rie** /ZHäk'rē/ ▸*n.* communal uprising or revolt.

**Ja·cuz·zi** /jə'kōōzē/ ▸*trademark* large bath with underwater jets of water to massage the body.

**jade** /jād/ ▸*n.* **1** hard, usu. green stone used for ornaments, etc. **2** green color of jade.

**jad·ed** /'jādid/ ▸*adj.* tired, bored, or lacking enthusiasm.

**jag** *inf.* ▸*n.* bout of unrestrained activity or emotion: *drinking jag* | *crying jag.*

**jag·ged** /'jagid/ ▸*adj.* **1** unevenly cut or torn. **2** deeply indented; with sharp points.

**ja·guar** /'jag,wär/ ▸*n.* large, flesh-eating spotted feline of Central and S. America.

**jai a·lai** /'hī (ə),lī/ ▸*n.* indoor court game similar to handball played with large curved wicker rackets.

**jail** /jāl/ ▸*n.* place to which persons are committed by a court for detention. ▸*v.* put in jail.

**ja·la·pe·ño** /,hälə'pānyō/ ▸*n.* hot pepper commonly used in Mexican cooking.

**ja·lop·y** /jə'läpē/ ▸*n.* (*pl.* **-ies**) *inf.* dilapidated old car.

**jal·ou·sie** /'jalə,sē/ ▸*n.* blind or shutter made of a row of angled slats.

**jam** /jam/ ▸*v.* (**jammed, jam·ming**) **1** squeeze or wedge into a space. **2** become wedged or immovable so that it cannot work. **3** push or crowd together. **4** apply forcefully or abruptly: *jam on the brakes.* **5** make (a radio transmission) unintelligible by interference. **6** *inf.* (in jazz, etc.) improvise with other musicians. ▸*n.* **1** crowded mass: *traffic jam.* **2** *inf.* predicament. **3** stoppage due to jamming. **4** (also **jam session**) informal gathering of jazz musicians improvising together. **5** preserve of fruit and sugar.

**jamb** /jam/ ▸*n.* side post or surface of a doorway, window, or fireplace.

**jam·bo·ree** /,jambə'rē/ ▸*n.* **1** celebration. **2** large rally of Boy Scouts or Girl Scouts.

**Jan.** ▸*abbr.* January.

**jan·gle** /'jaNGgəl/ ▸*v.* **1** cause (a bell, etc.) to make a harsh metallic sound. **2** irritate (the nerves, etc.) by discord, etc.

▶*n.* harsh metallic sound.

**jan·i·tor** /ˈjanitər/ ▶*n.* caretaker of a building. —**jan·i·to·ri·al** *adj.*

**Jan·u·ar·y** /ˈjanyo͝oˌerē/ ▶*n.* (*pl.* **-ies**) first month of the year.

**Jap·a·nese** /ˌjapəˈnēz/ ▶*n.* (*pl.* same) **1 a** native or national of Japan. **b** person of Japanese descent. **2** language of Japan.

▶*adj.* of or relating to Japan, its people, or its language.

**Jap·a·nese bee·tle** ▶*n.* iridescent green and brown beetle that is a garden and crop pest.

**jape** /jāp/ ▶*n.* practical joke.

▶*v.* say or do something in jest or mockery.

**jar** ▶*v.* (**jarred, jar·ring**) **1** (of sound, manner, etc.) sound discordant or grating (on the nerves, etc.). **2** strike or cause to strike with vibration or shock. **3** send a shock through (a part of the body).

▶*n.* **1** jarring sound or sensation. **2** shock or jolt. **3 a** container of glass, plastic, etc., usu. cylindrical. **b** contents of this.

**jar·gon** /ˈjärgən/ ▶*n.* words or expressions used by a particular group or profession: *medical jargon.*

**jas·mine** /ˈjazmən/ (also **jes·sa·mine**) ▶*n.* a fragrant ornamental shrub usu. with white or yellow flowers.

**jas·per** /ˈjaspər/ ▶*n.* opaque quartz, usu. red, yellow, or brown.

**jaun·dice** /ˈjôndis/ ▶*n.* **1** yellowing of the skin or whites of the eyes, often caused by obstruction of the bile duct or by liver disease. **2** bitterness or resentment. —**jaun·diced** *adj.*

**jaunt** /jônt/ ▶*n.* short excursion for enjoyment.

▶*v.* take a jaunt.

**jaunt·y** ▶*adj.* (**-i·er, -i·est**) lively, cheerful, and self-confident.

**jav·e·lin** /ˈjav(ə)lin/ ▶*n.* light spear thrown in a competitive sport or as a weapon.

**jaw** /jô/ ▶*n.* **1 a** upper or lower bony structure in vertebrates forming the framework of the mouth and containing the teeth. **b** corresponding parts of certain invertebrates. **2 a** (**jaws**) mouth with its bones and teeth. **b** narrow mouth of a valley, channel, etc. **c** gripping parts of a tool or machine.

▸*v. inf.* speak, esp. at tedious length.

**jaw·bone** ▸*n.* lower jaw in most mammals.

**jay** /jā/ ▸*n.* noisy chattering bird of the crow family with patterned plumage, often having blue feathers.

**jay·walk** ▸*v.* cross or walk in the street or road without regard for traffic.

**jazz** /jaz/ ▸*n.* music of American origin characterized by improvisation, syncopation, and usu. a regular or forceful rhythm. ☐ **jazz up** brighten or enliven.

**jazz·y** ▸*adj.* (**-i·er, -i·est**) **1** of or like jazz. **2** vivid; unrestrained.

**jeal·ous** /ˈjeləs/ ▸*adj.* **1** envious or resentful: *jealous of her success.* **2** afraid, suspicious, or resentful of rivalry in love. **3** fiercely protective (of rights, etc.). —**jeal·ous·y** *n.*

**jeans** /jēnz/ ▸*pl. n.* casual pants made of denim.

**Jeep** /jēp/ ▸*trademark* rugged, all-purpose motor vehicle incorporating four-wheel drive.

**jeer** /ji(ə)r/ ▸*v.* make rude and scoffing remarks. ▸*n.* scoff or taunt.

**Je·ho·vah** /jəˈhōvə/ ▸*n.* Hebrew name of God in the Old Testament.

**je·june** /jiˈjoon/ ▸*adj.* **1** naive, simplistic, and superficial. **2** dull. —**je·june·ly** *adv.*

**jell** /jel/ *inf.* ▸*v.* **1** set, as jelly. **2** take a definite form; cohere.

**jel·ly** /ˈjelē/ ▸*n.* (*pl.* **-lies**) **1** gelatinous preparation of fruit juice, etc., for use as a jam or a condiment: *grape jelly.* **2** any similar substance. ▸*v.* (**-lied**) set (food) in a jelly: *jellied eggs.*

**jel·ly·bean** ▸small, bean-shaped candy with a hard sugar coating and a gelatinous filling.

**jel·ly·fish** ▸*n.* (*pl.* usu. same) sea animal with a jellylike body and stinging tentacles.

**jel·ly roll** ▸*n.* rolled sponge cake with a jelly filling.

**jeop·ar·dize** /ˈjepərˌdīz/ ▸*v.* endanger.

**jeop·ar·dy** /ˈjepərdē/ ▸*n.* danger, esp. of harm or loss.

**jer·e·mi·ad** /ˌjerəˈmīəd; -ˌad/ ▸*n.* long, mournful complaint or lamentation; a list of woes.

**jerk** /jərk/ ▸*n.* **1** quick, sharp, sudden movement. **2** *inf.* obnoxious person. ▸*v.* **1** move or make something move with a jerk. **2** cure (beef, etc.) by cutting it in long slices and drying it in the sun.

**jer·kin** /'jərkin/ ▶*n.* sleeveless jacket, often of leather.

**jer·ky** ▶*n.* meat, esp. beef, that has been cured in the sun.
▶*adj.* (**-ki·er, -ki·est**) **1** characterized by sharp, sudden movement. **2** *inf.* silly; ridiculous; obnoxious.

**jer·sey** /'jərzē/ ▶*n.* (*pl.* **-seys**) **1 a** knitted, usu. woolen sweater. **b** knitted fabric. **2** (**Jersey**) light brown dairy cow from the island of Jersey.

**jest** /jest/ ▶*n.* **1** joke. **2** banter.
▶*v.* **1** joke. **2** fool around.
□ **in jest** in fun.

**jest·er** ▶*n.* professional clown at a medieval court, etc.

**Je·sus** /'jēzəs/ (also **Jesus Christ, Jesus of Nazareth**) ▶*n.* the name of the source of the Christian religion, died *c.* AD 30.

**jet** /jet/ ▶*n.* **1** stream of water, gas, etc., shot out esp. from a small opening. **2** spout or nozzle for this purpose. **3 a** (also **jet engine**) engine using jet propulsion. **b** (also **jet plane**) plane with jet engines. **4** hard black variety of lignite capable of being carved and highly

polished. **5** (also **jet-black**) deep glossy black color.
▶*v.* (**jet·ted, jet·ting**) **1** spurt out in jets. **2** travel by jet plane.

**jet lag** ▶*n.* extreme tiredness after a long flight across time zones.

**jet pro·pul·sion** ▶*n.* propulsion by the backward ejection of a high-speed jet of gas, etc.

**jet·sam** /'jetsəm/ ▶*n.* discarded material washed ashore, esp. that thrown overboard to lighten a ship, etc.

**jet set** ▶*n.* *inf.* wealthy people frequently traveling for pleasure. —**jet-set·ter** *n.*

**jet·ti·son** /'jetisən/ ▶*v.* **1 a** throw (esp. heavy material) overboard to lighten a ship, etc. **b** drop (goods) from an aircraft. **2** abandon; get rid of.

**jet·ty** /'jetē/ ▶*n.* (*pl.* **-ties**) **1** pier or breakwater constructed to protect or defend a harbor, coast, etc. **2** landing pier.

**jeu d'es·prit** /ˌᴢʜœ dəˈsprē/ ▶*n.* lighthearted display of wit and cleverness, esp. in a work of literature.

**Jew** /jo͞o/ ▶*n.* person of Hebrew descent or whose religion is Judaism. —**Jew·ish** *adj.*

**jew·el** /'jo͞oəl/ ▶*n.* **1** precious

stone. **2** jeweled personal ornament. **3** precious person or thing.

**jew·el box** ▶*n.* **1** small box in which jewelry is kept. **2** plastic case for a compact disc or CD-ROM.

**jew·el·ry** /ˈjo͞oəlrē/ ▶*n.* jewels, esp. of gold, silver, or precious stones, used for personal adornment.

**Jew's harp** (or **Jews' harp**) ▶*n.* small lyre-shaped musical instrument held between the teeth and struck with the finger.

**jib** /jib/ ▶*n.* **1** triangular sail set forward of a mast. **2** projecting arm of a crane.
▶*v.* (**jibbed**, **jib·bing**) jibe.

**jibe** /jīb/ ▶*v.* **1** (of a fore-and-aft sail or boom) swing or cause to swing across the vessel. **2** (of a ship or its crew) change course so that this happens. **3** (**jibe with**) agree with; be in accord with.
▶*n.* change of course causing jibing.

**jif·fy** /ˈjifē/ *inf.* ▶*n.* short time: *in a jiffy.*

**jig** /jig/ ▶*n.* **1 a** lively leaping dance. **b** music for this. **2** device that holds a piece of work and guides the tools operating on it.

▶*v.* (**jigged**, **jig·ging**) **1** dance a jig. **2** move quickly and jerkily up and down.

**jig·ger** /ˈjigər/ ▶*n.* measure or small glass of spirits, etc.

**jig·gle** /ˈjigəl/ ▶*v.* **1** shake lightly; rock jerkily. **2** fidget. —**jig·gly** *adj.*

**jig·saw** ▶*n.* **1** (also **jig·saw puz·zle**) picture on board or wood cut into irregular interlocking pieces to be reassembled. **2** machine saw with a fine blade for cutting on a curve.

**ji·had** /jiˈhäd/ ▶*n.* holy war undertaken by Muslims against unbelievers.

**jilt** /jilt/ ▶*v.* abruptly reject or abandon (a lover, etc.).

**jim crow** /ˈjim ˈkrō/ ▶*n. hist.* (also **Jim Crow**) practice of segregating blacks.

**jim·my** /ˈjimē/ ▶*n.* (*pl.* **-mies**) burglar's short crowbar, usu. made in sections.
▶*v.* (**-mied**) force open with a jimmy.

**jin·gle** /ˈjiNGgəl/ ▶*n.* **1** mixed noise as of bells or light metal objects being shaken together. **2 a** repetition of the same sound in words, esp. as an aid to memory or to attract attention.

**b** short verse of this kind used in advertising, etc.
▶*v.* make or cause to make a jingling sound. **—jin·gly** *adj.*

**jin·go·ism** /ˈjiNGgōˌizəm/ ▶*n.* extreme patriotism, esp. in the form of aggressive or warlike foreign policy.

**jinn** /jin/ (also **djinn** or **jin·ni** /jiˈnē; ˈjinē/) ▶*n.* (*pl.* same or **jinns**) (in Arabian and Muslim mythology) an intelligent spirit of lower rank than the angels, able to appear in human and animal forms and to possess humans.

**jinx** /jiNGks/ *inf.* ▶*n.* person or thing that seems to cause bad luck.
▶*v.* subject (a person) to an unlucky force.

**jit·ters** /ˈjitərz/ ▶*pl. n.* extreme nervousness **—jit·ter·y** *adj.*

**jive** /jīv/ ▶*n.* **1** jerky lively style of dance esp. popular in the 1950s. **2** music for this. **3** *inf.* talk or conversation, esp. when misleading or pretentious.

**job** /jōb/ ▶*n.* **1** piece of work to be done; task. **2** paid position of employment.

**job ac·tion** ▶*n.* any action, esp. a strike, taken by employees as a protest.

**job·ber** ▶*n.* **1** wholesaler.

**2** person who does casual or occasional work.

**job-shar·ing** ▶*n.* sharing of a full-time job by several part-time employees.

**jock** /jäk/ ▶*n. inf.* athlete.

**jock·ey** /ˈjäkē/ ▶*n.* (*pl.* **-eys**) rider in horse races, esp. professional.
▶*v.* **1** trick or cheat (a person). **2** outwit.

**jo·cose** /jōˈkōs/ ▶*adj.* playful; jocular.

**joc·u·lar** /ˈjäkyələr/ ▶*adj.*
**1** merry; fond of joking.
**2** humorous. **—joc·u·lar·i·ty** *n.*

**joc·und** /ˈjäkənd; ˈjō-/ ▶*adj.* cheerful and lighthearted.

**jodh·purs** /ˈjädpərz/ ▶*pl. n.* long breeches for riding, etc., close-fitting from the knee to the ankle.

**jog** /jäg/ ▶*v.* (**jogged, jog·ging**)
**1** run slowly, esp. as exercise.
**2** (of a horse) move at a slow trot. **3** nudge (a person), esp. to arouse attention; shake; push.
**4** stimulate (a person's or one's own memory).
▶*n.* **1** a shake, push, or nudge.
**2** slow walk or trot. **—jog·ger** *n.*

**joie de vivre** /ˌZHwä də ˈvēvrə/ ▶*n.* feeling of healthy and exuberant enjoyment of life.

**join** /join/ ▶*v.* **1** put together;

fasten; unite. **2** connect (points) by a line, etc. **3** become a member of. **4** take one's place with or in. **5** share the company of for a specified occasion: *may I join you for lunch?* **6** take part in. ▸*n.* point, line, or surface at which things are joined. □ **join forces** combine efforts. □ **join hands** hold each other's hands. □ **join up** enlist for military service.

**join·er** ▸*n.* person who makes furniture and light woodwork. —**join·er·y** *n.*

**joint** /joint/ ▸*n.* **1 a** place at which two or more things are joined. **2** point at which two bones fit together. **3** *inf.* place of meeting for drinking, etc. **4** *inf.* marijuana cigarette. ▸*adj.* held or done by, or belonging to, two or more persons working together: *joint action.* ▸*v.* **1** connect by joints. **2** divide (a body) at a joint or into joints. □ **out of joint 1** (of a bone) dislocated. **2** in a state of disorder.

**join·ture** /'joinCHər/ ▸*n.* estate settled on a wife for the period during which she survives her husband, in lieu of a dower.

**joist** /joist/ ▸*n.* supporting beam in floors, ceilings, etc. —**joist·ed** *adj.*

**joke** /jōk/ ▸*n.* **1 a** thing said or done to excite laughter. **b** witticism or jest. **2** ridiculous thing, person, or circumstance. ▸*v.* make jokes; banter.

**jok·er** ▸*n.* **1** person who jokes. **2** extra playing card with no fixed value.

**jol·ly** /'jälē/ ▸*adj.* (**-li·er, -li·est**) **1** happy and cheerful. **2** festive; jovial. **3** slightly drunk. ▸*v.* (**-lied**) *inf.* encourage in a friendly way.

**jolt** /jōlt/ ▸*v.* **1** move, disturb, or shake (esp. in a moving vehicle) with a jerk. **2** shock; perturb. ▸*n.* **1** a jerking movement. **2** surprise; shock.

**jon·quil** /'jänkwəl/ ▸*n.* narcissus with small fragrant yellow or white flowers.

**jo·rum** /'jôrəm/ ▸*n.* large bowl or jug used for serving drinks such as tea or punch.

**josh** /jäSH/ *inf.* ▸*v.* tease; banter.

**jos·tle** /'jäsəl/ ▸*v.* push, elbow, or bump against roughly. ▸*n.* jostling.

**jot** /jät/ ▸*v.* (**jot·ted, jot·ting**) write briefly or hastily. ▸*n.* very small amount: *not one jot.*

**joule** /jo͞ol/ ▶n. SI unit of work or energy. (Abbr.: **J**)

**jour·nal** /'jərnl/ ▶n. **1** newspaper or periodical. **2** daily record of events, or of financial transactions.

**jour·nal·ism** ▶n. business or practice of writing and producing newspapers. —**jour·nal·ist** n. —**jour·nal·is·tic** adj.

**jour·ney** /'jərnē/ ▶n. (pl. -**neys**) **1** act of going from one place to another. **2** distance traveled in a specified time: *day's journey.* ▶v. (-**neyed**) make a journey.

**jour·ney·man** ▶n. (pl. -**men**) trained craftsman employed by someone else.

**joust** /joust/ hist. ▶n. combat between two knights on horseback with lances. ▶v. engage in a joust.

**jo·vi·al** /'jōvēəl/ ▶adj. merry; convivial.

**jowl** /joul/ ▶n. (often **jowls**) lower part of the cheek, esp. when fleshy.

**joy** /joi/ ▶n. **1** pleasure; extreme gladness. **2** thing that causes joy. —**joy·ous** adj.

**joy·ride** inf. ▶n. a reckless ride in a car, with no destination. ▶v. (past -**rode**; past part. -**rid·den**) go for a joy ride.

**joy·stick** ▶n. **1** inf. control column of an aircraft. **2** lever controlling movement of a computer image.

**JP** ▶abbr. **1** justice of the peace. **2** jet propulsion.

**Jr.** ▶abbr. junior.

**ju·bi·lant** /'jo͞obələnt/ ▶adj. exultant; rejoicing. —**ju·bi·lance** n.

**ju·bi·la·tion** /ˌjo͞obə'lāsнən/ ▶n. feeling of great happiness and triumph.

**ju·bi·lee** /'jo͞obəˌlē/ ▶n. **1** time of rejoicing. **2** anniversary, esp. the 25th or 50th.

**Ju·da·ism** /'jo͞odeˌizəm/ ▶n. religion of the Jews, with a belief in one god and a basis in Mosaic and rabbinical teachings. —**Ju·da·ic** adj.

**judge** /jəj/ ▶n. **1** public official elected or appointed to hear and try cases in a law court. **2** person who decides a dispute or contest. ▶v. **1** form an opinion about; appraise. **2 a** try a legal case. **b** pronounce sentence on.

**judg·ment** /'jəjmənt/ (also **judge·ment**) ▶n. **1** ability to make considered decisions or arrive at sensible conclusions: *poor judgment.* **2** decision of a law court. **3** monetary or other obligation awarded by a court.

□ **pass judgment** give a decision in a legal matter. □ **reserve judgment** delay giving one's opinion.

**judg·men·tal** /jəj'mentl/ (also **judge·men·tal**) ▸*adj.* condemning; critical.

**ju·di·cial** /jōō'dishəl/ ▸*adj.* **1** of, done by, or proper to a court of law. **2** impartial.

**ju·di·ci·ar·y** /jōō'dishē,erē/ ▸*n.* (*pl.* **-ies**) judges of a judicial branch collectively.

**ju·di·cious** /jōō'dishəs/ ▸*adj.* sensible; wise; prudent. —**ju·di·cious·ly** *adv.*

**ju·do** /'jōōdō/ ▸*n.* sport of unarmed combat derived from jujitsu.

**jug** /jəg/ ▸*n.* **1** large container for liquids, with a handle and a narrow opening for pouring. **2** *inf.* prison.

**jug·ger·naut** /'jəgər,nôt/ ▸*n.* overwhelming force or object.

**jug·gle** /'jəgəl/ ▸*v.* **1** toss objects into the air and catch them, keeping several in the air at the same time. **2** deal with (several activities) at once.

**3** misrepresent (something) so as to deceive.

**jug·u·lar** /'jəgyələr/ ▸*adj.* of the neck or throat.

▸*n.* short for **JUGULAR VEIN.**

□ **go for the jugular** attack aggressively.

**jug·u·lar vein** ▸*n.* any of several large veins of the neck, carrying blood from the head.

**juice** /jōōs/ ▸*n.* **1** liquid part of fruit or vegetables. **2** (**juices**) fluid secreted by the body. **3** *inf.* fuel or electricity. **4** *inf.* alcoholic drink. —**juic·y** *adj.*

**juic·er** ▸*n.* device for extracting juice from fruits and vegetables.

**ju·jit·su** /,jōō'jitsōō/ (also **jiu·jit·su**) ▸*n.* Japanese system of unarmed combat and physical training.

**juke·box** /'jōōk,bäks/ ▸*n.* coin-operated machine for playing selected music.

**Jul.** ▸*abbr.* July.

**ju·li·enne** /,jōōlē'en/ ▸*adj.* cut into thin strips.

**Ju·ly** /jōō'lī/ ▸*n.* (*pl.* **Ju·lys**) seventh month of the year.

**jum·ble** /'jəmbəl/ ▸*v.* **1** confuse; mix up. **2** move about in disorder.

▸*n.* confused state or heap. —**jumb·ly** *adj.*

**jum·bo** /'jəmbō/ ▸adj. inf. very large.

**jump** /jəmp/ ▸v. **1** move off the ground by sudden muscular effort in the legs. **2** move suddenly or hastily. **3** rise suddenly: *prices jumped.* **4** pass over (an obstacle, etc.) by jumping.
▸n. **1** act of jumping. **2** abrupt rise in amount, value, status, etc. **3** obstacle to be jumped. **4 a** sudden transition. **b** gap in a series, logical sequence, etc.
□ **get** (or **have**) **a jump on** *inf.* get (or have) an early advantage over. □ **jump at** accept eagerly.

**jump·er** ▸n. **1** person or animal that jumps. **2** (also **jumper cable**) one of a pair of cables attached to a battery and used to start a motor vehicle with a weak or discharged battery. **3** sleeveless one-piece dress worn over a blouse. **4** loose jacket.

**jump-start** ▸v. start (a car with a dead battery) with jumper cables.
▸n. starting a car in such a way.

**jump·suit** ▸n. one-piece garment for the whole body.

**jump·y** ▸adj. (**-i·er, -i·est**) **1** nervous; easily startled. **2** making sudden movements.

**Jun.** ▸abbr. **1** June. **2** Junior.

**junc·tion** /'jəNGkSHən/ ▸n. **1** joint; joining point. **2** place where railroad lines or roads meet or cross. **3** joining.

**junc·tion box** ▸n. box containing a junction of electric cables, etc.

**junc·ture** /'jəNG(k)CHər/ ▸n. **1** critical moment of time: *at this juncture.* **2** place where things join. **3** joining.

**June** /jōōn/ ▸n. sixth month of the year.

**June bug** ▸n. large brown scarab beetle.

**jun·gle** /'jəNGgəl/ ▸n. **1** land with dense vegetation, esp. in the tropics. **2** place of vicious struggle.

**jun·gle gym** ▸n. playground structure with bars, ladders, etc., for climbing.

**jun·ior** /'jōōnyər/ ▸adj. **1** of or referring to younger people. **2** the younger (esp. appended to the name of a son with his father's name). **3** lower in age, standing, or position.
▸n. **1** person a specified number of years younger than another. **2** third-year high school or college student. **3** one's inferior in length of service, etc.

**jun·ior col·lege** ▸*n.* two-year college.

**jun·ior high school** ▸*n.* school for grades seven, eight, and sometimes nine.

**ju·ni·per** /ˈjo͞onəpər/ ▸*n.* evergreen shrub or tree with prickly leaves and dark purple berrylike cones.

**junk** /jəNGk/ ▸*n.* **1** discarded articles; rubbish. **2** thing of little value. **3** *inf.* narcotic drug. **4** flat-bottomed sailing vessel in the China seas.
▸*v.* discard as junk.

**junk bond** ▸*n.* high-interest bond deemed to be a risky investment.

**jun·ket** /ˈjəNGkit/ ▸*n.* **1** pleasure outing. **2** official's tour at public expense.
▸*v.* go on a junket.

**junk food** ▸*n.* food with low nutritional value.

**junk·ie** /ˈjəNGkē/ ▸*n.* *inf.* drug addict.

**junk mail** ▸*n.* unsolicited advertising matter sent through the mail.

**Ju·no·esque** /ˌjo͞onōˈesk/ ▸*adj.* (of a woman) imposingly tall and shapely.

**jun·ta** /ˈho͞ontə/ ▸*n.* political or military clique taking power in a coup d'état.

**Ju·pi·ter** /ˈjo͞opitər/ ▸*n.* largest planet of the solar system, fifth from the sun.

**ju·ris·dic·tion** /ˌjo͞orisˈdikSHən/ ▸*n.* **1** legal or other authority. **2** extent of this authority. —**ju·ris·dic·tion·al** *adj.*

**ju·ris·pru·dence** /ˌjo͞oris-ˈpro͞odns/ ▸*n.* science or philosophy of law.

**ju·rist** /ˈjo͞orist/ ▸*n.* expert in law.

**ju·ror** /ˈjo͞orər/ ▸*n.* member of a jury.

**ju·ry** /ˈjo͞orē/ ▸*n.* (*pl.* **-ries**) **1** body of persons sworn to give a verdict in a court of justice. **2** body of persons awarding prizes in a competition.

**just** /jəst/ ▸*adj.* **1** morally right or fair. **2** (of treatment, etc.) deserved: *just reward.* **3** right in amount, etc.; proper.
▸*adv.* **1** exactly: *just what I need.* **2** a little time ago: *have just seen them.* **3** *inf.* simply; merely: *just good friends.* **4** barely; no more than: *just a minute.* **5** *inf.* positively: *just splendid.* —**just·ness** *n.*
□ **just about** *inf.* almost exactly; almost completely. □ **just in case** as a precaution.

**jus·tice** /ˈjəstis/ ▶n. **1** just behavior or treatment. **2** exercise of authority in the maintenance of the law. **3** judge or magistrate.

**jus·tice of the peace** ▶n. magistrate who hears minor cases, grants licenses, performs marriages, etc.

**jus·ti·fy** /ˈjəstəˌfī/ ▶v. (-fied) **1** show the justice, rightness, or correctness of. **2** demonstrate adequate grounds for (conduct, a claim, etc.). **3** vindicate. **4** [as *adj.* **justified**] just; right. **5** *Printing* adjust (a line of type) to fill a space evenly.
—**jus·ti·fi·a·ble** *adj.*
—**jus·ti·fi·ca·tion** *n.*

**jut** /jət/ ▶v. (**jut·ted**, **jut·ting**) protrude; project.

**jute** /jo͞ot/ ▶n. rough fiber from the bark of an E. Indian plant, used for sacking, mats, etc.

**ju·ve·nes·cence** /ˌjo͞ovə-ˈnesəns/ ▶n. state or period of being young.

**ju·ve·nile** /ˈjo͞ovənl/ ▶adj. **1** of or for young people. **2** immature. ▶n. **1** young person. **2** *Law* person below the age at which ordinary criminal prosecution is possible.

**ju·ve·nile de·lin·quen·cy** ▶n. offenses committed by minors.
—**ju·ve·nile de·lin·quent** *n.*

**ju·ve·nil·i·a** /ˌjo͞ovəˈnilēə/ ▶pl. n. works produced by an author or artist while still young.

**jux·ta·pose** /ˈjəkstəˌpōz/ ▶v. place (things) side by side.
—**jux·ta·po·si·tion** *n.*

# Kk

**K**[1] /kā/ (also **k**) ▶*n.* (*pl.* **Ks** or **K's**; **k's**) eleventh letter of the alphabet.

**K**[2] (also **K.**) ▶*abbr.* **1** kelvin(s). **2** King; King's. **3** *Computing* **a** unit of 1,024 ($2^{10}$) bytes or bits, or loosely 1,000. **b** kilobyte(s). **4** 1,000. **5** *Baseball* strikeout.

**K**[3] ▶*symb. Chem.* potassium.

**k** ▶*abbr.* **1** karat(s). **2** kilogram(s). **3** kilometer(s). **4** knot(s).

**ka·bu·ki** /kəˈbo͞okē/ ▶*n.* form of traditional Japanese drama.

**kai·ser** /ˈkīzər/ *hist.* ▶*n.* emperor, esp. of Germany, Austria, or the Holy Roman Empire.

**ka·ke·mo·no** /ˌkäkəˈmōnō/ ▶*n.* (*pl.* **-nos**) Japanese unframed painting made on paper or silk and displayed as a wall hanging.

**kale** /kāl/ ▶*n.* variety of dark-green wrinkle-leafed cabbage.

**ka·lei·do·scope** /kəˈlīdəˌskōp/ ▶*n.* **1** tube containing mirrors and pieces of colored glass, etc., producing changing patterns when rotated. **2** constantly changing group of bright or interesting objects. —**ka·lei·do·scop·ic** *adj.*

**kame** /kām/ ▶*n.* steep-sided mound of sand and gravel deposited by a melting ice sheet.

**kan·ga·roo** /ˌkaNGgəˈro͞o/ ▶*n.* Australian marsupial with a long tail and strong back legs that travels by jumping.

**kan·ga·roo court** ▶*n.* improperly constituted or illegal court held by a group of people.

**Kans.** ▶*abbr.* Kansas.

**ka·o·lin** /ˈkāəlin/ ▶*n.* fine, soft, white clay used esp. for porcelain.

**ka·pok** /ˈkāˌpäk/ ▶*n.* fibrous, cottonlike substance from a tropical tree, used for stuffing cushions, etc.

**ka·put** /kəˈpo͝ot/ ▶*adj. inf.* broken; ruined; done for.

**ka·ra·o·ke** /ˌkarēˈōkē/ ▶*n.* entertainment in which people sing against prerecorded popular song tracks.

**ka·rat** /ˈkarət/ ▶*n.* measure of purity of gold, pure gold being 24 karats. (Abbr.: **k**)

**ka·ra·te** /kəˈrätē/ ▶*n.* Japanese system of unarmed combat using the hands and feet as weapons.

**kar·ma** /'kärmə/ ▶*n.* **1** (in Hinduism and Buddhism) sum of a person's actions in previous lives, viewed as deciding fate in future existences. **2** *inf.* destiny. —**kar·mic** *adj.*

**ka·ty·did** /'kātē,did/ ▶*n.* N. American insect related to the grasshopper.

**kay·ak** /'kī,ak/ ▶*n.* small, enclosed canoe for one paddler.

**ka·zoo** /kə'zoo/ ▶*n.* toy musical instrument into which the player sings or hums.

**KB** ▶*abbr.* kilobyte(s).

**kc** ▶*abbr.* kilocycle(s).

**ked·ger·ee** /'kejə,rē/ ▶*n.* **1** Indian dish consisting chiefly of rice, lentils, onions, and eggs. **2** European dish consisting chiefly of fish, rice, and hard-boiled eggs.

**keel** /kēl/ ▶*n.* main lengthwise structure along the centerline at the bottom of a ship, etc. ▶*v.* (**keel over**) **a** (of a vessel) turn over on its side. **b** *inf.* (of a person) fall over.

**keen** /kēn/ ▶*adj.* **1** eager; ardent. **2** (**keen on**) fond of; enthusiastic about. **3** (of the senses) sharp. **4 a** intellectually acute. **b** (of a remark, etc.) sharp; biting. **5** having a sharp edge or point. ▶*n.* Irish funeral song accompanied with wailing. ▶*v.* utter the keen; mourn by wailing. —**keen·ly** *adv.*

**keep** /kēp/ ▶*v.* (*past* and *past part.* **kept**) **1** have continuous charge of; retain possession of. **2** retain or reserve for a future occasion. **3** retain or remain in a specified condition, position, etc.: *keep cool* **4** put or store in a regular place. **5** detain: *what kept you?* **6** observe, honor, etc. (a law, custom, etc.). **7** maintain (a house, business, accounts, etc.) regularly and in proper order. **8** guard or protect (a person or place). **9** continue. *he kept singing | keeps saying that.* **10** continue to follow (a way or course). **11** remain fresh; not spoil. ▶*n.* **1** maintenance, food, etc.: *hardly earn your keep.* **2** *hist.* tower or stronghold. —**keep·er** *n.*

□ **for keeps** *inf.* (esp. of something received or won) permanently; indefinitely. □ **keep at** persist or cause to persist with. □ **keep back 1** remain at a distance. **2** retard the progress of.

**3** withhold: *kept back $50.* □ **keep down** **1** hold in subjection. **2** keep low in amount. **3** lie low; stay hidden. **4** not vomit (food eaten). □ **keep in mind** take into account having remembered. □ **keep on** continue to do something: *kept on laughing.* □ **keep out** exclude. □ **keep to oneself** **1** avoid contact with others. **2** refuse to disclose. □ **keep up** **1** maintain (progress, morale, etc.). **2** keep in repair, etc. **3** carry on (a correspondence, etc.). **4** not fall behind: *he had trouble keeping up because she was walking so fast.*

**keep·sake** ▶*n.* souvenir, esp. of the giver.

**keg** /keg/ ▶*n.* small barrel.

**kelp** /kelp/ ▶*n.* brown seaweed used as a food and mineral source.

**kel·vin** /ˈkelvin/ ▶*n.* unit of thermodynamic temperature, equal in magnitude to the degree celsius. (Abbr.: **K**). □ **Kelvin scale** scale of temperature with absolute zero as zero.

**ken** /ken/ ▶*n.* range of sight or knowledge.

**Ken.** ▶*abbr.* Kentucky.

**ken·nel** /ˈkenl/ ▶*n.* **1** small shelter for a dog. **2** breeding or boarding place for dogs. ▶*v.* (**-neled**, **-nel·ing**) put or go into; keep or live in a kennel.

**Ken·te** /ˈkentā/ (or **Ken·te cloth**) ▶*n.* colorful woven fabric of Ghanaian origin.

**ker·chief** /ˈkərCHif/ ▶*n.* **1** cloth used to cover the head or neck. **2** handkerchief. —**ker·chiefed** *adj.*

**kerf** /kərf/ ▶*n.* **1** slit made by cutting, esp. with a saw. **2** cut end of a felled tree.

**ker·nel** /ˈkərnl/ ▶*n.* **1** center within the hard shell of a nut, fruit stone, seed, etc. **2** whole seed of a cereal. **3** essence of anything.

**ker·o·sene** /ˈkerəˌsēn/ ▶*n.* petroleum distillate used as a fuel, solvent, etc.

**kes·trel** /ˈkestrəl/ ▶*n.* small hovering falcon.

**ketch·up** /ˈkeCHəp/ (also **cat·sup**) ▶*n.* spicy tomato-based condiment.

**ket·tle** /ˈketl/ ▶*n.* vessel for boiling or cooking. □ **a fine** (or **pretty**) **kettle of fish** *inf.* awkward state of affairs.

**ket·tle·drum** ▶*n.* large bowl-shaped drum.

**key** /kē/ ▸*n.* (*pl.* **keys**)
**1** instrument, usu. metal, for moving the bolt of a lock to lock or unlock. **2** similar implement for winding a clock, etc. **3** finger-operated button or lever on a piano, flute, typewriter, computer terminal, etc. **4** low-lying island or reef, esp. off Florida. **5 a** solution or explanation. **b** word or system for solving a cipher or code. **c** explanatory list of symbols used in a map, table, etc. **6** *Mus.* system of notes related to each other and based on a particular note: *key of C major.*
▸*adj.* essential; of vital importance.
▸*v.* (**keys**, **keyed**) **1** enter (data) by means of a keyboard. **2** fasten with a pin, bolt, etc. **3** align or link (one thing to another). **4** regulate the pitch of the strings of (a violin, etc.).
☐ **keyed up** nervous or tense.

**key·board** ▸*n.* **1** set of keys on a computer, piano, etc. **2** piano-like electronic musical instrument.
▸*v.* enter (data) by means of a keyboard. —**key·board·er** *n.* —**key·board·ist** *n.*

**key·hole** ▸*n.* hole for inserting a key in a lock or clock.

**key·note** ▸*n.* **1** prevailing tone or idea: *keynote address.* **2** *Mus.* note on which a key is based.

**key·stone** ▸*n.* **1** central locking stone of an arch. **2** central principle of a system, policy, etc.

**kg** ▸*abbr.* kilogram(s).

**kha·ki** /'kakē/ ▸*adj.* dull brownish-yellow.
▸*n.* (*pl.* **kha·kis**) **1 a** khaki fabric of twilled cotton or wool. **b** (**khakis**) pants or a military uniform made of this fabric. **2** dull brownish-yellow color.

**khan** /kän/ ▸*n.* title of rulers and officials in Central Asia, Afghanistan, etc. —**khan·ate** *n.*

**kHz** ▸*abbr.* kilohertz.

**kib·butz** /ki'bo͞ots/ ▸*n.* (*pl.* **kib·but·zim**) communal, esp. farming, settlement in Israel.

**ki·bosh** /kə'bäsh; 'kī,bäsh/ ▸*n.* (in phrase **put the kibosh on**) put an end to; dispose of decisively.

**kick** /kik/ ▸*v.* **1** strike or propel forcibly with the foot or hoof, etc. **2** *inf.* give up (a habit). **3** (**kick oneself**) be annoyed with oneself: *I could kick myself.*
▸*n.* **1** blow with the foot or hoof, etc. **2** *inf.* **a** sharp stimulant effect, esp. of alcohol.

**b** pleasurable thrill: *did it for kicks.* **3** *inf.* temporary interest: *on a jogging kick.* **4** recoil of a fired gun.

□ **kick around** *inf.* **1** drift idly from place to place. **2 a** treat roughly or scornfully. **b** discuss (an idea) unsystematically. □ **kick in 1** knock down (a door, etc.) by kicking. **2** *inf.* pay one's share. □ **kick in the pants** (or **teeth**) *inf.* surprise that prompts a fresh effort. □ **kick off 1 a** *Football, etc.* begin or resume play. **b** *inf.* begin. **2** remove (shoes, etc.) by kicking. □ **kick out** expel or dismiss forcibly. □ **kick up one's heels** frolic.

**kick·back** *inf.* ▶*n.* **1** recoil. **2** (usu. illegal) payment for collaboration.

**kick·off** ▶*n.* **1** *Football & Soccer* kick that starts play. **2** start of a campaign, drive, project, etc.

**kick·stand** ▶*n.* rod for supporting a bicycle or motorcycle when stationary.

**kid** /kid/ ▶*n.* **1** *inf.* child or young person. **2** young goat. **3** leather from its skin.

▶*v. inf.* **1** deceive (someone) in a playful or teasing way: *only kidding.* **2** deceive or fool

(someone): *she's kidding herself if she thinks nothing has changed.* □ **handle with kid gloves** treat carefully. □ **no kidding** *inf.* that is the truth.

**kid broth·er** (or **sister**) ▶*n. inf.* younger brother (or sister).

**kid·nap** /'kid,nap/ ▶*v.* (**-napped, -nap·ping; -naped, -nap·ing**) abduct (someone), esp. to obtain a ransom. —**kid·nap·per** *n.*

**kid·ney** /'kidnē/ ▶*n.* (*pl.* **-neys**) either of two organs in the abdominal cavity of vertebrates that remove wastes from the blood and excrete urine.

**kid·ney bean** ▶*n.* red-skinned kidney-shaped bean.

**kid·ney stone** ▶*n.* an accretion of minerals sometimes found in the kidney.

**kill** /kil/ ▶*v.* **1** cause the death of. **2** destroy; put an end to (feelings, etc.). **3** switch off (a light, engine, etc.). **4** pass (time, or a specified period) usu. while waiting. **5** defeat (legislation, etc.). **6** render ineffective (taste, sound, color, etc.): *thick carpet killed the sound of footsteps.*

▶*n.* **1** act of killing. **2** animal or animals killed, esp. by a hunter. **3** *inf.* destruction or disablement of an enemy aircraft, submarine, etc. —**kill·er** *n.*

□ **dressed to kill** dressed alluringly or impressively. □ **in at the kill** present at or benefiting from the successful conclusion of an enterprise. □ **kill two birds with one stone** achieve two aims at once. □ **kill with kindness** spoil (a person) with overindulgence.

**kill·er whale** ▶*n.* a predatory dolphin with a prominent dorsal fin.

**kill·ing** ▶*n.* **1 a** causing of death. **b** instance of this. **2** great (esp. financial) success: *she made a killing in real estate.*
▶*adj. inf.* exhausting.

**kill·joy** ▶*n.* gloomy person, esp. at a party, etc.

**kiln** /kiln/ ▶*n.* furnace or oven for baking bricks, pottery, etc.

**ki·lo** /ˈkēlō/ ▶*n.* (*pl.* **-los**) **1** kilogram. **2** kilometer.

**kilo-** /ˈkilō; ˈkilə/ ▶*comb. form* denoting a factor of 1,000 (esp. in metric units). (Abbr.: **k, K**)

**kil·o·byte** *Computing* ▶*n.* 1,024 (2$^{10}$ bytes) as a measure of data storage.

**kil·o·gram** ▶*n.* metric unit of mass, approx. 2.205 lb. (Abbr.: **kg**).

**kil·o·hertz** ▶*n.* 1,000 hertz; 1,000 cycles per second. (Abbr.: **kHz**).

**kil·o·li·ter** ▶1,000 liters. (Abbr.: **kl**).

**kil·o·me·ter** /kiˈlämitər/ ▶*n.* 1,000 meters (approx. 0.62 miles). (Abbr.: **km**). —**kil·o·met·ric** *adj.*

**kil·o·watt** ▶*n.* 1,000 watts. (Abbr.: **kW**).

**kilt** /kilt/ ▶*n.* knee-length skirt, usu. of pleated tartan, traditionally worn by Scottish Highland men.

**ki·mo·no** /kəˈmōnō/ ▶*n.* (*pl.* **-nos**) **1** long, loose Japanese robe worn with a sash. **2** similar dressing gown.

**kin** /kin/ ▶*n.* one's relatives or family.

**-kin** ▶*suffix* forming diminutive nouns: *catkin* | *manikin.*

**kind** /kīnd/ ▶*n.* **1** race, species, or natural group of animals, plants, etc. **2** class; type; sort; variety.
▶*adj.* of a friendly, generous, or gentle nature. —**kind·ness** *n.*

□ **in kind 1** in the same form; likewise: *replied in kind.* **2** (of payment) in goods or labor, not money. □ **nothing of the kind 1** not at all like the thing in question. **2** (expressing denial) not at all.

**kin·der·gar·ten** /ˈkindərˌgärtn/ ▸*n.* school or class preparing children for first grade.

**kind·heart·ed** ▸*adj.* of a kind disposition.

**kin·dle** /ˈkindl/ ▸*v.* **1** light or catch on fire. **2** arouse; inspire.

**kin·dling** /ˈkindliNG/ ▸*n.* small sticks, etc., for lighting fires.

**kind·ly** /ˈkīndlē/ ▸*adv.* **1** in a kind manner. **2** please: *kindly leave me alone.*
▸*adj.* (**-lier, -liest**) kind; warmhearted.
□ **not take kindly to** not be pleased by.

**kin·dred** /ˈkindrid/ ▸*n.* one's relations, collectively.
▸*adj.* related, allied, or similar: *I longed to find a kindred spirit.*

**ki·net·ic** /kiˈnetik/ ▸*adj.* of or due to motion. —**ki·net·i·cal·ly** *adv.*

**king** /kiNG/ ▸*n.* **1** male sovereign, esp. a hereditary ruler. **2** person preeminent in a specified field, etc. **3** large (or the largest) kind of plant, animal, etc.: *king penguin.* **4** *Chess* piece that must be checkmated for a win. **5** crowned piece in checkers. **6** playing card depicting a king.

**king·dom** /ˈkiNGdəm/ ▸*n.*
**1** territory subject to a king or queen. **2** spiritual reign attributed to God. **3** domain; sphere. **4** province of nature: *vegetable kingdom.*

**king·fish·er** ▸*n.* long-beaked, brightly colored bird that dives for fish in rivers, etc.

**king-size** (or **-sized**) ▸*adj.* larger than normal; very large.

**kink** /kiNGk/ ▸*n.* **1 a** twist or bend in wire, etc. **b** tight wave in hair. **2** mental twist or quirk.
▸*v.* form or cause to form a kink.

**kin·ship** ▸*n.* **1** blood relationship. **2** sharing of characteristics or origins.

**ki·osk** /ˈkēˌäsk/ ▸*n.* **1** open-fronted booth from which food, newspapers, tickets, etc., are sold. **2** columnar structure for posting notices, etc.

**kip·per** /ˈkipər/ ▸*n.* kippered fish, esp. herring.
▸*v.* cure by splitting, salting, and drying.

**kis·met** /ˈkizmit; -ˌmet/ ▸*n.* destiny; fate.

**kiss** /kis/ ▸*v.* **1** touch with the lips, esp. as a sign of love, affection, greeting, or reverence. **2** lightly touch.
▸*n.* **1** touch with the lips. **2** light

touch. **3** droplet-shaped piece of candy, etc.

□ **kiss and tell** recount one's sexual exploits. □ **kiss of death** action or event that causes certain failure.

**kit** /kit/ ▸*n.* **1** articles, equipment, etc., for a specific purpose. **2** set of parts needed to assemble an item. **3** kitten. **4** young fox, badger, etc.

□ **kit bag** usu. cylindrical bag used for carrying equipment, etc.

**kitch·en** /ˈkiCHən/ ▸*n.* room or area where food is prepared and cooked.

□ **everything but the kitchen sink** everything imaginable.

**kite** /kīt/ ▸*n.* **1** light framework with thin covering, flown on a string in the wind. **2** soaring bird of prey with long wings and usu. a forked tail.

**kith** /kiTH/ ▸*n.* (in phrase **kith and kin** or **kith or kin**) one's friends, acquaintances, and relations.

**kitsch** /kiCH/ ▸*n.* garish, pretentious, or vulgar art.

**kit·ten** /ˈkitn/ ▸*n.* young cat.

□ **have kittens** *inf.* be extremely upset or anxious.

**kit·ten·ish** ▸*adj.* **1** playful; lively. **2** flirtatious.

**kit·ty** ▸*n.* (*pl.* **-ties**) **1** kitten.

**2** pool of money collected from a number of people and designated for a particular purpose.

**ki·va** /ˈkēvə/ ▸*n.* chamber, built wholly or partly underground, used by male Pueblo Indians for religious rites.

**ki·wi** /ˈkēwē/ ▸*n.* (*pl.* **ki·wis**) **1** flightless long-billed New Zealand bird. **2** (**Kiwi**) *inf.* New Zealander. **3** (**kiwi fruit**) fuzzy-skinned, green-fleshed fruit.

**KKK** ▸*abbr.* Ku Klux Klan.

**kl** ▸*abbr.* kiloliter(s).

**klatch** /kläCH; klaCH/ (also **klatsch**) ▸*n.* social gathering, esp. for coffee and conversation.

**Klee·nex** /ˈklēneks/ ▸*trademark* a brand of disposable paper tissue for blowing the nose.

**klep·to·ma·ni·a** /ˌkleptəˈmānēə/ ▸*n.* recurrent urge to steal. —**klep·to·ma·ni·ac** *n. & adj.*

**klieg** /klēg/ (usu. **klieg light**) ▸*n.* powerful electric lamp used in filming.

**klutz** /kləts/ ▸*n. inf.* clumsy, awkward, or foolish person. —**klutz·y** *adj.*

**km** ▸*abbr.* kilometer(s).

**knack** /nak/ ▸*n.* acquired faculty of doing a thing.

**knap·sack** /'nap,sak/ ▸n. bag of supplies, etc., carried on the back.

**knave** /nāv/ ▸n. **1** rogue; scoundrel. **2** JACK (playing card). —**knav·er·y** n. —**knav·ish** adj.

**knead** /nēd/ ▸v. **1** prepare dough, paste, etc., by pressing and folding. **2** massage (muscles, etc.) as if kneading.

**knee** /nē/ ▸n. **1** joint between the thigh and the lower leg in humans and other animals. **2** part of a garment covering the knee.
□ **bring a person to his** or **her knees** reduce a person to submission.

**knee-jerk** ▸adj. predictable; automatic: *knee-jerk reaction*.

**knee·cap** ▸n. bone in front of the knee joint; patella.

**kneel** /nēl/ ▸v. (*past* and *past part.* **knelt** or **kneeled**) fall or rest on the knees or a knee.

**knell** /nel/ ▸n. **1** sound of a bell, esp. for a death or funeral. **2** announcement, event, etc., regarded as an ill omen.
▸v. (of a bell) ring solemnly.

**knick·ers** /'nikərz/ ▸pl. n. loose-fitting pants gathered at the knee or calf.

**knick·knack** /'nik,nak/ ▸n. trinket or small, dainty article.

**knife** /nīf/ ▸n. (*pl.* **knives**) cutting tool, usu. with a sharp-edged blade in a handle.
▸v. cut or stab with a knife.
□ **under the knife** undergoing surgery.

**knight** /nīt/ ▸n. **1** (in the Middle Ages) man who served his lord as an armored mounted soldier. **2** chess piece usu. shaped like a horse's head.
□ **knight in shining armor** chivalrous rescuer or helper, esp. of a woman.

**knit** /nit/ ▸v. (**knit·ting; knit·ted** or **knit**) **1** make (a garment, etc.) by interlocking loops of yarn with knitting needles or a knitting machine. **2** contract (the forehead) in vertical wrinkles. **3** make or become close or compact: *a close-knit group*.
▸n. knitted material or garment.

**knob** /näb/ ▸n. rounded protuberance, esp. at the end or on the surface of a thing as the handle of a door, drawer, etc. —**knob·by** adj.

**knock** /näk/ ▸v. **1** strike or thump against a surface with an audible sharp blow. **2** collide with someone or something, giving a sharp blow: *he ran into her, knocking her shoulder.* **3** force to move by a blow: *knocked her hand away.* **4** *inf.* criticize: *don't knock it!* **5** (of an engine) make a thumping or rattling noise.

▶*n.* **1** sudden short sound caused by a blow: *there was a loud knock on the back door.* **2** blow or collision. **3** injury caused by a blow or collision: *a knock on the head.* **4** sound of knocking in an engine.

□ **knock around** travel without a specific purpose. □ **knock down 1** strike (esp. a person) to the ground. **2** demolish. **3** *inf.* lower the price of (an article). □ **knock off 1** finish work. **2** rapidly produce (a work of art, etc.). **3** deduct (a sum) from a price, etc. **4** *inf.* steal from: *knocked off a liquor store.* **5** *inf.* kill. □ **knock on** (or **knock**) **wood** knock something wooden with the knuckles to avert bad luck. □ **knock out 1** make unconscious by a blow on the head. **2** *inf.* astonish. **3** *inf.* exhaust: *knocked themselves out swimming.* □ **knock together** assemble hastily or roughly. □ **knock up 1** make hastily. **2** *vulgar, inf.* make pregnant.

**knock·out** ▶*n.* **1** *Boxing* blow that knocks an opponent out. **2** *inf.* outstanding or irresistible person or thing.

**knoll** /nōl/ ▶*n.* small hill or mound.

**knot** /nät/ ▶*n.* **1 a** intertwining of rope, string, hair, etc., with another, itself, or something else to join or fasten together. **b** tangle in hair, knitting, etc. **2** unit of a ship's or aircraft's speed, equivalent to one nautical mile per hour. **3** hard mass in a tree trunk at the intersection with a branch.

▶*v.* (**knot·ted**, **knot·ting**) **1** tie in a knot. **2** entangle.

□ **tie the knot** get married.

**knout** /nout/ ▶*n.* (in imperial Russia) a whip used to inflict punishment, often causing death.

▶*v.* flog (someone) with such a whip.

**know** /nō/ ▶*v.* (*past* **knew**; *past part.* **known**) **1 a** have in the mind; have learned; be able to recall: *knows what to do.* **b** have a good command of: *knew German.* **2** be acquainted with. **3** recognize; identify: *I knew him at once.* **4** [as *adj.* **known**] **a** publicly acknowledge: *a known* thief. **b** *Math.* (of a quantity, etc.) have a value that can be stated.

▶*n.* (in phrase **in the know**) *inf.* well-informed; having special knowledge.

□ **know-it-all** *inf.* person who acts as if he or she knows everything. □ **know of** be aware of: *not that I know of.* □ **you know** *inf.* expression implying something generally known: *you know, the store on the corner.* □ **you never know** nothing in the future is certain.

**know-how** ▶*n.* **1** practical knowledge. **2** natural skill or invention.

**know·ing** ▶*n.* state of being aware or informed of any thing.

▶*adj.* excessively or prematurely shrewd: *today's society is too knowing, too corrupt.* —**know·ing·ly** *adv.*

**knowl·edge** /'nälij/ ▶*n.* **1** awareness or familiarity (of a person, fact, or thing): *have no knowledge of their character.* **2** understanding of a subject, language, etc.: *good knowledge of Greek.*

□ **to (the best of) my knowledge** so far as I know.

**knowl·edge·a·ble** ▶*adj.* well-informed. —**knowl·edge·a·bly** *adv.*

**know-noth·ing** ▶*n.* **1** ignorant person. **2** (**Know-Nothing**) member of a political party in the U.S., prominent from 1853 to 1856, that was antagonistic toward Roman Catholics and recent immigrants and whose members preserved its secrecy by denying its existence.

**knuck·le** /'nəkəl/ ▶*n.* **1** bone at a finger joint, esp. that adjoining the hand. **2** knee or ankle joint of an animal, used as food.

▶*v.* strike, press, or rub with the knuckles.

□ **knuckle down** apply oneself seriously to a task, etc. □ **knuckle under** give in; submit.

**knuck·le·head** ▶*n. inf.* slow-witted or stupid person.

**knurl** /nərl/ ▶*n.* small projecting knob or ridge, esp. in a series around the edge of something.

**KO** ▶*abbr.* knockout.

**ko·a·la** /kōˈälə/ ▶*n.* Australian bearlike marsupial with thick gray fur.

**kohl·ra·bi** /kōlˈräbē/ ▶*n.* (*pl.* **-bies**) cabbage with an edible turniplike stem.

**koi·no·ni·a** /ˌkoinəˈnēə/ ▶*n.* Christian fellowship or

communion, with God or, more commonly, with fellow Christians.

**kook** /kook/ *inf.* ▶*n.* crazy or eccentric person. —**kook·y** *adj.*

**Ko·ran** /kə'rän/ ▶*n.* the sacred book of Islam. —**Ko·ran·ic** *adj.*

**ko·re** /'kôrē; 'kôrā/ ▶*n.* (*pl.* **ko·rai** /'kôrī/) archaic Greek statue of a young woman, standing and clothed in long loose robes.

**Ko·re·an** /kə'rēən/ ▶*n.* **1** native or national of N. or S. Korea in SE Asia. **2** language of Korea. ▶*adj.* of or relating to Korea or its people or language.

**ko·sher** /'kōsHər/ ▶*adj.* **1** (of food, etc.) fulfilling the requirements of Jewish law. **2** *inf.* correct; genuine; legitimate.

**kow·tow** /'kou'tou/ ▶*n. hist.* Chinese custom of kneeling and touching the ground with the forehead in worship or submission. ▶*v.* act in a subservient manner.

**kryp·ton** /'krip,tän/ ▶*n. Chem.* inert gaseous element used in fluorescent lamps, etc. (Symb.: **Kr**).

**KS** ▶*abbr.* Kansas (in official postal use).

**ku·dos** /'k(y)oo,dōs/ ▶*n. inf.* glory; renown.

**kum·quat** /'kəm,kwät/ ▶*n.* **1** small orangelike fruit. **2** shrub or small tree yielding this.

**kung fu** /'kəNG 'foo/ ▶*n.* Chinese martial art similar to karate.

**kvell** /k(ə)vel/ ▶*v.* feel happy and proud.

**kvetch** /kvecH/ *inf.* ▶*n.* someone who complains a lot. ▶*v.* complain; whine.

**kW** ▶*abbr.* kilowatt(s).

**Kwan·zaa** /'kwänzə/ ▶*n.* secular festival observed by many African Americans from December 26 to January 1 as a celebration of their cultural heritage and traditional values.

**kwash·i·or·kor** /,kwäsHē'ôrkôr; -kər/ ▶*n.* form of malnutrition caused by protein deficiency in the diet, typically affecting young children in the tropics.

**KY** ▶*abbr.* Kentucky (in official postal use).

**Ky.** ▶*abbr.* Kentucky.

# Ll

**L**[1] /el/ (also **l**) ▸*n.* (*pl.* **Ls** or **L's**; **l's**)
**1** twelfth letter of the alphabet.
**2** (as a Roman numeral) 50.
**3** thing shaped like an L, as a joint connecting two pipes at right angles.

**L**[2] (also **L.**) ▸*abbr.* **1** Lake. **2** Latin.
**3** large.

**l** (also **l.**) ▸*abbr.* **1** left. **2** line.
**3** liter(s). **4** length.

**LA** ▸*abbr.* **1** Los Angeles.
**2** Louisiana (in official postal use).

**La** ▸*symb. Chem.* lanthanum.

**La.** ▸*abbr.* Louisiana.

**la** /lä/ *Mus.* ▸*n.* sixth note of a major scale.

**lab** /lab/ *inf.* ▸*n.* laboratory.

**la·bel** /ˈlābəl/ ▸*n.* **1** usu. small piece of paper, etc., attached to an object to give information about it. **2** short classifying phrase applied to a person, a work of art, etc.
▸*v.* **1** attach a label to. **2** assign to a category: *labeled them stupid.*

**la·bi·a** /ˈlābēə/ ▸*pl. n.* inner and outer folds of the vulva, at either side of the vagina.

**la·bi·um** /ˈlābēəm/ ▸*n.* (*pl.* **la·bi·a**)

each fold of skin enclosing the vulva.

**la·bor** /ˈlābər/ ▸*n.* **1** physical or mental work; exertion.
**2** workers, esp. manual, considered as a class or political force. **3** process of childbirth.
**4** particular task.
▸*v.* **1** work hard; exert oneself.
**2** strive for a purpose. **3** belabor.
**4** [as *adj.* **labored**] done with great effort; not spontaneous.
—**la·bor·er** *n.*
□ **labor-intensive** needing a large workforce. □ **labor of love** task done for pleasure, not reward.

**lab·o·ra·to·ry** /ˈlabrəˌtôrē/ ▸*n.* (*pl.* **-ries**) room or building for scientific experiments, research, etc.

**La·bor Day** ▸*n.* first Monday in September (or in some countries May 1), celebrated in honor of working people.

**la·bo·ri·ous** /ləˈbôrēəs/ ▸*adj.*
**1** needing hard work or toil.
**2** (esp. of literary style) showing signs of toil; not fluent.

**la·bor un·ion** ▸*n.* association of workers formed to protect and further their rights and interests.

**la·bret** /ˈlābret; -brit/ ▶*n.* object such as a small piece of shell, bone, or stone inserted into the lip as an ornament in some cultures.

**lab·y·rinth** /ˈlab(ə)ˌrinTH/ ▶*n.* complicated network of passages or paths. —**lab·y·rin·thi·an** *adj.* —**lab·y·rin·thine** *adj.*

**lace** /lās/ ▶*n.* **1** fine open fabric, made by weaving thread in patterns. **2** cord, etc., passed through eyelets or hooks for fastening shoes, etc.

▶*v.* **1** fasten or tighten with a lace or laces. **2** flavor (a drink) with liquor.

**lac·er·ate** /ˈlasəˌrāt/ ▶*v.* mangle or tear (esp. flesh or tissue). —**lac·er·a·tion** *n.*

**lach·es** /ˈlaCHiz/ ▶*n.* unreasonable delay in making an assertion or claim, such as asserting a right, claiming a privilege, or making an application for redress, which may result in refusal.

**lach·ry·mal** /ˈlakrəməl/ (also **lac·ri·mal**) ▶*adj. formal* or *poet./lit.* connected with tears or weeping.

**lach·ry·mose** /ˈlakrəˌmōs/ ▶*adj.* given to weeping; tearful.

**lack** /lak/ ▶*n.* want; deficiency: *lack of talent.*

▶*v.* be without or deficient in: *lacks courage.* —**lack·ing** *adj.*

**lack·a·dai·si·cal** /ˌlakəˈdāzikəl/ ▶*adj.* unenthusiastic; listless; idle.

**lack·ey** /ˈlakē/ ▶*n.* (*pl.* **-eys**) **1** servile follower; toady. **2** *hist.* footman; manservant.

**lack·lus·ter** ▶*adj.* **1** lacking in vitality, etc. **2** (of the hair or eyes) dull.

**la·con·ic** /ləˈkänik/ ▶*adj.* using few words.

**lac·quer** /ˈlakər/ ▶*n.* varnish made of shellac or synthetic substances.

▶*v.* coat with lacquer.

**la·crosse** /ləˈkrôs/ ▶*n.* game like field hockey, but with a ball passed using sticks having a netted pocket.

**lac·tate** /ˈlakˌtāt/ ▶*v.* secrete milk.

**lac·tose** /ˈlakˌtōs/ ▶*n.* sugar that occurs in milk.

**la·cu·na** /ləˈk(y)o͞onə/ ▶*n.* (*pl.* **-nae** or **-nas**) hiatus; gap.

**la·cus·trine** /lə'kəstrin/ ▸*adj.* of, relating to, or associated with lakes.

**lad** /lad/ ▸*n.* boy; youth.

**lad·der** /'ladər/ ▸*n.* set of horizontal bars fixed between two uprights and used for climbing.

**lad·en** /'lādn/ ▸*adj.* burdened; loaded down.

**lad·ing** ▸*n.* goods transported; freight; cargo.

**la·dle** /'lādl/ ▸*n.* long-handled spoon with a cup-shaped bowl for serving liquids. ▸*v.* transfer with a ladle.

**la·dy** /'lādē/ ▸*n.* (*pl.* **-dies**) **1** (as old-fashioned or polite term of reference) woman. **2** woman regarded as being of superior social status or as having refined manners. **3** (**Lady**) British title for a noblewoman. □ **ladies' room** women's restroom.

**la·dy·bug** ▸*n.* small beetle, usu. red-orange, with black spots.

**la·dy·fin·ger** ▸*n.* finger-shaped sponge cake.

**la·dy's-slip·per** ▸*n.* orchid with a small slipper-shaped lip on its flowers.

**lag** /lag/ ▸*v.* (**lagged**, **lag·ging**) fall behind; not keep pace. ▸*n.* delay.

**lag·an** /'lagən/ ▸*n.* (in legal contexts) goods or wreckage lying on the bed of the sea.

**la·ger** /'lägər/ ▸*n.* dry, light-colored, mild-flavored beer.

**lag·gard** /'lagərd/ ▸*n.* person who makes slow progress and falls behind others. —**lag·gard·ly** *adj. & adv.*

**la·goon** /lə'go͞on/ ▸*n.* **1** stretch of salt water separated from the sea by a sandbank, reef, etc. **2** shallow lake near a larger lake or river.

**la·ic** /'lāik/ ▸*adj.* nonclerical; lay. ▸*n.* layperson; a noncleric.

**la·i·cize** /'lāə,sīz/ ▸*v.* withdraw clerical character, control, or status from (someone or something); secularize.

**lair** /le(ə)r/ ▸*n.* **1** wild animal's resting place. **2** person's hiding place.

**laird** /le(ə)rd/ ▸*n.* (in Scotland) a person who owns a large estate.

**lais·sez-faire** /,lesā 'fe(ə)r/ (also **lais·ser-faire**) ▸*n.* policy of non-interference, esp. by a government.

**la·it·y** /'lāitē/ ▸*n.* lay people, as distinct from the clergy.

**lake** /lāk/ ▸*n.* large body of water surrounded by land.

**lam** /lam/ *inf.* ▶*n.* (in phrase **on the lam**) in flight, esp. from the police.

**la·ma** /ˈlämə/ ▶*n.* Tibetan or Mongolian Buddhist monk.

**La·maze meth·od** /ləˈmäz/ ▶*n.* *Med.* method for childbirth in which breathing exercises and relaxation techniques are used to control pain and facilitate delivery.

**lamb** /lam/ ▶*n.* **1** young sheep. **2** mild or gentle person.
▶*v.* give birth to a lamb.

**lam·baste** /lamˈbāst/ (also **lam·bast**) ▶*v. inf.* criticize severely.

**lam·bent** /ˈlambənt/ ▶*adj.* softly radiant. —**lam·ben·cy** *n.*

**lam·bre·quin** /ˈlambərkin; -brə-/ ▶*n.* **1** short piece of decorative drapery hung over the top of a door or window or draped from a shelf or mantelpiece. **2** piece of cloth covering the back of a medieval knight's helmet.

**lame** /lām/ ▶*adj.* **1** disabled, esp. in the foot or leg; limping. **2** (of an excuse, etc.) unconvincing; weak.
▶*v.* make lame; disable.
□ **lame duck** official in the final period of office, after the election of a successor.

**la·mé** /läˌmā/ ▶*n.* fabric with gold or silver threads woven in.

**la·ment** /ləˈment/ ▶*n.*
**1** passionate expression of grief. **2** song or poem of mourning or sorrow.
▶*v.* express or feel grief for or about; regret. —**lam·en·ta·tion** *n.*

**lam·i·na** /ˈlamənə/ ▶*n.* (*pl.* **-nae** /-ˌnē; -ˌnī/) thin layer, plate, or scale of sedimentary rock, organic tissue, or other material.

**lam·i·nate** /ˈlaməˌnāt/ ▶*v.*
**1** overlay with metal plates, a plastic layer, etc. **2** manufacture by placing layer on layer.
▶*n.* laminated structure, esp. of layers fixed together.
▶*adj.* in the form of laminate.
—**lam·i·na·tion** *n.*
—**lam·i·na·tor** *n.*

**lamp** /lamp/ ▶*n.* **1** device for giving light. **2** device producing ultraviolet or infrared radiation.

**lam·poon** /lamˈpo͞on/ ▶*n.* satirical attack on a person, etc.
▶*v.* satirize.

**lam·prey** /ˈlamprē/ ▶*n.* (*pl.* **-preys**) eellike fish with a sucker mouth, horny teeth, and a rough tongue.

**lance** /lans/ ▶*n.* **1** long spear, esp. one used by a horseman.
**2** LANCET.

▶*v.* **1** prick or cut open with a lancet. **2** pierce with a lance.

**lan·cet** /ˈlansit/ ▶*n.* small, two-edged surgical knife with a sharp point.

**land** /land/ ▶*n.* **1** solid part of the earth's surface. **2** expanse of country; ground; soil. **3** country; nation; state. **4** estate.

▶*v.* **1** set or go ashore. **2** alight on or bring (an aircraft, etc.) to the ground. **3** catch (a fish). **4** bring to, reach, or find oneself in a certain situation or place: *landed in jail.* **5** *inf.* win or obtain (a prize, job, etc.).

**land·ed** ▶*adj.* owning land: *landed gentry.*

**land·fall** ▶*n.* approach to land, esp. for the first time on a sea or air journey.

**land·fill** ▶*n.* **1** waste material, etc., used to landscape or reclaim land. **2** place where garbage is buried.

**land·ing** ▶*n.* **1 a** coming to land. **b** place where ships, etc., land. **2** platform between two flights of stairs, or at the top or bottom of a flight.

**land·ing craft** ▶*n.* craft designed for putting troops and equipment ashore.

**land·ing gear** ▶*n.* undercarriage of an aircraft.

**land·ing strip** ▶*n.* strip of land for taking off or landing an aircraft.

**land·locked** ▶*adj.* almost or entirely enclosed by land.

**land·lord** (*fem.* **land·la·dy**, *pl.* **-dies**) ▶*n.* **1** person who rents land or premises to a tenant. **2** person who keeps a boardinghouse, an inn, etc.

**land·lub·ber** /ˈlandˌləbər/ ▶*n.* person unfamiliar with the sea.

**land·mark** ▶*n.* **1 a** conspicuous object in a district, etc. **b** object marking a boundary, etc. **2** prominent or critical event, etc.

**land·mass** ▶*n.* large area of land.

**land mine** ▶*n.* explosive mine laid in or on the ground.

**land·scape** /ˈlandˌskāp/ ▶*n.* **1** scenery, as seen in a broad view from one place. **2** picture representing this; this genre of painting.
▶*v.* improve (a piece of land) by planned plantings, etc.

**land·slide** ▶*n.* **1** sliding down of a mass of land from a mountain. **2** overwhelming victory in an election.

**lane** /lān/ ▸*n.* **1** narrow road or path. **2** division of a road for a stream of traffic.

**lan·guage** /ˈlaɴɢgwij/ ▸*n.* **1** use of words as a method of human communication. **2** language of a particular community or country, etc. **3** system of symbols and rules for writing computer programs. **4** any method of expression: *sign language.*
□ **speak the same language** have a similar outlook, manner of expression, etc.

**lan·guid** /ˈlaɴɢgwid/ ▸*adj.* lacking vigor; idle; inert.

**lan·guish** /ˈlaɴɢgwish/ ▸*v.* **1** lose vitality. **2** droop or pine for.

**lan·guor** /ˈlaɴɢgər/ ▸*n.* **1** lack of energy or vitality. **2** listlessness.

**lank** /laɴɢk/ ▸*adj.* long, limp, and straight.

**lank·y** ▸*adj.* (**-i·er, -i·est**) tall and thin.

**lan·o·lin** /ˈlanl-in/ ▸*n.* fat from sheep's wool used for cosmetics, etc.

**lan·tern** /ˈlantərn/ ▸*n.* lamp with a transparent case protecting a flame, etc.

**lan·tern fish** ▸*n.* marine fish with small light organs on the head and body.

**lan·tern-jawed** ▸*adj.* having a long, thin jaw and prominent chin.

**lan·tha·num** /ˈlanтнənəm/ ▸*n.* a rare-earth metallic element, allied to aluminum. (Symb.: **La**)

**lan·yard** /ˈlanyərd/ ▸*n.* **1** cord worn around the neck or shoulder to which a knife, etc., may be attached. **2** *Naut.* short line for securing, tightening, etc.

**lap** ▸*n.* **1 a** one circuit of a racetrack, etc. **b** section of a journey, etc. **2** front of the body from the waist to the knees of a sitting person.
▸*v.* (**lapped, lap·ping**) **1** coil, fold, or wrap around or enfold in. **2** (usu. of an animal) drink using the tongue. **3** move or beat upon (a shore) with a rippling sound.
□ **in the lap of luxury** in extremely luxurious surroundings.

**lap·a·ros·co·py** /ˌlapəˈräskəpē/ ▸*n.* (*pl.* **-pies**) surgical procedure in which a fiber-optic instrument is inserted through the abdominal wall to view the organs in the abdomen or to permit a surgical procedure.

**la·pel** /ləˈpel/ ▸*n.* part of a coat, jacket, etc., folded back against the front around the neck opening.

**lap·i·dar·y** /ˈlapiˌderē/ ▸*adj.* concerned with stone(s).

▸*n.* (*pl.* **-ies**) cutter, polisher, or engraver of gems.

**lap·is laz·u·li** /ˈlapis ˈlazyəˌlē/ ▸*n.* bright blue semiprecious stone.

**lap·pet** /ˈlapit/ ▸*n.* small flap or fold, in particular:**a** fold or hanging piece of flesh in some animals.**b** loose or overlapping part of a garment.

**lap robe** ▸*n.* blanket, etc., used for warmth, esp. on a journey.

**lapse** /laps/ ▸*n.* **1** slight error. **2** weak decline into an inferior state. **3** passage of time: *after a lapse of three years.*

▸*v.* **1** fail to maintain a position or standard. **2** fall back into (an inferior or previous state): *lapsed into chaos.* **3** become invalid due to disuse, failure to renew, etc.: *her driver's license has lapsed.*

**lap·top** ▸*n.* (also **laptop computer**) portable computer suitable for use while resting on the user's legs.

**lar·ce·ny** /ˈlärs(ə)nē/ ▸*n.* (*pl.* **-nies**) theft of personal property. —**lar·ce·nous** *adj.*

□ **grand larceny** *Law* larceny in which the value of the stolen property exceeds a certain legally established limit. □ **petty larceny***Law* larceny in which the value of the stolen property is less than a certain legally established limit.

**larch** /lärCH/ ▸*n.* deciduous coniferous tree with bright foliage and tough wood.

**lard** /lärd/ ▸*n.* pig fat used in cooking, etc.

▸*v.* **1** insert strips of fat or bacon in (meat, etc.) before cooking. **2** embellish (talk or writing) with foreign or technical terms: *larded with literary allusions.*

**lar·der** /ˈlärdər/ ▸*n.* room or cupboard for storing food.

**large** /lärj/ ▸*adj.* **1** of relatively great size or extent. **2** of wide range; comprehensive.

▸*n.* (**at large**) **1** at liberty. **2** as a body or whole: *popular with the people at large.* **3** without a specific target: *scatters insults at large.* —**large·ness** *n.* —**larg·ish** *adj.*

**large·ly** ▸*adv.* to a great extent.

**lar·gess** /lärˈjes/ (also **lar·gesse**) ▸*n.* generous gifts or gift-giving.

**lar·go** /ˈlärgō/ *Mus.* ▸*adv. & adj.* in a slow tempo and dignified in style.

▶*n.* (*pl.* **-gos**) largo passage or movement.

**lar·i·at** /ˈlarēət/ ▶*n.* **1** lasso. **2** tethering rope.

**lark** /lärk/ ▶*n.* **1** small bird with a tuneful song, esp. the skylark. **2** *inf.* amusing adventure or escapade.

**lark·spur** ▶*n.* plant with a spur-shaped calyx.

**lar·va** /ˈlärvə/ ▶*n.* (*pl.* **-vae**) stage of development of an insect between egg and pupa. —**lar·val** *adj.*

**lar·yn·gi·tis** /ˌlarənˈjītis/ ▶*n.* inflammation of the larynx, often with a loss of voice.

**lar·ynx** /ˈlariNGks/ ▶*n.* (*pl.* **la·ryn·ges** or **lar·ynx·es**) hollow organ in the throat holding the vocal cords.

**la·sa·gna** /ləˈzänyə/ (also **la·sa·gne**) ▶*n.* pasta in wide strips, esp. as cooked and served with cheese, tomato sauce, etc.

**las·civ·i·ous** /ləˈsivēəs/ ▶*adj.* **1** lustful. **2** inciting to or evoking lust.

**la·ser** /ˈlāzər/ ▶*n.* device that generates an intense beam of coherent light.

**lash** /laSH/ ▶*v.* **1** make a sudden whiplike movement. **2** beat with a whip, etc. **3** fasten with a cord, etc.

▶*n.* **1** sharp blow by a whip, etc. **2** flexible end of a whip. **3** eyelash.

□ **lash out** speak or hit out angrily.

**lass** /las/ ▶*n.* girl or young woman.

**las·si·tude** /ˈlasiˌt(y)o͞od/ ▶*n.* languor; weariness.

**las·so** /ˈlaso͞/ ▶*n.* (*pl.* **-sos** or **-soes**) rope with a noose at one end, esp. for catching cattle, etc.

▶*v.* (**-soed**) catch with a lasso.

**last** /last/ ▶*adj.* **1** after all others; coming at or belonging to the end. **2 a** most recent: *last year.* **b** preceding: *got on at the last station.* **3** only remaining: *our last chance.* **4** (**the last**) least likely. **5** lowest in rank: *last place.*

▶*adv.* **1** after all others. **2** on the most recent occasion. **3** lastly.

▶*n.* **1** person or thing that is last. **2** (**the last**) **a** end. **b** death. **3** model for shaping a shoe or boot.

▶*v.* **1** continue for a specified period of time. **2** continue to function or be in good condition.

□ **at last** (or **long last**) in the end; after much delay. □ **last name** surname. □ **last straw** slight addition to a burden that makes it finally unbearable. □ **last word** 1 final or definitive statement: *always has the last word.* 2 latest fashion.

**last·ing** ▸*adj.* 1 continuing; permanent. 2 durable.
—**last·ing·ly** *adv.*

**lat.** ▸*abbr.* latitude.

**latch** /lacH/ ▸*n.* 1 fastening for a gate, etc. 2 lock needing a key to be opened from the outside.
▸*v.* fasten or be fastened with a latch.
□ **latch on/onto** *inf.* 1 attach oneself to (someone). 2 take up (an idea) enthusiastically.

**late** /lāt/ ▸*adj.* 1 after the due, usual, or proper time. 2 far on in a specified period. 3 no longer alive or functioning: *her late husband.* 4 (**latest**) of recent date.
▸*adv.* 1 after the due or usual time. 2 far on in time. 3 at or till a late hour.

**late·ly** /'lātlē/ ▸*adv.* not long ago; recently.

**la·tent** /'lātnt/ ▸*adj.* 1 concealed; dormant. 2 undeveloped.
—**la·ten·cy** *n.*

**lat·er·al** /'latərəl/ ▸*adj.* of, at, toward, or from the side or sides.

**lat·er·al·i·ty** /ˌlatəˈralətē/ ▸*n.* dominance of one side of the brain in controlling particular activities or functions, or of one of a pair of organs such as the eyes or hands.

**la·tex** /'lā,teks/ ▸*n.* (*pl.* **lat·i·ces** or **la·tex·es**) 1 milky fluid of esp. the rubber tree. 2 synthetic product resembling this.

**lath** /laTH/ ▸*n.* (*pl.* **laths**) thin flat strip of wood.
▸*v.* attach laths to.

**lathe** /lāTH/ ▸*n.* machine for shaping wood, metal, etc., by rotating it against a cutting tool.

**lath·er** /'laTHər/ ▸*n.* 1 froth produced by agitating soap, etc., and water. 2 frothy sweat, esp. of a horse. 3 state of agitation.
▸*v.* 1 form a lather. 2 cover with lather.

**Lat·in** /'latn/ ▸*n.* 1 language of ancient Rome and its empire. 2 person who speaks a language derived from Latin.
▸*adj.* 1 of or in Latin. 2 of the countries or peoples using languages developed from Latin.

**Lat·in A·mer·i·can** ▸*adj.* of or relating to Latin America.
▸*n.* native of Latin America.

**La·ti·no** /ləˈtēnō/ ▸*n.* (*pl.* **-nos**); (*fem.* **La·ti·na**) (*pl.* **-nas**) 1 native or inhabitant of Latin America. **2** person of Spanish-speaking or Latin American descent.

**lat·i·tude** /ˈlatiˌt(y)o͞od/ ▸*n.* **1 a** angular distance on a meridian north or south of the equator. **b** (**latitudes**) regions. **2** freedom of action or opinion: *was allowed much latitude.* —**lat·i·tu·di·nal** *adj.*

**lat·i·tu·di·nar·i·an** /ˌlatə-ˌt(y)o͞odnˈe(ə)rēən/ ▸*adj.* allowing latitude in religion; showing no preference among varying creeds and forms of worship. ▸*n.* person with a latitudinarian attitude.

**la·trine** /ləˈtrēn/ ▸*n.* communal toilet, esp. in a camp or barracks.

**lat·ter** /ˈlatər/ ▸*adj.* **1** second-mentioned of two. **2** nearer to the end: *latter part of the year.* **3** recent. ☐ **latter-day** modern.

**lat·tice** /ˈlatis/ ▸*n.* **1** structure of crossed laths with spaces between, used as a screen, fence, etc. **2** (also **latticework**) laths arranged in lattice formation.

**laud** /ˈlôd/ ▸*v.* praise. —**laud·a·to·ry** *adj.*

**lau·da·num** /ˈlôdn-əm; ˈlôdnəm/ ▸*n.* alcoholic solution containing morphine, prepared from opium and formerly used as a narcotic painkiller.

**laud·a·to·ry** /ˈlôdəˌtôrē/ ▸*adj.* (of speech or writing) expressing praise and commendation.

**laugh** /laf/ ▸*v.* **1** make sounds and movements in expressing amusement, scorn, etc. **2** (**laugh at**) ridicule; make fun of. ▸*n.* **1** sound, act, or manner of laughing. **2** *inf.* comical person or thing. —**laugh·ter** *n.* ☐ **have the last laugh** be ultimately the winner.

**laugh·a·ble** ▸*adj.* ludicrous; amusing. —**laugh·a·bly** *adv.*

**laugh·ing·stock** ▸*n.* person or thing ridiculed.

**laugh track** ▸*n.* recorded laughter added to a comedy show.

**launch** /lônCH/ ▸*v.* **1** set (a vessel) afloat. **2** hurl or send forth (a weapon, rocket, etc.). **3** set in motion (an enterprise, attack, etc.). ▸*n.* **1** act of launching. **2** motorboat, used esp. for pleasure. ☐ **launching pad 1** LAUNCHPAD. **2** SPRINGBOARD.

**launch·pad** ▸*n.* platform with a

supporting structure, from which rockets are launched.

**laun·der** /ˈlôndər/ ▶*v.* **1** wash and iron (clothes, etc.). **2** *inf.* transfer (funds) to conceal their origin.

**Laun·dro·mat** /ˈlôndrəˌmat/ ▶*trademark* establishment with coin-operated washing machines and dryers.

**laun·dry** /ˌlôndrē/ ▶*n.* (*pl.* **-dries**) **1** place for washing clothes, etc. **2** clothes or linen for laundering or newly laundered.

**lau·re·ate** /ˈlôrēit/ ▶*n.* person honored for outstanding creative or intellectual achievement: *Nobel laureate.*

**lau·rel** /ˈlôrəl/ ▶*n.* **1** (**laurels**) honor or distinction. **2** evergreen plant with dark-green glossy leaves; bay.

□ **rest on one's laurels** be complacent with one's success.

**la·va** /ˈlävə/ ▶*n.* matter flowing from a volcano that solidifies as it cools.

**la·vage** /ləˈväzH; ˈlavij/ ▶*n.* washing out of a body cavity, such as the colon or stomach, with water or a medicated solution.

**lav·a·to·ry** /ˈlavəˌtôrē/ ▶*n.* (*pl.* **-ries**) room with a toilet and wash basin.

**lave** /lāv/ ▶*v. poet./lit.* wash; bathe.

**lav·en·der** /ˈlavəndər/ ▶*n.* **1** evergreen shrub with aromatic purple flowers. **2** pale purplish-blue color.

**lav·ish** /ˈlaviSH/ ▶*adj.* abundant; profuse.

▶*v.* bestow or spend (money, effort, praise, etc.) abundantly.

**law** /lô/ ▶*n.* **1 a** rule enacted or customary in a community and recognized as enjoining or prohibiting certain actions. **b** body of such rules. **2** binding force or effect: *their word is law.* **3** (**the law**) **a** the legal profession. **b** *inf.* the police. **4** regularity in natural occurrences: *law of gravity.*

□ **law-abiding** obedient to the laws. □ **lay down the law** be dogmatic or authoritarian.

**law·ful** ▶*adj.* conforming with or recognized by law; not illegal.

**law·less** ▶*adj.* contrary to or without regard for the law; illegal.

**lawn** /lôn/ ▶*n.* **1** piece of grass kept mown in a yard, park, etc. **2** fine linen or cotton fabric.

**lawn mow·er** ▸*n.* machine for cutting the grass on a lawn.

**law·suit** ▸*n.* process or instance of making a claim in a court of law.

**law·yer** /ˈlɔiər/ ▸*n.* member of the legal profession.

**lax** /laks/ ▸*adj.* **1** lacking care, concern, etc. **2** loose; not compact. —**lax·i·ty** *n.*

**lax·a·tive** /ˈlaksətiv/ ▸*adj.* easing evacuation of the bowels. ▸*n.* laxative medicine.

**lay**¹ /lā/ ▸*v.* (*past* and *past part.* **laid**) **1** place on a surface, esp. horizontally or in the proper or specified place. **2** (of a bird) produce (an egg). **3** attribute or impute to. **4** prepare (a table) for a meal. **5** *vulgar, inf.* have sexual intercourse with. ▸*n.* way, position, or direction in which something lies. ▸*adj.* **1** not ordained into or belonging to the clergy: *lay preacher.* **2** not professionally qualified, esp. in law or medicine. □ **laid-back** *inf.* relaxed; unbothered. □ **laid up** confined to bed or the house. □ **lay claim to** claim as one's own. □ **lay down 1** put on the ground. **2** formulate (a rule or principle). **3** set down on paper. **4** sacrifice (one's life). □ **lay one's hands on** obtain; locate. □ **lay hands on** seize or attack. □ **lay hold of** seize or grasp. □ **lay into** *inf.* punish or scold severely. □ **lay off 1** discharge (workers) temporarily. **2** *inf.* desist. □ **lay of the land** current state of affairs. □ **lay out 1** spread out; expose to view. **2** prepare (a corpse) for burial. **3** *inf.* knock unconscious. **4** expend (money). □ **lay to rest** bury in a grave. □ **lay up 1** store; save. **2** put (a ship, etc.) out of service.

**lay**² ▸past of LIE.

**lay·er** /ˈlāər/ ▸*n.* **1** thickness of matter, esp. one of several, covering a surface. **2** person or thing that lays: *bricklayer.* ▸*v.* arrange in layers. —**lay·ered** *adj.*

**lay·ette** /lāˈet/ ▸*n.* set of clothing, etc., for a newborn child.

**lay·man** ▸*n.* (*fem.* **lay·wom·an**) **1** person who is not a member of the clergy; one of the laity. **2** person who is not a member of a given profession, as law or medicine.

**lay·off** ▶*n.* **1** temporary discharge of workers. **2** period when this is in force.

**lay·out** ▶*n.* way in which plans, printed matter, etc., are arranged or set out.

**lay·per·son** ▶*n.* **1** person who is not a member of the clergy; one of the laity. **2** person who is not a member of a given profession, as law or medicine.

**laz·ar** /'lazər; 'lāzər/ ▶*n.* poor and diseased person, esp. one afflicted by a feared, contagious disease such as leprosy.

**laze** /lāz/ ▶*v.* spend time lazily or idly.

**la·zy** /'lāzē/ ▶*adj.* (**-zi·er, -zi·est**) **1** disinclined to work; doing little work. **2** of or inducing idleness.

**lb.** ▶*abbr.* pound (weight).

**LC** (also **L.C.** or **l.c.**) ▶*abbr.* **1** landing craft. **2** Library of Congress. **3** lowercase.

**lea** /lē/ (also **ley**) ▶*n. poet.* meadow; pasture land.

**leach** /lēCH/ ▶*v.* **1** make (a liquid) percolate through some material. **2** (**leach away**) remove (soluble matter) or be removed in this way.

**lead**[1] /lēd/ ▶*v.* (*past* and *past part.* **led**) **1** cause to go with one, esp. by guiding or going in front. **2** direct or guide the actions or opinions of. **3** provide access to: *the road leads to Atlanta.* **4** go through (a life of a specified kind): *led a miserable existence.* **5 a** be ahead in a race or game. **b** be preeminent in some field. **6** be in charge of: *leads a team.* **7** begin a round of play at cards by playing (a card) or a card of (a particular suit). **8** (**lead to**) result in: *lead to the closing of the factory.* **9** (**lead with**) (of a newspaper) use (a particular item) as the main story.

▶*n.* **1** guidance given by going in front; example. **2 a** leading place; leadership. **b** amount by which a competitor is ahead of the others. **3** clue: *first real lead in the case.* **4** leash. **5** chief part in a play, etc. **6** (Also **lead story**) item of news given the greatest prominence. —**lead·er** *n.* —**lead·er·ship** *n.*

□ **lead-in** introduction, opening, etc. □ **lead off** begin. □ **lead on** entice deceptively. □ **lead time** time between the initiation and completion of a production process. □ **lead up to** precede; prepare for.

**lead**[2] /led/ ▶*n.* **1** *Chem.* heavy,

bluish-gray soft ductile metallic element. (Symb.: **Pb**) **2** graphite, esp. in a pencil **3** (also **lead·ing**) blank space between lines of print. —**lead·en** *adj.*

**lead·ed** /'ledid/ ▸*adj.* **1** (of windowpanes or a roof) framed, covered, or weighted with lead. **2** (of gasoline) containing tetraethyl lead. **3** (of type) having the lines separated by leads.

**leaf** /lēf/ ▸*n.* (*pl.* **leaves**) **1** each of several flattened usu. green structures of a plant, usu. on the side of a stem or branch. **2** single thickness of paper. **3** very thin sheet of metal, etc. **4** hinged or insertable part of a table, etc. ▸*v.* **1** put forth leaves. **2** (**leaf through**) turn over the pages of (a book, etc.). —**leaf·y** *adj.*

**leaf·let** /'lēflit/ ▸*n.* **1** printed sheet of paper giving information. **2** young leaf.

**league** /lēg/ ▸*n.* **1** people, countries, groups, etc., combining for a purpose. **2** group of sports teams that compete for a championship. **3** former measure of distance, usu. about three miles. ▫ **in league** allied; conspiring.

**leak** /lēk/ ▸*n.* **1** hole through which liquid or gas passes accidentally in or out. **2** disclosure of secret information.
▸*v.* **1** pass or lose through a leak. **2** disclose (secret information). —**leak·age** *n.* —**leak·y** *adj.*
▫ **take a leak** *inf.* urinate.

**lean** /lēn/ ▸*v.* (*past* and *past part.* **leaned** or **leant**) **1** be or place in a sloping position. **2** incline from upright: *leaned against the wall.* **3** rest or cause to rest for support against something: *he leaned his elbows on the table.* **4** (**lean on**) rely on. **5** (**lean to**) be partial to.
▸*n.* **1** inclination: *a decided lean to the right.* **2** meat that has little fat.
▸*adj.* **1** thin; having little fat. **2** meager; of poor quality: *lean crop.*
▫ **lean on** *inf.* put pressure on (a person) to act in a certain way. ▫ **lean years** years of scarcity.

**lean-to** ▸*n.* (*pl.* **-tos**) **1** building with its roof leaning against a wall. **2** shed with an inclined roof usu. leaning against trees, posts, etc.

**leap** /lēp/ ▸*v.* (*past* and *past part.*

leaped or **leapt**) **1** jump or spring forcefully. **2** jump across.

▶*n.* forceful jump.

□ **by leaps and bounds** with startlingly rapid progress. □ **leap at** accept eagerly. □ **leap of faith** accepting something on the basis of trust not reason.

**leap·frog** ▶*n.* game in which players vault with parted legs over others bending down.

▶*v.* (**-frogged, -frog·ging**) overtake to move into a leading position: *leapfrog into a sales position.*

**leap year** ▶*n.* year, occurring once in four, with 366 days (adding Feb. 29).

**learn** /lərn/ ▶*v.* (*past* and *past part.* **learned** or **learnt**) **1** gain knowledge of or skill in. **2** memorize. **3** (**learn of**) be informed about. **4** (**learn that**) become aware of.

**learn·ed** /ˈlərnid/ ▶*adj.* having or showing much learning.

**learn·ing dis·a·bil·i·ty** ▶*n.* disorder where a person has normal intelligence but difficulty with understanding or using written or spoken language.

**lease** /lēs/ ▶*n.* agreement by which the owner of property rents it for a specified time.

▶*v.* grant or take on a lease.

**leash** /lēSH/ ▶*n.* strap for holding a dog, etc.

▶*v.* put a leash on.

**least** /lēst/ ▶*adj.* smallest; slightest.

▶*n.* least amount.

▶*adv.* in the least degree.

□ **at least 1** at any rate. **2** (also **at the least**) not less than. □ **in the least** in the smallest degree: *not in the least offended.*

**leath·er** /ˈleT͟Hər/ ▶*n.* material made from the skin of an animal by tanning, etc.

▶*adj.* made of leather. —**leath·er·y** *adj.*

**leath·er·neck** ▶*n. inf.* U.S. Marine.

**leave** /lēv/ ▶*v.* (*past* and *past part.* **left**) **1 a** go away (from). **b** abandon. **2** allow to remain. **3** have remaining after one's death: *he leaves three children.* **4** bequeath.

▶*n.* **1** permission. **2** (also **leave of absence**) permission to be absent from duty.

□ **leave out** omit; not include. □ **on leave** legitimately absent from duty. □ **take one's leave (of)** bid farewell (to).

**leav·en** /ˈlevən/ ▶n. 1 substance added to dough to make it ferment and rise.
2 transforming influence.
▶v. 1 ferment with leaven.
2 permeate and transform for the better.

**lech·er** /ˈlecHər/ ▶n. lecherous man.

**lech·er·ous** /ˈlecHərəs/ ▶adj. full of or provoking lust.
—**lech·er·ous·ly** adv.
—**lech·er·y** n.

**lec·tern** /ˈlektərn/ ▶n. stand for holding a book for a lecturer, etc.

**lec·tion** /ˈleksHən/ ▶n. reading of a text found in a particular copy or edition.

**lec·ture** /ˈlekcHər/ ▶n.
1 educational talk to an audience. 2 long reprimand.
▶v. 1 deliver a lecture.
2 reprimand.

**ledge** /lej/ ▶n. narrow horizontal or shelflike projection. —**ledged** adj.

**led·ger** /ˈlejər/ ▶n. principal record of the accounts of a business.

**lee** /lē/ ▶n. 1 shelter. 2 (also **lee side**) side away from the wind.

**leech** /lēcH/ ▶n. bloodsucking worm formerly used medically.

**leek** /lēk/ ▶n. plant with a cylindrical bulb used in cooking.

**leer** /li(ə)r/ ▶v. look lasciviously or slyly and maliciously.
▶n. leering look.

**leer·y** /ˈli(ə)rē/ ▶adj. (-i·er, -i·est) cautious or wary: *leery of gang violence.*

**lee·ward** /ˈlēwərd/ ▶adj. & adv. on or toward the side away from the wind.

**lee·way** ▶n. 1 available amount of freedom to move or act.
2 sideways drift of a ship or aircraft to leeward.

**left** /left/ ▶adj. 1 on or toward the west side of the human body or any object when facing north.
2 referring to those favoring liberal, socialistic, or radical views.
▶adv. on or to the left side.
▶n. 1 left-hand part, region, or direction. 2 (often **the Left**) group or section favoring liberalism, social reform, etc.
□ **have two left feet** be clumsy.
□ **left-hand** adj. 1 on or toward the left side of a person or thing: *left-hand drive.* 2 done with the left hand. □ **left-handed** 1 using the left hand by preference. 2 (of a tool, etc.)

made to be used with the left hand

**left²** ▶past and past part. of LEAVE.

**left·o·ver** ▶n. something remaining when the rest is finished.

**leg** /leg/ ▶n. **1** each of the limbs on which a person or animal walks and stands. **2** part of a garment covering a leg. **3** support of a chair, table, etc. **4** section of a journey, relay race, etc.

□ **not have a leg to stand on** be unable to support one's argument. □ **on one's last legs** near death or the end of one's usefulness, etc.

**leg·a·cy** /ˈlegəsē/ ▶n. (pl. **-cies**) **1** gift left in a will. **2** thing handed down by a predecessor.

**le·gal** /ˈlēgəl/ ▶adj. **1** of or based on law. **2** appointed or required by law. **3** permitted by law. **—le·gal·ly** adv.

□ **legal holiday** public holiday established by law. □ **legal tender** currency that cannot legally be refused in payment of a debt.

**le·gal·ese** /ˌlēgəˈlēz/ ▶n. inf. technical language of legal documents.

**le·ga·tion** /liˈgāsHən/ ▶n. office and staff or headquarters of a diplomatic minister.

**le·ga·to** /liˈgätō/ Mus. ▶adv. & adj. in a smooth flowing manner.

▶n. (pl. **-tos**) legato passage or playing.

**leg·end** /ˈlejənd/ ▶n. **1 a** traditional story; myth. **b** such stories collectively. **2** inf. famous or remarkable person or event. **3 a** inscription. **b** caption. **c** wording on a map, etc., explaining the symbols used. **—leg·end·ar·y** adj.

**leg·er·de·main** /ˌlejərdəˈmān/ ▶n. trickery.

**leg·gings** ▶pl. n. tight-fitting stretch pants.

**leg·i·ble** /ˈlejəbəl/ ▶adj. clear enough to read; readable. **—leg·i·bly** adv.

**le·gion** /ˈlējən/ ▶n. **1** division of 3,000–6,000 men in the ancient Roman army. **2** large organized body.

▶adj. great in number: *his supporters are legion.*

□ **American Legion** association of ex-servicemen formed in 1919. □ **foreign legion** body of foreign volunteers in a modern, esp. French, army.

**leg·is·late** /ˈlejisˌlāt/ ▸v. make laws. —**leg·is·la·tion** n.

**leg·is·la·ture** /ˈlejisˌlāCHər/ ▸n. law-making body. —**leg·is·la·tive** adj.

**le·git·i·mate** /liˈjitəmit/ ▸adj. **1** (of a child) born of parents married to each other. **2** lawful; proper; regular. —**le·git·i·ma·cy** n. —**le·git·i·ma·tion** n.

**le·git·i·mism** /liˈjitəˌmizəm/ ▸n. support for a ruler whose claim to a throne is based on direct descent.

**le·git·i·mize** /liˈjitəˌmīz/ ▸v. **1** make legitimate. **2** serve as a justification for. —**le·git·i·mi·za·tion** n.

**leg·ume** /ˈlegˌyo͞om/ ▸n. plant of a family having seeds in pods, as peas and beans. —**le·gu·mi·nous** adj.

**lei** /lā/ ▸n. Polynesian garland of flowers.

**lei·sure** /ˈlēzHər/ ▸n. free time, as for recreation.

**lei·sure·ly** ▸adj. unhurried; relaxed. ▸adv. deliberately, without hurry.

**leit·mo·tif** /ˈlītmōˌtēf/ (also **leit·mo·tiv**) ▸n. recurring theme in music, literature, etc.

**lem·ma** /ˈlemə/ ▸n. (pl. **lem·mas** or **lem·ma·ta** /ˈlemətə/) **1** subsidiary or intermediate theorem in an argument or proof. **2** heading indicating the subject or argument of a literary composition, an annotation, or a dictionary entry.

**lem·ming** /ˈlemiNG/ ▸n. small arctic rodent.

**lem·on** /ˈlemən/ ▸n. **1** yellow, oval, sour citrus fruit, or the tree on which it grows. **2** pale-yellow color. **3** inf. unsatisfactory or disappointing thing, esp. a car. —**lem·on·y** adj.

**lem·on·ade** /ˌleməˈnād/ ▸n. drink made from lemon juice, sweetener, and water.

**le·mur** /ˈlēmər/ ▸n. long-tailed primate of Madagascar that lives in trees.

**lend** /lend/ ▸v. (past and past part. **lent**) **1** grant temporary use of. **2** allow the use of (money) at interest. —**lend·ing** n.
□ **lend an ear** listen. □ **lend itself to** (of a thing) be suitable for.

**length** /leNG(k)TH/ ▸n. **1** extent from end to end. **2** extent in or of time. **3** length of a horse, boat, etc., as a measure of the lead in a race. —**length·en** v. —**length·wise** adj. —**length·y** adj.
□ **at length 1** in detail. **2** at last.

**le·ni·ent** /'lēnēənt/ ▸*adj.* merciful; tolerant; not severe. —**le·ni·en·cy** *n.*

**len·i·ty** /'lenətē/ ▸*n.* kindness; gentleness.

**lens** /lenz/ ▸*n.* **1** piece of a transparent substance with one or both sides curved for concentrating or dispersing light rays, esp. in optical instruments. **2** device for focusing or otherwise modifying the direction of movement of light, sound, electrons, etc.

**Lent** /lent/ ▸*n.* Christian period of fasting and penitence preceding Easter. —**Lent·en** *adj.*

**lent** ▸past and past part. of LEND.

**-lent** ▸*suffix* forming adjectives: *pestilent* | *violent.*

**len·til** /'lent(ə)l/ ▸*n.* the edible seed of a pealike plant.

**le·o·nine** /'lēə,nīn/ ▸*adj.* about or like lions.

**leop·ard** /'lepərd/ (*fem.* **leop·ard·ess**) ▸*n.* large African or Asian feline with a black-spotted, yellowish, or all black coat; panther.

**le·o·tard** /'lēə,tärd/ ▸*n.* **1** close-fitting one-piece garment worn by dancers, acrobats, etc. **2** TIGHTS.

**lep·er** /'lepər/ ▸*n.* person suffering from leprosy.

**lep·re·chaun** /'leprə,kän/ ▸*n.* small mischievous sprite in Irish folklore.

**lep·ro·sy** /'leprəsē/ ▸*n.* contagious deforming disease that affects skin and nerves. —**lep·rous** *adj.*

**les·bi·an** /'lezbēən/ ▸*n.* homosexual woman. ▸*adj.* of or relating to female homosexuality. —**les·bi·an·ism** *n.*

**le·sion** /'lēzнən/ ▸*n.* injury to an organ, etc., affecting its function.

**less** /les/ ▸*adj.* **1** smaller in extent, degree, duration, number, etc. **2** of smaller quantity. ▸*adv.* to a smaller extent. ▸*n.* smaller amount. ▸*prep.* minus: *made $1,000 less tax.* —**less·en** *v.*

**-less** ▸*suffix* forming adjectives and adverbs: **1** from nouns, meaning 'not having, without, free from': *doubtless.* **2** from verbs, meaning 'not affected by or doing the action of the verb': *tireless.* — **-lessly** *suffix* — **-lessness** *suffix*

**less·ee** /le'sē/ ▶ n. person who holds a property by lease.

**less·er** /'lesər/ ▶ adj. not so great as the other or the rest: *lesser evil | lesser egret.*

**les·son** /'lesən/ ▶ n. **1** amount of teaching given at one time. **2** systematic instruction: *lessons in French.* **3** experience that serves to warn or encourage: *let that be a lesson to you.*

**les·sor** /'les,ôr/ ▶ n. person who lets a property by lease.

**lest** /lest/ ▶ conj. *formal* to avoid the risk of; for fear that: *lest we forget.*

**let** /let/ ▶ v. (**let·ting**; *past* and *past part.* **let**) **1 a** allow to. **b** cause to: *let me know.* **2** rent (rooms, land, etc.). **3** award (a contract for work).

▶ *aux. v.* supplying the first and third persons of exhortations (*let us pray*), commands (*let there be light*), assumptions (*let AB be equal to CD*), and permission or challenge (*let him do his worst*)

□ **let alone** not to mention: *hasn't got a TV, let alone a VCR.* □ **let be** not interfere with or do. □ **let down 1** lower. **2** disappoint. □ **let go 1** release. **2** cease to think or talk about. □ **let in 1** allow to enter: *let the dog in.* **2** (**let in on**) allow (a person) to share privileges, information, etc. □ **let off** allow to alight from a vehicle, etc. □ **let on** *inf.* **1** reveal a secret. **2** pretend: *let on that he had won.* □ **let out 1** make (a garment) looser. **2** emit (a sound, etc.). □ **let up** *inf.* become less intense or severe. □ **to let** for rent.

**-let** ▶ *suffix* **1** forming nouns, usu. diminutives: *droplet | leaflet* **2** denoting articles of ornament or dress: *anklet.*

**let·down** ▶ n. disappointment.

**le·thal** /'lēтнəl/ ▶ adj. causing death.

**leth·ar·gy** /'leтнərjē/ ▶ n. lack of energy. —**le·thar·gic** *adj.*

**let·ter** /'lctor/ ▶ n. **1** alphabetic character. **2** written or printed communication, usu. sent by mail.

▶ *v.* inscribe letters on.

□ **man** (or **woman**) **of letters** scholar or author. □ **to the letter** with adherence to every detail.

**let·tered** ▶ adj. well-read or educated.

**let·ter·head** ▶ n. printed heading on stationery.

**let·ter·per·fect** ▶ adj. precise; verbatim.

**let·tuce** /'letəs/ ▶ n. plant with usu. green leaves used in salads.

**let·up** *inf.* ▶*n.* **1** reduction in intensity. **2** relaxation of effort.

**leu·ke·mi·a** /lōō'kēmēə/ ▶*n.* malignant disease in which too many leukocytes are produced. —**leu·ke·mic** *adj.*

**leu·ko·cyte** /'lōōkə,sīt/ ▶*n.* white blood cell. —**leu·ko·cyt·ic** *adj.*

**lev·ee** /'levē/ ▶*n.* embankment against river floods.

**lev·el** /'levəl/ ▶*n.* **1** horizontal line or plane. **2** height or value reached: *eye level | sugar level.* **3** social, moral, or intellectual standard. **4** instrument giving a horizontal line. **5** floor or story in a building, ship, etc.
▶*adj.* **1** flat and even. **2** horizontal.
▶*v.* **1** make level. **2** raze. **3** aim (a gun, etc.). **4** direct (an accusation, etc.). **5** *inf.* (**level with**) be frank or honest with.
□ **do one's level best** *inf.* do one's utmost. □ **level off** make or become level or smooth. □ **on the level** *inf.* without deception.

**lev·el·head·ed** ▶*adj.* mentally well-balanced; sensible.

**lev·er** /'levər/ ▶*n.* **1** bar used to pry. **2** bar pivoted on a fixed point, used to move a load.

**3** handle moved to operate a mechanism.
▶*v.* use a lever.

**lev·er·age** /'lev(ə)rij/ ▶*n.* **1** action or power of a lever. **2** means of accomplishing a purpose; power.

**le·vi·a·than** /lə'vīəTHən/ ▶*n.* **1** (in biblical use) sea monster. **2** anything very large or powerful, esp. a ship.

**lev·i·tate** /'levi,tāt/ ▶*v.* rise and float in the air (esp. with reference to spiritualism). —**lev·i·ta·tion** *n.*

**lev·i·ty** ▶*n.* lack of serious thought; frivolity.

**lev·y** /'levē/ ▶*v.* (**-ied**) **1** impose or collect (payment, etc). **2** enlist or enroll (troops, etc.). **3** proceed to make (war).
▶*n.* (*pl.* **-ies**) **1** collecting of a tax; tax collected. **2 a** act of enrolling troops, etc. **b** (usu. **levies**) persons enrolled.

**lewd** /lōōd/ ▶*adj.* indecent; obscene.

**lex·i·cog·ra·phy** /,leksi'kägrəfē/ ▶*n.* compiling of dictionaries. —**lex·i·cog·ra·pher** *n.* —**lex·i·co·graph·i·cal** *adj.*

**lex·i·con** /'leksi,kän/ ▶*n.* **1** dictionary. **2** vocabulary of a person, language, branch of knowledge, etc.

**lex lo·ci** /ˈleks ˈlōsī; -sē/ ▸*n.* law of the country in which a transaction is performed, a tort is committed, or a property is situated.

**li·a·bil·i·ty** /ˌlīəˈbilitē/ ▸*n.* (pl. **-ties**) **1** being responsible for something, esp. legally. **2** (usu. **liabilities**) something for which one is responsible. **3** troublesome responsibility.

**li·a·ble** /ˈlī(ə)bəl/ ▸*adj.* **1** responsible by law. **2** subject to (a tax or penalty). **3** likely to do or be something: *areas liable to flooding.*

**li·ai·son** /ˈlēəˌzän/ ▸*n.* **1 a** communication or cooperation. **b** person who initiates such. **2** illicit sexual relationship.

**li·ar** /ˈlīər/ ▸*n.* person who lies, esp. habitually.

**li·bel** /ˈlībəl/ ▸*n. Law* a published false statement damaging to a person's reputation. ▸*v.* defame by libelous statements. —**li·bel·ous** *adj.*

**lib·er·al** /ˈlib(ə)rəl/ ▸*adj.* **1** ample; full. **2** generous. **3** open-minded. **4** not strict. **5** favoring political and social reform. ▸*n.* person of liberal views. —**lib·er·al·i·ty** *n.*

**lib·er·al arts** ▸*pl. n.* academic subjects such as literature, philosophy, etc., as distinct from professional and technical subjects.

**lib·er·ate** /ˈlibəˌrāt/ ▸*v.* set free. —**lib·er·a·tion** *n.* —**lib·er·a·tor** *n.*

**lib·er·tar·i·an** /ˌlibərˈte(ə)rēən/ ▸*n.* **1** advocate of minimal state intervention in citizens' lives. **2** *Philos.* believer in free will.

**lib·er·tine** /ˈlibərˌtēn/ ▸*n.* dissolute or immoral person.

**lib·er·ty** /ˈlibərtē/ ▸*n.* (pl. **-ties**) **1** freedom from captivity, slavery, etc. **2** freedom to do as one pleases. □ **at liberty 1** free. **2** entitled or allowed to do something. □ **take liberties** behave in an unduly familiar manner.

**li·bi·do** /ləˈbēdō/ ▸*n.* (pl. **-dos**) sexual desire. —**li·bid·i·nal** *adj.*

**li·brar·y** /ˈlīˌbrerē/ ▸*n.* (pl. **-ies**) **1** collection of books; its housing. **2** similar collection of films, records, computer software, etc.

**li·bret·to** /liˈbretō/ ▸*n.* (pl. **-tos** or **-ti**) text of an opera, etc. —**li·bret·tist** *n.*

**li·cense** /ˈlīsəns/ ▸*n.* **1** official permit to own, use, or do

something. **2** liberty of action, esp. when excessive.
▶*v.* **1** grant a license to. **2** authorize. —**li·cens·er** *n.* —**li·cen·sor** *n.*

**li·cen·see** /ˌlīsən'sē/ ▶*n.* holder of a license.

**li·cense plate** ▶*n.* plate on a motor vehicle that attests to its registration.

**li·cen·tious** /lī'senSHəs/ ▶*adj.* promiscuous and immoral in sexual matters.

**li·chen** /'līkən/ ▶*n.* plant composed of a fungus and an alga, growing on rocks, tree trunks, etc.

**lic·it** /'lisit/ ▶*adj.* not forbidden; lawful.

**lick** /lik/ ▶*v.* **1** pass the tongue over. **2** bring into a specified condition by licking: *licked it clean.* **3** (of a flame, waves, etc.) play lightly over; move gently. **4** *inf.* defeat; excel. **5** *inf.* thrash.
▶*n.* **1** act of licking with the tongue. **2** *inf.* small amount: *a lick of paint.*
□ **lick and a promise** *inf.* hasty performance of a task. □ **lick one's wounds** be in retirement after defeat.

**lick·e·ty·split** /'likitē 'split/ ▶*adv.* *inf.* at full speed; headlong.

**lick·ing** ▶*n. inf.* heavy defeat or beating.

**lick·spit·tle** /'lik,spitl/ ▶*n.* person who behaves obsequiously to those in power.

**lic·o·rice** /'lik(ə)risH/ ▶*n.* **1** black root extract used in candy and medicine. **2** candy made from this.

**lictor** /'liktər/ ▶*n.* (in ancient Rome) an officer attending the consul or other magistrate, bearing the fasces, and executing sentences on offenders.

**lid** /lid/ ▶*n.* **1** hinged or removable cover, esp. for a container. **2** EYELID.
□ **put a lid on** *inf.* be quiet about; keep secret. □ **take the lid off** *inf.* expose (a scandal, etc.).

**lie**[1] /lī/ ▶*v.* (**ly·ing**; *past* **lay**; *past part.* **lain**) **1** be in or assume a horizontal position. **2** rest flat on a surface. **3 a** be kept or remain or be in a specified state or place: *money is lying in the bank.* **b** (of abstract things) exist; reside: *my sympathies lie with the family.*
▶*n.* **1** way, direction, or position in which a thing lies. **2** place of cover of an animal or a bird.
□ **lie ahead** be going to happen.

◻ **lie down** assume a lying position; have a short rest. ◻ **lie low 1** keep quiet or unseen. **2** be discreet about one's intentions.

**lie**² ▸*n.* intentionally false statement. ▸*v.* (**lied, ly·ing**) **1 a** tell a lie or lies. **b** (of a thing) be deceptive: *cameras don't lie.* **2** get (oneself) into or out of a situation by lying: *lied my way out of danger.*

**lief** /lēf/ ▸*adv.* (**as lief**) as happily; as gladly.

**lien** /ˈlē(ə)n/ ▸*n. Law* a right over another's property to protect a debt charged on that property.

**lieu** /lōō/ ▸*n.* (in phrase **in lieu**) instead: *gave money in lieu of presents.*

**lieu·ten·ant** /lōōˈtenənt/ ▸*n.* **1** deputy. **2 a** army officer next in rank below captain. **b** naval officer next in rank below lieutenant commander. **3** police officer next in rank below captain. —**lieu·ten·an·cy** *n.*

**life** /līf/ ▸*n.* (*pl.* **lives**) **1** capacity for growth, functional activity, and continual change until death. **2** living things: *insect life.* **3 a** period from birth to the present or from the present to death: *will regret it all my life.* **b** duration of a thing's existence or ability to function. **4 a** state of existence as a living individual: *gave his life.* **b** living person: *no lives were lost.* **5** individual's actions or fortunes; manner of one's existence: *start a new life.* **6** energy; liveliness: *full of life.* **7** biography. **8** *inf.* sentence of imprisonment for life. —**life·less** *adj.*

◻ **come to life 1** emerge from inactivity. **2** (of an inanimate object) assume an imaginary animation. ◻ **large as life** *inf.* in person, esp. prominently: *stood there large as life.* ◻ **larger than life** exaggerated. ◻ **life-and-death** vitally important; desperate: *a life-and-death struggle.* ◻ **not on your life** *inf.* most certainly not. ◻ **take one's life in one's hands** take a crucial personal risk.

**life·blood** ▸*n.* **1** blood, as being necessary to life. **2** vital factor or influence.

**life·boat** ▸*n.* small boat for use in an emergency.

**life·care** ▸*adj.* catering to the needs of the elderly: *life-care residence.*

**life cy·cle** ▶*n.* series of changes in the life of an organism.

**life ex·pec·tan·cy** ▶*n.* average period that a person at a specified age may expect to live.

**life·guard** ▶*n.* expert swimmer employed to rescue bathers from drowning.

**life in·sur·ance** ▶*n.* insurance for a sum to be paid on the death of the insured.

**life in·ter·est** ▶*n.* right to property that a person holds for life but cannot dispose of further.

**life·long** ▶*adj.* lasting all one's life.

**life part·ner** ▶*n.* a member of a long-term monogamous relationship.

**life pre·serv·er** ▶*n.* buoyant or inflatable device to keep someone afloat in water.

**lif·er** /ˈlīfər/ ▶*n. inf.* **1** person serving a life sentence. **2** person committed to a very long career, esp. in the military.

**life·sav·er** ▶*n.* person or thing that saves one from serious difficulty. —**life·sav·ing** *n. & adj.*

**life sci·enc·es** ▶*pl. n.* biology and related subjects.

**life sen·tence** ▶*n.* sentence of imprisonment for life.

**life-size** (also **life-sized**) ▶*adj* of the same size as the person or thing represented.

**life·style** ▶*n.* way of life of a person or group.

**life sup·port** ▶*n.* maintenance of vital functions of a critically ill patient.

**life·time** ▶*n.* the duration of a person's life.

**life·work** ▶*n.* task, profession, etc., pursued throughout one's lifetime.

**lift** /lift/ ▶*v.* **1** raise or go up to a higher position. **2** elevate to a higher plane of thought or feeling: *the news lifted their spirits.* **3** (of a cloud, fog, etc.) rise; disperse. **4** remove (a barrier or restriction). **5** *inf.* **a** steal. **b** plagiarize (a passage of writing, etc.).
▶*n.* **1** lifting or being lifted. **2** ride in another person's vehicle. **3** apparatus for carrying persons up or down a mountain, etc. **4** transport by air. **5** upward pressure that air exerts on an airfoil. **6** feeling of elation.
☐ **not lift a finger** (or **hand**) not make the slightest effort: *didn't lift a finger to help.*

**lift·off** ▶*n.* vertical takeoff of a spacecraft or rocket.

**lig·a·ment** /ˈligəmənt/ ▶*n.* band of tough, fibrous tissue linking bones.

**li·ga·tion** /līˈgāSHən/ ▶*n.* **1** surgical procedure of closing off a blood vessel or other duct or tube in the body by means of a ligature or clip. **2** joining of two DNA strands or other molecules by a phosphate ester linkage.

**lig·a·ture** /ˈligəCHər/ ▶*n.* **1** tie; bandage. **2** *Mus.* slur; tie. **3** two or more letters joined, e.g., æ.

**light**[1] /līt/ ▶*n.* **1** electromagnetic radiation that stimulates sight and makes things visible, or its source. **2** traffic light. **3 a** flame or spark serving to ignite. **b** device producing this: *have you got a light?* **4** aspect in which a thing is regarded: *appeared in a new light.* **5** eminent person: *leading light.*
▶*v.* (*past* **lit**; *past part.* **lit** or **light·ed**) **1** ignite. **2** provide with light or lighting. **3** (of the face or eyes) brighten with animation.
▶*adj.* **1** well provided with light; not dark. **2** (of a color) pale: *light blue.*
□ **bring** (or **come**) **to light** reveal or be revealed. □ **in a good** (or bad) **light** giving a favorable (or unfavorable) impression. □ **light of one's life** much-loved person. □ **out like a light** deeply asleep or unconscious. □ **throw** (or **shed**) **light on** help to explain.

**light**[2] ▶*adj.* **1** not heavy. **2** relatively low in weight, amount, intensity, etc.: *light arms* | *light traffic.* **3** (of food) easy to digest. **4** (of entertainment, music, etc.) intended for amusement only; not profound. **5** (of sleep or a sleeper) easily disturbed. **6** nimble; quick-moving: *light step.* **7 a** unburdened: *light heart.* **b** giddy: *light in the head.*

□ **light touch** delicate or tactful treatment. □ **make light of** treat as unimportant. □ **make light work of** do a thing quickly and easily. □ **travel light** travel with a minimum load.

**light**[3] ▶*v.* (*past* and *past part.* **lit** or **light·ed**) **1** (**light on/upon**) come upon by chance. **2** (**light on**) fall and settle on. **3** (**light into**) *inf.* attack.

**light·en** /ˈlītn/ ▶*v.* **1 a** make or become lighter in weight. **2** bring relief to (the heart, mind, etc.). **3 a** shed light on.

**b** make or grow lighter or brighter.

**light·er** /'līter/ ▸*n.* **1** device for lighting cigarettes, etc. **2** boat for transferring goods from a ship.

**light-fin·gered** ▸*adj.* given to stealing.

**light-head·ed** ▸*adj.* giddy and slightly faint.

**light-heart·ed** ▸*adj.* **1** cheerful. **2** (unduly) casual; thoughtless.

**light·house** ▸*n.* tower or other structure containing a beacon light to warn or guide ships at sea.

**light in·dus·try** ▸*n.* manufacture of small articles.

**light me·ter** ▸*n.* instrument for measuring light intensity, esp. for correct photographic exposure.

**light·ning** /'lītniNG/ ▸*n.* flash of bright light produced by an electric discharge between clouds or between clouds and the ground.
▸*adj.* very quick.

**light·ning bug** ▸*n.* FIREFLY.

**light·ning rod** ▸*n.* metal rod or wire fixed to a building, mast, etc., to divert lightning.

**lights** /līts/ ▸*pl. n.* lungs of sheep or pigs used as food, esp. for pets.

**light·some** /'lītsəm/ ▸*adj.* **1** merry and carefree. **2** gracefully nimble.

**light·weight** ▸*adj.* **1** not heavy. **2** not important, serious, or consequential; trivial.
▸*n.* person of little consequence.

**light year** ▸*n.* distance light travels in one year, nearly 6 trillion miles.

**lig·ne·ous** /'lignēəs/ ▸*adj.* like wood; woody.

**lig·nite** /'lig,nīt/ ▸*n.* soft brown coal showing traces of plant structure, intermediate between bituminous coal and peat.
—**lig·nit·ic** *adj.*

**like** /līk/ ▸*adj.* (**more like, most like**) having some or all of the qualities of; alike: *in like manner.*
▸*prep.* in the manner of; to the same degree as: *acted like an idiot.*
▸*conj. inf.* **1** as: *he can't do it like you do.* **2** as if: *ate like they were starving.*
▸*n.* **1** counterpart; equal. **2** (**likes**) things one prefers: *likes and dislikes.*
▸*v.* **1** find agreeable or enjoyable. **2 a** choose to have; prefer: *like my coffee black.* **b** wish for: *would*

*like tea.* **3** feel about; regard.
—**lik·a·ble** or **like·a·ble** *adj.*

□ **and the like** and similar things; et cetera: *music, painting, and the like.* □ **like-minded** having the same tastes, opinions, etc. □ **like so** *inf.* like this; in this manner. □ **the likes of** *inf.* a person such as.

**-like** ▸*comb. form* forming adjectives from nouns, meaning 'similar to, characteristic of': *doglike.*

**like·ly** /ˈlīklē/ ▸*adj.* **1** probable. **2** reasonably expected: *likely to rain.* **3** promising; suitable: *three likely candidates.*
▸*adv.* probably. —**like·li·hood** *n.*

**lik·en** /ˈlīkən/ ▸*v.* point out the resemblance of: *likened the king to a god.*

**like·ness** ▸*n.* **1** resemblance: *her likeness to her cousin is amazing.* **2** semblance or guise: *in the likeness of a ghost.*

**like·wise** ▸*adv.* **1** also. **2** similarly.

**li·lac** /ˈlī,lək/ ▸*n.* **1** shrub with fragrant pinkish-violet or white blossoms. **2** pale pinkish-violet color.

**lil·li·pu·tian** /ˌlilə'pyo͞osHən/ (also **Lil·li·pu·tian**) ▸*adj.* diminutive.

**lilt** /lilt/ ▸*n.* **1** a light springing rhythm. **2** (of the voice) characteristic cadence.
▸*v.* [usu. as *adj.* **lilting**] move or speak, etc., with a lilt: *lilting melody.*

**lil·y** /ˈlilē/ ▸*n.* (*pl.* **-ies**) **1** plant with trumpet-shaped flowers on a tall stem. **2** similar plant, as the water lily.

**lil·y-liv·ered** ▸*adj.* cowardly.

**lil·y of the val·ley** ▸*n.* plant with white, bell-shaped, fragrant flowers.

**lil·y-white** ▸*adj.* **1** pure white. **2** faultless; totally innocent. **3** consisting only of white people: *lily-white suburb.*

**li·ma bean** /ˈlīmə/ ▸*n.* **1** plant with broad, flat, edible seeds. **2** seed of this plant.

**limb** /lim/ ▸*n.* **1** arm, leg, or wing. **2** large branch of a tree.

□ **out on a limb 1** isolated; stranded. **2** at a disadvantage.

**lim·ber** /ˈlimbər/ ▸*adj.* **1** lithe. **2** flexible.
▸*v.* make or become limber.

**lim·bo** /ˈlimbō/ ▸*n.* (*pl.* **-bos**) **1** (in some Christian beliefs) abode of the souls of unbaptized infants, and of the just who died before Christ. **2** intermediate state or condition. **3** W. Indian dance in which the dancer bends backward to pass under a horizontal bar that is progressively lowered.

**lime** /līm/ ▶*n.* **1** (also **quick·lime**) white substance (calcium oxide) obtained by heating limestone. **2** calcium hydroxide obtained by reacting quicklime with water. **3** citrus fruit like a lemon but green, smaller, and more acid, or the tree on which it grows. **4** pale green color. ▶*v.* treat with lime. —**lim·y** *adj.*

**lime·light** ▶*n.* **1** intense white light used formerly in theaters. **2** glare of publicity.

**li·men** /'līmən/ ▶*n.* (*pl.* **li·mens** or **lim·i·na** /'limənə/) threshold below which a stimulus is not perceived or is not distinguished from another.

**lim·er·ick** /'lim(ə)rik/ ▶*n.* humorous five-line stanza with a rhyme scheme *aabba.*

**lime·stone** ▶*n.* rock composed mainly of calcium carbonate.

**lim·i·nal** /'limənl/ ▶*adj.* **1** of or relating to a transitional or initial stage of a process. **2** occupying a position at, or on both sides of, a boundary or threshold.

**lim·it** /'limit/ ▶*n.* **1** point, line, or level beyond which something does not or may not extend. **2** greatest or smallest amount permissible. ▶*v.* set or serve as a limit to. —**lim·i·ta·tion** *n.*

□ **off limits** out of bounds.

**lim·it·ed** ▶*adj.* **1** confined. **2** not great in scope or talents: *limited experience.* **3** scanty; restricted.

**lim·nol·o·gy** /lim'näləjē/ ▶*n.* study of the biological, chemical, and physical features of lakes and other bodies of fresh water.

**lim·o** /'limō/ ▶*n.* (*pl.* **-os**) *inf.* LIMOUSINE.

**lim·ou·sine** /'limə,zēn/ ▶*n.* large, luxurious automobile, esp. with a chauffeur.

**limp** /limp/ ▶*v.* walk lamely. ▶*n.* lame walk. ▶*adj.* **1** not stiff or firm. **2** without energy or will. —**limp·ly** *adv.* —**limp·ness** *n.*

**lim·pet** /'limpit/ ▶*n.* small shellfish that sticks tightly to rocks.

**lim·pid** /'limpid/ ▶*adj.* clear; transparent.

**linch·pin** /'linCH,pin/ ▶*n.* **1** pin through the end of an axle to keep a wheel on. **2** person or thing vital to an enterprise, etc.

**lin·den** /'lindən/ ▶*n.* tree with

heart-shaped leaves and fragrant flowers.

**line** /līn/ ▸*n.* **1** long, narrow mark or band. **2** *Math.* straight or curved continuous extent of length without breadth. **3** wrinkle in the face. **4** contour or outline. **5** limit or boundary. **6** row of persons or things. **7 a** row of printed or written words. **b** portion of verse written in one line. **8** (**lines**) words of an actor's part: *learned her lines quickly.* **9** short letter or note: *drop me a line.* **10** cord, rope, etc. **11 a** wire or cable for a telephone or telegraph. **b** connection by means of this. **12** branch or route of a railroad system, or a whole system under one management. **13 a** regular succession of buses, ships, aircraft, etc., plying between certain places. **b** company conducting this: *shipping line.* **14** lineage. **15** course or manner of procedure, conduct, thought, etc.: *did it along these lines.* **16** course or channel: *lines of communication.* **17** business or occupation. **18** class of commercial goods: *new line of hats.* **19** *inf.* false or exaggerated account: *gave me a line about missing the bus.* **20** arrangement of soldiers or ships side by side. ▸*v.* **1** mark with lines. **2** stand at intervals along: *crowds lined the route.* **3** cover the inside surface of (a garment, box, etc.). ▢ **in line for** likely to receive. ▢ **line up 1** arrange or be arranged in a line or lines. **2** have ready: *had a job lined up.* ▢ **on the line 1** at risk: *put my reputation on the line.* **2** speaking on the telephone. ▢ **out of line** inappropriate.

**lin·e·age** /ˈlinēij/ ▸*n.* lineal descent; ancestry; pedigree.

**lin·e·al** /ˈlinēəl/ ▸*adj.* **1** in the direct line of descent or ancestry. **2** linear.

**lin·e·a·ment** /ˈlinēəmənt/ ▸*n.* (usu. **lineaments**) distinctive feature or characteristic, esp. of the face.

**lin·e·ar** /ˈlinēər/ ▸*adj.* **1 a** of or in lines. **b** of length. **2** long and narrow and of uniform breadth. —**lin·e·ar·i·ty** *n.*

**line drive** ▸*n.* hard-hit baseball that travels nearly parallel to the ground.

**line·man** ▸*n.* (*pl.* **-men**) **1 a** person who repairs and maintains telephone or power lines. **b** person who tests the safety of railroad lines.  **2** *Football* player on the line of scrimmage.

**lin·en** /'linin/ ▸*n.* **1** cloth woven from flax.  **2** sheets, towels, tablecloths, etc.
▸*adj.* made of linen.

**lin·er** /'līnər/ ▸*n.* **1** ship, aircraft, etc., carrying passengers on a regular line.  **2** removable lining.

**line·up** ▸*n.* **1** line of people.  **2** list of participants in a game, etc.

**-ling** ▸*suffix* denoting a diminutive: *duckling*.

**lin·ger** /'liNGgər/ ▸*v.* **1** loiter.  **2** dally.  **3** (esp. of an illness) be protracted.

**lin·ge·rie** /ˌlänzHə'rā/ ▸*n.* women's underwear and nightclothes.

**lin·go** /'liNGgō/ ▸*n.* (*pl.* **-goes**) *inf.* **1** foreign language.  **2** vocabulary of a special subject or group of people.

**lin·guist** /'liNGgwist/ ▸*n.* person skilled in languages or linguistics.

**lin·guis·tic** /liNG'gwistik/ ▸*adj.* of or relating to language or linguistics.

**lin·guis·tics** /liNG'gwistiks/ ▸*n.* study of language and its structure.  **—lin·guis·tic** *adj.*

**lin·i·ment** /'linəmənt/ ▸*n.* medication rubbed into the skin.

**lin·ing** /'līniNG/ ▸*n.* material that covers an inside surface.

**link** /liNGk/ ▸*n.* **1** loop or ring of a chain.  **2** connecting part; one in a series.
▸*v.* **1** connect or join (two things or one to another).  **2** be joined; attach oneself to (a system, etc.).

**links** ▸*pl. n.* golf course.

**link·up** ▸*n.* act or result of linking up.

**lin·net** /'linit/ ▸*n.* finch with brown and gray plumage.

**li·no·le·um** /lə'nōlēəm/ ▸*n.* canvas-backed floor covering coated with linseed oil, powdered cork, etc.

**lin·seed** /'lin,sēd/ ▸*n.* seed of flax.
□ **linseed oil** oil extracted from linseed and used esp. in paint and varnish.

**lint** /lint/ ▸*n.* fluff.  **—lint·y** *adj.*

**lin·tel** /'lintl/ ▸*n.* horizontal supporting piece of wood, stone, etc., across the top of a door or window.

**li·on** /'līən/ ▸*n.* **1** (*fem.* **li·on·ess**) large feline of Africa and S. Asia, with a tawny coat and, in the male, a flowing shaggy mane. **2** celebrated person.

□ **lion's share** largest part.

**li·on·ize** ▸*v.* treat as a celebrity. —**li·on·i·za·tion** *n.*

**lip** /lip/ ▸*n.* **1** either of the two fleshy parts forming the edges of the mouth opening. **2** edge of a vessel, etc. **3** *inf.* impudent talk.

□ **pay lip service to** express support of without taking action.

**li·po·suc·tion** /ˈlipōˌsəksHən/ ▸*n.* surgical removal of excess fat from under the skin by suction.

**lip·read·ing** ▸*n.* practice of understanding (speech) from observing a speaker's lip movements. —**lip·read** *v.*

**lip·stick** ▸*n.* stick of cosmetic for coloring the lips.

**li·que·fy** /ˈlikwəˌfī/ ▸*v.* (**-fied**) make or become liquid. —**li·que·fa·cient** *adj. & n.* —**li·que·fac·tion** *n.*

**li·queur** /liˈkər/ ▸*n.* any of several sweet alcoholic liquors, variously flavored.

**liq·uid** /ˈlikwid/ ▸*adj.* **1** having a consistency like that of water or oil. **2** (of sounds) clear and pure; fluent. **3** (of assets) easily converted into cash. ▸*n.* **1** liquid substance. **2** *Phonet.* sound of *l* or *r*. —**li·quid·i·ty** *n.*

□ **liquid crystal** turbid liquid with some order in its molecular arrangement. □ **liquid crystal display** visual display in electronic devices in which liquid crystals respond to signals.

**liq·ui·date** /ˈlikwiˌdāt/ ▸*v.* **1** wind up the affairs of (a business) by paying debts and distributing assets. **2** pay off (a debt). **3** convert into cash. **4** kill. —**liq·ui·da·tion** *n.*

**liq·uor** /ˈlikər/ ▸*n.* **1** alcoholic (esp. distilled) drink. **2** other liquid, esp. that produced in cooking.

**lisle** /līl/ ▸*n.* fine cotton thread or fabric made from it.

**lisp** /lisp/ ▸*n.* speech in which *s* and *z* are not pronounced correctly. ▸*v.* speak or utter with a lisp.

**lis·some** /ˈlisəm/ (also **lis·som**) ▸*adj.* lithe; supple; agile.

**list** /list/ ▸*n.* **1** number of items, names, etc., written or printed together as a record. **2** process or instance of listing. ▸*v.* **1** make a list of. **2** enter in a list. **3** (of a ship) lean over to one side. —**list·ing** *n.*

**lis·ten** /ˈlisən/ ▸*v.* **1** make an

effort to hear. **2** take notice of; heed.

□ **listen in** eavesdrop.

**list·less** ▸*adj.* lacking energy or enthusiasm.

**list price** ▸*n.* price of something as shown in a published list.

**lit** /lit/ ▸past and past part. of LIGHT.

**lit·a·ny** /ˈlitn-ē/ ▸*n.* (*pl.* **-nies**) **1** series of petitions to God recited by the clergy with set responses by the people. **2** tedious recital: *a litany of woes.*

**li·ter** /ˈlētər/ ▸*n.* metric unit of capacity equal to about 1.057 quarts.

**lit·er·al** /ˈlitərəl/ ▸*adj.* **1** taking words in their basic sense without metaphor or allegory. **2** following exactly the original wording: *literal translation.* **3** so called without exaggeration: *literal extermination.*
—**lit·er·al·ize** *v.*

**lit·er·ar·y** /ˈlitəˌrerē/ ▸*adj.* **1** concerning the writing, study, or content of literature. **2** well-read.

**lit·er·ate** /ˈlitərit/ ▸*adj.* **1** able to read and write. **2** educated; literary; well-read.

**li·te·ra·ti** /ˌlitəˈrätē/ ▸*pl. n.* well-educated people.

**lit·er·a·ture** /ˈlit(ə)rəˌCHər/ ▸*n.* **1** written works, esp. those of lasting artistic merit. **2** writings of a country, period, or particular subject. **3** *inf.* printed matter, leaflets, etc.

**lithe** /līTH/ ▸*adj.* flexible; supple.

**lith·i·um** /ˈliTHēəm/ ▸*n. Chem.* soft, silver-white metallic element. (Symb.: **Li**)

**lith·o·graph** /ˈliTHəˌgraf/ ▸*n.* lithographic print.
▸*v.* **1** print by lithography. **2** write or engrave on stone.

**li·thog·ra·phy** /liˌTHägrəfē/ ▸*n.* process of printing from a plate so treated that ink adheres only to what is to be printed.
—**li·thog·ra·pher** *n.*
—**li·tho·graph·ic** *adj.*

**lit·i·gant** /ˈlitəgənt/ ▸*n.* party to a lawsuit.

**lit·i·gate** /ˈlitəˌgāt/ ▸*v.* **1** be a party to a lawsuit. **2** contest (a point) in a lawsuit. —**lit·i·ga·tion** *n.* —**lit·i·ga·tor** *n.*

**li·ti·gious** /liˈtijəs/ ▸ **1** given to litigation. **2** quarrelsome.

**lit·mus** /ˈlitməs/ ▸*n.* dye that turns red under acid conditions and blue under alkaline conditions.

□ **litmus test** test to establish true character.

**Litt.D** ▸*abbr.* Doctor of Literature; Doctor of Letters.

**lit·ter** /ˈlitər/ ▸*n.* **1 a** refuse, esp. paper, discarded in an open or public place. **b** odds and ends lying about. **2** young animals brought forth at a birth. **3** stretcher for the sick and wounded. **4** (also **cat litter**) granulated material for a cat's waste.

▸*v.* **1** make untidy with litter. **2** scatter carelessly.

**lit·ter·bug** ▸*n.* person who leaves litter in a public place.

**lit·tle** /ˈlitl/ ▸*adj.* (**lit·tler, lit·tlest; less** or **les·ser; least**) **1** small in size, amount, degree, stature, distance, duration, etc. **2** trivial. **3** young or younger: *little boy | my little sister.* **4** paltry; contemptible: *you little sneak.*

▸*n.* **1** not much; only a small amount or distance: *got very little out of it.* **2** short time or distance: *after a little.*

▸*adv.* (**less, least**) **1** to a small extent only: *little more than speculation.* **2** not at all; hardly: *they little thought.* **3** somewhat: *is a little deaf.*

☐ **little by little** by degrees; gradually.

**lit·to·ral** /ˈlitərəl/ ▸*adj.* of or by the shore.

**lit·ur·gy** /ˈlitərjē/ ▸*n.* (*pl.* **-gies**) prescribed form of public worship. —**li·tur·gi·cal** *adj.*

**liv·a·ble** /ˈlivəbəl/ (also **live·a·ble**) ▸*adj.* **1** (of a house, climate, etc.) fit to live in. **2** (of a life) worth living.

**live**[1] /liv/ ▸*v.* **1** have life; be or remain alive. **2** subsist or feed: *lives on fruit | lives off the family.* **3** conduct oneself in a specified way: *live quietly.* **4** survive. **5** enjoy life to the fullest.

☐ **live down** cause (past guilt, embarrassment, etc.) to be forgotten. ☐ **live it up** *inf.* live gaily and extravagantly. ☐ **live up to** honor; fulfill.

**live**[2] /līv/ ▸*adj.* **1** that is alive; living. **2** (of a broadcast) heard or seen at the time of its performance. **3** of current importance: *a live issue.* **4 a** (of coals) glowing. **b** (of a wire, etc.) connected to electrical power.

**live·li·hood** /ˈlīvlē,hŏŏd/ ▸*n.* means of living; sustenance.

**live·long** /ˈliv,lôNG/ ▸*adj.* entire: *the livelong day.*

**live·ly** /ˈlīvlē/ ▸*adj.* (**-li·er, -li·est**) **1** energetic; brisk. **2** brisk: *a lively pace.* **3** vivacious; sociable.

**4** bright and vivid.
—**live·li·ness** *n.*

**liv·er** /ˈlivər/ ▶*n.* **1** large glandular organ in the abdomen of vertebrates. **2** flesh of an animal's liver as food.

**liv·er·wurst** /ˈlivərˌwərst/ ▶*n.* sausage of ground cooked liver, etc.

**liv·er·y** /ˈliv(ə)rē/ ▶*n.* (*pl.* -**ies**) **1** distinctive marking or outward appearance: *birds in their winter livery.* **2 a** place where horses can be hired. **b** company that has vehicles for hire. **3** distinctive uniform of a servant, etc. —**liv·er·ied** *adj.*

**live·stock** /ˈlīvˌstäk/ ▶*n.* [usu. treated as *pl.*] farm animals.

**live wire** ▶*n. inf.* energetic and forceful person.

**liv·id** /ˈlivid/ ▶*adj.* **1** *inf.* furiously angry. **2 a** of a bluish leaden color. **b** discolored as by a bruise. —**li·vid·i·ty** *n.*

**liv·ing** /ˈliviNG/ ▶*n.* **1** livelihood. **2** manner of life.
▶*adj.* **1** contemporary; now existent: *greatest living poet.* **2** (of a likeness) exact. **3** (of a language) still in use.

**liv·ing room** ▶*n.* room for general day use.

**liv·ing will** ▶*n.* written statement of a person's desire not to be kept alive by artificial means.

**liz·ard** /ˈlizərd/ ▶*n.* slender reptile having usu. a long tail, four legs, movable eyelids, and a rough or scaly hide.

**lla·ma** /ˈlämə/ ▶*n.* S. American ruminant, kept as a beast of burden and for its soft, woolly fleece.

**lla·no** /ˈlänō; ˈyä-/ ▶*n.* (*pl.* -**nos**) (in South America) a treeless grassy plain.

**LLB** ▶*abbr.* Bachelor of Laws.

**LLD** ▶*abbr.* Doctor of Laws.

**load** /lōd/ ▶*n.* **1** what is carried or is to be carried at one time. **2** burden or commitment of work, responsibility, etc. **3** *inf.* (**loads**) plenty; a lot: *loads of money.* **4** amount of power carried by an electric circuit.
▶*v.* **1** put or take a load on or aboard. **2 a** make (someone or something) carry a large amount of heavy things: *he was loaded down with luggage.* **b** burden (someone) with. **3** insert (the required operating medium) in a device, e.g., film in a camera, etc. **4** give a bias to (dice, etc.) with weights.

**loaf** /lōf/ ▸n. (pl. **loaves**) **1** unit of baked bread. **2** other food formed in the shape of a bread loaf: *meatloaf.*
▸v. spend time idly.

**loam** /lōm/ ▸n. fertile soil of clay, sand, and humus. —**loam·y** adj.

**loan** /lōn/ ▸n. **1** thing lent, esp. money. **2** lending or being lent.
▸v. lend.

**loan shark** ▸n. inf. person who lends money at exorbitant rates of interest.

**loan·word** ▸n. word adopted from a foreign language.

**loath** /lōTH/ ▸adj. disinclined; reluctant.

**loathe** /lōTH/ ▸v. detest.
—**loath·ing** n.

**lob** /läb/ ▸v. (**lobbed, lob·bing**) hit or throw (a ball, etc.) slowly or in a high arc.
▸n. **1** ball struck in a high arc. **2** stroke producing this result.

**lob·by** /ˈläbē/ ▸n. (pl. **-bies**) **1** entrance hall. **2** body of persons seeking to influence legislators on behalf of a particular interest: *tobacco lobby.*
▸v. (**-bied**) **1** solicit the support of (an influential person). **2** seek to influence (the members of a legislature). —**lob·by·ist** n.

**lobe** /lōb/ ▸n. **1** roundish and flattish pendulous part, often one of a pair: *lobes of the brain.* **2** EARLOBE. —**lo·bar** adj.

**lo·bot·o·my** /ləˈbätəmē/ ▸n. (pl. **-mies**) incision into the frontal lobe of the brain.

**lob·ster** /ˈläbstər/ ▸n. edible marine crustacean with stalked eyes and two pincerlike claws.
▸v. catch lobsters.

**lo·cal** /ˈlōkəl/ ▸adj. **1** belonging to, peculiar to, or existing in a particular place. **2** of or affecting only a part. **3** (of a train, bus, etc.) stopping at all stations.
▸n. **1** inhabitant of a particular place. **2** local train, bus, etc. **3** local anesthetic. **4** local branch of a labor union. —**lo·cal·ly** adv.

**lo·cal ar·e·a net·work** ▸n. system for linking telecommunications or computer equipment in several offices, a group of buildings, etc. (Abbr.: **LAN**)

**lo·cale** /lōˈkal/ ▸n. scene or locality of an event or occurrence.

**lo·cal·i·ty** /lōˈkalitē/ ▸n. (pl. **-ties**) **1** district. **2** site or scene of something.

**lo·cal·ize** /ˈlōkəˌlīz/ ▸v. restrict or assign to a particular place.
—**lo·cal·i·za·tion** n.

**lo·cate** /'lō‚kāt/ ▸*v.* **1** discover the place of. **2** establish or situate in a place.

**lo·ca·tion** /lō'kāsHən/ ▸*n.* **1** place. **2** locating. **3** natural setting in which film is made, as distinct from studio simulation: *they are filming on location.*

**loc. cit.** ▸*abbr.* in the passage already cited.

**lock** /läk/ ▸*n.* **1** mechanism for fastening a door, lid, etc., that requires a key or a combination to work it. **2** section of a canal or river within gates for raising and lowering the water level. **3** tress of hair. **4** (**locks**) the hair of the head.

▸*v.* **1 a** fasten with a lock. **b** (**lock up**) shut and secure by locking. **2** (**lock up/in**) enclose (a person or thing) by or as if by locking. **3** make or become rigidly fixed. **4** become or cause to become jammed or caught. **5** entangle; interlock.

☐ **lock out 1** keep (a person) out by locking the door. **2** (of an employer) submit (employees) to a lockout.

**lock·er** ▸*n.* lockable cupboard or compartment, esp. for public use.

☐ **locker room** room containing lockers, esp. in a sports facility.

**lock·et** /'läkit/ ▸*n.* small ornamental case usu. holding a portrait, and usu. worn on a necklace.

**lock·jaw** ▸*n.* TETANUS.

**lock·out** ▸*n.* employer's exclusion of employees from their workplace until certain terms are agreed to.

**lock·smith** ▸*n.* maker and repairer of locks.

**lock·step** ▸*n.* **1** a way of marching with close precision. **2** rigidly inflexible pattern or process.

**lock·up** ▸*n.* holding cell for police suspects.

**lo·co** /'lōkō/ ▸*adj. inf.* crazy.

**lo·co·mo·tion** /‚lōkə'mōsHən/ ▸*n.* motion or the power of motion from one place to another.

**lo·co·mo·tive** /‚lōkə'mōtiv/ ▸*n.* engine for pulling trains. ▸*adj.* of, relating to, or effecting locomotion: *locomotive power.*

**lo·co·weed** /'lōkō‚wēd/ ▸*n.* poisonous plant of the southwestern U.S., causing disease in livestock.

**lo·cus clas·si·cus** /'lōkəs

'klasikəs/ ▸n. (pl. **lo·ci clas·si·ci**
/'lō,sī 'klasə,sī/) passage
considered to be the best known
or most authoritative on a
particular subject.

**lo·cust** /'lōkəst/ ▸n. **1** kind of
grasshopper that migrates in
swarms, destroying vegetation.
**2** cicada. **3** (also **locust tree**) N.
American flowering tree yielding
durable wood.

**lo·cu·tion** /lō'kyo͞osʜən/ ▸n.
word, phrase, or idiom.

**lode** /lōd/ ▸n. vein of metal ore.

**lode·star** ▸n. **1** star that a ship,
etc., is steered by, esp. the pole
star. **2 a** guiding principle.
**b** object of pursuit.

**lode·stone** (also **load·stone**) ▸n.
**1** magnetic oxide of iron.
**2** thing that attracts.

**lodge** /läj/ ▸n. **1** small house
occupied by a gatekeeper,
gardener, etc. **2** house or hotel
in a resort. **3** house occupied in
the season for skiing, hunting,
etc. **4** beaver's or otter's lair.
▸v. **1** submit (a complaint).
**2** make or become fixed or
caught. **3** live as a paying guest.

**lodg·ing** ▸n. **1** temporary
accommodations. **2** (**lodgings**)
room or rooms rented for
lodging.

**loft** /lôft/ ▸n. **1** attic. **2** room over
a stable, esp. for hay, etc.
**3** height of an airborne ball.
▸v. send (a ball, etc.) high up.

**loft·y** ▸adj. (**-i·er, -i·est**) **1** (of
things) of imposing height.
**2** haughty; aloof. **3** exalted;
noble.

**log** /lôg/ ▸n. **1** unhewn piece of a
felled tree. **2** device for gauging
the speed of a ship. **3** (also
**log·book**) record of events
during the voyage of a ship or
aircraft. **4** logarithm.
▸v. (**logged, log·ging**) **1** enter
(data) in a logbook. **2** (of a ship,
etc.) achieve (a certain distance,
speed, etc.). **3** cut into logs.
□ **log on** (or **off**) go through the
procedures to begin (or
conclude) use of a computer
system.

**lo·gan·ber·ry** /'lōgən,berē/ ▸n.
(pl. **-ries**) **1** hybrid of a
blackberry and a raspberry. **2** its
dark red fruit.

**log·a·rithm** /'lôgə,riᴛʜəm/ ▸n.
the power to which a number
must be raised to produce a
given number: *the logarithm of
1,000 to base 10 is 3.*
—**log·a·rith·mic** adj.

**loge** /lōzʜ/ ▸n. (in a theater, etc.)
front section of the first balcony.

**log·ger·heads** /ˈlôɡərˌhedz/ ▸*pl. n.* (in phrase **at loggerheads**) disagreeing or disputing; at odds.

**log·ic** /ˈläjik/ ▸*n.* **1** science of reasoning. **2** particular scheme of or treatise on this. —**lo·gi·cian** *n.*

**-logic** (also **-logical**) ▸*comb. form* forming adjectives corresponding esp. to nouns ending in *-logy: analogic | theological.*

**log·i·cal** ▸*adj.* following naturally or sensibly; reasonable: *a logical conclusion.* —**log·i·cal·ly** *adv.*

**lo·gis·tics** /ləˈjistiks/ ▸*pl. n.* planning for and provision of services and supplies for an operation, program, etc. —**lo·gis·ti·cal** *adj.*

**log·jam** ▸*n.* **1** crowded mass of logs in a river. **2** deadlock.

**lo·go** /ˈlōgō/ ▸*n.* (*pl.* **-gos**) design adopted by an organization to identify its product, etc.

**lo·go·cen·tric** /ˌlōgəˈsentrik/ ▸*adj.* regarding words and language as a fundamental expression of an external reality (esp. applied as a negative term to traditional Western thought by postmodernist critics).

**log·o·gram** /ˈlôɡəˌgram/ ▸*n.* sign or character representing a word or phrase, such as those used in shorthand and some writing systems.

**log·o·griph** /ˈlôɡəˌgrif/ ▸*n.* puzzle involving anagrams, esp. one in which a number of words that can be spelled using a group of letters are to be identified from their synonyms introduced into a set of verses.

**lo·gom·a·chy** /lōˈgäməkē/ ▸*n.* (*pl.* **-chies**) argument about words.

**log·or·rhe·a** /ˌlôɡəˈrēə/ ▸*n.* tendency to extreme loquacity.

**log·roll·ing** ▸*n.* **1** *inf.* exchanging favors, esp. for political gain. **2** sport in which two people stand on and rotate a floating log until one loses by falling off. —**log·roll** *v.*

**-logy** ▸*comb. form* forming nouns denoting: **1** (usu. as **-ology**) subject of study or interest: *archaeology | zoology.* **2** characteristic of speech or language: *tautology.*

**loin** /loin/ ▸*n.* **1** (**loins**) the part of the body on both sides of the spine between the ribs and the hipbones. **2** meat from this part of an animal.

**loin·cloth** ▸*n.* cloth worn around the hips as a garment.

**loi·ter** /ˈloitər/ ▸*v.* hang around; linger idly.

**loll** /läl/ ▸*v.* **1** stand, sit, or recline in a lazy attitude. **2** (**loll out**) hang loosely.

**lol·la·pa·loo·za** /ˌläləpəˈlo͞ozə/ ▸*n.* person or thing that is particularly impressive or attractive.

**lol·li·pop** /ˈlälēˌpäp/ ▸*n.* hard, usu. round candy on a stick.

**lone** /lōn/ ▸*adj.* **1** (of a person) solitary; without a companion. **2** (of a place) unfrequented; uninhabited.
□ **lone wolf** person who prefers to act alone.

**lone·ly** /ˈlōnlē/ ▸*adj.* (**-li·er, -li·est**) **1** solitary. **2** (of a place) unfrequented. **3** sad because without friends.

**lon·er** ▸*n.* person who prefers to be alone.

**lone·some** /ˈlōnsəm/ ▸*adj.* **1** solitary. **2** feeling lonely.

**long** /lôNG/ ▸*adj.* (**-er, -est**) **1** measuring much from end to end in space or time. **2** in length or duration: *three miles long | two months long.* **3** elongated. **4** lasting much time: *long friendship.* **5** (of a vowel) having the pronunciation shown in the name of the letter. **6** (of odds or a chance) of low probability.
▸*n.* long interval or period: *will not take long.*
▸*adv.* (**-er, -est**) **1** by or for a long time: *long before.* **2** throughout a specified time: *all day long.*
▸*v.* have a strong wish or desire for.
□ **as** (or **so**) **long as** provided that.
□ **before long** soon.

**long.** ▸*abbr.* longitude.

**long-dis·tance** ▸*adj.* (of a telephone call) between distant places.

**lon·gev·i·ty** /lônˈjevətē/ ▸*n.* long life.

**long·hand** ▸*n.* ordinary handwriting.

**long·ing** ▸*n.* strong wish or desire. —**long·ing·ly** *adv.*

**lon·gi·tude** /ˈlänjiˌt(y)o͞od-/ ▸*n.* angular distance east or west from the prime meridian. —**lon·gi·tu·di·nal** *adj.*

**long jump** ▸*n.* track-and-field contest of jumping as far as possible along the ground in one leap.

**long-lived** /līvd/ ▸*adj.* **1** having a long existence or duration. **2** lasting a long time.

**long-range** ▸*adj.* **1** extending

into the future. **2** designed to extend or operate over a long distance.

**long·shore** /'lôNG,SHôr; 'läNG-/ ▸*adj.* existing on, frequenting, or moving along the seashore.

**long·shore·man** ▸*n.* (*pl.* **-men**) person employed to load and unload ships.

**long shot** ▸*n.* **1** wild guess or venture. **2** bet at long odds. □ **not by a long shot** by no means.

**long-term** ▸*adj.* covering a relatively long period of time.

**long-wind·ed** /'windid/ ▸*adj.* **1** (of speech or writing) tediously lengthy. **2** able to run a long distance without rest.

**look** /lo͝ok/ ▸*v.* **1 a** use one's sight. **b** (**look at**) turn one's eyes on; examine. **2** (**look at**) consider; examine: *look at the facts.* **3** (**look for**) **a** search for. **b** expect. **4** have a specified appearance; seem. **5** (**look into**) investigate.
▸*n.* **1** act of looking; glance: *scornful look.* **2** expression. **3** appearance.
▸*interj.* (also **look here!**) calling attention, expressing a protest, etc.
□ **look after** take care of. □ **look out** be vigilant and take notice:

*look out for the early warning signs.*
□ **look over** inspect; examine.
□ **look up 1** search for (esp. information in a book). **2** improve: *things are looking up.*
□ **look up to** respect; venerate.

**look-a·like** ▸*n.* person or thing closely resembling another.

**look·ing glass** ▸*n.* mirror.

**look·out** ▸*n.* **1** person or party stationed to keep watch. **2** *inf.* person's own concern: *that's his lookout.*

**loom** /lo͞om/ ▸*n.* apparatus for weaving.
▸*v.* **1** appear dimly, esp. as a threatening shape. **2** (of an event or prospect) be ominously close.

**loon** /lo͞on/ ▸*n.* aquatic diving bird.

**loon·y** ▸*n.* (*pl.* **-ies**) *inf.* mad or silly person; lunatic.
▸*adj.* (**-i·er, -i·est**) crazy; silly. —**loo·ni·ness** *n.*

**loop** /lo͞op/ ▸*n.* **1 a** figure produced by a curve, or a doubled thread, etc., that crosses itself. **b** anything forming this figure. **2** endless strip of tape or film allowing continuous repetition. **3** sequence of computer instructions that is repeated until a condition is satisfied.

▸*v.* **1** form or form into a loop. **2** fasten with a loop or loops. **3** move in looplike patterns.

**loop·hole** ▸*n.* means of evading a law or rule: *tax loopholes.*

**loose** /lo͞os/ ▸*adj.* **1** free from bonds or restraint. **2** not tightly held, fixed, etc. **3** slack; relaxed. **4** not compact or dense. **5** inexact. **6** morally lax.
▸*n.* state of freedom, esp. as an escapee: *on the loose.*
▸*v.* **1** release; set free; untie. **2** discharge (a missile, etc.). —**loos·en** *v.*
☐ **at loose ends** uncertain; disorganized.

**loot** /lo͞ot/ ▸*n.* **1** spoil; booty. **2** *inf.* money.
▸*v.* plunder.

**lop** /läp/ ▸*v.* (**lopped, lop·ping**) **1** cut or remove (a part or parts) from a whole, esp. branches from a tree. **2** hang limply.
☐ **lop-eared** (of an animal) having drooping ears.

**lope** /lōp/ ▸*v.* run with a long bounding stride.
▸*n.* long bounding stride.

**lop·sid·ed** /ˈläpˌsīdid/ ▸*adj.* unevenly balanced.
—**lop·sid·ed·ly** *adv.*

**lo·qua·cious** /lōˈkwāsнəs/ ▸*adj.* talkative. —**lo·quac·i·ty** *n.*

**lord** /lôrd/ ▸*n.* **1** master or ruler. **2** (**Lord**) **a** God or Christ. **b** British title for a nobleman.
▸*interj.* (**Lord!**) expressing surprise, dismay, etc.
☐ **lord it over** domineer.

**lore** /lôr/ ▸*n.* traditions and knowledge on a subject.

**lor·gnette** /lôrnˈyet/ (also **lor·gnettes**) ▸*n.* pair of glasses or opera glasses held in front of a person's eyes by a long handle at one side.

**lose** /lo͞oz/ ▸*v.* (*past* and *past part.* **lost**) **1** be deprived of or cease to have, esp. by negligence. **2** be deprived of by death. **3** become unable to follow, grasp, or find. **4** be defeated in (a game, lawsuit, battle, etc.). **5** evade: *lost our pursuers.* **6** disappear; perish: *lost at sea.*
☐ **lose heart** be discouraged.
☐ **lose out** be disadvantaged: *children who lost out on regular schooling.* ☐ **losing battle** effort in which failure seems certain.

**loss** /lôs/ ▸*n.* **1** losing; being lost. **2** person, thing, or amount lost. **3** detriment or disadvantage resulting from losing.
☐ **at a loss 1** (sold, etc.) for less

than was paid for it. **2** puzzled; uncertain. □ **be at a loss for words** not know what to say.

**loss lead·er** ▸*n.* item sold at a loss to attract customers.

**lost** /lôst/ ▸ past and past part. of LOSE.

▸*adj.* **1** unable to find one's way; not knowing where one is. **2** having strayed. **3** gone and not recoverable.

□ **be lost on** be wasted on or not appreciated by. □ **be lost without** have great difficulty if deprived of. □ **lost cause** **1** enterprise, etc., with no chance of success. **2** person one can no longer hope to influence.

**lot** /lät/ ▸*n.* **1** *inf.* **a** large number or amount: *a lot of people* | *lots of fun.* **b** *inf.* much: *a lot warmer.* **2 a** each of a set of objects used in making a chance selection. **b** this method of deciding: *chosen by lot.* **3** destiny, fortune, or condition. **4** allotment of land. **5** article or set of articles for sale at an auction, etc.

**lo·thar·i·o** /lōˈTHe(ə)rē͜ō/ ▸*n.* (*pl.* -os) rake or libertine.

**lo·tion** /ˈlōSHən/ ▸*n.* thick, smooth liquid applied to the skin for medicinal or cosmetic purposes.

**lot·ter·y** /ˈlätərē/ ▸*n.* (*pl.* -ies) game in which numbered tickets are sold and prizes are won by the holders of numbers drawn at random.

**lot·to** /ˈlätō/ ▸*n.* **1** game of chance involving the drawing of numbers. **2** lottery.

**lo·tus** /ˈlōtəs/ ▸*n.* type of water lily.

**lo·tus-eat·er** ▸*n.* person who spends time indulging in pleasure and luxury rather than dealing with practical concerns.

**lo·tus po·si·tion** ▸*n.* cross-legged position of meditation with the feet resting on the thighs.

**louche** /lōōSH/ ▸*adj.* disreputable or sordid in a rakish or appealing way.

**loud** /loud/ ▸*adj.* **1** strongly audible; noisy. **2** (of colors, etc.) gaudy; obtrusive.

▸*adv.* loudly. —**loud·ly** *adv.*
□ **out loud** aloud.

**loud·mouth** ▸*n. inf.* noisily self-assertive, vociferous person. —**loud·mouthed** *adj.*

**loud·speak·er** ▸*n.* apparatus that converts electrical impulses into sound, esp. music and voice.

**lounge** /lounj/ ▸*v.* **1** recline

comfortably; loll. **2** stand or move about idly.

▸*n.* **1** place for lounging. **2** waiting room.

**louse** /lous/ ▸*n.* **1** (*pl.* **lice**) parasitic insect. **2** *inf.* (*pl.* **lous·es**) contemptible person.

□ **louse up** *inf.* spoil or ruin.

**lous·y** /ˈlouzē/ ▸*adj.* (**-i·er, -i·est**) **1** *inf.* very bad; disgusting. **2** infested with lice. **3** *inf.* (**lousy with**) teeming with.

**lout** /lout/ ▸*n.* boorish person. —**lout·ish** *adj.*

**lou·ver** /ˈlo͞ovər/ ▸*n.* each of a set of overlapping slats that admit air and light and exclude rain. —**lou·vered** *adj.*

**love** /ləv/ ▸*n.* **1** deep affection; fondness. **2** deep romantic or sexual attachment. **3** great interest and pleasure in something. **4** beloved one; sweetheart. **5** (in some games) no score; nil.

▸*v.* **1** feel deep fondness for. **2** delight in; admire; greatly cherish.

□ **fall in love** develop a great (esp. sexual) love (for). □ **for love** for pleasure not profit. □ **love seat** small sofa for two. □ **make love** have sexual intercourse (with).

**love·lorn** /ˈləv,lôrn/ ▸*adj.* pining from unrequited love.

**love·ly** /ˈləvlē/ ▸*adj.* (**-li·er, -li·est**) **1** exquisitely beautiful. **2** *inf.* pleasing; delightful.

**love·sick** ▸*adj.* languishing with romantic love. —**love·sick·ness** *n.*

**low** /lō/ ▸*adj.* **1** not high or tall. **2** not elevated. **3** of or in humble rank. **4** small or less than normal in amount or extent or intensity. **5** dejected; lacking vigor. **6** not shrill or loud. **7** commonplace; vulgar. **8** unfavorable: *low opinion.*

▸*n.* **1** low or the lowest level or number. **2** area of low pressure. **3** sound made by cattle; moo.

▸*adv.* **1** in or to a low position or state. **2** in a low pitch or tone.

▸*v.* moo. —**low·ish** *adj.*

**low·brow** ▸*adj.* not intellectual or cultured.

▸*n.* lowbrow person. —**low·browed** *adj.*

**low-class** ▸*adj.* of low quality or social class.

**low com·e·dy** ▸*n.* comedy in which the subject and the treatment border on farce.

**low-down** ▸*adj.* abject; dishonorable.

▶*n. inf.* relevant information about something.

**low·er** ▶*adj.* **1** less high in position or status. **2** situated below another part. **3 a** situated on less high land: *Lower Egypt.* **b** situated to the south: *Lower California.*

▶*adv.* in or to a lower position, etc.

▶*v.* **1** let or haul down. **2** make or become lower. **3** degrade.

**low·er·case** ▶*n.* small letters.

▶*adj.* of or having small letters.

**low fre·quen·cy** ▶any frequency, esp. in radio, between 30 and 300 kilohertz.

**low-key** ▶*adj.* lacking intensity; restrained.

**low·ly** /ˈlōlē/ ▶*adj.* (**-li·er, -li·est**) humble; unpretentious. **—low·li·ness** *n.*

**low-mind·ed** ▶*adj.* having vulgar tastes or interests.

**low-pitched** ▶*adj.* **1** (of a sound) low. **2** (of a roof) having only a slight slope.

**low pres·sure** ▶ **1** little demand for activity or exertion. **2** (of atmospheric pressure) below average.

**low pro·file** ▶*n.* avoidance of attention or publicity.

**low tide** ▶*n.* time or level of the tide at its ebb.

**lox** /läks/ ▶*n.* **1** liquid oxygen. **2** smoked salmon.

**loy·al** /ˈloiəl/ ▶*adj.* faithful. **—loy·al·ty** *n.*

**loz·enge** /ˈläzənj/ ▶*n.* **1** sweet or medicinal tablet, for dissolving in the mouth. **2** diamond-shaped figure.

**LPN** ▶*abbr.* licensed practical nurse.

**LSD** ▶*abbr.* lysergic acid diethylamide, a powerful hallucinogenic drug.

**Lt.** ▶*abbr.* lieutenant.

**Ltd.** ▶*abbr.* limited.

**lu·au** /ˈlo͞oˌou/ ▶*n.* (*pl.* same or **lu·aus**) Hawaiian party or feast, esp. one accompanied by entertainment.

**lu·bri·cant** /ˈlo͞obrikənt/ ▶*n.* substance used to reduce friction.

▶*adj.* lubricating.

**lu·bri·cate** /ˈlo͞obriˌkāt/ ▶*v.* **1** apply oil or grease, etc. **2** make slippery. **—lu·bri·ca·tion** *n.* **—lu·bri·ca·tive** *adj.*

**lu·bri·cious** /lo͞oˈbrisHəs/ (also **lu·bri·cous** /ˈlo͞obrikəs/) ▶*adj.* **1** offensively displaying or intended to arouse sexual desire.

**2** smooth and slippery with oil or a similar substance.

**lu·cent** /ˈloōsənt/ ▸*adj.* glowing with or giving off light.

**lu·cid** /ˈloōsid/ ▸*adj.* **1** expressing or expressed clearly. **2** sane. —**lu·cid·i·ty** *n.*

**luck** /lək/ ▸*n.* **1** good or bad fortune. **2** circumstances of life (beneficial or not) brought by this. **3** good fortune; success due to chance.

**luck·y** ▸*adj.* (**-i·er, -i·est**) having, bringing, or resulting from good luck.

**lu·cra·tive** /ˈloōkrətiv/ ▸*adj.* profitable; yielding financial gain.

**lu·cre** /ˈloōkər/ ▸*n.* financial profit or gain.

**lu·dic** /ˈloōdik/ ▸*adj.* showing spontaneous and undirected playfulness.

**lu·di·crous** /ˈloōdikrəs/ ▸*adj.* absurd; ridiculous; laughable.

**lug** /ləg/ ▸*v.* (**lugged, lug·ging**) drag or carry with effort.
▸*n.* (also **lug nut**) nut that fastens a wheel to an axle.

**luge** /loōzн/ ▸*n.* toboggan ridden in a supine position down a chute.
▸*v.* ride on a luge.

**lug·gage** /ˈləgij/ ▸*n.* traveler's suitcases, bags, etc.

**lu·gu·bri·ous** /ləˈg(y)oōbrēəs/ ▸*adj.* doleful; mournful; dismal.

**luke·warm** /ˈloōkˈwôrm/ ▸*adj.* **1** moderately warm; tepid. **2** unenthusiastic; indifferent.

**lull** /ləl/ ▸*v.* **1** soothe or send to sleep. **2** cause to feel deceptively secure or confident. **3** (of noise, a storm, etc.) abate or fall quiet.
▸*n.* calm period.

**lul·la·by** /ˈlələ,bī/ ▸*n.* (*pl.* **-bies**) soothing song to send a child to sleep.

**lum·ba·go** /ˌləmˈbāgō/ ▸*n.* rheumatic pain in the lower back.

**lum·bar** /ˈləmbər/ ▸*adj.* of the lower back area.

**lum·ber** /ˈləmbər/ ▸*v.* move in a low, awkward way.
▸*n.* timber cut and prepared for use. —**lum·ber·ing** *adj.*

**lum·ber·jack** ▸*n.* one who fells, prepares, or conveys lumber.

**lum·ber·yard** ▸*n.* place where lumber is cut and stored for sale.

**lu·mi·nar·y** /ˈloōmə,nerē/ ▸*n.* (*pl.* **-ies**) **1** eminent person, esp. one who inspires others. **2** natural light-giving body.

**lu·mi·nes·cence** /ˌloōmə-

'nesəns/ ▶*n.* emission of light without heat. **—lu·mi·nes·cent** *adj.*

**lu·mi·nous** /'lōōmənəs/ ▶*adj.* bright or shining: *luminous glow* | *luminous dial.* **—lu·mi·nos·i·ty** *n.*

**lum·mox** /'ləməks/ ▶*n. inf.* clumsy or stupid person.

**lump** /ləmp/ ▶*n.* **1** compact shapeless mass. **2** tumor; swelling. **3** heavy or dull person.
▶*v.* **1** mass together or group indiscriminately. **2** become lumpy. **3** *inf.* put up with ungraciously: *like it or lump it.* **—lump·y** *adj.*

**lu·na·cy** /'lōōnəsē/ ▶*n.* (*pl.* **-cies**) **1** insanity. **2** great folly.

**lu·nar** /'lōōnər/ ▶*adj.* of, relating to, or determined by the moon.

**lu·nar mod·ule** ▶*n.* small craft for traveling between the moon and an orbiting spacecraft.

**lu·nar month** ▶*n.* interval between new moons (about 29 1/2 days).

**lu·nate** /'lōō,nāt/ ▶*adj.* crescent-shaped.
▶*n.* (also **lu·nate bone**) crescent-shaped carpal bone situated in the center of the wrist and articulating with the radius.

**lu·na·tic** /'lōōnə,tik/ ▶*n.* **1** insane person. **2** someone foolish or eccentric.
▶*adj.* mad; foolish or eccentric.
□ **lunatic fringe** extreme or eccentric minority group.

**lunch** /lənCH/ ▶*n.* midday meal.
▶*v.* eat lunch.

**lung** /ləNG/ ▶*n.* either of the pair of respiratory organs in humans and many other vertebrates.

**lunge** /lənj/ ▶*n.* **1** sudden movement forward. **2** basic attacking move in fencing.
▶*v.* drive a weapon violently in some direction.

**lu·pine** /'lōōpin/ ▶*n.* plant with long tapering spikes of blue, purple, pink, white, or yellow flowers.

**lu·pine**[2] /'lōōpīn/ ▶*adj.* of or like a wolf or wolves.

**lu·pus** /'lōōpəs/ ▶*n.* any of various ulcerous skin diseases, esp. tuberculosis of the skin.

**lurch** /lərCH/ ▶*n.* stagger; sudden unsteady movement.
▶*v.* stagger; move suddenly and unsteadily.
□ **leave someone in the lurch** desert (a friend, etc.) in difficulties.

**lure** /lŏŏr/ ▶*v.* **1** entice, usu. by baiting. **2** attract with the promise of a reward.

▸*n.* thing used to entice.  —**lur·ing** *adj.*

**lu·rid** /ˈlo͝orid/ ▸*adj.* **1** vivid or glowing in color. **2** sensational; horrifying. **3** ghastly; wan: *lurid complexion.*

**lurk** /lərk/ ▸*v.* **1** linger furtively. **2** lie in ambush. **3** [as *adj.* **lurking**] be latent; linger: *a lurking suspicion.*

**lus·cious** /ˈləsHəs/ ▸*adj.* **1** richly pleasing to the senses. **2** voluptuously attractive.

**lush** /ləsH/ ▸*adj.* **1** (of vegetation) luxuriant and succulent. **2** luxurious.
▸*n. inf.* alcoholic; drunkard.

**lust** /ləst/ ▸*n.* **1** strong sexual desire. **2** passionate desire for.
▸*v.* have a strong desire.

**lus·ter** /ˈləstər/ ▸*n.* **1** gloss; brilliance. **2** shining surface. **3** splendor; glory. —**lus·trous** *adj.*

**lus·tral** /ˈləstrəl/ ▸*adj.* relating to or used in ceremonial purification.

**lus·trate** /ˈləsˌtrāt/ ▸*v.* purify by expiatory sacrifice, ceremonial washing, or some other ritual action.

**lust·y** ▸*adj.* (**-i·er, -i·est**) **1** healthy and strong. **2** vigorous.

**lu·sus na·tu·rae** /ˈlo͞osəs nəˈt(y)o͝orˌē; -ˈt(y)o͝orˌī/ ▸*n.* (*pl.* same or **lu·sus·es na·tu·rae**) freak of nature.

**lute** /lo͞ot/ ▸*n.* guitarlike instrument with a long neck and pear-shaped body.

**lu·te·nist** /ˈlo͞otn-ist/ (also **lu·ta·nist**) ▸*n.* lute player.

**Lu·ther·an** /ˈlo͞oTH(ə)rən/ ▸*n.* member of the Lutheran Church.
▸*adj.* of or characterized by the theology of Martin Luther.

**luxe** /ləks; lo͝oks/ ▸*n.* luxury.

**lux·u·ri·ant** /ləɡˈzho͝orēənt/ ▸*adj.* **1** profuse in growth; exuberant. **2** richly ornate. —**lux·u·ri·ance** *n.*

**lux·u·ri·ate** /ləɡˈzho͝orēˌāt/ ▸*v.* **1** enjoy in a luxurious manner. **2** relax in comfort.

**lux·u·ry** /ˈləksHərē; ˈləɡzhə-/ ▸*n.* (*pl.* **-ries**) **1** choice or costly surroundings, possessions, etc. **2** inessential but costly and desirable item. —**lux·u·ri·ous** *adj.*

**-ly** ▸*suffix* **1** forming adjectives esp. from nouns, meaning: **a** having the qualities of: *princely.* **b** recurring at intervals of: *daily.* **2** forming adverbs from adjectives, denoting esp.

manner or degree: *boldly* | *happily* | *miserably* | *deservedly*.

**ly·cée** /lē'sā/ ▶*n. (pl.* **-cées** pronunc. same) secondary school in France that is funded by the government.

**lye** /lī/ ▶*n.* strong alkaline solution, esp. for washing.

**Lyme dis·ease** /'līm/ ▶*n.* disease transmitted by ticks, characterized by rash, fever, fatigue, and joint pain.

**lymph** /limf/ ▶*n.* colorless fluid from body tissues. —**lym·phoid** *adj.* —**lym·phous** *adj.*

□ **lymph node** (or **gland**) small mass of tissue that conveys lymph.

**lym·phat·ic** /lim'fatik/ ▶*adj.* **1** of or relating to lymph or its secretion. **2** (of a person) pale, flabby, or sluggish.
▶*n.* veinlike vessel conveying lymph in the body.

**lymph·o·cyte** /'limfə,sīt/ ▶*n.* type of white blood cell.

**lynch** /linCH/ ▶*v.* (of a mob) put (a person) to death without a legal trial. —**lynch·er** *n.* —**lynch·ing** *n.*

**lynx** /liNGks/ ▶*n.* wild cat with a short tail, spotted fur, and tufted ear tips.

**lyre** /lī(ə)r/ ▶*n.* ancient U-shaped harplike instrument.

**lyr·ic** /'lirik/ ▶*adj.* **1** (of poetry) expressing the writer's emotions. **2** meant to be sung; songlike.
▶*n.* **1** lyric poem. **2** (**lyrics**) words of a song.

# Mm

**M**[1] /em/ ▸*n.* (*pl.* **Ms** or **M's**; **m's**)
**1** thirteenth letter of the alphabet. **2** (as a Roman numeral) 1,000.

**M**[2] (also **M.**) ▸*abbr.* **1** Master.
**2** *Monsieur.* **3** mega-. **4** Mach.

**m** (also **m.**) ▸*abbr.* **1** male.
**2** married. **3** mile(s). **4** meter(s).
**5** million(s). **6** minute(s).
**7** milli-.

**MA** ▸*abbr.* **1** Master of Arts.
**2** Massachusetts (in official postal use).

**ma** /mä/ ▸*n. inf.* mother.

**ma'am** /mam/ ▸*n.* madam.

**ma·ca·bre** /mə'käb(rə)/ ▸*adj.* grim, gruesome.

**mac·ad·am** /mə'kadəm/ ▸*n.* broken stone used for road building.

**mac·a·ro·ni** /ˌmakə'rōnē/ ▸*n.* tubular variety of pasta.

**mac·a·ron·ic** /ˌmakə'ränik/ ▸*adj.* denoting language, esp. burlesque verse, containing words or inflections from one language introduced into the context of another.
▸*n.* (usu. **macaronics**) macaronic verse, esp. that which mixes the vernacular with Latin.

**mac·a·roon** /ˌmakə'rōōn/ ▸*n.* small light cake or cookie made with egg white, sugar, and ground almonds or coconut.

**ma·caw** /mə'kô/ ▸*n.* long-tailed brightly colored parrot native to S. and Central America.

**Mace** /mās/ ▸*trademark* aerosol spray used to disable an attacker temporarily.

**mace** /mās/ ▸*n.* **1** heavy spiked club used esp. in the Middle Ages. **2** ceremonial staff of office. **3** fibrous layer between a nutmeg's shell and its husk, dried and ground as a spice.

**mac·er·ate** /'masəˌrāt/ ▸*v.* make or become soft by soaking.

**ma·chet·e** /mə'ꜱHetē/ ▸*n.* heavy knife used in Central America and the W. Indies as a tool and weapon.

**Mach·i·a·vel·li·an** /ˌmakēə-'velēən/ ▸*adj.* elaborately cunning; scheming; unscrupulous.
—**Mach·i·a·vel·li·an·ism** *n.*

**mach·i·nate** /ˈmakəˌnāt; ˈmasHə-/ ▸v. engage in plots and intrigues; scheme.

**ma·chine** /məˈsHēn/ ▸n. **1** apparatus using or applying mechanical power, having several interrelated parts. **2** controlling system of an organization, etc.: *the party machine.*

**ma·chine gun** ▸n. automatic gun giving continuous, rapid fire.

**ma·chin·er·y** ▸n. (pl. **-ies**) **1** machines collectively. **2** components of a machine; mechanism. **3** means devised or available: *machinery for decision making.*

**ma·chin·ist** ▸n. person who operates a machine, esp. a nonportable power tool.

**ma·chis·mo** /məˈcHēzmō/ ▸n. exaggeratedly assertive manliness; show of masculinity.

**ma·cho** /ˈmäcHō/ ▸adj. showily manly or virile.

**mack·er·el** /ˈmak(ə)rəl/ ▸n. (pl. same or **-els**) N. Atlantic marine fish used for food.

**mack·in·tosh** /ˈmakənˌtäsH/ (also **mac·in·tosh**) ▸n. waterproof, esp. rubberized, coat.

**mac·ra·mé** /ˈmakrəˌmā/ ▸n. art of knotting cord or string to make decorative articles.

**macro-** ▸comb. form **1** long. **2** large; large-scale.

**mac·ro·bi·ot·ic** /ˌmakrōbīˈätik/ ▸adj. of a diet intended to prolong life, comprising pure vegetable foods, brown rice, etc. ▸n. (**macrobiotics**) theory of such a diet.

**mac·ro·cosm** /ˈmakrəˌkäzəm/ ▸n. **1** universe. **2** the whole of a complex structure.

**mac·ro·ec·o·nom·ics** /ˈmakrō-ˌekəˈnämiks; -ˌēkə-/ ▸pl. n. part of economics concerned with large-scale or general economic factors, such as interest rates and national productivity.

**ma·cron** /ˈmāˌkrän/ ▸n. diacritical mark (ˉ) over a long or stressed vowel.

**mac·u·late** ▸adj. /ˈmakyəˌlit/ spotted or stained. ▸v. /-ˌlāt/ mark with a spot or spots; stain.

**mad** /mad/ ▸adj. (**mad·der**, **mad·dest**) **1** insane; having a disordered mind. **2** wildly foolish. **3** wildly excited or infatuated: *chess-mad.* **4** *inf.* angry. **5** (of an animal) rabid. —**mad·ly** adj. —**mad·ness** n.

**mad·am** /ˈmadəm/ ▶n. 1 polite or respectful form of address or mode of reference to a woman. 2 woman who runs a brothel.

**mad·cap** ▶adj. wildly impulsive.

**made** /mād/ ▶past and past part. of MAKE.

**mad·e·leine** /ˈmadl-ən; ˌmadl-ˈān/ ▶n. small rich cake, typically baked in a shell-shaped mold and often decorated with coconut and jam.

**Mad·e·moi·selle** /ˌmad(ə)m(w)əˈzel/ ▶n. (pl. **Mad·e·moi·selles** or **Mes·de·moi·selles**) French title or form of address used of or to an unmarried woman; Miss.

**mad·man** ▶n. (pl. **-men**) man who is insane or who behaves insanely.

**Ma·don·na** /məˈdänə/ ▶n. 1 name for the Virgin Mary. 2 picture or statue of the Madonna.

**mad·ras** /madˈrəs/ ▶n. strong, lightweight cotton fabric with colored or white stripes, checks, etc.

**mad·ri·gal** /ˈmadrigəl/ ▶n. usu. 16th-c. or 17th-c. part song for several voices, usu. unaccompanied.

**mael·strom** /ˈmālˌsträm/ ▶n. 1 great whirlpool. 2 state of confusion.

**mae·nad** /ˈmēˌnad/ ▶n. (in ancient Greece) a female follower of Bacchus, traditionally associated with divine possession and frenzied rites.

**maes·tro** /ˈmīstrō/ ▶n. (pl. **-tri** or **-tros**) 1 distinguished musician, esp. a conductor or performer. 2 great performer in any sphere.

**Ma·fi·a** /ˈmäfēə/ ▶n. organized international body of criminals.

**mag·a·zine** /ˌmagəˈzēn/ ▶n. 1 periodical publication containing articles, stories, etc. 2 chamber for holding a supply of cartridges in a firearm. 3 similar device feeding a camera, slide projector, etc. 4 military store for arms, ammunition, etc.

**mage** /māj/ ▶n. magician or learned person.

**ma·gen·ta** /məˈjentə/ ▶n. light purplish red.

**mag·got** /ˈmagət/ ▶n. soft-bodied larva of certain two-winged insects, esp. the housefly or bluebottle. —**mag·got·y** adj.

**ma·gi** /ˈmājī/ ▶pl. of MAGUS.

**mag·ic** /ˈmajik/ ▶n. 1 supposed

art of influencing the course of events supernaturally.
**2** conjuring tricks. **3** enchanting quality or phenomenon.
▸*adj.* using or used in magic.
—**mag·i·cal** *adj.* —**mag·i·cal·ly** *adv.* —**ma·gi·cian** *n.*

**mag·ic lan·tern** ▸*n.* simple form of image projector used for showing photographic slides.

**mag·is·te·ri·al** /ˌmajəˈsti(ə)rēəl/ ▸*adj.* **1** imperious. **2** of or conducted by a magistrate.

**mag·is·trate** /ˈmajəˌstrāt/ ▸*n.* **1** civil officer administering the law. **2** official conducting a court for minor cases and preliminary hearings: *magistrate's court.*
—**mag·is·tra·cy** *n.*

**mag·ma** /ˈmagmə/ ▸*n.* (*pl.* **-ma·ta** or **-mas**) molten rock under the earth's crust, which forms igneous rock.

**mag·nan·i·mous** /magˈnanəməs/ ▸*adj.* nobly generous; not petty in feelings or conduct.
—**mag·na·nim·i·ty** *n.*
—**mag·nan·i·mous·ly** *adv.*

**mag·nate** /ˈmagˌnāt/ ▸*n.* wealthy and influential person, esp. in business: *shipping magnate.*

**mag·ne·sia** /magˈnēzHə/ ▸*n.*

magnesium oxide used as an antacid and laxative.

**mag·ne·si·um** /magˈnēzēəm/ ▸*n.* silvery lightweight metallic element used in alloys. (Symb.: Mg).

**mag·net** /ˈmagnit/ ▸*n.* piece of iron, steel, ore, etc., having properties of attracting or repelling iron.

**mag·net·ic** /magˈnetik/ ▸*adj.* **1 a** having the properties of a magnet. **b** producing, produced by, or acting by magnetism. **2** very attractive or alluring: *a magnetic personality.*
—**mag·net·i·cal·ly** *adv.*

**mag·net·ism** /ˈmagniˌtizəm/ ▸*n.* **1** magnetic phenomena and their study. **2** property of producing these phenomena. **3** attraction; personal charm.

**mag·ne·to** /magˈnētō/ ▸*n.* (*pl.* **-tos**) electric generator using permanent magnets and producing high voltage.

**mag·nif·i·cent** /magˈnifəsənt/ ▸*adj.* **1** splendid; stately. **2** sumptuously or lavishly constructed or adorned. **3** fine; excellent. —**mag·nif·i·cence** *n.*
—**mag·nif·i·cent·ly** *adv.*

**mag·ni·fy** /ˈmagnəˌfī/ ▸*v.* (**-fied**) **1** make (a thing) appear larger

than it is, as with a lens.
**2** intensify. —**mag·ni·fi·ca·tion** *n.*

**mag·nil·o·quent** /mag-ˈniləkwənt/ ▸*adj.* using high-flown or bombastic language.

**mag·ni·tude** /ˈmagnəˌt(y)o͞od/ ▸*n.* **1** largeness. **2** size. **3** importance.

**mag·no·lia** /magˈnōlyə/ ▸*n.* tree with dark-green foliage and large waxlike flowers.

**mag·num o·pus** /ˈmagnəm ˈōpəs/ ▸*n.* **1** great work of art, literature, etc. **2** most important work of an artist, writer, etc.

**mag·pie** /ˈmagˌpī/ ▸*n.* kind of crow with a long pointed tail, black-and-white plumage, and noisy behavior.

**ma·gus** /ˈmāgəs/ ▸*n.* (*pl.* **-gi**) **1** member of a priestly caste of ancient Persia. **2** sorcerer.

**ma·ha·ra·ja** /ˌmähəˈräjə; -ˈräzHə/ (also **ma·ha·ra·jah**) ▸*n.* an Indian prince.

**ma·hat·ma** /məˈhätmə/ ▸*n.* (esp. in India) revered person.

**mah-jongg** /ˌmä ˈzHäNG/ (also **mah·jong**) ▸*n.* Chinese game for four resembling rummy and played with 136 or 144 pieces called tiles.

**ma·hog·a·ny** /məˈhägənē/ ▸*n.* (*pl.* **-nies**) reddish-brown wood used for furniture.

**maid** /mād/ ▸*n.* female domestic servant.

**maid·en** /ˈmādn/ ▸*n.* young unmarried woman.
▸*adj.* **1** unmarried: *maiden aunt.* **2** first: *maiden voyage.*
—**maid·en·ly** *adj.*
□ **maiden name** wife's surname before marriage.

**maid·en·hair** ▸*n.* (also **maid·en·hair fern**) fern with fine hairlike stalks and delicate fronds.

**mail** /māl/ ▸*n.* **1** letters and parcels, etc., conveyed by the postal system. **2** postal system. **3** one complete delivery or collection of mail. **4** armor made of rings, chains, or plates, joined together flexibly.
▸*v.* send by mail.

**maim** /mām/ ▸*v.* cripple, disable, or mutilate.

**main** /mīn/ ▸*adj.* **1** chief in size, importance, etc.; principal: *the main part.* **2** exerted to the full: *by main force.*
▸*n.* principal duct, etc., for water, sewage, etc.: *water main.*
—**main·ly** *adj.*

**main·frame** ▸*n.* large-scale computer system.

**main·land** ▸*n.* large continuous extent of land, excluding neighboring islands, etc.

**main line** ▸*n.* chief railway line. ▸*v.* (**mainline**) *inf.* inject (a drug) intravenously.

**main·stay** ▸*n.* **1** chief support. **2** cable securing the principal mast of a ship.

**main·stream** ▸*n.* prevailing trend in opinion, fashion, etc.

**main·tain** /mān'tān/ ▸*v.* **1** cause to continue; keep up (an activity, etc.). **2** support by work, expenditure, etc. **3** assert as true. **4** preserve in good repair. —**main·tain·a·ble** *adj.*

**main·te·nance** /'māntənəns/ ▸*n.* **1** maintaining or being maintained. **2** provision of the means to support life.

**ma·iol·i·ca** /mī'äləkə/ ▸*n.* fine earthenware with colored decoration on an opaque white tin glaze, originating in Italy during the Renaissance.

**mai·son·ette** /ˌmāzə'net/ ▸*n.* set of rooms for living in, typically on two stories of a larger building and with its own entrance from outside.

**maî·tre d'hô·tel** /ˌmātrə dō'tel/ ▸*n.* (*pl.* **maî·tres d'hôtel** *pronunc.* same) (also **maitre d'** /ˌmātrə 'dē/) headwaiter.

**maize** /māz/ ▸*n.* **1** corn. **2** yellow.

**ma·jes·tic** /mə'jestik/ ▸*adj.* stately and dignified; grand; imposing.

**maj·es·ty** /'majəstē/ ▸*n.* (*pl.* **-ties**) **1** impressive stateliness, dignity, or authority, esp. of bearing, language, the law, etc. **2** (**Majesty**) part of several titles given to a sovereign or a sovereign's wife or widow or used in addressing them.

**ma·jor** /'mājər/ ▸*adj.* **1** important, large, serious, or significant. **2** *Music* **a** (of a scale) having intervals of a semitone between the third and fourth, and seventh and eighth degrees. **b** (of a key) based on a major scale.

▸*n.* **1** army officer next below lieutenant colonel and above captain. **2 a** student's most emphasized subject or course. **b** student specializing in a specified subject.

▸*v.* study or qualify in as a special subject: *to major in history.*

□ **major general** officer next below a lieutenant general.

**ma·jor·do·mo** /ˌmājərˈdōmō/ ▶n. (pl. **-mos**) chief steward of a great household.

**ma·jor·i·tar·i·an** /məˌjôriˈte(ə)rēən; -ˌjär-/ ▶adj. governed by or believing in decision by a majority.

▶n. person who is governed by or believes in decision by a majority.

**ma·jor·i·ty** /məˈjôrətē/ ▶n. (pl. **-ties**) **1** greater number or part. **2** number by which the votes cast for one party, candidate, etc., exceed those of the next in rank: won by a majority of 151. **3** full legal age: attained his majority.

**make** /māk/ ▶v. (past and past part. **made**) **1** construct; create; form from parts or other substances. **2** cause or compel. **3 a** bring about: made a noise. **b** cause to become or seem: made him angry. **4** compose; prepare: made her will. **5** constitute; amount to: 2 and 2 make 4. **6 a** undertake: made a promise. **b** perform (a bodily movement, a speech, etc.). **7** gain; acquire; procure. **8** prepare. **9** inf. **a** arrive at (a place) or in time for (a train, etc.). **b** manage to attend: I'm not sure if I'll make the meeting. **c** achieve a place in: made the first team. **10** consider to be; estimate as. **11** accomplish (a distance, speed, score, etc.). **12** form in the mind: I make no judgment.

▶n. **1** type, origin, brand, etc., of manufacture. **2** kind of mental, moral, or physical structure or composition. **—mak·er** n.

**make-be·lieve** ▶n. pretending; imagining.

▶adj. pretend.

▶v. pretend; imagine.

**make·shift** ▶adj. temporary; serving for the time being.

▶n. temporary substitute or device.

**make·up** ▶n. **1** cosmetics for the face, etc., either generally or to create an actor's appearance or disguise. **2** person's character, temperament, etc. **3** composition of a thing.

**mal-** /mal/ ▶comb. form **1 a** bad, badly: malpractice | maltreat. **b** faulty, faultily: malfunction. **2** not: maladroit.

**mal·a·chite** /ˈmaləˌkīt/ ▶n. bright green mineral consisting of copper hydroxyl carbonate.

**mal·ad·just·ed** ▸*adj.* **1** not correctly adjusted. **2** (of a person) unable to adapt to or cope with the demands of a social environment.
—**mal·ad·just·ment** *n.*

**mal·a·droit** /ˌmaləˈdroit/ ▸*adj.* clumsy; bungling.

**mal·a·dy** /ˈmalədē/ ▸*n.* (*pl.* **-dies**) ailment; disease.

**ma·laise** /məˈlāz/ ▸*n.* **1** nonspecific bodily discomfort. **2** feeling of uneasiness.

**mal·a·mute** /ˈmaləˌmyo͞ot/ ▸*n.* any of an Alaskan breed of large sled dogs.

**mal·a·prop·ism** /ˈmaləpräpˌizəm/ (also **mal·a·prop**) ▸*n.* use of a word in mistake for one sounding similar, to comic effect, e.g., *allegory* for *alligator*.

**ma·lar·i·a** /məˈle(ə)rēə/ ▸*n.* recurrent fever caused by a parasite introduced by the bite of a mosquito. —**ma·lar·i·al** *adj.*

**mal·con·tent** /ˌmalkənˈtent/ ▸*n.* discontented person; rebel. ▸*adj.* discontented or rebellious.

**mal du siè·cle** /ˌmal də sē-ˈek(lə)/ ▸*n.* world-weariness.

**male** /māl/ ▸*adj.* **1** of the sex that can beget offspring by fertilization or insemination. **2** of men or male animals, plants, etc.; masculine. **3** (of plants or their parts) containing only fertilizing organs. **4** (of parts of machinery, etc.) designed to enter or fill the corresponding female part: *a male plug.*
▸*n.* male person or animal.
—**male·ness** *n.*

**mal·e·dic·tion** /ˌmaliˈdiksHən/ ▸*n.* curse. —**mal·e·dic·to·ry** *adj.*

**mal·e·fac·tor** /ˈmaləˌfaktər/ ▸*n.* criminal; evildoer.

**ma·lef·ic** /məˈlefik/ ▸*adj.* causing or capable of causing harm or destruction, esp. by supernatural means. —**ma·lef·i·cent** /-ˈlefəsənt/ *adj.*

**ma·lev·o·lent** /məˈlevələnt/ ▸*adj.* wishing evil to others.
—**ma·lev·o·lence** *n.*
—**ma·lev·o·lent·ly** *adv.*

**mal·fea·sance** /malˈfēzəns/ ▸*n.* *Law* evildoing.

**mal·ice** /ˈmalis/ ▸*n.* intention to harm others. —**ma·li·cious** *adj.*
—**ma·li·cious·ly** *adv.*

**ma·lign** /məˈlīn/ ▸*adj.* **1** (of a thing) injurious. **2** (of a disease) malignant. **3** malevolent.
▸*v.* speak ill of; slander.

**ma·lig·nant** /məˈlignənt/ ▸*adj.* **1 a** (of a disease) very virulent or infectious. **b** cancerous.

**2** harmful; feeling or showing intense ill will. —**ma·lig·nan·cy** *n.* —**ma·lig·nant·ly** *adv.*

**ma·lin·ger** /məˈliNGgər/ ▶*v.* exaggerate or feign illness in order to escape duty, work, etc. —**ma·lin·ger·er** *n.*

**mall** /môl/ ▶*n.* **1** enclosed shopping center. **2** sheltered walk or promenade.

**mal·lard** /ˈmalərd/ ▶*n.* wild duck or drake of the northern hemisphere.

**mal·le·a·ble** /ˈmalēəbəl/ ▶*adj.* **1** (of metal, etc.) that can be shaped by hammering. **2** adaptable; pliable or flexible. —**mal·le·a·bil·i·ty** *n.*

**mal·let** /ˈmalit/ ▶*n.* **1** hammer, usu. of wood. **2** long-handled wooden hammer for striking a croquet or polo ball.

**mal·nu·tri·tion** ▶*n.* dietary condition resulting from the absence of healthful foods.

**mal·o·dor·ous** /malˈōdərəs/ ▶*adj.* having an unpleasant smell.

**mal·prac·tice** ▶*n.* improper, negligent, or criminal professional conduct.

**malt** /môlt/ ▶*n.* **1** barley or other grain that is steeped, germinated, and dried, esp. for brewing or distilling and vinegar making. **2** malt whiskey; malt liquor.
▶*v.* convert (grain) into malt.
□ **malted milk** drink combining milk, a malt preparation, and ice cream or flavoring.

**mal·treat** ▶*v.* ill-treat. —**mal·treat·ment** *n.*

**mal·ver·sa·tion** /ˌmalvərˈsāsHən/ ▶*n.* corrupt behavior in a position of trust, esp. in public office.

**ma·ma** /ˈmämə/ ▶*n.* mother.

**mam·mal** /ˈmaməl/ ▶*n.* warm-blooded vertebrate of the class secreting milk for the nourishment of its young. —**mam·ma·li·an** *adj. & n.*

**mam·ma·ry** /ˈmamərē/ ▶*adj.* of the breasts.

**mam·mo·gram** /ˈmaməˌgram/ ▶*n.* x-ray image of a breast, used to detect tumors.

**mam·mon** /ˈmamən/ (also **Mam·mon**) ▶*n.* wealth regarded as a god or as an evil influence.

**mam·moth** /ˈmaməTH/ ▶*n.* large extinct elephant with a hairy coat and curved tusks.
▶*adj.* huge.

**man** /man/ ▶*n.* (*pl.* **men**) **1** adult human male. **2 a** human being; person: *no man is perfect.* **b** the human race: *man is mortal.*

**3 a** worker; employee.
**b** manservant or valet. **4** (usu.
**men**) soldiers, sailors, etc., esp.
nonofficers. **5** any one of a set of
pieces used in playing chess,
checkers, etc.
▶*v.* (**manned, man·ning**) **1** supply
with a person or people for work
or defense, etc. **2** work or
service or defend: *man the pumps.*

**man·a·cle** /ˈmanəkəl/ ▶*n.* (usu.
**manacles**) **1** handcuff.
**2** restraint.
▶*v.* fetter with manacles.

**man·age** /ˈmanij/ ▶*v.* **1** organize;
regulate; be in charge of.
**2** succeed in achieving; contrive.
**3 a** succeed in one's aim, esp.
against heavy odds. **b** meet one's
needs with limited resources,
etc. —**man·ag·er** *n.*
—**man·a·ge·ri·al** *adj.*

**man·age·ment** ▶*n.*
**1** managing or being managed.
**2** professional administration of
business concerns, public
undertakings, etc.

**ma·ña·na** /mənˈyänə/ ▶*adv.* in
the indefinite future.
▶*n.* an indefinite future time.

**man·a·tee** /ˈmanəˌtē/ ▶*n.* large
aquatic plant-eating mammal.

**man·da·mus** /manˈdāməs/ ▶*n.*
judicial writ issued as a
command to an inferior court or
ordering a person to perform a
public or statutory duty.

**man·da·rin** /ˈmandərin/ ▶*n.*
**1** (**Mandarin**) most widely spoken
form of Chinese and the official
language of China. **2** official in
any of nine top grades of the
former imperial Chinese civil
service.

**man·date** /ˈmanˌdāt/ ▶*n.*
**1** official command or
instruction by an authority.
**2** support given by electors to a
government, labor union, etc.,
for a policy or course of action.
▶*v.* instruct (a delegate) to act or
vote in a certain way.

**man·da·to·ry** /ˈmandəˌtôrē/
▶*adj.* compulsory.

**man·di·ble** /ˈmandəbəl/ ▶*n.* jaw
or jawlike part. —**man·dib·u·lar**
*adj.*

**man·do·lin** /ˌmandlˈin/ ▶*n.*
musical instrument resembling
a lute, having paired metal
strings plucked with a plectrum.

**man·drake** /ˈmanˌdrāk/ ▶*n.*
poisonous plant having emetic
and narcotic properties and
possessing a root once thought
to resemble the human form.

**mane** /mān/ ▶*n.* long hair on the
neck of a horse, lion, etc.

**ma·neu·ver** /mə'no͞ovər/ ▸n. **1** planned and controlled movement or series of moves. **2** skillful plan. **3** (**maneuvers**) large-scale exercise of troops, warships, etc.

▸v. **1** perform or cause to perform a maneuver. **2** handle adroitly. —**ma·neu·ver·a·ble** adj. —**ma·neu·ver·a·bil·i·ty** n.

**man·ga·nese** /'maNGgə,nēz/ ▸n. gray metallic transition element used with steel to make alloys. (Symb.: **Mn**).

**mange** /mānj/ ▸n. skin disease in hairy and woolly animals. —**mang·y** adj.

**man·ger** /'mānjər/ ▸n. long open box or trough in a stable, etc., for horses or cattle to eat from.

**man·gle** /'maNGgəl/ ▸v. hack, cut, or mutilate by blows, etc.

**man·go** /'maNGgō/ ▸n. (pl. **-goes** or **-gos**) fleshy yellowish-red fruit of an E. Indian evergreen tree.

**man·grove** /'man,grōv/ ▸n. tropical tree or shrub with many tangled roots above ground.

**man·han·dle** ▸v. inf. handle roughly.

**man·hat·tan** /man'hatn/ ▸n. cocktail made of vermouth and whiskey, usu. flavored with bitters.

**man·hole** ▸n. covered opening in a floor, pavement, sewer, etc., for workers to gain access.

**man·hood** ▸n. **1** state of being a man rather than a child or woman. **2** manliness; courage. **3** a man's sexual potency.

**man·hunt** ▸n. search for a person, esp. a criminal.

**ma·ni·a** /'mānēə/ ▸n. **1** mental illness marked by periods of great excitement and violence. **2** excessive enthusiasm; obsession: *has a mania for jogging.*

**-mania** ▸comb. form **1** denoting a special type of mental abnormality or obsession: *megalomania.* **2** denoting extreme enthusiasm or admiration: *bibliomania.*

**ma·ni·ac** /'mānē,ak/ ▸n. **1** inf. person exhibiting extreme symptoms of wild behavior, etc.; madman. **2** inf. obsessive enthusiast: *gambling maniac.* —**ma·ni·a·cal** adj.

**man·ic** /'manik/ ▸adj. of or affected by mania.

▸n. person having such a disorder.

□ **manic-depressive** affected by or relating to a mental disorder with alternating periods of elation and depression.

**man·i·cure** /ˈmaniˌkyo͝or/ ▶*n.* cosmetic treatment of the hands and fingernails.

▶*v.* give a manicure to (the hands or a person). **—man·i·cur·ist** *n.*

**man·i·fest** /ˈmanəˌfest/ ▶*adj.* clear or obvious.

▶*v.* show plainly to the eye or mind.

▶*n.* cargo or passenger list. **—man·i·fes·ta·tion** *n.* **—man·i·fest·ly** *adv.*

**man·i·fes·to** /ˌmanəˈfestō/ ▶*n.* (*pl.* **-tos** or **-toes**) public declaration of policy and aims, esp. political or social.

**man·i·fold** /ˈmanəˌfōld/ ▶*adj.* **1** many and various. **2** having various forms, parts, applications, etc.

▶*n.* **1** manifold thing. **2** pipe or chamber branching into several openings.

**man·i·kin** /ˈmanikən/ (also **man·ni·kin**) ▶*n.* **1** little man; dwarf. **2** anatomical model of the body.

**ma·nip·u·late** /məˈnipyəˌlāt/ ▶*v.* **1** handle, esp. skillfully. **2** manage (a person, situation, etc.) to one's own advantage, esp. unfairly. **3** manually

examine and treat (a part of the body). **—ma·nip·u·la·tion** *n.* **—ma·nip·u·la·tive** *adj.*

**man·i·tou** /ˈmaniˌto͞o/ ▶*n.* (among certain Algonquian Indians) a good or evil spirit as an object of reverence.

**man·kind** ▶*n.* **1** human species. **2** male people, as distinct from female.

**man·ly** ▶*adj.* (**-li·er, -li·est**) **1** having qualities regarded as admirable in a man, such as courage, frankness, etc. **2** befitting a man. **—man·li·ness** *n.*

**man·na** /ˈmanə/ ▶*n.* **1** substance miraculously supplied as food to the Israelites in the wilderness (Exod. 16). **2** unexpected benefit, esp. as: *manna from heaven.*

**man·ne·quin** /ˈmanikən/ ▶*n.* **1** fashion model. **2** window dummy.

**man·ner** /ˈmanər/ ▶*n.* **1** way a thing is done or happens. **2 a** social behavior: *it is bad manners to stare.* **b** polite or well-bred behavior: *he has no manners.* **3** person's outward bearing, way of speaking, etc. **4** style in literature, art, etc.: *in the manner of Rembrandt.*

**man·ner·ism** ▸*n.* habitual gesture or way of speaking, etc.; idiosyncrasy.

**man·ner·ly** ▸*adj.* well-mannered; polite.
▸*adv.* politely.
—**man·ner·li·ness** *n.*

**ma·no a ma·no** /ˌmänō ä 'mänō/ (also **ma·no-a-ma·no**) ▸*adj.* (of combat or competition) hand-to-hand.
▸*adv.* in the manner of hand-to-hand combat or a duel.
▸*n.* (*pl.* **-nos**) intense fight or contest between two adversaries; a duel.

**man·or** /'manər/ ▸*n.* large country house with lands.
—**ma·no·ri·al** *adj.*

**man·pow·er** ▸*n.* number of people available or required for work, service, etc.

**man·qué** /mäNG'kā/ ▸*adj.* that might have been but is not; unfulfilled: *a comic actor manqué.*

**man·sard** /'man,särd/ ▸*n.* roof that has four sloping sides, each of which becomes steeper halfway down.

**manse** /mans/ ▸*n.* house of a minister.

**man·ser·vant** ▸*n.* (*pl.* **men·ser·vants**) male servant.

**man·sion** /'manSHən/ ▸*n.* large house.

**man·slaugh·ter** ▸*n.* unlawful and unintentional killing of a human being.

**man·sue·tude** /'manswi,tood; man'sooə-/ ▸*n.* meekness; gentleness.

**man·tel·piece** /'mantl,pēs/ (also **man·tel**) ▸*n.* structure of wood, marble, etc., above and around a fireplace.

**man·tic** /'mantik/ ▸*adj.* of or relating to divination or prophecy.

**man·til·la** /man'tē(y)ə/ ▸*n.* lace scarf worn by Spanish women over the hair and shoulders.

**man·tis** /'mantis/ (also **pray·ing man·tis**) ▸*n.* (*pl.* same or **-tis·es**) predatory insect that holds its forelegs in a position suggestive of hands folded in prayer.

**man·tle** /'mantl/ ▸*n.* **1** loose sleeveless cloak. **2** covering: *mantle of snow.*
▸*v.* clothe; conceal; envelop.

**man·tra** /'mantrə/ ▸*n.* word or sound repeated to aid concentration in meditation, orig. in Hinduism and Buddhism.

**man·u·al** /'manyooəl/ ▸*adj.* **1** of or done with the hands: *manual* *labor.* **2** (of a machine, etc.) worked by hand, not automatically.

▸*n.* book of instructions; handbook. —**man·u·al·ly** *adv.*

**man·u·fac·ture** /ˌmanyə'fakchər/ ▸*n.* making of articles, esp. in a factory, etc.

▸*v.* **1** make (articles), esp. on an industrial scale. **2** invent or fabricate (evidence, a story, etc.). —**man·u·fac·tur·er** *n.*

**man·u·mit** /ˌmanyə'mit/ ▸*v.* (**-mit·ted, -mit·ting**) *hist.* set (a slave) free. —**man·u·mis·sion** *n.*

**ma·nure** /mə'noor/ ▸*n.* fertilizer, esp. dung.

**man·u·script** /'manyə,skript/ ▸*n.* **1** book, piece of music, etc., written by hand. **2** author's text that has not yet been published.

▸*adj.* written by hand.

**man·y** /'menē/ ▸*adj.* (**more, most**) great in number; numerous.

▸*n.* a large number: *many went.*

**map** /map/ ▸*n.* **1** flat representation of the earth's surface, or part of it. **2** two-dimensional representation of the stars, the heavens, the moon, etc.

▸*v.* (**mapped, map·ping**) represent on a map.

**ma·ple** /'māpəl/ ▸*n.* any of various trees grown for shade, ornament, wood, or its sugar.

□ **maple sugar** sugar produced by evaporating the sap of the sugar maple, etc. □ **maple syrup** syrup produced from the sap of the sugar maple, etc.

**ma·qui·la·do·ra** /ˌmakilə'dôrə/ ▸*n.* factory in Mexico run by a foreign company and exporting its products to the country of that company.

**Mar.** ▸*abbr.* March.

**mar** /mär/ ▸*v.* (**marred, mar·ring**) spoil; disfigure.

**ma·ra·ca** /mə'räkə/ ▸*n.* gourd or gourd-shaped container filled with beans, etc., shaken as a percussion instrument.

**mar·a·thon** /'marə,thän/ ▸*n.* **1** long-distance running race, usu. of 26 miles 385 yards (42.195 km). **2** long-lasting or difficult task, operation, etc.: *a marathon shopping expedition.* —**mar·a·thon·er** *n.*

**ma·raud** /mə'rôd/ ▸*v.* make a plundering raid. —**ma·raud·er** *n.*

**mar·ble** /'märbəl/ ▸*n.* **1** crystalline limestone capable of taking a polish, used in sculpture and architecture. **2** anything made of marble: *marble clock.* **3 a** small ball of marble, glass, clay, etc., used as a toy. **b** (**marbles**) [treated as *sing.*] game using these. **4** (**marbles**) *inf.* one's mental faculties.

▶*v.* **1** [usu. as *adj.* **marbled**] stain or color (paper, soap, etc.) to look like marble. **2** [as *adj.* **marbled**] (of meat) streak with alternating layers of lean and fat.

**March** /märCH/ ▶*n.* third month of the year.

**march** ▶*v.* **1** walk in a military manner with a regular tread. **2** cause to march or walk: *marched him out of the room.* **3** walk or proceed steadily.

▶*n.* **1** act of marching. **2** progress or continuity. **3** piece of music composed to accompany a march. —**march·er** *n.*

**Mar·di Gras** /ˈmärdē ˌgrä/ ▶*n.* last day before Lent, celebrated as a carnival in some places, as New Orleans; Shrove Tuesday.

**mare**[1] /me(ə)r/ ▶*n.* female of any equine animal, esp. the horse.
□ **mare's nest** illusory discovery.

**ma·re**[2] /ˈmärā/ ▶*n.* (*pl.* **-ri·a** or **-res**) large dark flat area on the moon.

**mar·ga·rine** /ˈmärjərin/ ▶*n.* butter substitute made from vegetable oils or animal fats with milk, etc.

**mar·ga·ri·ta** /ˌmärgəˈrētə/ ▶*n.* cocktail made with tequila and citrus fruit juice.

**mar·gin** /ˈmärjin/ ▶*n.* **1** edge or border. **2** blank border on each side of the print on a page, etc. **3** amount (of time, money, etc.) by which a thing exceeds, falls short, etc.: *margin of profit.* **4** amount deposited with a stockbroker by the customer when borrowing from the broker to purchase securities.

**mar·gin·al** ▶*adj.* of secondary or minor importance.
—**mar·gin·al·ly** *adv.*

**mar·gin·al·ize** /ˈmärjənəˌlīz/ ▶*v.* treat (a person, group, or concept) as insignificant or peripheral.

**mar·grave** /ˈmärˌgrāv/ ▶*n.* hereditary title of some princes of the Holy Roman Empire.

**mar·i·cul·ture** /ˈmariˌkəlCHər/ ▶*n.* cultivation of fish or other marine life for food.

**mar·i·gold** /ˈmariˌgōld/ ▶*n.* plant with bright yellow, orange, or maroon flowers.

**ma·ri·jua·na** /ˌmarəˈ(h)wänə/ (also **ma·ri·hua·na**) ▶*n.* dried leaves, etc., of hemp, smoked or ingested as a drug.

**ma·rim·ba** /məˈrimbə/ ▸n. type of xylophone.

**ma·ri·na** /məˈrēnə/ ▸n. harbor for pleasure yachts, etc.

**mar·i·nade** /ˌmarəˈnād/ ▸n. mixture of wine, vinegar, oil, spices, etc., in which meat, fish, etc., is soaked before cooking.

**mar·i·nate** /ˈmarəˌnāt/ ▸v. soak (meat, fish, etc.) in a marinade. —**mar·i·na·tion** n.

**ma·rine** /məˈrēn/ ▸adj. **1** of, found in, or produced by the sea. **2** of or relating to shipping or naval matters: *marine insurance.* ▸n. **1** country's shipping, fleet, or navy: *merchant marine.* **2 a** member of the U.S. Marine Corps. **b** member of a body of troops trained to serve on land or sea.

**mar·i·ner** /ˈmarənər/ ▸n. sailor.

**mar·i·on·ette** /ˌmarēəˈnet/ ▸n. puppet worked by strings.

**mar·i·tal** /ˈmaritl/ ▸adj. of marriage or the relations between husband and wife.

**mar·i·time** /ˈmariˌtīm/ ▸adj. **1** connected with the sea or shipping: *maritime insurance.* **2** living or found near the sea.

**mar·jo·ram** /ˈmärjərəm/ ▸n. aromatic herb of the mint family used in cooking.

**mark** /märk/ ▸n. **1** trace, sign, stain, etc., on a surface, etc. **2 a** written or printed symbol: *question mark.* **b** number or letter denoting excellence, conduct, proficiency, etc.: *black mark.* **3** sign or indication of quality, character, feeling, etc. **4** target, object, goal, etc. **5** line, etc., indicating a position; marker. ▸v. **1** make a mark on (a thing or person), esp. by writing, cutting, scraping, etc. **2** allot marks to; correct (a student's work, etc.). **3** characterize: *day was marked by storms.* —**mark·er** n.

**mark·down** ▸n. reduction in price.

**marked** ▸adj. **1** having a visible mark. **2** clearly noticeable; evident: *a marked difference.* —**mark·ed·ly** adv.

**mar·ket** /ˈmärkit/ ▸n. **1** gathering of people for the purchase and sale of provisions, livestock, etc. **2** grocery store. **3** demand for a commodity. **4** conditions as regards, or opportunity for, buying or selling. **5** trade in a specified commodity: *the grain market.* ▸v. buy or sell. —**mar·ket·er** n.

☐ **market research** study of consumers' needs and preferences.

**mar·ket·place** ▸*n.* **1** open space where a market is held in a town. **2** world of trade. **3** forum or sphere for the exchange of ideas, etc.

**marks·man** ▸*n.* (*pl.* **-men**) person skilled in shooting, esp. with a pistol or rifle. —**marks·man·ship** *n.*

**mark·up** ▸*n.* amount added to cost for profit.

**mar·lin** /ˈmärlin/ ▸*n.* large long-nosed marine fish.

**mar·lin·spike** /ˈmärlən,spīk/ (also **mar·line·spike**) ▸*n.* pointed metal tool used by sailors to separate strands of rope or wire, esp. in splicing.

**mar·ma·lade** /ˈmärmə,lād/ ▸*n.* preserve of citrus fruit, usu. bitter oranges, made like jam.

**mar·mite** /ˈmär,mīt/ ▸*n.* earthenware cooking container.

**mar·mo·re·al** /märˈmôrēəl/ ▸*adj.* made of or likened to marble.

**mar·mo·set** /ˈmärmə,set/ ▸*n.* small tropical American monkey having a long bushy tail.

**mar·mot** /ˈmärmət/ ▸*n.* burrowing rodent with a heavyset body and short bushy tail.

**ma·roon** /məˈro͞on/ ▸*adj. & n.* brownish-crimson.
▸*v.* leave (a person) isolated in a desolate place (esp. an island).

**marque** /märk/ ▸*n.* make of car, as distinct from a specific model.

**mar·quee** /märˈkē/ ▸*n.* projecting roof over an entry.

**mar·que·try** /ˈmärkitrē/ ▸*n.* inlaid work in wood, ivory, etc.

**mar·quis** /ˈmärkwis/ ▸*n.* nobleman ranking between duke and count.

**mar·riage** /ˈmarij/ ▸*n.* **1** legal union of a man and a woman. **2** wedding. **3** intimate union: *marriage of true minds.* —**mar·riage·a·ble** *adj.*

**mar·row** /ˈmarō/ ▸*n.* soft fatty substance in the cavities of bones.

**mar·ry** /ˈmarē/ ▸*v.* (**-ried**) **1** take as one's wife or husband in marriage. **2** join or give in marriage. **3** unite intimately.

**Mars** /märz/ ▸*n.* reddish planet, fourth in order of distance from the sun and next beyond the earth.

**marsh** /märsH/ ▸*n.* low land flooded in wet weather and usu.

watery at all times. —**marsh·y** *adj.*

□ **marsh gas** methane.

**mar·shal** /ˈmärsHəl/ ▶*n.* **1** officer of a judicial district, similar to a sheriff. **2** officer arranging ceremonies, controlling procedure at races, etc.
▶*v.* arrange in due order.

**marsh·mal·low** /ˈmärsH,melō/ ▶*n.* spongy confection made of sugar, egg white, gelatin, etc.

**mar·su·pi·al** /märˈso͞opēəl/ ▶*n.* mammal characterized by being born incompletely developed and usu. carried and suckled in a pouch.
▶*adj.* of or like a marsupial.

**mart** /märt/ ▶*n.* market.

**mar·ten** /ˈmärtn/ ▶*n.* weasellike carnivore having valuable fur.

**mar·tial** /ˈmärsHəl/ ▶*adj.* **1** of or appropriate to warfare. **2** warlike; brave; fond of fighting.
□ **martial arts** fighting sports such as judo and karate. □ **martial law** military government, involving the suspension of ordinary law.

**mar·tin** /ˈmärtn/ ▶*n.* kind of swallow.

**mar·ti·net** /ˌmärtnˈet/ ▶*n.* strict (esp. military) disciplinarian.

**mar·ti·ni** /märˈtēnē/ ▶*n.* cocktail made of gin and dry vermouth, often garnished with a green olive, lemon peel, etc.

**mar·tyr** /ˈmärtər/ ▶*n.* **1** person who suffers or is put to death for refusing to renounce a faith or belief. **2** constant sufferer.
▶*v.* put to death as a martyr.
—**mar·tyr·dom** *n.*

**mar·vel** /ˈmärvəl/ ▶*n.* wonderful thing or person.
▶*v.* feel surprise or wonder.

**mar·vel·ous** ▶*adj.* amazing; extraordinary.

**Marx·ism** /ˈmärk,sizəm/ ▶*n.* anticapitalist political and economic theories of Karl Marx, advocating communism and socialism. —**Marx·ist** *n. & adj.*

**mar·zi·pan** /ˈmärzə,pan/ ▶*n.* paste of ground almonds, sugar, etc., used in confectionery.

**mas·car·a** /masˈkarə/ ▶*n.* cosmetic for darkening the eyelashes.

**mas·cot** /ˈmas,kät/ ▶*n.* person, animal, or thing that is supposed to bring good luck.

**mas·cu·line** /ˈmaskyəlin/ ▶*adj.* **1** of or characteristic of men. **2** manly; vigorous. **3** *Gram.* of or denoting the male gender.
▶*n. Gram.* masculine gender;

masculine word.
—**mas·cu·lin·i·ty** *n.*

**ma·ser** /ˈmāzər/ ▸*n.* device for amplifying or generating electromagnetic radiation in the microwave range (acronym of *m*icrowave *a*mplification by *s*timulated *e*mission of *r*adiation).

**MASH** /mash/ ▸*abbr.* Mobile Army Surgical Hospital.

**mash** ▸*n.* **1** soft mixture. **2** mixture of boiled grain, bran, etc., given warm to horses, etc. **3** mixture of malt and hot water used in brewing.
▸*v.* reduce (potatoes, etc.) to a uniform mass by crushing.

**mas·jid** /ˈməsjid; ˈmas-/ ▸*n.* Arabic word for a mosque.

**mask** /mask/ ▸*n.* **1** covering for all or part of the face as a disguise or for protection. **2** likeness of a person's face, esp. one made by taking a mold from the face: *death mask.* **3** disguise or pretense: *throw off the mask.*
▸*v.* **1** cover (the face, etc.) with a mask. **2** disguise or conceal (a taste, one's feelings, etc.).

**mas·och·ism** /ˈmasəˌkizəm/ ▸*n.* **1** form of (esp. sexual) perversion involving one's own pain or humiliation. **2** *inf.*

enjoyment of what appears to be painful or tiresome.
—**mas·och·ist** *n.*

**ma·son** /ˈmāsən/ ▸*n.* person who builds with stone or brick.

**ma·son·ry** ▸*n.* stonework.

**mas·quer·ade** /ˌmaskəˈrād/ ▸*n.* **1** false show or pretense. **2** masked ball.
▸*v.* pretend to be someone one is not: *masquerading as a journalist.*

**Mass.** ▸*abbr.* Massachusetts.

**mass** /mas/ ▸*n.* **1** coherent body of matter of indefinite shape. **2** dense aggregation of objects: *a mass of fibers.* **3** large number or amount. **4** (**the masses**) ordinary people. **5** *Physics* quantity of matter a body contains. **6** (often **Mass**) celebration of the Eucharist, esp. in the Roman Catholic Church.
▸*v.* assemble into a mass.

**mas·sa·cre** /ˈmasəkər/ ▸*n.* general slaughter (of persons or animals).
▸*v.* slaughter in large numbers.

**mas·sage** /məˈsäzʜ/ ▸*n.* rubbing, kneading, etc., of the body with the hands for therapeutic benefit.
▸*v.* apply massage to.

**mas·sif** /maˈsēf/ ▸*n.* compact group of mountains, esp. one that is separate from other groups.

**mas·sive** /ˈmasiv/ ▸*adj.* **1** large and heavy or solid.
**2** exceptionally large.
**3** substantial; impressive: *a massive reputation.*

**mass mar·ket** ▸*n.* market for goods that are produced in large quantities.

**mass noun** ▸*n.* noun that is not countable and cannot be used with the indefinite article or in the plural (e.g., *happiness*).

**mass-pro·duce** /ˈmas prəˈdoōs/ ▸*v.* produce large amounts of (an article) by an automated mechanical process. —**mass-pro·duc·tion** *n.*

**mast** /mast/ ▸*n.* **1** long upright post for supporting a ship's sails. **2** post or latticework upright for supporting a radio or television antenna. **3** flagpole: *half-mast.*

**mas·tec·to·my** /maˈstektəmē/ ▸*n.* (*pl.* **-mies**) surgical removal of all or part of a breast.

**mas·ter** /ˈmastər/ ▸*n.* **1** person having control or ownership: *master of the house.* **2** person who has or gets the upper hand: *we shall see which of us is master.* **3** skilled practitioner: *master of disguise* [as *adj.*] *master carpenter.*

**4** person who holds a second or further degree from a university: *master's degree* | *Master of Arts.*
**5** great artist. **6** *Chess, etc.* player of proven ability at international level. **7** original version (e.g., of a film or audio recording) from which a series of copies can be made.

▸*adj.* **1** commanding; superior: *a master spirit.* **2** main; principal: *master bedroom.* **3** controlling others: *master plan.*

▸*v.* **1** overcome; defeat. **2** acquire complete knowledge of or skill in.

**mas·ter class** ▸*n.* class, esp. in music, given by an expert to highly talented students.

**mas·ter·ful** ▸*adj.* **1** imperious; domineering. **2** masterly.

**mas·ter·ly** /ˈmastərlē/ ▸*adj.* very skillful.

**mas·ter·mind** ▸*n.* **1** person with an outstanding intellect. **2** person directing an intricate operation.

▸*v.* plan and direct (a scheme or enterprise).

**mas·ter of cer·e·mo·nies** ▸*n.* person who introduces speakers, entertainers, etc., at a public occasion.

**mas·ter·piece** ▶*n.* **1** outstanding piece of artistry or workmanship. **2** person's best work.

**mas·ter·stroke** ▶*n.* outstandingly skillful act of policy, etc.

**mas·ter·y** ▶*n.* **1** dominion; sway. **2** comprehensive knowledge or skill.

**mas·tic** /'mastik/ ▶*n.* **1** aromatic gum or resin exuded from the bark of a Mediterranean tree, used in making varnish and chewing gum and as a flavoring. **2** puttylike waterproof filler and sealant used in building.

**mas·ti·cate** /'masti,kāt/ ▶*v.* grind or chew (food) with one's teeth. —**mas·ti·ca·tion** *n.*

**mas·tiff** /'mastif/ ▶*n.* large strong breed of dog.

**mas·to·don** /'mastə,dän/ ▶*n.* large extinct mammal resembling the elephant.

**mas·toid** /'mas,toid/ ▶*n.* conical prominence on the temporal bone behind the ear.

**mas·tur·bate** /'mastər,bāt/ ▶*v.* arouse oneself sexually or cause (another person) to be aroused by manual stimulation of the genitals. —**mas·tur·ba·tion** *n.*

**mat** /mat/ ▶*n.* **1** piece of coarse material for wiping shoes on, esp. a doormat. **2** piece of cork, rubber, plastic, etc., for protecting a surface. **3** piece of resilient material for landing on in gymnastics, wrestling, etc.
▶*v.* (**mat·ted**, **mat·ting**) **1** [esp. as *adj.* **matted**] entangle in a thick mass: *matted hair.* **2** become matted.
▶*adj.* var. of MATTE.

**mat·a·dor** /'matə,dôr/ ▶*n.* bullfighter whose task is to kill the bull.

**match** /maCH/ ▶*n.* **1** contest or game of skill. **2 a** equal contender. **b** person or thing exactly like or corresponding to another. **3** marriage. **4** short, thin piece of flammable material tipped with a composition that can be ignited by friction.
▶*v.* **1** be equal to or harmonious with; correspond (to). **2** place in conflict, contest, or competition with. **3** find material, etc., that matches (another). **4** find (a person or thing) suitable for another: *matching unemployed workers to available jobs.*

**match·less** ▶*adj.* without an equal; incomparable.

**match·mak·er** ▶*n.* person who tries to arrange an agreement or relationship between two parties, esp. a marriage partnership.

**mate** /māt/ ▸*n.* **1** each of a pair, esp. of animals, birds, or socks. **2** officer on a merchant ship subordinate to the master. **3** husband or wife. **4** friend or fellow worker.

▸*v.* come or bring together for marriage or breeding.

**ma·te·ri·al** /mə'ti(ə)rēəl/ ▸*n.* **1** matter from which a thing is made. **2** cloth; fabric. **3** things needed for an activity: *building materials.* **4** information, etc., to be used in writing a book, etc.: *experimental material.*

▸*adj.* **1** of matter; corporeal. **2** concerned with bodily comfort, etc.: *material well-being.* **3** important; essential; relevant: *at the material time.*
—**ma·te·ri·al·ly** *adv.*

**ma·te·ri·al·ism** ▸*n.* **1** tendency to prefer material possessions and physical comfort to spiritual values. **2** theory that nothing exists but matter and its movements and modifications.
—**ma·te·ri·al·ist** *n.*
—**ma·te·ri·al·is·tic** *adj.*

**ma·te·ri·al·ize** ▸*v.* **1** cause to appear in bodily or physical form. **2** become actual fact. **3** appear or be present when expected: *the train didn't materialize.*

**ma·ter·ni·ty** /mə'tərnitē/ ▸*n.* motherhood.
▸*adj.* of or for women during pregnancy and childbirth.

**math** /maTH/ ▸*n.* mathematics.

**math·e·mat·ics** /maTH(ə)'matiks/ ▸*n.* **1** abstract science of number, quantity, and space. **2** [*pl. n.*] mathematical aspects of something. —**math·e·ma·ti·cal** *adj.* —**math·e·ma·ti·cal·ly** *adv.* —**math·e·ma·ti·cian** *n.*

**mat·i·née** /ˌmatn'ā/ (also **mat·i·nee**) ▸*n.* afternoon performance in a theater, etc.

**mat·ins** /'matnz/ ▸*n.* morning church service.

**ma·tri·arch** /'mātrē,ärk/ ▸*n.* female head of a family or tribe. —**ma·tri·ar·chal** *adj.* —**ma·tri·ar·chy** *n.*

**mat·ri·cide** /'matrə,sīd/ ▸*n.* **1** killing of one's mother. **2** person who does this. —**mat·ri·cid·al** *adj.*

**ma·tric·u·late** /mə'trikyə,lāt/ ▸*v.* **1** be enrolled at a college or university. **2** admit (a student) to membership of a college or university. —**ma·tric·u·la·tion** *n.*

**mat·ri·lin·e·al** /ˌmatrəˈlinēəl; ˌmā-/ ▸*adj.* of or based on kinship with the mother or the female line.

**mat·ri·mo·ny** /ˈmatrəˌmōnē/ ▸*n.* (*pl.* **-nies**) **1** rite of marriage. **2** state of being married. —**mat·ri·mo·ni·al** *adj.*

**ma·trix** /ˈmātriks/ ▸*n.* (*pl.* **-tri·ces** or **-trix·es**) mold in which a thing is cast or shaped.

**ma·tron** /ˈmātrən/ ▸*n.* **1** woman supervisor, as in an institution. **2** married woman, esp. a dignified and sober one. —**ma·tron·ly** *adj.*

**matte** /mat/ (also **matt** or **mat**) ▸*adj.* (of a color, surface, etc.) dull; without luster.

**mat·ter** /ˈmatər/ ▸*n.* **1 a** physical substance in general, as distinct from mind and spirit. **b** that which has mass and occupies space. **2** particular substance: *coloring matter.* **3** thing that is amiss: *what is the matter?* **4** affair or situation being considered, esp. in a specified way: *a serious matter.*
▸*v.* be of importance; have significance.

**mat·ter-of-fact** ▸*adj.*
**1** unimaginative; prosaic.
**2** unemotional. —**mat·ter-of-fact·ly** *adv.*

**mat·tock** /ˈmatək/ ▸*n.* agricultural tool for digging.

**mat·tress** /ˈmatris/ ▸*n.* fabric case stuffed with soft, firm, or springy material, or a similar case filled with air or water, used on or as a bed.

**ma·ture** /məˈCHo͝or/ ▸*adj.* **1** with fully developed powers of body and mind; adult. **2** complete in natural development; ripe. **3** (of thought, intentions, etc.) duly careful and adequate. **4** (of a bond, etc.) due for payment.
▸*v.* **1** develop fully; ripen. **2** (of a bond, etc.) become due for payment. —**ma·ture·ly** *adv.* —**ma·tu·ri·ty** *n.*

**mat·zo** /ˈmätsə/ ▸*n.* (*pl.* **-zos**) unleavened bread, served esp. at Passover.

**maud·lin** /ˈmôdlin/ ▸*adj.* weakly or tearfully sentimental.

**maul** /môl/ ▸*v.* **1** beat and bruise. **2** handle roughly or carelessly.
▸*n.* heavy hammer.

**maun·der** /ˈmôndər/ ▸*v.* talk in a rambling manner.

**mau·so·le·um** /ˌmôzəˈlēəm/ ▸*n.* large and grand tomb.

**mauve** /mōv/ ▸*adj.* pale purple.

▸*n.* **1** this color. **2** bright but delicate pale purple dye.

**ma·ven** /ˈmāvən/ ▸*n.* expert.

**mav·er·ick** /ˈmav(ə)rik/ ▸*n.* **1** unbranded calf or yearling. **2** unorthodox or independent-minded person.

**maw** /mô/ ▸*n.* **1** stomach of an animal. **2** jaws or throat of a voracious animal.

**mawk·ish** /ˈmôkiSH/ ▸*adj.* sentimental in a feeble or sickly way. —**mawk·ish·ly** *adv.* —**mawk·ish·ness** *n.*

**maxi-** ▸*comb. form* very large or long: *maxicoat.*

**max·im** /ˈmaksim/ ▸*n.* general truth or rule of conduct expressed in a sentence.

**max·i·mum** /ˈmaksəməm/ ▸*n.* (*pl.* **-ma** or **-mums**) highest possible or attainable amount. ▸*adj.* that is a maximum. —**max·i·mal** *adj.*

**May** /mā/ ▸*n.* fifth month of the year. ▢ **May Day** May 1, esp. as a festival with dancing, or as an international holiday in honor of workers.

**may** /mā/ ▸*aux. v.* (*3rd sing. present* **may**; *past* **might**) **1** expressing possibility: *it may be true.* **2** expressing permission: *may I*

come in? **3** expressing a wish: *may he live to regret it.* **4** expressing uncertainty or irony in questions: *who may you be?*

**may·be** ▸*adv.* perhaps; possibly.

**May·day** ▸*n.* international radio distress signal.

**may·flow·er** ▸*n.* any of various flowers that bloom in May.

**may·fly** ▸*n.* (*pl.* **-flies**) insect with four delicate wings, the adult of which lives briefly in spring.

**may·hem** /ˈmā(h)em/ ▸*n.* violent or damaging action.

**may·on·naise** /ˈmāəˌnāz/ ▸*n.* thick creamy dressing made of egg yolks, oil, vinegar, etc.

**may·or** /ˈmāər/ ▸*n.* chief executive of a city or town. —**may·or·al** *adj.*

**maze** /māz/ ▸*n.* **1** complex network of paths or passages; labyrinth. **2** confusion, confused mass, etc.

**ma·zu·ma** /məˈzo͞omə/ ▸*n.* money; cash.

**MB** (also **Mb**) ▸*abbr.* megabyte.

**MD** ▸*abbr.* **1** Doctor of Medicine. **2** Maryland (in official postal use). **3** muscular dystrophy.

**Md** ▸*symb.* mendelevium.

**Md.** ▸*abbr.* Maryland.

**ME** ▸*abbr.* Maine (in official postal use).

**Me.** ▸*abbr.* Maine.

**me** ▸*pron.* objective case of **I**: *he saw me.*

**mead** /mēd/ ▸*n.* alcoholic drink of fermented honey and water.

**mead·ow** /ˈmedō/ ▸*n.* **1** piece of grassland, esp. one used for hay. **2** piece of low well-watered ground, esp. near a river.

**mead·ow·lark** ▸*n.* ground-dwelling songbird with a brown streaky back.

**mea·ger** /ˈmēgər/ ▸*adj.* **1** lacking in amount or quality: *a meager salary.* **2** (of a person or animal) lean; thin. —**mea·ger·ly** *adv.* —**mea·ger·ness** *n.*

**meal** /mēl/ ▸*n.* **1** occasion when food is eaten. **2** the food eaten on one occasion. **3** grain or pulse ground to powder. —**meal·y** *adj.*

**mean** /mēn/ ▸*v.* (*past* and *past part.* **meant**) **1** have as one's purpose or intention. **2** design or destine for a purpose. **3** intend to convey or indicate or refer to. **4** be of some specified importance to.
▸*adj.* **1** not generous or liberal. **2** (of an action) ignoble; small-minded. **3** shabby. **4** malicious; ill-tempered. **5** (of a quantity) equally far from two extremes.
▸*n.* something midway between extremes. —**mean·ing·ful** *adj.* —**mean·ing·less** *adj.* —**mean·ly** *adv.* —**mean·ness** *n.*

**me·an·der** /mēˈandər/ ▸*v.* **1** (of a stream) wind about. **2** (of a person) wander at random.

**mean·ing** ▸*n.* **1** what is meant. **2** significance.
▸*adj.* expressive; significant. —**mean·ing·ful** *adj.* —**mean·ing·less** *adj.* —**mean·ing·ly** *adv.*

**mean·time** ▸*n.* intervening period.
▸*adv.* (also **mean·while**) in the time between: *in the meantime, I'll make some inquiries of my own.*

**mea·sles** /ˈmēzəlz/ ▸*n.* acute infectious viral disease marked by red spots on the skin.

**mea·sly** /ˈmēzlē/ ▸*adj.* (**-sli·er, -sli·est**) *inf.* inferior; contemptible; meager.

**meas·ure** /ˈmeZHər/ ▸*v.* **1** ascertain the extent or quantity of (a thing) by comparison with a standard. **2** be of a specified size: *it measures six inches.* **3** mark (a line, etc., of a given length).
▸*n.* **1** suitable action to achieve

some end: *cost-cutting measures.*
**2** legislative act. **3** system of or instrument for measuring.
**4** *Mus.* bar or the time content of a bar.

**meas·ured** ▸*adj.* **1** rhythmical; regular. **2** (of language) carefully considered.

**meas·ure·ment** ▸*n.*
**1** measuring. **2** size determined by measuring.

**meat** /mēt/ ▸*n.* **1** flesh of animals (esp. mammals) as food.
**2** essence or chief part of.
**3** edible part of nuts, shellfish, etc. —**meat·less** *adj.*

**meat·y** ▸*adj.* (**meat·i·er**, **meat·i·est**) **1** consisting of meat.
**2** full of substance: *he was finally offered a meaty role.*
—**meat·i·ness** *n.*

**me·chan·ic** /mi'kanik/ ▸*n.* skilled worker, esp. one who makes or uses or repairs machinery.

**me·chan·i·cal** ▸*adj.* **1** of machines or mechanisms.
**2** working or produced by machinery. **3** (of a person or action) like a machine; automatic; lacking originality.
—**me·chan·i·cal·ly** *adv.*

**me·chan·ics** ▸*n.* **1** branch of applied mathematics dealing with motion and tendencies to motion. **2** science of machinery.
**3** [*pl. n.*] method of construction or routine operation of a thing.

**mech·an·ism** /'mekə,nizəm/ ▸*n.*
**1** system of mutually adapted parts working together.
**2** structure or adaptation of parts of a machine. **3** mode of operation of a process.

**mech·a·nize** ▸*v.* **1** give a mechanical character to.
**2** introduce machines in.
**3** equip with tanks, armored cars, etc. —**mech·a·ni·za·tion** *n.*

**med·al** /'medl/ ▸*n.* piece of metal, usu. in the form of a disk, struck or cast with an inscription or device to commemorate an event, etc., or awarded as a distinction to a soldier, athlete, etc.

**med·al·ist** ▸*n.* recipient of a (specified) medal: *Olympic gold medalist.*

**me·dal·lion** /mə'dalyən/ ▸*n.*
**1** large medal. **2** thing shaped like this, e.g., a decorative panel or tablet, portrait, etc.

**med·dle** /'medl/ ▸*v.* interfere in or busy oneself unduly with others' concerns. —**med·dler** *n.*
—**med·dle·some** *adj.*

**me·di·a** /ˈmēdēə/ ▸n. **1** pl. of MEDIUM. **2** (**the media**) [treated as *sing.* or *pl.*] main means of mass communication (esp. newspapers and broadcasting) regarded collectively.

**me·di·a·cy** /ˈmēdēəsē/ ▸n. quality of being mediate.

**me·di·an** /ˈmēdēən/ ▸adj. situated in the middle. ▸n. **1** straight line drawn from any vertex of a triangle to the middle of the opposite side. **2** middle value of a series. **3** (also **median strip**) center divider separating opposing lanes on a divided highway.

**me·di·ate** /ˈmēdēˌāt/ ▸v. intervene (between parties in a dispute) to produce agreement or reconciliation. —**me·di·a·tion** *n.* —**me·di·a·tor** *n.*

**med·ic** /ˈmedik/ ▸n. *inf.* medical practitioner or student, esp. a member of a military medical corps.

**Med·i·caid** /ˈmediˌkād/ ▸n. federal system of health insurance for those requiring financial assistance.

**med·i·cal** /ˈmedikəl/ ▸adj. of medicine. —**med·i·cal·ly** *adv.*

**Med·i·care** /ˈmediˌke(ə)r/ ▸n. federal government program of health insurance for persons esp. over 65 years of age.

**med·i·cate** /ˈmediˌkāt/ ▸v. **1** treat medically. **2** impregnate with a medicinal substance. —**med·i·ca·tion** *n.*

**me·dic·i·nal** /məˈdisənl/ ▸adj. **1** (of a substance) having healing properties: *medicinal herbs.* **2** of or involving medicines or drugs. —**me·dic·i·nal·ly** *adv.*

**med·i·cine** /ˈmedisən/ ▸n. **1** science or practice of the diagnosis, treatment, and prevention of disease. **2** drug or preparation used for the treatment or prevention of disease.

**me·di·e·val** /ˌmēd(ē)ˈēvəl/ ▸adj. of the Middle Ages. —**me·di·e·val·ist** *n.*

**me·di·o·cre** /ˌmēdēˈōkər/ ▸adj. **1** of middling quality; neither good nor bad. **2** second-rate. —**me·di·oc·ri·ty** *n.*

**med·i·tate** /ˈmediˌtāt/ ▸v. engage in deep thought; reflect. —**med·i·ta·tion** *n.*

**me·di·um** /ˈmēdēəm/ ▸n. (*pl.* **-di·a** or **-di·ums**) **1** middle quality, degree, etc., between extremes. **2** means by which something is communicated or conveyed. **3** material or form used by an

artist, composer, etc. **4** (*pl.* **-ums**) person claiming to communicate with the dead.
▸*adj.* between two qualities, degrees, etc.

**med·ley** /ˈmedlē/ ▸*n.* (*pl.* **-leys**) collection of tunes, etc., played as one piece.

**meed** /mēd/ ▸*n.* deserved share or reward.

**meek** /mēk/ ▸*adj.* **1** humble and submissive. **2** piously gentle in nature. —**meek·ly** *adv.* —**meek·ness** *n.*

**meer·schaum** /ˈmi(ə)r͵SHôm/ ▸*n.* **1** soft white claylike substance. **2** tobacco pipe with the bowl made from this.

**meet** /mēt/ ▸*v.* (*past* and *past part.* **met**) **1 a** encounter; come face to face with. **b** (of two or more people) come into each other's company. **2** be present at the arrival of (a person, train, etc.). **3** come together or into contact (with): *where the road meets the river.* **4** come together or come into contact with for the purposes of conference, worship, etc.: *the committee meets every week.* **5 a** deal with or answer: *met the proposal with hostility.* **b** satisfy or conform with: *met the requirements.*

**6** experience, encounter, or receive: *met their death.*
▸*n.* assembly of competitors, etc.

**meet·ing** ▸*n.* **1** coming together. **2** assembly of people; gathering.

**meg** ▸*n.* (*pl.* same or **megs**) short for MEGABYTE.

**mega-** /ˈmegə/ ▸*comb. form* **1** large. **2** one million. (Abbr.: **M**).

**meg·a·byte** /ˈmegə͵bīt/ ▸*n.* unit of information equal to $2^{20}$ bytes or, loosely, one million bytes. (Abbr.: **MB** or **Mb**)

**meg·a·hertz** /ˈmegə͵hərts/ ▸*n.* one million hertz. (Abbr.: **MHz**).

**meg·a·lith** /ˈmegə͵liTH/ ▸*n.* large stone that forms a prehistoric monument (e.g., a menhir) or part of one (e.g., a stone circle).

**meg·a·lo·ma·ni·a** /͵megəlō-ˈmānēə/ ▸*n.* **1** mental disorder producing delusions of grandeur. **2** passion for grandiose schemes. —**meg·a·lo·ma·ni·ac** *adj. & n.* —**meg·a·lo·ma·ni·a·cal** *adj.*

**meg·a·lop·o·lis** /͵megəˈläpələs/ ▸*n.* very large, heavily populated city or urban complex.

**meg·a·phone** ▸*n.* large funnel-shaped device for amplifying the sound of the voice.

**meg·a·ton** ▸*n.* unit of explosive power equal to one million tons of TNT.

**mel·a·mine** /'melə,mēn/ ▸*n.* **1** white crystalline compound producing resins. **2** (also **melamine resin**) plastic made from this and used esp. for laminated coatings.

**mel·an·cho·li·a** /,melən'kōlēə/ ▸*n.* severe depression; anxiety.

**mel·an·chol·y** /'melən,kälē/ ▸*n.* (*pl.* **-ies**) **1** pensive sadness. **2** depression.
▸*adj.* sad; depressing; expressing sadness. **—mel·an·chol·ic** *adj.*

**mé·lange** /mā'länj/ ▸*n.* mixture; medley.

**mel·a·nin** /'melənin/ ▸*n.* dark-brown to black pigment occurring in the hair, skin, and iris of the eye.

**mel·a·no·ma** /,melə'nōmə/ ▸*n.* malignant tumor of melanin-forming cells, usu. in the skin.

**meld** /meld/ ▸*v.* merge; blend; combine.

**mel·io·rism** /'mēlēə,rizəm/ ▸*n.* belief that the world can be made better by human effort.

**mel·lif·lu·ous** /mə'liflŏŏəs/ ▸*adj.* (of a voice or words) pleasing; musical; flowing.
**—mel·lif·lu·ence** *n.*
**—mel·lif·lu·ous·ly** *adv.*

**mel·low** /'melō/ ▸*adj.* **1** (of sound, color, light) soft and rich; free from harshness. **2** (of character) softened or matured by age or experience. **3** genial; jovial. **4** (of wine) well-matured; smooth.
▸*v.* make or become mellow.
**—mel·low·ness** *n.*

**me·lo·di·ous** /mə'lōdēəs/ ▸*adj.* **1** of, producing, or having melody. **2** sweet-sounding.
**—me·lo·di·ous·ly** *adv.*
**—me·lo·di·ous·ness** *n.*

**mel·o·dra·ma** /'melə,drämə/ ▸*n.* **1** sensational dramatic piece with crude appeals to the emotions. **2** genre of drama of this type. **3** language, behavior, or an occurrence suggestive of this. **—mel·o·dra·mat·ic** *adj.*

**mel·o·dy** /'melədē/ ▸*n.* (*pl.* **-dies**) **1** arrangement of single notes in a musically expressive succession. **2** principal part in harmonized music; tune.

**mel·on** /'melən/ ▸*n.* sweet fruit of various gourds.

**melt** /melt/ ▸*v.* **1** (cause to) become liquefied by heat. **2** dissolve. **3** soften or be softened as a result of pity, love, etc. **4** change or merge imperceptibly into.

**melt·down** ▶*n.* **1** melting of a structure, esp. the overheated core of a nuclear reactor. **2** disastrous event.

**melt·ing point** ▶*n.* temperature at which any given solid will melt.

**melt·ing pot** ▶*n.* place where races, theories, etc., are mixed.

**mem·ber** /'membər/ ▶*n.* **1** person, animal, plant, etc., belonging to a society, team, taxonomic group, etc. **2** constituent portion of a complex structure. **3** any part or organ of the body, esp. a limb. —**mem·ber·ship** *n.*

**mem·brane** /'mem,brān/ ▶*n.* **1** any pliable sheetlike structure acting as a boundary, lining, or partition in an organism. **2** thin pliable sheet or skin of various kinds. —**mem·bra·nous** *adj.*

**meme** /mēm/ ▶*n.* element of a culture or system of behavior that may be considered to be passed from one individual to another by nongenetic means, esp. imitation.

**me·men·to** /mə'men,tō/ ▶*n.* (*pl.* **-tos** or **-toes**) object kept as a reminder or a souvenir of a person or an event.

**me·men·to mo·ri** /mə'men,tō 'môrē/ ▶*n.* (*pl.* same) object serving as a warning or reminder of death, such as a skull.

**mem·o** /'memō/ ▶*n.* written message, esp. in business.

**mem·oir** /'mem,wär/ ▶*n.* **1** historical account or biography written from personal knowledge or special sources. **2** (**memoirs**) autobiography.

**mem·o·ra·bil·i·a** /,mem(ə)rə-'bilēə/ ▶*pl. n.* souvenirs of memorable events.

**mem·o·ra·ble** /'mem(ə)rəbəl/ ▶*adj.* **1** worth remembering; not to be forgotten. **2** easily remembered. —**mem·o·ra·bil·i·ty** *n.* —**mem·o·ra·bly** *adv.*

**mem·o·ran·dum** /,memə-'randəm/ ▶*n.* (*pl.* **-da** or **-dums**) **1** note or record made for future use. **2** informal written message, esp. in business, etc.

**me·mo·ri·al** /mə'môrēəl/ ▶*n.* object, institution, or custom established in memory of a person or event. ▶*adj.* intending to commemorate a person or thing: *memorial service.*

**mem·o·rize** /ˈmeməˌrīz/ ▸v. commit to memory.
—**mem·o·ri·za·tion** n.

**mem·o·ry** /ˈmem(ə)rē/ ▸n. (pl. **-ries**) 1 mental faculty by which things are recalled. 2 store of things remembered.
3 recollection or remembrance. 4 reputation of a dead person. 5 length of time over which people continue to remember a person or event: *the worst slump in recent memory.* 6 act of remembering: *deed worthy of memory.* 7 storage capacity of a computer, etc.

**men·ace** /ˈmenəs/ ▸n. threat.
▸v. threaten, esp. in a malignant or hostile manner. —**men·ac·ing** adj. —**men·ac·ing·ly** adv.

**me·nag·er·ie** /məˈnajərē/ ▸n. small zoo.

**men·ar·che** /ˈmenˌärkē/ ▸n. first occurrence of menstruation.

**mend** /mend/ ▸v. 1 restore to a sound condition; repair.
2 regain health.
▸n. darn or repair.

**men·da·cious** /menˈdāSHəs/ ▸adj. lying; untruthful.
—**men·da·cious·ly** adv.
—**men·da·cious·ness** n.
—**men·dac·i·ty** n.

**men·dac·i·ty** /menˈdasitē/ ▸n. untruthfulness.

**men·di·cant** /ˈmendikənt/ ▸adj. 1 begging. 2 (of a friar) living solely on alms.
▸n. 1 beggar. 2 mendicant friar.
—**men·di·can·cy** n.

**men·hir** /ˈmenˌhi(ə)r/ ▸n. tall upright stone of a kind erected in prehistoric times in western Europe.

**me·ni·al** /ˈmēnēəl/ ▸adj. degrading; servile.
▸n. domestic servant.
—**me·ni·al·ly** adv.

**me·nin·ges** /məˈninjēz/ ▸pl. n. (sing. **me·ninx**) the three membrances enclosing the brain and spinal cord.

**men·in·gi·tis** /ˌmenənˈjītis/ ▸n. infection and inflammation of the meninges. —**men·in·git·ic** adj.

**men·o·pause** /ˈmenəˌpôz/ ▸n. ceasing of menstruation.
—**men·o·pau·sal** adj.

**me·nor·ah** /məˈnôrə/ ▸n. seven- or nine-armed candelabrum used in Jewish worship, esp. as a symbol of Judaism.

**mensch** /menCH/ ▸n. (pl. **mensch·en** /ˈmenCHən/ or **mensch·es**) person of integrity and honor.

**men·stru·ate** /ˈmenstroōˌāt/ ▶v. discharge blood and other materials from the uterus, usu. at monthly intervals from puberty until menopause, except during pregnancy. —**men·stru·a·tion** n.

**mens·wear** ▶n. clothes for men.

**-ment** /mənt/ ▶suffix **1** forming nouns expressing the means or result of the action of a verb: *abridgment* | *embankment*. **2** forming nouns from adjectives: *merriment* | *oddment*.

**men·tal** /ˈmentl/ ▶adj. **1** of, in, or done by the mind. **2** relating to or suffering from disorders of the mind. —**men·tal·ly** adv.

**men·tal·i·ty** /menˈtalitē/ ▶n. (pl. **-ties**) **1** mental character or disposition. **2** kind or degree of intelligence.

**men·ta·tion** /menˈtāsHən/ ▶n. mental activity.

**men·thol** /ˈmenˌTHôl/ ▶n. mint-tasting organic alcohol found in oil of peppermint, etc., used as a flavoring and to relieve local pain. —**men·tho·lat·ed** adj.

**men·tion** /ˈmensHən/ ▶v. **1** refer to briefly. **2** reveal or disclose. ▶n. reference.

**men·tor** /ˈmenˌtər/ ▶n. experienced and trusted adviser.

**men·u** /ˈmenyoō/ ▶n. **1 a** list of dishes available in a restaurant, etc. **b** list of items to be served at a meal. **2** *Computing* list of options showing the commands or facilities available.

**me·ow** /mēˈou/ ▶n. characteristic cry of a cat. ▶v. make this cry.

**mer·can·tile** /ˈmərkənˌtēl/ ▶adj. of or relating to trade or commerce. —**mer·can·til·ism** n.

**mer·ce·nar·y** /ˈmərsəˌnerē/ ▶adj. primarily concerned with money or other reward: *mercenary motives*. ▶n. (pl. **-ies**) hired soldier in foreign service.

**mer·chan·dise** /ˈmərcHənˌdīz/ ▶n. goods for sale. ▶v. **1** trade or traffic (in). **2** put on the market; promote; publicize. —**mer·chan·dis·er** n.

**mer·chant** /ˈmərcHənt/ ▶n. retail trader; dealer; storekeeper.

**mer·chant ma·rine** ▶n. a nation's commercial shipping.

**mer·cu·ri·al** /mərˌkyoōrēəl/ ▶adj. **1** (of a person) sprightly; ready-witted; volatile. **2** of or containing mercury. —**mer·cu·ri·al·ly** adv.

**mer·cu·ry** /ˈmərkyərē/ ▶n.
**1** silvery-white heavy liquid metallic element used in barometers, thermometers, etc. (Symb.: **Hg**). **2** (**Mercury**) planet nearest to the sun.

**mer·cy** /ˈmərsē/ ▶n. (pl. **-cies**)
**1** compassion or forbearance shown to enemies or offenders in one's power. **2** quality of compassion. **3** act of mercy. **4** something to be thankful for. —**mer·ci·ful** adj. —**mer·ci·less** adj.
□ **at the mercy of** wholly in the power of.

**mere** /mi(ə)r/ ▶adj. (**mer·est**) that is solely or no more or better than what is specified: questions that cannot be answered by mere mortals. —**mere·ly** adv.

**mer·e·tri·cious** /merəˈtrishəs/ ▶adj. **1** apparently attractive but having in reality no value or integrity. **2** of, relating to, or characteristic of a prostitute.

**merge** /mərj/ ▶v. **1 a** combine or be combined. **b** join or blend gradually. **2** lose or cause to lose character and identity in (something else). —**merg·er** n.

**me·rid·i·an** /məˈridēən/ ▶n. any of the great semicircles on the globe, passing through a given place and the North and South Poles.

**me·ringue** /məˈraNG/ ▶n. confection of sugar, egg whites, etc., baked crisp.

**me·ri·no** /məˈrēnō/ ▶n. (pl. **-nos**) **1** variety of sheep with long fine wool. **2** wool of this sheep, or cloth made from this.

**mer·it** /ˈmerit/ ▶n. **1** quality of being particularly good or worthy, so as to deserve praise or reward. **2** feature or fact that deserves reward or gratitude. **3** (**merits**) esp. Law intrinsic rights and wrongs.
▶v. deserve or be worthy of.

**mer·kin** /ˈmərkən/ ▶n. artificial covering of hair for the pubic area.

**mer·maid** /ˈmər,mād/ ▶n. imaginary sea creature, with the head and trunk of a woman and the tail of a fish.

**mer·o·nym** /ˈmerə,nim/ ▶n. term that denotes part of something but which is used to refer to the whole of it, e.g., faces when used to mean people in I see several familiar faces present.

**mer·ry** /ˈmerē/ ▶adj. (**-ri·er, -ri·est**) **1** joyous. **2** full of laughter or gaiety. —**mer·ri·ly** adv. —**mer·ri·ment** n. —**mer·ri·ness** n.

**mer·ry-go-round** ▸*n.* revolving machine with wooden horses or other animals, etc., for riding on at an amusement park, etc.

**mer·ry·mak·ing** ▸*n.* festivity; fun. —**mer·ry·mak·er** *n.*

**mes·ca·line** /ˈmeskəlin/ ▸*n.* hallucinogenic intoxicating compound from the peyote cactus.

**mesh** /meSH/ ▸*n.* **1** fabric or structure made of a network of fiber or thread. **2** each of the open spaces between the strands of a net or sieve, etc. ▸*v.* **1** (of the teeth of a wheel) be engaged (with others). **2** be harmonious.

**me·shu·ga** /məˈSHŏŏgə/ ▸*adj. inf.* (of a person) mad; idiotic.

**me·shu·gaas** /məSHŏŏˈgäs/ ▸*n. inf.* mad or idiotic ideas or behavior.

**mes·mer·ize** /ˈmezməˌrīz/ ▸*v.* fascinate; spellbind.

**mesne** /mēn/ ▸*adj.* intermediate.

**Mes·o·zo·ic** /ˈmezəˈzōik/ ▸*adj. Geol.* of or relating to an era of geological time marked by the development of dinosaurs, and with evidence of the first mammals, birds, and flowering plants. ▸*n.* this era.

**mes·quite** /məˈskēt/ ▸*n.* wood of a thorny leguminous tree, used in grilling food.

**mess** /mes/ ▸*n.* **1** dirty or untidy state. **2** state of confusion, embarrassment, or trouble. **3** something causing a mess, e.g., spilled liquid, etc. **4** disagreeable concoction. ▸*v.* (**mess up**) make a mess of; dirty; muddle. —**mess·y** *adj.*

**mes·sage** /ˈmesij/ ▸*n.* **1** oral or written communication sent by one person to another. **2** central import or meaning of an artistic work, etc.

**mes·sen·ger** /ˈmesənjər/ ▸*n.* person who carries a message.

**mess hall** ▸*n.* communal, esp. military, dining area.

**Mes·si·ah** /məˈsīə/ ▸*n.* **1** (also **messiah**) liberator of an oppressed people or country. **2 a** promised deliverer of the Jews. **b** (usu. **the Messiah**) Jesus Christ regarded as this. —**Mes·si·an·ic** *adj.*

**mes·ti·zo** /meˈstēzō/ ▸*n.* (*pl.* **-zos**) (in Latin America) a man of mixed race, esp. the offspring of a Spaniard and an American Indian.

**meta-** /ˈmetə/ (usu. **met-** before a vowel or *h*) ▸*comb. form*

**1** denoting change of position or condition: *metabolism*.
**2** denoting position: **a** behind. **b** after or beyond: *metaphysics*. **c** of a higher or second-order kind: *metalanguage*.

**me·tab·o·lism** /məˈtabəˌlizəm/ ▶*n.* all the chemical processes that occur within a living organism, resulting in energy production and growth. —**met·a·bol·ic** *adj.*

**met·al** /ˈmetl/ ▶*n.* **1** any of a class of chemical elements such as gold, silver, iron, and tin, usu. lustrous ductile solids and good conductors of heat and electricity. **2** alloy of any of these. ▶*adj.* made of metal.

**me·tal·lic** /meˈtalik/ ▶*adj.* of or like metal.

**met·al·lur·gy** /ˈmetlˌərjē/ ▶*n.* science concerned with the production, purification, and properties of metals and their application. —**met·al·lur·gic** *adj.* —**met·al·lur·gi·cal** *adj.* —**met·al·lur·gist** *n.*

**met·a·mor·phose** /ˌmetəˈmôr-ˌfōz/ ▶*v.* change in form or nature.

**met·a·mor·pho·sis** /ˌmetə-ˈmôrfəsis/ ▶*n.* (*pl.* **-ses**) **1** change of character, conditions, etc. **2** change of form in an animal, e.g., from a pupa to an insect, etc.

**met·a·noi·a** /ˌmetəˈnoiə/ ▶*n.* change in one's way of life resulting from penitence or spiritual conversion.

**met·a·phor** /ˈmetəˌfôr/ ▶*n.* application of a name or descriptive term or phrase to an object or action to which it is not literally applicable (e.g., *killing him with kindness*). —**met·a·phor·i·cal** *adj.* —**met·a·phor·i·cal·ly** *adv.*

**met·a·phys·ics** ▶*n.* **1** branch of philosophy dealing with concepts of being, knowing, cause, time, space, etc. **2** abstract theory with no basis in reality. —**met·a·phys·i·cal** *adj.* —**met·a·phy·si·cian** *n.*

**me·tas·ta·sis** /meˈtastəsis/ ▶*n.* development of secondary malignant growths at a distance from a primary site of cancer. —**me·tas·ta·size** *v.* —**met·a·stat·ic** *adj.*

**mete** /mēt/ ▶*v.* (**mete something out**) dispense or allot (justice, punishment, etc.).

**me·te·or** /ˈmētēər/ ▶*n.* **1** small body of matter from outer space that becomes incandescent as a result of friction with the earth's atmosphere. **2** streak of light emanating from a meteor.

**me·te·or·ic** /ˌmētē'ôrik/ ▶*adj.* **1** of meteors. **2** rapid like a meteor; dazzling; transient.

**me·te·or·ite** /'mētēəˌrīt/ ▶*n.* fallen meteor that reaches the earth's surface from outer space. —**me·te·or·it·ic** *adj.*

**me·te·or·ol·o·gy** /ˌmētēə'räləjē/ ▶*n.* study of the processes and phenomena of the atmosphere, esp. as a means of forecasting the weather. —**me·te·or·o·log·i·cal** *adj.* —**me·te·or·ol·o·gist** *n.*

**me·ter** /'mētər/ (also *Brit.* **me·tre**) ▶*n.* **1** basic metric measure of length, equal to about 39.4 inches. **2** instrument that measures, esp. one for recording a quantity of gas, electricity, postage, etc., supplied, present, or needed. **3** poetic rhythm, determined by the number and length of feet in a line.

**-meter** ▶*comb. form* **1** forming nouns denoting measuring instruments: *barometer.* **2** forming nouns denoting lines of poetry with a specified number of measures: *pentameter.*

**meth·a·done** /'meᴛʜəˌdōn/ ▶*n.* potent narcotic analgesic drug used esp. as a substitute for morphine or heroin.

**meth·ane** /'meᴛʜˌān/ ▶*n.* colorless, odorless, flammable gas, the main constituent of natural gas.

**meth·a·nol** /'meᴛʜəˌnôl/ ▶*n.* colorless, volatile, flammable liquid, used as a solvent. (Also called **methyl alcohol**).

**meth·od** /'meᴛʜəd/ ▶*n.* **1** special form of procedure esp. in any branch of mental activity. **2** orderliness; regular habits.

**me·thod·i·cal** /mə'ᴛʜädikəl/ ▶*adj.* orderly; systematic. —**me·thod·i·cal·ly** *adv.*

**Meth·od·ist** ▶*n.* member of a Christian Protestant church based on the teachings of John Wesley. —**Meth·od·ism** *n.*

**meth·od·ol·o·gy** /ˌmeᴛʜə'däləjē/ ▶*n.* (*pl.* **-gies**) system or science of methods.

**me·tic·u·lous** /mə'tikyələs/ ▶*adj.* **1** giving great or excessive attention to details. **2** very careful and precise. —**me·tic·u·lous·ly** *adv.*

**mé·tier** /me'tyā/ (also **me·tier**) ▶*n.* **1** one's trade, profession, or department of activity. **2** one's forte.

**me·ton·y·my** /məˈtänəmē/ ▶*n.* (*pl.* **-mies**) substitution of the name of an attribute or adjunct for that of the thing meant, for example *suit* for *business executive*, or *the track* for *horse racing*.

**met·ric** /ˈmetrik/ ▶*adj.* of or based on the meter.

**-metric** (also **-metrical**) ▶*comb. form* forming adjectives corresponding to nouns in *-meter* and *-metry*: *geometric*.
—**-metrically** *comb. form* forming adverbs.

**met·ri·cal** ▶*adj.* **1** of, relating to, or composed in rhythmic meter. **2** of or involving measurement.
—**met·ri·cal·ly** *adv.*

**me·tric sys·tem** ▶*n.* decimal measuring system with the meter, liter, and gram (or kilogram) as units of length, volume, and mass.

**met·ro·nome** /ˈmetrəˌnōm/ ▶*n.* *Mus.* instrument marking time at a selected rate by giving a regular tick.

**met·ro·plex** /ˈmetrəˌpleks/ ▶*n.* very large metropolitan area, esp. one that is an aggregation of two or more cities.

**me·trop·o·lis** /məˈträp(ə)ləs/ ▶*n.* very large and densely populated industrial and commercial city.

**met·ro·pol·i·tan** /ˌmetrəˈpälitn/ ▶*adj.* of or relating to a city, often including the surrounding areas: *the New York metropolitan area.*

**met·tle** /ˈmetl/ ▶*n.* strength of character; spirit; courage.

**mew** /myo͞o/ ▶*v.* (of a cat, gull, etc.) utter its characteristic cry. ▶*n.* this sound.

**mews** /myo͞oz/ ▶*n.* (*pl.* same) set of stables around an open yard or along a lane, now often converted into dwellings.

**Mex·i·can** /ˈmeksikən/ ▶*n.* **1** native or national of Mexico, a country in southern N. America. **2** language spoken in Mexico. ▶*adj.* of or relating to Mexico or its people.

**me·zu·zah** /məˈzo͞ozə/ (also **me·zu·za**) ▶*n.* (*pl.* **-zahs** or **-zas** or **-zot** or **-zoth** /-zōt/) parchment inscribed with religious texts and attached in a case to the doorpost of a Jewish house as a sign of faith.

**mez·za·nine** /ˈmezəˌnēn/ ▶*n.* low story between two others (usu. between the first and second floors).

**M.F.A.** ▸*abbr.* Master of Fine Arts.

**MI** ▸*abbr.* Michigan (in official postal use).

**mi** /mē/ ▸*n. Mus.* third tone of the diatonic scale.

**mi.** ▸*abbr.* mile(s).

**mi·as·ma** /mī'azmə/ ▸*n.* (pl. **-mas** of **-ma·ta**) highly unpleasant and unhealthy smell or vapor.

**mi·ca** /'mīkə/ ▸*n.* any of a group of silicate minerals with a layered structure.

**Mich.** ▸*abbr.* Michigan.

**micro-** /'mīkrō/ ▸*comb. form* **1** small: *microchip.* **2** denoting a factor of one millionth (10⁶): *microgram.* (Symb.: **μ**).

**mi·crobe** /'mī‚krōb/ ▸*n.* minute living being; microorganism (esp. bacteria causing disease and fermentation). —**mi·cro·bi·al** *adj.*

**mi·cro·brew·er·y** ▸*n.* limited-production brewery, often selling only locally.

**mi·cro·chip** ▸*n.* small piece of semiconductor (usu. silicon) used to carry electronic circuits.

**mi·cro·com·put·er** ▸*n.* small computer that contains a microprocessor as its central processor.

**mi·cro·cosm** /'mīkrə‚käzəm/ ▸*n.* **1** miniature representation. **2** mankind viewed as the epitome of the universe. **3** any community or complex unity viewed in this way. —**mi·cro·cos·mic** *adj.*

**mi·cro·fiche** /'mīkrə‚fēsH/ ▸*n.* (pl. same or **-fich·es**) flat rectangular piece of microfilm bearing miniaturized photographs of a printed text or document.

**mi·cro·film** ▸*n.* length of film bearing miniaturized photographs of documents, etc.

**mi·cro·man·age** /‚mīkrō'manij/ ▸*v.* control every part, however small, of (an enterprise or activity).

**mi·crom·e·ter** /mī'krämitər/ ▸*n.* gauge for accurately measuring small distances, thicknesses, etc.

**mi·cron** /'mī‚krän/ ▸*n.* one-millionth of a meter.

**mi·cro·or·gan·ism** ▸*n.* microscopic organism, e.g., algae, bacteria, fungi, protozoa, and viruses.

**mi·cro·phone** ▸*n.* instrument for converting sound waves into electrical currents.

**mi·cro·proc·es·sor** ▸*n.* integrated circuit that contains all the functions of a central processing unit of a computer.

**mi·cro·scope** ▸*n.* instrument magnifying small objects by means of a lens or lenses.

**mi·cro·scop·ic** /ˌmīkrəˈskäpik/ ▸*adj.* **1** visible only with a microscope. **2** extremely small.

**mi·cro·sur·ger·y** ▸*n.* intricate surgery performed using microscopes.

**mi·cro·wave** ▸*n.* **1** electromagnetic wave with a wavelength in the range 0.001–0.3m. **2** (also **microwave oven**) oven that uses microwaves to cook or heat food quickly. ▸*v.* cook in a microwave oven.

**mic·tu·rate** /ˈmikCHəˌrāt/ ▸*v.* urinate.

**mid** /mid/ ▸*adj.* of or in the middle part: *midsummer* | *in midair.*

**mid·day** ▸*n.* middle of the day; noon.

**mid·dle** /ˈmidl/ ▸*adj.* **1** at an equal distance from the extremities of a thing. **2** (of a member of a group) so placed as to have the same number of members on each side. **3** intermediate in rank, quality, etc. **4** average: *of middle height.* ▸*n.* **1** middle point or position or part. **2** waist.

**Mid·le Ag·es** ▸*pl. n.* period of European history between ancient times and the Renaissance, from *c.* 476 to 1453.

**Mid·dle A·mer·i·ca** ▸*n.* middle class in the U.S., esp. as a conservative political force.

**mid·dle class** ▸*n.* class of society between the upper and the lower, socially, economically, etc.

**Mid·dle Eng·lish** ▸*n.* the English language from *c.* 1150 to 1500.

**mid·dle·man** ▸*n.* (*pl.* -men) **1** any of the traders who handle a commodity between its producer and its consumer. **2** intermediary.

**mid·dle-of-the-road** ▸*adj.* moderate; avoiding extremes.

**mid·dle school** ▸*n.* school for children usu. in grades 5 to 8.

**mid·dling** /ˈmidliNG/ ▸*adj.* moderately good (esp. in phrase *fair to middling*). ▸*adv.* fairly or moderately.

**midge** /mij/ ▸*n. inf.* gnatlike insect.

**midg·et** /ˈmijit/ ▸*n.* extremely small person or thing.

**mid·land** /'midlənd/ ▸n. middle part of a country.

▸adj. of or in the midland.

**mid·night** ▸n. 12 o'clock at night.

**mid·riff** /'mid,rif/ ▸n. region of the front of the body between the thorax and abdomen.

**mid·ship·man** ▸n. (pl. -men) cadet in the U.S. Naval Academy.

**midst** /midst/ ▸prep. in the middle of.

**mid·sum·mer** ▸n. period of or near the summer solstice, around June 21.

**mid·term** ▸n. 1 middle of a period of office, academic term, etc. 2 exam in the middle of an academic term.

**mid·way** ▸n. area for concessions and amusements at a carnival, fair, etc.

▸adv. in or toward the middle of the distance between two points.

**mid·wife** ▸n. (pl. -wives) person trained to assist at childbirth. —**mid·wife·ry** n.

**mid·win·ter** ▸n. period of or near the winter solstice, around Dec. 22.

**mien** /mēn/ ▸n. person's look or bearing.

**miff** /mif/ ▸v. inf. (usu. **be miffed**) annoy: *she was miffed at not being invited.*

**might** /mīt/ ▸v. past of MAY, used esp.: 1 in reported speech, expressing possibility (*said he might come*) or permission (*asked if I might leave*). 2 expressing a possibility based on a condition not fulfilled: *if you'd looked you might have found it.* 3 expressing complaint that an obligation or expectation is not or has not been fulfilled: *they might have asked.* 4 expressing a request: *you might call in at the butcher's.*

▸n. impressive strength or power.

**might·y** ▸adj. (-i·er, -i·est) 1 powerful; strong. 2 massive; bulky.

▸adv. inf. extremely. —**might·i·ly** adv.

**mi·graine** /'mī,grān/ ▸n. intense headache that often affects vision.

**mi·grate** /'mī,grāt/ ▸v. 1 (of people) move from one place of abode to another, esp. in a different country. 2 (of a bird or fish) change its area of habitation with the seasons. —**mi·gra·tion** n. —**mi·gra·to·ry** adj.

**mi·ka·do** /mi'kädō/ ▸*n.* (*pl.* **-dos**) *hist.* title of the emperor of Japan.

**mike** /mīk/ ▸*n. inf.* microphone.

**mil** /mil/ ▸*n.* one-thousandth of an inch.

**mild** /mīld/ ▸*adj.* **1** gentle and conciliatory. **2** moderate; not severe. **3** (of food, tobacco, etc.) not sharp or strong in taste, etc. **4** tame; feeble; lacking energy or vivacity. —**mild·ly** *adv.* —**mild·ness** *n.*

**mil·dew** /'mil,d(y)o͞o/ ▸*n.* destructive growth of minute fungi on plants, damp paper, leather, etc. ▸*v.* taint or be tainted with mildew.

**mile** /mīl/ ▸*n.* unit of linear measure equal to 1,760 yards (approx. 1.609 kilometers).

**mile·age** /'mīlij/ ▸*n.* **1** number of miles traveled, used, etc. **2** number of miles traveled by a vehicle per unit of fuel. **3** traveling expenses (per mile). **4** *inf.* use; advantage: *he was getting a lot of mileage out of the mix-up.*

**mile·stone** ▸*n.* **1** stone marking a distance in miles. **2** significant event or stage in a life, history, project, etc.

**mi·lieu** /mil'yo͞o/ ▸*n.* (*pl.* **-lieus** or **-lieux**) one's environment or social surroundings.

**mil·i·tant** /'militənt/ ▸*adj.* combative; aggressively active, esp. in support of a (usu. political) cause. ▸*n.* militant person. —**mil·i·tan·cy** *n.* —**mil·i·tant·ly** *adv.*

**mil·i·ta·rism** /'militə,rizəm/ ▸*n.* **1** military spirit. **2** undue prevalence of the military spirit or ideals. —**mil·i·ta·ris·tic** *adj.*

**mil·i·ta·rize** ▸*v.* **1** equip with military resources. **2** make military or warlike.

**mil·i·tar·y** /'mili,terē/ ▸*adj.* of, relating to, or characteristic of soldiers or armed forces. ▸*n.* (**the military**) members of the armed forces, as distinct from civilians and the police. —**mil·i·tar·i·ly** *adv.*

**mil·i·tate** /'milə,tāt/ ▸*v.* (of facts or evidence) have force or effect (against): *these fundamental differences will militate against the two communities coming together.*

**mi·li·tia** /mə'lisнə/ ▸*n.* military force, esp. one raised from the civil population and supplementing a regular army in an emergency.

**milk** /milk/ ▸*n.* **1** opaque white

fluid secreted by female mammals for the nourishment of their young. **2** milk of cows, goats, or sheep as food. **3** milklike juice of plants, e.g., in the coconut.

▸*v.* **1** draw milk from (a cow, ewe, goat, etc.). **2** exploit (a person or situation). —**milk·y** *adj.*

**milk·sop** /'milk,säp/ ▸*n.* person who is indecisive and lacks courage.

**milk·weed** ▸*n.* plant with milky sap.

**Milk·y Way** ▸*n.* faintly luminous band of light emitted by countless stars encircling the heavens; the Galaxy.

**mill** /mil/ ▸*n.* **1 a** building fitted with a mechanical apparatus for grinding grain. **b** such an apparatus. **2** apparatus for grinding any solid substance to powder or pulp: *pepper mill.* **3** factory. **4** one-thousandth of a U.S. dollar.

▸*v.* **1** grind (grain), produce (flour), or hull (seeds) in a mill. **2** produce regular ribbed markings on the edge of (a coin). **3** cut or shape (metal) with a rotating tool. **4** move aimlessly (around).

**mil·len·ni·um** /mi'lenēəm/ ▸*n.* (*pl.* -**ni·a** or -**ni·ums**) **1** one-thousandth anniversary. **2** a period of 1,000 years. **3** the 1,000-year period of Christ's prophesied reign in person on earth. —**mil·len·ni·al** *adj.*

**mil·let** /'milit/ ▸*n.* cereal plant bearing a large crop of small nutritious seeds.

**milli-** /'milə/ ▸*comb. form* one thousandth.

**mil·li·gram** ▸*n.* one-thousandth of a gram.

**mil·li·li·ter** ▸*n.* one-thousandth of a liter.

**mil·li·me·ter** ▸*n.* one-thousandth of a meter.

**mil·li·ner** /'milənər/ ▸*n.* person who makes or sells women's hats. —**mil·li·ner·y** *n.*

**mil·lion** /'milyən/ ▸*n.* a thousand thousand. —**mil·lionth** *adj. & n.*

**mil·lion·aire** /,milyə'ne(ə)r/ ▸*n.* person who has over one million dollars, pounds, etc.

**mill·race** ▸*n.* current of water that drives a mill wheel.

**mill·stone** ▸*n.* **1** each of two circular stones used for grinding grain. **2** heavy burden or responsibility.

**milque·toast** /'milk,tōst/ (also

**Milque·toast**) ▸*n.* person who is timid or submissive.

**mime** /mīm/ ▸*n.* **1** acting using only gestures. **2** practitioner of mime.
▸*v.* convey by gesture without words.

**mim·ic** /'mimik/ ▸*v.* (**-icked**, **-ick·ing**) **1** imitate (a person, gesture, etc.) esp. to entertain or ridicule. **2** copy minutely or servilely. **3** (of a thing) resemble closely.
▸*n.* person skilled in imitation.
—**mim·ic·ry** *n.*

**mi·mo·sa** /mə'mōsə/ ▸*n.* **1** shrub having globular usu. yellow flowers. **2** acacia plant with showy yellow flowers. **3** cocktail of champagne and orange juice.

**mi·na·cious** /mə'nāsHəs/ ▸*adj.* menacing; threatening.

**min·a·ret** /ˌminə'ret/ ▸*n.* slender turret connected to a mosque.

**mince** /mins/ ▸*v.* **1** cut up or grind into very small pieces. **2** [usu. as *adj.* **mincing**] speak or walk with an affected delicacy.
☐ **mince words** use polite expressions, etc.: *she does not mince words when she's angry.*

**mince·meat** ▸*n.* mixture of currants, raisins, sugar, apples, candied peel, spices, often suet, and sometimes meat.

**mind** /mīnd/ ▸*n.* **1** seat of consciousness, thought, volition, and feeling. **2** attention; concentration. **3** intellect; reason. **4** remembrance; memory. **5** way of thinking or feeling: *shocking to the Victorian mind.*
▸*v.* **1** object to: *do you mind if I smoke?* **2** remember; heed; take care to: *mind you come on time.* **3** have charge of temporarily: *mind the house while I'm away.*

**mind·ful** ▸*adj.* taking heed or care; being conscious.

**mind·less** ▸*adj.* **1** not requiring thought or skill: *totally mindless work.* **2** showing no thought or skill. —**mind·less·ly** *adv.* —**mind·less·ness** *n.*

**mine** /mīn/ ▸*pron.* the one or ones of or belonging to me: *it is mine.*
▸*n.* **1** excavation in the earth for extracting metal, coal, salt, etc. **2** abundant source (of information, etc.). **3** military explosive device placed in the ground or in the water.
▸*v.* **1** obtain (metal, coal, etc.) from a mine. **2** dig in (the earth, etc.) for ore, etc. **3** tunnel. **4** lay

explosive mines under or in.
—**min·ing** *n.*

**min·er·al** /ˈmin(ə)rəl/ ▶*n.* **1** any of the species into which inorganic substances are classified. **2** substance obtained by mining.

**min·er·al·o·gy** /ˌminəˈräləjē/ ▶*n.* scientific study of minerals.
—**min·er·al·o·gist** *n.*

**min·er·al oil** ▶*n.* colorless, odorless, oily liquid obtained from petroleum and used as a laxative, in manufacturing cosmetics, etc.

**min·er·al wa·ter** ▶*n.* natural or processed water containing some dissolved salts, usu. bottled for drinking.

**min·e·stro·ne** /ˌminəˈstrōnē/ ▶*n.* thick vegetable soup.

**mine·sweep·er** ▶*n.* ship for clearing away floating and submerged mines.

**min·gle** /ˈmiNGgəl/ ▶*v.* **1** mix; blend. **2** (**mingle with**) (of a person) move about; associate.

**min·i** /ˈminē/ ▶*adj.* denoting a miniature version of something.

**mini-** ▶*comb. form* miniature.

**min·i·a·ture** /ˈmin(ē)əˌCHər/ ▶*adj.* **1** much smaller than normal. **2** represented on a small scale.
▶*n.* **1** any object reduced in size.

**2** small-scale minutely finished portrait.

**min·i·a·tur·ize** ▶*v.* produce in a smaller version; make small.

**min·i·mize** /ˈminəˌmīz/ ▶*v.* **1** reduce to, or estimate at, the smallest possible amount or degree. **2** estimate or represent at less than the true value or importance. —**min·i·mi·za·tion** *n.*

**min·i·mum** /ˈminəməm/ ▶*n.* (*pl.* **min·i·ma**) least possible or attainable amount.
▶*adj.* that is a minimum.
□ **minimum wage** lowest wage permitted by law.

**min·ion** /ˈminyən/ ▶*n.* follower or underling of a powerful person, esp. a servile or unimportant one.

**min·is·ter** /ˈminəstər/ ▶*n.* **1** member of the clergy. **2** head of a government department (in some countries). **3** diplomatic agent, usu. ranking below an ambassador.
▶*v.* render aid or service to.
—**min·is·te·ri·al** *adj.*

**min·is·try** /ˈminəstrē/ ▶*n.* (*pl.* **-tries**) **1** vocation office, tenure, or profession of a religious minister: *he is training for the ministry.* **2** body of ministers of a government or of a religion.

**3** government department headed by a minister.

**min·i·van** ▸*n.* vehicle, smaller than a full-sized van, for passengers, cargo, etc.

**mink** /miNGk/ ▸*n.* semiaquatic stoatlike animal bred for its thick brown fur.

**Minn.** ▸*abbr.* Minnesota.

**min·now** /ˈminō/ ▸*n.* small freshwater fish.

**mi·nor** /ˈmīnər/ ▸*adj.* **1** lesser or comparatively small in size or importance: *minor poet.* **2** *Mus.* less by a semitone than a corresponding major.
▸*n.* **1** person under the legal age limit or majority. **2** student's subsidiary subject or course.
▸*v.* (of a student) undertake study in (a subject) as a subsidiary: *she is majoring in physics and minoring in math.*

**mi·nor·i·ty** /məˈnôrətē/ ▸*n.* (pl. **-ties**) **1** smaller number or part, esp. within a political party or structure; less than half. **2** relatively small group of people differing from others in race, religion, language, political persuasion, etc. **3** being under full legal age.

**min·strel** /ˈminstrəl/ ▸*n.* **1** medieval singer or musician.

**2** member of a band of public entertainers with blackened faces, etc., performing songs and music ostensibly of African-American origin.

**mint** /mint/ ▸*n.* **1** aromatic plant used for flavoring. **2** peppermint or spearmint candy or lozenge. **3** place where money is coined. **4** vast sum of money.
▸*v.* **1** make (coin) by stamping metal. **2** invent or coin (a word, phrase, etc.). —**mint·age** *n.* —**mint·y** *adj.*

**min·u·et** /ˌminyoōˈet/ ▸*n.* slow stately dance for two in triple time.

**mi·nus** /ˈmīnəs/ ▸*prep.* **1** with the subtraction of: *7 minus 4 equals 3.* (Symb.: −). **2** (of temperature) below zero: *minus 2°.* **3** *inf.* lacking; deprived of: *returned minus their cash.*
▸*adj.* negative.
▸*n.* **1** *Math.* negative quantity. **2** disadvantage: *the plan has no minuses.*
□ **minus sign** the symbol (−) indicating subtraction or a negative value.

**mi·nus·cule** /ˈminəˌskyoōl/ *inf.*
▸*adj.* extremely small or unimportant.

**min·ute**[1] /ˈminit/ ▸*n.* **1** sixtieth part of an hour. **2** distance covered in one minute: *twenty minutes from the station.* **3** moment. **4** sixtieth part of an angular degree. (Symb.: ′) **5** (**minutes**) official memorandum or brief summary of a meeting, etc.

**mi·nute**[2] /mīˈn(y)o͞ot/ ▸*adj.* (**mi·nut·est**) **1** very small. **2** accurate; detailed. —**min·ute·ly** *adv.*

**mi·nu·ti·ae** /məˈn(y)o͞osHē,ē/ (also **mi·nu·ti·a** /-sHē,ə; -sHə/) ▸*pl. n.* small, precise, or trivial details of something.

**mir·a·cle** /ˈmirəkəl/ ▸*n.* **1** extraordinary event attributed to some supernatural agency. **2** remarkable occurrence. **3** remarkable specimen: *the plan was a miracle of ingenuity.* —**mi·rac·u·lous** *adj.* —**mi·rac·u·lous·ly** *adv.*

**mir·a·dor** /ˈmirəˌdôr/ ▸*n.* turret or tower attached to a building and providing an extensive view.

**mi·rage** /məˈräzH/ ▸*n.* **1** optical illusion caused by atmospheric conditions. **2** illusory thing.

**mire** /mī(ə)r/ ▸*n.* stretch of swampy or boggy ground.

▸*v.* **1** plunge or sink in a mire. **2** involve in difficulties.

**mir·ror** /ˈmirər/ ▸*n.* **1** polished surface, usu. of amalgam-coated glass or metal, which reflects an image. **2** anything reflecting truly or accurately.

▸*v.* reflect as in a mirror.

**mirth** /mərTH/ ▸*n.* merriment; laughter. —**mirth·ful** *adj.* —**mirth·less** *adj.*

**MIS** ▸*abbr. Computing* management information system.

**mis-** ▸*prefix* added to verbs, verbal derivatives, and nouns, meaning 'amiss,' 'badly,' 'wrongly,' 'unfavorably,' or having negative force: *mislead | misshapen | mistrust | misadventure.*

**mis·ad·ven·ture** /ˌmisəd-ˈvenCHər/ ▸*n.* bad luck; misfortune.

**mis·an·thrope** /ˈmisənˌTHrōp/ ▸*n.* person who hates or avoids human society. —**mis·an·throp·ic** *adj.* —**mis·an·thro·py** *n.*

**mis·ap·ply** ▸*v.* (**-plied**) apply (esp. funds) wrongly. —**mis·ap·pli·ca·tion** *n.*

**mis·ap·pre·hend** ▶*v.* misunderstand. —**mis·ap·pre·hen·sion** *n.*

**mis·ap·pro·pri·ate** /ˌmisə-ˈprōprēˌāt/ ▶*v.* take (funds, etc.) for one's own use; embezzle. —**mis·ap·pro·pri·a·tion** *n.*

**mis·be·got·ten** ▶*adj.* badly planned or designed.

**mis·be·have** ▶*v.* behave badly. —**mis·be·hav·ior** *n.*

**misc.** ▶*abbr.* miscellaneous.

**mis·car·riage** ▶*n.* **1** spontaneous premature abortion. **2** failure (of a plan, system, etc.).

**mis·car·ry** ▶*v.* (-ried) **1** have a miscarriage. **2** (of a business, plan, etc.) fail; be unsuccessful.

**mis·cast** ▶*v.* (*past* and *past part.* **-cast**) allot an unsuitable part to (an actor).

**mis·ceg·e·na·tion** /miˌsejə-ˈnāSHən; ˌmisəjə-/ ▶*n.* interbreeding of people considered to be of different racial types.

**mis·cel·la·ne·ous** /ˌmisə-ˈlānēəs/ ▶*adj.* of various kinds; assorted.

**mis·cel·la·ny** /ˈmisəˌlānē/ ▶*n.* mixture.

**mis·chance** ▶*n.* **1** bad luck. **2** instance of this.

**mis·chief** /ˈmisCHif/ ▶*n.* **1** pranks; scrapes. **2** playful malice; archness. **3** harm; injury. **4** person or thing responsible for harm or annoyance.

**mis·chie·vous** /ˈmisCHəvəs/ ▶*adj.* full of mischief.

**mis·ci·ble** /ˈmisəbəl/ ▶*adj.* (of liquids) forming a homogeneous mixture when added together.

**mis·con·ceive** ▶*v.* **1** have a wrong idea or conception. **2** [as *adj.* **misconceived**] plan, organize, etc. badly. —**mis·con·cep·tion** *n.*

**mis·con·duct** /misˈkändəkt/ ▶*n.* **1** improper or unprofessional behavior. **2** bad management.

**mis·con·strue** ▶*v.* interpret wrongly. —**mis·con·struc·tion** *n.*

**mis·cre·ant** /ˈmiskrēənt/ ▶*n.* vile wretch; villain.

**mis·deed** ▶*n.* evil deed; wrongdoing; crime.

**mis·de·mean·or** /ˈmisdiˌmēnər/ ▶*n.* **1** offense; misdeed. **2** *Law* indictable offense, less heinous than a felony.

**mi·ser** /ˈmīzər/ ▶*n.* person who hoards wealth greedily. —**mi·ser·ly** *adj.*

**mis·er·a·ble** /ˈmiz(ə)rəbəl/ ▶*adj.*
**1** wretchedly unhappy or
uncomfortable. **2** causing
wretchedness or discomfort:
*miserable weather.* **3** inadequate:
*miserable hovel.* **4** contemptible:
*you miserable creep!*
—**mis·er·a·bly** *adv.*

**mis·er·y** /ˈmiz(ə)rē/ ▶*n.* (*pl.* **-ies**)
**1** wretched state of mind, or of
outward circumstances. **2** thing
causing this.

**mis·fea·sance** /misˈfēzəns/ ▶*n.*
transgression, esp. the wrongful
exercise of lawful authority.

**mis·fire** ▶*v.* **1** (of a gun, motor
engine, etc.) fail to go off or start
or function regularly. **2** (of an
action, etc.) fail to have the
intended effect.
▶*n.* such a failure.

**mis·fit** ▶*n.* **1** person unsuited to
an environment, occupation, etc.
**2** garment, etc., that does not fit.

**mis·for·tune** ▶*n.* bad luck.

**mis·giv·ing** ▶*n.* feeling of
mistrust or apprehension: *I have
serious misgivings about his ability
to do the job.*

**mis·han·dle** ▶*v.* **1** deal with
incorrectly or ineffectively.
**2** handle roughly or rudely; ill-
treat.

**mis·hap** /ˈmisˌhap/ ▶*n.* unlucky
accident.

**mish·mash** /ˈmiSHˌmaSH/ ▶*n.*
confused mixture.

**mis·in·form** ▶*v.* give wrong
information to; mislead.
—**mis·in·for·ma·tion** *n.*

**mis·in·ter·pret** ▶*v.* **1** interpret
wrongly. **2** draw a wrong
inference from.
—**mis·in·ter·pre·ta·tion** *n.*

**mis·judge** ▶*v.* **1** have a wrong
opinion of. **2** make an incorrect
assessment of.
—**mis·judg·ment** *n.*

**mis·lay** ▶*v.* (*past* and *past part.*
**-laid**) unintentionally put (a
thing) where it cannot readily be
found.

**mis·lead** /misˈlēd/ ▶*v.* (*past* and
*past part.* **-led**) cause (a person) to
have a wrong idea or
impression: *the government misled
the public about the state of the
economy.*

**mis·man·age** ▶*v.* manage badly
or wrongly.
—**mis·man·age·ment** *n.*

**mis·match** ▶*v.* match
unsuitably or incorrectly.
▶*n.* bad match.

**mis·no·mer** /misˈnōmər/ ▶*n.*
name or term used wrongly.

**mi·sog·a·my** /məˈsägəmē/ ▸n. hatred of marriage.

**mi·sog·y·ny** /məˈsäjənē/ ▸n. hatred of women.
—**mi·sog·y·nist** n.

**mis·place** ▸v. **1** put in the wrong place. **2** bestow (affections, confidence, etc.) on an inappropriate object.
—**mis·place·ment** n.

**mis·print** ▸n. mistake in printing.
▸v. print wrongly.

**mis·prize** /misˈprīz/ ▸v. fail to appreciate the value of (something); undervalue.

**mis·pro·nounce** ▸v. pronounce (a word, etc.) wrongly.
—**mis·pro·nun·ci·a·tion** n.

**mis·quote** ▸v. quote wrongly.
—**mis·quo·ta·tion** n.

**mis·read** /misˈrēd/ ▸v. (*past* and *past part.* **-read** /-ˈred/) read or interpret (text, a situation, etc.) wrongly.

**mis·rep·re·sent** ▸v. represent wrongly; give a false or misleading account or idea of.
—**mis·rep·re·sen·ta·tion** n.

**mis·rule** /misˈro͞ol/ ▸n. bad government; disorder.
▸v. govern badly.

**Miss.** ▸abbr. Mississippi.

**miss** /mis/ ▸v. **1** fail to hit, reach, find, catch, see, meet, hear, etc. **2** fail to seize (an opportunity, etc.): *I missed my chance.* **3** notice or regret the loss or absence of. **4** avoid: *go early to miss the traffic.*

▸n. **1** failure to hit, reach, attain, connect, etc. **2** girl or unmarried woman. **3** (**Miss**) respectful title of an unmarried woman or girl.

**mis·sal** /ˈmisəl/ ▸n. book containing the texts used in Catholic Mass throughout the year.

**mis·shap·en** ▸adj. ill-shaped, deformed, distorted.

**mis·sile** /ˈmisəl/ ▸n. object or weapon suitable for throwing or propelling, esp. one directed by remote control or automatically.

**mis·sion** /ˈmisHən/ ▸n. **1** particular task or goal assigned to or assumed by a person or group. **2** military or scientific operation or expedition. **3** body of persons sent to conduct negotiations, etc., or to propagate a religious faith. **4** missionary post.

**mis·sion·ar·y** /ˈmisHəˌnerē/ ▸adj. of, concerned with, or characteristic of religious missions.

▶*n.* (*pl.* **-ies**) person doing missionary work.

**mis·sive** /'misiv/ ▶*n.* letter; message.

**mis·spell** ▶*v.* (*past* and *past part.* **-spelled** or **-spelt**) spell wrongly.

**mis·spend** ▶*v.* (*past* and *past part.* **-spent**) spend amiss or wastefully.

**mis·state** ▶*v.* state wrongly or inaccurately. —**mis·state·ment** *n.*

**mis·step** ▶*n.* **1** wrong step or action. **2** faux pas.

**mist** /mist/ ▶*n.* **1** water vapor near the ground in minute droplets limiting visibility. **2** condensed vapor obscuring glass, etc. **3** anything resembling or obscuring like mist. ▶*v.* cover or become covered with mist or as with mist. —**mist·y** *adj.*

**mis·take** /mə'stāk/ ▶*n.* **1** action or judgment that is misguided or wrong. **2** inaccuracy. ▶*v.* (*past* **mis·took**; *past part.* **mis·tak·en**) **1** misunderstand. **2** identify wrongly.

**mis·ter** /'mistər/ ▶*n.* title or form of address for a man.

**mis·tle·toe** /'misəl,tō/ ▶*n.* parasitic plant growing on apple and other trees and bearing white glutinous berries.

**mis·treat** ▶*v.* treat badly. —**mis·treat·ment** *n.*

**mis·tress** /'mistris/ ▶*n.* **1** female head of a household. **2** woman in authority. **3** woman (other than his wife) with whom a married man has a (usu. prolonged) sexual relationship.

**mis·tri·al** ▶*n.* trial rendered invalid by procedural error.

**mis·trust** ▶*v.* **1** be suspicious of. **2** feel no confidence in. ▶*n.* **1** suspicion. **2** lack of confidence.

**mis·un·der·stand** ▶*v.* (*past* and *past part.* **-un·der·stood**) **1** fail to understand correctly. **2** misinterpret. —**mis·un·der·stand·ing** *n.*

**mis·use** ▶*v.* /mis'yo͞oz/ **1** use wrongly; apply to the wrong purpose. **2** ill-treat. ▶*n.* /mis'yo͞os/ wrong or improper use or application.

**mite** /mīt/ ▶*n.* **1** small, often parasitic arachnid. **2** small sum of money. **3** small object or person.

**mi·ter** /'mītər/ ▶*n.* **1** tall, pointed, deeply cleft headdress worn by bishops and senior abbots as a symbol of office. **2** joint of two pieces of wood or other material at an angle of 90°.

▶ *v.* join with a miter. —**mi·tered** *adj.*

**mit·i·gate** /ˈmitəˌgāt/ ▶ *v.* make milder or less intense or severe: *your offer certainly mitigated their hostility.* —**mit·i·ga·tion** *n.*

**mi·to·sis** /mīˈtōsəs/ ▶ *n.* type of cell division that results in two nuclei each having the full number of chromosomes.

**mitt** /mit/ ▶ *n.* mitten.

**mit·ten** /ˈmitn/ ▶ *n.* glove with two sections, one for the thumb and the other for all four fingers.

**mix** /miks/ ▶ *v.* **1** combine; blend; put together. **2** be compatible.
▶ *n.* **1 a** mixing; mixture. **b** proportion of materials, etc., in a mixture. **2** ingredients prepared commercially for making a cake, concrete, etc. **3** merging of film pictures or sound.
□ **mix up 1** mix thoroughly. **2** confuse; mistake the identity of. □ **mix-up** confusion, misunderstanding, or mistake.

**mix·ol·o·gist** /mikˈsäləjist/ ▶ *n.* person who is skilled at mixing cocktails and other drinks.

**mix·ture** /ˈmiksCHər/ ▶ *n.* **1** process of mixing or being

mixed. **2** result of mixing; something mixed; combination of ingredients, qualities, characteristics, etc.

**ml** ▶ *abbr.* milliliter(s).

**mm** ▶ *abbr.* millimeter(s).

**MM.** ▶ *abbr.* Messieurs.

**MN** ▶ *abbr.* Minnesota (in official postal use).

**Mn** ▶ *symb. Chem.* manganese.

**mne·mon·ic** /nəˈmänik/ ▶ *adj.* of or designed to aid the memory.
▶ *n.* mnemonic device.

**MO** ▶ *abbr.* **1** Missouri (in official postal use). **2** money order.

**Mo** ▶ *symb. Chem.* molybdenum.

**Mo.** ▶ *abbr.* Missouri.

**moan** /mōn/ ▶ *n.* **1** long, low plaintive sound. **2** complaint; grievance.
▶ *v.* **1** make a moan or moans. **2** *inf.* complain or grumble: *he's always moaning about something.*

**moat** /mōt/ ▶ *n.* deep defensive ditch around a castle, town, etc., usu. filled with water.

**mob** /mäb/ ▶ *n.* disorderly crowd; rabble.
▶ *v.* (**mobbed, mob·bing**) crowd around in order to attack or admire.

**mo·bile** ▶ *adj.* /ˈmōbəl/
**1** movable; able to move easily.

**2** readily changing its expression. **3** (of a person) able to change his or her social status.

▸*n.* /ˈmōˌbēl/ decorative structure that may be hung so as to turn freely. **—mo·bil·i·ty** *n.*

□ **mobile home** transportable structure usu. parked and used as a residence.

**mo·bi·lize** /ˈmōbəˌlīz/ ▸*v.* organize or be organized for service or action (esp. troops in time of war). **—mo·bi·li·za·tion** *n.*

**Mö·bi·us strip** /ˈmōbēəs/ ▸*n.* surface with one continuous side formed by joining the ends of a rectangular strip after twisting one end through 180°.

**mob·ster** /ˈmäbstər/ ▸*n. inf.* gangster.

**moc·ca·sin** /ˈmäkəsin/ ▸*n.* soft, flat-soled leather slipper or shoe.

**mo·cha** /ˈmōkə/ ▸*n.* **1** coffee of fine quality. **2** beverage or flavoring made with this, often with chocolate added.

**mock** /mäk/ ▸*v.* **1** ridicule; scoff at. **2** mimic contemptuously.
▸*adj.* sham; imitation; pretended: *a large mock-Tudor house.*
**—mock·ing·ly** *adv.*
□ **mock-up** experimental model

or replica of a proposed structure, etc.

**mock·er·y** /ˈmäk(ə)rē/ ▸*n.* (*pl.* -ies) **1** derision; ridicule. **2** absurdly inadequate or futile action, etc.

**mock·ing·bird** ▸*n.* bird that mimics the notes of other birds.

**mode** /mōd/ ▸*n.* **1** way or manner in which a thing is done; method of procedure. **2** prevailing fashion or custom. **3** *Mus.* any of several types of scale.

**mod·el** /ˈmädl/ ▸*n.*
**1** representation in three dimensions of an existing person or thing or of a proposed structure, esp. on a smaller scale. **2** simplified description of a system, etc., to assist calculations and predictions. **3** particular design or style, esp. of a car. **4** exemplary person or thing. **5** person employed to pose for an artist or photographer or to display clothes, etc., by wearing them.
▸*v.* **1** fashion, shape, or form a model. **2 a** act or pose as a model. **b** display (a garment).

**mo·dem** /ˈmōdəm/ ▸*n.* device for transmitting data between computers, e.g., over a telephone line, cable, etc.

**mod·er·ate** ▸*adj.* /ˈmäd(ə)rit/ **1** avoiding extremes; temperate in conduct or expression. **2** fairly or tolerably large or good. **3** calm.
▸*n.* person who holds moderate views.
▸*v.* /ˈmädəˌrāt/ **1** make or become moderate. **2** act as a moderator of or to. —**mod·er·ate·ly** *adv.* —**mod·er·a·tion** *n.*

**mod·er·a·tor** /ˈmädəˌrātər/ ▸*n.* **1** arbitrator or mediator. **2** presiding officer, esp. of a debate.

**mod·ern** /ˈmädərn/ ▸*adj.* **1** of the present and recent times. **2** in current fashion; not antiquated.
▸*n.* person living in modern times. —**mo·der·ni·ty** *n.*

**mod·ern Eng·lish** ▸*n.* English from about 1500 onward.

**mod·ern·ism** ▸*n.* **1** modern ideas, methods, or practices. **2** style or movement in the arts that aims to break with classical and traditional forms. —**mod·ern·ist** *n.*

**mod·est** /ˈmädist/ ▸*adj.* **1** humble; not vain. **2** diffident; bashful; retiring. **3** decorous. **4** restrained; not excessive or

exaggerated; unpretentious. —**mod·est·ly** *adv.* —**mod·es·ty** *n.*

**mod·i·cum** /ˈmädikəm/ ▸*n.* small quantity.

**mod·i·fy** /ˈmädəˌfī/ ▸*v.* (**-fied**) **1** make less severe or extreme. **2** make partial changes in. **3** *Gram.* (esp. of an adjective) restrict or add to the sense of (a word, etc.). —**mod·i·fi·ca·tion** *n.*

**mod·ish** /ˈmōdisн/ ▸*adj.* fashionable; stylish.

**mod·u·late** /ˈmäjəˌlāt/ ▸*v.* **1 a** regulate or adjust. **b** moderate. **2** adjust or vary the tone or pitch of (the speaking voice). **3** alter the amplitude or frequency of (a wave). **4** change or cause to change from one musical key to another. —**mod·u·la·tion** *n.*

**mod·ule** /ˈmäjōōl/ ▸*n.* **1** standardized part or independent unit used in construction. **2** independent self-contained unit of a spacecraft. **3** unit or period of training or education. —**mod·u·lar** *adj.*

**mo·dus op·e·ran·di** /ˈmōdəs ˌäpəˈrandē/ ▸*n.* (*pl.* **mo·di op·e·ran·di** /ˈmōdī/) method of working.

**mo·gul** /'mōgəl/ ▸*n. inf.* important or influential person: *Hollywood mogul.*

**mo·hair** /'mō,he(ə)r/ ▸*n.* **1** hair of the angora goat. **2** yarn or fabric from this, either pure or mixed with wool or cotton.

**mo·hel** /moil; 'mō(h)el/ ▸*n.* person who performs the Jewish rite of circumcision.

**moi·re** /mô'rā/ ▸*n.* silk fabric that has been subjected to heat and pressure to give it a rippled effect.

**moist** /moist/ ▸*adj.* **1** slightly wet; damp. **2** (of the season, etc.) rainy. —**moist·en** *v.* —**moist·ly** *adv.* —**moist·ness** *n.*

**mois·ture** /'moischər/ ▸*n.* water or other liquid causing slight dampness.

**mois·tur·ize** ▸*v.* make less dry (esp. the skin by use of a cosmetic). —**mois·tur·iz·er** *n.*

**mo·lar** /'mōlər/ ▸*n.* back tooth with a broad top.

**mo·las·ses** /mə'lasiz/ ▸*n.* uncrystallized syrup extracted from raw sugar during refining.

**mold** /mōld/ ▸*n.* **1** hollow container into which a substance is poured or pressed to harden into a required shape. **2** something made in this way.

**3** distinctive style, form, or character. **4** woolly or furry growth of minute fungi occurring esp. in moist warm conditions.
▸*v.* **1** form into a particular shape or from certain ingredients. **2** influence the development of. —**mold·y** *adj.*

**mold·er** ▸*v.* decay to dust; deteriorate.

**mold·ing** ▸*n.* ornamentally shaped plaster or woodwork as an architectural feature.

**mole** /mōl/ ▸*n.* **1** small burrowing insect-eating mammal with dark velvety fur. **2** *inf.* spy established deep within an organization in a position of trust. **3** small often dark blemish on the skin.

**mol·e·cule** /'mälə,kyōōl/ ▸*n.* **1** smallest fundamental unit of an element or compound. **2** small particle. —**mo·lec·u·lar** *adj.*

**mole·hill** ▸*n.* small mound thrown up by a mole in burrowing.

**mole·skin** ▸*n.* **1** skin of a mole used as fur. **2** kind of cotton fustian with its surface shaved before dyeing.

**mo·lest** /mə'lest/ ▸*v.* **1** annoy or

pester in a hostile or injurious way. **2** attack or interfere with (a person), esp. sexually.
—**mo·les·ta·tion** *n.*
—**mo·lest·er** *n.*

**mol·li·fy** /'mälə,fī/ ▸*v.* (**-fied**) appease the anger or anxiety of (someone).

**mol·lusk** /'mäləsk/ ▸*n.* invertebrate with a soft body and usu. a hard shell, e.g., a snail or oyster.

**mol·ly·cod·dle** /'mälē,kädl/ ▸*v.* coddle; pamper.

**molt** /mōlt/ ▸*v.* shed feathers, hair, a shell, etc., in the process of renewing plumage, a coat, etc.

**mol·ten** /'mōltn/ ▸*adj.* melted, esp. made liquid by heat.

**mo·lyb·de·num** /mə'libdənəm/ ▸*n. Chem.* silver-white brittle metallic element used in steel. (Symb.: **Mb**)

**mom** /mäm/ ▸*n. inf.* mother.

**mo·ment** /'mōmənt/ ▸*n.* **1** very brief portion of time. **2** exact or particular point of time: *at last the moment arrived.*
**3** importance. **4** product of force and the distance from its line of action to a point.

**mo·men·tar·y** /'mōmən,terē/ ▸*adj.* lasting only a moment.
—**mo·men·tar·i·ly** *adv.*

**mo·men·tous** /mō'mentəs/ ▸*adj.* having great importance.
—**mo·men·tous·ly** *adv.*
—**mo·men·tous·ness** *n.*

**mo·men·tum** /mō'mentəm/ ▸*n.* (*pl.* **mo·men·ta**) **1** quantity of motion of a moving body, the product of its mass and velocity. **2** the impetus gained by movement. **3** strength or continuity derived from an initial effort.

**mom·my** /'mämē/ ▸*n.* (*pl.* **-mies**) *inf.* mother.

**Mon.** ▸*abbr.* Monday.

**mon·arch** /'mänərk/ ▸*n.* **1** ruler of a country, esp. hereditary, as a king, queen, etc. **2** large orange and black butterfly.
—**mo·nar·chic** *adj.*
—**mo·nar·chi·cal** *adj.*

**mon·ar·chy** /'mänərkē/ ▸*n.* (*pl.* **-chies**) **1** form of government with a monarch at the head. **2** a nation with this.

**mon·as·ter·y** /'mänə,sterē/ ▸*n.* (*pl.* **-ies**) residence of a religious community, esp. of monks living in seclusion.

**mo·nas·tic** /mə'nastik/ ▸*adj.* of, relating to, or resembling monks and nuns and their way of life.
▸*n.* follower of a monastic rule.

**Mon·day** /ˈməndā/ ▸n. second day of the week, following Sunday.

**mon·e·ta·rism** /ˈmänitəˌrizəm; ˈmən-/ ▸n. theory or practice of controlling the supply of money as the chief method of stabilizing the economy.

**mon·e·tar·y** /ˈmäniˌterē/ ▸adj. 1 of the currency in use. 2 of or consisting of money.
—**mon·e·tar·i·ly** adv.

**mon·ey** /ˈmənē/ ▸n. 1 current medium of exchange in the form of coins and paper currency. 2 wealth.

**mon·eyed** /ˈmənēd/ ▸adj. having much money; wealthy.

**mon·ey mar·ket** ▸n. trade in short-term stocks, loans, etc.

**mon·ey or·der** ▸n. order for payment of a specified sum, issued by a bank or post office.

**mon·ger** /ˈməNGgər/ ▸n. [in comb.] dealer; trader; promoter: warmonger.

**mon·goose** /ˈmänˌgo͞os/ ▸n. (pl. **mon·goos·es** or **mon·geese**) small flesh-eating civetlike mammal.

**mon·grel** /ˈmäNGgrəl/ ▸n. dog or other animal or plant of mixed breed.

▸adj. of mixed origin, nature, or character.

**mon·i·ker** /ˈmänikər/ (also **mon·ick·er**) ▸n. inf. name.

**mon·i·tor** /ˈmänitər/ ▸n. 1 any of various persons or devices for checking or warning about a situation, operation, etc. 2 school pupil with disciplinary or other special duties. 3 cathode-ray tube used as a television receiver or computer display device.
▸v. 1 act as a monitor of. 2 maintain regular surveillance over; check.

**mon·i·to·ry** /ˈmänəˌtôrē/ ▸adj. giving or serving as a warning.
▸n. (pl. **-ries**) (in church use) a letter of admonition from the pope or a bishop.

**monk** /məNGk/ ▸n. member of a religious community of men living under vows.

**mon·key** /ˈməNGkē/ ▸n. (pl. **-keys**) 1 any of various primates, including marmosets, baboons, apes, etc. 2 mischievous person, esp. a child: young monkey.
▸v. (pl. **-keys**, **-keyed**) tamper; fool around.

**mon·key busi·ness** ▸n. inf. mischief.

**mon·key wrench** ▸*n.* wrench with an adjustable jaw.

**mon·o** /'mänō/ *inf.* ▸*n.* infectious mononucleosis.
▸*adj.* monophonic.

**mono-** ▸*comb. form* one; alone; single: *monorail.*

**mon·o·chrome** ▸*n.* photograph or picture done in one color or different tones of this, or in black and white only.
▸*adj.* having or using only one color or in black and white only. —**mon·o·chro·mat·ic** *adj.*

**mon·o·cle** /'mänəkəl/ ▸*n.* single eyeglass.

**mon·o·coque** /'mänə,kōk; -,käk/ ▸*n.* aircraft or vehicle structure in which the chassis is integral with the body.

**mon·o·cot·y·le·don** /,mänə-,kätl'ēdn/ ▸*n.* any flowering plant with a single embryonic leaf. —**mon·o·cot·y·le·don·ous** *adj.*

**mon·oc·u·lar** /mə'näkyələr/ ▸*adj.* with or for one eye.

**mon·o·cul·ture** /'mänə,kəlcHər/ ▸*n.* cultivation of a single crop in a given area.

**mon·o·dy** /'mänədē/ ▸*n.* (*pl.* **-dies**) **1** ode sung by a single actor in a Greek tragedy. **2** poem lamenting a person's death. **3** music with only one melodic line.

**mo·nog·a·my** /mə'nägəmē/ ▸*n.* practice or state of being married to one person at a time. —**mo·nog·a·mist** *n.* —**mo·nog·a·mous** *adj.*

**mon·o·gram** /'mänə,gram/ ▸*n.* two or more letters, esp. a person's initials, interwoven as a device.

**mon·o·graph** ▸*n.* separate treatise on a single subject.

**mon·o·lith** /'mänl-iTH/ ▸*n.* **1** single block of stone, esp. shaped into a pillar or monument. **2** massive, immovable, or solidly uniform person or thing. —**mon·o·lith·ic** *adj.*

**mon·o·logue** /'mänl,ôg/ ▸*n.* long speech by one person.

**mon·o·ma·ni·a** /,mänə'mānēə/ ▸*n.* obsession of the mind by one idea or interest. —**mon·o·ma·ni·ac** *n. & adj.* —**mon·o·ma·ni·a·cal** *adj.*

**mon·o·nu·cle·o·sis** /,mänə-,n(y)ōōklē'ōsəs/ ▸*n.* infectious disease characterized by fever, swollen lymph nodes, and an abnormally high number of certain leukocytes in the blood.

**mon·o·phon·ic** ▸*adj.* using only one transmission channel for reproducing sound.

**mo·nop·o·ly** /məˈnäpəlē/ ▸*n.* (*pl.* **-lies**) **1 a** exclusive possession or control of the trade in a commodity or service. **b** this conferred as a privilege by the government. **2** commodity or service that is subject to a monopoly. —**mo·nop·o·lize** *v.*

**mon·o·rail** ▸*n.* railway with a single track.

**mon·o·so·di·um glu·ta·mate** /ˌmänəˌsōdēəm ˈglo̅o̅təˌmāt/ ▸*n. Chem.* white crystalline powder used to flavor food. (Abbr.: **MSG**).

**mon·o·syl·la·ble** ▸*n.* word of one syllable. —**mon·o·syl·lab·ic** *adj.*

**mon·o·the·ism** /ˈmänəˌTHē-ˌizəm/ ▸*n.* doctrine that there is only one God. —**mon·o·the·is·tic** *adj.*

**mon·o·tone** ▸*n.* **1** sound or utterance continuing or repeated on one note without change of pitch. **2** sameness of style in writing.
▸*adj.* without change of pitch.

**mo·not·o·ny** /məˈnätn-ē/ ▸*n.* **1** state of being monotonous.

**2** dull or tedious routine. —**mo·not·o·nous** *adj.*

**mon·o·treme** /ˈmänəˌtrēm/ ▸*n. Zool.* a primitive mammal that lays eggs and has a common opening for the urogenital and digestive systems. The platypus is a monotreme.

**Mon·sieur** /məsˈyœ(r)/ ▸*n.* (*pl.* **Mes·sieurs**) **1** French title corresponding to Mr. or sir. **2** Frenchman.

**Mon·si·gnor** /mänˈsēnyər/ ▸*n.* (*pl.* **-gnors** or **-gno·ri**) title of various Roman Catholic prelates, officers of the papal court, etc.

**mon·soon** /mänˈso̅o̅n/ ▸*n.* **1** seasonal wind in S. Asia, esp. in the Indian Ocean. **2** rainy season accompanying the summer monsoon.

**mon·ster** /ˈmänstər/ ▸*n.* **1** imaginary creature, usu. large and frightening. **2** inhumanly cruel or wicked person. **3** large, usu. ugly or misshapen animal or thing. **4** huge: *this is a monster of a book.*

**mon·strous** /ˈmänstrəs/ ▸*adj.* **1** like a monster; abnormally formed. **2** huge: *that is a monstrous waste of money.* **3 a** outrageously wrong or absurd. **b** atrocious.

—**mon·stros·i·ty** *n.*

—**mon·strous·ly** *adv.*

**Mont.** ▸*abbr.* Montana.

**mon·tage** /män'täzɥ/ ▸*n.*
**1** technique of producing a new composite whole from fragments of pictures, words, music, etc. **2** composition produced in this way.

**month** /mənɥ/ ▸*n.* **1 a** each of usu. twelve periods into which a year is divided. **b** period of time between the same dates in successive calendar months.
**2** period of 28 days or of four weeks.

**month·ly** ▸*adj.* done, produced, or occurring once a month.

▸*adv.* once a month; from month to month.

▸*n.* (*pl.* **-lies**) monthly periodical.

**mon·u·ment** /'mänyəmənt/ ▸*n.*
**1** anything enduring that serves to commemorate or make celebrated, esp. a structure or building. **2** ancient building or site. **3** typical or outstanding example: *a monument of indiscretion.*

**mon·u·men·tal** /ˌmänyə'mentl/ ▸*adj.* **1** extremely great; stupendous: *a monumental achievement.* **2** of or serving as a monument. —**mon·u·men·tal·ly** *adv.*

**moo** /moō/ ▸*v.* (**moos, mooed**) make the vocal sound of cattle; low.

▸*n.* (*pl.* **moos**) this sound.

**mooch** /moōcɥ/ *inf.* ▸*v.* beg; impose upon. —**mooch·er** *n.*

**mood** /moōd/ ▸*n.* **1** state of mind or feeling. **2** (**moods**) fits of melancholy or bad temper.
**3** *Gram.* form or set of forms of a verb serving to indicate whether it is to express fact, command, wish, etc.: *subjunctive mood.*

**mood·y** ▸*adj.* (**-i·er, -i·est**) given to changes of mood; gloomy; sullen. —**mood·i·ly** *adv.*
—**mood·i·ness** *n.*

**moon** /moōn/ ▸*n.* **1** the natural satellite of the earth, orbiting it monthly. **2** satellite of any planet.

▸*v.* behave dreamily or listlessly.
—**moon·less** *adj.*

**moon·light** ▸*n.* light of the moon.

▸*v.* (**-lighted**) *inf.* have two paid occupations, esp. one by day and one by night: *many instructors moonlight as professional consultants.*

**moon·shine** ▸*n.* **1** foolish talk or ideas. **2** *inf.* illicitly distilled or smuggled alcoholic liquor. **3** moonlight.

**moon·stone** ▸*n.* feldspar of pearly appearance.

**moon·y** /ˈmoonē/ ▸*adj.* (**moon·i·er, moon·i·est**) **1** dreamy and unaware of one's surroundings, for example because one is in love. **2** of or like the moon.

**Moor** /moor/ ▸*n.* member of a Muslim people inhabiting NW Africa. —**Moor·ish** *adj.*

**moor** /moor/ ▸*n.* tract of open uncultivated upland, esp. when covered with heather.
▸*v.* attach (a boat, buoy, etc.) to a fixed object.

**moor·ing** (often **moorings**) ▸*n.* **1** place where a boat, etc., is moored. **2** set of permanent anchors and chains laid down for ships to be moored to. **3** ideas, beliefs, etc., to which one is accustomed and from which one gains stability: *they have lost their spiritual moorings.*

**moose** /moos/ ▸*n.* (*pl.* same) largest variety of N. American deer.

**moot** /moot/ ▸*adj.* debatable; undecided.
▸*n. Law* discussion of a hypothetical case as an academic exercise.

**mop** /mäp/ ▸*n.* **1** wad or bundle of cotton or synthetic material fastened to the end of a stick, for cleaning floors, etc. **2** similarly shaped large or small implement for various purposes. **3** thick mass of hair.
▸*v.* (**mopped, mop·ping**) wipe or clean with or as with a mop.
□ **mop up** *inf.* finish a task.

**mope** /mōp/ ▸*v.* be gloomily depressed or listless; behave sulkily. —**mop·i·ness** *n.* —**mop·y** *adj.*

**mo·ped** /ˈmō,ped/ ▸*n.* lightweight motorized bicycle with pedals.

**mor·al** /ˈmôrəl/ ▸*adj.* **1 a** concerned with the distinction between right and wrong. **b** concerned with accepted rules and standards of human behavior. **2** virtuous; capable of moral action. **3** concerned with or leading to a psychological effect associated with confidence in a right action: *moral courage.*
▸*n.* **1** moral lesson (esp. at the end) of a fable, story, event, etc. **2** (**morals**) moral behavior, e.g.,

in sexual conduct. —**mor·al·ly** *adv.*

**mo·rale** /mə'ral/ ▸*n.* mental attitude or bearing of a person or group, esp. as regards confidence, discipline, etc.

**mo·ral·i·ty** /mə'ralətē/ ▸*n.* (*pl.* **-ties**) **1** degree of conformity to moral principles. **2** right moral conduct. **3** particular system of morals: *commercial morality.*

**mor·al·ize** /'môrə,līz/ ▸*v.* indulge in moral reflection or talk. —**mor·al·is·tic** *adj.*

**mo·rass** /mə'ras/ ▸*n.* **1** bog or marsh. **2** entanglement; disordered situation, esp. one impeding progress.

**mor·a·to·ri·um** /,môrə'tôrēəm/ ▸*n.* (*pl.* **-ri·ums** or **-ri·a**) temporary prohibition or suspension (of an activity).

**mor·bid** /'môrbid/ ▸*adj.* **1** unwholesome; macabre. **2** *Med.* of the nature of or indicative of disease. —**mor·bid·i·ty** *n.*

**mor·da·cious** /môr'dāsʜəs/ ▸*adj.* **1** denoting or using biting sarcasm or invective. **2** (of a person or animal) given to biting.

**mor·dant** /'môrdnt/ ▸*adj.* **1** caustic; biting: *he has a mordant sense of humor.* **2** serving to fix dye. —**mor·dant·ly** *adv.*

**more** /môr/ ▸*adj.* greater in quantity or degree; additional.
▸*n.* greater quantity, number, or amount.
▸*adv.* **1** to a greater degree or extent. **2** forming the comparative of some adjectives and adverbs.
□ **more or less 1** in a greater or less degree. **2** approximately; as an estimate.

**more·o·ver** ▸*adv.* further; besides.

**mo·res** /'môr,āz/ ▸*pl. n.* customs or conventions regarded as essential to or characteristic of a community.

**mor·ga·nat·ic** /,môrgə'natik/ ▸*adj.* of or denoting a marriage in which neither the spouse of lower rank nor any children have any claim to the possessions or title of the spouse of higher rank.

**morgue** /môrg/ ▸*n.* **1** place where bodies are kept, esp. to be identified or claimed. **2** (in a newspaper office, etc.) room or file of miscellaneous information.

**mor·i·bund** /'môrə,bənd/ ▸*adj.*

**1** at the point of death.
**2** lacking vitality.

**morn** /môrn/ ▶*n. poet.* morning.

**morn·ing** /'môrniNG/ ▶*n.* early part of the day, esp. from sunrise to noon.

**morn·ing glo·ry** ▶*n.* twining plant with trumpet-shaped flowers that open in the morning.

**morn·ing sick·ness** ▶*n.* nausea felt in the morning during pregnancy.

**mo·roc·co** /məˈräkō/ ▶*n. (pl.* **-cos**) fine flexible leather made (orig. in Morocco) from goatskins tanned with sumac.

**mo·ron** /'môrän/ ▶*n. inf.* stupid person. —**mo·ron·ic** *adj.*

**mo·rose** /məˈrōs/ ▶*adj.* sullen and ill-tempered. —**mo·rose·ly** *adv.*

**mor·pheme** /'môr,fēm/ ▶*n.* smallest meaningful morphological unit of a language.

**mor·phine** /'môr,fēn/ ▶*n.* narcotic drug from opium used to relieve pain.

**mor·phol·o·gy** /môrˈfäləjē/ ▶*n.* the study of the forms or structures of things. —**mor·pho·log·i·cal** *adj.* —**mor·phol·o·gist** *n.*

**mor·sel** /'môrsəl/ ▶*n.* mouthful; small piece (esp. of food).

**mor·tal** /'môrtl/ ▶*adj.* **1** subject to death. **2** causing death; fatal. **3** intense; very serious; implacable. ▶*n.* human being. —**mor·tal·ly** *adv.*

**mor·tal·i·ty** /môrˈtalitē/ ▶*n. (pl.* **-ties**) **1** being subject to death. **2** loss of life on a large scale. **3** death rate.

**mor·tar** /'môrtər/ ▶*n.* **1** mixture of lime with cement, sand, and water, used in building to bond bricks or stones. **2** short large-bore cannon for firing shells at high angles. **3** vessel in which ingredients are pounded with a pestle.

**mor·tar·board** ▶*n.* **1** academic cap with a stiff, flat square top. **2** flat board for holding mortar.

**mort·gage** /'môrgij/ ▶*n.* **1** conveyance of property to a creditor as security for a debt. **2 a** debt secured by a mortgage. **b** loan resulting in such a debt. ▶*v.* convey (a property) by mortgage.

**mor·ti·cian** /môrˈtiSHən/ ▶*n.* UNDERTAKER.

**mor·ti·fy** /'môrtə,fī/ ▶*v.* (**-fied**) **1** shame; humiliate. **2** bring (the flesh, the passions, etc.) into

subjection by discipline.
—**mor·ti·fi·ca·tion** n.
—**mor·ti·fy·ing** adj.

**mor·tise** /ˈmôrtis/ ▶n. hole in a framework designed to receive another part, esp. a tenon.

**mor·tu·ar·y** /ˈmôrCHŌŌˌerē/ ▶n. (pl. **-ies**) room or building in which dead bodies may be kept until burial or cremation.
▶adj. of or concerning death or burial.

**Mo·sa·ic** /mōˈzāik/ ▶adj. of Moses (in the Old Testament).

**mo·sa·ic** ▶n. picture or pattern produced by an arrangement of small variously colored pieces of glass or stone, etc.

**mo·sey** /ˈmōzē/ ▶v. (**-seys**, **-seyed**) inf. (**mosey along**) walk in a leisurely or aimless manner.

**Mos·lem** /ˈmäzləm/ ▶var. of MUSLIM.

**mosque** /mäsk/ ▶n. Muslim place of worship.

**mos·qui·to** /məˈskētō/ ▶n. (pl. **-toes** or **-tos**) insect, the female of which sucks the blood of humans and other animals.

**moss** /môs/ ▶n. small, flowerless plant growing in dense clusters on the surface of the ground, in bogs, on trees, on stones, etc.
—**moss·y** adj.

**most** /mōst/ ▶adj. 1 existing in the greatest quantity or degree. 2 the majority of.
▶n. 1 greatest quantity or number. 2 the majority.
▶adv. 1 in the highest degree. 2 forming the superlative of some adjectives and adverbs. 3 inf. almost: *most everyone understood.*

**-most** ▶suffix forming superlative adjectives and adverbs from prepositions and other words indicating relative position: *foremost | uttermost.*

**most·ly** ▶adv. 1 as regards the greater part. 2 usually.

**mote** /mōt/ ▶n. speck of dust.

**mo·tel** /mōˈtel/ ▶n. roadside hotel for motorists.

**moth** /môTH/ ▶n. 1 nocturnal insect having a stout body and without clubbed antennae. 2 small insect of this type, the larva of which feeds on cloth, etc.

**moth·ball** /ˈmôTHˌbôl/ ▶n. ball of camphor, naphthalene, etc., placed in stored clothes to keep away moths.

**moth·er** /ˈməTHər/ ▶n. 1 female parent. 2 quality or condition, etc., that gives rise to another.

**3** (also **Moth·er Su·pe·ri·or**) head of a female religious community. ▸*v.* act as a mother. —**moth·er·hood** *n.* —**moth·er·less** *adj.* □ **mother-in-law** mother of one's husband or wife.

**moth·er·land** ▸*n.* native country.

**moth·er-of-pearl** ▸*n.* smooth iridescent inner layer of the shell of some mollusks.

**mo·tif** /mō'tēf/ ▸*n.* **1** distinctive feature or dominant idea in an artistic or literary composition. **2** short succession of musical notes producing a single impression, out of which longer passages are developed.

**mo·tile** /'mōtl/ ▸*adj.* capable of motion. —**mo·til·i·ty** *n.*

**mo·tion** /'mōSHən/ ▸*n.* **1** moving; changing position. **2** gesture. **3** formal proposal put to a committee, legislature, etc. ▸*v.* **1** direct (a person) by a sign or gesture. **2** make a gesture directing: *motioned to me to leave.* —**mo·tion·less** *adj.*

**mo·tion pic·ture** ▸*n.* movie.

**mo·ti·vate** /'mōtə,vāt/ ▸*v.* **1** supply a motive to; be the motive of. **2** stimulate the interest of (a person in an activity). —**mo·ti·va·tion** *n.* —**mo·ti·va·tion·al** *adj.*

**mo·tive** /'mōtiv/ ▸*n.* **1** factor or circumstance that induces a person to act in a particular way. **2** MOTIF. ▸*adj.* causing or concerned with movement.

**mot·ley** /'mätlē/ ▸*adj.* (**-li·er, -li·est**) **1** diversified in color. **2** of varied character: *a motley crew.*

**mo·tor** /'mōtər/ ▸*n.* **1** thing that imparts motion. **2** engine, esp. one using electricity or internal combustion. ▸*adj.* **1** giving, imparting, or producing motion. **2** driven by a motor. **3** of or for motor vehicles. **4** relating to muscular movement or the nerves activating it.

**mo·tor·bike** ▸*n.* **1** lightweight motorcycle. **2** motorized bicycle.

**mo·tor·boat** ▸*n.* recreational boat powered by a motor.

**mo·tor·cade** /'mōtər,kād/ ▸*n.* procession of motor vehicles.

**mo·tor·cy·cle** ▸*n.* two-wheeled motor-driven road vehicle without pedal propulsion. —**mo·tor·cy·clist** *n.*

**mo·tor·ist** ▸*n.* driver of an automobile.

**mo·tor·ize** ▸*v.* **1** provide with a motor. **2** equip (troops, etc.) with motor transport.

**mot·tle** /ˈmätl/ ▸*v.* [usu. as *adj.* **mottled**] mark with spots or smears of color.

**mot·to** /ˈmätō/ ▸*n.* (*pl.* **-toes** or **-tos**) maxim adopted as a rule of conduct, etc.

**moue** /mo͞o/ ▸*n.* pouting expression used to convey annoyance or distaste.

**mound** /mound/ ▸*n.* heap or pile of earth, stones, etc.

**mount** /mount/ ▸*v.* **1** ascend; climb on. **2** set on horseback. **3** increase; accumulate. **4** place (an object) on a support or in a backing, frame, etc. **5** arrange; organize; set in motion. ▸*n.* **1** backing, setting, or other support on which a picture, etc., is set for display. **2** horse for riding. **3** mountain; hill: *Mount Everest | Mount of Olives.*

**moun·tain** /ˈmountn/ ▸*n.* **1** large natural elevation of the earth's surface. **2** large heap or pile; huge quantity. —**moun·tain·ous** *adj.*

**moun·tain bike** ▸*n.* bicycle with a light sturdy frame for riding on mountainous terrain.

**moun·tain·eer** /ˌmountnˈi(ə)r/ ▸*n.* person skilled in mountain climbing.

**moun·tain goat** ▸*n.* white goatlike animal of the Rocky Mountains, etc.

**moun·tain li·on** ▸*n.* large American wildcat; cougar; puma.

**moun·tain range** ▸*n.* line of mountains connected by high ground.

**moun·te·bank** /ˈmounti‚baNGk/ ▸*n.* swindler; charlatan.

**mourn** /môrn/ ▸*v.* feel or show deep sorrow or regret for (a dead person, a lost thing, etc.). —**mourn·er** *n.* —**mourn·ful** *adj.* —**mourn·ful·ly** *adv.*

**mouse** /mous/ ▸*n.* (*pl.* **mice**) **1** common small rodent. **2** timid or feeble person. **3** *Computing* small hand-held device that controls the cursor on a computer monitor.

**mousse** /mo͞os/ ▸*n.* **1 a** dessert of whipped cream, eggs, etc., usu. flavored with fruit or chocolate. **b** meat or fish purée made with whipped cream, etc. **2** preparation applied to the hair enabling it to be styled more easily.

**mous·tache** /ˈməs‚tasH/ ▸var. of **MUSTACHE**.

**mous·y** /ˈmousē/ ▸*adj.* (**-i·er,**

-i·est) **1** of or like a mouse. **2** shy or timid; ineffectual. **3** nondescript light brown.

**mouth** /mouᴛʜ/ ▸*n.* (*pl.* **mouths**) **1** external opening in the head, through which most animals admit food and emit communicative sounds. **2** opening of a container, cave, trumpet, etc. **3** place where a river enters the sea. ▸*v.* **1** utter or speak solemnly or with affectations; rant; declaim. **2** form words silently with the lips.

**mouth·piece** ▸*n.* part of a musical instrument, telephone, etc. placed next to or near the mouth.

**mouth·wash** ▸*n.* liquid antiseptic, etc., for rinsing the mouth or gargling.

**mouth·wa·ter·ing** ▸*adj.* having a delicious smell or appearance.

**move** /mo͞ov/ ▸*v.* **1** change one's position, posture, or place, or cause to do this. **2** put or keep in motion; rouse; stir. **3** go; proceed; make progress. **4** affect (a person) with emotion. **5** stimulate; provoke; prompt or incline. **6** propose in a meeting, deliberative assembly, etc. ▸*n.* **1** act or instance of moving.

**2** change of house, business premises, etc. **3** step taken to secure some action or effect; initiative. **4** the changing of the position of a piece in a board game. —**mov·a·ble** *adj.*

**move·ment** ▸*n.* **1** moving or being moved. **2** moving parts of a mechanism (esp. a clock or watch). **3** body of persons with a common object. **4** (usu. **movements**) person's activities and whereabouts, esp. at a particular time. **5** principal division of a longer musical work.

**mov·ie** /'mo͞ovē/ ▸story or event recorded by a camera as a set of moving images and shown on a screen in a theater; motion picture.

**mow** /mō/ ▸*v.* (*past part.* **mowed** or **mown**) cut down (grass, hay, etc.) with a scythe or machine. —**mow·er** *n.*

**mox·ie** /'mäksē/ ▸*n.* force of character, determination, or nerve.

**MP** ▸*abbr.* **1** military police. **2** Member of Parliament.

**m.p.h.** ▸*abbr.* miles per hour.

**Mr.** /'mistər/ ▸*n.* (*pl.* **Messrs.**) **1** title for a man. **2** title prefixed to a designation of office, etc.: *Mr. President.*

**MRI** ▶*abbr.* magnetic resonance imaging.

**Mrs.** /'misiz/ ▶*n.* (*pl.* same or **Mes·dames**) title for a married woman.

**MS** ▶*abbr.* **1** Mississippi (in official postal use). **2** Master of Science. **3** multiple sclerosis. **4** (also **ms.**) manuscript.

**Ms.** /miz/ ▶*n.* title for a married or unmarried woman.

**MSG** ▶*abbr.* monosodium glutamate.

**MT** ▶*abbr.* Montana (in official postal use).

**Mt** ▶*abbr.* meitnerium.

**Mt.** ▶*abbr.* **1** mount. **2** mountain.

**much** /məCH/ ▶*adj.* existing or occurring in a great quantity.

▶*n.* **1** great quantity. **2** noteworthy or outstanding example: *not much to look at.*

▶*adv.* **1** in a great degree. **2** for a large part of one's time: *is much away from home.*

**mu·ci·lage** /'myo͞os(ə)lij/ ▶*n.* **1** viscous substance obtained from plants. **2** adhesive gum; glue. —**mu·ci·lag·i·nous** *adj.*

**muck** /mək/ ▶*n.* **1** farmyard manure. **2** *inf.* dirt or filth; anything disgusting.

▶*v.* **1** (**muck out**) clean (a stable). **2** *inf.* (**muck up**) bungle (a job). **3** make dirty or untidy. —**muck·y** *adj.*

**muck·rake** ▶*v.* search out and reveal scandal. —**muck·rak·er** *n.* —**muck·rak·ing** *n.*

**muck·rak·ing** /'mək,rākiNG/ ▶*n.* action of searching out and publicizing scandalous information about famous people in an underhanded way.

**mu·cous** /'myo͞okəs/ ▶*adj.* of or covered with mucus. —**mu·cos·i·ty** *n.*

□ **mucous membrane** mucus-secreting epithelial tissue lining many body cavities and tubular organs.

**mu·cus** /'myo͞okəs/ ▶*n.* **1** slimy substance secreted by a mucous membrane. **2** gummy substance found in all plants.

**mud** /məd/ ▶*n.* wet, soft, earthy matter.

□ **fling** (or **sling** or **throw**) **mud** speak disparagingly or slanderously.

**mud·dle** /'mədl/ ▶*v.* **1** bring into disorder. **2** bewilder; confuse.

▶*n.* **1** disorder. **2** muddled condition.

**mu·ez·zin** /m(y)oo'ezin/ ▶*n.* Muslim crier who proclaims the hours of prayer, usu. from a minaret.

**muff** /məf/ ▶*n.* tube made of fur or other material for keeping the hands warm.
▶*v. inf.* **1** handle (a situation) clumsily or badly. **2** miss (a catch, ball, etc.).

**muf·fin** /'məfin/ ▶*n.* small cake or quick bread made from batter or dough and baked in a muffin pan.

**muf·fle** /'məfəl/ ▶*v.* **1** wrap or cover for warmth or to deaden sound. **2** [usu. as *adj.* **muffled**] stifle (an utterance, e.g., a curse). **3** prevent from speaking.

**muf·fler** ▶*n.* **1** wrap or scarf worn for warmth. **2** noise-reducing device on a motor vehicle's exhaust system.

**muf·ti** /'məftē/ ▶*n.* civilian clothes: *in mufti.*

**mug** /məg/ ▶*n.* drinking vessel, usu. cylindrical with a handle.
▶*v.* (**mugged**, **mug·ging**) **1** rob (a person) with violence, esp. in a public place. **2** *inf.* make faces, esp. before an audience, a camera, etc. —**mug·ger** *n.* —**mug·ging** *n.*
□ **mug shot** *inf.* photograph of a face for official purposes, esp. police records.

**mug·gy** /'məgē/ ▶*adj.* (**-gi·er**, **-gi·est**) oppressively damp and warm; humid. —**mug·gi·ness** *n.*

**mu·lat·to** /m(y)oo'lätō/ ▶*n.* (*pl.* **-toes** or **-tos**) person of mixed white and black parentage.

**mul·ber·ry** /'məl,berē/ ▶*n.* (*pl.* **-ries**) **1** deciduous tree bearing edible dark-red or white berries. **2** its fruit. **3** dark-red or purple color.

**mulch** /məlCH/ ▶*n.* mixture of straw, leaves, etc., spread around or over a plant to enrich or insulate the soil.
▶*v.* treat with mulch.

**mule** /myool/ ▶*n.* **1** offspring (usu. sterile) of a male donkey and a female horse. **2** stupid or obstinate person. **3** light shoe or slipper without a back. —**mul·ish** *adj.* —**mul·ish·ly** *adv.* —**mul·ish·ness** *n.*

**mu·li·eb·ri·ty** /ˌmyoolē'ebrətē/ ▶*n.* womanly qualities; womanhood.

**mull** /məl/ ▶*v.* **1** ponder or consider: *I'd like to mull it over for a while.* **2** warm (wine or cider, etc.) with added sugar, spices, etc.

**mul·lah** /'moolə; 'moolə/ ▶*n.*

Muslim learned in Islamic theology and sacred law.

**mul·let** /ˈməlit/ ▶*n.* any of several kinds of marine fish commonly used as food.

**mul·li·ga·taw·ny** /ˌməligəˈtônē/ ▶*n.* highly seasoned soup orig. from India.

**mul·lion** /ˈməlyən/ ▶*n.* vertical bar dividing the panes in a window. —**mul·lioned** *adj.*

**multi-** /ˈməltē; -tī/ ▶*comb. form* many; more than one.

**mul·ti·cul·tur·al** ▶*adj.* of or involving several cultural or ethnic groups.

**mul·ti·far·i·ous** /ˌməltiˈfe(ə)rēəs/ ▶*adj.* **1** many and various. **2** diverse. —**mul·ti·far·i·ous·ly** *adv.* —**mul·ti·far·i·ous·ness** *n.*

**mul·ti·me·di·a** ▶*adj.* involving several media.

▶*n.* combined use of several media, such as film, print, sound, etc.

**mul·ti·na·tion·al** ▶*adj.* **1** operating in several countries. **2** of several nationalities or ethnic groups.

▶*n.* multinational company.

**mul·ti·ple** /ˈməltəpəl/ ▶*adj.* **1** having several or many parts, elements, or individual components. **2** many and various.

▶*n.* number that contains another without a remainder: *56 is a multiple of 7.*

☐ **multiple-choice** (of a question in an examination) accompanied by several possible answers from which the correct one has to be chosen.

**mul·ti·ple scle·ro·sis** ▶*n.* chronic, progressive disease involving damage to the sheaths of nerve cells in the brain and spinal cord.

**mul·ti·plic·i·ty** /ˌməltəˈplisitē/ ▶*n.* (*pl.* **-ties**) **1** manifold variety. **2** great number.

**mul·ti·ply** /ˈməltəˌplī/ ▶*v.* (**-plied**) **1** obtain from (a number) another that is a specified number of times its value: *multiply 6 by 4.* **2** increase in number.

**mul·ti·task·ing** /ˌməltiˈtaskiNG; ˌməltī-/ ▶*n.* **1** simultaneous execution of more than one program or task by a single computer processor. **2** handling of more than one task at the same time by a single person.

**mul·ti·tude** /ˈməltiˌt(y)o͞od/ ▶*n.* great number; crowd.

**mul·ti·tu·di·nous** /ˌməlti-

't(y)o͞odn-əs/ ▸*adj.* **1** very numerous. **2** consisting of many individuals or elements.

**mum** /məm/ ▸*adj. inf.* silent: *keep mum.*
▸*n.* chrysanthemum.
☐ **mum's the word** say nothing.

**mum·ble** /'məmbəl/ ▸*v.* speak or utter indistinctly.
▸*n.* indistinct utterance.

**mum·bo jum·bo** /'məmbō 'jəmbō/ ▸*n.* (*pl.* **jum·bos**) *inf.* meaningless or ignorant ritual or language.

**mum·mer** /'məmər/ ▸*n.* actor in a traditional mime.

**mum·my** /'məmē/ ▸*n.* (*pl.* **-mies**) body of a human being or animal embalmed for burial, esp. in ancient Egypt.

**mumps** /məmps/ ▸*n.* infectious viral disease with swelling of the neck and face.

**munch** /mənCH/ ▸*v.* eat steadily with a marked action of the jaws.

**mun·dane** /ˌmən'dān/ ▸*adj.* **1** dull; routine. **2** of this world; worldly.

**mu·nic·i·pal** /myo͞o'nisəpəl/ ▸*adj.* of or concerning a municipality or its self-government.
—**mu·nic·i·pal·ly** *adv.*

**mu·nic·i·pal bond** ▸*n.* bond issued by a city, county, state, etc., to finance public projects.

**mu·nic·i·pal·i·ty** /myo͞oˌnisə-'palətē/ ▸*n.* (*pl.* **-ties**) town or district having local government.

**mu·nif·i·cent** /myo͞o'nifəsənt/ ▸*adj.* splendidly generous; bountiful. —**mu·nif·i·cence** *n.*

**mu·ni·ment** /'myo͞onəmənt/ ▸*n.* (usu. **muniments**) document or record, esp. one kept in an archive.

**mu·ni·tion** /myo͞o'nisHən; myə-/ ▸*pl. n.* (**munitions**) military weapons, ammunition, equipment, and stores.
▸*v.* supply with munitions.

**mu·ral** /'myo͞orəl/ ▸*n.* painting executed directly on a wall.
▸*adj.* of, like, or on a wall.
—**mu·ral·ist** *n.*

**mur·der** /'mərdər/ ▸*n.* **1** unlawful premeditated killing of a human being by another. **2** *inf.* unpleasant, troublesome, or dangerous state of affairs.
▸*v.* **1** kill (a human being) intentionally and unlawfully. **2** *inf.* utterly defeat or spoil by a bad performance, mispronunciation, etc.
—**mur·der·er** *n.*

**murk** /mərk/ ▸*n.* darkness; poor visibility.

**murk·y** ▸*adj.* (**-i·er, -i·est**) **1** dark; gloomy. **2** (of darkness) thick; dirty. **3** suspiciously obscure; shady: *murky past.* —**murk·i·ly** *adv.* —**murk·i·ness** *n.*

**mur·mur** /ˈmərmər/ ▸*n.* **1** subdued continuous sound, as made by waves, a brook, etc. **2** softly spoken or nearly inarticulate utterance. ▸*v.* **1** make a murmur. **2** utter (words) in a low voice, esp. as a complaint.

**mur·rain** /ˈmərən/ ▸*n.* **1** infectious disease affecting cattle or other animals. **2** plague, epidemic, or crop blight.

**mus·cat** /ˈmesˌkät/ (also **mus·ca·tel**) ▸*n.* sweet fortified white wine made from musk-flavored grapes.

**mus·cle** /ˈməsəl/ ▸*n.* **1** fibrous tissue with the ability to contract, producing movement in or maintaining the position of an animal body. **2** physical power or strength. ▸*v. inf.* force oneself on others; intrude: *muscling his way into meetings.* □ **muscle-bound** with muscles stiff and inelastic through excessive exercise or training.

**Muse** /myōōz/ ▸*n.* (in Greek and Roman mythology) one of the nine goddesses, the daughters of Zeus and Mnemosyne, who inspire poetry, music, drama, etc.

**muse** ▸*v.* ponder; reflect.

**mu·se·um** /myōōˈzēəm/ ▸*n.* building used for storing and exhibiting objects of historical, scientific, or cultural interest.

**mush** /məsH/ ▸*n.* **1** soft pulp. **2** feeble sentimentality. **3** boiled cornmeal dish. ▸*v.* **1** used as a command to encourage sled dogs. **2** travel across snow with a dogsled. —**mush·y** *adj.* —**mush·i·ly** *adv.* —**mush·i·ness** *n.*

**mush·room** /ˈməsHˌrōōm/ ▸*n.* edible fungus with a stem and domed cap. ▸*v.* appear or develop rapidly.

**mu·sic** /ˈmyōōzik/ ▸*n.* **1** art of combining vocal or instrumental sounds (or both) to produce beauty of form, harmony, and expression of emotion. **2** sounds so produced. **3** musical compositions. **4** pleasant natural sounds.

**mu·si·cal** ▸*adj.* **1** of or relating to music. **2** melodious;

harmonious. **3** fond of or skilled in music.
▶*n.* movie or drama that features songs.

**mu·si·cian** /myoŏ'zisHən/ ▶*n.* person skilled in music.

**mu·si·col·o·gy** /ˌmyoŏzi'käləjē/ ▶*n.* the academic study of music. —**mu·si·col·o·gist** *n.*

**musk** /məsk/ ▶*n.* substance produced by a gland in the male of an Asian deer and used as an ingredient in perfumes. —**musk·y** *adj.* —**musk·i·ness** *n.*

**mus·ket** /'məskit/ ▶*n.* smooth-bored light gun.

**mus·ket·eer** /ˌməski'ti(ə)r/ ▶*n.* *hist.* soldier armed with a musket.

**musk ox** ▶*n.* shaggy goat-antelope native to N. America.

**musk·rat** ▶*n.* large aquatic rodent native to N. America, having a musky smell.

**Mus·lim** /'məzlim/ (also **Mos·lem**) ▶*n.* follower of the Islamic religion.
▶*adj.* of or relating to the Muslims or their religion.

**mus·lin** /'məzlin/ ▶*n.* strong, woven cotton fabric.

**muss** /məs/ ▶*v. inf.* make someone's hair or clothes untidy.

**mus·sel** /'məsəl/ ▶*n.* bivalve mollusk often used for food.

**must** /məst/ ▶*aux. v.* (*3rd sing. present* **must**; *past* **had to** or (in indirect speech) **must**) **1** be obliged to. **2** be certain to. **3** ought to.
▶*n. inf.* thing that should not be missed.

**mus·tache** /'məs,tasH/ (also **mous·tache**) ▶*n.* hair left to grow on a man's upper lip.

**mus·tang** /'məs,taNG/ ▶*n.* small wild horse native to Mexico and California.

**mus·tard** /'məstərd/ ▶*n.* **1** plant with slender pods and yellow flowers. **2** seeds of this which are crushed, made into a paste, and used as a spicy condiment. **3** brownish-yellow color.

**mus·tard gas** ▶*n.* colorless oily liquid whose vapor is a powerful irritant.

**mus·ter** /'məstər/ ▶*v.* **1** summon. **2** collect; gather together.
□ **pass muster** be accepted as adequate.

**mus·ty** /'məstē/ ▶*adj.* (**-ti·er**, **-ti·est**) **1** moldy; stale. **2** lacking originality. —**must·i·ness** *n.*

**mu·ta·ble** /'myoŏtəbəl/ ▶*adj.* liable to change. —**mu·ta·bil·i·ty** *n.*

**mu·tant** /'myo͞otnt/ ▸*adj.* resulting from mutation. ▸*n.* mutant form.

**mu·ta·tion** /myo͞o'tāsʜən/ ▸*n.* **1** change; alteration. **2** genetic, heritable change. **3** mutant. —**mu·tate** *v.*

**mu·ta·tis mu·tan·dis** /m(y)o͞o'tātəs m(y)o͞o'tändəs; -'tātəs; -'tandəs/ ▸*adv.* (used when comparing two or more cases or situations) making necessary alterations while not affecting the main point at issue.

**mute** /myo͞ot/ ▸*adj.* **1** silent; refraining from speech. **2** (of a person or animal) dumb; speechless. ▸*n.* **1** dumb person: *a deaf mute.* **2** device for damping the sound of a musical instrument. ▸*v.* **1** deaden, muffle, or soften the sound, color, etc., of. **2** [as *adj.* **muted**] subdue.

**mu·ti·late** /'myo͞otl,āt/ ▸*v.* disfigure or destroy, esp. by cutting. —**mu·ti·la·tion** *n.*

**mu·ti·ny** /'myo͞otn-ē/ ▸*n.* (*pl.* -**nies**) open revolt, esp. by soldiers or sailors against their officers. ▸*v.* (-**nied**) revolt; engage in mutiny. —**mu·ti·neer** *n.* —**mu·ti·nous** *adj.*

**mutt** /mət/ ▸*n.* dog, esp. a mongrel.

**mut·ter** /'mətər/ ▸*v.* speak low in a barely audible manner. ▸*n.* muttered words or sounds.

**mut·ton** /'mətn/ ▸*n.* flesh of sheep as food.

**mu·tu·al** /'myo͞ocʜo͞oəl/ ▸*adj.* **1** (of feelings, actions, etc.) experienced or done by each of two or more parties with reference to the other or others: *mutual affection.* **2** held in common by two or more persons. —**mu·tu·al·ly** *adv.*

**mu·tu·al fund** ▸*n.* investment program funded by shareholders that trades in diversified holdings and is professionally managed.

**muz·zle** /'məzəl/ ▸*n.* **1** projecting part of an animal's face, including the nose and mouth. **2** guard fitted over an animal's nose and mouth to stop it from biting or feeding. **3** open end of a firearm. ▸*v.* **1** put a muzzle on. **2** impose silence upon.

**my** /mī/ ▸*pron.* of or belonging to me.

**my·col·o·gy** /mī'käləjē/ ▸*n.* **1** the study of fungi. **2** fungi of a particular region.

—**my·co·log·i·cal** *adj.*

—**my·col·o·gist** *n.*

**my·ol·o·gy** /mī'äləjē/ ▶*n.* study of the structure, arrangement, and action of muscles.

**my·o·pia** /mī'ōpēə/ ▶*n.* **1** nearsightedness. **2** lack of imagination or intellectual insight. —**my·op·ic** *adj.*

**myr·i·ad** /'mirēəd/ ▶*n.* indefinitely great number. ▶*adj.* of an indefinitely great number.

**myrrh** /mər/ ▶*n.* gum resin used, esp. in the Near East, in perfumery, incense, etc.

**myr·tle** /'mərtl/ ▶*n.* **1** evergreen shrub with aromatic foliage and white flowers. **2** PERIWINKLE.

**my·self** ▶*pron.* **1** emphatic form of I or ME: *I saw it myself.* **2** reflexive form of ME: *I was angry with myself.*

**mys·ta·gogue** /'mistə,gäg/ ▶*n.* teacher or propounder of mystical doctrines.

**mys·ter·y** /'mist(ə)rē/ ▶*n.* (*pl.* -**ies**) **1** secret, hidden, or inexplicable matter: *the reason remains a mystery.* **2** secrecy or obscurity: *wrapped in mystery.* **3** (also **mystery story**) fictional work dealing with a puzzling event, esp. a crime.

**mys·tic** /'mistik/ ▶*n.* person who seeks spiritual truths or experiences. —**mys·ti·cism** *n.*

**mys·ti·cal** ▶*adj.* **1** of mystics or mysticism. **2** inspiring a sense of spiritual mystery and awe.

**mys·ti·fy** /'mistə,fī/ ▶*v.* (-**fied**) **1** bewilder; confuse. **2** wrap up in mystery.

**mys·tique** /mis'tēk/ ▶*n.* atmosphere of mystery and veneration attending some activity or person.

**myth** /miTH/ ▶*n.* **1** traditional narrative usu. involving supernatural or imaginary persons and embodying popular ideas on natural or social phenomena, etc. **2** widely held but false notion. **3** fictitious person, thing, or idea. —**myth·i·cal** *adj.*

**my·thol·o·gy** /mi'THäləjē/ ▶*n.* (*pl.* -**gies**) collection of myths, esp. one belonging to a particular tradition: *Greek mythology.* —**myth·o·log·i·cal** *adj.* —**myth·o·log·i·cal·ly** *adv.*

**myth·o·ma·ni·a** /,miTHə'mānēə/ ▶*n.* abnormal or pathological tendency to exaggerate or tell lies.

# Nn

**N**[1] /en/ (also **n**) ▸*n.* (*pl.* **Ns** or **N's**; **n's**) fourteenth letter of the alphabet.

□ **to the nth (degree)** **1** *Math.* to any required power. **2** to any extent; to the utmost.

**N**[2] (also **N.**) ▸*abbr.* **1** north; northern. **2** noon.

**N**[3] ▸*symb. Chem.* nitrogen.

**n** (also **n.**) ▸*abbr.* **1** born. **2** name. **3** neuter. **4** noon. **5** number. **6** noun.

**nab** /nab/ ▸*v.* (**nabbed, nab·bing**) *inf.* **1** arrest; catch in wrongdoing. **2** seize; grab.

**na·bob** /'nābäb/ ▸*n.* wealthy person of influence.

**na·cre** /'nākər/ ▸*n.* mother-of-pearl. —**na·cre·ous** *adj.*

**na·dir** /'nādər/ ▸*n.* **1** part of the celestial sphere directly below an observer. **2** lowest point.

**nag** /nag/ ▸*v.* (**nagged, nag·ging**) **1 a** persistently annoy, irritate, scold, urge, etc., (a person). **b** find fault, complain, or urge, esp. persistently. **2** (of a pain) ache dully but persistently. **3 a** worry or preoccupy (a person, the mind, etc.): *his mistake nagged him.* **b** worry or gnaw: *his words nagged at her all day.*

▸*n.* **1** persistently nagging person. **2** horse, esp. an old or worthless one.

**nai·ad** /'nāad/ ▸*n.* (*pl.* **-ads** or **-a·des**) (in Greek mythology) water nymph.

**na·if** /nī'ēf/ (also **na·ïf**) ▸*adj.* naive or ingenuous.

▸*n.* naive or ingenuous person.

**nail** /nāl/ ▸*n.* **1** small usu. sharpened metal spike with a broadened flat head, driven in with a hammer to join things or to serve as a peg, protection, or decoration. **2** horny covering at the tip of the human finger or toe.

▸*v.* **1** fasten with a nail or nails. **2** fix or keep (a person, attention, etc.) fixed. **3 a** secure, catch, or get hold of (a person or thing). **b** expose or discover (a lie or a liar).

**na·ive** /nī'ēv/ (also **na·ïve**) ▸*adj.* **1** innocent; unaffected. **2** credulous; simple. —**na·ïve·ly** *adv.* —**na·ïve·té** *n.*

**na·ked** /'nākid/ ▸*adj.* **1** without clothes; nude. **2** undisguised: *naked truth.* **3** defenseless. **4** without addition, comment, support, evidence, etc. **5** devoid; without. **6** without leaves, hairs, scales, shell, etc. —**na·ked·ly** *adv.* —**na·ked·ness** *n.*

**name** /nām/ ▸*n.* **1 a** a word by which an individual person, animal, place, or thing is known, spoken of, etc. **b** all who go under one name; family, clan, or people in terms of its name: *the Scottish name.* **2** famous person. **3** reputation, esp. a good one.

▸*v.* **1** give a name to. **2** call (a person or thing) by the right name: *named the man in the photograph.* **3** mention; specify; cite. **4** nominate, appoint, etc. —**name·a·ble** *adj.*

**name·less** ▸*adj.* **1** having or showing no name. **2** inexpressible; indefinable. **3** unnamed; anonymous, esp. deliberately. **4** too horrific to be named.

**name·ly** /'nāmlē/ ▸*adv.* that is to say; in other words.

**name·sake** ▸*n.* person or thing having the same name as another.

**nan·ny** /'nanē/ ▸*n.* (*pl.* **-nies**) **1** child's nursemaid. **2** (also **nan·ny goat**) female goat.

**nan·o·sec·ond** /'nanə,sekənd/ (abbr.: **ns**) ▸*n.* one billionth of a second.

**nap** /nap/ ▸*v.* (**napped, nap·ping**) sleep lightly or briefly.

▸*n.* **1** short sleep or doze, esp. by day. **2** raised pile on textiles, esp. velvet.

**na·palm** /'nāpäm/ ▸*n.* jellied incendiary substance used in bombs.

▸*v.* attack with napalm bombs.

**nape** /nāp/ ▸*n.* back of the neck.

**naph·tha** /'nafтнə; 'nap-/ ▸*n.* flammable oil obtained by the dry distillation of organic substances such as coal, etc.

**nap·kin** /'napkin/ ▸*n.* square piece of linen, paper, etc., used for wiping the lips, fingers, etc., at meals.

**nar·cis·sism** /'närsə,sizəm/ ▸*n.* excessive or erotic interest in oneself, one's physical features, etc. —**nar·cis·sist** *n. & adj.* —**nar·cis·sis·tic** *adj.*

**nar·cis·sus** /när'sisəs/ ▸*n.* (*pl.* **-cis·si** or **-cis·sus·es**) any of several bulbous plants bearing a single flower with an undivided corona, as the daffodil.

**nar·co·sis** /närˈkōsis/ ▸*n.* state of stupor, drowsiness, or unconsciousness produced by drugs.

**nar·cot·ic** /närˈkätik/ ▸*adj.* **1** (of a substance) inducing drowsiness, sleep, or stupor. **2** (of a drug) affecting the mind.

▸*n.* narcotic substance, drug, or influence.

**nar·rate** /ˈnarāt/ ▸*v.* **1** give a story or account of. **2** provide a spoken accompaniment for (a film, etc.). —**nar·ra·tion** *n.* —**nar·ra·tor** *n.*

**nar·ra·tive** /ˈnarətiv/ ▸*n.* spoken or written account of connected events in order of happening.

▸*adj.* in the form of, or concerned with, narration: *narrative verse.*

**nar·row** /ˈnarō/ ▸*adj.* (**-er**, **-est**) **1 a** of small width. **b** confined or confining. **2** of limited scope. **3** with little margin.

▸*n.* (usu. **narrows**) narrow part of a strait, river, pass, street, etc.

▸*v.* **1** become narrow; diminish; contract; lessen. **2** make narrow; constrict; restrict. —**nar·row·ly** *adv.* —**nar·row·ness** *n.*

**nar·row-mind·ed** ▸*adj.* rigid or restricted in one's views; intolerant. —**nar·row-mind·ed·ness** *n.*

**nar·whal** /ˈnärwəl/ ▸*n.* Arctic white whale, the male of which has a long straight tusk.

**NASA** /ˈnasə/ ▸*abbr.* National Aeronautics and Space Administration.

**na·sal** /ˈnāzəl/ ▸*adj.* **1** of, for, or relating to the nose. **2** pronounced or spoken with the breath passing through the nose.

▸*n.* nasal letter or sound. —**na·sal·ize** *v.* —**na·sal·i·za·tion** *n.* —**na·sal·ly** *adv.*

**nas·cent** /ˈnāsənt/ ▸*adj.* just coming into existence. —**nas·cen·cy** *n.*

**nas·tur·tium** /nəˈstərSHəm/ ▸*n.* trailing plant with round leaves and bright orange, yellow, or red flowers.

**nas·ty** /ˈnastē/ ▸*adj.* (**-ti·er**, **-ti·est**) **1 a** highly unpleasant. **b** annoying; objectionable. **2** difficult to negotiate; dangerous; serious. **3** (of a person or animal) ill-natured; offensive. **4 a** obscene. **b** delighting in obscenity. —**nas·ti·ly** *adv.* —**nas·ti·ness** *n.*

**na·tal** /ˈnātl/ ▸*adj.* of or from one's birth.

**na·tion** /'nāsHən/ ▸n.
**1** community of people of mainly common descent, history, language, etc., forming a unified government or inhabiting a territory. **2** tribe or confederation of tribes of Native Americans. —**na·tion·al** adj. —**na·tion·al·ly** adv. —**na·tion·hood** n.

**na·tion·al·ism** /'nasHənə,lizəm/ ▸n. **1** patriotic feeling, principles, etc. **2** policy of national independence. —**na·tion·al·ist** n. & adj. —**na·tion·al·is·tic** adj.

**na·tion·al·i·ty** /,nasHə'nalitē/ ▸n. (pl. **-ties**) **1 a** status of belonging to a particular nation. **b** nation: *people of all nationalities.* **2** ethnic group forming a part of one or more political nations.

**na·tion·al·ize** /'nasHənə,līz/ ▸v. **1** take (industry, land, etc.) into government control or ownership. **2 a** make national. **b** make into a nation. —**na·tion·al·i·za·tion** n.

**na·tion·wide** /'nāsHən'wīd/ ▸adj. & adv. extending over the whole nation.

**na·tive** /'nātiv/ ▸n. **1 a** person born in a specified place. **b** local inhabitant. **2** indigenous animal or plant.
▸adj. **1** inherent; innate. **2** of one's birth: *native dress.* **3** belonging to a specified place: *the anteater is native to S. America.* **4 a** indigenous. **b** of the natives of a place. **5** in a natural state; unadorned; simple.
□ **Native American** member of the indigenous peoples of America or their descendants.

**na·tiv·ism** /'nāti,vizəm/ ▸n. **1** policy of protecting the interests of native-born or established inhabitants against those of immigrants. **2** return to or emphasis on traditional or local customs, in opposition to outside influences. **3** theory or doctrine that concepts, mental capacities, and mental structures are innate rather than acquired or learned.

**na·tiv·i·ty** /nə'tivitē/ ▸n. (pl. **-ties**) **1** (**the Nativity**) **a** the birth of Christ. **b** Christmas. **2** birth.

**NATO** /'nātō/ ▸abbr. North Atlantic Treaty Organization.

**nat·ter** /'natər/ ▸v. talk casually, esp. about unimportant matters; chatter.
▸n. casual and leisurely conversation.

**nat·ty** /ˈnatē/ *inf.* ▸*adj.* (**-ti·er,**
**-ti·est**) **1** smartly or neatly
dressed. **2** trim; smart: *a natty*
*blouse.* —**nat·ti·ly** *adv.*

**nat·u·ral** /ˈnaCHərəl/ ▸*adj.*
**1 a** existing in or caused by
nature. **b** uncultivated; wild.
**2** in the course of nature; not
exceptional. **3** (of human
nature, etc.) not surprising; to be
expected. **4** (of a person or a
person's behavior) unaffected,
easy, or spontaneous. **5 a** (of
qualities, etc.) inherent; innate.
**b** (of a person) having such
qualities: *a natural linguist.* **6** not
disguised or altered (as by
makeup, etc.). **7** likely by its or
their nature to be such: *natural*
*enemies.* **8** *Mus.* **a** (of a note) not
sharpened or flatted. **b** (of a scale)
not containing sharps or flats.
▸*n.* **1** *inf.* person or thing
naturally suitable, adept, expert,
etc. **2** *Mus.* **a** sign (♮) denoting a
return to natural pitch. **b** natural
note. —**nat·u·ral·ly** *adv.*
—**nat·u·ral·ness** *n.*

**nat·u·ral child·birth** ▸*n.*
childbirth with minimal medical
or technological intervention.

**nat·u·ral gas** ▸*n.* flammable
mainly methane gas extracted
from the earth.

**nat·u·ral his·to·ry** ▸*n.* **1** study
of animals or plants.
**2** aggregate of the facts
concerning the flora and fauna,
etc., of a particular place or
class.

**nat·u·ral·ism** ▸*n.* **1** realistic
representation in art and
literature of nature, character,
etc. **2 a** *Philos.* theory of the
world that excludes the
supernatural or spiritual.
**b** moral or religious system
based on this theory.
—**nat·u·ral·is·tic** *adj.*

**nat·u·ral·ist** ▸*n.* **1** expert in
natural history. **2** adherent of
naturalism.

**nat·u·ral·ize** ▸*v* **1** admit (a
foreigner) to citizenship.
**2** successfully introduce (an
animal, plant, etc.) into another
region. —**nat·u·ral·i·za·tion** *n.*

**nat·u·ral re·sources** ▸*pl. n.*
materials or conditions
occurring in nature and capable
of economic exploitation.

**nat·u·ral se·lec·tion** ▸*n.*
Darwinian theory of the survival
and propagation of organisms
best adapted to their
environment.

**na·ture** /ˈnāCHər/ ▸*n.* **1** innate or
essential qualities or character:

*is the nature of iron to rust.*
**2** (often **Nature**) **a** physical power causing all material phenomena. **b** these phenomena. **3** kind, sort, or class: *things of this nature.* **4** natural world.

**na·tur·ism** /ˈnāCHəˌrizəm/ ▶*n.* **1** practice of wearing no clothes in a vacation camp or for other leisure activities; nudism. **2** worship of nature or natural objects.

**naught** /nôt/ ▶*n.* zero.

**naugh·ty** /ˈnôtē/ ▶*adj.* (**-ti·er,** **-ti·est**) **1** (esp. of children) disobedient; badly behaved. **2** *inf.* mildly indecent. —**naugh·ti·ly** *adv.* —**naugh·ti·ness** *n.*

**nau·se·a** /ˈnôzēə/ ▶*n.* **1** feeling of sickness with an inclination to vomit. **2** loathing; revulsion.

**nau·se·ate** /ˈnôzēˌāt/ ▶*v.* **1** affect with nausea: *was nauseated by the smell.* **2** feel sick.

**nau·seous** ▶*adj.* **1** causing nausea; offensive to the taste or smell. **2** affected with nausea.

**nau·ti·cal** /ˈnôtikəl/ ▶*adj.* of sailors or navigation; naval; maritime. —**naut·i·cal·ly** *adv.*
□ **nautical mile** unit of approx.

2,025 yards (1,852 meters): (also called **sea mile**).

**nau·ti·lus** /ˈnôtl-əs/ ▶*n.* (*pl.* **-lus·es** or **-li**) cephalopod with a spiral shell, esp. one having a chambered shell.

**Nav·a·jo** /ˈnavəˌhō/ ▶*n.* (also **Nav'a·ho**) **1** member of a N. American Indian people native to New Mexico and Arizona. **2** language of this people.

**na·val** /ˈnāvəl/ ▶*adj.* **1** of, in, for, etc., the navy or a navy. **2** of or concerning ships: *a naval battle.*

**nave** /nāv/ ▶*n.* central part of a church, usu. from the west door to the chancel and excluding the side aisles.

**na·vel** /ˈnāvəl/ ▶*n.* depression in the center of the belly caused by detachment of the umbilical cord.
□ **navel orange** large seedless orange with a navellike formation at the top.

**na·vel-gaz·ing** ▶*n.* complacent self-absorption; concentration on a single issue at the expense of a wider view.

**nav·i·gate** /ˈnaviˌgāt/ ▶*v.* **1** manage or direct the course of (a ship, aircraft, etc.). **2 a** sail on (a sea, etc.). **b** fly through (the air). **3** assist the driver by map-

reading, etc. **4** sail a ship; sail in a ship. —**nav·i·ga·tion** *n.*
—**nav·i·ga·tion·al** *adj.*
—**nav·i·ga·tor** *n.*

**na·vy** /ˈnāvē/ ▶*n.* (*pl.* **-vies**)
**1** (often **the Navy**) **a** a nation's ships of war, including crews, maintenance systems, etc.
**b** officers and enlisted personnel of a navy. **2** (also **navy blue**) dark-blue color.
□ **navy bean** small white kidney bean.

**nay** /nā/ ▶*adv.* or rather; and even; and more than that: *impressive, nay, magnificent.*
▶*n.* **1** the word 'nay.' **2** negative vote: *counted 16 nays.*

**Na·zi** /ˈnätsē/ ▶*n.* (*pl.* **-zis**) **1** *hist.* member of the German National Socialist party. **2** adherent of this party's tenets.
▶*adj* of Nazis, Nazism, etc.
—**Na·zi·ism** or **Na·zism** *n.*

**NB** ▶*abbr.* **1** New Brunswick. **2** nota bene.

**Nb** ▶*symb. Chem.* niobium.

**NC** ▶*abbr.* North Carolina (in official postal use).

**ND** ▶*abbr.* North Dakota (in official postal use).

**Nd** ▶*symb. Chem.* neodymium.

**n.d.** ▶*abbr.* no date.

**N.Dak.** ▶*abbr.* North Dakota.

**NE** ▶*abbr.* **1** Nebraska (in official postal use). **2** northeast. **3** northeastern.

**Ne** ▶*symb. Chem.* neon.

**neap tide** /ˈnēp ˌtīd/ ▶*n.* tide when there is the least difference between high and low water.

**near** /ni(ə)r/ ▶*adv.* **1** to or at a short distance in space or time: *the time drew near | dropped near to them.* **2** closely: *as near as one can guess.*
▶*prep.* **1** to or at a short distance (in space, time, condition, or resemblance) from. **2 a** that is almost: *near-hysterical.*
**b** intended as a substitute for; resembling: *near beer.*
▶*adj.* **1** close to, in place or time: *the man nearest you.* **2 a** closely related. **b** intimate. **3** close; narrow: *near escape.*
▶*v.* **1** approach; draw near to. **2** draw near. —**near·ness** *n.*

**near·by** ▶*adj.* near, in position.
▶*adv.* close; not far away.

**near·ly** ▶*adv.* **1** almost. **2** closely.

**near·sight·ed** ▶*adj.* unable to see distant objects clearly.
—**near·sight·ed·ness** *n.*

**neat** /nēt/ ▶*adj.* **1** tidy and methodical. **2** elegantly simple.

**3** brief, clear, and pointed.
**4 a** cleverly executed. **b** deft;
dexterous. **5** (of esp. alcoholic
liquor) undiluted. **6** *inf.* (as a
general term of approval) good,
pleasing, excellent. —**neat·ly**
*adv.* —**neat·ness** *n.*

**neb·bish** /'nebisH/ ▸*n.* person,
esp. a man, who is regarded as
pitifully ineffectual, timid, or
submissive.

**Nebr.** ▸*abbr.* Nebraska.

**neb·u·la** /'nebyələ/ *Astron.* ▸*n.* (*pl.*
**-lae** or **-las**) **1** cloud of gas and
dust, glowing or appearing as a
dark silhouette against other
glowing matter. **2** bright area
caused by a galaxy, or a large
cloud of distant stars.
—**neb·u·lar** *adj.*

**neb·u·lous** /'nebyələs/ ▸*adj.* **1** in
the form of a cloud or haze.
**2** hazy, indistinct, or vague: *put
forward a few nebulous ideas.*

**nec·es·sar·y** /'nesə,serē/ ▸*adj.*
**1** requiring to be done, achieved,
etc.; requisite; essential.
**2** determined, existing, or
happening by natural laws,
predestination, etc., not by free
will; inevitable.
▸*n.* (*pl.* **-ies**) (usu. **necessaries**)
basic requirements.
—**nec·es·sar·i·ly** *adv.*

**ne·ces·si·tate** /nə'sesə,tāt/ ▸*v.*
make necessary (esp. as a result):
*will necessitate some sacrifice.*

**ne·ces·si·tous** /nə'sesitəs/
▸*adj.* (of a person) lacking the
necessities of life; needy.

**ne·ces·si·ty** ▸*n.* (*pl.* **-ties**)
**1 a** indispensable thing.
**b** indispensability. **2** imperative
need. **3** want; poverty; hardship.
□ **of necessity** unavoidably.

**neck** /nek/ ▸*n.* **1 a** part of the
body connecting the head to the
shoulders. **b** part of a garment
around or close to the neck.
**2** something resembling a neck,
e.g., the narrow part of a cavity
or vessel, a passage, channel,
etc.
▸*v. inf.* kiss and caress amorously.

**neck·er·chief** /'nekər,CHif/ ▸*n.*
square of cloth worn around the
neck.

**neck·lace** /'neklis/ ▸*n.* chain or
string of beads, precious stones,
links, etc., worn as an ornament
around the neck.

**neck·tie** ▸*n.* TIE.

**ne·crol·o·gy** /ne'kräləjē/ ▸*n.* (*pl.*
**-gies**) **1** obituary notice. **2** list of
deaths.

**nec·ro·man·cy** /'nekrə,mansē/
▸*n.* prediction of the future by

supposed communication with the dead. —**nec·ro·man·cer** *n.*

**ne·cro·sis** /ne'krōsis/ ▶*n. Physiol.* death of tissue caused by disease or injury, esp. as one of the symptoms of gangrene or pulmonary tuberculosis. —**ne·crot·ic** *adj.*

**nec·tar** /'nektər/ ▶*n.* **1** sugary substance produced by plants and made into honey by bees. **2** *Gk. & Rom. mythol.* the drink of the gods. **3** thick fruit juice. —**nec·tar·ous** *adj.*

**nec·tar·ine** /ˌnektə'rēn/ ▶*n.* variety of peach with a thin brightly colored smooth skin and firm flesh.

**née** /nā/ (also **nee**) ▶*adj.* born: *Mrs. Ann Smith, née Jones.*

**need** /nēd/ ▶*v.* **1** stand in want of; require: *needs a new coat.* **2** be under the necessity or obligation. ▶*n.* **1** requirement. **2** circumstances requiring action; necessity. **3** destitution; poverty. **4** crisis; emergency. —**need·less** *adj.* —**need·less·ly** *adv.*

**nee·dle** /'nēdl/ ▶*n.* **1 a** very thin small piece of smooth steel, etc., pointed at one end and with a slit (eye) for thread at the other, used in sewing. **b** larger plastic, wooden, etc., slender stick without an eye, used in knitting. **c** slender hooked stick used in crochet. **2** pointer on a dial. **3** end of a hypodermic syringe. **4** pointed rock or peak. **5** leaf of a fir or pine tree. ▶*v. inf.* incite or irritate; provoke: *I just said that to needle him.*

**nee·dle·point** ▶*n.* decorative needlework or lace made with a needle.

**nee·dle·work** ▶*n.* sewing or embroidery.

**need·y** ▶*adj.* (**need·i·er**, **need·i·est**) **1** (of a person) poor; destitute. **2** (of circumstances) characterized by poverty. **3** emotionally impoverished or demanding. —**need·i·ness** *n.*

**ne·far·i·ous** /ni'fe(ə)rēəs/ ▶*adj.* wicked; iniquitous. —**ne·far·i·ous·ly** *adv.* —**ne·far·i·ous·ness** *n.*

**ne·gate** /nə'gāt/ ▶*v.* **1** nullify; invalidate. **2** deny.

**neg·a·tive** /'negətiv/ ▶*adj.* **1** expressing or implying denial, prohibition, or refusal. **2** (of a person or attitude) lacking positive attributes. **3** marked by the absence of qualities: *a negative reaction.* **4** opposite to a

thing regarded as positive: *debt is negative capital.* **5** (of a quantity) less than zero, to be subtracted from others or from zero.
**6** *Electr.* **a** of the kind of charge carried by electrons.
**b** containing or producing such a charge.
▶*n.* **1** negative statement, reply, or word. **2** photographic image with black and white reversed or colors replaced by complementary ones.
**3** developed film or plate bearing such an image.
—**neg·a·tive·ly** *adv.*
—**neg·a·tiv·i·ty** *n.*

**ne·glect** /ni'glekt/ ▶*v.* **1** fail to care for or to do; be remiss about: *neglected their duty.* **2** not pay attention to; disregard: *neglected the obvious warning.*
▶*n.* **1** lack of caring; negligence: *the house suffered from neglect.* **2 a** neglecting. **b** being neglected: *the house fell into neglect.* —**ne·glect·ful** *adj.*
—**ne·glect·ful·ly** *adv.*

**neg·li·gee** /'neglə,ZHā/ ▶*n.* woman's dressing gown of sheer fabric.

**neg·li·gence** ▶*n.* **1** lack of proper care and attention. **2** *Law* failure to use reasonable care,

resulting in injury or damage.
—**neg·li·gent** *adj.*

**neg·li·gi·ble** /'neglijəbəl/ ▶*adj.* not worth considering; insignificant. —**neg·li·gi·bly** *adv.*

**ne·go·ti·ate** /nə'gōsHē,āt/ ▶*v.* **1** discuss in order to reach an agreement. **2** arrange (an affair) or bring about (a result) by negotiating. **3** find a way over, through, etc. (an obstacle, difficulty, etc.). **4** convert (a check, etc.) into money.
—**ne·go·tia·ble** *adj.*
—**ne·go·ti·a·tion** *n.*
—**ne·go·ti·a·tor** *n.*

**Ne·gro** /'nēgrō/ ▶*n.* (*pl.* **-groes**) member of a dark-skinned race orig. native to Africa.
▶*adj.* of black people. —**Ne·groid** *adj.*

**neigh** /nā/ ▶*n.* high whinnying sound of a horse.
▶*v.* make such a sound.

**neigh·bor** /'nābər/ ▶*n.* **1** person or thing near or living next door to or near or nearest another.
**2** fellow human being.
▶*v.* border on; adjoin.
—**neigh·bor·ly** *adj.*

**neigh·bor·hood** ▶*n.*
**1 a** district, esp. one forming a community within a town or city. **b** people of a district; one's

neighbors. **2** neighborly feeling or conduct.

**nei·ther** /ˈnēᴛʜər/ ▶*adj. & pron.* not the one nor the other of two people or things; not either.

▶*adv.* **1** not either; not on the one hand. *neither knowing nor caring.* **2** also not: *if you do not, neither shall I.*

**nem·e·sis** /ˈneməsis/ ▶*n.* (*pl.* **-ses**) **1** retributive justice. **2 a** downfall caused by this. **b** agent of such a downfall. **3** something that one cannot conquer, achieve, etc.

**neo-** ▶*comb. form* **1** new; modern. **2** new form of.

**ne·o·con·serv·a·tive** /ˌnēōkənˈsərvətiv/ ▶*adj.* of or relating to an approach to politics, literary criticism, theology, history, or any other branch of thought, that represents a return to a modified form of a traditional viewpoint, in contrast to more radical or liberal schools of thought.

▶*n.* person with neoconservative views.

**ne·o·lib·er·al** /ˌnēōˈlibərəl/ ▶*adj.* relating to or denoting a modified form of liberalism

tending to favor free-market capitalism.

▶*n.* person holding such views.

**ne·o·lith·ic** /ˌnēəˈliᴛʜik/ ▶*adj.* of the later Stone Age, when ground or polished stone weapons and implements prevailed.

**ne·ol·o·gism** /nēˈäləˌjizəm/ ▶*n.* **1** new word or expression. **2** coining or use of new words.

**ne·on** /ˈnēän/ ▶*n. Chem.* inert gaseous element giving an orange glow when electricity is passed through it: *neon light* | *neon sign.* (Symb.: **Ne**)

**ne·o·na·tal** /ˌnēəˈnātl/ ▶*adj.* of or relating to newborn children or animals.

**ne·o·phyte** /ˈnēəˌfīt/ ▶*n.* **1** new convert, esp. to a religious faith. **2** beginner; novice.

**ne·o·ter·ic** /ˌnēəˈterik/ ▶*adj.* recent; new; modern.

▶*n.* modern person; a person who advocates new ideas.

**neph·ew** /ˈnefyo͞o/ ▶*n.* son of one's brother or sister, or of one's brother-in-law or sister-in-law.

**ne·phri·tis** /nəˈfrītis/ ▶*n.* inflammation of the kidneys. (Also called **Bright's disease**).

**ne plus ul·tra** /ˈnē ˌpləs ˈəltrə/ ▶*n.* **1** furthest attainable point. **2** culmination, acme, or perfection.

**nep·o·tism** /ˈnepəˌtizəm/ ▶*n.* favoritism to relatives in conferring offices or privileges.

**Nep·tune** /ˈnept(y)o͞on/ ▶*n.* eighth planet from the sun.

**nerd** /nərd/ ▶*n. inf.* **1** foolish, feeble, or uninteresting person. **2** person intellectually talented but socially unskilled. **—nerd·y** *adj.*

**nerve** /nərv/ ▶*n.* **1** fiber or bundle of fibers that transmits impulses of sensation or motion between the brain or spinal cord and other parts of the body. **2 a** coolness in danger; bravery. **b** *inf.* impudence. **3** (**nerves**) heightened nervousness or sensitivity; mental or physical stress.
▶*v.* give strength, vigor, or courage to.
□ **nerve-rack·ing** (also **nerve-wrack·ing**) stressful; frightening.

**nerve gas** ▶*n.* poisonous gas affecting the nervous system.

**ner·vous** ▶*adj.* **1** timid or anxious. **2 a** excitable; highly strung. **b** resulting from this: *nervous headache.* **3** affecting or acting on the nerves.
**—ner·vous·ly** *adv.*
**—ner·vous·ness** *n.*

**ner·vous sys·tem** ▶*n.* the body's network of specialized cells that transmit nerve impulses between parts of the body.

**nerv·y** ▶*adj.* (**nerv·i·er, nerv·i·est**) bold; impudent; pushy.

**-ness** /nes/ ▶*suffix* forming nouns from adjectives, etc., expressing state or condition, or an instance of this: *happiness.*

**nest** /nest/ ▶*n.* **1** structure or place where a bird lays eggs and shelters its young. **2** any creature's breeding place or lair. **3** snug retreat or shelter. **4** group or set of similar objects, often of different sizes and fitting together for storage: *nest of tables.*
▶*v.* **1** use or build a nest. **2** (of objects) fit together or one inside another.

**nest egg** ▶*n.* sum of money saved for the future.

**nes·tle** /ˈnesəl/ ▶*v.* **1** settle oneself comfortably. **2** press oneself against another in affection, etc. **3** push (a head or shoulder, etc.) affectionately or snugly. **4** lie half hidden or embedded.

**net** /net/ ▶*n.* **1** open-meshed fabric of cord, rope, etc. **2** piece of net used esp. to restrain, contain, or delimit, or to catch fish, etc. **3** structure with net used in various games, esp. forming the goal in soccer, hockey, etc., and dividing the court in tennis, etc.
▶*v.* (**net·ted, net·ting**) **1** cover, confine, or catch with a net. **2** gain or yield as profit, weight, etc.
▶*adj.* **1** remaining after all necessary deductions. **2** (of an effect, result, etc.) ultimate; effective.

**neth·er** /ˈneT͟Hər/ ▶*adj.* lower in position. —**neth·er·most** *adj.*

**net·tle** /ˈnetl/ ▶*n.* plant with jagged leaves covered with stinging hairs.
▶*v.* **1** irritate; provoke. **2** sting with nettles.

**net·tle·some** ▶*adj.* **1** difficult. **2** annoying.

**net·work** ▶*n.* **1** arrangement of intersecting horizontal and vertical lines. **2** complex system of railways, roads, people, computers, etc., that interconnect or communicate.

**3** group of broadcasting stations connected for simultaneous broadcast of a program. **4** group of people who exchange information, contacts, etc., for professionsl or social purposes.
▶*v.* **1** link (machines, esp. computers) to operate interactively. **2** establish a network. **3** interact with other people to exchange information and develop contacts.

**neu·ral** /ˈn(y)o͝orəl/ ▶*adj.* of or relating to a nerve or the central nervous system.

**neu·ral·gia** /n(y)o͝oˈraljə/ ▶*n.* intense intermittent pain along a nerve, esp. in the head or face. —**neu·ral·gic** *adj.*

**neu·ri·tis** /n(y)o͝oˈrītis/ ▶*n.* inflammation of a nerve or nerves. —**neu·rit·ic** *adj.*

**neu·rol·o·gy** /n(y)o͝oˈräləjē/ ▶*n.* study of the nervous system. —**neu·ro·log·i·cal** *adj.* —**neu·rol·o·gist** *n.*

**neu·ron** /ˈn(y)o͝orän/ ▶*n.* specialized cell transmitting nerve impulses; nerve cell.

**neu·ro·sis** /n(y)o͝oˈrōsis/ ▶*n.* (*pl.* **neu·ro·ses**) mental illness marked by anxiety, obsessions, compulsive acts, etc., caused by a disorder of the nervous system

usu. without organic change.
—**neu·rot·ic** *adj.*

**neu·ro·sur·ger·y** ▶*n.* surgery performed on the brain or spinal cord. —**neu·ro·sur·geon** *n.* —**neu·ro·sur·gi·cal** *adj.*

**neu·ro·trans·mit·ter** ▶*n.* chemical substance that is released at the end of a nerve fiber and causes the transfer of the impulse to another nerve, muscle, etc.

**neu·ter** /'n(y)ōōtər/ ▶*adj.* **1** *Gram.* (of a noun, etc.) neither masculine nor feminine. **2** (of a plant) having neither pistils nor stamen. **3** (of an insect, animal, etc.) sexually undeveloped; castrated or spayed.
▶*v.* castrate or spay.

**neu·tral** /'n(y)ōōtrəl/ ▶*adj.* **1** not helping or supporting either of two sides; impartial. **2** indistinct; vague; indeterminate. **3** (of a gear) in which the engine is disconnected from the driven parts. **4** (of colors) not strong or positive; gray or beige. **5** *Chem.* neither acid nor alkaline. **6** *Electr.* neither positive nor negative.
▶*n.* **1 a** neutral nation, person, etc. **b** subject of a neutral nation.

**2** neutral gear. —**neu·tral·i·ty** *n.* —**neu·tral·ize** *v.* —**neu·tral·ly** *adv.*

**neu·tron** /'n(y)ōōträn/ ▶*n.* uncharged elementary particle of about the same mass as a proton.

**Nev.** ▶*abbr.* Nevada.

**nev·er** /'nevər/ ▶*adv.* **1** at no time; on no occasion; not ever. **2** not at all.

**nev·er·the·less** ▶*adv.* in spite of that; notwithstanding; all the same.

**ne·vus** /'nēvəs/ ▶*n.* (*pl.* **-vi** /-ˌvī/) birthmark or a mole on the skin, esp. a birthmark in the form of a raised red patch.

**new** /n(y)ōō/ ▶*adj.* **1 a** of recent origin or arrival. **b** made, invented, discovered, acquired, or experienced recently or now for the first time. **2** in original condition; not worn or used. **3 a** renewed or reformed. **b** reinvigorated. **4** different from a recent previous one. **5** unfamiliar or strange. **6 a** modern. **b** newfangled. **7** advanced in method or theory.
▶*adv.* [usu. in *comb.*] **1** newly; recently. **2** anew; afresh. —**new·ness** *n.*

**New Age** ▶*n.* set of beliefs intended to replace traditional

Western culture, with alternative approaches to religion, medicine, the environment, music, etc.

**new·el** /'n(y)o͞oəl/ ▸n.
**1** supporting central post of winding stairs. **2** top or bottom supporting post of a stair rail.

**new·fan·gled** /'n(y)o͞o'faNGgəld/ ▸adj. derog. different from what one is used to; objectionably new.

**new·ly** ▸adv. **1** recently. **2** afresh, anew. **3** in a new or different manner.

**new moon** ▸n. moon when first seen as a crescent after conjunction with the sun.

**news** /n(y)o͞oz/ ▸n. **1** information about important or interesting recent events, esp. when published or broadcast. **2** broadcast report of news: *shall we turn on the news?* **3** newly received or noteworthy information.

**news·cast** ▸n. radio or television broadcast of news reports. —**news·cast·er** n.

**news·let·ter** ▸n. concise periodical of news, events, etc., of special interest.

**news·pa·per** ▸n. printed publication (usu. daily or weekly) containing news, advertisements, correspondence, etc.

**new·speak** /'n(y)o͞o,spēk/ ▸n. ambiguous euphemistic language used chiefly in political propaganda.

**news·print** ▸n. low-quality paper on which newspapers are printed.

**news·stand** ▸n. stall for the sale of newspapers, magazines, etc.

**news·wor·thy** ▸adj. noteworthy as news.

**newt** /n(y)o͞ot/ ▸n. small amphibian having a well-developed tail.

**New Tes·ta·ment** ▸n. part of the Bible concerned with the life and teachings of Christ and his earliest followers.

**new·ton** /'n(y)o͞otn/ ▸n. Physics SI unit of force that, acting on a mass of one kilogram, increases its velocity by one meter per second every second. (Abbr.: **N**)

**New Year's Day** ▸n. January 1.

**next** /nekst/ ▸adj. **1** being or positioned or living nearest. **2** nearest in order of time.
▸adv. **1** in the nearest place or degree: *put it next to mine.* **2** on the first or soonest occasion.

▸*n.* next person or thing.

□ **next door** in the next house or room.

**nex·us** /ˈneksəs/ ▸*n.* (*pl.* same) connected group or series.

**NH** ▸*abbr.* New Hampshire (in official postal use).

**ni·a·cin** /ˈnīəsin/ ▸*n.* vitamin of the B complex, found in milk, liver, and yeast.

**nib** /nib/ ▸*n.* pen point.

**nib·ble** /ˈnibəl/ ▸*v.* **1 a** take small bites at. **b** eat in small amounts. **c** bite at gently or cautiously or playfully. **2** show cautious interest in. ▸*n.* very small amount of food.

**nice** /nīs/ ▸*adj.* **1** pleasant; satisfactory. **2** (of a person) kind; good-natured. **3** fine or subtle: *nice distinction.* —**nice·ly** *adv.* —**nice·ness** *n.*

**ni·ce·ty** /ˈnīsitē/ ▸*n.* (*pl.* -**ties**) **1** subtle distinction or detail: *she was not interested in the niceties of Greek and Latin.* **2** precision; accuracy. **3** detail of etiquette.

**niche** /niCH/ ▸*n.* **1** shallow recess, esp. in a wall to contain a statue, etc. **2** comfortable or suitable position in life or employment.

**nick** /nik/ ▸*n.* small cut or notch. ▸*v.* make a nick or nicks in.

□ **in the nick of time** only just in time.

**nick·el** /ˈnikəl/ ▸*n.* **1** *Chem.* malleable silver-white metallic element used in special steels, in magnetic alloys, and as a catalyst. (Symb.: **Ni**) **2** five-cent coin.

**nick·name** ▸*n.* familiar or humorous name given to a person or thing instead of or as well as the real name. ▸*v.* give a nickname to.

**nic·o·tine** /ˈnikəˌtēn/ ▸*n.* poisonous alkaloid present in tobacco.

**nic·o·tin·ic a·cid** ▸*n.* NIACIN.

**niece** /nēs/ ▸*n.* daughter of one's brother or sister, or of one's brother-in-law or sister-in-law.

**nif·ty** /ˈniftē/ ▸*adj.* (-**ti·er**, -**ti·est**) *inf.* **1** clever; adroit. **2** smart; stylish.

**nig·gard·ly** /ˈnigərdlē/ ▸*adj.* not generous; stingy. —**nig·gard·li·ness** *n.*

**nig·gling** ▸*adj.* causing slight annoyance or discomfort.

**nigh** /nī/ ▸*adv., prep., & adj.* near.

**night** /nīt/ ▸*n.* **1** period of darkness between one day and the next; time from sunset to sunrise. **2** nightfall. **3** darkness of night.

**night·cap** ▸*n.* **1** *hist.* cap worn in bed. **2** hot or alcoholic drink taken at bedtime.

**night·club** ▸*n.* club that is open at night and provides refreshment and entertainment.

**night·fall** ▸*n.* onset of night; end of daylight.

**night·gown** ▸*n.* woman's or child's loose garment worn in bed.

**night·hawk** ▸*n.* nocturnal bird related to the whippoorwill.

**night·in·gale** /ˈnītnˌgāl/ ▸*n.* small reddish-brown bird, of which the male sings melodiously, esp. at night.

**night·ly** ▸*adj.* **1** happening, done, or existing in the night. **2** recurring every night. ▸*adv.* every night.

**night·mare** /ˈnītˌme(ə)r/ ▸*n.* **1** frightening dream. **2** terrifying or very unpleasant experience or situation. **3** haunting or obsessive fear. —**night·mar·ish** *adj.*

**night·shade** ▸*n.* plant related to the potato, having poisonous black or red berries.

**night·shirt** ▸*n.* long shirt worn in bed.

**night·stick** ▸*n.* policeman's club.

**ni·hil·ism** /ˈnīəˌlizəm/ ▸*n.* rejection of all religious and moral principles. —**ni·hil·ist** *n.* —**ni·hil·is·tic** *adj.*

**nil** /nil/ ▸*n.* nothing; no number or amount.

**nim·ble** /ˈnimbəl/ ▸*adj.* (**-bler**, **-blest**) **1** quick and light in movement or action; agile. **2** (of the mind) quick to comprehend; clever; versatile. —**nim·bly** *adv.*

**nim·bus** /ˈnimbəs/ ▸*n.* (*pl.* **-bi** or **-bus·es**) **1** bright cloud or halo surrounding a supernatural being or saint or a person or thing. **2** large gray rain cloud.

**nIm·rod** /ˈnimräd/ ▸*n.* skillful hunter.

**nin·com·poop** /ˈninkəmˌpo͞op/ ▸*n.* simpleton; fool.

**nine** /nīn/ ▸*n.* **1** one more than eight, or one less than ten. **2** symbol for this (9, ix, IX). ▸*adj.* that amount to nine. —**ninth** *n. & adj.*

**nine·teen** ▸*n.* **1** one more than eighteen, or nine more than ten. **2** symbol for this (19, xix, XIX). ▸*adj.* that amount to nineteen. —**nine·teenth** *n. & adj.*

**nine·ty** ▸*n.* (*pl.* **-ties**) **1** product of nine and ten. **2** symbol for this (90, xc, XC). **3** (**nineties**) numbers from 90 to 99, esp. years. —**nine·ti·eth** n. & adj.

**nin·ny** /ˈninē/ ▸n. (pl. **-nies**) inf. foolish or simpleminded person.

**nip** /nip/ ▸v. (**nipped**, **nip·ping**) **1** pinch, squeeze, or bite sharply. **2** (of the cold, etc.) cause pain or harm to. **3** take a sip of liquor. ▸n. **1 a** pinch; sharp squeeze. **b** bite. **2** biting cold. **3** small quantity of liquor.

**nip·ple** /ˈnipəl/ ▸n. **1** small projection in which the mammary ducts of either sex of mammals terminate and from which in females milk is secreted for the young. **2** mouthpiece of a feeding bottle or pacifier. **3** device like a nipple in shape or function.

**nip·py** ▸adj. (**-pi·er**, **-pi·est**) inf. chilly or cold.

**nir·va·na** /nərˈvänə/ ▸n. (in Buddhism) perfect bliss attained by the extinction of individuality.

**nit** /nit/ ▸n. egg or young form of a louse or other parasitic insect.

**ni·ter** /ˈnītər/ ▸n. saltpeter; potassium nitrate.

**nit·pick** ▸v. inf. find fault in a petty manner. —**nit·pick·er** n.

**ni·trate** /ˈnītrāt/ ▸n. **1** any salt or ester of nitric acid. **2** potassium or sodium nitrate as a fertilizer. —**ni·tra·tion** n. —**ni·tric** adj. —**ni·trous** adj.

**nit·ric ac·id** ▸n. corrosive acid containing nitrogen.

**ni·tro·gen** /ˈnītrəjən/ ▸n. Chem. colorless, tasteless, odorless gaseous element that forms four-fifths of the atmosphere. (Symb.: N) —**ni·trog·e·nous** adj.

**ni·tro·glyc·er·in** /ˌnītrōˈglisərin/ (also **ni·tro·glyc·er·ine**) ▸n. explosive yellow liquid made by reacting glycerol with sulfuric and nitric acids.

**nit·ty-grit·ty** /ˈnitē ˈgritē/ ▸n. inf. realities or practical details of a matter.

**nit·wit** ▸n. inf. silly or foolish person.

**niv·e·ous** /ˈnivēəs/ ▸adj. snowy or resembling snow.

**nix** /niks/ ▸n. inf. nothing. ▸v. cancel.

**NJ** ▸abbr. New Jersey (in official postal use).

**NM** ▸abbr. New Mexico (in official postal use).

**N.Mex.** ▸abbr. New Mexico.

**No** ▸symb. Chem. nobelium.

**No.** ▸abbr. **1** number. **2** North.

**no** /nō/ ▸adj. **1** not any: there is no excuse | no two of them are alike.

**2** not a; quite other than: *is no fool* | *is no part of my plan.*
**3** hardly any: *did it in no time.*
**4** used elliptically as a slogan, notice, etc., to forbid, reject, or deplore the thing specified: *no parking.*

▶*adv.* **1** equivalent to a negative sentence: the answer to your question is negative; your request or command will not be complied with; the statement made or course of action intended or conclusion arrived at is not correct or satisfactory; the negative statement made is correct. **2** by no amount; not at all: *no better than before.*

▶*n.* (*pl.* **noes** or **nos**) **1** utterance of the word *no.* **2** denial or refusal. **3** negative vote.

**no·bil·i·ar·y** /nōˈbilēˌerē; -ˈbilyərē/ ▶*adj.* of or relating to the nobility.

**no·bil·i·ty** /nōˈbilitē/ ▶*n.* (*pl.* **-ties**) **1** nobleness of character, mind, birth, or rank. **2** class of nobles; aristocracy.

**no·ble** /ˈnōbəl/ ▶*adj.* (**-bler, -blest**) **1** belonging by rank, title, or birth to the aristocracy. **2** of excellent character; magnanimous. **3** of imposing appearance; splendid. **4** excellent; admirable.

▶*n.* nobleman or noblewoman. —**no·ble·ness** *n.* —**no·bly** *adv.*

**no·ble·man** ▶*n.* (*pl.* **-men**) man of noble rank or birth; peer.

**no·blesse o·blige** /nōˈbles ōˈblēzн/ ▶privilege entails responsibility.

**no·ble·wo·man** ▶*n.* (*pl.* **-wo·men**) woman of noble rank or birth; peeress.

**no·bod·y** ▶*pron.* no person.
▶*n.* (*pl.* **-ies**) person of no importance, authority, or position.

**no-brain·er** ▶*n.* something that requires or involves little or no mental effort.

**noc·tam·bu·list** /näkˈtambyəlist/ ▶*n.* sleepwalker.

**noc·tur·nal** /näkˈtərnəl/ ▶*adj.* of or in the night; done or active by night.

**noc·turne** /ˈnäktərn/ ▶*n. Mus.* short romantic composition, usu. for piano.

**noc·u·ous** /ˈnäkyo͞oəs/ ▶*adj.* noxious, harmful, or poisonous.

**nod** /näd/ ▶*v.* (**nod·ded, nod·ding**) **1** incline one's head slightly and briefly in greeting, assent, or command. **2** let one's head fall forward in drowsiness. **3** incline (one's head). **4** signify (assent, etc.) by a nod.

▸*n.* nodding of the head, esp. as a sign to proceed, etc.

**node** /nōd/ ▸*n.* **1** point at which lines or pathways intersect. **2** component in a computer network. **3** *Math.* point at which a curve intersects itself. **4** *Bot.* part of a plant stem from which leaves emerge. **5** *Anat.* natural swelling in an organ or part of the body. **6** *Physics* point of minimum disturbance in a standing wave system. —**nod·al** *adj.*

**nod·ule** /'näjōōl/ ▸*n.* **1** small, rounded lump. **2** small swelling or aggregation of cells, e.g., a small tumor, node, or ganglion. —**nod·u·lar** *adj.*

**No·el** /nō'el/ ▸*n.* Christmas.

**noir** /nwär/ ▸*adj.* black; dark: *film noir.*

**noise** /noiz/ ▸*n.* **1** sound, esp. a loud or unpleasant or undesired one. **2** irregular fluctuations accompanying a transmitted signal but not relevant to it.

▸*v.* spread abroad (rumors, etc.). —**nois·i·ly** *adv.* —**nois·i·ness** *n.* —**nois·y** *adj.*

**noi·some** /'noisəm/ ▸*adj.* **1** evil-smelling. **2** harmful; noxious.

**no·lens vo·lens** /'nōlənz 'vōlənz/ ▸*adv.* whether a person wants or likes something or not.

**no·mad** /'nō,mad/ ▸*n.* **1** member of a tribe roaming place to place for pasture. **2** wanderer.

▸*adj.* **1** living as a nomad. **2** wandering. —**no·mad·ic** *adj.*

**no man's land** ▸*n.* **1** disputed ground, as between two opposing armies. **2** area that is unowned or uninhabited.

**nom de guerre** /,näm də 'ger/ ▸*n.* (*pl.* **noms de guerre** *pronunc.* same) assumed name under which a person engages in combat or some other activity or enterprise.

**nom de plume** /,näm də ' plōōm/ ▸*n.* (*pl.* **noms de plume** *pronunc.* same) pen name.

**no·men·cla·ture** /'nōmən-,klācHər/ ▸*n.* **1** person's or community's system of names for things. **2** terminology of a science, etc.

**nom·i·nal** /'näminl/ ▸*adj.* **1** existing in name only; not real or actual: *nominal ruler.* **2** (of a sum of money, rent, etc.) virtually nothing; much below the actual value of a thing. **3** of or in names: *nominal and* essential distinctions. **4** of or as or like a noun. —**nom·i·nal·ly** *adv.*

**nom·i·nate** /'nämə,nāt/ ▶*v.* **1** propose (a candidate) for election. **2** appoint to an office. **3** name or appoint (a date or place). —**nom·i·na·tion** *n.* —**nom·i·na·tor** *n.*

**nom·i·na·tive** /'nämənətiv/ ▶*n. Gram.* **1** case of nouns, pronouns, and adjectives, expressing the subject of a verb. **2** word in this case. ▶*adj. Gram.* of or in this case.

**nom·i·nee** /,nämə'nē/ ▶*n.* person who is nominated for an office or as the recipient of a grant, etc.

**non-** /nän/ ▶*prefix* giving the negative sense of words with which it is combined, esp.: **1** not doing or having or involved with: *nonattendance* | *nonpayment* | *nonproductive.* **2 a** not of the kind or class described: *nonalcoholic* | *nonmember.* **b** forming terms used adjectivally: *nonunion* | *nonparty.* **3** lack of: *nonaccess.* **4** [with *adverbs*] not in the way described: *nonaggressively.* **5** forming adjectives from verbs, meaning 'that does not' or 'that is not meant to (or to be)':

*nonskid* | *noniron.* **6** used to form a neutral negative sense when a form in *in-* or *un-* has a special sense or (usu. unfavorable) connotation: *noncontroversial* | *noneffective* | *nonhuman.*

**non·age** /'nänij; 'nō-/ ▶*n.* period of immaturity or youth.

**no·na·ge·nar·i·an** /,nänəjə'nerēən/ ▶*n.* person from 90 to 99 years old. ▶*adj.* of this age.

**non·cha·lant** /,nänsHə'länt/ ▶*adj.* calm and casual; unmoved; indifferent. —**non·cha·lance** *n.* —**non·cha·lant·ly** *adv.*

**non·com** /'nän,käm/ ▶*n.* noncommissioned officer.

**non·com·ba·tant** /,nänkəm'batnt/ ▶*n.* person not fighting in a war, esp. a civilian, army chaplain, etc.

**non·com·mis·sioned** /,nänkə'misHənd/ ▶*adj. Mil.* (of an officer) not holding a commission. (Abbr.: **NCO**)

**non·com·mit·tal** /,nänkə'mitl/ ▶*adj.* avoiding commitment to a definite opinion or course of action.

**non compos men·tis** /,nän 'kämpəs 'mentis/ ▶*adj.* not in one's right mind.

**non·con·duc·tor** ▶*n.* substance

that does not conduct heat or electricity.

**non·con·form·ist** ▶*n.* person who does not conform to a prevailing principle. —**non·con·form·i·ty** *n.*

**non·de·script** /ˌnändəˈskript/ ▶*adj.* lacking distinctive characteristics; not easily classified.

**none** /nən/ ▶*pron.* **1 a** not any: *none of this concerns me.* **b** not any one of: *none were recovered.* **2** no persons: *none but fools have ever believed it.*
▶*adj.* no; not any: *you have money and I have none.*
▶*adv.* by no amount; not at all: *am none the wiser.*

**non·en·ti·ty** /nänˈentitē/ ▶*n.* (*pl.* -**ties**) **1** person or thing of no importance. **2** nonexistent thing; figment.

**none·such** /ˈnənˌsəCH/ (also **non·such**) ▶*n.* person or thing that is regarded as perfect or excellent.

**none·the·less** /ˌnənTHəˈles/ ▶*adv.* nevertheless.

**non·pa·reil** /ˌnänpəˈrel/ ▶*adj.* unrivaled or unique.
▶*n.* **1** such a person or thing. **2** candy made from a chocolate disk, decorated with sugar pellets.

**non·par·ti·san** ▶*adj.* not affiliated with or favoring one political party.

**non·plus** ▶*v.* (-**plussed**, -**plus·sing**; -**plused**, -**plus·ing**) completely perplex.

**non·prof·it** /ˈnänˈpräfit/ ▶*adj.* not involving nor making a profit.

**non·sec·tar·i·an** /ˌnänsek-ˈte(ə)rēən/ ▶*adj.* not affiliated with a specific religious group.

**non·sense** /ˈnänˌsens/ ▶*n.* absurd or meaningless words or ideas; foolish or extravagant conduct. —**non·sen·si·cal** *adj.* —**non·sen·si·cal·ly** *adv.*

**non se·qui·tur** /ˌnän ˈsekwitər/ ▶*n.* conclusion that does not logically follow from the premises.

**non·stop** ▶*adj.* **1** (of a train, etc.) not stopping at intermediate places. **2** (of a journey, performance, etc.) done without a stop or intermission.
▶*adv.* without stopping or pausing.

**non·suit** /nänˈso͞ot/ ▶*v.* (of a judge or court) subject (a plaintiff) to the stoppage of their suit on the grounds of failure to make a legal case or bring sufficient evidence.

**non·u·nion** /nän'yo͞onyən/ ▶*adj.* **1** not belonging to a labor union. **2** not done or produced by members of a labor union.

**non·vi·o·lence** ▶*n.* avoidance of violence, esp. as a principle. —**non·vi·o·lent** *adj.*

**noo·dle** /'no͞odl/ ▶*n.* **1** strip or ring of pasta. **2** *inf.* head.

**nook** /no͝ok/ ▶*n.* corner or recess; secluded place.

**noon** /no͞on/ ▶*n.* twelve o'clock in the day; midday.

**no one** ▶*n.* no person; nobody.

**noose** /no͞os/ ▶*n.* **1** loop with a slip knot, tightening when pulled, esp. in a snare, lasso, or hangman's halter. **2** snare or bond.
▶*v.* catch with or enclose in a noose; ensnare.

**nor** /nôr/ ▶*conj.* **1** and not; and not either: *can neither read nor write.* **2** and no more; neither: *"I cannot go" — "Nor can I".*

**Nor·dic** /'nôrdik/ ▶*adj.* **1** of the tall blond Germanic people in northern Europe, esp. in Scandinavia. **2** of or relating to Scandinavia or Finland.
▶*n.* Nordic person.

**norm** /nôrm/ ▶*n.* **1** standard or pattern or type. **2** customary behavior, etc.

**nor·mal** /'nôrməl/ ▶*adj.* **1** conforming to a standard; regular; usual; typical. **2** free from mental or emotional disorder.
▶*n.* **1** normal value of a temperature, etc., esp. that of blood. **2** usual state, level, etc. —**nor·mal·cy** *n.* —**nor·mal·i·ty** *n.* —**nor·mal·ize** *v.* —**nor·mal·ly** *adv.*

**nor·ma·tive** /'nôrmətiv/ ▶*adj.* of or establishing a norm.

**Norse** /nôrs/ ▶*n.* **1 a** Norwegian language. **b** Scandinavian language group. **2** (**the Norse**) **a** Norwegians. **b** Vikings.
▶*adj.* of ancient Scandinavia, esp. Norway.

**north** /nôrᴛʜ/ ▶*n.* **1 a** a point of the horizon 90° counterclockwise from east. **b** compass point corresponding to this. **2** (usu. **the North**) **a** part of the world or a country or a town lying to the north. **b** the arctic.
▶*adj.* **1** toward, at, near, or facing north. **2** from the north: *north wind.*
▶*adv.* **1** toward, at, or near the north. **2** further north than. —**north·er·ly** *adj. & adv.*

—**north·ern** *adj.* —**north·ward** *adj.*

**north·east** ▶*n.* **1** point of the horizon midway between north and east. **2** direction in which this lies.

▶*adj.* of, toward, or coming from the northeast.

▶*adv.* toward, at, or near the northeast. —**north·east·er·ly** *adj. & adv.* —**north·east·ern** *adj.*

**north pole** (also **North Pole**) ▶*n.* northernmost point of the earth's axis of rotation.

**North Star** ▶*n.* another name for Polaris.

**north·west** ▶*n.* **1** point of the horizon midway between north and west. **2** direction in which this lies.

▶*adj.* of, toward, or coming from the northwest.

▶*adv.* toward, at, or near the northwest. —**north·west·er·ly** *adj. & adv.* —**north·west·ern** *adj.*

**nose** /nōz/ ▶*n.* **1** organ above the mouth of a human or animal, used for smelling and breathing. **2 a** sense of smell. **b** ability to detect a particular thing: *a nose for scandal.* **3** front end or projecting part of a thing, e.g., of a car or aircraft.

▶*v.* **1 a** perceive the smell of; discover by smell. **b** detect. **2** pry or search. **3 a** make one's way cautiously forward. **b** make (one's or its way).

**nose cone** ▶*n.* cone-shaped nose of a rocket, etc.

**nose·dive** ▶*n.* **1** steep downward plunge by an airplane. **2** sudden plunge or drop.

▶*v.* make a nosedive.

**nose·gay** ▶*n.* sweet-scented bunch of flowers.

**nosh** /näsн/ *inf.* ▶*v.* eat, esp. between meals.

▶*n.* snack.

**nos·tal·gia** /nä'staljə/ ▶*n.* **1** sentimental yearning for a period of the past. **2** evocation of these feelings. —**nos·tal·gic** *adj.* —**nos·tal·gi·cal·ly** *adv.*

**nos·tril** /'nästrəl/ ▶*n.* either of two openings in the nose.

**nos·trum** /'nästrəm/ ▶*n.* **1** quack remedy. **2** pet scheme or favorite remedy, esp. for political or social reform.

**nos·y** /'nōzē/ (also **nos·ey**) *inf.* ▶*adj.* (**nos·i·er**, **nos·i·est**) inquisitive; prying. —**nos·i·ly** *adv.* —**nos·i·ness** *n.*

**not** /nät/ ▶*adv.* **1** expressing negation, esp.: **2** (also **n't** joined to a preceding verb) following an auxiliary verb or *be* or (in a question) the subject of such a verb: *she isn't there.* Use with other verbs is now archaic (*fear not*), except with participles and infinitives (*not knowing, I cannot say; we asked them not to come*). **3** used elliptically for a negative sentence or verb or phrase: *Do you want it? — Certainly not!* **4** used to express the negative of other words: *not a single one was left.*

**no·ta be·ne** /'nōtə 'benē/ ▸*v.* note well (that which follows). (Abbr.: **NB**)

**no·ta·ble** /'nōtəbəl/ ▸*adj.* worthy of note; striking; remarkable; eminent.

▸*n.* eminent person.
 —**no·ta·bil·i·ty** *n.* —**no·ta·bly** *adv.*

**no·ta·rize** /'nōtə,rīz/ ▸*v.* certify (a document) as a notary.

**no·ta·ry** /'nōtərē/ (also **no·ta·ry pub·lic**) ▸*n.* (*pl.* **-ries**) person authorized to perform certain legal formalities, esp. to draw up or certify contracts, deeds, etc. —**no·tar·i·al** *adj.*

**no·ta·tion** /nō'tāsHən/ ▸*n.* **1** representation of numbers, quantities, musical notes, etc., by symbols. **2** any set of such symbols.

**notch** /näcH/ ▸*n.* **1** V-shaped indentation on an edge or surface. **2** deep, narrow mountain pass or gap.

▸*v.* make notches in.

**note** /nōt/ ▸*n.* **1** brief written record as an aid to memory, for use in writing, public speaking, etc.: *spoke without notes.* **2** observation, usu. unwritten, of experiences, etc.: *compare notes.* **3** short or informal letter. **4** short annotation or additional explanation in a book, etc.; footnote or endnote. **5** written promise of payment. **6 a** notice; attention. **b** distinction; eminence. **7 a** written sign representing the pitch and duration of a musical sound. **b** single musical tone of definite pitch.

▸*v.* **1** observe; notice; give or draw attention to. **2** record as a thing to be remembered or observed. **3** be famous or well known: *were noted for their generosity.*

**note·book** ▸*n.* small book for making notes.

**note·wor·thy** ▸*adj.* worthy of attention; remarkable.

**noth·ing** /'nəTHiNG/ ▸*n.* **1** not anything. **2** no thing: *can find nothing useful.* **3** person or thing of no importance. **4** nonexistence; what does not exist. **5** (in calculations) no amount: *a third of nothing is nothing.*

▶*adv.* not at all; in no way.

**noth·ing·ness** ▶*n.* **1** nonexistence. **2** worthlessness, triviality, or insignificance.

**no·tice** /ˈnōtis/ ▶*n.* **1** attention; observation. **2** displayed sheet, etc., bearing an announcement. **3 a** intimation or warning: *give notice.* **b** formal declaration of intention to end an agreement, leave employment, etc. **4** short published review or comment about a new play, book, etc.

▶*v.* perceive; observe. —**no·tice·a·ble** *adj.* —**no·tice·a·bly** *adv.*

**no·ti·fy** /ˈnōtəˌfī/ ▶*v.* (-fied) **1** inform or give notice to (a person). **2** make known. —**no·ti·fi·ca·tion** *n.*

**no·tion** /ˈnōsHən/ ▶*n.* **1 a** concept or idea. **b** opinion. **c** vague view or understanding. **2** inclination, impulse, or intention. **3** (**notions**) small, useful articles, esp. thread, needles, buttons, etc.

**no·to·ri·ous** /nəˈtôrēəs/ ▶*adj.* well-known, esp. unfavorably:

notorious criminal. —**no·to·ri·e·ty** *n.* —**no·to·ri·ous·ly** *adv.*

**not·with·stand·ing** /ˌnätwiTH-ˈstandiNG/ ▶*prep.* in spite of.

▶*adv.* nevertheless; all the same.

**nought** /nôt/ ▶*var.* of NAUGHT.

**noun** /noun/ ▶*n. Gram.* word (other than a pronoun) used to name a person, place, thing, or concept (*common noun*), or a particular one of these (*proper noun*).

**nour·ish** /ˈnəriSH/ ▶*v.* **1 a** sustain with food. **b** enrich. **c** provide with intellectual or emotional sustenance or enrichment. **2** foster or cherish (a feeling, etc.). —**nour·ish·ing** *adj.* —**nour·ish·ment** *n.*

**nou·veau riche** /ˈnoōvō ˈrēSH/ ▶*n.* (*pl.* **nou·veaux riches** *pronunc.* same) person who has recently acquired (usu. ostentatious) wealth.

**nou·velle cui·sine** /noōˈvel kwiˈzēn/ ▶*n.* modern style of cooking that avoids rich, heavy foods and emphasizes the freshness of the ingredients and the presentation of the dishes.

**nou·velle vague** /noōˈvel ˌväg/ ▶*n.* grouping of French movie directors in the late 1950s and 1960s (including Jean-Luc

Godard and François Truffaut) who reacted against established French cinema and sought to make more innovative films.

**Nov.** ▶*abbr.* November.

**no·va** /ˈnōvə/ ▶*n.* (*pl.* **-vas** or **-vae**) star showing a sudden burst of brightness that then subsides.

**no·va·tion** /nōˈvāsʜən/ ▶*n.* substitution of a new contract in place of an old one.

**nov·el** /ˈnävəl/ ▶*n.* **1** fictitious prose story of book length. **2** of a new kind or nature; strange.

**nov·el·ty** ▶*n.* (*pl.* **-ties**) **1** newness. **2** new or unusual thing or occurrence. **3** small toy or decoration, etc. **4** [as *adj.*] having novelty: *novelty toys.*

**No·vem·ber** /nōˈvembər/ ▶*n.* eleventh month of the year.

**no·ve·na** /nōˈvēnə/ ▶*n.* (in the Roman Catholic Church) devotion consisting of special prayers or services on nine successive days.

**nov·ice** /ˈnävis/ ▶*n.* **1 a** probationary member of a religious order. **b** new convert. **2** beginner; inexperienced person.

**no·vi·ti·ate** /nōˈvisʜēit/ ▶*n.* **1** period of being a novice.

**2** religious novice. **3** novices' quarters.

**No·vo·caine** /ˈnōvəˌkān/ ▶*trademark* local anesthetic derived from benzoic acid.

**now** /nou/ ▶*adv.* **1** at the present or mentioned time. **2** immediately. **3** under the present circumstances. **4** on this further occasion. **5** (esp. in a narrative) then; next.
▶*conj.* as a consequence.
▶*n.* this time; the present.

**now·a·days** /ˈnouəˌdāz/ ▶*adv.* at the present time or age; in these times.
▶*n.* the present time.

**no·where** /ˈnō(h)wer/ ▶*adv.* in or to no place.
▶*pron.* no place.

**nox·ious** /ˈnäksʜəs/ ▶*adj.* harmful; unwholesome.

**noz·zle** /ˈnäzəl/ ▶*n.* spout on a hose, etc., from which a jet issues.

**nth** /enʈʜ/ ▶see **N.**

**nu·ance** /ˈn(y)o͞oˌäns/ ▶*n.* subtle shade of meaning, feeling, color, etc.

**nub** /nəb/ ▶*n.* **1** (**the nub**) central point of a matter: *the nub of the problem lies elsewhere.* **2** small lump of metal or rock. —**nub·by** *adj.*

**nu·bile** /ˈn(y)o͞o‚bīl/ ▶*adj.* (of a woman) marriageable or sexually attractive.

**nu·cle·ar** /ˈn(y)o͞oklēər/ ▶*adj.* **1** of, relating to, or constituting a nucleus. **2** using nuclear energy.

**nu·cle·ar en·er·gy** ▶*n.* energy obtained by nuclear fission or fusion.

**nu·cle·ar fam·i·ly** ▶*n.* couple and their children, regarded as a basic social unit.

**nu·cle·ar med·i·cine** ▶*n.* medical specialty that uses radioactive materials for diagnosis and treatment.

**nu·cle·ar phys·ics** ▶*n.* physics of atomic nuclei and their interactions, esp. in the generation of nuclear energy.

**nu·cle·on** /ˈn(y)o͞oklē‚än/ ▶*n.* *Physics* proton or neutron.

**nu·cle·us** /ˈn(y)o͞oklēəs/ ▶*n.* (*pl.* **-cle·i**) **1 a** central part or thing around which others are collected. **b** kernel of an aggregate or mass. **2** initial part meant to receive additions. **3** *Physics* positively charged central core of an atom. **4** *Biol.* specialized, often central part of a cell, containing the genetic material.

**nude** /n(y)o͞od/ ▶*adj.* naked; bare; unclothed.
▶*n.* **1** painting, sculpture, photograph, etc., of a nude human figure; such a figure. **2** nude person. —**nu·di·ty** *n.*

**nudge** /nəj/ ▶*v.* **1** prod gently with the elbow to attract attention. **2** give a reminder or encouragement to (a person).
▶*n.* prod; gentle push.

**nug·get** /ˈnəgit/ ▶*n.* **1** lump of gold, etc., as found in the earth. **2** something valuable for its size: *nugget of information.*

**nui·sance** /ˈn(y)o͞osəns/ ▶*n.* person, thing, or circumstance causing trouble or annoyance.

**nuit blanche** /‚nwē ˈblänSH/ ▶*n.* (*pl.* **nuits blanches** *pronunc.* same) sleepless night.

**nuke** /n(y)o͞ok/ ▶*v. inf.* **1** bomb or destroy with nuclear weapons. **2** cook (something) in a microwave oven.

**null** /nəl/ ▶*adj.* **1** (esp. **null and void**) invalid. **2** nonexistent; amounting to nothing. **3** without character or expression.

**nul·li·fy** /ˈnələ‚fī/ ▶*v.* (**-fied**) neutralize; invalidate; cancel. —**nul·li·fi·ca·tion** *n.*

**numb** /nəm/ ▶*adj.* deprived of

feeling or the power of motion: *numb with cold.*

▸*v.* **1** make numb. **2** stupefy; paralyze. —**numb·ness** *n.*

**num·ber** /'nəmbər/ ▸*n.* **1 a** arithmetical value representing a particular quantity and used in counting and calculating. **b** word, symbol, or figure representing this; numeral. **c** arithmetical value showing position in a series. **2** total count or aggregate: *the number of accidents has decreased.* **3** (**numbers**) arithmetic. **4 a** quantity or amount; total; count: *large number of people.* **b** numerical preponderance: *force of numbers.* **5 a** person or thing having a place in a series, esp. a single issue of a magazine, an item in a program, etc. **b** song, dance, musical item, etc. **6** company, collection, or group: *among our number.* **7** *Gram.* classification of words by their singular or plural forms.

▸*v.* **1** include. **2** assign a number or numbers to. **3** amount to (a specified number). **4 a** count. **b** comprise: *numbering forty thousand men.*

**num·ber·less** ▸*adj.* innumerable.

**nu·men** /'n(y)o͞omən/ ▸*n.* (*pl.* **-mi·na** /-mənə/) spirit or divine power presiding over a thing or place.

**nu·mer·al** /'n(y)o͞om(ə)rəl/ ▸*n.* figure or group of figures denoting a number.

**nu·mer·ate** /'n(y)o͞om(ə)rət/ ▸*adj.* acquainted with the basic principles of mathematics.

**nu·mer·a·tor** ▸*n.* number above the line in a common fraction showing how many of the parts indicated by the denominator are taken (e.g., 2 in $^2/_3$).

**nu·mer·i·cal** /n(y)o͞o'merikəl/ (also **nu·mer·ic**) ▸*adj.* of or relating to a number or numbers. —**nu·mer·i·cal·ly** *adv*

**nu·mer·ol·o·gy** /ˌn(y)o͞omə-'räləjē/ ▸*n.* (*pl.* **-gies**) study of the supposed occult significance of numbers.

**nu·mer·ous** ▸*adj.* **1** great in number; many. **2** consisting of many: *the rose family is a numerous one.*

**nu·mi·nous** /'n(y)o͞omənəs/ ▸*adj.* having a strong religious or spiritual quality; indicating or suggesting the presence of a divinity.

**nu·mis·mat·ics** /ˌn(y)o͞oməz-'matiks/ ▸*n.* study of coins or

medals. —**nu·mis·mat·ic** *adj.*
—**nu·mis·ma·tist** *n.*

**num·skull** /'nəm,skəl/ ▶*n.* stupid or foolish person.

**nun** /nən/ ▶*n.* member of a community of women living apart under religious vows.

**nun·ci·o** /'nənsē,ō; 'nŏŏn-/ ▶*n.* (*pl.* **-os**) (in the Roman Catholic Church) a papal ambassador to a foreign court or government.

**nun·cu·pa·tive** /'nəNGkyə,pātiv/ ▶*adj.* (of a will or testament) declared orally as opposed to in writing, esp. by a mortally wounded soldier or sailor.

**nun·ner·y** /'nən(ə)rē/ ▶*n.* (*pl.* **-ies**) religious house of nuns; convent.

**nup·tial** /'nəpSHəl/ ▶*adj.* of or relating to marriage or weddings.
▶*n.* (usu. **nuptials**) wedding.

**nurse** /nərs/ ▶*n.* **1** person trained to care for the sick or infirm. **2** (formerly) person employed or trained to take charge of young children.
▶*v.* **1 a** work as a nurse. **b** attend to (a sick person). **2** feed or be fed at the breast. **3** hold or treat carefully: *sat nursing my feet.* **4 a** foster; promote the development of (the arts, plants, etc.). **b** harbor or nurture (a grievance, hatred, etc.). **5** consume slowly.

□ **nurse-practitioner** registered nurse with advanced training in diagnosing and treating illness.

**nur·ser·y** /'nərs(ə)rē/ ▶*n.* (*pl.* **-ies**) **1 a** room or place equipped for young children. **b** day-care facility for children. **2** place where plants, trees, etc., are reared for sale or transplantation.

**nur·ser·y school** ▶*n.* school for children from the age of about three to five.

**nur·ture** /'nərCHər/ ▶*n.* **1** process of bringing up or training (esp. children). **2** nourishment. **3** sociological factors as an influence on or determinant of personality.
▶*v.* **1** bring up; rear. **2** nourish.
—**nur·tur·er** *n.*

**nut** /nət/ ▶*n.* **1 a** fruit consisting of a hard or tough shell around an edible kernel. **b** this kernel. **2** pod containing hard seeds. **3** small usu. hexagonal piece of metal, etc., with a threaded hole through it for securing a bolt. **4** *inf.* **a** crazy or eccentric person. **b** obsessive enthusiast or devotee: *health-food nut.*

☐ **nuts and bolts** *inf.* practical details.

**nut·hatch** ▸*n.* small bird that climbs trees and feeds on nuts, insects, etc.

**nut·meg** /ˈnətˌmeg/ ▸*n.* hard aromatic spheroidal seed used as a spice and in medicine.

**nu·tri·ent** /ˈn(y) o͞otrēənt/ ▸*n.* substance that provides essential nourishment.
▸*adj.* nutritious.

**nu·tri·ment** /ˈn(y)o͞otrəmənt/ ▸*n.* anything nourishing; food.

**nu·tri·tion** /n(y)o͞oˈtrisHən/ ▸*n.* **1** food; nourishment. **2** study of diet and its relation to health. —**nu·tri·tion·al** *adj.* —**nu·tri·tion·ist** *n.* —**nu·tri·tious** *adj.* —**nu·tri·tive** *adj.*

**nuts** /nəts/ ▸*adj. inf.* crazy, mad.
▸*interj. inf.* expression of contempt: *nuts to you.*

**nut·ty** ▸*adj.* (**-ti·er, -ti·est**) **1 a** full of nuts. **b** tasting like nuts. **2** *inf.* peculiar: *he has a lot of nutty ideas.* —**nut·ti·ness** *n.*

**nuz·zle** /ˈnəzəl/ ▸*v.* **1** rub or push against gently with the nose: *the foal nuzzled its mother.* **2** (**nuzzle up to/against**) lean or snuggle against: *the cat nuzzled up against me.*

**NV** ▸*abbr.* Nevada (in official postal use).

**NW** ▸*abbr.* **1** northwest. **2** northwestern.

**NY** ▸*abbr.* New York (in official postal use).

**ny·lon** /ˈnīˌlän/ ▸*n.* **1** tough, lightweight, elastic synthetic polymer used in industry and for textiles, etc. **2** nylon fabric. **3** (**nylons**) stockings of nylon.

**nymph** /nimf/ ▸*n.* **1** mythological female spirit associated with aspects of nature, esp. rivers and woods. **2** *poet./lit.* beautiful young woman. **3** immature form of some insects.

**nym·pho·ma·ni·a** /ˌnimfə-ˈmānēə/ ▸*n.* uncontrollable or excessive sexual desire in a woman.

**nys·tag·mus** /nəˈstagməs/ ▸*n.* rapid involuntary movements of the eyes.

# Oo

**O**[1] /ō/ (also **o**) ▸*n.* (*pl.* **Os** or **O's**; **o's**) **1** fifteenth letter of the alphabet. **2** human blood type.

**O**[2] ▸*symb. Chem.* oxygen.

**O**[3] ▸*interj.* var. of **OH**.

**o'** ▸*prep.* of; on: *o'clock | will-o'-the-wisp.*

**-o** /ō/ ▸*suffix* forming usu. slang variants or derivatives: *weirdo | wino.*

**oaf** /ōf/ ▸*n.* (*pl.* **oafs**) **1** awkward lout. **2** stupid person. **—oaf·ish** *adj.* **—oaf·ish·ly** *adv.* **—oaf·ish·ness** *n.*

**oak** /ōk/ ▸*n.* **1** tree having lobed leaves and bearing acorns. **2** durable wood of this tree, used esp. for furniture and in building. **3** [as *adj.*] made of oak: *oak table.* **—oak·en** *adj.*

**oar** /ôr/ ▸*n.* pole with a blade used for rowing or steering a boat by leverage against the water.

**oar·lock** ▸*n.* device for holding an oar in position while rowing.

**o·a·sis** /ō'āsis/ ▸*n.* (*pl.* **-ses**) **1** fertile spot in a desert. **2** area or period of calm in the midst of turbulence.

**oat** /ōt/ ▸*n.* **1** cereal plant, cultivated in cool climates. **2** (**oats**) grain yielded by this, used as food. **—oat·en** *adj.*

**oath** /ōTH/ ▸*n.* (*pl.* **oaths**) **1** solemn declaration (often naming God) as to the truth of something or as a commitment to future action. **2** profane or blasphemous utterance; curse.

**oat·meal** ▸*n.* **1** meal made from ground or rolled oats used esp. in cereal, cookies, etc. **2** cooked breakfast cereal made from this.

**ob·du·rate** /'äbd(y)ərit/ ▸*adj.* **1** stubborn. **2** hardened against persuasion or influence. **—ob·du·ra·cy** *n.*

**o·bei·sance** /ō'bāsəns/ ▸*n.* **1** bow, curtsy, or other respectful or submissive gesture. **2** homage; deference: *pay obeisance.* **—o·bei·sant** *adj.*

**ob·e·lisk** /'äbə‚lisk/ ▸*n.* tapering, usu. four-sided stone pillar set up as a monument or landmark, etc.

**o·bese** /ō'bēs/ ▸*adj.* very fat. **—o·be·si·ty** *n.*

**o·bey** /ō'bā/ ▸v. **1 a** carry out the command of: *you will obey me.* **b** carry out (a command): *obey orders.* **2** do what one is told to do. **3** be actuated by (a force or impulse). **—o·be·di·ence** *n.* **—o·be·di·ent** *adj.*

**ob·fus·cate** /'äbfə,skāt/ ▸v. **1** obscure or confuse. **2** stupefy, bewilder. **—ob·fus·ca·tion** *n.*

**o·bit·u·ar·y** /ō'bichoo,erē/ ▸n. (*pl.* **-ies**) notice of a death esp. in a newspaper.

**obj.** ▸abbr. **1** object. **2** objective. **3** objection.

**ob·ject** ▸n. /'äbjikt/ **1** material thing that can be seen or touched. **2** person or thing to which action or feeling is directed: *the object of our study.* **3** thing sought or aimed at; purpose. **4** *Gram.* noun or its equivalent governed by an active transitive verb or by a preposition.
▸v. /əb'jekt/ **1** express or feel opposition, disapproval, or reluctance; protest. **2** state as an objection. **—ob·jec·tor** *n.*

**ob·jec·tion** /əb'jekshən/ ▸n. **1** expression or feeling of opposition or disapproval. **2** adverse reason or statement.

**ob·jec·tion·a·ble** ▸adj. **1** open to objection. **2** unpleasant or offensive. **—ob·jec·tion·a·bly** *adv.*

**ob·jec·tive** ▸adj. **1** (of a person, writing, art, etc.) not dealing with personal opinions or feelings in dealing with facts. **2** external to the mind; actually existing. **3** *Gram.* (of a case or word) constructed as or appropriate to the object of a transitive verb or preposition.
▸n. something sought or aimed at; goal. **—ob·jec·tive·ly** *adv.* **—ob·jec·tive·ness** *n.* **—ob·jec·tiv·i·ty** *n.*

**ob·jec·tiv·ism** ▸n. **1** tendency to lay stress on what is external to or independent of the mind. **2** belief that certain things, esp. moral truths, exist independently of human knowledge or perception of them.

**ob·jet d'art** /,ôbzhä 'där/ ▸n. (*pl.* **ob·jets d'art** *pronunc.* same) small object of artistic worth.

**ob·jet trou·vé** /ôb,zhä troo'vä/ ▸n. (*pl.* **ob·jets trou·vés** *pronunc.* same) object found or picked up at random and considered aesthetically pleasing.

**ob·jur·gate** /'äbjər,gāt/ ▸v. rebuke severely; scold.

**ob·la·tion** /əˈblāsHən/ ▸n. thing presented to God or a god.

**ob·li·gate** /ˈäbliˌgāt/ ▸v. bind or compel (a person), esp. legally or morally: *he is obligated to answer the investigator's questions.* —**ob·li·ga·tion** n.

**ob·lig·a·to·ry** /əˈbligəˌtôrē/ ▸adj. 1 legally or morally binding. 2 compulsory. —**ob·lig·a·to·ri·ly** adv.

**o·blige** /əˈblīj/ ▸v. 1 constrain; compel. 2 be binding on. 3 a make indebted by conferring a favor. b gratify: *oblige me by leaving.* c perform a service for: *will you oblige?* 4 be indebted: *am obliged to you for your help.*

**o·blig·ing** ▸adj. courteous or accommodating; ready to do a service or kindness. —**o·blig·ing·ly** adv.

**o·blique** /əˈblēk/ ▸adj. 1 a slanting. b diverging from a straight line or course. 2 not going straight to the point; indirect.
▸n. oblique muscle. —**ob·lique·ly** adv. —**o·blique·ness** n.

**ob·lit·er·ate** /əˈblitəˌrāt/ ▸v. 1 a blot out; destroy. b leave no clear traces of. 2 deface (a postage stamp, etc.) to prevent further use. —**ob·lit·er·a·tion** n.

**ob·liv·i·on** /əˈblivēən/ ▸n. state of having or being forgotten.

**ob·liv·i·ous** /əˈblivēəs/ ▸adj. not aware of or not concerned about what is happening around one.

**ob·long** /ˈäbˌlôNG/ ▸adj. rectangular with adjacent sides unequal.
▸n. oblong figure or object.

**ob·nox·ious** /əbˈnäksHəs/ ▸adj. offensive; objectionable; disliked. —**ob·nox·ious·ly** adv. —**ob·nox·ious·ness** n.

**o·boe** /ˈōbō/ ▸n. woodwind double-reed instrument of treble pitch and plaintive tone. —**o·bo·ist** n.

**ob·scene** /əbˈsēn/ ▸adj. 1 offensively indecent, esp. by offending accepted sexual morality. 2 offensive to moral principles: *using animals' skins for fur coats is obscene.* —**ob·scene·ly** adv. —**ob·scen·i·ty** n.

**ob·scure** /əbˈskyo͝or/ ▸adj. 1 not discovered or known about: *its origins are obscure.* 2 not clearly expressed or easily understood. 3 not important or well known. 4 vague; indistinct. 5 dim or dingy.
▸v. make obscure, dark, indistinct, or unintelligible. —**ob·scure·ly** adv. —**ob·scu·ri·ty** n.

**ob·se·cra·tion** /ˌäbsəˈkrāsHən/ ▶*n.* earnest pleading or supplication.

**ob·se·quies** /ˈäbsəkwēz/ ▶*pl. n.* funeral rites.

**ob·se·qui·ous** /əbˈsēkwēəs/ ▶*adj.* servilely obedient or attentive. —**ob·se·qui·ous·ly** *adv.* —**ob·se·qui·ous·ness** *n.*

**ob·serv·ance** /əbˈzərvəns/ ▶*n.* **1** keeping or performing of a law, duty, custom, ritual, etc. **2** ceremony; rite.

**ob·serv·ant** ▶*adj.* **1** acute or diligent in taking notice. **2** attentive in esp. religious observances: *an observant Jew.* —**ob·serv·ant·ly** *adv.*

**ob·ser·va·to·ry** /əbˈzərvəˌtôrē/ ▶*n.* (*pl.* **-ries**) building for astronomical or other observation.

**ob·serve** /əbˈzərv/ ▶*v.* **1** perceive; become conscious of. **2** watch carefully. **3 a** follow or adhere to (a law, command, method, principle, etc.). **b** keep or adhere to (an appointed time). **c** maintain (silence). **d** perform (a rite). **e** celebrate (an anniversary). **4** examine and note scientifically. **5** say, esp. by way of comment. **6** remark.

—**ob·serv·a·tion** *n.* —**ob·serv·er** *n.*

**ob·sess** /əbˈses/ ▶*v.* **1** preoccupy or fill the mind of: *he was obsessed with thoughts of suicide.* **2** be preoccupied in this way: *he obsessed about the wrong she had done him.* —**ob·ses·sion** *n.* —**ob·ses·sive** *adj. & n.* —**ob·ses·sive·ly** *adv.* —**ob·ses·sive·ness** *n.*

**ob·so·les·cent** /ˌäbsəˈlesənt/ ▶*adj.* becoming obsolete; going out of use or date. —**ob·so·les·cence** *n.*

**ob·so·lete** /ˌäbsəˈlēt/ ▶*adj.* disused; discarded; antiquated.

**ob·sta·cle** /ˈäbstəkəl/ ▶*n.* person or thing that obstructs progress.

**ob·stet·rics** /əbˈstetriks/ ▶*pl. n.* [usu. treated as *sing.*] branch of medicine concerned with pregnancy and childbirth. —**ob·stet·ric** *adj.* —**ob·ste·tri·cian** *n.*

**ob·sti·nate** /ˈäbstənit/ ▶*adj.* stubborn; intractable. —**ob·sti·na·cy** *n.* —**ob·sti·nate·ly** *adv.*

**ob·strep·er·ous** /əbˈstrepərəs; äb-/ ▶*adj.* noisy and difficult to control. —**ob·strep·er·ous·ly** *adv.* —**ob·strep·er·ous·ness** *n.*

**ob·struct** /əbˈstrəkt/ ▶v. **1** block up. **2** prevent or retard the progress of. —**ob·struc·tion** n. —**ob·struc·tive** adj. —**ob·struc·tive·ness** n. —**ob·struc·tor** n.

**ob·struc·tion·ism** /əb-ˈstrəksHəˌnizəm/ ▶n. practice of deliberately impeding or delaying the course of legal, legislative, or other procedures.

**ob·tain** /əbˈtān/ ▶v. **1** acquire; secure. **2** formal be prevalent or established. —**ob·tain·a·ble** adj. —**ob·tain·ment** n.

**ob·trude** /əbˈtro͞od/ ▶v. **1** stick out; push forward. **2** thrust forward (oneself, one's opinion, etc.) importunately. —**ob·tru·sion** n. —**ob·tru·sive** adj. —**ob·tru·sive·ly** adv. —**ob·tru·sive·ness** n.

**ob·tru·sive** /əbˈtro͞osiv/ ▶adj. noticeable or prominent in an unwelcome or intrusive way.

**ob·tuse** /əbˈt(y)o͞os/ ▶adj. **1** dull-witted. **2** blunt; not sharp. **3** (of an angle) between 90° and 180°. —**ob·tuse·ly** adv. —**ob·tuse·ness** n.

**ob·verse** /ˈäbˌvərs/ ▶n. **1 a** side of a coin or medal, etc., bearing the head or principal design. **b** this design. **2** front or proper or top side of a thing. **3** counterpart of a fact or truth.

**ob·vi·ate** /ˈäbvēˌāt/ ▶v. get around or do away with (a need, inconvenience, etc.). —**ob·vi·a·tion** n.

**ob·vi·ous** /ˈäbvēəs/ ▶adj. easily seen or recognized or understood. —**ob·vi·ous·ly** adv. —**ob·vi·ous·ness** n.

**oc·ca·sion** /əˈkāzHən/ ▶n. **1 a** special or noteworthy event or happening. **b** time of this: on the occasion of their marriage. **2** reason, ground(s), or justification. **3** juncture suitable for doing something; opportunity. ▶v. **1** be the cause of. **2** cause (a person or thing to do something). —**oc·ca·sion·al** adj. —**oc·ca·sion·al·ly** adv.

**Oc·ci·dent** /ˈäksidənt; -ˌdent/ poet. ▶n. **1** (**the Occident**) West. **2** Europe, America, or both, as distinct from the Orient. —**oc·ci·den·tal** adj.

**oc·ci·put** /ˈäksəpət/ ▶n. (pl. **oc·ci·puts** or **oc·cip·i·ta** /äkˈsipitə/) back of the head or skull.

**oc·cult** /əˈkəlt/ ▶adj. **1** supernatural; mystical. **2** kept secret; esoteric.

**oc·cu·pa·tion** /ˌäkyəˈpāSHən/ ▶*n.* **1** what occupies one; means of passing one's time. **2** person's employment. **3 a** act of taking or holding possession of (a country, district, etc.) by military force. **b** state or time of this. —**oc·cu·pa·tion·al** *adj.*

**oc·cu·py** /ˈäkyəˌpī/ ▶*v.* (**-pied**) **1** reside in. **2** take up or fill (space or time or a place). **3** hold (a position or office). **4** keep (someone) busy or engaged. **5** take military possession of (a country, region, town, or strategic position). —**oc·cu·pant** *n.*

**oc·cur** /əˈkər/ ▶*v.* (**-curred, -cur·ring**) **1** come into being; happen. **2** exist or be encountered. **3** come into the mind of. —**oc·cur·rence** *n.*

**o·cean** /ˈōSHən/ ▶*n.* **1** large expanse of sea, esp. the Atlantic, Pacific, Indian, Arctic, and Antarctic Oceans. **2** very large expanse or quantity of anything: *oceans of time.* —**o·ce·an·ic** *adj.*

**o·cea·nog·ra·phy** /ˌōSHə-ˈnägrəfē/ ▶*n.* branch of science dealing with the sea. —**o·cea·nog·ra·pher** *n.* —**o·cea·no·graph·ic** *adj.*

**o·ce·lot** /ˈäsəˌlät; ˈōsə-/ ▶*n.* **1** medium-sized feline native to S. and Central America, having a deep yellow or orange coat with black striped and spotted markings. **2** its fur.

**o·cher** /ˈōkər/ ▶*n.* **1** mineral of clay and ferric oxide, used as a pigment varying from light yellow to brown or red. **2** pale brownish yellow.

**o'clock** /əˈkläk/ ▶*adv.* of the clock: *6 o'clock.*

**Oct.** ▶*abbr.* October.

**oc·ta·gon** /ˈäktəˌgän/ ▶*n.* plane figure with eight sides and angles. —**oc·tag·o·nal** *adj.*

**oc·tane** /ˈäktān/ ▶*n.* colorless flammable hydrocarbon present in gasoline.

**oc·tave** /ˈäktəv/ ▶*n.* **1** *Mus.* **a** eight notes occupying the interval between (and including) two notes, one having twice or half the frequency of vibration of the other. **b** this interval. **c** each of the two notes at the extremes of this interval. **2** group of eight.

**oc·tet** /äkˈtet/ ▶*n.* **1** *Mus.* **a** composition for eight voices or instruments. **b** performers of such a piece. **2** group of eight. **3** first eight lines of a sonnet.

**Oc·to·ber** /äk'tōbər/ ▸n. tenth month of the year.

**oc·to·ge·nar·i·an** /ˌäktəjə-'ne(ə)rēən/ ▸n. person from 80 to 89 years old.
▸adj. of this age.

**oc·to·pus** /'äktəpəs/ ▸n. (pl. **-pus·es**) cephalopod mollusk having eight suckered arms, a soft saclike body, and strong beaklike jaws.

**oc·u·lar** /'äkyələr/ ▸adj. of or connected with the eyes or sight; visual.

**OD**[1] ▸abbr. **1** doctor of optometry. **2** overdraft.

**OD**[2] inf. ▸v. (**OD's**, **OD'd**, **OD'ing**) take an overdose.
▸n. overdose, esp. of a narcotic drug.

**o.d.** ▸abbr. outside diameter.

**odd** /äd/ ▸adj. **1** strange, remarkable or eccentric. **2** casual; occasional: *odd jobs.* **3** not normally noticed or considered; unpredictable. **4** additional; besides the calculated amount: *a few odd cents.* **5 a** (of numbers) not integrally divisible by two. **b** bearing such a number: *no parking on odd dates.* **6** one item of a pair. **7** (appended to a number, sum, weight, etc.) somewhat more than: *forty-odd people.* **8** by which a round number, given sum, etc., is exceeded: *we have 102—what shall we do with the odd 2?*
—**odd·ly** adv. —**odd·ness** n.

**odd·ball** inf. ▸n. eccentric person.
▸adj. strange; bizarre.

**odd·i·ty** ▸n. (pl. **-ties**) **1** strange person, thing, or occurrence. **2** peculiar trait. **3** state of being odd.

**odd·ment** /'ädmənt/ ▸n. (usu. **oddments**) remnant or part of something, typically left over from a larger piece or set.

**odds** ▸pl. n. **1** ratio between the amounts staked by the parties to a bet, based on the expected probability either way. **2** balance of probability in favor of or against some result: *the odds are that it will rain.*

**ode** /ōd/ ▸n. lyric poem in the form of an address to a particular subject, often in elevated style and written in varied or irregular meter.

**o·de·um** /'ōdēəm/ ▸n. (pl. **o·de·ums** or **o·de·a** /'ōdēə/) (esp. in ancient Greece or Rome) a building used for musical performances.

**o·di·ous** /ˈōdēəs/ ▸*adj.* hateful; repulsive. —**o·di·ous·ly** *adv.* —**o·di·ous·ness** *n.*

**o·di·um** /ˈōdēəm/ ▸*n.* widespread dislike or disapproval.

**o·dor** /ˈōdər/ ▸*n.* **1** property of a substance that has an effect on the nasal sense of smell. **2** quality or trace: *odor of intolerance.* —**o·dor·less** *adj.*

**o·dor·if·er·ous** /ˌōdəˈrifərəs/ ▸*adj.* diffusing a scent, esp. an agreeable one; fragrant.

**od·ys·sey** /ˈädəsē/ ▸*n.* (*pl.* **-seys**) long adventurous journey.

**o'er** /ô(ə)r/ ▸*adv. & prep. poet.* OVER.

**oeu·vre** /ˈœvrə/ ▸*n.* works of an author, painter, composer, etc., esp. regarded collectively.

**of** /əv/ ▸*prep.* connecting a noun (often a verbal noun) or pronoun with a preceding noun, adjective, adverb, or verb, expressing a wide range of relations broadly describable as follows: **1** origin or cause: *paintings of Turner | died of malnutrition.* **2** material or substance: *house of cards | built of bricks.* **3** belonging or connection: *thing of the past | articles of clothing.* **4** identity or close relation: *city of Rome | pound of apples.* **5** removal or separation: *north of the city |* robbed us of $500. **6** reference or direction: *beware of the dog | short of money.* **7** partition, classification, or inclusion: *no more of that | part of the story | this sort of book.* **8** description, quality, or condition: *person of tact | girl of ten.* **9** time in relation to the following hour: *quarter of three.*

**o·fay** /ˈōˌfā/ ▸*n.* offensive term for a white person, used by black people.

**off** /ôf/ ▸*adv.* **1** away; at or to a distance: *is three miles off.* **2** out of position; not on or touching or attached: *take your coat off.* **3** so as to be rid of: *sleep it off.* **4** so as to be discontinued or stopped: *turn off the radio.* **5** to the end; so as to be clear: *clear off | pay off.* **6** situated as regards money, supplies, etc.: *is not very well off.*

▸*prep.* **1 a** from; away or down or up from: *fell off the chair.* **b** not on: *was already off the stage.* **2 a** (temporarily) relieved of or abstaining from: *off duty.* **b** not achieving or doing one's best in: *off one's game.* **3** using as a source or means of support: *live off the land.* **4** leading from; not far from: *a street off 1st Avenue.*

▸*adj.* far, further: *the off side of the wall.*

**of·fal** /ˈôfəl/ ▸*n.* less valuable edible parts of a carcass, esp. the entrails and internal organs.

**off·beat** ▸*adj.* **1** *Mus.* not coinciding with the beat. **2** *inf.* eccentric; unconventional.

▸*n. Mus.* any of the unaccented beats in a bar.

**of·fend** /əˈfend/ ▸*v.* **1** cause offense to; wound the feelings of. **2** displease or anger. **3** do wrong; transgress. —**of·fend·er** *n.* —**of·fend·ing** *adj.*

**of·fense** /əˈfens/ ▸*n.* **1** illegal act; transgression or misdemeanor. **2** wounding of the feelings: *no offense was meant.* **3** aggressive action. **4** /ˈôfens/ *Sports* team in possession of the ball, puck, etc.

**of·fen·sive** ▸*adj.* **1** giving or meant or likely to give offense; insulting. **2** disgusting. **3 a** aggressive, attacking. **b** (of a weapon) for attacking. **4** *Sports* designating the team in possession of the ball, puck, etc.

▸*n.* **1** aggressive action or attitude. **2** attack; offensive campaign. —**of·fen·sive·ly** *adv.* —**of·fen·sive·ness** *n.*

**of·fer** /ˈôfər/ ▸*v.* **1** present for

acceptance, refusal, or consideration: *offered me a drink.* **2** express readiness or show intention: *offered to take the children.* **3** provide; give an opportunity for. **4** present itself; occur: *as opportunity offers.*

▸*n.* **1** expression of readiness to do or give if desired, or to buy or sell. **2** amount offered. **3** bid.

**off·hand** ▸*adj.* curt or casual in manner.

▸*adv.* without preparation or premeditation: *I can't think of an answer offhand.* —**off·hand·ed** *adj.* —**off·hand·ed·ly** *adv.* —**off·hand·ed·ness** *n.*

**of·fice** /ˈôfis/ ▸*n.* **1** room or building used as a place of business, esp. for clerical or administrative work. **2** position with duties attached to it. **3** tenure of an official position, esp. that of government. **4** kindness or attention; service, esp. as: *through the good offices of.* **5** religious service.

**of·fi·cer** ▸*n.* **1** person holding a position of authority or trust, esp. one with a commission in the armed services, etc. **2** policeman or policewoman. **3** holder of a post in a society or business (e.g., the president or secretary). **4** holder of a public, civil, or ecclesiastical office.

**of·fi·cial** /ə'fisHəl/ ▸*adj.* **1** of or relating to an office or its tenure or duties. **2** characteristic of officials and bureaucracy. **3** properly authorized.

▸*n.* person holding office or engaged in official duties. —**of·fi·cial·ly** *adv.*

**of·fi·ci·ate** /ə'fisHē,āt/ ▸*v.* **1** act in an official capacity. **2** conduct a religious service.

**of·fi·cious** /ə'fisHəs/ ▸*adj.* **1** asserting one's authority aggressively; domineering. **2** intrusive; meddlesome. —**of·fi·cious·ly** *adv.* —**of·fi·cious·ness** *n.*

**off·set** ▸*n.* **1** compensation; consideration or amount neutralizing the effect of a contrary one. **2** [as *adj.*] method of printing in which ink is transferred from a plate or stone to a rubber surface and from there to paper, etc.: *offset lithography.*

▸*v.* (**-set·ting**; *past* and *past part.* **-set**) **1** counterbalance; compensate. **2** print by the offset process.

**off·shoot** ▸*n.* **1 a** side shoot or branch. **b** descendant of a family. **2** something derivative.

**off·shore** ▸*adj.* **1** at sea some distance from the shore. **2** (of goods, funds, etc.) made or registered abroad.

**off·spring** ▸*n.* (*pl.* same) children; descendant(s).

**off·stage** ▸*adj. & adv.* not on the stage and so not visible to the audience.

**oft** /ôft/ ▸*adv. poet.* often: *oft-recurring.*

**of·ten** /'ôf(t)ən/ ▸*adv.* (**-er, -est**) **1** frequently; many times. **2** at short intervals.

**o·gee** /ō'jē/ ▸*adj.* having a double continuous S-shaped curve.

▸*n.* S-shaped line or molding.

**o·gle** /'ōgəl/ ▸*v.* eye amorously or lecherously.

▸*n.* amorous or lecherous look. —**o·gler** *n.*

**o·gre** /'ōgər/ ▸*n.* **1** human-eating giant in folklore, etc. **2** terrifying person.

**OH** ▸*abbr.* Ohio (in official postal use).

**oh** /ō/ (also **O**) ▸*interj.* expressing surprise, pain, entreaty, etc.

**ohm** /ōm/ ▸*n.* unit of electrical resistance, transmitting a current of one ampere when subjected to a potential difference of one volt. (Symb.: Ω)

**-oid** ▶*suffix* forming adjectives and nouns, denoting form or resemblance: *asteroid* | *rhomboid* | *thyroid*. — **-oidal** *suffix*. — **-oidally** *suffix*.

**oil** /oil/ ▶*n.* **1** any of various thick, viscous, usu. flammable liquids insoluble in water. **2** petroleum. **3 a** oil paint: *a portrait in oils*. **b** picture painted in oil paints. ▶*v.* **1** apply oil to; lubricate. **2** impregnate or treat with oil. —**oil·y** *adj.*

**oil·cloth** ▶*n.* **1** fabric waterproofed with oil. **2** canvas coated with oil and used to cover a table or floor.

**oint·ment** /'ointmənt/ ▶*n.* greasy healing or cosmetic preparation for the skin.

**OK**[1] /'ō'kā/ (also **o·kay**) *inf.* ▶*adj.* all right; satisfactory. ▶*adv.* well; satisfactorily: *that worked out OK*. ▶*n.* (*pl.* **OKs**) approval; sanction. ▶*v.* (**OK's, OK'd, OK'ing**) approve; sanction.

**OK**[2] ▶*abbr.* Oklahoma (in official postal use).

**Okla.** ▶*abbr.* Oklahoma.

**ok·ra** /'ōkrə/ ▶*n.* **1** plant yielding long ridged seed pods. **2** seed pods eaten as a vegetable and used to thicken soups and stews.

**old** /ōld/ ▶*adj.* (**-er, -est**) **1 a** advanced in age. **b** not young or near its beginning. **2** made long ago. **3** long in use. **4** worn or dilapidated or shabby from age or use. **5** having the characteristics (experience, feebleness, etc.) of age. **6** practiced, inveterate. **7** belonging to the past; lingering on; former: *old times*. **8** dating from far back; ancient; primeval: *old friends*. **9** (appended to a period of time) of age: *is four years old*.

**Old Eng·lish** ▶*n.* English language up to *c.* 1150.

**old-fash·ioned** ▶*adj.* in or according to a fashion or tastes no longer current; antiquated.

**old guard** ▶*n.* original or past or conservative members of a group.

**old hat** ▶*adj. inf.* hackneyed.

**old mas·ter** ▶*n.* **1** great artist of former times, esp. of the 13th–17th c. in Europe. **2** painting by such a painter.

**old school** ▶*n.* **1** traditional attitudes. **2** people having such attitudes.

**Old Tes·ta·ment** ▸*n.* part of the Christian Bible containing the scriptures of the Hebrews.

**old-tim·er** ▸*n.* person with long experience or standing.

**Old World** ▸*n.* Europe, Asia, and Africa.

**o·le·ag·i·nous** /ˌōlē'ajənəs/ ▸*adj.* like or producing oil.

**o·le·an·der** /'ōlēˌandər/ ▸*n.* evergreen poisonous shrub native to the Mediterranean and bearing clusters of white, pink, or red flowers.

**o·le·o·mar·ga·rine** /ˌōlēō-'märj(ə)rən/ ▸*n.* margarine made from vegetable oils.

**ol·fac·to·ry** /äl'fakt(ə)rē/ ▸*adj.* of or relating to the sense of smell.

**ol·i·gar·chy** /'äliˌgärkē/ ▸*n.* (*pl.* -chies) **1** government or nation governed by a small group of people. **2** members of such a government. —**ol·i·garch** *n.* —**ol·i·gar·chic** *adj.*

**ol·ive** /'äləv/ ▸*n.* **1** (also **ol·ive tree**) evergreen tree having dark-green, lance-shaped leathery leaves with silvery undersides. **2** small oval fruit of this, having a hard stone and bitter flesh, green when unripe and bluish-black when ripe. **3** grayish-green color of an unripe olive.

▸*adj.* **1** colored like an unripe olive. **2** (of the complexion) yellowish-brown; sallow.

**om·buds·man** /'ämbədzmən/ ▸*n.* (*pl.* -men) official appointed to investigate complaints against public authorities, etc.

**o·me·ga** /ō'māgə/ ▸*n.* **1** last (24th) letter of the Greek alphabet (Ω, ω). **2** last of a series; final development.

**om·e·let** (also **om·e·lette**) ▸*n.* beaten eggs cooked in a frying pan, served folded over, often with a sweet or savory filling.

**o·men** /'ōmən/ ▸*n.* occurrence or object regarded as portending good or evil.

**om·i·nous** /'ämənəs/ ▸*adj.* **1** threatening. **2** of evil omen. —**om·i·nous·ly** *adv.*

**o·mit** /ō'mit/ ▸*v.* (**o·mit·ted**, **o·mit·ting**) **1** leave out; not insert or include. **2** leave undone. **3** fail or neglect. —**o·mis·sion** *n.*

**omni-** ▸*comb. form* **1** all. **2** in all ways or places.

**om·ni·bus** /'ämnəˌbəs/ ▸*n.* volume containing several items previously published separately. ▸*adj.* comprising several items.

**om·nip·o·tent** /äm'nipətənt/ ▸*adj.* **1** having great or absolute

power. **2** having great influence.
—**om·nip·o·tence** *n.*

**om·ni·pres·ent** /ˌämnəˈpreznt/
▶*adj.* **1** present everywhere.
**2** widely or constantly
encountered.
—**om·ni·pres·ence** *n.*

**om·ni·scient** /ämˈnisHənt/ ▶*adj.*
knowing everything.
—**om·ni·science** *n.*

**om·ni·um-gath·er·um**
/ˌämnēəm ˈgaTHərəm/ ▶*n.*
collection of miscellaneous
people or things.

**om·niv·o·rous** /ämˈniv(ə)rəs/
▶*adj.* **1** feeding on both plants
and flesh. **2** making use of
everything available.
—**om·ni·vore** *n.*
—**om·niv·o·rous·ly** *adv.*

**on** /än/ ▶*prep.* **1** supported by or
attached to or covering or
enclosing: *sat on a chair* | *stuck on
the wall* | *rings on her fingers* |
*leaned on his elbow.* **2** (of time)
exactly at; during: *on the hour* |
*working on Tuesday.* **3** as a result
of: *on further examination I found
this.* **4** (so as to be) having
membership, etc., of or
residence at or in: *she is on the
board of directors* | *lives on the
waterfront.* **5** close to: *a house on
the sea.* **6** in the direction of.

**7** having as a basis or motive: *on
good authority* | *did it on purpose.*
**8** concerning: *writes on finance.*
**9** using or engaged with: *is on the
pill* | *here on business.* **10** at the
expense of: *drinks are on me.*
**11** added to: *disaster on disaster.*
**12** in a specified manner or
style: *on the cheap* | *on the run.*
▶*adv.* **1** (so as to be) wearing: *put
your boots on.* **2** in the
appropriate direction; toward:
*look on.* **3** further forward: *is
getting on in years.* **4** with
continued action or operation:
*went plodding on* | *light is on.*
**5** due to take place as planned: *is
the party still on?*

**once** /wəns/ ▶*adv.* **1** on one
occasion only: *did not once say
please* | *have read it once.* **2** at
some time in the past: *could once
play chess.* **3** ever or at all: *if you
once forget it.*
▶*conj.* as soon as: *once they have
gone we can relax.*
▶*n.* one time or occasion: *just the
once.*

**on·col·o·gy** /änˈkäləjē; äNG-/ ▶*n.*
*Med.* study and treatment of
tumors.

**on·com·ing** ▶*adj.* approaching
from the front.

**one** /wən/ ▶*adj.* **1** single and

integral in number. **2** (with a noun implied) single person or thing of the kind expressed or implied: *one of the best.* **3** particular but undefined, esp. as contrasted with another: *that is one view.* **4** only such: *the one man who can do it.* **5** forming a unity: *one and undivided.* **6** identical; the same.

▸*n.* **1 a** lowest cardinal number. **b** thing numbered with it. **2** unity; a unit. **3** single thing or person or example: often referring to a noun previously expressed or implied: *the big dog and the small one.*

▸*pron.* **1** person of a specified kind: *loved ones.* **2** used to refer to any person as representing people in general: *one must admire him for his courage.*

**o·nei·ro·man·cy** /ō'nīrə,mansē/ ▸*n.* interpretation of dreams in order to foretell the future.

**one·ness** ▸*n.* **1** singleness. **2** uniqueness. **3** agreement. **4** sameness.

**on·er·ous** /'ōnərəs/ ▸*adj.* burdensome.
—**on·er·ous·ness** *n.*

**one·self** ▸*pron.* reflexive and (in apposition) emphatic form of one: *dress oneself* | *one has to do it oneself.*

**one-sid·ed** ▸*adj.* unfair; partial.

**one·time** ▸*adj. & adv.* former.

**one-track mind** ▸*n.* mind preoccupied with one subject.

**one-way** ▸*adj.* allowing movement or travel in one direction only.

**one-world** ▸*adj.* of, relating to, or holding the view that the world's inhabitants are interdependent and should behave accordingly.

**on·go·ing** ▸*adj.* **1** continuing. **2** in progress: *ongoing discussions.*

**on·ion** /'ənyən/ ▸*n.* edible bulb with a pungent taste and smell, composed of many concentric layers.

**on·look·er** ▸*n.* spectator.
—**on·look·ing** *adj.*

**on·ly** /'ōnlē/ ▸*adv.* **1** solely; merely; exclusively. **2** no longer ago than: *saw them only yesterday.* **3** with no better result than: *hurried home only to find her gone.*

▸*adj.* **1** existing alone of its or their kind: *their only son.* **2** best or alone worth knowing: *the only place to eat.*

▸*conj. inf.* except that; but: *he is still a young man, only he seems older.*

**on·o·ma·si·ol·o·gy** /ˌänəˌmāsē-ˈäləjē; -ˌmāzē-/ ▸*n.* branch of knowledge that deals with terminology, in particular contrasting terms for similar concepts.

**on·o·mas·tic** /ˌänəˈmastik/ ▸*adj.* of or relating to the study of the history and origin of proper names.

**on·o·mat·o·poe·ia** /ˌänəˌmatə-ˈpēə/ ▸*n.* formation of a word from a sound associated with what is named (e.g., *cuckoo*, *sizzle*). —**on·o·mat·o·poe·ic** *adj.* —**o·no·mat·o·po·et·ic** *adj.*

**on·rush** ▸*n.* onward rush.

**on·set** ▸*n.* beginning of something, esp. something unpleasant: *the onset of the flu.*

**on·slaught** ▸*n.* fierce attack.

**on·tic** /ˈäntik/ ▸*adj.* of or relating to entities and the facts about them; relating to real as opposed to phenomenal existence.

**on·to** /ˈänˌtoo/ ▸*prep.* moving to a location on (the surface of something).

**o·nus** /ˈōnəs/ ▸*n.* (*pl.* **o·nus·es**) burden, duty, or responsibility.

**on·ward** /ˈänwərd/ ▸*adv.* (also **on·wards**) **1** further on. **2** with advancing motion. ▸*adj.* directed onward.

**on·yx** /ˈäniks/ ▸*n.* semiprecious variety of agate with colored layers.

**o·ol·o·gy** /ōˈäləjē/ ▸*n.* study or collecting of birds' eggs.

**ooze** /ooz/ ▸*v.* **1** trickle or leak slowly out. **2** (of a substance) exude. **3** exude or exhibit (a feeling) liberally: *oozed sympathy.* ▸*n.* **1** wet mud or slime, esp. at the bottom of a river, lake, or estuary. **2** sluggish flow. —**ooz·y** *adj.*

**o·pal** /ˈōpəl/ ▸*n.* iridescent mineral often used as a gemstone. —**o·pal·es·cence** *n.* —**o·pal·es·cent** *adj.*

**o·paque** /ōˈpāk/ ▸*adj.* (**o·paqu·er**, **o·paqu·est**) **1** not transmitting light. **2** impenetrable to sight. **3** obscure; not lucid. **4** obtuse; dull-witted. —**o·pac·i·ty** *n.* —**o·paque·ly** *adv.* —**o·paque·ness** *n.*

**op. cit.** ▸*abbr.* in the work already quoted.

**OPEC** /ˈōpek/ ▸*abbr.* Organization of Petroleum Exporting Countries.

**o·pen** /ˈōpən/ ▸*adj.* **1** not closed, locked, or blocked up; allowing access. **2** unenclosed; unconfined; unobstructed. **3** uncovered; exposed.

**4** undisguised; public.
**5** unfolded or spread out: *had the map open on the table.* **6** (of a fabric) with gaps or intervals.
**7** (of a person) frank and communicative. **8** (of the mind) accessible to new ideas; unprejudiced. **9** (of an exhibition, shop, etc.) accessible to visitors or customers. **10** (of a meeting) admitting all. **11** (of a race, competition, scholarship, etc.) unrestricted as to who may compete. **12 a** willing to receive: *is open to offers.* **b** (of a choice, offer, or opportunity) still available: *there are three courses open to us.* **c** likely to suffer from or be affected by: *open to abuse.*

▶*v.* **1** make or become open or more open. **2 a** change from a closed or fastened position so as to allow access: *opened the door.* **b** (of a door, lid, etc.) have its position changed to allow access: *the door opened slowly.* **3** (of a door, room, etc.) afford access as specified: *opened on to a large garden.* **4 a** start or establish or get going (a business, activity, etc.). **b** be initiated; make a start.

▶*n.* **1** open space or country or air. **2** public notice or view;

general attention, esp. as: *into the open.* —**o·pen·er** *n.*
—**o·pen·ly** *adv.* —**o·pen·ness** *n.*

**o·pen-and-shut** ▶*adj.* (of an argument, case, etc.) straightforward and conclusive.

**o·pen-end·ed** ▶*adj.* having no predetermined limit.

**o·pen·hand·ed** /ˈōpənˈhandid/ ▶*adj.* generous.

**o·pen·ing** ▶*n.* **1** aperture or gap, esp. allowing access. **2** opportunity. **3** beginning; initial part.

▶*adj.* initial; first.

**o·pen·mind·ed** ▶*adj.* willing to consider new ideas; unprejudiced.

**o·pe·ra**[1] /ˈäp(ə)rə/ ▶*n.* dramatic work in one or more acts, set to music for singers (usu. in costume) and instrumentalists.
—**op·er·at·ic** *adj.*
—**op·er·at·i·cal·ly** *adv.*

**o·pe·ra**[2] /ˈōp(ə)rə/ ▶pl. of OPUS.

**op·er·a·ble** /ˈäp(ə)rəbəl/ ▶*adj.*
**1** that can be operated.
**2** suitable for treatment by surgery.

**op·er·ant** /ˈäpərənt/ ▶*adj.* involving the modification of behavior by the reinforcing or inhibiting effect of its own consequences (instrumental conditioning).

▶*n.* item of behavior that is initially spontaneous, rather than a response to a prior stimulus, but whose consequences may reinforce or inhibit recurrence of that behavior.

**op·er·ate** /ˈäpəˌrāt/ ▶*v.* **1** control the functioning of (a machine, etc.). **2** be in action; function. **3** perform a surgical operation. **4** function; work. —**op·er·a·tion** *n.* —**op·er·a·tor** *n.*

**op·er·at·ing sys·tem** ▶*n.* basic software that enables the running of a computer program.

**op·er·a·tion·al** ▶*adj.* **1** in or ready for use. **2** relating to the routine functioning of a business, etc. —**op·er·a·tion·al·ly** *adv.*

**op·er·a·tive** /ˈäp(ə)ritiv/ ▶*adj.* **1** functioning; having effect. **2** having the principal relevance: *"may" is the operative word.* **3** of or relating to surgery. ▶*n.* detective; spy.

**op·er·et·ta** /ˌäpəˈretə/ ▶*n.* light opera.

**op·er·ose** /ˈäpəˌrōs/ ▶*adj.* involving or displaying much industry or effort.

**oph·thal·mol·o·gy** /ˌäfThə(l)ˈmäləjē/ ▶*n.* branch of medicine concerned with the study and treatment of the eye. —**oph·thal·mol·o·gist** *n.*

**o·pi·ate** /ˈōpē-it/ ▶*adj.* **1** containing opium. **2** narcotic; soporific.

▶*n.* **1** drug containing opium, usu. to ease pain or induce sleep. **2** thing that soothes or stupefies.

**o·pine** /ōˈpīn/ ▶*v.* hold or express as an opinion.

**o·pin·ion** /əˈpinyən/ ▶*n.* **1** unproven belief or assessment. **2** view held as probable. **3** what one thinks about something. **4** professional advice: *get a second opinion before having surgery.*

**o·pin·ion·at·ed** /əˈpinyəˌnātid/ ▶*adj.* conceitedly assertive or dogmatic in one's opinions.

**o·pi·um** /ˈōpēəm/ ▶*n.* **1** addictive drug prepared from the juice of the opium poppy, used as an analgesic and narcotic. **2** anything regarded as soothing or stupefying.

**o·pos·sum** /əˈpäsəm/ ▶*n.* tree-living American marsupial having a prehensile tail and hind feet with an opposable thumb.

**op·po·nent** /ə'pōnənt/ ▶*n.* person who opposes or belongs to an opposing side.

**op·por·tune** /ˌäpər't(y)o͞on/ ▶*adj.* **1** (of a time) well-chosen or especially favorable. **2** (of an action or event) well-timed.

**op·por·tu·nism** ▶*n.* adaptation to circumstances, esp. regardless of principle. —**op·por·tun·ist** *n. & adj.* —**op·por·tu·nis·tic** *adj.* —**op·por·tu·nis·ti·cal·ly** *adv.*

**op·por·tu·ni·ty** /ˌäpər't(y)o͞onilē/ ▶*n.* (*pl.* **-ties**) favorable chance or opening offered by circumstances.

**op·pose** /ə'pōz/ ▶*v.* **1** disapprove of and attempt to prevent. **2** actively resist. **3** compete against (someone) in a contest. —**op·po·si·tion** *n.*

**op·po·site** /'äpəzit/ ▶*adj.* **1** having a position on the other side; facing: *the opposite side of the street.* **2** contrary; diametrically different: *a word that is opposite in meaning.* ▶*n.* anything opposite. ▶*adv.* **1** in an opposite position: *the tree stands opposite.* **2** in a complementary role to (another actor, etc.). ▶*prep.* in a position opposite to: *opposite the house is a tree.*

**op·press** /ə'pres/ ▶*v.* **1** keep in subservience. **2** govern or treat harshly. —**op·pres·sion** *n.* —**op·pres·sive** *adj.* —**op·pres·sive·ly** *adv.* —**op·pres·sor** *n.*

**op·pro·bri·um** /ə'prōbrēəm/ ▶*n.* harsh criticism or censure.

**opt** /äpt/ ▶*v.* decide; make a choice.

**op·tic** /'äptik/ ▶*adj.* of or relating to the eye or vision: *optic nerve.*

**op·ti·cal** /'äptlkəl/ ▶*adj.* **1** of sight; visual. **2 a** of or concerning sight or light in relation to each other. **b** belonging to optics. **3** (esp. of a lens) constructed to assist sight. —**op·ti·cal·ly** *adv.*
□ **optical illusion** image that deceives the eye.

**op·ti·cian** /äp'tisHən/ ▶*n.* maker or seller of eyeglasses, contact lenses, etc.

**op·tics** /'äptiks/ ▶*n.* scientific study of sight and the behavior of light.

**op·ti·mal** /'äptəməl/ ▶*adj.* best or most favorable.

**op·ti·mism** /'äptə,mizəm/ ▶*n.* inclination to hopefulness and confidence. —**op·ti·mist** *n.* —**op·ti·mis·tic** *adj.* —**op·ti·mis·ti·cal·ly** *adv.*

**op·ti·mum** /'äptəməm/ ▸n. (pl. -ma or -mums) 1 most favorable conditions (for growth, reproduction, etc.). 2 best possible compromise.
▸adj. OPTIMAL.

**op·tion** /'äpSHən/ ▸n. 1 a choosing; choice. b thing chosen. 2 liberty to choose. 3 right to buy or sell a particular thing at a specified price within a set time.

**op·tion·al** /'äpSHənl/ ▸adj. available to be chosen but not obligatory.

**op·tom·e·try** /äp'tämitrē/ ▸n. practice or profession of testing the eyes for defects in vision and prescribing corrective lenses or exercises. —**op·tom·e·trist** n.

**op·u·lent** /'äpyələnt/ ▸adj. ostentatiously rich and lavish. —**op·u·lence** n.

**o·pus** /'ōpəs/ ▸n. (pl. **op·er·a** or **op·us·es**) 1 Mus. a musical composition. b used before a number given to a composer's work, usu. indicating the order of publication: *Beethoven, op. 15.* 2 any artistic work.

**OR** ▸abbr. 1 Oregon (in official postal use). 2 operating room.

**or** /ôr/ ▸conj. 1 introducing an alternative: *white or black.* 2 introducing a synonym or explanation of a preceding word, etc.: *suffered from vertigo or dizziness.* 3 otherwise: *run or you'll be late.*

☐ **or else** 1 otherwise: *do it now, or else you will have to do it tomorrow.* 2 inf. expressing a warning or threat: *hand over the money or else.*

**-or** ▸suffix 1 forming nouns denoting an agent: *actor | escalator.* 2 forming nouns denoting state or condition: *error | horror.*

**or·a·cle** /'ôrəkəl/ ▸n. 1 ancient shrine where a god was believed to answer questions through a priest or priestess. 2 person or thing regarded as an infallible guide on something. —**or·ac·u·lar** adj.

**o·ral** /'ôrəl/ ▸adj. 1 by word of mouth; spoken; not written: *the oral tradition.* 2 done or taken by mouth: *oral contraceptive.*
▸n. inf. spoken examination, test, etc. —**o·ral·ly** adv.

**or·ange** /'ôrənj/ ▸n. 1 a round juicy citrus fruit with a bright reddish-yellow tough rind. b tree or shrub bearing fragrant white flowers and yielding this fruit.

**2** reddish-yellow color of an orange.
▶*adj.* orange-colored; reddish-yellow.

**o·rang·u·tan** /ə'raNG(g)ə,tan/ ▶*n.* large tree-living ape of Borneo and Sumatra, with characteristic long arms and hooked hands and feet and long reddish hair.

**o·ra·tion** /ô'rāsHən/ ▶*n.* formal speech, etc., esp. when ceremonial.

**or·a·tor** /'ôrətər/ ▶*n.* **1** person making a speech. **2** eloquent public speaker.

**or·a·to·ri·o** /,ôrə'tôrē,ō/ ▶*n.* (*pl.* **-os**) semidramatic work for orchestra and voices, esp. on a sacred theme.

**or·a·to·ry** /'ôrə,tôrē/ ▶*n.* (*pl.* **-ries**) **1** art or practice of formal speaking, esp. in public. **2** exaggerated, eloquent, or highly colored language. **3** small chapel, esp. for private worship. **—or·a·tor·i·cal** *adj.*

**orb** /ôrb/ ▶*n.* **1** globe surmounted by a cross, esp. carried by a sovereign at a coronation. **2** sphere; globe.

**or·bit** /'ôrbit/ ▶*n.* **1** curved path of a celestial object or spacecraft around a star, planet, or moon.

**2** one complete passage around an orbited body. **3** range or sphere of action.
▶*v.* **1** (of a satellite, etc.) go around in orbit. **2** move in orbit around. **3** put (a satellite) into orbit. **—or·bit·al** *adj.* **—or·bit·er** *n.*

**or·chard** /'ôrcHərd/ ▶*n.* piece of land with fruit trees.

**or·ches·tra** /'ôrkistrə/ ▶*n.* **1** group of instrumentalists, esp. combining strings, woodwinds, brass, and percussion: *symphony orchestra.* **2** (also **or·ches·tra pit**) part of a theater, etc., where the orchestra plays, usu. in front of the stage. **3** main-floor seating area in a theater. **—or·ches·tral** *adj.*

**or·ches·trate** /'ôrki,strāt/ ▶*v.* **1** arrange or compose for an orchestra. **2** arrange (elements of a situation, etc.) for maximum effect. **—or·ches·tra·tion** *n.*

**or·chid** /'ôrkid/ ▶*n.* **1** plant bearing flowers in fantastic shapes and brilliant colors, usu. having one petal larger than the others and variously spurred, lobed, pouched, etc. **2** flower of these plants.

**or·dain** /ôr'dān/ ▶*v.* **1** confer holy orders on; appoint to the

Christian ministry. **2 a** decree: *ordained that he should go.* **b** (of God, fate, etc.) destine; appoint: *has ordained us to die.*

**or·deal** /ôr'dēl/ ▸*n.* painful or horrific experience; severe trial.

**or·der** /'ôrdər/ ▸*n.* **1 a** condition in which every part, unit, etc., is in its right place; tidiness. **b** specified sequence, succession, etc.: *alphabetical order.* **2** authoritative command, direction, etc. **3** state of peaceful harmony under a constituted authority. **4** kind; sort: *talents of a high order.* **5 a** direction to a manufacturer, tradesman, waiter, etc., to supply something. **b** goods, etc., supplied. **6** constitution or nature of the world, society, etc.: *the moral order.* **7** *Biol.* taxonomic rank below a class and above a family. **8** (also **Order**) fraternity of monks and friars, or formerly of knights, bound by a common rule of life: *the Franciscan order.* **9 a** any of the grades of the Christian ministry. **b** status of a member of the clergy: *Anglican orders.* **10** any of the classical styles of architecture (Doric, Ionic, Corinthian, Tuscan, and Composite).

▸*v.* **1** command; bid; prescribe. **2** command or direct (a person) to a specified destination. **3** direct a manufacturer, waiter, tradesman, etc., to supply: *ordered dinner.* **4** put in order; regulate.

**or·der·ly** ▸*adj.* **1** methodically arranged; regular. **2** obedient to discipline; well-behaved.

▸*n.* (*pl.* **-lies**) **1** hospital attendant with nonmedical duties, esp. cleaning, moving equipment, escorting patients, etc. **2** soldier who carries orders for an officer, etc. —**or·der·li·ness** *n.*

**or·di·nal** /'ôrdn-əl/ ▸*n.* (in full **or·di·nal num·ber**) number defining a thing's position in a series, e.g., "first," "second," "third," etc.

**or·di·nance** /'ôrdn-əns/ ▸*n.* **1** authoritative order; decree. **2** statute, esp. by a local authority.

**or·di·nar·y** /'ôrdn,erē/ ▸*adj.* **1** regular; normal; usual: *in the ordinary course of events.* **2** uninteresting; commonplace. —**or·di·nar·i·ly** *adv.* —**or·di·nar·i·ness** *n.*

**or·di·na·tion** /ˌôrdnˈāsHən/ ▸*n.*
**1** conferring holy orders, esp. on a priest or deacon. **2** admission of a priest, etc., to church ministry.

**ord·nance** /ˈôrdnəns/ ▸*n.*
**1** artillery; military supplies.
**2** branch of the armed forces dealing esp. with military stores and materials.

**or·dure** /ˈôrjər/ ▸*n.* **1** dung.
**2** something regarded as vile.

**Ore.** ▸*abbr.* Oregon.

**ore** /ôr/ ▸*n.* naturally occurring solid material from which metal or other valuable minerals may be extracted.

**o·re·ad** /ˈôrēˌad/ ▸*n.* nymph believed to inhabit mountains.

**o·reg·a·no** /əˈregəˌnō/ ▸*n.* aromatic herb, the fresh or dried leaves of which are used as a flavoring in cooking.

**or·gan** /ˈôrgən/ ▸*n.* **1 a** usu. large musical instrument having pipes supplied with air from bellows, sounded by keys, and distributed into sets or stops that form partial organs, each with a separate keyboard. **b** smaller instrument without pipes, producing similar sounds electronically. **2** *Biol.* usu. self-contained part of an organism

having a special vital function: *vocal organs* | *digestive organs.*
**3** medium of communication, esp. a newspaper, company periodical, etc. —**or·gan·ist** *n.*

**or·gan·dy** /ˈôrgəndē/ ▸*n.* (*pl.* **-dies**) fine translucent cotton muslin, usu. stiffened.

**or·gan·ic** /ôrˈganik/ ▸*adj.* **1** of, relating to, or derived from living matter. **2** *Chem.* (of a compound, etc.) containing carbon. **3** *Agriculture* produced without the use of chemical fertilizers, pesticides, etc.: *organic farming.* **4 a** *Physiol.* of a bodily organ(s). **b** *Med.* (of a disease) affecting an organ.
**5 a** structural; inherent.
**b** constitutional; fundamental.
**6** organized; systematic: *an organic whole.* —**or·gan·i·cal·ly** *adv.*

**or·gan·ism** /ˈôrgəˌnizəm/ ▸*n.*
**1** living individual consisting of a single cell or of a group of interdependent parts sharing the life processes. **2** individual live plant or animal.

**or·gan·ize** /ˈôrgəˌnīz/ ▸*v.* **1** give an orderly structure to; systematize. **2** arrange for or initiate (a plan, etc.). **3 a** enroll (new members) in a labor union, political party, etc. **b** form (a labor union or other political group). **—or·gan·i·za·tion** *n.* **—or·gan·iz·er** *n.*

**or·ga·non** /'ôrgə,nän/ ▶*n.* instrument of thought, esp. a means of reasoning or a system of logic.

**or·gan·za** /ôr'ganzə/ ▶*n.* thin stiff transparent silk or synthetic dress fabric.

**or·gasm** /'ôr,gazəm/ ▶*n.* climax of sexual excitement. **—or·gas·mic** *adj.*

**or·gone** /'ôrgōn/ ▶*n.* (in the theory of Wilhelm Reich) a supposed sexual energy or life force distributed throughout the universe that can be collected and stored for therapeutic use.

**or·gy** /'ôrjē/ ▶*n.* (*pl.* **-gies**) **1** wild drunken festivity, esp. one at which indiscriminate sexual activity takes place. **2** excessive indulgence in an activity.

**o·ri·el** /'ôrēəl/ ▶*n.* projecting window of an upper story.

**o·ri·ent** /'ôrē,ənt/ ▶*n. poet./lit.* (**the Orient**) countries E. of the Mediterranean, esp. E. Asia. ▶*v.* **1** align or position (something) relative to specified positions. **2** adjust or tailor (something) to specified

circumstances. **3** (**orient oneself**) find one's position in relation to new surroundings. **—O·ri·en·tal** *adj.* **—o·ri·en·ta·tion** *n.*

**o·ri·en·teer·ing** /,ôriən'ti(ə)riNG/ ▶*n.* cross-country race in which participants use a map and a compass to navigate along an unfamiliar course.

**or·i·fice** /'ôrəfis/ ▶*n.* opening, esp. the mouth of a cavity.

**o·ri·ga·mi** /,ôrə'gämē/ ▶*n.* Japanese art of folding paper into decorative shapes.

**or·i·gin** /'ôrijən/ ▶*n.* **1** beginning or starting point; source. **2** person's ancestry: *what are his origins?*

**o·rig·i·nal** /ə'rijənl/ ▶*adj.* **1** existing from the beginning; innate. **2** inventive; creative. **3** not derivative or imitative; firsthand. ▶*n.* **1** original model, pattern, picture, etc., from which another is copied or translated. **2** eccentric or unusual person. **—o·rig·i·nal·i·ty** *n.* **—o·rig·i·nal·ly** *adv.*

**o·rig·i·nate** /ə'rijə,nāt/ ▶*v.* **1** have as an origin; begin: *the word originated in a marketing term.* **2** cause (something) to begin; initiate. **—o·rig·i·na·tion** *n.* **—o·rig·i·na·tive** *adj.* **—o·rig·i·na·tor** *n.*

**o·ri·ole** /ˈôrēˌōl/ ▸*n.* American bird with black and orange plumage in the male.

**or·mo·lu** /ˈôrməˌlōō/ ▸*n.* **1** gilded bronze or gold-colored alloy of copper, zinc, and tin used to decorate furniture, make ornaments, etc. **2** articles made of or decorated with these.

**or·na·ment** /ˈôrnəmənt/ ▸*n.* **1** thing used to adorn, esp. a trinket, vase, figure, etc. **2** quality or person conferring adornment, grace, or honor: *an ornament to her profession.* ▸*v.* adorn; beautify. **—or·na·men·tal** *adj.* **—or·na·men·ta·tion** *n.*

**or·nate** /ôrˈnāt/ ▸*adj.* elaborately adorned; highly decorated. **—or·nate·ly** *adv.* **—or·nate·ness** *n.*

**or·ner·y** /ˈôrn(ə)rē/ ▸*adj. inf.* cantankerous; unpleasant. **—or·ner·i·ness** *n.*

**or·ni·thol·o·gy** /ˌôrnəˈTHäləjē/ ▸*n.* the scientific study of birds. **—or·ni·tho·log·i·cal** *adj.* **—or·ni·thol·o·gist** *n.*

**o·rog·e·ny** /ôˈräjənē/ ▸*n.* process in which a section of the earth's crust is folded and deformed by lateral compression to form a mountain range.

**o·rog·ra·phy** /ôˈrägrəfē/ ▸*n.* branch of physical geography dealing with mountains.

**o·ro·tund** /ˈôrəˌtənd/ ▸*adj.* **1** (of the voice) round; imposing. **2** (of writing, style, etc.) pompous; pretentious.

**or·phan** /ˈôrfən/ ▸*n.* **1** child whose parents are dead. **2** young animal that has lost its mother. **3** person or thing bereft of previous protection, support, advantages, etc. ▸*v.* bereave (a child) of its parents.

**or·phan·age** /ˈôrfənij/ ▸*n.* residential institution for orphans.

**or·rer·y** /ˈôrərē/ ▸*n.* (*pl.* **-rer·ies**) mechanical model of the solar system, or of just the sun, earth, and moon, used to represent their relative positions and motions.

**ort** /ôrt/ (usu. **orts**) ▸*n.* or scrap or remainder of food from a meal.

**or·tho·don·tics** /ˌôrTHəˈdäntiks/ (also **or·tho·don·tia**) ▸*n.* treatment of irregularities in the teeth and jaws. **—or·tho·don·tic** *adj.* **—or·tho·don·tist** *n.*

**or·tho·dox** /ˈôrTHəˌdäks/ ▸*adj.*
**1** holding correct or currently accepted opinions, esp. on religious doctrine, morals, etc. **2** not independent-minded; unoriginal; unheretical. **3** (usu. **Orthodox**) (of Judaism) strictly keeping to traditional doctrine and ritual. —**or·tho·dox·y** *n.*

□ **Orthodox Church** Eastern Christian Church, separated from the Western Christian Church in the 11th c., having the Patriarch of Constantinople as its head, and including the national churches of Russia, Romania, Greece, etc.

**or·thog·ra·phy** /ôrˈTHägrəfē/ ▸*n.* (*pl.* **-phies**) **1** correct or conventional spelling. **2** spelling with reference to its correctness: *dreadful orthography.* **3** study or science of spelling. —**or·tho·graph·ic** *adj.*

**or·tho·pe·dics** /ˌôrTHəˈpēdiks/ ▸*n.* branch of medicine dealing with the correction of deformities of bones or muscles. —**or·tho·pe·dic** *adj.* —**or·tho·pe·dist** *n.*

**-ory** ▸*suffix* **1** forming nouns denoting a place for a particular function: *dormitory | refectory.* **2** forming adjectives (and occasionally nouns) relating to or involving a verbal action: *accessory | compulsory | directory.*

**os·cil·late** /ˈäsəˌlāt/ ▸*v.* **1 a** swing back and forth like a pendulum. **b** move back and forth between points. **2** vacillate; vary between extremes of opinion, action, etc. —**os·cil·la·tion** *n.* —**os·cil·la·tor** *n.*

**os·cu·late** /ˈäskyəˌlāt/ ▸*v.* kiss.

**o·sier** /ˈōZHər/ ▸*n.* willows used in basketwork.

**-osis** ▸*suffix* (*pl.* **-os·es**) denoting a process or condition, esp. a pathological state: *apotheosis | metamorphosis | acidosis | neurosis.*

**os·mic** /ˈäzmik/ ▸*adj.* relating to odors or the sense of smell.

**os·mo·sis** /äzˈmōsis; äs-/ ▸*n.* **1** *Biol. & Chem.* passage of a solvent through a semipermeable partition into a more concentrated solution. **2** process of gradual or unconscious assimilation of ideas, etc. —**os·mot·ic** *adj.*

**os·prey** /ˈäsprē/ ▸*n.* large bird of prey, with a brown back and white markings, feeding on fish.

**os·se·ous** /ˈäsēəs/ ▸*adj.* consisting of or turned into bone; ossified.

**os·si·fy** /ˈäsəˌfī/ ▸*v.* (**-fied**) **1** turn

into bone; harden. **2** make or become rigid, callous, or unprogressive.
—**os·si·fi·ca·tion** *n.*

**os·su·ar·y** /ˈäsHŏŏˌerē; ˈäs(y)ŏŏ-/ ▶*n.* (*pl.* **-ar·ies**) container or room into which the bones of dead people are placed.

**os·ten·si·ble** /äˈstensəbəl/ ▶*adj.* apparent; professed.
—**os·ten·si·bly** *adv.*

**os·ten·ta·tion** /ˌästənˈtāSHən/ ▶*n.* pretentious display, esp. of wealth and luxury.
—**os·ten·ta·tious** *adj.*
—**os·ten·ta·tious·ly** *adv.*

**os·ten·ta·tious** /ˌästənˈtāSHəs/ ▶*adj.* characterized by vulgar or pretentious display; designed to impress or attract notice.

**os·te·o·ar·thri·tis** /ˌästēˌōärˈTHrītis/ ▶*n.* degeneration of joint cartilage and the underlying bone, causing pain and stiffness.
—**os·te·o·ar·thrit·ic** *adj.*

**os·te·op·a·thy** /ˌästēˈäpəTHē/ ▶*n.* treatment of disease through manipulation of bones, esp. the spine, displacement of these being the supposed cause.
—**os·te·o·path** *n.*

**os·te·o·po·ro·sis** /ˌästēˌōpəˈrōsis/ ▶*n.* condition of brittle bones caused by loss of bony

tissue, esp. as a result of hormonal changes, or deficiency of calcium or vitamin D.

**os·tra·cize** /ˈästrəˌsīz/ ▶*v.* **1** exclude (a person) from a society, favor, common privileges, etc.; refuse to associate with. **2** banish.
—**os·tra·cism** *n.*

**os·trich** /ˈästriCH/ ▶*n.* large African swift-running flightless bird with long legs and two toes on each foot.

**oth·er** /ˈəTHər/ ▶*adj.* **1** not the same as one or some already mentioned or implied; separate in identity or distinct in kind. **2 a** further; additional. **b** alternative of two: *open your other eye.*
▶*n. & pron.* **1** additional, different, or extra person, thing, example, etc. (see **ANOTHER**). **2** the ones remaining: *where are the others?*

**oth·er·wise** ▶*adv.* **1** else; or else; in different circumstances. **2** in other respects: *he is somewhat unkempt, but otherwise very suitable.* **3** in a different way: *could not have acted otherwise.*
▶*adj.* in a different state: *the matter is quite otherwise.*

**oth·er·world·ly** ▶*adj.* **1** of or relating to an imaginary or spiritual world. **2** impractical.

**ot·ter** /'ätər/ ▶*n.* **1** aquatic fish-eating mammal having strong claws and webbed feet. **2** its fur or pelt.

**ot·to·man** /'ätəmən/ ▶*n.* upholstered seat or footstool.

**ou·bli·ette** /ˌo͞oblē'et/ ▶*n.* secret dungeon with access only through a trapdoor in its ceiling.

**oud** /o͞od/ ▶*n.* form of lute or mandolin played principally in Arab countries.

**ought** /ôt/ ▶*aux. v.* **1** expressing duty or rightness: *we ought to love our neighbors.* **2** expressing advisability or prudence: *you ought to go for your own good.* **3** expressing esp. strong probability: *he ought to be there by now.*

**ounce** /ouns/ ▶*n.* **1 a** unit of weight of one-sixteenth of a pound avoirdupois. (Abbr.: **oz**). **b** unit of one-twelfth of a pound troy. **2** small quantity. □ **fluid ounce** unit of capacity equal to one-sixteenth of a pint.

**our** /ou(ə)r/ ▶*pron.* **1** of or belonging to us or ourselves: *our house | our own business.* **2** of or belonging to all people: *our children's future.*

**ours** ▶*pron.* the one or ones belonging to or associated with us: *it is ours | ours are over there.*

**our·selves** ▶*pron.* **1 a** emphatic form of WE or US: *we ourselves did it | made it ourselves.* **b** reflexive form of US: *are pleased with ourselves.* **2** in our normal state of body or mind: *not quite ourselves today.*

**-ous** ▶*suffix* forming adjectives meaning 'abounding in, characterized by, of the nature of': *envious | glorious | mountainous | poisonous.*

**oust** /oust/ ▶*v.* **1** drive out or expel, esp. by forcing oneself into the place of. **2** dispossess.

**oust·er** ▶*n.* **1** ejection as a result of physical action, judicial process, or political upheaval. **2** expulsion.

**out** /out/ ▶*adv.* **1** away from or not in or at a place, etc.: *keep him out.* **2** forming part of phrasal verbs indicating: **a** dispersal away from a center, etc.: *hire out.* **b** coming or bringing into the open: *stand out.* **c** need for attentiveness: *look out.* **3 a** not in one's house, office, etc. **b** no longer in prison. **4** to or at an

end; completely: *out of bananas.*
**5** (of a fire, candle, etc.) not
burning. **6** *inf.* unconscious.
**7** (of a party, politician, etc.) not
in office. **8** unfashionable.
**9** *Sports* (of a batter, base runner,
etc.) no longer taking part as
such, having been tagged, struck
out, caught, etc. **10 a** not worth
considering; rejected. **b** not
allowed. **11** (of a stain, mark,
etc.) not visible; removed.
▸*prep.* out of: *looked out the*
*window.*
▸*n.* **1** *inf.* way of escape; excuse.
**2** *Baseball* play in which a batter
or base runner is retired from an
inning.
▸*v.* **1** come or go out; emerge.
**2** *inf.* expose the homosexuality
of (esp. a prominent person).
**out-** ▸*prefix* added to verbs and
nouns, meaning: **1** so as to
surpass or exceed: *outdo* |
*outnumber.* **2** external; separate:
*outline* | *outhouse.* **3** out of; away
from; outward: *outgrowth.*
**out·age** /ˈoutij/ ▸*n.* period of
time during which a power
supply, etc., is not operating.
**out·back** ▸*n.* (**the outback**)
remote and usu. uninhabited
inland regions of Australia.
**out·board** ▸*adj.* **1** (of a motor)

attachable to the outside of a
boat. **2** (of a boat) having an
outboard motor.
▸*n.* **1** outboard engine. **2** boat
with an outboard engine.
**out·break** ▸*n.* sudden eruption
of war, disease, rebellion, etc.
**out·build·ing** ▸*n.* detached
shed, barn, etc., within the
grounds of a main building.
**out·burst** ▸*n.* **1** verbal
explosion of anger, etc.
**2** bursting out.
**out·cast** ▸*n.* person rejected by
his or her home, country,
society, etc.
▸*adj.* rejected; homeless;
friendless.
**out·class** ▸*v.* **1** surpass in
quality. **2** defeat easily.
**out·come** ▸*n.* result; visible
effect.
**out·cry** ▸*n.* (*pl.* **-cries**) strong
public protest.
**out·dat·ed** ▸*adj.* out of date;
obsolete.
**out·dis·tance** ▸*v.* leave (a
competitor) behind completely.
**out·do** ▸*v.* (*past* **-did**; *past part.*
**-done**) exceed or excel; surpass.
**out·door** ▸*adj.* done, existing, or
used out of doors.
**out·er** ▸*adj.* **1** outside; external:

*pierced the outer layer.* **2** farther from the center or inside. —**out·er·most** *adj.*

□ **outer space** universe beyond the earth's atmosphere.

**out·field** ▸*n.* outer part of a playing area, esp. a baseball field. —**out·field·er** *n.*

**out·fit** ▸*n.* **1** set of clothes esp. designed to be worn together. **2** set of equipment, etc. **3** *inf.* group of people regarded as a unit, etc.; team. ▸*v.* (**-fit·ted**, **-fit·ting**) provide with an outfit, esp. of clothes.

**out·go·ing** ▸*adj.* **1** friendly. **2** retiring from office: *the outgoing governor.* **3** going out or away: *outgoing calls.*

**out·grow** ▸*v.* (*past* **-grew**; *past part.* **-grown**) **1** grow too big for. **2** leave behind (a childish habit, etc.). **3** grow faster or taller than.

**out·growth** ▸*n.* **1** offshoot; natural product. **2** the process of growing out.

**out·house** ▸*n.* **1** outbuilding used as a toilet, usu. with no plumbing. **2** building, esp. a shed, etc., built next to or on the grounds of a house.

**out·ing** ▸*n.* pleasure trip; excursion.

**out·land·ish** /outˈlandiSH/ ▸*adj.* bizarre; strange; unfamiliar. —**out·land·ish·ly** *adv.* —**out·land·ish·ness** *n.*

**out·last** ▸*v.* last longer than.

**out·law** ▸*n.* **1** person who has broken the law, esp. one who remains a fugitive. **2** *hist.* person denied protection of the law. ▸*v.* declare or make illegal.

**out·lay** ▸*n.* what is spent on something.

**out·let** ▸*n.* **1** means of exit or escape. **2** means of expression (of a talent, emotion, etc.). **3** agency, distributor, or market for goods: *a new retail outlet in China.* **4** electrical power receptacle.

**out·line** ▸*n.* **1** rough draft of a diagram, plan, proposal, etc. **2** summary of main features. **3** sketch containing only contour lines. **4** line or set of lines enclosing or indicating an object. ▸*v.* **1** draw or describe in outline. **2** mark the outline of.

**out·live** ▸*v.* **1** live longer than (another person). **2** live beyond (a specified date or time).

**out·look** ▸*n.* **1** prospect for the future. **2** mental attitude.

**out·ly·ing** ▸*adj.* situated far from a center; remote.

**out·mod·ed** /ˌout'mōdid/ ▸*adj.* **1** out of fashion. **2** obsolete.

**out·num·ber** ▸*v.* exceed in number.

**out·pa·tient** ▸*n.* hospital patient whose treatment does not require overnight hospitalization.

**out·place·ment** ▸*n.* assistance in finding new employment for workers who have been dismissed.

**out·post** ▸*n.* **1** detachment set at a distance from the main body of an army, esp. to prevent surprise. **2** distant branch or settlement.

**out·put** ▸*n.* **1** product of a process, esp. of manufacture, or of mental or artistic work. **2** quantity or amount of this. **3** printout, results, etc., supplied by a computer. **4** power, etc., delivered by an apparatus.
▸*v.* (-put·ting; *past* and *past part.* -put or -put·ted) **1** put or send out. **2** (of a computer) supply (results, etc.).

**out·rage** ▸*n.* **1** extremely strong reaction of anger, shock, etc. **2** something causing such a reaction.
▸*v.* **1** (usu. **be outraged**) arouse fierce anger, indignation, etc., in (someone). **2** violate or infringe flagrantly: *their behavior outraged all civilized standards.*

**out·ra·geous** /out'rājəs/ ▸*adj.* **1** shockingly bad or excessive. **2** wildly exaggerated. **3** very bold and startling.
—**out·ra·geous·ly** *adv.*

**ou·tré** /ōō'trā/ ▸*adj.* unconventional; eccentric.

**out·reach** ▸*n.* **1** extent or length of reaching out. **2** organization's involvement with activity in the community.

**out·right** ▸*adv.* **1** altogether; entirely: *proved outright.* **2** without reservation; openly.
▸*adj.* **1** downright; direct; complete. **2** undisputed; clear.
—**out·right·ness** *n.*

**out·run** ▸*v.* (-run·ning; *past* -ran; *past part.* -run) **1** run faster or farther than. **2** go beyond.

**out·sell** ▸*v.* (*past* and *past part.* -sold) **1** sell more than. **2** be sold in greater quantities than.

**out·set** ▸*n.* start; beginning.

**out·shine** ▸*v.* (*past* and *past part.* -shone) shine brighter than; surpass in ability, excellence, etc.

**out·side** ▸*n.* **1** external side or

surface; outer parts. **2** external appearance; outward aspect.

▸*adj.* **1** of, on, or nearer the outside; outer. **2 a** not belonging: *outside help.* **b** not a part of. **3** (of a chance, etc.) remote; very unlikely. **4** (of an estimate, etc.) greatest or highest possible.

▸*adv.* **1** on or to the outside. **2** in or to the open air. **3** not within or enclosed or included.

▸*prep.* **1** not in; to or at the exterior of. **2** external to; not included in; beyond the limits of: *outside the law.*

**out·sid·er** ▸*n.* **1** nonmember of some circle, party, profession, etc. **2** competitor, applicant, etc., thought to have little chance of success.

**out·sid·er art** ▸*n.* art produced by self-taught artists who are not part of the artistic establishment.

**out·skirts** ▸*pl. n.* outer area of a town, etc.

**out·smart** ▸*v. inf.* outwit; be cleverer than.

**out·spo·ken** ▸*adj.* frank in stating one's opinions.
—**out·spo·ken·ly** *adv.*
—**out·spo·ken·ness** *n.*

**out·spread** ▸*adj.* spread out; extended or expanded.

**out·stand·ing** ▸*adj.*
**1 a** conspicuous; eminent, esp. because of excellence.
**b** remarkable in (a specified field). **2** (esp. of a debt) not yet settled: *$200 still outstanding.*
—**out·stand·ing·ly** *adv.*

**out·strip** ▸*v.* (**-stripped, -strip·ping**) **1** pass in running, etc. **2** surpass, esp. competitively.

**out·take** ▸*n.* length of film or tape rejected in editing.

**out·ward** /ˈoutwərd/ ▸*adj.*
**1** situated on or directed toward the outside. **2** going out.
**3** bodily; external; apparent.

▸*adv.* (also **out·wards**) in an outward direction.

▸*n.* outward appearance of something; exterior.
—**out·ward·ly** *adv.*

**out·weigh** ▸*v.* exceed in weight, value, importance, or influence.

**out·wit** ▸*v.* (**-wit·ted, -wit·ting**) be too clever or crafty for; deceive by greater ingenuity.

**o·va** /ˈōvə/ ▸*pl.* of OVUM.

**o·val** /ˈōvəl/ ▸*adj.* having a rounded and slightly elongated outline or shape; egg-shaped.

▸*n.* body, object, or design with such a shape.

**o·va·ry** /ˈōvərē/ ▸*n.* (*pl.* **-ries**) **1** each of the female reproductive organs in which ova are produced. **2** hollow base of the carpel of a flower, containing one or more ovules.
—**o·var·i·an** *adj.*

**o·va·tion** /ōˈvāSHən/ ▸*n.* enthusiastic reception, esp. spontaneous and sustained applause.

**ov·en** /ˈəvən/ ▸*n.* **1** enclosed compartment of brick, stone, or metal for cooking food. **2** chamber for heating or drying.

**o·ver** /ˈōvər/ ▸*prep.* **1** above, in, or to a position higher than; upon. **2** out and down from; down from the edge of. **3** so as to cover: *a hat over his eyes.* **4** above and across: *flew over the North Pole.* **5** on the subject of: *heated debate over unemployment.* **6 a** superior to; in charge of. **b** in preference to. **7** so as to deal with completely: *went over the plans.*
▸*adv.* **1** expressing passage across an area: *he leaned over and touched my hand.* **2** beyond and hanging from a point: *listing over at an acute angle.* **3** in or to the place indicated: *over here.* **4** used to express action and result: *the car flipped over.* **5** finished: *the game is over.* **6** used to express repetition of a process: *you will have to do that over.* **7** with motion above something; so as to pass across something: *climb over.*

**over-** ▸*prefix* added to verbs, nouns, adjectives, and adverbs, meaning: **1** excessively: *overheat* | *overdue.* **2** upper; outer; extra: *overcoat* | *overtime.* **3** 'over' in various senses: *overhang* | *overshadow.* **4** completely; utterly: *overawe* | *overjoyed.*

**over·a·chieve** ▸*v.* **1** do more than might be expected (esp. scholastically). **2** achieve more than (an expected goal or objective, etc.).
—**o·ver·a·chieve·ment** *n.*
—**o·ver·a·chiev·er** *n.*

**o·ver·act** ▸*v.* act in an exaggerated manner.

**o·ver·all** ▸*adj.* **1** from end to end. **2** total; inclusive of all.
▸*adv.* in all parts; taken as a whole.
▸*pl. n.* (**overalls**) protective trousers, dungarees, or a combination suit, worn by workmen, etc.

**o·ver·awe** ▸*v.* overcome with awe.

**o·ver·bear·ing** ▸*adj.*
1 domineering; masterful.
2 overpowering.

**o·ver·bite** ▸*n.* condition in which the teeth of the upper jaw project forward over those of the lower jaw.

**o·ver·blown** ▸*adj.* excessively inflated or pretentious.

**o·ver·board** ▸*adv.* from a ship into the water: *fall overboard.*
□ **go overboard** behave immoderately; go too far.

**o·ver·cast** ▸*adj.* 1 (of the sky, weather, etc.) covered with cloud; dull and gloomy. 2 (in sewing) edged with stitching to prevent fraying.

**o·ver·charge** ▸*v.* 1 charge too high a price to (a person) or for (a thing). 2 put too much electric charge into (a battery). 3 put exaggerated or excessive detail into (a description, picture, etc.).
▸*n.* excessive charge for goods or a service.

**o·ver·coat** ▸*n.* 1 heavy coat, esp. one worn over indoor clothes for warmth outdoors in cold weather. 2 protective coat of paint, etc.

**o·ver·come** ▸*v.* (*past* **-came**; *past part.* **-come**) 1 succeed in dealing with; master. 2 defeat (an opponent). 3 affected by (emotion, etc.): *she was overcome with joy.*

**o·ver·do** ▸*v.* (*past* **-did**; *past part.* **-done**) 1 carry to excess; take too far: *I think you overdid the sarcasm.* 2 [usu. as *adj.* **overdone**] cook for too long.

**o·ver·dose** ▸*n.* excessive dose (of a drug, etc.).
▸*v.* take an excessive dose (of a drug, etc.): *he was admitted to the hospital after overdosing on cocaine.*

**o·ver·draft** ▸*n.* 1 deficit in a bank account caused by drawing more money than is credited to it. 2 amount of this.

**o·ver·draw** ▸*v.* (*past* **-drew**; *past part.* **-drawn**) 1 draw a sum of money in excess of the amount credited to (one's bank account). 2 overdraw one's account.

**o·ver·drive** ▸*n.* 1 mechanism in a motor vehicle providing a gear ratio higher than that of the usual gear. 2 state of high activity.

**o·ver·due** ▸*adj.* past the time due for payment, arrival, return, etc.

**o·ver·flow** ▸*v.* **1** flow over (the brim, limits, etc.). **2 a** (of a receptacle, etc.) be so full that the contents overflow it. **b** (of contents) overflow a container. **3** (of a crowd, etc.) extend beyond the limits of (a room, etc.). **4** flood (a surface or area). **5** (of kindness, a harvest, etc.) be very abundant.
▸*n.* **1** what overflows or is superfluous. **2** outlet for excess water, etc.

**o·ver·grown** ▸*adj.* **1** covered with plants that have been allowed to grow wild. **2** grown too large.

**o·ver·hand** ▸*adj. & adv.* (in tennis, baseball, etc.) thrown or played with the hand above the shoulder.

**o·ver·hang** ▸*v.* (*past* and *past part.* **-hung**) project or hang over.
▸*n.* **1** overhanging part of a structure or rock formation. **2** amount by which this projects.

**o·ver·haul** ▸*v.* **1** thoroughly examine and repair as necessary. **2** overtake.
▸*n.* thorough examination, with repairs if necessary.

**o·ver·head** ▸*adv.* **1** above one's head. **2** in the sky or on the floor above.

▸*adj.* **1** placed overhead. **2** (of expenses) arising from general operating costs.
▸*n.* overhead expenses.

**o·ver·hear** ▸*v.* (*past* and *past part.* **-heard**) hear as an eavesdropper or unintentionally.

**o·ver·joyed** /ˌōvərˈjoid/ ▸*adj.* filled with great joy.

**o·ver·kill** ▸*n.* **1** amount by which the capacity for destruction exceeds what is necessary for victory or annihilation. **2** excess.
▸*v.* kill or destroy to a greater extent than necessary.

**o·ver·land** ▸*adj. & adv.* by land.

**o·ver·lap** ▸*v.* (**-lapped**, **-lap·ping**) **1** partly cover (another object). **2** cover and extend beyond. **3** (of two things) partly coincide: *where psychology and philosophy overlap.*
▸*n.* **1** extension over. **2** amount of this.

**o·ver·lay** ▸*v.* (*past* and *past part.* **-laid**) **1** lay over. **2** cover the surface of (a thing) with (a coating, etc.).
▸*n.* **1** thing laid over another. **2** (in printing, map reading, etc.) transparent sheet superimposed on another.

**o·ver·look** ▸*v.* **1** fail to notice;

ignore, condone (an offense, etc.). **2** have a view from above. **3** supervise.

▸*n.* commanding position or view.

**o·ver·ly** /ˈōvərlē/ ▸*adv.* excessively; too.

**o·ver·night** ▸*adv.* **1** for a night. **2** during a night. **3** suddenly; immediately.

▸*adj.* **1** for use overnight: *overnight bag.* **2** done, etc., overnight.

**o·ver·pass** ▸*n.* road or railroad line that passes over another by means of a bridge.

**o·ver·play** ▸*v.* give undue importance to; overemphasize.

**o·ver·pow·er** ▸*v.* **1** subdue. **2** (of heat, emotion, etc.) be too intense for; overwhelm.
—**o·ver·pow·er·ing** *adj.*
—**o·ver·pow·er·ing·ly** *adv.*

**o·ver·rate** ▸*v.* assess too highly.

**o·ver·reach** ▸*v.* outwit; get the better of by cunning or artifice.

**o·ver·re·act** ▸*v.* respond more forcibly, etc., than is justified.
—**o·ver·re·ac·tion** *n.*

**o·ver·ride** ▸*v.* (*past* -**rode**; *past part.* -**rid·den**) **1** [often as *adj.* **overriding**] have or claim precedence or superiority over: *an overriding consideration.* **2 a** intervene and make

ineffective. **b** interrupt the action of (an automatic device), esp. to take manual control.

▸*n.* **1** suspension of an automatic function. **2** device for this.

**o·ver·rule** ▸*v.* set aside (a decision, etc.) by exercising a superior authority.

**o·ver·run** ▸*v.* (-**run·ning**; *past* -**ran**; *past part.* -**run**) **1** (of pests, weeds, etc.) swarm or spread over. **2** conquer or ravage (territory) by force. **3** (of time, expenditure, etc.) exceed (a fixed limit).

▸*n.* excess of produced items.

**o·ver·seas** ▸*adv.* abroad: *was sent overseas for training.*

▸*adj.* foreign.

**o·ver·see** ▸*v.* (*past* -**saw**; *past part.* -**seen**) officially supervise (workers, work, etc.).
—**o·ver·se·er** *n.*

**o·ver·shad·ow** ▸*v.* **1** appear much more prominent or important than. **2** shelter from the sun.

**o·ver·shoe** ▸*n.* shoe of rubber, etc., worn over another as protection from wet, cold, etc.

**o·ver·shoot** ▸*v.* (*past* and *past part.* -**shot**) **1** pass or send beyond (a target or limit). **2** (of an aircraft) fly or taxi beyond (the runway) when landing or taking off.

**o·ver·sight** ▸*n.* **1** failure to notice something. **2** inadvertent mistake.

**o·ver·sleep** ▸*v.* (*past* and *past part.* **-slept**) sleep beyond the intended time of waking.

**o·ver·state** ▸*v.* **1** state (esp. a case or argument) too strongly. **2** exaggerate.

**o·ver·stay** ▸*v.* stay longer than (one's welcome, a time limit, etc.).

**o·ver·step** ▸*v.* (**-stepped, -step·ping**) **1** pass beyond (a boundary or mark). **2** violate (certain standards of behavior, etc.).

**o·vert** /ōˈvərt; ˈōvərt/ ▸*adj.* unconcealed; done openly. **—o·vert·ly** *adv.*

**o·ver·take** ▸*v.* (*past* **-took**; *past part.* **-tak·en**) **1** catch up with and pass. **2** (of a storm, misfortune, etc.) come suddenly upon.

**o·ver·throw** ▸*v.* (*past* **-threw**; *past part.* **-thrown**) **1** remove forcibly from power. **2** conquer; overcome. **3** *Baseball* **a** (of a fielder) throw beyond the intended place. **b** (of a pitcher) throw too vigorously. ▸*n.* defeat or downfall.

**o·ver·time** ▸*n.* **1** time worked in addition to regular hours. **2** payment for this. **3** *Sports* additional period of play at the end of a game when the scores are equal. ▸*adv.* in addition to regular hours.

**o·ver·tone** ▸*n.* subtle quality or implication: *sinister overtones.*

**o·ver·ture** /ˈōvərˌCHŏŏr/ ▸*n.* **1** orchestral piece opening an opera, etc. **2** introduction to something more substantial.

**o·ver·turn** ▸*v.* **1** cause to turn over; upset. **2** reverse; subvert. **3** turn over; fall over.

**o·ver·view** ▸*n.* general survey.

**o·ver·ween·ing** /ˌōvərˈwēniNG/ ▸*adj.* showing excessive confidence or pride.

**o·ver·weight** ▸*adj.* beyond an allowed or suitable weight.

**o·ver·whelm** /ˌōvərˈ(h)welm/ ▸*v.* **1** overpower with emotion. **2** overpower with an excess of business, etc. **3** bury or drown beneath a huge mass; submerge utterly. **—o·ver·whelm·ing** *adj.*

**o·ver·work** ▸*v.* **1** work too hard. **2** cause (another person) to work too hard. **3** weary or exhaust with too much work. **4** make excessive use of. ▸*n.* excessive work.

**o·ver·wrought** ▸*adj.*
**1** overexcited; nervous; distraught. **2** too elaborate.

**o·vi·duct** /ˈōviˌdəkt/ ▸*n.* tube through which an ovum passes from the ovary.

**o·vine** /ˈōˌvīn/ ▸*adj.* of, relating to, or resembling sheep.

**o·void** /ˈōˌvoid/ ▸*adj.* (of a solid or of a surface) egg-shaped. ▸*n.* ovoid body or surface.

**ov·u·late** /ˈävyəˌlāt/ ▸*v.* produce ova or ovules, or discharge them from the ovary. —**ov·u·la·tion** *n.*

**ov·ule** /ˈävyo͞ol/ ▸*n.* part of the ovary of seed plants that contains the germ cell; unfertilized seed. —**ov·u·lar** *adj.*

**o·vum** /ˈōvəm/ ▸*n.* (*pl.* **o·va**) **1** mature reproductive cell of female animals, produced by the ovary. **2** egg cell of plants.

**owe** /ō/ ▸*v.* **1 a** be under obligation. **b** be in debt: *still owe for my car.* **2** be under obligation to render (gratitude, honor, etc.): *owe grateful thanks to all.* **3** be indebted to a person or thing for: *we owe to Newton the principle of gravitation.*

**owl** /oul/ ▸*n.* nocturnal bird of prey with large eyes and a hooked beak. —**owl·ish** *adj.*

**own** /ōn/ ▸*adj.* [prec. by possessive] **1** belonging to oneself or itself. **2** individual; peculiar; particular. ▸*v.* **1** have as property; possess. **2 a** confess; admit as valid, true, etc.: *owns he did not know.* **b** confess to: *owned up to a prejudice.* **3** acknowledge. —**own·er** *n.* —**own·er·ship** *n.*

**ox** /äks/ ▸*n.* (*pl.* **ox·en**) **1** large usu. horned domesticated ruminant used for draft, for supplying milk, and for eating as meat. **2** castrated male of a domesticated species of cattle.

**ox·ford** /ˈäksfərd/ ▸*n.* **1** low-heeled shoe that laces over the instep. **2** cotton fabric made in a basket weave, used for shirts and sportswear.

**ox·ide** /ˈäkˌsīd/ ▸*n.* binary compound of oxygen.

**ox·i·dize** /ˈäksiˌdīz/ ▸*v.* **1** combine or cause to combine with oxygen. **2** cover (metal) or (of metal) become covered with a coating of oxide; make or become rusty. —**ox·i·da·tion** *n.* —**ox·i·diz·er** *n.*

**ox·y·gen** /ˈäksijən/ ▸*n. Chem.* colorless, tasteless, odorless gaseous element, occurring naturally in air, water, and most minerals and organic substances, and essential to plant and animal life. (Symb.: O)

**ox·y·gen·ate** /'äksijə‚nāt/ ▶v. **1** supply, treat, or mix with oxygen; oxidize. **2** charge (blood) with oxygen by respiration. —**ox·y·gen·a·tion** n.

**ox·y·mo·ron** /‚äksə'môrän/ ▶n. figure of speech in which apparently contradictory terms appear in conjunction (e.g., *faith unfaithful kept him falsely true*).

**oys·ter** /'oistər/ ▶n. **1** bivalve mollusk, esp. edible kinds, sometimes producing a pearl. **2** something regarded as containing all that one desires: *the world is my oyster.*

**oz.** ▶*abbr.* ounce(s).

**o·zone** /'ō‚zōn/ ▶n. *Chem.* colorless unstable gas with a pungent odor and powerful oxidizing properties, used for bleaching, etc.

□ **ozone layer** layer of ozone in the stratosphere that absorbs most of the sun's ultraviolet radiation.

**o·zone lay·er** ▶n. layer in the earth's stratosphere at an altitude of about 6.2 miles (10 kilometers) containing a high concentration of ozone, which absorbs most of the ultraviolet radiation reaching the earth from the sun.

# Pp

**P**[1] /pē/ (also **p**) ▶*n.* (*pl.* **Ps** or **P's**; **p's**) sixteenth letter of the alphabet.

**P**[2] ▶*symb. Chem.* phosphorus.

**p**(also **p.**) ▶*abbr.* **1** page. **2** piano (softly).

**PA** ▶*abbr.* **1** Pennsylvania (in official postal use). **2** public address, esp. as: *PA system.*

**Pa** ▶*symb. Chem.* protactinium.

**pa** /pä/ ▶*n. inf.* father.

**p.a.** ▶*abbr.* per annum.

**PAC** /pak/ ▶*abbr.* political action committee.

**pace** /pās/ ▶*n.* **1** single step in walking or running. **2** rate at which something happens.
▶*v.* **1** traverse by pacing, esp. as an expression of anxiety: *she paced the hall for an hour.* **2** measure (a distance) by walking it. □ **keep pace (with)** advance at an equal rate (as).

**pace·mak·er** ▶*n.* device for stimulating heart contractions.

**pace·set·ter** ▶*n.* leader.

**pach·y·derm** /ˈpakəˌdərm/ ▶*n.* any thick-skinned mammal, esp. an elephant or rhinoceros.

**pa·cif·ic** /pəˈsifik/ ▶*adj.* peaceful; tranquil.

**pac·i·fism** /ˈpasəˌfizəm/ ▶*n.* belief that war and violence are morally unjustifiable.
—**pac·i·fist** *n. & adj.*

**pac·i·fy** /ˈpasəˌfī/ ▶*v.* (**-fied**) appease.

**pack** /pak/ ▶*n.* **1** set of items packaged for use or disposal together. **2** backpack. **3** set of playing cards. **4** group, esp. of wild animals.
▶*v.* **1** fill (a suitcase, bag, etc.) with clothes and other items. **2** crowd or cram; fill tightly. **3** (of animals, etc.) form a pack. **4** select (a jury, etc.) or fill (a meeting) so as to secure a decision in one's favor. □ **pack animal** animal used for carrying packs. □ **pack ice** area of large crowded pieces of floating ice in the sea.

**pack·age** /ˈpakij/ ▶*n.* **1** box, parcel, etc., in which things are packed. **2** (also **pack·age deal**) set of proposals or items offered or agreed to as a whole.

▶ *v.* make up into or enclose in a package.

**pack·et** ▶*n.* small package.

**pact** /pakt/ ▶*n.* agreement or a treaty.

**pad** /pad/ ▶*n.* **1** piece of soft material used to reduce friction or jarring, fill out hollows, hold or absorb liquid, etc. **2** sheets of blank paper fastened together at one edge, for writing or drawing on. **3** fleshy underpart of an animal's foot or of a human finger. **4** flat surface for helicopter takeoff or rocket launching. **5** floating leaf of a water lily.

▶ *v.* (**pad·ded, pad·ding**) **1** provide with a pad or padding; stuff. **2** lengthen or fill out with unnecessary material. **3** walk with a soft dull steady step. —**pad·ding** *n.*

**pad·dle** /'padl/ ▶*n.* **1** short broad-bladed oar. **2** paddle-shaped instrument.

▶ *v.* **1** move on water or propel a boat by means of paddles. **2** *inf.* spank.

□ **paddle wheel** wheel with radiating paddles around it for propelling a ship.

**pad·dock** /'padək/ ▶*n.* **1** small field, esp. for keeping horses in. **2** turf enclosure at a racetrack.

**pad·dy** /'padē/ ▶*n.* (*pl.* **-dies**) field where rice is grown.

**pad·lock** ▶*n.* detachable lock hanging by a pivoted hook on the object fastened.

▶ *v.* secure with a padlock.

**pa·dre** /'pädrā/ ▶*n. inf.* chaplain in any of the armed services.

**pae·an** /'pēən/ ▶*n.* song of praise or triumph.

**pa·gan** /'pāgən/ ▶*n.* person holding religious beliefs other than those of the main world religions.

▶ *adj.* of or relating to such people or beliefs. —**pa·gan·ism** *n.*

**page** /pāj/ ▶*n.* **1** leaf of a book, periodical, etc. **2** person employed to run errands, attend to a door, etc.

▶ *v.* **1** summon by making an announcement or by sending a messenger. **2** summon by a pager.

**pag·eant** /'pajənt/ ▶*n.* public entertainment consisting of a procession of elaborately costumed people or an outdoor performance illustrating historical events. —**pag·eant·ry** *n.*

**pag·er** /ˈpājər/ ▶n. electronic device that receives messages and notifies the user by beeping.

**pag·i·nate** /ˈpajəˌnāt/ ▶v. assign numbers to the pages of a book, etc. —**pag·i·na·tion** n.

**pag·i·na·tion** /ˌpajəˈnāsʜən/ ▶n. sequence of numbers assigned to pages in a book or periodical.

**pa·go·da** /pəˈgōdə/ ▶n. Hindu or Buddhist temple, esp. a many-tiered tower, in India and the Far East.

**pail** /pāl/ ▶n. bucket.

**pain** /pān/ ▶n. **1** physical suffering or discomfort resulting from illness, injury, etc. **2** mental suffering or distress. **3** careful effort: *take pains.* **4** (also **pain in the neck**, etc.) *inf.* troublesome person or thing; nuisance. ▶v. cause pain to. —**pain·ful** *adj.* □ **on** (or **under**) **pain of** with (death, etc.) as the penalty.

**pain·kill·er** ▶n. medicine or drug for alleviating pain.

**pains·tak·ing** ▶adj. careful, industrious, or thorough.

**paint** /pānt/ ▶n. coloring matter, esp. in liquid form for imparting color to a surface. ▶v. **1** cover (a surface) with paint. **2** depict (an object, scene, etc.) with paint; produce (a picture) by painting.

**paint·er** ▶n. **1** person who paints, esp. an artist or decorator. **2** rope attached to the bow of a boat for tying it to a dock.

**paint·ing** ▶n. **1** process or art of using paint. **2** painted picture.

**pair** /pe(ə)r/ ▶n. **1** set of two persons or things used together or regarded as a unit: *a pair of gloves.* **2** article (e.g., scissors) consisting of two joined or corresponding parts. ▶v. arrange or be arranged in couples.

**pais·ley** /ˈpāzlē/ ▶n. distinctive detailed pattern of curved feather-shaped figures.

**pa·ja·mas** /pəˈjäməz/ ▶pl. n. suit of loose pants and jacket for sleeping in.

**pal** /pal/ ▶n. *inf.* friend.

**pal·ace** /ˈpalis/ ▶n. **1** official residence of a president or sovereign. **2** mansion.

**pal·at·a·ble** /ˈpalitəbəl/ ▶adj. **1** (of food or drink) pleasant to taste. **2** (of an idea, suggestion, etc.) acceptable; satisfactory. —**pal·at·a·bil·i·ty** n.

**pal·ate** /ˈpalit/ ▶n. **1** structure closing the upper part of the mouth cavity in vertebrates. **2** taste; liking.

**pa·la·tial** /pəˈlāSHəl/ ▸*adj.* (of a building) like a palace, esp. spacious and magnificent.

**pa·la·ver** /pəˈlavər/ ▸*n.* prolonged and idle discussion.

**pa·laz·zo** /pəˈlätsō/ ▸*n.* (*pl.* **-laz·zos** or **-laz·zi** /-ˈlätsē/) palatial building, esp. in Italy.

**pale** /pāl/ ▸*adj.* **1** diminished in coloration; of a whitish or ashen appearance. **2** of faint luster; dim.
▸*v.* **1** grow or make pale. **2** become feeble in comparison (with).
▸*n.* **1** pointed piece of wood for fencing, etc.; stake. **2** boundary or enclosed area.

**Pa·le·o·lith·ic** /ˌpālēəˈliTHik/ ▸*adj.* of or relating to the early part of the Stone Age.

**pa·le·on·tol·o·gy** /ˌpālē,ənˈtäləjē/ ▸*n.* branch of science concerned with fossil animals and plants.
—**pa·le·on·tol·o·gist** *n.*

**Pa·le·o·zo·ic** /ˌpālēəˈzōik/ ▸*adj.* of an era of geological time marked by the appearance of marine and terrestrial plants and animals, esp. invertebrates.

**pal·ette** /ˈpalit/ ▸*n.* **1** thin board or slab or other surface, usu. with a hole for the thumb, on which an artist holds and mixes colors. **2** range of colors, etc., used by an artist.

**pal·frey** /ˈpôlfrē/ ▸*n.* (*pl.* **-freys**) docile horse used for ordinary riding, esp. by women.

**pal·i·mony** /ˈpalə,mōnē/ ▸*n. inf.* compensation made by one member of an unmarried couple to the other after separation.

**pa·limp·sest** /ˈpalimp,sest/ ▸*n.* writing material or manuscript on which the original writing has been erased for reuse.

**pal·in·drome** /ˈpalin,drōm/ ▸*n.* word or phrase that reads the same backward as forward (**e.g.,** *rotator*).

**pal·ing** /ˈpāliNG/ ▸*n.* fence made of pointed wooden or metal stakes.

**pal·i·node** /ˈpalə,nōd/ ▸*n.* poem in which the poet retracts a view or sentiment expressed in a former poem.

**pal·i·sade** /ˌpaləˈsād/ ▸*n.* **1** fence of pales or iron railings. **2** (**palisades**) line of high cliffs.

**pall** /pôl/ ▸*n.* **1** cloth spread over a coffin, hearse, or tomb. **2** dark covering: *pall of darkness* | *pall of smoke.*

▸*v.* become less interesting or appealing.

**pall·bear·er** ▸*n.* person helping to carry or officially escorting a coffin at a funeral.

**pal·let** /'palit/ ▸*n.* **1** straw mattress. **2** makeshift bed. **3** portable platform for transporting and storing loads.

**pal·li·ate** /'palē,āt/ ▸*v.* **1** make (a disease or its symptoms) less severe without removing the cause. **2** moderate (fears or suspicions). —**pal·li·a·tive** *n. & adj.*

**pal·lid** /'palid/ ▸*adj.* pale, esp. from illness.

**pal·lor** /'palər/ ▸*n.* paleness, esp. resulting from illness.

**palm** /päm/ ▸*n.* **1** any usu. tropical tree with no branches and a mass of large leaves at the top. **2** inner surface of the hand between the wrist and fingers. ▸*v.* conceal in the hand. □ **palm off** impose on or dispose of fraudulently.

**pal·met·to** /pal'metō/ ▸*n.* small palm tree.

**palm·ist·ry** /'päməstrē/ ▸*n.* supposed divination from lines and other features on the palm of the hand. —**palm·ist** *n.*

**Palm Sun·day** ▸*n.* Sunday before Easter, celebrating Christ's entry into Jerusalem.

**pal·o·mi·no** /,palə'mēnō/ ▸*n.* golden or tan-colored horse with a light-colored mane and tail.

**pal·pa·ble** /'palpəbəl/ ▸*adj.* **1** that can be touched or felt. **2** obvious. —**pal·pa·bly** *adv.*

**pal·pate** /'pal,pāt/ ▸*v.* examine (esp. medically) by touch. —**pal·pa·tion** *n.*

**pal·pi·tate** /'palpi,tāt/ ▸*v.* (of the heart) beat strongly, rapidly, or irregularly. —**pal·pi·ta·tion** *n.*

**pal·sy** /'pôlzē/ ▸*n.* (*pl.* **-sies**) paralysis with involuntary tremors.

**pal·ter** /'pôltər/ ▸*v.* **1** equivocate or prevaricate in action or speech. **2** (**palter with**) trifle with.

**pal·try** /'pôltrē/ ▸*adj.* (**-tri·er**, **-tri·est**) worthless; contemptible; trifling. —**pal·tri·ness** *n.*

**pa·lu·dal** /pə'lōōdl; 'palyədl/ ▸*adj.* (of a plant, animal, or soil) living or occurring in a marshy habitat.

**pam·pas** /'pampəz/ ▸*pl. n.* large treeless plains in S. America.

**pam·per** /'pampər/ ▸*v.* overindulge; spoil.

**pam·phlet** /'pamflit/ ▸*n.* small,

usu. unbound booklet or leaflet. —**pam·phlet·eer** n. & v.

**pan** /pan/ ▶n. **1** vessel of metal, earthenware, etc., usu. broad and shallow, used for cooking, heating, etc. **2** any similar shallow container.
▶v. (**panned, pan·ning**) **1** inf. criticize severely. **2** wash (gold-bearing gravel) in a pan. **3** (of a video or movie camera) move or be moved horizontally to give a panoramic effect or to follow a moving object.

**pan-** ▶comb. form **1** all; the whole of. **2** relating to or comprising the whole: *pan-American.*

**pan·a·ce·a** /ˌpanəˈsēə/ ▶n. universal remedy.

**pa·nache** /pəˈnaSH/ ▶n. assertiveness or flamboyant confidence of style or manner.

**pan·cake** ▶n. thin flat cake of batter usu. fried in a pan or on a griddle.

**pan·cre·as** /ˈpaNGkrēəs/ ▶n. gland near the stomach supplying the duodenum with digestive fluid and secreting insulin. —**pan·cre·at·ic** adj. —**pan·cre·a·ti·tis** n.

**pan·da** /ˈpandə/ ▶n. **1** (also **gi·ant pan·da**) large bearlike mammal, native to China and Tibet,

having characteristic black and white markings. **2** (also **red pan·da**) Himalayan raccoon-like mammal with reddish-brown fur.

**pan·dem·ic** /panˈdemik/ ▶adj. (of a disease) prevalent over a whole country or the world.

**pan·de·mo·ni·um** /ˌpandəˈmōnēəm/ ▶n. uproar; utter confusion.

**pan·der** /ˈpandər/ ▶v. (**pander to**) gratify or indulge (an immoral or distasteful desire or habit): *pandering to public greed.*

**pane** /pān/ ▶n. single sheet of glass in a window or door.

**pan·e·gy·ric** /ˌpanəˈjirik/ ▶n. laudatory discourse; eulogy.

**pan·el** /ˈpanl/ ▶n. **1** distinct, usu. rectangular, section of a surface (e.g., of a wall or door). **2** strip of material as part of a garment. **3** group of people gathered for a discussion, as advisors, etc.
▶v. fit, cover, or decorate with panels.
☐ **panel truck** small enclosed delivery truck.

**pan·el·ist** ▶n. member of a panel.

**pang** /paNG/ ▶n. sudden sharp pain or painful emotion.

**pan·han·dle** ▶n. narrow strip of

territory extending from one state into another.

▶ *v. inf.* beg for money in the street. —**pan·han·dler** *n.*

**pan·ic** /ˈpanik/ ▶*n.* sudden uncontrollable fear or alarm.

▶ *v.* (**-icked, -ick·ing**) affect or be affected with panic. —**pan·ic-strick·en** (or **panic-struck**) *adj.* —**pan·ick·y** *adj.*

**pan·nier** /ˈpanyər/ ▶*n.* basket, bag, or box, esp. one of a pair for transporting loads.

**pan·o·ply** /ˈpanəplē/ ▶*n.* (*pl.* -**plies**) complete or magnificent array.

**pan·op·tic** /paˈnäptik/ ▶*adj.* showing or seeing the whole at one view.

**pan·o·ra·ma** /ˌpanəˈramə/ ▶*n.* **1** unbroken view of a surrounding region. **2** complete survey or presentation of a subject, sequence of events, etc. —**pan·o·ram·ic** *adj.*

**pan·sy** /ˈpanzē/ ▶*n.* (*pl.* -**sies**) garden plant with flowers of various rich colors.

**pant** /pant/ ▶*v.* breathe with short quick breaths.

▶*n.* panting breath.

**pan·the·ism** /ˈpanTHēˌizəm/ ▶*n.* belief that God is identifiable with the forces of nature and with natural substances. —**pan·the·ist** *n.*

**pan·the·on** /ˈpanTHēˌän; -THēən/ ▶*n.* **1** building in which illustrious dead are buried or have memorials. **2** the deities of a people collectively. **3** temple dedicated to all the gods, esp. the circular one at Rome. **4** group of esteemed persons.

**pan·ther** /ˈpanTHər/ ▶*n.* leopard, esp. with black fur.

**pant·ies** /ˈpantēz/ ▶*pl. n. inf.* short-legged or legless underpants worn by women and girls.

**pan·to·graph** /ˈpantəˌgraf/ ▶*n.* **1** instrument for copying a drawing or plan on a different scale by a system of hinged and jointed rods. **2** jointed framework conveying a current to a train, streetcar, or other electric vehicle from overhead wires.

**pan·to·mime** /ˈpantəˌmīm/ ▶*n.* use of gestures and facial expression to convey meaning without speech, esp. in drama and dance.

▶*v.* convey meaning without speech using only gestures. —**pan·to·mim·ic** *adj.*

**pan·try** /ˈpantrē/ ▶*n.* (*pl.* -**tries**)

small room or cupboard for storage of kitchen supplies, groceries, etc.

**pants** /pants/ ▸*pl. n.* outer garment reaching from the waist usu. to the ankles, divided into two parts to cover the legs.

**pan·ty·hose** /ˈpantē,hōz/ ▸*pl. n.* usu. sheer one-piece garment combining panties and stockings.

**pan·zer** /ˈpanzər/ ▸*n.* German armored vehicle, esp. a tank.

**pap** /pap/ ▸*n.* **1** soft or semiliquid food for infants or invalids. **2** light or trivial reading matter; nonsense.

**pa·pa** /ˈpäpə/ ▸*n.* father.

**pa·pa·cy** /ˈpāpəsē/ ▸*n.* (*pl.* **-cies**) pope's office or tenure.

**pa·pal** /ˈpāpəl/ ▸*adj.* of a pope or the papacy.

**pa·pa·ya** /pəˈpīə/ ▸*n.* edible yellow fruit with orange flesh.

**pa·per** /ˈpāpər/ ▸*n.* **1** material manufactured in thin sheets from the pulp of wood or other fibrous substances, used for writing or drawing or printing on, or as wrapping material, etc. **2** newspaper. **3 a** printed document. **b** (**papers**) identification or other legal documents. **4** wallpaper. **5** essay or dissertation.
▸*v.* **1** apply paper to, esp. decorate (a wall, etc.) with wallpaper. **2** (**paper over**) disguise or try to hide. —**pa·per·er** *n.* —**pa·per·less** *adj.* —**pa·per·y** *adj.*
□ **paper clip** clip of bent wire or of plastic for holding several sheets of paper together.
□ **paper trail** documentation of transactions, etc.

**pa·per·back** ▸*adj.* (of a book) bound in stiff paper. ▸*n.* paperback book.

**pa·per chase** ▸*n.* **1** action of processing forms and other paperwork, esp. when considered excessive. **2** attempt to gain academic qualifications, esp. a law degree.

**pa·per ti·ger** ▸*n.* apparently threatening, but ineffectual, person or thing.

**pa·per trail** ▸*n.* written evidence of someone's activities.

**pa·per·weight** ▸*n.* small heavy object for keeping loose papers in place.

**pa·pier mâ·ché** /ˌpāpər məˈSHā/ ▸*n.* paper pulp used for molding into boxes, trays, etc.

**pa·pri·ka** /pəˈprēkə/ ▸*n.* **1** red

pepper. **2** powdery condiment made from it.

**pa·py·rus** /pə'pīrəs/ ▸*n.* (*pl.* **-ri**) writing material prepared in ancient Egypt from the pithy stem of a water plant.

**par** /pär/ ▸*n.* **1** average or normal amount, degree, condition, etc.: *be up to par.* **2** equality; equal footing. **3** number of strokes a skilled golfer should normally require for a hole or course. **4** face value of stocks and shares, etc. **5** (also **par of exchange**) recognized value of one country's currency in terms of another's.
□ **par for the course** *inf.* what is normal or to be expected.

**par-** ▸*prefix* var. of PARA- before a vowel or *h*: *paraldehyde* | *parody* | *parhelion.*

**para-** /'parə/ ▸*prefix* **1** beside: *paramilitary.* **2** beyond: *paranormal.*

**par·a·ble** /'parəbəl/ ▸*n.* narrative of imagined events used to illustrate a moral or spiritual lesson.

**pa·rab·o·la** /pə'rabələ/ ▸*n.* open plane curve formed by the intersection of a cone with a plane parallel to its side.

**par·a·chute** /'parə,SHoot/ ▸*n.* rectangular or umbrella-shaped apparatus allowing a slow and safe descent, esp. from an aircraft.
▸*v.* convey or descend by parachute. —**par·a·chut·ist** *n.*

**pa·rade** /pə'rād/ ▸*n.* **1** public procession, usu. celebrating a special day or event. **2** formal or ceremonial muster of troops for inspection. **3** distasteful display of a particular kind of behavior.
▸*v.* **1** march ceremonially in procession. **2** display ostentatiously.

**par·a·digm** /'parə,dīm/ ▸*n.* **1** example or pattern. **2** *Gram.* representative set of the inflections of a noun, verb, etc. —**par·a·dig·mat·ic** *adj.*

**par·a·dise** /'parə,dīs/ ▸*n.* **1** heaven. **2** place or state of complete happiness. **3** abode of Adam and Eve; garden of Eden. —**par·a·di·si·a·cal** *adj.*

**par·a·dox** /'parə,däks/ ▸*n.* **1** seemingly absurd or contradictory statement, even if actually well-founded. **2** person or thing having contradictory qualities, etc. —**par·a·dox·i·cal** *adj.*

**par·af·fin** /'parəfin/ ▸*n.* waxy

mixture of hydrocarbons used in candles, waterproofing, etc.

**par·a·gon** /ˈparəˌgän/ ▶*n.* model of excellence.

**par·a·graph** ▶*n.* distinct section of a piece of writing, beginning on a new usu. indented line. ▶*v.* arrange in paragraphs.

**par·a·keet** /ˈparəˌkēt/ ▶*n.* small usu. long-tailed parrot.

**par·a·le·gal** ▶*n.* person trained in subsidiary legal matters.

**par·al·lax** /ˈparəˌlaks/ ▶*n.* apparent difference in the position or direction of an object caused when the observer's position is changed. —**par·al·lac·tic** *adj.*

**par·al·lel** /ˈparəˌlel/ ▶*adj.* **1** (of lines or planes) having the same distance continuously between them. **2** existing at the same time and corresponding; simultaneous. ▶*n.* **1** person or thing similar to another. **2** comparison. **3** (also **parallel of latitude**) each of the imaginary parallel circles of constant latitude on the earth's surface. ▶*v.* **1** be parallel to; correspond to. **2** represent as similar; compare. —**par·al·lel·ism** *n.*

**par·al·lel·o·gram** ▶*n.* four-sided plane rectilinear figure with opposite sides parallel.

**pa·ral·y·sis** /pəˈraləsis/ ▶*n.* (*pl.* **-ses**) **1** impairment or loss of esp. the motor function of the nerves. **2** state of utter powerlessness. —**par·a·lyt·ic** *adj.* & *n.*

**par·a·lyze** /ˈparəˌlīz/ ▶*v.* **1** affect with paralysis. **2** render powerless.

**par·a·med·ic** ▶*n.* person trained in emergency medical procedures. —**par·a·med·i·cal** *adj.*

**pa·ram·e·ter** /pəˈramitər/ ▶*n.* **1** limit or boundary that defines the scope of an activity: *they set the parameters of the debate.* **2** numerical quantity constant in the case considered but varying in different cases.

**par·a·mil·i·tar·y** ▶*adj.* (of forces) ancillary to and similarly organized to military forces.

**par·a·mount** ▶*adj.* supreme; requiring first consideration.

**par·a·mour** /ˈparəˌmoŏr/ ▶*n.* illicit lover of a married person.

**par·a·noi·a** /ˌparəˈnoiə/ ▶*n.* **1** personality disorder esp. characterized by delusions of persecution and exaggerated self-importance. **2** abnormal tendency to suspect and mistrust others. —**par·a·noi·ac** adj. —**par·a·noid** adj.

**par·a·nor·mal** ▸adj. supernatural.

**par·a·pet** /'parəpit/ ▸n. **1** low wall at the edge of a roof, balcony, etc., or along the sides of a bridge. **2** defense of earth or stone to conceal and protect troops.

**par·aph** /'parəf; pə'raf/ ▸n. flourish after a signature, originally as a precaution against forgery.

**par·a·pher·na·li·a** /ˌparəfə(r)-'nālyə/ ▸pl. n. miscellaneous belongings, equipment, accessories, etc.

**par·a·phrase** ▸n. free rendering or rewording of a passage. ▸v. express the meaning of (a passage) in other words. —**par·a·phras·tic** adj.

**par·a·ple·gi·a** /ˌparə'plēj(ē)ə/ ▸n. paralysis of the legs and part or the whole of the trunk. —**par·a·ple·gic** adj. & n.

**par·a·psy·chol·o·gy** ▸n. study of mental phenomena outside the sphere of ordinary psychology.

—**par·a·psy·cho·log·i·cal** adj. —**par·a·psy·chol·o·gist** n.

**par·a·site** /'parəˌsīt/ ▸n. **1** organism living in or on another and benefiting at the expense of the other. **2** person who lives off or exploits another or others. —**par·a·sit·ic** adj.

**par·a·sol** /'parəˌsôl/ ▸n. light umbrella used to give shade from the sun.

**par·a·troops** ▸pl. n. troops equipped to be dropped by parachute from aircraft. —**par·a·troop·er** n.

**par·boil** /'pärˌboil/ ▸v. partly cook by boiling.

**par·cel** /'pärsəl/ ▸n. **1** goods, etc., wrapped in a package. **2** piece of land. ▸v. (**parcel something out**) divide into portions and distribute.

**parch** /pärCH/ ▸v. make or become hot and dry.

**parch·ment** ▸n. **1** animal skin, esp. that of a sheep or goat, prepared as a writing or painting surface. **2** high-grade paper made to resemble parchment.

**par·don** /'pärdn/ ▸n. **1** act of excusing or forgiving an offense, error, etc. **2** (also **full par·don**) remission of the legal consequences of a crime or conviction.

▸*v.* **1** release from the consequences of an offense, error, etc. **2** forgive; excuse.
—**par·don·a·ble** *adj.*

**pare** /pe(ə)r/ ▸*v.* **1** trim by cutting away the surface or edge. **2** diminish little by little.

**par·ent** /ˈpe(ə)rənt/ ▸*n.* person who has or adopts a child; a father or mother.
▸*v.* be or act as a parent of.
—**par·en·tal** *adj.*
—**par·ent·hood** *n.*
□ **parent company** company of which other companies are subsidiaries.

**par·ent·age** /ˈpe(ə)rəntij/ ▸*n.* lineage; descent from or through parents: *their parentage is unknown.*

**pa·ren·the·sis** /pəˈrenTHəsis/ ▸*n.* (*pl.* **-ses**) **1** explanatory or qualifying word, clause, or sentence. **2** (usu. **parentheses**) one of a pair of rounded brackets ( ) used to include such a word, etc.

**par ex·cel·lence** /ˌpär ˌeksəˈläns/ ▸*adv.* as having special excellence; being the supreme example of its kind.

**par·fait** /pärˈfā/ ▸*n.* layers of ice cream, fruit, etc., served in a tall glass.

**pa·ri·ah** /pəˈrīə/ ▸*n.* social outcast.

**par·i·mu·tu·el** /ˌparə ˈmyo͞oCHo͞oəl/ ▸*n.* form of betting in which those backing the first three places divide the losers' stakes.

**pa·ri pas·su** /ˌpärē ˈpäˌso͞o/ ▸*adv.* side by side; at the same rate or on an equal footing.

**par·ish** /ˈpariSH/ ▸*n.* **1** area having its own church and clergy. **2** county in Louisiana.

**par·i·ty** /ˈparitē/ ▸*n.* **1** equality; equal status or pay. **2** equivalence of one currency with another; being at par.

**park** /pärk/ ▸*n.* **1** public land set aside for recreation or as a preserve. **2** gear position or function in an automatic transmission that immobilizes the drive wheels. **3** area devoted to a specified purpose: *industrial park.*
▸*v.* **1** leave (a vehicle) usu. temporarily. **2** *inf.* deposit and leave, usu. temporarily.
□ **parking meter** coin-operated meter that receives payment for vehicles parked in the street and indicates the time available.

**par·ka** /ˈpärkə/ ▸n. hooded winter jacket.

**Par·kin·son's dis·ease** /ˈpärkinsənz/ (also **Par·kin·son·ism**) ▸n. progressive disease of the nervous system with tremor, muscular rigidity, and emaciation.

**park·way** ▸n. open landscaped highway.

**par·lance** /ˈpärləns/ ▸n. particular idiom.

**par·ley** /ˈpärlē/ ▸n. conference for debating points in a dispute, esp. a discussion of terms for an armistice, etc. ▸v. hold a parley.

**par·lia·ment** /ˈpärləmənt/ ▸n. legislature of various countries, as the United Kingdom.

**par·lia·men·tar·i·an** /ˌpärlə-ˌmenˈterēən/ ▸n. **1** member of a parliament. **2** person who is well-versed in parliamentary procedures.

**par·lia·men·ta·ry** /ˌpärlə-ˈment(ə)rē/ ▸adj. **1** of or relating to a parliament. **2** enacted or established by a parliament.

**par·lor** /ˈpärlər/ ▸n. **1** sitting room in a private house. **2** store providing specified goods or services: *beauty parlor.*

**par·lous** /ˈpärləs/ ▸adj. or full of danger or uncertainty; precarious. ▸adv. greatly or excessively.

**Par·me·san** /ˈpärməˌzän/ ▸n. a kind of hard dry cheese made orig. at Parma and used esp. in grated form.

**pa·ro·chi·al** /pəˈrōkēəl/ ▸adj. **1** of or concerning a parish. **2** local, narrow, or restricted in scope. —**pa·ro·chi·al·ism** n. —**pa·ro·chi·al·ly** adv.

□ **parochial school** school run or supported by a church.

**par·o·dy** /ˈparədē/ ▸n. (pl. **-dies**) **1** humorous exaggerated imitation of an author, literary work, style, etc. **2** feeble imitation; travesty. ▸v. (**-died**) compose a parody of. —**pa·rod·ic** adj. —**par·o·dist** n.

**pa·role** /pəˈrōl/ ▸n. release of a prisoner temporarily for a special purpose or completely before the fulfillment of a sentence, on the promise of good behavior. ▸v. put (a prisoner) on parole. —**pa·rol·ee** n.

**par·o·no·ma·sia** /ˌparənō-ˈmāzн(ē)ə/ ▸n. play on words; a pun.

**par·ox·ysm** /ˈparəkˌsizəm/ ▸n. sudden attack or outburst.

**par·quet** /pär'kā/ ▸n. flooring of wooden blocks arranged in a pattern.

**par·quet·ry** /'pärkitrē/ ▸n. inlaid work of blocks of various woods arranged in a geometric pattern, esp. for flooring or furniture.

**par·ri·cide** /'parə,sīd-/ ▸n. 1 killing of a near relative, esp. of a parent. 2 person who commits parricide. —**par·ri·ci·dal** adj.

**par·rot** /'parət/ ▸n. 1 mainly tropical bird with a short hooked bill, often vivid plumage, and the ability to mimic the human voice. 2 person who mechanically repeats the words or actions of another. ▸v. repeat mechanically.

**par·ry** /'parē/ ▸v. (-ried) 1 avert or ward off, esp. with a countermove. 2 deal skillfully with (an awkward question, etc.). ▸n. (pl. -ries) act of parrying.

**parse** /pärs/ ▸v. 1 describe the function and forms (of a sentence or a word in context) grammatically. 2 Computing analyze (a string or text) into logical syntactic components.

**par·sec** /'pär,sek/ (abbr.: **pc**) ▸n. unit of distance used in astronomy, equal to about 3.25 light years (3.08 × 10¹⁶ meters). One parsec corresponds to the distance at which the mean radius of the earth's orbit subtends an angle of one second of arc.

**par·si·mo·ny** /'pärsə,mōnē/ ▸n. stinginess. —**par·si·mo·ni·ous** adj.

**pars·ley** /'pärslē/ ▸n. biennial herb, with crinkly or flat aromatic leaves, used for seasoning and garnishing food.

**pars·nip** /'pärsnip/ ▸n. plant with a large pale yellow tapering root eaten as a vegetable.

**par·son** /'pärsən/ ▸n. any (esp. Protestant) member of the clergy.

**par·son·age** /'pärsənij/ ▸n. church house provided for a parson.

**part** /pärt/ ▸n. 1 some but not all of a thing or number of things. 2 essential member, constituent, or component. 3 division of a book, broadcast serial, etc. 4 each of several equal portions of a whole: *has 3 parts sugar to 2 parts flour*. 5 person's share in an action, etc. 6 character assigned to an actor on stage. 7 melody, etc., assigned to a particular voice or instrument. **8** each of the sides in an agreement or dispute. **9** region or district: *not from these parts.* **10** dividing line in combed hair.

▶*v.* **1** divide or separate into parts. **2** leave; say good-bye to. **3** (**part with**) give up possession of; hand over. **4** comb hair to form a part.

☐ **for one's part** as far as one is concerned. ☐ **in part** to some extent; partly. ☐ **part-time** occupying or using only part of one's working time. ☐ **take part (in)** assist or have a share (in).

**par·take** /pär'tāk/ ▶*v.* (*past* **-took**; *past part.* **-tak·en**) **1** take a share or part. **2** eat or drink something. —**par·tak·er** *n.*

**par·the·no·gen·e·sis** /ˌpärTHənō'jenəsis/ ▶*n.* reproduction by a female gamete without fertilization.

**par·tial** /'pärSHəl/ ▶*adj.* **1** not complete; forming only part. **2** (**partial to**) biased; having a liking for. —**par·ti·al·i·ty** *n.* —**par·tial·ly** *adv.*

**par·tic·i·pate** /pär'tisə,pāt/ ▶*v.* take a part or share (in). —**par·tic·i·pa·tion** *n.* —**par·tic·i·pant** *n.* —**par·tic·i·pa·to·ry** *adj.*

**par·ti·ci·ple** /'pärtə,sipəl/ ▶*n.* word formed from a verb (*going, gone, being, been*), and used in compound verb forms (*is going, has been*), or as an adjective (*working woman, burned toast*). —**par·ti·cip·i·al** *adj.*

**par·ti·cle** /'pärtikəl/ ▶*n.* **1** very small portion of matter. **2** minor part of speech, esp. a short indeclinable one.

**par·tic·u·lar** /pə(r)'tikyələr/ ▶*adj.* **1** relating to or considered as one thing or person as distinct from others; individual. **2** more than is usual; special: *use particular care in packing the glassware.* **3** scrupulously exact; fastidious.

▶*n.* **1** detail; item. **2** (**particulars**) points of information; detailed account. —**par·tic·u·lar·i·ty** *n.*

☐ **in particular** especially; specifically.

**par·tic·u·lar·ly** ▶*adv.* **1** especially; very. **2** specifically: *they particularly asked for you.*

**part·ing** ▶*n.* **1** leave-taking or departure. **2** division; separating.

**par·ti pris** /ˌpärtē 'prē/ ▶*n.* (*pl.* **par·tis pris** *pronunc.* same) preconceived view; a bias.

▶*adj.* prejudiced; biased.

**par·ti·san** /ˈpärtəzən/ (also
**par·ti·zan**) ▶n. **1** strong, esp.
unreasoning, supporter of a
party, cause, etc. **2** guerrilla.
▶adj. of or like partisans.
—**par·ti·san·ship** n.

**par·ti·tion** /pärˈtiSHən/ ▶n.
**1** division into parts. **2** structure
dividing a space into two parts,
esp. a light interior wall.
▶v. **1** divide into parts. **2** separate
with a partition.

**part·ly** ▶adv. to some extent; not
entirely.

**part·ner** /ˈpärtnər/ ▶n. **1** person
who shares or takes part with
another or others. **2** companion
in dancing. **3** player on the
same side in a game. **4** either
member of a married or
unmarried couple.
▶v. be the partner of.
—**part·ner·ship** n.

**par·tridge** /ˈpärtrij/ ▶n. (pl. same
or **-tridg·es**) any of various
species of game bird.

**par·tu·ri·ent** /pärˈt(y)o͞orēənt/
▶adj. (of a woman or female
mammal) about to give birth; in
labor.
▶n. parturient woman.

**par·tu·ri·tion** /ˌpärCHo͞oˈriSHən/
▶n. act of bringing forth young;
childbirth.

**par·ty** /ˈpärtē/ ▶n. (pl. **-ties**)
**1** social gathering. **2** body of
persons engaged in an activity or
traveling together: *search party*.
**3** group of people united in a
cause, opinion, etc., esp. an
organized political group.
**4** each side in an agreement or
dispute.
▶v. (**-tied**) entertain at or attend a
party.
□ **party line 1** policy adopted by a
political party. **2** shared
telephone line.

**par·ve·nu** /ˈpärvəˌn(y)o͞o/ (fem.
**par·ve·nue**) ▶n. person who has
recently gained wealth or
position.

**pas·chal** /ˈpaskəl/ ▶adj. **1** of or
relating to Easter. **2** of or
relating to the Jewish Passover.

**pas·quin·ade** /ˌpaskwəˈnād/ ▶n.
satire or lampoon, originally one
displayed or delivered publicly
in a public place.

**pass** /pas/ ▶v. (*past part.* **passed**)
**1** move onward; proceed past.
**2** overtake, esp. in a vehicle.
**3** be transferred or cause to be
transferred from one person or
place to another. **4** surpass;
exceed. **5** be accepted as.
**6** move; cause to go. **7** be
successful (in school, etc.).

**8 a** cause or allow (a bill) to proceed to further legislative processes. **b** (of a bill or proposal) be approved. **9** spend or use up (a certain time or period). **10** send (the ball) to another player of one's own team. **11** forgo one's turn or chance in a game, etc. **12** discharge from the body. **13** pronounce (judicial sentence) on.

▸*n.* **1** act or instance of passing. **2** permission giving free entry, access, leave, etc. **3** transference of the ball to another player on the same side. **4** narrow passage through mountains.

□ **in passing 1** by the way. **2** in the course of conversation, etc. □ **pass away 1** die. **2** cease to exist; come to an end. □ **pass the buck** *inf.* deny or shift responsibility. □ **pass by 1** go past. **2** disregard; omit. □ **pass out 1** become unconscious. **2** distribute.

**pass·a·ble** ▸*adj.* **1** barely satisfactory; just adequate. **2** (of a road, pass, etc.) that can be passed. —**pass·a·bly** *adv.*

**pas·sage** /ˈpasij/ ▸*n.* **1** process or means of passing; transit. **2** corridor. **3** liberty or right to pass through. **4** journey by sea or air. **5** transition. **6** short extract from a book, piece of music, etc.

**pass·book** ▸*n.* book issued by a bank, etc., to an account holder for recording deposits and withdrawals.

**passé** /paˈsā/ ▸*adj.* old-fashioned.

**pas·sel** /ˈpasəl/ ▸*n.* large group of people or things of indeterminate number; a pack.

**pas·sen·ger** /ˈpasinjər/ ▸*n.* traveler in or on a public or private conveyance (other than the driver, pilot, crew, etc.).

**pas·ser·by** ▸*n.* (*pl.* **pas·sers·by**) person who goes past, esp. by chance.

**pas·ser·ine** /ˈpasərin; -ˌrīn/ ▸*adj.* of, relating to, or denoting birds of a large order distinguished by feet that are adapted for perching, including all songbirds.

**pas·sim** /ˈpasim/ ▸*adv.* (of allusions or references in a published work) to be found at various places throughout the text.

**pass·ing** ▸*adj.* **1** going past: *passing cars.* **2** transient;

fleeting. **3** cursory; incidental: *a passing reference.*

▶*n.* **1** passage of something; *the passing of the years.* **2** death.

**pas·sion** /ˈpasHən/ ▶*n.* **1** strong emotion or enthusiasm. **2** emotional outburst. **3** object arousing passion. **4** (**the Passion**) suffering of Christ during his last days.
—**pas·sion·ate** *adj.*
—**pas·sion·less** *adj.*

**pas·sive** /ˈpasiv/ ▶*adj.* **1** suffering action; acted upon. **2** offering no opposition; submissive. **3** not active; inert. **4** *Gram.* designating the voice in which the subject undergoes the action of the verb. —**pas·sive·ly** *adv.* —**pas·siv·i·ty** *n.*
□ **passive resistance** nonviolent refusal to cooperate. □ **passive smoking** involuntary inhaling of smoke from others' cigarettes, etc.

**pass·key** ▶*n.* **1** private key to a gate, etc., for special purposes. **2** skeleton key or master key.

**Pass·o·ver** ▶*n.* Jewish spring festival commemorating the liberation of the Israelites from Egyptian bondage.

**pass·port** ▶*n.* **1** official document issued by a government certifying the holder's identity and citizenship, and authorizing travel abroad. **2** thing that ensures admission or attainment: *a passport to success.*

**pass·word** ▶*n.* prearranged word or phrase securing recognition, admission, etc.

**past** /past/ ▶*adj.* **1** gone by in time. **2** recently completed or gone by: *the past month.* **3** relating to a former time. **4** *Gram.* expressing a past action or state.
▶*n.* **1** past time or events. **2** person's past life, esp. if discreditable. **3** past tense or form.
▶*prep.* **1** beyond in time or place. **2** beyond the range, duration, or compass of.
▶*adv.* so as to pass by: *hurried past.*
□ **past master** expert.

**pas·ta** /ˈpästə/ ▶*n.* dried flour paste produced in various shapes and cooked in boiling water.

**paste** /pāst/ ▶*n.* **1** any moist fairly stiff mixture. **2** dough of flour with fat, water, etc. **3** liquid adhesive for sticking paper, etc. **4** hard vitreous composition used in making imitation gems.

▸*v.* fasten or coat with paste.

**paste·board** ▸*n.* stiff material made by pasting together sheets of paper.

**pas·tel** /pa'stel/ ▸*n.* **1** crayon of powdered pigments bound with a gum solution. **2** work of art in pastel. **3** light and subdued shade of a color.

**pas·teur·ize** /'pasснǝ,rīz/ ▸*v.* sterilize (milk, etc.) by heating. —**pas·teur·i·za·tion** *n.*

**pas·tiche** /pa'stēsн/ ▸*n.* literary or artistic work from or imitating various sources.

**pas·time** /'pas,tīm/ ▸*n.* pleasant recreation or hobby.

**pas·tor** /'pastǝr/ ▸*n.* priest or minister in charge of a church or a congregation. —**pas·tor·ate** *n.*

**pas·tor·al** /'pastǝrǝl/ ▸*adj.* **1** of shepherds or flocks and herds. **2** of or portraying country life. **3** of a pastor.
▸*n.* poem, play, picture, etc., giving an idealized version of country life. —**pas·to·ral·ism** *n.*

**pas·tra·mi** /pǝ'strämē/ ▸*n.* seasoned smoked beef.

**pas·try** /'pāstrē/ ▸*n.* (*pl.* **-tries**) **1** dough of flour, fat, and water baked and used as a base and covering for pies, etc. **2** food, made wholly or partly of this.

**pas·ture** /'pasснǝr/ ▸*n.* grassland suitable for grazing.
▸*v.* put (animals) to pasture.

**past·y** /'pastē/ ▸*adj.* (**-i·er, -i·est**) unhealthily pale (esp. in complexion). —**past·i·ness** *n.*

**pat** /pat/ ▸*v.* (**pat·ted, pat·ting**) **1** strike gently with the hand or a flat surface. **2** flatten or mold by patting.
▸*n.* **1** light stroke or tap, esp. with the hand in affection, etc. **2** small mass (esp. of butter).
▸*adj.* somewhat glib or unconvincing.
□ **stand pat** stick stubbornly to one's opinion or decision.

**patch** /pacн/ ▸*n.* **1** piece of material or metal, etc., used to mend a hole or as reinforcement. **2** pad worn to protect an injured eye. **3** dressing, etc., put over a wound. **4** large or irregular distinguishable area on a surface. **5** piece of ground. **6** scrap or remnant.
▸*v.* **1** repair with a patch or patches. **2** (of material) serve as a patch to. **3** put together, esp. hastily. **4** settle (a quarrel, etc.): *they patched up their differences.*

**patch test** ▸*n.* test for allergy in which skin patches

containing allergenic substances are applied to the skin.

**patch·y** ▸*adj.* (**-i·er, -i·est**)
1 uneven in quality. 2 having or existing in patches.
—**patch·i·ness** *n.*

**pâ·té** /paˈtā/ ▸*n.* rich paste or spread of finely chopped and spiced meat or fish, etc.

**pa·tel·la** /pəˈtelə/ ▸*n.* (*pl.* **-lae**) kneecap.

**pat·ent** /ˈpatnt/ ▸*n.* 1 official document conferring a right or title, esp. the sole right to make or use or sell some invention. 2 invention or process so protected.
▸*adj.* 1 obvious; plain. 2 conferred or protected by patent.
▸*v.* obtain a patent for.
—**pat·ent·a·ble** *adj.* —**pat·ent·ly** *adv.*

**pa·tent leath·er** ▸*n.* glossy leather.

**pa·tent med·i·cine** ▸*n.* trademarked medicine usu. available without prescription.

**pa·ter·nal** /pəˈtərnl/ ▸*adj.* 1 fatherly. 2 related through the father. 3 (of a government, etc.) limiting freedom and responsibility by well-meaning regulations.

**pa·ter·nal·ism** ▸*n.* policy of governing or behaving in a paternal way. —**pa·ter·nal·is·tic** *adj.*

**pa·ter·ni·ty** /pəˈternitē/ ▸*n.* 1 fatherhood. 2 one's paternal origin. 3 the source or authorship of a thing.

**path** /paTH/ ▸*n.* 1 way or track made for or by walking. 2 line along which a person or thing moves: *flight path.* 3 course of action.

**pa·thet·ic** /pəˈTHetik/ ▸*adj.* 1 arousing pity, sadness, or contempt. 2 *inf.* miserably inadequate. —**pa·thet·i·cal·ly** *adv.*

**pa·thet·ic fal·la·cy** ▸*n.* attribution of human feelings and responses to inanimate things or animals, esp. in art and literature.

**path·o·gen** /ˈpaTHəˌjen/ ▸*n.* agent causing disease. —**path·o·gen·ic** *adj.*

**path·o·log·i·cal** /ˌpaTHəˈläjikəl/ ▸*adj.* 1 of pathology. 2 caused by or of the nature of a physical or mental disorder: *pathological changes associated with senile dementia.* —**path·o·log·i·cal·ly** *adv.*

**pa·thol·o·gy** /pəˈTHäləjē/ ▸*n.* 1 science of the causes and effects of diseases. **2** symptoms of a disease. —**pa·thol·o·gist** *n.*

**pa·thos** /'pā,THäs/ ▶*n.* quality in speech, writing, events, etc., that evokes pity or sadness.

**-pathy** ▶*comb. form* forming nouns denoting: **1** curative treatment: *allopathy* | *homeopathy.* **2** feeling: *telepathy.*

**pa·tience** /'pāSHəns/ ▶*n.* perseverance; ability to endure; forbearance.

**pa·tient** /'pāSHənt/ ▶*adj.* having or showing patience. ▶*n.* person receiving medical treatment. —**pa·tient·ly** *adv.*

**pa·ti·na** /pə'tēnə/ ▶*n.* **1** film, usu. green, formed on old bronze. **2** similar film or gloss on other surfaces.

**pa·ti·o** /'patē,ō/ ▶*n.* **1** paved usu. roofless area adjoining and belonging to a house. **2** roofless inner court.

**pa·tri·arch** /'pātrē,ärk/ ▶*n.* **1** male head of a family or tribe. **2** chief bishop in the Orthodox Church. **3** venerable old man. —**pa·tri·ar·chal** *adj.*

**pa·tri·ar·chy** ▶*n.* (*pl.* **-chies**) system of society, government, etc., ruled by a man or men and with descent through the male line.

**pa·tri·ate** /'pātrē,āt/ ▶*v.* transfer control over (a constitution) from a mother country to its former dependency.

**pa·tri·cian** /pə'trisHən/ ▶*n.* **1** aristocrat. **2** member of a long-established wealthy family. **3** member of the ancient Roman nobility. ▶*adj.* aristocratic; well-bred.

**pat·ri·cide** ▶*n.* **1** killing of one's father. **2** person who kills his or her father.

**pat·ri·lin·e·al** /,patrə'linēəl/ ▶*adj.* of, relating to, or based on relationship to the father or descent through the male line.

**pat·ri·mo·ny** /'patrə,mōnē/ ▶*n.* (*pl.* **-nies**) property inherited from one's father or ancestor. —**pat·ri·mo·ni·al** *adj.*

**pa·tri·ot** /'pātrēət/ ▶*n.* person who is devoted to and ready to support or defend his or her country. —**pa·tri·ot·ic** *adj.* —**pa·tri·o·tism** *n.*

**pa·trol** /pə'trōl/ ▶*n.* **1** act of walking or traveling around an area in order to protect or supervise it. **2** guards, police, troops, etc., sent out to watch or protect. ▶*v.* (**-trolled, -trol·ling**) carry out a patrol (of). —**pa·trol·ler** *n.*

**pa·trol car** ▸*n.* police car used in patrolling roads and streets.

**pa·trol·man** ▸*n.* (*pl.* **-men**) police officer assigned to or patrolling a specific route.

**pa·tron** /'pātrən/ (*fem.* **pa·tron·ess**) ▸*n.* **1** person who gives financial or other support to a person, cause, work of art, etc. **2** habitual customer.

**pa·tron·age** /'pātrənij/ ▸*n.* **1** patron's or customer's support. **2 a** power to appoint others to government jobs. **b** distribution of such jobs.

**pa·tron·ize** ▸*v.* **1** treat condescendingly. **2** act as a patron toward (a person, cause, artist, etc.); support; encourage. **3** be a customer of.

**pa·tron saint** ▸*n.* protecting or guiding saint of a person, place, etc.

**pa·troon** /pə'trōōn/ ▸*n.* person given land and granted certain manorial privileges under the former Dutch governments of New York and New Jersey.

**pat·sy** /'patsē/ ▸*n.* (*pl.* **-sies**) person who is deceived, ridiculed, tricked, etc.

**pat·ter** /'patər/ ▸*n.* **1** rapid succession of taps, short light steps, etc. **2** rapid speech used by a comedian or salesperson.

**pat·tern** /'patərn/ ▸*n.* **1** decorative design. **2** regular or logical form, order, etc. **3** model or design, e.g., of a garment, from which copies can be made. **4** example of excellence; ideal; model: *a pattern of elegance.*
▸*v.* **1** model (a thing) on a design, etc. **2** decorate with a pattern.

**pat·ty** /'patē/ ▸*n.* (*pl.* **-ties**) small flat cake of food.

**pat·u·lous** /'pacHələs/ ▸*adj.* (esp. of the branches of a tree) spreading.

**pau·ci·ty** /'pôsitē/ ▸*n.* smallness of number or quantity.

**paunch** /pônCH/ ▸*n.* belly or stomach, esp. when protruding. —**paunch·y** *adj.*

**pau·per** /'pôpər/ ▸*n.* person without means; beggar.

**pause** /pôz/ ▸*n.* temporary stop; silence.
▸*v.* make a pause; wait.

**pave** /pāv/ ▸*v.* cover (a street, floor, etc.) with flat stones, bricks, etc. —**pav·ing** *n.*
□ **pave the way for** prepare for.

**pa·vil·ion** /pə'vilyən/ ▸*n.* **1** tent, esp. a large one at a show, fair, etc. **2** building or stand used for entertainments, exhibits, etc.

**3** detached building that is part of a connected set of buildings, as at a hospital.

**paw** /pô/ ▶*n.* foot of an animal having claws or nails.

▶*v.* scrape the ground with a paw or hoof.

**pawn** /pôn/ ▶*n.* **1** chess piece of the smallest size and value. **2** person used by others for their own purposes.

▶*v.* deposit an object with a pawnbroker, as security for money lent.

**pawn·broker** ▶*n.* person who lends money at interest on the security of personal property pawned.

**paw·paw** /'pô‚pô/ (also **pa'paw**) ▶*n.* N. American tree with purple flowers and edible fruit.

**pay** /pā/ ▶*v.* (*past* and *past part.* **paid**) **1** give (a person, etc.) what is due for services done, goods received, debts incurred, etc. **2** give (a sum) for work done, a debt, etc. **3** give, bestow, or express. **4** be profitable or advantageous. **5** let out (a rope) by slackening it.

▶*n.* wages.

▶*adj.* requiring payment of a coin, a set fee, etc., for use.

—**pay·ee** *n.*

□ **in the pay of** employed by.
□ **pay back** **1** repay. **2** punish or be revenged on. □ **pay off** **1** dismiss (workers) with a final payment. **2** *inf.* yield good results; succeed. **3** pay (a debt) in full.

**pay·load** ▶*n.* **1** part of an aircraft's load from which revenue is derived, as paying passengers. **2** explosive warhead carried by an aircraft or rocket.

**pay·mas·ter** ▶*n.* official who pays troops, workers, etc.

**pay·ment** ▶*n.* **1** act or instance of paying. **2** amount paid.

**pay·off** ▶*n.* **1** *inf.* payment made to someone, esp. as a bribe or reward. **2** return on an investment. **3** final outcome.

**pay·roll** ▶*n.* list of employees receiving regular pay.

**PC** ▶*abbr.* **1** personal computer. **2** politically correct.

**PE** ▶*abbr.* physical education.

**pea** /pē/ ▶*n.* **1** hardy climbing plant, with seeds growing in pods and used for food. **2** its seed.

**peace** /pēs/ ▶*n.* **1** quiet; tranquillity. **2** freedom from or the cessation of war. **3** freedom from civil disorder.

□ **hold one's peace** keep silent.

**peace·ful** ▸*adj.* **1** characterized by peace; tranquil. **2** not involving war or violence.

**peach** /pēCH/ ▸*n.* **1** round juicy fruit with downy cream or yellow skin flushed with red. **2** *inf.* attractive person or thing. —**peach·y** *adj.*

**pea·cock** ▸*n.* male peafowl, having brilliant plumage and an erectile fanlike tail (with eyelike markings).

**pea·fowl** ▸*n.* large crested pheasant.

**pea·hen** ▸*n.* female peafowl.

**pea jack·et** (also **pea·coat**) ▸*n.* short double-breasted woolen overcoat.

**peak** /pēk/ ▸*n.* **1** projecting usu. pointed part, esp.: **a** the pointed top of a mountain. **b** stiff brim at the front of a cap. **2 a** highest point. **b** time of greatest success. ▸*v.* reach the highest value, quality, etc.

**peak·ed** /ˈpēkid/ ▸*adj.* pale; sickly.

**peal** /pēl/ ▸*n.* **1 a** the loud ringing of a bell or bells, esp. a series of changes. **b** set of bells. **2** loud repeated sound, esp. of thunder, laughter, etc. ▸*v.* sound forth in a peal.

**pea·nut** ▸*n.* **1** leguminous plant, bearing pods that ripen underground and containing seeds used as food and yielding oil. **2** seed of this plant. **3** (**peanuts**) *inf.* paltry or trivial thing or amount, esp. of money. □ **peanut butter** paste of ground roasted peanuts.

**pear** /pe(ə)r/ ▸*n.* yellowish or brownish green fleshy fruit, tapering toward the stalk.

**pearl** /pərl/ ▸*n.* **1** usu. white or bluish gray hard mass formed within the shell of certain oysters, highly prized as a gem for its luster: *pearl necklace.* **2** precious thing; finest example. **3** anything resembling a pearl, e.g., a dewdrop, tear, etc. —**pear·ly** *adj.*

**peas·ant** /ˈpezənt/ ▸*n.* small farmer; agricultural worker. —**peas·ant·ry** *n.*

**peat** /pēt/ ▸*n.* vegetable matter decomposed in water and partly carbonized, used for fuel, in horticulture, etc. —**peat·y** *adj.*

**peb·ble** /ˈpebəl/ ▸*n.* small smooth stone worn by the action of water. —**peb·bly** *adj.*

**pe·can** /piˈkän; ˈpēˌkan/ ▸*n.* **1** pinkish brown smooth nut with an edible kernel. **2** hickory of the southern U.S., producing this.

**pec·ca·ble** /'pekəbəl/ ▶*adj.* capable of sinning.

**pec·ca·dil·lo** /ˌpekə'dilō/ ▶*n.* (*pl.* **-loes** or **-los**) trifling offense; venial sin.

**peck** /pek/ ▶*v.* **1** strike, bite, or pick up with a beak. **2** kiss hastily or perfunctorily.
▶*n.* **1 a** a stroke or bite with a beak. **b** mark made by this. **2** hasty or perfunctory kiss. **3** dry measure equal to 8 quarts.
□ **pecking order** social hierarchy.

**pec·tin** /'pektin/ ▶*n.* substance found in ripe fruits, etc., used as a gelling agent in jams and jellies.

**pec·to·ral** /'pektərəl/ ▶*adj.* of or worn on the breast or chest: *the bishop wears a pectoral cross.*
▶*n.* pectoral muscle or fin.

**pec·u·late** /'pekyəˌlāt/ ▶*v.* embezzle or steal (money, esp. public funds).

**pe·cu·liar** /pə'kyo͞olyər/ ▶*adj.* **1** strange; odd; unusual. **2** belonging exclusively to the individual. **3** particular; special. —**pe·cu·li·ar·i·ty** *n.* —**pe·cu·liar·ly** *adv.*

**pe·cu·ni·ar·y** /pə'kyo͞onēˌerē/ ▶*adj.* of, concerning, or consisting of money: *pecuniary aid.*

**ped·a·gogue** /'pedəˌgäg/ ▶*n.* schoolmaster or teacher, esp. a pedantic one. —**ped·a·gog·ic** *adj.* —**ped·a·gog·i·cal** *adj.* —**ped·a·gog·i·cal·ly** *adv.*

**ped·al** /'pedl/ ▶*n.* lever or control operated by the foot, esp. in a vehicle, on a bicycle, etc.
▶*v.* **1** operate (a cycle, etc.) by using the pedals. **2** ride a bicycle.

**ped·ant** /'pednt/ ▶*n.* person who insists on strict adherence to formal rules or literal meaning at the expense of a wider view. —**pe·dan·tic** *adj.* —**pe·dan·ti·cal·ly** *adv.* —**ped·ant·ry** *n.*

**ped·dle** /'pedl/ ▶*v.* **1** sell (goods) while traveling. **2** advocate or promote. **3** engage in selling. —**ped·dler** *n.*

**ped·er·as·ty** /'pedəˌrastē/ ▶*n.* sexual activity involving a man and a boy.

**ped·es·tal** /'pedəstl/ ▶*n.* **1** base supporting a column or pillar. **2** stone, etc., base of a statue, etc.

**pe·des·tri·an** /pə'destrēən/ ▶*n.* person who is walking.
▶*adj.* prosaic; dull; uninspired.

**pe·di·at·rics** /ˌpēdēˈatriks/ ▶n. branch of medicine dealing with children and their diseases.
—**pe·di·at·ric** adj.
—**pe·di·a·tri·cian** n.

**ped·i·cure** /ˈpediˌkyo͝or/ ▶n. care or treatment of the feet, esp. of the toenails.

**ped·i·gree** /ˈpedəˌgrē/ ▶n.
**1** recorded line of descent.
**2** genealogical table.

**ped·i·ment** /ˈpedəmənt/ ▶n. triangular front part of a building, esp. over a doorway, etc.

**pe·dom·e·ter** /pəˈdämitər/ ▶n. instrument for estimating distance traveled on foot by recording the number of steps taken.

**pe·do·phile** /ˈpedəˌfīl/ ▶n. person who is sexually attracted to children.

**peek** /pēk/ ▶v. look slyly; peep.
▶n. quick or sly look.

**peel** /pēl/ ▶v. **1** strip the skin, rind, bark, wrapping, etc., from.
**2** become bare of bark, skin, paint, etc.
▶n. outer covering of a fruit, vegetable, shrimp, etc.; rind.
—**peel·er** n.

**peep** /pēp/ ▶v. **1** look through a narrow opening; look furtively.

**2** come slowly into view; emerge. **3** make a shrill feeble sound as of young birds, mice, etc.; squeak; chirp.
▶n. **1** furtive or peering glance.
**2** peeping sound; cheep.
**3** slightest sound or utterance, esp. of protest, etc.

**peer** /pi(ə)r/ ▶v. look keenly or with difficulty.
▶n. **1** person who is equal in ability, standing, rank, or value; a contemporary: *tried by a jury of his peers.* **2** (*fem.* **peer·ess**) member of the British nobility.
—**peer·age** n. —**peer·less** adj.

**peeve** /pēv/ *inf.* ▶v. [usu. as *adj.* **peeved**] annoy; vex; irritate.
▶n. cause of annoyance: *his pet peeve is the imprecise use of words.*

**peev·ish** ▶adj. querulous; irritable.

**peg** ▶n. usu. cylindrical pin or bolt of wood or metal, used for holding, hanging, or supporting things.
▶v. (**pegged, peg·ging**) **1** fix (a thing) with a peg. **2** fix (a price, rate, etc.) at a particular level.
**3** throw (a ball) hard and low.

**pe·jo·ra·tive** /pəˈjôrətiv/ ▶adj. expressing contempt or disapproval.
▶n. word expressing contempt or

disapproval. —**pe·jo·ra·tive·ly**
*adv.*

**Pe·king·ese** /ˈpēkəˌnēz/ (also
**Pe·kin·ese**) ▸*n.* (*pl.* same) short-
legged lapdog with long hair and
a snub nose.

**pelf** /pelf/ ▸*n.* money, esp. when
gained in a dishonest or
dishonorable way.

**pel·i·can** /ˈpelikən/ ▸*n.* large
gregarious waterfowl with a
large bill and a pouch in the
throat for storing fish.

**pel·la·gra** /pəˈlagrə/ ▸*n.* disease
caused by deficiency of nicotinic
acid, characterized by cracking
of the skin and often resulting in
insanity.

**pel·let** /ˈpelit/ ▸*n.* **1** small
compressed ball of paper, bread,
etc. **2** pill. **3** piece of small shot.

**pell-mell** /ˈpel ˈmel/ ▸*adv.*
**1** headlong; recklessly: *rushed
pell-mell out of the room.* **2** in
disorder or confusion.

**pel·lu·cid** /pəˈloosid/ ▸*adj.*
transparent; clear; not confused.

**pelt** /pelt/ ▸*v.* strike repeatedly
with thrown objects.
▸*n.* undressed skin of a fur-
bearing mammal.

**pel·vis** /ˈpelvis/ ▸*n.* (*pl.* **-vis·es** or
**-ves**) basin-shaped cavity at the
lower end of the torso of most
vertebrates, formed from the hip
bones, sacrum, and other
vertebrae.

**pen** /pen/ ▸*n.* **1** instrument for
writing or drawing with ink.
**2** small enclosure for cows,
sheep, poultry, etc.
▸*v.* (**penned, pen·ning**) **1** write.
**2** enclose or shut in a pen.
**3** (**pen someone up/in**) confine
someone in a restricted space:
*we had been penned up in the house
for three days.*
□ **pen name** literary pseudonym.

**pe·nal** /ˈpēnl/ ▸*adj.* **1** of or
concerning punishment or its
infliction. **2** (of an offense)
punishable, esp. by law.

**pen·al·ty** /ˈpenlˌtē/ ▸*n.* (*pl.* **-ties**)
**1** punishment, esp. a fine, for a
breach of law, contract, etc.
**2** disadvantage, loss, etc., esp. as
a result of one's own actions:
*paid the penalty for his
carelessness.* **3** disadvantage
imposed on a competitor or
team for a breach of the rules,
etc.

**pen·ance** /ˈpenəns/ ▸*n.* act of
self-punishment as reparation
for guilt, sins, etc.

**pen·chant** /ˈpenCHənt/ ▸*n.*
inclination or liking.

**pen·cil** /ˈpensəl/ ▸*n.* instrument

for writing or drawing, usu. consisting of a thin rod of graphite, etc., enclosed in a wooden cylinder or metal case.

▶v. (**-ciled, -cil·ing; -cilled, -cil·ling**) **1** tint or mark with or as if with a pencil. **2** write, esp. tentatively or provisionally.

**pen·dant** /'pendənt/ (also **pen·dent**) ▶n. hanging jewel, etc., esp. one attached to a necklace, bracelet, etc.

**pen·dent** /'pendənt/ (also **pen·dant**) ▶adj. **1 a** hanging. **b** overhanging. **2** undecided; pending.

**pend·ing** ▶adj. awaiting decision or settlement; undecided: *a settlement was pending.*

▶prep. **1** during: *pending these negotiations.* **2** until: *pending his return.*

**pen·du·lous** /'penjələs/ ▶adj. hanging down; drooping and esp. swinging. —**pen·du·lous·ly** adv.

**pen·du·lum** /'penjələm/ ▶n. weight suspended so as to swing freely, esp. a rod with a weighted end regulating the movement of a clock's works.

**pe·ne·plain** /'pēnə,plān/ (also **pe·ne·plane**) ▶n. more or less level land surface produced by erosion over a long period.

**pen·e·tra·li·a** /,peni'trālēə/ ▶pl. n. innermost parts of a building; a secret or hidden place.

**pen·e·trate** /'peni,trāt/ ▶v. **1** find access into or through, esp. forcibly. **2** see into, find out, or discern (a person's mind, the truth, a meaning, etc.). **3** be absorbed by the mind. **4** [as adj. **penetrating**] **a** insightful; sensitive. **b** easily heard; piercing. —**pen·e·trat·ing·ly** adv. —**pen·e·tra·tion** n.

**pen·guin** /'peŋgwin/ ▶n. flightless sea bird of the southern hemisphere, with wings developed into scaly flippers for swimming underwater.

**pen·i·cil·lin** /,penə'silən/ ▶n. any of various antibiotics produced naturally by molds or synthetically.

**pe·nile** /'pēnəl; -nīl/ ▶adj. of, relating to, or affecting the penis.

**pen·in·su·la** /pə'ninsələ/ ▶n. piece of land almost surrounded by water. —**pen·in·su·lar** adj.

**pe·nis** /'pēnis/ ▶n. (pl. **-nis·es** or **-nes**) male organ of copulation

and (in mammals) urination.
—**pe·nile** *adj.*

**pen·i·tent** /'penitnt/ ▸*adj.*
repentant.
▸*n.* repentant sinner.
—**pen·i·tence** *n.* —**pen·i·ten·tial**
*adj.* —**pen·i·tent·ly** *adv.*

**pen·i·ten·tia·ry** /ˌpeni'tensHərē/
▸*n.* (*pl.* **-ries**) state or federal
prison.

**Penn.** (also **Penna.**) ▸*abbr.*
Pennsylvania.

**pen·nant** /'penənt/ ▸*n.* **1** long
tapering flag. **2 a** flag denoting a
sports championship, etc.
**b** sports championship.

**pen·ny** /'penē/ ▸*n.* (*pl.* **-nies**)
**1** (in the U.S., Canada, etc.) one-
cent coin. **2** British coin equal to
one hundredth of a pound.
□ **penny-pincher** very frugal
person.

**pen·ny·weight** ▸*n.* unit of
weight, 24 grains or one
twentieth of an ounce troy.

**pe·nol·o·gy** /pē'näləjē/ ▸*n.* study
of the punishment of crime and
of prison management.

**pen·sée** /ˌpän'sā/ ▸*n.* thought or
reflection put into literary form;
an aphorism.

**pen·sion** /'pensHən/ ▸*n.* regular
payment made to the disabled,
retirees, etc.

▸*v.* grant a pension to.
—**pen·sion·a·ble** *adj.*
—**pen·sion·er** *n.*

**pen·sive** /'pensiv/ ▸*adj.* **1** deep
in thought. **2** sorrowfully
thoughtful. —**pen·sive·ly** *adv.*

**penta-** ▸*comb. form* five.

**pen·ta·gon** /'pentəˌgän/ ▸*n.*
**1** plane figure with five sides
and angles. **2** (**the Pentagon**)
pentagonal headquarters
building of the U.S. Department
of Defense, located near
Washington, DC.
—**pen·tag·o·nal** *adj.*

**pen·ta·gram** ▸*n.* five-pointed
star.

**pen·tam·e·ter** /pen'tamitər/ ▸*n.*
verse of five feet, e.g., English
iambic verse of ten syllables.

**Pen·ta·teuch** /'pentəˌt(y)o͞ok/
▸*n.* first five books of the Old
Testament.

**pen·tath·lon** /pen'taTHˌlän/ ▸*n.*
athletic event comprising five
different events for each
competitor. —**pen·tath·lete** *n.*

**Pen·te·cost** /'pentiˌkôst/ ▸*n.*
**1** festival celebrating the descent
of the Holy Spirit on the
disciples of Jesus, celebrated on
the seventh Sunday after Easter.
(Also called **Whitsunday**.)
**2** Jewish harvest festival, on the

fiftieth day after the second day of Passover.

**Pen·te·cos·tal** (also **pen·te·cos·tal**) ▸*adj.* of or designating esp. fundamentalist Christian sects and individuals who emphasize the gifts of the Holy Spirit and express religious feelings by clapping, shouting, dancing, etc.
—**Pen·te·cos·tal·ism** *n.*
—**Pen·te·cos·tal·ist** *adj. & n.*

**pent·house** /'pent,hous/ ▸*n.* house or apartment on the roof or the top floor of a tall building.

**pen·ti·men·to** /ˌpentə'mentō/ ▸*n.* (*pl.* **-men·ti** /-'mentē/) visible trace of earlier painting beneath a layer or layers of paint on a canvas.

**pent-up** ▸*adj.* closely confined or held back: *pent-up feelings.*

**pen·ul·ti·mate** /pe'nəltəmit/ ▸*adj. & n.* last but one.

**pen·um·bra** /pe'nəmbrə/ ▸*n.* (*pl.* **-brae** or **-bras**) **1 a** partly shaded region around the shadow of an opaque body, esp. that around the total shadow of the moon or earth in an eclipse. **b** less dark outer part of a sunspot. **2** partial shadow. —**pen·um·bral** *adj.*

**pe·nu·ri·ous** /pə'n(y)o͝orēəs/ ▸*adj.* **1** stingy; grudging.

**2** extremely poor.
—**pe·nu·ri·ous·ness** *n.*

**pen·u·ry** /'penyərē/ ▸*n.* (*pl.* **-ries**) extreme poverty; destitution.

**pe·on** /'pē,än/ ▸*n.* drudge.

**pe·o·ny** /'pēənē/ ▸*n.* (*pl.* **-nies**) herbaceous plant with large globular red, pink, or white flowers.

**peo·ple** /'pēpəl/ ▸*n.* **1 a** persons composing a community, tribe, race, nation, etc.: *the American people.* **b** group of persons of a usu. specified kind: *the chosen people.* **2** the mass of people in a country, etc. **3** parents or other relatives. **4** subjects, armed followers, congregation, etc. **5** persons in general: *people do not like rudeness.*
▸*v.* populate; inhabit.

**pep** /pep/ *inf.* ▸*n.* vigor; go; spirit.
▸*v.* (**pepped, pep·ping**) (**pep up**) fill with vigor.
□ **pep talk** usu. short talk intended to enthuse, encourage, etc.

**pep·per** ▸*n.* **1** hot aromatic condiment from the dried berries of certain plants. **2** plant with a red, green, or yellow many-seeded fruit grown as a vegetable.
▸*v.* **1** sprinkle or treat with or as

if with pepper. **2** pelt with missiles.

**pep·per·corn** ▶*n.* dried pepper berry.

**pep·per mill** ▶*n.* device for grinding pepper by hand.

**pep·per·mint** ▶*n.* **1** mint plant grown for its strong-flavored oil. **2** candy flavored with peppermint.

**pep·per·o·ni** /ˌpepəˈrōnē/ ▶*n.* spicy sausage seasoned with pepper.

**pep·sin** /ˈpepsin/ ▶*n.* enzyme contained in the gastric juice.

**pep·tic** /ˈpeptik/ ▶*adj.* concerning or promoting digestion. ☐ **peptic ulcer** ulcer in the stomach or duodenum.

**per** /pər/ ▶*prep.* **1** for each. **2** by means of; by; through: *per rail.* **3** (also **as per**) in accordance with.

**per-** /pər/ ▶*prefix* **1** forming verbs, nouns, and adjectives meaning 'through; all over'. **2** completely; very.

**per·ad·ven·ture** /ˌpərəd-ˈvenCHər; ˌper-/ ▶*adv.* or perhaps. ▶*n.* or uncertainty or doubt as to whether something is the case.

**per·am·bu·late** /pəˈrambyəˌlāt/ ▶*v.* walk from place to place.

—**per·am·bu·la·tion** *n.*
—**per·am·bu·la·to·ry** *adj.*

**per·am·bu·la·tor** ▶*n.* baby carriage.

**per an·num** /pər ˈanəm/ ▶*adv.* for each year.

**per cap·i·ta** /pər ˈkapitə/ ▶*adv. & adj.* for each person.

**per·ceive** /pərˈsēv/ ▶*v.* **1** apprehend, esp. through the sight; observe. **2** apprehend with the mind; understand; regard. —**per·ceiv·a·ble** *adj.*

**per·cent** ▶*adv.* in every hundred. ▶*n.* **1** percentage. **2** one part in every hundred.

**per·cent·age** /pərˈsentij/ ▶*n.* **1** rate or proportion; percent. **2** proportion or share.

**per·cen·tile** /pərˈsenˌtīl/ ▶*n.* one of 99 values of a variable dividing a population into 100 equal groups as regards the value of that variable.

**per·cep·ti·ble** /pərˈseptəbəl/ ▶*adj.* capable of being perceived. —**per·cep·ti·bly** *adv.*

**per·cep·tion** ▶*n.* **1** act or faculty of perceiving. **2** intuitive recognition of a truth, aesthetic quality, etc.

**per·cep·tive** ▶*adj.* sensitive; discerning; observant: *perceptive*

*remark.* —**per·cep·tive·ly** *adv.*
—**per·cep·tive·ness** *n.*
—**per·cep·tiv·i·ty** *n.*

**perch** /pərCH/ ▶*n.* **1** bar, branch, etc., used by a bird to rest on. **2** high or precarious place for a person or thing to rest on. **3** (*pl.* same or **perch·es**) spiny-finned freshwater edible fish.
▶*v.* settle or rest, or cause to settle or rest, on or as if on a perch.

**per·chance** ▶*adv.* **1** by chance. **2** possibly; maybe.

**per·cip·i·ent** /pər'sipēənt/ ▶*adj.* (of a person) having a good understanding of things; perceptive.
▶*n.* (esp. in philosophy or with reference to psychic phenomena) a person who is able to perceive things.

**per·co·late** /'pərkə,lāt/ ▶*v.* **1** (of liquid, etc.) filter or ooze gradually. **2** (of an idea, etc.) permeate gradually.
—**per·co·la·tion** *n.*

**per·co·la·tor** ▶*n.* machine for making coffee by circulating boiling water through ground beans.

**per·cus·sion** /pər'kəsHən/ ▶*n.* **1 a** playing of music by striking instruments with sticks, etc.: *a percussion band.* **b** such

instruments collectively. **2** forcible striking of one esp. solid body against another.
—**per·cus·sion·ist** *n.*
—**per·cus·sive** *adj.*

□ **percussion cap** small amount of explosive powder contained in metal or paper and exploded by striking.

**per di·em** /pər 'dēəm/ ▶*adv. & adj.* for each day.
▶*n.* allowance or payment for each day.

**per·di·tion** /pər'disHən/ ▶*n.* eternal death; damnation.

**per·dur·a·ble** /pər'd(y)o͝orəbəl/ ▶*adj.* enduring continuously; imperishable.

**per·dure** /pər'd(y)o͝or/ ▶*v.* remain in existence throughout a substantial period of time; endure.

**pe·remp·to·ry** /pə'remptərē/ ▶*adj.* **1** admitting no denial or refusal. **2** dogmatic; imperious; dictatorial. —**pe·remp·to·ri·ly** *adv.*

**pe·ren·ni·al** /pə'renēəl/ ▶*adj.* **1** lasting through a year or several years. **2** (of a plant) lasting several years. **3** lasting a long time or forever.
▶*n.* perennial plant.
—**per·en·ni·al·ly** *adv.*

**per·fect** ▸*adj.* /ˈpərfikt/
**1** complete; not deficient.
**2** faultless: *a perfect diamond.*
**3 a** very satisfactory: *a perfect evening.* **b** most appropriate; suitable: *she is perfect for the job.*
**4** exact; precise: *a perfect circle.*
**5** entire; unqualified: *a perfect stranger.* **6** *Gram.* (of a tense) denoting a completed action or event in the past.
▸*v.* /pərˈfekt/ **1** make perfect; improve. **2** carry through; complete.
▸*n.* /ˈpərfikt/ *Gram.* the perfect tense. —**per·fect·i·ble** *adj.*
—**per·fec·tion** *n.* —**per·fect·ly** *adv.*

**per·fec·tion·ism** /pərˈfekSHə-ˌnizəm/ ▸*n.* uncompromising pursuit of excellence.
—**per·fec·tion·ist** *n.*

**per·fect pitch** ▸*n.* ability to recognize the pitch of a note or produce any given note.

**per·fer·vid** /pərˈfərvid/ ▸*adj.* intense and impassioned.

**per·fi·dy** /ˈpərfidē/ ▸*n.* breach of faith; treachery. —**per·fid·i·ous** *adj.* —**per·fid·i·ous·ly** *adv.*

**per·fo·rate** /ˈpərfəˌrāt/ ▸*v.*
**1** make a hole or holes through; pierce. **2** make a row of small holes in (paper, etc.) so that a part may be torn off easily.
—**per·fo·ra·tion** *n.*

**per·force** ▸*adv. formal* unavoidably; necessarily.

**per·form** ▸*v.* **1** do; execute.
**2** act in a play; play an instrument or sing, etc.
**3** operate; function.
—**per·form·ance** *n.*
—**per·form·er** *n.*

**per·form·ing arts** ▸*pl. n.* drama, music, and dance, etc.

**per·fume** /ˈpərˌfyo͞om/ ▸*n.*
**1** fragrant liquid containing the essence of flowers, etc.; scent.
**2** pleasant smell.
▸*v.* impart a sweet scent to; impregnate with a sweet smell.

**per·func·to·ry** /pərˈfəNGktərē/ ▸*adj.* done merely out of duty; superficial. —**per·func·to·ri·ly** *adv.* —**per·func·to·ri·ness** *n.*

**per·haps** /pərˈhaps/ ▸*adv.* it may be; possibly.

**peri-** ▸*prefix* around; about.

**per·i·car·di·um** /ˌperiˈkärdēəm/ ▸*n.* (*pl.* **-di·a**) membranous sac enclosing the heart.
—**per·i·car·di·al** *adj.*
—**per·i·car·di·tis** *n.*

**per·il** /ˈperəl/ ▸*n.* serious and immediate danger. —**per·il·ous** *adj.*

**pe·rim·e·ter** /pə'rimitər/ ▶*n.* **1** circumference or outline of a closed figure. **2** outer boundary of an enclosed area.

**per·i·ne·um** /ˌperə'nēəm/ ▶*n.* region of the body between the anus and the scrotum or vulva. —**per·i·ne·al** *adj.*

**pe·ri·od** /'piərēəd/ ▶*n.* **1** length or portion of time: *periods of rain.* **2** distinct portion of history, a person's life, etc.: *the Federal period.* **3** time forming part of a geological era. **4** interval between recurrences of an event. **5** time allowed for a lesson or other activity in school. **6** occurrence of menstruation. **7** punctuation mark (.) used at the end of a sentence or an abbreviation.

▶*adj.* characteristic of some past period: *period furniture.*

**pe·ri·od·ic** /ˌpi(ə)rē'ädik/ ▶*adj.* appearing or occurring at regular intervals. —**pe·ri·od·ic·i·ty** *n.*

**pe·ri·od·i·cal** ▶*n.* newspaper, magazine, etc., issued at regular intervals, usu. monthly or weekly. —**pe·ri·od·i·cal·ly** *adv.*

**pe·ri·od·ic ta·ble** ▶*n.* arrangement of elements in order of increasing atomic number.

**per·i·pa·tet·ic** /ˌperipə'tetik/ ▶*adj.* going from place to place; itinerant.

**pe·riph·er·al** /pə'rifərəl/ ▶*adj.* **1** of minor importance; marginal. **2** of the periphery; on the fringe. **3** (of equipment) used with a computer, etc., but not an integral part of it.

▶*n.* peripheral device or piece of equipment. —**pe·riph·er·al·ly** *adv.*

☐ **peripheral vision** **1** area seen around the outside of one's field of vision. **2** ability to perceive in this area.

**pe·riph·er·y** ▶*n.* (*pl.* **-ies**) **1** boundary of an area or surface. **2** outer or surrounding region.

**pe·riph·ra·sis** /pə'rifrəsis/ ▶*n.* (*pl.* **-ses**) roundabout way of speaking; circumlocution. —**per·i·phras·tic** *adj.*

**per·i·scope** /'peri,skōp/ ▶*n.* apparatus with a tube and mirrors or prisms, by which an observer can see things otherwise out of sight.

**per·ish** /'perisн/ ▶*v.* be destroyed; suffer death or ruin.

**per·ish·a·ble** ▶*adj.* **1** (of food) likely to go bad quickly.

**2** having a brief life or significance.

▶*pl. n.* (**perishables**) food that is likely to go bad quickly.

**per·i·to·ne·um** /ˌperitnˈēəm/ ▶*n.* (*pl.* **-ne·ums** or **-ne·a**) membrane lining the cavity of the abdomen. —**per·i·to·ne·al** *adj.*

**per·i·to·ni·tis** /ˌperitnˈītis/ ▶*n.* inflammation of the peritoneum.

**per·i·win·kle** /ˈperiˌwiNGkəl/ ▶*n.* **1** evergreen trailing plant with blue or white flowers. **2** intertidal saltwater snail.

**per·jure** /ˈpərjər/ ▶*v.* (**perjure oneself**) willfully tell an untruth when under oath.

**per·ju·ry** /ˈpərjərē/ ▶*n.* (*pl.* **-ries**) offense of willfully telling an untruth when under oath.

**perk** /pərk/ ▶*v.* (**perk up**) become or cause to become more lively, cheerful, or interesting.

▶*n. inf.* perquisite.

**perk·y** ▶*adj.* (**-i·er, -i·est**) **1** self-assertive; cocky; pert. **2** lively; cheerful.

**per·ma·frost** /ˈpərməˌfrôst/ ▶*n.* subsoil that remains frozen throughout the year, as in polar regions.

**per·ma·nent** /ˈpərmənənt/ ▶*adj.* lasting, or intended to last or function, indefinitely.

▶*n.* PERMANENT WAVE.

—**per·ma·nence** *n.*

□ **permanent press** process applied to a fabric to make it wrinkle-free. □ **permanent wave** chemically set wave in the hair, intended to last for many months.

**per·me·a·ble** /ˈpərmēəbəl/ ▶*adj.* capable of being permeated. —**per·me·a·bil·i·ty** *n.*

**per·me·ate** /ˈpərmēˌāt/ ▶*v.* **1** penetrate throughout; pervade; saturate. **2** diffuse itself. —**per·me·a·tion** *n.*

**per·mis·sion** /pərˈmiSHən/ ▶*n.* consent; authorization.

**per·mis·sive** ▶*adj.* **1** tolerant; liberal. **2** giving permission. —**per·mis·sive·ly** *adv.* —**per·mis·sive·ness** *n.*

**per·mit** ▶*v.* /pərˈmit/ (**-mit·ted, -mit·ting**) **1** give permission or consent to; authorize; allow. **2** give an opportunity (to).

▶*n.* /ˈpərmit/ document giving permission, allowing entry, etc.

**per·mu·ta·tion** /ˌpərmyo͞oˈtāSHən/ ▶*n.* **1** one of the possible ordered arrangements or groupings of a set of numbers, items, etc. **2** any combination or selection of a specified number of things from a larger group.

**per·ni·cious** /pər'nisHəs/ ▶*adj.* destructive; ruinous; fatal.

**per·ox·ide** /pə'räksīd/ ▶*n.* **1** compound of oxygen with another element containing the greatest possible proportion of oxygen. **2** hydrogen peroxide, esp. as used to bleach the hair or as an antiseptic.

**per·pen·dic·u·lar** /ˌpərpən-'dikyələr/ ▶*adj.* **1** at right angles (to a given line, plane, or surface). **2** upright; vertical. **3** (of a slope) very steep. ▶*n.* perpendicular line, plane, or direction.

**per·pe·trate** /'pərpiˌtrāt/ ▶*v.* commit (a crime, blunder, etc.). —**per·pe·tra·tion** *n.* —**per·pe·tra·tor** *n.*

**per·pet·u·al** /pər'pecHooəl/ ▶*adj.* **1** eternal; lasting forever or indefinitely. **2** continuous; uninterrupted. —**per·pet·u·al·ly** *adv.*

**per·pe·tu·i·ty** /ˌpərpi't(y)ooitē/ ▶*n.* (*pl.* -**ties**) state or quality of being perpetual. □ **in perpetuity** forever.

**per·plex** /pər'pleks/ ▶*v.*

**1** puzzle; bewilder; disconcert. **2** complicate or confuse (a matter).

**per·qui·site** /'pərkwəzit/ ▶*n.* **1** extra profit or allowance additional to a main income, etc. **2** customary extra right or privilege. **3** incidental benefit attached to employment, etc.

**per se** /pər 'sā/ ▶*adv.* by or in itself; intrinsically.

**per·se·cute** /'pərsiˌkyoot/ ▶*v.* subject to hostility or ill-treatment, esp. on the grounds of political or religious belief. —**per·se·cu·tion** *n.* —**per·se·cu·tor** *n.* —**per·se·cu·to·ry** *adj.*

**per·se·vere** /ˌpərsə'vi(ə)r/ ▶*v.* continue steadfastly or determinedly; persist. —**per·se·ver·ance** *n.*

**per·sim·mon** /pər'simən/ ▶*n.* tropical evergreen tree bearing edible tomato-like fruits.

**per·sist** /pər'sist/ ▶*v.* **1** continue firmly or obstinately. **2** continue in existence; survive. —**per·sist·ence** *n.* —**per·sist·ent** *adj.*

**per·son** /'pərsən/ ▶*n.* **1** individual human being. **2** living body of a human being: *hidden somewhere about your* person. **3** *Gram.* any of three classes of personal pronouns, verb forms, etc.: the person speaking (**first person**); the person spoken to (**second person**); the person spoken of (**third person**). **4** used to replace *-man* in words referring to either sex: *salesperson.*

□ **in person** physically present.

**per·son·a·ble** ▸*adj.* pleasing in appearance and behavior.

**per·son·age** /ˈpərsənij/ ▸*n.* **1** person, esp. of rank or importance. **2** character in a play, etc.

**per·son·al** /ˈpərsənəl/ ▸*adj.* **1** one's own; individual; private. **2** done or made in person: *my personal attention.* **3** directed to or concerning an individual: *personal letter.* **4** close; intimate: *a personal friend.* **5** of the body and clothing: *personal hygiene.*

□ **personal computer** computer designed for use by a single individual. □ **personal pronoun** pronoun replacing the subject, object, etc., e.g., *I*, *we*, *you*, *them*, *us*.

**per·son·al·i·ty** /ˌpərsəˈnalitē/ ▸*n.* (*pl.* **-ties**) **1** distinctive character or qualities of a person, often as distinct from

others: *an attractive personality.* **2** famous person.

**per·son·al·ize** /ˈpərsənlˌīz/ ▸*v.* make personal, esp. by marking with one's name, etc.

**per·so·na non gra·ta** /pər-ˈsōnə nän ˈgrätə/ ▸*n.* (*pl.* **per·so·nae non gra·tae** /pərˈsōnē nän ˈgrätē/) unacceptable or unwelcome person.

**per·son·i·fy** /pərˈsänəˌfī/ ▸*v.* (**-fied**) **1** represent (an abstraction or thing) as human. **2** [usu. as *adj.* **personified**] embody (a quality) in one's own person; exemplify typically. —**per·son·i·fi·ca·tion** *n.*

**per·son·nel** /ˌpərsəˈnel/ ▸*n.* body of employees in an organization or in the armed forces.

**per·spec·tive** /pərˈspektiv/ ▸*n.* **1** apparent relation between visible objects as to position, distance, etc. **2** mental view of the relative importance of things: *keep the right perspective.* **3** geographical or imaginary prospect.

**per·spi·ca·cious** /ˌpərspiˈkāsHəs/ ▸*adj.* having mental penetration or discernment. —**per·spi·cac·i·ty** *n.*

**per·spire** /pər'spī(ə)r/ ▶v. sweat.
—**per·spi·ra·tion** n.

**per·suade** /pər'swād/ ▶v.
**1** cause to believe; convince.
**2** induce.

**per·sua·sion** ▶n. **1** persuading.
**2** persuasiveness. **3** belief or
conviction, or the group holding
it.

**per·sua·sive** ▶adj. able to
persuade. —**per·sua·sive·ly** adv.
—**per·sua·sive·ness** n.

**pert** /pərt/ ▶adj. saucy; impudent.

**pert.** ▶abbr. pertaining.

**per·tain** /pər'tān/ ▶v. be
appropriate, related, or
applicable: *matters pertaining to
the organization of the government.*

**per·ti·na·cious** /ˌpərtn'āsHəs/
▶adj. holding firmly to an
opinion or a course of action.

**per·ti·nent** /'pərtn-ənt/ ▶adj.
relevant. —**per·ti·nence** n.

**per·turb** /pər'tərb/ ▶v. **1** throw
into confusion or disorder.
**2** disturb mentally; agitate.
—**per·tur·ba·tion** n.

**pe·rus·al** /pə'roozəl/ ▶n. action
of reading or examining
something.

**pe·ruse** /pə'rooz/ ▶v. read or
study carefully. —**pe·rus·al** n.

**per·vade** /pər'vād/ ▶v. spread
throughout; permeate.
—**per·va·sive** adj.

**per·va·sive** /pər'vāsiv/ ▶adj.
(esp. of an unwelcome influence
or physical effect) spreading
widely throughout an area or a
group of people.

**per·verse** /pər'vərs/ ▶adj. **1** (of a
person or action) deliberately or
stubbornly departing from what
is reasonable or required: *her
perverse decision not to cooperate.*
**2** contrary to the expected
standard or practice.
**3** perverted; wicked.
—**per·verse·ly** adv.
—**per·verse·ness** n.
—**per·ver·si·ty** n.

**per·ver·sion** ▶n. **1** alteration of
something from its original
meaning or state: *a scandalous
perversion of the law.* **2** sexual
behavior or desire that is
considered abnormal.

**per·vert** /pər'vərt/ ▶v. **1** turn (a
person or thing) aside from its
proper use or nature. **2** misapply
(words, etc.). **3** lead astray from
right opinion or conduct.
▶n. perverted person, esp.
sexually.

**pes·ky** /'peskē/ ▶adj. (**-ki·er**,
**-ki·est**) troublesome; annoying.
—**pesk·i·ness** n.

**pe·so** /'pāsō/ ▸n. chief monetary unit of several Latin American countries and of the Philippines.

**pes·si·mism** /'pesə,mizəm/ ▸n. tendency to be gloomy or expect the worst. —**pes·si·mist** n. —**pes·si·mis·tic** adj.

**pest** /pest/ ▸n. **1** destructive insect or other animal. **2** troublesome or annoying person or thing; nuisance.

**pes·ter** ▸v. trouble or annoy, esp. with frequent or persistent requests.

**pes·ti·cide** /'pestə,sīd/ ▸n. substance used for destroying pests, esp. insects. —**pes·ti·cid·al** adj.

**pes·ti·lence** /'pestl-əns/ ▸n. fatal epidemic disease; plague.

**pes·tle** /'pesəl/ ▸n. **1** club-shaped instrument for pounding substances in a mortar. **2** appliance for pounding, etc.

**pes·to** /'pestō/ ▸n. sauce made of fresh chopped basil, garlic, olive oil, and Parmesan cheese, used for pasta, fish, etc.

**pet** /pet/ ▸n. **1** domestic or tamed animal kept for pleasure or companionship. **2** darling; favorite. ▸adj. **1** kept as a pet. **2** of or for pet animals. **3** favorite or particular. **4** expressing fondness or familiarity: pet name. ▸v. (**pet·ted, pet·ting**) **1** stroke or pat (an animal) affectionately. **2** engage in sexually stimulating touching.

**pet·al** /'petl/ ▸n. each of the parts of the corolla of a flower.

**pe·ter** /'pētər/ ▸v. diminish; come to an end: the storm has petered out.

**pet·it** /'petē/ ▸adj. (of a crime) petty.

**pe·tite** /pə'tēt/ ▸adj. (of a woman) small and trim.

**pe·ti·tion** /pə'tisнən/ ▸n. **1** supplication or request. **2** formal written request, esp. one signed by many people. **3** application to a court for a writ, etc. ▸v. **1** make or address a petition to. **2** appeal earnestly or humbly. —**pe·ti·tion·er** n.

**pet·rel** /'petrəl/ ▸n. sea bird, usu. flying far from land.

**pet·ri·fy** /'petrə,fī/ ▸v. (**-fied**) **1** (of organic matter) change into a stony substance. **2** paralyze with fear, astonishment, etc. —**pet·ri·fac·tion** n.

**pet·ro·chem·i·cal** /,petrō-'kemikəl/ ▸n. substance

industrially obtained from petroleum or natural gas.

**pet·ro·glyph** /'petrə,glif/ ▸*n.* rock carving, esp. a prehistoric one.

**pe·tro·le·um** /pə'trōlēəm/ ▸*n.* hydrocarbon oil found in the upper strata of the earth, refined for use as fuel, etc.

□ **petroleum jelly** (also **pet·ro·la·tum**) translucent solid mixture of hydrocarbons used as a lubricant, ointment, etc.

**pet·ti·coat** /'petē,kōt/ ▸*n.* woman's or girl's skirted undergarment hanging from the waist or shoulders.

**pet·tish** /'petiSH/ ▸*adj.* peevish; petulant; easily put out.

**pet·ty** ▸*adj.* (-ti·er, -ti·est) **1** unimportant; trivial. **2** mean; small-minded; contemptible. —**pet·ti·ness** *n.*

**pet·ty cash** ▸*n.* money from or for small items of receipt or expenditure.

**pet·u·lant** /'pecHələnt/ ▸*adj.* peevishly impatient or irritable. —**pet·u·lance** *n.* —**pet·u·lant·ly** *adv.*

**pe·tu·nia** /pə't(y)o͞onyə/ ▸*n.* plant with white, purple, red, etc., funnel-shaped flowers.

**pew** /pyo͞o/ ▸*n.* (in a church) long bench with a back.

**pew·ter** /'pyo͞otər/ ▸*n.* gray alloy of tin with lead, copper, antimony, or various other metals.

**pe·yo·te** /pā'yōtē/ ▸*n.* hallucinogenic drug prepared from a small, soft, blue-green, spineless cactus, native to Mexico and the southern U.S., containing mescaline.

**PG** ▸*abbr.* (of movies) classified as suitable for children subject to parental guidance.

**pg.** ▸*abbr.* page.

**pH** ▸*n.* numerical scale measuring the relative acidity or alkalinity of a solution.

**phal·an·ster·y** /'falən,sterē/ ▸*n.* (*pl.* -ster·ies) group of people living together in community, free of external regulation and holding property in common.

**pha·lanx** /'fālaNGks/ ▸*n.* (*pl.* -lanx·es or -lan·ges) **1** set of people, etc., forming a compact mass, or banded for a common purpose. **2** (in ancient Greece) line of battle, esp. a body of Macedonian infantry drawn up in close order.

**phal·lic** /'falik/ ▸*adj.* of, relating

to, or resembling a phallus or erect penis.

**phal·lus** /'faləs/ ▶n. (pl. **-li** or **-lus·es**) **1** (esp. erect) penis. **2** image of this as a symbol of generative power in nature. —**phal·lic** adj.

**phan·tasm** /'fan,tazəm/ ▶n. illusion; phantom. —**phan·tas·mal** adj.

**phan·tas·ma·go·ri·a** /fan-,tazmə'gôrēə/ ▶n. shifting series of real or imaginary figures as seen in a dream. —**phan·tas·ma·gor·ic** adj.

**phan·tom** /'fantəm/ ▶n. **1** ghost; apparition; specter. **2** mental illusion.
▶adj. merely apparent; illusory.

**Pha·raoh** /'fe(ə),rō/ ▶n. title of rulers of ancient Egypt.

**Phar·i·see** /'farə,sē/ (also **phar·i·see**) ▶n. **1** member of an ancient Jewish sect, distinguished by strict observance of the traditional and written law. **2** self-righteous person; hypocrite.

**phar·ma·ceu·ti·cal** /,färmə-'sōōtikəl/ ▶adj. of the use, preparation, or sale of medicinal drugs.
▶n. **1** medicinal drug. **2** (usu.

pharmaceuticals) companies manufacturing medicinal drugs.

**phar·ma·col·o·gy** /,färmə-'käləjē/ ▶n. the science of the action of drugs on the body. —**phar·ma·co·log·i·cal** adj. —**phar·ma·col·o·gist** n.

**phar·ma·cy** /'färməsē/ ▶n. (pl. **-cies**) **1** preparation and (esp. medicinal) dispensing of drugs. **2** drugstore. —**phar·ma·cist** n.

**phar·ynx** /'fariNGks/ ▶n. (pl. **-yn·ges** or **-ynx·es**) cavity behind the nose and mouth, and connecting them to the esophagus. —**pha·ryn·ge·al** adj. —**phar·yn·gi·tis** n.

**phase** /fāz/ ▶n. **1** distinct stage in a process of change or development. **2** each of the aspects of the moon or a planet, according to the amount of its illumination.
▶v. carry out (a program, etc.) in phases or stages.
□ **phase in** (or **out**) bring gradually into (or out of) use.

**phat·ic** /'fatik/ ▶adj. denoting or relating to language used for general purposes of social interaction, rather than to convey information or ask questions.

**Ph.D.** ▸*abbr.* Doctor of Philosophy.

**pheas·ant** /ˈfezənt/ ▸*n.* long-tailed game bird, orig. from Asia.

**phe·no·bar·bi·tal** /ˌfēnōˈbärbiˌtôl/ ▸*n.* narcotic and sedative barbiturate drug used esp. to treat epilepsy.

**phe·nol** /ˈfēˌnôl/ ▸*n.* derivative of benzene used in dilute form as an antiseptic and disinfectant.

**phe·nom·e·non** /fəˈnäməˌnän/ ▸*n.* (*pl.* **-na**) **1** fact or occurrence that appears or is perceived. **2** remarkable person or thing. —**phe·nom·e·nal** *adj.*

**pher·o·mone** /ˈferəˌmōn/ ▸*n.* chemical substance secreted and released by an animal for detection and response by another usu. of the same species. —**pher·o·mo·nal** *adj.*

**phil-** ▸*comb. form* var. of PHILO-.

**-phil** ▸*comb. form* var. of -PHILE.

**phi·lan·der** /fəˈlandər/ ▸*v.* flirt or have casual affairs with women. —**phi·lan·der·er** *n.*

**phi·lan·thro·py** /fəˈlanᴛʜrəpē/ ▸*n.* practical benevolence, esp. charity on a large scale. —**phi·lan·thro·pist** *n.*

**phi·lat·e·ly** /fəˈlatl-ē/ ▸*n.* collection and study of postage stamps. —**phi·lat·e·list** *n.*

**-phile** (also **-phil**) ▸*comb. form* forming nouns and adjectives denoting fondness for what is specified: *bibliophile* | *Francophile*.

**phil·har·mon·ic** /ˌfilhärˈmänik/ ▸*adj.* fond of music (used characteristically in the names of orchestras, choirs, etc.).

**phi·lip·pic** /fəˈlipik/ ▸*n.* bitter attack or denunciation, esp. a verbal one.

**Phi·lis·tine** /ˈfiləˌstēn/ ▸*n.* **1** member of a people opposing the Israelites in ancient Palestine. **2** (usu. **philistine**) person who is hostile or indifferent to culture. ▸*adj.* hostile or indifferent to culture. —**phil·is·tin·ism** *n.*

**philo-** ▸*comb. form* denoting a liking for a specific thing: *philology* | *philosophy*.

**phil·o·den·dron** /ˌfiləˈdendrən/ ▸*n.* (*pl.* **-drons** or **-dra**) climbing plant with bright foliage.

**phi·log·y·nist** /fəˈläjənist/ ▸*n.* person who likes or admires women.

**phi·lol·o·gy** /fəˈläləjē/ ▸*n.* science of language, esp. in its historical and comparative aspects. —**phi·lol·o·gist** *n.*

**phi·los·o·pher** /fəˈläsəfər/ ▸*n.* **1** person engaged or learned in philosophy.  **2** person who lives by philosophy.

**phi·los·o·pher's stone** ▶*n.* (**the philosopher's stone**) mythical substance supposed to change any metal into gold or silver and, according to some, to cure all diseases and prolong life indefinitely. Its discovery was the supreme object of alchemy.

**phi·los·o·phy** /fə'läsəfē/ ▶*n.* (*pl.* **-phies**) **1** use of reason and argument in seeking truth and knowledge of reality, esp. of the causes and nature of things and of the principles governing existence.  **2** particular system or set of beliefs reached by this; personal rule of life. —**phil·o·soph·i·cal** *adj.*

**phle·bi·tis** /flə'bītis/ ▶*n.* inflammation of the walls of a vein.

**phlegm** /flem/ ▶*n.* thick viscous substance secreted by the mucous membranes of the respiratory passages, discharged by coughing.

**phleg·mat·ic** /fleg'matik/ ▶*adj.* stolidly calm; unexcitable; unemotional.

**phlo·em** /'flō,em/ ▶*n.* tissue conducting food material in plants.

**phlo·gis·ton** /flō'jistän; -tən/ ▶*n.* substance supposed by 18th-century chemists to exist in all combustible bodies, and to be released in combustion.

**phlox** /fläks/ ▶*n.* cultivated plant with scented clusters of esp. white, blue, and red flowers.

**-phobe** ▶*comb. form* forming nouns and adjectives denoting a person with a specified fear or dislike: *xenophobe.*

**pho·bi·a** /'fōbēə/ ▶*n.* abnormal or morbid fear or aversion. —**pho·bic** *adj. & n.*

**-phobia** ▶*comb. form* forming abstract nouns denoting a fear or dislike of what is specified: *agoraphobia* | *xenophobia.*

**phoe·be** /'fēbē/ ▶*n.* American flycatcher with gray-brown or black plumage.

**phoe·nix** /'fēniks/ ▶*n.* mythical bird, the only one of its kind, that burned itself on a funeral pyre and rose from the ashes to live through another cycle.

**phone** /fōn/ ▶*n. & v.* telephone.

**pho·neme** /'fōnēm/ ▶*n.* any of the units of sound in a specified language that distinguish one word from another (e.g., *p, b, d, t* as in *pad, pat, bad, bat,* in English).

**pho·net·ics** /fəˈnetiks/ ▸n.
**1** [treated as *pl.*] vocal sounds.
**2** the study of these.
—**pho·ne·ti·cian** *n.*

**phon·ics** /ˈfäniks/ ▸n. method of teaching people to read by correlating sounds with letters or groups of letters in an alphabetic writing system.

**phono-** ▸*comb. form* denoting sound.

**pho·no·graph** /ˈfōnəˌgraf/ ▸n. record player.

**pho·nol·o·gy** /fəˈnäləjē/ ▸n. the study of sounds in a language.

**pho·ny** /ˈfōnē/ (also **pho·ney**) ▸*adj.* (**-ni·er, -ni·est**) *inf.* **1** sham; counterfeit. **2** fictitious; fraudulent.
▸*n.* (*pl.* **-nies** or **-neys**) phony person or thing.

**phos·phate** /ˈfäsfāt/ ▸n. salt or ester of phosphoric acid, esp. used as a fertilizer.

**phos·phor** /ˈfäsfər/ ▸n. synthetic fluorescent or phosphorescent substance esp. used in cathode-ray tubes.

**phos·pho·res·cence** /ˌfäsfə-ˈresəns/ ▸n. **1** radiation similar to fluorescence but detectable after excitation ceases. **2** emission of light without combustion or perceptible heat.
—**phos·pho·res·cent** *adj.*

**phos·pho·rus** /ˈfäsfərəs/ ▸n. nonmetallic chemical element, existing as a poisonous whitish waxy substance burning slowly at ordinary temperatures and so appearing luminous in the dark. (Symb.: **P**) —**pos·phor·ic** *adj.* —**phos·pho·rous** *adj.*

**pho·to** /ˈfōtō/ ▸n. photograph.

**photo-** ▸*comb. form* denoting:
**1** light. **2** photography.

**pho·to·cop·y** ▸n. (*pl.* **-ies**) photographic copy of printed or written material.
▸*v.* (**-ied**) make a photocopy of.
—**pho·to·cop·i·er** *n.*

**pho·to·e·lec·tric** ▸*adj.* marked by or using emissions of electrons from substances exposed to light.
□ **photoelectric cell** device using this effect to generate current.

**pho·to fin·ish** ▸n. close finish of a race or contest, esp. one where the winner is only distinguishable on a photograph.

**pho·to·ge·nic** /ˌfōtəˈjenik/ ▸*adj.* (esp. of a person) having an appearance that looks pleasing in photographs.

**pho·to·graph** ▸n. picture taken by means of the chemical action of light or other radiation on sensitive film.

▶*v.* take a photograph of (a person, etc.). —**pho·tog·ra·pher** *n.* —**pho·to·graph·ic** *adj.*

**pho·tog·ra·phy** /fə'tägrəfē/ ▶*n.* taking and processing of photographs.

**pho·ton** /'fōtän/ ▶*n.* quantum of electromagnetic radiation energy, proportional to the frequency of radiation.

**pho·to op·por·tu·ni·ty** (also **pho·to-op**) ▶*n.* occasion on which celebrities, etc., pose for photographers by arrangement.

**pho·to·re·al·ism** /'fōtō'rēə-,lizəm/ ▶*n.* **1** detailed and unidealized representation in art, esp. of banal, mundane, or sordid aspects of life. **2** detailed visual representation, like that obtained in a photograph, in a nonphotographic medium such as animation or computer graphics.

**pho·to·sen·si·tive** ▶*adj.* reacting chemically, electrically, etc., to light.

**pho·to·syn·the·sis** ▶*n.* process in which the energy of sunlight is used by organisms, esp. green plants, to synthesize carbohydrates from carbon dioxide and water.

**phrase** /frāz/ ▶*n.* **1** group of words forming a conceptual unit, but not a sentence. **2** idiomatic or short pithy expression. **3** group of musical notes forming a distinct unit within a larger piece.

▶*v.* express in words. —**phras·al** *adj.*

**phra·se·ol·o·gy** /,frāzē'äləjē/ ▶*n.* (*pl.* **-gies**) mode of expression.

**phra·try** /'frātrē/ ▶*n.* (*pl.* **-tries**) descent group or kinship group in some tribal societies.

**phre·nol·o·gy** /fre'näləjē/ ▶*n.* *hist.* the study of the shape and size of the cranium as a supposed indication of character and mental faculties. —**phren·o·log·i·cal** *adj.* —**phre·nol·o·gist** *n.*

**phy·lac·ter·y** /fī'laktərē/ ▶*n.* (*pl.* **-ter·ies**) small leather box containing Hebrew texts on vellum, worn by Jewish men at morning prayer as a reminder to keep the law.

**phy·lum** /'fīləm/ ▶*n.* (*pl.* **phy·la**) taxonomic rank below kingdom comprising a class or classes and subordinate taxa.

**phys·i·cal** /'fizikəl/ ▸*adj.* **1** of or concerning the body: *physical exercise.* **2** of matter; material: *both mental and physical force.* **3 a** of, or according to, the laws of nature: *a physical impossibility.* **b** belonging to physics: *physical science.* ▸*n.* (also **physical examination**) medical examination. —**phys·i·cal·i·ty** *n.* —**phys·i·cal·ly** *adv.*

**phys·i·cal sci·enc·es** ▸*pl. n.* sciences used in the study of inanimate natural objects.

**phys·i·cal ther·a·py** ▸*n.* treatment of disease, injury, deformity, etc., by massage, infrared heat treatment, remedial exercise, etc.

**phy·si·cian** /fi'zisHən/ ▸*n.* medical doctor; M.D.

**phys·ics** /'fiziks/ ▸*n.* science dealing with the properties and interactions of matter and energy. —**phys·i·cist** *n.*

**phys·i·og·no·my** /ˌfizē-'ä(g)nəmē/ ▸*n.* (*pl.* **-mies**) cast or form of a person's features, expression, body, etc.

**phys·i·ol·o·gy** /ˌfizē'äləjē/ ▸*n.* **1** science of the functions of living organisms and their parts. **2** these functions.

—**phys·i·o·log·i·cal** *adj.* —**phys·i·ol·o·gist** *n.*

**phy·sique** /fi'zēk/ ▸*n.* bodily structure; build.

**pi** /pī/ ▸*n.* **1** sixteenth letter of the Greek alphabet (Π, π). **2** the symbol of the ratio of the circumference of a circle to its diameter (approx. 3.14159).

**pi·ac·u·lar** /pī'akyələr/ ▸*adj.* making or requiring atonement.

**pi·a·nis·si·mo** /ˌpēə'nisiˌmō/ ▸*adv. Music* very softly.

**pi·an·o** /pē'anō/ ▸*n.* (*pl.* **-nos**) large musical instrument played by pressing down keys on a keyboard and causing hammers to strike metal strings. ▸*adv. Music* softly. —**pi·an·ist** *n.*

**pi·az·za** /pē'ätsə/ ▸*n.* public square or marketplace.

**pi·ca** /'pīkə/ ▸*n.* unit of type size (1/6 inch).

**pi·ca·resque** /ˌpikə'resk/ ▸*adj.* (of a style of fiction) dealing with the episodic adventures of rogues, etc.

**pic·a·yune** /ˌpikə'yoon/ ▸*adj. inf.* of little value; trivial.

**pic·co·lo** /'pikəˌlō/ ▸*n.* small flute sounding an octave higher than the ordinary one.

**pick** /pik/ ▸*v.* **1** choose: *picked a*

*team.* **2** detach or pluck (a flower, fruit, etc.). **3** probe with the finger, an instrument, etc., to remove unwanted matter. **4** open (a lock) with an instrument other than a key. **5** steal, as from a person's pocket.

▶ *n.* **1** act or instance of picking. **2** selection or choice. **3** the best: *pick of the bunch.* **4** long-handled tool having a usu. curved iron bar pointed at one or both ends, used for breaking up hard ground, masonry, etc. **5** *inf.* plectrum.

□ **pick and choose** select fastidiously. □ **pick off 1** pluck (leaves, etc.) off. **2** shoot (people, etc.) one by one. **3** *Baseball* put out a base runner caught off base. □ **pick up 1 a** grasp and raise: *picked up his hat.* **b** clean up; straighten up. **2** acquire: *picked up a cold.* **3 a** fetch (a person, animal, or thing) left in another person's charge. **b** stop for and take along with one, esp. in a vehicle. **4** make the acquaintance of (a person) casually, esp. as a sexual overture. **5** recover; prosper; improve.

**pick·et** ▶ *n.* **1** person or group of people outside a place of work, intending to persuade esp. workers not to enter during a strike, etc. **2** pointed stake or peg driven into the ground to form a fence, etc.: *picket fence.*
▶ *v.* beset or guard with a picket or pickets. —**pick·et·er** *n.*
□ **picket line** boundary established by workers on strike.

**pick·le** /'pikəl/ ▶ *n.* **1** vegetable, esp. a cucumber, preserved in brine, vinegar, mustard, etc. **2** *inf.* plight: *a fine pickle we are in!*
▶ *v.* preserve in vinegar, brine, etc.

**pick·pock·et** ▶ *n.* person who steals from the pockets of others.

**pick·up** ▶ *n.* **1** small truck with an enclosed cab and open back. **2** act of collecting a person or goods. **3** *inf.* person met casually, esp. for sexual purposes.

**pick·y** ▶ *adj.* (**-i·er, -i·est**) *inf.* excessively fastidious; choosy. —**pick·i·ness** *n.*

**pic·nic** /'pik,nik/ ▶ *n.* outing or excursion including a packed meal eaten out of doors.
▶ *v.* (**-nicked, -nick·ing**) take part in a picnic.

**pic·ture** /'pikCHər/ ▶ *n.* **1** painting, drawing,

photograph, etc. **2** total visual or mental impression produced; scene: *the picture looks bleak.* **3** movie.

▶*v.* **1** represent in a picture. **2** imagine. **3** describe graphically.

□ **picture window** very large window consisting of one pane of glass.

**pic·tur·esque** /ˌpikCHəˈresk/ ▶*adj.* **1** (of landscape, etc.) beautiful or striking, as in a picture. **2** (of language, etc.) strikingly graphic; vivid.

**pid·gin** /ˈpijən/ ▶*n.* simplified language used for communication between people not having a common language.

**pie** /pī/ ▶*n.* **1** baked dish of fruit, meat, custard, etc., usu. with a top and base of pastry. **2** anything resembling a pie in form: *mud pie.*

**pie·bald** /ˈpīˌbôld/ ▶*adj.* (usu. of an animal, esp. a horse) having irregular patches of two colors, esp. black and white.

**piece** /pēs/ ▶*n.* **1** distinct portion forming part of or broken off from a larger object. **2** usu. short literary or musical composition; picture. **3** item. **4** object moved in a board game.

**5** definite quantity in which a thing is sold.

▶*v.* (**piece something together**) form into a whole; put together; join.

□ **go to pieces** collapse emotionally. □ **piece of one's mind** sharp rebuke or lecture.

**pièce de ré·sis·tance** /pēˈes də ˌreziˈstäns/ ▶*n.* (*pl.* **pièces de ré·sis·tance** *pronunc.* same) most important or remarkable item.

**piece·meal** ▶*adv.* piece by piece; gradually.

▶*adj.* partial; gradual; unsystematic.

**piece·work** ▶*n.* work paid for by the amount produced.

**pie chart** ▶*n.* circle divided into sections to represent relative quantities.

**pied** /pīd/ ▶*adj.* parti-colored.

**pied-à-terre** /pēˌyäd ə ˈte(ə)r/ ▶*n.* (*pl.* **pieds-à-terre** *pronunc.* same) usu. small residence for occasional use.

**pier** /pi(ə)r/ ▶*n.* **1** structure of iron or wood raised on piles and leading out to sea, a lake, etc., used as a promenade and landing place. **2** support of an arch or of the span of a bridge; pillar.

**pierce** /pi(ə)rs/ ▶*v.* **1** prick with a

sharp instrument, esp. to make a hole in. **2** pass through or into; penetrate.

**pierc·ing** ▸*adj.* **1** (of eyes or a look) appearing to see through someone. **2** (of a sound) extremely loud or shrill. **3** (of wind or cold) seeming to cut through one.

**pie·tà** /ˌpēäˈtä/ (often **Pie·tà**) ▸*n.* picture or sculpture of the Virgin Mary holding the dead body of Jesus Christ on her lap or in her arms.

**pi·e·ty** /ˈpīətē/ ▸*n.* (*pl.* **-ties**) **1** quality of being pious. **2** pious act.

**pig** /pig/ ▸*n.* **1** omnivorous hoofed bristly mammal, esp. a domesticated kind. **2** *inf.* greedy, dirty, obstinate, sulky, or annoying person. **3** oblong mass of metal (esp. iron or lead) from a smelting furnace. **—pig·let** *n.*

**pi·geon** /ˈpijən/ ▸*n.* large usu. gray and white bird often domesticated and bred and trained to carry messages, etc.; dove.

**pi·geon·hole** ▸*n.* each of a set of compartments in a cabinet or on a wall for papers, letters, etc. ▸*v.* assign to a preconceived category.

**pi·geon-toed** ▸*adj.* (of a person) having the toes turned inward.

**pig·gy·back** /ˈpigēˌbak/ ▸*n.* ride on the back and shoulders of another person. ▸*adv.* **1** on the back and shoulders of another person. **2 a** on the back or top of a larger object. **b** in addition to; along with.

**pig·head·ed** ▸*adj.* obstinate. **—pig·head·ed·ness** *n.*

**pig i·ron** ▸*n.* crude iron from a smelting furnace.

**pig·ment** /ˈpigmənt/ ▸*n.* **1** coloring matter used as paint or dye. **2** natural coloring matter of animal or plant tissue, e.g., chlorophyll, hemoglobin, etc.

**pig·men·ta·tion** /ˌpigmənˈtāsHən/ ▸*n.* natural coloring of plants, animals, etc.

**pig·my** /ˈpigmē/ ▸var. of **PYGMY**.

**pig·pen** /ˈpigˌpen/ ▸*n.* **1** enclosure for pigs. **2** *inf.* very dirty room or house.

**pig·tail** ▸*n.* braid hanging from the back of the head.

**pike** /pīk/ ▸*n.* (*pl.* same) **1** large voracious freshwater fish, with a long narrow snout and sharp teeth. **2** weapon with a pointed steel or iron head on a long wooden shaft.

**pi·laf** /pē'läf/ ▸*n.* dish of seasoned rice or wheat with meat, fish, vegetables, etc.

**pi·las·ter** /pi'lastər/ ▸*n.* rectangular column, esp. one projecting from a wall.
—**pi·las·tered** *adj.*

**pil·chard** /'pilCHərd/ ▸*n.* small marine fish, of the herring family.

**pile** /pīl/ ▸*n.* **1** heap of things laid or gathered upon one another: *a pile of leaves.* **2** large imposing building: *a stately pile.* **3** *inf.* large quantity. **4** heavy support beam driven vertically into the bed of a river, soft ground, etc. **5** soft projecting surface on velvet, plush, etc., or esp. on a carpet; nap.
▸*v.* heap up.

**pil·fer** /'pilfər/ ▸*v.* steal (objects) esp. in small quantities.
—**pil·fer·age** *n.*

**pil·grim** /'pilgrəm/ ▸*n.* **1** person who journeys to a sacred place. **2** traveler. **3** (**Pilgrim**) one of the English Puritans who founded the colony of Plymouth, Massachusetts, in 1620.

**pill** /pil/ ▸*n.* **1 a** solid medicine formed into a ball or a flat disk for swallowing whole. **b** (**the pill**) contraceptive pill. **2** *inf.* difficult or unpleasant person.

**pil·lage** /'pilij/ ▸*v.* plunder; sack (a place or a person).
▸*n.* pillaging, esp. in war.
—**pil·lag·er** *n.*

**pil·lar** /'pilər/ ▸*n.* **1** usu. slender vertical structure of wood, metal, or esp. stone used as a support or for ornament. **2** person regarded as a mainstay or support: *a pillar of strength.* **3** upright mass of air, water, rock, etc.
□ **from pillar to post** (driven, etc.) from one place to another; to and fro.

**pill·box** ▸*n.* **1** small shallow cylindrical box for holding pills. **2** hat of a similar shape. **3** small partly underground enclosed concrete fort used as an outpost.

**pil·lo·ry** /'pilərē/ ▸*n.* (*pl.* **-ries**) *hist.* wooden framework with holes for the head and hands, enabling the public to assault or ridicule a person so imprisoned.
▸*v.* (**-ried**) attack or ridicule publicly.

**pil·low** /'pilō/ ▸*n.* soft support or cushion, as under the head in sleeping.
▸*v.* **1** rest on or as if on a pillow.

**2** serve as a pillow for: *moss pillowed her head.*

**pi·lot** /'pīlət/ ▸*n.* **1** person who operates the flying controls of an aircraft. **2** person qualified to take charge of a ship entering or leaving a harbor. **3** guide. ▸*adj.* done as an experimental undertaking or test: *a pilot project.* ▸*v.* **1** act as a pilot on (a ship) or of (an aircraft). **2** conduct, lead, or initiate as a pilot: *piloted the new scheme.*

**pi·lot light** ▸*n.* small gas burner kept alight to light another.

**pi·mien·to** /pi'm(y)entō/ (also **pi·men·to**) ▸*n.* red, ripe bell pepper.

**pimp** /pimp/ ▸*n.* man who lives off the earnings of a prostitute or a brothel; pander.

**pim·ple** /'pimpəl/ ▸*n.* **1** small hard inflamed spot on the skin. **2** anything resembling a pimple, esp. in relative size.

**PIN** /pin/ ▸*n.* personal identification number.

**pin** ▸*n.* **1 a** small thin pointed piece of esp. steel wire used (esp. in sewing) for holding things in place, attaching one thing to another, etc. **2** small brooch. **3** peg of wood or metal for various purposes. ▸*v.* (**pinned, pin·ning**) **1** fasten with a pin or pins: *pinned up the hem.* **2** fix (blame, responsibility, etc.) on a person, etc. **3** seize and hold fast. □ **pin down 1** force (a person) to declare his or her intentions. **2** specify (a thing) precisely. □ **pin money** very small sum of money, esp. for spending on inessentials. □ **pins and needles** tingling sensation in a limb recovering from numbness.

**pin·a·fore** /'pinə,fôr/ ▸*n.* sleeveless apronlike garment worn over a child's dress.

**pin·ball** ▸*n.* game in which small metal balls are shot across a board and score points by striking pins with lights, etc.

**pince-nez** /'pans ,nā/ ▸*n.* (*pl.* same) pair of eyeglasses with a nose-clip instead of earpieces.

**pin·cers** /'pinsərz/ ▸*pl. n.* **1** gripping tool resembling scissors but with blunt usu. concave jaws. **2** front claws of lobsters and some other crustaceans.

**pinch** /pinCH/ ▸*v.* **1 a** grip tightly, esp. between finger and thumb. **b** (of a shoe, garment, etc.)

constrict painfully. **2** (of cold, hunger, etc.) grip painfully: *she was pinched with cold.* **3** *inf.* steal.

▶*n.* **1** act of pinching. **2** small amount: *pinch of snuff.* **3** stress or pain caused by poverty, cold, hunger, etc.

□ **in a pinch** in an emergency; if necessary. □ **pinch-hit 1** *Baseball* bat instead of another player. **2** fill in as a substitute, esp. at the last minute.

**pinch·beck** /ˈpinCH,bek/ ▶*n.* alloy of copper and zinc resembling gold, used for watches and costume jewelry.

▶*adj.* appearing valuable, but actually cheap or tawdry.

**pine** /pīn/ ▶*n.* **1** evergreen tree native to northern temperate regions, with needle-shaped leaves. **2** soft timber of this.

▶*v.* **1** long eagerly; yearn. **2** decline or waste away, esp. from grief, disease, etc.

□ **pine cone** cone-shaped fruit of the pine tree.

**pine·ap·ple** ▶*n.* **1** tropical plant with a spiral of sword-shaped leaves and a thick stem bearing a large fruit developed from many flowers. **2** fruit of this, consisting of yellow flesh surrounded by a tough segmented skin.

**ping** /pinG/ ▶*n.* single short high ringing sound.

▶*v.* make a ping.

**Ping-Pong** /ˈpinG ,pônG/ ▶*trademark* another name for TABLE TENNIS.

**pin·guid** /ˈpinGgwid/ ▶*adj.* of the nature of or resembling fat; oily or greasy.

**pin·head** ▶*n.* **1** flattened head of a pin. **2** *inf.* stupid or foolish person.

**pin·ion** /ˈpinyən/ ▶*n.* **1** outer part of a bird's wing. **2** small toothed gear engaging with a larger one.

▶*v.* **1** cut off the pinion of (a wing or bird) to prevent flight. **2** bind the arms of (a person).

**pink** /pinGk/ ▶*n.* **1** pale red color: *decorated in pink.* **2** cultivated plant with sweet-smelling white, pink, crimson, etc., flowers. **3** most perfect condition, etc.: *the pink of health.*

▶*adj.* of a pale red color.

▶*v.* cut a scalloped or zigzag edge on.

□ **pink slip** notice of layoff or termination from one's job.

**pink·ing shears** ▶*pl. n.* dressmaker's serrated shears for cutting a zigzag edge.

**pin·nace** /ˈpinis/ ▸n. small boat, with sails or oars, forming part of the equipment of a warship or other large vessel.

**pin·na·cle** /ˈpinəkəl/ ▸n. 1 natural peak. 2 small ornamental turret usu. ending in a pyramid or cone, crowning a buttress, roof, etc. 3 culmination: *he had reached the pinnacle of his career.*

**pin·nate** /ˈpināt/ ▸adj. (of a compound leaf) having leaflets arranged on either side of the stem.

**pin·point** ▸n. tiny dot or point. ▸v. locate with precision.

**pin·stripe** ▸n. 1 very narrow stripe in cloth. 2 fabric or garment with this.

**pint** /pīnt/ ▸n. measure of capacity for liquids, one half of a quart or 16 fluid ounces (.41 liter). □ **pint-sized** (also **pint-size**) *inf.* very small, esp. of a person.

**pin·up** ▸n. 1 photograph of a movie star, etc., for display. 2 person in such a photograph.

**pin·wheel** ▸n. 1 stick with vanes that twirl in the wind. 2 fireworks device that whirls and emits colored fire.

**Pin·yin** /ˈpinˈyin/ ▸n. system of romanized spelling for transliterating Chinese.

**pi·o·neer** /ˌpīəˈni(ə)r/ ▸n. 1 initiator of a new enterprise, inventor, etc. 2 explorer or settler; colonist. ▸v. initiate or originate (an enterprise, etc.).

**pi·ous** /ˈpīəs/ ▸adj. 1 devout; religious. 2 hypocritically virtuous; sanctimonious.

**pip** /pip/ ▸n. 1 seed of an apple, pear, orange, grape, etc. 2 any of the spots on playing cards, dice, or dominos.

**pipe** /pīp/ ▸n. 1 tube used to convey water, gas, etc. 2 narrow wooden or clay, etc., tube with a bowl at one end containing burning tobacco, etc., for smoking. 3 a wind instrument consisting of a single tube. b any of the tubes by which sound is produced in an organ. c (usu. **pipes**) bagpipes. 4 tubal organ, vessel, etc., in an animal's body. ▸v. 1 play (a tune, etc.) on a pipe or pipes. 2 convey (oil, water, gas, etc.) by pipes. 3 transmit (music, a radio program, etc.) by wire or cable. □ **pipe down** *inf.* be quiet or less insistent. □ **pipe organ** organ using pipes instead of or as well as reeds.

**pipe dream** ▶*n.* unattainable or fanciful hope or scheme.

**pipe·line** ▶*n.* **1** long, usu. underground, pipe for conveying esp. oil. **2** channel supplying goods, information, etc.

□ **in the pipeline** awaiting completion or processing.

**pip·ing** ▶*n.* **1** thin pipelike fold used to edge hems or frills on clothing, seams on upholstery, etc. **2** lengths of pipe, or a system of pipes, esp. in domestic use.

□ **piping hot** very or suitably hot (esp. as required of food, water, etc.).

**pip·pin** /ˈpipin/ ▶*n.* type of apple.

**pip·squeak** ▶*n.* *inf.* insignificant or contemptible person or thing.

**pi·quant** /ˈpēkənt/ ▶*adj.* **1** agreeably pungent, sharp, or appetizing. **2** pleasantly stimulating, or disquieting, to the mind. —**pi·quan·cy** *n.*

**pique** /pēk/ ▶*n.* ill-feeling; enmity; resentment: *in a fit of pique.*

▶*v.* (**piqued, piqu·ing**) **1** stimulate (curiosity, interest, etc.). **2** wound the pride of; irritate.

**pi·ra·cy** /ˈpīrəsē/ ▶*n.* (*pl.* **-cies**)

**1** practice or an act of robbery of ships at sea. **2** similar practice or act in other forms, esp. hijacking. **3** infringement of copyright.

**pi·ra·nha** /piˈränə/ ▶*n.* freshwater predatory fish native to S. America.

**pi·rate** /ˈpīrit/ ▶*n.* **1** person who attacks and robs ships at sea. **2** person who infringes another's copyright or other business rights.

▶*v.* reproduce (the work, ideas, etc., of another) without permission.

**pi·rogue** /piˈrōg/ ▶*n.* long narrow canoe made from a single tree trunk, esp. in Central America and the Caribbean.

**pir·ou·ette** /ˌpiro͞oˈet/ ▶*n.* dancer's spin on one foot or the point of the toe.

▶*v.* perform a pirouette.

**pis·cine** /ˈpīsēn; ˈpisīn/ ▶*adj.* of or concerning fish.

**pis·mire** /ˈpisˌmī(ə)r/ ▶*n.* ant.

**piss·ant** /ˈpisˌant/ ▶*n.* insignificant or contemptible person or thing.

▶*adj.* worthless; contemptible.

**pis·tach·i·o** /piˈstasHēˌō/ ▶*n.* **1** tree bearing small brownish green flowers and ovoid reddish fruit. **2** edible pale green seed of this.

**pis·til** /ˈpistl/ ▸n. female organs of a flower, comprising the stigma, style, and ovary. —**pis·til·late** adj.

**pis·tol** /ˈpistl/ ▸n. small hand-held firearm.

**pis·ton** /ˈpistn/ ▸n. disk or short cylinder fitting closely within a tube in which it moves up and down, as in an internal combustion engine, pump, etc. ▢ **piston ring** sealing ring on a piston. ▢ **piston rod** rod attached to a piston to impart motion.

**pit** /pit/ ▸n. **1** usu. large deep hole in the ground. **2** hollow or indentation on a surface. **3** short for ORCHESTRA PIT. **4** (**the pits**) inf. wretched or the worst imaginable place, situation, person, etc. **5** stone of a fruit. ▸v. (**pit·ted**, **pit·ting**) **1** (**pit someone/something against**) set (one's wits, strength, etc.) in opposition or rivalry. **2** make pits, esp. scars, in. **3** remove pits from (fruit).

**pi·ta** /ˈpētə/ (also **pit·ta**) ▸n. flat, hollow, unleavened bread that can be split and filled.

**pitch** /piCH/ ▸n. **1** that quality of a sound that is governed by the rate of vibrations producing it; degree of highness or lowness of a tone. **2** height, degree, intensity, etc.: *the pitch of despair.* **3** degree of a slope, esp. of a roof. **4** delivery of a baseball by a pitcher. **5** inf. salesman's advertising or selling approach. **6** sticky resinous black or dark brown substance obtained by distilling tar or turpentine, used for caulking the seams of ships, etc. ▸v. **1** *Baseball* deliver (the ball) to the batter. **2** express in a particular style or at a particular level. **3** erect and fix (a tent, camp, etc.). **4** (of a boat, etc.) rock or oscillate so that the front and back move up and down. **5** fall heavily, esp. headlong. ▢ **pitch in** inf. **1** set to work vigorously. **2** assist; cooperate.

**pitch·er** ▸n. **1** large jug with a lip and a handle, for holding liquids. **2** *Baseball* player who delivers the ball to the batter.

**pitch·fork** ▸n. long-handled two-pronged fork for pitching hay, etc.

**pitch·pipe** ▸n. small reed pipe blown to set the pitch for singing or tuning an instrument.

**pit·e·ous** /ˈpitēəs/ ▸adj.

deserving or causing pity; wretched. —**pit·e·ous·ly** *adv.*

**pit·fall** ▶*n.* unsuspected snare, danger, or drawback.

**pith** /piTH/ ▶*n.* **1** spongy white tissue lining the rind of an orange, lemon, etc. **2** spongy cellular tissue in the stems and branches of plants. **3** essential part. **4** physical strength; vigor. —**pith·y** *adj.*

**pith·y** /'piTHē/ ▶*adj.* (**pith·i·er,** **pith·i·est**) **1** (of language or style) concise and forcefully expressive. **2** (of a fruit or plant) containing much pith.

**pit·i·a·ble** /'pitēəbəl/ ▶*adj.* **1** deserving or arousing pity. **2** contemptibly poor or small.

**pit·i·ful** /'pitifəl/ ▶*adj.* **1** deserving or arousing pity. **2** very small or poor. —**pit·i·ful·ly** *adv.*

**pit·tance** /'pitns/ ▶*n.* scanty or meager allowance, wage, etc.

**pi·tu·i·tar·y** /pə't(y)ōōə,terē/ (also **pi·tu·i·tar·y gland** or **body**) ▶*n.* (*pl.* **-ies**) small ductless gland at the base of the brain.

**pit·y** /'pitē/ ▶*n.* (*pl.* **-ies**) **1** sorrow and compassion aroused by another's condition: *felt pity for the child.* **2** grounds for regret: *what a pity!* ▶*v.* (**-ied**) feel pity for.

**piv·ot** /'pivət/ ▶*n.* **1** short shaft or pin on which something turns or oscillates. **2** crucial or essential person, point, etc. ▶*v.* **1** turn on or as if on a pivot. **2** hinge on; depend on. —**piv·ot·al** *adj.*

**pix·el** /'piksəl/ ▶*n.* any of the minute dots, etc., that comprise an image on a display screen.

**pix·i·lat·ed** /'piksə,lātid/ ▶*adj.* **1** crazy; confused. **2** drunk.

**piz·za** /'pētsə/ ▶*n.* flat round base of dough baked with a topping of tomatoes, cheese, onions, etc.

**piz·ze·ri·a** /,pētsə'rēə/ ▶*n.* place where pizzas are made or sold.

**piz·zi·ca·to** /,pitsi'kätō/ ▶*adv.* *Mus.* plucking the strings of a violin, cello, etc., with the finger.

**pkg.** ▶*abbr.* package.

**pl.** ▶*abbr.* **1** plural. **2** place.

**plac·ard** /'plakärd/ ▶*n.* large poster, esp. for advertising.

**pla·cate** /'plākāt/ ▶*v.* pacify; conciliate.

**place** /plās/ ▶*n.* **1 a** particular portion of space. **b** proper or natural position: *take your places.* **2** city, town, village, etc.: *was born in this place.* **3** residence; dwelling. **4** rank; status. **5** space, esp. a seat, for a person:

*two places in the coach.* **6** point reached in a book, etc.: *lost my place.* **7** particular spot on a surface. **8** employment or office.

▸*v.* **1** put (a thing, etc.) in a particular place or state; arrange. **2** identify, classify, or remember correctly. **3** assign to a particular place; locate. **4** assign rank, importance, or worth to. **5** make (an order for goods, etc.). —**place·ment** *n.*

**pla·ce·bo** /pləˈsēbō/ ▸*n.* **1** harmless pill, etc., prescribed more for psychological benefit than for any physiological effect. **2** substance having no therapeutic effect, used as a control in testing new drugs, etc.

**pla·cen·ta** /pləˈsentə/ ▸*n.* (*pl.* **-tae** or **-tas**) organ in the uterus of pregnant mammals that nourishes and maintains the fetus. —**pla·cen·tal** *adj.*

**plac·er** /ˈplāsər/ ▸*n.* deposit of sand or gravel in the bed of a river or lake, containing particles of valuable minerals.

**plac·id** /ˈplasid/ ▸*adj.* **1** (of a person) not easily aroused or disturbed; peaceful. **2** mild; calm; serene. —**pla·cid·i·ty** *n.* —**plac·id·ly** *adv.*

**plack·et** /ˈplakit/ ▸*n.* opening or slit in a garment.

**pla·gia·rize** /ˈplājəˌrīz/ ▸*v.* **1** take and use (the thoughts, writings, inventions, etc., of another person) as one's own. **2** pass off the thoughts, etc., of (another person) as one's own. —**pla·gia·rism** *n.*

**plague** /plāg/ ▸*n.* **1** deadly contagious disease. **2** unusual infestation of a pest, etc. ▸*v.* (**plagued**, **plagu·ing**) pester or harass continually.

**plaid** /plad/ ▸*n.* **1** any cloth with a tartan pattern. **2** this pattern.

**plain** /plān/ ▸*adj.* **1** clear; evident: *is plain to see.* **2** readily understood; simple: *in plain words.* **3** uncomplicated; unembellished; simple. **4** straightforward. ▸*adv.* **1** clearly. **2** simply: *that is plain stupid.* ▸*n.* level tract of esp. treeless country. —**plain·ly** *adv.* —**plain·ness** *n.*

**plain clothes** ▸*pl. n.* ordinary clothes rather than a uniform: *a detective in plain clothes.*

**plain·song** ▸*n.* unaccompanied church music sung in unison in medieval modes and in free rhythm.

**plain·tiff** /'plāntif/ ▸n. person who brings a case against another into court.

**plaint·ive** /'plāntiv/ ▸adj. 1 expressing sorrow; mournful. 2 mournful-sounding. —**plain·tive·ly** adv. —**plaint·ive·ness** n.

**plait** /plāt/ ▸n. single length of hair, etc., made up of three or more strands; braid. ▸v. form (hair, etc.) into a plait.

**plan** /plan/ ▸n. 1 method or procedure by which a thing is to be done; design or scheme. 2 drawing or diagram of a structure. ▸v. (**planned, plan·ning**) 1 arrange (a procedure, etc.) beforehand; form a plan. 2 design (a building, new town, etc.). 3 make plans. —**plan·ner** n. —**plan·ning** n.

**pla·nar** /'plānər/ ▸adj. of, relating to, or in the form of a plane.

**plane** /plān/ ▸n. 1 airplane. 2 level surface. 3 level of attainment, thought, knowledge, etc. 4 tool used to smooth a usu. wooden surface by paring shavings from it. 5 (also **plane tree**) tree with broad leaves and bark that peels in uneven patches. ▸v. smooth (wood, metal, etc.) with a plane. ▸adj. 1 (of a surface, etc.) perfectly level. 2 (of an angle, figure, etc.) lying in a plane.

**plan·et** /'planit/ ▸n. 1 celestial body moving in an elliptical orbit around a star. 2 the earth. —**plan·e·tar·y** adj.

**plan·e·tar·i·um** /ˌplani-'te(ə)rēəm/ ▸n. (pl. **-i·ums** or **-i·a**) domed building in which images of stars, planets, constellations, etc., are projected for public entertainment or education.

**plan·gent** /'planjənt/ ▸adj. (of a sound) loud, reverberating, and often sad. —**plan·gen·cy** n.

**plank** /plaNGk/ ▸n. 1 long flat piece of timber used esp. in building, flooring, etc. 2 item of a political or other program: *there was considerable opposition to several planks in the party's platform.*

**plank·ton** /'plaNGktən/ ▸n. chiefly microscopic organisms drifting or floating in the sea or fresh water.

**plant** /plant/ ▸n. 1 living organism usu. containing chlorophyll enabling it to live wholly on inorganic substances and lacking specialized sense organs and the power of voluntary movement. **2** factory.

▶*v.* **1** place (a seed, bulb, or growing thing) in the ground so that it may take root and flourish. **2** put or fix in position. **3** cause (an idea, etc.) to be established esp. in another person's mind. **4** deliver (a blow, kiss, etc.) with a deliberate aim.

**plan·tain** /ˈplantən/ ▶*n.* kind of banana plant widely grown for its starchy fruit.

**plan·tar** /ˈplantər/ ▶*adj.* of or relating to the sole of the foot.

**plan·ta·tion** /planˈtāsʜən/ ▶*n.* **1** estate on which cotton, tobacco, etc., is cultivated. **2** area planted with trees, etc.

**plaque** /plak/ ▶*n.* **1** ornamental or commemorative tablet. **2** deposit on teeth where bacteria proliferate.

**plas·ma** /ˈplazmə/ (also **plasm**) ▶*n.* **1** colorless fluid part of blood, lymph, or milk. **2** another term for **PROTOPLASM**. **3** gas of positive ions and free electrons in about equal numbers.

**plas·ter** /ˈplastər/ ▶*n.* soft pliable mixture, esp. of lime putty and sand or cement, for spreading on walls, ceilings, etc., to form a smooth hard surface when dried.

▶*v.* **1** cover (a wall, etc.) with plaster or a similar substance. **2** stick or apply (a thing) thickly like plaster. **3** make (esp. hair) smooth with water, gel, etc.

☐ **plaster of Paris** fine white plaster made of gypsum and used for making plaster casts, etc.

**plas·ter·board** ▶*n.* type of board with a center filling of plaster, used for partitions, walls, etc.

**plas·tic** /ˈplastik/ ▶*n.* **1** any of a number of synthetic polymeric substances that can be given any required shape. **2** *inf.* credit card, charge card, etc.

▶*adj.* **1** made of plastic: *plastic bag.* **2** capable of being molded; pliant; supple. —**plas·tic·i·ty** *n.*

**plas·tic sur·ger·y** ▶*n.* process of reconstructing or repairing parts of the body by the transfer of tissue, either in the treatment of injury or for cosmetic reasons.

**plate** /plāt/ ▶*n.* **1** shallow vessel from which food is eaten or served. **2** similar vessel used esp. for making a collection in a church, etc. **3 a** utensils of silver, gold, or other metal.

**b** objects of plated metal.
**4** piece of metal with a name or inscription for affixing to a door, container, etc. **5** illustration on special paper in a book. **6** thin sheet of metal, glass, etc., coated with a sensitive film for photography. **7** *inf.* denture. **8** each of several rigid sheets of rock thought to form the earth's outer crust. **9** *Baseball* base at which the batter stands and which a runner touches to scores.
▶*v.* **1** apply a thin coat esp. of silver, gold, or tin to (another metal). **2** cover (esp. a ship) with plates of metal, esp. for protection.

**pla·teau** /pla'tō/ ▶*n.* (*pl.* **-teaux** or **-teaus**) **1** area of fairly level high ground. **2** state of little variation after a time of activity.

**plate glass** ▶*n.* thick, fine-quality glass for storefront windows, etc., orig. cast in plates.

**plat·en** /'platn/ ▶*n.* plate in a printing press that presses the paper against the type.

**plat·er·esque** /ˌplatə'resk/ ▶*adj.* (esp. of Spanish architecture) richly ornamented in a low-relief style suggesting silver work.

**plate tec·ton·ics** ▶*n.* study of the earth's surface based on the concept of moving plates forming its structure.

**plat·form** /'plat,fôrm/ ▶*n.* **1** raised level surface, as for a speaker, for freight loading, etc. **2** declared policy of a political party.

**plat·i·num** /'platn-əm/ ▶*n.* ductile malleable silvery-white metallic element unaffected by simple acids and fusible only at a very high temperature. (Symb.: Pt)

**plat·i·tude** /'plati,t(y)ōod/ ▶*n.* trite or commonplace remark, esp. one solemnly delivered. —**plat·i·tu·di·nous** *adj.*

**Pla·ton·ic** /plə'tänik/ ▶*adj.* **1** of or associated with the Greek philosopher Plato (d. 347 BC) or his ideas. **2** (**platonic**) (of love or friendship) not sexual. —**Pla·ton·i·cal·ly** *adv.*

**pla·toon** /plə'tōon/ ▶*n.* **1** subdivision of a military company. **2** group of persons acting together.

**plat·ter** /'platər/ ▶*n.* large flat dish or plate, esp. for food.

**plat·y·pus** /'plati,pŏos/ ▶*n.* Australian aquatic egg-laying mammal having a pliable ducklike bill. (Also called **duck·bill**).

**plau·dits** ▸*pl. n.* tribute; applause.

**plau·si·ble** /ˈplôzəbəl/ ▸*adj.* **1** (of an argument, statement, etc.) seeming reasonable or probable. **2** (of a person) persuasive but deceptive. —**plau·si·bil·i·ty** *n.* —**plau·si·bly** *adv.*

**play** /plā/ ▸*v.* **1** occupy or amuse oneself pleasantly or idly. **2** act lightheartedly or flippantly (with feelings, etc.). **3 a** perform on or be able to perform on (a musical instrument). **b** perform (a piece of music, etc.). **c** cause (a record, radio, etc.) to produce sounds. **4** perform (a drama or role) on stage, or in a movie or broadcast. **5** behave or act as: *play the fool.* **6** perform (a trick or joke, etc.) on (a person). **7 a** take part in (a game or recreation). **b** occupy (a specified position) in a team for a game. ▸*n.* **1** recreation or amusement, esp. as the spontaneous activity of children and young animals. **2 a** playing of a game. **b** action or manner of this. **3** dramatic piece for the stage, etc. —**play·er** *n.* —**play·ful** *adj.* —**play·ful·ness** *n.*

**play·back** ▸*n.* act or instance of replaying recorded audio or video from a tape, etc.

**play·bill** ▸*n.* poster or program for a play.

**play·boy** ▸*n.* irresponsible pleasure-seeking man.

**play·ground** ▸*n.* outdoor area set aside for children to play.

**play·house** ▸*n.* **1** theater. **2** toy house for children to play in.

**play·mate** ▸*n.* child's companion in play.

**play·pen** ▸*n.* portable enclosure for young children to play in.

**play·thing** ▸*n.* toy.

**play·wright** /ˈplāˌrīt/ ▸*n.* person who writes plays.

**pla·za** /ˈpläzə/ ▸*n.* marketplace or open square (esp. in a town).

**plea** /plē/ ▸*n.* **1** earnest appeal or entreaty. **2** formal statement by or on behalf of a defendant.

**plea bar·gain** ▸*n.* arrangement between prosecutor and defendant whereby the defendant pleads guilty to a lesser charge in the expectation of leniency.

**plead** /plēd/ ▸*v.* (*past* and *past part.* **plead·ed** or **pled**) **1** make an earnest appeal. **2** *Law* address a court. **3** maintain (a cause) esp. in a court. **4** declare to be one's state as regards guilt in or responsibility for a crime: *plead guilty* | *plead insanity*.

**pleas·ance** /ˈplezəns/ ▶*n.* secluded enclosure or part of a garden, esp. one attached to a large house.

**pleas·ant** /ˈplezənt/ ▶*adj.* pleasing to the mind, feelings, or senses.

**pleas·ant·ry** ▶*n.* (*pl.* **-ries**) pleasant or amusing remark, esp. made in casual conversation.

**please** /plēz/ ▶*v.* **1** be agreeable to; give pleasure to. **2** think fit; have the will or desire: *take as many as you please.* **3** used in polite requests: *come in, please.*

**pleas·ur·a·ble** /ˈplezʜərəbəl/ ▶*adj.* causing pleasure; agreeable.

**pleas·ure** ▶*n.* **1** feeling of satisfaction or joy. **2** enjoyment. **3** source of pleasure or gratification. **4** a person's will or desire: *what is your pleasure?*

**pleat** /plēt/ ▶*n.* fold or crease, esp. a flattened fold in cloth doubled upon itself. ▶*v.* make a pleat or pleats in.

**ple·be·ian** /pliˈbēən/ ▶*adj.* **1** uncultured. **2** coarse; ignoble.

**pleb·i·scite** /ˈplebəˌsīt/ ▶*n.* direct, popular vote on an issue.

**plec·trum** /ˈplektrəm/ ▶*n.* (*pl.* **-trums** or **-tra**) thin flat piece of plastic or horn, etc., held in the hand and used to pluck a string, esp. of a guitar.

**pledge** /plej/ ▶*n.* **1** solemn promise or undertaking. **2** thing given as security for the fulfillment of a contract, the payment of a debt, etc. **3** thing given as a token. ▶*v.* **1** deposit as security. **2** promise solemnly by the pledge of (one's honor, word, etc.). **3** bind by a solemn promise.

**ple·iad** /ˈplēəd/ ▶*n.* outstanding group of seven people or things.

**ple·na·ry** /ˈplenərē/ ▶*adj.* **1** entire; unqualified; absolute. **2** (of an assembly) to be attended by all members.

**plen·i·po·ten·ti·ar·y** /ˌplenipəˈtensʜēˌerē/ ▶*n.* (*pl.* **-ies**) person (esp. a diplomat) invested with the full power of independent action. ▶*adj.* having this power.

**plen·i·tude** /ˈpleniˌt(y)ōōd/ ▶*n.* **1** fullness; completeness. **2** abundance.

**plen·ty** /ˈplentē/ ▶*n.* **1** great or

sufficient quantity or number. **2** abundance.

▸*adv. inf.* fully; entirely. —**plen·ti·ful** *adj.*

**ple·o·nasm** /'plēə,nazəm/ ▸*n.* use of more words than are necessary to convey meaning (e.g., *see with one's eyes*), either as a fault of style or for emphasis.

**pleth·o·ra** /'pleᴛʜərə/ ▸*n.* oversupply; glut; excess.

**pleu·ra** /'plŏŏrə/ ▸*n.* (pl. **-rae**) membrane enveloping the lungs.

**pleu·ri·sy** /'plŏŏrəsē/ ▸*n.* inflammation of the pleura, marked by pain in the chest or side, fever, etc.

**Plex·i·glas** /'pleksi,glas/ ▸*trademark* tough, clear thermoplastic used instead of glass.

**pli·a·ble** /'plīəbəl/ ▸*adj.* **1** bending easily; supple. **2** yielding; compliant.

**pli·ant** /'plīənt/ ▸*adj.* pliable.

**pli·ers** /'plīərz/ ▸*pl. n.* pincers with parallel flat usu. serrated surfaces for holding small objects, bending wire, etc.

**plight** /plīt/ ▸*n.* condition or state, esp. an unfortunate one.

▸*v. archaic* pledge or promise (one's loyalty).

**PLO** ▸*abbr.* Palestine Liberation Organization.

**plod** /pläd/ ▸*v.* (**plod·ded, plod·ding**) **1** walk doggedly or laboriously; trudge. **2** work slowly and steadily. —**plod·der** *n.* —**plod·ding·ly** *adv.*

**plop** /pläp/ ▸*n.* **1** sound as of a smooth object dropping into water without a splash. **2** act of falling with this sound.

▸*v.* fall or drop with a plop.

**plot** /plät/ ▸*n.* **1** conspiracy or secret plan. **2** interrelationship of the main events in a play, novel, movie, etc. **3** defined and usu. small piece of ground.

▸*v.* (**plot·ted, plot·ting**) **1** make a plan or map of. **2** plan or contrive secretly (a crime, conspiracy, etc.). **3** mark (a point or course, etc.) on a chart or diagram.

**plotz** /pläts/ ▸*v. inf.* collapse or be beside oneself with frustration, annoyance, or other strong emotion.

**plo·ver** /'pləvər; 'plō-/ ▸*n.* plump-breasted shorebird, e.g., the lapwing, the sandpiper, etc.

**plow** /plou/ ▸*n.* **1** implement for cutting furrows in the soil and turning it up. **2** implement resembling this: *snowplow.*

▸*v.* **1** turn up (the earth) with a plow, esp. before sowing. **2** advance laboriously, esp. through work, a book, etc.

**plow·share** ▸*n.* cutting blade of a plow.

**ploy** /ploi/ ▸*n.* cunning maneuver to gain advantage.

**pluck** /plək/ ▸*v.* **1** take hold of (something) and quickly remove from its place. **2** strip (a bird) of feathers. **3** catch hold of and pull quickly: *she plucked at his sleeve.* **4** sound (the string of a musical instrument) with the finger or plectrum, etc.

▸*n.* courage; spirit.

**pluck·y** /ˈpləkē/ ▸*adj.* (**-i·er**, **-i·est**) brave; spirited.

**plug** /pləg/ ▸*n.* **1** piece of solid material fitting tightly into a hole. **2** device fitting into holes in a socket for making an electrical connection. **3** *inf.* piece of (often free) publicity for an idea, product, etc. **4** cake or stick of tobacco; piece of this for chewing.

▸*v.* (**plugged**, **plug·ging**) **1** stop up (a hole, etc.) with a plug. **2** *inf.* shoot or hit (a person, etc.). **3** *inf.* mention (a product, establishment, etc.) publicly to promote it. **4** *inf.* work steadily away (at).

**plum** /pləm/ ▸*n.* **1** oval fleshy fruit with sweet pulp and a flattish stone. **2** reddish-purple color. **3** something especially prized.

**plum·age** /ˈplo͞omij/ ▸*n.* bird's feathers.

**plumb** /pləm/ ▸*n.* ball of lead or other heavy material, esp. one attached to the end of a line for finding the depth of water or determining the vertical on an upright surface.

▸*adv.* exactly: *plumb in the center.*

▸*v.* **1** sound or test with a plumb. **2** learn in detail the facts about (a matter).

**plumb·er** ▸*n.* person who fits and repairs the apparatus of a water-supply system.

**plumb·ing** ▸*n.* **1** system or apparatus of water supply, heating, etc., in a building. **2** work of a plumber.

**plume** /plo͞om/ ▸*n.* **1** feather, esp. a large one used for ornament. **2** ornament of feathers, etc., attached to a helmet or hat or worn in the hair. **3** something resembling this: *plume of smoke.*

▸*v.* (of a bird) preen (itself or its feathers).

**plum·met** /ˈpləmit/ ▶v. fall or plunge rapidly.

▶n. steep and rapid fall.

**plump** /pləmp/ ▶adj. having a full rounded shape; fleshy.

▶v. make or become plump.
—**plump·ly** adv. —**plump·ness** n.

**plun·der** /ˈpləndər/ ▶v. steal goods from (a person or place), typically using force and in a time of civil disorder.

▶n. **1** violent and dishonest acquisition of property. **2** property acquired illegally and violently.

**plunge** /plənj/ ▶v. **1** thrust forcefully or abruptly. **2** immerse completely. **3** move suddenly and dramatically downward.

▶n. plunging action or movement; dive.

**plung·er** ▶n. **1** part of a mechanism that works with a plunging or thrusting movement. **2** rubber cup on a handle for clearing blocked pipes.

**plu·ral** /ˈplo͝orəl/ ▶adj. **1** more than one in number. **2** Gram. (of a word or form) denoting more than one.

▶n. Gram. plural word or form.
—**plu·ral·ly** adv.

**plu·ral·ism** ▶n. form of society in which the members of minority groups maintain their independent cultural traditions.
—**plu·ral·is·tic** adj.

**plu·ral·i·ty** /plo͝oˈralitē/ ▶n. (pl. -ties) **1** state of being plural. **2** large number of people or things. **3** number of votes cast for a candidate who receives more than any other but not an absolute majority.

**plus** /pləs/ ▶prep. **1** with the addition of. **2** inf. together with.

▶adj. **1** (after a number) at least: *fifteen plus.* **2** (after a grade, etc.) somewhat better than. **3** having a positive electrical charge. **4** additional; extra.

▶n. **1** mathematical operation of addition. **2** advantage: *speaking a second language is a plus.*

□ **plus sign** the symbol + indicating addition or a positive value.

**plus ça change** /ˈplo͞o sä ˈSHäNZH/ ▶exclam. used to express resigned acknowledgment of the fundamental immutability of human nature and institutions.

**plush** /pləSH/ ▶n. cloth of silk, cotton, etc., with a long soft nap.

▸*adj.* **1** made of plush.
**2** luxurious.

**Plu·to** /ˈplo͞otō/ ▸*n.* outermost known planet of the solar system.

**plu·to·ni·um** /plo͞oˈtōnēəm/ ▸*n.* dense silvery radioactive metallic transuranic element. (Symb.: **Pu**)

**plu·vi·al** /ˈplo͞ovēəl/ ▸*adj.* of rain or caused by rain.

**ply** /plī/ ▸*n.* (*pl.* **plies**) **1** thickness or layer of wood, cloth, etc.: *three-ply.* **2** strand of yarn or rope, etc.
▸*v.* (**plied**) **1** use or wield vigorously (a tool, weapon, etc.). **2** work steadily at (one's business or trade). **3** supply (a person) continuously (with food, drink, etc.): *the flight attendant plied them with champagne.*

**ply·wood** ▸*n.* strong thin board consisting of two or more layers glued and pressed together.

**Pm** ▸*symb. Chem.* promethium.

**p.m.** ▸*abbr.* between noon and midnight (Latin *post meridiem*).

**PMS** ▸*abbr.* premenstrual syndrome.

**pneu·mat·ic** /n(y)o͞oˈmatik/ ▸*adj.* **1** filled with air or wind. **2** operated by compressed air. —**pneu·mat·i·cal·ly** *adv.*

**pneu·mo·nia** /n(y)o͞oˈmōnēə/ ▸*n.* bacterial or viral lung inflammation in which the air sacs fill with pus and may become solid.

**PO** ▸*abbr.* **1** Post Office. **2** postal order. **3** Petty Officer.

**Po** ▸*symb. Chem.* polonium.

**poach** /pōCH/ ▸*v.* **1** cook (an egg) without its shell in or over boiling water. **2** cook (fish, etc.) by simmering in a small amount of liquid.
▸*v.* **1** catch (game or fish) illegally. **2** trespass or encroach (on another's property, ideas, etc.). —**poach·er** *n.*

**pock·et** /ˈpäkit/ ▸*n.* **1** small bag sewn into or on clothing, for carrying small articles. **2** pouchlike compartment or holder. **3** isolated group or area: *pockets of resistance.*
▸*adj.* of a suitable size and shape for carrying in a pocket.
▸*v.* **1** put into one's pocket. **2** appropriate, esp. dishonestly.

**pock·et·book** ▸*n.* purse or handbag.

**pock·et knife** ▸*n.* knife with a folding blade or blades, for carrying in the pocket.

**pock·et ve·to** ▸*n.* executive

veto of a legislative bill by allowing it to go unsigned.

**pock·marked** ▶*adj.* marked by scars from smallpox, chicken pox, etc.

**pod** /päd/ ▶*n.* **1** long seed vessel esp. of a leguminous plant, e.g., a pea. **2** cocoon of a silkworm. **3** small herd of marine animals, esp. whales.

**po·di·a·try** /pə'dīətrē/ ▶*n.* treatment of the feet and their ailments. —**po·di·a·trist** *n.*

**po·di·um** /'pōdēəm/ ▶*n.* (*pl.* -**di·ums** or -**di·a**) platform or rostrum.

**po·em** /'pōəm/ ▶*n.* piece of creative writing expressing feelings, etc., through the use of metaphor, rhythm, meter, and sometimes rhyme.

**po·et** /'pōit/ ▶*n.* person who writes poetry.

**po·et·as·ter** /'pōət,astər/ ▶*n.* person who writes inferior poetry.

**po·et·ic** /pō'etik/ ▶*adj.* of or like poetry.

**po·et·ry** /'pōətrē/ ▶*n.* **1** art or work of a poet. **2** poems collectively. **3** poetic or tenderly pleasing quality.

**po·grom** /'pōgrəm/ ▶*n.* organized massacre (orig. of Jews in Russia).

**poign·ant** /'poinyənt/ ▶*adj.* **1** painfully sharp to the emotions or senses; deeply moving. **2** arousing sympathy. —**poign·an·cy** *n.*

**poin·set·ti·a** /poin'set(ē)ə/ ▶*n.* shrub with large usu. scarlet bracts surrounding small yellow flowers.

**point** /point/ ▶*n.* **1** sharp or tapered end of a tool, weapon, pencil, etc. **2** tip or extreme end. **3** that which in geometry has position but not magnitude. **4** particular place or position. **5** precise or critical moment. **6** very small mark on a surface. **7** decimal point. **8** stage or degree in progress or increase. **9** temperature at which a change of state occurs: *freezing point.* **10** single item; detail or particular. **11** unit of scoring in games or of measuring value, etc. **12** sense or purpose; advantage or value.

▶*v.* **1** direct or aim (a finger, weapon, etc.). **2** aim or be directed to. **3** indicate; be evidence of: *it all points to murder.*

**point·ed** ▶*adj.* **1** sharpened or

tapering to a point. **2** (of a remark, etc.) penetrating; cutting. —**point·ed·ly** *adv.*

**point·er** ▸*n.* **1** thing that points, e.g., the index hand of a gauge, etc. **2** rod for pointing to features on a map, chart, etc. **3** hint, clue, or indication. **4** dog of a breed that on scenting game stands rigid looking toward it.

**point·less** ▸*adj.* lacking force, purpose, or meaning.

**poise** /poiz/ ▸*n.* **1** composure. **2** equilibrium. **3** carriage (of the head, etc.). ▸*v.* balance or be balanced.

**poi·son** /'poizən/ ▸*n.* **1** substance causing an organism death or injury, esp. in a small quantity. **2** harmful influence. ▸*v.* **1** administer poison to. **2** kill, injure, or infect with poison. **3** corrupt; pervert; spoil. —**poi·son·ous** *adj.*

**poi·son i·vy** ▸*n.* climbing plant secreting an irritant oil from its leaves.

**poke** /pōk/ ▸*v.* **1 a** thrust or push with the hand, point of a stick, etc. **b** be thrust forward. **2** produce (a hole, etc., in a thing) by poking. ▸*n.* thrust; jab.

**pok·er** /'pōkər/ ▸*n.* **1** stiff metal rod for stirring an open fire. **2** card game in which bluff is used as players bet on the value of their hands.

**pok·y** /'pōkē/ ▸*adj.* (**-i·er, -i·est**) slow.

**po·lar** /'pōlər/ ▸*adj.* **1** of or near a pole of the earth. **2** having magnetic or electric polarity. **3** directly opposite in character. —**po·lar·i·ty** *n.*

□ **polar bear** white bear of the Arctic regions.

**Po·lar·is** /pō'le(ə)ris/ ▸*n.* fairly bright star within one degree of the north celestial pole in the constellation Ursa Minor. (Also called **North Star, pole·star.**)

**po·lar·i·ty** /pō'larilē; pə-/ ▸*n.* (*pl.* **-ties**) the property of having poles or being polar.

**po·lar·ize** /'pōlə,rīz/ ▸*v.* **1** restrict the vibrations of (a transverse wave, esp. light) wholly or partially to one direction. **2** cause (something) to acquire polarity. **3** divide or cause to divide into two sharply contrasting groups or sets of opinions or beliefs.

**pol·der** /'pōldər/ ▸*n.* piece of low-lying land reclaimed from the sea or a river and protected by dikes, esp. in the Netherlands.

**Pole** /pōl/ ▶*n.* **1** native or national of Poland. **2** person of Polish descent.

**pole** /pōl/ ▶*n.* **1** long slender rounded piece of wood or metal. **2** (also **north pole, south pole**) **a** each of the two points in the celestial sphere about which the stars appear to revolve. **b** each of the extremities of the axis of rotation of the earth or another body. **3** each of the two opposite points on the surface of a magnet at which magnetic forces are strongest. **4** each of two terminals (positive and negative) of an electric cell, battery, etc.

**pole·cat** ▶*n.* **1** small European brownish black, flesh-eating mammal of the weasel family. **2** skunk.

**po·lem·ics** /pə'lemiks/ ▶*n.* [sometimes treated as *pl.*] art or practice of disputation.

**pole vault** ▶*n.* sport of vaulting over a high bar with the aid of a long flexible pole.

▶*v.* take part in this sport.

**po·lice** /pə'lēs/ ▶*n.* **1** civil force of a government, responsible for maintaining public order. **2** its members. **3** force with similar functions: *transit police.*

▶*v.* **1** control (a country or area) by means of police. **2** provide with police. **3** keep order in; control; monitor.

**pol·i·cy** /'päləsē/ ▶*n.* (*pl.* **-cies**) **1** course or principle of action adopted or proposed by a government, party, business, individual, etc. **2** insurance contract.

**po·li·o·my·e·li·tis** /ˌpōlēōˌmīə-'lītis/ (also **po·li·o**) ▶*n.* infectious viral disease that affects the central nervous system and can cause temporary or permanent paralysis.

**Po·lish** /'pōlisH/ ▶*adj.* **1** of or relating to Poland. **2** of the Poles or their language.

▶*n.* language of Poland.

**pol·ish** /'pälisH/ ▶*v.* **1** make or become smooth or glossy, esp. by rubbing. **2** refine or improve; add finishing touches to.

▶*n.* **1** substance used for polishing. **2** smoothness or glossiness produced by friction. **3** refinement; elegance.

**po·lite** /pə'līt/ ▶*adj.* (**-lit·er, -lit·est**) **1** having good manners; courteous. **2** cultivated; cultured. **3** refined; elegant: *polite letters.* —**po·lite·ly** *adv.* —**po·lite·ness** *n.*

**pol·i·tesse** /ˌpälə'tes/ ▸n. formal politeness or etiquette.

**pol·i·tic** /'päliˌtik/ ▸adj. 1 (of an action) judicious; expedient. 2 (of a person) prudent; sagacious.
▸v. (**-ticked, -tick·ing**) engage in politics.

**po·lit·i·cal** ▸adj. 1 of or concerning government, or public affairs generally. 2 taking or belonging to a side in politics. 3 concerned with seeking status, authority, etc.: *political decision.* —**po·lit·i·cal·ly** *adv.*

**pol·i·ti·cian** /ˌpäli'tisʜən/ ▸n. 1 person who is professionally involved in politics, esp. as the holder of an elective office. 2 person who acts in a manipulative and devious way to gain advancement.

**po·lit·i·cize** /pə'litəˌsiz/ ▸v. give a political character to.

**pol·i·tics** /'päliˌtiks/ ▸n. 1 a art and science of government. b public life and affairs. 2 [treated as *pl.*] a particular set of ideas, principles, or commitments in politics: *what are his politics?* b activities concerned with seeking power, status, etc.

**pol·ka** /'pō(l)kə/ ▸n. lively dance of Bohemian origin in duple time.

**pol·ka dot** ▸n. round dot as one of many forming a regular pattern on a textile fabric, etc.

**poll** /pōl/ ▸n. 1 process of voting. 2 result of voting or number of votes recorded. 3 survey of opinion.
▸v. 1 record the opinion or vote of. 2 (of a candidate) receive (so many votes). —**poll·ster** *n.*

**pol·lard** /'pälərd/ ▸v. cut off the top and branches of (a tree) to encourage new growth at the top.
▸n. 1 tree whose top and branches have been cut off for this reason. 2 animal, e.g., a sheep or deer, that has lost its horns or cast its antlers.

**pol·len** /'pälən/ ▸n. fine dustlike grains discharged from the male part of a flower containing the gamete that fertilizes the female ovule. —**pol·li·na·tion** *n.*
☐ **pollen count** index of the amount of pollen in the air.

**poll tax** ▸n. tax levied on every adult, without reference to their income or resources.

**pol·lute** /pə'lo͞ot/ ▸v. 1 contaminate or defile (the environment). 2 make foul or filthy. **3** destroy the purity or sanctity of. **—pol·lu·tant** *adj. & n.* **—pol·lut·er** *n.* **—pol·lu·tion** *n.*

**po·lo** /ˈpōlō/ ▸*n.* game of Asian origin played on horseback with a long-handled mallet and wooden ball.

**po·lo·ni·um** /pəˈlōnēəm/ ▸*n.* rare radioactive metallic element. (Symb.: **Po**)

**pol·ter·geist** /ˈpōltərˌgīst/ ▸*n.* noisy mischievous ghost, esp. one manifesting itself by physical damage.

**pol·troon** /pälˈtro͞on/ ▸*n.* spiritless coward.

**poly-** /ˈpälē/ ▸*comb. form* **1** denoting many or much. **2** polymerized: *polyester.*

**pol·y·es·ter** /ˌpälēˈestər/ ▸*n.* type of synthetic fiber or resin.

**pol·y·eth·yl·ene** /ˌpälēˈeᴛʜəlēn/ ▸*n.* plastic polymer of ethylene used for packaging and insulating materials.

**po·lyg·a·my** /pəˈligəmē/ ▸*n.* practice of having more than one spouse at a time. **—po·lyg·a·mist** *n.* **—po·lyg·a·mous** *adj.*

**pol·y·gon** /ˈpäliˌgän/ ▸*n.* plane figure with many (usu. a minimum of three) sides and angles. **—po·lyg·o·nal** *adj.*

**pol·y·graph** ▸*n.* machine designed to detect and record changes in physiological characteristics (e.g., rates of pulse and breathing), used esp. as a lie-detector.

**pol·y·he·dron** /ˌpäliˈhēdrən/ ▸*n.* (*pl.* **-dra**) solid figure with many (usu. more than six) faces.

**pol·y·math** ▸*n.* **1** person of much or varied learning. **2** great scholar.

**pol·y·mer** /ˈpäləmər/ ▸*n.* compound composed of one or more large molecules that are formed from repeated units of smaller molecules. **—pol·y·mer·ic** *adj.* **—pol·y·mer·i·za·tion** *n.*

**pol·y·no·mi·al** /ˌpäləˈnōmēəl/ ▸*n.* expression of more than two algebraic terms. ▸*adj.* of or being a polynomial.

**pol·yp** /ˈpäləp/ ▸*n.* **1** simple organism with a tube-shaped body. **2** small growth on a mucous membrane.

**po·lyph·o·ny** /pəˈlifənē/ ▸*n.* (*pl.* **-nies**) contrapuntal music. **—pol·y·phon·ic** *adj.* **—po·lyph·o·nous** *adj.*

**po·ly·se·my** /ˈpäliˌsemē/ ▸*n.* coexistence of many possible meanings for a word or phrase.

**pol·y·sty·rene** /ˌpäliˈstīrēn/ ▶*n.* plastic polymer of styrene used for insulation and in packaging.

**pol·y·syn·thet·ic** /ˌpäləsinˈTHetik/ ▶*adj.* denoting or relating to a language characterized by complex words consisting of several morphemes, in which a single word may function as a whole sentence. Many American Indian languages are polysynthetic.

**pol·y·tech·nic** /ˌpäliˈteknik/ ▶*n.* institution of higher education offering courses in many esp. vocational or technical subjects. ▶*adj.* dealing with or devoted to various vocational or technical subjects.

**pol·y·the·ism** /ˈpälēTHēˌizəm/ ▶*n.* belief in or worship of more than one god. —**pol·y·the·ist** *n.*

**pol·y·un·sat·u·rat·ed** /ˌpälēənˈsaCHəˌrātid/ ▶*adj.* (of a compound, esp. a fat or oil molecule) containing several double or triple bonds and therefore capable of further reaction.

**po·made** /päˈmād/ ▶*n.* scented dressing for the hair and the skin of the head.

**pome·gran·ate** /ˈpäm(ə)ˌgranit/ ▶*n.* orange-sized fruit with a tough reddish outer skin and containing many seeds in a red pulp.

**pom·mel** /ˈpäməl/ ▶*n.* **1** knob, esp. at the end of a sword hilt. **2** upward projecting front part of a saddle.

▶*v.* another term for PUMMEL.

**pomp** /pämp/ ▶*n.* **1** splendid display; splendor. **2** vainglory: *pomps and vanities of this wicked world.*

**pom·pom** /ˈpämˌpäm/ (also **pom·pon**) ▶*n.* ornamental ball or tuft often worn on hats or clothing.

**pomp·ous** /ˈpämpəs/ ▶*adj.* self-important; affectedly grand or solemn. —**pom·pos·i·ty** *n.* —**pom·pous·ly** *adv.*

**pon·cho** /ˈpänCHō/ ▶*n.* (*pl.* **-chos**) blanket-like cloak with a slit in the middle for the head.

**pond** /pänd/ ▶*n.* fairly small body of still water formed naturally or by hollowing or embanking.

**pon·der** /ˈpändər/ ▶*v.* think (over); muse (about).

**pon·der·ous** ▶*adj.* **1** heavy; unwieldy. **2** laborious. **3** (of style, etc.) dull; tedious. —**pon·der·ous·ly** *adv.* —**pon·der·ous·ness** *n.*

**pon·ti·fex** /ˈpäntəˌfeks/ ▶n. (pl. **pon·tif·i·ces** /pänˈtifəˌsēz/) (in ancient Rome) a member of the principal college of priests.

**pon·tiff** /ˈpäntəf/ ▶n. pope.

**pon·tif·i·cate** /pänˈtifiˌkāt/ ▶v. be pompously dogmatic.

**pon·toon** /ˌpänˈto͞on/ ▶n. **1** flat-bottomed boat. **2** each of several boats, hollow metal cylinders, etc., used to support a temporary bridge. **3** float for a seaplane.

**po·ny** /ˈpōnē/ ▶n. (pl. **-nies**) **1** horse of any small breed. **2** small drinking glass. **3** (**the ponies**) inf. racehorses: *he spent his inheritance playing the ponies.*

**po·ny·tail** ▶n. person's hair drawn back, tied, and hanging down like a pony's tail.

**poo·dle** /ˈpo͞odl/ ▶n. dog of a breed with a curly coat that is usually clipped.

**pooh-bah** /ˈpo͞o ˌbä/ (also **Pooh-Bah**) ▶n. person having much influence or holding many offices at the same time, esp. one perceived as pompously self-important.

**pool** /po͞ol/ ▶n. **1** small body of water or other liquid. **2** pool for swimming. **3** common supply of persons, vehicles, commodities, etc., for sharing by a group: *car pool.* **4 a** joint commercial venture. **b** common funding for this. **5** any of several games similar to billiards played on a pool table with usu. 16 balls.

▶v. **1** put (resources, etc.) into a common fund. **2** share (things) in common.

**poop** /po͞op/ ▶n. stern of a ship; aftermost and highest deck.

**poor** /po͝or/ ▶adj. **1** lacking adequate money or means to live comfortably. **2** (**poor in**) deficient in (a possession or quality). **3 a** scanty; inadequate: *a poor crop.* **b** less good than is usual or expected: *poor visibility.* —**poor·ly** adv.

**pop** /päp/ ▶n. **1** sudden sharp explosive sound as of a cork when drawn. **2** inf. effervescent soft drink. **3** inf. father.

▶v. (**popped, pop·ping**) **1** make or cause to make a pop. **2** put or move quickly or suddenly. **3** (of a ball) rise up into the air.

▶adj. inf. **1** in a popular or modern style. **2** performing popular music, etc.: *pop star.*

▶n. pop music.

□ **pop art** art based on modern popular culture and the mass media. □ **pop culture** commercial culture based on popular taste.

**pop.** ▶*abbr.* population.

**pop·corn** ▶*n.* **1** corn whose kernels burst open when heated. **2** these kernels when popped.

**pope** /pōp/ (also **Pope**) ▶*n.* head of the Roman Catholic Church.

**pop·in·jay** /ˈpäpənˌjā/ ▶*n.* fop; conceited person.

**pop·lar** /ˈpäplər/ ▶*n.* tree with a usu. rapidly growing trunk and tremulous leaves.

**pop·lin** /ˈpäplən/ ▶*n.* plain woven fabric usu. of cotton, with a corded surface.

**pop·o·ver** ▶*n.* light puffy hollow muffin made from an egg-rich batter.

**pop·py** ▶*n.* (*pl.* **-pies**) plant with showy often red flowers and a milky sap.

**pop·u·lace** /ˈpäpyələs/ ▶*n.* the common people.

**pop·u·lar** /ˈpäpyələr/ ▶*adj.* **1** liked or admired by many people or by a specified group: *a popular hero.* **2 a** of or carried on by the general public: *popular meetings.* **b** prevalent among the general public: *popular discontent.* **3** adapted to the understanding, taste, or means of the people: *popular science.*

—**pop·u·lar·i·ty** *n.* —**pop·u·lar·ly** *adv.*

**pop·u·late** /ˈpäpyəˌlāt/ ▶*v.* **1** inhabit; form the population of (a town, country, etc.). **2** supply with inhabitants.

**pop·u·la·tion** ▶*n.* **1** inhabitants. **2** total number of these or any group of living things.

**pop·u·lous** /ˈpäpyələs/ ▶*adj.* thickly inhabited.

**por·ce·lain** /ˈpôrs(ə)lən/ ▶*n.* **1** hard vitrified translucent ceramic. **2** objects made of this.

**porch** /pôrCH/ ▶*n.* **1** covered shelter for the entrance of a building. **2** veranda.

**por·cu·pine** /ˈpôrkyəˌpīn/ ▶*n.* rodent having defensive spines or quills.

**pore** /pôr/ ▶*n.* minute opening in a surface through which gases, liquids, or fine solids may pass. ▶*v.* (**pore over/through**) be absorbed in studying (a book, etc.).

**pork** /pôrk/ ▶*n.* the (esp. unsalted) flesh of a pig, used as food.

**pork bar·rel** ▶*n. inf.* use of government funds for projects designed to gain votes.

**por·nog·ra·phy** /pôrˈnägrəfē/ ▶*n.* explicit description or

exhibition of sexual activity in literature, films, etc.
—**por·nog·ra·pher** *n.*
—**por·no·graph·ic** *adj.*

**po·rous** /'pôrəs/ ▸*adj.* **1** full of pores. **2** letting through air, water, etc. —**po·ros·i·ty** *n.*
—**po·rous·ly** *adv.*

**por·poise** /'pôrpəs/ ▸*n.* sea mammal of the whale family with a low triangular dorsal fin and a blunt rounded snout.

**por·ridge** /'pôrij/ ▸*n.* dish consisting of oatmeal or another cereal boiled in water or milk.

**por·rin·ger** /'pôrənjər/ ▸*n.* small bowl, often with a handle, for soup, stew, etc.

**port** /pôrt/ ▸*n.* **1** harbor. **2** town with a harbor. **3** opening in the side of a ship for entrance, loading, etc. **4** left side (looking forward) of a ship, boat, or aircraft. **5** strong, sweet, dark red (occas. brown or white) fortified wine of Portugal.
□ **port of call** place where a ship or a person stops on a journey.

**por·ta·ble** /'pôrtəbəl/ ▸*adj.* easily movable; convenient for carrying.
▸*n.* portable object, e.g., a television, computer, etc.
—**por·ta·bil·i·ty** *n.*

**por·tage** /'pôrtij/ ▸*n.* **1** carrying of boats or goods between two navigable waters. **2** place at which this is necessary.

**por·tal** /'pôrtl/ ▸*n.* doorway, gate, etc., esp. a large and elaborate one.

**port·cul·lis** /pôrt'kələs/ ▸*n.* strong heavy grating lowered to block a gateway in a fortress, etc.

**por·tend** /pôr'tend/ ▸*v.* foreshadow as an omen.
—**por·tent** *n.*

**por·ter** ▸*n.* **1** person employed to carry luggage, etc., at an airport, hotel, etc. **2** gatekeeper or doorkeeper.

**port·fo·li·o** /pôrt'fōlē,ō/ ▸*n.* (*pl.* **-os**) **1** case for keeping loose sheets of paper, drawings, etc. **2** range of investments held by a person, a company, etc. **3** samples of an artist's work.

**port·hole** ▸*n.* glassed-in aperture in a ship's or aircraft's side for the admission of light.

**por·ti·co** /'pôrti,kō/ ▸*n.* (*pl.* **-coes** or **-cos**) roof supported by columns, usu. attached as a porch to a building.

**por·tière** /,pôrtē'er; -'tye(ə)r/ (also **por·tiere**) ▸*n.* curtain hung over a door or doorway.

**por·tion** /ˈpôrsʜən/ ▸n. **1** part or share. **2** amount of food allotted to one person. **3** one's destiny or lot.

**port·ly** ▸adj. (**-li·er, -li·est**) corpulent; stout. **—port·li·ness** n.

**port·man·teau** /pôrtˈmantō/ ▸n. (pl. **-teaus** or **-teaux**) leather trunk for clothes, etc., opening into two equal parts.

**port·man·teau word** ▸n. word blending the sounds and combining the meanings of two others, for example *motel* (from 'motor' and 'hotel') or *brunch* (from 'breakfast' and 'lunch').

**por·trait** /ˈpôrtrət; -ˌtrāt/ ▸n. **1** representation of a person or animal, esp. of the face, made by drawing, painting, photography, etc. **2** verbal picture; graphic description. **3** (in graphic design, etc.) format in which the height of an illustration, etc., is greater than the width.

**por·trait·ist** ▸n. person who makes portraits.

**por·tray** /pôrˈtrā/ ▸v. **1** make a likeness of. **2** describe graphically. **—por·tray·al** n.

**Por·tu·guese** /ˈpôrcʜəˌgēz/ ▸n. (pl. same) **1 a** native or national of Portugal. **b** person of Portuguese descent. **2** language of Portugal.

▸adj. of or relating to Portugal or its people or language.

**pose** /pōz/ ▸v. **1** assume a certain attitude of body, esp. when being photographed or being painted for a portrait. **2** pretend to be (another person, etc.): *posing as a celebrity.* **3** behave affectedly in order to impress others. **4** put forward or present (a question, etc.).

▸n. **1** attitude of body or mind. **2** affectation; pretense.

**po·seur** /pōˈzər/ (fem. **po·seuse**) ▸n. person who poses for effect or behaves affectedly.

**posh** /päsʜ/ ▸adj. inf. elegant; stylish.

**pos·it** /ˈpäzit/ ▸v. **1** assume as a fact; postulate. **2** put in place or position.

**po·si·tion** /pəˈziSʜən/ ▸n. **1** place occupied by a person or thing. **2** placement or arrangement. **3** proper place: *in position.* **4** advantage: *jockey for position.* **5** viewpoint. **6** person's situation in relation to others. **7** rank; status. **8** paid employment.

▸v. place in position.

**pos·i·tive** /ˈpäzitiv/ ▶*adj.*
**1** explicit; definite: *positive proof.*
**2** (of a person) convinced, confident, or overconfident in his or her opinion.
**3 a** constructive; directional. **b** optimistic. **4** (of a test or experiment) indicating the presence of something.
**5** tending toward increase or progress. **6** greater than zero.
**7** of, containing, or producing the kind of electrical charge opposite to that carried by electrons. **8** (of a photographic image) showing lights and shades or colors true to the original.

▶*n.* positive photograph, quantity, etc. —**pos·i·tive·ly** *adv.*

**pos·i·tiv·ism** /ˈpäzətivˌizəm; ˈpäztiv-/ ▶*n.* **1** philosophical system that holds that every rationally justifiable assertion can be scientifically verified or is capable of logical or mathematical proof, and that therefore rejects metaphysics and theism. **2** theory that laws are to be understood as social rules, valid because they are enacted by authority or derive logically from existing decisions, and that ideal or moral considerations (e.g., that a rule is unjust) should not limit the scope or operation of the law. **3** state or quality of being positive.

**pos·i·tron** /ˈpäziˌträn/ ▶*n.* elementary particle with a positive charge equal to the negative charge of an electron and having the same mass as an electron.

**po·sol·o·gy** /pəˈzäləjē/ ▶*n.* part of medicine concerned with dosage.

**pos·se** /ˈpäsē/ ▶*n.* (also **pos·se co·mi·ta·tus**) body of armed men summoned by a sheriff to enforce the law.

**pos·sess** /pəˈzes/ ▶*v.* **1** hold as property; own. **2** have a faculty, quality, etc. **3** occupy; dominate the mind of: *possessed by fear.* —**pos·ses·sor** *n.*

**pos·ses·sion** ▶*n.* **1** owning. **2** something owned. **3** being possessed by an evil spirit.

**pos·ses·sive** ▶*adj.* **1** having a desire to possess or retain what one already owns. **2** jealous and domineering. **3** *Gram.* indicating possession.
▶*n. Gram.* (also **possessive case**) case of nouns and pronouns expressing possession.

—pos·ses·sive·ly *adv.*
—pos·ses·sive·ness *n.*

**pos·set** /'päsət/ ▶*n.* drink made of hot milk curdled with ale, wine, or other alcoholic liquor and typically flavored with spices, drunk as a delicacy or as a remedy for colds.

**pos·si·ble** /'päsəbəl/ ▶*adj.* **1** capable of existing, happening, being done, etc. **2** potential: *possible way of doing it.*
—pos·si·bil·i·ty *n.* —pos·si·bly *adj.*

**pos·sum** /'päsəm/ ▶*n. inf.* opossum.
□ **play possum** pretend to be asleep or unconscious.

**post** /pōst/ ▶*n.* **1** piece of timber or metal set upright in the ground, etc., used as a support, marker, etc. **2** mail. **3** place where a soldier is stationed or which he or she patrols. **4** place of duty.
▶*v.* **1** attach (a paper, etc.) in a prominent place. **2** announce or advertise by placard or in a published text. **3** place or station (soldiers, an employee, etc.).

**post-** ▶*prefix* after in time or order: *postwar.*

**post·age** /'pōstij/ ▶*n.* amount charged for sending a letter, etc., by mail.
□ **postage stamp** official stamp affixed to a letter, etc., indicating the amount of postage paid.

**post·al** /'pōstəl/ ▶*adj.* of or by mail.

**post·card** ▶*n.* card for sending by mail.

**post·date** ▶*v.* affix a date later than the actual one to (a document, etc.)

**post·er** ▶*n.* **1** placard in a public place. **2** large printed picture.

**pos·te·ri·or** /pä'sti(ə)rēər; pō-/ ▶*adj.* **1** later; coming after in series, order, or time. **2** at the back.
▶*n.* buttocks.

**pos·ter·i·ty** /pä'sterətē/ ▶*n.* **1** all succeeding generations. **2** descendants of a person.

**post·grad·u·ate** ▶*adj.* **1** (of a course of study) carried on after receiving a high school or college degree. **2** of or relating to postgraduate students.

**post·haste** ▶*adv.* with great speed.

**post·hu·mous** /'päsCHəməs/ ▶*adj.* **1** occurring after death. **2** (of a child) born after the death of its father. **3** (of a book, etc.) published after the author's death. —**post·hu·mous·ly** *adv.*

**post·man** ▸*n.* (*pl.* **-men**) person employed to deliver and collect letters, etc.

**post·mark** ▸*n.* official dated postage cancellation mark stamped on a letter.

▸*v.* mark (an envelope, etc.) with this.

**post·mas·ter** ▸*n.* person in charge of a post office.

**post·mor·tem** /pōst'môrtəm/ ▸*n.* **1** (also **post·mor·tem ex·am·i·na·tion**) examination made after death, esp. to determine its cause. **2** discussion analyzing the course and result of a game, election, etc.

▸*adv. & adj.* happening after death.

**post·na·tal** ▸*adj.* characteristic of or relating to the period after childbirth.

**post of·fice** ▸*n.* public department or corporation responsible for postal services.

**post·paid** ▸*adj.* on which postage has been paid.

**post·par·tum** /ˌpōst'pärtəm/ ▸*adj.* following childbirth.

**post·pone** /pōst'pōn/ ▸*v.* cause or arrange (an event, etc.) to take place at a later time. —**post·pone·ment** *n.*

**post·script** ▸*n.* additional paragraph or remark, usu. at the end of a letter, introduced by 'P.S.'

**pos·tu·lant** /'päsCHələnt/ ▸*n.* candidate, esp. one seeking admission into a religious order.

**pos·tu·late** /'päsCHəˌlāt/ ▸*v.* assume as a necessary condition, esp. as a basis for reasoning; take for granted.

▸*n.* fundamental prerequisite or condition. —**pos·tu·la·tion** *n.*

**pos·ture** /'päsCHər/ ▸*n.* **1** bodily carriage or bearing. **2** mental or spiritual attitude or condition. **3** condition or state (of affairs, etc.): *in more diplomatic postures.*

▸*v.* assume a mental or physical attitude, esp. for effect.

**po·sy** /'pōzē/ ▸*n.* (*pl.* **-sies**) small bunch of flowers.

**pot** /pät/ ▸*n.* **1** vessel, usu. rounded, for holding liquids or solids or for cooking in. **2** total amount of the bet in a game, etc. **3** *inf.* large sum: *pots of money.* **4** *inf.* marijuana.

▸*v.* (**pot·ted**, **pot·ting**) place in a pot.

**po·ta·ble** /'pōtəbəl/ ▸*adj.* drinkable. —**po·ta·bil·i·ty** *n.*

**po·tage** /pô'täzh/ ▶*n.* thick soup.

**pot·ash** /'pät,ash/ ▶*n.* alkaline potassium compound.

**po·tas·si·um** /pə'tasēəm/ ▶*n.* soft silvery white metallic element. (Symb.: **K**)

**po·ta·to** /pə'tātō/ ▶*n.* (*pl.* **-toes**) **1** starchy plant tuber that is cooked and used for food. **2** plant bearing this.

**pot·bel·ly** ▶*n.* (*pl.* **-ies**) **1** protruding stomach. **2** person with this. **3** (also **pot·bel·ly stove**) small bulbous wood-burning stove.

**pot·boil·er** ▶*n.* work of literature or art done merely to make the writer or artist a living.

**po·tent** /'pōtnt/ ▶*adj.* **1** powerful; strong. **2** (of a reason) cogent; forceful. **3** (of a male) capable of sexual erection or orgasm. —**po·ten·cy** *n.*

**po·ten·tate** /'pōtn,tāt/ ▶*n.* monarch or ruler.

**po·ten·tial** /pə'tenchəl/ ▶*adj.* capable of coming into being or action; latent. ▶*n.* capacity for use or development; possibility. —**po·ten·ti·al·i·ty** *n.* —**po·ten·tial·ly** *adv.*

**po·ten·ti·ate** /pə'tenchē,āt/ ▶*v.* increase the power, effect, or likelihood of (something, esp. a drug or physiological reaction).

**pot·hole** ▶*n.* **1** deep hole, as in rock. **2** hole in a road surface.

**po·tion** /'pōshən/ ▶*n.* liquid medicine, drug, poison, etc.

**pot·latch** /'pät,lach/ ▶*n.* (among North American Indian peoples of the northwest coast) an opulent ceremonial feast at which possessions are given away or destroyed to display wealth or enhance prestige. ▶*v.* hold such a feast or ceremony.

**pot·luck** ▶*n.* **1** whatever (hospitality, food, etc.) is available. **2** meal to which each guest brings a dish to share.

**pot·pour·ri** /pōpŏo'rē/ ▶*n.* mixture of dried petals and spices used to perfume a room, etc.

**pot·sherd** /'pät,shərd/ ▶*n.* broken piece of ceramic material, esp. one found on an archaeological site.

**pot·shot** ▶*n.* random shot.

**pot·ter** ▶*n.* maker of ceramic vessels. □ **potter's wheel** horizontal revolving disk on which wet clay is shaped into round ceramic vessels.

**pot·ter's field** ▸*n.* burial place for paupers, strangers, etc.

**pot·ter·y** ▸*n.* (*pl.* **-ies**) **1** vessels, etc., made of fired clay. **2** potter's work. **3** potter's workshop.

**pouch** /pouCH/ ▸*n.* **1** small bag or detachable outside pocket. **2** pocketlike receptacle of kangaroos, etc.

**poul·tice** /ˈpōltis/ ▸*n.* soft medicated and usu. heated mass applied to the body for relieving soreness and inflammation.

**poul·try** /ˈpōltrē/ ▸*n.* domestic fowls (ducks, geese, turkeys, chickens, etc.), esp. as a source of food.

**pounce** /pouns/ ▸*v.* **1** spring or swoop, esp. as in capturing prey. **2** (**pounce on/upon**) make a sudden attack.

**pound** /pound/ ▸*n.* **1** unit of weight equal to 16 oz. avoirdupois or 12 oz. troy. (Abbr.: **lb.**) **2** (also **pound sterling**) (*pl.* same or **pounds**) chief monetary unit of the UK and several other countries. **3** enclosure where stray animals or officially removed vehicles are kept until redeemed.

▸*v.* **1** crush or beat with repeated heavy blows. **2** (of the heart) beat heavily. —**pound·age** *n.*

□ **pound sign 1** the sign #. **2** the sign £, representing pound sterling.

**pour** /pôr/ ▸*v.* **1** flow or cause to flow, esp. downward. **2** fall heavily: *it poured all night.* **3** come or go in profusion or rapid succession: *letters poured in.*

**pout** /pout/ ▸*v.* push the lips forward as an expression of displeasure or sulking. ▸*n.* such an action or expression. —**pout·y** *adj.*

**pov·er·ty** /ˈpävərtē/ ▸*n.* **1** being poor; need. **2** scarcity or lack.

**POW** ▸*abbr.* prisoner of war.

**pow·der** /ˈpoudər/ ▸*n.* **1** substance in the form of fine dry particles. **2** medicine or cosmetic in this form. ▸*v.* **1** apply powder to. **2** reduce to a fine powder: *powdered milk.* —**pow·der·y** *adj.*

**pow·er** /ˈpouər/ ▸*n.* **1** the ability to do or act: *will do all in my power.* **2** government, influence, or authority; control: *the party in power.* **3** authorization; delegated authority: *police powers.* **4** influential person, body, government, etc. **5** vigor; energy. **6** active property or function. **7** mechanical or electrical energy as distinct from hand labor: *power tools.* **8** public supply of (esp. electrical) energy. **9** product obtained when a number is multiplied by itself a certain number of times: *2 to the power of 3 = 8.* **10** magnifying capacity of a lens.

▸*v.* supply with mechanical or electrical energy. —**pow·er·ful** *adj.* —**pow·er·ful·ly** *adv.* —**pow·er·less** *adj.*

**pow·er·house** ▸*n. inf.* person or thing of great energy.

**pow·er of at·tor·ney** ▸*n.* legal authority to act for another person in specified matters.

**pow·er plant** ▸*n.* **1** facility producing esp. electrical power. **2** source of power, as an engine.

**pow·wow** /'pouˌwou/ ▸*n.* a meeting for discussion (orig. among Native Americans).

▸*v.* hold a powwow.

**pox** /päks/ ▸*n.* **1** any virus disease producing a rash of pimples that leave pockmarks on healing. **2** *inf.* SYPHILIS.

**pp** ▸*abbr.* pianissimo.

**pp.** ▸*abbr.* pages.

**ppd.** ▸*abbr.* **1** postpaid. **2** prepaid.

**PPS** ▸*abbr.* additional postscript.

**PR** ▸*abbr.* **1** public relations. **2** Puerto Rico.

**Pr** ▸*symb. Chem.* praseodymium.

**pr.** ▸*abbr.* pair.

**prac·ti·ca·ble** /'praktikəbəl/ ▸*adj.* **1** that can be done or used. **2** possible in practice.

**prac·ti·cal** ▸*adj.* **1** of or concerned with practice or use rather than theory. **2** useful; functional. **3** (of a person) inclined to action rather than speculation; able to make things function well. **4** feasible; concerned with what is actually possible: *practical politics.* —**prac·ti·cal·i·ty** *n.*

**prac·ti·cal joke** ▸*n.* humorous trick played on a person.

**prac·ti·cal·ly** ▸*adv.* **1** virtually; almost: *practically nothing.* **2** in a practical way.

**prac·tice** /'praktəs/ ▸*n.* **1** habitual action or performance. **2** habit or custom: *has been my regular practice.* **3 a** repeated exercise in an activity requiring the development of skill. **b** session of this. **4** action or execution as opposed to theory. **5** the professional work or business of a doctor, lawyer, etc.

▶ *v.* **1** perform habitually; carry out in action. **2** do repeatedly as an exercise to improve a skill; exercise oneself in or on (an activity requiring skill). **3** pursue or be engaged in (a profession, religion, etc.).

**prac·ti·tio·ner** /prak'tisHənər/ ▶ *n.* person practicing a profession, esp. medicine: *general practitioner.*

**prag·mat·ic** /prag'matik/ ▶ *adj.* dealing with matters with regard to their practical requirements or consequences. —**prag·ma·tist** *n.*

**prag·ma·tism** /'pragmə,tizəm/ ▶ *n.* **1** pragmatic attitude or policy. **2** approach that assesses the truth of meaning of theories or beliefs in terms of the success of their practical application.

**prai·rie** /'pre(ə)rē/ ▶ *n.* large area of usu. treeless grassland esp. in central N. America.

□ **prairie dog** N. American rodent living in burrows and making a barking sound.

**praise** /prāz/ ▶ *v.* **1** express warm approval or admiration of. **2** glorify (God) in words.

▶ *n.* praising; commendation: *won high praise.*

**praj·na** /'prazHnə/ ▶ *n.* direct insight into the truth taught by the Buddha, as a faculty required to attain enlightenment.

**pra·line** /'prā,lēn/ ▶ *n.* any of several candies made with almonds, pecans, etc., and sugar.

**prance** /prans/ ▶ *v.* **1** (of a horse) raise the forelegs and spring from the hind legs. **2** walk or behave in an arrogant manner. —**pranc·er** *n.*

**prank** /praNGk/ ▶ *n.* practical joke; piece of mischief.

**pra·se·o·dym·i·um** /,prāzēō-'dimēəm/ ▶ *n.* metallic element. (Symb.: **Pr**)

**prat·tle** /'pratl/ ▶ *v.* chatter or say in a childish or inconsequential way.

▶ *n.* **1** childish chatter. **2** inconsequential talk.

**prawn** /prôn/ ▶ *n.* edible shrimplike shellfish.

**pray** /prā/ ▶ *v.* **1** say prayers (to God, etc.); make devout supplication. **2** ask earnestly; entreat; beseech.

□ **praying mantis** see MANTIS.

**prayer** /'pre(ə)r/ ▶ *n.* **1** solemn request or thanksgiving to God. **2** formula used in praying: *the*

*Lord's prayer.* **3** act of praying: *be at prayer.* **4** entreaty to a person. —**prayer·ful** *adj.*

**pre-** /prē/ ▶*prefix* before (in time, place, order, degree, or importance).

**preach** /prēCH/ ▶*v.* **1** deliver (a sermon); proclaim or expound. **2** give moral advice in an obtrusive way. **3** advocate or inculcate (a quality or practice, etc.). —**preach·er** *n.*

**pre·am·ble** /'prē,ambəl/ ▶*n.* **1** preliminary statement or introduction. **2** introductory part of a constitution, statute, or deed, etc.

**pre·can·cer·ous** ▶*adj.* having the tendency to develop into a cancer.

**pre·car·i·ous** /pri'ke(ə)rēəs/ ▶*adj.* **1** uncertain; dependent on chance: *makes a precarious living.* **2** insecure; perilous: *precarious health.* —**pre·car·i·ous·ly** *adv.*

**pre·cau·tion** /pri'kôSHən/ ▶*n.* **1** action taken beforehand to avoid risk or ensure a good result. **2** caution exercised beforehand; prudent foresight. —**pre·cau·tion·ary** *adj.*

**pre·cede** /pri'sēd/ ▶*v.* come or go before in time, order, importance, etc.

**prec·e·dence** /'presidəns/ ▶*n.* priority in time, order, or importance, etc.

**prec·e·dent** /'president/ ▶*n.* **1** earlier event or action regarded as an example to be considered in subsequent similar circumstances. **2** previous case or legal decision, etc., taken as a guide for subsequent cases. ▶*adj.* preceding in time, order, importance, etc.

**pre·cept** /'prē,sept/ ▶*n.* rule or guide, esp. for conduct.

**pre·cep·tor** ▶*n.* teacher or instructor.

**pre·cinct** /'prē,siNGkt/ ▶*n.* **1** enclosed or specially designated area. **2** (**precincts**) environs. **3** official district, esp. for police or electoral purposes.

**pre·cious** /'preSHəs/ ▶*adj.* **1** of great value or worth. **2** beloved; much prized: *precious memories.* **3** affectedly refined. □ **precious metals** gold, silver, and platinum.

**prec·i·pice** /'presəpəs/ ▶*n.* vertical or steep face of a rock, cliff, mountain, etc.

**pre·cip·i·tate** ▶*v.* /pri'sipi,tāt/ **1** hasten the occurrence of; cause to occur prematurely. **2** throw down headlong. **3** cause (a substance) to be deposited in solid form from a solution. **4 a** condense (vapor) into drops and so deposit it. **b** fall as rain, snow, etc.

▶*adj.* /pri'sipitit/ **1** headlong; violently hurried: *precipitate departure.* **2** (of a person or act) hasty; rash; inconsiderate.

▶*n.* /pri'sipitit/ **1** substance precipitated from a solution. **2** moisture condensed in the form of rain, snow, etc. —**pre·cip·i·tate·ly** *adv.* —**pre·cip·i·ta·tion** *adv.*

**pre·cip·i·tous** ▶*adj.* **1** dangerously high or steep. **2** (of a change) sudden and dramatic. **3** (of an action) done suddenly and without careful consideration. —**pre·cip·i·tous·ly** *adv.*

**précis** /'prāsē/ ▶*n.* (*pl.* same) summary; abstract.

**pre·cise** /pri'sīs/ ▶*adj.* **1 a** accurately expressed. **b** definite; exact. **2** scrupulous in being exact. —**pre·cise·ly** *adv.* —**pre·cise·ness** *n.* —**pre·ci·sion** *n.*

**pre·clude** /pri'klo͞od/ ▶*v.* prevent from happening.

**pre·co·cious** /pri'kōsHəs/ ▶*adj.* **1** (of a person, esp. a child)

prematurely developed in some faculty or characteristic. **2** (of an action, etc.) indicating such development. —**pre·coc·i·ty** *n.*

**pre·cog·ni·tion** /ˌprēkäg-'nisHən/ ▶*n.* (supposed) foreknowledge, esp. of a supernatural kind. —**pre·cog·ni·tive** *adj.*

**pre·con·ceive** ▶*v.* form (an idea or opinion, etc.) beforehand.

**pre·con·di·tion** ▶*n.* prior condition that must be fulfilled before other things can be done.

**pre·cur·sor** /'prēˌkərsər/ ▶*n.* **1** harbinger. **2** forerunner.

**pre·da·cious** /pri'dāsHəs/ (also **pre·da·ceous**) ▶*adj.* (of an animal) predatory.

**pred·a·tor** /'predətər/ ▶*n.* animal naturally preying on others.

**pred·a·to·ry** /'predəˌtôrē/ ▶*adj.* **1** (of an animal) preying naturally upon others. **2** plundering or exploiting others.

**pred·e·ces·sor** /'predəˌsesər/ ▶*n.* person or thing coming before, e.g., a former holder of an office or position.

**pre·des·tine** /pri'destin/ ▶*v.* **1** determine beforehand. **2** ordain in advance by divine

will or as if by fate.
—**pre·des·ti·na·tion** n.

**pre·de·ter·mine** ▸v.
**1** determine or decree
beforehand. **2** predestine.
—**pre·de·ter·mi·na·tion** n.

**pre·dic·a·ment** /pri'dikəmənt/
▸n. difficult, unpleasant, or
embarrassing situation.

**pred·i·cate** ▸v. /'predi,kāt/
**1** assert or affirm as true or
existent. **2** found or base (a
statement, etc.) on.
▸n. /'predikit/ *Gram.* & *Logic* what is
said about the subject of a
sentence or proposition, etc.
(e.g., *went home* in *John went
home*).

**pre·dict** /pri'dikt/ ▸v. foretell;
prophesy. —**pre·dic·ta·ble** adj.

**pred·i·lec·tion** /,predl'eksHən/
▸n. preference or special liking.

**pre·dis·pose** ▸v. **1** influence
favorably in advance. **2** render
liable or inclined beforehand:
*poor diet and lack of exercise
predisposed him to heart disease.*
—**pre·dis·po·si·tion** n.

**pre·dom·i·nate** ▸v. **1** be the
strongest or main element;
preponderate: *garden in which
dahlias predominate.* **2** have or
exert control or power: *private
interest predominated over the*

*public good.* —**pre·dom·i·nant** adj.
—**pre·dom·i·nant·ly** adv.

**pre·em·i·nent** ▸adj.
**1** surpassing others.
**2** outstanding. —**pre·em·i·nence**
n. —**pre·em·i·nent·ly** adv.

**pre·empt** /prē'empt/ ▸v.
**1 a** forestall. **b** acquire or
appropriate in advance. **2** obtain
by preemption. —**pre·emp·tion**
n. —**pre·emp·to·ry** adj.

**preen** /prēn/ ▸v. **1** (of a bird)
straighten (the feathers or itself)
with its beak. **2** (of a person)
primp or admire (oneself, one's
hair, clothes, etc.).

**pre·fab·ri·cate** ▸v.
manufacture sections of (a
building, etc.) prior to their
assembly on a site.
—**pre·fab·ri·ca·tion** n.

**pref·ace** /'prefəs/ ▸n.
introduction to a book.
▸v. **1** (**preface something with/by**)
introduce or begin (a speech or
event) by doing something.
**2** provide (a book, etc.) with a
preface. —**pref·a·to·ry** adj.

**pre·fect** /'prē,fekt/ ▸n.
administrator; overseer.

**pre·fer** /pri'fər/ ▸v. (**-ferred,
-fer·ring**) **1** choose; like better.
**2** *formal* submit (information, an

accusation, etc.) for consideration.

**pref·er·able** /ˈpref(ə)rəbəl/ ▸*adj.* **1** to be preferred. **2** more desirable. —**pref·er·a·bly** *adv.*

**pref·er·ence** /ˈpref(ə)rəns/ ▸*n.* **1** greater liking of one alternative over another. **2** thing preferred. **3** favoring of one person, etc., before others. —**pref·er·en·tial** *adj.*

**pre·fer·ment** /priˈfərmənt/ ▸*n.* promotion to a higher office.

**pre·fig·ure** ▸*v.* **1** represent beforehand by a figure or type. **2** imagine beforehand.

**pre·fix** ▸*n.* element at the beginning of a word to adjust or qualify its meaning (e.g., *ex-*, *non-*, *re-*). ▸*v.* add as an introduction.

**preg·nant** /ˈpregnənt/ ▸*adj.* **1** having a child or young developing in the uterus. **2** full of meaning; significant or suggestive: *a pregnant pause.* —**preg·nan·cy** *n.*

**pre·hen·sile** /prēˈhensəl; -ˌsīl/ ▸*adj.* (of a tail or limb) capable of grasping.

**pre·his·tor·ic** ▸*adj.* **1** of or relating to the period before written records. **2** *inf.* utterly out of date. —**pre·his·to·ry** *n.*

**pre·judge** ▸*v.* form a premature judgment on (a person, issue, etc.). —**pre·judg·ment** *n.*

**prej·u·dice** /ˈprejədəs/ ▸*n.* **1** preconceived and irrational opinion. **2** bias or partiality based on this. **3** harm to a person's rights. ▸*v.* **1** cause to have a prejudice. **2** impair the validity or force of (a right, claim, statement, etc.). —**prej·u·diced** *adj.*

**prej·u·di·cial** /ˌprejəˈdisHəl/ ▸*adj.* harmful to someone or something; detrimental.

**pre·lap·sar·i·an** /ˌprēlap-ˈse(ə)rēən/ ▸*adj.* characteristic of the time before the Fall of Man; innocent and unspoiled.

**prel·ate** /ˈprelət/ ▸*n.* bishop or other high ecclesiastical dignitary.

**pre·lim·i·nar·y** /priˈliməˌnerē/ ▸*adj.* introductory; preparatory. ▸*n.* (*pl.* **-ies**) (usu. **preliminaries**) **1** preliminary action or arrangement: *dispense with the preliminaries.* **2** preliminary trial or contest.

**prel·ude** /ˈprelˌ(y)o͞od/ ▸*n.* **1** action, event, or situation serving as an introduction. **2** beginning introductory part of a poem, etc. **3** introductory piece of music to a fugue, suite, or an act of an opera.

**pre·ma·ture** /ˌpreməˈCHŏŏr/ ▸*adj.* **1** occurring or done before the usual or proper time; too early: *premature decision.* **2** (of a baby) born (esp. three or more weeks) before the end of the full term of gestation.
—**pre·ma·ture·ly** *adv.*

**pre·med·i·tate** ▸*v.* think out or plan (an action) beforehand: *premeditated murder.*
—**pre·med·i·ta·tion** *n.*

**pre·men·stru·al** ▸*adj.* occurring before a menstrual period.

**pre·mier** /prēˈmi(ə)r/ ▸*n.* prime minister or other head of government in certain countries. ▸*adj.* first in importance, order, or time.

**pre·miere** /prēˈmi(ə)r/ (also **pre·mière**) ▸*n.* first performance or showing. ▸*v.* give a premiere of.

**prem·ise** /ˈpreməs/ ▸*n.* **1** previous statement from which another is inferred. **2** (**premises**) house or building with its grounds and appurtenances.

**pre·mi·um** /ˈprēmēəm/ ▸*n.* **1** amount to be paid for a

contract of insurance. **2** sum added to interest, wages, price, etc. **3** reward or prize. **4** (of a commodity) of the best quality and therefore more expensive.
□ **at a premium 1** highly valued. **2** scarce and in demand.

**prem·o·ni·tion** /ˌpreməˈnisHən; ˌprem-/ ▸*n.* forewarning; presentiment. —**pre·mon·i·to·ry** *adj.*

**pre·oc·cu·py** ▸*v.* (**-pied**) (of a thought, etc.) dominate or engross the mind of (a person).
—**pre·oc·cu·pa·tion** *n.*

**pre·or·dain** /ˌprēôrˈdān/ ▸*v.* ordain or determine beforehand.

**prep** /prep/ *inf.* ▸*v.* prepare (something or oneself). ▸*n.* preparation (esp. of a patient before surgery).

**prep.** ▸*abbr.* preposition.

**pre·par·a·to·ry school** /ˈprepərəˌtôrē/ (also **prep school**) ▸*n.* private school preparing students for college.

**pre·pare** /priˈpe(ə)r/ ▸*v.* **1** make or get ready for use, consideration, etc. **2** make ready or assemble (food, a meal, etc.). **3** make (a person or oneself) ready or disposed in some way.
—**prep·ar·a·tion** *n.*
—**pre·par·a·to·ry** *adj.*

**pre·pay** ▸v. (*past* and *past part.* -**paid**) pay (a charge) in advance.

**pre·pense** /pri'pens/ ▸*adj.* deliberate; intentional.

**pre·pon·der·ance** /pri-'pändərəns/ ▸*n.* quality or fact of being greater in number, quantity, or importance.

**pre·pon·der·ant** /pri'pändərənt/ ▸*adj.* predominant; having great numbers, influence, etc. —**pre·pon·der·ance** *n.* —**pre·pon·der·ant·ly** *adv.*

**prep·o·si·tion** /ˌprepə'zisHən/ ▸*n.* word governing (and usu. preceding) a noun or pronoun and expressing a relation to another word or element, as in: 'the man *on* the platform,' 'came *after* dinner', 'what did you do it *for*?' —**prep·o·si·tion·al** *adj.*

**pre·pos·sess·ing** /ˌprepə-'zesiNG/ ▸*adj.* attractive or appealing in appearance.

**pre·pos·ter·ous** /pri'päst(ə)rəs/ ▸*adj.* utterly absurd; outrageous.

**prep·py** /'prepē/ *inf.* ▸*n.* (*pl.* -**pies**) person attending an expensive private school. ▸*adj.* (-**pi·er**, -**pi·est**) of or typical of such a person.

**pre·puce** /'prē,pyo͞os/ ▸*n.* foreskin.

**pre·req·ui·site** /prē'rekwəzit/ ▸*adj.* required as a precondition. ▸*n.* prerequisite thing.

**pre·rog·a·tive** /p(r)i'rägətiv/ ▸*n.* right or privilege exclusive to an individual or class.

**pres·age** /'presij/ ▸*v.* portend; foreshadow.

**pres·by·o·pi·a** /ˌprezbē'ōpēə; ˌpres-/ ▸*n.* farsightedness caused by loss of elasticity of the lens of the eye, occurring typically in middle and old age.

**Pres·by·te·ri·an** /ˌprezbə-'ti(ə)rēən/ ▸*adj.* (of a church) governed by elders all of equal rank. ▸*n.* member of a Presbyterian Church. —**Pres·by·te·ri·an·ism** *n.*

**pre·school** ▸*adj.* of or relating to the time before a child is old enough to go to school. ▸*n.* nursery school. —**pre·school·er** *n.*

**pre·scient** /'presHənt/ ▸*adj.* having foreknowledge or foresight. —**pre·science** *n.*

**pre·scribe** /pri'skrīb/ ▸*v.* **1** advise and authorize the use of (a medicine, etc.). **2** recommend as beneficial. **3** lay down or impose authoritatively.

**pre·scrip·tion** /pri'skripsHən/ ▸*n.* **1** act or instance of prescribing. **2** doctor's instruction for the preparation and use of a medicine.

**pre·scrip·tive** ▶*adj.* laying down rules to be followed.

**pres·ence** /'prezəns/ ▶*n.* **1** being present. **2** person or thing that is present without being seen. **3** person's appearance or bearing, esp. when imposing.

**pres·ent**[1] /'prezənt/ ▶*adj.* **1** being in the place in question: *how many were present at the meeting?* **2** now existing, occurring, or being such. **3** *Gram.* expressing an action, etc., now going on or habitually performed.
▶*n.* **1** the time now passing: *no time like the present.* **2** *Gram.* present tense. **3** gift; thing given or presented.

**pre·sent**[2] /pri'zent/ ▶*v.* **1** introduce, offer, or exhibit. **2** offer, give, or award as a gift. **3** put (a form of entertainment) before the public. **4** introduce: *may I present my fiancé?* **5** (of an idea, etc.) offer or suggest itself.
—**pres·en·ta·tion** *n.*
—**pre·sent·er** *n.*

**pre·sent·a·ble** /pri'zentəbəl/ ▶*adj.* **1** of good appearance; fit

to be presented. **2** fit for presentation.

**pre·sen·ti·ment** /pri'zentəmənt/ ▶*n.* vague expectation; foreboding (esp. of misfortune).

**pres·ent·ism** /'prezən,tizəm/ ▶*n.* uncritical adherence to present-day attitudes, esp. the tendency to interpret past events in terms of modern values and concepts.

**pres·ent·ly** /'prezəntlē/ ▶*adv.* **1** soon; after a short time. **2** at the present time; now.

**pres·er·va·tion** /,prezər-'vāsHən/ ▶*n.* **1** action of preserving. **2** state of being preserved. —**pres·er·va·tion·ist** *n.*

**pre·ser·va·tive** /pri'zərvətiv/ ▶*n.* substance used to preserve food, wood, etc., against decay.
▶*adj.* acting to preserve something.

**pre·serve** /pri'zərv/ ▶*v.* **1** keep safe or free from harm, decay, etc. **2** maintain or retain. **3** treat or refrigerate (food) to prevent decomposition or fermentation.
▶*n.* **1** preserved fruit; jam. **2** place where game or fish, etc., are preserved. **3** sphere or area of activity regarded as a person's own.

**pre·side** /pri'zīd/ ▸v. **1** be chairperson or president of a meeting, etc. **2** exercise control or authority.

**pres·i·dent** /'prezidənt/ ▸n. **1** elected head of a republican government. **2** head of a college, university, company, society, etc. —**pres·i·den·tial** adj.

**press** /pres/ ▸v. **1** apply steady force to (a thing in contact). **2** compress or squeeze a thing to flatten, shape, or smooth it. **3** be urgent; demand immediate action. **4** make an insistent demand: *press for campaign finance reform.* **5** continue in one's action: *they pressed on in spite of the foul weather.* **6** urge or entreat.
▸n. **1** act or instance of pressing. **2** device for compressing, flattening, shaping, extracting juice, etc. **3** printing press. **4** (**the press**) newspapers, journalists, etc., generally or collectively. **5** publicity.

**press a·gent** ▸n. person employed to obtain publicity.

**press con·fer·ence** ▸n. interview given to a number of journalists by a prominent person.

**press·ing** ▸adj. urgent.

**press re·lease** ▸n. official statement issued to newspapers.

**pres·sure** /'preSHər/ ▸n. **1 a** exertion of continuous force on or against a body by another in contact with it. **b** force exerted. **2** urgency: *work under pressure.* **3** affliction or difficulty: *under financial pressure.* **4** constraining influence: *if pressure is brought to bear.*
▸v. **1** coerce. **2** persuade.

**pres·sure cook·er** ▸n. airtight pot for cooking quickly under steam pressure.

**pres·sure group** ▸n. group formed to influence public policy.

**pres·sur·ize** /'preSHə,rīz/ ▸v. maintain normal atmospheric pressure in (an aircraft cabin, etc.) at a high altitude. —**pres·sur·i·za·tion** n.

**pres·ti·dig·i·ta·tion** /ˌprestə-ˌdijə'tāSHən/ ▸n. magic tricks performed as entertainment.

**pres·tige** /pres'tēZH/ ▸n. respect, reputation, or influence derived from achievements, power, associations, etc.

**pres·to** /'prestō/ ▸adv. Mus. in quick tempo.

**pre·sume** /pri'zoōm/ ▸v. **1** suppose to be true; take for granted. **2** dare; venture: *may I presume to ask?* **3** be presumptuous. —**pre·sum·a·bly** *adv.*

**pre·sump·tion** /pri'zəmpsнən/ ▸*n.* **1** arrogance; presumptuous behavior. **2** act of presuming a thing to be true. **3** thing that is or may be presumed to be true.

**pre·sump·tu·ous** ▸*adj.* (of a person or behavior) failing to observe the limits of what is appropriate. —**pre·sump·tu·ous·ly** *adv.* —**pre·sump·tu·ous·ness** *n.*

**pre·sup·pose** ▸*v.* **1** assume beforehand. **2** require as a precondition; imply.

**pre·tend** /pri'tend/ ▸*v.* **1** claim or assert falsely so as to deceive. **2** imagine to oneself in play: *pretended to be monsters.* **3 a** lay claim to (a right or title, etc.). **b** profess to have (a quality, etc.). —**pre·tend·er** *n.*

**pre·tend·er** /pri'tendər/ ▸*n.* person who claims or aspires to a title or position.

**pre·tense** ▸*n.* **1** pretending; make-believe. **2** false show of intentions or motives. **3** claim, esp. a false or ambitious one.

**pre·ten·sion** ▸*n.* **1** assertion of a claim. **2** pretentiousness.

**pre·ten·tious** ▸*adj.* **1** making an excessive claim to great merit or importance. **2** ostentatious. —**pre·ten·tious·ness** *n.*

**pret·er·it** /'pretərit/ (also **pret·er·ite**) *Gram.* ▸*adj.* expressing a past action or state. ▸*n.* preterit tense or form.

**pre·ter·nat·u·ral** /ˌprētər-'naCH(ə)rəl/ ▸*adj.* outside the ordinary course of nature; supernatural. —**pre·ter·nat·u·ral·ly** *adv.*

**pre·text** ▸*n.* **1** ostensible or alleged reason or intention. **2** excuse offered.

**pret·ty** /'pritē/ ▸*adj.* (**-ti·er, -ti·est**) **1** attractive in a fine or charming way. **2** fine or good of its kind. ▸*adv. inf.* fairly; moderately; considerably. ▸*v.* (**-tied**) make pretty or attractive: *she's all prettied up and ready to go.* —**pret·ti·ly** *adv.* —**pret·ti·ness** *n.*

**pret·zel** /'pretsəl/ ▸*n.* crisp or chewy knot-shaped or stick-shaped bread, usu. salted.

**pre·vail** /pri'vāl/ ▸*v.* **1** be victorious or gain mastery. **2** be the more usual or predominant. **3** exist or occur in general use or experience; be current.

**4** (**prevail on/upon**) persuade: *she was prevailed upon to give an account of her trip.* —**pre·vail·ing·ly** *adv.*

**prev·a·lent** /ˈprevələnt/ ▸*adj.*
**1** generally existing or occurring.
**2** predominant. —**prev·a·lence**
*n.* —**prev·a·lent·ly** *adv.*

**pre·var·i·cate** /priˈvariˌkāt/ ▸*v.*
**1** speak or act evasively or misleadingly. **2** quibble; equivocate. —**pre·var·i·ca·tion** *n.*
—**pre·var·i·ca·tor** *n.*

**pre·vent** /priˈvent/ ▸*v.* stop from happening or doing something; hinder; make impossible.
—**pre·vent·a·ble** *adj.*
—**pre·ven·tion** *n.* —**pre·ven·tive** *adj.*

**pre·view** ▸*n.* showing of a movie, play, exhibition, etc., before it is seen by the general public.
▸*v.* see or show in advance.

**pre·vi·ous** /ˈprēvēəs/ ▸*adj.* coming before in time or order.
—**pre·vi·ous·ly** *adv.*

**prey** /prā/ ▸*n.* **1** animal that is hunted or killed by another for food. **2** person or thing that is influenced by or vulnerable to (something undesirable): *prey to morbid fears.*
▸*v.* (**prey on/upon**) **1** seek or take as prey. **2** (of a disease, emotion, etc.) exert a harmful influence.

**pri·a·pism** /ˈprīəˌpizəm/ ▸*n.* persistent and painful erection of the penis.

**price** /prīs/ ▸*n.* **1** amount of money or goods for which a thing is bought or sold. **2** what is or must be given, done, sacrificed, etc., to obtain or achieve something.
▸*v.* fix or find the price or value of (a thing for sale).
□ **at a price** at a high cost.

**price·less** ▸*adj.* **1** invaluable.
**2** *inf.* very amusing or absurd.

**pric·ey** /ˈprīsē/ (also **pric·y**) ▸*adj.*
(**pric·i·er**, **pric·i·est**) *inf.* expensive.

**prick** /prik/ ▸*v.* **1** pierce slightly; make a small hole in. **2** provoke to action.
▸*n.* **1** act or instance of pricking.
**2** small hole or mark made by pricking.

**prick·le** /ˈprikəl/ ▸*n.* **1** small thorn. **2** hard pointed spine of a hedgehog, etc. **3** prickling sensation.
▸*v.* affect or be affected with a sensation as of pricking.
—**prick·ly** *adj.*

**prick·ly heat** ▸*n.* itchy skin inflammation, common in hot, damp weather.

**pride** /prīd/ ▸*n.* **1 a** elation or satisfaction at one's achievements, qualities, or possessions, etc., or those of somone close to one. **b** source of this feeling. **2** sense of dignity; self-respect. **3** group or company (of animals, esp. lions).

▸*v.* (**pride oneself on**) be proud of. —**pride·ful** *adj.*

□ **take pride** (or **a pride**) **in 1** be proud of. **2** maintain in good condition or appearance.

**prie-dieu** /prē 'dyœ/ ▸*n.* (*pl.* **prie-dieux** /'dyœ(z)/) piece of furniture for use during prayer, consisting of a kneeling surface and a narrow upright front with a rest for the elbows or for books.

**priest** /prēst/ ▸*n.* **1** ordained minister of hierarchical Christian churches. **2** official minister of a non-Christian religion. —**priest·hood** *n.* —**priest·ly** *adj.*

**priest·ess** ▸*n.* female priest of a non-Christian religion.

**prig** /prig/ ▸*n.* self-righteous or moralistic person. —**prig·gish** *adj.*

**prim** /prim/ ▸*adj.* (**prim·mer, prim·mest**) **1** stiffly formal and precise. **2** prudish. —**prim·ly** *adv.* —**prim·ness** *n.*

**pri·ma·cy** /'prīməsē/ ▸*n.* (*pl.* **-cies**) **1** preeminence. **2** office of an ecclesiastical primate.

**pri·ma don·na** /ˌprimə 'dänə/ ▸*n.* **1** chief female singer in an opera or opera company. **2** temperamentally self-important person.

**pri·ma fa·cie** /ˌprīmə 'fāsнē/ ▸*adj.* (of evidence) based on the first impression.

**pri·mal** /'prīməl/ ▸*adj.* **1** primitive; primeval. **2** chief; fundamental.

**pri·mar·y** /'prī,merē/ ▸*adj.* **1 a** of the first importance; chief. **b** fundamental; basic. **2** earliest; original. **3** designating any of the colors from which all other colors can be obtained by mixing.

▸*n.* (*pl.* **-ies**) **1** thing that is primary. **2** (also **pri·mar·y e·lec·tion**) preliminary election to appoint delegates or to select candidates. —**pri·mar·i·ly** *adv.*

**pri·mate** /'prī,māt/ ▸*n.* **1** member of the highest order of mammals, including lemurs, apes, monkeys, and human beings. **2** archbishop.

**prime** /prīm/ ▸*adj.* **1** chief; most

important. **2** (esp. of beef) first-rate; excellent. **3** primary; fundamental. **4** (of a number) divisible only by itself and 1 (e.g., 2, 3, 5, 7, 11).

▶*n.* **1** state of the highest perfection: *prime of life*. **2** the best part.

▶*v.* **1** prepare (a thing) for use or action. **2** equip (a person) with information, etc.

**prime me·rid·i·an** ▶*n.* meridian passing through Greenwich, England.

**prime min·is·ter** ▶*n.* head of an elected parliamentary government.

**prim·er** /'primər/ ▶*n.* **1** elementary textbook for teaching children to read. **2** introductory book.

**prime time** ▶*n.* time at which a television audience is the largest.

**pri·me·val** /prī'mēvəl/ ▶*adj.* **1** of or relating to the earliest age of the world. **2** ancient; primitive.

**prim·i·tive** /'primitiv/ ▶*adj.* **1** at an early stage of civilization. **2** undeveloped; crude; simple: *primitive methods.*

▶*n.* primitive person or thing.

**prim·i·tiv·ism** /'primətiv,izəm/ ▶*n.* **1** belief in the value of what

is simple and unsophisticated, expressed as a philosophy of life or through art or literature. **2** unsophisticated behavior that is unaffected by objective reasoning.

**pri·mo·gen·i·ture** /,prīmō'jeni-,CHər/ ▶*n.* **1** fact or condition of being the firstborn child. **2** (also **right of primogeniture**) right of inheritance of the firstborn.

**pri·mor·di·al** /prī'môrdēəl/ ▶*adj.* **1** existing at or from the beginning; primeval. **2** original; fundamental. —**pri·mor·di·al·ly** *adv.*

**primp** /primp/ ▶*v.* **1** make (the hair, one's clothes, etc.) neat or overly tidy. **2** groom (oneself) painstakingly.

**prim·rose** /'prim,rōz/ ▶*n.* plant bearing pale yellow flowers in the early spring.

**pri·mum mo·bi·le** /,prīməm 'mōbə,lē; ,prē-/ ▶*n.* central or most important source of motion or action.

**prince** /prins/ ▶*n.* **1** male member of a royal family other than a reigning king. **2** ruler of a small nation. **3** nobleman in some countries. **4** chief or greatest: *the prince of novelists.*

**prince·ly** ▶*adj.* (**-li·er, -li·est**) **1** of

or worthy of a prince.
**2** generous; splendid.
—**prince·li·ness** *n.*

**prin·cess** ▶*n.* **1** daughter of a monarch. **2** wife or widow of a prince. **3** female ruler of a small state. **4** *inf.* spoiled young woman.

**prin·ci·pal** /ˈprinsəpəl/ ▶*adj.* **1** first in rank or importance; chief. **2** main; leading.
▶*n.* **1** head, ruler, or superior. **2** head of a school. **3** leading performer. **4** capital sum as distinguished from interest or income.

**prin·ci·pal·i·ty** /ˌprinsəˈpalitē/ ▶*n.* (*pl.* **-ties**) **1** nation ruled by a prince. **2** government of a prince.

**prin·ci·ple** /ˈprinsəpəl/ ▶*n.* **1** fundamental truth or law as the basis of reasoning or action. **2 a** personal code of conduct. **b** (**principles**) such rules of conduct. **3** general law in physics, etc. **4** law of nature or science.

**print** /print/ ▶*n.* **1** indentation or residual mark: *fingerprint*. **2** printed lettering or writing. **3** picture or design printed from a block or plate. **4** positive picture produced on paper from

a negative. **5** printed design, picture, or fabric.
▶*v.* **1** produce or cause (a book, picture, etc.) to be produced by applying inked types, blocks, or plates, to paper, vellum, etc. **2** (**print on/in**) impress or stamp. **3** write (words or letters) without joining, in imitation of typography. **4** produce (a positive picture) from a photographic negative. **5** express or publish in print. **6** (usu. **print out**) (of a computer, etc.) produce output in printed form. —**print·er** *n.*

**print·ing press** ▶*n.* machine for printing text or pictures from type or plates.

**print·out** ▶*n.* computer output in printed form.

**pri·or** /ˈprīər/ ▶*adj.* **1** earlier. **2** coming before in time, order, or importance.
▶*adv.* (**prior to**) before.
▶*n.* superior officer of a religious house or order. —**pri·or·ess** *n.*

**pri·or·i·ty** /prīˈôritē/ ▶*n.* (*pl.* **-ties**) **1** precedence in rank, importance, etc. **2** interest having prior claim to consideration. —**pri·or·i·tize** *v.*

**prism** /ˈprizəm/ ▶*n.* **1** solid geometric figure whose two ends are similar, equal, and parallel rectilinear figures, and whose sides are parallelograms. **2** transparent body in this form, usu. triangular, that separates white light into a spectrum of colors. —**pris·mat·ic** *adj.*

**pris·on** /ˈprizən/ ▸*n.* **1** place of confinement for convicted criminals or persons awaiting trial. **2** custody; confinement. —**pris·on·er** *n.*

☐ **prison camp** camp for prisoners of war or political prisoners.

**pris·sy** /ˈprisē/ ▸*adj.* (**-si·er, -si·est**) prim; prudish. —**pris·si·ness** *n.*

**pris·tine** /ˈpris,tēn; priˈstēn/ ▸*adj.* **1** in its original condition; unspoiled. **2** spotless; fresh as if new.

**pri·vate** /ˈprīvit/ ▸*adj.* **1** belonging to an individual; one's own; personal: *private property.* **2** confidential: *private talks.* **3** not open to the public. **4** secluded. ▸*n.* soldier with a rank below corporal. —**pri·va·cy** *n.* —**pri·vate·ly** *adv.*

**pri·vate de·tec·tive** ▸*n.* detective engaged privately, outside an official police force.

**pri·va·tion** /prīˈvāsʜən/ ▸*n.* lack of the comforts or necessities of life: *suffered many privations.*

**priv·et** /ˈprivit/ ▸*n.* deciduous or evergreen shrub bearing small white flowers and much used for hedges.

**priv·i·lege** /ˈpriv(ə)lij/ ▸*n.* **1** right, advantage, or immunity. **2** special benefit or honor: *a privilege to meet you.* ▸*v.* invest with a privilege. —**priv·i·leged** *adj.*

**priv·i·ty** /ˈprivitē/ ▸*n.* (*pl.* **-ties**) relation between two parties that is recognized by law, such as that of blood, lease, or service.

**priv·y** /ˈprivē/ ▸*adj.* (**privy to**) sharing in the secret of (a person's plans, etc.). ▸*n.* (*pl.* **-ies**) toilet, esp. an outhouse.

**prize** /prīz/ ▸*n.* **1** something that can be won in a competition, lottery, etc. **2** reward given as a symbol of victory or superiority. **3** something worth striving for. ▸*adj.* supremely excellent or outstanding of its kind. ▸*v.* **1** value highly. **2** force open or out by leverage.

**pro** /prō/ ▸*adj.* for; in favor. ▸*n.* (*pl.* **pros**) **1** *inf.* professional. **2** reason or argument for or in favor.

▸*prep.* in favor of.

**pro-** ▸*prefix* **1** favoring or supporting: *pro-government.* **2** acting as a substitute or deputy for: *proconsul.* **3** forward: *produce.* **4** forward and downward: *prostrate.* **5** onward: *progress.* **6** in front of: *protect.*

**pro·ac·tive** /prō'aktiv/ ▸*adj.* (of a person, policy, or action) creating or controlling a situation by causing something to happen rather than responding to it after it has happened.

**prob·a·ble** /'präbəbəl/ ▸*adj.* expected to happen or prove true; likely. ▸*n.* probable candidate, member of a team, etc. —**prob·a·bil·i·ty** *n.* —**prob·a·bly** *adv.*

**pro·bate** /'prō‚bāt/ ▸*v.* establish the validity of (a will).

**pro·ba·tion** ▸*n.* **1** system of suspending the sentence of a criminal offender subject to a period of good behavior under supervision. **2** period of testing, as for a new employee. —**pro·ba·tion·al** *adj.* —**pro·ba·tion·ary** *adj.*

**pro·ba·tive** /'prōbətiv/ ▸*adj.* having the quality or function of proving or demonstrating something; affording proof or evidence.

**probe** /prōb/ ▸*n.* **1** penetrating investigation. **2** small device for measuring, testing, etc. **3** blunt surgical exploratory instrument. **4** (also **space probe**) unmanned exploratory spacecraft. ▸*v.* **1** examine or inquire into closely. **2** explore with a probe. —**prob·ing·ly** *adv.*

**pro·bi·ty** /'prōbitē/ ▸*n.* uprightness; honesty.

**prob·lem** /'präbləm/ ▸*n.* **1** doubtful or difficult matter requiring a solution: *the problem of ventilation.* **2** something hard to understand, accomplish, or deal with.

**pro bo·no** /'bōnō/ ▸*adj. & adv.* relating to a service, esp. legal work, for which no fee is charged.

**pro·bos·cis** /prə'bäsəs/ ▸*n.* **1** long flexible trunk or snout of some mammals, e.g., an elephant or tapir. **2** elongated mouth parts of some insects.

**pro·ce·dure** /prə'sējər/ ▸*n.* **1** way of proceeding, esp. a mode of conducting business or a legal action. **2** mode of performing a task. **3** series of actions conducted in a certain order or

manner. —**pro·ce·dur·al** *adj.*
—**pro·ce·dur·al·ly** *adv.*

**pro·ceed** /prəˈsēd/ ▸*v.* **1** go forward or on further; make one's way. **2** continue; go on with an activity. **3** (of an action) be carried on or continued. **4** adopt a course of action. **5** go on to say.

**pro·ceed·ing** ▸*n.* **1** action or piece of conduct. **2** (**proceedings**) (also **legal proceedings**) lawsuit. **3** (**proceedings**) published report of discussions or a conference.

**pro·cess**[1] /ˈpräˌses/ ▸*n.* **1** course of action or proceeding, esp. as a series of stages. **2** natural evolution or change: *process of growing old.* **3** series of operations performed in manufacturing something. ▸*v.* **1** handle or deal with by a particular process. **2** treat (food, esp. to prevent decay): *processed cheese.* —**pro·cess·or** *n.*

**pro·cess**[2] /prəˈses/ ▸*v.* walk in procession.

**pro·ces·sion** /prəˈseSHən/ ▸*n.* **1** number of people or vehicles, etc., moving forward in orderly or ceremonial succession. **2** movement of such a group.

**pro·ces·sion·al** ▸*adj.* used, carried, or sung in processions. ▸*n.* music sung or played during a procession.

**pro·choice** ▸*adj.* in favor of the right to legal abortion.

**pro·claim** ▸*v.* **1** announce or declare publicly or officially. **2** declare (a person) to be (a king, traitor, etc.). —**proc·la·ma·tion** *n.*

**pro·clit·ic** /prōˈklitik/ ▸*n.* word pronounced with so little emphasis that it is shortened and forms part of the following word, for example, *you* in *y'all.*

**pro·cliv·i·ty** /prōˈklivətē/ ▸*n.* (*pl.* **-ties**) tendency or inclination.

**pro·cras·ti·nate** /prəˈkrastəˌnāt/ ▸*v.* delay or postpone action. —**pro·cras·ti·na·tion** *n.* —**pro·cras·ti·na·tor** *n.*

**pro·cre·ate** /ˈprōkrēˌāt/ ▸*v.* produce offspring. —**pro·cre·a·tive** *adj.* —**pro·cre·a·tion** *n.*

**proc·tor** /ˈpräktər/ ▸*n.* supervisor of students in an examination, etc.

**pro·cure** /prəˈkyo͝or; prō-/ ▸*v.* **1** obtain, esp. by care or effort; acquire. **2** bring about. **3** obtain (people) for prostitution. —**pro·cur·a·ble** *adj.* —**pro·cure·ment** *n.*

**prod** /präd/ ▶v. (**prod·ded, prod·ding**) **1** poke with the finger or a pointed object. **2** stimulate to action. ▶n. **1** poke or thrust. **2** stimulus to action.

**prod·i·gal** /'prädigəl/ ▶adj. **1** wastefully extravagant. **2** having or giving on a lavish scale. ▶n. prodigal person. —**prod·i·gal·i·ty** n. —**prod·i·gal·ly** adv.

**pro·di·gious** /prə'dijəs/ ▶adj. **1** marvelous or amazing. **2** enormous. —**pro·di·gious·ly** adv.

**prod·i·gy** /'prädəjē/ ▶n. (pl. -**gies**) **1** person endowed with exceptional qualities or abilities, esp. a precocious child. **2** marvelous, esp. extraordinary, thing.

**pro·drome** /'prō,drōm/ ▶n. early symptom indicating the onset of a disease or illness.

**pro·duce** ▶v. /prə'd(y)o͞os/ **1** bring forward for consideration, inspection, or use. **2** manufacture (goods) from raw materials, etc. **3** bear or yield (offspring, fruit, a harvest, etc.). **4** bring into existence. **5** cause or bring about.

**6** supervise the production of (a movie, broadcast, etc.). ▶n. /'prōd(y)o͞os/ **1** what is produced, esp. agricultural products. **2** fruits and vegetables collectively. —**pro·duc·er** n.

**prod·uct** /'prädəkt/ ▶n. **1** thing or substance produced by natural process or manufacture. **2** result. **3** numerical quantity obtained by multiplying quantities together.

**pro·duc·tion** ▶n. **1** producing or being produced. **2** total yield. **3** thing produced, esp. a movie, broadcast, play, etc.

**pro·duc·tive** ▶adj. producing things, esp. in large quantities.

**pro·duc·tiv·i·ty** ▶n. **1** capacity to produce. **2** effectiveness of productive effort, esp. in industry. **3** production per unit of effort.

**pro·em** /'prō,em; -əm/ ▶n. preface or preamble to a book or speech.

**pro·fane** /prə'fān/ ▶adj. **1** not sacred; secular. **2** irreverent; blasphemous. ▶v. **1** treat (a sacred thing) with irreverence or disregard. **2** violate or pollute (something entitled to respect). —**pro·fa·na·tion** n.

**pro·fan·i·ty** /prəˈfanətē/ ▸*n.* (*pl.* **-ties**) **1** profane act. **2** profane language; blasphemy.

**pro·fess** /prəˈfes/ ▸*v.* **1** claim openly to have (a quality or feeling). **2** declare: *profess ignorance.* **3** affirm one's faith in or allegiance to.

**pro·fes·sion** ▸*n.* **1** work that involves some branch of advanced learning or science. **2** people engaged in a profession. **3** declaration or avowal.

**pro·fes·sion·al** ▸*adj.* **1** of or belonging to or connected with a profession. **2 a** skillful. **b** worthy of a professional: *professional conduct.* **3** engaged in a specified activity as one's main paid occupation. ▸*n.* a professional person. —**pro·fes·sion·al·ly** *adv.*

**pro·fes·sor** ▸*n.* **1** (often as a title) university academic of the highest rank. **2** university teacher. —**pro·fes·so·ri·al** *adj.*

**prof·fer** /ˈpräfər/ ▸*v.* offer.

**pro·fi·cient** /prəˈfisHənt/ ▸*adj.* adept; expert. —**pro·fi·cien·cy** *n.* —**pro·fi·cient·ly** *adv.*

**pro·file** /ˈprōˌfīl/ ▸*n.* **1** outline (esp. of a human face) as seen from one side. **2** short biographical or character sketch. ▸*v.* represent or describe by a profile. —**pro·fil·er** *n.*

**prof·it** /ˈpräfit/ ▸*n.* **1** advantage or benefit. **2** financial gain; excess of returns over expenditures. ▸*v.* **1** be beneficial to. **2** obtain an advantage or benefit. —**prof·it·a·bil·i·ty** *n.* —**prof·it·a·ble** *adj.*

**prof·i·teer** ▸*v.* make or seek to make excessive profits, esp. illegally. ▸*n.* person who profiteers.

**prof·li·gate** /ˈpräfligit/ ▸*adj.* **1** licentious; dissolute. **2** recklessly extravagant. ▸*n.* profligate person. —**prof·li·ga·cy** *n.*

**pro for·ma** /prō ˈfôrmə/ ▸*adv. & adj.* as or being a matter of form; for the sake of form.

**pro·found** /prəˈfound/ ▸*adj.* (**-er, -est**) **1** having or demanding great knowledge or insight. **2** deep; intense; unqualified: *profound indifference.* **3** deeply felt. —**pro·found·ly** *adv.* —**pro·fun·di·ty** *n.*

**pro·fuse** /prəˈfyo͞os/ ▸*adj.* **1** lavish; extravagant. **2** exuberantly plentiful;

abundant: *a profuse variety.*
—**pro·fuse·ly** *adv.*
—**pro·fu·sion** *n.*

**pro·gen·i·tive** /prə'jenətiv; prō-/
▶*adj.* having the quality of
producing offspring; having
reproductive power.

**pro·gen·i·tor** /prə'jenətər/ ▶*n.*
**1** ancestor. **2** person who
originates an artistic, political,
etc., movement.

**prog·e·ny** /'präjənē/ ▶*n.*
**1** offspring of a person or other
organism. **2** descendant or
descendants.

**pro·ges·ter·one** /prō'jestə,rōn/
▶*n.* steroid hormone that
stimulates the preparation of
the uterus for pregnancy.

**prog·no·sis** /präg'nōsəs/ ▶*n.* (*pl.*
**-ses**) forecast, as of a process or
the course of a disease.

**prog·nos·ti·cate** /präg'nästə-
,kāt/ ▶*v.* foretell; foresee;
prophesy. —**prog·nos·ti·ca·tion**
*n.* —**prog·nos·ti·ca·tor** *n.*

**pro·gram** /'prō,gram/ ▶*n.* **1** list
of a series of events, performers,
etc., at a public function, etc.
**2** radio or television broadcast.
**3** plan of future events. **4** course
or series of studies, lectures, etc.;
syllabus. **5** series of coded
instructions to control the
operation of a computer or other
machine.

▶*v.* (**-grammed, -gram·ming;
-gramed, -gram·ing**) **1** make a
program of. **2** express (a
problem) or instruct (a
computer) by means of a
program. —**pro·gram·ma·ble** *adj.*
—**pro·gram·mat·ic** *adj.*
—**pro·gram·mat·i·cal·ly** *adv.*
—**pro·gram·mer** *n.*

**pro·gram trad·ing** ▶*n.*
simultaneous purchase and sale
of many different stocks, or of
stocks and related futures
contracts, with the use of a
computer program to exploit
price differences in different
markets.

**prog·ress** ▶*n.* /'prägres/
**1** forward or onward movement
toward a destination. **2** advance;
improvement.

▶*v.* /prə'gres/ **1** move or be moved
forward or onward; continue.
**2** advance, develop, or improve:
*science progresses.*
□ **in progress** developing; going
on.

**pro·gres·sion** ▶*n.*
**1** progressing: *mode of
progression.* **2** succession; series.

**pro·gres·sion·ist** /prə-
'gresHənist/ ▶*n.* **1** supporter of

the theory that all life forms gradually progress or evolve to a higher form. **2** advocate of or believer in political or social progress.

▶*adj.* (of a person or theory) supporting or based on the theory that all life forms progress or evolve to a higher form.

**pro·gres·sive** ▶*adj.* **1** moving forward. **2** proceeding step-by-step; cumulative. **3 a** favoring or implementing rapid progress or social reform. **b** modern. **4** (of disease, violence, etc.) increasing in severity or extent. **5** *Gram.* (of an aspect) expressing an action in progress, e.g., *am writing, was writing.*

▶*n.* (**Progressive**) advocate of progressive political policies. —**pro·gres·sive·ly** *adv.* —**pro·gres·sive·ness** *n.* —**pro·gres·siv·ism** *n.*

**pro·hib·it** /prə'hibit/ ▶*v.* **1** forbid. **2** prevent.

**pro·hi·bi·tion** /ˌprō(h)ə'bisHən/ ▶*n.* **1** forbidding or being forbidden. **2** *Law* edict or order that forbids. **3** (**Prohibition**) period (1920–33) in the U.S. when the manufacture and sale of alcoholic beverages was

prohibited by law. —**pro·hi·bi·tion·ist** *n.*

**pro·hib·i·tive** /prə'hibitiv/ ▶*adj.* **1** (of prices, taxes, etc.) extremely high. **2** (of a law) prohibiting. —**pro·hib·i·tive·ly** *adv.*

**proj·ect** ▶*n.* /'präjekt/ **1** plan; scheme. **2** extensive undertaking, academic assignment, etc.

▶*v.* /prə'jekt/ **1** protrude; jut out. **2** throw. **3** extrapolate (results, etc.); forecast. **4** cause (light, shadow, images, etc.) to fall on a surface. **5** cause (a sound, esp. the voice) to be heard at a distance. —**pro·jec·tor** *n.*

**pro·jec·tile** /prə'jektl/ ▶*n.* **1** missile, esp. fired by a rocket. **2** object propelled through the air.

**pro·jec·tion** ▶*n.* **1** estimate of future situations based on a study of present ones. **2** presentation of an image, etc., on a surface or screen. **3** presenting a particular image of oneself, etc. **4** thing that projects from a surface.

**pro·le·gom·e·non** /ˌprōlə-'gämə,nän; -nən/ ▶*n.* (*pl.* **-na** /-nə/) critical or discursive introduction to a book.

**pro·le·tar·i·at** /ˌprōləˈte(ə)rēət/
▸*n.* **1** the working class.
**2** lowest, esp. uneducated, class.
—**pro·le·tar·i·an** *adj.*
—**pro·le·tar·i·an·ism** *n.*

**pro-life** ▸*adj.* opposed to the
right to legal abortion.

**pro·lif·er·ate** /prəˈlifəˌrāt/ ▸*v.*
reproduce; increase rapidly in
numbers. —**pro·lif·er·a·tion** *n.*

**pro·lif·ic** /prəˈlifik/ ▸*adj.*
**1** producing many offspring or
much output. **2** abundantly
productive. —**pro·lif·i·cal·ly** *adv.*

**pro·lix** /prōˈliks/ ▸*adj.* (of speech,
writing, etc.) lengthy; tedious.
—**pro·lix·i·ty** *n.*

**pro·logue** /ˈprōˌlôg/ (also
**pro·log**) ▸*n.* **1** preliminary
speech, poem, etc., esp. of a play.
**2** introductory event.

**pro·long** /prəˈlôNG/ ▸*v.* extend in
time or space.
—**pro·lon·ga·tion** *n.*

**prom** /präm/ ▸*n.* school or college
formal dance.

**prom·e·nade** /ˌpräməˈnād/ ▸*n.*
paved public walk, esp. along a
body of water.

**prom·i·nent** /ˈprämənənt/ ▸*adj.*
**1** jutting out; projecting.
**2** conspicuous. **3** distinguished;
important. —**prom·i·nence** *n.*
—**prom·i·nent·ly** *adv.*

**pro·mis·cu·ous** /prəˈmiskyo͞oəs/
▸*adj.* **1** having frequent and
diverse sexual relationships, esp.
transient ones. **2** random or
indiscriminate. —**prom·is·cu·i·ty**
*n.* —**prom·is·cu·ous·ly** *adj.*

**prom·ise** /ˈpräməs/ ▸*n.*
**1** assurance that one will or will
not undertake a certain action,
behavior, etc. **2** potential for
achievement.
▸*v.* **1** assure someone that one
will do something. **2** seem likely
to: *is promising to rain.*

**prom·is·so·ry** /ˈpräməˌsôrē/
▸*adj.* conveying a promise.
□ **promissory note** signed
document containing a written
promise to pay a stated sum.

**pro·mon·to·ry** /ˈprämənˌtôrē/
▸*n.* (*pl.* **-ries**) point of high land
jutting out into the sea, etc.;
headland.

**pro·mote** /prəˈmōt/ ▸*v.* **1** raise (a
person) to a higher office, rank,
grade, etc. **2** encourage (a cause,
process, desired result, etc.).
**3** publicize and sell (a product).
—**pro·mo·tion** *n.* —**pro·mo·tion·al**
*adj.*

**prompt** /prämpt/ ▸*adj.* made,
done, etc., readily or at once.
▸*adv.* punctually.
▸*v.* **1** incite; urge: *prompted them*

*to action.* **2** assist (an actor or hesitating speaker) with a cue or suggestion. **3** give rise to; inspire.

▶*n.* **1** something that prompts. **2** *Computing* indication or sign on a computer screen to show that the system is waiting for input. —**promp·ti·tude** *n.* —**prompt·ly** *adv.* —**prompt·ness** *n.*

**pro·mul·gate** /ˈprämˌəlˌgāt/ ▶*v.* **1** make known to the public; disseminate; promote. **2** proclaim (a decree, news, etc.). —**prom·ul·ga·tion** *n.*

**prone** /prōn/ ▶*adj.* **1** disposed or liable. **2** lying flat, esp. face downward.

**prong** /prôNG/ ▶*n.* each of two or more projections at the end of a fork, etc.

**pro·nom·i·nal** /prōˈnämənl/ ▶*adj.* of, relating to, or serving as a pronoun.

**pro·noun** /ˈprōˌnoun/ ▶*n.* word used instead of and to indicate a noun already mentioned or known, esp. to avoid repetition (e.g., *we, their, this, ourselves*).

**pro·nounce** /prəˈnouns/ ▶*v.* **1** utter or speak (words, sounds, etc.) in a certain way. **2** utter or deliver (a judgment, sentence, curse, etc.) officially or formally.

**3** state as being one's opinion. —**pro·nounce·a·ble** *adj.* —**pro·nounce·ment** *n.* —**pro·nun·ci·a·tion** *n.*

**pro·nounced** /prəˈnounst/ ▶*adj.* strongly marked; decided: *pronounced flavor.*

**pron·to** /ˈpräntō/ ▶*adv. inf.* promptly; quickly.

**pro·nun·ci·a·men·to** /prō-ˌnənsēəˈmentō/ ▶*n.* (*pl.* **-tos**) (esp. in Spain and Spanish-speaking countries) a political manifesto or proclamation.

**proof** /pro͞of/ ▶*n.* **1** facts, evidence, argument, etc., establishing or helping to establish a fact. **2** demonstration; proving. **3** test or trial: *put them to the proof.* **4** standard of strength of distilled alcoholic spirits. **5** trial impression before final printing. **6** stage in the resolution of a mathematical or philosophical problem. **7** photographic print made for selection, etc.

▶*adj.* impervious to penetration, ill effects, etc.: *proof against the harshest weather.*

**proof·read** /ˈpro͞ofˌrēd/ ▶*v.* (*past* and *past part.* **-read** /-ˌred/) read (esp. printer's proofs) and mark

any errors. —**proof·read·er** n.
—**proof·read·ing** n.

**prop** /präp/ ▸n. **1** rigid, esp.
separate, support. **2** person who
supplies support, assistance,
comfort, etc. **3** portable object
used on the set of a play or
movie.
▸v. (**propped**, **prop·ping**) support
with or as if with a prop.

**pro·pa·gan·da** /ˌpräpəˈgandə/
▸n. **1** organized program of
publicity, selected information,
etc., used to propagate a
doctrine, etc. **2** ideas, etc., so
propagated.

**prop·a·gate** /ˈpräpəˌgāt/ ▸v.
**1** (of a plant, animal, etc.) breed
or reproduce from the parent
stock. **2** spread (a statement,
belief, theory, etc.).
—**prop·a·ga·tion** n.
—**prop·a·ga·tive** adj.
—**prop·a·ga·tor** n.

**pro·pane** /ˈprōˌpān/ ▸n. gaseous
hydrocarbon of the alkane series
used as bottled fuel.

**pro·pel** /prəˈpel/ ▸v. (**-pelled**,
**-pel·ling**) **1** drive or push
forward. **2** urge on; encourage.
—**pro·pel·lant** n. & adj.

**pro·pel·ler** ▸n. revolving shaft
with blades, esp. for propelling a
ship or aircraft.

**pro·pen·si·ty** /prəˈpensitē/ ▸n.
(pl. **-ties**) inclination or tendency:
has a propensity for wandering.

**prop·er** /ˈpräpər/ ▸adj.
**1 a** accurate; correct. **b** fit;
suitable; right: at the proper time.
**2** decent; respectable, esp.
excessively so. **3** belonging or
relating: respect proper to them.
**4** strictly so called; real; genuine:
this is the crypt, not the cathedral
proper. —**prop·er·ly** adv.

☐ **proper noun** (or **name**) Gram.
name used for an individual
person, place, animal, country,
title, etc., e.g., Jane, London,
Everest.

**prop·er·ty** /ˈpräpərtē/ ▸n. (pl.
**-ties**) **1** something owned; a
possession, esp. a house, land,
etc. **2** attribute, quality, or
characteristic. **3** movable object
used on a theater stage, in a
movie, etc.

**proph·e·cy** /ˈpräfəˌsē/ ▸n. (pl.
**-cies**) prophetic utterance, esp.
biblical.

**proph·e·sy** /ˈpräfəˌsī/ ▸v. (**-sied**)
foretell (future events, etc.).

**proph·et** /ˈpräfit/ (fem.
**proph·et·ess**) ▸n. **1** person who
foretells events. **2** religious
teacher inspired by God.

**pro·phe·sy** /prəˈfetik/ ▸*adj.* prophesying.

**pro·phy·lax·is** /ˌprōfəˈlaksəs/ ▸*n.* (*pl.* **-lax·es**) preventive treatment against disease. —**pro·phy·lac·tic** *adj. & n.*

**pro·pin·qui·ty** /prəˈpiNGkwitē/ ▸*n.* **1** nearness in space; proximity. **2** close kinship. **3** similarity.

**pro·pi·ti·ate** /prəˈpisHē,āt/ ▸*v.* appease (an offended person, etc.). —**pro·pi·ti·a·tion** *n.* —**pro·pi·ti·a·to·ry** *adj.*

**pro·pi·tious** /prəˈpisHəs/ ▸*adj.* **1** favorable. **2** (of the weather, etc.) suitable. —**pro·pi·tious·ly** *adv.* —**pro·pi·tious·ness** *n.*

**pro·po·nent** /prəˈpōnənt/ ▸*n.* person advocating a motion, theory, or proposal.

**pro·por·tion** /prəˈpôrsHən/ ▸*n.* **1 a** comparative part or share. **b** comparative ratio: *proportion of births to deaths.* **2** correct or pleasing relation of things or parts of a thing. **3** dimensions; size: *large proportions.* **4** *Math.* equality of ratios between two pairs of quantities, e.g., 3:5 and 9:15. ▸*v.* make proportional. —**pro·por·tioned** *adj.* —**pro·por·tion·ate** *adj.*

**pro·por·tion·al** ▸*adj.* corresponding in size or amount to something else.

**pro·pos·al** /prəˈpōzəl/ ▸*n.* **1** act or an instance of proposing something. **2** course of action, etc., so proposed: *the proposal was never carried out.* **3** offer of marriage.

**pro·pose** /prəˈpōz/ ▸*v.* **1** put forward for consideration or as a plan. **2** make an offer of marriage. **3** nominate. —**pro·pos·er** *n.*

**prop·o·si·tion** /ˌpräpəˈzisHən/ ▸*n.* **1** statement or assertion. **2** plan proposed; proposal. **3** project, etc., considered in terms of its likely success: *difficult proposition.* **4** formal statement of a theorem or problem. **5** *inf.* sexual proposal. ▸*v. inf.* make a proposal (esp. of sexual intercourse) to. —**prop·o·si·tion·al** *adj.*

**pro·pound** /prəˈpound/ ▸*v.* offer for consideration; propose.

**pro·pri·e·tor** /prəˈprīətər/ ▸*n.* owner of a business, hotel, etc. —**pro·pri·e·to·ri·al** *adj.* —**pro·pri·e·tor·ship** *n.*

**pro·pri·e·ty** /prəˈprīitē/ ▸*n.* (*pl.* **-ties**) **1** fitness; rightness.

**2** correctness of behavior or morals. **3** (**proprieties**) details or rules of correct conduct.

**pro·pul·sion** /prə'pəlsHən/ ▸*n.* **1** driving or pushing forward. **2** impelling influence. —**pro·pul·sive** *adj.*

**pro·rate** ▸*v.* allocate or distribute proportionally.

**pro·sa·ic** /prō'zāik/ ▸*adj.* **1** like prose; lacking poetic beauty. **2** unromantic; dull; commonplace: *took a prosaic view of life.* —**pro·sa·i·cal·ly** *adv.*

**pro·sce·ni·um** /prə'sēnēəm/ ▸*n.* (*pl.* -**ni·ums** or -**ni·a**) vertical arched opening to the stage.

**pro·scribe** /prō'skrīb/ ▸*v.* **1** banish; exile. **2** put (a person) outside the protection of the law. **3** reject or denounce.

**prose** /prōz/ ▸*n.* **1** written or spoken language in its ordinary form. **2** plain or dull writing.

**pros·e·cute** /'präsi,kyōōt/ ▸*v.* **1** institute legal proceedings against (a person). **2** carry on (a trade, pursuit, etc.). —**pros·e·cu·tion** *n.* —**pros·e·cu·tor** *n.*

**pros·e·lyte** /'präsə,līt/ ▸*n.* person converted, esp. recently,

from one opinion, creed, party, etc., to another. —**pros·e·ly·tism** *n.*

**pro·sit** /'prōzit; -sit/ ▸*interj.* expression used as a toast when drinking to a person's health.

**pros·pect** /'präs,pekt/ ▸*n.* **1** something anticipated. **2** extensive view of landscape, etc.: *striking prospect.* **3** possible or probable customer, subscriber, etc.
▸*v.* explore (a region) for gold, etc. —**pros·pec·tive** *adj.* —**pros·pec·tor** *n.*

**pro·spec·tus** /prə'spektəs/ ▸*n.* printed document advertising or describing a school, commercial enterprise, etc.

**pros·per** /'präspər/ ▸*v.* succeed; thrive.

**pros·per·ous** ▸*adj.* financially successful. —**pros·per·i·ty** *n.*

**pros·tate** /'präs,tāt/ (also **pros·tate gland**) ▸*n.* gland surrounding the neck of the bladder in male mammals and releasing part of the semen.

**pros·the·sis** /präs'THēsis/ ▸*n.* (*pl.* -**ses**) artificial part supplied to replace a missing body part. —**pros·thet·ic** *adj.*

**pros·ti·tute** /'prästi,t(y)ōōt/ ▸*n.*

person who engages in sexual activity for payment.
▶*v.* **1** make a prostitute of (esp. oneself). **2** misuse (one's talents, skills, etc.) for money. —**pros·ti·tu·tion** *n.*

**pros·trate** /'präs,trāt/ ▶*adj.* **1 a** lying face downward, esp. in submission. **b** lying horizontally. **2** overcome, esp. by grief, exhaustion, etc.
▶*v.* **1** (**prostrate oneself**) throw oneself down in submission, etc. **2** reduce (someone) to extreme physical weakness: *she was prostrated by a migraine.* —**pros·tra·tion** *n.*

**pro·tag·o·nist** /prō'tagənist/ ▶*n.* chief person in a drama, story, etc.

**pro tan·to** /prō 'tan,tō/ ▶*adj. & adv.* to such an extent; to that extent.

**pro·te·an** /'prōtēən/ ▶*adj.* variable; taking many forms.

**pro·tect** /prə'tekt/ ▶*v.* keep (a person, thing, etc.) safe; defend; guard: *goggles protected her eyes from dust.* —**pro·tec·tive** *adj.* —**pro·tec·tor** *n.*

**pro·tec·tion** ▶*n.* **1** protecting or being protected; defense. **2** thing, person, or animal that provides protection.

**pro·tec·tor·ate** /prə'tektərit/ ▶*n.* nation that is controlled and protected by another.

**pro·té·gé** /'prōtə,zHā/ ▶*n.* person under the protection, patronage, tutelage, etc., of another.

**pro·tein** /'prō,tēn/ ▶*n.* any of a group of organic compounds composed of amino acids and forming an essential part of all living organisms.

**pro tem** /prō 'tem/ ▶*adv. & adj.* for the time being.

**pro tem·po·re** /'prō 'tempərē/ (also **pro tem**) ▶*adj. & adv.* for the time being.

**pro·test** ▶*n.* /'prō,test/ statement or act of dissent or disapproval.
▶*v.* /prə'test/ **1** make a protest. **2** affirm (one's innocence, etc.) solemnly. **3** object (to a decision, etc.). —**pro·test·er** *n.* —**pro·test·ing·ly** *adv.*

**Prot·es·tant** /'prätəstənt/ ▶*n.* member or follower of a Christian Church separated from the Roman Catholic Church after the Reformation.
▶*adj.* of the Protestant Churches or their members, etc. —**Prot·es·tant·ism** *n.*

**proto-** ▶*comb. form* first: *prototype.*

**pro·to·col** /'prōtə,kôl/ ▶*n.*

**1** official formality and etiquette. **2** original draft of a diplomatic document, esp. of the terms of a treaty. **3** formal statement of a transaction.

**pro·ton** /ˈprōˌtän/ ▶*n.* stable elementary particle with a positive electric charge, occurring in all atomic nuclei.

**pro·to·plasm** /ˈprōtəˌplazəm/ ▶*n.* material comprising the living part of a cell. —**pro·to·plas·mic** *adj.*

**pro·to·type** /ˈprōtəˌtīp/ ▶*n.* **1** original as a pattern for imitations, improved forms, etc. **2** trial model or preliminary version. —**pro·to·typ·i·cal** *adj.*

**pro·to·zo·an** /ˌprōtəˈzōən/ ▶*n.* (*pl.* **-zo·a** or **-zo·ans**) unicellular microscopic organism. ▶*adj.* (also **pro·to·zo·ic**) of this group.

**pro·tract** /prəˈtrakt/ ▶*v.* **1** prolong or lengthen. **2** draw (a plan, etc.) to scale.

**pro·tract·ed** ▶*adj.* of excessive length or duration. —**pro·tract·ed·ly** *adv.* —**pro·tract·ed·ness** *n.*

**pro·trac·tor** /ˈprōˌtraktər/ ▶*n.* instrument for measuring angles, usu. in the form of a graduated semicircle.

**pro·trude** /prəˈtro͞od/ ▶*v.* thrust or cause to thrust forth. —**pro·tru·sion** *n.*

**pro·tu·ber·ant** /prə-ˈt(y)o͞ob(ə)rənt/ ▶*adj.* bulging out; prominent: *protuberant eyes.* —**pro·tu·ber·ance** *n.*

**proud** /proud/ ▶*adj.* **1** feeling greatly honored or pleased. **2** haughty; arrogant. **3** (of an occasion, etc.) justly arousing pride.: *a proud day for us.* **4** (of a thing) imposing; splendid. —**proud·ly** *adv.* —**proud·ness** *n.*

**prove** /pro͞ov/ ▶*v.* (*past part.* **proved** or **prov·en**) **1** demonstrate the truth of by evidence or argument. **2** turn out to be: *it proved to be untrue.* **3** test the accuracy of (a calculation). □ **prove oneself** show one's abilities, courage, etc.

**prov·e·nance** /ˈprävənəns/ ▶*n.* origin or place of origin.

**prov·erb** /ˈprävˌərb/ ▶*n.* short pithy saying in general use, held to embody a general truth. —**pro·ver·bi·al** *adj.*

**pro·vide** /prəˈvīd/ ▶*v.* **1** supply; furnish; make available (to). **2** stipulate in a will, statute, etc. —**pro·vid·er** *n.*

**pro·vid·ed** ▶*conj.* on the

condition or understanding (that).

**prov·i·dence** /'prävə,dens/ ▸n. 1 protective care of God or nature. 2 timely care or preparation; foresight; thrift.

**prov·i·dent** ▸adj. having or showing foresight; thrifty. —**prov·i·dent·ly** adv.

**prov·i·den·tial** ▸adj. 1 of or by divine foresight or interposition. 2 opportune; lucky. —**prov·i·den·tial·ly** adv.

**prov·ince** /'prävins/ ▸n. 1 principal administrative division of some countries. 2 (**the provinces**) whole of a country outside major cities, esp. regarded as uncultured, unsophisticated, etc. 3 field, area or sphere of action.

**pro·vin·cial** /prə'vinchəl/ ▸adj. 1 of a province or provinces. 2 unsophisticated or uncultured. ▸n. 1 inhabitant of a province or the provinces. 2 unsophisticated or uncultured person. —**pro·vin·cial·ism** n. —**pro·vin·cial·ly** adv.

**pro·vi·sion** /prə'vizHən/ ▸n. 1 act or an instance of providing: *made no provision for his future.* 2 (**provisions**) food, drink, etc., esp. for an expedition. 3 clause of a legal or formal statement. ▸v. supply with provisions.

**pro·vi·sion·al** ▸adj. providing for immediate needs only; temporary. —**pro·vi·sion·al·ly** adv.

**pro·vi·so** /prə'vīzō/ ▸n. (pl. -sos) 1 stipulation. 2 clause of stipulation or limitation in a document.

**pro·voke** /prə'vōk/ ▸v. 1 rouse or incite. 2 call forth; instigate; cause. 3 irritate or anger. —**pro·vo·ca·tion** n. —**pro·voc·a·tive** adj.

**pro·vost** /'prō,vōst/ ▸n. high administrative officer of a church or university.

**prow** /prou/ ▸n. bow of a ship adjoining the stem.

**prow·ess** /'prouəs/ ▸n. 1 skill; expertise. 2 valor; gallantry.

**prowl** /proul/ ▸v. move about stealthily as if in search of prey, plunder, etc. ▸n. act or an instance of prowling. —**prowl·er** n.

**prox·e·mics** /präk'sēmiks/ ▸n. branch of knowledge that deals with the amount of space that people feel it necessary to set between themselves and others.

**prox·im·i·ty** /präk'simitē/ ▸*n.* nearness in space, time, etc.

**prox·y** /'präksē/ ▸*n.* (*pl.* **-ies**) **1** authorization given to a substitute or deputy: *a proxy vote.* **2** person authorized to act as a substitute, etc.

**prude** /prŏŏd/ ▸*n.* person having or affecting an attitude of extreme propriety or modesty, esp. in sexual matters. —**prud·er·y** *n.* —**prud·ish** *adj.*

**pru·dent** /'prŏŏdnt/ ▸*adj.* acting with care and thought for the future. —**pru·dence** *n.*

**pru·den·tial** /prŏŏ'denchəl/ ▸*adj.* involving or showing care and forethought, typically in business.

**prune** /prŏŏn/ ▸*n.* dried plum. ▸*v.* **1** trim (a tree, etc.) by cutting away dead or overgrown branches, etc. **2** remove (superfluous matter).

**pru·ri·ent** /'prŏŏrēənt/ ▸*adj.* **1** having an unhealthy obsession with sexual matters. **2** encouraging such an obsession. —**pru·ri·ence** *n.*

**pry** /prī/ ▸*v.* (**pried**) **1** inquire too inquisitively: *I'm tired of your prying into my personal life.* **2** use force to open something: *he used* a screwdriver to pry open the window.

**PS** ▸*abbr.* postscript.

**psalm** /säm/ ▸*n.* (also **Psalm**) sacred song esp. from the Book of Psalms (Old Testament). —**psalm·ist** *n.*

**pse·phol·o·gy** /sē'fäləjē/ ▸*n.* statistical study of elections and trends in voting.

**pseud·e·pig·ra·pha** /ˌsŏŏdə'pigrəfə/ ▸*pl. n.* spurious or pseudonymous writings, esp. Jewish writings ascribed to various biblical patriarchs and prophets but composed within approximately 200 years of the birth of Jesus Christ.

**pseudo-** (also **pseud-** before a vowel) ▸*comb. form* **1** false; not genuine: *pseudointellectual.* **2** resembling or imitating (often in technical applications): *pseudomalaria.*

**pseu·do·nym** /'sŏŏdn-im/ ▸*n.* fictitious name, esp. one assumed by an author.

**pso·ri·a·sis** /sə'rīəsis/ ▸*n.* skin disease marked by red scaly patches.

**psych** /sīk/ (also **psyche**) ▸*v. inf.* **1** prepare (oneself or another person) mentally for an ordeal, etc. **2** influence a person psychologically, esp. negatively; intimidate; frighten.

**psych.** (also **psychol.**) ▸*abbr.*
**1** psychological. **2** psychology.

**psy·che** /ˈsīkē/ ▸*n.* **1** soul; spirit.
**2** mind.

**psy·che·del·ic** /ˌsīkiˈdelik/ ▸*adj.*
**1** expanding the mind's awareness, etc., esp. through the use of hallucinogenic drugs.
**2** *inf.* hallucinatory in effect, color, design, etc.
▸*n.* hallucinogenic drug.

**psy·chi·a·try** /səˈkīətrē/ ▸*n.* the study and treatment of mental illness. —**psy·chi·at·ric** *adj.*
—**psy·chi·a·trist** *n.*

**psy·chic** /ˈsīkik/ ▸*adj.* **1** (of a person) considered to have occult powers, such as telepathy, clairvoyance, etc. **2** of the soul or mind.
▸*n.* person considered to have psychic powers; medium.

**psy·cho·ac·tive** /ˌsīkōˈaktiv/
▸*adj.* (chiefly of a drug) affecting the mind.

**psy·cho·a·nal·y·sis** /ˌsīkōə-ˈnaləsis/ ▸*n.* therapeutic method of treating mental disorders by discussion and analysis of repressed fears and conflicts.
—**psy·cho·an·a·lyze** *v.*

—**psy·cho·an·a·lyst** *n.*
—**psy·cho·an·a·lyt·ic** *adj.*

**psy·cho·gen·ic** /ˌsīkōˈjenik/
▸*adj.* having a psychological origin or cause rather than a physical one.

**psy·chol·o·gy** /sīˈkäləjē/ ▸*n.* (*pl.* -gies) **1** scientific study of the human mind. **2** treatise on or theory of this. **3** mental characteristics, etc., of a person, group, situation, etc.
—**psy·cho·log·i·cal** *adj.*
—**psy·chol·o·gist** *n.*

**psy·chom·e·try** /sīˈkämətrē/ ▸*n.* supposed ability to discover facts about an event or person by touching inanimate objects associated with them.

**psy·cho·sis** /sīˈkōsis/ ▸*n.* (*pl.* -ses) severe mental derangement with loss of contact with external reality.

**psy·cho·so·mat·ic** /ˌsīkōsə-ˈmatik/ ▸*adj.* (of an illness, etc.) mental, not physical, in origin.

**psy·cho·ther·a·py** ▸*n.* the treatment of mental disorder by psychological means.
—**psy·cho·ther·a·pist** *n.*

**PT** ▸*abbr.* physical therapy.

**Pt** ▸*symb. Chem.* platinum.

**pt.** ▸*abbr.* **1** part. **2** pint. **3** point.

**ptar·mi·gan** /ˈtärmigən/ ▸*n.*

grouse with black or gray plumage in the summer and white in the winter.

**pter·o·dac·tyl** /ˌterəˈdaktil/ ▸n. large extinct flying reptile.

**pto·maine** /ˈtōˌmān/ ▸n. any of various amine compounds, some toxic, in putrefying animal and vegetable matter.

**pub** /pəb/ ▸n. tavern or bar.

**pub.** (also **publ.**) ▸abbr. **1** public. **2** publication. **3** published. **4** publisher. **5** publishing.

**pu·ber·ty** /ˈpyo͞obərtē/ ▸n. period during which adolescents reach sexual maturity.

**pu·bes** /ˈpyo͞obēz/ ▸n. (pl. same) lower part of the abdomen at the front of the pelvis, covered with hair from puberty.

**pu·bes·cent** /pyo͞oˈbesənt/ ▸adj. **1** relating to or denoting a person at or approaching the age of puberty. **2** covered with short soft hair; downy.
▸n. person at or approaching the age of puberty.

**pu·bic** /ˈpyo͞obik/ ▸adj. of or near the genitalia.

**pub·lic** /ˈpəblik/ ▸adj. **1** of the people as a whole. **2** open to or shared by all. **3** done or existing openly: *public protest.* **4** (of a service, funds, etc.) provided by, concerning, or serving government.
▸n. **1** community in general, or members of the community. **2** specified section of the community: *reading public.*
—**pub·lic·ly** adv.

**pub·li·ca·tion** ▸n. **1** preparation and issuing of a book, newspaper, etc. **2** book, journal, etc., issued for public sale. **3** making something publicly known.

**pub·lic de·fen·der** ▸n. lawyer employed at public expense to represent a defendant who is unable to pay for legal assistance.

**pub·lic·i·ty** /pəˈblisitē/ ▸n. **1 a** advertising. **b** material or information used for this. **2** public exposure.

**pub·li·cize** /ˈpəbləˌsīz/ ▸v. advertise; make publicly known.

**pub·lic re·la·tions** ▸pl. n. [often treated as *sing.*] **1** professional maintenance of a favorable public image, esp. by a company, etc. **2** state of the relationship between the public and a company, etc.

**pub·lic school** ▸ **1** free, government-supported school. **2** *Brit.* private boarding school.

**pub·lic u·til·i·ty** ▸*n.* organization supplying water, gas, etc., to the community.

**pub·lish** /ˈpəbliSH/ ▸*v.* **1** prepare and issue (a book, newspaper, etc.) for public sale. **2** make generally known. **—pub·lish·er** *n.*

**puce** /pyo͞os/ ▸*adj.* of a dark red or purple-brown color. ▸*n.* dark red or purple-brown color.

**puck** /pək/ ▸*n.* rubber disk used in ice hockey.

**puck·er** ▸*v.* gather or cause to gather into wrinkles, folds, or bulges: *puckered her eyebrows.* ▸*n.* such a wrinkle, bulge, fold, etc.

**puck·ish** /ˈpəkiSH/ ▸*adj.* playful, esp. in a mischievous way.

**pud·ding** /ˈpo͝odiNG/ ▸*n.* any of various dessert dishes, usu. containing flavoring, sugar, milk, etc.

**pud·dle** /ˈpədl/ ▸*n.* small pool, esp. of rainwater. ▸*v.* (of liquid) form a small pool. **—pud·dly** *adj.*

**pudg·y** /ˈpəjē/ ▸*adj.* (**-i·er, -i·est**) *inf.* (esp. of a person) plump; slightly overweight.

**pu·er·ile** /ˈpyo͞o(ə)rəl/ ▸*adj.* trivial; childish; immature.

**pu·er·pe·ri·um** /ˌpyo͞oər-ˈpi(ə)rēəm/ ▸*n.* period of about six weeks after childbirth during which the mother's reproductive organs return to their original nonpregnant condition.

**puff** /pəf/ ▸*n.* **1** short quick blast of breath, wind, vapor, etc. **2** draw of smoke from a cigarette, pipe, etc. **3** light pastry containing jam, cream, etc. **4** extravagantly enthusiastic review of a book, etc., esp. in a newspaper. ▸*v.* **1** emit a puff of air or breath; blow with short blasts. **2** become or cause to become inflated; swell: *his eye was inflamed and puffed up.* **3** [usu. as *adj.* **puffed up**] elate; make proud or boastful. **—puf·fy** *adj.*

**puf·fin** /ˈpəfin/ ▸*n.* northern seabird with a large head, brightly colored triangular bill, and black and white plumage.

**pug** /pəg/ ▸*n.* dog of a dwarf breed with a broad flat nose and deeply wrinkled face.

**pu·gi·list** /ˈpyo͞ojəlist/ ▸*n.* boxer, esp. a professional one.

**pug·na·cious** /pəgˈnāSHəs/ ▸*adj.* quarrelsome; disposed to fight. **—pug·na·cious·ly** *adv.* **—pug·nac·i·ty** *n.*

**pug nose** ▶*n.* short squat or snub nose.

**pu·is·sant** /ˈpwisənt/ ▶*adj.* having great power or influence.

**pul·chri·tude** /ˈpəlkriˌt(y) o͞od/ ▶*n.* beauty.

**pule** /pyo͞ol/ ▶*v.* cry querulously or weakly; whimper.

**pull** /po͝ol/ ▶*v.* **1** exert force upon (a thing) tending to move it to oneself or the origin of the force: *stop pulling my hair.* **2** cause to move in this way. **3** extract; pluck out. **4** damage (a muscle, etc.) by abnormal strain.
▶*n.* **1** act of pulling. **2** force exerted by this. **3** influence; advantage. **4** something that attracts or draws attention.

**pul·let** /ˈpo͝olit/ ▶*n.* young hen, esp. one less than one year old.

**pul·ley** /ˈpo͝olē/ ▶*n.* (*pl.* **-leys**) grooved wheel or set of wheels for a rope, etc., to pass over, set in a block and used for changing the direction of a force.

**Pull·man** /ˈpo͝olmən/ ▶*n.* railroad sleeping car.

**pull·o·ver** ▶*n.* garment put on over the head and covering the top half of the body.

**pul·mo·nar·y** /ˈpo͝olməˌnerē/ ▶*adj.* of or relating to the lungs.

**pulp** /pəlp/ ▶*n.* **1** soft fleshy part of fruit, etc. **2** soft shapeless mass derived from rags, wood, etc., used in papermaking.
▶*v.* reduce to or become pulp. —**pulp·y** *adj.*

**pul·pit** /ˈpo͝olpit/ ▶*n.* raised enclosed platform in a church, etc., from which the preacher delivers a sermon.

**pul·sar** /ˈpəlˌsär/ ▶*n.* cosmic source of regular and rapid pulses of radiation, e.g., a rotating neutron star.

**pul·sate** /ˈpəlˌsāt/ ▶*v.* **1** expand and contract rhythmically; throb. **2** vibrate; quiver; thrill. —**pul·sa·tion** *n.*

**pulse** /pəls/ ▶*n.* **1** rhythmical throbbing of the arteries, esp. as felt in the wrists, temples, etc. **2** each successive beat of the arteries or heart. **3** throb or thrill of life or emotion. **4** single vibration of sound, electric current, light, etc. **5** rhythmical beat, esp. of music.
▶*v.* pulsate.

**pul·ver·ize** /ˈpəlvəˌrīz/ ▶*v.* reduce or be reduced to fine particles. —**pul·ver·i·za·tion** *n.*

**pu·ma** /ˈp(y)o͞omə/ ▶*n.* large

American wild cat. (Also called **cougar**, **panther**, **mountain lion**).

**pum·ice** /ˈpəmis/ (in full **pumice stone**) ▸n. **1** light porous volcanic rock often used as an abrasive in cleaning or polishing substances. **2** piece of this used for removing callused skin, etc.

**pum·mel** /ˈpəməl/ (also **pom·mel**) ▸v. strike repeatedly, esp. with the fist.

**pump** /pəmp/ ▸n. **1** machine for raising or moving liquids, compressing gases, inflating tires, etc. **2** low-cut shoe without ties, straps, etc.
▸v. **1** raise or remove (liquid, gas, etc.) with a pump. **2** fill (a tire, etc.) with air. **3** question (a person) persistently to obtain information. **4** move vigorously up and down.

**pum·per·nick·el** /ˈpəmpər-ˌnikəl/ ▸n. type of dark rye bread.

**pump·kin** /ˈpəm(p)kən/ ▸n. rounded orange edible gourd of a vine.

**pun** /pən/ ▸n. humorous use of a word to suggest different meanings, or of words of the same sound and different meanings.
▸v. (**punned**, **pun·ning**) make a joke exploiting the different meanings of a word.

**punch** /pənCH/ ▸v. **1** strike bluntly, esp. with a closed fist. **2** pierce (a hole).
▸n. **1** blow with a fist. **2** tool or machine for punching holes in or impressing a design or stamping a die on a material. **3** drink of fruit juices, sometimes mixed with wine or liquor, served cold or hot.

**punch line** ▸n. words giving the point of a joke or story.

**punch·y** ▸adj. (**-i·er**, **-i·est**) having punch or vigor; forceful.

**punc·til·i·o** /ˌpəNGKˈtilē,ō/ ▸n. (pl. **-os**) fine or petty point of conduct or procedure.

**punc·til·i·ous** /ˌpəNGKˈtilēəs/ ▸adj. attending to details, esp. in behavior. —**punc·til·i·ous·ly** adv. —**punc·til·i·ous·ness** n.

**punc·tu·al** /ˈpəNGKCHo͞oəl/ ▸adj. observant of the appointed time; prompt. —**punc·tu·al·i·ty** n. —**punc·tu·al·ly** adv.

**punc·tu·ate** /ˈpəNGKCHo͞o,āt/ ▸v. **1** insert punctuation marks in. **2** interrupt at intervals. **3** emphasize.

**punc·tu·a·tion** ▸n. **1** system or arrangement of marks used to punctuate a written passage.

**2** practice or skill of punctuating.

□ **punctuation mark** any of the marks (e.g., the period and comma) used in writing to separate sentences, etc., and to clarify meaning.

**punc·ture** /ˈpəNGkCHər/ ▶n. **1** piercing, as of a tire. **2** hole made in this way.

▶v. **1** make a puncture in or become punctured. **2** prick, pierce, or deflate.

**pun·dit** /ˈpəndit/ ▶n. learned expert or teacher. —**pun·dit·ry** n.

**pun·gent** /ˈpənjənt/ ▶adj. **1** having a sharp or strong taste or smell. **2** (of remarks) penetrating; biting; caustic. **3** having a sharp point. —**pun·gen·cy** n.

**pun·ish** /ˈpəniSH/ ▶v. **1** cause (an offender) to suffer for an offense. **2** inflict a penalty for (an offense). **3** hurt, abuse, or treat improperly. —**pun·ish·a·ble** adj. —**pun·ish·ment** n.

**pu·ni·tive** /ˈpyo͞onitiv/ (also **pu·ni·to·ry**) ▶adj. inflicting or intended to inflict punishment. —**pu·ni·tive·ly** adv.

**punk** /pəNGk/ ▶n. **1 a** worthless person or thing (often as a general term of abuse).

**b** nonsense. **2** (also **punk rock**) loud fast-moving form of rock music with crude and aggressive effects. **3** hoodlum or ruffian.

**punt**[1] /pənt/ ▶n. flat-bottomed boat, square at both ends, propelled by a long pole. ▶v. travel or convey in a punt.

**punt**[2] ▶v. kick (a football) after it has dropped from the hands and before it reaches the ground. ▶n. such a kick. —**punt·er** n.

**pu·ny** /ˈpyo͞onē/ ▶adj. (**-ni·er**, **-ni·est**) **1** small. **2** weak; feeble.

**pup** /pəp/ ▶n. **1** young dog. **2** young wolf, rat, seal, etc.

**pu·pa** /ˈpyo͞opə/ ▶n. (pl. **-pae**) insect in the stage of development between larva and imago. —**pu·pal** adj.

**pu·pil** /ˈpyo͞opəl/ ▶n. **1** person who is taught by another. **2** dark circular opening in the center of the iris of the eye.

**pup·pet** /ˈpəpit/ ▶n. **1** small figure moved by various means as entertainment. **2** person controlled by another. —**pup·pet·ry** n.

**pup·py** ▶n. (pl. **-pies**) **1** young dog. **2** conceited or arrogant young man.

**pur·chase** /ˈpərCHəs/ ▶v. **1** buy. **2** obtain or achieve at some cost.

▸*n.* **1** buying. **2** something bought. —**pur·chas·er** *n.*

**pure** /pyŏor/ ▸*adj.* **1** not mixed or adulterated with any other substance. **2** without any unnecessary elements. **3** free of contamination. **4** not morally corrupt. **5** (of a subject of study) abstract; not applied.

**pure·bred** /ˈpyŏorˌbred/ ▸*adj.* belonging to a recognized breed of unmixed lineage.

▸*n.* purebred animal.

**pu·rée** /pyŏoˈrā/ ▸*n.* smooth pulp of vegetables, fruit, etc.

▸*v.* (**-réed**) make a purée of.

**pur·ga·tive** /ˈpərgətiv/ ▸*adj.* strongly laxative.

▸*n.* purgative substance.

**pur·ga·to·ry** /ˈpərgəˌtôrē/ ▸*n.* (*pl.* **-ries**) **1** condition or supposed place of spiritual cleansing, esp. in Roman Catholic belief, of those dying in the grace of God but having to expiate venial sins, etc. **2** place or state of temporary suffering or expiation.

**purge** /pərj/ ▸*v.* **1** remove by cleansing. **2** rid (an organization, party, etc.) of persons regarded as undesirable. **3** empty (the bowels).

▸*n.* **1** act of purging. **2** purgative.

**pu·ri·fy** /ˈpyŏorəˌfī/ ▸*v.* (**-fied**) **1** cleanse or make pure. **2** make ceremonially clean. **3** clear of extraneous elements. —**pu·ri·fi·ca·tion** *n.* —**pu·ri·fi·er** *n.*

**pu·ri·tan** /ˈpyŏoritn/ ▸*n.* **1** (**Puritan**) member of a group of English Protestants who sought to simplify and regulate forms of worship. **2** person practicing extreme strictness in religion or morals.

▸*adj.* **1** of the Puritans. **2** scrupulous and austere in religion or morals. —**pu·ri·tan·i·cal** *adj.* —**pu·ri·tan·ism** *n.*

**pu·ri·tan·i·cal** /ˌpyŏoriˈtanikəl/ ▸*adj.* practicing or affecting strict religious or moral behavior.

**pu·ri·ty** /ˈpyŏoritē/ ▸*n.* pureness; cleanness.

**purl** /pərl/ ▸*n.* type of inverted knitting stitch.

▸*v.* knit with a purl stitch.

**pur·lieu** /ˈpərl(y)ŏo/ ▸*n.* (*pl.* **-lieus** or **-lieux** /-l(y)ŏo(z)/) **1** area near or surrounding a place. **2** person's usual haunts.

**pur·loin** /pərˈloin/ ▸*v.* steal; pilfer.

**pur·ple** /ˈpərpəl/ ▸*n.* color intermediate between red and blue.

▶*adj.* of a purple color.

**pur·port** /pər'pôrt/ ▶*v.* **1** profess; be intended to seem. **2** (of a document or speech) have as its meaning; state.
▶*n.* **1** ostensible meaning. **2** sense or tenor.
—**pur·port·ed·ly** *adv.*

**pur·pose** /'pərpəs/ ▶*n.* **1** object to be attained; thing intended. **2** intention to act. **3** resolution; determination. —**pur·pose·ful** *adj.* —**pur·pose·ful·ly** *adv.* —**pur·pose·ly** *adv.*

**pur·pos·ive** /'pərpəsiv/ ▶*adj.* having, serving, or done with a purpose.

**purr** /pər/ ▶*v.* **1** (of a cat) make a low vibratory sound expressing contentment. **2** (of machinery, etc.) make a similar sound.
▶*n.* purring sound.

**purse** /pərs/ ▶*n.* **1** small pouch for carrying money on the person. **2** handbag. **3** money; funds. **4** sum as a present or prize in a contest.
▶*v.* pucker or contract (the lips).

**purs·er** ▶*n.* officer on a ship who keeps accounts, esp. the head steward in a passenger vessel.

**pur·su·ant** /pər'so͞oənt/ ▶*adv.* *formal* (**pursuant to**) conforming

to or in accordance with.
—**pur·su·ant·ly** *adv.*

**pur·sue** /pər'so͞o/ ▶*v.* (**-sued**, **-su·ing**) **1** follow with intent to overtake or capture or do harm to. **2** continue or proceed along (a route or course of action). **3** follow or engage in (study or other activity). **4** proceed in compliance with (a plan, etc.). **5** continue to investigate or discuss (a topic). **6** seek the attention or acquaintance of (a person) persistently.
—**pur·su·er** *n.*

**pur·suit** /pər'so͞ot/ ▶*n.* **1** act or an instance of pursuing. **2** occupation or activity pursued.
□ **in pursuit of** pursuing.

**pu·ru·lent** /'pyo͞or(y)ələnt/ ▶*adj.* consisting of, containing, or discharging pus.

**pur·vey** /pər'vā/ ▶*v.* provide or supply (articles of food) as one's business. —**pur·vey·ance** *n.*
—**pur·vey·or** *n.*

**pus** /pəs/ ▶*n.* thick yellowish or greenish liquid produced from infected tissue.

**push** /po͝osH/ ▶*v.* **1** exert a force on (a thing) to move it or cause it to move away. **2 a** thrust forward or upward. **b** project or cause to project: *pushes out new* *roots.* **3** exert oneself, esp. to surpass others. **4** urge, impel, or press (a person) hard. **5** pursue or demand persistently: *pushed for reform.* **6** *inf.* sell (a drug) illegally.

▶*n.* **1** act or instance of pushing; shove or thrust. **2** force exerted in this. **3** vigorous effort. **4** enterprise; determination to succeed.

**push·o·ver** *inf.* ▶*n.* **1** something that is easily done. **2** person easily overcome, persuaded, etc.

**push·y** *inf.* ▶*adj.* (**-i·er, -i·est**) excessively self-assertive. —**push·i·ness** *n.*

**pu·sil·lan·i·mous** /ˌpyōōsə-ˈlanəməs/ ▶*adj.* lacking courage; timid. —**pu·sil·la·nim·i·ty** *n.* —**pu·sil·lan·i·mous·ly** *adv.*

**puss·y** /ˈpo͝osē/ ▶*n.* (*pl.* **-ies**) (also **puss, puss·y·cat**) *inf.* cat.

**puss·y·foot** ▶*v.* **1** move stealthily or warily. **2** act cautiously or noncommittally.

**puss·y wil·low** ▶*n.* willow with furry catkins.

**pus·tule** /ˈpəsCHo͞ol/ ▶*n.* pimple containing pus. —**pus·tu·lar** *adj.*

**put** /po͝ot/ ▶*v.* (**put·ting;** *past* and *past part.* **put**) **1** move to or cause to be in a specified place or position. **2** bring into a specified condition, relation, or state. **3** cause (a person) to go or be, habitually or temporarily: *put them at their ease.* **4** imagine (oneself) in a specified situation: *put yourself in my shoes.* **5** express in a specified way: *to put it mildly.* **6** submit for consideration or attention: *put it to a vote.*

▶*adj.* stationary; fixed: *stay put.*

**pu·ta·tive** /ˈpyōōtətiv/ ▶*adj.* reputed; supposed: *his putative father.*

**pu·tre·fy** /ˈpyōōtrəˌfī/ ▶*v.* (**-fied**) become or make putrid; go bad.

**pu·tres·cent** /pyōōˈtresənt/ ▶*adj.* in the process of rotting. —**pu·tres·cence** *n.*

**pu·trid** /ˈpyōōtrid/ ▶*adj.* **1** decomposed; rotten. **2** foul; noxious.

**putt** /pət/ ▶*v.* strike (a golf ball) gently on a putting green. ▶*n.* putting stroke. —**put·ter** *n.*

**put·ter** /ˈpətər/ ▶*v.* **1** work or occupy oneself in a desultory but pleasant manner. **2** go slowly; dawdle; loiter. —**put·ter·er** *n.*

**put·ty** /ˈpətē/ ▶*n.* (*pl.* **-ties**) soft, pliable mixture used for fixing panes of glass, filling holes in woodwork, etc.

▸*v.* (**-tied**) cover, fix, join, or fill up with putty.

**puz·zle** /ˈpəzəl/ ▸*n.* **1** difficult or confusing problem; enigma. **2** problem or toy designed to test knowledge or ingenuity. ▸*v.* **1** confound or disconcert mentally. **2** be perplexed (about). —**puz·zle·ment** *n.* —**puz·zling·ly** *adv.*

**Pvt.** ▸*abbr.* private.

**PX** ▸*abbr.* post exchange.

**pyg·my** /ˈpigmē/ (also **pig·my**) ▸*n.* (*pl.* **-mies**) **1** member of a small people of equatorial Africa and parts of SE Asia. **2** very small person, animal, or thing.

**py·lon** /ˈpīˌlän/ ▸*n.* tall structure erected as a support (esp. for electric power cables) or boundary or decoration.

**pyr·a·mid** /ˈpirəˌmid/ ▸*n.* **1** monumental structure, usu. of stone, with a square base and sloping sides meeting centrally at an apex, esp. an ancient Egyptian royal tomb. **2** solid of this type with a base of three or more sides. —**py·ram·i·dal** *adj.*

**pyre** /pī(ə)r/ ▸*n.* heap of combustible material, esp. a funeral pile for burning a corpse.

**py·rite** /ˈpīˌrīt/ ▸*n.* shiny yellow mineral.

**py·ro·ma·nia** /ˌpīrōˈmānēə/ ▸*n.* obsessive desire to set fire to things. —**py·ro·ma·ni·ac** *n.*

**py·ro·tech·nics** /ˌpīrəˈtekniks/ ▸*pl. n.* **1** [treated as *sing.*] art of making fireworks. **2** display of fireworks. **3** any brilliant display. —**py·ro·tech·nic** *adj.* —**py·ro·tech·ni·cal** *adj.*

**py·thon** /ˈpīˌтнän/ ▸*n.* large tropical constricting snake.

**pyx** /piks/ ▸*n.* container in which the consecrated bread of the Eucharist is kept.

# Qq

**Q** /kyōō/ (also **q**) ▸*n.* (*pl.* **Qs** or **Q's**; **q's**) seventeenth letter of the alphabet.

**QED** ▸*abbr.* which was to be demonstrated, from Latin *quod erat demonstrandum*.

**qt.** ▸*abbr.* quart(s).

**qty.** ▸*abbr.* quantity.

**qua** /kwä/ ▸*conj.* in the capacity of; as being.

**quack** /kwak/ ▸*n.* **1** harsh sound made by ducks. **2** unqualified practitioner, esp. of medicine. ▸*v.* utter this sound. —**quack·er·y** *n.*

**quad** /kwäd/ ▸*n. inf.* quadrangle.

**quad·ran·gle** /ˈkwä,draNGgəl/ ▸*n.* **1** four-sided plane figure, esp. a square or rectangle. **2** four-sided courtyard. —**quad·ran·gu·lar** *adj.*

**quad·rant** /ˈkwädrənt/ ▸*n.* **1** quarter of a circle's circumference. **2** instrument for taking angular measurements.

**quad·ri·lat·er·al** /ˌkwädrə-ˈlatərəl/ ▸*adj.* having four sides. ▸*n.* four-sided figure.

**qua·drille** /kwäˈdril/ ▸*n.* square dance containing usu. five figures.

**quad·ri·ple·gia** /ˌkwädrə-ˈplēj(ē)ə/ ▸*n.* paralysis of all four limbs. —**quad·ri·ple·gic** *adj. & n.*

**quad·roon** /kwäˈdrōōn/ ▸*n.* person whose parents are a mulatto and a white person and who is therefore one-quarter black by descent.

**quad·ru·ped** /ˈkwädrə,ped/ ▸*n.* four-footed animal, esp. a mammal.

**qua·dru·ple** /kwäˈdrōōpəl/ ▸*adj.* **1** fourfold. **2** having four parts. ▸*n.* fourfold number or amount. ▸*v.* multiply by four.

**qua·dru·plet** /kwäˈdrōōplit/ ▸*n.* each of four children born at one birth.

**qua·dru·pli·cate** /kwä-ˈdrōōplikit/ ▸*adj.* **1** fourfold. **2** of which four copies are made.

**quag·mire** /ˈkwag,mī(ə)r/ ▸*n.* **1** soft boggy or marshy area that gives way underfoot. **2** hazardous situation.

**quail** /kwāl/ ▸*n.* (*pl.* same or **quails**) small game bird related to the partridge.

▸*v.* be apprehensive with fear.

**quaint** /kwānt/ ▸*adj.* piquantly or attractively odd or old-fashioned. —**quaint·ly** *adj.* —**quaint·ness** *n.*

**quake** /kwāk/ ▸*v.* shake; tremble. ▸*n. inf.* earthquake.

**Quak·er** ▸*n.* member of the Society of Friends, a Christian movement devoted to peaceful principles and eschewing formal ritual. —**Quak·er·ism** *n.*

**qual·i·fi·ca·tion** /ˌkwäləfi-ˈkāSHən/ ▸*n.* **1** act or instance of qualifying. **2** quality, skill, or accomplishment fitting a person for a position or purpose. **3** thing that modifies or limits.

**qual·i·fy** /ˈkwälə.fī/ ▸*v.* (**-fied**) **1** make or be competent or fit for a position or purpose. **2** make legally entitled. **3** add reservations to; modify or make less absolute (a statement or assertion). —**qual·i·fi·er** *n.*

**qual·i·ta·tive** /ˈkwäli.tātiv/ ▸*adj.* of or concerned with quality.

**qual·i·ty** /ˈkwälitē/ ▸*n.* (*pl.* **-ties**) **1** degree of excellence. **2** general excellence. **3** distinctive attribute or faculty. **4** relative nature or kind or character of a thing.

**qualm** /kwäm/ ▸*n.* uneasy doubt esp. about one's own conduct; misgiving.

**quan·da·ry** /ˈkwänd(ə)rē/ ▸*n.* (*pl.* **-ries**) **1** state of perplexity. **2** difficult situation; practical dilemma.

**quan·ti·fy** /ˈkwäntə.fī/ ▸*v.* (**-fied**) **1** determine the quantity of. **2** measure or express as a quantity. —**quan·ti·fi·a·ble** *adj.* —**quan·ti·fi·ca·tion** *n.*

**quan·ti·ty** /ˈkwäntitē/ ▸*n.* (*pl.* **-ties**) **1** property of things that is measurable. **2** amount; number. **3** specified or considerable portion or number or amount. **4** (**quantities**) large amounts or numbers: *quantities of food.* **5** value, component, etc., that may be expressed in numbers. —**quan·ti·ta·tive** *adj.*

**quan·tum** /ˈkwäntəm/ ▸*n.* (*pl.* **-ta**) **1** discrete quantity of radiant energy. **2** required or allowed amount.
□ **quantum leap** sudden large increase or advance. □ **quantum theory** theory of physics based on the assumption that energy exists in discrete units.

**quan·tum me·ru·it** /ˌkwäntəm ˈmero͞oit/ ▸*n.* reasonable sum of money to be paid for services rendered or work done when the amount due is not stipulated in a legally enforceable contract.

**quar·an·tine** /ˈkwôrənˌtēn/ ▶n. 1 isolation imposed on persons or animals to prevent infection or contagion. 2 period of this. ▶v. put in quarantine.

**quark** /kwôrk/ ▶n. component of elementary particles.

**quar·rel** /ˈkwôrəl/ ▶n. angry argument or disagreement. ▶v. have an angry argument. —**quar·rel·some** adj.

**quar·ry** /ˈkwôrē/ ▶n. (pl. **-ries**) 1 place from which stone, etc., may be extracted. 2 object of pursuit by a bird of prey, hunters, etc. ▶v. (**-ried**) extract (stone) from a quarry.

**quart** /kwôrt/ ▶n. 1 liquid measure equal to a quarter of a gallon; two pints (.95 liter). 2 unit of dry measure, equivalent to one thirty-second of a bushel (1.1 liter).

**quar·ter** /ˈkwôrtər/ ▶n. 1 each of four equal parts into which a thing is or might be divided: *the first quarter of the year.* 2 coin worth 25 cents. 3 district or section. 4 (**quarters**) lodgings; abode. ▶v. 1 divide into quarters.

2 station or lodge in a specified place.

**quar·ter·back** ▶n. player who directs offensive play in football.

**quar·ter·ly** ▶adj. produced, payable, or occurring once every quarter of a year. ▶adv. once every quarter of a year. ▶n. (pl. **-lies**) quarterly publication.

**quar·tet** /kwôrˈtet/ ▶n. 1 *Mus.* a composition for four performers. b group of four performers. 2 any group of four.

**quartz** /kwôrts/ ▶n. mineral form of silica that crystallizes as hexagonal prisms.

**qua·sar** /ˈkwāˌzär/ ▶n. starlike celestial object that emits radio waves and light.

**quash** /kwôsH/ ▶v. 1 annul; reject as not valid, esp. by a legal procedure. 2 suppress; crush (a rebellion, etc.).

**quasi-** /ˈkwāzī/ ▶comb. form 1 seemingly; not really: *quasi-scientific.* 2 almost: *quasi-independent.*

**quat·rain** /ˈkwäˌtrān/ ▶n. stanza of four lines.

**qua·ver** /ˈkwāvər/ ▶v. (esp. of a voice or musical sound) vibrate; shake; tremble. ▶n. trembling sound.

—**qua·ver·ing·ly** *adv.* —**qua·ver·y** *adj.*

**quay** /kē/ ▶*n.* solid, stationary, artificial landing place for loading and unloading ships.

**quea·sy** /ˈkwēzē/ ▶*adj.* (**-si·er, -si·est**) (of a person) feeling nausea. —**quea·si·ly** *adv.* —**quea·si·ness** *n.*

**queen** /kwēn/ ▶*n.* **1** female sovereign. **2** (also **queen consort**) king's wife. **3** woman, country, or thing preeminent of its kind: *tennis queen.* **4** fertile female among ants, bees, etc. **5** most powerful piece in chess. **6** playing card with a picture of a queen.

**queer** /kwi(ə)r/ ▶*adj.* **1** strange; odd; eccentric. **2** *inf., usu. offensive* homosexual.

▶*n. inf., usu. offensive* homosexual. —**queer·ly** *adv.* —**queer·ness** *n.*

**quell** /kwel/ ▶*v.* **1** crush or put down (a rebellion, etc.). **2** suppress (fear, anger, etc.).

**quench** /kwenCH/ ▶*v.* **1** satisfy (thirst) by drinking. **2** extinguish (a fire or light, etc.).

**que·rist** /ˈkwi(ə)rist/ ▶*n.* person who asks questions; a questioner.

**quer·u·lous** /ˈkwer(y)ələs/ ▶*adj.* complaining; peevish.

—**quer·u·lous·ly** *adj.* —**quer·u·lous·ness** *n.*

**que·ry** /ˈkwi(ə)rē/ ▶*n.* (*pl.* **-ries**) question.

▶*v.* (**-ried**) **1** ask or inquire. **2** call (a thing) into question.

**quest** /kwest/ ▶*n.* search or the act of seeking. —**quest·er** *n.* —**quest·ing·ly** *adv.*

**ques·tion** /ˈkwesCHən/ ▶*n.* **1** sentence worded or expressed so as to seek information. **2** doubt or dispute about a matter. **3** matter to be discussed or decided or voted on. **4** problem requiring an answer or solution.

▶*v.* **1** ask questions of; interrogate. **2** throw doubt upon; raise objections to. —**ques·tion·a·ble** *adj.* —**ques·tion·er** *n.* —**ques·tion·ing·ly** *adv.*

☐ **question mark** punctuation mark (?) indicating a question.

**ques·tion·naire** /ˌkwesCHəˈne(ə)r/ ▶*n.* written series of questions, esp. for statistical study.

**queue** /kyo͞o/ ▶*n. chiefly Brit.* line or sequence of persons, vehicles, etc., awaiting their turn.

▶*v.* (**queued, queu·ing** or **queue·ing**) line (up).

**quib·ble** /ˈkwibəl/ ▶n. slight objection or criticism. ▶v. raise objections about a trivial matter.

**quiche** /kēSH/ ▶n. unsweetened custard pie with a savory filling.

**quick** /kwik/ ▶adj. 1 taking only a short time. 2 arriving after a short time; prompt. 3 with only a short interval: *in quick succession.* 4 (of a person) lively; intelligent; alert. ▶adv. quickly. ▶n. 1 soft flesh below the fingernails or toenails. 2 seat of feeling or emotion: *cut to the quick.* —**quick·ly** *adv.* —**quick·ness** *n.*

**quick·en** ▶v. 1 make or become quicker. 2 spring to life. 3 stimulate: *her words quickened my interest.*

**quick·ie** ▶n. *inf.* thing done or made quickly.

**quick·sand** ▶n. loose wet sand that sucks in anything placed or falling into it.

**quick·sil·ver** ▶n. mercury.

**quid·nunc** /ˈkwidˌnəNGk/ ▶n. inquisitive and gossipy person.

**quid pro quo** /ˈkwid ˌprō ˈkwō/ ▶n. 1 thing given as compensation. 2 return made (for a gift, favor, etc.).

**qui·es·cent** /kwēˈesnt/ ▶adj. 1 inert. 2 silent; dormant. —**qui·es·cence** *n.*

**qui·et** /ˈkwīit/ ▶adj. (-er, -est) 1 with little or no sound or motion. 2 of gentle or peaceful disposition. 3 unobtrusive; not overt. 4 undisturbed; uninterrupted. ▶n. 1 silence; stillness. 2 undisturbed state; tranquillity. ▶v. make or become quiet or calm; soothe. —**qui·et·ly** *adv.* —**qui·et·ness** *n.*

**quill** /kwil/ ▶n. 1 large feather in a wing or tail. 2 hollow stem of this. 3 spine of a porcupine.

**quilt** /kwilt/ ▶n. bedcovering made of padding enclosed between layers of cloth, etc., and kept in place by patterned stitching. ▶v. make quilts.

**quince** /kwins/ ▶n. hard acidic pear-shaped fruit used chiefly in preserves.

**quin·cunx** /ˈkwinˌkəNGks/ ▶n. (pl. **quin·cunx·es**) arrangement of five objects with four at the corners of a square or rectangle and the fifth at its center, used for the five on dice or playing cards, and in planting trees.

**qui·nine** /ˈkwīˌnīn/ ▶n. bitter

crystalline compound, used as a tonic and formerly to treat malaria.

**quin·sy** /ˈkwinzē/ ▸*n.* inflammation of the throat, esp. an abscess in the region of the tonsils.

**quin·tes·sence** /kwinˈtesəns/ ▸*n.* purest and most perfect, or most typical, form, manifestation, or embodiment of some quality or class. —**quin·tes·sen·tial** *adj.* —**quin·tes·sen·tial·ly** *adv.*

**quin·tet** /kwinˈtet/ ▸*n.* **1** *Mus.* **a** composition for five. **b** group of five performers. **2** any group of five.

**quin·tu·plet** /kwinˈtəplit/ ▸*n.* each of five children born at one birth.

**quip** /kwip/ ▸*n.* clever saying; epigram. ▸*v.* (**quipped, quip·ping**) make quips. —**quip·ster** *n.*

**quirk** /kwərk/ ▸*n.* **1** peculiarity of behavior. **2** trick of fate; freak. —**quirk·y** *adj.*

**quit** /kwit/ ▸*v.* (**quit·ting;** *past* and *past part.* **quit** or **quit·ted**) **1** give up; let go; abandon (a task, etc.). **2** cease; stop. —**quit·ter** *n.*

**quit·claim** /ˈkwitˌklām/ ▸*n.* formal renunciation or relinquishing of a claim. ▸*v.* renounce or relinquish a claim.

**quite** /kwīt/ ▸*adv.* **1** completely; entirely. **2** rather; to some extent.

**quits** /kwits/ ▸*adj.* (of two people) on even terms. □ **call it quits** agree that terms are now equal: *take this check, and we'll call it quits.*

**quiv·er** /ˈkwivər/ ▸*v.* tremble or vibrate with a slight rapid motion. ▸*n.* **1** quivering motion or sound. **2** case for holding arrows. —**quiv·er·y** *adj.*

**qui vive** /ˌkē ˈvēv/ ▸*n.* (in phrase **on the qui vive**) on the alert or lookout.

**quix·ot·ic** /kwikˈsätik/ ▸*adj.* extremely idealistic; pursuing lofty but unattainable ideals. —**quix·ot·i·cal·ly** *adv.*

**quiz** /kwiz/ ▸*n.* (*pl.* **quiz·zes**) quick or informal test. ▸*v.* (**quizzed, quiz·zing**) examine by questioning.

**quiz·zi·cal** /ˈkwizikəl/ ▸*adj.* expressing or done with mild or amused perplexity. —**quiz·zi·cal·ly** *adv.*

**quod·li·bet** /ˈkwädlə,bet/ ▸n.
**1** topic for or exercise in philosophical or theological discussion. **2** lighthearted medley of well-known tunes.

**quoin** /k(w)oin/ ▸n. **1** external angle of a building. **2** cornerstone. **3** wedge.

**quoit** /k(w)oit/ ▸n. **1** ring of rope or metal, etc., thrown to encircle a peg. **2** (**quoits**) game using these.

**quo·rum** /ˈkwôrəm/ ▸n. minimum number of members that must be present to constitute a valid meeting.

**quo·ta** /ˈkwōtə/ ▸n. **1** share that an individual person, group, or company is bound to contribute to or entitled to receive from a total. **2** number of goods, people etc., stipulated or permitted.

**quo·ta·tion** /kwōˈtāSHən/ ▸n. **1** act or instance of quoting or being quoted. **2** passage or remark quoted. **3** formal statement of cost or price.
☐ **quotation mark** one of a pair of raised marks, single (' ') or double (" "), used to mark a quoted passage, for emphasis, etc.

**quote** /kwōt/ ▸v. **1** cite or appeal to (an author, book, etc.) in confirmation of some view. **2** repeat or copy out a passage from. **3** state the price of.
▸n. inf. **1** passage quoted. **2** price quoted. **3** (**quotes**) quotation marks.

**quo·tid·i·an** /kwōˈtidēən/ ▸adj. **1** daily; of every day. **2** commonplace; trivial.

**quo·tient** /ˈkwōSHənt/ ▸n. result of a division.

# Rr

**R**[1] /är/ (also **r**) ▶*n.* (*pl.* **Rs** or **R's**; **r's**) eighteenth letter of the alphabet.

**R**[2] ▶*abbr.* **1** (also **R.**) river. **2** *Chess* rook. **3** (of movies) classified as prohibited to children under age 17 unless accompanied by an adult.

**r.** (also **r**) ▶*abbr.* **1** right. **2** recto. **3** run(s). **4** radius.

**rab·bi** /ˈrabˌī/ ▶*n.* (*pl.* **-bis**) Jewish religious leader. —**rab·bin·i·cal** *adj.* —**rab·bin·ate** *n.*

**rab·bin·i·cal** /rəˈbinikəl; ra-/ ▶*adj.* of or relating to rabbis or to Jewish law or teachings.

**rab·bit** /ˈrabit/ ▶*n.* long-eared, burrowing, plant-eating mammal related to the hare.

**rab·bit ears** ▶*pl. n.* television antenna consisting of two movable rods, usu. on top of the set.

**rab·ble** /ˈrabəl/ ▶*n.* disorderly crowd; mob.
□ **rabble-rouser** person who stirs up the rabble or a crowd.

**ra·bid** /ˈrabid/ ▶*adj.* **1** having a fanatical belief in something.

**2** affected with rabies. —**ra·bid·i·ty** *n.*

**ra·bies** /ˈrābēz/ ▶*n.* contagious and fatal viral disease, esp. of dogs, cats, raccoons, etc., transmissible through saliva to humans; hydrophobia.

**rac·coon** /raˈko͞on/ ▶*n.* N. American nocturnal mammal with a bushy, ringed tail and masklike band across the eyes.

**race** /rās/ ▶*n.* **1** contest of speed between runners, horses, vehicles, etc. **2** competition to be first to achieve something. **3** strong sea or river current. **4** each of the major divisions of humankind, having distinct physical characteristics. **5** fact or concept of division into races.
▶*v.* **1** take part in a race (with). **2** (cause to) go at full or excessive speed. —**rac·er** *n.*

**race·horse** ▶*n.* horse bred or kept for racing.

**race·track** ▶*n.* place where horse races are held.

**ra·cial** /ˈrāsHəl/ ▶*adj.* of, concerning, or based on race.

**rac·ism** /ˈrāsizəm/ ▶*n.* **1** belief in

the superiority of a particular race; prejudice based on this. **2** antagonism toward other races. —**rac·ist** *n. & adj.*

**rack** /rak/ ▸*n.* **1** framework usu. with rails, bars, etc., for holding things. **2** cogged or toothed bar or rail engaging with a wheel or pinion, etc. **3** cut of lamb, etc., including the front ribs.
▸*v.* **1** (of disease or pain) inflict suffering on. **2** place in or on a rack.

**rack·et** /'rakit/ ▸*n.* **1** (also **rac·quet**) hand-held implement with a round or oval frame strung with catgut, nylon, etc., used in tennis, squash, etc. **2** uproar; din. **3** *inf.* scheme for obtaining money, etc., by fraudulent and often violent means.

**rack·e·teer** /ˌrakiˈti(ə)r/ ▸*n.* person who operates an illegal business, as gambling, extortion, etc. —**rack·et·eer·ing** *n.*

**rack rent** ▸*n.* very high rent, esp. an annual rent equivalent to the full value of the property to which it relates.
▸*v.* (**rack-rent**) exact an excessive or extortionate rent from (a tenant) or for (a property).

**ra·con·teur** /ˌrakänˈtər/ ▸*n.* teller of interesting anecdotes.

**rac·quet·ball** /'rakit,bôl/ ▸*n.* racket game played on a four-walled court.

**rac·y** /'rāsē/ ▸*adj.* (**-i·er**, **-i·est**) **1** lively and vigorous in style. **2** risqué; suggestive. —**rac·i·ness** *n.*

**ra·dar** /'rā,där/ ▸*n.* system for detecting the direction, range, or presence of objects by reflection of transmitted radio waves (acronym of *r*adio *d*etecting *a*nd *r*anging).

**ra·di·al** /'rādēəl/ ▸*adj.* **1** of rays or radii. **2** arranged in spokes like rays or radii. **3** (of a tire) having fabric layers laid radially at right angles to the center of the tread. —**ra·di·al·ly** *adv.*

**ra·di·ant** /'rādēənt/ ▸*adj.* **1** emitting rays of light or energy. **2** looking bright or happy. —**ra·di·ance** *n.* —**ra·di·ant·ly** *adv.*
□ **radiant heat** heat transmitted by radiation.

**ra·di·ate** /'rādē,āt/ ▸*v.* **1 a** (of light or heat) emit or be emitted in rays. **2** emit (light, heat, or sound) from a center. **3** transmit or demonstrate (joy, etc.).

**4** diverge or cause to diverge or spread from a center.

**ra·di·a·tion** ▶*n.* **1** emission of energy as electromagnetic waves or as moving subatomic particles, esp. high-energy particles that cause ionization. **2** energy transmitted in this way. **3** (also **ra·di·a·tion ther·a·py**) treatment of disease using radiation, such as X rays or ultraviolet light.

**ra·di·a·tor** ▶*n.* **1** device through which hot water or steam circulates to heat a room, etc. **2** engine-cooling device in a motor vehicle, etc.

**rad·i·cal** /'radikəl/ ▶*adj.* **1** primary; fundamental. **2** extreme; thorough. **3** representing or holding extreme political views; revolutionary.
▶*n.* person holding radical views.

**ra·di·o** /'rādē͵ō/ ▶*n.* (*pl.* **-os**) **1 a** transmission and reception of sound messages, etc., by electromagnetic waves of radio frequency. **b** apparatus for this. **2** sound broadcasting: *prefers the radio.*
▶*v.* (**-oed**) **1** send (a message) by radio. **2** communicate or broadcast by radio.

**radio-** ▶*comb. form* **1** denoting radio or broadcasting. **2** connected with radioactivity. **3** connected with rays or radiation.

**ra·di·o·ac·tive** ▶*adj.* of or exhibiting radioactivity. —**ra·di·o·ac·tive·ly** *adv.*

**ra·di·o·ac·tiv·i·ty** ▶*n.* spontaneous disintegration of atomic nuclei, with emission of radiation or particles.

**ra·di·o·graph** /'rādēō͵graf/ ▶*n.* image produced on a sensitive plate or film by X-rays or other radiation.
▶*v.* produce an image of (something) on a sensitive plate or film by X-rays, gamma rays, or similar radiation.

**ra·di·ol·o·gy** /͵rādē'äləjē/ ▶*n.* the study of X rays and other high-energy radiation, esp. as used in medicine. —**ra·di·o·log·i·cal** *adj.* —**ra·di·ol·o·gist** *n.*

**ra·di·om·e·ter** /͵rādē'ämitər/ ▶*n.* instrument for detecting or measuring the intensity or force of radiation.

**ra·di·os·co·py** /͵rādē'äskəpē/ ▶*n.* examination by X-rays or similar radiation of objects opaque to light.

**ra·di·o·sonde** /ˈrādēōˌsänd/ ▶n. instrument carried by balloon or other means to various levels of the atmosphere and transmitting measurements by radio.

**rad·ish** /ˈradiSH/ ▶n. 1 plant with a fleshy pungent root. 2 this root, eaten esp. raw.

**ra·di·um** /ˈrādēəm/ ▶n. radioactive metallic element orig. obtained from pitchblende, etc. (Symb.: **Ra**).

**ra·di·us** /ˈrādēəs/ ▶n. (pl. **-di·i** or **-di·us·es**) 1 straight line from the center to the circumference of a circle or sphere. 2 distance from a center: *within a radius of 20 miles.* 3 thicker and shorter of the two bones in the human forearm.

**ra·don** /ˈrāˌdän/ ▶n. gaseous radioactive inert element arising from the disintegration of radium. (Symb.: **Rn**)

**RAF** ▶abbr. (in the UK) Royal Air Force.

**raf·fi·a** /ˈrafēə/ ▶n. 1 palm tree native to Madagascar, having very long leaves. 2 fiber from its leaves used for weaving, tying plants, etc.

**raf·fish** /ˈrafiSH/ ▶adj. disreputable; rakish. —**raf·fish·ly** adv. —**raf·fish·ness** n.

**raf·fle** /ˈrafəl/ ▶n. fund-raising lottery with prizes.
▶v. sell by means of a raffle.

**raft** /raft/ ▶n. 1 flat floating structure of logs or other materials for conveying persons or things. 2 lifeboat or small (often inflatable) boat. 3 large amount of something.
▶v. cross (water) on a raft.

**raf·ter** ▶n. each of the sloping beams forming the framework of a roof.

**rag** /rag/ ▶n. 1 torn, frayed, or worn piece of woven material. 2 (**rags**) old or worn clothes. 3 ragtime composition or tune. 4 *inf.* newspaper.
▶v. (**rag·ged**, **rag·ging**) tease; play rough jokes on.

**rag·a·muf·fin** /ˈragəˌməfin/ ▶n. child in ragged dirty clothes.

**rage** /rāj/ ▶n. 1 fierce or violent anger. 2 violent action of a natural force. 3 temporary enthusiasm; fad.
▶v. 1 be full of anger. 2 speak furiously or madly. 3 (of wind, battle, fever, etc.) be violent; be at its height; continue unchecked.

**ra·gout** /raˈgoō/ ▶n. dish of

highly seasoned meat stewed with vegetables.

**rag·time** ▶*n.* form of highly syncopated early jazz, esp. for the piano.

**rag·weed** ▶*n.* any of various plants with allergenic pollen.

**raid** /rād/ ▶*n.* rapid surprise attack, esp.: **1** in warfare. **2** to commit a crime or do harm. **3** by police, etc., to arrest suspects or seize illicit goods. ▶*v.* make a raid on. —**raid·er** *n.*

**rail** /rāl/ ▶*n.* **1** level or sloping bar or series of bars: **a** used to hang things on. **b** as the top of a banister. **c** forming part of a fence or barrier. **2** steel bar or continuous line of bars laid on the ground, usu. as a railroad. ▶*v.* complain using abusive language; rant.

**rail·ing** ▶*n.* fence or barrier made of rails.

**rail·ler·y** /ˈrālərē/ ▶*n.* (*pl.* **-ies**) good-humored ridicule.

**rail·road** ▶*n.* **1** track or set of tracks of steel rails upon which trains run. **2** system of such trains. ▶*v.* rush or coerce (a person or thing): *railroaded me into going.*

**rail·way** ▶*n. Chiefly Brit.* **RAILROAD.**

**rai·ment** /ˈrāmənt/ ▶*n. archaic* clothing.

**rain** /rān/ ▶*n.* **1 a** condensed atmospheric moisture falling in drops. **b** fall of such drops. **2** rainlike falling of liquid, particles, objects, etc. ▶*v.* send down or fall like rain. —**rain·y** *adj.*

□ **rain check 1** ticket given for later use when an outdoor event is canceled by rain. **2** promise that an offer will be maintained though deferred. □ **rain forest** luxuriant tropical forest with heavy rainfall.

**rain·bow** /ˈrānˌbō/ ▶*n.* arch of colors formed by reflection, refraction, and dispersion of the sun's rays in rain or mist. ▶*adj.* many-colored.

**rain·coat** ▶*n.* waterproof or water-resistant coat.

**rain·fall** ▶*n.* **1** fall of rain. **2** quantity of rain falling within a given area in a given time.

**raise** /rāz/ ▶*v.* **1** put or take into a higher position. **2** cause to rise, stand, or be vertical. **3** increase the amount, value, or strength of. **4** levy, collect, or bring together: *raise money.* **5** cause to be heard or considered: *raise an objection.*

**6** bring into being; arouse: *raise hopes.* **7** bring up; educate.
▶*n.* **1** increase in salary. **2** increase in a stake or bid.

**rai·sin** /ˈrāzin/ ▶*n.* partially dried grape.

**rai·son d'ê·tre** /rāˈzôN ˈdetr(ə)/ ▶*n.* (*pl.* **rai·sons d'ê·tre** *pronunc.* same) purpose or reason for a thing's existence.

**rake** /rāk/ ▶*n.* **1** implement consisting of a pole with a toothed crossbar at the end, used for gathering loose material, smoothing soil, etc. **2** dissolute man of fashion.
▶*v.* **1** collect or make smooth with or as with a rake. **2** scratch or scrape.

**rak·ish** /ˈrākiSH/ ▶*adj.* dashing; jaunty. —**rak·ish·ness** *n.*

**rale** /räl; ral/ ▶*n.* (usu. **rales**) abnormal rattling sound heard when examining unhealthy lungs with a stethoscope.

**ral·ly** /ˈralē/ ▶*v.* (**-lied**) **1** bring or come together as support or for action. **2** revive (courage, etc.). **3** recover after illness, etc.; revive. **4** (of share prices, etc.) increase after a fall.
▶*n.* (*pl.* **-lies**) **1** rallying or being rallied. **2** mass meeting for a cause.

**RAM** /ram/ ▶*abbr. Computing* random-access memory; internally stored software or data that is directly accessible.

**ram** ▶*n.* male sheep.
▶*v.* (**rammed, ram·ming**) **1** force or squeeze into place by pressure. **2** strike violently; crash against.

**ra·ma·da** /rəˈmädə; -ˈmadə/ ▶*n.* arbor or porch.

**Ram·a·dan** /ˈräməˌdän; ˈraməˌdan/ ▶*n.* ninth month of the Muslim year, during which strict fasting is observed from sunrise to sunset.

**ram·ble** /ˈrambəl/ ▶*v.* **1** walk for pleasure. **2** talk or write disconnectedly.
▶*n.* walk taken for pleasure. —**ram·bling** *adj.*

**ram·bunc·tious** /ramˈbəNGkSHəs/ ▶*adj. inf.* **1** uncontrollably exuberant. **2** unruly.

**ram·i·fi·ca·tion** /ˌraməfiˈkāSHən/ ▶*n.* **1** subdivision of a complex structure or process. **2** consequence.

**ramp** /ramp/ ▶*n.* **1** slope, esp. joining two levels of ground, floor, etc. **2** movable stairs for entering or leaving an aircraft.

**ram·page** /ˈramˌpāj/ ▶*v.* **1** rush

wildly or violently about. **2** rage; storm.

▶*n.* wild or violent behavior.

**ram·pant** /ˈrampənt/ ▶*adj.*
**1** unchecked; flourishing excessively. **2** violent or unrestrained.

**ram·part** /ˈramˌpärt/ ▶*n.*
**1** defensive wall with a broad top and usu. a stone parapet. **2** walkway on top of such a wall.

**ram·rod** ▶*n.* **1** rod for ramming a charge into a firearm. **2** thing that is very straight or rigid.

**ram·shack·le** ▶*adj.* tumbledown; rickety.

**ranch** /ranCH/ ▶*n.* **1** farm where animals are bred, e.g., cattle, sheep, etc. **2** (also **ranch house**) single-story house.

▶*v.* farm on a ranch. —**ranch·er** *n.*

**ran·cid** /ˈransid/ ▶*adj.* smelling or tasting like rank, stale fat. —**ran·cid·i·ty** *n.*

**ran·cor** /ˈraNGkər/ ▶*n.* inveterate bitterness; malignant hate. —**ran·cor·ous** *adj.*

**rand** /rand/ ▶*n.* chief monetary unit of South Africa.

**ran·dom** /ˈrandəm/ ▶*adj.* made, done, etc., without method or conscious choice. —**ran·dom·ly** *adv.*

**ran·dy** /ˈrandē/ ▶*adj.* (**-di·er, -di·est**) *inf.* lustful.

**rang** /raNG/ ▶ past of RING.

**range** /rānj/ ▶*n.* **1** region between limits of variation; extent; scope. **2** series of mountains. **3** open or enclosed area with targets for shooting. **4** cooking stove. **5** maximum distance that can be covered by a vehicle, weapon, aircraft, etc. **6** distance between a camera and the subject to be photographed. **7** large area of open land for grazing or hunting.

▶*v.* **1** reach; lie spread out; extend. **2** place or arrange in a row or ranks or in a specified situation, order, etc.: *trees ranged in ascending order of height.*

**rang·er** ▶*n.* **1** keeper of a national park or forest. **2** member of a body of armed men.

**rang·y** /ˈrānjē/ ▶*adj.* (**-i·er, -est**) tall and slim.

**rank** /raNGk/ ▶*n.* **1 a** position in a hierarchy. **b** high social position. **2** single line of soldiers or police officers drawn up abreast.

▶*v.* **1** have rank or place: *ranks next to the chief of staff.* **2** classify; grade.

▶*adj.* **1** (of vegetation) growing

too thickly or too luxuriantly. **2** (of air or water) having a foul or offensive smell. **3** flagrant; complete: *rank stupidity.*

□ **rank and file** ordinary undistinguished people.

**ran·kle** /ˈraNGkəl/ ▸v. (of envy, disappointment, etc., or their cause) cause persistent annoyance or resentment.

**ran·sack** /ˈran,sak/ ▸v. pillage or plunder (a house, country, etc.).

**ran·som** /ˈransəm/ ▸n. money demanded or paid for the release of a captive.

▸v. pay ransom for.

**rant** /rant/ ▸v. speak loudly, bombastically, violently, or theatrically.

▸n. piece of ranting.

**rap** /rap/ ▸n. **1** smart, slight blow. **2** sharp tapping sound. **3 a** rhythmic monologue recited to music. **b** (also **rap mu·sic**) style of pop music with words recited rather than sung. **4** *inf.* criminal charge: *a murder rap.*

▸v. (**rapped**, **rap·ping**) **1** strike smartly, esp. with a short tapping sound. **2** criticize adversely. **3** *inf.* talk. —**rap·per** *n.*

**ra·pa·cious** /rəˈpāSHəs/ ▸adj. grasping; predatory.
—**ra·pac·i·ty** *n.*

**rape** /rāp/ ▸n. **1** act of forcing a person to have sexual intercourse. **2** violent assault; forcible interference. **3** plant with oil-rich seeds.

▸v. commit rape on. —**rap·ist** *n.*

**rap·id** /ˈrapid/ ▸adj. quick; swift; brief.

▸n. (**rapids**) fast-flowing and turbulent part of a river's course. —**ra·pid·i·ty** *n.* —**rap·id·ly** *adv.*

**ra·pi·er** /ˈrāpēər/ ▸n. light slender sword for thrusting.

**rap·ine** /ˈrapin/ ▸n. plundering; robbery.

**rap·pel** /rəˈpel/ ▸v. (**-pelled, -pel·ling**) descend a rock face or other near-vertical surface by using a doubled rope coiled around the body and fixed at a higher point.

**rap·port** /raˈpôr/ ▸n. relationship or communication, esp. when useful and harmonious.

**rap·proche·ment** /ˌrap,rōSH-ˈmäN/ ▸n. resumption of harmonious relations, esp. between nations.

**rapt** /rapt/ ▸adj. fully absorbed or intent. —**rapt·ly** *adv.* —**rapt·ness** *n.*

**rap·tor** /ˈraptər/ ▸n. bird of prey, e.g., an eagle, hawk, falcon, or owl.

**rap·ture** /'rapCHər/ ▶*n.* **1** ecstatic delight. **2** (**raptures**) great pleasure or enthusiasm or the expression of it. —**rap·tur·ous** *adj.*

**rare** /re(ə)r/ ▶*adj.* (**rar·er, rar·est**) **1** seldom done or found or occurring; uncommon; unusual. **2** exceptionally good: *had a rare time.* **3** (of meat) cooked lightly, so as to be still red inside. —**rare·ly** *adj.* —**rare·ness** *n.* —**rar·i·ty** *n.*

**rare·bit** /'re(ə)rbit/ (also **Welsh rare·bit**) ▶*n.* dish of melted and seasoned cheese on toast.

**rar·ee-show** /'re(ə)rē ˌSHŌ/ ▶*n.* form of entertainment, esp. one carried in a box, such as a peep show.

**rar·e·fy** /'re(ə)rəˌfī/ ▶*v.* (**-fied**) make or become less dense or solid: *rarefied air.*

**rar·ing** ▶*adj. inf.* enthusiastic; eager: *raring to go.*

**ras·cal** /'raskəl/ ▶*n.* mischievous or impudent person.

**rash** /raSH/ ▶*adj.* reckless; impetuous; hasty.
▶*n.* **1** eruption of the skin in spots or patches. **2** sudden widespread appearance. —**rash·ly** *adv.* —**rash·ness** *n.*

**rash·er** ▶*n.* portion or serving of bacon or ham.

**rasp** /rasp/ ▶*n.* **1** coarse kind of file. **2** rough grating sound.
▶*v.* **1** scrape with or as with a rasp. **2** make a grating sound. —**rasp·ing·ly** *adv.* —**rasp·y** *adj.*

**rasp·ber·ry** /'razˌberē/ ▶*n.* (*pl.* **-ries**) **1** juicy red or black berry. **2** *inf.* sound made with the lips, expressing dislike, derision, or disapproval.

**rat** /rat/ ▶*n.* **1** rodent like a large mouse. **2** *inf.* unpleasant or treacherous person.
▶*v.* (**rat·ted, rat·ting**) *inf.* (**rat on**) inform on.
□ **rat race** hectic work routine; struggle to succeed.

**ratch·et** /'raCHit/ ▶*n.* **1** set of teeth on the edge of a bar or wheel with a catch permitting motion in one direction only. **2** (also **ratchet wheel**) wheel with a rim so toothed.

**rate** /rāt/ ▶*n.* **1** numerical proportion expressed in units (*rate of 50 miles per hour*) or as the basis of calculating (*rate of taxation*). **2** fixed or appropriate charge, cost, or value: *postal rates.* **3** pace of movement or change.
▶*v.* **1** assign a standard or value to

according to a scale. **2** consider to be of a certain quality, rank, etc.: *the program has been rated a great success.* **3** be regarded in a specific way: *he rates as one of the nicest people I have ever met.* **4** be worthy of; deserve.

**rath·er** /'raᴛʜər/ ▶*adv.* **1** by preference: *would rather stay.* **2** as a more likely alternative: *is stupid rather than honest.* **3** more precisely: *a book, or rather, a pamphlet.* **4** slightly; to some extent: *rather drunk.*

**rat·i·fy** /'ratə,fī/ ▶*v.* (-fied) confirm or accept by formal consent, signature, etc. —**rat·i·fi·ca·tion** *n.*

**ra·ti·o** /'rāsʜ(ē)ō/ ▶*n.* (*pl.* **-os**) quantitative relation between two comparable magnitudes: *a ratio of three to two.*

**ra·ti·o de·ci·den·di** /'rätē,ō ˌdesə'dendē/ ▶*n.* (*pl.* **ra·ti·o·nes de·ci·den·di** /ˌrätē'ōnēz/) rule of law on which a judicial decision is based.

**ra·tion** /'rasʜən/ ▶*n.* official allowance of food, clothing, etc., in a time of shortage. ▶*v.* limit (persons or provisions) to a fixed ration.

**ra·tion·al** /'rasʜənl/ ▶*adj.* **1** of or based on reason. **2** sensible;

sane. **3** able to reason. —**ra·tion·al·i·ty** *n.* —**ra·tion·al·ly** *adv.*

**ra·tion·ale** /ˌrasʜə'nal/ ▶*n.* fundamental reason; logical basis.

**ra·tion·al·ism** ▶*n.* practice of treating reason as the basis of knowledge and belief.

**ra·tion·al·ize** ▶*v.* offer a rational but specious explanation of (one's behavior or attitude). —**ra·tion·al·i·za·tion** *n.*

**rat·tan** /ra'tan/ ▶*n.* E. Indian climbing palm with long, thin, jointed pliable stems, used for furniture, etc.

**rat·tle** /'ratl/ ▶*v.* **1** give out a rapid succession of short, sharp, hard sounds. **2** (**rattle something off**) say or recite something rapidly: *he rattled off the instructions.* **3** (**rattle on**) talk in a lively thoughtless way. **4** *inf.* disconcert; alarm: *she turned quickly, rattled by his answer.* ▶*n.* **1** rattling sound. **2** device or plaything made to rattle. **3** set of horny rings in a rattlesnake's tail.

**rat·tle·snake** ▶*n.* poisonous American snake with rattling horny rings in its tail.

**rat·ty** /ˈratē/ ▸*adj.* (**-ti·er, -ti·est**) *inf.* shabby; seedy.

**rau·cous** /ˈrôkəs/ ▸*adj.* harsh sounding; loud and hoarse. **—rau·cous·ness** *n.*

**raun·chy** /ˈrônCHē/ ▸*adj.* (**-chi·er, -chi·est**) *inf.* earthy and sexually explicit: *a raunchy new novel.*

**rav·age** /ˈravij/ ▸*v.* do great damage to: devastate. ▸*n.* devastation; destructive effect: *the ravages of winter.*

**rave** /rāv/ ▸*v.* **1** talk wildly or furiously in or as in delirium. **2** speak with rapturous admiration (about). ▸*n. inf.* highly enthusiastic review of a film, play, etc.

**rav·el** /ˈravəl/ ▸*v.* **1** entangle or become entangled or knotted. **2** disentangle; separate into threads.

**ra·ven** /ˈrāvən/ ▸*n.* large glossy blue-black crow with a hoarse cry.

**rav·en·ing** /ˈravəniNG/ ▸*adj.* voraciously seeking prey.

**rav·en·ous** ▸*adj.* extremely hungry.

**ra·vine** /rəˈvēn/ ▸*n.* deep narrow gorge.

**rav·i·o·li** /ˌravēˈōlē/ ▸*n.* small pasta envelopes containing cheese, ground meat, etc.

**rav·ish** /ˈraviSH/ ▸*v.* **1** rape (a woman). **2** fill with intense delight; enrapture.

**rav·ish·ing** ▸*adj.* entrancing; delightful; very beautiful.

**raw** /rô/ ▸*adj.* **1** uncooked. **2** in the natural state; not processed or manufactured. **3** inexperienced; untrained. **4** (of the atmosphere, day, etc.) chilly and damp.

**raw·boned** ▸*adj.* gaunt and bony.

**raw·hide** ▸*n.* **1** untanned hide. **2** rope or whip of this.

**ray** /rā/ ▸*n.* **1** narrow beam of light from a small or distant source. **2** promising trace: *ray of hope.* **3** any of a set of radiating lines, parts, or things. **4** marine fish with a broad flat body and a long slender tail.

**ray·on** /ˈrāˌän/ ▸*n.* textile fiber or fabric made from cellulose.

**raze** /rāz/ ▸*v.* completely destroy; tear down.

**ra·zor** /ˈrāzər/ ▸*n.* instrument with a sharp blade used in cutting hair, esp. from the skin.

**RC** ▸*abbr.* Roman Catholic.

**RD** ▸*abbr.* Rural Delivery.

**Rd.** ▸*abbr.* Road (in names).

**Re** ▸*symb. Chem.* rhenium.

**re**[1] ▶*prep.* /rē/ **1** in the matter of (as the first word in a heading). **2** *inf.* about; concerning.

**re**[2] /rā/ ▶*n. Mus.* second note of a major scale.

**re-** /rē/ ▶*prefix* **1** attachable to almost any verb or its derivative, meaning: **a** once more; afresh; anew: *readjust.* **b** back; with return to a previous state: *reassemble.* **2** in verbs and verbal derivatives denoting: **a** in return; mutually: *react.* **b** opposition: *repel.* **c** behind or after: *remain.* **d** retirement or secrecy: *recluse.* **e** off; away; down: *recede | repress.* **f** frequentative or intensive force: *redouble | refine.* **g** negative force: *recant.*

**reach** /rēCH/ ▶*v.* **1** stretch out; extend. **2** stretch out the hand, etc.; make a reaching motion or effort. **3** get to or attain: *temperature reached 90°.* **4** make contact with the hand, etc., or by telephone, etc. ▶*n.* **1** extent to which something can reach, influence, etc. **2** act of reaching out. **—reach·a·ble** *adj.*

**re·act** /rē'akt/ ▶*v.* **1** respond (to a stimulus, etc.). **2** (of a substance or particle) be the cause of chemical activity or interaction with another: *nitrous oxide reacts with the metal.* **—re·act·ive** *adj.*

**re·ac·tion** ▶*n.* **1** action performed or a feeling experienced in response to a situation or event. **2** adverse bodily response to a drug, etc. **3** response in a reverse or contrary way. **4** interaction of substances undergoing chemical change.

**re·ac·tion·ar·y** /rē'akSHə,nerē/ ▶*adj.* opposing political or social liberalization or reform. ▶*n.* (*pl.* **-ar·ies**) a person who holds such views.

**re·ac·tor** ▶*n.* **1** person or thing that reacts. **2** (also **nu·cle·ar re·ac·tor**) apparatus or structure in which a controlled nuclear chain reaction releases energy.

**read** /rēd/ ▶*v.* (*past* and *past part.* **read** /red/) **1** reproduce mentally or vocally written or printed words. **2** convert or be able to convert (characters, symbols, etc.) into the intended words or meaning. **3** (of a recording instrument) show (a specified figure, etc.): *the thermometer reads 20°.* **4** *Computing* access (data), as to copy or display. **5** understand or interpret by hearing words or seeing signs,

gestures, etc. —**read·a·ble** *adj.*
—**read·a·bil·i·ty** *n.* —**read·er** *n.*

**read·ing** /ˈrēdiNG/ ▶*n.* **1** act or skill of reading. **2** knowledge of literature. **3** piece of literature or passage that is read aloud. **4** interpretation: *your reading of the situation is correct.* **5** figure or data shown by a recording instrument.

**read-on·ly** ▶*adj. Computing* (of a memory) able to be read at high speed but not capable of being changed by program instructions.

**read·y** /ˈredē/ ▶*adj.* (**-i·er, -i·est**) **1** with preparations complete: *dinner is ready.* **2** in a fit state: *are you ready?* **3** willing, inclined, or resolved: *ready for anything.* **4** within reach; easily secured: *ready cash.* **5** immediate; unqualified: *found ready acceptance.* **6** about to do something: *a bud just ready to burst.*
▶*adv.* beforehand; immediately usable: *ready-to-eat.*
▶*v.* (**-ied**) make ready; prepare.
—**read·i·ly** *adv.* —**read·i·ness** *n.*
□ **ready-made** **1** (esp. of clothes) made in a standard size, not to measure. **2** already available; convenient: *ready-made excuse.*

**re·a·gent** /rēˈājənt/ ▶*n.* substance used to cause a chemical reaction, esp. to detect another substance.

**re·al** /ˈrē(ə)l/ ▶*adj.* **1** actually existing or occurring. **2** genuine; rightly so called; not artificial. **3** consisting of immovable property such as land or houses: *real estate.* **4** appraised by purchasing power: *real value.*
▶*adv. inf.* really; very.
□ **real estate** property, esp. land and buildings.

**re·al·ism** ▶*n.* **1** practice of regarding things in their true nature and dealing with them as they are. **2** fidelity to nature in representation. —**re·al·ist** *n.* —**re·al·is·tic** *adj.*

**re·al·i·ty** /rēˈalitē/ ▶*n.* **1** what is real or existent or underlies appearances. **2** the real nature (of). **3** state of being real.

**re·al·ize** /ˈrē(ə)ˌlīz/ ▶*v.* **1** become fully aware of; conceive as real. **2** understand clearly. **3** convert into actuality: *realized a childhood dream.* **4** make (money or a profit) from a transaction. —**re·al·i·za·tion** *n.*

**re·al·ly** ▶*adv.* **1** in reality. **2** positively. **3** indeed; truly.

**4** an expression of mild protest or surprise.

**realm** /relm/ ▶*n.* **1** kingdom. **2** domain.

**re·al·po·li·tik** /rā'äl,pōli,tēk/ ▶*n.* system of politics or principles based on practical rather than moral or ideological considerations.

**re·al·tor** /'rē(ə)ltər; -,tôr/ ▶*n.* person who acts as an agent for the sale and purchase of buildings and land; a real estate agent.

**ream** /rēm/ ▶*n.* **1** twenty quires (or 500 sheets) of paper. **2** large quantity: *wrote reams about it.*
▶*v.* widen (a hole in metal, etc.) with a special tool.

**reap** /rēp/ ▶*v.* **1** cut or gather (esp. grain) as a harvest. **2** harvest the crop of (a field, etc.). **3** receive as the consequence of one's own or others' actions.

**rear** /ri(ə)r/ ▶*n.* **1** back part of anything. **2** space behind, or position at the back of, anything. **3** *inf.* buttocks.
▶*adj.* at the back.
▶*v.* **1 a** bring up and educate (children). **b** breed and care for (animals). **2** (of a horse, etc.) raise itself on its hind legs.

**rear ad·mir·al** ▶*n.* naval officer ranking below vice admiral.

**rear·most** ▶*adj.* furthest back.

**rear·ward** ▶*adj.* to the rear.
▶*adv.* (also **rear·wards**) toward the rear.

**rea·son** /'rēzən/ ▶*n.* **1** motive, cause, or justification. **2** fact adduced or serving as this. **3** intellectual faculty by which conclusions are drawn from premises. **4** sanity: *has lost his reason.* **5** sense; moderation.
▶*v.* **1** form or try to reach conclusions by connected thought. **2** use an argument (with) by way of persuasion. **3** conclude or assert in argument. —**rea·son·ing** *n.*

**rea·son·a·ble** ▶*adj.* **1** having sound judgment. **2** not absurd. **3** not excessive; inexpensive. **4** tolerable; fair. —**rea·son·a·bly** *adv.*

**re·as·sure** /,rēə'SHŏŏr/ ▶*v.* **1** restore confidence to; dispel the apprehensions of. **2** confirm in an opinion or impression. —**re·as·sur·ance** *n.* —**re·as·sur·ing·ly** *adv.*

**re·bate** /'rē,bāt/ ▶*n.* partial refund.
▶*v.* pay back as a rebate.

**re·bec** /'rēbek; 'reb,ek/ ▶*n.*

medieval stringed instrument played with a bow, typically having three strings.

**reb·el** ▶*n.* /'rebəl/ person who fights against or resists established authority.

▶*v.* /ri'bel/ (-**belled**, -**bel·ling**) **1** act as a rebel; revolt. **2** feel or display repugnance.

**re·bel·lion** ▶*n.* **1** act of violent or open resistance to an established government. **2** act or process of resisting authority, convention, etc. —**re·bel·lious** *adj.*

**re·bound** ▶*v.* /ri'bound/ spring back after impact.

▶*n.* /'rē,bound/ act of rebounding; recoil.

□ **on the rebound** while still recovering from an emotional shock, esp. rejection by a lover.

**re·buff** /ri'bəf/ ▶*n.* rejection of another's advances, help, sympathy, request, etc.

▶*v.* reject ungraciously.

**re·buke** /ri'byo͞ok/ ▶*v.* reprove sharply; subject to protest or censure.

▶*n.* rebuking or being rebuked; reproof.

**re·bus** /'rēbəs/ ▶*n.* representation of a word or phrase by pictures, etc., suggesting its parts.

**re·but** /ri'bət/ ▶*v.* (-**but·ted**, -**but·ting**) refute or disprove (evidence or a charge). —**re·but·tal** *n.*

**re·cal·ci·trant** /ri'kalsitrənt/ ▶*adj.* objecting to restraint. —**re·cal·ci·trance** *n.*

**re·call** ▶*v.* /ri'kôl/ **1** summon to return. **2** (of a product) request return to fix a defect. **3** recollect; remember. **4** revoke or annul (an action or decision).

▶*n.* /'rē,kôl/ act or instance of recalling.

**re·cant** /ri'kant/ ▶*v.* disavow a former opinion. —**re·can·ta·tion** *n.*

**re·cap** /'rē,kap/ ▶*v.* (-**capped**, -**cap·ping**) *inf.* recapitulate.

▶*n.* recapitulation.

**re·ca·pit·u·late** /,rekə'pichə,lāt/ ▶*v.* go briefly through again; summarize. —**re·ca·pit·u·la·tion** *n.*

**re·cap·ture** ▶*v.* **1** capture again. **2** regain (something that has been lost). **3** experience again.

▶*n.* act of recapturing.

**re·cede** /ri'sēd/ ▶*v.* **1** go or shrink back or further off. **2** diminish; fade: *a receding hairline.*

**re·ceipt** /ri'sēt/ ▶*n.* **1** receiving or being received. **2** written acknowledgment of payment. **3** (usu. **receipts**) amount of money, etc., received.

**re·ceive** /ri'sēv/ ▶*v.* **1** take or accept. **2** acquire; be provided with. **3** have conferred or inflicted on one. **4** greet or welcome, esp. in a specified manner.

**re·ceiv·er** ▶*n.* **1** person or thing that receives. **2** telephone earpiece. **3** person appointed by a court to receive funds, administer property of a bankrupt, etc. **4** radio or television apparatus that converts (broadcast signals) into sound or pictures.

**re·cen·sion** /ri'senCHən/ ▶*n.* revised edition of a text; an act of making a revised edition of a text.

**re·cent** /'rēsənt/ ▶*adj.* **1** not long past. **2** not long established; lately begun. —**re·cent·ly** *adv.*

**re·cep·ta·cle** /ri'septəkəl/ ▶*n.* containing vessel, place, or space.

**re·cep·tion** /ri'sepSHən/ ▶*n.* **1** receiving or being received. **2** manner in which a person or thing is received. **3** social occasion for receiving guests. **4 a** receiving of broadcast signals. **b** quality of this.

**re·cep·tion·ist** ▶*n.* person employed to receive guests, answer the telephone, etc.

**re·cep·tive** ▶*adj.* able or quick to receive impressions or ideas. —**re·cep·tiv·i·ty** *n.*

**re·cess** /'rē,ses; ri'ses/ ▶*n.* **1** space set back in a wall. **2** inner or remote place. **3** temporary cessation from proceedings, school, etc. ▶*v.* take a recess; adjourn.

**re·ces·sion** /ri'seSHən/ ▶*n.* **1** temporary decline in economic activity or prosperity. **2** receding or withdrawal from a place or point. —**re·ces·sion·ar·y** *adj.*

**re·ces·sive** ▶*adj.* **1** tending to recede. **2** appearing in offspring only when not masked by an inherited dominant characteristic.

**ré·chauf·fé** /,rā,SHō'fā -'SHō,fā/ ▶*n.* dish of warmed-up food left over from a previous meal.

**re·cher·ché** /rə,SHer'SHā/ ▶*adj.* rare, exotic, or obscure.

**re·cid·i·vist** /rə'sidəvist/ ▶*n.* person who relapses into crime, etc. —**re·cid·i·vism** *n.*

**rec·i·pe** /'resə,pē/ ▶*n.*

**1** ingredients and procedure for preparing cooked food. **2** device for achieving something: *recipe for success.*

**re·cip·i·ent** /ri'sipēənt/ ▶*n.* person who receives something.

**re·cip·ro·cal** /ri'siprəkəl/ ▶*adj.* in return: *reciprocal greeting.*

**re·cip·ro·cate** /-ˌkāt/ ▶*v.* respond to (a gesture, etc.) by making a corresponding one.

**re·cip·ro·cat·ing en·gine** ▶*n.* engine in which one or more pistons move up and down in cylinders; a piston engine.

**rec·i·proc·i·ty** /ˌresə'präsitē/ ▶*n.* practice of exchanging things with others for mutual benefit.

**re·cit·al** /ri'sītl/ ▶*n.* **1** reciting or being recited. **2** performance by a solo instrumentalist, dancer, or singer or by a small group.

**rec·i·ta·tive** /ˌresitə'tēv/ ▶*n.* musical declamation in the narrative and dialogue parts of opera and oratorio.

**re·cite** /ri'sīt/ ▶*v.* **1** repeat aloud or declaim (a poem or passage) from memory. **2** enumerate. —**rec·i·ta·tion** *n.*

**reck·less** /'reklis/ ▶*adj.* without thinking or caring about an action's consequences.

—**reck·less·ly** *adv.*

—**reck·less·ness** *n.*

**reck·on** /'rekən/ ▶*v.* **1** count; compute. **2** consider or regard. **3** (**reckon with**) take into account.

□ **to be reckoned with** of considerable importance; not to be ignored.

**reck·on·ing** ▶*n.* **1** counting or calculating. **2** settlement of an account.

**re·claim** /ri'klām/ ▶*v.* **1** take action to recover possession. **2** bring (land) under cultivation, esp. after being under water.

**re·cline** /ri'klīn/ ▶*v.* (cause to) be in a horizontal or leaning position.

**re·clin·er** ▶*n.* comfortable chair for reclining in.

**rec·luse** /'rekˌlo͞os/ ▶*n.* person given to or living in seclusion or isolation; hermit. —**re·clu·sive** *adj.*

**rec·og·ni·tion** /ˌrekəg'nisʜən/ ▶*n.* recognizing or being recognized.

**re·cog·ni·zance** /ri'kä(g)nə-zəns/ ▶*n.* pledge to a law court to observe some condition, e.g., to appear when summoned.

**rec·og·nize** /'rek(ə)gˌnīz/ ▶*v.* **1** identify as already known.

**2** realize or discover the nature of. **3** acknowledge the existence, validity, etc., of. **4** show appreciation of; reward. —**rec·og·niz·a·ble** *adj.*

**re·coil** /rē'koil/ ▸*v.* **1** suddenly move or spring back in fear, horror, or disgust. **2** shrink mentally in this way. **3** (of a gun) be driven backward by its discharge. ▸*n.* act or sensation of recoiling.

**rec·ol·lect** /ˌrekə'lekt/ ▸*v.* remember. —**rec·ol·lec·tion** *n.*

**rec·om·mend** /ˌrekə'mend/ ▸*v.* **1** suggest as fit for some purpose or use. **2** advise as a course of action, etc. —**rec·om·men·da·tion** *n.*

**rec·om·pense** /'rekəm,pens/ ▸*v.* compensate; repay. ▸*n.* compensation.

**rec·on·cile** /'rekən,sīl/ ▸*v.* **1** make friendly again after an estrangement. **2** make acquiescent or contentedly submissive to (something disagreeable). **3** make or show to be compatible. —**rec·on·cil·i·a·tion** *n.*

**re·con·dite** /'rekən,dīt/ ▸*adj.* **1** (of a subject or knowledge) abstruse; little known. **2** (of an author or style) obscure.

**re·con·nais·sance** /ri'känə-zəns/ ▸*n.* survey of a region, esp. to locate an enemy or ascertain strategic features.

**re·con·noi·ter** /ˌrēkə'noitər/ ▸*v.* make a reconnaissance.

**re·con·si·der** ▸*v.* consider again, esp. for a possible change. —**re·con·si·der·a·tion** *n.*

**rec·ord** ▸*n.* /'rekərd/ **1 a** information set down in writing. **b** document preserving this. **2** state of being set down or preserved in writing, etc. **3** thin plastic disk carrying recorded sound in grooves on each surface, for reproduction by a record player. **4** best performance or most remarkable event of its kind. ▸*v.* /ri'kôrd/ **1** set down in writing, etc., for later reference. **2** convert (sound, a broadcast, etc.) into permanent form for later reproduction.

**re·cord·er** ▸*n.* **1** apparatus for recording, esp. a tape recorder. **2** keeper of records. **3** wind instrument like a flute but blown through the end.

**re·count**[1] /ri'kount/ ▸*v.* **1** narrate. **2** tell in detail.

**re·count**[2] /'rē,kount/ ▸*v.* count again.

▶*n.* recounting, esp. of votes in an election.

**re·coup** /ri'kōōp/ ▶*v.* recover or regain (a loss).

**re·course** /rē'kôrs/ ▶*n.*
**1** resorting to a possible source of help. **2** person or thing resorted to.

**re·cov·er** /ri'kəvər/ ▶*v.* **1** regain possession, use, or control of. **2** return to health, consciousness, or to a normal state or position. **3** obtain or secure by legal process. —**re·cov·er·y** *n.*

**rec·re·ant** /'rekrēənt/ ▶*adj.*
**1** cowardly. **2** unfaithful to a belief; apostate.
▶*n.* **1** coward. **2** person who is unfaithful to a belief; an apostate.

**re·cre·ate** /ˌrēkrē'āt/ ▶*v.*
**1** create again. **2** reenact.

**rec·re·a·tion** /ˌrekrē'āsHən/ ▶*n.*
**1** process or means of refreshing or entertaining oneself. **2** pleasurable activity. —**rec·re·a·tion·al** *adj.*

**re·crim·i·nate** /ri'krimə,nāt/ ▶*v.* make mutual or counter accusations. —**re·crim·i·na·tion** *n.* —**re·crim·i·na·to·ry** *adj.*

**re·cru·desce** /ˌrēkrōō'des/ ▶*v.* break out again; recur.

**re·cruit** /ri'krōōt/ ▶*n.* **1** newly enlisted serviceman or servicewoman. **2** new member; beginner.
▶*v.* **1** enlist (a person) as a recruit. **2** get or seek recruits. —**re·cruit·ment** *n.*

**rec·tan·gle** /'rek,taNGgəl/ ▶*n.* plane figure with four straight sides and four right angles. —**rec·tan·gu·lar** *adj.*

**rec·ti·fy** /'rektə,fī/ ▶*v.* (-fied) adjust; make right.

**rec·ti·lin·e·ar** /ˌrektə'linēər/ ▶*adj.* bounded or characterized by straight lines.

**rec·ti·tude** /'rekti,t(y)ōōd/ ▶*n.* moral uprightness.

**rec·to** /'rektō/ ▶*n.* right-hand page of an open book.

**rec·tor** /'rektər/ ▶*n.* **1** clergy member in charge of a church or religious institution. **2** head of some schools, universities, and colleges.

**rec·to·ry** /'rektərē/ ▶*n.* (*pl.* -ries) rector's house.

**rec·tum** /'rektəm/ ▶*n.* (*pl.* -tums or -ta) lowest section of the large intestine, terminating at the anus.

**re·cum·bent** /ri'kəmbənt/ ▶*adj.* lying down; reclining.

**re·cu·per·ate** /ri'kōōpə,rāt/ ▶*v.*

recover from illness, exhaustion, loss, etc. —**re·cu·per·a·tion** *n.*

**re·cur** /ri'kər/ ▸*v.* (**-curred, -cur·ring**) occur again; be repeated.

**re·curve** /rē'kərv/ ▸*v.* bend backward.

▸*n.* bow that curves forward at the ends, which straighten out under tension when the bow is drawn.

**re·cy·cle** /rē'sīkəl/ ▸*v.* convert (waste) to reusable material. —**re·cy·cla·ble** *adj.*

**red** /red/ ▸*adj.* **1** of a color like blood. **2** flushed in the face with shame, anger, etc. **3** (of the eyes) bloodshot or red-rimmed. **4** (of the hair) reddish-brown; tawny.

▸*n.* **1** red color or pigment. **2** debit side of an account: *in the red.* —**red·den** *v.* —**red·ness** *n.*

**re·dact** /ri'dakt/ ▸*v.* edit (text) for publication.

**red·cap** ▸*n.* baggage porter.

**re·deem** /ri'dēm/ ▸*v.* **1** convert (tokens or bonds, etc.) into goods or cash. **2** deliver from sin and damnation. **3** make up for; compensate for. **4** save (oneself) from blame.

**red-eye** ▸*n.* late-night or overnight flight.

**red-faced** ▸*adj.* embarrassed; ashamed.

**red flag** ▸*n.* warning of danger.

**red-hand·ed** ▸*adv.* in the act of committing a crime, doing wrong, etc.

**red·head** ▸*n.* person with red hair.

**red her·ring** ▸*n.* misleading clue.

**red·in·te·grate** /ri'dintə,grāt/ ▸*v.* restore (something) to a state of wholeness, unity, or perfection.

**red·i·vi·vus** /,redə'vīvəs; -'vēvəs/ ▸*adj.* come back to life; reborn.

**red-let·ter day** ▸day that is pleasantly noteworthy or memorable.

**red light** ▸ **1** signal to stop on a road, etc. **2** warning or refusal.

**red-light dis·trict** ▸*n.* district containing many brothels.

**red·neck** /'red,nek/ ▸*n.* working-class white person, esp. a politically reactionary one from a rural area.

**red·o·lent** /'redl-ənt/ ▸*adj.* (**redolent of**) strongly suggestive or smelling of. —**red·o·lence** *n.*

**re·doubt·a·ble** /ri'doutəbəl/ ▸*adj.* formidable, esp. as an opponent.

**re·dress** ▸*v.* /ri'dres/ remedy or rectify (a wrong, grievance, etc.). ▸*n.* /'rē,dres/ reparation for a wrong.

**red tape** ▸excessive bureaucracy or formality, esp. in public business.

**re·duce** /ri'd(y)ŏŏs/ ▸*v.* **1** make or become smaller or less. **2** convert to another (esp. simpler) form: *reduced it to a powder.* **3** convert (a fraction) to the form with the lowest terms. **4** make lower in status, rank, price, etc. **5** lessen one's weight or size. —**re·duc·tion** *n.*

**re·dun·dant** /ri'dəndənt/ ▸*adj.* **1** superfluous. **2** that can be omitted without any loss of significance. —**re·dun·dan·cy** *n.*

**re·dux** /rē'dəks; 'rē'dəks/ ▸*adj.* brought back; revived.

**red·wood** ▸*n.* very large California conifer yielding red wood.

**reed** /rēd/ ▸*n.* **1 a** water or marsh plant with a firm stem. **b** tall straight stalk of this. **2 a** the vibrating, sound-producing part of the mouthpiece of some wind instruments. **b** reed instrument.

**reef** /rēf/ ▸*n.* ridge of rock, coral, etc., at or near the surface of the sea.

**reef·er** ▸*n.* **1** *inf.* marijuana cigarette. **2** thick close-fitting double-breasted jacket.

**reek** /rēk/ ▸*v.* **1** smell strongly and unpleasantly. **2** have unpleasant or suspicious associations: *reeks of corruption.* ▸*n.* foul or stale smell.

**reel** /rēl/ ▸*n.* **1** cylindrical device on which something is wound. **2** lively folk dance. ▸*v.* **1** wind on a reel. **2** stand or move unsteadily. □ **reel off** say or recite very rapidly and without apparent effort.

**re·en·try** /rē 'entrē/ ▸*n.* (*pl.* **-tries**) act of entering again, esp. (of a spacecraft, missile, etc.) into the earth's atmosphere.

**ref** /ref/ ▸*n.* *inf.* referee in sports.

**re·fec·to·ry** /ri'fekt(ə)rē/ ▸*n.* (*pl.* **-ries**) dining room, esp. in a monastery or college.

**re·fer** /ri'fər/ ▸*v.* (**-ferred, -fer·ring**) **1** send on or direct (a person, or a question for decision). **2** appeal or have recourse (to some authority or source of information): *referred to his notes.* **3** make an allusion or direct the hearer's attention: *did not refer to our problems.* —**re·fer·ral** *n.*

**ref·er·ee** /,refə'rē/ ▸*n.* **1** umpire, esp. in football, basketball, and soccer. **2** person consulted in a dispute, etc.

▶*v.* (**-eed**) act as referee in (a game, etc.).

**ref·er·ence** /ˈref(ə)rəns/ ▶*n.* **1** referring of a matter to some authority. **2 a** direction to a book, passage, etc. **b** book or passage so cited. **3 a** written testimonial supporting an applicant for employment, etc. **b** person giving this. —**ref·er·en·tial** *adj.*

**ref·er·en·dum** /ˌrefəˈrendəm/ ▶*n.* (*pl.* **-dums** or **-da**) direct popular vote on a political question.

**re·fill** ▶*v.* /rēˈfil/ fill again. ▶*n.* /ˈrēˌfil/ **1** new filling. **2** material for this.

**re·fine** /riˈfīn/ ▶*v.* **1** free from impurities or defects. **2** make or become more polished, elegant, or cultured. —**re·fined** *adj.* —**re·fine·ment** *n.*

**re·fin·er·y** /riˈfīnərē/ ▶*n.* (*pl.* **-ies**) plant where oil, etc., is refined.

**re·fit** ▶*v.* /rēˈfit/ (**-fit·ted, -fit·ting**) replace or repair machinery, equipment, and fittings in (a ship, building, etc.). ▶*n.* /ˈrēˌfit; rēˈfit/ restoration or repair of machinery, equipment, or fittings.

**re·flect** /riˈflekt/ ▶*v.* **1** (of a surface or body) throw back (heat, light, sound, etc.). **2** (of a mirror) show an image of. **3** testify to: *their behavior reflects a wish to succeed.* **4** (of an action, result, etc.) show or bring (credit, discredit, etc.). **5** meditate or consider. —**re·flec·tion** *n.*

**re·flec·tiv·i·ty** /ri̩flekˈtivətē; ̩rē-̩flek-/ ▶*n.* property of reflecting light or radiation.

**re·flex** /ˈrēˌfleks/ ▶*adj.* **1** (of an action) independent of will, as an automatic response to the stimulation of a nerve. **2** (of an angle) exceeding 180°. ▶*n.* reflex action.

**re·flex·ive** *Gram.* ▶*adj.* **1** (of a word or form) referring back to the subject of a sentence (esp. of a pronoun, e.g., *myself*). **2** (of a verb) having a reflexive pronoun as its object (as in *to wash oneself*).

**re·form** ▶*v.* /riˈfôrm/ **1** make or become better by the removal of faults and errors. **2** abolish or cure (an abuse or malpractice). ▶*n.* /ˈrēˌfôrm/ **1** removal of faults or abuses, esp. moral, political, or social. **2** improvement.

**re·fract** /riˈfrakt/ ▶*v.* (of water, air, or glass) make (a ray of light) change direction when it enters at an angle. —**re·frac·tion** n. —**re·frac·tive** adj.

**re·frac·to·ry** /ri'fraktərē/ ▶adj. stubborn; unmanageable; rebellious.

**re·frain** /ri'frān/ ▶v. stop oneself from doing something: *she refrained from comment.*
▶n. recurring phrase or lines, esp. at the ends of stanzas.

**re·fresh** ▶v. **1** give fresh spirit or vigor to. **2** revive or stimulate (the memory).

**re·fresh·ment** ▶n. **1** (**refreshments**) food and drink. **2** giving of fresh mental or physical energy.

**re·frig·er·ate** /ri'frijə,rāt/ ▶v. make or become cool or cold. —**re·frig·er·ant** n. —**re·frig·er·a·tion** n.

**re·frig·er·a·tor** ▶n. cabinet or room in which food, etc., is kept cold.

**ref·uge** /'ref,yooj/ ▶n. **1** shelter from pursuit, danger, or trouble. **2** person or place, etc., offering this.

**ref·u·gee** /,refyoo'jē/ ▶n. person taking refuge, esp. in a foreign country, from war, persecution, or natural disaster.

**re·ful·gent** /ri'fooljənt; -'fəl-/ ▶adj. shining brightly.

**re·fund** ▶v. /ri'fənd/ **1** pay back (money or expenses). **2** reimburse (a person). ▶n. /'rē,fənd/ **1** act of refunding. **2** sum refunded. —**re·fund·a·ble** adj.

**re·fur·bish** /ri'fərbiSH/ ▶v. **1** brighten up. **2** restore and redecorate.

**re·fuse**[1] /ri'fyooz/ ▶v. **1** indicate unwillingness or inability to do something. **2** indicate that one is not willing to accept or grant (something offered or requested). —**re·fus·al** n.

**ref·use**[2] /'refyoos/ ▶n. items rejected as worthless; waste.

**re·fute** /ri'fyoot/ ▶v. **1** prove the falsity or error of (a statement, etc.). **2** rebut by argument. —**re·fu·ta·tion** n.

**re·gain** ▶v. obtain possession or use of after loss.

**re·gal** /'rēgəl/ ▶adj. **1** royal; of or by a monarch or monarchs. **2** fit for a monarch; magnificent; majestic. —**re·gal·ly** adv.

**re·gale** /ri'gāl/ ▶v. entertain well.

**re·ga·li·a** /ri'gālyə/ ▶pl. n. **1** insignia of royalty. **2** elaborate clothes, accouterments, etc.; trappings; finery.

**re·gard** /ri'gärd/ ▸v. **1** gaze on steadily (usu. in a specified way): *regarded them suspiciously.* **2** heed; take into account. **3** think of in a specified way: *I regard them kindly.*

▸n. **1** attention or care. **2** esteem; kindly feeling. **3** (**regards**) expression of friendliness in a letter, etc.; compliments: *sent my best regards.*

**re·gard·ing** ▸prep. about; concerning; in respect of.

**re·gard·less** ▸adj. without regard or consideration for: *regardless of cost.*

▸adv. no matter what: *carried on regardless.*

**re·gat·ta** /ri'gätə/ ▸n. sporting event consisting of a series of boat or yacht races.

**re·gen·er·ate** /ri'jenə,rāt/ ▸v. **1** generate again. **2** impart new, more vigorous, and spiritually greater life to. —**re·gen·er·a·tion** n. —**re·gen·er·a·tive** adj.

**re·gent** /'rējənt/ ▸n. **1** person appointed to rule when a monarch is a minor or is absent or incapacitated. **2** member of a governing body, as of a university.

**reg·gae** /'regā/ ▸n. W. Indian style of music with a strongly accented subsidiary beat.

**reg·i·cide** /'rejə,sīd/ ▸n. **1** act of killing a king. **2** person who kills a king. —**reg·i·cid·al** adj.

**re·gime** /rā'ZHēm/ (also **ré·gime**) ▸n. **1** government, esp. an authoritarian one. **2** system.

**reg·i·men** /'rejəmən/ ▸n. prescribed course of exercise, way of life, and diet.

**reg·i·ment** /'rejəmənt/ ▸n. **1** military unit below division level. **2** large array or number.

▸v. organize (esp. oppressively) in groups or according to a strict system. —**reg·i·men·tal** adj. —**reg·i·men·ta·tion** n.

**re·gion** /'rējən/ ▸n. **1** area or division: *mountainous region.* **2** part of the body: *lumbar region.* —**re·gion·al** adj.

**re·gis·seur** /,rāZHē'sər/ ▸n. person who stages a theatrical production, esp. a ballet.

**reg·is·ter** /'rejistər/ ▸n. **1** official list, e.g., of births, marriages, property transactions, etc. **2** book in which items are recorded for reference. **3** range of a voice or instrument.

▸v. **1** set down (a name, fact, etc.) formally; record in writing. **2** enter or cause to be entered in a particular register. **3** express (an emotion) facially or by gesture: *registered surprise.* —**reg·is·tra·tion** *n.*

**reg·is·trar** /'reji,strär/ ▶*n.* official responsible for keeping records.

**reg·is·try** /'rejistrē/ ▶*n.* (*pl.* **-tries**) **1** place where registers or records are kept. **2** nationality of a merchant ship.

**reg·nant** /'regnənt/ ▶*adj.* **1** reigning; ruling. **2** currently having the greatest influence; dominant.

**re·gress** /ri'gres/ ▶*v.* **1** move backward, esp. return to a former state. **2** *Psychol.* return or cause to return mentally to a former stage of life. —**re·gres·sion** *n.* —**re·gres·sive** *adj.*

**re·gret** /ri'gret/ ▶*v.* (**-gret·ted, -gret·ting**) feel or express sorrow, repentance, or distress over (an action, loss, etc.).

▶*n.* **1** feeling of sorrow, repentance, or disappointment over an action, loss, etc. **2** (**regrets**) (esp. polite or formal) expression of disappointment or sorrow at an occurrence, inability to comply, etc. —**re·gret·ful** *adj.* —**re·gret·ful·ly**

*adv.* —**re·gret·ta·ble** *adj.* —**re·gret·ta·bly** *adv.*

**re·group** ▶*v.* group or arrange again or differently.

**reg·u·lar** /'regyələr/ ▶*adj.* **1** conforming to a rule or principle; systematic. **2** harmonious; symmetrical: *regular features.* **3** acting, done, or recurring uniformly or calculably in time or manner; habitual; constant. ▶*n. inf.* regular customer, visitor, etc. —**reg·u·lar·i·ty** *n.* —**reg·u·lar·ly** *adv.*

**reg·u·late** /'regyə,lāt/ ▶*v.* **1** control or maintain the rate of speed of (a machine or process) so that it operates properly. **2** control by means of rules or regulations. —**reg·u·la·to·ry** *adj.*

**reg·u·la·tion** ▶*n.* rule or directive made by an authority.

**re·gur·gi·tate** /rē'gərji,tāt/ ▶*v.* **1** bring (swallowed food) up again to the mouth. **2** cast or pour out again: *regurgitate the facts.* —**re·gur·gi·ta·tion** *n.*

**re·ha·bil·i·tate** /,rē(h)ə'bili,tāt/ ▶*v.* **1** restore to effectiveness or normal life by training, etc., esp. after imprisonment or illness. **2** restore to former privileges, proper condition, etc.

—re·ha·bil·i·ta·tion *n.*
—re·ha·bil·i·ta·tive *adj.*

**re·hash** ▸*v.* put (old material) into a new form without significant change or improvement. ▸*n.* material rehashed.

**re·hears·al** /ri'hərsəl/ ▸*n.* practice or trial performance of a play, concert, etc.

**re·hearse** /ri'hərs/ ▸*v.* practice (a play, recital, etc.) for later public performance.

**re·i·fy** /'rēə,fī/ ▸*v.* (**-fies, -fied**) make (something abstract) more concrete or real.

**reign** /rān/ ▸*v.* **1** be king or queen. **2** prevail: *confusion reigns.* **3** [usu. as *adj.* **reigning**] (of a winner, champion, etc.) currently hold the title, etc. ▸*n.* period during which a sovereign rules.

**re·im·burse** /,rēim'bərs/ ▸*v.* repay (a person who has expended money). —re·im·burse·ment *n.*

**rein** /rān/ ▸*n.* **1** long narrow strap with each end attached to the bit, used to guide or check a horse, etc. **2** means of control or guidance. ▸*v.* **1** check or manage with or as

with reins. **2** govern; restrain; control.

**re·in·car·na·tion** /,rēinkär-'nāsʜən/ ▸*n.* rebirth of a soul in a new body. —re·in·car·nate *adj.*

**rein·deer** /'rān,di(ə)r/ ▸*n.* subarctic deer of which both sexes have large antlers.

**re·in·force** /,rēin'fôrs/ ▸*v.* strengthen or support, esp. with additional personnel, material, etc. —re·in·force·ment *n.*

**re·in·state** /,rēin'stāt/ ▸*v.* restore to a former position. —re·in·state·ment *n.*

**re·in·sure** /,rē-in'sʜo͝or/ ▸*v.* (of an insurer) transfer (all or part of a risk) to another insurer to provide protection against the risk of the first insurance.

**re·it·er·ate** /rē'itə,rāt/ ▸*v.* say or do again or repeatedly. —re·it·er·a·tion *n.* —re·it·er·a·tive *adj.*

**re·ject** ▸*v.* /ri'jekt/ **1** dismiss as inadequate, inappropriate, etc. **2** refuse to agree to. **3** fail to show concern or affection for (a person). **4** show an immune response to (a transplanted organ or tissue) so that it fails to survive. ▸*n.* /'rē,jekt/ thing or person rejected as unfit or below standard. —**re·jec·tion** *n.*

**re·joice** /ri'jois/ ▸*v.* feel great joy; be glad.

**re·join** ▸*v.* **1** join together again; reunite. **2** say in answer; retort. —**re·join·der** *n.*

**re·ju·ve·nate** /ri'jo͞ovə,nāt/ ▸*v.* make (as if) young again. —**re·ju·ve·na·tion** *n.*

**re·lapse** /ri'laps; 'rē,laps/ ▸*v.* fall back or sink again (into a worse state after improvement). ▸*n.* relapsing, esp. a deterioration in a patient's condition after partial recovery.

**re·late** /ri'lāt/ ▸*v.* **1** narrate or recount. **2** be connected by blood or marriage: *he was related to my mother.* **3** connect (two things) in thought or meaning. —**re·lat·a·ble** *adj.*

**re·lat·ed** ▸*adj.* connected.

**re·la·tion** ▸*n.* **1** what one person or thing has to do with another. **2** relative. **3** (**relations**) way in which two or more people, countries, etc., regard each others. **4** (**relations**) sexual intercourse. —**re·la·tion·ship** *n.*

**rel·a·tive** /'relətiv/ ▸*adj.* **1** considered in relation to something else: *relative velocity.* **2** comparative: *their relative*

advantages. **3** having reference or relating: *the facts relative to the issue.* ▸*n.* **1** person connected by blood or marriage. **2** species related to another by common origin. —**rel·a·tive·ly** *adv.*

**rel·a·tiv·i·ty** /,relə'tivitē/ ▸*n.* **1** being relative. **2** *Physics* **a** (**special theory of relativity**) theory based on the principle that all motion is relative and that light has constant velocity. **b** (**general theory of relativity**) theory extending this to gravitation and accelerated motion.

**re·lax** /ri'laks/ ▸*v.* **1** make or become less stiff, rigid, tense, or formal. **2** cease work or effort. —**re·lax·a·tion** *n.*

**re·lay** /'rē,lā/ ▸*n.* **1** fresh set of people, material, etc. **2** device activating an electric circuit, etc., in response to changes affecting itself. **3** device to receive, reinforce, and transmit a message, broadcast, etc. ▸*v.* receive (a message, broadcast, etc.) and transmit it to others. □ **relay race** team race in which each member in turn covers part of the distance.

**re·lease** /ri'lēs/ ▸*v.* **1** set free;

liberate. **2** allow to move from a fixed position. **3** make (information, a film, etc.) publicly available.

▶*n.* **1** liberation from restriction, duty, or difficulty. **2** handle or catch that frees a mechanism. **3** document or item of information made available for publication: *press release.* **4** film, recording, etc., that is released.

**rel·e·gate** /ˈreliˌgāt/ ▶*v.* consign or dismiss to an inferior position. —**rel·e·ga·tion** *n.*

**re·lent** /riˈlent/ ▶*v.* abandon a harsh intention; yield to compassion; relax severity.

**re·lent·less** ▶*adj.* **1** oppressively constant. **2** harsh; inflexible. —**re·lent·less·ly** *adv.* —**re·lent·less·ness** *n.*

**rel·e·vant** /ˈreləvənt/ ▶*adj.* bearing on or having reference to the matter in hand. —**rel·e·vance** *n.*

**re·li·a·ble** /riˈlīəbəl/ ▶*adj.* **1** dependable. **2** of sound and consistent character or quality. —**re·li·a·bil·i·ty** *n.* —**re·li·a·bly** *adv.*

**re·li·ance** /riˈlīəns/ ▶*n.* trust; confidence. —**re·li·ant** *adj.*

**rel·ic** /ˈrelik/ ▶*n.* **1** object interesting because of its age or association. **2** surviving custom or belief, etc., from a past age. **3** (**relics**) fragments, ruins, etc.

**rel·ict** /ˈrelikt/ ▶*n.* **1** thing that has survived from an earlier period or in a primitive form. **2** widow.

**re·lief** /riˈlēf/ ▶*n.* **1 a** alleviation of pain, distress, anxiety, etc. **b** feeling resulting from such alleviation. **2** assistance to those in need. **3** replacing of a person or persons on duty. **4** sculpture, carving, etc., in which the design stands out from the surface.

**re·lieve** /riˈlēv/ ▶*v.* **1** bring or give relief to. **2** mitigate the tedium or monotony of. **3** release (a person) from a duty by acting as or providing a substitute.

**re·li·gion** /riˈlijən/ ▶*n.* **1** belief in and worship of a personal God or superhuman controlling power. **2** particular system of faith and worship. **3** thing that one is devoted to.

**re·lig·ious** ▶*adj.* **1** devoted to religion; devout. **2** of or concerned with religion. **3** scrupulous; conscientious.

**re·lin·quish** /riˈliNGkwish/ ▶*v.* **1** surrender or resign (a right or possession). **2** relax hold of (an object held).

—**re·lin·quish·ment** n.

**rel·ish** /'reliSH/ ▸n. **1** great liking or enjoyment. **2** attractive quality. **3** condiment eaten with plainer food to add flavor.

▸v. get pleasure out of; enjoy greatly.

**re·live** /rē'liv/ ▸v. live (an experience, etc.) over again, esp. in the imagination.

**re·lo·cate** ▸v. locate in a new place. —**re·lo·ca·tion** n.

**re·luc·tant** /ri'ləktənt/ ▸adj. unwilling or disinclined.

—**re·luc·tance** n. —**re·luc·tant·ly** adv.

**re·ly** /ri'lī/ ▸v. (**-lied**) (**rely on/upon**) depend on with confidence or assurance.

**REM** /rem/ ▸abbr. rapid eye movement.

**re·main** /ri'mān/ ▸v. **1** be left over after others or other parts have been removed, used, etc. **2** stay; be left behind: *remained at home.* **3** continue to be: *remained calm.*

**re·main·der** /ri'māndər/ ▸n. **1** part remaining or left over. **2** remaining persons or things. **3** number left after division or subtraction.

**re·mains** ▸pl. n. **1** what remains after other parts have been removed or used, etc. **2** relics of antiquity, esp. of buildings. **3** dead body.

**re·mand** /ri'mand/ ▸v. return (a prisoner) to custody, esp. to allow further inquiries to be made.

**re·mark** /ri'märk/ ▸v. **1** make a comment. **2** take notice of.

▸n. **1** written or spoken comment; anything said. **2** noticing or noting: *worthy of remark.*

**re·mark·a·ble** ▸adj. worth notice; exceptional; striking. —**re·mark·a·bly** adv.

**re·me·di·al** /ri'mēdēəl/ ▸adj. **1** affording or intended as a remedy. **2** (of teaching) for those in need of improvement in a particular discipline.

**rem·e·dy** /'remidē/ ▸n. (pl. **-dies**) **1** medicine or treatment. **2** means of counteracting or removing anything undesirable.

▸v. (**-died**) rectify; make good.

**re·mem·ber** /ri'membər/ ▸v. **1** keep in the memory; not forget. **2** bring back into one's thoughts. **3** convey greetings from (one person) to (another): *remember me to your mother.*

**re·mem·brance** ▶*n.*
1 remembering or being remembered. 2 memory; recollection. 3 keepsake; souvenir.

**re·mind** /ri'mīnd/ ▶*v.* cause (a person) to remember or think of (something or someone).
—**re·mind·er** *n.*

**rem·i·nisce** /ˌremə'nis/ ▶*v.* talk or think about past events.
—**rem·i·ni·scence** *n.*

**re·miss** /ri'mis/ ▶*adj.* careless of duty; lax; negligent.

**re·mis·sion** ▶*n.* 1 forgiveness (of sins, etc.). 2 remitting of a debt or penalty, etc.
3 diminution of force, effect, or degree (esp. of disease or pain).

**re·mit** /ri'mit/ ▶*v.* (-**mit·ted**, -**mit·ting**) 1 cancel or refrain from exacting or inflicting (a debt, punishment, etc.). 2 abate or slacken; cease partly or entirely. 3 send (money, etc.) in payment. 4 refer (a matter for decision, etc.) to some authority.

**re·mit·tance** ▶*n.* payment sent, esp. by mail.

**rem·nant** /'remnənt/ ▶*n.* 1 small remaining quantity. 2 piece of leftover cloth, etc.

**re·mod·el** /rē'mädl/ ▶*v.* model again or differently.

**re·mon·strate** /ri'män,strāt/ ▶*v.* make a protest; argue forcibly: *he turned angrily to remonstrate with Tommy.* —**re·mon·strance** *n.*

**re·morse** /ri'môrs/ ▶*n.* 1 deep regret for a wrong committed. 2 compassion, esp. as: *without remorse.* —**re·morse·ful** *adj.*

**re·mote** /ri'mōt/ ▶*adj.* (-**mot·er**, -**mot·est**) 1 far away in place or time. 2 isolated; secluded. 3 slight; faint: *not the remotest chance.* 4 aloof; not friendly.
—**re·mote·ly** *adv.*
—**re·mote·ness** *n.*

□ **remote control** control of an apparatus from a distance by means of signals transmitted from a radio or electronic device.

**re·move** /ri'mo͞ov/ ▶*v.* 1 take off or away from the place occupied. 2 get rid of; eliminate: *will remove all doubts.* 3 dismiss (from office, etc.). 4 distant or remote in condition: *not far removed from anarchy.*
—**re·mov·al** *n.*

**re·moved** ▶*adj.* (esp. of cousins) separated by a specified number of steps of descent: *a first cousin twice removed = a grandchild of a first cousin.*

**re·mu·ner·ate** /ri'myo͞onə,rāt/ ▶v. serve as or provide recompense for (toil, etc.) or to (a person). —**re·mu·ner·a·tion** n. —**re·mu·ner·a·tive** adj.

**Ren·ais·sance** /'renə,säns/ ▶n. 1 revival of art and literature in the 14th–16th c. 2 culture and style of art, architecture, etc., developed during this era. 3 (**renaissance**) any similar revival.

**re·nal** /'rēnl/ ▶adj. of or concerning the kidneys.

**re·nas·cent** /ri'nasənt; -'nāsənt/ ▶adj. becoming active or popular again.

**rend** /rend/ ▶v. (past and past part. **rent**) tear or wrench forcibly.

**rend·er** ▶v. 1 cause to be or become: rendered us helpless. 2 give or pay (money, service, etc.), esp. in return or as a thing due: render thanks. 3 represent or portray. 4 melt (fat, etc.).

**ren·dez·vous** /'rändi,vo͞o/ ▶n. (pl. same) 1 meeting at an agreed time and place, esp. between two people. 2 place used for such a meeting. ▶v. meet at an agreed time and place.

**ren·e·gade** /'reni,gād/ ▶n. person who deserts a party or principles. ▶adj. traitorous; heretical.

**re·nege** /ri'neg/ ▶v. go back on one's word, etc.

**re·new** /ri'n(y)o͞o/ ▶v. 1 revive; restore. 2 reinforce; resupply; replace. 3 reestablish; resume. 4 grant or be granted a continuation of (a license, lease, etc.). —**re·new·al** n.

**ren·net** /'renit/ ▶n. preparation used in making cheese.

**re·nounce** /ri'nouns/ ▶v. 1 formally abandon (a claim, right, etc.). 2 repudiate; reject. —**re·nounce·ment** n.

**ren·o·vate** /'renə,vāt/ ▶v. restore to good condition; repair. —**ren·o·va·tion** n.

**re·nown** /ri'noun/ ▶n. fame; high distinction. —**re·nowned** adj.

**re·nowned** /ri'nound/ ▶adj. known or talked about by many people; famous.

**rent** /rent/ ▶n. 1 tenant's periodical payment to an owner for the use of land or premises. 2 payment for the use of a service, equipment, etc. 3 large tear in a garment, etc. ▶v. pay or receive rent for. —**rent·er** n.

**rent·al** /'rentl/ ▶n. 1 amount paid

or received as rent. **2** act of renting. **3** rented house, etc.

**re·nun·ci·a·tion** /ri͵nənsē-'āsHən/ ▸*n.* **1** renouncing or giving up. **2** self-denial.

**Rep.** ▸*abbr.* **1** Representative. **2** Republican. **3** Republic.

**rep** /rep/ ▸*n. inf.* **1** representative, esp. a salesperson. **2** repertory theater or company.

**re·pair** /ri'pe(ə)r/ ▸*v.* **1** restore to good condition after damage or wear. **2** set right or make amends for (a loss, wrong, etc.). **3** go to (a place), esp. in company: *we repaired to the bar on the corner.*
▸*n.* **1** restoring to sound condition: *in need of repair.* **2** result of this: *the repair is hardly visible.* **3** relative condition for working or using: *in good repair.*

**rep·a·ra·tion** /͵repə'rāsHən/ ▸*n.* **1** making amends. **2** (**reparations**) compensation for war damage paid by a defeated state.

**rep·ar·tee** /͵repär'tē/ ▸*n.* witty banter.

**re·past** /ri'past/ ▸*n.* meal.

**re·pa·tri·ate** /rē'pātrē͵āt/ ▸*v.* restore (a person) to his or her native land. —**re·pa·tri·a·tion** *n.*

**re·pay** ▸*v.* (*past* and *past part.* **-paid**) pay back. —**re·pay·ment** *n.*

**re·peal** /ri'pēl/ ▸*v.* revoke or annul (a law, etc.).
▸*n.* repealing.

**re·peat** /ri'pēt/ ▸*v.* **1** say or do over again. **2** say again something said or written by someone else. **3** recur; appear again.
▸*n.* **1** repeating. **2** thing repeated, e.g., a repeated broadcast. —**re·peat·ed·ly** *adv.*

**re·pê·chage** /͵repə'sHäzH/ (also **re·pe·chage**) ▸*n.* (in rowing and other sports) a contest in which the runners-up in the eliminating heats compete for a place in the final.

**re·pel** /ri'pel/ ▸*v.* (**-pelled**, **-pel·ling**) **1** drive back; ward off. **2** be repulsive or distasteful to. —**re·pel·lent** *adj. & n.*

**re·pent** /ri'pent/ ▸*v.* **1** feel deep sorrow about one's actions, etc. **2** wish one had not done; resolve not to continue (a wrongdoing, etc.). —**re·pent·ance** *n.* —**re·pent·ant** *adj.*

**re·per·cus·sion** /͵rēpər'kəsHən/ ▸*n.* indirect effect or reaction.

**rep·er·toire** /'repə(r)͵twär/ ▸*n.* stock of pieces, plays, etc., that a performer, company, etc., is prepared to perform.

**rep·er·to·ry** /ˈrepərˌtôrē/ ▸*n.* (*pl.* **-ries**) **1** performance of various plays for short periods by one company. **2** repertoire.

**rep·e·ti·tion** /ˌrepiˈtishən/ ▸*n.* **1** repeating or being repeated. **2** thing repeated. —**rep·e·ti·tious** *adj.* —**re·pet·i·tive** *adj.*

**re·pine** /riˈpīn/ ▸*v.* feel or express discontent; fret.

**re·place** /riˈplās/ ▸*v.* **1** put back in place. **2** provide or be a substitute for. —**re·place·a·ble** *adj.* —**re·place·ment** *n.*

**re·play** ▸*v.* play (a match, recording, etc.) again.
▸*n.* act or instance of replaying a match, recording, or recorded incident in a game, etc.

**re·plen·ish** /riˈplenish/ ▸*v.* **1** fill up again. **2** renew (a supply, etc.). —**re·plen·ish·ment** *n.*

**re·plete** /riˈplēt/ ▸*adj.* **1** filled or well-supplied. **2** stuffed; gorged; sated. —**re·ple·tion** *n.*

**rep·li·ca** /ˈreplikə/ ▸*n.* **1** exact copy or likeness. **2** copy or model, esp. on a smaller scale. —**rep·li·ca·tion** *n.*

**re·ply** /riˈplī/ ▸*v.* (**-plied**) answer; respond.
▸*n.* (*pl.* **-plies**) answer.

**re·port** /riˈpôrt/ ▸*v.* **1 a** give an account of. **b** state as fact or news. **c** relate as spoken by another. **2** make an official or formal statement about. **3** name or specify (an offender or offense). **4** present oneself as having returned or arrived. **5** (**report to**) be responsible to (a supervisor, etc.).
▸*n.* **1** account given or opinion formally expressed after investigation or consideration. **2** account of an event, esp. for publication or broadcast. **3** common talk; rumor. **4** sound of an explosion. —**re·port·ed·ly** *adv.* —**re·port·er** *n.*
□ **report card** official report of a student's grades, progress, etc.

**re·pose** /riˈpōz/ ▸*n.* **1** cessation of activity. **2** sleep. **3** peaceful state; tranquility.
▸*v.* lie, be lying, or be laid, esp. in sleep or death.

**re·pos·i·to·ry** /riˈpäziˌtôrē/ ▸*n.* (*pl.* **-ries**) **1** place where things are stored, esp. a warehouse or museum. **2** book, person, etc., regarded as a store of information, etc.

**re·pos·sess** ▸*v.* regain possession of (esp. property or goods on which repayment of a

debt is in arrears).
—re·pos·ses·sion n.

**rep·re·hen·si·ble** /ˌrepri-
'hensəbəl/ ▶adj. deserving
censure; blameworthy.

**rep·re·sent** /ˌrepri'zent/ ▶v.
**1** stand for or correspond to.
**2** be a specimen or example of.
**3** describe; depict; delineate;
symbolize. **4** be a substitute or
deputy for; be entitled to act or
speak for. —**rep·re·sent·a·ble** adj.

**rep·re·sen·ta·tion** ▶n.
**1** representing or being
represented. **2** thing that
represents another. **3** (often
**representations**) allegation or
opinion. —**rep·re·sen·ta·tion·al**
adj.

**rep·re·sen·ta·tive** /ˌrepri-
'zentətiv/ ▶adj. **1** typical of a class
or as a specimen. **2** consisting of
or based on representation by
elected deputies, etc. **3** serving
as a portrayal or symbol (of).
▶n. **1** sample, specimen, or
typical embodiment. **2** agent,
spokesperson, etc. **3** legislative
delegate, deputy, etc.

**re·press** /ri'pres/ ▶v. **1** check;
restrain; keep under (control);
quell. **2** actively exclude (an
unwelcome thought) from
conscious awareness.

—**re·pres·sion** n. —**re·pres·sive**
adj.

**re·prieve** /ri'prēv/ ▶v. **1** remit or
postpone the execution of (a
condemned person). **2** give
respite to.
▶n. **1** cancellation or
postponement of a punishment.
**2** respite.

**rep·ri·mand** /'reprə,mand/ ▶n.
official or sharp rebuke.
▶v. rebuke, esp. officially.

**re·pri·sal** /ri'prīzəl/ ▶n. (act of)
retaliation.

**re·proach** /ri'prōCH/ ▶v. express
disapproval to (a person) for a
fault, etc.
▶n. **1** rebuke or censure. **2** thing
that brings disgrace or discredit.
**3** disgraced or discredited state.

**rep·ro·bate** /'reprə,bāt/ ▶n.
unprincipled or immoral person.
▶adj. immoral.

**re·pro·duce** ▶v. **1** produce a
copy or representation of.
**2** cause to be seen or heard, etc.,
again: *reproduce the sound exactly.*
**3** produce further members of
the same species by natural
means. —**re·pro·duc·i·ble** adj.
—**re·pro·duc·tion** n.
—**re·pro·duc·tive** adj.

**re·proof** /ri'prōōf/ ▶n. expression

of blame or disapproval.
—**re·prove** *v.* —**re·prov·ing·ly** *adv.*

**rep·tile** /ˈreptl/ ▶*n.* cold-blooded scaly animal of the class including snakes, lizards, crocodiles, turtles, tortoises, etc. —**rep·til·i·an** *adj.*

**re·pub·lic** /riˈpəblik/ ▶*n.* nation in which power is held by the people or their elected representatives.

**re·pub·li·can** ▶*adj.* of, characteristic of, or advocating a republic.
▶*n.* **1** person advocating or supporting republican government. **2** (**Republican**) supporter of the Republican Party. —**re·pub·li·can·ism** *n.*

**re·pu·di·ate** /riˈpyo͞odēˌāt/ ▶*v.* **1** disown; disavow; reject. **2** refuse to recognize or obey (authority or a treaty). —**re·pu·di·a·tion** *n.*

**re·pug·nance** /riˈpəgnəns/ ▶*n.* antipathy; aversion. —**re·pug·nant** *adj.*

**re·pulse** /riˈpəls/ ▶*v.* **1** drive back by force of arms. **2** rebuff. **3** be repulsive to.
▶*n.* repulsing or being repulsed.

**re·pul·sion** ▶*n.* **1** aversion; disgust. **2** *Physics* tendency of bodies to repel each other.

**re·pul·sive** ▶*adj.* causing aversion or loathing; disgusting.

**re·pur·chase** /rēˈpərCHəs/ ▶*v.* buy (something) back.
▶*n.* action of buying something back.

**rep·u·ta·ble** /ˈrepyətəbəl/ ▶*adj.* of good repute; respectable. —**rep·u·ta·bly** *adv.*

**rep·u·ta·tion** /ˌrepyəˈtāSHən/ ▶*n.* **1** what is generally said or believed about a person's or thing's character or standing: *a reputation for dishonesty.* **2** good repute; respectability.

**re·pute** /riˈpyo͞ot/ ▶*n.* **1** opinion generally held of someone or something: *pollution could bring the company's name into bad repute.* **2** state of being highly thought of: *chefs of international repute.*
▶*v.* [often as *adj.* **reputed**] to be generally considered; to be said to be. —**re·put·ed·ly** *adv.*

**re·quest** /riˈkwest/ ▶*n.* **1** act of asking politely for something. **2** thing asked for.
▶*v.* **1** politely or formally ask for. **2** ask a person to do something. **3** ask (that).

**re·qui·em** /ˈrekwēəm/ ▶*n.* **1** mass for the repose of the souls of the dead. **2** music for this.

**re·qui·es·cat** /ˌrekwēˈesˌkät; ˌrā-/ ▶*n.* wish or prayer for the repose of a dead person.

**re·quire** /riˈkwī(ə)r/ ▶*v.* **1** need; depend on. **2** lay down as an imperative: *required by law.* **3** command; instruct; insist on. —**re·quire·ment** *n.*

**req·ui·site** /ˈrekwəzət/ ▶*adj.* required by circumstances; necessary.
▶*n.* thing needed (for some purpose).

**req·ui·si·tion** ▶*n.* **1** official order for supplies. **2** formal demand or request.
▶*v.* demand the use or supply of, esp. by requisition order.

**re·quite** /riˈkwīt/ ▶*v.* **1** make appropriate return for (a service). **2** reward or avenge (a favor or injury). —**re·quit·al** *n.*

**rere·dos** /ˈrerəˌdäs; ˈri(ə)rə-/ ▶*n.* (*pl.* same) ornamental screen covering the wall at the back of an altar.

**re·run** ▶*v.* (**-run·ning**; *past* **-ran**; *past part.* **-run**) run (a broadcast, etc.) again.
▶*n.* television program, etc., shown again.

**re·scind** /riˈsind/ ▶*v.* revoke, cancel, or repeal.
—**re·scind·a·ble** *adj.*

**res·cue** /ˈreskyo͞o/ ▶*v.* (**-cued, -cu·ing**) save or set free from danger, harm, etc.
▶*n.* rescuing or being rescued.
—**res·cu·er** *n.*

**re·search** /riˈsərCH/ ▶*n.* systematic investigation into and study of materials, sources, etc., in order to establish facts and reach new conclusions.
▶*v.* do research into or for.
—**re·search·er** *n.*

**re·sem·ble** /riˈzembəl/ ▶*v.* be like; have a similarity to.
—**re·sem·blance** *n.*

**re·sent** /riˈzent/ ▶*v.* feel indignation at; be aggrieved by.
—**re·sent·ful** *adj.*
—**re·sent·ment** *n.*

**res·er·va·tion** /ˌrezərˈvāSHən/ ▶*n.* **1** reserving or being reserved. **2** thing booked, e.g., a room in a hotel. **3** express or tacit limitation to an agreement, etc.: *had reservations about the plan.* **4** area of land reserved for a particular group, as a tract federally designated for Native Americans.

**re·serve** /riˈzərv/ ▶*v.* **1** put aside; keep back for a later occasion or special use. **2** order to be

specially retained or allocated for a particular person or at a particular time. **3** retain or secure: *reserve the right to.*
▸*n.* **1** thing reserved for future use; extra amount. **2** self-restraint; reticence; lack of cordiality. **3** assets kept readily available. **4** land reserved for special use, esp. as a habitat.

**re·served** ▸*adj.* **1** reticent; uncommunicative. **2** set apart; destined for some use or fate. —**re·serv·ed·ly** *adv.*

**re·serv·ist** ▸*n.* member of the military reserve forces.

**res·er·voir** /ˈrezə(r)ˌvwär/ ▸*n.* **1** large lake used as a source of water supply. **2** receptacle for or of fluid. **3** reserve or supply, esp. of information.

**re·side** /riˈzīd/ ▸*v.* **1** have one's home; dwell permanently. **2** (of power, a right, etc.) rest or be vested in. **3** (**reside in**) (of a quality) be present or inherent in.

**res·i·dence** /ˈrez(ə)dəns/ ▸*n.* **1** a person's house. **2** fact of living in a particular place.

**res·i·den·cy** ▸*n.* (*pl.* **-cies**) **1** fact of living in a place. **2** period of hospital staff training for a physician.

**res·i·dent** ▸*n.* **1** permanent inhabitant. **2** medical school graduate engaged in specialized practice under supervision in a hospital.
▸*adj.* **1** residing; in residence. **2** having quarters at one's workplace. **3** located in.

**res·i·den·tial** /ˌreziˈdenCHəl/ ▸*adj.* **1** suitable for or occupied by private houses. **2** relating to or used as a residence.

**res·i·due** /ˈreziˌd(y)o͞o/ ▸*n.* what is left over or remains; remainder. —**re·sid·u·al** *adj.*

**re·sid·u·um** /riˈzijo͞oəm/ ▸*n.* (*pl.* **-sid·u·a** /-ˈzijo͞oə/) substance or thing that remains or is left behind, in particular, a chemical residue.

**re·sign** /riˈzīn/ ▸*v.* **1** give up office, one's employment, etc. **2** surrender; hand over (a right, charge, task, etc.). **3** reconcile (oneself) to the inevitable. —**res·ig·na·tion** *n.*

**re·signed** ▸*adj.* having resigned oneself; submissive; acquiescent. —**re·sign·ed·ly** *adv.*

**re·sile** /riˈzīl/ ▸*v.* abandon a position or a course of action.

**re·sil·ient** /riˈzilyənt/ ▸*adj.* **1** resuming its original shape after bending, compression, etc.

**2** readily recovering from a setback. —**re·sil·ience** *n.*

**res·in** /'rezin/ ▸*n.* **1** adhesive substance secreted by some plants. **2** (also **syn·thet·ic res·in**) organic compound made by polymerization, etc., and used in plastics, etc. —**res·in·ous** *adj.*

**re·sist** /ri'zist/ ▸*v.* **1** withstand the action or effect of. **2** abstain from (pleasure, temptation, etc.). **3** strive against; refuse to comply (with).

▸*n.* protective coating of a resistant substance. —**re·sist·ant** *adj.*

**re·sis·tance** ▸*n.* **1** resisting; refusal to comply. **2** power of resisting: *resistance to wear and tear.* **3** ability to withstand disease. **4** impeding or stopping the effect exerted by one thing on another. **5** *Physics* property or measure of hindering the conduction of electricity, heat, etc.

**re·sis·tor** ▸*n.* device having resistance to the passage of an electrical current.

**res ju·di·ca·ta** /ˌrēz ˌjōōdi'kätə; ˌräs/ ▸*n.* (*pl.* **res ju·de·ca·tae** /ˌjōōdi'kätē; -tī/) matter that has been adjudicated by a competent court and may not be pursued further by the same parties.

**res·o·lute** /'rezəˌlōōt/ ▸*adj.* determined; firm of purpose. —**res·o·lute·ly** *adv.* —**res·o·lute·ness** *n.*

**res·o·lu·tion** ▸*n.* **1** resolute temper or character. **2** thing resolved on; intention: *New Year's resolutions.* **3** formal expression of opinion or intention by a legislative body, etc. **4** solving of a problem, doubt, or question. **5** optical clarity or sharpness.

**re·solve** /ri'zälv/ ▸*v.* **1** make up one's mind; decide firmly. **2** separate or cause to separate into constituent parts. **3** solve; explain; settle (doubt, argument, etc.).

▸*n.* firm mental decision or intention.

**res·o·nant** /'rezənənt/ ▸*adj.* **1** (of sound or a place) echoing; resounding. **2** (of a body, room, etc.) tending to reinforce or prolong sounds. —**res·o·nance** *n.*

**res·o·nate** /'rezəˌnāt/ ▸*v.* **1** produce or be filled with a deep, full, reverberating sound. **2** evoke or suggest images or emotions.

**re·sort** /ri'zôrt/ ▶*n.* **1** place frequented for recreation, health, etc. **2 a** thing to which one has recourse; expedient; measure. **b** recourse (to).
▶*v.* turn (to) as an expedient: *resorted to threats.*

**re·sound** /ri'zound/ ▶*v.* fill or be filled with sound; echo.

**re·sound·ing** ▶*adj.* **1** (of a sound) loud enough to reverberate. **2** unmistakable; emphatic: *a resounding success.*

**re·source** /ri'sôrs; -'zôrs/ ▶*n.* **1** expedient or device. **2** (usu. **resources**) means available; asset. **3** (**resources**) country's collective wealth.
—**re·source·ful** *adj.*
—**re·source·ful·ly** *adv.*
—**re·source·ful·ness** *n.*

**re·spect** /ri'spekt/ ▶*n.* **1** deferential esteem felt or shown toward a person or quality. **2** heed or regard. **3** aspect, particular, etc. **4** reference; relation.
▶*v.* **1** regard with deference, esteem, or honor. **2** avoid interfering with, harming, etc.

**re·spect·a·ble** ▶*adj.* **1** decent and proper in appearance and behavior. **2** reasonably good in condition, appearance, number, size, etc.: *a respectable salary.*
—**re·spect·a·bil·i·ty** *n.*
—**re·spect·a·bly** *adv.*

**re·spect·ful** ▶*adj.* showing deference: *stood at a respectful distance.* —**re·spect·ful·ly** *adv.*
—**re·spect·ful·ness** *n.*

**re·spect·ing** ▶*prep.* with regard to; concerning.

**re·spec·tive** ▶*adj.* concerning or appropriate to each of several individually: *go to your respective places.* —**re·spec·tive·ly** *adv.*

**res·pi·ra·tion** /ˌrespə'rāsʜən/ ▶*n.* **1** breathing; a breath. **2** in organisms, absorption of oxygen and release of energy and carbon dioxide. —**res·pi·ra·to·ry** *adj.*

**res·pi·ra·tor** /ˌrespə'rātor/ ▶*n.* **1** apparatus worn over the face to purify, warm, etc., inhaled air. **2** apparatus for maintaining artificial respiration.

**res·pite** /'respit/ ▶*n.* **1** interval of rest or relief. **2** delay permitted before discharge of obligation or suffering of penalty.

**re·splen·dent** /ri'splendənt/ ▶*adj.* brilliant; dazzlingly or gloriously bright.
—**re·splen·dence** *n.*

**re·spond** /ri'spänd/ ▶*v.* **1** answer; reply. **2** react.

**re·spon·dent** ▶*n.* defendant, esp. in an appeal or divorce case.

**re·sponse** /ri'späns/ ▶*n.* **1** answer given in word or act; reply. **2** feeling, movement, change, etc., caused by a stimulus or influence.

**re·spon·si·bil·i·ty** /ri,spänsə-'bilitē/ ▶*n.* (*pl.* **-ties**) **1 a** being responsible. **b** authority and obligation. **2** person or thing for which one is responsible.

**re·spon·si·ble** ▶*adj.* **1** liable to be called to account (to a person or for a thing). **2** morally accountable for one's actions; capable of rational conduct. **3** of good credit, position, or repute; respectable. **4** being the primary cause. **—re·spon·si·bly** *adv.*

**re·spon·sive** ▶*adj.* **1** responding readily (to some influence). **2** sympathetic. **3** answering. **—re·spon·sive·ly** *adv.* **—re·spon·sive·ness** *n.*

**res·sen·ti·ment** /rə,säntē'män/ ▶*n.* psychological state arising from suppressed feelings of envy and hatred that cannot be acted upon, frequently resulting in some form of self-abasement.

**rest** /rest/ ▶*v.* **1** cease, abstain, or be relieved from exertion, action, etc. **2** be still or asleep, esp. to refresh oneself or recover strength. **3** lie (on); be supported (by). **4** place for support. **5** be left without further investigation or discussion: *let the matter rest.* **6** be left in the hands or charge of: *final arrangements rest with you.*
▶*n.* **1** repose or sleep. **2** cessation of exertion, activity, etc. **3** period of resting. **4** support for holding or steadying something. **5** (**the rest**) the remaining part or parts; the others; the remainder. **6** *Mus.* **a** interval of silence. **b** sign denoting this. **—rest·ful** *adj.*

**res·tau·rant** /'restərənt/ ▶*n.* place where people pay to sit and eat meals that are cooked and served on the premises.

**res·tau·ra·teur** /,restərə'tər/ ▶*n.* restaurant owner or manager.

**res·ti·tu·tion** /,resti't(y)o͞oSHən/ ▶*n.* **1** restoring of a thing to its proper owner. **2** reparation.

**res·tive** /'restiv/ ▶*adj.* **1** fidgety; restless. **2** unmanageable; rejecting control. **—res·tive·ly** *adv.* **—res·tive·ness** *n.*

**rest·less** ▶*adj.* **1** finding or affording no rest. **2** uneasy;

agitated. —**rest·less·ly** *adv.*
—**rest·less·ness** *n.*

**res·to·ra·tion** /ˌrestəˈrāsʜən/
▶*n.* **1** restoring or being
restored. **2** model or
representation of the supposed
original form of a thing.

**re·store** /riˈstôr/ ▶*v.* **1** bring back
to the original state by
rebuilding, repairing, etc.
**2** bring back to health, etc.
**3** give back to the original
owner. **4** replace; put back;
bring back. —**re·stor·a·tive** *adj.*
& *n.*

**re·strain** /riˈstrān/ ▶*v.* **1** check or
hold in; keep in check or under
control or within bounds.
**2** repress; keep down.

**re·straint** ▶*n.* **1** restraining or
being restrained. **2** controlling
agency or influence. **3** self-
control; moderation. **4** reserve
of manner.

**re·strict** /riˈstrikt/ ▶*v.* **1** confine;
limit. **2** withhold from general
circulation or disclosure.
—**re·stric·tion** *n.* —**re·stric·tive**
*adj.*

**rest room** ▶*n.* public toilet.

**re·sult** /riˈzəlt/ ▶*n.*
**1** consequence, issue, or
outcome of something.
**2** satisfactory outcome: *gets*

*results.* **3** end product of
calculation.

▶*v.* **1** arise as the actual or follow
as a logical consequence. **2** have
a specified end or outcome:
*resulted in a large profit.*
—**re·sult·ant** *adj.*

**re·sume** /riˈzo͞om/ ▶*v.* **1** begin
again or continue after an
interruption. **2** begin to speak,
work, or use again;
recommence. **3** get back; take
back: *resume one's seat.*
—**re·sump·tion** *n.*

**ré·su·mé** /ˌrezəˈmā/ (also
**re·su·mé, re·su·me**) ▶*n.*
summary, esp. of a person's
employment history.

**re·sur·face** ▶*v.* **1** lay a new
surface on (a road, etc.). **2** rise or
arise again; turn up again.

**re·sur·gent** /riˈsərjənt/ ▶*adj.*
**1** rising or arising again.
**2** tending to rise again.
—**re·sur·gence** *n.*

**re·sur·rect** /ˌrezəˈrekt/ ▶*v.* bring
back to life, use, memory, etc.
—**re·sur·rec·tion** *n.*

**re·sus·ci·tate** /riˈsəsəˌtāt/ ▶*v.*
**1** revive from unconsciousness
or apparent death. **2** restore to
vogue, vigor, or vividness.
—**re·sus·ci·ta·tion** *n.*

**ret** /ret/ ▶*v.* (**ret·ted, ret·ting**) soak (flax or hemp) in water to soften it and separate the fibers.

**re·tail** /ˈrēˌtāl/ ▶*n.* sale of goods in small quantities to the public. ▶*v.* (of goods) sell or be sold in retail trade. —**re·tail·er** *n.*

**re·tain** /riˈtān/ ▶*v.* **1** keep possession of; not lose. **2** not abolish, discard, or alter. **3** secure the services of (a person, esp. an attorney) with a preliminary payment.

**re·tain·er** ▶*n.* **1** fee for retaining an attorney, etc. **2** faithful servant: *old retainer.*

**re·take** ▶*v.* /rēˈtāk/ (*past* **-took**; *past part.* **-tak·en**) **1** take again. **2** recapture. ▶*n.* /ˈrēˌtāk/ **1** act of filming a scene or recording music, etc., again. **2** scene or recording obtained in this way.

**re·tal·i·ate** /riˈtalēˌāt/ ▶*v.* repay an injury, insult, etc., in kind; attack in return. —**re·tal·i·a·tion** *n.* —**re·tal·i·a·to·ry** *adj.*

**re·tard** /riˈtärd/ ▶*v.* **1** make slow or late. **2** delay the progress or accomplishment of. —**re·tard·ant** *adj. & n.* —**re·tar·da·tion** *n.*

**re·tard·ed** ▶*adj.* backward in mental or physical development.

**retch** /reCH/ ▶*v.* make a motion of vomiting, esp. involuntarily and without effect.

**re·ten·tion** /riˈtenCHən/ ▶*n.* retaining; being retained. —**re·ten·tive** *adj.*

**ret·i·cence** /ˈretəsəns/ ▶*n.* **1** personal hesitancy or avoidance; reluctance. **2** disposition to silence. —**ret·i·cent** *adj.*

**re·tic·u·late** ▶*v.* /riˈtikyəˌlāt/ divide or mark (something) in such a way as to resemble a net or network. ▶*adj.* /-lət; -ˌlāt/ reticulated.

**ret·i·cule** /ˈretiˌkyo͞ol/ ▶*n.* woman's small handbag, typically having a drawstring and decorated with embroidery or beads.

**ret·i·na** /ˈretnə/ ▶*n.* (*pl.* **-nas** or **-nae**) layer at the back of the eyeball sensitive to light. —**ret·i·nal** *adj.*

**ret·i·nue** /ˈretnˌ(y)o͞o/ ▶*n.* body of attendants accompanying an important person.

**re·tire** /riˈtī(ə)r/ ▶*v.* **1** leave office or employment, esp. because of age. **2** withdraw; go away; retreat. **3** go to bed. —**re·tir·ee** *n.* —**re·tire·ment** *n.*

**re·tort** /ri'tôrt/ ▸n. **1** incisive or witty or angry reply. **2** vessel with a long downward-turned neck used in distilling liquids. ▸v. make a witty or angry reply.

**re·touch** ▸v. improve (a picture, photograph, etc.) by minor alterations.

**re·trace** ▸v. **1** go back over (one's steps, etc.). **2** trace back to a source or beginning.

**re·tract** /ri'trakt/ ▸v. **1** withdraw (a statement or undertaking). **2** draw or be drawn back or in. —**re·trac·tion** n.

**re·tread** ▸v. (*past* -**trod**; *past part.* -**trod·den**) **1** tread (a path, etc.) again. **2** put a fresh tread on (a tire). ▸n. retreaded tire.

**re·treat** /ri'trēt/ ▸v. **1** move back or withdraw. **2** change one's decision, plans, etc., because of criticism from others. ▸n. **1** act of moving back or withdrawing. **2** act of changing one's plans, etc., because of criticism. **3** withdrawal into privacy or security. **4** place of shelter, seclusion, or meditation.

**re·trench** /ri'trenCH/ ▸v. cut down expenses. —**re·trench·ment** n.

**ret·ri·bu·tion** /ˌretrə'byo͞osHən/ ▸n. punishment considered morally right and fully deserved.

**re·trieve** /ri'trēv/ ▸v. **1** regain possession of; recover. **2** obtain (information stored in a computer, etc.). **3** rescue (esp. from a bad state). —**re·triev·al** n.

**ret·ro** /'retrō/ ▸adj. imitative of a style, fashion, or design from the recent past. ▸n. clothes or music whose style or design is imitative of those of the recent past.

**ret·ro·ac·tive** /ˌretrō'aktiv/ ▸adj. taking effect from a date in the past. —**ret·ro·ac·tive·ly** adv.

**ret·ro·fit** ▸v. (-**fit·ted**, -**fit·ting**) modify machinery, vehicles, etc., to incorporate changes and developments introduced after manufacture.

**ret·ro·grade** ▸adj. **1** directed backward; retreating. **2** inverse; reversed: *retrograde order.*

**ret·ro·gress** /ˌretrə'gres/ ▸v. return to an earlier and worse state. —**ret·ro·gres·sion** n. —**ret·ro·gres·sive** adj.

**ret·ro·spect** /'retrə,spekt/ ▸n. regard or reference to previous conditions. —**ret·ro·spec·tion** n. —**ret·ro·spec·tive** adj. & n.

**ret·ro·spec·tion** /ˌretrə-ˈspekSHən/ ▶n. action of looking back on or reviewing past events or situations, esp. those in one's own life.

**ret·rous·sé** /rəˌtrooˈsā ˌretroo-/ ▶adj. (of a person's nose) turned up at the tip, esp. in an attractive way.

**re·turn** /riˈtərn/ ▶v. **1** come or go back. **2** bring or put or send back. **3** pay back or reciprocate; give or say in response. **4** yield (a profit).
▶n. **1** coming or going back. **2 a** giving, sending, putting, or paying back. **b** thing given or sent back. **3** key on a computer or typewriter to start a new line. **4** proceeds or profit of an undertaking.

**Rev.** ▶abbr. Reverend.

**rev** /rev/ inf. ▶n. a revolution of an engine per minute.
▶v. (**revved**, **rev·ving**) **1** increase the running speed of (an engine). **2** (of an engine) operate with increasing speed when the accelerator is pressed.

**re·vamp** ▶v. renovate; revise; improve.

**re·vanch·ism** /rəˈvänˌSHizəm/ ▶n. policy of seeking to retaliate, esp. to recover lost territory.

**re·veal** /riˈvēl/ ▶v. **1** disclose; divulge; betray: *revealed his plans.* **2** cause or allow to be seen. —**re·veal·ing·ly** adv.

**re·vealed re·li·gion** ▶n. religion based on divine revelation rather than reason.

**rev·eil·le** /ˈrevəlē/ ▶n. military wake-up signal.

**rev·el** /ˈrevəl/ ▶v. **1** have a good time; be extravagantly festive. **2** take keen delight (in).
▶n. reveling. —**rev·el·er** n. —**rev·el·ry** n.

**rev·e·la·tion** /ˌrevəˈlāSHən/ ▶n. **1** surprising and previously unknown fact: *revelations about his personal life.* **2** divine or supernatural disclosure to humans.

**rev·el·ry** /ˈrevəlrē/ ▶n. (pl. **-ries**) (also **revelries**) lively and noisy festivities, esp. when these involve drinking a large amount of alcohol.

**rev·e·nant** /ˈrevəˌnän; -nənt/ ▶n. person who has returned, esp. supposedly from the dead.

**re·venge** /riˈvenj/ ▶n. **1** retaliation for an offense or injury. **2** desire for this; vindictive feeling.
▶v. inflict retaliation on behalf of (someone else): *it's a pity he chose*

*that way to revenge his sister.*
—**re·venge·ful** *adj.*

**rev·e·nue** /'revə,n(y)oō/ ▶*n.* income, esp. of a business or government.

**re·ver·ber·ate** /ri'vərbə,rāt/ ▶*v.* **a** (of sound, light, or heat) be returned, echoed, or reflected repeatedly. **b** return (a sound, etc.) in this way.
—**re·ver·ber·a·tion** *n.*

**re·vere** /ri'vi(ə)r/ ▶*v.* hold in deep or religious respect.
—**rev·er·ence** *n.* —**rev·er·ent** *adj.*
—**rev·er·en·tial** *adj.*

**Rev·er·end** /'rev(ə)rənd/ ▶*n. inf.* title of a member of the clergy.

**rev·er·ent** /'rev(ə)rənt/ ▶*adj.* feeling or showing deep and solemn respect.

**rev·er·en·tial** /,revə'renCHəl/ ▶*adj.* of the nature of, due to, or characterized by reverence.

**rev·er·ie** /'revərē/ ▶*n.* spell of abstracted musing.

**re·verse** /ri'vərs/ ▶*v.* **1** turn the other way around or up or inside out. **2** change to the opposite character or effect: *reversed the decision.* **3** travel or cause to travel backward.
▶*adj.* **1** backward or upside-down. **2** opposite or contrary in character or order; inverted.

▶*n.* **1** opposite or contrary: *the reverse is the case.* **2** occurrence of misfortune; defeat. **3** reverse gear or motion. **4** reverse side.
—**re·ver·sal** *n.* —**re·vers·i·ble** *adj.*

**re·vert** /ri'vərt/ ▶*v.* return to a former state, practice, opinion, etc. —**re·ver·sion** *n.*

**re·vet** /ri'vet/ ▶*v.* (**-vet·ted**, **-vet·ting**) face (a rampart, wall, etc.) with masonry, esp. in fortification.

**re·view** /ri'vyoō/ ▶*n.* **1** general survey or assessment of a subject or thing. **2** survey of the past. **3** criticism of a book, play, etc.
▶*v.* **1** survey or look back on. **2** reconsider or revise. **3** write a review of (a book, play, etc.).
—**re·view·er** *n.*

**re·vile** /ri'vīl/ ▶*v.* abuse; criticize abusively.

**re·vise** /ri'vīz/ ▶*v.* **1** examine and improve or amend (esp. written or printed matter). **2** consider and alter (an opinion, etc.).
—**re·vi·sion** *n.*

**re·vi·sion·ism** /ri'vizHə,nizəm/ ▶*n.* departure from or modification of an accepted doctrine, theory, view of history, etc. —**re·vi·sion·ist** *n. & adj.*

**re·viv·al** /ri'vīvəl/ ▶*n.* **1** improvement in condition or strength. **2** new production of an old play, etc. **3** reawakening of religious fervor. **—re·viv·al·ism** *n.* **—re·viv·al·ist** *n.*

**re·vive** /ri'vīv/ ▶*v.* **1** come or bring back to consciousness, life, or strength. **2** come or bring back to existence, use, notice, etc.

**re·voke** /ri'vōk/ ▶*v.* rescind, withdraw, or cancel (a decree, promise, etc.). **—rev·o·ca·tion** *n.*

**re·volt** /ri'vōlt/ ▶*v.* **1** rise in rebellion. **2** feel or affect with strong disgust. ▶*n.* act of rebelling. **—re·volt·ing** *adj.*

**rev·o·lu·tion** /ˌrevə'lōōSHən/ ▶*n.* **1** forcible overthrow of a government or social order. **2** any fundamental change or reversal of conditions. **3** revolving. **4** completion of an orbit or rotation. **—rev·o·lu·tion·ar·y** *adj. & n.*

**rev·o·lu·tion·ize** ▶*v.* introduce fundamental change to.

**re·volve** /ri'välv/ ▶*v.* **1** turn or cause to turn around, esp. on an axis; rotate. **2** move in a circular orbit.

**re·volv·er** ▶*n.* pistol with revolving chambers enabling several shots to be fired without reloading.

**re·vue** /ri'vyōō/ ▶*n.* theatrical entertainment of a series of short usu. satirical sketches and songs.

**re·vul·sion** /ri'vəlSHən/ ▶*n.* abhorrence; sense of loathing.

**re·ward** /ri'wôrd/ ▶*n.* **1 a** return or recompense for service or merit. **b** requital for good or evil; retribution. **2** sum offered for the detection of a criminal, restoration of lost property, etc. ▶*v.* give a reward to (a person) or for (a service, etc.).

**re·ward·ing** ▶*adj.* (of an activity, etc.) worthwhile; satisfying.

**re·word** ▶*v.* change the wording of.

**re·write** ▶*v.* (*past* **-wrote**; *past part.* **-writ·ten**) write again, esp. differently.

**RFD** ▶*abbr.* rural free delivery.

**rhab·do·man·cy** /'rabdə-ˌmansē/ ▶*n.* dowsing with a rod or stick.

**rhap·so·dize** /'rapsəˌdīz/ ▶*v.* talk or write about someone or something with great enthusiasm.

**rhap·so·dy** /'rapsədē/ ▶*n.* (*pl.* **-dies**) **1** enthusiastic, ecstatic, or extravagant utterance or

composition. **2** piece of music in one extended movement, usu. emotional in character.
—**rhap·sod·ic** *adj.*

**rhe·ni·um** /ˈrēnēəm/ ▶*n.* rare metallic element. (Symb.: **Rh**)

**rhe·o·stat** /ˈrēəˌstat/ ▶*n.* device used to control an electrical current by varying the resistance.

**rhet·o·ric** /ˈretərik/ ▶*n.* **1** art of effective or persuasive speaking or writing. **2** language designed to persuade or impress.
—**rhe·tor·i·cal** *adj.*
—**rhe·tor·i·cal·ly** *adv.*

□ **rhetorical question** question asked not for information but for an effect, e.g., *who cares?* meaning *nobody cares.*

**rheum** /rōōm/ ▶*n.* watery fluid that collects in or drips from the nose or eyes.

**rheu·ma·tism** /ˈrōōməˌtizəm/ ▶*n.* disease marked by inflammation and pain in the joints, muscles, or fibrous tissue, esp. rheumatoid arthritis.
—**rheu·mat·ic** *adj.*

**rheu·ma·toid arth·ri·tis** /ˈrōōməˌtoid/ ▶*n.* chronic progressive disease causing inflammation in the joints and resulting in painful deformity.

**Rh fac·tor** ▶antigen occurring in the red blood cells of most humans.

**rhine·stone** /ˈrīnˌstōn/ ▶*n.* imitation diamond.

**rhi·noc·er·os** /rīˈnäs(ə)rəs/ ▶*n.* (*pl.* same or **-os·es**) large thick-skinned ungulate of Africa and S. Asia, with one or two horns on the nose.

**rhi·zome** /ˈrīzōm/ ▶*n.* underground rootlike stem bearing both roots and shoots.

**rho·do·den·dron** /ˌrōdə-ˈdendrən/ ▶*n.* evergreen shrub with large clusters of bell-shaped flowers.

**rhom·boid** /ˈrämˌboid/ ▶*adj.* (also **rhom·boid·al**) like a rhombus.
▶*n.* quadrilateral of which only the opposite sides and angles are equal.

**rhom·bus** /ˈrämbəs/ ▶*n.* (*pl.* **-bus·es** or **-bi**) parallelogram with oblique angles and equal sides.

**rhu·barb** /ˈrōōˌbärb/ ▶*n.* **1** plants producing long fleshy dark-red stalks used cooked as food. **2** *inf.* heated dispute.

**rhyme** /rīm/ ▶*n.* **1** identity of sound between words or the endings of words, esp. in verse.

**2** verse or poem having rhymes. **3** word providing a rhyme. ▶*v.* **1 a** (of words or lines) produce a rhyme. **b** (**rhyme with**) act as a rhyme with (another). **2** make or write rhymes; versify. □ **rhyme or reason** sense; logic.

**rhythm** /ˈriᴛʜəm/ ▶*n.* **1** measured regular flow of verse or prose determined by the length of stress and syllables. **2** pattern of accent and duration of notes in music. —**rhyth·mi·cal** *adj.*

**rhythm meth·od** ▶*n.* birth control by avoiding sexual intercourse when ovulation is likely to occur.

**RI** ▶*abbr.* Rhode Island (in official postal use).

**rib** /rib/ ▶*n.* **1** each of the curved bones joined in pairs to the spine and protecting the chest. **2** supporting ridge, timber, rod, etc. ▶*v.* (**ribbed, rib·bing**) **1** provide with ribs. **2** *inf.* make fun of; tease.

**rib·ald** /ˈribəld/ ▶*adj.* referring to sexual matters in an amusingly rude way: *a ribald comment.*

**rib·ald·ry** /ˈribəldrē; ˈrī-/ ▶*n.* ribald talk or behavior.

**rib·bon** /ˈribən/ ▶*n.* **1** narrow strip or band of fabric, used esp. for trimming or decoration. **2** long, narrow strip of anything. **3** (**ribbons**) ragged strips: *his shirt was torn to ribbons.*

**ri·bo·fla·vin** /ˈrībəˌflāvin/ ▶*n.* vitamin of the B complex, found in liver, milk, eggs, etc. (Also called **vitamin B₂**).

**rice** /rīs/ ▶*n.* **1** cereal grass cultivated in marshes, esp. in Asia. **2** grains of this, used as food. ▶*v.* sieve (cooked potatoes, etc.) into thin strings. —**ric·er** *n.*

**rich** /rich/ ▶*adj.* **1** having much wealth. **2** splendid; costly; elaborate. **3** copious; abundant; fertile. **4** (of food or diet) containing much fat, sugar, spice, etc. **5** (of color or sound or smell) mellow and deep; strong and full. —**rich·ly** *adv.* —**rich·ness** *n.*

**rich·es** /ˈrichiz/ ▶*pl. n.* abundant means; valuable possessions.

**Rich·ter scale** /ˈriktər/ ▶*n.* scale of 0 to 10 for representing the strength of an earthquake.

**rick·ets** /ˈrikits/ ▶*n.* bone-softening disease of children, caused by a deficiency of vitamin D.

**rick·et·y** /ˈrikitē/ ▶*adj.* insecure; shaky.

**ric·o·chet** /'rikə,SHā/ ▶*n.* action of a projectile, esp. a shell or bullet, in rebounding off a surface.

▶*v.* (**-cheted**; **-chet·ing**) (of a projectile) make a ricochet.

**ri·cot·ta** /ri'kätə/ ▶*n.* soft Italian cheese resembling cottage cheese.

**ric·tus** /'riktəs/ ▶*n.* fixed grimace or grin.

**rid** /rid/ ▶*v.* (**rid·ding**; *past* and *past part.* **rid**) free (a person or place) of something unwanted.

□ **be** (or **get**) **rid of** dispose of.

**rid·dle** /'ridl/ ▶*n.* **1** question or statement testing ingenuity in divining its answer or meaning. **2** puzzling fact, thing, or person.

▶*v.* **1** make many holes in, esp. with gunshot. **2** spread through; permeate: *riddled with errors.*

**ride** /rīd/ ▶*v.* (*past* **rode**; *past part.* **rid·den**) **1** travel or be carried on (a bicycle, etc.) or in (a vehicle). **2** sit on and control or be carried by (a horse, etc.). **3** be carried or supported by: *the ship rides the waves.*

▶*n.* **1** journey or spell of riding. **2** amusement for riding on at a carnival, etc.

**rid·er** /'rīdər/ ▶*n.* **1** person who rides (esp. a horse). **2** addition to a document.

**ridge** /rij/ ▶*n.* **1** long, narrow hilltop, mountain range, or watershed. **2** any narrow elevation.

▶*v.* mark with ridges.

**rid·i·cule** /'ridi,kyōol/ ▶*n.* derision; mockery.

▶*v.* mock.

**ri·dic·u·lous** /ri'dikyələs/ ▶*adj.* **1** deserving or inviting ridicule. **2** unreasonable; absurd. —**ri·dic·u·lous·ly** *adv.*

**rife** /rīf/ ▶*adj.* **1** of common occurrence; widespread. **2** abounding in; teeming with: *the book was rife with factual errors.*

**riff** /rif/ ▶*n.* short repeated phrase in jazz, etc.

**riff-raff** /'rif,raf/ ▶*n.* rabble; disreputable persons.

**ri·fle** /'rīfəl/ ▶*n.* gun with a long, rifled barrel, esp. one fired from shoulder level.

▶*v.* search through something in a hurry in order to find or steal something.

**rift** /rift/ ▶*n.* **1** crack; split; opening. **2** disagreement; breach.

**rig** /rig/ ▶*v.* (**rigged**, **rig·ging**) **1** provide (a sailing ship) with sails, rigging, etc. **2** fit out; equip. **3** set up as a makeshift. **4** manage or conduct fraudulently: *rigged the election.*

▸*n.* **1** arrangement of a vessel's masts, sails, etc. **2** equipment for a special purpose.

**rig·ging** /ˈrigiNG/ ▸*n.* vessel's spars, ropes, etc.

**right** /rīt/ ▸*adj.* **1** morally good, justified, or accptable **2** true; not mistaken. **3** suitable; preferable. **4** sound or normal; healthy; satisfactory. **5** on or toward the east side when facing north.

▸*n.* **1** that which is correct or just. **2** justification or fair claim. **3** legal or moral authority to act. **4** right-hand part, region, or direction. **5** (often **Right**) conservative political group.

▸*v.* **1** restore to a proper, straight, or vertical position. **2** correct or avenge (mistakes, wrongs, etc.).

▸*adv.* **1** straight: *go right on.* **2** *inf.* immediately: *I'll be right back.* **3** all the way; completely. **4** exactly; quite: *right in the middle.* **5** correctly: *he had guessed right.* **6** on or to the right side. —**right·ly** *adv.*

**right an·gle** ▸*n.* angle of 90°.

**right·eous** /ˈrīCHəs/ ▸*adj.* morally right; virtuous; law-abiding. —**right·eous·ly** *adv.* —**right·eous·ness** *n.*

**right·ful** /ˈrītfəl/ ▸*adj.* **1** having a legitimate right to property, etc. **2** legitimate. —**right·ful·ly** *adv.*

**right of way** ▸*n.* **1** right of one vehicle to proceed before another. **2** right established by usage to pass over another's ground.

**right wing** ▸*n.* conservative section of a political party or system. —**right-wing** *adj.*

**rig·id** /ˈrijid/ ▸*adj.* **1** not flexible; unbendable. **2** not able to be changed or adapted. **3** (of a person) not adaptable in outlook, belief, etc. —**ri·gid·i·ty** *n.* —**rig·id·ly** *adv.*

**rig·ma·role** /ˈrigmə,rōl/ ▸*n.* **1** lengthy, complicated procedure. **2** rambling speech.

**rig·or** /ˈrigər/ ▸*n.* severity; strictness. —**rig·or·ous** *adj.* —**rig·or·ous·ly** *adv.* —**rig·or·ous·ness** *n.*

☐ **rigor mortis** stiffening of the body after death.

**rile** /rīl/ ▸*v. inf.* anger; irritate.

**rill** /ril/ ▸*n.* small stream.

**rille** /ˈril/ (also **rill**) ▸*n.* fissure or narrow channel on the moon's surface.

**rim** /rim/ ▸n. outer edge or border.
▸v. (**rimmed**, **rim·ming**) provide
with a rim; edge.

**rime** /rīm/ ▸n. light covering of
frost.

**rind** /rīnd/ ▸n. tough outer skin of
fruit, vegetables, cheese, etc.

**ring**¹ /riNG/ ▸n. **1** circular band,
usu. of metal, worn on a finger.
**2** something circular.
**3** enclosure for a circus
performance, boxing, etc.
**4** group of people combined
illicitly for profit, etc.
▸v. make or draw a circle around;
surround.

**ring**² ▸v. (*past* **rang**; *past part.*
**rung**) **1** give a clear resonant or
vibrating sound of or as of a bell.
**2** cause (a bell) to do this.
**3** resound with a sound: *theater
rang with applause.* **4** convey a
specified impression: *words rang
hollow.*
▸n. **1** ringing sound or tone.
**2** telephone call. **3** specified
feeling conveyed by words: *a
melancholy ring.*

**ring·lead·er** ▸n. leading
instigator of a crime, etc.

**ring·let** ▸n. curly lock of hair.

**ring·mas·ter** ▸n. director of a
circus performance.

**ring·worm** ▸n. fungal infection
of the skin causing circular
inflamed patches.

**rink** /riNGk/ ▸n. enclosed area of
floor or ice for skating.

**rinse** /rins/ ▸v. **1** wash
(something) with clean water to
remove soap or detergent.
**2** wash lightly without soap.
**3** clean (one's mouth) by swilling
around water or mouthwash and
then spitting it out.
▸n. **1** act of rinsing. **2** solution
for cleansing the mouth.
**3** preparation for conditioning
or coloring the hair.

**ri·ot** /ˈrīət/ ▸n. **1** disturbance of
the peace by a crowd.
**2** uncontrolled revelry. **3** lavish
display or sensation: *riot of
emotion.*
▸v. engage in a riot. **—ri·ot·ous**
*adj.*

**RIP** ▸*abbr.* may he or she or they
rest in peace (acronym of Latin
*requiescat* (pl. *requiescant*) *in pace*).

**rip** /rip/ ▸v. (**ripped**, **rip·ping**)
**1** tear or cut (a thing) quickly or
forcibly away or apart. **2** make a
tear in. **3** come violently apart;
split.
▸n. **1** long tear. **2** act of ripping.
□ **let rip** *inf.* act or proceed
without restraint. □ **rip into**
attack (a person) verbally. □ **rip**

**off** *inf.* defraud; steal. □ **rip-off** *inf.* fraud; swindle.

**rip cord** ▸*n.* cord for releasing a parachute from its pack.

**ripe** /rīp/ ▸*adj.* **1** (of grain, fruit, cheese, etc.) ready to be reaped, picked, or eaten. **2** mature; fully developed. **3** fit or ready: *land ripe for development.* —**rip·en** *v.* —**ripe·ness** *n.*

**ri·poste** /ri'pōst/ ▸*n.* quick retort.

**rip·ple** /'ripəl/ ▸*n.* **1** ruffling of the water's surface. **2** gentle lively sound, e.g., of laughter or applause. **3** brief wave of emotion, etc.: *a ripple of interest.* ▸*v.* (cause to) form or flow in ripples.

**rip·rap** /'rip,rap/ ▸*n.* loose stone used to form a foundation for a breakwater or other structure. ▸*v.* (**-rapped, -rap·ping**) strengthen with such a structure.

**rip-roar·ing** ▸*adj.* **1** wildly noisy or boisterous. **2** excellent; first-rate.

**rip·saw** ▸*n.* saw for sawing wood along the grain.

**rip·tide** ▸*n.* disturbance in the sea where opposing tidal currents meet.

**rise** /rīz/ ▸*v.* (*past* **rose**; *past part.* **ris·en**) **1** come or go up. **2** grow, project, expand, or incline upward; become higher. **3** appear above the horizon. **4** get up from lying, sitting, or kneeling. **5** come to life again: *rise from the ashes.* **6** (of dough) swell by the action of yeast, etc. **7** rebel. **8** originate; have as its source. ▸*n.* **1** upward movement or slope. **2** instance of social, political, etc., advancement. **3** increase in amount, size, numbers, etc.

**risk** /risk/ ▸*n.* **1** chance or possibility of danger, loss, injury, etc. **2** person or thing regarded in relation to risk: *is a poor risk.* ▸*v.* **1** expose to risk. **2** accept the chance of. —**risk·i·ness** *n.* —**risk·y** *adj.*

**ris·qué** /ri'skā/ ▸*adj.* slightly indecent.

**rite** /rīt/ ▸*n.* religious or solemn observance, act, or procedure. □ **rite of passage** event marking a stage of life, e.g., marriage.

**rit·u·al** /'riCHo͞oəl/ ▸*n.* **1** prescribed order of performing rites. **2** procedure regularly followed. ▸*adj.* of or done as a ritual or rite. —**rit·u·al·ism** *n.* —**rit·u·al·is·tic** *adj.* —**rit·u·al·ly** *adv.*

**ri·val** /'rīvəl/ ▸*n.* **1** person

competing with another.
**2** person or thing that equals another in quality.
▶*v.* **1** be the rival of. **2** seem or claim to be as good as. —**ri·val·ry** *n.*

**ri·ver** /'rivər/ ▶*n.* **1** copious natural stream of water flowing to the sea, a lake, etc. **2** copious flow: *river of lava.*

**riv·et** /'rivit/ ▶*n.* bolt for joining parts with its headless end being beaten out or pressed down when in place.
▶*v.* **1** join or fasten with rivets. **2** fix; make immovable. **3** direct intently (one's eyes or attention, etc.). **4** [often as *adj.* **riveting**] engross (a person or the attention).

**riv·u·let** /'riv(y)əlit/ ▶*n.* small stream.

**RN** ▶*abbr.* registered nurse.

**Rn** ▶*symb. Chem.* radon.

**RNA** ▶*abbrev. Chem.* ribonucleic acid: involved in controlling the synthesis of proteins.

**roach** /rōCH/ ▶*n. inf.* **1** cockroach. **2** butt of a marijuana cigarette.

**road** /rōd/ ▶*n.* **1** path or way with a prepared surface leading from one place to another, used by vehicles, pedestrians, etc. **2** particular course or direction

taken. **3** series of events that will lead to a certain conclusion.

**road·block** ▶*n.* barrier on a road, esp. one set up to stop and examine traffic.

**road·run·ner** ▶*n.* fast-running species of cuckoo of Mexican and U.S. deserts.

**road·stead** /'rōd,sted/ ▶*n.* sheltered stretch of water near the shore in which ships can ride at anchor.

**roam** /rōm/ ▶*v.* ramble; wander.

**roan** /rōn/ ▶*adj.* (of esp. a horse) having a coat thickly interspersed with another color.
▶*n.* roan animal.

**roar** /rôr/ ▶*n.* **1** loud, deep, hoarse sound. **2** loud laugh.
▶*v.* utter or make a roar.

**roast** /rōst/ ▶*v.* **1** cook in an oven or by open heat. **2** criticize severely. **3** offer a mocking tribute to someone at a roast.
▶*adj.* roasted.
▶*n.* **1** roast meat. **2** piece of meat for roasting. **3** banquet at which the honoree is subjected to good-natured mockery.

**rob** /räb/ ▶*v.* (**robbed, rob·bing**) **1** take unlawfully from, esp. by force or threat. **2** deprive of what is due or normal: *was robbed of my sleep.* **3** commit

robbery. **4** *inf.* cheat; swindle.
—**rob·ber** *n.* —**rob·ber·y** *n.*

**robe** /rōb/ ▸*n.* **1** long, loose outer garment. **2** long outer garment worn as an indication of rank, office, profession, etc.
▸*v.* **1** clothe in a robe; dress. **2** put on one's robes or vestments.

**rob·in** /ˈräbin/ ▸*n.* (also **rob·in red·breast**) red-breasted thrush.

**ro·bot** /ˈrō,bät/ ▸*n.* **1** machine with a human appearance or functioning like a human. **2** person who works mechanically but insensitively. —**ro·bot·ic** *adj.*

**ro·bot·ics** /rōˈbätiks/ ▸*n.* the study of robots; art or science of their design and operation.

**ro·bust** /rōˈbəst/ ▸*adj.* strong and healthy or sturdy, esp. in physique or construction. —**ro·bust·ly** *adv.* —**ro·bust·ness** *n.*

**rock** /räk/ ▸*n.* **1** hard mineral material of the earth's crust. **2** stone of any size. **3** firm and dependable support or protection.
▸*v.* **1** move gently to and fro; set or maintain such motion. **2** (cause to) sway from side to side; shake; reel. —**rock·y** *adj.*

□ **on the rocks** *inf.* **1** short of money. **2** broken down. **3** (of a drink) served over ice cubes.

**rock and roll** ▸*n.* popular music originating in the 1950s, characterized by a heavy beat and simple melodies, often with a blues element.

**rock-bot·tom** ▸*adj.* (of prices, etc.) the very lowest.

**rock·er** ▸*n.* **1** person or thing that rocks. **2** curved bar, etc., on which something can rock. **3** rocking chair. **4** performer of rock music.

**rock·et** /ˈräkit/ ▸*n.* **1** cylindrical projectile that can be propelled to a great height or distance by combustion of its contents. **2** engine using a similar principle. **3** rocket-propelled missile, spacecraft, etc.
▸*v.* **1** move rapidly upward or away. **2** increase rapidly: *prices rocketed.*

**rock·et·ry** ▸*n.* science or practice of rocket propulsion.

**rock·ing chair** ▸*n.* chair mounted on rockers for gently rocking in.

**rock salt** ▸*n.* common salt occurring naturally as a mineral.

**ro·co·co** /rəˈkōkō/ ▸*adj.* **1** of a late baroque style of decoration.

**2** (of literature, music, architecture, etc.) highly ornamented; florid.

**rod** /räd/ ▸*n.* **1** slender straight bar, esp. of wood or metal. **2** fishing rod. **3** measure of length equal to 5½ yards.

**ro·dent** /ˈrōdnt/ ▸*n.* mammal with strong incisors, e.g., the rat, mouse, squirrel, beaver, porcupine, etc.

**ro·de·o** /ˈrōdē͵ō/ ▸*n.* (*pl.* **-os**) exhibition of cowboys' skills in handling animals.

**roe** /rō/ ▸*n.* **1** fish eggs. **2** (*pl.* same or **roes**) (also **roe deer**) small European and Asian deer.

**rog·er** /ˈräjər/ ▸*interj.* your message has been received and understood (used in radio communication, etc.).

**rogue** /rōg/ ▸*n.* **1** dishonest, unprincipled, or mischievous person. **2** wild animal driven away or living apart from others. —**ro·guish** *adj.*

**rogues' gal·ler·y** ▸*n. inf.* collection of photographs of known criminals, used by police to identify suspects.

**roil** /roil/ ▸*v.* **1** make (a liquid) muddy by disturbing the sediment. **2** another term for RILE.

**role** /rōl/ ▸*n.* **1** actor's part in a play, motion picture, etc. **2** function.
□ **role model** person looked to by others as an example.

**roll** /rōl/ ▸*v.* **1** move or go in some direction by turning on an axis. **2** move or advance on or (of time, etc.) as if on wheels, etc. **3** turn over and over on itself to form a more or less cylindrical or spherical shape. **4** show or go with an undulating surface: *rolling hills | waves roll in.*
▸*n.* **1** rolling motion or gait. **2** rolling. **3** rhythmic sound of thunder, etc. **4** cylinder formed by turning material over and over on itself. **5** small portion of bread individually baked. **6** official list or register.

**roll·back** ▸*n.* reduction or decrease, as in prices.

**roll call** ▸*n.* process of calling out a list of names to establish who is present.

**roll·er** ▸*n.* **1** cylinder rolled over things to flatten or spread them. **2** cylinder on which something is wound.

**Rol·ler·blade** ▸*trademark* (**Rollerblades**) brand of in-line skates.

▸*v.* skate on Rollerblades.

**roll·er skate** ▸*n.* metal frame with small wheels, fitted to a shoe for gliding across a hard surface. —**roller-skate** *v.*

**roll·ing pin** ▸*n.* cylinder for rolling out pastry, dough, etc.

**roll·over** ▸*n.* extension or transfer of a debt or other financial relationship.

**ro·ly-po·ly** /ˈrōlē ˈpōlē/ ▸*adj.* pudgy; plump.

**ROM** /räm/ ▸*abbr. Computing* read-only memory: memory not capable of being changed by program instruction.

**Rom.** ▸*abbr.* **1** Roman. **2** Romania.

**ro·maine** /rōˈmān/ ▸*n.* long-leafed lettuce.

**Ro·man** /ˈrōmən/ ▸*adj.* **1** of ancient or modern Rome, its territory, people, etc. **2** (**roman**) (of type) plain and upright, used in ordinary print. **3** based on the ancient Roman alphabet.
▸*n.* **1** native or inhabitant of Rome. **2** (**roman**) roman type.

**ro·man à clef** /rōˌmän ä ˈklā/ (also **ro·man-à-clef**) ▸*n.* (*pl.* **ro·mans à clef** *pronunc.* same) novel in which real people or events appear with invented names.

**Ro·man can·dle** ▸*n.* firework discharging colored balls and sparks.

**Ro·man Cath·o·lic Church** ▸*n.* the part of the Christian Church that acknowledges the pope as its head.

**ro·mance** /rōˈmans/ ▸*n.* **1** quality or feeling characterized by mystery, excitement, or idealization of everyday life. **2** love affair. **3** sentimental or idealized love. **4** literary genre with romantic love or highly imaginative unrealistic episodes.
▸*adj.* (**Romance**) of any of the languages descended from Latin (French, Italian, Spanish, etc.).
▸*v.* court; woo.

**ro·man·ize** /ˈrōməˌnīz/ (also **Ro·man·ize**) ▸*v.* **1** bring (something, esp. a region or people) under Roman influence or authority. **2** make Roman Catholic in character. **3** put (text) into the Roman alphabet or into roman type.

**Roman num·er·al** ▸*n.* any of the Roman letters representing numbers: I = 1, V = 5, X = 10, L = 50, C = 100, D = 500, M = 1000.

**ro·man·tic** /rōˈmantik/ ▶*adj.*
**1** of, characterized by, or
suggestive of love or romance.
**2** (of a person) imaginative;
visionary; idealistic. **3** (of style
in art, music, etc.) concerned
more with feeling and emotion
than with form and aesthetic
qualities. **4** (also **Romantic**) of
the 18th–19th-c. movement or
style in the European arts.
—**ro·man·ti·cal·ly** *adv.*

**ro·man·ti·cism** /rōˈmantə-
ˌsizəm/ ▶*n.* (also **Ro·man·ti·cism**)
adherence to a romantic style in
art, music, etc.
—**ro·man·ti·cist** *n.*

**ro·man·ti·cize** ▶*v.* make or
render romantic or unreal.

**romp** /rämp/ ▶*v.* play
energetically.
▶*n.* spell of romping.

**rood** /rood/ ▶*n.* crucifix.

**roof** /roof; roŏf/ ▶*n.* **1** upper
covering of a building. **2** top of
any enclosed space.
▶*v.* cover with or as with a roof.
—**roofed** *adj.* —**roof·er** *n.*

**rook** /roŏk/ ▶*n.* **1** black European
and Asiatic bird of the crow
family. **2** chess piece with its
top in the shape of a battlement.
▶*v.* defraud.

**rook·ie** ▶*n. inf.* **1** new recruit,
e.g., police, etc. **2** first-year
player.

**room** /room; roŏm/ ▶*n.* **1** space
for or occupied by something;
capacity. **2** part of a building
enclosed by walls, floor, and
ceiling.
▶*v.* lodge; board.

**room ser·vice** ▶(in a hotel,
etc.) service of food or drink
taken to a guest's room.

**room·y** ▶*adj.* (**room·i·er**,
**room·i·est**) having plenty of
space.

**roost** /roost/ ▶*n.* branch or perch
for a bird, esp. to sleep.
▶*v.* settle for rest or sleep.

**roost·er** ▶*n.* male domestic
chicken; cock.

**root** /root; roŏt/ ▶*n.* **1** part of a
plant normally below the
ground, conveying nourishment
from the soil. **2** (**roots**)
attachment, esp. to one's place
of origin. **3** embedded part of a
hair, tooth, nail, etc. **4** basic
cause, source, or origin.
**5** number that when multiplied
by itself a specified number of
times gives a specified number
or quantity: *cube root of eight is
two.* **6** (of an animal, esp. a pig)
turn up the ground with the
snout, beak, etc., in search of

food. **7** rummage. **8** *inf.* (**root for**) encourage by applause or support.

▶*v.* **1** (cause to) take root or grow roots. **2** fix firmly; establish. **3** (**root out**) **a** drag or dig up by the roots. **b** find and get rid of.

**root beer** ▶*n.* carbonated drink made from an extract of roots.

**root ca·nal** ▶*n.* **1** pulp-filled cavity in the root of a tooth. **2** procedure to replace infected pulp with an inert substance.

**rope** /rōp/ ▶*n.* **1** stout cord made by twisting together strands of hemp, nylon, wire, etc. **2** quantity of roughly spherical objects strung together.
▶*v.* fasten, secure, or catch with rope.

**Roque·fort** /'rōkfərt/ ▶*trademark* soft blue-veined cheese made from sheep's milk.

**ro·sar·i·an** /rō'ze(ə)rēən/ ▶*n.* person who cultivates roses, esp. as an occupation.

**ro·sa·ry** /'rōzərē/ ▶*n.* (*pl.* -**ries**) **1** (in the Roman Catholic Church) repeated sequence of prayers, usu. said while counting them on a string of beads. **2** string of beads used for this.

**rose** /rōz/ ▶past of RISE.
▶*n.* **1** prickly bush or shrub bearing usu. fragrant red, pink, yellow, or white flowers. **2** this flower. **3** reddish-pink color.

**ro·sé** /rō'zā/ ▶*n.* light pink wine.

**rose·mary** /'rōz,me(ə)rē/ ▶*n.* evergreen fragrant shrub used as an herb.

**ro·sette** /rō'zet/ ▶*n.* rose-shaped ornament of ribbon.

**rose wa·ter** ▶*n.* perfume made from roses.

**ros·ter** /'rästər/ ▶*n.* list or plan of turns of duty, players available, etc.

**ros·trum** /'rästrəm/ ▶*n.* (*pl.* -**tra** or -**trums**) platform for public speaking, conducting an orchestra, etc.

**ros·y** /'rōzē/ ▶*adj.* (**ros·i·er, ros·i·est**) **1** pink; red. **2** optimistic; hopeful.

**rot** /rät/ ▶*v.* (**rot·ted, rot·ting**) decompose; decay.
▶*n.* process or state of rotting.

**ro·ta·ry** /'rōtərē/ ▶*adj.* acting by rotation.

**ro·tate** /'rō,tāt/ ▶*v.* **1** move or cause to move around an axis or center; revolve. **2** pass to each member of a group in a regularly recurring order: *the chairmanship will rotate.*
—**ro·ta·tion** *n.*

**ROTC** /'är'ō'tē'sē; 'rät,sē/ ▶abbr. Reserve Officers Training Corps.

**rote** /rōt/ ▶n. mechanical or habitual repetition.

**ro·tis·ser·ie** /rō'tisərē/ ▶n. rotating spit for roasting or barbecuing meat.

**ro·tor** /'rōtər/ ▶n. **1** rotary part of a machine. **2** rotary airfoil on a helicopter.

**rot·ten** /'rätn/ ▶adj. (-er, -est) **1** rotting or rotted. **2** morally, socially, or politically corrupt. **3** inf. very unpleasant.

**ro·tund** /rō'tənd/ ▶adj. plump; round. —**ro·tun·di·ty** n.

**ro·tun·da** /rō'təndə/ ▶n. circular building, hall, or room, esp. one with a dome.

**rou·é** /roo'ā/ ▶n. corrupt or dissolute man; rake.

**rouge** /roozH/ ▶n. red cosmetic for coloring the cheeks. ▶v. color with rouge.

**rough** /rəf/ ▶adj. (-er, -est) **1** uneven; bumpy; not smooth. **2** not mild, quiet, or gentle; boisterous; coarse. **3** harsh; insensitive. **4** unpleasant; severe; demanding. **5** incomplete; rudimentary; approximate. ▶adv. in a rough manner. ▶n. **1** hard aspect of life; hardship: take the rough with the smooth. **2** Golf rough ground. **3** unfinished or natural state. —**rough·ly** adv. —**rough·ness** n.

**rough·age** /'rəfij/ ▶n. coarse, fibrous material in food.

**rough·cast** /'rəf,kast/ ▶n. plaster of lime, cement, and gravel, used on outside walls. ▶adj. **1** (of a building or part of a building) coated with roughcast. **2** (of a person) lacking refinement. ▶v. coat (a wall) with roughcast.

**rough·en** ▶v. make or become rough.

**rough·shod** ▶adj. (in phrase **ride roughshod over**) treat inconsiderately or arrogantly.

**rou·lade** /roo'läd/ ▶n. dish cooked or served in the form of a roll, typically made from a flat piece of meat, fish, or sponge cake, spread with a soft filling and rolled up into a spiral.

**rou·lette** /roo'let/ ▶n. gambling game in which a ball is dropped on to a revolving numbered wheel.

**round** /round/ ▶adj. **1** shaped like a circle, sphere, or cylinder; convex; circular; curved. **2** (of a number) expressed for convenience as a whole number:

*spent $297.32, or in round figures $300.*

▸*n.* **1** round object or form. **2** recurring series of activities, functions, etc. **3** single provision of drinks, etc., to each member of a group. **4** ammunition to fire one shot. **5** set, series, or sequence of actions in turn. **6** song overlapping at intervals.

▸*adv.* around.

▸*prep.* around.

▸*v.* **1** give a round shape to. **2** double or pass around (a corner, cape, etc.). **3** express (a number) approximately for brevity.

**round·a·bout** ▸*adj.* circuitous; indirect.

**roun·del** /'roundl/ ▸*n.* **1** small disk, esp. a decorative medallion. **2** picture or pattern contained in a circle.

**round·house** ▸*n.* circular repair shed for railroad locomotives, built around a turntable.

**round·ly** ▸*adv.* bluntly; in plain language: *was roundly criticized.*

**round trip** ▸*n.* trip to one or more places and back again.

**round·up** ▸*n.* **1** systematic rounding up of people or things. **2** summary of facts or events.

**rouse** /rouz/ ▸*v.* **1** wake (up). **2** make or become active or excited. **3** provoke to anger: *is terrible when roused.*

**roust·a·bout** /'roustə,bout/ ▸*n.* unskilled or casual laborer, as in a circus.

**rout** /rout/ ▸*n.* **1** disorderly retreat. **2** heavy defeat.

▸*v.* put to flight; defeat utterly.

**route** /r$\overline{oo}$t; rout/ ▸*n.* way or course taken (esp. regularly).

▸*v.* send, forward, or direct by a particular route.

**rou·tine** /r$\overline{oo}$'tēn/ ▸*n.* **1** regular course or procedure. **2** set sequence in a dance, comedy act, etc.

▸*adj.* **1** performed as part of a routine. **2** of a customary or standard kind. —**rou·tine·ly** *adv.*

**rove** /rōv/ ▸*v.* wander; roam. —**rov·er** *n.*

**row**[1] /rō/ ▸*n.* **1** line of persons or things. **2** line of seats across a theater, etc.

▸*v.* **1** propel (a boat) with oars. **2** convey (a passenger) in this way.

□ **in a row** *inf.* in succession: *two Sundays in a row.*

**row**[2] /rou/ ▸*n. inf.* commotion; quarrel.

**row·boat** /'rō,bōt/ ▸*n.* small boat propelled by oars.

**row·dy** /ˈroudē/ ▸*adj.* (**-di·er,
-di·est**) noisy and disorderly.
▸*n.* (*pl.* **-dies**) rowdy person.
—**row·di·ly** *adv.* —**row·di·ness** *n.*

**row·el** /ˈrou(ə)l/ ▸*n.* spiked
revolving disk at the end of a
spur.

**roy·al** /ˈroiəl/ ▸*adj.* **1** of, suited to,
or worthy of a king or queen;
majestic. **2** in the service or
under the patronage of a king or
queen. —**roy·al·ly** *adv.*

**roy·al·ist** /ˈroiəlist/ ▸*n.* supporter
of monarchy.

**roy·al·ty** /ˈroiəltē/ ▸*n.* (*pl.* **-ties**)
**1** office, dignity, or power of a
king or queen; sovereignty.
**2** royal person(s). **3** percentage
of profit from a patent, song,
book, etc., paid to the creator.

**rpm.** (also **r.p.m.**) ▸*abbr.*
revolutions per minute.

**RR** ▸*abbr.* **1** railroad. **2** rural
route.

**RSVP** ▸*abbr.* (in an invitation,
etc.) please answer, (French
*répondez s'il vous plaît*).

**rub** /rəb/ ▸*v.* (**rubbed, rub·bing**)
**1** move one's hand or another
object with firm pressure over
the surface of. **2** apply (one's
hand, etc.) in this way. **3** clean,
polish, make dry, chafe, make
sore, etc., by rubbing.
▸*n.* spell or instance of rubbing.

**rub·ber** /ˈrəbər/ ▸*n.* **1** tough
elastic substance made from the
latex of plants or synthetically.
**2** (**rubbers**) galoshes. —**rub·ber·y**
*adj.*

□ **rubber band** loop of rubber for
holding papers, etc., together.
□ **rubber stamp** device for inking
and imprinting on a surface.
□ **rubber-stamp** **1** use a rubber
stamp. **2** approve automatically.

**rub·ber·neck** *inf.* ▸*n.* person
who turns their head to stare at
something in a foolish way.
▸*v.* act in this way.

**rub·bish** /ˈrəbiSH/ ▸*n.* waste or
worthless material or articles.

**rub·ble** /ˈrəbəl/ ▸*n.* rough
fragments of stone, brick, etc.

**ru·bel·la** /roōˈbelə/ ▸*n.* German
measles.

**ru·bi·cund** /ˈroōbəˌkənd/ ▸*adj.*
(esp. of someone's face) having a
ruddy complexion; high-colored.

**ru·ble** /ˈroōbəl/ ▸*n.* chief
monetary unit of Russia and
some other former republics of
the USSR.

**ru·bric** /ˈroōbrik/ ▸*n.* **1** heading
or passage in red or special
lettering. **2** explanatory words.

**ru·by** /ˈroōbē/ ▸*n.* (*pl.* **-bies**)
**1** rare precious stone varying

from deep crimson or purple to pale rose. **2** glowing, purple-tinged red color.

▸*adj.* of this color.

**ruck·sack** /ˈrək,sak; ˈroŏk-/ ▸bag with shoulder straps that allow it to be carried on a person's back; backpack.

**ruck·us** /ˈrəkəs/ ▸*n.* fracas or commotion.

**rud·der** /ˈrədər/ ▸*n.* **1** flat piece hinged vertically to the stern of a ship for steering. **2** vertical airfoil pivoted from the stabilizer of an aircraft, for controlling horizontal movement.

**rud·dy** /ˈrədē/ ▸*adj.* (**-di·er, -di·est**) **1** (of a person or complexion) freshly or healthily red. **2** reddish.

**rude** /roŏd/ ▸*adj.* (**rud·er, rud·est**) **1** impolite; offensive. **2** roughly made or done: *rude shelter.* **3** abrupt; startling: *rude awakening.* —**rude·ly** *adv.* —**rude·ness** *n.*

**ru·di·ment** /ˈroŏdəmənt/ ▸*n.* **1** elements or first principles of a subject. **2** imperfect beginning of something yet to develop. —**ru·di·men·ta·ry** *adj.*

**rue** /roŏ/ ▸*v.* (**rued, ru·ing** or **rue·ing**) regret greatly.

▸*n.* perennial evergreen shrub with bitter strong-scented leaves. —**rue·ful** *adj.*

**ruff** /rəf/ ▸*n.* **1** projecting, starched, frilly collar of the 16th c. **2** projecting or colored ring of feathers or hair around a bird's or animal's neck.

**ruf·fi·an** /ˈrəfēən/ ▸*n.* violent, lawless person.

**ruf·fle** /ˈrəfəl/ ▸*v.* **1** disturb the smoothness or tranquility of. **2** gather (fabric, etc.) into a ruffle.

▸*n.* frill of fabric, lace, etc.

**ru·fous** /ˈroŏfəs/ ▸*adj.* reddish brown in color.

▸*n.* reddish-brown color.

**rug** /rəg/ ▸*n.* floor covering of shaggy material or thick pile.

**rug·by** /ˈrəgbē/ ▸*n.* team game played with an oval ball that may be kicked, carried, and passed.

**rug·ged** /ˈrəgid/ ▸*adj.* **1** rough; uneven; wrinkled. **2** unpolished; lacking refinement. **3** robust; sturdy.

**ru·gose** /ˈroŏ,gōs/ ▸*adj.* wrinkled; corrugated.

**ru·in** /ˈroŏin/ ▸*n.* **1** destroyed or wrecked state. **2** utter destruction. **3** (**ruins**) remains of a destroyed building, etc.

**4** cause of ruin: *will be the ruin of us.*

▶*v.* bring or reduce to ruin or ruins. —**ru·in·ous** *adj.*

**rule** /rool/ ▶*n.* **1** principle to which an action conforms or is required to conform. **2** custom; standard. **3** government; dominion. **4** straight measure; ruler.

▶*v.* **1** dominate; keep under control. **2** have sovereign control of. **3** pronounce authoritatively. **4** make parallel lines across (paper).

**rul·er** ▶*n.* **1** person exercising government or dominion. **2** strip of wood, metal, etc., with straight edge used to draw lines or measure distance.

**rum** /rəm/ ▶*n.* spirit distilled from sugar cane or molasses.

**rum·ba** /'rəmbə/ ▶*n.* ballroom dance originating in Cuba.

**rum·ble** /'rəmbəl/ ▶*v.* **1** make a continuous deep resonant sound as of distant thunder. **2** move with a rumbling noise.

▶*n.* **1** rumbling sound. **2** *inf.* street fight between gangs.

**ru·mi·nant** /'roomənənt/ ▶*n.* cud-chewing animal.

**ru·mi·nate** /'roomə,nāt/ ▶*v.* **1** meditate; ponder. **2** (of ruminants) chew the cud. —**ru·mi·na·tion** *n.* —**ru·mi·na·tive** *adj.*

**rum·mage** /'rəmij/ ▶*v.* search, esp. unsystematically.

□ **rummage sale** sale of miscellaneous usu. secondhand articles, esp. for charity.

**rum·my** ▶*n.* any of various card games in which the players try to form sets and sequences of cards.

**ru·mor** /'roomər/ ▶*n.* general talk or hearsay of doubtful accuracy.

▶*v.* report by way of rumor: *it is rumored that you are leaving.*

**rump** /rəmp/ ▶*n.* hind part of a mammal or bird, esp. the buttocks.

**rum·ple** /'rəmpəl/ ▶*v.* make or become crumpled or untidy.

**rum·pus** /'rəmpəs/ ▶*n. inf.* disturbance; brawl; uproar.

**run** /rən/ ▶*v.* (**run·ning**; *past* **ran**; *past part.* **run**) **1** go with quick steps on alternate feet. **2** flee. **3** go hurriedly, briefly, etc. **4** advance by or as by rolling or on wheels, or smoothly or easily. **5** be in action or operation: *left the engine running.* **6** be current or operative: *the lease runs for 99 years.* **7** (of a play, etc.) be staged or presented. **8** extend; have a

course, order, or tendency.
**9** compete in a race. **10** seek election: *ran for president.*
**11** cause (water, etc.) to flow.
**12** direct or manage (a business, etc.).
▸*n.* **1** running. **2** short excursion. **3** distance traveled. **4** spell or course: *run of bad luck.* **5** high general demand. **6** quantity produced in one period of production. **7** *Baseball* point scored by a runner reaching home plate. **8** free use of or access to: *had the run of the house.* **9** line of unraveled stitches, esp. in hosiery.
□ **run-down 1** decayed after prosperity. **2** enfeebled through overwork, etc. □ **run-of-the-mill** ordinary.

**run·a·round** ▸*n.* deceit or evasion.

**run·a·way** ▸*n.* **1** fugitive. **2** animal or vehicle that is running out of control.
▸*adj.* that is running away or out of control: *runaway inflation.*

**run·down** ▸*n.* summary or brief analysis.

**rune stone** ▸*n.* **1** large stone carved with runes by ancient Scandinavians or Anglo-Saxons. **2** small stone, piece of bone, etc.,

marked with a rune and used in divination.

**rung** /rəNG/ ▸past part. of RING.
▸*n.* **1** step of a ladder.
**2** strengthening crosspiece in a chair, etc.

**run·ner** ▸*n.* **1** person, horse, etc., that runs, esp. in a race.
**2** creeping plant stem that can take root. **3** rod, groove, or blade on which a thing (e.g., a sled) slides.
□ **runner-up** competitor or team taking second place.

**run·ning dog** ▸*n.* **1** servile follower, esp. of a political system. **2** dog bred to run, esp. for racing or pulling a sled.

**run·ny** ▸*adj.* (-ni·er, -ni·est) tending to flow or exude fluid; semi-liquid.

**run·off** ▸*n.* **1** additional election, race, etc., after a tie. **2** surface water not absorbed by the ground.

**runt** /rənt/ ▸*n.* **1** smallest animal in a litter. **2** weakling; undersized person. —**runt·y** *adj.*

**run·way** ▸*n.* **1** surface along which aircraft take off and land.
**2** narrow walkway extending out from a stage into an auditorium.

**rup·ture** /ˈrəpCHər/ ▸n.
1 breaking; breach. 2 abdominal hernia.
▸v. 1 break or burst (a cell or membrane, etc.). 2 undergo a rupture.

**ru·ral** /ˈro͝orəl/ ▸adj. in, of, or suggesting the country.

**ruse** /ro͞oz/ ▸n. stratagem; trick.

**rush** /rəSH/ ▸v. 1 go, move, or act precipitately or with great speed. 2 move or transport with great haste. 3 perform or deal with hurriedly: *don't rush your dinner.* 4 force (a person) to act hastily. 5 attack or capture by sudden assault.
▸n. 1 rushing. 2 great activity; commotion. 3 marsh plant with slender stems, used for making chair seats, baskets, etc.

**rusk** /rəsk/ ▸n. slice of sweet bread rebaked as a light biscuit.

**rus·set** /ˈrəsit/ ▸n. reddish-brown color.

**Rus·sian** /ˈrəSHən/ ▸n. 1 native or national of Russia or the former Soviet Union. 2 language of Russia.
▸adj. of Russia, its people, or their language.

**rust** /rəst/ ▸n. 1 reddish corrosive coating formed on iron, steel, etc., by oxidation, esp. when wet. 2 fungal plant disease with rust-colored spots.
▸v. 1 affect or be affected with rust. 2 lose quality or efficiency by disuse or inactivity.

**rus·tic** /ˈrəstik/ ▸adj. 1 having the characteristics of or associations with the country or country life. 2 unsophisticated. 3 rude; rough.
▸n. country person. —**rus·tic·i·ty** n.

**rus·tle** /ˈrəsəl/ ▸v. 1 make or cause to make a gentle sound as of dry, blown leaves. 2 steal (cattle or horses).
▸n. rustling sound. —**rus·tler** n.

**rust·y** ▸adj. (**rust·i·er**, **rust·i·est**)
1 rusted or affected by rust. 2 impaired by neglect.

**rut** /rət/ ▸n. 1 deep track made by the passage of wheels. 2 established (esp. tedious) procedure. 3 periodic sexual excitement of male deer and other animals.
▸v. (**rut·ted**, **rut·ting**) mark with ruts.
□ **in a rut** following a fixed (esp. tedious or dreary) pattern of behavior.

**ru·ta·ba·ga** /ˈro͞otəˌbāgə/ ▸n. large yellow-fleshed turnip.

**ruth·less** /ˈro͞oTHlis/ ▸adj. having

no pity nor compassion.
—**ruth·less·ly** *adv.*
—**ruth·less·ness** *n.*
**ru·ti·lant** /ˈro͞otl-ənt/ ▶*adj.* glowing or glittering with red or golden light.
**RV** ▶*abbr.* **1** Revised Version (of the Bible). **2** recreational vehicle.
**rye** /rī/ ▶*n.* **1 a** cereal plant. **b** grains of this used for bread and fodder. **2** (also **rye whis·key**) whiskey distilled from fermented rye.

# Ss

**S**[1] /es/ (also **s**) ▶*n.* (*pl.* **Ss** or **S's**; **s's**) **1** nineteenth letter of the alphabet. **2** S-shaped object or curve.

**S**[2] (also **S.**) ▶*abbr.* **1** Saint. **2** society. **3** south, southern.

**S**[3] ▶*symb. Chem.* sulfur.

**s.** ▶*abbr.* **1** second(s). **2** singular. **3** son.

**'s** ▶*abbr.* **1** is; has: *he's.* **2** us: *let's.*

**sab·bath** /ˈsabəTH/ ▶*n.* (often **Sabbath**) religious day of rest kept by Christians on Sunday and Jews on Saturday.

**sab·bat·i·cal** /səˈbatikəl/ ▶*adj.* (of leave) granted at intervals from one's usual work, as to a teacher for study or travel. ▶*n.* period of sabbatical leave.

**sa·ber** /ˈsābər/ ▶*n.* **1** curved cavalry sword. **2** tapered fencing sword.

**sa·ble** /ˈsābəl/ ▶*n.* small, brown-furred mammal of N. Europe and N. Asia.

**sab·ot** /saˈbō; ˈsabō/ ▶*n.* kind of simple shoe, shaped and hollowed out from a single block of wood, traditionally worn by French peasants.

**sab·o·tage** /ˈsabəˌtäzH/ ▶*n.* deliberate damage to productive capacity, esp. as a political act. ▶*v.* commit sabotage on. —**sab·o·teur** *n.*

**sa·bra** /ˈsäbrə/ ▶*n.* Jew born in Israel (or before 1948 in Palestine).

**SAC** /sak/ ▶*abbr.* Strategic Air Command.

**sac** /sak/ ▶*n.* baglike structure in an animal or plant.

**sac·cha·rin** /ˈsak(ə)rin/ ▶*n.* sugar substitute.

**sac·cha·rine** /ˈsak(ə)rin/ ▶*adj.* **1** sugary. **2** unpleasantly overpolite, sentimental, etc.

**sa·chet** /saˈsHā/ ▶*n.* small bag or packet containing dry perfume, etc.

**sack** /sak/ ▶*n.* **1 a** large, strong bag for storing or conveying goods. **b** quantity contained in a sack. **2** (**the sack**) *inf.* dismissal from employment. ▶*v.* **1** put into a sack or sacks. **2** *inf.* dismiss from employment. **3** plunder and destroy (a captured town, etc.). —**sack·ful** *n.*

**sack·but** /ˈsak,bət/ ▸ *n.* early form of trombone used in Renaissance music.

**sack·cloth** ▸ *n.* **1** coarse fabric of flax or hemp. **2** clothing for penance and mourning: *sackcloth and ashes.*

**sac·ra·ment** /ˈsakrəmənt/ ▸ *n.* symbolic Christian ceremony, e.g., baptism and the Eucharist. —**sac·ra·ment·al** *adj.*

**sa·cred** /ˈsākrid/ ▸ *adj.* **1 a** dedicated to a god. **b** connected with religion. **2** safeguarded or required by religion, reverence, or tradition. —**sa·cred·ly** *adv.* —**sa·cred·ness** *n.*
□ **sacred cow** *inf.* hallowed idea or institution.

**sac·ri·fice** /ˈsakrə,fīs/ ▸ *n.* **1 a** voluntary giving up of something valued. **b** thing given up. **c** the loss entailed. **2 a** slaughter of an animal or person or surrender of a possession, as an offering to a deity. **b** animal, person, or thing offered.
▸ *v.* give up (a thing) as a sacrifice. —**sac·ri·fi·cial** *adj.*

**sac·ri·lege** /ˈsakrəlij/ ▸ *n.* violation or misuse of what is regarded as sacred.

—**sac·ri·le·gious** *adj.*
—**sac·ri·le·gious·ly** *adv.*

**sac·ris·ty** ▸ *n.* place in a church where vestments, etc., are kept.

**sac·ro·il·i·ac** /,sakrōˈilē,ak/ ▸ *n.* rigid joint at the back of the pelvis.

**sac·ro·sanct** /ˈsakrō,saNGkt/ ▸ *adj.* (of a person, place, law, etc.) most sacred; inviolable.

**sac·rum** /ˈsakrəm; ˈsā-/ ▸ *n.* (*pl.* **-ra** or **-rums**) *Anat.* triangular bone formed from fused vertebrae and situated between the two hipbones of the pelvis.

**sad** /sad/ ▸ *adj.* (**sad·der, sad·dest**) **1** unhappy; feeling sorrow or regret. **2** causing sorrow. **3** regrettable. **4** shameful; deplorable. —**sad·ly** *adv.* —**sad·ness** *n.*

**sad·dle** /ˈsadl/ ▸ *n.* **1** seat of leather, etc., fastened on a horse, etc., for riding. **2** seat on a bicycle, etc. **3** cut of meat consisting of the two loins.
▸ *v.* **1** put a saddle on (a horse, etc.). **2** (**saddle with**) burden with (a task).
□ **in the saddle** in office or control.

**sad·dle·bag** ▸ *n.* **1** each of a pair of bags laid across a horse, etc. **2** bag attached to a bicycle saddle, etc.

**sa·dism** /ˈsāˌdizəm/ ▶n. pleasure derived from inflicting cruelty on others. —**sad·ist** n. —**sa·dis·tic** adj. —**sa·dis·ti·cal·ly** adv.

**sa·do·mas·och·ism** /ˌsādō- ˈmasəˌkizəm/ ▶n. combination of sadism and masochism in one person. —**sa·do·mas·o·chist** n. —**sa·do·mas·o·chis·tic** adj.

**sa·fa·ri** /səˈfärē/ ▶n. (pl. **-ris**) expedition, esp. in E. Africa, to hunt or observe animals.

**safe** /sāf/ ▶adj. **1** free of danger or injury. **2** secure; not risky. **3** reliable; certain. **4** (also **safe and sound**) uninjured. ▶n. strong, lockable cabinet, etc., for valuables. —**safe·ly** adv.

**safe con·duct** ▶n. privilege of immunity from arrest or harm.

**safe-de·pos·it box** ▶n. secured box (esp. in a bank vault) for storing valuables.

**safe·guard** ▶n. proviso, stipulation, quality, or circumstance that tends to prevent something undesirable. ▶v. guard; protect.

**safe sex** ▶n. sexual activity in which precautions are taken against sexually transmitted diseases.

**safe·ty** ▶n. being free from risk or danger.

**safe·ty pin** ▶n. doubled pin with a guarded point.

**safe·ty ra·zor** ▶n. razor with a guard to prevent cutting the skin.

**saf·flow·er** /ˈsafˌlouər/ ▶n. thistlelike plant yielding a red dye and edible oil.

**saf·fron** /ˈsafrən/ ▶n. **1** bright yellow-orange food coloring and flavoring made from dried crocus stigmas. **2** color of this.

**sag** /sag/ ▶v. (**sagged, sag·ging**) **1** sink or subside, esp. unevenly. **2** bulge or curve downward in the middle. ▶n. sagging. —**sag·gy** adj.

**sa·ga** /ˈsägə/ ▶n. **1** long, heroic story of achievement, esp. medieval Icelandic or Norwegian. **2** any long, involved story.

**sa·ga·cious** /səˈgāSHəs/ ▶adj. showing insight, good judgment, or wisdom. —**sa·ga·cious·ly** adv. —**sa·gac·i·ty** n.

**sage**[1] /sāj/ ▶n. aromatic herb with dull grayish-green leaves. —**sag·y** adj.

**sage**[2] ▶n. wise person.

▶*adj.* of or indicating profound wisdom. —**sage·ly** *adv.*

**sage·brush** ▶*n.* shrubby aromatic plant of western N. America.

**sag·it·tate** /ˈsajəˌtāt/ ▶*adj.* shaped like an arrowhead.

**sa·go** /ˈsāgō/ ▶*n.* (*pl.* **-gos**) **1** edible starch made from the sago palm. **2** (**sago palm**) tropical palm from which sago is made.

**said** /sed/ ▶past and past part. of SAY.

**sail** /sāl/ ▶*n.* **1** piece of material extended on rigging to catch the wind and propel a vessel. **2** voyage or excursion in a sailing ship, etc. **3** wind-catching apparatus of a windmill.
▶*v.* **1** travel on water by the use of sails or engine power. **2 a** navigate (a ship, etc.). **b** travel on (a sea). **3** glide or move smoothly. **4** *inf.* succeed easily: *sailed through the exams.*

**sail·board** ▶*n.* board with a mast and sail, used for windsurfing.

**sail·boat** ▶*n.* boat driven by sails.

**sail·cloth** ▶*n.* canvas or canvaslike material for sails, upholstery, tents, etc.

**sail·fish** ▶*n.* large marine fish with a large dorsal fin.

**sail·or** ▶*n.* **1** member of a ship's crew. **2** person who enjoys boating.

**saint** /sānt/ ▶*n.* **1** holy or (in some churches) canonized person regarded as having a place in heaven. **2** very virtuous person. —**saint·hood** *n.* —**saint·like** *adj.* —**saint·ly** *adj.*

**sake**[1] /sāk/ ▶*n.* **1** benefit; advantage. **2** cause; purpose.

**sa·ke**[2] /ˈsäkē/ ▶*n.* Japanese rice wine.

**sa·la·cious** /səˈlāsHəs/ ▶*adj.* lustful; lecherous. —**sa·la·cious·ly** *adv.* —**sa·la·cious·ness** *n.*

**sal·ad** /ˈsaləd/ ▶*n.* mixture of usu. cold vegetables, and sometimes eggs, meats, pasta, etc., often with dressing.

**sal·a·man·der** /ˈsaləˌmandər/ ▶*n.* tailed newtlike amphibian.

**sa·la·mi** /səˈlämē/ ▶*n.* (*pl.* **-mis**) highly seasoned orig. Italian sausage often flavored with garlic.

**sal·a·ried** ▶*adj.* receiving a salary.

**sal·a·ry** /ˈsalərē/ ▸n. (pl. **-ries**) fixed regular wages.

**sale** /sāl/ ▸n. **1** exchange of a commodity for money, etc.; act or instance of selling. **2** amount sold. **3** event at which goods are sold, esp. at reduced prices.
—**sales·man** n.
—**sales·man·ship** n.
—**sales·per·son** n.
□ **for sale** offered for purchase.
□ **on sale** available for purchase, esp. at a reduced price.

**sa·lient** /ˈsālyənt/ ▸adj. most noticeable or important.
—**sa·li·ent·ly** adv.

**sa·line** /ˈsāˌlēn/ ▸adj. containing or like salt. —**sa·lin·i·ty** n.
—**sal·i·ni·za·tion** n.

**sa·li·va** /səˈlīvə/ ▸n. liquid secreted into the mouth by glands. —**sal·i·var·y** adj.

**sal·low** /ˈsalō/ ▸adj. (**-er, -est**) (of the skin or complexion, or of a person) of a sickly yellow or pale brown. —**sal·low·ness** n.

**sal·ly** /ˈsalē/ ▸n. (pl. **-lies**)
**1** sudden charge; sortie.
**2** witticism; piece of banter.
▸v. (**-lied**) (**sally forth**) go for a walk, set out on a journey, etc.

**salm·on** /ˈsamən/ ▸n. (pl. same or **-ons**) edible fish with characteristic pink flesh.

**sal·mo·nel·la** /ˌsalməˈnelə/ ▸n. (pl. **-lae**) bacterium causing food poisoning.

**sa·lon** /səˈlän/ ▸n. **1** reception room. **2** room or establishment of a hairdresser, beautician, etc.

**sa·loon** /səˈlo͞on/ ▸n. bar; tavern.

**sal·sa** /ˈsälsə/ ▸n. **1** dance and music of Cuban origin, with jazz and rock elements. **2** spicy sauce made from tomatoes, chilies, onions, etc.

**SALT** /sôlt/ ▸abbr. Strategic Arms Limitation Talks (or Treaty).

**salt** /sôlt/ ▸n. **1** sodium chloride, esp. mined or evaporated from seawater. **2** chemical compound formed from the reaction of an acid with a base. **3** substance resembling salt in taste, form, etc.: *bath salts.* **4** (also **old salt**) experienced sailor.
▸adj. **1** impregnated with, containing, or tasting of salt. **2** (of a plant) growing in the sea or in salt marshes.
▸v. **1** cure or preserve with salt or brine. **2** season with salt. **3** make (a narrative, etc.) piquant. **4** sprinkle (the ground, etc.) with salt, esp. in order to melt snow, etc. —**salt·y** adj.
□ **salt of the earth** person or people of great worthiness,

reliability, honesty, etc. (Matt. 5:13). □ **take with a grain of salt** regard as exaggerated; believe only part of. □ **worth one's salt** efficient; capable.

**salt·cel·lar** ▶*n.* vessel holding salt for table use.

**sal·tine** /sôl'tēn/ ▶*n.* lightly salted, square, flat cracker.

**salt·pe·ter** /sôlt'pētər/ ▶*n.* potassium nitrate, used in preserving meat and in gunpowder.

**salt·wa·ter** ▶*adj.* of or living in the sea.

**sa·lu·bri·ous** /sə'lōōbrēəs/ ▶*adj.* **1** health-giving; healthy. **2** (of surroundings, etc.) pleasant; agreeable.

**sal·u·tar·y** /'salyə,terē/ ▶*adj.* **1** producing good effects; beneficial. **2** health-giving.

**sal·u·ta·tion** /ˌsalyə'tāSHən/ ▶*n.* expression of greeting, spoken or written. —**sal·u·ta·tion·al** *adj.*

**sa·lute** /sə'lōōt/ ▶*n.* **1** gesture of respect, homage, greeting, etc. **2** *Mil. & Naut.* prescribed gesture or use of weapons or flags as a sign of respect or recognition. **3** ceremonial discharge of a gun or guns.

▶*v.* **1** make or perform a salute. **2** greet.

**sal·vage** /'salvij/ ▶*n.* **1** rescue of property, from the sea, fire, etc. **2** property saved in this way.

▶*v.* save from a wreck, fire, adverse circumstances, etc. —**sal·vage·a·ble** *adj.* —**sal·vag·er** *n.*

**sal·va·tion** /sal'vāSHən/ ▶*n.* **1** saving or being saved. **2** deliverance from sin and damnation. **3** person or thing that saves.

**salve** /sav/ ▶*n.* **1** healing ointment. **2** thing that is soothing or consoling.

▶*v.* soothe.

**sal·ver** /'salvər/ ▶*n.* metal serving tray.

**sal·vo** /'sal,vō/ ▶*n.* (*pl.* **-voes** or **-vos**) simultaneous firing of artillery.

**sa·ma·dhi** /sə'mädē/ ▶*n.* (*pl.* **-dhis**) a state of intense concentration achieved through meditation.

**sam·ba** /'sambə; 'säm-/ ▶*n.* ballroom dance of Brazilian and African origins.

▶*v.* (**-baed, -ba·ing**) dance the samba.

**same** /sām/ ▶*adj.* **1** identical; not different. **2** unvarying; uniform. **3** just mentioned.

▸*pron.* the same person or thing: *asked for the same.*

▸*adv.* similarly; in the same way: *we all feel the same.*
—**same·ness** *n.*

**Sa·mhain** /ˈsouən/ ▸*n.* first day of November, celebrated by the ancient Celts as a festival marking the beginning of winter and the Celtic new year.

**sam·iz·dat** /ˈsämiz‚dät; səmyiz-ˈdät/ ▸*n.* clandestine copying and distribution of literature banned by the state, esp. formerly in the communist countries of eastern Europe.

**sam·ple** /ˈsampəl/ ▸*n.* **1** small representative part or quantity. **2** illustrative or typical example. ▸*v.* take, give, or try samples of.

**sam·pler** /ˈsamplər/ ▸*n.* **1** collection of representative items, etc. **2** piece of embroidery worked in various stitches as a specimen of proficiency.

**sam·u·rai** /ˈsamə‚rī/ ▸*n.* (*pl.* same) member of a former military caste in Japan.

**san·a·tive** /ˈsanətiv/ ▸*adj.* conducive to physical or spiritual health and well-being; healing.

**sanc·ti·fy** /ˈsaNG(k)tə‚fī/ ▸*v.*

(-**fied**) make sacred or holy.
—**sanc·ti·fi·ca·tion** *n.*
—**sanc·ti·fi·er** *n.*

**sanc·ti·mo·ni·ous** /‚saNG(k)tə-ˈmōnēəs/ ▸*adj.* making a show of sanctity or piety.
—**sanc·ti·mo·ni·ous·ly** *adv.*
—**sanc·ti·mo·ni·ous·ness** *n.*

**sanc·tion** /ˈsaNG(k)sHən/ ▸*n.* **1** approval or encouragement given to an action, etc., by custom or tradition. **2** penalty for disobeying a law or rule. **3** (**sanctions**) usu. economic action by a nation to coerce another to conform to norms of conduct. ▸*v.* authorize, countenance, or agree to (an action, etc.).

**sanc·ti·ty** /ˈsaNG(k)titē/ ▸*n.* holiness; sacredness; inviolability.

**sanc·tu·ar·y** /ˈsaNG(k)CHŌŌ‚erē/ ▸*n.* (*pl.* -**ies**) **1** holy place; church, temple, etc. **2** place of refuge for birds, wild animals, etc.

**sanc·tum** /ˈsaNG(k)təm/ ▸*n.* (*pl.* -**tums** or -**ta**) **1** holy place. **2** private place.

**sand** /sand/ ▸*n.* loose grains resulting from the erosion of rocks and found on the seashore, riverbeds, deserts, etc.

▶*v.* smooth with sandpaper.
—**sand·y** *adj.*

**san·dal** /ˈsandl/ ▶*n.* shoe with an openwork upper or no upper, attached to the foot usu. by straps.

**san·dal·wood** ▶*n.* scented wood of an Asian tree.

**sand·bag** ▶*n.* bag filled with sand used for fortifications, ballast, etc.
▶*v.* (**-bagged**, **-bag·ging**) **1** barricade or defend with sandbags. **2** fell with a blow from a sandbag. **3** coerce.
—**sand·bag·ger** *n.*

**sand·bar** ▶*n.* bank of sand at the mouth of a river or on the coast.

**sand·blast** ▶*v.* roughen, treat, or clean with a jet of sand driven by compressed air or steam.
—**sand·blast·er** *n.*

**sand·box** ▶*n.* large container of sand for children to play in.

**sand dol·lar** ▶*n.* round, flat sea urchin.

**sand dune** ▶*n.* mound or ridge of sand formed by the wind.

**sand·lot** ▶*n.* piece of unoccupied sandy land used for children's games.

**sand·man** ▶*n.* personification of tiredness causing children's eyes to smart toward bedtime.

**sand·pa·per** ▶*n.* paper with an abrasive coating for smoothing or polishing.
▶*v.* smooth with sandpaper.

**sand·pip·er** ▶*n.* wading shore bird with a piping call.

**sand·stone** ▶*n.* sedimentary rock of consolidated sand.

**sand·storm** ▶*n.* storm of wind with clouds of sand.

**sand·wich** /ˈsan(d)wich/ ▶*n.* two or more slices of bread with a filling of meat, cheese, etc.
▶*v.* **1** put (a thing, statement, etc.) between two of another character. **2** squeeze in between others: *sat sandwiched in the middle.*

**sane** /sān/ ▶*adj.* **1** of sound mind; not mad. **2** (of views, etc.) moderate; sensible. —**sane·ly** *adv.* —**sane·ness** *n.*

**sang-froid** /säNGˈfrwä/ ▶*n.* composure, coolness, etc., in danger or under agitating circumstances.

**san·gri·a** /saNGˈgrēə/ ▶*n.* drink of red wine with lemon juice, fruit, spices, etc.

**san·gui·nar·y** /ˈsaNGgwə,nerē/ ▶*adj.* bloody; bloodthirsty.

**san·guine** /ˈsaŋɡwin/ ▸*adj.*
1 optimistic; confident. 2 (of the complexion) florid; ruddy.
—**san·guine·ly** *adv.*
—**san·guine·ness** *n.*

**san·i·tar·i·um** /ˌsaniˈte(ə)rēəm/
▸*n.* (*pl.* **-i·ums** or **-i·a**)
establishment for the restoration of health.

**san·i·tar·y** /ˈsaniˌterē/ ▸*adj.* 1 of conditions that affect health, esp. with regard to dirt and infection. 2 hygienic; free from or designed to kill germs, infection, etc. —**san·i·tar·i·ly** *adv.*

**san·i·tar·y nap·kin** ▸*n.* absorbent pad used during menstruation.

**san·i·ta·tion** /ˌsaniˈtāsHən/ ▸*n.*
1 sanitary conditions.
2 maintenance or improving of these. 3 disposal of sewage and refuse.

**san·i·tize** /ˈsaniˌtīz/ ▸*v.* 1 make sanitary; disinfect. 2 render (information, etc.) more acceptable by removing improper or disturbing material.
—**san·i·tiz·er** *n.*

**san·i·ty** /ˈsanitē/ ▸*n.* condition of being sane.

**San·skrit** /ˈsanˌskrit/ ▸*n.* ancient and sacred language of the Hindus in India.

▸*adj.* of or in this language.

**sans ser·if** /ˌsan(z) ˈserəf/ ▸*n.* style of type without serifs.
▸*adj.* without serifs.

**sap** /sap/ ▸*n.* 1 vital juice circulating in plants. 2 vigor; vitality.
▸*v.* (**sapped, sap·ping**) 1 drain of sap. 2 undermine; weaken.

**sa·pi·ent** /ˈsāpēənt/ ▸*adj.* wise.
—**sa·pi·ence** *n.* —**sa·pi·ent·ly** *adv.*

**sap·ling** /ˈsapliNG/ ▸*n.* 1 young tree. 2 youth.

**sap·o·na·ceous** /ˌsapəˈnāsHəs/
▸*adj.* of, like, or containing soap; soapy.

**sap·phire** /ˈsaˌfī(ə)r/ ▸*n.*
1 transparent, bright blue precious stone. 2 its color.
▸*adj.* of sapphire blue.

**sar·casm** /ˈsärˌkazəm/ ▸*n.*
1 bitter or wounding remark.
2 taunt, esp. one ironically worded. —**sar·cas·tic** *adj.*
—**sar·cas·ti·cal·ly** *adv.*

**sar·co·ma** /särˈkōmə/ ▸*n.* (*pl.* **-mas** or **-ma·ta**) malignant tumor of connective tissue.

**sar·coph·a·gus** /särˈkäfəgəs/
▸*n.* (*pl.* **-gi**) stone coffin.

**sar·dine** /särˈdēn/ ▸*n.* small edible fish, usu. sold tightly packed in cans.

**sar·don·ic** /sär'dänik/ ▸*adj.*
**1** grimly jocular. **2** bitterly
mocking or cynical.
—**sar·don·i·cal·ly** *adv.*

**sa·ri** /'särē/ ▸*n.* (*pl.* **-ris**) length of
cloth draped around the body,
traditionally worn by women of
India.

**sa·rong** /sə'rôNG/ ▸*n.* Malay and
Javanese garment of a long strip
of cloth wrapped around the
body.

**sar·sa·pa·ril·la** /ˌsärs(ə)pə'rilə;
ˌsaspə-/ ▸*n.* preparation of the
dried roots of various plants,
used to flavor a carbonated
drink.

**sar·to·ri·al** /sär'tôrēəl/ ▸*adj.* of
men's clothes or tailoring.
—**sar·to·ri·al·ly** *adv.*

**s.a.s.e.** ▸*abbr.* self-addressed
stamped envelope.

**sash** /saSH/ ▸*n.* **1** long strip or
loop of cloth, etc., worn over one
shoulder or around the waist.
**2** frame holding the glass in a
fixed or sliding window.
—**sashed** *adj.*

**sass** /sas/ *inf.* ▸*n.* impudence;
disrespectful mannerism or
speech.
▸*v.* be impudent to.

**sas·sa·fras** /'sasəˌfras/ ▸*n.*
**1** small tree native to N.

America. **2** medicinal
preparation from its leaves or
bark.

**Sa·tan** /'sātn/ ▸*n.* the devil.

**satch·el** /'saCHəl/ ▸*n.* bag with a
handle for carrying books, etc.

**sate** /sāt/ ▸*v.* satisfy completely.

**sa·teen** /sa'tēn/ ▸*n.* cotton fabric
woven like satin with a glossy
surface.

**sat·el·lite** /'satlˌīt/ ▸*n.*
**1** celestial body orbiting the
earth or another planet.
**2** artificial body placed in orbit
around the earth or another
planet. **3** small country
controlled by another.
▸*adj.* transmitted by satellite:
*satellite communications.*

**sat·el·lite dish** ▸concave dish-
shaped antenna for receiving
broadcasting signals transmitted
by satellite.

**sat·in** /'satn/ ▸*n.* fabric with a
glossy surface on one side.
▸*adj.* smooth as satin. —**sat·in·y**
*adj.*

**sat·ire** /'saˌtī(ə)r/ ▸*n.* **1** use of
ridicule, irony, sarcasm, etc., to
expose folly or vice or to
lampoon an individual. **2** work
using this. —**sa·tir·i·cal** *adj.*
—**sa·tir·i·cal·ly** *adv.*

**sat·i·rize** /'satəˌrīz/ ▸*v.* deride

and criticize by means of satire. **—sat·i·ri·za·tion** *n.*

**sat·is·fac·to·ry** /ˌsatisˈfakt(ə)rē/ ▶*adj.* adequate; causing or giving satisfaction. **—sat·is·fac·to·ri·ly** *adv.*

**sat·is·fy** /ˈsatisˌfī/ ▶*v.* (**-fied**) **1** meet the expectations or desires of; comply with (a demand). **2** be adequate. **3** pay (a debt or creditor). **4** provide with adequate information or proof; convince. **—sat·is·fac·tion** *n.* **—sat·is·fy·ing** *adj.*

**sat·u·rate** /ˈsaCHəˌrāt/ ▶*v.* **1** make very wet. **2** fill to capacity or excess. **—sat·u·ra·tion** *n.*

**Sat·ur·day** /ˈsatərˌdā/ ▶*n.* seventh day of the week, following Friday.

**Sat·urn** /ˈsatərn/ ▶*n.* sixth planet from the sun, with a system of broad flat rings circling it.

**sat·ur·nine** /ˈsatərˌnīn/ ▶*adj.* having a gloomy appearance or temperament.

**sa·tyr** /ˈsatər; ˈsātər/ ▶*n.* **1** (in Greek and Roman mythology) woodland god with some manlike and goatlike features. **2** lustful or sensual man.

**sauce** /sôs/ ▶*n.* **1** liquid or semisolid preparation taken as a relish with food; the liquid constituent of a dish. **2** something adding piquancy or excitement. **3** *inf.* impudence; impertinence.

**sauce·pan** ▶*n.* cooking pan, usu. with a lid and a long handle.

**sau·cer** ▶*n.* shallow circular dish for holding a cup.

**sau·cy** /ˈsôsē/ ▶*adj.* (**-ci·er, -ci·est**) impudent. **—sau·ci·ly** *adv.* **—sau·ci·ness** *n.*

**sau·er·kraut** /ˈsou(ə)rˌkrout/ ▶*n.* chopped cabbage that has been pickled in brine.

**sau·na** /ˈsônə/ ▶*n.* Finnish-style steam bath.

**saun·ter** /ˈsôntər/ ▶*v.* walk slowly; stroll. ▶*n.* leisurely ramble.

**sau·sage** /ˈsôsij/ ▶*n.* seasoned ground meat, often in a tube-shaped edible casing.

**sau·té** /sôˈtā/ ▶*adj.* quickly cooked or browned in a little hot fat. ▶*v.* (**-téed** or **-téd**) cook in this way.

**sav·age** /ˈsavij/ ▶*adj.* **1** fierce; cruel. **2** wild; primitive. **3** *inf.* angry; bad-tempered. ▶*n.* **1** *hist.* or *poet.* member of a primitive tribe. **2** cruel or barbarous person.

▶v. **1** (esp. of a dog, wolf, etc.) attack and bite or trample. **2** (of a critic, etc.) attack fiercely.
—**sav·age·ly** adv.

**sa·van·na** /sə'vanə/ (also **sa·van·nah**) ▶n. grassy plain in tropical and subtropical regions.

**sa·vant** /sa'vänt/ (fem. **sa·vante**) ▶n. learned person.

**save** /sāv/ ▶v. **1** rescue, preserve, protect, or deliver from danger, harm, etc. **2** keep for future use. **3** avoid wasting.
▶n. Hockey, soccer, etc. preventing an opponent's scoring.
—**sav·a·ble** or **save·a·ble** adj.
—**sav·er** n.

**sav·ing** ▶adj. [in comb.] making economical use of: labor-saving.
▶n. **1** anything saved; an economy. **2** (**savings**) money saved.

**sav·ior** /'sāvyər/ ▶n. **1** person who saves from danger, destruction, etc. **2** (**the/our Savior**) Christ.

**sa·voir faire** /ˌsavwär 'fe(ə)r/ ▶n. ability to act suitably in any situation; tact.

**sa·vor** /'sāvər/ ▶n. characteristic taste, flavor, etc.
▶v. **1 a** appreciate and enjoy the taste of (food). **b** enjoy or appreciate (an experience, etc.). **2** suggest by taste, smell, etc.: savors of mushrooms.
—**sa·vor·less** adj.

**sa·vor·y** /'sāv(ə)rē/ ▶n. (pl. **-vor·ies**) aromatic herb used esp. in cooking.
▶adj. **1** having an appetizing taste or smell. **2** salty or spicy rather than sweet.

**sav·vy** /'savē/ ▶n. shrewdness; understanding.
▶adj. (**-vi·er**, **-vi·est**) knowing; wise.

**saw**[1] /sô/ ▶n. **1** hand tool having a toothed blade or disk used to cut hard materials. **2** proverb; maxim: that's just an old saw.
▶v. (past part. **sawed** or **sawn**) **1** cut (wood, etc.) with a saw. **2** use a saw. —**saw·like** adj.

**saw**[2] ▶past of SEE.

**saw·dust** ▶n. powdery particles of wood produced in sawing.

**saw·horse** ▶n. rack supporting wood for sawing.

**sax** /saks/ ▶n. inf. SAXOPHONE.

**Sax·on** /'saksən/ ▶n. **1** hist. member of the Germanic people that conquered parts of England in the 5th–6th c. **2** (usu. **Old Sax·on**) language of the Saxons.

**sax·o·phone** /ˈsaksəˌfōn/ ▶n. keyed brass reed instrument. —**sax·o·phon·ist** n.

**say** /sā/ ▶v. (*3rd sing. present* **says**; *past* and *past part.* **said**) **1 a** utter (specified words); remark. **b** express. **2** state; promise. **3** be asserted or described: *they were said to be training freedom fighters.* **4** repeat (a lesson, etc.); recite. ▶n. **1 a** opportunity for stating one's opinion, etc. **b** stated opinion. **2** share in a decision. □ **say-so 1** power of decision. **2** mere assertion. □ **that is to say 1** in other words. **2** or at least.

**say·ing** ▶n. maxim, proverb, adage, etc. □ **go without saying** be too well known or obvious to need mention.

**sa·yo·na·ra** /ˌsīəˈnärə/ ▶exclam. goodbye.

**SC** ▶abbr. South Carolina (in official postal use).

**Sc** ▶symb. Chem. the element scandium.

**s.c.** ▶abbr. small capitals.

**scab** /skab/ ▶n. **1** dry rough crust formed over a healing cut, sore, etc. **2** inf., derog. person who refuses to strike or join a labor union, or who tries to break a strike by working. ▶v. (**scabbed**, **scab·bing**) form a scab; heal over. —**scabbed** adj. —**scab·by** adj. —**scab·like** adj.

**scab·bard** /ˈskabərd/ ▶n. hist. sheath for a sword, etc.

**sca·bies** /ˈskābēz/ ▶n. contagious skin disease causing severe itching.

**scads** ▶pl. n. inf. large number or quantity.

**scaf·fold** /ˈskafəld/ ▶n. raised wooden platform used formerly for the execution of criminals, esp. by hanging.

**scaf·fold·ing** ▶n. temporary structure of wooden planks and metal poles providing a platform for workers on the outside of a building.

**scald** /skôld/ ▶v. **1** injure with very hot liquid or steam. **2** heat (esp. milk) to near boiling point. **3** immerse briefly in boiling water.

**scale**[1] /skāl/ ▶n. **1** each of the small, thin, bony or horny overlapping plates protecting the skin of fish and reptiles. **2** deposit formed in a kettle, boiler, etc. ▶v. **1** remove scale(s). **2** form,

come off in, or drop scales.
—**scal·y** *adj.*

**scale**[2] ▶*n.* **1** (also **scales**) weighing device. **2** graded classification system. **3** *Geog.* & *Archit.* ratio of size in a map, model, picture, etc. **4** relative dimensions or degree: *generosity on a grand scale.* **5** *Mus.* arrangement of all the notes in any system of music in ascending or descending order. **6 a** set of marks on a line used in measuring. **b** piece of metal, apparatus, etc., on which these are marked.

▶*v.* climb (a wall, height, etc.).

□ **tip the scales** be the decisive factor.

**scal·lion** /ˈskalyən/ ▶*n.* any long-necked onion with a small bulb.

**scal·lop** /ˈskäləp; ˈskal-/ ▶*n.* **1** bivalve mollusk much prized as food. **2** (also **scal·lop shell**) single shell of a scallop, with a toothed edge. **3** (**scallops**) ornamental edging cut in material in imitation of a scallop edge.

▶*v.* (-**loped**, -**lop·ing**) ornament (an edge or material) with scallops.
—**scal·lop·ing** *n.*

**scalp** /skalp/ ▶*n.* skin covering the top of the head, with the hair, etc., attached.

▶*v.* **1** *hist.* take the scalp of (an enemy). **2** *inf.* resell (shares, tickets, etc.) at a high or quick profit. —**scalp·er** *n.*

**scal·pel** /ˈskalpəl/ ▶*n.* surgeon's sharp knife.

**scam** /skam/ ▶*n. inf.* trick or swindle; fraud.

**scam·per** /ˈskampər/ ▶*v.* run quickly.

▶*n.* act or instance of scampering.

**scam·pi** /ˈskampē/ ▶*pl. n.* large shrimp, esp. sautéed in garlic butter.

**scan** /skan/ ▶*v.* (**scanned**, **scan·ning**) **1** look at intently or quickly. **2** (of a verse, etc.) be metrically correct: *this line doesn't scan.* **3** resolve (a picture) into its elements of light and shade in a prearranged pattern.

▶*n.* **1** scanning. **2** image obtained by scanning or with a scanner.
—**scan·na·ble** *adj.*

**scan·dal** /ˈskandl/ ▶*n.* **1** thing or person causing general public outrage or indignation. **2** outrage, etc., so caused. **3** malicious gossip.
—**scan·dal·ous** *adj.*
—**scan·dal·ous·ly** *adv.*

**scan·dal·ize** ▶ *v.* offend morally; shock.

**scan·ner** ▶ *n.* **1** device for obtaining an electronic image of something. **2** device for monitoring radio frequencies, esp. police or emergency frequencies.

**scan·sion** /ˈskansHən/ ▶ *n.* metrical scanning of verse.

**scant** /skant/ (also **scant·y**) ▶ *adj.* barely sufficient; deficient. —**scant·i·ly** *adv.* —**scant·ness** *n.*

**scape·goat** /ˈskāpˌgōt/ ▶ *n.* person blamed for the wrongdoing of others.

**scar** /skär/ ▶ *n.* usu. permanent mark on the skin from a healed wound, burn, or sore. ▶ *v.* (**scarred, scar·ring**) form or mark with a scar. —**scar·less** *adj.*

**scar·ab** /ˈskarəb/ ▶ *n.* **1** sacred dung beetle of ancient Egypt. **2** ancient Egyptian gem cut in the form of a beetle.

**scarce** /ske(ə)rs/ ▶ *adj.* **1** insufficient for the demand; scanty. **2** rare. —**scarce·ness** *n.* —**scar·ci·ty** *n.*
□ **make oneself scarce** *inf.* keep out of the way.

**scarce·ly** ▶ *adv.* **1** hardly; barely; only just. **2** surely not.

**scare** /ske(ə)r/ ▶ *v.* **1** frighten or become frightened, esp. suddenly. **2** (**scare away/off**) drive away by frightening. ▶ *n.* **1** sudden attack of fright. **2** alarm.

**scare·crow** ▶ *n.* human figure dressed in old clothes and set up in a field to scare birds away.

**scared** ▶ *adj.* frightened; terrified.

**scarf** /skärf/ ▶ *n.* (*pl.* **scarfs** or **scarves**) **1** square, triangular, or long, narrow strip of material worn around the neck, over the shoulders, or tied around the head for warmth or ornament. **2** joint made by scarfing. ▶ *v.* **1** join the beveled ends of lumber, etc., by bolting, gluing, etc. **2** *inf.* eat or drink enthusiastically: *he scarfed down the waffles.* —**scarfed** *adj.*

**scar·i·fy** /ˈskarəˌfī/ ▶ *v.* (**-fied**) make superficial incisions in. —**scar·i·fi·ca·tion** *n.*

**scar·let** /ˈskärlit/ ▶ *n.* brilliant red color tinged with orange. ▶ *adj.* of a scarlet color.
□ **scarlet fever** infectious bacterial fever with a scarlet rash.

**scar·y** /ˈske(ə)rē/ ▶ *adj.* (**-i·er, -i·est**) *inf.* frightening. —**scar·i·ly** *adv.*

**scat** /skat/ *inf.* ▶*v.* (**scat·ted**, **scat·ting**) depart quickly.
▶*interj.* go!
▶*n.* improvised jazz singing using sounds imitating instruments, instead of words.

**scath·ing** /'skāT͟HiNG/ ▶*adj.* scornful; severely critical.

**scat·ter** /'skatər/ ▶*v.* **1** throw here and there; strew. **2** disperse or cause (animals, clouds, etc.) to disperse. **3** (**be scattered**) be found at intervals rather than all together.

**scat·ter·brain** ▶*n.* person lacking concentration.
—**scat·ter·brained** *adj.*

**scat·ter·ing** ▶*n.* small amount scattered.

**scav·enge** /'skavənj/ ▶*v.* **1** search for and collect (discarded items). **2** feed on carrion, refuse, etc.

**sce·nar·i·o** /sə'ne(ə)rē,ō/ ▶*n.* (*pl.* **-os**) **1** outline of the plot of a play, film, opera, etc. **2** postulated sequence of future events.

**sce·nar·ist** /sə'ne(ə)rist/ ▶*n.* screenwriter.

**scene** /sēn/ ▶*n.* **1** place where events occur. **2 a** incident in real life, fiction, etc. **b** description or representation of an incident, etc. **3** public display of emotion, temper, etc. **4** portion of a play in a fixed setting. **5** landscape or a view.
—**scen·ic** *adj.*

☐ **behind the scenes 1** offstage. **2** unknown to the public; secret(ly).

**scen·er·y** /'sēn(ə)rē/ ▶*n.* **1** natural features of a landscape. **2** painted representations of landscape, rooms, etc., used as the background in a play, etc.

**scent** /sent/ ▶*n.* **1** distinctive, esp. pleasant, smell. **2** perceptible scent trail left by an animal. **3** PERFUME.
▶*v.* **1 a** discern by scent. **b** sense the presence of. **2** make fragrant. —**scent·ed** *adj.*

**scep·ter** /'septər/ ▶*n.* staff as a symbol of sovereignty.

**scha·den·freu·de** /'SHädən-ˌfroidə/ (also **Scha·den·freu·de**) ▶*n.* pleasure derived by someone from another person's misfortune.

**sched·ule** /'skejo͞ol/ ▶*n.* **1** list or plan of intended events, times, etc. **2** list of rates or prices. **3** timetable.
▶*v.* include in a schedule.

**scheme** /skēm/ ▶*n.* **1** proposed

or operational systematic plan or arrangement. **2** cunning plot.

▶*v.* plan, esp. secretly or deceitfully. —**schem·er** *n.* —**schem·ing** *adj. & n.*

**scher·zo** /'skertsō/ ▶*n. (pl.* **-zos**) *Mus.* vigorous, light, or playful composition, usu. as a movement in a symphony, sonata, etc.

**schism** /'s(k)izəm/ ▶*n.* division of a group (esp. religious) into opposing sects or parties usu. over doctrine. —**schis·mat·ic** *adj. & n.*

**schis·mat·ic** /s(k)iz'matik/ ▶*adj.* of, characterized by, or favoring schism.

▶*n.* (esp. in the Christian Church) a person who promotes schism; an adherent of a schismatic group.

**schist** /SHist/ ▶*n.* layered crystalline rock.

**schiz·o·phre·ni·a** /ˌskitsə'frēnēə; -'fren-/ ▶*n.* mental disease marked by a breakdown in the relation between thoughts, feelings, and actions, frequently accompanied by delusions and retreat from society. —**schiz·o·phren·ic** *adj. & n.*

**schle·miel** /SHlə'mēl/ ▶*n. inf.* foolish or unlucky person.

**schlep** /SHlep/ (also **schlepp**) *inf.* ▶*v.* (**schlepped, schlep·ping**) **1** carry; drag. **2** go or work tediously or effortfully.

▶*n.* (also **schlep·per**) person or thing that is tedious, awkward, or slow.

**schlock** /SHläk/ ▶*n. inf.* inferior goods; trash.

**schlock·meis·ter** /'SHläk-ˌmīstər/ ▶*n. inf.* purveyor of cheap or trashy goods.

**schlub** /SHləb/ (also **shlub**) ▶*n. inf.* talentless, unattractive, or boorish person.

**schlump** /SHlo͝omp/ (also **shlump**) ▶*n. inf.* slow, slovenly, or inept person.

**schmaltz** /SHmälts/ ▶*n. inf.* excessive sentimentality. —**schmaltz·y** *adj.*

**schmo** /SHmō/ (also **shmo**) ▶*n.* (*pl.* **schmoes**) *inf.* fool or a bore.

**schnapps** /SHnäps/ ▶*n.* any of various alcoholic drinks, often flavored.

**schnor·rer** /'SHnôrər/ (also **shnor·rer**) ▶*n. inf.* beggar or scrounger; a lazy person.

**schol·ar** /'skälər/ ▶*n.* **1** learned person; academic. **2** pupil.

—**schol·ar·ly** *adj.*
—**schol·ar·li·ness** *n.*
**schol·ar·ship** ▸*n.* **1 a** academic achievement; learning of a high level. **b** standards of a good scholar. **2** payment from the funds of a school, university, local government, etc., to maintain a student in full-time education, awarded on the basis of scholarly achievement.
**scho·las·tic** /skə'lastik/ ▸*adj.* of or concerning schools, education, etc.
—**scho·las·ti·cal·ly** *adv.*
**scho·li·ast** /'skōlē,ast/ ▸*n.* commentator on ancient or classical literature.
**school** /skool/ ▸*n.* **1** educational institution. **2** university division. **3 a** group of artists, etc., whose works share distinctive characteristics. **b** group of people sharing a cause, principle, method, etc.: *school of thought.* **4** group of fish, porpoises, whales, etc.
▸*v.* discipline; train.
**schoo·ner** /'skoonər/ ▸*n.* fore-and-aft rigged ship with two or more masts, the foremast being smaller than the other masts.
**schuss** /shoos; shŏos/ ▸*n.* straight downhill run on skis.

▸*v.* make a straight downhill run on skis.
**schwa** /shwä/ ▸*n. Phonet.* **1** indistinct unstressed vowel sound as in *a* mom*e*nt *a*go. **2** symbol representing this.
**sci·at·i·ca** /sī'atikə/ ▸*n.* neuralgia of the hip and thigh.
**sci·ence** /'sīəns/ ▸*n.* **1** systematic study of the structure and behavior of the physical and natural world through observation and experimentation. **2** systematic and formulated knowledge, esp. on a specified subject.
—**sci·en·tif·ic** *adj.*
**sci·ence fic·tion** ▸fiction based on imagined future scientific discoveries, frequently dealing with space travel, life on other planets, etc.
**sci-fi** /'sī 'fī/ ▸*n. inf.* science fiction.
**scim·i·tar** /'simətər/ ▸*n.* Oriental curved sword.
**scin·til·la** /sin'tilə/ ▸*n.* trace or spark.
**scin·til·late** /'sintl,āt/ ▸*v.* **1** talk cleverly or wittily; be brilliant. **2** sparkle; twinkle.
—**scin·til·lat·ing** *adj.*
—**scin·til·la·tion** *n.*
**sci·on** /'sīən/ ▸*n.* **1** descendant.

**2** shoot of a plant, etc., esp. for grafting or planting.

**scis·sors** /ˈsizərz/ (also **pair of scis·sors**) ▸*pl. n.* manual cutting instrument having two pivoted blades with finger and thumb holes in the handles.

**scle·ro·sis** /skləˈrōsis/ ▸*n.* abnormal hardening of body tissue. —**scle·rot·ic** *adj. & n.*

**scoff** /skôf/ ▸*v.* speak derisively; mock; be scornful.
▸*n.* mocking words; taunt.
—**scoff·er** *n.* —**scoff·ing·ly** *adv.*

**scold** /skōld/ ▸*v.* rebuke.
—**scold·er** *n.* —**scold·ing** *n.*

**sconce** /skäns/ ▸*n.* wall bracket for candles or electric lights.

**scone** /skōn; skän/ ▸*n.* biscuitlike cake, esp. served with tea.

**scoop** /skoop/ ▸*n.* **1** any of various objects resembling a spoon, esp.: **a** short-handled deep shovel used for transferring grain, sugar, etc. **b** long-handled ladle used for transferring liquids. **c** excavating part of a digging machine, etc.
**2** scooping movement.
**3** exclusive news item.
▸*v.* **1** hollow out with or as if with a scoop. **2** lift with or as if with a scoop. **3** precede (a rival newspaper, etc.) with news.
—**scoop·er** *n.* —**scoop·ful** *n.*

**scoot** /skoot/ ▸*v. inf.* dart away quickly.

**scoot·er** ▸*n.* **1** light vehicle consisting of a footboard on two wheels and a long steering handle. **2** light two-wheeled motorized bicycle with a shieldlike protective front.

**scope** /skōp/ ▸*n.* **1** range; opportunity. **2** reach of mental activity, observation, or outlook.

**scorch** /skôrCH/ ▸*v.* burn or become burned on the surface with dry heat. —**scorch·er** *n.*

**scorch·ing** ▸*adj. inf.* **1** (of the weather) very hot. **2** (of criticism, etc.) stringent; harsh.
—**scorch·ing·ly** *adv.*

**score** /skôr/ ▸*n.* **1 a** number of points made by a player, team, etc., in some games. **b** total number of points, etc., at the end of a game. **2** (*pl.* same or **scores**) twenty or a set of twenty. **3** (**scores**) a great many. **4** reason or motive: *rejected on the score of absurdity.* **5** *Mus.* **a** copy of a composition showing all the vocal and instrumental parts arranged one below the other. **b** music for a film or play.

**6** notch, line, etc., cut or scratched into a surface. ▸*v.* **1** win or gain (a goal, run, success, etc.). **2 a** make a score in a game. **b** keep the tally of points, runs, etc., in a game. **3** mark with notches, incisions, lines, etc. **4** *Mus.* orchestrate or arrange (a piece of music).

**scorn** /skôrn/ ▸*n.* **1** disdain; contempt; derision. **2** object of contempt, etc.: *the scorn of all onlookers.* ▸*v.* hold in contempt. **—scorn·ful** *adj.* **—scorn·ful·ly** *adv.*

**scor·pi·on** /ˈskôrpēən/ ▸*n.* arachnid with lobsterlike pincers and a jointed stinging tail.

**Scot** /skät/ ▸*n.* **1** native of Scotland or person of Scottish descent. **2** member of a Gaelic people that migrated from Ireland to Scotland around the 6th c.

**Scotch** /skäCH/ ▸*adj.* old-fashioned term for **SCOTTISH**. ▸*n.* (also **Scotch whiskey**) whiskey distilled in Scotland, esp. from malted barley.

**scotch** ▸*v.* put an end to; frustrate.

**scot-free** ▸*adv.* without punishment or injury.

**Scots** /skäts/ ▸*adj.* **SCOTTISH**. ▸*n.* form of English spoken in (esp. Lowlands) Scotland.

**Scot·tish** /ˈskätiSH/ ▸*adj.* of or relating to Scotland or its inhabitants.

**scoun·drel** /ˈskoundrəl/ ▸*n.* unscrupulous villain; rogue.

**scour** /skour/ ▸*v.* **1** cleanse or brighten by rubbing, esp. with soap, chemicals, sand, etc. **2** clear out (a pipe, channel, etc.) by flushing through. **3** subject (a place, etc.) to a thorough search in order to locate something: *scoured the newspaper.* **—scour·er** *n.*

**scourge** /skərj/ ▸*n.* **1** whip used for punishment. **2** anything regarded as a cause of suffering: *scourge of famine.* ▸*v.* **1** whip. **2** punish harshly; oppress. **—scourg·er** *n.*

**scout** /skout/ ▸*n.* **1** person, esp. a soldier, sent ahead to get information about the enemy's position, strength, etc. **2 TALENT SCOUT**. **3** (**Scout**) Boy Scout or Girl Scout. ▸*v.* **1** make a search in various places. **2** explore to get information about (territory, etc.). **3** look for talented people

for recruitment. **—scout·er** *n.*
**—scout·ing** *n.*

**scowl** /skoul/ ▶*n.* frowning or sullen expression.
▶*v.* make a scowl or frown.

**scrab·ble** /'skrabəl/ ▶*v.* scratch or grope to find or collect or hold on to something.

**scrag·gly** /'skraglē/ ▶*adj.* sparse and irregular.

**scram** /skram/ ▶*v.* (**scrammed**, **scram·ming**) *inf.* go away quickly.

**scram·ble** /'skrambəl/ ▶*v.*
**1** make one's way over rough ground, rocks, etc., by clambering, crawling, etc.
**2** struggle with competitors (for a thing or share). **3** mix together indiscriminately. **4** cook (beaten eggs). **5** make (a broadcast transmission or telephone conversation) unintelligible.
**6** move hastily.
▶*n.* **1** act of scrambling.
**2** difficult climb or walk.
**3** eager struggle or competition.

**scrap** /skrap/ ▶*n.* **1** small detached piece; fragment.
**2** rubbish or waste material.
**3** (**scraps**) **a** odds and ends.
**b** bits of uneaten food. **4** *inf.* fight or quarrel.

▶*v.* (**scrapped**, **scrap·ping**)
**1** discard as useless. **2** *inf.* have a fight or quarrel.

**scrap·book** ▶*n.* book of blank pages for sticking clippings, drawings, etc., in.

**scrape** /skrāp/ ▶*v.* **1 a** move a hard or sharp edge across (a surface), esp. to make smooth.
**b** apply (a hard or sharp edge) in this way. **2 a** rub (a surface) harshly against another.
**b** scratch or damage by scraping.
**3 a** move with a sound of scraping. **b** emit or produce such a sound. **4** barely manage (to achieve, amass, etc.).
▶*n.* **1** act or sound of scraping.
**2** abrasion. **3** *inf.* awkward predicament. **—scrap·er** *n.*

**scratch** /skraCH/ ▶*v.* **1** score or mark the surface of with a sharp object. **2** scrape, esp. with the nails to relieve itching. **3** cancel or strike (out) with a pencil, etc.
**4** withdraw (a competitor, candidate, etc.).
▶*n.* **1** mark or wound made by scratching. **2** sound of scratching. **3** *inf.* superficial wound.
▶*adj.* collected by chance.
**—scratch·y** *adj.*
□ **from scratch** from the

beginning. ☐ **up to scratch** up to the required standard.

**scrawl** /skrôl/ ▶v. write in a hurried untidy way.

▶n. piece of hurried writing.

**scraw·ny** /'skrônē/ ▶adj. (**-ni·er, -ni·est**) lean; skinny. —**scrawn·i·ness** n.

**scream** /skrēm/ ▶n. loud, high-pitched, piercing cry of fear, pain, etc.

▶v. emit or utter with a loud, high-pitched cry.

**screech** /skrēCH/ ▶n. harsh, high-pitched scream.

▶v. utter with or make a high-pitched noise. —**screech·er** n. —**screech·y** adj.

**screen** /skrēn/ ▶n. **1** fixed or movable upright partition for separating, concealing, or sheltering. **2** thing used to conceal or shelter. **3 a** blank surface on which a photographic image is projected. **b** movies or the motion-picture industry. **4** frame with fine wire netting to keep out flies, mosquitoes, etc.

▶v. **1** shelter; hide. **2 a** show (a film, etc.). **b** broadcast (a television program).

☐ **screen test** audition for a part in a motion picture.

**screen·play** ▶n. script of a

motion picture or television show.

**screw** /skrōō/ ▶n. **1** thin metal cylinder or cone with a spiral ridge or thread running around the outside or the inside. **2** (also **screw pro·pel·ler**) propeller with twisted blades acting like a screw on the water or air.

▶v. **1** fasten or tighten with a screw or screws. **2** turn (a screw). **3** twist or turn around like a screw. **4** extort (consent, money, etc.) from (a person).

☐ **put the screws on** inf. pressure; intimidate. ☐ **screw up 1** contract or contort (one's face, etc.). **2** summon up (one's courage, etc.). **3** inf. bungle.

**screw·driv·er** ▶n. tool with a shaped tip to fit into the head of a screw to turn it.

**scrib·ble** /'skribəl/ ▶v. write carelessly or hurriedly.

▶n. something written carelessly or hurriedly. —**scrib·bler** n. —**scrib·bly** adj.

**scribe** /skrīb/ ▶n. ancient or medieval copyist of manuscripts.

**scrim·mage** /'skrimij/ ▶n. **1** rough or confused struggle; brawl. **2** Sports **a** Football action from the moment the ball is in play till it is dead. **b** practice game.

▶*v.* engage in a scrimmage.

**scrimp** /skrimp/ ▶*v.* be sparing or parsimonious. —**scrimp·y** *adj.*

**scrip** /skrip/ ▶*n.* provisional certificate of money subscribed to a bank or company, etc., entitling the holder to a formal certificate and dividends.

**script** /skript/ ▶*n.* **1** handwriting; written characters. **2** type imitating handwriting. **3** alphabet or system of writing: *Russian script.* **4** text of a play, film, or broadcast.

▶*v.* write a script for (a motion picture, etc.).

**scrip·to·ri·um** /ˌskrip'tôrēəm/ ▶*n.* (*pl.* **-to·ri·a** /-'tôrēə/ or **-to·ri·ums**) room set apart for writing, esp. one in a monastery where manuscripts were copied.

**scrip·ture** /'skripCHər/ ▶*n.* **1** sacred writings. **2** (**Scripture** or **the Scriptures**) the Bible.

**scrive·ner** /'skriv(ə)nər/ ▶*n.* clerk, scribe, or notary.

**scrod** /skräd/ ▶*n.* young cod or haddock, esp. as food.

**scroll** /skrōl/ ▶*n.* **1** roll of parchment or paper esp. with writing on it. **2** ornamental design or carving imitating a roll of parchment.

▶*v.* move (a display on a computer screen) vertically.

**scro·tum** /'skrōtəm/ ▶*n.* (*pl.* **-ta** or **-tums**) pouch of skin containing the testicles. —**scro·tal** *adj.*

**scrounge** /skrounj/ ▶*v. inf.* **1** obtain (things) illicitly or by cadging. **2** search about to find something at no cost. —**scroung·er** *n.*

**scrub** /skrəb/ ▶*v.* (**scrubbed, scrub·bing**) **1** rub hard so as to clean. **2** use a chemical process to remove impurities from (gas, etc.).

▶*n.* **1** scrubbing or being scrubbed. **2** brushwood or stunted forest growth. —**scrub·ber** *n.*

**scruff** /skrəf/ ▶*n.* back of the neck.

**scruff·y** /'skrəfē/ ▶*adj.* (**-i·er, -i·est**) *inf.* shabby; slovenly; untidy. —**scruff·i·ness** *n.*

**scrump·tious** /'skrəmpSHəs/ *inf.* ▶*adj.* delicious. —**scrump·tious·ly** *adv.* —**scrump·tious·ness** *n.*

**scru·ple** /'skro͞opəl/ ▶*n.* (usu. **scruples**) moral concern; doubt caused by this.

▸*v.* be reluctant because of scruples.

**scru·pu·lous** /ˈskro͞opyələs/ ▸*adj.* **1** conscientious or thorough. **2** careful to avoid doing wrong. —**scru·pu·lous·ly** *adv.* —**scru·pu·lous·ness** *n.*

**scru·ti·nize** /ˈskro͞otn̩ˌīz/ ▸*v.* look closely at; examine closely or thoroughly. —**scru·ti·niz·er** *n.* —**scru·ti·ny** *n.*

**scu·ba** /ˈsko͞obə/ ▸*n.* (*pl.* **-bas**) gear that provides an air supply from a portable tank for swimming underwater (acronym for *s*elf-*c*ontained *u*nderwater *b*reathing *a*pparatus).

**scuff** /skəf/ ▸*v.* **1** graze or brush against. **2** mark or wear down (shoes) in this way.

▸*n.* mark of scuffing.

**scuf·fle** /ˈskəfəl/ ▸*n.* confused struggle or disorderly fight at close quarters.

▸*v.* engage in a scuffle.

**scull** /skəl/ ▸*n.* **1** either of a pair of small oars used by a single rower. **2** racing rowboat.

▸*v.* propel (a boat) with sculls.

**scul·ler·y** /ˈskəl(ə)rē/ ▸*n.* (*pl.* **-ler·ies**) small kitchen or room at the back of a house for washing dishes, etc.

**sculp·ture** /ˈskəlpCHər/ ▸*n.* **1** art of making three-dimensional or relief forms. **2** work of sculpture.

▸*v.* practice or represent in sculpture. —**sculp·tur·al** *adj.*

**scum** /skəm/ ▸*n.* **1** layer of dirt, froth, etc., at the top of liquid. **2** *inf.* worthless person or group.

▸*v.* (**scummed, scum·ming**) **1** (of a liquid) become covered with a layer or dirt or froth. **2** form a scum on (a liquid). —**scum·my** *adj.*

**scup·per** /ˈskəpər/ ▸*n.* hole at the edge of a boat's deck to allow water to run off.

**scur·ri·lous** /ˈskərələs/ ▸*adj.* grossly or indecently abusive. —**scur·ril·ous·ly** *adv.* —**scur·ril·ous·ness** *n.*

**scur·ry** /ˈskərē/ ▸*v.* (**-ried**) run or move hurriedly; scamper.

▸*n.* (*pl.* **-ries**) **1** act or sound of scurrying. **2** bustle; haste.

**scur·vy** /ˈskərvē/ ▸*n.* disease caused by a deficiency of vitamin C.

**scu·tage** /ˈsk(y)o͞otij/ ▸*n.* (in a feudal society) money paid by a vassal to his lord in lieu of military service.

**scut·tle** /ˈskətl/ ▸*n.* **1** receptacle for carrying and holding a small supply of coal. **2** hole with a lid in a ship's deck or side.

▶*v.* **1** run hurriedly or furtively. **2** let water into (a ship) to sink it.

**scut·tle·butt** ▶*n. inf.* rumor; gossip.

**scut work** (also **scut·work**) ▶*n.* tedious, menial work.

**scythe** /sīTH/ ▶*n.* mowing and reaping implement with a long curved blade swung over the ground by a long pole with two short handles projecting from it.
▶*v.* cut with a scythe.

**SD** ▶*abbr.* South Dakota (in official postal use).

**S.Dak.** ▶*abbr.* South Dakota.

**SE** ▶*abbr.* **1** southeast. **2** southeastern.

**Se** ▶*symb. Chem.* selenium.

**sea** /sē/ ▶*n.* **1** expanse of salt water that covers most of the earth's surface or a part of this. **2** particular (usu. named) tract of salt water partly or wholly enclosed by land: *North Sea.* **3** large inland lake: *Sea of Galilee.* **4** waves of the sea; their motion or state: *choppy sea.* **5** vast quantity or expanse.
□ **at sea** **1** in a ship on the sea. **2** perplexed; confused.

**sea·bed** ▶*n.* ground under the sea; ocean floor.

**sea·food** ▶*n.* edible sea fish or shellfish.

**sea·go·ing** ▶*adj.* (of a ship) suitable or designed for voyages on the sea

**sea·gull** ▶*n.* GULL.

**sea·horse** (also **sea horse**) ▶*n.* small upright marine fish with a head like that of a horse.

**seal** /sēl/ ▶*n.* **1** fish-eating amphibious sea mammal with flippers and webbed feet. **2** piece of wax, lead, paper, etc., with a stamped design, attached to a document as a guarantee of authenticity or security. **3** engraved piece of metal, gemstone, etc., for stamping a design on a seal. **4** substance or device to close a gap. **5** act or gesture regarded as a guarantee.
▶*v.* **1** close or fasten securely. **2** stamp or fasten with a seal. **3** fix a seal to. **4** certify as correct with a seal or stamp.

**sea legs** ▶*pl. n.* ability to keep one's balance and avoid seasickness when at sea.

**sea li·on** ▶*n.* eared seal.

**seam** /sēm/ ▶*n.* **1** line where two edges join, esp. of cloth or boards. **2** fissure between

parallel edges. **3** wrinkle.
**4** stratum of coal, etc.
▸ *v.* join with a seam. —**seam·less**
*adj.*

**sea·man** /ˈsēmən/ ▸*n.* (*pl.* **-men**)
sailor, esp. one below the rank
of officer.

**seam·stress** /ˈsēmstris/ ▸*n.*
woman who sews professionally.

**seam·y** ▸*adj.* (**-i·er, -i·est**)
unpleasant; disreputable.
—**seam·i·ness** *n.*

**se·ance** /ˈsāˌäns/ (also **sé·ance**)
▸*n.* meeting at which
spiritualists attempt to make
contact with the dead.

**sea·plane** ▸*n.* aircraft designed
to take off from and land and
float on water.

**sea·port** ▸*n.* town with a harbor
for seagoing ships.

**sear** /si(ə)r/ ▸*v.* **1 a** scorch or
burn. **b** cauterize; brand.
**2** brown (meat) quickly at a high
temperature.

**search** /sərCH/ ▸*v.* **1** look
through or go over thoroughly
to find something. **2** examine or
feel over (a person) to find
anything concealed. **3 a** probe.
**b** examine or question (one's
mind, conscience, etc.)
thoroughly.
▸*n.* searching; investigation.

—**search·er** *n.* —**search·ing·ly**
*adv.*

**search·light** ▸*n.* **1** powerful
outdoor electric light with a
concentrated directional beam.
**2** beam from this.

**sea·shell** ▸*n.* shell of a
saltwater mollusk.

**sea·shore** ▸*n.* land next to the
sea.

**sea·sick** ▸*adj.* nauseated from
the motion of the sea.
—**sea·sick·ness** *n.*

**sea·son** /ˈsēzən/ ▸*n.* **1** each of
the four divisions of the year
(spring, summer, fall, and
winter). **2** time of year
characterized by climatic or
other features: *dry season.*
**3** time of year when something
is plentiful, active, etc. **4** proper
or suitable time.
▸*v.* **1** flavor (food) with salt,
herbs, etc. **2 a** make or become
suitable or in the desired
condition, esp. by exposure to
the air or weather. **b** [usu. as *adj.*
**seasoned**] make or become
experienced. —**sea·son·al** *adj.*
☐ **in season 1** (of food) available
in plenty and in good condition.
**2** (of an animal) in heat.
**3** timely. ☐ **season ticket** ticket
entitling the holder to any

number of journeys, admittances, etc., in a given period.

**sea·son·a·ble** ▶*adj.* **1** suitable to or usual in the season. **2** opportune. **3** meeting the needs of the occasion. —**sea·son·a·bly** *adv.*

**sea·son·ing** ▶*n.* spice or flavoring added to food.

**seat** /sēt/ ▶*n.* **1** thing made or used for sitting on. **2** buttocks. **3** part of a garment covering the buttocks. **4** part of a chair, etc., on which the sitter's weight directly rests. **5** place for one person to sit. **6** right to occupy a seat, esp. as a member of Congress, etc. **7** site or location of something specified: *seat of learning.*
▶*v.* **1** cause to sit. **2** provide seating for. **3** (**be seated**) sit down. **4** put or fit in position.

**seat belt** ▶*n.* belt securing a person in the seat of a car, aircraft, etc.

**seat·ing** ▶*n.* **1** seats collectively. **2** sitting accommodations.

**sea·way** ▶*n.* inland waterway open to seagoing ships.

**sea·weed** ▶*n.* algae growing in the sea in the form of leafy or branching plants.

**sea·wor·thy** ▶*adj.* (esp. of a ship) fit to put to sea. —**sea·wor·thi·ness** *n.*

**se·ba·ceous** /sə'bāsHəs/ ▶*adj.* of or relating to oily secretions or fat.

**seb·or·rhe·a** /ˌsebə'rēə/ ▶*n.* excessive discharge from the sebaceous glands.

**se·cede** /si'sēd/ ▶*v.* withdraw formally from an alliance, organization, etc: *the kingdom of Belgium seceded from the Netherlands in 1830.* —**se·ces·sion** *n.*

**se·clude** /si'klōōd/ ▶*v.* **1** keep (a person or place) away from company. **2** [usu. as *adj.* **secluded**] hide or screen from view. —**se·clu·sion** *n.*

**sec·ond** /'sekənd/ ▶*n.* **1** sixtieth of a minute of time. **2** (also **se·cond of arc**) sixtieth of a minute of angular distance. (Symb.: ″) **3** *inf.* very short time: *wait a second.* **4** position in a sequence corresponding to that of the number 2 in the sequence 1–2. **5** runner-up. **6** next to lowest in a sequence of gears. **7** another person or thing in addition to one previously mentioned or considered.

**8** (**seconds**) inferior goods.
**9** (**seconds**) *inf.* a second helping.
▶*adj.* **1** next after first.
**2** additional. **3** subordinate;
inferior.
▶*v.* support; back up.
□ **second hand** hand in some
watches and clocks, recording
seconds.

**sec·ond·ar·y** /ˈsekənˌderē/ ▶*adj.*
**1** coming after or next below
what is primary. **2** derived from
or depending on or
supplementing what is primary.
**3** (of education, a school, etc.) for
those who have had primary
education, usu. from 11 to 18
years.
▶*n.* (*pl.* **-ies**) secondary thing.
—**sec·ond·ar·i·ly** *adv.*

**sec·ond-guess** ▶*v. inf.* judge or
criticize with hindsight.

**sec·ond·hand** ▶*adj.* **1 a** (of
goods) having had a previous
owner; not new. **b** (of a store,
etc.) where such goods can be
bought. **2** (of information, etc.)
accepted on another's authority
and not from original
investigation.
▶*adv.* **1** on a secondhand basis.
**2** indirectly.

**sec·ond na·ture** ▶*n.* acquired
tendency that has become

instinctive: *is second nature to
him.*

**sec·ond per·son** ▶*n. Gram.* see
PERSON.

**sec·ond-rate** ▶*adj.* mediocre;
inferior.

**sec·ond string** ▶*n.* alternative
available in case of need.

**sec·ond thoughts** ▶*pl. n.*
revised opinion or resolution.

**sec·ond wind** ▶*n.* renewed
energy to continue an effort.

**se·cret** /ˈsēkrit/ ▶*adj.* **1** kept or
meant to be kept private,
unknown, or hidden. **2** acting or
operating secretly.
▶*n.* **1** thing to be kept secret.
**2** thing known only to a few.
**3** valid but not commonly
known or recognized method of
achieving or maintaining
something: *what's their secret?*
—**se·cre·cy** *n.* —**se·cret·ly** *adv.*

**sec·re·tar·i·at** /ˌsekrəˈte(ə)rēət/
▶*n.* administrative office or
department, esp. a
governmental one.

**sec·re·tar·y** /ˈsekrəˌterē/ ▶*n.* (*pl.*
**-ies**) **1** employee who assists
with correspondence, records,
making appointments, etc.
**2** official appointed by a society,
etc., to conduct its

correspondence, keep its records, etc. —**sec·re·tar·i·al** *adj.*

**se·crete** /si'krēt/ ▸*v.* **1** (of a cell, organ, etc.) produce by secretion. **2** conceal; put into hiding. —**se·cre·tor** *n.*

**se·cre·tion** ▸*n.* **1** process by which substances are produced and discharged from a cell for a function in the organism or for excretion. **2** substance discharged in such a way.

**se·cre·tive** /'sēkritiv/ ▸*adj.* inclined to make secrets; uncommunicative. —**se·cre·tive·ly** *adv.* —**se·cre·tive·ness** *n.*

**sect** /sekt/ ▸*n.* **1** group subscribing to (sometimes unorthodox) religious, political, or philosophical doctrines. **2** religious denomination.

**sec·tion** /'seksHən/ ▸*n.* **1** part cut off or separated from something. **2** each of the parts into which a thing is divided (actually or conceptually) or divisible or out of which a structure can be fitted together. **3** distinct group or subdivision of a larger body of people. **4** *Surgery* separation by cutting. **5 a** cutting of a solid by a plane. **b** resulting figure.

▸*v.* arrange in or divide into sections. —**sec·tion·al** *adj.*

**sec·tor** /'sektər/ ▸*n.* **1** distinct part of an enterprise, society, the economy, etc. **2** subdivision of an area. **3** plane figure enclosed by two radii of a circle, ellipse, etc., and the arc between them.

**sec·u·lar** /'sekyələr/ ▸*adj.* **1** not spiritual or sacred. **2** (of education, etc.) not concerned with religion or religious belief. —**sec·u·lar·ism** *n.* —**sec·u·lar·ize** *v.* —**sec·u·lar·i·za·tion** *n.*

**se·cure** /si'kyŏŏr/ ▸*adj.* **1** untroubled by danger or fear; safe. **2** reliable; certain not to fail. **3** fixed or fastened.

▸*v.* **1** make secure or safe. **2** fasten, close, or confine securely. **3** succeed in obtaining. —**se·cur·a·ble** *adj.* —**se·cure·ly** *adv.*

**se·cu·ri·ty** ▸*n.* (*pl.* -**ties**) **1** secure condition or feeling. **2** thing that guards or guarantees. **3** thing deposited or pledged as a guarantee of a loan, etc. **4** (often **securities**) certificate attesting credit or the ownership of stock, bonds, etc.

**se·dan** /si'dan/ ▸*n.* enclosed

automobile for four or more people.

**se·date**[1] /si'dāt/ ▶*adj.* tranquil and dignified; equable; serious. —**se·date·ly** *adv.* —**se·date·ness** *n.*

**se·date**[2] ▶*v.* treat with a sedative drug. —**se·da·tion** *n.*

**sed·a·tive** /'sedətiv/ ▶*n.* calming drug, influence, etc. ▶*adj.* calming; soothing; inducing sleep.

**sed·en·tar·y** /'sedn,terē/ ▶*adj.* 1 sitting. 2 (of work, etc.) done while sitting and with little physical exercise.

**Se·der** /'sādər/ ▶*n.* Jewish ritual service and ceremonial dinner for the first night or first two nights of Passover.

**sedge** /sej/ ▶*n.* grasslike plant usu. growing in wet areas.

**sed·i·ment** /'sedəmənt/ ▶*n.* 1 matter that settles to the bottom of a liquid; dregs. 2 *Geol.* matter deposited by water or wind. —**sed·i·men·ta·ry** *adj.* —**sed·i·men·ta·tion** *n.*

**se·di·tion** /si'disHən/ ▶*n.* conduct or speech inciting to rebellion. —**se·di·tious** *adj.* —**se·di·tious·ly** *adv.*

**se·duce** /si'd(y) oōs/ ▶*v.* 1 entice into sexual activity or

wrongdoing. 2 tempt: *seduced by the smell of coffee.* —**se·duc·er** *n.* —**se·duc·tion** *n.* —**se·duc·tive** *adj.* —**se·duc·tive·ly** *adv.*

**sed·u·lous** /'sejələs/ ▶*adj.* (of a person or action) showing dedication and diligence.

**see** /sē/ ▶*v.* (*past* **saw**; *past part.* **seen**) 1 discern by use of the eyes or have the power to do this. 2 understand. 3 learn; find out. 4 meet and recognize. 5 a meet socially. b meet regularly as a boyfriend or girlfriend. 6 consider; decide (on). 7 experience. 8 (**see to**) ensure.
▶*n.* office or jurisdiction of a bishop or archbishop.
□ **see about** 1 attend to. 2 consider; look into. □ **see through** 1 not be deceived by; detect the true nature of. 2 penetrate visually.

**seed** /sēd/ ▶*n.* 1 flowering plant's unit of reproduction capable of developing into another such plant. 2 semen. 3 fundamental or underlying cause. 4 descendants.
▶*v.* 1 sow seeds (in). 2 produce or drop seed. —**seed·less** *adj.*
□ **go to seed** 1 cease flowering as

seed develops. **2** become unkempt; deteriorate.

**seed·ling** ▸*n.* plant raised from seed.

**seed mon·ey** ▸*n.* money allocated to initiate a project.

**seed·y** ▸*adj.* (**-i·er, -i·est**) **1** full of seed. **2** going to seed. **3** shabby looking. —**seed·i·ly** *adv.* —**seed·i·ness** *n.*

**see·ing** ▸*conj.* considering that; inasmuch as; because.

**seek** /sēk/ ▸*v.* (*past* and *past part.* **sought**) **1** make a search or inquiry (for). **2 a** try or want to find or get. **b** ask for: *sought help from him.* **3** endeavor. —**seek·er** *n.*

**seem** /sēm/ ▸*v.* appear to be.

**seem·ing** ▸*adj.* apparent but perhaps not real: *with seeming sincerity.* —**seem·ing·ly** *adv.*

**seem·ly** ▸*adj.* (**-li·er, -li·est**) conforming to propriety or good taste; decorous; suitable. —**seem·li·ness** *n.*

**seep** /sēp/ ▸*v.* ooze out; percolate slowly. —**seep·age** *n.*

**seer** /si(ə)r/ ▸*n.* prophet; visionary.

**seer·suck·er** /'si(ə)r,səkər/ ▸*n.* material of linen, cotton, etc., with a puckered surface.

**see·saw** /'sē,sô/ ▸*n.* **1** long plank balanced on a central support for children to sit on at each end and move up and down by pushing the ground with their feet. **2** up-and-down or to-and-fro motion.

▸*v.* **1** play on a seesaw. **2** move up and down as on a seesaw. **3** vacillate in policy, emotion, etc.

▸*adj. & adv.* with up-and-down or backward-and-forward motion.

**seethe** /sēTH/ ▸*v.* **1** boil; bubble over. **2** be very agitated, esp. with anger.

**seg·ment** /'segmənt/ ▸*n.* **1** each part into which a thing is or can be divided. **2** *Geom.* part of a circle or sphere cut off by a line or plane intersecting it.

▸*v.* divide into segments. —**seg·men·tal** *adj.* —**seg·men·tar·y** *adj.* —**seg·men·ta·tion** *n.*

**seg·re·gate** /'segri,gāt/ ▸*v.* **1** isolate. **2** enforce racial separation on (persons) or in (a community, etc.). —**seg·re·ga·tion** *n.*

**se·gue** /'segwā/ ▸*v.* (**-gued, -gue·ing**) move without interruption from one song, scene, topic, item, etc., to another.

▶*n.* uninterrupted transition from one song, scene, topic, item, etc., to another.

**seine** /sān/ ▶*n.* fishing net for encircling fish, usu. hauled ashore.

**seis·mic** /ˈsīzmik/ (also **seis·mal**) ▶*adj.* of or relating to earthquakes. —**seis·mi·cal·ly** *adv.*

**seis·mo·graph** /ˈsīzmə,graf/ ▶*n.* instrument that records the force, direction, etc., of earthquakes. —**seis·mo·graph·ic** *adj.*

**seis·mol·o·gy** /sīzˈmäləjē/ ▶*n.* the study of earthquakes. —**seis·mo·log·i·cal** *adj.* —**seis·mol·o·gist** *n.*

**seize** /sēz/ ▶*v.* **1** take hold of forcibly or suddenly. **2** take possession of forcibly. **3 a** take possession of (contraband goods, etc.) by warrant or legal right; confiscate; impound. **b** arrest or apprehend (a person). **4** affect suddenly. **5** take advantage of (an opportunity). **6** comprehend quickly or clearly. **7** (of a moving part in a machine) become jammed.

**sei·zure** /ˈsēZHər/ ▶*n.* **1** taking possession legally or by force. **2** sudden violent attack of an illness.

**sel·dom** /ˈseldəm/ ▶*adv.* rarely; not often.

▶*adj.* rare.

**se·lect** /səˈlekt/ ▶*v.* choose, esp. as the best or most suitable.

▶*adj.* **1** chosen for excellence or suitability; choice. **2** (of a society, etc.) exclusive. —**se·lec·tion** *n.* —**se·lec·tive** *adj.* —**se·lec·tive·ly** *adv.*

**self** /self/ ▶*n.* (*pl.* **selves**) **1** individuality; essence; personality. **2** person or thing as the object of introspection or reflexive action: *the consciousness of self.* **3 a** one's own interests or pleasure. **b** concentration on these: *self is a bad guide to happiness.*

**self-** ▶*comb. form* expressing reflexive action: **1** of or directed toward oneself or itself: *self-respect.* **2** by oneself or itself, esp. without external agency: *self-evident.* **3** on, in, for, or relating to oneself or itself: *self-confident.*

**self-ad·dressed** ▶*adj.* (of an envelope, etc.) having one's own address on for return communication.

**self-cen·tered** ▸*adj.* preoccupied with one's own personality or affairs.

**self-con·scious** ▸*adj.* socially inept through embarrassment or shyness. —**self-con·scious·ly** *adv.* —**self-con·scious·ness** *n.*

**self-con·tained** ▸*adj.* **1** (of a person) uncommunicative or reserved; independent; self-possessed. **2** complete in itself. —**self-con·tain·ment** *n.*

**self-con·trol** ▸*n.* power of controlling one's external reactions, emotions, etc.; equanimity.

**self-de·fense** ▸*n.* **1** aggressive act, speech, etc., intended as defense. **2** skills for defending oneself.

**self-de·ni·al** ▸*n.* negation of one's interests, needs, or wishes, esp. in favor of those of others; self-control; forbearance. —**self-de·ny·ing** *adj.*

**self-de·ter·mi·na·tion** ▸*n.* **1** nation's right to determine its own government, etc. **2** ability to act with free will.

**self-ef·fac·ing** ▸*adj.* retiring; modest; timid.

**self-ev·i·dent** ▸*adj.* obvious; without the need of evidence or further explanation.

**self-im·age** ▸*n.* one's own idea or picture of oneself.

**self-in·ter·est** ▸*n.* one's personal interest or advantage. —**self-in·ter·est·ed** *adj.*

**self·ish** /ˈselfiSH/ ▸*adj.* concerned chiefly with one's own personal profit or pleasure. —**self·ish·ly** *adv.* —**self·ish·ness** *n.*

**self·less** ▸*adj.* unselfish. —**self·less·ly** *adv.* —**self·less·ness** *n.*

**self-made** ▸*adj.* **1** successful or rich by one's own effort. **2** made by oneself.

**self-pos·sessed** ▸*adj.* habitually exercising self-control; poised; composed. —**self-pos·ses·sion** *n.*

**self-pres·er·va·tion** ▸*n.* **1** preservation of one's own life, safety, etc. **2** this as a basic instinct of humans and animals.

**self-re·spect** ▸*n.* respect for oneself. —**self-re·spect·ing** *adj.*

**self-right·eous** ▸*adj.* smugly sure of one's rectitude, correctness, etc. —**self-right·eous·ly** *adv.* —**self-right·eous·ness** *n.*

**self·same** ▸*adj.* very same: *the selfsame village.*

**self-seek·ing** ▸*adj. & n.* seeking

one's own welfare before that of others.

**self-serv·ice** ▶*adj.* (of a store, restaurant, gas station, etc.) where customers serve themselves.

**self-styled** ▶*adj.* called so by oneself.

**self-suf·fi·cient** ▶*adj.*
1 needing nothing; independent.
2 (of a person, nation, etc.) able to supply one's own needs.
—**self-suf·fi·cien·cy** *n.* —**self-suf·fi·cient·ly** *adv.*

**sell** /sel/ ▶*v.* (*past* and *past part.* **sold**) 1 make over or dispose of in exchange for money. 2 offer for sale. 3 (of goods) be purchased: *will never sell.* 4 have a specified price.
▶*n. inf.* manner of selling: *soft sell.*
—**sell·a·ble** *adj.* —**sell·er** *n.*
□ **sell off** sell the remainder of (goods) at reduced prices. □ **sell out** 1 sell all one's stock, shares, etc. 2 **a** betray. **b** be treacherous or disloyal.

**sel·vage** /'selvij/ ▶*n.* edging that prevents cloth from unraveling.

**se·man·tics** /sə'mantiks/ ▶*n.* branch of linguistics concerned with meaning.
—**se·man·ti·cist** *n.*

**sem·a·phore** /'seməˌfôr/ ▶*n.* system of signaling with the arms or two flags.
▶*v.* signal or send by semaphore.

**sem·blance** /'sembləns/ ▶*n.* outward or superficial appearance of something: *semblance of anger.*

**se·men** /'sēmən/ ▶*n.* reproductive fluid of males.

**se·mes·ter** /sə'mestər/ ▶*n.* half of an academic year.

**semi-** /'semē, 'semī/ ▶*prefix*
1 half: *semicircle.* 2 partly.
3 almost: *a semismile.*
4 occurring or appearing twice in a specified period: *semiannual.*

**sem·i·cir·cle** ▶*n.* half of a circle or of its circumference.
—**sem·i·cir·cu·lar** *adj.*

**sem·i·co·lon** ▶*n.* punctuation mark (;) indicating a division in a sentence.

**sem·i·con·duc·tor** ▶*n.* substance that has conductivity intermediate between insulators and metals.

**sem·i·fi·nal** ▶*n.* match or round immediately preceding the final.
—**sem·i·fi·nal·ist** *n.*

**sem·i·nal** /'semənl/ ▶*adj.* 1 of seed, semen, or reproduction.
2 rudimentary; undeveloped.
3 (of ideas, etc.) providing the

basis for future development.
**—sem·i·nal·ly** *adv.*

**sem·i·nar** /'semə,när/ ▶*n.*
**1** small class at a university, etc.,
for discussion and research.
**2** conference of specialists.

**sem·i·nar·y** /'semə,nerē/ ▶*n.* (*pl.*
**-ies**) **1** training college for
priests, rabbis, etc. **2** place of
education or development.
**—sem·i·nar·i·an** *n.*

**Sem·i·nole** /'semə,nōl/ ▶*n.*
**1 a** N. American Indian people
native to Florida. **b** member of
this people. **2** language of this
people.

**se·mi·ot·ics** /,sēmē'ätiks;
,semē-; ,sem,ī-/ ▶*n.* study of signs
and symbols and their use or
interpretation.

**sem·i·pre·cious** ▶*adj.* (of a
gem) less valuable than a
precious stone.

**Se·mit·ic** /sə'mitik/ ▶*adj.* **1** of or
relating to the Semites, esp. the
Jews. **2** of or relating to the
languages of the family
including Hebrew and Arabic.

**sem·i·tone** ▶*n. Mus.* half a tone.

**sem·pi·ter·nal** /,sempə'tərnl/
▶*adj.* eternal and unchanging;
everlasting.

**sen·ate** /'senit/ ▶*n.* **1** legislative
body. **2** (**Senate**) upper and
smaller assembly in the U.S.,
France, and other countries, in
the states of the U.S., etc.
**—sen·a·tor** *n.*

**send** /send/ ▶*v.* (*past* and *past
part.* **sent**) **1** order or cause to go
or be conveyed. **2** propel; cause
to move: *sent him flying.*
**3** dismiss with or without force:
*sent her away.* **—send·er** *n.*

□ **send for 1** summon. **2** order by
mail. □ **send off 1** get (a letter,
parcel, etc.) dispatched. **2** attend
the departure of (a person) as a
sign of respect, etc. □ **send-off**
demonstration of goodwill, etc.,
at the departure of a person, the
start of a project, etc.

**se·nile** /'sē,nīl/ ▶*adj.* of or
characteristic of old age, esp. its
weaknesses or diseases.
**—se·nil·i·ty** *n.*

**se·nior** /'sēnyər/ ▶*adj.* **1** more or
most advanced in age or
standing. **2** of high or highest
position. **3** of the final year at a
university, high school, etc.

▶*n.* **1** person of advanced age or
comparatively long service, etc.
**2** one's elder, or one's superior
in length of service,
membership, etc. **3** senior
student. **—sen·ior·i·ty** *n.*

**se·nior cit·i·zen** ▶*n.* elderly person, esp. a retiree.

**sen·sa·tion** /sen'sāsʜən/ ▶*n.* **1** feeling in one's body detected by the senses. **2 a** intense interest, etc., esp. among a large group of people. **b** person, event, etc., causing such interest.

**sen·sa·tion·al** ▶*adj.* **1** causing or intended to cause great public excitement, etc. **2** dazzling; wonderful. —**sen·sa·tion·al·ism** *n.* —**sen·sa·tion·al·ize** *v.*

**sense** /sens/ ▶*n.* **1** any of the five bodily faculties by which sensation is roused: *dull sense of smell.* **2** ability to perceive or feel. **3** consciousness; intuitive awareness. **4** quick or accurate appreciation, understanding, or instinct. **5** common sense. **6 a** meaning of a word. **b** intelligibility or coherence. ▶*v.* **1** perceive by a sense or senses. **2** be vaguely aware of.

**sen·si·bil·i·ty** /ˌsensə'bilitē/ ▶*n.* (*pl.* **-ties**) **1** capacity to feel. **2** (**sensibilities**) emotional capacities or feelings.

**sen·si·ble** /'sensəbəl/ ▶*adj.* **1** having or showing wisdom or common sense. **2** (of clothing, etc.) practical and functional. —**sen·si·bly** *adv.*

**sen·si·tive** /'sensitiv/ ▶*adj.* **1** acutely affected by external stimuli or mental impressions; having sensibility. **2** (of a person) easily offended. **3** (of an instrument, film, etc.) responsive to or recording slight changes. **4** (of a topic, etc.) requiring tactful treatment or secrecy. —**sen·si·tive·ly** *adv.* —**sen·si·tiv·i·ty** *n.*

**sen·si·tize** ▶*v.* make sensitive. —**sen·si·ti·za·tion** *n.* —**sen·si·tiz·er** *n.*

**sen·sor** /'sensər/ ▶*n.* device for the detection or measurement of a physical property to which it responds.

**sen·so·ry** ▶*adj.* of sensation or the senses.

**sen·su·al** /'sensʜo͞oəl/ ▶*adj.* **1 a** of or depending on the senses only and not on the intellect or spirit; carnal; fleshly. **b** given to the pursuit of sensual pleasures or the gratification of the appetites. **2** of sense or sensation; sensory. —**sen·su·al·ist** *n.* —**sen·su·al·i·ty** *n.* —**sen·su·al·ly** *adv.*

**sen·su·ous** ▶*adj.* **1** relating to the senses rather than the intellect. **2** physically gratifying. —**sen·su·ous·ly** *adv.*

**sen·tence** /'sentns/ ▸*n.* **1** set of words complete in itself as the expression of a thought, containing or implying a subject and predicate, and conveying a statement, question, exclamation, or command. **2 a** decision of a court of law, esp. the punishment allotted to a person convicted in a criminal trial. **b** declaration of this.
▸*v.* **1** declare the sentence of (a convicted criminal, etc.). **2** declare (such a person) to be condemned to a specified punishment: *sentenced to 20 years in prison.*

**sen·ten·tious** /sen'tencHəs/ ▸*adj.* **1** pompously moralizing. **2** affectedly formal. —**sen·ten·tious·ly** *adv.* —**sen·ten·tious·ness** *n.*

**sen·tient** /'sencH(ē)ənt/ ▸*adj.* having the power of perception by the senses. —**sen·tience** *n.* —**sen·tient·ly** *adv.*

**sen·ti·ment** /'sentəmənt/ ▸*n.* **1** mental feeling. **2 a** what one feels. **b** verbal expression of this. **3** mawkish tenderness.

**sen·ti·men·tal** ▸*adj.* **1** of or characterized by sentiment. **2** showing or affected by emotion rather than reason.

—**sen·ti·men·tal·i·ty** *n.*
—**sen·ti·men·tal·ize** *v.*
—**sen·ti·men·tal·ly** *adv.*

**sen·ti·nel** /'sentn-əl/ ▸*n.* sentry; lookout.

**sen·try** /'sentrē/ ▸*n.* (*pl.* **-tries**) soldier standing guard.

**se·pal** /'sēpəl/ ▸*n. Bot.* division or leaf of the calyx.

**sep·a·rate** ▸*adj.* /'sep(ə)rit/ forming a unit by itself; physically disconnected, distinct, or individual.
▸*pl. n.* (**separates**) /'sep(ə)rits/ separate articles of clothing suitable for wearing together in various combinations.
▸*v.* /'sepə,rāt/ **1** make separate; sever. **2** prevent union or contact of. **3** go different ways; disperse. **4** divide or sort (milk, ore, fruit, etc.) into constituent parts or sizes. —**sep·a·ra·ble** *adj.* —**sep·a·rate·ly** *adv.* —**sep·a·ra·tion** *n.*

**sep·a·rat·ist** ▸*n.* person who favors separation, esp. political independence. —**sep·a·ra·tism** *n.*

**sep·a·ra·tor** ▸*n.* machine for separating, e.g., cream from milk.

**se·pi·a** /'sēpēə/ ▸*n.* **1** dark reddish-brown color or paint.

**2** brown tint used in photography.

**sep·sis** /ˈsepsis/ ▸n. **1** state of being septic. **2** blood poisoning.

**Sept.** ▸abbr. September.

**Sep·tem·ber** /sepˈtembər/ ▸n. ninth month of the year.

**sep·tet** /sepˈtet/ ▸n. **1** Mus. **a** composition for seven performers. **b** the performers. **2** any group of seven.

**sep·tic** /ˈseptik/ ▸adj. infected with harmful bacteria.

**sep·ti·ce·mi·a** /ˌseptiˈsēmēə/ ▸n. blood poisoning. —**sep·ti·ce·mic** adj.

**sep·tu·a·ge·nar·i·an** /ˌsepCHo͞oəjəˈne(ə)rēən/ ▸n. person from 70 to 79 years old. ▸adj. of this age.

**sep·ul·cher** /ˈsepəlkər/ (also **sep·ul·chre**) ▸n. tomb or burial place. —**sep·ul·chral** adj.

**seq.** ▸abbr. (pl. **seqq.**) the following.

**se·qua·cious** /siˈkwāSHəs/ ▸adj. (of a person) lacking independence or originality of thought.

**se·quel** /ˈsēkwəl/ ▸n. **1** what follows (esp. as a result). **2** novel, motion picture, etc.,

that continues the story of an earlier one.

**se·que·la** /siˈkwelə/ ▸n. (pl. **-que·lae** /-ˈkwelē; -ˈkwelī/) (usu. **sequelae**) condition that is the consequence of a previous disease or injury.

**se·quence** /ˈsēkwəns/ ▸n. **1** (order of) succession. **2** set of things belonging next to one another. **3** part of a motion picture, etc., dealing with one scene or topic. ▸v. arrange in a definite order. —**se·quen·tial** adj. —**se·quen·tial·ly** adv.

**se·quent** /ˈsēkwənt/ ▸adj. following in a sequence or as a logical conclusion.

**se·ques·ter** /siˈkwestər/ ▸v. seclude; isolate; set apart.

**se·quin** /ˈsēkwin/ ▸n. circular spangle for attaching to clothing as an ornament. —**se·quined** adj.

**se·quoi·a** /səˈk(w)oi-ə/ ▸n. Californian evergreen coniferous tree of very great height.

**se·rac** /səˈrak/ ▸n. pinnacle or ridge of ice on the surface of a glacier.

**ser·aph** /ˈserəf/ ▸n. (pl. **-a·phim** or **-aphs**) angelic being of the highest order of the celestial hierarchy. **—se·raph·ic** *adj.*

**ser·e·nade** /ˌserə'nād/ ▶*n.* piece of music sung or played at night, esp. by a lover under his lady's window.
▶*v.* sing or play a serenade to.

**ser·en·dip·i·ty** /ˌserən'dipitē/ ▶*n.* occurrence of events by chance in a happy way. **—ser·en·dip·i·tous** *adj.* **—ser·en·dip·i·tous·ly** *adv.*

**se·rene** /sə'rēn/ ▶*adj.* (**-ren·er, -ren·est**) **1 a** clear and calm. **b** unruffled. **2** placid; tranquil; unperturbed. **—se·rene·ly** *adv.* **—se·ren·i·ty** *n.*

**serf** /sərf/ ▶*n.* agricultural laborer bound under the feudal system to work a lord's estate. **—serf·dom** *n.*

**serge** /sərj/ ▶*n.* durable twilled worsted, etc., fabric.

**ser·geant** /'särjənt/ ▶*n.* **1** noncommissioned army, marine, or air force officer next below warrant officer. **2** police officer ranking below captain.

**se·ri·al** /'si(ə)rēəl/ ▶*n.* story, play, etc., published, broadcast, or shown in regular installments.
▶*adj.* **1** of or in or forming a series. **2** (of a story, etc.) in the form of a serial. **—se·ri·al·ize** *v.*

**—se·ri·al·i·za·tion** *n.* **—se·ri·al·ly** *adv.*

**ser·i·cul·ture** /'seri,kəlcHər/ ▶*n.* production of silk and the rearing of silkworms for this purpose.

**se·ries** /'si(ə)rēz/ ▶*n.* (*pl.* same) **1** number of things of which each is similar to the preceding or in which each successive pair are similarly related; sequence, succession, order, row, or set. **2** set of successive games between the same teams. **3** set of related but individual television programs.

**ser·if** /'serif/ ▶*n.* slight projection extending from the main part of a letter, as in the top and bottom of I.

**ser·i·graph** /'seri,graf/ ▶*n.* printed design produced by means of a silkscreen.

**se·ri·ous** /'si(ə)rēəs/ ▶*adj.* **1** thoughtful; earnest; sober. **2** important; demanding consideration. **3** not slight nor negligible. **4** sincere; not ironic nor joking. **—se·ri·ous·ly** *adv.* **—se·ri·ous·ness** *n.*

**ser·mon** /'sərmən/ ▶*n.* **1** spoken or written discourse on a religious or moral subject, esp. a discourse based on a text or passage of Scripture and delivered in a place of worship. **2** piece of admonition or reproof; lecture. —**ser·mon·ize** v.

**se·ro·neg·a·tive** /ˌsi(ə)rō-ˈnegətiv/ ▶adj. giving a negative result in a test of blood serum, e.g., for the presence of a virus.

**se·ro·pos·i·tive** /ˌsi(ə)rōˈpäzitiv/ ▶adj. giving a positive result in a test of blood serum, e.g., for the presence of a virus.

**ser·pent** /ˈsərpənt/ ▶n. **1 a** snake, esp. large. **b** scaly limbless reptile. **2** sly or treacherous person.

**ser·pen·tine** /ˈsərpənˌtēn; -ˌtīn/ ▶adj. **1** of or like a serpent. **2** coiling; tortuous; sinuous; meandering; writhing. **3** cunning; subtle; treacherous.

**ser·rat·ed** /səˈrātid/ ▶adj. having an edge with sawlike teeth, for cutting.

**ser·ried** /ˈserēd/ ▶adj. (of rows of people or things) standing close together.

**se·rum** /ˈsi(ə)rəm/ ▶n. (pl. **-ra** or **-rums**) **1** liquid that separates from a clot when blood coagulates, used esp. in inoculations. **2** watery fluid in animal bodies.

**serv·ant** /ˈsərvənt/ ▶n. **1** person employed to do domestic duties. **2** devoted follower; person willing to serve another.

**serve** /sərv/ ▶v. **1** do a service for (a person, community, etc.). **2** be a servant (to). **3** carry out duties. **4 a** be employed (in an organization, the armed forces, etc.). **b** be a member of the armed forces. **5** be useful; meet requirements (of); perform a function. **6** attend to (a customer). **7** deliver (a subpoena, etc.) to (someone). **8** Sports deliver (a ball, etc.) to begin or resume play.

▶n. Sports act or instance of serving. —**serv·er** n.

□ **serve a person right** be a person's deserved punishment or misfortune.

**serv·ice** /ˈsərvis/ ▶n. **1** helping or doing work for another or for a community, etc. **2** work done in this way. **3** assistance or benefit given. **4** supplying of a public need, e.g., water, gas, etc. **5** employment as a servant. **6** state or period of employment. **7** public department or organization: civil service. **8** (**services**) the armed forces. **9** ceremony of worship. **10** maintenance of a machine,

etc. **11** serving of food, drinks, etc. **12** set of dishes, etc., for serving meals. **13** *Sports* **a** act or instance of serving. **b** person's turn to serve.
▶*v.* **1** provide a service. **2** maintain or repair (a car, machine, etc.). —**serv·ice·man** *n.*
□ **at a person's service** ready to serve a person. □ **service industry** one providing services not goods.

**serv·ice·a·ble** ▶*adj.* **1** useful or usable. **2** able to render service. **3** durable but plain. —**serv·ice·a·bil·i·ty** *n.*

**ser·vile** /ˈsərvīl/ ▶*adj.* slavish; fawning; completely dependent. —**ser·vil·i·ty** *n.*

**ser·vi·tude** /ˈsərviˌt(y) o͞od/ ▶*n.* **1** slavery. **2** subjection (esp. involuntary); bondage.

**ses·a·me** /ˈsesəmē/ ▶*n.* seed of an E. Indian plant, used as food and yielding an edible oil.

**ses·sion** /ˈseSHən/ ▶*n.* **1** assembly of a deliberative or judicial body to conduct its business. **2** single meeting for this purpose. **3** period during which such meetings are regularly held.

**set**[1] /set/ ▶*v.* (**set·ting**; *past* and *past part.* **set**) **1** put, lay, or stand (a thing) in a certain position or location. **2 a** make ready or fix in position. **b** dispose suitably for use, action, or display. **3** adjust (a clock, watch, alarm, etc.) to show or sound at the right time. **4** insert (a jewel) in a ring, framework, etc. **5** lay (a table) for a meal. **6** arrange (the hair) while damp so that it dries in the required style. **7** harden or solidify. **8** (of the sun, moon, etc.) appear to move below the horizon. **9** represent (a story, etc.) as happening in a certain time or place. **10** establish (a record, etc.). **11 a** put parts of (a broken or dislocated bone, limb, etc.) into the correct position for healing. **b** deal with (a fracture or dislocation) in this way. **12** provide (words, etc.) with music for singing. **13 a** arrange or produce (type, film, etc.) as required. **b** arrange the type, film, etc., for (a book, etc.). **14 a** cause (a hen) to sit on eggs. **b** place (eggs) for a hen to sit on.

□ **set about** begin. □ **set down 1** record in writing. **2** land an aircraft. □ **set forth 1** begin a journey. **2** make known. □ **set out 1** begin a journey. **2** (**set out to**) intend. □ **set up 1** place in position or view. **2** organize or start (a business, etc.).

**set**[2] ▸*n.* **1** group of linked, related, or similar persons or things. **2** collection of implements, vessels, etc., regarded collectively and needed for a specified purpose. **3** radio or television receiver. **4** (in tennis, etc.) group of games counting as a unit toward a match. **5** setting, including stage furniture, etc., for a play, etc.

▸*adj.* **1** fixed or arranged in advance. **2** unlikely to change. **3** ready, prepared, or likely to do something.

**set·back** ▸*n.* **1** reversal or arrest of progress. **2** relapse.

**set·tee** /seˈtē/ ▸*n.* seat (usu. upholstered), with a back and usu. arms, for more than one person.

**set·ter** ▸*n.* **1** dog of a large, long-haired breed trained to stand rigid when scenting game. **2** this breed.

**set·ting** ▸*n.* **1** position or manner in which a thing is set. **2** immediate surroundings (of a house, etc.). **3** surroundings of any object regarded as its framework; the environment of

a thing. **4** place and time, scenery, etc., of a story, drama, etc. **5** mounting in which a jewel is set. **6** set of cutlery and other accessories for one person at a table.

**set·tle** /ˈsetl/ ▸*v.* **1** establish or become established in an abode or way of life. **2 a** cease or cause to cease from wandering, disturbance, movement, etc. **b** adopt a regular or secure style of life. **3 a** sit or come down to stay for some time. **b** cause to do this. **4** bring to or attain fixity, certainty, composure, or quietness. **5** determine or decide or agree upon. **6** resolve (a dispute, etc.) or terminate (a lawsuit). **7** pay (a debt, an account, etc.). **8** colonize. **9** subside. —**set·tle·ment** *n.* —**set·tler** *n.*

**set·up** ▸*n.* **1** arrangement or organization. **2** manner, structure, or position of this. **3** *inf.* trick or conspiracy, esp. to make an innocent person appear guilty.

**sev·en** /ˈsevən/ ▸*n.* **1** one more than six. **2** symbol for this (7, vii, VII). —**sev·enth** *adj. & n.*

**sev·en·teen** ▸*n.* **1** one more than sixteen. **2** symbol for this

(17, xvii, XVII). —**sev·en·teenth** *adj. & n.*

**sev·en·ty** ▶*n. (pl.* **-ties**) **1** seven times ten. **2** symbol for this (70, lxx, LXX). **3** (**seventies**) the numbers from 70 to 79, esp. the years of a century or of a person's life. —**sev·en·ti·eth** *adj. & n.* —**sev·en·ty·fold** *adj. & adv.*

**sev·er** /ˈsevər/ ▶*v.* **1** divide, break, or make separate, esp. by cutting. **2** part; divide: *severed our friendship.* —**sev·er·a·ble** *adj.* —**sev·er·ance** *n.*

**sev·er·al** /ˈsev(ə)rəl/ ▶*adj.* **1** more than two but not many. **2** separate or respective. ▶*n.* some; a few.

**se·vere** /səˈvi(ə)r/ ▶*adj.* **1** rigorous, strict, and harsh. **2** serious; critical. **3** unadorned; plain in style. —**se·vere·ly** *adv.* —**se·ver·i·ty** *n.*

**sew** /sō/ ▶*v.* (*past part.* **sewn** or **sewed**) fasten, join, etc., by making stitches with a needle and thread or a sewing machine. —**sew·er** *n.* —**sew·ing** *n. & adj.* □ **sew something up** *inf.* bring something to a satisfactory conclusion.

**sew·age** /ˈsōōij/ ▶*n.* waste matter conveyed in sewers.

**sew·er** /ˈsōōər/ ▶*n.* conduit, usu. underground, for carrying off drainage water and waste matter.

**sex** /seks/ ▶*n.* **1** either of the main divisions (male and female) into which living things are placed on the basis of their reproductive functions. **2** sexual instincts, desires, etc., or their manifestation. **3** *inf.* sexual intercourse. ▶*adj.* of or relating to sex: *sex education.* —**sex·less** *adj.*

**sex·a·ge·nar·i·an** /ˌseksəjəˈne(ə)reən/ ▶*n.* person from 60 to 69 years old. ▶*adj.* of this age.

**sex·ism** ▶*n.* prejudice or discrimination, esp. against women, on the grounds of sex. —**sex·ist** *adj. & n.*

**sex·tant** /ˈsekstənt/ ▶*n.* instrument for measuring the angular distance of objects by means of mirrors.

**sex·tet** /seksˈtet/ ▶*n.* **1** *Mus.* composition for six voices or instruments. **2** performers of such a piece. **3** any group of six.

**sex·ton** /ˈsekstən/ ▶*n.* person who looks after a church and churchyard.

**sex·u·al** /ˈsekshōōəl/ ▶*adj.* of or relating to sex, to the sexes, or

to the relations between them.
—**sex·u·al·i·ty** *n.* —**sex·u·al·ly** *adv.*

**sex·u·al ha·rass·ment** ▸*n.* harassment in a workplace, etc., involving unwanted sexual advances.

**sex·u·al in·ter·course** ▸*n.* insertion of a man's erect penis into a woman's vagina, usu. followed by the ejaculation of semen.

**sex·y** ▸*adj.* (**-i·er**, **-i·est**) **1** sexually attractive or stimulating. **2** sexually aroused. —**sex·i·ly** *adv.* —**sex·i·ness** *n.*

**Sgt.** (also **SGT**) ▸*abbr.* Sergeant.

**shab·by** /ˈSHabē/ ▸*adj.* (**-bi·er**, **-bi·est**) **1** in bad repair or condition; faded and worn. **2** contemptible; dishonorable. —**shab·bi·ly** *adv.* —**shab·bi·ness** *n.*

**shack** /SHak/ ▸*n.* roughly built hut or cabin.

**shack·le** /ˈSHakəl/ ▸*n.* **1** metal loop or link, closed by a bolt, to connect chains, etc. **2** (**shackles**) pair of fetters enclosing the ankles or wrists. **3** (**shackles**) something that restrains or impedes. ▸*v.* fetter; impede; restrain.

**shad** /SHad/ ▸*n.* (*pl.* same or

shads) edible marine fish spawning in fresh water.

**shade** /SHād/ ▸*n.* **1** comparative darkness (and usu. coolness) caused by shelter from direct light. **2** area so sheltered. **3** color, esp. as distinguished from one nearly like it. **4** slight amount. **5** screen excluding or moderating light. **6** (**shades**) *inf.* sunglasses. ▸*v.* **1** screen from light. **2** cover, moderate, or exclude the light of. **3** darken, esp. with parallel pencil lines to represent shadow, etc. —**shade·less** *adj.*

**shad·ow** /ˈSHadō/ ▸*n.* **1** shade; patch of shade projected by a body intercepting light. **2** slightest trace; weak or insubstantial remnant. **3** shaded part of a picture. **4** gloom or sadness. ▸*v.* **1** cast a shadow over. **2** secretly follow and watch. —**shad·ow·er** *n.* —**shad·ow·less** *adj.* —**shad·ow·y** *adj.*

**shad·y** /ˈSHādē/ ▸*adj.* (**-i·er**, **-i·est**) **1** giving shade. **2** situated in shade. **3** (of a person or behavior) disreputable; of doubtful honesty. —**shad·i·ly** *adv.* —**shad·i·ness** *n.*

**shaft** /SHaft/ ▸*n.* **1 a** arrow or

spear. **b** long slender stem of these. **2** remark intended to hurt or provoke. **3** stem or handle of a tool, implement, etc. **4** long narrow space, usu. vertical, for access to a mine, for ventilation, etc. **5** long and narrow part transmitting motion between other parts. **6** central stem of a feather.

▸*v. inf.* treat unfairly.

**shag** /SHag/ ▸*n.* **1** rough growth or mass of hair, carpet pile, etc. **2** coarse kind of cut tobacco. —**shag·gi·ness** *n.* —**shag·gy** *adj.*

**shah** /SHä/ ▸*n.* title of the former monarch of Iran.

**shake** /SHāk/ ▸*v.* (*past* **shook**; *past part.* **shak·en**) **1** move forcefully or quickly up and down or to and fro. **2** tremble or vibrate markedly or cause to do this. **3** *inf.* astonish or upset the composure of.

▸*n.* **1** shaking; being shaken. **2** (**the shakes**) *inf.* fit of trembling or shivering. **3** shingle made by splitting sections from a log.

□ **shake hands** clasp right hands at meeting or parting, in reconciliation or congratulation, etc. □ **shake off** get rid of (something unwanted). □ **shake**

**up 1** mix (ingredients) by shaking. **2** make uncomfortable. **3** rouse from lethargy, apathy, conventionality, etc. □ **shake-up** upheaval or drastic reorganization.

**shake·down** ▸*n. inf.* **1** radical change or restructuring. **2** thorough search. **3** extortion.

**shak·y** ▸*adj.* (**-i·er, -i·est**) **1** unsteady; trembling. **2** unsound; infirm. **3** unreliable. —**shak·i·ly** *adv.* —**shak·i·ness** *n.*

**shale** /SHāl/ ▸*n.* soft rock of consolidated mud or clay that splits easily. —**shal·y** *adj.*

**shall** /SHal/ ▸*v.* (*3rd sing. present* **shall**; *past* **should**) **1** (in the 1st person) expressing the future tense (*I shall return soon*) or (with *shall* stressed) emphatic intention (*I shall have a party*). **2** (in the 2nd and 3rd persons) expressing strong assertion or command rather than a wish (see **WILL**): *you shall not catch me again.*

**shal·lot** /SHə'lät; 'SHalət/ ▸*n.* onionlike plant with a cluster of small edible bulbs.

**shal·low** /'SHalō/ ▸*adj.* **1** of little depth. **2** superficial; trivial.

▸*pl. n.* (**shallows**) shallow place. —**shal·low·ness** *n.*

**sham** /sham/ ▸*v.* (**shammed, sham·ming**) feign; pretend.

▸*n.* **1** imposture; pretense. **2** person or thing pretending or pretended to be what he or she or it is not.

▸*adj.* counterfeit.

**sham·ble** /ˈshambəl/ ▸*v.* walk or run with a shuffling or awkward gait.

▸*n.* **1** shambling gait. **2** (**shambles**) [treated as *sing.*] **a** scene of destruction. **b** condition of disorder.

**shame** /shām/ ▸*n.* **1** distress or humiliation caused by consciousness of one's guilt or folly. **2** capacity for experiencing this feeling, esp. as imposing a restraint on behavior: *has no sense of shame.* **3** state of disgrace, discredit, or intense regret. **4 a** person or thing that brings disgrace, etc. **b** thing or action that is wrong or regrettable.

▸*v.* **1** bring shame on; make ashamed. **2** force by shame. —**shame·ful** *adj.* —**shame·ful·ly** *adv.* —**shame·ful·ness** *n.* —**shame·less** *adj.* —**shame·less·ness** *n.*

**shame·faced** ▸*adj.* **1** showing shame. **2** bashful; diffident.

**sham·poo** /sham'poo/ ▸*n.* **1** substance used to wash hair, a car, a carpet, etc. **2** act or instance of cleaning with shampoo.

▸*v.* (**-poos, -pooed**) wash with shampoo.

**sham·rock** ▸*n.* plant with trifoliate leaves; national emblem of Ireland.

**shang·hai** /ˈshang'hī/ ▸*v.* (**-hais, -haied, -hai·ing**) trick or force (a person) into working.

**shank** /shangk/ ▸*n.* **1** lower part of the leg. **2** shaft or stem. **3** long narrow part of a tool, etc., joining the handle to the working end.

**shanks' mare** (also **shanks' pony**) ▸*n.* used to refer to one's own legs and the action of walking as a means of conveyance.

**shan·ty** /ˈshantē/ ▸*n.* (*pl.* **-ties**) hut or cabin.

**shape** /shāp/ ▸*n.* **1** external form or appearance; outline: *a shape emerged from the mist.* **2** condition: *the building was in poor shape.* **3** definite or orderly arrangement.

▸*v.* **1** give a certain shape or form to; fashion. **2** have a great

influence on. **—shape·less** *adj.*
**—shape·less·ness** *n.*

□ **shape up** show promise; make good progress.

**shape·ly** ▸*adj.* (**-li·er, -li·est**) having an attractive shape. **—shape·li·ness** *n.*

**shape·shift·er** /'SHāp,SHiftər/ ▸*n.* (chiefly in fiction) a person or being with the ability to change their physical form at will.

**shard** /SHärd/ ▸*n.* fragment of pottery.

**share** /SHe(ə)r/ ▸*n.* **1** portion that a person receives from or gives to a common amount. **2 a** part contributed by an individual to an enterprise or commitment. **b** part received by an individual from this. ▸*v.* **1** get or have or give a share (of). **2** use or benefit from jointly with others. **3** (**share in**) participate in. **—shar·er** *n.*

**sha·ri·a** /SHä'rēə/ (also **sha·ri·ah** or **sha·ri·at** /-ät/) ▸*n.* Islamic canonical law based on the teachings of the Koran and the traditions of the Prophet, prescribing both religious and secular duties and sometimes retributive penalties for lawbreaking.

**shark** /SHärk/ ▸*n.* **1** large, usu. voracious marine fish with a long body and prominent dorsal fin. **2** *inf.* swindler; profiteer.

**sharp** /SHärp/ ▸*adj.* **1** having an edge or point able to cut or pierce. **2** tapering to a point or edge. **3** abrupt; steep. **4** well-defined; clean-cut. **5** severe or intense. **6** (of a voice or sound) shrill and piercing. **7** (of words, etc.) harsh or acrimonious: *had a sharp tongue.* **8** acute; quick to comprehend. **9** quick to take advantage; artful. **10** *Mus.* raised by a semitone. **11** *inf.* stylish. ▸*n.* **1** *Mus.* **a** note raised a semitone above natural pitch. **b** the sign (♯) indicating this. **2** *inf.* swindler; cheat. ▸*adv.* **1** punctually. **2** *Mus.* above true pitch. **—sharp·ly** *adv.* **—sharp·ness** *n.*

**sharp·en** ▸*v.* make or become sharp or sharper. **—sharp·en·er** *n.*

**sharp·shoot·er** ▸*n.* skilled marksman.

**shat·ter** /'SHatər/ ▸*v.* **1** break suddenly in pieces. **2** severely damage or utterly destroy. **3** greatly upset. **—shat·ter·ing** *adj.* **—shat·ter·ing·ly** *adv.* **—shat·ter-proof** *adj.*

**shave** /SHāv/ ▸*v.* (*past part.*

**shaved** or **shav·en**) **1** remove (bristles or hair) with a razor. **2** reduce by a small amount. **3** pass close to without touching; miss narrowly.
▶*n.* shaving or being shaved.
—**shav·er** *n.*

**shav·ing** ▶*n.* sliver of wood.

**shawl** /SHôl/ ▶*n.* piece of fabric, usu. rectangular, worn over the shoulders or head.

**she** /SHē/ ▶*pron.* (*obj.* **her**; *poss.* **her**; *pl.* **they**) **1** woman or girl or female animal previously named or in question. **2** thing regarded as female, as a vehicle or ship.
▶*n.* female; woman.

**sheaf** /SHēf/ ▶*n.* (*pl.* **sheaves**) group of things laid lengthwise together and usu. tied, esp. grain stalks, etc.

**shear** /SHi(ə)r/ ▶*v.* (*past* **sheared**; *past part.* **shorn** or **sheared**) **1** cut with scissors, shears, etc. **2** remove by cutting.
▶*pl. n* (**shears**) large scissors.
—**shear·er** *n.*

**sheath** /SHēTH/ ▶*n.* (*pl.* **sheaths**) **1** close-fitting cover for the blade of a knife or sword. **2** structure in living tissue that closely envelops another. **3** woman's close-fitting dress. **4** condom.

**sheathe** /SHēTH/ ▶*v.* **1** put into a sheath. **2** encase; protect with a sheath.

**she·bang** /SHə'baNG/ ▶*n. inf.* matter; set of circumstances: *the whole shebang.*

**shed** /SHed/ ▶*n.* one-story structure, usu. of wood, used for storage, as a shelter for animals, etc., or as a workshop.
▶*v.* (**shed·ding**; *past* and *past part.* **shed**) **1** let or cause to fall off. **2** take off (clothes). **3** cause to fall or flow: *shed blood.* **4** disperse; diffuse; radiate: *shed light.*

**sheen** /SHēn/ ▶*n.* **1** gloss or luster. **2** radiance; brightness.

**sheep** /SHēp/ ▶*n.* (*pl.* same) **1** ruminant mammal with a thick woolly coat, esp. kept in flocks for its wool or meat. **2** bashful, timid, or silly person.

**sheep·dog** ▶*n.* **1** dog trained to guard and herd sheep. **2** dog of various breeds suitable for this.

**sheep·fold** ▶*n.* enclosure for sheep.

**sheep·ish** ▶*adj.* **1** bashful; shy; reticent. **2** embarrassed, esp. because of shame.
—**sheep·ish·ly** *adv.*
—**sheep·ish·ness** *n.*

**sheer** /SHi(ə)r/ ▶*adj.* **1** unqualified; absolute: *sheer* *luck.* **2** (of a cliff, ascent, etc.) perpendicular. **3** (of a textile) diaphanous.

▶*adv.* **1** directly; outright. **2** perpendicularly.

▶*v.* swerve or change course.
—**sheer·ly** *adv.* —**sheer·ness** *n.*

**sheet** /SHēt/ ▶*n.* **1** large rectangular piece of cotton or other fabric, used for bedclothes. **2** broad usu. thin flat piece of material (e.g., paper or metal). **3** wide continuous surface or expanse of water, ice, flame, falling rain, etc. **4** rope attached to the lower corner of a sail for securing or controlling it.

□ **sheet music** music published on unbound pages.

**sheik** /SHēk; SHāk/ ▶*n.* Arab ruler.
—**sheik·dom** *n.*

**shek·el** /'SHekəl/ ▶*n.* **1** chief monetary unit of modern Israel. **2** (**shekels**) *inf.* money; riches.

**shelf** /SHelf/ ▶*n.* (*pl.* **shelves**) **1** flat piece of wood or metal, etc., projecting from a wall, or as part of a unit, used to support books, etc. **2** ledge or recess.
—**shelved** *adj.*

□ **on the shelf** postponed, as a plan or project.

**shelf life** ▶*n.* amount of time for which a stored item remains usable.

**shell** /SHel/ ▶*n.* **1** hard outer case of many marine mollusks, tortoises, eggs, nuts, etc. **2** explosive projectile for use in a gun or mortar. **3** outer structure, esp. when hollow.

▶*v.* **1** remove the shell or pod from. **2** bombard with shells.
—**shelled** *adj.* —**shell-like** *adj.*

□ **shell out** *inf.* pay (money).

**shel·lac** /SHə'lak/ ▶*n.* lac resin used for making varnish.

▶*v.* (**-lacked, -lack·ing**) **1** coat with shellac. **2** *inf.* defeat or thrash soundly.

**shell·fish** ▶*n.* **1** shelled mollusk, e.g., an oyster or mussel. **2** crustacean, e.g., a crab or shrimp.

**shell shock** ▶*n.* nervous breakdown resulting from exposure to battle. —**shell-shocked** *adj.*

**shel·ter** /'SHeltər/ ▶*n.* **1** protection from danger, bad weather, etc. **2** place of refuge.

▶*v.* **1** serve as or provide with shelter to; protect. **2** find refuge; take cover.

**shelve** /SHelv/ ▶*v.* **1** put (books, etc.) on a shelf. **2** abandon or defer (a plan, etc.).

**shep·herd** /ˈSHepərd/ ▶*n.* person employed to tend sheep.
▶*v.* **1** tend (sheep, etc.) as a shepherd. **2** guide (followers, etc.).

**sher·bet** /ˈSHərbit/ ▶*n.* fruit-flavored ice confection.

**sher·iff** /ˈSHerif/ ▶*n.* civil law-enforcement officer.

**sher·ry** /ˈSHerē/ ▶*n.* (*pl.* **-ries**) fortified wine.

**shib·bo·leth** /ˈSHibəliTH/ ▶*n.* long-standing formula, doctrine, phrase, etc., held to be true by a party or sect.

**shield** /SHēld/ ▶*n.* **1** broad piece of metal, etc., used as protection against blows or a missile. **2** something shaped like a shield. **3** person or thing serving to protect.
▶*v.* protect or screen.

**shift** /SHift/ ▶*v.* **1** change or move or cause to change or move from one position to another. **2** manage as best one can. **3** change gear in a vehicle.
▶*n.* **1** act or instance of shifting. **2** substitution of one thing for another; rotation. **3** periods in which different groups of workers do the same jobs in relays: *the night shift.* **4** woman's straight unwaisted dress. **5** (also

**shift key**) key on a keyboard used to switch between lowercase and uppercase, etc. **6** gear lever in a motor vehicle.

**shift·less** ▶*adj.* lacking resourcefulness; lazy; inefficient. —**shift·less·ly** *adv.* —**shift·less·ness** *n.*

**shift·y** ▶*adj.* (**-i·er, -i·est**) *inf.* evasive; deceitful. —**shift·i·ly** *adv.* —**shift·i·ness** *n.*

**shik·sa** /ˈSHiksə/ ▶*n.* (used esp. by Jews) a gentile girl or woman.

**shill** /SHil/ ▶*n.* person employed to decoy or entice others into buying, gambling, etc.

**shil·ling** /ˈSHiliNG/ ▶*n.* former British coin and monetary unit worth one-twentieth of a pound.

**shil·ly-shal·ly** /ˈSHilē ˌSHalē/ ▶*v.* (**-lied**) be undecided; vacillate.

**shim** /SHim/ ▶*n.* washer or thin strip of material used to align parts, make them fit, or reduce wear.
▶*v.* (**shimmed, shim·ming**) wedge (something) or fill up (a space) with a shim.

**shim·mer** /ˈSHimər/ ▶*v.* shine with a tremulous or faint diffused light.
▶*n.* such a light. —**shim·mer·ing·ly** *adv.* —**shim·mer·y** *adj.*

**shin** /SHin/ ▸n. **1** front of the leg below the knee. **2** cut of beef from the lower foreleg.
▸v. (**shinned shin·ning**) climb quickly by clinging with the arms and legs: *he shinned up the pole.*

**shin·dig** ▸n. inf. festive, esp. noisy, party.

**shine** /SHīn/ ▸v. (*past* and *past part.* **shone** or **shined**) **1** emit or reflect light; be bright; glow. **2** (of the sun, a star, etc.) be visible. **3** cause (a lamp, etc.) to shine. **4** (*past* and *past part.* **shined**) polish. **5** be brilliant; excel.
▸n. **1** light; brightness, esp. reflected. **2** high polish; luster. —**shin·ing** *adj.* —**shin·y** *adj.*

**shin·gle** /ˈSHiNGgəl/ ▸n. **1** rectangular tile used on roofs, spires, or esp. walls. **2** small signboard, esp. of a doctor, lawyer, etc. **3** area of small pebbles on a beach. **4** (**shingles**) [treated as *sing.*] *Med.* acute, painful inflammation of the nerve ganglia, causing a rash of small blisters.
▸v. roof or clad with shingles.

**Shin·to** /ˈSHintō/ ▸n. official religion of Japan, incorporating the worship of ancestors and nature spirits. —**Shin·to·ism** *n.* —**Shin·to·ist** *n.*

**ship** /SHip/ ▸n. **1** large seagoing vessel. **2** aircraft. **3** spaceship.
▸v. (**shipped, ship·ping**) put, take, or send in a ship, etc. —**ship·pa·ble** *adj.* —**ship·per** *n.*

**-ship** ▸suffix forming nouns denoting: **1** quality or condition: *hardship.* **2** status, office, or tenurer: *authorship* | *chairmanship.* **3** collective individuals of a group: *membership.*

**ship·ment** ▸n. **1** shipping of goods. **2** goods shipped.

**ship·shape** ▸adv. & adj. in good order; trim and neat.

**ship·wreck** ▸n. **1 a** destruction of a ship by a storm, foundering, etc. **b** ship so destroyed. **2** destruction of hopes, dreams, etc.

**ship·yard** ▸n. place where ships are built, repaired, etc.

**shire** /SHī(ə)r/ ▸n. county in Great Britain.

**shirk** /SHərk/ ▸v. avoid (duty, work, responsibility, fighting, etc.). —**shirk·er** *n.*

**shirt** /SHərt/ ▸n. upper-body garment, often having a collar and sleeves.

**shiv** /SHiv/ ▸*n.* knife or razor used as a weapon.

**shiv·a·ree** ▸*n.* variant spelling of CHARIVARI.

**shiv·er** /'SHivər/ ▸*v.* **1** tremble with cold, fear, etc. **2** break into shivers.
▸*n.* **1** momentary shivering movement. **2** (**the shivers**) attack of shivering: *got the shivers in the dark.* **3** (usu. **shivers**) small piece or splinter. —**shiv·er·y** *adj.*

**shoal** /SHōl/ ▸*n.* **1** great number of fish swimming together. **2** area of shallow water.
▸*v.* (of fish) form shoals.

**shock** /SHäk/ ▸*n.* **1** violent collision, impact, tremor, etc. **2** sudden and disturbing effect on the emotions, etc. **3** acute state of prostration following a wound, pain, etc., esp. when much blood is lost. **4** discharge of electricity through a person. **5** unkempt or shaggy mass of hair.
▸*v.* **1 a** horrify; outrage. **b** cause shock. **2** affect with an electric or pathological shock. —**shock·ing** *adj.*

**shock jock** ▸*n.* disc jockey on a talk-radio show who expresses opinions in a deliberately offensive or provocative way.

**shod·dy** /'SHädē/ ▸*adj.* (**-di·er, -di·est**) trashy; shabby; poorly made. —**shod·di·ly** *adv.* —**shod·di·ness** *n.*

**shoe** /SHo͞o/ ▸*n.* **1** outer foot covering having a sturdy sole and not reaching above the ankle. **2** metal rim nailed to the hoof of a horse, etc.; horseshoe. **3** (also **brake shoe**) part of a brake that presses against a wheel rim or drum.
▸*v.* (**shoe·ing**; *past* and *past part.* **shod**) **1** fit (esp. a horse, etc.) with a shoe or shoes. **2** (**be shod**) be wearing shoes of a specified kind. —**shoe·less** *adj.*

**shoe·horn** ▸*n.* curved piece of horn, metal, etc., for easing one's heel into a shoe.

**shoe·lace** ▸*n.* cord for fastening shoes.

**shoe·mak·er** ▸*n.* maker of boots and shoes. —**shoe·mak·ing** *n.*

**shoe·string** ▸*n.* **1** *inf.* small or inadequate budget. **2** shoelace.

**shoe tree** ▸*n.* shaped block for keeping a shoe in shape when not worn.

**sho·far** /'SHōfər; SHō'fär/ ▸*n.* (*pl.* **sho·fars** or **sho·froth** /SHō'frōt; -'frōs/) ram's-horn trumpet used by ancient Jews in religious ceremonies and as a battle signal, now sounded at Rosh Hashanah and Yom Kippur.

**sho·gun** /ˈSHōgən/ ▶*n.* any of a succession of Japanese hereditary commanders in chief and virtual rulers before 1868.

**shone** /SHōn/ ▶*v.* past and past part. of SHINE.

**shook** /SHŏŏk/ ▶*v.* past of SHAKE.

**shoot** /SHōōt/ ▶*v.* (*past* and *past part.* shot) **1 a** cause (a gun, bow, etc.) to fire. **b** discharge (a bullet, arrow, etc.) from a gun, bow, etc. **c** kill or wound (a person, animal, etc.) with a bullet, arrow, etc. **2** send out, discharge, come, go, etc., esp. swiftly. **3** (of a plant, etc.) put forth buds, etc. **4** film or photograph. **5** *Basketball, etc.* take a shot at (the goal). **6** (of a pain) pass with a stabbing sensation. **7** (**shoot up**) *inf.* inject, esp. oneself with (a drug). ▶*n.* **1** act or instance of shooting. **2** young branch or new growth of a plant. —**shoot·er** *n.* —**shoot·ing** *n. & adj.* □ **shoot-out** *inf.* decisive gunfight; showdown.

**shoot·ing star** ▶*n.* small, rapidly moving meteor.

**shop** /SHäp/ ▶*n.* **1** place for the retail sale of goods or services; store. **2** place for manufacture or repair; workshop: *my car is in the shop.* ▶*v.* (**shopped, shop·ping**) go to buy goods. —**shop·per** *n.* □ **shop around** look for the best bargain.

**shop·lift·er** ▶*n.* person who steals goods while appearing to shop. —**shop·lift·ing** *n.*

**shore** /SHôr/ ▶*n.* land that adjoins the sea or a large body of water. ▶*v.* (usu. **shore up**) support with or as if with a prop or beam; hold up.

**shorn** /SHôrn/ ▶past part. of SHEAR.

**short** /SHôrt/ ▶*adj.* **1 a** measuring little; not long from end to end. **b** not long in duration. **2** of small height; not tall. **3 a** (**short of/on**) deficient in. **b** *inf.* in insufficient supply: *food is short.* **c** not far-reaching. **4 a** concise; brief. **b** curt; uncivil. **5** (of pastry) crumbling; flaky. ▶*adv.* **1** abruptly. **2** rudely; uncivilly. ▶*n.* **1** short circuit. **2** short movie. ▶*v.* short-circuit. —**short·ness** *n.* □ **be caught short 1** be put at a

disadvantage. **2** be unprepared.
□ **short for** abbreviation for.

**short·age** /ˈsHôrtij/ ▸*n.*
deficiency; lack.

**short·bread** ▸*n.* crisp, rich,
crumbly type of cookie made
with butter, flour, and sugar.

**short·cake** ▸*n.* cake, pastry, or
biscuit with fruit and whipped
cream.

**short·change** ▸*v.* rob or cheat
by giving insufficient money as
change.

**short cir·cuit** ▸*n.* electric
circuit through low resistance,
esp. instead of the resistance of a
normal circuit.
—**short-cir·cuit** *v.*

**short·com·ing** ▸*n.* failure to
come up to a standard; defect.

**short cut** ▸*n.* **1** route
shortening the distance traveled.
**2** quick way of accomplishing
something.

**short·en** ▸*v.* make or become
shorter.

**short·en·ing** ▸*n.* fat used for
making pastry, bread, etc.

**short·fall** ▸*n.* deficit.

**short·hand** ▸*n.* method of rapid
writing.

**short·hand·ed** ▸*adj.*
understaffed.

**short list** (also **short·list**) ▸*n.*
selective list of candidates from
which a final choice is made.
▸*v.* (**short-list**) put (someone) on a
short list.

**short-lived** /-ˈlīvd; -ˈlivd/ ▸*adj.*
ephemeral; not long-lasting.

**short·ly** ▸*adv.* **1** soon. **2** briefly.
**3** curtly.

**short shrift** /sHrift/ ▸*n.* rapid
and unsympathetic dismissal: *the
judge gave the argument short
shrift.*

**short·sight·ed** ▸*adj.* lacking
imagination or foresight.

**short·stop** ▸*n.* baseball fielder
positioned between second and
third base.

**short sto·ry** ▸*n.* story with a
fully developed theme but
shorter than a novella.

**short·wave** ▸*n.* radio that
receives long-distance signals
carried by waves shorter than
those used for commercial
broadcasts.

**Sho·sho·ne** /sHōˈsHōnē/ (also
**Sho·sho·ni**) ▸*n.* **1 a** N. American
Indian people native to the
western U.S. **b** member of this
people. **2** language of this
people.

**shot** /sHät/ ▸*n.* **1** firing of a gun,
cannon, etc. **2** attempt to hit by
shooting or throwing, etc.

**3 a** single nonexplosive missile for a cannon, gun, etc. **b** small lead pellet used in quantity in a single charge or cartridge in a shotgun. **4 a** photograph. **b** film sequence photographed continuously by one camera. **5 a** stroke or kick in a ball game. **b** *inf.* an attempt to guess or do something: *let her have a shot at it.* **6** launch of a space rocket: *a moon shot.* **7** *inf.* **a** drink of liquor. **b** hypodermic injection.

▶*v.* past and past part. of **SHOOT**.

▶*adj. inf.* exhausted; finished.

**shot·gun** ▶*n.* gun for firing small shot.

**should** /sнŏŏd/ ▶*v. aux.* (*3rd sing.* **should**) **1** past of **SHALL**, used esp.: **a** to express a duty, obligation, or likelihood; ought to: *you should be more careful.* **b** (in the 1st person) to express a tentative suggestion: *I should like to say something.* **2** forming an indefinite clause: *if you should see him.*

**shoul·der** /'sнōldər/ ▶*n.* **1 a** part of the body at which the arm, foreleg, or wing is attached. **b** the top of the upper arm. **c** either of the two projections below the neck from which the arms hang. **2** upper foreleg and

shoulder blade of a pig, lamb, etc., when butchered. **3** (often **shoulders**) **a** the upper part of the back and arm. **b** this part of the body regarded as capable of bearing a burden or blame, providing comfort, etc. **4** strip of land next to a paved road.

▶*v.* **1 a** push with the shoulder. **b** make one's way by jostling. **2** take on (a burden, etc.).

☐ **shoulder blade** either of the large flat bones of the upper back.

**shout** /sноut/ ▶*v.* **1** speak or cry loudly. **2** say or express loudly.

▶*n.* loud cry. —**shout·er** *n.*

**shove** /sнəv/ ▶*v.* **1** push vigorously. **2** make one's way by pushing. **3** *inf.* put somewhere: *shoved it in the drawer.*

▶*n.* act of shoving.

☐ **shove off 1** start from the shore in a boat. **2** *inf.* depart; go away: *told him to shove off.*

**shov·el** /'sнəvəl/ ▶*n.* spadelike tool with raised sides for shifting quantities of earth, snow, etc.

▶*v.* **1** shift or clear (coal, etc.) with or as if with a shovel. **2** *inf.* move (esp. food) in large quantities or roughly: *shoveled peas into his mouth.*

**show** /sнō/ ▶*v.* (*past part.* **shown**

or **showed**) **1** be, allow, or cause to be visible; manifest. **2** offer, exhibit, or produce for scrutiny, etc. **3** indicate or reveal (one's feelings). **4** (of feelings, etc.) be manifest. **5 a** demonstrate. **b** cause (a person) to understand. **6** conduct or lead.

▶*n.* **1** act or instance of showing; state of being shown. **2 a** spectacle, display, exhibition, etc. **b** collection of things, etc., shown for public entertainment or in competition: *flower show.* **3 a** play, etc., esp. a musical. **b** entertainment program on television, etc. **c** any public entertainment or performance. **4** outward appearance or display. □ **show off 1** display to advantage. **2** *inf.* act pretentiously. □ **show-off** *inf.* person who shows off.

**show·case** ▶*n.* **1** glass case used for exhibiting goods, etc. **2** event, etc., for presenting (esp. attractively) to general attention. ▶*v.* display in or as if in a showcase.

**show·down** ▶*n.* final test or confrontation; decisive situation.

**show·er** /'shouər/ ▶*n.* **1** brief fall of esp. rain, hail, sleet, or snow. **2 a** brisk flurry of bullets,

dust, etc. **b** similar flurry of gifts, honors, etc. **3 a** cubicle, bath, etc., in which one bathes under a spray of water. **b** apparatus used for this. **c** act of bathing in a shower. **4** party for giving presents to a prospective bride, expectant mother, etc. ▶*v.* **1 a** discharge (water, missiles, etc.) in a shower. **b** make wet with or as if with a shower. **2** bathe in a shower. **3** lavishly bestow (gifts, etc.). **4** descend in a shower. —**show·er·y** *adj.*

**show·piece** ▶*n.* **1** item presented for exhibition or display. **2** outstanding specimen.

**show·place** ▶*n.* house, etc., that tourists go to see.

**show·y** ▶*adj.* (**-i·er, -i·est**) **1** brilliant; gaudy, esp. vulgarly so. **2** striking. —**show·i·ly** *adv.* —**show·i·ness** *n.*

**shrap·nel** /'shrapnəl/ ▶*n.* fragments of an exploded artillery shell, bomb, etc.

**shred** /shred/ ▶*n.* **1** scrap, fragment, or bit. **2** least amount. ▶*v.* (**shred·ded, shred·ding**) tear or cut into shreds. —**shred·der** *n.*

**shrew** /shrōō/ ▶*n.* **1** small, usu. insect-eating, mouselike mammal with a long pointed snout. **2** bad-tempered or scolding woman. —**shrew·ish** *adj.*

**shrewd** /SHrōōd/ ▶*adj.* astute; clever and judicious. —**shrewd·ly** *adv.* —**shrewd·ness** *n.*

**shriek** /SHrēk/ ▶*v.* **1** utter a shrill screeching sound. **2** utter (sounds or words) by shrieking: *shrieked his name.* ▶*n.* high-pitched piercing cry or scream.

**shrill** /SHril/ ▶*adj.* **1** piercing and high-pitched in sound. **2** (esp. of a protester) sharp; unrestrained; unreasoning. —**shril·ly** *adv.* —**shrill·ness** *n.*

**shrimp** /SHrimp/ ▶*n.* **1** (*pl.* same or **shrimps**) small (esp. marine) edible crustacean. **2** *inf.* small person.

**shrine** /SHrīn/ ▶*n.* **1** sacred or revered place. **2** place associated with or containing memorabilia of a particular event, etc.

**shrink** /SHriNGk/ ▶*v.* (*past* **shrank**; *past part.* **shrunk** or **shrunk·en**) **1** make or become smaller, esp. from moisture, heat, or cold. **2 a** retire; recoil; flinch; cower. **b** (**shrink from**) be averse to doing. ▶*n.* **1** act or instance of shrinking;

shrinkage. **2** *inf.* psychiatrist. —**shrink·a·ble** *adj.* —**shrink·proof** *adj.*

□ **shrink-wrap** enclose (an article) in plastic film. □ **shrink wrap** plastic film used to shrink-wrap.

**shrink·age** /ˈSHriNGkij/ ▶*n.* **1 a** process or fact of shrinking. **b** degree or amount of shrinking. **2** allowance made for loss due to wastage, theft, etc.

**shriv·el** /ˈSHrivəl/ ▶*v.* contract or wither into a wrinkled, folded, rolled-up, contorted, or dried-up state.

**shroud** /SHroud/ ▶*n.* **1** sheetlike garment for wrapping a corpse for burial. **2** anything that conceals. **3** (**shrouds**) *Naut.* ropes supporting the mast or topmast. ▶*v.* **1** clothe (a body) for burial. **2** cover, conceal, or disguise.

**shrub** /SHrəb/ ▶*n.* any woody plant smaller than a tree; bush. —**shrub·by** *adj.*

**shrub·ber·y** /ˈSHrəbərē/ ▶*n.* (*pl.* **-ies**) area planted with shrubs.

**shrug** /SHrəg/ ▶*v.* (**shrugged**, **shrug·ging**) **1** slightly and momentarily raise the shoulders to express indifference, helplessness, contempt, etc. **2** shrug the shoulders to express (indifference, etc.): *shrugged his consent.*

▶*n.* act or instance of shrugging.

□ **shrug off** dismiss as unimportant.

**shtetl** /ˈsʜtetl; ˈsʜtätl/ ▶*n. (pl.* **shtet·lach** /ˈsʜtetläкʜ; ˈsʜtätläкʜ/ or **shtetls**) small Jewish town or village in eastern Europe.

**shtick** /sʜtik/ ▶*n. inf.* theatrical routine, gimmick, etc.

**shuck** /sʜək/ ▶*n.* husk, pod, or shell.

▶*v.* **1** remove the shucks of; shell. **2** peel off or remove.

**shud·der** /ˈsʜədər/ ▶*v.* **1** shiver, esp. convulsively, from fear, cold, repugnance, etc. **2** feel strong repugnance.

▶*n.* act or instance of shuddering. —**shud·der·ing·ly** *adv.* —**shud·der·y** *adj.*

**shuf·fle** /ˈsʜəfəl/ ▶*v.* **1** drag (the feet) in walking. **2** rearrange or intermingle (playing cards, papers, etc.).

▶*n.* **1** shuffling movement. **2** act or instance of shuffling cards. **3** general change of relative positions.

**shuf·fle·board** ▶*n.* game played by pushing disks with a long-handled cue over a marked surface.

**shul** /sʜo͞ol; sʜo͝ol/ ▶*n.* synagogue.

**shun** /sʜən/ ▶*v.* (**shunned, shun·ning**) avoid; keep clear of.

**shunt** /sʜənt/ ▶*v.* **1** redirect or cause (a train) to be redirected, esp. onto a siding. **2** *Electr.* provide (a current) with a shunt. **3 a** postpone or evade. **b** divert (a decision, etc.) onto another person, etc.

▶*n.* **1** act or instance of shunting. **2** *Electr.* bypass for diverting current. **3** *Surgery* bypass for the circulation of the blood.

**shut** /sʜət/ ▶*v.* (**shut·ting**; *past* and *past part.* **shut**) **1 a** move (a door, window, lid, etc.) to block an aperture. **b** close (a room, window, box, eye, mouth, etc.) by moving a door, etc. **2** become closed. **3** fold or contract (a book, hand, telescope, etc.). **4** (**shut in/out**) keep (a person, sound, etc.) in or out of a room, etc.

□ **shut down 1** stop (a factory, nuclear reactor, etc.) from operating. **2** (of a factory, etc.) stop operating. □ **shut-in** invalid confined to home, bed, etc. □ **shut off 1** stop the flow of (water, gas, etc.). **2** separate from society, etc. □ **shut out 1** exclude. **2** prevent (an opponent) from scoring. □ **shut up** **1** close all doors and windows. **2** imprison. **3** *inf.* stop talking.

**shut·ter** ▶*n.* **1 a** movable, often louvered, cover for a window. **b** structure of slats on rollers used for the same purpose. **2** device that exposes the film in a camera. ▶*v.* put up the shutters of.

**shut·tle** /ˈSHətl/ ▶*n.* **1** bobbin with two pointed ends used for carrying the weft thread across between the warp threads in weaving. **2** train, bus, etc., going back and forth over a short route continuously. **3** SPACE SHUTTLE. ▶*v.* **1** move or cause to move back and forth. **2** transport by or travel in a shuttle.

**shut·tle·cock** ▶*n.* feathered object struck in badminton.

**shy** /SHī/ ▶*adj.* (**shy·er**, **shy·est** or **shi·er**, **shi·est**) **1 a** diffident or uneasy in company; timid. **b** (of an animal, bird, etc.) easily startled; timid. **2** wary; reluctant. **3** [in *comb.*] showing fear of or distaste for: *gun-shy*. ▶*v.* (**shied**) **1** (esp. of a horse) start suddenly aside in fright. **2** (**shy at/away from**) avoid.

▶*n.* sudden startled movement. —**shy·ly** *adv.* —**shy·ness** *n.*

**shy·ster** /ˈSHīstər/ ▶*n. inf.* unscrupulous lawyer.

**SI** ▶*abbr.* the international system of units of measurement.

**Si** ▶*symb. Chem.* silicon.

**sib·i·lant** /ˈsibələnt/ ▶*adj.* **1** sounded with a hiss. **2** hissing. ▶*n.* sibilant letter or sound. —**sib·i·lance** *n.*

**sib·i·late** /ˈsibəˌlāt/ ▶*v.* utter with a hissing sound.

**sib·ling** /ˈsibliNG/ ▶*n.* brother or sister.

**sib·yl** /ˈsibəl/ ▶*n.* pagan prophetess. —**sib·yl·line** *adj.*

**sic** /sik/ ▶*adv.* (usu. in brackets) used, spelled, etc., as written. ▶*v.* (**sicced**, **sic·cing**) urge (a dog) to attack.

**sick** /sik/ ▶*adj.* **1** affected by physical or mental illness. **2** [often in *comb.*] vomiting or tending to vomit: *seasick*. **3** (of an emotion) so intense as to cause one to feel unwell. **4** (**sick of**) intensely annoyed with or bored by: *I'm sick of your moods*. **5** *inf.* (of humor, etc.) jeering at misfortune, etc.; morbid: *a sick joke*. —**sick·en** *v.* —**sick·ness** *n.* □ **sick leave** leave granted because of illness.

**sick·le** /ˈsikəl/ ▸n. **1** short-handled tool with a semicircular blade, used for cutting grain, lopping, or trimming. **2** anything sickle-shaped, esp. the crescent moon.

**sick·le cell a·ne·mi·a** (also **sick·le cell dis·ease**) ▸n. severe hereditary form of anemia in which a mutated form of hemoglobin distorts the red blood cells into a crescent shape at low oxygen levels.

**sick·ly** ▸adj. (-li·er, -li·est) **1** often ill; in poor health. **2** (of a person's complexion) faint or pale. **3** (of a flavor, smell, color, etc.) so unpleasant as to cause nausea. **4** sentimental or mawkish. —**sick·li·ness** n.

**side** /sīd/ ▸n. **1 a** each of the surfaces bounding an object. **b** inner or outer surface. **c** such a surface as distinct from the top or bottom, front or back. **2 a** half of a person or animal that is on the right or the left, esp. of the torso. **b** left or right half or a specified part of a thing, etc. **c** position next to a person or thing: *seaside*. **3** either surface of a thing having two surfaces. **4** any of several aspects of a question, character, etc. **5** each of two sets of opponents in war, politics, games, etc. **6 a** part or region near the edge and remote from the center. **b** subordinate, peripheral, or detached part. **7** each of the bounding lines of a plane figure. **8** line of hereditary descent through the father or the mother.

▸v. be on the same side as a disputant, etc.: *sided with his father.* —**side·less** adj.

□ **on the side 1** as a sideline. **2** secretly or illicitly. **3** as a side dish. □ **side dish** extra dish subsidiary to the main course. □ **take sides** support one cause, etc., in a dispute.

**side·bar** ▸n. short article in a newspaper, magazine, etc., placed next to a main article and providing additional information.

**side·board** ▸n. flat-topped cupboard for dishes, table linen, decanters, etc.

**side·burns** ▸pl. n. hair grown by a man down the sides of his face.

**side·kick** ▸n. inf. close associate.

**side·light** ▸n. incidental information, etc.

**side·line** ▸n. **1** work, etc., done

in addition to one's main activity. **2** (**sidelines**) **a** line bounding the side of a football field, tennis court, etc. **b** space next to these where spectators, etc., sit.

▸*v.* remove (a player) from a team through injury, suspension, etc.

**side·long** ▸*adj.* oblique. ▸*adv.* obliquely.

**si·de·re·al time** ▸*n.* time reckoned from the motion of the earth (or a planet) relative to the distant stars (rather than with respect to the sun).

**side·sad·dle** ▸*n.* saddle having supports for both feet on the same side of the horse.

▸*adv.* riding in this position on a horse.

**side·show** ▸*n.* minor show or attraction in an exhibition or entertainment.

**side·split·ting** ▸*adj.* causing violent laughter.

**side·step** ▸*v.* (-**stepped**, -**step·ping**) **1** avoid by stepping sideways. **2** evade.

**side·track** ▸*v.* **1** postpone, evade, or divert consideration of. **2** divert (a person) from considering, etc.

**side·walk** ▸*n.* paved walk for pedestrians.

**side·ways** ▸*adv. & adj.* **1** to or from a side. **2** with one side facing forward.

**sid·ing** ▸*n.* **1** short track at the side of a railroad line, used for switching trains. **2** material for the outside of a building, e.g., clapboards, shingles, etc.

**si·dle** /ˈsīdl/ ▸*v.* walk in a timid, furtive, stealthy, or cringing manner.

**SIDS** /sidz/ ▸*abbr.* sudden infant death syndrome; crib death.

**siege** /sēj/ ▸*n.* **1** military action of surrounding and blockading a town, building, etc. **2** period during which a siege lasts. □ **lay siege to** conduct the siege of.

**si·er·ra** /sēˈerə/ ▸*n.* long jagged mountain chain.

**si·es·ta** /sēˈestə/ ▸*n.* afternoon sleep or rest esp. in hot countries.

**sieve** /siv/ ▸*n.* utensil having a perforated or meshed bottom for separating solids or coarse material from liquids or fine particles.

▸*v.* put through a sieve.

**sift** /sift/ ▸*v.* **1** put (material) through a sieve to remove lumps or large particles. **2** examine (evidence, facts, etc.) thoroughly to isolate that which is most important. **—sift·er** *n.*

**sigh** /sī/ ▶*v.* **1** emit a long, deep, audible breath expressive of sadness, weariness, relief, etc. **2** (of the wind, etc.) make a sound like sighing.
▶*n.* act or instance of sighing.

**sight** /sīt/ ▶*n.* **1 a** faculty of seeing. **b** act or instance of seeing; state of being seen. **2** thing seen. **3** range of vision. **4** (**sights**) noteworthy features of a town, etc. **5 a** device on a gun or optical instrument for assisting the precise aim or observation. **b** aim or observation so gained.
▶*v.* **1** get sight of, esp. by approaching: *they sighted land.* **2** observe (esp. aircraft, animals, etc.): *sighted buffalo.*
□ **at** (or **on**) **sight** as soon as seen: *liked him on sight.*

**sight·ed** ▶*adj.* **1** not blind. **2** having a specified kind of sight: *farsighted.*

**sight-read** ▶*v.* read and perform (music) at sight.

**sign** /sīn/ ▶*n.* **1** thing indicating a quality, state, etc.; thing perceived as indicating a future state or occurrence; portent: *violence is a sign of weakness.* **2** mark, symbol, etc. **3** gesture or action conveying information, an order, etc. **4** signboard or signpost. **5** any of the twelve divisions of the zodiac.
▶*v.* **1 a** write (one's name, initials, etc.). **b** sign (a document) as authorization. **2** communicate by gesture, esp. using sign language. **3** engage or be engaged by signing a contract, etc. **4** mark with a sign.
□ **sign for** acknowledge receipt of by signing. □ **sign language** system of communication by hand gestures, used esp. by the hearing impaired. □ **sign off 1** end work, broadcasting, a letter, etc. **2** acknowledge by signature. □ **sign up 1** engage or employ (a person). **2 a** commit (another person or oneself) by signing, etc. **b** enroll.

**sig·nal** /ˈsignəl/ ▶*n.* **1 a** usu. prearranged sign conveying information, guidance, etc. **b** message made up of such signs: *signals made with flags.* **2** *Electr.* electrical impulse or impulses or radio waves transmitted as a signal.
▶*v.* **1** make signals. **2 a** make

signals to; direct. **b** transmit by signal; announce.

**sig·na·to·ry** /'signə,tôrē/ ▶ *n.* (*pl.* **-ries**) party or esp. a nation that has signed an agreement or esp. a treaty.

**sig·na·ture** /'signəCHər/ ▶ *n.* **1 a** person's name, initials, or mark used in signing. **b** act of signing a document, etc. **2** *Mus.* **a** group of sharps or flats indicating the key. **b** notation showing tempo. **3** section of a book made from one folded sheet.

**sig·net** /'signit/ ▶ *n.* small seal, as on a ring.

**sig·nif·i·cant** ▶ *adj.* **1** having a meaning; indicative. **2** noteworthy; important. —**sig·nif·i·cance** *n.*

**sig·nif·i·cant oth·er** ▶ *n.* person with whom someone has an established romantic or sexual relationship.

**sig·ni·fy** /'signə,fī/ ▶ *v.* (**-fied**) **1** be a sign or indication of. **2** mean. **3** make known. **4** be of importance; matter. —**sig·ni·fi·ca·tion** *n.* —**sig·ni·fier** *n.*

**si·lage** /'sīlij/ ▶ *n.* green fodder stored in a silo.

**si·lence** /'sīləns/ ▶ *n.* **1** absence of sound. **2** abstinence from speech or noise. **3** avoidance of mentioning a thing, betraying a secret, etc. ▶ *v.* make silent, esp. by coercion or superior argument. —**si·lent** *adj.* —**si·lent·ly** *adv.*

**si·lenc·er** ▶ *n.* device for reducing the noise emitted by a gun, etc.

**sil·hou·ette** /,siloo'et/ ▶ *n.* **1** representation of a person or thing showing the outline only, usu. in solid black on white or cut from paper. **2** dark shadow or outline against a lighter background. ▶ *v.* represent or show in silhouette.

**sil·i·ca** /'silikə/ ▶ *n.* silicon dioxide, occurring as quartz, etc. □ **silica gel** hydrated silica in a hard granular form used in packaging to absorb moisture.

**sil·i·cate** /'sili,kāt; -kit/ ▶ *n.* compound of a metal with silicon and oxygen.

**sil·i·con** /'sili,kän/ ▶ *n. Chem.* nonmetallic element occurring widely in silica and silicates. (Symb.: **Si**)

**sil·i·cone** /'sili,,kōn/ ▶ *n.* any organic compound of silicon.

**silk** /silk/ ▶ *n.* **1** fine, strong, soft

lustrous fiber produced by silkworms. **2** thread or cloth from this. —**silk·y** *adj.*

**silk·worm** ▸*n.* caterpillar that spins its cocoon of silk.

**sill** /sil/ ▸*n.* slab of stone, wood, or metal at the foot of a window or doorway.

**sil·ly** /'silē/ ▸*adj.* (**-li·er, -li·est**) **1** lacking sense; foolish; imprudent; unwise. **2** ridiculous.
▸*n.* (*pl.* **-lies**) *inf.* foolish person. —**sil·li·ness** *n.*

**si·lo** /'sīlō/ ▸*n.* (*pl.* **-los**) **1** pit or airtight structure in which green crops are stored for fodder. **2** pit or tower for the storage of grain, cement, etc. **3** underground storage chamber for a guided missile.

**silt** /silt/ ▸*n.* sediment deposited by water in a channel, harbor, etc.
▸*v.* choke or be choked with silt. —**silt·y** *adj.*

**sil·ver** /'silvər/ ▸*n. Chem.* **1** grayish-white, lustrous, precious metallic element. (Symb.: **Ag**) **2** color of silver. **3** silver coins. **4** household cutlery.
▸*adj.* **1** made wholly or chiefly of silver. **2** colored like silver.

▸*v.* coat or plate with silver. —**sil·ver·y** *adj.*

**sil·ver·fish** ▸*n.* (*pl.* same or **-fish·es**) silvery wingless insect.

**sil·ver ju·bi·lee** ▸*n.* 25th anniversary of a significant event.

**sil·ver med·al** ▸*n.* medal of silver, usu. awarded as second prize.

**sil·ver·ware** ▸*n.* **1** articles of or coated with silver. **2** tableware of any metal.

**sil·vi·cul·ture** /'silvi,kəlcHər/ ▸*n.* growing and cultivation of trees.

**sim·i·an** /'simēən/ ▸*adj.* **1** of or concerning the anthropoid apes. **2** like an ape or monkey.
▸*n.* ape or monkey.

**sim·i·lar** /'simələr/ ▸*adj.* having a resemblance in appearance, kind, quantity, etc. —**sim·i·lar·i·ty** *n.* —**sim·i·lar·ly** *adv.*

**sim·i·le** /'siməlē/ ▸*n.* comparison of one thing with another of a different kind, as an illustration or ornament (e.g., *as brave as a lion*).

**si·mil·i·tude** /si'milə,t(y)ood/ ▸*n.* likeness, guise, or outward appearance.

**sim·mer** /'simər/ ▸*v.* **1** be or keep bubbling or boiling gently.

**2** be in a state of suppressed anger or excitement. ▶*n.* simmering condition. □ **simmer down** become calm or less agitated.

**sim·per** /ˈsimpər/ ▶*v.* smile in a silly or affected way. ▶*n.* such a smile. —**sim·per·ing·ly** *adv.*

**sim·ple** /ˈsimpəl/ ▶*adj.* **1** easily understood or done. **2** not complicated or elaborate; without luxury or sophistication. **3** not compound. **4** absolute; unqualified; straightforward. **5** foolish or ignorant; gullible; feeble-minded. —**sim·ply** *adv.*

**sim·ple·mind·ed** ▶*adj.* **1** natural; unsophisticated. **2** feeble-minded. —**sim·ple·mind·ed·ly** *adv.* —**sim·ple·mind·ed·ness** *n.*

**sim·ple·ton** /ˈsimpəltən/ ▶*n.* fool.

**sim·pli·fy** ▶*v.* (**-fied**) make simple or simpler. —**sim·pli·fi·ca·tion** *n.*

**sim·plis·tic** /simˈplistik/ ▶*adj.* **1** excessively or affectedly simple. **2** oversimplified so as to conceal or distort difficulties. —**sim·plis·ti·cal·ly** *adv.*

**sim·u·late** /ˈsimyəˌlāt/ ▶*v.* **1 a** pretend to have or feel (an attribute or feeling). **b** pretend to be. **2** imitate or counterfeit. —**sim·u·la·ted** *adj.* —**sim·u·la·tion** *n.*

**si·mul·ta·ne·ous** /ˌsīməlˈtānēəs/ ▶*adj.* occurring or operating at the same time. —**si·mul·ta·ne·ous·ly** *adv.*

**sin** /sin/ ▶*n.* **1 a** breaking of divine or moral law, esp. by a conscious act. **b** such an act. **2** offense against good taste or propriety, etc. ▶*v.* (**sinned, sin·ning**) commit a sin. —**sin·ful** *adj.* —**sin·ful·ly** *adv.* —**sin·ful·ness** *n.* —**sin·less** *adj.* —**sin·less·ly** *adv.* —**sin·less·ness** *n.* —**sin·ner** *n.*

**since** /sins/ ▶*prep.* throughout or during the period after: *must have happened since yesterday.* ▶*conj.* **1** during or in the time after: *has not spoken since the dog died.* **2** because; inasmuch as. ▶*adv.* **1** from that time or event until now. **2** ago.

**sin·cere** /sinˈsi(ə)r/ ▶*adj.* (**-cer·er, -cer·est**) **1** free from pretense or deceit. **2** genuine; honest; frank. —**sin·cere·ly** *adv.* —**sin·cer·i·ty** *n.*

**si·ne·cure** /ˈsīnəˌkyo͝or/ ▶*n.* position that requires little or no work but usu. yields profit or honor.

**si·ne di·e** /ˈsinā ˈdēā/ ▸*adv.* (with reference to business or proceedings that have been adjourned) with no appointed date for resumption.

**si·ne qua non** /ˌsinā ˌkwä ˈnōn/ ▸*n.* indispensable condition or qualification.

**sin·ew** /ˈsinyo͞o/ ▸*n.* **1** tough fibrous tissue uniting muscle to bone; tendon. **2** (**sinews**) muscles; bodily strength; wiriness. —**sin·ew·y** *adj.*

**sing** /siNG/ ▸*v.* (*past* **sang**; *past part.* **sung**) **1** utter musical sounds, esp. words with a set tune. **2** (of the wind, a kettle, etc.) make humming, buzzing, or whistling sounds.
▸*n.* act or spell of singing.
—**sing·er** *n.*

**singe** /sinj/ ▸*v.* (**singe·ing**) burn superficially or lightly.
▸*n.* superficial burn.

**sin·gle** /ˈsiNGgəl/ ▸*adj.* **1** one only. **2** united or undivided. **3 a** designed or suitable for one person: *single room.* **b** used or done by one person, etc. **4** one by itself; not one of several. **5** separately. **6** not married.
▸*n.* **1** single thing, or item in a series. **2** *Baseball* hit that allows the batter to reach first base safely. **3** unmarried person.
▸*v.* **1** (**single out**) choose as an example or as distinguishable or to serve some purpose. **2** *Baseball* hit a single. —**sin·gly** *adv.*

**sin·gle file** ▸*n.* line of people or things arranged one behind another.

**sin·gle-hand·ed** ▸*adv. & adj.* **1** done without help from anyone else. **2** done or designed to be used with one hand. —**sin·gle-hand·ed·ly** *adv.*

**sin·gle-mind·ed** ▸*adj.* having or intent on only one purpose.

**sin·gle par·ent** ▸*n.* person bringing up a child or children without a partner.

**sing·song** ▸*adj.* uttered with a monotonous rhythm or cadence.
▸*n.* singsong manner.

**sin·gu·lar** /ˈsiNGgyələr/ ▸*adj.* **1** unique; much beyond the average; extraordinary. **2** eccentric or strange. **3** *Gram.* (of a word or form) denoting a single person or thing.
▸*n. Gram.* **1** singular word or form. **2** singular number. —**sin·gu·lar·i·ty** *n.* —**sin·gu·lar·ly** *adv.*

**sin·is·ter** /'sinistər/ ▸*adj.*
**1** suggestive of evil; looking malignant or villainous.
**2** wicked or criminal: *a sinister motive.* **3** ominous.

**sink** /siNGk/ ▸*v.* (*past* **sank** or **sunk**; *past part.* **sunk** or **sunk·en**)
**1** fall or come slowly downward.
**2** disappear below the horizon.
**3 a** go or penetrate below the surface esp. of a liquid. **b** (of a ship) go to the bottom of the sea, etc. **4** settle down comfortably: *sank into a chair.* **5** gradually lose strength or value or quality, etc.; decline.
▸*n.* **1** basin with a water supply and outflow pipe. **2** place where foul liquid collects. **3** place of vice or corruption. —**sink·age** *n.*
□ **sink in 1** penetrate or make its way in. **2** become gradually comprehended.

**sin·u·ous** /'sinyo͞oəs/ ▸*adj.* with many curves; tortuous; undulating. —**sin·u·ous·ly** *adv.* —**sin·u·ous·ness** *n.*

**si·nus** /'sīnəs/ ▸*n.* cavity of bone or tissue, esp. in the skull connecting with the nostrils.

**sip** /sip/ ▸*v.* (**sipped, sip·ping**) drink in small amounts or by spoonfuls.

▸*n.* **1** small mouthful of liquid. **2** act of taking this.

**si·phon** /'sīfən/ ▸*n.* tube for conveying liquid from a container to a lower level by atmospheric pressure.
▸*v.* **1** conduct or flow through a siphon. **2** divert or set aside (funds, etc.). —**si·phon·age** *n.*

**sir** /sər/ ▸*n.* **1** polite form of address or reference to a man. **2** (**Sir**) titular prefix to the forename of a knight or baronet.

**sire** /sī(ə)r/ ▸*n.* **1** male parent of an animal, esp. a stallion. **2** father or male ancestor.
▸*v.* beget.

**si·ren** /'sīrən/ ▸*n.* **1** device for making a loud prolonged signal or warning sound. **2** (in Greek mythology) woman or winged creature whose singing lured unwary sailors onto rocks. **3** dangerously fascinating woman.

**sir·loin** /'sər,loin/ ▸*n.* choicer part of a loin of beef.

**si·sal** /'sīsəl/ ▸*n.* fiber used for making ropes.

**sis·sy** /'sisē/ *inf.* ▸*n.* (*pl.* **-sies**) effeminate or cowardly person.
▸*adj.* (**-si·er, -si·est**) effeminate; cowardly. —**sis·si·fied** *adj.* —**sis·sy·ish** *adj.*

**sis·ter** /ˈsistər/ ▶*n.* **1** woman or girl in relation to sons and other daughters of her parents. **2** female fellow member of a labor union, class, race, etc. **3** nun. —**sis·ter·hood** *n.* —**sis·ter·ly** *adj.* —**sis·ter·li·ness** *n.*

□ **sister-in-law 1** sister of one's spouse. **2** wife of one's brother or brother-in-law.

**sit** /sit/ ▶*v.* (**sit·ting;** *past* and *past part.* **sat**) **1** rest the buttocks on the ground or a raised seat, etc., with the torso upright. **2** cause to sit; place in a sitting position. **3 a** (of a bird) perch or remain on its nest to hatch its eggs. **b** (of an animal) rest with the hind legs bent and the body close to the ground. **4** (of a committee, etc.) be in session. **5** pose (for a portrait). —**sit·ter** *n.*

□ **sit in on** be present as a guest or observer at (a meeting, etc.). □ **sit out** take no part in (a dance, etc.). □ **sit tight** *inf.* remain firmly in one's place. □ **sit-up** physical exercise in which a person sits up without raising the legs from the ground.

**si·tar** /siˈtär/ ▶*n.* long-necked E. Indian lute with movable frets. —**si·tar·ist** *n.*

**site** /sīt/ ▶*n.* place; location. ▶*v.* locate or place.

**sit·u·ate** /ˈsiCHo͞o͞oˌāt/ ▶*v.* **1** put in a certain position or circumstances. **2** establish or indicate the place of; put in a context.

**sit·u·a·tion** ▶*n.* **1** place and its surroundings. **2** circumstances; position; state of affairs. —**sit·u·a·tion·al** *adj.*

**sit·u·a·tion·ism** /ˌsiCHo͞o͞oˈāSHəˌnizəm/ ▶*n.* theory that human behavior is determined by surrounding circumstances rather than by personal qualities.

**sitz·krieg** /ˈsitsˌkrēg/ ▶*n.* war, or a phase of a war, in which there is little or no active warfare.

**six** /siks/ ▶*n.* **1** one more than five, or four less than ten. **2** symbol for this (6, vi, VI). —**sixth** *adj. & n.*

**six·teen** ▶*n.* **1** one more than fifteen, or six more than ten. **2** symbol for this (16, xvi, XVI). —**six·teenth** *adj. & n.*

**six·ty** ▶*n.* (*pl.* **-ties**) **1** six times ten. **2** symbol for this (60, lx, LX). **3** (**sixties**) numbers from 60 to 69, esp. the years of a century or of a person's life. —**six·ti·eth** *adj. & n.* —**six·ty·fold** *adj. & adv.*

**siz·a·ble** /ˈsīzəbəl/ (also **size·a·ble**) ▸*adj.* large or fairly large. —**siz·a·bly** *adv.*

**size** /sīz/ ▸*n.* **1** relative dimensions; magnitude. **2** each of the classes, usu. numbered, into which similar things are divided according to size. **3** gelatinous solution used in glazing paper, stiffening textiles, etc.

▸*v.* **1** sort or group in sizes or according to size. **2** glaze, stiffen, etc.

□ **size up 1** estimate the size of. **2** *inf.* form a judgment of.

**siz·zle** /ˈsizəl/ ▸*v.* **1** sputter or hiss, esp. in frying. **2** *inf.* be in a state of great heat or excitement, etc.

▸*n.* **1** sizzling sound. **2** *inf.* state of great heat or excitement. —**siz·zler** *n.* —**siz·zling** *adj. & adv.*

**skald** /skôld; skäld/ (also **scald**) ▸*n.* (in ancient Scandinavia) a composer and reciter of poems honoring heroes and their deeds.

**skate**[1] /skāt/ ▸*n.* ice skate or roller skate.

▸*v.* move or perform (a specified figure) on skates. —**skat·er** *n.*

**skate**[2] ▸*n.* (*pl.* same or **skates**) large, flat, raylike marine fish used as food.

**skate·board** ▸*n.* short narrow board on roller-skate wheels for riding on while standing.

▸*v.* ride on a skateboard. —**skate·board·er** *n.*

**ske·dad·dle** /skiˈdadl/ ▸*v. inf.* run away; depart quickly; flee.

**skein** /skān/ ▸*n.* **1** loosely-coiled bundle of yarn or thread. **2** flock of wild geese, etc., in flight.

**skel·e·ton** /ˈskelitn/ ▸*n.* **1 a** hard internal or external framework of bones, cartilage, woody fiber, etc., supporting or containing the body of an animal or plant. **b** dried bones of a human being or other animal fastened together in the same relative positions as in life. **2** supporting framework or structure of a thing. —**skel·e·tal** *adj.* —**skel·e·tal·ly** *adv.*

□ **skeleton key** key designed to fit many locks by having the interior of the bit hollowed.

**skep·tic** /ˈskeptik/ ▸*n.* person inclined to doubt all accepted opinions; cynic. —**skep·ti·cal** *adj.* —**skep·ti·cal·ly** *adv.* —**skep·ti·cism** *n.*

**sketch** /skeCH/ ▸*n.* **1** rough or unfinished drawing, painting,

outline, etc. **2** very short play, usu. humorous and limited to one scene.
▶*v.* **1** make a sketch (of). **2** indicate briefly or in outline.

**sketch·y** ▶*adj.* (**-i·er, -i·est**) **1** giving only a slight or rough outline, like a sketch. **2** *inf.* unsubstantial or imperfect, esp. through haste. —**sketch·i·ly** *adv.* —**sketch·i·ness** *n.*

**skew** /skyoō/ ▶*adj.* oblique; slanting.
▶*v.* change direction; distort.

**skew·er** /'skyoōər/ ▶*n.* long pin designed for holding meat compactly together while cooking.
▶*v.* fasten together or pierce with or as if with a skewer.

**ski** /skē/ ▶*n.* (*pl.* **skis** or **ski**) each of a pair of long narrow pieces of wood, etc., for traveling over snow or water.
▶*v.* (**skied, ski·ing**) travel on skis. —**ski·er** *n.*
□ **ski lift** device for carrying skiers up a slope, usu. on seats hung from an overhead cable.

**skid** /skid/ ▶*v.* (**skid·ded, skid·ding**) (of a vehicle, a wheel, or a driver) slide or cause to slide on slippery ground, esp. sideways or obliquely.

▶*n.* **1** skidding movement. **2** strong base for supporting heavy objects during moving.
□ **on the skids** *inf.* about to be discarded or defeated.

**skid row** ▶*n. inf.* part of a town frequented by vagrants, alcoholics, etc.

**skiff** /skif/ ▶*n.* light rowboat or scull.

**skill** /skil/ ▶*n.* expertness; practiced ability; facility in an action; dexterity or tact. —**skilled** *adj.* —**skill·ful** *adj.* —**skill·ful·ly** *adv.* —**skill·ful·ness** *n.*

**skil·let** /'skilit/ ▶*n.* frying pan.

**skim** /skim/ ▶*v.* (**skimmed, skim·ming**) **1** take a floating layer from the surface of (a liquid). **2** keep touching lightly or nearly touching (a surface) in passing over. **3** go or glide lightly. **4** read or look over cursorily.
▶*n.* act or instance of skimming. —**skim·mer** *n.*

**skim milk** ▶*n.* milk from which the cream has been removed.

**skimp** /skimp/ ▶*v.* be stingy.
▶*adj.* scanty.

**skimp·y** ▶*adj.* (**-i·er, -i·est**) meager; not ample or sufficient.

—**skimp·i·ly** *adv.*
—**skimp·i·ness** *n.*

**skin** /skin/ ▶*n.* **1** flexible continuous covering of a human or other animal body. **2** outer layer or covering, esp. of a plant, fruit, or sausage.
▶*v.* (**skinned, skin·ning**) remove the skin from. —**skin·less** *adj.*
□ **skin-deep** superficial; not deep or lasting.

**skin di·ver** ▶*n.* person who swims underwater without a diving suit, usu. with scuba, flippers, etc.

**skin·flint** ▶*n.* miserly person.

**skin·ny** ▶*adj.* (**-ni·er, -ni·est**) thin or emaciated. —**skin·ni·ness** *n.*

**skin·ny dip·ping** ▶*n. inf.* swimming in the nude.

**skip** /skip/ ▶*v.* (**skipped, skip·ping**) **1 a** move along lightly, esp. with alternate hops. **b** jump lightly from the ground, esp. so as to clear a jump rope. **2** move quickly from one point, subject, etc., to another. **3** omit in dealing with a series or in reading: *skip every tenth row.* **4** *inf.* not participate in.
▶*n.* **1** skipping movement or action. **2** *Computing* action of passing over part of a sequence of data or instructions.

**skip·per** ▶*n.* sea captain, esp. of a small trading or fishing vessel.
▶*v.* act as captain of.

**skir·mish** /ˈskərmiSH/ ▶*n.* minor battle.
▶*v.* engage in a skirmish.

**skirt** /skərt/ ▶*n.* **1** woman's outer garment hanging from the waist. **2** part of a dress or other garment that hangs below the waist.
▶*v.* **1** go along or past the edge of. **2** avoid. —**skirt·ed** *adj.*
—**skirt·less** *adj.*

**skit** /skit/ ▶*n.* light, usu. short, piece of satire or burlesque.

**skit·tish** /ˈskitiSH/ ▶*adj.* **1** lively; playful. **2** (of a horse, etc.) nervous; inclined to shy.
—**skit·tish·ly** *adv.*
—**skit·tish·ness** *n.*

**skoal** /skōl/ (also **skol**) ▶*exclam.* used to express friendly feelings toward one's companions before drinking.

**skul·dug·ger·y** /skəlˈdəgərē/ (also **skull·dug·ger·y**) ▶*n.* trickery; unscrupulous behavior.

**skulk** /skəlk/ ▶*v.* move stealthily, lurk, or keep oneself concealed. —**skulk·er** *n.*

**skull** /skəl/ ▶*n.* **1** bony case of the brain of a vertebrate. **2** the head as the seat of intelligence.

**skull·cap** ▸*n.* small, close-fitting, brimless cap.

**skunk** /skəNGk/ ▸*n.* **1** black cat-sized mammal with white stripes on the back that emits a powerful stench as a defense. **2** *inf.* thoroughly contemptible person.

**sky** /skī/ ▸*n.* (*pl.* **skies**) atmosphere and outer space seen from the earth. □ **sky-high** very high.

**sky·light** ▸*n.* window in a roof or ceiling.

**sky·line** ▸*n.* outline of buildings, etc., defined against the sky.

**sky·rock·et** ▸*n.* fireworks rocket. ▸*v.* (esp. of prices, etc.) rise very rapidly.

**sky·scrap·er** ▸*n.* very tall building.

**sky·writ·ing** ▸*n.* writing traced in the sky by an airplane's smoke trails.

**slab** /slab/ ▸*n.* flat, broad, fairly thick piece of solid material.

**slack** /slak/ ▸*adj.* **1** (of rope, etc.) not taut. **2** inactive or sluggish. **3** negligent or remiss. **4** (of tide, etc.) neither ebbing nor flowing. ▸*n.* **1** slack part of a rope. **2** slack

period. **3** (**slacks**) trousers. —**slack·ly** *adv.* —**slack·ness** *n.*

**slack·en** ▸*v.* make or become slack.

**slack·er** ▸*n.* shirker; indolent person.

**slag** /slag/ ▸*n.* refuse left after smelting.

**slake** /slāk/ ▸*v.* satisfy (thirst, desire, etc.).

**sla·lom** /'släləm/ ▸*n.* ski race down a zigzag obstacle course.

**slam** /slam/ ▸*v.* (**slammed, slam·ming**) **1** shut forcefully and loudly. **2** move violently: *the car slammed into the tree.* **3** *inf.* criticize severely. ▸*n.* **1** sound or action of slamming. **2** winning of every trick in a card game.

**slan·der** /'slandər/ ▸*n.* **1** malicious, false, and injurious statement spoken about a person. **2** uttering of such statements. ▸*v.* utter slander about. —**slan·der·ous** *adj.* —**slan·der·ous·ly** *adv.*

**slang** /slaNG/ ▸*n.* words, phrases, and uses that are regarded as very informal or taboo or are peculiar to a specified profession, class, etc.: *racing*

*slang.* —**slang·i·ly** *adv.*
—**slang·i·ness** *n.* —**slang·y** *adj.*

**slant** /slant/ ▶*v.* **1** (cause to) slope; lie or go at an angle. **2** [often as *adj.* **slanted**] present (information), esp. in a biased or unfair way.
▶*n.* **1** slope; oblique position. **2** point of view, esp. a biased one.

**slap** /slap/ ▶*v.* (**slapped, slap·ping**) **1** strike with the palm or a flat object, so as to make a similar noise. **2** lay forcefully: *slapped the money on the table.*
▶*n.* **1** blow with the palm or a flat object. **2** rebuke; insult.

**slap·dash** ▶*adj.* hasty and careless.
▶*adv.* in a slapdash manner.

**slap·hap·py** ▶*adj. inf.* cheerfully casual or flippant.

**slap·stick** ▶*n.* boisterous knockabout comedy.

**slash** /slasн/ ▶*v.* **1** make a sweeping cut or cuts with a knife, etc., (at). **2** reduce (prices, etc.) drastically.
▶*n.* **1 a** slashing cut or stroke. **b** wound or slit made by this. **2** oblique stroke or line.
—**slash·er** *n.*

**slat** /slat/ ▶*n.* thin, narrow piece of wood, etc.

**slate** /slāt/ ▶*n.* **1** fine-grained, esp. bluish-gray, rock easily split into flat smooth plates. **2** piece of this used as roofing or paving material or for writing on. **3** color of slate. **4** list of nominees for office, etc.
▶*v.* **1** cover with slates esp. as roofing. **2** (usu. **be slated**) schedule; plan: *renovations are slated to begin next week.*
▶*adj.* made of slate. —**slat·y** *adj.*

**slat·tern** /ˈslatərn/ ▶*n.* slovenly woman.

**slaugh·ter** /ˈslôtər/ ▶*n.* **1** killing of animals for food. **2** killing of many people or animals at once or continuously; carnage; massacre.
▶*v.* **1** kill in a ruthless manner or on a great scale. **2** kill for food; butcher. —**slaugh·ter·er** *n.*
—**slaugh·ter·house** *n.*

**slave** /slāv/ ▶*n.* **1** person who is the legal property of and has to serve another. **2** drudge; hard worker. **3** helpless victim of some dominating influence: *slave to duty.*
▶*v.* work very hard. —**slav·er·y** *n.*
☐ **slave driver** person who makes others work hard.

**sla·ver** /ˈslavər/ ▸n. **1** saliva running from the mouth. **2** drivel; nonsense.
▸v. drool; dribble.

**Slav·ic** /ˈslävik/ ▸adj. **1** of or relating to the group of Indo-European languages including Russian, Polish, and Czech. **2** of or relating to the peoples of eastern and central Europe who speak these languages.
▸n. Slavic language group.

**slav·ish** /ˈslāviSH/ ▸adj. **1** like slaves. **2** without originality. —**slav·ish·ly** adv. —**slav·ish·ness** n.

**slay** /slā/ ▸v. (past **slew**; past part. **slain**) kill. —**slay·er** n.

**slea·zy** /ˈslēzē/ ▸adj. (**-zi·er, -zi·est**) **1** squalid; tawdry. **2** (of textiles, etc.) flimsy. —**slea·zi·ly** adv. —**slea·zi·ness** n.

**sled** /sled/ ▸n. vehicle on runners for use on snow.
▸v. (**sled·ded, sled·ding**) ride on a sled.

**sledge** /slej/ ▸n. **1** large, heavy sled. **2** (also **sledge·ham·mer**) heavy hammer with a long handle.

**sleek** /slēk/ ▸adj. **1** (of hair, fur, skin, etc.) smooth and glossy. **2** looking well-fed and comfortable.
▸v. make sleek, esp. by stroking or pressing down. —**sleek·ly** adv. —**sleek·ness** n.

**sleep** /slēp/ ▸n. natural condition of rest with suspended consciousness, the eyes closed, and the muscles relaxed.
▸v. (past and past part. **slept**) **1 a** be in a state of sleep. **b** fall asleep. **2** provide sleeping accommodations for. **3** (**sleep with**) have sexual intercourse with. —**sleep·less** adj. —**sleep·less·ly** adv. —**sleep·less·ness** n. —**sleep·y** adj.
□ **put to sleep 1** anesthetize. **2** kill (an animal) mercifully.
□ **sleeping bag** padded bag to sleep in esp. when camping, etc.
□ **sleeping car** railroad car with berths; Pullman.

**sleep·er** ▸n. **1** person or animal that sleeps. **2** movie, etc., that achieves sudden unexpected success. **3** sleeping car.

**sleep·walk·ing** ▸n. walking while asleep. —**sleep·walk** v. —**sleep·walk·er** n.

**sleet** /slēt/ ▸n. snow and rain falling together.
▸v. fall as sleet: *it is sleeting.*

**sleeve** /slēv/ ▸n. **1** part of a garment that covers an arm.

**2** tube enclosing something.
—**sleeved** adj. —**sleeve·less** adj.

□ **up one's sleeve** concealed but in reserve.

**sleigh** /slā/ ▸n. sled drawn by horses or reindeer.

**slen·der** /'slendər/ ▸adj. (-er, -est) **1 a** of small girth or breadth. **b** gracefully thin. **2** relatively small or scanty; inadequate. —**slen·der·ly** adv. —**slen·der·ness** n.

**sleuth** /slo͞oTH/ ▸n. inf. detective.

**slew** /slo͞o/ ▸v. **1** turn or swing forcibly to a new position. **2** past of SLAY.

▸n. inf. large number or quantity.

**slice** /slīs/ ▸n. **1** thin piece or wedge cut off or out. **2** share; part. **3** Golf & Tennis slicing stroke.

▸v. **1** cut into slices. **2** cut (a piece) off. **3** cut (as with a knife). **4 a** Golf strike (the ball) so that it deviates away from the striker. **b** (in other sports) propel (the ball) forward at an angle. —**slic·er** n.

**slick** /slik/ ▸adj. inf. **1 a** skillful or efficient. **b** superficially or pretentiously smooth and dexterous. **c** glib. **2 a** sleek; smooth. **b** slippery.

▸n. patch of oil, etc., esp. on the sea.

▸v. inf. **1** make sleek or smart. **2** flatten (one's hair, etc.). —**slick·ly** adv. —**slick·ness** n.

**slick·er** ▸n. **1** swindler. **2** (also **city slick·er**) smart and sophisticated city dweller. **3** raincoat of smooth material.

**slide** /slīd/ ▸v. (past and past part. **slid**) **1** (cause to) move along a smooth surface with continuous contact. **2** move quietly; glide.

▸n. **1 a** act or instance of sliding. **b** decline. **2** inclined plane down which children, goods, etc., slide. **3** piece of glass holding an object for a microscope. **4** mounted transparency viewed with a projector. —**slid·er** n.

□ **let things slide** be negligent; allow deterioration.

**slid·ing scale** ▸n. scale of fees, taxes, wages, etc., that varies according to some standard.

**slight** /slīt/ ▸adj. **1 a** inconsiderable; of little significance. **b** barely perceptible. **c** inadequate; scanty. **2** slender; frail-looking.

▸v. treat disrespectfully; neglect.

▸n. failure to show due respect. —**slight·ly** adv. —**slight·ness** n.

**slim** /slim/ ▸*adj.* (**slim·mer,
slim·mest**) **1 a** of long, narrow
shape. **b** gracefully thin.
**2** slight; insufficient. —**slim·ly**
*adv.* —**slim·ming** *n. & adj.*
—**slim·ness** *n.*

**slime** /slīm/ ▸*n.* thick slippery or
sticky substance.

▸*v.* cover with slime. —**slim·i·ly**
*adv.* —**slim·i·ness** *n.* —**slim·y**
*adj.*

**sling** /sliNG/ ▸*n.* **1** strap, etc., to
support or raise a hanging
weight. **2** bandage looped
around the neck to support an
injured arm. **3** straplike device
for flinging a stone or other
missile.

▸*v.* (*past* and *past part.* **slung**) **1** *inf.*
throw. **2** suspend with a sling.

**sling·shot** ▸*n.* forked stick, etc.,
with elastic for shooting stones,
etc.

**slink** /sliNGk/ ▸*v.* (*past* and *past
part.* **slunk**) move in a stealthy or
guilty manner.

**slip** /slip/ ▸*v.* (**slipped, slip·ping**)
**1** slide unintentionally, esp. for a
short distance; lose one's footing
or balance. **2** go or move with a
sliding motion. **3** escape by
being slippery or hard to hold.
**4** go unobserved or quietly.
**5 a** make a careless or casual

mistake. **b** fall below standard.
**6** (**slip on/off**) pull (a garment)
hastily on or off.

▸*n.* **1** act or instance of slipping.
**2** accidental or slight error.
**3** woman's skirted
undergarment. **4** bay in a dock
for mooring a vessel. **5** small
piece of paper. **6** cutting taken
from a plant for grafting or
planting; scion. **7** clay in a
creamy mixture with water, for
decorating earthenware.

□ **let slip** utter inadvertently.
  □ **slip up** *inf.* make a mistake.

**slip·cov·er** ▸*n.* removable fabric
covering for usu. upholstered
furniture.

▸*v.* cover with a slipcover.

**slip·knot** ▸*n.* knot that can be
undone by a pull.

**slip·per** ▸*n.* **1** light, loose,
comfortable indoor shoe. **2** light
slip-on shoe for dancing, etc.

**slip·per·y** ▸*adj.* **1** difficult to
hold. **2** (of a surface) causing
sliding or slipping by its
smoothness or slickness.
**3** unreliable; unscrupulous.
—**slip·per·i·ness** *n.*

**slip·shod** ▸*adj.* **1** careless;
unsystematic. **2** slovenly.

**slip-up** ▸*n.* mistake; blunder.

**slit** /slit/ ▶*n.* straight, narrow incision or opening.

▶*v.* (**slit·ting**; *past and past part.* **slit**) **1** make a slit in. **2** cut into strips.

**slith·er** /ˈsliᴛʜər/ ▶*v.* slide unsteadily. —**slith·er·y** *adj.*

**sli·ver** /ˈslivər/ ▶*n.* long, thin piece cut or split off; splinter.

▶*v.* **1** break off as a sliver. **2** break or form into slivers.

**slob** /släb/ ▶*n. inf.* lazy, untidy person.

**slob·ber** ▶*v.* **1** slaver. **2** show excessive sentiment.

▶*n.* saliva running from the mouth; slaver. —**slob·ber·y** *adj.*

**sloe** /slō/ ▶*n.* shrub with small bluish-black fruit with a sharp sour taste.

**sloe-eyed** ▶*adj.* having attractive dark, typically almond-shaped eyes.

**slog** /släg/ ▶*v.* (**slogged**, **slog·ging**) walk or work doggedly.

▶*n.* hard steady work or walking. —**slog·ger** *n.*

**slo·gan** /ˈslōgən/ ▶*n.* **1** short catchy phrase used in advertising, etc. **2** party cry; watchword or motto.

**sloop** /slo͞op/ ▶*n.* small sailboat with one mast.

**slop** /släp/ ▶*v.* (**slopped**, **slop·ping**) (allow to) spill or flow over the edge of a vessel.

▶*n.* **1** unappetizing liquid. **2** (**slops**) dirty waste water.

**slope** /slōp/ ▶*n.* **1** inclined position, state, or direction. **2** difference in level between the two ends or sides of a thing.

▶*v.* lie or put at an angle; slant.

**slop·py** /ˈsläpē/ ▶*adj.* (**-pi·er**, **-pi·est**) **1** watery and disagreeable. **2** unsystematic; careless. **3** weakly emotional; maudlin. —**slop·pi·ly** *adv.* —**slop·pi·ness** *n.*

**slosh** /släsʜ/ ▶*v.* splash or flounder about; move with a splashing sound.

**slot** /slät/ ▶*n.* **1** slit in a machine for a coin. **2** allotted place in an arrangement or schedule.

▶*v.* (**slot·ted**, **slot·ting**) place or be placed into or as if into a slot.

**sloth** /slôᴛʜ/ ▶*n.* **1** laziness or indolence. **2** slow-moving nocturnal mammal of S. America that hangs upside down in trees. —**sloth·ful** *adj.* —**sloth·ful·ly** *adv.* —**sloth·ful·ness** *n.*

**slot ma·chine** ▶*n.* gambling machine worked by the insertion of a coin in a slot.

**slouch** /slouCH/ ▸v. stand, move, or sit in a drooping fashion. ▸n. **1** slouching posture or movement. **2** inf. incompetent or indifferent worker. —**slouch·y** adj.

**slough** /slou; sloo/ ▸n. **1** swamp; marshy pond. **2** state of hopeless depression. ▸v. shed dead skin.

**slov·en·ly** ▸adj. untidy and careless. —**slov·en·li·ness** n.

**slow** /slō/ ▸adj. **1 a** taking a relatively long time to do a thing. **b** not quick; acting or moving or done without speed. **2** gradual. **3** (of a clock, etc.) showing a time earlier than is the case. **4** (of a person) not understanding or learning readily. **5** slack or sluggish. ▸adv. slowly: *slow-moving traffic.* ▸v. reduce one's speed or the speed of (a vehicle, etc.). —**slow·ly** adv. —**slow·ness** n. ☐ **slow motion** speed of a film in which actions, etc., appear much slower than usual.

**slow·down** ▸n. deliberate slowing down of productivity.

**sludge** /sləj/ ▸n. **1** thick, greasy mud or sediment. **2** sewage. —**sludg·y** adj.

**slug** /sləg/ ▸n. **1** hard blow. **2** small shell-less mollusk destructive to plants. **3** bullet. **4** shot of liquor. **5** counterfeit coin. ▸v. (**slugged**, **slug·ging**) strike with a hard blow. —**slug·ger** n.

**slug·gard** /'sləgərd/ ▸n. lazy, sluggish person. —**slug·gard·ly** adj.

**slug·gish** ▸adj. slow-moving; indolent. —**slug·gish·ly** adv. —**slug·gish·ness** n.

**sluice** /sloos/ ▸n. sliding gate, etc., for controlling the flow of water, etc.

**slum** /sləm/ ▸n. **1** overcrowded and squalid back street, district, etc., usu. in a city. **2** house or building unfit for human habitation. ▸v. (**slummed**, **slum·ming**) **1** live in slumlike conditions. **2** visit slums, as out of curiosity.

**slum·ber** /'sləmbər/ ▸v. & n. sleep. —**slum·ber·ous** adj.

**slump** /sləmp/ ▸n. sudden fall in prices and trade. ▸v. **1** undergo a slump; fail. **2** sit or fall heavily or limply. **3** lean or subside.

**slur** /slər/ ▸v. (**slurred**, **slur·ring**) **1** pronounce indistinctly so that the sounds run into one another. **2** Mus. perform (notes) legato.

**3** put a slur on (a person or a person's character).  **4** (**slur over**) pass over (a fact, fault, etc.) lightly.

▸ *n.* **1** imputation of wrongdoing.  **2** act or instance of slurring.  **3** *Mus.* curved line joining notes to be slurred.

**slurp** /slərp/ ▸ *v.* eat or drink noisily.

▸ *n.* sound of this.

**slush** /sləSH/ ▸ *n.* **1** thawing, muddy snow.  **2** silly sentiment. —**slush·y** *adj.* —**slush·i·ness** *n.*

**slush fund** ▸ *n.* reserve fund, esp. for political bribery.

**slut** /slət/ ▸ *n.* slovenly or promiscuous woman. —**slut·tish** *adj.* —**slut·tish·ness** *n.*

**sly** /slī/ ▸ *adj.* (**sli·er**, **sli·est** or **sly·er**, **sly·est**)  **1** cunning; crafty; wily.  **2 a** (of a person) practicing secrecy or stealth.  **b** (of an action, etc.) done, etc., in secret.  **3** mischievous; knowing; insinuating. —**sly·ly** (also **sli·ly**) *adv.* —**sly·ness** *n.*

☐ **on the sly** secretly; covertly.

**smack** /smak/ ▸ *n.* **1** sharp slap or blow.  **2** loud kiss.  **3** *inf.* heroin.

▸ *v.* **1** slap.  **2** have a flavor of; taste of.  **3** suggest the presence or effects of.

▸ *adv. inf.* **1** with a smack.  **2** suddenly; directly; violently.

**small** /smôl/ ▸ *adj.* **1** not large or big.  **2** slender; thin.  **3** not great in importance, amount, number, strength, or power.  **4** young.

▸ *n.* slenderest part of something: *small of the back.*

▸ *adv.* into small pieces. —**small·ness** *n.*

☐ **small fry** *inf.* **1** young child or children.  **2** insignificant things or people.  ☐ **small talk** light social conversation.  ☐ **small-time** *inf.* unimportant or petty.

**small-mind·ed** ▸ *adj.* petty; narrow in outlook. —**small-mind·ed·ness** *n.*

**small·pox** ▸ *n.* acute contagious viral disease, usu. leaving permanent scars.

**smarm·y** /ˈsmärmē/ ▸ *adj.* (**smarm·i·er**, **smarm·i·est**) ingratiating and wheedling in a way that is perceived as insincere or excessive.

**smart** /smärt/ ▸ *adj.* **1** clever; ingenious; quickwitted.  **2** well-groomed; neat.  **3** stylish; fashionable.  **4** quick; brisk.

▸ *v.* **1** feel or give pain.  **2** (of an insult, grievance, etc.) rankle.

▸ *n.* sharp pain.

▸ *adv.* smartly; in a smart manner.

—**smart·ing·ly** *adv.* —**smart·ly** *adv.* —**smart·ness** *n.*

**smart bomb** ▸*n.* bomb that can be guided directly to its target by use of radio waves, television, or lasers.

**smart·en** ▸*v.* make or become smart.

**smash** /smasH/ ▸*v.* **1 a** break into pieces; shatter. **b** bring or come to sudden destruction, defeat, or disaster. **2** move with great force and impact. ▸*n.* **1** act or instance of smashing; violent fall, collision, or disaster. **2** sound of this. **3** (also **smash hit**) very successful play, song, performer, etc.

**smashed** ▸*adj. inf.* drunk.

**smear** /smi(ə)r/ ▸*v.* **1** daub or mark with a greasy or sticky substance. **2** smudge. **3** defame; slander. ▸*n.* **1** act or instance of smearing. **2** *Med.* **a** material smeared on a microscopic slide, etc., for examination. **b** specimen taken from this. —**smear·y** *adj.*

**smeg·ma** /'smegmə/ ▸*n.* sebaceous secretion in the folds of the skin, esp. under a man's foreskin.

**smell** /smel/ ▸*n.* **1** faculty or power of perceiving odors.

**2** quality perceived by this. **3** unpleasant odor. **4** act of inhaling to ascertain smell. ▸*v.* (*past* and *past part.* **smelled** or **smelt**) **1** perceive or detect the odor of. **2** emit odor. **3** have or use a sense of smell.

**smelt** /smelt/ ▸*v.* **1** separate metal from (ore) by melting. **2** extract or refine (metal) in this way. ▸*n.* (*pl.* same or **smelts**) small edible green and silver fish. —**smelt·er** *n.*

**smid·gen** /'smijin/ (also **smid·gin**) ▸*n. inf.* small bit.

**smile** /smīl/ ▸*v.* **1** relax the features into a pleased or kind or gently skeptical expression, with the lips parted and the corners of the mouth turned up. **2** (**smile on/upon**) encourage. ▸*n.* **1** act or instance of smiling. **2** smiling expression or aspect. —**smil·ing·ly** *adv.*

**smirch** /smərCH/ ▸*v.* mark, soil, or discredit. ▸*n.* spot or stain.

**smirk** /smərk/ ▸*n.* affected, conceited, or silly smile. ▸*v.* make such a smile. —**smirk·ing·ly** *adv.* —**smirk·y** *adj.*

**smite** /smīt/ ▸*v.* (*past* **smote**; *past part.* **smit·ten**) **1** strike with a firm blow. **2** (**be smitten**) be strongly attracted to: *he was smitten with the young woman.*

**smith** /smiTH/ ▸*n.* **1** worker in metal: *goldsmith.* **2** blacksmith.

**smith·er·eens** /ˌsmiTHəˈrēnz/ ▸*pl. n.* small fragments: *smash into smithereens.*

**smith·y** /ˈsmiTHē/ ▸*n.* (*pl.* **-ies**) blacksmith's workshop; forge.

**smock** /smäk/ ▸*n.* loose shirtlike garment for protecting the clothing.

**smog** / smäg/ ▸*n.* fog intensified by smoke. —**smog·gy** *adj.*

**smoke** /smōk/ ▸*n.* **1** visible vapor from a burning substance. **2** act of smoking tobacco. ▸*v.* **1** emit smoke or visible vapor. **2** inhale and exhale the smoke of a cigarette, etc. **3** preserve by the action of smoke. —**smoke·less** *adj.* —**smok·er** *n.* —**smok·i·ly** *adv.* —**smok·i·ness** *n.* —**smok·y** *adj.*

**smoke de·tec·tor** ▸*n.* fire protection device that detects and warns of the presence of smoke.

**smoke screen** (also **smoke·screen**) ▸*n.* **1** cloud of smoke diffused to conceal (esp. military) operations. **2** ruse for disguising one's activities.

**smoke·stack** ▸*n.* chimney.

**smol·der** /ˈsmōldər/ ▸*v.* **1** burn slowly without a flame. **2** (of emotions, etc.) exist in a suppressed state. **3** (of a person) show silent anger, hatred, etc.

**smooch** /smōocH/ *inf.* ▸*n. & v.* kiss. —**smooch·er** *n.* —**smooch·y** *adj.*

**smooth** /smōoTH/ ▸*adj.* **1** having an even and regular surface. **2** not wrinkled, pitted, scored, or hairy. **3** (of a journey, etc.) untroubled by difficulties. **4** suave; conciliatory. **5** (of movement, etc.) not suddenly varying; not jerky. ▸*v.* **1** make or become smooth. **2** reduce or get rid of (differences, faults, difficulties, etc.). ▸*n.* smoothing touch or stroke. ▸*adv.* smoothly. —**smooth·ly** *adv.* —**smooth·ness** *n.*

**smor·gas·bord** /ˈsmôrgəsˌbôrd/ ▸*n.* buffet offering a variety of hot and cold foods.

**smoth·er** /ˈsmeTHər/ ▸*v.* **1** suffocate; stifle. **2** overwhelm with (kisses, kindness, etc.). **3** cover entirely in or with. **4** extinguish (a fire) by covering it.

**smudge** /sməj/ ▸*n.* **1** blurred or

smeared spot, stain, or mark; blot. **2** stain or blot on a person's character, etc.
▶*v.* **1** make a smudge on. **2** become smeared or blurred. **3** smear or blur the lines of (writing, drawing, etc.). —**smudge·less** *adj.* —**smudg·i·ly** *adv.* —**smudg·i·ness** *n.* —**smudg·y** *adj.*

**smug** /sməg/ ▶*adj.* (**smug·ger, smug·gest**) self-satisfied; complacent. —**smug·ly** *adv.* —**smug·ness** *n.*

**smug·gle** /ˈsməgəl/ ▶*v.* **1** import or export (goods) illegally, esp. without payment of customs duties. **2** convey secretly. —**smug·gler** *n.* —**smug·gling** *n.*

**smut** /smət/ ▶*n.* **1** small flake of soot, etc. **2** spot or smudge made by this. **3** obscene or lascivious talk, pictures, or stories. **4** fungal disease of cereals. —**smut·ty** *adj.* —**smut·ti·ly** *adv.* —**smut·ti·ness** *n.*

**snack** /snak/ ▶*n.* **1** light, casual, or hurried meal. **2** small amount of food eaten between meals. ▶*v.* eat a snack.

**snaf·fle** /ˈsnafəl/ ▶*n.* (also **snaffle bit**) (on a bridle) a simple bit, typically a jointed one, used with a single set of reins.

**snag** /snag/ ▶*n.* **1** unexpected obstacle or drawback. **2** jagged or projecting point. **3** tear in material, etc. ▶*v.* (**snagged, snag·ging**) catch or tear on a snag. —**snagged** *adj.* —**snag·gy** *adj.*

**snail** /snāl/ ▶*n.* slow-moving mollusk with a spiral shell.

**snake** /snāk/ ▶*n.* **1 a** long, limbless reptile. **b** limbless lizard or amphibian. **2** (also **snake in the grass**) treacherous person or secret enemy. **3** plumber's snakelike device for clearing obstructed pipes. ▶*v.* move or twist like a snake. —**snak·y** *adj.*

**snap** /snap/ ▶*v.* (**snapped, snap·ping**) **1** break suddenly or with a snap. **2** emit or cause to emit a sudden sharp crack. **3 a** (**snap at**) speak irritably or spitefully to (a person). **b** say irritably or spitefully. **4** (esp. of a dog, etc.) make a sudden audible bite. **5** move quickly. **6** take a snapshot of. ▶*n.* **1** act or sound of snapping. **2** crisp cookie: *gingersnap*. **3** snapshot. **4** (also **cold snap**) sudden brief spell of cold weather. **5** vigor or liveliness; zest. **6** *inf.* easy task: *it was a snap.* **7** fastener for clothing, etc.

▶*adv.* with the sound of a snap.

▶*adj.* made or done on the spur of the moment. **—snap·per** *n.* **—snap·pish** *adj.*

**snap·drag·on** ▶*n.* plant with a bag-shaped flower like a dragon's mouth.

**snap·py** ▶*adj.* (**-pi·er, -pi·est**) *inf.* **1** irritable; ill-tempered. **2** cleverly concise. **3** neat and elegant. **—snap·pi·ly** *adv.* **—snap·pi·ness** *n.*
□ **make it snappy** be quick.

**snap·shot** ▶*n.* casual photograph.

**snare** /sne(ə)r/ ▶*n.* **1** trap for catching birds or animals. **2** trick or temptation.

▶*v.* **1** catch (a bird, etc.) in a snare. **2** ensnare; lure or trap (a person).

**snarl** /snärl/ ▶*v.* **1** (of a dog) growl with bared teeth. **2** (of a person) speak cynically or angrily. **3** become entangled, congested, or confused.

▶*n.* act or sound of snarling. **—snarl·y** *adj.*

**snatch** /snaCH/ ▶*v.* **1** seize quickly, eagerly, or unexpectedly. **2** steal (a wallet, handbag, etc.) by grabbing. **3** *inf.* kidnap. **4** (**snatch at**) **a** try to seize. **b** take (an offer, etc.) eagerly.

▶*n.* **1** act of snatching. **2** fragment. **—snatch·er** *n.*

**sneak** /snēk/ ▶*v.* **1** go or convey furtively; slink. **2** *inf.* steal unobserved; make off with.

▶*n.* mean-spirited, underhanded person.

▶*adj.* acting or done without warning; secret. **—sneak·i·ly** *adv.* **—sneak·ing·ly** *adv.* **—sneak·i·ness** *n.* **—sneak·y** *adj.*

**sneak·er** ▶*n.* rubber-soled shoe for sport or casual wear.

**sneer** /sni(ə)r/ ▶*n.* derisive smile or remark.

▶*v.* **1** smile derisively. **2** say sneeringly. **—sneer·ing·ly** *adv.*

**sneeze** /snēz/ ▶*n.* **1** sudden involuntary expulsion of air from the nose and mouth. **2** sound of this.

▶*v.* make a sneeze. **—sneez·er** *n.* **—sneez·y** *adj.*

**snick·er** /'snikər/ ▶*n.* half-suppressed laugh.

▶*v.* to utter such a laugh. **—snick·er·ing·ly** *adv.*

**snide** /snīd/ ▶*adj.* sneering; slyly

derogatory. —**snide·ly** *adv.*
—**snide·ness** *n.*

**sniff** /snif/ ▸*v.* **1** draw up air audibly through the nose. **2** draw in (a scent, drug, liquid, or air) through the nose.
▸*n.* act or sound of sniffing. —**sniff·er** *n.* —**sniff·ing·ly** *adv.*
☐ **sniff at** show contempt for.
☐ **sniff out** detect.

**snif·fle** ▸*v.* sniff slightly or repeatedly.
▸*n.* sound of this.

**snif·ter** /'sniftər/ ▸*n.* balloon-shaped glass for brandy.

**snig·ger** /'snigər/ ▸*n.* smothered or half-suppressed laugh.
▸*v.* give such a laugh.

**snip** /snip/ ▸*v.* (**snipped, snip·ping**) cut with scissors, esp. in small, quick strokes.
▸*n.* act of snipping.

**snipe** /snīp/ ▸*n.* (*pl.* same or **snipes**) wading bird with a long, straight bill.
▸*v.* **1** fire shots from hiding, usu. at long range. **2** make a sly critical attack. —**snip·er** *n.*

**snip·pet** /'snipit/ ▸*n.* **1** small piece cut off. **2** scrap or fragment (of information).

**snip·py** ▸*adj.* (**-pi·er, -pi·est**) *inf.* fault-finding and snappish.

—**snip·pi·ly** *adv.*
—**snip·pi·ness** *n.*

**snit** /snit/ ▸*n. inf.* sulk.

**snitch** /snɪCH/ *inf.* ▸*v.* **1** steal. **2** inform on a person.
▸*n.* informer.

**sniv·el** /'snivəl/ ▸*v.* **1** cry and sniffle. **2** complain in a whining or tearful way.
▸*n.* slight sniff. —**sniv·el·er** *n.*
—**sniv·el·ing** *adj.* —**sniv·el·ing·ly** *adv.*

**snob** /snäb/ ▸*n.* person who despises those considered socially, intellectually, etc., inferior. —**snob·ber·y** *n.*
—**snob·bish** *adj.* —**snob·bish·ly** *adv.* —**snob·bish·ness** *n.*
—**snob·by** *adj.*

**snoop** /snoop/ *inf.* ▸*v.* pry.
▸*n.* **1** act of snooping. **2** person who snoops. —**snoop·er** *n.*
—**snoop·y** *adj.*

**snooze** /snooz/ *inf.* ▸*n.* short sleep, esp. in the daytime.
▸*v.* take a snooze. —**snooz·er** *n.*
—**snooz·y** *adj.*

**snore** /snôr/ ▸*n.* snorting or grunting sound in breathing during sleep.
▸*v.* make this sound. —**snor·er** *n.*

**snor·kel** /'snôrkəl/ ▸*n.*
**1** breathing tube for an underwater swimmer. **2** device

for supplying air to a submerged submarine.

▶*v.* use a snorkel. **—snor·kel·er** *n.*

**snort** /snôrt/ ▶*n.* **1** explosive sound made by the sudden forcing of breath through the nose. **2** *inf.* inhaled dose of a (usu. illegal) powdered drug.

▶*v.* **1** make a snort. **2** *inf.* inhale (esp. cocaine or heroin).

**snot** /snät/ ▶*n. inf.* **1** nasal mucus. **2** contemptible person.

**snout** /snout/ ▶*n.* projecting nose and mouth of an animal. **—snout·ed** *adj.* **—snout·y** *adj.*

**snow** /snō/ ▶*n.* **1** frozen atmospheric vapor falling to earth in light white flakes. **2** fall or layer of this. **3** *inf.* cocaine.

▶*v.* **1** fall as snow: *it is snowing.* **2** *inf.* deceive or charm with plausible words.

☐ **be snowed under** be overwhelmed, esp. with work.

**snow·ball** ▶*n.* **1** snow pressed together into a ball, esp. for throwing in play. **2** anything that increases rapidly like a snowball rolled on snow.

▶*v.* increase rapidly.

**snow·board** ▶*n.* board similar to a wide ski, ridden over snow in an upright or surfing position. **—snow·board·er** *n.*

**snow·drop** ▶*n.* bulbous plant bearing white drooping flowers in the early spring.

**snow·flake** ▶*n.* small crystal of snow.

**snow·man** ▶*n.* (*pl.* **-men**) figure resembling a human, made of compressed snow.

**snow·mo·bile** /-mō,bēl/ ▶*n.* motor vehicle, esp. with runners or revolving treads, for traveling over snow.

**snow·shoe** ▶*n.* racket-shaped attachment to a boot for walking on snow without sinking in. **—snow·sho·er** *n.*

**snow·storm** ▶*n.* heavy fall of snow.

**snub** /snəb/ ▶*v.* (**snubbed, snub·bing**) rebuff or humiliate.

▶*n.* act of snubbing; rebuff.

▶*adj.* short and blunt in shape. **—snub·ber** *n.*

**snuff** ▶*v.* put out (a candle).

▶*n.* powdered tobacco or medicine taken by sniffing.

☐ **up to snuff** *inf.* up to standard.

**snug** /snəg/ ▶*adj.* (**snug·ger, snug·gest**) **1** cozy; comfortable; sheltered. **2** close-fitting. **—snug·ly** *adv.* **—snug·ness** *n.*

**snug·gle** ▶*v.* settle or draw into a warm comfortable position.

**so** /sō/ ▶*adv.* **1** to such an extent.

**2** to the degree or in the manner implied: *so expensive that few can afford it.* **3** (adding emphasis) to that extent; in that or a similar manner: *I want to leave and so does she.* **4** very: *I am so glad.* **5** (with verb of saying or thinking, etc.) as previously mentioned or described: *I think so.*

▶*conj.* **1** with the result that: *there was none left, so we had to go without.* **2** in order that: *came home early so that I could see you.* **3** and then; as the next step.

□ **and so on** (or **and so forth**) **1** and others of the same kind. **2** and in other similar ways. □ **so-called** commonly designated or known as, often incorrectly. □ **so-so** indifferent; not very good. □ indifferently.

**soak** /sōk/ ▶*v.* **1** make or become thoroughly wet through saturation with or in liquid. **2** (**soak up**) **a** absorb (liquid). **b** acquire (knowledge, etc.) copiously. **3** (of liquid) make its way or penetrate by saturation.

▶*n.* soaking. —**soak·age** *n.* —**soak·ing** *n. & adj.*

**so-and-so** ▶*n.* (*pl.* **so-and-sos**) **1** particular person or thing not needing to be specified: *told me*

to do so-and-so. **2** *inf.* person disliked or regarded with disfavor.

**soap** /sōp/ ▶*n.* cleansing agent yielding lather when rubbed in water.

▶*v.* apply soap to. —**soap·i·ly** *adv.* —**soap·i·ness** *n.* —**soap·less** *adj.* —**soap·y** *adj.*

□ **soap opera** broadcast melodrama, usu. serialized in many episodes.

**soap·box** ▶*n.* makeshift stand for a public speaker.

**soar** /sôr/ ▶*v.* **1** fly or rise high. **2** reach a high level. —**soar·ing·ly** *adv.*

**sob** /säb/ ▶*v.* (**sobbed, sob·bing**) draw breath in convulsive gasps usu. with weeping.

▶*n.* convulsive drawing of breath, esp. in weeping. —**sob·bing·ly** *adv.*

**so·ber** /ˈsōbər/ ▶*adj.* (**-er, -est**) **1** not affected by alcohol. **2** not given to excessive drinking of alcohol. **3** moderate; tranquil; sedate; serious.

▶*v.* (often **sober up**) make or become sober. —**so·ber·ly** *adv.*

**so·bri·quet** /ˈsōbrə,kā; -,ket/ ▶*n.* **1** nickname. **2** assumed name.

**soc·cer** /ˈsäkər/ ▶*n.* game played by two teams of eleven players with a round ball that cannot be touched with the hands during play except by the goalkeepers.

**so·cia·ble** /ˈsōsHəbəl/ ▸*adj.* liking the society of other people; gregarious; friendly. —**so·cia·bil·i·ty** *n.* —**so·cia·ble·ness** *n.* —**so·cia·bly** *adv.*

**so·cial** /ˈsōsHəl/ ▸*adj.* **1** of or relating to society or its organization. **2** concerned with the mutual relations of human beings or of classes of human beings. **3** living in organized communities. **4** needing companionship; gregarious; interdependent.

▸*n.* social gathering, esp. one organized by a club, congregation, etc. —**so·cial·ly** *adv.*

**so·cial gos·pel** ▸*n.* Christian faith practiced as a call not just to personal conversion but to social reform.

**so·cial·ism** ▸*n.* **1** political and economic theory of social organization advocating state ownership and control of the means of production, distribution, and exchange. **2** policy or practice based on this

theory. —**so·cial·ist** *n. & adj.* —**so·cial·is·tic** *adj.*

**so·cial·ist re·al·ism** ▸*n.* theory of art, literature, and music officially sanctioned by the state in some communist countries (esp. in the Soviet Union under Stalin), by which artistic work was supposed to reflect and promote the ideals of a socialist society.

**so·cial·ite** ▸*n.* person prominent in fashionable society.

**so·cial·ize** ▸*v.* **1** act in a sociable manner. **2** organize on socialistic principles. —**so·cial·i·za·tion** *n.*

**so·cial sci·ence** ▸*n.* study of human society and social relationships. —**so·cial sci·en·tist** *n.*

**So·cial Se·cur·i·ty** ▸*n.* federal program of assistance to the elderly, disabled, etc.

**so·cial work** ▸*n.* work of benefit to those in need of help or welfare, esp. done by specially trained personnel. —**so·cial work·er** *n.*

**so·ci·e·ty** /səˈsīətē/ ▸*n.* (*pl.* **-ties**) **1** sum of human conditions and activity regarded as a whole functioning interdependently.

2 social community. **3 a** social mode of life. **b** customs and organization of an ordered community. **4** socially advantaged or prominent members of a community. **5** companionship; company. **6** association; club. —**so·ci·e·tal** adj. —**so·ci·e·tal·ly** adv.

**so·ci·o·bi·ol·o·gy** /ˌsōsēōˌbī-ˈäləjē/ ▸n. scientific study of the biological (esp. ecological and evolutionary) aspects of social behavior in animals and humans.

**so·ci·ol·o·gy** /ˌsōsēˈäləjē/ ▸n. study of society and social problems. —**so·ci·o·log·i·cal** adj. —**so·ci·o·log·i·cal·ly** adv. —**so·ci·ol·o·gist** n.

**so·ci·om·e·try** /ˌsōsēˈämətrē/ ▸n. quantitative study and measurement of relationships within a group of people.

**sock** /säk/ ▸n. **1** short knitted covering for the foot, usu. not reaching the knee. **2** hard blow. ▸v. inf. hit forcefully.

**sock·et** /ˈsäkit/ ▸n. hollow for something to fit into.

**sod** /säd/ ▸n. grass or a section of grass with its roots.

**so·da** /ˈsōdə/ ▸n. **1** sodium bicarbonate. **2** (also **soda pop**) a sweet effervescent soft drink. **b** (also **soda water**) effervescent water for drinking. □ **soda fountain** counter for preparing and serving sodas, sundaes, and ice cream.

**sod·den** /ˈsädn/ ▸adj. saturated with liquid; soaked through; soggy. —**sod·den·ly** adv.

**so·di·um** /ˈsōdēəm/ ▸n. soft silver white reactive metallic element. (Symb.: **Na**) □ **sodium bicarbonate** white soluble powder used in the manufacture of fire extinguishers and effervescent drinks. □ **sodium chloride** common salt. □ **sodium hydroxide** deliquescent compound that is strongly alkaline and used in the manufacture of soap and paper.

**sod·om·y** /ˈsädəmē/ ▸n. sexual intercourse involving anal or oral copulation. —**sod·om·ize** v.

**so·fa** /ˈsōfə/ ▸n. long upholstered seat with a back and arms. □ **sofa bed** sofa that can be converted into a bed.

**sof·fit** /ˈsäfit/ ▸n. underside of an architectural structure, such as an arch, a balcony, or overhanging eaves.

**soft** /sôft/ ▸adj. **1** lacking

hardness or firmness; yielding to pressure; easily cut. **2** (of cloth, etc.) smooth; not rough or coarse. **3** (of air, etc.) mellow; mild. **4** (of water) free from mineral salts. **5** (of a light, color, etc.) not brilliant or glaring. **6** gentle and pleasing. **7** (of an outline, etc.) not sharply defined. **8** gentle; conciliatory; complimentary; amorous.

▶*adv.* softly: *play soft.* —**soft·ly** *adv.* —**soft·ness** *n.*

☐ **soft-boiled** (of an egg) lightly boiled with the yolk soft or liquid. ☐ **soft drink** nonalcoholic usu. effervescent drink. ☐ **soft palate** rear part of the palate. ☐ **soft sell** restrained, low key or subtly persuasive salesmanship. ☐ **soft touch** *inf.* gullible person, esp. over money.

**soft·ball** ▶*n.* **1** ball like a baseball but larger and pitched underhand. **2** form of baseball using this.

**soft·en** /ˈsôfən/ ▶*v.* make or become soft or softer.

**soft·heart·ed** ▶*adj.* tender; compassionate; easily moved. —**soft·heart·ed·ness** *n.*

**soft tar·get** ▶*n.* person or thing that is relatively unprotected or vulnerable, esp. to military or terrorist attack.

**soft·ware** ▶*n.* programs for a computer.

**sog·gy** /ˈsägē/ ▶*adj.* (**-gi·er, -gi·est**) sodden; saturated; dank. —**sog·gi·ly** *adv.* —**sog·gi·ness** *n.*

**soi·gné** /swänˈyā/ ▶*adj.* (*fem.* **-gnée** *pronunc.* same) dressed very elegantly; well groomed.

**soil** /soil/ ▶*n.* **1** upper layer of earth in which plants grow. **2** ground belonging to a nation; territory: *on British soil.* **3** dirty mark. **4** filth; refuse.
▶*v.* **1** make dirty; smear or stain with dirt. **2** tarnish; defile; bring discredit to.

**soi·rée** /swäˈrā/ ▶*n.* evening party.

**so·journ** /ˈsōjərn/ ▶*n.* temporary stay.
▶*v.* stay temporarily. —**so·journ·er** *n.*

**sol·ace** /ˈsälis/ ▶*n.* comfort.
▶*v.* give comfort to.

**so·lar** /ˈsōlər/ ▶*adj.* of, relating to, or reckoned by the sun: *solar time.*

☐ **solar system** the sun and the celestial bodies whose motion it governs.

**so·lar·i·um** /səˈle(ə)rēəm/ ▶*n.* (*pl.* **-i·ums** or **-i·a**) room with extensive areas of glass for admitting sunlight.

**so·lar plex·us** /ˈpleksəs/ ▶*n.* complex of radiating nerves at the pit of the stomach.

**sol·der** /ˈsädər/ ▶*n.* fusible alloy used to join metal parts.
▶*v.* join with solder.
—**sol·der·er** *n.*

**sol·dier** /ˈsōljər/ ▶*n.* person serving in or having served in an army.
▶*v.* serve as a soldier: *was off soldiering.* —**sol·dier·ly** *adj.*
□ **soldier on** *inf.* persevere doggedly.

**sole** /sōl/ ▶*n.* **1** undersurface of the foot. **2** part of a shoe, sock, etc., under the foot (esp. excluding the heel). **3** flatfish used as food.
▶*v.* provide (a shoe, etc.) with a sole.
▶*adj.* one and only; single; exclusive. —**soled** *adj.* —**sole·ly** *adv.*

**sol·emn** /ˈsäləm/ ▶*adj.* **1** serious and dignified. **2** formal. **3** grave; sober. —**so·lem·ni·ty** *n.*
—**sol·emn·ly** *adv.*
—**sol·emn·ness** *n.*

**sol·em·nize** /ˈsäləmˌnīz/ ▶*v.* perform or mark with a ceremony, esp. of marriage.
—**sol·em·ni·za·tion** *n.*

**so·lic·it** /səˈlisit/ ▶*v.* **1** ask repeatedly or earnestly for or seek or invite (business, etc.). **2** accost as a prostitute.
—**so·lic·i·ta·tion** *n.*

**so·lic·i·tor** ▶*n.* **1** person who solicits. **2** canvasser.

**so·lic·i·tous** ▶*adj.* showing interest or concern.
—**so·lic·i·tous·ly** *adv.*

**sol·id** /ˈsälid/ ▶*adj.* (**-er, -est**) **1** firm and stable in shape; not liquid or fluid: *solid food.* **2** of a single material throughout, not hollow or containing cavities: *solid sphere.* **3** of the same substance throughout: *solid silver.* **4** strong; sound; reliable. **5** three dimensional. **6** uninterrupted; continuous.
▶*n.* solid substance or body.
—**so·lid·i·fy** *v.* —**so·lid·i·fi·ca·tion** *n.* —**so·lid·i·ty** *n.* —**sol·id·ly** *adv.*

**sol·i·dar·i·ty** /ˌsäləˈdaritē/ ▶*n.* unity or agreement of feeling or action, esp. among individuals with a common interest.

**sol·id state** ▶*n.* state of matter in which materials are not fluid but retain their boundaries without support, the atoms or molecules occupying fixed positions with respect to one another and unable to move freely.

▶*adj.* (**sol·id-state**) (of a device) making use of the electronic properties of solid semiconductors.

**so·lil·o·quy** /sə'liləkwē/ ▶*n.* (*pl.* **-quies**) speech made aloud to oneself, esp. in drama.
—**so·lil·o·quist** *n.*
—**so·lil·o·quize** *v.*

**sol·i·taire** /'säli,tə(ə)r/ ▶*n.* **1** diamond or other gem set by itself. **2** any of several card games for one player.

**sol·i·tar·y** /'sälə,terē/ ▶*adj.* **1** living alone; not gregarious. **2** secluded or unfrequented. **3** single or sole: *solitary instance.*
—**sol·i·tar·i·ly** *adv.* —**sol·i·tude** *n.*

**so·lo** /'sōlō/ ▶*n.* **1** (*pl.* **-los** or **-li**) vocal or instrumental piece or passage, or dance, performed by one person. **2** (*pl.* **-los**) **a** unaccompanied flight by a pilot in an aircraft. **b** anything done by one person unaccompanied.
▶*v.* (**-loed**) perform a solo.
▶*adv.* unaccompanied; alone.
—**so·lo·ist** *n.*

**sol·stice** /'sōlstis/ ▶*n.* time or date, about June 21 (**summer** solstice) and December 22 (**winter solstice**), at which the sun's path is farthest from the equator. —**sol·sti·tial** *adj.*

**sol·u·ble** /'sälyəbəl/ ▶*adj.* that can be dissolved, esp. in water. —**sol·u·bil·i·ty** *n.*

**sol·ute** /'säl,yo͞ot/ ▶*n.* minor component in a solution, dissolved in the solvent.

**so·lu·tion** /sə'lo͞osHən/ ▶*n.* **1** act or a means of solving a problem or difficulty. **2 a** conversion of a solid or gas into a liquid by mixture with a liquid. **b** mixture produced by this.

**solve** /sälv/ ▶*v.* answer or effectively deal with (a problem or difficulty). —**solv·a·ble** *adj.* —**solv·er** *n.*

**sol·vent** /'sälvənt/ ▶*adj.* **1** able to dissolve or form a solution with something. **2** having enough money to meet one's liabilities.
▶*n.* solvent liquid, etc.
—**sol·ven·cy** *n.*

**som·ber** /'sämbər/ ▶*adj.* dark; gloomy; dismal. —**som·ber·ly** *adv.* —**som·ber·ness** *n.*

**som·bre·ro** /säm'bre(ə)rō/ ▶*n.* (*pl.* **-ros**) broad-brimmed felt or straw hat worn esp. in Mexico and the southwest U.S.

**some** /səm/ ▸*adj.* **1** unspecified amount or number of: *some apples.* **2** that is unknown or unnamed: *some day.* **3** denoting an approximate number: *some twenty minutes.* **4** considerable: *went to some trouble.* **5** at least a small amount of: *have some consideration.*
▸*pron.* some number or amount: *I have some already.*
▸*adv.* to some extent: *do it some more.*

**-some** ▸*suffix* **1** forming adjectives meaning: **a** productive of: *fearsome.* **b** characterized by being: *lithesome.* **2** forming nouns from numerals, meaning 'a group of (so many)': *foursome.*

**some·bod·y** ▸*pron.* some person.
▸*n.* (*pl.* **-ies**) person of importance.

**some·day** ▸*adv.* at some time in the future.

**some·how** ▸*adv.* for some unstated reason or way.

**some·one** ▸*pron. & n.* somebody.

**som·er·sault** /'səmər,sôlt/ ▸*n.* leap or roll in which a person turns head over heels and lands on the feet.
▸*v.* perform a somersault.

**some·thing** ▸*n. & pron.* **1** some unspecified or unknown thing: *something has happened.* **2** unexpressed quantity, quality, or extent: *something of a fool.*
□ **something else 1** something different. **2** *inf.* something exceptional.

**some·time** ▸*adv.* at some unspecified time.
▸*adj.* former: *sometime mayor.*

**some·times** ▸*adv.* at some times; occasionally.

**some·what** ▸*adv.* to some extent.

**some·where** ▸*adv.* in or to some place.
▸*pron.* some unspecified place.

**som·nam·bu·lism** /säm-'nambyə,lizəm/ ▸*n.* sleepwalking.
—**som·nam·bu·list** *n.*

**som·nif·er·ous** /säm'nifərəs/ ▸*adj.* tending to induce sleep; soporific.

**som·no·lent** /'sämnələnt/ ▸*adj.* **1** sleepy; drowsy. **2** inducing drowsiness. **3** *Med.* in a state between sleeping and waking.
—**som·no·lence** *n.*
—**som·no·lent·ly** *adv.*

**son** /sən/ ▸*n.* **1** boy or man in relation to his parents. **2** male descendant.

□ **son-in-law** husband of one's daughter.

**so·nar** /ˈsōˌnär/ ▶n. **1** system for the underwater detection of objects by reflected sound. **2** apparatus for this.

**so·na·ta** /səˈnätə/ ▶n. composition for one or two instruments, usu. in several movements.

**song** /sôNG/ ▶n. **1** words set to music or meant to be sung. **2** singing or vocal music. **3** musical cry of some birds. □ **song and dance** inf. fuss or commotion.

**song·bird** ▶n. bird with a musical call.

**son·ic** /ˈsänik/ ▶adj. of or relating to or using sound or sound waves. □ **sonic boom** loud explosive noise made when an aircraft surpasses the speed of sound.

**son·ics** /ˈsäniks/ ▶pl. n. musical sounds artificially produced or reproduced.

**son·net** /ˈsänit/ ▶n. poem of 14 lines using any of a number of rhyme schemes and usu. having ten syllables per line.

**so·no·rous** /ˈsänərəs/ ▶adj. **1** having a loud, full, or deep sound; resonant. **2** (of a speech, style, etc.) imposing; grand. —**so·nor·i·ty** n. —**so·no·rous·ly** adv. —**so·no·rous·ness** n.

**soon** /sōon/ ▶adv. **1** in a short time. **2** quickly; before long. **3** readily or willingly: would as soon stay behind. □ **sooner or later** at some future time; eventually.

**soot** /sōot/ ▶n. black powdery deposit from smoke.

**soothe** /sōoTH/ ▶v. **1** calm (a person or feelings). **2** soften or mitigate (pain). —**sooth·er** n. —**sooth·ing** adj. —**sooth·ing·ly** adv.

**sooth·say·er** /ˈsōoTHˌsāər/ ▶n. diviner or seer.

**SOP** (also **S.O.P.**) ▶abbr. standard operating procedure.

**sop** /säp/ ▶n. **1** piece of bread, etc., dipped in gravy, etc. **2** thing given or done to pacify or bribe. ▶v. (**sopped, sop·ping**) **1** be drenched. **2** (**sop up**) absorb (liquid) in a towel, etc.

**soph·ism** /ˈsäfizəm/ ▶n. fallacious argument, esp. one used deliberately to deceive.

**so·phis·ti·cat·ed** /səˈfistiˌkātid/ ▶adj. **1** (of a person) educated and refined; worldly-wise. **2** (of a thing, idea, etc.) highly

developed and complex.
—**so·phis·ti·ca·tion** *n.*

**soph·ist·ry** /ˈsäfəstrē/ ▶*n.* (*pl.* **-ries**) clever and subtle reasoning that is intended to deceive.

**soph·o·more** /ˈsäf(ə)ˌmôr/ ▶*n.* second year college or high school student.

**sop·o·rif·ic** /ˌsäpəˈrifik/ ▶*adj.* inducing sleep.
▶*n.* soporific drug or influence.
—**sop·o·rif·er·ous** *adj.*
—**sop·o·rif·i·cal·ly** *adv.*

**sop·py** /ˈsäpē/ ▶*adj.* (**-pi·er, -pi·est**) *inf.* mawkishly sentimental.

**so·pran·o** /səˈpranō/ ▶*n.* (*pl.* **-pran·os** or **-pran·i**) **1 a** highest pitched singing voice. **b** singer with this voice. **c** part written for it. **2 a** instrument of a high or the highest pitch in its family. **b** its player.

**sor·bet** /sôrˈbā; ˈsôrbit/ ▶*n.* sweetened frozen confection, usu. with fruit flavoring.

**sor·cer·er** /ˈsôrsərər/ (*fem.* **sor·cer·ess**) ▶*n.* magician; wizard. —**sor·cer·y** *n.*

**sor·did** /ˈsôrdid/ ▶*adj.* dirty or squalid. —**sor·did·ly** *adv.*
—**sor·did·ness** *n.*

**sore** /sôr/ ▶*adj.* **1** (of a part of the body) painful. **2** (of a person) suffering pain. **3** angry or vexed. **4** grievous or severe: *in sore need.*
▶*n.* sore place on the body.
—**sore·ly** *adv.* —**sore·ness** *n.*
□ **sore point** subject causing distress or annoyance.

**sor·ghum** /ˈsôrgəm/ ▶*n.* tropical cereal grass.

**so·ro·ral** /səˈrôrəl/ ▶*adj.* of or like a sister or sisters.

**so·ror·i·ty** /səˈrôritē/ ▶*n.* (*pl.* **-ties**) female students' society in a university or college, usu. for social purposes.

**sor·rel** /ˈsôrəl/ ▶*adj.* of a light reddish-brown color.
▶*n.* **1** this color. **2** sharp-tasting herb.

**sor·row** /ˈsärō/ ▶*n.* **1** mental distress caused by loss or disappointment, etc. **2** cause of sorrow.
▶*v.* **1** feel sorrow. **2** mourn.
—**sor·row·er** *n.* —**sor·row·ing** *adj.*

**sor·ry** /ˈsärē/ ▶*adj.* (**-ri·er, -ri·est**) **1** pained or regretful or penitent. **2** (**sorry for**) feeling pity or sympathy for. **3** wretched; in a poor state.
—**sor·ri·ly** *adv.*

**sort** /sôrt/ ▶*n.* **1** group of things, etc., with common attributes; class or kind. **2** roughly of the kind specified: *is some sort of doctor.*

▶*v.* arrange systematically or according to type, class, etc. —**sort·a·ble** *adj.* —**sort·er** *n.* —**sort·ing** *n.*

□ **of a sort** (or **of sorts**) *inf.* not fully deserving the name: *a holiday of sorts.* □ **out of sorts** slightly unwell. □ **sort of** *inf.* as it were; to some extent.

**sor·tie** /ˌsôr'tē/ ▶*n.* **1** attack by troops from a besieged garrison. **2** operational flight by a single military aircraft.

**SOS** ▶*n.* (*pl.* **SOSs**) international code signal of extreme distress, used esp. by ships at sea.

**sot·to vo·ce** /'sätō 'vōchē/ ▶*adv.* in an undertone or aside.

**sou·brette** /soo'bret/ ▶*n.* minor female role in a comedy, typically that of a pert maidservant.

**souf·flé** /soo'flā/ ▶*n.* light dish usu. made with beaten egg whites and baked.

**sough** /səf; sou/ ▶*v.* (of the wind in trees, the sea, etc.) make a moaning, whistling, or rushing sound. ▶*n.* sound of this type.

**sought** /sôt/ ▶past and past part. of SEEK.

**soul** /sōl/ ▶*n.* **1** spiritual or immaterial part of a human being, often regarded as immortal. **2** moral or emotional or intellectual nature of a person or animal. **3** personification or pattern of something: *the very soul of discretion.* **4** individual: *not a soul in sight.* **5** animating or essential part. **6** African-American culture, music, ethnic pride, etc.

□ **soul mate** person ideally suited to another.

**sound**[1] /sound/ ▶*n.* **1** sensation caused in the ear by the vibration of air or other medium. **2** vibrations causing this sensation. **3** what is or may be heard. **4** idea or impression conveyed by words: *don't like the sound of that.*

▶*v.* **1** emit or cause to emit sound. **2** utter or pronounce: *sound a note of alarm.* **3** convey an impression when heard: *you sound worried.* **4** test the depth or quality of the bottom of (the sea or a river, etc.). **5** (**sound out**) inquire (esp. cautiously or discreetly) into the opinions or feelings of (a person). —**sound·er** *n.* —**sound·less** *adj.*

—**sound·less·ly** *adv.*
—**sound·less·ness** *n.*

**sound**[2] ▸*adj.* **1** healthy; not diseased, injured, or rotten. **2** (of an opinion or policy, etc.) correct; judicious; legally valid. **3** restful; undisturbed.

▸*adv.* soundly: *sound asleep.*

▸*n.* **1** narrow passage of water connecting two seas or a sea with a lake, etc. **2** arm of the sea. —**sound·ly** *adv.*
—**sound·ness** *n.*

**sound bar·ri·er** ▸*n.* high resistance of air to objects moving at speeds near that of sound.

**sound bite** ▸*n.* short extract from a recorded interview, chosen for its pungency or appropriateness.

**sound ef·fect** ▸*n.* sound other than speech or music made artificially for use in a play, movie, etc.

**sound·proof** ▸*adj.* impervious to sound.

▸*v.* make soundproof.

**sound·track** ▸*n.* sound element of a movie, television broadcast, etc.

**soup** /soop/ ▸*n.* liquid dish made by boiling meat, fish, or vegetables, etc., in stock or water.

▸*v. inf.* (**soup up**) increase the power and effectiveness of.
□ **in the soup** *inf.* in difficulties.

**soup·çon** /soop'sôN/ ▸*n.* very small quantity of something.

**soup·y** /'soopē/ ▸*adj.* (**-i·er, -i·est**) of or resembling soup.
—**soup·i·ness** *n.*

**sour** /'sou(ə)r/ ▸*adj.* **1** acid in taste or smell. **2** (of food, esp. milk) bad because of fermentation. **3** (of a person, temper, etc.) harsh; morose; bitter. **4** (of a thing) unpleasant; distasteful.

▸*v.* make or become sour: *soured the cream.* —**sour·ly** *adv.*
—**sour·ness** *n.*
□ **sour grapes** resentful disparagement of something one cannot personally acquire.

**source** /sôrs/ ▸*n.* **1** place, person, or thing from which something issues or originates. **2** person, document, etc., providing evidence: *reliable sources of information.*

**south** /souTH/ ▸*n.* **1** point of the horizon 90° clockwise from east. **2** compass point corresponding to this. **3** direction in which this lies. **4** (usu. **the South**) a part of the world or a country or a town lying to the south. **b** southern states of the U.S., especially those that were part of the Confederacy.

▶*adj.* **1** toward, at, near, or facing the south. **2** coming from the south: *south wind.*

▶*adv.* **1** toward, at, or near the south. **2** (**south of**) further south than. —**south·er·ly** *adj. & adv.* —**south·ern** *adj.* —**south·ward** *adj. & adv.*

**South Af·ri·can** ▶*adj.* of or relating to the Republic of South Africa.

▶*n.* native or inhabitant of South Africa.

**South A·mer·i·can** ▶*adj.* of or relating to South America.

▶*n.* native or inhabitant of South America.

**south·east** ▶*n.* **1** point midway between south and east. **2** direction in which this lies.

▶*adj. & adv.* of, toward, or coming from the southeast. —**south·east·er·ly** *adj. & adv.* —**south·east·ern** *adj.*

**south·paw** ▶*n. inf.* left-handed person.

**south pole** (also **South Pole**) ▶*n.* southernmost point of the earth's axis of rotation.

**south·west** ▶*n.* **1** point midway between south and west. **2** direction in which this lies.

▶*adj. & adv.* of, toward, or coming from the southwest. —**south·west·er·ly** *adj. & adv.* —**south·west·ern** *adj.*

**sou·ve·nir** /ˌsoovəˈni(ə)r/ ▶*n.* memento of an occasion, place, etc.

**sov·er·eign** /ˈsäv(ə)rin/ ▶*n.* supreme ruler, esp. a monarch.

▶*adj.* **1** supreme. **2** possessing independent national authority: *a sovereign state.* —**sov·er·eign·ty** *n.*

**so·vi·et** /ˈsōvēit/ ▶*n.* **1** (in the former USSR) elected local, district, or national council. **2** (**Soviet**) citizen of the former USSR.

▶*adj.* (usu. **Soviet**) of or concerning the former Soviet Union.

**sow**[1] /sō/ ▶*v.* (*past* **sowed**; *past part.* **sown** or **sowed**) **1 a** scatter or put (seed) on or in the earth. **b** plant (a field, etc.) with seed. **2** initiate; arouse. —**sow·er** *n.*

**sow**[2] /sou/ ▶*n.* female adult pig.

**soy·bean** /ˈsoiˌbēn/ (also **soy**) ▶*n.* **1** leguminous plant cultivated for the edible oil and flour it yields and used as a replacement for animal protein in certain foods. **2** seed of this.

**soy·sauce** ▶*n.* sauce made with fermented soybeans, used esp. in Asian cooking.

**spa** /spä/ ▶*n.* resort or facility offering use of exercise equipment, steam baths, etc.

**space** /spās/ ▶*n.* **1 a** continuous unlimited area or expanse that may or may not contain objects, etc. **b** interval between points or objects. **c** empty area; room. **2** (also **outer space**) physical universe beyond the earth's atmosphere. **3** place, seat, berth, etc., made available: *no space on the bus.* **4** interval of time.
▶*v.* set or arrange at intervals.
—**spac·er** *n.*

**space·craft** (also **space·ship**) ▶*n.* vehicle for traveling in space.

**space shut·tle** ▶*n.* rocket-launched spacecraft used to make repeated journeys between the earth and earth orbit.

**space sta·tion** ▶*n.* large artificial satellite used as a base for operations in space.

**spa·cious** /'spāSHəs/ ▶*adj.* having ample space; covering a large area; roomy.

—**spa·cious·ly** *adv.*
—**spa·cious·ness** *n.*

**spade** /spād/ ▶*n.* **1** tool used for digging or cutting the ground, etc., with a sharp-edged metal blade and a long handle. **2** playing card of a suit denoted by black inverted heart-shaped figures with small stalks.
▶*v.* dig over (ground) with a spade.

**spa·ghet·ti** /spə'getē/ ▶*n.* pasta made in long thin strings.

**span** /span/ ▶*n.* **1** full extent of something from end to end. **2** each arch or part of a bridge between piers or supports.
▶*v.* (**spanned, span·ning**) stretch from side to side of; extend across.

**span·gle** /'spaNGgəl/ ▶*n.* **1** sequin. **2** small sparkling object.
▶*v.* [usu. as *adj.* **spangled**] cover with or as if with spangles: *spangled costume.* —**span·gly** *adj.*

**span·iel** /'spanyəl/ ▶*n.* **1** dog of any of various breeds with a long silky coat and drooping ears. **2** any of these breeds.

**Span·ish** /'spaniSH/ ▶*adj.* of or relating to Spain or its people or language.
▶*n.* **1** language of Spain and

Spanish America. **2** (**the Spanish**) the people of Spain.

**spank** /spaNGk/ ▸*v. & n.* slap, esp. on the buttocks, with the open hand.

**spank·ing** ▸*adj.* **1** brisk or lively. **2** *inf.* striking; excellent.
▸*adv. inf.* very; exceedingly: *spanking clean.*
▸*n.* slapping on the buttocks.

**spar** /spär/ ▸*n.* stout pole, esp. as a ship's mast, etc.
▸*v.* (**sparred, spar·ring**) **1** make the motions of boxing without landing heavy blows. **2** argue.

**spare** /spe(ə)r/ ▸*adj.* **1** extra. **2** lean; thin. **3** scanty; frugal; not copious: *spare diet.*
▸*n.* **1** spare part. **2** *Bowling* knocking down of all the pins with the first two balls.
▸*v.* **1** afford to give to someone: *can spare you a couple.* **2** refrain from killing, hurting, inflicting, etc. —**spare·ly** *adv.*
—**spare·ness** *n.* —**spar·ing·ly** *adv.*

**spark** /spärk/ ▸*n.* **1** fiery particle from a fire. **2** particle of a quality, etc.: *not a spark of life.* **3** flash of electricity. **4** flash of wit, etc.
▸*v.* **1** emit sparks of fire or electricity. **2** stir into activity;

initiate (a process) suddenly.
—**spark·y** *adj.*

**spar·kle** /'spärkəl/ ▸*v.* **1** emit or seem to emit sparks; glitter; scintillate. **2** (of wine, etc.) effervesce.
▸*n.* **1** gleam or spark. **2** vivacity; liveliness. —**spark·ly** *adj.*

**spark plug** ▸*n.* device for firing the explosive mixture in an internal combustion engine.

**spar·row** /'sparō/ ▸*n.* small brownish-gray bird.

**sparse** /spärs/ ▸*adj.* thinly dispersed or scattered; not dense. —**sparse·ly** *adv.*
—**sparse·ness** *n.* —**spar·si·ty** *n.*

**Spar·tan** /'spärtn/ ▸*adj.* **1** of Sparta in ancient Greece. **2** (**spartan**) rigorous; frugal; austere.
▸*n.* citizen of Sparta.

**spasm** /'spazəm/ ▸*n.* **1** sudden involuntary muscular contraction. **2** sudden, brief spell of an activity or sensation.

**spas·mod·ic** /spaz'mädik/ ▸*adj.* **1** of, caused by, or subject to, a spasm or spasms. **2** occurring or done by fits and starts: *spasmodic efforts.* —**spas·mod·i·cal·ly** *adv.*

**spas·tic** /'spastik/ ▸*adj.* of or afflicted with spasms.

—**spas·ti·cal·ly** adv.

—**spas·tic·i·ty** n.

**spat** /spat/ ▶past and past part. of SPIT.

▶n. inf. petty quarrel.

**spate** /spāt/ ▶n. large or excessive amount.

**spa·tial** /ˈspāsHəl/ ▶adj. of or concerning space. —**spa·tial·ly** adv.

**spat·ter** /ˈspatər/ ▶v. **1** splash. **2** (of rain, etc.) fall here and there.

▶n. **1** splash; drop. **2** quick pattering sound.

**spat·u·la** /ˈspacHələ/ ▶n. broad-bladed flat implement used for spreading, stirring, mixing, etc.

**spawn** /spôn/ ▶n. eggs of fish, frogs, etc.

▶v. **1** deposit spawn. **2** produce or generate. —**spawn·er** n.

**spay** /spā/ ▶v. sterilize (a female animal) by removing the ovaries.

**speak** /spēk/ ▶v. (past **spoke**; past part. **spok·en**) **1** make articulate verbal utterances. **2** utter (words, the truth, etc.). **3** have a conversation. **4** make a speech. **5** use or be able to use (a specified language).

**speak·eas·y** ▶n. (pl. **-ies**) illicit liquor store or drinking club during Prohibition in the U.S.

**speak·er** /ˈspēkər/ ▶n. **1** person who speaks, esp. in public. **2** person who speaks a specified language: *French speaker.* **3** (usu. **Speaker**) presiding officer in a legislative assembly, esp. the U.S. House of Representatives. **4** LOUDSPEAKER.

**spear** /spi(ə)r/ ▶n. **1** weapon with a pointed usu. steel tip and a long shaft. **2** pointed stem of asparagus, etc.

▶v. pierce or strike with or as if with a spear: *speared an olive.*

**spear·head** ▶n. **1** point of a spear. **2** individual or group chosen to lead a thrust or attack.

▶v. act as the spearhead of (an attack, etc.).

**spear·mint** ▶n. common garden mint used in flavoring.

**spe·cial** /ˈspesHəl/ ▶adj. **1 a** particularly good; exceptional. **b** peculiar; specific. **2** for a particular purpose. **3** denoting education for children with particular needs, e.g., the disabled.

▶n. special edition of a newspaper, dish on a menu, etc. —**spe·cial·ly** adv. —**spe·cial·ness** n.

□ **special delivery** delivery of mail in advance of the regular delivery. □ **special effects** movie or television illusions created by props, camera work, etc.

**spe·cial·ist** ▶*n.* person who is highly skilled in a specific field.

**spe·cial·ize** ▶*v.* devote oneself to a particular area of interest, skill, etc. —**spe·cial·i·za·tion** *n.*

**spe·cial·ty** ▶*n.* (*pl.* **-ties**) special pursuit, product, operation, etc., to which a company or a person gives special attention.

**spe·cie** /'spēsHē/ ▶*n.* coin as opposed to paper money.

**spe·cies** /'spēsēz; -sHēz/ ▶*n.* (*pl.* same) **1** class of things having some characteristics in common. **2** *Biol.* category in the system of classification of living organisms consisting of similar individuals capable of exchanging genes or interbreeding. **3** kind or sort.

**spe·cies·Ism** /'spēsHē,zizəm; spēsē-/ ▶*n.* assumption of human superiority leading to the exploitation of animals.

**spe·cif·ic** /spə'sifik/ ▶*adj.* **1** clearly defined; definite. **2** relating to a particular subject; peculiar: *a style specific to that.* ▶*n.* specific aspect or factor: *shall we discuss specifics?* —**spe·cif·i·cal·ly** *adv.* —**spec·i·fic·i·ty** *n.*

**spec·i·fi·ca·tion** /,spesəfi'kāsHən/ ▶*n.* **1** act of specifying. **2** (**specifications**) detailed description of the construction, workmanship, materials, etc., of work done or to be done.

**spec·i·fy** /'spesə,fī/ ▶*v.* (**-fied**) **1** name or mention expressly or as a condition. **2** include in specifications. —**spec·i·fi·er** *n.*

**spec·i·men** /'spesəmən/ ▶*n.* **1** individual or part taken as an example of a class or whole. **2** *Med.* sample of fluid or tissue for testing.

**spe·cious** /'spēsHəs/ ▶*adj.* plausible but wrong. —**spe·ci·os·i·ty** *n.* —**spe·cious·ly** *adv.* —**spe·cious·ness** *n.*

**speck** /spek/ ▶*n.* **1** small spot or stain. **2** particle.

**speck·le** /'spekəl/ ▶*n.* speck, esp. one of many. ▶*v.* [often as *adj.* **speckled**] mark with speckles or patches.

**specs** /'speks/ ▶*pl. n. inf.* **1** pair of eyeglasses. **2** specifications.

**spec·ta·cle** /'spektəkəl/ ▶*n.* **1** public show, ceremony, etc. **2** anything attracting public attention. **3** (**spectacles**) pair of eyeglasses.

**spec·tac·u·lar** /spek'takyələr/ ▶*adj.* striking; amazing; lavish.

▸*n.* spectacular show.
—**spec·tac·u·lar·ly** *adv.*

**spec·ta·tor** /'spek͵tātər/ ▸*n.* person who looks on at a show, game, incident, etc.

**spec·ter** ▸*n.* **1** ghost. **2** haunting presentiment.

**spec·trum** /'spektrəm/ ▸*n.* (*pl.* **-tra**) **1** band of colors, as seen in a rainbow, etc. **2** distribution of visible electromagnetic radiation arranged in a progressive series according to wavelength. **3** entire range or a wide range of anything arranged by degree or quality, etc.

**spec·u·lar** /'spekyələr/ ▸*adj.* of, relating to, or having the properties of a mirror.

**spec·u·late** /'spekyə͵lāt/ ▸*v.* **1** form a theory or conjecture. **2** invest in stocks, etc., in the hope of gain but with the possibility of loss. —**spec·u·la·tion** *n.* —**spec·u·la·tor** *n.*

**speech** /spēCH/ ▸*n.* **1** faculty, act, or manner of speaking. **2** formal public address. **3** language of a nation, region, group, etc. —**speech·less** *adj.*

**speed** /spēd/ ▸*n.* **1** rapidity of movement. **2** rate of progress or motion over a distance in time.

**3** arrangement of gears yielding a specific ratio in a bicycle or automobile transmission. **4 a** sensitivity of film to light. **b** light-gathering power of a lens. **c** duration of an exposure. **5** *inf.* amphetamine drug. ▸*v.* (*past* and *past part.* **sped**) **1** go fast. **2** (*past* and *past part.* **speed·ed**) travel at an illegal or dangerous speed. **3** send fast or on its way. —**speed·er** *n.* —**speed·i·ly** *adv.* —**speed·y** *adj.*
□ **speed up** move or work at greater speed.

**speed·om·e·ter** /spi'dämitər/ ▸*n.* instrument on a motor vehicle, etc., indicating its speed to the driver.

**spe·le·ol·o·gy** /͵spēlē'äləjē/ ▸*n.* study of caves. —**spe·le·o·log·i·cal** *adj.* —**spe·le·ol·o·gist** *n.*

**spell** /spel/ ▸*v.* (*past* and *past part.* **spelled** or **spelt**) **1** write or name correctly the letters that form (a word, etc.). **2** (of letters) form (a word, etc.). **3** result in; involve: *spell ruin.* **4** relieve or take the place of (a person) in work, etc. ▸*n.* **1** form of words used as a magical charm or incantation. **2** attraction or fascination exercised by a person, activity, quality, etc. **3** short or fairly short period: *a cold spell in April.* **4** turn of work: *did a spell of woodwork.*

□ **spell out 1** make out (words, writing, etc.) letter by letter. **2** explain in detail.

**spell·bound** ▸*adj.* entranced.

**spe·lunk·er** /spiˈlənGkər/ ▸*n.* person who explores caves, esp. as a hobby. **—spe·lunk·ing** *n.*

**spe·lunk·ing** /spiˈlənGkiNG/ ▸*n.* exploration of caves, esp. as a hobby.

**spend** /spend/ ▸*v.* (*past* and *past part.* **spent**) **1** pay out (money). **2 a** use or consume (time or energy). **b** use up; exhaust; wear out.

**spend·thrift** ▸*n.* extravagant person; prodigal. ▸*adj.* extravagant; prodigal.

**sperm** /spərm/ ▸*n.* (*pl.* same or **sperms**) **1** SPERMATOZOON. **2** male reproductive fluid containing spermatozoa; semen.

□ **sperm whale** large whale yielding valuable oil.

**sper·ma·cet·i** /ˌspərməˈsetē/ ▸*n.* white waxy substance produced by the sperm whale, formerly used in candles and ointments. It is present in a rounded organ in the head, where it focuses acoustic signals and aids in the control of buoyancy.

**sper·ma·to·zo·on** /ˌspərmətəˈzōən/ ▸*n.* (*pl.* **-zo·a**) mature motile sex cell in animals. **—sper·ma·to·zo·an** *adj.*

**sper·mi·cide** /ˈspərməˌsīd/ ▸*n.* substance able to kill spermatozoa. **—sper·mi·cid·al** *adj.*

**spew** /spyo͞o/ ▸*v.* (**spew out**) expel or be expelled rapidly and forcibly.

**sphere** /sfi(ə)r/ ▸*n.* **1** solid figure, or its surface, with every point on its surface equidistant from its center. **2** object having this shape; ball or globe. **3** field of action, influence, etc. **—spher·i·cal** *adj.*

**spher·oid** /ˈsfi(ə)roid/ ▸*n.* spherelike but not perfectly spherical body. **—sphe·roi·dal** *adj.*

**sphinc·ter** /ˈsfiNGktər/ ▸*n.* Anat. ring of muscle surrounding and serving to guard or close an opening or tube, esp. the anus.

**sphinx** /sfiNGks/ ▸*n.* ancient Egyptian stone figure having a lion's body and a human or animal head.

**spice** /spīs/ ▶*n.* **1** aromatic or pungent vegetable substance used to flavor food. **2** interesting or piquant quality. ▶*v.* flavor with spice. —**spic·i·ness** *n.* —**spic·y** *adj.*

**spick-and-span** /'spik ən 'span/ ▶*adj.* **1** fresh and new. **2** neat and clean.

**spi·der** /'spīdər/ ▶*n.* arachnid, many species of which spin webs for the capture of insects as food.

**spiel** /spēl; ʃpēl/ ▶*n. inf.* glib speech or story, esp. a salesman's patter.

**spif·fy** /'spifē/ ▶*adj.* (**-fi·er, -fi·est**) *inf.* stylish; smart. —**spif·fi·ly** *adv.*

**spig·ot** /'spigət/ ▶*n.* **1** faucet. **2** small peg or plug, esp. in a cask.

**spike** /spīk/ ▶*n.* **1** thin pointed piece of metal. **2** any of several metal points set into the sole of a running shoe to prevent slipping. **3** large stout nail. **4** flower cluster formed of many flower heads attached closely on a long stem. ▶*v.* **1** fasten or provide with spikes. **2** make useless; put an end to; thwart (an idea, etc.). **3** *inf.* lace (a drink) with alcohol, a drug, etc. —**spik·i·ly** *adv.* —**spik·i·ness** *n.* —**spik·y** *adj.*

**spill** /spil/ ▶*v.* (*past* and *past part.* **spilled** or **spilt**) fall or run or cause (a liquid, powder, etc.) to fall or run out of a vessel, esp. unintentionally. ▶*n.* **1** spilling or being spilled. **2** tumble or fall, esp. from a horse, etc. —**spil·lage** *n.*
□ **spill the beans** *inf.* divulge information, etc., esp. unintentionally or indiscreetly.

**spin** /spin/ ▶*v.* (**spin·ning**; *past* and *past part.* **spun**) **1** turn or cause to turn or whirl around quickly. **2** draw out and twist (wool, cotton, etc.) into threads. **3** (of a spider, silkworm, etc.) make (a web, gossamer, cocoon, etc.) by extruding a fine viscous thread. **4** tell or write (a story, essay, article, etc.). **5** (of a person's head, etc.) be dizzy through excitement, astonishment, etc. ▶*n.* **1** spinning motion; whirl. **2** revolving motion through the air. **3** interpretation. **4** *inf.* brief drive, esp. in a car.
□ **spin doctor** political operative who attempts to influence press coverage of events. □ **spin off 1** throw off by centrifugal force

in spinning. **2** create or establish as a by-product or derivative endeavor.

**spin·ach** /'spinicH/ ▸*n.* dark green vegetable with edible leaves.

**spin·dle** /'spindl/ ▸*n.* **1** pin in a spinning wheel used for twisting and winding the thread. **2** pin or axis that revolves or on which something revolves.

**spin doc·tor** ▸*n.* spokesperson employed to give a favorable interpretation of events to the media, esp. on behalf of a political party.

**spine** /spīn/ ▸*n.* **1** series of vertebrae extending from the skull to the small of the back; backbone. **2** any hard pointed process or structure. **3** sharp ridge or projection. **4** part of a book's jacket or cover that encloses the fastened edges of the pages. —**spi·nal** *adj.*

**spine·less** ▸*adj.* **1** having no spine; invertebrate. **2** lacking resolve; weak.

**spin·et** /'spinit/ ▸*n.* small upright piano.

**spin·ning wheel** ▸*n.* apparatus for spinning yarn or thread with a spindle driven by a wheel attached to a crank or treadle.

**spin·ster** /'spinstər/ ▸*n.* unmarried woman.

**spi·ral** /'spīrəl/ ▸*adj.* coiled in a plane or as if around a cylinder or cone.
▸*n.* **1** plane or three-dimensional spiral curve. **2** spiral thing. **3** progressive rise or fall.
▸*v.* **1** move in a spiral course. **2** (of prices, wages, etc.) rise or fall, esp. rapidly. —**spi·ral·ly** *adv.*

**spire** /spī(ə)r/ ▸*n.* tapering cone- or pyramid-shaped structure, esp. on a church tower.

**spi·re·a** /spī'rēə/ ▸*n.* shrub with clusters of small white or pink flowers.

**spir·it** /'spirit/ ▸*n.* **1** vital animating essence of a person or animal; soul. **2** ghost. **3** prevailing mental or moral condition or attitude; mood; tendency: *public spirit.* **4** (**spirits**) strong distilled liquor. **5** courage; energy; vivacity. **6** real meaning: *spirit of the law.*
▸*v.* (**spirit away**) convey rapidly and secretly by or as if by spirits.

**spir·i·tu·al** /'spiri,cHŌŌəl/ ▸*adj.* **1** of or concerning the spirit as opposed to matter. **2** religious; divine; inspired.
▸*n.* religious song derived from the musical traditions of African-

American people.
—spir·i·tu·al·i·ty *n.* —spir·i·tu·al·ly
*adv.* —spir·i·tu·al·ness *n.*

**spir·i·tu·al·ism** ▶*n.* belief that
the spirits of the dead can
communicate with the living,
esp. through mediums.
—spir·i·tu·al·ist *n.*

**spit** /spit/ ▶*v.* (**spit·ting**; *past* and
*past part.* **spat** or **spit**) **1** eject
saliva from the mouth. **2** eject
(saliva, blood, food, etc.) from
the mouth: *spit the meat out.*
**3** utter (oaths, threats, etc.)
vehemently. **4** (of a fire, pen,
pan, etc.) send out sparks, ink,
hot fat, etc.
▶*n.* **1** spittle. **2** act or an instance
of spitting. **3** rod on which meat
is skewered before being roasted
on a fire, etc. **4** small point of
land projecting into the sea.

**spite** /spīt/ ▶*n.* feeling of ill will;
malice.
▶*v.* thwart; mortify; annoy: *does it
to spite me.* —spite·ful *adj.*
—spite·ful·ly *adv.*
□ **in spite of** notwithstanding.

**spit·fire** ▶*n.* person with a fiery
temper.

**spit·tle** /ˈspitl/ ▶*n.* saliva.

**splash** /splasH/ ▶*v.* **1** spatter or
cause (liquid) to spatter in small
drops. **2** (of a person) cause

liquid to spatter: *was splashing
about in the bath.* **3** display
(news) prominently.
▶*n.* **1** act or an instance of
splashing. **2** quantity of liquid
splashed. **3** spot or patch of dirt,
etc., splashed onto a thing.
—splash·y *adj.*
□ **make a splash** attract much
attention.

**splash·down** ▶*n.* landing of a
spacecraft in the sea.

**splat** ▶*n. inf.* sharp cracking or
slapping sound.

**splat·ter** ▶*v.* splash, esp. with a
continuous noisy action.

**splay** /splā/ ▶*v.* spread out.

**spleen** /splēn/ ▶*n.* abdominal
organ involved in maintaining
the proper condition of blood in
most vertebrates.

**splen·did** /ˈsplendid/ ▶*adj.*
**1** magnificent; sumptuous.
**2** dignified; impressive.
**3** excellent; fine. —splen·did·ly
*adv.* —splen·did·ness *n.*

**splen·dor** ▶*n.* splendid
appearance.

**splice** /splīs/ ▶*v.* **1** join the ends
of (ropes) by interweaving
strands. **2** join (pieces of timber,
tape, film, etc.) in an
overlapping position.

▶*n.* joint made by splicing. —**splic·er** *n.*

**splint** /splint/ ▶*n.* **1** strip of rigid material used for holding a broken bone, etc., when set. **2** rigid or flexible strip of esp. wood used in basketwork, etc.

**splin·ter** ▶*v.* break into fragments.

▶*n.* small, thin, sharp-edged piece broken off from wood, glass, etc. —**splin·ter·y** *adj.*

**split** /split/ ▶*v.* (**split·ting**; *past* and *past part.* **split**) **1 a** break or cause to break forcibly into parts, esp. with the grain or into halves. **b** divide into parts, esp. equal shares. **2** remove or be removed by breaking, separating, or dividing. **3** separate, esp. through discord. **4** *inf.* leave, esp. suddenly.

▶*n.* **1** act or result of splitting. **2** separation into parties; schism. **3** acrobatic position with the legs stretched fully apart. —**split·ter** *n.*

**split·ting** ▶*adj.* very painful; acute: *splitting headache.*

**splotch** /spläch  / *inf.* ▶*n.* daub, blot, or smear.

▶*v.* make a splotch on. —**splotch·i·ness** *n.* —**splotch·y** *adj.*

**splurge** /splərj/ *inf.* ▶*n.* act of spending money freely or extravagantly.

▶*v.* spend money freely or extravagantly.

**splut·ter** /ˈsplətər/ ▶*v.* **1** speak rapidly or incoherently. **2** make rapid spitting sounds.

▶*n.* rapid, incoherent speech. —**splut·ter·ing·ly** *adv.*

**spoil** /spoil/ ▶*v.* (*past* and *past part.* **spoiled** or **spoilt**) **1 a** damage; diminish the value of. **b** reduce a person's enjoyment, etc., of. **2** overindulge (esp. a child, pet, etc.). **3** (of food) go bad; decay.

▶*pl. n.* (**spoils**) goods stolen or taken forcibly from a person or place. —**spoil·age** *n.*

**spoke** ▶past of SPEAK.

▶*n.* each of the bars running from the hub to the rim of a wheel.

**spokes·man** /ˈspōksmən/ (*pl.* **-men**; *fem.* **spokes·wom·an**, *pl.* **-wom·en**) (also **spokes·per·son**) ▶*n.* person speaking for a group, etc.

**spo·li·a·tion** /ˌspōlēˈāSHən/ ▶*n.* **1** action of ruining or destroying something. **2** action of taking goods or property from somewhere by illegal or unethical means.

**sponge** /spənj/ ▶*n.* **1** any aquatic

animal with pores in its body wall and a rigid internal skeleton. **2** skeleton of a sponge, or an artificial version, used for cleaning. **3** thing of spongelike absorbency or consistency. **4** (also **spong·er**) person who lives off another's means.

▸*v.* **1** wipe, clean, or absorb with or as if with a sponge. **2** live as a parasite. —**spong·y** *adj.* —**spong·i·ness** *n.*

☐ **sponge cake** very light cake made with eggs.

**spon·sor** /'spänsər/ ▸*n.* **1** person who supports an activity; backer. **2** business organization that pays the cost of producing a broadcast program in return for advertising time. **3** godparent at baptism or a person who presents a candidate for confirmation.

▸*v.* be a sponsor for. —**spon·sor·ship** *n.*

**spon·ta·ne·ous** /spän'tānēəs/ ▸*adj.* **1** acting or done or occurring without external cause. **2** instinctive; automatic; natural. —**spon·ta·ne·i·ty** *n.* —**spon·ta·ne·ous·ly** *adv.*

☐ **spontaneous combustion** ignition of a mineral or

vegetable substance from internal heat.

**spoof** /spoof/ ▸*n. & v. inf.* **1** parody. **2** hoax.

**spook** /spook/ *inf.* ▸*n.* ghost. ▸*v.* **1** frighten; unnerve; alarm. **2** take fright; become alarmed.

**spool** /spool/ ▸*n.* **1** reel for winding magnetic tape, yarn, etc. **2** revolving cylinder of an angler's reel.

▸*v.* wind on a spool.

**spoon** /spoon/ ▸*n.* utensil consisting of an oval or round bowl and a handle for conveying food (esp. liquid) to the mouth, for stirring, etc.

▸*v.* take (liquid, etc.) with a spoon. —**spoon·ful** *n.*

**spoon·feed** ▸*v.* (*past* and *past part.* **-fed**) **1** feed with a spoon. **2** provide help, information, etc., to (a person) without requiring any effort on the recipient's part.

**spoor** /spoor/ ▸*n.* track or scent left by an animal.

**spo·rad·ic** /spə'radik/ ▸*adj.* occurring only here and there or occasionally; separate; scattered. —**spo·rad·i·cal·ly** *adv.*

**spore** /spôr/ ▸*n.* **1** specialized reproductive cell of many plants and microorganisms. **2** these collectively.

**sport** /spôrt/ ▶*n.* **1 a** game or competitive activity, esp. an outdoor one involving physical exertion, e.g., baseball, football, racing, hunting, etc. **b** (**sports**) such activities collectively: *world of sports.* **2** amusement; diversion; fun. **3** *inf.* fair or generous person.

▶*v.* **1** divert oneself; take part in a pastime. **2** wear, exhibit, or produce, esp. ostentatiously.

**sport·ive** ▶*adj.* playful. —**sport·ive·ly** *adv.*

**sports car** ▶*n.* low-built fast car.

**sports·man** ▶*n.* person who is fair and generous, esp. in winning and defeat. —**sports·man·ship** *n.*

**sports·wear** ▶*n.* clothes worn for casual use or sports.

**sport·y** ▶*adj.* (**-i·er, -i·est**) *inf.* rakish; showy. —**sport·i·ly** *adv.* —**sport·i·ness** *n.*

**spot** /spät/ ▶*n.* **1 a** small roundish part of the surface of a thing distinguished by color, texture, etc. **b** blemish; defect. **2** particular place; definite locality. **3** SPOTLIGHT. **4** *inf.*

awkward or difficult situation: *in a tight spot.*

▶*v.* (**spot·ted, spot·ting**) **1** *inf.* identify; recognize; catch sight of. **2** mark or become marked with spots. —**spot·less** *adj.* —**spot·less·ly** *adv.*

□ **on the spot** at the scene of an action or event.

**spot·light** ▶*n.* **1** beam of light directed on a small area. **2** lamp projecting this. **3** full attention or publicity.

**spous·al** /ˈspouzəl/ ▶*adj.* of or relating to marriage or to a husband or wife.

**spouse** /spous/ ▶*n.* husband or wife.

**spout** /spout/ ▶*n.* projecting tube or lip through which a liquid, etc., is poured or issues from.

▶*v.* discharge or issue forcibly in a jet. —**spout·er** *n.*

**Sprach·ge·fühl** /ˈSHpräkgəˌfŏŏl/ ▶*n.* intuitive feeling for the natural idiom of a language.

**sprain** /sprān/ ▶*v.* wrench (an ankle, wrist, etc.) so as to cause pain and swelling.

▶*n.* such a wrench.

**sprat** /sprat/ ▶*n.* small European herring-like fish, used as food.

**sprawl** /sprôl/ ▶*v.* **1** sit or lie or fall with limbs flung out or in an

ungainly way. **2** (of handwriting, a plant, a town, etc.) be of irregular or straggling form.
▶*n.* sprawling movement, position, or mass.
—**sprawl·ing·ly** *adv.*

**spray** /sprā/ ▶*n.* **1** water or other liquid flying in small drops. **2** sprig of flowers or leaves.
▶*v.* **1** throw (liquid) in the form of spray. **2** sprinkle (an object) with small drops or particles.
—**spray·a·ble** *adj.* —**spray·er** *n.*

**spread** /spred/ ▶*v.* (*past* and *past part.* **spread**) **1 a** open or extend the surface of. **b** cause to cover a larger surface. **2** have a wide or increasing extent: *spreading trees.* **3** become or make widely known, felt, etc.: *rumors are spreading.*
▶*n.* **1** act, instance, or extent of spreading. **2** diffusion; expanse: *spread of learning.* **3** *inf.* elaborate meal. **4** food for spreading on bread, etc. **5** bedspread.
**6** printed matter spread across more than one column. **7** ranch or farm with extensive land.
—**spread·er** *n.*

**spread·ea·gled** ▶*adj.* with arms and legs extended.

**spread·sheet** ▶*n.* **1** computer program that manipulates

figures for calculation. **2** report generated by such a program.

**spree** /sprē/ ▶*n. inf.* **1** lively extravagant outing: *shopping spree.* **2** bout of fun or drinking, etc.

**sprig** /sprig/ ▶*n.* small branch or shoot.

**spright·ly** /ˈsprītlē/ ▶*adj.* (**-li·er, -li·est**) vivacious; lively; brisk.
—**spright·li·ness** *n.*

**spring** /spriNG/ ▶*v.* (*past* **sprang** or **sprung**; *past part.* **sprung**) **1** jump; move rapidly or suddenly: *sprang from his seat.* **2** move rapidly as from a constrained position or by the action of a spring. **3** originate or arise: *springs from an old family.* **4** produce or develop or make known suddenly or unexpectedly: *loves to spring surprises.*
▶*n.* **1** resilient device usu. of bent or coiled metal used esp. to drive clockwork or for cushioning in furniture or vehicles. **2** season after winter. **3** place where water, oil, etc., wells up from the earth. **4** jump: *took a spring.* **5** elasticity. —**spring·y** *adj.*

**spring·board** ▶*n.* **1** springy board giving impetus in leaping, diving, etc. **2** point of departure.

**springe** /sprinj/ ▶*n.* noose or snare for catching small game.

**sprin·kle** /ˈspriNGkəl/ ▶*v.* **1** scatter in small drops or particles. **2** subject to sprinkling with liquid, etc. **3** distribute in small amounts.
▶*n.* **1** light shower. **2** sprinkling. —**sprin·kler** *n.*

**sprint** /sprint/ ▶*v.* run a short distance at full speed.
▶*n.* **1** short, fast run. **2** similar short spell of maximum effort in cycling, swimming, auto racing, etc. —**sprint·er** *n.*

**sprite** /sprīt/ ▶*n.* elf, fairy, or goblin.

**sprock·et** /ˈspräkit/ ▶*n.* each of several teeth on a wheel engaging with links of a chain.

**sprout** /sprout/ ▶*v.* begin to grow; put forth (shoots).
▶*n.* shoot of a plant.

**spruce** /sproōs/ ▶*adj.* neat in dress and appearance; smart.
▶*v.* (**spruce up**) make or become neat and fashionable.
▶*n.* cone-bearing fir with dense foliage.

**spry** /sprī/ ▶*adj.* (**spry·er, spry·est**) active; lively. —**spry·ly** *adv.* —**spry·ness** *n.*

**spud** /spəd/ ▶*n. inf.* potato.

**spume** /spyoōm/ ▶*n. & v.* froth; foam. —**spum·y** *adj.*

**spunk** /spəNGk/ ▶*n. inf.* courage; mettle; spirit. —**spunk·y** *adj.* —**spunk·i·ness** *n.*

**spur** /spər/ ▶*n.* **1** device with a small spike or a spiked wheel worn on a rider's heel for urging a horse forward. **2** stimulus or incentive. **3** projection.
▶*v.* (**spurred, spur·ring**) **1** prick (a horse) with spurs. **2** incite; stimulate.
□ **on the spur of the moment** on a momentary impulse; impromptu.

**spu·ri·ous** /ˈspyoōrēəs/ ▶*adj.* not genuine; not being what it purports to be. —**spu·ri·ous·ly** *adv.* —**spu·ri·ous·ness** *n.*

**spurn** /spərn/ ▶*v.* reject with disdain; treat with contempt. —**spurn·er** *n.*

**spurt** /spərt/ ▶*v.* **1 a** gush out in a jet or stream. **b** cause (liquid, etc.) to do this. **2** make a sudden effort.
▶*n.* **1** sudden gushing out; jet. **2** short sudden effort or increase of pace, esp. in racing.

**sput·ter** /ˈspətər/ ▶*v.* **1** emit (with) spitting sounds. **2** speak or utter in a hurried or vehement fashion.

▶*n.* sputtering.

**spu·tum** /'spyo͞otəm/ ▶*n.* (*pl.* **-ta**) saliva; spittle.

**spy** /spī/ ▶*n.* (*pl.* **spies**) **1** person who secretly collects and reports information on the activities, movements, etc., of an enemy, competitor, etc. **2** person who keeps watch on others, esp. furtively.
▶*v.* (**spied**) **1** discern; see. **2** act as a spy. —**spy·ing** *n.*

**spy·glass** ▶*n.* small telescope.

**squab** /skwäb/ ▶*n.* young pigeon or other bird.

**squab·ble** /'skwäbəl/ ▶*n.* petty or noisy quarrel.
▶*v.* engage in a squabble. —**squab·bler** *n.*

**squad** /skwäd/ ▶*n.* small group of people sharing a task, etc., esp. of soldiers or police.

**squad·ron** /'skwädrən/ ▶*n.* unit of aircraft, warships, etc.

**squal·id** /'skwälid/ ▶*adj.* **1** filthy. **2** mean or poor. —**squa·lid·i·ty** *n.* —**squal·id·ly** *adv.* —**squal·id·ness** *n.*

**squall** /skwôl/ ▶*n.* **1** sudden or violent wind, esp. with rain or snow. **2** discordant cry; scream (esp. of a baby).
▶*v.* utter a squall; scream. —**squal·ly** *adj.*

**squa·lor** /'skwälər/ ▶*n.* state of being filthy or squalid.

**squan·der** /'skwändər/ ▶*v.* spend (money, time, etc.) wastefully. —**squan·der·er** *n.*

**square** /skwe(ə)r/ ▶*n.* **1** equilateral rectangle. **2** open area surrounded by buildings. **3** product of a number multiplied by itself: *81 is the square of 9.* **4** *inf.* conventional or old-fashioned person.
▶*adj.* **1** having the shape of a square. **2** having or in the form of a right angle: *table with square corners.* **3** designating the area of a square whose side is the length of the unit specified: *square mile.* **4** equal; settled. **5** fair and honest. **6** *inf.* conventional or old-fashioned.
▶*adv.* squarely.
▶*v.* **1** make square. **2** multiply (a number) by itself: *3 squared is 9.* **3** reconcile: *the results do not square with your conclusions.* —**square·ly** *adv.* —**square·ness** *n.*

□ **square dance** dance with usu. four couples facing inward from four sides. □ **square meal** substantial and satisfying meal. □ **square root** number that multiplied by itself gives a specified number.

**squash**[1] /skwäSH/ ▶v. **1** crush or squeeze flat or into pulp. **2** dismiss (a proposal, etc.).
▶n. game played with rackets and a small ball against the walls of a closed court. —**squash·y** adj. —**squash·i·ly** adv. —**squash·i·ness** n.

**squash**[2] ▶n. (pl. same or **squash·es**) plant with gourdlike fruit that may be used as a vegetable.

**squat** /skwät/ ▶v. (**squat·ted**, **squat·ting**) **1** sit on one's heels or on the ground with the knees drawn up. **2** occupy (a building) as a squatter.
▶adj. (**squat·ter**, **squat·test**) (of a person, etc.) short and thick; dumpy.
▶n. squatting posture.

**squat·ter** ▶n. person who unlawfully occupies an uninhabited building.

**squawk** /skwôk/ ▶n. **1** loud harsh cry, esp. of a bird. **2** complaint.
▶v. utter with or make a squawk. —**squawk·er** n.

**squeak** /skwēk/ ▶n. short shrill cry or sound.
▶v. **1** make or utter with a squeak. **2** (**squeak by/through**) inf. pass or escape narrowly. —**squeak·i·ly** adv. —**squeak·i·ness** n. —**squeak·y** adj.

**squeal** /skwēl/ ▶n. prolonged shrill sound.
▶v. **1** make or utter with a squeal. **2** inf. become an informer. —**squeal·er** n.

**squeam·ish** /ˈskwēmiSH/ ▶adj. **1** easily nauseated or disgusted. **2** fastidious; sensitive. —**squeam·ish·ly** adv. —**squeam·ish·ness** n.

**squee·gee** /ˈskwēˌjē/ ▶n. rubber-edged implement often set on a long handle and used for cleaning windows, etc.

**squeeze** /skwēz/ ▶v. **1** exert pressure on. **2** force (a person or thing) into or through a small or narrow space. **3 a** harass by exactions; bring pressure to bear on. **b** obtain (money, etc.) by extortion, entreaty, etc.
▶n. **1** squeezing; being squeezed. **2** close embrace. **3** crowd or crowded state; crush. **4** restriction on borrowing, investment, etc., in a financial crisis.

**squelch** /skwelCH/ ▶v. suppress; silence.

▶*n.* instance of squelching.

**squib** /skwib/ ▶*n.* **1** small hissing firework that finally explodes. **2** short satirical composition; lampoon.

**squid** /skwid/ ▶*n.* sea creature with tentacles, used for food.

**squig·gle** /'skwigəl/ ▶*n.* short curly line, esp. in handwriting or doodling.

▶*v.* make such lines. —**squig·gly** *adj.*

**squint** /skwint/ ▶*v.* **1** look obliquely or with half closed eyes. **2** have the eyes turned in different directions.

▶*n.* **1** stealthy or sidelong glance. **2** permanent deviation in the direction of one eye. —**squint·er** *n.* —**squint·y** *adj.*

**squire** /'skwī(ə)r/ ▶*n.* **1** English country gentleman. **2** knight's attendant.

▶*v.* (of a man) attend upon or escort (a woman).

**squirm** /skwərm/ ▶*v.* **1** wriggle; writhe. **2** show or feel embarrassment.

▶*n.* squirming movement. —**squirm·y** *adj.*

**squir·rel** /'skwər(ə)l/ ▶*n.* tree-dwelling rodent with a bushy tail.

▶*v.* hoard.

**squirt** /skwərt/ ▶*v.* **1** eject or be ejected in a jet. **2** splash with liquid or powder ejected by squirting.

▶*n.* **1 a** jet of water, etc. **b** small quantity produced by squirting. **2** *inf.* insignificant but presumptuous person.

**squish** /skwiSH/ ▶*n.* slight squelching sound.

▶*v.* move with a squish. —**squish·y** *adj.*

**Sr** ▶*symb. Chem.* strontium.

**Sr.** ▶*abbr.* **1** Senior. **2** Señor. **3** Signor. **4** *Eccl.* Sister.

**SRO** ▶*abbr.* standing room only.

**SS** ▶*abbr.* **1** steamship. **2** *hist.* Nazi special police force.

**SST** ▶*abbr.* supersonic transport.

**St.** ▶*abbr.* **1** Street. **2** Saint.

**stab** /stab/ ▶*v.* (**stabbed, stab·bing**) pierce or wound with a knife or other pointed instrument.

▶*n.* **1** blow or thrust with a knife, etc. **2** sharp pain. **3** *inf.* attempt; try: *I'll have a stab at it.*

**sta·bile** /'stā,bēl/ ▶*n.* freestanding abstract sculpture or structure, typically of wire or sheet metal, in the style of a mobile but rigid and stationary.

**sta·bi·lize** /'stābə,līz/ ▶*v.* make

or become stable. —**sta·bi·liz·er**
n. —**sta·bi·li·za·tion** n.

**sta·ble**[1] /ˈstābəl/ ▸adj. (**sta·bler,
sta·blest**) **1** firmly fixed or
established. **2** (of a person) well-
adjusted; sane; reliable; sensible.
—**sta·bil·i·ty** n. —**sta·ble·ness** n.
—**sta·bly** adv.

**sta·ble**[2] ▸n. **1** building for
horses. **2** persons, products, etc.,
having a common origin or
affiliation.
▸v. put or keep in a stable.

**stac·ca·to** /stəˈkätō/ ▸adv. & adj.
chiefly Mus. with each sound or
note sharply detached or
separated from the others.

**stack** /stak/ ▸n. **1** pile or heap,
esp. in orderly arrangement.
**2** inf. large quantity. **3** (**the
stacks**) part of a library where
books are compactly stored.
▸v. **1** pile in a stack or stacks.
**2 a** arrange (cards) secretly for
cheating. **b** manipulate
(circumstances, etc.) to one's
advantage. —**stack·a·ble** adj.

**sta·di·um** /ˈstādēəm/ ▸n. (pl.
-**di·ums** or -**di·a**) arena with tiers
of seats for spectators.

**staff** /staf/ ▸n. **1** (pl. **staffs** or
**staves**) **a** stick or pole for use in
walking or climbing or as a
weapon. **b** stick or pole as a sign

of office or authority. **2** [treated
as sing. or pl.] body of persons
employed in a business, etc.
**3** (pl. **staffs** or **staves**) Mus. set of
usu. five parallel lines on which
music is written.
▸v. provide (an institution, etc.)
with a staff. —**staffed** adj.

**stag** /stag/ ▸n. adult male deer.
▸adj. for men only, e.g., a party,
etc.

**stage** /stāj/ ▸n. **1** point or period
in a process or development: is
in the larval stage. **2 a** raised
floor or platform, esp. one on
which plays, etc., are performed.
**b** (**the stage**) theatrical
profession. **c** scene of action.
**3 a** regular stopping place on a
route. **b** distance between two
stopping places. **4** section of a
rocket with a separate engine.
▸v. **1** present (a play, etc.) on
stage. **2** arrange the occurrence
of: staged a comeback.
□ **stage fright** nervousness on
facing an audience.

**stage·coach** ▸n. large enclosed
horse-drawn coach running
regularly between two places.

**stage·hand** ▸n. person
handling scenery, etc., during a
performance on stage.

**stag·ger** /ˈstagər/ ▸v. **1** walk

unsteadily; totter. **2** shock; confuse. **3** arrange (events, hours of work, etc.) so that they do not coincide. **4** arrange (objects) so that they are not in line.

▸*n.* tottering movement.

**stag·ger·ing** ▸*adj.* **1** astonishing; bewildering. **2** that staggers. —**stag·ger·ing·ly** *adv.*

**stag·nant** /'stagnənt/ ▸*adj.* **1** (of liquid) motionless; having no current. **2** (of life, action, the mind, etc.) showing no activity; dull; sluggish. —**stag·nan·cy** *n.* —**stag·nant·ly** *adv.* —**stag·nate** *v.*

**staid** /stād/ ▸*adj.* of quiet and steady character; sedate. —**staid·ly** *adv.* —**staid·ness** *n.*

**stain** /stān/ ▸*v.* **1** discolor or be discolored by the action of liquid sinking in. **2** damage (a reputation, character, etc.). **3** color (wood, glass, etc.) by a process other than painting or covering the surface.

▸*n.* **1** discoloration; spot; mark. **2 a** blot or blemish. **b** damage to a reputation, etc. **3** substance used in staining. —**stain·less** *adj.*

□ **stained glass** dyed or colored glass, esp. in a lead framework in a window: *stained-glass window.*

**stain·less steel** ▸*n.* steel alloy not liable to rust or tarnish under ordinary conditions.

**stair** /ste(ə)r/ ▸*n.* **1** each of a set of fixed steps. **2** (**stairs**) set of steps: *passed him on the stairs.*

**stair·case** ▸*n.* (also **stair·way**) set of stairs and its surrounding structure.

**stair·well** ▸*n.* shaft in which a staircase is built.

**stake** /stāk/ ▸*n.* **1** stout, sharpened stick or post driven into the ground as a support, boundary mark, etc. **2** sum of money, etc., wagered. **3** interest or concern, esp. financial. **4** (**stakes**) prize money, esp. in a horse race.

▸*v.* **1** fasten, secure, or support with a stake or stakes. **2** (**stake off/out**) mark off (an area) with stakes. **3** establish (a claim). **4** wager. **5** support, esp. financially.

**stake·out** ▸*n.* inf. surveillance.

**sta·lac·tite** /stə'lak,tīt/ ▸*n.* deposit of calcium carbonate having the shape of a large icicle hanging from the roof of a cave, cliff overhang, etc.

**sta·lag·mite** /stə'lag,mīt/ ▸*n.*

deposit of calcium carbonate in the shape of a large inverted icicle rising from the floor of a cave, etc.

**stale** /stāl/ ▸*adj.* (**stal·er, stal·est**) **1** not fresh; musty; insipid. **2** trite or unoriginal. —**stale·ness** *n.*

**stale·mate** ▸*n.* **1** drawn position in chess. **2** position where progress is impossible.

**stalk** /stôk/ ▸*n.* main stem of a plant; leaf, flower, fruit, etc. ▸*v.* **1** pursue stealthily. **2** walk in a stately or haughty manner. —**stalked** *adj.* —**stalk·er** *n.*

**stall** /stôl/ ▸*n.* **1** trader's stand or booth in a market, etc. **2** compartment for one animal in a stable, etc. **3** compartment for one person in a shower, toilet, etc. ▸*v.* **1** (of a vehicle or its engine) stop or lose power. **2** stop making progress. **3** be obstructive or evasive.

**stal·lion** /ˈstalyən/ ▸*n.* uncastrated adult male horse.

**stal·wart** /ˈstôlwərt/ ▸*adj.* **1** strongly built; sturdy. **2** courageous; resolute; determined. ▸*n.* stalwart person, esp. a loyal partisan. —**stal·wart·ly** *adv.*

**sta·men** /ˈstāmən/ ▸*n.* male fertilizing organ of a flowering plant, including the anther containing pollen.

**stam·i·na** /ˈstamənə/ ▸*n.* physical or mental endurance.

**stam·mer** /ˈstamər/ ▸*v.* speak with halting articulation, esp. with pauses or rapid repetitions of the same syllable, or utter in this way: *stammered out an excuse.* ▸*n.* **1** tendency to stammer. **2** instance of stammering. —**stam·mer·er** *n.* —**stam·mer·ing·ly** *adv.*

**stamp** /stamp/ ▸*v.* **1** bring down (one's foot) heavily on the ground, etc. **2** impress (a pattern, mark, etc.) on (a surface). **3** affix a postage or other stamp to. ▸*n.* **1** instrument for stamping. **2** mark or pattern made by this, esp. as an official authorization or certification. **3** small adhesive piece of paper indicating that a price, fee, or tax has been paid, esp. a postage stamp. **4** heavy downward blow with the foot or sound of this. **5** characteristic mark or impression: *bears the stamp of genius.*

□ **stamp out** put an end to; crush; destroy.

**stam·pede** /stam'pēd/ ▸ *n.*
**1** sudden flight or hurried movement of animals or people. **2** spontaneous response of many persons to a common impulse.
▸ *v.* **1** take part in a stampede. **2** cause to do this.

**stance** /stans/ ▸ *n.* **1** attitude or position of the body, esp. when hitting a ball, etc. **2** standpoint; attitude of mind.

**stanch** /stônCH; stanCH/ (also **staunch**) ▸ *v.* **1** restrain the flow of (esp. blood). **2** restrain the flow from (esp. a wound).

**stan·chion** /ˈstanCHən/ ▸ *n.* post or pillar; upright support; vertical strut.

**stand** /stand/ ▸ *v.* (*past* and *past part.* **stood**) **1** have or take or maintain an upright position, esp. on the feet or a base. **2** be situated: *here once stood a village.* **3** be in a specified condition: *stands accused.* **4** place or set in an upright or specified position: *stood it against the wall.* **5** move to and remain in a specified position or attitude: *stand aside | stand aloof.* **6** remain valid or unaltered. **7** endure; tolerate.
▸ *n.* **1** resistance to attack or compulsion, esp. as: *make a stand.* **2** rack, set of shelves, etc. **3** small open-fronted structure for a trader outdoors or in a market, etc. **4** raised structure to sit or stand on. **5** group of growing plants: *stand of trees.*

□ **stand by 1** look on without interfering. **2** uphold; support (a person). **3** adhere to (terms or promises). **4** wait; stand ready for. □ **stand for** represent; signify; imply: *"U.S." stands for "United States."* □ **stand-in** deputy or substitute. □ **stand off** move or keep away; keep one's distance. □ **stand out** be prominent or conspicuous or outstanding. □ **stand up 1** come to or remain in or place in a standing position. **2** (of an argument, etc.) be valid. **3** *inf.* fail to keep an appointment with. □ **stand up for** support; side with; maintain (a person or cause). □ **stand up to 1** meet or face (an opponent) courageously. **2** be resistant to the harmful effects of (wear, use, etc.).

**stan·dard** /ˈstandərd/ ▸ *n.*
**1** object or quality or measure serving as a basis or example or principle by which others are judged. **2** the degree of

excellence, etc., required for a particular purpose. **3** distinctive flag. **4** upright support.
▶*adj.* **1** serving or used as a standard. **2** of a normal or prescribed but not exceptional quality, size, etc. **3** having recognized and permanent value; authoritative.
—**stand·ard·ize** *v.*
—**stand·ard·i·za·tion** *n.*
☐ **standard of living** degree of material comfort available to a person or class or community.
☐ **standard time** uniform time for places in approximately the same longitude, established in a country or region by law or custom.

**stand·by** ▶*n.* (*pl.* **-bys**) **1** person or thing ready if needed in an emergency, etc. **2** readiness for duty: *on standby.*

**stand·ing** ▶*n.* **1** esteem or repute, esp. high; status; position. **2** duration: *long standing.*
▶*adj.* **1** upright. **2** established; permanent: *standing rule.*

**stand·off·ish** ▶*adj.* cold or distant in manner.
—**stand·off·ish·ly** *adv.*
—**stand·off·ish·ness** *n.*

**stand·pipe** ▶*n.* vertical pipe extending from a water supply.

**stand·point** ▶*n.* point of view.

**stand·still** ▶*n.* stoppage; inability to proceed.

**stan·za** /ˈstanzə/ ▶*n.* section of a poem, typically of four or more lines.

**sta·ple** /ˈstāpəl/ ▶*n.* **1** U-shaped metal bar or piece of wire with pointed ends for driving into and holding together papers, etc. **2** principal or important product or food.
▶*v.* provide or fasten with a staple.
▶*adj.* main or principal: *staple commodities.* —**sta·pler** *n.*

**star** /stär/ ▶*n.* **1** celestial body appearing as a luminous point in the night sky. **2** figure or object with radiating points esp. as a decoration or mark of rank, or to show a category of excellence: *five-star hotel.* **3** famous or brilliant person; principal performer.
▶*v.* (**starred, star·ring**) **1** (of a movie, etc.) feature as a principal performer. **2** (of a performer) be featured in a movie, etc. —**star·dom** *n.*
—**star·ry** *adj.*

**star·board** ▸*n. Naut., Aeron.* right-hand side of a ship, boat, or aircraft.

**starch** /stärCH/ ▸*n.* **1** carbohydrate obtained chiefly from cereals and potatoes. **2** preparation of this used for stiffening fabric. ▸*v.* stiffen with starch. —**starch·y** *adj.*

**star·dust** /ˈstärˌdəst/ ▸*n.* (esp. in the context of success in the world of entertainment or sports) a magical or charismatic quality or feeling.

**stare** /ste(ə)r/ ▸*v.* look fixedly with eyes open, esp. as the result of curiosity, surprise, horror, etc.: *stared in amazement.* ▸*n.* staring gaze.

**star·fish** ▸*n.* sea creature with five or more radiating arms.

**stark** /stärk/ ▸*adj.* **1** desolate; bare: *stark landscape.* **2** sharply evident; downright: *in stark contrast.* ▸*adv.* completely; wholly: *stark naked.* —**stark·ly** *adv.* —**stark·ness** *n.*

**star·let** /ˈstärlit/ ▸*n.* promising young performer, esp. a woman.

**star·ling** ▸*n.* small bird with blackish-brown, speckled, iridescent plumage.

**start** /stärt/ ▸*v.* **1** begin; commence. **2** set or be set in motion or action. **3** make a sudden movement from surprise, pain, etc. ▸*n.* **1** beginning. **2** place from which a race, etc., begins. **3** sudden movement of surprise, pain, etc.

**star·tle** /ˈstärtl/ ▸*v.* shock; surprise.

**starve** /stärv/ ▸*v.* **1** die or cause to die of hunger or suffer from malnourishment. **2** (**be starving** or **starved**) *inf.* feel very hungry. **3** feel a strong need or craving (for): *starved for attention.* —**star·va·tion** *n.*

**starve·ling** /ˈstärvliNG/ ▸*n.* undernourished or emaciated person or animal. ▸*adj.* (of a person or animal) lacking enough food; emaciated.

**stash** /staSH/ ▸*v. inf.* **1** conceal; put in a safe or hidden place. **2** hoard. ▸*n.* **1** hiding place. **2** thing hidden.

**stat.** ▸*abbr.* **1** at once. **2** statistics. **3** statute.

**state** /stāt/ ▸*n.* **1** existing condition or position of a person or thing. **2** civil government. **3** political community under one government or forming part of a federation. **4** *inf.* excited, anxious, or agitated mental condition.

▶*v.* **1** express in speech or writing. **2** specify.
—**state·hood** *n.*

□ **state of the art** current stage of development of a practical or technological subject. □ **state-of-the-art** using the latest techniques or equipment: *state-of-the-art weaponry.*

**state·craft** /'stāt,kraft/ ▶*n.* skillful management of state affairs; statesmanship.

**state·less** ▶*adj.* (of a person) having no nationality or citizenship. —**state·less·ness** *n.*

**state·ly** ▶*adj.* (-li·er, -li·est) dignified; imposing; grand.
—**state·li·ness** *n.*

**state·ment** /'stātmənt/ ▶*n.* **1** stating or being stated; expression in words. **2** formal account of facts. **3** record of financial transactions.

**state·room** ▶*n.* private compartment in a passenger ship or train.

**states·man** ▶*n.* (*pl.* -men; *fem.* **states·wom·an**, *pl.* -wom·en) distinguished and capable politician or diplomat.

—**states·man·like** *adj.*
—**states·man·ship** *n.*

**stat·ic** /'statik/ ▶*adj.* **1** stationary; not acting or changing; passive. **2** *Physics* concerned with bodies at rest or forces in equilibrium.

▶*n.* electrical disturbances in the atmosphere or the interference with telecommunications caused by this.

□ **static electricity** electricity that is not flowing as a current and is produced by friction.

**sta·tion** /'stāsHən/ ▶*n.* **1** place where trains, buses, etc., stop at a regular time. **2** place or building, etc., where a someone stands or a particular activity is carried on. **3** radio or television broadcasting channel. **4** position in life; rank or status.

▶*v.* **1** assign a station to. **2** put in position.

□ **station wagon** car with passenger seating and storage or an extra seating area in the rear.

**sta·tion·ar·y** /'stāsHə,nerē/ ▶*adj.* **1** remaining in one place. **2** not changing.

**sta·tion·er·y** /'stāsHə,nerē/ ▶*n.* **1** writing materials. **2** writing paper, esp. with matching envelopes.

**stat·ism** /ˈstātˌizəm/ ▶*n.* political system in which the state has substantial centralized control over social and economic affairs.

**sta·tis·tic** /stəˈtistik/ ▶*n.* **1** numerical fact or item. **2** (**statistics**) [treated as *sing.*] science of collecting and analyzing numerical data. **3** (**statistics**) any systematic collection or presentation of such facts. —**sta·tis·ti·cal** *adj.* —**sta·tis·ti·cal·ly** *adv.* —**stat·is·ti·cian** *n.*

**stat·u·ar·y** /ˈstacho͞oˌerē/ ▶*n.* (*pl.* **-ies**) statues collectively.

**stat·ue** /ˈstacho͞o/ ▶*n.* sculptured figure of a person or animal.

**stat·u·esque** /ˌstacho͞oˈesk/ ▶*adj.* tall or dignified.

**stat·u·ette** ▶*n.* small statue.

**stat·ure** /ˈstachər/ ▶*n.* **1** height of a (esp. human) body. **2** degree of eminence, social standing, or advancement: *recruit someone of his stature.*

**sta·tus** /ˈstātəs; ˈstatəs/ ▶*n.* **1** rank; social position; relative importance: *not sure of their status in the hierarchy.* **2** present condition.

**sta·tus quo** /ˈkwō/ ▶*n.* existing state of affairs.

**stat·ute** /ˈstacho͞ot/ ▶*n.* written law. —**stat·u·to·ry** *adj.*

**staunch** /stônCH/ ▶*adj.* trustworthy; loyal. ▶var. of STANCH. —**staunch·ly** *adv.* —**staunch·ness** *n.*

**stave** /stāv/ ▶*n.* each of the curved pieces of wood forming the sides of a cask, barrel, etc. ▶*v.* (*past* and *past part.* **stove** or **staved**) break a hole in.

**stay** /stā/ ▶*v.* **1** continue to be in the same place or condition; not depart or change. **2** have temporary residence. **3** postpone (a judgment, decision, execution, etc.). ▶*n.* **1 a** act or an instance of staying. **b** duration of this: *just a ten-minute stay.* **2** suspension or postponement of a sentence, judgment, etc.: *stay of execution.* **3** prop or support. □ **staying power** endurance; stamina.

**STD** ▶*abbr.* sexually transmitted disease.

**std.** ▶*abbr.* standard.

**stead** /sted/ ▶*n.* place or role someone or something should have or fill: *she was appointed in her husband's stead.* □ **stand in good stead** be advantageous or serviceable to:

*his early training stood him in good stead.*

**stead·fast** ▸*adj.* constant; firm; unwavering. —**stead·fast·ly** *adv.* —**stead·fast·ness** *n.*

**stead·y** ▸*adj.* (**-i·er, -i·est**) **1** firmly fixed or supported; unwavering. **2** regular and continuous; constant. **3** (of a person) serious and dependable. **4** not changing; established: *steady girlfriend.*
▸*v.* (**-ied**) make or become steady: *steady the boat.*
▸*adv.* steadily: *hold it steady.*
▸*n.* (*pl.* **-ies**) *inf.* regular boyfriend or girlfriend. —**stead·i·ly** *adv.* —**stead·i·ness** *n.*

**stead·y state** ▸*n.* unvarying condition in a physical process, esp. as in the theory that the universe is eternal and maintained by constant creation of matter.

**steak** /stāk/ ▸*n.* thick slice of meat or fish.

**steal** /stēl/ ▸*v.* (*past* **stole**; *past part.* **sto·len**) **1** take (another person's property) illegally or without right or permission, esp. in secret. **2** obtain surreptitiously or by surprise: *stole a kiss.* **3** move, esp. silently or stealthily.
▸*n. inf.* unexpectedly easy task or good bargain.

**stealth** /stelTH/ ▸*n.* secrecy; secret procedure. —**stealth·i·ly** *adv.* —**stealth·y** *adj.*

**steam** /stēm/ ▸*n.* **1** vapor from heated water. **2 a** power obtained from steam. **b** *inf.* power or energy generally.
▸*v.* **1** cook or treat with steam. **2** give off steam.

**steam·er** ▸*n.* **1** (also **steam·ship**) vessel propelled by steam, esp. a ship. **2** vessel for steaming food in.

**steam·roll·er** ▸*n.* **1** heavy slow-moving vehicle with a roller, used to flatten newly laid asphalt, etc. **2** crushing power or force.
▸*v.* crush or move forcibly or indiscriminately.

**ste·at·o·py·gi·a** /ˌslēətəˈpijēə; stēˌatə-/ ▸*n.* accumulation of large amounts of fat on the buttocks, esp. as a normal condition in certain peoples of arid parts of southern Africa.

**steed** /stēd/ ▸*n.* horse.

**steel** /stēl/ ▸*n.* **1** alloy of iron and carbon with other elements increasing strength and malleability, much used for making tools, weapons, etc.

**2** strength; firmness: *nerves of steel.*

▶*adj.* of or like steel.

▶*v.* harden or make resolute. —**steel·y** *adj.*

**steel wool** ▶*n.* abrasive substance consisting of a mass of fine steel shavings.

**steep** /stēp/ ▶*adj.* **1** sloping sharply. **2** *inf.* (of prices) unreasonably high; exorbitant.

▶*v.* soak or bathe in liquid. —**steep·en** *v.* —**steep·ly** *adv.* —**steep·ness** *n.*

**stee·ple** /ˈstēpəl/ ▶*n.* tall tower, esp. one surmounted by a spire. —**stee·pled** *adj.*

**stee·ple·chase** ▶*n.* race with ditches, hedges, etc., to jump.

**stee·ple·jack** ▶*n.* person who climbs tall chimneys, steeples, etc., to do repairs, etc.

**steer** /sti(ə)r/ ▶*v.* **1** direct the course of; be directed. **2** guide.

▶*n.* castrated ox that is raised for beef.

□ **steer clear of** avoid.

**steer·age** /ˈsti(ə)rij/ ▶*n.* part of a ship allotted to passengers traveling at the cheapest rate.

**steer·age·way** /ˈsti(ə)rij،wā/ (also **steer·age-way**) ▶*n.* (of a vessel) the minimum speed required for proper response to the helm.

**stein** /stīn/ ▶*n.* mug, esp. for beer.

**ste·la** /ˈstēlə/ ▶*n.* (*pl.* **-lae** /-،lē/) upright stone slab or column typically bearing a commemorative inscription or relief design, often serving as a gravestone.

**stel·lar** /ˈstelər/ ▶*adj.* **1** of a star or stars. **2** *inf.* exceptionally good.

**stem** /stem/ ▶*n.* **1** main body or stalk of a plant, fruit, flower, leaf, etc. **2** stem-shaped part of an object. **3** *Gram.* root or main part of a noun, verb, etc., to which inflections are added.

▶*v.* (**stemmed**, **stem·ming**) **1** spring or originate from. **2** check or stop. —**stem·med** *adj.*

**stench** /stenCH/ ▶*n.* offensive or foul smell.

**sten·cil** /ˈstensəl/ ▶*n.* **1** thin sheet of plastic, metal, etc., in which a pattern or lettering is cut, used to produce a pattern on the surface beneath it by applying ink, paint, etc. **2** pattern so produced.

▶*v.* (**-ciled**, **-cil·ing**; **-cilled**, **-cil·ling**) **1** produce (a pattern) with a stencil. **2** decorate or mark (a surface) in this way.

**ste·nog·ra·phy** /stəˈnägrəfē/ ▸n. shorthand. —**ste·nog·ra·pher** n. —**sten·o·graph·ic** adj.

**sten·tor** /ˈstenˌtôr; ˈstentər/ ▸n. person with a powerful voice.

**sten·to·ri·an** /stenˈtôrēən/ ▸adj. (of a voice) loud and powerful.

**step** /step/ ▸n. **1** complete movement of one leg in walking or running. **2** unit of movement in dancing. **3** measure taken, esp. one of several. **4** surface of a stair, stepladder, etc.; tread. **5** short distance.
▸v. (**stepped, step·ping**) **1** lift and set down one's foot or alternate feet in walking. **2** move a short distance by stepping.
□ **step-by-step** gradually; cautiously. □ **step in** intervene to help or hinder. □ **step up** increase; intensify.

**step-** ▸comb. form denoting a relationship resulting from a parent's remarriage.

**step·lad·der** ▸n. short ladder with flat steps and a folding support.

**steppe** /step/ ▸n. level grassy unforested plain.

**-ster** ▸suffix denoting a person engaged in or associated with a particular activity or thing: *gangster* | *trickster*.

**ste·re·o** /ˈsterē-ō; ˈsti(ə)r-/ ▸n. (pl. -**os**) stereophonic sound system or reproduction.

**ster·e·og·ra·phy** /ˌsterēˈägrəfē; ˌsti(ə)r-/ ▸n. depiction or representation of three-dimensional things by projection onto a two-dimensional surface, e.g., in cartography.

**ster·e·o·phon·ic** /-fänik/ ▸adj. (of sound reproduction) using two or more channels giving the effect of naturally distributed sound. —**ster·e·o·phon·i·cal·ly** adv.

**ster·e·op·ti·con** /ˌsterēˈäptiˌkän; ˌsti(ə)r-/ ▸n. slide projector that combines two images to create a three-dimensional effect, or makes one image dissolve into another.

**ster·e·o·type** ▸n. **a** person or thing that conforms to a widely accepted type. **b** such a type, idea, or attitude.
▸v. standardize; cause to conform to a type. —**ster·e·o·typ·i·cal** adj. —**ster·e·o·typ·i·cal·ly** adv.

**ster·ile** /ˈsterəl/ ▸adj. **1** not able to produce fruit or (of an animal) young; barren. **2** free from living microorganisms, etc. —**ste·ril·i·ty** n.

**ster·il·ize** ▸*v.* **1** make sterile. **2** deprive of the power of reproduction. —**ster·i·li·za·tion** *n.* —**ster·i·liz·er** *n.*

**ster·ling** /ˈstərliNG/ ▸*n.* **1** British money: *paid in sterling.* **2** (also **sterling silver**) silver of 92½% purity.
▸*adj.* of solid worth; genuine; reliable.

**stern** /stərn/ ▸*adj.* severe; grim; strict; authoritarian: *stern treatment.*
▸*n.* rear part of a ship or boat. —**stern·ly** *adv.* —**stern·ness** *n.*

**ster·num** /ˈstərnəm/ ▸*n.* (*pl.* **-nums** or **-na**) breastbone.

**ster·nu·ta·tion** /ˌstərnyə-ˈtāSHən/ ▸*n.* action of sneezing.

**ster·oid** /ˈsteroid; ˈsti(ə)r-/ ▸*n.* any of a group of organic compounds including many hormones, alkaloids, and vitamins. —**ster·oid·al** *adj.*

**ster·to·rous** /ˈstərtərəs/ ▸*adj.* (of breathing) noisy and labored.

**stet** /stet/ ▸*v.* (**stet·ted, stet·ting**) (usu. as an instruction written on printed text, etc.) ignore or cancel the correction or alteration; let the original form stand.

**steth·o·scope** /ˈsteTHəˌskōp/ ▸*n.* instrument used in listening to the action of the heart, lungs, etc.

**ste·ve·dore** /ˈstēvəˌdôr/ ▸*n.* person employed in loading and unloading ships.

**stew** /st(y)o͞o/ ▸*v.* **1** cook by long simmering. **2** *inf.* fret or be anxious.
▸*n.* **1** dish of stewed meat, etc. **2** *inf.* agitated or angry state: *be in a stew.*

**stew·ard** /ˈst(y)o͞oərd/ ▸*n.* **1** passengers' attendant on a ship or aircraft or train. **2** person responsible for supplies of food, etc., for a college or club, etc. **3** property manager. —**stew·ard·ship** *n.*

**sthen·ic** /ˈsTHenik/ ▸*adj.* of or having a high or excessive level of strength and energy.

**sti·cho·myth·i·a** /ˌstikəˈmiTHēə/ ▸*n.* dialogue in which two characters speak alternate lines of verse, used as a stylistic device in ancient Greek drama.

**stick** ▸*n.* **1** short slender branch or length of wood. **2** implement used to propel the ball in hockey, polo, etc.
▸*v.* (*past* and *past part.* **stuck**) **1** insert or thrust (a thing or its point) into or through

something: *stuck a finger in my eye.* **2** attach or become or remain fixed by or as by adhesive, etc.: *stick a label on it.* **3** endure: *the name stuck.* **4** not open, release, etc.; jam. **5** *inf.* remain in a place: *stuck indoors.*
□ **stick to** remain close to or fixed on or to. □ **stick up for** support or defend.

**stick·er** ▸*n.* adhesive label, notice, etc.

**stick·ler** ▸*n.* person who insists on something: *stickler for accuracy.*

**stick shift** ▸*n.* manual transmission.

**stick·y** /ˈstikē/ ▸*adj.* (**-i·er, -i·est**) **1** tending or intended to stick or adhere. **2** humid.
—**stick·i·ness** *n.*

**stiff** /stif/ ▸*adj.* **1** rigid; not flexible. **2** hard to bend, move, or turn. **3** formal; constrained.
▸*n. inf.* corpse. —**stiff·en** *v.*
—**stiff·en·er** *n.* —**stiff·ly** *adv.*
—**stiff·ness** *n.*

**sti·fle** /ˈstīfəl/ ▸*v.* **1** suppress: *the administration attempted to stifle dissent.* **2** experience or cause to experience constraint of breathing: *stifling heat.*
—**sti·fling·ly** *adv.*

**stig·ma** /ˈstigmə/ ▸*n.* (*pl.* **-mas,**

**-ma·ta**) **1** mark or sign of disgrace or discredit. **2** part of a flower pistil that receives the pollen in pollination.
**3** (**stigmata**) (in Christian belief) marks resembling those left on Christ's body by the Crucifixion.

**stig·ma·tize** ▸*v.* describe or regard as worthy of disgrace.

**stile** /stīl/ ▸*n.* arrangement of steps over a fence or wall.

**sti·let·to** /stəˈletō/ ▸*n.* (*pl.* **-tos**) **1** short dagger with a thick blade. **2** (also **stiletto heel**) long tapering heel of a woman's shoe or a shoe with such a heel.

**still** /stil/ ▸*adj.* **1** not or hardly moving. **2** with little or no sound; calm and tranquil: *a still evening.*
▸*n.* **1** deep silence: *still of the night.* **2** static photograph, esp. a single shot from a movie or videotape. **3** apparatus for distilling alcohol, etc.
▸*adv.* **1** without moving: *stand still.* **2** even now or at a particular time: *why are you still here?* **3** nevertheless. **4** even; yet; increasingly: *still greater efforts.* —**still·ness** *n.*
□ **still life** painting or drawing of inanimate objects, e.g., fruit or flowers.

**still·born** ▶*adj.* born dead.

**stilt** /stilt/ ▶*n.* **1** either of a pair of poles with supports for the feet for walking with the body elevated. **2** each of a set of piles or posts supporting a building, etc.

**stilt·ed** ▶*adj.* stiff and unnatural; bombastic. —**stilt·ed·ness** *n.*

**stim·u·lant** /'stimyələnt/ ▶*n.* stimulating substance or influence.

**stim·u·late** ▶*v.* **1** act as a stimulus to. **2** animate; excite; arouse. —**stim·u·lat·ing** *adj.* —**stim·u·la·tion** *n.* —**stim·u·la·tive** *adj.*

**stim·u·lus** /'stimyələs/ ▶*n.* (*pl.* **-li**) **1** thing that rouses to activity or energy. **2** stimulating or rousing effect.

**sting** /stiNG/ ▶*v.* (*past* and *past part.* **stung**) **1** wound or pierce with a sharp organ as of a bee. **2** feel or cause to feel a sharp pain.
▶*n.* wound or pain caused by stinging. —**sting·er** *n.* —**sting·ing·ly** *adv.*

**stin·gy** /'stinjē/ ▶*adj.* (**-gi·er**, **-gi·est**) ungenerous; mean. —**stin·gi·ly** *adv.* —**stin·gi·ness** *n.*

**stink** /stiNGk/ ▶*v.* (*past* **stank** or **stunk**; *past part.* **stunk**) emit a strong offensive smell.
▶*n.* **1** strong or offensive smell. **2** *inf.* fuss.

**stint** /stint/ ▶*v.* **1** restrict to a small allowance. **2** be thrifty or mean.
▶*n.* allotted amount of work: *do one's stint.*

**sti·pend** /'stī,pend/ ▶*n.* fixed regular allowance or salary.

**stip·ple** /'stipəl/ ▶*v.* draw, paint, engrave, etc., with dots instead of lines. —**stip·pling** *n.*

**stip·u·late** /'stipyə,lāt/ ▶*v.* demand or specify as part of an agreement. —**stip·u·la·tion** *n.* —**stip·u·la·tor** *n.*

**stir** /stər/ ▶*v.* (**stirred**, **stir·ring**) **1** mix by moving an implement around and around in (a liquid, etc.). **2** move or cause to move, esp. slightly. **3** arouse or inspire or excite (the emotions, a person, etc.).
▶*n.* **1** act of stirring. **2** commotion or excitement. —**stir·rer** *n.*
□ **stir up 1** incite (trouble, etc.). **2** stimulate; excite; arouse.

**stir-fry** ▶*v.* (**-fried**) fry rapidly while stirring and tossing.

**stir·rup** /'stərəp; 'stir-/ ▶*n.* each of a pair of devices attached to each side of a horse's saddle, in the form of a loop with a flat base to support the rider's foot.

**stitch** /stiCH/ ▶n. 1 (in sewing, knitting, or crocheting) single pass of a needle, or the thread or loop resulting from this. 2 least bit of clothing: *hadn't a stitch on.* 3 acute pain in the side.
▶v. sew; make stitches (in).
—**stitch·er** *n.* —**stitch·er·y** *n.*
□ **in stitches** *inf.* laughing uncontrollably.

**stoat** /stōt/ ▶n. mammal of the weasel family.

**sto·chas·tic** /stə'kastik/ ▶adj. randomly determined; having a random probability distribution or pattern that may be analyzed statistically but may not be predicted precisely.

**stock** /stäk/ ▶n. 1 store of goods, etc., ready for sale or distribution, etc. 2 supply; quantity. 3 equipment or raw material for manufacture or trade, etc. 4 farm animals or equipment. 5 a capital of a business company. b shares in this. 6 line of ancestry. 7 liquid made by stewing bones, vegetables, fish, etc., as a basis for soup, gravy, sauce, etc.
▶adj. 1 kept in stock and so

regularly available: *stock sizes.* 2 hackneyed; conventional: *stock answer.*
▶v. 1 have or keep (goods) in stock. 2 supply.
□ **stock brok·er** dealer who buys and sells stock. □ **stock-in-trade** 1 requisites of a trade or profession. 2 ready supply of characteristic phrases, attitudes, etc. □ **stock up** provide with or get stocks or supplies.

**stock·ade** /stä'kād/ ▶n. 1 line or enclosure of upright stakes. 2 military prison.
▶v. fortify with a stockade.

**stock ex·change** ▶n. place where stocks and shares are bought and sold.

**stock·ing** ▶n. knitted fabric covering for the leg and foot.

**stock mar·ket** ▶n. stock exchange.

**stock·pile** ▶n. accumulated stock of goods, materials, weapons, etc., held in reserve.
▶v. accumulate a stockpile of.

**stock·y** ▶adj. (-i·er, -i·est) short and strongly built; thickset.
—**stock·i·ly** *adv.* —**stock·i·ness** *n.*

**stock·yard** ▶n. enclosure with pens, etc., for the sorting or temporary keeping of cattle.

**stodg·y** /'stäjē/ ▸*adj.* (**-i·er, -i·est**) dull; uninteresting; old-fashioned. —**stodg·i·ly** *adv.* —**stodg·i·ness** *n.*

**sto·ic** /'stōik/ ▸*n.* person who endures pain or hardship without showing their feelings. ▸*adj.* (also **sto·i·cal**) enduring pain or hardship without complaint. —**sto·i·cal·ly** *adv.* —**sto·i·cism** *n.*

**stoke** /stōk/ ▸*v.* feed and tend (a fire or furnace).

**stole** /stōl/ ▸*n.* woman's long, wide scarf, worn around the shoulders. ▸past of STEAL.

**stol·id** /'stälid/ ▸*adj.* **1** lacking or concealing emotion or animation. **2** not easily excited or moved. —**sto·lid·i·ty** *n.* —**stol·id·ly** *adv.* —**stol·id·ness** *n.*

**stom·ach** /'stəmək/ ▸*n.* **1** internal organ in which food is digested. **2** lower front of the body. **3** appetite or inclination. ▸*v.* **1** find sufficiently palatable to swallow or keep down. **2** endure: *cannot stomach it.*

**stomp** /stämp/ ▸*v.* tread or stamp heavily. —**stomp·er** *n.*

**stone** /stōn/ ▸*n.* **1** solid nonmetallic mineral matter, of which rock is made. **2** gem. **3 a** thing resembling stone in hardness or form, e.g., the hard case of the kernel in some fruits. **b** *Med.* (often **stones**) hard mass forming in certain body organs. **4** (*pl.* same) British unit of weight equal to 14 lb. (6.35 kg). ▸*v.* pelt with stones. —**ston·y** *adj.* □ **leave no stone unturned** try all possible means. □ **stone's throw** short distance.

**stoned** ▸*adj. inf.* under the influence of alcohol or drugs.

**stone·wall** ▸*v.* obstruct (a discussion or investigation) or be obstructive with evasive answers, denials, etc.

**stood** /sto͝od/ ▸ past and past part. of STAND.

**stooge** /sto͞oj/ ▸*n. inf.* **1** butt or foil, esp. for a comedian; straight man. **2** assistant or subordinate, esp. for routine or unpleasant work.

**stool** /sto͞ol/ ▸*n.* **1** single seat without a back or arms. **2** FOOTSTOOL. **3** piece of feces. □ **stool pigeon** police informer or decoy.

**stoop** /sto͞op/ ▸*v.* **1** bend forward and downward. **2** condescend. **3** descend or lower oneself (to some conduct): *has stooped to crime.* ▸*n.* **1** stooping posture. **2** porch or set of steps in front of a house.

**stop** /stäp/ ▶*v.* (**stopped, stop·ping**) **1** bring or come to an end; completely check the progress or motion or operation (of). **2** block or close up (a hole or leak, etc.).
▶*n.* **1** stopping; being stopped. **2** place designated for a bus, train, etc., to stop. **3** device for stopping motion at a particular point. **4** (in an organ) row of pipes of one character. —**stop·page** *n.*
□ **stop at nothing** be ruthless.

**stop·gap** ▶*n.* temporary solution to a problem.

**stop·o·ver** ▶*n.* break in one's journey.

**stop·per** ▶*n.* plug for closing a bottle, etc.

**stop·watch** ▶*n.* watch with a mechanism for recording elapsed time, used to time races, etc.

**stor·age** /ˈstôrij/ ▶*n.* **1 a** storing of goods, etc. **b** space available for storing. **2** cost of storing. **3** electronic retention of data in a computer, etc.
□ **storage battery** (or **storage cell**) battery (or cell) for storing electricity.

**store** /stôr/ ▶*n.* **1** quantity of something kept available for use. **2** (**stores**) **a** articles for a particular purpose accumulated for use. **b** supply of these or the place where they are kept. **3** retail outlet or shop.
▶*v.* **1** put (furniture, etc.) in storage. **2** accumulate for future use. **3** enter or retain (data) for retrieval. —**store·keep·er** *n.*

**store·house** ▶*n.* place where things are stored.

**stork** /stôrk/ ▶*n.* long-legged large wading bird with white plumage, black wingtips, and a long reddish beak.

**storm** /stôrm/ ▶*n.* **1** violent disturbance of the atmosphere with strong winds and usu. with thunder and rain or snow, etc. **2** violent political, etc., disturbance. **3** outbreak of applause, indignation, hisses, etc.: *the announcement was met by a storm of opposition.*
▶*v.* **1** rage; bluster. **2** move violently or angrily: *stormed out.* **3** attack or capture by storm. —**storm·proof** *adj.* —**storm·y** *adj.*
□ **take by storm 1** capture by direct assault. **2** rapidly captivate.

**sto·ry** /ˈstôrē/ ▶*n.* (*pl.* **-ries**)

**1** account of imaginary or past events; narrative, tale, or anecdote. **2** (also **story line**) narrative or plot of a novel or play, etc. **3** horizontal division of a building.

**sto·ry·board** /ˈstôrēˌbôrd/ ▶n. sequence of drawings, typically with some directions and dialogue, representing the shots planned for a movie or television production.

**stout** /stout/ ▶adj. **1** somewhat fat; corpulent; bulky. **2** thick; strong. **3** brave; resolute.
▶n. strong, dark brown beer.
—**stout·ly** adv. —**stout·ness** n.

**stout·heart·ed** ▶adj. courageous. —**stout·heart·ed·ly** adj.

**stove** /stōv/ ▶n. closed apparatus burning fuel or electricity for heating or cooking.

**stow** /stō/ ▶v. pack (goods, etc.) tidily and compactly.

**stow·a·way** ▶n. person who hides on a ship or airplane to travel free of charge.

**stra·bis·mus** /strəˈbizməs/ ▶n. abnormal alignment of the eyes; the condition of having a squint.

**strad·dle** /ˈstradl/ ▶v. **a** sit or stand across (a thing) with the legs wide apart. **b** be situated across or on both sides of.
—**strad·dler** n.

**strafe** /strāf/ ▶v. harass with gunfire.

**strag·gle** /ˈstragəl/ ▶v. **1** lack or lose compactness or tidiness. **2** be or become dispersed or sporadic. **3** trail behind others in a march or race, etc.
—**strag·gler** n. —**strag·gly** adj.

**straight** /strāt/ ▶adj. **1** extending uniformly in the same direction; without a curve or bend. **2** successive; uninterrupted: *three straight wins*. **3** honest; candid. **4 a** unmodified. **b** (of a drink) undiluted. **5** inf. **a** (of a person, etc.) conventional or respectable. **b** heterosexual.
▶n. **1** part of something that is not curved: *he pulled away in the straight*. **2** sequence of five cards in poker.
▶adv. **1** in a straight line; direct; without deviation or hesitation or circumlocution. **2** correctly.
—**straight·en** v.
—**straight·ness** n.

**straight ar·row** ▶n. inf. honest person.

**straight·a·way** ▶n. straight part of a course, track, road, etc.

**straight-faced** ▶adj. with a

blank or serious facial expression.

**straight·for·ward** ▶*adj.* **1** honest or frank. **2** (of a task, etc.) uncomplicated. —**straight·for·ward·ly** *adv.* —**straight·for·ward·ness** *n.*

**strain** /strān/ ▶*v.* **1** stretch tightly; make or become taut or tense. **2** press to extremes. **3** clear (a liquid) of solid matter by passing it through a sieve, etc.; filter. ▶*n.* **1** act or an instance of straining. **2** injury caused by straining a muscle, etc. **3** severe demand on physical strength or resources. **4** snatch or spell of music or poetry. **5** breed or stock of animals, plants, etc. **6** tendency in a person's character.

**strained** ▶*adj.* constrained; forced; artificial.

**strait** /strāt/ ▶*n.* **1** narrow passage of water connecting two seas or large bodies of water. **2** (usu. **straits**) difficulty; distress.

**strait·jack·et** ▶*n.* **1** strong garment with long arms for confining a violent person. **2** restrictive measures.

**strait·laced** ▶*adj.* puritanical.

**strand** /strand/ ▶*v.* **1** run aground. **2** leave helpless, esp. without money or means of transport. ▶*n.* **1** each of the threads or wires twisted around each other to make a rope or cable. **2** element or strain in any composite whole. **3** shore; beach.

**strange** /strānj/ ▶*adj.* **1** unusual; peculiar; surprising; eccentric; novel. **2** unfamiliar; alien; foreign. **3** not at ease; out of one's element: *felt strange in such company.* —**strange·ly** *adv.* —**strange·ness** *n.*

**strang·er** ▶*n.* **1** person new to a particular place or company. **2** person one does not know. **3** person entirely unaccustomed to (a feeling, experience, etc.).

**stran·gle** /ˈstraNGɡəl/ ▶*v.* **1** squeeze the windpipe or neck of, esp. so as to kill. **2** hamper or suppress. —**stran·gler** *n.*

**stran·gle·hold** ▶*n.* **1** deadly grip. **2** complete and exclusive control.

**stran·gu·late** /ˈstraNGɡyə,lāt/ ▶*v. Med.* prevent circulation through (a vein, intestine, etc.) by compression.

**strap** /strap/ ▶*n.* **1** strip of leather, etc., often with a buckle or other fastening for holding things together, etc. **2** thing like this for keeping a garment in place.

▶*v.* (**strapped**, **strap·ping**) secure or bind with a strap.

□ **strapped for** *inf.* short of: *strapped for cash.*

**strat·a·gem** /ˈstratəjəm/ ▶*n.* cunning plan or scheme, esp. for deceiving an enemy.

**strat·e·gy** /ˈstratəjē/ ▶*n.* (*pl.* **-gies**) **1** art of war or military deployment. **2** plan of action or policy in business, politics, etc.: *economic strategy.* —**stra·te·gic** *adj.* —**strat·e·gist** *n.*

**strat·i·fy** /ˈstratəˌfī/ ▶*v.* (**-fied**) **1** [usu. as *adj.* **stratified**] arrange in strata. **2** construct in layers, social grades, etc. —**strat·i·fi·ca·tion** *n.*

**strat·o·sphere** /ˈstratəˌsfi(ə)r/ ▶*n.* layer of atmospheric air above the troposphere extending to about 30 miles above the earth's surface. —**strat·o·spher·ic** *adj.*

**stra·tum** /ˈstrātəm; ˈstrat-/ ▶*n.* (*pl.* **-ta** or **-tums**) **1** *Geol.* or *Archaeol.* layer or set of layers of any deposited substance. **2** atmospheric layer. **3** social class.

**straw** /strô/ ▶*n.* **1** dry cut stalks of grain for use as fodder or as material for packing, etc. **2** single stalk or piece of straw. **3** thin tube for sucking a drink from a glass, etc.

□ **straw vote** (or **straw poll**) unofficial ballot as a test of opinion.

**straw·ber·ry** ▶*n.* (*pl.* **-ries**) **1** plant with white flowers, trifoliate leaves, and runners. **2** pulpy, red, edible fruit of this.

**stray** /strā/ ▶*v.* **1** wander from the right place or from one's companions, etc.; go astray. **2** deviate morally.

▶*n.* person or thing that has strayed, esp. a domestic animal.

▶*adj.* **1** strayed or lost. **2** isolated; found or occurring occasionally: *hit by a stray bullet.*

**streak** /strēk/ ▶*n.* **1** long, thin, usu. irregular line or band, esp. of color. **2** strain or element in a person's character. **3** spell or series: *winning streak.*

▶*v.* **1** mark with streaks. **2** move very rapidly. —**streak·y** *adj.*

**stream** /strēm/ ▶*n.* **1** flowing body of water, esp. a small river. **2** flow of a fluid, a mass of people, questions, etc.

**3** current; direction: *against the stream.*

▶*v.* flow or move as a stream.

**stream·er** ▶*n.* **1** long narrow flag. **2** long narrow strip of ribbon or paper.

**stream·line** ▶*v.* **1** give (a vehicle, etc.) the form that presents the least resistance to motion. **2** make simple or more efficient or better organized.

**street** /strēt/ ▶*n.* public road in a city, town, or village, lined with buildings.

**street·car** ▶*n.* commuter vehicle that operates on rails in city streets.

**street·smart** ▶*adj. inf.* having the skills and knowledge necessary for dealing with modern urban life.

**street·walk·er** ▶*n.* prostitute seeking customers on the street.

**strength** /streNG(k)TH/ ▶*n.* **1** being strong; degree or manner of this. **2** person or thing affording strength. **3** positive attribute. **4** number of persons present or available. **5** full complement.

**strength·en** ▶*v.* make or become stronger. —**strength·en·er** *n.*

**stren·u·ous** /ˈstrenyo͞oəs/ ▶*adj.* **1** requiring or using great effort. **2** energetic. —**stren·u·ous·ly** *adv.* —**stren·u·ous·ness** *n.*

**strep throat** /strep/ ▶*n.* acute sore throat caused by streptococci.

**strep·to·coc·cus** /ˌstreptə-ˈkäkəs/ ▶*n.* (*pl.* -**coc·ci**) bacterium of a type often causing infectious diseases. —**strep·to·coc·cal** *adj.*

**stress** /stres/ ▶*n.* **1** pressure; tension. **2** physical or mental strain or distress. **3** emphasis.

▶*v.* **1** emphasize. **2** subject to stress. **3** become tense or anxious. —**stress·ful** *adj.* —**stress·ful·ly** *adv.*

**stretch** /strecH/ ▶*v.* **1** draw or be drawn or admit of being drawn out into greater length or size. **2** make or become taut. **3** place or lie at full length or spread out. **4** thrust out one's limbs. **5** strain; exaggerate: *stretch the truth.*

▶*n.* **1** continuous extent or expanse or period. **2** stretching or being stretched. —**stretch·a·ble** *adj.* —**stretch·a·bil·i·ty** *n.* —**stretch·y** *adj.* —**stretch·i·ness** *n.*

**stretch·er** ▶*n.* framework for carrying a person in a lying position.

**strew** /strōō/ ▶*v.* (*past part.* **strewn** or **strewed**) **1** scatter or spread about over a surface. **2** spread a surface with scattered things.

**strick·en** /ˈstrikən/ ▶*adj.* affected or overcome with illness, misfortune, etc.: *stricken with measles.*

**strict** /strikt/ ▶*adj.* **1** precisely limited or defined; undeviating. **2** requiring complete compliance or exact performance: *gave strict orders.* —**strict·ly** *adv.* —**strict·ness** *n.*

**stric·ture** /ˈstrikCHər/ ▶*n.* **1** (usu. **strictures**) critical or censorious remark. **2** restriction.

**stride** /strīd/ ▶*v.* (*past* **strode**; *past part.* **strid·den**) walk with long firm steps. ▶*n.* **1 a** single long step. **b** length of this. **2** manner of striding. **3** (usu. **strides**) progress: *great strides.* □ **take in one's stride** manage without difficulty.

**stri·dent** /ˈstrīdnt/ ▶*adj.* loud and harsh. —**stri·den·cy** *n.* —**stri·dent·ly** *adv.*

**strid·u·late** /ˈstrijəˌlāt/ ▶*v.* (of an insect, esp. a male cricket or grasshopper) make a shrill sound by rubbing the legs, wings, or other parts of the body together.

**strife** /strīf/ ▶*n.* conflict; struggle.

**strike** /strīk/ ▶*v.* (*past* **struck**; *past part.* **struck** or **strick·en**) **1** deliver (a blow) or inflict a blow on; hit. **2** come or bring sharply into contact with: *ship struck a rock.* **3** propel or divert with a blow: *struck the ball into the pond.* **4** (**strike at**) try to hit. **5** ignite (a match) or produce (sparks, etc.) by rubbing. **6** (of a clock) indicate (the time) with a chime, etc. **7** attack, affect, or afflict suddenly. **8** agree on (a bargain). **9** discover or find. **10** (of employees) engage in a strike. ▶*n.* **1** act or instance of striking. **2** organized refusal by employees to work until some grievance is remedied. **3** sudden find or success: *lucky strike.* **4** an attack, esp. from the air. **5** *Baseball* pitched ball counted against a batter, either for failure to hit it fair or because it passes through the strike zone. —**strik·er** *n.*

□ **strike out** *Baseball* **a** dismiss (a batter) by means of three strikes. **b** be dismissed in this way.
□ **strike up** **1** start (an acquaintance, conversation, etc.) off-handedly or casually. **2** begin playing (a tune, etc.).

**strike zone** ▸*n. Baseball* area above home plate extending from the batter's armpits to knees.

**strik·ing** ▸*adj.* impressive; attracting attention. —**strik·ing·ly** *adv.*

**string** /striNG/ ▸*n.* **1** twine or narrow cord. **2** piece of this. **3** length of catgut or wire on a musical instrument, producing a note by vibration. **4** (**strings**) stringed instruments in an orchestra, etc. **5** (**strings**) condition; complication: *offer has no strings.* ▸*v.* (*past* and *past part.* **strung**) **1** supply with a string or strings. **2** thread (beads, etc.) on a string. **3** arrange in or as a string. —**stringed** *adj.* —**string·less** *adj.*

**string bean** ▸*n.* kind of bean with an edible pod.

**strin·gent** /ˈstrinjənt/ ▸*adj.* strict; precise. —**strin·gen·cy** *n.* —**strin·gent·ly** *adv.*

**strip** /strip/ ▸*v.* (**stripped,**

**strip·ping**) **1** remove the clothes or covering from. **2** undress oneself. **3** deprive (a person) of property or titles. **4** take apart or leave bare. **5** tear the thread from (a screw) or the teeth from (a gearwheel). ▸*n.* **1** act of stripping, esp. of undressing in striptease. **2** long narrow piece: *strip of land.*

**stripe** /strīp/ ▸*n.* **1** long narrow band or strip differing in color or texture from the surface on either side of it: *black with a red stripe.* **2** chevron, etc., denoting military rank.

**strip·ling** /ˈstripliNG/ ▸*n.* youth not yet fully grown.

**strip mall** ▸*n.* shopping mall consisting of stores, etc., in one-story buildings along a main road.

**strip mine** ▸*n.* mine worked by removing the material that overlies the ore, etc. —**strip-mine** *v.*

**strive** /strīv/ ▸*v.* (*past* **strove**; *past part.* **striv·en**) **1** try hard. **2** struggle or contend. —**striv·er** *n.*

**stroke** /strōk/ ▸*n.* **1** act of striking; blow or hit. **2** sudden disabling attack caused esp. by thrombosis. **3** action or movement esp. as one of a series. **4** whole of the motion (of a wing, oar, etc.) until the starting position is regained. **5** mode of moving the arms and legs in swimming. **6** mark made by the movement in one direction of a pen or pencil or paintbrush. **7** sound made by a striking clock.

▶*v.* caress lightly.

**stroll** /strōl/ ▶*v.* saunter or walk in a leisurely way.

▶*n.* short leisurely walk: *go for a stroll.*

**stroll·er** ▶*n.* chairlike conveyance on wheels, for pushing a child in.

**strong** /strÔNG/ ▶*adj.* (**-er, -est**) **1** having the power of resistance; not easily damaged, overcome, or disturbed. **2** healthy. **3** capable of exerting great force or of doing much; muscular; powerful. **4** forceful or powerful in effect: *strong wind.* **5** decided or firmly held: *strong views.* **6** intense; concentrated.

▶*adv.* strongly. **—strong·ly** *adv.*

**strong·box** ▶*n.* strongly made small chest for valuables.

**strong·hold** ▶*n.* **1** fortified place. **2** secure refuge. **3** center of support for a cause, etc.

**stron·ti·um** /ˈstränCHēəm; -tēəm/ *Chem.* ▶*n.* soft silver white metallic element occurring naturally in various minerals. (Symb.: **Sr**)

□ **strontium 90** radioactive isotope of strontium.

**strop** /sträp/ ▶*n.* device, esp. a strip of leather, for sharpening razors.

**struc·ture** /ˈstrəkCHər/ ▶*n.* **1 a** constructed unit, esp. a building. **b** way in which a building, etc., is constructed. **2** framework.

▶*v.* give structure or shape to; organize; frame. **—struc·tur·al** *adj.* **—struc·tured** *adj.*

**stru·del** /ˈstroōdl/ ▶*n.* confection of thin pastry rolled up around a filling and baked: *apple strudel.*

**strug·gle** /ˈstrəgəl/ ▶*v.* **1** make forceful or violent efforts to get free of restraint or constriction. **2** try hard under difficulties. **3** (**struggle with/against**) contend with; fight against.

▶*n.* **1** act or spell of struggling. **2** hard or confused contest. **3** determined effort under difficulties.

**strum** /strəm/ ▶*v.* (**strummed, strum·ming**) **1** play on (a guitar, etc.) by sweeping the thumb or a

plectrum up or down the strings. **2** play (a tune, etc.) in this way.
▶*n.* sound made by strumming.
—**strum·mer** *n.*

**strum·pet** /ˈstrəmpət/ ▶*n.* female prostitute or a promiscuous woman.

**strut** /strət/ ▶*n.* **1** bar forming part of a framework and designed to resist compression. **2** strutting gait.
▶*v.* (**strut·ted, strut·ting**) walk with a pompous or affected stiff, erect gait.

**strych·nine** /ˈstrikˌnin; -ˌnēn/ ▶*n.* vegetable alkaloid, bitter and highly poisonous, formerly used as a stimulant and (in small amounts) a medication.

**stub** /stəb/ ▶*n.* **1** shortened remnant of a pencil, cigarette, etc., after use. **2** part of a check, receipt, etc., retained as a record.
▶*v.* (**stubbed, stub·bing**) strike (one's toe) against something.

**stub·ble** ▶*n.* **1** cut stalks of cereal plants left sticking up after the harvest. **2 a** cropped hair or cropped beard. **b** short growth of unshaven hair.
—**stub·bly** *adj.*

**stub·born** /ˈstəbərn/ ▶*adj.* obstinate; inflexible.

—**stub·born·ly** *adj.*
—**stub·born·ness** *n.*

**stuc·co** /ˈstəkō/ ▶*n.* (*pl.* **-coes** or **-cos**) plaster or cement for coating walls.
▶*v.* (**-coed**) coat with stucco.

**stuck-up** ▶*adj. inf.* conceited.

**stud** /stəd/ ▶*n.* **1** large-headed nail or knob, esp. for ornament. **2** double button for a collar, shirt front, etc. **3** stallion. **4** *inf.* young man, esp. one noted for sexual prowess.
▶*v.* (**stud·ded, stud·ding**) **1** set with or as if with studs. **2** (usu. **be studded**) set thickly or strew (with): *the handle of the dagger was studded with jewels.*

**stu·dent** /ˈst(y)o͞odnt/ ▶*n.* person who is studying, esp. at school, college, etc.

**stud·ied** ▶*adj.* deliberate; affected.

**stu·di·o** /ˈst(y)o͞odēˌō/ ▶*n.* (*pl.* **-os**) **1** workroom of a painter, photographer, etc. **2** place where movies, recordings, or broadcast programs are made.

**stud·y** /ˈstədē/ ▶*n.* (*pl.* **-ies**) **1** acquisition of knowledge, esp. from books. **2** (**studies**) pursuit of academic knowledge. **3** room used for reading, writing, etc. **4** piece of work, esp. a drawing, done for practice or as an experiment: *a study of a head.* **5** thing worth observing or investigating.

▸*v.* (**-ied**) **1** make a study of; investigate or examine (a subject): *study law.* **2** apply oneself to study. **3** scrutinize or earnestly contemplate: *studied their faces.* —**stu·di·ous** *adj.*

**stuff** /stəf/ ▸*n.* **1** material or constituents of something. **2** things; belongings.

▸*v.* **1** pack (a receptacle) tightly or force into a confined space. **2** fill out the skin of (a preserved animal or bird, etc.) to restore the original shape. **3** (**stuff oneself**) eat greedily.

**stuff·ing** ▸*n.* **1** padding used to stuff cushions, etc. **2** mixture used to stuff food, esp. before cooking.

**stuff·y** ▸*adj.* (**-i·er, -i·est**) **1** (of a room, etc.) lacking fresh air. **2** (of a person's nose, etc.) stuffed up. **3** dull and conventional. —**stuff·i·ly** *adv.* —**stuff·i·ness** *n.*

**stul·ti·fy** /'stəltə,fī/ ▸*v.* (**-fied**) make ineffective, useless, or futile, esp. as a result of tedious routine: *stultifying boredom.* —**stul·ti·fi·ca·tion** *n.*

**stum·ble** /'stəmbəl/ ▸*v.*

**1** involuntarily lurch forward or have a partial fall. **2** make a mistake or repeated mistakes in speaking, etc. **3** find by chance: *stumbled on an abandoned well.*

▸*n.* act of stumbling. —**stum·bling·ly** *adv.*

□ **stumbling block** obstacle.

**stump** /stəmp/ ▸*n.* **1** projecting remnant of a cut or fallen tree. **2** cut off or worn down remnant of something.

▸*v.* **1** (of a question, etc.) be too hard for; puzzle. **2** travel through a state, etc., making political speeches. —**stump·y** *adj.*

**stun** /stən/ ▸*v.* (**stunned, stun·ning**) **1** knock senseless; stupefy. **2** bewilder or shock. **3** (of a sound) deafen temporarily.

**stun·ning** ▸*adj. inf.* extremely impressive or attractive. —**stun·ning·ly** *adv.*

**stunt** /stənt/ ▸*v.* hinder the growth or development of.

▸*n.* something unusual done to attract attention; trick or daring maneuver. —**stunt·ed·ness** *n.*

**stu·pe·fy** /'st(y)ōōpə,fī/ ▸*v.* (**-fied**) **1** make stupid or insensible. **2** stun with astonishment. —**stu·pe·fa·cient** *adj. & n.*

—**stu·pe·fac·tion** *n.*

—**stu·pe·fy·ing** *adj.*

—**stu·pe·fy·ing·ly** *adv.*

**stu·pen·dous** /st(y)oo'pendəs/ ▶*adj.* amazing or prodigious, esp. in terms of size or degree.
—**stu·pen·dous·ly** *adv.*
—**stu·pen·dous·ness** *n.*

**stu·pid** /'st(y)oopid/ ▶*adj.* (-**er**, -**est**) unintelligent; slow-witted; foolish. —**stu·pid·i·ty** *n. adv.*
—**stu·pid·ly** *adv.*

**stu·por** /'st(y)oopər/ ▶*n.* dazed, torpid, or helplessly amazed state. —**stu·por·ous** *adj.*

**stur·dy** /'stərdē/ ▶*adj.* (-**di·er**, -**di·est**) **1** robust; strongly built. **2** vigorous: *sturdy resistance.*
—**stur·di·ly** *adv.* —**stur·di·ness** *n.*

**stur·geon** /'stərjən/ ▶*n.* large sharklike fish used as food and a source of caviar.

**stut·ter** /'stətər/ ▶*v.* stammer, esp. by involuntarily repeating the first consonants of words.
▶*n.* act or habit of stuttering.
—**stut·ter·er** *n.* —**stut·ter·ing·ly** *adv.*

**sty** /stī/ ▶*n.* (*pl.* **sties**) **1** pen or enclosure for pigs. **2** *inf.* filthy room or dwelling. **3** inflamed swelling on the edge of an eyelid.

**style** /stīl/ ▶*n.* **1** kind or sort, esp. in regard to appearance and form: *elegant style of house.* **2** manner of writing or speaking or performing. **3** distinctive manner of a person or school or period. **4** superior quality or manner: *do it in style.* **5** fashion in dress, etc.
▶*v.* **1** design or make, etc., in a particular (esp. fashionable) style. **2** designate in a specified way.

**styl·ish** ▶*adj.* **1** fashionable; elegant. **2** having a superior quality, manner, etc.
—**styl·ish·ly** *adv.*
—**styl·ish·ness** *n.*

**styl·ist** ▶*n.* **1 a** designer of fashionable styles, etc. **b** hairdresser. **2** stylish writer or performer. —**sty·lis·tic** *adj.*

**sty·lis·tics** /stī'listiks/ ▶*n.* study of the distinctive styles found in particular literary genres and in the works of individual writers.

**sty·lite** /'stī,līt/ ▶*n.* ascetic living on top of a pillar, esp. in ancient or medieval Syria, Turkey, and Greece in the 5th century AD.

**styl·ize** ▶*v.* [usu. as *adj.* **stylized**] paint, draw, etc., in a conventional nonrealistic style.
—**styl·i·za·tion** *n.*

**sty·lus** /ˈstīləs/ ▶*n.* (*pl.* **-li** or **-lus·es**) **1** phonograph needle. **2** pointed tool.

**sty·mie** /ˈstīmē/ ▶*v.* (**-mied, -my·ing** or **-mie·ing**) obstruct; thwart.

**styp·tic** /ˈstiptik/ ▶*adj.* (of a drug, etc.) that checks bleeding. ▶*n.* styptic drug or substance.

**sty·ro·foam** /ˈstīrəˌfōm/ ▶*trademark* brand of expanded rigid lightweight polystyrene plastic.

**sua·sion** /ˈswāzHən/ ▶*n.* persuasion as opposed to force or compulsion.

**suave** /swäv/ ▶*adj.* smooth; polite; sophisticated. —**suave·ly** *adv.* —**suave·ness** *n.* —**suav·i·ty** *n.*

**sub** /səb/ ▶*n. inf.* **1** submarine. **2** substitute. ▶*v.* (**subbed, sub·bing**) act as a substitute.

**sub-** ▶*prefix* **1** at or to or from a lower position: *subordinate* | *submerge* | *subtract.* **2** secondary or inferior position: *subclass* | *subtotal.* **3** nearly; more or less: *subarctic.*

**sub·a·tom·ic** ▶*adj.* occurring in or smaller than an atom.

**sub·com·mit·tee** ▶*n.* committee formed from another committee for a specialized task.

**sub·con·scious** ▶*adj.* of or concerning the part of the mind that is not fully conscious but influences actions, etc. ▶*n.* this part of the mind. —**sub·con·scious·ly** *adv.* —**sub·con·scious·ness** *n.*

**sub·con·ti·nent** ▶*n.* extensive landmass, smaller than a continent. —**sub·con·ti·nent·al** *adj.*

**sub·con·tract** ▶*v.* assign or do work outside one's company.

**sub·cul·ture** ▶*n.* distinct cultural group within a larger culture. —**sub·cul·tur·al** *adj.*

**sub·cu·ta·ne·ous** ▶*adj.* under the skin. —**sub·cu·ta·ne·ous·ly** *adv.*

**sub·di·vide** ▶*v.* divide again after a first division. —**sub·di·vi·sion** *n.*

**sub·duc·tion** /səbˈdəksHən/ ▶*n.* sideways and downward movement of the edge of a plate of the earth's crust into the mantle beneath another plate.

**sub·due** /səbˈd(y)oo/ ▶*v.* (**-dued, -du·ing**) conquer, subjugate, or tame.

**sub·dued** ▶*adj.* softened;

lacking in intensity; toned down: *subdued light.*

**sub·head** (also **sub·head·ing**) ▶*n.* subordinate heading or title in a chapter, article, etc.

**sub·ject** ▶*n.* /'səbjikt/ **1** matter, theme, etc., to be discussed, described, represented, dealt with, etc. **2** field of study. **3** *Gram.* noun or its equivalent about which a sentence is predicated and with which the verb agrees. **4** any person living under a government. **5** person or animal undergoing treatment, examination, or experimentation.

▶*adj.* /'səbjikt/ **1** owing obedience to a government, colonizing power, force, etc. **2** (**subject to**) liable, exposed, or prone to: *subject to infection.* **3** (**subject to**) under the power or authority of.

▶*adv.* /'səbjikt/ (**subject to**) conditionally upon: *subject to your consent, I propose to try again.*

▶*v.* /səb'jekt/ make liable; expose; treat: *subjected us to hours of waiting.* —**sub·jec·tion** *n.*

**sub·jec·tive** /səb'jektiv/ ▶*adj.* **1** (of art, literature, written history, a person's views, etc.) personal; not impartial or literal. **2** of the individual consciousness or perception; imaginary, partial, or distorted. —**sub·jec·tive·ly** *adv.* —**sub·jec·tive·ness** *n.* —**sub·jec·tiv·i·ty** *n.*

**sub·ju·gate** /'səbjə,gāt/ ▶*v.* bring into subjection; subdue; vanquish. —**sub·ju·ga·tion** *n.*

**sub·junc·tive** /səb'jəNG(k)tiv/ *Gram.* ▶*adj.* of a verb mood) denoting what is imagined or wished or possible, e.g., *were* in *if I were you.*

▶*n.* subjunctive mood or a verb in this mood.

**sub·lease** ▶*n.* lease of a property by a tenant to someone else.

▶*v.* lease to someone by a tenant.

**sub·let** ▶*v.* (-**let·ting**; *past* and *past part.* -**let**) lease (an apartment, etc.) to someone by a tenant.

**sub·li·mate** /'səblə,māt/ ▶*v.* **1** divert (the energy of a primitive impulse, esp. sexual) into a culturally more acceptable activity. **2** *Chem.* convert (a substance) from the solid state directly to its vapor by heat, and usu. allow it to solidify again. **3** refine; purify; idealize. —**sub·li·ma·tion** *n.*

**sub·lime** /sə'blīm/ ▶*adj.* (-**lim·er**,

-lim·est) **1** of the most exalted, grand, or noble kind; awe-inspiring: *sublime genius*. **2** arrogantly unruffled; extreme: *sublime ignorance*. —**sub·lime·ly** *adv.* —**sub·lim·i·ty** *n.*

**sub·li·mi·nal** /səˈblimənl/ ▸*adj.* *Psychol.* (of a stimulus, etc.) below the threshold of sensation or consciousness. —**sub·lim·in·al·ly** *adv.*

**sub·ma·chine gun** ▸*n.* hand-held lightweight machine gun.

**sub·ma·rine** ▸*n.* vessel, esp. an armed warship, capable of operating under water. ▸*adj.* existing, occurring, done, or used under the surface of the sea: *submarine cable*. □ **submarine sandwich** sandwich made with a long bread roll.

**sub·merge** ▸*v.* place, go, or dive under water. —**sub·mer·gence** *n.*

**sub·merse** ▸*v.* submerge. —**sub·mer·sion** *n.*

**sub·mis·sive** /səbˈmisiv/ ▸*adj.* humble; obedient. —**sub·mis·sive·ly** *adv.* —**sub·mis·sive·ness** *n.*

**sub·mit** ▸*v.* (-mit·ted, -mit·ting) **1** (usu. **submit to**) cease resistance; give way; yield. **2** present for consideration.

**3** subject (a person or thing) to an operation, process, treatment, etc. —**sub·mis·sion** *n.*

**sub·nor·mal** ▸*adj.* (esp. as regards intelligence) below or less than normal. —**sub·nor·mal·i·ty** *n.*

**sub·or·di·nate** ▸*adj.* /səˈbôrdn-it/ of inferior importance or rank; secondary; subservient. ▸*n.* /səˈbôrdn-it/ person working under another. ▸*v.* /səˈbôrdn-ˌāt/ make or treat as subordinate. —**sub·or·di·nate·ly** *adv.* —**sub·or·di·na·tion** *n.* □ **subordinate clause** clause modifying or dependent on a main clause.

**sub·orn** /səˈbôrn/ ▸*v.* induce by bribery, etc., to commit perjury, etc. —**sub·or·na·tion** *n.*

**sub·plot** ▸*n.* subordinate plot in a play, etc.

**sub·poe·na** /səˈpēnə/ ▸*n.* writ ordering a person to appear in court. ▸*v.* (*past* and *past part.* **-naed**) serve a subpoena on.

**sub·ro·ga·tion** /ˌsəbrəˈgāSHən/ ▸*n.* substitution of one person or group by another in respect of a debt or insurance claim, accompanied by the transfer of any associated rights and duties.

**sub ro·sa** /'rōzə/ ▶*adj. & adv.* in secrecy or confidence.

**sub·scribe** /səb'skrīb/ ▶*v.*
**1** contribute (a specified sum) or make or promise a contribution to a fund, project, charity, etc., esp. regularly. **2** express one's agreement with an opinion, resolution, etc.: *cannot subscribe to that.* **3** arrange to receive a periodical, cable television service, etc., regularly. —**sub·scrib·er** *n.*

**sub·script** ▶*adj.* written or printed below the line.
▶*n.* subscript number or symbol.

**sub·scrip·tion** ▶*n.*
**1** subscribing. **2** agreement to take and pay for usu. a specified number of issues of a newspaper, magazine, etc.

**sub·se·quent** /'səbsəkwənt/ ▶*adj.* following a specified event, etc., in time, esp. as a consequence. —**sub·se·quent·ly** *adv.*

**sub·ser·vi·ent** /səb'sərvēənt/ ▶*adj.* **1** prepared to obey others unquestioningly. **2** less important. —**sub·ser·vi·ence** *n.* —**sub·ser·vi·ent·ly** *adv.*

**sub·side** /səb'sīd/ ▶*v.* **1** become

tranquil; abate: *excitement subsided.* **2** (of water, etc.) sink to a lower level. —**sub·sid·ence** *n.*

**sub·sid·i·ar·y** /səb'sidē‚erē/ ▶*adj.* **1** supplementary; auxiliary. **2** (of a company) controlled by another.
▶*n.* (*pl.* -**ies**) subsidiary thing, person, or company.

**sub·si·dy** /'səbsidē/ ▶*n.* (*pl.* -**dies**) grant of money, esp. by the government.

**sub·sist** /səb'sist/ ▶*v.* **1** keep oneself alive; be kept alive. **2** remain in being; exist. —**sub·sist·ent** *adj.*

**sub·soil** ▶*n.* soil immediately under the surface soil.

**sub·son·ic** ▶*adj.* relating to speeds less than that of sound. —**sub·son·i·cal·ly** *adv.*

**sub·stance** /'səbstəns/ ▶*n.* **1** particular kind of material having uniform properties. **2** reality; solidity. **3** content or essence as opposed to form, etc. **4** wealth and possessions.

**sub·stand·ard** ▶*adj.* of less than the required or normal quality or size; inferior.

**sub·stan·tial** /səb'stanCHəl/ ▶*adj.* **1** of considerable importance, size, value, or validity. **2** solid; stout:

*substantial house.* **3** commercially successful; wealthy. **4** essential; true in large part. **5** real rather than imaginary. —**sub·stan·tial·ly** *adv.*

**sub·stan·ti·ate** /səb'stanCHē-ˌāt/ ▸*v.* prove the truth of (a charge, claim, etc.). —**sub·stan·ti·a·tion** *n.*

**sub·stan·tive** /'səbstəntiv/ ▸*adj.* having separate and independent existence. ▸*n. Gram.* noun. —**sub·stan·ti·val** *adj.* —**sub·stan·tive·ly** *adv.*

**sub·sti·tute** /'səbstiˌt(y)o͞ot/ ▸*n.* person or thing acting or serving in place of another. ▸*v.* act or cause to act as a substitute. —**sub·sti·tut·a·ble** *adj.* —**sub·sti·tu·tion** *n.*

**sub·struc·ture** ▸*n.* underlying or supporting structure. —**sub·struc·tur·al** *adj.*

**sub·sume** /səb'so͞om/ ▸*v.* include (an instance, idea, category, etc.) in a rule, class, category, etc. —**sub·sum·a·ble** *adj.*

**sub·tend** /'səb'tend/ ▸*v.* **1** (of a line, arc, or figure) form (an angle) at a particular point when straight lines from its extremities are joined at the point. **2** (of an angle or chord)

have bounding lines or points that meet or coincide with those of (a line or arc).

**sub·ter·fuge** /'səbtərˌfyo͞oj/ ▸*n.* **1** evasive or conspiratorial lying or deceit. **2** statement, etc., used for such a purpose.

**sub·ter·ra·ne·an** /ˌsəbtə-'rānēən/ ▸*adj.* underground; concealed.

**sub·text** ▸*n.* underlying theme.

**sub·ti·tle** ▸*n.* **1** secondary or additional title of a book, etc. **2** caption at the bottom of a movie, etc., esp. translating dialogue. ▸*v.* provide with a subtitle or subtitles.

**sub·tle** /'sətl/ ▸*adj.* (-tler, -tlest) **1** evasive or mysterious; hard to grasp: *subtle charm.* **2** (of scent, color, etc.) faint; delicate: *subtle perfume.* **3 a** perceptive: *subtle senses.* **b** ingenious: *subtle device.* —**sub·tle·ness** *n.* —**sub·tle·ty** *n.* —**sub·tly** *adv.*

**sub·to·tal** ▸*n.* total of one part of a group of figures to be added.

**sub·tract** /səb'trakt/ ▸*v.* deduct (a part, quantity, or number) from another. —**sub·trac·tion** *n.* —**sub·trac·tive** *adj.*

**sub·trop·ics** ▸*pl. n.* regions

bordering on the tropics.
—**sub·trop·i·cal** adj.

**sub·urb** /'səbərb/ ▶ n. outlying district of a city.  —**sub·ur·ban** adj.

**sub·ur·bi·a** /sə'bərbēə/ ▶ n. suburbs, their inhabitants, and their way of life.

**sub·vent** /səb'vent/ ▶ v. support or assist by the payment of a grant of money, esp. from the government.

**sub·vert** /səb'vərt/ ▶ v. overturn, overthrow, or upset (religion, government, morality, etc.).
—**sub·ver·sive** adj.

**sub·way** ▶ n. underground, usu. electrically powered commuter railroad.

**sub·ze·ro** ▶ adj. (of temperature) lower than zero.

**suc·ce·da·ne·um** /ˌsəksi-'dānēəm/ ▶ n. (pl. -ne·a /-nēə/) substitute, esp. for a medicine or drug.

**suc·ceed** /sək'sēd/ ▶ v. **1** have success; be successful. **2** come next in order. **3** come by an inheritance, office, title, or property: *succeeded to the throne.* **4** take over an office, property, inheritance, etc., from: *succeeded his father.*

**suc·cès d'es·time** /sook,sā

des'tēm/ ▶ n. (pl. same) success through critical appreciation, as opposed to popularity or commercial gain.

**suc·cess** /sək'ses/ ▶ n. **1** accomplishment of an aim; favorable outcome. **2** attainment of wealth, fame, or position. **3** thing or person that turns out well.  —**suc·cess·ful** adj.  —**suc·cess·ful·ly** adv.

**suc·ces·sion** ▶ n. **1 a** process of following in order; succeeding. **b** series or sequence. **2** succeeding to a throne, office, inheritance, etc.
—**suc·ces·sion·al** adj.
—**suc·ces·sive** adj.
—**suc·ces·sive·ly** adv.
□ **in succession** one after another.

**suc·ces·sor** ▶ n. person or thing that succeeds another.

**suc·cinct** /sə(k)'sing(k)t/ ▶ adj. briefly expressed; terse; concise.
—**suc·cinct·ly** adv.
—**suc·cinct·ness** n.

**suc·cor** /'səkər/ ▶ n. aid; assistance, esp. in time of need. ▶ v. give succor to.

**suc·cu·bus** /'səkyəbəs/ ▶ n. (pl. -bi /-,bī/) female demon believed to have sexual intercourse with sleeping men.

**suc·cu·lent** /ˈsəkyələnt/ ▸*adj.* **1** juicy; palatable. **2** *Bot.* (of a plant, its leaves, or stems) thick and fleshy.
▸*n. Bot.* succulent plant.
—**suc·cu·lence** *n.*
—**suc·cu·lent·ly** *adv.*

**suc·cumb** /səˈkəm/ ▸*v.* **1** surrender; be overcome. **2** die.

**suc·cur·sal** /səˈkərsəl/ ▸*adj.* (of a religious establishment such as a monastery) subsidiary to a principal establishment.

**such** /səCH/ ▸*adj.* **1** of the kind or degree indicated: *such people | people such as these.* **2** so great; in such high degree: *not such a fool as to believe them.* **3** of a more than normal kind or degree: *such crude language.*
▸*pron.* such a person; such a thing.
□ **as such** as being what has been indicated or named: *there is no theater as such.* □ **such as** for example.

**suck** /sək/ ▸*v.* **1** draw (a fluid) into the mouth by suction. **2** draw fluid from (a thing) in this way. **3** engulf, smother, or drown in a sucking movement. **4** *inf.* be or seem very unpleasant, contemptible, or unfair.
▸*n.* act or instance of sucking.

□ **suck up** *inf.* behave obsequiously.

**suck·er** ▸*n.* **1** *inf.* gullible person. **2 a** rubber cup, etc., that adheres to a surface by suction. **b** similar organ of an organism. **3** *Bot.* shoot springing from a root, stem, or axil.

**suck·le** /ˈsəkəl/ ▸*v.* **1 a** feed (young) from the breast or udder. **b** nourish: *suckled his talent.* **2** feed by sucking the breast, etc.

**suck·ling** ▸*n.* unweaned child or animal.

**su·crose** /ˈso͞oˌkrōs/ ▸*n. Chem.* sugar from sugar cane, sugar beet, etc.

**suc·tion** /ˈsəksHən/ ▸*n.* **1** act or instance of sucking. **2 a** production of a partial vacuum by the removal of air, etc., in order to force in liquid, etc., or procure adhesion. **b** force produced by this process: *suction keeps the lid on.*

**sud·den** /ˈsədn/ ▸*adj.* occurring or done unexpectedly or without warning; abrupt; hurried; hasty: *sudden storm.* —**sud·den·ly** *adv.*
—**sud·den·ness** *n.*
□ **all of a sudden** suddenly.
□ **sudden death** *inf.* decision in a tied game, etc., dependent on

one move, card, toss of a coin, etc. □ **sudden infant death syndrome** *Med.* death of a seemingly healthy infant from an unknown cause; crib death. (Abbr.: **SIDS**)

**su·dor·if·ic** /ˌsoodəˈrifik/ ▸*adj.* relating to or causing sweating. ▸*n.* drug that induces sweating.

**suds** /sədz/ ▸*pl. n.* froth of soap and water. —**suds·y** *adj.*

**sue** /soo/ ▸*v.* (**sued, su·ing** or **sue·ing**) institute legal proceedings against (a person).

**suede** /swād/ ▸*n.* **1** leather with a soft nap on one side. **2** cloth resembling suede.

**su·et** /ˈsooit/ ▸*n.* hard white fat from the kidneys or loins of cattle, etc., used in cooking, etc.

**suf·fer** /ˈsəfər/ ▸*v.* **1** undergo or experience (pain, loss, grief, defeat, change, etc.): *suffered banishment.* **2** undergo pain, grief, damage, etc. **3** tolerate: *does not suffer fools gladly.* —**suf·fer·er** *n.* —**suf·fer·ing** *n.*

**suf·fer·ance** ▸*n.* tacit consent.

**suf·fice** /səˈfīs/ ▸*v.* be enough or adequate (for).

**suf·fi·cient** /səˈfishənt/ ▸*adj.* sufficing; adequate; enough: *is sufficient for a family.* —**suf·fi·cient·ly** *adv.*

**suf·fix** /ˈsəfiks/ ▸*n.* verbal element added at the end of a word to form a derivative (e.g., *-ation, -fy, -ing, -itis*).

**suf·fo·cate** /ˈsəfəˌkāt/ ▸*v.* **1** choke or kill by stopping breathing, esp. by pressure, fumes, etc. **2** produce a choking or breathlessness in. **3** be or feel suffocated. —**suf·fo·cat·ing** *adj.* —**suf·fo·ca·tion** *n.*

**suf·frage** /ˈsəfrij/ ▸*n.* right to vote in political elections. —**suf·fra·gist** *n.*

**suf·fuse** /səˈfyooz/ ▸*v.* (of color, moisture, etc.) overspread throughout. —**suf·fu·sion** *n.*

**Su·fi** /ˈsoofē/ ▸*n.* Muslim ascetic and mystic. —**Su·fism** *n.*

**sug·ar** /ˈSHoogər/ ▸*n.* **1** sweet crystalline substance obtained from various plants, esp. the sugar cane and sugar beet, used in cooking, etc.; sucrose. **2** *Chem.* soluble usu. sweet-tasting crystalline carbohydrate, e.g., glucose. ▸*v.* sweeten or coat with sugar. —**sug·ar·less** *adj.* —**sug·ar·y** *adj.* □ **sugar-coated 1** (of food) enclosed in sugar. **2** made superficially attractive.

**sug·ar beet** ▸*n.* beet from which sugar is extracted.

**sug·ar cane** ▸*n.* tropical grass from which sugar is made.

**sug·ar ma·ple** ▸*n.* maple from whose sap sugar and syrup are made.

**sug·ar plum** ▸*n.* candy of flavored boiled sugar.

**sug·gest** /sə(g)'jest/ ▸*v.* **1** propose (a theory, plan, or hypothesis). **2 a** evoke, etc.: *this poem suggests peace.* **b** hint at.

**sug·gest·i·ble** ▸*adj.* open to suggestion; easily swayed.

**sug·ges·tion** ▸*n.* **1** suggesting or being suggested. **2** theory, plan, etc., suggested: *made an excellent suggestion.* **3** slight trace; hint.

**sug·ges·tive** ▸*adj.* **1** conveying a suggestion; evocative. **2** (esp. of a remark, joke, etc.) indecent; improper; racy.
  —**sug·ges·tive·ly** *adv.*
  —**sug·ges·tive·ness** *n.*

**su·i·cide** /'sooi,sīd/ ▸*n.* **1 a** intentional killing of oneself. **b** person who commits suicide. **2** self-destructive action or course: *political suicide.*

**su·i ge·ne·ris** /'soo,ē 'jenərəs/ ▸*adj.* of its own kind; unique.

**suit** /soot/ ▸*n.* **1** set of dress clothes of matching material, usu. of a jacket and trousers, or a jacket and a skirt; set of clothes for a special occasion, etc. **2** any of the four sets (spades, hearts, diamonds, clubs) in a pack of cards. **3** lawsuit.
▸*v.* **1** go well with (a person's figure, features, etc.). **2** meet the demands or requirements of; satisfy. **3** make fitting; accommodate.

**suit·a·ble** ▸*adj.* well fitted for the purpose; appropriate.
  —**suit·a·bil·i·ty** *n.*
  —**suit·a·ble·ness** *n.* —**suit·a·bly** *adv.*

**suit·case** ▸*n.* usu. oblong case with a handle for carrying clothes, etc.

**suite** /swēt/ ▸*n.* **1** set of things belonging together, as rooms or furniture. **2** *Mus.* set of instrumental compositions to be played as a unit. **3** set of people in attendance; retinue.

**suit·or** /'sootər/ ▸*n.* man seeking to marry a specified woman; wooer.

**sul·fate** /'səl,fāt/ ▸*n.* salt or ester of sulfuric acid.

**sul·fide** /'səl,fīd/ ▸*n. Chem.* binary compound of sulfur.

**sul·fur** /'səlfər/ ▸*n. Chem.* pale yellow nonmetallic element burning with a blue flame and a

suffocating smell. (Symb.: **S**)
—**sul·fur·ous** adj. —**sul·fur·y** adj.
□ **sulfur dioxide** colorless pungent gas formed by burning sulfur in air and used as a food preservative.

**sul·fu·ric ac·id** /səl'fyŏŏrik/ ▶n. dense, oily, colorless, highly corrosive acid.

**sul·fur·ous** /'səlfərəs/ ▶adj. **1** (chiefly of vapor or smoke) containing or derived from sulfur. **2** marked by bad temper, anger, or profanity.

**sulk** /səlk/ ▶v. be sulky.
▶n. period of sullen, esp. resentful, silence.

**sulk·y** ▶adj. (**-i·er, -i·est**) sullen, morose, or silent, esp. from resentment. —**sulk·i·ly** adv.
—**sulk·i·ness** n.

**sul·len** /'sələn/ ▶adj. **1** morose; resentful; sulky. **2** dismal; melancholy. —**sul·len·ly** adv.
—**sul·len·ness** n.

**sul·ly** ▶v. (**-lied**) disgrace; tarnish.

**sul·tan** /'səltn/ ▶n. Muslim sovereign. —**sul·tan·ate** n.

**sul·ta·na** /səl'tanə/ ▶n. **1** seedless raisin. **2** mother, wife, concubine, or daughter of a sultan.

**sul·try** /'səltrē/ ▶adj. (**-tri·er, -tri·est**) **1** (of the atmosphere or the weather) hot or oppressive; close. **2** (of a person, etc.) passionate; sensual. —**sul·tri·ly** adv. —**sul·tri·ness** n.

**sum** /səm/ ▶n. **1** total resulting from addition. **2** particular amount of money.
▶v. (**summed, sum·ming**) find the sum of.
□ **sum up** express an opinion of; summarize.

**su·mac** /'soŏmak; 'SHoŏ-/ ▶n. **1** shrub having reddish cone-shaped fruits used as a spice in cooking. **2** dried and ground leaves of this used in tanning and dyeing.

**sum·ma·rize** /'səmə,rīz/ ▶v. make or be a summary of.
—**sum·ma·ri·za·tion** n.

**sum·ma·ry** ▶n. (pl. **-ries**) brief statement of the main points of something.
▶adj. dispensing with needless details or formalities; brief.
—**sum·mar·i·ly** adv.

**sum·ma·tion** /sə'māsHən/ ▶n. **1** finding of a total or sum; an addition. **2** adding up.
—**sum·ma·tion·al** adj.

**sum·mer** /'səmər/ ▶n. warmest season of the year.
▶v. pass the summer.
—**sum·mer·y** adj.

**sum·mit** /'səmit/ ▶n. **1** highest point; apex. **2** highest degree. **3** discussion between heads of government.

**sum·mon** /'səmən/ ▶v. **1** call upon to appear, esp. at a court of law. **2** call upon: *summoned her to assist.* **3** call together.
□ **summon up** gather (courage, spirits, resources, etc.).

**sum·mons** /'səmənz/ ▶n. (pl. **-mons·es**) authoritative or urgent call to attend on some occasion or do something.

**sum·mum bo·num** /'so͞oməm 'bōnəm/ ▶n. highest good, esp. as the ultimate goal according to which values and priorities are established in an ethical system.

**su·mo** /'so͞omō/ ▶n. style of Japanese wrestling practiced by very heavy competitors.

**sump** /səmp/ ▶n. pit, well, hole, etc., to collect liquid.

**sump·tu·ary** /'səm(p)CHo͞o,erē/ ▶adj. relating to or denoting laws that limit private expenditure on food and personal items.

**sump·tu·ous** /'səm(p)CHo͞oəs/ ▶adj. rich; lavish; costly.
—**sump·tu·ous·ly** adv.
—**sump·tu·ous·ness** n.

**Sun.** ▶abbr. Sunday.

**sun** /sən/ ▶n. **1** star around which the earth orbits and from which it receives light and warmth. **2** any similar star.
▶v. (**sunned sun·ning**) bask in the sun.

**sun·bathe** ▶v. bask in the sun, esp. to tan the body.

**sun·block** ▶n. cream or lotion that protects the skin from sunburn and also prevents most tanning.

**sun·burn** ▶n. reddening and inflammation of the skin caused by overexposure to the sun.
▶v. suffer from sunburn.

**sun·dae** /'sən,dā/ ▶n. dish of ice cream with fruit, nuts, syrup, etc.

**Sun·day** ▶n. first day of the week, the Christian sabbath and day of worship.

**sun·der** /'səndər/ ▶v. archaic separate; sever.

**sun·dial** ▶n. instrument showing the time by the shadow of a pointer cast by the sun onto a graduated disk.

**sun·dry** /'səndrē/ ▶adj. various; several.
▶pl. n. (**sundries**) items or oddments not mentioned individually.

**sun·fish** ▶n. almost spherical fish, esp. a large ocean variety.

**sun·flow·er** ▸*n.* very tall plant with large, showy, golden-rayed flowers.

**sun·glass·es** ▸*pl. n.* glasses tinted to protect the eyes from sunlight or glare.

**sun·light** ▸*n.* light from the sun.

**sun·lit** ▸*adj.* illuminated by sunlight.

**sun·ny** ▸*adj.* (**-ni·er, -ni·est**) **1** bright with or warmed by sunlight. **2** cheery and bright in temperament. —**sun·ni·ness** *n.*

**sun·rise** ▸*n.* **1** rising of the sun. **2** time of this.

**sun·roof** ▸*n.* section of an automobile roof that can be slid open.

**sun·screen** ▸*n.* cream or lotion that protects the skin from ultraviolet rays.

**sun·set** ▸*n.* **1** setting of the sun. **2** sky full of color at sunset. **3** time of this.

**sun·shine** ▸*n.* **1** light of the sun. **2** good weather. **3** cheerfulness.

**sun·spot** ▸*n.* one of the dark patches, lasting for varying periods, observed on the sun's surface.

**sun·stroke** ▸*n.* illness from excessive exposure to the sun.

**sun·tan** ▸*n.* brownish coloring of skin caused by exposure to the sun.

**sup** /səp/ ▸*v.* (**supped, sup·ping**) eat supper.

**su·per** /ˈso͞opər/ ▸*adj. inf.* exceptional; splendid. ▸*n. inf.* superintendent.

**super-** ▸*comb. form* forming nouns, adjectives, and verbs, meaning: **1** above, beyond, or over in place or time or conceptually: *superstructure* | *supernormal.* **2** to a great or extreme degree: *superabundant.* **3** extra good or large of its kind: *supertanker.* **4** of a higher kind: *superclass.*

**su·per·a·bun·dant** ▸*adj.* abounding beyond what is normal or right. —**su·per·a·bun·dance** *n.* —**su·per·a·bun·dant·ly** *adv.*

**su·per·an·nu·a·ted** ▸*adj.* **1** retired because of age. **2** obsolete.

**su·perb** /so͞oˈpərb/ ▸*adj.* **1** splendid; grand: *superb courage.* **2** excellent; fine. —**su·perb·ly** *adv.*

**su·per·car·go** /ˈso͞opərˌkärgō/ ▸*n.* (*pl.* **-goes** or **-gos**) representative of the ship's owner on board a merchant ship, responsible for overseeing the cargo and its sale.

**su·per·charge** ▸*v.* **1** charge (the atmosphere, etc.) with energy, emotion, etc. **2** use a supercharger on (an internal combustion engine).

**su·per·cil·i·ous** /-'silēəs/ ▸*adj.* contemptuous; haughty.
—**su·per·cil·i·ous·ly** *adv.*
—**su·per·cil·i·ous·ness** *n.*

**su·per·con·duc·tiv·i·ty** ▸*n.* *Physics* property of zero electrical resistance in some substances at very low absolute temperatures.
—**su·per·con·duc·tive** *adj.*

**su·per·e·go** ▸*n.* (*pl.* **-gos**) *Psychol.* part of the mind that acts as a conscience.

**su·per·er·o·ga·tion** /ˌsōōpər-ˌerə'gāsHən/ ▸*n.* performance of more work than duty requires.

**su·per·fi·cial** /-'fisHəl/ ▸*adj.* **1** of or on the surface; lacking depth: *superficial wounds.* **2** swift or cursory. **3** apparent but not real: *superficial resemblance.* **4** (esp. of a person) shallow.
—**su·per·fi·ci·al·i·ty** *n.*
—**su·per·fi·cial·ly** *adv.*

**su·per·flu·ous** /sōō'pərflōōəs/ ▸*adj.* more than enough; redundant; needless.
—**su·per·flu·ous·ly** *adv.*
—**su·per·flu·ous·ness** *n.*

**su·per·high·way** ▸*n.* multilane, limited-access divided highway.

**su·per·hu·man** ▸*adj.* **1** beyond normal human capability. **2** above what is human.
—**su·per·hu·man·ly** *adv.*

**su·per·im·pose** ▸*v.* lay (a thing) on something else.
—**su·per·im·po·si·tion** *n.*

**su·per·in·tend** /ˌsōōp(ə)rin'tend/ ▸*v.* supervise; direct.
—**su·per·in·tend·ence** *n.*
—**su·per·in·tend·en·cy** *n.*

**su·per·in·ten·dent** ▸*n.* **1** person who manages or supervises an organization, activity, etc. **2** caretaker of a building.

**su·pe·ri·or** /sə'pi(ə)rēər/ ▸*adj.* **1** in a higher position; of higher rank. **2 a** above the average in quality, etc.: *made of superior leather.* **b** supercilious; haughty. **3** better or greater in some respect.
▸*n.* person superior to another in rank, character, etc.: *is her superior in courage.*
—**su·pe·ri·or·i·ty** *n.*

**su·per·la·tive** /sə'pərlətiv/ ▸*adj.*

**1** of the highest quality or degree: *superlative wisdom.* **2** *Gram.* (of an adjective or adverb) expressing the highest degree of a quality (e.g., *bravest, most fiercely*).
▸*n.* **1** *Gram.* superlative expression or form of an adjective or adverb. **2** exaggerated or excessive statement, comment, expression, etc.
—**su·per·la·tive·ly** *adv.*
—**su·per·la·tive·ness** *n.*

**su·per·lu·na·ry** /ˌso͞opər-ˈlo͞onərē/ ▸*adj.* belonging to a higher world; celestial.

**su·per·man** ▸*n.* (*pl.* -**men**) *inf.* man of exceptional strength or ability.

**su·per·mar·ket** ▸*n.* large self-service store selling foods, household goods, etc.

**su·per·nat·u·ral** ▸*adj.* attributed to or thought to reveal some force above the laws of nature; magical; mystical.

**su·per·no·va** ▸*n.* (*pl.* -**no·vae** or -**no·vas**) *Astron.* star that suddenly increases very greatly in brightness because of an explosion ejecting most of its mass.

**su·per·nu·mer·ar·y** /ˌso͞opər-ˈn(y)o͞oməˌrerē/ ▸*adj.* in excess of the normal number; extra.
▸*n.* (*pl.* -**ies**) **1** extra or unwanted person or thing. **2** actor without a speaking part; extra.

**su·per·pow·er** ▸*n.* extremely powerful nation.

**su·per·script** ▸*adj.* written or printed above the line.
▸*n.* superscript number or symbol.

**su·per·sede** /-ˈsēd/ ▸*v.* **1 a** adopt or appoint another person or thing in place of. **b** set aside; cease to employ. **2** (of a person or thing) take the place of. —**su·per·sed·ence** *n.*

**su·per·son·ic** ▸*adj.* designating or having a speed greater than that of sound.
—**su·per·son·i·cal·ly** *adv.*

**su·per·star** ▸*n.* extremely famous or renowned actor, movie star, athlete, etc.
—**su·per·star·dom** *n.*

**su·per·sti·tion** /-ˈstiSHən/ ▸*n.* **1** credulity regarding the supernatural. **2** irrational fear of the unknown. **3** practice, opinion, or religion based on these tendencies.
—**su·per·sti·tious** *adj.*
—**su·per·sti·tious·ly** *adv.*

**su·per·struc·ture** ▸*n.* **1** part

of a building above its foundations. **2** structure built on top of something else. —**su·per·struc·tur·al** *adj.*

**su·per·vene** /-'vēn/ ▶*v.* occur as an interruption in or a change from some state. —**su·per·ven·tion** *n.*

**su·per·vise** /-ˌvīz/ ▶*v.* superintend; oversee. —**su·per·vi·sion** *n.* —**su·per·vi·sor** *n.* —**su·per·vi·so·ry** *adj.*

**su·per·wo·man** ▶*n.* (*pl.* **-women**) *inf.* woman of exceptional strength or ability, esp. one who manages a home, brings up children, and has a full-time job.

**su·pine** /'soo͞ˌpīn/ ▶*adj.* lying face upward. —**su·pine·ly** *adv.* —**su·pine·ness** *n.*

**sup·per** /'səpər/ ▶*n.* evening meal.

**sup·plant** /sə'plant/ ▶*v.* dispossess and take the place of, esp. by underhand means. —**sup·plant·er** *n.*

**sup·ple** /'səpəl/ ▶*adj.* (**-pler, -plest**) **1** flexible; pliant; easily bent. **2** compliant; avoiding overt resistance; artfully or servilely submissive. —**sup·ple·ness** *n.*

**sup·ple·ment** /'səpləmənt/ ▶*n.* **1** thing or part added to improve or provide further information. **2** separate section of a newspaper or periodical.
▶*v.* provide a supplement for. —**sup·ple·men·tal** *adj.* —**sup·ple·men·ta·ry** *adj.* —**sup·ple·men·ta·tion** *n.*

**sup·pli·ant** /'səplēənt/ ▶*n.* person making a humble plea to someone in power or authority.
▶*adj.* making or expressing a plea, esp. to someone in power or authority.

**sup·pli·cate** /'səpliˌkāt/ ▶*v.* **1** petition humbly to (a person) or for (a thing). **2** make a petition. —**sup·pli·cant** *adj. & n.* —**sup·pli·ca·tion** *n.*

**sup·ply** /sə'plī/ ▶*v.* (**-plied**) **1** provide or furnish (a thing needed). **2** provide (a person, etc., with a thing needed). **3** meet or make up for (a deficiency or need).
▶*n.* (*pl.* **-plies**) **1** stock, store, amount, etc. **2** (**supplies**) provisions; equipment. —**sup·pli·er** *n.*

**sup·ply-side** ▶*adj.* denoting a policy designed to increase output and employment by reducing taxation and other government restrictions.

**sup·port** /sə'pôrt/ ▶v. **1** carry all or part of the weight of. **2** provide for (a family, etc.). **3** bear out; substantiate. **4** give help or countenance to; further. **5** speak in favor of.

▶n. **1** supporting or being supported. **2** person or thing that supports.

**sup·pose** /sə'pōz/ ▶v. **1** assume; be inclined to think. **2** take as a possibility or hypothesis.
—**sup·pos·ed** adj.
—**sup·pos·ed·ly** adv.
—**sup·po·si·tion** n.

**sup·po·si·tion** /ˌsəpə'ziSHən/ ▶n. uncertain belief.

**sup·pos·i·ti·tious** /sə,päzə-'tiSHəs/ ▶adj. **1** substituted for the real thing; not genuine. **2** suppositious.

**sup·pos·i·to·ry** /sə'päzə,tôrē/ ▶n. (pl. **-ries**) medical preparation that is inserted in the rectum or vagina.

**sup·press** /sə'pres/ ▶v. **1** put an end to, esp. forcibly. **2** prevent from being done, seen, heard, or known. —**sup·pres·sion** n.

**sup·pu·rate** /'səpyə,rāt/ ▶v. **1** form pus. **2** fester.

—**sup·pu·ra·tion** n.
—**sup·pu·ra·tive** adj.

**supra-** ▶prefix **1** above. **2** beyond; transcending.

**su·prem·a·cist** /sə'premə,sist/ ▶n. advocate of the supremacy of a particular group: *white supremacist.*

**su·prem·a·cy** ▶n. state of being superior to all others in power, status, etc.

**su·preme** /sə'prēm/ ▶adj. **1** highest in authority or rank. **2** greatest; most important. **3** (of a penalty, sacrifice, etc.) involving death. —**su·preme·ly** adv. —**su·preme·ness** n.
□ **Supreme Court** highest judicial court in a nation, etc.

**su·ra** /'soorə/ (also **su·rah**) ▶n. chapter or section of the Koran.

**su·ral** /'soorəl/ ▶adj. of or relating to the calf of the leg.

**sur·charge** /'sər,CHärj/ ▶n. additional charge or payment.
▶v. exact a surcharge from.

**surd** /sərd/ ▶adj. (of a number) irrational.

**sure** /SHoor/ ▶adj. **1** having or seeming to have adequate reason for a belief or assertion. **2** confident. **3** reliable or unfailing: *there is one sure way to*

*find out.* **4** certain.
**5** undoubtedly true or truthful.
▸*adv. inf.* certainly. —**sure·ly** *adv.*
—**sure·ness** *n.*
▢ **sure-footed** never stumbling or
making a mistake.

**sur·e·ty** /ˈsHŏŏritē/ ▸*n.* (*pl.* **-ties**)
**1** person who takes
responsibility for another's debt,
obligation, etc. **2** certainty.

**surf** /sərf/ ▸*n.* **1** swell of the sea
breaking on the shore or reefs.
**2** foam produced by this.
▸*v.* **1** ride the surf, with or as
with a surfboard. **2** switch
between or search through
(television channels or Internet
sites). —**surf·er** *n.*

**sur·face** /ˈsərfis/ ▸*n.* **1** outside
or uppermost layer of a material
body. **2** upper boundary of a
liquid, the ground, etc.
**3** outward or superficial aspect
of anything.
▸*v.* **1** give the required surface to
(a road, paper, etc.). **2** rise or
bring to the surface. **3** become
visible or known.

**surf·board** ▸*n.* long narrow
board used in surfing.

**sur·feit** /ˈsərfit/ ▸*n.* **1** excess,
esp. in eating or drinking.
**2** feeling of being overfilled or
disgust resulting from this.

▸*v.* be or cause to be wearied
through an excess of something.

**sur·fi·cial** /sərˈfisHəl/ ▸*adj.* of or
relating to the earth's surface.

**surge** /sərj/ ▸*n.* **1** sudden rush.
**2** heavy forward or upward
motion. **3** rapid increase in
price, activity, etc. **4** sudden
marked increase in voltage.
▸*v.* **1** (of the sea, etc.) swell.
**2** move suddenly and powerfully
forward. **3** increase suddenly.

**sur·geon** /ˈsərjən/ ▸*n.* medical
practitioner qualified to practice
surgery.

**sur·ger·y** /ˈsərjərē/ ▸*n.* (*pl.* **-ies**)
medical treatment of injuries or
disorders by cutting or
manipulation of affected parts of
the body. —**sur·gi·cal** *adj.*
—**sur·gi·cal·ly** *adv.*

**sur·ly** /ˈsərlē/ ▸*adj.* (**-li·er, -li·est**)
bad-tempered and unfriendly;
churlish. —**sur·li·ness** *n.*

**sur·mise** /sərˈmīz/ ▸*n.*
conjecture.
▸*v.* suppose that something is
true without having evidence to
confirm it.

**sur·mount** /sərˈmount/ ▸*v.*
overcome or get over (a difficulty
or obstacle). —**sur·mount·a·ble**
*adj.*

**sur·name** /ˈsərˌnām/ ▶n. family or last name.

**sur·pass** /sərˈpas/ ▶v. outdo; be greater or better than.

**sur·plice** /ˈsərplis/ ▶n. loose white linen vestment worn over a cassock by clergy and choristers.

**sur·plus** /ˈsərˌpləs/ ▶n. **1** amount left over. **2** excess of revenue over expenditure. ▶adj. exceeding what is needed or used.

**sur·prise** /sə(r)ˈprīz/ ▶n. **1** unexpected or astonishing event or circumstance. **2** emotion caused by this. **3** catching or being caught unawares. ▶v. **1** turn out contrary to the expectations of: *your answer surprised me.* **2** shock; scandalize: *I am surprised at you.* **3** capture or attack by surprise. **4** come upon (a person) unawares. —**sur·pris·ing** adj. —**sur·pris·ing·ly** adv.

**sur·re·al·ism** /səˈrēəˌlizəm/ ▶n. 20th-c. movement in art and literature aiming at expressing the subconscious mind, e.g., by the irrational juxtaposition of images. —**sur·re·al·ist** n. & adj. —**sur·re·al·is·tic** adj.

**sur·ren·der** /səˈrendər/ ▶v. **1** hand over; relinquish. **2** submit, esp. to an enemy. **3** give oneself over to a habit, emotion, influence, etc. ▶n. act or an instance of surrendering.

**sur·rep·ti·tious** /ˌsərəpˈtisHəs/ ▶adj. done by stealth; clandestine. —**sur·rep·ti·tious·ly** adv.

**sur·ro·gate** /ˈsərəgit/ ▶n. **1** substitute. **2** judge in charge of probate, inheritance, and guardianship. —**sur·ro·ga·cy** n.
□ **surrogate mother** woman who bears a child on behalf of another woman.

**sur·round** /səˈround/ ▶v. come or be all around; encircle; enclose.

**sur·round·ings** ▶pl. n. things in the neighborhood of, or conditions affecting, a person or thing.

**sur·tax** /ˈsərˌtaks/ ▶n. additional tax.

**sur·veil·lance** /sərˈvāləns/ ▶n. close observation, esp. of a suspected person.

**sur·vey** ▶v. /sərˈvā/ **1** take or present a general view of. **2** examine the condition of (a building, etc.). **3** determine the

boundaries, extent, ownership, etc., of (a district, etc.).
▸ *n.* /'sərvā/ **1** general view or consideration. **2** map or plan made by surveying.
—**sur·vey·or** *n.*

**sur·viv·al·ism** /sər'vīvə,lizəm/
▸ *n.* **1** policy of trying to ensure one's own survival or that of one's social or national group.
**2** practicing of outdoor survival skills as a sport or hobby.

**sur·vive** /sər'vīv/ ▸ *v.* **1** continue to live or exist; be still alive or existent. **2** live or exist longer than. **3** remain alive in spite of (a danger, accident, etc.).
—**sur·vi·val** *n.* —**sur·vi·vor** *n.*

**sus·cep·ti·ble** /sə'septəbəl/
▸ *adj.* easily affected or influenced. —**sus·cep·ti·bly** *adv.*

**su·shi** /'sooshē/ ▸ *n.* Japanese dish of balls of cold rice flavored and garnished, esp. with raw fish or shellfish.

**sus·pect** ▸ *v.* /sə'spekt/ **1** have an impression of the existence or presence of. **2** mistrust. **3** be inclined to think. **4** doubt the genuineness or truth of.
▸ *n.* /'səs,pekt/ person under suspicion.
▸ *adj.* /'səs,pekt/ subject to or deserving suspicion.

**sus·pend** /sə'spend/ ▸ *v.* **1** hang up. **2** keep inoperative or undecided for a time; defer. **3** bar temporarily from a school, function, office, privilege, etc.

**sus·pend·ers** ▸ *pl. n.* straps worn across the shoulders and supporting trousers, a skirt, etc.

**sus·pense** /sə'spens/ ▸ *n.* state of anxious uncertainty or expectation. —**sus·pense·ful** *adj.*

**sus·pen·sion** ▸ *n.* **1** suspending or being suspended. **2** means by which a vehicle is supported on its axles. **3** substance consisting of particles suspended in a medium.
□ **suspension bridge** bridge with a roadway suspended from cables supported by structures at each end.

**sus·pi·cion** /sə'spishən/ ▸ *n.*
**1** feeling or thought of a person who suspects. **2** suspecting or being suspected. **3** slight trace of something.

**sus·pi·cious** /sə'spishəs/ ▸ *adj.*
**1** prone to or feeling suspicion.
**2** prompting suspicion: *suspicious lack of surprise.* —**sus·pi·cious·ly** *adv.*

**sus·pire** /sə'spī(ə)r/ ▸ *v.* breathe.

**sus·tain** /sə'stān/ ▸ *v.* **1** support or bear the weight of, esp. for a long period. **2** encourage; support. **3** (of food) give nourishment to. **4** undergo or suffer (defeat or injury, etc.). **5** (of a court, etc.) uphold or decide in favor of (an objection, etc.). —**sus·tain·ment** *n.*

**sus·te·nance** /'səstənəns/ ▶*n.* **1** nourishment; food. **2** means of support; livelihood.

**sus·ten·ta·tion** /ˌsəst(ə)n-'tāSHən/ ▶*n.* support or maintenance of someone or something, esp. through the provision of money.

**su·sur·rus** /sŏŏ'sərəs/ (also **su·sur·ra·tion** /ˌsŏŏsə'rāSHən/) ▶*n.* whispering, murmuring, or rustling.

**sut·ler** /'sətlər/ ▶*n.* person who followed an army and sold provisions to the soldiers.

**su·ture** /'sŏŏCHər/ ▶*n.* **1** joining of the edges of a wound or incision by stitching. **2** thread or wire used for this. —**su·tured** *adj.*

**svelte** /svelt/ ▶*adj.* slender; graceful.

**SW** ▶*abbr.* **1** southwest. **2** southwestern.

**swab** /swäb/ ▶*n.* absorbent pad used for cleaning or applying medicaton.

▶*v.* (**swabbed**, **swab·bing**) clean with a swab.

**swad·dle** /'swädl/ ▶*v.* swathe (esp. an infant) tightly.

**swag** /swag/ ▶*n.* ornamental display of flowers, drapery, etc., hanging decoratively in a curve.

**swag·ger** ▶*v.* walk or behave arrogantly.

▶*n.* swaggering gait or manner. —**swag·ger·ing·ly** *adv.*

**Swa·hi·li** /swä'hēlē/ ▶*n.* (*pl.* same) **1** member of a Bantu people of Zanzibar and adjacent coasts. **2** their language, widely spoken in E. Africa.

**swale** /swāl/ ▶*n.* low or hollow place, esp. a marshy depression between ridges.

**swal·low** /'swälō/ ▶*v.* **1** cause or allow (food, etc.) to pass down the throat. **2** accept meekly or credulously. **3** repress: *swallow one's pride.* **4** engulf or absorb.

▶*n.* **1** act of swallowing. **2** amount swallowed in one action. **3** migratory, swift-flying, insect-eating bird with a forked tail and long pointed wings.

**swamp** /swämp/ ▶*n.* piece of waterlogged ground.

▶*v.* **1** overwhelm, flood, or soak with water. **2** overwhelm with an excess or large amount of something. **—swamp·y** *adj.*

**swan** /swän/ ▸*n.* large, usu. white, water bird having a long flexible neck and webbed feet. □ **swan song** person's last work or act before death or retirement, etc.

**swank** /swaNGk/ ▸*n. inf.* **1** ostentation; swagger. **2** style; elegance. **—swank·y** *adj.*

**swap** /swäp/ ▸*v.* (**swapped**, **swap·ping**) exchange or barter (one thing for another). ▸*n.* **1** act of swapping. **2** thing swapped.

**swarm** /swôrm/ ▸*n.* **1** cluster of bees leaving the hive with the queen to establish a new colony. **2** large cluster of insects, birds, or people. **3** (**a swarm/swarms of**) great numbers. ▸*v.* **1** move in or form a swarm. **2** (of a place) be overrun, crowded, or infested.

**swarth·y** /ˈswôrT͟Hē/ ▸*adj.* (**-i·er**, **-i·est**) dark; dark-complexioned. **—swarth·i·ness** *n.*

**swash·buck·ling** /ˈswôsH-ˌbəkling/ ▸*adj. & n.* showing flamboyant daring.

**swas·ti·ka** /ˈswästikə/ ▸*n.* **1** ancient symbol formed by an equal-armed cross with each arm

continued at a right angle. **2** this with clockwise continuations as the symbol of Nazi Germany.

**swat** /swät/ ▸*v.* (**swat·ted**, **swat·ting**) hit hard and abruptly. ▸*n.* sharp blow.

**swatch** /swäcH/ ▸*n.* sample, esp. of cloth or fabric.

**swath** /swäTH/ ▸*n.* strip cut in one sweep as by a mower.

**swathe** /swäT͟H; swāT͟H/ ▸*v.* bind or enclose in bandages or garments, etc. ▸*n.* bandage or wrapping.

**sway** /swā/ ▸*v.* **1** (cause to) move gently to and fro. **2** control or influence. ▸*n.* **1** rule, influence, or government: *hold sway.* **2** swaying motion or position.

**swear** /swe(ə)r/ ▸*v.* (*past* **swore**; *past part.* **sworn**) **1** state or promise solemnly or on oath. **2** use profane or indecent language. **3** (**swear to**) admit the certainty of: *could not swear to it.* □ **swear off** *inf.* promise to abstain from (drink, etc.).

**sweat** /swet/ ▸*n.* **1** moisture exuded through the pores of the skin; perspiration. **2** state or period of anxiety. ▸*v.* (*past* and *past part.* **sweat** or

**sweat·ed)** **1** give off sweat or as sweat; perspire. **2** be anxious, terrified, suffering, etc. **3** (cause to) drudge or toil. —**sweat·y** *adj.*

**sweat·er** ▸*n.* knitted garment for the upper body.

**sweat lodge** ▸*n.* hut, typically dome-shaped and made with natural materials, used by North American Indians for ritual steam baths as a means of purification.

**sweat·pants** ▸*pl. n.* loose pants of absorbent cotton material worn for exercise, etc.

**sweat·shirt** ▸*n.* pullover shirt of absorbent material.

**Swed·ish** /'swēdisH/ ▸*adj.* of or relating to Sweden or its people or language.
▸*n.* language of Sweden.

**sweep** /swēp/ ▸*v.* (*past* and *past part.* **swept**) **1** clean or clear with or as with a broom. **2** collect or remove (dirt, etc.) by sweeping. **3** carry or drive along with force. **4** remove or clear forcefully. **5** traverse or glide swiftly or lightly.
▸*n.* **1** act or motion of sweeping. **2** range or scope. —**sweep·er** *n.*

**sweep·ing** ▸*adj.* **1** wide in range or effect: *sweeping changes.* **2** taking no account of particular cases or exceptions: *sweeping statement.* —**sweep·ing·ly** *adv.*

**sweep·stakes** ▸*n.* form of gambling in which all the stakes are divided among the winners.

**sweet** /swēt/ ▸*adj.* **1** tasting of sugar. **2** fragrant. **3** melodious or harmonious. **4** amiable; pleasant; charming.
▸*n.* **1** something sweet. **2** sweetness. **3** candy. —**sweet·en** *v.* —**sweet·ly** *adv.* —**sweet·ness** *n.*
□ **sweet tooth** liking for sweet-tasting foods.

**sweet·bread** ▸*n.* pancreas or thymus of an animal, esp. as food.

**sweet·bri·er** ▸*n.* wild rose of Europe and central Asia with small fragrant pink flowers.

**sweet·en·er** ▸*n.* substance used to sweeten food or drink.

**sweet·heart** ▸*n.* **1** lover or darling. **2** term of endearment (esp. as a form of address).

**sweet pea** ▸*n.* any dwarf or climbing plant with fragrant flowers.

**sweet po·ta·to** ▸*n.* tropical climbing plant with sweet tuberous roots used for food.

**sweet wil·liam** ▸*n.* fragrant

garden pink with clusters of white, pink, or red flowers.

**swell** /swel/ ▶*v.* (*past part.* **swol·len** or **swelled**) **1** grow or cause to grow bigger or louder or more intense. **2** rise or raise up. **3** bulge. **4** feel full of joy, pride, relief, etc.
▶*n.* **1** act or state of swelling. **2** heaving of the sea with waves that do not break. **3** crescendo.
▶*adj. inf.* fine; splendid; excellent.

**swel·ter** /'sweltər/ ▶*v.* [usu. as *adj.* **sweltering**] be uncomfortably hot.
▶*n.* sweltering atmosphere or condition.

**swerve** /swərv/ ▶*v.* change or cause to change direction, esp. abruptly.
▶*n.* swerving movement.

**swift** /swift/ ▶*adj.* quick; rapid.
▶*n.* swift-flying, insect-eating bird with long wings. —**swift·ly** *adv.* —**swift·ness** *n.*

**swig** /swig/ *inf.* ▶*v.* (**swigged**, **swig·ging**) drink in large swallows.
▶*n.* swallow of drink, esp. a large amount.

**swill** /swil/ ▶*v.* drink greedily.
▶*n.* mainly liquid refuse as pig food.

**swim** /swim/ ▶*v.* (**swim·ming**; *past* swam; *past part.* **swum**) **1** propel the body through water with the limbs, fins, or tail. **2** traverse (a stretch of water or its distance) by swimming. **3** have a dizzy effect or sensation. **4** (**swim in/with**) be flooded with.
▶*n.* spell or act of swimming. —**swim·mer** *n.*

**swim·suit** ▶*n.* garment worn for swimming.

**swin·dle** /'swindl/ ▶*v.* cheat (a person) of money, possessions, etc.
▶*n.* act of swindling. —**swin·dler** *n.*

**swine** /swīn/ ▶*n.* (*pl.* same) **1** pig. **2** *inf.* (*pl.* **swine** or **swines**) contemptible person. —**swin·ish** *adj.* —**swin·ish·ly** *adv.*

**swing** /swiNG/ ▶*v.* (*past* and *past part.* **swung**) **1 a** move or cause to move with a to-and-fro or curving motion; sway. **b** hang so as to be free to sway. **2** move by gripping something and leaping, etc. **3** go with a swinging gait: *swung out of the room.* **4** (**swing around**) move around to the opposite direction. **5** change from one opinion or mood to another. **6** (**swing at**) attempt to hit. **7** *inf.* deal with or achieve; manage.

▶*n.* **1** act, motion, or extent of swinging. **2** swinging or smooth gait or rhythm or action. **3** seat slung by ropes, etc., for swinging on or in. **4** rhythmic jazz or dance music.

**swinge** /swinj/ ▶*v.* (**swinge·ing**) strike hard; beat.

**swipe** /swīp/ *inf.* ▶*v.* **1** hit hard and recklessly. **2** steal.
▶*n.* reckless hard hit or attempted hit.

**swirl** /swərl/ ▶*v.* move or flow or carry along with a whirling motion.
▶*n.* **1** swirling motion. **2** twist or curl, esp. as part of a pattern or design. —**swirl·y** *adj.*

**swish** /swisH/ ▶*v.* **1** swing (a scythe, stick, etc.) audibly through the air, grass, etc. **2** move with or make a swishing sound.
▶*n.* swishing action or sound.

**switch** /swicH/ ▶*n.* **1** device for making and breaking the connection in an electric circuit. **2 a** transfer, changeover, or deviation. **b** exchange. **3** slender flexible shoot cut from a tree. **4** device at the junction of railroad tracks for transferring a train from one track to another.
▶*v.* **1** turn (an electrical device) on

or off. **2** change or transfer (position, subject, etc.). **3** exchange.

**switch·back** ▶*n.* railroad or road with alternate sharp ascents and descents.

**switch·board** ▶*n.* apparatus for varying connections between electric circuits, esp. in telephony.

**swiv·el** /ˈswivəl/ ▶*n.* coupling between two parts enabling one to revolve without turning the other.
▶*v.* turn on or as on a swivel.

**swiv·et** /ˈswivit/ ▶*n.* fluster or panic.

**swol·len** /ˈswōlən/ ▶past part. of SWELL.

**swoon** /swōōn/ *lit.* ▶*v.* faint.
▶*n.* occurrence of fainting.

**swoop** /swōōp/ ▶*v.* **1** descend rapidly like a bird of prey. **2** make a sudden attack.
▶*n.* swooping or snatching movement or action.

**sword** /sôrd/ ▶*n.* weapon usu. of metal with a long blade and hilt with a handguard.

**sword·fish** ▶*n.* large marine fish with an extended swordlike upper jaw.

**syb·a·rite** /ˈsibəˌrīt/ ▶*n.* person who is self-indulgent or devoted to sensuous luxury. **—syb·a·rit·ic** *adj.*

**syc·a·more** /ˈsikəˌmôr/ ▸*n.* plane tree of N. America or its wood.

**syc·o·phant** /ˈsikəfənt/ ▸*n.* flatterer; toady. **—syc·o·phan·cy** *n.* **—syc·o·phan·tic** *adj.* **—syc·o·phan·ti·cal·ly** *adv.*

**syl·la·ble** /ˈsiləbəl/ ▸*n.* **1** unit of pronunciation forming the whole or a part of a word and usu. having one vowel sound. **2** character or characters representing a syllable.

**syl·la·bus** /ˈsiləbəs/ ▸*n.* (*pl.* **-bus·es** or **-bi**) program or outline of a course of study, teaching, etc.

**syl·lo·gism** /ˈsiləˌjizəm/ ▸*n.* reasoning in which a conclusion is drawn from two given or assumed propositions. **—syl·lo·gis·tic** *adj.* **—syl·lo·gis·ti·cal·ly** *adv.*

**sylph** /silf/ ▸*n.* **1** elemental spirit of the air. **2** slender, graceful woman or girl.

**syl·van** /ˈsilvən/ (also **sil·van**) ▸*adj.* **1 a** of the woods. **b** having woods; wooded. **2** rural.

**sym·bi·o·sis** /ˌsimbēˈōsis/ ▸*n.* (*pl.* **-ses**) **1** close coexistence and interaction of two different organisms, usu. to the advantage of both. **2** mutually advantageous association. **—sym·bi·ot·ic** *adj.* **—sym·bi·ot·i·cal·ly** *adv.*

**sym·bol** /ˈsimbəl/ ▸*n.* **1** thing conventionally regarded as typifying, representing, or recalling something. **2** representative mark, sign, logo, etc. **—sym·bol·ic** *adj.* **—sym·bol·i·cal·ly** *adv.*

**sym·bol·ism** ▸*n.* **1 a** use of symbols to represent ideas. **b** symbols collectively. **2** artistic and poetic movement or style using symbols and indirect suggestion to express ideas, emotions, etc. **—sym·bol·ist** *n.* **—sym·bol·is·tic** *adj.* **—sym·bol·ize** *v.*

**sym·me·try** /ˈsimitrē/ ▸*n.* (*pl.* **-tries**) **1** correct or beautiful proportion of parts; balance; harmony. **2** repetition of exactly similar parts facing each other or a center. **—sym·met·ri·cal** *adj.* **—sym·met·ri·cal·ly** *adv.*

**sym·pa·thize** /ˈsimpəˌTHīz/ ▸*v.* **1** feel or express sympathy. **2** agree. **—sym·pa·thiz·er** *n.*

**sym·pa·thy** /-THē/ ▸*n.* (*pl.* **-thies**) **1 a** state of being simultaneously affected with the same feeling as another. **b** capacity for this.

**2** compassion or commiseration; condolences. **3** agreement in opinion or desire. —**sym·pa·thet·ic** *adj.*

**sym·pho·ny** /'simfənē/ ▶*n.* (*pl.* **-nies**) elaborate composition usu. for full orchestra, and in several movements. —**sym·phon·ic** *adj.* —**sym·phon·i·cal·ly** *adv.*

**sym·po·si·um** /sim'pōzēəm/ ▶*n.* (*pl.* **-si·ums** or **-po·si·a**) conference or meeting to discuss a particular subject.

**symp·tom** /'sim(p)təm/ ▶*n.* **1** *Med.* physical or mental sign of disease. **2** sign of the existence of something.

**syn·a·gogue** /'sinə,gäg/ ▶*n.* **1** house of worship where a Jewish assembly or congregation meets for religious observance and instruction. **2** assembly itself. —**syn·a·gog·i·cal** *adj.*

**syn·apse** /'sin,aps/ ▶*n.* minute gap between two nerve cells, across which impulses pass by diffusion of a neurotransmitter.

**sync** /siNGk/ (also **synch**) *inf.* ▶*n.* synchronization. ▶*v.* synchronize. □ **in** (or **out of**) **sync** harmonizing or agreeing well (or badly).

**syn·chro·nize** /'siNGkrə,nīz/ ▶*v.*

**1** occur or cause to occur at the same time. **2** make the sound and picture of (a movie, etc.), coincide. **3** cause (clocks, etc.) to show a standard or uniform time. —**syn·chro·ni·za·tion** *n.*

**syn·chro·nous** /'siNGkrənəs/ ▶*adj.* **1** existing or occurring at the same time. **2** (of a satellite or its orbit) making or denoting an orbit around the earth or another celestial body in which one revolution is completed in the period taken for the body to rotate around its axis.

**syn·co·pate** /'siNGkə,pāt/ ▶*v.* *Mus.* displace the beats or accents in (a passage) so that strong beats become weak and vice versa. —**syn·co·pa·tion** *n.*

**syn·co·pe** /'siNGkəpē/ ▶*n.* **1** temporary loss of consciousness caused by a fall in blood pressure. **2** omission of sounds or letters from within a word, e.g., when *probably* is pronounced /'präblē/.

**syn·dic** /'sindik/ ▶*n.* **1** government official in various countries. **2** (in the UK) a business agent of certain universities and corporations.

**syn·di·cate** ▶*n.* /'sindikit/ **1** combination of individuals or businesses to promote a common interest. **2** agency supplying features, columns, etc. to newspapers, etc.

▸*v.* /'sindi͵kāt/ **1** form into a syndicate. **2** publish (material) through a syndicate.
—**syn·di·ca·tion** *n.*

**syn·drome** /'sin͵drōm/ ▸*n.* **1** group of concurrent symptoms of a disease. **2** characteristic combination of opinions, emotions, behavior, etc.
—**syn·drom·ic** *adj.*

**syn·er·gism** /'sinər͵jizəm/ (also **syn·er·gy**) ▸*n.* combined effect of drugs, organs, etc., that exceeds the sum of their individual effects. —**syn·er·get·ic** *adj.*
—**syn·er·gic** *adj.* —**syn·er·gist** *n.*
—**syn·er·gis·tic** *adj.*
—**syn·er·gis·ti·cal·ly** *adv.*

**syn·er·gy** /'sinərjē/ (also **syn·er·gism** /-͵jizəm/) ▸*n.* interaction or cooperation of two or more organizations, substances, or other agents to produce a combined effect greater than the sum of their separate effects.

**syn·es·the·sia** /͵sinəs'THēzhə/ ▸*n.* **1** production of a sense impression relating to one sense or part of the body by stimulation of another sense or part of the body. **2** poetic description of a sense impression in terms of another sense, as in "a loud perfume" or "an icy voice."

**syn·od** /'sinəd/ ▸*n.* church council of delegated clergy and sometimes laity.

**syn·o·nym** /'sinə͵nim/ ▸*n.* word or phrase that means the same as another (e.g., *shut* and *close*).
—**syn·on·y·mous** *adj.*

**syn·op·sis** /sə'näpsis/ ▸*n.* (*pl.* **-ses**) summary; outline; brief general survey. —**syn·op·size** *v.*

**syn·tac·tic** /sin'taktik/ ▸*adj.* of or according to syntax.

**syn·tax** /'sin͵taks/ ▸*n.* **1** grammatical arrangement of words. **2** rules for or analysis of this. —**syn·tac·tic** *adj.*
—**syn·tac·ti·cal·ly** *adv.*

**syn·the·sis** /'sinTHəsis/ ▸*n.* (*pl.* **-ses**) **1** combining of elements into a whole. **2** *Chem.* artificial production of compounds from their constituents.

**syn·the·size** /-͵sīz/ ▸*v.* **1** make a synthesis of. **2** combine into a coherent whole.

**syn·the·siz·er** ▸*n.* electronic console or keyboard, producing a variety of instrumental sounds.

**syn·thet·ic** /sin'THetik/ ▶*adj.*
  **1** made by chemical synthesis,
  esp. to imitate a natural product.
  **2** affected; insincere.
  ▶*n.* synthetic substance.
  —**syn·thet·i·cal·ly** *adv.*

**syph·i·lis** /'sifəlis/ ▶*n.* contagious
  venereal disease. —**syph·i·lit·ic**
  *adj.*

**sy·ringe** /sə'rinj/ ▶*n.* device for
  sucking in and ejecting liquid in
  a fine stream.

**syr·up** /'sirəp/ ▶*n.* **1** sweet sauce
  of sugar dissolved in water.
  **2** any thick, esp. sweet liquid.
  **3** excessive sweetness of style or
  manner. —**syr·up·y** *adj.*

**sys·tem** /'sistəm/ ▶*n.* **1** complex
  whole; set of connected things
  or parts. **2** organized
  arrangement; network; plan or
  procedure. **3** set of organs in
  the body with a common
  structure or function: *digestive
  system.*

**sys·tem·at·ic** /ˌsistə'matik/ ▶*adj.*
  done or acting according to a
  fixed plan or system.
  —**sys·tem·at·i·cal·ly** *adv.*

**sys·tem·a·tize** ▶*v.* **1** make
  systematic. **2** devise a system
  for. —**sys·tem·a·ti·za·tion** *n.*

**sys·tem·ic** /sə'stemik/ ▶*adj.* of
  or concerning the whole body.
  —**sys·tem·i·cal·ly** *adv.*

**sys·to·le** /'sistəlē/ ▶*n.* normal
  rhythmic contraction of the
  heart. —**sys·tol·ic** *adj.*

# Tt

**T**[1] /tē/ (also **t**) ▶*n.* (*pl.* **Ts** or **T's**; **t's**) **1** twentieth letter of the alphabet. **2** T-shaped thing: *T-joint.*
□ **to a T** exactly; to perfection.

**T**[2] ▶*abbr.* **1** tablespoon. **2** temperature.

**T**[3] ▶*symb. Chem.* tritium.

**t.** ▶*abbr.* **1** ton(s). **2** teaspoon. **3** temperature.

**tab** /tab/ ▶*n.* **1** small flap or strip attached for grasping, fastening, or hanging up, or for identification. **2** *inf.* bill; check: *picked up the tab.* **3** facility in a computer program or device on a typewriter for advancing to a sequence of set positions.
▶*v.* (**tabbed, tab·bing**) provide with a tab or tabs.
□ **keep tabs on** *inf.* have under observation.

**Ta·bas·co** /təˈbaskō/ ▶*trademark* pungent hot pepper sauce.

**tab·by** /ˈtabē/ ▶*n.* (*pl.* **-bies**) gray, orange, or brownish cat with dark stripes.

**tab·er·na·cle** /ˈtabərˌnakəl/ ▶*n.* **1** large place of worship. **2** niche or receptacle esp. for the Eucharistic elements. **3** tent used as a sanctuary by the Israelites during the Exodus.

**ta·bes·cent** /təˈbesənt/ ▶*adj.* wasting away.

**tab·la·ture** /ˈtabləCHər; -ˌCHŏŏr/ ▶*n.* form of musical notation indicating fingering rather than the pitch of notes, written on lines corresponding to, for example, the strings of a lute or the holes on a flute.

**ta·ble** /ˈtābəl/ ▶*n.* **1** flat surface with one or more legs, used for eating, working at, etc. **2** set of facts or figures in columns, etc.: *a table of contents.*
▶*v.* postpone consideration of (a matter).
□ **turn the tables** reverse circumstances to one's advantage. □ **under the table** *inf.* (esp. of a payment) covertly; secretly.

**tab·leau** /ˌtaˈblō/ ▶*n.* (*pl.* **-leaux**) **1** picturesque presentation. **2** silent and motionless group of people arranged to represent a scene.

**ta·ble·land** ▶*n.* plateau.

**ta·ble·spoon** ▶*n.* **1** large spoon for serving food. **2** unit of measure equal to ¹/₂ fl. oz. —**ta·ble·spoon·ful** *n.*

**tab·let** /'tablit/ ▶*n.* **1** writing pad. **2** flat slab of stone or wood, usu. inscribed. **3** solid dose of a medicine, etc.

**ta·ble ten·nis** ▶*n.* indoor game played with paddles and a ball bounced on a table divided by a net.

**ta·ble·ware** ▶*n.* dishes, utensils, etc., used for serving and eating.

**tab·loid** /'tab,loid/ ▶*n.* small-sized, usu. sensationalized newspaper.

**ta·boo** /tə'bōō/ ▶*n.* prohibition imposed by religion or social custom.
▶*adj.* avoided or prohibited, esp. by social custom: *taboo words.*

**tab·u·lar** /'tabyələr/ ▶*adj.* of or arranged in tables or lists.

**ta·bu·late** ▶*v.* arrange (figures or facts) in tabular form. —**tab·u·la·tion** *n.* —**tab·u·la·tor** *n.*

**ta·cet** /'tāsit; 'tas-; 'täket/ ▶*v.* (as a direction) indicating that a voice or instrument is silent.

**ta·chom·e·ter** /ta'kämitər/ ▶*n.* instrument measuring the speed of an engine.

**tach·y·car·di·a** /,takē'kärdēə/ ▶*n.* abnormally rapid heart rate.

**tac·it** /'tasit/ ▶*adj.* understood or implied without being stated: *tacit consent.* —**tac·it·ly** *adv.*

**tac·i·turn** /'tasi,tərn/ ▶*adj.* saying little; uncommunicative. —**tac·i·tur·ni·ty** *n.* —**tac·i·turn·ly** *adv.*

**tack** /tak/ ▶*n.* **1** small sharp broad-headed nail. **2** long stitch for fastening fabrics, etc., lightly or temporarily together. **3** direction or temporary change of direction in sailing to take advantage of a side wind, etc. **4** course of action or policy. **5** saddle, bridle, etc., of a horse.
▶*v.* **1** fasten with tacks. **2** stitch lightly together. **3** (**tack on**) annex (a thing). **4** change a ship's course by turning its head to the wind.

**tack·le** ▶*n.* **1** equipment for a task or sport: *fishing tackle.* **2** mechanism, esp. of ropes, pulley blocks, etc., for lifting weights, etc. **3** act of tackling in football, etc.
▶*v.* **1** try to deal with (a problem or difficulty). **2** *Football* stop (a player with the ball).

**tack·y** ▶*adj.* (**-i·er, -i·est**) **1** (of glue, paint, etc.) still slightly

sticky after application.
**2** showing poor taste or style.
—**tack·i·ness** *n.*

**ta·co** /'täkō/ ▶*n.* (*pl.* **-cos**) tortilla filled with meat, cheese, lettuce, tomatoes, etc.

**tact** /takt/ ▶*n.* adroitness in dealing with others, esp. in delicate situations; intuitive social grace. —**tact·ful** *adj.* —**tact·ful·ly** *adv.* —**tact·ful·ness** *n.* —**tact·less** *adj.* —**tact·less·ly** *adv.*

**tac·tic** ▶*n.* **1** (**tactics**) [often treated as *sing.*] disposition of armed forces, esp. in war. **2** procedure to achieve an end. —**tac·ti·cian** *n.*

**tac·tile** /'taktl/ ▶*adj.* **1** of the sense of touch. **2** perceived by touch. —**tac·til·i·ty** *n.*

**tad** /tad/ *inf.* ▶*n.* small amount: often used adverbially: *a tad salty.*

**tad·pole** ▶*n.* larva of an amphibian, esp. a frog or toad.

**taf·fe·ta** /'tafitə/ ▶*n.* fine lustrous silk or synthetic fabric.

**taf·fy** /'tafē/ ▶*n.* (*pl.* **-fies**) chewy boiled sugar or molasses candy.

**tag** /tag/ ▶*n.* **1** label or marker, esp. attached to an object. **2** children's chasing game.
▶*v.* (**tagged, tag·ging**) **1** provide

with a tag or tags. **2** touch in or as in a game of tag.
□ **tag along** follow without being invited. □ **tag on** add at the end.

**t'ai chi ch'uan** /'tī ˌCHē 'CHwän/ (also **t'ai chi**) ▶*n.* Chinese martial art and system of calisthenics consisting of sequences of very slow controlled movements.

**tail** /tāl/ ▶*n.* **1** hindmost part of an animal, esp. extending beyond the rest of the body. **2** thing like a tail, esp. a rear extension. **3** rear part of an airplane, rocket, or vehicle. **4** part of a shirt or coat below the waist at the back. **5** (**tails**) reverse of a coin. **6** *inf.* person following another.
▶*v. inf.* shadow or follow closely.

**tail·gate** ▶*n.* hinged or removable flap or door at the rear of a motor vehicle.
▶*v. inf.* drive too closely behind (another vehicle). —**tail·gat·er** *n.*

**tail·light** ▶*n.* rear light of a vehicle.

**tai·lor** /'tālər/ ▶*n.* maker or fitter of clothes.
▶*v.* **1** make (clothes) as a tailor. **2** make or adapt for a special purpose.
□ **tailor-made 1** made to order by a tailor. **2** made or suited for a

particular purpose: *a job tailor-made for me.*

**tail·pipe** ▶*n.* rear exhaust pipe.

**tail·spin** ▶*n.* dive by an aircraft with the tail spiraling.

**taint** /tānt/ ▶*n.* spot or trace of decay, infection, corruption, etc. ▶*v.* affect or become affected with a taint.

**take** /tāk/ ▶*v.* (**took**; **tak·en**) **1** lay hold of; get into one's hands. **2** occupy: *take a chair.* **3** make use of: *take precautions.* **4** consume as food or medicine. **5** be effective: *inoculation did not take.* **6** carry; convey: *bus will take you.* **7** remove; steal. **8** experience: *take pleasure.* **9** accept: *take the offer.* **10** subtract: *take 3 from 9.* **11** make; undertake; perform: *take notes | take an oath.* ▶*n.* **1** amount taken or caught in one session, attempt, etc. **2** film sequence photographed continuously at one time. **3** money received by a business. □ **take after** resemble (a parent, etc.). □ **take five** (or **ten**) take a break, esp. from work. □ **take heart** be encouraged. □ **take out** escort; date. □ **take-out** (of food) bought cooked for eating elsewhere.

**take·off** ▶*n.* **1** act of becoming airborne. **2** *inf.* act of mimicking.

**take·o·ver** ▶*n.* assumption of control (esp. of a business).

**talc** /talk/ ▶*n.* **1** talcum powder. **2** magnesium silicate used as a lubricant, etc.

**tal·cum pow·der** ▶*n.* powdered talc for toilet and cosmetic use, usu. perfumed.

**tale** /tāl/ ▶*n.* **1** narrative or story, esp. fictitious. **2** lie; falsehood.

**tal·ent** /'talənt/ ▶*n.* special aptitude or faculty. —**tal·ent·ed** *adj.*

**tal·is·man** /'talismən/ ▶*n.* (*pl.* **-mans**) ring, stone, etc., supposed to have magic powers, esp. of bringing good luck. —**tal·is·man·ic** *adj.*

**talk** /tôk/ ▶*v.* **1** converse or communicate by spoken words. **2** express; utter; discuss: *talking nonsense.* **3** reveal secrets. ▶*n.* **1** conversation; talking. **2** particular mode of speech: *baby talk.* **3** address or lecture. **4** (often **talks**) discussion; negotiation. —**talk·er** *n.* □ **talk shop** talk about one's occupation, etc.

**talk·a·tive** /'tôkətiv/ ▶*adj.* talking a lot.

**talk·ing-to** ▶*n.* scolding.

**tall** /tôl/ ▸*adj.* **1** of more than average height. **2** of a specified height: *about six feet tall.* —**tall·ness** *n.*

**tal·low** /'talō/ ▸*n.* hard (esp. animal) fat melted down to make candles, soap, etc.

**tal·ly** /'talē/ ▸*n.* (*pl.* **-lies**) **1** reckoning of a debt or score. **2** total score or amount. ▸*v.* (**-lied**) **1** (**tally with**) agree; correspond. **2** record or reckon by tally.

**Tal·mud** /'täl,mŏŏd/ ▸*n.* body of Jewish civil and ceremonial law and tradition.

**tal·on** /'talən/ ▸*n.* claw, esp. of a bird of prey.

**tam** /tam/ ▸*n.* tam-o'-shanter.

**ta·ma·le** /tə'mälē/ ▸*n.* Mexican food of seasoned meat and corn flour steamed or baked in corn husks.

**tam·a·rack** /'tamə,rak/ ▸*n.* slender N. American larch.

**tam·a·rind** /'tamə,rind/ ▸*n.* tropical evergreen tree or its juicy, edible fruit.

**tam·bou·rine** /,tambə'rēn/ ▸*n.* percussion instrument consisting of a hoop with parchment stretched over one side and jingling disks around the hoop.

**tame** /tām/ ▸*adj.* **1** (of an animal) domesticated; not wild or shy. **2** insipid; dull. ▸*v.* make tame; domesticate; subdue. —**tame·ly** *adv.* —**tame·ness** *n.*

**tam-o'-shanter** /'tam ə ,SHan(t)ər/ ▸*n.* round woolen or cloth beret of Scottish origin.

**tamp** /tamp/ ▸*v.* ram down tightly by a series of taps.

**tam·per** /'tampər/ ▸*v.* (**tamper with**) meddle with or make unauthorized changes in.

**tam·pon** /'tam,pän/ ▸*n.* plug of soft material used to absorb fluid, esp. blood.

**tan** /tan/ ▸*n.* **1** brown skin color from exposure to ultraviolet light. **2** yellowish-brown color. ▸*adj.* yellowish-brown. ▸*v.* (**tanned, tan·ning**) **1** make or become brown by exposure to ultraviolet light. **2** convert (raw hide) into leather. —**tan·na·ble** *adj.* —**tan·ning** *n.* —**tan·nish** *adj.*

**tan·dem** /'tandəm/ ▸*n.* set of two with one following the other. □ **in tandem** arranged one behind another.

**tang** /taNG/ ▸*n.* strong taste or smell. —**tang·y** *adj.*

**tan·ge·lo** /'tanjə,lō/ ▸*n.* (*pl.* **-los**)

hybrid of tangerine and grapefruit.

**tan·gent** /ˈtanjənt/ ▸*n.* **1** straight line, curve, or surface that meets a curve but does not intersect it. **2** ratio of the sides opposite and adjacent to an angle in a right triangle. —**tan·gen·cy** *n.*

□ **on a tangent** diverging from a previous course of action or thought, etc.

**tan·gen·tial** /tanˈjenCHəl/ ▸*adj.* **1** of or along a tangent. **2** peripheral. —**tan·gen·tial·ly** *adv.*

**tan·ger·ine** /ˌtanjəˈrēn/ ▸*n.* small sweet orange-colored citrus fruit with a thin skin.

**tan·gi·ble** /ˈtanjəbəl/ ▸*adj.* **1** perceptible by touch. **2** definite; clearly intelligible; not elusive: *tangible proof.* —**tan·gi·bil·i·ty** *n.* —**tan·gi·bly** *adv.*

**tan·gle** /ˈtaNGgəl/ ▸*v.* **1** intertwine or become intertwined in a confused mass. **2** (**tangle with**) *inf.* become involved (esp. in conflict) with. ▸*n.* **1** confused mass of intertwined threads, etc. **2** confused or complicated state.

**tan·go** /ˈtaNGgō/ ▸*n.* (*pl.* **-gos**)

slow S. American ballroom dance or the music for this. ▸*v.* (**-goed**) dance the tango.

**tank** /taNGk/ ▸*n.* **1** large container usu. for liquid or gas. **2** heavy armored fighting vehicle moving on a tracked carriage.

**tan·kard** /ˈtaNGkərd/ ▸*n.* tall mug with a handle and sometimes a hinged lid, esp. for beer.

**tank·er** ▸*n.* ship, aircraft, or truck for carrying liquids or gases in bulk.

**tank top** ▸*n.* sleeveless, close-fitting, collarless upper garment.

**tan·nin** /ˈtanin/ ▸*n.* substance found in tree bark and in tea, used in tanning.

**tan·ta·lize** /ˈtan(t)l̩ˌīz/ ▸*v.* torment or tease by the sight or promise of what is unobtainable. —**tan·ta·liz·er** *n.* —**tan·ta·liz·ing·ly** *adv.*

**tan·ta·mount** /ˈtantəˌmount/ ▸*adj.* equivalent (to).

**tan·tiv·y** /tanˈtivē/ ▸*n.* (*pl.* **-tiv·ies**) rapid gallop or ride. ▸*exclam.* used as a hunting cry. ▸*adj.* moving or riding swiftly.

**tant mieux** /ˈtäN ˈmyə/ ▸*exclam.* so much the better.

**tant pis** /ˈtäN ˈpē/ ▸*exclam.* so much the worse; the situation is regrettable but now beyond retrieval.

**tan·trum** /'tantrəm/ ▸*n.* outburst of bad temper or petulance.

**tap** /tap/ ▸*n.* **1** device for drawing liquid in a controlled flow. **2** wiretapping. **3** light blow; rap. **4** metal attachment on a tap dancer's shoe. **5** (**taps**) [treated as *sing.* or *pl.*] military bugle call.
▸*v.* (**tapped, tap·ping**) **1** let out (liquid) by means of, or as if by means of, a tap. **2** obtain information or supplies from. **3** connect a secret listening device to. **4** strike gently but audibly.
□ **on tap** *inf.* ready for immediate use.

**tap dance** ▸*n.* dance where the feet tap out an elaborate rhythm. —**tap-dance** *v.*

**tape** /tāp/ ▸*n.* **1** narrow strip of material for tying up, fastening, etc. **2** long narrow flexible material with magnetic properties, used for recording sounds, pictures, or computer data.
▸*v.* **1** tie up, join, seal, mark off, etc., with tape. **2** record on tape.
□ **tape deck** device for playing and recording magnetic tape.
□ **tape measure** strip of tape or

flexible metal marked for measuring lengths. □ **tape recorder** apparatus for recording and replaying sounds on magnetic tape.

**ta·per** /'tāpər/ ▸*n.* slender candle.
▸*v.* make or become gradually less or narrower.

**tap·es·try** /'tapistrē/ ▸*n.* (*pl.* **-tries**) thick fabric in which colored weft threads are woven to form pictures or designs.

**tape·worm** /'tāp‚wərm/ ▸*n.* ribbonlike parasitic intestinal worm with a segmented body.

**tap·i·o·ca** /‚tapē'ōkə/ ▸*n.* starchy substance in hard white grains, obtained from cassava and used for puddings, etc.

**ta·pir** /'tāpər/ ▸*n.* nocturnal hoofed mammal of Central and S. America and Malaysia, with a short flexible snout.

**tap root** ▸*n.* main root tapering downward.

**tar** /tär/ ▸*n.* **1** dark, thick, flammable liquid distilled from wood, coal, etc., used as a preservative of wood and iron, in making roads, etc. **2** similar substance formed in the combustion of tobacco, etc. **3** sailor.
▸*v.* (**tarred, tar·ring**) cover with tar.

**tar·an·tel·la** /ˌtarənˈtelə/ ▶n. whirling S. Italian dance or the music for it.

**tar·ant·ism** /ˈtarənˌtizəm/ ▶n. psychological illness characterized by an extreme impulse to dance, prevalent in southern Italy from the 15th to the 17th c., and widely believed at the time to have been caused by the bite of a tarantula.

**ta·ran·tu·la** /təˈranCHələ/ ▶n. large, black, hairy spider.

**tar·dy** /ˈtärdē/ ▶adj. (**-di·er, -di·est**) slow to act, come, or happen. —**tar·di·ly** adv. —**tar·di·ness** n.

**tare** /te(ə)r/ ▶n. **1** vetch, esp. as a weed or fodder. **2** allowance made for the container or vehicle weighed with the goods it holds.

**tar·get** /ˈtärgit/ ▶n. **1** mark fired or aimed at, esp. an object marked with concentric circles. **2** person or thing aimed or fired at. **3** objective: *target date.* **4** butt for criticism, abuse, etc.
▶v. **1** identify or single out (a person or thing) as an object of attention or attack. **2** aim or direct: *target our efforts.*

**tar·iff** /ˈtarif/ ▶n. **1** table of fixed charges. **2** duty on a particular class of goods.

**tar·nish** /ˈtärniSH/ ▶v. **1** lose or cause (metal) to lose luster. **2** sully or blemish (a reputation).
▶n. **1** loss of luster, esp. as a film on a metal's surface. **2** blemish; stain.

**ta·ro** /ˈtarō/ ▶n. (pl. **-ros**) tropical plant with edible tuberous roots.

**ta·rot** /ˈtarō/ ▶n. pack of mainly picture cards used in fortune-telling.

**tar·pau·lin** /tärˈpôlən; ˈtärpə-/ (also **tarp**) ▶n. heavy-duty waterproof cloth, esp. of canvas or plastic.

**tar·ra·gon** /ˈtarəˌgän/ ▶n. bushy herb with leaves used as a flavoring.

**tar·ry** /ˈtärē/ ▶v. (**-ried**) linger; stay; wait.

**tart** /tärt/ ▶n. **1** small pie containing fruit, jam, etc. **2** prostitute; promiscuous woman.
▶adj. **1** sharp or acid in taste. **2** (of a remark, etc.) cutting; bitter. —**tart·ly** adv. —**tart·ness** n. —**tart·y** adj.

**tar·tan** /ˈtärtn/ ▶n. **1** plaid pattern, esp. denoting a Scottish Highland clan. **2** woolen fabric woven in this pattern.

**tar·tar** /ˈtärtər/ ▶n. **1** hard deposit that forms on the teeth. **2** deposit that forms a hard crust in wine. **3** violent-tempered or intractable person.

**tar·tar sauce** ▶n. sauce of mayonnaise and chopped pickles, etc.

**task** /task/ ▶n. piece of work to be done.
□ **take to task** rebuke; scold.
□ **task force** group specially organized for a task.

**task·mas·ter** ▶n. person who makes others work hard.

**tas·sel** /ˈtasəl/ ▶n. decorative tuft of loosely hanging threads or cords. —**tas·seled** adj.

**taste** /tāst/ ▶n. **1** sensation caused in the mouth by contact of the taste buds with a substance. **2** small sample of food or drink. **3** liking or predilection: *expensive tastes.* **4** aesthetic discernment in art, conduct, etc.
▶v. **1** sample or perceive the flavor of (food, etc.). **2** experience: *never tasted failure.* **3** have a specified flavor: *tastes of onions.* —**taste·ful** adj. —**taste·ful·ly** adv. —**taste·less** adj.
□ **taste bud** cell or nerve ending

on the surface of the tongue, by which things are tasted.

**tast·y** /ˈtāstē/ ▶adj. (**-i·er, -i·est**) (of food) pleasing in flavor; appetizing. —**tast·i·ness** n.

**tat·ter** /ˈtatər/ ▶n. (usu. **tatters**) irregularly torn cloth or paper, etc. —**tat·tered** adj.
□ **in tatters** inf. (of a negotiation, etc.) ruined; demolished.

**tat·tle** /ˈtatl/ ▶v. **1** chatter; gossip. **2** reveal (secrets).

**tat·too** /taˈtoo/ ▶v. **1** mark (skin) by puncturing it and inserting pigments. **2** make (a design) in this way.
▶n. **1** tattooed pattern. **2** military display or pageant. **3** rhythmic tapping or drumming.

**tat·ty** /ˈtatē/ ▶adj. shabby and untidy; ragged. —**tat·ti·ness** n.

**taunt** /tônt/ ▶n. insult; provocation.
▶v. insult; reproach (a person) contemptuously. —**taunt·ing·ly** adv.

**taupe** /tōp/ ▶adj. & n. dark, brownish gray.

**taut** /tôt/ ▶adj. **1** (of a rope, muscles, etc.) tight; not slack. **2** (of nerves) tense. —**taut·ly** adv. —**taut·ness** n.

**tau·tol·o·gy** /tôˈtäləjē/ ▶n. (pl. **-gies**) saying of the same thing

twice in different words, esp. as a fault of style (e.g., *arrived one after the other in succession*).
—**tau·to·log·i·cal** *adj.*

**tav·ern** /ˈtavərn/ ▸*n.* inn or bar.

**taw·dry** /ˈtôdrē/ ▸*adj.* (**-dri·er, -dri·est**) **1** showy but worthless. **2** gaudy; vulgar.
—**taw·dri·ness** *n.*

**taw·ny** /ˈtônē/ ▸*adj.* (**-ni·er, -ni·est**) orangish or yellowish brown.

**tax** /taks/ ▸*n.* **1** government revenue compulsorily levied on individuals, property, or businesses. **2** strain; heavy demand; burdensome obligation.
▸*v.* **1** impose a tax on. **2** make heavy demands on (a person's powers, resources, etc.).
—**tax·a·ble** *adj.* —**tax·a·tion** *n.*

**tax·i** /ˈtaksē/ ▸*n.* (*pl.* **-is** or **-ies**) (also **tax·i·cab**) automobile licensed for hire and usu. fitted with a meter.
▸*v.* (**-ied, -i·ing** or **-y·ing**) **1** (of an aircraft) move along the ground before takeoff or after landing. **2** go or convey in a taxi.

**tax·i·der·my** /ˈtaksəˌdərmē/ ▸*n.* art of preparing, stuffing, and mounting the skins of animals.
—**tax·i·der·mist** *n.*

**tax·on·o·my** /takˈsänəmē/ ▸*n.* scientific classification of organisms. —**tax·o·nom·ic** *adj.*
—**tax·on·o·mist** *n.*

**tax·pay·er** ▸*n.* person who pays taxes.

**tax shel·ter** ▸*n.* arrangement made to avoid or minimize taxes.

**TB** ▸*abbr.* **1** tubercle bacillus. **2** tuberculosis.

**Tb** ▸*symb. Chem.* terbium.

**tbs.** (also **tbsp.**) ▸*abbr.* tablespoon.

**T cell** ▸*n.* lymphocyte involved in the immune system's response.

**tea** /tē/ ▸*n.* **1** leaves of an evergreen shrub of Asia. **2** drink made by infusing dried tea leaves in boiling water. **3** infusion of herbal or other leaves. **4** afternoon party or light meal.
□ **tea bag** small porous bag holding tea leaves for infusion.

**teach** /tēCH/ ▸*v.* (*past* and *past part.* **taught**) give systematic information to (a person) or about (a subject or skill).
—**teach·er** *n.*

**tea·cup** ▸*n.* cup for serving tea.

**teak** /tēk/ ▸*n.* large deciduous

tree of East India or its hard durable wood.

**tea ket·tle** ▸*n.* kettle with a spout, handle, and cover, used for boiling water.

**teal** /tēl/ ▸*n.* (*pl.* same) **1** small freshwater duck. **2** dark, greenish blue color.

**team** /tēm/ ▸*n.* **1** set of players forming one side in a game, debate, etc. **2** two or more persons or animals working together.
▸*v.* join in a team or in common action.

**team·ster** /'tēmstər/ ▸*n.* driver of a truck or a team of animals.

**tea·pot** ▸*n.* usu. ceramic pot with a handle, spout, and lid, for brewing and serving tea.

**tear**[1] /te(ə)r/ ▸*v.* (*past* **tore**; *past part.* **torn**) **1** pull apart or to pieces with some force. **2** pull violently: *tore off the cover.* **3** violently disrupt or divide: *torn by conflicting emotions.* **4** *inf.* go hurriedly. **5** undergo tearing: *the curtain tore down the middle.*
▸*n.* hole or split caused by tearing.

**tear**[2] /ti(ə)r/ ▸*n.* **1** drop of clear salty liquid secreted by glands in the eye. **2** tearlike thing; drop.
—**tear·ful** *adj.* —**tear·ful·ly** *adv.*

□ **in tears** crying; shedding tears.
□ **tear gas** gas that disables by causing severe irritation to the eyes.

**tear·jerk·er** ▸*n. inf.* sentimental story, film, etc.

**tease** /tēz/ ▸*v.* **1 a** make fun of playfully, unkindly, or annoyingly. **b** tempt or allure, esp. sexually. **2** pick (wool, hair, etc.) into separate fibers.
▸*n.* **1** *inf.* person fond of teasing. **2** instance of teasing.
—**teas·ing·ly** *adv.*

**tea·spoon** ▸*n.* **1** spoon for stirring tea, etc. **2** amount held by this, approx. $1/6$ fl. oz.
—**tea·spoon·ful** *n.*

**teat** /tēt/ ▸*n.* mammary nipple, esp. of an animal.

**tech·ni·cal** /'teknikəl/ ▸*adj.* **1** of the mechanical arts and applied sciences: *technical college.* **2** of a particular subject, etc., or its techniques. **3** strictly or legally interpreted. —**tech·ni·cal·ly** *adv.* —**tech·ni·cian** *n.*

**tech·ni·cal·i·ty** /ˌtekni'kalitē/ ▸*n.* (*pl.* **-ties**) **1** technical expression. **2** technical point or detail.

**Tech·ni·col·or** /'tekniˌkələr/ ▸*trademark* process of color cinematography.

**tech·nique** /tek'nēk/ ▸*n.*
**1** mechanical skill; applicable method. **2** manner of artistic execution in music, painting, etc.

**tech·noc·ra·cy** /tek'näkrəsē/ ▸*n.* (*pl.* **-cies**) rule or control by technical experts. —**tech·no·crat** *n.* —**tech·no·crat·ic** *adj.*

**tech·nol·o·gy** /tek'näləjē/ ▸*n.* (*pl.* **-gies**) **1** study or use of the mechanical arts and applied sciences. **2** these subjects collectively. —**tech·no·log·i·cal** *adj.* —**tech·nol·o·gist** *n.*

**tec·ton·ics** /tek'täniks/ ▸*pl. n.* [treated as *sing.*] large-scale processes affecting the structure of the earth's crust.

**ted·dy bear** ▸*n.* stuffed toy bear.

**te·di·ous** /'tēdēəs/ ▸*adj.* tiresomely long; wearisome. —**te·di·ous·ly** *adv.* —**te·di·ous·ness** *n.* —**te·di·um** *n.*

**tee** /tē/ ▸*n. Golf* **1** cleared space from which a golf ball is struck at the beginning of play for each hole. **2** small wood or plastic support for a golf ball.
▸*v.* (**teed**) *Golf* place (a ball) on a tee.
□ **tee off** *Golf* play a ball from a tee.

**teem** /tēm/ ▸*v.* **1** be abundant. **2** (**teem with**) be full of or swarming with: *teeming with ideas.*

**teens** /tēnz/ ▸*pl. n.* years of age from 13 to 19. —**teen·ag·er** *n.*

**tee·ter** /'tētər/ ▸*v.* totter; move unsteadily.

**teethe** /tēTH/ ▸*v.* grow or cut teeth.

**tee·to·tal·er** /tē'tōtələr/ ▸*n.* person who abstains totally from alcohol.

**te·fil·lin** /tə'filin; -fē'lēn/ ▸*pl. n.* collective term for Jewish phylacteries.

**Tef·lon** /'tef,län/ ▸*trademark* nonstick coating for kitchen utensils, etc.

**teg·u·ment** /'tegyəmənt/ ▸*n.* integument of an organism, esp. a parasitic flatworm.

**tel.** ▸*abbr.* **1** telephone. **2** telegraph.

**tel·e·cast** /'telə,kast/ ▸*n.* television broadcast.
▸*v.* transmit by television. —**tel·e·cast·er** *n.*

**tel·e·com·mu·ni·ca·tions** (also **tel·e·com·mu·ni·ca·tion**) ▸*n.* technology of communication over a distance by cable, telephone, broadcasting, etc.

**tel·e·con·fer·ence** ▶*n.* conference with participants linked by telecommunication devices. —**tel·e·con·fer·enc·ing** *n.*

**tel·e·gen·ic** /ˌteləˈjenik/ ▶*adj.* having an appearance or manner that is appealing on television.

**tel·e·graph** ▶*n.* system or device for transmitting messages or signals over a distance esp. by making and breaking an electrical connection.

▶*v.* send (a message) to by telegraph. —**tel·e·graph·ic** *adj.* —**te·leg·ra·phy** *n.*

**tel·e·mar·ket·ing** ▶*n.* marketing by unsolicited telephone calls. —**tel·e·mar·ket·er** *n.*

**te·lep·a·thy** /təˈlepəTHē/ ▶*n.* supposed paranormal communication of thoughts. —**tel·e·path·ic** *adj.* —**tel·e·path·i·cal·ly** *adv.* —**te·lep·a·thist** *n.*

**tel·e·phone** /ˈteləˌfōn/ ▶*n.* apparatus for transmitting and receiving sound (esp. speech) over a distance by using optical or electrical signals.

▶*v.* speak to or send (a message) by telephone. —**tel·e·phon·ic** *adj.*

—**tel·e·phon·i·cal·ly** *adv.* —**tel·e·phon·y** *n.*

**tel·e·pho·to** ▶*n.* (*pl.* **-tos**) (in full **telephoto lens**) photographic lens producing a large image of a distant object. —**tel·e·pho·tog·ra·phy** *n.*

**tel·e·scope** ▶*n.* optical instrument using lenses or mirrors to magnify distant objects.

▶*v.* **1** press or drive (sections of a tube, etc.) together so that one slides into another. **2** compress in space or time. —**tel·e·scop·ic** *adj.* —**tel·e·scop·i·cal·ly** *adv.*

**tel·e·thon** /ˈteləˌTHän/ ▶*n.* television program to raise money for a charity.

**tel·e·van·ge·list** /ˌteləˈvanjəlist/ ▶*n.* evangelical preacher who appears regularly on television.

**tel·e·vi·sion** ▶*n.* **1** system for reproducing on a screen visual images transmitted by radio waves. **2** (also **television set**) device with a screen for receiving these signals. (Abbr.: **TV**) —**tel·e·vise** *v.*

**tell** /tel/ ▶*v.* (*past* and *past part.* **told**) **1** relate in speech or writing. **2** make known; express in words: *tell me what you want.* **3** reveal or signify to (a person):

*your face tells me everything.*
**4** divulge information, etc.; reveal a secret.
☐ **tell apart** distinguish between.

**tell·er** ▸*n.* person employed to receive and pay out money in a bank, etc.

**tell·tale** ▸*adj.* revealing.

**tel·lu·ri·an** /təˈloŏrēən/ ▸*adj.* of or inhabiting the earth.
▸*n.* inhabitant of the earth.

**tem·blor** /ˈtemblər; -ˌblôr/ ▸*n.* earthquake.

**te·mer·i·ty** /təˈmeritē/ ▸*n.* audacity; rashness.

**temp** /temp/ ▸*n. inf.* temporary employee.

**temp.** ▸*abbr.* **1** temperature. **2** temporary.

**tem·per** /ˈtempər/ ▸*n.* **1** mood; mental disposition. **2** irritation; anger: *fit of temper.* **3** composure; calmness: *lose one's temper.*
▸*v.* **1** bring (metal or clay) to a proper hardness or consistency. **2** moderate: *temper justice with mercy.*

**tem·per·a** /ˈtempərə/ ▸*n.* method of painting using an emulsion, e.g., of pigment with egg, esp. on canvas.

**tem·per·a·ment** /ˈtemp(ə)rəmənt/ ▸*n.* person's or animal's nature and character.

**tem·per·a·men·tal** ▸*adj.* moody; unreliable.

**tem·per·ance** /ˈtemp(ə)rəns/ ▸*n.* **1** moderation, esp. in eating and drinking. **2** abstinence from alcohol.

**tem·per·ate** /ˈtemp(ə)rit/ ▸*adj.* **1** moderate. **2** (of a region or climate) mild. —**tem·per·ate·ly** *adv.* —**tem·per·ate·ness** *n.*
☐ **temperate zone** each of the two belts of latitude between the torrid zone and the northern and southern frigid zones.

**tem·per·a·ture** /ˈtemp(ə)rə-ˌCHər/ ▸*n.* **1** measured or perceived degree of heat or cold of a body, thing, region, etc. **2** body temperature above normal: *have a temperature.*

**tem·pest** /ˈtempist/ ▸*n.* violent storm or agitation. —**tem·pes·tu·ous** *adj.* —**tem·pes·tu·ous·ly** *adv.* —**tem·pes·tu·ous·ness** *n.*

**tem·plate** /ˈtemplit/ ▸*n.* **1** piece of thin board or metal plate used as a pattern in cutting, drilling, etc. **2** *Computing* preset format for a document or file, used so that the format does not have to be recreated each time it is needed.

**tem·ple** /'tempəl/ ▸ *n.* **1** building for the worship of a god or gods. **2** flat part of either side of the head between the forehead and the ear.

**tem·po** /'tempō/ ▸ *n.* (*pl.* **-pos** or **-pi**) speed at which music is or should be played.

**tem·po·ral** /'temp(ə)rəl/ ▸ *adj.* **1** worldly as opposed to spiritual; secular. **2** of time. **3** of the temples of the head: *temporal artery.*

**tem·po·rar·y** /'tempə,rerē/ ▸ *adj.* lasting or meant to last only for a limited time. **—tem·po·rar·i·ly** *adv.*

**tem·po·rize** /'tempə,rīz/ ▸ *v.* avoid committing oneself so as to gain time. **—tem·po·ri·za·tion** *n.*

**tempt** /tem(p)t/ ▸ *v.* **1** entice or incite (a person) to do a wrong or forbidden thing. **2** risk provoking (fate, etc.). **—temp·ta·tion** *n.*

**tem·pu·ra** /tem'pŏŏrə/ ▸ *n.* Japanese dish of fish, shellfish, or vegetables, dipped in batter and deep-fried.

**ten** /ten/ ▸ *n.* **1** one more than nine. **2** symbol for this (10, x, X). **3** ten-dollar bill. **—ten·fold** *adj.*

**ten·a·ble** /'tenəbəl/ ▸ *adj.* maintainable or defensible against attack or objection: *tenable position.* **—ten·a·bil·i·ty** *n.*

**te·na·cious** /tə'nāsʜəs/ ▸ *adj.* **1** keeping a firm hold. **2** (of memory) retentive. **3** persistent; resolute. **—te·na·cious·ly** *adv.* **—te·na·cious·ness** *n.* **—te·nac·i·ty** *n.*

**ten·an·cy** /'tenənsē/ ▸ *n.* (*pl.* **-cies**) use of land or a building as a tenant.

**ten·ant** /'tenənt/ ▸ *n.* **1** person who rents land or property from a landlord. **2** occupant of a place.

**ten·ant·ry** /'tenəntrē/ ▸ *n.* **1** [treated as *sing.* or *pl.*] tenants of an estate. **2** tenancy.

**tend** /tend/ ▸ *v.* **1** be apt or inclined. **2** be moving; hold a course: *tends to the same conclusion.* **3** take care of; look after.

**ten·den·cy** /'tendənsē/ ▸ *n.* (*pl.* **-cies**) leaning; inclination.

**ten·den·tious** /ten'densʜəs/ ▸ *adj.* (of writing, etc.) calculated to promote a particular cause or viewpoint; having an underlying purpose. —**ten·den·tious·ly** *adv.* —**ten·den·tious·ness** *n.*

**ten·der** /'tendər/ ▶*adj.* (**-er, -est**) **1** easily cut or chewed; not tough. **2** susceptible to pain or grief; sensitive: *tender heart.* **3** loving; affectionate.
▶*v.* offer; present (one's services, payment, resignation, etc.).
▶*n.* offer, esp. in writing, to execute work or supply goods at a fixed price. —**ten·der·ly** *adv.* —**ten·der·ness** *n.*

**ten·der·foot** /'tendər,foŏt/ ▶*n.* newcomer or novice.

**ten·der·loin** /'tendər,loin/ ▶*n.* tender cut of beef or pork loin.

**ten·di·ni·tis** /,tendə'nītis/ ▶*n.* inflammation of a tendon.

**ten·don** /'tendən/ ▶*n.* cord of strong tissue attaching a muscle to a bone, etc.

**ten·dril** /'tendrəl/ ▶*n.* slender leafless shoot by which some climbing plants cling.

**ten·e·brous** /'tenəbrəs/ ▶*adj.* dark; shadowy or obscure.

**ten·e·ment** /'tenəmənt/ ▶*n.* overcrowded or run-down apartment house.

**ten·et** /'tenit/ ▶*n.* doctrine; dogma; principle.

**Tenn.** ▶*abbr.* Tennessee.

**ten·nis** /'tenis/ ▶*n.* game in which two or four players strike a ball with rackets over a net stretched across a court.

**ten·on** /'tenən/ ▶*n.* projecting piece of wood made for insertion into a cavity (esp. a mortise) in another piece.

**ten·or** /'tenər/ ▶*n.* **1 a** male singing voice between baritone and alto or countertenor. **b** singer with this voice. **2** general purport or drift. **3** prevailing course, esp. of a person's life or habits.

**ten·pins** ▶*n.* bowling game using ten pins.

**tense** /tens/ ▶*adj.* **1** stretched tight; strained. **2** causing tenseness: *tense moment.*
▶*v.* make or become tense.
▶*n. Gram.* form taken by a verb to indicate the time (also the continuance or completeness) of the action, etc.: *present tense* | *imperfect tense.* —**tense·ly** *adv.* —**tense·ness** *n.*

**ten·sile** /'tensəl/ ▶*adj.* **1** of tension. **2** capable of being stretched.

**ten·sion** /'tensHən/ ▶*n.* **1** stretching; being stretched; tenseness. **2** mental strain or excitement.

**ten·sive** /ˈtensiv/ ▸*adj.* causing or expressing tension.

**tent** /tent/ ▸*n.* portable shelter or dwelling of canvas, cloth, etc., supported by poles and ground pegs.

**ten·ta·cle** /ˈtentəkəl/ ▸*n.* long, slender, flexible appendage of an (esp. invertebrate) animal, used for feeling, grasping, or moving.

**ten·ta·tive** /ˈtentətiv/ ▸*adj.* **1** provisional; not certain: *tentative suggestion.* **2** hesitant. —**ten·ta·tive·ly** *adv.* —**ten·ta·tive·ness** *n.*

**ten·ter·hook** /ˈtentər,ho͝ok/ ▸(in phrase **on tenterhooks**) in a state of anxiety or uncertainty.

**tenth** /tenTH/ ▸*n.* **1** next after ninth. **2** each of ten equal parts of a thing. ▸*adj.* that is the tenth. —**tenth·ly** *adv.*

**ten·u·ous** /ˈtenyo͞oəs/ ▸*adj.* weak or slight; insubstantial. —**ten·u·ous·ly** *adv.* —**ten·u·ous·ness** *n.*

**ten·ure** /ˈtenyər/ ▸*n.* **1** holding of an office or of land or accommodations, etc. **2** guaranteed permanent employment, esp. as a teacher or professor. —**ten·ured** *adj.*

**te·pee** /ˈtē,pē/ (also **tee·pee**) ▸*n.* conical tent orig. used by Native Americans.

**tep·id** /ˈtepid/ ▸*adj.* **1** slightly warm. **2** unenthusiastic.

**te·qui·la** /təˈkēlə/ ▸*n.* Mexican liquor made from an agave.

**ter·a·tol·o·gy** /ˌterəˈtäləjē/ ▸*n.* **1** scientific study of congenital abnormalities and abnormal formations. **2** mythology relating to fantastic creatures and monsters.

**ter·cen·ten·ni·al** ▸*n.* 300th anniversary or its celebration. —**ter·cen·ten·ar·y** *n.*

**ter·gi·ver·sate** /tərˈjivər,sāt; ˈtərjivər-/ ▸*v.* **1** make conflicting or evasive statements; equivocate. **2** change one's loyalties; be apostate.

**term** /tərm/ ▸*n.* **1** word for a definite concept, esp. specialized. **2** (**terms**) stipulations: *cannot accept your terms.* **3** limited, usu. specified, period: *term of five years.* ▸*v.* call; assign a term to: *the music termed classical.* □ **come to terms with 1** reconcile oneself to (a difficulty, etc.). **2** conclude an agreement with.

**ter·ma·gant** /ˈtərməgənt/ ▸*n.* harsh-tempered or overbearing woman.

**ter·mi·nal** /'tərmənl/ ▸*adj.* **1 a** (of a disease) leading to death. **b** (of a patient) dying. **2** of or forming a limit or terminus. ▸*n.* **1** terminating thing; extremity. **2** terminus for planes, trains, or long-distance buses. **3** point of connection for closing an electric circuit. **4** apparatus for transmission of messages between a user and a computer, communications system, etc. —**ter·mi·nal·ly** *adv.*

**ter·mi·nate** /'tərmə,nāt/ ▸*v.* bring or come to an end. —**ter·mi·na·tion** *n.* —**ter·mi·na·tor** *n.*

**ter·mi·nol·o·gy** /,tərmə'näləjē/ ▸*n.* (*pl.* **-gies**) technical terms of a subject.

**ter·mi·nus** /'tərmənəs/ ▸*n.* (*pl.* **-ni** or **-nus·es**) end of a bus route, pipeline, etc.; end point.

**ter·mite** /'tər,mīt/ ▸*n.* antlike social insect destructive to wood.

**tern** /tərn/ ▸*n.* marine bird like a gull but usu. smaller and with a long forked tail.

**ter·race** /'teris/ ▸*n.* **1** flat area formed on a slope. **2** paved area beside a house.

**ter·ra-cot·ta** /'terə 'kätə/ ▸*n.* **1** unglazed usu. brownish red earthenware. **2** its color.

**ter·ra fir·ma** /'terə 'fərmə/ ▸*n.* dry land; firm ground.

**ter·rain** /tə'rān/ ▸*n.* land with regard to its natural features.

**ter·ra·pin** /'terə,pin/ ▸*n.* N. American edible freshwater turtle.

**ter·rar·i·um** /tə're(ə)rēəm/ ▸*n.* (*pl.* **-i·ums** or **-i·a**) usu. glass enclosure for plants or small land animals.

**ter·res·tri·al** /tə'restrēəl/ ▸*adj.* **1** of or on the earth; earthly. **2** of or living on land.

**ter·ri·ble** /'terəbəl/ ▸*adj.* **1** shockingly bad or serious. **2** *inf.* very unpleasant. —**ter·ri·bly** *adv.*

**ter·ri·er** /'terēər/ ▸*n.* small dog.

**ter·rif·ic** /tə'rifik/ ▸*adj.* **1** huge; intense. **2** *inf.* excellent: *did a terrific job.* —**ter·rif·i·cal·ly** *adv.*

**ter·ri·fy** /'terə,fī/ ▸*v.* (**-fied**) fill with terror. —**ter·ri·fy·ing** *adj.* —**ter·ri·fy·ing·ly** *adv.*

**ter·ri·to·ry** /'terə,tôrē/ ▸*n.* (*pl.* **-ries**) **1** extent of land under a ruler, nation, city, etc. **2** sphere of action or thought; province. —**ter·ri·to·ri·al** *adj.*

**ter·ror** /'terər/ ▸*n.* **1** extreme fear. **2** use of organized intimidation.

**ter·ror·ism** ▶*n.* use of violence and intimidation for political purposes. —**ter·ror·ist** *n.*

**ter·ror·ize** ▶*v.* fill with terror.

**ter·ry** /ˈterē/ (also **ter·ry cloth**) ▶*n.* (*pl.* **-ries**) pile fabric with the loops uncut, used esp. for towels.

**terse** /tərs/ ▶*adj.* (**ters·er, ters·est**) brief; concise; curt. —**terse·ly** *adv.* —**terse·ness** *n.*

**ter·ti·ar·y** /ˈtərSHē,erē/ ▶*adj.* third in order, rank, etc.

**ter·ti·um quid** /ˈtərSHēəm ˈkwid; ˈtərtēəm/ ▶*n.* third thing that is indefinite and undefined but is related to two definite or known things.

**tes·sel·late** (also **tes·se·late**) ▶*v.* decorate (a floor) with mosaics.

**test** /test/ ▶*n.* **1** critical examination or trial of a person's or thing's qualities. **2** means of so examining. **3** oral or written examination. ▶*v.* subject to a test.

**Test.** ▶*abbr.* Testament.

**tes·ta·ment** /ˈtestəmənt/ ▶*n.* **1** will, esp. as: *last will and testament.* **2** evidence; proof: *testament to his loyalty.* **3 a** (**Testament**) division of the Christian Bible (see **OLD TESTAMENT, NEW TESTAMENT**).

**tes·tate** /ˈtes,tāt/ ▶*adj.* having left a valid will at death.

**tes·ti·cle** /ˈtestikəl/ (also **tes·tis**) ▶*n.* male organ that produces spermatozoa, etc., esp. one of a pair in the scrotum of a man and most mammals. —**tes·tic·u·lar** *adj.*

**tes·ti·fy** /ˈtestə,fī/ ▶*v.* (**-fied**) **1** (of a person or thing) bear witness: *testified to the facts.* **2** give evidence.

**tes·ti·mo·ni·al** /ˌtestəˈmōnēəl/ ▶*n.* statement of character, conduct, or qualifications.

**tes·ti·mo·ny** ▶*n.* (*pl.* **-nies**) **1** witness's statement under oath. **2** declaration or statement of fact.

**tes·tos·ter·one** /tesˈtästə,rōn/ ▶*n.* sex hormone formed in the testicles.

**test tube** ▶*n.* thin glass tube closed at one end, used for chemical tests, etc.

**tes·ty** ▶*adj.* (**-ti·er, -ti·est**) irritable; touchy. —**tes·ti·ly** *adv.* —**tes·ti·ness** *n.*

**tet·a·nus** /ˈtetn-əs/ ▶*n.* bacterial disease causing painful spasm of the voluntary muscles.

**tête-à-tête** /ˈtāt ə ˈtāt/ ▶*n.* private conversation between two persons.

▶*adv.* together in private: *dined tête-à-tête.*

**teth·er** /ˈteTHər/ ▶*n.* rope, etc., confining an animal.

▶*v.* tie (an animal) with a tether.

☐ **at the end of one's tether** having reached the limit of one's patience, resources, abilities, etc.

**tetra-** ▶*comb. form* four.

**tet·ra·gram** /ˈtetrəˌgram/ ▶*n.* word consisting of four letters or characters.

**tet·ra·he·dron** /ˌtetrəˈhēdrən/ ▶*n.* (*pl.* **-he·dra** or **-he·drons**) four-sided solid; triangular pyramid. —**tet·ra·he·dral** *adj.*

**Tex.** ▶*abbr.* Texas.

**text** /tekst/ ▶*n.* **1** main body of a book as distinct from notes, etc. **2** original words of an author or document. **3** passage from Scripture, esp. as the subject of a sermon. —**tex·tu·al** *adj.*

**text·book** /ˈteks(t)ˌbŏŏk/ ▶*n.* book for use in studying, esp. a standard account of a subject.

**tex·tile** /ˈteksˌtīl/ ▶*n.* any woven material or cloth.

▶*adj.* of weaving or cloth: *textile industry.*

**tex·tu·al·i·ty** /ˌteksCHŏŏˈalitē/ ▶*n.* **1** quality or use of language characteristic of written works as opposed to spoken usage.

**2** strict adherence to a text; textualism.

**tex·ture** /ˈteksCHər/ ▶*n.* **1** feel or appearance of a surface or substance. **2** quality or style of music, writing, etc., resulting from composition. —**tex·tur·al** *adj.*

**thal·a·mus** /ˈTHaləməs/ ▶*n.* (*pl.* **-mi**) *Anat.* either of two masses in the forebrain, serving as relay stations for sensory information.

**tha·lid·o·mide** /THəˈlidəˌmīd/ ▶*n.* sedative drug found to cause fetal malformation when taken early in pregnancy.

**thal·li·um** /ˈTHalēəm/ ▶*n. Chem.* rare soft white metallic element. (Symb.: **Tl**)

**than** /THan/ ▶*conj.* **1** introducing a comparison: *you are older than he.* **2** introducing an element of difference: *anyone other than me.*

**than·a·tol·o·gy** /ˌTHanəˈtäləjē/ ▶*n.* scientific study of death and the practices associated with it, including the study of the needs of the terminally ill and their families.

**thank** /THangk/ ▶*v.* **1** express gratitude to. **2** hold responsible: *you can thank yourself for that.*

▶*pl. n.* (**thanks**) **1** expression or

feeling of gratitude: *give thanks.* **2** thank you. —**thank·ful** *adj.*

**thank·less** ▸*adj.* (of a task, etc.) unpleasant and unlikely to inspire the appreciation of others.

**thanks·giv·ing** ▸*n.* **1** expression of gratitude, esp. to God. **2** (**Thanksgiving**) national holiday for giving thanks, celebrated on the fourth Thursday in November in the U.S.

**that** /THat/ ▸*pron.* (*pl.* **those**) **1** person or thing indicated, named, or understood: *who is that in the yard?* **2** (contrasted with *this*) the further or less immediate or obvious, etc., of two: *this is much heavier than that.* **3** action, behavior, or circumstances just observed or mentioned: *don't do that again.* **4** the one, the person, etc., specified in some way: *those who have cars.* **5** (*pl.* **that**) used instead of *which* or *whom* to introduce a defining clause: *there is nothing here that matters.*

▸*adj.* (*pl.* **those**) **1** designating the person or thing indicated, named, understood, etc.: *look at that dog.* **2** contrasted with *this*: *this is heavier than that one.*

▸*adv.* **1** to such a degree; so: *have done that much.* **2** *inf.* very: *not that good.* **3** at which, on which, etc.: *the day that I first met her.*

▸*conj.* introducing a subordinate clause indicating: **1** statement or hypothesis: *they say that he is better.* **2** purpose: *we live that we may eat.* **3** result: *am so sleepy that I cannot think.*

**thatch** /THaCH/ ▸*n.* roofing material of straw, reeds, palm leaves, or similar material.

▸*v.* cover with thatch.

**thau·ma·turge** /ˈTHômə,tərj/ ▸*n.* worker of wonders and performer of miracles; a magician.

**thaw** /THô/ ▸*v.* **1** (of a frozen thing) pass or cause to pass into a liquid or unfrozen state. **2** become warm enough to melt ice, etc.

▸*n.* **1** thawing. **2** warmth of weather that thaws.

**the** /THə; THē/ ▸*adj.* [called the *definite article*] **1** denoting one or more persons or things already mentioned, under discussion, implied, or familiar: *gave the man a wave.* **2** describing as unique: *the president.* **3** best known: *no relation to the Hemingway.* **4** indicating a following defining

clause or phrase: *the best I can do.*
**5** speaking generically: *plays the harp well.*
▸*adv.* in or by that (or such a) degree: *the more the merrier.*

**the·an·throp·ic** /ˌTHēən-ˈTHräpik/ ▸*adj.* embodying deity in a human form; both divine and human.

**the·ar·chy** /ˈTHēˌärkē/ ▸*n.* (*pl.* **-chies**) rule by a god or gods.

**the·a·ter** /ˈTHēətər/ (esp. Brit. **the·a·tre**) ▸*n.* **1** building or outdoor area for dramatic performances, showing movies, etc. **2** writing and production of plays. **3** scene or field of action: *theater of war.* —**the·at·ri·cal** *adj.* —**the·at·ri·cal·ly** *adv.*

**thee** /THē/ ▸*pron.* objective case of **THOU**.

**theft** /THeft/ ▸*n.* act of stealing.

**their** /THe(ə)r/ ▸*poss. pron.* of or belonging to them.

**theirs** ▸*poss. pron.* the one or ones belonging to them.

**the·ism** /ˈTHēˌizəm/ ▸*n.* belief in gods or a god. —**the·ist** *n.* —**the·is·tic** *adj.*

**them** /THem/ ▸*pron.* **1** *objective case* of **THEY**: *I saw them.* **2** *inf.* they: *it's them again.*

**theme** /THēm/ ▸*n.* **1** subject, topic, or recurrent focus. **2** *Mus.*

prominent melody in a composition. **3** school exercise, esp. an essay, on a given subject. —**the·mat·ic** *adj.* —**the·mat·i·cal·ly** *adv.*

**them·selves** ▸*pron.*
**1 a** emphaic form of **THEY** or **THEM**. **b** reflexive form of **THEM**.
**2** in their normal state of body or mind: *are quite themselves again.*

**then** /THen/ ▸*adv.* **1** at that time. **2 a** next; after that. **b** and also. **3** in that case: *then you should have said so.*
▸*adj.* such at the time in question: *the then senator.*
▸*n.* that time: *until then.*
□ **then and there** immediately and on the spot.

**thence** /THens/ ▸*adv.* **1** from that place. **2** for that reason.

**thence·forth** ▸*adv.* from that time onward.

**the·og·o·ny** /THēˈägənē/ ▸*n.* (*pl.* **-nies**) genealogy of a group or system of gods.

**the·ol·o·gy** /THēˈäləjē/ ▸*n.* (*pl.* **-gies**) study of God; system of religious beliefs. —**the·o·log·i·cal** *adj.* —**the·o·log·i·cal·ly** *adv.* —**the·o·lo·gian** *n.*

**the·o·rem** /ˈTHi(ə)rəm/ ▸*n. chiefly Math.* **1** general proposition not self-evident but proved by reasoning. **2** rule in algebra, etc., esp. one expressed by symbols or formulae.

**the·o·ret·i·cal** /ˌTHēə'retikəl/ ▸*adj.* **1** concerned with the theory of a subject rather than its practical application. **2** based on theory rather than experience. —**the·o·ret·i·cal·ly** *adv.*

**the·o·ry** /'THi(ə)rē/ ▸*n.* (*pl.* **-ries**) **1** supposition or system of ideas explaining something, esp. one based on general principles. **2** set of principles on which the practice of an activity is based. **3** idea used to account for a situation or justify a course of action.

**ther·a·peu·tics** /ˌTHerə-'pyo͞otiks/ ▸*pl. n.* [treated as *sing.*] branch of medicine concerned with the treatment of disease and the action of remedial agents.

**ther·a·py** /'THerəpē/ ▸*n.* (*pl.* **-pies**) nonsurgical treatment of physical or mental disorders. —**ther·a·peu·tic** *adj.* —**ther·a·pist** *n.*

**there** /ˌT͟He(ə)r/ ▸*adv.* **1** in, at, or to that place or position: *lived there for years.* **2** at that point (in speech, performance, writing, etc.). **3** in that respect: *I agree with you there.* **4** used to indicate the fact or existence of something: *there is a house on the corner.*
▸*n.* that place: *lives near there.*
▸*interj.* expressing confirmation, triumph, dismay, etc.: *there! what did I tell you?*

**there·by** ▸*adv.* by that means.

**there·fore** ▸*adv.* for that reason; consequently.

**there·in** ▸*adv. formal* in that place.

**there·of** ▸*adv.* of that or it.

**there·on** ▸*adv. formal* following from the thing just mentioned.

**there·up·on** ▸*adv.* immediately after that.

**ther·mal** /'THərməl/ ▸*adj.* **1** of, for, or producing heat. **2** promoting the retention of heat: *thermal underwear.* —**ther·mal·ly** *adv.*

**ther·mo·dy·nam·ics** /ˌTHərmōdī'namiks/ ▸*n.* science of the relations between heat and other forms of energy. —**ther·mo·dy·nam·ic** *adj.* —**ther·mo·dy·nam·i·cal·ly** *adv.*

**ther·mom·e·ter** /THər'mämitər/ ▸*n.* instrument for measuring temperature.

**ther·mo·nu·cle·ar** ▸*adj.* relating to nuclear reactions that occur only at very high temperatures.

**Ther·mos** /'THərməs/ ▸*trademark* bottle, etc., with a double wall enclosing a vacuum, used to keep liquids hot or cold.

**ther·mo·sphere** ▸*n.* region of the atmosphere in which temperature increases with height.

**ther·mo·stat** /-ˌstat/ ▸*n.* device that automatically regulates or responds to temperature. —**ther·mo·stat·ic** *adj.*

**the·sau·rus** /THə'sôrəs/ ▸*n.* (*pl.* **-ri** or **-rus·es**) book that categorizes or lists synonyms and related concepts.

**these** /THēz/ ▸pl. of **THIS**.

**the·sis** /'THēsis/ ▸*n.* (*pl.* **-ses**) **1** proposition to be maintained or proved. **2** dissertation, esp. by a candidate for a doctoral degree.

**thes·pi·an** /'THespēən/ ▸*adj.* of drama. ▸*n.* actor or actress.

**they** /THā/ ▸*pron.* (*obj.* **them**; *poss.* **their, theirs**) **1** pl. of **HE, SHE, IT. 2** people in general: *they say we are wrong.* **3** those in authority: *they have raised the fees.*

**thi·a·mine** /'THīəmin/ (also **thi·a·min**) ▸*n.* vitamin of the B complex, found in unrefined cereals, beans, and liver, a deficiency of which causes beriberi. (Also called **vitamin B1**).

**thick** /THik/ ▸*adj.* **1 a** of great or specified extent between opposite surfaces: *thick wall.* **b** of large diameter. **2** (of a line, etc.) broad; not fine. **3** arranged closely; crowded together; dense. **4** densely covered or filled: *air thick with snow.* **5** *inf.* stupid; dull. ▸*n.* **1** thick part of anything. **2** (**the thick**) busiest or most intense part. —**thick·en** *v.* —**thick·ly** *adv.* —**thick·ness** *n.*

**thick·et** /'THikit/ ▸*n.* tangle of shrubs or trees.

**thick·set** ▸*adj.* **1** heavily or solidly built. **2** set or growing close together.

**thief** /THēf/ ▸*n.* (*pl.* **thieves**) person who steals, esp. secretly.

**thigh** /THī/ ▸*n.* part of the leg between the hip and the knee.

**thim·ble** /'THimbəl/ ▸*n.* metal or plastic cap worn to protect the finger and push the needle in sewing.

**thin** /THin/ ▸*adj.* (**thin·ner, thin·nest**) **1** having opposite surfaces close together; of small thickness. **2** (of a line, etc.) narrow or fine. **3** lean; not plump. **4** not dense or copious: *thin hair.* **5** weak. **6** flimsy or transparent.

▶*v.* (**thinned, thin·ning**) make or become thin or thinner. —**thin·ly** *adv.* —**thin·ness** *n.*

**thing** /THiNG/ ▶*n.* **1** entity, idea, action, etc., that is or may be thought about or perceived. **2** inanimate material object. **3** unspecified item: *a few things to buy.* **4** act, idea, or utterance: *silly thing to do.* **5** *inf.* fashion: *latest thing in footwear.* **6** (**things**) personal belongings or clothing: *where are my things?* **7** (**things**) affairs in general: *not in the nature of things.* **8** (**things**) circumstances; conditions: *things look good.*

**think** /THiNGk/ ▶*v.* (*past* and *past part.* **thought**) **1** be of the opinion. **2** judge or consider: *is thought to be a fraud.* **3** exercise the mind: *let me think.* **4** (**think about**) consider; imagine. —**think·er** *n.*

**think tank** ▶*n.* body of experts providing advice and ideas on specific national or commercial problems.

**thin·ner** ▶*n.* solvent used to make paints, etc., less viscous.

**third** /THərd/ ▶*n.* **1** next after the second. **2** each of three equal parts of a thing.

▶*adj.* that is the third. —**third·ly** *adv.*

□ **third-class** lower quality; inferior. □ **Third World** developing countries of Asia, Africa, and Latin America.

**thirst** /THərst/ ▶*n.* **1** need to drink liquid; feeling of discomfort caused by this. **2** strong desire; craving: *thirst for power.*

▶*v.* **1** feel thirst. **2** have a strong desire. —**thirst·y** *adj.* —**thirst·i·ly** *adv.* —**thirst·i·ness** *n.*

**thir·teen** /ˌTHərˈtēn/ ▶*n.* **1** one more than twelve, or three more than ten. **2** symbol for this (13, xiii, XIII).

▶*adj.* that amount to thirteen. —**thir·teenth** *adj. & n.*

**thir·ty** /ˈTHərtē/ ▶*n.* (*pl.* **-ties**) **1** product of three and ten. **2** symbol for this (30, xxx, XXX). **3** (**thirties**) numbers from 30 to 39, esp. the years of a century or of a person's life. —**thir·ti·eth** *adj. & n.*

**this** /THis/ ▶*pron.* (*pl.* **these**) **1** person or thing close at hand or indicated or already named or understood: *this is my cousin.* **2** (contrasted with *that*) person or thing nearer to hand or more immediately in mind.

▶*adj.* (*pl.* **these**) **1** designating the person or thing close at hand, etc. **2** (of time): the present or current: *am busy all this week.*

▶*adv.* to this degree or extent: *knew him when he was this high.*

□ **this and that** *inf.* various unspecified things.

**this·tle** /ˈTHisəl/ ▶*n.* prickly plant, usu. with globular heads of purple flowers.

**thith·er** /ˈTHiTHər/ ▶*adv. archaic* to or toward that place.

**thong** /THÔNG/ ▶*n.* narrow strip of hide or leather.

**tho·rax** /ˈTHôraks/ ▶*n.* (*pl.* **tho·rax·es** or **tho·ra·ces** /ˈTHôrəsēz/) *Anat. & Zool.* part of the trunk between the neck and the abdomen. **—tho·rac·ic** /THə-ˈrasik/ *adj.*

**thorn** /thôrn/ ▶*n.* **1** sharp-pointed projection on a plant. **2** thorn-bearing shrub or tree. **—thorn·y** *adj.*

□ **thorn in one's side** (or **flesh**) constant annoyance.

**thor·ough** /ˈTHərō/ ▶*adj.* **1** complete and unqualified; not superficial. **2** acting or done with great care and completeness. **—thor·ough·ly** *adv.* **—thor·ough·ness** *n.*

**thor·ough·bred** ▶*adj.* of pure breeding.

▶*n.* thoroughbred animal, esp. a horse.

**thor·ough·fare** ▶*n.* road or path open at both ends, esp. for traffic.

**thor·ough·go·ing** ▶*adj.* complete; uncompromising; not superficial.

**those** /THōz/ ▶pl. of **THAT**.

**thou** /THou/ ▶*pron.* (*obj.* **thee**; *poss.* **thy** or **thine**; *pl.* **ye** or **you**) *archaic* second person singular pronoun.

**though** /THō/ ▶*conj.* **1** in spite of being; despite the fact that. **2** even if: *ask him, though he may refuse.* **3** and yet; nevertheless.

▶*adv. inf.* however; all the same: *I wish you had told me, though.*

**thought** /THôt/ ▶past and past part. of **THINK**.

▶*n.* **1** process or power of thinking; the faculty of reason. **2** way of thinking associated with a particular time, people, etc.: *medieval European thought.* **3** reflection; consideration; regard. **4** idea or piece of reasoning produced by thinking.

**5** (**thoughts**) what one is thinking; one's opinion.

**thought·ful** ▸*adj.* **1** engaged in or given to meditation. **2** (of a book, writer, remark, etc.) giving signs of serious thought. **3** considerate. —**thought·ful·ly** *adv.* —**thought·ful·ness** *n.*

**thought·less** ▸*adj.* **1** careless of consequences or of others' feelings. **2** due to lack of thought. —**thought·less·ly** *adv.* —**thought·less·ness** *n.*

**thou·sand** /ˈTHouzənd/ ▸*n.* (*pl.* **-sands** or same) **1** product of a hundred and ten. **2** symbol for this (1,000; m; M). **3** *inf.* large number.
▸*adj.* that amount to a thousand. —**thou·sand·fold** *adj. & adv.* —**thou·sandth** *adj. & n.*

**thrall** /THrôl/ ▸*n.* bondage; slavery: *in thrall.*

**thrash** /THraSH/ ▸*v.* **1** beat or whip severely. **2** (**thrash about/around**) move or fling the limbs about violently or in panic. —**thrash·ing** *n.*

**thread** /THred/ ▸*n.* **1** spun cotton, silk, glass, etc.; yarn. **2** thin cord of twisted yarns used esp. in sewing and weaving. **3** continuous aspect of a thing:

*the thread of life.* **4** spiral ridge of a screw.
▸*v.* **1** pass a thread through (a needle). **2** put on a thread. **3** insert (a strip of film, tape, etc.) into equipment. **4** make (one's way) carefully through a crowded place, etc.

**thread·bare** ▸*adj.* **1** thin and tattered. **2** shabbily dressed.

**threat** /THret/ ▸*n.* **1** declaration of an intention to punish or hurt. **2** imminence of something undesirable: *threat of war.* **3** person or thing as a likely cause of harm, etc. —**threat·en** *v.*

**three** /THrē/ ▸*n.* **a** one more than two, or seven less than ten. **b** symbol for this (3, iii, III).
▸*adj.* that amount to three.
□ **three-dimensional** having or appearing to have length, breadth, and depth.

**three·fold** ▸*adj. & adv.* **1** three times as much or as many. **2** consisting of three parts.

**thren·o·dy** /ˈTHrenədē/ ▸*n.* (*pl.* **-dies**) lament.

**thresh** /THreSH/ ▸*v.* beat out or separate grain from (wheat, etc.). —**thresh·er** *n.*

**thresh·old** /ˈTHreSH,(h)ōld/ ▸*n.* **1** strip of wood or stone forming the bottom of a doorway. **2** point of entry or beginning: *threshold of a new century.* **3** limit: *pain threshold.*

**thrice** /THrīs/ ▶*adv. chiefly formal, poet.* three times.

**thrift** /THrift/ ▶*n.* economical management of resources; frugality. —**thrift·i·ly** *adv.* —**thrift·i·ness** *n.* —**thrift·y** *adj.*
□ **thrift shop** store selling secondhand items.

**thrill** /THril/ ▶*n.* **1** wave or nervous tremor of emotion or sensation: *thrill of joy.* **2** thrilling experience.
▶*v.* feel or cause to feel a thrill. —**thrill·ing** *adj.* —**thrill·ing·ly** *adv.*

**thrill·er** ▶*n.* exciting or sensational story or play.

**thrive** /THrīv/ ▶*v.* (*past* **throve** or **thrived**; *past part.* **thriv·en** or **thrived**) **1** prosper; flourish. **2** grow vigorously.

**throat** /THrōt/ ▶*n.* **1** windpipe or gullet. **2** front part of the neck.

**throat·y** ▶*adj.* (**-i·er, -i·est**) (of a voice) hoarsely resonant. —**throat·i·ly** *adv.* —**throat·i·ness** *n.*

**throb** /THräb/ ▶*v.* (**throbbed, throb·bing**) **1** pulsate, esp. forcefully or rapidly. **2** vibrate

with a persistent rhythm or with emotion or pain.
▶*n.* throbbing.

**throes** ▶*pl. n.* violent pang, esp. of childbirth or death.
□ **in the throes of** struggling with the task of.

**throm·bo·sis** /THräm'bōsis/ ▶*n.* (*pl.* **-ses**) coagulation of the blood in a blood vessel or organ.

**throne** /THrōn/ ▶*n.* ceremonial seat for a sovereign, bishop, etc.

**throng** /THrôNG/ ▶*n.* crowd, esp. of people.
▶*v.* **1** come in great numbers. **2** flock into or crowd around.

**throt·tle** /'THrätl/ ▶*n.* device controlling flow of fuel, steam, etc., in an engine.
▶*v.* choke; strangle.

**through** /THro͞o/ ▶*prep.* **1** from end to end or from side to side of. **2** between or among. **3** from beginning to end of: *read through the letter.* **4** because of: *lost it through carelessness.* **5** up to and including: *Monday through Friday.*
▶*adv.* through a thing; from side to side, end to end, or beginning to end.
▶*adj.* (of traffic) going through a place to its destination.

**through·out** ▸*prep. & adv.* right through; from beginning to end.

**throw** /THrō/ ▸*v.* (*past* **threw**; *past part.* **thrown**) **1** propel with force through the air. **2** force violently into a specified position or state. **3** cause to be in a specified state: *thrown out of work.* **4** operate (a switch or lever). **5** *inf.* lose (a contest or race, etc.) intentionally.
▸*n.* **1** act of throwing or being thrown. **2** distance a thing is or may be thrown. **3** light cover or blanket.
□ **throw away 1** discard as useless or unwanted. **2** waste or fail to make use of. □ **throw out 1** put out forcibly or suddenly. **2** discard as unwanted. □ **throw up** *inf.* vomit.

**throw·a·way** /'THrōə,wā/ ▸*adj.* meant to be thrown away after (one) use.
▸*n.* thing to be thrown away after (one) use.

**throw·back** /'THrō,bak/ ▸*n.* reversion to an earlier type.

**thru** /THrōō/ ▸var. of **THROUGH**.

**thrush** /THrəSH/ ▸*n.* **1** any of various songbirds. **2** fungal disease, esp. one marked by whitish vesicles in the mouth and throat.

**thrust** /THrəst/ ▸*v.* (*past* and *past part.* **thrust**) **1** push with a sudden impulse or with force. **2** (**thrust on/upon**) impose (a thing) forcibly. **3** stab; lunge suddenly.
▸*n.* **1** thrusting movement or force. **2** chief theme or gist of remarks, etc.

**thru·way** /'THrōō,wā/ ▸*n.* highway.

**thud** /THəd/ ▸*n.* low dull sound.
▸*v.* (**thud·ded**, **thud·ding**) make or fall with a thud. —**thud·ding·ly** *adv.*

**thug** /THəg/ ▸*n.* vicious ruffian. —**thug·ger·y** *n.* —**thug·gish** *adj.*

**thumb** /THəm/ ▸*n.* short thick finger on the human hand, set apart from the other four.
▸*v.* **1** manipulate with or as with a thumb. **2** request or obtain (a ride) by signaling with a raised thumb.

**thumb·nail** ▸*n.* **1** nail of a thumb. **2** *Computing* small picture of an image.
▸*adj.* brief and concise.

**thumb·tack** ▸*n.* tack with a flat head, pressed in with the thumb.

**thump** /THəmp/ ▸*v.* beat or strike heavily, esp. with the fist.
▸*n.* heavy blow.

**thun·der** /ˈTHəndər/ ▶n. **1** loud noise heard after a lightning flash. **2** resounding, loud, deep noise.

▶v. **1** produce sounds of or like thunder. **2** utter loudly.

**thun·der·bolt** ▶n. **1** flash of lightning with a simultaneous crash of thunder. **2** unexpected occurrence or item of news.

**thun·der·clap** ▶n. crash of thunder.

**thun·der·cloud** ▶n. cumulus cloud charged with electricity and producing thunder and lightning.

**thun·der·head** ▶n. rounded cumulus cloud projecting upward and heralding a thunderstorm.

**thun·der·storm** ▶n. storm accompanied by thunder and lightning.

**thun·der·struck** ▶adj. amazed; surprised.

**thu·ri·ble** /ˈTHo͝orəbəl/ ▶n. censer.

**thu·ri·fer** /ˈTHo͝orəfər/ ▶n. acolyte carrying a censer.

**Thurs.** ▶abbr. Thursday.

**Thurs·day** /ˈTHərzdā/ ▶n. fifth day of the week, following Wednesday.

**thus** /THəs/ ▶adv. **1** in this way. **2** as a result or inference. **3** to this extent; so.

**thwack** /THwak/ ▶v. strike with a sharp blow.

▶n. sharp blow.

**thwart** /THwôrt/ ▶v. frustrate or foil.

**thy** /THī/ (also **thine** before a vowel) ▶pron. archaic of or belonging to thee.

**thyme** /tīm/ ▶n. any of several aromatic herbs used for flavoring.

**thy·mus** /ˈTHīməs/ ▶n. (pl. **-mus·es** or **-mi**) lymphoid organ situated in the neck of vertebrates.

**thy·roid** /ˈTHī,roid/ ▶n. (also **thyroid gland**) large ductless gland in the neck of vertebrates, secreting a hormone that regulates growth and development.

**thy·self** /THīˈself/ ▶pron. emphatic & reflexive form of **THOU** or **THEE**.

**ti·ar·a** /tēˈärə/ ▶n. jeweled ornamental band worn on the head.

**Ti·bet·an** /təˈbetn/ ▶n. **1 a** native of Tibet. **b** person of Tibetan descent. **2** language of Tibet.

▸*adj.* of or relating to Tibet or its language.

**tib·i·a** /'tibēə/ ▸*n.* (*pl.* **-i·ae**) inner of two bones extending from the knee to the ankle.

**tic** /tik/ ▸*n.* involuntary muscular twitch.

**tick** /tik/ ▸*n.* **1** slight recurring click, esp. that of a watch or clock. **2** parasitic arachnid on the skin of warm-blooded vertebrates.
▸*v.* (of a clock, etc.) make a tick.

**tick·er** ▸*n.* **1** *inf.* heart. **2** machine that receives and prints telegraphed messages onto paper tape.

**tick·et** /'tikit/ ▸*n.* **1** written or printed piece of paper or card entitling the holder to admittance, travel by public transport, etc. **2** notification of a traffic offense, etc. **3** label giving price, etc. **4** list of a political party's candidates.
▸*v.* attach or serve a ticket to.

**tick·ing** ▸*n.* stout material used to cover mattresses, etc.

**tick·le** /'tikəl/ ▸*v.* **1 a** apply light touches or strokes to (a person, etc.) so as to produce laughter and spasmodic movement. **b** feel this sensation: *my foot tickles.* **2** excite agreeably; amuse.

▸*n.* tickling sensation. **—tick·lish** *adj.* **—tick·ly** *adj.*

**tick-tack-toe** (also **tic-tac-toe**) ▸*n.* game of marking Xs or Os in a nine-square grid.

**tid·al wave** /'tīdl/ ▸*n.* exceptionally large ocean wave, as caused by an underwater earthquake, etc.

**tid·bit** /'tid,bit/ ▸*n.* **1** small morsel. **2** choice item of news, etc.

**tid·dly·winks** /'tidlē ,wiNGks/ ▸*n.* game played by flicking counters into a cup, etc.

**tide** /tīd/ ▸*n.* **1** periodic rise and fall of the sea due to the attraction of the moon and sun. **2** marked trend of fortune, events, etc.: *the tide of public opinion.* **—tid·al** *adj.*

**ti·dings** ▸*pl. n.* news; information.

**ti·dy** /'tīdē/ ▸*adj.* (**-di·er, -di·est**) **1** neat; orderly. **2** considerable: *tidy sum.*
▸*v.* (**-died**) put in good order; make tidy. **—ti·di·ly** *adv.* **—ti·di·ness** *n.*

**tie** /tī/ ▸*v.* (**ty·ing**) **1 a** attach or fasten with string, cord, etc. **b** link conceptually. **2** form into a knot or bow. **3** restrict (a person) as to conditions, place, etc.: *tied to his job.* **4** achieve the same score or place as another competitor.

▸*n.* **1** cord, line, etc., used for fastening. **2** strip of material worn around the collar and tied in a knot at the front. **3** bond: *family ties.* **4** equal score among competitors. **5** beam laid horizontally as a support for railroad rails.

□ **tie-in** connection or association. □ **tie-up** temporary stoppage.

**tier** /ti(ə)r/ ▸*n.* vertical or sloped row, rank, or unit of structure. —**tiered** *adj.*

**tiff** /tif/ ▸*n.* slight or petty quarrel.

**ti·ger** /ˈtīgər/ ▸*n.* **1** large, striped Asian feline. **2** fierce, energetic, or formidable person.

**tight** /tīt/ ▸*adj.* **1** closely held, drawn, fastened, stretched, etc. **2** too closely fitting. **3** [usu. in *comb.*] impermeable; impervious to a specified thing: *watertight.* **4** (of money or materials) not easily obtainable.

▸*adv.* tightly: *hold tight!* —**tight·en** *v.* —**tight·ly** *adv.* —**tight·ness** *n.*

□ **tight-fisted** stingy. □ **tight-lipped** secretive; taciturn.

**tight·rope** ▸*n.* rope stretched tightly high above the ground, on which acrobats perform.

**tights** ▸*pl. n.* thin but not sheer, close-fitting wool, nylon, etc., garment covering the legs and lower body.

**tight·wad** /ˈtīt,wäd/ ▸*n. inf.* person who is miserly or stingy.

**til·de** /ˈtildə/ ▸*n.* mark (˜), put over a letter to mark a change in pronunciation.

**tile** /tīl/ ▸*n.* **1** thin slab of baked clay, etc., used for covering roofs, walls, or floors. **2** thin flat piece used in a game.

▸*v.* cover with tiles.

**till** /til/ ▸*prep. & conj.* up to (a specified time or event); until.

▸*n.* drawer for money in a store, bank, etc.

▸*v.* cultivate (land). —**till·a·ble** *adj.*

**till·er** /ˈtilər/ ▸*n.* horizontal bar fitted to a boat's rudder to turn it in steering.

**tilt** /tilt/ ▸*v.* assume or cause to assume a sloping position; heel over.

▸*n.* **1** tilting. **2** sloping position. **3** inclination or bias.

□ **at full tilt** at full speed or with full force.

**tim·ber** /ˈtimbər/ ▸*n.* **1** standing trees suitable for lumber. **2** piece of wood or beam, esp. as the rib of a vessel.

**tim·ber·line** ▸*n.* line or level above which no trees grow.

**tim·ber wolf** ▸*n.* large N. American gray wolf.

**tim·bre** /'tambər/ ▸*n.* distinctive character of a musical sound or voice.

**time** /tīm/ ▸*n.* **1** indefinite continued progress of existence, events, etc., in past, present, and future, regarded as a whole. **2** progress of this as affecting persons or things: *stood the test of time.* **3** portion of time; period. **4** point of time, esp. in hours and minutes: *the time is 7:30.* **5** indefinite period: *waited for a time.* **6** particular reckoning of time: *in record time | eight o'clock Eastern time.* **7** occasion: *last time.* **8** expressing multiplication: *five times six is thirty.* **9** any of several rhythmic patterns of music.
▸*v.* **1** choose the time for. **2** do at a chosen or correct time. **3** arrange the time of arrival of. **4** ascertain the time taken by. **5** regulate the duration or interval of. □ **ahead of time** earlier than expected. □ **all the time 1** throughout. **2** constantly. □ **at the same time 1** simultaneously.

**2** nevertheless. □ **for the time being** until some other arrangement is made. □ **in time 1** punctual. **2** eventually. □ **time after time** repeatedly; on many occasions.

**time bomb** ▸*n.* bomb designed to explode at a preset time.

**time cap·sule** ▸*n.* box, etc., containing objects typical of the present time, buried for discovery in the future.

**time clock** ▸*n.* clock with a device for recording workers' hours of work.

**time·keep·er** ▸*n.* person who records time, esp. of workers or in a game.

**time·less** ▸*adj.* not affected by the passage of time; eternal. —**time·less·ly** *adv.* —**time·less·ness** *n.*

**time line** ▸*n.* graphic representation of the passage of time as a line.

**time·ly** /'tīmlē/ ▸*adj.* (**-li·er, -li·est**) opportune; coming at the right time. —**time·li·ness** *n.*

**time·piece** ▸*n.* clock or watch.

**time-serv·er** ▸*n.* **1** person who changes their views to suit the prevailing circumstances or fashion. **2** person who makes very little effort at work because they are waiting to leave or retire.

**time·ta·ble** ▶*n.* schedule, esp. of arrivals and departures of buses, trains, etc.

**time·worn** ▶*adj.* damaged or made less attractive by the passage of time.

**time zone** ▶*n.* range of longitudes where a common standard time is used.

**tim·id** /'timid/ ▶*adj.* easily frightened; apprehensive; shy. —**ti·mid·i·ty** *n.* —**tim·id·ly** *adv.* —**tim·id·ness** *n.*

**tim·ing** ▶*n.* control of an action or process.

**tim·o·rous** /'timərəs/ ▶*adj.* timid; fearful. —**tim·or·ous·ly** *adv.* —**tim·or·ous·ness** *n.*

**tim·pa·ni** /'timpənē/ ▶*pl. n.* set of kettledrums. —**tim·pa·nist** *n.*

**tin** /tin/ ▶*n.* silvery white metallic element used esp. in alloys and to form tin plate. (Symb.: **Sn**)

▶*v.* (**tinned, tin·ning**) cover or coat with tin.

**tinc·ture** /'tiNG(k)CHər/ ▶*n.* medicinal solution (of a drug) in alcohol: *tincture of quinine.*

**tin·der** /'tindər/ ▶*n.* dry substance that readily catches fire from a spark.

**tin·der·box** ▶*n.* **1** box for tinder. **2** explosive situation.

**tine** /'tīn/ ▶*n.* prong, tooth, or point of a fork, comb, antler, etc. —**tined** *adj.*

**tinge** /tinj/ ▶*v.* (**tinge·ing** or **ting·ing**) **1** color slightly. **2** affect slightly.

▶*n.* slight color or trace.

**tin·gle** /'tiNGgəl/ ▶*v.* feel or cause to feel a slight prickling, stinging, or throbbing sensation.

▶*n.* tingling sensation. —**tin·gly** *adj.*

**tin·ker** /'tiNGkər/ ▶*n.* mender of kettles, pans, etc.

▶*v.* (**tinker at/with**) work or repair in an amateurish or desultory way. —**tin·ker·er** *n.*

**tin·kle** /'tiNGkəl/ ▶*v.* make or cause to make a succession of short, light, ringing sounds.

▶*n.* tinkling sound.

**tin·sel** /'tinsəl/ ▶*n.* **1** glittering metallic strips, threads, etc., used as decoration. **2** superficial brilliance or splendor.

**tint** /tint/ ▶*n.* **1** light or delicate variety of a color. **2** hair dye.

▶*v.* apply a tint to; color.

**tin·tin·nab·u·la·tion** /ˌtintə-ˌnabyəˈlāsHən/ ▶*n.* ringing or tinkling of bells.

**ti·ny** /'tīnē/ ▸*adj.* (-ni·er, -ni·est) very small or slight.

**-tion** ▸*suffix* forming nouns of action, condition, etc.

**tip** /tip/ ▸*n.* **1** extremity or end, esp. of a small or tapering thing. **2** slight push or tilt. **3** small gift of money for a service given. **4** small or casual piece of advice.
▸*v.* (**tipped, tip·ping**) **1** provide with a tip. **2** (cause to) lean or slant. **3** make a small present of money to, esp. for a service given.

**tip·ple** /'tipəl/ ▸*v.* drink intoxicating liquor habitually. —**tip·pler** *n.*

**tip·sy** ▸*adj.* (-si·er, -si·est) slightly intoxicated. —**tip·si·ness** *n.*

**tip·toe** ▸*v.* (-toed, -toe·ing) walk quietly or stealthily on the balls of ones feet.

**tip-top** *inf.* ▸*adj. & adv.* highest in excellence.
▸*n.* highest point.

**ti·rade** /'tī,rād/ ▸*n.* long vehement denunciation or declamation.

**tire** /tī(ə)r/ ▸*v.* make or grow weary or bored.
▸*n.* rubber covering, usu. inflatable, that fits around a wheel rim. —**tire·less** *adj.*
—**tire·less·ly** *adv.*

**tired** /tī(ə)rd/ ▸*adj.* **1** weary; ready for sleep. **2** (**tired of**) bored with. —**tired·ness** *n.*

**tire·some** ▸*adj.* annoying or tedious.

**tis·sue** /'tisHŌŌ/ ▸*n.* **1** any coherent mass of specialized cells of which animals or plants are made. **2** disposable piece of thin, soft, absorbent paper for wiping, drying, etc. **3** fine, gauzy fabric.

**ti·tan** /'tītn/ ▸*n.* person of very great strength, intellect, or importance.

**ti·ta·ni·um** /tī'tānēəm/ ▸*n.* gray metallic element. (Symb.: **Ti**)

**tithe** /tīTH/ ▸*n.* one tenth of the annual product of land or labor, formerly taken as a church tax.
▸*v.* pay tithes.

**ti·tian** /'tisHən/ ▸*adj.* (of hair) bright, golden auburn.

**tit·il·late** /'titl,āt/ ▸*v.* **1** excite pleasantly. **2** tickle. —**tit·il·la·tion** *n.*

**ti·tle** /'tītl/ ▸*n.* **1** name of a book, work of art, etc. **2** caption or credit in a movie, broadcast, etc. **3** nomenclature indicating a person's status (e.g., *professor, queen*) or used as a form of address (e.g., *Mr.*). **4** championship. **5** *Law* right to ownership of property with or without possession.

▶*v.* give a title to.

**tit·mouse** /ˈtitˌmous/ ▶*n.* (*pl.* -**mice**) any of various small birds.

**tit·ter** /ˈtitər/ ▶*v.* laugh furtively; giggle.

▶*n.* furtive laugh.

**tit·tle** /ˈtitl/ ▶*n.* small thing.

**tit·u·ba·tion** /ˌtiCHəˈbāSHən/ ▶*n.* nodding movement of the head or body, esp. as caused by a nervous disorder.

**tit·u·lar** /ˈtiCHələr/ ▶*adj.* **1** of or relating to a title. **2** in name or title only: *titular ruler.*

**tiz·zy** /ˈtizē/ ▶*n.* (*pl.* -**zies**) state of nervous agitation: *in a tizzy.*

**tme·sis** /təˈmēsis/ ▶*n.* (*pl.* -**ses** /-sēz/) separation of parts of a compound word by an intervening word or words, heard mainly in informal speech (e.g., *shove it back any-old-where in the pile*).

**TN** ▶*abbr.* Tennessee (in official postal use).

**TNT** ▶*abbr.* trinitrotoluene, a high explosive.

**to** /to͞o/ ▶*prep.* **1** introducing a noun expressing: **a** what is reached, approached, or touched: *fell to the ground.* **b** as far as: *went on to the end.* **c** what

is followed: *made to order.*
**d** what is considered or affected: *am used to that.* **e** what is caused or produced: *turn to stone.* **f** what is compared: *won by three to two.*
**2** introducing the infinitive: **a** as a verbal noun: *to get there.*
**b** expressing purpose, consequence, or cause: *we eat to live.* **c** as a substitute for *to* + infinitive: *wanted to come but was unable to.*

▶*adv.* **1** in the normal or required position or condition: *come to* | *heave to.* **2** in a nearly closed position.

☐ **to and fro** backward and forward.

**toad** /tōd/ ▶*n.* **1** froglike amphibian breeding in water but living chiefly on land.
**2** repulsive or detestable person.

**toad·stool** ▶*n.* mushroom-like fungus, usu. poisonous.

**toad·y** ▶*n.* (*pl.* -**ies**) sycophant.

▶*v.* (-**ied**) behave servilely to; fawn upon.

**toast** /tōst/ ▶*n.* **1** sliced bread browned on both sides by radiant heat. **2** words introducing a drink in honor of someone or something.

▶*v.* **1** brown or become browned by radiant heat. **2** warm (one's feet, oneself, etc.) at a fire, etc. **3** drink to the health or in honor of.

**toast·er** ▶*n.* electrical device for making toast.

**to·bac·co** /təˈbakō/ ▶*n.* (*pl.* **-cos**) **1** plant with leaves used for smoking, chewing, or snuff. **2** its leaves, esp. as prepared for smoking.

**to·bog·gan** /təˈbägən/ ▶*n.* narrow, runnerless sled for use on snow. ▶*v.* ride on a toboggan.

**to·day** /təˈdā/ ▶*adv.* **1** on this present day. **2** nowadays. ▶*n.* **1** this present day. **2** modern times.

**tod·dle** /ˈtädl/ ▶*v.* walk with short unsteady steps. ▶*n.* toddling walk.

**todd·ler** ▶*n.* child who has recently learned to walk.

**tod·dy** /ˈtädē/ ▶*n.* (*pl.* **-dies**) drink of liquor with hot water, sugar, etc.

**to-do** /təˈdoo/ ▶*n.* commotion or fuss.

**toe** /tō/ ▶*n.* **1** any of the five digits of the foot. **2** part of footwear that covers the toes.

**toe·hold** ▶*n.* **1** small place where a person's foot can be lodged, as when climbing. **2** position from which progress can be made.

**toe·nail** ▶*n.* nail at the tip of each toe.

**tof·fee** /ˈtôfē/ ▶*n.* firm or hard candy made by boiling sugar, butter, etc.

**to·fu** /ˈtōfoo/ ▶*n.* curd made from soybeans.

**to·ga** /ˈtōgə/ ▶*n.* ancient Roman citizen's loose flowing outer garment.

**to·geth·er** /təˈgeT͟Hər/ ▶*adv.* **1** in company or conjunction: *walking together*. **2** simultaneously: *both shouted together*. **3** so as to unite: *tied them together*.

**to·geth·er·ness** ▶*n.* **1** being together. **2** feeling of comfort from being together.

**togs** /tägz/ ▶*pl. n. inf.* clothes.

**toil** /toil/ ▶*v.* work laboriously or incessantly. ▶*n.* prolonged or intensive labor; drudgery.

**toi·let** /ˈtoilit/ ▶*n.* **1 a** fixture, as in a bathroom, etc., for defecating and urinating. **b** bathroom; lavatory. **2** (also **toilette**) process of washing oneself, dressing, etc. □ **toilet water** diluted perfume.

**toi·let·ry** ▶*n.* (*pl.* **-ries**) any of

various articles or cosmetics used in washing, dressing, etc.

**to·ken** /'tōkən/ ▸*n.* **1** thing serving as a symbol, reminder, or mark: *token of affection.* **2** anything used to represent something else, esp. a metal disk, etc., used instead of money. ▸*adj.* **1** nominal or perfunctory: *token effort.* **2** chosen to represent a particular group: *token woman on the committee.* □ **by the same token 1** similarly. **2** moreover.

**to·ken·ism** ▸*n.* granting of minimum concessions, esp. to appease radical demands, etc.

**tol·er·a·ble** /'tälərəbəl/ ▸*adj.* **1** endurable. **2** fairly good. —**tol·er·a·bly** *adv.*

**tol·er·ance** /'tälərəns/ ▸*n.* **1** willingness or ability to tolerate; forbearance. **2** capacity to tolerate. **3** allowable variation in any measurable property. —**tol·er·ant** *adj.*

**tol·er·ate** /'tälə,rāt/ ▸*v.* **1** allow the existence or occurrence of without interference. **2** endure (suffering, etc.).

**toll** /tōl/ ▸*n.* **1** charge to use a bridge, road, etc. **2** cost or damage caused by a disaster, etc. **3** stroke or sound of a bell.

▸*v.* (of a bell) sound or cause to sound with slow, uniform strokes.

**toll·booth** ▸*n.* booth from which tolls are collected.

**tom** /täm/ ▸*n.* male animal, esp. a cat or a turkey.

**tom·a·hawk** /'tämə,hôk/ ▸*n.* Native American war ax.

**to·ma·to** /tə'mātō; -'mätō/ ▸*n.* (*pl.* **-toes**) **1** glossy red or yellow, pulpy edible fruit. **2** plant bearing this.

**tomb** /to͞om/ ▸*n.* **1** burial vault. **2** grave.

**tom·boy** ▸*n.* girl who behaves in a traditionally boyish way. —**tom·boy·ish** *adj.*

**tomb·stone** ▸*n.* stone over a grave, usu. with an epitaph.

**tom·cat** ▸*n.* male domestic cat.

**tome** /tōm/ ▸*n.* large heavy book or volume.

**tom·fool·er·y** /täm'fo͞ol(ə)rē/ ▸*n.* foolish behavior.

**to·mog·ra·phy** /tə'mägrəfē/ ▸*n.* technique for displaying a representation of a cross section through a human body or other solid object using X-rays or ultrasound.

**to·mor·row** /təˈmôrō/ ▶*adv. & n.*
**1** (on) the day after today. **2** (in)
the near future.

**tom-tom** ▶*n.* early drum beaten
with the hands.

**ton** /tən/ ▶*n.* **1** (**short ton**) unit of
weight equal to 2,000 lb. (907.19
kg). **2** (**long ton**) *Brit.* unit of
weight equal to 2,240 lb.
(1016.05 kg). **3** (usu. **a ton
of/tons of**) *inf.* large number or
amount: *tons of money.*

**to·nal·i·ty** /tōˈnalitē/ ▶*n.* (*pl.* **-ties**)
relationship between the tones
of a musical scale.

**tone** /tōn/ ▶*n.* **1** musical or vocal
sound, esp. with reference to its
pitch, quality, and strength.
**2** manner of expression in
writing or speaking. **3** proper
firmness of bodily organs.
▶*v.* give the desired tone to.

**tongs** /tôNGz/ ▶*pl. n.* instrument
with two arms for grasping and
holding.

**tongue** /təNG/ ▶*n.* **1** fleshy
muscular organ in the mouth
used in tasting, licking, and
swallowing, and (in humans) for
speech. **2** faculty of or tendency
in speech: *a sharp tongue.*
**3** particular language: *the
German tongue.* **4** thing like a
tongue in shape or position.

□ **tongue-and-groove** applied to
boards in which a tongue along
one edge fits into a groove along
the edge of the next. □ **tongue-
in-cheek** ironic; slyly humorous.
□ **tongue-tied** too shy,
embarrassed, or surprised to
speak. □ **tongue twister**
sequence of words difficult to
pronounce quickly and correctly.

**ton·ic** /ˈtänik/ ▶*n.* **1** invigorating
medicine. **2** anything serving to
invigorate.
□ **tonic water** carbonated water
containing quinine.

**to·night** /təˈnīt/ ▶*adv.* on the
present or approaching evening
or night.
▶*n.* the evening or night of the
present day.

**ton·nage** /ˈtənij/ ▶*n.* ship's
internal cubic volume or freight-
carrying capacity.

**ton·sil** /ˈtänsəl/ ▶*n.* either of two
small organs, one on each side
of the root of the tongue.

**ton·sil·lec·to·my** /ˌtänsə-
ˈlektəmē/ ▶*n.* (*pl.* **-mies**) surgical
removal of the tonsils.

**ton·sil·li·tis** /ˌtänsəˈlītis/ ▶*n.*
inflammation of the tonsils.

**ton·so·ri·al** /tänˈsôrēəl/ ▶*adj.* of
or relating to a barber or
hairdressing.

**ton·sure** /ˈtänsHər/ ▸*n.* shaved crown of the head or the entire head, esp. of a person entering a monastic order.

**too** /to͞o/ ▸*adv.* **1** to a greater extent than is desirable, permissible, etc.: *too large.* **2** *inf.* extremely: *too kind.* **3** in addition: *are they coming, too?*

**tool** /to͞ol/ ▸*n.* **1** implement used to carry out mechanical functions manually or by machine. **2** thing used in an occupation or pursuit: *tools of one's trade.* **3** person used as a mere instrument by another.
▸*v.* **1** shape or decorate with a tool. **2** impress a design on (leather).

**toot** /to͞ot/ ▸*n.* short sharp sound as made by a horn.
▸*v.* make or cause to make a short sharp sound.

**tooth** /to͞oTH/ ▸*n.* (*pl.* **teeth**) **1** each of a set of hard, bony, enamel-coated structures in the jaws of most vertebrates, used for biting and chewing. **2** toothlike part or projection, e.g., the cog of a gearwheel, point of a saw or comb, etc. ☐ **tooth and nail** fiercely.

**tooth·ache** ▸*n.* pain in the tooth or teeth.

**tooth·brush** ▸*n.* brush for cleaning the teeth.

**tooth·paste** ▸*n.* preparation for cleaning the teeth.

**tooth·pick** ▸*n.* small, sharp instrument for removing food from between the teeth.

**tooth·some** ▸*adj.* **1** delicious. **2** attractive.

**tooth·y** ▸*adj.* (**-i·er, -i·est**) having large, numerous, or prominent teeth.

**top** /täp/ ▸*n.* **1** highest point, part, rank, etc. **2** upper part or surface. **3** garment for the upper part of the body. **4** lid of a jar, saucepan, etc. **5** twirling toy that spins on a point.
▸*adj.* **1** highest in position: *top shelf.* **2** highest in degree or importance: *top speed.*
▸*v.* (**topped, top·ping**) **1** provide with a top, cap, etc. **2** be higher or better than; surpass: *topped the list.* **—top·most** *adj.*

**to·paz** /ˈtōpaz/ ▸*n.* transparent or translucent mineral, usu. yellow, used as a gem.

**top·coat** ▸*n.* **1** overcoat. **2** outer coat of paint, etc.

**tope** /tōp/ ▸*v.* drink alcohol to excess, esp. on a regular basis.

**top hat** ▸*n.* man's tall hat worn with formal dress.

**top·heav·y** ▶*adj.*
**1** disproportionately heavy at the top. **2** (of an organization, etc.) having a disproportionately large number of people in administrative positions.

**top·ic** /'täpik/ ▶*n.* subject of a discourse, conversation, argument, etc.

**top·i·cal** ▶*adj.* **1** dealing with the news, current affairs, etc. **2** (of medicine, etc.) applied to or affecting a part of the body.

**top·mast** ▶*n.* mast next above the lower mast on a sailing ship.

**top·most** ▶*adj.* highest.

**to·pog·ra·phy** /tə'pägrəfē/ ▶*n.* **1** detailed description, mapping, etc., of the features of a town, district, etc. **2** such features. —**top·o·graph·i·cal** *adj.* —**top·o·graph·i·cal·ly** *adv.*

**to·pos** /'tōpōs/ ▶*n.* (*pl.* **-poi** /-poi/) traditional theme or formula in literature.

**top·ping** ▶*n.* thing that tops another thing, as on cake, ice cream, pizza, etc.

**top·ple** /'täpəl/ ▶*v.* **1** fall or cause to fall. **2** overthrow.

**top·soil** ▶*n.* fertile top layer of soil.

**top·sy-tur·vy** /'täpsē 'tərvē/ ▶*adv. & adj.* **1** upside down. **2** in utter confusion.

**tor** /tôr/ ▶*n.* hill or rocky peak.

**To·rah** /'tōrə/ ▶*n.* law of God as revealed to Moses and recorded in the first five books of the Hebrew Scriptures.

**torch** /tôrCH/ ▶*n.* thing lit for illumination.
▶*v. inf.* set alight with or as with a torch.

**torch·bear·er** ▶*n.* **1** person who carries a ceremonial torch. **2** person who leads others toward a valued goal.

**tor·e·a·dor** /'tôrēə,dôr/ ▶*n.* bullfighter.

**tor·ment** ▶*n.* /'tôrment/ **1** severe physical or mental suffering. **2** cause of this.
▶*v.* /tôr'ment/ **1** subject to torment. **2** tease or worry excessively. —**tor·men·tor** *n.*

**tor·na·do** /tôr'nādō/ ▶*n.* (*pl.* **-does**) violent, usu. localized storm with whirling winds in a funnel-shaped cloud.

**tor·pe·do** /tôr'pēdō/ ▶*n.* (*pl.* **-does**) cigar-shaped, self-propelled, underwater explosive missile.
▶*v.* (**-doed**) **1** destroy or attack with a torpedo. **2** destroy (a policy, institution, plan, etc.).

**tor·pid** /ˈtôrpid/ ▸*adj.* sluggish; inactive; dull; apathetic. —**tor·pid·i·ty** *n.* —**tor·pid·ly** *adv.*

**tor·por** /ˈtôrpər/ ▸*n.* sluggish condition.

**torque** /tôrk/ ▸*n. Mech.* force that produces rotation.

**tor·rent** /ˈtôrənt/ ▸*n.* **1** rushing stream of liquid. **2** (usu. **torrents**) great downpour of rain. —**tor·ren·tial** *adj.* —**tor·ren·tial·ly** *adv.*

**tor·rid** /ˈtôrəd/ ▸*adj.* **1** (of the weather) very hot and dry. **2** passionate; intense. —**tor·rid·ly** *adv.* —**tor·rid·ness** *n.*

**tor·sion** /ˈtôrSHən/ ▸*n.* twisting, esp. of one end of a body while the other is held fixed.

**tor·so** /ˈtôrsō/ ▸*n.* (*pl.* **-sos** or **-si**) trunk of the human body.

**tort** /tôrt/ ▸*n. Law* breach of duty (other than under contract) leading to liability for damages.

**torte** /tôrt/ ▸*n.* elaborate sweet cake.

**tor·ti·lla** /tôrˈtē(y)ə/ ▸*n.* thin, flat, Mexican corn or wheat bread eaten with or without a filling.

**tor·toise** /ˈtôrtəs/ ▸*n.* turtle, esp. a land turtle.

**tor·toise·shell** ▸*n.* yellowish brown, mottled or clouded outer shell of some turtles, used for jewelry and ornaments.

**tor·tu·ous** /ˈtôrCHo͞oəs/ ▸*adj.* **1** full of twists and turns. **2** devious; circuitous. —**tor·tu·ous·ly** *adv.* —**tor·tu·ous·ness** *n.*

**tor·ture** /ˈtôrCHər/ ▸*n.* **1** infliction of severe bodily pain, esp. as a punishment or a means of persuasion. **2** severe physical or mental suffering. ▸*v.* inflict severe pain upon. —**tor·tur·er** *n.* —**tor·tur·ous** *adj.* —**tor·tur·ous·ly** *adv.*

**toss** /tôs/ ▸*v.* **1** throw lightly or carelessly. **2** roll about, throw, or be thrown, restlessly or from side to side. **3** throw (a coin) into the air to decide a choice, etc., by the side on which it lands. **4** prepare or coat by mixing or shaking. ▸*n.* act of tossing (a coin, etc.). □ **toss-up 1** doubtful matter; even chance: *it's a toss-up whether he wins.* **2** tossing of a coin.

**tot** /tät/ ▸*n.* small child.

**to·tal** /ˈtōtl/ ▸*adj.* **1** complete; comprising the whole. **2** absolute: *in total ignorance.* ▸*n.* total number or amount. ▸*v.* (**-taled, -tal·ing; -talled, -tal·ling**) **1 a** amount in number to: *they totaled 131.* **b** calculate the total of. **2** *inf.* demolish. —**to·tal·i·ty** *n.* —**to·tal·ly** *adv.*

**to·tal·i·tar·i·an** /tō͵talə'terēən/ ▸*adj.* of a dictatorial government requiring complete subservience. —**to·tal·i·tar·i·an·ism** *n.*

**tote** /tōt/ ▸*v. inf.* carry; convey.

**to·tem** /'tōtəm/ ▸*n.* **1** natural object or animal adopted as an emblem of a clan or individual. **2** image of this. —**to·tem·ic** *adj.* —**to·tem·ism** *n.*

□ **totem pole** pole on which totems are carved or hung.

**tot·ter** /'tätər/ ▸*v.* stand or walk unsteadily or feebly. ▸*n.* unsteady or shaky movement. —**tot·ter·y** *adj.*

**tou·can** /'tōō͵kan/ ▸*n.* tropical American fruit-eating bird with an immense beak and brightly colored plumage.

**touch** /təCH/ ▸*v.* **1** come into or be in physical contact with (another thing). **2** (of two things, etc.) be in or come into contact. **3** rouse tender or painful feelings in: *touched by his appeal.* **4** approach in excellence, etc.: *can't touch him for style.* ▸*n.* **1** act of touching. **2** faculty of perception through physical contact, esp. with the fingers. **3** small amount; slight trace.

□ **in touch (with) 1** in communication. **2** up to date, esp. regarding news, etc. **3** aware. □ **lose touch 1** cease to be informed. **2** cease to be in contact. □ **out of touch 1** not in correspondence. **2** not up to date. **3** lacking in awareness: *out of touch with his son's beliefs.* □ **touch and go** risky. □ **touch up** give finishing touches to or retouch.

**touch·down** ▸*n.* **1** act of landing by an aircraft. **2** *Football* act or instance of scoring by crossing the goal line.

**tou·ché** /tōō'SHā/ ▸*interj.* **1** acknowledgment of a hit by a fencing opponent. **2** acknowledgment of a justified accusation, witticism, or point made in reply to one's own.

**touch·stone** ▸*n.* criterion.

**touch·y** ▸*adj.* (**-i·er, -i·est**) apt to take offense; overly sensitive. —**touch·i·ness** *n.*

**tough** /təf/ ▸*adj.* **1** hard to break, cut, tear, or chew. **2** able to endure hardship; hardy. **3** unyielding; difficult. **4** *inf.* **a** acting sternly. **b** (of circumstances, luck, etc.) severe; hard.

▸*n.* tough person, esp. a hoodlum. —**tough·en** *v.* —**tough·ness** *n.*

**tou·pee** /tोo'pā/ ▸*n.* hairpiece to cover a bald spot.

**tour** /tो͝or/ ▸*n.* **1** pleasure journey from place to place. **2** term of military or diplomatic duty. **3** series of performances, games, etc., at different places.
▸*v.* make a tour (of).

**tour de force** /də 'fôrs/ ▸*n.* feat of strength or skill.

**tour·ism** ▸*n.* commercial organization and operation of visits to places of interest.

**tour·ist** ▸*n.* person traveling for pleasure.

**tour·na·ment** /'to͝ornəmənt/ ▸*n.* **1** large contest of many rounds. **2** medieval pageant with jousting.

**tour·ni·quet** /'tərnəkət/ ▸*n.* device for stopping arterial blood flow.

**tou·sle** /'touzəl/ ▸*v.* make untidy; rumple.

**tout** /tout/ ▸*v.* solicit patronage persistently.
▸*n.* person who touts.

**tout de suite** /ˌto͞ot 'swēt/ ▸*adv.* immediately; at once.

**to·va·rish** /tə'värisн/ (also **to·va·rich**) ▸*n.* (in the former USSR) a comrade (often used as a form of address).

**tow** /tō/ ▸*v.* pull along by a rope, etc.
▸*n.* towing; being towed.

**toward** /t(w)ôrd/ (also **towards**) ▸*prep.* **1** in the direction of: *set out toward town.* **2** as regards; in relation to: *attitude toward death.* **3** as a contribution to; for: *toward your expenses.*

**tow·el** /'tou(ə)l/ ▸*n.* piece of absorbent cloth or paper used for drying after washing.
▸*v.* wipe or dry with a towel. —**tow·el·ing** *n.*

**tow·er** /'tou(ə)r/ ▸*n.* tall structure.
▸*v.* reach or be high or above; be superior.

**tow·head** /'tō,hed/ ▸*n.* person with very light blond hair. —**tow·head·ed** *adj.*

**town** /toun/ ▸*n.* **1** defined area between a village and a city in size. **2** central business area in a neighborhood: *going into town.*

**town hall** ▸*n.* building for the administration of local government.

**town house** ▸*n.* house in a development sharing a wall with another house.

**town meet·ing** ▸*n.* meeting of the voters of a town to transact public business.

**town·ship** ▸*n.* division of a county in some states, having limited corporate powers.

**tow·path** ▸*n.* path beside a river or canal, used as a pathway for horses towing barges.

**tox·e·mi·a** /täk'sēmēə/ ▸*n.* blood poisoning.

**tox·ic** /'täksik/ ▸*adj.* **1** of poison. **2** poisonous. —**tox·ic·i·ty** *n.*

**tox·i·col·o·gy** /ˌtäksi'käləjē/ ▸*n.* scientific study of poisons. —**tox·i·co·log·i·cal** *adj.* —**tox·i·col·o·gist** *n.*

**tox·in** /'täksin/ ▸*n.* poison produced by a living organism.

**tox·oph·i·lite** /täk'säfəˌlīt/ ▸*n.* student or lover of archery. ▸*adj.* of or relating to archers and archery.

**toy** /toi/ ▸*n.* **1** plaything. **2** thing regarded as providing amusement. **3** diminutive breed of dog, etc. ▸*v.* (**toy with**) trifle, amuse oneself, or flirt with.

**trace** /trās/ ▸*v.* **1** observe, or find vestiges or signs of, by investigation. **2** copy (a drawing, etc.) by drawing over its lines on superimposed translucent paper. **3** pursue one's way along (a path, etc.). ▸*n.* **1** indication of something having existed; vestige. **2** very small quantity. —**trace·a·ble** *adj.* —**trace·a·bil·i·ty** *n.*

☐ **trace element** chemical element occurring or required in minute amounts.

**trac·er·y** ▸*n.* (*pl.* **-ies**) fine decorative pattern.

**tra·che·a** /'trākēə/ ▸*n.* (*pl.* **-che·ae** or **-che·as**) windpipe. —**tra·che·al** *adj.*

**tra·che·ot·o·my** /ˌtrākē'ätəmē/ ▸*n.* (*pl.* **-mies**) incision in the trachea to relieve an obstruction.

**track** /trak/ ▸*n.* **1** mark or marks left by a person, animal, or thing in passing. **2** rough path, esp. one beaten by use. **3** continuous line of railroad rails. **4** course for running or racing. **5** section of a record, compact disc, etc., containing one song, etc. ▸*v.* **1** follow the track of. **2** trace (a course, development, etc.). **3** make a track with (dirt, etc.) from the feet.

☐ **keep** (or **lose**) **track of** follow (or fail to follow) the course of.

**track·ball** ▸*n.* small ball than

can be rotated by hand to move a cursor on a computer screen.

**tract** /trakt/ ▶*n.* **1** region or area of indefinite, esp. large, extent. **2** bodily organ or system: *respiratory tract.* **3** pamphlet, esp. political or religious.

**trac·ta·ble** ▶*adj.* easily handled; manageable. **—trac·ta·bil·i·ty** *n.*

**trac·tion** /'trakSHən/ ▶*n.* **1** act of pulling or being pulled. **2** gripping power on a surface.

**trac·tive** /'traktiv/ ▶*adj.* relating to or denoting the power exerted in pulling, esp. by a vehicle or other machine.

**trac·tor** ▶*n.* vehicle used for hauling machinery, heavy loads, etc.

**trade** /trād/ ▶*n.* **1 a** buying and selling. **b** business conducted for profit (esp. as distinct from a profession). **c** business of a specified nature or time: *tourist trade.* **2** skilled professional craft. **3** transaction, esp. a swap. ▶*v.* **1** engage in trade; buy and sell. **2** exchange in commerce; barter (goods). **—trad·er** *n.* **—trades·man** *n.*
□ **trade in** exchange (esp. a used car, etc.) in part payment for another. □ **trade off** exchange, esp. as a compromise. □ **trade**

**on** take advantage of (a person's reputation, etc.).

**trade·mark** ▶*n.* **1** device, word, or words secured by law or custom as representing a company, product, etc. **2** distinctive characteristic, etc.

**tra·di·tion** /trə'disHən/ ▶*n.* **1** custom, opinion, or belief handed down to posterity. **2** valued convention or observance. **—tra·di·tion·al** *adj.* **—tra·di·tion·al·ly** *adv.*

**tra·duce** /trə'd(y)oōs/ ▶*v.* speak ill of; misrepresent.

**traf·fic** /'trafik/ ▶*n.* **1** vehicles moving on a public highway, in the air, or at sea. **2** trade. **3** comings and goings. ▶*v.* (**-ficked, -fick·ing**) (**traffic in**) deal in (something). **—traf·fick·er** *n.*
□ **traffic circle** road junction at which traffic moves in one direction around a central island. □ **traffic light** signal with colored lights to control road traffic.

**tra·ge·di·an** /trə'jēdēən/ ▶*n.* writer of or actor in tragedies.

**trag·e·dy** /'trajidē/ ▶*n.* (*pl.* **-dies**) **1** serious accident, crime, or disaster; great misfortune. **2** play dealing with tragic events and with an unhappy ending. —**trag·ic** *adj.*

**trail** /trāl/ ▶*n.* **1** track left by a moving thing, person, etc. **2** beaten path or track, esp. through a wild region. **3** part dragging behind a thing or person: *trail of smoke.*
▶*v.* **1** draw or be drawn along behind, esp. on the ground. **2** walk wearily (behind); lag. **3** follow the trail of; pursue.

**trail·blaz·er** ▶*n.* pioneer.

**trail·er** ▶*n.* **1** scenes from a movie, etc., used to advertise it in advance. **2** vehicle towed by another. **3** mobile home.

**train** /trān/ ▶*v.* **1** teach (a person, animal, oneself, etc.) a specified skill, esp. by practice. **2** bring or come into a state of physical fitness by exercise, diet, etc. **3** [usu. as *adj.* **trained**] make (the mind, eye, etc.) discerning through practice. **4** point or aim (a gun, camera, etc.).
▶*n.* **1** series of railroad cars drawn by an engine. **2** thing dragged along behind or forming the back part of a dress, robe, etc. **3** succession or series of people, things, events, etc. —**train·ee** *n.* —**train·er** *n.* —**train·ing** *n.*

**traipse** /trāps/ ▶*v.* tramp or trudge wearily.

**trait** /trāt/ ▶*n.* distinguishing feature or characteristic.

**trai·tor** /ˈtrātər/ ▶*n.* person who is treacherous or disloyal, esp. to his or her country. —**trai·tor·ous** *adj.* —**trai·tor·ous·ly** *adv.*

**tra·jec·to·ry** /trəˈjektərē/ ▶*n.* (*pl.* **-ries**) path of an object moving under given forces.

**tram** ▶*n.* cable car.

**tram·mel** /ˈtraməl/ ▶*v.* hamper.

**tramp** /tramp/ ▶*v.* **1** walk heavily and firmly. **2** tread on; trample; stamp on.
▶*n.* **1** itinerant vagrant or beggar. **2** sound of a person, or esp. people, walking, marching, etc., or of horses' hooves. **3** long walk. **4** *inf., derog.* promiscuous woman.

**tram·ple** /ˈtrampəl/ ▶*v.* tread underfoot.

**tram·po·line** /ˈtrampəˌlēn/ ▶*n.* strong canvas sheet connected by springs to a horizontal frame, used for gymnastic jumping. —**tram·po·lin·ist** *n.*

**trance** /trans/ ▶*n.* **1** sleeplike state without response to stimuli. **2** state of rapture; ecstasy.

**tran·quil** /ˈtraNGkwəl/ ▶*adj.* calm;

serene; unruffled. —**tran·quil·i·ty** or **tran·quil·li·ty** *n.* —**tran·quil·ly** *adv.*

**tran·quil·iz·er** ▶*n.* drug used to diminish anxiety.

**trans-** /tranz; trans/ ▶*prefix* **1** across; beyond: *transcontinental.* **2** into another state or place: *transform.*

**trans.** ▶*abbr.* **1** transaction. **2** transfer. **3** transitive. **4** translated; translation; translator. **5** transmission. **6** transportation.

**trans·act** ▶*v.* perform or carry out (business). —**trans·ac·tion** *n.*

**trans·at·lan·tic** ▶*adj.* **1** beyond the Atlantic Ocean. **2** crossing the Atlantic: *a transatlantic flight.*

**trans·ceiv·er** /tran'sēvər/ ▶*n.* device that can both transmit and receive communications.

**tran·scend** /tran'send/ ▶*v.* **1** be beyond the range or grasp of (human experience, reason, belief, etc.). **2** excel; outdo; surpass. —**tran·scend·ence** *n.* —**tran·scend·ent** *adj.* —**tran·scend·ent·ly** *adv.*

**tran·scen·den·tal** /ˌtransen-'dentl/ ▶*adj.* of a spiritual realm; mystical.

**trans·con·ti·nen·tal** ▶*adj.* (of a railroad, etc.) extending across a continent.

**tran·scribe** ▶*v.* **1** make a copy of, esp. in writing; write out. **2** arrange (music) for a different instrument, etc. —**tran·scrib·er** *n.* —**tran·scrip·tion** *n.*

**trans·duc·er** /trans'd(y)o͞osər; tranz-/ ▶*n.* device for converting a nonelectrical signal into an electrical one, e.g., pressure into voltage.

**tran·sept** /'tran,sept/ ▶*n.* either arm of a cross-shaped church at right angles to the nave.

**trans·fer** ▶*v.* /trans'fər/ (-**ferred**, -**fer·ring**) **1** convey, remove, or hand over. **2** move from one position to another. **3** change from one station, route, etc., to another on a journey.

▶*n.* /'transfər/ **1** transferring or being transferred. **2** design, etc., conveyed or to be conveyed from one surface to another. **3** conveyance of property, a right, etc. **4** ticket for transferring during travel.

**trans·fig·ure** ▶*v.* change in form or appearance, esp. so as to elevate or idealize. —**trans·fig·u·ra·tion** *n.*

**trans·fix** ▶*v.* **1** pierce with a

sharp implement. **2** paralyze with horror or astonishment.

**trans·form** ▶*v.* make a thorough or dramatic change in the form, appearance, character, etc., of. —**trans·for·ma·tion** *n.*

**trans·form·er** ▶*n.* apparatus for reducing or increasing the voltage of an electrical current.

**trans·fuse** /trans'fyoo͞z/ ▶*v.* **1** permeate. **2** transfer (blood) from one person to another. —**trans·fu·sion** *n.*

**trans·gress** /trans'gres; tranz-/ ▶*v.* go beyond the bounds or limits set by (a commandment, law, etc.); violate. —**trans·gres·sion** *n.* —**trans·gres·sor** *n.*

**tran·sient** /'transHənt/ ▶*adj.* of short duration; passing. ▶*n.* temporary visitor, worker, etc. —**tran·sience** *n.*

**tran·sis·tor** /tran'zistər/ ▶*n.* **1** small semiconductor device that controls the flow of an electric current. **2** (also **tran·sis·tor ra·dio**) portable radio using transistors.

**transit** /'tranzit/ ▶*n.* going, conveying, or being conveyed, esp. over a distance.

**tran·si·tion** ▶*n.* passing or change from one place, state, condition, style, etc., to another.

**tran·si·tive** /'transitiv/ ▶*adj.* (of a verb) that takes a direct object, e.g., *saw* in *saw the donkey.*

**tran·si·to·ry** ▶*adj.* not permanent; transient. —**tran·si·to·ri·ness** *n.*

**trans·late** /trans'lāt/ ▶*v.* **1** express the sense of (a word, text, etc.) in another language. **2** express in another form. —**trans·la·tion** *n.* —**trans·la·tor** *n.*

**trans·lit·er·ate** /trans'litə,rāt/ ▶*v.* represent (a word, etc.) in the closest corresponding characters of a different language. —**trans·lit·er·a·tion** *n.*

**trans·lu·cent** /trans'loo͞sənt/ ▶*adj.* allowing light to pass through; semitransparent. —**trans·lu·cence** *n.*

**trans·mi·grate** /trans'mī,grāt; tranz-/ ▶*v.* **1** (of the soul) pass into a different body after death. **2** migrate.

**trans·mi·gra·tion** ▶*n.* passage of the soul into a different body after death.

**trans·mis·sion** /trans'misHən/ ▶*n.* **1** transmitting; being transmitted. **2** broadcast program. **3** mechanism by which power is transmitted from an engine to the axle in a vehicle.

**trans·mit** /trans'mit/ ▶v. (-mit·ted, -mit·ting) **1** pass or hand on; transfer. **2** allow to pass through; conduct. **3** broadcast (a radio or television program). —**trans·mit·ta·ble** adj. —**trans·mit·tal** n. —**trans·mit·ter** n.

**trans·mog·ri·fy** /trans'mägrə‚fī/ ▶v. (-fied) transform, esp. in a magical or surprising manner.

**trans·mute** /trans'myoot/ ▶v. change in form, nature, or substance. —**trans·mut·a·ble** adj. —**trans·mut·a·bil·i·ty** n. —**trans·mu·ta·tion** n.

**trans·oce·an·ic** ▶adj. crossing the ocean: transoceanic flight.

**tran·som** /'transəm/ ▶n. **1** horizontal bar of wood or stone across a window or the top of a door. **2** window above a door or larger window.

**tran·son·ic** /tran'sänik/ (also **trans·son·ic**) ▶adj. denoting or relating to speeds close to that of sound.

**trans·pa·cif·ic** ▶adj. crossing the Pacific.

**trans·par·ent** /tran'spe(ə)rənt/ ▶adj. **1** easily seen through.

**2** easily understood or detected. —**trans·par·en·cy** n. —**trans·par·ent·ly** adv.

**tran·spire** /tran'spī(ə)r/ ▶v. **1** occur; happen. **2** emit (vapor, sweat, etc.), or be emitted, through the skin, lungs, or leaves. —**tran·spi·ra·tion** n.

**trans·plant** ▶v. **1** plant in or move to another place. **2** surgically transfer (living tissue or an organ) to another part of the body or to another body.

▶n. **1** transplanting of an organ or tissue. **2** thing, esp. a plant, transplanted. —**trans·plan·ta·tion** n.

**trans·port** ▶v. **1** take or carry to another place. **2** affect with strong emotion.

▶n. **1** system or vehicle for conveyance. **2** (usu. **transports**) vehement emotion: transports of joy. —**trans·port·a·ble** adj. —**trans·por·ta·tion** n. —**trans·port·er** n.

**trans·pose** ▶v. **1** cause (two or more things) to change places. **2** put (music) into a different key. —**trans·pos·er** n. —**trans·po·si·tion** n.

**trans·sex·u·al** ▶n. **1** person having the physical

characteristics of one sex but psychological identification with the other. **2** person whose sex has been changed by surgery. —**trans·sex·u·al·ism** *n.*

**tran·sub·stan·ti·a·tion** ▶*n.* doctrine that the bread and wine in the Euchartist are transformed at the consecration into the body and blood of Christ.

**trans·verse** ▶*adj.* situated or extending across something. —**trans·verse·ly** *adv.*

**trans·ves·tite** /trans'ves,tīt/ ▶*n.* person who derives pleasure from wearing clothes of the opposite sex.

**trap** /trap/ ▶*n.* **1** device, often baited, for catching animals. **2** trick betraying a person into speech or an act. **3** arrangement to catch an unsuspecting person. **4** curve in a downpipe, etc., that fills with liquid and forms a seal against the upward passage of gases. ▶*v.* (**trapped, trap·ping**) catch or hold in a trap.

**tra·peze** /tra'pēz/ ▶*n.* crossbar suspended by ropes used as a swing for acrobatics, etc.

**trap·e·zoid** /'trapi,zoid/ ▶*n.* quadrilateral with only one pair of sides parallel. —**trap·e·zoi·dal** *adj.*

**trap·pings** ▶*pl. n.* **1** ornamental accessories. **2** outward forms or symbols of status.

**trash** /trasн/ ▶*n.* something worthless; rubbish. ▶*v. inf.* wreck; vandalize; discard. —**trash·y** *adj.*

**trau·ma** /'troumə; 'trô-/ ▶*n.* (*pl.* -**ma·ta** or -**mas**) **1** physical injury or shock. **2** profound emotional shock. —**trau·ma·tic** *adj.* —**trau·ma·tize** *v.* —**trau·ma·ti·za·tion** *n.*

**tra·vail** /trə'vāl/ ▶*n.* painful or laborious effort.

**trav·el** /'travəl/ ▶*v.* **1** go from one place to another; make a journey, esp. of some length or abroad. **2** journey along or through (a country). **3** move or proceed as specified: *light travels faster than sound.* ▶*n.* traveling, esp. in foreign countries. —**trav·el·er** *n.* —**trav·el·ing** *adj.*

**tra·verse** ▶*v.* /trə'vərs/ travel or lie across: *traversed the country.* ▶*n.* /'travərs/ **1** traversing. **2** thing that crosses another. —**tra·vers·al** *n.*

**trav·er·tine** /'travər,tēn; -tin/ ▶*n.* white or light-colored calcareous rock deposited from mineral springs, used in building.

**trav·es·ty** /'travistē/ ▶n. (pl. -ties) grotesque misrepresentation or imitation: *travesty of justice.*

▶v. (-tied) make or be a travesty of.

**trawl** /trôl/ ▶n. large wide-mouthed fishing net dragged by a boat along the sea bottom.

▶v. fish or catch with a trawl.

**tray** /trā/ ▶n. flat receptacle, usu. with a raised rim, for carrying small articles.

**treach·er·y** /'trecHərē/ ▶n. violation of faith or trust; betrayal. —**treach·er·ous** adj. —**treach·er·ous·ly** adv.

**tread** /tred/ ▶v. (**trod**; **trod·den** or **trod**) set down one's foot; walk; step.

▶n. **1** manner or sound of walking. **2** top surface of a step or stair. **3** surface pattern on a tire.

□ **tread water** maintain an upright position in the water by moving the feet and hands.

**trea·dle** /'tredl/ ▶n. lever worked by the foot and imparting motion to a machine.

**tread·mill** ▶n. device for producing motion by the treading on endless moving steps or a belt.

**trea·son** /'trēzən/ ▶n. betrayal of one's nation. —**trea·son·a·ble** adj. —**trea·son·ous** adj.

**treas·ure** /'trezHər/ ▶n. **1** precious metals or gems. **2** thing valued for its rarity, workmanship, associations, etc.

▶v. value highly.

□ **treasure trove** discovered treasure of unknown ownership.

**treas·ur·y** ▶n. (pl. -ies) **1** place for storing public or private funds. **2** funds or revenue of a nation, institution, or society. **3** (**Treasury**) department managing the public revenue of a country. —**treas·ur·er** n.

**treat** /trēt/ ▶v. **1** act or behave toward or deal with in a certain way. **2** apply a process to: *treat with acid.* **3** apply medical care or attention to. **4** pay for food, drink, entertainment, etc.

▶n. **1** delightful event or circumstance. **2** meal, entertainment, etc., paid for by another. —**treat·ment** n.

**trea·tise** /'trētis/ ▶n. written work dealing formally and systematically with a subject.

**trea·ty** /'trētē/ ▶n. (pl. -ties) formal agreement between nations.

**tre·ble** /'trebəl/ ▸*adj.* threefold; triple.

▸*n.* highest musical voice, instrument, or part.

▸*v.* make or become three times as much or many; increase threefold.

**tree** /trē/ ▸*n.* **1** branched perennial plant with a woody, self-supporting main stem or trunk. **2** something shaped like a tree.

**tre·foil** /'trē,foil/ ▸*n.* **1** plant with leaves divided into three parts. **2** design resembling this.

**trek** /trek/ ▸*v.* (**trekked, trek·king**) travel or make one's way arduously.

▸*n.* journey made by trekking. —**trek·ker** *n.*

**trel·lis** /'trelis/ ▸*n.* lattice of light wooden or metal bars, esp. as a support for climbing plants.

**trem·ble** /'trembəl/ ▸*v.* **1** shake involuntarily from weakness, etc.; quiver. **2** be in a state of extreme apprehension.

▸*n.* trembling; quiver. —**trem·bly** *adj.*

**tre·men·dous** /trə'mendəs/ ▸*adj.* **1** immense; overpowering. **2** *inf.* remarkable; considerable; excellent. —**tre·men·dous·ly** *adv.*

**trem·o·lo** /'tremə,lō/ ▸*n.* (*pl.* **-los**) *Mus.* vibrating effect in an instrument or voice.

**trem·or** /'tremər/ ▸*n.* **1** shaking; quivering. **2** slight earthquake.

**trem·u·lous** /'tremyələs/ ▸*adj.* trembling. —**trem·u·lous·ly** *adv.* —**trem·u·lous·ness** *n.*

**trench** /trenCH/ ▸*n.* long, narrow, usu. deep ditch.

☐ **trench coat** loose belted raincoat.

**tren·chant** /'trenCHənt/ ▸*adj.* (of style or language, etc.) incisive; terse; vigorous. —**tren·chan·cy** *n.* —**tren·chant·ly** *adv.*

**trend** /trend/ ▸*n.* general direction and tendency (esp. of events, fashion, or opinion).

**trend·y** *inf.* ▸*adj.* (**-i·er, -i·est**) fashionable. —**trend·i·ly** *adv.* —**trend·i·ness** *n.*

**tre·pan** /trə'pan/ ▸*n.* saw used by surgeons for perforating the skull.

▸*v.* (**-panned, -pan·ning**) perforate (a person's skull) with a trepan.

**trep·i·da·tion** /,trepi'dāSHən/ ▸*n.* fear; anxiety.

**tres·pass** /'trespəs/ ▸*v.* **1** make an unlawful or unauthorized intrusion (esp. on land or property). **2** encroach: *trespass on your hospitality.*

▶*n.* act of trespassing.
—**tres·pass·er** *n.*

**tress** /tres/ ▶*n.* long lock of human hair.

**tres·tle** /ˈtresəl/ ▶*n.*
**1** supporting structure for a table, etc., usu. consisting of a bar with two divergent pairs of legs. **2** open braced framework to support a bridge, etc.

**tret** /tret/ ▶*n.* allowance of extra weight made to purchasers of certain goods to compensate for waste during transportation.

**tri-** ▶*comb. form* three or three times.

**tri·ad** /ˈtrīˌad/ ▶*n.* group of three (esp. notes in a chord).

**tri·age** /trēˈäzн/ ▶*n.* assignment of priorities for treatment of wounds, illnesses, etc.

**tri·al** /ˈtrīəl/ ▶*n.* **1** judicial examination and determination of issues between parties by a judge with or without a jury. **2** tryout; test.
☐ **on trial** **1** being tried in a court of law. **2** to be proved or tested.

**tri·an·gle** /ˈtrīˌaнɡɡəl/ ▶*n.*
**1** plane figure with three sides and angles. **2** triangular steel musical instrument struck with a small steel rod. —**tri·an·gu·lar** *adj.*

**tribe** /trīb/ ▶*n.* **1** group of (esp. primitive) families or communities, usu. linked by cultural ties and having a recognized leader. **2** any similar natural or political division.
—**trib·al** *adj.* —**trib·al·ism** *n.*

**tri·bol·o·gy** /trīˈbäləjē/ ▶*n.* study of friction, wear, lubrication, and the design of bearings; the science of interacting surfaces in relative motion.

**trib·u·la·tion** /ˌtribyəˈlāsнən/ ▶*n.* great affliction.

**tri·bu·nal** /trīˈbyoōnl/ ▶*n.* **1** board appointed to adjudicate in some matter. **2** court of justice. **3** place of judgment.

**trib·u·tar·y** /ˈtribyəˌterē/ ▶*n.* (*pl.* **-ies**) river or stream flowing into a larger river or lake.

**trib·ute** /ˈtribyoōt/ ▶*n.* **1** thing said, done, or given as a mark of respect or affection. **2** formerly, periodic payment by one nation or ruler to another.

**trice** /trīs/ ▶*n.* (in phrase **in a trice**) in a moment; instantly.

**tri·cen·ten·ni·al** ▶*n.* three-hundredth anniversary of an important event.

**tri·ceps** /ˈtrīˌseps/ ▶*n.* muscle (esp. in the upper arm) with three points of attachment at one end.

**trick** /trik/ ▸*n.* **1** action or scheme to fool, outwit, or deceive. **2** illusion: *trick of the light.* **3** special technique; knack. **4** feat of skill or dexterity. **5** practical joke. **6 a** cards played in one round of a card game. **b** point gained in this.
▸*v.* **1** deceive by a trick; outwit. **2** swindle: *tricked out of their savings.* —**trick·er·y** *n.* —**trick·y** *adj.*

**trick·le** /'trikəl/ ▸*v.* **1** flow or cause to flow in drops or a small stream. **2** come or go slowly or gradually: *information trickles out.*
▸*n.* trickling flow.

**tri·col·or** /'trī,kələr/ ▸*n.* flag of three colors.
▸*adj.* (also **tri·col·ored**) having three colors.

**tri·cy·cle** /'trīsikəl/ ▸*n.* three-wheeled pedal-driven vehicle.

**tri·dent** /'trīdnt/ ▸*n.* three-pronged spear.

**tried** /trīd/ ▸past and past part. of TRY.

**tri·en·ni·al** /trī'enēəl/ ▸*adj.* lasting or recurring every three years. —**tri·en·ni·al·ly** *adv.*

**tri·fle** /'trīfəl/ ▸*n.* **1** thing of slight value or importance. **2** small amount, esp. of money.
▸*v.* **1** talk or act frivolously. **2** (**trifle with**) treat or deal with frivolously.

**tri·fling** /'trīf(ə)liNG/ ▸*adj.* unimportant or trivial.

**trig·ger** /'trigər/ ▸*n.* **1** movable device for releasing a spring or catch and so setting off a mechanism (esp. that of a gun). **2** event, occurrence, etc., that sets off a chain reaction.
▸*v.* set (an action or process) in motion; precipitate.

**trig·o·nom·e·try** /,trigə'nämitrē/ ▸*n.* branch of mathematics dealing with the relations of the sides and angles of triangles and with the relevant functions of angles. —**trig·o·no·met·ric** *adj.* —**trig·o·no·met·ri·cal** *adj.*

**trill** /tril/ ▸*n.* **1** quavering sound, esp. a rapid alternation of sung or played notes. **2** bird's warbling. **3** pronunciation of *r* with a vibration of the tongue.
▸*v.* **1** produce a trill. **2** warble.

**tril·lion** /'trilyən/ ▸*n.* (*pl.* same or **-lions**) a million million (1,000,000,000,000 or $10^{12}$). —**tril·lionth** *adj. & n.*

**tril·o·gy** /ˈtriləjē/ ▸n. (pl. **-gies**) group of three related literary or operatic works.

**trim** /trim/ ▸v. (**trimmed, trim·ming**) **1** make neat or of the required size or form, esp. by cutting. **2** cut off (unwanted parts). **3** ornament; decorate. **4** arrange (sails) to suit the wind.

▸n. **1** ornament; decorative material. **2** cutting of a person's hair.

▸adj. **1** neat, slim, or tidy. **2** in good condition. **—trim·ly** adv. **—trim·ness** n.

**tri·mes·ter** /trīˈmestər/ ▸n. **1** period of three months, esp. of human gestation. **2** one of three terms in an academic year.

**trim·ming** /ˈtrimiNG/ ▸n. **1** ornamentation or decoration. **2** (**trimmings**) usual accompaniments, esp. of the main course of a meal. **3** (**trimmings**) pieces cut off in trimming.

**trin·i·ty** /ˈtrinitē/ ▸n. (pl. **-ties**) **1** state of being three. **2** group of three. **3** (**Trinity** or **Holy Trinity**) the three persons of the Christian Godhead (Father, Son, and Holy Spirit).

**trin·ket** /ˈtriNGkit/ ▸n. trifling ornament, esp. a piece of jewelry.

**tri·o** /ˈtrē-ō/ ▸n. (pl. **-os**) **1** group of three. **2** Mus. a composition for three performers. **b** group of three performers.

**trip** /trip/ ▸v. (**tripped, trip·ping**) **1** move with quick light steps. **2 a** stumble or cause to stumble, esp. by catching the feet. **b** (**trip up**) make or cause to make a slip or blunder. **3** release (part of a machine) suddenly by knocking aside a catch, etc.

▸n. **1** journey or excursion, esp. for pleasure. **2** tripping or being tripped or tripped up. **3** nimble step. **4** inf. hallucinatory experience caused by a drug.

**tri·par·tite** /trīˈpärˌtīt/ ▸adj. **1** consisting of three parts. **2** shared by or involving three parties.

**tripe** /trīp/ ▸n. **1** stomach of a ruminant, esp. an ox, as food. **2** inf. nonsense; rubbish.

**tri·ple** /ˈtripəl/ ▸adj. **1** consisting of three usu. equal parts or things; threefold. **2** involving three parties. **3** three times as much or many.

▸n. **1** threefold number or amount. **2** set of three.

**3** *Baseball* hit on which the batter reaches third base. ▸*v.* multiply by three.

**trip·let** /'triplit/ ▸*n.* each of three children or animals born at one birth.

**trip·li·cate** ▸*adj.* /'triplikit/ existing in three examples or copies. ▸*v.* /'tripli,kāt/ make three copies of. —**trip·li·ca·tion** *n.*

**tri·pod** /'trīpäd/ ▸*n.* three-legged stand for a camera, etc.

**trip·tych** /'triptik/ ▸*n.* picture or relief carving on three usu. hinged panels.

**tri·reme** /'trī,rēm/ ▸*n.* ancient Greek or Roman war galley with three banks of oars. The rowers are believed to have sat in threes on angled benches, rather than in three superimposed banks.

**tris·kai·dek·a·pho·bi·a** /,triskī,dekə'fōbēə; ,triskə-/ ▸*n.* extreme superstition regarding the number thirteen.

**tris·tesse** /trē'stes/ ▸*n.* state of melancholy sadness.

**trite** /trīt/ ▸*adj.* (of a phrase, opinion, etc.) hackneyed; overused. —**trite·ly** *adv.* —**trite·ness** *n.*

**tri·umph** /'trīəmf/ ▸*n.* **1 a** state of victory or success. **b** great success or achievement. **2** supreme example: *a triumph of engineering.* ▸*v.* **1** gain a victory; be successful. **2** (often **triumph over**) exult. —**tri·umph·ant** *adj.*

**tri·um·phal·ism** /trī'əmfə,lizəm/ ▸*n.* excessive exultation over one's success or achievements (used esp. in a political context).

**tri·um·vir** /trī'əmvər/ ▸*n.* (*pl.* **-virs** or **-vi·ri** /-və,rī/) (in ancient Rome) each of three public officers jointly responsible for overseeing any of the administrative departments.

**tri·um·vi·rate** /trī'əmvərit/ ▸*n.* ruling group of three persons.

**tri·une** /'trī,(y) o͞on/ ▸*adj.* consisting of three in one (used esp. with reference to the Trinity).

**triv·et** /'trivit/ ▸*n.* tripod or bracket for a hot pot, kettle, or dish to stand on.

**triv·i·a** /'trivēə/ ▸*pl. n.* trifles or trivialities.

**triv·i·al** /'trivēəl/ ▸*adj.* of small value or importance; trifling. —**triv·i·al·i·ty** *n.* —**triv·i·al·ly** *adv.*

**trog·lo·dyte** /'träglə,dīt/ ▸*n.* cave dweller, esp. of prehistoric times. —**trog·lo·dyt·ic** *adj.*

**troi·ka** /'troikə/ ▸*n.* **1** Russian

vehicle with a team of three horses abreast. **2** group of three people, esp. as an administrative council.

**troil·ism** /ˈtroiˌlizəm/ ▸*n.* sexual activity involving three participants.

**troll** /trōl/ ▸*n.* giant or dwarf in Scandinavian folklore.
▸*v.* fish by drawing bait along in the water.

**trol·ley** /ˈträlē/ ▸*n.* (*pl.* **-leys**) **1** (also **trolley car**) streetcar powered by electricity obtained from an overhead cable. **2** large cart or table on wheels.

**trol·lop** /ˈträləp/ ▸*n.* promiscuous or disreputable woman.

**trom·bone** /trämˈbōn/ ▸*n.* brass wind instrument with a sliding tube. —**trom·bon·ist** *n.*

**troop** /troōp/ ▸*n.* **1** assembled company; assemblage of people or animals. **2** (**troops**) soldiers; armed forces. **3** cavalry unit under a captain. **4** unit of Girl Scouts, Boy Scouts, etc.
▸*v.* come together or move in large numbers.

**tro·phy** /ˈtrōfē/ ▸*n.* (*pl.* **-phies**) **1** cup, statuette, etc., awarded as a prize in a contest. **2** memento or souvenir taken in hunting, war, etc.

**trop·ic** /ˈträpik/ ▸*n.* **1** parallel of latitude 23°27′ north (**tropic of Cancer**) or south (**tropic of Capricorn**) of the Equator. **2** (**the tropics**) warm-weather region between the tropics of Cancer and Capricorn. —**trop·i·cal** *adj.*

**tro·pism** /ˈtrōˌpizəm/ ▸*n.* turning of all or part of an organism in a particular direction in response to an external stimulus.

**tro·po·sphere** /ˈträpəˌsfi(ə)r/ ▸*n.* lowest layer of the atmosphere extending upward from the earth's surface. —**tro·po·spher·ic** *adj.*

**trot** /trät/ ▸*v.* (**trot·ted**, **trot·ting**) **1** run at a moderate pace. **2** (of a horse) proceed at a steady pace faster than a walk.
▸*n.* action or exercise of trotting.

**troth** /trôth/ ▸*n. archaic* faithfulness to a promise.

**trou·ba·dour** /ˈtroōbəˌdôr/ ▸*n.* French medieval lyric poet.

**trou·ble** /ˈtrəbəl/ ▸*n.* **1** difficulty or distress; vexation; affliction. **2** inconvenience; bother. **3** perceived failing: *that's the trouble with you.* **4** dysfunction: *engine trouble.* **5** strife; disturbance.
▸*v.* **1** cause distress or anxiety to; disturb; afflict. **2** subject or be

subjected to inconvenience or unpleasant exertion: *sorry to trouble you.* —**trou·ble·some** *adj.*

**trou·bled** ▶*adj.* beset by problems or conflict.

**trou·ble·mak·er** ▶*n.* person who habitually causes trouble. —**trou·ble·mak·ing** *n.*

**trou·ble·shoot·er** ▶*n.* **1** mediator in a dispute. **2** person who corrects faults in machinery, etc. —**trou·ble·shoot·ing** *n.*

**trough** /trôf/ ▶*n.* **1** long, narrow open receptacle for water, animal feed, etc. **2** channel or hollow like this. **3** elongated region of low barometric pressure.

**trounce** /trouns/ ▶*v.* defeat heavily. —**trounc·er** *n.* —**trounc·ing** *n.*

**troupe** /trōōp/ ▶*n.* company of actors, acrobats, etc.

**trou·sers** /ˈtrouzərz/ ▶*pl. n.* outer garment covering the body from the waist to the ankles, with a separate part for each leg.

**trous·seau** /ˈtrōō,sō/ ▶*n.* (*pl.* **-seaus** or **-seaux**) bride's collection of clothes, linens, etc.

**trout** /trout/ ▶*n.* (*pl.* same or **trouts**) food fish related to the salmon.

**tro·ver** /ˈtrōvər/ ▶*n.* common-law action to recover the value of personal property that has been wrongfully disposed of by another person.

**trow·el** /ˈtrouəl/ ▶*n.* **1** small flat-bladed tool used to spread mortar, etc. **2** scoop for lifting plants or earth.

**troy** /troi/ (also **troy weight**) ▶*n.* system of weights used for precious metals and gems.

**tru·ant** /ˈtrōōənt/ ▶*n.* child who stays away from school without permission. —**tru·an·cy** *n.*

**truce** /trōōs/ ▶*n.* temporary agreement to cease hostilities.

**truck** /trək/ ▶*n.* **1** vehicle for carrying loads. **2** handcart. **3** dealings. ▶*v.* convey on or in a truck. —**truck·er** *n.*

**tru·cu·lent** /ˈtrəkyələnt/ ▶*adj.* aggressively defiant. —**truc·u·lence** *n.* —**truc·u·lent·ly** *adv.*

**trudge** /trəj/ ▶*v.* go on foot, esp. laboriously. ▶*n.* trudging walk.

**true** /trōō/ ▶*adj.* **1** in accordance with fact or reality. **2** genuine; authentic. **3** loyal; faithful. **4** exact; accurate. —**tru·ly** *adj.*

**truf·fle** /ˈtrəfəl/ ▶*n.* **1** edible, rich-flavored underground fungus. **2** candy made of chocolate.

**tru·ism** /'troo͞,izəm/ ▶*n.* obviously true or hackneyed statement.

**trull** /trəl/ ▶*n.* prostitute.

**trump** /trəmp/ ▶*n.* playing card of a suit ranking above the others.

▶*v.* **1** play a trump card (on) when another suit has been led. **2** *inf.* gain a surprising advantage over.

**trum·per·y** ▶*n.* (*pl.* **-ies**) **1** worthless finery. **2** worthless article; junk.

**trum·pet** /'trəmpit/ ▶*n.* **1** brass instrument with a flared bell and a bright penetrating tone. **2** trumpet-shaped thing: *ear trumpet.*

▶*v.* proclaim loudly (a person's or thing's merit). **—trum·pet·er** *n.*

**trun·cate** /'trəNG,kāt/ ▶*v.* cut the top or the end from; shorten. **—trun·ca·tion** *n.*

**trun·cheon** /'trənCHən/ ▶*n.* short club carried esp. by a police officer.

**trun·dle** /'trəndl/ ▶*v.* roll or move heavily or noisily, esp. on or as on wheels.

□ **trundle bed** wheeled bed stored under a larger bed.

**trunk** /trəNGk/ ▶*n.* **1** main stem of a tree. **2** body apart from the limbs and head. **3** main part of any structure. **4** large box with a hinged lid for luggage, storage, etc. **5** usu. rear storage compartment of an automobile. **6** elephant's elongated prehensile nose. **7** (**trunks**) men's shorts worn for swimming, etc.

**truss** /trəs/ ▶*n.* **1** framework supporting a roof, bridge, etc. **2** surgical appliance worn to support a hernia.

▶*v.* **1** tie up (a fowl) for cooking. **2** support (a roof, bridge, etc.) with a truss or trusses.

**trust** /trəst/ ▶*n.* **1** firm belief in the reliability, truth, strength, etc., of a person or thing. **2** confident expectation. **3** responsibility: *in a position of trust.* **4** *Law* **a** arrangement whereby a person or group manages property on another's behalf. **b** property so held. **5** body of trustees. **6** association of companies for reducing competition, etc.

▶*v.* **1** place trust in; believe in. **2** allow to have or use (a thing): *trust them with my books.* **3** have faith, confidence, or hope that a thing will take place. **4** place reliance (in): *we trust in you.* **—trust·wor·thy** *adj.*

**trus·tee** ▶*n.* **1** *Law* person managing property in trust. **2** member of an administrative board.

**trust fund** ▶*n.* assets belonging to a trust, held by the trustees for the beneficiaries,

**trust·y** ▶*adj.* (**-i·er, -i·est**) loyal; faithful.

**truth** /trōōTH/ ▶*n.* **1** quality or state of being true. **2** what is true. **—truth·ful** *adj.* **—truth·ful·ly** *adv.* **—truth·ful·ness** *n.*

**try** /trī/ ▶*v.* (**tried**) **1** make an effort with a view to success. **2** make an effort to achieve: *tried my best.* **3** test by use or experiment. **4** tax: *tries my patience.* **5 a** investigate and decide (a case or issue) judicially. **b** subject (a person) to trial: *tried for murder.* ▶*n.* (*pl.* **tries**) effort to accomplish something. □ **tried and true** proved reliable by experience.

**try·ing** ▶*adj.* annoying; hard to endure.

**try·out** ▶*n.* test of ability, fitness, etc.

**tryst** /trist/ ▶*n.* meeting, esp. a secret one of lovers.

**tsar** /zär/ ▶var. of CZAR.

**T-shirt** (also **tee shirt**) ▶*n.* short-sleeved, collarless casual top having the form of a T when spread out.

**tsp.** ▶*abbr.* (*pl.* **tsps.**) teaspoon; teaspoonful.

**T square** ▶*n.* T-shaped instrument for drawing or testing right angles.

**tsu·na·mi** /(t)sōō'nämē/ ▶*n.* (*pl.* same or **-mis**) long high sea wave caused by an earthquake, submarine landslide, or other disturbance.

**tub** /təb/ ▶*n.* **1** open, flat-bottomed, usu. round container for various purposes. **2** bathtub.

**tu·ba** /'t(y)ōōbə/ ▶*n.* (*pl.* **-bas**) low-pitched brass wind instrument.

**tub·by** /'təbē/ ▶*adj.* (**-bi·er, -bi·est**) short and fat. **—tub·bi·ness** *n.*

**tube** /t(y)ōōb/ ▶*n.* **1** long, hollow cylinder. **2** pliable cylinder sealed at one end for holding a semiliquid substance: *tube of toothpaste.* **3** hollow, cylindrical organ in the body. **—tu·bal** *adj.* **—tub·ing** *n.* **—tu·bu·lar** *adj.*

**tu·ber** ▶*n.* thick, rounded part of a stem or rhizome, usu. found underground, e.g., a potato. **—tu·ber·ous** *adj.*

**tu·ber·cle** /'t(y)ōōbərkəl/ ▶*n.* small, rounded swelling on the body or in an organ, esp. as characteristic of tuberculosis.

**tu·ber·cu·lo·sis** /tə,bərkyə-'lōsis/ ▶*n.* infectious disease characterized by tubercles, esp. in the lungs. **—tu·ber·cu·lar** *adj.* **—tu·ber·cu·lous** *adj.*

**tu·bule** /'t(y)oo̅,byoo̅l/ ▶*n.* small tube in a plant or animal body.

**tuck** /tək/ ▶*v.* **1** draw, fold, or turn the outer or end parts of (cloth or clothes, etc.) close together so as to be held; thrust in the edge of (a thing). **2** stow: *tucked it in a corner.* **3** make a stitched fold in (material, a garment, etc.). ▶*n.* flattened, usu. stitched fold in material, etc.

**tuck·er** ▶*v. inf.* (usu. in phrase **be tuckered out**) exhaust; wear out.

**Tues.** (also **Tue.**) ▶*abbr.* Tuesday.

**Tues·day** /'t(y)oo̅z,dā/ ▶*n.* third day of the week, following Monday.

**tuft** /təft/ ▶*n.* bunch or collection of threads, grass, feathers, hair, etc., held or growing together at the base. **—tuft·ed** *adj.* **—tuft·y** *adj.*

**tug** /təg/ ▶*v.* (**tugged, tug·ging**) **1** pull hard or violently; jerk. **2** tow (a ship, etc.) with a tugboat.

▶*n.* **1** hard, violent, or jerky pull. **2** sudden strong emotion. **3** TUGBOAT.

☐ **tug-of-war 1** trial of strength between two sides pulling against each other on a rope. **2** decisive or severe contest.

**tug·boat** ▶*n.* small, powerful boat for towing or pushing ships, barges, etc.

**tu·i·tion** /t(y)oo̅'isHən/ ▶*n.* fee charged for instruction by a school, college, etc.

**tu·lip** /'t(y)oo̅ləp/ ▶*n.* bulbous spring-flowering plant with showy cup-shaped flowers.

**tulle** /tool/ ▶*n.* soft, fine silk, etc., net for veils and dresses.

**tum·ble** /'təmbəl/ ▶*v.* **1** fall or cause to fall suddenly, clumsily, or headlong. **2** perform acrobatic feats, esp. somersaults. ▶*n.* **1** sudden or headlong fall. **2** somersault or other acrobatic feat.

**tum·ble·down** ▶*adj.* falling or fallen into ruin.

**tum·bler** ▶*n.* **1** drinking glass. **2** acrobat. **3** pivoted piece in a lock that holds the bolt until lifted by a key or a combination.

**tum·ble·weed** ▶*n.* plant whose globular bush breaks off in late summer and is tumbled about by the wind.

**tum·brel** /'təmbrəl/ (also **tum·bril**) ▸*n.* open cart in which condemned persons were taken to the guillotine during the French Revolution.

**tu·mid** /'t(y)o͞omid/ ▸*adj.* **1** swollen; inflated. **2** bombastic; pompous. —**tu·mid·i·ty** *n.* —**tu·mid·ly** *adv.*

**tum·my** /'təmē/ ▸*n.* (*pl.* -**mies**) *inf.* stomach.

**tu·mor** /'t(y)o͞omər/ ▸*n.* swelling, esp. from an abnormal growth of tissue. —**tu·mor·ous** *adj.*

**tu·mult** /'t(y)o͞o͟,məlt/ ▸*n.* **1** uproar or din, esp. of a disorderly crowd. **2** emotional agitation. —**tu·mul·tu·ous** *adj.*

**tu·mu·lus** /'t(y)o͞omyə,ləs/ ▸*n.* (*pl.* -**li** /-,lī/) ancient burial mound; a barrow.

**tun** /tən/ ▸*n.* large beer or wine cask.

**tu·na** /'t(y)o͞onə/ ▸*n.* (*pl.* same or **tu·nas**) large edible marine fish.

**tun·dra** /'təndrə/ ▸*n.* vast, level, treeless Arctic region usu. with underlying permafrost.

**tune** /t(y)o͞on/ ▸*n.* melody. ▸*v.* **1** adjust (a musical instrument) to the true pitch. **2** adjust (a radio, etc.) to the frequency of a signal. **3** adjust (an engine, etc.) to run smoothly and efficiently. —**tune·ful** *adj.* —**tun·er** *n.*

**tune-up** ▸*n.* adjustment, as of the engine of a car, to improve performance.

**tung·sten** /'təNGstən/ ▸*n.* dense metallic element with a very high melting point. (Symb.: **W**)

**tu·nic** /'t(y)o͞onik/ ▸*n.* **1** blouselike garment extending to the hips, sometimes belted. **2** loose, often sleeveless garment, esp. as worn in ancient Greece and Rome.

**tun·ing fork** ▸*n.* two-pronged steel device that vibrates when struck to give a note of specific pitch.

**tun·nel** /'tənl/ ▸*n.* **1** underground passage dug through a hill or under a road, river, etc., esp. for a railroad or road. **2** underground passage dug by an animal. ▸*v.* **1** make a tunnel through. **2** make (one's way) by tunneling. □ **tunnel vision 1** vision that is normal only in a small central area. **2** *inf.* inability to grasp a situation's wider implications.

**tur·ban** /'tərbən/ ▸*n.* headdress

of fabric wound around a cap or the head. **—tur·baned** *adj.*

**tur·bid** /ˈtərbid/ ▶*adj.* **1** muddy; thick; not clear. **2** (of a style, etc.) confused; disordered. **—tur·bid·i·ty** *n.*

**tur·bine** /ˈtərˌbīn/ ▶*n.* rotary motor driven by a flow of water, steam, gas, wind, etc.

**tur·bo·jet** /ˈtərbōˌjet/ ▶*n.* **1** jet engine in which the jet also operates a turbine-driven air compressor. **2** aircraft powered by this.

**tur·bo·prop** ▶*n.* **1** jet engine in which a turbine is used as in a turbojet and also to drive a propeller. **2** aircraft powered by this.

**tur·bot** /ˈtərbət/ ▶*n.* any of various flatfishes prized as food.

**tur·bu·lent** /ˈtərbyələnt/ ▶*adj.* **1** disturbed; in commotion. **2** (of a flow of air, etc.) varying irregularly. **3** tumultuous; riotous. **—tur·bu·lence** *n.* **—tur·bu·lent·ly** *adv.*

**tu·reen** /t(y)o͞oˈrēn/ ▶*n.* deep covered dish for soup, etc.

**turf** /tərf/ ▶*n.* **1** layer of grass, etc., with earth and its roots. **2** (**the turf**) horse racing generally. **3** *inf.* person's territory or sphere of influence.

▶*v.* cover (ground) with turf.

**tur·gid** /ˈtərjid/ ▶*adj.* **1** swollen; inflated. **2** (of language) pompous; bombastic. **—tur·gid·i·ty** *n.*

**tur·key** /ˈtərkē/ ▶*n.* **1** large bird orig. of N. America, wild or bred for food. **2** *inf.* theatrical failure; flop.

□ **talk turkey** *inf.* talk frankly; get down to business.

**tur·mer·ic** /ˈtərmərik/ ▶*n.* **1** E. Indian plant of the ginger family. **2** its rhizome, powdered and used for yellow dye or as a spice, esp. in curry powder.

**tur·moil** /ˈtərˌmoil/ ▶*n.* **1** confusion; agitation. **2** din and bustle.

**turn** /tərn/ ▶*v.* **1** move around a point or axis; give or receive a rotary motion. **2** change in position or direction; invert; reverse. **3** change in nature, form, or condition: *turned into a dragon.* **4 a** set about: *turned to doing the ironing.* **b** have recourse to: *turned to me for help.* **c** go on to consider next: *we'll now turn to your report.* **5** become or cause to become: *turned sour.* **6 a** make or become hostile to: *turned them against us.* **b** become hostile to; attack: *suddenly turned* on them. **7** move to the other side of; go around: *turned the corner.*

▶*n.* **1** turning; rotary motion. **2** change of direction or tendency: *sudden turn to the left.* **3** point at which a turning or change occurs. **4** tendency or disposition: *mechanical turn of mind.* **5** opportunity, obligation, etc., that comes successively: *my turn to read.* **6** service of a specified kind: *did me a good turn.*

□ **at every turn** continually; at each new stage, etc. □ **in turn** in succession. □ **take turns** act alternately. □ **turn down** reject (a proposal, application, etc.). □ **turn in** hand in; deliver.

**turn·a·bout** ▶*n.* **1** act of turning about. **2** abrupt change of policy, etc.

**turn·coat** ▶*n.* person who changes sides in a conflict, dispute, etc.

**turn·ing point** ▶*n.* time at which a decisive change occurs.

**tur·nip** /ˈtərnəp/ ▶*n.* **1** plant with a large white globular root. **2** its root as a vegetable.

**turn·off** ▶*n.* **1** turning off a main road. **2** *inf.* something that repels or causes a loss of interest.

**turn·out** ▶*n.* number of people attending a meeting, etc.

**turn·o·ver** ▶*n.* **1** amount of money taken in a business. **2** rate at which people enter and leave employment, etc. **3** small pastry made by folding crust over a filling. **4** rate at which goods are sold and replaced.

**turn·pike** ▶*n.* highway on which a toll is usu. charged.

**turn·stile** ▶*n.* gate with revolving arms, allowing people through singly.

**turn·ta·ble** ▶*n.* circular revolving platform.

**tur·pen·tine** /ˈtərpənˌtīn/ ▶*n.* oil made from resin, used for thinning paint and as a solvent.

**tur·pi·tude** /ˈtərpiˌt(y)o͞od/ ▶*n.* depravity; wickedness.

**tur·quoise** /ˈtərˌk(w)oiz/ ▶*n.* **1** semiprecious stone, usu. opaque and greenish blue or blue. **2** greenish blue color. ▶*adj.* of this color.

**tur·ret** /ˈtərit/ ▶*n.* **1** small tower, esp. decorating a building. **2** low, flat, usu. revolving armored tower for a gun and gunners in a ship, aircraft, fort, or tank. **—tur·ret·ed** *adj.*

**tur·tle** /ˈtərtl/ ▶*n.* terrestrial or aquatic reptile encased in a shell of bony plates, and having flippers or webbed toes.

**tur·tle·dove** ▶*n.* wild dove noted for its soft cooing and affection for its mate.

**tur·tle·neck** ▶*n.* **1** high, close-fitting, turned over collar on a garment. **2** garment with such a collar.

**tusk** /təsk/ ▶*n.* long, pointed tooth, esp. protruding from a closed mouth, as in the elephant, walrus, etc. —**tusked** *adj.*

**tus·sive** /ˈtəsiv/ ▶*adj.* relating to coughing.

**tus·sle** /ˈtəsəl/ ▶*n.* scuffle. ▶*v.* engage in a tussle.

**tus·sock** /ˈtəsək/ ▶*n.* clump of grass, etc. —**tus·sock·y** *adj.*

**tu·te·lage** /ˈt(y)o͞otl-ij/ ▶*n.* **1** guardianship. **2** instruction.

**tu·tor** /ˈt(y)o͞otər/ ▶*n.* private teacher. ▶*v.* act as a tutor to.

**tu·tu** /ˈto͞oˌto͞o/ ▶*n.* ballet dancer's short skirt of stiffened frills.

**tux·e·do** /təkˈsēdō/ (also **tux**) ▶*n.* (*pl.* **-dos** or **-does**) man's short black formal jacket.

**TV** ▶*abbr.* television.

**twad·dle** /ˈtwädl/ ▶*n.* silly writing or talk.

**twain** /twān/ ▶*adj. & n. archaic* two.

**twang** /twaNG/ ▶*n.* **1** sound made by the plucked string of a musical instrument or bow. **2** nasal quality of a voice. ▶*v.* emit or cause to emit this sound. —**twang·y** *adj.*

**tweak** /twēk/ ▶*v.* pinch and twist sharply. ▶*n.* instance of tweaking.

**tweed** /twēd/ ▶*n.* rough-surfaced woolen cloth, usu. of mixed colors.

**tweet** /twēt/ ▶*n.* chirp of a small bird. ▶*v.* make a chirping noise.

**tweez·ers** /ˈtwēzərz/ ▶*pl. n.* small pair of pincers for picking up small objects, plucking out hairs, etc.

**twelve** /twelv/ ▶*n.* **1** one more than eleven. **2** symbol for this (12, xii, XII). —**twelfth** *adj. & n.*

**twen·ty** /ˈtwentē/ ▶*n.* (*pl.* **-ties**) **1** product of two and ten. **2** symbol for this (20, xx, XX). **3** (**twenties**) numbers from 20 to 29, esp. the years of a century or of a person's life. —**twen·ti·eth** *adj. & n.*

□ **twenty-twenty** (or **20/20**) **1** vision of normal acuity. **2** *inf.*

denoting clear perception or hindsight.

**twerp** /twərp/ ▸ *n. inf.* stupid or objectionable person.

**twice** /twīs/ ▸ *adv.* **1** two times; on two occasions. **2** double in degree or quantity: *twice as good.*

**twid·dle** /'twidl/ ▸ *v.* twirl, adjust, or play with randomly or idly.
▸ *n.* act of twiddling. **—twid·dly** *adj.*
□ **twiddle one's thumbs 1** make one's thumbs rotate around each other. **2** have nothing to do.

**twig** /twig/ ▸ *n.* small branch or shoot of a tree or shrub. **—twig·gy** *adj.*

**twi·light** /'twī,līt/ ▸ *n.* **1** light from the sky when the sun is below the horizon, esp. in the evening. **2** period of this.

**twill** /twil/ ▸ *n.* fabric so woven as to have a surface of diagonal parallel ridges. **—twilled** *adj.*

**twin** /twin/ ▸ *n.* **1** each of a closely related or associated pair, esp. of children or animals born at one birth. **2** exact counterpart of a person or thing.
□ **twin bed** each of a pair of single beds.

**twine** /twīn/ ▸ *n.* **1** strong string of twisted strands of fiber. **2** coil; twist.
▸ *v.* coil; wind.

**twinge** /twinj/ ▸ *n.* sharp momentary local pain or pang.

**twin·kle** /'twiNGkəl/ ▸ *v.* **1** (of a star, light, etc.) shine with rapidly intermittent gleams. **2** (of the eyes) sparkle.
▸ *n.* **1** sparkle or gleam of the eyes. **2** slight flash of light; glimmer. **3** short, rapid movement.
□ **in a twinkling** in an instant; very quickly.

**twirl** /twərl/ ▸ *v.* spin, swing, or twist quickly and lightly around.
▸ *n.* twirling motion. **—twirl·er** *n.* **—twirl·y** *adj.*

**twist** /twist/ ▸ *v.* **1** change the form (of) by rotating one end and not the other, or the two ends in opposite directions. **2** wrench or pull out of shape with a twisting action: *twisted my ankle.* **3** wind (strands, etc.) around each other. **4** take or cause to take a spiral form. **5** (**twist off**) break off by twisting.
▸ *n.* **1** act of twisting. **2** twisted state. **3** thing formed by twisting. **4** unexpected development. **—twist·y** *adj.*

**twist·er** ▸ *n. inf.* tornado.

**twit** /twit/ ▸ *n. inf.* silly or foolish person.

▸*v.* (**twit·ted, twit·ting**) reproach or taunt, usu. good-humoredly.

**twitch** /twiCH/ ▸*v.* **1** (of features, muscles, etc.) move or contract spasmodically. **2** pull sharply at. ▸*n.* **1** sudden involuntary contraction or movement. **2** sudden pull or jerk.

**twit·ter** ▸*v.* (of or like a bird) emit a succession of light tremulous sounds. ▸*n.* **1** twittering sound. **2** *inf.* tremulously excited state. —**twit·ter·y** *adj.*

**two** /too/ ▸*n.* **1** one more than one. **2** symbol for this (2, ii, II). ▸*adj.* that amount to two.

□ **two-bit** *inf.* cheap; petty. □ **two-dimensional 1** having or appearing to have length and breadth but no depth. **2** lacking depth or substance; superficial. □ **two-faced** insincere; deceitful.

**two·fold** ▸*adj. & adv.* **1** twice as much or as many. **2** consisting of two parts.

**two·some** ▸*n.* two persons together.

**twp.** ▸*abbr.* township.

**TX** ▸*abbr.* Texas (in official postal use).

**-ty** ▸*suffix* **1** forming nouns denoting quality or condition: *cruelty* | *plenty*. **2** denoting tens: *twenty* | *thirty* | *ninety.*

**ty·chism** /'tī‚kizəm/ ▸*n.* doctrine that account must be taken of the element of chance in reasoning or explanation of the universe.

**ty·coon** /tī'koon/ ▸*n.* business magnate.

**tyke** /tīk/ ▸*n.* small child.

**tym·pa·num** /'timpənəm/ ▸*n.* (*pl.* -**nums** or -**pa·na**) **1** middle ear. **2** eardrum. —**tym·pan·ic** *adj.*

**type** /tīp/ ▸*n.* **1** class; kind; sort. **2** person, thing, or event exemplifying a group or class. **3** printed characters or letters. ▸*v.* **1** write with a typewriter or keyboard. **2** assign to a type; classify.

**type·cast** ▸*v.* (*past* and *past part.* -**cast**) assign (an actor or actress) repeatedly to the same type of role.

**type·script** ▸*n.* typewritten document.

**type·set·ter** ▸*n.* **1** person who composes type. **2** composing machine. —**type·set** *v.* —**type·set·ting** *n.*

**type·writ·er** ▸*n.* machine with keys for producing printlike characters on paper inserted around a roller. —**type·writ·ten** *adj.*

**ty·phoid** /'tī,foid/ (also **ty·phoid fe·ver**) ▶*n.* infectious bacterial fever attacking the intestines.

**ty·phoon** /tī'foon/ ▶*n.* violent hurricane.

**ty·phus** /'tīfəs/ ▶*n.* infectious fever with a purple rash, headaches, and usu. delirium. —**ty·phous** *adj.*

**typ·i·cal** /'tipikəl/ ▶*adj.* **1** serving as a characteristic example; representative. **2** characteristic; to be expected. —**typ·i·cal·ly** *adv.*

**typ·i·fy** /'tipə,fī/ ▶*v.* (**-fied**) **1** be typical of. **2** represent by or as a type or symbol.

**ty·po** /'tīpō/ ▶*n.* (*pl.* **-pos**) *inf.* typographical error.

**ty·pog·ra·phy** /tī'pägrəfē/ ▶*n.* **1** art or process of printing. **2** style and appearance of printed matter. —**ty·pog·ra·pher** *n.* —**ty·po·graph·i·cal** *adj.* —**ty·po·graph·i·cal·ly** *adv.*

**tyr·an·ny** /'tirənē/ ▶*n.* (*pl.* **-nies**) **1** cruel and arbitrary use of authority. **2** rule by a tyrant. —**ty·ran·ni·cal** *adj.* —**tyr·an·nize** *v.*

**ty·rant** /'tīrənt/ ▶*n.* **1** oppressive or cruel ruler. **2** person exercising power arbitrarily or cruelly.

**ty·ro** /'tīrō/ ▶*n.* (*pl.* **-ros**) beginner; novice.

# Uu

**U**[1] /yōo/ (also **u**) ▸*n.* (*pl.* **Us** or **U's**; **u's**) **1** twenty-first letter of the alphabet. **2** U-shaped object or curve.

**U**[2] (also **U.**) ▸*abbr.* university.

**U**[3] ▸*symb. Chem.* uranium.

**u·biq·ui·tous** /yōoˈbikwətəs/ ▸*adj.* present everywhere or in several places simultaneously. —**u·biq·ui·tous·ly** *adv.* —**u·biq·ui·tous·ness** *n.* —**u·biq·ui·ty** *n.*

**ud·der** /ˈədər/ ▸*n.* baglike mammary gland of cattle, sheep, etc., with several teats.

**UFO** (also **ufo**) ▸*n.* (*pl.* **UFOs** or **ufos**) unidentified flying object.

**ug·ly** /ˈəglē/ ▸*adj.* (**-li·er, -li·est**) **1** unpleasing or repulsive to see or hear. **2** threatening; dangerous: *the sky has an ugly look.* —**ug·li·ness** *n.*

**u·ku·le·le** /ˌyōokəˈlālē/ ▸*n.* small, four-stringed guitar.

**ul·cer** /ˈəlsər/ ▸*n.* open sore on or in the body, often forming pus. —**ul·cer·ate** *v.* —**ul·cer·a·tion** *n.* —**ul·cer·ous** *adj.*

**ul·na** /ˈəlnə/ ▸*n.* (*pl.* **-nas** or **-nae**) the thinner and longer of the two forearm bones. —**ul·nar** *adj.*

**ul·te·ri·or** /əlˈti(ə)rēər/ ▸*adj.* existing in the background; hidden; secret: *ulterior motive.*

**ul·ti·mate** /ˈəltəmit/ ▸*adj.* **1** last or last possible; final. **2** fundamental; primary: *ultimate truths.* **3** maximum: *ultimate tensile strength.* —**ul·ti·mate·ly** *adj.* —**ul·ti·mate·ness** *n.*

**ul·ti·ma·tum** /ˌəltəˈmātəm/ ▸*n.* (*pl.* **-tums** or **-ta**) final demand or statement of terms in negotiations.

**ul·tra** /ˈəltrə/ ▸*adj.* favoring extreme views or measures, esp. in religion or politics.

**ultra-** ▸*comb. form* **1** beyond; on the other side of. **2** extreme(ly), excessive(ly): *ultraconservative | ultramodern.*

**ul·tra·high fre·quen·cy** ▸*n.* radio frequency in the range 300 to 3,000 MHz. (Abbr.: **UHF**)

**ul·tra·ma·rine** ▸*n.* brilliant blue pigment or color.

**ul·tra·son·ic** /ˌəltrəˈsänik/ ▸*adj.* of or involving sound waves with a frequency above the upper limit of human hearing.

**ul·tra·sound** ▶n. ultrasonic waves, esp. as used in medicine.

**ul·tra·vi·o·let** ▶adj. of or using radiation with a wavelength shorter than that of visible light rays.

**ul·tra vi·res** /ˌəltrə ˈvīrēz/ ▶adj. & adv. beyond one's legal power or authority.

**ul·u·late** /ˈəlyəˌlāt; ˈyo͞ol-/ ▶v. howl or wail as an expression of strong emotion, typically grief.

**um·ber** /ˈəmbər/ ▶n. brownish natural pigment or color.

**um·bil·i·cal cord** /ˌəmˈbilikəl/ ▶n. flexible cordlike structure attaching a human or other mammalian fetus to the placenta during gestation.

**um·bil·i·cus** /ˌəmˈbilikəs/ ▶n. (pl. -ci or -cus·es) navel.

**um·brage** /ˈəmbrij/ ▶n. offense; sense of slight or injury.

**um·brel·la** /ˌəmˈbrelə/ ▶n. **1** light, portable device for protection against rain, strong sun, etc., consisting of a usu. circular canopy of cloth mounted by means of a collapsible metal frame on a central stick. **2** protection or patronage.

**u·mi·ak** /ˈo͞omēˌak/ ▶n. Eskimo open boat made with skin stretched over a wooden frame.

**um·laut** /ˈo͞omˌlout/ ▶n. mark (··) used over a vowel, esp. in Germanic languages, to indicate a vowel change.

**ump** /əmp/ ▶n. inf. umpire.

**um·pire** /ˈəmˌpī(ə)r/ ▶n. person appointed to enforce the rules and settle disputes esp. in various sports. ▶v. act as umpire.

**ump·teen** /ˈəm(p)ˌtēn/ inf. ▶adj. indefinitely many; a lot of. ▶pron. indefinitely many. —**ump·teenth** adj.

**UN** ▶abbr. (also **U.N.**) United Nations.

**un-**[1] ▶prefix **1** added to adjectives and participles and their derivative nouns and adverbs, meaning: **a** not; denoting the absence of a quality or state: *unusable* | *unhappiness*. **b** reverse of, usu. with an implication of approval or disapproval: *unselfish* | *unscientific*. **2** (less often) added to nouns, meaning 'a lack of': *unrest* | *untruth*.

**un-**[2] ▶prefix added to verbs and (less often) nouns, forming verbs denoting: **1** reversal or cancellation of an action or

state: *undress* | *unsettle.*
**2** deprivation or separation: *unmask.* **3** release from: *unburden.* **4** causing to be no longer: *unman.*

**un·a·ble** /ˌənˈābəl/ ▸*adj.* lacking the skill, means, etc., to do something.

**un·ac·count·a·ble** ▸*adj.* **1** unable to be explained. **2** not responsible.
—**un·ac·count·a·bil·i·ty** *n.*
—**un·ac·count·a·bly** *adv.*

**un·af·fect·ed** ▸*adj.* **1** not affected. **2** free from affectation; genuine; sincere.
—**un·af·fect·ed·ly** *adv.*
—**un·af·fect·ed·ness** *n.*

**u·nan·i·mous** /yo͞oˈnanəməs/ ▸*adj.* **1** all in agreement: *the committee was unanimous.* **2** (of an opinion, vote, etc.) held or given by general consent: *the unanimous choice.* —**u·na·nim·i·ty** *n.* —**u·nan·i·mous·ly** *adv.*

**un·as·sum·ing** ▸*adj.* not pretentious or arrogant; modest.
—**un·as·sum·ing·ly** *adv.*

**un·at·tached** ▸*adj.* **1** not attached, esp. to a particular body, organization, etc. **2** not engaged or married.

**un·a·vail·ing** ▸*adj.* not availing; achieving nothing; ineffectual.
—**un·a·vail·ing·ly** *adv.*

**un·a·wares** ▸*adv.*
**1** unexpectedly: *met them unawares.* **2** inadvertently: *dropped it unawares.*

**un·bal·anced** ▸*adj.* **1** not keeping an even balance. **2** (of a person) mentally disturbed.

**un·bear·a·ble** ▸*adj.* not bearable. —**un·bear·a·bly** *adv.*

**un·be·com·ing** ▸*adj.* **1** not flattering a person. **2** not fitting; unsuitable.

**un·bend** ▸*v.* (*past* and *past part.* **-bent**) **1** straighten. **2** relax from strain or severity; become affable.

**un·bend·ing** ▸*adj.* inflexible; firm; austere: *unbending rectitude.*

**un·bid·den** ▸*adj.* without having been invited or commanded.

**un·blush·ing** ▸*adj.* not feeling or showing embarrassment or remorse.

**un·bos·om** ▸*v.* **1** disclose (thoughts, etc.). **2** unburden (oneself) of one's thoughts, etc.

**un·bowed** /ˌənˈboud/ ▸*adj.* not having submitted to pressure.

**un·bri·dled** ▸*adj.* uncontrolled; unrestrained.

**un·bro·ken** ▶*adj.* **1** not broken.
**2** not tamed: *unbroken horse.*
**3** not interrupted: *unbroken sleep.*
**4** not surpassed: *unbroken record.*

**un·bur·den** ▶*v.* **1** relieve of a
burden. **2** relieve (oneself, one's
conscience, etc.) by confession,
etc.

**un·called for** ▶*adj.* undesirable
and unnecessary: *uncalled-for
remarks.*

**un·can·ny** ▶*adj.* (**-ni·er, -ni·est**)
seemingly supernatural;
mysterious. —**un·can·ni·ly** *adv.*

**un·cer·e·mo·ni·ous** ▶*adj.*
**1** informal. **2** abrupt;
discourteous.
—**un·cer·e·mo·ni·ous·ly** *adv.*

**un·chart·ed** ▶*adj.* not mapped
or surveyed.

**un·cle** /ˈəNGkəl/ ▶*n.* **1** brother of
one's father or mother. **2** aunt's
husband.
□ **Uncle Sam** *inf.* federal
government personified: *will
fight for Uncle Sam.*

**un·com·pro·mis·ing** ▶*adj.*
unwilling to compromise;
stubborn; unyielding.

**un·con·cern** ▶*n.* indifference;
apathy.

**un·con·di·tion·al** ▶*adj.* not
subject to conditions; complete:

*unconditional surrender.*
—**un·con·di·tion·al·ly** *adv.*

**un·con·scion·a·ble** ▶*adj.*
**1** not right or reasonable.
**2** unreasonably excessive: *an
unconscionable length of time.*
—**un·con·scion·a·bly** *adv.*

**un·con·scious** ▶*adj.* not
conscious: *unconscious of any
change* | *fell unconscious on the
floor.*
▶*n.* that part of the mind that is
inaccessible to the conscious
mind but that affects behavior,
emotions, etc.
—**un·con·scious·ly** *adv.*
—**un·con·scious·ness** *n.*

**un·couth** /ˌənˈko͞oTH/ ▶*adj.* (of a
person, manners, appearance,
etc.) lacking in ease and polish;
uncultured; rough: *uncouth voices*
| *behavior was uncouth.*

**unc·tion** /ˈəNG(k)SHən/ ▶*n.*
anointing with oil, etc., as a
religious rite.

**unc·tu·ous** /ˈəNG(k)CHo͞oəs/ ▶*adj.*
**1** unpleasantly flattering;
ingratiating. **2** having a greasy
or soapy feel; oily.
—**unc·tu·ous·ly** *adv.*

**un·cut** ▶*adj.* **1** complete;
uncensored. **2** not shaped by
cutting.

**un·daunt·ed** ▸*adj.* not discouraged by difficulty, danger, etc.

**un·de·mon·stra·tive** ▸*adj.* not expressing feelings, etc., outwardly; reserved.

**un·der** /ˈəndər/ ▸*prep.* **1 a** in or to a position lower than; below; beneath: *fell under the table.* **b** on the inside of (a surface, etc.): *vest under his jacket.* **2 a** inferior to; less than: *a captain is under a major* | *is under 18.* **b** at or for a lower cost than: *under $20.* **3** subject to; controlled by: *lives under oppression* | *the country prospered under him.*
▸*adv.* **1** in or to a lower position or condition: *kept him under.* **2** *inf.* in a state of unconsciousness: *put her under for the operation.*

**under-** ▸*prefix* **1** below; beneath: *underground.* **2** lower in status; subordinate: *undersecretary.* **3** insufficiently; incompletely: *undercook* | *underdeveloped.*

**un·der·a·chieve** ▸*v.* do less well than might be expected (esp. scholastically).
—**un·der·a·chiev·er** *n.*

**un·der·age** ▸*adj.* not old enough, esp. not yet of adult status.

**un·der·bel·ly** ▸*n.* (*pl.* **-lies**) underside of an animal, vehicle, etc., esp. as an area vulnerable to attack.

**un·der·brush** ▸*n.* undergrowth in a forest.

**un·der·car·riage** ▸*n.* **1** wheeled, retractable structure beneath an aircraft used for landing, etc. **2** supporting frame of a vehicle.

**un·der·class** /ˈəndərˌklas/ ▸*n.* lowest social stratum in a country or community, consisting of the poor and unemployed.

**un·der·clothes** ▸*pl. n.* clothes worn under others, esp. next to the skin.

**un·der·cov·er** ▸*adj.* **1** surreptitious. **2** spying, esp. by infiltration: *undercover agent.*

**un·der·cur·rent** ▸*n.* underlying, often contrary, feeling, activity, or influence: *undercurrent of protest.*

**un·der·cut** ▸*v.* (**-cut·ting**; *past* and *past part.* **-cut**) **1** sell or work at a lower price than. **2** render unstable or less firm; undermine.

**un·der·de·vel·oped** ▸*adj.* **1** not fully developed; immature.

**2** (of a country, etc.) below its potential economic level.

**un·der·dog** ▸*n.* **1** oppressed person. **2** person whose loss in a contest, etc., is expected.

**un·der·done** ▸*adj.* not sufficiently cooked.

**un·der·es·ti·mate** ▸*v.* form too low an estimate of. —**un·der·es·ti·mation** *n.*

**un·der·ex·pose** ▸*v.* expose (film) for too short a time. —**un·der·ex·po·sure** *n.*

**un·der·gar·ment** ▸*n.* piece of underwear.

**un·der·go** ▸*v.* (*past* **-went**; *past part.* **-gone**) be subjected to; suffer; endure.

**un·der·grad·u·ate** /-ˈgrajo͞oit/ ▸*n.* student at a college or university who has not yet received a degree.

**un·der·ground** ▸*adv.* **1** beneath the ground. **2** in or into secrecy or hiding. ▸*adj.* **1** situated underground. **2** secret; subversive. **3** unconventional; experimental: *underground press.* ▸*n.* secret subversive group or activity.

**un·der·growth** ▸*n.* dense growth of shrubs, etc., esp. under large trees.

**un·der·hand** ▸*adj.* made with the arm or hand below shoulder level: *underhand serve.*

**un·der·hand·ed** ▸*adj.* secret; deceptive; crafty.

**un·der·line** ▸*v.* **1** draw a line under. **2** emphasize; stress.

**un·der·ling** /ˈəndərliNG/ ▸*n.* subordinate.

**un·der·mine** ▸*v.* injure, weaken, or wear out secretly or insidiously.

**un·der·neath** /-ˈnēTH/ ▸*prep.* **1** at or to a lower place than; below. **2** on the inside of; within. ▸*adv.* **1** at or to a lower place. **2** inside. ▸*n.* lower surface or part. ▸*adj.* lower.

**un·der·pass** ▸*n.* road, etc., passing under a railroad, another road, etc.

**un·der·pin·ning** ▸*n.* **1** solid underground foundation to support a building. **2** ideas, etc., that justify or form the basis for something.

**un·der·priv·i·leged** ▸*adj.* not enjoying the normal standard of living or rights in a society.

**un·der·score** ▸*v.* underline.

**un·der·sec·re·tar·y** ▸*n.* (*pl.* **-ies**) subordinate official, esp. a junior minister or senior civil servant.

**un·der·signed** ▶*adj.* [usu. as *pl. n.* **the undersigned**] who has or have signed this document.

**un·der·staffed** ▶*adj.* having too few staff.

**un·der·stand** ▶*v.* (*past* and *past part.* **-stood**) **1** perceive the meaning of (words, a person, a language, etc.): *understood you perfectly* | *cannot understand French.* **2** perceive the significance or explanation or cause of: *do not understand why he came.* **3** sympathize with; know how to deal with: *understand your difficulty* | *cannot understand him at all.* **4** infer esp. from information received; take as implied; take for granted: *I understand that it begins at noon.* —**un·der·stand·a·ble** *adj.* —**un·der·stand·a·bly** *adv.*

**un·der·stand·ing** ▶*n.* **1** ability to understand or think; intelligence. **2** power of abstract thought. **3** individual's perception of a situation, etc. **4** informal agreement. **5** sympathy or tolerance. ▶*adj.* **1** having understanding, insight, or good judgment. **2** sympathetic.

**un·der·state** ▶*v.* **1** express in greatly restrained terms. **2** represent as being less than it actually is. —**un·der·stat·ed** *adj.* —**un·der·state·ment** *n.*

**un·der·stud·y** ▶*n.* (*pl.* **-ies**) person ready to act at short notice in the absence of another. ▶*v.* (**-ied**) act as an understudy to (a person).

**un·der·take** ▶*v.* (*past* **-took**; *past part.* **-tak·en**) **1** bind oneself to perform; make oneself responsible for; engage in; enter upon (work, an enterprise, a responsibility, etc.). **2** accept an obligation; promise.

**un·der·tak·er** ▶*n.* person whose business is to organize funerals.

**un·der·tak·ing** ▶*n.* **1** work, etc., undertaken; enterprise: *a serious undertaking.* **2** pledge or promise.

**un·der·tone** ▶*n.* undercurrent of feeling.

**un·der·tow** ▶*n.* current below the surface of the sea moving in the opposite direction to the surface current.

**un·der·wear** ▶*n.* underclothes.

**un·der·whelm** /ˌəndər'(h)welm/ ▶*v.* (usu. **be underwhelmed**) fail to impress or make a positive impact on (someone); disappoint.

**un·der·world** ▸*n.* **1** those who live by organized crime and immorality. **2** mythical abode of the dead under the earth.

**un·der·write** ▸*v.* (*past* **-wrote;** *past part.* **-writ·ten**) **1** sign and accept liability under (an insurance policy, etc.). **2** undertake to finance or support. —**un·der·writ·er** *n.*

**un·dine** /ˌənˈdēn; ˈənˌdēn/ ▸*n.* female spirit or nymph inhabiting water.

**un·do** ▸*v.* (*past* **-did;** *past part.* **-done**) **1** unfasten or untie (a coat, button, package, etc.). **2** annul; cancel: *cannot undo the past.* **3** ruin or destroy.

**un·do·ing** ▸*n.* **1** ruin or cause of ruin. **2** reversing what has been done. **3** opening or unfastening.

**un·dress** ▸*v.* take clothes off.

**un·du·late** /ˈənjəˌlāt/ ▸*v.* have or cause to have a wavy motion or look. —**un·du·la·tion** *n.*

**un·dy·ing** ▸*adj.* **1** immortal. **2** never-ending: *undying love.* —**un·dy·ing·ly** *adv.*

**un·earned** ▸*adj.* not earned. □ **unearned income** income from investments, etc., as opposed to salary, etc.

**un·earth** ▸*v.* discover by searching, digging, or rummaging.

**un·earth·ly** ▸*adj.* supernatural; mysterious. —**un·earth·li·ness** *n.*

**un·eas·y** ▸*adj.* (**-i·er, -i·est**) nervous; anxious. —**un·eas·i·ly** *adv.* —**un·eas·i·ness** *n.*

**un·ed·i·fy·ing** /ˌənˈedəˌfī-iNG/ ▸*adj.* (esp. of an event taking place in public) distasteful; unpleasant.

**un·e·quiv·o·cal** ▸*adj.* not ambiguous; plain; unmistakable. —**un·e·quiv·o·cal·ly** *adv.*

**un·ex·cep·tion·al** ▸*adj.* not out of the ordinary; usual; normal. —**un·ex·cep·tion·al·ly** *adv.*

**un·feel·ing** ▸*adj.* unsympathetic; harsh. —**un·feel·ing·ly** *adv.*

**un·flap·pa·ble** /ˌənˈflapəbəl/ *inf.* ▸*adj.* imperturbable; calm. —**un·flap·pa·bil·i·ty** *n.* —**un·flap·pa·bly** *adv.*

**un·fledged** /-ˈflejd/ ▸*adj.* **1** (of a bird) not yet having enough feathers for flight. **2** immature; inexperienced.

**un·fold** ▸*v.* reveal or be revealed.

**un·found·ed** ▸*adj.* having no foundation: *unfounded hopes* | *unfounded rumor.*

**un·gain·ly** /-'gānlē/ ▸*adj.* awkward; clumsy. —**un·gain·li·ness** *n.*

**un·guent** /'əNGgwənt/ ▸*n.* soft substance used as ointment or for lubrication.

**un·hand** ▸*v. archaic* let go of.

**un·hinge** ▸*v.* **1** [usu. as *adj.* **unhinged**] make (someone) mentally unbalanced. **2** take (a door, etc.) off its hinges.

**uni-** ▸*comb. form* one; having or consisting of one.

**u·ni·cam·er·al** /,yo͞onə-'kam(ə)rəl/ ▸*adj.* (of a legislative body) having a single legislative chamber.

**u·ni·corn** /'yo͞onə,kôrn/ ▸*n.* mythical animal with a horse's body and a single straight horn.

**u·ni·form** ▸*adj.* **1** not changing in form or character; unvarying: *present a uniform appearance | of uniform size.* **2** conforming to the same standard, rules, or pattern. ▸*n.* distinctive clothing worn by members of the same body, e.g., by soldiers, police, and schoolchildren. —**u·ni·for·mi·ty** *n.* —**u·ni·form·ly** *adv.*

**u·ni·fy** /'yo͞onə,fī/ ▸*v.* (**-fied**) reduce to unity or uniformity. —**u·ni·fi·ca·tion** *n.*

**u·ni·lat·er·al** ▸*adj.* **1** performed by or affecting only one person or party: *unilateral disarmament.* **2** one-sided. —**u·ni·lat·er·al·ly** *adv.*

**un·im·peach·a·ble** ▸*adj.* beyond reproach or question. —**un·im·peach·a·bly** *adv.*

**un·in·hib·it·ed** ▸*adj.* expressing one's thoughts or feelings without restraint.

**un·in·ter·est·ed** ▸*adj.* **1** not interested. **2** unconcerned; indifferent.

**u·nion** /'yo͞onyən/ ▸*n.* **1** uniting; being united. **2** whole resulting from the combination of parts or members. **3** LABOR UNION. **4** concord; agreement: *lived together in perfect union.*

**u·nique** /yo͞o'nēk/ ▸*adj.* of which there is only one; unequaled; having no like, equal, or parallel: *this vase is considered unique.* —**u·nique·ly** *adv.* —**u·nique·ness** *n.*

**u·ni·sex** ▸*adj.* (of clothing, hairstyles, etc.) designed to be suitable for both sexes.

**u·ni·son** /'yo͞onəsən/ ▸*n.* **1** singing or playing the same melody. **2** agreement; concord: *acted in perfect unison.*

**u·nit** /'yo͞onit/ ▸*n.* **1** individual thing, person, or group regarded as single and complete.

**2** quantity as a standard in terms of which other quantities may be expressed: *unit of heat* | *mass per unit volume*. **3** device with a specified function forming part of a complex mechanism.

**U·ni·tar·i·an** /ˌyo͞oniˈte(ə)rēən/ ▶n. **1** person who believes that God is not a Trinity but one being. **2** member of a religious body maintaining this and advocating freedom from formal dogma or doctrine. —**U·ni·tar·i·an·ism** *n.*

**u·nite** /yo͞oˈnīt/ ▶v. **1** join together; combine. **2** form or cause to form a physical or chemical whole: *oil will not unite with water.*

**u·ni·ty** /ˈyo͞onitē/ ▶n. (*pl.* **-ties**) **1** oneness; being one, single, or individual; being formed of parts that constitute a whole: *disturbs the unity of the idea* | *national unity.* **2** harmony or concord between persons, etc. **3** thing forming a complex whole: *a person regarded as a unity.*

**u·ni·ver·sal** /ˌyo͞onəˈvərsəl/ ▶adj. of, belonging to, done, etc., by all; applicable to all cases: *met with universal approval.* —**u·ni·ver·sal·i·ty** *n.* —**u·ni·ver·sal·ly** *adv.*

**u·ni·verse** /ˈyo͞onəˌvərs/ ▶n. **1** all existing things; the cosmos. **2** sphere of existence, influence, activity, etc.

**u·ni·ver·si·ty** ▶n. (*pl.* **-ties**) educational institution designed for instruction, examination, or both, of students in many branches of advanced learning, conferring degrees in various disciplines, and often embodying colleges and similar institutions.

**un·kempt** /ˌənˈkem(p)t/ ▶adj. untidy; of neglected appearance.

**un·lead·ed** /ənˈledid/ ▶adj. (of gasoline, etc.) without added lead.

**un·less** /ənˈles/ ▶conj. if not; except when: *shall go unless I hear from you.*

**un·let·tered** ▶adj. illiterate.

**un·man** /ˌənˈman/ ▶v. (**-manned, -man·ning**) deprive of qualities traditionally associated with men, such as self-control or courage.

**un·mit·i·gat·ed** ▶adj. **1** not modified. **2** absolute; unqualified: *an unmitigated disaster.*

**un·nerve** ▶v. deprive of strength or resolution. —**un·nerv·ing·ly** *adv.*

**un·par·al·leled** ▸*adj.* having no parallel or equal.

**un·plumbed** ▸*adj.* not fully explored or understood.

**un·prin·ci·pled** ▸*adj.* lacking or not based on good moral principles.

**un·print·a·ble** ▸*adj.* that cannot be printed, esp. because too indecent or libelous or blasphemous.

**un·rav·el** ▸*v.* **1** cause to be no longer raveled, tangled, or intertwined. **2** probe and solve (a mystery, etc.). **3** undo (a fabric, esp. a knitted one). **4** become disentangled or unknitted.

**un·re·con·struct·ed** ▸*adj.* not reconciled to the current political theory.

**un·re·mit·ting** ▸*adj.* never relaxing or slackening; incessant. —**un·re·mit·ting·ly** *adv.*

**un·re·quit·ed** /ˌənriˈkwītid/ ▸*adj.* (of a feeling, esp. love) not returned or rewarded.

**un·rest** ▸*n.* restlessness; disturbance; agitation.

**un·ruf·fled** ▸*adj.* not agitated or disturbed; calm.

**un·rul·y** ▸*adj.* (**-i·er, -i·est**) not easily controlled or disciplined; disorderly. —**un·rul·i·ness** *n.*

**un·sa·vor·y** ▸*adj.*
**1** disagreeable; disgusting.
**2** morally offensive.

**un·scru·pu·lous** ▸*adj.* having no moral principles.
—**un·scru·pu·lous·ly** *adv.*

**un·sea·son·a·ble** ▸*adj.* **1** not appropriate to the season.
**2** untimely; inopportune.
—**un·sea·son·a·bly** *adv.*

**un·seat** ▸*v.* **1** remove from a position of authority. **2** dislodge from a seat, esp. on horseback.

**un·seem·ly** ▸*adj.* (**-li·er, -li·est**)
**1** indecent. **2** unbecoming.
—**un·seem·li·ness** *n.*

**un·seen** ▸*adj.* not seen; invisible.

**un·set·tle** ▸*v.* cause to feel anxious or uneasy; disturb.
—**un·set·tling** *adj.*

**un·sound** ▸*adj.* **1** unhealthy; diseased. **2** rotten; weak. **3** ill-founded; fallacious.
—**un·sound·ness** *n.*

**un·spar·ing** ▸*adj.* **1** lavish; profuse. **2** merciless.
—**un·spar·ing·ly** *adv.*

**un·speak·a·ble** ▸*adj.* **1** that cannot be expressed in words.
**2** indescribably bad or objectionable. —**un·speak·a·bly** *adv.*

**un·sta·ble** ▸*adj.* (**-bler, -blest**)
**1** not stable. **2** changeable.
**3** showing a tendency to sudden mental or emotional changes.

**un·strung** ▸*adj.* unnerved.

**un·sung** ▸*adj.* not celebrated; unknown; unappreciated.

**un·ten·a·ble** ▸*adj.* not tenable; that cannot be defended.

**un·think·a·ble** ▸*adj.* **1** that cannot be imagined or grasped by the mind. **2** *inf.* highly unlikely or undesirable.

**un·ti·dy** ▸*adj.* (**-di·er, -di·est**) not neat or orderly. —**un·ti·di·ly** *adv.* —**un·ti·di·ness** *n.*

**un·tie** ▸*v.* (*pres. part.* **-ty·ing**)
**1** undo (a knot, the cords of a package, etc.). **2** release from bonds or attachment.

**un·til** /ˌənˈtil/ ▸*prep. & conj.* up to the time of the event mentioned: *he held the position until his death | you don't know what you can do until you try.*

**un·to** /ˈəntoō/ ▸*prep.* archaic term for **TO** : *do unto others | faithful unto death | take unto oneself.*

**un·told** ▸*adj.* not (able to be) counted or measured: *untold misery.*

**un·touch·a·ble** ▸*adj.* that may not or cannot be touched.

**un·to·ward** ▸*adj.*
**1** inconvenient; unexpected.
**2** unseemly.

**un·u·su·al** ▸*adj.* not usual; remarkable; rare. —**un·u·su·al·ly** *adv.*

**un·well** ▸*adj.* not in good health; (somewhat) ill.

**un·wield·y** /ˌənˈwēldē/ ▸*adj.* (**-i·er, -i·est**) cumbersome, or hard to manage, owing to size, shape, etc. —**un·wield·i·ness** *n.*

**un·will·ing** ▸*adj.* reluctant. —**un·will·ing·ly** *adv.* —**un·will·ing·ness** *n.*

**un·wit·ting** /-ˈwitiNG/ ▸*adj.*
**1** unaware: *unwitting offender.*
**2** unintentional. —**un·wit·ting·ly** *adv.* —**un·wit·ting·ness** *n.*

**un·wont·ed** /-ˈwôntid/ ▸*adj.* not customary or usual. —**un·wont·ed·ly** *adv.*

**up** /əp/ ▸*adv.* **1** at, in, or toward a higher place or position: *jumped up in the air | what are they doing up there?* **2** to or in a place regarded as higher, esp. northward: *up in New England.* **3** *inf.* ahead, etc., as indicated: *went up front.* **4 a** to or in an erect position or condition: *stood it up.* **b** to or in a prepared or required position: *wound up the watch.* **c** in or into a condition of efficiency, activity, or progress: *stirred up trouble* | *the house is up for sale.* **5** (of a computer, machine, etc.) running and available for use. **6** at or to a higher price or value: *our costs are up.* **7** completely or effectually: *burn up* | *eat up* | *use up.* **8** completed; past: *time is up.* **9** awake or out of bed: *are you up yet?* **10** (of the sun, etc.) having risen. **11** happening, esp. unusually or unexpectedly: *something is up.* **12** (**up on**) informed about. **13** *Baseball* at bat: *he struck out his last time up.*

▶*prep.* **1** upward along, through, or into: *climbed up the ladder.* **2** along: *walked up the road.* **3** at or in a higher part of: *is situated up the street.*

▶*v.* (**upped**, **up·ping**) increase or raise, esp. abruptly: *upped all their prices.*

☐ **ups and downs** mixed fortune.

**up-** ▶*prefix* added: **1** as an adverb to verbs and verbal derivations, meaning 'upward': *update.* **2** as a preposition to nouns forming adverbs and adjectives: *up-country* | *uphill.* **3** as an adjective to nouns: *upland* | *upstroke.*

**up·beat** ▶*n.* unaccented beat in music.

▶*adj. inf.* optimistic or cheerful.

**up·braid** ▶*v.* chide or reproach (a person).

**up·bring·ing** ▶*n.* care and education of a child.

**UPC** ▶*abbr.* Universal Product Code.

**up·com·ing** ▶*adj.* forthcoming; about to happen.

**up·coun·try** ▶*adv. & adj.* toward the interior of a region.

**up·date** ▶*v.* bring up to date. ▶*n.* updated information, etc.

**up·end** ▶*v.* set or rise up on end.

**up·grade** ▶*v.* **1** raise in rank, etc. **2** improve (equipment, etc.). ▶*n.* **1** upgrading. **2** improvement. **3** upward slope.

**up·heav·al** /ˌəpˈhēvəl/ ▶*n.* violent or sudden change or disruption.

**up·hill** ▶*adv.* up a hill, slope, etc. ▶*adj.* **1** sloping up; ascending. **2** arduous; difficult: *an uphill task.*

**up·hold** ▶*v.* (*past* and *past part.* **-held**) **1** confirm. **2** support (a person, practice, etc.).

**up·hol·ster·y** /əpˈhōlstərē/ ▶*n.* soft, padded textile covering affixed to furniture such as sofas, chairs, etc. —**up·hol·ster** *v.* —**up·hol·ster·er** *n.*

**up·keep** ▸*n.* **1** maintenance in good condition. **2** cost or means of this.

**up·land** ▸*n. & adj.* (of) the higher or inland parts of a country.

**up·lift** ▸*v.* **1** raise; lift up. **2** elevate morally or spiritually.
▸*n. inf.* morally or spiritually elevating influence. —**up·lift·ing** *adj.*

**up·link** /ˈəpˌliNGk/ ▸*n.* communications link to a satellite.
▸*v.* provide (someone) with or send (something) by such a link.

**up·mar·ket** /ˌəpˈmärkit; ˈəp-ˌmär-/ (also **up-mar·ket**) ▸*adj. & adv.* upscale.

**up·on** /əˈpän/ ▸*prep.* another term for ON. *Upon* is sometimes more formal, and is preferred in *once upon a time* and *upon my word*, and in uses such as *row upon row of seats* and *Christmas is almost upon us.*

**up·per** ▸*adj.* **1** higher in place; situated above: *upper lip.* **2** higher in rank or dignity, etc.: *upper class.*
▸*n.* **1** part of a boot or shoe above the sole. **2** *inf.* stimulant drug, esp. an amphetamine.
□ **upper hand** dominance or control.

**up·per·case** ▸*adj.* (of letters) capital.
▸*n.* capital letters.

**up·pish** /ˈəpiSH/ ▸*adj.* arrogantly self-assertive.

**up·pi·ty** /ˈəpətē/ ▸*adj. inf.* arrogant; snobbish.

**up·right** ▸*adj.* **1** erect; vertical: *an upright posture.* **2** honorable or honest.
▸*n.* vertical part or support. —**up·right·ly** *adv.* —**up·right·ness** *n.*

**up·ris·ing** ▸*n.* rebellion or revolt.

**up·roar** ▸*n.* tumult; violent disturbance.

**up·roar·i·ous** /ˌəpˈrôrēəs/ ▸*adj.* **1** characterized by or provoking loud noise or uproar. **2** very funny.

**up·root** ▸*v.* **1** pull (a plant, etc.) up from the ground. **2** displace.

**up·scale** ▸*adj. & adv.* toward or relating to the more affluent or upper sector of society or the market.

**up·set** ▸*v.* (-set·ting; *past* and *past part.* -set) **1** overturn or be overturned. **2** overcome; defeat. **3** disturb or disrupt.
▸*n.* **1** condition of upsetting or being upset: *a stomach upset.*

**2** surprising result in a game, etc.

▶*adj.* disturbed: *upset stomach.* —**up·set·ting·ly** *adv.*

**up·shot** ▶*n.* outcome or conclusion.

**up·side down** ▶*adv.* **1** with the upper part where the lower part should be; inverted. **2** in or into total disorder.

▶*adj.* (also **up·side-down**) inverted.

**up·stage** ▶*adj. & adv.* nearer the back of a stage.

▶*v.* divert attention from (a person) to oneself; outshine.

**up·stairs** /ˌəp'ste(ə)rz/ ▶*adv. & adj.* to or on an upper floor.

▶*n.* upper floor.

**up·start** ▶*n.* newly successful, esp. arrogant, person.

**up-to-date** ▶*adj.* modern; fashionable.

**up·ward** ▶*adv.* (also **up·wards**) toward what is higher, superior, larger in amount, or more important.

▶*adj.* moving, extending, pointing, or leading upward.

**u·ra·ni·um** /yoŏ'rānēəm/ ▶*n. Chem.* radioactive, gray, dense metallic element, capable of nuclear fission and used as a source of nuclear energy. (Symb.: U) —**u·ran·ic** *adj.*

**U·ra·nus** /'yoŏrənəs/ ▶*n.* seventh planet from the sun.

**ur·ban** /'ərbən/ ▶*adj.* of, living in, or situated in a town or city: *an urban population.*

**ur·bane** /ər'bān/ ▶*adj.* courteous; suave; elegant and refined in manner. —**ur·bane·ly** *adv.* —**ur·ban·i·ty** *n.*

**ur·chin** /'ərchin/ ▶*n.* mischievous child, esp. young and raggedly dressed.

**u·re·a** /yoŏ'rēə/ ▶*n.* soluble, nitrogenous compound contained esp. in urine. —**u·re·al** *adj.*

**u·re·ter** /'yoŏrətər; yoŏ'rētər/ ▶*n.* duct by which urine passes from the kidney to the bladder.

**u·re·thra** /yoŏ'rēthrə/ ▶*n.* (*pl.* **-thras** or **-thrae**) duct by which urine is discharged from the bladder.

**urge** /ərj/ ▶*v.* **1** drive forcibly; impel: *urged the horses forward.* **2** encourage or entreat earnestly or persistently: *urged them to go.* **3** advocate (an action or argument, etc.) emphatically (to a person).

▶*n.* **1** urging impulse or tendency. **2** strong desire.

**ur·gent** /'ərjənt/ ▶*adj.* **1** requiring immediate action or attention. **2** persistent in demand. —**ur·gen·cy** *n.* —**ur·gent·ly** *adv.*

**u·ri·nal** /ˈyo͝orənl/ ▶*n.* place or receptacle for urination by men.

**u·ri·nate** /ˈyo͝orəˌnāt/ ▶*v.* discharge urine. —**u·ri·na·tion** *n.*

**u·rine** /ˈyo͝orən/ ▶*n.* pale-yellow fluid secreted as waste from the blood by the kidneys, stored in the bladder, and discharged through the urethra. —**u·ri·na·ry** *adj.*

**urn** /ərn/ ▶*n.* **1** vase with a foot and usu. a rounded body, esp. for storing the ashes of the dead. **2** large vessel with a tap, in which tea or coffee is made or kept hot.

**u·rol·o·gy** /yo͝oˈräləjē/ ▶*n.* scientific study of the urinary system. —**u·ro·log·ic** *adj.* —**u·rol·o·gist** *n.*

**ur·sine** /ˈərˌsin; -ˌsēn/ ▶*adj.* of, relating to, or resembling bears.

**ur·text** /ˈo͝orˌtekst/ ▶*n.* (*pl.* **-tex·te** /-ˌtekstə/) original or the earliest version of a text, to which later versions can be compared.

**ur·ti·cate** /ˈərtiˌkāt/ ▶*v.* cause a stinging or prickling sensation like that given by a nettle.

**U.S.** (also **US**) ▶*abbr.* United States (of America).

**us** /əs/ ▶*pron.* objective case of WE: *they saw us.*

**us·age** /ˈyo͞osij/ ▶*n.* **1** use; treatment: *damaged by rough usage.* **2** habitual or customary practice, esp. as creating a right, obligation, or standard.

**use** ▶*v.* /yo͞oz/ **1 a** cause to act or serve for a purpose; bring into service: *rarely uses the car.* **b** consume or take (alcohol, a drug, etc.), esp. habitually. **2** exploit for one's own ends: *they are just using you* | *used his position.* **3** (**used to**) did or had in the past (but no longer) as a customary practice or state: *I used to be an archaeologist.* **4** (**be/get used to**) be or become familiar with by habit; accustomed: *I am not used to hard work.*

▶*n.* /yo͞os/ **1** using or being used: *put it to good use* | *worn and polished with use.* **2** right or power of using: *lost the use of my right arm.* **3 a** ability to be used: *a flashlight would be of use.* **b** purpose for which a thing can be used. **4** custom or usage: *long use has reconciled me to it.* —**us·a·ble** *adj.* —**use·ful** *adj.* —**use·less** *adj.* —**us·er** *n.*

**used** /yo͞ozd/ ▶*adj.* secondhand.

**us·er-friend·ly** ▸*adj.* (of a machine or system) designed to be easy to use.

**ush·er** /ˈəSHər/ ▸*n.* person who shows people to their seats in a theater, church, etc.

▸*v.* **1** act as usher to. **2** announce or show in, etc.: *ushered us into the room.*

**u·su·al** /ˈyo͞oZHo͞oəl/ ▸*adj.* customary; habitual: *the usual formalities | it is usual to tip them | forgot my keys as usual.*

▸*n.* (**the usual**) *inf.* person's usual drink, meal, etc. —**u·su·al·ly** *adv.*

**u·surp** /yo͞oˈsərp/ ▸*v.* seize or assume (a throne or power, etc.) wrongfully. —**u·surp·er** *n.*

**u·su·ry** /ˈyo͞oZHərē/ ▸*n.* **1** lending of money at an exorbitant or illegal rate of interest. **2** interest at this rate. —**u·su·rer** *n.* —**u·su·ri·ous** *adj.*

**UT** ▸*abbr.* Utah (in official postal use).

**u·ten·sil** /yo͞oˈtensəl/ ▸*n.* implement or vessel, esp. for domestic use: *cooking utensils.*

**u·ter·us** /ˈyo͞otərəs/ ▸*n.* (*pl.* **-ter·i** or **-ter·us·es**) the womb. —**u·ter·ine** *adj.*

**u·tile** /ˈyo͞otl; ˈyo͞oˌtīl/ ▸*adj.* advantageous.

**u·til·i·tar·i·an** /yo͞oˌtiləˈte(ə)rēən/ ▸*adj.* designed to be useful rather than attractive; severely practical.

**u·til·i·ty** /yo͞oˈtilətē/ ▸*n.* (*pl.* **-ties**) **1** being useful or profitable. **2** PUBLIC UTILITY.

**u·ti·lize** ▸*v.* make practical use of; use effectively. —**u·ti·li·za·tion** *n.* —**u·ti·liz·er** *n.*

**ut·most** /ˈətˌmōst/ ▸*adj.* furthest, extreme, or greatest: *showed the utmost reluctance.*

**U·to·pi·a** /yo͞oˈtōpēə/ ▸*n.* imaginary place or state where everything is perfect. —**U·to·pi·an** *adj.*

**ut·ter** /ˈətər/ ▸*v.* **1** emit audibly. **2** express in words.

▸*adj.* complete; total; absolute: *utter misery | saw the utter absurdity of it.* —**ut·ter·ly** *adv.*

**u·vu·la** /ˈyo͞ovyələ/ ▸*n.* (*pl.* **-las** or **-lae**) fleshy extension of the soft palate hanging above the throat. —**u·vu·lar** *adj.*

**ux·o·ri·al** /ˌəkˈsôrēəl; əgˈzôr-/ ▸*adj.* of or relating to a wife.

# Vv

**V**¹ /vē/ (also **v**) ▶*n.* (*pl.* **Vs** or **V's**; **v's**) **1** twenty-second letter of the alphabet. **2** V-shaped thing. **3** (as a Roman numeral) five.

**V**² (also **V.**) ▶*abbr.* volt(s).

**V**³ ▶*symb. Chem.* vanadium.

**v.** ▶*abbr.* **1** verse. **2** verso. **3** versus. **4** very.

**VA** ▶*abbr.* **1** Veterans Administration. **2** Virginia (in official postal use).

**Va.** ▶*abbr.* Virginia.

**va·can·cy** /'vākənsē/ ▶*n.* (*pl.* **-cies**) **1** being vacant or empty. **2** unoccupied position or job: *there are three vacancies for computer specialists.* **3** available room in a hotel, etc.

**va·cant** /'vākənt/ ▶*adj.* not filled nor occupied; empty. —**va·cant·ly** *adv.*

**va·cate** /'vā,kāt/ ▶*v.* **1** leave vacant or cease to occupy (a room, etc.). **2** give up (a post, etc.).

**va·ca·tion** /vā'kāsHən/ ▶*n.* time of rest, recreation, etc., esp. spent away from home.
▶*v.* take a vacation, esp. away from home for pleasure and recreation.

**vac·ci·nate** /'vaksə,nāt/ ▶*v.* inoculate to immunize against a disease. —**vac·ci·na·tion** *n.*

**vac·cine** /vak'sēn/ ▶*n.* substance used to stimulate the production of antibodies and procure immunity from disease.

**vac·il·late** /'vasə,lāt/ ▶*v.* be irresolute; keep changing one's mind. —**vac·il·la·tion** *n.*

**vac·u·ous** /'vakyo͞oəs/ ▶*adj.* unintelligent; mindless; inane. —**va·cu·i·ty** *n.*

**vac·u·um** /'vak,yo͞o(ə)m/ ▶*n.* (*pl.* **-u·ums** or **-u·a**) **1** space entirely devoid of matter. **2** space from which the air has been completely or partly removed by a pump, etc. **3** absence of the normal or previous content, activities, etc. **4** (*pl.* **-u·ums**) *inf.* vacuum cleaner.
▶*v. inf.* use or clean with a vacuum cleaner.
□ **vacuum cleaner** apparatus for removing dust, etc., by suction.
□ **vacuum-packed** sealed after partial removal of air. □ **vacuum**

**tube** *Electr.* tube with a near-vacuum that regulates electric current.

**va·de me·cum** /ˌvädē ˈmākəm; ˌvädē ˈmē-/ ▶*n.* handbook or guide that is kept constantly at hand for consultation.

**vag·a·bond** /ˈvagəˌbänd/ ▶*n.* wanderer, esp. an idle one. ▶*adj.* wandering.

**va·ga·ry** /ˈvāgərē/ ▶*n.* (*pl.* **-ries**) caprice; eccentric idea or act: *the vagaries of Fortune.*

**va·gi·na** /vəˈjīnə/ ▶*n.* (*pl.* **-nas** or **-nae**) canal between the uterus and vulva in female mammals. —**vag·i·nal** *adj.*

**va·gi·na den·ta·ta** /denˈtätə/ ▶*n.* motif of a vagina with teeth, occurring in folklore and fantasy and said to symbolize male fears of the dangers of sexual intercourse, esp. of castration.

**vag·i·nis·mus** /ˌvajəˈnizməs/ ▶*n.* painful spasmodic contraction of the vagina in response to physical contact or pressure (esp. in sexual intercourse).

**va·grant** /ˈvāgrənt/ ▶*n.* person without a settled home or regular work. ▶*adj.* wandering or roving: *a vagrant musician.* —**va·gran·cy** *n.*

**vague** /vāg/ ▶*adj.* (**va·guer**, **va·guest**) uncertain, indefinite, or unclear: *gave a vague answer.* —**vague·ly** *adv.* —**vague·ness** *n.*

**vain** /vān/ ▶*adj.* (**-er**, **-est**)
**1** excessively proud or conceited, esp. about one's own attributes.
**2** empty; trivial: *vain boasts.*
**3** useless; futile. —**vain·ly** *adv.* —**vain·ness** *n.*
□ **in vain** without success: *it was in vain that we protested.*

**vain·glo·ry** ▶*n.* boastfulness; extreme vanity. —**vain·glo·ri·ous** *adj.*

**val·ance** /ˈvaləns/ ▶*n.* short curtain around the frame or canopy of a bed, above a window, or under a shelf.

**vale** /vāl/ ▶*n.* valley: *the Vale of Glamorgen.*

**val·e·dic·to·ri·an** /ˌvalidikˈtôrēən/ ▶*n.* person who gives a valedictory, esp. the highest-ranking member of a graduating class.

**val·e·dic·to·ry** /ˌvaliˈdikt(ə)rē/ ▶*adj.* serving as a farewell.
▶*n.* (*pl.* **-ries**) farewell address.

**va·lence** /ˈvāləns/ ▶*n.* *Chem.* combining power of an atom measured by the number of hydrogen atoms it can displace or combine with.

**val·en·tine** /ˈvalənˌtīn/ ▶n.
1 card or gift sent as a mark of love or affection on St. Valentine's Day (Feb. 14).
2 sweetheart greeted on this day.

**va·let** /vaˈlā/ ▶n. man's personal attendant.
▶v. act as a valet to.

**val·iant** /ˈvalyənt/ ▶adj. brave; courageous. —**val·iant·ly** adv.

**val·id** /ˈvalid/ ▶adj. 1 (of a reason, objection, etc.) sound or defensible. 2 legally acceptable: valid passport. —**val·i·date** v. —**va·lid·i·ty** n. —**val·id·ly** adv.

**val·ise** /vəˈlēs/ ▶n. small suitcase; traveling bag.

**val·ley** /ˈvalē/ ▶n. low area between hills and usu. with a stream flowing through it.

**val·or** /ˈvalər/ ▶n. courage, esp. in battle.

**val·u·able** /ˈvaly(oo)əbəl/ ▶adj. of great value, price, or worth.
▶pl. n. (**valuables**) valuable things.

**val·u·a·tion** /ˌvalyooˈāsHən/ ▶n.
1 estimation (esp. by a professional) of a thing's worth.
2 worth estimated. —**val·u·ate** v.

**val·ue** /ˈvalyoo/ ▶n. 1 worth, desirability, or utility: the value of regular exercise. 2 amount of money or goods for which a thing can be exchanged in the open market. 3 (**values**) one's principles or standards; one's judgment of what is valuable or important in life. 4 Math. amount denoted by an algebraic term.
▶v. (**-ued, -u·ing**) 1 estimate the value of (esp. professionally): valued the property at $200,000.
2 have a high or specified opinion of: a valued friend.

**valve** /valv/ ▶n. 1 device controlling the flow of fluid through a pipe, etc. 2 part of an organ, etc., allowing a flow of blood, etc., in one direction only. 3 device to vary the effective length of the tube in a brass musical instrument. 4 each of the two shells of an oyster, mussel, etc.

**vamp** /vamp/ ▶n. 1 upper front part of a boot or shoe. 2 (in popular music) short, simple introductory passage. 3 inf. woman who uses sexual attraction to exploit men.

**vam·pire** /ˈvamˌpī(ə)r/ ▶n. supposedly reanimated corpse that sucks the blood of sleeping persons.

**van** /van/ ▶n. 1 covered vehicle for conveying goods, etc., esp. a large truck or trailer: moving van.

**2** smaller such vehicle, similar to a panel truck and used esp. for carrying passengers, etc.

**van·dal** /ˈvandl/ ▸*n.* person who willfully or maliciously damages property. —**van·dal·ism** *n.* —**van·dal·ize** *v.*

**vane** /vān/ ▸*n.* **1** (also **weather vane**) revolving pointer on a roof or other high place to show the direction of the wind. **2** blade of a propeller, sail of a windmill, etc.

**van·guard** ▸*n.* **1** foremost part of an advancing army, etc. **2** leaders of a movement, etc.

**va·nil·la** /vəˈnilə/ ▸*n.* **1 a** tropical climbing orchid with fragrant flowers. **b** (**vanilla bean**) fruit of these. **2** flavoring obtained from the vanilla bean.

**van·ish** /ˈvaniSH/ ▸*v.* disappear completely.

**van·i·ty** /ˈvanitē/ ▸*n.* (*pl.* **-ties**) **1** conceit about one's appearance or attainments. **2** futility or unsubstantiality: *the vanity of human achievement.*

**van·quish** /ˈvaNGkwiSH/ ▸*v.* conquer or overcome.

**van·tage** /ˈvantij/ ▸*n.* (also **van·tage point**) place affording a good view or prospect.

**vap·id** /ˈvapid/ ▸*adj.* insipid; lacking interest; flat; dull. —**va·pid·i·ty** *n.* —**vap·id·ly** *adv.* —**vap·id·ness** *n.*

**va·por** /ˈvāpər/ ▸*n.* **1** moisture or another substance diffused or suspended in air, e.g., mist or smoke. **2** *Physics* gaseous form of a substance. —**va·por·ous** *adj.*

**va·por·ize** ▸*v.* convert or be converted into vapor. —**va·por·i·zer** *v.*

**va·ri·a·ble** /ˈv(ə)rēəbəl/ ▸*adj.* **1** changeable; adaptable. **2** apt to vary; not constant: *variable fortunes.* **3** *Math.* (of a quantity) indeterminate; able to assume different numerical values.

▸*n.* variable thing or quantity. —**var·i·a·bil·i·ty** *n.* —**var·i·a·bly** *adv.*

**var·i·ance** /ˈve(ə)rēəns/ ▸*n.* **1** difference of opinion; dispute; lack of harmony: *a theory at variance with all known facts.* **2** discrepancy. **3** officially allowed exception to regulations, zoning laws, etc.

**var·i·ant** ▸*adj.* **1** differing in form or details from the main one: *variant spelling.* **2** having different forms.

▸*n.* variant form, spelling, type, etc.

**var·i·a·tion** /ˌve(ə)rē'āsHən/ ▶n. **1** varying. **2** departure from a former or normal condition, action, or amount, or from a standard or type: *prices are subject to variation.* **3** variant.

**var·i·col·ored** ▶adj. of various colors.

**var·i·cose** /'varəˌkōs/ ▶adj. permanently and abnormally dilated: *varicose veins.*

**va·ri·e·tal** /və'rīətl/ ▶adj. **1** (of a wine or grape) made from or belonging to a single specified variety of grape. **2** of, relating to, characteristic of, or forming a variety.
▶n. varietal wine.

**va·ri·e·ty** /və'rīətē/ ▶n. (pl. **-ties**) **1** diversity; absence of uniformity: *not enough variety in our lives.* **2** quantity or collection of different things: *for a variety of reasons.* **3** different form of a thing, quality, etc. **4** *Biol.* subspecies.

**var·i·ous** /'ve(ə)rēəs/ ▶adj. **1** different; diverse. **2** more than one; several. —**var·i·ous·ly** adv.

**var·nish** /'värnisH/ ▶n. resinous solution used to give a hard shiny transparent coating.
▶v. **1** apply varnish to. **2** gloss over (a fact).

**var·y** /'ve(ə)rē/ ▶v. (**-ied**) make, become, or be different; modify; diversify.

**vas·cu·lar** /'vaskyələr/ ▶adj. of or containing vessels for conveying blood, sap, etc.: *vascular tissue.*

**vase** /vās; vāz; väz/ ▶n. vessel used as an ornament or container, esp. for flowers.

**va·sec·to·my** /va'sektəmē/ ▶n. (pl. **-mies**) surgical removal of part of the ducts that carry semen from the testicles, esp. as a method of birth control.

**vas·sal** /'vasəl/ ▶n. person subordinate to another.

**vast** /vast/ ▶adj. immense; huge. —**vast·ly** adv. —**vast·ness** n.

**vat** /vat/ ▶n. large tank or other vessel, esp. for holding liquids.

**vat·ic** /'vatik/ ▶adj. describing or predicting what will happen in the future.

**va·tic·i·nate** /və'tisəˌnāt/ ▶v. foretell the future.

**vaude·ville** /'vôd(ə)ˌvil/ ▶n. stage show of dances, songs, comedy acts, etc. —**vaude·vil·li·an** adj. & n.

**vault** /vôlt/ ▶n. **1** arched roof. **2** vaultlike covering: *the vault of heaven.* **3** underground chamber: **a** as a place of storage.

**b** as a place of interment. **4** act of vaulting.

▶ *v.* leap or spring over, esp. using the hands or a pole.

**vaunt** /vônt/ ▶ *v.* boast about or praise excessively.
— **vaunt·ing·ly** *adv.*

**vav·a·sour** /ˈvavəˌsôr/ ▶ *n.* vassal owing allegiance to a powerful lord and having other vassals under him.

**VCR** ▶ *abbr.* videocassette recorder.

**VD** ▶ *abbr.* venereal disease.

**V-Day** ▶ *n.* Victory Day, esp. with reference to the Allied victories in World War II.

**VDT** ▶ *abbr.* video display terminal.

**veal** /vēl/ ▶ *n.* calf's flesh as food.

**vec·tor** /ˈvektər/ *Math., Physics* ▶ *n.* quantity having direction as well as magnitude: *radius vector.*

**veer** /vi(ə)r/ ▶ *v.* change direction.

**ve·gan** /ˈvēgən/ ▶ *n.* person who eats no meat or animal products.

**veg·e·ta·ble** /ˈvej(i)təbəl/ ▶ *n.* herbaceous plant used for food, e.g., a cabbage, potato, turnip, bean, etc.
▶ *adj.* of, derived from, relating to, or comprising plant life.

**veg·e·tar·i·an** /ˌvejiˈte(ə)rēən/ ▶ *n.* person who eats no meat or fish.
▶ *adj.* excluding animal food, esp. meat: *vegetarian diet.*
— **veg·e·tar·i·an·ism** *n.*

**veg·e·tate** /ˈvejiˌtāt/ ▶ *v.* **1 a** live an uneventful or monotonous life. **b** spend time lazily or passively. **2** grow as plants do.
— **veg·e·ta·tive** *adj.*

**veg·e·ta·tion** ▶ *n.* plants collectively; plant life.

**ve·he·ment** /ˈvēəmənt/ ▶ *adj.* showing or caused by strong feeling; forceful; ardent.
— **ve·he·mence** *n.*
— **ve·he·ment·ly** *adv.*

**ve·hi·cle** /ˈvēəkəl/ ▶ *n.* **1** conveyance for transporting people, goods, etc., esp. on land. **2** medium for thought, feeling, or action: *the stage is the best vehicle for their talents.* **3** liquid, etc., as a medium for suspending pigments, drugs, etc.
— **ve·hic·u·lar** *adj.*

**veil** /vāl/ ▶ *n.* **1 a** a piece of usu. transparent fabric concealing the face. **b** piece of fabric covering the head and shoulders. **2** thing that conceals: *under the veil of friendship | a veil of mist.*
▶ *v.* **1** cover with a veil. **2** [usu. as

*adj.* **veiled**] partly conceal: *veiled threats.*

**vein** /vān/ ▶*n.* **1** any of the blood vessels conveying blood to the heart. **2** rib of an insect's wing or of a leaf. **3** streak of a different color in wood, marble, cheese, etc. **4** fissure in rock filled with ore. **5** distinctive character or tendency; mood: *spoke in a sarcastic vein.*

**Vel·cro** /'velkrō/ ▶*trademark* fastener for clothes, etc., consisting of two strips of nylon fabric, one looped and one burred, which adhere when pressed together.

**vel·le·i·ty** /və'lēətē; ve-/ ▶*n. (pl.* **-ties**) wish or inclination not strong enough to lead to action.

**vel·lum** /'veləm/ ▶*n.* **1** fine parchment. **2** smooth writing paper.

**ve·loc·i·ty** /və'läsətē/ ▶*n. (pl.* **-ties**) speed, esp. of an inanimate object in a given direction.

**ve·lour** /və'lŏŏr/ ▶*n.* plushlike woven fabric.

**vel·vet** /'velvit/ ▶*n.* woven fabric of silk, cotton, etc., with a thick short pile. —**vel·vet·y** *adj.*

**vel·ve·teen** /'velvi,tēn/ ▶*n.* cotton fabric with a pile like velvet.

**ve·nal** /'vēnl/ ▶*adj.* able to be bribed or corrupted. —**ve·nal·i·ty** *n.* —**ve·nal·ly** *adv.*

**vend** /vend/ ▶*v.* offer (small wares) for sale. —**ven·dor** *n.*

□ **vending machine** machine that dispenses small articles for sale when a coin or token is inserted.

**ven·det·ta** /ven'detə/ ▶*n.* prolonged bitter quarrel.

**ven·due** /ven'd(y)ŏŏ/ ▶*n.* public auction.

**ve·neer** /və'ni(ə)r/ ▶*n.* **1** thin covering layer of fine wood. **2** deceptive outward appearance of a quality.

**ven·er·a·ble** /'ven(ə)rəbəl/ ▶*adj.* entitled to respect on account of character, age, associations, etc. —**ven·er·a·bil·i·ty** *n.* —**ven·er·a·bly** *adv.*

**ven·er·ate** /'venə,rāt/ ▶*v.* regard with deep respect. —**ven·er·a·tion** *n.*

**ve·ne·re·al** /və'ni(ə)rēəl/ ▶*adj.* of or transmitted by sexual intercourse.

**ven·er·y** /'venərē/ ▶*n.* sexual indulgence.

**ve·ne·tian blind** /və'nēSHən/ ▶*n.* window blind of adjustable horizontal slats to control the light.

**venge·ance** /'venjəns/ ▶*n.* retaliation; revenge.
□ **with a vengeance** in an extreme degree.

**venge·ful** /'venjfəl/ ▶*adj.* vindictive; seeking vengeance. **—venge·ful·ly** *adv.*

**ve·ni·al** /'vēnēəl/ ▶*adj.* (of a sin or fault) pardonable.

**ven·i·son** /'venəsən/ ▶*n.* deer's flesh as food.

**ven·om** /'venəm/ ▶*n.* **1** poisonous fluid of snakes, scorpions, etc., usu. transmitted by a bite or sting. **2** malignity. **—ven·om·ous** *adj.* **—ven·om·ous·ly** *adv.*

**ve·nous** /'vēnəs/ ▶*adj.* of, full of, or contained in veins.

**vent** /vent/ ▶*n.* **1** opening allowing the passage of air, etc. **2** outlet; free expression: *gave vent to their indignation.* **3** slit in a garment, esp. in the lower edge of the back of a coat.
▶*v.* give free expression to: *vented my anger on the cat.*

**ven·ti·late** /'ventl,āt/ ▶*v.* **1** cause air to enter or circulate freely in. **2** air (a question, grievance, etc.). **—ven·ti·la·tion** *n.*

**ven·tral** /'ventrəl/ ▶*adj.* of or on the abdomen. **—ven·tral·ly** *adv.*

**ven·tri·cle** /'ventrikəl/ ▶*n.* hollow part of an organ, esp. in the brain or heart. **—ven·tric·u·lar** *adj.*

**ven·tril·o·quism** /ven'trilə‐ ,kwizəm/ ▶*n.* skill of speaking without moving the lips, esp. as entertainment. **—ven·tril·o·quist** *n.*

**ven·ture** /'venCHər/ ▶*n.* **1** risky undertaking. **2** commercial speculation.
▶*v.* dare to do or say something or go somewhere: *did not venture to stop them.*

**ven·ture cap·i·tal** ▶*n.* capital invested in a project in which there is a substantial element of risk, typically a new or expanding business.

**ven·ture·some** /'venCHərsəm/ ▶*adj.* willing to take risks or embark on difficult or unusual courses of action.

**ven·ue** /'ven,yoo/ ▶*n.* **1** place for a sports event, meeting, concert, etc. **2** *Law* place where a jury must be gathered and a cause tried (orig. the neighborhood of the crime, etc.).

**Ve·nus** /'vēnəs/ ▶*n.* planet second from the sun in the solar system.

**ve·ra·cious** /vəˈrāsHəs/ ▸*adj.* speaking or representing the truth.

**ve·rac·i·ty** /vəˈrasitē/ ▸*n.* 1 accuracy. 2 habitual truthfulness.

**ve·ran·da** /vəˈrandə/ ▸*n.* roofed platform along the outside of a house, level with the ground floor.

**verb** /vərb/ ▸*n. Gram.* word used to indicate an action, state, or occurrence (e.g., *hear, become, happen*).

**ver·bal** /ˈvərbəl/ ▸*adj.* 1 of words: *made a verbal distinction.* 2 oral; not written: *gave a verbal statement.* —**ver·bal·ly** *adv.*

**ver·bal·ize** ▸*v.* express in words. —**ver·bal·i·za·tion** *n.* —**ver·bal·i·zer** *n.*

**ver·ba·tim** /vərˈbātəm/ ▸*adv. & adj.* in exactly the same words; word for word: *copied it verbatim.*

**ver·be·na** /vərˈbēnə/ ▸*n.* plant bearing clusters of fragrant flowers.

**ver·bi·age** /ˈvərbēij/ ▸*n.* needless accumulation of words.

**ver·bose** /vərˈbōs/ ▸*adj.* using more words than are needed. —**ver·bose·ly** *adv.* —**ver·bos·i·ty** *n.*

**ver·dant** /ˈvərdnt/ ▸*adj.* green, esp. bright and fresh-colored. —**ver·dant·ly** *adv.*

**ver·dict** /ˈvərdikt/ ▸*n.* 1 decision on an issue of fact in a civil or criminal cause or an inquest. 2 opinion or judgment.

**ver·di·gris** /ˈvərdiˌgrē/ ▸*n.* green substance that forms on copper and its alloys.

**ver·dure** /ˈvərjər/ ▸*n.* green vegetation.

**verge** /vərj/ ▸*n.* 1 edge or border. 2 extreme limit beyond which something happens: *on the verge of tears.* ▸*v.* 1 incline downward or in a specified direction: *the now verging sun* | *verge to a close.* 2 (**verge on**) border on; approach closely: *verging on the ridiculous.*

**ver·glas** /verˈglä/ ▸*n.* thin coating of ice or frozen rain on an exposed surface.

**ver·i·fy** /ˈverəˌfī/ ▸*v.* (**-fied**) establish the truth or correctness of by examination: *must verify the statement* | *verified my figures.* —**ver·i·fi·a·ble** *adj.* —**ver·i·fi·ca·tion** *n.*

**ver·i·ly** /ˈverəlē/ ▸*adv. archaic* really; truly.

**ver·i·si·mil·i·tude** /ˌverəsəˈmiliˌt(y)o͞od/ ▸*n.* appearance of being true or real.

**ver·i·ta·ble** /ˈveritəbəl/ ▶*adj.* real; rightly so called: *a veritable feast.* —**ver·i·ta·bly** *adv.*

**vé·ri·té** /ˌveriˈtā/ ▶*n.* genre of film, television, and radio programs emphasizing realism and naturalism.

**ver·i·ty** /ˈveritē/ ▶*n.* (*pl.* -ties) **1** true statement, esp. one of fundamental import. **2** truth.

**ver·mi·form** /ˈvərməˌfôrm/ ▶*adj.* resembling or having the form of a worm.

**ver·mil·ion** /vərˈmilyən/ ▶*n.* brilliant red pigment or color.

**ver·min** /ˈvərmin/ ▶*pl. n.* **1** mammals, insects, and birds injurious to game, crops, etc. **2** vile persons. —**ver·min·ous** *adj.*

**ver·mouth** /vərˈmo͞oTH/ ▶*n.* wine flavored with aromatic herbs.

**ver·nac·u·lar** /vərˈnakyələr/ ▶*n.* language spoken by the ordinary people of a particular country, district, etc.

**ver·nal** /ˈvərnl/ ▶*adj.* of, in, or appropriate to spring: *vernal breezes.* —**ver·nal·ly** *adv.*

**ver·nis·sage** /ˌvərnəˈsäzH/ ▶*n.* (*pl.* same) private viewing of paintings before public exhibition.

**ver·sa·tile** /ˈvərsətl/ ▶*adj.* capable of doing or being used for many different things: *a versatile mind* | *a versatile sewing machine.* —**ver·sa·til·i·ty** *n.*

**verse** /vərs/ ▶*n.* **1 a** poetry. **b** particular type of poetry: *English verse.* **2** stanza of a poem or song. **3** each of the short numbered divisions of the Bible or other scripture.

**versed** ▶*adj.* (**versed in**) experienced or skilled in; knowledgeable about: *she is well versed in medieval literature.*

**ver·si·fy** /ˈvərsəˌfī/ ▶*v.* (-fied) express in or compose verse. —**ver·si·fi·ca·tion** *n.*

**ver·sion** /ˈvərzHən/ ▶*n.* **1** account of a matter from a particular point of view: *told them my version of the incident.* **2** book, etc., in a particular edition or translation: *Authorized Version.* **3** form or variant of a thing as performed, adapted, etc.

**ver·so** /ˈvərsō/ ▶*n.* left-hand page of an open book.

**ver·sus** /ˈvərsəs/ ▶*prep.* against. (Abbr.: **v**, **vs.**)

**ver·te·bra** /ˈvərtəbrə/ ▶*n.* (*pl.* -brae) each segment of the backbone. —**ver·te·bral** *adj.*

**ver·te·brate** ▶*n.* animal having

a spinal column, including mammals, birds, reptiles, amphibians, and fishes.

**ver·tex** /'vər,teks/ ▸*n.* (*pl.* **-ti·ces** or **-tex·es**) **1** highest point; top or apex. **2** meeting point of lines that form an angle.

**ver·ti·cal** /'vərtikəl/ ▸*adj.* **1** at right angles to a horizontal plane; perpendicular. **2** in a direction from top to bottom. ▸*n.* vertical line or plane. —**ver·ti·cal·ly** *adv.*

**ver·tig·i·nous** /vər'tijənəs/ ▸*adj.* of or causing vertigo.

**ver·ti·go** /'vərtəgō/ ▸*n.* dizziness.

**verve** /vərv/ ▸*n.* enthusiasm; vigor.

**ver·y** /'verē/ ▸*adv.* **1** in a high degree: *did it very easily* | *had a very bad cough.* **2** in the fullest sense: *at the very latest* | *my very own room.* ▸*adj.* **1** actual; truly such (emphasizing identity, significance, or extreme degree): *the very thing we need* | *those were his very words.* **2** mere; sheer: *the very idea of it was horrible.*

**ves·i·cant** /'vesəkənt/ ▸*adj.* tending to cause blistering. ▸*n.* agent that causes blistering.

**ves·i·cle** /'vesikəl/ ▸*n.* fluid- or air-filled sac; blister. —**ve·sic·u·lar** *adj.*

**ves·pers** /'vespərz/ ▸*n.* evening prayer service.

**ves·per·tine** /'vespər,tīn; -,tēn/ ▸*adj.* **1** of, relating to, occurring, or active in the evening. **2** (of a flower) opening in the evening. **3** active in the evening.

**ves·pine** /'ves,pīn; -pin/ ▸*adj.* of or relating to wasps.

**ves·sel** /'vesəl/ ▸*n.* **1** hollow receptacle, esp. for liquid. **2** ship or boat, esp. a large one. **3** duct or canal holding or conveying blood or other fluid.

**vest** /vest/ ▸*n.* waist-length close-fitting, sleeveless garment, often worn under a suit jacket, etc. ▸*v.* **1** (usu. **be vested in**) bestow (powers, authority, etc.) on a person: *executive power is vested in the president.* **2** (**vest in**) (of property, a right, etc.) come into the possession of (a person): *the bankrupt's power vests in his trustee.*
□ **vest-pocket** small enough to fit into a pocket.

**ves·ti·bule** /'vestə,byōōl/ ▸*n.* hall or lobby next to the outer door of a building.

**ves·tige** /'vestij/ ▸*n.* **1** trace or

sign: *vestiges of an earlier civilization* | *found no vestige of their presence.* **2** slight amount; particle: *without a vestige of clothing.* —**ves·tig·i·al** *adj.*

**vest·ment** /'vestmənt/ ▸*n.* official robe, esp of clergy or the choir during a service.

**ves·try** /'vestrē/ ▸*n.* (*pl.* **-tries**) **1** church room or building, used as an office and for keeping vestments in. **2** committee of parishioners chosen to conduct temporal business in the Episcopal Church.

**vet** /vet/ ▸*n. inf.* **1** veterinarian. **2** veteran.
▸*v.* (**vet·ted, vet·ting**) make a critical examination of (a plan, work, candidate, etc.).

**vetch** /veCH/ ▸*n.* plant of the pea family largely used for silage or fodder.

**vet·er·an** /'vet(ə)rən/ ▸*n.* **1** person with long experience in an occupation: *war veteran.* **2** person who has served in the armed forces.

**vet·er·i·nar·i·an** /ˌvet(ə)rə-'ne(ə)rēən/ ▸*n.* doctor qualified to treat diseased or injured animals.

**vet·er·i·nar·y** /'vet(ə)rəˌnerē/ ▸*adj.* of or for the treatment of diseases and injuries of animals.

**ve·to** /'vētō/ ▸*n.* (*pl.* **-toes**) **1 a** consitutional right to reject a bill, resolution, etc. **b** such a rejection. **2** prohibition: *put one's veto on a proposal.*
▸*v.* (**-toed**) **1** exercise a veto against (a measure, etc.). **2** forbid authoritatively.

**vex** /veks/ ▸*v.* anger by a petty annoyance; irritate. —**vex·a·tion** *n.* —**vex·ing** *adj.* —**vex·ing·ly** *adv.*

**vi·a** /'vīə/ ▸*prep.* by way of; through.

**vi·a·ble** /'vīəbəl/ ▸*adj.* **1** (of a plan, etc.) feasible; practicable esp. from an economic standpoint. **2** (of a fetus or newborn child) capable of maintaining life. —**vi·a·bil·i·ty** *n.* —**vi·a·bly** *adv.*

**vi·a·duct** ▸*n.* long bridge, esp. a series of arches, carrying a road or railroad across a valley, etc.

**Vi·ag·ra** /vī'agrə/ ▸*trademark* synthetic compound used to enhance male potency.

**vi·al** /'vī(ə)l/ ▸*n.* small vessel esp. for medicines.

**vi·and** /'vīənd/ ▸*n.* (usu. **viands**) item of food.

**vi·at·i·cum** /vī'atikəm; vē-/ ▶*n.* (*pl.* **-ca** /-kə/) **1** Eucharist as given to a person near or in danger of death. **2** supply of provisions or an official allowance of money for a journey.

**vibes** /vībz/ ▶*pl. n. inf.* **1** person's emotional state or the atmosphere of a place as felt by others. **2** VIBRAPHONE.

**vi·brant** /'vībrənt/ ▶*adj.* **1** full of energy or enthusiasm: *vibrant with emotion.* **2** (of sound) resonant. **3** (of color) vivid. —**vi·bran·cy** *n.* —**vi·brant·ly** *adv.*

**vi·bra·phone** /'vībrə,fōn/ ▶*n.* percussion instrument of tuned metal bars with motor-driven resonators and metal tubes giving a vibrato effect. —**vi·bra·phon·ist** *n.*

**vi·brate** /'vī,brāt/ ▶*v.* **1** move or cause to move continuously and rapidly to and fro; oscillate. **2** resonate. —**vi·bra·tor** *n.* —**vi·bra·tor·y** *adj.*

**vi·bra·tion** ▶*n.* **1** vibrating. **2** (**vibrations**) characteristic atmosphere or feelings in a place, as communicable to people present in it.

**vi·bra·to** /və'brätō/ ▶*n.* rapid slight variation in pitch in singing or playing an instrument, producing a tremulous effect.

**vic·ar** /'vikər/ ▶*n.* member of the clergy.

**vic·ar·age** /'vikərij/ ▶*n.* residence of a vicar.

**vi·car·i·ous** /vī'ke(ə)rēəs/ ▶*adj.* **1** experienced in the imagination through another person: *vicarious pleasure.* **2** acting or done for another: *vicarious suffering.* —**vi·car·i·ous·ly** *adv.* —**vi·car·i·ous·ness** *n.*

**vice** /vīs/ ▶*n.* **1** evil or immoral conduct or a particular form of this. **2** defect of character or behavior: *drunkenness was not among his vices.* ▶*prep.* in the place of; in succession to.

**vice-** ▶*comb. form* forming nouns meaning: as a substitute or deputy for: *vice chancellor.*

**vice pres·i·dent** ▶*n.* official ranking below and deputizing for a president.

**vice·roy** /'vīs,roi/ ▶*n.* sovereign's deputy ruler in a colony, province, etc.

**vi·ce ver·sa** /'vīsə 'vərsə/ ▶*adv.* with the order of the terms changed; the other way around: *from left to right or vice versa.*

**vi·cin·i·ty** /vəˈsinitē/ ▶*n.* (*pl.* **-ties**) surrounding district.

**vi·cious** /ˈvisHəs/ ▶*adj.* **1** bad-tempered; spiteful. **2** violent; dangerous. **3** evil. —**vi·cious·ly** *adv.* —**vi·cious·ness** *n.*

☐ **vicious circle** self-perpetuating, harmful sequence of cause and effect.

**vi·cis·si·tude** /vəˈsisiˌt(y)o͞od/ ▶*n.* (usu. **vicissitudes**) change of circumstances, esp. variation of fortune.

**vic·tim** /ˈviktəm/ ▶*n.* **1** person injured or killed as a result of an event or circumstance. **2** person or thing injured or destroyed in pursuit of an object or in gratification of a passion, etc. **3** prey; dupe: *fell victim to a con man.*

**vic·tor** /ˈviktər/ ▶*n.* winner in battle or in a contest.

**vic·to·ry** /ˈvikt(ə)rē/ ▶*n.* (*pl.* **-ries**) defeat of an enemy or an opponent.

**vict·uals** /ˈvitlz/ ▶*pl. n.* food, provisions, esp. as prepared for use.

**vi·de** /ˈvēdē; ˈvēˌdā; ˈvīdē/ ▶*v.* see; consult (used as an instruction in a text to refer the reader to a specified passage, book, author, etc., for fuller or further information).

**vid·e·o** /ˈvidēˌō/ ▶*adj.* **1** relating to the recording, reproducing, or broadcasting of visual images, and usu. sound, on magnetic tape. **2** relating to the broadcasting of television pictures.
▶*n.* (*pl.* **-os**) **1** such recording, reproducing, or broadcasting. **2** movie, etc., on videotape.
▶*v.* (**-oed**) make a video recording of.

☐ **video display terminal** *Computing* monitor. ☐ **video game** game played by electronically manipulating images produced by a computer program on a television or other screen.

**vid·e·o·cas·sette** ▶*n.* cassette of videotape.

☐ **videocassette recorder** apparatus for recording and playing videotapes.

**vid·e·o·tape** ▶*n.* magnetic tape for recording moving pictures and sound.
▶*v.* record on this.

**vie** /vī/ ▶*v.* (**vied, vy·ing**) compete; strive for superiority: *vied with each other for recognition.*

**view** /vyo͞o/ ▶*n.* **1** range of vision:

*came into view.* **2** what is seen from a particular point; scene or prospect: *room with a view.* **3 a** opinion: *holds strong views on morality.* **b** manner of considering a thing: *took a long-term view of it.*

▸*v.* look at; inspect; examine; consider: *we are going to view the house | different ways of viewing a subject.*

**view·point** ▸*n.* point of view.

**vig·il** /ˈvijəl/ ▸*n.* keeping awake during the night, etc., esp. to keep watch or pray: *keep vigil.*

**vig·i·lance** ▸*n.* watchfulness; caution. —**vig·i·lant** *adj.*

**vig·i·lan·te** /ˌvijəˈlantē/ ▸*n.* member of a self-appointed group maintaining order.

**vi·gnette** /vinˈyet/ ▸*n.* short description or character sketch.

**vig·or** /ˈvigər/ ▸*n.* physical or mental strength or energy. —**vig·or·ous** *adj.* —**vig·or·ous·ly** *adv.*

**vile** /vīl/ ▸*adj.* **1** disgusting. **2** morally base; depraved. **3** *inf.* abominably bad: *vile weather.* —**vile·ness** *n.*

**vil·i·fy** /ˈviləˌfī/ ▸*v.* (**-fied**) defame; speak evil of. —**vil·i·fi·ca·tion** *n.*

**vil·la** /ˈvilə/ ▸*n.* country house, esp. a luxurious one.

**vil·lage** /ˈvilij/ ▸*n.* small municipality with limited corporate powers. —**vil·lag·er** *n.*

**vil·lain** /ˈvilən/ ▸*n.* person guilty or capable of great wickedness. —**vil·lain·ous** *adj.* —**vil·lain·y** *n.*

**vim** /vim/ ▸*n. inf.* vigor.

**vin·ai·grette** /ˌviniˈgret/ ▸*n.* salad dressing of oil, vinegar, and seasoning.

**vin·di·cate** /ˈvindiˌkāt/ ▸*v.* **1** clear of blame or suspicion. **2** establish the existence, merits, or justice of (one's courage, conduct, assertion, etc.). **3** justify. —**vin·di·ca·tion** *n.* —**vin·dic·a·tive** *adj.*

**vin·dic·tive** /vinˈdiktiv/ ▸*adj.* **1** tending to seek revenge. **2** spiteful. —**vin·dic·tive·ly** *adv.* —**vin·dic·tive·ness** *n.*

**vine** /vīn/ ▸*n.* climbing or trailing woody-stemmed plant, esp. one bearing grapes.

**vin·e·gar** /ˈvinigər/ ▸*n.* sour liquid obtained from wine, cider, etc., by fermentation and used as a condiment or for pickling. —**vin·e·gar·y** *adj.*

**vine·yard** /ˈvinyərd/ ▸*n.* plantation of grapevines, esp. for wine-making.

**vin·tage** /ˈvintij/ ▸*n.* **1** season's produce of grapes or wine.

**2** wine of high quality from a particular year and district. **3** year, etc., when a thing was made, etc. ▶*adj.* **1** of high quality, esp. from the past or characteristic of the best period of a person's work. **2** of a past season.

**vint·ner** /'vintnər/ ▶*n.* wine merchant.

**vi·nyl** /'vīnl/ ▶*n.* plastic made by polymerization.

**vi·o·la** /vē'ōlə/ ▶*n.* string instrument larger than the violin and of lower pitch.

**vi·o·late** /'vīə‚lāt/ ▶*v.* **1** disregard; fail to comply with (an oath, treaty, law, etc.). **2** treat (a sanctuary, etc.) profanely or with disrespect. **3** disturb (a person's privacy, etc.). **4** rape. —**vi·o·la·tion** *n.*

**vi·o·lence** /'vī(ə)ləns/ ▶*n.* **1** behavior involving physical force intended to hurt or kill someone or something. **2** strength of emotion or destructive natural force. **3** *Law* unlawful exercise of physical force or intimidation by the exhibition of this.

**vi·o·lent** ▶*adj.* **1** involving or using great physical force: *violent person* | *violent storm.* **2** intense; vehement; passionate; furious: *violent contrast* | *violent dislike.* **3** resulting from or caused by violence. —**vi·o·lent·ly** *adv.*

**vi·o·let** /'vī(ə)lət/ ▶*n.* **1** plant, esp. the sweet violet, with usu. purple, blue, or white flowers. **2** bluish-purple color seen at the end of the spectrum opposite red. ▶*adj.* of this color.

**vi·o·lin** /‚vīə'lin/ ▶*n.* musical instrument with four strings of treble pitch played with a bow. —**vi·o·lin·ist** *n.*

**vi·o·lon·cel·lo** /‚vīələn'CHelō/ ▶*n.* (*pl.* -**los**) CELLO.

**VIP** ▶*abbr.* very important person.

**vi·per** /'vīpər/ ▶*n.* **1** small venomous snake, esp. the common viper. **2** treacherous person. —**vi·per·ous** *adj.*

**vi·ra·go** /və'rägō; -'rā-/ ▶*n.* (*pl.* -**gos**) fierce or abusive woman.

**vi·ral** /'vīrəl/ ▶*adj.* of or caused by a virus. —**vi·ral·ly** *adv.*

**vi·res·cent** /və'resənt; vī-/ ▶*adj.* greenish.

**vir·gin** /'vərjən/ ▶*n.* **1** person who has never had sexual intercourse. **2** (**the Virgin**) Mary, mother of Christ. ▶*adj.* **1** never having had sexual intercourse. **2** untouched; not yet used or tried. —**vir·gin·al** adj. —**vir·gin·i·ty** n.

**vir·gule** /'vər,gyo͞ol/ ▶n. slanting line used to mark division of words or lines.

**vir·ile** /'virəl/ ▶adj. of a man; having masculine vigor or strength. —**vi·ril·i·ty** n.

**vi·rol·o·gy** /vī'räləjē/ ▶n. the scientific study of viruses. —**vi·ro·log·i·cal** adj. —**vi·rol·o·gist** n.

**vir·tu·al** /'vərCHo͞oəl/ ▶adj. that is such for practical purposes though not in name or according to strict definition: *is the virtual manager of the business.* —**vir·tu·al·ly** adv.

**vir·tu·al re·al·i·ty** ▶n. generation by computer software of an image or environment that appears real to the senses.

**vir·tue** /'vərCHo͞o/ ▶n. **1** moral excellence; goodness. **2** chastity. **3** good quality: *has the virtue of being adjustable.*

**vir·tu·o·so** /,vərCHo͞o'ōsō/ ▶n. (pl. **-si** or **-sos**) person highly skilled in the technique of a fine art, esp. music. —**vir·tu·os·i·ty** n.

**vir·u·lent** /'vir(y)ələnt/ ▶adj. **1** strongly poisonous. **2** (of a disease) violent or malignant. **3** bitterly hostile: *virulent animosity.* —**vir·u·lence** n. —**vir·u·lent·ly** adv.

**vi·rus** /'vīrəs/ ▶n. **1** microscopic organism often causing diseases. **2** COMPUTER VIRUS.

**vi·sa** /'vēzə/ ▶n. endorsement on a passport, etc., esp. allowing the holder to enter or leave a country.

**vis·age** /'vizij/ ▶n. poet. face. —**vis·aged** adj.

**vis·à·vis** /'vēz ə 'vē/ ▶prep. **1** in relation to. **2** opposite to. ▶adv. facing one another.

**vis·cer·a** /'visərə/ ▶pl. n. interior organs of the body (e.g., brain, heart, liver, etc.), esp. in the abdomen (e.g., the intestines).

**vis·cer·al** ▶adj. **1** of the viscera. **2** relating to deep feelings rather than reasoning.

**vis·cid** /'visid/ ▶adj. glutinous; sticky.

**vis·count** /'vī,kount/ ▶n. British nobleman ranking between an earl and a baron.

**vis·cous** /'viskəs/ (also **vis·cid**) ▶adj. **1** glutinous; sticky. **2** semifluid. —**vis·cos·i·ty** n.

**vise** /vīs/ ▶n. instrument, esp. attached to a workbench, with two movable jaws holding an object so as to leave the hands free to work on it.

**vis·i·bil·i·ty** /ˌvizəˈbilitē/ ▶*n.* **1** state of being able to see or be seen. **2** distance one can see as determined by weather conditions.

**vis·i·ble** /ˈvizəbəl/ ▶*adj.* **1** that can be seen by the eye. **2** that can be perceived or ascertained: *has no visible means of support* | *spoke with visible impatience.* —**vis·i·bly** *adv.*

**vi·sion** /ˈvizHən/ ▶*n.* **1** act or faculty of seeing: *impaired his vision.* **2 a** thing or person seen in a dream or trance. **b** supernatural or prophetic apparition. **3** thing or idea perceived vividly in the imagination: *romantic visions of youth.*

**vi·sion·ar·y** /ˈvizHəˌnerē/ ▶*adj.* **1** given to seeing visions; indulging in fanciful theories. **2** of a vision or the imagination. ▶*n.* (*pl.* **-ies**) visionary person.

**vi·sion quest** ▶*n.* attempt to achieve a vision of a future guardian spirit, traditionally undertaken at puberty by boys of the Plains Indian peoples, typically through fasting or self-torture.

**vis·it** /ˈvizit/ ▶*v.* **1** go or come to see (a person, place, etc.) as an act of friendship or ceremony, on business or for a purpose, or from interest. **2** reside temporarily with (a person) or at (a place). **3** (of a disease, calamity, etc.) come upon; attack.
▶*n.* **1 a** act of visiting; call on a person or at a place. **b** temporary stay with a person or at a place. **2** occasion of going to a doctor, dentist, etc. **3** formal or official call. **4** chat. —**vis·i·tor** *n.*

**vis·i·ta·tion** ▶*n.* **1** formal visit. **2** divine punishment.

**vi·sor** /ˈvīzər/ ▶*n.* **1 a** movable part of a helmet covering the face. **b** projecting front part of a cap. **2** shield (fixed or movable) to protect the eyes from unwanted light, esp. at the top of a vehicle windshield.

**vis·ta** /ˈvistə/ ▶*n.* extensive view as through a long opening.

**vis·u·al** /ˈvizHo͞oəl/ ▶*adj.* of or used in seeing.
▶*n.* (usu. **visuals**) visual image or display; picture. —**vis·u·al·ly** *adv.*

**vis·u·al·ize** ▶*v.* imagine visually. —**vis·u·al·i·za·tion** *n.*

**vi·tal** /ˈvītl/ ▶*adj.* **1** essential. **2** full of life or activity. —**vi·tal·ly** *adv.*

□ **vital signs** pulse rate, rate of respiration, and body temperature considered as signs of life. □ **vital statistics** number of births, marriages, deaths, etc.

**vi·tal·ism** /ˈvītlˌizəm/ ▶*n.* theory that the origin and phenomena of life are dependent on a force or principle distinct from purely chemical or physical forces.

**vi·tal·i·ty** /vīˈtalitē/ ▶*n.* **1** liveliness; animation. **2** (of an institution, language, etc.) ability to endure and to perform its functions.

**vi·tal sta·tis·tics** ▶*pl. n.* **1** quantitative data concerning a population, such as the number of births, marriages, and deaths. **2** measurements of a woman's bust, waist, and hips.

**vit·a·min** /ˈvītəmin/ ▶*n.* any of various organic compounds essential for many living organisms to maintain normal health and development.

**vi·ti·ate** /ˈvisHēˌāt/ ▶*v.* **1** impair; corrupt; debase. **2** make invalid or ineffectual. —**vi·ti·a·tion** *n.*

**vit·i·cul·ture** /ˈvitiˌkəlCHər/ ▶*n.* cultivation of grapevines.

—**vit·i·cul·tur·al** *adj.*
—**vit·i·cul·tur·ist** *n.*

**vit·re·ous** /ˈvitrēəs/ ▶*adj.* of or like glass.

□ **vitreous humor** transparent jellylike tissue filling the eyeball.

**vit·ri·fy** /ˈvitrəˌfī/ ▶*v.* (**-fied**) convert or be converted into glass or a glasslike substance, esp. by heat. —**vit·ri·fac·tion** *n.* —**vit·ri·fi·ca·tion** *n.*

**vit·ri·ol** /ˈvitrēəl/ ▶*n.* **1** sulfuric acid or a sulfate, orig. one of glassy appearance. **2** caustic or hostile speech, criticism, or feeling. —**vit·ri·ol·ic** *adj.*

**vi·tu·per·ate** /vīˈt(y)o͞opəˌrāt/ ▶*v.* revile; abuse. —**vi·tu·per·a·tion** *n.* —**vi·tu·per·a·tive** *adj.*

**vi·va·cious** /viˈvāsHəs/ ▶*adj.* lively; sprightly; animated. —**vi·va·cious·ly** *adv.* —**vi·va·cious·ness** *n.* —**vi·vac·i·ty** *n.*

**vi·va vo·ce** /ˌvēvə ˈvōCHā; ˌvīvə ˈvōsē/ ▶*adj.* (esp. of an examination) oral rather than written.
▶*adv.* orally rather than in writing.

**viv·id** /ˈvivid/ ▶*adj.* **1** (of color) strong; intense: *vivid green.* **2** (of a mental faculty, impression, or description) clear; lively;

graphic: *vivid imagination* | *vivid recollection of the scene.* —**viv·id·ly** *adv.* —**viv·id·ness** *n.*

**viv·i·fy** /ˈvivəˌfī/ ▶*v.* (-**fied**) enliven; animate; make lively or living. —**viv·i·fi·ca·tion** *n.*

**viv·i·sect** /ˈvivəˌsekt; ˌvivəˈsekt/ ▶*v.* perform vivisection on (an animal) (used only by people who are opposed to the practice).

**viv·i·sec·tion** /ˌvivəˈsekSHən/ ▶*n.* surgery on living animals for purposes of scientific research.

**vix·en** /ˈviksən/ ▶*n.* **1** female fox. **2** spiteful woman.

**viz.** /viz/ or said as /ˈnāmlē/ ▶*adv.* namely; in other words (used esp. to introduce a gloss or explanation).

**viz·ard** /ˈvizərd/ ▶*n.* mask or disguise.

**vi·zier** /vəˈzi(ə)r/ ▶*n. hist.* high official in the Ottoman Empire. —**vi·zier·i·al** *adj.*

**vo·cab·u·lar·y** /vōˈkabyəˌlerē/ ▶*n.* (*pl.* -**ies**) **1** words used by a particular language, individual, book, branch of science, etc., or by a particular author. **2** list of these, arranged alphabetically with definitions or translations.

**vo·cal** /ˈvōkəl/ ▶*adj.* **1** of or uttered by the voice: *vocal communication.* **2** outspoken: *was very vocal about her rights.* —**vo·cal·ly** *adv.*

□ **vocal cords** folds of the lining membrane of the larynx near the opening of the glottis, with edges vibrating in the air stream to produce the voice.

**vo·cal·ist** ▶*n.* singer, esp. of jazz or popular songs.

**vo·cal·ize** ▶*v.* form (a sound); utter (a word); sing.

**vo·ca·tion** /vōˈkāSHən/ ▶*n.* **1** strong feeling of fitness for a particular career (in religious contexts, a divine call). **2** trade or profession. —**vo·ca·tion·al** *adj.*

**voc·a·tive** /ˈväkətiv/ *Gram.* ▶*n.* case of nouns used in addressing a person or thing. ▶*adj.* of or in this case.

**vo·cif·er·ate** /vōˈsifəˌrāt/ ▶*v.* utter (words, etc.) noisily; shout. —**vo·cif·er·a·tion** *n.*

**vo·cif·er·ous** ▶*adj.* vehement or clamorous.

**vod·ka** /ˈvädkə/ ▶*n.* alcoholic spirit distilled chiefly from rye.

**vogue** /vōg/ ▶*n.* **1** prevailing fashion. **2** popularity: *has had a great vogue.*

**voice** /vois/ ▸n. **1** sound formed in the larynx and uttered by the mouth, esp. by a person. **2 a** spoken or written words, esp. as: *give voice*. **b** opinion so expressed. **c** right to express an opinion: *I have no voice in the matter*. **3** set of verb forms showing the relation of the subject to the action: *active voice | passive voice*. **4** vocal ability, esp. in singing.
▸v. express: *the letter voices our opinion*.
□ **voice mail** automatic telephone answering system that records messages from callers.

**void** /void/ ▸adj. **1 a** empty; vacant. **b** lacking; free from: *a style void of affectation*. **2** invalid; not binding: *null and void*.
▸n. empty space; vacuum: *cannot fill the void made by death*.
▸v. **1** render invalid. **2** excrete.

**voile** /voil/ ▸n. thin, semitransparent dress material.

**vol.** ▸abbr. volume.

**vol·a·tile** /'välətl/ ▸adj. **1** evaporating rapidly: *volatile salts*. **2** changeable; fickle. **3** apt to break out into violence.
**—vol·a·til·i·ty** n.

**vol·ca·no** /väl'kānō/ ▸n. (pl. -noes) mountain from which lava, cinders, steam, gases, etc., escape through openings in the earth's crust.

**vole** /vōl/ ▸n. small plant-eating rodent.

**vo·li·tion** /və'lisHən/ ▸n. **1** exercise of the will. **2** power of willing.

**vol·ley** /'välē/ ▸n. **1 a** simultaneous discharge of a number of weapons. **b** bullets, etc., discharged in a volley. **2** torrent of oaths, etc. **3** *Tennis* return of a ball in play before it touches the ground.
▸v. **1** return or send (a ball) by a volley. **2** discharge (bullets, abuse, etc.) in a volley.

**vol·ley·ball** ▸n. game for two teams of six hitting a large ball by hand over a net.

**volt** /vōlt/ ▸n. unit of electromotive force, the difference of potential that would carry one ampere of current against one ohm resistance. (Abbr.: **V**)

**volt·age** /'vōltij/ ▸n. electromotive force expressed in volts.

**volt·me·ter** ▸n. instrument for measuring electric potential in volts.

**vol·u·ble** /'välyəbəl/ ▸adj.

speaking or spoken at length.
—**vol·u·bil·i·ty** *n.* —**vol·u·bly** *adv.*

**vol·ume** /'välyoom/ ▶*n.* **1** single book forming part or the whole of a work. **2 a** solid content; bulk. **b** space occupied by a gas or liquid. **3** quantity or power of sound.

**vo·lu·mi·nous** /və'loomənəs/ ▶*adj.* large in volume; bulky.
—**vo·lu·mi·nous·ly** *adv.*

**vol·un·tar·y** /'välən,terē/ ▶*adj.* **1** done, acting, or able to act of one's own free will; not compulsory. **2** unpaid. **3** brought about, produced, etc., by voluntary action.
—**vol·un·tar·i·ly** *adv.*

**vol·un·teer** /,välən'ti(ə)r/ ▶*n.* person who voluntarily undertakes a task or enters military service.
▶*v.* **1** undertake or offer voluntarily. **2** make a voluntary offer of one's services; be a volunteer.

**vo·lup·tu·ous** /və'ləpchooəs/ ▶*adj.* **1** of, tending to, occupied with, or derived from, sensuous or sensual pleasure. **2** full of sexual promise, esp. through shapeliness or fullness.
—**vo·lup·tu·ous·ly** *adv.*
—**vo·lup·tu·ous·ness** *n.*

**vo·lute** /və'loot/ ▶*n. Archit.* spiral-shaped ornamental scroll.
—**vo·lut·ed** *adj.*

**vo·lu·tion** /və'looshən/ ▶*n.* **1** rolling or revolving motion. **2** single turn of a spiral or coil.

**vom·it** /'vämit/ ▶*v.* **1** eject (matter) from the stomach through the mouth. **2** eject violently; belch (forth).
▶*n.* matter vomited from the stomach.

**vom·i·tus** /'vämətəs/ ▶*n.* matter that has been vomited.

**voo·doo** /'voo,doo/ ▶*n.* form of religion based on witchcraft, esp. as practiced in the W. Indies. —**voo·doo·ism** *n.*

**vo·ra·cious** /və'rāshəs/ ▶*adj.* greedy; ravenous.
—**vo·ra·cious·ly** *adv.*
—**vo·ra·cious·ness** *n.*
—**vo·rac·i·ty** *n.*

**vor·tex** /'vôr,teks/ ▶*n.* (*pl.* **-ti·ces** or **-tex·es**) **1** whirlpool or whirlwind. **2** any whirling motion or mass. **3** thing viewed as swallowing up or engrossing.

**vo·ta·ry** /'vōtərē/ ▶*n.* (*pl.* **-ries**) **1** person vowed to religious service. **2** devoted follower, adherent, or advocate of a person, system, occupation, etc.

**vote** /vōt/ ▶*n.* **1** formal

expression of choice or opinion by a ballot, show of hands, etc. **2** right to vote. **3** votes given by or for a particular group.
▶*v.* **1** give or register a vote. **2** cause (someone) to gain or lose a particular post or honor by means of a vote. —**vot·er** *n.*

**vo·tive** /ˈvōtiv/ ▶*adj.* offered or consecrated in fulfillment of a vow.
▶*n.* object offered in this way, such as a candle used as a vigil light.

**vouch** /voucH/ ▶*v.* answer for; be surety for.

**vouch·er** ▶*n.* **1** document exchangeable for goods or services. **2** receipt.

**vouch·safe** ▶*v. formal* condescend to grant or allow.

**vow** /vou/ ▶*n.* solemn promise, esp. in the form of an oath to God.
▶*v.* promise solemnly.

**vow·el** /ˈvouəl/ ▶*n.* **1** speech sound made with vibration of the vocal cords but without audible friction. **2** letter representing this, as *a, e, i, o, u.*

**voy·age** /ˈvoi-ij/ ▶*n.* journey, esp. a long one by sea or in space.
▶*v.* make a voyage. —**voy·ag·er** *n.*

**voy·eur** /voiˈyər/ ▶*n.* person who obtains sexual gratification from

watching others having sex or undressing. —**vo·yeur·ism** *n.* —**voy·eur·is·tic** *adj.*

**VP** ▶*abbr.* vice president.

**VS** ▶*abbr.* veterinary surgeon.

**vs.** ▶*abbr.* versus.

**VT** ▶*abbr.* Vermont (in official postal use).

**Vt.** ▶*abbr.* Vermont.

**vug** /vəg/ ▶*n.* cavity in rock, lined with mineral crystals.

**vul·can·ize** /ˈvəlkəˌnīz/ ▶*v.* treat (rubber, etc.) with sulfur at a high temperature to increase its strength. —**vul·can·i·za·tion** *n.*

**vul·gar** /ˈvəlgər/ ▶*adj.* **1** of or characteristic of the common people. **2** coarse in manners; low. —**vul·gar·i·ty** *n.* —**vul·gar·ly** *adv.*

**vul·ner·a·ble** /ˈvəln(ə)rəbəl/ ▶*adj.* **1** easily wounded or harmed. **2** exposed to damage by a weapon, criticism, etc. —**vul·ner·a·bil·i·ty** *n.* —**vul·ner·a·bly** *adv.*

**vul·ture** /ˈvəlCHər/ ▶*n.* **1** large carrion-eating bird of prey. **2** rapacious person. —**vul·tur·ous** *adj.*

**vul·va** /ˈvəlvə/ ▶*n.* (*pl.* **-vas** or **-vae**) external female genitals.

**vy·ing** /ˈvī-iNG/ ▶*pres. part.* of **VIE**.

# Ww

**W¹** /ˈdəbəl,yōō/ (also **w**) ▸*n.* (*pl.* **Ws** or **W's; w's**) twenty-third letter of the alphabet.

**W²** (also **W.**) ▸*abbr.* **1** watt(s). **2** West; Western.

**W³** ▸*symb. Chem.* tungsten.

**w.** ▸*abbr.* **1** wide(s). **2** with. **3** watt(s).

**WA** ▸*abbr.* Washington (state) (in official postal use).

**wack·y** /ˈwakē/ ▸*adj.* (**-i·er, -i·est**) *inf.* crazy. —**wack·i·ly** *adv.* —**wack·i·ness** *n.*

**wad** /wäd/ ▸*n.* **1** lump of soft material. **2** number of bills of currency or documents placed together.
▸*v.* (**wad·ded, wad·ding**) **1** stop up or keep in place with a wad. **2** press (cotton, etc.) into a wad or wadding.

**wad·dle** /ˈwädl/ ▸*v.* walk with short steps and a swaying motion.
▸*n.* waddling gait.

**wade** /wād/ ▸*v.* **1** walk through water, mud, etc., esp. with difficulty. **2** make one's way with difficulty. **3** (**wade through**) read (a book, etc.) in spite of its dullness, etc. —**wad·a·ble** or **wade·a·ble** *adj.*

**wa·di** /ˈwädē/ ▸*n.* (*pl.* **-dis** or **-dies**) (in certain Arabic-speaking countries) a valley, ravine, or channel that is dry except in the rainy season.

**wa·fer** /ˈwāfər/ ▸*n.* **1** very thin, light, crisp cake, cookie, or biscuit. **2** thin disk of unleavened bread used in the Eucharist.

**waf·fle** /ˈwäfəl/ *inf.* ▸*v.* fail to make up one's mind.
▸*n.* **1** failure to make up one's mind. **2** small, crisp batter cake with an indented lattice pattern. —**waf·fler** *n.* —**waf·fly** *adj.*
□ **waffle iron** utensil, usu. of two shallow metal pans hinged together, for cooking waffles.

**waft** /waft/ ▸*v.* convey or travel easily as through air or over water.
▸*n.* whiff or scent.

**wag** /wag/ ▸*v.* (**wagged, wag·ging**) shake or wave rapidly to and fro.
▸*n.* **1** wagging motion. **2** facetious person; joker.

**wage** /wāj/ ▶*n.* (usu. **wages**)
**1** fixed regular payment to an employee, esp. to a manual or unskilled worker. **2** return; recompense.
▶*v.* carry on (a war, etc.).

**wa·ger** ▶*n. & v.* BET.

**wag·on** /'wagən/ ▶*n.* four-wheeled vehicle for heavy loads.
□ **on the wagon** *inf.* abstaining from drinking alcohol.

**waif** /wāf/ ▶*n.* homeless and helpless person, esp. an abandoned child.

**wail** /wāl/ ▶*n.* prolonged and plaintive loud, high-pitched cry of pain, grief, etc.
▶*v.* **1** utter a wail. **2** lament or complain persistently or bitterly.

**wain·scot** /'wān,skōt/ ▶*n.* wooden paneling on the lower part of an interior wall.

**waist** /wāst/ ▶*n.* **1** part of the human body below the ribs and above the hips. **2** part of a garment encircling or covering the waist.

**waist·band** ▶*n.* strip of cloth forming the waist of a garment.

**waist·line** ▶*n.* size of a person's body at the waist.

**wait** /wāt/ ▶*v.* **1** defer action or departure for a specified time or until some event occurs. **2** be expectant or on the watch. **3** serve food, drinks, etc., (at). **4** (**wait on**) act as an attendant to.
▶*n.* period of waiting.

**wait·er** ▶*n.* person who serves food or drinks in a hotel or restaurant, etc.

**wait·ing list** ▶*n.* list of people waiting for something, as admission to a school, etc.

**waive** /wāv/ ▶*v.* refrain from insisting on or using (a right, claim, opportunity, legitimate plea, rule, etc.).

**waiv·er** ▶*n. Law* act or an instance of waiving.

**wake** /wāk/ ▶*v.* (*past* **woke** or **waked**; *past part.* **wok·en** or **waked**) **1** cease or cause to cease to sleep. **2** become or cause to become alert, attentive, or active.
▶*n.* **1** watch beside a corpse before burial. **2** track left on the water's surface by a moving ship. **3** turbulent air left behind a moving aircraft, etc.

**wake·ful** ▶*adj.* **1** unable to sleep. **2** (of a night, etc.) passed with little or no sleep.
—**wake·ful·ness** *n.*

**wak·en** ▶*v.* make or become awake.

**wale** /wāl/ ▸n. **1** mark left on the skin by a rod or whip; weal. **2** ridge on corduroy.

**walk** /wôk/ ▸v. **1** (of a person or other biped) progress by lifting and setting down each foot in turn, never having both feet off the ground at once. **2** travel or go on foot. **3** *Baseball* **a** reach first base on balls. **b** allow to do this.
▸n. **1** act or manner of walking; the ordinary human gait. **2 a** distance walked. **b** excursion on foot. **3** place, track, or route intended or suitable for walking. **4** *Baseball* four pitched balls advancing a batter to base.

**walk·ie-talk·ie** /ˈwôkē ˈtôkē/ ▸n. two-way radio carried on the person, esp. by police officers, etc.

**walk·ing stick** ▸n. **1** stick used for support in walking. **2** long, slender insect that resembles a twig.

**walk·out** ▸n. sudden angry departure, esp. as a protest or strike.

**wall** /wôl/ ▸n. vertical structure of usu. brick or stone, esp. enclosing, protecting, or dividing a space or supporting a roof.
▸v. surround, block off, or protect with a wall.

**wall·board** ▸n. type of wall covering made from wood pulp, plaster, etc.

**wal·let** /ˈwälit/ ▸n. usu. pocket-size case for holding money, credit cards, etc.

**wall·eye** ▸n. **1 a** eye with a streaked or opaque white iris. **b** eye squinting outward. **2** (also **wall·eyed pike**) American perch with large prominent eyes.

**wall·flow·er** ▸n. inf. person who feels shy, awkward, or excluded at a party.

**wal·lop** /ˈwäləp/ inf. ▸v. thrash; beat.
▸n. heavy blow.

**wal·low** /ˈwälō/ ▸v. **1** (esp. of an animal) roll about in mud, etc. **2** (usu. **wallow in**) indulge in unrestrained pleasure, misery, etc.
▸n. **1** act or instance of wallowing. **2** place used for wallowing.

**wall·pa·per** ▸n. decorative paper for pasting onto interior walls.

**wal·nut** /ˈwôlˌnət/ ▸n. **1** tree with aromatic leaves and drooping catkins. **2** edible nut of this tree. **3** its timber, used for furniture.

**wal·rus** /ˈwôlrəs/ ▸*n.* large, amphibious, long-tusked arctic mammal related to the seal and sea lion.

**waltz** /wôlts/ ▸*n.* ballroom dance in triple time or the music for this.

▸*v.* **1** dance a waltz. **2** *inf.* (**waltz around/in/out/**) move lightly, casually, etc.

**wan** /wän/ ▸*adj.* pale; exhausted, weak; worn. —**wan·ly** *adv.*

**wand** /wänd/ ▸*n.* **1** stick used by a magician for effect. **2** staff symbolizing some officials' authority. **3** handheld electronic device that can be passed over a bar code to read the data this represents.

**wan·der** /ˈwändər/ ▸*v.* **1** go from place to place aimlessly. **2** stray; digress.

**wan·der·lust** ▸*n.* eagerness for traveling or wandering.

**wane** /wān/ ▸*v.* **1** (of the moon) decrease in apparent size after the full moon. **2** decrease in power, vigor, etc.

**wan·gle** /ˈwaNGgəl/ ▸*v. inf.* obtain (a favor, etc.) by scheming, etc.

**wan·na·be** /ˈwänəbē/ ▸*n. inf.* anyone who would like to be someone or something else.

**want** /wänt/ ▸*v.* **1** desire; wish for possession of; need. **2** lack. **3** (usu. **be wanted**) (of the police) desire to apprehend (a suspected criminal).

▸*n.* **1 a** lack or deficiency. **b** poverty; need. **2** craving.

**want·ing** ▸*adj.* lacking; not equal to requirements.

**wan·ton** /ˈwäntn/ ▸*adj.* **1** licentious; lewd. **2** luxuriant; unrestrained. —**wan·ton·ly** *adv.* —**wan·ton·ness** *n.*

**war** /wôr/ ▸*n.* **1 a** armed hostilities, esp. between nations; conflict. **b** specific period or instance of this. **2 a** hostility or contention between people, groups, etc. **b** sustained campaign against crime, disease, poverty, etc.

▸*v.* (**warred, war·ring**) make war.

**war·ble** /ˈwôrbəl/ ▸*v.* sing in a gentle, trilling manner.

▸*n.* warbling sound. —**war·bler** *n.*

**ward** /wôrd/ ▸*n.* **1** division of a hospital, prison, etc. **2** administrative division of a city or town, esp. an electoral district. **3** minor under the care of a guardian or a court.

□ **ward off** **1** parry (a blow). **2** avert (danger, etc.).

**-ward** /wərd/ (also **-wards**) ▶*suffix* added to nouns of place or destination and to adverbs of direction and forming: **1** adverbs meaning 'toward the place, etc.': *moving backward.* **2** adjectives meaning 'turned or tending toward': *downward look.* **3** nouns meaning 'the region toward or about': *look to the eastward.*

**war·den** /ˈwôrdn/ ▶*n.* **1** chief administrator of a prison. **2** supervising official: *game warden.*

**ward·er** ▶*n.* guard; caretaker.

**ward·robe** ▶*n.* **1** large cupboard for storing clothes. **2** person's entire stock of clothes. **3** costume department or costumes of a theater, a movie company, etc.

**ware** /we(ə)r/ ▶*n.* **1** things of the same kind made usu. for sale: *chinaware | hardware.* **2** (**wares**) articles for sale. **3** ceramics, etc., of a specified material, factory, or kind: *Wedgwood ware | delftware.*

**ware·house** ▶*n.* building in which goods are stored.

▶*v.* store, esp. temporarily, in a repository.

**war·fare** ▶*n.* campaigning or engaging in war.

**war·head** ▶*n.* explosive head of a missile, torpedo, or similar weapon.

**war·horse** ▶*n. inf.* veteran soldier, politician, etc.

**war·lock** ▶*n.* male witch.

**warm** /wôrm/ ▶*adj.* **1** of or at a moderately high temperature. **2** (clothes, etc.) affording warmth. **3** sympathetic; friendly.

▶*v.* **1** make or become warm or cheerful. **2** (**warm to**) become animated about or sympathetic toward. —**warm·ly** *adv.* —**warm·ness** *n.* —**warmth** *n.*

□ **warm-blooded** having blood that maintains a warm temperature. □ **warm-up** period of preparatory exercise for a contest or performance.

**warm·heart·ed** ▶*adj.* kind; friendly. —**warm·heart·ed·ly** *adv.* —**warm·heart·ed·ness** *n.*

**war·mon·ger** ▶*n.* person who seeks to bring about or promote war.

**warn** /wôrn/ ▶*v.* **1** inform of possible danger, problem, etc. **2** give cautionary advice.

**warp** /wôrp/ ▸v. **1** make or become twisted out of shape. **2** make or become perverted or strange.
▸n. **1** state of being warped; distortion. **2** lengthwise threads in a loom. —**warp·age** n.

**war·rant** /'wôrənt/ ▸n. **1** authorization; justification. **2** written authorization allowing police to search premises, arrest a suspect, etc.
▸v. **1** justify. **2** guarantee or attest to. —**war·rant·er** or **war·ran·tor** n.

**war·ran·ty** ▸n. (pl. -ties) guarantee of the quality of a thing sold, etc., often accepting responsibility for defects or repairs.

**war·ren** /'wôrən/ ▸n. network of interconnecting rabbit burrows.

**war·ri·or** /'wôrēər/ ▸n. person experienced or distinguished in fighting.

**war·ship** ▸n. armored ship used in war.

**wart** /wôrt/ ▸n. small, hard, round growth on the skin. —**wart·y** adj.

**war·y** /'we(ə)rē/ ▸adj. (-i·er, -i·est) on one's guard; cautious. —**war·i·ly** adv. —**war·i·ness** n.

**was** /wəz; wäz/ ▸1st & 3rd sing. past of BE.

**Wash.** ▸abbr. Washington.

**wash** /wäsH/ ▸v. **1** cleanse with liquid, esp. water. **2** (**wash off/out**) (of a stain, etc.) be removed by washing. **3** sweep, move, or splash. **4** brush a thin coat of watery paint or ink over.
▸n. **1** act or instance of washing. **2** clothes for washing or just washed. **3** visible or audible motion of agitated water or air, esp. due to the passage of a ship or aircraft. **4** thin coating of watercolor, wall paint, or metal. —**wash·a·ble** adj.
☐ **washed out 1** faded. **2** pale. ☐ **washed up** inf. defeated; having failed. ☐ **wash one's hands of** renounce responsibility for.

**wash·ba·sin** (also **wash·bowl**) ▸n. basin, usu. fixed to a wall, for washing one's hands and face.

**wash·board** ▸n. ribbed board on which clothes are scrubbed.

**wash·cloth** ▸n. cloth of absorbent material made for washing one's face and body.

**wash·er** ▸n. **1** person or machine that washes. **2** flat ring of rubber, metal, etc., placed under the head of a screw, etc., to disperse its pressure.

**wash·room** ▸*n.* bathroom.

**was·n't** /'wəzənt; 'wäz-/ ▸*contr.* was not.

**WASP** /wäsp/ (also **Wasp**) ▸*n.* white Anglo-Saxon Protestant. —**Wasp·y** *adj.*

**wasp** ▸*n.* stinging insect with a black and yellow striped body.

**wasp·ish** ▸*adj.* irritable; petulant; sharp in retort.

**was·sail** /'wäsəl; -ˌsāl/ *archaic* ▸*n.* **1** spiced ale or cider drunk at celebrations of Christmas Eve or Twelfth Night. **2** festive occasion with drinking. ▸*v.* celebrate; sing carols.

**waste** /wāst/ ▸*v.* **1** use more of (something) than is needed. **2** use or spend to no purpose. **3** fail to use. **4** wear away gradually; make or become weak. ▸*adj.* **1** superfluous. **2** not inhabited or cultivated. ▸*n.* **1** act or instance of wasting. **2** waste material or food. **3** waste region. —**wast·age** *n.* —**waste·ful** *adj.*
□ **lay waste** ravage; devastate.

**waste·land** ▸*n.* **1** unproductive or useless area of land. **2** place

or time considered spiritually or intellectually barren.

**wast·rel** /'wāstrəl/ ▸*n.* good-for-nothing person.

**watch** /wäCH/ ▸*v.* **1** keep the eyes fixed on. **2** keep under observation. **3** (**watch for**) be on an alert for; be vigilant about. **4** (**watch over**) look after; take care of. ▸*n.* **1** small portable timepiece for carrying on one's person. **2** state of alert or constant observation or attention. **3** period of watching. **4** guard; security officer. —**watch·ful** *adj.*
□ **watch out** be on one's guard.

**watch·dog** ▸*n.* **1** dog kept to guard property, etc. **2** person or body monitoring others' rights, etc.

**watch·man** ▸*n.* (*pl.* **-men**) person employed to look after an empty building, etc., at night.

**watch·tow·er** ▸*n.* tower from which observation can be kept.

**watch·word** ▸*n.* phrase summarizing a guiding principle.

**wa·ter** /'wôtər/ ▸*n.* **1** colorless, transparent, odorless, tasteless liquid compound of oxygen and hydrogen. **2** liquid consisting chiefly of this and found in seas, lakes, rivers, and rain. **3** body or expanse of water. **4** (**waters**) part of a sea or river. **5** liquid secretion.

▸*v.* **1** sprinkle, supply, or soak with water. **2** (of the mouth or eyes) secrete water.

□ **make one's mouth water** cause one's saliva to flow; stimulate one's appetite or anticipation.

□ **water-repellent** not easily penetrated by water.

**wa·ter buf·fa·lo** ▸*n.* common domestic E. Indian buffalo.

**wa·ter chest·nut** ▸*n.* nutlike tuber from a sedge, used esp. in Chinese cooking.

**wa·ter·col·or** ▸*n* **1** pigment diluted with water. **2** picture painted with this.

**wa·ter·course** ▸*n.* **1** brook, stream, or artificial water channel. **2** bed along which this flows.

**wa·ter·cress** ▸*n.* pungent edible plant growing in running water.

**wa·ter·fall** ▸*n.* stream of water flowing over a precipice or down a steep hillside.

**wa·ter·fowl** ▸*pl. n.* birds frequenting water, esp. swimming game birds.

**wa·ter·front** ▸*n.* part of a town or city adjoining a river, lake, harbor, etc.

**wa·ter lil·y** ▸*n.* aquatic plant with broad flat floating leaves and flowers.

**wa·ter·line** ▸*n.* line along which the surface of water touches a ship's side.

**wa·ter·logged** ▸*adj.* saturated or filled with water.

**wa·ter·mark** ▸*n.* faint identifying design in some paper.

▸*v.* mark with this.

**wa·ter·mel·on** ▸*n.* large, smooth, green melon with sweet, juicy red pulp.

**wa·ter moc·ca·sin** ▸*n.* venomous snake of the southern U.S.; cottonmouth.

**wa·ter·proof** ▸*adj.* impervious to water.

▸*v.* make waterproof.

**wa·ter·shed** ▸*n.* **1** line of separation between waters flowing to different rivers, basins, or seas. **2** turning point in affairs.

**wa·ter ski** ▸*n.* each of a pair of skis for skimming the surface of the water when towed by a motorboat.

**wa·ter·spout** ▸*n.* gyrating column of water and spray

formed by a whirlwind between sea and cloud.

**wa·ter ta·ble** ▸*n.* level below which the ground is saturated with water.

**wa·ter·tight** ▸*adj.* **1** closely fastened or fitted to prevent the passage of water. **2** (of an argument, etc.) unassailable.

**wa·ter·way** ▸*n.* navigable channel.

**wa·ter·wheel** ▸*n.* large wheel driven by flowing water, used to drive machinery.

**wa·ter·works** ▸*n.* establishment for managing a water supply.

**wa·ter·y** ▸*adj.* **1** containing too much water. **2** of or consisting of water. **3** (of the eyes) suffused or running with water.

**watt** /wät/ ▸*n.* the SI unit of electrical power, equivalent to one joule per second. (Symb.: **W**)

**wat·tle** /'wätl/ ▸*n.* **1** interlaced rods and split rods used for fences, etc. **2** loose fleshy appendage on the head or throat of a turkey or other birds.

**wave** /wāv/ ▸*v.* **1** (often **wave to**) move a hand, etc., to and fro in greeting or as a signal. **2** show or cause to show a sinuous or sweeping motion as of a flag, tree, or wheat field in the wind. **3** express (a greeting, instruction, etc.) by waving. **4** (of hair, etc.) be wavy.

▸*n.* **1** ridge of water between two depressions. **2** fluctuating motion, etc. **3** gesture of waving. **4** undulating form, as in the hair. **5** *Physics* **a** disturbance of the particles of a fluid medium for the propagation or direction of motion, heat, light, sound, etc. **b** single curve in the course of this motion. —**wav·y** *adj.*

□ **make waves** *inf.* cause trouble.

**wave·length** ▸*n.* **1** distance between successive crests of a wave. (Symb.: $\lambda$) **2** *inf.* particular mode or range of thinking: *she and I are not on the same wavelength.*

**wa·ver** ▸*v.* **1** be or become unsteady. **2** be irresolute. **3** (of a light) flicker. —**wa·ver·ing·ly** *adv.*

**wax**[1] /waks/ ▸*n.* **1** sticky, plastic yellowish substance secreted by bees as the material of honeycomb cells; beeswax. **2** this used for candles, modeling, etc. **3** any similar substance, e.g., earwax.

▸*v.* cover or treat with wax.

—**wax·i·ly** adv. —**wax·i·ness** n. —**wax·y** adj.

□ **wax bean** yellow-podded snap bean. □ **wax paper** (also **waxed paper**) paper waterproofed with a layer of wax.

**wax**2 ▶v. **1** (of the moon between new and full) increasing in apparent size. **2** become larger or stronger.

□ **wax and wane** undergo alternate increases and decreases.

**wax·wing** ▶n. any of various birds with small tips like red sealing wax on some wing feathers.

**way** /wā/ ▶n. **1** road, track, path, etc. **2** course or route for reaching a place. **3** place of passage into a building, through a door, etc. **4** method or plan for attaining an object. **5 a** person's desired or chosen course of action. **b** custom or manner of behaving. **6** normal course of events. **7** traveling distance. **8** specified direction.

□ **by the way** incidentally. □ **way-out** inf. **1** unusual; eccentric. **2** excellent. □ **ways and means** methods of achieving something, esp. of raising government revenue.

**way·far·er** /'wā,fe(ə)rər/ ▶n. traveler, esp. on foot.

**way·lay** ▶v. (past and past part. **-laid**) **1** lie in wait for. **2** stop to rob or interview.

**way·side** ▶n. side of a road.

**way·ward** ▶adj. childishly self-willed or perverse. —**way·ward·ly** adv. —**way·ward·ness** n.

**we** /wē/ ▶pron. (obj. **us**; poss. **our**, **ours**) **1** pl. of I used by and with reference to more than one person. **2** used for or by a royal person, an editor, etc., when speaking.

**weak** /wēk/ ▶adj. **1** deficient in strength, power, vigor, or number. **2** unconvincing. —**weak·en** v. —**weak·ly** adj. —**weak·ness** n.

□ **weak moment** time when one is unusually compliant or temptable.

**weak·ling** ▶n. feeble person or animal.

**weal** /wēl/ ▶n. ridge raised on the flesh by a stroke of a rod or whip.

**wealth** /welTH/ ▶n. **1** riches. **2** state of being rich. **3** abundance. —**wealth·y** adj.

**wean** /wēn/ ▶v. **1** accustom (an infant or other young mammal) to food other than (esp. its mother's) milk. **2** disengage (from a habit, etc.).

**weap·on** /ˈwepən/ ▶*n.* **1** thing designed or used or usable for inflicting bodily harm. **2** means for trying to gain the advantage in a conflict.

**weap·on·ry** ▶*n.* weapons collectively.

**wear** /we(ə)r/ ▶*v.* (*past* **wore**; *past part.* **worn**) **1** have on one's person as clothing, an ornament, etc. **2** exhibit or present (a facial expression, etc.). **3 a** injure the surface of, or partly obliterate or alter, by rubbing, stress, or use. **b** undergo such injury or change. **4** (**wear off/away**) rub or be rubbed off. **5** exhaust. **6** (**wear down**) overcome by persistence. **7** endure continued use or life.

▶*n.* **1** wearing or being worn. **2** things worn; clothing: *sportswear.* **3** (also **wear and tear**) damage sustained from continuous use. —**wear·a·ble** *adj.* —**wear·a·bil·i·ty** *n.* —**wear·ing·ly** *adv.*

□ **wear off** lose effectiveness or intensity. □ **wear out** use or be used until no longer usable.

**wea·ri·some** /ˈwi(ə)rēsəm/ ▶*adj.* tedious; tiring by monotony or length. —**wea·ri·some·ly** *adv.* —**wea·ri·some·ness** *n.*

**wea·ry** /ˈwi(ə)rē/ ▶*adj.* (**-ri·er,** **-ri·est**) **1** very tired. **2** impatient of.

▶*v.* (**-ried**) make or grow weary. —**wea·ri·ly** *adv.* —**wea·ri·ness** *n.*

**wea·sel** /ˈwēzəl/ ▶*n.* small, flesh-eating mammal related to the stoat and ferret.

**weath·er** /ˈweT͟Hər/ ▶*n.* state of the atmosphere at a place and time as regards heat, cloudiness, dryness, sunshine, wind, rain, etc.

▶*v.* **1** discolor or partly disintegrate by exposure to air. **2** come safely through (a storm, difficult period, etc.).

□ **under the weather** *inf.* indisposed or out of sorts.

**weath·er·ize** ▶*v.* make resistant to cold weather.

**weath·er·proof** ▶*adj.* resistant to the effects of bad weather, esp. rain.

▶*v.* make weatherproof.

**weath·er vane** ▶*n.* see VANE.

**weave** /wēv/ ▶*v.* (*past* **wove**; *past part.* **wo·ven** or **wove**) **1** form (fabric) by interlacing long threads in two directions.

**2** make fabric in this way.
**3** make (a basket or wreath, etc.) by interlacing rushes or flowers, etc. **4** make (facts, etc.) into a story or connected whole.
**5** move repeatedly from side to side.

▶*n.* style of weaving. —**weav·er** *n.*

**web** /web/ ▶*n.* **1** woven fabric.
**2** connected series: *web of lies.*
**3** cobweb, gossamer, or similar product of a spinning creature.
**4** membrane between the toes of a swimming animal or bird.
**5** (**the Web**) short for WORLD WIDE WEB.
□ **web-footed** having the toes connected by webs.

**Web·mas·ter** (also **web·mas·ter**) ▶*n.* person who designs and develops Web sites.

**Web site** (also **web site** or **web·site**) ▶*n.* location connected to the Internet that maintains one or more pages on the World Wide Web.

**Wed.** ▶*abbr.* Wednesday.

**wed** /wed/ ▶*v.* (**wed·ding**; *past* and *past part.* **wed·ded** or **wed**)
**1** marry. **2** unite; combine.

**we'd** /wēd/ ▶*contr.* **1** we had.
**2** we should; we would.

**wed·ding** ▶*n.* marriage ceremony.

**wedge** /wej/ ▶*n.* **1** piece of wood, metal, etc., tapering to a sharp edge, driven between two objects or parts to secure or separate them. **2** anything resembling a wedge.

▶*v.* **1** secure or fasten by means of a wedge. **2** force open or apart with a wedge. **3** pack or thrust (a thing or oneself) tightly in or into.

**wed·lock** ▶*n.* married state.

**Wednes·day** /'wenz,dā/ ▶*n.* fourth day of the week, following Tuesday.

**wee** /wē/ ▶*adj.* (**we·er**; **we·est**) little; tiny.

**weed** /wēd/ ▶*n.* **1** plant growing where it is not wanted. **2** *inf.* **a** marijuana. **b** tobacco.

▶*v.* **1** clear (an area) of weeds. **2** (**weed out**) sort out (inferior or unwanted parts, etc.) for removal.

**weeds** ▶*pl. n.* (also **widow's weeds**) black mourning clothing worn by a widow.

**week** /wēk/ ▶*n.* **1** period of seven days, often reckoned from Sunday to Saturday. **2** working period during a week. *stay for a week.*

**week·day** ▶*n.* day other than

Saturday or Sunday: *a weekday afternoon.*

**week·end** ▸*n.* Saturday and Sunday.

▸*v.* spend a weekend.

**week·ly** ▸*adj.* done, produced, or occurring once a week.

▸*adv.* once a week.

▸*n.* (*pl.* **-lies**) weekly newspaper or periodical.

**weep** /wēp/ ▸*v.* (*past* and *past part.* **wept**) **1** shed tears. **2** exude liquid. —**weep·y** *adj.*

**wee·vil** /'wēvəl/ ▸*n.* destructive beetle feeding esp. on grain, cotton, etc.

**weft** /weft/ ▸*n.* threads woven across a warp to make fabric.

**weigh** /wā/ ▸*v.* **1** find the weight of. **2** compare or consider. **3** be equal to (a specified weight). **4** exert an influence. **5** (**weigh on**) be heavy or burdensome to.

□ **weigh down 1** bring or keep down. **2** be oppressive.

**weight** /wāt/ ▸*n.* **1** *Physics* force experienced by a body as a result of the earth's gravitation. **2** heaviness of a body. **3** quantitative expression of a body's weight. **4** body of a known weight for use in weighing. **5** heavy object or load. **6** influence; importance; preponderance.

▸*v.* **1 a** attach a weight to. **b** hold down with a weight. **2** impede or burden. —**weight·y** *adj.*

**weir** /wi(ə)r/ ▸*n.* **1** dam built across a river to raise the level of water upstream or regulate its flow. **2** enclosure of stakes, etc., set in a stream as a trap for fish.

**weird** /wi(ə)rd/ ▸*adj.* **1** uncanny; supernatural. **2** *inf.* very strange; bizarre. —**weird·ly** *adv.* —**weird·ness** *n.*

**weird·o** /'wi(ə)r,dō/ ▸*n.* (*pl.* **-os**) *inf.* odd or eccentric person.

**wel·come** /'welkəm/ ▸*n.* act of greeting or receiving gladly; kind or glad reception.

▸*interj.* expressing such a greeting.

▸*v.* receive with a welcome.

▸*adj.* **1** received with pleasure. **2** allowed or invited. —**wel·com·ing·ly** *adv.*

**weld** /weld/ ▸*v.* **1 a** hammer or press (heated pieces of metal) into one piece. **b** join by fusion with an electric arc, etc. **2** unite; join.

▸*n.* welded joint. —**weld·er** *n.*

**wel·fare** /'wel,fe(ə)r/ ▸*n.* **1** well-being; happiness; health and prosperity. **2** financial support given by a government to the unemployed, disadvantaged, etc.

**wel·kin** /ˈwelkin/ ▶*n.* sky or heaven.

**well** /wel/ ▶*adv.* (**better**, **best**) **1** in a satisfactory way. **2** in the right way. **3** with some distinction. **4 a** thoroughly; carefully. **b** intimately; closely. **5** with approval; favorably. **6** probably; reasonably.

▶*adj.* (**better**, **best**) **1** in good health. **2 a** satisfactory. **b** advisable.

▶*interj.* expressing surprise, resignation, insistence, etc.

▶*n.* **1** shaft sunk into the ground to obtain water, oil, etc. **2** enclosed space like a well shaft. **3** source.

▶*v.* spring as from a fountain.

□ **as well as** in addition to.

□ **well-advised** prudent. □ **well-appointed** having all the necessary equipment. □ **well-balanced** sane; sensible. □ **well-being** state of being well, healthy, contented, etc. □ **well-bred** having or showing good breeding or manners. □ **well-disposed (toward)** having a good disposition or friendly feeling (for). □ **well-done 1** (of meat, etc.) thoroughly cooked. **2** (of a

task, etc.) performed well. □ **well-founded** based on good evidence. □ **well-grounded** having good knowledge of the groundwork of a subject. □ **well-heeled** *inf.* wealthy. □ **well-informed** having much knowledge or information about a subject. □ **well-known 1** known to many. **2** known thoroughly. □ **well-meaning** (or **well-meant**) having good intentions. □ **well-off 1** wealthy. **2** in a fortunate situation. □ **well-read** knowledgeable through much reading. □ **well-rounded** having or showing a fully developed personality, ability, etc. □ **well-spoken** articulate or refined in speech. □ **well-to-do** prosperous. □ **well-worn 1** much worn by use. **2** (of a phrase, etc.) trite.

**we'll** /wēl/ ▶*contr.* we shall; we will.

**well·born** ▶*adj.* of a good or esteemed family.

**well·spring** ▶*n.* original and bountiful source of something.

**Welsh** /welsʜ/ ▶*adj.* of or relating to Wales or its people or language.

▶*n.* **1** Celtic language of Wales. **2** (**the Welsh**) the people of

Wales. —**Welsh·man** n.
—**Welsh·wom·an** n.

□ **Welsh rabbit** (or **Welsh rarebit**) another term for RAREBIT.

**welsh** (also **welch**) ▸v. (**welsh on**) evade (an obligation, debt, promise, etc.)

**welt** /welt/ ▸n. **1** leather rim sewn around the edge of a shoe upper for the sole to be attached to. **2** WEAL. **3** trimming.

**wel·ter** ▸n. **1** state of general confusion. **2** disorderly mixture or contrast of beliefs, policies, etc.
▸v. roll; wallow.

**wen** /wen/ ▸n. benign tumor on the skin, esp. of the scalp.

**wench** /wenCH/ ▸n. girl or young woman.

**wend** /wend/ ▸v. (in phrase **wend one's way**) make one's way.

**went** /went/ ▸past of GO.

**were** /wər/ ▸2nd sing. past, pl. past, and past subj. of BE.

**we're** /wi(ə)r/ ▸contr. we are.

**were·n't** /wər(ə)nt/ ▸contr. were not.

**were·wolf** /'we(ə)r,wŏŏlf/ ▸n. (pl. **-wolves**) mythical being who at times changes from a person to a wolf.

**west** /west/ ▸n. **1 a** point of the horizon where the sun sets at the equinoxes. **b** compass point corresponding to this. **c** direction in which this lies. **2** (usu. **the West**) **a** European civilization. **b** the nations of western Europe and N. America. **c** western part of a country, etc., esp. the American West.
▸adj. & adv. toward, at, near, or from the west. —**wes·ter·ly** adj. —**wes·tern** adj.

**west·er·ing** /'westəriNG/ ▸adj. (esp. of the sun) nearing the west.

**west·ern·ize** (also **Wes·tern·ize**) ▸v. influence with or convert to the ideas, customs, etc., of the West. —**west·ern·i·za·tion** n.

**west·ward** ▸adj. & adv. (also **west·wards**) toward the west.
▸n. westward direction or region.

**wet** /wet/ ▸adj. (**wet·ter**, **wet·test**) **1** soaked, covered, or dampened with water or other liquid. **2** rainy.
▸v. (**wet·ting**; past and past part. **wet** or **wet·ted**) **1** make wet. **2** urinate in or on.
▸n. **1** liquid that wets something. **2** rainy weather. —**wet·ly** adv. —**wet·ness** n.

**whack** /(h)wak/ inf. ▸v. strike or beat forcefully.

►*n.* sharp or resounding blow.

□ **have a whack at** *inf.* attempt.

□ **out of whack** *inf.* out of order; malfunctioning.

**whale** /(h)wāl/ ►*n.* (*pl.* same or **whales**) large marine mammal having a streamlined body and horizontal tail, and breathing through a blowhole on the head. ►*v. inf.* beat; thrash.

**whale·bone** ►*n.* elastic horny substance growing in thin parallel plates in the upper jaw of some whales.

**wharf** /(h)wôrf/ ►*n.* (*pl.* **wharves** or **wharfs**) level quayside area to which a ship may be moored to load and unload.

**what** /(h)wət; (h)wät/ ►*adj.* **1** asking for a choice from an indefinite number or for a statement of amount, number, or kind. **2** whatever: *will give you what help I can.* **3** [usu. in *interj.*] how great or remarkable: *what luck!* ►*pron.* **1** what thing or things? **2** (asking for a remark to be repeated) = what did you say? **3** that or those which: *what followed was worse.* ►*adv.* to what extent: *what does it matter?*

**what·ev·er** ►*adj. & pron.* **1** WHAT (in relative uses) with the emphasis on indefiniteness. **2** though anything: *we are safe whatever happens.* **3** at all; of any kind: *there is no doubt whatever.*

**what·so·ev·er** ►*adj. & pron.* WHATEVER.

**wheat** /(h)wēt/ ►*n.* **1** cereal plant bearing dense four-sided seed spikes. **2** its grain, used in making flour, etc.

□ **wheat germ** embryo of the wheat grain, extracted as a source of vitamins.

**whee·dle** /'(h)wēdl/ ►*v.* coax, influence, or get by flattery or endearments.

**wheel** /(h)wēl/ ►*n.* **1** circular frame or disk that revolves on an axle. **2** something round. **3** (**wheels**) *inf.* car. ►*v.* **1** turn on an axis or pivot. **2** push, pull, or move on wheels.

**wheel·bar·row** ►*n.* small cart with one wheel and two shafts for carrying garden loads, etc.

**wheel·base** ►*n.* distance between the front and rear axles of a vehicle.

**wheel·chair** ►*n.* chair on wheels for an invalid or disabled person.

**wheeze** /(h)wēz/ ►*v.* breathe with an audible whistling sound.

▶*n.* sound of wheezing.
—**wheez·y** *adj.*

**whelp** /(h)welp/ ▶*n.* young dog; puppy.

▶*v.* give birth to (a whelp or whelps).

**when** /(h)wen/ ▶*adv.* **1** at what time? **2** on what occasion? **3** (time) at or on which: *there are times when I could cry.*

▶*conj.* **1** at the or any time that; as soon as: *come when you like.* **2** although. **3** after which; and then; but just then: *was nearly asleep when the bell rang.*

▶*pron.* what time?: *till when can you stay?*

**whence** /(h)wens/ ▶*adv. & conj. formal* from where; from which.

**when·ev·er** ▶*conj. & adv.* **1** at whatever time; on whatever occasion. **2** every time that.

**where** /(h)we(ə)r/ ▶*adv.* **1** in or to what place or position?: *where is the milk?* **2** in what respect?: *where does the argument lead?* **3** in what book, etc.?; from whom?: *where did you read that?* **4** in or to which: *places where they meet.*

▶*conj.* wherever: *go where you like.*

▶*pron.* what place?

**where·a·bouts** ▶*adv.* approximately where?: *whereabouts are they?*

▶*n.* [treated as *sing.* or *pl.*] person's or thing's location.

**where·as** ▶*conj.* **1** in contrast or comparison with the fact that. **2** seeing that.

**where·by** ▶*conj.* by what or which means.

**where·fore** ▶*adv. archaic* **1** for what reason? **2** for which reason.

**where·in** ▶*conj. formal* in what or which place or respect.

**where·of** ▶*conj. formal* of what or which: *the means whereof.*

**where·up·on** ▶*conj.* immediately after which.

**wher·ev·er** ▶*adv. & conj.* in or to whatever place.

**where·with·al** /-wiTH,ôl/ ▶*n.* money, etc., needed for a purpose: *has not the wherewithal to do it.*

**wher·ry** /'(h)werē/ ▶*n.* (*pl.* **-ries**) light rowboat used chiefly for carrying passengers.

**whet** /(h)wet/ ▶*v.* (**whet·ted, whet·ting**) **1** sharpen (a tool). **2** stimulate (the appetite or a desire, etc.).

**wheth·er** /'(h)weTHər/ ▶*conj.* introducing the first or both of alternative possibilities: *I do not know whether they have arrived or not.*

**whet·stone** ▶*n.* fine-grained stone for sharpening knives, etc.

**whey** /(h)wā/ ▶*n.* watery liquid left when milk forms curds.

**which** /(h)wɪCH/ ▶*adj.* **1** asking for choice from a definite set of alternatives: *which John do you mean?* **2** being the one just referred to: *ten years, during which time they admitted nothing.* ▶*pron.* **1** what person or thing. **2** used in place of *that* after *in* or *that: the house in which I was born.*

**which·ev·er** ▶*adj. & pron.* **1** any which: *whichever one you like.* **2** no matter which: *whichever one wins, they both get a prize.*

**whiff** /(h)wif/ ▶*n.* puff or breath of air, odor, etc.

**while** /(h)wīl/ ▶*n.* period of time: *waited a while.* ▶*conj.* **1** during the time that. **2** although: *while I want to believe it, I cannot.* ▶*v.* (**while away**) pass (time, etc.) in a leisurely or interesting manner. □ **worth one's while** worth the time or effort spent.

**whi·lom** /'(h)wīləm/ ▶*adv.* formerly; in the past.

▶*adj.* former; erstwhile.

**whim** /(h)wim/ ▶*n.* sudden fancy; caprice.

**whim·per** /'(h)wimpər/ ▶*v.* make or utter with feeble, querulous, or frightened sounds. ▶*n.* whimpering sound.

**whim·sy** /'(h)wimzē/ (also **whim·sey**) ▶*n.* (*pl.* **-sies** or **-seys**) fanciful behavior or idea; whim. —**whim·si·cal** *adj.*

**whine** /(h)wīn/ ▶*n.* **1** complaining, long-drawn wail as of a dog. **2** similar shrill, prolonged sound. **3** querulous tone or complaint. ▶*v.* **1** emit or utter a whine. **2** complain in a querulous tone. —**whin·er** *n.* —**whin·ing·ly** *adv.* —**whin·y** *adj.*

**whin·ny** /'(h)winē/ ▶*n.* (*pl.* **-nies**) gentle or joyful neigh. ▶*v.* (**-nied**) give a whinny.

**whip** /(h)wip/ ▶*n.* **1** lash attached to a handle for urging on animals, punishing, etc. **2** legislative member of a political party appointed to control discipline, tactics, etc. ▶*v.* (**whipped, whip·ping**) **1** beat or urge on with a whip. **2** beat (cream, eggs, etc.) into a froth. **3** move suddenly, unexpectedly, or rapidly.

**whip·lash** ▶*n.* **1** flexible end of a whip. **2** injury to the neck caused by a jerk of the head, esp. as in a motor vehicle accident.

**whip·pet** /'(h)wipit/ ▶*n.* crossbred dog of the greyhound type used for racing.

**whip·poor·will** /'(h)wipər,wil/ ▶*n.* nocturnal N. American bird, named for its call.

**whir** /(h)wər/ ▶*n.* continuous rapid buzzing or softly clicking sound.

▶*v.* (**whirred, whir·ring**) make this sound.

**whirl** /(h)wərl/ ▶*v.* **1** swing around and around; revolve rapidly. **2** move with bewildering speed.

▶*n.* **1** whirling movement. **2** state of intense activity. **3** state of confusion.

—**whirl·ing·ly** *adv.*

**whirl·pool** ▶*n.* powerful circular eddy in the sea, etc., often causing suction to its center.

**whirl·wind** ▶*n.* **1** mass or column of air whirling rapidly in a funnel shape over land or water. **2** confused tumultuous process.

**whisk** /(h)wisk/ ▶*v.* **1** brush away lightly. **2** whip (cream, eggs, etc.). **3** convey or go quickly.

▶*n.* **1** whisking action or motion. **2** utensil for whisking eggs, cream, etc. **3** (also **whisk broom**) small short-handled broom.

**whisk·er** ▶*n.* **1** (**whiskers**) hair growing on a man's face, esp. on the cheeks. **2** each of the bristles on the face of a cat, etc.

**whis·key** /'(h)wiskē/ (also **whis·ky**) ▶*n.* (*pl.* **-keys** or **-kies**) alcoholic liquor distilled esp. from grain, e.g., corn or malted barley.

**whis·per** /'(h)wispər/ ▶*v.* **1** speak very softly without vibration of the vocal cords. **2** rustle or murmur.

▶*n.* **1** whispering speech or sound. **2** whispered remark.

**whist** /(h)wist/ ▶*n.* card game usu. for four players.

**whis·tle** /'(h)wisəl/ ▶*n.* **1** clear shrill sound made by forcing breath through a small hole between nearly closed lips. **2** similar sound made by a bird, the wind, a missile, etc. **3** instrument used to produce such a sound.

▶*v.* **1** emit a whistle. **2** produce (a tune) by whistling.

**whis·tle·blow·er** ▶*n.* one who publicizes wrongdoing in a workplace or organization.

**whit** /(h)wit/ ▸*n.* particle; least possible amount: *she had not changed a whit.*

**white** /(h)wīt/ ▸*adj.* **1** resembling a surface reflecting sunlight without absorbing any of the visible rays; of the color of milk or fresh snow. **2** approaching such a color; pale. **3** having light-colored skin.

▸*n.* **1** white color or pigment. **2** visible part of the eyeball around the iris. **3** white or light-colored person or thing.
—**whit·en** *v.* —**whit·en·ing** *adj.*
—**white·ness** *n.*
□ **white cell** leukocyte. □ **white-collar** (of a worker) clerical; professional. □ **white elephant** useless possession. □ **white lie** harmless or trivial untruth. □ **white light** colorless light, e.g., ordinary daylight. □ **white water** rapids; foamy stretch of water.

**white-bread** ▸*adj.* belonging to or representative of the white middle class.

**white·out** /'(h)wīt,out/ ▸*n.* **1** blizzard, esp. in polar regions, that reduces visibilities to near zero. **2** weather condition in which the features and horizon of snow-covered country are indistinguishable due to uniform light diffusion. **3** white correction fluid for covering typing or writing mistakes. **4** loss of color vision due to rapid acceleration, often before a loss of consciousness.

**white slave** ▸*n.* woman tricked or forced into prostitution, typically one taken to a foreign country for this purpose.

**white·wash** ▸*n.* **1** solution of lime or ground chalk for whitening walls, etc. **2** means employed to conceal mistakes or faults.
▸*v.* **1** cover with whitewash. **2** attempt by concealment to clear the reputation of.

**whith·er** /'(h)wiTHər/ ▸*adv.* to what place, position, or state?
▸*conj.* to which place; to whatever place.

**whit·ing** /'(h)wītiNG/ ▸*n.* small, white-fleshed fish used as food.

**Whit·sun·day** ▸seventh Sunday after Easter, commemorating Pentecost.

**whit·tle** /'(h)witl/ ▸*v.* **1** carve or pare (wood, etc.) with a knife. **2** (**whittle down**) reduce by repeated subtractions.

**whiz** /(h)wiz/ ▸*n.* (*pl.* **whiz·zes**) **1** sound made by an object moving through the air at great speed. **2** *inf.* genius; expert.

▶*v.* (**whizzed**, **whiz·zing**) move with or make a whiz.

□ **whiz kid** *inf.* brilliant or highly successful young person.

**WHO** ▶*abbr.* World Health Organization.

**who** /hōō/ ▶*pron.* (*obj.* **whom**; *poss.* **whose**) **1 a** what or which person or persons?: *who called?* **b** what sort of person or persons?: *who am I to object?* **2** (a person) that: *anyone who wishes can come.*

**whoa** /(h)wō/ ▶*interj.* command to stop or slow a horse, etc.

**who·dun·it** /hōō'dənit/ (also **who·dun·nit**) ▶*n. inf.* story or play about the detection of a crime, etc., esp. murder.

**who·ev·er** ▶*pron.* (*obj.* **whom·ev·er**; *poss.* **whos·ev·er**) **1** the or any person or persons who. **2** regardless of who: *come out, whoever you are.*

**whole** /hōl/ ▶*adj.* **1** uninjured; unbroken; intact; undiminished. **2** not less than; all there is of. ▶*n.* **1** thing complete in itself. **2** all there is of a thing. **3** all members, etc., of. —**whol·ly** *adv.* —**whole·ness** *n.*

**whole·heart·ed** ▶*adj.*

**1** completely devoted. **2** done with all possible effort or sincerity. —**whole·heart·ed·ly** *adv.* —**whole·heart·ed·ness** *n.*

**whole·sale** ▶*n.* selling of things in large quantities to be retailed by others. ▶*adj. & adv.* **1** by wholesale. **2** on a large scale. ▶*v.* sell wholesale. —**whole·sal·er** *n.*

**whole·some** ▶*adj.* promoting or indicating physical, mental, or moral health. —**whole·some·ness** *n.*

**whole·wheat** ▶*adj.* made of wheat with none of the bran or germ removed.

**whom** /hōōm/ ▶objective case of **WHO**.

**whom·ev·er** ▶objective case of **WHOEVER**.

**whoop** /(h)wōōp/ ▶*n.* **1** loud cry of or as of excitement, etc. **2** long, rasping, indrawn breath in whooping cough. ▶*v.* utter a whoop.

□ **whooping cough** infectious bacterial disease with a series of short, violent coughs followed by a whoop.

**whop·per** /'(h)wäpər/ ▶*n. inf.* **1** something big of its kind. **2** great lie.

**whop·ping** ▸*adj. inf.* huge: *whopping lie.*

**whore** /hôr/ ▸*n.* prostitute.

**whore·son** /'hôrsən/ ▸*n.* unpleasant or greatly disliked person.

**whorl** /(h)wôrl/ ▸*n.* **1** circular arrangement. **2** one turn of a spiral.

**whose** /ho͞oz/ ▸*pron.* of or belonging to which person?: *whose is this book?*
▸*adj.* of whom or which: *whose book is this?*

**who·so·ev·er** ▸*pron.* (*obj.* **whom·so·ev·er**; *poss.* **whose·so·ev·er**) WHOEVER.

**why** /(h)wī/ ▸*adv.* **1** for what reason or purpose?: *why did you do it?* **2** for which: *reasons why I did it.*
▸*interj.* expressing: surprised discovery or recognition: *why, it's you!*
▸*n.* (*pl.* **whys**) reason or explanation: *whys and wherefores.*

**WI** ▸*abbr.* Wisconsin (in official postal use).

**wick** /wik/ ▸*n.* strip or thread of fibrous or spongy material feeding a flame with fuel in a candle, lamp, etc.
▸*v.* draw (moisture) away by capillary action.

**wick·ed** /'wikid/ ▸*adj.* (**-ed·er**, **-ed·est**) **1** evil or morally wrong. **2** playfully mschievous. **3** *inf.* extremely unpleasant.
—**wick·ed·ly** *adv.*
—**wick·ed·ness** *n.*

**wick·er** ▸*n.* braided twigs, etc., as material for chairs, baskets, mats, etc.

**wick·et** ▸*n.* **1** small door or gate, esp. beside or in a larger one. **2** croquet hoop.

**wide** /wīd/ ▸*adj.* (**wid·er**, **wid·est**) **1** having sides far apart; broad, not narrow. **2** considerable; more than is needed: *wide margin.* **3** in width: *foot wide.*
▸*adv.* **1** widely. **2** to the full extent. **3** far from the target, etc. —**wid·en** *v.* —**wide·ly** *adv.*
□ **wide awake 1** fully awake. **2** *inf.* wary; knowing. □ **wide-eyed** surprised or naive.

**wide·spread** ▸*adj.* widely distributed.

**wid·ow** /'widō/ ▸*n.* woman who has lost her husband by death and has not married again.
▸*v.* make into a widow or widower. —**wid·ow·hood** *n.*

**wid·ow·er** ▸*n.* man who has lost his wife by death and has not married again.

**width** /widTH/ ▶*n.*
**1** measurement from side to side. **2** large extent.
**3** something of a specific width.

**wield** /wēld/ ▶*v.* **1** hold and use. **2** exert or command.

**wield·y** /'wēldē/ ▶*adj.* (**wield·i·er**, **wield·i·est**) easily controlled or handled.

**wie·ner** /'wēnər/ ▶*n.*
FRANKFURTER.

**wife** /wīf/ ▶*n.* (*pl.* **wives**) married woman, esp. in relation to her husband. —**wife·ly** *adj.*

**wig** /wig/ ▶*n.* artificial covering of hair for the head.

**wig·gle** /'wigəl/ ▶*v.* move or cause to move quickly from side to side, etc.
▶*n.* act of wiggling. —**wig·gler** *n.*

**wig·wam** /'wig,wäm/ ▶*n.* Native American hut or tent.

**wild** /wīld/ ▶*adj.* **1** in its original natural state; not domesticated nor cultivated. **2** not civilized; barbarous. **3** unrestrained; disorderly. **4** tempestuous. **5** haphazard; ill-aimed.
▶*adv.* in a wild manner.
▶*n.* wild tract; wilderness.
—**wild·ly** *adv.* —**wild·ness** *n.*
□ **wild card 1** playing card having a rank chosen by the player holding it. **2** *Computing*

character that will match any character or sequence of characters. □ **wild-goose chase** foolish or hopeless quest. □ **wild rice** N. American aquatic grass with edible grains.

**wild·cat** /'wīld,kat/ ▶*n.* **1** hot-tempered or violent person. **2** any of various smallish undomesticated cats, e.g., the lynx, bobcat, etc.
▶*adj.* **1** reckless; financially unsound. **2** (of a strike) sudden and unofficial.

**wil·de·beest** /'wildə,bēst/ ▶*n.* GNU.

**wil·der·ness** /'wildərnis/ ▶*n.* uncultivated and uninhabited region.

**wild·fire** ▶*n.* rapidly spreading fire.

**wild·ing** /'wīldiNG/ ▶*n.* activity by a gang of youths of going on a protracted and violent rampage in a public place, attacking people at random.

**wild·life** ▶*n.* wild animals collectively.

**wiles** /wīlz/ ▶*pl. n.* cunning; trickery.

**will**[1] /wil/ ▶*v.* (*3rd sing. present* **will**; *past* **would**) **1** expressing the future tense in statements, commands, or questions: *you will* *regret this.* **2** (in the 1st person) expressing intention: *I will return soon.* **3** expressing desire, consent, or inclination: *will you have a sandwich?* **4** expressing habitual or inevitable tendency: *accidents will happen.*

**will²** ▶*n.* **1** faculty by which a person decides what to do. **2** self-control; willpower. **3** strong desire or intention. **4** power of effecting one's intentions or dominating others. **5** directions (usu. written) in legal form for the disposition of one's property after death. ▶*v.* **1** intend; desire. **2** exercise willpower. **3** bequeath by the terms of a will. □ **at will** whenever one pleases.

**will·ful** ▶*adj.* **1** intentional; deliberate. **2** obstinate; headstrong. —**will·ful·ly** *adv.* —**will·ful·ness** *n.*

**wil·lies** /ˈwilēz/ ▶*pl. n. inf.* nervous discomfort.

**will·ing** ▶*adj.* **1** ready to consent or undertake. **2** given or done, etc., by a willing person. —**will·ing·ly** *adv.* —**will·ing·ness** *n.*

**wil·li·waw** /ˈwilēˌwô/ ▶*n.* sudden violent squall blowing offshore from a mountainous coast.

**will-o'-the-wisp** /ˈwil ə T͟Hə ˈwisp/ ▶*n.* **1** phosphorescent light seen on marshy ground. **2** delusive hope or plan.

**wil·low** /ˈwilō/ ▶*n.* tree, usu. near water, yielding wood and pliant branches for furniture, baskets, etc.

**wil·low·y** ▶*adj.* (**-i·er, -i·est**) lithe and slender.

**will·pow·er** ▶*n.* self-control.

**wil·ly-nil·ly** /ˈwilē ˈnilē/ ▶*adv.* whether one likes it or not.

**wilt** /wilt/ ▶*v.* droop; become limp.

**wil·y** /ˈwīlē/ ▶*adj.* (**-i·er, -i·est**) full of wiles; crafty; cunning. —**wil·i·ness** *n.*

**wimp** /wimp/ ▶*n. inf.* feeble or ineffectual person. —**wimp·y** *adj.*

**wim·ple** /ˈwimpəl/ ▶*n.* cloth headdress covering the head, the neck, and the sides of the face, formerly worn by women and still worn by some nuns.

**win** /win/ ▶*v.* (**win·ning;** *past* and *past part.* **won**) **1** acquire or secure as a result of a fight, contest, bet, effort, etc. **2** be victorious (in). ▶*n.* victory in a game, etc.

**wince** /wins/ ▶*n.* start or involuntary shrinking

movement showing pain or distress.

▸ *v.* give a wince.

**winch** /winCH/ ▸*n.* **1** crank of a wheel or axle. **2** windlass.

▸ *v.* lift with a winch.

**wind**¹ /wind/ ▸*n.* **1** air in more or less rapid natural motion. **2** breath or breathing. **3** mere empty words. **4** gas generated in the bowels, etc. **5** (**winds**) wind instruments of an orchestra collectively.

▸ *v.* cause to be out of breath. —**wind·y** *adj.*

□ **in the wind** happening or about to happen. □ **wind instrument** musical instrument in which sound is produced by a current of air, esp. the breath. □ **wind sock** canvas cylinder or cone on a mast to show the direction of the wind at an airfield, etc.

**wind**² /wīnd/ ▸*v.* (*past* and *past part.* **wound**) **1** go in a circular, spiral, curved, or crooked course. **2** wrap closely; surround with or as with a coil. **3** coil (into a ball). **4** tighten the coiled spring of (a clock, etc.).

▸ *n.* bend or turn.

**wind·bag** /'wind,bag/ ▸*n. inf.* person who talks a lot but says little of any value.

**wind·break** /'wind,brāk/ ▸*n.* row of trees or a fence or wall, etc., serving to break the force of the wind.

**wind·chill** /'win(d),CHil/ (also **wind·chill fac·tor**) ▸*n.* quantity expressing the effective lowering of the air temperature caused by the wind, esp. as affecting the rate of heat loss from an object or human body or as perceived by an exposed person.

**wind·chill fac·tor** /'wind,CHil/ ▸*n.* quantity expressing the perceived lowering of the air temperature caused by the wind.

**wind·ed** /'windid/ ▸*adj.* breathless.

**wind·fall** /'wind,fôl/ ▸*n.* **1** fruit blown to the ground by the wind. **2** unexpected good fortune.

**win·di·go** /'windi,gō/ ▸*n.* (*pl.* **-gos** or **-goes**) (in the folklore of some northern Algonquian peoples) a cannibalistic giant; a person who has been transformed into a monster by the consumption of human flesh.

**wind·lass** /'windləs/ ▶n. machine with a horizontal axle for hauling or hoisting.
▶v. hoist or haul with a windlass.

**wind·mill** /'wind,mil/ ▶n. mill worked by the action of the wind on its sails.

**win·dow** /'windō/ ▶n. **1 a** opening in a wall, etc., usu. with glass in fixed, sliding, or hinged frames, to admit light or air, etc., and allow the occupants to see out. **b** glass filling this opening. **2** *Computing* framed area on a display screen for viewing information. **3** interval or opportunity for action.

**win·dow·pane** ▶n. pane of glass in a window.

**win·dow·sill** ▶n. sill below a window.

**wind·pipe** /'wind,pīp/ ▶n. air passage from the throat to the lungs; trachea.

**wind shear** /wind/ ▶n. variation in wind velocity occurring along a direction at right angles to the wind's direction and tending to exert a turning force.

**wind·shield** /'wind,SHēld/ ▶n. shield of glass at the front of a motor vehicle.

**wind·storm** /'wind,stôrm/ ▶n. storm with very strong wind but little precipitation.

**wind·surf·ing** /'wind,sərfiNG/ ▶n. sport of riding on water on a sailboard. —**wind·surf** v. —**wind·surf·er** n.

**wind·swept** /'wind,swept/ ▶adj. **1** (of a place) exposed to strong winds. **2** (of a person) untidy after exposure to the wind.

**wind·up** /'wīnd,əp/ ▶n. **1** conclusion; finish. **2** *Baseball* motions made by a pitcher, esp. arm swinging, in preparation for releasing a pitch.

**wind·ward** /'windwərd/ ▶adj. & adv. on the side from which the wind is blowing.
▶n. windward direction.

**wine** /wīn/ ▶n. **1** fermented grape juice as an alcoholic drink. **2** fermented drink resembling this made from other fruits, etc. **3** dark-red color of red wine. —**win·y** adj.

**win·er·y** /'wīnərē/ ▶n. (pl. **-ies**) establishment where wine is made.

**wing** /wiNG/ ▶n. **1** each of the limbs or organs by which a bird, bat, or insect is able to fly. **2** winglike structure forming a supporting part of an aircraft.

**3** part of a building, etc., extended in a certain direction. **4** section of a political party in terms of the extremity of its views.

▶*v.* **1** travel or traverse on wings or in an aircraft. **2** wound in a wing or an arm. —**winged** *adj.*

☐ **take under one's wing** treat as a protégé. ☐ **wing it** improvise.

**wink** /wiNGk/ ▶*v.* **1** quickly close and open one eye as a signal or greeting. **2** (of a light, etc.) twinkle; shine or flash intermittently.

▶*n.* act or instance of winking.

☐ **wink at** **1** purposely avoid seeing. **2** connive at (a wrongdoing, etc.).

**win·kle** /'wiNGkəl/ ▶*n.* small herbivorous shore-dwelling mollusk with a spiral shell.

**win·ner** ▶*n.* person, racehorse, etc., that wins.

**win·ning** ▶*adj.* **1** having or bringing victory or an advantage. **2** attractive; persuasive.

▶*pl. n.* (**winnings**) money won.

**win·now** /'winō/ ▶*v.* **1** blow (grain) free of chaff, etc. **2** sift; separate; examine.

**win·some** /'winsəm/ ▶*adj.* attractive; engaging.
—**win·some·ly** *adv.*
—**win·some·ness** *n.*

**win·ter** /'wintər/ ▶*n.* coldest season of the year.

▶*adj.* characteristic of or suitable for winter.

▶*v.* pass the winter.

**win·ter·green** ▶*n.* evergreen plant with red berries, source of an aromatic flavoring oil.

**win-win** ▶*adj.* denoting a situation in which each party benefits in some way.

**wipe** /wīp/ ▶*v.* **1** clean or dry by rubbing. **2** rub (a cloth) over a surface. **3** spread or remove by wiping.

▶*n.* **1** act of wiping. **2** piece of material for wiping. —**wip·er** *n.*

☐ **wipe out** destroy; annihilate.
☐ **wiped out** *inf.* tired out; exhausted.

**wire** /wī(ə)r/ ▶*n.* metal drawn out into a thread or thin flexible rod.

▶*v.* **1** provide, attach, fasten, strengthen, etc., with wire. **2** *Electr.* install electrical circuits in.

**wire·less** ▶*adj.* operating without wires, esp. by electromagnetic waves.

**wire·tap** ▸*v.* (-tapped, -tap·ping) connect a listening device to (a telephone or telegraph line) to listen to a call or transmission.

**wir·ing** /ˈwī(ə)riNG/ ▸*n.* system or installation of wires providing electrical circuits.

**wir·y** /ˈwī(ə)rē/ ▸*adj.* (-i·er, -i·est) **1** tough and flexible as wire. **2** (of a person) thin and sinewy.

**Wis.** ▸*abbr.* Wisconsin.

**wis·dom** /ˈwizdəm/ ▸*n.* **1** quality of having experience, knowledge, and good judgment. **2** wise sayings, thoughts, etc.
□ **wisdom tooth** each of the four hindmost molars, which usu. appear at about the age of 20.

**wise** /wīz/ ▸*adj.* **1** having experience, knowledge, and sound judgment. **2** prudent; sensible.
▸*v. inf.* (**wise up**) become aware of something.
▸*n.* (in phrase **in no wise**) not at all. —**wise·ly** *adv.*
□ **wise guy** *inf.* know-it-all.

**-wise** ▸*suffix* forming adjectives and adverbs of manner (*crosswise, lengthwise*) or respect (*moneywise*).

**wise·a·cre** ▸*n.* person who affects a wise manner; wise guy.

**wise·crack** ▸*n. inf.* smart pithy remark.

**wish** /wiSH/ ▸*v.* **1** have or express a desire or aspiration for. **2** have as a desire or aspiration. **3** want or demand.
▸*n.* **1** desire, request, or aspiration. **2** thing desired.

**wish·bone** ▸*n.* forked bone between the neck and breast of a fowl.

**wish·y-wash·y** /ˈwiSHē ˈwäSHē/ ▸*adj.* **1** feeble, insipid, or indecisive in quality or character. **2** weak; watery.

**wisp** /wisp/ ▸*n.* small thin or twisted bunch, piece, or amount of something. —**wisp·y** *adj.* —**wisp·i·ness** *n.*

**wis·te·ri·a** /wiˈsti(ə)rēə/ ▸*n.* climbing plant with hanging clusters of blue, purple, or white flowers.

**wist·ful** ▸*adj.* yearningly or mournfully expectant. —**wist·ful·ly** *adv.* —**wist·ful·ness** *n.*

**wit** /wit/ ▸*n.* **1** mental sharpness and inventiveness. **2** aptitude for the quick, unexpected, and humorous combining or contrasting of ideas or expressions. **3** person possessing such an aptitude.

□ **at one's wits' end** utterly at a loss or in despair. □ **to wit** namely.

**witch** /wiCH/ ▶*n.* **1** woman thought to have evil magic powers. **2** follower or practitioner of modern witchcraft.

□ **witch doctor** tribal magician of primitive people. □ **witch-hunt** campaign directed against a particular group of those holding unpopular or unorthodox views.

**witch·craft** ▶*n.* **1** use of magic. **2** use of spells and the invocation of spirits.

**witch·er·y** ▶*n.* **1** practice of magic. **2** power exercised by beauty or eloquence or the like.

**witch ha·zel** ▶*n.* **1** American shrub with bark yielding an astringent lotion. **2** this lotion.

**with** /wiTH; wiTH/ ▶*prep.* expressing: **1** instrument or means used: *cut with a knife.* **2** association or company: *lives with his mother.* **3** cause: *shiver with fear.* **4** possession: *vase with handles.* **5** circumstances: *sleep with the window open.* **6** manner: *behaved with dignity.* **7** reference or regard: *how are things with you?*

**with·draw** ▶*v.* (*past* **-drew;** *past part.* **-drawn**) **1** pull or take aside or back. **2** remove; retract; take away. **3** take (money) out of an account. **4** retire or go away; move away or back. —**with·draw·al** *n.*

**with·drawn** ▶*adj.* unusually shy and unsociable.

**with·er** /ˈwiTHər/ ▶*v.* **1** make or become dry and shriveled. **2** deprive of or lose vigor, vitality, freshness, or importance.

**with·ers** /ˈwiTHərz/ ▶*pl. n.* ridge between a horse's shoulder blades.

**with·hold** ▶*v.* (*past* and *past part.* **-held**) **1** refuse to give, grant, or allow. **2** deduct, esp. from a paycheck.

**with·in** ▶*prep.* **1** inside; enclosed or contained by. **2** inside the range of (an area, boundary, etc.). **3** not further off than. ▶*adv.* inside; indoors.

**with·out** ▶*prep.* **1** in the absence of. **2** not having the use or benefit of. ▶*adv. archaic* outside.

**with·stand** ▶*v.* (*past* and *past part.* **-stood**) oppose; hold out against.

**wit·less** ▶*adj.* foolish; stupid.

**wit·ling** /'witliNG/ ▸n. person who considers themselves to be witty.

**wit·ness** /'witnis/ ▸n. **1** person who sees an event take place. **2** person giving sworn testimony. **3** person attesting another's signature to a document. ▸v. **1** be a witness of (an event, etc.). **2** be witness to the authenticity of. **3** give or serve as evidence or an indication of.

**wit·ti·cism** /'witi,sizəm/ ▸n. witty remark.

**wit·ty** ▸adj. (**-ti·er, -ti·est**) showing verbal wit. —**wit·ti·ly** adv. —**wit·ti·ness** n.

**wiz·ard** /'wizərd/ ▸n. **1** sorcerer; magician. **2** person of remarkable powers; genius. —**wiz·ard·ry** n.

**wiz·ened** /'wizənd/ ▸adj. shriveled-looking.

**wob·ble** /'wäbəl/ ▸v. **1** (cause to) move unsteadily from side to side. **2** stand or go unsteadily; stagger. **3** waver; vacillate. **4** (of the voice or sound) quaver; pulsate. ▸n. **1** unsteady movement from side to side. **2** instance of vacillation or pulsation. —**wob·bly** adj.

**woe** /wō/ ▸n. **1** affliction; bitter grief. **2** (**woes**) calamities; troubles.

**woe·be·gone** /'wōbi,gôn/ ▸adj. dismal-looking.

**wok** /wäk/ ▸n. bowl-shaped metal pan used in Chinese cooking.

**wolf** /woolf/ ▸n. (pl. **wolves**) **1** wild, flesh-eating mammal related to the dog, and hunting in packs. **2** inf. man given to seducing women. ▸v. devour (food) greedily. —**wolf·ish** adj. —**wolf·ish·ly** adv. □ **cry wolf** raise repeated false alarms (so that a genuine one is disregarded).

**wol·ver·ine** /,woolvə'rēn/ ▸n. voracious carnivorous mammal of the weasel family.

**wom·an** /'woomən/ ▸n. (pl. **wom·en** /'wimən/) **1** adult human female. **2** women in general.

**womb** /woom/ ▸n. organ of conception and gestation in a woman and other female mammals; uterus.

**wom·bat** /'wäm,bat/ ▸n. burrowing, plant-eating Australian marsupial resembling a small bear, with short legs.

**won·der** /'wəndər/ ▸n. **1** emotion excited by what is unexpected, unfamiliar, or inexplicable. **2** strange or remarkable person, thing, event, etc.

▶*v.* **1** be filled with wonder. **2** be surprised to find. **3** desire or be curious to know.

**won·der·ful** ▶*adj.* very remarkable or admirable. **—won·der·ful·ly** *adv.*

**won·drous** /'wəndrəs/ *poet./lit.* ▶*adj.* wonderful.
▶*adv.* wonderfully: *wondrous kind.*

**wont** /wônt/ ▶*adj. poet./lit.* accustomed: *as we were wont to say.*
▶*n. formal* what is customary; one's habit: *as is my wont.*

**won't** /wōnt/ ▶*contr.* will not.

**woo** /wōō/ ▶*v.* (**woos, wooed**) **1** court; seek the love of. **2** seek the favor or support of. **—woo·er** *n.*

**wood** /wŏŏd/ ▶*n.* **1 a** hard fibrous material that forms the main substance of the trunk or branches of a tree or shrub. **b** this cut for lumber, fuel, etc. **2** (also **woods**) growing trees densely occupying a tract of land. **—wood·ed** *adj.* **—wood·y** *adj.*
☐ **out of the woods** out of danger or difficulty.

**wood·bine** /'wŏŏd,bīn/ ▶*n.* wild honeysuckle.

**wood·chuck** ▶*n.* reddish-brown and gray N. American marmot. (Also called **groundhog.**)

**wood·cut** ▶*n.* **1** relief cut on a block of wood. **2** print made from this.

**wood·en** ▶*adj.* **1** made of or like wood. **2** stiff; clumsy; expressionless. **—wood·en·ly** *adv.*

**wood·land** ▶*n.* wooded country, woods: *woodland scenery.*

**wood·note** /'wŏŏd,nōt/ ▶*n.* natural and untrained musical note resembling the song of a bird.

**wood·peck·er** ▶*n.* bird that taps tree trunks with its beak in search of insects.

**wood·pile** ▶*n.* pile of wood, esp. for fuel.

**wood·shed** ▶*n.* shed where wood for fuel is stored.

**woods·man** ▶*n.* (*pl.* **-men**) person who lives in or is familiar with woodland.

**wood·wind** ▶*n.* **1** wind instruments that were orig. made mostly of wood, e.g., the flute and clarinet. **2** individual instrument of this kind or its player: *the woodwinds are out of tune.*

**wood·work** ▶*n.* things made of

wood, esp. paneling, moldings, etc. —**wood·work·ing** n.

**woof**[1] /wŏŏf/ ▶n. gruff bark of a dog.
▶v. bark.

**woof**[2] /wŏŏf; wŏŏf/ ▶n. WEFT.

**woof·er** /ˈwŏŏfər/ ▶n. loudspeaker designed to reproduce low frequencies.

**wool** /wŏŏl/ ▶n. **1** fine, soft, wavy hair from the fleece of sheep, goats, etc. **2 a** yarn produced from this hair. **b** cloth or clothing made from it. **3** substance resembling wool: *steel wool.* —**wool·en** adj.

**wool·gath·er·ing** ▶n. daydreaming or absentmindedness.

**wool·ly** ▶adj. (**-li·er, -li·est**) **1** bearing or naturally covered with wool or woollike hair. **2** resembling or suggesting wool: *woolly clouds.* **3** vague or confused. —**wool·li·ness** n.

**word** /wərd/ ▶n. **1** sound or combination of sounds forming a meaningful element of speech, writing, or printing. **2** speech, esp. as distinct from action. **3** one's promise or assurance: *he gave me his word.* **4** (usu. **words**) remark or conversation. **5** (**words**) text of a song or an actor's part. **6** (**words**) angry talk. **7** news; intelligence; message. **8** command.
▶v. put into words; select words to express. —**word·less** adj. —**word·less·ly** adv. —**word·less·ness** n.

□ **word of mouth** spoken, not written language.

**word·ing** ▶n. **1** form of words used. **2** way in which something is expressed.

**word·play** ▶n. witty use of words, esp. punning.

**word proc·ess·ing** ▶n. production, storage, and manipulation of text on a word processor.

**word proc·es·sor** ▶n. computer software program for electronically storing text entered from a keyboard, incorporating corrections, and providing a printout.

**word·y** ▶adj. (**-i·er, -i·est**) using or expressed in too many words; verbose. —**word·i·ness** n.

**work** /wərk/ ▶n. **1** application of mental or physical effort to a purpose; use of energy. **2** task to be undertaken. **3** thing done or made by work; result of an action. **4** employment or occupation. **5 a** literary or musical composition. **b** (**works**) all such by an author, composer, etc. **6** (**works**) operative part of a clock or machine. **7** (**works**) *inf.* all that is available; everything needed.

▶ *v.* (*past* and *past part.* **worked** or esp. as *adj.* **wrought**) **1** do work; be engaged in bodily or mental activity. **2** be employed in certain work. **3** operate or function, esp. effectively. **4** carry on, manage, or control. **5** bring about; produce as a result. **6** knead; bring to a desired shape or consistency. **7** do, or make by, needlework, etc. **8** (**work on**) exert influence on. —**work·er** *n.*

**work·a·hol·ic** /ˌwərkəˈhôlik/ ▶*n.* *inf.* person addicted to working.

**work·fare** /ˈwərkˌfe(ə)r/ ▶*n.* welfare system that requires those receiving benefits to perform some work or to participate in job training.

**work·horse** ▶*n.* horse, person, or machine that performs hard work.

**work·load** ▶*n.* amount of work to be done.

**work·man** ▶*n.* (*pl.* -**men**) person employed to do manual labor.

**work·man·like** ▶*adj.* showing practiced skill.

**work·man·ship** ▶*n.* degree of skill in doing a task or quality of the product made.

**work·out** ▶*n.* session of physical exercise or training.

**work·shop** ▶*n.* **1** room or building in which goods are manufactured. **2** meeting for concerted discussion or activity.

**work·sta·tion** ▶*n.* **1** location of a stage in a manufacturing process. **2** computer terminal or the desk, etc., where this is located.

**world** /wərld/ ▶*n.* **1 a** the earth, or a planetary body like it. **b** its countries and their inhabitants. **c** all people; the earth as known or in some particular respect. **2** the universe or all that exists; everything. **3** secular interests and affairs. **4** human affairs; active life. **5** specified class, time, domain, or sphere of activity: *world of baseball.* **6** vast amount.
□ **world-class** of a quality or standard regarded as high throughout the world.

**world·ling** /ˈwərldliNG/ ▶*n.* cosmopolitan and sophisticated person.

**world·ly** ▶*adj.* (-**li·er**, -**li·est**) **1** temporal or earthly.

2 sophisticated.
—**world·li·ness** n.

**World Wide Web** ▸n. global computer network for exchange of text, hypertext, graphics, audio, etc. (Abbr.: **WWW**)

**worm** /wərm/ ▸n. **1** any of various types of creeping or burrowing invertebrate animals with long, slender bodies and no limbs. **2** long, slender larva of an insect. **3** (**worms**) intestinal or other internal parasites. **4** insignificant or contemptible person.
▸v. **1** move with a crawling motion. **2** insinuate oneself into a person's favor, confidence, etc. **3** rid of intestinal worms.
—**worm·y** adj.
□ **worm gear** arrangement of a toothed wheel worked by a revolving spiral.

**worm·wood** ▸n. woody plant with a bitter aromatic taste.

**worn** /wôrn/ ▸past part. of WEAR.
▸adj. **1** damaged by use or wear. **2** looking tired and exhausted.

**worn out** ▸adj. **1** extremely tired; exhausted. **2** damaged or shabby.

**wor·ry** /'wərē/ ▸v. (-ried) **1** give way to anxiety. **2** harass; be a trouble or anxiety to. **3** (of a

dog, etc.) shake or pull about with the teeth. **4** make uneasy; disturb.
▸n. (pl. **-ries**) **1** thing that causes anxiety. **2** disturbed state of mind; anxiety.

**worse** /wərs/ ▸adj. (compar. of **bad**) **1** more bad. **2** in or into worse health or a worse condition.
▸adv. (compar. of **badly**) more badly or more ill.
▸n. **1** worse thing or things. **2** worse condition: *change for the worse.* —**wors·en** v.

**wor·ship** /'wərSHip/ ▸n. **1 a** homage or reverence paid to a deity. **b** acts, rites, or ceremonies of worship. **2** adoration or devotion: *worship of wealth.*
▸v. (**-shiped, -ship·ing; -shipped, -ship·ping**) **1** adore as divine; honor with religious rites. **2** idolize. —**wor·ship·er** (or **wor·ship·per**) n.

**worst** /wərst/ ▸adj. (superl. of **bad**) most bad.
▸adv. (superl. of **badly**) most badly.
▸n. worst part, event, circumstance, or possibility.
▸v. get the better of; defeat.

**wors·ted** /'wo͝ostid/ ▶*n.* **1** fine smooth yarn spun from combed long, stapled wool. **2** fabric made from this.

**worth** /wərth/ ▶*adj.* **1** of a value equivalent to. **2** such as to justify or repay; deserving. **3** possessing or having property amounting to.
▶*n.* **1** what a person or thing is worth; the (usu. specified) merit of. **2** equivalent of money in a commodity.

**worth·less** ▶*adj.* having no value or merit.
—**worth·less·ness** *n.*

**worth·while** ▶*adj.* worth the time or effort spent; of value or importance.

**wor·thy** /'wərthē/ ▶*adj.* (**-thi·er, -thi·est**) deserving effort, attention, or respect.
▶*n.* (*pl.* **-thies**) worthy person.
—**wor·thi·ness** *n.*

**would** /wo͝od/ ▶*aux. v.* (past of **will**) used esp.: **1 a** in reported speech: *he said he would be home by evening.* **b** to express the conditional mood: *they would have been killed if they had gone.* **2** to express habitual action: *would wait every evening.* **3** to express a question or polite request: *would you come in,*

please? **4** to express consent: *they would not help.*
□ **would-be** desiring or aspiring to be.

**wound**[1] /wo͝ond/ ▶*n.* **1** injury done to living tissue by a cut, blow, etc. **2** injury to a person's reputation or a pain inflicted on a person's feelings.
▶*v.* inflict a wound on.

**wound**[2] /wound/ ▶past and past part. of **WIND**.

**wrack** ▶*n.* **RACK.**

**wraith** /rāth/ ▶*n.* ghost.

**wran·gle** /'raNGgəl/ ▶*n.* noisy argument, altercation, or dispute.
▶*v.* **1** engage in a wrangle. **2** herd (cattle). —**wran·gler** *n.*

**wrap** /rap/ ▶*v.* (**wrapped, wrap·ping**) **1** envelop in folded or soft encircling material. **2** arrange or draw (a pliant covering) around.
▶*n.* **1** shawl, scarf, etc. **2** material used for wrapping.
□ **under wraps** in secrecy. □ **wrap up** finish off.

**wrap·per** ▶*n.* **1** that which wraps; cover. **2** loose enveloping robe or gown.

**wrath** /rath/ ▶*n.* extreme anger.
—**wrath·ful** *adj.*
—**wrath·ful·ness** *n.*

**wreak** /rēk/ ▶v. **1** express (vengeance or one's anger, etc.). **2** cause (damage, etc.).

**wreath** /rēTH/ ▶n. **1** flowers or leaves fastened in a ring. **2** curl or ring of smoke or cloud.

**wreathe** /rēT͟H/ ▶v. **1** encircle as, with, or like a wreath. **2** (of smoke, etc.) move in the shape of wreaths.

**wreck** /rek/ ▶n. **1** destruction or disablement, esp. of a ship or automobile. **2** ship or automobile, etc., that has suffered a wreck. **3** greatly damaged thing. ▶v. **1** cause the wreck of. **2** completely ruin (hopes, chances, etc.). **3** suffer a wreck.

**wreck·age** /'rekij/ ▶n. **1** wrecked material. **2** remnants of a wreck. **3** action of wrecking.

**wreck·er** ▶n. **1** person or thing that wrecks or destroys. **2** vehicle used to remove disabled cars, etc.

**wren** /ren/ ▶n. small, usu. brown, songbird having an erect tail.

**wrench** /rencH/ ▶n. **1** violent twist or oblique pull or tearing off. **2** tool for gripping and turning nuts, etc. **3** painful uprooting or parting.

▶v. **1 a** twist or pull violently around or sideways. **b** injure (a limb, etc.) by undue straining; sprain. **2** pull off with a wrench.

**wrest** /rest/ ▶v. **1** wrench away from a person's grasp. **2** obtain by effort or with difficulty.

**wres·tle** /'resəl/ ▶v. **1** take part in a fight, either as a sport or in earnest, that involves grappling with one's opponent and trying to force them to the ground. **2** struggle; contend. —**wres·tler** n. —**wres·tling** n.

**wretch** /recH/ ▶n. unfortunate or pitiable person.

**wretch·ed** /'recHid/ ▶adj. (**-ed·er**, **-ed·est**) **1** unhappy or miserable. **2** of bad quality or no merit; contemptible. **3** unsatisfactory; displeasing. —**wretch·ed·ly** adv. —**wretch·ed·ness** n.

**wrig·gle** /'rigəl/ ▶v. **1** twist or turn with short, writhing movements. **2** move or go in this way. **3** practice evasion. ▶n. act of wriggling. —**wrig·gly** adj.

**wring** /riNG/ ▶v. (past and past part. **wrung**) **1** squeeze and twist, esp. to remove liquid. **2** squeeze (someone's hand) tightly. **3** obtain by pressure or importunity; extort.

**wrin·kle** /ˈriNGkəl/ ▸*n.* **1** slight crease in the skin such as is produced by age. **2** similar mark in a flexible surface.
▸*v.* **1** make wrinkles in. **2** form or become marked with wrinkles. —**wrin·kly** *adj.*

**wrist** /rist/ ▸*n.* **1** joint connecting the hand with the forearm. **2** part of a garment covering the wrist.

**writ** /rit/ ▸*n.* legal document commanding or forbidding action.

**write** /rīt/ ▸*v.* (*past* **wrote**; *past part.* **writ·ten**) **1** mark paper or some other surface by means of a pen, pencil, etc., with symbols, letters, or words. **2** form or mark (such symbols, etc.). **3** fill out or complete (a form, check, etc.). **4** put (data) into a computer store. **5** compose.

**writ·er** ▸*n.* person who writes; author.

**writhe** /rīTH/ ▸*v.* **1** twist or roll oneself about in or as if in acute pain. **2** suffer severe mental discomfort or embarrassment.
▸*n.* act of writhing.

**writ·ing** ▸*n.* **1** handwriting. **2** literary work.

**wrong** /rôNG/ ▸*adj.* **1** mistaken; not true; in error. **2** unsuitable;

less or least desirable. **3** contrary to law or morality. **4** amiss; out of order.
▸*adv.* in a wrong manner or direction; with an incorrect result.
▸*n.* **1** what is morally wrong. **2** injustice.
▸*v.* treat unjustly; do wrong to. —**wrong·ly** *adv.*

**wrong·do·ing** ▸*n.* illegal or dishonest behavior. —**wrong·do·er** *n.*

**wrong·ful** ▸*adj.* not fair, just, or legal. —**wrong·ful·ly** *adv.*

**wrong·head·ed** ▸*adj.* perverse and obstinate. —**wrong·head·ed·ness** *n.*

**wroth** /rôTH/ ▸*adj.* angry.

**wrought** /rôt/ ▸*adj.* (of metals) beaten out or shaped by hammering.
☐ **wrought iron** tough malleable form of iron. ☐ **wrought up** upset and anxious.

**wry** /rī/ ▸*adj.* (**wry·er**, **wry·est**; **wri·er**, **wri·est**) **1** distorted. **2** contorted in disgust, disappointment, or mockery. **3** (of humor) dry and mocking. —**wry·ly** *adv.* —**wry·ness** *n.*

**wuss** /wŏŏs/ ▸*n.* inf. weak or ineffectual person.

**WV** ▸*abbr.* West Virginia (in official postal use).

**WWW** ▸*abbr.* World Wide Web.

**WY** ▸*abbr.* Wyoming (in official postal use).

**WYSIWYG** /ˈwizēˌwig/ (also **wysiwyg**) ▸*adj. Computing* denoting the representation of text onscreen in a form exactly corresponding to its appearance on a printout (acronym of *what you see is what you get*).

# Xx

**X**¹ /eks/ (also **x**) ▶*n.* (*pl.* **Xs** or **X's**; **x's**) twenty-fourth letter of the alphabet.

**X**² ▶ **1** (as a Roman numeral) ten. **2** extra. **3** extraordinary. **4** cross-shaped symbol esp. used to indicate position: *X marks the spot,* or incorrectness, or to symbolize a kiss or a vote, or as the signature of a person who cannot write. **5** (also **X-rated**) (of a movie) classified as suitable for adults only.

**x** ▶*symb.* **1** excess. **2** *Math.* unknown quantity or variable. **3** *Math.* horizontal-axis coordinate.

**X chro·mo·some** ▶*n.* sex chromosome of which the number in female cells is twice that in male cells.

**xe·no·pho·bi·a** /ˌzēnəˈfōbēə/ ▶*n.* deep dislike of foreigners. —**xe·no·phobe** *n.* —**xe·no·pho·bic** *adj.*

**xe·rog·ra·phy** /ziˈrägrəfē/ ▶*n.* dry copying process in which black or colored powder adheres to electrically charged parts of a surface. —**xe·ro·graph·ic** *adj.*

**Xe·rox** /ˈzi(ə)rˌäks/ ▶*trademark* **1** machine for copying by xerography. **2** copy thus made. ▶*v.* reproduce by this process.

**X·mas** /ˈkrisməs; ˈeksməs/ ▶*n. inf.* CHRISTMAS.

**X ray** (also **x-ray**) ▶*n.* **1** electromagnetic radiation of short wavelength, able to pass through opaque bodies. **2** photograph made by X rays. ▶*v.* photograph, examine, or treat with X rays.

**xy·lo·phone** /ˈzīləˌfōn/ ▶*n.* musical instrument of graduated wooden or metal bars struck with small wooden hammers. —**xy·lo·phon·ist** *n.*

# Yy

**Y**[1] /wī/ (also **y**) ▸*n.* (*pl.* **Ys** or **Y's**; **y's**) twenty-fifth letter of the alphabet.

**Y**[2] ▸*symb. Chem.* yttrium.

**y** ▸*symb. Math.* **1** vertical-axis coordinate. **2** unknown quantity or variable.

**y.** ▸*abbr.* **1** yard(s). **2** year(s).

**-y** ▸*suffix* **1** forming adjectives: **a** from nouns and adjectives, meaning: full of; having the quality of: *messy.* **b** from verbs, meaning 'inclined to,' 'apt to': *runny.* **2** forming diminutives, pet names, etc.: *Mickey.* **3** forming nouns denoting state, condition, or quality: *modesty.*

**yacht** /yät/ ▸*n.* sailing vessel for racing, cruising, etc., esp. for pleasure.
▸*v.* race or cruise in a yacht.
—**yacht·ing** *n.*

**ya·hoo** /'yä,hoo/ ▸*n.* coarse, boorish person.

**yahr·zeit** /'yär,tsīt; 'yôr-/ ▸*n.* (among Jews) the anniversary of someone's death, esp. a parent's.

**yak** /yak/ ▸*n.* long-haired, humped Tibetan ox.

**yam** /yam/ ▸*n.* **1 a** tropical or subtropical climbing plant. **b** edible starchy tuber of this. **2** sweet potato.

**yam·mer** /'yamər/ *inf.* ▸*n.* loud and sustained or repetitive noise.
▸*v.* **1** make a loud repetitive noise. **2** talk volubly.
—**yam·mer·er** *n.*

**yank** /yaNGk/ *inf.* ▸*v.* pull with a jerk.
▸*n.* **1** sudden hard pull. **2** (**Yank**) American.

**Yan·kee** /'yaNGkē/ ▸*n. inf.* **1** inhabitant of the U.S. **2** inhabitant of New England or one of the other northern states. **3** Union soldier in the American Civil War.

**yap** /yap/ ▸*v.* (**yapped**, **yap·ping**) **1** bark shrilly. **2** *inf.* talk noisily, foolishly, or complainingly.
▸*n.* sound of yapping.

**yard** /yärd/ ▸*n.* **1** unit of linear measure equal to 3 feet (0.9144 meter). **2** square or cubic yard, esp. (in building) of sand, etc. **3** spar slung across a mast for a sail to hang from. **4** piece of ground, esp. attached to a building or used for a particular purpose. **5** lawn and garden area of a house.

**yard·age** /'yärdij/ ▸*n.* number of yards of material, etc.

**yard·arm** ▸*n.* outer extremity of a ship's yard.

**yard·stick** ▸*n.* **1** standard used for comparison. **2** measuring rod a yard long, usu. divided into inches, etc.

**yare** /yär; ye(ə)r/ ▸*adj.* (of a ship) easy to steer; easily manageable.

**yar·mul·ke** /'yä(r)mə(l)kə/ ▸*n.* skullcap worn by Orthodox Jewish men.

**yarn** /yärn/ ▸*n.* **1** spun thread, esp. for knitting, weaving, etc. **2** *inf.* long or rambling story or discourse.

**yar·row** ▸*n.* plant with feathery leaves and heads of white, yellow, or pink flowers.

**yash·mak** /yäsH'mäk; 'yasH-,mak/ ▸*n.* veil concealing all of the face except the eyes, worn by some Muslim women in public.

**yaw** /yô/ ▸*v.* (of a ship or aircraft, etc.) fail to hold a straight course; go unsteadily. ▸*n.* yawing of a ship, etc., from its course.

**yawl** /yôl/ ▸*n.* small sailboat.

**yawn** /yôn/ ▸*v.* **1** (as a reflex) open the mouth wide and inhale, esp. when sleepy or bored. **2** gape; be wide open. ▸*n.* act of yawning.

**yaws** /yôz/ ▸*n.* contagious disease of tropical countries, caused by a bacterium that enters skin abrasions and gives rise to small crusted lesions that may develop into deep ulcers.

**Y chro·mo·some** ▸*n.* sex chromosome occurring only in male cells.

**ye** /yē/ ▸*pron. archaic* pl. of THOU.

**yea** /yā/ ▸*adv.* **1** yes. **2** indeed. ▸*n.* affirmative vote or voter.

**year** /yi(ə)r/ ▸*n.* **1** time occupied by the earth in one revolution around the sun, 365 days, 5 hours, 48 minutes, and 46 seconds in length. **2** (also **calendar year**) period of 365 days (or 366 days in leap years) from Jan. 1 to Dec. 31. **3 a** period of the same length as this starting at any point: *four years ago.* **b** such a period in terms of a particular activity, etc., occupying its duration: *school year.* **4** (**years**) age or time of life. **5** (usu. **years**) *inf.* very long time. —**year·ly** *adj. & adv.*

**year·book** ▸*n.* annual

publication dealing with events or aspects of the (usu. preceding) year.

**year·ling** ▸*n.* **1** animal between one and two years old. **2** racehorse in the calendar year after the year of foaling.

**yearn** /yərn/ ▸*v.* **1** have a strong emotional longing. **2** be filled with compassion or tenderness. —**yearn·ing·ly** *adv.*

**year-round** ▸*adj. & adv.* happening or continuing throughout the year.

**yeast** /yēst/ ▸*n.* grayish-yellow fungus used to cause fermentation in making beer, to raise bread, etc.

**yegg** /yeg/ ▸*n.* burglar or safecracker.

**yell** /yel/ ▸*n.* **1** loud sharp cry of pain, anger, etc. **2** shout. ▸*v.* utter with or make a yell.

**yel·low** /'yelō/ ▸*adj.* **1** of the color between green and orange in the spectrum, as of lemons, egg yolks, or gold. **2** having a yellow skin or complexion. **3** *inf.* cowardly. ▸*n.* yellow color or pigment. ▸*v.* make or become yellow. □ **yellow fever** tropical virus disease with fever and jaundice. □ **yellow jacket** any of various

wasps or hornets with yellow and black bands.

**yelp** /yelp/ ▸*n.* sharp, shrill cry of or as of a dog in pain or excitement. ▸*v.* utter a yelp.

**yen**[1] /yen/ ▸*n.* (*pl.* same) chief monetary unit of Japan.

**yen**[2] ▸*n. inf.* longing or yearning.

**yen·ta** /'yentə/ ▸*n.* woman who is a gossip or busybody.

**yeo·man** /'yōmən/ ▸*n.* (*pl.* -**men**) **1** *hist.* man holding and cultivating a small landed estate. **2** in the U.S. Navy, petty officer performing clerical duties on board ship.

**yes** /yes/ ▸*adv.* **1** indicating affirmation, consent, assent, etc. **2** (in answer to a summons or address) an acknowledgment of one's presence. ▸*n.* (*pl.* **yes·ses**) utterance of the word *yes*. □ **yes-man** *inf.* weakly acquiescent person.

**ye·shi·va** ▸*n.* Orthodox Jewish school, college, or seminary.

**yes·ter·day** /'yestər,dā/ ▸*adv.* **1** on the day before today. **2** in the recent past. ▸*n.* **1** day before today. **2** the recent past.

**yet** /yet/ ▸*adv.* **1** as late as; until;

now or then. **2** so soon as; by; now or then. **3** again; in addition. **4** still: *I will do it yet.* **5** even: *a yet more difficult task.*
▶*conj.* but nevertheless.

**yet·i** /'yetē/ ▶*n.* large hairy creature resembling a human or bear, said to live in the highest part of the Himalayas.

**yew** /yoo/ ▶*n.* dark-leaved evergreen coniferous tree with red berrylike cones.

**yield** /yēld/ ▶*v.* **1** produce or return as a fruit, profit, or result. **2** give up; surrender. **3** submit; defer to. **4** give right of way to (other traffic, etc).
▶*n.* amount yielded or produced.

**yo·del** /'yōdl/ ▶*v.* sing with melodious inarticulate sounds and frequent changes between falsetto and the normal voice.
▶*n.* yodeling cry. —**yo·del·er** *n.*

**yo·ga** /'yōgə/ ▶*n.* Hindu system of philosophic meditation and exercise. —**yo·gic** *adj.*

**yo·gi** /'yōgē/ ▶*n.* teacher of yoga.

**yo·gurt** /'yōgərt/ ▶*n.* semisolid food prepared from milk fermented by added bacteria.

**yoke** /yōk/ ▶*n.* **1** wooden crosspiece fastened over the necks of two oxen, etc., and attached to the plow or wagon

to be drawn. **2** object like a yoke in form or function. **3** dominion or servitude. **4** part of a garment fitting over the shoulders.
▶*v.* **1** put a yoke on. **2** couple or unite (a pair).

**yolk** /yōk/ ▶*n.* yellow internal part of an egg.

**Yom Kip·pur** /'yäm ki'poor/ ▶*n.* most solemn religious holiday of the Jewish year.

**yon·der** /'yändər/ ▶*adv.* over there; at some distance in that direction.
▶*adj.* situated yonder.

**yore** /yôr/ ▶*n.* (**of yore**) long ago; formerly.

**you** /yoo/ ▶*pron.* (*obj.* **you**; *poss.* **your, yours**) person or persons addressed.

**young** /yəNG/ ▶*adj.* (**-er; -est**) **1** not far advanced in life, development, or existence; not yet old. **2** immature; inexperienced. **3** of or characteristic of youth.
▶*n.* offspring.

**young·ster** /'yəNGstər/ ▶*n.* child or young person.

**your** /yôr/ ▶*poss. pron.* of or belonging to you.

**you're** /yoor/ ▶*contr.* you are.

**your·self** ▶*pron.* (*pl.* **-selves**) **1 a** emphatic form of **YOU**.

**b** reflexive form of **YOU**. **2** in your normal state of body or mind: *are quite yourself again.*

**youth** /yo͞oTH/ ▶*n.* **1** being young; period between childhood and adult age. **2** young person. **3** young people collectively.

**yowl** /youl/ ▶*n.* loud, wailing cry. ▶*v.* utter a yowl.

**yo-yo** /ˈyō ˌyō/ ▶*n.* (*pl.* **yo-yos**) **1** toy consisting of a pair of disks that can be made to fall and rise on a string. **2** thing that repeatedly falls and rises. ▶*v.* (**-yoed, -yoing**) **1** play with a yo-yo. **2** move up and down; fluctuate.

**yr.** ▶*abbr.* (*pl.* **yrs.**) **1** year(s). **2** yours. **3** younger.

**yuc·ca** /ˈyəkə/ ▶*n.* N. American white-flowered plant with swordlike leaves.

**yule** /yo͞ol/ ▶*n.* (also **yule·tide**) Christmas festival.

**yum·my** /ˈyəmē/ ▶*adj.* (**-mi·er, -mi·est**) *inf.* tasty; delicious.

**yup·pie** /ˈyəpē/ (also **yup·py**) *inf.* ▶*n.* (*pl.* **-pies**) young, ambitious professional person working in a city. ▶*adj.* characteristic of a yuppie or yuppies. (from *y*oung *u*rban *p*rofessional.).

**yup·pi·fy** /ˈyəpəˌfī/ ▶*v.* (**-fies, -fied**) make more affluent and upmarket in keeping with the taste and lifestyle of yuppies.

# Zz

**Z** /zē/, (also **z**) ▸*n.* (*pl.* **Zs** or **Z's**; **z's**) twenty-sixth letter of the alphabet.

**z** ▸*symb.* **1** *Math.* **a** unknown quantity or variable. **b** coordinate of the third-dimensional axis. **2** *Chem.* (usu. **Z**) atomic number.

**za·ny** /'zānē/ ▸*adj.* (**-ni·er, -ni·est**) comically idiotic; crazily ridiculous. **—za·ni·ly** *adv.* **—za·ni·ness** *n.*

**zap** /zap/ *inf.* ▸*v.* (**zapped, zap·ping**) **1 a** kill or destroy. **b** send an electric current, radiation, etc., through (someone or something). **2** *Computing* erase or change (an item in a program). ▸*n.* strong emotional effect.

**zeal** /zēl/ ▸*n.* **1** earnestness or fervor. **2** hearty and persistent endeavor. **—zeal·ous** *adj.* **—zeal·ous·ly** *adv.* **—zeal·ous·ness** *n.*

**zeal·ot** /'zelət/ ▸*n.* extreme partisan; fanatic.

**zeal·ous** /'zeləs/ ▸*adj.* having or showing zeal.

**ze·bra** /'zēbrə/ ▸*n.* (*pl.* same or **-bras**) black and white striped African quadruped related to the ass and horse.

**Zen** /zen/ ▸*n.* form of Buddhism emphasizing the value of meditation and intuition.

**ze·nith** /'zēniTH/ ▸*n.* **1** part of the sky directly above an observer. **2** any peak or highest point.

**zeph·yr** /'zefər/ ▸*n. poet./lit.* mild gentle breeze.

**zep·pe·lin** /'zep(ə)lin/ ▸*n.* large dirigible airship of the early 20th c., orig. for military use.

**ze·ro** /'zi(ə)rō/ ▸*n.* (*pl.* **-ros**) **1 a** the figure 0. **b** no quantity or number; nil. **2** point on the scale from which a positive or negative quantity is reckoned. ☐ **zero in on 1** take aim at. **2** focus one's attention on.

**ze·ro-sum** ▸*adj.* (of a game or situation) in which whatever is gained by one side is lost by the other.

**zest** /zest/ ▸*n.* **1** piquancy; stimulating flavor or quality. **2 a** keen enjoyment or interest. **b** relish. **c** gusto. **3** scraping of orange or lemon peel as flavoring. —**zest·ful** *adj.* —**zest·ful·ly** *adv.* —**zest·i·ness** *n.* —**zest·y** *adj.*

**zig·zag** /ˈzigˌzag/ ▶*n.* line or course having abrupt alternate right and left turns.
▶*adj.* having the form of a zigzag.
▶*adv.* with a zigzag course.
▶*v.* (**-zagged**, **-zag·ging**) move in a zigzag course.

**zilch** /zilCH/ ▶*n. inf.* nothing.

**zil·lion** /ˈzilyən/ ▶*n. inf.* indefinite large number.
—**zil·lionth** *adj. & n.*

**zinc** /ziNGk/ ▶*n.* white metallic element used as a component of brass, in galvanizing, in electric batteries, and in printing plates. (Symb.: **Zn**)

**zing** /ziNG/ ▶*n. inf.* vigor; energy.
▶*v.* move swiftly or with a shrill sound. —**zing·er** *n.* —**zing·y** *adj.*

**zin·ni·a** /ˈzinēə/ ▶*n.* composite plant with showy rayed flowers of various colors.

**Zi·on·ism** /ˈzīəˌnizəm/ ▶*n.* movement for the development and protection of a Jewish nation in what is now Israel.
—**Zi·on·ist** *n.*

**zip** /zip/ ▶*n.* **1** light fast sound, as of a bullet passing through air. **2** energy; vigor.

▶*v.* (**zipped**, **zip·ping**) **1** fasten with a zipper. **2** move with zip or at high speed.

**zip code** (also **ZIP code**) ▶*n.* assigned numeric postal code to speed the sorting and delivering of mail.

**zip·per** ▶*n.* fastening device of two flexible strips with interlocking projections closed or opened by pulling a slide along them.
▶*v.* fasten with a zipper.

**zip·py** /ˈzipē/ ▶*adj.* (**-pi·er**, **-pi·est**) *inf.* **1** bright; fresh; lively. **2** fast; speedy. —**zip·pi·ly** *adv.* —**zip·pi·ness** *n.*

**zir·con** /ˈzərˌkän/ ▶*n.* zirconium silicate of which some translucent varieties are cut into gems.

**zir·co·ni·um** /ˌzərˈkōnēəm/ ▶*n.* gray metallic element. (Symb.: **Zr**)

**zit** /zit/ ▶*n. inf.* pimple.

**zith·er** /ˈziTHər/ ▶*n.* musical instrument consisting of a flat wooden sound box with numerous strings stretched across it, placed horizontally and played with the fingers and a plectrum.

**zo·di·ac** /ˈzōdēˌak/ ▶*n.* **1** imaginary belt of the heavens including all apparent positions of the sun, moon, and planets divided into twelve equal parts. **2** diagram of these signs. —**zo·di·a·cal** *adj.*

**zom·bie** /ˈzämbē/ ▶*n.* **1** *inf.* dull or apathetic person. **2** corpse said to be revived by witchcraft.

**zone** /zōn/ ▶*n.* **1** area having particular features, properties, purpose, or use: *danger zone.* **2** (also **time zone**) range of longitudes where a common standard time is used. **3** *Geog.* latitudinal division of the earth.
▶*v.* **1** encircle as or with a zone. **2** assign as or to a particular area. —**zon·al** *adj.* —**zon·ing** *n.*

**zonk** /zäNGk; zôNGk/ ▶*v.* **1** hit or strike. **2** fall or cause to fall suddenly and heavily asleep or lose consciousness.

**zonked** /zäNGkt/ ▶*adj. inf.* (often **zonked out**) exhausted; intoxicated.

**zoo** /zoo/ ▶*n.* park with a collection of animals for exhibition or study.

**zo·ol·o·gy** /zōˈäləjē/ ▶*n.* the scientific study of animals. —**zo·o·log·i·cal** *adj.* —**zo·ol·o·gist** *n.*

**zoom** /zoom/ ▶*v.* **1** move quickly, esp. with a buzzing sound. **2 a** (of an airplane) to climb at high speed and a steep angle. **b** cause (an airplane) to do this. **3 a** (of a camera) move rapidly from a long shot to a close-up. **b** cause (a lens or camera) to do this.
▶*n.* **1** airplane's steep climb. **2** zooming camera shot.
□ **zoom lens** lens allowing a camera to zoom by varying the focal length.

**zo·o·phyte** /ˈzōəˌfīt/ ▶*n.* plantlike animal, esp. a coral, sea anemone, or sponge. —**zo·o·phyt·ic** *adj.*

**zuc·chi·ni** /zooˈkēnē/ ▶*n.* (*pl.* same or **-nis**) green variety of smooth-skinned summer squash.

**zwie·back** /ˈzwīˌbak/ ▶*n.* rusk or sweet cake toasted in slices.

**zy·de·co** /ˈzīdəˌkō/ ▶*n.* kind of black American dance music originally from southern Louisiana, typically featuring accordion and guitar.

**zy·gote** /ˈzīˌgōt/ ▶*n. Biol.* cell formed by the union of two gametes. —**zy·got·ic** *adj.*

**zy·mur·gy** /ˈzīˌmərjē/ ▶*n.* study or practice of fermentation in brewing, winemaking, or distilling.

# Language Guide

# Guide to Spelling

Any reader or writer knows that spelling is an important component of writing. Some individuals seem to have little or no trouble spelling words correctly, while others seem to struggle with spelling, often with the same words over and over.

For those who have experienced the struggle, it is important to remember that spelling is a skill that improves with practice. Regular reading and writing, accompanied by a dictionary for consultation, are the best methods for improving one's spelling. Anyone who has encountered trouble with spelling knows that the English language contains numerous irregularities. Even so, there are a number of basic spelling rules that can be followed in most cases.

*[For spelling guidelines for plural nouns and possessive nouns, refer to the "Noun" section under "Parts of Speech."]*

---

**TIP**

Keep a list of words that you find difficult to spell. Use a dictionary to confirm the correct spellings. Add to your list whenever you encounter a troublesome word. Refer to your list often, and quiz yourself. Make up sentences that include words from the list, writing them without going back and forth to double-check the spelling. Compare the words in your sentences to the words on your list. Make a note of the words that continue to give you trouble, and write these words in sentences every day until you have learned to spell them.

---

## COMPOUND ADJECTIVES AND NOUNS

A compound adjective or noun is a single term formed from two or more distinct words. There are three spelling formats for compounds: open, hyphenated, and closed.

In an **open compound**, the component words are separate, with no hyphen (*well fed; wagon train*).

In a **hyphenated compound**, the component words are joined by a hyphen (*half-baked; city-state*).

In a **closed compound**, the component words are joined into a single word (*hardheaded; campfire*).

## Compound adjectives

For most cases of open compound adjectives, there is a general rule of thumb: the compound is left open when it is not followed by the modified noun; the compound is hyphenated when it is followed by the modified noun.

She was well known in the South for her poetry.
[The compound *well known* is open because it is not followed by the modified noun *She*.]

In the South, she was a well-known poet.
[The compound *well-known* is hyphenated because it is followed by the modified noun *poet*.]

A notable exception occurs when the first part of the compound adjective is an adverb that ends in *–ly*. In this case, the compound remains open, even when it is followed by the noun.

The woman who met us in the lobby was beautifully dressed.
A beautifully dressed woman met us in the lobby.

## Compound nouns

For spellers, the least troublesome compound nouns are familiar closed compounds.

briefcase
cupcake
downstairs
fireplace

Other compound nouns can be troublesome. Although certain ones, such as *mother-in-law*, are always hyphenated, many compound nouns commonly occur in more than one acceptable format, such as *ice cap* or *icecap* and *vice president* or *vice-president*. For most spelling questions, the best resource is a dictionary; for questions pertaining specifically to compounds, an unabridged edition is recommended.

---

**TIP**

Different dictionaries often disagree on the preferred spelling formats for a number of compounds, so writers are well advised to consult just one dictionary when establishing a spelling style.

---

## PREFIXES

A prefix is a group of letters added to the beginning of a word to adjust its meaning.

In most cases, prefixes are affixed to the root word without hyphenation.

> antibacterial
> postwar
> semicircle

Often, however, a hyphen is customary, necessary, or preferable.

Certain prefixes almost always take a hyphen: *all-, ex-, full-, quasi-, self-*.

> all-encompassing
> ex-partner
> full-bodied
> quasi-liberal
> self-confidence

When the root word begins with a capital letter, the prefix takes a hyphen:

> anti-American
> pre-Conquest

Sometimes, without a hyphen, a word could be easily confused with another.

> We <u>recovered</u> our furniture.

Does this mean we *found* our *missing* furniture? Or did we *put new coverings on our furniture?* If the latter is meant, a hyphen would have avoided confusion:

> We <u>re-covered</u> our furniture.

Sometimes, a hyphen is not necessary but preferable. Without it, the word may look awkward. One such circumstance is when the last letter of the prefix and the first letter of the root word are both vowels. For each of the following pairs of words, either spelling is acceptable.

> antiknock / anti-knock
> preadapt / pre-adapt
> semiindependent / semi-independent

---

**TIP**

Regarding the use of optional hyphens, the writer should establish a preferred style. Keeping a running list of hyphenated terms can help writers keep track of which spellings they have already used in their text, thus making the style consistent.

---

## SUFFIXES

A suffix is group of letters added to the end of a word to create a derivative of the word.

There are exceptions to the following guidelines on how to spell with suffixes, but in most cases these rules apply:

A root word that ends in *e* drops the *e* when the suffix begins with a vowel.

> rehearse / rehearsing

However, most words that end in *ce* or *ge* keep the *e* when the suffix begins with *a* or *o*.

> service / serviceable
> advantage / advantageous

A root word that ends in *e* keeps the *e* when the suffix begins with a consonant.

> wise / wisely

A root word that ends in a *y* preceded by a consonant changes the *y* to *i* when the suffix begins with any letter other than *i*.

> satisfy / satisfies / satisfying

A root word that ends in *ie* changes the *ie* to *y* when the suffix is *–ing*.

> lie / lying

A root word that ends in *oe* keeps the *e* when the suffix begins with a vowel, unless the vowel is *e*.

> toe / toeing / toed

A one-syllable root word that ends in a single consonant preceded by a single vowel doubles the consonant when the suffix is *–ed, -er,* or *–ing*. This rule also applies to root words with two or more syllables if the accent is on the last syllable.

> stir / stirred
> refer / referring

## WORD DIVISION

Sometimes it is necessary to "break" a word when the line on the page has run out of space. Dividing a word at the end of a line is perfectly acceptable, as long as two conditions are met: the word must be divisible, and the division must be made in the right place.

When a word is properly divided, a hyphen is attached to its first part, so that the hyphen is at the end of the line.

> At the conclusion of the interview, I was given
> two minutes to summarize my manage-
> ment experiences.

| What words are never divisible? | *for example:* |
|---|---|
| • one-syllable words | catch; flutes; strange; through |
| • contractions | didn't; doesn't; wouldn't; you're |
| • abbreviations | Calif.; NASCAR; RSVP; YMCA |
| • numbers written as numerals | 1776; $2,800; 9:45; 0.137 |

## Where is a correct place to divide a word?

| | *good break:* | *bad break:* |
|---|---|---|
| • after a prefix | inter-national | interna-tional |
| • before a suffix that has more than two letters | govern-ment | gov-ernment |
| • between the main parts of a closed compound | nut-cracker | nutcrack-er |
| • at the hyphen of a hyphenated compound | gender-neutral | gen-der-neutral |
| • after double consonants if the root word ends in the double consonants | address-ing | addres-sing |
| • otherwise, between double consonants | rib-bon | ribb-on |
| • in general (for words that don't fall into the previous categories), between syllables | whis-per | whi-sper |

## Where is an incorrect place to divide a word?

| | *good break:* | *bad break:* |
|---|---|---|
| • before a two-letter suffix | —— | odd-ly |
| • after the first syllable if it has only one letter | Ameri-can | A-merican |
| • before the last syllable if it has only one letter | nu-tria | nutri-a |
| • before the ending –*ed* if the –*ed* is not pronounced | —— | abash-ed |

---

**TIP**

When dividing a word at the end of a line, it is always a good idea to use a dictionary to verify the word's proper syllabification.

# NUMBERS

Numbers are an important part of everyday communication, yet they often cause the writer to stumble, particularly over questions of spelling and style. The guidelines on *how* to spell out a number are fairly straightforward. The guidelines on *when* to spell out a number are not so precise.

## How to spell out numbers

### Cardinal numbers

The most common problem associated with the spelling of whole cardinal numbers is punctuation. The rules are actually quite simple: Numeric amounts that fall between twenty and one hundred are always hyphenated. No other punctuation should appear in a spelled-out whole number, regardless of its size.

| | |
|---|---|
| 26 | twenty-six |
| 411 | four hundred eleven |
| 758 | seven hundred fifty-eight |
| 6,500 | six thousand five hundred |
| 33,003 | thirty-three thousand three |
| 972,923 | nine hundred seventy-two thousand nine hundred twenty-three |

Note: the word *and* does not belong in the spelling of a number. For example, "758" should not be spelled "seven hundred and fifty-eight."

### Ordinal numbers

The punctuation of spelled-out ordinal numbers typically follows the rules for cardinal numbers.

What should we do for their <u>fifty-fifth</u> anniversary?
He graduated <u>two hundred twenty-ninth</u> out of a class of two hundred thirty.

When ordinal numbers appear as numerals, they are affixed with *–th*, with the exception of those ending with the ordinal *first*, *second*, or *third*.

| | |
|---|---|
| 1st | 581st |
| 2nd | 32nd |
| 3rd | 73rd |
| 4th | 907th |

Note: Sometimes *2nd* is written as *2d*, and *3rd* as *3d*.

## Fractions

A fraction can appear in a number of formats, as shown here:

| | |
|---|---|
| $\frac{3}{8}$ | case fraction (*or* split fraction) |
| 3/8 | fraction with solidus |
| 0.375 | decimal fraction |
| three-eighths | spelled-out fraction |

When acting as an adjective, a spelled-out fraction should always be hyphenated.

> The Serbian democrats have won a <u>two-thirds</u> majority.

When acting as a noun, a spelled-out fraction may or may not be hyphenated, according to the writer's or publisher's preferred style.

> At least <u>four-fifths</u> of the supply has been depleted.
>    *or*
> At least <u>four fifths</u> of the supply has been depleted.

# When to spell out numbers

When to spell out a number, whole or fractional, is as much a matter of sense as of style. Text that is heavy with numbers, such as scientific or statistical material, could become virtually unreadable if the numbers were all spelled out. Conversely, conventional prose that occasionally makes mention of a quantity may look unbalanced with an occasional numeral here and there.

Often, the decision to spell or not to spell comes down to simple clarity.

> Our standard paper size is 8½ by 11.
> Our standard paper size is 8 1/2 by 11.
> Our standard paper size is eight and a half by eleven.
> Our standard paper size is eight and one-half by eleven.

The preceding four sentences say exactly the same thing, but the best choice for readability is the first.

Even the most comprehensive books of style and usage do not dictate absolute rules regarding the style of numbers in text. When writing, it is most important to be as consistent as possible with a style once one has been established. For example, some writers or publishers may adopt a policy of spelling out the numbers zero through ten. Others may prefer to spell out the numbers zero through ninety-nine. Either style is perfectly acceptable, as long as the style is followed throughout the written work.

Sometimes, even after adopting a basic number style, the writer may wish to incorporate certain style allowances and exceptions. Perhaps the decision has been made to spell out only the numbers zero though ninety-nine. But in one paragraph, a sentence reads, "There must have been more than 1,000,000 people there." In this case, it may be better to write, "There must have been more than a million people there."

## SYMBOLS

In most contexts of formal writing, the use of symbols should be strictly limited, but there are occasions when a symbol may be a better choice than a word. Text that deals largely with commerce, for instance, may rely on the use of various monetary symbols to keep the text organized and readable. In any text, mathematical equations and scientific formulas are much easier to read if written with symbols rather than words. Also, it is usually appropriate to use symbols within tables and charts; as symbols conserve space, they prevent a "cluttered look."

Here are some of the most common symbols found in print:

| | | | |
|---|---|---|---|
| @ | at | ≈ | is approximately equal to |
| c/o | care of | ≠ | is not equal to |
| $ | dollar | < | is less than |
| ¢ | cent | > | is greater than |
| Can$ | Canadian dollar | ≤ | is less than or equal to |
| £ | pound | ≥ | is greater than or equal to |
| ¥ | yen | √ | square root of |
| # | number or pound | ∞ | infinity |
| / | per | © | copyright |
| % | percent | ® | registered |
| ° | degree | ™ | trademark |
| + | plus | ¶ | paragraph |
| − | minus | § | section |
| ÷ | divided by | * | asterisk |
| × | times | † | dagger |
| ± | plus or minus | ‡ | double dagger |
| = | equals | ‖ | parallels *or* pipes |

Symbols are sometimes used to point out note references to the reader. In a table or chart, for instance, the writer may wish to indicate that an item is further explained or identified elsewhere on the page. A symbol placed with the item signals the reader to look for an identical symbol, which precedes the additional information. Sometimes, numerals are the symbols of choice, but if the material within the table or chart consists of numerals, it is probably better to use non-numeric symbols for the note references. The conventional set of symbols used for this purpose, in the conventional sequence in which to use them, is *, †, ‡, §, ||, #.

---

### TIP

Numerals and other symbols should never begin a sentence. If the symbol should not or cannot be spelled out, the sentence needs to be reworded.

19 students have become mentors.
*should be:*
Nineteen students have become mentors.

2004 is the year we plan to get married.
*should be:*
We plan to get married in 2004.

$10 was found on the stairs.
*should be:*
Ten dollars was found on the stairs.

6:00 is the earliest I can leave.
*should be:*
Six o'clock is the earliest I can leave.
*or:*
The earliest I can leave is 6:00.

$y = 2x + 1$ is a line with a slope of 2.
*should be:*
The line $y = 2x + 1$ has a slope of 2.

---

# COMMONLY MISSPELLED WORDS

| | | |
|---|---|---|
| absence | amateur | because |
| absolutely | analysis | beggar |
| acceptance | analyze | beginning |
| accessible | anesthetic | behavior |
| accidentally | angel | believe |
| accommodate | angle | benefit |
| accompany | annually | benefited |
| accuracy | answer | bicycle |
| ache | anticipate | bouillon |
| achieve | anxiety | boundary |
| achievement | apartheid | bulletin |
| acquaintance | aperitif | bureau |
| acquire | apology | buried |
| acre | apparatus | business |
| across | apparent | cafeteria |
| actually | appearance | calendar |
| administration | appetite | campaign |
| admittance | appreciate | cancellation |
| adolescent | approach | captain |
| advantageous | appropriate | carburetor |
| advertisement | approximately | career |
| advisable | argue | ceiling |
| affectionate | argument | cemetery |
| affidavit | arrangement | census |
| aficionado | ascend | certificate |
| afraid | ascertain | chamois |
| again | assistant | changeable |
| aggravate | athletic | character |
| aghast | attendance | characteristic |
| aisle | authority | chauffeur |
| allege | auxiliary | chic |
| allotment | available | chief |
| allotment | awkward | chocolate |
| ally | bachelor | choice |

## Commonly Misspelled Words (cont.)

| | | |
|---|---|---|
| choose | criticism | embarrass |
| chose | criticize | eminent |
| Christian | cruelly | emphasize |
| clothes | curiosity | encouragement |
| collateral | curious | encumbrances |
| colonel | cylinder | enforceable |
| color | dealt | entirely |
| column | debtor | entourage |
| commercial | deceive | envelope |
| commission | decision | environment |
| committee | definite | equipped |
| community | dependent | escape |
| compel | describe | especially |
| competitor | despair | essential |
| completely | desperate | exaggerate |
| conceivable | despise | excellent |
| concentrate | develop | exciting |
| condemn | difference | exercise |
| confidence | dilemma | exhilarating |
| confidential | disappearance | exhort |
| confusion | disappoint | existence |
| connoisseur | disastrous | expense |
| conscience | discipline | experience |
| conscious | discrepancy | experiment |
| continuous | disease | extraordinary |
| controlled | doctor | extremely |
| controversial | duplicate | facsimile |
| convertible | easily | familiar |
| cooperate | ecclesiastical | fantasy |
| copyright | ecstasy | fascinate |
| corps | effect | fashionable |
| correspondence | efficient | fasten |
| counterfeit | eighth | fatal |
| courageous | elementary | favorite |
| courteous | eligible | February |

| | | |
|---|---|---|
| field | height | knowledge |
| fiery | heinous | laboratory |
| finally | heroine | laborer |
| financial | hors d'oeuvre | laid |
| forehead | hospital | legitimate |
| foreign | humor | leisure |
| forfeit | humorous | liaison |
| fortunately | hungrily | library |
| forty | hygiene | license |
| forward | hypocrisy | lieutenant |
| fourth | hypocrite | lightning |
| freight | ignorance | likely |
| friend | illiterate | liquefy |
| fulfill | imagine | liquidate |
| further | immediately | listener |
| gauge | impossible | literature |
| genius | incidentally | livelihood |
| gourmet | increase | lively |
| government | indefinite | loneliness |
| governor | independent | luxury |
| gracious | indictment | magazine |
| grammar | indispensable | magnificent |
| guarantee | individually | maintenance |
| guerrilla | inevitable | maneuver |
| guess | influence | manufacturer |
| guidance | ingredient | marriage |
| gymnasium | innocence | marvelous |
| gypsy | inoculate | mathematics |
| handsome | insurance | meant |
| hangar | intelligence | mechanic |
| hanger | interference | medical |
| happened | interrupt | medicine |
| happiness | iridescent | melancholy |
| harass | irrelevant | merchandise |
| Hawaii | itinerary | millionaire |
| heavily | jealous | miniature |

## Commonly Misspelled Words (cont.)

| | | |
|---|---|---|
| minimum | organization | prejudice |
| minuscule | originally | preparation |
| minute | outrageous | presence |
| miscellaneous | pageant | pressure |
| mischief | paid | pretension |
| mischievous | parallel | privilege |
| misspell | paralleled | probably |
| mortgage | paralyze | procedure |
| muscle | parliament | proceed |
| mysterious | particular | procure |
| narrative | pastime | professor |
| naturally | peaceful | proffered |
| necessary | peculiar | promissory |
| nickel | performance | pronunciation |
| niece | permanent | propaganda |
| ninety | perseverance | psychology |
| noisily | personality | pursuit |
| non sequitur | personnel | questionnaire |
| noticeable | perspiration | quiet |
| obstacle | persuade | quite |
| occasionally | pessimistic | realize |
| occurrence | phenomenal | really |
| offensive | Philippines | realtor |
| official | philosophy | realty |
| often | physical | receipt |
| omission | picnicking | recognize |
| omit | pleasant | recommend |
| omitted | politician | referred |
| once | Portuguese | reign |
| operate | possession | relevant |
| opponent | possibility | relieve |
| opportunity | practically | religious |
| optimistic | practice | removal |
| orchestra | prairie | rendezvous |
| ordinarily | preferred | repertoire |

repetition
rescind
reservoir
resistance
resource
responsibility
restaurant
rheumatism
rhythm
ridiculous
roommate
sachet
sacrifice
sacrilegious
safety
satisfied
scarcely
scarcity
scene
schedule
scholar
scissors
scurrilous
seance
secretary
seize
semester
separate
sergeant
shepherd
siege
similar
sincerely
skein

skiing
skillful
sophomore
soufflé
source
souvenir
specifically
specimen
sponsor
statistics
straight
strength
stretch
strictly
stubborn
substitute
subtle
succeed
successful
suede
sufficient
summary
superintendent
supersede
surgeon
surprise
susceptible
suspense
swimming
sympathetic
synonym
temperamental
temperature
tendency

therefore
thorough
though
thoughtful
tomorrow
tragedy
transferred
tremendous
truly
twelfth
typical
unanimous
unnecessary
useful
useless
usually
vacillate
vacuum
vague
valuable
variety
various
vegetable
vengeance
vilify
villain
warrant
weather
Wednesday
weird
whether
whole
yacht
yield

# Commonly Confused Words

Certain words in the English language are commonly confused with other words that are in some way similar. Some of the most frequently confused terms are listed here, accompanied by brief usage notes.

| confused terms | proper usage |
| --- | --- |
| accept | *Accept* is a verb, meaning "consent to receive" or "agree to undertake."<br>   I am pleased to <u>accept</u> your generous offer. |
| except | *Except* is usually a preposition, meaning "not including" or "other than."<br>   Everyone <u>except</u> Ursula has made reservations. |
| advice | *Advice* is a noun meaning "guidance" or "recommendations."<br>   May I ask your <u>advice</u> on a personal matter? |
| advise | *Advise* is a verb meaning "offer suggestions," "give an opinion," or "warn."<br>   We were <u>advised</u> to take an alternate route. |
| affect | *Affect* is a verb meaning "influence" or "produce an effect on."<br>   The rise in gas prices has <u>affected</u> our travel plans. |
| effect | *Effect*, as a noun, means "the result or consequence of an action."<br>   The rise in gas prices has had an <u>effect</u> on our travel plans. |

| confused terms | proper usage |
| --- | --- |
| | *Effect*, as a verb, means "bring about" or "cause to occur."<br><br>Exactly what circumstances have <u>effected</u> these rising gas prices? |
| already | *Already* means "before now" or "by now."<br><br>Evelyn <u>already</u> fixed the leak. |
| all ready | *All ready* means "completely ready."<br><br>Are you <u>all ready</u> to leave? |
| all together | *All together* means "all in one place" or "all at once."<br><br>For the first time in years, we were <u>all together</u>. |
| altogether | *Altogether* means "in total."<br><br><u>Altogether</u>, there are six bedrooms. |
| allusion | *Allusion* is used to refer indirectly to someone or something.<br><br>The *allusion* to Jesus in his poetry is fairly obvious. |
| illusion | *Illusion* means "a false or misleading appearance or impression."<br><br>His mother created the <u>illusion</u> of a happy family. |
| adverse | *Adverse* means "unfavorable" or "harmful."<br><br>Drought has had an <u>adverse</u> effect on the crops. |
| averse | *Averse* means "having a strong dislike of or opposition to."<br><br>I am not <u>averse</u> to the idea of moving. |
| as | *As* is sometimes a preposition, used to refer to function or character.<br><br>He landed a job <u>as</u> an editor.<br><br>*As* is sometimes a conjunction, used to indicate the concurrence of events.<br><br>The fans went wild <u>as</u> Elvis walked onto the stage. |

| confused terms | proper usage |
| --- | --- |
| like | *Like*, as a preposition, takes an object. It means "similar to."<br>    That dog looks <u>like</u> a bear.<br><br>*Like* is not a conjunction, yet it is frequently used as one. Especially in formal speech or writing, be careful to avoid this incorrect usage:<br>    I don't have a big kitchen <u>like</u> you do. [incorrect]<br>    I don't have a big kitchen <u>like</u> yours. [correct]<br><br>    Sammy goes to bed by eight, just <u>like</u> children should. [incorrect]<br>    Sammy goes to bed by eight, just <u>as</u> children should. [correct] |
| beside | *Beside* is a preposition meaning "next to" or "alongside."<br>    Please put the tray on the table <u>beside</u> my bed. |
| besides | *Besides*, as a preposition, means "in addition to."<br>    <u>Besides</u> the free room, we were given a lavish breakfast.<br><br>*Besides*, as an adverb, means "furthermore."<br>    I'm too tired to go to a restaurant. <u>Besides</u>, I'm not hungry. |
| can | *Can* expresses ability<br>    Cheetahs <u>can</u> run at a remarkable speed. |
| may | *May* expresses permission or possibility.<br>    The children <u>may</u> have more pizza. [permission]<br>    I <u>may</u> join you later. [possibility]<br><br>Note: In most informal contexts, the use of *can* to express permission is generally accepted as standard usage.<br>    The children <u>can</u> have more pizza. |

| confused terms | proper usage |
|---|---|
| capital | *Capital* refers to uppercase letters, money, administrative cities, or crimes punishable by death.<br>    The first word should begin with a <u>capital</u> Q. [letters]<br>    The <u>capital</u> expenditures exceeded our budget. [money]<br>    Vilnius is the <u>capital</u> of Lithuania. [cities]<br>    Treason is a <u>capital</u> offense. [crimes] |
| capitol | *Capitol* refers only to a building that houses a legislature. The proper name *the Capitol* refers specifically to the building that houses the U.S. Congress in Washington, D.C.<br>    We met on the steps of the Virginia state <u>capitol</u>. |
| could have/ should have | *Could have* and *should have* are grammatically correct verb forms.<br>    I <u>could have</u> gone to Harvard. |
| could of/should of | *Could of* and *should of* are meaningless forms that should never be used. They are mistakenly used because they sound like *could have* and *should have*. |
| elicit | *Elicit* is a verb meaning "draw out (a response, answer, or fact) from someone."<br>    The police were unable to <u>elicit</u> a confession from the suspect. |
| illicit | *Illicit* is an adjective meaning "forbidden by law" or "improper."<br>    Ray's <u>illicit</u> use of the funds led to his dismissal. |
| emigrate | *Emigrate* means "move out of a country."<br>    Her grandfather <u>emigrated</u> from Poland in 1926. |
| immigrate | *Immigrate* means "move into a country."<br>    Gerda <u>immigrated</u> to Australia with her second husband. |

| confused terms | proper usage |
|---|---|
| good | *Good* is an adjective meaning "favorable" or "appropriate" or "pleasing." <br>    The dance performance was <u>good</u>. |
| well | *Well* is an adverb meaning "in a good or satisfactory way." <br>    She dances <u>well</u>. |
| lend | *Lend* is a verb meaning "grant the temporary use of." Lend is always a verb. <br>    I will <u>lend</u> my car to you. |
| loan | *Loan*, as a verb, means "grant the temporary use of." Hence, it can be a synonym of lend. <br>    I will <u>loan</u> my car to you. <br><br> *Loan*, as a noun, means "a thing that is borrowed" or "an act of lending something." <br>    He thanked me for the <u>loan</u> of my car. |
| lay, laid | *Lay* is a verb meaning "put (something) down." The past tense of *lay* is *laid*. <br>    Let's <u>lay</u> our towels in a sunny spot. <br>    We are <u>laying</u> our towels in a sunny spot. <br>    We <u>laid</u> our towels in a sunny spot. |
| lie, lay | *Lie* is a verb meaning "assume a horizontal or resting position." The past tense of *lie* is *lay*. <br>    Let's <u>lie</u> on our towels. <br>    We are <u>lying</u> on our towels. <br>    Earlier today, we <u>lay</u> on our towels. <br><br> Note: The base *lay* and the past tense *lay* are two different words with distinctly different usages. |
| personal | *Personal* is an adjective that refers to a person's private or individual affairs. <br>    I will give this matter my <u>personal</u> attention. |

| confused terms | proper usage |
|---|---|
| personnel | *Personnel* is plural noun that refers to the people employed by an organization.<br>　　All <u>personnel</u> are invited to attend the reception.<br><br>*Personnel* is often used as a shortened form of *personnel department.*<br>　　Ask someone in <u>personnel</u> for a copy of the form. |
| principal | *Principal*, as an adjective, means "most important."<br>　　Our <u>principal</u> concerns are food and shelter.<br><br>*Principal*, as a noun, refers to a person in charge or to a sum of money on which interest is paid.<br>　　The <u>principal</u> of Franklin High School is Mr. Barnes. [person]<br>　　I still owe most of the <u>principal</u> on my student loan. [money] |
| principle | *Principle* is a noun meaning "rule" or "basis for conduct."<br>　　He strictly adhered to the principles of his faith. |
| real | *Real* is an adjective meaning "actual" or "genuine."<br>　　Is that painting a <u>real</u> Picasso? |
| really | *Really* is an adverb used to mean "in actual fact" or as an emphasis to a statement.<br>　　She and I are not <u>really</u> related. ["in actual fact"]<br>　　Do you <u>really</u> want to go? [emphasis]<br><br>Note: The word *real* is sometimes used adverbially for emphasis, in place of the adverb *really*. In informal contexts, such usage may be acceptable, but it should be strictly avoided in formal contexts.<br>　　He is a <u>real</u> nice salesman. [informal]<br>　　He is a <u>really</u> nice salesman. [formal] |

| confused terms | proper usage |
| --- | --- |
| than | *Than* is used in comparisons.<br>The original movie was much better <u>than</u> the sequel. |
| then | *Then* is usually used to indicate a relative time.<br>We saw the movie, and <u>then</u> we went home.<br><br>*Then* sometimes means "also" or "in that case."<br>The hours are great, and <u>then</u> there's the overtime. ["also"]<br>You don't want salad? <u>Then</u> don't stop at the store. ["in that case"] |
| there | *There* is an adverb meaning "at that place."<br>The tomatoes are over <u>there</u>. |
| their | *Their* is a possessive pronoun meaning "belonging to them."<br>I wonder if they still have tomatoes in <u>their</u> garden. |
| they're | *They're* is the contracted form of "they are."<br>I wonder if <u>they're</u> going to grow tomatoes this year. |
| to | *To* is a preposition that expresses motion in a particular direction or indicates a point reached.<br>I've never been <u>to</u> Japan.<br><br>*To* is also used as the mark of an infinitive.<br>Would you like me <u>to</u> help? |
| too | *Too* is an adverb meaning "also" or "excessively."<br>Is Arlene coming <u>too</u>? ["also"]<br>He's driving <u>too</u> fast. ["excessively"] |
| two | *Two* is a number.<br>There are <u>two</u> candles in the drawer. |
| waive | *Waive* is a verb meaning "give up (a right or claim)" or "refrain from enforcing."<br>Sidney refused to <u>waive</u> his parental rights. |

# Commonly Confused Words

| confused terms | proper usage |
|---|---|
| wave | *Wave*, as a verb, means "move one's hands to and fro, especially to signal a message such as a greeting."<br>Sidney <u>waved</u> to reporters as he left the courthouse. |
| we | *We* is a subjective pronoun. It is used as a subject of a verb, either by itself or with a noun that expresses the category to which the *we* belongs.<br><u>We</u> received our schedules on Monday.<br><u>We teachers</u> received our schedules on Monday. |
| us | *Us* is an objective pronoun. It is used as an object of a verb.<br>The schedules were distributed to <u>us</u> on Monday.<br><br>Note: Especially in informal speech, the pronoun *us* is frequently used subjectively, but such usage is never correct.<br>When Dr. Wilson retired, <u>us students</u> gave her a party. [incorrect]<br>When Dr. Wilson retired, <u>we students</u> gave her a party. [correct] |
| who | *Who* is used as a subject.<br>This is the woman <u>who</u> found your wallet. |
| whom | *Whom* is used as the object of a verb or preposition.<br>For <u>whom</u> did you make the card? |
| whose | *Whose* is the possessive form of *who*.<br>We're not sure <u>whose</u> money this is. |
| who's | *Who's* is the contracted form of *who is* and *who has*.<br><u>Who's</u> the new accountant? [*who is*]<br><u>Who's</u> got change for a ten? [*who has*] |
| your | *Your* is the possessive form of *you*.<br>Why is Owen wearing <u>your</u> coat? |
| you're | *You're* is the contracted form of *you are*.<br>If <u>you're</u> going home now, I'll lock up. |

# Usage Notes

## aggravate

**Aggravate** in the sense 'annoy or exasperate' dates back to the 17th century and has been so used by respected writers ever since. This use is still regarded as incorrect by some traditionalists on the grounds that it is too radical a departure from the etymological meaning of 'make heavy.' It is, however, comparable to meaning changes in hundreds of other words which have long been accepted without comment.

## alternate, alternative

**Alternate** can be a verb, noun, or adjective, while **alternative** can be a noun or adjective. In both American and British English, the adjective **alternate** means 'every other' (*there will be a dance on **alternate** Saturdays*) and the adjective **alternative** means 'available as another choice' (*an **alternative** route; **alternative** medicine; **alternative** energy sources*). In American usage, however, **alternate** can also be used to mean 'available as another choice': *an **alternate** plan called for construction to begin immediately rather than waiting for spring.* Likewise, a book club may offer an 'alternate selection' as an alternative to the main selection.

Some traditionalists maintain, from an etymological standpoint, that you can have only two alternatives (from the Latin *alter* 'other (of two); the other') and that uses of more than two alternatives are erroneous. Such uses are, however, normal in modern standard English.

## altogether, all together

Note that **altogether** and **all together** do not mean the same thing. **Altogether** means 'in total, totally' as in *there are six bedrooms **altogether***, or *that is a different matter **altogether***, whereas **all together** means 'all in one place' or 'all at once,' as in *it was good to have a group of friends all together*, or *they came in all together*.

## anticipate

**Anticipate** in the sense 'expect, foresee' is well established in informal use (*he anticipated a restless night*), but is regarded as a weakening of the meaning by many traditionalists. The formal sense is more specific in its meaning, 'be aware of and deal with beforehand' (*the doctor anticipated the possibility of a relapse by prescribing new medications*).

## anyone, any one

**Any one** is not the same as **anyone**, and the two forms should not be used interchangeably. **Any one**, meaning 'any single (person or thing),' is written as two words to emphasize singularity: *any one of us could do the job*; *not more than ten new members are chosen in any one year*. Otherwise it is written as one word: *anyone who wants to come is welcome*.

## Asian, Asiatic

The standard and accepted term when referring to individual people is **Asian** rather than **Asiatic**, which can be offensive. However, **Asiatic** is standard in scientific and technical use, for example in biological and anthropological classifications. See note for **oriental**.

## author, coauthor

In the sense 'be the author of,' the verb **author** is objected to by some traditionalists who regard it as an awkward or pretentious substitute for *write* or *compose*. This usage is widespread and well established though, and has been in use since the end of the 16th century. The verb **coauthor**, for which there is no common synonym, is useful and unobjectionable.

## bad, badly

Confusion in the use of **bad** versus **badly** usually has to do with verbs called copulas, such as *feel* or *seem*. Thus, standard usage calls for *I feel bad*, not *I feel badly*. As a precise speaker or writer would explain, *I feel badly* means 'I do not have a good sense of touch.'

## beg the question

The original meaning of the phrase **beg the question** belongs to the field of logic. It is a translation of the Latin rhetorical term *petitio principii*, literally meaning 'laying claim to a principle,' that is, assuming something that ought to be proved first, as in the following sentence: *dogs should be locked up, otherwise attacks by wild dogs on children will continue to increase.* This **begs the question** (among other questions) whether, in fact, such attacks are increasing. Usually such a statement will give the impression that the problem of proving the argument has been sidestepped. From this impression of sidestepping, a new meaning has developed: 'avoid the question, evade the issue,' as in *they said he **begged the question** by criticizing his opponent's program.* Also, over the last 100 years or so another, more general use has arisen: 'invite an obvious question,' as in *some definitions of mental illness **beg the question** of what constitutes normal behavior.* Both of these newer meanings are widely accepted in modern standard English, although they have been criticized as being misunderstandings of the Latin rhetorical term. To some traditionalists, the sense of 'assume the truth of an argument to be proved' is still the only correct meaning of **beg the question**. Both of the newer meanings of **beg** are used not only with *question*, but with other words as well: *beg the point, beg the issue, beg the difficulties.*

## between, among
**Between** is used in speaking of only two things, people, etc.: *we must choose between two equally unattractive alternatives.* **Among** is used for collective and undefined relations of usually three or more: *agreement on landscaping was reached among all the neighbors.* But where there are more than two parties involved, **between** may be used to express one-to-one relationships of pairs within the group or the sense 'shared by': *there is close friendship between the members of the club*; *diplomatic relations between the U.S., Canada, and Mexico.*

## between you and me
*Between you and I, between you and he,* etc., are incorrect; **between** should be followed only by the objective case: *between you and me, between you and him,* etc.

## bimonthly
The meaning of **bimonthly** (and other similar words such as **biweekly** and **biyearly**) is ambiguous. The only way to avoid this ambiguity is to use alternative expressions like *every two months* and *twice a month.* In the publishing world, the meaning of **bimonthly** is more fixed and is invariably used to mean 'every two months.'

## black

**Black**, designating Americans of African heritage, became the most widely used and accepted term in the 1960s and 1970s, replacing **Negro**. It is not usually capitalized: *black Americans.*

Through the 1980s, the more formal *African American* replaced **black** in much usage, but both are now generally acceptable. *Afro-American*, first recorded in the 19th century and popular in the 1960s and 1970s, is now heard mostly in anthropological and cultural contexts. See note for **colored.**

## blonde, blond

The spellings **blonde** and **blond** correspond to the feminine and masculine forms in French. Although the distinction is usually retained in Britain, American usage since the 1970s has generally preferred the gender-neutral **blond**. The adjective **blonde** may still refer to a woman's (but not a man's) hair color, though use of the noun risks offense (*See that blonde over there?*): the offense arises from the fact that the color of hair is not the person. The adjective applied to inanimate objects (wood, beer) is typically spelled **blond**.

## both and

When **both** is used in constructions with **and**, the structures following 'both' and 'and' should be symmetrical in well-formed English. Thus, *studies of zebra finches, **both** in the wild **and** in captivity* is stronger and clearer than *studies of zebra finches, **both** in the wild **and** captivity.* In the second example, the symmetry or parallelism of 'in the wild' and 'in captivity' has been lost.

## Caribbean

There are two possible pronunciations of the word **Caribbean**, and both are used widely and acceptably in the U.S. In the Caribbean itself, the preferred pronunciation puts the stress on the **-rib-**. In Britain, speakers more often put the stress on the **-be-**, although in recent years, the other pronunciation has gained ground in Britain as the more 'up-to-date' and, to some, the more 'correct' pronunciation.

## co-

In modern American English, the tendency increasingly is to write compound words beginning with **co-** without hyphenation, as in *costar, cosignatory,* and *coproduce.* British usage generally tends more often to show a preference for the older, hyphenated, spelling, but even in Britain the trend seems to be in favor of less hyphenation than in the past. In both the U.S. and the UK, for example, the spellings of *coordinate* and *coed* are encountered with or without hyphenation, but the more common choice for either word in either country is without the hyphen.

**Co-** with the hyphen is often used in compounds that are not yet standard (*co-golfer*), or to prevent ambiguity (*co-driver*—because *codriver* could be mistaken for *cod river*), or simply to avoid an awkward spelling (*co-own* is clearly preferable to *coown*). There are also some relatively less common terms, such as *co-respondent* (in a divorce suit), where the hyphenated spelling distinguishes the word's meaning and pronunciation from that of the more common *correspondent*.

## colored

**Colored** referring to skin color is first recorded in the early 17th century and was adopted in the U.S. by emancipated slaves as a term of racial pride after the end of the Civil War. The word is still used in the National Association for the Advancement of Colored People (NAACP), but otherwise **colored** sounds old-fashioned at best, and is usually offensive.

*People of color*, has gained some favor, but is also used in reference to other nonwhite ethnic groups: *a gathering spot for African Americans and other **people of color** interested in reading about their cultures.*

In South Africa, the term **colored** (normally written **Coloured**) has a different history. It is used to refer to people of mixed-race parentage rather than, as elsewhere, to refer to African peoples and their descendants, i.e., as a synonym for *black*. In modern use in this context, the term is not considered offensive or derogatory. See note for **black.**

## compare to, compare with

Traditionally, **compare to** is used when similarities are noted in dissimilar things: *shall I **compare** thee **to** a summer's day?* To **compare with** is to look for either differences or similarities, usually in similar things: ***compare** the candidate's claims **with** his actual performance.* In practice, however, this distinction is rarely maintained.

## comprise

According to traditional usage, **comprise** means 'consist of,' as in *the country **comprises** twenty states*, and should not be used to mean 'constitute or make up (a whole),' as in *this single breed comprises 50 percent of the Swiss cattle population*. But confusion has arisen because of uses in the passive, which have been formed by analogy with words like *compose*: when **comprise** is used in the active (as in *the country comprises twenty states*) it is, oddly, more or less synonymous with the passive use of the second sense (as in *the country is comprised of twenty states*). Such passive uses of **comprise** are common and are fast becoming part of standard English.

### continual, continuous

In precise usage, **continual** means 'frequent, repeating at intervals' and **continuous** means 'going on without pause or interruption': *we suffered from the continual attacks of mosquitoes; the waterfall's continuous flow creates an endless roar*. The most common error is the use of **continuous** where **continual** is meant: *continual* (that is, 'intermittent') *rain or tantrums can be tolerated; continuous* (that is, 'uninterrupted') *rain or tantrums cannot be tolerated*. To prevent misunderstanding, some careful writers use *intermittent* instead of **continual**, and *uninterrupted* in place of **continuous**. **Continuous** is the word to use in describing spatial relationships, as in *a continuous series of rooms* or *a continuous plain of arable land*. Avoid using **continuous** (or *continuously*) as a way of describing something that occurs at regular or seasonal intervals: in the sentence, *our synagogue's Hanukkah candle-lighting ceremony has been held continuously since 1925*, the word *continuously* should be replaced with *annually*.

### data

**Data** was originally the plural of the Latin word *datum*, 'something (e.g., a piece of information) given.' **Data** is now used as a singular where it means 'information': *this data was prepared for the conference*. It is used as a plural in technical contexts and when the collection of bits of information is stressed: *all recent data on hurricanes are being compared*. Avoid *datas* and *datae*, which are false plurals, neither English nor Latin.

### deaf-mute

In modern use, **deaf-mute** has acquired offensive connotations (implying, wrongly, that such people are without the capacity for communication). It should be avoided in favor of other terms such as *profoundly deaf*.

## decimate

Historically, the meaning of the word **decimate** is 'kill one in every ten of (a group of people).' This sense has been superseded by the later, more general sense 'kill or destroy a large percentage or part of,' as in *the virus has decimated the population*. Some traditionalists argue that this and other later senses are incorrect, but it is clear that these extended senses are now part of standard English. It is sometimes also argued that **decimate** should refer to people and not to things or animals such as weeds or insects. It is generally agreed that **decimate** should not be used to mean 'defeat utterly.'

## due to

The use of **due to** as a prepositional phrase meaning 'because of,' as in *he had to retire* **due to** *an injury* first appeared in print in 1897, and traditional grammarians have opposed this prepositional usage for more than a century on the grounds that it is a misuse of the adjectival phrase **due to** in the sense of 'attributable to, likely or expected to' (*the train is* **due to** *arrive at 11:15*), or 'payable or owed to' (*render unto Caesar what is* **due to** *Caesar*). Nevertheless, this prepositional usage is now widespread and common in all types of literature and must be regarded as standard English.

The phrase *due to the fact that* is very common in speech, but it is wordy, and, especially in writing, one should use the simple word 'because.'

## dumb

Although **dumb** meaning 'not able to speak' is the older sense, it has been overwhelmed by the newer sense (meaning 'stupid') to such an extent that the use of the first sense is now almost certain to cause offense. Alternatives such as *speech-impaired* should be used instead.

## dwarf

In the sense 'an abnormally small person,' **dwarf** is normally considered offensive. However, there are no accepted alternatives in the general language, since terms such as *person of restricted growth* have gained little currency.

## either ... or

In good English writing style, it is important that **either** and **or** are correctly placed so that the structures following each word balance and mirror each other. Thus, sentences such as *either I accompany you* **or** *I wait here* and *I'm going* *to buy **either** a new camera **or** a new video* are correct, whereas sentences such as **either** *I accompany you **or** John* and *I'm **either** going to buy a new camera **or** a video* are not well-balanced sentences and should not be used in written English.

### enormity

This word is imprecisely used to mean 'great size,' as in *it is difficult to comprehend the **enormity** of the continent,* but the original and preferred meaning is 'extreme wickedness,' as in *the **enormity** of the mass murders.* To indicate enormous size, the words *enormousness, immensity, vastness, hugeness,* etc., are preferable.

### enthuse

The verb **enthuse** is formed as a back-formation from the noun *enthusiasm* and, like many verbs formed from nouns in this way, it is regarded by traditionalists as unacceptable. It is difficult to see why: back-formation is a perfectly established means for creating new words in the language (verbs like *classify, commentate,* and *edit* were also formed as back-formations from nouns, for example). **Enthuse** itself has been in the language for more than 150 years.

### equal, unique

It is widely held that adjectives such as **equal** and **unique** have absolute meanings and therefore can have no degrees of comparison. Hence they should not be modified, and it is incorrect to say *more equal* or *very unique* on the grounds that these are adjectives that refer to a logical or mathematical absolute.

### equally, equally as

The construction **equally as**—as in *follow-up discussion is **equally as** important*—is relatively common but is sometimes criticized on the grounds of redundancy. **Equally** used alone is adequate: *follow-up discussion is **equally** important.*

### Eskimo

In recent years, **Eskimo** has come to be regarded as offensive because of one of its possible etymologies (Abnaki *askimo* 'eater of raw meat'), but this descriptive name is accurate since Eskimos traditionally derived their vitamins from eating raw meat. Another etymology (*Montnais* 'netter of snowshoes') is possible, but the etymological problem is still unresolved.

The peoples inhabiting the regions from northwestern Canada to western Greenland call themselves *Inuit*. Since there are no Inuit living in the U.S., **Eskimo** is the only term that can be properly applied to all of the peoples as a whole, and it is still widely used in anthropological and archaeological contexts. The broader term *Native American* is sometimes used to refer to Eskimo and Aleut peoples. See note for **Inuit.**

## espresso
The often-occurring variant spelling *expresso*—and its pronunciation /ik'spresō/—is incorrect and was probably formed by analogy with *express*.

## everyday, every day
The adjective **everyday**, 'pertaining to every day, ordinary,' is correctly spelled as one word (*carrying out their everyday activities*), but the adverbial phrase **every day**, meaning 'each day,' is always spelled as two words (*it rained every day*).

## everyone, every one
The pronoun **everyone,**meaning 'every person,' is correctly spelled as one word: *everyone had a great time at the party*. The pronoun **every one**, meaning 'each one,' is spelled as two words: *every one of the employees got a bonus at the end of the year*. The word *everybody* is substitutable in the first example but not in the second example.

## exceptionable, exceptional
**Exceptionable** means 'open to objection' and is usually found in negative contexts: *there was nothing exceptionable in the evidence*. It is sometimes confused with the much more common **exceptional**, meaning 'unusual, outstanding.' Their opposites, *unexceptionable* ('unobjectionable, beyond criticism') and *unexceptional* ('ordinary'), are also sometimes confused.

## feasible
The primary meaning of **feasible** is 'capable of being done or effected.' There is rarely a need to use **feasible** to mean 'likely' or 'probable' when those words can do the job. There are cases, however, in which a careful writer finds that the sense of likelihood or probability (as with an explanation or theory) is more naturally or idiomatically expressed with **feasible** than with *possible* or *probable*.

## first, second, third

**First**, **second**, **third**, etc., are adverbs as well as adjectives: *first*, *dice three potatoes*; *second*, *add the bouillon*. *Firstly, secondly*, etc., are also correct, but make sure not to mix the two groups: *first, second, third*; not *first, secondly, thirdly*.

## fortuitous

The traditional, etymological meaning of **fortuitous** is 'happening by chance': a *fortuitous meeting* is a chance meeting, which might turn out to be either a good thing or a bad thing. In modern uses, however, **fortuitous** tends more often to be used to refer to fortunate outcomes, and the word has become more or less a synonym for 'lucky' or 'fortunate.' This use is frowned upon as being not etymologically correct and is best avoided except in informal contexts.

## go and

The use of **go** followed by **and**, as in *I must go and change* (rather than *I must go to change*), is extremely common but is regarded by some grammarians as an oddity. *Go* used in the sense of *say* (*She goes, "No way!"*) is informal, on a par with *I'm like, "No way!"*

## good, well

The adverb corresponding to the adjective **good** is **well**: *she is a good swimmer who performs well in meets*. Confusion sometimes arises because **well** is also an adjective meaning 'in good health, healthy,' for which **good** is widely used informally as a substitute: *I feel well*, meaning 'I feel healthy'—versus the informal *I feel good*, meaning either 'I feel healthy' or 'I am in a good mood.'

## graduate, graduate from

The traditional use is "be graduated from": *she will be graduated from medical school in June*. However, it is now more common to say **graduate from**: *she will graduate from medical school in June*. The use of **graduate** as a transitive verb, as in *he graduated high school last week*, is increasingly common, especially in speech, but is considered incorrect by most traditionalists.

## grow

Although **grow** is typically intransitive, as in *he grew two inches taller over the summer*, its use as a transitive verb has long been standard in such phrases as *grow crops* and *grow a beard*.

Recently, however, **grow** has extended its transitive sense and has become trendy in business, economics, and government contexts: *growing the industry*, **growing** *your business*, **growing** *your investment*, and so on. Many people stumble over this extended sense and label it 'jargon.'

## handicapped, disabled

**Handicapped** in the sense referring to a person's mental or physical disabilities is first recorded in the early 20th century. For a brief period in the second half of the 20th century, it looked as if **handicapped** would be replaced by **disabled**, but both words are now acceptable and interchangeable in standard American English, and neither word has been overtaken by newer coinages such as *differently abled* or *physically challenged*.

## harass

Traditionally, the word **harass** has been pronounced with stress on the first syllable, as **har-**." But the newer pronunciation that puts the stress on the second syllable **-ass** is increasingly more widespread and is considered standard. This pronunciation fact is also true for *harassment*.

## he

Until recently, **he** was used uncontroversially to refer to a person of unspecified sex, as in *every child needs to know that* **he** *is loved*. This use has become problematic and is a hallmark of old-fashionedness and sexism in language. Use of **they** as an alternative to **he** in this sense *(everyone needs to feel that* **they** *matter)* has been in use since the 16th century in contexts where it occurs after an indefinite pronoun such as *everyone* or *someone*. It is becoming more and more accepted both in speech and in writing. Another acceptable alternative is *he or she*, although this can become tiresomely long-winded when used frequently. See note for **they.**

## hopefully

The traditional sense of **hopefully**, 'in a hopeful manner' (*he stared* **hopefully** *at the trophy*), has been used since 1593. The first recorded use of **hopefully** as a sentence adverb, meaning 'it is to be hoped that' (**hopefully**, *we'll see you tomorrow*), appears in 1702 in the *Magnalia Christi Americana*, written by Massachusetts theologian and writer Cotton Mather. This use of **hopefully** is now the most common one. Sentence adverbs in general (*frankly, honestly, regrettably, seriously*) are found in English since at least the 1600s, and their use has become common in recent decades. However, most traditionalists take the view that all sentence adverbs are inherently suspect. Although they concede that the battle over **hopefully** is lost on the popular front, they continue to withhold approval of its use as a sentence adverb. Attentive ears are particularly bothered when the sentence that follows does not match the promise of the introductory adverb, as when *frankly* is followed not by an expression of honesty but by a self-serving proclamation (*frankly, I don't care if you go or not*). See note for **thankfully.**

### however, how ever
When **ever** is used as an intensifier after *how, what, when, where,* or *why,* it should be separated by a space. Thus, *how ever did you find her?* could be rephrased, with no change of meaning, *how did you ever find her?* This rule tends to be more often followed—or more widely understood—in Britain than in the U.S.

   **However** in the sense of 'no matter how' (**however** *gently you correct him, Peter always takes offense*) should be spelled as one word.

### humanitarian
**Humanitarian** is not synonymous with *human,* but usage often belies this fact, as evident in this sentence: *Red Cross volunteers rushed to the scene of what may be the the worst* **humanitarian** *disaster this country has seen.* This use of **humanitarian** to mean 'human' is quite common, esp. in 'live reports' on television, but is not generally considered good English style. Strictly speaking, it could be argued that *a* **humanitarian** *disaster* would more accurately refer to "a catastrophe to which no relief agencies responded."

### Indian, Native American
**Indian,** meaning 'native of America before the arrival of Europeans,' is objected to by many who now favor **Native American**. There are others (including many members of these ethnic groups), however, who see nothing wrong with **Indian** or *American Indian,* which are long-established terms, although the preference where possible is to refer to specific peoples, as *Apache, Delaware,* and so on.

   The terms *Amerind* and *Amerindian,* once proposed as alternatives to **Indian,** are used in linguistics and anthropology, but have never gained widespread use. Newer alternatives, not widely used or established, include *First Nation* (esp. in Canada) and the more generic *aboriginal peoples.*

   It should be noted that **Indian** is held by many not to include some

American groups, for example, Aleuts and Eskimos. A further consideration is that **Indian** also (and in some contexts primarily) refers to inhabitants of India or their descendants, who may be referred to as *Asian Indians* to prevent misunderstanding.

## innocent, not guilty

**Innocent** properly means 'harmless,' but it has long been extended in general language to mean 'not guilty.' The jury (or judge) in a criminal trial does not, strictly speaking, find a defendant **innocent**. Rather, a defendant may be *guilty* or *not guilty* of the charges brought. In common use, however, owing perhaps to the concept of the *presumption of innocence*, which instructs a jury to consider a defendant free of wrongdoing until proven guilty on the basis of evidence, **not guilty** and **innocent** have come to be thought of as synonymous.

## interface

The word **interface** is a relatively new word, having been in the language (as a noun) since the 1880s. However, in the 1960s it became widespread in computer use and, by analogy, began to enjoy a vogue as both a noun and a verb in many other spheres. Traditionalists object to it on the grounds that there are plenty of other words that are more exact and sound less like trendy jargon.

## Inuit

The peoples inhabiting the regions from northwestern Canada to western Greenland speak **Inuit** languages and call themselves **Inuit** (not *Eskimo*), and **Inuit** now has official status in Canada. By analogy, **Inuit** is also used in the U.S., usually in an attempt to be politically correct, as a general synonym for *Eskimo*. This, however, is inaccurate because there are no **Inuit** in Alaska and **Inuit** therefore cannot include people from Alaska. Only *Eskimo* includes all of these peoples.

## last, latest

In precise usage, **latest** means 'most recent' (*my* **latest** *project is wallpapering my dining room*), and **last** means 'final' (*the* **last** *day of the school year will be June 18*). But **last** is often used in place of **latest**, esp. in informal contexts: *I read his last novel.*

### latter

**Latter** means 'the second-mentioned of two.' Its use to mean 'the last-mentioned of three or more' is common, but is considered incorrect by some because **latter** means 'later' rather than 'latest.' *Last* or *last-mentioned* is preferred where three or more things are involved.

### less, fewer

In standard English, **less** should be used only with uncountable things (*less money*; *less time*). With countable things, it is incorrect to use **less**: thus, *less people* and *less words* should be corrected to *fewer people* and *fewer words*..

### literally

In its standard use, **literally** means 'in a literal sense, as opposed to a nonliteral or exaggerated sense,': *I told him I never wanted to see him again, but I didn't expect him to take it* **literally**. In recent years, an extended use of **literally** (and also *literal*) has become very common, where **literally** (or *literal*) is used deliberately in nonliteral contexts, for added effect: *they bought the car and* **literally** *ran it into the ground*. This use can lead to unintentional humorous effects (*we were* **literally** *killing ourselves laughing*) and is not acceptable in formal English.

### locate

In formal English, one should avoid using **locate** to mean 'find (a missing object)': *he can't seem to* **locate** *his keys*. In precise usage, **locate** means 'discover the exact place or position of' or 'fix the position of, put in place': *the doctors hope to* **locate** *the source of the bleeding; the studio should be* **located** *on a north-facing slope*.

### a lot of, lots of

**A lot of** and **lots of** are very common in speech and writing, but they still have a distinctly informal feel and are generally not considered acceptable for formal English, where alternatives such as *many* or *a large number* are used instead.

Written as one word, *alot* is incorrect, although not uncommon.

### man

Traditionally, the word **man** has been used to refer not only to adult males but also to human beings in general, regardless of sex. There is a historical explanation for this: in Old English, the principal sense of **man** was 'a human being,' and the words *wer* and *wif* were used to refer specifically to 'a male person' and 'a female person,' respectively. Subsequently, **man** replaced *wer* as the normal term for 'a male person,' but at the same time the older sense 'a human being' remained in use.

In the second half of the 20th century, the generic use of **man** to refer to 'human beings in general' (*reptiles were here long before* **man** *appeared on the earth*) became problematic; the use is now often regarded as sexist or old-fashioned. In some contexts, terms such as *the human race* or *humankind* may be used instead of **man** or *mankind*. However, in other cases, particularly in compound forms, alternatives have not yet become established: there are no standard accepted alternatives for *manpower* or the verb **man**, for example.

### -man

Traditionally, the form **-man** was combined with other words to create a term denoting an occupation or role, as in *fireman, layman, chairman,* and *mailman.* As the role of women in society has changed, with the result that women are now more likely to be in roles previously held exclusively by men, many of these terms ending in **-man** have been challenged as sexist and out of date. As a result, there has been a gradual shift away from **-man** compounds except where referring to a specific male person. Gender-neutral terms such as *firefighter* and *mail carrier* are widely accepted alternatives. And new terms such as *chairperson, layperson,* and *spokesperson*, which only a few decades ago seemed odd or awkward, are common today.

### may, might

Traditionalists insist that one should distinguish between **may** (present tense) and **might** (past tense) in expressing possibility: *I* **may** *have some dessert after dinner if I'm still hungry; I* **might** *have known that the highway would be closed because of the storm.* In casual use, though, **may** and **might** are generally interchangeable: *they* **might** *take a vacation next month; he* **may** *have called earlier, but the answering machine was broken.*

### Myriad

**Myriad** is derived from a Greek noun and adjective meaning 'ten thousand.' It was first used in English as a noun in reference to a great but indefinite number. The adjectival sense of 'countless, innumerable' appeared much later. In modern English, use of **myriad** as a noun and adjective are equally standard and correct, despite the fact that some traditionalists consider the adjective as the only acceptable use of the word.

## native

In contexts such as *a native of Boston*, the use of the noun **native** is quite acceptable. But when used as a noun without qualification, as in *this dance is a favorite with the natives*, it is more problematic. In modern use, it is used humorously to refer to the local inhabitants of a particular place: *that bar is no longer popular with the natives*. In other contexts, it has an old-fashioned feel and, because of being closely associated with a colonial European outlook on nonwhite peoples living in remote places, it may cause offense.

## neither ... nor

When **neither** is followed by **nor**, it is important in good English style that the two halves of the structure mirror each other: *she saw herself as **neither** wife nor mother* rather than *she **neither** saw herself as wife **nor** mother*.

## normalcy

**Normalcy** has been criticized as an uneducated alternative to *normality*, but actually is a common American usage and can be taken as standard: *we are anticipating a return to* **normalcy**.

## octopus

The standard English plural of **octopus** is **octopuses**. However, the word **octopus** comes from Greek, and the Greek plural form is **octopodes** (/ˌäk'täpə,dēz/). Modern usage of **octopodes** is so infrequent that many people mistakenly create the erroneous plural form *octopi*, formed according to rules for Latin plurals.

## older, oldest; younger, youngest

Where two, and no more, are involved, they may be **older** and **younger**: *the **older** of the twins, by ten minutes, is Sam; the **younger** is Pamela*. Where there are more than two, one may be the **oldest** or **youngest**: *I have four siblings, of whom Jane is the **oldest***.

## Oriental

The term **Oriental**, denoting a person from the Far East, is regarded as offensive by many Asians, esp. Asian Americans. It has many associations with

European imperialism in Asia. Therefore, it has an out-of-date feel and tends to be associated with a rather offensive stereotype of the people and their customs as inscrutable and exotic. *Asian* and more specific terms such as *East Asian*, *Chinese*, and *Japanese* are preferred. See note for **Asian.**

## ought, ought not

The verb **ought** is a modal verb, which means that, grammatically, it does not behave like ordinary verbs. In particular, the negative is formed with the word **not** by itself, without auxiliary verbs such as *do* or *have*. Thus the standard construction for the negative is *he **ought not** to go*. Note that the preposition *to* is required in both negative and positive statements: *we **ought** to accept her offer*, or *we **ought not** to accept her offer* (not *we **ought** accept* or *we **ought not** accept*). The alternative forms *he **didn't ought** to have gone* and *he **hadn't ought** to have gone*, formed as if **ought** were an ordinary verb rather than a modal verb, are not acceptable in formal English.

Reserve **ought** for expressing obligation, duty, or necessity, and use *should* for expressing suitability or appropriateness.

## plus

The use of **plus** as a conjunction meaning 'furthermore' (***plus**, we will be pleased to give you personal financial advice*) is considered informal and should be avoided in formal writing.

## prove

For complex historical reasons, **prove** developed two past participles: **proved** and **proven**. Both are correct and can be used more or less interchangeably: *this hasn't been **proved** yet*; *this hasn't been **proven** yet*. **Proven** is the more common form when used as an adjective before the noun it modifies: *a **proven** talent* (not *a **proved** talent*). Otherwise, the choice between **proved** and **proven** is not a matter of correctness, but usually of sound and rhythm—and often, consequently, a matter of familiarity, as in the legal idiom *innocent until **proven** guilty*.

## rob

In law, to **rob** is to take something from someone by causing fear of harm, whether or not actual harm occurs. The term is widely, but incorrectly, used to refer to *theft*: *our house was **robbed** while we were away*. Technically, the more correct statement would be *our house was burglarized while we were away*.

## Scottish, Scot, Scots, Scotch

The terms **Scottish**, **Scot**, **Scots**, and **Scotch** are all variants of the same word. They have had different histories, however, and in modern English they have developed different uses and connotations.

The normal everyday word used to mean 'of or relating to Scotland or its people' is **Scottish**: *Scottish* people; *Scottish* hills; *Scottish* Gaelic; *she's English, not Scottish.*

The normal, neutral word for 'a person from Scotland' is **Scot**, along with *Scotsman*, *Scotswoman*, and the plural form **the Scots** (or, less commonly, **the Scottish**).

**Scots** is also used, like **Scottish**, as an adjective meaning 'of or relating to Scotland.' However, it tends to be used in a narrower sense to refer specifically to the form of English used in Scotland: *Scots accent; the Scots word for 'night.'*

The word **Scotch**, meaning either 'of or relating to Scotland' or 'a person/the people from Scotland,' was widely used in the past by Scottish writers such as Robert Burns and Sir Walter Scott. In the 20th century, it became less common. It is disliked by many Scottish people (as being an 'English' invention) and is now regarded as old-fashioned in most contexts. It survives in certain fixed phrases, as, for example, *Scotch* broth and *Scotch* whisky.

## sink

In modern English, the past tense of **sink** is generally **sank** (less commonly **sunk**), and the past participle is always **sunk**. The form **sunken** now survives only as an adjective: *a sunken garden; sunken cheeks.*

## spastic

**Spastic**, usually used as an adjective, has been used in medical senses since the 18th century and is still a neutral term for conditions like *spastic colon* or *spastic paraplegia*. In the 1970s and 1980s, **spastic**, usually used as a noun, became a term of abuse and was directed toward anyone regarded as incompetent or physically uncoordinated. Nowadays, this latter use of **spastic**, whether as a noun or as an adjective, is likely to cause offense, and even in medical use it is preferable to use phrasing such as *person with cerebral palsy* instead of the noun **spastic**.

## spinster

The development of the word **spinster** is a good example of the way in which a word acquires strong connotations to the extent that it can no longer be used in a neutral sense. From the 17th century, the word was appended to names as the official legal description of an unmarried woman: *Elizabeth Harris of Boston, Spinster.* This type of use survives today in some legal and religious contexts. In modern everyday English, however, **spinster** cannot be used to mean simply 'unmarried woman'; it is now always a derogatory term, referring or alluding to a stereotype of an older woman who is unmarried, childless, prissy, and repressed.

## split infinitive

Is it wrong to use a **split infinitive**, separating the infinitive marker **to** from the verb? If so, then these statements are grammatically incorrect: *you have to really watch him*; *to boldly go where no one has gone before.* Writers who long ago insisted that English could be modeled on Latin created the "rule" that the English infinitive must not be split: *to clearly state* violates this rule; one must say *to state clearly.* But the Latin infinitive is one word (e.g., *amare*, 'to love') and cannot be split, so the rule is not firmly grounded, and treating two English words as one can lead to awkward, stilted sentences. In particular, the placing of an adverb in English is extremely important in giving the appropriate emphasis. Consider, for example, the "corrected" forms of the previous examples: *you really have to watch him*; *to go boldly where no one has gone before.* The original, intended emphasis of each statement has been changed, and for no other reason than to satisfy an essentially unreasonable rule. Some traditionalists may continue to hold up the split infinitive as an error, but in standard English, the principle of allowing split infinitives is broadly accepted as both normal and useful.

## thankfully

**Thankfully** has been used for centuries to mean 'in a thankful manner,' as in *she accepted the offer* **thankfully**. Since the 1960s, it has also been used as a sentence adverb to mean 'fortunately,' as in **thankfully**, *we didn't have to wait.* Although this use has not attracted the same amount of attention as *hopefully*, it has been criticized for the same reasons. It is, however, far more common now than is the traditional use. See note for **hopefully.**

## that, who, which

The word **that** can be omitted in standard English where it introduces a *subordinate* clause, as in *she said (that) she was satisfied.* **That** can also be dropped in a *relative* clause where it is the *object* of the clause, as in *the book (that) I've just written.* **That**, however, is obligatory when it is the *subject* of the relative clause, as in *the company that employs Jack.*

It is sometimes argued that, in relative clauses, **that** should be used for *nonhuman* references and **who** should be used for *human* references: *a house that overlooks the park*, but *the woman who lives next door.* In practice, while it is true to say that **who** is restricted to human references, the function of **that** is flexible. It has been used for both human and nonhuman references since at least the 11th century. In standard English, it is interchangeable with **who** in this context.

Is there any difference between the use of **that** and **which** in sentences such as *any book that gets children reading is worth having*, and *any book which gets children reading is worth having?* The general rule is that, in *restrictive* relative clauses, where the relative clause serves to define or restrict the reference to the particular one described, **that** is the preferred relative pronoun. However, in *nonrestrictive* relative clauses, where the relative clause serves only to give additional information, **which** must be used: *this book, which is set in the last century, is very popular with teenagers*, but not *this book, that is set in the last century, is very popular with teenagers.*

## they

The word **they** (with its counterparts *them, their,* and *themselves*) as a singular pronoun to refer to a person of unspecified sex has been used since at least the 16th century. In the late 20th century, as the traditional use of **he** to refer to a person of either sex came under scrutiny on the grounds of sexism, this use of **they** has become more common. It is now generally accepted in contexts where it follows an indefinite pronoun such as *anyone, no one, someone,* or *a person:* **anyone** *can join if* **they** *are a resident;* **each** *to* **their** *own.* In other contexts, coming after singular nouns, the use of **they** is now common, although less widely accepted, esp. in formal contexts. Sentences such as *ask a friend if they could help* are still criticized for being ungrammatical. Nevertheless, in view of the growing acceptance of **they** and its obvious practical advantages, **they** is used in many cases where **he** would have been used formerly. See note for **he.**

## thus, thusly

The expansion of the adverb **thus** to **thusly** is usually considered unnecessary, but it can serve a distinct function, as in introducing a direct quotation: *He answered her* **thusly**: *"your evidence is lacking and your conclusions are just plain wrong!"*

## transpire

The common use of **transpire** to mean 'occur, happen' (*I'm going to find out exactly what transpired*) is a loose extension of an earlier meaning, 'come to be known' (*it transpired that Mark had been baptized a Catholic*). This loose sense of 'happen,' which is now more common in American usage than the sense of 'come to be known,' was first recorded in U.S. English toward the end of the 18th century and has been listed in U.S. dictionaries from the 19th century. Careful writers should note, however, that in cases where *occur* or *happen* would do just as well, the use of **transpire** may strike readers as an affectation or as jargon.

## utilize

**Utilize**, borrowed in the 19th century from the French *utiliser*, means 'make practical or effective use of.' Because it is a more formal word than *use* and is often used in contexts (as in business writing) where the ordinary verb *use* would be simpler and more direct, **utilize** may strike readers as pretentious jargon and should therefore be used sparingly.

## various, various of

In standard English, the word **various** is normally used as an adjective. It is best reserved for contexts indicating variety, and should not be used as a synonym for *several*. In colloquial American speech, **various** is sometimes also used (as though it were a pronoun) followed by *of*, as in *various of her friends had called*—another way of saying *some of* or *several of*. This use is discouraged by some traditionalists, however, because **various** is properly an adjective, not a pronoun, and **various of** erodes the sense of variety, diversity, and distinctness. This erosion or blurring of meaning is further evident in the use of *various different*, as in **various different** *kinds of oak*, a redundant wording that should be avoided.

## vis-à-vis

The expression **vis-à-vis** literally means 'face to face.' Avoid using it to mean 'about, concerning,' as in *he wanted to talk to me* **vis-à-vis** *next weekend*. In the sense 'in contrast, comparison, or relation to,' however, **vis-à-vis** is generally acceptable: *let us consider government regulations* **vis-à-vis** *employment rates.*

## well

The adverb **well** is often used in combination with past participles to form compound adjectives: *well-adjusted, well-intentioned, well-known,* and so on. As far as hyphenation is concerned, there are three general rules: (1) if the compound adjective is placed before the noun (i.e., in the attributive position), it should be hyphenated (*a* **well-intentioned** *remark*); (2) if the compound adjective is preceded by an adverb (*much, very, surprisingly,* etc.), the compound adjective is open (*a* **thoroughly well prepared** *student*); (3) if the compound adjective is placed after the noun or verb (i.e., in the predicate position), it may, but need not, be hyphenated (*her remark was* **well-intentioned** or *her remark was* **well intentioned**). Likewise, other, similar compounds with *better, best, ill, little, lesser, least,* etc., are hyphenated before the noun (*a* **little-known** *author*), often open after a noun or verb (*the author was* **little known**), and open if modified by an adverb (*a* **very little known** *author*).

## whatever, what ever

In the sentence *I will do* **whatever** *you ask of me* (in which **whatever** means 'anything'), **whatever** is correctly spelled as one word. But in the interrogative sense (**what ever** *was Mary thinking?*), the emphasis is on *ever,* and it should be spelled as the two words **what ever** because *ever* is serving as an intensifier to the pronoun *what.*

## while, whereas

**While** is sometimes used, without causing any misunderstandings, in the sense of **whereas** ('although,' 'by contrast,' 'in comparison with the fact that'). This usage is frowned on by some traditionalists, but **while** is sometimes preferable, as in contexts in which **whereas** might sound inappropriately formal: *while you say you like her, you've never stood up for her*). **Whereas** is preferable, however, for preventing ambiguity in contexts in which **while** might be read as referring to time, or might falsely suggest simultaneity: *whereas Burton promised to begin at once, he was delayed nine months for lack of funding; whereas Jonas was an excellent planter and cultivator, Julius was a master harvester.*

## worthwhile

The adjective **worthwhile** is used both attributively (that is, before the noun) and predicatively (that is, when it stands alone and comes after the verb). In both positions, it is almost always written as one word: *a **worthwhile** book, the book was **worthwhile***. But it is occasionally hyphenated (*a **worth-while** book*) or written as two words (*the book was **worth while***).

## wrought havoc

The phrase **wrought havoc**, as in *they **wrought havoc** on the countryside*, is an acceptable variant of *wreaked havoc*. Here, **wrought** is an archaic past tense of *work*. It is not, as is sometimes assumed, a past tense of *wreak*.

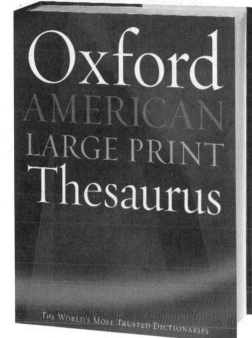

**gath·er** /ˈgaTHər/ ▸v. **1** bring or come together; assemble. **2** acquire by gradually collecting; amass. **3** harvest. **4** infer or understand. **5** increase: *gather speed*. **6** summon up (one's thoughts, energy, etc.) for a purpose. **7** draw (material, or one's brow) together in folds or wrinkles. ▸n. (**gathers**) part of a garment that is gathered or drawn in. —**gath·er·er** *n.*

**gauche** /gōSH/ ▸adj. **1** lacking ease or grace; socially awkward. **2** tactless.

**gau·cho** /ˈgouCHō/ ▸n. (*pl.* **-chos**) cowboy of the South American pampas.

**gaud·y** /ˈgôdē/ ▸adj. (**-i·er, -i·est**) tastelessly or extravagantly bright or showy. —**gaud·i·ly** *adv.* —**gaud·i·ness** *n.*

**gauge** /gāj/ (also **gage**) ▸n. **1** standard measure to which certain things must conform, esp. in thickness or diameter. **2** instrument for measuring. **3** distance between a pair of rails or the wheels on one axle. ▸v. **1** measure exactly. **2** estimate.

**gaunt** /gônt/ ▸adj. **1** lean; haggard. **2** grim or desolate in appearance. —**gaunt·ly** *adv.* —**gaunt·ness** *n.*

**gaunt·let** /ˈgôntlit/ ▸n. stout glove with a long loose wrist. □ **run the gauntlet** be subjected to harsh criticism. □ **throw down the gauntlet** make a challenge.

**gauze** /gôz/ ▸n. thin transparent fabric of silk, cotton, etc. —**gauz·y** *adj.*

**ga·vage** /gəˈväzH/ ▸n. administration of food or drugs by force, esp. to an animal, typically through a tube leading down the throat to the stomach.

**gav·el** /ˈgavəl/ ▸n. small hammer used by an auctioneer, or for calling a meeting, courtroom, etc., to order.

**gawk** /gôk/ ▸v. stare stupidly.

**gawk·y** /ˈgôkē/ ▸adj. (**-i·er, -i·est**) awkward or ungainly. —**gawk·i·ly** *adv.*

**gay** /gā/ ▸adj. **1 a** homosexual. **b** intended for or used by homosexuals: *gay bar*. **2** lighthearted and carefree; cheerful **3** brightly colored. ▸n. homosexual, esp. male.

**gaze** /gāz/ ▸v. look fixedly. ▸n. intent look. —**gaz·er** *n.*

**ga·ze·bo** /gəˈzēbō/ ▸n. (*pl.* **-bos** or **-boes**) open-sided structure giving a wide view.

**ga·zelle** /gəˈzel/ ▶n. any of various graceful soft-eyed antelopes of Asia or Africa.

**ga·zette** /gəˈzet/ ▶n. newspaper, esp. the official one of an organization or institution: *University Gazette.*

**gaz·et·teer** /ˌɡazəˈti(ə)r/ ▶n. geographical index or dictionary.

**gaz·pa·cho** /ɡäˈspäCHō/ ▶n. (*pl.* **-chos**) Spanish soup made with tomatoes, oil, garlic, onions, etc., and served cold.

**gear** /ɡi(ə)r/ ▶n. **1** (**gears**) set of toothed wheels that work together, as in a vehicle. **2** particular setting of these: *low gear.* **3** equipment or tackle for a special purpose. **4** possessions in general.
▶v. **1** adjust or adapt (something) to. **2** (**gear up**) make ready or prepared.

**gear·shift** ▶n. lever used to engage or change gear.

**geck·o** /ˈɡekō/ ▶n. (*pl.* **-os** or **-oes**) tropical lizard.

**gee** /jē/ (also **gee whiz**) ▶interj. mild expression of surprise, discovery, etc.

**geek** /ɡēk/ ▶n. **1** unfashionable or socially inept person. **2** person with an eccentric devotion to a particular interest.

**3** carnival performer who does wild or disgusting acts.

**gee·zer** /ˈɡēzər/ ▶n. inf. person, esp. an old man.

**Gei·ger count·er** /ˈɡīɡər/ ▶n. device for measuring radioactivity by detecting and counting ionizing particles.

**gei·sha** /ˈɡāSHə/ ▶n. (*pl.* same or **gei·shas**) Japanese hostess trained in entertaining men with dance and song.

**gel** /jel/ ▶n. **1** semisolid colloidal suspension or jelly. **2** gelatinous hairstyling preparation.
▶v. (**gelled**, **gel·ling**) form a gel.

**gel·a·tin** /ˈjelətn/ (also **gel·a·tine**) ▶n. transparent water-soluble protein derived from collagen and used in food preparation, photography, etc. —**ge·lat·i·nous** *adj.*

**geld** /ɡeld/ ▶v. castrate.

**geld·ing** ▶n. gelded animal, esp. a male horse.

**gel·id** /ˈjelid/ ▶adj. icy; extremely cold.

**gem** /jem/ ▶n. **1** precious stone, esp. when cut and polished. **2** object or person of great beauty or worth. —**gem·like** *adj.*

**ge·müt·lich·keit** /ɡəˈmo͞otlik-ˌkīt/ (also **Ge·müt·lich·keit**) ▶n. geniality; friendliness.

**Gen.** ▶*abbr.* **1** General.
**2** Genesis (Old Testament).

**-gen** ▶*comb. form* **1** *Chem.* that which produces: *hydrogen* | *antigen*. **2** *Bot.* growth: *endogen* | *exogen* | *acrogen*.

**gen·der** /ˈjendər/ ▶*n.*
**1 a** grammatical classification corresponding to the two sexes and sexlessness. **b** each of these classes of nouns. **2** a person's sex.

**gene** /jēn/ ▶*n.* unit of heredity composed of DNA or RNA and forming part of a chromosome, that alone or in conjunction with other genes determines a particular characteristic of an individual.

**ge·ne·al·o·gy** /ˌjēnēˈäləjē; -ˈal-/ ▶*n.* (*pl.* **-gies**) **1** descent traced continuously from an ancestor. **2** study of family descent. —**ge·ne·a·log·i·cal** *adj.* —**ge·ne·a·log·i·cal·ly** *adv.* —**ge·ne·al·o·gist** *n.*

**gen·er·al** /ˈjen(ə)rəl/ ▶*adj.*
**1** completely or almost universal; including or affecting all or nearly all parts or cases of things. **2** prevalent; widespread; usual. **3** not limited in application; not restricted, specialized, or detailed: *a general idea.*

▶*n.* **1** commander of an army. **2** tactician or strategist of specified merit: *a great general.* —**gen·er·al·ly** *adv.*

□ **in general 1** as a normal rule; usually. **2** for the most part.

**gen·er·al·is·si·mo** /ˌjenərəˈlisəˌmō/ ▶*n.* (*pl.* **-mos**) commander of a combined military force consisting of army, navy, and air force units.

**gen·er·al·i·ty** /ˌjenəˈralitē/ ▶*n.* (*pl.* **-ties**) **1** statement or principle having general validity or force. **2** vagueness; lack of detail.

**gen·er·al·ize** ▶*v.* **1** speak in general or indefinite terms. **2** infer (a law or conclusion) by induction. —**gen·er·al·i·za·tion** *n.*

**gen·er·ate** /ˈjenəˌrāt/ ▶*v.* **1** bring into existence; produce; evolve. **2** produce (electricity). —**gen·er·at·ive** *adj.*

**gen·er·a·tion** /ˌjenəˈrāsHən/ ▶*n.* **1** all the people born at a particular time, regarded collectively: *my generation.* **2** single step in descent or pedigree. **3** stage in (esp. technological) development:

*fourth-generation computers.*
**4** procreation.

**gen·er·a·tor** /ˈjenəˌrātər/ ▸*n.* machine for converting mechanical into electrical energy.

**ge·ner·ic** /jəˈnerik/ ▸*adj.* **1** characteristic of a class; general, not specific or special. **2** (of goods, esp. a drug) having no trade or brand name. —**ge·ner·i·cal·ly** *adv.*

**gen·er·ous** /ˈjenərəs/ ▸*adj.* **1** giving or given freely. **2** noble-minded; unprejudiced. **3** abundant. —**gen·er·os·i·ty** *n.* —**gen·er·ous·ly** *adv.*

**gen·e·sis** /ˈjenəsis/ ▸*n.* **1** origin. **2** (**Genesis**) first book of the Old Testament.

**ge·net·ics** /jəˈnetiks/ ▸*n.* the study of heredity and inherited characteristics. —**ge·net·i·cist** *n.*

**gen·ial** /ˈjēnyəl; -nēəl/ ▸*adj.* sociable; kindly; cheerful. —**ge·ni·al·i·ty** *n.* —**ge·nial·ly** *adv.*

**ge·nie** /ˈjēnē/ ▸*n.* (*pl.* usu. **ge·ni·i**) spirit of Arabian folklore.

**genital** /ˈjenitl/ ▸*adj.* of or relating to human or animal reproductive organs. ▸*pl. n.* (**genitals**) external reproductive organs.

**gen·i·ta·li·a** /ˌjeniˈtālēə/ ▸*pl. n.* genitals.

**gen·i·tive** /ˈjenitiv/ ▸*n.* grammatical case indicating possession or association. ▸*adj.* of or in the genitive.

**gen·ius** /ˈjēnyəs/ ▸*n.* **1** exceptional intellectual or creative power or other natural ability or tendency. **2** person having this.

**gen·o·cide** /ˈjenəˌsīd/ ▸*n.* deliberate extermination of a people or nation. —**gen·o·ci·dal** *adj.*

**ge·nome** /ˈjēˌnōm/ ▸*n.* complete set of genes or genetic material present in a cell or organism.

**gen·re** /ˈzhänrə/ ▸*n.* kind or style of art, literature, etc.

**gen·teel** /jenˈtēl/ ▸*adj.* **1** affectedly or ostentatiously refined or stylish. **2** well-bred; upper-class. —**gen·teel·ly** *adv.*

**gen·tian** /ˈjenchən/ ▸*n.* mountain plant usu. with violet or vivid blue flowers.

**Gen·tile** /ˈjentīl/ ▸*adj.* not Jewish; heathen. ▸*n.* person who is not Jewish.

**gen·tle** /ˈjentl/ ▸*adj.* (**-tler, -tlest**) **1** not rough; mild or kind, esp. in temperament. **2** moderate;